T0397515

The Law of U.S. Foreign Relations

The Law of U.S. Foreign Relations

SEAN D. MURPHY
Manatt/Ahn Professor of International Law
The George Washington University
School of Law

EDWARD T. SWAINE
Charles Kennedy Poe Research Professor of Law
The George Washington University
School of Law

OXFORD
UNIVERSITY PRESS

OXFORD
UNIVERSITY PRESS

Oxford University Press is a department of the University of Oxford. It furthers the University's objective of excellence in research, scholarship, and education by publishing worldwide. Oxford is a registered trade mark of Oxford University Press in the UK and certain other countries.

Published in the United States of America by Oxford University Press
198 Madison Avenue, New York, NY 10016, United States of America.

© Sean D. Murphy and Edward T. Swaine 2023

Library of Congress Cataloging-in-Publication Data
Names: Murphy, Sean D., author. | Swaine, Edward T., author.
Title: The law of U.S. foreign relations / Sean D. Murphy, Edward T. Swaine.
Other titles: Law of US foreign relations
Description: New York : Oxford University Press, 2023. |
Includes bibliographical references and index. |
Identifiers: LCCN 2022051679 (print) | LCCN 2022051680 (ebook) |
ISBN 9780199361977 (hardback) | ISBN 9780199361984 (updf) |
ISBN 9780190067700 (epub) | ISBN 9780199361991 (online)
Subjects: LCSH: United States—Foreign relations—Law and legislation.
Classification: LCC KF4651 .M87 2023 (print) | LCC KF4651 (ebook) |
DDC 342.73/0412—dc23/eng/20230105
LC record available at https://lccn.loc.gov/2022051679
LC ebook record available at https://lccn.loc.gov/2022051680

DOI: 10.1093/law/9780199361977.001.0001

Printed by Integrated Books International, United States of America

Note to Readers
This publication is designed to provide accurate and authoritative information in regard to the subject matter covered. It is based upon sources believed to be accurate and reliable and is intended to be current as of the time it was written. It is sold with the understanding that the publisher is not engaged in rendering legal, accounting, or other professional services. If legal advice or other expert assistance is required, the services of a competent professional person should be sought. Also, to confirm that the information has not been affected or changed by recent developments, traditional legal research techniques should be used, including checking primary sources where appropriate.

(Based on the Declaration of Principles jointly adopted by a Committee of the American Bar Association and a Committee of Publishers and Associations.)

You may order this or any other Oxford University Press publication by visiting the Oxford University Press website at www.oup.com.

Contents

Foreword by Judge Stephen M. Schwebel   xv
General Preface   xvii
Methodological Preface   xix
Acknowledgments   xxvii
Table of Short Forms for Commonly Cited Authorities   xxix

1. Allocating and Balancing Foreign Relations Powers   1
   I. Allocating Foreign Relations Powers   2
     A. Congress   3
     B. President   5
     C. Judiciary   9
     D. Foreign Relations Powers Not Derived from the Constitution?   11
     E. Federalism   17
   II. Balancing Foreign Relations Powers   19
     A. Balancing in the Shadow of the President's Institutional
       Advantages   20
       1. President's Advantages Generally   20
       2. President's Advantages Unique to Foreign Relations   23
     B. Balancing and the President's Posture vis-à-vis Congress   30
   III. Foreign Relations Powers in Times of National Emergency   42

2. Legislating Foreign Relations   51
   I. Enumerated and Non-Enumerated Powers to Legislate   52
     A. Congress' Enumerated Powers to Legislate on Foreign Relations   52
     B. Congress' Non-Enumerated Power to Legislate on Foreign
       Relations   54
   II. Procedural and Other Cross-Cutting Aspects of the Power to
     Legislate   59
     A. House and Senate Committees   59
     B. Presentment and the Legislative Veto   61
     C. Presidential Signing Statements   63
     D. Congressional Reporting and Consultation Requirements   68
     E. Presumptions Regarding the Interpretation of Foreign Relations
       Statutes   69
     F. Congressional Oversight of Foreign Relations   71
       1. Methods for Oversight   72
       2. Subpoenas and Contempt   73

3. Withholding of Information by the Executive Branch 74
    a. Classified Information 74
    b. Executive Privilege 76
III. Power of the Purse 80
IV. Power to Regulate Commerce with Foreign Nations 88
  A. Scope of the Foreign Commerce Power 89
  B. Trade in Goods and Services 94
  C. Foreign Investment 96
  D. Other Activities and Instrumentalities Connected to Foreign
    Commerce 98
  E. Presidential Emergency Economic Powers 99
V. Power to Regulate the Value of Foreign Coin 101

3. Conducting Foreign Relations 105
  I. Power to Conduct Foreign Relations 108
    A. Pre-Constitutional Experience 108
    B. Constitutional Design 110
    C. Early Practice Under the Constitution 115
    D. Solidification of the President's Power to Conduct
      Foreign Relations 121
  II. Receiving Foreign Ambassadors and Other Public Ministers 125
    A. Receiving Foreign Ambassadors 125
    B. Establishing Foreign Missions in the United States 126
    C. Declaring Foreign Diplomats *Persona Non Grata* 131
  III. Appointing U.S. Ambassadors, Ministers, and Consuls 132
    A. Selection of Ambassadors, Ministers, and Consuls 133
    B. Ineligibility Clause 136
    C. Removal 138
    D. Ambassadors Not Subject to Senate Consent 139
    E. Regulation of Diplomatic Posts and Positions 140
  IV. Recognition Power and Collateral Effects 144
    A. Recognition of a New Foreign State 144
      1. Presidential Prerogative 144
      2. Congress' Limited Role 147
      3. Nonrecognition 149
    B. Recognition of a Foreign Government Coming to Power
      Extraconstitutionally 151
    C. Collateral Effects of Nonrecognition in U.S. Courts 156
      1. Inability to Have Access to U.S. Courts as a Foreign State/
        Government 156
      2. Inability to Claim Foreign Sovereign Immunity from Suit 159
      3. Inability to Control Foreign State Property Located in the
        United States 161

4. Public/External Acts of the Nonrecognized Foreign Entity Not
   Given Effect by U.S. Courts   161
D. Conclusion of Executive Agreements Incidental to Recognition   163
E. Recognition of Foreign Belligerency and Insurgency   167
F. Altering Treaties to Accommodate Newly Created Foreign States   169
V. Foreign Emoluments Clause   171

4. Judging Foreign Relations   175
  I. Historical Role of the Judiciary in Foreign Relations   176
    A. Pre-Constitutional Experience   176
    B. Constitutional Design   178
    C. Subsequent History   181
  II. Nonjusticiability and Foreign Affairs   184
    A. Political Question Doctrine   184
     1. Background and Scope   184
     2. Applying the Doctrine   187
    B. Other Nonjusticiability Doctrines   193
     1. Standing   193
     2. Ripeness and Mootness   195
  III. Act of State Doctrine   199
  IV. Applying U.S. Law Abroad   210
    A. Jurisdictional Bases   211
     1. Prescriptive Jurisdiction   212
      a. Territorial and Effects Jurisdiction   213
      b. Nationality (Active Personality) Jurisdiction   216
      c. Passive Personality Jurisdiction   219
      d. Protective Jurisdiction   222
      e. Universal Jurisdiction   224
       i. General Approach   225
       ii. U.S. Practice   227
      f. Constitutional Limits   230
     2. Adjudicative Jurisdiction   231
     3. Enforcement Jurisdiction   234
    B. Presumption Against Extraterritoriality   235
     1. Background, Purpose, and Scope   235
     2. Two-Step Approach   238
    C. Prescriptive Comity and Reasonableness   242
  V. Immunity from U.S. Jurisdiction   246
    A. Foreign Sovereign Immunity   246
     1. Early Development   247
     2. Nature and Scope of the FSIA   252
     3. "Foreign States"   258
      a. Foreign State *Stricto Sensu* and Political Subdivisions   258
      b. Agencies or Instrumentalities   261

4. Immunity from Suit	264
a. Waiver (and Related Exceptions)	265
b. Commercial Activity Exception	268
c. Expropriation Exception	273
d. Property and Tort Exceptions	276
e. Terrorism-Related Exceptions	279
5. Immunity from Attachment and Execution	285
B. International Organizations, Officials, and Premises	287
C. Diplomatic and Consular Officials and Premises	295
D. Other Foreign Officials	302
1. Head-of-State (Status-Based) Immunity	305
2. Official (Conduct-Based) Immunity	312
3. Special Mission Immunity	319
5. Customary International Law	**323**
I. Customary International Law Under the Constitution	324
A. Pre-Constitutional Experience and Its Diagnosis	324
B. Constitutional Design	327
1. Law of Nations and the Congress	327
2. Law of Nations and the President	329
3. Law of Nations and the Judiciary	330
4. General Reflections	333
II. Incorporating Customary International Law into U.S. Law	335
A. Legislative Incorporation	335
1. Piracies and Felonies	336
2. Offenses Against the Law of Nations	338
3. Residual Authority	344
B. Executive Incorporation	346
1. Generally	346
2. Making and Interpreting Customary International Law	348
3. Take Care Authority	352
C. Judicial Incorporation	356
1. Customary International Law as General Common Law	357
2. Customary International Law as Federal Common Law	361
III. Limits on Incorporation	370
A. Relationship with the Constitution	371
B. Relationship with Federal Statutes	373
1. Later-in-Time Statutes	373
2. Later-in-Time Customary International Law	379
3. Presumption of Consistency	382
C. Relationship with Treaties	387
D. Relationship with Executive Branch Conduct	389
IV. Contemporary Issue Areas	395
A. Piracy and Terrorism	396
1. Piracy	396
2. Terrorism	400

      B. Human Rights   401
          1. Alien Tort Statute (ATS)   401
          2. Other Human Rights Statutes   411

6. Treaties and Other International Agreements   415
  I. Historical Emergence of the Treaty Power   418
      A. Pre-Constitutional Experience   418
          1. Pre-Articles Experience   418
          2. Experience Under the Articles of Confederation   420
      B. Constitutional Design   426
          1. Separation of Treaty Powers   426
          2. Treaties and the States   429
          3. Evaluation During Ratification   432
      C. Subsequent History   434
  II. Making Treaties   436
      A. Making Treaties Under International Law   437
          1. Capacity and Authority   437
          2. Consent and Entry into Force   440
          3. Reservations to Treaties   440
          4. Impact of National Law on Treaty Law   442
      B. Treaty-Making Under Article II   444
          1. Negotiation (and Advice)   444
          2. Consent by the Senate   451
          3. U.S. Reservations and Other Conditions   453
          4. Ratification by the President   458
      C. Obligations Arising Prior to Entry into Force of the Treaty   460
          1. Obligation Not to Defeat the Object and Purpose of the Treaty   460
          2. Obligations from Provisional Application of the Treaty   464
      D. Constitutional Limits on Treaty-Making   469
          1. Subject-Matter Limits   470
          2. Other Constitutional Limits   475
  III. Interpreting International Agreements   483
      A. International (and Domestic) Elements   484
          1. Text and Context   484
          2. Subsequent Agreements, Subsequent Practice, and
             Relevant Rules   491
          3. Preparatory Work and Other Supplementary Means   495
      B. Deference by U.S. Courts When Interpreting Treaties   497
          1. Judicial Deference to the Executive Branch   497
          2. Judicial Deference to the Senate   500
          3. Judicial Deference to International Tribunals   506
  IV. Incorporation, Implementation, and Hierarchical Status   510
      A. Incorporation by Treaty Self-Execution   510
          1. Beginnings of Self-Execution and Non-Self-Execution   511
          2. Consequences of Self-Execution   516
          3. Consequences of Non-Self-Execution   520

4. Treaty-Based Inquiry   524
5. Constitution-Based Inquiry   530
6. Justiciability-Based Inquiry   533
7. Declarations by the Treaty-Makers   535
B. Implementation of Treaty Obligations by Other Means   540
C. Hierarchical Status   545
  1. Conflicts Between Treaties and the Constitution   545
  2. Conflicts Between Treaties and Statutes   547
  3. Conflicts Between Treaties and Other International Law   552
  4. Conflicts Between Treaties and State and Local Law   553
V. Agreements Other than Article II Treaties   556
A. Congressional-Executive Agreements   561
  1. *Ex Ante* Agreements   562
  2. *Ex Post* Agreements   567
  3. Constitutional Limits   569
B. Executive Agreements Pursuant to Treaty   573
C. Sole Executive Agreements   575
D. Nonbinding Agreements   580
E. Establishing Commitments by Means Other than Agreement   584
VI. Exiting Treaties   587
A. Exit Under International Law   588
B. Presidential Authority to Bring About Exit   589
C. Congressional Regulation of Exit   596

7. International Organizations   601
I. Historical Perspectives   602
A. Articles of Confederation   603
B. Constitutional Design   606
C. Subsequent Practice   607
II. U.S. Participation in International Organizations   615
A. Method for Admission   615
B. Method for Withdrawal/Suspension   618
C. Method for Engaging in Rulemaking   620
D. Method for Engaging in Dispute Resolution   625
III. Incorporation of International Organization Lawmaking into U.S. Law   629
A. Treaty Changes   630
B. International Legislation   634
C. International Dispute Resolution   637
D. Execution by International Organizations   638
E. Delegation Concerns   639
  1. Delegation of Authority to Change U.S. Treaty Obligations   641
  2. Delegation of Legislative Authority   644
  3. Delegation of Judicial Authority   647
  4. Delegation of Executive Authority   656

8. War Powers   659

   I. Power to Resort to Armed Force   662
      A. Pre-Constitutional Origins of the Power   662
      B. Power as Expressed in the U.S. Constitution   664
      C. Historical Practice   670
         1. Early Precedents: 1789 to the Civil War   670
         2. Civil War to 1950: Emergence as a Global Military Power   679
         3. Cold War: Swing to Executive Dominance   691
         4. Congress' Efforts to Reclaim Authority: War Powers Resolution   697
         5. Post-Cold War Uses of Force   704
            a. Emergence of the U.N. Security Council as a Factor   705
            b. Uses of Force in Response to Terrorist Threats   710
            c. Uses of Force Principally for Humanitarian Objectives   717
         6. Threatening Armed Conflict   724
      D. Contemporary Issues   725
         1. Method and Consequences of Congressional Authorization   725
         2. Consequences of International Law   729
         3. Theories of Balancing   731
            a. President May Not Use Armed Force Without
               Congressional Authorization Except to "Repel
               Sudden Attacks"   732
            b. In Addition to Repelling Attacks, the President May Use
               Armed Force to Address Low-Intensity Armed Conflict,
               Subject to Congressional Restrictions   734
            c. In Addition to Repelling Attacks, the President May
               Use Armed Force When Authorized by the U.N. Security
               Council   742
            d. President May Resort to Any Armed Force (Including
               Large-Scale Deployments), Subject to Congressional
               Restrictions   746
            e. President Has Preclusive Authority to Resort to Armed
               Conflict, But Can Be Impeached or Denied Funding   748
  II. Power to Conduct Armed Conflict   751
      A. Consequences of International Law   751
      B. Commander-in-Chief Power   754
      C. Power to Make Rules Concerning Captures on Land and Water   764
      D. Power to Grant Letters of Marque and Reprisal   768
 III. Power to Establish and Regulate the Military   771
      A. Power to Raise Revenues to Provide for the Common Defense,
         to Raise and Support the Military, and to Purchase and Regulate
         Military Installations   771
      B. Power to Regulate the Military   775
      C. Power to Call Forth, Organize, Arm, and Discipline the Militia   782

9. Federalism and Foreign Relations 787

I. Role of States in Foreign Relations 788
II. Methods of Preempting State Law 800
  A. Preemption by Federal Statute 802
  B. Preemption by Treaty 812
  C. Preemption by Presidential Action 819
  D. Preemption by Dormant Foreign Commerce Clause 825
  E. Preemption by Dormant Foreign Affairs Power 829
  F. Preemption by Customary International Law 836
III. Compact Clause 839

10. Individual Rights and Foreign Relations 849

I. Types of Persons and Places 850
  A. Noncitizens in the United States 850
  B. Persons in Unincorporated U.S. Territories 854
  C. Citizens and Noncitizens Abroad 857
  D. U.S. Obligations Under International Law as a Backdrop 860
II. Rights Arising Under the Bill of Rights and Fourteenth
  Amendment 867
  A. Speech, Religion, and the Press (First Amendment) 869
    1. Regulation of Protests Near Embassies or Consulates 872
    2. Right to Receive Foreign Speech 872
    3. Denial of Entry of Noncitizens with Respect to Religion and
       Free Exercise 874
    4. Access to and Unlawful Disclosure of Foreign Relations
       Information 878
    5. Provision of Support to Terrorist Groups 881
  B. Keep and Bear Arms (Second Amendment) 882
    1. Defense Against a Foreign Attack 883
    2. Right of Noncitizens to Bear Arms in the United States 884
    3. Relationship to U.S. Arms Controls Treaties 886
  C. Unreasonable Searches and Seizures (Fourth Amendment) 888
    1. Foreign Intelligence Surveillance in the United States 889
    2. Searches and Seizures of Noncitizens in the United States 892
    3. Searches and Seizures of Citizens and Noncitizens Abroad 894
    4. *Bivens* Actions by Noncitizens Against the U.S. Government 900
    5. Inspection Regimes Required by Arms Control Treaties 902
  D. Due Process, Equal Protection, and Taking of Property (Fifth
     Amendment) 905
    1. U.S. Criminal Investigation of Noncitizens Abroad 907
    2. U.S. Abduction of Noncitizens Abroad for U.S. Prosecution 910
    3. U.S. Civil or Criminal Actions Against Noncitizens Located
       Abroad 914
    4. Equal Protection for Noncitizens in the United States 916

	5.	Taking of Property Without Just Compensation	919
	6.	Liberty of Travel to and from the United States	929
	7.	Military Detention of Noncitizens Abroad	931
E.	Trials (Sixth Amendment)		935
	1.	Right to a Speedy U.S. Trial for Noncitizen Located Abroad	937
	2.	Post-Indictment Right of Counsel for Noncitizen Located Abroad	938
	3.	Right to Confront and Compel Testimony of Witnesses Located Abroad	938
	4.	Trial by Military Commission	940
F.	Prohibition on Cruel and Unusual Punishment (Eighth Amendment)		942
G.	Equal Protection Under the Law (Fourteenth Amendment)		945
	1.	Lawful Permanent Residents	946
	2.	Nonimmigrant Noncitizens	949
	3.	Undocumented Noncitizens	950
	4.	Possible Application of Rational Basis Review	951

III. Rights Arising in Certain Subject-Matter Areas   953

A.	Immigration Law		953
	1.	Constitutional Underpinnings	953
	2.	Admission of Nonimmigrants and Immigrants	961
	3.	Refugees and Asylum Seekers	968
		a. Refugees	968
		b. Asylum Seekers	970
	4.	Removal and Non-refoulement	974
	5.	Loss of U.S. Citizenship	979
B.	Transnational Family Law		982
	1.	International Child Abduction	982
	2.	International Adoption	985
	3.	International Child Support and Maintenance Obligations	987
C.	Extradition		989

Index   997

Foreword

The Law of U.S. Foreign Relations is extraordinary in every respect. It is a comprehensive and necessarily lengthy exposition and analysis of that law, whose complexity is set forth with lucid clarity. The well-written main text is a pleasure to read; the supporting footnotes enrich the text. Its unflinching judgments are balanced and sound. The tensions between presidential authority and senatorial advice and consent are fairly and fully examined. No significant issue of the law of U.S. foreign relations is overlooked.

All this is not to say that the practice of the United States in applying its foreign relations law is sound. A glaring deficiency is the decay in its ratification of treaties. The United States plays a leading part in the negotiation of treaties, bilateral and multilateral. But its failure to ratify treaties has reached disheartening proportions. Two examples out of scores are these.

The Vienna Convention on the Law of Treaties (VCLT) was the product of the International Law Commission of the United Nations in its early years when its membership glowed with distinction.[1] British special rapporteurs of outstanding capacity—Brierly, Lauterpacht, Fitzmaurice, and Waldock—produced a series of reports and a draft convention that stimulated intense study by international lawyers the world over, including a study group of the American Society of International Law that comprised international legal luminaries of the nation. The VCLT was duly completed and adopted by sessions of a conference of plenipotentiaries. The president of the United States submitted it to the Senate for its advice and consent. No consequential objection to any of its provisions emerged then or thereafter. It has been ratified by the great majority of states. But not by the United States, for unaccountable reasons. The State Department has been reduced to stating that provisions of the VCLT reflect customary international law.

The U.N. Convention on the Law of the Sea is the product of the most extensive and intensive process of treaty-making in world history.[2] The United States played a leading role—if not the leading role—in that demanding process. Outstanding Republican statesmen and international lawyers, such as John

---

[1] Vienna Convention on the Law of Treaties, May 23, 1969, 8 I.L.M. 679, 1155 U.N.T.S. 331 (entered into force Jan. 27, 1980, not ratified).

[2] U.N. Convention on the Law of the Sea, Dec. 10, 1982, S. TREATY DOC. No. 103-39 (1994), 1833 U.N.T.S. 397 (entered into force Nov. 16, 1994, not ratified).

R. Stevenson, Elliot Richardson, Professor Bernard Oxman (who was chairman of the Convention's English-language drafting committee), and Professor John Norton Moore, led U.S. participation. It is rumored that a sole, obscure opponent of U.S. ratification on deep seabed exploitation grounds has been able to block Senate ratification, despite vigorous support of the U.S. Navy for ratification. The United States criticizes the People's Republic of China for violating provisions of a treaty that the United States seems unable to ratify.

Difficulties of ratification in these and too many other instances go back to fundamental provisions of the U.S. Constitution that require a positive vote of two-thirds of the Senate present and voting (a proposed requirement of three-quarters was put aside during the Constitution's enactment). The Constitution affords each state two senators, regardless of population. The upshot is that ratification of treaties is hostage to a fraction of the population of the United States.

To a significant extent, this blockage has been sidestepped by other modes of U.S. adherence to international accords—ways examined searchingly by the authors of this volume. But the impasse on treaty ratification so famously illustrated by U.S. failure to ratify the 1919 Treaty of Versailles retains its importance, as the foregoing two examples indicate. The painful fact is that adherence to international treaties by the United States is singularly crippled. There is ground to ask how long the influence of the United States in the negotiation of treaties can last in the face of this expanding record of failure to ratify.

The failure to ratify treaties and the development of alternative modes of agreement are an important characteristic of U.S. foreign relations law practice, but of course there exists a wide array of complex issues in this area of the law, each of which require close scrutiny of constitutional text, statutes, case law, and associated practice. By providing that scrutiny, *The Law of U.S. Foreign Relations* is certain to become a handbook of the executive branch, especially within the Office of the Legal Adviser of the State Department, and of Congress, notably for the Senators and staff of the Senate Committee on Foreign Relations. It will be the source of first and often last resort of national and international judges, foreign ministries the world over, and other practitioners and scholars in the field. All will find it to be an indispensable guide to understanding the subtleties of the law of the foreign relations of the United States.

STEPHEN M. SCHWEBEL
Former President of the International Court of Justice
Former Deputy Legal Adviser, U.S. Department of State

General Preface

Since the founding of the American republic, law has governed the foreign relations of the United States. While a discrete field of "U.S. foreign relations law" was not widely recognized until the second half of the twentieth century,[1] the topics it addresses have always been indispensable to nationhood. The powers to go to war, to seize foreign nationals and property, to regulate immigration, or to impose economic sanctions on foreign states have obvious consequences for the present and future well-being of the nation. The same is true for the powers to conclude arms control or environmental treaties, to recognize new foreign entities as "states" (or new foreign governments that seize power unconstitutionally), to open U.S. courts for the vindication of human rights claims, to join or withdraw from international organizations, or to accept as binding decisions of those organizations or of international courts.

What powers may the federal government exercise in this area of the law? To which branch of government are such powers assigned? If shared, how are such powers to be balanced? When, if at all, may the federal courts intercede to arbitrate as between the political branches, or to check them when acting in concert? Where do the several states fit into this scheme? When are treaties "self-executing" in the United States and what consequences flow from that status? When is customary international law a part of U.S. law? How do such sources fit within the hierarchy of U.S. legal sources?

In recent decades, various treatises and countless law review articles have addressed these and related questions from theoretical, doctrinal, and practical perspectives. In writing this volume, we benefited greatly from such works and sought to synthesize and build upon them. An especially influential treatise was Louis Henkin's *Foreign Affairs and the Constitution*, first published in 1972 at the height of U.S. involvement in the Vietnam War, and reissued in a second edition in 1996 under the title *Foreign Affairs and the United States Constitution*. We are not so presumptuous as to aim at succeeding Professor Henkin's work,

---

[1] The term "U.S. foreign relations law" became more broadly recognized with the project resulting in the *Restatement (Second) of the Foreign Relations Law of the United States*. See *Evolution of International Law in the 20th Century: Reports on Regional Meetings: American Points of View and Practice: Report*, 50 AM. SOC'Y INT'L L. PROC. 26, 27 (1956) (remarks of Covey Oliver) (describing project's initiation, and explaining "foreign relations law of the United States" as "being an amalgam of some aspects of constitutional law, of public international law, plain old corridor practice and 'international lawyering'").

but our objective in this treatise is similar: to provide a thorough single-volume source of guidance to government lawyers, judges, scholars, practitioners, and advanced students interested in the foreign relations law of the United States. As even Professor Henkin found, it is impossible to discuss all of U.S. foreign relations law in a single volume. We were selective in the topics we address and with respect to the issues within those topics.

Having spent years researching and writing this volume, we are very glad to see it finally come to print. We hope that it proves of use to its readers and welcome suggestions for its improvement.

SEAN D. MURPHY
EDWARD T. SWAINE

Methodological Preface

Our principal objective in this volume was to describe U.S. foreign relations law and only secondarily to provide our normative perspective on the path that law should take. This descriptive focus simplified our task. For example, if Supreme Court precedent addressed a question or the lower courts established a stable consensus, we sought to describe the cases and their holdings. Of course, a case, or a constitutional or statutory provision, may pose difficult interpretive questions; there, we aimed to highlight the issue and, where appropriate, suggested what seemed to us the better answer. For better or for worse, the field of foreign relations law also involves many questions that have not been resolved by courts (and may never be). Here, too, we tried to provide tentative and balanced answers.

Given our descriptive objectives, we did not attempt to establish or describe any comprehensive methodology. Nevertheless, it may be useful to disclose some of our overarching methodological approaches in writing this volume.

I. Constitutional Law

This is not a treatise on the U.S. Constitution or constitutional theory, but constitutional law is a fundamental component of U.S. foreign relations law. As indicated, our initial guide on these matters was judicial doctrine. Not only is precedent a widely accepted basis for resolving legal questions in U.S. law, including for the political branches, but it tends to approximate the results that would follow from other mainstream interpretive methods.[1]

At least where matters are not resolved by precedent, it is common to turn to the constitutional text, even if that leaves many critical questions unresolved,[2] and then to history. Pre-constitutional experience surely matters. The founding generation often looked to British practice: it is sometimes hard to say with

---

[1] To use Akhil Amar's terms, then, the approach we take is closer to doctrinarism than documentarian. Akhil Reed Amar, *Foreword: The Document and the Doctrine*, 114 Harv. L. Rev. 26, 26–27 (2000).

[2] This is a common impression. *See, e.g.,* Henkin, Foreign Affairs, at 13–14, 15 ("[W]here foreign relations are concerned the Constitution seems a strange, laconic document . . . many powers of government are not mentioned"). For an invaluable, comprehensive attempt to find textual answers, see Michael D. Ramsey, The Constitution's Text in Foreign Affairs (2007).

confidence whether Americans were seeking to break from that experience or to ensure continuity, but it certainly informed their terminology and understanding of legal alternatives. The founding generation was also influenced by more immediate matters, notably the experiences of the colonies prior to independence, of the Continental Congresses, and under the Articles of Confederation.[3] From the founding itself, a variety of materials might illuminate the text. The records of the 1787 Constitutional Convention, while a primary reference for lawyers and constitutional scholars, have important deficiencies. The official records of the convention were incomplete and largely unavailable during the founding period (having been deposited with the Department of State in 1796 and first published only in 1819).[4] Madison's notes, while more detailed, were revised by him over a longer period of time and only published fifteen years after his death, and thus are less salient to public understanding in 1787 and its immediate aftermath.[5] While potentially informative, neither of these two sources was intended to function (nor could they function) as authoritative guides to constitutional interpretation.[6]

Publications that sought to influence subsequent consideration of the Constitution, like the *Federalist Papers* and Anti-Federalist rejoinders, sometimes provide insight, though they are obviously partisan and were not uniformly read by all those involved in ratifying the Constitution.[7] Last, and definitely not least, are records of the state ratification conventions, which despite their own deficiencies may be favored over those of the constitutional convention itself.[8] This and other indicia of what might be called the "original understanding" may be probative, even if not determinative.[9]

---

[3] *See, e.g.*, Gregory E. Maggs, *A Concise Guide to the Articles of Confederation as a Source for Determining the Original Meaning of the Constitution*, 85 Geo. Wash. L. Rev. 397 (2017) (discussing various types of claims that might be made about the interpretive significance of the Articles).

[4] Journal, Acts and Proceedings of the Convention, Assembled at Philadelphia, Monday, May 14, and Dissolved Monday, September 17, 1787, which Formed the Constitution of the United States (John Quincy Adams ed., 1819).

[5] The Papers of James Madison (1841).

[6] *See* Mary Sarah Bilder, Madison's Hand: Revising the Constitutional Convention (2015); Mary Sarah Bilder, *How Bad Were the Official Records of the Federal Convention?*, 80 Geo. Wash. L. Rev. 1620 (2012); Gregory E. Maggs, *A Concise Guide to the Records of the Federal Constitutional Convention of 1787 as a Source of the Original Meaning of the U.S. Constitution*, 80 Geo. Wash. L. Rev. 1707 (2012).

[7] Gregory E. Maggs, *A Concise Guide to the Federalist Papers as a Source of the Original Meaning of the United States Constitution*, 87 B.U. L. Rev. 801 (2007).

[8] *See* Jack Rakove, Original Meanings: Politics and Ideas in the Making of the Constitution 16–18 (2010). Some of the qualifications are discussed in Gregory E. Maggs, *A Concise Guide to the Records of the State Ratifying Conventions as a Source of the Original Meaning of the U.S. Constitution*, 2009 U. Ill. L. Rev. 457; *see also* H. Jefferson Powell, *The Modern Misunderstanding of Original Intent*, 54 U. Chi. L. Rev. 1513, 1531–42 (1987) ("[T]he records of the Constitution's framing and ratification vary wildly in their reliability . . .").

[9] *Cf.* H. Jefferson Powell, *The Original Understanding of Original Intent*, 98 Harv. L. Rev. 885, 903–04 (1985) (noting that the Framers themselves expected that future interpretation would be guided by constitutional text rather than extratextual records).

We used subsequent political practice, embedded in the historical de-velopment of the nation since its founding, recognizing that this, too, may confront methodological challenges.[10] Courts often do not have the opportunity or inclination to resolve foreign-relations issues, so the po-litical branches are often left to sort things out for themselves.[11] Early en-gagement by the political branches illuminates both their understanding of the Constitution and their attempts to transform it.[12] Longstanding accommodations between the political branches almost certainly con-tribute to constitutional meaning, though it may be difficult to determine when these practices should be viewed as establishing legal constraints on future behavior.[13]

In assessing such practices, we prioritized public, authoritative declarations from either branch, such as presidential statements, legislation, and resolutions, over positions expressed by lower-level executive officials, congressional committees, or individual members of Congress. We also favored positions that were consistently expressed (or at least implied) across administrations and periods of history, rather than occurring in isolation. Implications from inac-tion, however, tend to be more fraught: while courts are often tempted to infer congressional acquiescence from inaction following executive branch practice, members of Congress face greater obstacles to expressing authoritative views on constitutional questions and relatively modest incentives to defend legislative prerogatives. As such, we generally attribute little significance to silence from either branch, but particularly little to congressional silence. Of course, there is a range of behavior between authoritative actions and acquiescence. Congress and the Senate may deny appropriations for activities that members regard as objectionable or refuse consent to the appointment of officials. The executive branch may underenforce legislative measures (or, for that matter, conform with measures to which it ostensibly objects). Finally, even executive and legislative materials that are of only modest interest in demonstrating acquiescence—for example, opinions of the Department of Justice's Office of Legal Counsel or

---

[10] For a thoughtful evaluation, see Curtis A. Bradley & Trevor W. Morrison, *Historical Gloss and the Separation of Powers*, 126 HARV. L. REV. 411 (2012).

[11] *See, e.g.*, Goldwater v. Carter, 444 U.S. 996, 1004 (1979) (Rehnquist, J., concurring in the judg-ment) (describing termination of treaties as "a dispute between coequal branches of our Government, each of which has resources available to protect and assert its interests").

[12] *See, e.g.*, JONATHAN GIENAPP, THE SECOND CREATION: FIXING THE AMERICAN CONSTITUTION IN THE FOUNDING ERA (2018) (emphasizing activities of the first Congress); *see also* DAVID P. CURRIE, THE CONSTITUTION IN CONGRESS: THE FEDERALIST PERIOD, 1789–1801 (1996).

[13] Thus, a widely referenced opinion in *Youngstown* adverted to "a systematic, unbroken, exec-utive practice, long pursued to the knowledge of the Congress and never before questioned"—an ostensibly demanding test, but without detail as to what constitutes an "executive practice" or what it means to have been "questioned." Youngstown Sheet & Tube Co. v. Sawyer, 343 U.S. 579, 610 (1952) (Frankfurter, J., concurring).

reports by the Congressional Research Service—may be valuable as syntheses of institutional positions or persuasive in their own right.

II. Statutory Law, Regulations, and Executive Orders

Once U.S. foreign relations legislation becomes law, it is published by the Archivist of the United States as "slip law" and in *U.S. Statutes at Large*, and then codified in scattered sections of the *U.S. Code* (though often in Title 22). Such law is also collected together in a publication of the Congressional Research Service entitled *Legislation on Foreign Relations*, a five-volume, annotated compendium of legislation that also includes relevant executive orders and international agreements. Although at one time prepared annually by the Congressional Research Service for the Senate Committee on Foreign Relations and House Committee on Foreign Affairs, the compendium is now updated less regularly. For the most part, however, we have cited to the *U.S. Statutes at Large* or to the *U.S. Code*, as appropriate; federal regulations implementing these laws have been cited to the *Code of Federal Regulations*,[14] while related executive orders and rules are cited to the *Federal Register*.

III. International Law

This volume is not about international law as such. Yet whether and how that law becomes a part of U.S. law and how it influences the conduct of U.S. foreign relations are central questions for U.S. foreign relations law. Two sources of international law play a particularly prominent role.

The first, customary international law, is formed by widespread, representative, and consistent state practice undertaken out of a sense of legal obligation. Customary international law historically has played a role with respect to U.S. law: sometimes used when interpreting the U.S. Constitution or U.S. statutes; sometimes directly incorporated into U.S. law by statute; or sometimes applied as part of federal common law. It is not necessary, for our purposes, to discuss the persistent methodological questions relating to the identification of customary international law, save to the extent they inform national rules regulating the roles of various U.S. actors. Nor is it necessary to examine the vast array of specific rules of customary international law, save for those that heavily

---

[14] *See especially* Title 8 (Aliens and Nationality); Title 15 (Commerce and Foreign Trade); Title 19 (Customs Duties); Title 22 (Foreign Relations); Title 32 (National Defense); Title 33 (Navigation and Navigable Waters); and Title 46 (Shipping).

influence U.S. law, such as rules concerning foreign sovereign and foreign official immunity.

The second source of international law, treaties, is relevant in much the same way. Our principal concern in this volume was whether and how treaties—a term we generally used interchangeably with "international agreements" (while using "Article II treaties" and similarly specific terms when discussing types of U.S. agreements)—become part of U.S. law or influence the conduct of U.S. foreign relations. We note, without discussing extensively, the international law of treaties as it bears on issues like the formation, operation, or termination of treaties. As to these and similar questions, we draw primarily on the Vienna Convention on the Law of Treaties (referred to herein as the "Vienna Convention" or "VCLT");[15] as discussed in Chapter 6, while the United States is not a party to the Vienna Convention, U.S. officials and courts (among others) generally regard it as reflecting customary international law. We do note instances in which international law remains unresolved or unclear notwithstanding the VCLT, and sometimes note instances in which the U.S. government has signaled its acceptance of a particular VCLT or other treaty-law rule, not least because those views may be highly influential for U.S. courts.

IV. Use of the American Law Institute's Restatements on U.S. Foreign Relations Law

The American Law Institute (ALI) has published three restatements on the "foreign relations law of the United States." The first of these restatements was a single volume published in 1965 during the period when the ALI was issuing its "second" restatement series, and hence was designated as the *Restatement (Second) of the Foreign Relations Law of the United States*. The second of these restatements was a two-volume edition published in 1987, entitled the *Restatement (Third) of the Foreign Relations Law of the United States*. In 2018, the ALI completed work on three discrete topics for the *Restatement (Fourth)*, on which one of us served as a reporter and the other as an advisor: that work addressed the status of treaties in U.S. law; exercise of U.S. jurisdiction (and recognition and enforcement of judgments); and immunity of foreign states from U.S. jurisdiction.[16] For topics not yet addressed by the *Restatement (Fourth)*, the

---

[15] Vienna Convention on the Law of Treaties, art. 2(1)(a), May 23, 1969, 8 I.L.M. 679, 681, 1155 U.N.T.S. 331 (entered into force Jan. 27, 1980, not ratified) [hereinafter VCLT]. A separate agreement addresses agreements involving international organizations. Vienna Convention on the Law of Treaties Between States and International Organizations or Between International Organizations, Mar. 21, 1986, 25 ILM 543, U.N. Doc. A/CONF.129/15.

[16] *See generally* G. Edward White, *From the Third to the Fourth Restatement of Foreign Relations: The Rise and Potential Fall of Foreign Affairs Exceptionalism, in* THE RESTATEMENT AND

relevant provisions of the *Restatement (Third)* remain the ALI's most recent, and most authoritative, position.[17]

These restatements skillfully describe rules of U.S. foreign relations law falling within the field as they perceive it.[18] As many of the same topics are discussed in this volume, and because the restatements are influential with U.S. officials and U.S. courts, we address relevant restatement provisions frequently. It should be noted, however, that while the restatements are prepared by a U.S. professional society, through a process in which U.S. government lawyers often participated, the restatements do not purport to codify rules accepted by the U.S. government and therefore should not be viewed themselves as evidence of U.S. government practice. Furthermore, the more comprehensive *Restatement (Third)* is also more than thirty years old at this point and so may be somewhat less reliable as a description of U.S. approaches, even if in many regards it is still highly persuasive. Finally, there are important topics of U.S. foreign laws addressed here, like war powers, that the restatements have never addressed.

V. Comparative Foreign Relations Law

Comparative foreign relations law can be a fruitful avenue of inquiry for understanding a given nation's system. Part of the reason is historical: for the United States, for example, British foreign relations law prior to 1776 or 1789 helps clarify what those framing the Articles of Confederation and the U.S. Constitution, respectively, would have evaluated when crafting the U.S. law of foreign relations. Beyond that, however, the contemporary foreign relations law of the United Kingdom and of other countries may illuminate approaches or techniques that are successful (or unsuccessful) elsewhere. For example, when considering the incorporation of international law into U.S. law, there may be value in considering whether and how foreign states do so through their own constitutions.[19]

Nonetheless, for reasons of space and clarity, this volume only infrequently compares U.S. foreign relations law to the foreign relations law of other countries

---

BEYOND: THE PAST, PRESENT, AND FUTURE OF U.S. FOREIGN RELATIONS LAW 23 (Paul B. Stephan & Sarah A. Cleveland eds., 2020).

[17] *E.g.*, RESTATEMENT (FOURTH), Part I (International Law and Its Relation to United States Law), Note at 3 (expressing this view with respect to Part I of the *Restatement (Third)*).

[18] *See* RESTATEMENT (THIRD) § 1; *see also* Edward T. Swaine, *Consider the Source: Evidence and Authority in the Fourth Restatement, in* THE RESTATEMENT AND BEYOND: THE PAST, PRESENT, AND FUTURE OF U.S. FOREIGN RELATIONS LAW, *supra* note 16, at 512–13 & nn.12–13 (noting potential variation in the approach taken by the *Restatement (Fourth)*, in view of the draft Reporters' Memorandum, Section 1: Definition of the Foreign Relations Law of the United States).

[19] *See, e.g.*, Tom Ginsburg et al., *Commitment and Diffusion: How and Why National Constitutions Incorporate International Law*, 2008 ILL. L. REV. 201.

and invokes the latter only infrequently. For readers interested in pursuing such issues further, *The Oxford Handbook of Comparative Foreign Relations Law* is a terrific compendium, edited by Curtis Bradley, that analyzes common topics addressed by a wide range of states worldwide.[20] Campbell McLachlan's treatise on *Foreign Relations Law* focuses on four Anglo-Commonwealth states, namely Australia, Canada, New Zealand, and the United Kingdom.[21] Hans Michelmann's *Foreign Relations in Federal Countries* provides a comparative perspective on the conduct of foreign relations and foreign policy in twelve federal countries.[22] The foreign relations law of the European Union, as a supranational institution, is the subject of numerous books and articles.[23] Other studies, like *National Treaty Law and Practice*, focus specifically on treaty practice in the national laws of various states.[24] Still other studies, like this volume, focus on the foreign relations law of a particular foreign state, such as the foreign relations law of China,[25] France,[26] Germany,[27] India,[28] Iran,[29] Japan,[30] Russia,[31] or the United Kingdom.[32]

---

[20] THE OXFORD HANDBOOK OF COMPARATIVE FOREIGN RELATIONS LAW (Curtis Bradley ed., 2019); *see also* William E. Butler, *Foreign Relations Law as State Practice, in* PERESTROIKA AND INTERNATIONAL LAW 109 (W.E. Butler ed., 1990) (discussing the definition of "foreign relations law" and the status it occupies among other fields of law).

[21] CAMPBELL MCLACHLAN, FOREIGN RELATIONS LAW (2014).

[22] HANS MICHELMANN, FOREIGN RELATIONS IN FEDERAL COUNTRIES (2009).

[23] *See, e.g.,* EU FOREIGN RELATIONS LAW: CONSTITUTIONAL FUNDAMENTALS (Marise Cremona & Bruno de Witte eds., 2008); ROBERT SCHÜTZE, FOREIGN AFFAIRS AND THE EU CONSTITUTION (2014).

[24] NATIONAL TREATY LAW AND PRACTICE (Duncan B. Hollis et al. eds., 2005); *see also* WILLIAM E. BUTLER, THE LAW OF TREATIES IN RUSSIA AND THE COMMONWEALTH OF INDEPENDENT STATES (2002).

[25] *See* BJÖRN AHL, DIE ANWENDUNG VÖLKERRECHTLICHER VERTRÄGE IN CHINA (2009); ERIC C. IP, COMPARATIVE SUBNATIONAL FOREIGN RELATIONS LAW IN THE CHINESE SPECIAL ADMINISTRATIVE REGIONS (2016); Chen Yifeng, *The Treaty-Making Power in China: Constitutionalization, Progress and Problems,* 15 ASIAN Y.B. INT'L L. 43 (2009); Eric C. Ip, *Comparative Subnational Foreign Relations Law in the Chinese Special Administrative Region,* 65 INT'L. & COMP. L.Q. 953 (2016).

[26] *See* RENAUD DEHOUSSE, FÉDÉRALISME ET RELATIONS INTERNATIONALES: UNE RÉFLEXION COMPARATIVE (1991); ELISABETH ZOLLER, DROIT DES RELATIONS EXTERIEURES (1992).

[27] *See* VOLKER RÖBEN, AUSSENVERFASSUNGSRECHT: EINE UNTERSUCHUNG ZUR AUSWÄRTIGEN GEWALT DES OFFENEN STAATES (2007).

[28] BIMAL N. PATEL, THE STATE PRACTICE OF INDIA AND THE DEVELOPMENT OF INTERNATIONAL LAW: DYNAMIC INTERPLAY BETWEEN FOREIGN POLICY AND JURISPRUDENCE (2016).

[29] Ramin Moschtaghi, *The Relation between International Law, Islamic Law and Constitutional Law of the Islamic Republic of Iran—A Multilayer System of Conflict?, in* 13 MAX PLANCK Y.B. OF U.N. LAW 375 (2009), https://perma.cc/6YJD-CR4E (analysis of the relationship between Islamic law and international law from the perspective of both international law and Iranian national law); *see also* MUHAMMAD IBN AL-HASAN SHAYBANI, THE ISLAMIC LAW OF NATIONS: SHAYBANI'S SIYAR (Majid Khadduri trans., 1966) (discussing law relating to the historical and contemporary relations among Islamic nations and other states); YITZHAK REITER, WAR, PEACE AND INTERNATIONAL RELATIONS IN ISLAM (2011) (analysis of rulings of Islamic law issued by religious sages and clerics on issues of war and peace).

[30] Hiroshi Oda, *International Relations, in* JAPANESE LAW 443 (3d ed. 2009).

[31] *See* WILLIAM E. BUTLER, RUSSIAN FOREIGN RELATIONS AND INVESTMENT LAW (2006).

[32] *See, e.g.,* F.A. MANN, FOREIGN AFFAIRS IN ENGLISH COURTS (1986) (focusing on the relationship of the executive and the judiciary in matters involving foreign relations); CYRIL M. PICCIOTTO, THE RELATION OF INTERNATIONAL LAW TO THE LAW OF ENGLAND AND OF THE UNITED STATES OF AMERICA (1915).

VI.   Terminology

To avoid confusion and uncertainty, we favored terms that were already widely in use and tried to use them as consistently as possible. One potentially problematic term for U.S. foreign relations law is "state," which for most U.S. lawyers conjures up the idea of the fifty states, but for an international lawyer typically connotes a nation or country. We used the word in both senses, but referred to a "foreign state" or to "the several states" if the context would otherwise be ambiguous; we occasionally used the term "nation" or "country" if it better suited a particular context.

When discussing the law of the United States, as contrasted to international law, we normally used "national law" rather than "domestic" or "internal" law; of course, it was often necessary to refer more particularly to "federal law" or "state law." Rather than referring to "American" or "America," we usually referred to "U.S." or "United States," in recognition that there are many states that are part of the American hemisphere.

In contemporary international law, the term "war" has been replaced with "armed conflict," but the former remains a salient aspect of the U.S. Constitution, and so we referred to and analyzed the "war powers," while acknowledging as appropriate the interface with international law in this area. As explained in Chapter 10, there is a distinction between a "national" and a "citizen" of the United States, but nevertheless we typically referred to "citizens" when speaking of U.S. nationals. Foreign nationals were referred to as "noncitizens" rather than "aliens," and those in the United States without permission were referred to as "undocumented" rather than "illegal" noncitizens, given that the terms "alien" and "illegal" are increasingly considered demeaning and dehumanizing. When relevant to the discussion, we distinguished noncitizens in the United States based on their status, specifically "lawful permanent residents," "non-immigrant noncitizens" (such as tourists), and "undocumented noncitizens."

SEAN D. MURPHY
EDWARD T. SWAINE

Acknowledgments

Professors Murphy and Swaine wish to thank their many assistants over the years who have provided outstanding research in support of this volume: Nathalie Baker, Jeff Brundage, Marta Bylica, Bonnie Chen, Alden DiIanni-Morton, Alexis Dorner, Kelly Dunn, Samuel Haack, Patrick Hynds, John Knoblett, Grace Lee, William Logsdon, Hayden Pendergrass, Emily Pierce, Eleanor Ross, Jillian Timko, Andreia Trifoi, Lexi Utech, Maxwell Weiss, and Laura Withers. In particular, they wish to thank Leah Calabro, John Catalfamo, Taylor Kilpatrick, George Mackie, and Ryan Migeed for comprehensive assistance during the project's final phase.

Professors Murphy and Swaine also thank the library staff at George Washington University Law School (especially Lori Fossum, Herb Somers, and Traci Spackey), and the law school's deans for their support and encouragement. They also wish to thank the participants at various workshops where draft chapters were presented, including at the law school's Potomac Foreign Relations Law Roundtable.

Table of Short Forms for Commonly Cited Authorities

The following short forms—in addition to those indicated in *The Bluebook: A Uniform System of Citation* (20th ed. 2020)—are used throughout this volume.

Short Form Used in This Volume	Authority
DIGEST OF U.S. PRACTICE	*Digest of United States Practice in International Law* (1973–present) (covers developments during the year or years indicated in title; published online exclusively since 2011)
HENKIN, FOREIGN AFFAIRS	Louis Henkin, *Foreign Affairs and the U.S. Constitution* (2d ed. 1996)
FARRAND'S RECORDS	*The Records of the Federal Convention of 1787* (Max Farrand ed., 1937)
HACKWORTH DIGEST	Green Haywood Hackworth, *Digest of International Law* (1940–44) (eight volumes covering developments from 1906 to 1939)
MOORE DIGEST	John Bassett Moore, *A Digest of International Law* (1906) (eight volumes covering developments from 1776 to 1906)
RESTATEMENT (SECOND)	*Restatement (Second) of the Foreign Relations Law of the United States* (Am. Law. Inst. 1965)
RESTATEMENT (THIRD)	*Restatement (Third) of the Foreign Relations Law of the United States* (Am. Law. Inst. 1987)
RESTATEMENT (FOURTH)	*Restatement (Fourth) of the Foreign Relations Law of the United States* (Am. Law. Inst. 2018)
WHARTON DIGEST	Francis Wharton, *A Digest of the International Law of the United States* (2d ed. 1887) (three volumes covering developments from 1789 to 1886)
WHITEMAN DIGEST	Marjorie M. Whiteman, *Digest of International Law* (1963–73) (fifteen volumes covering developments from 1940 to 1960)

1

Allocating and Balancing Foreign Relations Powers

U.S. foreign relations law concerns the domestic law of the United States that has substantial significance for U.S. foreign affairs, as well as the incorporation of international law (principally in the form of treaties, customary international law, and certain acts of international organizations) into U.S. law.[1] Much of this law takes conventional forms easily recognized by any U.S. lawyer—provisions of the U.S. Constitution, federal statutes, executive branch orders and other actions, and judicial decisions, and sometimes also the laws operating in the several states. Moreover, these and more diverse sources contain concrete rules capable of driving outcomes in very predictable ways. Yet U.S. foreign relations law also reflects principles that are less conspicuous and where the outcome, in a given context, is less certain and more susceptible to political or national security concerns. As such, to understand fully this area of the law, it is important to consider not just its determinate, substantive rules, but also the procedures by which rules are formed and the practices of the relevant actors over time.[2]

This chapter provides an overall context for the field of U.S. foreign relations law. Section I considers the allocation of foreign relations powers, taking account of each of the key players: Congress, the president, the courts, and the states. The starting point is the U.S. Constitution, which grants to the federal government virtually all the relevant foreign relations powers, and concomitantly denies them to the several states.[3] Yet the Constitution leaves much unsaid, including at times which branch of the federal government is expected to exercise national authority. Such uncertainties are not necessarily due to a faulty constitutional design; many have observed that the Framers fully intended the sharing of power in many areas, including that of foreign relations, to be an enduring source of conflict among the branches. As Edwin Corwin famously observed,

---

[1] RESTATEMENT (THIRD) § 1.

[2] *See generally* CURTIS A. BRADLEY, INTERNATIONAL LAW IN THE U.S. LEGAL SYSTEM (3d ed. 2021); MICHAEL J. GLENNON, CONSTITUTIONAL DIPLOMACY (1990); HENKIN, FOREIGN AFFAIRS; JORDAN J. PAUST, INTERNATIONAL LAW AS LAW OF THE UNITED STATES (1996); MICHAEL D. RAMSEY, THE CONSTITUTION'S TEXT IN FOREIGN AFFAIRS (2007); JOHN M. ROGERS, INTERNATIONAL LAW AND UNITED STATES LAW (1999); PHILLIP R. TRIMBLE, INTERNATIONAL LAW: UNITED STATES FOREIGN RELATIONS LAW (2002).

[3] *See* Chapter 9.

"The Constitution, considered only for its affirmative grants of power capable of affecting the issue, is an invitation to struggle for the privilege of directing American foreign policy."[4]

. Given the sharing of foreign relations powers, Section II addresses their balancing. Due to certain inherent institutional advantages, the president is the dominant actor in the field of U.S. foreign relations law, but operates subject to important checks available to Congress and the courts. In balancing the exercise of foreign relations powers, much appears to depend on the posture of Congress vis-à-vis the president's action; does Congress support or oppose the president's action, or is Congress' position not manifest? Moreover, such balancing may unfold through a sequence of events that leaves a public record of the constitutional perspectives of the political branches, but that also has a less formal dimension. For example, Congress may adopt a law bearing on foreign relations; the president may respond by issuing a signing statement that rejects a particular provision of that law on constitutional grounds; Congress may follow by threatening to deny funds or other support; and the president may acquiesce, or the two branches may reach a behind-the-scenes compromise. Even if the two political branches are operating in lockstep, there are constitutional limits to the exercise of their power, most notably in relation to powers reserved to the several states and rights possessed by individuals.

Section III considers whether, in practice, the allocation and balancing of foreign affairs powers changes in a time of national crisis or emergency. In such situations, including an international armed conflict or a major terrorist attack, one might ask whether special latitude is accorded to the federal government that normally would not exist and, if so, what implications that may have for a constitutional democracy.

I. Allocating Foreign Relations Powers

The Constitution accords to Congress the larger share of enumerated powers directly or indirectly relating to foreign relations, while the president is accorded relatively few, some of which are shared with Congress. Even so, certain general powers of the president, in particular the vesting of the "executive power," loom large in this area. To a degree, foreign relations powers are also accorded to the courts, allowing them to decide disputes arising in this area, though they have also developed (and invoked) doctrines of abstention. In addition to the enumerated specific and general powers set forth in the Constitution, at times there has been reliance upon what appears to be "extraconstitutional" power in this area,

---

[4] EDWARD S. CORWIN, THE PRESIDENT: OFFICE AND POWERS 201 (5th ed. 1984).

derived from the existence of the United States as a sovereign nation. And while U.S. foreign relations powers are largely denied to the several states, they retain a robust role in this area, especially in the implementation of U.S. obligations under international law.

A. Congress

Scholars of the Constitution often observe that it accords to Congress far more enumerated powers over foreign relations as compared with those of the president.[5] First, the Constitution has several powers that focus directly on foreign affairs. For example, the power to regulate commerce with foreign nations,[6] like its counterpart relating to interstate commerce, "underlies a tremendously broad and varied array of U.S. legislation."[7] Congress also has the power to establish a uniform rule of naturalization;[8] the power to regulate the value of foreign coin;[9] and the power to define and punish piracies and felonies committed on the high seas and offenses against the law of nations.[10] The last of these powers, with its reference to the "law of nations," is the only place in the U.S. Constitution where specific mention is made of what we today refer to as "customary international law," though international law also informs the meaning of various words (such as "piracy" and "high seas") contained in the Constitution's enumerated powers.[11]

Second, Congress has a series of powers that fall generally under the rubric of "war powers."[12] These powers include the power to declare war;[13] the power to grant letters of marque and reprisal;[14] the power to make rules concerning captures on land and water;[15] the power to raise and support armies, subject to the limit that "no Appropriation of Money to that Use shall be for a longer Term than two Years";[16] the power to provide and maintain a navy;[17] the power to

---

[5] *See, e.g.,* Francis D. Wormuth & Edwin B. Firmage, To Chain the Dog of War: The War Power of Congress in History and Law 177 (1986). *See generally* Henkin, Foreign Affairs, at 63–82; Ramsey, *supra* note 2, at 197–256.

[6] U.S. Const. art. I, § 8, cl. 3; *see* Chapter 2 § IV.

[7] Anthony J. Colangelo, *The Foreign Commerce Clause*, 96 Va. L. Rev. 949, 950 (2010).

[8] U.S. Const. art. I, § 8, cl. 4; *see* Chapter 10 § III(A).

[9] U.S. Const. art. I, § 8, cl. 5; *see* Chapter 2 § V.

[10] U.S. Const. art. I, § 8, cl. 10; *see* Chapter 5 § I(B), § II(A), § IV.

[11] For a theory as to how the Constitution interacts with distinct branches of the law of nations, see Anthony J. Bellia, Jr. & Bradford R. Clark, The Law of Nations and the United States Constitution (2017); *see also* Anthony J. Bellia, Jr. & Bradford R. Clark, *The International Law Origins of American Federalism*, 120 Colum. L. Rev. 835 (2020). *See generally* Chapter 5.

[12] *See generally* Chapter 8.

[13] U.S. Const. art. I, § 8, cl. 11.

[14] *Id.*

[15] *Id.*

[16] *Id.,* cl. 12.

[17] *Id.,* cl. 13.

make rules for the government and regulation of the land and naval forces;[18] the power to provide for calling forth the militia to execute the laws of the union, suppress insurrections, and repel invasions;[19] the power to provide for organizing, arming, training, and disciplining the militia;[20] and the power to exercise exclusive authority over all federal forts, magazines, arsenals, dockyards, and other "needful" buildings.[21] Given that, at the time of the framing, the United States had only recently secured independence by means of war, and given the contemporary significance of war for settling international disputes and redressing violations of international law, the fact that the Constitution entrusted Congress with such comprehensive authority over war and peace speaks volumes about its central role in U.S. foreign relations more generally.[22]

Finally, Congress has certain broad constitutional powers that play a significant role in U.S. foreign relations. Thus, the broad constitutional power "to lay and collect Taxes, Duties, Imposts and Excises"[23] supports the taxation of U.S. nationals and corporations located or doing business abroad. Congress' power to "provide for the common Defence and general Welfare of the United States,"[24] often referred to as the "spending power," can be used to appropriate funds for a wide range of foreign relations activities, such as foreign aid. Congress also has the power to enact all laws "necessary and proper" to execute any federal power.[25] The broad powers of Congress to legislate for the nation (and to conduct oversight of the executive) allow it to participate extensively in the regulation of matters that concern U.S. foreign relations.[26]

As in other areas of law, U.S. courts have interpreted these congressional foreign affairs powers broadly whenever Congress chooses to act, unless there is an encroachment upon the president's power, or a specific constitutional limitation on congressional power or on federal power generally. For example, the Constitution specifically provides that the privilege of the writ of habeas corpus may not be suspended by Congress except in cases of rebellion "or Invasion,"[27] and that no preference shall be given in regulating commerce or raising revenue

---

[18] *Id.*, cl. 14.

[19] *Id.*, cl. 15.

[20] *Id.*, cl. 16.

[21] *Id.*, cl. 17.

[22] *See* ABRAHAM D. SOFAER, WAR, FOREIGN AFFAIRS, AND CONSTITUTIONAL POWER: THE ORIGINS 2–3 (1976).

[23] U.S. CONST. art. I, § 8, cl. 1.

[24] *Id.; see id.* § 9, cl. 7 ("No Money shall be drawn from the Treasury, but in Consequence of Appropriations made by Law . . ."); *see also* Chapter 2 § III.

[25] U.S. CONST. art. I, § 18.

[26] *See* Phillip R. Trimble, *The President's Foreign Affairs Power, in* FOREIGN AFFAIRS AND THE U.S. CONSTITUTION 39, 40 (Louis Henkin et al. eds., 1990).

[27] U.S. CONST. art. I, § 9, cl. 2.

to the ports of one state over another.[28] Federal power more generally, of course, is limited by the Bill of Rights.[29]

B. President

In contrast to Congress, the president is expressly allocated relatively few foreign relations powers under the Constitution.[30] The president serves as commander in chief of the armed forces and of the "Militia of the several States" (now the National Guard, which is under the dual control of the state governments and federal government).[31] Further, the president has the power to make treaties, provided that two-thirds of the senators present concur;[32] these treaties create U.S. rights and obligations under international law, but also become part of the "supreme Law of the Land" of the United States.[33] The president has the power to appoint ambassadors and other public ministers and consuls (again with the advice and consent of the Senate)[34] and the power to receive ambassadors and other public ministers.[35] These powers to "appoint" and "receive" serve as the foundation of a general power to conduct the foreign relations of the United States,[36] making the president both the "voice" and "ears" for U.S. interaction with foreign states and, of increasing importance, with international organizations.[37] Together with the power to make treaties, they also establish the president as the focal point for the making, interpreting, and terminating of international law as it relates to the United States, which in turn can have important effects on the U.S. legal system.[38]

To these specific foreign relations powers of the president may be added two general responsibilities: the vesting in the president of the "executive power"[39] and the president's duty to "take Care that the Laws be faithfully executed."[40]

---

[28] *Id.*, cl. 6.

[29] *See* Chapter 10 § II.

[30] *See generally* HENKIN, FOREIGN AFFAIRS, at 31–62; RAMSEY, *supra* note 2, at 135–93.

[31] U.S. art. II, § 2, cl. 1; *see* Chapter 8 § II(B).

[32] U.S. CONST. art. II, § 2, cl. 2.

[33] *Id.* art. VI, cl. 2. *See generally* Chapter 6.

[34] U.S. CONST. art. II, § 2, cl. 2.

[35] *Id.*, § 3.

[36] *See generally* Chapter 3.

[37] *See generally* Chapter 7.

[38] *See, e.g.,* MARK WESTON JANIS, AMERICA AND THE LAW OF NATIONS 1776–1939 (2010); MARK WESTON JANIS, THE AMERICAN TRADITION OF INTERNATIONAL LAW: GREAT EXPECTATIONS, 1789–1914 (2004). Presidential control of U.S. engagement with international law raises important issues regarding transparency and accountability. *See* Curtis A. Bradley & Jack L. Goldsmith, *Presidential Control over International Law*, 131 HARV. L. REV. 1201 (2018); Oona A. Hathaway, Curtis A. Bradley, & Jack L. Goldsmith, *The Failed Transparency Regime for Executive Agreements: An Empirical and Normative Analysis*, 134 HARV. L. REV. 629 (2020).

[39] U.S. CONST. art. II, § 1, cl. 1.

[40] *Id.*, § 3.

These provisions loom particularly large in the field of U.S. foreign relations law because many of the president's contemporary activities are difficult to attribute to more topical constitutional authorities, making it habitual for the executive to fall back on generalities.

With respect to the vesting of the executive power, the debate between Alexander Hamilton (as Pacificus) and James Madison (as Helvidius) over President George Washington's power to proclaim U.S. neutrality set the stage for conflicting views that remain today.[41] The Constitution provides Congress only with the "legislative Powers herein granted" by Article I, while Article II says the "executive Power shall be vested" in the president. For Hamilton, that indicated a grant of broad power to the president, to include not just executing laws adopted by Congress but also authority over foreign relations subject to a few exceptions (such as the Senate's role in the making of treaties).[42] At the same time, there is scant evidence that the Framers intended broadly to vest foreign affairs powers in the president, and the Supreme Court has declined to view the vesting clause in this way.[43] Even so, the vesting of executive power has been relied upon in other contexts,[44] and Hamilton's approach provides a basis

---

[41] *Compare* Curtis A. Bradley & Martin S. Flaherty, *Executive Power Essentialism and Foreign Affairs*, 102 MICH. L. REV. 545 (2004) (concluding that the "executive Power" was essentially a power to execute the laws), *and* Julian Davis Mortenson, *Article II Vests Executive Power, Not the Royal Prerogative*, 119 COLUM. L. REV. 1169 (2019) (finding that the power is solely to implement legal rules created by some other authority and provides no substantive foreign affairs authority to the president), *with* Steven G. Calabresi & Saikrishna B. Prakash, *The President's Power to Execute the Laws*, 104 YALE L.J. 541 (1994) (taking the contrary position); *see also* Ilan Wurman, *In Search of Prerogative*, 70 DUKE L.J. 93 (2020) (suggesting that the "executive power" plausibly included additional powers related to law execution, such as the ability to promulgate related regulations).

[42] Alexander Hamilton, Pacificus No. 1 (June 29, 1793), *reprinted in* 15 THE PAPERS OF ALEXANDER HAMILTON 33–43 (Harold C. Syrett & Jacob E. Cooke eds., 1969); *cf.* James Madison, Letters of Helvidius No. II, *in* 6 THE WRITINGS OF JAMES MADISON 152 (Gaillard Hunt ed., 1900–1910); *see* Chapter 8 § I(C)(1).

[43] *See infra* this chapter text accompanying notes 199–265 (discussing *Youngstown Sheet & Tube Co. v. Sawyer*); *see also* HENKIN, FOREIGN AFFAIRS, at 16. Disagreement about the scope of the Article II Vesting Clause was evident in *Morrison v. Olson*, 487 U.S. 654 (1988), where the Court upheld the constitutionality of a statute requiring the attorney general to apply for the appointment of an independent counsel after receiving a request from Congress, unless he or she determines that "there are no reasonable grounds to believe that further investigation or prosecution is warranted." 28 U.S.C. § 592(b)(1) (2018). Justice Scalia, alone in dissent, invoked the Vesting Clause, finding that the conduct of a criminal investigation is an exercise of purely executive power and that the statute deprived the president of exclusive control over the exercise of that power. *Id.* at 705–07 (Scalia, J., dissenting). The majority responded that such an argument "depends upon an extrapolation from general constitutional language which we think is more than the text will bear." *Id.* at 690 n.29.

[44] *See, e.g.*, United States v. Arthrex, Inc., 141 S. Ct. 1970 (2021) (invoking the Article II Vesting Clause when finding that statutory restrictions may not insulate administrative patent judges from the direction and supervision of the director of the Patent and Trademark Office); Seila Law LLC v. Consumer Financial Protection Bureau, 140 S. Ct. 2183, 2197, 2204–05 (2020) (holding that for-cause restriction of president's authority to remove the director of the Consumer Financial Protection Bureau violated the separation of powers, and invoking the vesting of executive power in the president, as well the president's "take care" responsibility); Myers v. United States, 272 U.S. 52 (1926) (relying on the Vesting Clause when holding that the president has the exclusive power of removing executive officers); *see also infra* this chapter notes 54–56. Of course, reliance upon a

for asserting the constitutionality of the vast foreign relations powers that the president, in fact, exercises in practice. In *Zivotofsky v. Kerry* (*Zivotofsky II*),[45] the Court was confronted with a statute providing that, when issuing a passport to a U.S. citizen born in the city of Jerusalem, the secretary of state shall, when requested, record the place of birth as "Israel."[46] The U.S. embassy in Israel was so requested, but declined to do so, citing the executive branch's longstanding position at that time of not recognizing any country as having sovereignty over Jerusalem. The Court found the statute as an unconstitutional encroachment upon the president's exclusive power to recognize a foreign sovereign.[47] After citing to constitutional clauses conferring this "recognition power" on the president, the Court stated that it "need not consider whether or to what extent the Vesting Clause, which provides that the 'executive Power' shall be vested in the President, provides further support for the President's action here."[48]

The president's duty to take care that U.S. laws are faithfully executed, for its part, appears to include many important forms of federal law relating to foreign relations: not just federal statutes but also relevant constitutional provisions and treaties.[49] Whether the duty extends to the faithful execution of particular executive lawmaking acts depends in part on whether they are consistent with other, hierarchically superior law. For example, a president's ability to act consistently with "take care" responsibilities, while acting inconsistently with a congressional statute, would depend on whether the law being "faithfully executed" can be directly supported by the Constitution.[50] Another potentially significant

---

"vesting" doctrine does not invariably favor the president, given that the legislative power is vested in Congress, U.S. Const. art. I, § 1 ("All legislative Powers herein granted shall be vested in a Congress . . ."), while the judicial power is vested in the courts. U.S. Const. art. III, § 1 ("The judicial power of the United States, shall be vested in one supreme Court, and in such inferior Courts as the Congress may from time to time ordain and establish.").

[45] 576 U.S. 1 (2015) (*Zivotofsky II*). For further discussion of *Zivotofsky II*, see *infra* this chapter §§ II(A)(2), II(C); Chapter 2 § II(C); and Chapter 3 § I(D). In an earlier decision, the Court found that the case was justiciable. *See* Zivotofsky v. Clinton, 566 U.S. 189 (2012) (*Zivotofsky I*). For further discussion of *Zivotofsky I*, see Chapter 4 § II(A).

[46] Foreign Relations Authorization Act, Fiscal Year 2003, § 214(d), Pub. L. No. 107-228, 116 Stat. 1350, 1366 (2002).

[47] *See* Chapter 3 § I(D).

[48] *Zivotofsky II*, 576 U.S. at 13–14. Justice Thomas, however, would have reached and applied the Article II Vesting Clause in support of upholding the president's power. *Id.*, 576 U.S. at 34–35, 40 (Thomas, J., concurring in the judgment in part and dissenting in part).

[49] *Cf.* Andrew Kent, Ethan J. Leib, & Jed Handelsman Shugerman, *Faithful Execution and Article II*, 132 Harv. L. Rev. 2111, 2136 (2019) (noting lack of any "confident answer to the question whether, in its original meaning, the faithful execution of 'the laws' commanded by the Take Care Clause encompasses only statutes of Congress, or something more—perhaps the Constitution, treaties, common law, or the law of nations, too"); Edward T. Swaine, *Taking Care of Treaties*, 108 Colum. L. Rev. 331, 342–59 (2008) (discussing general scope, but with particular regard to treaties).

[50] *Compare Zivotofsky II*, 576 U.S. at 28–32 (upholding executive branch refusal to list a U.S. citizen's place of birth as "Israel" on his U.S. passport, notwithstanding statutory mandate, on the basis that the statute unconstitutionally interferes with the president's recognition power under

qualification, relating to treaties, concerns whether a treaty provision's non-self-executing character, at least to the extent anticipated by the Senate and president, implicitly forecloses any "take care" authority.[51] Probably the greatest uncertainty concerns whether the "take care" duty includes faithfully implementing customary international law within the domestic sphere. Given the president's ability on the international plane to shape an emerging rule of customary international law, and (in principle) to persistently object to the application of an emerging rule to the United States, much may turn on whether the president is declining to implement domestically an applicable rule of customary international law, or instead is interpreting the rule as not applicable to the United States or as not susceptible to domestic incorporation.[52] In any event, the president's general duty to faithfully execute the law places him or her in a unique position for recognizing, interpreting, and applying law relevant to foreign relations.[53]

In some instances, the executive branch has argued that power also resides amid the "unitary executive" theory of the presidency. This theory is grounded in the vesting of the executive power in the president and the Take Care Clause, but its exact scope and meaning are contested. The less controversial claim is that, in order for the president to carry out his or her constitutional responsibilities, the president must be able to rely upon the faithful service of subordinate officials. To the extent that Congress or the courts interfere with the president's right to control or receive effective service from his or her subordinates within the executive branch, those other branches unconstitutionally limit the ability of the president to perform his or her constitutional function.[54] The more controversial claim is that the theory also supports an unenumerated but inherent executive

---

Article II), *with id.* at 79, 83–84 (Scalia, J., dissenting) (stressing, instead, presidential obligation to "take Care" that congressional legislation be faithfully executed).

[51] *See* Medellín v. Texas, 552 U.S. 491, 532 (2008). *See generally* Chapter 6 § IV(A)(3).

[52] *See generally* Chapter 5 §§ I(B)(2), II(B)(3), III(D).

[53] *But cf.* Jack Goldsmith & John F. Manning, *The Protean Take Care Clause*, 164 U. PA. L. REV. 1835, 1867 (2016) (concluding that "the Take Care Clause has been a placeholder for broad judicial judgments about the appropriate relations among the branches in our constitutional system," and faulting integrity of Supreme Court's jurisprudence); Swaine, *Taking Care of Treaties, supra* note 49, at 349–53 (suggesting "antiplenary principle" for construing Take Care Clause, so as to limit unfettered presidential invocation of related constitutional authority).

[54] *See, e.g.,* Seila Law LLC v. Consumer Financial Protection Bureau, 140 S. Ct. 2183, 2197, 2204–05 (2020); Opinion on Statute Limiting the President's Authority to Supervise the Director of the Centers for Disease Control in the Distribution of an AIDS Pamphlet, 12 Op. O.L.C. 47, 48 (1988); Steven G. Calabresi & Kevin H. Rhodes, *The Structural Constitution: Unitary Executive, Plural Judiciary*, 105 HARV. L. REV. 1153, 1165–68 (1992). For the theory in relation to congressional reporting requirements, see Chapter 2 § II(D). The theory's historical grounding is debatable. *Compare* STEVEN G. CALABRESI & CHRISTOPHER S. YOO, THE UNITARY EXECUTIVE PRESIDENTIAL POWER FROM WASHINGTON TO BUSH (2008) (finding historical support for the theory), *with* Lawrence Lessig & Cass R. Sunstein, *The President and the Administration*, 94 COLUM. L. REV. 1 (1994) (finding only limited historical basis for the unitary executive theory, but some normative appeal).

power of undefined but broad scope,[55] which some have dismissed as essentially advocating a "monarchical executive."[56]

Even if such aggressive interpretation of executive powers is untenable, it remains the case (as discussed in Sections II and III following) that an extraordinary amount of day-to-day U.S. governmental authority in the field of foreign relations is exercised by the executive branch. There are myriad factors that favor presidential power in this area, not the least of which are that the president alone controls the modern regulatory state[57] and further represents the United States in diplomatic relations and before U.S., foreign, and international courts.

C. Judiciary

The Constitution provides that the federal judicial power extends to all cases arising under treaties; cases affecting ambassadors, other public ministers and counsels; cases of admiralty and maritime jurisdiction; and controversies between a state (or its citizens) and foreign states (or their citizens).[58] Further, federal courts are vested with jurisdiction over matters arising under the Constitution and federal statutes, including as these relate to foreign relations. When interpreting statutes, federal courts will use certain presumptions or doctrines that call for consideration of international law, such as a presumption that Congress has not intended to violate international law.[59] Federal courts also apply federal common law in the interstices of codified law; one of the limited enclaves for doing so involves customary international law, at least in certain circumstances.[60]

Thus, U.S. courts regularly are called upon to decide matters touching on foreign relations, as seen in the numerous U.S. cases cited throughout this volume.[61]

---

[55] *See, e.g.*, JOHN YOO, THE POWERS OF WAR AND PEACE: THE CONSTITUTION AND FOREIGN AFFAIRS AFTER 9/11, at 18–19 (2005).

[56] FREDERICK A.O. SCHWARZ, JR. & AZIZ Z. HUQ, UNCHECKED AND UNBALANCED: PRESIDENTIAL POWER IN A TIME OF TERROR 157 (2007); *see* Martin S. Flaherty, *The Most Dangerous Branch*, 105 YALE L.J. 1725 (1996).

[57] *See, e.g.*, Kathryn A. Watts, *Controlling Presidential Control*, 114 MICH. L. REV. 683 (2016); Elena Kagan, *Presidential Administration*, 114 HARV. L. REV. 2245 (2001); Harold H. Bruff, *Presidential Management of Agency Rulemaking*, 57 GEO. WASH. L. REV. 533 (1989).

[58] U.S. CONST. art. III, § 2.

[59] Referred to as the "Charming Betsy doctrine." *See* Chapter 2 § II(E), Chapter 4 § IV(B)(1), and Chapter 5 § III(B)(3).

[60] *See* Chapter 5 § II.

[61] For general discussion of the role of U.S. courts in the context of foreign relations, see David Gray Adler, *Court, Constitution and Foreign Affairs, in* THE CONSTITUTION AND THE CONDUCT OF AMERICAN FOREIGN POLICY 19 (David Gray Adler & Larry N. George eds., 1996); JOSEPH D. BECKER, THE AMERICAN LAW OF NATIONS: PUBLIC INTERNATIONAL LAW IN AMERICAN COURTS (2001); STEPHEN BREYER, THE COURT AND THE WORLD: AMERICAN LAW AND THE NEW GLOBAL REALITIES (2015); HENKIN, FOREIGN AFFAIRS, at 131–48; INTERNATIONAL LAW IN THE U.S. SUPREME COURT: CONTINUITY AND CHANGE (David L. Sloss et al. eds., 2011); RAMSEY, *supra* note 2, at 321–76.

Yet U.S. courts are also urged to apply doctrines of abstention to avoid addressing on the merits cases concerning foreign relations.[62] In particular, U.S. courts may be called upon to invoke the "political question" doctrine to avoid second-guessing actions of Congress or the president in the field of foreign relations, leaving resolution of disputes between those branches to the political process.[63] Such arguments at times work, given that the Supreme Court has maintained that "the conduct of foreign relations is committed by the Constitution to the political departments of the Federal Government"[64] and that "[m]atters intimately related to foreign policy and national security are rarely proper subjects for judicial intervention."[65] Pursuant to the "act of state" doctrine, U.S. courts have declined to pass upon the legality of acts taken by foreign governments within their own territory, albeit subject to certain limitations.[66] Under the doctrine of "international comity," U.S. courts will sometimes defer to the judgment of a foreign forum, just as foreign fora at times will defer to U.S. courts.[67] The doctrine of *forum non conveniens* may be invoked by a court to dismiss a case when a foreign forum has jurisdiction to hear the case, and "trial in the chosen forum would establish . . . oppressiveness and vexation to a defendant . . . out of all proportion to plaintiff's convenience, or . . . the chosen forum [is] inappropriate because of considerations affecting the court's own administrative and legal problems."[68] Such abstention doctrines have sometimes been viewed as an aspect of "foreign relations exceptionalism," whereby courts refrain from addressing such disputes because, unlike cases involving domestic affairs, foreign relations disputes present issues for which courts are not well suited.[69]

---

[62] *See* BRADLEY, *supra* note 2, at 1–31; Jonathan I. Charney, *Judicial Deference in Foreign Relations*, in FOREIGN AFFAIRS AND THE U.S. CONSTITUTION, *supra* note 26, at 98; HAROLD HONGJU KOH, THE NATIONAL SECURITY CONSTITUTION: SHARING POWER AFTER THE IRAN-CONTRA AFFAIR 134–49 (1990); Jonathan L. Entin, *War Powers, Foreign Affairs, and the Courts: Some Institutional Considerations*, 45 CASE W. RES. J. INT'L L. 443 (2012).

[63] *See* Chapter 4 § II(A).

[64] United States v. Pink, 315 U.S. 203, 222–23 (1942); *see* Michael J. Glennon, *Foreign Affairs and the Political Question Doctrine*, in FOREIGN AFFAIRS AND THE U.S. CONSTITUTION, *supra* note 26, at 107; Linda Champlin & Alan Schwarz, *Political Question Doctrine and Allocation of the Foreign Affairs Power*, 13 HOFSTRA L. REV. 215 (1985); Lisa Rudikoff Price, *Banishing the Specter of Judicial Foreign Policymaking: A Competence-Based Approach to the Political Question Doctrine*, 38 N.Y.U. J. INT'L L. & POL. 323 (2006).

[65] Haig v. Agee, 453 U.S. 280, 292 (1981).

[66] *See* Chapter 4 § III.

[67] *See* Chapter 4 § IV(C).

[68] Sinochem Int'l Co. v. Malay. Int'l Shipping Corp., 549 U.S. 422, 429 (2007) (citing Am. Dredging Co. v. Miller, 510 U.S. 443, 447–48 (1994)).

[69] *See, e.g.*, Curtis A. Bradley, *Breard, Our Dualist Constitution, and the Internationalist Conception*, 51 STAN. L. REV. 529, 539 n.51 (1999); Jean Galbraith, *Treaty Termination as Foreign Affairs Exceptionalism*, 92 TEX. L. REV. 121, 123 (2014); John O. McGinnis, *Constitutional Review by the Executive in Foreign Affairs and War Powers: A Consequence of Rational Choice in the Separation of Powers*, 56 LAW & CONTEMP. PROBS. 293, 306–08 (1993).

Yet, as the numerous cases cited throughout this volume demonstrate, courts often *do* address on the merits cases relating to foreign relations, in the context of interbranch disputes, federalism disputes, and disputes concerning individual rights. Even the foundational case for the political question doctrine stressed that "it is error to suppose that every case or controversy which touches foreign relations lies beyond judicial cognizance."[70] Indeed, when the courts are being asked not "to supplant a foreign policy decision of the political branches" but, rather, to interpret the Constitution or a statute relating to a matter of foreign relations, then, in principle, they are being called upon to engage in a "familiar judicial exercise" for which they are well equipped.[71] Thus, while courts may at times act as a bystander, they also at times serve as umpire or protector, suggesting that the claims for "foreign relations exceptionalism" in this area may be overstated.[72]

D. Foreign Relations Powers Not Derived from the Constitution?

The idea that foreign relations powers not expressly enumerated in the Constitution nevertheless reside in the federal government has a pedigree in U.S. constitutional law.[73] When President Thomas Jefferson in 1803 concluded the Louisiana Purchase, whereby the United States nominally acquired a vast swath of the central part of the United States, he did so with the full support of Congress. Yet the power of the U.S. government to purchase or otherwise acquire territory is not expressly enumerated in the Constitution,[74] leading Jefferson himself to have doubts as to the constitutionality of his action.[75] Such acquisitions, when constitutionally challenged, have been upheld not only by reference to enumerated powers (such as on war or making of treaties), or to the "necessary and proper" clause or some other constitutional theory, but as

---

[70] Baker v. Carr, 369 U.S. 186, 211 (1962).

[71] Zivotofsky v. Clinton, 566 U.S. 189, 196 (2012) (*Zivotofsky I*). For further discussion of *Zivotofsky I*, see Chapter 4 § II(A).

[72] Ganesh Sitaraman & Ingrid Wuerth, *The Normalization of Foreign Relations Law*, 128 HARV. L. REV. 1897, 1906–19 (2015); Ernest A. Young, *Dual Federalism, Concurrent Jurisdiction, and the Foreign Affairs Exception*, 69 GEO. WASH. L. REV. 139, 140–41 (2001). *But see* Carlos M. Vázquez, *The Abiding Exceptionalism of Foreign Relations Doctrine*, 128 HARV. L. REV. F. 305 (2015) (finding that Sitaraman and Wuerth's "claim that exceptionalism is now exceptional seems overstated").

[73] HENKIN, FOREIGN AFFAIRS, at 16.

[74] The Constitution does provide for the admission of new states, U.S. CONST. art. IV, § 3, cl. 2, and for the administration of territory of the United States, *id.*, cl. 3. Such provisions might be read as extending beyond just power to administer existing territory, and to admit new states from that territory, to encompass implicitly a power to acquire new territory.

[75] Letter to John Breckenridge, 10 THE WRITINGS OF THOMAS JEFFERSON 407, 411; *see* Donald L. Robinson, *Presidential Prerogative and the Spirit of American Constitutionalism, in* THE CONSTITUTION AND THE CONDUCT OF AMERICAN FOREIGN POLICY, *supra* note 61, at 116; *see also* Chapter 6 § II(D)(2).

an attribute of U.S. sovereignty. Thus, when considering the constitutionality of a statute declaring U.S. acquisition of islands discovered by U.S. citizens that contain guano (an important source of fertilizer in the nineteenth century), the Supreme Court did not look to the expressly enumerated powers set forth in the Constitution. Rather, it said:

> By the law of nations, recognized by all civilized states, dominion of new territory may be acquired by discovery and occupation as well as by cession or conquest, and when citizens or subjects of one nation, in its name, and by its authority or with its assent, take and hold actual, continuous, and useful possession . . . of territory unoccupied by any other government or its citizens, the nation to which they belong may exercise such jurisdiction and for such period as it sees fit over territory so acquired. *This principle affords ample warrant for the legislation of Congress* concerning guano islands.[76]

Partial reliance on inherent sovereign powers also may be observed with respect to the federal government's authority to govern such territories (and the District of Columbia as well).[77]

In *Chae Chan Ping v. United States* (more widely known as the *Chinese Exclusion Case*), the Supreme Court was confronted with a challenge to a congressional statute that restricted the entry of Chinese laborers into the United States.[78] No such power to restrict immigration was expressly accorded to Congress in the Constitution; the closest was Congress' power to establish a uniform rule of naturalization (a power that, on its terms, solely encompasses how a noncitizen becomes a U.S. citizen). Nevertheless, the Court decided that the power to exclude noncitizens must be a federal power, given that "[j]urisdiction over its own territory to that extent is an incident of every independent nation. It is a part of its independence. If it could not exclude aliens it would be to that

---

[76] Jones v. United States, 137 U.S. 202, 212 (1890) (emphasis added); *see* Am. Ins. Co. v. Canter, 26 U.S. (1 Pet.) 511, 542 (1828).

[77] Sere v. Pitot, 10 U.S. (6 Cranch) 332, 336–37 (1810); Am. Ins. Co. v. Canter, 26 U.S. (1 Pet.) 511, 546 (1828); Late Corp. of Church of Jesus Christ of Latter-Day Saints v. United States, 136 U.S. 1, 42 (1890); *see also* U.S. CONST. art. IV, § 3, cl. 2 (regulation of territories); *id. art.* I, § 8, cl. 17 (regulation of the District). The presence of such inherent sovereign powers may explain why the power to govern territories is not bound by the Vesting Clauses of Articles I, II, and III. *See* Benner v. Porter, 50 U.S. (9 How.) 235, 242 (1850) (finding that territorial governments set up by Congress "are not organized under the Constitution, nor subject to its complex distribution of the powers of government, as the organic law; but are the creations, exclusively, of the legislative department.").

[78] Chae Chan Ping v. United States, 130 U.S. 581 (1889). The Page Act of 1875, ch. 141, Pub. L. No. 43-141, 18 Stat. 477 (1875) (also known as the Asian Exclusion Act), was the first restrictive U.S. immigration law, and effectively barred the entry of women from China (and of any "Oriental country"). The Chinese Exclusion Act of 1882, ch. 126, Pub. L. No. 47-126, 22 Stat. 58 (1882), at issue in *Chae Chan Ping*, curtailed immigration by Chinese men as well. For discussion of the case in the context of U.S. immigration law, see Chapter 10 § III(A). For an interesting reference in this case to the war power, see Chapter 8 § I(C)(1).

extent subject to the control of another power. . . ."[79] Such reasoning is grounded in the idea that the federal government, ultimately, is responsible for protecting the United States in its foreign relations; consequently, the government has the discretion to call forth certain powers to address perceived threats, whether relating to actual or potential armed conflict, or in lesser forms. According to the Court, moreover, the federal government also has the authority to decide when those powers should be invoked.[80]

The *Chinese Exclusion Case* and others like it, however, left important questions unanswered. For example, the conclusion that regulation of immigration is an inherent sovereign authority does not necessarily lead to the conclusion that such power must be exclusive to the national government, nor to the conclusion that such power be plenary. Moreover, as critics of the *Chinese Exclusion Case* have observed, the racial animus present in the adoption of the "Chinese exclusion" statutes of the time casts some amount of disrepute on the case.[81] Even Justice Field's majority opinion sought to distance itself from whether such exclusion was appropriate, viewing it as a matter for political and not judicial determination.[82]

In *United States v. Curtiss-Wright Export Corp.*, discussed further later,[83] the Supreme Court (per Justice George Sutherland) articulated a theory of the foreign relations power that was predicated on a distinctive historical narrative.[84] According to the Court, at the time of the American Revolution, the foreign relations power pertinent to the thirteen colonies transferred from the British government to the Continental Congress, and then in 1781, from the Second Continental Congress to the Congress of the Articles of Confederation. Upon ratification of the U.S. Constitution, such foreign relations power transferred from the Confederation Congress to the government created by the U.S. Constitution.[85]

---

[79] *Chae Chan Ping*, 130 U.S. at 603–04; *see also* Nishimura Ekiu v. United States, 142 U.S. 651, 659 (1892) ("It is an accepted maxim of international law, that every sovereign nation has the power, as inherent in sovereignty, and essential to self-preservation, to forbid the entrance of foreigners within its dominions . . . . In the United States this power is vested in the national government . . . .").

[80] *Chae Chan Ping*, 130 U.S. at 606.

[81] Louis Henkin, *The Constitution and United States Sovereignty: A Century of* Chinese Exclusion *and Its Progeny*, 100 HARV. L. REV. 853, 857 (1987); *see also id.* at 863 (concluding that "*Chinese Exclusion*—its very name is an embarrassment—must go"); T. Alexander Aleinikoff, *Citizens, Aliens, Membership and the Constitution*, 7 CONST. COMMENT 9, 11–12 (1990) (suggesting that *Chinese Exclusion* is "an embarrassment to constitutional law," part of a series of decisions that "upheld the shameful laws that excluded and deported Chinese laborers").

[82] *Chae Chan Ping*, 130 U.S. at 602–03.

[83] *See infra* this chapter text accompanying notes 168–191.

[84] United States v. Curtiss-Wright Export Corp., 299 U.S. 304, 315 (1936); *see* David M. Levitan, *The Foreign Relations Power: An Analysis of Mr. Justice Sutherland's Theory*, 55 YALE L.J. 467, 478 (1946).

[85] *Curtiss-Wright Export Corp.*, 299 U.S. at 316–17.

Two important consequences flowed from this narrative. First, since the foreign relations power was never possessed by each of the several states, it is not a power that was "delegated" to the federal government by those states. The Court maintained that "since the states severally never possessed international powers, such powers could not have been carved from the mass of state powers but obviously were transmitted to the United States from some other source."[86] As such, any elements of this foreign relations power not enumerated in the Constitution cannot be "reserved to" the states under the Tenth Amendment.

Second, the U.S. foreign relations power is *not* comprised solely of the various powers enumerated in the Constitution; other powers inextricably associated with "external sovereignty" also reside in the federal government and do "not depend upon the affirmative grants of the Constitution."[87] According to the Court, "the power to acquire territory by discovery and occupation, the power to expel undesirable aliens, the power to make such international agreements as do not constitute treaties in the constitutional sense, none of which is expressly affirmed by the Constitution, nevertheless exist as inherently inseparable from the conception of nationality."[88] In fact, the Court stated that the "powers to declare and wage war, to conclude peace, to make treaties, to maintain diplomatic relations with other sovereignties, if they had never been mentioned in the Constitution, would have vested in the federal government as necessary concomitants of nationality."[89] As such, while the Constitution's foreign relations powers enumerated in the Constitution are important, they do not exhaust the federal government's power in this area.

The Court's historical narrative in *Curtiss-Wright* has been sharply contested.[90] The Articles of Confederation that were crafted in the period prior to ratification

---

[86] *Id.* at 316.

[87] *Id.* at 318.

[88] *Id.* (citations omitted). The Court cited inter alia to Jones v. United States, 137 U.S. 202, 212 (1890) (the power to acquire territory); Fong Yue Ting v. United States, 149 U.S. 698, 705 (1893) (the power to expel undesirable noncitizens); B. Altman & Co. v. United States, 224 U.S. 583, 600–01 (1912) (the power to make international agreements that are not "treaties"). For a more recent indication of such powers, see Arizona v. United States, 567 U.S. 387, 394–95 (2012) (finding that the federal government's "power over the subject of immigration and the status of aliens" rests in part on "its inherent power as sovereign to control and conduct relations with foreign nations").

[89] *Curtiss-Wright Export Corp.*, 299 U.S. at 318. Left unexplained is why the Framers would have decided to mention many important foreign affairs powers in the Constitution if doing so was unnecessary. The answer might lie in the need to clarify which political branch was expected to exercise such power. Yet if that is the case, then presumably all relevant foreign affairs powers should be mentioned in the Constitution so as to clarify their allocation, unless there is an unstated presumption that any unmentioned foreign affairs powers simply require some form of collaboration by the political branches.

[90] *See* Ramsey, *supra* note 2, at 13–30; Charles A. Lofgren, United States v. Curtiss-Wright Export Corporation: *An Historical Reassessment*, 83 Yale L.J. 1, 32 (1973); *see also* Henkin, Foreign Affairs, at 19. *But see* Chisholm v. Georgia, 2 U.S. (2 Dall.) 419, 470–71 (1793); Richard B. Morris, *The Forging of the Union Reconsidered: A Historical Refutation of State Sovereignty over Seabeds*, 74 Colum. L. Rev. 1056, 1061–62 (1974).

of the Constitution are probably best understood as establishing a confederacy of thirteen sovereign states, not a single sovereign state to which Great Britain might feasibly have transferred external sovereignty. Indeed, the Articles expressly refer to a "confederacy" or "confederation" constituting a "firm league of friendship," one in which "each state *retains* its sovereignty, freedom and independence."[91] Rather than evidencing a single sovereign state, structural aspects of the Articles were akin to those of multilateral treaties among multiple sovereign states: delegates to the Congress were compensated by their own state governments;[92] each state had a single vote, rather than each representative having a vote;[93] and amendments required unanimous consent by all states.[94] While it is true that the Confederation Congress was given authority to speak and act on behalf of the states in foreign relations, such also was the case—as Akhil Amar has noted—for other eighteenth-century leagues of sovereign states, notably the Dutch and Swiss confederacies.[95] Further, the state constitutions enacted during this period support the view that the thirteen states viewed themselves as being sovereign and independent, not as a portion of a single sovereign state.[96]

The views expressed in *Curtiss-Wright* are not necessarily contingent on its historical account. To the extent a foreign relations power attaches to each sovereign state when it is formed, such power is not necessarily "received" or "delegated" from some other state. Rather, the power arguably arises as a necessary incident of the sovereignty of that particular state, operating within the realm of international law, and thus—in the case of the United States—did not depend on a delegation by the several states nor any express constitutional grant. Yet even on this approach, the Framers might be understood as having allocated many of these inherent foreign affairs powers to the federal government, but leaving all others to the several states. In other words, the fact that foreign affairs powers exist as a necessary incident of sovereignty does not resolve how the Constitution approaches their distribution as between the federal government and the states.

On balance, the express granting of important foreign affairs powers to the federal government, the denial of certain foreign affairs powers to the states (as discussed later), and the concerns from the Articles of Confederation period that drove the development of the Constitution all support the view that any

---

[91] ARTICLES OF CONFEDERATION OF 1781, arts. I, II, III (emphasis added).

[92] *Id.* art. V (prohibiting state delegates from holding any office under the United States).

[93] *Id.* art. V (providing "each State shall have one vote").

[94] *Id.* art. XIII.

[95] AKHIL REED AMAR, AMERICA'S CONSTITUTION: A BIOGRAPHY 27–28 (2005). For other accounts, see MERRILL JENSEN, THE ARTICLES OF CONFEDERATION 176 (1970); Claude H. Van Tyne, *Sovereignty in the American Revolution: An Historical Study*, 12 AM. HIST. REV. 529 (1907).

[96] *See, e.g.*, MASS. CONST. pt. I, art. IV ("The people of this commonwealth have the sole and exclusive right of governing themselves, as a free, sovereign, and independent state."); N.H. CONST. pt. I, art. VII (virtually identical).

unmentioned foreign affairs powers were likely intended to reside with the federal government. And that conclusion appears supported by subsequent practice in which the federal government exercised arguably "extraconstitutional" foreign relations powers.[97] Yet this leaves much unresolved about the nature and scope of those powers. An enduring uncertainty, as Louis Henkin cautioned, is that "we are not told [in the Constitution] how the undifferentiated bundle of federal powers inherent in sovereignty is distributed among the federal branches."[98] Often, as in the context of the Louisiana Purchase or the *Chinese Exclusion Case*, the assumption appears to have been that both political branches have a role to play in exercising the power, much as they participate in the exercise of a typical enumerated power. *Curtiss-Wright*, however, famously exalted the president's role, as discussed further later.[99] More certain is that any "extraconstitutional" powers are subject to constitutional prohibitions. For example, since the *Chinese Exclusion Case*, the Court has considered exercise of Congress' power relating to immigration as fully subject to the constitutional constraints of the Bill of Rights.[100]

Significantly, the prospect that national authority is estranged from the Constitution's text tends to enhance the role for international law in both enabling and in limiting such power. If an inherent power arises as "an incident of every independent nation,"[101] then it invites consideration of the attributes accorded to such power under international law. Moreover, in the *Chinese Exclusion Case*, the Court noted that the "sovereign powers" of the United States are restricted by "considerations of public policy and justice which control, more or less, the conduct of all civilized nations . . . ."[102] That oblique reference appears to acknowledge that any reliance on extraconstitutional power invariably must look to some source as a reference point for the power's existence and scope, which is best understood today as the rules present in international law.[103]

---

[97] *See, e.g.*, Chapter 2 § I(B) and Chapter 6 § V.

[98] HENKIN, FOREIGN AFFAIRS, at 22.

[99] *See infra* this chapter text accompanying notes 168–191.

[100] Chae Chan Ping v. United States, 130 U.S. 581, 604 (1889) (indicating that the sovereign power over immigration is "restricted . . . by the Constitution itself"); *see* Chapter 10 § III(A). That is not to say that the understanding of constitutional limits is necessarily generous or even consistent. *See* Sarah H. Cleveland, *The Plenary Power Background of* Curtiss-Wright, 70 U. COLO. L. REV. 1127, 1145–47 (1999).

[101] *Chae Chan Ping*, 130 U.S. at 603.

[102] *Id.* at 604.

[103] Sarah H. Cleveland, *Our International Constitution*, 31 YALE J. INT'L L. 1, 39 (2006); *see* Sarah H. Cleveland, *Powers Inherent in Sovereignty: Indians, Aliens, Territories, and the Nineteenth Century Origins of Plenary Power over Foreign Affairs*, 81 TEX. L. REV. 1, 7 (2002) (further elaboration of the thesis); *see also* Rebecca Ingber, *International Law Constraints as Executive Power*, 57 HARV. INT'L L. J. 49 (2016).

E. Federalism

This chapter is focused on the balancing of the federal foreign relations powers, not the relationship of the federal government to the several states, which is addressed extensively in Chapter 9. Still, in assessing that balance, it is important to acknowledge that the Constitution explicitly inhibited the role of the states in exercising foreign relations powers, thus appearing to reaffirm the residue of authority left to the federal government. The Constitution provides that no state shall enter into any "Treaty, Alliance, or Confederation," nor shall any state grant letters of marque and reprisal.[104] Further, no state without the consent of Congress may lay imposts or duties on imports or exports, except as necessary for its inspection laws.[105] Finally, no state shall, without the consent of Congress, "keep Troops, or Ships of War in time of Peace, enter into any Agreement or Compact with another State, or with a foreign Power, or engage in War, unless actually invaded, or in such imminent Danger as will not admit of delay."[106] To this must be added, of course, that federal law (including treaties and customary international law in the form of federal common law) binds the several states as "the supreme Law of the Land."[107]

These admonitions to the states, in conjunction with the express and implied foreign relations powers accorded to the federal government under the Constitution, might lead one to conclude that the states were expected to play little or no role in the exercise of foreign relations powers.[108] Certainly, U.S. constitutional history makes clear that important matters concerning foreign relations were intended to be dealt with under federal law. Those who gathered at the constitutional convention in Philadelphia were reacting, in large part, to the lack of effective control by the central government over foreign relations, to include the regulation of foreign commerce. Further, they were concerned with the resistance of state courts to the enforcement of the 1783 Treaty of Paris with Great Britain, which protected persons who had remained loyal to Britain and called for repayment of U.S. debts to them. The new federal government was designed to correct these and other deficiencies.[109]

---

[104] U.S. Const. art. I, § 10, cl. 1.

[105] *Id.*, cl. 2.

[106] *Id.*, cl. 3.

[107] *Id.* art. VI, cl. 2; *see* Chapters 6 § (I)(B)(2) and 7 § (I)(B).

[108] *See, e.g.,* Zschernig v. Miller, 389 U.S. 429, 436 (1968) (suggesting that "foreign affairs and international relations [are] matters which the Constitution entrusts solely to the Federal Government"); Hines v. Davidowitz, 312 U.S. 52, 63 (1941) ("The Federal Government . . . is entrusted with full and exclusive responsibility for the conduct of affairs with foreign sovereignties.").

[109] *See, e.g.,* The Federalist Nos. 1, 6, 8–9, 11, 21 (Alexander Hamilton), Nos. 2–5 (John Jay), No. 49 (James Madison); *see* Richard B. Bilder, *The Role of States and Cities in Foreign Relations*, 83 Am. J. Int'l L. 821, 821 (1989), *reprinted in* Foreign Affairs and the U.S. Constitution, *supra* note 26, at 115.

Even so, it is a mistake to view the several states (and substate entities, such as cities) as irrelevant to the exercise of U.S. foreign relations powers; indeed, the Constitution expressly envisages a role for the states in certain respects.[110] For example, states are permitted to enter into "compacts" with foreign states and substate entities, such as for the construction or maintenance of a transboundary bridge or road.[111] Moreover, as a practical matter, the states are deeply involved in aspects of U.S. foreign relations, such as the implementation of U.S. obligations under international law.[112] Treaties adhered to by the United States relating to human rights, transnational family law, international commercial law, or foreign investment are almost exclusively implemented by means of state and local law, since such issues mostly have not been federalized in the United States.[113] For example, when an individual is detained by police in the United States, the obligations owed by the United States under the International Covenant on Civil and Political Rights (including to respect the rights not to be arbitrarily arrested and to be informed promptly of any charges) are usually fulfilled through the actions of local police, prosecutors, and courts.[114] Likewise, because protection of foreign investment in the United States relies almost entirely on state and local law, arbitration claims brought by foreign investors against the United States under bilateral investment treaties or free trade agreements almost always concern actions adverse to the foreign investor that were taken at the state or local level.[115] For that reason, the federal government must carefully consider whether state and local law operates in a manner that allows the United States to ratify or accede to a treaty, and to monitor carefully the development of customary international law in relation to local law in the United States.

Further, states and cities regularly pursue initiatives that concern foreign relations.[116] Sometimes those initiatives are criticism or condemnation of a federal foreign relations policy, whether it be the 1798 Virginia and Kentucky Resolutions that protested the U.S. "undeclared war" with France or the numerous resolutions adopted by cities criticizing the 2003 U.S. intervention in

---

[110]   *See generally* HENKIN, FOREIGN AFFAIRS, at 149–69; RAMSEY, *supra* note 2, at 259–317.

[111]   *See* Chapter 9 § III.

[112]   *See* MICHAEL J. GLENNON & ROBERT D. SLOANE, FOREIGN AFFAIRS FEDERALISM: THE MYTH OF NATIONAL EXCLUSIVITY (2016).

[113]   *See* Julian G. Ku, *The State of New York Does Exist: How the States Control Compliance with International Law*, 82 N.C. L. REV. 457 (2004).

[114]   International Covenant on Civil and Political Rights, arts. 9(1) & 14(3)(a), Dec. 16, 1966, SENATE TREATY DOC. NO. 95-20, 999 U.N.T.S. 171 (entered into force Mar. 23, 1976).

[115]   *See* Chapter 2 § IV(C).

[116]   *See, e.g.*, Julian G. Ku, *Gubernatorial Foreign Policy*, 115 YALE L.J. 2380 (2006); Edward T. Swaine, *The Undersea World of Foreign Relations Federalism*, 2 CHI. J. INT'L L. 337 (2001); EARL H. FRY, THE EXPANDING ROLE OF STATE AND LOCAL GOVERNMENTS IN U.S. FOREIGN AFFAIRS (1998).

Iraq. Other initiatives attempt to adopt state or local laws that implement a rule or standard of international law, such as regional, state, and municipal controls on carbon-based emissions as might be called for by climate change agreements.[117] These steps often go unaddressed by the federal government (and sometimes are even affirmatively permitted),[118] but in some instances challenges will be brought against the state or local government on preemption grounds, in which case the action may be struck down as being expressly or implicitly preempted by a federal statute or treaty,[119] by the "dormant" foreign commerce clause,[120] or possibly by a more inchoate federal foreign relations power.[121]

II. Balancing Foreign Relations Powers

While the constitutional text would seem to accord the balance of foreign relations powers to Congress, in fact the president dominates U.S. engagement in foreign relations. Such dominance is a product of institutional advantages that the president enjoys generally as compared with Congress as well as advantages that are unique to foreign relations.[122] Edwin Corwin strikes the right note when he says: "The verdict of history, in short, is that the power to determine the substantive content of American foreign policy is a divided power, with the lion's share falling usually, though by no means always, to the President."[123] Even so, Congress (and the courts) play an important role in this area, serving as formal and informal checks on presidential action, such that foreign relations powers are regularly being balanced among the federal branches.

[117] *See* Judith Resnik et al., *Ratifying Kyoto at the Local Level: Sovereigntism, Federalism, and Translocal Organizations of Local Actors (TOGAs)*, 50 ARIZ. L. REV. 709 (2008).

[118] *See, e.g.,* Comprehensive Anti-Apartheid Act of 1986, Pub. L. No. 99-440, § 606, 100 Stat. 1086 (2018) (preserving state and local measures against South Africa).

[119] *See* Chapter 6 §§ I(B)(2), (IV)(C)(4) and Chapter 9 § (II)(A)–(B).

[120] *See* Chapter 2 § (IV) and Chapter 9 § (II)(D).

[121] *See* Chapter 9 § (II)(E).

[122] THE FEDERALIST No. 70, at 423 (Alexander Hamilton) ("Decision, activity, secrecy, and dispatch will generally characterize the proceedings of one man in a much more eminent degree than the proceedings of any greater number; and in proportion as the number is increased, these qualities will be diminished."); *see* KOH, *supra* note 62, at 118–23; Eric A. Posner & Cass R. Sunstein, *Chevronizing Foreign Relations Law*, 116 YALE L.J. 1170, 1202 (2007); Robert Knowles, *American Hegemony and the Foreign Affairs Constitution*, 41 ARIZ. ST. L.J. 87, 128 (2009); Ganesh Sitaraman & Ingrid Wuerth, *The Normalization of Foreign Relations Law*, 128 HARV. L. REV. 1897, 1935–49 (2015). Surveying the literature a half century ago, Professor Monaghan found: "Not surprisingly, . . . most writers recognize that the respective ambits of congressional and executive powers in controlling the direction of American policy cannot be resolved simply by an appeal to the constitutional text." Henry P. Monaghan, *Presidential War-Making*, 50 B.U. L. REV. 19, 24 (1970).

[123] EDWARD S. CORWIN, THE PRESIDENT: OFFICE AND POWERS 201 (5th ed. 1984).

A. Balancing in the Shadow of the President's Institutional Advantages

1. President's Advantages Generally

Many of the Framers of the U.S. Constitution appear to have assumed that, while the political branches would share powers, Congress would be the more powerful and influential of the two political branches. Yet the office of the president has from the outset possessed considerable advantages that were not obvious from the text of the Constitution, and those advantages have grown more significant as the United States itself has grown in size, in population, and in economic, military, and political strength. The president's capacity to direct the government in ways not prescribed by Article II of the Constitution animated Richard E. Neustadt's seminal 1960 study on *Presidential Power and the Modern Presidents*,[124] which emphasized the importance of the president's professional reputation, personal persuasion, and public prestige in wielding power. The president's ability to veto (or threaten to veto) legislation, to command the attention of his or her party in Congress (which is typically divided[125] or reticent if not compliant on major issues), and to pursue initiatives from the "bully pulpit" of the White House (as the only government official elected by the entire nation) often combine to place Congress in a reactive posture to the president.[126] At times, the president has even asserted a right not to enforce, not to defend, or to delay implementation of a validly enacted statute due to the president's view that it was unconstitutional.[127]

Further, the complexity of governing the modern United States has played to the president's advantage, notwithstanding a great expansion in the scope and detail of congressional lawmaking. First, the efficient and effective implementation of such laws and policies demands a well-organized and hierarchical

---

[124] RICHARD E. NEUSTADT, PRESIDENTIAL POWER AND THE MODERN PRESIDENTS: THE POLITICS OF LEADERSHIP (1960).

[125] On the advantages that accrue to the president from political polarization, see Jody Freeman & David B. Spence, *Old Statutes, New Problems*, 163 U. PA. L. REV. 1, 7 (2014).

[126] *See* Philip B. Kurland, *The Impotence of Reticence*, 1968 DUKE. L.J. 619, 634–36 (suggesting reasons for the overall gravitation of power from the legislative to the executive branch); Phillip R. Trimble, *The President's Foreign Affairs Power*, *in* FOREIGN AFFAIRS AND THE U.S. CONSTITUTION, *supra* note 26, at 39, 41–43. *See generally* JOHN P. BURKE, PRESIDENTIAL POWER: THEORIES AND DILEMMAS (2018); MATTHEW CRENSON & BENJAMIN GINSBERG, PRESIDENTIAL POWER: UNCHECKED AND UNBALANCED (2007); LOUIS FISHER, THE LAW OF THE EXECUTIVE BRANCH: PRESIDENTIAL POWER (2014); KOH, *supra* note 62, at 117–33; ARTHUR M. SCHLESINGER, JR., THE IMPERIAL PRESIDENCY (1973); PRESIDENTIAL POWER: FORGING THE PRESIDENCY FOR THE TWENTY-FIRST CENTURY (Robert Y. Shapiro et al. eds., 2000).

[127] *See* Chapter 2 § II(C); *see also* Dawn E. Johnsen, *Presidential Non-Enforcement of Constitutionally Objectionable Statutes*, 63 L. & CONTEMP. PROBS. (Winter/Spring 2000), at 7; Saikrishna Bangalore Prakash, *The Executive's Duty to Disregard Unconstitutional Laws*, 96 GEO. L.J. 1613 (2008); Neal Devins & Saikrishna Prakash, *The Indefensible Duty to Defend*, 112 COLUM. L. REV. 507 (2012); Michael Sant'Ambrogio, *The Extra-legislative Veto*, 102 GEO. L.J. 351, 351 (2014).

bureaucracy headed, of course, by the president. Each president appoints those who lead the various executive departments and agencies; they in turn, owe fidelity to the president, and marshal the extensive resources of their offices and personnel to advance the president's preferences, within the bounds of the law, but also interpreting that law so as to bend it toward the president's objectives.[128]

Second, the complexity of U.S. governance, including the need for expertise to develop detailed rules and the desire to adjust quickly when confronted with evolving situations, has required Congress, in practice, to delegate vast amounts of power to the executive. While Congress typically adopts a broad, framework law for regulating in a particular area, an extensive amount of detailed decision-making must then be left to the executive for implementation of that law through agency rules and regulations.[129] This delegation of "legislative" power prompted a clash during the New Deal era with the nondelegation doctrine, by which the Supreme Court declared that "Congress is not permitted to abdicate or to transfer to others the essential legislative functions with which it is thus vested."[130] Per the Court, a statute may assign responsibility to the executive only so long as it sets out an "intelligible principle" for the exercise of that authority.[131] Whether prior to the New Deal the nondelegation doctrine actually constrained expansive delegations of power to the president is contested,[132] but in any event, the Supreme Court has not struck down any statute on that basis since the New Deal.[133] While not all observers are happy with this state of affairs,[134] and others maintain that the doctrine still has

---

[128] *See, e.g.*, Kagan, *supra*, note 57, at 2384.

[129] Monaghan, *supra* note 122, at 22; Kathryn A. Watts, *Rulemaking as Legislating*, 103 Geo. L.J. 1003, 1013 (2015).

[130] A.L.A. Schechter Poultry Corp. v. United States, 295 U.S. 495, 529 (1935); Panama Refining Co. v. Ryan, 293 U.S. 388, 421 (1935); *see* Industrial Union Dep't, AFL-CIO v. Am. Petroleum Inst., 448 U.S. 607, 675 (1986) (finding that the delegation decisions require that Congress "lay down the general policy and standards that animate the law, leaving the agency to refine those standards, [to] 'fill in the blanks,' or [to] apply those standards to particular cases"). *See generally* Cass R. Sunstein, *Constitutionalism After the New Deal*, 101 Harv. L. Rev. 421, 494 (1987).

[131] J. W. Hampton, Jr., & Co. v. United States, 276 U.S. 394, 409 (1928); *accord* Gundy v. United States, 139 S. Ct. 2116, 2123 (2019).

[132] *See* Keith E. Whittington & Jason Iuliano, *The Myth of the Nondelegation Doctrine*, 165 U. Pa. L. Rev. 379 (2017).

[133] The Court has noted, repeatedly, that "'[W]e have "almost never felt qualified to second-guess Congress regarding the permissible degree of policy judgment that can be left to those executing or applying the law."'" *Gundy*, 139 S. Ct. at 2129 (quoting Whitman v. Am. Trucking Ass'ns, 531 U.S. 457, 474–75 (2001) (quoting Mistretta v. United States, 488 U.S. 361, 416 (1989) (Scalia, J., dissenting))); *but cf.* Clinton v. City of New York, 524 U.S. 417, 447–48 (1998) (holding that the Line Item Veto Act of 1996, 110 Stat. 1200, authorizing the president to selectively void portions of appropriation bills, violated Article I, § 7 of the Constitution, and declining to reach nondelegation challenge). By contrast, the Court regularly overturns lower court decisions that have invoked the doctrine to strike down a statute. *See, e.g.*, Dep't of Transp. v. Ass'n of Am. R.Rs., 575 U.S. 43, 55 (2015) (reversing a D.C. Circuit decision regarding delegation under the Passenger Railroad Investment and Improvement Act of 2008).

[134] *See, e.g.*, David Schoenbrod, Power without Responsibility: How Congress Abuses the People through Delegation (1993); Gary Lawson, *The Rise and Rise of the Administrative*

vitality,[135] the reality is that the scope of executive regulatory power has dramatically expanded over the past century concomitant with the expansion of federal power generally in day-to-day U.S. affairs.[136]

Congress has sought to reclaim some of this transferred power by cabining presidential discretion, and the breadth of its efforts are evident even in the foreign relations context.[137] Notably, Congress has also tried to shore up its authority by including in various statutes a provision commonly referred to as the "legislative veto," which entailed Congress delegating authority to the executive on the basis that, if an executive decision when implementing such authority is opposed by a resolution adopted in one or both houses of Congress, the decision is overturned. In *INS v. Chadha*,[138] however, the Supreme Court declared the legislative veto to be unconstitutional. In that case, Congress had authorized, in a section of the Immigration and Nationality Act, that either house could invalidate and suspend deportation rulings of the attorney general. The Court concluded that even though such a provision might enhance governmental efficiency, it violated the "explicit constitutional standards" regarding lawmaking, and in particular that Congress must present legislative acts to the president for his or her signature.[139] Dissenting, Justice Byron White described the Court as presenting Congress "with a Hobson's choice" between the "hopeless task" of writing legislation with sufficient specificity and simply "abdicat[ing] its lawmaking function to the Executive Branch" for it to employ without constraint.[140] Justice White also listed a number of legislative veto provisions in statutes, some longstanding, that would now be unconstitutional, including many in the area of foreign affairs and national security.[141]

State, 107 HARV. L. REV. 1231, 1237–41 (1994); PHILIP HAMBURGER, IS ADMINISTRATIVE LAW UNLAWFUL? (2014); Ilan Wurman, *Constitutional Administration*, 69 STAN. L. REV. 359, 362–63 (2017). Others have argued that the doctrine should be put out of its misery. *See* Eric A. Posner & Adrian Vermeule, *Interring the Nondelegation Doctrine*, 69 U. CHI. L. REV. 1721 (2002).

[135] *See* Larry Alexander & Saikrishna Prakash, *Reports of the Nondelegation Doctrine's Death are Greatly Exaggerated*, 70 U. CHI. L. REV. 1297 (2003) (critiquing Posner & Vermeule argument); Cary Coglianese, *Dimensions of Delegation*, 167 U. PA. L. REV. 1849 (2019).

[136] *See* Sunstein, *supra* note 130, at 447–48.

[137] There are numerous examples of such efforts. At the height of political conflict over the Vietnam War, the Senate in 1969 adopted a nonbinding National Commitments Resolution expressing its sense that a national commitment of U.S. armed forces or financial resources to assist a foreign country could only be undertaken pursuant to a treaty, statute, or concurrent resolution of both houses of Congress. S. Res. 85, 91st Cong., 2d Sess. (1969). In 1973, Congress adopted over the president's veto the War Powers Resolution, which inter alia provided that the president may only introduce U.S. forces into hostilities where there exists a declaration of war, specific statutory authorization, or a national emergency meeting statutorily defined criteria. H.R.J. Res. 542, Pub. L. No. 93-148, 87 Stat. 555, 555 (codified at 50 U.S.C. § 1541(c) (2018)); *see* Chapter 8 § I(C)(4).

[138] 462 U.S. 919 (1983).

[139] *Id.* at 959.

[140] *See id.* at 968 (White, J., dissenting).

[141] *See id.* at 1003–05 (White, J., dissenting) (Appendix § A). For further discussion, see Chapter 2 § II(B).

Simultaneously, the Court has developed *Chevron* deference,[142] a doctrine providing that courts should defer to executive agency interpretations of a statute that accords authority to the agency. Such deference is inappropriate if the statute is clear and unambiguous as to the matter at issue,[143] or if the executive's interpretation is unreasonable,[144] and it is accorded only to agency actions reached through formal proceedings that have the force of law (such as adjudications or notice-and-comment rulemaking).[145] The overall effect of *Chevron* deference, where applicable, is to strengthen further the power of the executive by granting it leeway in determining the scope of its statutory authority.[146]

The *Chevron* doctrine, however, is not entirely stable. One potentially significant development, for example, is the possibility of not deferring to the executive with respect to so-called "major questions." The Supreme Court has recently held that in certain "extraordinary cases," where an administrative agency asserts unusually broad authority over matters of distinctive economic and political significance, the agency "must point to 'clear congressional authorization' for the power it claims." Whatever the scope of this doctrine as applied to agencies, the Court's reasoning may not extend to statutes that delegate authority directly to the president, and its application to a foreign relations matter (even one of great significance) is uncertain in light of the relatively significant authority assigned to the executive branch in this area.[147]

2. President's Advantages Unique to Foreign Relations

In crafting his *Two Treatises of Government*, John Locke acknowledged that public authority contained two powers—legislative and executive—but to these

---

[142] *See* Chevron U.S.A., Inc. v. Natural Resources Defense Council, Inc., 467 U.S. 837 (1984). For analysis of the doctrine, see KRISTIN E. HICKMAN & RICHARD J. PIERCE, ADMINISTRATIVE LAW TREATISE §§ 3.2–3.6 (6th ed. 2018).

[143] *See Chevron*, 467 U.S. at 842–43.

[144] *See id.* at 844.

[145] *See* Christensen v. Harris County, 529 U.S. 576 (2000). Less formal measures may nonetheless be entitled to a measure of deference. *See, e.g.,* Coeur Alaska, Inc. v. Se. Alaska Conservation Council, 557 U.S. 261, 283–84 (2009) (agency memorandum); United States v. Mead Corp., 533 U.S. 218, 234–38 (2001) (noting alternative forms of deference).

[146] *Compare* Brett Kavanaugh, *Fixing Statutory Interpretation*, 129 HARV. L. REV. 2118, 2150 (2016) (arguing that *Chevron* is "nothing more than a judicially orchestrated shift of power from Congress to the Executive Branch") (reviewing ROBERT A. KATZMANN, JUDGING STATUTES (2014)), *with* Cass R. Sunstein, Chevron *as Law*, 107 GEO. L.J. 1613 (2019) (finding that if Congress implicitly has instructed courts, through the governing provision of the Administrative Procedure Act, 5 U.S.C. § 706 (2018), to defer to reasonable agency interpretations of genuinely ambiguous law, there is no constitutional problem with the *Chevron* doctrine).

[147] West Virginia v. Envtl. Prot. Agency, 142 S. Ct. 2587, 2609 (2022) (quoting Utility Air Regulatory Group v. EPA, 573 U.S. 302, 324 (2014)); *see id.* (relating doctrine to case law and concerns involving agency action). A concurrence seconded the political and economic significance of agency regulation as factors in determining whether a major question was presented, adding that the doctrine might also be triggered when regulation touched a traditional state domain—something less likely in the foreign relations context. *Id.* at 2620–21 (Gorsuch, J., concurring).

Locke added a third power, which he referred to as "federative" power. For Locke, federative power contained "the Power of War and Peace, Leagues and Alliances, and all the Transactions with all Persons and Communities without the Commonwealth . . . ."[148] A hallmark of this power is not just that it dealt with external relations but that it was "much less capable to be directed by antecedent, standing, positive Laws, than the Executive; and so must necessarily be left to the Prudence and Wisdom of those whose hands it is in, to be managed for the publick good."[149]

Indeed, both the "executive" and "federative" powers required recognition of certain "prerogatives," whereby actions may be taken that are outside the framework of the laws if such actions advance the society's best interest.[150] While the two types of power were distinct, Locke regarded it as impracticable for them to be placed in different hands, as doing so would lead to "disorder and ruine."[151] There is no evidence that Locke's "federative power" had any positive influence on the drafting of the U.S. Constitution and its allocation of foreign relations powers.[152] Even so, Locke's intuition that external or foreign relations required a special form of power, one best exercised by the executive, appears borne out in practice for U.S. foreign relations. Indeed, there are certain functional (or institutional) advantages enjoyed by the president that are unique or largely unique to the field of foreign relations, and that play to his or her dominance in exercising foreign relations powers.

First, building upon the fact that the president leads the massive executive bureaucracy, the president's foreign relations powers to "appoint" and "receive" ambassadors, and to negotiate treaties (including those by which the United States might join an international organization), establish the president as a crucial focal point for formulating and implementing U.S. foreign policy.[153] For example, it is the president who decides whether the United States should accept Kosovo[154] or South Sudan[155] as a newly independent country, or that the communist government in Beijing represents the country of China rather than the nationalist government on Taiwan.[156] It is the president who decides to

---

[148] JOHN LOCKE, TWO TREATISES OF GOVERNMENT ch. XII, § 146 (Peter Laslett ed., 2d ed. 1967).

[149] Id. § 147.

[150] Id. at ch. XIV, §§ 159–68.

[151] Id. at ch. XII, § 148.

[152] See, e.g., JACK N. RAKOVE, ORIGINAL MEANINGS: POLITICS AND IDEAS IN THE MAKING OF THE CONSTITUTION 250 (1996); Robinson, supra note 75, at 114, 115.

[153] See generally Chapter 3.

[154] Letter to President Fatmir Sejdiu of Kosovo Recognizing Kosovo as an Independent and Sovereign State, 1 PUB. PAPERS 228–29 (Feb. 18, 2008).

[155] Statement Recognizing South Sudan as an Independent and Sovereign State, 2 PUB. PAPERS 845 (July 9, 2011).

[156] Statement on Diplomatic Relations Between the United States and the People's Republic of China, 2 PUB. PAPERS 2266 (Dec. 18, 1978).

conclude[157] (or to terminate[158]) an agreement with allies that seeks to contain Iran's nuclear program, who decides whether to seek election to (or to abandon) a position on the U.N. Human Rights Council,[159] or whether to appear in cases brought against the United States at the International Court of Justice.[160] Indeed, through the extensive executive branch personnel based in Washington, D.C., and at U.S. embassies and consulates worldwide, it is the president who is able to obtain extensive information about foreign states and the work of international organizations, including on their leadership and their policies, or about foreign events, crises, or threats. Having received such information, the president is uniquely situated to marshal the executive bureaucracy to analyze such information from a range of sources, develop a considered view as to the U.S. policy response, and to communicate that policy back through these myriad channels, along the way engaging allies, challenging foes, and even litigating outcomes before international courts and tribunals.[161]

Second, and relatedly, for the United States to have a *coherent* foreign policy, at least on a day-to-day basis, it is commonly asserted that there must be a "sole voice" or "one voice" for articulating that policy externally to the rest of the world.[162] As a single voice (rather than the constellation of voices found in Congress), the president is said to be in the superior position to articulate a clear, cogent, and consistent U.S. foreign policy and, in so doing, to make commitments to foreign governments that they perceive as dependable. For example, when deciding whether to recognize a new foreign state, the president is best equipped to

---

[157] Remarks on the Joint Comprehensive Plan of Action to Prevent Iran from Obtaining a Nuclear Weapon, 2 PUB. PAPERS 896 (July 14, 2015).

[158] National Security Presidential Memorandum on Ceasing United States Participation in the Joint Comprehensive Plan of Action and Taking Additional Action to Counter Iran's Malign Influence and Deny Iran All Paths to a Nuclear Weapon, 2018 DAILY PRES. DOC. 311 (May 8, 2018). For discussion of the conclusion and termination of international agreements generally, see Chapter 6.

[159] Remarks to the Press, Mike Pompeo, Secretary of State, and Nikki Haley, U.S. Permanent Representative to the United Nations, Remarks on the UN Human Rights Council (June 19, 2018); Press Statement, Antony J. Blinken, Secretary of State, U.S. Decision to Reengage with the UN Human Rights Council (Feb. 8, 2021).

[160] For example, the United States during the Trump administration decided to participate in two cases brought against the United States by Iran, but reportedly is not participating in a third case brought against the United States by Palestine. The cases are: *Alleged Violations of the 1955 Treaty of Amity, Economic Relations, and Consular Rights (Iran v. United States)*; *Certain Iranian Assets (Iran v. United States)*; and *Relocation of the United States Embassy to Jerusalem (Palestine v. United States)*.

[161] David. L. Sloss et al., *Continuity and Change over Two Centuries, in* INTERNATIONAL LAW IN THE U.S. SUPREME COURT: CONTINUITY AND CHANGE 589, 591–92 (David L. Sloss et al. eds., 2011); HENKIN, FOREIGN AFFAIRS, at 31–34; GLENNON, *supra* note 2, at 27–30.

[162] *See* Arizona v. United States, 567 U.S. 387, 409 (2012); Zivotofsky v. Clinton, 566 U.S. 189, 214 (2012) (*Zivotofsky I*) (Breyer, J., dissenting); MICHAEL D. RAMSEY, THE CONSTITUTION'S TEXT IN FOREIGN AFFAIRS 32–46 (2007). *But see* Sarah H. Cleveland, Crosby *and the "One-Voice" Myth in U.S. Foreign Relations*, 46 VILL. L. REV. 975 (2001); David H. Moore, *Beyond One Voice*, 98 MINN. L. REV. 953 (2014).

act decisively, one way or the other, on behalf of the United States.[163] The need for decisive action, and a coherent voice, will differ by issue area, and in many circumstances it will even be difficult for the modern executive branch to manifest a unified position. As a general matter, though, Congress will certainly find it more difficult to establish a single, collective view, including in vital areas of foreign relations such as the deployment of U.S. forces. Of course, often Congress is supportive of the president's policy, in which case the "one voice" may well be that of the political branches working together.[164]

Third, in matters of foreign relations, there is sometimes—though not always—a need to act and to react expeditiously, often with a detailed position or robust execution. That need may be most apparent in matters that threaten U.S. national security, such as the attacks of 9/11, but it may be discerned even in other contexts: proposals by a foreign state to cooperate on a particular initiative; negotiation of treaty text at a multilateral conference; statements at and adoption of resolutions by an international organization; submission of a pleading before an international tribunal; and so on. Certainly, many issues of foreign relations, such as whether the United States should ratify a treaty, whether the United States should fund an international organization and if so to what degree, or the legal framework by which the United States imposes sanctions on foreign states do not require speed (or "despatch"); rather, considered judgment by a constellation of political actors is not only possible but desirable.[165] Yet in an international system of some 193 coequal sovereigns, the field of foreign relations presents a unique situation whereby regular interactions of the United States with foreign states likely could not occur in an effective manner if all or most matters were habitually referred to Congress for consideration.

Fourth, the domain of foreign relations is also one in which the ability to operate with secrecy is sometimes of great importance. Most foreign relations information is public, reported regularly in the press and other media, including information on armed conflict, humanitarian crises, trade imbalances, climate change, and cyberthreats. At the same time, the United States operates a very large foreign intelligence collection apparatus, spearheaded by the Central Intelligence Agency and the National Security Agency, which provides classified

---

[163] *See, e.g.*, Zivotofsky v. Kerry, 576 U.S. 1, 14 (2015) (*Zivotofsky II*) ("Recognition is a topic on which the Nation must 'speak . . . with one voice.' That voice must be the President's.") (quoting Am. Ins. Assn. v. Garamendi, 539 U.S. 396, 424 (2003)).

[164] *See, e.g.*, Munaf v. Geren, 553 U.S. 674, 702 (2008) (noting that for the judiciary "to second-guess" determinations about the likelihood that foreign governments will torture transferees would "undermine the Government's ability to speak with one voice in this area"). Indeed, from its inception, the political question doctrine has embraced the idea that foreign relations is an area where the political branches should not be second-guessed by the courts. *See* Baker v. Carr, 369 U.S. 186, 211 (1962) (indicating that foreign relations issues may be political questions because "many such questions uniquely demand [a] single-voiced statement of the Government's views").

[165] *See generally* Chapter 2.

analysis for use in U.S. government interactions with foreign states, including in relation to counterespionage and terrorism. Further, U.S. interactions with foreign states (and sometimes international organizations) also are often done in a confidential manner, allowing for frank and sensitive exchanges of views that would not be possible if fully transparent. While classified information is shared with Congress through highly regulated means,[166] full disclosure to Congress of such information is regarded as infeasible for its adequate protection, as well as protection of sources and methods of collection. Consequently, the need for careful handling of such information again places the executive in the driver's seat for important aspects of U.S. foreign relations.

The degree to which these functional advantages should be pertinent in assessing the president's constitutional powers has been questioned.[167] But Justice Sutherland's opinion in *Curtiss-Wright* famously suggested that these functional advantages were significant in evaluating the president's constitutional authority—and that this authority was substantial indeed.[168] In that case, Congress adopted a statute authorizing the president to prohibit certain arms sales if the president believed doing so would help resolve an armed conflict in South America.[169] Thereafter, the president issued a proclamation prohibiting such sales.[170] When defendants were indicted for violating the prohibition, they challenged the ability of Congress to delegate such power to the president.[171] That challenge may seem insubstantial from a contemporary standpoint, but in 1936, the nondelegation doctrine was at its zenith, at least with respect to legislation governing domestic matters.

The first part of Justice Sutherland's analysis for the Court, as previously noted,[172] advanced a theory to the effect that foreign relations powers are an inescapable element of U.S. sovereignty that do "not depend upon the affirmative grants of the Constitution."[173] The second part then considered *who* gets to exercise this power and concluded that it was principally the president. According to the Court, "[i]n this vast external realm [of external affairs], with its important, complicated, delicate and manifold problems, the President alone has the power to speak or listen as a representative of the nation."[174] Recounting the

---

[166] *See* Chapter 2 § II(F)(1).

[167] *See, e.g.*, Larry N. George, *Democratic Theory and the Conduct of American Foreign Policy, in* THE CONSTITUTION AND THE CONDUCT OF AMERICAN FOREIGN POLICY, *supra* note 61, at 57; Sitaraman & Wuerth, *supra* note 72, at 1935–49; Harlan Grant Cohen, *Formalism and Distrust: Foreign Affairs in the Roberts Court*, 83 GEO. WASH. L. REV. 380 (2015).

[168] United States v. Curtiss-Wright Export Corp., 299 U.S. 304 (1936).

[169] *Curtiss-Wright*, 299 U.S. at 312.

[170] *Id.* at 312–13.

[171] *Id.* at 314–15.

[172] *See supra* this chapter text accompanying notes 83–89.

[173] *Curtiss-Wright*, 299 U.S. at 318.

[174] *Id.* at 319.

various functional advantages enjoyed by the president, *Curtiss-Wright* went on to discuss the need to accord the president "discretion and freedom from statutory restriction" beyond what would be admissible for "domestic affairs."[175] On this account, "the very delicate, plenary and exclusive power of the President as the sole organ of the federal government in the field of international relations" did "not require as a basis for its exercise an act of Congress"—though it was otherwise to "be exercised in subordination to the applicable provisions of the Constitution."[176] In short, the president's functional advantages closely informed, if not determined, the scope of constitutional authority that the judiciary should afford the executive branch.

For obvious reasons, the executive branch regularly invoked *Curtiss-Wright* in the ensuing years, as U.S. power in global affairs—and presidential power in directing U.S. foreign relations—steadily expanded, and the case remains influential today.[177] *Curtiss-Wright*'s detractors, however, rightly note several problems with treating the decision as an authoritative pronouncement on presidential authority.[178] Much of what Justice Sutherland said seems to extend well beyond the issue presented to the Court, so much so that key aspects of the opinion are often characterized as dicta, including by the Supreme Court.[179] In *Curtiss-Wright*, Congress had legislated in an area expressly within its constitutional power (foreign commerce); there was no need to rely on any extraordinary federal powers. Further, Congress had instructed the president as to the zone of discretion and the president acted within that zone. The case did not, accordingly, present any issue of the president acting solely on his own authority, and certainly not acting in conflict with the wishes of Congress.

The sources cited by Justice Sutherland also provided little support for unilateral presidential authority. The opinion drew on a speech in 1800 by (then

---

[175] *Id.* at 320.

[176] *Id.* For criticisms, see KOH, *supra* note 62, at 94; David Gray Adler, *The Steel Seizure Case and Inherent Presidential Power*, 19 CONST. COMMENT. 155, 190 (2002); Michael J. Glennon, *Two Views of Presidential Foreign Affairs Power: Little v. Barreme or Curtiss-Wright?*, 13 YALE J. INT'L L. 5, 13 (1988); David M. Levitan, *The Foreign Relations Power: An Analysis of Mr. Justice Sutherland's Theory*, 55 YALE L.J. 467, 489 (1946).

[177] *See, e.g.*, Office of the Legal Counsel, U.S. Dep't of Justice, Authority to Withdraw from the North American Free Trade Agreement 5 (Oct. 17, 2018), https://perma.cc/7VJF-FTA7; *Zivotofsky II*, 576 U.S. at 66 (Roberts, C.J., dissenting) (observing that "[t]he expansive language in *Curtiss-Wright* casting the President as the 'sole organ' of the Nation in foreign affairs certainly has attraction for members of the Executive Branch," and noting that "[t]he Solicitor General invokes the case no fewer than ten times in his brief"); *see also* KOH, *supra* note 62, at 94.

[178] *See, e.g.*, GLENNON, *supra* note 2, at 20–34; HENKIN, FOREIGN AFFAIRS, at 19–20; KOH, *supra* note 62, at 93–95; Lofgren, *supra* note 90, at 30.

[179] *Zivotofsky II*, 576 U.S. at 20–21 (noting, after quoting the description of the president's power as "sole organ" in external relations, that "[t]his description of the President's exclusive power was not necessary to the holding of *Curtiss-Wright*—which, after all, dealt with congressionally authorized action, not a unilateral Presidential determination"); *see also* GLENNON, *supra* note 2, at 20; Robinson, *supra* note 75, at 121.

Representative) John Marshall in the House of Representatives, in which he stated that "[t]he President is the sole organ of the nation in its external relations, and its sole representative with foreign nations."[180] The speech concerned whether President John Adams should be impeached or censured for turning over to Britain an individual charged with murder before a U.S. court.[181] Marshall's position was that the president was the appropriate authority not only for carrying out legislative policy in the form of statutes but also for carrying out treaties, and in that case for fulfilling an extradition treaty according to obligations owed the British.[182] Marshall was not advocating (nor was Adams) in favor of regarding the president as the "sole organ" for *making* foreign policy but, rather, for *implementing* a policy previously laid down by Congress.[183]

The final and most basic problem with Sutherland's approach is that, even if the opinion correctly identifies the president's dominant role in the field of foreign relations (and the reasons for that dominance), it failed to justify a reading of the Constitution under which Congress and the courts lack authority altogether. The idea that the president is the "one voice" for articulating U.S. foreign policy is not the same thing as the president having *exclusive* power in this area; many commentators have referred to the metaphor as an inaccurate myth or slogan.[184] Although Congress may not play a substantial role in any day-to-day sense, it has always been significant in formulating and driving U.S. foreign policy, from trade policy to military funding to immunity of foreign states and their officials. In *Crosby v. National Foreign Trade Council*,[185] for example, the Supreme Court concluded that a congressional mandate was consistent with, rather than hindering, the president's "effective voice" in "dealing with other governments."[186] More recently, in *Zivotofsky II*, the Court rejected "that unbounded power"

---

[180] *Curtiss-Wright*, 299 U.S. at 319–20.

[181] For an extensive discussion of the background, see Ruth Wedgwood, *The Revolutionary Martyrdom of Jonathan Robbins*, 100 YALE L.J. 229, 286–311 (1990).

[182] The House debate between Marshall and Representative Gallatin appears to have turned not on different views as to the president's ability to execute treaties or to exercise any broader power, but rather concerned whether the treaty in question was fit for presidential execution without additional congressional or judicial measures. *See id.* at 333–53.

[183] *See* Louis Fisher, *The Staying Power of Erroneous Dicta: from Curtiss-Wright to Zivotofsky*, 31 CONST. COMMENT. 149, 163–64 (2016); GLENNON, *supra* note 2, at 8; HENKIN, FOREIGN AFFAIRS, at 41.

[184] *See, e.g.*, Curtis A. Bradley, *The Treaty Power and American Federalism*, 97 MICH. L. REV. 390, 446 (1998); Sarah H. Cleveland, *Crosby and the "One-Voice" Myth in U.S. Foreign Relations*, 46 VILL. L. REV. 975, 975 (2001); David H. Moore, *Beyond One Voice*, 98 MINN. L. REV. 953, 1038 (2014); Michael D. Ramsey, *International Law as Non-Preemptive Federal Law*, 42 VA. J. INT'L L. 555, 561 (2002); Ernest A. Young, *Sorting Out the Debate over Customary International Law*, 42 VA. J. INT'L L. 365, 449 (2002).

[185] 530 U.S. 363 (2000). For further discussion, see *supra* this chapter § I(B); *infra* this chapter § II(B); Chapter 2 § II(C); and Chapter 3 § I(D).

[186] *Id.* at 381.

suggested by the "sole organ" language in *Curtiss-Wright*.[187] Instead, it stressed that "whether the realm is foreign or domestic, it is still the Legislative Branch, not the Executive Branch, that makes the law," and that "[i]t is not for the President alone to determine the whole content of the Nation's foreign policy."[188] Indeed, even the states—found in *Crosby* to be interfering with the "one voice" of the president and Congress in establishing sanctions policy—have room to participate, as previously noted,[189] unless otherwise preempted by federal law.[190]

The fact that *Curtiss-Wright* involved a situation of delegated power to the president is not incidental, either to the decision in that case or to the post–World War II expansion of executive power in the field of foreign relations. Presidential power increased in large part as a function of permanent and interlocking *ex ante* statutory authorizations, which charge the president with taking action that was deemed necessary. While open-ended statutory authorizations raise legitimate questions about an "imperial presidency," they also signal a continuing relevance of Congress, creating opportunities for congressional oversight and restraint, as well as judicial intervention when presidential action lacks either a constitutional or statutory basis.[191]

B. Balancing and the President's Posture vis-à-vis Congress

Given the role of both political branches in the formation, interpretation, and execution of foreign relations law—albeit with considerable institutional advantages to the executive—a central preoccupation has been balancing of such powers as between those branches. Of course, politics is a vital element, so much so that it has been argued that the Constitution does nothing more than establish a framework within which political discourse over foreign relations powers may unfold.[192]

Yet the constitutional framework has certain substantive consequences when approaching the balancing of powers. Various constitutional provisions seem

---

[187] *Zivotofsky II*, 576 U.S. at 20; *see id.* at 66 (Roberts, C.J., dissenting) (agreeing that "our precedents have never accepted such a sweeping understanding of executive power").

[188] *Id.* at 21. For an important qualification, suggesting that *Zivotofsky II* is largely compatible with *Curtiss-Wright*, see Jean Galbraith, Zivotofsky v. Kerry *and the Balance of Power*, 109 AJIL UNBOUND 16 (2015).

[189] *See supra* this chapter text accompanying notes 104–121.

[190] Chief Justice Roberts noted in *Zivotovsky II* that "the President's so-called general foreign relations authority does not permit him to countermand a State's lawful action." *Zivotofsky II*, 576 U.S. at 66 (Roberts, C.J., dissenting) (citing Medellín v. Texas, 552 U.S. 491, 523–32 (2008)); *see* Jack L. Goldsmith, *Federal Courts, Foreign Affairs, and Federalism*, 83 VA. L. REV. 1617, 1688 (1997).

[191] *See generally* Andrew Kent & Julian Davis Mortenson, *The Search for Authorization: Three Eras of the President's National Security Power*, in THE CAMBRIDGE COMPANION TO THE UNITED STATES CONSTITUTION (Karen Orren & John W. Compton eds., 2018).

[192] H. JEFFERSON POWELL, THE PRESIDENT'S AUTHORITY OVER FOREIGN AFFAIRS 6 (2002).

to establish a foreign relations authority in one of the political branches, and thus implicitly to deny the other branch authority to exercise that power on its own. The president on his or her own cannot plausibly decide, for example, the rules by which a noncitizen may become a U.S. citizen or that unappropriated funds shall be given in aid to a foreign state, because the Constitution expressly allocates those powers to Congress. Likewise, Congress on its own cannot plausibly decide to command the army or to receive a new foreign ambassador, as those powers are expressly allocated to the president.

More often, though, an authority of keen relevance to foreign relations is not expressly allocated by the Constitution to one or the other political branch, leaving it unclear whether it is an entailment of another, closely related power. While the president may receive a foreign ambassador, does this imply that the president may recognize the existence of a new foreign state?[193] While the Senate may prevent the president from entering into a treaty by declining to provide consent, does this imply that the Senate's consent is required before the president may terminate or withdraw from a treaty?[194]

Assuming that a power is assigned to Congress, Congress may have acted in a manner that serves as a basis for presidential action. Thus, if Congress has established rules by which a noncitizen may become a U.S. citizen, or has authorized and appropriated funds for aid to a foreign State, the president acquires authority to execute those acts of Congress.[195] Here, the issue that arises is not whether the president has been assigned by the Constitution a foreign relations power, but whether Congress has expressly or impliedly granted authority to the president on a matter of foreign relations that he or she would not otherwise have.[196]

Beyond circumstances in which the Constitution assigns authority to one of the branches, which it may elect to share, there may be others in which the power to act (including the prevention of action) with respect to an aspect of foreign relations does not reside solely in one of the political branches but, rather, is a shared or concurrent power between the two political branches. Such shared power may be of the type where both branches must act, such as for the making of a treaty or the appointing of an ambassador, as acts by both the president and the Senate are contemplated. But there are significant areas of foreign relations where, due to the silence of the Constitution, either political branch is capable of acting, and arguments that only the president or only Congress may act are misguided.[197] For example, it is possible to argue that, while the president may not

---

[193] *See* Chapter 3 § IV(A).
[194] *See* Chapter 6 § VI.
[195] *See* Chapter 2 § III and Chapter 10 § III(A).
[196] *See* HENKIN, FOREIGN AFFAIRS, at 15.
[197] *See, e.g.,* Monaghan, *supra* note 122, at 25. For a sustained thesis that "the power to conduct American foreign policy is not exclusively presidential, but rather a power shared by the president,

declare war between the United States and a foreign state, he or she may never-theless project low-intensity U.S. military force abroad (measured by its nature, scope, and duration) without congressional approval, while at the same time Congress may act to prevent such force, such as by denying funds for it.[198] If so, the foreign relations power to decide whether to project U.S. military force of that scale abroad does not reside solely in one or the other political branch.

A popular analytical framework for thinking about the roles of Congress and the president, which often arises in the context of foreign relations,[199] is found in *Youngstown Sheet & Tube Co. v. Sawyer* (also known as the *Steel Seizure* case).[200] The Korean War entailed a large-scale deployment of U.S. forces abroad without a formal declaration of war by Congress. The administration of President Harry Truman maintained that support for the U.S. deployment required a steady supply of steel from U.S. mills, but laborers in the steel industry were on the verge of a strike. Consequently, President Truman issued an executive order, without express statutory authority, directing his secretary of commerce to seize and operate U.S. steel mills.[201] The executive order was claimed to be constitution-ally grounded in the president's power as commander in chief and more gen-erally in the executive power of the president. The mill owners, however, sued complaining that the seizures were authorized neither by Congress nor by the Constitution.[202] The executive branch argued that the seizure enjoyed both leg-islative authorization and constitutional authority; in the lower courts, it also

the Congress, and the courts," and that the "constitutional system of checks and balances is not sus-pended simply because foreign affairs are at issue," see KOH, *supra* note 62, at 4.

[198] *See* Chapter 8 § I(D)(3)(b).

[199] *See* Patricia L. Bellia, *Executive Power in* Youngstown's *Shadow*, 19 CONST. COMMENT. 87, 90 (2002).

[200] 343 U.S. 579 (1952). Though the framework is intended for use by courts, it may also be relevant for how the president and Congress generally should approach consideration of their powers. *See, e.g.*, Samuel Estreicher & Steven Menashi, *Taking* Steel Seizure *Seriously: The Iran Nuclear Agreement and the Separation of Powers*, 86 FORDHAM L. REV. 1199 (2017). On whether Justice Jackson's frame-work might be used, *mutatis mutandis*, to assess the constitutionality of conduct taken by the courts or Congress (rather than by the executive) that directly affects foreign relations, see Kristen Eichensehr, *Courts, Congress, and the Conduct of Foreign Relations*, 85 U. CHI. L. REV. 609 (2018). On whether the framework could be helpful when considering other dimensions that may arise, such as federalism or protection of individual rights, see Laurence H. Tribe, *Transcending the* Youngstown *Triptych: A Multidimensional Reappraisal of Separation of Powers Doctrine*, 126 YALE L.J.F. 86 (2016). The literature on the case is copious. *See, e.g.*, Patricia L. Bellia, *The Story of the Steel Seizure Case*, *in* PRESIDENTIAL POWER STORIES 233 (Christopher H. Schroeder & Curtis A. Bradley eds., 2008); GLENNON, *supra* note 2, at 8–18; Edward S. Corwin, *The Steel Seizure Case: A Judicial Brick Without Straw*, 53 COLUM. L. REV. 53 (1953); Edward T. Swaine, *The Political Economy of* Youngstown, 83 S. CAL. L. REV. 263 (2010); Symposium, *President Truman and the Steel Seizure Case: A 50-Year Retrospective*, 41 DUQ. L. REV. 667 (2003); Symposium, Youngstown *at Fifty*, 19 CONST. COMMENT. 1 (2002). For further discussion of *Youngstown*, see Chapter 8 § II(B).

[201] Exec. Order No. 10,340, 17 Fed. Reg. 3,139 (Apr. 8, 1952).

[202] *Youngstown*, 343 U.S. at 582–83.

argued that Congress lacked any capacity to restrict the president's action, but it abandoned that argument before the Supreme Court.[203]

The Supreme Court, per Justice Black, found the president's order unconstitutional. Justice Black's formalist approach asked whether Congress had authorized the president's action and, if not, whether a specific presidential power supported the action. The Court found that the executive order was not authorized by Congress;[204] to the contrary, such an authorization was rejected during the course of adopting the Taft-Hartley Act on labor-management relations,[205] when Congress failed to adopt an amendment authorizing such seizure in times of emergency.[206] Further, the commander-in-chief power did not provide authority for the president to take such action with respect to a labor dispute.[207] Finally, the Court stated that "the President's power to see that the laws are faithfully executed refutes the idea that he is to be a lawmaker."[208]

While the majority's judgment has been celebrated as a resounding statement that the president is governed by the law (and by the courts), even amid wartime exigencies,[209] Justice Jackson's concurrence is by far the more influential.[210] Justice Jackson wrote in part to provide a functional framework for considering the relationship of the political branches, with an eye to protecting Congress' role from an increasingly active and powerful executive.[211] Rather than view power as anchored exclusively in one or the other branch, Justice Jackson suggested a

---

[203] *See* Swaine, *supra* note 200, at 276.

[204] *Youngstown*, 343 U.S. at 585.

[205] Labor Management Relations (Taft-Hartley) Act of 1947, ch. 120, Pub. L. No. 80-101, §§ 206, 210, 61 Stat. 136, 155–56 (1947) (codified at 29 U.S.C. §§ 141–97 (2018)).

[206] *Youngstown*, 343 U.S. at 586. Justice Clark's concurrence emphasized the incompatibility of the executive order with the Taft-Hartley Act. *See id.* at 660–67 (Clark, J., concurring).

[207] *Id.* at 587; *see* Swaine, *supra* note 200, at 306 & n.181.

[208] *Youngstown*, 343 U.S. at 587. Justice Douglas concurred in Justice Black's formalist approach, but other concurring opinions emphasized different factors. For example, Justice Frankfurter's concurrence emphasized history, saying that, notwithstanding implications from the constitutional text, the president might be said to have a power to take certain action in light of a long course of conduct unobjected to by Congress. Yet here Justice Frankfurter found the opposite: "Congress has frequently—at least 16 times since 1916—specifically provided for executive seizure of production, transportation, communications, or storage facilities," but "[i]n every case it has qualified this grant of power with limitations and safeguards." Given such history, Congress had to be understood as withholding such authority when adopting the Taft-Hartley Act. *Id.* at 597–99 (J. Frankfurter, concurring).

[209] *See, e.g.*, David Gray Adler, *The Steel Seizure Case and Inherent Presidential Power*, 19 CONST. COMMENT. 155, 156 (2002). Not everyone celebrated; Chief Justice Vinson, joined by Justices Reed and Minton, dissented, citing various factors for why the president's power should be upheld. *Youngstown*, 343 U.S. at 667–710 (Vinson, C.J., dissenting, joined by Reed and Minton, JJ.).

[210] *See, e.g.*, Zivotofsky v. Kerry, 576 U.S. 1, 10 (2015) (*Zivotofsky II*); Medellín v. Texas, 552 U.S. 491, 494 (2015); Hamdan v. Rumsfeld, 548 U.S. 557 (2006) (Kennedy, J., concurring in part); Crosby v. Nat'l Foreign Trade Council, 530 U.S. 363, 375, 380–81 (2000); *see also* HENKIN, FOREIGN AFFAIRS, at 84–96; KOH, *supra* note 62, at 105.

[211] *See, e.g.*, William N. Eskridge, Jr., *Relationships Between Formalism and Functionalism in Separation of Powers Cases*, 22 HARV. J.L. & PUB. POL. 21, 23–24 (1998); ABRAHAM D. SOFAER, WAR, FOREIGN AFFAIRS AND CONSTITUTIONAL POWER: THE ORIGINS 382 n.18 (1976).

three-tiered approach that turns on the posture of Congress in relation to the president's conduct:

> [*Category One*:] When the President acts pursuant to an express or implied authorization of Congress, his authority is at its maximum, for it includes all that he possesses in his own right plus all that Congress can delegate. In these circumstances, and in these only, may he be said (for what it may be worth) to personify the federal sovereignty. If his act is held unconstitutional under these circumstances, it usually means that the Federal Government as an undivided whole lacks power. A seizure executed by the President pursuant to an Act of Congress would be supported by the strongest of presumptions and the widest latitude of judicial interpretation, and the burden of persuasion would rest heavily upon any who might attack it.[212]
>
> [*Category Two*:] When the President acts in absence of either a congressional grant or denial of authority, he can only rely upon his own independent powers, but there is a zone of twilight in which he and Congress may have concurrent authority, or in which its distribution is uncertain. Therefore, congressional inertia, indifference or quiescence may sometimes, at least as a practical matter, enable, if not invite, measures on independent presidential responsibility. In this area, any actual test of power is likely to depend on the imperatives of events and contemporary imponderables rather than on abstract theories of law.[213]
>
> [*Category Three*:] When the President takes measures incompatible with the expressed or implied will of Congress, his power is at its lowest ebb, for then he can rely only upon his own constitutional powers minus any constitutional powers of Congress over the matter. Courts can sustain exclusive Presidential control in such a case only by disabling the Congress from acting upon the subject. Presidential claim to a power at once so conclusive and preclusive must be scrutinized with caution, for what is at stake is the equilibrium established by our constitutional system.[214]

Applying this framework, Justice Jackson concluded that President Truman's seizure of the steel mills was not authorized by Congress, and therefore could not fall within category one.[215] Further, category two was not available since "Congress has not left seizure of private property an open field"; rather, there were three statutory policies enacted by Congress that authorized seizures of property, none of which were invoked in this context.[216] The seizure, therefore,

---

[212] Youngstown Sheet & Tube Co. v. Sawyer, 343 U.S. 579, 635–37 (1952) (Jackson, J. concurring).
[213] *Id*. at 637.
[214] *Id*. at 637–38.
[215] *Id*. at 639.
[216] *Id*.

could only fall within category three. Yet the seizure of private property in the United States could not be justified as an executive power vested in the president,[217] the commander-in-chief power,[218] or more "nebulous, inherent powers . . . said to have accrued to the office from the customs and claims of preceding administrations."[219]

Each of Justice Jackson's categories raises difficult questions. Given that an express or implied authorization of Congress places the presidential action in the first, optimal category, defining when such authorization exists is critical. Express authorization may be relatively easy to identify, but it is also the least likely to generate a dispute (at least between the political branches). For example, in *Crosby v. National Foreign Trade Council*, a private party argued that a federal statute imposing sanctions on Myanmar (Burma) preempted Massachusetts law. In agreeing that it did, the Court (per Justice Souter) recalled Justice Jackson's category one, since the statute expressly authorized the president to terminate such sanctions, to impose new types of sanctions, and to waive sanctions for national security reasons.[220]

But what of implied authorization? Simple inaction by Congress in the face of presidential action is probably inadequate to support deeming a matter to fall in category one, as that congressional posture seems to be contemplated in category two. Perhaps congressional authorizations and appropriations tangentially related to the president's actions may, in a particular context, constitute implied authorization. In that spirit, the three *Youngstown* dissenters argued that Congress had appropriated billions for U.S. involvement in the Korean War, and further had granted the president authority not just to requisition property, and to allocate and fix priorities for scarce goods, but also "to stabilize prices and wages and to provide for settlement of labor disputes arising in the defense program."[221] According to them: "The President has the duty to execute the foregoing legislative programs. Their successful execution depends upon continued production of steel and stabilized prices for steel."[222] Yet such tangential acts apparently were not sufficient for Justice Jackson (or for the other members of the majority). While the majority's view that Congress had not implied authorization for the president to seize the steel mills seems correct, the method of determining when

---

[217] *Id.* at 640–41.

[218] *Id.* at 641–46.

[219] *Id.* at 646–54.

[220] Crosby v. Nat'l Foreign Trade Council, 530 U.S. 363, 375–76 (2000); *see also* Hamdi v. Rumsfeld, 542 U.S. 507, 583–84 (2004) (Thomas, J., dissenting) (invoking category one to support the president's authority to detain a U.S. citizen as an enemy combatant; with the plurality, this provided a majority in support of the proposition).

[221] *Youngstown*, 343 U.S. at 671–72 (Vinson, C.J., dissenting, joined by Reed and Minton, JJ.).

[222] *Id.* at 672.

authorization is implied and when it is not—though perhaps central for many disputes of this kind—was left opaque.

In category two, in which Congress has neither authorized the action nor denied such authorization, the president may only rely on his or her independent authority—enabled or invited, possibly, by congressional inaction—if the area is one in which the president "and Congress . . . have concurrent authority, or in which its distribution is uncertain."[223] Though Justice Jackson rejected the idea of nebulous, inherent executive powers, this "zone of twilight" potentially affords much the same opportunity, at least in areas where the action at issue is not grounded in a power deemed exclusive to Congress.[224] It also suggests that presidential power is variable, depending not only on whether Congress is silent, but also based on "events and contemporary imponderables" derived from the context at hand[225]—perhaps the nature of the executive action, or the needs of the nation, or the risk to civil liberties or property rights. The contrast with Justice Black's more rigid approach seems stark, and the scope for judicial discretion in evaluating these circumstances vast. The import, moreover, is that courts are entitled to play a lesser role in policing the president's exercise of power, potentially contributing to its further growth.[226] If this same framework is to be applied by the political branches in cases not presented for judicial review, it might license even greater confidence by the executive in its entitlements.

For example, category two appeared to license dramatic executive action in *Dames & Moore v. Regan*.[227] During 1979 to 1981, U.S. diplomatic and consular personnel were held hostage in Iran, a crisis that only ended with the entry into force of the Iran–U.S. Algiers Accords, concluded by President Jimmy Carter as executive agreements without congressional approval.[228] Among other things, the Algiers Accords required the United States to nullify all attachments of Iranian property in the United States, to transfer Iranian assets from the United States to Iran, and to terminate claims that had been filed by U.S. nationals in U.S. courts against Iran, all in exchange for Iran's release of the hostages.[229] Some of those U.S. claimants, who already had judgments and attachments of assets in

---

[223] *Id.* at 674 (Jackson, J., concurring).
[224] *Id.*
[225] *Id.*·
[226] *See* Adler, *supra* note 61, at 19.
[227] 453 U.S. 654 (1981); *see* Harold H. Bruff, *The Story of Dames & Moore: Resolution of An International Crisis by Executive Agreement, in* PRESIDENTIAL POWER STORIES (Christopher H. Schroeder & Curtis A. Bradley eds., 2009). The author of the *Dames & Moore* majority opinion, Justice Rehnquist, was a former clerk of Justice Jackson. A few years after penning *Dames & Moore*, Justice Rehnquist would reiterate the overall importance of *Youngstown* for U.S. constitutional law. *See* William H. Rehnquist, *Constitutional Law and Public Opinion*, 20 SUFFOLK U. L. REV. 751, 753 (1986) (describing *Youngstown* as a "very important constitutional case").
[228] *Dames & Moore*, 453 U.S. at 664.
[229] *Id.* at 665.

the United States, challenged the constitutionality of the executive orders that sought to implement the Algiers Accords, arguing that the president lacked statutory or constitutional authority.[230]

The Court—deciding the matter on an expedited schedule (about a week from argument to decision)—invoked Justice Jackson's *Youngstown* framework as "analytically useful"[231] and held that the nullification of attachments and transfer of Iranian assets abroad fell within the scope of preexisting statutes, notably the International Emergency Economic Powers Act (IEEPA)[232] and the Hostage Act.[233] The more difficult issue was the president's action in suspending claims in U.S. courts, which the Court found was not specifically authorized by IEEPA (because such claims are not "transactions" regulated by that statute), nor by the Hostage Act (which contained broad language relating to hostage situations).[234] These two statutes were nevertheless "highly relevant in the looser sense of indicating congressional acceptance of a broad scope for executive action in circumstances such as those presented in this case."[235] Moreover, there was "a longstanding practice of settling such claims by executive agreement,"[236] and Congress had implicitly approved such practice by adopting statutes allowing for the receipt of funds and their distribution to U.S. citizens.[237] Based on these factors (inferences from laws in this area and the history of acquiescence in executive claims settlement), the Court concluded that the president "was authorized to suspend pending claims" in U.S. court.[238] The Court went on to note that "Congress has not disapproved of the action taken here."[239] The Court did not expressly say which category of Justice Jackson's framework it saw relevant for resolving the matter, but it signaled that it regarded the situation as falling within category two.[240]

---

[230] *Id.* at 666–67.

[231] *Id.* at 669 (quoting Youngstown Sheet & Tube Co. v. Sawyer, 343 U.S. 579, 635 (1952) (Jackson, J., concurring)); *see also id.* ("[I]t is doubtless the case that executive action in any particular instance falls, not neatly in one of three pigeonholes, but rather at some point along a spectrum running from explicit congressional authorization to explicit congressional prohibition. This is particularly true as respects cases such as the one before us, involving responses to international crises the nature of which Congress can hardly have been expected to anticipate in any detail.").

[232] International Emergency Economic Powers Act, tit. II, Pub. L. No. 95-223, 91 Stat. 1626 (1977) (codified at 50 U.S.C. § 1701 (2018)) (IEEPA); *see* Chapter 2 § IV(E).

[233] Hostage Act, 22 U.S.C. § 1732.

[234] *Dames & Moore*, 453 U.S. at 675–77. Although the Algiers Accords obligated the United States to terminate claims against Iran in U.S. courts, the executive orders initially just suspended such claims, on the basis that only once the claim was adjudicated on the merits at the Claims Tribunal would it be terminated in U.S. courts. *Id.* at 666.

[235] *Id.* at 677.

[236] *Id.* at 679. For further discussion of sole executive agreements, see Chapter 6 § V(C).

[237] *Dames & Moore*, 453 U.S. at 680–82.

[238] *Id.* at 686.

[239] *Id.* at 687.

[240] *See, e.g., id.* at 678.

Yet the opinion made the lines drawn between Justice Jackson's categories seem less clear. Congress' posture in *Dames & Moore* was not entirely one of "inertia, indifference or quiescence" but rather constituted active engagement in issues relating to economic crises, hostage-taking, and claims settlements; its statutes were "highly relevant in the looser sense of indicating congressional acceptance of a broad scope for executive action in circumstances such as those presented in this case," yet seemingly did not constitute implied authorization under category one.[241] At the same time, notwithstanding its attention to the relevant subjects, at no point did Congress ever authorize the suspension or termination of claims in U.S. courts, arguably the kind of implicit opposition that was divined in *Youngstown* and which might have placed the situation for *Dames & Moore* in category three.[242] If an objective of Justice Jackson's framework in *Youngstown* was to be protective of Congress' role in the face of an increasingly powerful executive, its application in *Dames & Moore* suggested that the malleability of the categories might defeat that objective.[243]

In category three, Congress' posture is that of opposition to the president's action. Any augmented power that the president would have received by Congress' authorization (category one) or through concurrent executive-congressional authority (category two) must now be subtracted, leaving the president alone with "his own constitutional powers."[244] But what powers are those? In *Youngstown* itself, the Court gave little weight to the vesting of the executive power in the president or to the president's power to see that the laws are faithfully executed; it may be that such powers were simply "scrutinized with caution" under the circumstances at hand and found inadequate to redeem President Truman's action, or that more specific powers are invariably needed in order to satisfy category three.[245] It is also unclear what circumstances warrant inclusion in category

---

[241] *Id.* at 677–78.

[242] *But see id.* at 677 (explaining that, given diversity of possible presidential actions, a congressional failure "specifically to delegate authority does not, 'especially . . . in the areas of foreign policy and national security,' imply 'congressional disapproval' of action taken by the Executive") (quoting Haig v. Agee, 453 U.S. 280, 291 (1981)); *id.* at 688 ("We are thus clearly not confronted with a situation in which Congress has in some way resisted the exercise of Presidential authority.").

[243] *See* KOH, *supra* note 62, at 142. *But see* Mark S. Rosen, *Revisiting* Youngstown: *Against the View that Jackson's Concurrence Resolves the Relation Between Congress and Commander-in-Chief*, 54 UCLA L. REV. 1703, 1711 n.22 (2007) (finding that *Dames & Moore* did not undermine Justice Jackson's reasoning).

[244] Youngstown Sheet & Tube Co. v. Sawyer, 343 U.S. 579, 637 (1952) (Jackson, J., concurring).

[245] Justice Black maintained that, "[i]n the framework of our Constitution, the President's power to see that the laws are faithfully executed refutes the idea that he is to be a lawmaker[,] . . . [a]nd the Constitution is neither silent nor equivocal about who shall make laws which the President is to execute." *Id.* at 587. In dismissing the president's reliance on the clause vesting the executive power in the president, Justice Jackson rejected "the view that this clause is a grant in bulk of all conceivable executive power, but regard[ed] it as an allocation to the presidential office of the generic powers thereafter stated." *Id.* at 641 (Jackson, J., concurring). As for the Take Care Clause, Justice Jackson said that it must be "matched against" the Fifth Amendment prohibition on the taking of property without due process of law. *Id.* at 646.

three in the first place. When a presidential measure is incompatible with the will of Congress is not self-evident. A statute that expressly prohibits certain presidential action would seem to qualify; it may be less obvious whether sufficient opposition is manifest in a statute that authorizes some presidential action but fails to address the kind of action in controversy. In *Youngstown* itself, the Court appears to have regarded such an omission as sufficient to relegate President Truman to category three—there was no statute prohibiting seizure of the steel mills, but there were related statutes that contained no such authorization[246]— yet this will often be difficult to assess.

A category three example arose in *Medellín v. Texas*.[247] That case concerned an effort by President George W. Bush to enforce, by presidential memorandum, a decision rendered by the International Court of Justice requiring Texas courts to review and reconsider the conviction and sentencing of certain Mexican nationals on death row.[248] When considering whether the president's action was authorized by certain treaties entered into by the United States, the U.S. Supreme Court saw the matter as falling into category three: the treaties at issue were not self-executing and therefore could not authorize the president to take action;[249] moreover, unilaterally enforcing a non-self-executing treaty would be against the "implied will" of Congress.[250] Having located the situation in category three, the Court somewhat abruptly found that the president's action was unsupportable,[251] an outcome that reinforced a sense that Congress' opposition, when exercising its foreign relations powers, invariably defeats the president's authority. The Court then considered whether the president's action could be based on a presidential foreign affairs power to settle international disputes. Here the Court eschewed any direct reference to the *Youngstown* framework, but its analysis suggested that it might have viewed the question as falling into category two. Unlike foreign claims settlement by executive agreement, which the Court had upheld in cases such as *Dames & Moore*, there was no substantial history of congressional acquiescence in favor of the president's capacity to resolve an international dispute by means of directing action by a state or its courts.[252] The Court's analysis showed the proximity, and fluidity, of categories one and two. If, to succeed in category two's "zone of twilight," the president must show

---

[246] An early example of this approach may be seen in the case of *Little v. Barreme*, where Chief Justice Marshall found that a statute authorizing the president to seize vessels sailing to a French port is an implicit prohibition on the president's seizure of vessels sailing from a French port. *Little v. Barreme*, 6 U.S. (2 Cranch) 170 (1804).

[247] 552 U.S. 491 (2008). For further discussion of this case, see Chapter 3 § I(D); Chapter 5 § II(B); Chapter 6 §§ III(B), IV(A); Chapter 7 § III(C); and Chapter 9 §§ II(B), II(C).

[248] *Avena and Other Mexican Nationals* (Mex. v. U.S.), Judgment, 2004 I.C.J. 12 (Mar. 31).

[249] *Medellín*, 552 U.S. at 527.

[250] *Id.*

[251] *Id.* at 527–30.

[252] *Id.* at 532.

a "systematic, unbroken, executive practice, long pursued to the knowledge of Congress and never before questioned," lest congressional acquiescence be insufficient in degree to support the president's independent powers, then that standard seems very close to the idea of implied authorization in category one.[253] Viewed differently, though, the Court may have been suggesting that the president had little claims settlement authority to speak of in the absence of congressional authorization.

The malleability of the categories, as well as the danger for the executive of being found in category three, were on full display in *Hamdan v. Rumsfeld*, a case holding unconstitutional a military commission established by President George W. Bush at Guantánamo Bay naval base to try alleged terrorist fighters.[254] In considering whether such a military commission was authorized by Congress or under the inherent powers of the president, four justices viewed the matter as falling within category three,[255] while three justices viewed it as engaging category one.[256] At the same time, the *Hamdan* majority took it as a given (at least when it came to war powers) that the president, even when possessing independent authority under the Constitution, lacks authority to disregard limits imposed by Congress when it is properly exercising *its* constitutional powers.[257] While Justice Jackson had advised that, within category three, the president could "rely only upon his own constitutional powers minus any constitutional powers of Congress over the matter,"[258] *Hamdan* suggested that this calculation was invariably fatal to the assertion of presidential authority.

By contrast, in *Zivotofsky II*, the Court unambiguously regarded as falling within category three a confrontation between Congress and the president over the birthplace notation on a passport for a U.S. citizen born in Jerusalem,[259] yet Congress did not prevail. In essence, the Court found that the president has the exclusive power to grant formal "recognition" to a foreign sovereign, which includes identifying the territory over which that sovereign rules.[260] Congress

---

[253] *See* Michael J. Turner, *Fade to Black: The Formalization of Jackson's Youngstown Taxonomy by Hamdan and Medellín*, 58 Am. U. L. Rev. 665, 690 (2009).

[254] Hamdan v. Rumsfeld, 548 U.S. 557 (2006). For further discussion, see Chapter 5 § II(A)(2); Chapter 8 §§ II(A), II(B), III(B); and Chapter 10 § II(E)(4).

[255] *Id.* at 638–39 (Kennedy, J., concurring, joined by Souter, Ginsburg, and Breyer, JJ.).

[256] *Id.* at 680–82 (Thomas, J., dissenting, joined by Scalia and Alito, JJ.).

[257] *Id.* at 593 n.23.

[258] Youngstown Sheet & Tube Co. v. Sawyer, 343 U.S. 579, 637 (1952) (Jackson, J., concurring).

[259] *Zivotofsky II*, 576 U.S. at 10 ("Because the President's refusal to implement [the statute] falls into Justice Jackson's third category, his claim must be 'scrutinized with caution,' and he may rely solely on powers the Constitution grants to him alone.") (quoting Youngstown Sheet & Tube Co. v. Sawyer, 343 U.S. 579, 638 (1952) (Jackson, J., concurring)). For further discussion of *Zivotofsky II*, see *supra* this chapter §§ I(B), II(B); Chapter 2 § II(C); and Chapter 3 § I(D).

[260] *Zivotofsky II*, 576 U.S. at 23 (finding that "the Executive Branch determines whether the United States will recognize foreign states and governments and their territorial bounds"); *id.* at 28 ("[H]istory confirms the Court's conclusion in the instant case that the power to recognize or decline

has related power, such as to enact passport legislation, but lacked power that would in essence command the president (and the secretary of state) to issue a formal statement that contradicts a prior formal position on recognition.[261] Thus, while the Court's decisions in *Hamdan* and *Medellín* might suggest that Congress always wins in category three, *Zivotofsky II* suggests to the contrary, so long as the power being exercised is exclusive to the president and thus Congress' effort to exercise power is not proper.[262] The significance of the decision was not lost on Chief Justice Roberts, who began his dissent by declaring that "[t]oday's decision is a first: Never before has this Court accepted a President's direct defiance of an Act of Congress in the field of foreign affairs."[263]

Despite these and other shortcomings, Justice Jackson's analytical framework continues to be favored by courts charged with tackling difficult issues relating to the president's exercise of authority concerning foreign relations.[264] The popularity of Justice Jackson's framework probably derives in part from its abandonment of a binary approach, in which the president either possesses or lacks authority as a general matter, in favor of a more pragmatic and context-sensitive approach. As a matter of *realpolitik*, the approach is probably also appealing to the political branches. Congress is permitted to stand on the sidelines as the president acts, without fully abandoning the field; at any point, Congress can enter the game if it has the political will to do so, thereby placing the president's power at its "lowest ebb." In the meantime, the president benefits by not being shackled solely to specific Article II powers or to authorizations from Congress: Congress' inaction opens up a twilight zone of opportunity for the president to exploit, so long as Congress is not provoked into contrary action. If the president's desire to keep Congress on the sidelines encourages presidential caution and consultation, then Justice Jackson's approach might help to constrain, at least to a degree, executive assertions of authority. Whether this outweighs the risk that a president will avoid seeking congressional authorization, for fear that any failure

---

to recognize a foreign state and its territorial bounds resides in the President alone."). On the recognition power more generally, see Chapter 3 § IV.

[261] *Id.* at 31–32 ("It was an improper act for Congress to 'aggrandiz[e] its power at the expense of another branch' by requiring the President to contradict an earlier recognition determination in an official document issued by the Executive Branch.") (citing to Freytag v. Comm'r, 501 U.S. 868, 878 (1991)).

[262] *Id.* at 29–30 ("As Justice Jackson wrote in *Youngstown*, when a Presidential power is 'exclusive,' it 'disabl[es] the Congress from acting upon the subject.' 343 U.S., at 637–38 ... (concurring opinion).").

[263] *Id.* at 61 (Roberts, C.J., dissenting).

[264] *See, e.g.*, KindHearts for Charitable Humanitarian Dev. v. Geithner, 647 F. Supp. 2d 857, 876–77 (N.D. Ohio 2009); Al-Bihani v. Obama, 619 F.3d 1, 48–52 (D.C. Cir. 2010) (Kavanaugh, J., concurring in the denial of rehearing en banc); Sierra Club v. Trump, 963 F.3d 874, 887 (9th Cir. 2020), *vacated*, No. 20-138 (U.S. July 2, 2021); Rosebud Sioux Tribe v. Trump, 495 F. Supp. 3d 968, 979–80 (D. Mont. 2020).

may be regarded as disapproval triggering category three scrutiny, undoubtedly depends on the president's political prospects in a given matter.[265]

All told, foreign relations cases such as *Youngstown* (where the president's power yields to that of Congress), *Dames & Moore* (where the president and Congress are viewed as acting in harmony), and *Zivotofsky II* (where Congress' power yields to that of the president) provide certain guideposts, but not bright lines, for understanding the balancing of foreign relations power. At either end of the spectrum are instances in which a specific power is considered to reside exclusively in one branch; in such instances, represented by *Zivotofsky II*, that power will be upheld and protected by the courts. Elsewhere on the spectrum, express or implied congressional support for—or longstanding congressional acquiescence to—the exercise of a particular power by the executive also will likely lead to it being upheld.

By contrast, presidential conduct in an area of concurrent power where Congress opposes (or has not acquiesced in) executive action places the president on weak footing. Thus, in *Hamdan*, the majority was willing to entertain the assumption that the power to structure military commissions was not exclusively held by Congress, but considered that its restrictions on the executive power sufficed to divest any presidential authority. In *Medellín*, even the implied limits on the domestic efficacy of treaties, inferred from the Senate's consent in view of U.S. judicial doctrine, sufficed to truncate presidential authority.

Yet such cases suggest that any true guide to the balancing of foreign relations powers cannot rest solely on abstract judicial formulas, or even on the synthesis of judicial precedent. Rather, the balancing of power is affected by the particular presidential action at issue being exercised at a particular time and in a particular way, against a historical backdrop of presidential and congressional conduct that may relate to that action—and hence informed by the interbranch process of action-reaction-accommodation that characterizes much of U.S. constitutional law on the separation of powers.

III. Foreign Relations Powers in Times of National Emergency

Unlike the constitutions of some foreign states and some human rights treaties, the U.S. Constitution does not contain a provision allowing the government to alter the normal constitutional order, including the suspension of certain civil liberties in a time of war or national emergency.[266] Where they exist, such

---

[265] *See* Swaine, *supra* note 200, at 264, 304–05.
[266] HENKIN, FOREIGN AFFAIRS, at 53.

"national emergency" provisions typically allow the government to take steps that transgress most (but not all) civil liberties, so long as the emergency is publicly declared, the transgression is proportionate to the emergency, and the declaration subsides once the emergency has passed.[267]

The sole U.S. constitutional provision that speaks directly and generally to emergencies is the Habeas Corpus Clause, which provides in Article I that the writ "shall not be suspended, unless when in cases of rebellion or invasion the public safety may require it."[268] That clause is understood as empowering Congress—but not the executive—to suspend the writ in the circumstances indicated.[269] Indeed, it has been noted that, while the Founding Fathers did not rule out the possibility that a "crisis might require the executive to act outside the Constitution," neither did they intend to confer constitutional legitimacy on such acts, believing that the "legal order would be better preserved if departures from it were frankly identified as such than if they were anointed with a factitious legality and thereby enabled to serve as constitutional precedents for future action."[270]

There do exist a few U.S. statutes that establish general frameworks for different kinds of emergencies, including national emergencies,[271] major disasters,[272] and public health emergencies.[273] Further, there are more than one hundred statutes containing provisions granting the executive power in particular subject-matter areas during a national emergency, such as regulation of financial and other commercial transactions of foreign entities "to deal with any unusual and extraordinary threat, which has its source in whole or in substantial part outside the United States" and "with respect to which a national emergency has been declared . . . ."[274] Such statutory authorizations establish Congress' support for

---

[267] For a theoretical, historical, and comparative perspective on emergency powers, see OREN GROSS & FIONNUALA NÍ AOLÁIN, LAW IN TIMES OF CRISIS: EMERGENCY POWERS IN THEORY AND PRACTICE (2006).

[268] U.S. CONST. art. I, § 9, cl. 2.

[269] Ex parte Bollman, 8 U.S. (4 Cranch) 75, 101 (1807) ("If at any time the public safety should require the suspension of the powers vested by this act in the courts of the United States, it is for the legislature to say so."); see also infra text accompanying notes 276–278 (discussing Ex parte Merryman, 17 F. Cas. 144 (C.C.D. Md. 1861)).

[270] ARTHUR SCHLESINGER, JR., THE IMPERIAL PRESIDENCY 9 (1973).

[271] National Emergencies Act of 1976, 50 U.S.C. §§ 1601–51 (2018). For historical accounts of the use of emergency powers since the founding, see Harold Relyea, A Brief History of Emergency Powers in the United States (Special Comm. on Nat'l Emergencies & Delegated Emergency Powers, Working Paper No. 36-612, 1974); L. ELAINE HALCHIN, CONG. RESEARCH SERV., 98-505, NATIONAL EMERGENCY POWERS (2021).

[272] Robert T. Stafford Disaster Relief and Emergency Assistance Act of 1988, 42 U.S.C. §§ 5121–5207.

[273] Public Health Service Act of 1944, 42 U.S.C. § 247d.

[274] International Emergency Economic Powers Act, tit. II, Pub. L. No. 95-223, 91 Stat. 1626 (1977) (codified at 50 U.S.C. § 1701) (IEEPA). For a useful compendium of 136 statutory grants of power to the president upon declaration of a national emergency, see BRENNAN CENTER FOR JUSTICE, A GUIDE TO EMERGENCY POWERS AND THEIR USE (2020).

particular types of presidential action in a time of crisis and allow for a degree of transparency in the activation of the power, its use, and its termination.

In some situations, however, the president or the political branches together have claimed authority to act in a time of war or national emergency that violates civil liberties.[275] A famous incident of this kind came early in the U.S. civil war, when President Abraham Lincoln ordered the army to suspend the writ of habeas corpus along the military line between Philadelphia and Washington, with the objective of detaining southern sympathizers who were impeding the movement of Union troops. Declared unconstitutional by Chief Justice Roger Taney (sitting as a circuit judge) in *Ex parte Merryman*,[276] President Lincoln rhetorically asked whether it made sense to adhere rigidly to the Constitution in situations where the Constitution's very existence was threatened: "Are all the laws *but one* to go unexecuted, and the Government itself go to pieces lest that one be violated?"[277] President Lincoln appears to have understood that his action was unconstitutional, but viewed it as necessary and was prepared to face whatever repercussions might arise from Congress (which later adopted a statute authorizing suspension of the writ) or the people of the United States (which later reelected the president to a second term).[278]

The Court at times has upheld similar denials of civil liberties in a time of crisis. After the Japanese attack on Pearl Harbor at the outset of World War II, the U.S. government ordered Japanese-Americans living on the West Coast to move to internment camps, purportedly as a matter of national security.[279] A U.S. citizen of Japanese ancestry living in California, Fred Korematsu, chose to stay at his residence rather than obey. Upon being arrested and convicted of violating the order, Korematsu sued, arguing that the government's action was a denial of liberty without due process of law in violation of the Fifth Amendment.[280] Despite recognizing that legal restrictions on persons of a single racial group are suspect and must be rigidly scrutinized, the Court in *Korematsu v. United States* upheld the action as an exercise of federal war powers for protection against espionage and sabotage. The Court elided the racial aspects of the case, asserting instead that Korematsu "was excluded because we are at war with the Japanese

---

[275] *See generally* Norman Dorsen, *Foreign Affairs and Civil Liberties, in* FOREIGN AFFAIRS AND THE U.S. CONSTITUTION, *supra* note 26, at 134.

[276] 17 F. Cas. 144 (C.C.D. Md. 1861).

[277] 6 A COMPILATION OF THE MESSAGES AND PAPERS OF THE PRESIDENTS 25 (James D. Richardson ed., 1909).

[278] For more detailed discussion, see Chapter 8 § I(C)(2).

[279] Such action was based upon statute, see Act of March 21, 1942, ch. 191, Pub. L. No. 77-503, 56 Stat. 173, on executive order, see Exec. Order No. 9,066, 7 Fed. Reg. 1407 (Feb. 19, 1942), later rescinded by Proclamation No. 4417, 41 Fed. Reg. 7741 (Feb. 19, 1976) (codified at 3 C.F.R. pt. 2714 (1977)), and on military orders, see, for example, Civilian Exclusion Order No. 34, Western Defense Command and Fourth Army Wartime Civil Control Administration (May 3, 1942).

[280] Korematsu v. United States, 323 U.S. 214, 218 (1944).

Empire" and because the authorities had "decided that the military urgency of the situation demanded that all citizens of Japanese ancestry be segregated from the West Coast temporarily."[281]

Even at the time of the decision, members of the Court recognized the government's action as an extraordinary aberration.[282] Justice Frank Murphy's dissent lamented that such action "goes over 'the very brink of constitutional power' and falls into the ugly abyss of racism."[283] Likewise, Justice Owen Roberts in dissent asserted that this was a "case of convicting a citizen as a punishment for not submitting to imprisonment in a concentration camp, based on his ancestry, and solely because of his ancestry, without evidence or inquiry concerning his loyalty and good disposition towards the United States."[284]

Justice Jackson's opinion may (again) have been the most prescient. Writing in dissent, he declared the action unconstitutional, because "a judicial construction of the due process clause that will sustain this order is a far more subtle blow to liberty than the promulgation of the order itself."[285] He warned that the precedent would "lie[] about like a loaded weapon ready for the hand of any authority that c[ould] bring forward a plausible claim of an urgent need."[286] At the same time, Justice Jackson apparently accepted that the military would act to protect the nation in a time of war, that military necessity was not an area in which the courts were equipped to judge, and that ultimately the courts could not be viewed as the means for controlling military action in time of war.[287] Rather, the "chief restraint upon those who command the physical forces of the country, in the future as in the past, must be their responsibility to the political judgments of their contemporaries and to the moral judgments of history."[288] Apparently, rigid adherence to the Constitution at all times could not be expected of the political branches; indeed, Justice Jackson would later assert the evocative maxim that the Constitution is not a "suicide pact."[289]

---

[281] *Id.* at 223.

[282] According to the executive branch itself, the Court's consideration of these issues may have been impaired by the government's misleading representations during the litigation. Neal Katyal, *Confession of Error: The Solicitor General's Mistakes During the Japanese-American Internment Cases*, U.S. DEP'T OF JUSTICE (May 20, 2011), https://perma.cc/24MR-56ML. For discussion, compare Charles Sheehan, *Solicitor General Charles Fahy and Honorable Defense of the Japanese-American Exclusion Cases*, 54 AM. J. LEGAL HIST. 469 (2014), with Peter Irons, *How Solicitor General Charles Fahey Misled the Supreme Court in the Japanese American Internment Cases: A Reply to Charles Sheehan*, 55 AM. J. LEGAL HIST. 208 (2015).

[283] *Korematsu*, 323 U.S. at 233 (Murphy, J., dissenting).

[284] *Id.* at 226 (Roberts, J., dissenting).

[285] *Id.* at 245–46 (Jackson, J., dissenting).

[286] *Id.* at 246.

[287] *Id.* at 247–48.

[288] *Id.* at 248.

[289] Terminiello v. Chicago, 337 U.S. 1, 37 (1949) (Jackson, J., dissenting).

Korematsu and an earlier case, *Hirabayashi v. United States*,[290] were heavily crit-icized outside the Court for an unwillingness to examine the true reasons that motivated the government's action (racial hostility and discrimination), and for dis-pensing with civil liberties in a time of crisis instead.[291] Yet the "loaded weapon" remained good law well into the twenty-first century, even after Congress pro-vided surviving detainees compensation and Fred Korematsu was awarded the Presidential Medal of Freedom.[292]

The terrorist attacks of 9/11 against the United States unleashed a wide range of executive action that also severely challenged, if not transgressed, civil liber-ties.[293] Such actions included: the establishment by presidential military order of special tribunals to try noncitizens suspected of involvement in terrorist activi-ties;[294] interrogation techniques used against such noncitizens abroad;[295] deten-tion of some U.S. nationals as "enemy combatants";[296] detention in the United States of thousands of noncitizens as a preventive strategy against future terrorist activity;[297] government monitoring of exchanges between suspected terrorists and their lawyers;[298] a vast expansion in the scope of government surveillance

[290] 320 U.S. 81 (1943).

[291] *See, e.g.,* Eugene V. Rostow, *The Japanese American Cases—A Disaster*, 54 YALE L.J. 489 (1945); Eric L. Muller, *The Japanese American Cases—A Bigger Disaster Than We Realized*, 49 How. L.J. 417 (2006); Jerry Kang, *Dodging Responsibility: The Story of* Hirabayashi v. United States, *in* RACE LAW STORIES (Devon Carbado & Rachel Moran eds., 2008). On the tribunals that judged the "loyalty" of these U.S. citizens of Japanese ancestry, see ERIC L. MULLER, AMERICAN INQUISITION: THE HUNT FOR JAPANESE AMERICAN DISLOYALTY IN WORLD WAR II (2017).

[292] *See* Civil Liberties Act of 1988, 50 U.S.C. §§ 1989–89b (2018) (apologizing for the detentions and granting personal compensation of $20,000 to each surviving prisoner or their spouse/parent); Remarks on Presenting the Presidential Medal of Freedom, 1 PUB. PAPERS 56-58 (Jan. 15, 1998).

[293] *See generally* JACK GOLDSMITH, THE TERROR PRESIDENCY: LAW AND JUDGMENT INSIDE THE BUSH ADMINISTRATION 81 (2007).

[294] Detention, Treatment, and Trial of Certain Non-Citizens in the War Against Terrorism, 66 Fed. Reg. 57,833 (Nov. 13, 2001); *see* Neal K. Katyal & Laurence H. Tribe, *Waging War, Deciding Guilt: Trying the Military Tribunals*, 111 YALE L.J. 1259 (2002). In *Hamdan v. Rumsfeld*, 548 U.S. 557 (2006), the Court found that the military commissions violated the Uniform Code of Military Justice (UCMJ), 10 U.S.C. §§ 801–946a, but left open the door for Congress to authorize such commissions, which it proceeded to do. *See* Military Commissions Act of 2006, Pub. L. No. 109-366, 120 Stat. 2600 (2006). The phenomenon is not unique to the United States; for a survey of the prosecution of terrorists in India, Israel, Russia, Spain, and the United States, see Amos N. Guiora, *Where Are Terrorists to Be Tried: A Comparative Analysis of Rights Granted to Suspected Terrorists*, 56 CATH. U. L. REV. 805 (2007).

[295] S. SELECT COMM. ON INTELLIGENCE, COMMITTEE STUDY OF THE CENTRAL INTELLIGENCE AGENCY'S DETENTION AND INTERROGATION PROGRAM, S. REP. NO. 113-288 (2014).

[296] Hamdi v. Rumsfeld, 542 U.S. 507, 519, 538–39 (2004); Rumsfeld v. Padilla, 542 U.S. 426 (2004); JENNIFER K. ELSEA, CONG. RESEARCH SERV., RL31724, DETENTION OF AMERICAN CITIZENS AS ENEMY COMBATANTS (2005).

[297] *See* Ctr. for Nat'l Sec. Studies v. U.S. Dep't of Justice, 331 F.3d 918, 927–28 (D.C. Cir. 2003); *see also* SEAN D. MURPHY, UNITED STATES PRACTICE IN INTERNATIONAL LAW: 1999–2001, at 437 (2002) (describing public information about the detentions).

[298] *See* National Security; Prevention of Acts of Violence and Terrorism, Interim Rule, 66 Fed. Reg. 55062 (Oct. 31, 2001); Final Rule, 72 Fed. Reg. 16271 (Apr. 4, 2007) (codified at 28 C.F.R. pts. 500–501).

within the United States;[299] and a mass detection program called the "Total Information Awareness" project that sought to analyze detailed information on persons to anticipate and prevent terrorist incidents.[300] A salient feature of what was declared as the "war on terror" was the idea that (in many cases) the existence of an "armed conflict" allowed special rules to apply that diminished civil liberties, while concomitantly the combatants in, and location and duration of, the conflict were unclear.

There appear to be three broad approaches for addressing federal foreign affairs powers in times of war or national emergency. First, one might regard the U.S. constitutional order as being the same whether or not a war or national emergency exists. Given that there are no "emergency" provisions in the Constitution, the Bill of Rights operates the same in time of war or terrorist attack as it does in peacetime. On this view, civil liberties do not diminish during a war or national emergency and, indeed, are needed even more in time of crisis than might otherwise be the case.[301]

Second, some scholars have advocated for an approach whereby the government would formally and publicly declare a national emergency, thereby providing special powers to the government for a limited period of time.[302] The advantage of this approach would be to make clear that deviations from the normal constitutional order are "extralegal" but are cabined by a specific time of crisis and thus cannot serve as a precedent for the use of powers and protection of civil liberties that usually exist.[303]

The third approach, which appears to be the one adopted by the Supreme Court, is to approach the Constitution as allowing, in context, for a balancing

[299] See ACLU v. U.S. Dep't of Justice, 265 F. Supp. 2d 20 (D.D.C. 2003); see also Tracey Topper Gonzalez, *Individual Rights Versus Collective Security: Assessing the Constitutionality of the USA PATRIOT Act*, U. MIAMI INT'L & COMP. L. REV. 75 (2003).

[300] See, e.g., Oren Gross, *Chaos and Rules: Should Responses to Violent Crises Always Be Constitutional?*, 112 YALE L.J. 1011, 1014–18 (2003); Anthony Lewis, *Civil Liberties in a Time of Terror*, 2003 WIS. L. REV. 257 (2003).

[301] See, e.g., David Cole, *Judging the Next Emergency: Judicial Review and Individual Rights in Times of Crisis*, 101 MICH. L. REV. 2565 (2003); David Cole, *The Priority of Morality: The Emergency Constitution's Blind Spot*, 113 YALE L.J. 1753 (2004).

[302] See, e.g., Bruce Ackerman, *The Emergency Constitution*, 113 YALE L.J. 1029, 1037 (2004); Gross, *supra* note 300, at 1023, 1096–1133.

[303] See Gross, *supra* note 300, at 1097. *But see* Kim Lane Scheppele, *Law in a Time of Emergency: States of Exception and the Temptations of 9/11*, 6 U. PA. J. CONST. L. 1001, 1082–83 (2004) (finding that much "of the international community that has entrenched both democracy and the rule of law has turned away from these extra-legal justifications for states of exception. Instead, such states have attempted to embed exceptionality as an instance of the normal, and not as a repudiation of the possibility of normality."); Kim Lane Scheppele, *Exceptions that Prove the Rule: Embedding Emergency Government in Everyday Constitutional Life*, in THE LIMITS OF CONSTITUTIONAL DEMOCRACY 124 (Jeffrey K. Tulis & Stephen Macedo eds., 2010) (analyzing various incidents of states of emergency worldwide and concluding that they share in common features damaging to constitutional governance). For comparative law on this issue, see CONSTITUTIONALISM UNDER EXTREME CONDITIONS (Richard Albert & Yaniv Ronzai eds., 2020).

between the government's need to protect the nation and the civil liberties guaranteed to the people. Thus, in times of war or national emergency, the balance shifts in favor of greater government power—and in particular executive power—at the expense of the protection of civil liberties.[304] Chief Justice Rehnquist, in his book on civil liberties in wartime, wrote: "In any civilized society the most important task is achieving a proper balance between freedom and order. In wartime, reason and history both suggest that this balance shifts to some degree in favor of order."[305] There is undoubtedly a strain in U.S. constitutional jurisprudence that tolerates government action during times of severe crisis, even if that action normally would be regarded as unconstitutional.

For example, in *Hamdi v. Rumsfeld*, the Court considered whether the government violated a U.S. national's Fifth Amendment right to due process by holding him indefinitely in the United States, without access to an attorney, based solely on an executive branch declaration that he was an "enemy combatant" who fought against the United States.[306] A plurality of the Court, per Justice O'Connor, approached the matter as a question of balancing, stating that it "is beyond question that substantial interests lie on both sides of the scale in this case."[307] On one side of the scale, "a state of war is not a blank check for the president when it comes to the rights of the Nation's citizens,"[308] and "Hamdi's 'private interest . . . affected by the official action' is the most elemental of liberty interests—the interest in being free from physical detention by one's own government."[309] But on "the other side of the scale are the weighty and sensitive governmental interests in ensuring that those who have in fact fought with the enemy during a war do not return to battle against the United States."[310] According to the Court, "the law of war and the realities of combat may render such detentions both necessary and appropriate, and our due process analysis need not blink at those realities."[311]

Ultimately, the Court found that the government's position on process for Hamdi had not struck the correct balance, and it crafted the contours

---

[304] *See, e.g.*, Rosa Ehrenreich Brooks, *War Everywhere: Rights, National Security Law, and the Law of Armed Conflict in the Age of Terror*, 153 U. PA. L. REV. 675, 695–702 (2004).

[305] WILLIAM H. REHNQUIST, ALL THE LAWS BUT ONE: CIVIL LIBERTIES IN WARTIME 222 (1998); *id.* at 224; *see* Padilla v. Rumsfeld, 352 F.3d 695, 714 (2d Cir. 2003) ("The Constitution envisions grave national emergencies and contemplates significant domestic abridgements of individual liberties during such times."), *rev'd and remanded*, 542 U.S. 426 (2004) (reversing on technical grounds).

[306] Hamdi v. Rumsfeld, 542 U.S. 507 (2004). For further discussion, see Chapter 10 § II(D)(7) and Chapter 8 § III(B).

[307] *Id.* at 529 (plurality op.).

[308] *Id.* at 536 (citing to Youngstown Sheet & Tube Co. v. Sawyer, 343 U.S. 579, 587 (1952)).

[309] *Id.* at 529 (citing to Foucha v. Louisiana, 504 U.S. 71, 80 (1992)).

[310] *Id.* at 531.

[311] *Id.*

of a specialized form of due process. While Hamdi was entitled to challenge his classification as an enemy combatant, and had a right to receive notice of the factual basis for his classification and a fair opportunity to rebut the government's factual assertions before a neutral decision maker, the enemy-combatant proceedings need not follow the normal due process in U.S. courts; rather, they "may be tailored to alleviate their uncommon potential to burden the Executive at a time of ongoing military conflict."[312] Thus, hearsay could be accepted as reliable evidence, there could be a presumption in favor of the government's evidence, and once the government advanced credible evidence the onus could shift to Hamdi to rebut it with more persuasive evidence.[313]

From *Hamdi* and comparable cases or incidents, it appears that in a time of war or national emergency, the federal government approaches the exercise of foreign relations powers as broader in scope than would normally be the case, and therefore capable of overcoming objections to reasonable and proportionate diminishment of civil liberties. Further, as with respect to foreign relations powers in normal times, deference to the president's need to act in time of crisis seem enhanced. Even so, as *Hamdi* suggests, a time of crisis does not accord to the president a "blank check" for the exercise of power; that power will continue to be checked, in some fashion, by the prerogatives of Congress and judicial protection of core individual rights and freedoms.[314] Perhaps with that in mind, the Court in 2018 explicitly repudiated *Korematsu*, with Chief Justice John Roberts stating that "*Korematsu* was gravely wrong the day it was decided, has been overruled in the court of history, and—to be clear—'has no place in law under the Constitution.'"[315]

---

[312] *Id.* at 533.

[313] *Id.* at 533–34.

[314] On the need for judicial review even in times of emergency, see Martin S. Flaherty, *Judicial Foreign Relations Authority After 9/11*, 56 N.Y. L. SCH. L. REV. 119, 122 (2011–2012); DAVID RUDENSTINE, THE AGE OF DEFERENCE: THE SUPREME COURT, NATIONAL SECURITY, AND THE CONSTITUTIONAL ORDER (2016); MARTIN S. FLAHERTY, RESTORING THE GLOBAL JUDICIARY: WHY THE SUPREME COURT SHOULD RULE IN U.S. FOREIGN AFFAIRS 5–7 (2019).

[315] Trump v. Hawaii, 138 S. Ct. 2392, 2423 (2018) (quoting Korematsu v. United States, 323 U.S. 214, 248 (1944) (Jackson, J., dissenting)). Ironically, the Court in *Trump* was criticized as engaging in a *Korematsu*-style unwillingness to analyze whether presidential orders prohibiting entry into the United States of persons from largely Muslim countries were based on racial animus. *See id.* at 2435, 2447–48 (Sotomayor, J., dissenting) (drawing parallels with *Korematsu*, and finding that the majority's "highly abridged account does not tell even half of the story" of the president's ban on travel, and greatly minimizes the evidence demonstrating that the ban "was motivated by hostility and animus toward the Muslim faith"); Richard A. Dean, Trump v. Hawaii *Is* Korematsu *All Over Again*, 29 GEO. MASON CIV. RTS. L.J. 175, 176 (2019); John Ip, *The Travel Ban, Judicial Deference, and the Legacy of* Korematsu, 63 HOW. L.J. 153, 154–55 (2020); Neal Kumar Katyal, Trump v. Hawaii: *How the Supreme Court Simultaneously Overturned and Revived* Korematsu, 128 YALE L.J.F. 641 (2019). On the travel ban and the First Amendment, see Chapter 10 § II(A)(2); on the travel ban and presidential discretion in immigration law, see Chapter 10 § III(A)(2).

2
Legislating Foreign Relations

As discussed in Chapter 1, the president historically has enjoyed certain inherent advantages in exercising power in the field of U.S. foreign relations, resulting in a role that goes well beyond what the U.S. Constitution itself expressly indicates. Even so, Congress has retained its own considerable power in this regard, serving as a critical check on (and partner with) the executive.

This chapter addresses Congress' power to legislate with respect to foreign relations. The Constitution vests in Congress legislative powers that are specific to foreign affairs and other, more general, powers that are important in the foreign affairs realm. Further, to the extent that there is an inherent general foreign affairs power that the U.S. government possesses arising from the sovereignty of the United States, that power might be shared by the political branches, supporting congressional action in circumstances where an enumerated power is lacking.[1] These powers, together, have been used to enact a wide array of federal statutes concerning U.S. foreign relations, and these statutes in turn are the source of extensive federal regulations. Many of these statutes concern issues central to U.S. national and economic security, including immigration, punishment of international and transnational crimes, the import and export of goods, foreign investment in the United States, and the provision of U.S. government goods and services to foreign governments. Indeed, a large degree of U.S. foreign policy is accomplished through the provision of foreign aid and through sales of military goods and services to allies, which may be conditioned upon a foreign government's fidelity to the rule of law, human rights obligations, or other matters.[2]

This chapter cannot address all such laws and regulations; nor, for that matter, does it address the full range of constitutional authority, some of which is covered elsewhere in this volume. Section I instead surveys and highlights the enumerated and possible unenumerated powers of Congress to legislate on foreign relations. Section II addresses important cross-cutting aspects of the legislative power that have recurrently featured with respect to foreign relations. Sections III and IV, respectively, focus on two key enumerated powers of Congress that

---

[1] *See* Chapter 1 § I(D) (especially discussions relating to the implications of *Curtiss-Wright* and *Chae Chan Ping*).
[2] *See generally* LEGISLATING FOREIGN POLICY (Hoyt Purvis & Steven J. Baker eds., 1984).

are not discussed elsewhere in this volume: the power to appropriate funds as it relates to foreign relations and the power to regulate commerce with foreign nations. Finally, Section V addresses the power to regulate the value of foreign coin.

I. Enumerated and Non-Enumerated Powers to Legislate

A. Congress' Enumerated Powers to Legislate on Foreign Relations

Congress possesses a variety of substantive powers relating to foreign relations that are enumerated in Article I, Section 8, of the Constitution.[3] Most significant are the power to regulate commerce with foreign nations;[4] the power to establish a uniform rule of naturalization throughout the United States;[5] the power to regulate the value of foreign coin;[6] the power to define and punish piracies and felonies committed on the high seas, and offenses against the law of nations;[7] various powers relating to war and national defense;[8] and the power to enact laws which shall be necessary and proper for carrying into execution these (and other) powers.[9] Other sections of Article I support Congress' power to enact laws on receipt of gifts or an office by U.S. government personnel from a foreign government[10] and to regulate the interaction of the several states with foreign countries, such as with respect to duties on imports or exports and relating to the approval of foreign agreements and compacts.[11]

Still other enumerated powers allow Congress to regulate matters that, in certain circumstances, may relate to foreign affairs.[12] Thus, the power to lay taxes can be used to support statutes that regulate taxation of U.S. nationals and corporations located abroad,[13] while Congress' power to "provide for the common Defence and general Welfare of the United States" (often referred to as the "spending power") can be used to support statutes that appropriate funds for U.S. foreign aid, the establishment of U.S. embassies and consulates abroad, and the operations of the Department of State and other government agencies

---

[3] HENKIN, FOREIGN AFFAIRS, at 63–70.
[4] U.S. CONST. art. I, § 8, cl. 3; *see infra* this chapter § IV(A).
[5] U.S. CONST. art. I, § 8, cl. 4; *see* Chapter 10 § III(A).
[6] U.S. CONST. art. I, § 8, cl. 5; *see infra* this chapter § V.
[7] U.S. CONST. art. I, § 8, cl. 10; *see* Chapter 5 § II(A)(1)–(2).
[8] U.S. CONST. art. I, § 8, cl. 11–16; *see* Chapter 8 § I(B).
[9] U.S. CONST. art. I, § 8, cl. 18; *see* Chapter 6 § IV(B) (with respect to implementation of treaties).
[10] U.S. CONST. art. I, § 9, cl. 8; *see* Chapter 3 § V.
[11] U.S. CONST. art. I, § 10, cl. 2–3; *see* Chapter 9 § III.
[12] HENKIN, FOREIGN AFFAIRS, at 72–75.
[13] U.S. CONST. art. I, § 8, cl. 1; *see, e.g.,* Tax Reform Act of 1986, Pub. L. No. 99-514, 100 Stat. 2085 (codified as amended in scattered sections of 26 U.S.C.).

engaged in foreign relations.[14] Congress' power to regulate with respect to the District of Columbia supports statutes addressing the treatment of foreign embassies, their property, and their personnel in the nation's capital.[15] Congress' power to enact laws creating and regulating the departments and agencies of the executive branch, implied from the president's power to make appointments to offices "which shall be established by law," supports extensive laws regulating the Department of State and other agencies involved in U.S. foreign relations.[16] Congress' power to ordain and establish inferior courts to the U.S. Supreme Court[17] sustains, for example, the creation of a Court of International Trade,[18] while its power to regulate the jurisdiction of federal courts, set forth in Article III,[19] supports the adoption of statutes that regulate such jurisdiction with respect to foreign relations.[20] Congress' power to punish treason,[21] which consists of waging war against the United States or giving aid and comfort to its enemies,[22] supports statutes criminalizing the commission and concealment of treason.[23] The Constitution expressly accords to Congress the power to admit new states, which can be an essential component of acquiring foreign territory (as in the admission of California following the Treaty of Guadalupe Hidalgo).[24] It also provides a power to dispose of property belonging to the United States, which supports statutes that, for example, authorize the sale, lease, or other transfer of excess defense articles to foreign states.[25]

Indeed, it is difficult to identify an enumerated power of Congress that cannot, at least in theory, have some connection to U.S. foreign relations. Ostensibly domestic legislative authority may become relevant to international affairs, for example, when the subject is regulated by an international agreement of the United

---

[14] U.S. CONST. art. I, § 8, cl. 1; *see also id.* § 9, cl. 7. *See infra* this chapter § III.

[15] U.S. CONST. art. I, § 8, cl. 17.

[16] *Id. art.* II, § 2, cl. 2.

[17] *Id.* art. III., § 1.

[18] The Court of International Trade, formerly known as the Customs Court, is an Article III court of nine judges located in New York, with nationwide jurisdiction over certain civil actions arising out of U.S. customs and international trade laws. For example, the court hears disputes relating to determinations by the Department of Commerce regarding anti-dumping and countervailing duties. *See* 28 U.S.C. §§ 251–58 (organization of the court), §§ 1581–85 (jurisdiction), §§ 2631–47 (procedures) (2018).

[19] U.S. CONST. art. III, § 2, cl. 1.

[20] For example, a statute instructing federal courts not to dismiss claims concerning a particular issue through invocation of the Act of State doctrine. *See* 22 U.S.C. § 2370 (2018) ("Second Hickenlooper amendment").

[21] U.S. CONST. art. III., § 3, cl. 2.

[22] *Id.* art. III., § 3, cl. 1.

[23] 18 U.S.C. §§ 2381–82 (2018); *see also* 38 U.S.C. § 6104 (forfeiture for treason).

[24] U.S. CONST. art. IV, § 3, cl. 1; *see* Treaty of Peace, Friendship, Limits, and Settlement with the Republic of Mexico, Mex.-U.S., Feb. 2, 1848, 9 Stat. 922; Act of Sept. 9, 1850, ch. 50, 9 Stat. 452; *see also* Chapter 6 § II(D)(2) (discussing use of treaty power to acquire territory).

[25] U.S. CONST. art. IV, § 3, cl. 2; *see* Foreign Assistance Act, Pub. L. No. 87-195, §§ 516, 644(g) (1961) (codified at 22 U.S.C. §§ 2321j, 2403g (2018)).

States and Congress is charged with implementing the agreement through its enumerated powers (including the Necessary and Proper Clause). Examples include laws on borrowing funds from foreign governments or banks,[26] on international standards for weights and measurements,[27] and on transnational postal or copyright matters.[28]

B. Congress' Non-Enumerated Power to Legislate on Foreign Relations

As discussed in Chapter 1, the broad vesting of the executive power in the president under Article II, Section 1, of the Constitution is often cited as the predicate for significant, otherwise unmentioned power in the field of foreign relations that the president in fact wields.[29] By contrast, Article I, Section 1 of the Constitution provides to Congress "[a]ll legislative powers herein granted shall be vested in a Congress of the United States,"[30] arguably implying that no legislative power is conferred on Congress by the Constitution apart from other powers specifically enumerated in other provisions. This has led some scholars to maintain that Congress possesses no general foreign affairs power; instead, it possesses only enumerated foreign affairs powers, and any other legislative foreign affairs powers remain with the several states (or with the people).[31] Other scholars, including Louis Henkin, have maintained that a general foreign affairs power exists as an inherent part of any country's government, that Congress has historically exercised such power through the adoption of certain types of statutes, and that such power has been recognized on occasion by the U.S. courts.[32]

The argument that Congress is limited to its enumerated powers depends on textualist claims (including the contrast with Article II, Section 1) and other constitutional arguments that transcend the foreign relations context. There are also broad counterarguments. For example, Article I, Section 1's reference to legislative powers may be understood as simply stressing that the listed powers were vested solely in Congress, not that they were confined in their substantive

---

[26] U.S. Const. art. I, § 8, cl. 2. *See, e.g.,* 12 U.S.C. §§ 3901–11 (2018) (international lending supervision).

[27] U.S. Const. art. I, § 8, cl. 5. *See, e.g.,* 15 U.S.C. §§ 201–205*l* (standards for weight and measurement and conversion of metric system).

[28] U.S. Const. *art.* I, § 8, cl. 7–8. *See e.g.,* Berne Convention Implementation Act of 1988, 17 U.S.C. § 101 note; 39 U.S.C. § 407 (implementing the Constitution of the Universal Postal Union, July 10, 1964, 16 U.S.T. 1291, 611 U.N.T.S. 7).

[29] U.S. Const. art. II, § 1 ("The executive Power shall be vested in a President of the United States . . ."); *see* Chapter 1 § I(B).

[30] *Id.* art. I, § 1.

[31] *See, e.g.,* Michael D. Ramsey, The Constitution's Text in Foreign Affairs 204 (2007).

[32] *See* Henkin, Foreign Affairs, at 70–72. *See generally* Chapter 1 § I(D).

scope.[33] The question of unenumerated congressional powers relating to foreign relations is subordinate to this larger question, and for the most part, resolving it seems unnecessary. Congress' extensive enumerated powers to legislate under Article I of the U.S. Constitution appear sufficient to support the adoption of a very wide range of legislation relating to foreign relations—especially when combined with Congress' capacity under the Necessary and Proper Clause to implement international agreements concluded by the United States.[34] As such, the need of Congress to rely on a general foreign affairs power appears *de minimis*.

Even so, Congress has adopted statutes that do not easily fit within the scope of its enumerated powers and might be construed as expressing a more general foreign affairs power. One class of such statutes concerns the acquisition of territory other than by admission of new states.[35] The 1856 Guano Islands Act provides that islands, rocks, or keys not within the jurisdiction of any other country should "be considered as appertaining to the United States" if a U.S. national discovers upon them a deposit of guano and provides notice of the discovery to the Department of State.[36] However unlikely it may seem, that statute, and acts taken in pursuance of it, at one time supported U.S. claims to about one hundred islands, and today still supports U.S. claims to about a dozen islands, such as Navassa Island located in the Caribbean Sea.[37] Similarly, other statutes regulate U.S. sovereign rights in maritime or air spaces located outside U.S. territory, such as in the U.S. exclusive economic zone[38] or in the U.S. continental shelf,[39] and establish U.S. control of air defense identification zones located beyond U.S. territorial airspace,[40] even though there are no enumerated powers that expressly

[33] See Richard Primus, *Herein of "Herein Granted": Why Article I's Vesting Clause Does Not Support the Doctrine of Enumerated Powers*, 35 CONST. COMMENT. 301 (2020); *see also id.* at 303 & 303 n.14.

[34] *See* Chapter 5 § II(A)(2). *Cf.* Alison L. LaCroix, *The Shadow Powers of Article I*, 123 YALE L.J. 2044, 2059–60 (2014).

[35] While the Constitution accords to Congress the power to admit new states, U.S. Const. art. IV, § 3, cl. 1, and to regulate territory belonging to the United States, *id. art.* IV, § 3, cl. 2, it does not expressly accord to Congress power to acquire new territory. *See* Chapter 1 § I(D). Once territory is acquired, constitutional doctrine acknowledges incorporated territories, which normally are territories on a path to statehood (as occurred with Alaska and Hawaii), or unincorporated territories, such as American Samoa, Guam, Northern Marianas Islands, Puerto Rico, or the U.S. Virgin Islands. On the application of constitutional rights in unincorporated territories, see Chapter 10 § I(B).

[36] 48 U.S.C. §§ 1411–19 (2018). The statute also authorizes the president to use military force to protect such islands and extends U.S. criminal jurisdiction to them. *See generally* JIMMY M. SKAGGS, THE GREAT GUANO RUSH: ENTREPRENEURS AND AMERICAN OVERSEAS EXPANSION (1994).

[37] Navassa Island (or La Navasse) is a small, uninhabited island located between Haiti and Jamaica that is administered by the United States (through the U.S. Fish and Wildlife Service) as an unorganized, unincorporated territory. The Supreme Court in 1890 affirmed that the United States had jurisdiction in three criminal cases that arose from events on the island in 1889. Jones v. United States, 137 U.S. 202 (1890); *see* Sovereignty Over Swan Islands, 34 Op. Att'y Gen. 507 (1925). For a dispute under U.S. law as to title to the island, see Warren v. United States, 234 F.3d 1331 (D.C. Cir. 2000).

[38] Magnuson-Stevens Fishery Conservation and Management Act, 16 U.S.C. §§ 1801–91d (2018).

[39] Outer Continental Shelf Lands Act, 43 U.S.C. §§ 1331–56.

[40] 49 U.S.C. § 40103(b)(3). The United States maintains four air defense identification zones: one contiguous to the forty-eight states; and ones contiguous to Alaska, Guam, and Hawaii. *See* 14 C.F.R. §§ 99.41–99.43, 99.45, 99.47, & 99.49 (2019).

address such issues.[41] A third set of examples concern the treatment of relations with foreign governments and foreign officials, at least in circumstances where the statute is not implementing an international agreement or is not related to Congress' powers to define and punish offenses against the law of nations or to regulate within the District of Columbia. For example, such statutes might include those that make it an offense to impersonate foreign diplomats, consuls, and officers,[42] or criminalizing conspiracy to injure the property of a foreign government.[43] A fourth class might be those regulating acts committed against U.S. nationals who are located abroad (again, in circumstances where the statute is not squarely grounded in the implementation of an international agreement or in Congress' power to define and punish offenses against the law of nations), such as statutes protecting U.S. nationals abroad from terrorism.[44] Likewise, such power might serve to sustain all statutes criminalizing overseas conduct of U.S. nationals involving foreign governments, nationals, or property.[45]

The Supreme Court's examination of other statutes, in additional areas, has sometimes suggested the possibility of unenumerated powers. For example, a general foreign affairs power might be invoked to support statutes requiring U.S. nationals who are located abroad to comply with obligations owed to the U.S. government. Thus, in *Blackmer v. United States*, involving the refusal of a U.S. national living abroad to return to the United States to serve as a witness, the Court said that it cannot "be doubted that the United States possesses the power *inherent in sovereignty* to require the return to this country of a citizen, resident elsewhere, whenever the public interest requires it, and to penalize him in case of refusal."[46] The Court further asserted that under the U.S. constitutional system there is "national authority which may be exercised by the Congress by virtue of the legislative power *to prescribe the duties of the citizens of the United States.*"[47] That same power may be the source of authority for Congress, as suggested in *Reid v. Covert*, to compel a civilian dependent,

---

[41] Though one might infer congressional power over maritime matters based on the grant of maritime jurisdiction to federal courts. U.S. CONST. art. III, § 2.

[42] 18 U.S.C. § 915 (2018).

[43] 18 U.S.C. § 956. For other statutes addressing treatment of foreign governments or officials, see, for example, 18 U.S.C. § 952 (criminalizing making false statements influencing foreign governments in certain circumstances); 18 U.S.C. § 953 (regulating correspondence with foreign governments or officials).

[44] 18 U.S.C. § 2332 (2018) (criminal penalties for terrorists who kill or attempt to kill U.S. nationals abroad); 18 U.S.C. § 2333 (civil remedies for terrorist victims).

[45] There are many examples of laws criminalizing actions of U.S. citizens abroad. *See* 18 U.S.C. § 1116 (granting the United States jurisdiction over murder or manslaughter of foreign officials, official guests, or internationally protected persons); 18 U.S.C. § 2261 (criminalizing domestic violence committed by someone who traveled in "foreign commerce"); PROTECT Act, 18 U.S.C. § 2423(c) (discussed *infra* note 284).

[46] Blackmer v. United States, 284 U.S. 421, 437 (1932) (emphasis added).

[47] *Id.* (emphasis added).

accompanying a member of the U.S. military, to return to the United States to stand trial for a crime committed abroad.[48] Power relating to such duties also might support the Logan Act, which makes it an offense for a U.S. national to carry on "correspondence or intercourse with any foreign government . . . with the intent to influence the measures or conduct of any foreign government . . . in relation to any disputes or controversies with the United States, or to defeat the measures of the United States."[49]

The Court has expressed similar views regarding immigration. While the power to establish a uniform rule of naturalization allows Congress to legislate with respect to the conditions by which persons can become U.S. nationals (as well as perhaps lose citizenship),[50] it does not expressly cover a wider array of issues concerning the entry, presence, and removal of non-nationals. Authority for legislation of that kind (discussed in Chapter 10) might be extrapolated from Congress' naturalization power or the Foreign Commerce Clause, but the Court has implied a broader, unenumerated congressional power over foreign relations. In *Hines v. Davidowitz*, for example, the Supreme Court upheld a statute requiring registration of noncitizens,[51] stating in part that "the regulation of aliens is . . . intimately blended and intertwined with responsibilities of the national government."[52] Thereafter, the Court has spoken sweepingly as to Congress' power in this area without reference to any enumerated power, such as: "The Federal Government has broad constitutional powers in determining what aliens shall be admitted to the United States, the period they may remain, regulation of their conduct before naturalization, and the terms and conditions of their naturalization."[53]

Other unenumerated powers might be invoked on future occasions. For example, Congress to this point has premised statutes allowing U.S. nationals to be extradited to another country to circumstances in which extradition is predicated on either a treaty or executive agreement.[54] Yet Congress'

---

[48] 354 U.S. 1, 7–8 (1957).

[49] 18 U.S.C. § 953 (2018). No one has been convicted under the Logan Act. *See* Daniel B. Price, *Nonenforcement by Accretion: The Logan Act and the Take Care Clause*, 55 HARV. J. LEGIS. 443, 445 (2018); *see also* Detlev F. Vagts, *The Logan Act: Paper Tiger or Sleeping Giant?*, 60 AM. J. INT'L L. 268 (1966).

[50] 8 U.S.C. § 1483.

[51] Although the statute in *Hines* was eventually repealed, current law also requires registration. *See* 8 U.S.C. §§ 1302–06.

[52] Hines v. Davidowitz, 312 U.S. 52, 66 (1941).

[53] *See* Takahashi v. Fish & Game Comm., 334 U.S. 410, 419 (1948); *see also* Chae Chan Ping v. United States, 130 U.S. 581, 603 (1889) (finding it not open to controversy that "the government of the United States, through the action of the legislative department, can exclude aliens from its territory"). For further discussion of *Chae Chan Ping* (also known as the *Chinese Exclusion Case*), see Chapter 1 § I(D); Chapter 8 § I(C)(1); and Chapter 10 § III(A)(1).

[54] 18 U.S.C. § 3184. On extradition generally, see Chapter 10 § III(C).

foreign affairs power might be said to support Congress' ability to enact a statute allowing a U.S. national to be extradited to another country even in other circumstances. Although there is no enumerated power to adopt statutes governing extradition, in *Valentine v. United States*, the Supreme Court stated that "the power to provide for extradition is a national power" that "is not confided to the Executive in the absence of treaty *or legislative provision.*"[55]

Of course, statutory enactments may be based on a combination of a general foreign affairs power and an enumerated power of Congress, whereby the enumerated power supports some but not all of the legislation. The legislative history of the Foreign Sovereign Immunities Act (FSIA), a comprehensive statute governing the immunity of foreign states in U.S. courts,[56] suggests that it was founded on a wide variety of premises:

> Constitutional authority for enacting such legislation derives from the constitutional power of the Congress to prescribe the jurisdiction of Federal courts (art. I, sec. 8, cl. 9; art. III, sec. 1); to define offenses against the "Law of Nations" (art. I, sec. 8, cl. 10); to regulate commerce with foreign nations (art. I, sec. 8, cl. 3); and "to make all Laws which shall be necessary and proper for carrying into Execution . . . all . . . Powers vested . . . in the Government of the United States," including the judicial power of the United States over controversies between "a State, or the Citizens thereof, and foreign States . . . ." (art. I, sec. 8, cl. 18; art. III, sec. 2, cl. 1).[57]

It is challenging to associate certain components of the FSIA with enumerated powers. For example, while the exception to foreign sovereign immunity relating to commercial activity would appear to be grounded in part on Congress' foreign commerce power,[58] other exceptions to immunity included in the FSIA may implicate a general congressional foreign affairs power. In *Verlinden B.V. v. Central Bank of Nigeria*, the Supreme Court noted Congress' "authority over foreign commerce *and foreign relations*," and further alluded to the fact that "[a]ctions against foreign sovereigns in our courts raise sensitive issues concerning the foreign relations of the United States, and the primacy of federal concerns is evident."[59]

---

[55] Valentine v. United States, 299 U.S. 5, 8 (1936) (emphasis added).
[56] 28 U.S.C. §§ 1330, 1332, 1391(f), 1441(d), 1602–11. For a fuller discussion of the FSIA, see Chapter 4 § V(A).
[57] H.R. REP. NO. 94-1487, at 12 (1976) (citing Nat'l Bank v. Republic of China, 348 U.S. 356, 370–71 (1955) (Reed, J., dissenting); Banco Nacional de Cuba v. Sabbatino, 376 U.S. 398, 425 (1964)).
[58] *See, e.g.*, 28 U.S.C. § 1605(a)(2).
[59] Verlinden B.V. v. Central Bank of Nigeria, 461 U.S. 480, 493 (1983) (emphasis added).

II. Procedural and Other Cross-Cutting Aspects of the Power to Legislate

A. House and Senate Committees

As with other subjects, foreign relations legislation originates in the House or Senate through bills proposed by members, which are then typically taken up by the relevant committees or subcommittees with jurisdiction over the subject matter of the bill.[60] Thus, the House Foreign Affairs Committee has jurisdiction over legislation related to a wide variety of issues, including: foreign assistance; strategic planning and agreements; national security developments affecting foreign policy; war powers; treaties and executive agreements; arms control and disarmament issues; international law enforcement issues, including narcotics control programs and activities; the United Nations and other international organizations, including assessed and voluntary contributions; international law; and the promotion of democracy. Matters relating to agencies of the executive branch with responsibilities for foreign relations also fall within the Committee's ambit, such as the Department of State, the Agency for International Development, and the Peace Corps Amendments to and implementation of organic statutes in the foreign relations field, such as the Foreign Assistance Act (FAA) or Arms Export Control Act (AECA), also come before the Committee, including export and licensing policy for munitions items and technology and dual-use equipment and technology.[61] A similar situation exists in the Senate, with the Senate Foreign Relations Committee exercising jurisdiction over a comparable range of foreign relations issues, and with further unique responsibilities relating to its role in consenting to the ratification of treaties[62] and to the appointment of ambassadors, other public ministers, and consuls.[63]

---

[60] VALERIE HEITSHUSEN, CONG. RESEARCH. SERV., 98–241, COMMITTEE TYPES AND ROLES 1 (2017).

[61] Additional House committees also address foreign relations matters, notably the committees on Appropriations, Armed Services, Energy and Commerce, Homeland Security, and Intelligence. Specific issues relating to foreign affairs may also be addressed by other committees. For instance, trade legislation originates in the House Committee on Ways and Means, which has a subcommittee designated to work on trade legislation. See IAN F. FERGUSSON, CONG. RESEARCH SERV., RL33743, TRADE PROMOTION AUTHORITY (TPA) AND THE ROLE OF CONGRESS IN TRADE POLICY (2015). For a discussion of the emergence during the 1970s of the contemporary system of committees and subcommittees in the House, and other reforms, see CHARLES W. WHALEN, JR., THE HOUSE AND FOREIGN POLICY (1982).

[62] See Chapter 6 §§ II(B)(2), III(B)(2).

[63] See Chapter 3 § III.

For both the House and the Senate, not all legislation relating to foreign affairs is necessarily taken up in the aforementioned committees, as other committees may be viewed as the proper venues. For example, the Justice Against Sponsors of Terrorism Act[64] —a statute enacted in 2016 over President Barack Obama's veto[65] that had significant ramifications for U.S.-Saudi relations[66]—originated in the Senate Judiciary Committee and was never taken up in the Senate Foreign Relations Committee.[67]

Moreover, some issues with considerable impact on foreign affairs, such as military and intelligence matters, are handled by multiple committees. This division of foreign affairs issues among congressional committees sometimes results in competition between them, even within each chamber,[68] in which case they must be resolved by the relevant chairpersons[69] or by other means.[70] Sometimes these differences mirror differences arising within the executive branch. For example, the provision of foreign assistance has long been a matter of developmental policy falling principally within the domain of the Department of State, and concomitantly of the House and Senate foreign affairs/relations committees. Yet increasingly the Department of Defense has had extensive operational involvement in the provision of such assistance (e.g., in Afghanistan and Iraq), thereby drawing greater attention by the armed services committees of the two houses, which are focused more on security than developmental objectives.[71]

---

[64] Pub. L. No. 114-222 (2016) (codified in scattered sections of 28 U.S.C.).

[65] Message to the Senate Returning without Approval the Justice Against Sponsors of Terrorism Act, 2016 DAILY COMP. PRES. DOC. 628 (Sept. 23, 2016).

[66] See, e.g., Katherine Holcombe, JASTA Straw Man? How the Justice Against Sponsors of Terrorism Act Undermines Our Security and its Stated Purpose, 25 AM. U. J. GENDER, SOC. POL'Y & L. 359, 379 (2017).

[67] For procedural background on the legislation, see Justice Against Sponsors of Terrorism Act, CONGRESS.GOV, https://perma.cc/DEQ6-8LDA.

[68] John J. Harter, Congress and Foreign Affairs, AMERICAN DIPLOMACY (Jan. 2011), https://perma.cc/WE3H-WS58.

[69] The individual serving as chair is an important factor in the committee's influence and effectiveness. See, e.g., Frédérick Gagnon, The Most Dynamic Club: Vandenberg, Fulbright, Helms, and the Activism of the Chairman of the US Senate Foreign Relations Committee, 14 FOREIGN POL'Y ANALYSIS 191 (2018). Of course, the speaker of the House or majority leader in the Senate can have a strong influence on U.S. foreign relations if he or she chooses to do so. See, e.g., Jordan T. Cash, "The Voice of America": The Speaker of the House and Foreign Policy Agenda-Setting, 53 POLITY 666 (2021).

[70] For example, disputes among committees in the House of Representatives may be resolved or addressed through a recommendation to the House by the Committee on Rules, when that Committee sets the terms of debate on a particular piece of legislation. See H. COMM. ON RULES, 117TH CONG., 2D SESS., SPECIAL RULES PROCESS ¶ 3 (2022), https://perma.cc/5TQ7-6NDH.

[71] On the differing roles of the departments, see NINA M. SERAFINO, CONG. RESEARCH SERV., R44444, SECURITY ASSISTANCE AND COOPERATION: SHARED RESPONSIBILITY OF THE DEPARTMENTS OF STATE AND DEFENSE (2016); see also William F.S. Miles, Deploying Development to Counter Terrorism: Post-9/11 Transformation of U.S. Foreign Aid to Africa, 55 AFR. STUDS. REV. 27, 33 (2012) (explaining an evolution in U.S. foreign aid by which development programs increasingly contain a security dimension).

B. Presentment and the Legislative Veto

As is the case with the enactment of any law, bills concerning foreign relations must pass both houses of Congress by a simple majority vote and be presented to the president.[72] Like other legislation, the president may sign the bill into law or veto it; following a veto, Congress sometimes chooses to let the legislation die (for example, this occurred with the Foreign Affairs Reform and Restructuring Act of 1998),[73] and sometimes successfully overrides the veto by two-thirds majority votes in both houses (as occurred with the Justice Against Sponsors of Terrorism Act).[74]

The requirement that Congress present legislation to the president before it can be enacted into law has been construed as rendering unconstitutional statutes in which Congress retains for itself the ability, through a conclusive vote within one or both houses, to alter the law—what is called a "legislative veto." *INS v. Chadha* involved a statute granting the executive branch discretion to allow a deportable noncitizen to remain in the United States, but reserving to either house the ability to countermand the executive's decision in any given case.[75] The Supreme Court found that such action by Congress was essentially legislative in character, and therefore required Congress to act bicamerally (not just by the action of the House or Senate alone) and by presentment to the president (excluding, thereby, even a two-house measure where there was no opportunity for a presidential veto).[76] Dissenting in *Chadha*, Justice White described the majority's decision as "sound[ing] the death knell for nearly 200 other statutory provisions" that had reserved to Congress a legislative veto;[77] he included a dozen foreign affairs and national security statutes among a list of those affected, such as the War Powers Resolution, which had been enacted to combat assertions of executive branch authority that Congress viewed as excessive.[78] Indeed, the case favoring the legislative veto in the foreign affairs context was arguably stronger than for domestic affairs, insofar as the presidential authority

---

[72] U.S. CONST. art. I, § 7.

[73] See H.R. 1757, 105th Cong. (1998); Message to the House of Representatives Returning Without Approval Foreign Affairs Reform and Restructuring Legislation, 2 PUB. PAPERS 1830 (Oct. 21, 1998); 144 CONG. REC. 27,404-05 (1998).

[74] See Message to the Senate Returning Without Approval the Justice Against Sponsors of Terrorism Act, 2016 DAILY COMP. PRES. DOC. 628 (Sept. 23, 2016). President Obama's veto was overridden in the Senate by a vote of 97 to 1 and in the House of Representatives by a vote of 348 to 77, resulting in the enactment of the Justice Against Sponsors of Terrorism Act, Pub. L. No. 114-222 (2016). 162 CONG. REC. H6032, S6173 (daily ed. Sept. 28, 2016).

[75] 462 U.S. 919 (1983).

[76] Id. at 951–59.

[77] Id. at 967 (White, J., dissenting).

[78] Id. at 1003–06 (appendix to opinion of White, J., dissenting).

that Congress sought to temper rested, at least to some degree, on power that Congress had not conferred at all.[79]

One reason the legislative veto emerged was a congressional desire to be able to reacquire, in particular instances, extensive authority that it had delegated to the executive branch.[80] The condition precedent was the capacity to delegate wide-ranging authority to the executive branch notwithstanding the nondelegation doctrine, which the Supreme Court had determined in its 1936 decision in *Curtiss-Wright* should apply less stringently in the field of foreign affairs[81]—and which had been relaxed more generally across the board since then.[82] A striking example of such delegation is a statute, adopted in 2005, which granted the secretary of homeland security unilateral authority to waive all local, state, and federal laws to expedite the construction of fences, concrete slabs, or other infrastructure at the U.S. border.[83]

If the circumstances occasioning *Chadha* are widely agreed by observers, the consequences are not. The conventional wisdom is that the decision unwound previous interbranch bargains and, prospectively, deprived Congress of an important tool for reclaiming delegated authority, leaving it with a "Hobson's choice": either attempt the "hopeless task" of drafting statutes so as to address potential future issues relating to a statute's administration or, alternatively, delegate authority without hope of recovering it.[84] As Curtis Bradley has suggested, this may be overstated. Prior to *Chadha*, Congress rarely exercised the legislative veto, and perhaps never in a foreign affairs context (putting aside individual deportation suspensions as in *Chadha* itself).[85] The mechanism proved to be of little value, for example, in the war powers setting.[86] To be sure, the prospect of a veto may well have tempered presidential adventurism,[87] but it seems likely that this would have become more attenuated the more dormant the power became.

---

[79]   *Id.; see* HENKIN, FOREIGN AFFAIRS, at 127; *id.* at 127 n.* (noting countervailing arguments).

[80]   For discussion of its origins generally, see JAMES M. LANDIS, THE ADMINISTRATIVE PROCESS (1938); Gary Lawson, *The Rise and Rise of the Administrative State*, 107 HARV. L. REV. 1231 (1994); Cass R. Sunstein, *Constitutionalism after the New Deal*, 101 HARV. L. REV. 421 (1987); for greater focus on the foreign affairs context, see Curtis A. Bradley, *Reassessing the Legislative Veto: The Statutory President, Foreign Affairs, and Congressional Workarounds*, 13 J. LEGAL ANALYSIS 439, 443–47 (2021).

[81]   United States v. Curtiss-Wright Export Corp., 299 U.S. 304, 319–20 (1936).

[82]   *See* Chapter 1 § II(A)(2).

[83]   Emergency Supplemental Appropriations Act for Defense, the Global War on Terror, and Tsunami Relief, 2005, div. B, Pub. L. No. 109-13, § 102 (2005) (codified at 8 U.S.C. § 1103 note (2018)) (delegating "the authority to waive all legal requirements such Secretary, in such Secretary's sole discretion, determines necessary to ensure expeditious construction of the barriers and roads under this section"); *see In re* Border Infrastructure Environmental Litigation, 284 F. Supp. 3d 1092, 1130–37 (S.D. Cal. 2018) (upholding § 102 against nondelegation challenge).

[84]   *Chadha*, 462 U.S. at 968 (White, J., dissenting).

[85]   *See* Bradley, *supra* note 80, at 453 (citing Robert S. Gilmour & Barbara Hinkson Craig, *After the Congressional Veto: Assessing the Alternatives*, 3 J. POL'Y ANALYSIS & MGMT. 373, 374 (1984)).

[86]   *See id.* at 466–72; *see also* Chapter 8 § I(C)(4).

[87]   *See* Bradley, *supra* note 80, at 453–56 (citing conflicting evidence).

Post-*Chadha*, moreover, Congress was not left defenseless. While some veto provisions were replaced with legislative mechanisms that were vulnerable to presidential veto,[88] Congress also turned to report-and-wait provisions that temporarily suspended the effect of executive branch measures while allowing a more pronounced opportunity for legislation, as with the Iran Nuclear Agreement Review Act of 2015, which delayed implementation of a multilateral agreement with Iran.[89] While Congress could turn to these and other innovative techniques,[90] the legislative veto itself has never truly been abandoned. Not only were many legislative veto provisions left on the books, but Congress adopted at least some additional provisions of the same type, supposing (with some reason) that they would induce at least a degree of voluntary compliance.[91] Indeed, by one estimate, more than 80 percent of all legislative veto provisions were enacted following *Chadha*.[92] The informal authority these provisions assert—coupled with the availability of other routine tools, like the capacity of either house to block appropriations, which has been aptly characterized as a "one-house veto"[93]—probably preserves a considerable amount of any leverage the legislative veto ever established.

C. Presidential Signing Statements

When signing foreign relations legislation into law, the president may make a statement that describes how the executive branch intends to interpret or apply the statute.[94] The president may merely advance a contestable interpretation of

---

[88] *See id.* at 457; *see, e.g.*, Pub. L. No. 99-247, 100 Stat. 9 (1986) (codified at 22 U.S.C. § 2776 (2018)) (substituting, in relation to authorizing arms sales, the enactment of "a joint resolution prohibiting" such a sale for adoption of "a concurrent resolution stating that [Congress] objects to" such sale).

[89] Pub. L. No. 1141-17, 129 Stat. 201 (codified at 42 U.S.C. § 2160e) (providing for the prompt notification to Congress of a concluded agreement with an accompanying report, the opportunity for congressional hearings, and a period of up to sixty days, during which the president could not alter statutory sanctions on Iran); *see* Bradley, *supra* note 80, at 459–60; *see also infra* this chapter § IV(F).

[90] *See* Bradley, *supra* note 80, at 463–65 (noting examples of sunset provision and other time-related provisions, among others).

[91] *See* Louis Fisher, *The Legislative Veto: Invalidated, It Survives*, L. & CONTEMP. PROBS. (Autumn 1993), at 273; *see also* Bradley, *supra* note 80, at 461–62.

[92] *See* MICHAEL J. BERRY, THE MODERN LEGISLATIVE VETO: MACROPOLITICAL CONFLICT AND THE LEGACY OF CHADHA 275 (2016); *see also* LOUIS FISHER, CONSTITUTIONAL CONFLICTS BETWEEN CONGRESS AND THE PRESIDENT 171 (6th rev. ed. 2014) (indicating that nearly one thousand legislative vetoes were enacted following *Chadha*).

[93] Matthew B. Lawrence, *Congress' Domain: Appropriations, Time, and Chevron*, 70 DUKE L.J. 1057, 1073 (2021) (noting, additionally, that this authority was part of the original design of the separation of powers).

[94] *See, e.g.*, Statement on Signing the Lord's Resistance Army Disarmament and Northern Uganda Recovery Act of 2009, 1 PUB. PAPERS 699 (May 24, 2010) (interpreting the law as expressing a U.S. commitment to oppose the Lord's Resistance Army); Statement on Signing the United States–India Nuclear Cooperation Approval and Nonproliferation Enhancement Act, 2 PUB. PAPERS 1290 (Oct. 8, 2008) (interpreting the law as implementing an executive agreement while remaining consistent with the provisions of the Atomic Energy Act, 42 U.S.C. § 2011 et seq.).

a statute based on an assertion about its purpose or some aspect of its legislative history. More controversially, the president may indicate that a statutory
mandate is unconstitutional and will not be heeded, or declare that a provision
has to be construed differently so as to ensure constitutionality.[95] While a constitutional objection might be on any basis,[96] the most common version is that
a provision infringes upon the president's own powers and that it will, therefore, be construed to operate only in a manner consistent with such powers.[97]
Naturally, such claims are not infrequently made in the foreign relations context, as the executive branch has been prone toward an expansive conception
of presidential authority that is then irregularly assessed in court. For example,
in 2005, President George W. Bush signed into law a wide-ranging defense
appropriations act that included a provision prohibiting the cruel, inhuman, or
degrading treatment or punishment of persons held in U.S. custody regardless of
nationality or physical location,[98] a provision designed to address U.S. government conduct in the wake of the September 11, 2001 (or "9/11") terrorist attacks
and the 2003 U.S. intervention in Iraq. In a signing statement, the president said
that the provision would be interpreted "in a manner consistent with the constitutional authority of the President to supervise the unitary executive branch and
as Commander in Chief."[99]

Although signing statements have been employed for much of U.S. history,[100]
their use during recent administrations has drawn particular scrutiny and inspired debate about whether they have become exceptional in degree or kind.[101]

---

[95] Statement on Signing the Office of National Drug Control Policy Reauthorization Act of 2006,
2 Pub. Papers 2226 (Dec. 29, 2006) (declaring unconstitutional several provisions of the statute
requiring consultation with Congress).

[96] See, e.g., Statement on Signing the Assisted Suicide Funding Restriction Act of 1997, 1 Pub.
Papers 515–16 (Apr. 30, 1997) (invoking First Amendment as basis for directing agencies to construe
the Act so as "not to restrict Federal funding for other activities, such as those that provide forums
for the free exchange of ideas"); Statement on Signing the Telecommunications Act of 1996, 1 Pub.
Papers 188, 190 (Feb. 8, 1996) (noting First Amendment concerns about restricting abortion-related
speech, and advising that the Department of Justice will decline to enforce the relevant provision).

[97] Statement on Signing the Sudan Accountability and Divestment Act of 2007, 2 Pub. Papers
1596 (Dec. 31, 2007); Statement on Signing the Palestinian Anti-Terrorism Act of 2006, 2 Pub.
Papers 2221 (Dec. 21, 2006).

[98] The provision is codified at 42 U.S.C. § 2000dd (2018).

[99] Statement on Signing the Department of Defense, Emergency Supplemental Appropriations
to Address Hurricanes in the Gulf of Mexico, and the Pandemic Influenza Act, 2006, 2 Pub. Papers
1901 (Dec. 30, 2005).

[100] See generally Christopher S. Yoo, Presidential Signing Statements: A New Perspective, 164 U. Pa.
L. Rev. 1801, 1805–07 (2016).

[101] This was especially pronounced during the George W. Bush administration. Compare, e.g.,
American Bar Association Task Force on Presidential Signing Statements and the
Separation of Powers Doctrine, Report and Recommendations 6, 10–18 (2006) (reviewing
use, and finding use by President George W. Bush to be exceptional), with Curtis A. Bradley & Eric
A. Posner, Presidential Signing Statements and Executive Power, 23 Const. Comment. 307, 312–34
(2006) (concluding that the George W. Bush administration did not necessarily exhibit a distinctive
view as to the function of signing statements or concerning the underlying positions they expressed).

Such debate has sharpened the distinct questions posed. The potential value of statements as a contribution to (or gloss on) legislative history seems limited: even if separation-of-powers objections might be useful in such regard,[102] neither the executive branch nor the courts have seemed so inclined.[103] More plausible is the potential value of signing statements in relation to a statute's constitutional predicates: not simply as an expression of the president's legal views but also as harbingers of the executive branch's execution of the statute (usually, but not exclusively, in the form of Justice Department enforcement or litigation policy).[104]

A host of objections have been raised to the use of such statements in this way, including that they circumvent the hard choices imposed by the Constitution's veto provisions.[105] More fundamentally, critics have maintained that relying on such statements to disregard a statutory provision violates the Constitution, given the president's obligation to faithfully execute the laws.[106] Other commentators,

---

See generally Symposium, *The Last Word? The Constitutional Implications of Presidential Signing Statements*, 16 WM. & MARY BILL RTS. J. 1 (2007).

[102] *See, e.g.*, Marc N. Garber & Kurt A. Wimmer, *Presidential Signing Statements as Interpretations of Legislative Intent: An Executive Aggrandizement of Power*, 24 HARV. J. ON LEGIS. 363 (1987); William D. Popkins, *Judicial Use of Presidential Legislative History: A Critique*, 66 IND. L.J. 699 (1991). *But see* Yoo, *supra* note 100 (arguing that the president is due "equal dignity" in the legislative process and as a contributor to legislative history).

[103] *See* John M. de Figueiredo & Edward H. Stiglitz, *Signing Statements and Presidentializing Legislative History*, 69 ADMIN. L. REV. 841 (2017) (concluding that courts rarely cite or substantially rely on presidential signing statements of any kind); Bradley & Posner, *supra* note 101, at 345 n.131 (noting concession by Department of Justice official that "[s]igning statements, of course, are not binding on the courts") (quoting *The Use of Presidential Signing Statements: Hearing Before the S. Comm. on the Judiciary*, 109th Cong. 6 (2006) (statement of Michelle Boardman, Deputy Assistant Att'y Gen., Dep't of Justice)). *Compare, e.g.*, United States v. Ruiz, 2021 WL 5235545 *3 (W.D. Tex. Nov. 10, 2021) (stating that presidential signing statements "are rarely used in statutory interpretation, but when used they are often used as confirmatory or supplemental evidence of congressional intent") (citing authorities), *with* United States v. Cleveland, 356 F. Supp. 3d 1215, 1242, 1250, 1260–61, 1265–66 (D.N.M. 2018) (emphasizing series of signing statements relating to criminal jurisdiction over tribal land).

[104] Other federal agencies, of course, may be implicated, directly or indirectly. For example, following the presidential signing statement concerning the Assisted Suicide Funding Restriction Act of 1997, *see supra* note 96, the Legal Services Corporation, though not regarding itself as subject to any executive decision, nonetheless evaluated application of the president's caveat to its own programs. Restriction on Assisted Suicide, Euthanasia, and Mercy Killing, 62 Fed. Reg. 67,746, 67,747–48 (Dec. 30, 1997). Even state officials may be affected. *See* Yakima Valley Mem'l Hosp. v. Washington State Dep't of Health, 654 F.3d 919, 934 (9th Cir. 2011).

[105] *See, e.g.*, AMERICAN BAR ASSOCIATION TASK FORCE, *supra* note 101, at 18–19 (depicting presidential signing statements as line-item vetoes).

[106] The American Bar Association, following a task force's recommendation, resolved that it "opposes, as contrary to the rule of law and our constitutional system of separation of powers, the misuse of presidential signing statements by claiming the authority or stating the intention to disregard or decline to enforce all or part of a law the President has signed," in addition to those that would "interpret such a law in a manner inconsistent with the clear intent of Congress." AMERICAN BAR ASSOCIATION, RECOMMENDATION 304 (2006), https://perma.cc/RVJ2-DZA2; *see* AMERICAN BAR ASSOCIATION TASK FORCE, *supra* note 101, at 18–19; Christopher N. May, *Presidential Defiance of Unconstitutional Laws: Reviving the Royal Prerogative*, 21 HASTINGS CONST. L.Q. 865, 873–74 (1994).

and the executive branch, have argued that signing statements are better understood as a method by which the president enforces the laws of the United States
in a manner more consistent with the Constitution.[107] Thus, a signing statement saying that the president views as advisory a congressional requirement
that a certain position be taken in negotiations with a foreign government, or in
dealings within an international organization, is a means by which the president
maintains his constitutional prerogative of representing the United States in foreign relations. For example, after Congress instructed the executive branch to
take certain positions with respect to actions being decided within international
financial institutions—as one part of appropriations legislation[108]—President
Obama stated that such instructions "would interfere with my constitutional
authority to conduct foreign relations by directing the Executive to take certain positions in negotiations or discussions with international organizations
and foreign governments," and therefore would not be treated "as limiting my
ability to engage in foreign diplomacy or negotiations."[109] Of course, stating
that principle did not mean that the president would act contrary to congressional instructions.[110] Indeed, on at least some occasions, presidential signing
statements have attested that, despite a statute's asserted constitutional infirmity,
the executive branch will adhere to the statute as written purely as a matter of
comity.[111]

A signing statement was an important part of the background to *Zivotofsky
v. Kerry* (*Zivotofsky II*), which was discussed in Chapter 1.[112] In 2002, Congress
adopted the Foreign Relations Authorization Act, Fiscal Year 2003, which provided in Section 214(d): "For purposes of the registration of birth, certification
of nationality, or issuance of a passport of a United States citizen born in the city

---

There is some support in case law for such concerns. *See* United States v. Smith, 27 F. Cas. 1192, 1230
(C.C.N.Y. 1806).

[107] *See, e.g.*, Bradley & Posner, *supra* note 101, at 340–44; *Presidential Signing Statements Under
the Bush Administration: A Threat to Checks and Balances and the Rule of Law?: Hearing Before
the H. Comm. on the Judiciary*, 110th Cong. 11–25 (2007) (statement of John P. Elwood, Deputy
Assistant Att'y Gen., Office of Legal Counsel, Dep't of Justice); *The Use of Presidential Signing
Statements: Hearing Before the S. Comm. on the Judiciary*, 109th Cong. 6–18 (2006) (statement of
Michelle Boardman, Deputy Assistant Att'y Gen., Dep't of Justice); Presidential Authority to Decline
to Execute Unconstitutional Statutes, 18 Op. O.L.C. 199 (1994); The Legal Significance of Presidential
Signing Statements, 17 Op. O.L.C. 131 (1993). For a general review of this debate, and possible
reforms, see Louis Fisher, *Signing Statements: Constitutional and Practical Limits*, 16 WM. & MARY
BILL RTS. J. 183 (2007).
[108] Supplemental Appropriations Act, Fiscal Year 2009, tit. XIV, Pub. L. No. 111-32, §§ 1403–04,
123 Stat. 1919 (2009).
[109] Statement on Signing the Supplemental Appropriations Act, 1 PUB. PAPERS 889 (June 24, 2009).
[110] *The Use of Presidential Signing Statements, supra* note 107, at 6 (statement of Michelle
Boardman, Deputy Assistant Att'y Gen., Dep't of Justice).
[111] *See, e.g.*, Statement on Signing Legislation Supporting the Participation of Taiwan in the World
Health Organization, 1 PUB. PAPERS 1044, 1045 (June 14, 2004).
[112] *See* Chapter 1 §§ I(B), II(A), II(B).

of Jerusalem, the Secretary [of State] shall, upon the request of the citizen or the citizen's legal guardian, record the place of birth as Israel."[113] Although President George W. Bush signed the legislation into law, he issued a statement indicating that Section 214(d) was an impermissible interference "with the President's constitutional authority to conduct the Nation's foreign affairs and to supervise the unitary executive branch."[114] Thereafter, the executive branch declined to issue passports in such circumstances recording the place of birth as Israel, such as was requested by the parents of Menachem Zivotofsky, who brought suit on his behalf. Ultimately, the Supreme Court agreed that the provision did violate the president's power to recognize foreign states and governments.[115]

In reaching its conclusion, the Court noted, but did not rely on, the president's signing statement.[116] In the lower court proceedings, the plaintiff asked that the signing statement be regarded as "invalid because [the president] should have instead vetoed the enactment to register his objection," but the court of appeals considered the potential inefficacy of the statement irrelevant in view of the court's own holding that the statutory provision to which it pertained was unconstitutional.[117] Neither decision regarded the signing statement as particularly consequential. Taken on its own, the president's use of signing statements to set aside or alter a statutory provision would presumably fall within Justice Jackson's third category in *Youngstown*, where the president's power is most suspect, given that the statement would by hypothesis be incompatible with the expressed will of Congress.[118] As *Zivotofsky II* indicated, the president's non-acquiescence would probably be subject to the same degree of scrutiny regardless, and a signing statement (at least when clear) may be most significant in simply illuminating the clash.[119]

Nonetheless, signing statements may be consequential in other ways. Some matters may not be readily justiciable; as to those, a signing statement may go far in establishing the relevant law.[120] Beyond that, such statements may influence

[113] 7 U.S.C. § 1765d-1 (2018) (now repealed).

[114] Statement on Signing the Foreign Relations Authorization Act, Fiscal Year 2003, 2 PUB. PAPERS 1697 (Sept. 30, 2002).

[115] Zivotofsky v. Kerry, 576 U.S. 1 (2015) (*Zivotofsky II*). For further discussion, see Chapter 3 § I(D).

[116] *Zivotofsky II*, 576 U.S. at 8.

[117] Zivotofsky *ex rel.* Zivotofsky v. Sec'y of State, 725 F.3d 197, 220 (D.C. Cir. 2013), *aff'd sub nom.* *Zivotofsky II*, 576 U.S. 1 (2015).

[118] Youngstown Sheet & Tube Co. v. Sawyer, 343 U.S. 579, 637 (1952) (Jackson, J., concurring) ("When the President takes measures incompatible with the expressed or implied will of Congress, his power is at its lowest ebb."). For further discussion of *Youngstown*, see Chapter 1 § II(B) and Chapter 8 § II(B).

[119] *Zivotofsky II*, 576 U.S. at 10.

[120] The legislation at issue in *Zivotofsky* was carefully (and successfully) crafted so as to establish a basis for challenging the president's position on the status of Jerusalem. *See* Zivotofsky v. Sec'y of State, 444 F.3d 614 (D.C. Circuit 2006) (upholding standing to challenge denial of requested passport).

the substance of judicial opinion. There has been some suggestion that presidential statements may be useful in rebutting claims that the executive branch has acquiesced in congressional assertions of authority,[121] or conversely, that the *absence* of objection indicates executive acquiescence.[122] These kinds of claims are likely to be common in foreign relations matters given the relative prevalence of arguments concerning the historical practice of the branches. In *Zivotofsky II* itself, the Court considered carefully whether historical practice supported the claim that the recognition power belonged to the president alone, or whether Congress was permitted to exert authority.[123] As to questions like these, an executive pattern established by signing statements might be quite germane, which may provide an additional motivation for their continued use.

D. Congressional Reporting and Consultation Requirements

One recurring objection in presidential signing statements has involved requirements that that executive branch officials report to or consult with Congress,[124] and requirements of this kind are frequently included in statutes relating to foreign relations. A well-known example is the annual *Country Reports on Human Rights Practices* produced by the Department of State, which report on the human rights practices of all U.N. member states and other countries receiving U.S. foreign assistance (such as Kosovo), and which are required under the Foreign Assistance Act of 1961 and the Trade Act of 1974, as amended.[125]

The executive branch has objected to some of these statutory requirements when they appear to touch on particularly sensitive matters or core presidential competences.[126] Another bone of contention is when provisions require a report or other communication to Congress from a specific executive branch official other than the president. The executive branch has sometimes objected to such provisions as impinging upon the "unitary executive," a reference to the vesting

---

[121] *See, e.g.*, INS v. Chadha, 462 U.S. 919, 942 n.13 (1983) (invoking a variety of presidential statements to illustrate recurring presidential objections to the constitutionality of the legislative veto); *cf.* Bowsher v. Synar, 478 U.S. 714, 719 n.1 (1986) (noting that the president's signing statement had expressed constitutional objections concerning the Comptroller General's encroachment on presidential authority).

[122] Free Enter. Fund v. Pub. Co. Acct. Oversight Bd., 561 U.S. 477, 523 (2010) (Breyer, J., dissenting).

[123] *Zivotofsky II*, 576 U.S. at 23–28.

[124] *See, e.g.*, Statement on Signing Legislation to Provide for Improvement of Federal Education Research, Statistics, Evaluation, Information, and Dissemination, and for Other Purposes, 2 PUB. PAPERS 2037, 2037–38 (Nov. 5, 2002).

[125] Foreign Assistance Act of 1961, Pub. L. No. 87-195, §§ 116(d), 502B(b), 75 Stat. 424 (codified as amended at 22 U.S.C. §§ 2151n(d), 2304(b) (2018)); Small Business Job Protection Act of 1996, Pub. L. No. 104-88, § 1952 (codified as amended at 19 U.S.C. §§ 2464).

[126] *See, e.g.*, Statement on Signing the Foreign Relations Authorization Act, Fiscal Years 1990 and 1991, 1 PUB. PAPERS 239, 240 (Feb. 16, 1990).

of the executive power in the president, which Congress impinges upon when it directs the activities of his subordinates.[127] In one memorandum, the Justice Department's Office of Legal Counsel (OLC) explained that, for the president to carry out his constitutional duties, he "must be able to rely upon the faithful service of subordinate officials," and to "the extent that Congress or the courts interfere with the President's right to control or receive effective service from his subordinates within the Executive Branch, those other branches limit the ability of the President to perform his constitutional function."[128]

Most presidential signing statements permit, by their nature, a degree of mutual accommodation. For example, President George W. Bush decided to construe as only advisory a statutory provision whereby Congress required consultations by the secretary of state with its appropriations committees prior to use of funds for a Middle East Partnership Initiative.[129] Nevertheless, the Department of State did consult with the relevant committees prior to the disbursement of the funds.[130]

E. Presumptions Regarding the Interpretation of Foreign Relations Statutes

As discussed in greater depth in Chapter 4, statutes concerning U.S. foreign relations are generally interpreted by the same methods appropriate to other statutes, but certain presumptions often arise when foreign relations are at issue.[131] The starting presumption is that Congress has intended that the statute apply only to acts occurring within U.S. territory[132] or under U.S. control, such as U.S. military bases.[133] Reasons for this presumption against extraterritorial application of statutes include the belief that Congress legislates with national (not international) concerns in mind,[134] that Congress seeks to avoid unintended clashes

---

[127] *See* Chapter 1 § I(B).

[128] Constitutionality of Statute Requiring Executive Agency to Report Directly to Congress, 6 Op. O.L.C. 632, 638–39 (1982).

[129] Statement on Signing the Foreign Operations, Export Financing, and Related Programs Appropriations Act, 2006, 2 PUB. PAPERS 1716 (Nov. 14, 2005).

[130] *See* Government Accountability Office, Presidential Signing Statements Accompanying the Fiscal Year 2006 Appropriations Acts, Study No. B-308603, at 20–21 (June 18, 2007), https://perma.cc/ETA7-3JA8.

[131] *See* Chapter 4 § IV(B); *see also* CURTIS A. BRADLEY, INTERNATIONAL LAW IN THE U.S. LEGAL SYSTEM 169–99 (2d ed. 2015).

[132] *See* RESTATEMENT (FOURTH) § 404.

[133] *See* Rasul v. Bush, 542 U.S. 466 (2004); Vermilya–Brown Co. v. Connell, 335 U.S. 377 (1948); RESTATEMENT (FOURTH) § 404 rptrs. note 11.

[134] *See* Microsoft Corp. v. AT&T Corp., 550 U.S. 437, 454 (2007).

between U.S. laws and those of foreign states,[135] and that Congress desires to avoid violations of international law.[136]

Notwithstanding the presumption against extraterritoriality, Congress has the authority to regulate conduct occurring abroad if it chooses to do so.[137] The requisite intent may be expressly stated by a statute's language, such as a provision criminalizing the murder of a U.S. national abroad or extraterritorial money laundering.[138] For example, the 1986 Maritime Drug Law Enforcement Act authorizes U.S. authorities to exercise jurisdiction not just in U.S. waters and not just over U.S.-registered vessels but also "beyond territorial jurisdiction" (on the high seas and even in foreign waters) over any vessel "registered in a foreign nation where the flag nation has consented or waived objection to the enforcement of the United States law by the United States."[139] Congress' intent may also be regarded as implicit in the statute given its overall purpose, such as where the prescribed conduct occurs abroad but has effects within the United States.[140]

Yet caution is warranted in readily implying such intent; there must be in the statute a "clear, affirmative indication that [the statute] applies extraterritorially"[141] (albeit not a "clear statement"). Thus, whereas a statute protecting the U.S. government from fraud may be viewed as implicitly extending to such fraudulent acts wherever located,[142] a statute likely will not be viewed as implicitly extending to acts abroad that have no connection with the

---

[135] See EEOC v. Arabian Am. Oil Co., 499 U.S. 244, 248 (1991); see also Smith v. United States, 507 U.S. 197, 204 (1993); John H. Knox, A Presumption Against Extrajurisdictionality, 104 AM. J. INT'L L. 351 (2010).

[136] RESTATEMENT (FOURTH) § 404 rptrs. notes 1–2. The Restatement, however, characterizes this third reason as an initial rationale that became less important over time as rules of customary international law on prescriptive jurisdiction became less territorial.

[137] See, e.g., RJR Nabisco, Inc. v. European Cmty., 579 U.S. 325, 339 (2016); Morrison v. National Australia Bank Ltd., 561 U.S. 247, 255 (2010); Microsoft Corp. 550 U.S. at 454–56. Whether there are constitutional limits to the ability of Congress to exercise extraterritorial jurisdiction is an unexplored issue. Arguably "the Constitution permits Congress to make acts committed abroad crimes under United States law only to the extent permitted by international law" and that, "especially when Congress acts under its power to define offenses against the law of nations, or exercises powers of sovereignty deriving from the law of nations, it cannot violate the territorial limitations imposed by that law." Andreas F. Lowenfeld, U.S. Law Enforcement Abroad: The Constitution and International Law, in FOREIGN AFFAIRS AND THE U.S. CONSTITUTION 176, 177–78 (Louis Henkin et al. eds., 1990).

[138] See 18 U.S.C. § 1119 (2018) (murder abroad); 18 U.S.C. § 1956 (extraterritorial money laundering).

[139] 46 U.S.C. §§ 70503 (b), 70502(c)(1)(C). For an analysis of whether, under Article I (and specifically under the Piracies and Felonies Clause), Congress constitutionally is able to regulate foreign nationals on foreign vessels in foreign waters, see Eugene Kontorovich, The "Define and Punish" Clause and the Limits of Universal Jurisdiction, 103 Nw. U. L. REV. 149 (2009); Eugene Kontorovich, Beyond the Article I Horizon: Congress' Enumerated Powers and Universal Jurisdiction over Drug Crimes, 93 MINN. L. REV. 1191 (2009).

[140] See, e.g., Spector v. Norwegian Cruise Line Ltd., 545 U.S. 119 (2005); Hartford Fire Ins. Co. v. California, 509 U.S. 764 (1993); United States v. Aluminum Co. of America, 148 F.2d 416 (2d Cir. 1945).

[141] RJR Nabisco, 579 U.S. at 337; see Kiobel v. Royal Dutch Petroleum Co., 569 U.S. 108, 118 (2013).

[142] United States v. Bowman, 260 U.S. 94 (1922).

United States.[143] In *Kiobel v. Royal Dutch Petroleum Co.*, the Court concluded that a statute according federal courts jurisdiction over claims by noncitizens for torts in violation of the law of nations, or of a treaty of the United States, was not intended to cover conduct occurring in foreign territory, though it could cover conduct on the high seas.[144] This reluctance to apply U.S. laws extraterritorially is understandable, though if the essential concern is potential conflict with the laws of other nations, then perhaps an inquiry into the nature of the U.S. law in that regard is merited. Arguably the presumption should not be applied in any situation where extraterritorial application of U.S. law helps implement *international law*, since doing so harmonizes U.S. laws with the laws of other nations rather than clashes with them.[145]

Under the *Charming Betsy* doctrine or canon, there is also a presumption that an act of Congress ought never be construed to violate international law, as well as foreign law, if any other possible construction remains.[146] Indeed, the U.S. Supreme Court "ordinarily construes ambiguous statutes to avoid unreasonable interference with the sovereign authority of other nations."[147] This presumption, in turn, invites an assessment of whether international law prohibits a country from exercising prescriptive jurisdiction in certain circumstances, a matter also addressed in greater depth in Chapter 4.[148]

F. Congressional Oversight of Foreign Relations

Because the executive branch exhibits a considerable amount of independence in conducting foreign relations, Congress' oversight tools are especially important: they allow Congress to gather information for enacting or amending foreign relations law, to scrutinize the executive branch's adherence to existing law, and to ascertain and influence U.S. foreign policy. Among the available tools are public and nonpublic hearings and meetings with executive branch officials, receipt of executive branch reports, and, when necessary, compulsion of executive branch documents or testimony through subpoena. Given that some information provided to Congress in the field of foreign relations is classified, steps must be taken to protect such information from disclosure.[149]

---

[143] *See, e.g.,* F. Hoffmann-LaRoche Ltd. v. Empagran S.A., 542 U.S. 155 (2004).

[144] *Kiobel*, 569 U.S. at 123–24. For further discussion, see Chapter 5 §§ II(A), IV(B)(1).

[145] *See* Anthony J. Colangelo, *A Unified Approach to Extraterritoriality*, 97 VA. L. REV. 1019 (2011).

[146] Murray v. Schooner Charming Betsy, 6 U.S. 64, 118 (1804). For further discussion, see Chapter 4 § IV(B)(1) and Chapter 5 § III(B)(3).

[147] *F. Hoffman-La Roche Ltd.*, 542 at 164–65 (citations omitted); *see* McCulloch v. Sociedad Nacional de Marineros de Honduras, 372 U.S. 10, 21–22 (1963).

[148] *See* Chapter 4 § IV(A).

[149] *See* JENNIFER K. ELSEA, CONG. RESEARCH SERV., RS21900, THE PROTECTION OF CLASSIFIED INFORMATION: THE LEGAL FRAMEWORK (2017).

1. Methods for Oversight

Congressional oversight typically occurs through the standing committees and subcommittees referred to earlier, which often issue reports summarizing their findings.[150] An important example was the 2012 report of the Senate Select Committee on Intelligence, entitled *Committee Study of the Central Intelligence Agency's Detention and Interrogation Program*.[151] The report—more than six thousand pages in length—was issued after a five-year investigation of the techniques used by U.S. intelligence officers to interrogate persons detained in the aftermath of the attacks of 9/11, based on extensive review of documents of the Central Intelligence Agency, testimony of government and nongovernmental officials, and other sources.[152] More recently, in 2020, the Senate Select Committee on Intelligence released a five-volume report on *Russian Active Measures Campaigns and Interference in the 2016 U.S. Election*; while overlapping with the better-known Mueller Report, a product of the Department of Justice, Congress' contribution was distinctively bipartisan.[153]

Yet in some situations, a special committee can be established by a resolution of the House or Senate to investigate a particular matter on a temporary basis. When this is done, the terms of membership and the mandate of the committee are determined in the resolution. Thus, to investigate a covert program operated from the White House during the Reagan administration that sold arms to Iran and transferred the proceeds to Nicaraguan rebels, the two houses of Congress established a "Joint Congressional Committee for the Iran-Contra Affair." The committee consisted of members from both houses of Congress and resulted in a lengthy report as to the incident, along with recommendations.[154] Although

---

[150] *See* Legislative Reorganization Act of 1946, 60 Stat. 812, § 136. On whether individual members of Congress may conduct such oversight, see Office of the Legal Counsel, U.S. Dep't of Justice, *Authority of Individual Members of Congress to Conduct Oversight of the Executive Branch* (May 1, 2017), https://perma.cc/5PLJ-RMN9.

[151] S. Select Comm. on Intelligence, 112th Cong., Committee Study of the Central Intelligence Agency's Detention and Interrogation Program (Dec. 13, 2012) [hereinafter Senate Detention Report]. Although the full report was classified, a declassified 528-page executive summary was publicly released. S. Select Comm. on Intelligence, 112th Cong., Committee Study of the Central Intelligence Agency's Detention and Interrogation Program (2014). Both Republicans on the Committee and the CIA issued responses. S. Select Comm. on Intelligence Minority Views, 112th Cong., Committee Study of the Central Intelligence Agency's Detention and Interrogation Program (2014); Press Release, Central Intelligence Agency, CIA Comments on Senate Select Committee on Intelligence Report on the Rendition, Detention, and Interrogation Program (June 27, 2013), https://perma.cc/S342-YMDE.

[152] *See* Senate Detention Report, Appendix 1: Terms of Reference, 457.

[153] S. Select Comm. on Intelligence, 116th Cong., Rep. on Russian Active Measures Campaigns and Interference in the 2016 U.S. Election (2020); *see also* U.S. Dep't of Justice, Report on the Investigation into Russian Interference in the 2016 Presidential Election, Special Counsel Robert S. Mueller, III (2019).

[154] House Select Comm. to Investigate Covert Arms Transactions with Iran and Senate Select Comm. on Secret Military Assistance to Iran and the Nicaraguan Opposition, Report of the Congressional Comms. Investigating the Iran-Contra Affair, S. Rep. No. 100-216, H.R. Rep. No. 100-433 (1987) [hereinafter Iran Contra Report].

the report and recommendations were an important complement to an executive branch review by the Tower Commission and to an independent counsel investigation into individual wrongdoing, critics contended that the House and Senate select committees failed to come to grips with the underlying constitutional conditions that led to the scandal.[155]

Congress also on occasion has established a body of independent experts to investigate a matter and to provide recommendations, as occurred with the creation of the "National Commission on Terrorist Attacks on the United States" (also known as the "9/11 Commission").[156] Established by a statute that set forth its mandate and working procedures, the commission consisted of ten independent experts (half appointed by the Democratic congressional leadership and half by the Republican congressional leadership), for the purpose of studying the origins of the 9/11 terrorist attacks and the U.S. readiness for and response to the those attacks.[157] The commission completed a lengthy public report in 2004 that contained forty-one recommendations for preventing future terrorist attacks and strengthening U.S. national security.[158]

2. Subpoenas and Contempt

While the Constitution does not expressly provide Congress with the power to conduct investigations, let alone issue subpoenas,[159] the Supreme Court has recognized that each house of Congress has the power "to secure needed information" by subpoena so as to legislate wisely and effectively.[160] That power, however, is subject to limitations. As the Court has recently indicated, a subpoena must relate to a "legitimate task" of Congress; it must serve a "valid legislative purpose"; it may not be "for the purpose of 'law enforcement,'" since that role is assigned to the executive and to the courts; and recipients of such subpoenas "retain their constitutional rights [and privileges] throughout the course of [Congress'] investigation."[161]

If witnesses refuse to cooperate with a congressional investigation, they are exposed to the possibility of being held in contempt (or, relatedly, in breach of

---

[155] See HAROLD HONGJU KOH, THE NATIONAL SECURITY CONSTITUTION: SHARING POWER AFTER THE IRAN-CONTRA AFFAIR ch. 1 (1990).

[156] National Commission on Terrorist Attacks Upon the United States, About the Commission (Aug. 21, 2004), https://perma.cc/37ZP-KSAE.

[157] Intelligence Authorization Act for Fiscal Year 2003, Pub. L. No. 107-306, §§ 601-11.

[158] NATIONAL COMMISSION ON TERRORIST ATTACKS UPON THE UNITED STATES, THE 9/11 COMMISSION REPORT: FINAL REPORT OF THE NATIONAL COMMISSION ON TERRORIST ATTACKS UPON THE UNITED STATES (2004), https://perma.cc/CU6M-QPUH.

[159] Trump v. Mazars USA, LLP, 140 S. Ct. 2019, 2031 (2020).

[160] McGrain v. Daugherty, 273 U.S. 135, 161 (1927).

[161] Mazars USA, 140 S. Ct. at 2031-32 (quoting Watkins v. United States, 354 U.S. 178, 187-88, 198 (1957); Quinn v. United States, 349 U.S. 155, 161 (1955)). See also id. at 2032-36 (suggesting more demanding test when a congressional subpoena seeks a president's personal, nonprivileged information); infra this chapter § II (F)(3).

congressional privilege).[162] Although the Constitution is silent on Congress holding nonmembers in contempt, such power has been exercised since the founding, and justified as necessary for the effective functioning of Congress.[163] In rare instances, Congress has sought to arrest and imprison an executive branch official, including those involved in foreign relations. For example, in 1879, the House of Representatives had its sergeant-at-arms arrest George F. Seward, the U.S. Minister to China, for failing to provide certain records to a House committee that was investigating alleged financial misfeasance relating to the U.S. consulate at Shanghai.[164] More commonly, however, Congress has sought to enforce its contempt citations by means of the courts.[165] Such measures are supplemented, of course, with the receipt of information from other sources, such as testimony by nongovernmental organizations or individuals.

3. Withholding of Information by the Executive Branch

As a general matter, information possessed by the executive branch concerning foreign relations has been viewed as protected from involuntary disclosure to the public. Although the Administrative Procedure Act generally requires that rulemaking by government agencies follow procedures of public notice and comment, such requirements do not apply "to the extent that there is involved . . . a military or foreign affairs function of the United States."[166] Likewise, although the Freedom of Information Act generally calls for the public disclosure of information upon demand, it exempts "matters that are . . . specifically under criteria established by an Executive order to be kept secret in the interest of national defense or foreign policy."[167]

During the legislative and oversight process, and especially in the context of foreign relations, the executive branch may assert that information cannot be disclosed to Congress, either because it is classified or because of an executive privilege. The following briefly addresses these two areas of friction between the political branches.

a. Classified Information

For decades, presidents have established the federal government's classification standards by executive order, citing to both constitutional and statutory

---

[162] Statutory contempt is based upon 2 U.S.C. § 192 (2018). Congress, however, also is regarded as having inherent constitutional power to hold a person in contempt. *See* Anderson v. Dunn, 19 U.S. 204, 228 (1821). *See generally* JOSH CHAFETZ, CONGRESS'S CONSTITUTION: LEGISLATIVE AUTHORITY AND THE SEPARATION OF POWERS 152–98 (2017).

[163] CHAFETZ, *supra* note 162, at 180.

[164] *Id.* at 176–77.

[165] *See* Chapter 4 § II(B)(1).

[166] 5 U.S.C. §§ 553(a)(1), 554(a)(4) (2018).

[167] 5 U.S.C. § 552(b)(1)(A).

authority.[168] The relevant executive order identifies certain categories of information the disclosure of which could reasonably be expected to damage national security, including "foreign government information" and information on "foreign relations or foreign activities of the United States, including confidential sources."[169]

The principal statute in this area sets forth procedures governing the granting and denial of access to classified material, but leaves with the president the authority to determine classification standards;[170] other statutes address related matters.[171] The extent to which Congress can regulate the executive in this regard, however, is not settled. On the one hand, the Supreme Court has stated in dicta that, considering the president's role as commander in chief, the "authority to classify and control access to information bearing on national security . . . flows primarily from this Constitutional investment of power in the President and exists quite apart from any explicit congressional grant."[172] On the other hand, the Court also has recognized Congress' ability to require the executive branch to adopt new classification procedures, or to establish Congress' own procedures, subject only to executive privilege.[173]

By contrast, sharing of classified information by the executive branch with courts for the purpose of national security prosecutions is highly regulated by the Classified Information Procedures Act (CIPA).[174] In certain cases, the prosecution may wish to introduce classified information in order to obtain a conviction, while in others (perhaps some of the same cases), the defendant may wish to do so to avoid one. At the outset of the case, CIPA permits either party to request a pretrial conference "to consider matters relating to classified information that may arise in connection with the prosecution."[175] Upon the government's request, a court is required to issue a protective order "against the disclosure of any classified information disclosed by the United States to any defendant in any criminal case."[176] Such disclosure then may be made to defendants or defense counsel who are cleared to access the information. Yet CIPA also allows the

---

[168] See, e.g., John F. Murphy, Knowledge Is Power: Foreign Policy and Information Interchange Among Congress, the Executive Branch, and the Public, 49 TUL. L. REV. 505, 508 (1975).

[169] See Exec. Order No. 13,526, §§ 1.1, 1.4(d), 3 C.F.R 298 (2009).

[170] See Counterintelligence and Security Enhancement Act of 1994, tit. VIII, Pub. L. No. 103-359 (codified at 50 U.S.C. §§ 3161, 3162–64 (2018)).

[171] For example, the Public Interest Declassification Act of 2000 establishes a Public Interest Declassification Board, which advises the president on declassification of certain information. 50 U.S.C. § 3161 note (2018). The Reducing Over-Classification Act requires the inspectors general of executive branch agencies to assess implementation of classification policies. Id.

[172] Dep't of the Navy v. Egan, 484 U.S. 518, 527 (1988) (citing Cafeteria Workers v. McElroy, 367 U.S. 886, 890 (1961)).

[173] EPA v. Mink, 410 U.S. 73, 83 (1973).

[174] 18 U.S.C. app. §§ 1–16 (2018).

[175] CIPA § 2.

[176] CIPA § 3.

government, "upon a sufficient showing" (which is typically made in an *ex parte*
and *in camera* hearing before the court), to delete certain classified items from
a discovery request or, if disclosure is required, to provide unclassified summaries or substitutions.[177] After reviewing the disclosed information, defendants
must provide timely pretrial notice of any intention to introduce the information at pretrial or trial proceedings.[178] Then, upon the government's request,
the court is required to hold a pretrial evidentiary hearing (which is typically
in camera but open to both parties to attend) "to make all determinations concerning the use, relevance, or admissibility of classified information that would
otherwise be made during the trial or pretrial proceeding."[179] CIPA also allows
the government to pursue an expedited, interlocutory appeal of any decision by
a trial court that forces the disclosure of classified information, denies a protective order, or penalizes government retention of classified information.[180] Such
procedures generally appear sound in balancing the interests of the government
as against the interest of defendants, but various proposals have been made for
improvements.[181]

b. Executive Privilege

The Constitution does not explicitly address the topic of executive privilege,
let alone whether it entails the right to withhold information from Congress.
Nonetheless, such a privilege has been asserted throughout U.S. history, including
with respect to matters of foreign relations.[182] The privilege is invoked often with respect to the release of documents to, or testimony before, congressional committees
or investigative bodies—sometimes with respect to communications with foreign
governments, or communications or deliberations among senior U.S. government
officials concerning foreign relations.

While debate has continued regarding whether executive privilege has a sound
constitutional basis,[183] the Supreme Court has accepted its assertion in certain

---

[177] CIPA § 4.

[178] CIPA § 5.

[179] CIPA § 6.

[180] CIPA § 7. For greater detail on how CIPA works, see U.S. Dep't of Justice, Synopsis of Classified
Information Procedures Act (CIPA), https://perma.cc/8J2N-NGQY (updated Jan. 2020); Saul M.
Pilchen & Benjamin B. Klubes, *Using the Classified Information Procedures Act in Criminal Cases: A
Primer for Defense Counsel*, 31 AM. CRIM. L. REV. 191 (1994). As applied, CIPA has been challenged
on Fifth and Sixth Amendment grounds. *See, e.g.*, United States v. Bin Laden, 2001 WL 66393
(S.D.N.Y. Jan. 25, 2001). For further discussion, see Chapter 10 § II(A)(3).

[181] *See, e.g.*, Afsheen John Radsan, *Remodeling the Classified Information Procedures Act (CIPA)*, 32
CARDOZO L. REV. 437 (2010) (calling for adjustments in three areas of CIPA's application); Richard P.
Salgado, Note, *Government Secrets, Fair Trials, and the Classified Information Procedures Act*, 98 YALE
L.J. 427 (1988).

[182] History of Refusals by Executive Branch Officials to Provide Information Demanded by
Congress, 6 Op. O.L.C. 751, 753 (1982) (citing historical examples).

[183] The classic criticism is RAOUL BERGER, EXECUTIVE PRIVILEGE: A CONSTITUTIONAL MYTH
(1974). For responses urging that the privilege be acknowledged but within limits, see George C.

contexts. Thus, with respect to disclosure to the courts, the Supreme Court has found that such "privilege is fundamental to the operation of Government and inextricably rooted in the separation of powers under the Constitution."[184] While the privilege is not absolute (thus it typically would not shield material needed for a criminal trial that could be provided under the protected conditions of *in camera* inspection), the Court indicated in *Nixon v. United States* that a claim of executive privilege is especially strong when it is invoked to protect military, diplomatic, or sensitive national security secrets, an area where the president's Article II responsibilities merit deference.[185] In the context of disclosure to the public, Justice Stewart's concurrence in *New York Times v. United States* stated that "it is the constitutional duty of the Executive . . . to protect the confidentiality necessary to carry out its responsibilities in the field[] of international relations . . . ."[186] More recently, in *Trump v. Mazars USA*, the president did not invoke executive privilege,[187] but the Court described it as a "constitutional privilege" applicable in appropriate cases deserving "the greatest protection consistent with the fair administration of justice."[188] While differentiating cases involving nonprivileged, private information about the president's finances, the Court stressed that "special" separation-of-powers concerns remained that required carefully balancing Congress' legislative interests against the need to protect the president's "unique constitutional position."[189]

Drawing upon such decisions, on several occasions, OLC has maintained the ability of the president to withhold foreign relations information from Congress.[190] For example, during the Clinton administration, Congress sought documentary information about the administration's policy toward death squads and other human rights violations in Haiti, in the form of records of diplomatic meetings or communications between the president, vice president, and

Calhoun, *Confidentiality and Executive Privilege, in* THE TETHERED PRESIDENCY: CONGRESSIONAL CONSTRAINTS ON EXECUTIVE POWER 173 (Thomas M. Franck ed., 1981); Mark J. Rozell, *Executive Privilege and the Clinton Presidency: Restoring Balance to the Debate Over Executive Privilege: A Response to Berger*, 8 WM. & MARY BILL OF RTS. J. 541 (2000). *See generally* Symposium, United States v. Nixon: *Presidential Power and Executive Privilege Twenty-Five Years Later*, 83 MINN. L. REV. 1061 (1999).

[184] United States v. Nixon, 418 U.S. 683, 708 (1974).

[185] *Id.* at 703–07.

[186] New York Times v. United States, 403 U.S. 713, 728–30 (Stewart, J., concurring).

[187] 140 S. Ct. 2019, 2028 (2020).

[188] *Id.* at 2032 (quoting United States v. Nixon, 418 U.S. 683, 715 (1974)).

[189] *Id.* at 2036.

[190] *See, e.g.,* Office of the Legal Counsel, U.S. Dep't of Justice, Publication of a Report to the President on the Effect of Automobile and Automobile-Part Imports on the National Security (Jan. 17, 2020), https://perma.cc/A2RH-AWYL; 6 Op. O.L.C. *supra* note 182; Memorandum from John R. Stevenson, Legal Adviser, Dep't of State, and William H. Rehnquist, Assistant Attorney Gen., Office of Legal Counsel, *Re: The President's Executive Privilege to Withhold Foreign Policy and National Security Information* (Dec. 8, 1969), https://perma.cc/W4WB-D76W.

national security adviser, and the president or prime minister of Haiti. The executive branch declined to provide most documents based on executive privilege. Among other things, OLC asserted that "[h]istory is replete with examples of the Executive's refusal to produce to Congress diplomatic communications and related documents because of the prejudicial impact such disclosure could have on the President's ability to conduct foreign relations."[191]

During the Trump administration, Congress faced obstacles when trying to obtain executive branch documents and testimony from the White House and several government agencies. In the fall of 2019, various House committees issued subpoenas for documents and testimony regarding allegations that President Trump had solicited foreign interference from the government of Ukraine for the purpose of helping his re-election in the 2020 U.S. presidential election. The executive branch declined to release responsive documents, asserting that the subpoenas sought information concerning internal presidential communications and executive branch deliberations, as well as diplomatic communications arising in connection with U.S. foreign relations with Ukraine, all of which were protected by executive privilege.[192] Further, OLC advised that the stated purpose of the subpoenas for documents was to assist the House in an impeachment investigation, but that when the subpoenas were issued there had not yet been a formal vote in the House to launch such an investigation.[193] With respect to witnesses, OLC advised that the committees' attempts to compel executive branch witness testimony without agency counsel would place information potentially protected by executive privilege in jeopardy and, therefore, subpoenas seeking such testimony could not be enforced.[194]

[191] Assertion of Executive Privilege for Documents Concerning Conduct of Foreign Affairs with Respect to Haiti, 20 Op. Att'y Gen. 5 (1996) (citing to 6 Op. O.L.C., *supra* note 182).

[192] *See* Letter from Pat A. Cipollone, Counsel to the President, to Nancy Pelosi, Speaker of the House of Representatives, Eliot L. Engel, Chairman of House Foreign Affairs Comm., Adam B. Schiff, Chairman of House Permanent Select Comm., & Elijah E. Cummings, Chairman of House Comm. on Oversight and Reform (Oct. 8, 2019), https://perma.cc/W54A-9TS6; *see also* Letter from President Donald J. Trump, to Nancy Pelosi, Speaker of the House of Representatives (Dec. 17, 2019), https://perma.cc/GJT7-E77T (protesting the impeachment proceedings). For a congressional subpoena seeking testimony from the former White House counsel on these issues, see Comm. on the Judiciary v. McGahn, 407 F. Supp. 3d 35 (D.D.C. 2019) (in House committee's civil action to enforce its subpoena, court finds that the committee had standing), *rev'd*, 951 F.3d 510 (D.C. Cir. Feb. 28, 2020) (finding that Article III "forbids federal courts from resolving this kind of interbranch information dispute"), *vacated*. en banc 968 F.3d 755 (D.C. Cir. 2020).

[193] According to OLC, such a vote must precede any attempt by the committee to compel the production of documents or testimony. While Congress did ultimately adopt a resolution authorizing the impeachment investigation, OLC maintained that the resolution did not cure the legal status of the prior subpoenas. Office of Legal Counsel, U.S. Dep't of Justice, House Committees' Authority to Investigate for Impeachment, 8, 53–54 (Jan. 19, 2020), https://perma.cc/DKC9-7HP2; *see* H.R. Res. 660, 116th Cong. (2019) (resolution of impeachment).

[194] Office of Legal Counsel, U.S. Dep't of Justice, Exclusion of Agency Counsel from Congressional Depositions in the Impeachment Context, 1–5 (Nov. 1, 2019), https://perma.cc/2BPX-S6NX.

The executive branch may refuse to disclose documents even when the congressional demand is linked to the use of appropriated funds. For example, at the time of the Mexican debt crisis in 1994, the House of Representatives sought certain documents from the executive branch concerning actions taken to strengthen the Mexican peso and stabilize the economy of Mexico.[195] While some documents were provided, others were not.[196] In Section 406 of the Mexican Debt Disclosure Act of 1995, Congress required the president to certify, before additional economic support funds could be provided to Mexico, that any document that was classified or privileged and not produced to the House of Representatives was nevertheless "produced to specified Members of Congress or their designees by mutual agreement" among the president and specified congressional leaders.[197] The executive branch interpreted the statute as allowing certification, while withholding sensitive information, without any such interbranch agreement.[198] After the General Counsel for the House of Representatives questioned the executive's interpretation of the statute, OLC found unconstitutional interpreting the statute "to require the President either to dishonor the United States' commitment to Mexico, thereby posing a threat that Mexico would default and jeopardize important U.S. interests, or to divulge all documents, even highly sensitive documents reflecting diplomatic negotiations, to at least some Members of Congress as a condition of aid to Mexico."[199]

As the Supreme Court has indicated, "disputes over congressional demands for presidential documents have not ended up in court,"[200] instead being resolved for the most part in the "hurly-burly, the give-and-take of the political process between the legislative and the executive."[201] Litigation by Congress to compel disclosure in the face of a claim of privilege has been rare and raises questions as to justiciability.[202] As the D.C. Circuit explained, courts will find that members

---

[195] See H. R. Res. 80; 141 CONG. REC. 6408 (1995).

[196] The documents consisted of documents withheld: (1) by the White House reflecting confidential communications between the president and foreign leaders; (2) by the White House revealing White House deliberations; and (3) by the Central Intelligence Agency that constituted daily briefings for the president or records of meetings at the National Security Council or with senior White House staff. See Presidential Certification Regarding the Provision of Documents to the House of Representatives Under the Mexican Debt Disclosure Act of 1995, 20 Op. O.L.C. 253, 259 (1996).

[197] Mexican Debt Disclosure Act of 1995, 31 U.S.C. § 5302 note, tit. IV, Pub. L. No. 104-6, § 406, 109 Stat. 73, 89, 91–92.

[198] 20 Op. O.L.C., supra note 196, at 253, 260–61.

[199] Id. at 264.

[200] Trump v. Mazars USA, LLP, 140 S. Ct. 2019, 2029 (2020).

[201] Id. (quoting Hearings on S. 2170 et al. Before the Subcomm. on Intergovernmental Rels. of the S. Comm. on Gov't Operations, 94th Cong. 87 (1975) (Antonin Scalia, Assistant Attorney General, Office of Legal Counsel)).

[202] See Senate Select Comm. on Presidential Campaign Activities v. Nixon, 366 F. Supp. 51 (D.D.C.), aff'd, 498 F.2d 725 (D.C. Cir. 1974); see also U.S. House of Representatives v. U.S. Dep't of Justice, 951 F.3d 589 (D.C. Cir. 2020) (finding authorization of redacted grand jury materials was proper because "judicial proceeding" exception in Federal Rules of Criminal Procedure extended to impeachment proceedings and Committee showed a "particularized need" for materials); Comm. on Judiciary of U.S. House of Representatives v. McGahn, 968 F.3d 755 (D.C. Cir. 2020) (en banc) (affirming

of Congress or congressional committees can bring such suits if: (1) the "institutional injury" alleged is not "wholly abstract and widely dispersed"; (2) the attempted litigation is consistent with historical practice; (3) the relevant house of Congress authorized the party to bring the suit; and (4) dismissing the suit would either prevent the party from accessing "an adequate remedy" or would insulate the action from constitutional challenge.[203] To the extent that the matter is litigated, Congress likely must show that the material sought is "demonstrably critical to the responsible fulfilment of the committee's functions"[204] and in furtherance of legitimate legislative responsibilities of Congress.[205] Yet resolution of situations where the privilege is invoked is most likely to occur through interbranch dialogue and accommodation, rather than through the courts.

III. Power of the Purse

One of the principal enumerated powers of Congress for legislating on foreign relations is the "spending power," meaning its power to "pay the Debts and provide for the common Defence and general Welfare of the United States,"[206] and relatedly its power to appropriate funds necessary and proper to carry out the activities of the U.S. government.[207] The Constitution reinforces this authority by specifying that no U.S. government funds may be expended except pursuant to an appropriations law.[208] Congress, of course, also enjoys the power "[t]o lay and collect Taxes."[209] Collectively these powers are often referred to as "the power

---

declaratory and injunctive relief for House Judiciary Committee in its effort to subpoena President Trump's former White House counsel as part of the Committee's investigations into Russian interference in the 2016 U.S. presidential election); U.S. House of Representatives v. Mnuchin, 969 F.3d 353 (D.C. Cir. 2020) (en banc) (remanded for further consideration in light of the holding in *McGahn* "that there is no general bar against the House of Representatives' standing in all cases involving purely interbranch disputes").

[203] *McGahn*, 968 F.3d at 775–76 (quoting Raines v. Byrd, 521 U.S. 811, 829 (1997)).

[204] Senate Select Comm. on Presidential Campaign Activities v. Nixon, 498 F.2d 725, 731 (D.C. Cir. 1974) (en banc).

[205] Barenblatt v. United States, 360 U.S. 109, 111–12 (1959); McGrain v. Daugherty, 273 U.S. 135, 160 (1927); *see also* Trump v. Thompson, 20 F.4th 10, 25 (D.C. Cir. 2021) (identifying both the requirement that materials be "demonstrably critical" and necessary for a legitimate congressional purpose as "carefully tailored balancing tests" that "courts have employed" to "weigh the competing constitutional concerns").

[206] U.S. Const. art. 1, § 8, cl. 1; *see also id. art.* 1, § 7, cl. 1 ("All Bills for raising Revenue shall originate in the House of Representatives; but the Senate may propose or concur with amendments as on other Bills.").

[207] *Id.* art. 1, § 8, cl. 18 (Necessary and Proper Clause).

[208] *Id.* art. 1, § 9, cl. 7 ("No Money shall be drawn from the Treasury, but in Consequence of Appropriations made by Law . . . ."); *see also* The Federalist No. 48 (James Madison) ("the legislative department alone has access to the pockets of the people").

[209] U.S. Const. art. 1, § 8, cl. 1.

of the purse."[210] Such power is wide-ranging in that the conducting of foreign relations by the executive branch typically entails some expenditure of funds, such as in the resort to armed force. At the same time, Congress' discretion when exercising the power to appropriate funds is limited; it cannot be used in violation of the Constitution, such as in a manner contrary to the First Amendment, and Congress must provide public funds for "constitutionally-mandated activities."[211] Thus, Congress cannot refuse to appropriate funds necessary for the president to send ambassadors, receive ambassadors, or make treaties.[212] One scholar has argued that funding constraints on the conduct of diplomacy should attract an anti-manipulation principle, modeled on federalism cases, whereby the power of the purse prevails except in narrow circumstances when it would unduly manipulate judgments properly left to the president alone.[213]

A proving ground for these principles in the area of foreign relations is the 1961 Foreign Assistance Act (FAA), which provides an overall framework and set of policy objectives for U.S. foreign aid, military assistance, and military education and training programs.[214] In essence, the FAA establishes a structure for the provision of U.S. bilateral economic assistance, humanitarian assistance, assistance to international organizations and programs, military assistance, and law enforcement assistance.[215] For example, FAA Section 117 authorizes the president to furnish assistance to developing countries to improve their capacity for environmental protection,[216] while FAA Section 133 authorizes the president to establish programs that combat corruption and promote good governance in Eastern Europe.[217]

At the same time, the FAA (as well as other statutes) imposes limits on foreign assistance. For example, countries with which the United States has no diplomatic relations are ineligible for aid,[218] and there are funding restrictions on international programs that support abortions and involuntary sterilizations[219]

---

[210] *See generally* CHAFETZ, *supra* note 162, 45–77; WILLIAM C. BANKS & PETER RAVEN-HANSEN, NATIONAL SECURITY LAW AND THE POWER OF THE PURSE (1994); HENKIN, FOREIGN AFFAIRS, at 112–15; Louis Fisher, *The Spending Power, in* THE CONSTITUTION AND THE CONDUCT OF AMERICAN FOREIGN POLICY 227 (David Gray Adler & Larry N. George eds., 1996). For a view that Congress, to a certain extent, has relinquished to the executive its spending power, see LOUIS FISHER, CONGRESSIONAL ABDICATION ON WAR AND SPENDING (2000); *see also* Louis Fisher, *How Tightly Can Congress Draw the Purse Strings?*, 83 AM. J. INT'L L. 758 (1989); LOUIS FISHER, PRESIDENTIAL SPENDING POWER (1975).

[211] *See* Kate Stith, *Congress' Power of the Purse*, 97 YALE L.J. 1343, 1350–51 (1988).

[212] *See id.* at 1351.

[213] *See* Zachary S. Price, *Funding Restrictions and Separation of Powers*, 71 VAND. L. REV. 357 (2018).

[214] Foreign Assistance Act of 1961, Pub. L. No. 87-195 (codified at 22 U.S.C. §§ 2151–52i (2018)).

[215] DIANNE E. RENNACK & SUSAN G. CHESSER, CONG. RESEARCH SERV., R40089, FOREIGN ASSISTANCE ACT OF 1961: AUTHORIZATIONS AND CORRESPONDING APPROPRIATIONS 2 (2011).

[216] 22 U.S.C. § 2151p (2018).

[217] 22 U.S.C. § 2152c.

[218] FAA § 620(t) (codified at 22 U.S.C. § 2370).

[219] FAA §104(f).

or support agricultural development activities that compete with commodities grown in the United States.[220] Some limitations are triggered when a foreign state recipient engages in proscribed conduct. For example, Section 116 of the FAA prohibits foreign assistance to a government that "engages in a consistent pattern of gross violations of internationally recognized human rights, . . . unless such assistance will directly benefit the needy people in such country."[221] Similarly, Section 620M prohibits the furnishing of assistance to any foreign security unit where there is credible information that the unit has committed a gross violation of human rights.[222]

Prior to 1985, authorizations embedded in the FAA were regularly updated either through amendment to the FAA or through new authorization statutes, but thereafter annual authorization acts were used instead to keep the FAA current, typically styled as the "Foreign Relations Authorization Act" for a given fiscal year.[223] Such acts fell within the purview of the foreign affairs committees of the House and Senate, giving them a significant role in the shaping of U.S. policy in this area. In theory, under this approach each significant expenditure of funds would first be authorized in one statute (which might permanently alter statutory authority) and then funds would be appropriated in pursuance of that authorization in a second statute (with the appropriation only relevant for one or two fiscal years), although in practice, the line between the two types of statutes was not always sharply drawn.[224] In recent years foreign affairs authorization legislation has not been adopted, effectively leaving broader policy issues to be addressed in appropriations legislation, which falls within the jurisdiction of the House and Senate appropriations committees.[225] At the same time, statutes have been adopted that both authorize and appropriate funds for specific functional issues[226] and for specific countries.[227]

---

[220] Foreign Operations, Export Financing, and Related Programs Appropriations Act, 2004, div. D, Pub. L. No. 108-199, §513 (known as the Bumpers amendment).

[221] Pub. L. No. 87-195 (codified at 22 U.S.C. § 2151n(a) (2018)).

[222] Pub. L. No. 87-195 (codified at 22 U.S.C. § 2378d).

[223] RENNACK & CHESSER, *supra* note 215.

[224] *See* Louis Fisher, *The Authorization-Appropriation Process in Congress: Formal Rules and Informal Practices*, 29 CATH. U.L. REV. 51, 72 (1979).

[225] Senate and House rules both contain provisions purporting to limit the ability to include policy provisions in appropriations bills. *See* RULES OF THE HOUSE OF REPRESENTATIVES, 117th Cong., Rule XXI(2)(b); STANDING RULES OF THE SENATE, S. DOC. NO. 113-18, Rule XVI(2).

[226] Examples include the United States Leadership Against HIV/AIDs, the Tuberculosis, and Malaria Act of 2003, Pub. L. No. 108-25, 117 Stat. 711 (codified at 22 U.S.C. §§ 7601–04) and the Energy Independence and Security Act of 2007, Pub. L. No. 110-140, 121 Stat. 1492 (codified at 42 U.S.C. §§ 17001–386).

[227] Examples include the Comprehensive Peace in Sudan Act of 2004, Pub. L. No. 108-497, 118 Stat. 4012, as amended by Darfur Peace and Accountability Act of 2006, Pub. L. No. 109-344, 120 Stat. 1869 (codified at 50 U.S.C. § 1701 note), and the Enhanced Partnership with Pakistan Act of 2009, Pub. L. No. 111-73, 123 Stat. 2060 (codified at 22 U.S.C. §§ 8401–42).

Foreign affairs appropriations legislation—usually styled as the "Department of State, Foreign Operations, and Related Programs Appropriations Act" for a given fiscal year, either as a stand-alone statute or as a title within an omnibus law covering a range of government agencies[228]—has become an increasingly important source of congressional authority over foreign affairs. The need for the executive branch to return for funding on a roughly annual basis (a practice that is not at all determined by the Constitution) allows Congress to exercise substantial influence through the allocation of money.[229] In addition, appropriations acts have become an important source of limits on foreign assistance. They may preclude use of funds in relation to specific countries, such as Cuba, Iran, North Korea, and Syria,[230] or they may be contingent on particular events. For example, omnibus appropriations acts in recent years have prohibited economic assistance to the Palestinian Authority if (1) "the Palestinians obtain the same standing as member states or full membership as a state in the United Nations or any specialized agency thereof outside an agreement negotiated between Israel and the Palestinians"; or (2) "the Palestinians initiate an International Criminal Court judicially authorized investigation, or actively support such an investigation, that subjects Israeli nationals to an investigation for alleged crimes against Palestinians."[231]

A more general, oft-salient provision in foreign appropriations legislation prohibits U.S. assistance "to the government of any country whose duly elected head of government is deposed by military coup or decree," although assistance may be resumed once a democratically elected government has taken office.[232] Executive branch adherence to this provision is sometimes grudging. For example, after a military coup in Thailand in 2014, the United States did cut off development assistance and military financing and training programs for the duration of the military's rule (about eighteen months), but maintained funding for law enforcement, counterterrorism and nonproliferation efforts, global health programs, and the Peace Corps.[233]

---

[228] Of course, various other appropriations acts are also relevant, such as those of the Department of Defense.

[229] *See* Price, *supra* note 213, at 367–68; Matthew B. Lawrence, *Subordination and Separation of Powers*, 131 YALE L.J. 78, 98 (2021).

[230] *See, e.g.*, Department of State, Foreign Operations, and Related Programs Appropriations Act, 2009, § 7007.

[231] *See* Consolidated and Further Continuing Appropriations Act, div. A, tit. VII, Pub. L. No. 113-235, § 7041(i)(2)(i) (2009).

[232] *Id.* § 7008. In 2021 alone, there were five successful coups in Chad, Mali, Guinea, Myanmar, and Sudan. *See Global Instances of Coups, 1950–Present*, ARRESTED DICTATORSHIP (regularly updated), https://perma.cc/4A4D-95F8.

[233] CONG. RESEARCH SERV., IF11267, COUP-RELATED RESTRICTIONS IN U.S. FOREIGN AID (2019); Jessica Schulberg, *The Military Coup in Thailand is Putting the U.S. in an Awkward Position*, NEW REPUBLIC (May 23, 2014), https://perma.cc/JZ7Z-ZBXR.

The executive branch has sometimes objected to appropriations restrictions as infringing upon the president's Article II powers. For example, Section 7054 of the Department of State, Foreign Operations, and Related Programs Appropriations Act, Fiscal Year 2009, prohibited all funds made available under FAA Title I from being used to pay the expenses for any U.S. delegation to a spe-cialized U.N. agency, body, or commission that is chaired or presided over by a country with a government that the secretary of state has determined supports international terrorism.[234] OLC took the position that the secretary of state was justified in disregarding Section 7054 as an impermissible interference "with the President's authority to manage the Nation's foreign diplomacy."[235] Another ex-ample is Section 1340(a) of the Department of Defense and Full-Year Continuing Appropriations Act, Fiscal Year 2011, which precluded the White House Office of Science and Technology Policy (OSTP) from using appropriated funds "to develop, design, plan, promulgate, implement, or execute a bilateral policy, program, order, or contract of any kind to participate, collaborate, or coordi-nate bilaterally in any way with China or any Chinese-owned company."[236] OLC again found that such a bar impaired the president's conduct of foreign affairs by means of restrictions targeting OSTP's expenditures for diplomatic purposes,[237] and further noted that "the fact that section 1340 is an appropriations restric-tion, rather than a direct prohibition of conduct," was irrelevant to its analysis of the provision's constitutionality.[238] By contrast, OLC signaled that a limitation focused on related domestic activity, such as a refusal "to appropriate funds for OSTP participation in a conference bringing together the U.S. business commu-nity to determine how to meet energy efficiency benchmarks," would be consti-tutional, "even if those benchmarks were articulated in agreements negotiated between OSTP and China."[239]

Consistent with the Constitution's insistence on congressional control of appropriations,[240] certain statutes seek to ensure that the U.S. government only uses funds as prescribed by Congress. The Budget and Impoundment Control Act (ICA) requires congressional approval of any executive decision to reduce

---

[234] Omnibus Appropriations Act, Fiscal Year 2009, div. H, Pub. L. No. 111-8, 123 Stat. 524, 831.

[235] Office of Legal Counsel, U.S. Dep't of Justice, Re: Constitutionality of Section 7054 of the Fiscal Year 2009 Department of State, Foreign Operations, and Related Programs Appropriations Act, at 4 (June 1, 2009) [hereinafter Section 7054 Opinion], https://perma.cc/HM8N-V8Q8. For analysis of the power to conduct foreign relations, see Chapter 3. For analysis of U.S. participation in interna-tional organizations, see Chapter 7 § II.

[236] Pub. L. No. 112-10, 125 Stat. 38, 123.

[237] Office of the Legal Counsel, U.S. Dep't of Justice, Unconstitutional Restrictions on Activities of the Office of Science and Technology Policy in Section 1340A of the Department of Defense and Full-Year Continuing Appropriations Act, 2011, at 3–11 (Sept. 19, 2011), https://perma.cc/P2AR-4ZX2.

[238] Id. at 6.

[239] Id. at 10.

[240] U.S. CONST. art. 1, § 9, cl. 7 ("No Money shall be drawn from the Treasury, but in Consequence of Appropriations made by Law. . . .").

or terminate a program for which Congress has authorized funds;[241] at the same time, government agencies often are granted limited authority to reprogram funding to take account of changed circumstances, provided that Congress is notified (and, in practice, provided that Congress concurs). The Anti-Deficiency Act prohibits federal employees, inter alia, from "mak[ing] or authoriz[ing] an expenditure or obligation exceeding an amount available in an appropriation or fund for the expenditure or obligation."[242] The Miscellaneous Receipts Act provides that generally all funds received by the United States, including through the receipt of taxes or the sale of land or other property, must be paid into the treasury and not expended by federal employees except as approved by Congress.[243] There are some exceptions to the latter rule in the field of foreign relations, such as for certain funds received by the Customs Service[244] or the Overseas Private Investment Corporation.[245]

Prosecutions under these statutes are rare, but their restrictions have featured in some notorious foreign relations controversies. Thus, the final report of the Joint Congressional Committee for the Iran-Contra Affair concluded that the collection of the funds by White House officials from arms sales to Iran without placing those funds in the treasury violated the Miscellaneous Receipts Act, while the expenditure of the funds to assist the Nicaraguan contras without congressional appropriation violated the Anti-Deficiency Act (as well as the Boland Amendments).[246]

More recently, the U.S. Government Accountability Office (GAO), an agency of the legislative branch, reviewed the decision by the Office of Management and Budget (OMB) to withhold from obligation funds that had been appropriated to the Department of Defense for security assistance to Ukraine.[247] In addition to affording the president a limited capacity to propose the rescission of funds, the ICA gives executive branch officials strictly circumscribed authority to defer

---

[241] 2 U.S.C. §§ 681–88 (2018); *see, e.g.,* Train v. City of New York, 420 U.S. 35 (1975) (finding that the president may not impound funds).

[242] 31 U.S.C. § 1341(a)(1)(A) (2018).

[243] 31 U.S.C. § 3302. For example, in 2012, a contractor working on a Mali development program pursued a claim against the U.S. government's Millennium Challenge Corporation (MCC) before an international arbitral tribunal. The tribunal dismissed the claim and ordered the contractor to pay costs. MCC was accorded $97,575 of those costs, which reflected the amounts it expended for outside counsel, labor, and travel. The Justice Department determined, however, that an arbitral award of legal costs does not qualify as a refund for purposes of the "refunds to appropriations" exception to the Miscellaneous Receipts Act, and therefore that the MCC had to deposit the monies in the general fund of the Treasury. *See* Office of the Legal Counsel, U.S. Dep't of Justice, Applicability of the Miscellaneous Receipts Act to an Arbitral Award of Legal Costs (Mar. 6, 2018), https://perma.cc/7NVX-MD7N.

[244] *See* 19 U.S.C. § 1524 (2018).

[245] *See* 22 U.S.C. § 2196.

[246] Iran Contra Report, *supra* note 154, at 349.

[247] U.S. Gov't Accountability Off., B-331564, Matter of Office of Management and Budget—Withholding of Ukraine Security Assistance (2020), https://perma.cc/KBJ5-5U28.

expenditures: Congress must be notified, the deferral cannot last beyond the end of the instant fiscal year, and the purposes of the deferral must be "to provide for contingencies," "to achieve savings" or efficiencies, or "as specifically provided by law."[248] In GAO's view, the reason that the funds were withheld—according to OMB, at least in part so that they would not be spent "in a manner that could conflict with the President's foreign policy"[249]—was unlawful, because deferral for policy reasons was not permitted under the ICA.[250] OMB and GAO evidently disagreed as to whether the delay in question amounted to a mere "programmatic delay" akin to an external factor causing an unavoidable delay,[251] and as to whether OMB's position was consistent with the president's duty to "take Care that the Laws be faithfully executed,"[252] but the funds were eventually obligated.

As previously noted, Congress' power to appropriate funds is limited by other parts of the Constitution, including the need for Congress to provide sufficient funds for the other branches to carry out their constitutionally mandated duties or prerogatives.[253] Thus, it would be unconstitutional for Congress to refuse to provide any funds for the operation of the Department of State or for the operation of U.S. embassies abroad, to the extent that doing so would effectively deny the president any meaningful ability to make treaties or to send and receive ambassadors. Denial of funds to open an embassy in a single country, subject to conditions imposed by Congress, might also be construed as an unconstitutional denial to the president of his power to recognize new states. When Congress enacted such a provision in 1996—denying funds for the opening or operating of a new embassy in the Socialist Republic of Vietnam absent a detailed certification[254]—the Clinton administration reacted by stating that the prohibition was "an unconstitutional condition on the exercise of the President's power to control the recognition and non-recognition of foreign governments—a power that flows directly from his textually-committed authority to receive ambassadors. . . ."[255]

Of course, providing no funds for such constitutionally envisaged duties or prerogatives is different from reducing funding, and also different from denying funding for an activity that implicates concurrent powers. One poignant way in

[248] 2 U.S.C. § 684.

[249] Letter from Mark R. Paoletta, Gen. Couns., Off. of Mgmt. & Budget, to Tom Armstrong, Gen. Couns., Gov't Accountability Off. 9 (Dec. 11, 2019), https://perma.cc/2MK3-FGCD.

[250] U.S. Gov't Accountability Off., supra note 247, at 6–7.

[251] Compare Letter from Mark R. Paoletta, supra note 249, at 5–9, with U.S. Gov't Accountability Off., supra note 247, at 7.

[252] Id.; cf. U.S. Const. art. II, § 3.

[253] See, e.g., Fisher, How Tightly Can Congress Draw the Purse Strings?, supra note 210; J. Gregory Sidak, The President's Power of the Purse, 1989 Duke L.J. 1162 (1989).

[254] Omnibus Consolidated Rescissions and Appropriations Act of 1996, Pub. L. No. 104-134, § 609, 110 Stat. 1321 (1996).

[255] Section 609 of the FY 1996 Omnibus Appropriations Act, 20 Op. O.L.C. 189, 193 (1996).

which this issue has presented itself is in the context of a statute requiring the president to withdraw military forces from the battlefield. For example, in 1971, President Richard Nixon signed into law a statute containing a provision that required withdrawal of all U.S. troops from Southeast Asia.[256] When signing, the president stated that the provision expressed Congress' "judgment about the manner in which the American involvement in the war should be ended," but was "without binding force or effect" due to the president's own constitutional authority, and that therefore he was under no obligation to carry out the provision.[257] A federal district court later found that the law established U.S. policy "to the exclusion of any different executive or administration policy, and had binding force and effect on every officer of the Government, no matter what their private judgments of that policy, and illegalized the pursuit of an inconsistent executive or administration policy."[258] At the same time, the court concluded that the statute provided "a very wide discretion" as to how, exactly, the policy was to be implemented, such that executive branch initiatives (and even the "very unfortunate" signing statement) did not ultimately diverge from the statutory statement of policy.[259]

While similar confrontations between Congress' power of the purse and the commander-in-chief power have periodically surfaced,[260] they are typically resolved through interbranch accommodation rather than litigation.[261] For example, in 2007 Congress adopted legislation that would have required a withdrawal of U.S. troops from Iraq in the absence of certain presidential determinations, but President George W. Bush vetoed the bill.[262] An attempt to override the veto failed in the House of Representatives. Thereafter both houses adopted and the president signed into law alternative legislation that inter alia: (1) established certain "benchmarks" that the Iraqi government was required to meet and provided that economic support funds would be denied to Iraq unless the president certified that the benchmarks were being met (though the law also allowed the president to waive this restriction); and (2) said the president "shall direct the

---

[256] Act of Nov. 17, 1971, Pub. L. No. 92-156, § 601, 85 Stat. 430 (known as the Mansfield amendment).

[257] Statement on Signing the Military Appropriations Authorization Bill, 1 PUB. PAPERS 1114 (Nov. 17, 1971).

[258] DaCosta v. Nixon, 55 F.R.D. 145, 146 (E.D.N.Y. 1972).

[259] Id.

[260] See, e.g., Exercising Congress' Constitutional Power to End a War Before the S. Comm. on the Judiciary, 110th Cong. (2007) (discussing Congress' ability to compel a withdrawal of U.S. armed forces from Iraq); Charles Tiefer, Can Appropriation Riders Speed Our Exit from Iraq?, 42 STAN. J. INT'L L. 291 (2006).

[261] See Peter Raven-Hansen & William C. Banks, Pulling the Purse Strings of the Commander in Chief, 80 VA. L. REV. 8333 (1994).

[262] See Remarks on Returning Without Approval to the House of Representatives the "U.S. Troop Readiness, Veterans' Care, Katrina Recovery, and Iraq Accountability Appropriations Act, 2007," 1 PUB. PAPERS 513 (May 1, 2007).

orderly redeployment of elements of U.S. forces from Iraq" if the Iraqi government so requested.[263] In accepting this interbranch accommodation, President Bush appears to have been particularly concerned that Congress not use its power to set "an artificial timetable for withdrawal."[264] Conversely, although as of 2021 Congress had not sought to force a withdrawal of U.S. troops from Afghanistan, and instead had continued to appropriate extensive funds for military operations there, President Joe Biden decided to withdraw all U.S. troops, leading to a collapse of the Afghan government and a rapid takeover of the country by the Taliban.[265]

IV. Power to Regulate Commerce with Foreign Nations

Another principal enumerated power of Congress that concerns foreign relations is the power to regulate commerce with foreign nations,[266] which is accompanied by the power to collect duties, imposts, and excises.[267] Establishing a national power to regulate foreign commerce and reduce the impediments that had been imposed by the several states was a key objective for the Framers.[268] As the Supreme Court has recalled, the Articles of Confederation essentially allowed the states to burden "commerce both among themselves and with foreign countries very much as they pleased. Before 1787 it was commonplace for seaboard States with port facilities to derive revenue to defray the costs of state and local governments by imposing taxes on imported goods destined for customers in other States."[269]

As discussed later, the constitutional limits on the foreign commerce power remain unclear, but it undoubtedly supports a vast array of laws. This section is necessarily confined to certain general categories of such legislation: laws

[263] U.S. Troop Readiness, Veterans' Care, Katrina Recovery, and Iraq Accountability Appropriations Act, 2007, Pub. L. No. 110–28, § 1314, 121 Stat. 112, 124–25.
[264] See Remarks, supra note 262, at 513 ("It makes no sense to tell the enemy when you plan to start withdrawing."); The President's News Conference, 1 PUB. PAPERS 379, 385 (Apr. 3, 2007) ("I think setting an artificial timetable for withdrawal is a significant mistake.").
[265] See CONG. RESEARCH SERV., R46879, U.S. MILITARY WITHDRAWAL AND TALIBAN TAKEOVER IN AFGHANISTAN: FREQUENTLY ASKED QUESTIONS (2021). For fiscal year 2020, the Department of Defense obligated some $40 billion for military operations and reconstruction activities in Afghanistan. Id. at 5.
[266] U.S. CONST. art. I, § 8, cl. 3.
[267] Id. art. I, § 8, cl. 1; see, e.g., Brown v. Maryland, 25 U.S. (12 Wheat.) 419 (1827), where Chief Justice Marshall found unconstitutional a Maryland statute requiring importers of foreign goods to purchase a Maryland license, due to Congress' powers both to lay imposts on imports and to regulate foreign commerce. On the "dormant" Foreign Commerce Clause, see Chapter 9 § II(D).
[268] See, e.g., HENKIN, FOREIGN AFFAIRS, at 65 ("From the beginning, the foreign trade of the United States was near the core of its foreign policy, and the power to regulate commerce with foreign nations gave Congress a major voice in it.").
[269] Michelin Tire Corp. v. Wages, 423 U.S. 276, 283 (1976).

regulating trade in goods and services; laws regulating foreign investment; laws regulating instrumentalities and activities that have some other connection to foreign commerce; and laws granting the president emergency economic powers. As discussed in Chapter 9, moreover, the import of the foreign commerce power is not limited to enabling Congress to enact legislation; even when the power is not exercised by Congress, the "dormant" foreign commerce power also has the effect of preempting state law.[270]

A. Scope of the Foreign Commerce Power

Since the early 1970s, the Supreme Court has summarized the general categories of legislation that Congress may enact under its commerce power as including (1) legislation regulating "the use of channels of interstate or foreign commerce"; (2) legislation regulating the "instrumentalities of interstate commerce, . . . or persons or things in [interstate] commerce"; and (3) legislation regulating activities that substantially affect interstate commerce.[271] Even since their advent, these categories (particularly the third) are not always predictably applied— unsurprisingly, given the fluid and evolutionary nature of the Court's Commerce Clause jurisprudence[272]—but they provide a starting point for most analyses.

No comparable framework exists for the foreign commerce power;[273] indeed, as one court of appeals observed, it is fair to say that the Supreme Court has never "thoroughly explored the scope of the Foreign Commerce Clause."[274] While some courts have analyzed statutes based on the foreign commerce power using the three-category approach,[275] the Supreme Court has indicated that, given the

[270] See, e.g., Barclays Bank PLC v. Franchise Tax Bd., 512 U.S. 298, 320 (1994). See generally Chapter 9 § II(D).
[271] Perez v. United States, 402 U.S. 146, 150 (1971); see, e.g., Gonzales v. Raich, 545 U.S. 1, 16 (2005); United States v. Morrison, 529 U.S. 598, 608–09 (2000); United States v. Lopez, 514 U.S. 549, 558–59 (1995).
[272] For summaries, see Morrison, 529 U.S. at 607–08; Lopez, 514 U.S. at 552–58; id. at 568–75 (Kennedy, J., concurring); id. at 584–85, 593–99 (Thomas, J., concurring); e.g., Lopez, 514 U.S. at 568 (Kennedy, J., concurring) (adverting to "[t]he history of the judicial struggle to interpret the Commerce Clause"); Raich, 545 U.S. at 33–34 (Scalia, J., concurring) (stating that for thirty years "our cases have mechanically recited that the Commerce Clause permits congressional regulation of three categories," but describing the third as "different in kind" and as recited tending toward being "misleading and incomplete").
[273] See Anthony J. Colangelo, The Foreign Commerce Clause, 96 VA. L. REV. 949, 983–86 (2010); Naomi Harlin Goodno, When the Commerce Clause Goes International: A Proposed Legal Framework for the Foreign Commerce Clause, 65 FLA. L. REV. 1139, 1161–63 (2013).
[274] The Eleventh Circuit Court of Appeals acknowledged that "[n]either this Court nor the Supreme Court" had done so. United States v. Baston, 818 F.3d 651, 667 (11th Cir. 2016).
[275] See, e.g., United States v. Cummings, 281 F.3d 1046, 1049 n.1 (9th Cir. 2002) (using the three-category framework when analyzing constitutionality of the International Parental Kidnapping Crime Act, 18 U.S.C. § 1204(a) (2012)); United States v. Homaune, 898 F. Supp. 2d 153, 159 (D.D.C. 2012) (same).

lack of federalism concerns, there "is evidence that the Founders intended the scope of the foreign commerce power to be greater" than with interstate commerce, due to the need for the United States to speak with "one voice" in its economic relations with other states.[276] If that is the case then, given the considerable (if not unlimited) expanse of the domestic commerce power, the foreign commerce power is capable of supporting a very wide array of legislation on matters related to such commerce.[277] Conversely, it has been noted that the Constitution speaks to a power to regulate commerce "with" foreign nations (thus, between the United States and a foreign nation), not "within" or even "among" foreign nations, arguably suggesting that the power actually may be narrower than the domestic Commerce Clause (which refers to commerce "among the several States").[278] Justice Thomas, who would prefer an originalist approach to both questions, has further cautioned that "even if the foreign commerce power were broader than the interstate commerce power as understood at the founding, it would not follow that the foreign commerce power is broader than the interstate commerce power as [the Supreme] Court now construes it."[279] Lower courts have disagreed about whether the foreign commerce power is broader, though many endorse approaches that are designed to be at least as easily satisfied as in cases involving interstate commerce.[280]

Even if the domestic commerce power and foreign commerce power are viewed as comparable in scope (one neither greater nor lesser than the other), the foreign commerce power must be viewed as quite broad. Contemporary international economic relations are such that a wide variety of previously local activities may well impinge upon international trade, foreign investment, international banking, finance, transportation or communication, maritime affairs, or other transnational transactions, opening the door to copious federal legislation if Congress chooses to exercise such power. Indeed, domestic and foreign commerce are often so intertwined that one cannot be considered as sealed off from the other. The challenge lies in describing the power over foreign commerce

---

[276] Japan Line, Ltd. v. County of Los Angeles, 441 U.S. 434, 448 (1979); *see id.* at 448 n.13 ("It has never been suggested that Congress' power to regulate foreign commerce could be" limited by "considerations of federalism and state sovereignty."); Atl. Cleaners & Dyers v. United States, 286 U.S. 427, 434 (1932) ("the power when exercised in respect of foreign commerce may be broader than when exercised as to interstate commerce"); United States v. Bredimus, 352 F.3d 200, 208 (5th Cir. 2003) ("The Supreme Court has long held that Congress's authority to regulate foreign commerce is even broader than its authority to regulate interstate commerce.").

[277] HENKIN, FOREIGN AFFAIRS, at 65–67.

[278] For a sustained argument in this regard, see Colangelo, *supra* note 272.

[279] Baston v. United States, 137 S. Ct. 850, 852 (2017) (Thomas, J., dissenting from denial of cert.).

[280] *See* United States v. Park, 938 F.3d 354, 372 (D.C. Cir. 2019). *But see* United States v. Al-Maliki, 787 F.3d 784, 793 (6th Cir. 2015) (expressing "skeptic[ism]" that "Congress has greater commerce power over conduct occurring in foreign countries than conduct occurring in the States").

so that it does not appear to "confer upon Congress a virtually plenary power over global economic activity."[281]

There appears to be little controversy that the power encompasses legislation that regulates trade in goods and services between the United States and other countries, as well as foreign investment in the United States, and other activities that have a connection with foreign commerce.[282] What has elicited some controversy is whether the power includes the ability to regulate conduct occurring solely within a foreign country that has little or no connection with or effects in the United States. An example for how this issue may arise concerns the penalties against sex tourism that are part of the Prosecutorial Remedies and Other Tools to end the Exploitation of Children Today (PROTECT) Act of 2003.[283] The PROTECT Act provides, in relevant part, that any U.S. citizen or permanent resident "who travels in foreign commerce" and engages in any illicit sexual conduct, such as with a minor, may be fined or imprisoned.[284] The statutory text and legislative history make it clear that Congress intended to justify the provision on the basis of its power over foreign commerce.[285] Criminal prosecution under this provision has led to challenges that it represents an unconstitutional exercise of the foreign commerce power by regulating conduct (sexual exploitation) abroad that would not, were it to occur within the United States, constitute interstate commerce regulable as such. Those challenges have not succeeded. For example, the Ninth Circuit in *United States v. Clark* took what it regarded as a "global, commonsense approach" to the circumstances, in which the question posed is "whether the statute bears a rational relationship to Congress' authority under the Foreign Commerce Clause."[286] Applying that approach, it concluded that the "illicit sexual conduct reached by the statute expressly includes commercial sex acts performed by a U.S. citizen on foreign soil," and "falls under the

Baston, 137 S. Ct. at 853 (Thomas, J., dissenting from denial of cert.).
[282] *See* Gibbons v. Ogden, 22 U.S. 1, 193 (1824); *see also* Kenneth M. Casebeer, *The Power to Regulate "Commerce with Foreign Nations" in a Global Economy and the Future of American Democracy: An Essay*, 56 U. Miami L. Rev. 25 (2001); Anthony J. Colangelo, *The Foreign Commerce Clause*, 96 Va. L. Rev. 949 (2010); Kathleen Claussen, *Regulating Foreign Commerce Through Multiple Pathways: A Case Study*, 130 Yale L.J.F. 266 (2020).
[283] Pub. L. 108-21, § 105, 117 Stat. 650, 654 (codified as amended at 18 U.S.C. § 2423(b)–(g) (2018)). There exist a variety of similar statutes. *See, e.g.*, Child Support Recovery Act of 1992 § 2(a), 18 U.S.C. § 228 (prohibiting traveling in interstate or foreign commerce with the intent to evade a support obligation); Violence Against Women Act of 1994 § 40221(a), 18 U.S.C. § 2261 (domestic violence statute prohibiting traveling in interstate or foreign commerce with the intent to kill, injure, harass, or intimidate a spouse).
[284] Pub. L. 108-21, § 105(c), 117 Stat. at 654.
[285] Previously proposed legislation with the same language had addressed the constitutional basis. *See* H.R. Rep. No. 107-525, at 5 (2002) (providing, in constitutional authority statement, that "the Committee finds the authority for this legislation in article I, section 8 of the Constitution"). The report accompanying the final PROTECT Act did not have a comparable section. *See* H.R. Rep. No. 108-66 (2003) (Conf. Rep.).
[286] United States v. Clark, 435 F.3d 1100, 1103, 1114 (9th Cir. 2006).

broad umbrella of foreign commerce and consequently within congressional authority under the Foreign Commerce Clause."[287]

The court in *Clark* viewed the close nexus between the defendant's decision to travel to Cambodia and his illicit activities as relevant, noting that whether "a longer gap between the travel and the commercial sex act could trigger constitutional or other concerns is an issue we leave for another day."[288] Further, the court made clear that, on the facts presented, there was a "commercial sex act" (the defendant paid for the act); the court was not addressing other illicit sexual conduct falling within the scope of the statute that was less commercial in nature, such as exploitation accomplished by the threat or use of force.[289] The potential elasticity of this approach was on display in *United States v. Bollinger*, in which the defendant had moved to Haiti in 2004 and began molesting young girls five years later.[290] In 2012, he was indicted under the PROTECT Act for engaging in an illicit sexual act after traveling in foreign commerce. In upholding the constitutionality of the statute as applied, the Fourth Circuit maintained that "the Foreign Commerce Clause allows Congress to regulate activities that demonstrably affect" foreign commerce,[291] and found that it was "eminently rational to believe that prohibiting the noncommercial sexual abuse of children by Americans abroad has a demonstrable effect on sex tourism and the commercial sex industry."[292]

By contrast, in *United States v. Pendleton*, the Third Circuit was confronted with a defendant U.S. national who travelled to Germany, where he molested a fifteen-year-old boy.[293] While the court was hesitant to adopt *Clark*'s relatively elastic approach to foreign commerce authority,[294] it upheld the prosecution as constitutionally permissible based on the capacity of Congress to regulate the use of channels of foreign commerce to keep them free of immoral or injurious uses, much as for interstate commerce. The court concluded that, in the PROTECT Act, Congress could "regulate persons who use the channels of commerce to circumvent local laws that criminalize child abuse and molestation."[295]

The original version of the PROTECT Act was understood to require only that a U.S. citizen travel in foreign commerce and thereafter engage in illicit

---

[287] *Id.* at 1103.
[288] *Id.* at 1107 n.11.
[289] *Id.* at 1110; *see* 18 U.S.C. § 2423(f) (2018).
[290] United States v. Bollinger, 798 F.3d 201, 203–04 (4th Cir. 2015).
[291] *Id.* at 215–16.
[292] *Id.* at 218.
[293] United States v. Pendleton, 658 F.3d 299, 301 (3d Cir. 2011).
[294] *Id.* at 307–08.
[295] *Id.* at 311; *see* United States v. Bredimus, 352 F.3d 200 (5th Cir. 2003) (affirming on similar reasoning conviction under 18 U.S.C. § 2423(b), which reaches any person who travels in foreign commerce "for the purpose of" engaging in illicit sexual conduct).

sexual conduct.[296] In 2013, however, the statute was amended so as to cover a U.S. citizen "who travels in foreign commerce *or resides, either temporarily or permanently,* in a foreign country, and engages in any illicit sexual conduct with another person."[297] In *United States v. Park*, which involved the revised PROTECT Act, the D.C. Circuit upheld as constitutional the prosecution of a U.S. citizen engaged in, among other things, what it portrayed as "non-commercial child sex abuse abroad" while residing in Vietnam.[298] In supporting the link to Congress' foreign commerce power, the court noted that such conduct could reinforce the acceptability of illicit behavior, allow traffickers "to entice patrons into . . . subsequent commercial behavior," encourage U.S. citizens to relocate to countries that lack the will or capacity to regulate child sex abuse, and resolve enforcement difficulties that would be created by requiring more overt commercial aspects, all of which established that "Congress had a rational basis to conclude that a law requiring proof of commercial activity would result in dramatic underenforcement" and that the defendant's activities, "when aggregated, ha[d] a substantial effect on the market for prostitution and sex trafficking of children."[299]

The court acknowledged that the question of the constitutionality of the PROTECT Act as applied to noncommercial abuse was "a closer one" than for other aspects of the defendant's conduct, and that other applications of the statute might exceed congressional authority.[300] Critically, however, the court held that the entire application of the PROTECT Act at issue in the case could be upheld on the basis of the treaty power, insofar as the act was rationally related to implementing the Optional Protocol on the Sale of Children, Child Prostitution and Child Pornography, a valid Article II treaty of the United States.[301] As noted in the next section, it is not uncommon for U.S. statutes potentially relying on the foreign commerce power to have an independent basis in an international agreement of the United States.

---

[296] *Clark*, 435 F.3d at 1107.

[297] Violence Against Women Reauthorization Act of 2013, Pub. L. No. 113-4, § 1211(b), 127 Stat. 54, 142 (codified at 18 U.S.C. § 2423(c) (2018)) (emphasis added). The Ninth Circuit regarded this amendment as casting doubt on its construction of the prior version of the statute—insofar as the new language implied that the statute "was previously inapplicable to U.S. citizens living abroad unless they were traveling . . . when they had illicit sex"—meaning that the original statute would be inapplicable to the conduct of a U.S. citizen residing in Cambodia. United States v. Pepe, 895 F.3d 679, 681–82 (9th Cir. 2018).

[298] United States v. Park, 938 F.3d 354, 373 (D.C. Cir. 2019).

[299] *Id.* at 373–74 (citing, inter alia, United States v. Lindsay, 931 F.3d 852, 863 (9th Cir. 2019)).

[300] *Id.*

[301] *Id.* at 363–70; *see* Optional Protocol to the Convention on the Rights of the Child on the Sale of Children, Child Prostitution and Child Pornography, May 25, 2000, T.I.A.S. No. 13,095, 2171 U.N.T.S. 227.

B. Trade in Goods and Services

Public controls on trade in goods and services between the United States and other countries are largely grounded in global, regional, and bilateral trade agreements, for which there are U.S. implementing statutes. The 1890 Tariff Act, although largely protectionist in nature, was the first statute to essentially empower the president to negotiate tariff arrangements with foreign states, allowing him or her by proclamation to raise or lower tariffs depending on the tariff practice of the foreign state.[302] In reaction to the high tariffs that contributed to the Depression, the 1934 Reciprocal Trade Agreements Act was much more oriented toward promotion of free trade, expressly authorizing the president to enter into trade agreements and permitting the president to reduce tariffs with a trading partner (on a reciprocal basis) up to 50 percent.[303] Pursuant to this statute, conclusion of international agreements became a central component of U.S. trade policy. The 1962 Trade Expansion Act established a new institutional element, which later became the Cabinet-level position of the U.S. Trade Representative, allowing for more centralized authority in pursuing trade initiatives.[304] Because trade agreements began to transition from dealing solely with tariffs to addressing as well limitations on regulatory barriers to trade, the 1974 Trade Act revamped congressional-executive relations in this area, returning considerable control to Congress over whether to conclude a trade agreement, and addressing the adoption of its implementing statute.[305]

These implementing statutes allow the United States to uphold its obligations under, for example, the 1994 Uruguay Round trade agreements,[306] the 1994 North American Free Trade Agreement (NAFTA),[307] the 2004 Central American Free Trade Agreement–Dominican Republic (CAFTA-DR),[308] the 2019 United States–Mexico–Canada Agreement (USMCA),[309] and bilateral

---

[302] Tariff Act of 1890, ch. 1244, § 3, 26 Stat. 567, 612 (also known as the McKinley Tariff).

[303] Reciprocal Trade Agreements Act of 1934, ch. 474, Pub. L. No. 73-316, 48 Stat. 943, 943–44 (codified as amended at 19 U.S.C. § 1351 (2018)).

[304] Trade Expansion Act of 1962, Pub. L. No. 87-794, § 241, 76 Stat. 872, 878 (creating the Special Trade Representative for Trade Negotiations; this section was repealed in 1975); Reorganization Plan No. 3 of 1979, § 1, 3 C.F.R. 513, 513 (1980) (redesignating the office as the Office of the United States Trade Representative).

[305] Trade Act of 1974, Pub. L. No. 93-618, 88 Stat. 1978 (1975). Various statutes have also allowed for conditional, nonreciprocal lower U.S. tariffs to certain developing states. *See, e.g.,* African Growth and Opportunity Act, tit. I, Pub. L. No. 106-200, 114 Stat. 251, 252 (2000) (codified as amended at scattered section of 19 U.S.C.).

[306] The Uruguay Round Agreements Act, Pub. L. No. 103-465, 108 Stat. 4809 (1994) (codified at 19 U.S.C. §§ 3501–3624 (2018)).

[307] North American Free Trade Agreement Implementation Act, 19 U.S.C. §§ 3331–3473.

[308] Dominican Republic–Central America–United States Free Trade Agreement Implementation Act, Pub. L. No. 109-53 (2005) (codified at 19 U.S.C. §§ 4001–4112).

[309] Agreement Between the United States of America, the United States of Mexico, and Canada (Dec. 13, 2019), https://perma.cc/RW2F-TRBR.

free trade agreements with other countries.[310] Such statutes might be viewed as supported by either the foreign commerce power[311] or as necessary and proper for implementing a treaty of the United States, although such agreements are formally concluded as congressional-executive agreements. As discussed in Chapter 6, congressional-executive agreements are not transmitted to the Senate for advice and consent by a two-thirds majority but, rather, are transmitted to both houses of Congress for a simple majority vote. Moreover, such trade agreements sometimes proceed pursuant to a "fast-track" or "trade promotion" process, which involves presidential consultation with Congress in advance of concluding the trade agreement in exchange for Congress, once the agreement is concluded, expeditiously deciding whether to approve it without amendment.[312]

As part of the implementing statute, Congress approves of the agreement, thereby allowing the president to ratify it.[313] At the same time, the statute typically provides that no provision of the agreement itself that is inconsistent with U.S. law has any effect, and that preemption of state law by the agreement is limited in nature. With respect to the latter, the implementing statute for the Uruguay Round trade agreements provided that no state law "may be declared invalid as to any person or circumstance on the ground that the provision or application is inconsistent with the Agreement, except in an action brought by the United States for the purpose of declaring such law or application invalid."[314] Thus, for purposes of domestic U.S. law, the implementing statute places the principal focus on the statute itself, rather than the agreement, as the governing law.

Additional statutes also provide the president with authority to implement U.S. obligations under its trade agreements. For example, the Omnibus Trade and Competitiveness Act of 1988 authorizes the president, whenever he or she determines that import restrictions of a foreign country or of the United States are unduly burdening and restricting U.S. foreign trade, to proclaim the modification of any existing duty, the continuance of existing duty-free or excise treatment, or the imposition of such additional duties, as he or she determines to be required or appropriate to carry out trade agreements.[315] Other statutes allow the president to grant preferential trade benefits to certain countries, typically developing countries. Thus, the Andean Trade Preference Act authorizes the

---

[310] As of 2022, the United States has bilateral free trade agreements with: Australia, Bahrain, Chile, Colombia, Israel, Jordan, Morocco, Oman, Panama, Peru, Singapore, and South Korea. An example of an implementing statute is the U.S.-Chile Free Trade Agreement Implementation Act, Pub. L. No. 108-77, 117 Stat. 909 (codified at 19 U.S.C. § 3805 note).

[311] Congress authorized the president to negotiate bilateral or multilateral tariff-reduction agreements in the 1934 Reciprocal Trade Agreements Act, 19 U.S.C. § 1351.

[312] See e.g., Bipartisan Congressional Trade Priorities and Accountability Act of 2015, tit. I, Pub. L. No. 114-26, 129 Stat. 319, 320; see Chapter 6 § V(A).

[313] See, e.g., 19 U.S.C. § 3511.

[314] See id. § 4012(b).

[315] Id. §§ 2902(a), 2902(e).

president to proclaim duty-free entry for all eligible articles, and duty reductions for certain other articles, that are the product of any beneficiary country designated under that act.[316]

The principal statute regulating the export of defense articles and services is the 1976 AECA.[317] Pursuant to the AECA, the United States conducts an extensive foreign military sales program whereby foreign governments purchase military goods and services, subject to end-use and retransfer limitations.[318] The statute has special rules controlling the export of missiles and missile equipment or technology[319] and on nuclear nonproliferation.[320] Of particular note is AECA Section 2778, which authorizes the president to control the import and the export of defense articles and services, and to provide foreign policy guidance to U.S. persons in that regard. Under this provision, the president may designate those items to be considered as "defense articles" and "defense services" (the U.S. Munitions List) and then regulate them, which has been done through a licensing system governed by the International Trafficking in Arms Regulations.[321]

C. Foreign Investment

As a general matter, Congress has not sought to regulate U.S. investment abroad, though U.S. treaties provide protections for U.S. investors in certain countries. Likewise, Congress generally has not sought to regulate foreign investment in the United States, leaving such matters to be regulated by laws at the federal and state level in the same manner as domestic-origin investment.[322] Therefore, U.S. obligations to protect foreign investment under national treatment, most-favored-nation treatment, or fair-and-equitable treatment standards (and to protect such investment from expropriation) that are contained in bilateral investment treaties,[323] in free trade agreements,[324] or in the older friendship, commerce, and navigation treaties[325] are implemented through existing U.S. constitutional and statutory rules that are highly protective of property in

---

[316] Id. §§ 3201–06. The countries are Bolivia, Colombia, Ecuador, and Peru.
[317] Arms Export Control Act (AECA) of 1976, tit. II, Pub. L. No. 94-329, 90 Stat. 729 (1976) (codified at 22 U.S.C. §§ 2751–99).
[318] Id. §§ 2761–67.
[319] Id. §§ 2797–97c.
[320] Id. §§ 2799aa–99aa-2.
[321] 22 C.F.R. pts. 120–30 (2019).
[322] Fred L. Morrison, *The Protection of Foreign Investment in the United States of America*, 58 Am. J. Comp. L. (Supplement) 437, 438 (2010).
[323] *See* U.S. Dep't of State, *United States Bilateral Investment Treaties*, https://perma.cc/VRP9-UP99.
[324] *See* Office of the U.S. Trade Representative, *Free Trade Agreements*, https://perma.cc/NGJ3-RSR7.
[325] *See, e.g.*, Treaty of Friendship, Commerce and Navigation, U.S.-Japan, Apr. 2, 1953, 4 U.S.T. 2063.

the United States. For example, investment by resident noncitizens "is protected by the equal protection and due process clauses [of the Constitution] and only reasonable discriminations are permitted."[326]

The federal government, however, does regulate and limit certain foreign investments and real estate transactions by foreign persons that may pose a risk to U.S. national security.[327] A 1988 amendment to the Defense Production Act of 1950 provided for the establishment of a federal interagency Committee on Foreign Investment in the United States (CFIUS),[328] which reviews on an expedited basis proposed transactions for investment in the United States that could result in control of a U.S. business by a foreign person. The purpose of looking at such "covered transactions" is to determine the effect of them on the national security of the United States.

If CFIUS finds that a covered transaction presents national security risks, and that other provisions of law do not provide adequate authority to address the risks, then CFIUS may enter into an agreement with, or impose conditions on, the parties to the transaction to mitigate such risks, or may refer the case to the president for action. For example, based on a CFIUS review in 2012, President Obama prohibited the acquisition and ownership of four wind-farm-project companies by a U.S. company, Ralls Corporation, and required it to divest its interests in any such companies. Ralls Corporation was owned by Chinese nationals, and the wind farm sites were near restricted air space at the Naval Weapons Systems Training Facility Boardman in Oregon.[329] Ralls Corporation challenged the prohibition, claiming inter alia that the president's order deprived Ralls of its constitutionally protected property interests in violation of the Due Process Clause of the Fifth Amendment. In 2014, the D.C. Circuit Court of Appeals found, in *Ralls Corporation v. CFIUS*, that there was no statutory bar to judicial review of the constitutional claim and that such claim was justiciable.[330] Further, the court agreed that the corporation's due process rights were violated, since it was not informed of the official action undertaken, was not given access to unclassified evidence on which the action was taken, and was not afforded an opportunity to rebut that evidence.[331] In 2015, Ralls Corporation and the government reached

---

[326] RESTATEMENT (THIRD) § 722 cmt. f.

[327] *See generally* Jonathan Masters & James McBride, *Foreign Investment and U.S. National Security*, COUNCIL ON FOREIGN RELATIONS (Aug. 28, 2018), https://perma.cc/VBY3-N6HR.

[328] Defense Production Act of 1950, § 721, 50 U.S.C. § 4565 (2018) (known as the "Exon-Florio amendment"). The original provision was substantially revised by the Foreign Investment and National Security Act of 2007, Pub. L. No. 110-49, 121 Stat. 246 (2007), and by the Foreign Investment Risk Review Modernization Act of 2018, Pub. L. No. 115-232, § 1701, 132 Stat. 1636, 2174 (2018). The statute is implemented by Exec. Order No. 11,858, 73 Fed. Reg. 4,677 (May 7, 1975), as amended, and by regulations at 31 C.F.R. pts. 800–02 (2021); *see also CFIUS Laws and Guidance*, U.S. DEP'T OF TREASURY, https://perma.cc/5AJS-S9V4.

[329] *CFIUS Annual Report to Congress for 2012*, at 2 (2013), https://perma.cc/Z53J-VPMG.

[330] 758 F.3d 296, 311, 314 (D.C. Cir. 2014).

[331] *Id.* at 325.

an undisclosed settlement in the case, which reportedly allowed the corporation to keep its acquisition of the wind farm project companies.[332]

An unresolved issue is whether state laws that seek to prohibit state government entities and companies from entering into investment-related agreements with companies that have ties to certain foreign states may be preempted by the CFIUS scheme. For example, Texas recently enacted the Lone Star Infrastructure Protection Act, which restricts the ability to engage in agreements relating to critical Texas infrastructure with companies that have ties to China, Iran, North Korea, or Russia.[333] Arguably such a statute should be preempted if it poses an obstacle to the federal CFIUS process.[334]

D. Other Activities and Instrumentalities Connected to Foreign Commerce

Congress may regulate other activities that, in some fashion, have a connection to foreign commerce. Thus, various statutes regulate or protect instrumentalities by which such commerce takes place, such as laws on sabotage of aircraft engaged in foreign commerce,[335] theft from shipments occurring in foreign commerce,[336] fraud in connection with computers used in foreign commerce,[337] and means or facilities of foreign commerce used to disseminate child pornography.[338] Other statutes address activities that may have adverse consequences for the U.S. economy, such as with respect to antitrust[339] or money laundering.[340]

A statute that has had a significant effect on U.S. business practices is the Foreign Corrupt Practices Act (FCPA), enacted in 1977, which makes it unlawful for certain classes of persons and entities to make payments to foreign government officials to assist in obtaining or retaining business.[341] In 1988, the statute was amended, inter alia, to introduce a "knowing" standard—that is,

---

[332] *See* Daniel C. Schwartz, Jennifer Kies Mammen, & Joshua A. James, *Ralls and CFIUS Reach Settlement Leaving Impact of Future CFIUS Reviews Uncertain*, BRYAN CAVE LEIGHTON PAISNER (Nov. 12, 2015), https://perma.cc/7VPE-MPWP.

[333] Lone Star Infrastructure Protection Act, S.B. 2116, 87th Leg., Reg. Sess. (Tex. 2021).

[334] *See* Kristen E. Eichensehr, *CFIUS Preemption*, 13 HARV. NAT'L SEC. J. 1 (2022).

[335] Aircraft Sabotage Act, 18 U.S.C. § 32 (2018) (prohibiting the destruction of aircraft in interstate or foreign commerce).

[336] 18 U.S.C. § 659.

[337] Computer Fraud and Abuse Act, 18 U.S.C. § 1030(e)(2)(b).

[338] 18 U.S.C. §§ 2252A(a)(1), 2252A(a)(2)(b).

[339] Sherman Antitrust Act, 15 U.S.C. § 1; Foreign Trade Antitrust Improvements Act, 15 U.S.C. § 6a.

[340] 18 U.S.C. § 1956(a)(2) (prohibiting international transportation or transmission, or attempted transportation or transmission, of funds).

[341] 15 U.S.C. §§ 78dd-1–dd-3. *See generally* MARTIN WEINSTEIN, ROBERT MEYER, & JEFFREY CLARK, THE FOREIGN CORRUPT PRACTICES ACT: COMPLIANCE, INVESTIGATIONS AND ENFORCEMENT (2018).

knowing that a thing of value is being provided in exchange for influencing the foreign official—and to provide affirmative defenses for lawful gifts under the foreign state's law and for compensating reasonable expenditures incurred by the foreign official.[342] While the act's anti-bribery provisions originally applied only to U.S. persons and certain foreign issuers of securities, in 1998 they were extended to apply to foreign firms and persons who cause an act in furtherance of a corrupt payment to take place within the territory of the United States.[343] Further, under the FCPA, companies whose securities are listed in the United States are required to meet certain accounting requirements.[344] The FCPA has been a robust area of U.S. practice and litigation, with U.S. courts addressing various aspects of the meaning of the statute.[345] Moreover, the FCPA has significantly influenced the adoption of anti-bribery conventions by the Organisation for Economic Co-operation and Development, the Organization of American States, and the United Nations, which require states parties to those conventions to adopt similar national laws.[346]

E. Presidential Emergency Economic Powers

In 1977, Congress enacted the International Emergency Economic Powers Act (IEEPA),[347] which authorizes the president to regulate commerce after declaring a national emergency, if necessary, for responding to "an unusual and extraordinary threat" to the United States from a foreign source. Among other things, the president may investigate, regulate, or prohibit any transactions in foreign exchange, bank transfers involving any interest of a foreign country or national, or the importing or exporting of currency or securities, by any person or

[342] Omnibus Trade and Competitiveness Act, tit. V, Pub. L. No. 100-418, 102 Stat. 1107, 1415, 1416–18 (1988).

[343] International Anti-Bribery and Fair Competition Act, Pub. L. 105-366, § 4, 112 Stat. 3302 (1998) (codified at 15 U.S.C. 78dd-3).

[344] 15 U.S.C. § 78m.

[345] For example, one interpretive issue has been what constitutes a foreign government or its instrumentality. See United States v. Esquenazi, 752 F.3d 912, 925 (11th Cir. 2014) (interpreting "instrumentality" in the FCPA to mean "an entity controlled by the government of a foreign country that performs a function the controlling government treats as its own"); see also United States v. Hoskins, 902 F.3d 69, 97 (2d Cir. 2018) (holding presumption against extraterritoriality prevents complicity and conspiracy statutes from being applied to a defendant who does not fall under an enumerated category of offenders in the FCPA).

[346] Convention on Combating Bribery of Foreign Public Officials in International Business Transactions, Dec. 17, 1997, S. TREATY DOC. No. 105-43; Inter-American Convention Against Corruption, Mar. 29, 1996, S. TREATY DOC. No. 105-39, 35 I.L.M. 724; United Nations Convention Against Corruption, Dec. 9, 2003, S. TREATY DOC. No. 109-6, 43 I.L.M. 37 (2004); see also Rachel Brewster & Christine Dryden, *Building Multilateral Anticorruption Enforcement: Analogies Between International Trade & Anti-Bribery Law*, 57 VA. J. INT'L L. 221, 237–38 (2018).

[347] International Emergency Economic Powers Act, tit. II, Pub. L. No. 95-223, 91 Stat. 1626 (1977) (codified at 50 U.S.C. § 1701).

with respect to any property subject to the jurisdiction of the United States.[348] Whenever he or she exercises such power, the president must immediately report to Congress on the circumstances necessitating the exercise of such power and periodically must keep Congress informed.[349]

IEEPA was first invoked in 1979 during the Iran hostage crisis to "freeze" accounts and property of Iran's government and its instrumentalities.[350] The constitutionality of the president's action was at issue in *Dames & Moore v. Regan*, as discussed in Chapter 1.[351] Since then, the president has invoked IEEPA (through 2021) on sixty-one occasions as the basis for declaring a national emergency, involving a variety of countries.[352] In some instances, the authority has been invoked against assets of nonstate actors; thus, in the aftermath of 9/11, IEEPA was invoked to block U.S.-held property of "specially designated global terrorists" that commit, threaten to commit, or support terrorism, including al-Qaeda.[353]

While IEEPA has been used to address major international crises and to target terrorists and narcotics traffickers, it has also been used in more unusual circumstances. For example, in 2020 President Trump issued an executive order invoking IEEPA to allow for various types of sanctions on foreign employees of an international tribunal, the International Criminal Court (ICC), who were directly involved in investigating or prosecuting current or former members of the armed forces of the United States or its allies.[354] Moreover, the executive order permitted sanctions against any foreign person who has "materially assisted, sponsored, or provided financial, material, or technological support for, or goods or services to or in support of" any such ICC actions.[355] The action followed on a decision by the ICC Appeals Chamber that authorized the initiation of an ICC investigation of atrocity crimes in Afghanistan.[356] The order was challenged

---

[348] *Id.* § 1702(a).

[349] *Id.* § 1703. For further discussion of IEEPA, see Chapter 10 § II(D)(5).

[350] Exec. Order No. 12,170, 44 Fed. Reg. 65,729 (Nov. 14, 1979).

[351] *See* Chapter 1 § II(B).

[352] *See* CHRISTOPHER A. CASEY ET AL., CONG. RESEARCH SERV., R45618, THE INTERNATIONAL EMERGENCY ECONOMIC POWERS ACT: ORIGINS, EVOLUTION, AND USE (2020); *see, e.g.,* Exec. Order No. 13,936, 3 C.F.R. 399 (2021); Exec. Order No. 13,953, 3 C.F.R. 451 (2021); Exec. Order No. 13,959, 3 C.F.R. 475 (2021); Exec. Order No. 14,014, 86 Fed. Reg. 9,429 (Feb. 12, 2021); Exec. Order No. 14,024, 86 Fed. Reg. 20,249 (Apr. 19, 2021); Exec. Order No. 14,046, 86 Fed. Reg. 52,389 (Sept. 17, 2021); Exec. Order No. 14,059, 86 Fed. Reg. 71,549 (Dec. 17, 2021).

[353] *See* Exec. Order No. 13,224, 50 Fed. Reg. 49,079 (Sept. 23, 2001); *see also* Elena Chachko, *Administrative National Security,* 108 GEO L.J. 1063, 1093–1102 (2020).

[354] Exec. Order No. 13,928, § 1(a)(i)(A)–(B), 3 C.F.R. 372, 373 (2020).

[355] *Id.* § 1(a)(i)(C).

[356] Judgment on the appeal against the decision on the authorization of an investigation into the situation in the Islamic Republic of Afghanistan, ICC-02/17-138 (Mar. 5, 2020). For a critique of the U.S. sanctions, see Adam M. Smith, *Dissecting the Executive Order of Int'l Criminal Court Sanctions: Scope, Effectiveness, and Tradeoffs,* JUST SECURITY (June 15, 2020), https://perma.cc/2AMJ-PZ3P.

by a public interest law organization and law professors regarding their potential designation under IEEPA, as well as on various constitutional grounds. A district court held that their concerns about potential designation under the order were too speculative to confer standing, yet granted a preliminary injunction on grounds that the order violated their right to free speech as a content- and viewpoint-based regulation.[357] The Biden administration dismissed the government's appeal of the preliminary injunction, revoked the executive order, and terminated the national emergency the United States had declared, and later terminated sanctions it had imposed against certain ICC officials.[358]

V. Power to Regulate the Value of Foreign Coin

Congress possesses the power to "coin Money, regulate the Value thereof, and of foreign coin."[359] The "foreign coin" element is not typically analyzed as a stand-alone power but, rather, as an aspect of Congress' general ability to make U.S. money and regulate its value, including in relation to foreign currency.[360] In addition, this clause is frequently read along with other clauses of the Constitution that deny the several states certain powers relating to regulation of tender,[361] which are construed as indicating positive powers of Congress.[362]

For many years, foreign coin played an important role in the monetary affairs of the United States. After declaring independence, the several states proceeded to coin their own money, as would later be authorized under the Articles of Confederation.[363] Meanwhile, the Continental Congress began issuing paper currency in the form of continental dollars, which were based on the value of the Spanish dollar.[364] Such "continentals," however, depreciated rapidly, becoming virtually worthless. Moreover, by the end of the Revolutionary War, there was virtually no gold or silver specie produced by the several states left in circulation

---

[357] Open Soc'y Just. Initiative v. Trump, 510 F. Supp. 3d 198 (S.D.N.Y. 2021).

[358] Kristen E. Eichensehr, *Contemporary Practice of the United States Relating to International Law*, 115 Am. J. Int'l L. 714, 729 (2021); *see* Exec. Order 14,022, 86 Fed. Reg. 17,895 (Apr. 1, 2021).

[359] U.S. Const. art. I, § 8, cl. 5

[360] Farley Grubb, *The US Constitution and Monetary Powers: An Analysis of the 1787 Constitutional Convention and the Constitutional Transformation of the US Monetary System*, 13 Fin. Hist. Rev. 43, 43 (2006); Richard Sylla, *The Transition to a Monetary Union in the United States, 1787–1795*, 13 Fin. Hist. Rev. 73, 73 (2006).

[361] U.S. Const. art. I, § 10, cl. 1 (denying to the several states the power to "coin money; emit Bills of Credit; make any Thing but gold and silver Coin a Tender in Payment of Debts").

[362] Sylla, *supra* note 360, at 73.

[363] *See* Articles of Confederation of 1781, art. IX, ¶ 4.

[364] David A. Martin, *The Changing Role of Foreign Money in the United States, 1782–1857*, 37 J. Econ. Hist. 1009, 1010 (1977). The influence of foreign coin may be seen in the selection of the term "dollar" to describe the new U.S. unit; that term had been in common usage since the colonial period, in reference to the Spanish eight-real coin or Spanish dollar (also referred to as "pieces of eight").

in the United States, having been exported to pay foreign debts.[365] As such, foreign currency became widely used and would remain in circulation in the United States for the next century.

During the Constitutional Convention in 1787, the focus of the delegates on issues relating to monetary policy principally involved the power to issue bills of credit and paper money, the power to determine what will constitute a legal tender, and the power to charter banks.[366] The main controversy was over treatment of state banks, the possibility of a federal bank, and the ability of the federal government to print paper money as opposed to minting specie.[367] Little discussion occurred as to regulating the value of money, including foreign currency in the United States, as it was apparently clear to the delegates that the federal government would have that power.

In 1789, the first Congress under the Constitution accorded legal status in the United States to foreign gold and silver coins.[368] In 1792, Congress established the U.S. dollar as the standard unit of currency and authorized the minting of U.S. coinage but did not do away with the legal status of foreign coins.[369] In due course, foreign coins received in payment to the U.S. government (such as for payment of taxes) were reminted by the federal government into U.S. specie,[370] enabling U.S. specie to increase in circulation while the use of foreign coin decreased.[371] Further, some foreign specie was stored to be used as bullion or sold at a profit back to the original country.[372] By the Coinage Act of 1857, Congress repealed prior laws authorizing the use of foreign coin as legal tender in the United States and instituted a program whereby foreign coins in circulation in the United States could be turned into the Treasury Department and reimbursed in U.S. currency.[373]

In 1832, President Andrew Jackson requested that Congress pass legislation to criminalize the counterfeiting of foreign currencies. That request was based on the secretary of state's view that there was a large market in foreign currencies and that it was embarrassing for the United States to admit, when other countries noted that counterfeit currency had arrived from the United States, that such acts were legal in the United States.[374] In addition, President Jackson pointed to

---

[365] *Id.* at 1010.
[366] Grubb, *supra* note 360, at 43.
[367] *Id.*
[368] Martin, *supra* note 364, at 1010.
[369] Coinage Act of 1792, 1 Stat. 246 (1792); *see* Martin, *supra* note 364, at 1010.
[370] H.R. Rep. No. 56-1512 (1st Sess. 1900).
[371] Martin, *supra* note 364, at 1018.
[372] H.R. Rep. No. 56-1512 (1st Sess. 1900); Martin, *supra* note 364, at 1018.
[373] Coinage Act of 1857, §§ 2–3, 34 Stat. 163 (Feb. 21, 1857); *see* Martin, *supra* note 364, at 1016, 1018.
[374] ANDREW JACKSON & EDWARD LIVINGSTON, COUNTERFEIT FOREIGN COINS, H.R. Doc. No. 214 (Apr. 23, 1832).

the benefits for promoting the protection of U.S. currency abroad, as well as its place among other nations, were the United States to adopt such legislation.[375] Legislation was enacted and thereafter supplemented, such that today the United States has criminalized in the United States the counterfeiting of foreign currency, as well as the possession of materials to counterfeit foreign currencies,[376] and criminalized the counterfeiting or circulating of foreign bank notes[377] and foreign obligations and securities.[378] Such statutes have been upheld by the Supreme Court, although the Court has relied on the Define and Punish the Law of Nations Clause and the Commerce Clause, rather than just the power to regulate foreign coin.[379]

---

[375] *Id.*

[376] 18 U.S.C. §§ 486, 488, 489 (2018).

[377] *Id.* §§ 482, 483.

[378] *Id.* §§ 478, 479.

[379] *See, e.g.,* United States v. Arjona, 120 U.S. 479 (1887) (upholding statutes criminalizing the counterfeiting of foreign currency based on Congress' power to define and punish the law of nations); United States v. Marigold, 50 U.S. 560 (1850) (upholding the validity of counterfeiting statutes generally under the power to regulate commerce and the power to make and regulate money and its value).

3

Conducting Foreign Relations

On a daily basis, the U.S. government is engaged in communications, negotiations, and other forms of interaction with foreign governments and international organizations, expressing the U.S. government's position on a range of legal and policy issues and, in return, receiving and considering the positions of others. Thus, the U.S. government lobbies other states bilaterally in support of its initiatives for addressing matters of peace and security; it attends diplomatic meetings in an effort to persuade foreign nations as to steps for pursuing human rights or cooperation on criminal matters; it files pleadings before foreign and international courts on behalf of the United States with respect to trade or investment matters; and so on. This power to represent the United States in the diplomatic arena might be referred to as the "power to conduct foreign relations," meaning the ability to implement U.S. foreign relations objectives in relations with other states and international organizations.

As noted in Section I, the U.S. Constitution does not expressly indicate in which branch resides this power to conduct foreign relations, but in practice it has been exercised almost exclusively by the executive branch. Article II, of course, vests the "executive power" with the president, and this assigns to the president the role of implementing foreign policy rules that either political branch establishes in the course of exercising its constitutional authorities.[1] Further, the president's powers to make treaties and as commander in chief necessarily involve representing the United States in particular matters with other states or international organizations. Most distinctly, the Constitution accords to the president two express powers that lay a significant foundation for presidential power in this area: first, the power to receive foreign ambassadors and public ministers (also known as the Reception Clause),[2] which is discussed in Section II; and second, the power to appoint U.S. ambassadors, other public ministers, and consuls with the consent of the Senate,[3] which is discussed in Section III. The constitutional prohibition on U.S. officials from accepting any emolument from foreign governments, except with the consent of Congress, is addressed in Section V.

---

[1] U.S. CONST. art. II, § 1.
[2] *Id.*, § 3.
[3] *Id.*, § 2.

While the enumerated powers to "receive" and "appoint" are well known as part of the cluster of constitutional powers that concern U.S. foreign relations, at the time of the founding little attention was given to them as a source of presidential power for conducting U.S. foreign relations. Indeed, key Framers tended to downplay the significance of these powers. Alexander Hamilton referred to them in the *Federalist Papers* as "without consequence in the administration of the government,"[4] and James Madison, during the first term of the Washington administration, described them as little more than "a particular mode of communication."[5]

Even so, from the Washington administration onward, there have been considerable consequences that flow from these powers that merit close attention. By expressly empowering the president alone to receive foreign ambassadors and public ministers, Article II places the president on the front line as the conduit through which the United States, as a nation, officially engages with foreign states, as well as international organizations. Likewise, by expressly empowering the president to choose the persons who represent the United States abroad (subject to consent of the Senate), Article II ensures that such ambassadors and consuls serve under, report to, and are accountable to the president and the president alone. Communications sent through such representatives, to or from the United States, are within the control of the president, whether in the context of U.S. embassies or missions abroad, or in the context of participation in the work of international organizations. While the Senate can reject persons nominated by the president as ambassadors, it cannot make those nominations itself, nor, once appointed, remove ambassadors with whom it disagrees. It is this unique position as the "voice" and "ears" of the nation that compels a widely accepted vision of the president as possessing the power to conduct U.S. foreign relations,[6] a vision that has been repeatedly recognized by the Supreme Court.[7]

This unique position has some further consequences. In conjunction with the president's power to make treaties, such powers accord to the president the ability to engage in negotiations with foreign governments and international organizations toward formal or informal agreements or other outcomes, including alliances with some states, disengagement with others, and pursuit of policies

---

[4] THE FEDERALIST NO. 69, at 420 (Alexander Hamilton); *see infra* this chapter § I(B).

[5] James Madison, Helvidius Number III (Sept. 7, 1793), *in* THE PACIFICUS-HELVIDIUS DEBATES OF 1793–1794: TOWARD THE COMPLETION OF THE AMERICAN FOUNDING 8, 74 (Morton J. Frisch ed., 2007) [hereinafter THE PACIFICUS-HELVIDIUS DEBATES]; *see infra* this chapter § I(C).

[6] This front-line role does not necessarily exclude significant congressional influence on presidential action vis-à-vis foreign governments and international organizations. *See, e.g.,* Jean Galbraith, *The Runaway Presidential Power over Diplomacy*, 108 VA. L. REV. 81 (2022); Kristina Daugirdas, *Congress Underestimated: The Case of the World Bank*, 107 AM. J. INT'L. L. 517, 518–19 (2013); *see also* Chapter 7 § II.

[7] *See, e.g.,* United States v. Louisiana, 363 U.S. 1, 35 (1960) ("The President . . . is the constitutional representative of the United States in its dealings with foreign nations.").

through international organizations.[8] This enables the president to play a critical role in shaping international law on behalf of the United States, not only by negotiating international agreements (to which the United States may or may not adhere) but also by conducting U.S. practice that contributes to the formation of customary international law[9]—and, once international law in the form of international agreements or customary rules is formed, by interpreting that law.[10]

Less obvious consequences also flow from these powers to receive and to appoint, which are discussed in Section IV. Of particular significance, is that the power to "receive" places the president in the front-line position of determining whether a foreign entity, as far as the United States is concerned, constitutes a foreign "state" or "government" of a foreign state, thereby triggering a particular relationship between the United States and that foreign entity regulated by international law. When President George Washington decided in 1793, without consulting Congress, that he would receive Edmond-Charles Genêt as the Ambassador of France, he immediately bestowed upon the revolutionary French government a certain status, one carrying significant political and legal ramifications both internationally and within the United States. Over time, this ability to determine whether a foreign state or foreign government merited "recognition" as such, accorded to the president a unique and powerful role, since determining whether a nation or a government existed was the first and most rudimentary element that made all other aspects of U.S. foreign relations with that entity possible. This "power of recognition," recently confirmed by the Supreme Court in *Zivotofsky v. Kerry*, is viewed as an exclusive power of the president, one that cannot be abridged by Congress.[11]

To be sure, this power may be overclaimed. As noted in Chapter 1, the Supreme Court in *United States v. Curtiss-Wright Export Corp.* characterized the president as the "sole organ of the federal government in the field of international relations,"[12] but that characterization has not withstood the test of time, even in the eyes of the Supreme Court itself. As even a cursory reading of the Constitution suggests, the foreign affairs powers are divided among the political branches, with Congress seemingly being accorded the greater share. Congress can check and has checked the president's power to conduct foreign relations in various ways, and the U.S. federal system also allows for some participation

---

[8] *See* Chapter 6 § II.

[9] *See* Chapter 5 §§ I(B)(2), II(B).

[10] *See* Chapter 5 § II(B)(2); Chapter 6 § III. For an analysis in the context of a single administration, see Jack Goldsmith, *The Contributions of the Obama Administration to the Practice and Theory of International Law*, 57 HARV. INT'L L.J. 455 (2016).

[11] *See infra* this chapter § I(D). For further discussion of *Zivotofsky v. Kerry*, see Chapter 1 §§ I(B), II(A)(2), II(B) and Chapter 2 § II(C).

[12] United States v. Curtiss-Wright Export Corp., 299 U.S. 304, 320 (1936). For detailed discussion of the case, see Chapter 1 §§ I(D), II(A)(2).

by the several states in the conduct of their own foreign relations. Even when Congress remains silent, the president's ability to rely on this power has limits, as was demonstrated in *Medellín v. Texas*.[13]

Still, even if the president is not the sole, or wholly independent, organ in conducting the foreign affairs of the United States, the authority to receive and appoint ambassadors has historically supported the president as the central player for conducting U.S. foreign relations. Hence, understanding the contours of presidential power in this area requires attention to history and associated case law.

I. Power to Conduct Foreign Relations

A. Pre-Constitutional Experience

Prior to the American Revolution, the British government took charge of significant diplomacy relevant to the American colonies, including the conclusion of virtually all treaties (such as those ending the Seven Years' War). Moreover, such powers were lodged with the king, who alone was able to make treaties, make war, and appoint or receive ambassadors or consuls.[14] Of course, in certain circumstances, the colonies were empowered by London to engage in diplomatic affairs, such as authorization by the British Board of Trade for several colonies to meet in Albany in 1754 to pursue and conclude a treaty establishing a defensive alliance with the nations of the Iroquois against the French.[15] Further, less formal contacts on matters of trade and security regularly occurred between colonial representatives and either the Indian tribes or other European powers present on the American continent, spurred on by a period of "benign neglect" by the mother country.[16] Agents representing individual colonies were also present abroad in the colonial period, including Benjamin Franklin as representative of multiple colonies in London just prior to the Revolution.[17] Yet it would not be

---

[13] *See infra* this chapter § I(D). For further discussion of *Medellín*, see Chapter 1 § II(B); Chapter 5 § II(B); Chapter 6 §§ III(B)(3), IV(A); Chapter 7 § III(C); and Chapter 9 §§ II(B), II(C).

[14] Blackstone noted that a king "has the sole power of sending ambassadors to foreign states, and receiving ambassadors at home." 1 WILLIAM BLACKSTONE, COMMENTARIES *253. Further, he indicated that the "rights, the powers, the duties and the privileges of ambassadors are determined by the law of nature and nations, and not by any municipal constitutions." *Id.*

[15] *See* TIMOTHY J. SHANNON, INDIANS AND COLONISTS AT THE CROSSROADS OF EMPIRE: THE ALBANY CONGRESS OF 1754 (2002); *see also* FRED ANDERSON, CRUCIBLE OF WAR: THE SEVEN YEARS' WAR AND THE FATE OF EMPIRE IN BRITISH NORTH AMERICA, 1754–1766, at 77–85 (2000).

[16] JOHN C. MILLER, ORIGINS OF THE AMERICAN REVOLUTION 30 (1943). In various ways, the colonies actually thwarted foreign relations initiatives of Britain, such as by disobeying the British blockade of the French and Spanish West Indies during the French and Indian War. *Id.* at 45.

[17] GORDON S. WOOD, THE AMERICANIZATION OF BENJAMIN FRANKLIN 105–51 (2004).

until the American Revolution that the colonies proved capable of embarking on common diplomatic action independent of direction from London.

After the Declaration of Independence, but before entry into force of the Articles of Confederation, the Continental Congress engaged persons formally and informally as its agents in dealing with foreign powers, initially through its Committee of Secret Correspondence and later a Committee of Foreign Affairs.[18] Hence, it retained Arthur Lee (who, in 1775, was acting as a colonial agent in London) to provide reports on "the disposition of foreign powers toward us."[19] In December 1776, Benjamin Franklin and Silas Deane, along with Lee, were appointed joint commissioners in Paris to liaise with the French government, to seek French recognition, and otherwise to gather intelligence.[20] Their efforts paid off in France's effective recognition of and defensive alliance with the United States through a 1778 treaty of amity.[21] Charles William Frederick Dumas, in a private capacity, as well as the commissioners in Paris, served a similar function for Congress with respect to the Netherlands.[22] Various other diplomatic and commercial agents were retained, including at least one—Edward Bancroft—who appears to have served as a double agent in representations with the British.[23]

Under the Articles of Confederation, which were adopted by the Second Continental Congress in November 1777 but only entered into force in 1781, there existed no executive authority. Rather, political authority rested with Congress, which, among other things, was expressly granted the powers to send and receive "ambassadors."[24] By contrast, the several states were expressly denied the power to send or receive any "embassy," except upon consent of the Congress.[25] Congress' ability to conduct foreign relations, however, was hampered by an inability to delegate: more particularly, it could not delegate to its committees any matter requiring approval by a supermajority of nine states, such as the entry into treaties and alliances.[26] Even so, a "Department of Foreign Affairs" was established, with Robert Livingston as its first secretary. Thereafter,

---

[18] *See* EDMUND CODY BURNETT, THE CONTINENTAL CONGRESS 118 (1941); H. JAMES HENDERSON, PARTY POLITICS IN THE CONTINENTAL CONGRESS 270 (1974); RICHARD B. MORRIS, THE FORGING OF THE UNION 1781–1789, at 95 (1987).

[19] HENRY MERRITT WRISTON, EXECUTIVE AGENTS IN AMERICAN FOREIGN RELATIONS 4 (1929) (quoting the Committee of Secret Correspondence, Dec. 12, 1775).

[20] *Id.* at 4–5; *see also* THOMAS A. BAILEY, A DIPLOMATIC HISTORY OF THE AMERICAN PEOPLE 27 (10th ed. 1980); SAMUEL FLAGG BEMIS, THE DIPLOMACY OF THE AMERICAN REVOLUTION 25–28 (1957) (1935).

[21] Treaty of Amity and Commerce, Fr.-U.S., Feb. 6, 1778, 8 Stat. 12.

[22] WRISTON, *supra* note 19, at 5–6. *See generally* FRIEDRICH EDLER, THE DUTCH REPUBLIC AND THE AMERICAN REVOLUTION (1911).

[23] WRISTON, *supra* note 19, at 8–10.

[24] ARTICLES OF CONFEDERATION OF 1781, art. IX, ¶ 1.

[25] *Id.* art. VI, ¶ 1.

[26] *Id.* art. IX, ¶ 6.

treaties were concluded by agents of Congress with the Netherlands, Sweden, and—after Yorktown—Great Britain that effectively recognized the United States.[27] Though the secretary was responsible for communications with the ministers of foreign powers, Livingston felt shackled to making only those communications that directly reflected public acts taken by Congress and disabled from frank exchanges on even trivial matters not expressly addressed by Congress.[28]

The secretary's role grew well beyond clerical matters after John Jay's assumption of the position in 1784. Among other things, Jay pursued an important treaty that would have recognized exclusive Spanish navigational rights on the Mississippi River for decades (the Jay-Gardoqui Treaty).[29] Notwithstanding Jay's considerable influence in Congress, however, that treaty failed to secure Congress' approval, and Jay as secretary remained squarely under the control of Congress, invariably forwarding to Congress correspondence received from persons abroad, such as the Marquis de La Fayette.[30] As such, the Confederation Congress gave little real authority to its secretary to act as an independent agent, nor to the other agencies or committees that it formed.[31]

B. Constitutional Design

Because Article II of the Constitution vests the "executive power" in the president, it has been argued this endows the president with the entirety of the executive power, including exclusive control over the conduct of U.S. foreign relations[32]—save as may be dictated by other constitutional provisions, like those expressly establishing a congressional role (including, for example, the Senate's right to consent to the making of treaties or Congress' right to declare war).[33]

---

[27] Definitive Treaty of Peace, Gr. Brit.-U.S., Sept. 3, 1783, 8 Stat. 80; Treaty of Amity and Commerce with Sweden, Swed.-U.S., Apr. 3, 1783, 8 Stat. 60; Treaty of Amity and Commerce, Neth.-U.S., Oct. 8, 1782, 8 Stat. 32. For an account of "recognition" in this period and its implications for understanding contemporary constitutional powers, see Robert Reinstein, *Recognition: A Case Study on the Original Understanding of Executive Power*, 45 U. RICH. L. REV. 801 (2011). *See also* Chapter 6 § I(A)(2) (discussing the Mississippi River negotiations).

[28] WRISTON, *supra* note 19, at 18–20.

[29] BAILEY, *supra* note 20, at 62.

[30] WRISTON, *supra* note 19, at 21–23.

[31] *See* 1 BRADFORD PERKINS, THE CREATION OF A REPUBLICAN EMPIRE, 1776–1865, at 54–55 (1993); JACK N. RAKOVE, THE BEGINNINGS OF NATIONAL POLITICS: AN INTERPRETIVE HISTORY OF THE CONTINENTAL CONGRESS 196 (1979).

[32] U.S. CONST. art. II, § 1; *see* Saikrishna B. Prakash & Michael D. Ramsey, *The Executive Power over Foreign Affairs*, 111 YALE L.J. 231, 256–57 (2001). *See generally* STEVEN G. CALABRESI & CHRISTOPHER S. YOO, THE UNITARY EXECUTIVE: PRESIDENTIAL POWER FROM WASHINGTON TO BUSH (2008); MICHAEL D. RAMSEY, THE CONSTITUTION'S TEXT IN FOREIGN AFFAIRS (2007); Steven G. Calabresi & Saikrishna B. Prakash, *The President's Power to Execute the Laws*, 104 YALE L.J. 541 (1994).

[33] U.S. CONST. art. II, § 2; *id.* art. I, § 8.

On this account, the president's power to conduct foreign relations need not depend on any more specific enumerated powers, such as the powers to appoint and receive ambassadors. One puzzle for that argument, however, is the development of those enumerated powers, and their separation from the "executive power," as the Constitution was being formulated.[34]

The principal proposals placed before the Constitutional Convention in May and June of 1787 did not expressly allocate to the president the power to appoint and receive ambassadors. The May 29 Pinckney Plan provided that "[t]he Executive Power of the United States shall be vested in a President,"[35] but apparently did not regard such authority as encompassing the appointment of ambassadors. Indeed, the president was not empowered under the Pinckney Plan to appoint *any* key officers, including his own Secretaries of State or War; rather, the "Senate and House of Delegates in Congress assembled" were to "institute offices and appoint officers for the Departments of foreign Affairs, War, Treasury and Admiralty."[36]

The Virginia Plan, introduced on the same day, also did not directly address the issue; it simply stated that the "National Legislature ought to be impowered to enjoy the Legislative Rights vested in Congress by the Confederation," while a National Executive—elected by the National Legislature—enjoyed "a general authority to execute the National laws" and "the Executive rights vested in Congress by the Confederation."[37] Conceivably that vesting of the "executive power" in the president signaled that the power to appoint and receive ambassadors was being given to the president, but there are reasons to doubt such an interpretation, including because some Virginia delegates apparently viewed the important foreign affairs powers as "legislative" in nature.[38]

The June 15 New Jersey plan stated that there should be created a federal executive, who shall have "general authority to execute the federal acts [and] ought to appoint all federal officers not otherwise provided for . . . ."[39] Yet the plan

---

[34] See Arthur Bestor, *Respective Roles of Senate and President in the Making and Abrogation of Treaties—The Original Intent of the Framers of the Constitution Historically Examined*, 55 WASH. L. REV. 1, 87 (1979). For broader objections to "executive power" claims, see, for example, Curtis A. Bradley & Martin S. Flaherty, *Executive Power Essentialism and Foreign Affairs*, 102 MICH. L. REV. 545 (2004); A. Michael Froomkin, *The Imperial Presidency's New Vestments*, 88 NW. L. REV. 1346 (1994); Henry P. Monaghan, *The Protective Power of the Presidency*, 93 COLUM. L. REV. 1 (1993); Julian Davis Mortenson, *Article II Vests the Executive Power, Not the Royal Prerogative*, 119 COLUM. L. REV. 1169 (2019); Robert J. Reinstein, *The Limits of Executive Power*, 59 AM. U. L. REV. 259 (2009); for discussion in relation to foreign relations balancing, see Chapter 1 § I(B).

[35] 3 FARRAND'S RECORDS, at app. D, art. 8; *see also* ABRAHAM D. SOFAER, WAR, FOREIGN AFFAIRS AND CONSTITUTIONAL POWER: THE ORIGINS 26 (1976).

[36] 3 FARRAND'S RECORDS, at app. D, art. X.

[37] 1 FARRAND'S RECORDS, at 21.

[38] Virginian George Mason, with respect to appointments matters, called for "the concurrence of the Senate to be required only in the appointment of Ambassadors, and in making treaties, which are more of a legislative nature." 2 FARRAND'S RECORDS, at 537.

[39] 1 FARRAND'S RECORDS, at 244.

stated that "in addition to the powers vested in the United States in Congress, by the present existing articles of Confederation," certain other powers should also be vested in Congress, apparently leaving the power to appoint and receive ambassadors with Congress as it had been under the Articles of Confederation.[40]

Only with Alexander Hamilton's speech of June 18, which advocated generally for strong executive powers, was the idea expressly introduced of the president having significant powers with respect to appointments, specifically the powers of "sole appointment of the heads or chief officers of the departments of Finance, War and Foreign Affairs [and] the nomination of all other officers (Ambassadors to foreign Nations included) subject to the approbation or rejection of the Senate . . . ."[41] Still, the August 6 draft by the Committee of Detail provided that, notwithstanding the creation of an executive vested with the executive power, the power of appointing ambassadors was to be accorded to Congress, which was vested with the legislative power. While the "Executive Power of the United States shall be vested in a single person,"[42] the draft constitution stated that the "Senate of the United States shall have power to make treaties, and to appoint Ambassadors, and Judges of the Supreme Court."[43] At the same time, the draft provided that the president "shall receive Ambassadors, and may correspond with the supreme Executives of the several States."[44]

Hence, as of early August 1787, the prevalent view was that the principal foreign affairs powers of treaty-making and appointment of ambassadors should reside with Congress, including the power to send ambassadors, with only the power of receiving ambassadors being assigned to the executive. In early September, language emerged from the Committee of Eleven by which the president would appoint ambassadors (as well as make treaties) with the "advice and consent" of at least two-thirds of the Senate.[45] This change in the location of the power evoked no recorded debate, which is perhaps surprising given that the power had been exercised solely by Congress under the Articles of Confederation and had been envisaged as a congressional power by virtually everyone at the convention up until this point.[46] One structural explanation might be that, since the opening of relations with a foreign government (such as with France in 1778) occurred by

---

[40] *Id.* at 243.
[41] *Id.* at 292. Only in late August did Gouverneur Morris make the first formal proposal along these lines for an executive "council of state," which also made little headway. *See* 2 FARRAND'S RECORDS, at 336, 342–43.
[42] James Madison, *August 6 Draft*, art. X [IX] § 1, *in* 2 FARRAND'S RECORDS, at 185.
[43] *Id.*, art. IX [VIII], § 1, at 183.
[44] *Id.*, art. X [IX], § 2, at 185.
[45] *Id.* at 495, 498–99. Certain Framers, such as Pinckney, continued to oppose placing this power with the president. *See id.* at 538 (Sept. 7).
[46] *See* SOFAER, *supra* note 35, at 36 (noting that the new proposal on the power to appoint important officers, including ambassadors, "marked a sharp break with all prior positions advanced except Hamilton's").

means of a treaty, which then entailed an exchange of ambassadors, ministers or consuls, it was thought best to keep those powers together, lodged with the president but with a role for the Senate.

In any event, in its final form, the powers to appoint and receive were located in Article II, Sections 2 and 3, of the Constitution. Section 2 provides: "The President . . . by and with the Advice and Consent of the Senate, shall appoint Ambassadors, other public Ministers and Consuls . . . ." Section 3 provides that the president "shall receive Ambassadors and other public Ministers . . . ."[47]

Neither power was the subject of sustained attention during the ratification debates; they featured mostly as aspects of the broader foreign affairs powers allocated to the federal government and divided between the Congress and the president.[48] As previously noted, Hamilton, in *Federalist No. 69*, sought to downplay the significance of the powers to appoint and receive ambassadors, characterizing them as largely ministerial functions, ones that were far less significant than had been accorded to the British king. Of the power to receive, he saw it as "more a matter of dignity than of authority" and "a circumstance which will be without consequence in the administration of the government"; indeed, "it was far more convenient that it should be arranged in this manner, than that there should be a necessity of convening the legislature, or one of its branches, upon every arrival of a foreign minister, though it were merely to take the place of a departed predecessor."[49] Anti-Federalists, for their part, saw the powers as among a range accorded to the president and denied to the states, which in combination threatened a return to royal prerogatives.[50] The Anti-Federalists, of course, lost the debate, and the U.S. Constitution was ratified with the lingering gloss placed upon the powers to appoint and receive ambassadors by the *Federalist Papers*.

One explanation that has been tendered for why the location of the appoint-and-receive powers garnered little attention, and why Hamilton characterized it as "more a matter of dignity than of authority," is that the Framers and state ratifying conventions regarded countries as obliged to act with some level of automaticity in such matters and that no significant public policy decisions arise when ambassadors are appointed or received.[51] On this view the law of nations, as taught by scholars well known to the Framers (like Hugo Grotius and Emer

---

[47] U.S. CONST. art. II, §§ 2, 3. On Congress' powers generally relating to appointment (and removal) of executive and judicial officials, see JOSH CHAFETZ, CONGRESS's CONSTITUTION: LEGISLATIVE AUTHORITY AND THE SEPARATION OF POWERS 78–151 (2017).

[48] For a survey of references to the "receive ambassadors" clause during the ratification debates, see Reinstein, *supra* note 27, at 845–51.

[49] THE FEDERALIST No. 69, at 420–21 (Alexander Hamilton).

[50] *See, e.g.*, Luther Martin, Genuine Information IX, MD. GAZETTE (BALT.), Jan. 29, 1788, reprinted in 15 THE DOCUMENTARY HISTORY OF THE RATIFICATION OF THE CONSTITUTION 494, 496 (John P. Kaminski et al. eds., 2009).

[51] *See* David Gray Adler, *The President's Recognition Power, in* THE CONSTITUTION AND THE CONDUCT OF AMERICAN FOREIGN POLICY 133 (David Gray Adler & Larry N. George eds., 1996).

de Vattel), had by the mid-1700s adopted a theory of recognition according to which was expected that whenever a usurper successfully wrested power within a state, other states were expected automatically to recognize that government and to exchange ambassadors with it. As such, locating the appoint-and-receive powers with the president was of no particular consequence, since the decision to "recognize" a new foreign government or foreign state was triggered by factual circumstances outside the president's control and entailed no independent policy decision. The post-ratification emergence of a significant "recognition" power vested in the president, then, would be an unexpected expansion of what was supposed to be a ministerial function.

This explanation falls short for two reasons. First, Grotius and Vattel cannot be regarded as endorsing, in such a pure form, a theory of automatic recognition.[52] The thrust of Grotius's theory was not to advocate a requirement that other states recognize automatically a usurper who seizes control of the state; the idea that other states would so legitimate a new government simply was not a feature of his times and would only emerge in the centuries that followed.[53] Vattel (writing in 1758) considered whether foreign nations should recognize a usurper regime, including by addressing whether foreign nations should receive or send ambassadors to such a regime, but his approach also does not appear to call for automatic recognition.[54] Second, this reading of Grotius and Vattel is not consistent with the actual practice of states at the time, including France's recognition of the United States during the Revolutionary War. There was no sense from the international discourse at the time that France was compelled automatically to recognize the United States upon its declaration of independence and seizure of territorial control, nor that France was precluded from recognizing the United States until such time as Britain no longer wielded authority over important areas of the colonies.[55]

[52] See JULIUS GOEBEL, THE RECOGNITION POLICY OF THE UNITED STATES 37 (1915).
[53] See HUGO GROTIUS, THE LAW OF WAR AND PEACE: DE JURE BELLI AC PACIS LIBRI TRES 103, 138–59 (Francis W. Kelsey trans., 1925) (1625) (advancing a theory of sovereignty whereby the people cannot "restrain and punish kings whenever they make a bad use of their power").
[54] Vattel emphasized that recognition was desirable in situations where an usurper had actual control of the state, but there is no express call for recognition of a revolutionary regime and no state practice existed at that time in support of such a notion upon which Vattel could rely. See GOEBEL, supra note 52, at 42. The lack of concern with international legitimation of the usurper is present as well in the work of Samuel von Pufendorf, writing in the 1670s. See id. at 40.
[55] As previously noted, France entered into a commercial treaty and treaty of alliance with the United States in February 1778, which in essence constituted recognition of the fledgling republic, followed in March by formal French communication of that recognition to the British Government and the reception of Deane, Franklin, and Lee by Louis XVI. Nothing in France's statements of the time, or the British reaction, indicate a belief that such recognition was an automatic result driven by congressional control over colonial territory; indeed, it occurred at a time when, despite the rebels' recent victory at Saratoga, Washington's army was generally weak and on the run and British troops were actually occupying key U.S. cities, including New York and Philadelphia, forcing the Congress to flee the latter. Rather, French Foreign Minister Comte de Vergennes acted out of a political desire to weaken Britain, shifting the balance of power in Europe in France's favor, not out of a sense that he

The more plausible explanation for why the Framers shifted the power to appoint and receive ambassadors to the president was not because the power was seen as merely ministerial; rather, the power might prove important, but it would in any event be exercised *concurrently* by the president and Senate. What can be gleaned from the debates at the convention, as well as in the process of ratification, is that the president was viewed by many as an agent of the Senate (or the Congress) on key matters of foreign policy, including the decision to appoint ambassadors.[56] While in hindsight it is clear that the Senate's role in consenting to the appointment of ambassadors (or, for example, the Congress as a whole in declaring war) is a less substantial check on the foreign affairs power that now has aggregated to the president, it seems likely that at the time few envisaged the direction this power would take in the centuries to come.

C. Early Practice Under the Constitution

Whatever the intention behind the constitutional design, at an early stage in the new American republic, a power to conduct foreign relations emerged and became centered on the president. Indeed, the general contours and implications of the power to appoint and receive ambassadors became apparent in the first term of President Washington's administration.[57] Following in the footsteps of the American Revolution, revolution broke out in France in 1789, leading to the fall of the French monarchy and a decade of political and social upheaval. A new French constitution in 1791 sought to establish a constitutional monarchy, while another in 1793 constituted France's first republican government, though both were short-lived features of a period of extreme turmoil. The reactions of President Washington to these developments served to illuminate several facets of the power to appoint and receive ambassadors.[58]

---

had no choice but to recognize the new republic due to the law of nations. *See* JONATHAN R. DULL, A DIPLOMATIC HISTORY OF THE AMERICAN REVOLUTION 107–09 (1985); RICHARD B. MORRIS, THE PEACEMAKERS: THE GREAT POWERS AND AMERICAN INDEPENDENCE 13–17 (1965); WILLIAM C. STINCHCOMBE, THE AMERICAN REVOLUTION AND THE FRENCH ALLIANCE 11–13 (1969); RICHARD W. VAN ALSTYNE, EMPIRE AND INDEPENDENCE: THE INTERNATIONAL HISTORY OF THE AMERICAN REVOLUTION 135–39 (1965).

[56] *See* Chapter 1 § II(B).
[57] As noted elsewhere, however, there are reasons not to weigh such practice too heavily, given the unique status of President Washington and the unique dangers for the country during his administration. *See* Chapter 1 § I(B) and Chapter 5 § II(B)(1).
[58] *See generally* ALEXANDER DECONDE, ENTANGLING ALLIANCE: POLITICS & DIPLOMACY UNDER GEORGE WASHINGTON 177–80 (1958); STANLEY ELKINS & ERIC MCKITRICK, THE AGE OF FEDERALISM: THE EARLY AMERICAN REPUBLIC, 1788–1800, at 303–73 (1993); GORDON S. WOOD, EMPIRE OF LIBERTY: A HISTORY OF THE EARLY REPUBLIC, 1789–1815, at 174–208 (2009).

One facet concerned how the United States should respond when faced with the outbreak of war among other states. On April 20, 1792, France declared war on Austria, leading to war with both Austria and Prussia. When Louis XVI was executed on January 21, 1793, it resulted in a uniting against France of all monarchies in Europe, including Spain, the Netherlands, and Great Britain, in what is sometimes referred to as the "First Coalition." The outbreak of war between Britain and France posed considerable danger for the nascent American Republic and led to President Washington's Proclamation of Neutrality of April 22, 1793, which announced the intention of the United States to "pursue a conduct friendly and impartial towards the belligerent powers" and to prosecute persons in the United States who supplied contraband of war to such powers.[59] A key effect of the proclamation was to annul or repudiate the 1778 France-U.S. treaty of alliance,[60] which would have obliged the United States to assist France against Britain.

By issuing the proclamation on his own authority, Washington provoked a debate over whether the president was encroaching upon the powers of the Senate (by annulling part of a treaty) and of the Congress generally (by potentially embroiling the nation in war with France). In his seven *Pacificus* essays in support of the Proclamation, Hamilton advanced his robust views on executive power in part through reference to the power to appoint and receive ambassadors.[61] For Hamilton, the overall imperative was for the president to carry out the foreign relations of the United States, including those policies previously consented to by Congress. To implement U.S. treaties of peace and to avoid war absent a congressional declaration, the president must be able to issue such proclamations of neutrality; so too, when a foreign government falls from power, the president must be able to clarify the status of treaty relationships with the foreign state.[62]

Of course, Hamilton's "outlines of a vigorous and competent" executive[63] did not go unanswered. Madison as *Helvidius* dismissed *Pacificus'* idea that the Constitution's clause granting the president the power to appoint and receive ambassadors implied a broad grant of authority, particularly if it intruded upon Congress' power to decide between war and peace. Noting among other things the way the power to appoint and receive ambassadors was downplayed

---

[59] Proclamation of Neutrality (Apr. 22, 1793), *in* 12 THE WRITINGS OF GEORGE WASHINGTON 281–82 (Worthington Chauncey Ford ed., 1891). For Washington's request for advice from his Cabinet, see Questions Submitted by the President (Apr. 18, 1793), *in id.* at 280. *See generally* CHARLES MARION THOMAS, AMERICAN NEUTRALITY IN 1793: A STUDY IN CABINET GOVERNMENT (2d ed. 1967).

[60] Treaty of Alliance Fr.-U.S., art. 11, Feb. 6, 1778, 8 Stat. 6, 10.

[61] The broader thrust of the essays emphasized the vesting of the executive power in the president, which the subsequent specific grants of power in Article II serve to illustrate, and that the direction of foreign policy is inherently an executive function.

[62] Alexander Hamilton, Pacificus Number 1 (June 29, 1793), *in* THE PACIFICUS-HELVIDIUS DEBATES *supra* note 5, at 14–15 (emphasis in original).

[63] ANDREW C. MCLAUGHLIN, A CONSTITUTIONAL HISTORY OF THE UNITED STATES 255 (1935).

by Hamilton in *Federalist No. 69*, Madison claimed that little more was intended by the clause than to point "out the department of the government, most proper for the ceremony of admitting public Ministers, of examining their credentials, and of authenticating their title to the privileges annexed to their character by the law of nations."[64]

Both sides' views were driven, no doubt, by the broader political climate (and the emergence of a two-party system), and neither side decisively won the debate. In support of Madison's general position, Congress entered the field in 1794 by adopting a neutrality statute, which (along with its successors) has since applied to situations of U.S. neutrality.[65] Yet the Hamiltonian position in favor of inherent presidential authority presented a compelling and popular vision for the situation at hand, given that war for the United States with any of the European powers at that time would have been perilous.[66] The British and Spanish presence posed threats from the north and south of the new republic; Britain harassed U.S. commerce on the high seas; frontier settlements, particularly in the northwest, remained under almost constant conflict with Indian tribes; and internal dissension would soon flower in the Whiskey Rebellion.[67] Hamilton's emphasis on an expansive reach of executive power in the field of foreign affairs, one largely independent of Congress and in part predicated on the power to appoint and receive ambassadors, was not without its appeal.

A second relevant facet of the U.S. reaction to the French Revolution concerned the Washington administration's decision to engage in diplomatic relations with the new French government. By 1792, the French monarchy had clearly been usurped, replaced by a political faction within the French Legislative Assembly and the National Convention known as the Girondists. The United States was thus confronted with whether it should officially "recognize" the new government, a decision that held important policy ramifications for the United States in its relations with France and with the monarchies of the rest of Europe.[68] A refusal to do so would indicate rejection or disapproval of the new regime in France and a potential betrayal of the democratic ideals for which the American Revolution had been fought; yet opening relations could indicate endorsement of the excesses of the French revolutionary regime, as well as antagonize European powers with whom the United States could not afford war.

---

[64] James Madison, Helvidius Number III (Sept. 7, 1793), *in* THE PACIFICUS-HELVIDIUS DEBATES, *supra* note 5, at 74, 75–76.

[65] *See* 18 U.S.C. §§ 959–61 (2018).

[66] *See* WOOD, *supra* note 58, at 188 (noting Jefferson's advice to Madison that, given public opinion, the Republicans "had to stop caviling about who was to constitutionally" declare neutrality).

[67] *See* McLAUGHLIN, *supra* note 63, at 257.

[68] Concern with such revolts ultimately led European monarchies, at the Congress of Vienna convened in 1814–15 after the Napoleonic wars, to agree that they would not recognize a government that came to power through rebellion. *See* TIM CHAPMAN, THE CONGRESS OF VIENNA 1814–1815, at 16–19 (1998).

The decision was taken, through the exercise of presidential authority incidental to the power to appoint and receive ambassadors, by opening official contacts in both Paris and Philadelphia, then the capital of the United States. There was a choice to be made; although Louis XVI was executed, he had a living male heir. Further, that choice could plausibly have entailed some level of congressional involvement. Indeed, if Madison was correct in *Helvidius* that the power to appoint and receive contained no "important prerogative,"[69] then the opening of relations with republican France should have been viewed as a significant policy decision for Congress to consider, with the president entrusted only with execution of any result. Instead, President Washington proceeded without formally consulting Congress at all. In doing so, the United States in effect recognized the revolutionary French government, presenting the first opportunity for the executive to articulate its theory of recognition. Secretary of State Thomas Jefferson famously instructed the U.S. minister to France, Gouverneur Morris, to open relations with the new government based on what became a touchstone for U.S. recognition policy for at least a century: "It accords with our principles to acknowledge any Government to be rightful which is formed by the will of the nation, substantially declared."[70]

The Girondists wound up appointing Edmond-Charles Genêt to serve as Ambassador of France to the United States. In April 1793, Genêt arrived in the United States at Charleston, where he proceeded to recruit and arm American privateers to join French expeditions against the British.[71] Genêt's conduct threatened U.S. neutrality and his appeal for creation of democratic-republic "societies" in the United States arguably threatened to create instability within the United States of the kind then unfolding in France.[72] Consequently, there was evident policy significance to the decision about whether to receive "citizen" Genêt as the ambassador from France when he arrived in Philadelphia; yet President Washington did so, again without officially consulting Congress.[73]

A third relevant facet of the U.S. reaction to the French Revolution involved the broader question of who speaks for the United States in the realm of foreign affairs. When Ambassador Genêt requested, on behalf of a French consul, an exequatur (a document which guarantees the consul's rights and privileges of the office), Secretary of State Thomas Jefferson noted that the commission for the

---

[69] James Madison, Helvidius Number III (Sept. 7, 1793), *in* THE PACIFICUS-HELVIDIUS DEBATES, *supra* note 5, at 75.

[70] Letter from Thomas Jefferson, Sec'y of State, to Gouverneur Morris, Am. Minister at Paris (Nov. 7, 1792), *in* 1 MOORE DIGEST, at 120; *see* Letter from Thomas Jefferson, Sec'y of State, to Gouverneur Morris, Am. Minister at Paris (March 12, 1793), *in id.*, at 120.

[71] *See generally* HARRY AMMON, THE GENET MISSION (1973).

[72] *See generally* EUGENE PERRY LINK, DEMOCRATIC-REPUBLICAN SOCIETIES, 1790–1800 (1942).

[73] Harry Ammon, *The Genet Mission and the Development of American Political Parties*, 52 J. AM. HIST. 725, 727–28 (1966).

consul issued by the French government was addressed to "the Congress of the United States," a holdover practice from the time of the Articles of Confederation. In rejecting the request, Jefferson referred to the president as "the only channel of communication between this country and foreign nations," such that "it is from him alone that foreign nations or their agents are to learn what is or has been the will of the nation; and whatever he communicates as such, they have a right and are bound to consider as the expression of the nation . . . ."[74]

Jefferson's conception of the executive branch as the voice of the United States was accepted by Congress even in the 1790s. By the end of the decade, Congress had adopted the Logan Act, forbidding unauthorized citizens from negotiating with foreign governments.[75] A year later came John Marshall's famous speech in Congress declaring the executive to be the "sole organ of the nation in its external relations, and its sole representative with foreign nations"[76]—a statement made in the context of a debate over whether, under Article 27 of the Jay Treaty,[77] President John Adams should extradite (to the United Kingdom) a murder suspect whose case was pending in U.S. court. While Marshall's speech is best understood as an argument that the president is authorized to execute U.S. foreign affairs power as duly authorized by the political branches, it is also a clear indication that it is the president who serves as the "mouthpiece" for the United States in the conduct of U.S. external relations, a view maintained by the president and Congress throughout the next century and beyond.[78]

A final facet of the U.S. reaction to the French Revolution relates to the possibility of declaring foreign ambassadors as *persona non grata*.[79] The power to appoint and receive is silent as to how an ambassador, once received, should be treated in terms of the length of their service. Is the president empowered unilaterally to terminate the tenure of the ambassador? Or

---

[74] To the French Minister (Edmond Charles Genêt), Nov. 22, 1793, *in* VIII THE WRITINGS OF THOMAS JEFFERSON 73 (Paul Leicester Ford ed., 1898). As late as 1833, communications from foreign states were still being received addressed to both the president and Congress, prompting President Jackson's Secretary of State, Edward Livingston, to send letters to various countries with instructions that communications only be addressed to the president. *See* QUINCY WRIGHT, THE CONTROL OF AMERICAN FOREIGN RELATIONS 28–29 (1922).

[75] Act of Jan. 30, 1799, ch. I, 1 Stat. 613 (codified at 18 U.S.C. § 953 (2018)). George Logan was a Pennsylvania state legislator (and later U.S. senator) who in 1798 had undertaken negotiations with the French government, hoping to avert war between the United States and France. For an account of the event and subsequent developments on this issue, see Kevin M. Kearney, *Private Citizens in Foreign Affairs: A Constitutional Analysis*, 36 EMORY L.J. 285 (1987).

[76] 10 ANNALS OF CONG. 613 (1800).

[77] Treaty of Amity, Commerce and Navigation, Gr. Brit.–U.S., Nov. 19, 1794, 8 Stat. 116, 129.

[78] *See, e.g.*, 54 CONG. REC. 663 (1897); for a fuller discussion, see Chapter 1 § I(B).

[79] When a foreign diplomat or consular official is no longer welcome in the host country, the person is declared *persona non grata* (literally "person not appreciated") and asked to leave. *See infra* this chapter § II(C). While such persons often enjoy immunity from the exercise of national jurisdiction (criminal or civil), *see* Chapter 4 § V, and therefore cannot be arrested, they can be expelled on short notice.

does such an act inherently trigger foreign policy repercussions that should be debated and consented to by the Senate? Given that the Senate plays no role in the initial decision to receive the ambassador, there seems to be little textual basis for arguing that the Senate plays a role in any subsequent treatment, but there remains potential force to Madison's concern that conduct of this nature risks war and hence intrudes upon a congressional power. In any event, having received Genêt, Washington and Jefferson urged him to refrain from efforts to arm privateers to capture British ships; when that failed, Washington demanded, without formally consulting Congress, that France recall Genêt. Ultimately, when the Jacobin faction seized power in France in early 1794, Genêt was recalled.[80] This appeared to set a precedent that the president could declare foreign ambassadors (and other diplomats) *persona non grata* without consulting with, let alone receiving authorization from, Congress.

The potential importance of *not* receiving an ambassador was amply demonstrated fifteen years later after Napoleon invaded Spain in his "Peninsula War."[81] Napoleon's usurpation in 1808 of the Spanish monarch, Charles IV, in favor of Napoleon's brother, provoked a popular uprising that eventually spread throughout Spain. The city of Cádiz served as the seat of the liberal *Cortes* (parliament) that favored restoration of the Spanish monarchy under a new constitution. For years war raged in Spain, without any definitive governmental regime. In 1809, the junta in Cádiz appointed Luis de Onís to serve as envoy to the United States.[82] President Madison, however, refused to receive him, stating that the crown of Spain was disputed and that the United States would not recognize either side of the belligerency. Ultimately, in 1813, Napoleon agreed to the restoration of Charles IV's son to the throne, though Ferdinand VII initially struggled to control internal democratic elements that threatened his rule. Only in December 1815, after events had settled, did President Madison decide to receive Onís, thereby recognizing the government of Ferdinand VII.[83]

---

[80] Sensing that he would likely be executed upon his return, Genêt asked and received asylum from President Washington and thereafter lived peacefully in the United States until his death in 1834. Eugene R. Sheridan, *The Recall of Edmond Charles Genet: A Study in Transatlantic Politics and Diplomacy*, 18 DIPLOMATIC HIST. 463, 486 (1994).

[81] For background, see CHARLES ESDAILE, THE PENINSULAR WAR: A NEW HISTORY (2002); DAVID GATES, THE SPANISH ULCER: A HISTORY OF THE PENINSULAR WAR (1986); CHARLES OMAN, HISTORY OF THE PENINSULAR WAR (1902–30) (seven volumes).

[82] Onís is now principally remembered in the United States for negotiating the Adams-Onís Treaty in 1819 (as Spanish foreign minister with U.S. Secretary of State John Quincy Adams), by which Florida was granted to the United States and the U.S.-Spanish border in the West was settled.

[83] *See* CHARLES C. GRIFFIN, THE UNITED STATES AND THE DISRUPTION OF THE SPANISH EMPIRE, 1810–1822, at 69–73 (1937).

D. Solidification of the President's Power to Conduct
Foreign Relations

Following the adoption of the Constitution and its immediate aftermath, the power to appoint and receive ambassadors was invoked frequently in support of the broader power of the president to conduct U.S. foreign relations vis-à-vis other nations and, more recently, international organizations. As the nation grew in size and importance over the nineteenth century, U.S. legations and then embassies spread globally, as did foreign representations in Washington, D.C. Diplomacy and intelligence gathering became integral parts of the U.S. emergence onto the international stage, first as an economic power and then as a military one. The executive's unique position as the "voice" and "ears" of the nation led over time to a widely accepted vision of the president as possessing the power to conduct U.S. foreign relations. Moreover, as discussed in Section IV, there continued to be numerous incidents in which the president's exercise of the recognition power lent U.S. support to a new country or new regime of an existing country, or denied it as much.[84] Sometimes Congress played a role as well, but only in limited situations, notably recognition associated with the gain or loss of U.S. territory, or recognition in the context of a declaration of war.

In view of the president's dominant role in conducting U.S. foreign relations (and Congress' relatively limited role), it is perhaps no surprise that Justice Sutherland's 1936 opinion in *Curtiss-Wright*, which described "the very delicate, plenary and exclusive power of the President as the sole organ of the federal government in the field of international relations," leaned heavily on the claim that "the President alone has the power to speak or listen as a representative of the nation."[85] While much of Sutherland's discourse relied on the president's functional advantages as a single actor (as compared with the multiple actors of Congress), it also emphasized the president's "confidential sources of information" and "his agents in the form of diplomatic, consular and other officials."[86] The president's posture as the conduit of information to and from foreign nations, inextricably linked to his power of appointing and receiving ambassadors, seems to lie at the core of arguments in favor of the general power of the executive to conduct U.S. foreign relations.

That general power, of course, is not limitless, and rote reference to the power to appoint and receive has not supported all executive claims. As in other areas of U.S. foreign relations law, executive power here is bounded by any prohibitions within the Constitution, restrictions falling within congressional authority, and the

---

[84] See *infra* this chapter § IV(A) (salient instances of U.S. recognition and nonrecognition of states, and instances of congressional involvement) and §IV(B) (recognition of governments).

[85] United States v. Curtiss-Wright Export Corp., 299 U.S. 304, 319, 320 (1936).

[86] *Id.* at 320; *see* Chapter I § II(A)(2).

constraints of federalism. The latter limitation at least was evident in the efforts by the executive branch in 2005 to compel Texas courts to give effect to the decision of the International Court of Justice (ICJ) in the *Avena* case,[87] by means of a memorandum issued by President George W. Bush.[88] Some of the arguments advanced by the executive branch to both the Texas criminal appeals court and the U.S. Supreme Court in *Medellín v. Texas* turned on the president's role in representing the United States internationally, including before international organizations such as the United Nations. The executive branch attempted to argue that, by virtue of being the U.S. diplomatic conduit to the rest of the world, the president could in effect deem a non-self-executing treaty to have domestic legal effect in state court proceedings. In addition to the president's own constitutional power, the executive branch noted the president's statutory responsibilities to represent the United States before the ICJ;[89] the president's representation of the United States at the U.N. Security Council, the organ charged with enforcing the Court's judgments; and the president's "established role" in litigating foreign policy issues.[90] The Court, however, rejected the use of the president's diplomatic role in this way—as a means of giving domestic effect to an international obligation—in the absence of congressional support, pointing out the role of Congress in making treaties and enacting legislation to implement any non-self-executing provisions.[91]

Other arguments pressed by the executive branch in *Medellín v. Texas* turned on a version of the power to conduct foreign relations as evidenced by cases such as *United States v. Belmont, United States v. Pink, Dames & Moore v. Regan*, and *American Insurance v. Garamendi*, which encompasses a presidential power to resolve international claims with foreign nations.[92] According to the executive, that expanded power included an ability to issue a presidential directive to state courts on matters relating to criminal law. The Supreme Court had little difficulty in pointing out that the *Belmont* line of cases involved a "narrow and strictly limited authority to settle international claims disputes pursuant to an executive agreement," not the kind of unilateral action at issue in *Medellín*.[93]

---

[87] Case Concerning Avena and Other Mexican Nationals (Mex. v. U.S.), Judgment, 2004 I.C.J. 12 (Mar. 31).

[88] Memorandum for the U.S. Attorney-General Regarding Compliance with the Decision of the International Court of Justice in Avena, 44 I.L.M. 964 (Feb. 28, 2005). For further discussion, see Chapter 9 § II(C).

[89] *See* 22 U.S.C. § 287 (2018).

[90] Brief for the United States as Amicus Curiae Supporting Petitioner at 17–19, Medellín v. Texas, 552 U.S. 491 (2008) (No. 06-984), 2007 WL 1909462; *see* Chapter 6 § IV(A)(3).

[91] Medellín v. Texas, 552 U.S. 491, 521–22 (2008). On the *Medellín* case generally, see Chapter 1 § II(B); Chapter 5 § II(B); Chapter 6 §§ III(B)(3), IV(A); Chapter 7 § III(C); and Chapter 9 §§ II(B), II(C).

[92] Am. Ins. v. Garamendi, 539 U.S. 396 (2003); Dames & Moore v. Regan, 453 U.S. 654 (1981); United States v. Pink, 315 U.S. 203, 229 (1942); United States v. Belmont, 301 U.S. 324 (1937). For discussion, see *infra* notes 359–368 and accompanying text; Chapter 6 § V(C); and Chapter 9 § II(C).

[93] *Medellín*, 552 U.S. at 532.

On other occasions, the Supreme Court has provided strong support to the president's power with respect to the conduct of U.S. foreign relations, notably in its 2015 decision in *Zivotofsky v. Kerry* (*Zivotofsky II*).[94] In that case, Menachem Zivotofsky was born to U.S. citizen parents in Jerusalem.[95] When they requested that the U.S. embassy list on his passport "Jerusalem, Israel" as his place of birth, the embassy declined, due to a Department of State policy recognizing no country as possessing sovereignty over the city of Jerusalem.[96] The family sued, noting that Congress had enacted legislation providing that, "[f]or purposes of the registration of birth, certification of nationality, or issuance of a passport of a United States citizen born in the city of Jerusalem, the Secretary shall, upon the request of the citizen or the citizen's legal guardian, record the place of birth as Israel."[97] While President George W. Bush had signed the legislation into law, he maintained in a signing statement that this provision was unconstitutional, including because it interfered with the president's power to conduct foreign relations.[98]

To resolve the conflict between the two political branches, the Court applied Justice Jackson's *Youngstown* test, recognizing that the conflict between the political branches placed the issue in Justice Jackson's third category.[99] In considering the president's power, the Court noted that the Reception Clause had become understood, despite initially being dismissed by Hamilton and others, as having accorded to the president a power of recognition.[100] As support, the Court cited "prominent international scholars [who] suggested that receiving an ambassador was tantamount to recognizing the sovereignty of the sending state."[101] It also cited incidents such as President Washington's recognition, without congressional involvement, of France's ambassador

---

[94] 576 U.S. 1 (2015) (*Zivotofsky II*). For further discussion of *Zivotofsky II*, see Chapter 1 §§ I(B), II(A)(2), II(B) and Chapter 2 § II(C). For discussion of the earlier decision of the Court on justiciability, see Zivotofsky *ex rel.* Zivotofsky v. Clinton, 566 U.S. 189 (2012) (*Zivotofsky I*); *see* Chapter 4 § II(A).

[95] *Zivotofsky II*, 576 U.S. at 8.

[96] *Id.* at 7–9. The Department's administrative rule requires it to record the place of birth on a passport as the "country [having] present sovereignty over the actual area of birth." U.S. Dep't of State, 7 Foreign Affairs Manual § 1383.4 (1987). If a citizen objects to the country listed as sovereign by the Department of State, he or she may list the city or town of birth, rather than the country. *See id.* § 1383.6. But the citizen cannot require the Department to list a country that the Department does not regard as sovereign over the place of birth.

[97] Foreign Relations Authorization Act, Fiscal Year 2003, Pub. L. No. 107-228, § 214(d), 116 Stat. 1350, 1366.

[98] Statement on Signing the Foreign Relations Authorization Act, Fiscal Year 2003, 2 PUB. PAPERS 1697, 1698 (Sept. 30, 2002).

[99] *Id.* at 10. For further discussion of *Youngstown*, see Chapter 1 § II(B) and Chapter 8 § II(B).

[100] U.S. CONST. art. II, § 3; *see Zivotofsky II*, 576 U.S. at 11–12 (noting government's reliance on the Reception Clause).

[101] *Zivotofsky II*, 576 U.S. at 12 (citing writings by Vattel, van Bynkershoek, and Grotius); *id.* (concluding that "[i]t is a logical and proper inference, then, that a Clause directing the President alone to receive ambassadors would be understood to acknowledge his power to recognize other nations").

(Edmond-Charles Genêt) after the French Revolution, which led Hamilton to change his views; for the Court, this evidence of practice so soon after adoption of the Constitution, combined with other indicia, suggested that the Reception Clause "provides support, although not the sole authority, for the President's power to recognize other nations."[102] The Court found further support for the president's power in this area in the Article II power to make treaties and to appoint ambassadors with the advice and consent of the Senate, observing in that regard that Congress has no equivalent constitutional power to initiate diplomatic relations.[103]

Having concluded that the power to recognize foreign governments lies with the president, the Court turned to whether this power is exclusive, or whether Congress has a role. Among other things, the Court held that "[r]ecognition is a topic on which the Nation must 'speak . . . with one voice'" and "[t]hat voice must be the President's."[104] Further, the executive branch has the exclusive "characteristic of unity at all times" and the capacity to make delicate and decisive diplomatic action,[105] as shown through extensive historical practice.[106] Given that, the Court concluded that an exclusive presidential recognition power was "necessary" for U.S. diplomatic relations,[107] an outcome that (in the Court's view) had implicitly been accepted by Congress.[108]

As such, the Court found that the statute unconstitutionally infringed on the president's recognition power, for "[i]f the power over recognition is to mean anything, it must mean that the President not only makes the initial, formal recognition determination but also that he may maintain that determination in his and his agent's statements."[109] Congress has various constitutional means of disagreeing with the president's recognition decisions, including declining to confirm ambassadors, instituting embargos, or declaring war, but enacting a law that contradicts the president's decision was not a permissible approach.[110]

---

[102] *Id.* at 13.

[103] *Id.* at 13–14.

[104] *Id.* at 14 (quoting Am. Ins. v. Garamendi, 539 U.S. 396, 424 (2003)).

[105] *Id.*

[106] *Id.* at 17–28. The Court found that "a fair reading of relevant precedent illustrates that this Court has long considered recognition to be the exclusive prerogative of the Executive." *Id.* at 3.

[107] *Id.* at 17.

[108] *Id.* at 28. *But see* Robert J. Reinstein, *Is the President's Recognition Power Exclusive?*, 86 TEMPLE L. REV. 1 (2013) (concluding that the constitutional text, original understanding, structure, and post-ratification evidence do not support an exclusive recognition power in the executive).

[109] *Zivotofsky II*, 576 U.S. at 29.

[110] *Id.* at 30. Though the executive prevailed in the case, two years after the Court's decision, in 2017, President Donald J. Trump decided to change U.S. policy by recognizing Jerusalem as the capital of Israel and relocating the U.S. Embassy in Israel from Tel Aviv to Jerusalem. Recognizing Jerusalem as the Capital of the State of Israel and Relocating the United States Embassy to Israel to Jerusalem, Proclamation No. 9683, 82 Fed. Reg. 58331 (Dec. 11, 2017).

II. Receiving Foreign Ambassadors and Other Public Ministers

As previously noted, Article II, Section 3, of the Constitution, sometimes called the Reception Clause, provides that the president "shall receive Ambassadors and other public Ministers . . . ."[111] This section discusses some of the most salient aspects of this power to receive.

A. Receiving Foreign Ambassadors

Under international law, the establishment of diplomatic relations between two states occurs based on mutual consent.[112] As the "receiving state," the United States is not obligated to establish diplomatic relations with another state; nor is it obligated, once diplomatic relations exist, to allow specific persons to represent that state in the United States.

Based on his or her Article II power, the president regularly receives foreign diplomats and consular officials and, when doing so, occasionally advances a U.S. policy of recognizing the existence of a new state or recognizing that a particular government that came to power extraconstitutionally (such as from a coup or a rebellion) is the *de jure* government of the state.[113] Exercise of the president's power to receive is discretionary; not only may the president receive or refuse to receive foreign officials but the president may also require such officials to depart the United States after they have been received.[114]

When the United States and another state have diplomatic relations, and the foreign state wishes to send an ambassador to represent it in Washington, D.C., the foreign state requests agreement for a particular individual to serve as its ambassador, which must then be approved by the Department of State. Once approved, the foreign state issues a formal diplomatic letter (a letter of credence or "diplomatic credentials"), which is addressed from the foreign head of state to the U.S. president. Upon arriving in Washington, D.C., the ambassador provides a copy of the letter to the secretary of state (or deputy secretary of state) and then,

---

[111] U.S. CONST. art. II, § 3.

[112] Vienna Convention on Diplomatic Relations, Apr. 18, 1961, art. 2, 23 U.S.T. 3227, 500 U.N.T.S. 95 ("The establishment of diplomatic relations between States, and of permanent diplomatic missions, takes place by mutual consent") [hereinafter VCDR]. *See generally* EILEEN DENZA, DIPLOMATIC LAW: COMMENTARY ON THE VIENNA CONVENTION ON DIPLOMATIC RELATIONS (4th ed. 2018); IVOR ROBERTS, SATOW'S DIPLOMATIC PRACTICE (7th ed. 2017).

[113] As previously noted, the authority under Article II § 3 to receive foreign ambassadors undergirds the president's power to "recognize" foreign states, a power that the Supreme Court has found exclusive to the president. *See supra* this chapter text accompanying notes 68–73 and notes 94–110; *see also infra* this chapter § IV.

[114] *See infra* this chapter § II(C).

at a credentialing ceremony at the White House, presents the letter to the president. The ambassador does not begin his or her duties in the United States until the credentials are presented. In the absence of an ambassador, the foreign state may be represented by the deputy chief of mission (deputy ambassador), serving as *chargé d'affaires*, whose credentials are signed by the foreign minister and presented to the secretary of state. A similar process exists for the ambassador from an international organization, such as the African Union or the League of Arab States, to the United States.

Other high-level diplomats, such as political, economic or legal counselors at an embassy, must also be accredited to the Department of State. All such high-level diplomats, once accredited, are identified (along with their spouses) on the Department's "Diplomatic List," also referred to as the "blue list."[115] Persons on this list enjoy the highest level of immunities provided under the Vienna Convention on Diplomatic Relations (VCDR).[116] Lower-level employees of the foreign state are also notified to the Department of State prior to taking up their posts. Such persons are identified on the Department's "Employees of Diplomatic Missions Not Printed in the Diplomatic List," also known as the "white list."[117] The majority of these individuals enjoy significant immunities, but less comprehensive immunity than diplomats.[118] Foreign consular officials, once accredited, are listed in the Department's "Foreign Consular Officers in the United States."[119] Such officials and their staffs generally enjoy immunities in accordance with the Vienna Convention on Consular Relations (VCCR); in some cases a bilateral agreement provides greater immunity.[120]

B. Establishing Foreign Missions in the United States

The 1982 Foreign Missions Act[121] sets forth various laws regulating the operation in the United States of foreign missions (embassies and consulates), as

[115] *See, e.g.,* U.S. Dep't of State, Office of the Chief of Protocol, *Diplomatic List* (Spring 2020), https://perma.cc/2XP3-U473. U.S. courts have held that certifications by the Department of State are conclusive as to the status, privileges, and immunities of foreign diplomatic personnel. *See In re* Baiz, 135 U.S. 403 (1890).

[116] VCDR, *supra* note 112, arts. 29, 31. The diplomat's family members are entitled to the same immunities, unless they are U.S. nationals. For further discussion of such immunities, see Chapter 4 § V(C).

[117] *See* Carrera v. Carrera, 174 F.2d 496, 497 (D.C. Cir. 1949).

[118] VCDR, *supra* note 112, art. 37. The diplomat's family members are entitled to the same immunities, unless they are U.S. nationals.

[119] The Department no longer produces in hard-copy form either "the white list" or the "Foreign Consular Officers" list and instead maintains them internally on electronic databases.

[120] Vienna Convention on Consular Relations, Apr. 24, 1963, arts. 43, 71, 21 U.S.T. 77, 596 U.N.T.S., 261 [hereinafter VCCR]. For further discussion of such immunities, see Chapter 4 § V(C).

[121] Foreign Missions Act, tit. II, Pub. L. No. 97-241, § 201, 96 Stat. 282 (1982) (codified at 22 U.S.C. §§ 4301–16 (2018)).

well as public international organizations and foreign missions to such organizations.[122] The United States fulfills its obligations regarding foreign missions under the VCDR and VCCR largely through this statute, while it accords to the secretary of state considerable discretion, recognizing that treatment of foreign missions in the United States should be done with an eye to whether reciprocity is being provided by foreign states to U.S. missions abroad.[123] The secretary is authorized to delegate his responsibilities to an office within the Department of State,[124] which is the Office of Foreign Missions.

When a foreign state acquires property for a mission in the United States, there are two possibilities. First, the secretary of state may "implement an exchange of property" between the United States and the foreign state, whereby each provides to the other premises that each will then use for the purposes of its mission in the other state.[125] The secretary must notify Congress fifteen days before such in-kind exchange.[126] Alternatively, the foreign state may acquire property on its own, either by purchase or rent, but must notify the secretary of state before doing so.[127] The secretary must notify the director of the FBI and the secretary of defense of such acquisitions, so that they can ensure that the foreign state is not using the property to "engage in intelligence activities directed against the United States."[128] The secretary may require divesture if the use or acquisition of such property does not comply with U.S. law, any relevant bilateral agreement, or when it is "otherwise necessary to protect the interests of the United States."[129]

While foreign embassies in the United States are typically located in Washington, D.C., foreign consulates may be located across the United States, especially in major cities. Such consulates are designed to "not only . . . include the provision of citizen services and the issuance of visas, but also further[] the development of commercial, economic, cultural and scientific relations between the sending State and the receiving State."[130] The rules set forth in the Foreign Missions Act generally apply to consulates as well, but are implemented in accordance with the VCCR. Consular posts can be classified as a consulate general, consulate, vice consulate, or consular agency, based on the size of the post, the scope of its functions, and the level of supervision from other consular posts.[131]

---

[122] *See* 22 U.S.C. § 4309 (2018) (international organizations generally); *id.* § 4309A (activities of U.N. employees).

[123] 22 U.S.C. § 4301(c).

[124] 22 U.S.C. § 4303(4).

[125] 22 U.S.C. § 4304(b)(5), (f).

[126] 22 U.S.C. § 4304(f)(4).

[127] 22 U.S.C. § 4305. Generally acceptable areas for establishing such missions in Washington, D.C., are set forth in 22 U.S.C. § 4306.

[128] 22 U.S.C. § 4305(d).

[129] *Id.*

[130] U.S. Dep't of State, Office of Foreign Missions, *Handbook for the Establishment of Consular Posts*, § II (May 23, 2017), https://perma.cc/9W24-JWT3.

[131] *Id.*, § III.

Once property for a mission is acquired by a foreign state, the United States is obligated under the VCDR and VCCR to respect and protect the premises of such missions,[132] even if the United States has severed diplomatic relations and the premises are not being used by the foreign state.[133] The same is true with respect to properties acquired by international organizations based in the United States, pursuant to the relevant headquarters agreement,[134] and with respect to properties of the missions of foreign states to those organizations. Protection of such missions is provided by the Department of State[135] and the U.S. Secret Service.[136]

When operating foreign missions, various privileges and immunities are accorded to the mission and its personnel, based on treaties, statutes, or regulation.[137] Such benefits, which are implemented by the Department of State,[138] can include exemption from taxation and customs fees, immunity from civil and criminal liability, and inviolability of diplomatic premises, archives, documents, and bags. At the same time, while the mission may be immune from civil jurisdiction, international law allows a receiving state to require that the sending state secure liability insurance, covering situations such as harm from a motor vehicle accident. The United States imposes such requirements on foreign missions.[139] Further, Congress has required the secretary of state to provide an annual "Report on Cases Involving Diplomatic Immunity" that, among other things, indicates the number of persons residing in the United States who enjoy full diplomatic immunity from U.S. criminal jurisdiction and each case involving such a person where there was reasonable cause to believe the person committed a serious criminal offense within the United States.[140] Moreover, the United States imposes travel restrictions within the United States on certain personnel of

---

[132] VCDR, *supra* note 112, art. 45 (the United States has a duty to "respect and protect the premises of the mission, together with its property and archives"); VCCR, *supra* note 120, art. 27 (the United States "shall . . . respect and protect the consular premises, together with the property of the consular post and the consular activities").

[133] Mousa v. Islamic Republic of Iran, No. 00-2096, 2003 U.S. Dist. LEXIS 25812, at *13–14 (D.D.C. Nov. 5, 2003) (holding that, under the VCCR and VCDR, the United States must protect Iranian diplomatic and consular property even when the properties at issue are not being used by Iran, and the property can therefore not be garnished as damages for a state-sponsored terrorism injury).

[134] *See, e.g.*, Agreement Regarding the Headquarters of the United Nations, U.N.-U.S., arts. VI, VII, June 26, 1947, T.I.A.S. 09-618, 11 U.N.T.S. 147 [hereinafter Headquarters Agreement]. The agreement was authorized by Pub. L. No. 80-357, 61 Stat. 756 (1947) (codified at 22 U.S.C. § 287 note (2018)). Article VI of the agreement is entitled "Police Protection of the Headquarters District," while Article VII is entitled "Public Services and Protection of the Headquarters District."

[135] 22 U.S.C. § 4314 (2018).

[136] 18 U.S.C. § 3056A.

[137] For discussion of related immunity issues, see Chapter 4 § V(C).

[138] 22 U.S.C. § 4304.

[139] 22 U.S.C. § 4304A.

[140] 22 U.S.C. § 4304B.

either international organizations based in the United States or foreign missions to such organizations.[141]

U.S. obligations owed to foreign embassies and missions are rarely litigated in U.S. courts.[142] In *United States v. Palestine Liberation Organization*,[143] however, the obligations of the United States under the U.N.-U.S. Headquarters Agreement[144] were at issue with respect to offices of the Palestine Liberation Organization (PLO) in the United States. Beginning in 1974,[145] the PLO had permanent observer status at the United Nations,[146] and to that end maintained a mission in New York. In 1987, however, Congress adopted the Anti-Terrorism Act (ATA),[147] which stated that the PLO is "a terrorist organization and a threat to the interests of the United States, its allies, and to international law and should not benefit from operating in the United States."[148] Consequently, the statute forbade the establishment or maintenance of "an office, headquarters, premises, or other facilities or establishments within the jurisdiction of the United States at the behest or direction of, or with funds provided by" the PLO, if the purpose is to further the PLO's interests.[149] Shortly before the ATA was to take effect, the attorney general informed the PLO mission that its presence was about to become unlawful. When the mission did not close, the government filed suit in U.S. court against the PLO seeking injunctive relief for closure of the mission.[150] Named individuals in the case (officials at the mission) responded that the United States was obligated under the Headquarters Agreement to allow the presence of foreign missions for representation at the United Nations[151] and, further, that any

[141] 22 U.S.C. § 4316.

[142] *See, e.g.,* 767 Third Ave. Assocs. v. Permanent Mission of Zaire to U.N., 988 F.2d 295, 297 (2d Cir. 1993) (holding that although a landlord was entitled to money damages, a foreign mission to the United Nations is inviolable and "international and U.S. law precludes the forcible eviction"); Concerned Jewish Youth v. McGuire, 621 F.2d 471, 474 (2d Cir. 1980) (holding that the government has "a substantial interest in protecting foreign officials and their property" and is therefore authorized to limit protests outside the Russian mission); Anti-Defamation League of B'nai B'rith v. Kissinger, Civil Action No. 74 C 1545 (E.D.N.Y. Nov. 1, 1974) (finding that, under the U.N.-U.S. Headquarters Agreement, the United States must allow PLO representatives access to, and presence in the vicinity of, the United Nations).

[143] 695 F. Supp. 1456 (S.D.N.Y. 1988).

[144] *See* Headquarters Agreement, *supra* note 134.

[145] G.A. Res. 3237 (XXIX) (Nov. 22, 1974).

[146] Permanent observers are not member states of the United Nations but are allowed to be present in U.N. proceedings and maintain "permanent observer missions" in New York. *See* U.N. Secretary-General, *Permanent Missions to the United Nations: Rep. of the Secretary-General*, U.N. Doc. A/939/Rev. 1 (1949).

[147] 22 U.S.C. §§ 5201–03 (2018).

[148] 22 U.S.C. § 5201(b).

[149] 22 U.S.C. § 5202(3).

[150] United States v. Palestine Liberation Organization, 695 F. Supp. 1456, 1460–61 (S.D.N.Y. 1988).

[151] *See* Headquarters Agreement, *supra* note 134, art. IV ("Communications and Transit" of representatives to the United Nations) and art. V ("Resident Representatives to the United Nations").

disputes under the agreement must be submitted to arbitration,[152] not resolved in U.S. courts.

The district court found that the obligation to arbitrate only concerned disputes under the Headquarters Agreement between the United States *and the United Nations*, which was not the case at hand.[153] As to the merits of the government's request for an injunction, the court reasoned that the ATA must be interpreted in light of U.S. obligations under the Headquarters Agreement. "Only where a treaty is irreconcilable with a later enacted statute and Congress has clearly evinced an intent to supersede a treaty by enacting a statute does the later enacted statute take precedence."[154] The court found that reading the ATA to require closure of a mission to the United Nations "would fly in the face of the Headquarters Agreement,"[155] and yet Congress evinced no express intent in the statute to supersede the treaty.[156] Consequently, the court decided that the ATA was not applicable to the PLO mission, but it "could effectively curtail any PLO activities in the United States, aside from the Mission to the United Nations."[157] The government chose not to appeal the decision and the PLO mission in New York continued in its operations.[158]

The PLO office in Washington, D.C., was closed but, based on a presidential waiver,[159] was re-established in 1994 as the PLO Mission to the United States, following the conclusion of the Oslo Accords and the creation of the Palestinian National Authority (commonly referred to as the Palestinian Authority).[160] In 2010, the executive branch acceded to a request that the office be renamed the

---

[152] *See id.*, art. VIII, § 21.

[153] *Palestine Liberation Organization*, 695 F. Supp., at 1461–64. Separately, the U.N. General Assembly sought advice from the ICJ as to whether the United States was obligated under the Headquarters Agreement to enter into arbitration to address the potential closure of the PLO mission. *See* G.A. Res. 42/229 A (Mar. 2, 1988); G.A. Res. 42/229 B (Mar. 2, 1988). The ICJ advised that the United States was bound to respect its obligation under the agreement to do so. Applicability of the Obligation to Arbitrate under Section 21 of the United Nations Headquarters Agreement of 26 June 1947, Advisory Opinion, 1988 I.C.J. 12 (April 26). No arbitration, however, thereafter occurred because the U.S. government allowed the PLO's mission to continue its operations.

[154] *Palestine Liberation Organization*, 695 F. Supp., at 1464. On the *Charming Betsy* doctrine, see Chapter 2 § II(E), Chapter 4 § IV(D), Chapter 5 § III(B)(3), and Chapter 6 § V(A)(2).

[155] *Palestine Liberation Organization*, 695 F. Supp., at 1464.

[156] *Id.* at 1465. The court noted that the text of the ATA never mentions the Headquarters Agreement, nor includes *treaties* in its statement that "notwithstanding any provision of law to the contrary," and that "no member of Congress, at any point, explicitly stated that the ATA was intended to override any international obligation of the United States." *Id.* at 1468–70.

[157] *Id.* at 1471.

[158] *See generally* W. Michael Reisman, *An International Farce: The Sad Case of the PLO Mission*, 14 YALE J. INT'L L. 412 (1989).

[159] Six-month waivers were permitted under various appropriations laws. *See, e.g.*, Waiver and Certification of Statutory Provisions of Section 1003 of Public Law 100-204 Regarding the Palestine Liberation Organization Office, 78 Fed. Reg. 1299 (Jan. 8, 2013).

[160] *See generally* GEOFFREY R. WATSON, THE OSLO ACCORDS: INTERNATIONAL LAW AND THE ISRAELI-PALESTINIAN PEACE AGREEMENTS (2000).

General Delegation of the PLO to the United States. In 2018, however, the executive branch ordered the closure of the office, saying that "the PLO has not taken steps to advance the start of direct and meaningful negotiations with Israel" and that the decision was "consistent with Administration and Congressional concerns with Palestinian attempts to prompt an investigation of Israel by the International Criminal Court."[161]

An impediment to the reopening of this office arises from the adoption of two statutes in 2018–2019: the Anti-Terrorism Clarification Act (ATCA)[162] and the Promoting Security and Justice for Victims of Terrorism Act (PSJVTA),[163] each of which amended the ATA. Among other things, the ATA provides a civil cause of action by which U.S. nationals injured by acts of international terrorism may sue responsible persons or entities for treble damages.[164] Prior to the ATCA and PSJVTA, the ATA did not purport to resolve personal jurisdiction over such persons or entities.[165] The amendments, however, provide that certain actions by the PLO or Palestinian Authority trigger consent to personal jurisdiction, one of which is maintaining or establishing any PLO or Palestine Authority office, headquarters, premises, or other facilities or establishments in the United States.[166] As such, reopening the office in Washington, D.C., could expose the PLO or Palestinian Authority to substantial civil judgments in U.S. courts.

C. Declaring Foreign Diplomats *Persona Non Grata*

After a foreign diplomatic or consular official has been received in the United States, the U.S. government may determine that the person's activities (e.g., espionage or criminal activity) are incompatible with his or her recognized functions, or that his or her presence is undesirable for political or other reasons (e.g., as a "tit for tat" response to expulsion of a U.S. diplomat abroad), such that the person

---

[161] U.S. Dep't of State Press Statement, *Closure of the PLO Office in Washington* (Sept. 10, 2018).

[162] Pub. L. No. 115-253 (2018) (codified at 18 U.S.C. 1 note (2018)).

[163] The PSJVTA was § 903 of the Further Consolidated Appropriations Act, Pub. L. No. 116-94 (2019). For background on the two amendments, see JIM ZANOTTI & JENNIFER K. ELSEA, CONG. RESEARCH SERV., R46274, THE PALESTINIANS AND AMENDMENTS TO THE ANTI-TERRORISM ACT: U.S. AID AND PERSONAL JURISDICTION (2020).

[164] 18 U.S.C. § 2333 (2018).

[165] For jurisdictional difficulties in civil litigation prior to enactment of the amendments, see Waldman v. Palestine Liberation Organization, 835 F.3d 317, 322 (2d Cir. 2016) (concluding that certain terrorist attacks were not sufficiently connected to the United States to create personal jurisdiction in U.S. federal courts).

[166] 18 U.S.C. § 2334(e)(1)(B)(i–ii) (West Supp. 2020). An exception exists for an office used exclusively to conduct official business with the United Nations. *Id.* § 2334(e)(3)(A).

should be expelled. The VCDR recognizes that "[t]he receiving State may at any time and without having to explain its decision, notify the sending State that the head of the mission or any member of the diplomatic staff . . . is *persona non grata* or that any other member of the staff . . . is not acceptable."[167]

For the United States, such a determination is made by the president, as an inherent aspect of the president's power to receive ambassadors[168] and as an aspect of the broad authority delegated to the president over nonresident noncitizens under the Immigration and Nationality Act.[169] Deeming someone *persona non grata*, or an "unwelcome or unacceptable person," is discretionary and can be done not only with respect to persons who have already been received in the United States but also those who have not yet entered.[170] If the person is already in the United States, upon being declared *persona non grata*, that person must depart within a "reasonable period" of time.[171] If the sending state does not comply, the president may use law enforcement personnel to compel compliance, but to date this has never been necessary.[172] The only protections available to such a person would appear to be when the person invokes a right *of non-refoulement* due to a credible fear of persecution or torture in the sending state[173] or, under the Due Process Clause of the Fifth Amendment,[174] challenges whether he or she is the person who has been ordered to be expelled.[175]

III. Appointing U.S. Ambassadors, Ministers, and Consuls

Article II, Section 2 of the Constitution provides that the president "by and with the Advice and Consent of the Senate, shall appoint Ambassadors, other public Ministers and Consuls . . . ."[176] This section discusses some of the most salient aspects of this power to appoint.

[167] VCDR, *supra* note 112, art. 9 (emphasis added); *see also* VCCR, *supra* note 120, art. 23.

[168] Presidential Power to Expel Diplomatic Personnel from the United States, 4A Op. O.L.C. 207, 208 (1980). A different outcome may arise for lawful permanent residents and noncitizens who seek asylum.

[169] *See id.* at 215–16.

[170] Ambassadors and Other Public Ministers of the United States, 7 Op. Att'y Gen. 186, 209 (1855).

[171] VCDR, *supra* note 112, art. 9(2).

[172] 4A Op. O.L.C., *supra* note 168, at 211 ("It has long been customary for the sending states to withdraw diplomats voluntarily when those diplomats have been declared persona non grata. Thus, . . . in American practice it has apparently never been necessary forcibly to expel such a diplomat").

[173] *See* Chapter 10 § III(A)(4).

[174] U.S. CONST. amend. V.

[175] 4A Op. O.L.C., *supra* note 168, at 222.

[176] U.S. CONST. art. II, § 2.

A. Selection of Ambassadors, Ministers, and Consuls

When selecting the persons to serve at U.S. missions abroad, the president has essentially unfettered discretion, subject only to the requirement of consent from the Senate. This authority has long been construed broadly. An 1855 opinion issued by Attorney General Caleb Cushing opined that the Appointments Clause accorded a presidential power to appoint diplomatic agents of whatever type, without any need for statutory authority nor subject to any limitations by Congress, but subject to the concurrence of the Senate.[177] Cushing was reacting to legislation that purported to require, among other things, that the president "appoint representatives of the grade of envoys extraordinary and ministers plenipotentiary" to designated countries.[178] According to Cushing, "Congress cannot by law constitutionally require the President to make removals or appointments of public ministers on a given day, or to make such appointments of a prescribed rank, or to make or not make them at this or that place . . . ."[179] Rather, the president had "the absolute discretion at all times . . . to appoint a public minister of such degree as he and [the Senate] might please for any particular mission, or not to appoint any."[180] Interestingly, the Cushing opinion placed emphasis on international law as a source of the president's power, stating that the president's authority "derived from the law of nations, and the authority to appoint from the Constitution."[181]

The president's capacity to appoint ambassadors and other public ministers serving abroad based simply on some combination of constitutional authority and international law—as opposed to depending upon statutory authorization for the creation of positions—remains both surprisingly unclear and little disputed. The president has continued to assert the constitutional authority to make such appointment (albeit with diminishing emphasis on the law of nations as a foundation).[182] At the same time, Congress has provided periodic

---

[177] 7 Op. Att'y Gen. *supra* note 170, at 193; *see* Byers v. United States, 22 Ct. Cl. 59, 63–64 (1887) (noting Cushing's opinion).

[178] An Act to Remodel the Diplomatic and Consular Systems of the United States, 10 Stat. 619, 623 (1855).

[179] 7 Op. Att'y Gen. *supra* note 170, at 217–18.

[180] *Id.* at 219.

[181] *Id.* at 194.

[182] For a rare modern emphasis on the law-of-nations premise, see Officers of the United States Within the Meaning of the Appointments Clause, 31 Op. O.L.C. 73, 117 n.17 (2007) (stating that "[t]he President has authority to appoint to diplomatic offices without an authorizing act of Congress, because the Constitution itself expressly recognizes such offices under the law of nations"). *See generally* Ryan M. Scoville, *Unqualified Ambassadors,* 69 DUKE L.J. 71, 158–63 (2019) (describing law-of-nations argument as "striking," but noting "substantial" evidence for it in early practice); *id.* at 163–64 (reporting that, by contrast, "[e]vidence of the law-of-nations view essentially disappears around the late 1800s," but noting the aforementioned opinion by the Department of Justice's Office of the Legal Counsel (OLC)). The greater emphasis has been on the president's authority. *See, e.g.,*

statutory authorization for positions without pushback from the executive branch.[183]

One of Congress' key contributions has been to regulate the overall *structure* of U.S. diplomatic representation, and executive branch acquiescence may be explained in part on that basis. Though the Constitution speaks of the power to appoint "Ambassadors, other public Ministers, and Consuls," the United States practice from 1789 until 1893 was only to appoint "ministers" and "consuls" to foreign countries, a stylistic way for the new republic to distance itself from the traditional European practice of using "ambassadors."[184] Two paths of diplomatic representation emerged during this period: a "diplomatic service," consisting of persons posted to U.S. embassies or legations, and a "consular service," consisting of persons posted to consulates who were focused on promoting U.S. commerce and assisting U.S. nationals abroad. Until 1856, such personnel earned no salary; ministers were normally wealthy individuals, while consular service personnel typically supported themselves through commercial activities within their host country or by collecting consular fees. Starting in 1856, Congress enacted a statute permitting consular personnel to receive a salary, while precluding them from engaging in commercial activity at their post. The 1924 Rogers Act merged the diplomatic and consular services into a single Foreign Service, creating competitive examinations for new personnel and providing for promotion only through merit.[185] By the 1970s, the presence of personnel at diplomatic posts from multiple federal agencies led Congress to mandate that the ambassador have full responsibility for the "direction, coordination, and supervision of all United States Government

Nomination of Sitting Member of Congress to be Ambassador to Vietnam, 20 Op. O.L.C. 284, 286 (1996) (stating that "the President has the inherent, constitutional power to create diplomatic offices" such as ambassadorships, without any need for statutory authorization). By its nature, this relies more heavily on a broad notion of executive authority and has potential implications for other offices. *Compare* Scoville, *Unqualified Ambassadors, supra*, at 152 & n.271 (criticizing broader claim founded on the Vesting Clause), *and id.* at 153–58 (discussing competing views concerning a basis in the Appointments Clause, but focusing on ambassadors and comparable diplomats), *with* James Durling & E. Garrett West, *Appointments Without Law*, 105 VA. L. REV. 1281 (2019) (arguing that diplomats and Supreme Court justices should be treated comparably for purposes of the Appointments Clause and that neither required statutory authorization), *and id.* at 1321–40 (evaluating, and ultimately rejecting, bases for distinguishing diplomats).

[183] Scoville, *Unqualified Ambassadors, supra* note 182, at 164–70.
[184] *See* STAFF OF S. COMM. ON FOREIGN RELATIONS, 97TH CONG., THE AMBASSADOR IN U.S. FOREIGN POLICY: CHANGING PATTERNS IN ROLES, SELECTION, AND DESIGNATIONS 1 (Comm. Print 1981). After 1893, with the rise of the United States as a major power on the international stage, appointment of ambassadors became routine.
[185] Act of May 24, 1924, ch. 182, 43 Stat. 140 (amended 1946); *see* ROBERT D. SCHULZINGER, THE MAKING OF THE DIPLOMATIC MIND: THE TRAINING, OUTLOOK, AND STYLE OF UNITED STATES FOREIGN SERVICE OFFICERS, 1908–1931 (1975).

officers and employees in that country, except for personnel under the command of a United States area military commander."[186]

Even so, Congress has asserted the ability to authorize discrete positions as well. The current statute regulating such matters is the Foreign Service Act of 1980, which states that "[t]he President may, by and with the advice and consent of the Senate, appoint an individual . . . as an ambassador at large, as an ambassador, [or] as a minister . . . ."[187] While such language might be interpreted as evidence of congressional authority to create the office of ambassador or minister, the prior practice of such offices being created by the president without explicit statutory authority, and the generality of the terms, suggest that the language may be best read as declaratory in nature. Other instances, however, suggest a degree of presidential acquiescence. For example, President Bill Clinton appeared to approve of legislation establishing the Ambassador at Large for International Religious Freedom while advising of his intention to nominate a particular individual "for the position of Ambassador at Large created under the Act."[188] The matter may be unresolved for so long as Congress and the president avoid academic disagreements concerning whether a particular position has received sufficient authorization by Constitution, statute, or otherwise.

Whether Congress may adopt a statute that purports to instruct the president on the *type* of person who may be appointed as an ambassador is more prone to being contested and is an area where some form of constitutional balancing is required. On the one hand, it appears generally accepted that Congress has a role in setting reasonable qualifications for office.[189] On the other hand, "[t]he President has the sole responsibility for nominating [principal officers] and the Senate has the sole responsibility of consenting to the President's choice."[190] Reconciling these authorities has not always been easy. For example, a provision of the Lobbying Disclosure Act of 1995 stated that anyone "who has directly represented, aided, or advised a foreign entity . . . in any trade negotiation, or trade dispute, with the United States may not be appointed as United States Trade Representative or as a Deputy United States Trade Representative" (both of whom have the rank of ambassador).[191] On behalf of the executive branch, the Department of Justice's Office of the Legal Counsel (OLC) took the position that this provision was an unconstitutional intrusion on the president's power

---

[186] State Department/USIA Authorization Act, Fiscal Year 1975, Pub. L. 93-475, § 12, 88 Stat. 1439, 1442 (1974) (prior to 1982 amendment).

[187] 22 U.S.C. § 3942(a)(1) (2018).

[188] Statement on Signing the International Religious Freedom Act of 1998, 2 PUB. PAPERS 1883–84 (Oct. 27, 1998); *see* Scoville, *Unqualified Ambassadors, supra* note 182, at 167.

[189] *See* Myers v. United States, 272 U.S. 52, 128–29 (1926).

[190] Pub. Citizen v. U.S. Dep't of Justice, 491 U.S. 440, 487 (1989) (Kennedy, J., concurring in the result).

[191] Lobbying Disclosure Act of 1995, Pub. L. No. 104-65, § 21(b)(3), 109 Stat. 691, 705 (1995) (codified at 19 U.S.C. § 2171(b)(4) (2018)).

of appointment because it would preclude appointment of "a broad group of the most knowledgeable and experienced practitioners in the field of international trade" to a position that "is especially close to the President."[192]

The potential tension may be ameliorated by careful statutory drafting. Some provisions of the Foreign Service Act of 1980, for example, signal the expectations of Congress concerning which type of person will be nominated to serve as an ambassador. In particular, the statute provides that a chief of mission "should possess clearly demonstrated competence to perform" his or her duties and that this competence includes "to the maximum extent practicable, a useful knowledge of the principal language or dialect of the country in which the individual is to serve, and knowledge and understanding of the history, the culture, the economic and political institutions, and the interests of that country and its people."[193] Other provisions emphasize that chief of mission positions "should" normally be given to career members of the Foreign Service, that political campaign contributions "should not" be a factor in the appointment process, and that the president "shall" provide the Senate Foreign Relations Committee with "a report on the demonstrated competence of that nominee to perform the duties of the position in which he or she is to serve."[194] The contrasting language suggests that the provisions regarding qualifications may be only advisory in character.

B. Ineligibility Clause

One potential constitutional limitation on who may be appointed as an ambassador or other diplomatic agent is the "Ineligibility Clause" of the U.S. Constitution,[195] which limits the appointment of members of Congress in certain limited circumstances. That clause provides: "No Senator or Representative shall, during the Time for which he was elected, be appointed to any civil Office under the Authority of the United States, which shall have been created, or the Emoluments whereof shall have been encreased during such time . . . ."[196] OLC has assumed, without deciding, that the position of ambassador is a "civil office" within the meaning of this clause. It has acknowledged, however, that the answer is unclear and that not all of the rule's purposes are served by such

---

[192] Constitutionality of Statute Governing Appointment of United States Trade Representative, 20 Op. O.L.C. 279, 279, 280 (1996); *see also* Statement on Signing the Lobbying Disclosure Act of 1995, 2 PUB. PAPERS 1907, 1907 (Dec. 19, 1995) ("The Congress may not, of course, impose broad restrictions on the President's constitutional prerogative to nominate persons of his choosing to the highest executive branch positions, and this is especially so in the area of foreign relations.").

[193] *Id.* § 3944(a)(1).

[194] *Id.* § 3944(a)(4).

[195] U.S. CONST. art. I, § 6, cl. 2.

[196] *Id.*

a construction: in particular, if the clause is intended to prevent "self-dealing" by Congress, that concern does not seem present when the office in question is being created by the president pursuant to his inherent constitutional powers.[197]

In any event, if the clause applies to appointments of ambassadors, then it precludes the appointment of a member of Congress to a newly created post, even if the member resigns from Congress. At the same time, the clause would not preclude appointment of the member after his or her term expires. In 1996, when the United States and the Socialist Republic of Vietnam established diplomatic relations, OLC opined that Representative Douglas Peterson was only eligible to be appointed ambassador to Vietnam if the president created the position *after* the expiration of the term for which Peterson was elected.[198] Consequently, after Peterson's term expired in January 1997, President Clinton appointed him as the first U.S. ambassador to the Socialist Republic of Vietnam. Further, when a diplomatic position is created, the Ineligibility Clause does not preclude the appointment to it of a member of that Congress at some point in the future after that session of Congress expires, even if the member remains in Congress. OLC has taken the position that "appointment of a Member of Congress to an office created by some previous Congress, of which he was also a member, has not been considered to be within the prohibition of the Constitution. Numerous such appointments have been made in the past."[199]

The same general principle applies with respect to increases in salary; a member of Congress appointed as ambassador could not benefit from any salary increase for that position approved by the Congress in which he or she was serving at the time of his appointment. In 1996, when Representative Bill Richardson was being considered to serve as U.S. Ambassador to the United Nations, OLC determined that the requirements of the Ineligibility Clause imposed no impediments, since neither the post nor salary increases for the position had been approved by the Congress in existence at that time.[200] Thereafter,

---

[197] 31 Op. O.L.C., *supra* note 182, at 93 n.7 (stating that "this Office has assumed, consistent with an 1895 opinion of the Attorney General and the text of the [Ineligibility] Clause, that an ambassador holds a 'civil Office' subject to the Clause, while also noting arguments to the contrary based on the specific purposes of that Clause"); 20 Op. O.L.C., *supra* note 182, at 285 & n.5 (noting prevention of self-dealing and other objectives). More formally, Madison opined in 1834 that "[t]he place of a foreign minister or consul is not an *office* in the constitutional sense of the term" since "[i]t cannot, as an office, be created by the mere appointment for it . . . ." *Power of the President to Appoint Public Ministers and Consuls in the recess of the Senate,* 4 LETTERS AND OTHER WRITINGS OF JAMES MADISON 350 (1865) (emphasis in original).

[198] 20 Op. O.L.C., *supra* note 182, at 285. OLC determined that the post is created "at the time of *appointment* of the first ambassador to a foreign State once the President establishes diplomatic relations with that State," not the point at which the person is nominated nor even when the Senate provides its consent. *Id.* at 292 (emphasis added).

[199] Memorandum from Norbert A. Schlei, Assistant Attorney Gen., Office of Legal Counsel, Re: *Effect Upon the Judicial Appointment of a Former Congressman of a Judicial Salary Increase, Enacted by the Congress from Which He has Resigned* 2 (Dec. 12, 1963), *quoted in* Application of the Ineligibility Clause, 20 Op. O.L.C. 410, 411 n.1 (1996).

[200] Application of the Ineligibility Clause, 20 Op. O.L.C. 410 (1996).

Richardson was nominated, consented to by the Senate, and served in that position.

C. Removal

Once the Senate has consented to the appointment of an ambassador, the president retains the discretion to refrain from actually making that appointment.[201] Further, it is commonly understood that, once an ambassador is appointed, the president is empowered to remove that ambassador at will, without any requirement that consent be secured from the Senate.[202] Congressional power to effect removal of an ambassador (or other appointed officials) appears to be more circumscribed. Past practice indicates that Congress can affect a removal in certain limited situations: by terminating the existence of a diplomatic post, by enacting limits on tenure, and by requiring removal when an ambassador has been convicted of civil or criminal offenses.

Yet Congress cannot affect a removal simply on policy grounds. Attorney General Cushing's 1855 opinion determined that "Congress cannot, by legislative act, appoint or remove consuls any more than ministers . . . ."[203] Over time, the Supreme Court appears to have developed doctrine in accord with that opinion. In *Bowsher v. Synar*[204] and *Myers v. United States*,[205] the Supreme Court determined that Congress could not normally remove officers who are charged with executing the law.[206] If that is correct, it would appear that Congress could also not take steps that in effect were designed to bring about a removal on policy grounds, such as abolishing an embassy solely for the purpose of removing an

---

[201] See Marbury v. Madison, 5 U.S. (1 Cranch) 137, 155–58 (1803) (discussing presidential appointments generally); Appointment of a Senate-Confirmed Nominee, Memorandum Opinion for the Counsel to the President (Oct. 12, 1999), https://perma.cc/GP7K-AB4H (emphasizing presidential discretion until the appointment is actually made); 3 JOSEPH STORY, COMMENTARIES ON THE CONSTITUTION OF THE UNITED STATES 404, § 1545 (1833) (same).

[202] See, e.g., 1 CORWIN ON THE CONSTITUTION: THE FOUNDATIONS OF AMERICAN CONSTITUTIONAL AND POLITICAL THOUGHT, THE POWERS OF CONGRESS, AND THE PRESIDENT'S POWER OF REMOVAL 317–71 (Richard Loss ed., 1981); Martin S. Flaherty, *Relearning Founding Lessons: The Removal Power and Joint Accountability*, 47 CASE W. RES. L. REV. 1563 (1997).

[203] Appointment of Consuls, 7 Op. Att'y Gen. 242, 248 (1855); see also Constitutionality of Proposed Legislation Requiring Renomination and Reconfirmation of Executive Branch Officers Upon the Expiration of a Presidential Term, 11 Op. O.L.C. 25, 26 (1987) ("[T]he power to remove officers of the Executive Branch is vested exclusively in the President . . . .").

[204] 478 U.S. 714, 726 (1986).

[205] 272 U.S. 52, 161 (1926).

[206] For an argument that the Court has excessively restricted congressional power in this area and that Congress can remove all appointees whose offices it created, see Saikrishna Prakash, *Removal and Tenure in Office*, 92 VA. L. REV. 1779, 1783 (2006) ("Although the Supreme Court and the executive branch have drawn the line when it comes to statutes that do nothing more than remove incumbent officers, nothing in the Constitution supports this artificial line drawing.").

ambassadorial appointment (perhaps evidenced by recreating the same embassy after the removal was affected).

D. Ambassadors Not Subject to Senate Consent

Most persons appointed to the rank of "ambassador" are placed before the Senate for consent prior to their appointment. Such persons may be destined to serve as the chief of mission at an embassy (in which case they also are accorded the rank of "ambassador extraordinary and plenipotentiary"); may serve as a representative to an international organization, international conference, or international negotiation; or may be accorded the rank in recognition of an exemplary career in the foreign service.[207] In nominating ambassadors, presidents are not limited to persons who have risen in the professional diplomatic corps. Unlike many other countries, U.S. presidents often nominate political and financial supporters, including to some of the most important embassies abroad.[208]

In addition, there exists a rank of "ambassador-at-large" (also subject to Senate confirmation) for persons who usually have a personal relationship with the president and are asked to perform a special assignment. Such rank has been used sporadically since 1949,[209] a notable recent example being its use since 1997 for the Ambassador-at-Large for Global Criminal Justice (previously the Ambassador-at-Large for War Crimes Issues).

There is yet a third type of ambassador, a person with a "personal rank of ambassador," who is not placed before the Senate for confirmation. Such rank has been used in a variety of circumstances for persons serving the diplomatic needs of the president: sometimes for routine matters (e.g., chief of protocol at the White House), but at other times for matters of considerable significance (e.g., mediating a dispute between the United Kingdom and Guatemala).[210] The legal theory for the existence of such a rank seems to be that this person is serving simply as a presidential agent, not as an officer of the government, and hence Senate confirmation is not required.[211] Still, a formalist reading of the Constitution would lead to a conclusion that most of these ad hoc ambassadors should be placed before the Senate for advice and consent.[212] Tensions between

---

[207] See 22 U.S.C. § 3942(a)(1)–(2)(A) (2018).

[208] For an empirical assessment of the qualifications of such appointees, see Scoville, *Unqualified Ambassadors, supra* note 182 (concluding that political appointees on average are much less qualified than their career counterparts).

[209] See LEE H. BURKE, AMBASSADOR AT LARGE: DIPLOMAT EXTRAORDINARY 16–19 (1972).

[210] See THE AMBASSADOR IN U.S. FOREIGN POLICY, *supra* note 184, at 9–10.

[211] See Wood v. United States, 107 U.S. 414, 416–17 (1883) (finding that presidential agents are not officers of the government).

[212] See Ryan M. Scoville, *Ad Hoc Diplomats*, 68 DUKE L.J. 907 (2019).

the Senate and the president in the 1960s concerning the use of this rank resulted in its more selective use,[213] but the practice continues today. For example, during his eight years in office, President Clinton appointed nineteen persons to serve with a personal rank of ambassador.[214] The Foreign Service Act and implementing regulations require that such persons only serve for a period of six months or less and that the president report to the Senate on the necessity for conferring the rank, the dates it will be held, the reason for not seeking Senate confirmation, and other relevant information.[215] Further, such persons do not receive any additional compensation by virtue of this rank.[216]

E. Regulation of Diplomatic Posts and Positions

Separate from the appointing of particular persons to a diplomatic post (e.g., ambassador, deputy chief of mission, political counselor, and so on) is the creation of the post itself and the positions at that post. Diplomatic posts have been classified in different ways. Up until World War II, the United States used the term "legation" to describe a diplomatic post of lesser significance than an embassy and the term "consulate" to denote a post supporting an important U.S. commercial presence in the host state or region. Since World War II, the United States has dropped the term "legation," but has also used a new type of post, "diplomatic mission," to represent U.S. interests before certain international organizations, such as the United Nations, the European Union, the North Atlantic Treaty Organization, and the various international organizations located in Geneva. Usually, every country where there is a U.S. diplomatic representation now has an embassy, while additional consulates are used in countries where there is an extensive U.S. commercial or tourist presence.[217] For countries with which the United States has no diplomatic relations (such as Cuba until 2015 or Iran), the United States at times has requested a third country (such as Switzerland) to allow operation of a U.S. "interests section" as a formal part of the third country's embassy. The interests section is, however, staffed by U.S. personnel and operates much as would an embassy or consulate, apart from matters of formal protocol.

---

[213] See THE AMBASSADOR IN U.S. FOREIGN POLICY, *supra* note 184, at 10–11.

[214] See History of the Department of State During the Clinton Presidency (1993–2001), app. 4, U.S. DEP'T OF STATE, https://perma.cc/F4G3-8643. An example is the appointment in 1995 of Michael J. Matheson while serving as Special Negotiator for the Negotiation of the Landmines Protocol to the Convention on Conventional Weapons.

[215] See 22 U.S.C. § 3942(a)(2)(B)(i)–(ii) (2018).

[216] See id. § 3942(a)(2)(C).

[217] In the spirit of the electronic age, the United States has also begun developing "virtual presence posts" in certain countries, such as Brazil and Mexico, whereby an internet site provides information tailored to that locale. See U.S. Embassies, Consulates, and Diplomatic Missions, U.S. DEP'T OF STATE, https://perma.cc/2342-CM64.

As a general matter, the creation of departments and agencies within the U.S. government, including those within the executive branch, along with specifications about the functions and operations of those offices, is accomplished by statute or some form of congressionally delegated authority. Further, at least the senior positions within that department or agency will also be established by statute or congressional delegation. As previously noted, however, the constitutional footing of diplomatic positions is somewhat different. Historically, the executive branch has maintained that the president has inherent constitutional power to create diplomatic positions and posts. This view emerged when establishment of a post and the positions at it often went hand in hand with the decision to appoint particular persons as the president's representatives to foreign nations. For example, before Congress even enacted legislation in 1789 creating the Department of Foreign Affairs (later the Department of State), President Washington nominated, and the Senate confirmed, William Short to serve in the position of *chargé d'affaires* in France.[218] For decades thereafter, "Congress did not interfere with executive establishment of diplomatic offices as the need arose."[219]

When Congress ultimately sought to exercise some control over certain diplomatic posts during the Grant administration, in the form of closures, it appeared to accomplish little lasting change in its authority. President Ulysses S. Grant declared in an 1876 signing statement that he would construe such legislation so as to avoid "implying a right in the legislative branch to direct the closing or discontinuing of any of the diplomatic or consular offices of the Government," because if Congress sought to do so, "it would be an invasion of the constitutional prerogatives and duty of the Executive."[220] The federal courts seemed to favor the executive's authority in this regard. In *Francis v. United States*, the Court of Claims stated that—unlike for most government offices—for the diplomatic service, "Congress seems to have practically conceded, whether on constitutional grounds rightly or wrongly . . . , the duty, power, or right of the Executive to appoint diplomatic agents, of any rank or title, at any time and at any place," though such persons are "subject to such compensation, or none at all, as the legislative branch of the Government should in its wisdom see fit to provide . . . ."[221]

Nevertheless, in recent times, Congress has occasionally sought to regulate presidential power in the opening, closing, expanding, or location of diplomatic

---

[218] *See* 1 A COMPILATION OF THE MESSAGES AND PAPERS OF THE PRESIDENTS 58 (James D. Richardson ed., Bureau Nat'l Literature & Art 1904) (1897) (letter from President George Washington to the Senate, dated June 15, 1789, nominating Short).

[219] HENRY BARTHOLOMEW COX, WAR, FOREIGN AFFAIRS, AND CONSTITUTIONAL POWER: 1829–1901, at 4 (1984).

[220] 7 A COMPILATION OF THE MESSAGES AND PAPERS OF THE PRESIDENTS 377–78 (James D. Richardson ed., Bureau Nat'l Literature & Art 1904) (1897).

[221] Francis v. United States, 22 Ct. cl. 403, 405 (1887).

posts in countries where congressional-executive policy preferences clash. For example, Congress has sought to control U.S. policy with respect to Israel through regulation of the U.S. diplomatic and consular presence in that country. In 1984, a bill was introduced in the House of Representatives that would have compelled the relocation of the U.S. Embassy from Tel Aviv to Jerusalem.[222] The Reagan administration, however, strongly objected, stating that any such decision was "so closely connected with the President's exclusive constitutional power and responsibility to recognize, and to conduct ongoing relations with, foreign governments as to, in our view, be beyond the proper scope of legislative action."[223] In 1995, a similar bill was introduced in the Senate (S. 770), declaring it U.S. policy that Jerusalem should be recognized as the capital of Israel, that groundbreaking for construction of a U.S. embassy in Jerusalem should begin no later than December 1996, and that the embassy should open no later than May 1999. Further, the bill would have limited the availability of funds for diplomatic representation in Israel until such steps were taken. OLC opined that the provision was unconstitutional, stating that "because the venue at which diplomatic relations occur is itself often diplomatically significant, Congress may not impose on the President its own foreign policy judgments as to the particular sites at which the United States' diplomatic relations are to take place."[224] Moreover, "Congress cannot trammel the President's constitutional authority to conduct the Nation's foreign affairs and to recognize foreign governments by directing the relocation of an embassy," especially "where, as here, the location of the embassy is not only of great significance in establishing the United States' relationship with a single country, but may well also determine our relations with an entire region of the world."[225]

Nevertheless, President Clinton allowed the bill to pass into law as the Jerusalem Embassy Act of 1995, in part because it contained a waiver provision allowing the president to suspend the funding constraints if necessary to protect U.S. national security interests.[226] Until late 2018, Presidents Clinton, Bush,

---

[222] H.R. 4376, 98th Cong. (1984).

[223] Letter from George P. Shultz, Sec'y of State, to Dante B. Fascell, Chairman, Comm. on Foreign Affairs, U.S. House of Representatives 2 (Feb. 13, 1984), in Bill to Relocate United States Embassy from Tel Aviv to Jerusalem, 19 Op. O.L.C. 123, 126 (1995).

[224] Bill to Relocate United States Embassy, 19 Op. O.L.C., supra note 223, at 125.

[225] Id.

[226] Jerusalem Embassy Act of 1995, Pub. L. No. 104-45, § 7, 109 Stat. 398, 400. The bill was not signed by the president, but passed into law after ten days given that Congress was in session. Relatedly, the Foreign Relations Authorization Act for 2003 urged the president to relocate the embassy, stated that none of its funds could be used for the "publication of any official government document which lists countries and their capital cities unless the publication identifies Jerusalem as the capital of Israel," and provided that, for "purposes of the registration of birth, certification of nationality, or issuance of a passport of a United States citizen born in the city of Jerusalem, the Secretary [of State] shall, upon the request of the citizen or the citizen's legal guardian, record the place of birth as Israel." Foreign Relations Authorization Act, Fiscal Year 2003, Pub. L. No. 107-228, § 214, 116 Stat. 1350, 1366 (2002). The Supreme Court declared invalid the passport provision in Zivotofsky v. Kerry,

Obama, and Trump exercised the waiver every six months.[227] Thereafter, based on President Trump's decision to recognize Jerusalem as the capital of Israel, the United States moved forward with relocating the U.S. Embassy to Jerusalem.[228]

Similarly, Congress sought to cabin presidential discretion in diplomatic representation with the Socialist Republic of Vietnam when the United States opened diplomatic relations with that country in 1995. Section 609 of the Fiscal Year 1996 Omnibus Appropriations Act prohibited the use of funds to open or expand diplomatic or consular posts in Vietnam or increase their personnel size, unless the president certified that Vietnam was cooperating on matters relating to Vietnam War-era prisoners of war or persons missing in action.[229] OLC took the view that such a prohibition "is an unconstitutional condition on the exercise of the President's power to control the recognition and non-recognition of foreign governments—a power that flows directly from his textually-committed authority to receive ambassadors, U.S. Const. art. II, § 3."[230] While Congress is assigned the power to appropriate funds for the U.S. government, OLC maintained that such power cannot be used to usurp the executive function of "recognition."[231] Interestingly, the OLC opinion did not rely on the power to appoint ambassadors (the power more directly relevant when discussing U.S. diplomatic activities in Vietnam), presumably because that power is shared with the Senate.

Sporadic other efforts at congressional control over diplomatic posts also have been rebuffed by the president through signing statements that treat such measures as advisory in nature. Thus, in 1987 President Ronald Reagan announced that he would construe provisions of the Foreign Relations Authorization Act for Fiscal Years 1988 and 1989 that forbade "the closing of any United States consular or diplomatic post abroad"[232] in a manner that would avoid unconstitutional interference with the president's authority with respect to diplomacy.[233] Similarly, when the Foreign Relations Authorization Act for Fiscal Years 1994 and 1995 contained provisions purporting to require the establishment of a diplomatic office in Lhasa, Tibet,[234] President Clinton stated that he would "implement them

---

576 U.S. 1 (2015) (*Zivotofsky II*). *See supra* this chapter § I(D); *see also* Chapter 1 §§ I(B), II(A)(2), II(B) and Chapter 2 § II(C).

[227] *See, e.g.*, Presidential Determination No. 2018-09 of Dec. 07, 2018, 83 Fed. Reg. 66,555 (Dec. 7, 2018).

[228] Proclamation No. 9683, 82 Fed. Reg. 58,331 (Dec. 6, 2017).

[229] Omnibus Consolidated Rescissions and Appropriations Act of 1996, Pub. L. No. 104-134, § 609, 110 Stat. 1321, 1321-063–1321-064; *see* Chapter 2 § III.

[230] Section 609 of the FY 1996 Omnibus Appropriations Act, 20 Op. O.L.C. 189, 193 (1996).

[231] *Id.*

[232] Pub. L. No. 100-204, § 122(a)(1), 101 Stat. 1331, 1339 (1987).

[233] Statement on Signing the Foreign Relations Authorization Act, Fiscal Years 1988 and 1989, 2 PUB. PAPERS 1541, 1542 (Dec. 22, 1987).

[234] Pub. L. No. 103-236, § 221, 108 Stat. 382, 421 (1994).

to the extent consistent with [his] constitutional responsibilities."[235] While such legislation might be interpreted as congressional rejection of the president's position on his plenary power to create, locate, or close diplomatic posts, it is also possible to interpret Congress as occasionally adopting provisions that lay claim to a congressional power that is now understood, even by Congress, not to exist.

IV. Recognition Power and Collateral Effects

A. Recognition of a New Foreign State

1. Presidential Prerogative

As noted in Section I, the presidential power to send and receive ambassadors in the early American Republic was seen to imply a further presidential power—that of recognizing an entity as constituting the government of an existing state.[236] This "recognition power" has arisen and been confirmed repeatedly over the course of U.S. history.

Thus, in the early nineteenth century, new South American states (Argentina, Chile, Colombia) sought recognition when they revolted against Spanish control. As those entities became increasingly independent as a matter of fact, Henry Clay, the longtime speaker of the House, sought on several occasions to exert congressional power to bring about U.S. recognition of them as states, but without success.[237] Clay's efforts were even resisted by some of his own colleagues, who criticized Clay's gambit as a violation of separation of powers principles.[238] Secretary of State (and later President) John Quincy Adams also expressed constitutional objections to Clay's proposal before President James Monroe's Cabinet, with reference back to the precedents set on recognition of a new government by the Washington and Madison administrations.[239] Based on such advice, President Monroe resisted an enhanced congressional role, though the administration did consult with Congress once the presidential decision to recognize such states had been made in order to ensure funding for the new U.S. diplomatic missions.[240] The episode also demonstrated the broader significance of the president's recognition power, as President Monroe's effectuation of

---

[235] Statement on Signing the Foreign Relations Authorization Act, Fiscal Years 1994 and 1995, 1 PUB. PAPERS 807, 808 (Apr. 30, 1994).

[236] See supra this chapter § I(C).

[237] For an account, see EDWARD S. CORWIN, THE PRESIDENT: OFFICE AND POWERS 1787–1984, at 214–18 (5th rev. ed. 1984).

[238] Id. at 216.

[239] Quoted in id. at 216–17.

[240] See FREDERIC L. PAXSON, THE INDEPENDENCE OF THE SOUTH AMERICAN REPUBLICS: A STUDY IN RECOGNITION AND FOREIGN POLICY 170–73 (1903).

that authority essentially coincided with the issuance in December 1923 of the "Monroe Doctrine," which asserted that the "American continents . . . are henceforth not to be considered as subjects for future colonization by any European powers."[241]

Presidential dominance was similarly demonstrated when the United States recognized the Republic of Texas as a sovereign nation in 1837. Henry Clay, once again, sought to assert congressional control over such recognition, but was again unsuccessful.[242] Rather, President Martin van Buren recognized Texas by appointing Alcée La Branche as U.S. Chargé d'Affaires, albeit with Senate consent.[243] As this and other episodes demonstrated, the growing stature of the United States meant that the significance of its recognition grew too, as did its appreciation that recognition could make or break the aspirations of an entity in its quest for statehood. As Secretary of State William Seward would muse in 1861, no doubt with an eye toward potential foreign recognition of the Confederacy, "to recognize the independence of a new state, and so favor, possibly determine, its admission into the family of nations, is the highest possible exercise of sovereign power."[244]

By the twentieth century, U.S. legal doctrine on recognition of states was well settled, even in situations where, as a factual matter, the existence of the state was tenuous at best. President Theodore Roosevelt recognized the new Republic of Panama a mere four days after insurgents sought to break away from Colombia.[245] In the midst of World War I, President Woodrow Wilson recognized the government of a Czechoslovakian state that did not actually exist (a part of Austria-Hungary); its government was located in Washington, D.C.[246] The executive branch alone decided to recognize as new states the myriad entities in the post–World War II era, many formed from the collapse of European colonial empires,[247] while others (such as Israel) emerged from the League of Nations mandate system or United Nations trusteeship system.[248]

---

[241] *See generally* GRETCHEN MURPHY, HEMISPHERIC IMAGININGS: THE MONROE DOCTRINE AND NARRATIVES OF U.S. EMPIRE (2005).

[242] L. THOMAS GALLOWAY, RECOGNIZING FOREIGN GOVERNMENTS: THE PRACTICE OF THE UNITED STATES 16–17 (1978).

[243] *See* STANLEY SIEGEL, A POLITICAL HISTORY OF THE TEXAS REPUBLIC 1836–1845, at 77–78, n.119 (1956).

[244] Quoted in LOUIS L. JAFFE, JUDICIAL ASPECTS OF FOREIGN RELATIONS 87 (1933).

[245] *See* 1903 PAPERS RELATING TO THE FOREIGN RELATIONS OF THE UNITED STATES 225, 230–31 (1904).

[246] Charles G. Fenwick, *Recognition of the Czechoslovak Nation*, 12 AM. POL. SCI. REV. 715 (1918).

[247] *See, e.g.*, Recognition of States: Solomon Islands, *reprinted in* 1978 DIGEST OF U.S. PRACTICE, at 86; Recognition of States: Djibouti, *reprinted in* 1977 DIGEST OF U.S. PRACTICE, at 15; Recognition of States: Mozambique, *reprinted in* 1975 DIGEST OF U.S. PRACTICE, at 34; Recognition of States: Surinam, *reprinted in id.* at 36.

[248] *See* Israel Proclaimed as an Independent Republic: Text of Letter From the Agent of the Provisional Government of Israel to the President of the U.S., May 15, 1948, 18 DEP'T ST. BULL., 1948, at 673.

Since the advent of the United Nations, admission of new states to member-ship in that organization has served as a form of "collective recognition" that an entity has achieved the status of statehood.[249] This has tended to further rein-force the president's authority relative to that of Congress. The U.S. vote in both the General Assembly and the Security Council regarding admission of a new member occurs solely upon instruction by the executive branch. Moreover, sig-nificant U.S. conditions that had to be met by the former republics of the Soviet Union and Yugoslavia prior to U.S. recognition were issued by the executive branch, without congressional approval.[250] Concomitant with such admission to the United Nations, the executive branch will typically recognize the new state, as when President Obama stated in 2011: "I am proud to declare that the United States formally recognizes the Republic of South Sudan as a sovereign and inde-pendent nation . . . ."[251] Yet in situations where collective recognition through international organizations is not possible, the executive branch goes it alone, as when President George W. Bush declared in 2008: "On behalf of the American people, I hereby recognize Kosovo as an independent and sovereign state."[252]

From the beginning, U.S. courts have acknowledged that the recognition of new states is a function for the political branches. In *Gelston v. Hoyt*, the Supreme Court stated that it is "the exclusive right of governments to acknowledge new states arising in the revolutions of the world, and until such recognition by our government, or by that to which the new state previously belonged, courts of justice are bound to consider the ancient order of things as remaining un-changed."[253] Moreover, over the course of the 1800s, decisions of the Supreme Court clearly accepted allocation of this power to the president. For example, in *Williams v. Suffolk Insurance Co.*, the Court rhetorically asked "can there be any doubt, that when the executive branch of the government, which is charged

---

[249] Under U.N. Charter Article 4(1), U.N. membership is only open to "states."

[250] *See* Testimony by Ralph Johnson, Deputy Secretary of State for European and Canadian Affairs, Oct. 17, 1991, 2 FOREIGN POL'Y BULL., Nov./Dec. 1991, at 39, 42; *see also* Edwin D. Williamson & John E. Osborn, *A U.S. Perspective on Treaty Succession and Related Issues in the Wake of the Breakup of the USSR and Yugoslavia*, 33 VA. J. INT'L L. 261 (1993).

[251] Statement Recognizing South Sudan as an Independent and Sovereign State, 2 PUB. PAPERS 845 (July 9, 2011).

[252] Letter to President Fatmir Sejdiu of Kosovo Recognizing Kosovo as an Independent and Sovereign State, 1 PUB. PAPERS 228 (Feb. 18, 2008).

[253] Gelston v. Hoyt, 16 U.S. (3 Wheat.) 246, 248 (1818); *see also* United States v. Palmer, 16 U.S. (3 Wheat.) 610, 643 (1818) (stating that "when a civil war rages in a foreign nation, one part of which separates itself from the old established government, and erects itself into a distinct government," U.S. courts "must view such newly constituted government as it is viewed by the legislative and ex-ecutive departments of the government of the United States"). As Chief Justice Marshall explained, in dicta, such a position could be maintained notwithstanding the views of publicists like Vattel, since their conception of a state's recognition obligations under international law were "addressed to *sovereigns*, not to *courts*." Rose v. Himely, 8 U.S. (4 Cranch) 241, 272 (1808) (emphasis in original), *overruled in part on other grounds*, Hudson v. Guestier, 10 U.S. (6 Cranch) 281 (1810); *see* Robert J. Reinstein, *Slavery, Executive Power and International Law: The Haitian Revolution and American Constitutionalism*, 53 AM. J. LEGAL HIST. 141, 217–21 (2013).

with our foreign relations, shall in its correspondence with a foreign nation assume a fact in regard to the sovereignty of any island or country, it is conclusive
on the judicial department?"[254] For the Court, there was to be no inquiry into
"whether the executive be right or wrong" for it was "enough to know that in
the exercise of his constitutional functions, he has decided the question. Having
done this under the responsibilities which belong to him, it is obligatory on the
people and government of the Union."[255] Ultimately, it is no surprise that both
the *Restatement (Second)* and *Restatement (Third)* by the American Law Institute
on U.S. foreign relations law would, without reservation, allocate to the president
the power to recognize new states.[256]

As suggested by *Zivotofsky v. Kerry*,[257] the issue of recognition of a state includes
whether particular territory is a part of a recognized state; that is, whether the
United States recognizes the sovereignty of an existing state over disputed territory. For example, in relation to the dispute between the United Kingdom and
Argentina over the Falkland/Malvinas Islands in the Atlantic, which has spanned
the last two centuries, the executive branch has driven the determination that the
islands are under U.K. sovereignty. When an issue concerning sovereignty over
those islands reached the Supreme Court in 1839, the Supreme Court had no
hesitation in finding the executive's position controlling.[258]

2. Congress' Limited Role

Presidential control over the recognition of new states may encounter limits in
light of powers allocated to, or shared concurrently with, Congress—in particular, when recognition of a new state occurs in the context of the acquisition or
loss of territory, or of a declaration of war.

One such circumstance arises when the United States adds territory. For example, in 1826, the United States recognized the independence of the Kingdom
of Hawaii, by means of the executive negotiating with the kingdom a treaty
of friendship, commerce, and navigation.[259] The first U.S. commissioner to
the kingdom was appointed by President Franklin Pierce in 1853 and the first
U.S. minister resident was appointed by President Lincoln in 1863.[260] The

---

[254] Williams v. Suffolk Ins., 38 U.S. 415, 420 (1839).

[255] *Id.*

[256] RESTATEMENT (THIRD) § 204. The *Restatement on Foreign Relations Law of the United States
(Fourth)*, as of 2022, does not address this area of U.S. foreign relations law.

[257] 576 U.S. 1 (2015) (*Zivotofsky II*). For further discussion of *Zivotofsky II*, see *supra* this chapter
§ I(D); Chapter 1 §§ I(B), II(Λ)(2), II(B); and Chapter 2 § II(C).

[258] Williams v. Suffolk Ins., 38 U.S. 415, 418 (1839).

[259] Robert H. Stauffer, *The Hawai'i–United States Treaty of 1826*, 17 HAW. J. OF HIST. 40, 55–58
(1983). The treaty was never ratified by the United States but served as an indirect means of recognizing Hawaii's sovereignty.

[260] *A Guide to the United States' History of Recognition, Diplomatic, and Consular Relations, by
Country, since 1776: Hawaii*, OFF. OF THE HISTORIAN, FOREIGN SERV. INST., U.S. DEP'T OF STATE,
https://perma.cc/8D3X-LZHE.

decision to annex Hawaii as part of the United States, however, brought Congress fully into the picture. It was Congress that dissolved U.S. relations with Hawaii as an independent state and adopted a joint resolution in 1898 annexing Hawaii, which President William McKinley signed into law.[261]

Likewise, Congress appears to play a potential when considering whether territory—rather than being recognized as part of another state—should be deemed a part of U.S. territory. Thus, the Supreme Court, in considering whether an island could be said to fall under U.S. sovereignty, viewed the existence of a statute on the matter as a permissible exercise of congressional power, stating: "Who is the sovereign, *de jure* or *de facto*, of a territory, is not a judicial, but a political, question, the determination of which by the legislative and executive departments of any government conclusively binds the judges, as well as all other officers, citizens, and subjects of that government."[262]

Conversely, the decision to cede territory may implicate Congress' role. After the United States defeated Spain in the Spanish-American War of 1898, the United States occupied the Philippines for nearly fifty years.[263] In 1934, Congress adopted the Philippine Independence Act, which set forth a ten-year transition plan for Philippine independence.[264] As a part of that statute, Congress instructed the president to "recognize the independence of the Philippine Islands as a separate and self-governing nation."[265] In 1946, President Harry Truman issued a proclamation expressing such recognition,[266] after which he appointed the first U.S. ambassador to the Philippines.[267]

The power of recognition may also operate in tandem with the power to declare war, giving Congress a greater say. The principal example arose in the context of steps leading up to the congressional declaration of war against Spain in 1898. On April 20, 1898, Congress adopted a joint resolution determining that the "people of the Island Cuba are, and of right ought to be, free and independent," declaring U.S. "recognition of the independence of the people of Cuba," calling for the withdrawal of all Spanish military personnel from Cuba, authorizing the president to use the U.S. armed forces to ensure that these conditions were met, and asserting that the Cuban people were to govern themselves.[268]

---

[261] Joint Resolution to Provide for annexing the Hawaiian Islands to the United States, 30 Stat. 750 (1898).

[262] Jones v. United States, 137 U.S. 202, 212 (1890).

[263] H.W. BRANDS, BOUND TO EMPIRE: THE UNITED STATES AND THE PHILIPPINES 24–25 (1992).

[264] 22 U.S.C. § 1394 (2018).

[265] *Id.* at § 1394(a).

[266] Proclamation No. 2695, 11 Fed. Reg. 7517 (July 4, 1946).

[267] *A Guide to the United States' History of Recognition, Diplomatic, and Consular Relations, by Country, since 1776: Philippines*, OFF. OF THE HISTORIAN, FOREIGN SERV. INST., U.S. DEP'T OF STATE, https://perma.cc/H25E-RNQH.

[268] H.R.J. Res. 24, 55th Cong. (1898).

Instead of expressing objections or reservations about the inability of Congress to "recognize" a new state of Cuba by means of a joint resolution,[269] President McKinley signed the joint resolution into law and transmitted that resolution to Spain, saying that the United States would intervene militarily if Cuban independence were not granted. On April 21, Spain terminated diplomatic relations with the United States. On April 25, President McKinley provided to Congress information on these events, along with a recommendation that Congress declare war. Again, the president expressed no reservation about Congress' recognition of Cuba in the April 20 joint resolution. Rather, the president asserted that once the demand of the joint resolution became law, it "became the duty of the Executive to address [the demand] to the Government of Spain in obedience to said resolution . . . ," and that the joint resolution generated "things which the President is thereby required and authorized to do."[270] Congress then declared war on April 25, with effect retroactive to April 21.[271] An outcome of the ensuing war, of course, was the creation of an independent state of Cuba.

3. Nonrecognition

As a complement to the recognition of states, it appears generally accepted in practice that the presidential power entails a power *not* to recognize an entity as constituting a new state. For example, in 1804, Haiti proclaimed its independence from France, becoming the second independent country in the Western Hemisphere, and the first free black republic—a symbol of the aspirations of enslaved people. President Thomas Jefferson (himself a slave owner) nonetheless declined to recognize Haiti, and continued to treat France as sovereign; his successors also declined to recognize Haitian independence, despite tensions with their approach to new Latin American states, until President Lincoln in 1862.[272] Lincoln appointed a U.S. commissioner and consul-general as the U.S. representative. Only in 1943, after a nineteen-year U.S. occupation of

---

[269] The McKinley administration's reaction may be contrasted with that of the second Cleveland administration's reaction to a similar gambit by Congress in 1896. In that incident, the Senate Foreign Relations Committee informed the executive branch that it proposed to report out a resolution recognizing the independence of a Republic of Cuba. Cleveland's Secretary of State, Richard Olney, responded that such a resolution, if adopted, could only be regarded as "another expression of opinion," because "[t]he power to recognize the so-called Republic of Cuba as an independent state rests exclusively with the Executive." *See* Eugene V. Rostow, *Great Cases Make Bad Law: The War Powers Act*, 50 TEX. L. REV. 833, 866 (1972) (citing HENRY JAMES, RICHARD OLNEY & HIS PUBLIC SERVICE 168–69 (1923)).

[270] 10 A COMPILATION OF THE MESSAGES AND PAPERS OF THE PRESIDENTS 154 (James D. Richardson ed., Bureau Nat'l Literature & Art 1904) (1897).

[271] Act of Apr. 25, 1898, Pub. L. No. 55-69, 30 Stat. 364.

[272] *A Guide to the United States' History of Recognition, Diplomatic, and Consular Relations, by Country, since 1776: Haiti*, OFF. OF THE HISTORIAN, FOREIGN SERV. INST., U.S. DEP'T OF STATE, https://perma.cc/H8EK-KMVZ; *see* Reinstein, *supra* note 253, at 194–217.

Haiti—and in the midst of World War II—did the United States elevate its legation to an embassy.[273]

Other examples of nonrecognition, as a policy controlled by the president,
abound. The Hoover administration refused to recognize the Japanese puppet
state of Manchukuo that was purportedly established in 1932.[274] Subsequent to
the seizure of the Baltic states of Estonia, Latvia, and Lithuania by the Union
of Soviet Socialist Republics (USSR) in 1940, the executive branch refused to
recognize that those states had been subsumed into the USSR, a decision accepted by various U.S. courts.[275] After the Allied invasion of Syria in July 1941,
the Free French declared it to be an independent state (no longer a mandate of
France), but the executive branch refused to recognize the new state until after
the end of the war.[276] More recently, the president has declined to recognize the
existence of a state of Palestine, even though 138 states voted in 2012 to accord
Palestine status as an observer *state* at the United Nations.[277] Various other entities aspiring to statehood today (such as Artsakh, Abkhazia, Somaliland, South
Ossetia, and Tibet) remain unrecognized by the United States.

Collective nonrecognition, in which the executive branch participates on behalf of the United States in a concerted effort to withhold recognition, is also
a feature of contemporary international law. After the minority racist regime
in Southern Rhodesia unilaterally declared independence from the United
Kingdom, the United States supported a resolution at the U.N. Security Council
calling upon "all States not to recognize this illegal authority and not to entertain any diplomatic or other relations with it."[278] When South Africa sought to
maintain its authority in Namibia (South West Africa) during the 1960s and
1970s, along with its policies of apartheid, the executive branch also voted at
the Security Council to, in effect, declare nonrecognition of South African authority over such territory.[279] Similarly, after Indonesia's invasion of East Timor

---

[273] *Id.*

[274] *See, e.g.*, Richard N. Current, *The Stimson Doctrine and the Hoover Doctrine*, 59 Am. Hist. Rev.
513 (1954).

[275] *See, e.g.*, The Maret, 145 F.2d 431, 442 (3d Cir. 1944); Estonian State Cargo & Passenger S.S. Line
v. United States, 116 F. Supp. 447 (Ct. Cl. 1953); Latvian State Cargo & Passenger S.S. Line v. Clark,
80 F. Supp. 683 (D.D.C. 1948), *aff'd*, 188 F.2d 1000 (D.C. Cir. 1951); A/S Merilaid & Co. v. Chase Nat'l
Bank, 71 N.Y.S.2d 377 (N.Y. Sup. Ct. 1947).

[276] *See* Thomas D. Grant, The Recognition of States: Law and Practice in Debate and
Evolution 133 (1999).

[277] *See* G.A. Res. 67/19, pmbl., ¶ 2 (Nov. 29, 2012) (acknowledging the right of the Palestinian
people to their independent state of Palestine, and according to Palestine nonmember observer state
status in the United Nations). The vote was 138 in favor, 9 against (including the United States), and
41 abstentions.

[278] S.C. Res. 217 (May 6, 1965); *see* U.S. Dep't of State, Memorandum on Southern Rhodesia, ¶ 7
(Jan. 23, 1967), in XXIV Foreign Relations of the United States, 1964–68 (1999) (Doc. 553).

[279] *See* S.C. Res. 276 (Jan. 30, 1970); S.C. Res. 264 (Mar. 20, 1969). The International Court of Justice
followed suit. Legal Consequences for States of the Continued Presence of South Africa in Namibia
(South West Africa) Notwithstanding Security Council Resolution 276 (1970), Advisory Opinion,
1971 I.C.J. 16, at 46 (June 21). For rejection by the U.N. General Assembly (with U.S. support) of

beginning in 1975, the Security Council adopted resolutions with U.S. support in effect denying Indonesia's authority over that territory.[280] After Turkey's 1974 invasion of Cyprus and the proclamation by Turkish Cypriots of a new state, the Turkish Republic of Northern Cyprus, the executive branch voted in favor of a Security Council resolution calling upon "all States not to recognize any Cypriot State other than the Republic of Cyprus."[281] In the face of efforts by Bosnian Serbs in 1992 to establish a Republika Srpska, the United States supported a Security Council resolution calling for respect of Bosnia's territorial integrity, and affirming that "any entities unilaterally declared or arrangements imposed in contravention thereof will not be accepted."[282]

The president's power to withdraw recognition of an existing state is perhaps more complicated. The United States is a party to the 1933 Montevideo Convention, which provides in Article 6 that recognition is "unconditional and irrevocable."[283] The president's charge to faithfully execute the law includes complying with U.S. treaty obligations, such that the Montevideo Convention, would appear to limit presidential discretion, at least as between states party to that convention. Moreover, the provisions of the U.N. Charter speak of its members as "states," such that a presidential decision to no longer regard a U.N. member as a "state" would likely be inconsistent with U.S. obligations under that treaty. Even so, in practice, the executive has in essence "derecognized" states in the context of state dissolution, such as in the breakup of the Socialist Federal Republic of Yugoslavia in 1991–1992.

B. Recognition of a Foreign Government Coming to Power Extraconstitutionally

The power to "recognize" is seen as comprising both the power to recognize an entity as a new state and the power to recognize which entity serves as the government of an existing state. The latter form of recognition arises in situations where a government has come to power through a process not contemplated by the state's internal constitutional process, such as through a military coup or an insurgency.

South Africa's effort to stand up a new state of the Transkei as a homeland for part of South Africa's black population, see G.A. Res. 31/6, ¶¶ 2–3 (Oct. 26, 1976).

[280] See S.C. Res. 384 (Dec. 22, 1975); see also G.A. Res. 3485 (Dec. 12, 1975).
[281] S.C. Res. 541 (Nov. 18, 1983); see also S.C. Res. 550 (May 11, 1984).
[282] S.C. Res. 787, ¶ 3 (Nov. 16, 1992).
[283] See Inter-American Convention on Rights and Duties of States art. 6, Dec. 26, 1933, 49 Stat. 3097, 165 L.N.T.S. 19 [hereinafter Montevideo Convention].

Starting with recognition of the republican government of the French Revolution, the power to recognize new governments has been considered to fall within the exclusive province of the president. President Wilson—himself a scholar on constitutional powers of the federal government—stated in a message to Congress in 1919 that "the initiative in directing the relations of our Government with foreign governments is assigned by the Constitution to the Executive, and to the Executive, only."[284] In *National City Bank of New York v. Republic of China*, the Supreme Court stated that the recognition of foreign governments is a function of the executive branch and is wholly outside the competence of the judiciary.[285] Similarly, in *Banco Nacional de Cuba v. Sabbatino*, the Supreme Court emphatically declared "[p]olitical recognition is exclusively a function of the Executive."[286]

The policy by which the executive branch has decided to recognize foreign governments, however, has evolved over time.[287] Jefferson's approach to recognition of the revolutionary government in France—as he put it in internal correspondence, that "[i]t accords with our principles to acknowledge any Government to be rightful which is formed by the will of the nation, substantially declared,"[288] such that "[t]he will of the nation is the only thing essential to be regarded"[289]—appears to contain within it two potentially different ideas. The first, that what matters is whether the entity in question in fact controls the territory that it purports to govern, is referred to as the *de facto* theory of recognition; U.S. recognition of the revolutionary French government was understood to embody this approach.[290] Yet Jefferson's reference to "the will of the nation" as "the only essential thing"—even if leavened, in his correspondence, with deference to the idea that every state "may govern itself according to whatever form it pleases, and change these forms at its own will"[291]—introduced the idea that the entity must, in some sense, reflect the nation's will, and perhaps that of its people.

The *de facto* approach was U.S. doctrine at least through the Civil War, and entailed little inquiry into whether a new government reflected the will of the

---

[284] Letter from Woodrow Wilson, President, to Albert B. Fall, Senator (Dec. 9, 1919), *in* STAFF OF S. COMM. ON FOREIGN AFFAIRS, 66TH CONG., REP. OF SENATOR ALBERT B. FALL EXAMINING INTO MEXICAN AFFAIRS 4 (Comm. Print 1920).

[285] Nat'l City Bank of N.Y. v. Republic of China, 348 U.S. 356, 358 (1955); *see also* Nat'l Union Fire Ins. Co. of Pittsburgh v. Republic of China, 254 F.2d 177 (4th Cir. 1958).

[286] Banco Nacional de Cuba v. Sabbatino, 376 U.S. 398, 410 (1964).

[287] In *United States v. Pink*, 315 U.S. 203, 229 (1942), the Supreme Court observed that the authority to recognize governments "is not limited to a determination of the government to be recognized. It includes the power to determine the policy which is to govern the question of recognition."

[288] *See* Letter from Thomas Jefferson (Nov. 7, 1792), *supra* note 70, at 120.

[289] *See* Letter from Thomas Jefferson (March 12, 1793), *supra* note 70, at 120.

[290] *See* Reinstein, *supra* note 108, at 11–12; Reinstein, *supra* note 253, at 196–98.

[291] *See* Letter from Thomas Jefferson (March 12, 1793), *supra* note 70, at 120.

people.[292] When considering the rise of yet another extraconstitutional government in France (ending the reign of King Louis-Philippe and creating the French Second Republic), Secretary of State (and later President) James Buchanan asserted in 1848 that the United States had "from its origin, always recognized *de facto* governments," that it recognized "the right of all nations to create and re-form their political institutions according to their own will and pleasure," and that it was "sufficient for us to know that a government exists capable of maintaining itself; and then its recognition on our part inevitably follows."[293] In such instances, the simple fact that the new government successfully seized control, and that the population was obeying it, was typically viewed as sufficient for establishing the "will" of the people in accepting the government.

As matters developed, presidential policy came at times to place heavier reliance on the notion that the government must have popular support, an approach typically associated with President Wilson's attitude toward the overthrow of governments in Latin American states during his administrations. Yet even beforehand, the inherent U.S. sentiment in favor of democratic governance influenced the recognition policy of some administrations. Secretary of State Seward, in considering whether the United States should recognize a new government in Peru, stated: "What we wait for in this case is the legal evidence that the existing administration has been deliberately accepted by the people of Peru. When a republican form of government is constitutionally established, we hasten to recognize the administration . . . ."[294] Interestingly, Seward seemed to believe that a U.S. recognition policy that did not concern itself with democracy "would necessarily tend to impair the constitutional vigor *of our own government*, and thus favor disorganization, disintegration, and anarchy throughout the American continent."[295]

Factors other than the entity's control and democratic pedigree have also played a role in U.S. recognition policy. Promoting stability in a country or region is sometimes of paramount interest, as appears to have been the case in the cautious approach of the Clinton administration to recognition of the former Yugoslavia republics. President Clinton also expressly stated that he was using the possibility of U.S. recognition of the government of Angola as "leverage towards promoting an end to the civil war and hostilities" in that country.[296]

---

[292] Reinstein, *supra* note 253, at 197–98; *see* 20 Op. O.L.C., *supra* note 230, at 194 n.11 (citing Construction of the Mesilla Treaty, 7 Op. Att'y Gen. 582, 587 (1855) for the proposition that U.S. recognition policy originally accepted "any foreign government existing *de facto*").

[293] Letter from James Buchanan, Sec'y of State, to Richard Rush, Am. Minister at Paris (Feb. 24, 1848), *in* 1 MOORE DIGEST, at 123, 124 (emphasis in original).

[294] 1868 PAPERS RELATING TO THE FOREIGN RELATIONS OF THE UNITED STATES 864 (1869).

[295] *Id.* (emphasis added).

[296] Remarks and an Exchange With Reporters Prior to Discussions With Archbishop Desmond Tutu, 1 PUB. PAPERS 704, 704 (May 19, 1993).

As with the nonrecognition of states, the power to recognize governments subsumes within it a presidential power *not* to recognize new governments.[297] For instance, in 1913 President Wilson refused to recognize the Huerta government of Mexico, since it had taken control in Mexico through revolution and force of arms. That lack of recognition apparently contributed to Victoriano Heurta's downfall in 1914. After the Russian revolution of 1917 and the establishment of Russia's communist government, U.S. presidents from Wilson to Hoover continued to recognize the provisional government and refused to recognize the communist regime. Only in 1933 did President Roosevelt formally recognize the communist regime.[298] Similarly, when the communist government of China came to power in 1949, presidents from Truman to Johnson declined to recognize that regime as the government of China, favoring instead the nationalist regime resident on Taiwan.[299] Only with President Nixon in 1972 was *de facto* recognition accorded to the Chinese communist government, followed by *de jure* recognition in 1978.[300] Political reasons have driven other incidents of nonrecognition; the United States explicitly refused to recognize the People's Movement for the Liberation of Angola government in Angola in 1979 due to its Marxist leanings,[301] while the government of Manuel Antonio Noriega that seized power in Panama was refused recognition in 1989 shortly before U.S. intervention.[302]

Practice confirms as well the power of the president to withdraw recognition from a government that was previously recognized by the United States, even if done during the pendency of a case before a U.S. court.[303] Recognition of the communist USSR government ran in tandem with the withdrawal of recognition from the Russian provisional government,[304] just as recognition of the communist government of China ran in tandem with withdrawal of recognition from the nationalist regime.[305] Reflecting on this historical practice, OLC has opined that the "Executive's recognition power necessarily subsumes within itself the power to withhold or deny recognition, to determine the conditions on which recognition will be accorded, and to define the nature and extent of diplomatic contacts with an as-yet unrecognized government."[306]

---

[297] *See, e.g.*, Gov't of Fr. v. Isbrandtsen-Moller Co., 48 F. Supp. 631 (S.D.N.Y. 1943).
[298] *See* JOHN LEWIS GADDIS, RUSSIA, THE SOVIET UNION, AND THE UNITED STATES: AN INTERPRETIVE HISTORY 111–22 (2d ed. 1978).
[299] *See* U.S. Policy on Nonrecognition of Communist China, 39 DEP'T ST. BULL. 385 (1958).
[300] *See* Diplomatic Relations Between the United States and the People's Republic of China, 2 PUB. PAPERS 2264 (Dec. 15, 1978).
[301] *See* Diplomatic Relations: Angola, 1979 DIGEST OF U.S. PRACTICE, at 110.
[302] *See* U.S. Severs Diplomatic Contact with Noriega Regime, 89 DEP'T ST. BULL. 69 (1989).
[303] *See* Republic of Vietnam v. Pfizer, Inc., 556 F.2d 892, 894 (8th Cir. 1977).
[304] *See* State of Russia v. Nat'l City Bank of N.Y., 69 F.2d 44 (2d Cir. 1934) (finding that the exchange of diplomatic notes in November 1933 establishing diplomatic relations between United States and Government of Union of Soviet Socialist Republics resulted in the former government of the state of Russia no longer being recognized).
[305] *See* Goldwater v. Carter, 617 F.2d 697, 707–08 (D.C. Cir. 1979).
[306] 20 Op. O.L.C., *supra* note 230, at 194 (citations omitted).

In the second half of the twentieth century, as various nondemocratic regimes came to power, principally in developing states, the executive branch began de-emphasizing the issuance of a formal statement of "recognition" when a new regime comes to power. This trend culminated in a 1977 announcement by the Department of State, which explained that formal recognition of new governments was creating "the impression among other nations that the United States approved of those governments it recognized and disapproved of those from which it withheld recognition," which in turn "affected our decisions in ways that have not always advanced U.S. interests."[307] Consequently, the Department said: "In recent years, U.S. practice has been to deemphasize and avoid the use of recognition in cases of changes of governments and to concern ourselves with the question of whether we wish to have diplomatic relations with the new governments."[308] In light of that that change, "establishment of relations does not involve approval or disapproval but merely demonstrates a willingness on our part to conduct our affairs with other governments directly."[309]

Consistent with that approach, the United States declined to issue formal statements of recognition in the 1960s with respect to various Latin American and African regimes; in the 1970s with respect to new governments in Afghanistan, Bangladesh, Cyprus, El Salvador, Greece, Sudan, and Vietnam; and in the 1980s with respect to Haiti, Nigeria, and Sudan.[310] Yet, somewhat confusingly, in some instances the United States *did* issue formal statements of recognition, such as in 1978 when U.S. policy switched with respect to the government of China,[311] or when the Aquino government was recognized in the Philippines in 1986.[312]

In general, however, the contemporary approach avoids a formal statement of "recognition" of a government in favor of other types of statements that indicate acceptance of a new regime. For example, in anticipation of Hamid Karzai's inauguration as Chairman of the Afghan Interim Authority (AIA) in December 2002, the Department of State simply announced that the United States would deal with the AIA when it assumed power.[313] After the toppling of Saddam Hussein's government in Iraq, the U.S. government announced in June 2004 that "full sovereignty was transferred to a new Iraqi interim government. The Coalition

---

[307] Diplomatic Recognition: A Foreign Relations Outline, 77 Dep't St. Bull. 462, 463 (1977). For a similar congressional statement that U.S. diplomatic relations should not signal approval of a new regime, see S. Rep. No. 91-338 (1969).

[308] Diplomatic Recognition: A Foreign Relations Outline, 77 Dep't St. Bull. 462, 463 (1977).

[309] *Id.*

[310] *See* Mary Beth West & Sean D. Murphy, *The Impact on U.S. Litigation of Non-Recognition of Foreign Governments*, 26 Stan. J. Int'l L. 435, 457 (1990).

[311] *See supra* text accompanying footnotes 299–300.

[312] *See* Secretary's Statement, Feb. 25, 1986, 86 Dep't St. Bull. 69 (Apr. 1986).

[313] *See* Press Release, Dep't of State, Afg.: Reopening of US Mission (Dec. 14, 2001), https://perma.cc/3QUB-WRQZ.

Provisional Authority, led by Ambassador Paul Bremer, ceased to exist. The Iraqi Government is now running the day-today [sic] operations of its country."[314]

C. Collateral Effects of Nonrecognition in U.S. Courts

U.S. recognition or nonrecognition of a foreign state or government has serious collateral consequences for the ability of an entity to participate in, to have its acts given effect by, or to obtain sovereign immunity from, U.S. courts. As noted previously, U.S. courts generally have viewed presidential decisions as dispositive on whether a foreign entity is a state or government. Nonetheless, in the area of collateral effects before U.S. courts, presidential power has not always been given full effect.

1. Inability to Have Access to U.S. Courts as a Foreign State/Government

Article III of the U.S. Constitution provides that the judicial power extends to all cases affecting "Ambassadors, other public Ministers and Consuls . . . to Controversies . . . between a State, or the Citizens thereof, and foreign States, Citizens or Subjects."[315] By statute, federal jurisdiction extends to civil actions by and against foreign states, regardless of the amount in controversy.[316] According to the Supreme Court in *Pfizer, Inc. v. Government of India*, "[i]t has long been established that only governments recognized by the United States and at peace with us are entitled to access to our courts, and that it is within the exclusive power of the Executive Branch to determine which nations are entitled to sue."[317] In that case, India—a recognized state—was held to be a "person" within the meaning of Section 4 of the Clayton Act, and hence entitled to sue in U.S. courts for treble damages under the federal antitrust laws to the same extent as any other plaintiff. Similarly, in *Guaranty Trust Co. v. United States*, the Court stated that the "rights of a sovereign state are vested in the state rather than in any particular government which may purport to represent it, and that suit in its behalf may be maintained in our courts only by that government which has been recognized by the political department of our own government . . . ."[318]

The fact that the recognized government has no actual power in its state—such as the lack of control over Panama by the government of

---

[314] *See* Bureau of Public Affairs, Fact Sheet, *Iraq's Transition to Self-Government*, U.S. DEP'T OF STATE (June 28, 2004), https://perma.cc/LWX3-7WEK.

[315] U.S. CONST. art. III, § 2, cl. 1.

[316] 28 U.S.C. § 1330 (2018).

[317] Pfizer, Inc. v. Gov't of India, 434 U.S. 308, 319–20 (1978).

[318] Guar. Tr. Co. v. United States, 304 U.S. 126, 137 (1938) (citations omitted).

President Eric Arturo Delvalle during 1988–1989 (after Delvalle was ousted by Noriega and his allies), or the lack of control over Haiti by the government of President Jean-Bertrand Aristide during 1991–1994 (after Aristide was ousted by military and police authorities)—has had no bearing on judicial determinations concerning access to U.S. courts.[319] By contrast, where the foreign state or government has not been recognized, it is denied access to U.S. courts even if it fully controls its state, such as occurred when the socialist governments of the USSR[320] and Vietnam[321] sought access prior to their formal recognition.

As this suggests, recognition is an important determinant, but it is not the only consideration. Access is not denied based solely on the lack of diplomatic relations: if relations have been severed, but the United States still recognizes the foreign government, that government can have access to U.S. courts.[322] Yet even the lack of formal "recognition" does not necessarily preclude access to U.S. courts. When, during the second half of the twentieth century, the executive branch began de-emphasizing formal recognition, courts were forced to surmise on their own whether the U.S. government accepted a new regime or not. If the U.S. government has opened up diplomatic relations with a new regime, the new regime is deemed to be entitled to access U.S. courts. Even if the United States does *not* open up diplomatic relations, it may undertake other acts that signal to U.S. courts that access is to be permitted. For example, in *Iran v. Gould*, the United States declined to indicate, one way or the other, whether it recognized the Islamic government of Iran, but it filed a statement of interest indicating that the "Executive Branch believes Iran should be afforded access to U.S. courts for the purpose of recognition and enforcement of [Iran-U.S. Claims] Tribunal awards rendered in its favor," and that this "express statement by the Executive should be treated as dispositive of the issue of the standing of the government of Iran, without regard to issues of recognition and diplomatic relations."[323] The district court deferred to this statement and allowed the Iranian government

[319] *See, e.g.,* Republic of Panama v. Citizens & S. Int'l Bank, 682 F. Supp. 1544 (S.D. Fla. 1988); Republic of Panama v. Republic Nat'l Bank, 681 F. Supp. 1066 (S.D.N.Y. 1988); Lafontant v. Aristide, 844 F. Supp. 128 (E.D.N.Y. 1994).

[320] *See* The Penza, 277 F. 91 (E.D.N.Y. 1921); The Rogdai, 278 F. 294 (N.D. Cal. 1920); Russian Socialist Federated Soviet Republic v. Cibrario, 139 N.E. 259 (N.Y. 1923).

[321] Republic of Vietnam v. Pfizer, Inc., 556 F.2d 892 (8th Cir. 1977).

[322] *See, e.g.,* Banco Nacional de Cuba v. Sabbatino, 376 U.S. 398, 408–12 (1964) (finding that the lack of diplomatic relations with Cuba did not mean the Cuban government was not recognized, nor that its state-owned bank was precluded from pursuing claims on its behalf); Japanese Gov't v. Commercial Cas. Ins. Co., 101 F. Supp. 243 (S.D.N.Y. 1951) (finding that Japan's lack of diplomatic representation in the United States following World War II did not alter its status as a sovereign government recognized as such by the United States).

[323] Statement of Interest of the United States at 7, Iran v. Gould, No. 87-03673 (C.D. Cal. Jan. 14, 1988), *quoted in* West & Murphy, *supra* note 310, at 461.

standing, saying that "the crystal-clear governing rule is that access to our courts is a matter strictly within the purview of the Executive Branch."[324]

A similar outcome occurred in *National Petrochemical Co. of Iran v. The M/ T Stolt Sheaf*, where the Second Circuit detected that the U.S. practice in recognizing governments had altered. Given that the U.S. Department of State "has sometimes refrained from announcing recognition of a new government because grants of recognition have been misinterpreted as pronouncements of approval," the court explained, it is now the case that "the absence of formal recognition cannot serve as the touchstone for determining whether the Executive Branch has 'recognized' a foreign nation for the purpose of granting that government access to United States courts."[325]

While the courts accept executive branch recognition (or its functional equivalent) as conclusive, the specific *legal consequences* that flow from such recognition under U.S. law remain to be decided by the courts. The Supreme Court noted in *Guaranty Trust Co.* that while the determination of *what* government represents a foreign state is a political question, once that determination has been made, courts "are free to draw for themselves its legal consequences in litigations pending before them."[326] Normally, the legal consequence of non-recognition of a foreign government (or its equivalent) is that the government will be denied access to a U.S. court, but there are some situations where access will not be denied. Thus, where the access is being sought by a corporation owned by the unrecognized entity, U.S. courts have allowed access in the same manner as access would be granted to any corporation.[327]

Moreover, given Congress' power to regulate the jurisdiction of federal courts, it would appear that Congress can accord access to unrecognized governments or states by statute, even though doing so might be construed as infringing upon executive power. The principal example is the Taiwan Relations Act, which provides in part that the "capacity of Taiwan to sue and be sued in courts in the United States, in accordance with the laws of the United States, shall not be abrogated, infringed, modified, denied, or otherwise affected in any way by the absence of diplomatic relations or recognition," and further that no "requirement,

---

[324] Iran v. Gould, No. 87-03673, slip. op. at 3–4 (C.D. Cal. Jan 14, 1988), *quoted in* West & Murphy, *supra* note 310, at 461–62. This portion of the district court's opinion was not appealed. *See* Iran v. Gould, Inc., 887 F.2d 1357, 1361 n.7 (9th Cir. 1989).

[325] Nat'l Petrochemical Co. of Iran v. M/T Stolt Sheaf, 860 F.2d 551, 554 (2d Cir. 1988) (citations omitted); *see also* Org. for Inv. Econ. & Tech. Assistance v. Shack & Kimball, No. 85-0437, 1988 WL 143323 (D.D.C. Dec. 28, 1988). Even where the executive branch has expressly stated that it does *not* recognize a foreign government, it may still call upon U.S. courts to allow access for that government. *See* Transportes Aereos de Angl. v. Ronair, Inc., 544 F. Supp. 858 (D. Del. 1982).

[326] Guar. Tr. Co. v. United States, 304 U.S. 126, 137–38 (1938); *see also* Bank of China v. Wells Fargo Bank & Union Tr., 92 F. Supp. 920 (N.D. Cal. 1950), *modified*, 209 F.2d 467 (9th Cir. 1953).

[327] *See* Russ. Volunteer Fleet v. United States, 282 U.S. 481 (1931); The Maret, 145 F.2d 431, 439 (3d Cir. 1944); The Tenbergen, 48 F.2d 363 (E.D.N.Y. 1930).

whether expressed or implied, under the laws of the United States with respect to maintenance of diplomatic relations or recognition shall be applicable with respect to Taiwan."[328] Presumably if Congress were to adopt a similar statute with respect to other entities not recognized as states or as a government, it too would be regarded as a permissible exercise of congressional powers, so long as it were consistent with Article III.

Finally, an exception to the general rule of non-access may arise with respect to access to U.S. courts *by the nationals* of a foreign entity. Normally a party before a U.S. court can invoke federal court jurisdiction by asserting that the action is between "citizens of a State and citizens or subjects of a foreign state,"[329] a basis that might be thought unavailable when the entity of the person's nationality is not a recognized foreign state. Yet the Supreme Court found in *J.P. Morgan Chase Bank v. Traffic Stream (BVI) Infrastructure Ltd.* that a foreign "national" is a "citizen or subject" of a foreign state even where that state is not formally recognized by the United States.[330] In that case, the court found that a corporation established under the laws of the British Virgin Islands is a "citizen or subject" of a foreign state, even though the British Virgin Islands is an overseas territory of the United Kingdom that has not been recognized by the United States as a state.[331] It may be that this case is best limited to situations where a corporate entity has status pursuant to incorporation in a substate entity, given that the United Kingdom was a recognized state and had permitted its overseas territory to create corporate structures. In situations where the entity is not a part of a recognized state, the result may be different, as in the 1947 case of *Klausner v. Levy*.[332] There, the district court concluded that it lacked the power to accept an instrumentality of Palestine for the purpose of determining whether diversity jurisdiction existed, seeing such recognition as constitutionally allocated to the executive branch.

2. Inability to Claim Foreign Sovereign Immunity from Suit

Just as an unrecognized state or government cannot ordinarily secure access to U.S. courts as a state or government, so too the unrecognized foreign entity typically is not allowed to invoke sovereign immunity from suit in U.S. courts.

As discussed in greater depth in Chapter 4,[333] the federal statute by which U.S. courts have jurisdiction over foreign states is the Foreign Sovereign

---

[328] 22 U.S.C. § 3303(b)(7)–(8) (2018).
[329] 28 U.S.C. § 1332(a)(2) (2018).
[330] 536 U.S. 88 (2002).
[331] For prior lower court decisions that had reached a contrary conclusion, see Koehler v. Bank of Berm. (N.Y.) Ltd., 209 F.3d 130 (2d Cir. 2000), *amended by*, 229 F.3d 424 (2d Cir. 2000); U.S. Fid. & Guar. Co. v. Braspetro Oil Servs. Co., 199 F.3d 94 (2d Cir. 1999).
[332] 83 F. Supp. 599 (E.D. Va. 1949).
[333] *See* Chapter 4 § V.

Immunities Act (FSIA).[334] When the FSIA was adopted, the House Committee's report noted that previously courts generally deferred to the executive branch as to whether an entity was entitled to sovereign immunity, but that such practice was inconsistent with that of other countries, which usually permitted courts to determine the issue as a matter of international law.[335] Hence, one purpose of the statute was to remove immunity decisions from the purview of the executive branch, since "decisions on claims by foreign states to sovereign immunity are best made by the judiciary on the basis of a statutory regime which incorporates standards recognized under international law."[336]

Since adoption of the FSIA, U.S. courts have tended, when the issue arises, to conduct their own assessment of whether a foreign entity constituted a state (or government of a state) within the meaning of international law, often relying upon the conditions set forth in sources such as the *Restatement (Third)*[337] or the Montevideo Convention.[338] In doing so, courts analyze international law as not requiring recognition by other states when determining whether a state exists and thereby adopt the declaratory theory of recognition.[339] For example, in *Morgan Guaranty Trust*, the Second Circuit used the four basic criteria found in both the *Restatement (Third)* and the Montevideo Convention when determining that "Palau simply does not have the attributes of statehood, and cannot be considered a foreign sovereign" within the meaning of the FSIA.[340] The same approach was taken by the First and Second Circuits in determining that the Palestine Liberation Organization was not a state for purposes of invoking immunity from suit in U.S. courts.[341]

While the courts have shown some independence in this area, the Supreme Court's decision in *Austria v. Altmann*[342] recognizes a continuing role for the executive branch. There the Court noted that, in FSIA cases, the Department of State has retained authority to file "statements of interest suggesting that courts decline to exercise jurisdiction in particular cases implicating foreign sovereign immunity."[343] The cautious language, however, confirms that it is the court's prerogative to make the final determination of whether immunity is warranted.

---

[334] *See* 28 U.S.C. §§ 1330, 1332, 1391(f), 1441(d), 1602–11 (2018).
[335] *See* H.R. REP. NO. 94-1487 at 7 (1976).
[336] *Id.* at 14.
[337] RESTATEMENT (THIRD) § 201.
[338] *See* Montevideo Convention, *supra* note 283.
[339] *See* RESTATEMENT (THIRD) § 202.
[340] Morgan Guar. Tr. Co. v. Republic of Palau, 924 F.2d 1237, 1244 (2d Cir. 1991).
[341] Ungar v. Palestine Liberation Org., 402 F.3d 274, 292 (1st Cir. 2005); Klinghoffer v. S.N.C. Achille Lauro Ed Altri, 937 F.2d 44, 47–49 (2d Cir. 1991). For further discussion, see Chapter 4 § V(A)(3)(a).
[342] 541 U.S. 677 (2004).
[343] *Id.* at 701.

3. Inability to Control Foreign State Property Located in the United States

A further significant effect of presidential recognition or nonrecognition concerns the ability of foreign entities to gain access to assets of the state that they purport to represent. This issue typically arises in the context of two or more entities vying against each other to gain the use of financial assets, such as reserves held with the Federal Reserve Bank of New York.

As a rule, whatever entity is recognized by the executive branch as the government of the state is the entity granted access to those assets.[344] For example, the post–World War II government in the Netherlands was precluded from recovering bonds held by the Federal Reserve Bank of New York, which had been seized from Dutch citizens by Germany during the war, because the executive branch still recognized the Dutch government-in-exile as the *de jure* government of the Netherlands.[345] Just prior to the U.S. intervention in Panama in 1989, the *de facto* government of Panama was led by Noriega, while the *de jure* government—recognized by the United States—was led by Guillermo Endara (who was elected in 1989, but prevented from assuming power by Noriega). When representatives of both governments sought to obtain control over funds and property located in the United States belonging to Panama's national airline, the court only accepted the status of the Endara government and refused to allow attorneys of the Noriega regime to intervene in the litigation.[346]

The executive's role is safeguarded by Congress, by a means that also safeguards U.S. financial institutions. U.S. law protects any federal reserve bank, or any bank insured by the Federal Deposit Insurance Corporation, by declaring that it is lawful for the bank that receives assets from a recognized foreign state to then deliver those assets to a person (or their designee) "who is recognized by the Secretary of State as being the accredited representative of such foreign state to the Government of the United States . . . ."[347] That provision was crafted during World War II to protect banks in their activities relating to European governments in exile.

4. Public/External Acts of the Nonrecognized Foreign Entity Not Given Effect by U.S. Courts

U.S. courts regularly give legal effect to the acts of recognized foreign governments, with particular deference given under the Act of State doctrine when those acts occur within the territory of the foreign state.[348] Even when a

---

[344] *See, e.g.*, Bank of China v. Wells Fargo Bank & Union Tr., 92 F. Supp. 920 (N.D. Cal. 1950), *modified*, 209 F.2d 467 (9th Cir. 1953).

[345] *See* State of the Netherlands v. Fed. Reserve Bank of N.Y., 99 F. Supp. 655 (S.D.N.Y. 1951).

[346] *See* Republic of Panama v. Air Pan. Internacional, S.A., 745 F. Supp. 669 (S.D. Fla. 1988).

[347] 12 U.S.C. § 632 (2018).

[348] For further discussion of the act of state doctrine, see Chapter 4 § III.

recognized foreign government loses U.S. recognition, U.S. courts still give its acts legal effect for the period during which the U.S. recognition existed.[349] In part, this approach is because certain types of legal acts, such as a contract entered into by a government, are viewed as binding *the state*, and hence still possessing legal effect even if that government is de-recognized and another takes its place.[350]

The acts of an entity that is not recognized as having sovereign authority at the relevant time are often not given effect by U.S. courts.[351] Thus, when the USSR seized control of Latvia and purported to nationalize Latvian ships, U.S. courts declined to accord any legal effect to the nationalization with respect to vessels that made their way to U.S. ports.[352] Indeed, courts seem reluctant to appear at cross purposes with the political branches by according legal significance to the acts of entities that have not been recognized. Yet there are exceptions. Thus, New York's highest state court gave effect to a nationalization decree when it related to property located in the unrecognized state. In *M. Salimoff v. Standard Oil Co.*, the court stated that the unrecognized communist regime in the USSR "may be objectionable in a political sense," but "is not unrecognizable as a real governmental power which can give title to property within its limits."[353] The *Salimoff* decision represents a strand in U.S. jurisprudence that, in certain circumstances, accepts the practical reality of an unrecognized government or state, where that entity is fully operating in a sovereign capacity within its territory, even if it is politically at odds with the executive branch. While U.S. courts as a general matter will support the executive's denial of status to the foreign entity, U.S. courts will nevertheless give effect to that entity's acts in situations where not doing so creates practical problems.

Exceptionally, then, when an unrecognized entity engages in acts that are local in nature (such as in *Salimoff*), concern private affairs, or would perpetrate an apparent injustice, U.S. courts may give those acts legal effect.[354] In *Upright*

---

[349] *See* Guar. Tr. Co. v. United States, 304 U.S. 126, 140 (1938) (finding that the later recognition of the Soviet government left unaffected those legal consequences of the previous recognition of the Provisional Government and its representatives).

[350] *See* Am. Bell Int'l, Inc. v. Iran, 474 F. Supp. 420, 423 (S.D.N.Y. 1979) (asserting that "American courts have traditionally viewed contract rights as vesting not in any particular government but in the state of which that government is an agent").

[351] *See, e.g.*, Fed. Republic Germany v. Elicofon, 358 F. Supp. 747 (E.D.N.Y. 1972), *aff'd*, 478 F.2d 231 (2d Cir. 1973); Stiftung v. V.E.B. Carl Zeiss, Jena, 293 F. Supp. 892, 900 (S.D.N.Y. 1968), *modified*, 433 F.2d 686 (2d Cir. 1970).

[352] *See* Latvian State Cargo & Passenger S.S. Line v. Clark, 80 F. Supp. 683 (D.D.C. 1948), *aff'd*, 188 F.2d 1000 (D.C. Cir. 1951).

[353] M. Salimoff & Co. v. Standard Oil Co., 186 N.E. 679, 682 (N.Y. 1933).

[354] *See, e.g.*, Daniunas v. Simutis, 481 F. Supp. 132 (S.D.N.Y. 1978); *In re* Estate of Bielinis, 284 N.Y.S.2d 819 (N.Y. Sur. Ct. 1967), *aff'd*, 292 N.Y.S.2d 363 (N.Y. App. Div. 1968); *In re* Luberg, 243 N.Y.S.2d 747 (N.Y. App. Div. 1963).

v. Mercury Business Machines Co.,[355] Mercury purchased typewriters from an East German government-owned manufacturer, but then refused to pay the debt on grounds that the government was not recognized by the United States. The New York court again rejected the argument, stating that even an unrecognized government "may nevertheless have *de facto* existence which is juridically cognizable," one that "may affect private rights and obligations arising either as a result of activity in, or with persons or corporations within, the territory controlled by such *de facto* government."[356] Notably, in some cases, such as *Upright*, the matter is being litigated in U.S. courts because the underlying debt or property has been assigned by the unrecognized entity to a U.S. national, and therefore the court's willingness to give legal effect to the act of the unrecognized entity is likely motivated in part by a desire to protect the interests of a U.S. national.

Here, too, it would appear that Congress can provide direction to the courts. In the Taiwan Relations Act, U.S. courts are instructed to give effect to Taiwan government acts notwithstanding the lack of U.S. recognition of that government. The statute provides in part that the absence of recognition "shall not abrogate, infringe, modify, deny, or otherwise affect in any way any rights or obligations (including but not limited to those involving contracts, debts, or property interests of any kind) under the laws of the United States heretofore or hereafter acquired by or with respect to Taiwan," nor "affect in any way the ownership of or other rights or interests in properties, tangible and intangible, and other things of value, owned or held on or prior to December 31, 1978, or thereafter acquired or earned by the governing authorities on Taiwan."[357] The Taiwan Relations Act is not *sui generis* on this point; under various U.S. statutes, such as on counterfeiting currency or murdering officials, U.S. courts are instructed to apply the statute "irrespective of recognition."[358]

D. Conclusion of Executive Agreements Incidental to Recognition

In the course of the twentieth century, the president has used the "recognition" power as a means of supporting sole executive agreements, which sometimes dispose of claims as an ancillary or incidental matter. Two cases relating to President Roosevelt's recognition of the communist government of the USSR

---

[355] 213 N.Y.S.2d 417 (N.Y. App. Div. 1961). For analysis, see Stanley Lubman, *The Unrecognized Government in American Courts*: Upright v. Mercury Business Machines, 62 COLUM. L. REV. 275 (1962).

[356] *Upright*, 213 N.Y.S.2d at 419 (emphasis in original).

[357] 22 U.S.C. § 3303(b)(3) (2018).

[358] *See, e.g.*, 18 U.S.C. §§ 11, 1116 (2018).

laid the groundwork for this incidental power, *United States v. Belmont*[359] and, five years later, *United States v. Pink*.[360]

In *Belmont*, the Soviet regime had nationalized a Russian corporation, which in turn owned a deposit held by a New York banker. Incidental to the U.S. recognition of the Soviet regime, the Roosevelt administration negotiated a sole executive agreement (one not submitted to the Senate for consent nor both Houses for a majority vote), typically referred to as the Litvinov Assignment, which assigned to the U.S. government all Soviet claims against U.S. nationals.[361] At the same time, the U.S. government espoused and settled all U.S. nationals' claims against the Soviet regime, with the intention of using proceeds from the Soviet assignment as a means of paying U.S. claimants. When the U.S. government sought to obtain the deposit from the New York banker, however, New York courts refused to recognize the assignment, finding that New York policy did not accept that the Soviet regime had good title to such assets, as the nationalization was an unlawful act. The Supreme Court overturned the New York courts, stating that, given the president's recognition of the Soviet government, the effect was to validate "all acts of the Soviet Government here involved from the commencement of its existence" and that "the negotiations, acceptance of the assignment and agreements and understandings in respect thereof were within the competence of the President may not be doubted."[362]

In the course of its decision, the Court issued its striking statement concerning foreign relations federalism, opining that "[i]n respect of all international negotiations and compacts, and in respect of our foreign relations generally, state lines disappear. As to such purposes the State of New York does not exist."[363] The willingness of the Court to see the recognition power as supporting a sole executive agreement that could trump state law was no doubt influenced by the deteriorating situation internationally (Hitler had by this time abrogated German obligations under the Treaty of Versailles, was sending German troops into the Rhineland, and the following year would annex Austria and move troops into the Sudetenland), as well as the expansive language concerning the power of the executive in the field of foreign affairs in its decision in *Curtiss-Wright*, decided just one year earlier.

Similar facts were at issue in *United States v. Pink*, where a Russian insurance company organized by the former government of Russia had assets in New York that were nationalized and expropriated by the communist regime of the USSR. The U.S. government initially tried to obtain control of the assets based on the

---

[359] 301 U.S. 324 (1937). For further discussion of *Belmont*, see Chapter 9 § II(C).
[360] 315 U.S. 203 (1942). For further discussion of *Pink*, see Chapter 9 § II(C).
[361] For discussion of sole executive agreements, see Chapter 6 § V(C).
[362] *Belmont*, 301 U.S. at 330.
[363] *Id.* at 331.

Litvinov Assignment through an action in federal court, but the Supreme Court found that the matter should first be addressed in New York courts.[364] Thereafter, efforts by the U.S. government to secure the assets in New York courts failed, resulting in the matter returning to the Supreme Court. Here, once again, the Supreme Court upheld the government's claims, saying that the "the powers of the President in the conduct of foreign relations included the power, without consent of the Senate, to determine the public policy of the United States with respect to the Russian nationalization decrees," that the president's "authority is not limited to a determination of the government to be recognized," and that the "[p]ower to remove such obstacles to full recognition as settlement of claims of our nationals certainly is a modest implied power of the President," given that "[u]nless such a power exists, the power of recognition might be thwarted or seriously diluted."[365]

Actions ancillary to the act of recognition are not confined to the settlement of claims. In *United States v. Arlington County*,[366] the United States asked the Fourth Circuit to uphold a 1979 sole executive agreement with the German Democratic Republic (GDR, or "East Germany"), which made a GDR-owned apartment building exempt from county tax, on grounds that the agreement related to the U.S. recognition of the GDR in 1974. The court upheld the agreement, finding that the "President is empowered to recognize the government of a foreign state" and this "authority is not confined to the act of recognition."[367] Given that the "genesis of the 1979 agreement was the President's recognition of the GDR in 1974," application "of the principles derived from *Belmont* and *Pink* establish that the executive branch was authorized to enter into the 1979 agreement.[368]

Moreover, some lower federal courts began extending the incidental power for settling claims to situations where recognition of the foreign government was not materially in doubt. Thus, in *Ozanic v. United States*, the Second Circuit was confronted with the assignment to a U.K. corporation of a claim against the United States that had been settled as part of a U.S.-Yugoslavia claims settlement agreement, which was concluded at a time when U.S. recognition of the Yugoslav government was not at issue.[369] In upholding the validity of this sole executive agreement, the Second Circuit stated that the "constitutional power of the President extends to the settlement of mutual claims between a foreign government and the United States, at least when it is an incident to the recognition of that government; *and it would be unreasonable to circumscribe it to such*

---

[364] United States v. Bank of N.Y. & Tr., 296 U.S. 463 (1936).

[365] *Pink*, 315 U.S. 203 at 229–30 (citations omitted).

[366] 669 F.2d 925 (4th Cir. 1982).

[367] *Id.* at 929.

[368] *Id.* at 930 (footnote omitted).

[369] 188 F.2d 228 (2d Cir. 1951).

controversies."[370] The court explained that the "continued mutual amity between
the nation and other powers again and again depends upon a satisfactory compromise of mutual claims; the necessary power to make such compromises has
existed from the earliest times and been exercised by the foreign offices of all civilized nations."[371]

The extension of the power to conclude sole executive agreements even when
recognition is not at issue was adopted in *Dames & Moore v. Regan.*[372] There,
the sole executive agreement, the Algiers Accords, was found constitutionally
permissible because it was the necessary incident to resolution of a major foreign policy dispute between the United States and Iran, the 1979 to 1981 hostage crisis. That agreement, and the executive orders implementing it, suspended
claims of U.S. nationals against Iran in U.S. courts and terminated such claims
through binding arbitration in an Iran–United States Claims Tribunal based in
The Hague. In upholding the agreement (and the executive orders), the Court
cited *Belmont* and *Pink* when emphasizing the historical executive practice of
settling claims of U.S. nationals against foreign countries by executive agreement, even though the earlier cases involved an agreement concluded concomitantly with an exercise of the recognition power, whereas *Dames & Moore* did
not. Importantly, the Court emphasized how such claims agreements had been
known to and acquiesced in by Congress,[373] thereby suggesting that presidential
action of such type, if opposed by Congress, might lead to a different result.

The zenith of this expanded use of the claims settlement power occurred in
American Insurance v. Garamendi,[374] a case in which neither an exercise of the
recognition power occurred nor the conclusion of an executive agreement directly settling claims. In this case, the Supreme Court considered a provision of
California's Holocaust Victim Insurance Relief Act which required any insurer
that did business in California and that sold insurance policies in Europe which
were in effect during the Holocaust-era to disclose certain information about
those policies to the California Insurance Commissioner. Failure to do so could
result in the insurer losing its California license. The Court found that the provision impermissibly interfered with the president's conduct of foreign affairs,
relying heavily on certain executive agreements between the United States and
Germany. In those agreements, Germany committed itself to a process for payment of Holocaust-era claims, including claims against German insurance companies, and in exchange the United States committed to seek from U.S. courts

---

[370] *Id.* at 231 (emphasis added).

[371] *Id.*

[372] Dames & Moore v. Regan, 453 U.S. 654 (1981); *see* Chapter 1 § II(B); *See also* Charles T. Main
Intern., Inc. v. Khuzestan Water & Power Auth., 651 F.2d 800 (1st Cir. 1981) (finding that the president had inherent power under the Constitution to settle the claims of the U.S. plaintiffs against Iran).

[373] *Dames & Moore*, 453 U.S., at 678–80.

[374] 539 U.S. 396 (2003).

dismissal of claims against German companies. The agreements, however, did not entail espousal of such claims by the U.S. government nor their official settlement by means of the executive agreements (reflecting doubt on the part of the federal government that it could constitutionally espouse claims by U.S. nationals against foreign *nationals*, as opposed to against a foreign state). In explaining why the California statute was impermissible, the Court acknowledged that the agreements differed from those in *Belmont*, *Pink*, and *Dames & Moore*, "insofar as they address claims associated with formerly belligerent states, but against corporations, not the foreign governments."[375] But the court said that such a distinction did not matter, since historically "wartime claims against even nominally private entities have become issues in international diplomacy, and three of the postwar settlements dealing with reparations implicating private parties were made by the Executive alone."[376] Such practice ran in tandem with pragmatism; "untangling government policy from private initiative during wartime is often so hard that diplomatic action settling claims against private parties may well be just as essential in the aftermath of hostilities as diplomacy to settle claims against foreign governments."[377]

E. Recognition of Foreign Belligerency and Insurgency

The outbreak of war between two foreign states creates a state of belligerency, which, under traditional international law, triggers various rights and duties by third states as neutrals.[378] The president's power of recognition has been construed as extending to recognition of the existence of such a belligerency, and doing so might be seen as a precursor to further decisions concerning the obligations of the United States as a neutral state. Yet in contemporary times, with the general prohibition on the use of military force except in self-defense, application of this law of neutrality has become uneven. Indeed, to the extent that one state is viewed as the aggressor state, third states (including the United States) have often acted to assist the defending

---

[375] *Id.* at 415–16.

[376] *Id.* at 416.

[377] *Id.* For further discussion of *Dames & Moore* and *Garamendi*, see Chapter 6 § V(C) and Chapter 9 §§ II(C), II(E).

[378] *See, e.g.,* Paul Seger, *The Law of Neutrality, in* THE OXFORD HANDBOOK OF INTERNATIONAL LAW IN ARMED CONFLICT 262 (Andrew Clapham & Paola Gaeta eds., 2014); Yves Sandoz, *Rights, Powers and Obligations of Neutral Powers under the Conventions, in* THE 1949 GENEVA CONVENTIONS: A COMMENTARY 90 (Andrew Clapham et al. eds., 2015); JAMES UPCHER, NEUTRALITY IN CONTEMPORARY INTERNATIONAL LAW (2020). For example, "[n]eutrals have the right to continue during war to trade with the belligerents, subject to the law relating to contraband and blockade. The existence of this right is universally admitted, although on certain occasions it has been in practice denied." 7A MOORE DIGEST 99.

state rather than assume a position of neutrality. For example, when armed conflict broke out between Russia and Georgia in 2008, the United States airlifted Georgian troops who were operating in Iraq back to Georgia, an act that normally would implicate U.S. neutrality obligations.[379] Likewise, the supply of weapons and other support by Western states for Ukraine after Russia's interventions in 2014 and 2022 belies any strict application of the traditional law of neutrality.

Similarly, when a rebel faction within a state succeeds in becoming a significant insurgency, that too can trigger various rights and obligations under traditional international law, including an obligation upon third states not to support the military efforts of either belligerent even if invited to do so. Yet, again, contemporary U.S. practice has sometimes eschewed such rules and turned instead (to a degree) on advancement of human rights and democratic governance, so as to favor one side rather than assume a position of neutrality.[380] For example, in the midst of the Syrian civil war in 2014–2015, President Obama had to consider whether to follow through on Congress' authorization to provide "assistance . . . and sustainment, to appropriately vetted elements of the Syrian opposition," for the purpose inter alia of "securing territory controlled by the Syrian opposition" and "[p]romoting the conditions for a negotiated settlement to end the conflict in Syria."[381] Again, the decision whether to recognize that an insurgency exists and, if so, what obligations arise under international law for the United States would appear to fall within the realm of presidential discretion.[382]

Today, formal statements recognizing a belligerency or insurgency are uncommon, particularly since the adoption of the U.N. Charter. Even so, the posture taken by the United States in the context of the 1980 to 1988 Iraq-Iran war suggests the continuing relevance of the law of neutrality in at least some circumstances.[383] Ultimately, all such practice confirms the central role of the president in determining for the United States whether such rules come into play.

---

[379] See White House Press Release, *Setting the Record Straight: President Bush Has Taken Action to Ensure Peace, Security and Humanitarian Aid in Georgia* (Aug. 13, 2008), https://perma.cc/8MZW-GTNR (noting that the United States had completed an airlift of Georgian troops from Iraq to Georgia).

[380] Contemporary practice with respect to the Syrian civil war reveals numerous examples of third-state assistance to both sides of a non-international armed conflict. *See, e.g.*, Luca Ferro & Nele Verlinden, *Neutrality During Armed Conflicts: A Coherent Approach to Third-State Support for Warring Parties*, 17 CHINESE J. INT'L L. 15, 22–27 (2018).

[381] Carl Levin and Howard P. "Buck" McKeon National Defense Authorization Act for Fiscal Year 2015, Pub. L. No. 113-291, § 1209(a), 128 Stat. 3292, 3541 (2014).

[382] *See* RESTATEMENT (SECOND) § 94 cmt. e.

[383] *See* John H. McNeill, *Neutral Rights and Maritime Sanctions: The Effect of Two Gulf Wars*, 31 VA. J. INT'L L. 632 (1991).

F. Altering Treaties to Accommodate Newly Created
Foreign States

The power to appoint and receive ambassadors may also be seen as supporting the president's ability to alter existing treaties as a means of accommodating new states that emerge from a predecessor state. When the USSR collapsed after 1990, forming Russia and several other states, the United States embarked on a nego- tiating process governed by a "continuity principle," whereby USSR treaty rights and obligations passed to the successor states unless the terms or the object and purpose of the treaty required a different result.[384]

While that approach was not controversial with regard to most treaties, the potential for the president to unilaterally alter the parties to the Anti-Ballistic Missile (ABM) Treaty[385] was of concern to many in Congress. Consequently, both the House and Senate made efforts to insert provisions addressing the matter into the Department of Defense Authorization Act for Fiscal Year 1997. For example, as reported to the floor of the Senate, Section 231(a) of the bill stated that "the United States shall not be bound by any international agree- ment entered into by the President that would substantively modify the ABM Treaty," to include "any agreement that would add one or more countries as sig- natories to the treaty or would otherwise convert the treaty from a bilateral treaty to a multilateral treaty, unless the agreement is entered pursuant to the treaty making power of the President under the Constitution."[386] OLC took the view that Section 223(a) was unconstitutional, in part because of the president's power to interpret and implement treaties, and in part due to the president's power to recognize foreign states and governments. With respect to the latter, OLC ad- vanced three basic propositions: (1) the "question of determining which States are the 'successors' to a State that, like the former Soviet Union, has been com- pletely dissolved, is a matter for the President alone to determine in the exercise of his recognition authority"; (2) "in determining which States are the successors of a dissolved State, the President may also determine which of the successors are bound by the former State's treaty obligations towards the United States, and the

---

[384] See Williamson & Osborn, *supra* note 250.

[385] Treaty on the Limitation of Anti-Ballistic Missile Systems, U.S.-U.S.S.R., May 26, 1972, 23 U.S.T. 3435 [hereinafter ABM Treaty].

[386] Department of Defense Authorization Act for Fiscal Year 1997, S. 1745, 104th Cong. § 231(a) (1996). As adopted by the Senate, the provision began with a clause stating: "It is the sense of the Senate that during fiscal year 1997 . . . ." *Id.* The House version provided: "Any addition of a new signatory party to the ABM Treaty (in addition to the United States and the Russian Federation) constitutes an amendment to the treaty that can only be agreed to by the United States through the treaty-making power of the United States." Department of Defense Authorization Act for Fiscal Year 1997, H.R. 3230, 104th Cong. § 234 (1996). The final version of the statute contained no such provisions. *See* National Defense Authorization Act for Fiscal Year 1997, Pub. L. No. 104-201, 110 Stat. 2422 (1996).

extent to which they are so bound"; and (3) "[o]ne of the elements of the recognition of these newly emergent States was and is their succession to applicable Soviet treaties," such that "the proposed legislation would act in derogation of the President's recognition power."[387] Among other things, OLC asserted that the "continuity" approach taken by the executive was "rooted, not only in the United States' past diplomatic practice, but in its understanding of international law."[388]

Yet OLC's position may not always appeal to courts, given that the treaty power is one concurrently exercised between the president and the Senate. In *Artukovic v. Boyle*,[389] decided in 1952, a federal district court considered whether a 1902 extradition treaty between the United States and the Kingdom of Serbia could still be regarded as being in effect as between the United States and Yugoslavia, a federal state of which Serbia was one republic. In that instance, the court accepted that the executive branch has the power to recognize new states and governments, but further asserted that the executive branch could not enter into treaties with such entities without the consent of the Senate. According to the court, "the question of whether or not a treaty exists between the United States and Yugoslavia is not a matter which lies exclusively within the Executive Department but is a judicial question to be decided by the courts."[390] Although the Department of State appeared to have taken a contrary view, the court concluded that the treaty had no continuing force.[391] The court of appeals, reversing, stated that its decision was based on its disagreement with the facts as they were perceived by the district court, but also stressed the importance of deferring to the decisions of both states concerned: "If their agreed decisions, when based upon supporting facts, are not conclusive, they should at least weigh very heavily."[392]

Arguably the "recognition" power might also be viewed as supporting a unilateral presidential power to terminate or withdraw from treaties. In *Goldwater v. Carter*,[393] the Supreme Court declined to pass upon the constitutionality of President Jimmy Carter's termination of the U.S.-Taiwan defense treaty.[394] Justice Brennan dissented, arguing that President Carter had the power to so terminate the treaty, a power he saw grounded in the recognition power and in prior cases such as *United States v. Pink*. According to Justice Brennan, "[a]brogation of the defense treaty with Taiwan was a necessary incident to Executive recognition

---

[387] Constitutionality of Legislative Provision Regarding ABM Treaty, 20 Op. O.L.C. 246, 251–52 (1996).

[388] *Id.* at 248.

[389] 107 F. Supp. 11 (S.D. Cal. 1952).

[390] *Id.* at 24.

[391] *Id.* at 33.

[392] Ivancevic v. Artukovic, 211 F.2d 565, 573–74 (9th Cir. 1954).

[393] 444 U.S. 996 (1979).

[394] For further discussion of the justiciability issues involved in *Goldwater*, see Chapter 4 §§ II(A)(2) and II(B)(2).

of the Peking Government, because the defense treaty was predicated upon the now-abandoned view that the Taiwan Government was the only legitimate political authority in China."[395]

V. Foreign Emoluments Clause

The Foreign Emoluments Clause of the Constitution prohibits any U.S. government "person holding any Office of Profit or Trust" from accepting "any present, Emolument, Office, or Title, of any kind whatever" from a foreign government, except with the consent of Congress.[396] The Department of Justice has interpreted the clause as applying not just to appointees to offices who exercise significant authority, but to all U.S. government employees, given that the clause was intended broadly to exclude corruption and foreign influence.[397] In general, the objective in the clause is to preclude foreign governments from bribing U.S. officials, including diplomats, or otherwise diverting their loyalty from the United States.

The 1966 Foreign Gifts and Decorations Act provides detailed guidance in this respect.[398] The statute prohibits employees from requesting or encouraging the tender of a "gift" (meaning a tangible or intangible present) or a "decoration" (meaning an order, device, medal, badge, insignia, emblem, or award).[399] Further, the statute prohibits accepting or retaining a gift unless it is "a gift of minimal value tendered and received as a souvenir or mark of courtesy."[400]

---

[395] *Goldwater*, 444 U.S. at 1007 (Brennan, J., dissenting) (citations omitted). For further discussion of the treaty termination issue in *Goldwater*, see Chapter 6 § VI(B).

[396] U.S. CONST. art. I, § 9, cl. 8. The Articles of Confederation had a similar provision, but contained no reference to the consent of Congress, and covered not just federal officials but state officials as well. *See* ARTICLES OF CONFEDERATION of 1781, art. VI, ¶ 1 ("[N]or shall any person holding any office of profit or trust under the United States, or any of them, accept any present, emolument, office or title of any kind whatever from any King, Prince or foreign State."). For analysis of the Foreign Emoluments Clause, see Amandeep S. Grewal, *The Purposes of the Foreign Emoluments Clause*, 59 S. TEX. L. REV. 167 (2017); Erik M. Jensen, *The Foreign Emoluments Clause*, 10 ELON L. REV. 73 (2018); Deborah Sills, *The Foreign Emoluments Clause: Protecting Our National Security Interests*, 26 BROOK. J. L. & POL'Y 63 (2018). The clause has also been referred to as the Emoluments Clause, Gifts Clause, or Foreign Gifts Clause. There is, however, separately a Domestic Emoluments Clause (also known as the Presidential Emoluments Clause) that is focused specifically on the president. It prohibits the president from receiving any emolument "from the United States, or any of them." U.S. CONST. art. II, § 1, cl. 7.

[397] Application of the Emoluments Clause of the Constitution and the Foreign Gifts and Decorations Act, 6 Op. O.L.C. 156, 157–58 (1982); *see* 2 FARRAND'S RECORDS, at 389 (notes of James Madison); 3 FARRAND'S RECORDS, at 327 (remarks by Edmund Randolph that it "was thought proper, in order to exclude corruption and foreign influence, to prohibit any one in office from receiving or holding any emoluments from foreign states.").

[398] Foreign Gifts and Decorations Act, 5 U.S.C. § 7342 (2018).

[399] 5 U.S.C. § 7342(a)(3), (a)(4), (b)(1).

[400] 5 U.S.C. § 7342(b)(2), (c)(1)(A). While Congress has consented to the receipt of gifts of minimal value from a foreign government, individual agencies of the executive branch may impose

"Minimal value" was defined in the statute as $100 or less, but the statute allows for adjustments over time to account for inflation.[401] If refusal of a gift offered by a foreign government "would likely cause offense or embarrassment or otherwise adversely affect the foreign relations of the United States," the gift may be accepted, but is "deemed to have been accepted on behalf of the United States and, upon acceptance, shall become the property of the United States."[402]

Congress has not consented to the acceptance by U.S. employees of other forms of payments or compensation from foreign governments, such as compensation for services rendered. For example, the Department of Justice determined that an employee of the U.S. Nuclear Regulatory Commission could not provide paid advice to a U.S. consulting firm that had been retained by an entity of the Mexican government to assist in the building of a nuclear power plant. Even though the U.S. government employee would have done the work on his own time and would have been paid by the U.S. firm, he would have been paid indirectly by the Mexican government through funds it provided to the firm. Further, the relationship of the employee with the firm was the principal reason that the firm was retained by the Mexican government.[403]

By contrast, the Department of Justice did not view the Emoluments Clause (or the Foreign Gifts and Decorations Act) as implicated in a situation where a large university provided expert consultants to a foreign government, and the foreign government had no control or influence over the selection of the experts or their pay from the university. In such a situation, even if one of the experts held a U.S. government position, there was no payment to that expert "from" a foreign government.[404] Similarly, an award relating to sustainable development granted to an employee of the national oceanic and atmospheric administration was permissible because the award was not from a foreign government but from a nongovernmental entity with very limited Swedish government involvement.[405] Although the city of Göteborg, Sweden, was involved in creation of the award, it was not involved in the selection of award recipients.

In academic commentary, there is some disagreement as to whether the Foreign Emoluments Clause addresses itself to elected officials.[406] In practice,

additional restrictions on the acceptance by their employees of such gifts. *See, e.g.*, 2 U.S. Dep't of State, Foreign Affairs Manual § 960, https://perma.cc/572R-YJ3X.

[401] 5 U.S.C. § 7342(a)(5).

[402] 5 U.S.C. § 7342(c)(1)(B).

[403] Application of the Emoluments Clause of the Constitution and the Foreign Gifts and Decorations Act, *supra* note 397, at 158.

[404] *Id.*

[405] Applicability of the Emoluments Clause and the Foreign Gifts and Decorations Act to the Göteborg Award for Sustainable Development, 34 Op. O.L.C. 1 (2010).

[406] *Compare* Zephyr Teachout, *Gifts, Offices and Corruption*, 107 Nw. L. Rev. 30 (2012) (finding that elected officers are covered by the clause), *with* Seth Barrett Tillman, *The Original Public Meaning of the Foreign Emoluments Clause: A Reply to Professor Zephyr Teachout*, 107 Nw. L. Rev. 180 (2013)

however, it appears that the Department of Justice regards elected officials, including the president, as covered by the clause, thereby requiring them to justify whether gifts, presents, or awards they receive are consistent with both the Constitution and the Foreign Gifts and Decorations Act.[407] For example, the awarding of the Nobel Peace Prize to President Obama in 2009 (which included a sum of approximately $1.4 million) was deemed by the Department of Justice as implicating but not violating the Emoluments Clause, because the Nobel Committee that awards the prize, while elected by the Norwegian Parliament, acts independently of the Norwegian government when selecting the prize recipient.[408]

President Trump's continued ownership of his business enterprises after assuming office prompted extensive commentary and some litigation as to whether such connections violated the Foreign Emoluments Clause.[409] The emoluments purportedly received included from foreign states leasing space in properties and paying for rooms and events at hotels of Trump-owned companies, as well as foreign states approving intellectual property rights to such companies. Defenders of the president maintained, however, that an "emolument" means only a payment or benefit received as a consequence of discharging the duties of an office, not ordinary business transactions conducted at arm's length.[410]

(finding that the clause's formulation of "holding any Office under" the United States refers only to appointed officers); Seth Barrett Tillman, *The Foreign Emoluments Clause—Where the Bodies Are Buried: "Idiosyncratic" Legal Positions*, 59 S. TEX. L. REV. 237 (2017) (same).

[407] Applicability of the Emoluments Clause and the Foreign Gifts and Decorations Act to the President's Receipt of the Nobel Peace Prize, 33 Op. O.L.C. 1, 4 (2009) ("The President surely 'hold[s] an[] Office of Profit or Trust'. . . ."); *see* Marissa L. Kibler, Note, *The Foreign Emoluments Clause: Tracing the Framers' Fears About Foreign Influence Over the President*, 74 N.Y.U. ANN. SURV. AM. L. 449 (2019).

[408] 33 Op. O.L.C., *supra* note 407, at 12. Prior to President Obama, the Nobel Peace Prize had been "received by two other sitting presidents—Theodore Roosevelt and Woodrow Wilson—by a sitting Vice President, Secretary of State and Senator, and by a retired General of the Army." *Id.* at 4.

[409] *See, e.g.*, Citizens for Resp. & Ethics in Washington (CREW) v. Trump, 953 F.3d 178 (2d Cir. 2020) (amended op.) (finding that a nonprofit government ethics group, along with various organizations and individuals involved with hospitality industries in New York and Washington, D.C., had standing to sue for violation of the Domestic and Foreign Emoluments Clauses, based on a theory of competitive harm resulting from the allegedly unlawful acts); District of Columbia v. Trump, 291 F. Supp. 3d 725 (D. Md. 2018) (similar action, in which the District of Columbia and the State of Maryland were found to have standing); Blumenthal v. Trump, 335 F. Supp. 3d 45 (D.D.C. 2018) (finding that members of Congress had standing to sue President Trump for violating the Foreign Emoluments Clause), *reversed*, 949 F.3d 14 (D.C. Cir. 2020) (holding that the members lacked standing because individual members of Congress may not sue based on alleged institutional injury to the legislature as a whole). After President Trump left office in January 2021, the U.S. Supreme Court dismissed appeals in two of these cases as moot. Adam Liptak, *Supreme Court Ends Emoluments Suits Against Trump*, N.Y. TIMES (Jan. 25, 2021), https://perma.cc/TBH2-K48U; *see* Trump v. District of Columbia, 141 S. Ct. 1262 (2021) (mem.); Trump v. Citizens for Resp. & Ethics in Washington, 141 S. Ct. 1262 (2021) (mem.).

[410] *See, e.g.*, Amandeep S. Grewal, *The Foreign Emoluments Clause and the Chief Executive*, 102 MINN. L. REV. 639 (2017).

4

Judging Foreign Relations

Although U.S. foreign relations is a field fully stocked with legal issues—involving not just treaties and customary international law but also conventional domestic material like the U.S. Constitution, statutes, executive orders, and state common law—the judiciary often seems secondary. Courts clearly played a foundational role in developing many basic rules of U.S. foreign relations law. Today, however, they are often assumed to be marginal players, rarely involved in resolving the field's more fundamental legal disputes. Louis Henkin's formulation was telling: "Foreign relations are political relations conducted by the political branches of the federal government," which "[a]t times . . . come into court."[1] With respect to the president, in particular, courts may be regarded as playing an oppositional, and losing, role.[2]

There is some truth in this depiction, but it is also incomplete. Courts do not attempt to manage foreign relations or to resolve rapidly evolving, detailed controversies (nor, for that matter, do they typically regulate financial markets or second-guess corporate boardrooms). Yet they do play an indispensable part in the architecture of foreign relations law. Whatever their limitations, courts are vital in articulating general legal principles and rules of foreign relations law and in taking account of foreign and international law, and when doing so perform tasks to the benefit of (and often at the behest of) the political branches.[3]

---

[1] HENKIN, FOREIGN AFFAIRS, at 131; *see also* QUINCY WRIGHT, THE CONTROL OF AMERICAN FOREIGN RELATIONS 134–35 (describing debate about whether the foreign relations power is essentially executive or essentially legislative, and that "[t]he courts have been perfectly clear that these powers are not of an essential judicial nature, and consequently have considered themselves incompetent to decide them").

[2] *See* Kevin Arlyck, *The Courts and Foreign Affairs at the Founding*, 2017 BYU L. REV. 1, 2 (noting that "modern readers" are "accustomed . . . to debate on the role of the courts in foreign affairs that generally presupposes an opposition between judicial decisionmaking and presidential policymaking").

[3] For a contemporary defense of this role, particularly with regard to the role of courts in considering foreign and international legal circumstances, see STEPHEN BREYER, THE COURT AND THE WORLD: AMERICAN LAW AND THE NEW GLOBAL REALITIES (2015).

I. Historical Role of the Judiciary in Foreign Relations

A. Pre-Constitutional Experience

Colonial-era courts were largely irrelevant to foreign affairs while matters were run by Great Britain. Independence initially did little to alter that, as early state constitutions generally neglected the opportunity to reorganize their judiciaries.[4] Admiralty was an exception. Prewar, courts charged with prosecuting smuggling and piracy had spirited accused Americans and apprehended vessels overseas without any jury trial. Beginning in 1775, however, the Continental Congress urged the states to take greater responsibility for adjudicating captures fairly. They gradually did, with varying structures and remits, while generally adhering to general maritime law and congressional measures and facilitating trial by jury.[5]

The next phase, under the Articles of Confederation, left the national government still dependent on state courts, with the result that the judiciary often neglected matters of keen import for foreign affairs. The Articles required the states to abide by laws enacted by Congress and to abide by the Articles themselves,[6] but (aside from foreclosing states from laying imposts or duties that interfered with certain treaties) they imposed no duty on states or their courts to abide by international law.[7] The Articles also required state courts to provide full faith and credit to one another and to accord privileges and immunities to one another's (free) inhabitants, but the interests of foreign parties were not mentioned.[8] Congress could arbitrate important types of disputes between states, but nothing was said of those involving foreign powers, officials, or citizens.[9]

Again, maritime matters were an exception. The Articles gave Congress power to establish courts to try "piracies and felonies committed on the high seas" and appellate courts to review state court decisions "in all cases of captures."[10] Congress delegated authority for the establishment of such trial courts back

---

[4] Erwin C. Surrency, *The Transition From Colonialism to Independence*, 46 Am. J. Legal Hist. 55, 59 (2004) (noting Pennsylvania as exceptional in this regard).

[5] William R. Casto, *The Origins of Federal Admiralty Jurisdiction in an Age of Privateers, Smugglers, and Pirates*, 37 Am. J. Legal Hist. 117, 123–25 (1993); Wythe Holt, *"To Establish Justice": Politics, the Judiciary Act of 1789, and the Invention of the Federal Courts*, 1989 Duke L.J. 1421, 1427–28 (1989) (citing Henry Bourguignon, The First Federal Court: The Federal Appellate Prize Court of the American Revolution, 1775–1787, at 44–48, 57–75, 101–34, 243–51, 297–343 (1977)); Surrency, *supra* note 4, at 60–62.

[6] Articles of Confederation of 1781, art. XIII.

[7] *Id.*, art. VI.

[8] *Id.*, art. IV.

[9] *Id.*, art. IX.

[10] Articles of Confederation of 1781, art. IX.

to the states,[11] with committees assuming appellate authority, even before the Articles formally took effect. In 1780, Congress established the first federal court to handle such appeals. Yet state legislatures still restricted the classes of potential appellants, and compliance with federal judgments still depended on the states.[12] Congress exhorted the states to direct their admiralty judges to carry out the federal court's decrees,[13] but state judges and other state officials remained erratic about it. Admiralty decrees from other states, too, were not always treated respectfully.[14]

The failure of the Articles of Confederation to address the judiciary more generally allowed prosaic matters to blossom into foreign relations controversies. The plight of British creditors, owed substantial monies by colonists, is the clearest illustration. Collecting debts during hostilities would have been difficult under the best of circumstances, but the states and their courts made it more so. The likelihood that postwar revival of debt collection efforts would meet a similar fate led to provisions in the 1783 Treaty of Paris that obligated the United States to remove impediments to recovery, to prevent confiscations of Loyalist property, and to recommend to the states measures to enable restitution.[15] Nonetheless, state resistance, fueled by an economic downturn and popular outrage, continued, and some states even closed their courts to British claims.[16] Such violations of U.S. treaty obligations undermined the international standing of the United States and reduced its ability to insist on Great Britain's fidelity to its own obligations, exciting interest in securing treaty supremacy in the new Constitution.[17] Such controversies also raised questions as to whether state courts would attend to national interests in other matters with international resonance.[18]

[11] *See* WILFRED J. RITZ, REWRITING THE HISTORY OF THE JUDICIARY ACT OF 1789: EXPOSING MYTHS, CHALLENGING PREMISES, AND USING NEW EVIDENCE, 99–101 (Wythe Holt & L. H. LaRue eds., 1990).

[12] *See* HENRY BOURGUIGNON, THE FIRST FEDERAL COURT: THE FEDERAL APPELLATE PRIZE COURT OF THE AMERICAN REVOLUTION, 1775–1787, at 57–75 (1977).

[13] 16 J. CONTINENTAL CONGRESS 61 (Jan. 14, 1780).

[14] *See* David J. Bederman, *Admiralty and the Eleventh Amendment*, 72 NOTRE DAME L. REV. 935, 942–43, 949–50 (1996); Casto, *supra* note 5, at 126–32; Holt, *supra* note 5, at 1428–29; Surrency, *supra* note 4, at 62, 66–67.

[15] Definitive Treaty of Peace, Gr. Brit.–U.S., Sept. 3, 1783, arts. 4–6, *in* 2 TREATIES AND OTHER INTERNATIONAL ACTS OF THE UNITED STATES OF AMERICA 151 (Hunter Miller ed., 1931).

[16] *See* Holt, *supra* note 5, at 1430–53.

[17] *See* Chapter 6 § I(A)(1). For discussion of the centrality of debt and related issues to transatlantic relations, and to the formation and development of the Constitution, see Daniel J. Hulsebosch, *Being Seen Like a State: How Americans (and Britons) Built the Constitutional Infrastructure of a Developing Nation*, 59 WM. & MARY L. REV. 1239 (2018).

[18] In the closely watched case of *Rutgers v. Waddington*, a New York court, pressed by Alexander Hamilton, largely accepted his argument that the Treaty of Paris and the law of nations prevented New York from nullifying the reliance of a British merchant on British military orders as a defense against a trespass action, to the evident displeasure of the New York Assembly. William Michael Treanor, *Judicial Review Before Marbury*, 58 STAN. L. REV. 455, 480–87 (2005); *see* 1 THE LAW PRACTICE OF ALEXANDER HAMILTON 282–543 (J. Goebel ed., 1964); *see, e.g.,* Letter from Thomas

B. Constitutional Design

The need for national courts with jurisdiction over matters like admiralty and treaties, which implicated interests external to particular states, may seem obvious to the modern gaze. But as compared to other topics, including some relating to foreign relations, the judiciary received little attention in the run-up to the constitutional convention.[19]

The inattention to courts changed a bit at the convention. The participants were inclined to sympathize with British creditors,[20] and interest in a national judiciary, responsible for sensitive foreign-relations matters, was evident.[21] James Madison and other Virginia delegates proposed "one or more supreme tribunals, and of inferior tribunals to be chosen by the National Legislature."[22] The inferior courts were to have trial jurisdiction, and the supreme tribunal final appellate jurisdiction, over not only core admiralty matters but also "cases in which foreigners or citizens of other States . . . may be interested" and "questions which may involve the national peace and harmony."[23] Later proposals varied as to whether some form of appellate jurisdiction sufficed,[24] and in how translating "national peace and harmony" into more sharply delineated heads of jurisdiction, such as that for cases involving ambassadors,[25] or involving treaties or the law of

---

Jefferson to George Hammond (May 29, 1792), *reprinted in* 1 AMERICAN STATE PAPERS: FOREIGN RELATIONS 201; Letter from Alexander Hamilton to Secretary of State (Apr. 19, 1792), *reprinted in id.* at 232; Alexander Hamilton, Philo Camillus No. 3 (Aug. 12, 1795), *reprinted in* 19 THE PAPERS OF ALEXANDER HAMILTON 124, 131–33 (Harold C. Syrett ed., 1973).

[19] Holt, *supra* note 5, at 1424 (noting "the astonishing lack of comment upon the need for a national court system in the period immediately before the Constitutional Convention.") (citing Henry J. Friendly, *The Historic Basis of Diversity Jurisdiction*, 41 HARV. L. REV. 483, 484 (1927)).

[20] Holt, *supra* note 5, at 1439, 1459 (describing pro-creditor alignment at the Convention).

[21] *See* Letter from George Mason to Arthur Lee (May 21, 1787), *reprinted in* 3 FARRAND'S RECORDS, at 24 (reporting, on the eve of the Convention, that "[t]he most prevalent idea," with respect to the courts, was for "a judiciary system with cognizance of all such matters as depend upon the law of nations," along with "such other objects as the local courts of justice may be inadequate to").

[22] 1 FARRAND'S RECORDS, at 21–22 (Madison) (May 29).

[23] *Id.* After the Committee of the Whole agreed on "one or more supreme tribunals, and . . . inferior tribunals," *id.*, the Convention rejected a proposal by Rutledge to eliminate inferior national courts (and continue relying on state courts), settling on the establishment of a supreme court and vesting the national legislature with the authority to create inferior courts. *See id.* at 95 (June 4) (Journal), 104–05 (Madison) (Committee of the Whole language); *id.* at 118 (June 5) (Journal), 119–24 (Madison) (debate).

[24] The surviving summaries of the Pinckney Plan shared an emphasis on such appellate jurisdiction, confining the use of national courts otherwise to admiralty and maritime matters. 2 FARRAND'S RECORDS, at 136; 3 *id.* at 600, 608. Hamilton's plan would have given a supreme tribunal original jurisdiction over cases involving capture, and appellate jurisdiction over national revenues cases and those concerning citizens of foreign states. 1 *id.* at 291 (June 18) (Madison). The New Jersey Plan likewise conferred appellate jurisdiction only over matters other than those involving the impeachment of federal officers. 1 *id.* at 244 (June 15) (Madison).

[25] The New Jersey Plan, for example, maintained jurisdiction over cases "in which foreigners may be interested," but dropped reference to "national peace and harmony" matters—instead

nations.[26] The attention to matters of external interest was unmistakable.

After little recorded debate, a Committee of Detail draft emerged in early August that largely anticipated Article III as it presently stands,[27] with jurisdiction over treaties being added later that month.[28] The final text detailed the federal judicial power—divided between the Supreme Court and inferior courts—over broad categories that might bear on foreign affairs, like cases arising under the Constitution or the laws of the United States, and controversies involving the United States as a party. Other bases for jurisdiction were squarely in the foreign affairs wheelhouse: all cases arising under "Treaties made, or which shall be made," "affecting Ambassadors, other public Ministers and Consuls" (assigned to the Supreme Court's original jurisdiction, and not subject to congressional exception and regulation), or concerning "admiralty and maritime Jurisdiction," and all controversies "between a State, or the Citizens thereof, and foreign States, Citizens or Subjects."[29] Direct reference to the "law of nations," however, disappeared in the Committee of Detail, leaving uncertainty as to whether it was intended to be among the cases "arising under . . . the Laws of the United States."[30] Still, the remaining heads of jurisdiction allowed national courts to resolve most law-of-nations disputes as that law was then understood.[31]

On the whole, Article III appeared to address not only cases in which international law might arise but also cases in which the failure to afford justice might violate obligations of the United States or create other conflicts with foreign states. Its supporters viewed this as a step toward a federal judiciary that

adding (appellate) jurisdiction over cases involving rights of ambassadors and treaty construction. 1 FARRAND'S RECORDS, at 244 (June 15) (Madison).

[26] The Pinckney Plan appeared to include jurisdiction over cases involving the construction of treaties or the law of nations. 2 FARRAND'S RECORDS, at 136; 3 id. at 608; 3 id. at 600 (varying depiction); see also 1 id. at 244 (Madison) (New Jersey Plan) (including cases involving "the construction of any treaty or treaties"); 3 id. at 157 (providing, in other notes of the New Jersey Plan, appellate jurisdiction over "all Cases in which Foreigners may be interested in the Construction of any Treaty").

[27] 2 FARRAND'S RECORDS, at 186–87 (Aug. 6) (Madison's notes). The lack of debate has been read as further evidence of disinterest. See, e.g., Henry J. Bourguignon, The Federal Key to the Judiciary Act of 1789, 46 S.C. L. REV. 647, 651–52 (1995) ("When one quickly surveys the debates at the Constitutional Convention, one might get the impression that Article III of the Constitution was practically an afterthought for the delegates.").

[28] This addition accorded with the evolving language of the Supremacy Clause. 2 FARRAND'S RECORDS, at 431 (Aug. 27) (Madison) (noting motion by Rutledge adding "and treaties made or which shall be made under their authority," made "conformably to a preceding amendment in another place"); id. at 423–24 (Aug. 27) (Journal) (same); see id. at 417 (Aug. 25) (Madison's notes) (noting Madison's motion to add, after "all treaties made," "the words 'or which shall be made' . . . to obviate all doubt concerning the force of treaties preexisting, by making the words 'all treaties made' to refer to them, as the words inserted would refer to future treaties"); id. at 409 (Aug. 25) (Journal) (same).

[29] U.S. CONST. art. III, § 2, cl. 1, 2.

[30] See Chapter 5 § I(B)(3).

[31] See, e.g., Stewart Jay, The Status of the Law of Nations in Early American Law, 42 VAND. L. REV. 819, 844 & n.115 (1989).

could, together with the political branches, enhance national security.[32] Having earlier described "the want of a judiciary power" as "crown[ing] the defects of the Confederation,"[33] Hamilton famously submitted "that the peace of the WHOLE ought not to be left at the disposal of a PART," because "[t]he union will undoubtedly be answerable to foreign powers for the conduct of its members."[34] In Hamilton's view, this warranted alienage jurisdiction, since "[s]o great a proportion of the cases in which foreigners are parties involve national questions, that it is by far most safe and most expedient to refer all those in which they are concerned to the national tribunals," as well as jurisdiction over admiralty and maritime matters, since even "[t]he most bigoted idolizers of state authority" understood that these involved the law of nations and implicated "the public peace."[35] Jay made a similar case for entrusting treaties to federal courts, stressing concerns about inconsistency and parochialism from the states.[36] Similar arguments, for other heads of jurisdiction, were pressed during ratification debates in Virginia and elsewhere.[37]

Naturally, the prospect of a national judiciary, one considerably expanded from its largely hypothetical roots in the Articles, engendered resistance. Elbridge Gerry, who refused to sign the proposed Constitution, highlighted its judiciary's "oppressive" character.[38] Others, including in Virginia, shared the sentiment,

---

[32] See generally ANTHONY J. BELLIA, JR. & BRADFORD R. CLARK, THE LAW OF NATIONS AND THE UNITED STATES CONSTITUTION (2017); David M. Golove & Daniel J. Hulsebosch, A Civilized Nation: The Early American Constitution, the Law of Nations, and the Pursuit of International Recognition, 85 N.Y.U. L. REV. 932, 1001–07 (2010); e.g., Thomas H. Lee, The Safe-Conduct Theory of the Alien Tort Statute, 106 COLUM. L. REV. 830, 840 (2006) (drawing attention to "the crucial role the founding group intended the newly created federal courts to play in ensuring national security, economic strength, and the peaceful conduct of the Republic's foreign affairs").

[33] THE FEDERALIST NO. 22, at 150 (Alexander Hamilton).

[34] THE FEDERALIST NO. 80, at 476 (Alexander Hamilton).

[35] Id.

[36] THE FEDERALIST NO. 3, at 42–44 (John Jay).

[37] Remarking on jurisdiction over cases involving foreign states, John Marshall stated that it was "the means of preventing disputes with foreign nations." 3 JONATHAN ELLIOT, THE DEBATES IN THE SEVERAL STATE CONVENTIONS, ON THE ADOPTION OF THE FEDERAL CONSTITUTION, AS RECOMMENDED BY THE GENERAL CONVENTION AT PHILADELPHIA IN 1787, at 557 (2d ed. 1996) (1891) [hereinafter ELLIOT'S DEBATES]. James Madison and others attributed a similar purpose to the creation of federal courts, and federal jurisdiction, generally. 3 id. at 530 (James Madison) (explaining goals "to prevent all occasions of having disputes with foreign powers, to prevent disputes between different states, and remedy partial decisions"); id. at 532–38 (offering similar defenses of particular grants); 3 id. at 570 (William Randolph) (describing federal judiciary as being "[s]elf-defence" of the national government against encroachment by the states, and "to perpetuate harmony between us and foreign powers"). For illustrations elsewhere, see, for example, 2 id. at 489–90 (Wilson) (noting significance of treaty jurisdiction to foreign relations); id. at 492–93 (hypothesizing, in justifying clause concerning jurisdiction over suits involving foreign citizens, a foreign sovereign stating that "'My subject has received a flagrant injury: do me justice, or I will do myself justice'"); 4 id. at 158 (William Davie) (supporting jurisdiction over treaties and the rights of foreigners, since "[i]f our courts of justice did not decide in favor of foreign citizens and subjects when they ought, it might involve the whole Union in a war").

[38] 1 ELLIOT'S DEBATES, supra note 37, at 492–93.

though some conceded the argument for federal authority over foreign-facing cases and controversies.[39] About one-fifth of the amendments proposed by the state ratifying conventions, and more than one-quarter of the amendments proposed in the first session of Congress, sought changes in Article III.[40] These were not successful, and the substantial addition of the Bill of Rights was not perceived as having any special relevance for foreign relations. The bigger influence on Article III was its early implementation.

C. Subsequent History

The First Congress, through the Judiciary Act of 1789,[41] illuminated the contemporary understanding of Article III and its ambitions.[42] After delicate compromises, the Act managed to establish federal courts capable of addressing matters touching on foreign affairs.[43] Federal question jurisdiction was limited, leaving most issues to state courts.[44] Diversity and alienage jurisdiction, too, was shared with state courts (subject, in certain cases, to possible removal), and governed by a high monetary threshold, without great regard to whether foreign

---

[39] Thus, for example, George Mason, in Virginia, protested "What is there left to the State Courts? . . . There is no limitation," but granted the propriety of federal jurisdiction over treaties, ambassadors, and maritime matters. 3 *id.* at 521, 523; *see also* Federal Farmer, No. 3 (Oct. 10, 1787), *in* 2 THE COMPLETE ANTI-FEDERALIST 41–43 (Herbert J. Storing ed., 1981) (objecting to forms of diversity jurisdiction, including those involving foreigners); Brutus No. 13 (Feb. 21, 1788), *in id.* at 159–65 (questioning authority in cases arising under treaties as potentially "dangerous and improper," but accepting propriety of jurisdiction over, among things, cases concerning ambassadors and admiralty and maritime matters).

[40] RUSSELL R. WHEELER & CYNTHIA E. HARRISON, FED. JUDICIAL CTR., CREATING THE FEDERAL JUDICIAL SYSTEM 2 (3d ed. 2005) (citing RICHARD H. FALLON, DANIEL J. MELTZER, & DAVID L. SHAPIRO, HART AND WECHSLER'S THE FEDERAL COURTS AND THE FEDERAL SYSTEM 20 (4th ed. 1996)).

[41] Act of Sept. 24, 1789, ch. 20, 1 Stat. 73.

[42] The Judiciary Act is often considered highly useful as a basis for interpreting Article III. 1 LAURENCE H. TRIBE, AMERICAN CONSTITUTIONAL LAW 276 (3d ed. 2000) (stating that the Judiciary Act of 1789 "is ordinarily thought to reflect an authoritative understanding of the meaning of Article III"); *e.g.*, William R. Casto, *The First Congress's Understanding of Its Authority Over the Federal Courts' Jurisdiction*, 26 B.C. L. REV. 1101, 1103 (1985). At the same time, its value in resolving particular questions may be constrained, including because it was highly politicized. *See* Daniel J. Meltzer, *The History and Structure of Article III*, 138 U. PA. L. REV. 1569, 1585 & n.55, 1608–13 & nn.139–63 (1990).

[43] *See, e.g.,* Holt, *supra* note 5, at 1515–18; Charles Warren, *New Light on the History of the Federal Judiciary Act of 1789*, 37 HARV. L. REV. 49, 52–54 (1923).

[44] Under the statute, the Supreme Court was charged with responsibility, via writs of error, only when a state's highest court had drawn into question the validity or supremacy of federal law. Judiciary Act of 1789, *supra* note 41, § 25, 1 Stat. at 85–86; *see* Warren, *supra* note 43, at 61–62 (noting reduction of federal-question jurisdiction in committee); Meltzer, *supra* note 42, at 1585–86 (noting that this would not fully be resolved until 1914).

citizens were involved.[45] Even so, some topics of foreign concern fared somewhat better. For example, while Article III had permitted admiralty and maritime matters, like most matters, to be left to the Supreme Court's appellate jurisdiction, the First Congress gave the new federal courts exclusive original jurisdiction over all such cases, including prize cases of potentially great sensitivity, with the exception of some common-law, *in personam* matters that had been folded into Article III when the terms were simplified during the Convention.[46]

Article III had also extended the federal judicial power "to all Cases affecting Ambassadors, other public Ministers and Consuls"—indeed, providing that "the Supreme Court shall have original Jurisdiction" over them, as with cases to which a U.S. state was party.[47] This was not completely fulfilled by the first Judiciary Act, but the compromises were relatively minor. The Supreme Court was given exclusive jurisdiction over suits or proceedings *against* ambassadors or other public ministers and nonexclusive jurisdiction over others, namely, those *by* ambassadors or other public ministers, or those brought by or against consuls or vice consuls. This approach meant that foreign officials had relatively ready recourse to the Supreme Court, and ensured that the Court could resolve suits against high-ranking emissaries that were especially likely to offend international obligations. Moreover, Congress only permitted those suits or proceedings "as a court of law can have or exercise consistently with the law of nations," which it buttressed a year later by criminalizing certain actions against ambassadors or other public ministers as violations of the law of nations.[48]

Last, but not least, the first Judiciary Act added concurrent federal jurisdiction over "all causes where an alien sues for a tort only in violation of the law of nations or a treaty of the United States."[49] This provision, which later became known as the Alien Tort Statute (ATS), had little early application that might

[45] Judiciary Act of 1789, *supra* note 41, § 11-12, 1 Stat. at 78–80. The high monetary threshold substantially compromised the direct recourse to federal courts of many British creditors. Casto, *supra* note 42, at 1110–14; Holt, *supra* note 5, at 1487–88.

[46] Judiciary Act of 1789, *supra* note 41, § 9, 1 Stat. at 76–77. For more extensive discussion, including the Act's "saving to suitors" clause permitting common law remedies, see Bradford R. Clark, *Federal Common Law: A Structural Reinterpretation*, 144 U. PA. L. REV. 1245, 1332–60 (1996); Meltzer, *supra* note 42, at 1585–86. *But see* Holt, *supra* note 5, at 1497 (describing exemption under the "saving to suitors" clause as "a startling breach of the general understanding that admiralty and maritime cases would be exclusively federal, to say nothing of article III's mandatory language").

[47] U.S. CONST. art. III, § 2.

[48] Judiciary Act of 1789, *supra* note 41, § 13, 1 Stat. at 80; Crimes Act of 1790, ch. 9, §§ 25–26, 1 Stat. 112, 117–18; *see* Clark, *supra* note 46, at 1311–21; *see also* Meltzer, *supra* note 42, at 1576, 1595–99; Warren, *supra* note 43, at 93–94.

[49] Judiciary Act of 1789, *supra* note 41, § 9, 1 Stat. at 76–77. Congress complemented this through statutory directions concerning the cause of action. *See* Act of Sept. 29, 1789, ch. 21, 1 Stat. 93 (repealed 1792); Act of May 8, 1792, ch. 36, 1 Stat. 275 (repealed 1872); Anthony J. Bellia, Jr. & Bradford R. Clark, *The Original Source of the Cause of Action in Federal Courts: The Example of the Alien Tort Statute*, 101 VA. L. REV. 609 (2015).

have clarified its intended use.[50] Notably, though, it appeared to assert federal jurisdiction over cases not obviously contemplated by Article III—to the extent the ATS applied to any cause of action arising under the law of nations (which were arguably not part of the "laws of the United States"), rather than being limited to cases predicated on other Article III heads of jurisdiction—without any surviving discussion of how this was compatible with the Constitution.[51] The First Congress also considered proposals that would have dramatically reduced the scope of federal jurisdiction generally, and also without much concern about constitutional objections.[52] Finer points aside, though, the first Judiciary Act succeeding in establishing a long-lasting, substantial role for national courts in foreign relations matters.

Early judicial practice is better discussed in particular doctrinal contexts. But on the whole, the founding generation seemed to welcome judicial engagement in foreign relations. During the Neutrality Crisis, for example, when the United States was pressed by Great Britain to remedy French predation on British shipping, the executive branch encouraged a substantial role for the courts; the objective was assuredly not to undermine the executive's own role in diplomacy, but rather to use admiralty and maritime jurisdiction to resolve legal disputes, the better to regulate a foreign-relations crisis. The Supreme Court declined any purely advisory role, but did accept the capacity of federal courts (at least in principle) to address privateering disputes.[53] The Neutrality Crisis is better known for helping to define the powers of the political branches, which potentially qualified the potential for judicial intervention, but it also validated some judicial function in foreign affairs.[54]

[50] Partly because the ATS was little applied, it presented a number of puzzles when it was revived late in the twentieth century. See infra this chapter § IV(A)(1)(e)(ii); see also Chapter 5 § IV(B).

[51] For discussion of the constitutional questions raised by the ATS, compare, e.g., Anthony J. Bellia, Jr. & Bradford R. Clark, The Alien Tort Statute and the Law of Nations, 78 U. Chi. L. Rev. 445 (2011), and Curtis A. Bradley, The Alien Tort Statute and Article III, 42 Va. J. Int'l L. 587 (2002), and John Harrison, The Constitution and the Law of Nations, 106 Geo. L.J. 1659 (2018), with William S. Dodge, The Constitutionality of the Alien Tort Statute: Some Observations on Text and Context, 42 Va. J. Int'l L. 687 (2002), and Carlos M. Vázquez, Customary International Law as U.S. Law: A Critique of the Revisionist and Intermediate Positions and a Defense of the Modern Position, 86 Notre Dame L. Rev. 1495 (2011). In Jesner v. Arab Bank, PLC, 138 S. Ct. 1386 (2018), Justice Gorsuch expressed the view—seemingly as a matter of statutory interpretation only—that "because Article III's diversity-of-citizenship clause calls for a U.S. party, and because the ATS clause requires an alien plaintiff, it follows that an American defendant was needed for an ATS suit to proceed." Id. at 1415 (Gorsuch, J., concurring in part and concurring in the judgment).

[52] See Wythe Holt, Federal Courts as the Asylum to Federal Interests: Randolph's Report, the Benson Amendment, and the Original Understanding of the Federal Judiciary, 36 Buff. L. Rev. 341 (1987) (describing two near-immediate, unsuccessful initiatives).

[53] See Arlyck, supra note 2; see also Golove & Hulsebosch, supra note 32, at 1023–27; David Sloss, Judicial Foreign Policy: Lessons from the 1790s, 53 St. Louis U. L.J. 145, 148 (2008). See generally William R. Casto, Foreign Affairs and the Constitution in the Age of Fighting Sail (2006).

[54] For other emphases, see, for example, Casto, supra note 53, at 3 (stating that "the federal courts played a relatively minor role" in resolving the crisis); Martin S. Flaherty, The Story of the Neutrality

II. Nonjusticiability and Foreign Affairs

Over time—due at least in part to changing visions of the judicial role, the greater breadth and depth of U.S. engagement in foreign affairs, or other factors—the degree to which judicial involvement in foreign relations controversies was accepted appears to have changed, leaving the impression that the judiciary plays a secondary role. Justiciability doctrines reflect that development and, to a degree, may have helped fuel it.

A. Political Question Doctrine

Every justiciability doctrine has potential purchase in cases touching on foreign relations, but the political question doctrine is the one with greatest prominence. The poor track record of the doctrine in Supreme Court litigation may temper its significance, but the doctrine continues to command attention, and is likely to continue to maintain an important role in the lower courts.

1. Background and Scope

The political question doctrine has a surprisingly limited pedigree. The seminal application was *Luther v. Borden*, which held that identifying the lawful government of Rhode Island—at issue due to a dispute between members of a popular movement claiming sovereignty and a militia acting on behalf of the state's legislature—"is a question to be settled by the political power[,] [a]nd when that power has decided, the courts are bound to take notice of its decision, and to follow it."[55] Chief Justice Taney likened the question to the recognition of foreign governments, in which "the government acknowledged by the President is always recognized in the courts of justice."[56] The Supreme Court later extended this approach, acknowledging that Congress, like the president, might sometimes be vested with authority to make the final judgment as to the constitutional scope of its powers.[57] In the main, these foundational cases described circumstances in

---

Controversy: Struggling Over Presidential Power Outside the Courts, in PRESIDENTIAL POWER STORIES 21 (Christopher H. Schroeder & Curtis A. Bradley eds., 2009) (emphasizing rise in presidential authority); *see also* Arlyck, *supra* note 2, at 2–4 & nn.3–7 (citing additional authorities).

[55]   Luther v. Borden, 48 U.S. (7 How.) 1, 47 (1849).
[56]   *Id.* at 44; *cf.* Oetjen v. Cent. Leather Co., 246 U.S. 297, 302 (1918) (addressing expropriation by Mexico as an act of state, and stating that recognition "'is not a judicial, but is a political question, the determination of which by the legislative and executive departments of any government conclusively binds the judges'") (quoting Jones v. United States, 137 U.S. 202, 212 (1890)).
[57]   Pac. States Tel. & Tel. Co. v. Oregon, 223 U.S. 118, 141–42, 146 (1912) (invoking doctrine to defer to Congress regarding whether the state government of Oregon, including its decisions adopted by popular initiative, was unrepublican).

which a court would regard a political actor's decision as final, even if that decision involved applying a legal rule.[58]

The linchpin of modern doctrine, *Baker v. Carr*,[59] arguably continued this approach,[60] but it also provided considerably more guidance. Examples from foreign relations were front and center, but the Court also stressed that "it is error to suppose that every case or controversy which touches foreign relations lies beyond judicial cognizance."[61] Rather, Justice Brennan's opinion described the need for "a discriminating analysis of the particular question posed, in terms of the history of its management by the political branches, of its susceptibility to judicial handling in the light of its nature and posture in the specific case, and of the possible consequences of judicial action." The Court described a series of factors, one or more of which marked a possible political question:

> Prominent on the surface of any case held to involve a political question is found [1] a textually demonstrable constitutional commitment of the issue to a coordinate political department; or [2] a lack of judicially discoverable and manageable standards for resolving it; or [3] the impossibility of deciding without an initial policy determination of a kind clearly for nonjudicial discretion; or [4] the impossibility of a court's undertaking independent resolution without expressing lack of the respect due coordinate branches of government; or [5] an unusual need for unquestioning adherence to a political decision already made; or [6] the potentiality of embarrassment from multifarious pronouncements by various departments on one question.[62]

The Supreme Court subsequently indicated that political question doctrine concerned subject-matter jurisdiction, thereby distinguishing it from nonjurisdictional constraints like the act of state doctrine.[63] One longstanding

---

[58] *See* John Harrison, *The Political Question Doctrines*, 67 Am. U. L. Rev. 457 (2018); *cf. id.* at 481–85 (noting secondary strand involving cases like Gilligan v. Morgan, 413 U.S. 1 (1973), in which the Court asserted limits to the judicial capacity to afford prospective relief against a political actor in military or national security contexts).

[59] 369 U.S. 186 (1962).

[60] *Compare* Harrison, *supra* note 58, at 497–504 (stressing continuity), *with* Tara Leigh Grove, *The Lost History of the Political Question Doctrine*, 90 N.Y.U. L. Rev. 1908 (2015) (distinguishing modern doctrine).

[61] 369 U.S. at 211. The Court noted as potential political questions cases involving treaty termination, judicial refusal to apply a treaty that was inconsistent with a subsequent statute, recognition of foreign governments, recognition of belligerency abroad, recognition of foreign official representatives, and immunity from seizure of vessels owned by friendly foreign governments, and the duration of hostilities. *Id.* at 211–14.

[62] *Id.* at 217 (enumeration added).

[63] Rucho v. Common Cause, 139 S. Ct. 2484, 2508 (2019) (vacating and remanding on political question grounds, "with instructions to dismiss for lack of jurisdiction"); Schlesinger v. Reservists Comm. to Stop the War, 418 U.S. 208, 215 (1974) (describing doctrine as an element of Article III jurisdictional limits). *But cf.* United States Department of Commerce v. Montana, 503 U.S. 442, 458 (1992) (describing doctrine as entailing "abstention from judicial review"). Lower courts generally

critique, however, is that the political question doctrine does not really restrain the judiciary much at all, given how similar it is to deciding on the merits
whether authority has been assigned by the Constitution to one or both of the
political branches.[64] And in practice, relatively few subsequent cases, even those
touching on foreign affairs, were regarded as presenting political questions.[65] For
example, while the Court applied the doctrine in a case involving relief against
the National Guard and in a case involving treaty termination,[66] it held it inapposite to a matter of statutory interpretation that involved monitoring treaty
performance.[67]

The Court's application of the political question doctrine in *Zivotofsky
v. Clinton (Zivotofsky I)*, in 2012,[68] was portrayed by some as signaling the
doctrine's end.[69] That case involved a suit by parents seeking to have their
Jerusalem-born son's place of birth listed as "Israel" on a consular report of birth
abroad and on his passport, as permitted by a federal statute.[70] Their request
was rejected by U.S. officials based on a Department of State policy that prohibited, for foreign policy reasons, any formal legal pronouncement concerning the
status of Jerusalem, consistent with President George W. Bush's position that
he would decline to enforce the statutory provision because it impermissibly

took the doctrine to limit Article III jurisdiction, and presumably will be encouraged by *Rucho. See,
e.g.*, Corrie v. Caterpillar, 503 F.3d 974, 979–82 (9th Cir. 2007); *accord* Spectrum Stores, Inc. v. Citgo
Petroleum Corp., 632 F.3d 938, 948 (5th Cir. 2011); *see also* Al-Tamimi v. Adelson, 916 F.3d 1, 7–8
n.4 (D.C. Cir. 2019) (treating doctrine as jurisdictional, but acknowledging "[p]erhaps the better
view is that ... some elements of the political question doctrine are jurisdictional and others are prudential"); *cf.* Harrison, *supra* note 58, at 485–504 (arguing, prior to *Rucho*, that the Court had never
formally held that the doctrine was a limit on Article III jurisdiction, and that doing so would be
misplaced).

[64] HENKIN, FOREIGN AFFAIRS, at 143–48; Louis Henkin, *Is There a "Political Question" Doctrine?*,
85 YALE L.J. 597 (1976); *e.g.*, El-Shifa Pharm. Indus. Co. v. United States, 607 F.3d 836, 857 (D.C. Cir.
2010) (en banc; Kavanaugh, J., concurring in the judgment) (political question doctrine should not
apply to cases alleging violations of statutes regulating executive conduct, because "the court would
be ruling (at least implicitly) that the statute intrudes impermissibly on the Executive's prerogatives
under Article II of the Constitution").

[65] *See El-Shifa Pharm. Indus. Co.*, 607 F.3d at 856 & n.3 (Kavanaugh, J., concurring in the judgment) (noting foreign relations controversies decided by the Supreme Court); *see also id.* at 841–42
(en banc; majority op.).

[66] See, respectively, Gilligan v. Morgan, 413 U.S. 1, 10–12 (1973) (holding that complaint alleging
violation of speech and assembly rights at Kent State presented nonjusticiable political question insofar as it sought judicial supervision of Ohio National Guard), and Goldwater v. Carter, 444 U.S.
996, 1002–06 (1979) (plurality op.) (holding that unilateral termination of a treaty presented a political question). For more extensive discussion of treaty termination, see Chapter 6 § VI.

[67] Japan Whaling Ass'n v. Am. Cetacean Soc'y, 478 U.S. 221, 229–30 (1986) (interpreting statutes
requiring the Secretary of Commerce to certify Japan for failing to abide by International Whaling
Convention quotas, like interpreting treaties, does not present a political question).

[68] 566 U.S. 189 (2012).

[69] *See, e.g.*, Gwynne Skinner, *Misunderstood, Misconstrued, and Now Clearly Dead: The "Political
Question Doctrine" as a Justiciability Doctrine*, 29 J.L. & POL. 427 (2014).

[70] Foreign Relations Authorization Act, Fiscal Year 2003, Pub. L. No. 107-228, § 214(d), 116 Stat.
1350, 1366 (2002).

interfered with the president's constitutional authority to "determine the terms on which recognition is given to foreign states."[71] The district court dismissed the suit on political question grounds, and the court of appeals affirmed,[72] but the Supreme Court reversed. The Court described the political question doctrine as a "narrow exception" to the judiciary's obligation to decide cases properly before it.[73] The Court emphasized the need to focus on the question posed, not on a decision's potential implications, and stressed that a statute's constitutionality was classically a question for the courts—a point it reconciled, or tried to reconcile, with the first two *Baker* factors.[74]

As stringent as *Zivotofsky I* may have seemed, the political question doctrine survived it. The Court subsequently held in *Rucho v. Common Cause* that political gerrymandering claims presented a political question,[75] making clear that the doctrine remains available where the nature of the question so warrants. The doctrine will almost certainly remain a force in the lower courts, which lack the luxury of discretionary review, and which may appreciate a means by which they can avoid resolving difficult foreign relations cases.[76]

2. Applying the Doctrine

The initial step in political question cases is to identify as precisely as possible the question that is purportedly nonjusticiable. While the inquiry is case-specific, some generalizations are possible. Particularly after *Zivotofsky I*, interbranch battles over a statute's constitutionality are likely to be regarded as susceptible to judicial review. Lower courts have also indicated that cases involving the due process rights of individuals are justiciable,[77] and the dissenters in *Rucho* went so

[71] Statement on Signing the Foreign Relations Authorization Act, Fiscal Year 2003, 38 WEEKLY COMP. PRES. DOC. 1658, 1659 (Sept. 30, 2002).
[72] Zivotofsky v. Sec'y of State, 571 F.3d 1227 (D.C. Cir. 2009), *aff'g* 511 F. Supp. 2d 97 (D.D.C. 2007).
[73] *Zivotofsky I*, 566 U.S. at 195.
[74] *Id.* at 195–201. Justice Sotomayor's concurrence would have emphasized the first three *Baker* factors (viewing the final three factors as influential on "[r]are occasions"), whereas Justice Breyer's dissent would have placed greater weight on the foreign affairs, and Middle East, context. *Id.* at 202–07 (Sotomayor, J., concurring in part and concurring in the judgment); *id.* at 212–20 (Breyer, J., dissenting).
[75] 139 S. Ct. 2484, 2508 (2019). This followed earlier, inconclusive indications that the political question doctrine applied. Vieth v. Jubelirer, 541 U.S. 267, 277–81 (2004) (plurality opinion).
[76] *See, e.g.*, Al-Tamimi v. Adelson, 916 F.3d 1, 7–14 (D.C. Cir. 2019); Jaber v. United States, 861 F.3d 241, 245–50 (D.C. Cir. 2017); Saldana v. Occidental Petroleum Corp., 774 F.3d 544, 551–54 (9th Cir. 2014); Center for Biological Diversity v. Trump, 453 F. Supp. 3d 11, 30–34 (D.D.C. 2020); Ahmed v. Cissna, 327 F. Supp. 3d 650, 668–70 (S.D.N.Y. 2018).
[77] Comm. of U.S. Citizens Living in Nicaragua v. Reagan, 859 F.2d 929, 935 (D.C. Cir. 1988) (noting that "the Supreme Court has repeatedly found that claims based on [due process] rights are justiciable, even if they implicate foreign policy decisions"); *see* Zaidan v. Trump, 317 F. Supp. 3d 8, 26–29 (D.D.C. 2018) (holding justiciable due process claims objecting to inclusion on terrorist "kill list," notwithstanding political question doctrine).

188 THE LAW OF U.S. FOREIGN RELATIONS

far as to imply that the doctrine was ill-suited to any constitutional violation.[78]
On that view, it is unclear whether a case like *Goldwater v. Carter*, in which a plurality of the Supreme Court decided that the president's unilateral termination of
a bilateral treaty presented a political question, would be decided the same way
nowadays.[79]

There remain, of course, a broad range of other claims to which the political
question doctrine might apply. At least some asserted statutory violations,[80]
treaty violations,[81] customary international law violations,[82] and common-law
torts[83] have been considered political questions. The *dramatis personae*, too, vary.
Cases typically involve challenges to federal or state action, but cases challenging
foreign governments and private companies have also been dismissed using the
doctrine, at least sometimes because they are tantamount to challenging official
U.S. policies.[84]

---

[78] *Rucho*, 139 S. Ct. at 2509 (Kagan, J., dissenting) (opening by declaring "[f]or the first time ever,
this Court refuses to remedy a constitutional violation because it thinks the task beyond judicial
capabilities").

[79] Goldwater v. Carter, 444 U.S. 996, 1002–06 (1979) (plurality op.); Harold Hongju Koh,
Presidential Power to Terminate International Agreements, 128 YALE L.J. FORUM 432, 445 (2018) (concluding that "[u]nder *Zivotofsky I*'s narrowed two-pronged political question test, treaty termination
is not a political question"). For further discussion of treaty termination, see Chapter 6 § VI.

[80] *See, e.g.*, *Zaidan*, 317 F. Supp. 3d at 25–26 (claim that the "kill list" failed to conform with
Presidential Policy Guidance, thereby constituting an arbitrary and capricious action violating the
Administrative Procedure Act); *see also* Wu Tien Li-Shou v. United States, 777 F. 3d 175, 181 (4th
Cir. 2015) (finding the Public Vessels Act standard insufficient to avoid political question concerning
sinking of fishing vessel during NATO exercise); *cf. Al-Tamimi*, 916 F.3d at 12 n.6 (noting that a statutory claim is less likely to present a political question, because it is generally directed to the judiciary
and provides courts with a judicially manageable standard, but "a statutory claim can present a political question if resolving [it] requires the court to make an integral policy choice").

[81] *See, e.g.*, Republic of the Marshall Islands v. United States, 865 F.3d 1187, 1200–01 (9th Cir.
2017) (claimed breaches of Treaty on the Non-Proliferation of Nuclear Weapons).

[82] *See, e.g.*, El-Shifa Pharm. Indus. Co. v. United States, 607 F.3d 836, 844–46 (D.C. Cir. 2009) (claim
that the United States violated an international norm against uncompensated property destruction,
following a cruise missile attack against a Sudanese pharmaceutical plant); Alperin v. Vatican Bank,
410 F.3d 532, 558–62 (9th Cir. 2005); Tel-Oren v. Libyan Arab Republic 726 F.2d 774, 823–27 (D.C.
Cir. 1984) (Robb, J., concurring) (international law claims relating to armed attack on civilians).
Post-*Zivotofsky I*, decisions have varied as to whether such claims are more cognizable if incorporated by statute. *Compare Al-Tamimi*, 916 F.3d at 11–12 (holding that a claim that Israeli settlers were
committing genocide did not present political question, in light of judicially manageable standard
afforded by the Alien Tort Statute), *with* Jaber v. United States, 861 F.3d 241, 245–49 (D.C. Cir.
2017) (holding that a claim that U.S. drone attack violated customary international law presented a
political question, notwithstanding the Alien Tort Statute and Torture Victim Protection Act).

[83] *See, e.g.*, *El-Shifa Pharm. Indus. Co.*, 607 F.3d at 846–48 (defamation claims, intertwined with
asserted basis for cruise missile attack); *cf.* Lane v. Halliburton, 529 F.3d 548, 557–68 (5th. Cir.
2008) (finding that fraudulent misrepresentation and negligence claims, alleging failure by a military contractor to protect its truck drivers against insurgent attacks in Iraq, might not be inextricable
from political question).

[84] *See, e.g.*, Saldana v. Occidental Petroleum Corp., 774 F.3d 544, 550–55 (9th Cir. 2014) (dismissing
on political question grounds Alien Tort Statute claims against oil company, in part because it was
impossible to advance a theory of liability that would not apply with equal force to foreign policy and
national security determinations by the U.S. government) (citing Corrie v. Caterpillar, 503 F.3d 974
(9th Cir. 2007)); *Alperin*, 410 F.3d at 560 (stressing that resolving allegations that the Vatican assisted
fleeing war criminals would necessarily bear on similar allegations against the United States).

After a potential political question is identified, the next challenge is choosing which multifactor test to apply. Some judges are attracted to the condensed test articulated by Justice Powell in *Goldwater v. Carter*.[85] Most, however, invoke the previously quoted *Baker v. Carr* approach—understanding both that, in theory, any one of the six *Baker* factors may suffice to establish a political question,[86] and also that the first two *Baker* factors (particularly after *Zivotofsky I*) are predominant or even necessary conditions.[87]

The *Baker* approach is not easy to apply. The first factor ("a textually demonstrable constitutional commitment of the issue" to one of the political branches) is sometimes addressed by reciting various powers held by the president or Congress, but that can say more about the merits than about whether the question is one the Constitution says is to be resolved by one of the other branches. It is the question which matters. Thus, as *Zivotofsky I* explained, asking the judiciary to decide whether a particular sovereign deserves recognition would present a political question, but asking whether a particular matter falls or does not fall within the president's recognition power is justiciable.[88] Constitutional text that describes conclusive political branch authority over matters of law-application and fact-finding is the most indicative, though evidence that no judicial role was contemplated is also helpful.[89] In contrast, claims about downstream consequences of a decision made by one of the political branches are much less probative.[90] If the political question doctrine speaks to such consequences, it can only be through the other (prudential) factors.

---

[85] Justice Powell would have condensed the inquiry into three factors: "(i) Does the issue involve resolution of questions committed by the text of the Constitution to a coordinate branch of Government? (ii) Would resolution of the question demand that a court move beyond areas of judicial expertise? (iii) Do prudential considerations counsel against judicial intervention?" Goldwater v. Carter, 444 U.S. 996, 998 (1979) (Powell, J., concurring in judgment); *see, e.g.,* Ramirez de Arellano v. Weinberger, 745 F. 2d 1500, 1511 (D.C. Cir. 1984) (citing approach).

[86] For example, political gerrymandering opinions focused on the second factor. Rucho v. Common Cause, 139 S. Ct. 2484, 2494 (2019); Vieth v. Jubelirer, 541 U.S. 267, 278 (2004) (plurality opinion); *see also* Schneider v. Kissinger, 412 F.3d 190, 194 (D.C. Cir. 2005) ("To find a political question, we need only conclude that one factor is present, not all."); *accord* Jaber v. United States, 861 F.3d 241, 245 (D.C. Cir. 2017); *cf.* Baker v. Carr, 369 U.S. 186, 217 (if "one of these formulations is inextricable from the case," a political question may be found).

[87] *Zivotofsky I,* 566 U.S. 189, 195 (2012) (focusing on first two factors); *Vieth,* 541 U.S. at 278 (plurality opinion) (describing *Baker* factors as "probably listed in descending order of both importance and certainty"); *see also* Nixon v. United States, 506 U.S. 224, 228 (1993); *Al Tamimi,* 916 F.3d at 10; Republic of the Marshall Islands v. United States, 865 F.3d 1187, 1200 (9th Cir. 2017); Hourani v. Mirtchev, 796 F.3d 1, 8 (D.C. Cir. 2015); *Alperin,* 410 F.2d at 545.

[88] *Zivotofsky I,* 566 U.S. at 196–97.

[89] *See Nixon,* 506 U.S. at 233–35.

[90] For example, the Ninth Circuit concluded that because "[d]etermining whether the Vatican Bank was unjustly enriched by profits derived from slave labor" during World War II would require examining the wartime conduct of an occupation regime, "[c]ondemning . . . a foreign government with which the United States was at war," the first *Baker* factor indicated a political question. *Alperin,* 410 F.3d at 561. But it is hard to see how the claim unsettled the finality either of a declaration of war or its cessation; at most, it would seem like the kind of "political implications" that *Zivotofsky I* distinguished. *Zivotofsky I,* 566 U.S. at 196 (internal quotations and citations omitted).

The second *Baker* factor ("a lack of judicially discoverable and manageable standards for resolving" the question) is itself largely unmanageable. *Zivotofsky I* indicated that the complexity or difficulty of resolving a legal inquiry does not by itself make a case nonjusticiable,[91] but the second factor is mostly just that. Courts have referred to the vagueness of statutory and treaty terms,[92] noted the challenge of assessing both "small-bore tactical decisions" and grand strategies,[93] and suggested an adverse presumption for foreign relations matters lacking statutory, administrative, or case law.[94] In a political gerrymandering case, the Supreme Court suggested that justiciable standards are ones that are not only "discernible" and "manageable" but also "limited and precise," "clear," and "politically neutral."[95] In foreign relations cases, analogously, courts have balked at claims that they perceive as involving whether a military or foreign policy decision was wise. Often, this is based on a surmise from the claim: for example, a claimant who invokes a law-of-nations standard may be taken to be asking whether U.S. military action was "mistaken and not justified," or a wrongful death action may be interpreted as questioning the wisdom of a covert intelligence action.[96] Courts should be careful lest their wariness of policy arguments in legal form lead them to recast reasonably precise claims as abstract questions.[97]

Prudential considerations, in the guise of the remaining *Baker* factors or otherwise,[98] are also hazardous. Courts deciding foreign affairs cases will likely continue to note when initial policy determinations are required, or if deciding a question might show a lack of respect for the political branches or potentially cause embarrassment. Still, given recent Supreme Court precedent, it is unlikely

---

[91] *Zivotofsky I*, 566 U.S. at 197, 200.

[92] As to statutes, see, for example, Ctr. for Biological Diversity v. Trump, 453 F. Supp. 3d 11, 32–33 (D.D.C. 2020) (acknowledging that courts routinely engage in statutory interpretation, but concluding that whether the president exceeded his authority under the National Emergency Act was not judicially manageable); California v. Trump, 407 F. Supp. 3d 869, 891 (N.D. Cal. 2019) (same); as to treaties, see, for example, Republic of the Marshall Islands v. United States, 865 F.3d 1187, 1201 (9th Cir. 2017) (negotiating obligations in the Nuclear Non-Proliferation Treaty). As the latter opinion noted, there is a likeness between treaty terms that fail the second *Baker* factor and those that courts may deem non-self-executing, see *id.* at 1201, but only the political question doctrine affects subject-matter jurisdiction. *See supra* this chapter text accompanying note 63.

[93] *E.g.*, Wu Tien Li-Shou v. United States, 777 F. 3d 175, 180–81 (4th Cir. 2015).

[94] *E.g.*, Spectrum Stores, Inc. v. Citgo Petroleum Corp., 632 F.3d 938, 952 (5th Cir. 2011).

[95] Rucho v. Common Cause, 139 S. Ct. 2484, 2500 (2019); *see also* Vieth v. Jubelirer, 541 U.S. 267, 278 (2004) (plurality opinion). *But see Rucho*, 139 S. Ct. at 2521 (Kagan, J., dissenting) ("The majority's 'how much is too much' critique fares no better than its neutrality argument. How about the following for a first-cut answer: This much is too much.").

[96] The examples are drawn from El-Shifa Pharmaceutical Industries Co. v. United States, 607 F.3d 836, 845 (D.C. Cir. 2010) (en banc), and Schneider v. Kissinger, 412 F.3d 190, 197 (D.C. Cir. 2005). In a later case, the D.C. Circuit characterized this approach as "functional." Jaber v. United States, 861 F.3d 241, 246 (D.C. Cir. 2017).

[97] *See, e.g., Spectrum Stores*, 632 F.3d at 952 (expressing "recasting" objection); *Schneider*, 412 F.3d at 197 (same).

[98] Baker v. Carr, 369 U.S. 186, 217 (1962). Professor Harrison has contended that these additional factors actually elaborate the first factor, properly understood. *See* Harrison, *supra* note 58, at 500–04.

that such grounds could sustain dismissal on political question grounds.[99] Some recent decisions have asked instead whether the questions involve "policy choices ... to be made by the political branches" or "purely legal issues ... to be decided by the courts,"[100] which is not necessarily an improvement.[101] Whether such an approach will invite or survive Supreme Court scrutiny remains to be seen.

Lower courts may also develop relevant variants of the political question doctrine. For example, some decisions, reflecting an intuition that military decisions are for the executive branch, suggest that military contractor cases should focus on whether the military exercises direct control over the contractor or whether the military's decisions regarding the contractor's conduct are closely intertwined with national defense interests.[102] Cases challenging the government's resort to the use of armed force often suggest a similar instinct, but without any distinctive formula. Some Vietnam-era war powers cases regarded challenges as categorically nonjusticiable on political question grounds,[103] while others suggested that whether congressional approval was required was justiciable, while the choice of how approval might be manifested was left to Congress.[104] Following enactment of the War Powers Resolution, some (but not all) decisions held that whether its application had been triggered presented a political question.[105] Because such

---

[99] *But see* Saldana v. Occidental Petroleum Corp., 774 F.3d 544, 552 (9th Cir. 2014) (appearing to rest on the fourth, fifth, and sixth *Baker* factors).

[100] Al-Tamimi v. Adelson, 916 F.3d 1, 11 (D.C. Cir. 2019). In *Al-Tamimi* itself, the court also applied the full slate of *Baker* factors. *See id.* at 11–12. For broader assessments, see *Jabar*, 861 F.3d at 246–49; *Wu Tien Li-Shou*, 777 F.3d at 180–82.

[101] Courts may have very different instincts about whether a particular claim (such as one concerning genocide) raises a purely legal issue. *Compare, e.g., Al-Tamimi*, 916 F.3d at 11–12 (regarding the question of whether Israeli settlers are presently committing genocide as justiciable, in light of statutory framing), *with* Davoyan v. Republic of Turkey, 116 F. Supp. 3d 1084, 1103–04 (C.D. Cal. 2013) (regarding allegations of Turkish genocide toward ethnic Armenians as essentially political).

[102] Metzgar v. KBR, Inc., 893 F.3d 241, 260 (4th Cir. 2018); *see also* Al Shimari v. CACI Premier Technology, Inc., 840 F.3d 147 (4th Cir. 2016).

[103] Massachusetts v. Laird, 451 F.2d 26, 32–34 (1st Cir. 1971) (regarding the war powers as constitutionally committed to both political branches, and not to the judiciary); *accord* Luftig v. McNamara, 373 F.2d 664, 665–66 (D.C. Cir. 1967); Atlee v. Laird, 347 F. Supp. 689, 703–07 (E.D. Pa. 1972), *aff'd without opinion sub nom.*, Atlee v. Richardson, 411 U.S. 911 (1973).

[104] Orlando v. Laird, 443 F.2d 1039, 1042–44 (2d Cir. 1971); *see also* DaCosta v. Laird, 448 F.2d 1368, 1370 (2d Cir. 1971) (noting, too, that means of winding down a conflict posed a political question); Berk v. Laird, 429 F.2d 302, 305 (2d Cir. 1970).

[105] These decisions usually involved both constitutional claims and claims under the War Powers Resolution. *Compare, e.g.*, Campbell v. Clinton, 203 F.3d 19, 25 (D.C. Cir. 2000) (Silberman, J., concurring) (whether the president's refusal to discontinue U.S. activities in Yugoslavia presented a political question given absence of justiciable standards for determining that the statute was triggered), *with id.* at 37–41 (Tatel, J., concurring) (concluding that it did not). For examples of cases found to pose political questions, Crockett v. Reagan, 720 F.2d 1355, 1356–57 (D.C. Cir. 1983) (U.S. military officials in El Salvador); Ange v. Bush, 752 F. Supp. 509, 514–15 (D.D.C. 1990) (pre-Iraq-Kuwait War buildup); Lowry v. Reagan, 676 F. Supp. 333, 340 n.53 (D.D.C.1987) (reflagging operations in the Persian Gulf); *see also* Sanchez-Espinoza v. Reagan, 770 F.2d 202, 209 (D.C. Cir. 1985) (citing prudential *Baker* factors in refusing remedy for aid to Contras).

cases involve constitutional and statutory interpretation, and have largely turned on prudential and remedial considerations, *Zivotofsky I* might suggest a sea change, but thus far that has not been apparent.[106]

Once a court has identified a political question, it must determine whether it is truly "inextricable from the case," or whether the court may instead exercise jurisdiction over remaining issues.[107] This is largely left to judicial discretion, as is the political question doctrine more generally. Congress may legislate so as to confer subject-matter jurisdiction on federal courts, and influence whether a statutory question is judicially manageable or separable, but it cannot override an Article III limitation.[108] As to the executive branch, courts may be interested in its views regarding the consequences of accepting jurisdiction, or concerning prudential factors,[109] but these factors appear to have less weight these days— and deferring to an interested participant may be unwise.[110]

Narrowing the political question doctrine, as in *Zivotofsky I*, might be expected to enhance judicial engagement with foreign affairs matters.[111] Moreover, at least in statutory cases, such narrowing might check the judicial tendency to acquiesce in presidential assertions of authority. That was not, however, how matters later played out in *Zivotofsky v. Kerry (Zivotofsky II)*, which proved to be an extraordinary vindication of the executive's prerogatives.[112]

---

[106] For example, in *Smith v. Obama*, 217 F. Supp. 3d 283 (D.D.C. 2016), *vacated as moot*, 731 Fed. Appx. 8 (D.C. Cir. 2018) (mem.), the district court dismissed a service member's claims that the U.S. campaign against the Islamic State of Iraq and the Levant (ISIL) exceeded commander-in-chief and statutory authority and violated the War Powers Resolution. It focused on the first two *Baker* factors, and distinguished *Zivotofsky I* primarily on the basis that the questions went "significantly beyond interpreting statutes and determining whether they are constitutional," as the court was asked "to second-guess the Executive's application of these statutes to specific facts on the ground in an ongoing combat mission halfway around the world." *Id.* at 299; *see also* Endeley v. U.S. Dep't of Defense, 268 F.Supp.3d 166, 176–78 (D.D.C. 2017) (dismissing on political question grounds claim that U.S. missile strike against Syrian target was unconstitutional and lacked statutory authority); *cf.* Jaber v. United States, 861 F.3d 241 (D.C. Cir. 2017) (dismissing, on political question grounds, international-law challenge by representatives of victims of drone strike in Yemen).

[107] Baker v. Carr, 369 U.S. 186, 217 (1962); *e.g.*, Al-Tamimi v. Adelson, 916 F.3d 1, 13–14 (D.C. Cir. 2019) (concluding that political question, while potentially relevant to the resolution of claims, was extricable); *cf.* Lane v. Halliburton, 529 F.3d 548, 565–69 (5th. Cir. 2008) (remanding for consideration of inextricability).

[108] *See, e.g., Jaber*, 861 F.3d at 246.

[109] *See, e.g., Al-Tamimi*, 916 F.3d at 13.

[110] *But see* Spectrum Stores, Inc. v. Citgo Petroleum Corp., 632 F.3d 938, 951–52 & n.14 (5th Cir. 2011). The failure of the United States to file a statement of interest should be considered as irrelevant. Saldana v. Occidental Petroleum Corp., 774 F.3d 544, 554 (9th Cir. 2014).

[111] *Cf.* Harrison, *supra* note 58, at 520–28 (defending narrower, substantive version of political question both as avoiding judicial interference with foreign relations and as facilitating the implementation of political branch decisions).

[112] *Compare El-Shifa Pharm. Indus. Co.*, 607 F.3d at 857 (en banc; Kavanaugh, J., concurring in the judgment) (arguing that "[a]pplying the political question doctrine in statutory cases . . . would not reflect benign deference to the political branches," but "would systematically favor the Executive Branch over the Legislative Branch . . ."), *with* Zivotofsky v. Kerry, 576 U.S. 1 (2015) (*Zivotofsky II*).

B. Other Nonjusticiability Doctrines

While foreign affairs cases are particularly closely associated with the political question doctrine, other nonjusticiability doctrines—like standing, ripeness, and mootness—apply largely as they do elsewhere.[113] Aspects that are more distinctive to the foreign relations context deserve at least brief discussion.

1. Standing

The limitation of federal jurisdiction in Article III, § 2, to "Cases" and "Controversies" means that in order to establish constitutional standing, a claimant must demonstrate an "injury in fact," "fairly traceable" to the complained-of conduct by the defendant, "that is likely to be redressed by a favorable judicial decision."[114] The injury must be personal and particularized to the plaintiff.[115] Historically, Article III's requirements have been supplemented by prudential standing, which is a "general prohibition on a litigant's raising another person's legal rights, the rule barring adjudication of generalized grievances more appropriately addressed in the representative branches, and the requirement that a plaintiff's complaint fall within the zone of interests protected by the law invoked."[116] Recent cases, however, have tended to integrate these prudential concerns into the constitutional doctrine—with the possible exception of the general bar on third-party standing, which limits the right of one party to assert the interests of another.[117]

Foreign relations cases are prone to standing issues. It is often hard to establish a particularized, personal injury when challenging foreign policy decisionmaking;[118] a "generalized grievance," "common to all members of the public," is common in foreign relations and national security contexts, but that is inadequate to establish standing.[119] Establishing injury can also be difficult due to insufficient

---

[113] RESTATEMENT (THIRD) § 1 rptrs. note 4 (observing that "[t]he jurisprudence of adjudication—principles as to jurisdiction, standing, mootness, ripeness, etc.—applies to foreign relations cases as to others," but distinguishing the political question doctrine).

[114] Bank of America Corp. v. City of Miami, 137 S. Ct. 1296, 1302 (2017) (quoting Spokeo, Inc. v. Robins, 578 U.S. 330, 338 (2016), and citing Lujan v. Defs. of Wildlife, 504 U.S. 555, 560–61 (1992)).

[115] Raines v. Byrd, 521 U.S. 811, 818–19 (1997) (citing, and quoting, Allen v. Wright, 468 U.S. 737, 751 (1984), and Lujan, 504 U.S. at 560–61 & n.1).

[116] Allen, 468 U.S. at 751; see Elk Grove Unified School Dist. v. Newdow, 542 U.S. 1, 12 (2004).

[117] Lexmark Int'l, Inc. v. Static Control Components, Inc., 572 U.S. 118, 126–27 & n.3 (2014).

[118] HENKIN, FOREIGN AFFAIRS, at 142–43.

[119] United States v. Richardson, 418 U.S. 166, 176–77 (1974) (dismissing on standing grounds a taxpayer suit challenging the failure to disclose CIA expenditures, allegedly in violation of art. I, § 9, cl. 7) (internal citations and quotations omitted); see Schlesinger v. Reservists Comm. to Stop the War, 418 U.S. 208, 217 (1974) (dismissing taxpayer suit concerning members of Congress holding commissions in the military reserves, alleging that it violated the Incompatibility Clause, art. I, § 6, cl. 2); see also Lujan, 504 U.S. at 573–78 (applying principle to violation of statutory rights).

information.[120] Courts are especially hesitant in potential separation-of-powers clashes. If standing doctrine serves to limit judicial usurpation of power belonging to the political branches, arguably it must be rigorously applied when reaching the merits would allow courts to decide whether one of the political branches has acted unconstitutionally.[121] (Also arguably, however, it would be better to let the merits speak to whether the action is constitutional, especially since judicial review may well sustain the political branch's authority.) Courts favoring a more rigorous approach often find a lack of standing in constitutional challenges touching on intelligence and foreign relations.[122]

Congress has some capacity to resolve prudential concerns by stipulating who has standing.[123] That capacity may be diminished nowadays, given that the Supreme Court relies less on any distinction between prudential and constitutional standing, and has shown signs of hostility toward Congress' ability to confer Article III standing.[124] Even so, abiding by legislative instructions diminishes the likelihood of separation-of-powers clashes with one of the political branches.[125] As a result, whether a plaintiff has the right to sue may turn on whether the plaintiff is among the class that Congress has authorized to sue by creating a cause of action.[126]

Congress, and its subsidiary institutions and members, may themselves be inhibited in bringing cases. In *Raines v. Byrd*, the Supreme Court took a narrow view of the circumstances in which individual legislators could show a sufficient personal stake.[127] The Court noted that the legislators in that matter had not

[120] *See, e.g.*, Clapper v. Amnesty Int'l. USA, 568 U.S. 398, 411–14 (2013) (noting, inter alia, dearth of actual knowledge concerning surveillance targeting and limited prospect of obtaining information from foreign intelligence agencies).

[121] *Clapper*, 568 U.S. at 408–09; Raines v. Byrd, 521 U.S. 811, 820 (1997).

[122] *Clapper*, 568 U.S. at 409 (citing *Richardson*, 418 U.S. at 167–70, *Schlesinger*, 418 U.S. at 209–11, and Laird v. Tatum, 408 U.S. 1, 111–16 (1972)).

[123] *Raines*, 521 U.S. at 820 n.3 (distinguishing, in this regard, Congress' inability to "erase" constitutional standing requirements from its ability to "eliminate[] any prudential standing limitations . . .") (citations omitted); *see also* Zivotofsky v. Secretary of State, 444 F.3d 614, 617 (D.C. Cir. 2006) (reversing dismissal based on lack of standing).

[124] In *TransUnion LLC v. Ramirez*, 141 S. Ct. 2190 (2021), a narrow majority of the Court held that plaintiffs alleging violation of the Fair Credit Reporting Act, 15 U.S.C. § 1681 *et seq.*, did not automatically satisfy the injury-in-fact requirement under Article III simply by identifying a statutory right and statutory authorization to sue. As the majority explained, while " 'Congress may "elevate" harms that "exist" in the real world before Congress recognized them to actionable legal status, it may not simply enact an injury into existence, using its lawmaking power to transform something that is not remotely harmful into something that is.' " *Id.* at 2205 (quoting Hagy v. Demers & Adams, 882 F.3d 616, 622 (6th Cir. 2018)). *But see id.* at 2220–21 (Thomas, J., dissenting) (stressing congressional power to create private or personal rights that confer standing).

[125] *Raines*, 521 U.S. at 820 n.3 (noting that when Congress statutorily confers standing, it "significantly lessens the risk of unwanted conflict with the Legislative Branch when that plaintiff brings suit").

[126] Lexmark Int'l, Inc. v. Static Control Components, Inc., 572 U.S. 118, 127–28 (2014).

[127] *Raines*, 521 U.S. at 820–30 (rejecting standing to challenge Line Item Veto Act); *see also* Va. House of Delegates v. Bethune-Hill, 139 S. Ct. 1945, 1953–54 & n.4 (2019) (stating that, under *Raines*, "individual members lack standing to assert the institutional interests of a legislature" much like "a single House of a bicameral legislature lacks capacity to assert interests belonging to the legislature as a whole"); *see also* Blumenthal v. Trump, 949 F.3d 14, 19–21 (D.C. Cir. 2020) (treating "*Raines* [as

been authorized to represent their houses of Congress, and that they and other litigants had alternative recourse, while acknowledging that such distinctions might not be dispositive.[128] Other circumstances may be more favorable. In a recent *en banc* decision, the D.C. Circuit explained that "a legislative *institution* may properly assert an institutional injury," even if "an individual *member* of that institution generally may not."[129] In the court's view, a House committee had suffered particularized injury, fairly traceable to a refusal to cooperate with one of its subpoenas, and likely to be redressed by a favorable judicial decision. The court stressed that the House had authorized the Committee's suit, that no alternative was practicable, and that it was consistent with established practice and constitutional structure.[130] Supreme Court case law concerning state legislatures, however, suggests that courts may continue to apply stringent standards to legislative standing.[131]

Private parties, at least those with personal stakes different from those of ordinary citizens, have an easier path to establishing standing. So do U.S. states, which are "entitled to special solicitude in . . . standing analysis."[132] As discussed in Chapter 9, while states have a limited role in U.S. foreign relations, they are not wholly estranged. In a number of instances, such as immigration, they may be able to establish standing as sovereigns to challenge federal policy.[133]

2. Ripeness and Mootness

As with standing, ripeness and mootness in foreign relations cases are highly derivative of case law developed in other contexts. These doctrines have been described, inexactly, as temporal versions of standing. Assuming a described injury would satisfy standing requirements, ripeness "asks whether an injury that

the] starting point when individual members of the Congress seek judicial remedies," and controlling, in dismissing standing in foreign emoluments suit); Spence v. Clinton, 942 F. Supp. 32 (D.D.C. 1996) (dismissing on standing grounds suit brought by House members alleging that the president had unconstitutionally failed to comply with statutory obligations to spend or obligate funds for certain missile defense systems).

[128] *Raines*, 521 U.S. at 829–30.
[129] Comm. on Judiciary of U.S. House of Representatives v. McGahn, 968 F.3d 755, 775 (D.C. Cir. 2020) (en banc) (emphases added).
[130] *Id.* at 763, 772; *see also* U.S. House of Representatives v. Mnuchin, 969 F.3d 353, 354 (D.C. Cir. 2020) (en banc) (remanding for further panel consideration, given that "*McGahn* . . . hold[s] that there is no general bar against the House of Representatives' standing in all cases involving purely interbranch disputes").
[131] *Compare* Ariz. State Legislature v. Ariz. Indep. Redistricting Comm'n, 576 U.S. 787, 799–804 (2015) (finding standing in lawsuit brought by the Arizona House and Senate, acting together), *with Bethune-Hill*, 139 S. Ct. at 1953–54 (distinguishing *Arizona State Legislature*, finding no standing in suit brought by a single state house, rather than the general assembly as a whole).
[132] Massachusetts v. EPA, 549 U.S. 497, 520 (2007).
[133] *See, e.g.*, California v. Trump, 963 F.3d 926 (9th Cir. 2020) (deeming California and New Mexico to have standing to challenge alleged diversion of federal funds for construction of border wall with Mexico).

has not yet happened is sufficiently likely to happen," and mootness concerns whether a past injury can still be properly remedied.[134]

Ripeness has both a constitutional basis (Article III's "case or controversy" requirement) and prudential elements, and although a court is only obligated to consider the former, the distinction between them is often unclear.[135] The question is usually whether "there is a substantial controversy, between parties having adverse legal interests, of sufficient immediacy and reality to warrant the issuance of a declaratory judgment."[136] Avoiding "abstract disagreements" requires looking at whether the issue is fit for judicial decision—including whether the prospective injury is remote or contingent—and considering the vices and virtues of deferring judicial intervention, including the potential hardship to the parties.[137]

These inquiries are highly fact-specific, defying generalization even in foreign relations cases.[138] The statutory context may matter: the Administrative Procedure Act (APA), for example, affords review of certain agency actions, but whether an APA-based challenge is ripe will turn in part on whether the relevant statutory provision calls for immediate judicial review.[139] Constitutional claims may be more likely to be deemed unripe for prudential reasons, given judicial leeriness about reaching constitutional issues, but that has had relatively little predictive value.[140] For example, challenges to legislative schemes protecting executive branch officials against removal by the president have been deemed

---

[134] 13B WRIGHT, MILLER, & COOPER, FEDERAL PRACTICE AND PROCEDURE: JURISDICTION AND RELATED MATTERS §3532.1 (3d ed. 2008); see, e.g., McInnis-Misenor v. Maine Medical Ctr., 319 F.3d 63, 69 (1st Cir. 2003) (citing prior Wright & Miller edition). The Supreme Court has described mootness as "the doctrine of standing set in a time frame," Arizonans for Official English v. Arizona, 520 U.S. 43, 68 n.22 (1997) (internal quotations and citations omitted), but it has also qualified that description, noting (for example) the distinctive "capable of repetition, yet evading review" exception for mootness. Friends of the Earth, Inc. v. Laidlaw Envtl. Servs., 528 U.S. 167, 189–90 (2000).

[135] Reno v. Catholic Soc. Servs., Inc., 509 U.S. 43, 58 n.18 (1993) (noting two dimensions); 13B WRIGHT, MILLER, & COOPER, supra note 134, § 3532.1 (asserting that "[t]he line [between constitutional and prudential ripeness] is so thin that no substantial benefit is to be gained by efforts to draw it, unless it be thought that prudential doctrines enable still greater case-specific discretion"). Even procedurally, the distinction is not outcome-determinative. Compare, e.g., Stolt-Nielsen S.A. v. AnimalFeeds Int'l Corp., 559 U.S. 662, 670 n.2 (2010) (treating prudential ripeness argument as waived), with Nat'l Park Hosp. Ass'n v. Dep't of Interior, 538 U.S. 803, 808 (2003) (noting that even a prudential ripeness argument may be considered on a court's own motion).

[136] Lake Carriers' Ass'n v. MacMullan, 406 U.S. 498, 506 (1972).

[137] Abbott Labs. v. Gardner, 387 U.S. 136, 148–49 (1967); see 13B WRIGHT, MILLER, & COOPER, supra note 134 §§ 3532.2–.3.

[138] Cf. Suitum v. Tahoe Reg'l Planning Agency, 520 U.S. 725, 733–34 (1997) (describing ripeness analysis particular to regulatory takings claims).

[139] Nat'l Park Hosp. Ass'n, 538 U.S. at 808; Lujan v. Nat'l Wildlife Fed'n, 497 U.S. 871, 891 (1990).

[140] The reluctance is often acknowledged on the way to addressing those questions. See, e.g., Clinton v. Jones, 520 U.S. 681, 690 (1997) ("[W]e have often stressed the importance of avoiding the premature adjudication of constitutional questions"); accord Matal v. Tam, 137 S. Ct. 1744, 1755 (2017). See generally 13B WRIGHT, MILLER, & COOPER, supra note 134 § 3532.1.

ripe even prior to any contested removal.[141] On the other hand, petitions seeking review of certificates of extradition based on a risk that the petitioner will be tortured upon return have been deemed not ripe prior to final approval of extradition by the secretary of state.[142]

Once a suit is ripe, it must remain so, lest it become moot; a case must remain an actual controversy throughout all stages of litigation.[143] Like ripeness, mootness doctrine is attributed to Article III as well as to prudential considerations involving remedial discretion and judicial administration.[144] Like ripeness, too, the doctrine's application is highly fact-dependent. Intervening events may make a case moot, by diminishing the utility of judicial remedies, but the nature of the claim, and that of the defendant, matter.[145] Voluntary cessation of conduct may also moot a challenge, if the defendant satisfies a heavy burden of showing that its conduct is unlikely to recur. The same basic approach governs when a U.S. official or agency is being sued, as is often true in foreign relations.[146] But unlike private defendants (who have little capacity to effect changes in the law),[147] a government defendant may not be able to invoke changes in official policy as having mooted an action against it, given the prospect that it may change the policy back again.[148] Statutory changes are regarded differently, presumably

---

[141] *See, e.g.*, Seila Law LLC v. Consumer Fin. Prot. Bureau, 140 S. Ct. 2183, 2196 (2020) (challenge to for-cause removal provision insulating director of the Consumer Financial Protection Bureau (CFPB) was not required to await contested removal, "because when such a provision violates the separation of powers it inflicts a 'here-and-now' injury on affected third parties that can be remedied by a court") (quoting Bowsher v. Synar, 478 U.S. 714, 727 n.5 (1986)).

[142] *See, e.g.*, Meza v. U.S. Atty. Gen., 693 F.3d 1350, 1356–57 (11th Cir. 2012) (holding habeas corpus action, following issuance of a certification of extraditability, not ripe prior to determination by the secretary of state as to whether the petitioner is likely to be tortured or should be extradited); Hoxha v. Levi, 465 F.3d 554, 564–65 (3d Cir. 2006) (holding unripe an APA claim, invoking the secretary of state's responsibility under the Foreign Affairs Reform and Restructuring Act for not extraditing persons in danger of being subject to torture, prior to a final decision on extradition). Such ripeness objections precede consideration of the rule of non-inquiry, which indicates the ultimate decision to extradite by the secretary would not be subject to judicial review. *See, e.g.*, Cornejo-Barreto v. Siefert, 379 F.3d 1075, 1087 (9th Cir. 2004). *But see* Aguasvivas v. Pompeo, 984 F.3d 1047, 1055 (1st Cir. 2021) (stating that "even though these issues could be mooted if the Secretary decides that Aguasvivas should not be extradited, that possibility . . . does not change the fact that the Secretary seeks to have Aguasvivas detained now"). For broader discussion of extradition, see Chapter 10 § III(C).

[143] *See* Already, LLC v. Nike, Inc., 568 U.S. 85, 91 (2013) (quoting Alvarez v. Smith, 558 U.S. 87, 93 (2009)); *accord* Kingdomware Techs., Inc. v. United States, 579 U.S. 162, 169 (2016).

[144] Insofar as Article III is concerned, mootness must be addressed. *See, e.g.*, Honig v. Doe, 484 U.S. 305 (1988). Cases increasingly focus on this constitutional component. *See* Campbell-Ewald Co. v. Gomez, 577 U.S. 153, 160–61 (2016); *Already*, 568 U.S. at 91; *Kingdomware*, 579 U.S. at 169–70; *accord* 13B WRIGHT, MILLER, & COOPER, *supra* note 134, § 3533.1.

[145] 13C WRIGHT, MILLER, & COOPER, *supra* note 134, § 3533.3.

[146] Friends of the Earth, Inc. v. Laidlaw Envtl. Servs., 528 U.S. 167, 189 (2000) (citing United States v. Concentrated Phosphate Export Assn., 393 U.S. 199, 203 (1968)).

[147] Courts perceive a general obligation to apply the law in effect at the time of the decision. Henderson v. United States, 568 U.S. 266, 271 (2013); *see* 13C WRIGHT, MILLER, & COOPER, *supra* note 134, § 3533.6.

[148] 13C WRIGHT, MILLER, & COOPER, *supra* note 134, § 3533.7; *see, e.g.*, West Virginia v. Envtl. Prot. Agency, 142 S. Ct. 2587, 2606–07 (2022) (concluding that a case was not moot notwithstanding

because they are more permanent.[149] More generally, because developments of all kinds may be temporary or even tactical, courts may (exceptionally) permit review of otherwise moot measures that are "capable of repetition, yet evading review."[150]

Mootness and ripeness have played a prominent and complex role in litigation objecting to U.S. uses of military force. Suits by service members protesting a near-imminent use of force have been deemed unripe prior to any actual deployment.[151] Congressional challenges have been deemed unripe on similar grounds,[152] and may even be unripe after force is employed so long as Congress as a whole has not fixed its view and decisively broken with the executive branch.[153] Courts tend to cite prudential considerations relating to military matters and the need to defer to the political branches.[154] Yet courts are also prone to dismiss challenges as moot if the conflict has nearly or wholly ceased.[155] Because

EPA's withdrawal of the contested emissions limits given the risk that the agency might reimpose them, considering the absence of any representation to the contrary and the agency's conviction that the limits were lawful).

[149] *See, e.g.*, Bowen v. Kizer, 485 U.S. 386 (1988); U.S. Dept. of Justice v. Provenzano, 469 U.S. 14 (1984). In one matter, a court of appeals deemed moot claims by congressional plaintiffs that executive branch assistance to groups that were attempting to overthrow the Nicaraguan government violated a statutory rider when the relevant appropriations, together with their limiting rider, expired. Sanchez-Espinoza v. Reagan, 770 F.2d 202, 210 (D.C. Cir. 1985).

[150] The exception applies only in the unusual case in which "the challenged action [is] in its duration too short to be fully litigated prior to cessation or expiration," and "there [is] a reasonable expectation that the same complaining party [will] be subject to the same action again." *Kingdomware*, 579 U.S. at 170 (quoting Spencer v. Kemna, 523 U.S. 1, 17 (1998)); *see* 13C WRIGHT, MILLER, & COOPER, *supra* note 134, § 3533.8. The same approach is used when a government defendant has ceased its complained-of conduct. *Spencer*, 523 U.S. at 18; *cf.* Padilla v. Hanft, 547 U.S. 1062, 1064 (2006) (Ginsburg, J., dissenting from denial of certiorari) ("A party's voluntary cessation does not make a case less capable of repetition or less evasive of review").

[151] *See, e.g.*, Ange v. Bush, 752 F. Supp. 509, 515–16 (D.D.C. 1990). *But see* Doe v. Bush, 323 F.3d 133, 138 n.4 (1st Cir. 2003) (resisting argument that "no claim can ever be ripe until an attack has actually occurred" because that "would seem to say that a case cannot be ripe on the basis of reasonably predictable future injury").

[152] *Doe v. Bush*, 323 F.3d at 139 (noting, in action brought by service members and members of Congress, that "[m]any important questions remain unanswered about whether there will be a war, and, if so, under what conditions").

[153] *Id.* at 137 (noting that there was no "constitutional impasse" between Congress and the president regarding the use of force against Iraq, and therefore the issue was not ripe for judicial review); *accord* Dellums v. Bush, 752 F. Supp. 1141, 1149–51 (D.D.C. 1990); *see also* Greenham Women Against Cruise Missiles v. Reagan, 755 F.2d 34, 37 (2d Cir. 1985) (per curiam); Sanchez–Espinoza v. Reagan, 770 F.2d 202, 210–11 (D.C. Cir. 1985) (Ginsburg, J., concurring) (rejecting, on ripeness grounds, action by congressional and noncongressional plaintiffs concerning U.S. support for forces bearing arms against the Nicaraguan government); *cf.* Lowry v. Reagan, 676 F. Supp. 333, 337–39 (D.D.C. 1987) (reaching similar conclusion, on basis of "remedial discretion" doctrine sounding in ripeness, concerning earlier Persian Gulf activities). *See generally* Goldwater v. Carter, 444 U.S. 996, 997 (1979) (Powell, J., concurring) (taking position in treaty termination matter that courts should decline, on ripeness grounds, to decide "issues affecting the allocation of power between the President and Congress until the political branches reach a constitutional impasse").

[154] *See, e.g., Ange*, 752 F. Supp. at 516; Dornan v. U.S. Sec'y of Def., 676 F. Supp. 6, 9–10 (D.D.C. 1987).

[155] *See, e.g.*, Conyers v. Reagan, 765 F.2d 1124, 1127–29 (D.C. Cir. 1985) (congressional challenge to invasion of Grenada was mooted when U.S. combat troops were withdrawn); Flynt v. Weinberger,

Congress may hesitate to intervene for political reasons, or simply find it hard to act quickly, a lack of ripeness—quickly followed by mootness—is a frequent risk.[156] The difficulty of steering between this Scylla and Charybdis, on top of potential standing and political question challenges, mean that judicial review is often hard to procure, leaving the legal judgment of executive branch officials to play an outsized role.[157]

III. Act of State Doctrine

The act of state doctrine is a mainstay of U.S. foreign relations law, but it has meant quite different things over the years. When applicable, it requires that courts treat an official act of a foreign sovereign as a rule of decision in U.S. judicial proceedings. The principle has revealed itself only gradually, and its limits are yet to be fully understood.

The act of state doctrine has sometimes been difficult to distinguish from other doctrines that prevent courts from second-guessing foreign sovereigns. The modern doctrine is attributed to *Underhill v. Hernandez*,[158] but that case was an imperfect vehicle. Because the claims in that action were against a foreign government official, they implicated distinguishable questions relating to the immunity of foreign state officials.[159] At the same time, *Underhill's* sweeping pronouncements (that "[e]very sovereign State is bound to respect the independence of every other sovereign State," such that "the courts of one country will not sit in judgment on the acts of the government of another done within its own territory") insinuated a broader principle of non-inquiry.[160]

762 F.2d 134, 135 (D.C. Cir. 1985) (action seeking to enable press coverage of Grenada invasion was mooted when sought-after press ban was lifted, lacking reasonable likelihood that particular controversy would recur). *But see* JB Pictures, Inc. v. Dep't of Def., 86 F.3d 236, 238 (D.C. Cir. 1996) (concluding that, because a policy of limiting press access to the arrival of the remains of deceased soldiers at an air force base continued and would apply to any returning deceased in ongoing U.S. conflicts, action was not moot).

[156] *See generally* John Hart Ely, WAR AND RESPONSIBILITY: CONSTITUTIONAL LESSONS OF VIETNAM AND ITS AFTERMATH 57–60 (1993) (criticizing ripeness approach); Peter D. Coffman, *Power and Duty: The Language of the War Power*, 80 CORNELL LAW REV. 1236, 1266 (1995) (book review) (noting concern, relative to congressional and judicial proceedings, that "the issue will not ripen until it is effectively moot").

[157] *See* Randolph D. Moss, *Executive Branch Legal Interpretation: A Perspective from the Office of Legal Counsel*, 52 ADMIN. L. REV. 1303, 1304 (2000).

[158] 168 U.S. 250 (1897); *see* Banco Nacional de Cuba v. Sabbatino, 376 U.S. 398, 416 (1964) (describing *Underhill* as "[t]he classic American statement of the act of state doctrine").

[159] *See infra* this chapter § V(D).

[160] *Underhill*, 168 U.S. at 252.

Eventually, several expropriations cases generated greater clarity.[161] In *Banco Nacional de Cuba v. Sabbatino*,[162] the Supreme Court held that a Cuban decree establishing rights in Cuba for a Cuban government entity was enforceable in U.S. court, notwithstanding allegations that the decree expropriated property of U.S. nationals in violation of international law. Stating the doctrine in circumscribed terms, the Court cautioned:

> [W]e decide only that the Judicial Branch will not examine the validity of a taking of property within its own territory by a foreign sovereign government, extant and recognized by this country at the time of the suit, in the absence of a treaty or other unambiguous agreement regarding controlling legal principles, even if the complaint alleges that the taking violates customary international law.[163]

Two other Supreme Court cases involving Cuba followed: one failed to produce a majority,[164] and in the other, the Court held the act of state doctrine inapplicable when the refusal of Cuban parties to pay demanded funds was not treated as an official sovereign repudiation of the debt.[165] The Court's next (and, still, latest) formative decision narrowed the doctrine a good bit. *W.S. Kirkpatrick & Co. v. Environmental Tectonics Corp., Int'l* involved allegations that Nigerian officials had accepted bribes, in violation of Nigerian and U.S. laws, before awarding a contract.[166] Notwithstanding the allegations' sensitivity, the Court held that the act of state doctrine was inapplicable where nothing required that the judiciary "declare invalid, and thus ineffective as 'a rule of decision for the courts of this country,' ... the official act of a foreign sovereign."[167] In other words, given that the U.S. court could award civil damages under U.S. statutes against a U.S. company and its chief executive officer for bribery of a foreign official without addressing the validity of such action under Nigerian law, the act of state doctrine was not implicated.

---

[161] There were a handful of intervening decisions. *See, e.g.,* Oetjen v. Cent. Leather Co., 246 U.S. 297, 302–03 (1918) (stating that U.S. government recognition of Mexico's revolutionary government as "validates all the actions and conduct of the government so recognized from the commencement of its existence," establishing validity of property title); Ricaud v. Amer. Metal Co., 246 U.S. 304, 310 (1918) (same).

[162] 376 U.S. 398 (1964).

[163] *Id.* at 428.

[164] First Nat'l City Bank v. Banco Nacional de Cuba, 406 U.S. 759 (1972). Five justices agreed on reversing and remanding the lower court's application of the act of state doctrine to preclude a counterclaim. *See infra* text accompanying note 219.

[165] Alfred Dunhill of London, Inc. v. Republic of Cuba, 425 U.S. 682 (1976).

[166] 493 U.S. 400 (1990).

[167] *Id.* at 405 (quoting Ricaud v. Am. Metal Co., 246 U.S. 304, 310 (1918)).

Nowadays, then, the act of state doctrine is distinct from other issues with which it shares common cause. Although the doctrine may arise in cases involving immunity defenses, it can also be relevant even when neither the foreign state nor its personnel (past or present) are parties.[168] Moreover, unlike the political question doctrine, the act of state doctrine is *substantive* rather than jurisdictional. Rather than result in the case simply being dismissed as nonjusticiable, application of the act of state doctrine permits a court to render a judgment on the merits, albeit on the basis of accepting the foreign act as valid.[169]

As the doctrine has gained autonomy, the lack of any well-defined foundation has become clearer. Newer cases indicate that it is not required by the Constitution, by international law, or by statute; instead, they characterize the doctrine as consistent with international comity, respect for foreign sovereigns acting within their territories, and appropriate judicial deference to the executive branch given the separation of powers.[170] The doctrine remains one of the best examples of federal common law in the foreign relations field,[171] notwithstanding the Supreme Court's misgivings about that body of law.[172] But the doctrine's vague foundation, coupled with its capacity to preempt state law, has contributed to it being narrowly read.

Three defining criteria are now apparent. First, a foreign official act (or "public act") of some type,[173] by "a recognized foreign sovereign power" (meaning, recognized by the United States, irrespective of whether friendly relations are being maintained),[174] must be at issue. The act must be attributable to a foreign

---

[168] RESTATEMENT (FOURTH) § 441 rptrs. note 3; *see, e.g.,* Konowaloff v. Metro. Museum of Art, 702 F.3d 140 (2d Cir. 2012) (affirming dismissal, on act of state grounds, of action against museum relating to Soviet Union's confiscation of private owner's painting).

[169] Republic of Austria v. Altmann, 541 U.S. 677, 700 (2004); *see also Alfred Dunhill,* 425 U.S. at 725–28 (Marshall, J., dissenting) (distinguishing act of state and sovereign immunity doctrines). *But see* Trajano v. Marcos, Nos. 86–2448, 86–15039, 1989 WL 76894, at *2 (9th Cir. July 10, 1989) (noted in table 878 F.2d 1439) ("The act of state doctrine is the foreign relations equivalent of the political question doctrine").

[170] *Kirkpatrick,* 493 U.S. at 408; RESTATEMENT (FOURTH) § 441 cmt. a & rptrs. note 1. Regarding international law, see Banco Nacional de Cuba v. Sabbatino, 376 U.S. 398, 422 (1964) (explaining that the doctrine is neither required nor limited by international law); *see also W.S. Kirkpatrick,* 493 U.S. at 404 (noting that "[w]e once viewed the doctrine as an expression of international law") (citing Oetjen v. Central Leather Co., 246 U.S. 297, 303–04 (1918)). Regarding constitutional law, see *Sabbatino,* 376 U.S. at 422–23 (stating that "[t]he text of the Constitution does not require the act of state doctrine," but stating that it has "'constitutional' underpinnings"); *see also infra* text accompanying notes 209–215 (discussing congressional capacity).

[171] *Sabbatino,* 376 U.S. at 427 ("[T]he scope of the act of state doctrine must be determined according to federal law"); *see* RESTATEMENT (FOURTH) § 441 cmt. b & rptrs. notes 2, 4.

[172] *See, e.g.,* Sosa v. Alvarez-Machain, 542 U.S. 692, 726 (2004) (citing *Sabbatino* as exceptional example of federal common law); Boyle v. United Techs. Corp., 487 U.S. 500, 504 (1988) (same); *see* Chapter 5 § II(C)(2) (discussing status of customary international law as federal common law).

[173] *See Sabbatino,* 376 U.S. at 401 (referring to "public acts"). Any *Sabbatino*-era theory that the doctrine was focused on determinations of title to property can no longer be maintained. RESTATEMENT (FOURTH) § 441 rptrs. note 1.

[174] *See Sabbatino,* 376 U.S. at 401 (referring to "public acts of a recognized foreign sovereign power"). As the *Restatement (Fourth)* notes, U.S. recognition, when given, appears to be retroactive

sovereign, but beyond that, some degree of authorization or ratification, making the decision a formal expression of sovereignty, may be required.[175] Acts of lower-level officials, not authorized or ratified by the government, have been excluded.[176] Significantly, the recognition and enforcement of judgments of foreign courts are also typically exempted from the act of state doctrine, and subject to their own detailed regime.[177]

Second, an act's validity must be directly at issue. As *Kirkpatrick* drove home, "[a]ct of state issues only arise when a court *must decide*—that is, when the outcome of the case turns upon—the effect of official action by a foreign sovereign."[178] Unfortunately, the explanation was unduly confusing. According to the Court, it was permissible to make "factual findings [about] the legality of the

in effect. RESTATEMENT (FOURTH) § 441 rptrs. note 8 (citing Oetjen v. Cent. Leather Co., 246 U.S. 297, 303 (1918)); *see also* Konowaloff v. Metro. Museum of Art, 702 F.3d 140, 146 (2d Cir. 2012) ("[T]he act of state doctrine applies retroactively to acts that were undertaken by the foreign state prior to official United States recognition."); Petroleos de Venezuela S.A. v. MUFG Union Bank, N.A., 495 F. Supp. 3d 257, 272–73 (S.D.N.Y. 2020) (rejecting argument that retroactivity was limited to circumstances where a new government had arisen due to civil war or revolution). That friendly relations are not required is clear from *Sabbatino*, given the state of U.S. relations at the time with Cuba, and surfaces again in contemporary cases involving Iran. *See Sabbatino*, 376 U.S. at 401.

[175] *Alfred Dunhill*, 425 U.S. at 692–93 (holding that refusal of Cuban government agents to repay or refund sums of money was not act of state, absent any showing that they "had been invested with sovereign authority to repudiate . . . the debts incurred"); *id.* at 695 (citing absence of any "statute, decree, order, or resolution of the Cuban Government itself" showing any sovereign determination); McKesson Corp. v. Islamic Republic of Iran, 672 F.3d 1066, 1074 (D.C. Cir. 2012) (noting that "Iran did not pass a law, issue an edict or decree, or engage in formal governmental action" to expropriate property); *cf.* RESTATEMENT (FOURTH) § 441 cmt. c (stating that "[n]ot all acts attributable to a foreign sovereign constitute official acts to which the act of state doctrine applies"). *But see Alfred Dunhill*, 425 U.S. at 718–20 (Marshall, J., dissenting) (resisting understanding that formal, or affirmative, acts are required to establish acts of state).
[176] *See, e.g., McKesson Corp.*, 672 F.3d at 1074 (holding that the act of state doctrine did not apply to "a pattern of conduct by Iran's agents that cannot fairly be characterized as public or official acts of a sovereign government"); Filártiga v. Peña-Irala, 630 F.2d 876, 889–90 (2d Cir. 1980) (suggesting doubts "whether action by a state official in violation of the Constitution and laws of the Republic of Paraguay, and wholly unratified by that nation's government, could properly be characterized as an act of state"); Filártiga v. Peña-Irala, 577 F. Supp. 860, 862 (E.D.N.Y. 1984) (agreeing, on remand, that Paraguay's failure to ratify acts "alone is sufficient to show that they were not acts of state").
[177] The *Restatement (Second)* and subsequent cases hedged somewhat on this question. *See, e.g.,* Timberlane Lumber Co. v. Bank of Am., N.T. & S.A., 549 F.2d 597, 607–08 (9th Cir. 1976) ("'A judgment of a court may be an act of state. Usually it is not, because it involves the interests of private litigants or because court adjudication is not the usual way in which the state exercises its jurisdiction to give effect to public interests.'") (quoting RESTATEMENT (SECOND) § 41 comment d)); *see also In re* Philippine Nat'l Bank, 397 F.3d 768, 772–74 (9th Cir. 2005) (stating that "there is no inflexible rule preventing a judgment sought by a foreign government from qualifying as an act of state," and holding that a forfeiture action by the Philippine government was an act of state). The *Restatement (Fourth)* stated more categorically that "[t]he act of state doctrine does not apply to the judgments of foreign courts." RESTATEMENT (FOURTH) § 441 cmt. c; *id.* rptrs. note 9 (citing RESTATEMENT (FOURTH) §§ 481–90 on foreign judgments). On its view, however, the fact of a foreign judgment would not preclude a U.S. court from giving effect to "the foreign official act on which the judgment rested," producing the same result in a case like *In re Philippine Nat'l Bank. Id.* rptrs. note 9.
[178] W.S. Kirkpatrick & Co. v. Envtl. Tectonics Corp., Int'l, 493 U.S. 400, 406 (1990) (emphasis in original).

Nigerian contract," because "its legality is simply not a question to be decided."[179] By this, the Court appears to have meant that it could determine whether the contract concluded by the Nigerian official entailed, factually, a bribe within the meaning of the Foreign Corrupt Practices Act, without deciding upon the legality of the contract under Nigerian law. If so, the Court used a quite restrictive meaning of "decided," particularly given that it conceded (*arguendo*) that the U.S. judicial proceedings would have to determine that the payments at issue violated Nigeria law in order to sustain the complaint.[180] The upshot is that a U.S. court may essentially determine the legality of a foreign sovereign's action, without triggering the act of state doctrine, so long as the court does not "decide" the legality of the foreign act in the sense of formally disregarding the act's efficacy. That approach seems roughly akin to the *Restatement (Fourth)*'s subsequent distinction between "impos[ing] legal consequences on a transaction or event," which is permissible, and "pass[ing] on the validity of the act," which is not.[181]

Understandably, lower courts have not reliably observed this subtle distinction.[182] In fact, doing so might dramatically reduce the doctrine's application in foreign relations cases. One oft-litigated issue concerns how the doctrine applies to alleged human rights violations, which typically involve a government acting within its own territory.[183] Courts often regard such litigation as potentially implicating the act of state doctrine, but may look for ways to set it aside. Thus, some lower court decisions have suggested that human rights violations may as a class fall within an exception to the doctrine, discussed later, for violation of treaties and other unambiguous agreements, at least so long as human rights law is sufficiently unambiguous about the existence of a violation.[184] Other decisions

---

[179] *Id.* at 406.

[180] *Id.*

[181] RESTATEMENT (FOURTH) § 441 cmt. d; *see also id.* rptrs. note 6.

[182] *See, e.g.*, Spectrum Stores, Inc. v. Citgo Petroleum Corp., 632 F.3d 938, 954–56 (5th Cir. 2011) (applying act of state doctrine in dismissing price fixing suit, on theory that granting relief would "sit in judgment of the acts of foreign sovereigns in their own territories" and "effectively" order a foreign government to alter its preferred natural resource policy); World Wide Minerals, Ltd. v. Republic of Kazakhstan, 296 F.3d 1154 (D.C. Cir. 2002) (holding that the act of state doctrine barred claim that Kazakhstan government's refusal to issue export permit constituted a breach of contract, although such a holding would render invalid neither the contract nor the denial of an export permit); *see also* RESTATEMENT (FOURTH) § 441 rptrs. note 6 (noting cases); John Harrison, *The American Act of State Doctrine*, 47 GEO. J. INT'L L. 507, 538–56 (2016) (critiquing these and other cases).

[183] The *Restatement (Fourth)* took no clear position on how human rights cases should be evaluated, instead noting several of the approaches taken by lower courts. RESTATEMENT (FOURTH) § 441 rptrs. note 5.

[184] *See* RESTATEMENT (THIRD) § 443 cmt. c (stating that "[a] claim arising out of an alleged violation of fundamental human rights," such as for torture or genocide, "would (if otherwise sustainable) probably not be defeated by the act of state doctrine, since the accepted international law of human rights is well established and contemplates external scrutiny of such acts"); *accord* Mamani v. Berzain, 2009 WL 10664387, at *11 (S.D. Fla. Nov. 25, 2009), *rev'd on other grounds*, 654 F.3d 1148 (11th Cir. 2011).

consider whether any such exception should be confined to violation of *jus cogens* norms (the handful of peremptory norms of general international law, such as the prohibition on genocide).[185] Still other decisions contemplate that the doctrine is not engaged because a human rights violation was not authorized or ratified by the government, and thus should not be regarded as an act of the sovereign.[186] Yet if the distinction indicated by *Kirkpatrick* is generalized, actions seeking damages for alleged human rights violations should not even raise act of state issues in the first place, since the validity of the foreign sovereign's act is not being directly decided by a U.S. court: under *Kirkpatrick*, the mere fact that the act's invalidity is a logical entailment of a finding that compensation is due under a U.S. tort statute should be insufficient to trigger the act of state doctrine.[187]

Third, the doctrine applies only to official acts "performed within [a foreign sovereign's] own territory."[188] This is sometimes described as an "extraterritorial exception" to the act of state doctrine.[189] Courts will defer to the U.S. government concerning the location of a foreign state's territorial borders, and in general, the limitation is easily applied to the expropriation of real property; application to foreign government measures affecting intangibles like debts or contractual rights, which may easily implicate the United States, is more complex.[190]

---

[185] *See, e.g.*, Sarei v. Rio Tinto, PLC, 671 F.3d 736, 757 (9th Cir. 2011) (en banc) (stating that "jus cogens norms are exempt from the [act of state] doctrine"), *vacated and remanded*, 569 U.S. 945 (2013), *rev'd on other grounds*, 722 F.3d 1109 (9th Cir. 2013) (en banc). This approach may be attributed to the view that they cannot be sovereign, or public acts. *See, e.g., id.* at 759 (stating that genocide claims "are not barred by the act of state doctrine because violations of jus cogens norms are not sovereign acts"); *accord* Warfaa v. Ali, 33 F. Supp. 3d 653, 661–62 (E.D. Va. 2014). It might also be due to a perceived prohibition on declaring valid violations of such norms, though that seems to overstate what U.S. courts decide when recognizing an act of state defense. Kashef v. BNP Paribas S.A., 925 F.3d 53, 61–62 (2d Cir. 2019) ("We are prohibited from deeming valid, for purposes of act-of-state deference, atrocities such as genocide, mass rape, and ethnic cleansing, which violate jus cogens norms.").

[186] *See, e.g.*, Kadic v. Karadžić, 70 F.3d 232, 250 (2d Cir. 1995) (indicating, in dictum, "we doubt that the acts of even a state official, taken in violation of a nation's fundamental law and wholly unratified by that nation's government, could properly be characterized as an act of state") (citing similar dictum in Filartiga v. Pena-Irala, 630 F.2d 876, 889 (2d Cir. 1980)); *cf.* Trajano v. Marcos, Nos. 86-2448, 86-15039, 1989 WL 76894, at *2 (9th Cir. July 10, 1989) (878 F.2d 1439 (table)) (holding that human rights claims against former Philippines president, to which neither the current government nor the United States objected, was not barred by act of state doctrine).

[187] Indeed, the indictment is more indirect than in *Kirkpatrick*, which was assumed to entail a finding that a Nigerian decision violated Nigerian law. *See supra* this chapter text accompanying notes 166–167. Similar reasoning was adopted by the Second Circuit in *Kashef*, 925 F.3d at 59–60, but that court appeared not to regard this reasoning as an independent basis for rejecting the act of state defense, instead exploring alternative grounds. *See supra* this chapter note 185.

[188] W.S. Kirkpatrick & Co. v. Envtl. Tectonics Corp., Int'l, 493 U.S. 400, 405 (1990); *see* Banco Nacional de Cuba v. Sabbatino, 376 U.S. 398, 401 (1964); *see also* RESTATEMENT (FOURTH) § 441 rptrs. note 7 (citing additional authority and comparable limitation under English law).

[189] *See, e.g.*, Villoldo v. Castro Ruz, 821 F.3d 196, 202 (1st Cir. 2016); Tchacosh Co. v. Rockwell Int'l Corp., 766 F.2d 1333, 1336–37 (9th Cir. 1985). Courts sometimes stress that this exception applies to property "located within the United States at the time of the confiscation." Sea Breeze Salt, Inc. v. Mitsubishi Corp., 899 F.3d 1064, 1075 n.5 (9th Cir. 2018). *See generally* Republic of Iraq v. First Nat'l City Bank, 353 F.2d 47, 51 (2d Cir. 1965) (Friendly, J.).

[190] RESTATEMENT (FOURTH) § 441 rptrs. note 7.

Should these three criteria be fulfilled, the task remaining to a court applying the act of state doctrine is surprisingly unclear. In *Sabbatino*, the Court advised that courts should consider certain additional factors that might counsel against applying the doctrine, like a greater "degree of codification or consensus concerning a particular area of international law," the fact that the government being challenged was no longer in existence, or the less significant nature of certain international rules for U.S. foreign relations (recognizing that "some aspects of international law touch much more sharply on national nerves than do others"). Several such factors will be considered later as possible exceptions. More broadly, the Court waxed eloquent about the need to maintain the doctrine's "continuing vitality" by balancing the functions assigned to the judiciary and the political branches, and to avoid "laying down or reaffirming an inflexible and all-encompassing rule."[191]

Twenty-five years later, *Kirkpatrick* set out a less flexible approach. Rejecting an argument that it acknowledged sounded "deceptively similar" to the *Sabbatino* opinion, the Court explained that case as merely having "suggested that a sort of balancing approach could be applied," and as merely noting possible instances in which such "balance shift[ed] against application of the doctrine."[192] *Kirkpatrick* suggested that balancing of other considerations could not generate any more expansive act of state doctrine without undermining the judicial role.[193] Lower courts still consider *Sabbatino*'s factors in assessing the act of state doctrine,[194] but it is not clear how the Court would regard any decision that relied on them to dismiss an otherwise appropriate action.

Beyond the three criteria ratified in *Kirkpatrick*, and any *Sabbatino*-type balancing that survives *Kirkpatrick*, many potential exceptions to the act of state doctrine have been posited. Fully seven deserve mention. The first, a possible exception for foreign government acts that are alleged human rights violations, has already been noted. A second potential exception would be for foreign government commercial activities. In *Alfred Dunhill of London, Inc. v. Republic of Cuba*, four Justices joined an opinion that would exclude from the doctrine "repudiation of a purely commercial obligation owed by a foreign sovereign or by

---

[191] *Sabbatino*, 376 U.S. at 427–28.
[192] *W.S. Kirkpatrick & Co.*, 493 U.S. at 409.
[193] *Id.* at 409.
[194] *See, e.g.*, Royal Wulff Ventures LLC v. Primero Mining Corp., 938 F.3d 1085, 1096–98 (9th Cir. 2019) (describing consideration of *Sabbatino* factors as discretionary, but regarding the factors as favoring application of the doctrine); *id.* at 1104–06 (Bennett, J., dissenting) (disputing application of factors); Ning Xianhua v. Oath Holdings, Inc., 536 F. Supp. 3d 535, 553–56 (N.D. Cal. 2021) (distinguishing between "mandatory" and "additional" (prudential) factors under *Sabbatino*, and after finding mandatory criteria are satisfied and balancing additional factors, holding that the act of state doctrine did not bar the suit).

one of its commercial instrumentalities," but four other Justices indicated resist-ance.[195] The *Restatement (Fourth)* noted that some lower courts have rejected such a broad exception, but the matter is also unresolved in most circuits.[196] Some decisions have, without explicitly adopting any such exception, treated commercial activities as more private than official in character, and thus ineli-gible for the act of state doctrine.[197]

A third exception, with firmer footing, concerns government acts that vio-late treaties. A government's act in its own territory that clearly violates inter-national law arguably deserves little deference, as a U.S. court is not exercising its own judgment in finding the foreign act invalid; rather, the court is simply recognizing an invalidity arising from the foreign state's own acceptance of cer-tain international obligations. In *Sabbatino*, the Supreme Court described itself as recognizing an act of state defense "in the absence of a treaty or other un-ambiguous agreement regarding controlling legal principles"—as distinct from the case before it, which involved a contested principle of customary interna-tional law."[198] *Sabbatino* itself may not have proposed this as a clear "treaty ex-ception," but lower courts have recognized one.[199] Although there are a range of applications,[200] the exception usually involves a government act that clearly

---

[195] 425 U.S. 682, 695 (1976) (White, J.). Justice Marshall, writing for himself and three others, questioned the wisdom of any such exception, and found it unwarranted on the facts. *Id.* at 724–30 (Marshall, J., dissenting).

[196] RESTATEMENT (FOURTH) § 441 rptrs. note 5. As the *Restatement (Fourth)* indicated, the Fifth and Eleventh Circuits have rejected such a "commercial activities" exception, at least any of a scope similar to that concerning foreign sovereign immunity. Spectrum Stores, Inc. v. Citgo Petroleum Corp., 632 F.3d 938, 954 n.16 (5th Cir. 2011); Honduras Aircraft Registry Ltd. v. Honduras, 129 F.3d 543, 550 (11th Cir. 1997). However, the Ninth Circuit, whatever it might once have implied, has treated the issue as unresolved. Sea Breeze Salt, Inc. v. Mitsubishi Corp., 899 F.3d 1064, 1074–75 (9th Cir. 2018). *But see* Int'l Ass'n of Machinists & Aerospace Workers v. OPEC, 649 F.2d 1354, 1360 (9th Cir. 1981) (appearing to reject any exception). Further, at least three other circuits are also unde-cided. *Sea Breeze Salt*, 899 F.3d at 1074 (citing Fed. Treasury Enter. Sojuzplodoimport v. Spirits Int'l B.V., 809 F.3d 737, 744 (2d Cir. 2016); Envtl. Tectonics v. W.S. Kirkpatrick, Inc., 847 F.2d 1052, 1059 & n.8 (3d Cir. 1988); Kalamazoo Spice Extraction Co. v. Provisional Military Gov't of Socialist Ethiopia, 729 F.2d 422, 425 n.3 (6th Cir. 1984)).

[197] *See, e.g.*, de Csepel v. Republic of Hung., 714 F.3d 591, 604 (D.C. Cir. 2013); McKesson Corp. v. Islamic Republic of Iran, 672 F.3d 1066, 1073–74 (D.C. Cir. 2012); *see also* RESTATEMENT (FOURTH) § 441 rptrs. note 5 (citing other cases).

[198] Banco Nacional de Cuba v. Sabbatino, 376 U.S. 398, 428 (1964).

[199] RESTATEMENT (FOURTH) § 441 cmt. g (stating that the Court has "suggested" such an exception, but noting its recognition in the lower courts); *id.* rptrs. note 11; *see also* Kalamazoo Spice Extraction Co. v. Provisional Military Gov't of Socialist Ethiopia, 729 F.2d 422, 425 (6th Cir. 1984) (examining requests that the court "recognize" such an exception).

[200] *See, e.g.*, Bodner v. Banque Paribas, 114 F. Supp. 2d 117, 130 n.11 (E.D.N.Y. 2000) (concluding that Nazi expropriation was ineligible for an act of state defense because, among other things, it was "clearly prohibited by international law, including the Hague Convention of 1907"); Faysound Ltd. v. Walter Fuller Aircraft Sales, Inc., 748 F. Supp. 1365, 1372 (E.D. Ark. 1990) (applying treaty exception in light of terms applicable to the United States and the Philippines as states parties to the Convention on the International Recognition of Rights in Aircraft); *see also* United States v. Labs of Va., Inc., 272 F. Supp. 2d 764, 771–72 (N.D. Ill. 2003) (concluding that the Convention on International Trade in Endangered Species of Wild Fauna and Flora (CITES) "established a framework that influenced, if

violates a bilateral treaty between the United States and the foreign state concerned.[201] Executive branch support for deciding the case helps.[202] In theory, customary international law also might establish sufficiently clear controlling rules, but to date the rules invoked have generally proven too indefinite or controversial to meet *Sabbatino*'s threshold.[203] Unlike treaties, moreover, customary international law—while binding on states—need not reflect a particular state's explicit consent, and so arguably does less to undermine a foreign state's claim for autonomy when engaging in governmental acts at home.[204]

Fourth, application of the doctrine may be waived. A foreign state may accomplish waiver by agreement, by failing to raise the issue in a timely fashion, or by treaty.[205] Waiver is assumed to be the prerogative of the foreign sovereign, but any party capable of benefiting may waive it during litigation.[206] For reasons just noted, a customary international law obligation that the government not engage in the act is probably insufficient to establish a particular state's waiver. Even as to treaty obligations, merely establishing a treaty-based duty should not suffice, at least not if waiver by treaty is to have any function distinct from the treaty exception. Rather, for waiver, the relevant treaty rule should specifically address the sovereign's acceptance of justiciability in local courts.

A fifth potential exception, implied by the reference in *Sabbatino* to foreign sovereign governments "extant and recognized by this country at the time of

not dictated, Indonesia's export decisions" so as to undermine their status as foreign government decisions).

[201] *See, e.g., Kalamazoo Spice*, 729 F.2d at 425–28 (U.S.-Ethiopia Treaty of Amity); Foremost McKesson, Inc. v. Islamic Republic of Iran, Civ. A. No. 82-0220, 1989 WL 44086, at *6 (D.D.C. Apr. 18, 1989) (U.S.-Iran Treaty of Amity); *see also* Ramirez de Arellano v. Weinberger, 745 F.2d 1500, 1540 (D.C. Cir. 1984) (stating in dicta that the act of state doctrine "was never intended to apply when an applicable bilateral treaty governs the legal merits of the controversy").

[202] *See Kalamazoo Spice*, 729 F.2d at 425–26, 427–28 (citing position by the executive branch that the treaty mooted application of the act of state doctrine). The views of international organizations may, for appropriate treaties, perform a comparable function. *See* Callejo v. Bancomer, S.A., 764 F.2d 1101, 1116–21 (5th Cir. 1985) (treating interpretation by the International Monetary Fund as persuasive authority in determining that its Articles of Agreement did not establish unambiguous, controlling legal principles limiting Mexican regulations).

[203] *Sabbatino*, 376 U.S. at 428.

[204] *Cf.* RESTATEMENT (FOURTH) § 441 cmt. f ("The implied consent by a state to an obligation under customary international law, however, does not by itself constitute a waiver of the act of state doctrine.").

[205] RESTATEMENT (FOURTH) § 441 cmt. f & rptrs. note 10; *see, e.g.*, Cabri v. Gov't of Republic of Ghana, 981 F. Supp. 129, 131 & n.2 (E.D.N.Y. 1997), *aff'd in part and rev'd in part on other grounds*, 165 F.3d 193 (2d Cir. 1999).

[206] Kadic v. Karadžić, 70 F.3d 232, 250 (2d Cir. 1995) (deeming act of state argument waived when not raised by self-proclaimed foreign official in district court). The *Restatement (Third)* ventured that making waiver by a foreign state decisive would be inappropriate in light of residual interest by the U.S. executive branch, see RESTATEMENT (THIRD) § 441 cmt. e, but that view was challenged in the *Restatement (Fourth)*. RESTATEMENT (FOURTH) § 441 cmt. f & rptrs. note 10.

suit,"[207] is put at issue when the foreign government responsible for an act of state has been replaced—presumably, through extraconstitutional or other extraordinary means. A successor government may indeed be less inclined to find objectionable a U.S. court decision treating as invalid acts of its predecessor government. That said, it might not, and any uncertainty could be resolved simply by making clear that a successor government may waive the act of the state defense. Consistent with that view, some decisions have refrained from applying any exception absent renunciation of the act of state by a successor government.[208]

Sixth, Congress may displace the act of state doctrine, just as it may modify other federal common law. The outcome in *Sabbatino* itself was swiftly altered by Congress through what is known as the Second Hickenlooper Amendment, which directed courts not to apply the act of state doctrine to post-1958 disputes involving claimed rights to property taken in violation of international law. The amendment was subject to certain exceptions, most notably for cases in which the president filed a suggestion indicating that applying the act of state doctrine was required by the foreign policy interests of the United States.[209] In practice, moreover, the amendment has been narrowly construed, including by applying it (and setting aside the act of state doctrine) only to disputes involving intangible property (or proceeds from the expropriated property) found in the United States at the time of suit.[210] Courts also have not applied the amendment to claims brought by nationals of the confiscating state, on the premise that takings by the foreign state of its own nationals' property does not violate international law (referred to as the "domestic takings rule").[211]

Whatever its precise scope, the Second Hickenlooper Amendment clearly demonstrates Congress' authority to set aside the act of state doctrine when it wishes to do so.[212] Congress has rarely taken that course since; interestingly, the

---

[207] *Sabbatino*, 376 U.S. at 428 (referencing acts "by a foreign sovereign government, extant and recognized by this country at the time of suit").

[208] Konowaloff v. Metro. Museum of Art, 702 F.3d 140, 147–48 (2d Cir. 2012) (noting that the present Russian government had not repudiated the relevant act of confiscation by the Soviet government in 1918). *But see* Republic of Iraq v. ABB AG, 920 F. Supp. 2d 517, 534 (S.D.N.Y. 2013) (distinguishing *Konowaloff* where the successor regime governing Iraq had, in fact, attempted to repudiate the acts of the preceding regime).

[209] Foreign Assistance Act of 1964 (Second Hickenlooper Amendment), Pub. L. No. 88-633, 77 Stat. 386 (codified at 22 U.S.C. § 2370(e)(2) (2018)).

[210] RESTATEMENT (FOURTH) § 441 cmt h & rptrs. note 12 (citing cases). *But see, e.g.*, West v. Multibanco Comermex, S.A., 807 F.2d 820, 829–30 (9th Cir. 1987) (rejecting as unduly formalistic the distinction between tangible and intangible property); Ramirez de Arellano v. Weinberger, 745 F.2d 1500, 1541 n.180 (D.C. Cir. 1984) (rejecting interpretation that the amendment "must invariably be limited to expropriated personal property located in the United States").

[211] RESTATEMENT (FOURTH) § 441 cmt h & rptrs. note 12; *see, e.g.*, Fogade v. ENB Revocable Trust, 263 F.3d 1274, 1294–95 (11th Cir. 2001). The domestic takings rule has recently been confirmed in the context of the Foreign Sovereign Immunities Act. *See* Federal Republic of Germany v. Philipp, 141 S. Ct. 703 (2021); *infra* this chapter text accompanying notes 628–633.

[212] Banco Nacional de Cuba v. Farr, 383 F.2d 166 (2d Cir. 1967).

few instances coincide roughly with a U.S. perception that certain types of government acts infringe international legal obligations.[213] Much the same result may be achieved indirectly, by statutorily authorizing certain types of lawsuits, such as those based on acts of torture or acts by state sponsors of terrorism. The language of the statute, or its legislative history, may evidence an intent that the act of state doctrine not be applied to such lawsuits, on the premise that such conduct was not defensible as a sovereign act.[214] However, the mere fact that a statute establishes liability for a foreign state or for foreign officials, standing alone, need not be construed as implicitly overriding the act of state doctrine.[215]

Seventh, there is a possible exception based on input from the executive branch. Courts defer to the executive branch when it comes to determining a foreign state's territorial borders, as may be necessary in assessing whether an act has been "performed within its own territory,"[216] or for determining whether "a recognized foreign sovereign power" is responsible for the public acts in question.[217] Deference as to such matters is a byproduct of familiar separation-of-powers principles. The more distinctive question is whether the executive branch is entitled, per the so-called *Bernstein* exception,[218] to cancel application of the doctrine altogether in a particular case. Three Justices of the Court joined

---

[213] *See, e.g.*, Pub. L. 104-114, Title III, § 302, 110 Stat. 815 (1996) (codified at 22 U.S.C. § 6082(a)(6) (2018)) (barring act of state defense in cases brought by U.S. nationals involving liability for trafficking in confiscated property). The Federal Arbitration Act provides broadly that "[e]nforcement of arbitral agreements, confirmation of arbitral awards, and execution upon judgments based on orders confirming such awards shall not be refused on the basis of the Act of State doctrine." Pub. L. 100-669, § 1, 102 Stat. 3969 (1988) (current version at 9 U.S.C. § 15); *see* Allied–Bruce Terminix Cos., Inc. v. Dobson, 513 U.S. 265, 272 (1995) (citing provision as "eliminating the Act of State doctrine as a bar to arbitration"). This broad exception to the doctrine does not formally reflect any treaty terms, but it is integral to the U.S. scheme for implementing the New York and Panama Conventions (cited *infra* this chapter, at note 587). Republic of Ecuador v. ChevronTexaco Corp., 376 F. Supp. 2d 334, 366 (S.D.N.Y. 2005).

[214] As to torture, see S. Rep. No. 102-249, pt. 4, at 8 (1991) (indicating that "the [Senate Committee on the Judiciary] does not intend the 'act of state' doctrine to provide a shield from lawsuit for former officials," while arguing that torture is not a public act to which the defense applies). *Compare* Lizarbe v. Rondon, 642 F. Supp. 2d 473, 488–89 (D. Md. 2009) (noting congressional views), *with* Doe v. Liu Qi, 349 F. Supp. 2d 1258, 1291 n.22 (N.D. Cal. 2004) (considering congressional action relevant to a balancing of factors, but that "[a]bsent a clearer indication from Congress . . . courts are not precluded from considering the act of state doctrine in adjudicating claims under the TVPA"). The position of courts regarding terrorism is more complex, given the convoluted history of legislation, but they have not generally endorsed the defense. *See, e.g.*, Owens v. Republic of Sudan, 374 F. Supp. 2d 1, 26–27 (D.D.C. 2005) (citing congressional and executive branch actions rejecting act of state defense); Daliberti v. Republic of Iraq, 97 F. Supp. 2d 38, 55 (D.D.C. 2000) (same).

[215] Restatement (Fourth) § 441 rptrs. note 14 (citing Sherman Act cases).

[216] W.S. Kirkpatrick & Co., Inc. v. Envtl. Tectonics Corp., Int'l, 493 U.S. 400, 405 (1990); Banco Nacional de Cuba v. Sabbatino, 376 U.S. 398, 401 (1964); *see supra* this chapter text accompanying notes 188–190.

[217] *Sabbatino*, 376 U.S. at 401; *see supra* this chapter text accompanying notes 173–177.

[218] *See* Bernstein v. Van Heyghen Freres, 163 F.2d 246 (2d Cir. 1947) (refraining from evaluating validity of Nazi property confiscation); Bernstein v. Nederlandsche-Amerikaansche Stoomvaart-Maatschappij, 210 F.2d 375 (2d Cir. 1954) (declining to apply the act of state doctrine in view of indication by the U.S. Department of State that application of the doctrine was not unnecessary).

an opinion to that effect, saying that "where the Executive Branch, charged as it is with primary responsibility for the conduct of foreign affairs, expressly represents to the Court that application of the act of state doctrine would not advance the interests of American foreign policy, that doctrine should not be applied by the courts," but the remainder of the Court differed.[219] In *Kirkpatrick*, the Court noted the proposed exception without reaching it.[220] At the same time, it quite directly rejected a related possibility: that the policy considerations underlying the act of state doctrine could be invoked, by the executive branch or otherwise, as "a doctrine unto themselves, justifying *expansion* of the act of state doctrine," which the Court regarded as detracting from the ordinary obligation of the judiciary to decide cases.[221] Basically, executive-informed foreign relations considerations might be used to narrow the doctrine's application, but not to expand it.

IV. Applying U.S. Law Abroad

Like other nations, the United States regulates persons, property, and conduct principally within its borders, but sometimes it also reaches abroad (more precisely, extraterritorially). When it does so, U.S. laws are more likely to conflict with the interests of foreign states, which may themselves be regulating the same conduct. The converse is also true: foreign states are not typically interested in regulating matters within the United States, but when they are, it is potentially at odds with U.S. interests.

Customary international law and, in a few contexts, treaties have posited rules that reduce the potential for interstate conflict. Some of these rules establish affirmative bases on which states may justify the exercise of jurisdiction. Other international rules, like international comity, attempt to restrain such exercises based on the relative interests of foreign sovereigns.

These international rules, while important, are not left to their own devices. If they were, their capacity to serve as constraints might be underwhelming, at least within the U.S. legal system. Congress generally prefers not to offend international law or foreign sovereigns. Still, as explored in other chapters, U.S. courts

---

[219] *Compare* First Nat'l City Bank v. Banco Nacional de Cuba, 406 U.S. 759, 768 (1972) (Rehnquist, J., joined by Burger, C.J., & White, J.), *with id.* at 773 (Douglas, J., concurring in result) (expressing concern that under a *Bernstein* exception, "the Court becomes a mere errand boy for the Executive Branch which may choose to pick some people's chestnuts from the fire, but not others"); *id.* at 773 (Powell, J., concurring in judgment) (noting separation of powers concerns); *id.* at 790–93 (Brennan, J., dissenting, joined by Stewart, Marshall, & Blackmun, JJ.) (elaborating criticism).

[220] *W.S. Kirkpatrick*, 493 U.S. at 405 ("find[ing] it unnecessary . . . to pursue those inquiries, since the factual predicate for application of the act of state doctrine does not exist").

[221] *Id.* at 408–10 (emphasis added).

will enforce a clear statutory provision, such as an assertion of jurisdiction, notwithstanding any inconsistent, preexisting international law limitations.[222] U.S. restraint, accordingly, is also a function of *domestic* legal rules that help to temper the reach of national law and avoid conflict with international law and foreign sovereigns. Together with diplomatic and political sensitivity, the combination of international and domestic legal rules ultimately provides some restraint on the exercise of U.S. regulation abroad.

A. Jurisdictional Bases

Practice elsewhere varies, but U.S. foreign relations law typically divides jurisdiction into three categories: (1) jurisdiction to prescribe, or legislative jurisdiction, which is the authority to make law for persons, property, or conduct; (2) jurisdiction to adjudicate, which is the authority to apply the law to persons or property; and (3) jurisdiction to enforce, which is the authority to compel obedience with the law.[223] Each type of jurisdiction is ordinarily exercised by a particular branch of the government—jurisdiction to prescribe by the legislature, jurisdiction to adjudicate by the judiciary, and jurisdiction to enforce by the executive. But that division is not inevitable. For example, administrative tribunals within the executive branch exercise jurisdiction to adjudicate, and executive rulemaking constitutes jurisdiction to prescribe.[224] Moreover, more than one type of jurisdiction may be exercised at the same time, and they can be difficult to tell apart, which may be one reason why international practice often does not recognize adjudicative jurisdiction as a discrete category.[225] As reflected in the following, jurisdiction to prescribe has attracted the most sustained interest under international law, probably because other assertions of jurisdiction are at least partly derivative.[226]

---

[222] *See* Chapter 5 § III(B) (customary international law); Chapter 6 § IV(C)(2) (treaties).

[223] RESTATEMENT (FOURTH) part IV, intro. note; *id.* § 401 cmt. b & rptrs. note 2. As the *Restatement (Fourth)* acknowledged, see *id.* rptrs. note 2, practice outside the United States varies, but there is certainly support for the three-part structure. *See, e.g.,* Int'l L. Comm'n, *Rep. to the General Assembly on the Work of Its Fifty-Eighth Session,* 61 U.N. GAOR Supp. No. 10, at 517–18 ¶ 5, U.N. Doc. A/61/10 (2006), *reprinted in* [2006] 2(2) Y.B. Int'l L. Comm'n 229–30 ¶ 5, U.N. Doc. A/CN.4/SER.A/2006/Add.1 (Part 2).

[224] RESTATEMENT (FOURTH) part IV, intro. note; *id.* § 401 cmt. b & rptrs. note 2. *See also id.* § 402 rptrs. note 3 (indicating how varied institutions exhibit prescriptive jurisdiction).

[225] RESTATEMENT (FOURTH) part IV, intro. note & § 401 cmt. b (describing categories); *id.* rptrs. note 2 (noting disagreement, particularly outside of United States, regarding recognizing a category of adjudicative jurisdiction).

[226] *Cf. id.* part IV, intro. note (noting international law bearing on various forms of jurisdiction).

1. Prescriptive Jurisdiction

In the absence of any general multilateral treaty on prescriptive jurisdiction, customary international law provides the basic rules.[227] In its 1927 *S.S. "Lotus" (Fr. v. Turk.)* judgment, the Permanent Court of International Justice (PCIJ) indicated that there was no general or presumptive prohibition on the exercise of extraterritorial jurisdiction. So long as a state avoids certain established prohibitions—in that case, any that would bar a state from exercising criminal jurisdiction over a collision on the high seas involving harm to a vessel flying its flag—the state enjoys "a wide measure of discretion" and "remains free to adopt the principles which it regards as best and most suitable."[228]

Nonetheless, today states usually disfavor the exercise of extraterritorial jurisdiction unless it can be justified by reference to certain recognized bases, which are addressed individually later.[229] Beyond these safe harbors, the exercise of prescriptive jurisdiction is subject to greater contestation. Put more generally, international law is said to permit prescriptive jurisdiction when there is a "genuine connection" between the state and the persons, property, or conduct being regulated.[230] That standard, while sound enough, may be of limited utility, and as detailed below the connection is certainly understood differently in different contexts.

There remain persistent challenges to aligning U.S. and other state practices. For example, under customary international law, the permissible bases of prescriptive jurisdiction may apply differently to different types of matters—so as to distinguish between criminal matters, private-party invocations of public law (such as private antitrust claims), and private-party litigation concerning private law—or leave this to the discretion of individual states.[231] (The *Restatement*

---

[227] *Id.* § 407 cmt b.

[228] S.S. "Lotus" (Fr. v. Turk.), 1927 P.C.I.J. (ser. A) No. 10, (Sept. 7), at 19. Although one portion of the decision seemed to say that jurisdiction could only be exercised within a state's territory, the question being addressed in that part of the judgment concerned enforcement jurisdiction (i.e., whether a state could enforce its decisions in another state). Christopher Staker, *Jurisdiction*, *in* INTERNATIONAL LAW 292 (Malcolm D. Evans, 5th ed. 2018); *see* S.S. "Lotus" (Fr. v. Turk.), 1927 P.C.I.J. (ser. A) No. 10, (Sept. 7), at 18–19 ("[T]he first and foremost restriction imposed by international law upon a State is that—failing the existence of a permissive rule to the contrary—it may not exercise its power in any form in the territory of another State. In this sense jurisdiction is certainly territorial; it cannot be exercised by a State outside its territory except by virtue of a permissive rule derived from international custom or from a convention.").

[229] These tensions are acknowledged, but not resolved, in many accounts. *See, e.g.*, Int'l L. Comm'n, *supra* note 223, at 520–21 ¶¶ 8–10; RESTATEMENT (FOURTH) § 407 rptrs. note 1.

[230] RESTATEMENT (FOURTH) § 407.

[231] For example, international law commentary quite frequently addresses criminal jurisdiction separately. *See, e.g.*, Int'l Law Comm'n, *supra* note 223, at 523–29, ¶¶ 18–27 (distinguishing between criminal and commercial jurisdiction); JAMES CRAWFORD, BROWNLIE'S PRINCIPLES OF PUBLIC INTERNATIONAL LAW 441–55 (9th ed. 2019) (criminal); *id.* at 455–60 (civil); *id.* at 455 (noting views that would minimize distinction). Civil law jurisdictions are more accustomed to regarding extraterritorial criminal jurisdiction as appropriate, which likely colors their perception of international law. *See* CEDRIC RYNGAERT, JURISDICTION IN INTERNATIONAL LAW 101–04 (2d ed. 2015).

(Fourth) took the position that in principle the same international-law princi-ples applied in all of these contexts.[232]) States also may not depict their domestic lawmaking in ways that correspond with international categories. In the United States, for example, whether a statute regulating particular conduct is premised on the Foreign Commerce Clause will not always be clear, but that is more likely to be addressed than whether it is an appropriate exercise of "territorial juris-diction" under customary international law. Even when Congress has been less attentive to the international law dimension, U.S. statutes may still be defended after the fact as resting on one or another of the generally accepted justifications for exercising jurisdiction to prescribe—to which the United States has gradually become more accustomed[233]—but an after-the-fact inquiry may be more provi-sional and complex.

a. Territorial and Effects Jurisdiction

Once it was established as a sovereign state, the United States regarded itself as ca-pable of adopting legislation effective throughout its territory.[234] The full import of this was not necessarily self-evident. Some early cases implied that, as a corollary, exercising authority extraterritorially would violate another, territorial sovereign's prerogatives.[235] Others, though, suggested that U.S. jurisdiction could be exercised on nonterritorial bases, like nationality,[236] or at least suggested that competing sov-ereign assertions of jurisdiction might be resolved diplomatically.[237]

The idea that territory could be an exclusive basis for prescriptive jurisdiction seems increasingly foreign today, but territory nonetheless remains the most widely employed and least controversial jurisdictional basis recognized under

---

[232] See RESTATEMENT (FOURTH) § 407 cmt. f & rptrs. note 5.

[233] RESTATEMENT (FOURTH) § 402 rptrs. note 2 (noting evolution of U.S. views).

[234] David L. Sloss, Michael D. Ramsey, & William S. Dodge, *International Law in the Supreme Court to 1860*, *in* INTERNATIONAL LAW IN THE U.S. SUPREME COURT: CONTINUITY AND CHANGE 38 (2011).

[235] See, e.g., The Schooner Exchange v. McFaddon, 11 U.S. (7 Cranch) 116, 136 (1812) (describing territorial jurisdiction as "necessarily exclusive and absolute," being "susceptible of no limitation not imposed by itself," and requiring that exceptions be derived from consent); *id.* at 137 (describing "[t]his full and absolute territorial jurisdiction being alike the attribute of every sovereign, and being incapable of conferring extra-territorial power"); *cf.* The Island of Palmas Case (or Miangas) (U.S. v. Neth.), 11 R.I.A.A. 813, 838 (Perm. Ct. Arb. 1928) (stating that "territorial sovereignty belongs always to one, or in exceptional circumstances to several States, to the exclusion of all others").

[236] The Apollon, 22 U.S. 362, 370 (1824) ("The laws of no nation can justly extend beyond its own territories, except so far as regards its own citizens."); Rose v. Himely, 8 U.S. 241, 279 (1808) ("It is conceded that the legislation of every country is territorial; that beyond its own territory, it can only affect its own subjects or citizens"), *overruled in part on other grounds*, Hudson v. Guestier, 10 U.S. (6 Cranch) 281 (1810).

[237] See, e.g., The Ship Richmond v. United States, 13 U.S. (9 Cranch.) 102, 104 (1815) ("The seizure of an American vessel within the territorial jurisdiction of a foreign power, is certainly an offence against that power, which must be adjusted between the two governments").

customary international law.[238] It is also highly germane to treaties. International agreements establish obligations that are quite often framed in territorial terms, proceeding on the predicate that a state party may regulate matters within its territory.[239] Some treaties, like the Convention on Genocide, require states parties to exercise criminal jurisdiction for acts committed within their territory, though this may can be understood as involving both prescriptive and enforcement jurisdiction.[240] While treaties also assert other bases, it is the exceptional agreement, like the Antarctic Treaty, that obstructs the ability of a state to regulate acts on a territorial basis.[241]

The foreign relations law of the United States is also reflexively territorial. Even if U.S. statutes do not refer to their geographic application, it may be assumed that they apply throughout the United States. Some, at least, are explicitly framed as applying to U.S. territory.[242] These statutes do not typically offer any definition of that territory, though there is, for example, a general-purpose definition in the federal criminal code[243] and another for immigration law.[244] Objects may be assimilated to U.S. territory for the purpose of regulating conduct on them, like the maritime vessels, aircraft, and spacecraft considered part of the "special maritime and territorial jurisdiction of the United States";[245] this is consistent

---

[238] CRAWFORD, *supra* note 231, at 440 ("The starting-point in this part of the law is the presumption that jurisdiction . . . is territorial"); *id.* at 442 (describing territoriality as "universally recognized"); *accord* Staker, *supra* note 228, at 296–97; Int'l L. Comm'n, *supra* note 223, at 522, 523 ¶¶ 14, 18; RESTATEMENT (FOURTH) part IV, intro. note; RYNGAERT, *supra* note 231, at 49.

[239] The Vienna Convention on the Law of Treaties, indeed, goes so far as to presume territorial scope. Vienna Convention on the Law of Treaties art. 29, May 23, 1969, 8 I.L.M. 679, 1155 U.N.T.S. 331.

[240] Convention on the Prevention and Punishment of the Crime of Genocide art. VI, Dec. 9, 1948, 28 I.L.M. 760, 78 U.N.T.S. 277; *see* Arrest Warrant of 11 April 2000 (Dem. Repub. Congo v. Belg.), Judgment, 2002 I.C.J. 11, 71 ¶ 27 (Feb. 14) (joint separate opinion by Higgins, Kooijmans, & Buergenthal, JJ.).

[241] Antarctic Treaty art. 4, Dec. 1, 1959, 12 U.S.T. 794, 402 U.N.T.S. 71 (disclaiming effect on existing territorial claims, but clarifying that treaty-related activities cannot establish territorial sovereignty); *see* Richard B. Bilder, *Control of Criminal Conduct in Antarctica*, 52 VA. L. REV. 231, 270 (1966) (concluding that this "precludes the United States from enacting legislation asserting criminal jurisdiction in Antarctica on a territorial basis," meaning that some other jurisdictional basis recognized in international law must be identified). Other treaties denounce sovereign claims in a manner inimical to territoriality. *See, e.g.*, Treaty on Principles Governing the Activities of States in the Exploration and Use of Outer Space, Including the Moon and Other Celestial Bodies art. 2, Jan. 27, 1967, 18 U.S.T. 2410, 610 U.N.T.S. 205.

[242] RESTATEMENT (FOURTH) § 402 rptrs. note 5 (citing examples).

[243] 18 U.S.C. § 5 (2018) ("The term 'United States', as used in this title in a territorial sense, includes all places and waters, continental or insular, subject to the jurisdiction of the United States, except the Canal Zone.").

[244] 8 U.S.C. § 1101(a)(38) ("The term 'United States', except as otherwise specifically herein provided, when used in a geographical sense, means the continental United States, Alaska, Hawaii, Puerto Rico, Guam, the Virgin Islands of the United States, and the Commonwealth of the Northern Mariana Islands.").

[245] 18 U.S.C. § 7(1), (5), (6) (2018); *see also id.* § 7(2) (U.S. vessels on the Great Lakes); *id.* § 7(3) (land acquired or used by the United States and subject to its concurrent or exclusive jurisdiction). Other provisions would be more problematic as a matter of territory, see *id.* § 7(4) (guano-containing rocks and islands, designated by the president as "appertaining to the United States"),

with the approach taken to "territory" under international law and construed in its light.[246]

Territorial jurisdiction becomes trickier once the territory of other states is involved.[247] The longest-running issue has concerned the circumstances in which a state may exercise such jurisdiction over matters that occur partially, but not *entirely*, within its territory. A state is said to be prescribing based on "subjective" territorial jurisdiction in relation to conduct that occurs within its territory—or which has at least been initiated within its territory, even if the conduct is completed in another state or has consequences there (for example, when the United States regulates the discharge of a weapon in the United States that harms someone across a border). By contrast, a state is said to be prescribing based on "objective" territorial jurisdiction in relation to conduct initiated elsewhere but completed or effectuated within its territory (for example, when U.S. law regulates the discharge of a weapon outside the United States that harms someone within the United States). Both forms of territorial jurisdiction are acceptable under international law,[248] although a treaty-based regime will make its own choices.[249] U.S. courts appear to regard international law as satisfied if at least some of the conduct occurs within the United States.[250]

"Effects" jurisdiction is a form of objective territoriality that was once greatly controversial and which today remains sensitive. Though often described (pejoratively) as a form of extraterritorial jurisdiction,[251] its predicate is territorial in character. An exercise of prescriptive jurisdiction by a state is properly based on effects jurisdiction when, even if no constituent element of the regulated matter takes place within that state's territory, conduct occurring outside that territory

---

or clearly invoke other jurisdictional predicates. *Id.* § 7(8)–(9) (passive personality and nationality jurisdiction).

[246] *See, e.g.*, Lauritzen v. Larsen, 345 U.S. 571 (1952); United States v. Flores, 289 U.S. 137, 155–59 (1933). Nonetheless, some courts would describe this as extraterritorial. Case of Hirsi Jamaa and Others v. Italy, App. No. 27765/09, 2012-II Eur. Ct. H.R. 97, 132–33, ¶¶ 75, 77–78 (2012).

[247] This is self-evident if territory changes hands. Early case law suggested, for example, that the exercise of U.S. revenue law would be "suspended" if another state had acquired full sovereignty over the area being regulated. United States v. Rice, 17 U.S. 246, 254 (1819) (suggesting that "the laws of the United States could no longer be rightfully enforced there or be obligatory upon the inhabitants who remained and submitted to the conquerors").

[248] RESTATEMENT (FOURTH) § 408 cmt. c & rptrs. note 4; RYNGAERT, *supra* note 231, at 77–79.

[249] Article 12(2) of the Rome Statute provides for International Criminal Court (ICC) jurisdiction if, among other things, "[t]he State on the territory of which the conduct in question occurred" is a party to the Statute. The pre-trial chamber has construed that provision in light of general international law, state practice, and other treaties, and held that criminal jurisdiction could be exercised if a legal element of the crime, or part of the crime, had occurred within a state's territory. Prosecutor v. People of Bangladesh, ICC-RoC46(3)-01/18, Decision on the Prosecutor's Request for a Ruling on Jurisdiction under Article 19(3) of the Statute, ¶ 66 (Sept. 6, 2018).

[250] RESTATEMENT (FOURTH) § 402 rptrs. note 5 (citing United States v. Neil, 312 F.3d 419, 422 (9th Cir. 2002), and United States v. Jordan, 223 F.3d 676, 693 (7th Cir. 2000)).

[251] *Cf.* RESTATEMENT (FOURTH) § 402 cmt. a.

has, or (perhaps) is intended to have, substantial effects within it (for example, regulation of two foreign companies conspiring to fix prices of a commodity in a foreign market, which has substantial collateral consequences for prices in the United States).[252] The United States was a pioneer in asserting effects-based territorial jurisdiction, particularly in antitrust and other economic matters, and it was initially a source of serious friction with European states.[253] The two approaches have since grown more similar.[254] There continues to be uncertainty about the threshold for the exercise of effects-based territorial jurisdiction—for example, whether a mere intention to produce substantial effects suffices even if substantial effects do not in fact materialize[255]—but fundamental objections to the principle of regulating conduct abroad that has effects within the territorial state are ebbing.

b. Nationality (Active Personality) Jurisdiction

The United States from its beginning has exercised jurisdiction over its citizens and residents, understanding it to be consistent with international law for a state to regulate its own nationals regardless of their whereabouts.[256] Nationality jurisdiction also seems consistent with international law today, and indeed indispensable for addressing matters arising in territories not subject to exclusive

---

[252] RESTATEMENT (FOURTH) § 409 & cmt a.

[253] See Edward T. Swaine, The Local Law of Global Antitrust, 43 WM. & MARY L. REV. 627, 643–46 (2001); e.g., id. at 644–45 & n.59 (citing claim by U.S. official that, as of 1981, "there have been five diplomatic protests of U.S. antitrust cases for every instance of express diplomatic support, and three blocking statutes for every cooperation agreement").

[254] See id. at 645–46 (stating, of effects jurisdiction, that "[b]y the end of the century it appeared as though the jurisdictional theory everywhere rejected had become nearly universal among active antitrust authorities"). There was for some time disagreement about whether the European Court of Justice's Wood Pulp decision, see Joined Cases 89, 104, 114, 116, 117 & 125–129/85, A. Ahlström Osakeyhtiö v. Comm'n ("Wood Pulp"), 1988 E.C.R. 5193, 5242–44, was entirely equivalent to the U.S. effects test. See Swaine, The Local Law of Global Antitrust, supra note 253, at 645 & n.65; compare RESTATEMENT (FOURTH) § 409 rptrs. note 2 (emphasizing similarity), with Joseph P. Griffin, Foreign Governmental Reactions to U.S. Assertions of Extraterritorial Jurisdiction, 6 GEO. MASON L. REV. 505, 512–23 (1998) (noting distinctions). The overlap has since become clearer. See Case C-413/14, Intel Corp. v. Euro. Comm'n, 2017 EUR-Lex CELEX LEXIS 632, ¶ 45 (Sept. 6, 2017) (upholding lower-court decision that either the implementation test or a "qualified effects" test would be consistent with international law, and noting that either aims at "preventing conduct which, while not adopted within the EU, has anticompetitive effects liable to have an impact on the EU market"); see also Case T-102/96, Gencor Ltd. v. Comm'n of the European Communities, 1999 E.C.R. II-753 (Court of First Instance).

[255] Courts in the United States have accepted jurisdiction based on intended effects and asserted (without much analysis) that it is consistent with international law. See, e.g., United States v. Yousef, 327 F.3d 56, 96–97 (2d Cir. 2003) (claiming that jurisdiction to prescribe was appropriate because "the defendants intended their actions to have an effect . . . on and within the United States"); RESTATEMENT (FOURTH) § 402 rptrs. note 6 (citing other examples). The Restatement (Fourth) did not take a clear position. Id. § 409 cmt. c & rptrs. note 4 (describing practice of "some states" in regulating conduct "that was intended to have, but did not have, a substantial effect within their territory," and citing U.S. and foreign examples).

[256] See supra this chapter note 236 (quoting The Apollon, 22 U.S. 362, 370 (1824), and Rose v. Himely, 8 U.S. (4 Cranch) 241, 279 (1808)).

territorial claims—such as on the high seas, in Antarctica, or on the International Space Station.[257] Contemporary discussion often describes this as "active personality" (in contrast to "passive personality" jurisdiction, discussed later).

Application to natural persons is often straightforward. International law leaves it to national law to define nationality and its application.[258] It is considered permissible, for example, for states to assert nationality-based jurisdiction even over conduct by a natural person who has since changed nationality, or who became a national after engaging in the conduct in question.[259] Although international law permits nationality jurisdiction to be asserted without regard to the nature of the offense, in practice it is more often asserted by states for matters like murder or hostage-taking.[260] The United States itself does not systematically assert jurisdiction over its nationals for all conduct abroad, but various statutes do regulate extraterritorial conduct (or conduct irrespective of location) based on U.S. citizenship[261] or nationality.[262]

Entities other than natural persons present their own definitional issues. Vessels and aircraft flying the flag of a state are generally regarded as nationals of that state, and hence their conduct may be regulated even when occurring abroad. According to widely subscribed multilateral conventions, states have the ability to determine how they will grant nationality to ships (and to determine whether they are entitled to fly that state's flag),[263] and likewise for

---

[257] CRAWFORD, *supra* note 231, at 444 & n.37. The Antarctic Treaty actually provides that authorized personnel shall only be subject to the jurisdiction of states parties of which they are nationals, and not on any other basis. Antarctic Treaty, *supra* note 241, art. VIII; *cf.* Smith v. United States, 507 U.S. 197 (1993) (construing "foreign country" to include Antarctica for purposes of limiting the waiver of claims against the United States under the Federal Tort Claims Act, based in part on the presumption against extraterritorial application of U.S. law). In contrast, for the International Space Station, passive personality jurisdiction plays a role subsidiary to nationality jurisdiction. Agreement Concerning Cooperation on the Civil International Space Station, art. 22, Jan. 29, 1998, T.I.A.S No. 12,927.

[258] RESTATEMENT (FOURTH) § 410 cmt. b & rptrs. note 2; CRAWFORD, *supra* note 231, at 443–44; Int'l Law Comm'n, *supra* note 223, at 523–24.

[259] RESTATEMENT (FOURTH) § 410 rptrs. note 1; RYNGAERT, *supra* note 231, at 104; *see* Harvard Research on International Law, Draft Convention on Jurisdiction with Respect to Crime, 29 AM. J. INT'L L. 439, 532 (1935) (arguing that criminal jurisdiction over one-time nationals avoided circumvention by any who might change nationality after the fact, and jurisdiction over those becoming nationals after the fact avoided impunity within states that as a matter of policy refused to extradite nationals).

[260] *See* Int'l Law Comm'n, *supra* note 223, at 524 ¶ 18 n.21.

[261] *See, e.g.,* 18 U.S.C. § 1956(f)(1) (criminalizing money laundering "by a United States citizen"); *see also* RESTATEMENT (FOURTH) § 402 rptrs. note 7 (citing additional examples).

[262] *See, e.g.,* 18 U.S.C. § 1203(b)(1)(A) (2018) (criminalizing hostage-taking outside the United States by "a national of the United States"); *see also* RESTATEMENT (FOURTH) § 402 rptrs. note 7 (citing additional examples). Nationals of the United States include both citizens and others who owe permanent allegiance to it, see Immigration and Nationality Act (INA) § 101(a)(22), 8 U.S.C. § 1102(a)(22), but the additional scope "has little practical impact today . . . for the only remaining noncitizen nationals are residents of American Samoa and Swains Island." Miller v. Albright, 523 U.S. 420, 467 n.2 (1998) (Ginsburg, J., dissenting); *see* Chapter 10 § I(A), n.5 and § III(A)(1), n.602.

[263] The 1958 U.N. Convention on the High Seas allows each state to fix the conditions for granting nationality to ships, and provides that "[s]hips have the nationality of the State whose flag they are

aircraft.[264] Corporations may also be nationals of a state and regulated for corporate conduct that occurs abroad. Nationality based on where a corporation is incorporated or has its seat is commonplace,[265] and the United States employs both approaches.[266]

Basing nationality jurisdiction on less formal relationships—like a degree of presence of a legal or natural person within the state—can be more controversial. For example, the United States sometimes asserts nationality jurisdiction based on whether a company is doing business in the United States.[267] Similarly, as regards natural persons, the United States sometimes asserts jurisdiction over foreign nationals who are residents; for example, the PROTECT Act criminalizes illicit sexual conduct not only by U.S. citizens but also by any noncitizen admitted for permanent residence.[268] The consistency of such approaches with customary international law may yet be challenged by other states, but practice seems to have grown more accommodating, at least in some areas.[269] For example, many states assert nationality jurisdiction over residents, determined based on a prior period of residency, for purposes of assessing income tax liability.[270] By contrast,

entitled to fly"; however, "[t]here must exist a genuine link between the State and the ship," and the state must exercise its jurisdiction effectively. Convention on the High Seas art. 5(1), Apr. 29, 1958, 13 U.S.T. 2312, 450 U.N.T.S. 11; *see also* U.N. Convention on the Law of the Sea art. 91, Dec. 10, 1982, 1833 U.N.T.S. 123 (providing similar rule, in treaty to which the United States not a party).

[264] Convention of Offences and Certain Other Acts Committed on Board Aircraft art. 3, Sept. 14, 1963, 20 U.S.T. 2941, 704 U.N.T.S. 219 (providing authority to state of registration); *id.* art. 4 (providing authority to other states); Convention on International Civil Aviation art. 17, Dec. 7, 1944, 61 Stat. 1180, 15 U.N.T.S. 295 ("Aircraft have the nationality of the State in which they are registered."); Convention for the Regulation of Aerial Navigation art. 6, Oct. 13, 1919, 11 L.N.T.S. 173 (similar); *see also supra* this chapter text accompanying notes 245–246 (noting capacity to regulate matters aboard national vessels as territorial in character).

[265] RESTATEMENT (FOURTH) § 410 cmt. b & rptrs. note 2 (citing examples).

[266] *Id.* § 402 rptrs. note 7 (citing examples).

[267] *Id.* § 402 rptrs. note 7.

[268] Prosecutorial Remedies and Other Tools to End the Exploitation of Children Today (PROTECT Act), 18 U.S.C. § 2423 (2018) (codified as amended); *cf.* United States v. Park, 938 F.3d 354 (2019) (upholding statute against constitutional challenge); for further discussion, see Chapter 2 § IV(A). As with the PROTECT Act, most such statutes are addressed to lawful permanent residents (or "alien admitted for permanent residence"). *See, e.g.,* 18 U.S.C. § 1837 (extending criminalization of economic espionage to conduct outside the United State, connected to acts within the United States, if by "a natural person who is a citizen or permanent resident alien of the United States"). In a few cases, residency is defined less formally. *See, e.g.,* 15 U.S.C. § 78dd-2(h)(1)(A) (subjecting to the Foreign Corrupt Practices Act "any individual who is a citizen, national, or resident of the United States").

[269] *See* RYNGAERT, *supra* note 231, at 104 (concluding that, in light of recent expansions of criminal jurisdiction by some states, "domicile or residence probably represents an adequate jurisdictional basis" under international law).

[270] *See, e.g.,* 26 U.S.C. § 7701(a)(30)(A) (treating "a citizen or resident of the United States" as U.S. persons subject to the Internal Revenue Code); *see also* Reuven S. Avi-Yonah, *International Tax as International Law*, 57 TAX. L. REV. 483, 485 (2004) (stating that "every country in the world (including the United States) has adopted a definition of nationality for tax purposes that is much broader than how nationality commonly is understood"); *id.* (expressing "doubt there is another substantive area of international law in which nationality jurisdiction for individuals rests on so flimsy a ground as mere physical presence").

the Military Extraterritorial Jurisdiction Act asserts what appears to be a distinct form of nationality jurisdiction not only over members of the U.S. armed forces but also all those employed by or accompanying such forces, including those who might be neither nationals nor residents of the United States.[271]

c. Passive Personality Jurisdiction

Prescriptive jurisdiction based on harm to a state's nationals, known as "passive personality" jurisdiction, was contested in the famous *S.S. Lotus* case, but the PCIJ viewed the circumstances as not requiring its resolution.[272] Since that time, states increasingly have exercised authority that is consistent with a passive personality basis, but usually only for serious offenses, such as terrorist acts that harm a state's nationals abroad.[273] It is hard to discern whether the limited way passive personality jurisdiction has been asserted is due to perceived international law limits, comity, or sovereign priorities.[274] Moreover, the exercise of passive personality jurisdiction by a state is sometimes invited by treaty, as with the Convention against Torture, which permits states parties to assert jurisdiction in cases where the victims are their nationals, and requires other states parties to cooperate in that regard through mutual legal assistance and extradition.[275]

The United States resisted exercising passive personality jurisdiction for some time.[276] But like France, another holdout, the United States became more

---

[271] 18 U.S.C. § 3261(a). In limiting the scope of this jurisdiction, Congress also reinforced its extraterritorial character. *Id.* (limiting jurisdiction to "an offense punishable by imprisonment for more than 1 year if the conduct had been engaged in within the special maritime and territorial jurisdiction of the United States"); *see* RESTATEMENT (FOURTH) § 402 rptrs. note 7. To be sure, particular applications of the statute may be justified in terms of other theories, as the facts may suggest. *See* United States v. Williams, 722 F. Supp. 2d 1313 (M.D. Ga. 2010) (suggesting relevance of objective territoriality, nationality, passive personality, and protective jurisdiction), *aff'd in part*, 509 Fed. Appx. 899 (11th Cir. 2013).

[272] S.S. Lotus (Fr. v. Turk.), Judgment, 1927 P.C.I.J. (ser. A) No. 10, at 22–23 ¶ 60 (Sept. 7).

[273] Arrest Warrant of 11 April 2000 (Dem. Rep. Congo v. Belg.), Judgment, 2002 I.C.J. 63, 76–77 ¶ 47 (joint separate opinion by Higgins, Kooijmans, & Buergenthal, JJ.) (Feb. 14) (stating that passive personality jurisdiction, "for so long regarded as controversial," now "meets with relatively little opposition, at least so far as a particular category of offences is concerned"); *see also* CRAWFORD, *supra* note 231, at 444–46; RESTATEMENT (FOURTH) § 411 & cmt. a. *But cf.* RYNGAERT, *supra* note 231, at 110 (stating that "[i]t is unclear whether the nationality of the victim . . . constitutes a sufficient jurisdictional link under international law," and regarding it as "quite likely . . . the most aggressive basis for extraterritorial jurisdiction (if universal jurisdiction *in absentia* is discounted)"); *id.* at 112 (noting that recent state practice supports such jurisdiction for a limited class of offenses).

[274] *See* CRAWFORD, *supra* note 231, at 444–46; RESTATEMENT (FOURTH) § 411 cmt. b & rptrs. notes 1–2.

[275] Convention against Torture and Other Cruel, Inhuman or Degrading Treatment or Punishment arts. 5(1)(c) & (2), Dec. 10, 1984, S. Treaty Doc. No. 100-20, 1485 U.N.T.S. 85, (elaborating *aut dedere aut judicare* principle, including as applied to victim nationals); *see also* Convention of Offences Committed on Board Aircraft, *supra* note 264, art. 4(b) (providing for jurisdiction over offenses against a state party's nationals); Convention for the Suppression of Unlawful Acts Against the Safety of Maritime Navigation art. 6(2)(b), Mar. 3, 1988, T.I.A.S. No. 95-306, 1678 U.N.T.S. 221 (same).

[276] In *Cutting's Case*, the United States objected after Mexico asserted jurisdiction over a U.S. citizen, recently resident in Mexico, concerning criminal libel against a Mexican national for

amenable in light of the principle's utility for addressing terrorism.[277] Successive editions of the *Restatement* also evolved in keeping with developments. The *Restatement (Second)* indicated that passive personality jurisdiction was not accepted under international law; the *Restatement (Third)* suggested its potential availability for certain offenses; most recently, the *Restatement (Fourth)* described it as a commonly accepted basis for prescriptive jurisdiction.[278] U.S. courts were hesitant initially in interpreting U.S. statutes so as to encompass such jurisdiction, but have since come to accept passive personality as an appropriate jurisdictional basis.[279]

A number of U.S. statutes now assert jurisdiction to protect U.S. nationals against offenses committed outside the United States.[280] Most involve relatively extreme offenses, like possession or use of weapons of mass destruction and hostage-taking,[281] but this is not always the case.[282] For example, part of the special maritime and territorial jurisdiction of the United States concerns unspecified offenses committed against a U.S. national who are on board vessels during a voyage with a scheduled departure from or arrival in the United States, "[t]o the

---

a publication made in the United States; Mexico ultimately dropped the charges. 1887 For. Rel. 751 (1888); *see* 2 MOORE DIGEST, at 228–42; *see also* 137 CONG. REC. 8677 (1991) (reprinting letter from the Assistant Secretary of State for Legislative Affairs, commenting on the proposed Murder of United States Nationals Act of 1991, and relating that "the United States has spoken against the assertion of 'passive personality' jurisdiction and has avoided its application under U.S. law").

[277] Eric Cafritz & Omer Tene, *Article 113-7 of the French Penal Code: The Passive Personality Principle*, 41 COLUM. J. TRANSNAT'L L. 585, 593–95 (2003); Int'l L. Comm'n, *supra* note 223, at 524 ¶ 19.

[278] RESTATEMENT (FOURTH) § 411 & rptrs. note 3; *see also* RESTATEMENT (SECOND) § 30(2) ("A state does not have jurisdiction to prescribe a rule of law attaching legal consequences to conduct of an alien outside its territory merely on the ground that the conduct affects one of its nationals."); RESTATEMENT (THIRD) § 402 cmt. g (observing that passive personality has been "increasingly accepted as applied to terrorist and other organized attacks on a state's nationals by reason of their nationality, or to assassination of a state's diplomatic representatives or other officials").

[279] *Compare, e.g.*, United States v. Columba-Colella, 604 F.2d 356, 360 (5th Cir. 1979) ("Congress would not be competent to attach criminal sanctions to the murder of an American by a foreign national in a foreign country, even if the victim returned home and succumbed to his injuries") (citing RESTATEMENT (SECOND)), *with* United States v. Yousef, 327 F.3d 56, 96 (2d Cir. 2003) (finding jurisdiction under passive personality principle over alleged plots to bomb U.S.-flag aircraft, carrying U.S. citizens and crews bound for the United States).

[280] Unlike for nationality jurisdiction, however, such statutes are typically limited to protection of nationals and not of all U.S. residents. *See* RESTATEMENT (FOURTH) § 402 rptrs. note 8.

[281] *E.g.*, 18 U.S.C. § 175(a) (2018) (asserting jurisdiction regarding possession and related offenses concerning biological weapons, and stating that "[t]here is extraterritorial Federal jurisdiction over an offense under this section committed by or against a national of the United States"); 18 U.S.C. § 229(c)(3) (use of chemical weapons outside the United States against a U.S. national); 18 U.S.C. § 1203(b)(1)(A) (seizing or detaining a U.S. national as hostage outside the United States); *see* RESTATEMENT (FOURTH) § 402 rptrs. note 8 (citing additional examples).

[282] Some statutes, moreover, have been upheld on that basis. *See, e.g.*, United States v. Neil, 312 F.3d 419, 422–23 (9th Cir. 2002) (treating passive personality as one of several available bases for jurisdiction over criminal sexual contact with a minor); United States v. Hill, 279 F.3d 731, 740 (9th Cir. 2002) (relying on passive personality as one basis for jurisdiction over offense of harboring a fugitive owing child support, when support would have benefited U.S. citizens).

extent permitted by international law."[283] Other statutes establish jurisdiction over a broad range of offenses against U.S. officers and employees.[284]

One question is whether passive personality jurisdiction may properly be exercised only when a state's nationals are targeted *by virtue of* their nationality. The link may be assumed or implied for offenses like terrorism or when diplomats or other state officials are targeted, but international law is not clear as to whether it is required. U.S. statutes perceived as exercising passive personality jurisdiction do not generally require purpose in this sense as a prerequisite, and courts have not implied it. One Ninth Circuit decision treated the passive personality principle as more tenable "when applied to terrorist activities and organized attacks on a state's nationals because of the victim's nationality," as contrasted with "a random murder of an American tourist."[285] Yet a later decision by the Ninth Circuit attributed this reasoning to the fact that the statute in question was not expressly extraterritorial, whereas a different statute that was expressly extraterritorial could be justified on the basis of passive personality without any need for a showing that U.S. nationality motivated the alleged offense.[286]

Somewhat distinctly, the United States bases not just criminal statutes but also civil liability statutes on passive personality jurisdiction, at least with respect to terrorism. The Anti-Terrorism Act (ATA) created a treble damages remedy for U.S. nationals suffering injury to person, property, or business due to an act of "international terrorism," defined as activities primarily outside the United States or transcending national boundaries.[287] The Foreign Sovereign Immunities Act (FSIA), as amended, provides jurisdiction and a private right of action against state sponsors of terrorism for certain acts of terrorism where the victim is a U.S. national, member of the U.S. armed forces, or a U.S. government employee or contractor.[288] Invoking, but not relying exclusively on, passive

[283] 18 U.S.C. § 7(8); *see, e.g.,* United States v. Neil, 312 F.3d 419, 23 (9th Cir. 2002) (upholding application of sexual conduct statute, premised on jurisdiction under 18 U.S.C. § 7(8), as consistent with passive personality jurisdiction); United States v. Roberts, 1 F. Supp. 2d 601, 607 (E.D. La. 1998) (invoking passive personality and objective territoriality).

[284] *E.g.,* 18 U.S.C. § 111 (assault against officer or employee of the United States); 18 U.S.C. § 1114 (murder of officer or employee of the United States); 18 U.S.C. § 351 (murder, kidnapping, and assault of members of Congress, members of Cabinet, and Supreme Court justices). These have been construed as exercising passive personality jurisdiction. *See* United States v. Benitez, 741 F.2d 1312, 1316 (11th Cir. 1984) (invoking protective and passive personality jurisdiction in support of prosecutions under, inter alia, 18 U.S.C. §§ 111, 1114, 1117, & 2112); *cf. Layton,* 509 F. Supp. at 216 & n.5 (noting, but not deciding, possible passive personality jurisdiction for prosecution under 18 U.S.C. § 351).

[285] United States v. Vasquez-Velasco, 15 F.3d 833, 841 n.7 (9th Cir. 1994) (citing RESTATEMENT (THIRD) § 402 cmt. g).

[286] *Neil,* 312 F.3d at 423; *see also* Biton v. Palestinian Interim Self-Government Auth., 510 F. Supp. 2d 144, 146 (D.D.C. 2007) (concluding that such jurisdiction remains germane "even though the victims were not targeted because of their U.S. citizenship," and citing case law).

[287] 18 U.S.C. § 2333 (2018); for the definition of international terrorism, see 18 U.S.C. § 2331(1).

[288] 28 U.S.C. § 1605A(c). For further discussion, see *infra* this chapter § V(A)(4)(e).

personality jurisdiction, U.S. courts have found such provisions to be consistent with (or at least, not clearly inconsistent with) international law.[289]

d. Protective Jurisdiction

Another sometimes controversial basis for exercising prescriptive jurisdiction is the protective principle, which justifies authority over serious offenses committed abroad that implicate state security or other vital interests. Such acts, though occurring abroad, are likely of genuine concern to the affected state, but of undependable interest to the state in which they occur—leaving the former in need of a jurisdictional basis to ensure that the conduct is addressed.[290]

States have long asserted jurisdiction over some such matters. The clear challenge for international law lies in describing the kinds of interests that qualify. Over time, they seem to have broadened—so that the protective principle is now asserted to cover not just espionage, currency counterfeiting, falsification of official documents, and conspiracy to violate immigration or customs laws, but also terrorism and cybercrime.[291] Assessing state practice is difficult, since some vital interests (like offenses against a state's officials) is also likely to implicate passive personality jurisdiction, and others (like terrorism) may also implicate universal jurisdiction.[292]

U.S. practice poses similar challenges. A number of statutes are plausibly premised on vital interests long recognized by other states, and courts have upheld them as such.[293] Assessing statutes predicated on more distinctive interests is

---

[289] Goldberg v. UBS AG, 690 F. Supp. 2d 92, 108–11 (E.D.N.Y. 2010) (invoking passive personality and objective territoriality, in relation to ATA); *Biton*, 510 F. Supp. 2d at 146–47 (invoking passive personality and universal jurisdiction, in relation to ATA); Flatow v. Islamic Republic of Iran, 999 F. Supp. 1, 15 n.7 (D.D.C. 1998) (invoking passive personality, protective, and universal jurisdiction in support of jurisdiction, in relation to predecessor state-sponsored terrorism provision).

[290] RYNGAERT, *supra* note 231, at 114.

[291] These and similar matters are sometimes described as being matters of external or internal security. *See* RESTATEMENT (FOURTH) § 412; *id.* § 412 cmt. a & rptrs. note 1; *see also* CRAWFORD, *supra* note 231, at 446; Int'l L. Comm'n, *supra* note 223, at 525 ¶ 20; RYNGAERT, *supra* note 231, at 112.

[292] RESTATEMENT (FOURTH) § 412 rptrs. note 2. For example, a provision that criminalized the killing of U.S. nationals overseas—but which limited prosecution to certified instances of terrorism-related circumstances—was understood to be warranted, at least in part, by protective jurisdiction. Omnibus Diplomatic Security and Antiterrorism Act of 1986, Pub. L. No. 99-399, tit. XII, § 1202(a), 100 Stat. 896 (1986) (codified as amended at 18 U.S.C. § 2332 (2018)); *see* 132 CONG. REC. 2355, 2356 (1986) (remarks of Sen. Specter); *Bills to Authorize Prosecution of Terrorists and Others Who Attack U.S. Government Employees and Citizens Abroad: Hearing Before the Subcomm. on Security and Terrorism of the S. Comm. on the Judiciary*, 99th Cong. 67–68 (1985) (statement of Abraham D. Sofaer, Department of State Legal Adviser). The focus on U.S. victims naturally engaged passive personality jurisdiction as well. *Cf. id.* at 41–42 (remarks of Sen. Specter); *id.* at 22–29 (Congressional Research Service analysis suggesting imperfect correlation between the approach of two draft bills and international bases of jurisdiction).

[293] *See, e.g.*, 18 U.S.C. § 470 (counterfeiting by persons outside the United States). Not infrequently, the statutes in question are not expressly extraterritorial, but their extension appears not to offend the presumption against extraterritoriality. *See, e.g.*, 18 U.S.C. § 1546 (fraud and misuse of visas, permits, and other documents); United States v. Pizzarusso, 388 F.2d 8, 10–11 (2d Cir. 1968) (upholding, on the basis of protective jurisdiction, conviction of foreign national for providing false statement on

more difficult. The United States has perceived protective jurisdiction as permitting criminal statutes directed at overseas terrorism that harms U.S. persons, and U.S. courts have upheld such statutes on that basis,[294] but such jurisdiction might instead be justified (including by other states) on the basis of passive personality jurisdiction. Statutes that sanction drug trafficking outside the United States may pose more acute complications. Congress made a point of claiming, when enacting the Maritime Drug Law Enforcement Act (MDLEA), that drug trafficking "presents a specific threat to the safety of maritime navigation and the security of the United States."[295] Courts have divided as to whether this is sufficient to warrant protective jurisdiction, such that the United States may exercise criminal jurisdiction over drug trafficking on the high seas—or in similar environments—based on an inchoate threat to the United States, and in the absence of any more direct connection.[296] There remain, too, residual concerns involving construing the scope of related statutory provisions and their consistency with constitutional principles.[297]

visa application to U.S. consular officer in Canada); 18 U.S.C. §§ 792–99 (criminal espionage); United States v. Zehe, 601 F. Supp. 196, 198 (D. Mass. 1985) (holding that foreign national may be prosecuted for extraterritorial espionage based on protective jurisdiction); 18 U.S.C. §§ 1114, 1117 (conspiracy to murder and murder of government officials); United States v. Benitez, 741 F.2d 1312, 1316–17 (11th Cir. 1984) (upholding conviction of foreign national for, inter alia, attempted murder of DEA agents abroad, as consistent with passive personality and protective jurisdiction); see RESTATEMENT (FOURTH) § 402, rptrs. note 9 (citing additional examples).

[294] See, e.g., United States v. Yousef, 327 F.3d 56, 110–11 (2d Cir. 2003) (concluding that jurisdiction under 18 U.S.C. § 32(b)(3), enacted as part of the Aircraft Sabotage Act of 1984, Pub. L. No. 98-473, 98 Stat. 1837, 2187–88, was proper based on protective jurisdiction); United States v. Bin Laden, 92 F. Supp. 2d 189, 221 (S.D.N.Y. 2000) (noting consistency of 18 U.S.C. §§ 2332–32a with protective jurisdiction); supra this chapter note 287 (discussing 18 U.S.C. § 2332). Congress also regarded protective jurisdiction as warranting broad implementation of the Convention for the Suppression of Unlawful Acts Against the Safety of Maritime Navigation, supra note 275 (discussing provisions codified, as amended, at 18 U.S.C. § 2280).

[295] Maritime Drug Law Enforcement Act, Pub. L. 109-304, § 10(2), 120 Stat. 1685 (2006) (codified as amended at 46 U.S.C. § 70501).

[296] RESTATEMENT (FOURTH) § 402 rptrs. note 9 (suggesting that U.S. courts "have divided on whether the protective principle properly extends to narcotics trafficking"). Compare United States v. Perlaza, 439 F.3d 1149, 1161–63 (9th Cir. 2006) (rejecting attempted invocation of the "drug trafficking protective principle"), and United States v. Wright-Barker, 784 F.2d 161, 167 n.5 (3d Cir. 1986) (same), with United States v. Dávila-Reyes, 937 F.3d 57, 62–63 (1st Cir. 2019) (concluding that application of the MDLEA was warranted under the protective principle), and United States v. Tinoco, 304 F.3d 1088, 1108 (11th Cir. 2002) (accepting that Congress "may assert extraterritorial jurisdiction over vessels in the high seas that are engaged in conduct that 'has a potentially adverse effect and is generally recognized as a crime by nations that have reasonably developed legal systems'") (quoting United States v. Gonzalez, 776 F.2d 931, 939 (11th Cir. 1985)). See also United States v. Lawrence, 727 F.3d 386, 394–95 (5th Cir. 2013) (upholding, on the basis of the protective principle, jurisdiction over conspiracy to possess illicit substances aboard an aircraft with intent to distribute, in violation of Comprehensive Drug Abuse Prevention and Control Act of 1970, § 1009(b), 21 U.S.C.A. § 959(b), but noting possible distinction where no actions took place in the United States or "where the conduct at issue was lawful in the jurisdictions in which it occurred but unlawful in the United States").

[297] The Ninth Circuit, among others, has maintained jurisdictional requirements for applying MDLEA extraterritorially, involving the relationship of the United States to the vessel and conduct

Future novel attempts to invoke protective jurisdiction may be just as difficult to evaluate. The broadening of acceptable security interests, including in international practice, suggests a big tent, but international law provides no general criteria or coherent limits.[298] Under the *Restatement (Second)*, the conduct subject to protective jurisdiction must be generally recognized as criminal and must threaten a state's security or "the operation of its governmental functions";[299] the *Restatement (Third)* was more or less consistent;[300] under the *Restatement (Fourth)*, the conduct must be that "directed against the security of the state or against a limited class of other fundamental state interests," and while the new version provides illustrations of those interests, finding common threads is challenging.[301] Courts seem quite likely to defer to the political branches in the absence of any more determinate meaning.

e. Universal Jurisdiction

Universal jurisdiction is both the least demanding and most stringent basis for prescriptive jurisdiction. On the one hand, it requires no connection between the state asserting jurisdiction and the persons or conduct concerned. On the other hand, it is relevant only for a very limited number of especially egregious offenses; as the *Restatement (Fourth)* puts it, only for "certain offenses of universal concern."[302] The idea, at its core, is that a state is permitted to exercise an

concerned, for which it considers protective jurisdiction relevant but by itself inadequate. United States v. Perlaza, 439 F.3d 1149, 1162–63 (9th Cir. 2006). Other decisions consider protective jurisdiction in the context of evaluating due process claims relating to jurisdiction over drug trafficking. *Tinoco*, 304 F.3d at 1109; United States v. Cardales, 168 F.3d 548, 553 (1st Cir. 1999).

[298] As James Crawford put it:

The categories of what may be considered a vital interest for the purposes of protective jurisdiction are not closed, and no criteria exist for determining such interests beyond a vague sense of gravity. Ultimately, the identification of exorbitant jurisdiction may be a matter of knowing it when one sees it.

CRAWFORD, *supra* note 231, at 446.

[299] RESTATEMENT (SECOND) § 33(1); *see, e.g.*, United States v. Zehe, 601 F. Supp. 196, 198 (D. Mass. 1985).

[300] RESTATEMENT (THIRD) § 402(3) ("certain conduct outside its territory by persons not its nationals that is directed against the security of the state or against a limited class of other state interests"); *id.* cmt. f (reiterating *Restatement (Second)* approach, including its reference to the "integrity of governmental functions" and generally recognized crimes, while also providing examples of "espionage, counterfeiting of the state's seal or currency, falsification of official documents, as well as perjury before consular officials, and conspiracy to violate the immigration or customs laws").

[301] RESTATEMENT (FOURTH) § 412 (noting examples "such as espionage, certain acts of terrorism, murder of government officials, counterfeiting of the state's seal or currency, falsification of official documents, perjury before consular officials, and conspiracy to violate immigration or customs laws").

[302] RESTATEMENT (FOURTH) § 413; *see also* THE PRINCETON PRINCIPLES ON UNIVERSAL JURISDICTION 28 (Stephen Macedo ed., 2001), https://perma.cc/UAL6-ZEDS (Principle 1) (describing "universal jurisdiction [a]s criminal jurisdiction based solely on the nature of the

additional degree of prescriptive jurisdiction to matters as to which it has no particular connection in pursuit of upholding and enforcing certain fundamental international values.[303]

i. General Approach At present, there is a workable consensus regarding the core offenses over which universal jurisdiction may be exercised. They are often described—with the understanding that any list may be non-exhaustive—as including genocide, crimes against humanity, torture, war crimes, piracy, and the slave trade.[304] Sometimes a more conservative view is taken, as in dicta in some of the *Arrest Warrant* opinions at the International Court of Justice (ICJ), where fewer eligible offenses were catalogued.[305] Others would add the crime of aggression to the list,[306] and (as noted later) the United States, at least, would include certain acts of terrorism.[307]

Whatever the qualifying offenses, the means by which eligible offenses are decided is quite unclear. Widely ratified treaties like the Convention against Torture, which requires states parties to exercise jurisdiction over offenders who turn up in their territory (even if the offense occurred abroad and did not involve the state party's nationals), are often invoked as evidencing universal jurisdiction.[308] Such claims seem tenuous, however, given that such

crime, without regard to where the crime was committed, . . . the nationality of the victim, or any other connection to the state exercising such jurisdiction").

---

[303] The vindication of international values is usually implicit, and not an essential criterion beyond the nature of the offenses. *But cf.* Int'l Law Comm'n, *supra* note 223, at 522–23, ¶ 16 (stressing that because "a State exercises such jurisdiction in the interest of the international community rather than exclusively in its own national interest," it falls outside the scope of extraterritorial jurisdiction exercised by sovereign states).

[304] RESTATEMENT (FOURTH) § 413; *see also* PRINCETON PRINCIPLES, *supra* note 302, at 29 (Principle 2).

[305] The judgment indicated that it was unnecessary to address universal jurisdiction. Arrest Warrant of 11 April 2000 (Dem. Rep. Congo v. Belg.), Judgment, 2002 I.C.J. 11, 19, ¶ 43 (Feb. 14). Still, several judges suggested that customary international law recognized such jurisdiction only for maritime piracy. *See id.* at 38, ¶¶ 4–5 & 42, ¶ 12 (separate opinion by President Guillame); *id.* at 55, ¶ 6 (declaration of Ranjeva, J.); *see also id.* at 92–94, ¶¶ 6–9 (separate opinion by Rezek, J.). Others, though, understood it to be permitted as to other offenses like war crimes and crimes against humanity. *See, e.g., id.* at 81–83, ¶¶ 60–62, 65 (joint separate opinion of Higgins, Kooijmans, & Buergenthal, JJ.); *id.* at 169–77 (dissenting opinion by van den Wyngaert, J.). Other cases also suggested divided views. *See, e.g.*, Questions Relating to the Obligation to Prosecute or Extradite (Belg. v. Sen.), Judgment, 2012 I.C.J. 422, 478–80, ¶¶ 30–32 (July 20) (separate opinion by Abraham, J.) (contending that, were the Court to accept jurisdiction, it would properly hold that there was no obligation to exercise universal jurisdiction over war crimes or crimes against humanity without additional bases); *id.* at 556–57 (separate opinion by Cançado Trindade, J.) (suggesting emergence of universal jurisdiction).

[306] *Compare* RESTATEMENT (FOURTH) § 413 (omitting aggression), *with* PRINCETON PRINCIPLES, *supra* note 302, at 29 (Principle 2) (including "crimes against peace"). *See generally* CRAWFORD, *supra* note 231, at 452 (noting addition of aggression to the crimes over which the ICC may exercise jurisdiction, but concluding that "[f]or now . . . it is questionable as to whether aggression can be considered a crime of universal jurisdiction," adding "[t]he better view may be that it is not").

[307] *See infra* this chapter text accompanying notes 332–338.

[308] *See, e.g.*, Questions Relating to the Obligation to Prosecute or Extradite, 2012 I.C.J. at 451, ¶¶ 74–75. *But see id.* at 616, ¶ 36 (dissenting opinion by Sur, J.) (noting that describing this as universal

jurisdiction is based on a mutual concession among states parties to a treaty, not on customary international law.[309] The better evidence may be national implementing legislation that permits the exercise of such jurisdiction even over nationals of nonparties to the treaty.[310] That evidence may be of limited value, however, if the states asserting jurisdiction did not deliberately legislate beyond other jurisdictional bases, if the state in practice does not act upon such jurisdiction, or if nonparty states have had little real occasion to protest. Methodological questions like these may be relevant as additional offenses are posited to fall within universal jurisdiction.

Universal jurisdiction, even for agreed offenses, is not unregulated. Criminal jurisdiction is widely accepted,[311] but there is not yet broad support for exercising civil jurisdiction absent other connections of the state with the persons or conduct concerned.[312] State practice also suggests potential disagreement as to whether universal jurisdiction permits trial *in absentia*, or instead requires that the accused be present within the state at some critical juncture (an issue that may more directly concern adjudicative (or enforcement) jurisdiction).[313] States may also limit universal jurisdiction to particular periods of time (to take account, for example, of when a state has adhered to a relevant treaty) or specific conflicts, or require that assertions of jurisdiction be approved by a high-level prosecutor or executive or judicial body. While such limits may be idiosyncratic national choices,[314] they may also suggest an essential element of reasonableness in employing this particular basis of jurisdiction.

Parsing state practice will likely remain difficult. As just suggested, one challenge lies in determining whether constraints on national practice are owed to perceived legal boundaries, or instead arise because states simply choose not to exercise jurisdiction to its fullest possible extent. A second problem is that state practice may be apparent only when other possible jurisdictional bases are

jurisdiction is "an overstatement, since it concerns only the parties"). For other examples, see CRAWFORD, *supra* note 231, at 454–55; RYNGAERT, *supra* note 231, at 123–25.

[309] RYNGAERT, *supra* note 231, at 124.

[310] RESTATEMENT (FOURTH) § 413 rptrs. note 2 ("It is the national legislation, rather than the treaty, that provides direct evidence of state practice on universal jurisdiction").

[311] RESTATEMENT (FOURTH) § 413 rptrs. note 3; RYNGAERT, *supra* note 231, at 129–31. For an extensive survey, see U.N. Secretary-General, *The Scope and Application of the Principle of Universal Jurisdiction*, U.N. Doc. A/66/93 (June 20, 2011) (supplemented by U.N. Doc. A/71/111, U.N. Doc. A/70/125, U.N. Doc. A/69/174, U.N. Doc. A/68/113, U.N. Doc. A/67/116, U.N. Doc. A/66/93 Add.1)); *see also* U.N. Secretary-General, *The Scope and Application of the Principle of Universal Jurisdiction*, U.N. Doc. A/65/181 (July 29, 2010) (initial overview).

[312] RESTATEMENT (FOURTH) § 413 rptrs. notes 3–4 (describing, respectively, international practice regarding criminal and civil jurisdiction).

[313] CRAWFORD, *supra* note 231, at 453.

[314] This position is taken by the RESTATEMENT (FOURTH) § 413 rptrs. note 5.

ruled out; some observers even define universal jurisdiction as state assertions "in the absence of any other generally recognized head of prescriptive jurisdiction."[315] Finally, it has long been perceived that actual use of universal jurisdiction is rare—consisting mainly of high-profile cases like Israel's prosecution of Eichmann[316] and Spain's (ultimately aborted) pursuit of Pinochet[317]—and often controversial. Some scholarship suggests that universal jurisdiction may be asserted more frequently than is usually perceived, often for persons already residing in the state at issue. If so, this may reflect growing expertise within domestic systems and attempts by states to fulfill their obligations under the Rome Statute.[318]

ii. U.S. Practice The United States has a long history itself of exercising what appears to be universal jurisdiction. Piracy on the high seas is subject to life imprisonment for whomever "is afterwards brought into or found in the United States," which courts have understood to assert universal jurisdiction.[319] (Indeed, predecessor statutes were amended so as to eliminate any required nexus to the United States.[320]) Slavery and slave-trading have also been prohibited by means of universal jurisdiction, as now are other forms of trafficking.[321] Consistent with its treaty obligations, the United States exercises jurisdiction over genocide and torture without requiring any U.S. nexus beyond the presence of the offender in the United States, and prosecutions of those offenses do not seem consistent with protective jurisdiction.[322] In other instances, like crimes against humanity and

---

[315] CRAWFORD, *supra* note 231, at 451.

[316] Attorney General of Israel v. Eichmann, 36 I.L.R. 277, 298–304 (Sup. Ct. Isr. 1962).

[317] The U.K. decision, which arose from a Spanish request for extradition, was issued by the House of Lords. *See* Regina v. Bow St. Metro. Stipendiary Magistrate, *Ex parte* Pinochet Ugarte, 2 WLR 827, 830 (HL 1999).

[318] Máximo Langer & Mackenzie Eason, *The Quiet Expansion of Universal Jurisdiction*, 30 EUR. J. INT'L L. 779 (2019).

[319] 18 U.S.C. § 1651 (2018); *see, e.g.*, United States v. Ali, 718 F.3d 929, 935 (D.C. Cir. 2013).

[320] *See* United States v. Dire, 680 F.3d 446, 455–56 (4th Cir. 2012); United States v. Hasan, 747 F. Supp. 2d 599, 612–14 (E.D. Va. 2010). Early U.S. decisions wrestled with whether a connection to the United States was necessary. *Compare* United States v. Palmer, 16 U.S. (3 Wheat.) 610, 631 (1818) (construing 1790 act as requiring citizenship or other U.S. nexus for the range of piracy-related offenses regulated), *with* United States v. Smith, 18 (5 Wheat.) U.S. 153, 162 (1820) (construing 1819 act to reference piracy as defined by the law of nations, which permitted states to punish "all persons, whether natives or foreigners, who have committed this offence against any persons whatsoever, with whom they are in amity"). While they ultimately determined that no connection to the United States was necessary, that did not mean that the capacity to exercise universal jurisdiction was actually exploited. *See* Eugene Kontorovich, *The Piracy Analogy: Modern Universal Jurisdiction's Hollow Foundation*, 45 HARV. INT'L L.J. 183, 192 & n.51 (2004) (citing ALFRED P. RUBIN, THE LAW OF PIRACY 302, 348 n.50 (2d. ed. 1998)).

[321] RESTATEMENT (FOURTH) § 402 rptrs. note 10.

[322] *See also id.* (detailing additional statutory provisions establishing forms of universal jurisdiction to implement treaties).

war crimes, the United States has not legislated to the full extent permitted by universal jurisdiction.[323]

Civil claims have been a recurring source of controversy in U.S. practice implicating universal jurisdiction. The Alien Tort Statute (ATS), originally enacted as part of the Judiciary Act of 1789, provides district courts with jurisdiction over "any civil action by an alien for a tort only, committed in violation of the law of nations or a treaty of the United States."[324] When the statute began to be used in earnest, just a few decades ago, it was sometimes described as an example of universal jurisdiction because it required no direct connection with the United States.[325] This understanding was largely consistent with the Supreme Court's first ATS decision, *Sosa v. Alvarez-Machain*,[326] but later application of the presumption against extraterritoriality resulted in a requirement that ATS causes of action must at a bare minimum "touch and concern" U.S. territory "with sufficient force."[327] A clearer example might be the Torture Victim Protection Act (TVPA), which establishes a cause of action for those who, "under actual or apparent authority, or color of law, of any foreign nation," commit torture or extrajudicial killing, and when it was enacted Congress appeared to rely on universal jurisdiction.[328]

As previously noted, using universal jurisdiction for civil claims remains unsettled.[329] While the *Restatement (Third)* regarded such jurisdiction as consistent

---

[323] *Id.* The United States is a party to no treaty, and has no statute, on crimes against humanity. As to war crimes, the 1949 Geneva Conventions, to which the United States is a party, provide: "Each High Contracting Party shall be under the obligation to search for persons alleged to have committed, or to have ordered to be committed, such grave breaches, and shall bring such persons, regardless of their nationality, before its own courts." *See, e.g.*, Geneva Convention (I) for the Amelioration of the ·Condition of the Wounded and Sick in Armed Forces in the Field art. 49, Aug. 12, 1949, 75 U.N.T.S. 31, 62. The U.S. implementing statute, however, only makes it an offense to commit any of a list of violations of such conventions if the crime was committed by or against a U.S. national, or a member of the U.S. armed forces. *See* War Crimes Act, 18 U.S.C. § 2441 (2018); *see also* Michael J. Matheson, *The Amendment of the War Crimes Act*, 101 AM. J. INT'L L. 48 (2007). However, Congress is actively considering legislation that would add jurisdiction over war crimes abroad even if neither the accused nor the victim is a U.S. national. Charlie Savage, *Russian Atrocities Prompt Bipartisan Push to Expand U.S. War Crimes Law*, N.Y. TIMES, May 17, 2022, at A7.

[324] 28 U.S.C. § 1350; *see supra* text accompanying notes 49–51 (describing innovative aspects of ATS at adoption); *see also* Chapter 5 § IV(B) (discussing ATS more generally).

[325] *Compare, e.g.*, Donald Francis Donovan & Anthea Roberts, *The Emerging Recognition of Universal Civil Jurisdiction*, 100 AM. J. INT'L L. 142, 146–48 (2006), *with* Curtis A. Bradley, *Universal Jurisdiction and U.S. Law*, 2001 U. CHI. LEGAL F. 323, 325 (2001).

[326] 542 U.S. 692 (2004); *see id.* at 762 (Breyer, J., concurring in part and concurring in the judgment) (describing the Court's approach as consistent with comity and principles of universal jurisdiction). For further discussion, see Chapter 5 §§ II(C)(2), IV(B)(1).

[327] Kiobel v. Royal Dutch Petroleum, 569 U.S. 108, 124–25 (2013). For further discussion of the presumption against extraterritoriality, see *infra* this chapter § IV(B).

[328] Pub. L. 102-256, Mar. 12, 1992, § 2(a), 106 Stat. 73 (codified at 28 U.S.C. § 1350 note); *see* Torture Victim Protection Act, S. REP. No. 102-249, at 5 (1991) (invoking "the doctrine of universal jurisdiction"). The House Report did not make any similar reference. Torture Victim Protection Act of 1991, H.R. REP. No. 102-367(I) (1991).

[329] *See supra* this chapter text accompanying note 312.

with international law, the *Restatement (Fourth)* was more equivocal, and noted amicus submissions by foreign states in ATS suits that objected to extraterritorial legislation.[330] Because private enforcement of the ATS, TVPA, and similar statutes is not subject to executive branch control, the judiciary plays an outsized role in moderating this form of prescriptive jurisdiction, and recent cases have shown the courts' restraining influence.[331]

Other U.S. statutes may also raise issues because of the type of conduct they would address. As previously noted, the Anti-Terrorism Act affords civil liability for acts of terrorism, but may be premised in whole or in part on passive personality jurisdiction;[332] jurisdiction over acts of terrorism affecting U.S. interests may also plausibly be based on the protective principle,[333] or it may predicated on treaties.[334] Still, in some instances, at least, universal jurisdiction seems like the most plausible premise: for example, for statutes criminalizing terrorism-related offenses against foreign officials and internationally protected persons, or addressing violence at international airports, if they rely solely on the basis that an offender is later found in the United States.[335]

To that extent, universal jurisdiction remains controversial. Although the *Restatement (Fourth)* suggested growing confidence that "certain acts of terrorism" are acts of universal concern, warranting universal jurisdiction,[336] U.S. courts are at odds with one another.[337] There is a similar disagreement regarding whether drug trafficking warrants the exercise of universal jurisdiction,

---

[330] *Compare* RESTATEMENT (THIRD) § 404 cmt. b (stating that "international law does not preclude the application of non-criminal law" on the basis of universal jurisdiction, such as by providing a civil remedy for piracy victims), *with* RESTATEMENT (FOURTH) § 413, cmt. d (commenting that "the permissibility and limits of universal civil jurisdiction remain controversial," and noting rarity of use and objection by some states), *and id.* § 413 rptrs. note 4 (noting amicus briefs opposing universal jurisdiction over civil actions, along with others suggesting qualified acceptance).

[331] *See* Chapter 5 § IV(B).

[332] *See supra* this chapter text accompanying note 287.

[333] *See supra* this chapter text accompanying note 292 (discussing 18 U.S.C. § 2332 (2018)).

[334] *See, e.g.,* Convention for the Suppression of Unlawful Seizure of Aircraft art. 4(2), Dec. 16, 1970, 22 U.S.T. 1641, 860 U.N.T.S. 105.

[335] Jurisdiction is also typically established (and perhaps more frequently prosecuted) when the activity takes place in the United States, or when the victim or offender is a U.S. national. *See, e.g.,* 18 U.S.C. § 37 (violence at international airports); 18 U.S.C. §§ 112(e)(3), 878(d)(3), and 1116(c)(3) (various offenses relating to foreign officials and internationally protected persons, as well as official guests); *see also* RESTATEMENT (FOURTH) § 402 rptrs. note 10 (citing additional examples).

[336] RESTATEMENT (FOURTH) §§ 402(1)(f) & 413; *see* RESTATEMENT (THIRD) § 404 (acknowledging universal jurisdiction over various offenses, "and perhaps certain acts of terrorism").

[337] *Compare, e.g.,* Waldman v. Palestine Liberation Organization, 835 F.3d 317, 330 n.10 (2d Cir. 2016) ("[T]errorism—unlike piracy, war crimes, and crimes against humanity—does not provide a basis for universal jurisdiction.") (quoting United States v. Yousef, 327 F.3d 56, 107–08 (2d Cir. 2003) (per curiam)), *and In re* Terrorist Attacks on September 11, 2001, 714 F.3d 118, 125 (2d Cir. 2013) (same), *with* United States v. Yunis, 924 F.2d 1086, 1092 (D.C. Cir. 1991) (concluding that "[a]ircraft hijacking may well be one of the few crimes so clearly condemned under the law of nations that states may assert universal jurisdiction to bring offenders to justice").

occasioned by the MDLEA, which criminalizes conduct by foreign nationals on foreign ships on the high seas.[338]

Such questions may have limited relevance in U.S. litigation. If Congress has the constitutional power to legislate extraterritorially, it can transgress any limits on the scope of universal jurisdiction under international law.[339] To be sure, limits on universal jurisdiction might inform the construction or application of Congress' constitutional power, as with the Offences Clause.[340] Such limits might also inform the interpretation of a federal statute that is unclear as to whether it is asserting universal jurisdiction.[341] But a statute may expressly regulate conduct abroad, and even foreclose international law inquiries, as appears to have been attempted in the MDLEA.[342] Discussing international law limits on prescriptive jurisdiction in such a situation may be unnecessary and unhelpful, given that they do not control the outcome of the case.

f. Constitutional Limits

As the preceding discussion suggests, while international law limits on prescriptive jurisdiction inform U.S. practice concerning prescriptive jurisdiction, they do not control it. If the United States adopts legislation asserting jurisdiction, the principal question is whether it was adopted pursuant to constitutional authority,[343] notably the power to regulate foreign commerce,[344] the power to define and punish offenses against the law of nations,[345] and the necessary and proper

---

[338] 46 U.S.C. §§ 70502(c), 70503. *Compare, e.g.,* United States v. Perlaza, 439 F.3d 1149, 1163 (9th Cir. 2006) (rejecting the government's reliance on universal jurisdiction), *with* United States v. Estupinan, 453 F.3d 1336, 1339 (11th Cir. 2006) ("[I]nasmuch as the trafficking of narcotics is condemned universally by law-abiding nations, we see no reason to conclude that it is 'fundamentally unfair' for Congress to provide for the punishment of persons apprehended with narcotics on the high seas." (quoting United States v. Martinez-Hidalgo, 993 F.2d 1052, 1056 (3d Cir. 1993))). For further discussion of MDLEA, see *supra* this chapter text accompanying notes 295–297.

[339] *See* Chapter 5 § III(B).

[340] *Compare, e.g.,* United States v. Bellaizac-Hurtado, 700 F.3d 1245, 1257–58 (11th Cir. 2012) (holding that it was unnecessary to decide whether drug trafficking was subject to universal jurisdiction, since regardless, "[b]ecause drug trafficking is not a violation of customary international law . . . Congress exceeded its power, under the Offences Clause, when it proscribed the defendants' conduct in the territorial waters of Panama"), *with id.* at 1258–59 (Barkett, J., specially concurring) (holding that, to be an "Offence[] against the Law of Nations," conduct must violate customary international law and be subject to U.S. jurisdiction under customary international law principles, including universal jurisdiction).

[341] *See infra* this chapter text accompanying notes 379–380 (discussing the *Charming Betsy* canon).

[342] *See* 46 U.S.C. § 70505 (stating that a person subject to criminal or civil enforcement "does not have standing to raise a claim of failure to comply with international law as a basis for a defense," that "[a] claim of failure to comply with international law in the enforcement of this chapter may be made only by a foreign nation," and that "[a] failure to comply with international law does not divest a court of jurisdiction and is not a defense to a proceeding under this chapter"). *E.g.,* United States v. Prado, 933 F.3d 121, 147 (2d Cir. 2019).

[343] *See* Chapter 2 § I; *see also* RESTATEMENT (FOURTH) § 403 (describing federal constitutional limits on prescriptive jurisdiction).

[344] U.S. CONST. art. 1, § 8, cl. 3; *see* Chapter 2 § I(A).

[345] U.S. CONST. art. 1, § 8, cl. 10; *see* Chapter 5 § I(B)(1).

power, including as it concerns implementing treaties.[346] Other power may be delegated to the executive branch, and the federal courts possess the power to make federal common law in discrete areas.[347] Subject to restrictions imposed by federal law, prescriptive jurisdiction is also exercised by state governments through their constitutions, state statutes, and state common law.[348]

Constitutional limits may be more generous than international law affords. Where that is the case, U.S. courts may find themselves obliged to enforce national law that puts the United States in breach of its international obligations. Of course, constitutional limits (and the relevant statute or common-law rule) may also be more restrictive than international law affords.[349] Notwithstanding calls for closer alignment between U.S. constitutional limits and international law limits bearing on prescriptive jurisdiction,[350] differences between the limits in the national and international spheres are likely to remain significant.

2. Adjudicative Jurisdiction

Adjudicative jurisdiction concerns the authority of courts (or administrative tribunals) to apply law to persons or property.[351] In the case of U.S. federal courts and tribunals, the scope of this authority is established by the Constitution and by Congress, while state courts and tribunals enjoy more general jurisdiction.[352] Most of these limitations transcend U.S. foreign relations law,[353] as do personal jurisdiction limits and personal service requirements.[354]

As this suggests, the most commonly invoked principles regarding adjudicative jurisdiction are familiar from domestic contexts. *Forum non conveniens*, for example, permits a court to dismiss an action where there is an available and adequate forum and the balance of private and public interests favors dismissal.[355] Different variants are practiced in federal and state court.[356] The federal version,

---

[346] U.S. CONST. art. 1, § 8, cl. 18; *see* Chapter 6 §§ I(C), IV(A)(7).

[347] *See* Chapter 5 § II(C).

[348] RESTATEMENT (FOURTH) § 403.

[349] *See, e.g.*, Fleming v. Page, 50 U.S. 603, 615 (1850); for discussion suggesting greater inconsistency in this case law, see Sloss, Ramsey, & Dodge, *supra* note 234, at 38.

[350] *See, e.g.*, KAL RAUSTIALA, DOES THE CONSTITUTION FOLLOW THE FLAG? THE EVOLUTION OF TERRITORIALITY IN AMERICAN LAW (2009); Sarah Cleveland, *Embedded International Law and the Constitution Abroad*, 110 COLUM. L. REV. 225 (2010).

[351] RESTATEMENT (FOURTH) part IV, intro. note; *id.* § 401 cmt. b & rptrs. note 2. As the *Restatement (Fourth)* acknowledged, see *id.* § 401 rptrs. note 2, practice outside the United States varies, but there is certainly some support for the three-part structure. *See, e.g.*, Int'l L. Comm'n, *supra* note 223, at 517–18, ¶ 5.

[352] RESTATEMENT (FOURTH) § 421.

[353] *See id.* § 421 rptrs. note 10 (observing that "[t]he Restatement Third did not address subject-matter jurisdiction as a condition for the exercise of jurisdiction to adjudicate") (citing RESTATEMENT (THIRD) § 421 cmt. j).

[354] RESTATEMENT (FOURTH) §§ 422–23.

[355] RESTATEMENT (FOURTH) § 424; *see, e.g.*, Gulf Oil Corp. v. Gilbert, 330 U.S. 501, 508–09 (1947).

[356] The Supreme Court has specifically declined to address the status of *forum non conveniens* under *Erie. See* Piper Aircraft Co. v. Reyno, 454 U.S. 235, 248 n.13 (1981). Generally, federal courts

though, was partly codified by Congress when it addressed transfers of venue within the federal system, so the common law standard continues to apply only when the alternative forum is in a foreign state.[357]

Case law in the foreign relations context varies these principles somewhat. For example, the strong presumption normally applied in favor of a plaintiff's choice of forum may be diminished when the United States is not a foreign plaintiff's home forum.[358] The assessment of interests, the adequacy of an available forum abroad, and various procedural aspects (like the enforcement of forum-selection clauses) are also largely conventional, but the application is distinct in some regards.[359] As one illustration, the deference owed a foreign plaintiff's choice of forum may be affected by a treaty obligation to ensure equal access to courts in the United States,[360] and criminal adjudication may be constrained by extradition treaties and the like.[361]

The role of customary international law in assessing adjudicative jurisdiction is disputed. The *Restatement (Fourth)* took the position that, apart from immunity, "modern customary international law generally does not impose limits on jurisdiction to adjudicate[;]"[362] thus, it "restate[d] rules of personal jurisdiction exclusively as domestic law of the United States."[363] Some regarded

treat the issue as one of federal law—regardless of the jurisdictional basis of the case before them—while state courts apply state common law rules of *forum non conveniens* in matters before them. These standards may differ, although a number of states adhere to approaches like those followed in federal court. RESTATEMENT (FOURTH) § 424 cmt. b & rptrs. notes 1–2.

[357] Am. Dredging Co. v. Miller, 510 U.S. 443, 449 n.2 (1994); *see also* Sinochem Int'l Co. v. Malaysia Int'l Shipping Corp., 549 U.S. 422, 430 (2007) (tentatively noting potential relevance to transfers to state or territorial courts); Atl. Marine Const. Co. v. Dist. Court, 571 U.S. 49, 60–61 (2013) (describing codification in 28 U.S.C. § 1404(a)).

[358] *Piper*, 454 U.S. at 255–56.

[359] For discussion, see, respectively, RESTATEMENT (FOURTH) § 424 rptrs. notes 5, 3, & 6. The *Restatement (Fourth)* also addresses antisuit injunctions and obtaining evidence, *id.* §§ 425–26, and in the criminal context, trials in absentia, *id.* § 427.

[360] *See* RESTATEMENT (FOURTH) § 424 rptrs. note 4; *see, e.g.*, Blanco v. Banco Industrial de Venezuela, S.A., 997 F.2d 974, 981 (2d Cir.1993) (stating, in dicta, that equal access provision in a United States–Venezuela treaty meant that "no discount may be imposed upon the plaintiff's initial choice of a New York forum in this case solely because [plaintiff] is a foreign corporation"). This obligation is liable to be satisfied if the same deference is afforded to the nonresident foreign plaintiff's choice as would be given a nonresident U.S. citizen choosing a U.S. forum. *See, e.g.*, Kisano Trade and Invest Ltd. v. Lemster, 737 F.3d 869, 874–75 (3d Cir. 2013) (applying United States–Israel treaty); *cf.* Pollux Holding Ltd. v. Chase Manhattan Bank, 329 F.3d 64, 73 (2d Cir. 2003) (stating that United States–Liberia treaty would, if requiring equal treatment, require "at best" the "lesser deference afforded a U.S. citizen living abroad who sues in a U.S. forum").

[361] RESTATEMENT (FOURTH) § 428; *see* Chapter 10 § III(C) (discussing extradition).

[362] RESTATEMENT (FOURTH) pt. IV, ch. 2 intr. note, at 219; *accord id.* § 422 rptrs. note 1; *id.* § 424 rptrs. note 10.

[363] *Id.* § 422 rptrs. note 11; *see also id.* § 422 rptrs. note 11 (contrasting this approach with that of the *Restatement (Third)* § 421, which had set out "some international rules and guidelines" while acknowledging that it was "not always clear whether the principles governing jurisdiction to adjudicate are applied as requirements of public international law or as principles of national law"); *see also* William S. Dodge, *Jurisdiction in the Fourth Restatement of Foreign Relations Law*, 18 Y.B. OF PRIVATE

this as marginalizing international law's relevance, including because it associated international practice with comity, and thus diminishing checks on state authority.[364] The disagreement turns on challenges typical for customary international law, such as whether exorbitant assertions of jurisdiction by states over persons or property demonstrate a lack of international law limits or, alternatively, simply breach them. Similarly, it can be challenging to decide whether the refusal by states to recognize a foreign judgment is due to concern that international law was violated in rendering the judgment, or stems from some other reason, such as a lack of reciprocity. These conventional challenges are probably compounded by the fact that, as previously noted, not all states or international lawyers recognize jurisdiction to adjudicate as a distinctive category, which may make discerning doctrinal limits more difficult.

It is hard, in any case, to identify any distinctive checking function that customary international law serves on adjudicative jurisdiction as it is exercised in the United States—again, putting aside immunity, various forms of which are addressed later in this chapter.[365] One unsettled (and unlikely) prospect would be a prudential exhaustion requirement, whereby civil claims based on an international law violation abroad must first be pursued in a foreign forum before they may be adjudicated in U.S. court, such as for ATS claims[366] or takings claims permitted under the FSIA.[367] If such a rule is asserted on the basis of international law, it seems to casually transpose a restriction on the diplomatic espousal of private claims to claims brought by individuals in U.S. court.[368]

INT'L L. 143, 147 (2017); William S. Dodge & Scott Dodson, *Personal Jurisdiction and Aliens*, 116 MICH. L. REV. 1205 (2018).

[364] *See, e.g.*, Alex Mills, *Private Interests and Private Law Regulation in Public International Law Jurisdiction, in* OXFORD HANDBOOK ON JURISDICTION IN INTERNATIONAL LAW 330 (Stephen Allen et al., eds., 2019); Austin Parrish, *Personal Jurisdiction: The Transnational Difference*, 59 VA. J. INT'L L. 97, 131–38 (2019); Lucas Roorda & Cedric Ryngaert, *Public International Law Constraints on the Exercise of Adjudicatory Jurisdiction, in* UNIVERSAL CIVIL JURISDICTION: WHICH WAY FORWARD? ch. 4 (Serena Forlati & Pietro Franzina eds., 2020).

[365] *See infra* this chapter § V.

[366] Sarei v. Rio Tinto, PLC, 550 F.3d 822, 828–32 (9th Cir. 2008) (en banc) (plurality opinion), *vacated on other grounds*, 569 U.S. 945 (2013); *cf.* Sosa v. Alvarez-Machain, 542 U.S. 692, 733 n.21 (2004) (suggesting that an exhaustion requirement for ATS claims "would certainly [be considered] in an appropriate case"). This is distinct from any statutory requirement, such as that explicitly provided in the Torture Victims Protection Act, 28 U.S.C. § 1350 (2018); *see Sarei*, 550 F.3d at 827–28 (noting suggestion in prior proceedings); *see also* Chapter 5 § IV(B).

[367] *See, e.g.*, Fischer v. Magyar Allamvasutak Zrt., 777 F.3d 847, 856–59 (7th Cir. 2015). An exhaustion requirement might also be derived as part of the inquiry into whether international law was violated in the first place. *Id.*; *see* Republic of Austria v. Altmann, 541 U.S. 677, 714 (2004) (Breyer, J., concurring) (stating that "a plaintiff may have to show an absence of remedies in the foreign country sufficient to compensate for any taking"). Other courts have resisted this step. *E.g.*, Cassirer v. Kingdom of Spain, 616 F.3d 1019, 1034–37 (9th Cir. 2010); *see infra* this chapter § V(A)(4)(c) (discussing expropriation exception).

[368] Philipp v. Federal Republic of Germany, 894 F.3d 406, 416 (D.C. Cir. 2018), *vacated and rev'd on other grounds*, 141 S. Ct. 703 (2021); de Csepel v. Republic of Hungary, 169 F. Supp. 3d 143, 169

3. Enforcement Jurisdiction

International law rules relating to enforcement jurisdiction—involving the authority to search, arrest, seize, and imprison, among other things—are relatively straightforward. Under international law, a state may conduct enforcement within its territory at its discretion, barring any contrary treaty obligation.[369] By contrast, a state may enforce its law in *another* state only with that other state's consent.[370] Naturally, this may require assessing whether a state has in fact exercised jurisdiction within another state's territory, or whether it was enforced consistent with the terms of a treaty entailing the territorial state's consent, like the consent granted among NATO members or the consent granted by Cuba with respect to Guantánamo Bay.[371]

Enforcement jurisdiction, like adjudicative jurisdiction, is downstream from prescriptive jurisdiction—and from adjudicative jurisdiction when judicial involvement is a predicate.[372] As such, limits on prescriptive or adjudicative jurisdiction cabin the scope of enforcement jurisdiction. For example, when the United States sought to enforce a warrant that would have required Microsoft to produce content stored on a server in Ireland, that issue was framed as one involving the extraterritorial application of a U.S. statute; that framing incidentally avoided any enforcement question, at least before Congress intervened to clarify that extraterritorial warrants in fact were authorized.[373]

As the *United States v. Microsoft* case illustrates, national law also looms large in relation to enforcement jurisdiction. Congress may authorize enforcement jurisdiction over and above what international law might countenance, but that is limited to a degree by presumptions discussed in the following sections.

(D.D.C. 2016), *aff'd in part and rev'd in part*, 859 F.3d 1094, 1109 (D.C. Cir. 2017); RESTATEMENT FOURTH § 424 rptrs. note 10.

[369] RESTATEMENT (FOURTH) § 432 rptrs. note 2; *see supra* this chapter text accompanying note 275 (discussing as *aut dedere aut judicare* obligations).

[370] RESTATEMENT (FOURTH) § 432; CRAWFORD, *supra* note 231, at 462; Staker, *supra* note 238, at 294.

[371] *See, e.g.*, Agreement between the Parties to the North Atlantic Treaty regarding the Status of their Forces art. VII, June 19, 1951, 4 U.S.T. 1792, 199 U.N.T.S. 67; Lease of Lands for Coaling and Naval Stations, Cuba-U.S., art. III, Feb. 16–23, 1903, T.S. No. 418.

[372] As the *Restatement (Fourth)* concisely summarized:

> A state may exercise jurisdiction to enforce its own law only when it has jurisdiction to prescribe. A state may exercise jurisdiction to enforce its own law through its courts only when it has jurisdiction to prescribe and jurisdiction to adjudicate. A state may exercise jurisdiction to enforce the laws of other states even if it lacks jurisdiction to prescribe or jurisdiction to adjudicate.

RESTATEMENT (FOURTH) § 432 cmt. c.

[373] Matter of Warrant to Search a Certain E-Mail Account Controlled and Maintained by Microsoft Corp., 829 F.3d 197 (2d Cir. 2016), *vacated and rev'd on other grounds sub nom.* United States v. Microsoft Corp., 138 S. Ct. 1186 (2018); *see* Consolidated Appropriations Act, Pub. L. 115-141, § 103(a), 132 Stat. 1214 (2018) (the Clarifying Lawful Overseas Use of Data Act, or CLOUD Act, codified at 18 U.S.C. § 2703 (2018)).

Otherwise, U.S. law typically constrains U.S. enforcement measures. Consistent with international principles, the authority to enforce may be limited by U.S. authority to prescribe.[374] Further, constitutional limitations (like the Due Process Clauses) or statutory provisions relating to the exercise of police authority may preclude extraterritorial enforcement.[375]

Absent such limits, self-restraint is not always exercised. In *United States v. Alvarez-Machain*, for example, the Supreme Court found that an extradition treaty between the United States and Mexico did not implicitly prohibit U.S. officials from abducting persons from Mexico, and left the question of whether "general international law principles" had been violated, as Mexico protested, to the executive branch.[376] The respondent did not directly raise in U.S. court the issue that his seizure violated customary international law, as opposed to violating a bilateral extradition treaty. The outcome, though perhaps anomalous, suggests real limits to judicial vigilance regarding U.S. violations of international limits on enforcement jurisdiction.

B. Presumption Against Extraterritoriality

As has been made clear, the judicial role in ensuring that the United States conforms to international limits—whether legal or political—is somewhat truncated, given that Congress has the final say. Nonetheless, the judiciary has assumed an active role in construing what it has said, and a key tool in recent decades has been the presumption against extraterritoriality. Such a presumption reduces the potential for conflict both with international law and with foreign sovereigns, but whether either objective is effectively pursued, consistent with congressional expectations, is a different matter.[377]

1. Background, Purpose, and Scope

What is now labeled as a presumption against extraterritoriality—the idea that federal courts should construe U.S. statutes to apply only within U.S. territory[378]— has appeared in a variety of guises. The *Charming Betsy* canon—discussed at greater length in Chapter 5—announced that "an act of Congress ought never to be construed to violate the law of nations if any other possible construction

---

[374] *See* RESTATEMENT (FOURTH) § 431 rptrs. note 7; Fed. Trade Comm'n v. Compagnie De Saint-Gobain-Pont-A-Mousson, 636 F.2d 1300, 1317 (D.C. Cir. 1980) (asserting that the United States may not "exercise its enforcement jurisdiction within foreign territory before its prescriptive jurisdiction over the investigated conduct has been proved to exist").

[375] *See* Chapter 10 § II(C).

[376] 504 U.S. 655, 669 (1992); *see* Chapter 10 § II(D)(2).

[377] *See also* Chapter 2 § II(E).

[378] RESTATEMENT (FOURTH) § 404.

remains."[379] Because international law generally restricted a state's jurisdiction to its territory, the Supreme Court occasionally applied the presumption to inhibit the reach of U.S. statutes from reaching the high seas.[380]

As international law grew more permissive, the *Charming Betsy* principle became less stringent as a jurisdictional restraint. In *American Banana v. United Fruit Co.*, the Supreme Court arrived at a similar result as *Charming Betsy*. Rather than relying on international law, however, the Court considered that conflict-of-laws principles and comity warranted presuming that Congress did not intend its statutes to apply beyond U.S. territory.[381] Cases thereafter continued to cite comity (as well as international law) as a reason to avoid jurisdictional disputes between the United States and foreign states,[382] but increasingly grew to emphasize statutory purpose, invoking "the assumption that Congress is primarily concerned with domestic conditions."[383] What became known as the presumption against extraterritoriality drove the Supreme Court's 1991 decision in *EEOC v. Arabian American Oil Co.*,[384] and figured prominently in Roberts Court cases like *Morrison v. National Australia Bank Ltd.*[385] and *RJR Nabisco, Inc. v. European Community.*[386]

International law seems to have been gradually de-emphasized,[387] but the reasons are unclear; possibly it was simply perceived as being less stringent than what comity or Congress demanded. The shift from international law, as well as a subtler shift from comity to congressional intent,[388] may also reflect less of an

[379] Murray v. Schooner Charming Betsy, 6 U.S. (2 Cranch) 64, 118 (1804); *see* Chapter 2 § II(E) and Chapter 5 § III(B)(3); *see also* Chapter 6 § IV(C)(2) (considering presumption in the context of treaties).

[380] *See, e.g.*, The Apollon, 22 U.S. (9 Wheat.) 362, 370–71 (1824) (construing customs law in view of presumption that "municipal laws . . . must always be restricted in construction, to places and persons, upon whom the Legislature have authority and jurisdiction," so as to avoid "a clear violation of the laws of nations"); *see also* Brown v. Duchesne, 60 U.S. (19 How.) 183, 195 (1857) (patent law); Rose v. Himely, 8 U.S. (4 Cranch) 241, 279 (1807) (prize law), *overruled in part on other grounds*, Hudson v. Guestier, 10 U.S. (6 Cranch) 281 (1810). For excellent discussions, see William S. Dodge, *The New Presumption Against Extraterritoriality*, 133 HARV. L. REV. 1582, 1589–91 (2020); John H. Knox, *A Presumption Against Extrajurisdictionality*, 104 AM. J. INT'L L. 351, 362–66 (2010); Sloss, Ramsey, & Dodge, *supra* note 234, at 38–39.

[381] 213 U.S. 347, 357 (1909).

[382] *See, e.g.*, EEOC v. Arabian Am. Oil Co. (Aramco), 499 U.S. 244, 248 (1991) (explaining that, in part, the presumption "serves to protect against unintended clashes between our laws and those of other nations which could result in international discord").

[383] Foley Bros. v. Filardo, 336 U.S. 281, 285 (1949).

[384] 499 U.S. 244 (1991); *see* Dodge, *supra* note 380, at 1597–98 (describing *Aramco* as "[t]he seminal case in the presumption's rebirth").

[385] 561 U.S. 247 (2010).

[386] 579 U.S. 325 (2016).

[387] *See, e.g.*, RESTATEMENT (FOURTH) § 404 rptrs. note 2 (describing shift).

[388] In *RJR Nabisco*, for example, the Court noted that the presumption "serves to avoid the international discord that can result when U.S. law is applied to conduct in foreign countries," while reflecting that "Congress generally legislates with domestic concerns in mind"—but notwithstanding the former rationale, made clear that the presumption applies "regardless of whether there is a risk of conflict between the American statute and a foreign law." *RJR Nabisco*, 579 U.S. at 335–36 (internal citations and quotations omitted).

evolution than a practical reality: whether the presumption against extraterritoriality is based on international law, comity, or something else, the congressional capacity to override any nonconstitutional consideration warrants inquiry into what Congress indicated when enacting a statute.

If the presumption against extraterritoriality is based on the "commonsense notion that Congress *generally* legislates with domestic concerns in mind,"[389] it is fair to ask whether there are categories of circumstances in which that expectation is misplaced. For example, the Supreme Court once suggested that the presumption might not apply to statutes criminalizing certain conduct, like fraud against the U.S. government, that Congress would likely wish to prevent regardless of location.[390] Some lower court cases have read this to suggest that presumption applies less readily to criminal statutes, but others have reached quite different conclusions.[391] It has also been questioned whether the presumption applied to provisions conferring jurisdiction upon courts. In *RJR Nabisco*, however, the Court made the presumption's intended breadth evident, stating that it applies "regardless of whether the statute in question regulates conduct, affords relief, or merely confers jurisdiction."[392] This raised concerns that the presumption might apply to broadly written subject-matter jurisdiction statutes, such as the jurisdiction of federal courts over federal questions, that could not (in part due to their generality) overcome it. Notwithstanding the language in *RJR Nabisco*, there is reason to think the Court did not mean to go so far.[393]

The presumption against extraterritoriality is federal in nature. Because it involves an assumption about the intent of the U.S. Congress, the presumption does not apply to state statutes. States may, however, elect to adopt their own presumptions against extraterritoriality, and may also choose whether to

---

[389] Smith v. United States, 507 U.S. 197, 204 n.5 (1993) (emphasis added).

[390] *See* United States v. Bowman, 260 U.S. 94, 97–98 (1922) (distinguishing between crimes that "affect the peace and good order of the community," like assault or arson, which were presumptively territorial, and statutory crimes "not logically dependent on their locality for the Government's jurisdiction, but are enacted because of the right of the Government to defend itself against obstruction, or fraud wherever perpetrated").

[391] For examples of cases suggesting that the presumption is inapplicable in criminal contexts, see, for example, United States v. Leija-Sanchez, 820 F.3d 899, 901 (7th Cir. 2016); United States v. Siddiqui, 699 F.3d 690, 700 (2d Cir. 2012). *But see* RESTATEMENT (FOURTH) § 404 rptrs. note 4 (suggesting comparable approaches to criminal and other statutes, taking into account statutory purposes); Julie Rose O'Sullivan, *The Extraterritorial Application of Federal Criminal Statutes: Analytical Roadmap, Normative Conclusions, and a Plea to Congress for Direction*, 106 GEO. L.J. 1021 (2018) (suggesting stronger presumption against extraterritoriality for criminal statutes).

[392] *RJR Nabisco*, 579 U.S. at 337.

[393] As has been noted, the Court has not applied the presumption to purely subject-matter jurisdiction statutes like 18 U.S.C. § 3231 (2018) ("all offenses against the laws of the United States"), 28 U.S.C. § 1331 (federal questions), and 28 U.S.C. § 1332 (diversity). RESTATEMENT (FOURTH) § 404 rptrs. note 3; *see also* Dodge, *supra* note 380, at 1620–23 (arguing that such application would be inappropriate).

construe state statutes in such a way as to mirror the geographic scope of any counterpart provisions under federal law.[394]

2. Two-Step Approach

As the presumption against extraterritoriality became more routine, the Supreme Court developed a two-step approach for the administering it. As explained in *RJR Nabisco*, the first step involves asking "whether the presumption against extraterritoriality has been rebutted—that is, whether the statute gives a clear, affirmative indication that it applies extraterritorially."[395] If it does not, and the statute is not extraterritorial, a court should proceed to the second step: "determin[ing] whether the case involves a domestic application of the statute ... by looking to the statute's 'focus.'" At this second step, "[i]f the conduct relevant to the statute's focus occurred in the United States, then the case involves a permissible domestic application even if other conduct occurred abroad." However, "if the conduct relevant to the focus occurred in a foreign country, then the case involves an impermissible extraterritorial application regardless of any other conduct that occurred in U.S. territory."[396]

These steps, and their relationship to one another, are worth examining in sequence. One challenge with step one concerns whether it establishes a reliable presumption at all. Although step one calls for a "clear, affirmative indication" of statutory scope, the Court has denied creating a "clear statement" rule—that is, one requiring that the statute specifically state that it is to apply extraterritorially.[397] Given that disavowal, and varied approaches to determining congressional intent, it is unclear how much the presumption necessarily differs from a routine inquiry into whether a statute applies to the matter at hand.[398]

---

[394] *See* RESTATEMENT (FOURTH) § 404 rptrs. note 5; William S. Dodge, *Presumptions Against Extraterritoriality in State Law*, 53 U.C. DAVIS L. REV. 1389 (2020).

[395] *RJR Nabisco*, 579 U.S. at 337.

[396] *Id.*

[397] *See id.* at 340 ("While the presumption can be overcome only by a clear indication of extraterritorial effect, an express statement of extraterritoriality is not essential."); Morrison v. Nat'l Australia Bank Ltd, 561 U.S. 247, 265 (2010) (explaining that "we do not say ... that the presumption against extraterritoriality is a 'clear statement rule' ... if by that is meant a requirement that a statute say 'this law applies abroad'"); Dodge, *supra* note 380, at 1610; RESTATEMENT (FOURTH) § 404 cmt. b. But for such caveats, one might have thought otherwise. *See, e.g., RJR Nabisco*, 579 U.S. at 337 (demanding "clear, affirmative indication"); *Morrison*, 561 U.S. at 265 (distinguishing a provision that overcame the presumption from one that did not, finding in the former "a clear statement of extraterritorial effect" consisting of "[i]ts explicit provision for a specific extraterritorial application"); *see also* EEOC v. Arabian Am. Oil Co., 499 U.S. 244, 258 (1991) (alluding to "Congress' awareness of the need to make a clear statement that a statute applies overseas").

[398] *See, e.g., Morrison*, 561 U.S. at 265 (allowing that "assuredly context can be consulted as well"); *see also* Sale v. Haitian Ctrs. Council, 509 U.S. 155, 177 (1993) (concluding based on "all available evidence about the meaning"). In *RJR Nabisco*, the Court found that its "unique structure makes [the Racketeer Influenced and Corrupt Organizations Act] the rare statute that clearly evidences extraterritorial effect despite lacking an express statement of extraterritoriality," at least with regard to predicate offenses committed abroad that also violated a predicate statute that itself applied (clearly) extraterritorially. 579 U.S. at 340; *see also* RESTATEMENT (FOURTH) § 404 rptrs. note 10 (describing

Other issues with step one concern its relation with step two. Step one will appear premature, and unnecessary, in at least some instances, since it requires examining whether Congress intended extraterritorial application of a provision,[399] although (as would be examined at step two) looking at the statutory focus might show that Congress would have regarded the case as purely domestic in character. It can also be hard to start with step one. While the Court conceives of the inquiries as quite distinct,[400] sometimes the issues at step one can only properly be resolved by considering matters involved in step two. Whether a provision was intended to apply extraterritorially involves what it is focused on; even if a provision happens to advert to something "outside the United States," one should determine whether that reference is a critical factor in the provision's operation before saying whether it demonstrates extraterritorial application.[401]

Such challenges may make step two analysis of a provision's focus, to learn whether its application in that case would be understood as domestic, an appealing place to start.[402] RJR Nabisco indeed allowed that courts may skip over step one "in appropriate cases,"[403] while evidencing how difficult it might be for a step two analysis to proceed independent of step one.[404] Step two itself

how a provision's nongeographic purpose may indicate that it applies extraterritorially). *But see, e.g.,* United States v. Napout, 963 F.3d 163, 178 (2d Cir. 2020) (deciding, summarily, that there was no "clear, affirmative statutory indication of extraterritoriality" with respect to wire fraud conspiracy statute).

[399] A court's inquiry at step one may have to go beyond examining a particular provision, and even encompass unrelated provisions of a statute, or the tendency in a class of statutes. *See, e.g.,* WesternGeco LLC v. ION Geophysical Corp., 138 S. Ct. 2129, 2136–37 (2018) (explaining that it was prudent to avoid resolving whether "the presumption against extraterritoriality should *never apply* to statutes . . . that merely provide a general damages remedy for conduct that Congress has declared unlawful," as "[r]esolving that question could implicate many other statutes besides the Patent Act") (emphasis added).

[400] *See, e.g., RJR Nabisco,* 579 U.S. at 337–38 (explaining that, when the presumption has been overcome at step one, its geographic scope "turns on the limits Congress has (or has not) imposed on the statute's foreign application, and not on the statute's 'focus' "); Morrison v. Nat'l Australia Bank Ltd, 561 U.S. 247, 267 n.9 (2010) ("If § 10(b) did apply abroad, we would not need to determine which transnational frauds it applied to; it would apply to all of them (barring some other limitation).").

[401] For example, as *RJR Nabisco* summarized another decision, "[b]ecause 'all the relevant conduct' regarding those violations 'took place outside the United States,' " assessing the "focus" was unnecessary. *RJR Nabisco,* 579 U.S. at 337 (quoting Kiobel v. Royal Dutch Petroleum Co., 569 U.S. 108, 124 (2013)). But it would seem like determining what conduct is "relevant" involved the statute's focus. This was also suggested in *Morrison,* where step two asked whether the focus of the relevant securities provision was "the place where the deception originated" or rather "purchases and sales of securities in the United States," 561 U.S. at 266, when its analysis at step one had already stretched to show that the latter was the focus. *Id.* at 262–65.

[402] *See, e.g.,* United States v. McClellan, 959 F.3d 442, 468 (1st Cir. 2020) (indicating that the court would skip to step two "when it is 'plain' that a domestic application is present but the statute itself gives rise to complex questions of congressional intent," and noting "difficult questions" in the case at hand) (citations omitted).

[403] *RJR Nabisco,* 579 U.S. at 338 n.5.

[404] In *RJR Nabisco,* the Court concluded that two provisions of RICO overcame the presumption. 579 U.S. at 340–41. However, with regard to another provision, RICO's private right of action, the Court concluded at step one there was no clear indication that Congress intended extraterritorial

poses separate challenges. As the Court has cautioned, step two cannot be satisfied by alleging a modicum of domestic contacts that are unrelated to the
statutory objective.[405] Instead, a court has to begin with a holistic analysis into
"'the objec[t] of [a statute's] solicitude,'" including "the parties and interests it
'seeks to "protec[t]"' or vindicate";[406] the focus this reveals might be conduct,
transactions, injuries, or something else, which a court will then use in assessing
whether the relevant ingredient happened domestically or not.[407] Postponing
these difficult questions to step two may be appealing.[408] But even if they can
be deferred, it is fair to ask whether such an open-ended inquiry attenuates any
benefit from an interpretive presumption, and whether some other test might be
devised.[409]

Whatever the proper steps, the presumption should be applied to particular
provisions, rather than to a statute as a whole—although construing the statute
as a whole may be instrumental at either step one or step two.[410] In addition,
case law indicates that the geographic scope of ancillary criminal provisions
(concerning conspiracy or aiding and abetting, for example) will generally be
supposed to track that of the underlying criminal offense.[411] It has also been

---

application, reasoning in part that the type of injury addressed by the provision suggested a different
(and possibly narrower) focus than elsewhere. *Id.* at 349–50. At step two, the Court simply stated that
the private-action provision "requires a civil RICO plaintiff to allege and prove a domestic injury to
business or property and does not allow recovery for foreign injuries." *Id.* at 354. This "focus" analysis
seemed entirely derived from the initial discussion at step one, and suggested no meaningful distinction. *See also* Dodge, *supra* note 380, at 1611.

[405] *Morrison*, 561 U.S. at 266 ("[T]he presumption against extraterritorial application would be a
craven watchdog indeed if it retreated to its kennel whenever some domestic activity is involved . . .");
id. at 266 (remonstrating against "such a timid sentinel").

[406] WesternGeco LLC v. ION Geophysical Corp., 138 S. Ct. 2129, 2137 (2018) (quoting *Morrison*,
561 U.S. at 267).

[407] RESTATEMENT (FOURTH) § 404 cmt. c; *see id.* rptrs. note 8 (citing cases). In *RJR Nabisco*, the
Court noted the application of 18 U.S.C. § 1957(d)(2) to an offense that "takes place outside the
United States" if U.S. persons were responsible, but presumably the language was salient because
the conduct establishing the offense (not the affiliation of the person) was the focus of the provision.
RJR Nabisco, 579 U.S. at 338.

[408] *See RJR Nabisco*, 579 U.S. at 338 n.5 (suggesting that the point of postponing step two is to potentially "obviate step two's 'focus' inquiry"). *But see In re* Picard, 917 F.3d 85 (2d Cir. 2019) (bypassing
step one, without explanation, in favor of complex inquiry into statutory focus).

[409] A court might instead evaluate whether the case would in theory require extraterritorial application of the statute, in light of a provision's focus and the relevant facts, then determine whether
Congress clearly indicated that it was intended to apply extraterritorially. These inquiries could be
bypassed if there were a clear, affirmative statement of extraterritoriality of a kind that would satisfy a
clear statement rule, thus avoiding the need for any searching analysis.

[410] RESTATEMENT (FOURTH) § 404 rptrs. note 9 (citing cases); *see, e.g.*, Prime Int'l Trading, Ltd.
v. BP P.L.C., 937 F.3d 94, 104 (2d Cir. 2019) (noting that step two requires examining the "focus" of
each provision individually, but also requires examining "how the 'statutory provision at issue works
with other provisions'") (quoting *WesternGeco*, 138 S. Ct. at 2137)).

[411] *See, e.g.*, United States v. Napout, 963 F.3d 163, 179 (2d Cir. 2020); United States v. Ali, 718 F.3d
929, 939 (D.C. Cir. 2013); *see also RJR Nabisco*, 579 U.S. at 341 ("assum[ing] without deciding" that
RICO's conspiracy provision's "extraterritoriality tracks that of the provision underlying the alleged
conspiracy"); RESTATEMENT (FOURTH) § 404 rptrs. note 10; Dodge, *supra* note 380, at 1616.

JUDGING FOREIGN RELATIONS   241

suggested that deference to agency interpretations concerning extraterritoriality is appropriate.[412] How such deference would be applied under current doctrine is unclear, and it may be doubted that it would accomplish much at step one.[413]

Prior to *RJR Nabisco*, the Court suggested a variant, or perhaps an alternative, to the second step. The majority in *Kiobel v. Royal Dutch Petroleum Co.*, having established that the presumption applied to the ATS and had not been overcome, stated simply that "all the relevant conduct took place outside the United States," adding that "even where the claims *touch and concern* the territory of the United States, they must do so with sufficient force to displace the presumption against extraterritorial application."[414] What this meant was unclear, other than establishing that "mere corporate presence" in the United States by a foreign corporation did not suffice in that case.[415] However, in a subsequent ATS case, *Nestlé USA v. Doe*, the Court applied the conventional two-step approach, with the justices agreeing, nearly unanimously, that the plaintiffs sought impermissibly extraterritorial application of the ATS to allegations of forced labor in Côte d'Ivoire (Ivory Coast).[416] Having previously settled that the statutory provision did not apply extraterritorially, the Court did not resolve a second-step dispute between the parties as to the ATS's "focus," reasoning that even on the plaintiff's position "nearly all" of the relevant conduct occurred abroad.[417] Neither corporate presence of the defendant in the United States, nor what the Court characterized as "general corporate activity" (or "operational decisions") there, provided the requisite nexus "between the cause of action . . . and domestic conduct."[418] Although such corporate activity seemed like conduct that might "touch and concern" the United States, that inquiry was abandoned.

---

[412] RESTATEMENT (FOURTH) § 404 cmt. e & rptrs. note 12. Like the case law, the *Restatement (Fourth)* is somewhat unclear as to when the envisioned deference is like that in Chevron, U.S.A., Inc. v. Nat. Res. Def. Council, 467 U.S. 837 (1984), or rather the lesser deference accorded under Skidmore v. Swift & Co., 323 U.S. 134 (1944)).

[413] *Cf.* EEOC v. Arabian Am. Oil Co., 499 U.S. 244, 257–58 (1991) (concluding, after assessing an inconsistent and belated EEOC interpretation, that it was "insufficiently weighty to overcome the presumption against extraterritorial application"); Valdus Reinsurance, Ltd. v. United States, 786 F.3d 1039, 1049 (D.C. Cir. 2015) (assuming, *arguendo*, that the issue of *Chevron* deference was before the court, and relevant following *Morrison*, "accord[ing] deference requires some indication that the agency has considered the effect of the presumption against extraterritoriality"); Liu Meng–Lin v. Siemens AG, 763 F.3d 175, 182 (2d Cir. 2014) ("[I]t is far from clear that an agency's assertion that a statute has extraterritorial effect, unmoored from any plausible statutory basis for rebutting the presumption against extraterritoriality, should be given deference").

[414] Kiobel v. Royal Dutch Petroleum Co., 569 U.S. 108, 124–25 (2013) (emphasis added). For further discussion of *Kiobel* and other ATS cases, see Chapter 5 §§ II(C)(2), IV(B)(1).

[415] For one discussion, see Edward T. Swaine, Kiobel *and Extraterritoriality: Here, (Not) There, (Not Even) Everywhere*, 69 OKLA. L. REV. 23 (2016).

[416] 141 S. Ct. 1931 (2021). Justice Alito dissented on the basis that he would have resolved the case on other grounds that he regarded as entailing fewer assumptions. *Id.* at 1950–51 (Alito, J., dissenting).

[417] 141 S. Ct. at 1937.

[418] *Id.*

C. Prescriptive Comity and Reasonableness

International comity evokes a rich (and richly confusing) set of doctrines applied by U.S. courts. It was famously described by the Supreme Court in *Hilton v. Guyot* as "the recognition which one nation allows within its territory to the legislative, executive or judicial acts of another nation, having due regard both to international duty and convenience, and to the rights of its own citizens or of other persons who are under the protection of its laws."[419] Subsequent U.S. cases and commentary distinguish between adjudicative comity and prescriptive comity. Adjudicative comity, or comity among courts, entails discretionary deference by a national court to exercise jurisdiction that it possesses, in favor of proceedings in a foreign state.[420] Viewed expansively, this includes doctrines like the recognition of foreign judgments, *forum non conveniens*, prudential exhaustion, and other forms of abstention based on international comity principles.[421] The case law is extensive and largely beyond the scope of this work.[422]

Prescriptive comity, in contrast, involves at its threshold whether U.S. law is potentially applicable to the case at hand, usually as a matter of statutory interpretation and, potentially, its presumption against extraterritoriality—though courts may also apply doctrines like the conflict of laws and the act of state doctrine.[423] Assuming that U.S. law is applicable, prescriptive comity also concerns whether it is reasonable to apply that law in context, given the alternative possibility of regulation under foreign law. This "reasonableness" inquiry has been through a lot.[424] Until the 1970s, the idea that the extraterritorial application of U.S. law should be tempered by a balancing of U.S. and foreign interests gained

---

[419]   Hilton v. Guyot, 159 U.S. 113, 163–64 (1895).

[420]   *See, e.g.,* Cooper v. Tokyo Power Co. Holdings, Inc., 960 F.3d 549, 566 (9th Cir. 2020) (distinguishing adjudicative and prescriptive comity, and applying adjudicative comity); *In re* Picard, 917 F.3d 85, 101 (2d Cir. 2019) (distinguishing adjudicative and prescriptive comity, and applying prescriptive comity); *In re* Maxwell Commc'n Corp., 93 F.3d 1036, 1047 (2d Cir. 1996) (distinguishing adjudicative and prescriptive comity, and applying adjudicative comity, but finding them "not inconsistent propositions" in the case at hand).

[421]   For expert description of these and other subtopics, see William S. Dodge, *International Comity in American Law*, 115 COLUM. L. REV. 2071, 2079 (2015). *Compare, e.g.,* Maggie Gardner, *Abstention at the Border*, 105 VA. L. REV. 63, 102 (2019) (distinguishing prescriptive comity, which "asks whether a jurisdiction's law applies," from adjudicative comity, which "asks whether the court should hear the case in order to apply that law," and critiquing latter), *with* Samuel Estreicher & Thomas H. Lee, *In Defense of International Comity*, 93 S. CAL. L. REV. 169, 175 (2020) (agreeing with distinction, but defending adjudicative comity).

[422]   *But see supra* this chapter text accompanying notes 355–357 (briefly noting *forum non conveniens*).

[423]   *See* Dodge, *supra* note 421, at 2079; *see also* Gardner, *supra* note 421, at 102–03 (distinguishing between positive and negative components of prescriptive comity); *see, e.g., In re* Picard, 917 F.3d at 101; *In re Maxwell Communication Corp.,* 93 F.3d at 1047.

[424]   *See generally* William S. Dodge, *Extraterritoriality and Conflict-of-Laws Theory: An Argument for Judicial Unilateralism*, 39 HARV. INT'L L.J. 101, 121–43 (1998) (reviewing developments); Swaine, *The Local Law of Global Antitrust, The Local Law of Global Antitrust, supra* note 253, at 671–83 (same).

little traction.[425] Antitrust suits, for example, simply were not dismissed on that basis.[426] Nonetheless, some decisions—like the Ninth Circuit's decision in *Timberlane Lumber Co. v. Bank of America*—articulated factors for U.S. courts to consider in evaluating whether to moderate extraterritorial application.[427] Despite pushback against *Timberlane* by other decisions,[428] the *Restatement (Third)* endorsed a similar balancing approach, urging the consideration of factors relating to U.S. interests, the foreign state's interests, the justified expectations of the regulated parties, and the interests of the international system, in determining whether it was reasonable for the United States to apply its law to that conduct.[429] The *Restatement (Third)* represented that this approach was required by customary international law, without identifying much state practice.[430]

In *Hartford Fire Ins. Co. v. California*, involving a private antitrust suit alleging an anticompetitive agreement among London reinsurers, the Supreme Court appeared to accept a comity inquiry—and looked to the *Restatement (Third)* approach—but marginalized it. In the majority's view, the conduct satisfied the "effects" doctrine and therefore fell within Sherman Act jurisdiction; once that was settled, a court could invoke comity and refuse to permit the exercise of jurisdiction only if there were a "true conflict" between U.S. law and foreign law, such that the London reinsurers could not comply simultaneously with U.K. and

---

[425] The *Restatement (Second)* did propose that two states should moderate their exercise of enforcement jurisdiction when it appeared to require inconsistent conduct from a person (a "true conflict"), but did not indicate that inhibited prescriptive jurisdiction. RESTATEMENT (SECOND) § 40; *see also* RESTATEMENT (SECOND) OF CONFLICTS, § 6 (AM. L. INST. 1971) (describing choice of law principles involving balancing of factors); *id.* § 145 (describing "most significant relationship" test).

[426] As the court acknowledged in *Timberlane Lumber Co. v. Bank of America*, "[i]n actual litigation, jurisdiction has not often been found lacking." 549 F.2d 597, 608 n.12 (9th Cir. 1976) (indicating that as of 1973, no government-initiated foreign trade antitrust cases had been dismissed for lack of jurisdiction) (citing WILBUR L. FUGATE, FOREIGN COMMERCE AND THE ANTITRUST LAWS, app. B, at 498 (2d ed. 1973)).

[427] 549 F.2d 597, 613–15 (9th Cir. 1976); *see also* Mannington Mills, Inc. v. Congoleum Corp., 595 F.2d 1287, 1296–98 (3d Cir. 1979) (adopting a similar balancing approach).

[428] *See, e.g.,* Laker Airways Ltd. v. Sabena, Belgian World Airlines, 731 F.2d 909 (D.C. Cir. 1984); *cf. In re* Uranium Antitrust Litigation, 617 F.2d 1248, 1255–56 (7th Cir. 1980) (avoiding issue).

[429] RESTATEMENT (THIRD) § 403; *see also id.* § 403 cmt. b (noting that there was no priority among these factors and that they were non-exhaustive). Other sections addressed the specific regulatory contexts of antitrust (*id.* § 415) and securities (*id.* § 416).

[430] RESTATEMENT (THIRD) § 403 cmt. a ("stat[ing] the principle of reasonableness as a rule of international law"). It was telling that the *Restatement (Third)* approach so closely resembled others that had not found a basis in international law. *See id.* rptrs. note 10 (adopting factors indicated in the *Restatement (Second) of Conflicts*, while adverting to state practice); RESTATEMENT (SECOND) OF CONFLICT OF LAWS, § 6(2) & cmt. c (describing factors as choice-of-law principles attributable to common law); *Timberlane,* 549 F.2d at 609 (stating that although the United States' exercise of extraterritorial jurisdiction should yield to foreign interests at some point, "[w]hat that point is or how it is determined is not defined by international law"). *See generally* RESTATEMENT (FOURTH) § 407 rptrs. note 6 (stating that *Restatement (Third)* § 403 "is not supported by state practice"); William S. Dodge, *Reasonableness in the Restatement (Fourth) of Foreign Relations Law,* 55 WILLAMETTE L. REV. 521, 524 (2019) (same); Swaine, *The Local Law of Global Antitrust, supra* note 253, at 689–93 (same).

U.S. laws.[431] Dissenting, Justice Scalia also invoked the *Restatement (Third)*, including as a statement of international law principles, but observed (correctly) that the majority had misunderstood it: reasonableness was a matter of prescriptive jurisdiction, not to be confused with discretionary, adjudicative comity, and in Justice Scalia's view this counseled against applying the Sherman Act.[432]

Justice Scalia's criticism prevailed in the *F. Hoffmann-La Roche Ltd. v. Empagran S.A.* decision.[433] Considering another antitrust action, this one alleging price-fixing, the Court invoked what it described as a "rule of statutory construction" that kept U.S. antitrust laws "reasonable, and hence consistent with principles of prescriptive comity": namely, that a U.S. court "ordinarily construes ambiguous statutes to avoid unreasonable interference with the sovereign authority of other nations."[434] Applying that rule, the Court had little difficulty concluding that an exception under the Foreign Trade Antitrust Improvements Act did not apply to claims by foreign purchasers, if based on foreign injury that was independent of adverse effects within the United States, because it would be unreasonable to risk interference with a foreign nation's approach to commercial regulation without U.S. harms.[435]

The basis and content of prescriptive comity, and the rule of reasonableness, remain works in progress. In *Empagran*, the Court stated that the rule "reflects principles of customary international law," and invoked both Justice Scalia's dissent and Section 403 of the *Restatement (Third)* (each of which had stated reasonableness as a principle of international law), as well as the principle that statutes should be construed wherever possible to avoid violating international law, thereby implying that prescriptive comity was required by international law.[436] The *Restatement (Fourth)*, however, backed away from Section 403, and appears to take the position that prescriptive comity is not required by international law, being instead a principle of statutory construction that is merely informed by international considerations.[437] Although either depiction puts prescriptive

---

[431] Hartford Fire Ins. Co. v. California, 509 U.S. 764, 798 (1993) (quoting Société Nationale Industrielle Aérospatiale v. United States Dist. Court for Southern Dist. of Iowa, 482 U.S. 522, 555 (1987) (Blackmun, J., concurring in part and dissenting in part)); *see generally id.* at 795–99.

[432] *Id.* at 814–21 (Scalia, J., dissenting); *see, e.g., id.* at 821 (arguing, after stating that "[l]iterally, the *only* support that the Court adduces for its position is § 403 of the Restatement (Third)," that "[t]he Court has completely misinterpreted this provision" by applying the "true conflict" approach without first determining whether the exercise of jurisdiction by the United States is not "unreasonable") (emphasis in original).

[433] 542 U.S. 155, 164 (2004).

[434] *Id.* at 164–65; *see also id.* at 169 (describing the rule as consistent with principles of prescriptive comity).

[435] *Id.* at 165–69 (construing Foreign Trade Antitrust Improvements Act of 1982 (FTAIA), 96 Stat. 1246, 15 U.S.C. § 6a (2018)).

[436] *Id.* at 164 (citing authorities).

[437] This is indirectly signaled. *See* RESTATEMENT (FOURTH) § 401 cmt. a (defining "international comity" as "reflect[ing] deference to foreign states that international law does not mandate); *id.* § 405 & cmt. a (stating principle of "prescriptive comity"); Dodge, *supra* note 430, at 527–28 (describing "domestic law rules adopted as matter of international comity").

comity on a mandatory footing, the uncertainty may reinforce its stereotype as a discretionary doctrine.[438]

As to the rule's content, both *Empagran* and the *Restatement (Fourth)* endorsed, on their different premises, the idea that courts should construe U.S. statutes so as to "avoid unreasonable interference with the sovereign authority" of other states.[439] Contrary to the "true conflict" test of *Hartford Fire*, it appears that "interference" can occur even when foreign authority is not being exercised (as it is equally a sovereign prerogative to leave a matter unregulated).[440] Further, whether interference is "reasonable" depends on whether it advances a legitimate interest of the United States; for example, where anticompetitive conduct solely affects another state's companies and customers, it would not.[441] Beyond this the inquiry is mysterious. *Empagran* invoked reasonableness without endorsing any particular set of factors,[442] and the *Restatement (Fourth)* was also indeterminate.[443] Unfortunately, a reasonableness standard may simply be better suited to adjudicatory comity than to statutory construction, even if that risks conferring excessive discretion in individual cases.[444]

Ultimately, any reasonableness inquiry should be clearer in its relation to other doctrines. Justice Scalia's *Hartford Fire* dissent noted how applying a U.S. statute might implicate any of several U.S. doctrines—the presumption against extraterritoriality, prescriptive comity, and the *Charming Betsy* presumption of conformity with international law—and suggested that the presumption against extraterritoriality might have priority.[445] For its part, the *Restatement (Fourth)* notes not only that the presumption against extraterritoriality may make other limits unnecessary but also that it may reflect *already* the interest protected by

---

[438] *See, e.g.*, Hilton v. Guyot, 159 U.S. 113, 163–64 (1895) ("'Comity,' in the legal sense, is neither a matter of absolute obligation, on the one hand, nor of mere courtesy and good will, upon the other."); *see* Dodge, *supra* note 421, at 2075 (noting uncertainties stemming from *Hilton v. Guyot*, in context of broader account of comity).

[439] *Empagran*, 542 U.S. at 164; RESTATEMENT (FOURTH) § 405 cmt. a & rptrs. note 2.

[440] RESTATEMENT (FOURTH) § 405 rptrs. note 2.

[441] *Empagran*, 542 U.S. at 165, 166; *see* RESTATEMENT (FOURTH) § 405 rptrs. note 2.

[442] The Court did reject taking "account of comity considerations case by case, abstaining where comity considerations, so dictate," as "too complex to prove workable." *Empagran*, 542 U.S. at 168. The Court also rejected varying a statute's interpretation depending upon the type of anticompetitive conduct at issue, see *id.* at 168–69, but it did not evaluate whether to apply Section 403's factors in a more general fashion.

[443] *See* RESTATEMENT (FOURTH) § 405 & cmt. a. The black letter provision provides, in full, that "[a]s a matter of prescriptive comity, courts in the United States *may* interpret federal statutory provisions to include *other limitations* on their applicability," presumably including reasonableness—a placeholder approach that may be wise without being instructive. *Id.* § 405 (emphases added).

[444] *See* Gardner, *supra* note 421, at 105 ("[B]alancing sovereign interests may make sense when determining whether to apply a statute to a given set of facts (a conflicts of law-type question), but not when interpreting a statute as it will apply across cases.").

[445] *See Hartford Fire Ins. Co.*, 509 U.S. at 812–18 (Scalia, J., dissenting); *e.g., id.* at 814–15 (Scalia, J., dissenting) (describing how once "the presumption against extraterritoriality has been overcome or is otherwise inapplicable," the *Charming Betsy* canon becomes relevant).

prescriptive comity.[446] Following renewed emphasis on the presumption against extraterritoriality, it will be important, but potentially difficult, to determine whether considering additional doctrines double-counts the interests of foreign states (or measures twice the countervailing interests of the United States). Existing case law provides little clarity.[447]

V. Immunity from U.S. Jurisdiction

Like much modern law, immunities doctrines are increasingly disaggregated and specialized. In part this tracks the way governance has evolved. Sovereign persons, such as a king or queen, have long enjoyed immunity from the local laws and courts of a foreign sovereign. The emergence of states as distinct entities required distinguishing the immunity of those entities from that of their sovereigns;[448] further differentiation followed, including among classes of state officials, and international law now addresses the immunity of international organizations and their officials as well.

How these immunities are expressed in U.S. law varies. As of the mid-1970s, the immunity of foreign states became wholly governed by a statute, the FSIA. The immunity of diplomats and consular officials, and that of international organizations and their officials, is driven by treaty, though also reflected in statutory provisions. Other foreign officials, in contrast, largely remain subject to customary international law and federal common law. These differences influence which U.S. institutions lead in the law's development and possible reform.

A. Foreign Sovereign Immunity

Foreign sovereign immunity—meaning, the immunity of foreign states, as distinct from the immunity of their officials—is one of the most frequently litigated areas in U.S. foreign relations law. After describing formative developments, and

---

[446] RESTATEMENT (FOURTH) § 405 rptrs. note 4.

[447] The *Restatement (Fourth)* notes as one of the "rare cases" combining these approaches *Parkcentral Glob. Hub Ltd. v. Porsche Auto. Holdings SE*, 763 F.3d 198 (2d Cir. 2014); *see* RESTATEMENT (FOURTH) § 405 rptrs. note 4. A subsequent decision critiqued *Parkcentral* as inconsistent with Supreme Court precedent regarding the presumption against extraterritoriality. Stoyas v. Toshiba Corporation, 896 F.3d 933, 950 (9th Cir. 2018).

[448] Arthur Watts, *The Legal Position in International Law of Heads of States, Heads of Governments and Foreign Ministers*, 247 RECUEIL DES COURS 21, 35–36 (1994); *see also* GAMAL MOURSI BADR, STATE IMMUNITY: AN ANALYTICAL AND PROGNOSTIC VIEW 9 (1984).

JUDGING FOREIGN RELATIONS   247

providing an overview of the FSIA, this section illustrates some of the issues with which courts continue to wrestle.[449]

1. Early Development

The American colonies did not universally insist on governmental immunity from suit in their own courts, and some charters even provided that the colonial government could sue and be sued.[450] That did not mean that the colonies accepted being sued in the courts of *other* colonies. The Eleventh Amendment, already ratified by 1795, rushed to clarify that the states did not welcome federal jurisdiction over suits against them by citizens of other states.[451]

It was probably clearer yet that suits in U.S. courts against unwilling foreign sovereigns could be highly sensitive. The Constitution, however, left unresolved the question of foreign sovereign immunity in U.S. courts.[452] Early legal skirmishes, principally involving suits by private parties against foreign sovereigns for their seizure of U.S. ships, made evident this sensitivity, including by highlighting the executive branch's uncertain role in protecting foreign sovereigns in such cases.[453]

---

[449] For more extensive, and expert, expositions, see JOSEPH W. DELLAPENNA, SUING FOREIGN GOVERNMENTS AND THEIR CORPORATIONS (2d ed. 2003); DAVID P. STEWART, FED. JUD. CTR., THE FOREIGN SOVEREIGN IMMUNITIES ACT: A GUIDE FOR JUDGES (2d ed. 2018); RESTATEMENT (FOURTH) §§ 451–64.

[450] Calvin R. Massey, *State Sovereignty and the Tenth and Eleventh Amendments*, 56 U. CHI. L. REV. 61, 87–97 (1989).

[451] U.S. CONST. AMEND. XI. Chief Justice Jay had noted that suits by citizens of another state were necessary to facilitate the enforcement of U.S. treaty obligations against states. Chisholm v. Georgia, 2 U.S. (2 Dall) 419, 474 (1793). But that view clearly did not endure. *See also* Hans v. Louisiana, 134 U.S. 1, 11 (1890) (suggesting that *Chisholm* had "created such a shock of surprise throughout the country"). The Supreme Court later held that state sovereign immunity barred suits by a state's own citizens, see *Hans*, 134 U.S. at 10–15, and then that such immunity limited abrogation in state courts as well. Alden v. Maine, 527 U.S. 706 (1999).

[452] Early *state* sovereign immunity debates did not appear to consider the matter settled by Article III, despite the fact that it described federal jurisdiction over suits against states. This would imply that Article III's grant of federal jurisdiction over suits involving *foreign* states was considered consistent with the possibility that foreign states might yet be deemed immune from suit. Chief Justice Jay made a similar point with regard to suits against the United States. *Chisholm*, 2 U.S. at 478 (Jay, C.J.); *see* Massey, *supra* note 450, at 106.

[453] *See generally* Chimène I. Keitner, *Between Law and Diplomacy: The Conundrum of Common Law Immunity*, 54 GA. L. REV. 217 (2019); Chimène I. Keitner, *The Forgotten History of Foreign Official Immunity*, 87 N.Y.U. L. REV. 704 (2012). Although two 1790s Attorney General opinions recorded the U.S. executive's refusal to intervene in judicial proceedings at the behest of foreign sovereigns, to raise what we would now classify as an official immunity issue, practice was not entirely consistent. Thus, in one 1796 episode, the U.S. government filed a "suggestion" objecting to a lawsuit that sought attachment of a French warship and which alleged that its captain, a commissioned French officer (and U.S. citizen), had acted unlawfully and owed damages. During the same episode, however, the executive also signaled discomfort with France's having called, "with no very clear conception of the constitutional powers of the Executive, for a direct interference to annul the judicial proceedings." *See* Keitner, *Between Law and Diplomacy, supra*, at 233–39 (discussing *The Cassius*).

Before long, the Supreme Court recognized foreign sovereign immunity from the jurisdiction of U.S. courts.[454] *The Schooner Exchange* involved a French naval warship that was forced by bad weather into port at Philadelphia, where an action was brought against it by former U.S. owners who claimed that the vessel had been unlawfully seized by the French. Chief Justice Marshall regarded the vessel's immunity from suit as unsettled.[455] Each nation had unlimited jurisdiction over persons, property, or conduct in its territory, including its harbors. At the same time, all nations enjoyed equal sovereignty, and interacted on that basis for their mutual benefit. This equality led to the "relaxation" of territorial jurisdiction when one sovereign entered another sovereign's territory with express or implied permission.[456] Reviewing comparable practices, the Court concluded that a nation's ports were presumptively open to a friendly nation's public ships, including its warships, which were then exempt from the jurisdiction of the local courts.[457] The Court perceived additional prudential reasons for this conclusion, but felt they were unnecessary to its conclusion.[458]

The Schooner Exchange suggested a cautious, context-dependent approach to foreign sovereign immunity. The Court seemed to seek state practice at a relatively granular level. The respect for "sovereign rights" also permitted a distinction between *acta jure imperii* (sovereign, or public, acts) and *acta jure gestionis* (private acts),[459] one soon elaborated in cases involving the immunity of the U.S. government before its own courts.[460] Importantly, immunity depended on the will of the territorial sovereign, meaning that the host state might choose to deny such immunity in particular circumstances.[461] Any denial of typical immunities would be by advance notice, ideally,[462] but the host state could at any point "destroy[] th[e] implication" of immunity by acting "in a manner not

---

[454] *The Schooner Exchange* is widely regarded as seminal, and not only for the United States. *See, e.g.*, BADR, *supra* note 448, at 9–10; Ian Sinclair, *The Law of Sovereign Immunity: Recent Developments*, 167 RECUEIL DES COURS 113, 121–22 (1980).

[455] Schooner Exchange v. McFaddon, 11 U.S. (7 Cranch) 116, 136 (1812) (claiming that "[i]n exploring an unbeaten path, with few, if any, aids from precedents or written law, the court has found it necessary to rely much on general principles, and on a train of reasoning, founded on cases in some degree analogous to this").

[456] *Id*. at 136–37.

[457] The Court cited as examples of recognized accommodations instances involving immunity of the foreign sovereign from arrest or detention, immunity for the sovereign's diplomats, and immunity for foreign troops permitted to pass through territory. *Id*. at 137–46.

[458] *Id*. at 146.

[459] *Id*. at 137. Although foreign public and private ships were treated alike in treaties, the Court considered that the susceptibility of merchant ships to jurisdiction was distinguishable. The Court speculated, without deciding, that merchant ships entering a port under exigent circumstances, consistent with treaty rights, might also have enjoyed immunity, but perhaps not if they were "attempting to trade." *Id*. at 142–43.

[460] Bank of the United States v. Planter's Bank, 22 U.S. (9 Wheat.) 904, 907–08 (1824) (stating that "when a government becomes a partner in any trading company, it devests itself, so far as concerns the transactions of that company, of its sovereign character, and takes that of a private citizen").

[461] *Schooner Exchange*, 11 U.S. at 136 ("All exceptions . . . to the full and complete power of a nation within its own territories, must be traced up to the consent of the nation itself.")

[462] *E.g., id*. at 141.

to be misunderstood."[463] In *The Schooner Exchange* itself, however, the U.S. executive branch had instead filed a "suggestion" that immunity was owed to the French vessel, which made clear the host state's desire that such immunity be respected.[464]

Over time, foreign sovereign immunity became broader and more generic, applying to all state organs and instrumentalities, without any particular focus on context. Courts in the United States also gravitated toward a generalized, "absolute" theory that made no distinction between a foreign state's public and private activities.[465] That theory seemed to be consistent with that practiced by foreign states in their own courts,[466] but also had idiosyncrasies distinctive to the United States that became increasingly pronounced.[467] Of particular note, the position of the United States as the territorial sovereign increasingly became synonymous with the case-specific views of the executive branch. For some time, these views were respected but not necessarily conclusive.[468] As litigated immunity claims became more varied and less traditional—such that case law provided less guidance, and sovereigns were more prone to differ with one another[469]—the Supreme Court also made it harder for foreign defendants to assert immunity in

[463] *Id.* at 146.

[464] *Id.* at 116, 118; *id.* at 147.

[465] This history is sometimes oversimplified: for example, the suggestion that the United States adhered to the "absolute" theory "[f]rom the Nation's founding until 1952." Brief for the United States as Amicus Curiae Supporting Petitioners at 2, Republic of Austria v. Altmann, 541 U.S. 677 (2004) (No. 03-13). Even at the time of *The Schooner Exchange*, the absolute theory might not have included immunity in relation to disputes over real property in the United States. *See Schooner Exchange*, 11 U.S. at 145 (noting that a foreign prince might then be "assuming the character of a private individual"). Commercial activities were not rigorously tested before U.S. courts. For example, the immunity of state-owned trading vessels under U.S. law was only settled in the early twentieth century. Berizzi Bros. Co. v. The Pesaro, 271 U.S. 562, 574 (1926); *see also id.* at 576 (acknowledging "some diversity of opinion on the question" among lower federal courts); *cf.* Verlinden B.V. v. Central Bank of Nigeria, 461 U.S. 480, 486 (1983) (stating that *The Schooner Exchange* "came to be regarded as extending virtually absolute immunity to foreign sovereigns," and citing *The Pesaro*); The Roseric, 254 F. 154, 158–62 (D.N.J. 1918) (reviewing case law); The Maipo, 259 F. 367 (S.D.N.Y. 1919) (indicating misgivings, but upholding immunity of Chilean steamship).

[466] *See* William W. Bishop, Jr., *New United States Policy Limiting Sovereign Immunity*, 47 AM. J. INT'L L. 93, 94–95 (1953) (noting support in state practice, but also noting unsettled views in the U.K. House of Lords).

[467] *See infra* this chapter text accompanying notes 478–482 (discussing Tate Letter). For example, notwithstanding "absolute" immunity, U.S. case law indicated by the early 1900s that state-owned enterprises did not share the foreign sovereign's immunity. *E.g.*, Molina v. Comision Reguladora del Mercado de Henequen, 103 A. 397, 399–400 (N.J. 1918); *see also* Bernard Fensterwald, Jr., *Sovereign Immunity and Soviet State Trading*, 63 HARV. L. REV. 614, 618–20 (1950) (suggesting that "American courts... almost universally have denied immunity to all corporate agents" of foreign sovereigns).

[468] *See* Robert M. Jarvis, *The Tate Letter: Some Words Regarding Its Authorship*, 55 AM. J. LEGAL HIST. 465, 470 (2015) (reprinting speech by Professor Jack B. Tate to the Association of the Bar of the City of New York, April 15, 1954) (noting that, in the case of the *Pesaro*, the Supreme Court disregarded the Department of State position); *see also* 2 GREEN HACKWORTH, DIGEST OF INTERNATIONAL LAW 437–38, 444–46 (1941) (providing additional background).

[469] *See, e.g.*, 2 HACKWORTH, *supra* note 468, at 424–28 (describing *Attualita* dispute, concerning steamship requisitioned by Italian government, as to which the executive branch intervened); The Attualita, 238 F. 909, 911 (4th Cir. 1916) (noting limited executive branch submission).

their own right,[470] so the significance of executive branch input increased.[471] By the late 1930s, the Court said that the executive's views were dispositive.[472] By 1945, the Court went further, affirming in *Republic of Mexico v. Hoffman* that executive branch suggestions of immunity, when proffered, were controlling, and adding that judicial discretion in other cases should be exercised in accord with "the principles accepted by the department of the government charged with the conduct of our foreign relations."[473]

The growing favor shown executive branch authority was unsurprising, given the Supreme Court's developing tendency to defer to the executive branch in foreign relations matters generally.[474] Deference might have been particularly appealing in view of cases coming before the Court, which typically involved private attempts to seize foreign sovereign vessels, not more anodyne suits for money damages.[475] The Court was also somewhat slower to concede finality to executive branch determinations that immunity was *not* due, perhaps because judicial second-guessing that had the effect of establishing immunity was less likely to offend foreign sovereigns.[476]

---

[470] *Ex Parte* Muir, 254 U.S. 522, 532–33 (1921) (requiring that the foreign sovereign, or its representative, had to appear as a suitor or, if it lacked standing, ensure that the U.S. executive branch certify the requisite public status and immunity to the court). The *Muir* procedure was developed for federal courts, but was also (generally) followed in state courts. Francis Deak, *The Plea of Sovereign Immunity and the New York Court of Appeals*, 40 COLUM. L. REV. 453 (1940).

[471] G. Edward White, *The Transformation of the Constitutional Regime of Foreign Relations*, 85 VA. L. REV. 1, 134–45 (1999).

[472] Companía Española de Navegación Marítima, S.A. v. The Navemar, 303 U.S. 68, 74–76 (1938); Deak, *supra* note 470, at 459–62.

[473] 324 U.S. 30, 35 (1945); *see also Ex parte* Republic of Peru, 318 U.S. 578, 588 (1943) ("[C]ourts are required to accept and follow the executive determination that [a] vessel is immune"); *id.* at 587–89.

[474] White, *supra* note 471, at 145.

[475] The Court observed that "the judicial seizure of the vessel of a friendly foreign state is so serious a challenge to its dignity, and may so affect our friendly relations with it," that executive determination was appropriate. *See Republic of Peru*, 318 U.S. at 588; *see also Hoffman*, 324 U.S. at 34–36 (cautioning about "[t]he judicial seizure of the property of a friendly state"). The Court was also of the view that uncompensated wrongs to plaintiffs, frustrated by immunity, were better "righted through diplomatic negotiations rather than by the compulsions of judicial proceedings." *Republic of Peru*, 318 U.S. at 589.

[476] Earlier cases generally acceded to executive branch recommendations of immunity. *E.g.*, *Republic of Peru*, 318 U.S. at 588. In *Hoffman*, the Court agreed with the Department of State's conclusion *against* immunity, but it seemed most concerned maintaining consistency: it emphasized that case law, and longstanding Department of State policy, had endorsed immunity for vessels in the possession and service of a foreign government, but not when a vessel was owned by a foreign government not in possession of it. 324 U.S. at 36–37. The Court resisted "enlarge[ing] an immunity to an extent which the government, although often asked, has not seen fit to recognize." *Id.* at 38; *accord id.* at 35. *Hoffman* may signify broader acceptance of executive branch authority. *See id.* at 39 (Frankfurter, J., concurring); White, *supra* note 471, at 143–45. But the Court simply stated the modest position that "we find no persuasive ground for allowing the immunity in this case, an important reason being that the State Department has declined to recognize it." *Hoffman*, 324 U.S. at 35 n.1.

As such, the courts stopped short of complete capitulation to executive preferences.[477]

The executive's first attempt at a comprehensive policy on sovereign immunity was its famous 1952 Tate Letter. Having long questioned whether immunity was required for a foreign sovereign's commercial activities,[478] perceiving an increase in those sovereign activities, and finding a wavering commitment by other states to the absolute theory of immunity, the Department of State announced a "restrictive theory of sovereign immunity," whereby immunity would be recognized only for sovereign or public acts (*acta jure imperii*).[479] The letter anticipated, correctly, that U.S. courts would respect the executive's views.[480] It explained that thereafter foreign sovereigns could bring immunity objections to the Department of State or raise them directly in court.[481] Where courts lacked a Department determination, they could attempt to apply on their own the government's general approach to the facts of the case.[482]

By the late 1960s, the Department of State had created an internal, adversarial hearing procedure, as a means of applying the general approach to particular disputes.[483] Nevertheless, the regime continued to be regarded as politicized and inconsistent,[484] with the Department too often finding immunity for allies

---

[477] *See, e.g.*, National City Bank of New York v. Republic of China, 348 U.S. 356, 360 (1955) (stating that the Department of State's "failure or refusal to suggest" sovereign immunity "has been accorded significant weight by this Court").

[478] *Compare* Letter from Secretary of State Lansing to Attorney General Gregory (Nov. 8, 1918), *excerpted in* 2 HACKWORTH, *supra* note 468, at 429 ("[W]here [government-owned] vessels were engaged in commercial pursuits, they should be subject to the obligations and restrictions of trade, if they were to enjoy its benefits and profits"), *with* Letter from Attorney General Gregory to Secretary of State Lansing (Nov. 25, 1918), *excerpted in id.* at 430 (reporting conviction of the Department of Justice that "that as the law now stands, these ships are immune"). Dicta often stresses, however, that the State Department generally adhered to absolute immunity. *See, e.g.*, Jam v. Int'l Fin. Corp., 139 S. Ct. 759, 766 (2019); Rubin v. Islamic Republic of Iran, 138 S. Ct. 816, 821 (2018); Verlinden B.V. v. Central Bank of Nigeria, 461 U.S. 480, 486 (1983).

[479] *See Changed Policy Concerning the Granting of Sovereign Immunity to Foreign Governments*, 26 DEP'T STATE BULL. 984 (1952) (reprinting Letter from Jack B. Tate, Acting Legal Adviser, U.S. Dep't of State, to Philip B. Perlman, Acting U.S. Att'y Gen. (May 19, 1952)). This letter followed an appraisal of the law of sovereign immunity by the Department of State's Committee on Sovereign Immunity, resulting in a 176-page report finalized in 1949. *See* Jarvis, *supra* note 468, at 466–69. Other undertakings helped set the stage. *See, e.g.*, Harvard Research in International Law, *Competence of Courts in Regard to Foreign States*, 26 AM. J. INT'L L. SUPP. 451, 597, 606 (1932) (distinguishing commercial activities, but acknowledging that this was "highly controversial").

[480] *Changed Policy, supra* note 479, at 985.

[481] *Sovereign Immunity Decisions of the Department of State, May 1952 to January 1977*, 1977 DIGEST OF U.S. PRACTICE, at 1019.

[482] CURTIS A. BRADLEY, INTERNATIONAL LAW IN THE U.S. LEGAL SYSTEM 243–45 (3d ed. 2021) (describing the Department of State's approach to immunity during this period).

[483] 1977 DIGEST OF U.S. PRACTICE, at 1019; *see also id.* at 1020–81.

[484] H.R. REP. NO. 94-1487, at 7 (1976), *reprinted in* 1976 U.S.C.C.A.N. 6604, 6606; *see also Jurisdiction of U.S. Foreign States: Hearing on H.R. 11315 Before the Subcomm. on Admin. Law of the H. Comm. on the Judiciary*, 94th Cong. 24, 25, 29 (1976) (testimony of Monroe Leigh, Legal Adviser, Department of State); *cf.* Adam S. Chilton & Christopher A. Whytock, *Foreign Sovereign Immunity and Comparative Institutional Competency*, 163 U. PA. L. REV. 411, 426–30 (2015) (summarizing

and denying it to foes, even when the issues were similar. Such behavior amplified concerns that deference to the executive abdicated the judiciary's responsibility.[485] The Department of State also came to regard the process as burdensome and prone to amplify, rather than quell, diplomatic controversy.[486]

By adopting the FSIA in 1976, Congress, with the executive's support, concluded that immunity would "henceforth be decided by courts of the United States and of the States."[487] The statute represented the first mutual attempt to exercise what *The Schooner Exchange* described as the territorial sovereign's authority to consent to "[a]ll exceptions" to territorial sovereignty, while acting "in a manner not to be misunderstood" in tempering the immunity of foreign sovereigns.[488] A key part of the exercise involved turning the keys back over to the courts.

2. Nature and Scope of the FSIA

The FSIA's provisions "work in tandem" to regulate jurisdiction.[489] Title 28, Section 1604 "bars federal and state courts from exercising jurisdiction when a foreign state *is* entitled to immunity," while Section 1330(a) establishes district court jurisdiction over suits "when a foreign state is *not* entitled to immunity."[490] Section 1330(b) makes personal jurisdiction track subject-matter jurisdiction.[491] Taken as a whole, the FSIA is the "sole basis for obtaining jurisdiction over a foreign state in our courts."[492] Generally, the FSIA proceeds on the basis that foreign sovereigns are entitled to immunity from the jurisdiction of U.S. courts (and from attachment of and execution against its property), unless that immunity is denied by one of several statutory exceptions, as discussed later.

Still, the FSIA is not merely jurisdictional. In *Verlinden B. V. v. Central Bank of Nigeria*,[493] the Court held that the FSIA established substantive federal law

concerns about prior regime, but also challenging idea that State Department immunity decisions were more prone to politicization than those made by courts under the FSIA).

[485] *See, e.g.*, Philip C. Jessup, *Has the Supreme Court Abdicated One of Its Functions?*, 40 AM. J. INT'L L. 168 (1946).

[486] H.R. REP. NO. 94-1487, *supra* note 484, at 9 (1976); *Immunities of Foreign States: Hearing on H.R. 3493 Before the Subcomm. on Claims and Governmental Relations of the H. Comm. on the Judiciary*, 93d Cong. 15 (1973) (statement of Charles N. Brower, Acting Legal Adviser, Department of State).

[487] 28 U.S.C. § 1602 (2018).

[488] The Schooner Exchange v. McFaddon, 11 U.S. (7 Cranch) 116, 136, 146 (1812).

[489] Argentine Republic v. Amerada Hess Shipping Corp., 488 U.S. 428, 434 (1989).

[490] *Id.* at 434 (emphases in original); *see* 28 U.S.C. § 1604; *id.* § 1330(a).

[491] 28 U.S.C. § 1330(b). Whether foreign sovereigns are entitled to invoke extra-statutory, constitutional restrictions on personal jurisdiction is a separate matter. *See* Chapter 10 § II(D)(3).

[492] *Amerada Hess*, 488 U.S. at 434. This exclusivity of the FSIA as the basis for jurisdiction over a foreign sovereign in U.S. courts means that a plaintiff may not instead invoke subject-matter jurisdiction under other grants of authority, like the Alien Tort Statute, as a means of circumventing foreign sovereign immunity. *Id.* at 437–39 (listing other examples).

[493] 461 U.S. 480 (1983).

sufficient for "arising under" jurisdiction under Article III.[494] The FSIA also applies in state court, while affording a basis for removal to federal court.[495] When applicable, it establishes immunity from jurisdiction and from particular remedies, while also identifying limits to that immunity for covered entities.[496] Even when an exception to immunity allows jurisdiction over a foreign state, the FSIA continues to govern procedural aspects of the litigation.[497] The FSIA's comprehensive scope was one basis for the Supreme Court's holding, in *Republic of Austria v. Altmann*, that the statute applied retroactively to conduct taking place before its enactment, and even before the United States fully endorsed the restrictive theory of immunity[498]—cementing the statute's wide-ranging temporal

---

[494] *Id.* at 497; *see id.* at 496–97. As the Court noted, a House Report indicated that "the primary purpose of the Act was to '[set] forth comprehensive rules governing sovereign immunity.'" *Id.* at 496 (quoting H.R. REP. No. 94-1487, at 12 (1976), *reprinted in* 1976 U.S.C.C.A.N. 6604, 6610); *id.* at 495 n.22 (quoting same passage). The act also applied to actions by foreign plaintiffs against foreign sovereigns, as in *Verlinden* itself, which exceeded the diversity clause of Article III. *Id.* at 489–91.

[495] 28 U.S.C. § 1604 (establishing immunity "from the jurisdiction of the courts of the United States and of the States," subject to exception); *id.* § 1441(d) (providing right of removal); *see Verlinden*, 461 U.S. at 489 (noting provisions); H.R. REP. No. 94-1487, at 32 (1976), *reprinted in* 1976 U.S.C.C.A.N. 6604, 6631 (noting importance of removal for foreign states).

[496] The "when applicable" caveat is necessary because persons or entities not covered by the FSIA might be able to invoke "foreign sovereign immunity under the common law." Samantar v. Yousuf, 560 U.S. 305, 324 (2010); *see infra* this chapter § V(D)(2) (discussing in relation to foreign official immunity).

[497] 28 U.S.C. §§ 1330(b), 1606, & 1608; *see* STEWART, *supra* note 449, at 2–3 (noting, inter alia, "extended time for answering complaints, a right of removal of the case from state court to federal court, entitlement to a non-jury trial, [and] limitations on award of punitive damages"); *id.* at 18–22 (discussing personal jurisdiction and venue); *id.* at 25–32 (miscellaneous procedural and evidentiary issues). While these issues may seem peripheral, they are often the source of litigation. *See, e.g.*, Republic of Sudan v. Harrison, 139 S. Ct. 1048 (2019) (addressing one of the three means of service identified in the FSIA).

Other procedural issues, like discovery, were nonetheless left to existing law, H.R. REP. No. 94-1487, at 23 (1976), *reprinted in* 1976 U.S.C.C.A.N. 6604, 6621–22, save for certain terrorism-related provisions. *See* 28 U.S.C. § 1605(g). A foreign state immune from suit is also immune from discovery. *E.g.*, Peninsula Asset Mgmt. (Cayman) Ltd. v. Hankook Tire Co., 476 F.3d 140, 143 (2d Cir. 2007); RESTATEMENT (FOURTH) § 462 cmt. c & e. U.S. courts, however, may order "jurisdictional discovery" as necessary to determine whether an entity is indeed a foreign state or whether one of the exceptions applies. *See* Packsys, S.A. de C.V. v. Exportadora de Sal, S.A. de C.V., 899 F.3d 1081 (9th Cir. 2018); Arch Trading Corp. v. Republic of Ecuador, 839 F.3d 193, 207 (2d Cir. 2016); RESTATEMENT (FOURTH) § 462, cmt. b & rptrs. note 2. Further, if a court decides that suit may proceed, discovery may be limited on comity grounds and in light of the burdens it might place on foreign sovereigns. *See* Republic of Argentina v. NML Capital, Ltd., 573 U.S. 134, 142–46 & n.6 (2014); RESTATEMENT (FOURTH) § 462 & rptrs. note 1. These factors may also be weighed in assessing post-judgment discovery about extraterritorial assets, which is not restricted by the FSIA itself. *NML Capital*, 573 U.S. at 144–45.

[498] 541 U.S. 677 (2004). The statute lacked characteristics of potentially problematic retroactive lawmaking—foreign sovereigns had no justifiable expectations of immunity, nor did the statute increase their liability for prior conduct, and no private rights were upset—but it had substantive effects. *Id.* at 694–96. The Court was persuaded in part by the fact that some FSIA provisions suggested its application to pre-enactment conduct. *Id.* at 697–98 (discussing, inter alia, preambular language in § 1602, and how the status of instrumentalities was determined at the time of suit irrespective of status at the time of conduct) (citing Dole Food Co. v. Patrickson, 538 U.S. 468 (2003)). Ultimately, the Court reasoned that the statute's "comprehensive" framework would be frustrated if it were not applied to pre-enactment conduct. *Id.* at 699–700. Notably, the Court suggested that

reach.[499]

Gaps in the FSIA regime are also noteworthy. First, the FSIA only concerns immunity of "states," not of persons, including state officials.[500] Second, the FSIA does not generally establish causes of action, meaning that plaintiffs suing a foreign state must ordinarily rely on some other substantive law (federal or more likely state law), with foreign sovereigns simply being "liable in the same manner and to the same extent as a private individual under like circumstances."[501] (Exceptionally, the FSIA does establish causes of action relating to terrorism.[502]) Third, the FSIA has not been understood to afford immunity to a foreign state against indictments or grand jury subpoenas, as might arise in criminal actions against a state-owned enterprise.[503] Civil proceedings predicated on criminal liability may be a different matter.[504]

---

the executive branch might be able to seek to prevent the FSIA's retroactive application in particular cases. *Id.* at 701.

[499] *See also* Opati v. Republic of Sudan, 140 S. Ct. 1601 (2020) (holding that FSIA amendments creating a cause of action for state-sponsored acts of terrorism and permitting recovery of punitive damages applied retroactively).

[500] *See infra* this chapter § V(D) (discussing, inter alia, Samantar v. Yousuf, 560 U.S. 305 (2010)).

[501] 28 U.S.C. § 1606; *see* First Nat'l City Bank v. Banco Para El Comercio Exterior de Cuba, 462 U.S. 611, 620 (1983) (concluding that the FSIA "was not intended to affect the substantive law determining the liability of a foreign state or instrumentality, or the attribution of liability among instrumentalities of a foreign state"); *id.* at 621–23 (applying principles "common to both international law and federal common law").

[502] *See infra* this chapter text accompanying notes 671–674.

[503] *See In re* Grand Jury Proceeding Related To M/V Deltuva, 752 F. Supp. 2d 173, 176–80 (D.P.R. 2010); *see also* United States v. Noriega, 117 F.3d 1206, 1212 (11th Cir. 1997); United States v. Hendron, 813 F. Supp. 973, 974–77 (E.D.N.Y. 1993); RESTATEMENT (FOURTH) § 451 rptrs. note 4 (although "Section 1604 does not explicitly limit its grant of immunity to civil cases," to this point "no reported court decision has dismissed an indictment or otherwise suppressed a criminal prosecution based on immunity conferred by the FSIA"); Chimène Keitner, *Prosecuting Foreign States*, 61 VA. J. INT'L L. 221 (2021) (concluding that the FSIA leaves the issue of immunity from criminal proceedings to the common law). The executive branch appears to agree. Brief for the United States in Opposition at 9–12, *In re* Grand Jury Subpoena, 139 S. Ct. 1378 (mem.) (2019) (No. 18-948); *id.* at 18–19 (citing prior prosecutions of state-owned enterprises).

·The dearth of cases applying the FSIA in criminal matters may have other explanations. Immunity will be irrelevant if a criminal statute does not apply to foreign sovereigns in the first place. Even if the FSIA applied to criminal proceedings, the statute's exceptions, like that for commercial activities, might apply too. *In re* Grand Jury Subpoena, 912 F.3d 623, 627–34 (D.C. Cir. 2019); Brief for the United States in Opposition at 12–16, *In re* Grand Jury Subpoena, 139 S. Ct. 1378 (mem.) (2019) (No. 18-948).

[504] Cases have wrestled with whether civil RICO claims against foreign sovereigns are foreclosed because immunity means the underlying acts are not "indictable" under 18 U.S.C. § 1961. *Compare, e.g.*, Southway v. Central Bank of Nigeria, 198 F.3d 1210, 121416 (10th Cir. 1999) (indicating doubt as to the FSIA's application in criminal contexts, but applying statutory exceptions), *with* Keller v. Central Bank of Nigeria, 277 F.3d 811, 818–21 (6th Cir. 2002) (concluding that the FSIA granted immunity from criminal prosecution for Nigerian central bank and bank officials, rendering acts non-indictable for purposes of civil RICO claims), *partially abrogated by* Samantar v. Yousuf, 560 U.S. 305 (2010).

As all this suggests, foreign sovereign immunity in the United States is statutory rather than constitutional.[505] Some Supreme Court decisions further imply that U.S. legal obligations in this regard are solely matters of national law, and that international considerations are simply matters of comity or diplomacy.[506] That view would be mistaken. The Court elsewhere has acknowledged, as have the political branches, that immunity from national jurisdiction arises under international law.[507] Indeed, there is a global consensus that where not the subject of treaty,[508] immunity is governed by customary international law.[509] The content of that law is less certain than the FSIA,[510] and state disagreements centered on international law continue to be litigated,[511] but the discourse among states

[505] *See, e.g.,* Verlinden B.V. v. Central Bank of Nigeria, 461 U.S. 480, 486 (1983) (stating that "foreign sovereign immunity is a matter of grace and comity on the part of the United States, and not a restriction imposed by the Constitution").

[506] Thus, the Court subsequently stated a more truncated view that immunity was "a matter of grace and comity on the part of the United States," implying that it was discretionary under international law. Rubin v. Islamic Republic of Iran, 138 S. Ct. 816, 821 (2018) (quoting *Verlinden,* 461 U.S. at 486); *see also Altmann,* 541 U.S. at 696 (describing foreign sovereign immunity as according "to foreign states and their instrumentalities " 'protection . . . as a gesture of comity' ") (quoting Dole Food Co. v. Patrickson, 538 U.S. 468, 479 (2003)).

[507] *See, e.g.,* Bolivarian Republic of Venezuela v. Helmerich & Payne Int'l Drilling Co., 137 S. Ct. 1312, 1319 (2017) (stating that the FSIA largely "embodies basic principles of international law long followed both in the United States and elsewhere"); Permanent Mission of India to the United Nations v. City of New York, 551 U.S. 193, 199 (2007) (noting the FSIA "codification of international law at the time of the FSIA's enactment"); H.R. REP. No. 94-1487, at 14 (1976), *reprinted in* 1976 U.S.C.C.A.N. 6604, 6613 (attributing restrictive theory to international law); *id.* at 14 (describing FSIA as "a statutory regime which incorporates standards recognized under international law"); Brief for the United States as Amicus Curiae at 2, 39, Alfred Dunhill of London, Inc. v. Republic of Cuba, 425 U.S. 682 (1976) (No. 73-1288) (depicting the restrictive theory as a principle of international law).

[508] The United Nations Convention on Jurisdictional Immunities of States and Their Property, G.A. Res. 59/38, Annex (Dec. 2, 2004), recognized in its preamble that "the jurisdictional immunities of States and their property are generally accepted as a principle of customary international law." That convention is not itself yet in force, however, and the United States is not a signatory. The European Convention on State Immunity, May 16, 1972, 1495 U.N.T.S. 181, E.T.S. 74, is in force, but has only eight states parties, and the United States is not among them.

[509] *See* HAZEL FOX & PHILIPPA WEBB, THE LAW OF STATE IMMUNITY 13–14 (3d ed. 2013); XIAODONG YANG, STATE IMMUNITY IN INTERNATIONAL LAW 35 & nn.1–7 (2012); *e.g.,* Jurisdictional Immunities of the State (Ger. v. It.: Greece Intervening), Judgment, 2012 I.C.J. 99, 123, ¶ 56 (Feb. 3) ("States generally proceed on the basis that there is a right to immunity under international law, together with a corresponding obligation on the part of other States to respect and give effect to that immunity"); Jones v. Ministry of Interior of Saudi Arabia, [2006] UKHL 26, [2007] 1 AC (HL) 270, ¶ 101 (appeal taken from Eng.) ("[S]tate immunity is not a 'self-imposed restriction on the jurisdiction of its courts which the United Kingdom has chosen to adopt' and which it can, as a matter of discretion, relax or abandon. It is imposed by international law").

[510] Jasper Finke, *Sovereign Immunity: Rule, Comity or Something Else?,* 21 EUR. J. INT'L L. 853, 874 (2010) ("All states, with a very few exceptions, accept sovereign immunity as something which is legally binding under international law. But that's basically it."); Wenhua Shan & Peng Wang, *Divergent Views on State Immunity in the International Community, in* THE CAMBRIDGE HANDBOOK OF IMMUNITIES AND INTERNATIONAL LAW 61–62, 78 (Tom Ruys, Nicolas Angelet, & Luca Ferro eds., 2019) (arguing that residual state commitment to absolute immunity undermines the restrictive approach, while accepting immunity as a rule of international law).

[511] *See, e.g.,* Jurisdictional Immunities of the State (Ger. v. It.: Greece intervening), Judgment, 2012 I.C.J. 99 (Feb. 3) (finding Germany immune from civil claims in Italian courts under customary international law); *see also* Certain Iranian Assets (Iran v. U.S.), Preliminary Objections, Judgment,

entails assertions of *legal* rights and obligations, not mere comity. That understanding is critical for protecting the U.S. government from actions in foreign
courts. The Supreme Court's references to comity in this context may simply
reflect its uncertainty as to whether the FSIA is more or less protective than
international law, and its desire to avoid highlighting statutory conflicts with international law that the judiciary cannot resolve.[512]

The practical question remains whether the FSIA fully accounts for any international limits or whether they remain relevant to courts when applying the
FSIA. Congress clearly intended, when enacting the FSIA, to align U.S. practice
with international law.[513] This suggests a basis for construing the FSIA in light
of international obligations, particularly for statutory terms designed to incorporate international law.[514] Still, some caution is required. U.S. case law most
clearly suggests attending to international law as it stood when the FSIA was
enacted—rather than commending interpretation according to current norms,
as the *Charming Betsy* canon would suggest.[515] Congress also retains the capacity
to abridge foreign sovereign immunity, as a matter of domestic law, even if it
would violate international law.[516] Naturally, to the extent that U.S. practice is not
dictated by a belief as to the scope of contemporary international law, it inhibits
the U.S. capacity to contribute through its practice to the formation of customary
international law.[517]

It bears emphasis, finally, that even taking contemporary international law
into account, foreign sovereign immunity is an essentially conservative enterprise. As explained in Chapter 5, states have increasingly recognized a limited
number of peremptory (or *jus cogens*) rules from which states are not permitted

---

2019 I.C.J. 7 (Feb. 13) (finding that the treaty over which the Court had jurisdiction did not incorporate customary rules on sovereign immunities).

[512] *But see* Fox & Webb, *supra* note 509, at 14 (contrasting view of immunity as an international-
law obligation with *Altmann*); Finke, *supra* note 510, at 856 (citing the U.S. Supreme Court as exemplifying those "reject[ing] ... legally binding effect under customary international law altogether").

[513] *See supra* this chapter text accompanying note 507 (citing authorities); *see, e.g.*, 28 U.S.C. § 1602
(2018) (invoking international law approach to commercial activities).

[514] RESTATEMENT (FOURTH) § 451 cmt. c.

[515] Permanent Mission of India to the United Nations v. City of New York, 551 U.S. 193, 199
(2007) (identifying as one "well-recognized" purpose of the FSIA "codification of international law
at the time of the FSIA's enactment"); *see also* RESTATEMENT (FOURTH) § 451 cmt. c (observing that
"Congress and the Department of State considered international law when the FSIA was drafted,
debated, and enacted"). Case law has been more attuned, in any event, to international law and practice at the time of enactment, and less to subsequent developments. *E.g.*, Federal Republic of Germany
v. Philipp, 141 S. Ct. 703, 712 (2021) (expropriations exception); Republic of Argentina v. Weltover,
Inc., 504 U.S. 607, 612–13 (1992) (commercial activity exception); Saudi Arabia v. Nelson, 507 U.S.
349, 359 (1993) (same); *Permanent Mission of India*, 551 U.S. at 199–202 (immovable property
exception).

[516] *See, e.g.*, *infra* this chapter text accompanying notes 689–692 (discussing terrorism exception).

[517] *But cf.* RESTATEMENT (FOURTH) § 451 cmt. c (noting that the FSIA and accompanying case law
may also influence "the content, interpretation, and development of international law").

to derogate, like the prohibitions on genocide and torture.[518] Even so, the ICJ has held that foreign states retain their immunity in national courts from claims that they have committed *jus cogens* offenses.[519] Two elements of the ICJ's decision deserve mention. First, it reasoned that "rules which determine the scope and extent of jurisdiction and when that jurisdiction may be exercised do not derogate from those substantive rules which possess *jus cogens* status, nor is there anything inherent in the concept of *jus cogens* which would require their modification or would displace their application."[520] Second, if "the mere allegation that the State had committed [serious violations of international law] were to be sufficient to deprive the State of its entitlement to immunity, immunity could, in effect be negated simply by skillful construction of the claim."[521]

U.S. decisions applying the FSIA are in accord. Lower courts have denied that there is a general exception for *jus cogens* offenses, or that states have implicitly waived immunity for such offenses.[522] The Supreme Court has also rejected arguments that the FSIA's expropriations exception may be applied so as to permit claims that property taken through forced sales amounts to an act of genocide.[523] The Court justified its reading of the exception as consistent with the international law of expropriation (which does not encompass takings by a foreign state from its own nationals) and with the international law of state immunity, citing ICJ case law.[524] Going further, the Court described what it termed "the reticulated boundaries Congress placed in the FSIA with regard to human rights violations," and said it had itself consistently "rejected efforts to insert modern human rights law into FSIA exceptions ill-suited to the task."[525] This wary

---

[518] *See* Chapter 5 § IV (B)(1).

[519] Jurisdictional Immunities of the State (Ger. v. It.), Judgment, 2012 I.C.J. 99, ¶¶ 81–97 (Feb. 3).

[520] *Id.* ¶ 95.

[521] *Id.* ¶ 82.

[522] RESTATEMENT (FOURTH) § 453 rptrs. note 10; *see, e.g.*, Matar v. Dichter, 563 F.3d 9, 14 (2d Cir. 2009) (stating that "there is no general *jus cogens* exception to FSIA immunity"); Sampson v. Federal Republic of Germany, 250 F.3d 1145, 1149–56 (7th Cir. 2001) (rejecting argument that violations of *jus cogens* amounts to an implied waiver); Princz v. Federal Republic of Germany, 26 F.3d 1166, 1173–74 (D.C. Cir. 1994) (same); Siderman de Blake v. Republic of Argentina, 965 F.2d 699, 714–19 (9th Cir. 1992) ("[W]e conclude that if violations of *jus cogens* committed outside the United States are to be exceptions to immunity, Congress must make them so"). Similar views were expressed in connection with suits against foreign heads of state and other foreign officials when those suits were evaluated (mistakenly) under the FSIA. *See infra* this chapter §§ V(D)(1) (head-of-state immunity), V(D)(2) (official immunity).

[523] Federal Republic of Germany v. Philipp, 141 S. Ct. 703 (2021).

[524] *Id.* at 712–13 (citing Jurisdictional Immunities of the State (Ger. v. It.), 2012 I.C.J. 99, 139 (Feb. 3)).

[525] *Id.* at 713–14; *see id.* at 714 (citing the limitation of the noncommercial torts exception to conduct in the United States and the limitations of the terrorism exception to certain human rights claims); *id.* (quoting conclusion in *Saudi Arabia v. Nelson* that the commercial activity exception did not include claims of illegal detention and torture in Saudi Arabia, "however monstrous such abuse undoubtedly may be") (quoting Saudi Arabia v. Nelson, 507 U.S. 349, 361 (1993)).

approach to international human rights law, even if warranted by the terms of the FSIA, may or may not keep pace with future developments in international law.

3. "Foreign States"

The threshold question under the FSIA is whether the entity invoking immunity is a "foreign state."[526] That term is not defined. Section 1603 indicates that this *includes* "a political subdivision of a foreign state" (also undefined) and an "agency or instrumentality of a foreign state" (which is defined), but nothing more comprehensive is attempted.[527]

Care in approaching this threshold question has its rewards. It is helpful first to identify the foreign state *stricto sensu*—evaluating statehood as it would be understood in diplomatic relations—not only because the state itself is eligible for immunity but also because a relationship to that entity is essential for establishing any *other* "foreign state" entity under the FSIA.[528] It is also helpful to understand the FSIA as distinguishing between (a) the foreign state *stricto sensu*, plus its "political subdivisions"; and (b) "agencies or instrumentalities." Because "agencies or instrumentalities" receive reduced immunity in some contexts,[529] it is sometimes important to know whether an entity falls within that category.[530]

a. *Foreign State* Stricto Sensu *and Political Subdivisions*

The foreign state *stricto sensu*—the threshold and, sometimes, ultimate question—is basically any "state" existing under international law other than the

---

[526] Courts encounter that threshold not just in assessing the basic question of immunity, see 28 U.S.C. § 1604 (2018), but also, for example, in assessing removal, see 28 U.S.C. § 1441(d)). As it typically arises, in considering subject-matter jurisdiction, the defendant must make a prima facie showing that it is a foreign sovereign, on which it retains the burden of persuasion. *See, e.g.*, Kelly v. Syria Shell Petroleum Dev. B.V., 213 F.3d 841, 847 (5th Cir. 2000). Not unreasonably, this burden-shifting approach may be necessary only "where the named defendant is not a sovereign state." Global Technology, Inc. v. Yubei (Xinxiang) Power Steering System Co., 807 F.3d 806, 811 (6th Cir. 2015).

[527] 28 U.S.C. § 1603(a). Because an "agency or instrumentality" is thus part of a "foreign state," one must take care in describing distinctions "between foreign states and their agencies and instrumentalities." *E.g.*, RESTATEMENT (FOURTH) § 452, rptrs. note 4.

[528] *Cf.* Ministry of Defense and Support for Armed Forces of Islamic Republic of Iran v. Elahi, 546 U.S. 450, 452 (2006) (per curiam) (noting Solicitor General's description of the issue "whether [Iran's Ministry of Defense] is simply a 'foreign state' (what the Ministry calls 'a foreign state *stricto sensu*') or whether the Ministry is an 'agency or instrumentality' of a foreign state (as the Ninth Circuit held)").

[529] *See* Dole Food Co. v. Patrickson, 538 U.S. 468, 471 (2003) (stating that "*[s]ome* of the Act's provisions also may be invoked by a corporate entity that is an 'instrumentality' of a foreign state as defined by the Act") (emphasis added). For example, only an agency or instrumentality may be liable for punitive damages. 28 U.S.C. § 1606. Moreover, the property of an agency or instrumentality of a foreign state is subject to attachment or execution under additional circumstances, "regardless of whether the property is or was involved in the act upon which the claim is based." *Id.* § 1610(b)(1)–(3).

[530] *See also* RESTATEMENT (FOURTH) § 452 cmt. d ("The distinction . . . is . . . significant in applying the exception to immunity based on property taken in violation of international law, and for determining the applicable rules for service of process, venue, execution of judgments, and punitive damages") (citing 28 U.S.C. §§ 1605(a)(3), 1606, 1608, 1610); STEWART, *supra* note 449, at 33.

United States. When statehood is in controversy, courts may apply criteria culled from customary international law,[531] or they can draw on relatively clear markers like membership in the United Nations.[532] Courts may also assess whether the executive branch has recognized the entity before the court as a "foreign state," such as through a formal statement or by commencing diplomatic relations, or they may solicit the Department of State's views.[533] The FSIA was designed to reduce executive branch control over immunity decisions,[534] but the case for deferring to executive branch positions on the antecedent question of whether a foreign sovereign is actually before the court is strong.[535] Because an entity's status as a "foreign state" under the FSIA is supposed to be determined at the time of suit,[536] attention to new circumstances, as to which the executive is likely

---

[531] Customary international law, reflected in the 1933 Montevideo Convention, requires a permanent population, defined territory, a government, and the capacity to enter into foreign relations. Convention on the Rights and Duties of States art. 1, Dec. 26, 1933, 49 Stat. 3097, 165 L.N.T.S. 19; *see also* RESTATEMENT (FOURTH) § 452 cmt. a. Courts have invoked versions of these criteria, usually attributed to a domestic source like the *Restatement*. *See, e.g.*, Samantar v. Yousuf, 560 U.S. 305, 314 (2010) (stating that "[t]he term 'foreign state' on its face indicates a body politic that governs a particular territory," relying on *Restatement (Second)* § 4, but noting broader scope of 28 U.S.C. § 1603); Ungar v. Palestine Liberation Organization, 402 F.3d 274, 283–84 (1st Cir. 2005) (noting Montevideo Convention, and concluding that the similar *Restatement (Third)* standard "controls the statehood question").

[532] While admission is a political decision, it does require a determination that an entity is a state, so it is a useful proxy. *See* U.N. Charter arts. 3–4. U.N. membership will also roughly correspond with judicial deference to the executive, since the United States, as a permanent member of the Security Council, would have had to recommended admission. *Id.* art. 4(2); Provisional Rules of Procedure of the Security Council, R. 60, U.N. Doc. S/96/Rev.7 (Dec. 21, 1982), https://perma.cc/F478-A7TA. Full membership is a better indicator than observer status or other, lesser rights of participation. STEWART, *supra* note 449, at 34.

[533] RESTATEMENT (FOURTH) § 452 cmt. a & rptrs. note 1; *see also* Chapter 3 § IV(A) (discussing recognition of foreign states). Courts may also be able to consult other materials, like Department of State publications that speak to statehood. *See, e.g.*, Eur. Community v. RJR Nabisco, 814 F. Supp. 2d 189, 196 (E.D.N.Y. 2011), *vacated & remanded on other grounds*, 764 F.3d 129 (2d Cir. 2014), *rev'd and remanded*, RJR Nabisco v. European Community, 579 U.S. 325 (2016). *But see, e.g.*, Kirschenbaum v. 650 Fifth Ave. & Related Props., 830 F.3d 107, 124–25 (2d Cir. 2016) (discounting reliance on definition of "Government of Iran" in an executive order for purposes of determining whether an Iranian entity was part of a "foreign state" under FSIA, in deference to international law criteria).

[534] As the *Restatement (Fourth)* recalled, the FSIA's legislative history "suggest[ed] that the [FSIA]'s application should be consistent with international law and that the views of the executive branch should not control the question of whether . . . a foreign state (or agency or instrumentality) is entitled to immunity." RESTATEMENT (FOURTH) § 452 rptrs. note 1 (citing H.R. REP. No. 94-1487, at 7 (1976), *reprinted in* 1976 U.S.C.C.A.N. 6604, 6605–06).

[535] One of the concerns about the Tate Letter regime, that foreign governments would apply pressure to produce a favorable submission by the executive, is also less persuasive—at least if one assumes that official U.S. policy regarding statehood is established.

[536] RESTATEMENT (FOURTH) § 451 rptrs. note 3 (citing Dole Food Co. v. Patrickson, 538 U.S. 468, 478 (2003)). *Dole Food* held that "instrumentality status [must] be determined at the time suit is filed," relying on 28 U.S.C. § 1603(b)(2), rather than addressing the foreign state *stricto sensu*. But courts are likely to take the same approach to ascertaining the existence of a "foreign state." *See* Republic of Austria v. Altmann, 541 U.S. 677, 696 (2004) (describing foreign sovereign immunity as "reflect[ing] current political realities and relationships," and affording "some *present* 'protection'") (emphasis in original; quoting *Dole Food*, 538 U.S. at 479); *cf.* O'Bryan v. Holy See, 556 F.3d 361, 372 n.3 (6th Cir. 2009) (holding that whether the relevant conduct "preceded the United States' recognition of the

to be informed, may be important.[537] Ordinarily the application of traditional criteria and executive branch submissions will coincide, allowing courts to cite available evidence without prioritizing it.[538]

Assuming a foreign state *stricto sensu* is identified, any part of it, including "a political subdivision," is entitled to immunity.[539] Political subdivisions include subnational governments like states, provinces, and cities.[540] The foreign state *stricto sensu* also includes government organs such as departments of defense (and branches of the armed services)[541] and ministries of foreign affairs (and embassies, consulates, and permanent missions),[542] among others.[543] It is usually easy to determine that subdivisions, departments, ministries, and the like are

Holy See as a foreign sovereign"—referring, in fact, to the beginning of diplomatic relations—was irrelevant, as immunity depended on current status).

[537] For example, courts have held that Palestine, the Palestinian Authority, and the PLO are not "foreign states" on a variety of grounds—but while noting international developments, including changing views by other sovereigns. *Compare, e.g., Klinghoffer*, 937 F.2d at 47–49 (holding that it was "quite clear" as of 1991 that the PLO did not qualify for statehood), *with* Ungar v. Palestine Liberation Organization, 402 F.3d 274, 288–92 (1st Cir. 2005) (distinguishing between claims for Palestinian statehood at various junctures). *See generally* Knox v. Palestine Liberation Organization, 306 F. Supp. 2d 424, 424–48 (S.D.N.Y. 2004).

[538] *See* RESTATEMENT (FOURTH) § 452 rptrs. note 1 (noting that "[i]n the cases to date, courts have acted consistently with the views of the executive branch and have not identified direct conflicts between the recognition of the entity by the executive branch and the criteria for statehood under international law"); *see, e.g., O'Bryan* 556 F.3d at 372–74 (concluding that, under any approach, the Holy See was a foreign state under the FSIA); *RJR Nabisco*, 814 F. Supp. 2d at 194–200 (noting, in considering FSIA definition while examining diversity jurisdiction, that the European Community was not a foreign state according either to international criteria or to the Department of State); *Knox*, 306 F. Supp. at 431–38 (concluding that there is no state of Palestine according to international criteria, including as indicated by the *Restatement (Third)*); *id.* at 446–48 (noting conflict with declared U.S. policy regarding Palestine).

[539] The inquiry typically should not be whether a political subdivision itself qualifies for statehood under international law; it should be enough that it is part of a polity that does. *See* Kirschenbaum v. 650 Fifth Ave. & Related Props., 830 F.3d 107, 125 (2d Cir. 2016).

[540] 28 U.S.C. § 1603(a) (2018); *see* H.R. REP. No. 94-1487, at 15 ("The term 'political subdivisions' includes all governmental units beneath the central government, including local governments"); RESTATEMENT (FOURTH) § 452, cmt. b & rptrs. note 2; *see, e.g.*, Big Sky Network Can., Ltd. v. Sichuan Provincial Gov't, 533 F.3d 1183, 1189 (10th Cir. 2008) (Sichuan Province and Qingyang District).

[541] *See, e.g.*, Wye Oak Tech., Inc. v. Republic of Iraq, 666 F.3d 205, 214 (4th Cir. 2011) (Iraq Ministry of Defense); Transaero, Inc. v. La Fuerza Aerea Boliviana, 30 F.3d 148, 153 (D.C. Cir. 1994) (Bolivian Air Force).

[542] Service of process frequently provokes immunity issues for embassies and consulates. 28 U.S.C. § 1608(a); *see, e.g.*, Nwoke v. Consulate of Nigeria, No. 17-cv-00140, 2018 WL 1071445 (N.D. Ill. Feb. 27, 2018) (Consulate of Nigeria in Chicago), *aff'd*, 729 F. App'x 478 (7th Cir. 2018). Permanent missions of foreign states to international organizations, such as those in New York to the United Nations, are also considered political subdivisions. *E.g.*, USAA Cas. Ins. Co. v. Permanent Mission of Republic of Namibia, 681 F.3d 103, 107 & n.18 (2d Cir. 2012) (Namibian mission to the United Nations); *see also* RESTATEMENT (FOURTH) § 452 rptrs. note 3 (supporting treatment of embassies, consulate, or foreign missions to international organizations as political subdivisions of foreign states, but critiquing decisions supposing that status to rest on their separate legal personality).

[543] *See, e.g.*, Magness v. Russian Federation, 247 F.3d 609, 613 n.7 (5th Cir. 2001) (Russian Ministry of Culture).

part of a "foreign state."[544] The trickier question, discussed later, is whether certain other organs or entities of the foreign state have a separate legal personality, so as to be classified as "agencies and instrumentalities" of a foreign state and subjected to a somewhat different set of rules.[545]

b. Agencies or Instrumentalities

"Agency or instrumentality of a foreign state" is the only foreign state entity defined by the FSIA, and the legislative history provides examples to illustrate the category's intended breadth.[546] Nonetheless, the category is the most litigated aspect of what constitutes a "foreign state." The statute defines an "agency of instrumentality of a foreign state" as a (1) "separate legal person, corporate or otherwise"; (2) "which is an organ of a foreign state or political subdivision thereof, or a majority of whose shares or other ownership interest is owned by a foreign state or political subdivision thereof"; and (3) which is not a U.S. citizen or created under the laws of any third country.[547] All three criteria apply as of the time suit is filed, not at the time of the relevant conduct.[548]

This definition, as elaborated by courts, serves to differentiate agencies or instrumentalities from the foreign state *stricto sensu*, and also from nongovernmental entities. Moreover, the definition helps to differentiate as *among* agencies and instrumentalities, so as to respect differences in form (and financial responsibility) while also respecting different degrees of immunity according to U.S. law.[549] The definition has little connection with international law, and it is

---

[544] Given that the FSIA does not govern official immunity, see *infra* this chapter text accompanying notes 803–807, political subdivisions are normally understood to be limited to entities not persons. One decision, however, held that the Minister of Finance of Trinidad and Tobago qualified as a political subdivision of a foreign state, and that an airline of which the minister was the majority owner therefore qualified as an agency or instrumentality. Singh *ex rel.* Singh v. Caribbean Airlines, Ltd., 798 F.3d 1355, 1358–59 (11th Cir. 2015).

[545] The significance of this distinction between a foreign state (and its political subdivisions) and the state's agencies and instrumentalities was recognized, for example, in *Ministry of Def. and Support for Armed Forces of Islamic Republic of Iraq v. Elahi*, 546 U.S. 450 (2006) (per curiam), which vacated a decision concerning the Iraqi Ministry of Defense in part on the hypothesis that the lower court might have "erroneously presumed that there was no relevant distinction between a foreign state and its agencies or instrumentalities." *Id.* at 453.

[546] The House Report indicates that the entities "could assume a variety of forms, including a state trading corporation, a mining enterprise, a transport organization such as a shipping line or airline, a steel company, a central bank, an export association, a governmental·procurement agency or a department or ministry which acts and is suable in its own name." H.R. REP. NO. 94-1487, at 15–16 (1976), *reprinted in* 1976 U.S.C.C.A.N. 6604, 6614.

[547] 28 U.S.C. § 1603.

[548] Dole Food Co. v. Patrickson, 538 U.S. 468, 478–80 (2003) (applying timing analysis in concluding that, even if an entity was an agency or instrumentality by virtue of its ownership by Israel, "[a]ny relationship recognized under the FSIA . . . had been severed before suit was commenced").

[549] STEWART, *supra* note 449, at 36–44. Some of these themes were suggested in *First National City Bank v. Banco Para El Comercio Exterior de Cuba*, 462 U.S. 611, 623–34 (1983) [hereinafter *Bancec*], which noted related FSIA policies. *See, e.g., id.* at 627–28 (discussing 28 U.S.C. § 1610(b), preventing execution against the property of one agency to satisfy the judgment against another).

understood to afford greater immunity before U.S. courts for foreign entities than is required of the United States.[550]

The first two criteria do the lion's share of the work.[551] The first (separate legal personality) requires that the entity be legally distinguishable from the rest of the foreign state.[552] It would include, for example, a trading enterprise established by a state to stabilize income for domestic producers in a particular commodity sector. "[D]uly created instrumentalities of a foreign state" are "accorded a presumption of independent status," rebuttable when the instrumentality is acting as the agent (or alter ego) of the foreign state or when a fraud or injustice would result.[553] When considering whether the entity is acting as an alter ego, courts have used various tests to determine whether the foreign state is exercising "day-to-day control or a high level of domination" over the entity so as to defeat any separate personality. The fraud-or-injustice inquiry focuses on abuse of the independent form, such as manipulating assets, rather than on conduct that is part of the underlying complaint.[554]

The second criterion, involving attribution to the foreign state, requires that an agency or instrumentality either be majority-owned by the foreign state or be an organ of it.[555] Majority ownership is often at issue in litigation against state-owned corporations and commercial banks;[556] it requires formal ownership rather than control, and it must also be direct, so the statute is not satisfied if a state owns the relevant entity through another agency or instrumentality.[557]

---

[550] See, e.g., RESTATEMENT (FOURTH) § 452 rptrs. note 12.

[551] The third criterion—excluding from an "agency or instrumentality of a foreign state" any entities that are U.S. citizens or created under the laws of third countries—tends to exclude entities that are not really part of that foreign state in any conventional sense. 28 U.S.C. § 1603(b)(3). This criterion has not posed many issues. See STEWART, supra note 449, at 44.

[552] 28 U.S.C. § 1603(b)(1); see RESTATEMENT (FOURTH) § 452 cmt. d & rptrs. note 3.

[553] Bancec, 462 U.S. at 627, 629. Bancec addressed a different question—when, as a matter of substantive law, particular conduct by one entity may be attributed to another—and the Supreme Court's reasoning is not entirely suitable for jurisdictional inquiries under the FSIA. Nonetheless, the Bancec presumption has been, and is, applied in the FSIA context. RESTATEMENT (FOURTH) § 452 rptrs. note 7; e.g., Doe v. Holy See, 557 F.3d 1066, 1077–80 (9th Cir. 2009) (applying Bancec approach to assess whether the actions of a corporation may be attributed to a state for purposes of establishing FSIA jurisdiction over the latter); see also RESTATEMENT (FOURTH) § 452 rptrs. note 7 (noting application to due process issues). Bancec and other cases have not provided great insight as to what the FSIA's term "duly created" means, nor the law by which it is to be determined. The better view is that while the FSIA provides the framework for examining legal personality, it necessarily draws on the laws of the foreign state. Id. § 452 rptrs. note 11. But see Wye Oak Tech., Inc. v. Republic of Iraq, 666 F.3d 205, 212–14 (4th Cir. 2011) (emphasizing application of FSIA standards, and marginalizing invocation of Iraqi law); Compagnie Noga D'Importation et D'Exportation, S.A. v. Russian Federation, 361 F.3d 676, 684–85 (2d Cir. 2004) (declining to resolve whether federal common law, public international law, or Russian law determined whether Russian government was separate from Russian Federation).

[554] RESTATEMENT (FOURTH) § 452 rptrs. notes 8–9 (discussing case law).

[555] The agency or instrumentality may also be an organ of a political subdivision, or majority owned by it. 28 U.S.C. § 1603(b)(2).

[556] See Kelly v. Syria Shell Petroleum Dev. B.V., 213 F.3d 841, 846 (5th Cir. 2000).

[557] Dole Food Co. v. Patrickson, 538 U.S. 468, 477 (2003) ("A corporation is an instrumentality of a foreign state under the FSIA only if the foreign state itself owns a majority of the corporation's shares"); see also id. at 474–77. A different result may obtain if the intermediary is a political

The question of whether an entity is an "organ" is more elusive. The idea was to capture public, commercial entities that had a degree of autonomy and a relationship with the foreign state that took a different form than conventional corporate ownership.[558] Lower courts have developed various multifactor tests,[559] but the gist is to determine whether a foreign state controls an entity that also performs a public function.[560] The distinction between an organ that is part of the foreign state *stricto sensu* and an organ of a state that, due to being a separate legal person, is an agency or instrumentality, can be challenging. The prevailing approach assesses whether a separate entity's "core functions" are governmental (in which case it is part of the foreign state *stricto sensu*) or commercial (in which case it may be an agency or instrumentality).[561] Courts sometimes ask whether the entity is "integral" to the state, but this may be understood as asking whether it is predominantly governmental.[562] The core function test yields some rules of

subdivision of the foreign state, since the statute expressly provides that agencies or instrumentalities of political subdivisions are entitled to immunity. *See, e.g.,* Singh *ex rel.* Singh v. Caribbean Airlines, Ltd., 798 F.3d 1355, 1358–59 (11th Cir. 2015) (distinguishing *Dole*). More exotically, courts have had to address the possibility of collective pooling, in which foreign states jointly own the majority of an entity's shares—even though no one of them owns more than half—and whether that ownership qualifies the entity as an agency or instrumentality. *See* European Cmty. v. RJR Nabisco, Inc., 764 F.3d 129, 147 (2d Cir. 2014) (noting share-pooling precedents), *rev'd on other grounds*, 579 U.S. 325 (2016); RESTATEMENT (FOURTH) § 452 rptrs. note 6 (reviewing cases).

[558] STEWART, *supra* note 449, at 41.

[559] *See, e.g., Kelly,* 213 F.3d at 847 (agreeing with other decisions that "there is no 'clear test' for determining agency or instrumentality status under the § 1603(b)(2) 'organ' prong") (citations omitted); RESTATEMENT (FOURTH) § 452 rptrs. note 5 (citing the five-factor test in *Kelly* as "the most influential and the most widely adopted"); *see also* EOTT Energy Operating Ltd. Partnership v. Winterthur Swiss Ins. Co., 257 F.3d 992, 997 (9th Cir. 2001) (detailing similar six-factor test); USX Corp. v. Adriatic Ins. Co., 345 F.3d 190, 209 (3d Cir. 2003) (seven-factor test).

[560] RESTATEMENT (FOURTH) § 452 cmt. e (indicating that "all [judicial tests] consider whether the foreign state created the entity for a public purpose and other circumstances around its creation; the degree of supervision or control of the entity by the foreign state; whether the foreign state requires the entity to hire public employees and pays their salaries; the entity's obligations and privileges under the foreign state's law; and whether the entity engages in public (governmental) activity on behalf of the foreign state"). As with majority ownership, it may be possible for an organ to be controlled by multiple states. *RJR Nabisco, Inc.,* 764 F.3d at 147 (concluding that the European Community qualifies as an "organ" under the FSIA, therefore satisfying 28 U.S.C. § 1332(a)(4) and diversity jurisdiction).

[561] RESTATEMENT (FOURTH) § 452 cmt. d & rptrs. note 4. This approach is usually traced to the D.C. Circuit decision in *Transaero, Inc. v. La Fuerza Aerea Boliviana,* 30 F.3d 148, 151 (D.C. Cir. 1994); *see also* Singh *ex rel.* Singh v. Caribbean Airlines, Ltd., 798 F.3d 1355, 1358–59 (11th Cir. 2015); Wye Oak Tech., Inc. v. Republic of Iraq, 666 F.3d 205, 214 (4th Cir. 2011); Ministry of Def. & Support for the Armed Forces of the Islamic Republic of Iran v. Cubic Def. Sys., Inc., 495 F.3d 1024, 1035 (9th Cir. 2007), *rev'd on other grounds sub nom.* Ministry of Def. & Support for the Armed Forces of the Islamic Republic of Iran v. Elahi, 556 U.S. 366 (2009); Garb v. Republic of Poland, 440 F.3d 579, 590–94 (2d Cir. 2006); Magness v. Russian Federation, 247 F.3d 609, 613 n.7 (5th Cir. 2001).

[562] *See, e.g., Transaero,* 30 F.3d at 151 (asking whether an entity "is an integral part of a foreign state's political structure" or instead "an entity whose structure and function is predominantly commercial") (quoting Segni v. Commercial Office of Spain, 650 F. Supp. 1040, 1041–42 (N.D. Ill. 1988)). Some cases do emphasize the centrality or significance of a subdivision. *See, e.g.,* USAA Cas. Ins. Co. v. Permanent Mission of Republic of Namibia, 681 F.3d 103, 107 (2d Cir. 2012) (describing Namibian permanent mission as the "embodiment" of a foreign state); Wultz v. Islamic Republic of Iran, 864

thumb—for example, a finance ministry is likely part of the foreign state *stricto sensu*, whereas central banks are usually agencies or instrumentalities—but even these may be contested.[563] It may be wise for courts to avoid resolving an entity's precise status as a "foreign state" *stricto sensu* or as an "agency or instrumentality" when the case involves FSIA provisions for which the distinction is irrelevant.[564]

4. Immunity from Suit

The FSIA confers immunity from suit on the foreign state, broadly conceived, unless the plaintiff establishes[565]—by presenting more than a nonfrivolous claim, even at the jurisdictional stage[566]—that one of the statute's exceptions applies.[567] Unsurprisingly, whether one of the exceptions applies, a question of federal law,[568] is often at the core of FSIA litigation. True to the restrictive approach, acts

F. Supp. 2d 24, 32 (D.D.C. 2012) (describing Iranian and Syrian entities as "essential parts of the political structure"). But these should not be understood to suggest a prerequisite, and less essential entities have been treated as subdivisions and "foreign states." *See supra* this chapter text accompanying notes 539–540.

[563] Central banks are cited as an example of an agency or instrumentality in the legislative history, see *supra* this chapter note 546 (quoting H.R. Rep. No. 94-1487), and the case law has aligned with that position. *See* Davoyan v. Republic of Turkey, No. CV 10-05636, 2010 WL 11507885 (C.D. Cal. Dec. 7, 2010) (reviewing cases). Finance ministries, by contrast, may be treated as political subdivisions. *See Garb*, 440 F.3d at 594–98 (treating Ministry of the Treasury of Poland was a political subdivision, not an agency or instrumentality); *see also* Chettri v. Nepal Rastra Bank, 834 F.3d 50, 54–55 (2d Cir. 2016) (noting common ground that while Nepal's Department of Revenue Investigation, part of its Ministry of Finance, was a political subdivision, bank acting as "Nepal's financial agent" was an agency or instrumentality). *But see Garb*, 440 F.3d at 598–604 (Straub, J., dissenting) (concluding that Poland's Ministry of Treasury was better regarded as an agency or instrumentality).

[564] The same approach may be adopted even for clearer cases. *See, e.g.,* CapitalKeys, LLC v. Democratic Republic of Congo, 278 F. Supp. 3d 265, 282 (D.D.C. 2017) (suggesting that a central bank might be characterized as an agency or instrumentality or, arguably, as the mere alter ego of the foreign state, before applying waiver and commercial activity exceptions). In other contexts the distinctions may be completely irrelevant. *See, e.g.,* Blocking Property of the Government of Iran and Iranian Financial Institutions, Exec. Order No. 13599, 3 C.F.R. 13599, § 7(d) (2013) (defining "Government of Iran" as "the Government of Iran, any political subdivision, agency, or instrumentality thereof, including the Central Bank of Iran").

[565] The plaintiff bears the burden of making a showing that an exception applies, and if that burden is satisfied, the foreign sovereign must persuade the court that it does not. *See, e.g.,* Petersen Energía Inversora S.A.U. v. Argentine Republic and YPF S.A., 895 F.3d 194, 204 (2d Cir. 2018).

[566] In Bolivarian Republic of Venezuela v. Helmerich & Payne Intern. Drilling Co., 137 S. Ct. 1312 (2017), the Supreme Court held (in the context of the expropriation exception, 28 U.S.C. § 1605(a)(3)) that a plaintiff "must make out a legally valid claim that a certain kind of right is at issue (property rights) and that the relevant property was taken in a certain way (in violation of international law)," and that more than a non-frivolous claim or "a good argument to that effect" was needed. *Id.* at 1316. That approach seems applicable to other FSIA exceptions, but it may be challenging to accomplish at the jurisdictional stage without resolving the merits. *See* Restatement (Fourth) § 455 rptrs. note 5.

[567] 28 U.S.C. § 1605(a)(1)–(6) (waiver, commercial activity, expropriations, immovable property, noncommercial torts, and arbitral award exceptions); *id.* § 1605(b)–(d) (exceptions for maritime liens and preferred mortgages); *id.* § 1605A (exception for state-sponsored terrorism); *id.* § 1607 (exception for counterclaims).

[568] Aquamar, S.A. v. Del Monte Fresh Produce N.A., Inc., 179 F.3d 1279, 1293–94 & n.36 (11th Cir. 1999) (citing cases). The terrorism-related exceptions, distinctly, draw on "generalized principles of tort law"—neither federal common law nor the forum state's law—for aspects of their causes of

that are *jure gestionis* account for some exceptions, but other exceptions target particular types of state conduct, like torts or acts relating to international arbitration, that were of concern to the United States in 1976 or (if the exception arose through an amendment) at a later time. Most of these exceptions are defined in a way consistent with, but not determined by, immunity rules of international law.[569] A few result from political decisions that are more difficult to associate with international law, such as the exception for certain acts of state-sponsored terrorism.[570]

a. Waiver (and Related Exceptions)

Section 1605(a)(1) denies immunity to a foreign state before U.S. courts in cases where that state has waived immunity, "either explicitly or by implication."[571] This is wholly consistent with ideas of sovereign consent articulated in *The Schooner Exchange*.[572] A foreign state may explicitly renounce immunity from jurisdiction in U.S. courts in an international agreement or a contract. For example, friendship, commerce, and navigation (FCN) may expressly waive the immunity of state-related entities or their property;[573] they will not be read to do so indirectly.[574] Contractual waivers are typically deemed sufficiently unambiguous when a forum-selection clause provides that disputes are to be resolved in U.S. courts.[575]

action. Stansell v. Republic of Cuba, 217 F. Supp. 3d 320, 341 (D.D.C. 2016); *see also* this chapter text accompanying notes 671–678 (discussing causes of action created for terrorism-related exceptions).

[569] For example, the United Nations Convention on Jurisdictional Immunities of States and Their Property art. 10, G.A. Res. 59/38, annex (Dec. 2, 2004), which the United States has not ratified and which is not yet in force, identifies the commercial transactions that lack immunity, but leaves nexus questions to be resolved by the forum state. *See* RESTATEMENT (FOURTH) § 454 rptrs. note 10.

[570] *Cf.* STEWART, *supra* note 449, at 47 (highlighting the exceptions for waiver, commercial activity, expropriations, noncommercial torts, and enforcement of arbitral awards—along with the terrorism-related exceptions—as the most frequently invoked).

[571] 28 U.S.C. § 1605(a)(1).

[572] *See supra* this chapter text accompanying notes 454–464.

[573] RESTATEMENT (FOURTH) § 453 rptrs. note 2 (providing examples).

[574] The treaty terms must "expressly conflict[t]" with the FSIA. Argentine Republic v. Amerada Hess Shipping Corp., 488 U.S. 428, 443 (1989) (internal quotation marks omitted; alteration in original); *see* Williams v. National Gallery of Art, London, No. 16-CV-6978, 2017 WL 4221084 (S.D.N.Y. Sept. 21, 2017) (reviewing case law). Agreements will also be construed as concerning only the entities addressed. RESTATEMENT (FOURTH) § 453 rptrs. note 2 (discussing case law interpreting the Treaty of Amity, Economic Relations, and Consular Rights, Treaty of Amity, Economic Relations, and Consular Rights, U.S.-Iran, Aug. 15, 1955, 8 U.S.T. 899, 284 U.N.T.S. 93).

[575] A provision submitting disputes to a particular court, not in the United States, should not suffice. *Compare, e.g.*, GDG Acquisitions LLC v. Government of Belize, 849 F.3d 1299, 1303, 1306 (11th Cir. 2017) (Florida-related provisions, including forum-selection clause), *with* CCM Pension-A, L.L.C. v. Republic of Argentina, No. 16-cv-1650 (TPG), 2016 WL 4154892 (S.D.N.Y. Aug. 2, 2016) (Italian bonds providing for application of Italian law, and submission to jurisdiction in courts of Milan, do not effectuate FSIA waiver), *and* SI Group Consort Ltd. v. Ukraine, Ivano-Frankivsk State Admin., No. 15 CV 3047-LTS, 2017 WL 398400 (S.D.N.Y. Jan. 30, 2017) (Ukraine-related provisions).

Waivers by implication are less straightforward. A foreign state must manifest a "clear and unambiguous" intent to waive,[576] even if that is hard to square with doing so implicitly. Three examples cited by the House Judiciary Committee report during the FSIA's enactment—namely, when foreign states "agreed to arbitration in another country," "agreed that the law of a particular country should govern a contract," or "filed a responsive pleading in an action without raising the defense of sovereign immunity"—have been taken as canon.[577] As to the first example, the effect of agreements to arbitrate is now largely addressed by a subsequently enacted section.[578] The second example, implying waiver from a contractual choice-of-law provision indicating that U.S. law governs, seems to rest on a faulty premise, as foreign courts can also apply U.S. law.[579] The third example, in which a foreign state is deemed to have waived (really, forfeited) immunity during litigation if it failed to raise the defense in its first responsive pleading,[580] should be understood to complement the more basic situation in which a foreign state, by initiating an action in U.S. court, implicitly waives its immunity for matters with the scope of the action.[581] Attempting to withdraw either an explicit or an implicit waiver is fruitless unless it is in keeping with the waiver's original terms.[582]

---

[576] RESTATEMENT (FOURTH) § 453 cmt. a; see, e.g., Architectural Ingenieria Siglo XXI, LLC v. Dominican Republic, 788 F.3d 1329, 1338 (11th Cir. 2015).

[577] H.R. REP. NO. 94-1487, at 18 (1976), reprinted in 1976 U.S.C.C.A.N. 6604, 6617; see RESTATEMENT (FOURTH) § 453 rptrs. note 1; see also id. § 453 cmts. a–b (suggesting that the distinction between explicit and implicit waivers tracks one between waivers in writing and waivers by conduct). Case law focuses on these three categories, without categorically shutting the door on others. See, e.g., Calzadilla v. Banco Latino Internacional, 413 F.3d 1285, 1287–88 (11th Cir. 2005); In re Republic of the Philippines, 309 F.3d 1143, 1151 (9th Cir. 2002); see also Af-Cap, Inc. v. Republic of Congo, 462 F.3d 417, 426–27 (5th Cir. 2006) (stating that "[i]f this Court wanted to go outside of the three ordinary circumstances, it must still 'narrowly construe' the implicit waiver clause") (citations omitted).

[578] 28 U.S.C. § 1605(a)(6) (2018); see RESTATEMENT (FOURTH) § 453 rptrs. note 4; for discussion, see infra this chapter text accompanying notes 586–591.

[579] Cf. RESTATEMENT (FOURTH) § 453 rptrs. note 3 (suggesting that whether intent to waive can be inferred simply from a contract's U.S. choice-of-law provision "remains unclear"). Regardless, the legislative history may be influential. See Transamerican Steamship Corp. v. Somali Democratic Republic, 767 F.2d 998, 1004–07 (D.C. Cir. 1985) (Wald, J., concurring) (suggesting that Congress may have misunderstood preexisting case law, but that its perception should nonetheless govern, and that it is appropriate for U.S. courts to assume a lead role); accord Eckert Int'l v. Gov't of the Sovereign Democratic Republic of Fiji, 32 F.3d 77 (4th Cir. 1994). But see Pere ex rel. Pere v. Nuovo Pignone, Inc., 150 F.3d 477, 482 (5th Cir. 1998) (suggesting that context did not support any implied intent to waive, notwithstanding choice-of-law clause).

[580] RESTATEMENT (FOURTH) § 453(3) & cmt. b & rptrs. note 5. Failure to raise immunity in a preliminary motion is not fatal, but a pleading like an answer is "the point of no return." Canadian Overseas Ores Ltd. v. Compania de Acero del Pacifico S.A., 727 F.2d 274, 277 (2d Cir. 1984). Like other forms of implied waiver, waiver from a failure to invoke is to be construed narrowly. See Drexel Burnham Lambert Grp. v. Committee of Receivers for A.W. Galadari, 12 F.3d 317, 325–28 (2d Cir. 1993) (explaining that immunity need not be deemed waived, even if absent from an answer, if it was raised beforehand).

[581] RESTATEMENT (FOURTH) § 453 rptrs. note 5; STEWART, supra note 449, at 50.

[582] 28 U.S.C. § 1605(a)(1); RESTATEMENT (FOURTH) § 453(5).

Three other exceptions operate somewhat like waiver. Section 1604, sometimes called the "treaty exception to immunity," provides that immunity from jurisdiction is "[s]ubject to existing international agreements to which the United States is a party at the time of [the FSIA's] enactment."[583] This functions more like a conflicts provision. A preexisting agreement may diminish immunity otherwise conferred by the FSIA, much as would a post-enactment agreement under the waiver exception,[584] but it may also preserve greater immunity than the FSIA would otherwise afford.[585]

The arbitration exception (§ 1605(a)(6)), added in 1988, incorporated a judicial practice of treating a foreign state's agreement to arbitrate as waiving its immunity against actions either to enforce the agreement or to confirm an award made pursuant to the agreement.[586] This exception applies when: (1) the subject matter is capable of settlement by arbitration under U.S. law and the place of arbitration is in the United States; (2) the basis for the arbitration is an international agreement in force for the United States;[587] or (3) the underlying claim

---

[583] 28 U.S.C. § 1604; cf. RESTATEMENT (FOURTH) § 455, rptrs. note 13 (discussing application of the treaty exception in the context of expropriation claims).

[584] See RESTATEMENT (FOURTH) § 453, rptrs. note 2. Not unlike waiver, an express conflict between the international agreement and immunity under the FSIA is required. Argentine Republic v. Amerada Hess Shipping Corp., 488 U.S. 428, 441–43 (1989) (citing H.R. REP. NO. 94-1487, at 17 (1976), reprinted in 1976 U.S.C.C.A.N. 6604, 6616). A recent district court case applying the treaty exception not only had to determine whether the sovereign defendant, clearly a "foreign state" for FSIA purposes, was an entity addressed by the FCN treaty between the United States and Ireland, but also whether the commercial activities that triggered the loss of immunity under the treaty were satisfied (assuming in the first place they were meaningfully distinct from those under the FSIA). Shelbourne N. Water St. Corp. v. Nat'l Asset Mgmt. Agency, 374 F. Supp. 3d 712, 725–26 (N.D. Ill. 2019).

[585] Thus, courts have reviewed (but generally rejected) claims that an agreement establishing a claims mechanism effectively establishes the exclusive means of obtaining redress against a foreign state. See, e.g., Simon v. Republic of Hungary, 812 F.3d 127, 135–36 (D.C. Cir. 2016) (citing Moore v. United Kingdom, 384 F.3d 1079, 1084–85 (9th Cir. 2004), and Abelesz v. Magyar Nemzeti Bank, 692 F.3d 661, 669 (7th Cir. 2012)). In an unpublished opinion, the D.C. Circuit considered arguendo whether Article 2(1) of the U.N. Charter offered greater immunity than the then existing terrorist exception, 28 U.S.C. § 1605(a)(7), and appeared to regard as a precondition that such a treaty would have to be self-executing. Wyatt v. Syrian Arab Republic, 266 F. App'x 1, 2 (D.C. Cir. 2008). Section 1604 itself does not seem to require that, and it is better read without any such qualification, for sake of consistency with U.S. treaty obligations.

[586] 28 U.S.C. § 1605(a)(6); see An Act to Implement the Inter-American Convention on International Commercial Arbitration, Pub. L. 100-669, § 2, 102 Stat 3969 (1988); see also RESTATEMENT (FOURTH) § 453 rptrs. notes 1–2 & § 458 cmt. a; RESTATEMENT (THIRD) OF U.S. L. OF INT'L COM. AND INV.-STATE ARB. §§ 2.25, 4.26 (AM. LAW INST., Proposed Final Draft, Apr. 24, 2019); STEWART, supra note 449, at 74–75.

[587] These conventions include the Convention on the Recognition and Enforcement of Foreign Arbitral Awards, June 10, 1958, 21 U.S.T. 2517, 330 U.N.T.S. 38 (New York Convention); the Inter-American Convention on International Commercial Arbitration, Jan. 30, 1975, 14 I.L.M. 336, 1438 U.N.T.S. 245 (Panama Convention); and the Convention on the Settlement of Investment Disputes between States and Nationals of Other States, Mar. 18, 1965, 4 I.L.M. 532, 575 U.N.T.S. 159 (ICSID Convention); as well as bilateral investment treaties. See RESTATEMENT (FOURTH) § 453 rptrs. notes 3–6. The application of the exception to ICSID is especially complex and unresolved in important respects. See RESTATEMENT (FOURTH) § 458 rptrs. note 5; RESTATEMENT (THIRD) OF U.S. L. OF INT'L COM. AND INV.-STATE ARB., supra note 586, §§ 5.4–5.6.

is one for which a FSIA exception would have been available but for the arbitration.[588] Perhaps unexpectedly, these terms enable jurisdiction even when the United States is not the place chosen for arbitration, and even when the foreign state subject to suit is not itself a party to any arbitration convention that would waive its immunity.[589] The exception applies to a variety of actions,[590] but does not allow relitigating the issue of arbitrability under international law or the substantive conclusions in arbitral awards.[591]

Finally, the counterclaim exception (§ 1607) provides that if a foreign state has initiated or intervened in U.S. proceedings, it cannot turn around and invoke immunity against counterclaims.[592] This exception is akin to implied waiver, though the loss of immunity may be wholly unintentional.[593] Regardless, the equitable argument for removing immunity from a foreign state that has deliberately availed itself of a U.S. court is strong.

b. Commercial Activity Exception

The commercial activity exception (28 U.S.C. § 1605(a)(2)) denies immunity to a foreign state before U.S. courts with respect to actions that are based on that state's commercial activities.[594] Unsurprisingly, given that the prevalence of such activities drove the U.S. shift to the restrictive approach to immunity, this is the most litigated FSIA exception.[595]

---

[588] This third component adverts to exceptions provided by other provisions in § 1605 or § 1607 (the counterclaim exception) but does not advert to the terrorism-related exceptions (§§ 1605A and 1605B), which had not been adopted when the arbitration exception was established. Terrorism-related arbitration is specifically contemplated in § 1605A(a)(2)(A)(iii)), and might qualify according to the waiver exception.

[589] The latter scenario may transpire if a foreign state—not itself party to a relevant convention—consents to arbitration in a third state that happens to be a party to such a convention. Moreover, the arbitration exception can apply even when the defendant state agreed to arbitrate before the FSIA's arbitration exception was adopted. Creighton Ltd. v. Gov't of State of Qatar, 181 F.3d 118, 123–24 (D.C. Cir. 1999) (New York Convention). By contrast, the waiver exception would not be applicable if the foreign state is not itself a party to the relevant convention; if it is a party, waiver may be available as an alternative ground. *Compare id.* at 122–23, *with* Seetransport Wiking Trader Schiffahrtsgesellschaft MBH & Co., Kommanditgesellschaft v. Navimpex Centrala Navala, 989 F.2d 572, 577–79 (2d Cir. 1993)).

[590] The statute specifically mentions actions to "enforce" an agreement to arbitrate or to "confirm" an award made. 28 U.S.C. § 1605(a)(6). Actions to "enforce" an award appear to be covered by analogy, as may other types of arbitration-related actions. RESTATEMENT (THIRD) OF U.S. L. OF INT'L COM. AND INV.-STATE ARB., *supra* note 586, § 4.26 rptrs. notes (a)(i).

[591] *See, e.g.,* Chevron Corp. v. Republic of Ecuador, 949 F. Supp. 2d 57, 63 (D.D.C. 2013).

[592] 28 U.S.C. § 1607.

[593] *See* RESTATEMENT (FOURTH) § 453(2), cmt. c & rptrs. note 6 (addressing counterclaims separately, but also describing them as an implied waiver of immunity).

[594] 28 U.S.C. § 1605(2).

[595] *See* H.R. REP. No. 94-1487, at 18 (1976), *reprinted in* 1976 U.S.C.C.A.N. 6604, 6617 (describing commercial activities as "probably the most important instance in which foreign states are denied immunity"). Another group of exceptions concerns a subclass of commercial activities: suits to enforce a maritime lien against a foreign state's vessel or cargo, if the "maritime lien is based upon a commercial activity of the foreign state." 28 U.S.C. § 1605(b). For discussion, see RESTATEMENT (FOURTH) § 459; DELLAPENNA, *supra* note 449, at 341–49.

The commercial activity exception provides that an action may proceed "based upon" circumstances falling into one of three types, described by separate clauses in the statute: (1) "a commercial activity carried on in the United States by the foreign state"; (2) "an act performed in the United States in connection with a commercial activity of the foreign state elsewhere"; or (3) "an act outside the territory of the United States in connection with a commercial activity of the foreign state elsewhere" where "that act causes a direct effect in the United States."[596] Like other FSIA exceptions, each clause hinges on a limited type of conduct by foreign sovereigns (here, a "commercial activity"), a relationship between that conduct and the action upon which the claim rests (here, "based upon"), and some kind of nexus (or "connection") with the United States.

The core concept of a "commercial activity" is only incompletely defined in the statute.[597] The FSIA does make clear that the activity may be transitory (not solely "a regular course of commercial conduct") and that whether it is "commercial" is determined by "the nature of the course of conduct or particular transaction or act, rather than by reference to its purpose."[598] The latter was intended to thwart attempts by foreign states to argue that activities could not be commercial if they were involved the pursuit of public ends.[599] Thus, a foreign state's purchase of boots for its army is a commercial activity; because the nature of purchasing boots is commercial, the fact that it is designed to facilitate national defense is irrelevant.[600] Nevertheless, arguments related to the "purpose" of the activity have persisted. Most prominently, in *Republic of Argentina v. Weltover*, Argentina claimed (unsuccessfully) that its issuance of bonds, to refinance its debt, distinguished it from a private debtor, including because its restructuring was designed to address a national economic crisis. The Court demurred, noting that private actors are capable of issuing bonds and resisting Argentina's attempt to distinguish its transaction's "context."[601] It is irrelevant, therefore, whether a foreign state had a profit motive—although the fact that an activity is ordinarily

---

[596] 28 U.S.C. § 1605(a)(2); *see also id.* § 1603(d)–(e).

[597] *See* Republic of Argentina v. Weltover, Inc., 504 U.S. 607, 612 (1992) (noting that statutory definition "leaves the critical term 'commercial' largely undefined").

[598] 28 U.S.C. § 1603(d). This definition is effectively modified elsewhere, for purposes outside the commercial activity exception. *See infra* this chapter text accompanying notes 636–638 (discussing Foreign Cultural Exchange Jurisdictional Immunity Clarification Act and 28 U.S.C. § 1605(h)).

[599] H.R. Rep. No. 94-1487, at 16, *reprinted in* 1976 U.S.C.C.A.N. 6604, 6615 ("As the definition indicates, the fact that goods or services to be procured through a contract are to be used for a public purpose is irrelevant; it is the essentially commercial nature of an activity or transaction that is critical.").

[600] *See Weltover*, 504 U.S. at 614–15.

[601] *Weltover*, 504 U.S. at 614–17; *see also id.* at 616 (rejecting Argentina's attempted distinction on the basis of its assertion that it did not receive fair market value); *cf.* Saudi Arabia v. Nelson, 507 U.S. 349, 361 (1993) (describing distinguishing "purpose" from "nature" as difficult, but required by the statute).

one pursued for profit may nonetheless be relevant in determining whether it is commercial.[602]

The basic question is whether a foreign state is acting "not as regulator of a market, but in the manner of a private player within it,"[603] an approach that reflects the restrictive theory's distinction between *acta jure imperii* and *acta jure gestionis*.[604] In *Saudi Arabia v. Nelson*, the Court held that Saudi Arabia's alleged wrongful arrest, imprisonment, and torture of an employee in Saudi Arabia fell outside the exception because such exercises of police power were "peculiarly sovereign in nature" (notwithstanding that, as Justice White stressed, a private employer could use private security personnel in much the same way).[605] Case law has also wrestled with whether an activity's criminal nature prevents it from being deemed commercial.[606] Cases based on commercial activities that occur in the United States tend toward more conventional, and predictable, fact patterns than when the commercial activity takes place abroad.[607]

---

[602] H.R. Rep. No. 94-1487, at 16, *reprinted in* 1976 U.S.C.C.A.N. 6604, 6615 ("Certainly, if an activity is customarily carried on for profit, its commercial nature could readily be assumed.").

[603] *Weltover*, 504 U.S. at 614. Another way of formulating the test is whether the foreign state's acts "are the type of actions by which a private party engages" in commerce. *Id.*

[604] *Nelson*, 507 U.S. at 359–60.

[605] *Compare id.* at 360–63, *and id.* at 362 ("Exercise of the powers of police and penal officers is not the sort of action by which private parties can engage in commerce."), *with id.* at 365–70 (White, J., concurring in judgment) (noting private employer parallels).

[606] There have been suggestions that illegality might be irrelevant to commercial character, see Cicippio v. Islamic Republic of Iran, 30 F.3d 164, 168 (D.C. Cir. 1994), or that criminal conduct is presumptively noncommercial. *See* Letelier v. Republic of Chile, 748 F.2d 790, 797–98 (2d Cir. 1984). Most courts steer a middle course, asking whether the criminal acts are themselves ones in which a private party might in practice engage and if they were rendered in a commercial context. *See* Restatement (Fourth) § 454 rptrs. note 3 (regarding treatment of criminal conduct as presumptively noncommercial as inconsistent with the majority approach). Thus, conduct comprising bribery, forgery, fraud or similar conduct may be deemed commercial, if it relates to commercial matters like contracting. *See, e.g.*, Keller v. Central Bank of Nigeria, 277 F.3d 811, 816 (6th Cir. 2002); Adler v. Federal Republic of Nigeria, 219 F.3d 869, 875 (9th Cir. 2000); Southway v. Cent. Bank of Nigeria, 198 F.3d 1210, 1217–18 (10th Cir. 1999). On the other hand, kidnapping and assassinations, see *Letelier*, 748 F.2d at 797—not unlike the wrongful arrest, detention, and torture at issue in *Nelson*, 507 U.S. at 360–63—have been excluded as activities that could not (legally) be pursued by private parties in commerce. In all events, the conclusion that an activity like money laundering is excluded from the exception is doubtful. *But see In re* Terrorist Attacks on September 11, 2001, 349 F. Supp. 2d 765, 793 (S.D.N.Y. 2005) (indicating that money laundering, because it is illegal, is noncommercial).

[607] The *Restatement (Fourth)* helpfully catalogs likely commercial activities:

> Activities that are generally deemed commercial include the production, sale, or purchase of goods; the borrowing or lending of money and the provision of standard banking services; the lease or bailment of property; the acquisition of, or trade in, intellectual property, including trade secrets; the ownership of shares and exercise of majority control of boards of directors; and contracts for most services and some forms of employment.

It also indicates unlikely commercial activities:

> Activities that are not generally considered commercial include the regulation of the market, such as the control of a foreign-currency exchange; the expulsion of an alien; the administration of a government health or welfare program; the operation of a police force or judicial system; the condemnation or taking of property through state authority; the employment of diplomats, civil servants, military personnel, or others who make policy decisions or exercise sovereign authority; and similar activities.

Assuming commercial activity is involved, courts must consider whether one of Section 1605(a)(2)'s three clauses is implicated, as these define the activity's connection to the United States. The first clause, where the foreign state's commercial activity is actually "carried on in the United States," entails the closest connection, and is the most clearly defined in the statute.[608] The second clause, involving an act performed in the United States in connection with a commercial activity abroad, is less litigated. The act in the United States need not itself be a commercial activity, so this clause requires establishing a substantive or causal relationship between that U.S. act and the foreign state's commercial activity elsewhere.[609]

The third clause requires that an act that is outside the United States, but which is connected with the foreign state's commercial activity elsewhere, must "cause[] a direct effect in the United States." Such acts have the most attenuated U.S. nexus, and it is not easy to discern the exact standard.[610] The Supreme Court has not established high thresholds for either "direct" or "effect." For example, in *Weltover*, it sufficed that Argentina's unilateral rescheduling of its payment obligations on the bonds resulted in the withholding of money that Argentina was contractually obligated to deposit in a New York bank: because those funds did not arrive in accordance with the contractual schedule, Argentina's actions had the requisite "effect" in the United States.[611] Some lower courts require either a legally significant act in the United States of some kind or that the conduct having direct effect in the United States itself be legally significant in some way; this is probably a mistake.[612]

RESTATEMENT (FOURTH) § 454, cmt. b; *see also id.* § 454 rptrs. notes 1–2 (discussing cases); STEWART, *supra* note 449, at 52–56.

[608] *See* 28 U.S.C. § 1603(e) ("A 'commercial activity carried on in the United States by a foreign state' means commercial activity carried on by such state and having substantial contact with the United States."). Case law establishes that single events—a meeting, a letter delivery, a telephone call, a transfer of funds—do not suffice. RESTATEMENT (FOURTH) § 454 rptrs. note 5.

[609] For cases in which this standard was found unsatisfied, see Anglo-Iberia Underwriting Mgmt. v. P.T. Jamsostek, 600 F.3d 171, 176 n.3, 178–79 (2d Cir. 2010); Garb v. Republic of Poland, 440 F.3d 579, 587 (2d Cir. 2006). For a counterexample, see Adler v. Federal Republic of Nigeria, 107 F.3d 720, 726 (9th Cir. 1997). The inquiry is closely related to (and sometimes conflated with) the "based upon" requirement. *See, e.g.*, Stena Rederi AB v. Comision de Contratos, 923 F.2d 380, 387–90 (5th Cir. 1991). The nexus, or connection, inquiry concerns the relationship between some act and the foreign state's commercial activity elsewhere, as opposed to whether the case is "based upon" that act.

[610] *See generally* STEWART, *supra* note 449, at 58–64.

[611] 504 U.S. 607, 617–19 (1992). In *Weltover*, the Court rejected any requirement of substantiality or foreseeability, purposefully departing from an approach taken by lower courts (other than the one on review) and suggested by the legislative history. *Id.* at 617–18. Instead, it held that more than "speculative" or "purely trivial" effect in the United States was needed, and that directness required that such effect was ". . . an immediate consequence of the defendant's . . . activity." *Id.* at 618 (internal quotations and citations omitted).

[612] The lower court decision in *Weltover*, for example, reported that "courts often look to the place where legally significant acts giving rise to the claim occurred," and concluded that "[t]he legally significant act was defendants' failure to abide by the contractual terms; i.e., to make payments in New York." Weltover, Inc. v. Republic of Argentina, 941 F.2d 145, 152, 153 (2d Cir. 1991), *aff'd*, 504

Finally, assuming a foreign state's commercial activity is in the United States, connects with an act in the United States, or connects with a foreign act causing a direct effect therein, any case must be "based upon" the activity or act establishing the U.S. nexus.[613] The Supreme Court held in *OBB Personenverkehr AG v. Sachs* that such activity or act must be "the 'particular conduct' that constitutes the 'gravamen' of the suit," not just one element of the case.[614] Notwithstanding the Court's phrasing, the "gravamen" should probably be determined on a claim-by-claim basis, not for the entire complaint.[615] Meeting the requirement entails assessing which acts are relevant to a claim and where they occur, and courts sometimes conclude that a case is not genuinely based upon the U.S.-related activity or act. Thus, while Austria's sale of a railroad pass in the United States may well be a commercial activity, that is insufficient if the claim is based upon Austrian negligence regarding the operation of a train in Austria.[616] At the same time, the gravamen of alleged illegal financial activity has been deemed to be where that misconduct occurs, even if the injury occurs elsewhere.[617]

U.S. 607 (1992); *see also* Guirlando v. T.C. Ziraat Bankasi A.S., 602 F.3d 69, 73–79 (2d Cir. 2010); Rush–Presbyterian–St. Luke's Med. Ctr. v. Hellenic Republic, 877 F.2d 574, 581–82 (7th Cir. 1989); Terenkian v. Republic of Iraq, 694 F.3d 1122, 1133–35 (9th Cir. 2012). Other courts, however, have rejected such approaches for reasons that seem persuasive: not only do these tests seem to add an unexpressed requirement to the statute but they also tend to make the third clause of § 1605(a)(2) overlap with the two other clauses. *See* Orient Mineral Co. v. Bank of China, 506 F.3d 980, 997–99 (10th Cir. 2007); Voest-Alpine Trading USA Corp. v. Bank of China, 142 F.3d 887, 894–95 (5th Cir. 1998); *see also* Am. Telecom Co. v. Republic of Lebanon, 501 F.3d 534, 539–40 (6th Cir. 2007) (acknowledging, without resolving, disagreement as to whether a legally significant act is required). Noting disagreement on this question, the *Restatement (Fourth)* took no position, observing that it would often make no difference—but noting possible exceptional circumstances. Restatement (Fourth) § 454 rptrs. note 8.

[613] In other words, the case must be based upon either the foreign state's commercial activity (for clause 1) or a connected act (for clauses 2 and 3).

[614] OBB Personenverkehr AG v. Sachs, 577 U.S. 27, 35 (2015) (quoting Nelson v. Saudi Arabia, 507 U.S. 349, 356–57 (1993)).

[615] Rodriguez v. Pan American Health Organization, 29 F.4th 706, 712–14 (D.C. Cir. 2022).

[616] *See OBB Personenverkehr AG*, 577 U.S. at 35–36 (deeming claims to be based on negligent conduct and unsafe railroad conditions in Austria, even when railroad pass was sold in the United States and linked to alleged failure to warn). The same type of analysis has been applied to contract actions. *See, e.g.*, Janini v. Kuwait Univ., 43 F.3d 1534, 1536 (D.C. Cir. 1995) (case held to be based upon "the conduct that caused the losses alleged, namely the termination of the employment contracts, and not upon pre-employment contact . . . in this country").

If an action seeks to satisfy the first clause, the "based upon" inquiry may occasion scrutiny as to whether a foreign state has engaged in any *relevant* "commercial activity" at all. In *Nelson*, the Court focused first on "identifying the particular conduct on which the [plaintiffs'] action is 'based' for purposes of the Act," which it understood to mean "something more than a mere connection with, or relation to, commercial activity." 507 U.S. at 357–58 & n.4. It then held that the activity on which the case was based was sovereign rather than commercial in character. *Id.* at 358–63. Justice White instead reasoned that the activity in question was commercial in character, but occurred in Saudi Arabia; there was also commercial activity in the United States, he noted, but the case was not "based upon" that. *Id.* at 370 (White, J., concurring in the judgment).

[617] Rodriguez, 29 F.4th at 715–17.

c. Expropriation Exception

The expropriation exception (§ 1605(a)(3)) denies immunity to a foreign state before U.S. courts with respect to certain actions against that state "in which rights in property taken in violation of international law are in issue."[618] The exception has some conventional features, like a required nexus with the United States (consisting, for example, of that property's presence in the United States in relation to a commercial activity carried out there by the foreign state).[619] Yet, unlike the commercial activity exception, which is oriented toward acts of a private nature, the expropriation exception is primarily concerned with acts that are only committed by a sovereign[620]—demanding a different approach to limiting a foreign state's immunity.

The expropriation exception is also a rare FSIA provision that tries to reconcile one international law rule (calling for immunity from the exercise of national jurisdiction) with another (proscribing the expropriation without compensation of a foreign national's property).[621] The exception itself, however, does not track international law: the idea that state immunity from foreign national jurisdiction yields to claims of expropriations violating international law has not been broadly accepted by other states.[622] The FSIA does not, however, establish any cause of action for expropriation of property, but merely permits jurisdiction over claims grounded on another legal basis, such as in contract or tort law.[623]

---

[618] 28 U.S.C. § 1605(a)(3) (2018).

[619] Alternatively, the exception applies if "that property or any property exchanged for such property is owned or operated by an agency or instrumentality of the foreign state and that agency or instrumentality is engaged in a commercial activity in the United States." The U.S. nexus thus turns on the presence, ownership, or operation of the property that is the subject of the taking or "any property exchanged for such property." 28 U.S.C. § 1605(a)(3); see RESTATEMENT (FOURTH) § 455 rptrs. note 7. Here (as elsewhere), care must be taken to distinguish between foreign states and their agencies or instrumentalities, as it takes less to establish jurisdiction over the latter: for agencies and instrumentalities, the relevant property (including property exchanged for taken property) need not be in the United States, and the commercial activity may be unrelated. RESTATEMENT (FOURTH) § 455 rptrs. notes 2 (citing H.R. REP. No. 94-1487, at 19–20 (1976), reprinted in 1976 U.S.C.C.A.N. 6604, 6618) & 9; STEWART, supra note 449, at 69–70; see De Csepel v. Republic of Hungary, 859 F.3d 1094, 1104–08 (D.C. Cir. 2017) (explaining alternative thresholds).

[620] RESTATEMENT (FOURTH) § 455 rptrs. note 4.

[621] Cf. Bolivarian Republic v. Helmerich & Payne, 137 S. Ct. 1312, 1319–22 (2017) (stressing fidelity of FSIA immunity and the expropriations exception to international law).

[622] Federal Republic of Germany v. Philipp, 141 S. Ct. 703, 713 (2021) (acknowledging that "the expropriation exception, because it permits the exercise of jurisdiction over some public acts of expropriation, goes beyond even the restrictive view," and that "no other country has adopted a comparable limitation on sovereign immunity") (citing RESTATEMENT (FOURTH) § 455 rptrs. note 15); see also id. at 713 (attributing U.S. approach to its "defense of America's free enterprise system").

[623] See, e.g., Cassirer v. Kingdom of Spain, 616 F.3d 1019, 1026 (9th Cir. 2010) (en banc). State law ordinarily provides FSIA-related causes of action. See supra this chapter text accompanying note 501. The D.C. Circuit has indicated (exceptionally) that a bilateral treaty may afford a basis for an expropriation claim. McKesson Corp. v. Islamic Republic of Iran, 672 F.3d 1066, 1077–81 (D.C. Cir. 2012) (holding that bilateral treaty with Iran provided a private right of action arising under Iranian law—as Iran had conceded—and that such claim was also enforceable in U.S. court).

At the threshold, an action invoking the expropriation exception must establish "a legally valid claim that a certain kind of right is at issue (property rights) and that the relevant property was taken in a certain way (in violation of international law)."[624] The property rights at issue may involve either tangible or intangible property, though the scope of the intangible property rights included is uncertain.[625] As to the requisite violation of international law, the exception aims to address nationalization or expropriation "without payment of the prompt, adequate and effective compensation required by international law" and "takings which are arbitrary or discriminatory in nature."[626] Based on international law, courts have also sometimes asked whether the taking was one not for a public purpose, though in practice that factor has not played a substantial role.[627]

Case law has wrestled with how best to conform the exception to relevant international law. In *Federal Republic of Germany v. Philipp*,[628] the Supreme Court expressly endorsed the position—previously recognized by Justice Breyer as the "consensus" view among U.S. courts[629]—that the expropriation exception did not cover expropriations of property that belonged to the foreign state's own nationals. This "domestic takings rule," the Court explained, was consistent with international law, with U.S. foreign policy, and with pre-FSIA congressional intervention to permit claims against foreign states for the expropriation of property owned by Americans.[630] The Court rejected, however, the argument that

---

[624] *Helmerich & Payne*, 137 S. Ct. at 1316. The Court held that more than a "non-frivolous" claim was required, given the inquiry's jurisdictional nature and the need to avoid embroiling foreign sovereigns in U.S. litigation, and likewise that courts should resolve necessary factual disputes "as near to the outset of the case as is reasonably possible." *Id.* at 1324. Lower courts have observed that the Court's approach "notably departs from the usual pleading standards" associated with a motion to dismiss. Comparelli v. Republica Bolivariana De Venezuela, 891 F.3d 1311, 1319 (11th Cir. 2018). Arguably the Court's "non-frivolous" standard may be generalized to other FSIA exceptions. RESTATEMENT (FOURTH) § 44 rptrs. note 5.

[625] *See, e.g.,* Abelesz v. Magyar Nemzeti Bank, 692 F.3d 661, 671–73 (7th Cir. 2012); Nemariam v. Federal Democratic Republic of Ethiopia, 491 F.3d 470, 475–80 (D.C. Cir. 2007); RESTATEMENT (FOURTH) § 455 cmt. d & rptrs. note 3 (endorsing inclusion of intangible property). This includes bank accounts (as in *Abelesz* and *Nemariam*), and may include contractual rights as well. Smith Rocke Ltd. v. Republica Bolivariana de Venezuela, No. 12 Cv. 7316(LGS), 2014 WL 288705 *5–*6 (S.D.N.Y. Jan. 27, 2014)). Even if contractual rights are property, however, mere breach would not constitute a taking. Zappia Middle E. Constr. Co. v. Emirate of Abu Dhabi, 215 F.3d 247, 251–52 (2d Cir. 2000).

[626] H.R. REP. No. 94-1487, at 19–20 (1976), *reprinted in* 1976 U.S.C.C.A.N. 6604, 6618; *see also* RESTATEMENT (FOURTH) § 455 cmt. c & rptrs. note 4.

[627] *See, e.g.,* Cassirer v. Kingdom of Spain, 616 F.3d 1019, 1027 (9th Cir. 2010) (en banc); RESTATEMENT (FOURTH) § 455 cmt. c & rptrs. note 4. The *Restatement (Third)* acknowledged that the "public purpose" criterion "has not figured prominently in international claims practice, perhaps because the concept of public purpose is broad and not subject to effective reexamination by other states." RESTATEMENT (THIRD) § 712 cmt. e.

[628] 141 S. Ct. 703, 709–11 (2021).

[629] Republic of Austria v. Altmann, 541 U.S. 677, 713 (2004) (Breyer, J., concurring); *see also* RESTATEMENT (FOURTH) § 455 rptrs. note 6 (citing cases).

[630] *Philipp*, 141 S. Ct. 703 at 711–13. As the Court explained, the Second Hickenlooper Amendment rejected the Court's application of the act of state doctrine, but did not correct its understanding of the international law basis for a claim, which rested on the contention that a state was

the exception of "rights in property taken in violation of international law" meant property taken in violation of *any* international law, such as allegations of forced sales of art by the Third Reich amounting to acts of genocide, concluding instead that Congress meant to address only takings in violation of the "international law *of expropriation*" (or derived from the "law of property," or involving "property and property-related rights").[631] The Court expressed concern that permitting the statutory term "taken in violation of international law" to include genocide and "any human rights abuses" (involving, presumably, the loss of property) would run afoul of international law that upholds sovereign immunity even against allegations of serious human rights abuses—and what the Court depicted as the FSIA's guarded reception of human rights claims.[632] The decision may be more broadly read as tempering lower court interest in whether claims alleging genocide-related wrongs and similarly severe abuses should be treated differently for FSIA purposes.[633]

Despite its relationship with international law, the expropriation exception's scope remains a matter of U.S. statutory law. Courts wrestle, for example, with whether exhaustion of local remedies in the foreign state is required before proceeding in U.S. court. While requiring exhaustion for claims in U.S. courts might make them better resemble international proceedings regarding takings, that reading is not invited by the FSIA, particularly given that other exceptions to immunity explicitly require exhaustion; that also makes it difficult to read

---

limited in its ability to expropriate the property of noncitizens. *Id.* at 711; *see* Banco Nacional de Cuba v. Sabbatino, 376 U.S. 398, 428 (1964); *see also* Foreign Assistance Act of 1964 (Second Hickenlooper Amendment), Pub. L. No. 88-633, 77 Stat. 386 (codified at 22 U.S.C. § 2370(e)(2) (2018)), discussed *supra* this chapter text accompanying notes 209–212.

[631] *Philipp*, 141 S. Ct. 703 at 712 (emphasis added). The Court did not explore potential exceptions to the domestic takings rule that might be more easily attributed to the international law of expropriation, such as whether jurisdiction might be properly exercised over domestic takings involving discrimination by the foreign state based on a domestic entity's foreign ownership. *See, e.g.*, Helmerich & Payne v. Bolivarian Republic of Venezuela, 784 F.3d 804, 812–13 (D.C. Cir. 2015), *vacated and remanded on other grounds*, 137 S. Ct. 1312 (2017).

[632] *Id.* at 713 (citing Jurisdictional Immunities of the State (Ger. v. Italy), Judgment, 2012 I.C.J. 99, 139 (Feb. 3)).

[633] *See, e.g.*, Abelesz v. Magyar Nemzeti Bank, 692 F.3d 661, 674–77 (7th Cir. 2012) (distinguishing allegations of expropriation funding a genocidal campaign); Simon v. Republic of Hungary, 812 F.3d 127, 142–44 (D.C. Cir. 2016) (distinguishing genocide-related claims). *But cf.* Mezerhane v. Republica Bolivariana de Venezuela, 785 F.3d 545, 551 (11th Cir. 2015) (distinguishing cases involving "unique context of a mass genocide perpetrated by Nazi Germany," and applying domestic takings principle notwithstanding allegations of resulting statelessness). The *Restatement (Fourth)* had expressed concern that any exception for egregious violations might "open[] courts in the United States to a wide range of property-related claims arising out of foreign internal (as well as international) conflicts characterized by widespread human-rights violations." RESTATEMENT (FOURTH) § 455 rptrs. note 6; *accord* STEWART, *supra* note 449, at 67–68. Congress has revisited the issue of expropriations in relation to certain violations. *See, e.g.*, Holocaust Expropriated Art Recovery Act of 2016, Pub. L. No. 114-308, 130 Stat. 1524 (2016) (adopting a statute of limitations in relation to actions to recover artwork and other property lost as result of Nazi persecution during World War II).

in an exhaustion requirement in order to maintain consistency with international law.[634] This has led some courts to deny any mandatory statutory exhaustion requirements, but others have suggested that the statutory requirement of showing a taking "in violation of international law" may itself require establishing through litigation in the host state that it has refused to pay compensation.[635]

Finally, because the expropriation exception is a creature of national law, Congress is quite capable of truncating it. In 2016, the Foreign Cultural Exchange Jurisdictional Immunity Clarification Act added a new section to the FSIA (§ 1605(h)) providing that importing foreign state–controlled art work into the United States for "certain art exhibition activities" at cultural or educational institutions, if affirmed by the executive branch as being in the national interest, would not be deemed to be "commercial activity" for purposes of the expropriation exception.[636] As the Court explained in *Federal Republic of Germany v. Philipp*, this "clarification" responded to lower court decisions that had opened up to U.S. litigation art-lending by foreign states, with the new section preserving foreign sovereign immunity.[637] The Court noted that Congress had left intact the expropriation exception (as a derogation from foreign sovereign immunity) for Nazi-era claims and comparable offenses, but stressed that Congress had not thereby disturbed the exception's overall focus on the taking of property and property-related rights, irrespective of whether any such conduct could be associated with other violations of international law.[638]

d. Property and Tort Exceptions

Two additional FSIA exceptions address common-law property and tort claims against a foreign state of the kind that might be made against any private actor.

---

[634] *See* 28 U.S.C. § 1605A(2)(A)(iii) (2018) (requiring an opportunity to arbitrate in relation to the exception for state-sponsored terrorism); *see infra* this chapter note 657.

[635] *See* Republic of Austria v. Altmann, 541 U.S. 677, 714 (2004) (Breyer, J., concurring) (noting that "a plaintiff may have to show an absence of remedies in the foreign country sufficient to compensate for any taking") (citing, inter alia, RESTATEMENT (THIRD) § 713 cmt. f). The lines are not completely clear. *Compare* Cassirer v. Kingdom of Spain, 616 F.3d 1019, 1034–37 (9th Cir. 2010) (en banc) (concluding that there is no statutory mandate of exhaustion, but conceding possibility that it may be required by the merits of a claim), *and* Agudas Chasidei Chabad of U.S. v. Russian Federation, 528 F.3d 934, 948–49 (D.C. Cir. 2008) (suggesting, without deciding, absence of an exhaustion requirement), *with* Abelesz v. Magyar Nemzeti Bank, 692 F.3d 661, 678–82 (7th Cir. 2012) (concluding that there is no statutory mandate of exhaustion, but stressing need to exhaust domestic remedies in order to state a valid claim of expropriation), *and* Fischer v. Magyar Allamvasutak ZRT, 777 F.3d 847, 852, 854–55 (7th Cir. 2015) (same). The *Restatement (Fourth)* concluded simply that "the interpretation of the statute that does not require exhaustion appears to be the proper one." RESTATEMENT (FOURTH) § 455 rptrs. note 11.

[636] Pub. L.114-319, § 2(a), Dec. 16, 2016, 130 Stat. 1618 (codified at 28 U.S.C. § 1605(h) (2018)); *see* STEWART, *supra* note 449, at 13. The provision also requires publication of the executive branch determination. 28 U.S.C. § 1605(h)(1).

[637] 141 S. Ct. 703, 714–15 (2021) (citing Malewicz v. Amsterdam, 362 F. Supp. 2d 298, 313–315 (D.D.C. 2005)).

[638] *Id.* at 715.

They are similar, in this respect, to the commercial activity exception, but more sharply constrained geographically.

For cases involving rights in property (§ 1605(a)(4)), the property must be "in the United States,"[639] and only certain rights are implicated. The first clause addresses cases when such property is "acquired by succession or gift"; the idea is that a foreign state is then standing in the shoes of a private litigant.[640] The second clause applies when "rights in immovable property" in the United States are in issue. The Supreme Court construed this as including claims involving key incumbrances on those rights, like on the right to convey, but not torts that happen incidentally to involve property.[641]

Garden-variety torts are more likely to proceed under what is often called the "noncommercial tort" exception (§ 1605(a)(5)), which allows actions seeking money for personal injury or death, or property damage or loss, such as suits against foreign sovereigns responsible for traffic accidents.[642] The potential reach of the exception is substantially narrowed by a requirement that the tort must "occur[] in the United States," which courts have taken to mean that the "entire tort," including the injury and the precipitating act, must occur domestically.[643]

The tort exception was intended to supplement the commercial activity exception, so commercial activity is not required; at the same time, the commercial nature of an alleged act does not take it out of this exception.[644] Instead, the core inquiry is whether a foreign state or its employee engaged in a "tortious act or

---

[639] 28 U.S.C. § 1605(a)(4) (2018); see RESTATEMENT (FOURTH) § 456 rptrs. note 3 (noting potential uncertainties regarding the situs of intangible property).

[640] H.R. REP. No. 94-1487, at 29 (1976), reprinted in 1976 U.S.C.C.A.N. 6604, 6628. The means by which the rights have been acquired is viewed expansively, but not so as to "open the courts to all suits involving inherited or donated property." Asociacion de Reclamantes v. United Mexican States, 561 F. Supp. 1190, 1197 (D.D.C. 1983), aff'd on other grounds, 735 F.2d 1517 (D.C. Cir. 1984).

[641] Permanent Mission of India to the United Nations v. City of New York, 551 U.S. 193, 198 (2007). The Court differentiated "claims incidental to property ownership, such as actions involving an 'injury suffered in a fall,'" to which the exception does not apply. Id. at 201.

[642] 28 U.S.C. § 1605(a)(5); see H.R. REP. No. 94-1487, at 20 (1976), reprinted in 1976 U.S.C.C.A.N. 6604, 6619 ("Section 1605(a)(5) is directed primarily at the problem of traffic accidents but is cast in general terms"); see generally STEWART, supra note 449, at 70–74.

[643] RESTATEMENT (FOURTH) § 457 rptrs. note 1 (citing cases). Conservatively construing "in the United States" is arguably consistent with the presumption against extraterritoriality. Argentine Republic v. Amerada Hess Shipping Corp., 488 U.S. 428, 439–41 (1989) (excluding torts occurring on the high seas). State law, which determines the elements of the tort, also determines more exactly where the tort occurs. See, e.g., Doe v. Federal Democratic Republic of Ethiopia, 851 F.3d 7, 9–12 (D.C. Cir. 2017) (applying Maryland intrusion-upon-seclusion tort).

[644] The tort exception is prefaced by a statement that it applies to any case "not otherwise encompassed in paragraph (2) above," 28 U.S.C. § 1605(a)(5), which suggests that a tortious activity is eligible to be deemed a "commercial activity" under § 1605(a)(2). Moreover, § 1605(a)(3) directly excludes "interference with contract rights," which suggests that commercial activities would otherwise be eligible for inclusion. See also RESTATEMENT (FOURTH) § 457 rptrs. note 3. But cf. Letelier v. Republic of Chile, 748 F.2d 790, 795 (2d Cir. 1984) (suggesting that commercial activity and tort exceptions are "mutually exclusive," such that it would be inconsistent, given a lower court holding that certain complained-of activities were "tortious, not commercial," to then "lift execution immunity based on a finding that the activities were commercial") (emphasis added).

omission" under state law.[645] Certain torts are excluded from the exception and remain subject to immunity.[646] Among these excluded claims, the most elusive class are those based on the exercise or performance by the foreign state of a "discretionary function."[647] Such functions relate to the initiation or execution of governmental, nonobligatory activities involving policy judgment, and will be construed (like misrepresentation claims) in light of similar exclusions of claims against the U.S. government under the Federal Tort Claims Act (FTCA).[648] The parallel treatment is natural at first glance, but ultimately it is hard to justify. Foreign sovereign immunity under the FSIA bears little relation to U.S. sovereign immunity before U.S. courts, and there is no need for one to mimic the other.[649] Moreover, the effect of a discretionary function exclusion under the FSIA is idiosyncratic: foreign state acts under other exceptions of the FSIA contain no such exclusion, and indeed an act excluded from the tort exception as a discretionary function may well be liable under another exception, such as for commercial activity.[650] Finally, even if the discretionary function exclusion in the FSIA tort exception could be kept parallel with the FTCA, it is not obvious why it should be. The more attractive aim would be to develop the U.S. law of foreign sovereign immunity in keeping with the overall objective of the restrictive approach and its particular sensitivities.[651]

---

[645] H.R. REP. No. 94-1487, at 21 (1976), *reprinted in* 1976 U.S.C.C.A.N. 6604, 6620. One challenge has been how to determine whether acts by an employee are within "the scope of his office or employment" and attributable to the sovereign. *See generally* RESTATEMENT (FOURTH) § 457 rptrs. note 2.

[646] *See* 28 U.S.C. § 1605(a)(5)(B) (excluding "any claim arising out of malicious prosecution, abuse of process, libel, slander, misrepresentation, deceit, or interference with contract rights").

[647] *See* 28 U.S.C. § 1605(a)(5)(A) (excluding "any claim based upon the exercise or performance or the failure to exercise or perform a discretionary function regardless of whether the discretion be abused").

[648] 28 U.S.C. § 2680(a), (h); O'Bryan v. Holy See, 556 F.3d 361, 383–85 (6th Cir. 2009). FSIA discretionary function cases, in particular, "draw heavily" on Federal Tort Claims Act (FTCA) precedent. USAA Cas. Ins. Co. v. Permanent Mission of Republic of Namibia, 681 F.3d 103, 112 n.43 (2d Cir. 2012); *see, e.g.,* Doe v. Holy See, 557 F.3d 1066, 1083–85 (9th Cir. 2009).

[649] The FSIA's legislative history suggests that the discretionary function provisions of the FSIA and FTCA "correspond" without directly stating that they should be interpreted alike. H.R. REP. No. 94-1487, at 21 (1976), *reprinted in* 1976 U.S.C.C.A.N. 6604, 6620.

[650] *See, e.g.,* Saudi Arabia v. Nelson, 507 U.S. 349 (1993) (considering tort, evidently not satisfying § 1605(a)(3), under §1605(a)(2)). Most courts have held that the exclusion of particular torts from § 1605(a)(5)(B) does not preclude such torts from falling within other FSIA exceptions, such as the commercial activity exception. *See, e.g.,* Exp. Grp. v. Reef Indus., Inc., 54 F.3d 1466, 1473–77 (9th Cir. 1995) (interference with contractual rights); Fagan v. Deutsche Bundesbank, 438 F. Supp. 2d 376, 389 (S.D.N.Y. 2006) (defamation); WMW Mach., Inc. v. Werkzeugmaschinenhandel GmbH, 960 F. Supp. 734, 741–42 (S.D.N.Y. 1997) (interference with contractual rights); *see generally* RESTATEMENT (FOURTH) § 457 rptrs. note 3; DELLAPENNA, *supra* note 449, at 434–36. *But see* Gregorian v. Izvestia, 871 F.2d 1515, 1522 n.4 (9th Cir. 1989) (stating, in dictum relating to libel claim, that "it is far more likely that Congress meant the clauses retaining immunity in section 1605(a)(5) (B) to deny jurisdiction over any claims alleging the torts listed"); Bryks v. Canadian Broad. Corp., 906 F. Supp. 204, 208–10 (S.D.N.Y. 1995) (same, for defamation claim).

[651] The *Restatement (Fourth)* cautioned against borrowing FTCA case law on discretionary functions, reasoning that it was concerned about judicial second-guessing of decision-making by the U.S. political branches, not anything involving foreign relations. RESTATEMENT (FOURTH) § 457

e. Terrorism-Related Exceptions

Two terrorism-related exceptions deny immunity to a foreign state before U.S. courts with respect to certain actions against that state for harm from terrorist acts that were sponsored or supported by the state.[652] Since being introduced in 1996, terrorism-related exceptions have been a fount of judicial and legislative activity.[653] Congress first created, and gradually extended, an exception for state-sponsored terrorism (originally § 1605(a)(7), now § 1605A).[654] In 2016, the Justice Against Sponsors of Terrorism Act (JASTA) added a companion provision (§ 1605B), principally to enable suit by U.S. victims of the 9/11 attacks, but having much wider potential.[655] The two exceptions operate differently and defy easy summary,[656] but each departs from the FSIA's ordinary approach and gives rise to distinct foreign relations issues.

The two terrorism-related exceptions limit their extent by fundamentally different means. The older exception (§ 1605A) has no territorial limits, unlike other FSIA exceptions.[657] Instead, Section 1605A limits the class of plaintiffs, who must be U.S. nationals or government officials,[658] and perhaps more significantly limits defendants: only a foreign state designated by the secretary of state

---

rptrs. note 4. But it appeared to accept borrowing FTCA precedents regarding misrepresentation. *See id.* § 457 rptrs. note 5.

[652] 28 U.S.C. §§ 1605(A), 1605(B).

[653] Antiterrorism and Effective Death Penalty Act of 1996, Pub. L. No. 104-132, § 221(a)(1)(C), 110 Stat. 1214, 1241 (formerly codified at § 1605(a)(7)). For detailed history, see *In re* Islamic Republic of Iran Terrorism Litigation, 659 F. Supp. 2d 31, 38–62 (D.D.C. 2009); STEWART, *supra* note 449, at 97–102.

[654] Then Section 1605(a)(7)) was repealed and replaced, not merely amended, in 2008. National Defense Authorization Act for fiscal Year 2008, Pub. L. No. 110-181, § 1083, 122 Stat. 3, 338–44 (codified at § 1605A).

[655] Justice Against Sponsors of Terrorism, Pub. L. No. 114-222, 130 Stat. 853 (2016); *see* 28 U.S.C. § 1605B. As to its central purpose, see, for example, 162 CONG. REC. H6025 (Sept. 28, 2016) (remarks of Rep. King); *id.* at 6026 (remarks of Rep. Adler).

[656] For example, § 1605A has a provision that applies only to a particular docket. 28 U.S.C. § 1605A(a)(2)(B) (providing that a court shall hear a claim if "the act described in paragraph (1) is related to Case Number 1:00CV03110 (EGS) in the United States District Court for the District of Columbia").

[657] The closest § 1605A comes to a territoriality limit is a requirement that a foreign state be permitted an opportunity to arbitrate cases in which the act occurred in the state's territory. 28 U.S.C. § 1605A(a)(2)(A)(iii). While plaintiffs in such circumstances must demonstrate to the court an offer to arbitrate, beyond that the requirement has proven irrelevant, as states to date have not availed themselves of the opportunity. *See* RESTATEMENT (FOURTH) § 460 rptrs. note 3; STEWART, *supra* note 449, at 121.

[658] Technically, the plaintiff must be a U.S. national, a member of the U.S. armed forces, or an employee or contractor of the U.S. government acting within the scope of his or her employment. 28 U.S.C. § 1605A(a)(2)(A)(ii). By referencing "the claimant or the victim," the provision is also understood to permit jurisdiction over claims by family members of victims—not merely those victims and their "legal representative[s]," as with the more narrowly drawn cause of action associated with § 1605A. *See* Owens v. Republic of Sudan, 864 F.3d 751, 805–07 (D.C. Cir. 2017) (distinguishing between § 1605A(a) and § 1605A(c)), *rev'd and remanded on other grounds*, Opati v. Republic of Sudan, 140 S. Ct. 1601 (2020).

as a "state sponsor of terrorism" may be sued,[659] and only a handful of foreign states have been so designated.[660] The newer exception (§ 1605B) has a more conventional territorial restriction, resembling the tort exception in requiring a U.S. injury and "an act of international terrorism in the United States."[661] Unlike the older exception, it is not limited to U.S. plaintiffs.[662] It also confers less authority on the executive branch, which cannot designate which foreign states are susceptible to suit—and instead may only seek a stay in proceedings[663] or seek additional discretion from Congress.[664] This lack of executive discretion prompted a presidential veto, but that was overridden by Congress.[665]

The terrorism-related exceptions also diverge on the wrongdoing at issue. Section 1605A governs claims based on "personal injury or death" caused by "an

---

[659] The term "state sponsor of terrorism" is defined by statute as "a government that has repeatedly provided support for acts of international terrorism," if it has been so designated. 28 U.S.C. § 1605A(h)(6). The state must have been designated at the time of, or as a result of, the relevant act, and must remain so designated at the time the claim is filed (or nearly so). 28 U.S.C. § 1605A(a)(2)(A)(i) (I); see also id. § 1605A(a)(2)(A)(i)(II) (providing separate rule for particular classes of actions).

[660] As of early 2022, Cuba, the Democratic People's Republic of Korea (North Korea), Iran, and Syria are designated. See State Sponsors of Terrorism, U.S. DEPARTMENT OF STATE, https://perma.cc/ GB8D-TDL5. In 2020, Sudan was removed based on its agreement to pay hundreds of millions of dollars in compensation to victims of al-Qaeda attacks on U.S. embassies in Kenya and Tanzania and on a U.S. Navy destroyer—reportedly, with the funds being held in escrow until Congress enacts legislation to give Sudan immunity for other terrorist attacks. Lara Jakes, Declan Walsh, & Eric Schmitt, State Dept. to Remove Sudan from List of Terrorist States, N.Y. TIMES, Oct. 20, 2020, at A14; see Certification of Rescission of the Determination regarding the Government of Sudan, WHITE HOUSE, Oct. 26, 2020, https://perma.cc/MEH6-N3NH (citing to presidential documents). States previously placed on, but then removed from, the designation include Iraq, Libya, and South Yemen (and Cuba, which was later returned).

[661] 28 U.S.C. § 1605B(b)(1). Indeed, it was originally conceived of as an amendment to the non-commercial tort exception. See Justice Against Sponsors of Terrorism Act, H.R. 3143, 113th Cong. (2013); accord S. 1535, 113th Cong. (2013). However, in assessing whether a foreign state (or its officials) have committed an act that is causally related to this terrorism, courts may consider acts regardless of where they occurred—unlike the tort exception's "entire tort" approach. Compare 28 U.S.C. § 1605B(b)(2), with supra this chapter text accompanying note 643. Moreover, the terrorist act, by virtue of the definition of "international terrorism," cannot have occurred solely within the United States. See 18 U.S.C. § 2331(1)(C); cf. Doe v. Bin Laden, 663 F.3d 64, 70 (2d Cir. 2011) ("The terrorism exception, far from limiting the preexisting noncommercial tort exception, is there to cover some injuries that the noncommercial tort exception does not reach.").

[662] But see infra this chapter text accompanying note 675 (describing scope of the associated cause of action).

[663] The secretary of state must certify that the United States is engaged in good-faith discussions with the foreign state regarding resolution of the claims. A court may issue such a stay for up to six months, renewably. Justice Against Sponsors of Terrorism Act, Pub. L. No. 114-222, § 5, 130 Stat. 853, 854 (2016) (28 U.S.C.A. § 1605B note).

[664] After the U.S. invasion of Iraq and the overthrow of President Saddam Hussein, Congress authorized the president to make inapplicable to Iraq provisions of law applicable to countries that have supported terrorism, seemingly including a preceding version of § 1605A (former 28 U.S.C. § 1605(a)(7)). See National Defense Authorization Act for Fiscal Year 2008 (NDAA), Pub. L. No. 110-181, § 1083(d), 122 Stat. 3, 343–44; 73 Fed. Reg. 6,571 (Feb. 5, 2008). The Supreme Court subsequently upheld the president's exercise of this waiver authority, including for cases pending at the time of enactment. Republic of Iraq v. Beaty, 556 U.S. 848 (2009).

[665] 162 CONG. REC. H6023-02 (2016) (reflecting veto message, Senate vote, and House reconsideration and vote).

act of torture, extrajudicial killing, aircraft sabotage, hostage taking," or material support for such an act.[666] The newer Section 1605B, in contrast, governs claims for "physical injury to person or property or death," in the United States, caused by an act of "international terrorism,"[667] which preexisting law defines capaciously.[668] The relative breadth of Section 1605B is deliberate.[669] So long as there is a sufficient U.S. nexus, U.S. courts may exercise jurisdiction over terrorism-related claims against foreign states that would be ineligible under Section 1605A because the claimant is not a U.S. national or affiliate, because the defendant is not a designated "state sponsor of terrorism," because property damage alone is at stake, or because the terrorism did not involve torture, extrajudicial killing, aircraft sabotage, or hostage-taking.[670]

Finally, quite unlike other FSIA exceptions, the terrorism-related exceptions each establish a federal cause of action. As originally adopted, Section 1605A lacked any cause of action, so claimants had to resort to existing tort law allowing suit against private individuals in similar circumstances, just as for other FSIA exceptions.[671] Existing tort law offered little that was directly germane to acts of terrorism committed abroad, and claimants (and then Congress) were discontent.[672] Section 1605A now provides expressly for a federal cause of action,[673]

---

[666] 28 U.S.C. § 1605A(a)(1). Each form of wrongdoing (rather than terrorism itself) is defined in reference to another statute or international agreement. See id. § 1605A(h)(1) (incorporating definition of "aircraft sabotage" from the Convention for the Suppression of Unlawful Acts Against the Safety of Civil Aviation, Sept. 23, 1971, 24 U.S.T. 564, 974 U.N.T.S. 177); id. § 1605A(a)(2) ("hostage taking" as under the International Convention Against the Taking of Hostages, Dec. 17, 1979, T.I.A.S. 11081, 1316 U.N.T.S. 205); id. § 1605A(a)(3) ("material support or resources" as under 18 U.S.C. § 2339); id. § 1605A(a)(7) ("torture" and "extrajudicial killing" as under the Torture Victim Protection Act, 28 U.S.C. § 1350 note).

[667] 28 U.S.C. § 1605B(b).

[668] The preexisting law encompasses violent or dangerous acts, of a kind that would be illegal under U.S. law, that are intended to intimidate or coerce civilians or governments or to use mass destruction, assassination, or kidnapping to affect government conduct. See 28 U.S.C. § 1605B(a) (incorporating definition of "international terrorism" from the Anti-Terrorism Act, 18 U.S.C. § 2331). Any "act of war," however, is specifically excluded from that definition. 28 U.S.C. § 1605B(a)(2); see 18 U.S.C. § 2331(4) (defining such acts).

[669] See Pub. L. No. 114-222 § 2(b), 130 Stat. 852, 853 (2016) (stating provision's purpose "to provide civil litigants with the broadest possible basis, consistent with the Constitution of the United States, to seek relief" against those directly or indirectly supporting terrorism against the United States).

[670] Conversely, jurisdiction under § 1605A may be uniquely available if the physical injury or death has not occurred in the United States.

[671] See 28 U.S.C. § 1606. Courts resisted the impulse to infer causes of action as a matter of federal common law. See, e.g., Cicippio-Puleo v. Islamic Republic of Iran, 353 F.3d 1024, 1032–36 (D.C. Cir. 2004).

[672] Congress' first attempt at a cause of action for what became § 1605A was the Flatow Amendment. See Pub. L. No. 104-208, § 589, 110 Stat. 3009, 3009–172 (1996) (codified at 28 U.S.C. § 1605 note). The Flatow Amendment was ultimately construed by courts to establish liability only for a foreign state's officials, not for states themselves. Cicippio-Puleo, 353 F.3d at 1036.

[673] 28 U.S.C. § 1605A(c); see National Defense Authorization Act for Fiscal Year 2008 (NDAA), Pub. L. No. 110-181, § 1083, 122 Stat. 3, 338–44 (2008) (codified at 28 U.S.C. § 1605A); Owens v. Republic of Sudan, 864 F.3d 751, 763–65 (D.C. 2017) (providing history), rev'd and remanded on other grounds, Opati v. Republic of Sudan, 140 S. Ct. 1601 (2020).

though curiously, not all claimants capable of establishing subject-matter jurisdiction under the exception are eligible under the statutory criteria for the cause
of action.[674] Likewise, Section 1605B establishes a cause of action, and likewise
only for some potential claimants—in its case, only U.S. nationals, which better
aligns the provision with Section 1605A.[675]

The consequence, for both provisions, is that some terrorism victims who can
surmount foreign sovereign immunity and establish subject-matter jurisdiction by
means of the terrorism-related exceptions must still depend on state-law tort claims
for their cause of action. For many claimants, though, the FSIA scheme is relatively
generous. Foreign states rarely defend themselves against such claims; if they fail to
appear, courts still must assess the merits (default rulings are not permitted), but
the prospects for recovery are probably enhanced. Moreover, punitive damages
are uniquely available against state sponsors of terrorism under Section 1605A,[676]
and treble damages against Section 1605B defendants.[677] The risk of high-value
judgments is now accentuated by FSIA provisions reducing the broad immunity ordinarily available against execution.[678]

One may doubt whether private litigation is the best way to compensate
victims of terrorism.[679] Further, the terrorism-related exceptions are not as
one with the FSIA's original objectives. Such suits do not treat foreign states
like private parties for comparable activities, but address distinctive acts.
Moreover, the terrorism-related exceptions have assigned less responsibility
to the judiciary, meaning that political choices will continue to invite foreign-
relations controversy. Indeed, Congress has repeatedly amended the terrorism-
related exceptions so as to dictate outcomes in the courts, and has deliberately

---

[674] *Compare* 28 U.S.C. § 1605A(a)(2)(A)(ii) (establishing subject-matter jurisdiction over cases in
which "the claimant or victim" is a U.S. national, a member of the U.S. armed forces, or an employee
or agent of the U.S. government), *with id.* § 1605A(c)(4) (extending liability to persons falling into
one of those three categories or their "legal representative").

[675] 28 U.S.C. § 1605B(c).

[676] The FSIA generally bars punitive damages against the foreign state *stricto sensu* while permitting them against state agencies or instrumentalities. 28 U.S.C. § 1606. Such damages are expressly
permitted, however, against foreign state sponsors of terrorism. *Id.* § 1605A(c).

[677] 28 U.S.C. § 1605B(c); 18 U.S.C. § 2333(a).

[678] *See infra* this chapter § V(A)(5) (discussing attachment and execution); *see, e.g.,* Certain Iranian
Assets (Iran v. U.S.), Application Instituting Proceedings, 2016 I.C.J. General List No. 164, app. 2,
tables 1–3 (June 14), https://perma.cc/4XZ2-PVT6 (compiling lawsuits, judgments, and enforcement proceedings, including approximately judgments for $26 billion in compensatory damages and
$30 billion dollars in punitive damages); Amduso v. Republic of Sudan, 61 F. Supp. 3d 42, 46 (D.D.C.
2014) (awarding total judgment against Sudan of over $1.7 billion).

[679] *See, e.g., Benefits for U.S. Victims of International Terrorism: Hearing Before the Senate
Comm. on Foreign Relations,* 108th Cong. 4 (2003) (statement of William H. Taft, IV, Legal
Adviser, Department of State) (describing the scheme as "inequitable, unpredictable, occasionally costly to the U.S. taxpayer and damaging to the foreign policy and national security goals of
this country").

(if inconsistently) charged the executive branch with making controversial decisions about its application.[680]

Despite some pushback, Congress has also not seriously evaluated whether these terrorism-related exceptions are compatible with international law.[681] As previously noted, U.S. antiterrorism laws pose challenging questions regarding prescriptive jurisdiction;[682] provisions abrogating foreign-state immunity are yet more difficult to defend. Only Canada has adopted comparable legislation,[683] and there is no general recognition that states engaged in terrorism—let alone terrorism as defined by U.S. law—surrender their immunity in foreign state courts. While those objecting to the exercise of jurisdiction in such circumstances might be tasked with showing that state practice and *opinio juris* support foreign sovereign immunity for terrorism,[684] the more persuasive view is that the lack of evidence favoring an exception for terrorist-related acts means that such conduct remains subject to an overarching backdrop of immunity. International conventions, for their part, state a general rule of immunity and compile specific exceptions without providing one for terrorism.[685]

---

[680] *See supra* this chapter text accompanying notes 660–669 (contrasting roles for the executive under §§ 1605A and 1605B).

[681] *See, e.g., Evaluating the Justice Against Sponsors of Terrorism Act, S. 2930: Hearing before the Subcomm. on Crime and Drugs of the Senate Comm. on the Judiciary*, 111th Cong., 2nd Sess., at 38 (2010) (testimony of John B. Bellinger III) (describing preexisting exception for state sponsors of terrorism as inconsistent with customary international law, and JASTA, as initially proposed, as a "decision to derogate further"); *Congress Overrides Obama's Veto to Pass Justice Against Sponsors of Terrorism Act*, 111 AM. J. INT'L L. 156, 159–61 (2017) (describing international law objections from, inter alia, the European Union, Saudi Arabia, Russia, and the United Arab Emirates). After enactment, the executive branch hesitated to describe the statute as violating international law, see *id.* at 161, but its initial veto message came close. Message to the Senate Returning Without Approval the Justice Against Sponsors of Terrorism Act, 2016 DAILY COMP. PRES. DOC. 628 (Sept. 23, 2016) (stating that JASTA "would upset longstanding international principles regarding sovereign immunity").

[682] *See supra* this chapter text accompanying notes 273, 277, 285–286, 289–292, 294, 307, 332–337.

[683] *See* State Immunity Act, R.S.C. 1985, c S-18, § 6.1 (Can.) (as amended by Justice for Victims of Terrorism Act, S.C. 2012, c. 1, s. 2, § 4 (Can.)). As a result, Canadian courts will recognize U.S. judgments respecting terrorism claims against foreign states. *See, e.g.,* Tracy v. Iran (Information and Security), 2017 O.N.C.A. 549 (Ont. Ct. App. 2017); *see also* Kazemi Estate v. Islamic Republic of Iran, 2014 SCC 62, [2014] 3 S.C.R. 176.

[684] *See, e.g.,* William S. Dodge, *Does JASTA Violate International Law?*, JUST SECURITY (Sept. 30, 2016), https://perma.cc/L4KS-5BZM; David P. Stewart, *Immunity and Terrorism, in* CAMBRIDGE HANDBOOK, *supra* note 510, at 651.

[685] Thus, terrorism-related offenses are not mentioned in the U.N. Convention on Jurisdictional Immunities of States and Their Property, G.A. Res. 59/38, annex (Dec. 2, 2004). That convention is not yet in force; moreover, its general statement of immunity was not intended as a definitive statement about prevailing customary international law. *See id.* art. 5; *see also* Int'l Law Comm'n, *Draft Articles on Jurisdictional Immunities of States and their Property and Commentaries Thereto,* U.N. Doc. A/46/10, *reprinted in* [1991] Y.B. Int'l L. Comm'n 22–23, A/CN.4/SER.A./1991/Add. 1 (Part 2). That said, its preamble reinforces the idea that immunity is presumed under international law, and its compilation of diverse exceptions might have added terrorism. *See* Convention on Jurisdictional Immunities of States and Their Property, *supra*, arts. 10–21. Much the same can be said of the European Convention on State Immunity, *supra* this chapter text accompanying note 508.

The ICJ has recently favored a similar approach. In the *Jurisdictional Immunities of the State* case, the ICJ essentially accepted state immunity for sovereign acts as a starting point from which exceptions would need to be established.[686] It rejected arguments that the conduct's illegality and gravity warranted a different approach, and even suggested that the FSIA exception for state sponsors of terrorism was anomalous.[687] In a different case, Iran claimed that various proceedings in U.S. courts against Iran that invoked the terrorism-related exceptions violated Iran's sovereign immunity under international law. The ICJ, however, held that the claim fell outside of the treaty conferring jurisdiction on the court, and therefore it did not reach the merits.[688]

Future cases might present U.S. courts with opportunities to evaluate the FSIA's compatibility with international law, but they are unlikely to produce any compromises. Objections to the FSIA on the ground that it departs from international law must confront Congress' ability to override international law regarding immunity for domestic law purposes, and given the statute's specificity there is limited potential for interpretive reconciliation using the *Charming Betsy* canon.[689] Other legal objections have been unsuccessful. Foreign state defendants have unsuccessfully argued that terrorism-related exceptions entail unequal treatment under international law.[690] Courts have also rejected arguments that they constitute an unconstitutional delegation of power.[691] The Supreme Court considered the Central Bank of Iran's argument that one statutory provision unconstitutionally directed the result in particular litigation, but upheld the provision as having sufficiently established "new substantive standards," a view which likely provided little comfort to foreign states concerned.[692]

---

[686] The parties had accepted "that immunity is governed by international law and is not a mere matter of comity." Jurisdictional Immunities of the State (Ger. v. It.), Judgment, 2012 I.C.J. 99, ¶ 53 (Feb. 3). The Court then seemed to accept immunity as a starting point for its analysis of terrorism, from which an exception would be necessary. *Id.* ¶¶ 55–57, 60–61. When construing the territorial tort exception, the Court looked to state practice and *opinio juris* relating to conduct by armed forces of a foreign state during an armed conflict. *Id.* ¶¶ 64–65, 73–74, 77.

[687] *Id.* ¶ 88; *see also id.* ¶¶ 81–91.

[688] Certain Iranian Assets (Iran v. U.S.), Preliminary Objections, Judgment, 2019 I.C.J. 7, ¶¶ 48–80 (Feb. 13).

[689] *See supra* this chapter text accompanying notes 381–386.

[690] *See* Wyatt v. Syrian Arab Republic, 266 F. App'x 1, 2 (D.C. Cir. 2008) (rejecting argument that 28 U.S.C. § 1605(a)(7), the predecessor to § 1605A, infringed on the "sovereign equality" principle, including because the United States was treating alike all states that happened to have been designated as state sponsors of terrorism); *accord* Wyatt v. Syrian Arab Republic, 736 F. Supp. 2d 106, 113 n.8 (D.D.C. 2010) (applying § 1605A); Wultz v. Islamic Republic of Iran, No. 08-cv-1460 (RCL), 2010 WL 4190277 at *2 (D.D.C. Oct. 20, 2010).

[691] *Wultz*, 2010 WL 4190277 at *3; *see also* Gates v. Syrian Arab Republic, 646 F.3d 1, 4 (D.C. Cir. 2011).

[692] *See* Bank Markazi v. Peterson, 578 U.S. 212, 231 (2016) (objections to Terrorism Risk Insurance Act (TRIA), Pub. L. 107-297, tit. II, § 201, 116 Stat. 2337 (2002) (codified at 28 U.S.C. § 1610 note), and Iran Threat Reduction and Syria Human Rights Act of 2012, Pub. L. No. 112-158, 125 Stat. 1298 (codified at 22 U.S.C. §§ 8701–95)); *accord In re* Terrorist Attacks, 298 F. Supp. 3d 631, 660–61 (S.D.N.Y. 2018) (rejecting similar argument by Saudi Arabia in relation to JASTA). *But see Bank Markazi*, 578

5. Immunity from Attachment and Execution

Under the FSIA, U.S. property of a foreign state is generally immune from attachment, arrest, or execution—"attachment immunity," for short—unless it is subject to a statutory exception or exempted by virtue of a preexisting international agreement.[693] This immunity may appear similar to the immunity from suit discussed previously, but appearances can be deceiving. Attachment immunity involves its own detailed rules that defy easy summary, with critical differences between pre-judgment and post-judgment actions,[694] among types of property,[695] and the like.[696]

Nevertheless, a few general points are warranted. First, attachment immunity presents a distinct, additional hurdle for claimants seeking to sue a foreign state before U.S. courts. Congress understood when enacting the FSIA that encroachments on a foreign state's property were more problematic than simply obtaining a judgment against that state.[697] Accordingly, a state's lack of immunity from suit does not necessarily put its U.S. property at risk,[698] and there may be instances in which a foreign state cannot be forced to relinquish assets to satisfy a judgment against it.[699]

Second, when it comes to attachment immunity, the foreign state *stricto sensu* is treated differently than its agencies and instrumentalities. If property of a foreign state *stricto sensu* is at issue, that property must have been used in a commercial activity and (generally) must relate to the claim giving rise to the

U.S. at 234 (citing approvingly congressional capacity to exercise authority "that governed one or a very small number of specific subjects").

[693] 28 U.S.C. § 1609 (general principle of immunity); *id.* § 1610(a) (exceptions for state *stricto sensu*); *id.* § 1610(b) (additional exceptions for agencies or instrumentalities of a foreign state).
[694] *See id.* § 1610(d) (restricting attachment prior to entry of judgment, as well as prior to reasonable period of notice provided for in § 1610(c)). Prejudgment attachment for purposes of acquiring jurisdiction is precluded. *See* RESTATEMENT (FOURTH) § 453 cmt. d & rptrs. note 9.
[695] *See, e.g.,* 28 U.S.C. § 1610(e) (addressing vessels of a foreign state); *id.* § 1611 (exempting designated property of international organizations, certain properties of foreign central banks, certain property of a military character, and inviolable property like embassies and consulates and their bank accounts).
[696] For detailed discussion of other essential issues, see RESTATEMENT (FOURTH) § 464; STEWART, *supra* note 449, at 81–96.
[697] Walters v. Industrial and Commercial Bank of China, Ltd., 651 F.3d 280, 289 (2d Cir. 2011); *see also* H.R. REP. No. 94-1487, at 27 (1976), *reprinted in* 1976 U.S.C.C.A.N. 6604, 6626 (noting controversial nature, but asserting that "there is a marked trend toward limiting the immunity from execution").
[698] The converse may also be true, at least in the case of waiver. *See* RESTATEMENT (FOURTH) § 453 (stating that "a waiver of immunity from suit does not imply a waiver of immunity from attachment of property, and a waiver of immunity from attachment of property does not imply a waiver of immunity from suit"); *cf.* 28 U.S.C. § 1610 (waiver of immunity from suit); *id.* § 1609 (waiver of attachment immunity).
[699] *See, e.g.,* Permanent Mission of India to the United Nations v. City of New York, 551 U.S. 193, 196 n.1 (2007) (noting that, even were the plaintiff to obtain a declaratory judgment of a lien, the Permanent Mission of India would be immune from foreclosure, and a remedy would require its voluntary cooperation or congressional coercion).

judgment.[700] Because less protection is afforded the property of a foreign state's agency or instrumentality[701]—and given that plaintiffs tend to target entities and assets they can successfully pursue—courts will often be called to assess whether a defendant is part of the foreign state *stricto sensu* (such as a political subdivision) or is instead an agency or instrumentality that enjoys a separate juridical status, and will permit attachment of an entity's property only after careful review.[702]

Third, it is difficult for Congress to resist statutory tinkering with attachment immunity as new issues arise in U.S. litigation. In *Rubin v. Islamic Republic of Iran*,[703] plaintiffs used Section 1605A to obtain a judgment against Iran, a designated state sponsor of terrorism, that they followed with a suit to attach Iranian antiquities on loan to the University of Chicago. This implicated terrorism-related provisions that Congress had repeatedly amended,[704] to the point of addressing specific assets in designated lawsuits.[705] As the Court recounted, Congress added Section 1610(g)(1) in order to identify property available to

---

[700] *See* 28 U.S.C. § 1610(a)(2).

[701] While eligible property of a foreign state must be "used for a commercial activity in the United States," 28 U.S.C. § 1610(a), there is no such requirement for the property of an agency or instrumentality (though it is quite likely that it will be so used in any event). *Id.* § 1610(b). Moreover, unlike § 1610(a)(2)—which requires that a foreign state's property be part of the commercial activity on which a claim is based—§ 1610(b)(2) provides that if an agency or instrumentality is not immune due to the commercial activity exception (among other things), its property is subject to attachment or execution regardless of whether the property was involved. The remaining exceptions, other than those for waiver and arbitral awards, track the same distinction. *See* RESTATEMENT (FOURTH) § 464 cmt. c.

[702] *See, e.g.,* Alejandre v. Telefonica Larga Distancia de Puerto Rico, Inc., 183 F.3d 1277, 1284–85 (11th Cir. 1999); De Letelier v. Republic of Chile, 748 F.2d 790, 795 (2d Cir. 1984). This distinction between the foreign state *stricto sensu* and the state's agencies or instrumentalities is reflected in the Supreme Court's decision in First Nat'l City Bank v. Banco Para El Comercio Exterior de Cuba, 462 U.S. 611 (1983), known as *Bancec*, which dealt with set-off and substantive liability.

[703] 138 S. Ct. 816 (2018).

[704] Congress added a provision when first adopting the terrorism-related exception in 1996 (that later became § 1605A). Pub. L. 104-132, tit. II, § 221(b), 110 Stat. 1242 (1996); *see* 28 U.S.C. § 1610(a) (7) (permitting attachment of or execution against foreign state property in aid of judgments relating to claims for which the foreign state lacked immunity under §1605A (or §1605(a)(7) as it was then in effect), regardless of whether the property was involved); *id.* § 1610(b)(3) (addressing property of agencies or instrumentalities in similar terms). In 1998, Congress adopted a provision that allowed execution or attachment against designated frozen or diplomatic assets of the state sponsors of terrorism, but also allowed the president to waive the provision, which thereafter regularly occurred. Pub. L. No. 105-277, § 117, 112 Stat. 2681 (1998) (codified at 28 U.S.C. § 1610(f)(1), (3)); *see* Presidential Determination No. 2001-03: Determination to Waive Attachment Provisions Relating to Blocked Property of Terrorist-List States: Memorandum for the Secretary of State [and] the Secretary of the Treasury, 65 Fed. Reg. 66,483 (Oct. 28, 2000). In 2002, the Terrorism Risk Insurance Act, Pub. L. 107-297, tit. II, § 201, 116 Stat. 2337 (2002) (codified at 28 U.S.C. § 1610 note), allowed execution against defined blocked assets "of the terrorist party" (both a state sponsor of terrorism and any of its agencies or instrumentalities), also providing for waiver. *See* STEWART, *supra* note 449, at 131–34. This was further modified in 2008, yielding the current text of 28 U.S.C. § 1610(g). *See* Pub. L. No. 110-181, div. A, tit. X, § 1083(b)(3), 122 Stat. 341 (2008); STEWART, *supra* note 449, at 134–36.

[705] A provision at issue in *Bank Markazi v. Peterson*, 578 U.S. 212 (2016), addressed execution against certain blocked assets belonging to Iran, identified in a designated lawsuit. *See* Pub. L. No. 112-158, tit. V, § 502, 126 Stat. 1258 (2012) (codified at 22 U.S.C. § 8772).

satisfy Section 1605A judgments, including by making available the property of the state sponsor's agencies or instrumentalities without regard to any separate juridical status they might otherwise deserve. But the Court unanimously held that the provision did not actually abrogate attachment immunity. That is, plaintiffs could dispense with any obligation to show that they were entitled to proceed against the property of a particular agency or instrumentality, but maintained their obligation to identify an exception to foreign sovereign immunity against suit and an obligation to find an exception to the foreign state's attachment immunity.[706]

B. International Organizations, Officials, and Premises

The immunity of international organizations, while a distinctive subject in many respects,[707] is indirectly governed under U.S. law by the FSIA. Unfortunately, how the FSIA translates into that context is unclear—partly because the FSIA's application to international organizations was only recently decided, but mostly because the FSIA was never designed to apply to international organizations.

The foundation for the immunity of international organizations in the United States is not actually the FSIA, but rather the International Organization Immunities Act (IOIA), enacted in 1945.[708] The mechanics of the IOIA are straightforward. If the United States participates in an international organization, the president may designate it as being entitled to privileges and immunities. The president may also withhold, withdraw, condition, or limit these privileges and immunities, or even revoke such designation if the organization or its officers or employees have abused its privileges, exemptions, or immunities.[709]

Under the IOIA, fully designated organizations, along with their property and their assets, generally "shall enjoy the same immunity from suit and every form of judicial process as is enjoyed by foreign governments," save where they have expressly waived it.[710] The meaning of "the same immunity . . . as is enjoyed by foreign governments" was, until recently, unresolved.[711] On one view—favored

---

[706] *Rubin*, 138 S. Ct. at 824.

[707] This section will consider not only the immunity owed international organizations but also (briefly) the immunity of current and former officials and employees, which is largely governed by the same instruments.

[708] International Organizations Immunities Act of 1945, 59 Stat. 669 (codified at 22 U.S.C. § 288 et seq.).

[709] 22 U.S.C. § 288. The presidential designation of immunity may take effect after the claims accrue, so long as it is before the complaint is filed. Garcia v. Sebelius, 867 F. Supp. 2d 125, 143–44 (D.D.C. 2012) (citing Weidner v. Int'l Telecomm. Satellite Org., 392 A.2d 508, 510 (D.C. 1978)), *vacated in part*, 919 F. Supp. 2d 43 (D.D.C. 2013).

[710] 22 U.S.C. § 288a(b).

[711] For a summary of the prior debate, see Aaron I. Young, *Deconstructing International Organization Immunity*, 44 GEO. J. INT'L L. 311 (2012).

in the D.C. Circuit, where many cases against international organizations were brought[712]—international organizations enjoyed the same immunity afforded foreign states when the IOIA was enacted in 1945 (when it was generally perceived that foreign sovereign immunity was absolute).[713] On another view, international organizations enjoyed the immunity *presently* enjoyed by foreign states, which reflects the development of restrictive immunity and its codification in the FSIA.[714] Other views were more nuanced.[715]

In 2019, the Supreme Court settled the matter in *Jam v. International Finance Corporation*.[716] Occasioned by a suit by farmers and fisherman in India against a member organization of the World Bank, claiming that its funding for a nearby project had harmed the environment, the Court held that IOIA immunity for international organizations was "continuously equivalent" with that conferred on foreign sovereigns.[717] It based this on the IOIA's text, as confirmed by the "reference canon," which indicates that when a statute invokes a general subject, it "adopts the law on that subject as it exists whenever a question under the statute arises".[718] The Court also cited executive branch views expressed following adoption of the FSIA.[719] Because the Court took the answer to be dictated by the IOIA, it showed little interest in contrasts between international organizations and foreign states, though it did suggest that restrictive immunity for international organizations would not necessarily give rise to excessive liability.[720] Ultimately, in a little-explained leap, the Court indicated that "updating" international organization immunity to keep pace with foreign sovereign immunity meant that the FSIA—a particular *embodiment* of restrictive immunity, salted

---

[712] This may be the case even more often, given the likely application of the FSIA's venue provisions. *See infra* this chapter note 729.

[713] Atkinson v. Inter-Am. Dev. Bank, 156 F.3d 1335 (D.C. Cir. 1998). A few other decisions followed this approach. *See* Price v. Unisea, Inc., 289 P.3d 914, 919–20 (Alaska 2012); Bro Tech Corp. v. Eur. Bank for Reconstruction and Dev., No. 00–CV–02160–CG, 2000 WL 1751094, at *3 (E.D. Pa. Nov. 29, 2000) (preceding *OSS Nokalva*).

[714] OSS Nokalva, Inc. v. Eur. Space Agency, 617 F.3d 756, 763–64 (3d Cir. 2010). Some pre-*Atkinson* decisions in the D.C. Circuit also applied the FSIA, either as an exclusive basis, see Rendall-Speranza v. Nassim, 932 F. Supp. 19, 23–24 (D.D.C. 1996), or as an alternative ground. Tuck v. Pan Am. Health Org., 668 F.2d 547, 550 (D.C. Cir. 1981); Broadbent v. Org. of Am. States, 628 F.2d 27, 32–33 (D.C. Cir. 1980).

[715] The *Restatement (Third)*, for example, considered that international organizations "generally" enjoyed functional immunity, see RESTATEMENT (THIRD) § 467(2), but it also suggested that until the scope of immunity under customary international law was "authoritatively resolved [international organizations] will probably be accorded only restricted immunity under the law of the United States." *Id.* § 467 cmt. d.

[716] Jam v. Int'l Fin. Corp., 139 S. Ct. 759 (2019).

[717] *Id.* at 768.

[718] *Id.* at 767–70.

[719] *Id.* at 770–71 & n.2 (citing authorities); *see, e.g.,* Letter from Roberts B. Owen, Legal Adviser, State Department, to Leroy D. Clark, General Counsel, Equal Employment Opportunity Commission (June 24, 1980), *reprinted in* Marian L. Nash, *Contemporary Practice of the United States Relating to International Law*, 74 AM. J. INT'L L. 917, 917–18 (1980); 1980 DIGEST U.S. PRACTICE 16.

[720] *Jam*, at 768–69, 771–72.

with references to foreign states—would be the touchstone. After *Jam*, it held, "the Foreign Sovereign Immunities Act governs the immunity of international organizations."[721]

Using the FSIA for international organizations may not be easy. Statutory provisions exemplifying the restrictive approach, like the commercial activity exception, may translate awkwardly to international organizations. For example, when an international bank based in Washington, D.C., lends funds to a developing country, is that a commercial activity and, if so, is it sufficiently connected to the United States? In *Jam* itself, the Court anticipated that the immunity of such organizations might prove durable, suggesting room for doubt as to whether lending activity by development banks would constitute "commercial activity," whether the activity would have a sufficient nexus to the United States, or whether such a lawsuit would be "based upon" either the U.S. commercial activity or related U.S. acts.[722] (And on remand, the lower court upheld the organization's immunity on the plausible premise that the complaint's gravamen was tortious activity taking place abroad.[723]) It is too early to perceive any broad pattern,[724] but lower courts may develop distinct approaches in applying FSIA exceptions to international organizations. Tests distinguishing commercial or private acts (*jure gestionis*) from those "peculiarly sovereign in nature" (*jure imperii*)[725] may apply awkwardly to organizations that lack sovereignty altogether[726]—for example, as concerns their lending to foreign states that are

---

[721] *Id.* at 772.

[722] *Id.*

[723] Jam v. Int'l Fin. Corp., 442 F. Supp. 3d 162 (D.D.C. 2020), *aff'd*, 3 F.4th 405 (D.C. Cir. 2021). The district court did not evaluate whether the activity was commercial in nature. *Id.* at 171 & n.2. In determining the gravamen of the complaint, the district employed a "holistic approach." *Id.* at 175. It concluded that the gravamen of the particular complaint was not the lending or any other U.S. activity but the pursuit of a power plant in India that resulted from it. *Id.* at 175–79; *accord Jam v. Int'l Fin. Corp.*, 3 F.4th at 409–11.

[724] *See, e.g.,* Rosenkrantz v. Inter-Am. Dev. Bank, 35 F.4th 854 (D.C. Cir. 2022) (holding that claims that the Inter-American Development Bank had improperly prohibited certain entities from participating in loans to Latin American and Caribbean states fell outside the commercial activity and waiver exceptions); Rodriguez v. Pan American Health Organization, 29 F.4th 706 (D.C. Cir. 2022) (holding that health organization's service as a financial intermediary between the Cuban and Brazilian governments, resulting in human trafficking of Cuban physicians, constituted an allegation of "commercial activity" warranting denial of motion to dismiss)); Francisco S. v. Aetna Life Ins. Co., No. 2:18-cv-00010, 2020 WL 1676353, at *6–7 (C.D. Utah Apr. 6, 2020) (holding that the World Bank's provision of health insurance to its employees, via a private third-party administrator, constituted commercial activity under FSIA approach). A few pre-*Jam* cases applied the FSIA exceptions scheme, at least as an alternative ground. *See, e.g.,* Askir v. Boutros-Ghali, 933 F. Supp. 368, 371–72 (S.D.N.Y. 1996) (concluding that, even under application of restrictive immunity and the FSIA, U.N. peacekeeping operations were not commercial activity).

[725] Saudi Arabia v. Nelson, 507 U.S. 349, 359–61 (1993).

[726] Charles H. Brower II, *International Immunities: Some Dissident Views on the Role of Municipal Courts*, 41 VA. J. INT'L L. 1, 16–17 (2001).

themselves fully sovereign,[727] or as to employment of a truly international civil service.[728]

Another set of issues involves assessing whether the "same immunity" requires applying the FSIA's terms that are ancillary to any theory of restrictive immunity, such as whether the FSIA's venue provision (for any "civil action against a foreign state") applies to actions against an international organization.[729] As previously noted, the FSIA's terrorism-related exceptions also have little to do with the restrictive theory; the exception for state sponsors (§ 1605A) in particular targets state-like rather than private (or international organization) behavior. To apply either terrorism-related exception to international organizations, the United States would have to be participating in, and refusing to revoke the IOIA designation for, the suspect international organization.[730]

Parallel IOIA provisions may also complicate the "same immunity" analysis. For example, as previously noted, FSIA provisions permit waiver "either explicitly or by implication," and indicate that international agreements may vary the level of foreign sovereign immunity.[731] The IOIA, by contrast, provides only that international organizations may waive immunity "expressly"—not, seemingly, by implication.[732] The charters of some organizations do seem to limit immunity,[733] but they have been read quite narrowly by U.S. courts to permit only the "*type of suit* by the *type of plaintiff* that 'would benefit the organization over the

---

[727] In *Jam*, the Supreme Court noted counsel's suggestion that lending by international organizations to sovereigns, on condition that their governments enact regulatory changes, was not the sort of a transaction into which a private party could enter. Jam v. Int'l Fin. Corp., 139 S. Ct. 759, 772 (2019); *see* Transcript of Oral Argument at 27–30, Jam v. Int'l Fin. Corp., 139 S. Ct. 759 (2019) (No. 17-1011).

[728] In foreign sovereign immunity cases, employment matters may be regarded as noncommercial if an employee is in the civil service or its equivalent, see El-Hadad v. United Arab Emirates, 496 F.3d 658, 663–68 (D.C. Cir. 2007), but may regard a foreign state's employment of non-nationals in the United States (even those in the civil service) as commercial in character. H.R. REP. NO. 94-1487, at 16 (1976), *reprinted in* 1976 U.S.C.C.A.N. 6604, 6615; *e.g.*, Lasheen v. Embassy of the Arab Rep. of Egypt, 485 Fed. Appx. 203, 206 (9th Cir. 2012). In a pre-*Jam* case, the D.C. Circuit stated that an international organization's employment relationship with its administrative staff is noncommercial, and suggested that any exception for non-national employees would effectively swallow the rule. Broadbent v. Org. of Am. States, 628 F.2d 27, 34–35 (D.C. Cir. 1980).

[729] The IOIA does not itself address venue and had left courts to apply provisions of general application. One court concluded, after exhaustive analysis, that 28 U.S.C. § 1391(f) (2018), governing civil actions against foreign states, was newly the exclusive venue provision for cases against international organizations—and as applied, required transfer of suit against Pan American Health Organization. Rodriguez v. Pan Am. Health Org., No. 18-cv-24995, 2020 WL 1666757 (S.D. Fla. Apr. 3, 2020).

[730] *See infra* this chapter text accompanying notes 748–752.

[731] 28 U.S.C. § 1604 (noting capacity of preexisting international agreements to vary immunity otherwise conferred by the FSIA); *id.* § 1605(a)(1) (addressing post-enactment waivers, including by international agreement); *see supra* this chapter § V(A)(4)(a).

[732] 22 U.S.C. § 288a(b).

[733] *See, e.g.*, Articles of Agreement of the International Finance Corporation art. 6 § 3(vi), May 25, 1955, 7 U.S.T. 2197, 264 U.N.T.S. 117.

long term.'"[734] This case law is less germane now that immunity may be defeated by the FSIA's commercial activity exception,[735] but it could be obviated completely if the FSIA's waiver exception adds to the IOIA's slightly different terms.[736] Regardless, courts will still have to construe charter-based waivers. Unlike U.S. immunity jurisprudence, which typically poses a choice between absolute and restrictive approaches, international practice often suggests a functional approach in which international organizations enjoy the immunity needed to fulfill their purposes.[737] The charters of major organizations may embody this approach, or presume a background of absolute immunity,[738] and it will be important to monitor how they are construed by U.S. courts in light of the conclusive U.S. shift to a restrictive approach.

Significantly, international agreements may also *enhance* an organization's immunity beyond what a restrictive approach would indicate.[739] The most important example is probably the Convention on the Privileges and Immunities of the United Nations ("General Convention"), which ensures absolute immunity for the United Nations,[740] including U.N. subsidiary bodies, like certain

---

[734] Jam v. Int'l Fin. Corp., 860 F.3d 703, 706 (D.C. Cir. 2017) (emphases in original; quoting Osseiran v. Int'l Fin. Corp., 552 F.3d 836, 840 (D.C. Cir. 2009)), *rev'd on other grounds*, Jam v. Int'l Fin. Corp., 139 S. Ct. 759 (2019).

[735] *Jam*, 860 F.3d at 707 (noting "superficial similarity" to a proposed commercial activities test, but further noting the greater breadth of such a test); *see also id.* at 712 (Pillard, J., concurring) (stating, inter alia, that "the cases in which we have applied *Mendaro* [v. World Bank, 717 F.2d 610 (D.C. Cir. 1983)] to hold that claims are not immunity-barred look remarkably like cases that would be allowed to proceed under the FSIA's commercial activity exception").

[736] *But see* Jam v. Int'l Fin. Corp., 442 F. Supp. 3d 162, 179 n.5 (D.D.C. 2020) (stating that the Supreme Court's opinion in *Jam* "did not overturn the D.C. Circuit's corresponding benefits test for waivers of immunity in international treaties, nor does the Supreme Court's interpretation of the IOIA provide any information as to what the drafters of the IFC Articles of Agreement intended").

[737] RESTATEMENT (THIRD) § 467(1); *see also* PETER H.F. BEKKER, THE LEGAL POSITION OF INTERGOVERNMENTAL ORGANIZATIONS: A FUNCTIONAL NECESSITY ANALYSIS OF THEIR LEGAL STATUS AND IMMUNITIES (1994); Michael Singer, *Jurisdictional Immunity of International Organizations: Human Rights and Functional Necessity Concerns*, 36 VA. J. INT'L L. 65 (1996). There is room for dispute as to whether international law has fully crystallized. Michael Wood, *Do International Organizations Enjoy Immunity Under Customary International Law?*, 10 INT'L ORG. L. REV. 287, 317 (2014).

[738] *See, e.g.*, Constitution of the World Health Organization art. 67(a), July 22, 1946, 62 Stat. 2679, 14 U.N.T.S. 185 ("The Organization shall enjoy in the territory of each Member such privileges and immunities as may be necessary for the fulfilment of its objective and for the exercise of its functions."). The immunities of some organizations must be ascertained according to more than one instrument, including any relevant reservations. *See* Statute of the International Atomic Energy Agency art. XV, July 29, 1957, 8 U.S.T. 1093, 276 U.N.T.S. 3 (establishing functional immunity for the IAEA, but also providing for further articulation in separate agreements with members).

[739] *Jam*, 139 S. Ct. at 771 (stating that "the privileges and immunities accorded by the IOIA are only default rules," and that "[i]f the work of a given international organization would be impaired by restrictive immunity, the organization's charter can always specify a different level of immunity").

[740] Convention on the Privileges and Immunities of the United Nations art. II(2), Feb. 13, 1946, 21 U.S.T. 1418, 1 U.N.T.S. 15 [hereinafter General Convention] (providing that the United Nations "shall enjoy immunity from every form of legal process except insofar as in any particular case it has expressly waived its immunity"). The Convention on the Privileges and Immunities of the Specialized Agencies ("Special Convention"), Nov. 21, 1947, 33 U.N.T.S. 261, governs the immunity of autonomous organizations that carry out various functions on behalf of the United Nations—such as the

peacekeeping missions and the U.N. Development Program.[741] Prior to *Jam*, lower courts applied the General Convention alongside the IOIA (under which the United Nations had been duly designated) by asserting that they both provided for absolute immunity or by applying the treaty in lieu of the statute.[742] Other agreements posed similar issues.[743] *Jam* did not elaborate how, precisely, such agreements should be applied now that "the [FSIA] governs the immunity of international organizations."[744] Presumably, pre-FSIA international agreements establishing absolute immunity can be accommodated through the FSIA's clause that grandfathers existing international agreements,[745] while post-FSIA international agreements would govern if they are considered self-executing and prevailed in U.S. law under a later-in-time analysis.[746] Like IOIA-based immunity, immunity under the General Convention or other agreements may be waived, but typically such waivers must be express.[747]

Finally, the IOIA has distinct features that operate independent of the FSIA. One is the IOIA's delegation of authority to the president to designate

International Monetary Fund (IMF), the World Health Organization (WHO), the International Finance Corporation (IFC), and the World Intellectual Property Organization (WIPO). However, the United States is not a party to the Special Convention.

[741] *See, e.g.,* Georges v. United Nations, 84 F. Supp. 3d 246, 249 (S.D.N.Y. 2015) (applying General Convention to the U.N. Stabilization Mission in Haiti (MINUSTAH), also subject to a Status of Forces Agreement), *aff'd,* Georges v. United Nations, 834 F.3d 88 (2d Cir. 2016); Lempert v. Rice, 956 F. Supp. 2d 17, 23–24 (D.D.C. 2013) (applying General Convention to the U.N. Development Program as a subsidiary organ).

[742] Exec. Order No. 9,698, 11 Fed. Reg. 1,809 (Feb. 19, 1946) (designating United Nations, among other organizations); *see, e.g.,* Brzak v. United Nations, 597 F.3d 107, 111–13 (2d Cir. 2010) (concluding that the United Nations was immune under the General Convention as a self-executing treaty, under the IOIA were that statute deemed to establish absolute immunity, and under the IOIA if read consistent with the FSIA); Van Aggelen v. United Nations, 311 Fed. Appx. 407, 409 (2d Cir. 2009) (assuming absolute immunity under the U.N. Charter, the General Convention, and the IOIA).

[743] *See, e.g., Jam,* 139 S. Ct. at 771–72 (citing example of the Articles of Agreement of the International Monetary Fund art. IX, § 3, Dec. 27, 1945, 60 Stat. 1413, 2 U.N.T.S. 39). To a degree, the development of immunity-enhancing agreements buttresses the holding in *Jam*. The U.S. government cited in this regard the example of the Organization of American States (OAS): while its charter appeared to establish functional immunity, see Charter of the Organization of American States art. 103, Dec. 13, 1951, 2 U.S.T. 2394, 119 U.N.T.S. 3, after the OAS was designated under the IOIA, the United States entered into a further agreement that afforded absolute immunity. Headquarters Agreement Between the Government of the United States of America and the Organization of American States art. IV, § 1, May 14, 1992, S. Treaty Doc. No. 102-40. This was evidently done to enhance the restrictive immunity thought due under the IOIA, in exchange for OAS's commitments. S. Treaty Doc. No. 102-40, *supra,* at VI (describing agreement as "afford[ing] the OAS full immunity from judicial process, thus going beyond the usual United States practice of affording restrictive immunity"); *see* Brief for the United States as Amicus Curiae Supporting Reversal at 28, Jam v. Int'l Fin. Corp., 139 S. Ct. 759 (2019) (No. 17-1011).

[744] 139 S. Ct. at 772.

[745] *See supra* text accompanying note 731.

[746] *See* Chapter 6 § IV(A)(2).

[747] *See, e.g., Brzak,* 597 F.3d at 113; *see also* Georges v. United Nations, 834 F.3d 88, 92–98 (2d Cir. 2016) (holding that the United Nations' alleged disregard of internal dispute procedures did not fatally undermine a condition precedent for immunity, nor constitute a material breach).

an international organization as entitled to privileges and immunities. In *Jam*, the Court rejected the argument that the president's capacity to thus "update" immunities for a particular organization undermined the Court's construction, in which the IOIA essentially updated itself; the Court described presidential authority as "retail rather than wholesale."[748] To the Court, the authority was comparable to what the recognition power affords for foreign sovereign immunity, one difference being that the executive's authority with respect to international organizations is delegated by Congress.[749] Likewise, the power to revoke such designation might be analogized to the capacity of the executive to derecognize a foreign state or its government.[750] Arguably the president's more graduated authority to condition or limit immunities of international organizations seems more like the Tate Letter regime that prevailed prior to the FSIA—and which the political branches were intent on renouncing when adopting the FSIA.[751] Of course, if an international organization's immunity is derived from an international agreement binding the United States, presidential authority is limited, barring lawful steps to terminate, suspend, or withdraw from the agreement in question.[752]

Another distinguishing feature of the IOIA concerns its relation to immunities of persons. The FSIA does not apply to suits against foreign government

---

[748] 139 S. Ct. at 770.

[749] Section 288 of the IOIA says that a designated organization must be one in which the legislature has authorized the United States to participate. This means, for example, that the president lacks authority to designate the Organization of the Petroleum Exporting Countries (OPEC), in which the United States does not participate. Prewitt Enter. v. Org. of Petroleum Exporting Countries, 353 F.3d 916, 922 n.9 (11th Cir. 2003). Prior legislative approval of U.S. participation may also help insulate the IOIA from constitutional challenges. See United States v. Harder, 168 F. Supp. 3d 732, 740–42 (E.D. Pa. 2016) (rejecting nondelegation objection to statutory provision prohibiting certain trade practices, identifying affected "public international organizations" in part according to presidential designation under 22 U.S.C. § 288). Congress does, however, occasionally extends executive branch authority under the IOIA to encompass organizations in which the United States does not participate. See, e.g., Extending Immunities to the Office of the High Representative in Bosnia and Herzegovina and the International Civilian Office in Kosovo Act of 2010 §§ 2, 17, 124 Stat. 1260 (2010) (codified at 22 U.S.C. § 288f-7); Exec. Order No. 13,568, 76 Fed. Reg. 13,497 (Mar. 8, 2011); Zuza v. Office of the High Representative, 857 F.3d 935, 936–37 (D.C. Cir. 2017).

[750] This authority has been exercised to reflect an organization's cessation, sometimes in connection with U.S. re-engagement with its successor. See, e.g., Exec. Order No. 11,767, 39 Fed. Reg. 6,603 (Feb. 21, 1974) (Organization of African Unity), revoked by Exec. Order No. 13,377, 70 Fed. Reg. 20,263 (Apr. 18, 2005) (revoking designation of the Organization of African Unity and designating the African Union, by virtue of IOIA and amendments thereto) (citing, inter alia 22 U.S.C. §§ 288, 288f-2).

[751] In *Jam* itself, the Supreme Court cited INTERPOL and INTELSAT as examples of international organizations accorded only limited immunity. 139 S. Ct. at 770 (citing Exec. Order No. 12,425, 3 C.F.R. 193 (1984) (INTERPOL); Exec. Order No. 11,718, 3 C.F.R. 177 (1974) (INTELSAT)). In each case, those limits were later removed. Exec. Order No. 13,524, 74 Fed. Reg. 67,803 (Dec. 16, 2009) (INTERPOL); Exec. Order No. 11,966, 42 Fed. Reg. 4,331 (Jan. 19, 1977) (INTELSAT); see also Exec. Order No. 12,359, 47 Fed. Reg. 17,791 (Apr. 26, 1982) (designating limited immunity for the International Food Policy Research Institute).

[752] See Chapter 6 § VI (addressing treaty termination).

officials.[753] The IOIA, in contrast, *does* apply to persons associated with international organizations, though it is not a self-contained regime.[754] The IOIA establishes—for the organizations' officers and employees, and for those representing foreign governments in international organizations[755]—immunity from suit and legal process "relating to acts performed by them in their official capacity and falling within their functions," absent waiver by the relevant entity.[756] This immunity for official acts, which is similar to one used for current and former officials of foreign states, is substantial but not unlimited.[757]

As elsewhere, this statutory scheme concerning officials of international organizations is supplemented by international agreements. The General Convention establishes for high-ranking U.N. officials the same immunities afforded diplomats, "in accordance with international law," which brings into play the Vienna Convention on Diplomatic Relations (discussed in the following subsection). More generally, it confers immunity from suit and legal process on U.N. officials for communications and acts performed in their official capacity, plus other privileges and immunities.[758] This scheme means that current and former officials are guaranteed functional immunity for their official

---

[753] *See infra* this chapter § V(D) (discussing Samantar v. Yousuf, 560 U.S. 305 (2010)).

[754] *See* United States v. Bahel, 662 F.3d 610, 623 (2d Cir. 2011) (rebutting attempt by a former U.N. employee to invoke the Diplomatic Relations Act, 22 U.S.C. § 254d, by observing that "the IOIA expressly applies to 'officers and employees of [international] organizations'") (quoting 22 U.S.C. § 288(d)(b)).

[755] The IOIA provides that to benefit, personnel must be notified to and designated by the secretary of state. 22 U.S.C. § 288e. While the person is immune, if such immunity is invoked, the secretary of state may order that the person leave the United States and no longer enjoy such benefits.

[756] 22 U.S.C. § 288d(b); *see also id.* § 288d(a) (establishing privileges and immunities with respect to entry and departure into the United States for specified personnel and their immediate families).

[757] *See infra* this chapter § V(D)(2) (discussing official immunity). A wide variety of acts are considered to be taken in an official capacity. *See, e.g.,* Rendall-Speranza v. Nassim, 107 F.3d 913, 919–20 (D.C. Cir. 1997) (alleged battery by employee of the International Finance Corporation deemed to fall within official capacity, and subject to immunity under the IOIA, on predicate that battery would have involved the protection of offices against trespass and of files from tampering or theft); Donald v. Orfila, 788 F.2d 36, 36 (D.C. Cir. 1986) (employment termination at the direction of the secretary general of the Organization of American States was within official capacity, and subject to IOIA immunity).

[758] General Convention, *supra* note 740, art. V, § 19 (addressing immunities of the U.N. secretary-general and all assistant secretaries-general); *id.* art. V, § 18(a) (addressing official capacity immunity); *id.* art. V, §§ 18(b)–(g) (detailing assorted privileges and immunities, such as tax exemption and national service exemptions); *see also id.* art. V, § 17 (authorizing U.N. secretary-general to specify eligible categories of officials). For descriptions of this regime, see Letter from Michael J. Garcia, U.S. Att'y, to Robert W. Sweet, U.S. Dist. J., S. Dist. N.Y., Re: Brzak; et al. v. United Nations, et al., 06 Civ. 3432 (RWS) at 3, (Oct. 2, 2007), https://perma.cc/U9S4-ALMY; Letter from Nicholas Cartier, U.S. Dep't Justice Trial Att'y, to Roanne L. Mann, Chief U.S. Mag. J., E. Dist. N.Y., Re: Laventure et al. v. United Nations et al., CV-14-1611 (Townes, J.) (Mann, C.M.J.) at 5–6, (May 24, 2017), https://perma.cc/GE7R-ELYZ. At U.S. insistence—reflected in a reservation to the General Convention, as well as well as statutory law—U.S. nationals or permanent residents who are also U.N. employees do not benefit from some privileges and immunities, such as those concerning national service and taxation. The same is the case for other international organizations. RESTATEMENT (THIRD) § 469 cmts. b & e & rptrs. notes 3, 5–7; *e.g.,* 26 U.S.C. § 893 (income tax exemption); U.S. Reservation to § 18(b) of the General Convention, *supra* note 740, https://perma.cc/5D79-K4AQ.

acts, much as they would be pursuant to application of the IOIA; such immunity encompasses acts as diverse as employment-related matters and the direction of peacekeeping troops.[759] The General Convention is supplemented by yet other agreements, such as the U.N.-U.S. Headquarters Agreement, which addresses the United Nations' physical presence in the United States.[760] Accordingly, that agreement not only protects U.N. officials while in transit, and establishes the inviolability of U.N. premises, but also provides diplomatic privileges and immunities to designated officials of U.N. member states serving as representatives to the United Nations (who are also covered by the IOIA).[761] Other international organizations also have immunity regimes based on international agreements, including headquarters agreements.[762]

C. Diplomatic and Consular Officials and Premises

Diplomatic and consular privileges and immunities are extensively regulated by two widely subscribed treaties to which the United States is a party: the Vienna Convention on Diplomatic Relations (VCDR) and the Vienna Convention on Consular Relations (VCCR).[763] Each has generated extensive international practice and commentary, some of it concerning immunity-related issues.[764]

---

[759] *See, e.g.*, Brzak v. United Nations, 597 F.3d 107, 113 (2d Cir. 2010) (employment-related claims); Laventure v. United Nations, 279 F. Supp. 3d 394, 400–01 (E.D.N.Y. 2017) (decisions concerning the deployment of cholera-infected U.N. peacekeeping troops to Haiti). As might be expected, such immunity may be waived, subject to standards set by the governing agreement. *See, e.g.*, Koumoin v. Ki-Moon, No. 16-cv-2111, 2016 WL 7243551 at *5 (S.D.N.Y. Dec. 14, 2016) (rejecting argument that the United Nations had impliedly waived the U.N. secretary-general's immunity by participating in internal review before the U.N. Administrative Tribunal).

[760] Agreement Between the United Nations and the United States Regarding the Headquarters of the United Nations, June 26, 1947, U.S.-U.N., 61 Stat. 758, 11 U.N.T.S. 11 [hereinafter Headquarters Agreement]; *see* RESTATEMENT (THIRD) § 467, cmt. f & rptrs. note 9.

[761] As regards U.N. officials in transit, see Headquarters Agreement, *supra* note 760, art. IV § 11; RESTATEMENT (THIRD) § 468 cmt. c & rptrs. notes 2, 5–6; *id.* § 469 rptrs. note 1; *see also id.* § 469 note 8 (distinguishing invitees); Kadic v. Karadzic, 70 F.3d 232, 247–48 (2d Cir. 1995) (same). As regards inviolability of premises, see Headquarters Agreement, art. III § 9; RESTATEMENT (THIRD) § 468 cmts. b–c & rptrs. notes 3, 7. As regards representatives of member states, see Headquarters Agreement, art. V § 15; RESTATEMENT (THIRD) § 470; Statement of Interest of the United States at 6–18, Begum v. Saleh, No. 99 Civ. 11834 (RMB) (S.D.N.Y. Mar. 31, 2000), excerpted at 2000 DIGEST OF U.S. PRACTICE, available at https://perma.cc/M3CC-D6L7 (describing application of the U.N. Charter, the Headquarters Agreement, and the General Convention to representatives to the United Nations and their families).

[762] *See generally* RESTATEMENT (THIRD) § 469.

[763] Vienna Convention on Diplomatic Relations, June 24, 1964, 23 U.S.T. 3227, 500 U.N.T.S. 95 [hereinafter VCDR]; Vienna Convention on Consular Relations, Apr. 24, 1963, 21 U.S.T. 77, 596 U.N.T.S. 261 [hereinafter VCCR].

[764] *See generally* EILEEN DENZA, DIPLOMATIC LAW: COMMENTARY ON THE VIENNA CONVENTION ON DIPLOMATIC RELATIONS (4th ed. 2016); LUKE T. LEE & JOHN QUIGLEY, CONSULAR LAW AND PRACTICE (3d ed. 2008). The distinction between immunity and "privileges" is not particularly rigorous. *See, e.g.*, LINDA S. FREY & MARSHA L. FREY, THE HISTORY OF DIPLOMATIC IMMUNITY 490–91

As discussed in Chapter 3, core provisions ensure the inviolability, in varying respects, of diplomatic and consular premises and officials in the United States.[765] As one measure of these rules' strength, obligations to respect and protect all such premises survive the severing of diplomatic relations and even armed conflict between the United States and the foreign state.[766] While such provisions are routinely observed without much invocation in U.S. courts, Chapter 9 discusses how the VCCR's provisions addressing consular functions on behalf of detained noncitizens have occasioned substantial international and domestic litigation for the United States.[767]

The VCDR and VCCR are incorporated differently. The VCDR entered into force for the United States in 1972. At first it existed alongside the old statutory regime, which had been enacted in 1790,[768] but eventually Congress enacted the Diplomatic Relations Act of 1978.[769] The result is that the VCDR, together with certain statutory provisions, sets forth U.S. law as to diplomatic privileges and immunities.[770] In contrast, because there is no comparable implementing

(1999) (describing range of diplomatic immunities and privileges recognized in the United States after passage of the Diplomatic Relations Act of 1978).

[765] See Chapter 3 § II(A) (diplomatic officials); Chapter 3 § II(B) (diplomatic premises). Diplomatic premises are absolutely inviolable. VCDR, supra note 763, art. 22; DENZA, supra note 764, at 110–48. Consular premises are inviolable to a somewhat lesser extent, including because of an exception for protective actions relating to fire or other disasters. VCCR, supra note 763, art. 31; see Lee & Quigley, supra note 764, at 353–84.

[766] VCDR, supra note 763, art. 15; VCCR, supra note 763, art. 27.

[767] See Chapter 9 § II(B)–(C). For the culmination of the U.S. proceedings, see Medellín v. Texas, 552 U.S. 491 (2008); for the culmination of the international proceedings, see Case Concerning Avena and Other Mexican Nationals (Mex. v. U.S.), Judgment, 2004 I.C.J. 12 (Mar. 31). For additional discussions of Medellín, see Chapter 1 § II(B); Chapter 3 § I(D); Chapter 5 § II(B); Chapter 6 §§ III(B) (3), IV; and Chapter 7 § III(C).

[768] See Letter from Robert G. Dixon, Jr., Assistant Att'y Gen., Office of Legal Counsel, Dep't of Justice, to Charles N. Brower, Acting Legal Adviser, Dep't of State (May 4, 1973), excerpted in Arthur W. Rovine, Contemporary Practice of the United States Relating to International Law, 67 AM. J. INT'L L. 760, 760–61 (1973) (noting shared assumption that the VCDR "is self-executing and therefore can be considered part of domestic law without further implementation," but also that "ratification . . . did not act to repeal existing legislation," given the possibility of applying broader statutory privileges and immunities).

[769] Ch. 9, §§ 25–27, 1 Stat. 117 (1790), superseded by Pub. L. No. 95-393, 92 Stat. 808 (1978) (codified at 22 U.S.C. §§ 254a–e); see Abdulazi v. Metropolitan Dade County, 741 F.2d 1328, 1330 (11th Cir. 1984); Barry Cohen, The Diplomatic Relations Act of 1978, 28 CATH. U. L. REV. 797, 797–818 (1979). Statutory implementation also enables the United States to extend the privileges and immunities in the VCDR to the missions of nonparty states—though that does not include mission staff. 22 U.S.C. § 254b; contrast id. § 254a (describing application for states parties).

[770] The statute itself does not expressly incorporate the VCDR and better attends to other matters not directly addressed by the treaty. Nonetheless, Congress apparently intended to "codify the privileges and immunities provisions of the Vienna Convention as the sole United States law on the subject," and repeal inconsistent legislation, while at the same time continuing to regard the treaty as self-executing. S. REP. No. 95-1108, at 1–2 (1978); e.g., 22 U.S.C. § 254d (entitling individuals to move to dismiss actions based on their entitlement to immunity under the VCDR; cf. RESTATEMENT (FOURTH) § 421 rptrs. note 6 (describing VCDR as self-executing, while noting that "Congress has additionally implemented [it] by statute").

legislation for the VCCR, U.S. consular relations law depends more directly on that treaty.[771] Most VCCR litigation has involved the rights of detained noncitizens, and in those cases, courts have generally assumed that the relevant treaty provisions are self-executing,[772] often while addressing whether (even if self-executing) the VCCR affords detained noncitizens enforceable rights.[773] Of course, some VCCR provisions may be self-executing, while others are not,[774] but it is also generally assumed that the VCCR may be directly invoked by foreign states in U.S. courts in relation to rights accorded consular officials.[775] The VCCR is supplemented by bilateral consular conventions, which provides for their application (even as between parties to the VCCR) if they afford more generous privileges and immunities.[776]

The VCDR and the Diplomatic Relations Act establish for diplomatic agents inviolability against arrest or detention, absolute immunity against criminal prosecution, and immunity against most exercises of civil and administrative jurisdiction.[777] There are exceptions for civil actions against diplomatic agents relating to personal real estate, succession, or professional or commercial activity outside official functions, but these exceptions have been narrowly construed by U.S. courts.[778] Other VCDR provisions concern regulatory matters, such as

[771] But cf. infra this chapter text accompanying notes 790–798 (discussing presidential authority).

[772] In Medellín v. Texas, the Supreme Court found it unnecessary to resolve either the issue of self-execution of the VCCR or the issue of individual rights. Medellín, 552 U.S. at 506 n.4; see Earle v. District of Columbia, 707 F.3d 299, 304 (D.C. Cir. 2012) (likewise declining to resolve them). A few opinions have been more forward-leaning. Medellín v. Dretke, 544 U.S. 660, 685–86 (2005) (O'Connor, J., dissenting) (concluding that Article 36 of the VCCR is self-executing, and noting agreement of the U.S. government); Breard v. Pruett, 134 F.3d 615, 622 (4th Cir. 1998) (Butzner, J. concurring) (VCCR is self-executing). But cf. Fernando v. Sareen, No. 3:15-cv-03039-JD, 2016 WL 556007, at *3 (N.D. Cal. Feb. 12, 2016) (construing Medellín, mistakenly, as "finding that the Vienna Convention is not self-executing").

[773] A few decisions state sweepingly that the VCCR does not confer individual rights. See, e.g., Cardenas v. Stephens, 820 F.3d 197, 203 & n.6 (5th Cir. 2016). Other opinions, defensibly, consider the matter according to individual provision. See, e.g., Sanchez-Llamas v. Oregon, 548 U.S. 331, 342–43 (2006) (assuming arguendo that Article 36 of the VCCR gives foreign nationals "an individually enforceable right to request that their consular officers be notified of their detention, and an accompanying right to be informed by authorities of the availability of consular notification"); accord Medellín, 552 U.S. at 506 n.4 (quoting Sanchez-Llamas).

[774] See Chapter 6 § IV.

[775] See, e.g., RESTATEMENT (FOURTH) § 421 rptrs. note 6 (describing jurisdiction over immunities cases on the basis that "[b]oth [the VCDR and the VCCR] are self-executing"). Indeed, the lack of implementing legislation may be due to expectations that the VCCR would be considered self-executing. See, e.g., S. EXEC. REP. NO. 91-9, at 5 (1969) (statement of J. Edward Lyerly, Deputy Legal Adviser, that the VCCR "is considered entirely self-executive and does not require any implementing or complementing legislation").

[776] VCCR, supra note 763, art. 73; RESTATEMENT (THIRD) § 465 rptrs. note 3.

[777] See VCDR, supra note 763, arts. 29 (inviolability generally), 30 (residence and papers), 31(1) (immunity); U.S. Dep't of State, 2 Foreign Affairs Manual 232.1, https://perma.cc/76U4-UW6T; RESTATEMENT (THIRD) § 464. As the Restatement (Third) advises, inviolability and immunity protect the affected parties from certain legal processes, but that does not mean they are free to ignore the governing law. RESTATEMENT (THIRD) § 464 cmt. c.

[778] See VCDR, supra note 763, art. 31(1)(a)–(c); RESTATEMENT (THIRD) § 464 cmt. f & rptrs. note 9; e.g., Tabion v. Mufti, 73 F.3d 535, 537–39 (4th Cir. 1996) (stressing narrowness of commercial

exemptions for diplomatic agents from taxes.[779] Former diplomatic agents retain immunity for acts performed in exercising their official functions,[780] and the VCDR provides some protection for other personnel.[781]

The VCCR affords consular officers a more modest form of inviolability (from arrest or detention only pending trial, and excluding judicially authorized proceedings involving grave crimes) and immunity resembling that accorded former diplomatic agents—that is, providing immunity for acts performed in the exercise of official functions.[782] Immunity for traffic accidents was a particular point of controversy. While the Diplomatic Relations Act struck a compromise for diplomats that required insurance and provided for direct suit against insurers, the VCCR instead established an accident-related exception to the immunity of

exception, and noting that commercial and contractual matters not involving the pursuit of a trade or business remain subject to immunity). Commercial activity is largely proscribed for such officials anyway, see VCDR, *supra* note 763, art. 42, meaning that any exception may be "minor" or even "meaningless." *Diplomatic Immunity: Hearings on S. 476, S. 477, S. 478, S. 1256, S. 1257 and H.R. 7819 Before the Subcomm. on Citizens and Shareholders Rights and Remedies of the Senate Comm. on the Judiciary*, 95th Cong., 2d Sess. 32 (1978) (testimony of Bruno A. Ristau, Chief, Foreign Litigation Unit, Civil Division); *see Tabion*, 73 F.3d at 538 & n.6 (citing this and related authority).

[779] VCDR, *supra* note 763, arts. 33–36 (addressing social security, tax, military and similar obligations, and customs); RESTATEMENT (THIRD) § 464 cmt. c & rptrs. note 3.

[780] VCDR, *supra* note 763, art. 39(1)–(2). The standard for residual immunity has been variously stated. *See, e.g.*, Swarna v. Al Awadi, 622 F.3d 123, 135 (2d Cir. 2010) (residual immunity applies to acts "incidental and indispensable to diplomatic activities includ[ing], in this context, only such acts as are directly imputable to the state or inextricably tied to a diplomat's professional activities").

[781] VCDR, *supra* note 763, art. 1 (defining affected personnel); 22 U.S.C. § 254a (2018) (defining "members of a mission" and included personnel). Family members in a diplomatic agent's household are generally treated like the agents themselves, but administrative and technical staff (and their families) enjoy somewhat reduced immunity from civil and administrative jurisdiction, and service staff enjoy immunity only for official functions. VCDR, *supra* note 763, arts. 37(1) & 39(2)–(3) (family); *id.* art. 37(2) (administrative and technical staff and families); *id.* art. 37(3) (service staff); *see also* art. 37(4) (addressing yet more limited privileges and immunities due personal servants); RESTATEMENT (THIRD) § 464 cmts. a, g.

[782] VCCR, *supra* note 763, art. 41 (inviolability); *id.* art. 43 (immunity); U.S. Dep't of State, 1 Foreign Affairs Manual 232.2, https://perma.cc/RL7V-2TL2; *see* Rana v. Islam, 305 F.R.D. 53, 59, 60 (S.D.N.Y. 2015) (contrasting VCDR and VCCR regimes, and noting that "[t]he standard for residual diplomatic immunity is virtually identical to that for consular immunity"); *cf.* RESTATEMENT (THIRD) § 465 cmt. a & rptrs. note 1 (stating that "[t]he immunity of consular officers from the receiving state's jurisdiction to prescribe is essentially the same as that of diplomatic agents," save that a consular officer's immunity is generally limited to official functions); *id.* § 465 cmt. c (describing criminal jurisdiction).

The first inquiry, therefore, is whether a consular function is implicated at all; employing persons for personal domestic work, for example, is not considered to be a consular function. *See, e.g.*, Park v. Shin, 313 F.3d 1138, 1141–43 (9th Cir. 2002); *Rana*, 305 F.R.D. at 59–62; *contrast* Ewald v. Royal Nor. Embassy, No. 11–2116 SRN/SER, 2012 WL 245244, at *4 (D. Minn. Jan. 26, 2012) (citing workplace decisions, protecting consular premises, and obtaining office space as consular functions) (citations omitted). If so, the question is then whether the acts for which immunity is sought were performed within the scope of that function. *Park*, 313 F.3d at 1141–42. The fact that something is unlawful or wrongful does not mean it falls outside the scope. *Ewald*, 2012 WL 245244, at *5; *e.g.*, Ford v. Clement, 834 F. Supp. 72, 75–77 (S.D.N.Y. 1993) (Sotomayor, J.) (dismissing on consular immunity grounds claims alleging employment discrimination, harassment, and wrongful termination).

consular officers.[783] Other exceptions for consular immunity include contractual matters,[784] a provision allowing members of a consular post to be called to serve as witnesses,[785] and various exemptions relating to obligations under domestic law, such as for residence or work permits.[786]

Significantly, the immunity for both diplomats and consular officials is subject to waiver by the foreign state concerned, as it is for the benefit of the state rather than the individual.[787] Such waiver must be express, although it may also be accomplished when a diplomat or consular official initiates proceedings.[788] Raising immunity, on the other hand, may be accomplished by the individual concerned, so long as the state concerned does not differ.[789]

More so than for foreign sovereign immunity or immunity of international organizations (and more like other forms of individual immunity, as discussed later), the executive branch plays a pervasive role in administering diplomatic and consular immunity. The Department of State accredits diplomatic and consular personnel assigned to duty in the United States, normally a condition precedent for whether such personnel may claim immunity.[790] U.S. courts consider

[783] For diplomats, see 22 U.S.C. § 254e; 28 U.S.C. § 1364; S. Rep. No. 95-1108, at 3–5 (1978); cf. Restatement (Third) § 464 rptrs. note 8 (noting that issuing traffic violations, for payment by a foreign mission, appears accepted). For consular officials, see VCCR, supra note 763, art. 43(2)(b); id. art. 56 (requiring compliance with receiving state regulations concerning insurance against third-party risks); Restatement (Third) § 465 cmt. d.

[784] VCCR, supra note 763, art. 43(2)(a); e.g., Rana, 305 F.R.D. at 62 (holding, alternatively, that action brought by domestic employee would, if qualifying as consular function, nonetheless be excluded from immunity as a contractual matter).

[785] VCCR, supra note 763, art. 44. As noted, this is not the case for diplomats. Restatement (Third) § 464 cmt. f. It is limited, however, in that (beyond avoiding interference with or inquiry into official matters) consular officials cannot be compelled to cooperate should they refuse. VCCR, supra note 763, art. 44; see id. art. 41 (discussing inviolability generally); Restatement (Third) § 465 cmt. e.

[786] VCCR, supra note 763, arts. 46–52, 71(2). Family members of consular personnel do not share their immunities (unlike the families of diplomats), but they do enjoy similar exemptions. Restatement (Third) § 465 rptrs. note 9.

[787] This is evident in the preambles to both treaties. The primary implication is that the individual may not block the relevant state's waiver. Restatement (Third) § 464 cmt. j. The United States, like other states, encourages states to waive immunity in criminal matters. U.S. Dep't of State, 2 Foreign Affairs Manual 232.5, https://perma.cc/4JZ8-UQ85; Text of 11-15-89 Circular Diplomatic Note to Chiefs of Diplomatic Missions in the United States, id. at Exhibit 233.4 (https://perma.cc/KY2D-29C7).

[788] As to diplomats, see VCDR, supra note 763, art. 32; Restatement (Third) § 464 cmt. j & rptrs. note 15; as to consular officials, see VCCR, supra note 763, art. 45; Restatement (Third) § 465 rptrs. note 11 (stating that "[t]he principles governing waiver of immunity of consular officials are the same as for diplomats"). The initiation of such proceedings precludes immunity as to counterclaims. VCDR, supra note 763, art. 32(3); VCCR, supra note 763, art. 45(2)–(3).

[789] United States v. Al Sharaf, 183 F. Supp. 3d 45, 51–52 (D.D.C. 2016) (diplomatic immunity). Corroboration from the state, however, may be necessary. Mazengo v. Mzengi, 542 F. Supp. 2d 96, 99–100 (D.D.C. 2008).

[790] See Chapter 3 § II(A); see also U.S. Dep't of State, 2 Foreign Affairs Manual 232.4, https://perma.cc/4JZ8-UQ85; Restatement (Third) § 464 rptrs. note 1 ("In the United States, a person's diplomatic status is established when it is recognized by the Department of State") (citing cases). As the Restatement (Third) notes, the Department of State's view is that its Diplomatic List (the "Blue List" of diplomatic officers and spouses), and presumably its other lists of foreign personnel (such as its

Department of State certification of diplomatic status to be conclusive,[791] and they also appear inclined to defer regarding whether that status requires immunity and dismissal of an action—although the latter seems more judicial in character.[792] In practice, judicial and executive determinations appear closely aligned.[793]

Beyond expressing its positions in judicial proceedings, the Department of State enjoys other remedial options, such as its general policy of requiring (where a foreign state has refused to waive immunity) that those benefiting from immunity but accused of serious criminal offenses must leave the country.[794] It also has more general authority. Under the Diplomatic Relations Act, the president is given authority, since delegated to the secretary of state, to specify privileges and immunities that afford "more favorable treatment or less favorable treatment" than under the VCDR, under terms or conditions of the president's choosing, so long as they are reciprocal. This appears to license executive agreements or even less formal arrangements by which immunities for a particular foreign

---

"White List" of other diplomatic personnel), is merely presumptive proof either that a listed individual is entitled to diplomatic status or that an unlisted individual is not. Restatement (Third) § 464 rptrs. note 1 (citing Trost v. Tompkins, 44 A.2d 226 (Mun. Ct. App. D.C. 1945); United States v. Dizdar, 581 F.2d 1031 (2d Cir. 1978)). But cf. Ali v. Dist. Dir., 209 F. Supp. 3d 1268, 1276 (S.D. Fla. 2016) (regarding nonexistence of an individual on the Blue List as probative of whether he enjoyed diplomatic immunity at the time of his son's birth). See generally Chapter 3 § II(A) (describing U.S. procedures for receiving foreign ambassadors and similar officials).

[791] See, e.g., United States v. Al-Hamdi, 356 F.3d 564, 570–73 (4th Cir. 2004) (giving "substantial deference" to the Department of State's interpretation of the family members entitled to immunity as part of a diplomat's household, noting that "no reviewing court has ever held that the State Department's certification is anything but conclusive," and holding that such certification "is conclusive evidence as to the diplomatic status of an individual"); see also In re Baiz, 135 U.S. 403, 421–22, 432 (1890) (indicating deference to "the decision of the executive in reference to the public character of a person claiming to be a foreign minister"); Restatement (Third) § 464 rptrs. note 1 ("A certification by the Department of State that an individual is, or is not, a diplomatic agent, communicated to a court in the United States, is binding on the court") (citing cases).

[792] One decision stated that "once the United States Department of State has regularly certified a visitor to this country as having diplomatic status, the courts are bound to accept that determination, and that the diplomatic immunity flowing from that status serves as a defense to suits already commenced." Abdulaziz v. Metropolitan Dade County, 741 F.2d 1328, 1329–30 (11th Cir. 1984).

[793] See, e.g., Rana v. Islam, 305 F.R.D. 53, 59 (S.D.N.Y. 2015) (holding, following legal analysis, that employment relationship fell outside consular functions and lacked consular immunity, without Department of State certification but where consular status was "unquestionabl[e]"); Swarna v. Al-Awadi, 622 F.3d 123, 133–40 (2d Cir. 2010) (holding, following legal analysis, that employment relationship fell outside residual diplomatic immunity, consistent with views submitted by the Department of State). In one case, a district court dismissed an indictment on diplomatic immunity grounds, holding that a Department of State submission asserted the wrong conclusion concerning immunity—without disputing the certification of status. United States v. Khobragade, 15 F. Supp. 3d 383, 387–88 (S.D.N.Y. 2014).

[794] See Chapter 3 § II(C); see also Text of 11-15-89 Circular Diplomatic Note, supra note 787; Presidential Power to Expel Diplomatic Personnel from the United States, 4A Op. O.L.C. 207 (1980) (describing constitutional and treaty bases for presidential authority to expel diplomats).

state's officials are enhanced.[795] A comparable provision was added much later for consular privileges and immunities.[796] Originally, the president also had the capacity to address, through conciliation or before the ICJ, disputes between the United States and other states parties concerning the VCDR and the VCCR,[797] but the United States has withdrawn from the optional protocols that enabled dispute resolution.[798]

One vital dimension to diplomatic and consular immunity, facilitated but by no means ensured by U.S. adherence to its VCDR and VCCR obligations, concerns application of such immunity to U.S. personnel abroad. In numerous instances, the Department of State has objected that the treatment of U.S. diplomatic and consular personnel abroad amounts to treaty violations,[799] and often such personnel have benefited from a receiving state's adherence. Occasionally such controversies have become prominent interstate disputes and even proceedings before international tribunals. Indeed, the United States has vindicated the rights of its personnel by securing orders from the ICJ that Iran had to release

---

[795] 22 U.S.C. § 254c(a); Exec. Order No. 12101, 43 Fed. Reg. 5195 (Nov. 19, 1978) (delegating authority to secretary of state); *e.g.*, Agreement on Privileges and Immunities of Embassy Staffs, Dec. 14, 1978, U.S.-U.S.S.R., 30 U.S.T. 2341, T.I.A.S. No. 9340. Less favorable treatment, even if reciprocal, is not expressly licensed by the VCDR. RESTATEMENT (THIRD) § 464 rptrs. note 12; *see* VCDR, *supra* note 763, art. 47(2)(b) (exempting agreements to afford more favorable bilateral arrangements from nondiscrimination provision).

[796] Department of State Authorities Act, Fiscal Year 2017, Pub. L. No. 114-323, tit. V, § 501, 130 Stat. 1935 (codified as amended at 22 U.S.C. § 254c(b)). Distinctively, the consular provision delegates authority to the secretary of state, with the concurrence of the attorney general, and requires consultation with Senate and House committees. Other comparable provisions were added to permit the secretary of state to regulate foreign missions and their members with the objective of securing similar treatment for U.S. missions and personnel overseas. Foreign Missions Act of 1982, Pub. L. No. 97-241, tit. II, §§ 201–04, 96 Stat. 273 (codified as amended at 22 U.S.C. §§ 4301–13).

[797] Optional Protocol to the Vienna Convention on Diplomatic Relations Concerning the Compulsory Settlement of Disputes, Apr. 18, 1961, 23 U.S.T. 3227, 500 U.N.T.S. 95; Optional Protocol to the Vienna Convention on Consular Relations, Apr. 24, 1963, 21 U.S.T. 77, 5596 U.N.T.S. 261.

[798] *Contemporary Practice of the United States Relating to International Law*, 113 AM. J. INT'L L. 131, 133–36 (2019) (noting both withdrawals in the context of the initiation of withdrawal from the Optional Protocol to the VCDR, and discussing potential vulnerability in terms of treaty law).

[799] For example, the United States asserted diplomatic immunity on behalf of Ray Davis, credentialed as a security officer with U.S. embassy staff in Pakistan (though reportedly a CIA officer) after Davis was arrested and detained following an incident in which he shot and killed two Pakistanis. Pakistani officials released him and allowed him to return to the United States after monetary compensation was provided to his victims. *Controversy Regarding Status of U.S. Official Involved in Shootings in Lahore: Contemporary Practice of the United States Relating to International Law*, 105 AM. J. INT'L L. 336 (2011). Official intervention is not a given, and the United States retains authority to decide whether to espouse the interests of its diplomats. Thus, a former Department of State employee alleged in U.S. court that the United States had violated her constitutional rights by failing to assert diplomatic and consular immunity on her behalf in Italian criminal proceedings regarding her alleged involvement in the extraordinary rendition of a suspected terrorist. The court concluded that such decisions were confined to the government's discretion, and that entitlement to "the assertion, non-assertion, or waiver of diplomatic or consular immunity by the United States *in a foreign judicial proceeding*" presented a nonjusticiable political questions. De Sousa v. Department of State, 840 F. Supp.2d 92, 108 (D.D.C. 2012) (emphasis in original).

U.S. hostages, return custody of the U.S. embassy, and pay financial damages.[800] Yet, at the same time, the United States has been chastised for its failure to observe in U.S. courts its own obligations, most prominently in the cases referred to previously involving the treatment under the VCCR of noncitizens on death row in the United States,[801] which prompted the U.S. withdrawal from the VCDR and VCCR's international dispute resolution mechanisms. It is not yet clear whether the protection of U.S. personnel abroad under the diplomatic and consular regimes will suffer in the wake of such withdrawals.

D. Other Foreign Officials

Historically, immunity issues involving other types of foreign officials (such as heads of state, heads of government, or ministers of foreign affairs) were less frequently litigated than the immunity of foreign states.[802] The rise of criminal and civil suits against such foreign officials may be traceable to developments in the international law of human rights, by which foreign officials were viewed as having international obligations vis-à-vis persons within the territory of the foreign state. In any event, over time the number of cases in U.S. courts against such officials has increased, adding some clarity to the immunity enjoyed by such officials—while also casting several points of conflict into sharp relief.

One of the biggest breakthroughs has been the Supreme Court's reaffirmation that the immunity of foreign officials is governed by federal common law. The common law had long regulated the immunity of foreign officials, just as with foreign states. But unlike foreign states (or, for that matter diplomats, consular officials, and international organizations), foreign officials never had a clear reckoning by statute or treaty. A number of lower courts applied the FSIA to foreign officials.[803] However, in 2010, in *Samantar v. Yousuf,* the Supreme Court

---

[800]   United States Diplomatic and Consular Staff in Tehran (U.S. v. Iran), Provisional Order, 1979 I.C.J. 7 (Dec. 15); United States Diplomatic and Consular Staff in Tehran (U.S. v. Iran), Judgment, 1980 I.C.J. 3 (May 24).

[801]   *See supra* this chapter note 767.

[802]   In *Samantar v. Yousuf,* the Supreme Court reported that pre-FSIA questions of official or head-of-state immunity before U.S. courts were rare and, thus, not on Congress' radar when adopting the FSIA. 560 U.S. 305, 323 n.18 (2010) (citing Department of State estimate that only 5 percent of its sovereign immunity decisions between 1952 and 1977 involved official or head-of-state immunity) (citations omitted); *accord id.* at 312. Cases concerning such immunities apparently surged after the FSIA's enactment. Joseph W. Dellapenna, *Head-of-State Immunity—Foreign Sovereign Immunities Act—Suggestion by the Department of State:* Lafontant v. Aristide, 88 Am. J. Int'l L. 528, 531 (1994) (highlighting "a rather remarkable number of suits (given the prior dearth of such suits) . . . filed against heads of foreign states" following the FSIA); Lewis S. Yelin, *Head of State Immunity as Sole Executive Lawmaking,* 44 Vand. J. Transnat'l L. 911, 951 (2011) (suggesting rise was "[c]oincident").

[803]   The leading case supporting application of the FSIA to individuals was Chuidian v. Phil. Nat'l Bank, 912 F. 2d 1095, 1103 (9th Cir. 1990); *see also In re* Terrorist Attacks on September 11, 2001, 538 F.3d 71, 83 (2d Cir. 2008); Keller v. Cent. Bank of Nigeria, 277 F.3d 811, 815 (6th Cir. 2002);

disagreed. In its view, while the FSIA was "clearly intended to supersede the common-law regime for claims against foreign states," nothing suggested "that Congress similarly wanted to codify the law of foreign official immunity."[804] The Court did little in *Samantar* to articulate the applicable common-law doctrine.[805] Though it adverted to pre–Tate Letter cases involving foreign sovereign immunity, and the role of the executive branch, in suggesting that some baseline existed,[806] the Court left the relationship between the common-law doctrine and international law unresolved. That relationship may be consequential, since relatively broad or relatively narrow constructions of immunity for these other foreign officials might affect U.S. compliance with international obligations.[807]

As things stand, common-law immunity does at least correspond with international distinctions between three different immunity types, which U.S. case law most often describes as "head-of-state" immunity, "official immunity," and "special mission immunity."[808] As discussed later, "head-of-state" immunity is very broad in what it accomplishes, covering both official and private acts, but— while not actually limited to heads of state—it is confined to a narrow group of senior government officials. The persons who benefit from this immunity obtain it from their current status as senior government officials, and only for their duration in those positions—hence the immunity's alternative depiction as "status-based" or "personal" immunity (immunity *ratione personae*). A second type of immunity is usually called "official" immunity, which broadly applies to all government officials, and even after they leave government, but only for their official (not private) acts. This term too can be confusing, since all three types of immunity involve "officials"; hence, this second type of immunity may be better described as "conduct-based" or "functional" immunity (immunity *ratione materiae*). Status-based and conduct-based immunity may apply simultaneously or sequentially.[809] A third type of immunity is "special mission" immunity, which

Byrd v. Corporacion Forestal y Industrial de Olancho S. A., 182 F.3d 380, 388 (5th Cir. 1999); El-Fadl v. Cent. Bank of Jordan, 75 F. 3d 668, 671 (D.C. Cir. 1996). *But see* Yousuf v. Samantar, 552 F.3d 371, 378–81 (4th Cir. 2009) (acknowledging "majority view," but holding that the FSIA does not apply to individual foreign officials), *aff'd*, Samantar v. Yousuf, 560 U.S. 305 (2010); Enahoro v. Abubakar, 408 F.3d 877, 881–82 (7th Cir. 2005).

[804] *Samantar v. Yousuf*, 560 U.S. at 325.

[805] *See id.* at 321 & n.15, 322, 325–26.

[806] *See, e.g., id.* at 311–12.

[807] If U.S. courts construe common-law immunity more narrowly than does international law, they risk offending the international law of immunity. If they recognize immunity where international law does not require it, that more generous view might obstruct rights established by international law— though that risk is less significant if a particular remedy is not required by international law.

[808] *See, e.g., Samantar v. Yousuf*, 560 U.S. at 312 & n.6; Lewis v. Mutond, 918 F.3d 142, 145 (2d Cir. 2019).

[809] *See, e.g.,* Yousuf v. Samantar, 699 F.3d 763, 768–69 (4th Cir. 2012) (describing potential application of both forms of immunity).

applies to foreign government officials and others who travel to another state for a diplomatic negotiation or meeting, typically having notified the host state and secured assent in advance.[810]

Procedural questions for handling immunity cases are largely left to national law, which in the United States is broadly similar across all three forms of immunity.[811] Such immunities are for the benefit of the foreign state rather than for the individual, which means that the foreign state can waive the immunity of present or former officials.[812] Foreign states wishing instead to assert immunity for their officials typically raise the issue directly with the Department of State; courts, in turn, are supposed to ensure that the Department has had an opportunity to opine before they decide the issue.[813] Any view the Department of State wishes to express, whether recognizing or opposing the recognition of immunity, is expressed through a "suggestion of immunity" filed on its behalf by the Justice Department.[814]

Courts generally confront immunity issues, when they need to decide them, in a fairly straightforward fashion.[815] As part of what has been described as a two-step process, courts first attend to any executive branch filing, which will often resolve the case; second, when the executive branch has been silent regarding immunity, a court is to decide the immunity question on its own.[816]

---

[810] See infra this chapter § V(D)(3).

[811] For a general description, see Harold Koh, Foreign Official Immunity After Samantar: A United States Government Perspective, 44 VAND. J. TRANSNAT'L L. 1141, 1149–55 (2011) (describing "New Samantar Process").

[812] See Arrest Warrant of 11 Apr. 2000 (Dem. Rep. Congo v. Belg.), Judgment, 2002 I.C.J. 3, ¶ 61 (Feb. 14) (a foreign official "cease[s] to enjoy immunity from foreign jurisdiction if the State which they represent or have represented decides to waive that immunity"). Such waiver must be clear and unequivocal. In re Doe, 860 F.2d 40, 46 (2d Cir. 1988). Waivers may also be comprehensive. See, e.g., Mamani v. Berzain, 654 F.3d 1148, 1151 n.4 (11th Cir. 2011) (accepting "that the present government of Bolivia has waived any immunity that [a former president and former defense minister] might enjoy"); In re Doe, 860 F.2d at 43, 45–46 (accepting waiver of "any residual sovereign, head of state, or diplomatic immunity" enjoyed by former Philippines president and spouse). Under some circumstances, a suit may implicate a foreign state more deeply, because the state is a required party or the real party in interest in the case, either of which might require dismissal if the foreign state is entitled to immunity under the FSIA. Samantar v. Yousuf, 560 U.S. at 324–25.

[813] Neither step, however, is obligatory. See, e.g., In re Terrorist Attacks on September 11, 2001, 122 F. Supp. 3d 181, 186–87 (S.D.N.Y. 2015) (rejecting objection that an official immunity defense was not before the court because Saudi Arabia had not requested a suggestion of immunity, nor had the Department of State volunteered its views).

[814] See 28 U.S.C. § 517 (2018) (providing that the United States, through the Department of Justice, may "attend to the interests of the United States" in pending proceedings in U.S. and state courts). Suggestions opposing immunity are less common. But see, e.g., Statement of Interest of the United States of America, Yousuf v. Samantar, No. 1:04 Civ. 1360, 2011 WL 7445583 (E.D. Va., Feb. 15, 2011) (suggesting absence of official immunity), aff'd, 699 F.3d 763 (4th Cir. 2012).

[815] Courts may ignore the issue if the case is properly resolved on other grounds, such as lack of personal jurisdiction or failure of service. See Statement of Interest and Suggestion of Immunity at 8 n.3, Rosenberg v. Lashkar-E-Taiba, 980 F. Supp. 2d 336 (E.D.N.Y. 2013) (Nos. 10-CV-5381 et al.).

[816] The Supreme Court's description of this two-step approach has been inexact. Judicial inquiry (the second step) was supposed to be appropriate "'in the absence of recognition of the immunity by the Department of State' . . .", see Samantar v. Yousuf, 560 U.S. at (2010) (quoting Ex parte Peru, 318 U.S. 578, 587 (1943)), but this left unclear whether courts were to proceed similarly when the

Courts conduct any "step two" inquiry in accordance with the common law and with Department of State practice in prior cases.[817]

Beyond this, the roles of the executive, judiciary, and legislature require more discriminating assessment. Executive branch suggestions in individual cases typically assert—regardless of the type of immunity—that U.S. courts must defer *completely* to the executive's suggestions.[818] Yet the case law seems to fall short of establishing automatic deference for all types of immunity of officials. In any given case, a court may well consider the type of immunity at issue, the basis for the executive's position, and the executive's fidelity to previously declared positions.[819] The proper role for Congress, too, may vary. Even if *Samantar v. Yousuf* was correct in concluding that the FSIA was not intended to codify the law of foreign official immunity,[820] it remains a fair question whether Congress *should* codify the common law, including by entrusting elements to the executive branch or by directly linking the U.S. approach with that taken by international law. Whether codification is a superior approach, or feasible, may depend on the type of immunity under consideration.

1. Head-of-State (Status-Based) Immunity

Under international law, heads of state (such as the king or queen of the United Kingdom or the president of France) and certain other high-ranking officials are immune from the exercise of jurisdiction by foreign states,[821] the better to lead and represent their states in international affairs.[822] This basic principle is the same in U.S. law,[823] yet difficult questions remain concerning its domestic administration.

executive branch clearly eschewed the chance to recommend, or recommended against, immunity. *See* Heaney v. Gov't of Spain, 445 F.2d 501, 503 & n.2 (2d Cir. 1971) (stating that "the State Department's failure or refusal to suggest immunity is a significant factor to be taken into consideration in determining if the case is one justifying derogation from the normal exercise of the court's jurisdiction").

[817] Koh, *supra* note 811, at 1161 (observing that because "the government need not, and should not, speak in every case," and that "[i]f the State Department says less but speaks clearly when it does speak, litigants and courts should be able to use our broader pronouncements to sort out government perspectives and revise their own positions accordingly").

[818] *See infra* this chapter text accompanying notes 825, 846, 852, 885–888.

[819] For comparable skepticism, and an in-depth discussion of the role of federal common law, see Ingrid Wuerth, *Foreign Official Immunity Determinations in U.S. Courts: The Case Against the State Department*, 51 VA. J. INT'L L. 915 (2011).

[820] *Samantar v. Yousuf*, 560 U.S. at 325.

[821] Arrest Warrant of 11 April 2000 (Dem. Rep. Congo v. Belg.), Judgment, 2002 I.C.J. 3, ¶ 51 (Feb. 14) (describing as "firmly established that . . . certain holders of high-ranking office in a State . . . enjoy immunities from jurisdiction in other States, both civil and criminal"). The application to other qualifying officials is discussed below. *See infra* this chapter text accompanying notes 837–844.

[822] *See, e.g.*, FOX & WEBB, *supra* note 509, at 54; Watts, *supra* note 448, at 31–32, 36–38.

[823] *See, e.g.*, RESTATEMENT (SECOND) § 66 (extending a foreign state's immunity to its head of state, head of government, foreign minister, and persons designated by any of those officials as a member of the official's party).

It seems well accepted that suggestions of head-of-state immunity by the executive, whether favoring or opposing immunity, are not reviewable by U.S. courts based on judicial disagreement with their factual basis.[824] Thus, it is for the executive to decide who is the U.K. monarch or the president of France. Moreover, the executive branch has insisted, and the lower courts have agreed, that the Department of State's legal conclusions concerning the application of head-of-state immunity are binding upon courts.[825] Some mid-twentieth-century foreign sovereign immunity cases, decided by the Supreme Court and referenced in *Samantar v. Yousuf*, lend support to that proposition. But those cases, which mostly addressed *in rem* immunity of foreign states, are distinguishable from head-of-state immunity cases arising today. Moreover, deference to the executive would have been particularly compelling at that time, in light of the uncertainty at the time surrounding the absolute and restrictive theories.[826]

The present-day inclination of courts to defer may be an attempt at continuity, but it also reflects changed jurisprudential assumptions. Courts appear more reluctant to presuppose that customary international law on immunity directly establishes a federal common law of immunity; rather than look to international law for the rule of decision, courts may prefer to look to the executive.[827] (Indeed, new caution about viewing customary international law as establishing federal common law might help explain the executive's reluctance to suggest that it is

---

[824] For example, in *LaFontant v. Aristide*, the district court—acceding to the executive branch's suggestion of head-of-state immunity—stressed that such immunity "extends only to the person the United States government acknowledges as the official head-of-state," which "is not a factual issue to be determined by the courts," and rejected attempts to suggest that the immunity had been waived by another, nonrecognized government. 844 F. Supp. 128, 132, 133–35 (E.D.N.Y. 1994). A rare case in which the executive branch (and thus the United States) denied immunity to a head of state involved General Manuel Noriega, at the relevant time the *de facto* head of Panama; from the U.S. perspective, it merely continued its policy of refraining from recognizing Noriega as the head of state, which made his lack of immunity straightforward. United States v. Noriega, 117 F.3d 1206, 1211–12 (11th Cir. 1997); *see* Dapo Akande & Sangeeta Shah, *Immunities of State Officials, International Crimes, and Foreign Domestic Courts*, 21 EUR. J. INT'L L. 815, 820 (2011).

[825] Among post-*Samantar v. Yousuf* cases, see, for example, Habyarimana v. Kagame, 696 F.3d 1029, 1032 (10th Cir. 2012); Yousuf v. Samantar, 699 F.3d 763, 769–73 (4th Cir. 2012) (holding, following remand from the Supreme Court, that the executive branch head-of-state immunity determinations—but not its determinations regarding official immunity—were owed absolute deference). The executive branch has stated that "we are not aware of any case in which a court has subjected a sitting head of state to suit after the Executive Branch issued a Suggestion of Immunity," without addressing whether executive branch suggestions of non-immunity have also been universally dispositive. Brief for the United States as Amicus Curiae Supporting Appellee at 7, Manoharan v. Rajapaksa, 711 F.3d 178 (D.C. Cir. 2013) (No. 12-5087). For a note of hesitation, see Tawfik v. Al-Sabah, No. 11 Civ. 6455 (ALC) (JCF), 2012 WL 3542209, at *2–3 (S.D.N.Y. Aug. 16, 2012) (agreeing with a Department of State suggestion of head-of-state immunity, but stating that the court "does not—and need not—adopt a broader holding that the Executive Branch's determination is perforce 'controlling' and 'not subject to judicial review.' ").

[826] *See supra* this chapter text accompanying notes 468–477. To be sure, some courts regard these distinctions as irrelevant, or conclude that the case for deference is greater "when the suggested immunity involves a foreign leader." Ye v. Zemin, 383 F.3d 620, 626 n.8 (7th Cir. 2004).

[827] *See also* this chapter § III (Act of State doctrine). *See generally* Chapter 5 § II(C).

bound by customary international law in its own determinations, though undoubtedly it prefers greater discretion regardless.[828]) However, absolute judicial deference to the executive branch, especially on matters involving established legal principles, may also be problematic given contemporary concerns about presidential lawmaking. Deference serves separation of powers by diminishing judicial involvement in foreign relations,[829] but a judicial decision to defer entirely in an area of federal common law, without a clear constitutional basis for doing so, strains the judiciary's role as well.[830]

If courts reflect further on the deference question, the Constitution permits a more nuanced approach. The recognition power vindicates presidential authority to decide whether an entity is a foreign state and, further, which entity is the government of that state, and it is buttressed by the president's general authority for conducting foreign relations.[831] The case for deference on recognition issues, however, does not necessarily justify deference in resolving all head-of-state immunity issues, if one supposes any judicial capacity to "draw for themselves [the] legal consequences in litigations pending before them."[832] Presumably diplomacy can also be served by judicial development of cogent and transparent doctrine that indicates where the lines are to be drawn. Case law could acknowledge international law's background role while identifying particular respects in which the courts accord great weight (or some other degree

---

[828] Executive branch submissions have suggested that customary international law is relevant to its internal assessment. *See, e.g.*, Suggestion of Immunity Submitted by the United States at 2, Habyarimana v. Kagame, 821 F. Supp. 2d 1244 (W.D. Okla. 2011) (No. 5:10-CV-00437), *aff'd*, 696 F.3d 1029 (10th Cir. 2012) (noting, inter alia, its "consideration of the relevant principles of customary international law"). But that is not the same as accepting that such law is binding on its determinations.

[829] The leading statement, still influential today, comes from Judge Wisdom's opinion in *Spacil v. Crowe*:

> Separation-of-powers principles impel a reluctance in the judiciary to interfere with or embarrass the executive in its constitutional role as the nation's primary organ of international policy. And the degree to which granting or denying a claim of immunity may be important to foreign policy is a question on which the judiciary is particularly ill-equipped to second-guess the executive. The executive's institutional resources and expertise in foreign affairs far outstrip those of the judiciary. Perhaps more importantly, in the chess game that is diplomacy only the executive has a view of the entire board and an understanding of the relationship between isolated moves.

489 F.2d 614, 619 (5th Cir. 1974) (citations omitted); *see, e.g.*, *Habyarimana*, 693 F.3d at 1032–33 (quoting passage).

[830] *Cf.* W.S. Kirkpatrick & Co. v. Envtl. Tectonics Corp., 493 U.S. 400, 409 (1990) (noting, in Act of State context, the obligation of courts "to decide cases and controversies properly presented to them," notwithstanding separation-of-powers considerations); Zivotofsky v. Clinton, 566 U.S. 189, 201 (2012) (stressing obligation of courts to evaluate merits of arguments concerning the passport and recognition powers, rather than deciding on political question grounds).

[831] *See* Chapter 3 § I.

[832] Guar. Trust Co. v. United States, 304 U.S. 126, 138 (1938); *id.* at 138–40 (distinguishing presidential authority "in recognizing a foreign government and in receiving its diplomatic representatives," which is "conclusive on all domestic courts," from judicial capacity to assess whether a state statute of limitations was tolled). For discussion, see Yelin, *supra* note 802, at 962–68.

of deference) to the executive's views, not unlike the approach taken to foreign sovereign immunity before and after enacting the FSIA.[833]

Even assuming that the executive branch is due complete deference for head-of-state immunity, U.S. courts may be left to apply such immunity independently if the executive fails to make any suggestion. One potential difficulty may concern the entity entitled to assert immunity. International law addresses statehood, but under U.S. law, whether the United States recognizes a particular entity as a foreign state or as the government of a foreign state are questions assigned to the president.[834] In the absence of any executive branch guidance, a court may be left to determine whether the person before it is an official of a recognized government of a recognized foreign state.[835] For example, whether head-of-state immunity is to be accorded to China's president depends initially on whether the United States recognizes the People's Republic of China as a state, and further whether the United States recognizes the communist regime based in Beijing as the government of that state; one or more of such issues may be left to the judiciary.[836]

---

[833] For the situation prior to enactment of the FSIA, see RESTATEMENT (SECOND) § 72(1) (explaining that an executive branch suggestion of foreign sovereign immunity is "conclusive as to issues determined by executive action within the exclusive constitutional competence of the executive branch of government and as to other issues directly affecting the conduct of foreign relations," but "[a]s to all other issues, such a suggestion will be given great weight"). Following the FSIA, U.S. submissions on matters of statutory construction are not entitled to deference (though they are of "considerable interest"). In contrast, Department of State opinions "on the implications of exercising jurisdiction over particular [foreign states] in connection with their alleged conduct . . . might well be entitled to deference as the considered judgment of the Executive on a particular question of foreign policy." Republic of Austria v. Altmann, 541 U.S. 677, 701–02 (2004).

[834] See Chapter 3 § I(D); e.g., Baker v. Carr, 369 U.S. 186, 212–13 (1962) (stating, in dicta, that "it is the executive that determines a person's status as representative of a foreign government," and "recognition of [a] foreign government[] so strongly defies judicial treatment that without executive recognition a foreign state has been called 'a republic of whose existence we know nothing'") (references omitted). The deference owed executive branch policy on such matters may be distinguishable from determinations of whether an entity is a "foreign state" under the FSIA, principally because that statute was intent on withdrawing authority from the executive branch and conferring it on the courts. See supra this chapter text accompanying notes 532–538.

[835] Unusually, Congress may weigh in. Thus, U.S. nonrecognition of Taiwan as a foreign state (or as the government of China) is not fatal to the assertion of head-of-state immunity on behalf of its president, because the Taiwan Relations Act provides that it will be deemed eligible for similar treatment. Weiming Chen v. Ying-jeou Ma, 2013 WL 4437607, *3 (S.D.N.Y. Aug. 19, 2013); see Taiwan Relations Act, Pub. L. 96-8, § 2, Apr. 10, 1979, 93 Stat. 14 (codified at 22 U.S.C. §§ 3303(b)(1) (2018) ("Whenever the laws of the United States refer or relate to foreign countries, nations, states, governments, or similar entities, such terms shall include and such laws shall apply with respect to Taiwan.").

[836] Compare, e.g., Ye v. Zemin, 383 F.3d 620, 627–30 (7th Cir. 2004) (treating as conclusive an executive branch suggestion of head-of-state immunity for the president of China), with First Am. Corp. v. Al-Nahyan, 948 F. Supp. 1107, 1121 (D.D.C. 1996) (holding that members of the ruling family of Dubai were not entitled to head-of-state immunity when the executive branch had not suggested immunity, the United States had not recognized Dubai as an independent foreign state, there was doubt whether it would meet international criteria, and that none of those asserting immunity could be deemed a head of such a state in any event).

A second issue that may arise concerns the officials eligible for head-of-state immunity, which as previously noted is a broader class than the name suggests. Under international law, heads of government (like the prime ministers of the United Kingdom or France), as well as ministers of foreign affairs, are entitled to the same immunity as heads of state.[837] Whether state practice will support including other officials, beyond this "troika," is uncertain.[838] Domestic U.S. practice supports extending head-of-state immunity to heads of government and ministers of foreign affairs, and to some members of their parties.[839] An executive branch decision to extend this status-based immunity to others, like a minister of defense or of trade, might fairly reflect the diplomatic role of such officials, but could test judicial deference.[840]

[837] Case Concerning Certain Questions of Mutual Assistance in Criminal Matters (Djib. v. Fr.), Judgment, 2008 I.C.J. 179, ¶ 170 (June 4) (heads of state); Arrest Warrant of 11 April 2000 (Dem. Rep. Congo v. Belg.), Judgment, 2002 I.C.J. 3, ¶ 51 (Feb. 14) (ministers of foreign affairs, and noting heads of state and heads of government); *accord* Int'l Law Comm'n, *Immunity of State officials from foreign criminal jurisdiction: Texts and titles of the draft articles adopting by the Drafting Committee on first reading,* at 2, A/CN.4/L.969 (2022).

[838] Most depictions of the "troika" imply a limit, but the ICJ, which was in the vanguard in extending head-of-state immunity to foreign ministers, has noted that it applies to officials "such as" those three. *Arrest Warrant of 11 April 2000,* 2002 I.C.J. ¶ 51. In *Case Concerning Certain Questions of Mutual Assistance in Criminal Matters,* however, the Court agreed with France that Djibouti's public prosecutor and head of national security did not enjoy personal immunities. 2008 I.C.J. ¶¶ 185–88, 194. The ILC has not to date supported expanding the range of officials. Int'l Law Comm'n, *Rep. on the Work of its Sixty-Fifth Session,* ch. V, at 43–47, A/68/10 (2013); *see also* Sean D. Murphy, *Immunity* Ratione Personae *of Foreign Government Officials and Other Topics: The Sixty-Fifth Session of the International Law Commission,* 108 AM. J. INT'L L. 41, 44–46 (2014); Muriel Ubéda-Saillard, *Foreign Officials Entitled to (Absolute) Personal Immunity During Their Time in Office, in* CAMBRIDGE HANDBOOK, *supra* note 510, at 484–87. State practice has not closed the door. *See, e.g.,* Re Mofaz, 128 I.L.R. 709, 712 (Bow St. Magis. Ct., 2004) (U.K.) (acknowledging "working in somewhat uncharted waters" but concluding that "a Defence Minister would automatically acquire State immunity in the same way as that pertaining to a Foreign Minister"). *See generally* JOANNE FOAKES, THE POSITION OF HEADS OF STATE AND SENIOR OFFICIALS IN INTERNATIONAL LAW 128–33 (2014); FOX & WEBB, *supra* note 509, at 566; RAMONA PEDRETTI, IMMUNITY OF HEADS OF STATES AND STATE OFFICIALS FOR INTERNATIONAL CRIMES 41–45 (2014). Members of the family of a head of state appear to have enjoyed immunity on the basis of international comity, not due to an international legal obligation. Roman Anatolevich Kolodkin (Special Rapporteur on Immunity of State Officials from Foreign Criminal Jurisdiction), *Preliminary Rep. on Immunity of State Officials from Foreign Criminal Jurisdiction,* ¶ 128, U.N. Doc. A/CN.4/601 (May 29, 2008).

[839] *See* RESTATEMENT (SECOND) § 66 (describing status-based immunity for "troika" and members of their parties); *e.g.,* Manoharan v. Rajapaksa, 711 F.3d 178, 179–80 (D.C. Cir. 2013) (sitting president of Sri Lanka); Force v. Sein, No. 15 Civ. 7772, 2016 WL 1261139, at *3 (S.D.N.Y. Mar. 30, 2016) (sitting president and foreign minister of Myanmar); Tachiona v. Mugabe, 169 F. Supp. 2d 259, 296–97 (S.D.N.Y. 2001) (sitting president and foreign minister of Zimbabwe)), *aff'd in part on other grounds, rev'd in part,* 386 F.3d 205 (2d Cir. 2004); Saltany v. Reagan, 702 F. Supp. 319, 320 (D.D.C. 1988) (prime minister of United Kingdom), *aff'd in part, rev'd in part,* 886 F.2d 438 (D.C. Cir. 1989); Kline v. Kaneko, 535 N.Y.S.2d 303 (Sup. Ct. 1988) (immunity for wife of president of Mexico).

[840] *Cf.* Hassen v. Nahyan, No. CV 09–01106 DMG, 2010 WL 9538408, at *5 (C.D. Cal. Sept. 17, 2010) (concluding, in the absence of a State Department submission, that a high-ranking military officer is "not entitled to absolute immunity as a head of state"); First Am. Corp., 948 F. Supp. at 1121 (noting absence of State Department suggestion of immunity, and uncertainty relating to statehood, but also declining to recognize head-of-state immunity for the Minister of Defense of the United Arab Emirates); El-Hadad v. Embassy of the U.A.E., 69 F. Supp. 2d 69, 82 n.10 (D.D.C. 1999) (stating in dicta, and absent a Department of State suggestion, that "head of state immunity . . . is limited only

A third issue, at least potentially, concerns the scope of head-of-state immunity. If a given person is eligible, in principle, for head-of-state immunity, such immunity (unlike "official," or conduct-based, immunity) extends to both private and official conduct, including conduct preceding the person's time in office.[841] Further, it extends to both criminal and civil matters,[842] and is equal to or exceeds diplomatic immunity in its scope.[843] The broad authority of the executive branch over immunity's administration helps secure this immunity. In particular, immunity for criminal matters is said to be resolved conclusively by prosecutors in deciding whether to bring charges. Since those prosecutors follow the executive branch's view of head-of-state immunity, their reluctance to charge sitting heads of state and other senior officials effectively establishes wide-ranging immunity for such officials before U.S. courts.[844]

International law and U.S. law agree that head-of-state immunity applies regardless of any alleged wrong's severity. Thus, the ICJ found that a sitting foreign minister is immune from foreign criminal jurisdiction even for alleged war crimes and crimes against humanity,[845] the prohibition of which are among the handful of peremptory norms of international law (*jus cogens*) from which no derogation is permitted. Lower courts in the United States have suggested

---

to the sitting official head of state," and does not "cover all agents of the head of state"), *rev'd in part on other grounds*, 216 F.3d 29 (D.C. Cir. 2000).

[841] *See, e.g.*, Arrest Warrant of 11 April 2000 (Dem. Rep. Congo v. Belg.), Judgment, 2002 I.C.J. 3, ¶ 55 (Feb. 14); Habyarimana v. Kagame, 696 F.3d 1029, 1032 (10th Cir. 2012) (noting application to suits concerning pre-office conduct).

[842] For its breadth in criminal matters, see Case Concerning Certain Questions of Mutual Assistance in Criminal Matters (Djib. v. Fr.), Judgment, 2008 I.C.J. 177, ¶ 174 (June 4); *Arrest Warrant of 11 April 2000*, 2002 I.C.J. ¶ 54; Fox & Webb, *supra* note 509, at 555–56 (and accompanying text); Watts, *supra* note 448, at 54; Ubéda-Saillard, *Foreign Officials Entitled to (Absolute) Personal Immunity During Their Time in Office*, in Cambridge Handbook, *supra* note 510, at 487–88. There remains some disagreement about whether, under international law, civil immunity extends to the pursuit of private ends or commercial matters, but U.S. practice is relatively broad and definitive. *See* Fox & Webb, *supra* note 509, at 553–55; Watts, *supra* note 448, at 52–53, 54–58.

[843] Fox & Webb, *supra* note 509, at 551 (and accompanying text).

[844] *See* 2007 Digest of U.S. Practice at 445, 449 (excerpting post by John B. Bellinger, Legal Adviser of the Department of State, stating that "[t]he Legal Adviser's office is not aware of any criminal charges having been brought against a sitting head of state by United States federal or state prosecutors."). *But cf.* United States v. Noriega, 117 F.3d 1206, 1212 (11th Cir. 1997) (stating, in relation to the alleged de jure and de facto leader of Panama, not acknowledged as such by the United States, that "by pursuing Noriega's capture and this prosecution, the Executive Branch has manifested its clear sentiment that Noriega should be denied head-of-state immunity").

Executive branch authority over civil matters is obviously less extensive. That said, courts have sometimes suggested exceptions to immunity for heads of state, but they also defer to the executive. *See* Plaintiffs A, B, C, D, E, F v. Zemin, 282 F. Supp. 2d 875, 885 (N.D. Ill. 2003) (suggesting "limited exceptions" to head-of-state immunity for "real property abroad, private services as an executor of an estate, or personal commercial activities," based on international law), *aff'd on other grounds sub. nom.* Ye v. Zemin, 383 F.3d 620, 627–30 (7th Cir. 2004) (agreeing that "there are exceptions to the immunity a head of state (as well as a foreign nation) is granted in this country's courts," but noting that determination whether those exceptions apply "is left to the Executive Branch").

[845] *Arrest Warrant of 11 April 2000*, 2002 I.C.J., ¶¶ 58, 61.

a similar approach, accepting executive-suggested immunity irrespective of the severity of the alleged claims.[846] (Foreign sovereign immunity under the FSIA is similarly unyielding.[847]) One rationale for maintaining immunity even for such allegations is that at an early stage in the proceedings (when a head of state might be arrested during a visit), the allegations are just that—allegations—and that immunity may be too easily subverted if it suffices to allege a particular type of offense.

This illustrates the disquieting potential of deference. On the approach favored by the executive branch, courts might be compelled to accept head-of-state immunity for serious offenses committed by *additional* officials of the executive branch's choosing.[848] Granting the immunity may be an important bulwark against as-yet unproven allegations that have the immediate potential to interfere with the governance of a foreign state, and which might complicate its diplomatic relations with the United States. At the same time, the cumulative effect deserves contemplation: the executive branch would have the discretionary capacity to establish immunity even if such official would not be eligible for immunity under international law, even if the U.S. government would not grant immunity for comparable officials from other states or request it for comparable U.S. officials, and even if the alleged offense was of a kind Congress made actionable under the TVPA or similar statute.[849] It may be more satisfactory were the judiciary to indicate that, in the absence of statutory direction, international law provides the basic principles for head-of-state, or status-based, immunity, and that executive branch suggestions are final as to certain issues left to domestic

---

[846] *See, e.g., Ye,* 383 F.3d at 625–27 (president of China); Force v. Sein, No. 15 Civ. 7772, 2016 WL 1261139, at *3 (S.D.N.Y. Mar. 30, 2016) (president and foreign minister of Myanmar); Devi v. Rajapaksa, No. 11 Civ. 6634, 2012 WL 3866495, at *3 (S.D.N.Y. Sept. 4, 2012) (president of Sri Lanka), *appeal dismissed,* Devi v. Rajapaksa, No. 12–4081, 2013 WL 3855583 (2d Cir. Jan. 30, 2013); Am. Justice Ctr. v. Modi, No. 14 Civ. 7780, 2015 U.S. Dist. LEXIS 177427 (S.D.N.Y. Jan. 14, 205) (prime minister of India). That result holds as well for TVPA-based claims against heads of state, given the presumption that statutes do not abrogate the common law. *See, e.g.,* Manohoran v. Rajapaksa, 711 F.3d 178, 180 (D.C. Cir. 2013).

[847] *See supra* this chapter text accompanying notes 519–525.

[848] As noted previously, there has been some judicial resistance to expanding the offices eligible for status-based immunity, albeit without executive branch guidance. *See supra* note 840 (citing cases). In one case, even the Department of State was resisted, but not in a way that changed the result. *See* Republic of Philippines v. Marcos, 665 F. Supp. 793, 797 (N.D. Cal. 1987) (distinguishing the Philippines solicitor general, while a "very high ranking official," from a foreign state's sovereign or foreign minister, the "two traditional bases for a recognition or grant of head-of-state immunity"); *id.* at 798 (describing it as "a radical departure from past custom" that "the government . . . seeks to expand the head-of-state doctrine to encompass all government officials of a foreign state to whom the State Department chooses to extend immunity"); Diplomatic Missions and Embassy Property, 1981–1988 DIGEST OF U.S. PRACTICE, at 988 (noting that the deposition subpoena was instead quashed on the ground of diplomatic immunity, a ground not argued by the Department of State).

[849] The TVPA may well not override head-of-state immunity established under the common law. *See infra* text accompanying notes 876–877 (noting comparable official immunity case law). That said, the ability to expand the range of officials eligible for head-of-state immunity is at least in tension with legislative policy.

authorities—like those concerning recognition of a foreign government or state—which are firmly rooted in the separation of powers.

2. Official (Conduct-Based) Immunity

Official immunity is probably the hardest form of individual immunity to sum-marize, because it is so diverse in its potential application. Unlike diplomatic, consular, or head-of-state immunity, official immunity is neither comprehensive nor attached to particular classes of officials. Instead, such immunity is conduct-based, attaching to a variety of officials for all their official acts. Because it is not status-based, it also may be asserted even after the individuals concerned have left their official posts or ceased to act on behalf of the state, with respect to official acts undertaken while in office. Thus, this type of immunity applies to former heads of state and other former senior officials who once may have benefited from status-based immunity, but who no longer do. Such immunity serves the interests of the foreign state, but the relationship is not entirely resolved.[850]

Official immunity under U.S. law adds another layer of complexity. Like head-of-state immunity, official immunity is governed by the common law. International rules inform the work of U.S. courts and that of the U.S. executive branch, but they are not necessarily controlling.[851]

A distinctive feature of U.S. law, unsurprisingly, is judicial deference to the executive branch. Courts treat executive branch suggestions concerning of-ficial immunity deferentially and accommodate those suggestions through a procedure like that for head-of-state immunity. But while the execu-tive branch insists, as with head-of-state immunity, that such suggestions are dispositive[852]—irrespective of any perceived conflict with international

[850] In one conception, official immunity is designed to prevent litigants from eroding foreign sovereign immunity by attacking those who act on the state's behalf; in another, official immunity prevents an individual from being held responsible for acts which are really those of a foreign state. See Akande & Shah, supra note 824, at 825–28; Rosanne van Alebeek, Functional Immunity of State Officials from the Criminal Jurisdiction of Foreign National Courts, in CAMBRIDGE HANDBOOK, supra note 510, at 498–502; cf. Brief for the United States as Amicus Curiae Supporting Affirmance at 27, Samantar v. Yousuf, 560 U.S. 305 (2010) (No. 08-1555) [U.S. Samantar Brief] ("[I]n some circumstances the immunity of officials under Executive Branch principles may be broader than (as in other circumstances it may be narrower than) that of the state under the FSIA").

[851] See, e.g., Samantar v. Yousuf, 560 U.S. 305, 320 n.14 (2010) (implying that another case might "determine whether declining to afford immunity . . . would be consistent with international law"); U.S. Samantar Brief, supra note 850, at I (alluding to "common law principles of immunity articulated by the Executive Branch, informed by customary international law"); id. at 27 (noting relevance of "background principles for . . . official acts, and fidelity to international norms and the protection of United States officials abroad are important factors" for executive branch consideration).

[852] The degree of requested deference is not always clear. See U.S. Samantar Brief, supra note 850, at 28 (describing "pre-existing practice" in which "courts defer to Executive suggestions and princi-ples of immunity with respect to foreign officials"); Koh, Foreign Official Immunity, supra note 811, at 1152 (statement by then–legal adviser that "when State Department determinations of immunity and non-immunity are made in particular cases, the courts should defer to those State Department deter-minations"). But the government has often claimed that any Department of State "determination" is "binding" on courts. See, e.g., Brief for the United States as Amicus Curiae Supporting Appellees

law[853]—the case law has not entirely cohered.[854] There is little foundation on which to rest. In the founding era, the executive seemed to respect the courts' own capacity to resolve cases against lower-ranking or former foreign officials on their merits.[855] Gradually, case law suggested broader deference to the executive

at 10, Yousuf v. Samantar, 699 F.3d 763 (4th Cir. 2012) (No. 11-1479); *id.* at 1 (same); *id.* at 18 ("that determination controls"). Explanations tend to invoke sovereign immunity precedent. *See, e.g., id.* at 12, citing *Ex Parte* Peru, 318 U.S. 578, 588 (1943) (stating that "courts are required to accept and follow the executive determination that the vessel is immune"); *id.* at 15 (citing Isbrandtsen Tankers, Inc. v. President of India, 446 F.2d 1198, 1201 (2d Cir. 1971) ("The State Department is to make this determination, in light of the potential consequences to our own international position. Hence once the State Department has ruled in a matter of this nature, the judiciary will not interfere.")).

[853] *See, e.g.*, Brief for the United States as Amicus Curiae Supporting Appellee at *12–13, Manoharan v. Rajapaksa, 711 F.3d 178 (D.C. Cir. 2013) (No. 12-5087) (stating that "[t]he United States takes principles of customary international law into account in considering a request for immunity," and "the Suggestion of Immunity in this case is fully consistent with customary international law," but also that deference is required regardless and "arguments about customary international law have no bearing on this case").

[854] *Compare, e.g.*, Doe v. De Leon, 555 Fed. Appx. 84, 85 (2d Cir. 2014) (treating as "dispositive" a Department of State suggestion of immunity for former president of Mexico), *and* Matar v. Dichter, 563 F.3d 9, 14 (2d Cir. 2009) (relying on Department of State suggestion of immunity for former head of Israeli Security Agency), *and* Ben-Haim v. Edri, 183 A.3d 252, 255–59 (N.J. App. Div. 2018) (treating as binding a Department of State suggestion of immunity for Israeli rabbinical judges and rabbinical official), *with* Yousuf v. Samantar, 699 F.3d 763, 773 (4th Cir. 2012) (concluding that, while courts should give absolute deference to the Department of State on its status-based immunity determinations, "such as head-of-state immunity," its "determination regarding conduct-based immunity . . . is not controlling, but it carries substantial weight in our analysis of the issue"). The D.C. Circuit indicated in dicta that a suggestion of immunity would be binding, but appears not to have resolved whether a suggestion of non-immunity would be. Lewis v. Mutond, 918 F.3d 142 (D.C. Cir. 2019); Manoharan v. Rajapaksa, 711 F.3d 178, 179, 180 n.* (D.C. Cir. 2013) (relying on executive branch suggestion of head-of-state immunity, but stating that "[t]his case does not require us to decide what deference we should give to the State Department when the Department indicates that a defendant, whether a sitting head of state or otherwise, should not receive immunity"). The Ninth Circuit—while at least affording "substantial weight" to suggestions of immunity—has not decided whether more is due. Dogan v. Barak, 932 F.3d 888, 893–94 (9th Cir. 2019) (declining to "decide the level of deference"—between "substantial weight" and absolute deference—"owed to the State Department's suggestion of immunity in this case").

[855] This willingness to allow such cases to run their course is best evidenced in a pair of Attorney General opinions. In one, Attorney General Bradford said that "[w]ith respect to his suability," the former governor of Guadeloupe was "on a footing with any other foreigner (not a public minister)"— i.e., those not entitled to status-based immunity—"who comes within the jurisdiction of our courts." Suits Against Foreigners, Case of Collot, 1 Op. Att'y Gen. 45 (1794). The opinion allowed, however, that "if the [former governor's] seizure of the vessel is admitted to have been an official act, done . . . by virtue, or under color, of the powers vested in him as governor," that would be dispositive; regardless, the U.S. government entrusted the matter to the courts alone. *Id.* ("[B]e this as it may, it is evident that this is not a case for the interposition of the government; and that Mr. Collot must defend himself by such means as his counsel shall advise."). A few years later, Attorney General Charles Lee, responding to diplomatic protests, agreed that Henry Sinclair, operating under a letter of marque from the British, was not amenable to liability "for what he does in pursuance of his commission, to any judicial tribunal in the United States," but again stated that "the Executive cannot interpose with the judiciary proceedings between an individual and Henry Sinclair, whose controversy is entitled to a trial according to law." Actions Against Foreigners, Case of Sinclair, 1 Op. Att'y Gen. 81 (1797). As Professor Keitner has emphasized, this practice appeared to respect a distinction between immunity as it would have operated for heads of state or diplomats, where it would have required dismissal for a lack of jurisdiction, and merits-based defenses available to other officials, who could claim not to be personally responsible for acts taken with the scope of the official's lawful powers. *See* Keitner,

branch, but very few cases directly involved foreign official immunity.[856] In much the same pattern, the executive branch paid little attention to foreign officials under the Tate Letter regime, and Congress ignored them when enacting the FSIA. Eventually, in *Samantar v. Yousuf*, the Supreme Court clarified that the common law governed official immunity, but it explicitly withheld comment on the law's substance, and may be understood to have left unaddressed the exact role for the executive branch.[857]

As with head-of-state immunity, official immunity is composed of distinct questions that may inform the degree of judicial deference that is warranted. Some cases may involve issues falling within the executive's exclusive competence, such as whether the foreign state was an entity entitled to invoke immunity in U.S. court, or whether a foreign government purporting to waive official immunity is entitled to do so. Suggestions of immunity based on such factual determinations should be regarded as conclusive,[858] notwithstanding that the executive appears to retain discretion as to whether such factors matter at all.[859]

Between Law and Diplomacy, supra note 453, at 227–33 (discussing attorney general opinions); Keitner, *The Forgotten History, supra* note 453, *passim* (exploring 1790s cases).

[856] The most prominent reported cases appear to be Heaney v. Gov't of Spain, 445 F.2d 501 (2d Cir. 1971) (dismissing action against Spanish consular official on immunity grounds); Greenspan v. Crosbie, No. 74 Civ. 4734 (GLG), 1976 WL 841, at *2 (S.D.N.Y. Nov. 23, 1976) (dismissing securities-related action against three Canadian provincial officials on immunity grounds); Waltier v. Thomson, 189 F. Supp. 319, 320–21 (S.D.N.Y. 1960) (dismissing action against Canadian consular officials on immunity grounds); *see* Samantar v. Yousuf, 560 U.S. 305, 311–12, 322 (2010); Sovereign Immunity Decisions of the Department of State, May 1952 to January 1977, 1977 DIGEST OF U.S. PRACTICE, at 1020, 1037, 1075–77 (adding related case); Koh, *supra* note 811, at 1144 n.13, 1147. Only *Greenspan* directly supports the dispositive nature of a Department of State determination of official immunity. *Greenspan*, 1976 WL 841, at *2. The other cases concerned consular immunity and its distinct legal bases; moreover, *Heaney* involved no suggestion of immunity, and in *Waltier* the suggestion of immunity was Canada's—with the U.S. submission apparently being limited to the scope of the Canadian officials' duties. *Heaney*, 445 F.2d at 502, 504–06; *Waltier*, 189 F. Supp. At 320–21. Other cases better describe principles more akin to the Act of State doctrine. *See* Underhill v. Hernandez, 168 U.S. 250, 252 (1897) (noting "[t]he immunity of individuals from suits brought in foreign tribunals for acts done within their own states, in the exercise of governmental authority, whether as civil officers or as military commanders").

[857] *See Samantar v. Yousuf*, 560 U.S. at 323 ("We have been given no reason to believe that Congress saw as a problem, or wanted to eliminate, the State Department's role in determinations regarding individual official immunity").

[858] *See supra* this chapter text accompanying notes 824, 831–833 (discussing issues in the context of head-of-state immunity). More hypothetical situations, like the potential inability of an unrecognized government to waive deference, do not seem to require equivalent deference—particularly not if an appropriate request was made initially by a recognized government. *But cf.* Statement of Interest of the United States of America, *supra* note 814, at 8. Likewise, difficulties in developing a determinate U.S. position (due, for example, to problems communicating with a government) might simply warrant letting a court decide immunity on its own. Warfaa v. Ali, 33 F. Supp. 3d 653, 657 (E.D. Va. 2014), *aff'd* 811 F.3d 653 (4ᵗʰ Cir. 2016) (noting report that, due to difficulties in communicating with the government of Somalia, the United States was unable to present its views to the court).

[859] For example, the Department of State has considered it relevant that a defendant is "a former official of a state with no currently recognized government to request immunity on his behalf, including by expressing a position on whether the acts in question were taken in an official capacity." Statement of Interest of the United States of America, *supra* note 814, at 8. Whatever the warrant

As with head-of-state immunity, it also appears accepted that official immunity for criminal matters is effectively regulated in the course of the government's decision to indict.[860]

At the opposite extreme are instances in which judicial determination involves a straightforward question about whether an act was undertaken in the person's official capacity.[861] Even relatively straightforward cases may require construing foreign law, including submissions on that subject by foreign governments. But similar questions under the FSIA are entrusted to the courts, and do not engage the executive branch's exclusive competence.[862] Indeed, for official immunity, the executive branch may elect to leave them to the courts, so they are not beyond judicial competence.

In between these extremes are some criteria suggested by the executive branch, being dictated neither by the nature of official immunity nor by international precedent. For example, the executive has asserted that a basis for denying official immunity in certain circumstances may be whether the person claiming immunity is a U.S. lawful permanent resident at the time of suit.[863] Assuming that residency is a reasonable consideration, it remains unclear why courts should permit the executive to decide whether and when it matters.[864] If such a factor is

for these factors, the U.S. position has been that they matter, but that it is also within the executive branch's discretion to decide that they do not. *See, e.g., id.* At 9; Brief for the United States as Amicus Curiae Supporting Appellees, *supra* note 852, at 6–7, 19; Statement of Interest of the United States of America at 8, Ahmed v. Magan, No. 2:10-cv-342, 2011 WL 13160129, at *2 (S.D. Ohio Nov. 7, 2011) ("In future cases presenting different circumstances, the Department could determine either that a former official of a state without a recognized government is immune from civil suit for acts taken in an official capacity, or that a former official of a state with a recognized government is not immune from civil suit for acts that were not taken in an official capacity.").

[860] *See supra* this chapter text accompanying note 844; U.S. Samantar Brief, *supra* note 850, at 12 n.6 ("In choosing to prosecute a foreign official, the Executive Branch has necessarily determined that the official is not properly protected by immunity"). Courts do not seem to regard convening a grand jury (or its related proceedings, like subpoenas) as likewise establishing such a conclusive determination. *See, e.g., In re* Grand Jury Proceedings, Doe No. 700, 817 F.2d 1108 (4ᵗʰ Cir. 1987) (resolving grand jury proceeding concerning former president on waiver grounds instead).

[861] *See, e.g.*, Mireskandari v. Mayne, No. CV 12-3861 JGB, 2016 WL 1165896, at *15–*20 (C.D. Cal. Mar. 23, 2016) (concluding that various officials of the Law Society of England and Wales were entitled to common-law immunity given absence of allegations involving any personal, non-official capacity); Richardson v. Att'y Gen. of the Virgin Is., No. 2008-144, 2013 WL 4494975, at *14–*17 (D. V.I. Aug. 20, 2013) (foreign customs officer entitled to common-law immunity for acts clearly taken in official capacity).

[862] *See, e.g.*, El-Hadad v. United Arab Emirates, 496 F.3d 658, 663–68 (D.C. Cir. 2007) (assessing, for purposes of the commercial activity exception, how the United Arab Emirates defined its civil service, the job title and duties of an employee, and the nature of the employee's work).

[863] *See, e.g.*, Statement of Interest of the United States of America, *supra* note 814, at 7 (describing as "[p]articularly significant" and "critical to the present Statement of Interest" that "U.S. residents like Samantar who enjoy the protections of U.S. law ordinarily should be subject to the jurisdiction of the courts, particularly when sued by U.S. residents").

[864] Nevertheless, the Fourth Circuit's decision in *Samantar v. Yousuf*—which rejected the view that State Department positions on immunity should be controlling, but thought they should be given "substantial weight"—duly weighed residency. 699 F.3d 763, 773, 777–78 (4ᵗʰ Cir. 2012) (noting Samantar's "binding tie to the United States and its court system").

a discretionary basis for ignoring an otherwise-valid immunity claim, perhaps it is inappropriate for courts to consider it on their own when no executive suggestion is filed;[865] however, making a criterion turn entirely on whether a suggestion is filed would be in tension with the idea that executive branch rules are to be mirrored by courts as part of a shared common law.[866]

With deference an incomplete solution—certainly, in the absence of suggestions—difficult issues also remain concerning the scope of official capacity. One recurring question is whether the act of the foreign official being litigated was an "official" act. Acts may be clearly official, or clearly private, in character. Yet at times the nature of the act is less clear, and a formal test for resolving the matter is difficult to identify. The leading candidate at present may be the pre-FSIA test in *Restatement (Second)* § 66, which asks whether an act was performed by a public minister, official, or agent, in an official capacity, such that the effect of exercising jurisdiction would be to enforce a rule against the foreign state itself.[867] That test probably functions best to exclude immunity for acts that are nominally in an official capacity, but that do not implicate sovereign policies.[868] Still, the test may be archaic: suits against officials that effectively enforce a rule against a foreign state itself now should be resolved under the FSIA as an action against the foreign state, rather than against an individual under common-law official immunity.[869] There have been hints by the executive

---

[865] *See, e.g.*, Statement of Interest of the United States of America at 9, Ahmed v. Magan, No. 2:10-cv-342, 2011 WL 13160129, at *2 (S.D. Ohio Nov. 7, 2011) (stressing that defendant "is a former official of a state with no currently recognized government to request immunity on his behalf, including by expressing a position on whether the acts in question were taken in an official capacity").

[866] *See supra* this chapter text accompanying notes 815–817 (discussing two-step approach).

[867] RESTATEMENT (SECOND) § 66. For recent, if guarded, invocation, see Samantar v. Yousuf, 560 U.S. 305, 321 (2010) (stating that the *Restatement* had been found "instructive" as to the "scope of an official's immunity at common law"); *id.* At 321 n.15 ("We express no view on whether Restatement § 66 correctly sets out the scope of the common-law immunity applicable to current or former foreign officials"); Lewis v. Mutond, 918 F.3d 142, 146 (D.C. Cir. 2016) (applying *Restatement (Second)* § 66 based on the shared assumption of the parties). *But see id.* At 148–49 (Randolph, J., concurring in the judgment) (doubting authority of the *Restatement (Second)*, and stressing difficulty of finding relevant rules).

[868] *See* RESTATEMENT (SECOND) § 66, illus. 3 ("X is an employee of the naturalization service of state A employed in state B for the purpose of inspecting the credentials of prospective migrants from B to A. While driving a car on an official mission, he injures Y, a national of B. Y sues X in B, alleging that his injury was due to the negligence of X. X is not entitled to the immunity of A …").

[869] *See, e.g.*, Nnaka v. Federal Republic of Nigeria, 238 F. Supp. 3d 17, 30–31 (D.D.C. 2017); Strange v. Islamic Republic of Iran, No. 14-435 (CKK), 2016 WL 10770678, at *5 (D.D.C. May 6, 2016); Mohammadi v. Islamic Republic of Iran, 947 F. Supp. 48, 71–73 (D.D.C. 2013); Gomes v. ANGOP, Angl. Press Agency, No. 11–CV–0580 (DLI)(JO), 2012 WL 3637453, at * 18 (E.D.N.Y. Aug. 22, 2012). It may be impossible in some circumstances to proceed "against an individual official alone" (or at all). *See Samantar v. Yousuf*, 560 U.S. at 324. First, "it may be the case that the foreign state itself, its political subdivision, or an agency or instrumentality is a required party," which may require dismissal as against the official, if the FSIA makes the foreign state immune. *Id.* at 324–25. Second, it is possible that in some actions the state should be treated as the real party in interest. *Id.* at 325. There may also be a nonstatutory form of foreign sovereign immunity, unless *Samantar v. Yousuf*'s reference to "foreign sovereign immunity" was to the common law of official immunity. *Id.* at 324 ("Even if a

branch, as yet without resonance in the case law, that it "generally presumes that actions taken by a foreign official exercising the powers of his or her office" are taken in an official capacity, and that this is strongest when a former head of state is involved, given that office's "wide-ranging responsibilities."[870] In any event, future decisions might afford a high degree of deference to executive branch suggestions when former heads of state are involved—given both the range of their responsibilities and more acute political sensitivities.[871]

A second issue is whether certain kinds of alleged acts are either incapable of being regarded as "official" in nature or are otherwise ineligible for official immunity. The asserted illegality of an act under foreign or international law that is the predicate for a claim cannot alone be sufficient for displacing official immunity; if that were the case, then basic allegations of crimes or civil wrongs would result in a loss of immunity. Whether courts should distinguish allegations of certain serious crimes under international law, including violations of peremptory or *jus cogens* norms, has been sharply debated. As with sovereign immunity and head-of-state immunity, compromising immunity based on skillful pleading may be problematic. The complexity is compounded for official immunity, which may require concluding that alleged conduct contrary to preemptory norms *can* be attributable to a foreign state (so as to engage the international responsibility of the state), while at the same time positing that the conduct *cannot* be regarded as an official act (so as to preclude immunity of the official). In any event, denial of immunity in such circumstances is not settled as a matter of international law.[872]

---

suit is not governed by the [FSIA], it may still be barred by foreign sovereign immunity under the common law.").

[870] Suggestion of Immunity Submitted by the United States of America at 5, Doe v. Zedillo, No. 3:11-cv-01433-AWT (D. Conn. Sept. 7, 2012) (No. 38-1), https://perma.cc/8WPY-9K77.

[871] In contrast, the executive branch view is that because each and every assessment of official capacity is potentially sensitive, every executive branch suggestion, when offered, should be treated as conclusive. *See, e.g.,* U.S. Samantar Brief, *supra* note 850, at 27–28.

[872] *See* Fox & Webb, *supra* note 509, at 571 (regarding exceptional treatment of *jus cogens* offenses to be highly uncertain); Akande & Shah, *supra* note 824, at 825–52 (criticizing prevailing justifications, but finding an exception justified by recent developments in international law); van Alebeek, *supra* note 850, at 502–24 (describing conflicting state practice, but favoring regarding such offenses as not official acts); William S. Dodge, *Foreign Official Immunity in the International Law Commission: The Meanings of "Official Capacity,"* 109 AJIL UNBOUND 156 (2015) (criticizing failure to recognize distinct meanings attributed to official capacity); Chimène I. Keitner, *Categorizing Acts by State Officials: Attribution and Responsibility in the Law Of Foreign Official Immunity,* 26 DUKE J. COMP. & INT'L L. 451 (2016) (same); *see also* Yousuf v. Samantar, 699 F.3d 763, 775–76 (4th Cir. 2012) (discussing theory and state practice). The issue of whether there are any exceptions to official immunity from foreign criminal jurisdiction for allegations of serious crimes under international law is presently before the ILC. Int'l Law Comm'n, *Immunity of State officials from foreign criminal jurisdiction: Texts and titles of the draft articles adopting by the Drafting Committee on first reading, supra* note 837, at 2 (providing, in draft article 7, that official immunity shall not apply when the official is alleged to have committed one of six specified international crimes). For an analysis of government reactions, see Janina Barkholdt & Julian Kulaga, *Analytical Presentation of the Comments and Observations by States on Draft Article 7, Paragraph 1, of the ILC Draft Articles on Immunity of State Officials From Foreign Criminal Jurisdiction, United Nations General Assembly, Sixth Committee,*

Domestically, U.S. cases generally favor maintaining official immunity even when violations of *jus cogens* or peremptory norms are alleged,[873] but that view has recently been questioned.[874] Even ignoring the uncertain international law footing, squaring an exception to immunity for allegations of *jus cogens* violations with other U.S. practice would present challenges. There is as yet no similar exception for foreign sovereign immunity or head-of-state immunity.[875] Further, at least some courts have favored the view that statutes such as the TVPA do not override official immunity, in light of a presumption for reading statutes to be consistent with the common law.[876] Vesting the executive branch with the power to decide whether current and former foreign officials deserve to be arrested and tried based on an allegation of a serious *jus cogens* violation is a considerable authority to contemplate. Still, it is arguably comparable to assigning it authority to determine conclusively whether or not such officials are entitled to immunity in the event of other serious offenses, such as the murder of U.S. nationals, so long as those acts are done while in office and for official reasons. Reconsideration is

2017, KFG Working Paper Series No. 14 (2018), http://dx.doi.org/10.2139/ssrn.3172104. Notably, it may be harder as a matter of state practice to justify the exercise of civil jurisdiction over officials alleged to have committed serious offenses, which is usually what is at issue in U.S. cases. van Alebeek, *supra* note 850, at 521–22.

[873] *See, e.g.,* Ye v. Zemin, 383 F.3d 620, 625–27 (7th Cir. 2004) (indicating, pre-*Samantar v. Yousuf*, that "[o]ur interpretation of the FSIA confirmed that Congress could grant immunity to a foreign state for acts that amounted to violations of *jus cogens* norms"); Matar v. Dichter, 563 F.3d 9, 14–15 (2d Cir. 2009) (extending the lack of a general *jus cogens* exception to the FSIA to common law official immunity, given deference to the executive branch); Giraldo v. Drummond Co., 493 Fed. Appx. 106 (D.C. Cir. 2012) (granting immunity to a foreign official even in the face of allegations of *jus cogens* violations); Saleh v. Bush, 848 F.3d 880, 892–94 (9th Cir. 2017) (holding claims of *jus cogens* violations did not alter immunity); Dogan v. Barak, 932 F.3d 888, 896–97 (9th Cir. 2019) (declining to recognize exception for *jus cogens* offenses where foreign state had ratified conduct and Department of State had suggested immunity).
[874] *See Yousuf v. Samantar*, 699 F.3d at 776–77 (concluding that "under international and domestic law," there is no entitlement "to foreign official immunity for jus cogens violations, even if the acts were performed in the defendant's official capacity"); *see also* Sarei v. Rio Tinto, PLC, 487 F.3d 1193, 1210 (9th Cir. 2007) (stating, in Act of State doctrine rather than an immunity context, that acts violating *jus cogens* norms acts "cannot constitute official sovereign acts") (citing Siderman de Blake, 965 F.2d 699, 718 (9th Cir. 1992)).
[875] *See supra* this chapter text accompanying notes 519–525 (foreign sovereign immunity); *supra* this chapter text accompanying notes 845–849 (head-of-state immunity). If official immunity but not head-of-state immunity could be denied for alleged *jus cogens* violations, it might reinforce the incentive of any head of state to cling to power.
[876] Torture Victim Protection Act of 1991, 28 U.S.C. § 1350 note, § 2(a)(1) (2018). The Ninth Circuit recently concluded that the TVPA creates a torture-related cause of action against "[a]n individual" without subjecting to suit individuals entitled to official immunity. Dogan v. Barak, 932 F.3d 888, 894–96 (9th Cir. 2019). The Second Circuit's view may be similar in effect. Matar v. Dichter, 563 F.3d 9, 15 (2d Cir 2009) (indicating that "because the extension of common-law immunity is discretionary, the TVPA will apply to any individual official whom the Executive declines to immunize"). The D.C. Circuit has disagreed. Lewis v. Muton, 918 F.3d 142, 148 (D.C. Cir. 2019) (Srinivasan, J., concurring) (finding that the TVPA "displaces any common-law, conduct-based immunity that might otherwise apply in the context of claims under that Act"); *id.* at 149–50 (Randolph, J., concurring) (same).

likely to succeed only if distinct and judicially administrable questions can be identified.

3. Special Mission Immunity

Special mission immunity is the least developed form of immunity for foreign officials, but it is highly consistent with broader U.S. immunities practice. A state may use a special mission as a temporary expedient for conducting relations with another state on a specific matter, having obtained the latter's consent (at least where it encroaches on the latter's territory). An example might be a negotiation of a bilateral agreement by the United States with a foreign state, where the foreign state's delegation comes to Washington, D.C., for a three-day meeting. In such a situation, the foreign state delegation typically would receive permission from the Department of State for the visit. Host state consent to the visit is particularly significant for immunity purposes because the member of such a mission may not possess a particular credential or position (unlike diplomats or a head of state); moreover, while the immunity is functional in origin, the member's immunity need not be limited to acts performed in an official capacity (in contrast to conduct-based immunity).[877]

Special mission immunity is the subject of the 1969 U.N. Convention on Special Missions, which has entered into force, but participation in that treaty is not widespread, and the United States has not signed or ratified it.[878] The U.S. position, which has support, has been that the Convention does not itself reflect customary international law.[879] At the same time, the United States has declared, in a qualified way, that it regards the doctrine of special mission immunity as having a basis in customary international law.[880]

---

[877] Andrew Sanger & Michael Wood, *The Immunities of Members of Special Missions*, in CAMBRIDGE HANDBOOK, *supra* note 510, at 452, 452–54, 464; Convention on Special Missions art. 1, Dec. 8, 1969, 1400 U.N.T.S. 231; *cf.* Michael Wood, *The Immunity of Official Visitors*, 16 MAX PLANCK Y.B. U.N. LAW 35, 40 & n.4 (2012) (suggesting alternative terminology).

[878] Convention on Special Missions, *supra* note 877; Further Statement of Interest of the United States in Support of the United States' Suggestion of Immunity at 3–5, Weixum v. Xilai, 568 F. Supp. 2d 35 (D.D.C. 2008) (Civ. No. 04-0649 (RJL)), https://perma.cc/CLA4-CAPA (elaborating U.S. view); *see also* Committee of Legal Advisers on Public International Law (CAHDI), *Replies by States to the Questionnaire on "Immunities of Special Missions"* at 137, CAHDI (2018) 6 prov, (July 11, 2018) (U.S. replies), https://perma.cc/S2UH-GKHU [hereinafter CAHDI, *Replies by States*] ("[T]he United States does not apply any international legal instruments specifically in the area of the immunities of special missions.").

[879] United States v. Sissoko, 995 F. Supp. 1469, 1471 (S.D. Fla. 1997). The general view appears to be that the Convention indicates broader privileges and immunities, for a narrower range of personnel, than would be available under customary international law. FOX & WEBB, *supra* note 509, at 567–68; Sanger & Wood, *supra* note 877, at 461; *cf.* RESTATEMENT (THIRD) § 464 rptrs. note 13 (stating that "the Convention on Special Missions reflects what is increasingly practiced and in many respects may emerge as customary international law").

[880] CAHDI, *Replies by States*, *supra* note 878, at 138 ("[W]hile the full extent of special missions immunity remains unsettled, there is a widespread consensus that, at a minimum, it is generally inappropriate for States to exercise jurisdiction over ministerial-level officials invited on a special diplomatic mission. . . . We are continuing to review and evaluate our practice in this area . . ."); *accord*

While a foreign delegation may be able to request and receive an express acknowledgment that special mission immunity of a particular scope is being granted to particular individuals, usually foreign delegations are simply granted permission to travel to the host state, potentially leaving unclear how the immunity is to be applied. There is no settled international practice as to the types of persons or missions to which special mission immunity applies, and state practice varies, but it seems reasonably clear that high-level delegations from a foreign state—not necessarily being members of the present government—can be deemed eligible if they represent the sending state with the consent of the receiving state.[881] There is greater uncertainty as to the scope of special mission immunity. Customary international law supports personal inviolability (including service of process) and immunity from criminal jurisdiction for members of a special mission, but the extension of such immunity to civil jurisdiction more generally is unclear.[882]

For its part, the United States has suggested that immunity applies at a minimum to certain "high-level" or "ministerial-level" or "senior" officials when visiting the United States (but not automatically to lower officials, nor simply by virtue of a temporary assignment to a foreign mission), and that this immunity applies to the exercise of jurisdiction by both federal and state courts.[883] In the few cases that have been litigated, U.S. courts have followed executive branch suggestions, without requiring any showing of prior consent to a special mission as such.[884]

Suggestion of Immunity and Statement of Interest of the United States, *supra* note 878, at 4; Further Statement of Interest, *supra* note 878, at 5, 7, 8–10; *see* The Freedom and Justice Party and Others v. The Secretary of State for Foreign and Commonwealth Affairs, [2018] EWCA Civ, 1719, ¶¶ 95–96 (Eng. C.A.) (noting lack of clarity in CAHDI submission by the United States); Wood, *supra* note 877, at 94–98 (discussing U.S. practice); Sanger & Wood, *supra* note 877, 474 (same).

[881] Sanger & Wood, *supra* note 877, at 478–79; Wood, *supra* note 877, at 67–72; *cf.* Convention on Special Missions, *supra* note 877, arts. 3–20.

[882] Sanger & Wood, *supra* note 877, at 465–78; Wood, *supra* note 877, at 71–72. Such immunity appears to apply regardless of the gravity of the alleged offenses. Re Bo Xilai, 128 I.L.R. 173 (Bow St. Magis. Ct., 2005) (U.K.) (applying special mission immunity in refusing application for arrest warrant relating to torture allegations); *see also* The Freedom and Justice Party and Others, [2018] EWCA Civ, ¶¶ 107–11. The Convention generally affords the same privileges and immunities as accorded diplomatic staff. Sanger & Wood, *supra* note 877, at 459–61.

[883] CAHDI, *Replies by States*, *supra* note 878, at 137–39.

[884] *Weixum*, 568 F. Supp. 2d at 38 (former provincial governor, and sitting Minister of Commerce, held immune from service of process and from civil jurisdiction following Department of State suggestion of a "special diplomatic mission to the United States that rendered Minister Bo immune from service of process"); Kilroy v. Charles Windsor, Prince of Wales, Civ. No. C-78-291 (N.D. Ohio, 1978), *excerpted in* 1978 DIGEST OF U.S. PRACTICE at 641, 641–43 (dismissing civil suit against the Prince of Wales, following suggestion by the Department of State that it regarded the prince's visit as "a special diplomatic mission and considers the Prince to have been an official diplomatic envoy while present in the United States on that special mission"); *cf.* Suggestion of Interest Submitted on Behalf of the United States, Chong Boon Kim v. Yim Yong Shik, Civ. No. 12565 (Haw. Cir. Ct. 1963), *excerpted in* 58 AM. J. INT'L L. 165, 186–87 (1964) (noting U.S. suggestion of immunity on behalf of the Korean foreign minister by virtue of his "diplomatic status"—but more closely resembling head-of-state

Absent widespread adherence to the U.N. Convention on Special Missions, international rules on special mission immunity are likely to remain hazy. Identifying state practice is difficult because the visits are short and ideally uneventful; any controversies may surface when immunity is initially disrespected, such as by an arrest, and states may then resolve the matter simply by releasing the individual and refusing to prosecute.[885] As a practical matter, this means that U.S. courts might have little international guidance in resolving any actual controversies other than that afforded through executive branch suggestions. Deference also seems warranted by the nature of special mission immunity, given presidential authority over recognition of foreign states and governments and over the conduct of diplomacy.[886] Allowing U.S. courts to confer special mission immunity in the absence of executive branch suggestions might materially undermine executive branch authority: it would be peculiar, for instance, if the executive could refuse to accredit a foreign diplomat (thereby denying diplomatic immunity) while the courts proceeded to afford immunity by determining her or his entitlement to special mission immunity.[887]

Special mission immunity may appear vestigial and useful only when a foreign official's status or acts are not otherwise protected. But its availability is nevertheless worth considering when evaluating the appropriate deference to be given executive branch suggestions in other immunity contexts. If courts defer completely to executive branch suggestions of special mission immunity, then that mechanism affords an important backstop for preserving the security of diplomacy within the United States, irrespective of whether a similar degree of deference is preserved elsewhere.

immunity—and its acceptance as the basis for dismissing jurisdiction). This appears consistent with state practice. Sanger & Wood, *supra* note 877, at 479–80. Yet, the particular U.S. procedure is hardly inevitable: in the United Kingdom, for example, the government is responsible for consenting in advance, but the ultimate question of immunities is left to the courts. *The Freedom and Justice Party and Others*, [2018] EWCA Civ, ¶ 9.

[885] Sanger & Wood, *supra* text accompanying note 877, at 462.
[886] *Cf. Kilroy v. Charles Windsor*, *supra* note 884, at 642 (explaining that immunity of foreign officials, "being based on foreign policy considerations and the Executive's desire to maintain amiable relations with foreign states, applies with even more force to live persons representing a foreign nation on an official visit").
[887] *Cf.* United States v. Sissoko, 995 F. Supp. 1469 (D. Fla. 1997) (rejecting invocation of special mission immunity for a special adviser to a foreign state mission absent diplomatic accreditation by the United States or any suggestion of immunity); Further Statement, *supra* note 878, at 6 (distinguishing *Sissoko*).

5

Customary International Law

Customary international law—the binding law arising from the practice of states, rather than from their formal agreement[1]—accounts for vital components of the international law binding the United States, including rules relating to immunity, jurisdiction, human rights, and the law of the sea. Nonetheless, the Constitution, federal statutes, and case law leave a number of very basic questions unresolved. The United States has long accepted that it is bound by customary international law on the international plane[2] and that it is part of our domestic law.[3] Still, its precise *place* in U.S. law has not been clearly resolved. To what extent are the political branches entrusted with incorporating customary international law into U.S. law and to what extent are they required to heed it? Under what circumstances do federal courts have jurisdiction over questions of customary international law, and when does it supply a rule of decision? Is customary international law supreme over the laws of the several states? The relative silence of the Constitution and case law on these questions has given rise to a kind of cacophony, in which forcefully expressed theories suggest very different answers to these fundamental questions.

This chapter discusses settled and open questions concerning customary international law, the contemporary term of choice, as well as comparable aspects

---

[1] Statute of the International Court of Justice art. 38(1)(b), June 26, 1945, 59 Stat. 1055, 1060, T.S. No. 993, at 25, 30 (providing that the International Court of Justice is to apply "international custom, as evidence of a general practice accepted as law"); Restatement (Third) § 102(2) (describing customary international law as resulting from "a general and consistent practice of states followed by them from a sense of legal obligation"). For leading contemporary guides, see Comm. on Formation of Customary (Gen.) Int'l Law, Int'l Law Ass'n, Final Report of the Committee: Statement of Principles Applicable to the Formation of General Customary International Law (2000), available at https://perma.cc/KUZ7-8Z2V; Int'l Law Comm'n, Rep. on the Work of its Seventieth Session, U.N. Doc. A/73/10, ch. V (2018) (draft conclusions and commentaries on the identification of customary international law).

[2] See, e.g., Chisholm v. Georgia, 2 U.S. (2 Dall.) 419, 474 (1793) (stating that "the United States had, by taking a place among the nations of the earth, become amenable to the laws of nations," such that "it was their interest as well as their duty to provide, that those laws should be respected and obeyed").

[3] See, e.g., Sosa v. Alvarez-Machain, 542 U.S. 692, 729 (2004) ("For two centuries we have affirmed that the domestic law of the United States recognizes the law of nations.") (citations omitted); The Paquete Habana, 175 U.S. 677, 700 (1900) (stating that "[i]nternational law is part of our law, and must be ascertained and administered by the courts of justice of appropriate jurisdiction, as often as questions of right depending upon it are duly presented for their determination."); The Nereide, 13 U.S. (9 Cranch) 388, 423 (1815) (explaining that in the absence of a congressional enactment, U.S. courts are "bound by the law of nations, which is a part of the law of the land").

of an older term, the "law of nations," which is the body of law actually referenced in the Constitution. Confusingly, the "law of nations" was sometimes used to refer to the entirety of international law,[4] but sometimes more narrowly and interchangeably with customary international law—with the modern Supreme Court favoring this more narrow understanding,[5] sometimes while stressing how the character of the norms within this category should be understood more narrowly still.[6] This chapter uses the term "law of nations" in reviewing earlier discourse and as appropriate in evaluating how it was used in the Constitution; otherwise, it focuses on the function of customary international law today.

I. Customary International Law Under the Constitution

A. Pre-Constitutional Experience and Its Diagnosis

The founding generation was keenly familiar with the law of nations. In part this was due to their education in the leading treatises, which were understood to be the best guides to its theory and practice.[7] For the Founders, though, an appreciation of the law of nations was not merely a matter of intellectual interest but also one of necessity. When Benjamin Franklin wrote in 1775 to thank the American agent in The Hague for sending three copies of Vattel's influential treatise[8] and to report that his copy "has been continually in the hands of the members of our

---

[4] Blackstone, for example, also included within his "law of nations" both treaty law and the law merchant (that concerning intercourse between individuals from different states). See MARK WESTON JANIS, THE AMERICAN TRADITION OF INTERNATIONAL LAW: GREAT EXPECTATIONS, 1789–1914, at 2–15 (2004) (describing Blackstone's usage and Bentham's coining of "international law"); see also Sarah H. Cleveland & William S. Dodge, Defining and Punishing Offenses Under Treaties, 124 YALE L.J. 2202, 2210–33 (2015) (arguing that the Framers understood "law of nations," including as it was used in the Offences Clause, as encompassing treaties and other forms of international law).

[5] See, e.g., Hartford Fire Ins. v. California, 509 U.S. 764, 815 (1993) (Scalia, J., dissenting); United States v. Percheman, 32 U.S. 51, 65 (1833); see also United States v. Bellaizac-Hurtado, 700 F.3d 1245, 1251–52 (11th Cir. 2012) (reviewing precedent).

[6] See infra this chapter text accompanying notes 235–255 (discussing Sosa v. Alvarez-Machain, 542 U.S. 692 (2004)).

[7] See Edwin D. Dickinson, Law of Nations as Part of the National Law of the United States, 101 U. PA. L. REV. 26, 35–36 (1952); Stewart Jay, The Status of the Law of Nations in Early American Law, 42 VAND. L. REV. 819, 823 (1989).

[8] EMER DE VATTEL, THE LAW OF NATIONS; OR PRINCIPLES OF THE LAW OF NATURE: APPLIED TO THE CONDUCT AND AFFAIRS OF NATIONS AND SOVEREIGNS (1759). Vattel's influence on the founding generation has been widely noted. See, e.g., PETER ONUF & NICHOLAS ONUF, FEDERAL UNION, MODERN WORLD: THE LAW OF NATIONS IN AN AGE OF REVOLUTIONS 1776–1814, at 11 (1993); Charles G. Fenwick, The Authority of Vattel (I), 7 AM. POL. SCI. REV. 395 (1913); Charles G. Fenwick, The Authority of Vattel (II), 8 AM. POL. SCI. REV. 375 (1914); Douglas J. Sylvester, International Law as Sword or Shield? Early American Foreign Policy and the Law of Nations, 32 N.Y.U. J. INT'L L. & POL. 1, 67 (1999). But cf. infra this chapter text accompanying notes 64–68 (evaluating reliance on Vattel·in modern discussions of original understanding).

[Continental] Congress," he explained that "the circumstances of a rising state make it necessary frequently to consult the law of nations."[9]

Franklin and his colleagues were intent in part, perhaps even primarily, on securing for the United States the rights of a new nation: recognition by other states, the capacity to enter into treaties and to secure free commerce and navigation, the security of neutrality and the rights of prize, and so forth.[10] But the founding generation was also anxious to ensure U.S. compliance with the law of nations. The states committed numerous violations of the Treaty of Paris with Great Britain—the very instrument that had acknowledged U.S. independence and its right to function as a state under international law—as John Jay, then Secretary of Foreign Affairs (and signatory of the treaty), laid out in a report for the Continental Congress.[11] There were also regular reports that U.S. citizens had violated the rights of noncitizens. The Continental Congress recommended in 1781 that the state legislatures provide for punishment of several specific violations of the law of nations and establish tribunals to hear cases involving other such offenses and provide for civil redress.[12] But problems persisted—most famously, in the 1784 assault in Philadelphia on Marbois, a member of the French embassy, by fellow French national Longchamps—and powerful foreign countries like France complained directly to their counterparts in the U.S. capital.[13] Congress was compelled to pass a resolution urging that the states arrest Longchamps,[14] later adopting a more general resolution urging the adoption of statutes providing for punishment of those offending foreign ministers or servants.[15]

Incidents of this type posed both direct and indirect problems for the United States. Assaulting an ambassador and similar misconduct constituted violations of the law of nations.[16] Moreover, U.S. condemnation of the attack might be

[9] Letter from Benjamin Franklin to Charles F.W. Dumas (Dec. 19, 1775), *reprinted in* 2 FRANCIS WHARTON, THE REVOLUTIONARY DIPLOMATIC CORRESPONDENCE OF THE UNITED STATES 64 (1889).

[10] *See generally* ONUF & ONUF, *supra* note 8; David M. Golove & Daniel J. Hulsebosch, *A Civilized Nation: The Early American Constitution, the Law of Nations, and the Pursuit of International Recognition*, 85 N.Y.U. L. REV. 932 (2010); Sylvester, *supra* note 8.

[11] 31 JOURNALS OF THE CONTINENTAL CONGRESS, at 781, 784–874. *See also* Chapter 6 § I(A)(2).

[12] 21 JOURNALS OF THE CONTINENTAL CONGRESS, at 1136–37 (setting out resolution and committee report); for discussion, see Anthony J. Bellia, Jr., & Bradford R. Clark, *The Alien Tort Statute and the Law of Nations*, 78 U. CHI. L. REV. 445, 494–98 (2011).

[13] *See* William R. Casto, *The Federal Courts' Protective Jurisdiction over Torts Committed in Violation of the Law of Nations*, 18 CONN. L. REV. 467, 491–94 (1986); Alfred Rosenthal, *The Marbois-Longchamps Affair*, 63 PA. MAG. HIST. & BIOGRAPHY 294 (1939). For discussion both of the Marbois incident and a contemporary incident involving the entry into the house of Van Berckel, a Dutch minister, and the arrest of one of his domestic servants, see Curtis A. Bradley, *The Alien Tort Statute and Article III*, 42 VA. J. INT'L L. 587, 638–42 (2002); Thomas H. Lee, *The Safe-Conduct Theory of the Alien Tort Statute*, 106 COLUM. L. REV. 830, 860–62 (2006).

[14] 27 JOURNALS OF THE CONTINENTAL CONGRESS, at 478.

[15] 28 JOURNALS OF THE CONTINENTAL CONGRESS, at 315; for discussion, see Bradley, *supra* note 13, at 639–41.

[16] *See, e.g.*, 2 VATTEL, *supra* note 8, book IV, § 81, at 142.

discredited in the absence of sufficient punishment and give rise to national responsibility if the offense were unremedied (indeed, under the law of nations as
they understood it, might provide cause for retaliation and war, if the offense
were particularly grave).[17] The seriousness of these issues was appreciated not
only by the Continental Congress, in its appeals to the states for reforms, but
seemingly by the states themselves. A few states enacted statutes facilitating jurisdiction over law-of-nations offenses,[18] and others (like Pennsylvania) exhibited
at least some capacity for prosecuting such offenses as common law crimes.[19]

Legitimate concerns remained, however, that the United States might be accused of indirectly offending the law of nations, and similar problems attended
other kinds of trespasses. For example, pre-constitutional struggles to abide
by international agreements (discussed more extensively in Chapter 6) also—
derivatively—risked giving cause for war according to the law of nations.[20] Even
wrongs against property and other interests of noncitizens, which had little to do
with the law of nations as an initial matter, might cause diplomatic contretemps—
and, if unaddressed, blossom into law of nations concerns in their own right.[21]

Those advocating for a new Constitution were keenly aware of these
challenges. Writing before the convention, James Madison observed that treaty
violations and other "frequent violations of the law of nations" might bring about
"the greatest of public calamities" for the nation as a whole.[22] George Mason
arrived in Philadelphia engaged with proposals to establish a federal judiciary
"with cognizance of all such matters as depend on the law of nations,"[23] and

---

[17] See 21 JOURNALS OF THE CONTINENTAL CONGRESS, at 1136. For a discussion of Vattel's "per-
fect rights," which permitted states to seek enforcement of their own accord, including by force, see
ANTHONY J. BELLIA, JR. & BRADFORD R. CLARK, THE LAW OF NATIONS AND THE UNITED STATES
CONSTITUTION 44–45 (2017); Anthony J. Bellia, Jr. & Bradford R. Clark, The Federal Common Law of
Nations, 109 COLUM. L. REV. 1, 15–19 (2009) (same).

[18] See Andrew Kent, Congress's Under-Appreciated Power to Define and Punish Offenses Against
the Law of Nations, 85 TEX. L. REV. 843, 881 n.180 (2007) (citing examples from Connecticut, South
Carolina, and Virginia).

[19] Respublica v. De Longchamps, 1 U.S. (1 Dall.) 111, 114 (1784); see Bradley, supra note 13, at
641–42 (discussing satisfactory resolution of Marbois and Van Berckel incidents); Kent, supra note
18, at 876–80 (casting doubt on significance of incidents for development of the Constitution). In the
Marbois incident itself, France was most disappointed over the failure to extradite Longchamps.

[20] See, e.g., 1 VATTEL, supra note 8, book II, § 164 (describing violation of a treaty as infringing a
perfect right of the other sovereign).

[21] 1 VATTEL, supra note 8, book II, §§ 72–78, at 136–37 (describing a nation's responsibility for the
acts of its citizens); see Bellia & Clark, The Alien Tort Statute and the Law of Nations, supra note 12, at
471–77, 501–03 (describing the then-prevalent understanding of state responsibility, and actual violence and property infringement against British and other foreign subjects).

[22] James Madison, Vices of the Political System of the United States (Apr. 1787), in 1 THE FOUNDER'S
CONSTITUTION 167 (Philip B. Kurland & Ralph Lerner eds., 1986).

[23] Letter from George Mason to Arthur Lee (May 21, 1787), in 3 FARRAND'S RECORDS, at 24
(discussing impressions of prevailing initiatives); see Amendments to the Articles of Confederation
Proposed by a Grand Committee of Congress (Aug. 7, 1786), in 1 THE DOCUMENTARY HISTORY OF
THE RATIFICATION OF THE CONSTITUTION 163, 67 (Merrill Jensen ed., 1976) (proposing creation of
a federal court with capacity to exercise review over "all Causes wherein questions Shall arise on the

Edmund Randolph echoed Madison's warning at the convention's beginning.[24] Later, mindful of the national government's assumption of responsibility under the new Constitution for both the law of nations and treaties, John Jay stressed that "it is of high importance to the peace of America that she observe the law of nations toward all these powers."[25] The subject of indirect violations was among the issues that remained seized. Alexander Hamilton, denying the value for juris- dictional purposes of distinguishing between "cases arising upon treaties and the laws of nations" and "those which may stand merely on the footing of municipal law," queried whether—insofar as the latter involved foreigners—they "would not if unredressed, be an aggression upon his sovereign, as well as one which violated the stipulations of a treaty or the general law of nations." The basic point, he famously stressed, was that "the peace of the *whole* ought not to be left at the disposal of a *part*."[26]

B. Constitutional Design

Given this background, the Constitution's superficial neglect of customary international law actually becomes easier to comprehend. Parts of the new Constitution explicitly addressed the law of nations, but it was generally addressed indirectly; that was less a sign of neglect than of the law's pervasive- ness, which commended broad solutions. It is worth describing the resulting design before turning, later in the chapter, to subsequent practice and controver- sies. Other constitutional provisions germane to the law of nations—for example, Congress' power to "declare war" and to "grant letters of marque and reprisal," or the president's power to "receive ambassadors" and to "make treaties," either of which implicate the understanding of those concepts under customary interna- tional law—are addressed in separate chapters.[27]

1. Law of Nations and the Congress
In keeping with the earlier exhortations to states to create tribunals charged with violations of the law of nations,[28] the Committee of Detail initially considered giving a national legislature the power "[t]o provide tribunals and punishment

---

meaning and construction of Treaties entered into by the United States with any foreign power, or on the Law of Nations").

[24] 1 FARRAND'S RECORDS, at 19 (May 29) (Madison); *id.* at 24–27 (McHenry).

[25] THE FEDERALIST No. 3, at 43 (John Jay).

[26] THE FEDERALIST No. 80, at 476–77 (Alexander Hamilton).

[27] See, respectively, Chapter 8 (war powers, including letters of marque and reprisal); Chapter 3 (power to send and receive ambassadors); and Chapter 6 (treaties).

[28] *See supra* this chapter text accompanying note 12.

for mere offences against the law of nations."[29] After the proposal of separate tribunals was dropped, and the jurisdiction of general federal courts (including as to the law of nations) evolved,[30] the Committee reported in early August a proposal in which Congress might "declare the law and punishment of piracies and felonies committed on the high seas, and the punishment of counterfeiting ... and of offences against the law of nations."[31]

These powers were then refined.[32] The capacity to punish was retained with only incidental changes in phrasing;[33] the main controversy instead concerned whether it was appropriate for Congress to "declare" or otherwise refine some or all of the offenses. After it was resolved that the power to punish felonies and piracies would be less vague and more uniform if Congress could also "define" them,[34] Gouverneur Morris proposed establishing parallel authority to "define and punish" law-of-nations offenses as well.[35] James Wilson objected that "[t]o pretend to define the law of nations which depended on the authority of all the Civilized Nations of the World, would have a look of arrogance[] that would make us ridiculous," and Morris responded that as far as "*offences*" were concerned definition was proper because the law of nations was "often too vague and deficient to be a rule."[36]

The result was the only explicit reference to what we would now describe as customary international law: Article I, Section 8, which gives Congress the power to "define and punish Piracies and Felonies committed on the high Seas, and Offences against the Law of Nations."[37] How the Supreme Court and the political branches have understood this authority—particularly that for "Offences against the Law of Nations," but also the separable authority over "Piracies" and "Felonies committed on the high Seas"—is discussed in the remainder of this chapter. There is no evidence, however, for the view that the clause was such a comprehensive grant to the legislature as to preclude executive or judicial authority over customary international law.[38] The evidence concerning the

---

[29] 2 FARRAND'S RECORDS, at 143 (Committee of Detail IV).

[30] *See infra* this chapter § II(C).

[31] 2 FARRAND'S RECORDS, at 181–82 (Madison).

[32] The authority over counterfeiting was also refined and relocated. U.S. CONST. art. I, § 8, cl. 6.

[33] The word "punish" was eventually substituted for "punishment." 2 FARRAND'S RECORDS, at 315–16 (Madison).

[34] 2 FARRAND'S RECORDS, at 316 (Madison).

[35] *Id.* at 614–15 (Madison). Morris was reacting to a Committee of Style draft that gave Congress the power to "punish" such offenses, rather than the power to "define and punish" piracies and high-seas felonies established in the immediately preceding clauses. *Id.* at 595 (Committee of Style); *see* Cleveland & Dodge, *supra* note 4, at 2225–26; Beth Stephens, *Federalism and Foreign Affairs: Congress's Power to "Define and Punish . . . Offenses Against the Law of Nations,"* 42 WM. & MARY L. REV. 447, 472–73 & n.94 (2000).

[36] 2 FARRAND'S RECORDS, at 615 (Madison) (emphasis in original).

[37] U.S. CONST. art. 1, § 8, cl. 10.

[38] *But see* Al Odah v. United States, 321 F.3d 1134, 1147 (D.C. Cir. 2003) (Randolph, J., concurring) (suggesting that the Offences Clause "makes it abundantly clear that Congress—not the Judiciary—is to determine, through legislation, what international law is and what violations of it

authority enjoyed by those branches may not be determinate as to its precise scope, but it is sufficient to undermine any suggestion that Congress occupied the field.

2. Law of Nations and the President

Article II undoubtedly affords some affirmative authority that was informed by the law of nations, like the powers relating to "Treaties" and "Ambassadors, other public Ministers and Consuls."[39] In addition, Article II imposed on the president the general responsibility to "take Care that the Laws be faithfully executed."[40] This reference to "the Laws" might be contrasted to references to "Laws of the United States" in Article III or Article VI, so as to suggest that the president must take heed of laws *not* "of the United States"—including the law of nations.[41] Such an inference is arguably buttressed by the drafting history, which shows a steady widening in executive responsibility from one for "the National Laws"[42] to the "the Laws of the United States"[43] to the eventual, unqualified "the Laws."[44]

There was near-immediate evidence as to what leading participants in the founding era thought, occasioned by President Washington's 1793 proclamation of neutrality in the conflict between Great Britain and France.[45] Hamilton (as Pacificus) and Madison (as Helvidius) publicly debated whether the proclamation fell within the president's authority—a dispute partly about the status of the Treaty of Alliance, and partly about the scope of the general grant of the "executive Power"—but they concurred as to the ambit of the Take Care Clause.[46]

ought to be cognizable in the courts"), *rev'd on other grounds*, Rasul v. Bush, 542 U.S. 466 (2004); Padilla v. Rumsfeld, 352 F.3d 695, 714 (2d Cir. 2003) ("The Constitution entrusts the ability to define and punish offenses against the law of nations to the Congress, not the Executive."), *rev'd on other grounds*, Rumsfeld v. Padilla, 542 U.S. 426 (2004); *see also* Brief for the United States as Amicus Curiae Supporting Petitioner at 8, Sosa v. Alvarez-Machain, 542 U.S. 692 (2004) (No. 03-339) (citing Judge Randolph's opinion with approval).

[39] *See infra* this chapter notes 141–150.
[40] U.S. CONST. art. II, § 3.
[41] For other examples from the constitutional text, see Edward Swaine, *Taking Care of Treaties*, 108 COLUM. L. REV. 331, 342–43 (2008).
[42] 1 FARRAND'S RECORDS, at 21 (Madison). This language or its equivalent persisted for a while. *Id.* at 63 (Journal); *id.* at 64, 67 (Madison) (referring to proceedings before Committee of the Whole); 2 FARRAND'S RECORDS, at 23 (Journal); *id.* at 145 (Committee of Detail); *see also* 1 FARRAND'S RECORDS, at 244 (Madison) (reporting New Jersey Plan and its reference to executive implementing "the federal acts"); *id.* at 292 (Madison) (relaying Hamilton Plan provision that executive would "have a negative on all laws about to be passed, and the execution of all laws passed").
[43] 2 FARRAND'S RECORDS, at 171 (Committee of Detail); *see also id.* at 158 (Committee of Detail) (reporting Pinckney Plan provision assigning president "to attend to the Execution of the Laws of the U.S.").
[44] *Id.* at 574, 600 (Committee of Style).
[45] Proclamation of Neutrality (Apr. 22, 1793), *in* 12 THE WRITINGS OF GEORGE WASHINGTON 281–82 (Worthington Chauncey Ford ed., 1891); *see also* Chapter 3 § I(C).
[46] William R. Casto, *Pacificus & Helvidius Reconsidered*, 28 N. KY. L. REV. 612, 617, 619, 621, 626, 627–28, 633 (2001).

Hamilton, defending the president's proclamation, stated that "[t]he executive is charged with the execution of all laws, the laws of Nations as well as the Municipal law, which recognises and adopts those laws."[47] Madison, demurring in other regards, agreed that "the executive is bound faithfully to execute the laws of neutrality, whilst those laws continue unaltered by the competent authority. . . . It is bound to the faithful execution of these as of all other laws internal and external. . . ."[48] To all appearances, neither distinguished between treaties and what we would now call customary international law, seeing both as germane to the international responsibility of the United States and to the laws the executive was required to execute. Perhaps they would have agreed that "take care" responsibility addressed only *supreme* federal law—but their understanding of international law's domestic status may not have permitted that distinction.[49] Such questions also implicate the contemplated role for the federal judiciary.

3. Law of Nations and the Judiciary

With the convention's turn away from special tribunals for law-of-nations matters, it confronted two questions: first, how to vest jurisdiction over the law of nations in the general national judiciary that was being contemplated; and second, the status of the law of nations relative to other sources of law for these courts (and for other actors). Neither question was clearly resolved, at least not so as to preclude present-day disputes.

The first question, concerning law-of-nations jurisdiction, was addressed at the convention. Randolph's Virginia Plan envisioned a federal judiciary with appellate jurisdiction over cases involving the rights of ambassadors, captures, acts of piracy and felonies on the high seas, and other cases in which foreigners may be interested—including "questions which may involve the national peace and harmony," which Randolph probably intended to include violations of the law of nations.[50] Paterson's New Jersey Plan, submitted later, lacked any explicit

---

[47] Alexander Hamilton, Pacificus No. I (June 29, 1793), *reprinted in* 15 THE PAPERS OF ALEXANDER HAMILTON 33, 40 (Harold R. Syrett & Jacob E. Cooke eds., 1851) [hereinafter Pacificus No. I]; *see also* Alexander Hamilton, *Message for Washington to Congress, in Reply to a Call for Papers Relating to the Treaty with Great Britain* (Mar. 29, 1796), *in* 7 THE WORKS OF ALEXANDER HAMILTON 556, 566 (John C. Hamilton ed., 1851) [hereinafter Hamilton's March 29, 1796 Draft Message] ("Treaties, therefore, in our government, of themselves and without any additional sanction, have full legal perfection as laws.").

[48] *See* James Madison, Letters of Helvidius No. II (Aug. 28, 1793), *reprinted in* 6 THE WRITINGS OF JAMES MADISON 151, 159 (Gaillard Hunt ed., 1906).

[49] *See infra* this chapter text accompanying notes 400–402 (discussing status of law of nations as federal law); Chapter 6 § IV(A) (discussing original understanding of self-executing and non-self-executing treaties).

[50] Just prior to proposing his resolutions, Randolph had cited as one of the Confederation's defects its failure to provide security against foreign invasion, including that Congress could not punish "infractions of treaties or of the law of nations." 1 FARRAND'S RECORDS, at 19 (May 29) (Madison). Discussion of the Virginia Plan and variants remained focused on the need to put matters involving national peace and harmony before a federal court. *See, e.g.*, 1 FARRAND'S RECORDS, at 22 (May

reference to this peace-and-harmony jurisdiction, but otherwise proceeded similarly, likewise including "all cases in which foreigners might be interested."[51] (Madison, responding, expressed concern that this would not do enough to address law of nations concerns.[52]) Most directly, the Pinckney Plan, put before the convention on the same day as the Virginia Plan, envisioned a federal judicial court with appellate jurisdiction over all cases arising from "the Law of Nations."[53]

None of these approaches was adopted, at least not directly. Some matters involving the law of nations were accommodated in discrete categories of Article III. Jurisdiction over cases arising under treaties, cases affecting ambassadors and similar foreign officials, admiralty and maritime matters, and diversity cases involving "foreign states, citizens or subjects" potentially enabled federal courts to address most of the direct or derivative law-of-nations offenses that had emerged under the Articles of Confederation.

The question, then, is whether customary international law matters *not* addressed by these more specific heads of jurisdiction were nonetheless supposed to be within Article III's grant of federal question jurisdiction.[54] That question is difficult to resolve.[55] The original language was broadened from "laws passed by the Legislature of the United States" to "laws of the United States,"[56]

---

29) (Madison) (reporting resolutions proposed by Randolph); *id.* at 238 (June 15) (Yates) (reporting unanimous approval of proposal by Randolph to resolve details on pending proposal based on principle that (inter alia) "questions which involve the national peace and harmony" were within the national judiciary's jurisdiction). *Cf.* 3 FARRAND's RECORDS, at 593–94 (discussing authenticity issues relating to versions of Virginia Plan).

[51]   1 FARRAND's RECORDS, at 244 (June 15) (Madison). *Cf.* 3 FARRAND's RECORDS, at 611–15 (discussing authenticity issues relating to versions of New Jersey Plan).

[52]   1 FARRAND's RECORDS, at 316 (June 19) (Madison) (asking, of New Jersey Plan, "Will it prevent those violations of the law of nations & Treaties which if not prevented must involve us in the calamities of foreign wars?").

[53]   3 FARRAND's RECORDS, at 608 (detailing reconstructed version of Pinckney Plan); *accord* 2 FARRAND's RECORDS, at 136 (outline of plan; Committee of Detail III); *id.* at 157 (extract of plan; Committee of Detail VII); *see also* 1 FARRAND's RECORDS, at 16 (May 29) (Journal) (noting introduction); *cf.* Charles Pinckney, *Observations on the Plan of Government* (May 28, 1787), *in* 3 FARRAND's RECORDS, at 106, 117 (noting importance of involvement by independent national judiciary). *But see* 3 FARRAND's RECORDS, at 600 (providing discrepant, probably inauthentic, version of Pinckney Plan omitting reference to the law of nations).

[54]   *Compare, e.g.,* Bradley, *supra* note 13, *with* William S. Dodge, *The Constitutionality of the Alien Tort Statute: Some Observations on Text and Context,* 42 VA. J. INT'L L. 687 (2002); *see also* Michael G. Collins, *The Diversity Theory of the Alien Tort Statute,* 42 VA. J. INT'L L. 649 (2002).

[55]   Whether and how Article III incorporates the law of nations in the guise of federal common law is addressed separately below. *See infra* this chapter § II(C)(2).

[56]   *Compare* 2 FARRAND's RECORDS, at 186 (Aug. 6) (Madison), *with id.* at 423–24 (August 27) (Journal); *id.* at 430–31 (Aug. 27) (Madison). Notably, though, the same change was urged for the Supremacy Clause, suggesting the possibility of a broader or merely editorial objective. *See* 2 FARRAND's RECORDS, at 389 (Aug. 23) (Madison); *see also id.* at 431 (Aug. 27) (Madison) (noting Rutledge amendments to jurisdictional provision, including as to references to the legislature, and noting attention to conformity between the clauses).

which might newly permit the law of nations, but the Framers had earlier seemed to assume that matters involving the peace of the nation—the most compelling components of any law-of-nations jurisdiction—fell into a different category.[57] A more piecemeal approach might have been considered tenable. As previously noted, other Article III heads of jurisdiction might well have allayed concerns about the inability to address either law-of-nations offenses or other matters giving rise to comparable concerns. Framing jurisdiction in terms of the law of nations (or as an implied part of the "laws of United States"), moreover, might have occasioned divisive debate about that subject's scope. Such a grant might well have folded in private components of the law of nations, like conflicts and the law merchant, and thus entailed federal jurisdiction over nondiversity cases involving commercial issues; more generally, there was doubt about the ease of defining the law of nations, as suggested by the dispute over Congress' power to punish offenses against the law of nations.[58] Notwithstanding, a number of participants conveyed their assumption that Article III as written would permit jurisdiction over all law-of-nations offenses.[59] Absent any definitive resolution of the matter within range of the framing,[60] the issue has been rejoined in modern debate over the status of international law as federal common law—a subject addressed later in this chapter.[61]

[57] See, e.g., 2 FARRAND'S RECORDS, at 39 (July 18) (Journal) (reporting unanimous passage of resolution separately noting jurisdiction over "cases arising under laws passed by the general Legislature" and "such other questions as involve the National peace and harmony"); id. at 132–33 (Committee of Detail I) (similar); id. at 146 (Committee of Detail IV) (similar); id. at 172 (Committee of Detail IX) (distinguishing instead between jurisdiction over "all Cases arising under Laws passed by the Legislature of the United States" and subcategories implicating law of nations offenses); id. at 186 (Aug. 6) (Madison) (same). This was all the more evident in Federalist No. 80, authored by Hamilton. THE FEDERALIST No. 80, at 476–77, 480–81 (Alexander Hamilton); see Collins, supra note 54, at 658–61 (reviewing Federalist No. 80 in this connection).

[58] Jay, supra note 7, at 832; Bradley, supra note 13, at 598–600; see infra this chapter § II(A)(2) (discussing Offences Clause).

[59] For example, John Jay wrote that "treaties and articles of treaties, as well as the laws of nations," would be expounded consistently by the national courts. See THE FEDERALIST No. 3, at 43 (John Jay). This and other statements were not always clear as to whether they assumed congressional action, and of what type. Compare Bradley, supra note 13, at 606–07, with Dodge, supra note 54, at 708–09. Some post-ratification statements suggested that the term "Laws of the United States," as it was used in Article III, included the law of nations. John Jay, now Chief Justice, instructed a grand jury in 1793 that "The Laws of Nations" was a separate classification among "the Laws of the united States" [sic]. At another point, he recalled that "the obligation of Treaties and the Laws of Nations . . . form a very important part of the Laws of our nation," having first scratched out that they were part of the laws of the United States—that is, they formed "a very important part of the Laws of ~~the united St~~ our nation" [sic]. John Jay, Charge to the Grand Jury of the Circuit Court for the District of Virginia (May 22, 1793), in 2 THE DOCUMENTARY HISTORY OF THE SUPREME COURT OF THE UNITED STATES, 1789–1800, at 380–82 (Maeva Marcus ed., 1988); see also Draft of John Jay's Charge to the Grand Jury of the Circuit Court for the District of Virginia (before Apr. 22, 1793), in 2 id. at 359, 360. For interpretations, see Bradley, supra note 13, at 607–16; Collins, supra note 54, at 667–70; Dodge, supra note 54, at 710–11.

[60] But see infra this chapter notes 141, 204 (discussing Am. Ins. Co. v. 356 Bales of Cotton, 26 U.S. (1 Pet.) 511 (1828)).

[61] See infra this chapter § II(C)(2).

Modern discourse also focuses on a second, related dimension—the authority of the law of nations in U.S. law—to which the framing's records speak even less directly. The Supremacy Clause refers to those "Laws of the United States ... made in Pursuance [of the Constitution]." There is dispute as to whether this additional language indicates a narrower scope for Article VI than for Article III—excluding from the Supremacy Clause a category of laws, including the law of nations, that is *not* excluded from federal jurisdiction under Article III—or instead clarifies Article VI without suggesting that the law of nations belongs within either provision.[62] In either event, because the law of nations is not "made" by the United States, let alone in pursuance of its Constitution, it seems unlikely to have been included within the Supremacy Clause proper. If customary international law now has force comparable to that bestowed by the Supremacy Clause, it may be by virtue of some other means, such as an expression of the judicial power.

4. General Reflections

Within these debates lurks a deeper question about the anticipated relationship between the new constitutional scheme and the older law of nations. Those in the founding era thought constitutional ambiguities would be worked out over time.[63] Given that the new Constitution's operation was dependent on the law of nations (not only as to what Congress could define and punish but also as to the meaning of terms like "ambassadors" or "war"), they likely expected that the law of nations would be part of this refinement.

Whether and to what extent they anticipated that the law of nations *itself* would evolve is harder to reckon. There was no canonical source for understanding the law of nations in 1789: lawyers sometimes treat Vattel's influential *The Law of Nations* as a definitive guide, but this may distort his significance[64] and that of the era's publicists more generally.[65] Even so, Vattel and his peers tended to attribute

---

[62] On the former view, see 1 WILLIAM WINSLOW CROSSKEY, POLITICS AND THE CONSTITUTION IN THE HISTORY OF THE UNITED STATES 620–22 (1953); Dodge, *supra* note 54, at 703–07. On the latter view, see Bradley, *supra* note 13, at 604–05; Collins, *supra* note 54, at 666.

[63] *See, e.g.,* Henry Paul Monaghan, *Supremacy Clause Textualism,* 110 COLUM. L. REV. 731, 785–88 (2010); Caleb Nelson, *Originalism and Interpretive Conventions,* 70 U. CHI. L. REV. 519, 525–29 (2003); H. Jefferson Powell, *The Original Understanding of Original Intent,* 98 HARV. L. REV. 885 (1985); Peter J. Smith, *The Marshall Court and the Originalist's Dilemma,* 90 MINN. L. REV. 612, 623–34 (2006).

[64] *See* Brian Richardson, *The Use of Vattel in the American Law of Nations,* 106 AM. J. INT'L L. 547 (2012) (arguing that the modern use of Vattel is at least partly due to modern preferences).

[65] *See* Jesse S. Reeves, *The Influence of the Law of Nature upon International Law in the United States,* 3 AM. J. INT'L L. 547 (1909). Nineteenth-century successors like Wheaton, Phillimore, Halleck, and Hall were quite influential in their day and not always easily reconciled with their predecessors, so relying on Vattel and his contemporaries depends on a theory about when constitutional meaning was fixed. *See* William S. Dodge, *Customary International Law, Congress and the Courts: Origins of the Later-in-Time Rule, in* MAKING TRANSNATIONAL LAW WORK IN THE GLOBAL ECONOMY: ESSAYS IN HONOUR OF DETLEV VAGTS 531, 545 n.93, 548–51 (Pieter H.F. Bekker, Rudolf Dolzer, & Michael Waibel eds., 2010) (noting reliance on these publicists by the Supreme Court).

the law of nations in whole or in part to natural law: revealed by the practice of states, but also fixed by human reason or something more transcendental.[66] Natural law theories deeply influenced early U.S. rhetoric on the law of nations,[67] and lingered well later, at least rhetorically.[68]

All this made little difference for particular rules. Since states were presumed to conform to natural law, judges could look to state practice either as being significant in its own right or as evidence of the natural order.[69] The more the Framers thought of the law of nations in natural law terms, though, the more fixed they likely expected it to be.[70] It might thus have been harder to imagine the breadth of matters that would eventually be addressed by customary international law, including the rights of citizens against their own governments (and harder, at the same time, to anticipate how matters already governed by the law of nations, such as the law of the sea, might become the subject of multilateral

[66] *See* Sylvester, *supra* note 8, at 67. Thus, both Vattel's "necessary" law of nations (unchanging and binding, if only on the sovereign's conscience) and his "voluntary" law of nations (refined in light of the fundamental principles of sovereignty) were grounded in natural law, as distinct from a "customary" law of nations (or "international custom") founded instead on state practice. *See* VATTEL, *supra* note 8, §§ 6–7, 25–27.

[67] *See, e.g., Draft of John Jay's Charge to the Grand Jury of the Circuit Court for the District of Virginia* (before Apr. 22, 1793), *in* 2 THE DOCUMENTARY HISTORY OF THE SUPREME COURT OF THE UNITED STATES, *supra* note 59, at 359, 361 ("It may be asked who made the Laws of Nations. The answer is he from whose will proceed all moral Obligations, and which will is made known to us by Reason or by Revelation."); *James Iredell's Charge to the Grand Jury of the Circuit Court for the District of South Carolina* (May 12, 1794), *in* 2 *id.* at 454, 459 (stating that "the only way to ascertain the duties which one nation owes to another, is to enquire what reason dictates, that attribute which the Almighty has bestowed upon all mankind"). *But cf.* Reeves, *supra* note 65 (describing diversity in U.S. views, and deviation in practice from natural law precepts).

[68] *See, e.g.,* The Prize Cases, 67 U.S. 635, 670 (1862) ("The law of nations is also called the law of nature; it is founded on the common consent as well as the common sense of the world.").

[69] The Supreme Court's reasoning relating to the rights of belligerents and neutrals is illustrative:

> To ascertain [the unwritten law of nations], we resort to the great principles of reason and justice: but, as these principles will be differently understood by different nations under different circumstances, we consider them as being, in some degree, fixed and rendered stable by a series of judicial decisions. . . . The decisions of the Courts of every country show how the law of nations, in the given case, is understood in that country, and will be considered in adopting the rule which is to prevail in this.

Thirty Hogsheads of Sugar v. Boyle, 13 U.S. (9 Cranch) 191, 198 (1815). The assumption that natural law and the law of nations were identical faded over time, as in Chief Justice Marshall's conclusion that the slave trade violated the former but not the latter. The Antelope, 23 U.S. (10 Wheat.) 66, 120–22 (1825); *see also* Shanks v. Dupont, 28 U.S. 242, 258 (1830) (Johnson, J., dissenting) (stating that, while he once favored a right of an individual to elect to change national allegiance, "I then gave too much weight to natural law and the suggestions of reason and justice; in a case which ought to be disposed of upon the principles of political and positive law, and the law of nations"). *See generally* Reeves *supra* note 65, at 554–61.

[70] George Nicholas, for example, characterized the law of nations as "permanent and general . . . superior to any act or law of any nation; it implied the consent of all, and was mutually binding on all." 3 THE DEBATES IN THE SEVERAL STATE CONVENTIONS ON THE ADOPTION OF THE FEDERAL CONSTITUTION 502 (J. Elliot ed., 1836). Vattel remarked that "since the natural law is not subject to change . . . it follows that the necessary Law of Nations is not subject to change." VATTEL, *supra* note 8, § 8.

treaties). In any event, the Framers built in capacity for the political branches to react to changes in the law of nations—by choosing to define and punish offenses, or by allocating Article III jurisdiction in matters concerning the law of nations. And regardless of their expectations, the contemporary law of U.S. foreign relations has undoubtedly evolved to keep pace (at least to some degree) with changes that upended the old law of nations.

II. Incorporating Customary International Law into U.S. Law

While the Constitution may have focused little direct attention on customary international law, it established national institutions each with authority that, to varying degrees, lent itself to incorporating that law—in the sense of making it part of U.S. law. This section will describe that authority, before Section III describes limitations on it.

A. Legislative Incorporation

Congress quickly took advantage of its newfound authority to legislate regarding the law of nations, including by enabling the lower courts to fulfill their role. Adopted in the first session of the first Congress, the Judiciary Act of 1789 vested newly created federal district courts with concurrent jurisdiction over "all causes where an alien sues for a tort only in violation of the law of nations or a treaty of the United States"—a provision that later became known as the Alien Tort Claims Act or Alien Tort Statute (ATS).[71] The act also gave federal district courts exclusive jurisdiction over minor crimes and offenses "cognizable under the authority of the United States" (including offenses committed on the high seas), admiralty and maritime matters, and suits against consuls or vice-consuls; gave to circuit courts concurrent alienage jurisdiction for significant cases and exclusive jurisdiction over major crimes cognizable under U.S. authority; and gave the Supreme Court exclusive jurisdiction over cases against ambassadors and other public ministers.[72] Less than a year later, Congress enacted, as part of its first comprehensive statute addressing federal crimes, provisions that criminalized piracy and attacks on

---

[71] Judiciary Act of 1789, ch. 20, § 9(b), 1 Stat. 73, 77; for the current version, see 28 U.S.C. § 1350 (2018). The Supreme Court appears to attribute no significance to the textual changes. *See* Sosa v. Alvarez-Machain, 542 U.S. 692, 713 n.10 (2004).

[72] Judiciary Act of 1789, ch. 20, §§ 9, 11, 13.

ambassadors.[73] The pace of activity slowed, but the early practice offered insight into the authority these provisions conferred.

1. Piracies and Felonies

Constitutional authority to "define and punish Piracies and Felonies committed on the high Seas" was little explained before ratification, and one of the critical issues that surfaced was how this related to the law of nations. In addition to punishing offenses like robbery on the high seas, which clearly constituted "general" piracy violating international law, the 1790 criminal statute punished as "a pirate and felon" persons committing various offenses (like murder, or "piratically and feloniously" taking goods or vessels not on the high seas, or causing insurrection on a ship) that would not count as piracy under the law of nations.[74] Such acts might, however, be addressable as "municipal" (or "statutory") piracy or otherwise fall within Article I authority over "Felonies committed on the high Seas."[75]

The dual character of the 1790 act, and Congress' ability to do more than was directly enabled by the law of nations, proved controversial. Early grand jury charges expressed uncertainty as to whether Congress could extend U.S. jurisdiction beyond "general" piracy without offending the law of nations.[76] Eventually this featured in the Jonathan Robbins affair, involving the extradition by the United States to Great Britain of a purported U.S. citizen (and, secondarily, the decision to eschew his prosecution under U.S. law).[77] Defending President John Adams's conduct, then-Representative John Marshall took the view that the 1790 act should not be read to assert universal jurisdiction over offenses other than general piracy.[78] This was roughly consistent with the position he later espoused

---

[73]   Crimes Act of 1790, ch. 9, §§ 8–13, 1 Stat. 112, 113–15 (establishing offenses for piracy and other offenses on the high seas); *id.* §§ 26, 28, at 118 (establishing offenses for interference with diplomatic immunity or safe conduct, as well as for assaults on ambassadors).

[74]   *Id.* §§ 8–13, 1 Stat. 113-15; *see* Anthony J. Colangelo, *A Unified Approach to Extraterritoriality*, 97 VA. L. REV. 1019, 1066–71 (2011).

[75]   DAVID P. CURRIE, THE CONSTITUTION IN CONGRESS: THE FEDERALIST PERIOD, 1789–1801, at 93–97 (1997); *see also* ALFRED P. RUBIN, THE LAW OF PIRACY 128–37 (1988).

[76]   *James Wilson's Charge to the Grand Jury* (May 23, 1791), *in* 2 THE DOCUMENTARY HISTORY OF THE SUPREME COURT OF THE UNITED STATES *supra* note 59, at 166, 179; James Iredell, *Charge to the Grand Jury of the Circuit Court for the District of New Jersey* (Apr. 2, 1793), *in id.* at 348, 355; Joseph Story, *A Charge Delivered to the Grand Juries of the Circuit Court* (1819), *reprinted in* 1 THE AFRICAN SLAVE TRADE AND AMERICAN COURTS 1, 2 (Paul Finkelman ed., 1988). For discussion, in particular with regard to the implications for universal jurisdiction over offenses other than the international offense of piracy, see Eugene Kontorovich, *The "Define and Punish" Clause and the Limits of Universal Jurisdiction*, 103 Nw. U. L. REV. 149, 176–79 (2009); *see also infra* text accompanying note 292.

[77]   A federal district court found that it had jurisdiction over Robbins and ordered that he should be extradited to Great Britain. United States v. Robins, 27 F. Cas. 825, 832–33 (D.S.C. 1799) (No. 16,175). Others in the group, however, were prosecuted under the 1790 act, including an American. Kontorovich, *supra* note 76, at 179–82. *See generally* Ruth Wedgwood, *The Revolutionary Martyrdom of Jonathan Robbins*, 100 YALE L.J. 229 (1990).

[78]   10 ANNALS OF CONG. 596 (1800); *see* Kontorovich, *supra* note 76, at 182–84 (reading Marshall's speech as implying that such authority could never be conferred by the Piracy Clause).

on the Supreme Court, even in *United States v. Palmer*, in which he narrowly construed the act (drawing sharp criticism) to avoid applying it to matters involving only foreign subjects on foreign ships.[79] In a case decided shortly afterward, *United States v. Furlong*, Justice Johnson suggested that in construing the 1790 act, Congress should be supposed to have intended both to legislate within its constitutional authority and to exhaust that authority, although he would still have excluded some offenses (like murder among foreign subjects on a foreign vessel) as falling outside the scope of general piracy.[80] On the whole, the cases suggest that the Court saw the constitutional authority to regulate "Felonies committed on the high Seas," including municipal piracy, as less robust in territorial reach than the universal jurisdiction to define and punish general piracy, which was established by and consistent with international law.[81]

Congress regularly employed international law both to establish the full reach of authority over "Piracies" and, at the same time, to cabin the other "Felonies" that might be regulated. As a more comprehensive remedy to the Supreme Court's decision in *Palmer*, Congress adopted in 1819 a provision establishing as a capital offense, for "any person or persons whatsoever," commission on the high seas of "the crime of piracy, as defined by the law of nations."[82] The Supreme Court held that this was constitutionally sufficient to "define" piracy, since piracy (unlike the other offenses subject to the clause) had a sufficiently determinate meaning in international law.[83] Other statutes reaching beyond general piracy, like those defining the slave trade as (municipal) piracy, tended to be of more limited reach, probably reflecting an understanding that, absent a widely recognized and determinate offense under international law, the United States could (or should) only regulate its own affairs.[84] Eventually, though, use of this

[79] United States v. Palmer, 16 U.S. (3 Wheat.) 610, 630–34 (1818) (construing the act not to apply to high-seas robberies involving foreign vessels and foreign subjects); *see also* United States v. Klintock, 18 U.S. (5 Wheat.) 144 (1820) (Marshall, C.J.) (distinguishing stateless vessels from the foreign vessels at issue in *Palmer*, in construing the 1790 statute). For discussion, see United States v. Hasan, 747 F. Supp. 2d 599, 612–14 (E.D. Va. 2010), *aff'd sub. nom.* United States v. Dire, 680 F.3d 446 (4th Cir. 2012); Colangelo, *supra* note 74, at 1061–66, 1071–72.

[80] United States v. Furlong, 18 U.S. (5 Wheat.) 184, 195–99 (1820).

[81] This was suggested as well by Justice Johnson's dissent in *Palmer*, in which he stated that Congress could "inflict punishment on offences committed on board the vessels of the United States, or by citizens of the United States, any where; but congress cannot make that piracy which is not piracy by the law of nations, in order to give jurisdiction to its own courts over such offences." *Palmer*, 16 U.S. at 641–42 (Johnson, J., dissenting).

[82] Act of Mar. 3, 1819, ch. 77, § 5, 3 Stat. 510, 513–14; *see also* RUBIN, *supra* note 75, at 144–51.

[83] United States v. Smith, 18 U.S. (5 Wheat.) 153 (1820).

[84] Act of May 15, 1820, ch. 113, §§ 4–5, 3 Stat. 600, 600–01 (limiting application to U.S. citizens engaged in the slave trade, or any person engaged in slave trade on a ship owned in whole or in part by U.S. citizens); *see* The Antelope, 23 U.S. (10 Wheat.) 66, 104 (1825) (asserting that "[t]he United States have done all in their power, consistently with their constitution, to abolish the trade"); *accord id.* at 111–12, 122–23; Letter from John Quincy Adams to Stratford Canning (June 24, 1823), *in* 7 WRITINGS OF JOHN QUINCY ADAMS 498, 502 (Worthington Chancey Ford ed., 1917); Kontorovich, *supra* note 76, at 194–98.

authority became less circumspect, and the distinction between "Piracies" and "Felonies committed on the high Seas" may no longer be well maintained.[85]

2. Offenses Against the Law of Nations

As compared to its authority over piracy, Congress' authority over "Offences against the Law of Nations" is potentially relevant to a wide variety of circumstances. In recent memory, for example, Congress has relied on this capacity in addressing foreign sovereign immunity,[86] the protection of foreign diplomats,[87] torture,[88] and the laws of war,[89] among others.[90]

There was little evident controversy at the founding as to whether Congress should have some kind of authority over such matters. The tension, rather, concerned whether Congress also needed authority to "define" the relevant offenses, which might otherwise be too vague for domestic purposes, or whether such authority was too substantial.[91] In practice, conferring the power to "define" offenses has meant Congress has the power, but not any obligation, to engage in any such refinement. Thus, Congress may choose simply to advert to a component of the law of nations or, as in the first Congress' torts provision, to refer to the law of nations *en toto*.[92] A statute may be upheld as a lawful exercise of Offences Clause authority even if Congress has not identified the offense as

---

[85] *See infra* this chapter § IV(A).

[86] Foreign Sovereign Immunities Act (FSIA), Pub. L. No. 94-583, 90 Stat. 2891 (codified as amended at 28 U.S.C. §§ 1602–11 (2018)); *see* H.R. REP. No. 94-1487, at 12 (1976), *reprinted in* 1976 U.S.C.C.A.N. 6604, 6611 (citing, inter alia, law of nations authority); Argentine Republic v. Amerada Hess Shipping Corp., 488 U.S. 428, 436 (1989).

[87] 18 U.S.C. § 112 (2018). In striking down part of a predecessor statute for the District of Columbia, the Supreme Court noted its basis in international law. *See* Boos v. Barry, 485 U.S. 312, 322–24 (1988).

[88] Torture Victim Protection Act (TVPA), Pub. L. No. 102-256, 106 Stat. 73 (1992) (codified at 28 U.S.C.A. § 1350 note); *see* S. REP. No. 102-249, at 5–6 (1991) (citing, inter alia, law of nations authority); *see also* 18 U.S.C. §§ 2340(1), 2340A (2018) (criminalizing certain acts of torture).

[89] Military Commissions Act of 2006, Pub. L. No. 109-366, 120 Stat. 2600; *see id.* § 4(a)(2), 120 Stat. 2631 (codified at 10 U.S.C. § 821 (2018)); H.R. REP. No. 109-664, pt. 1, at 24, 25 (2006) (citing law of nations authority).

[90] For other examples, see Kent, *supra* note 18, at 861–68; Michael H. Posner & Peter J. Spiro, *Adding Teeth to United States Ratification of the Covenant on Civil and Political Rights: The International Human Rights Conformity Act of 1993*, 42 DEPAUL L. REV. 1209, 1225 n.75 (1993). It is commonly assumed that Congress relied at least in part on the Offences Clause in enacting the ATS. *See, e.g.*, Cleveland & Dodge, *supra* note 4, at 2235; HENKIN, FOREIGN AFFAIRS, at 359 n.20.

[91] *See supra* this chapter text accompanying notes 34–37.

[92] *See infra* this chapter § IV(B)(1) (discussing the ATS); *see also Ex parte* Quirin, 317 U.S. 1, 29 (1942) (explaining, with respect to Article 15 of the Articles of War, predecessor to Article 21 of the Uniform Code of Military Justice (10 U.S.C. § 821 (2018)), that "[i]t is no objection that Congress in providing for the trial of such offenses [of the law of war] has not itself undertaken to codify that branch of international law or to mark its precise boundaries, or to enumerate or define by statute all the acts which that law condemns"); *In re* Yamashita, 327 U.S. 1, 7, 17–18 (1946). The assumption in such cases is that the "law of war," or analogous phrase, alludes to international law. *See* Hamdan v. United States, 696 F.3d 1238, 1248–49 (D.C. Cir. 2012) (citing authority), *overruled on other grounds*, Al Bahlul v. United States, 767 F.3d 1 (D.C. Cir. 2014) (en banc).

one violating the law of nations. In *United States v. Arjona*, the Supreme Court upheld on the basis of law-of-nations authority a statute that criminalized the counterfeiting of foreign notes, bonds, and other securities within the United States, without any evidence that Congress intended to invoke that authority. The Court rejected the defendant's submission that "it is necessary, in order to 'define' the offense, that it be declared in the statute itself to be 'an offense against the law of nations.'" Rather, the Court explained, "[w]hether the offense as defined is an offense against the law of nations depends on the thing done, not on any declaration to that effect by Congress."[93]

The potential absence of any statutory declaration does place greater stress on the capacity of courts to assess "the thing done" and its relation to international law. In order for a statute to be sustained under the Offences Clause, it must concern a violation of international law: that much is implied by *Arjona*, and it is consistent with the original understanding that the power to define was essentially one to refine separately established wrongs.[94] The focus, moreover, appears to be contemporary. That is, the putative offense need not be one that would have violated the law of nations at the time the Constitution was adopted.[95] Instead, the question concerns whether there was such an offense at the time Congress legislated or, at any rate, at the time of any statutory violation.[96]

Statutes enacted under the Offences Clause sort into roughly three different categories. In the first and least controversial category, a statute addresses a specific offense, like torture, that corresponds directly to a recognized rule of customary international law; Congress may even allude to the Offences Clause. In such cases, courts can more readily defer to the judgment of the political branches that this authority is well founded.

---

[93] United States v. Arjona, 120 U.S. 479, 488 (1887).

[94] For a nice discussion of these points, see United States v. Bellaizac-Hurtado, 700 F.3d 1245, 1249–51 (11th Cir. 2012).

[95] *Arjona* acknowledged freely that the fraudulent practices with which Congress was concerned in the late nineteenth century had less significance at the Constitution's founding. *Arjona*, 120 U.S. at 484 (discussing Vattel and subsequent developments); *id.* at 485–86 (discussing changes in global commerce). *See also* Sosa v. Alvarez-Machain, 542 U.S. 692, 724–25 (2004) (acknowledging similarly that the ATS allowed causes of action "based on the present-day law of nations"). *But cf. Bellaizac-Hurtado*, 700 F.3d at 1253–54 (suggesting, without resolving, that there might be bounds to incorporating modern customary international law).

[96] This is particularly clear when Congress refers generally to international law. *See* Sosa, 542 U.S. at 724–25; *see also Ex parte Quirin*, 317 U.S. at 30 (explaining that the Offences Clause affords Congress the choice between "crystallizing in permanent form and in minute detail every offense against the law of war," or instead adopting a common-law method permitting development by military tribunals and courts). For discussion in relation to contemporary piracy, see *infra* this chapter § IV(A)(1). For a very broad argument for congressional authority—including the proposition that a statute may be sustained even though it addresses an offense that is no longer regarded as an offense under international law—see Alex H. Loomis, *The Power to Define Offenses Against the Law of Nations*, 40 HARV. J.L. & PUB. POL'Y 417 (2017).

In a second category, exemplified by *Arjona*, courts must assess whether a statute identifying a particular offense—but one lacking a self-evident correlate under, or attribution to, international law—can nonetheless be justified under the Offences Clause. *Arjona* suggests that courts may defer under these circumstances as well. The Court described the international consensus expansively, so as to include counterfeiting and "any fraud upon a foreign nation or its subjects,"[97] and devoted less attention to whether counterfeiting violated international law than it did to whether international law gave foreign nations the right to demand that the United States seek punishment of an offense so injurious to their security.[98] This was consistent with founding-era concerns,[99] but it swept quite broadly absent clear evidence that either the original wrong or a failure to remedy the wrong would violate international law (let alone "furnish sufficient cause for war," which the Court accepted might not be the case).[100] A stricter view was evidenced in a court of appeals decision holding that Congress lacked authority under the Offences Clause to punish drug trafficking in another state's territory because it was not recognizable as a violation of customary international law.[101]

A third category is also at least potentially problematic: statutes in which Congress, by virtue of broad references to "international law" or the like, delegates substantial authority to the executive branch to determine whether an offense is actually one violating customary international law.[102] Congress is expressly entrusted with power to "define" the offenses in question,[103] but it is also

---

[97] *Arjona*, 120 U.S. at 485 (quoting EMER DE VATTEL, THE LAW OF NATIONS 46 n.50 (Joseph Chitty ed., 4th ed. 1835)). In general, the Court relied heavily on secondary authority (particularly Vattel) describing the offense in broad, thematic terms, without citing evidence of state practice. *Id.* at 484–88.

[98] *Id.* at 486–87.

[99] *See supra* this chapter text accompanying notes 22–26.

[100] *Arjona*, 120 U.S. at 487. The Supreme Court took a more skeptical approach in *Boos v. Barry*, 485 U.S. 312 (1988), while reconciling Offences Clause authority with the constitutional right to engage in First Amendment expressive activities near foreign embassies in the District of Columbia. On the one hand, the Court noted that "that the United States has a vital national interest in complying with international law," citing the Offences Clause—which it appeared to consider as the constitutional basis for the statute, though that was not directly at issue. *Id.* at 323. But the Court concluded that the statute was not narrowly tailored to serve a compelling interest, indicating skepticism that international law required the statute in light of the different regime adopted for the rest of the country. *Id.* at 323–27. The lower court decision, however, had expressly stated that the Offences Clause served as the statute's basis and concluded that international law required such measures. Finzer v. Barry, 798 F.2d 1450, 1455–58 (D.C. Cir. 1986).

[101] *See* United States v. Bellaizac-Hurtado, 700 F.3d 1245 (11th Cir. 2012) (holding unconstitutional the application of the Maritime Drug Law Enforcement Act, 46 U.S.C. §§ 70503(a), 70506, to drug trafficking activity in Panama's territorial sea).

[102] For extensive discussion, see Eugene Kontorovich, *Discretion, Delegation, and Defining in the Constitution's Law of Nations Clause*, 106 NW. L. REV. 1675 (2012).

[103] *See, e.g.*, United States v. Bin Ladin, 92 F. Supp. 2d 189, 220 (S.D.N.Y. 2000) (stating that the Offences Clause "does not merely give Congress the authority to punish offenses against the law of nations; it also gives Congress the power to 'define' such offenses").

regarded as having the capacity to delegate to the executive branch in matters involving foreign affairs.[104] Courts are reluctant to substitute their judgment,[105] but sometimes read such delegations narrowly. World War II–era cases upheld Offences Clause authority to delegate to the executive branch the creation of military commissions responsible for hearing violations of the "laws of war," at least so long as U.S. courts recognized the acts charged as constituting such offenses.[106] More recent cases exhibited greater ambivalence. In *Hamdan v. Rumsfeld*, a plurality of the Supreme Court rejected the argument that conspiracy fell within a broad statutory grant concerning the "law of war." The justices did not address the scope of potential congressional authority, but reasoned that "[w]hen ... neither the elements of the offense nor the range of permissible punishments is defined by statute or treaty, the precedent must be plain and unambiguous."[107] Subsequent decisions, relying on subsequently enacted legislative authority, upheld the capacity to try such offenses by military commission without clearly departing from the plurality's cautious approach or even relying directly on the Offences Clause.[108]

The Offences Clause may have other limits, but it also has untapped potential. One set of questions involves criminality. It is generally presumed that an "offence" against international law need not be a *criminal* offense under

---

[104] *See* Chicago & So. Air Lines v. Waterman S.S. Corp., 333 U.S. 103, 109 (1948); United States v. Curtiss-Wright Export Corp., 299 U.S. 304 (1936); *see also* Chapter 1 §§ I(D), II(A) and Chapter 2 § II(B).

[105] Hamdan v. Rumsfeld, 548 U.S. 557, 655 (2006) (Kennedy, J., concurring, joined by Souter, Ginsburg, and Breyer, J.J.) (stating that "Congress, not the Court, is the branch in the better position to undertake the sensitive task of establishing a principle not inconsistent with the national interest or international justice") (internal quotation marks and citation omitted); *accord Finzer*, 798 F.2d at 1458–59 (citing *Chicago & So. Air Lines*, 333 U.S. at 111), *aff'd in part sub nom. Boos* v. Barry, 485 U.S. 312 (1988).

[106] *See Ex parte* Quirin, 317 U.S. 1, 29 (1942) (noting lack of statutory specification, but inquiring "whether any of the acts charged is an offense against the law of war"); *id.* at 30–37 (citing international conventions, state practice, and multiple publicists); *compare, e.g., In re* Yamashita, 327 U.S. 1, 7, 13, 15–16 (1946) (citing limited authority supporting the obligations of a commander in chief for his troops), *with id.* at 28 (Murphy, J., dissenting) (asserting that "[t]he recorded annals of warfare and the established principles of international law afford not the slightest precedent for such a charge").

[107] Hamdan v. Rumsfeld, 548 U.S. at 602 (plurality op.). *But see id.* at 690 (Thomas, J., dissenting) (criticizing this as inconsistent with a presumption favoring congressional authority and the actions of military commissions). For further discussions of *Hamdan*, see Chapter 1§ II(B); Chapter 8 §§ II(A), II(B), III(B); and Chapter 10 § II(E)(4).

[108] After enactment of the Military Commissions Act of 2006, Pub. L. No. 109-336, 120 Stat. 2600, the D.C. Circuit upheld conspiracy convictions. *See* Bahlul v. United States, 840 F.3d 757 (D.C. Cir. 2016) (en banc). Three members of the six-judge majority found it unnecessary to reach the issue, given Congress' war powers and associated authority, see *id.* at 761 (Kavanaugh, J., concurring), but one member would have upheld the conviction based in part on the Offences Clause. *See id.* at 759 (Henderson, J., concurring) (citing Al Bahlul v. United States, 792 F.3d 1, 44–55 (D.C. Cir. 2015) (Henderson, J., dissenting)); *see also* Al Bahlul v. United States, 767 F.3d 1, 53–62 (D.C. Cir. 2014) (en banc) (Brown, J., concurring in the judgment in part and dissenting in part).

international law in order to be redressed by Congress under the Offences Clause.[109] It is a separate question whether "punish[ment]" under the Offences Clause licenses Congress to adopt noncriminal, as well as well as criminal, penalties. Congress appears to have assumed as much, for example, in enacting civil remedies under the Torture Victim Protection Act, though the point was not uncontroversial—in part because of executive branch skepticism.[110] Other statutes, like the Foreign Sovereign Immunities Act (FSIA), may also have authorized civil liability at least in part based on Offences Clause authority.[111] Executive branch hesitancy about expanding beyond criminal liability seemed most concerned at the prospect that Offences Clause authority might be used to regulate asserted presidential prerogatives, like military commissions,[112] and civil liability itself may be less of an issue.[113]

Even if the Offences Clause is not confined to criminal offenses under international law, it has been proposed that Congress' capacity to define and punish offenses is limited by other international law principles, such as rules limiting the permissible scope of national prescriptive jurisdiction. Thus, for example, it is suggested that the United States may not generally punish conduct with which it lacks any connection, because the Offences Clause only permits pursuing

[109] However, criminality under international law has been considered relevant in construing the intended scope of congressional statutes. *See, e.g.,* G. Edward White, *A Customary International Law of Torts*, 41 VAL. U. L. REV. 755, 763 (2007) (comparing, in addressing ATS, "Blackstone's discussion of 'offenses against the law of nations' (by which he meant criminal offenses) with his treatment of torts"); Stephens, *supra* note 35, at 484–504 (describing less narrow use by Blackstone and in other eighteenth-century work).

[110] *Compare* S. REP. NO. 102-249, at 5–6 (1991) (citing Offences Clause authority for the TVPA), *with id.* at 13–14 (minority views of Sens. Simpson and Grassley) (citing testimony that "[i]t is a difficult and unresolved question . . . whether that power [under the Offences Clause] extends to creating a civil cause of action in this country for disputes that have no factual nexus with the United States or its citizens") (quoting *Torture Victim Protection Act of 1989: Hearings on S. 1629 and H.R. 1662 Before the Subcomm. on Immigration and Refugee Affairs of the Senate Judiciary Comm.*, 101st Cong., 13–14 (1990) (statement of John O. McGinnis, Deputy Assistant Attorney General, Office of Legal Counsel)); *see also* Memorandum for Daniel J. Bryan, Assistant Attorney General, Office of Legislative Affairs, from Patrick F. Philbin, Deputy Assistant Attorney General, Office of Legal Counsel, *Swift Justice Authorization Act*, 2002 WL 34482989 at *15 (Apr. 8, 2002) (advising that, as originally envisioned, Offences Clause authority was to be limited to "the ordinary power to set the punishment for violations of criminal laws").

[111] *See, e.g.,* Cleveland & Dodge, *supra* note 4, at 2236 & n.196.

[112] Memorandum for Daniel J. Bryan, *supra* note 110, at *15–16; *see also* Legality of the Use of Military Commissions to Try Terrorists, 25 Op. O.L.C. 238, 244 (2001). *But see* Memorandum for the Files from Steven G. Bradbury, Principal Deputy Assistant Attorney General, Re: Status of Certain OLC Opinions Issued in the Aftermath of the Terrorist Attacks of September 11, 2001, at 2, 4–5 (Jan. 15, 2009), https://perma.cc/ALE3-XP7V (qualifying the Swift Justice Authorization Act memorandum and other contemporaneous opinions memoranda as unduly restrictive of congressional authority).

[113] *Cf.* Brief for the United States as Respondent Supporting Petitioner at 33 n.9, Sosa v. Alvarez-Machain, 542 U.S. 692 (2004) (No. 03-339) (acknowledging that the same considerations that led to the Offences Clause would warrant vesting the decision to provide civil liability in the national legislature).

offenses consistent with international law.[114] While such a constraint may seem straightforward and consistent with the authority's internationalist premises, it is in potential tension with the general principle that U.S. courts will apply a duly enacted statute even if it violates international law limits.[115] Assuming the Offences Clause authority is insufficient where any international law limits would be exceeded, other authority like the Necessary and Proper Clause might be invoked, on the premise that Congress may determine whether broad federal legislation is necessary to avoid or remedy widely recognized wrongs.[116] The significance of any constrained view of the Offences Clause, then, will turn on the evolving parameters of other doctrines.[117]

Finally, Sarah Cleveland and William Dodge have argued that a common supposition about the Offences Clause, that it concerns what we might call the *unwritten* law of nations, is erroneous, and that treaty offenses were also encompassed within the "law of nations" offenses that Congress was entitled to address.[118] As noted previously, the "law of nations" was variously used by the Framers and the treatises they consulted—sometimes narrowly, to describe what we would now call customary international law, and sometimes more capaciously, so as to sweep in treaties[119]—and there is evidence for both usages in relation to the Offences Clause. Evaluating the evidence is challenging. The broader reading has to confront the clear focus on unwritten violations, including

---

[114] *See, e.g.*, United States v. Bellaizac-Hurtado, 700 F.3d 1245, 1259 (11th Cir. 2012) (Barkett, J., specially concurring) ("Only conduct that violates a norm of customary international law *and* is subject to United States jurisdiction under customary international law principles may be prosecuted in United States courts as an 'Offence[] against the Law of Nations.'") (emphasis in original).

[115] *See infra* this chapter text accompanying notes 281–296. *See generally* Chapter 4 § IV(A)(1).

[116] As the Supreme Court noted in *United States v. Arjona*:

> A right secured by the law of nations to a nation, or its people, is one the United States as the representatives of this nation are bound to protect. Consequently, a law which is necessary and proper to afford this protection is one that congress may enact, because it is one that is needed to carry into execution a power conferred by the Constitution on the Government of the United States exclusively. . . . [T]he United States must have the power to pass it and enforce it themselves, or be unable to perform a duty which they may owe to another nation, and which the law of nations has imposed on them as part of their international obligations.

120 U.S. 479, 487 (1887); *see also* Brief for the United States at 50–51, Hamdan v. United States, 696 F.3d 1238 (D.C. Cir. 2012) (No. 11-1257) (arguing that, even if material support for terrorism was not established as an existing offense against international law, it was within "the heartland of the type of activity condemned by the international community," and that, "consistent with the latitude it possesses under the Define and Punish Clause," Congress had "determined that punishing the provision of material support to terrorism is necessary and proper to fulfill our nation's international responsibilities to prevent and to punish terrorism itself.").

[117] *Cf.* Nat'l Fed'n of Indep. Bus. v. Sebelius, 567 U.S. 519, 558–61 (2012) (concluding that individual mandate component of health care reform legislation was an invalid exercise of the Necessary and Proper Clause as one not "narrow in scope" nor "incidental" to the exercise of the Commerce Clause). For discussion in relation to treaties, see Chapter 6 § IV(B).

[118] *See generally* Cleveland & Dodge, *supra* note 4; *id.* at 2205 & n.11 (noting prevalence of contrary assumption).

[119] *See supra* this chapter text accompanying note 4.

the perceived need for Congress to "define" such offenses.[120] Even on a narrow reading, treaty offenses would have warranted mention, insofar as unremedied breaches implicated U.S. responsibility and might constitute indirect violations of unwritten international law.[121] Subsequent practice offers modest but inconclusive evidence that treaties are included.[122] The question of whether treaty violations may be redressed under the Offences Clause is significant, in any case, only if the Necessary and Proper Clause is narrowly construed so as to limit federal legislation to powers found elsewhere in Article I. To this point, the Supreme Court has not clearly adopted such a reading.

3. Residual Authority

Whatever the expected breadth of the Offences Clause, including as supplemented by the Necessary and Proper Clause, Congress has other means to encourage U.S. conformity with customary international law.[123] Probably most obviously, the United States is party to international agreements that incorporate standards established (or at least informed) by customary international law, such as the minimum standard of treatment guaranteed by numerous bilateral treaties,[124] as well as the North American Free Trade Agreement (NAFTA)

---

[120] *See supra* this chapter text accompanying notes 32–36 (noting Convention discussion, including colloquy between Morris and Wilson); *see also* Cleveland & Dodge, *supra* note 4, at 2226–27 (concluding that this exchange, while focused on unwritten law, did not necessarily suggest the exclusion of treaties).

[121] *See supra* this chapter text accompanying notes 20–21. This may help explain some discussion of treaty violations in relation to the Offences Clause. *See* Cleveland & Dodge, *supra* note 4, at 2224–30 (describing references in convention and ratification debates).

[122] On a number of occasions, Congress appeared to rely in part on the Offences Clause in relation to provisions implementing treaty obligations. *See* Cleveland & Dodge, *supra* note 4, at 2234–52 (citing examples including the ATS, the Crimes Act of 1790, the Submarine Cable Act of 1888, and the Foreign Sovereign Immunities Act). Few instances involved direct invocations of the Offences Clause solely, and many involved what could be described as violations of customary international law. As for judicial precedent, some cases mention the Offences Clause in relation to international law and U.S. compliance generally. Probably the most relevant cases involved military commissions, which discussed the use of the Offences Clause to punish violations of the law of war, arguably including treaty violations. *Id.* at 2252–55; *see, e.g., Ex parte* Quirin, 317 U.S. 1, 30 nn.7 & 35 (1942) (identifying unlawful belligerents); Application of Yamashita, 327 U.S. 1, 8, 15–16 (1946) (command responsibility); *see also* Hamdan v. Rumsfeld, 548 U.S. 557, 610 (2006) (plurality op.) (concluding that conspiracy was not a violation of the law of nations, and noting incidentally in that connection that it did not violate any of the major treaties governing the law of war); Cleveland & Dodge, *supra* note 4, at 2252–58 (discussing these and other cases).

[123] For historical examples, see QUINCY WRIGHT, THE CONTROL OF AMERICAN FOREIGN RELATIONS 179–83 (1922).

[124] *See* U.S. Dep't of State, *U.S. Model Bilateral Investment Treaty*, art. 5(1), (2) & Annexes A, B (2012), https://perma.cc/KMJ2-ASRQ (defining minimum standard of treatment in terms of customary international law). The minimum treatment standard expressed in these and similar international obligations may not be precisely that required by customary international law: its inclusion helped to avoid controversy on that point, and to secure dispute settlement. *See, e.g.,* George K. Foster, *Recovering "Protection and Security": The Treaty Standard's Obscure Origins, Forgotten Meaning, and Key Current Significance,* 45 VAND. J. TRANSNAT'L L. 1095, 1145–49 (2012).

(now the United States–Mexico–Canada Agreement, or USMCA).[125] In such instances, Congress' authority is mingled with power shared with the executive branch to enter into treaties and congressional-executive agreements. Nor is the agreement of other states necessary. Thus, the FSIA, which incorporates the restrictive theory of sovereign immunity, was premised on the Foreign Commerce Clause as well as on the Offences Clause.[126] Were a case like *United States v. Arjona* decided today, it seems likely the congressional authority could be fully supported on Foreign Commerce Clause grounds alone.[127]

The role this residual authority serves in incorporating customary international law is easy to overlook. When Congress can exercise authority on such grounds, the incentive to advert to international law is doubtful. U.S. law may have preceded custom's development, or might secure conformity without any need to incorporate an international law standard (or make U.S. law turn on such standards as they may evolve). This may explain in part why the U.S. Code adverts only infrequently to the law of nations or customary international law.[128] References in state codes are even less common.[129]

The diverse constitutional authority available to Congress is generally constructive for U.S. compliance; states may discharge their obligations under customary international law by any and all suitable means, so long as they manage to avoid breaches. Particularly given that Congress and other actors may implement international law without adverting to it, however, this undermines U.S. capacity to track its means for compliance. If this obscures the legislative voice on

---

[125] North American Free Trade Agreement, Can.-Mex.-U.S., Dec. 17, 1992, art. 1105(1), 32 I.L.M. 296 (1993); *see* NAFTA Free Trade Comm'n, Notes of Interpretation of Certain Chapter 11 Provisions, 2001 DIGEST OF U.S. PRACTICE, at 568–70 (providing that "the concepts of 'fair and equitable treatment' and 'full protection and security' do not require treatment in addition to or beyond that which is required by the customary international law minimum standard of treatment of aliens."). The scope of Chapter 11 is altered under Chapter 14 of the USMCA. *See* Chapter 7 § III(E) (3).

[126] *See infra* this chapter note 153.

[127] United States v. Arjona, 120 U.S. 479, 488 (1887); *see supra* this chapter text accompanying notes 93–98; Chapter 2 § IV. *But cf.* Baston v. United States, 137 S. Ct. 850 (2017) (Thomas, J., dissenting from denial of certiorari) (describing, critically, Supreme Court and lower court case law construing the Foreign Commerce Clause expansively).

[128] Most codified references to "customary international law" as such concern the law of the sea. *See, e.g.*, 18 U.S.C. § 2281 (2018); 33 U.S.C. §§ 857–19, 1503, 1902; 42 U.S.C. § 9111; *see also* 16 U.S.C. § 1435 (providing that chapter governing marine sanctuaries "shall be applied in accordance with generally recognized principles of international law," in addition to international agreements to which the United States is party). Codified references to the "law of nations"—while dwindling—are more varied. *See, e.g.*, 18 U.S.C. § 1651 (criminalizing piracy); 18 U.S.C. § 3058 (limits to internment of enemy belligerents); 28 U.S.C. § 1350 (actions by noncitizens for torts).

[129] *But see, e.g.*, CONN. GEN. STAT. § 50a-203 (2019) (deeming admissible evidence of principles of customary international law). This relative infrequency may be due in part to the diminished need for states to identify a particular basis for exercising authority (let alone one framed in international terms) or to the sense that national government is primarily responsible for such matters. *See* Chapter 9 § I.

international law, it also tends to diminish a potential channel for influencing its development abroad.

B. Executive Incorporation

1. Generally

The president's role in implementing international law was not mentioned expressly in the Constitution and may well have been considered subordinate to that of Congress. Legislative authorization, whether by statute or treaty (or other congressionally approved agreement), remains the most straightforward basis for executive branch engagement. The president is required by statute, for example, to treat adversely certain states or international organizations complicit in expropriations or nationalizations that violate international law.[130] Congress has also required attention to these customary standards in the negotiation of bilateral investment treaties.[131] In such instances, the presidential authority to incorporate customary international law derives from the power of Congress (or, in relation to treaties, from a shared power), and claims that the president lacks sufficient authority are quite unlikely to arise. Rather, constitutional objections are likely to be premised on the claim that legislation interferes with plenary and exclusive executive branch prerogatives.[132]

Yet the president's role has never been entirely derivative. As previously noted, the Crimes Act of 1790 created authority for the executive branch to prosecute as "violaters of the laws of nations" persons committing several specific offenses, such as crimes against ambassadors.[133] But the executive branch also assumed the capacity to prosecute violations of the law of nations even in the absence of any congressional enactment. When President Washington declared neutrality during the war between England and France—in itself an assertion of executive power[134]—he gave instructions to prosecute "all persons, who shall, within

---

[130] One early example is the so-called first Hickenlooper Amendment. Foreign Assistance Act of 1962, Pub. L. No. 87-565, § 301(d)(3), 76 Stat. 255, 260–61 (1962) (codified at 22 U.S.C. § 2370(e)(1), (2) (2018)) (providing that the president is to suspend assistance to countries expropriating in violation of international law, barring presidential waiver); see Davis R. Robinson, *U.S. Foreign Relations Law and Expropriation*, 83 DEP'T OF STATE BULL. 52, 52 (1983) (describing role of executive agencies); see also Chapter 7 § II(C) (noting comparable examples in the context of international organizations).

[131] See Bipartisan Congressional Trade Priorities and Accountability Act of 2015, tit. I, Pub. L. 114-26, § 102, 129 Stat. 320 (2015) (codified at 19 U.S.C. § 4201(b) (2018)) (describing as negotiating objectives, inter alia, fulfilling international law regarding treatment of investors and consistency with "internationally recognized core labor standards").

[132] See infra this chapter § III(D).

[133] Crimes Act of 1790, ch. 9, § 26, 1 Stat. 112, 118; see also id. § 28, 1 Stat. at 118 (describing violations of safe conduct, among other offenses, as "infract[ions of] the law of nations"); supra this chapter text accompanying note 73.

[134] See supra this chapter text accompanying notes 45–48.

the cognizance of the courts of the United States, violate the law of nations."[135] Secretary of State Jefferson explained to his French counterpart that it would violate the law of nations, and thus "the laws of the land, of which the law of nations makes an integral part," were France to arm vessels in the United States to deploy against England.[136] Alexander Hamilton, writing in support of presidential authority, described the law of nations as part of the law of the land, as salient for the executive as for the courts.[137] To buttress presidential authority to police neutrality, Congress in 1794 enacted a statute criminalizing certain acts giving military assistance to foreign states;[138] before long, the capacity to prosecute federal common-law crimes was generally unsettled.[139] But the broader premise— that the law of nations, as part of the law of the land, commanded the executive branch's attention, even in the absence of legislative incorporation—was not directly challenged.[140]

Apart from the Take Care Clause, addressed separately later, the constitutional text itself provides only limited bases for this authority. Some authority

---

[135] See Proclamation of Neutrality, supra note 45.

[136] Mr. Jefferson, Secretary of State, to Mr. Genet, Minister Plenipotentiary of France (June 15, 1793), in Proclamation of Neutrality (April 22, 1793), in 1 AMERICAN STATE PAPERS: FOREIGN RELATIONS 150 (Walter Lowrie & Matthew St. Clair Clarke eds., 1833).

[137] Pacificus No. 1 (June 29, 1793), in 15 THE PAPERS OF ALEXANDER HAMILTON 33, 34, 43 (Harold C. Syrett ed., 1969) (describing the law of nations as part of the law of the land, to which penalties attach for acts of contravention). Later, writing as Camillus, Hamilton explained that the confiscatory acts violating the Jay Treaty would also violate the law of nations, and "'Tis indubitable that the customary law of European Nations is as a part of the common law and by adoption that of the U States." From Alexander Hamilton To Defence No. XX (Oct. 23–24, 1795), in 19 id. at 342.

[138] Act of June 5, 1794, ch. 50, 1 Stat. 381 (1794). This followed unsuccessful prosecution in Henfield's Case, 11 F. Cas. 1099 (C.C.D. Pa. 1793) (No. 6360).

[139] See United States v. Coolidge, 14 U.S. (1 Wheat.) 415 (1816); United States v. Hudson & Goodwin, 11 U.S. (7 Cranch) 32, 34 (1812). Those decisions might suggest that prior belief in federal common-law crimes was flatly mistaken, see Robert C. Palmer, The Federal Common Law of Crime, 4 LAW & HIST. REV. 267 (1986); Kathryn Preyer, Jurisdiction to Punish: Federal Authority, Federalism and the Common Law of Crimes in the Early Republic, 4 LAW & HIST. REV. 223 (1986), and repudiate contrary depictions of the law of nations as common law. See BELLIA & CLARK, THE LAW OF NATIONS AND THE UNITED STATES CONSTITUTION, supra note 17, at 66–67, 157–61; Bellia & Clark, The Federal Common Law of Nations, supra note 17, at 55. Yet it is plausible to attribute the decisions to a changed view in light of highly charged circumstances, including controversial indictments for seditious libel. See 2 GEORGE L. HASKINS & HERBERT A. JOHNSON, HISTORY OF THE SUPREME COURT OF THE UNITED STATES—FOUNDATIONS OF POWER: JOHN MARSHALL, 1801–1815, at 633–46 (1981); 1 CHARLES WARREN, THE SUPREME COURT IN UNITED STATES HISTORY 433–41 (1922); Stewart Jay, Origins of Federal Common Law: Part One, 133 U. PA. L. REV. 1003 (1985); Stephen B. Presser, The Supra-Constitution, the Courts, and the Federal Common Law of Crimes: Some Comments on Palmer and Preyer, 4 LAW & HIST. REV. 325 (1986); Gary D. Rowe, Note, The Sound of Silence: United States v. Hudson & Goodwin, The Jeffersonian Ascendancy, and the Abolition of Federal Common Law Crimes, 101 YALE L.J. 919 (1992).

[140] See also Who Privileged from Arrest, 1 Op. Att'y Gen. 26, 27 (1792) (stating, in regard to alleged violation of ministerial immunity falling outside the terms of a congressional measure, that "[t]he law of nations, although not specially adopted by the constitution or any other municipal act, is essentially a part of the law of the land"); Territorial Rights—Florida, 1 Op. Att'y Gen. 68, 69 (1797) (stating that although "Congress has passed no act yet upon the subject," criminal prosecution could be maintained because "[t]he common law has adopted the law of nations in its fullest extent, and made it a part of the law of the land").

may be invited by the Constitution's use in Article II of internationally informed terms. The power to "make Treaties," for example, was understood as referencing an authority ultimately defined by the law of nations, and as such to encompass subjects like the acquisition of territory and extradition;[141] it was also understood to communicate potential limits on that authority.[142] The president's role as "Commander in Chief" likewise alludes to powers articulated and limited by international law.[143] The power to "receive Ambassadors and other public Ministers" is, for similar reasons, informed by international law.[144] Interestingly, it has been maintained that the offices of "Ambassadors, other public Ministers and Consuls" need not be established by Congress, as the law of nations had itself created offices that were available for presidential appointment.[145]

2. Making and Interpreting Customary International Law

As a matter of practice, the president also makes and interprets customary international law for the United States. Unlike for treaties, there is no constitutional provision for the president to "make" customary international law (or the "law of nations").[146] Nevertheless, the array of foreign affairs authorities detailed in Article II, the Constitution's overall structure, and the president's long-recognized role as "the sole organ of the nation in its external relations, and its

---

[141] U.S. CONST. art. II, § 2, cl. 2; *see* Ware v. Hylton, 3 U.S. (3 Dall.) 199, 261 (1796) (Iredell, J.) ("The subject of treaties, Gentlemen truly say, is to be determined by the law of nations."); *e.g.*, Am. Ins. Co. v. 356 Bales of Cotton, 26 U.S. (1 Pet.) 511, 542 (1828) (territory); Holmes v. Jennison, 39 U.S. (14 Pet.) 540, 569 (1840) (plurality op.) (extradition). For careful discussion of these and other examples, see Sarah H. Cleveland, *Our International Constitution*, 31 YALE J. INT'L L. 1, 14–17 (2006).

[142] *See, e.g.*, Foster v. Neilson, 27 U.S. (2 Pet.) 253, 314 (1829) (describing nature of treaties).

[143] U.S. CONST. art. II, § 2, cl. 1 (Commander-in-Chief authority); *see* David Golove, *Military Tribunals, International Law, and the Constitution: A Franckian-Madisonian Approach*, 35 N.Y.U. J. INT'L L. & POL. 363, 365 (2003) (stating that, "[i]n designating [the president] commander in chief, the Constitution grants him the power to exercise (at least some of) the belligerent rights of the United States under international law," which is "a very great power, but it is not a power without limits"). *See generally* Chapter 8 § II(B).

[144] U.S. CONST. art. II, § 3 (send and receive authority); *In re* Baiz, 135 U.S. 403, 419 (1890) (explaining that constitutional references to appointment and reception of "ambassadors, other public ministers and consuls" describe "a class existing by the law of nations"); Public Ministers, 2 Op. Att'y Gen. 290, 291 (1829) (describing diplomatic privileges as guided by the law of nations and the U.S. Constitution); *see* Chapter 3 § II.

[145] U.S. CONST. art II, § 2, cl. 2; *see, e.g.*, United States *ex rel.* Goodrich v. Guthrie, 58 U.S. (17 How.) 284, 290–91 (1854) ("All offices under the government of the United States are created, either by the law of nations, such as ambassadors and other public ministers, or by the constitution and the statutes."); Ambassadors and Other Public Ministers of the U.S., 7 Op. Att'y Gen. 186, 193 (1855) (explaining that the Appointments Clause empowers the president to appoint public ministers as recognized by the law of nations, without requiring an authorizing act of Congress). *But cf. id.* at 194 ("[T]he designation of the officer was derived from the law of nations, and the authority to appoint from the Constitution."). For discussion, see James Durling & E. Garrett West, *Appointments Without Law*, 105 VA. L. REV. 1281, 1321–29 (2019).

[146] *Contrast* U.S. CONST. art. II, § 2, cl. 2 (providing that the president "shall have Power, by and with the Advice and Consent of the Senate, to make Treaties, provided two-thirds of the Senators present concur . . .").

sole representative with foreign nations,"[147] have been understood to confer a leading international role for the president in relation to customary international law. Congress may have originally been envisioned as defining and punishing offenses that are essentially preexisting, but the president is accepted as a participant in the law's creation.[148] "When articulating principles of international law in its relations with other states," the Supreme Court remarked in *Banco Nacional de Cuba v. Sabbatino*, "the Executive Branch speaks not only as an interpreter of generally accepted and traditional rules, as would the courts, but also as an advocate of standards it believes desirable for the community of nations and protective of national concerns."[149] This role is encouraged by international approach to state practice, which (while crediting the contributions of legislatures and courts) tends to emphasize the kinds of diplomatic activities and "executive conduct" in which the president and other Article II officials engage.[150]

The domestic significance of the president's role is more elusive and, perhaps, problematic. In practice, the executive branch's determination that a norm is established as a rule of customary international law has been highly influential.[151] For example, President Truman's announcement that the United States had the right under customary international law to exploit its continental shelf not only established U.S. policy and influenced the emergence of a new international rule, but swayed U.S. courts as well.[152] Similarly, U.S. advocacy of the restrictive theory had a substantial impact on the scope of foreign sovereign immunity both under

---

[147] United States v. Curtiss-Wright Exp. Corp., 299 U.S. 304, 319 (1936) (quoting Rep. John Marshall, 10 Annals of Cong. 613 (1800)); *see also* Medellín v. Texas, 552 U.S. 491, 524 (2008), *citing* First Nat. City Bank v. Banco Nacional de Cuba, 406 U.S. 759, 767 (1972) (plurality op.) ("The President has 'the lead role . . . in foreign policy' "); American Ins. Assn. v. Garamendi, 539 U.S. 396, 414 (2003) ("Article II of the Constitution places with the President the 'vast share of responsibility for the conduct of our foreign relations' ") (quoting Youngstown Sheet & Tube Co. v. Sawyer, 343 U.S. 579, 610–11 (1952) (Frankfurter, J., concurring)). *See generally* Chapter 3.

[148] *See, e.g.*, RESTATEMENT (THIRD) § 1 rptrs. note 2 (describing U.S. role in developing customary international law as "largely, though not exclusively, the work of the President and those acting on his behalf"); Curtis A. Bradley & Jack L. Goldsmith, *Presidential Control over International Law*, 131 HARV. L. REV. 1201, 1226–30 (2018).

[149] Banco Nacional de Cuba v. Sabbatino, 376 U.S. 398, 432–33 (1964).

[150] Int'l L. Comm'n, Rep. on the Work of its Seventieth Session, *supra* note 1, at 120 (conclusions 5 and 6, describing forms of state practice); COMM. ON FORMATION OF CUSTOMARY (GEN.) INT'L LAW, *supra* note 1, at 17–18 (same).

[151] RESTATEMENT (THIRD) § 111 rptrs. note 1 (1987) (explaining that the "[t]he President's authority and duty to take care that a principle of customary law be faithfully executed," and "the doctrine that a new customary law becomes United States law automatically and supersedes at least State law," both "depend on an authoritative determination that the particular principle has in fact become part of customary law").

[152] Policy of the United States with Respect to the Natural Resources of the Subsoil and Sea Bed of the Continental Shelf, Proclamation No. 2667, 10 Fed. Reg. 12,303 (Oct. 2, 1945); *see* RESTATEMENT (THIRD) § 102 rptrs. note 2 (describing Truman declaration as immediately effective in customary international law terms); *see, e.g.*, United States v. California, 332 U.S. 19, 33 n.18 (1947) (citing Truman declaration).

international law and in domestic legal practice.[153] While this role is significant, there is little if any support for the proposition that executive branch recognition of a rule of customary international law is necessary or, by itself, sufficient for the rule's recognition by the judiciary or other U.S. actors.

In addition to helping make customary international law, the president also plays a major role in interpreting it—again, not merely in state-to-state interactions on the international plane. Notwithstanding the absence of any explicit constitutional assignment, U.S. courts tend to defer to the executive branch interpretations of which they are made aware.[154] Several rationales have been proffered. Most obviously, it may be desirable for the United States to speak with one voice on such matters. As to why that voice should be the president's, it may be thought to follow from the fact that the president is most likely to be held directly accountable by foreign states for any perceived deviations. In addition, the president is likely to have greater command of state practice and *opinio juris* than would a court (or, for that matter, Congress).[155]

How *much* deference is the more difficult question. The *Restatement (Third)* advised that courts give "particular weight" to the U.S. position on customary international law. This arguably sounds like less than the "great weight" often recited for executive views regarding treaty interpretation, but apparently little distinction was intended.[156] In practice, both the professed and apparent degree of deference varies. Naturally, a court inclined to disagree with the executive

---

[153] *See, e.g.*, Alfred Dunhill of London, Inc. v. Cuba, 425 U.S. 682, 698–705 (1976) (describing executive branch influence in refinement of sovereign immunity doctrine); Republic of Argentina v. Weltover, Inc., 504 U.S. 607, 612 (1992) (suggesting that commercial activities exception in the Foreign Sovereign Immunities Act should be construed on assumption that Congress incorporated restrictive theory of immunity previously endorsed by executive branch).

[154] RESTATEMENT (THIRD) § 112, cmt. c; Bradley & Goldsmith, *supra* note 148, at 1230–33; Julian G. Ku, *Structural Conflicts in the Interpretation of Customary International Law*, 45 SANTA CLARA L. REV. 857, 862–64 (2005).

[155] The *Restatement (Third)* suggested the first two rationales. RESTATEMENT (THIRD) § 112 cmt. c. For emphasis on expertise, see, for example, Curtis A. Bradley, *Chevron Deference and Foreign Affairs*, 86 VA. L. REV. 649, 661–62, 707–15 (2000); Julian Ku & John Yoo, Hamdan v. Rumsfeld: *The Functional Case for Foreign Affairs Deference to the Executive Branch*, 23 CONST. COMMENT. 179, 197–205 (2006). *See generally* Ingrid Wuerth, *The Alien Tort Statute and Federal Common Law: A New Approach*, 85 NOTRE DAME L. REV. 1931, 1956–57 (2010) (suggesting deference based on the executive's "expertise and informational advantages, as well as its general role in the formation of customary international law and its related function as bearing the primary responsibility for treaty negotiation"). *But cf.* Ganesh Sitaraman & Ingrid Wuerth, *The Normalization of Foreign Relations Law*, 128 HARV. L. REV. 1897, 1936–38 (2015) (criticizing degree of deference to executive branch expertise generally).

[156] RESTATEMENT (THIRD) § 112 cmt. c; *see id.* (indicating that "these various expressions are not used with precision and do not necessarily imply different degrees of deference"); *id.* § 326, rptrs. note 4 (citing cases). The executive branch perceives the deference as equivalent. *See, e.g.*, Brief for the United States as Amicus Curiae at 15, Domingues v. Nevada, 528 U.S. 963 (1999) (No. 98-8327) (submitting that "the courts should defer to the position of the Executive Branch as to whether a rule of customary international law is presently binding on the United States in its relations with other Nations, just as they give great weight to the Executive Branch's interpretation of a treaty").

branch's position may be inclined to state the degree of deference owed in more modest terms, and vice versa. Beyond this, it is possible to hypothesize factors that may help predict stronger and weaker versions of deference. When the United States has played a leading role in establishing the rule, deference to the executive branch—as partly responsible for the rule's making—may be more inviting; this might help explain pre-FSIA deference to suggestions of sovereign immunity.[157] More generally, public and consistent interpretations are more likely to engage the credibility of the United States and concern the president's foreign affairs function, as will issues of obvious national interest.[158] As this suggests, deference as to the president's interpretation of customary international law may be closely associated with the deference to separation-of-powers principles. In the official immunity context, for example, the executive branch has forthrightly stated that its principles in making official immunity determinations are "informed by" customary international law but bind U.S. courts because of separation of powers principles, and it has the same view with regard to head-of-state immunity; courts have widely agreed.[159]

Conversely, inconsistency in the U.S. position, or distance from core executive functions, may cut against deference. Furthermore, more mature rules, with easily discerned guidance from U.S. and foreign courts, should depend less on executive branch reckonings.[160] Finally, when the United States is a party or has its sovereign interests directly at issue, courts may be more skeptical in according deference. This may help explain cases that exhibit less deference, involving the jurisdiction of military commissions[161] and wrongdoing by the U.S.

[157] *See, e.g.,* Samantar v. Yousuf, 560 U.S. 305, 311 (2010) (describing pre-FSIA deference, including following the adoption by the executive branch of the restrictive immunity principle); Republic of Austria v. Altmann, 541 U.S. 677, 689–91 (2004) (same); Verlinden B.V. v. Central Bank of Nigeria, 461 U.S. 480, 486–88 (1983) (same). *See generally* Chapter 4 § V(A)(1).

[158] *See, e.g.,* United States v. County of Arlington, 702 F.2d 485, 487–88 (4th Cir. 1983) (finding persuasive the Department of State position that a foreign sovereign was immune from local taxes under customary international law, and that where such views were "at least as tenable as those to the contrary . . . the position adopted by the Department of State in an area of particular sensitivity and importance to the responsibilities conferred on it as the weight which tips the scale").

[159] *See, e.g.,* Brief for the United States as Amicus Curiae Supporting Affirmance at 8–9, 27–28, Samantar v. Yousuf, 560 U.S. 305 (2010) (No. 08-1555) (official immunity); Brief for the United States as Amicus Curiae Supporting Appellee at 2, 7, Manoharan v. Rajapaksa, 711 F.3d 178 (D.C. Cir. 2013) (No. 12-5087) (head-of-state immunity). Judicial endorsement of executive branch views has been "'overwhelming,'" based on separation of powers considerations that largely transcend forms of immunity. Habyarimana v. Kagame, 696 F.3d 1032 (10th Cir. 2012) (quoting Spacil v. Crowe, 489 F.2d 614, 617 (5th Cir.1974) (Wisdom, J.)); *see* Chapter 4 § V(D)(1)–(2). *But cf.* Yousuf v. Samantar, 699 F.3d 763, 773 (4th Cir. 2012) (indicating that the court would "give absolute deference to the State Department's position on status-based immunity doctrines such as head-of-state immunity," but only "substantial weight" on conduct-based official immunity).

[160] *See* Wuerth, *The Alien Tort Statute and Federal Common Law, supra* note 155, at 1956–58 (suggesting "modest" or "some" deference to executive branch views relating to the content of customary international law when that law is in development, but "little" deference to such views when the law was already well developed).

[161] *See supra* this chapter text accompanying notes 106–112.

military.[162] In the classic case of *The Paquete Habana*, the Supreme Court deferred little to the executive branch's construction of international law, at least not in any conventional sense; the Court's interest in citing U.S. practice appeared to have been hoisting the government by its own petard.[163]

3. Take Care Authority

Assume a clear rule of customary international law, neither implemented by Congress nor directly germane to one of the international responsibilities assigned by the Constitution, such as making treaties. What effect does such a rule have on presidential authority? This largely turns on the president's constitutional obligation to "take Care that the Laws be faithfully executed"[164]—which, as the Supreme Court has stressed, also gives him "the power to do so."[165] As noted earlier, the relatively broad cast of Article II over "the Laws" (as opposed to the "Laws of the United States" used in Article III and Article VI) and its drafting evolution (from "the National Laws" to the "the Laws of the United States" to the "the Laws") suggest that the law of nations would be included, and the Pacificus-Helvidius debate suggests that Hamilton and Madison shared this assumption as well.[166]

The Supreme Court soon signaled greater ambivalence. In *Brown v. United States*, decided in 1814, Chief Justice Marshall declined to endorse the president's power to seize enemy property within the United States at the time war was declared, rejecting the proposition that "in executing the laws of war, the executive may seize and the Courts condemn all property which, according to the modern law of nations, is subject to confiscation."[167] As Marshall explained, such a proposition mistakenly assumed that "modern usage constitutes a rule which acts directly upon the thing itself by its own force, and not through the sovereign power." Instead, he perceived the seizure rule as more of "a guide which

---

[162] *See, e.g., In re* "Agent Orange" Product Liability Litigation, 373 F. Supp. 2d 7, 110 (E.D.N.Y. 2005) (rejecting request for deference "insofar as it suggests that the executive's statement of the law is controlling," while allowing that "the courts will often be influenced by the executive's interpretation since its expertise in international law is substantial").

[163] The Paquete Habana, 175 U.S. 677, 690–91, 696–97, 698–99, 709–10 (1900) (describing U.S. practice); *id.* at 712 (stating that "[t]he position taken by the United States during the recent war with Spain was quite in accord with the rule of international law, now generally recognized by civilized nations, in regard to coast fishing vessels," while in practice violating that rule). For whatever reason, the executive branch also made no claim for deference. *See* William S. Dodge, The Paquete Habana: *Customary International Law as Part of Our Law, in* INTERNATIONAL LAW STORIES 175, 181 n.50 (John E. Noyes, Laura A. Dickinson, & Mark W. Janis eds., 2007). For further discussion of *The Paquete Habana,* see *infra* this chapter §§ II(B)(3), II(C)(1), and III(D).

[164] U.S. CONST. art. II, § 3.

[165] Free Enterprise Fund v. Public Co. Accounting Oversight Bd., 561 U.S. 477, 513 (2010).

[166] *See supra* this chapter text accompanying notes 45–49.

[167] Brown v. United States, 12 U.S. (8 Cranch) 110, 128 (1814). The argument contemplated that "it might require an act of the legislature to justify the condemnation of that property which, according to modern usage, ought not to be confiscated." *Id.*

the sovereign follows or abandons at his will," "subject to infinite modification" and dependent on "political considerations" making it more suitable for the legislature than for the executive or the judiciary.[168] In contrast, Justice Story's dissent stressed that the president was bound by the customary international law of seizure.[169] However, while concluding that the president had, under the circumstances, discretionary authority to condemn British property that was in the United States, Justice Story relied on implied congressional and constitutional authority and disclaimed the view that customary international law had directly established such capacity in the president.[170] In short, neither opinion endorsed the view that permissive international law rules, which allowed but did not obligate actions by states, conferred power on the president. By the same token, neither addressed the effect of an obligatory customary international law rule in the absence of congressional authorization.

Subsequent decisions kept alive the idea that the president had an obligation to execute customary international law without entirely resolving these questions. While some cases described the Take Care Clause in extremely broad terms, going well beyond international obligations,[171] decisions like *Youngstown Sheet & Tube Co. v. Sawyer* and *Medellín v. Texas* stressed that it did not encompass authority that the president could employ or ignore at will.[172] The leading

---

[168] *Id.* at 128–29.

[169] *Id.* at 153 (Story, J., dissenting) (indicating that "he cannot lawfully transcend the rules of warfare established among civilized nations," nor "lawfully exercise powers or authorize proceedings which the civilized world repudiates and disclaims"). Chief Justice Marshall's majority opinion may be read to imply that the authority to deviate from customary international law was also vested, if at all, in Congress only. *See* Dodge, *supra* note 163, at 200; David L. Sloss, Michael D. Ramsey, & William S. Dodge, *International Law in the Supreme Court to 1860, in* INTERNATIONAL LAW IN THE U.S. SUPREME COURT: CONTINUITY AND CHANGE 34–35 (2011). In the case at hand, though, the presence of continually varying political conditions meant that the rule was "not an immutable rule of law"—suggesting that it served neither to authorize or constrain the executive branch absent legislative intervention. *Brown*, 12 U.S. at 128.

[170] Justice Story's opinion suggested that customary international law helped legitimate executive action, where it did not constrain it. *Brown*, 12 U.S. at 149 (Story, J., dissenting) (explaining that, absent legislation, the executive was guided by "the law of nations as applied to a state of war," because "with him the sovereignty of the nation rests as to the execution of the laws"). But he distanced himself from the authority-conferring view also rejected by the majority, *id.* at 153, adding that "[t]he modern usage of nations is resorted to merely as a limitation of this discretion, not as conferring the authority to exercise it," because "[t]he sovereignty to execute it is supposed already to exist in the president, by the very terms of the constitution," where (he thought) the majority would have to concede it rested—absent restriction by Congress or international law. *Id.* at 154.

[171] *See, e.g., In re* Neagle, 135 U.S. 1, 64 (1890) (suggesting, in upholding issuance of writ of habeas corpus for deputy U.S. marshal charged with murder committed in defense of Supreme Court justice, that Take Care authority extended to "the rights, duties, and obligations growing out of the Constitution itself, our international relations, and all the protection implied by the nature of the government under the Constitution").

[172] Medellín v. Texas, 552 U.S. 491, 532 (2008) ("This authority allows the President to execute the laws, not make them."); Youngstown Sheet & Tube Co. v. Sawyer, 343 U.S. 579, 588 (1952) (rejecting president's invocation of Take Care Clause authority on the ground that "[t]he President's order does not direct that a congressional policy be executed in a manner prescribed by Congress—it directs

U.S. decision on customary international law, *The Paquete Habana*, is often read as striking inconsistent notes. The decision's famous pronouncement that "[i]nternational law is part of our law" arose as part of a holding that the United States had unlawfully violated an international custom exempting coastal fishing vessels from capture as prizes of war. To that extent, the decision suggested that the judiciary can invoke customary international law as a basis for constraining the executive branch (assisted by the fact that the president, too, had ordered officials to abide by international law, and by the secretary of navy's incorporation of customary rules in instructions to subordinates).[173] But the judiciary was described as giving effect to international law "where there is no treaty, and no controlling executive or legislative act or judicial decision,"[174] which was easily taken to mean that customary international law would be stymied by a "controlling executive act." The *Restatement (Third) of Foreign Relations Law* acknowledged this complexity, but concluded that international law—including, but not limited to, "agreements of the United States"—is "law of the United States," from which it followed that "the President has the obligation and the necessary authority to take care that they be faithfully executed."[175]

Executive branch legal views have also been qualified. Early legal opinions describing the law of nations as part of U.S. law did not emphasize the Take Care Clause or describe it as establishing significant ancillary authority.[176] Later invocations were usually incidental to the invocation of other powers, such as commander-in-chief authority.[177] The subordination of the Take Care Clause

that a presidential policy be executed in a manner prescribed by the President"). For discussion of this "anti-plenary" reading of the Clause, see Swaine, *Taking Care of Treaties, supra* note 41, at 349–52.

[173] The Paquete Habana, 175 U.S. 677, 700, 712–14 (1900). Both prior to and after the declaration of war, the president instructed that international law was to be followed. *See* Proclamation No. 6, 30 Stat. 1769, 1769 (Apr. 22, 1898); Proclamation No. 8, 30 Stat. 1770, 1770–71 (Apr. 26, 1898). As discussed below, this may suggest the possibility of a different outcome when the president has not called for compliance, see *infra* this chapter § III(D), but it signaled the significance attributed to customary obligations in executive branch practice.

[174] *The Paquete Habana*, 175 U.S. at 700; *accord id.* at 708 ("This rule of international law is one which prize courts, administering the law of nations, are bound to take judicial notice of, and to give effect to, in the absence of any treaty or other public act of their own government in relation to the matter."); *see infra* this chapter § III (D) (discussing alternative readings, in relation to the president's capacity to disregard customary international law).

[175] RESTATEMENT (THIRD) § 111 cmt. c. For some qualifications in the *Restatement (Third)* regarding customary international law's status, see *infra* note 294.

[176] Thus, Attorney General Lee's opinion relating to an alleged violation of Spanish territorial integrity by U.S. residents, while emphasizing that it violated the law of nations (and that this was part of U.S. law, and bound the United States to comply), also acknowledged that the United States lacked the capacity to deliver any offender in the absence of a particular law enabling compliance. Territorial Rights—Florida, 1 Op. Att'y. Gen. 68, 69–70 (1797).

[177] *See, e.g.*, Presidential Power to Use the Armed Forces Abroad Without Statutory Authorization, 4A Op. O.L.C. 185, 186 (1980) (noting that president may use take care authority to enforce both treaties and customary international law); *see infra* this chapter note 291 (discussing additional acts of incorporation in war powers context).

was evident following the September 11, 2001, terrorist attacks, when executive branch memoranda denied that customary international law was binding federal law in part out of concern that it might inhibit the president's war powers.[178] Although these memoranda have little continuing authority,[179] they reflect enduring concerns that construing the Take Care Clause as encompassing customary international law might do little to enhance executive branch authority, and merely result in an unwelcome loss of executive discretion.[180]

The Supreme Court has not reconciled the constraining and conferring aspects of the Take Care Clause.[181] Were the executive branch to claim additional authority on that basis, problems of bootstrapping could loom large. The mere fact that the executive branch has decided to regard an international norm as binding international law for the United States should not, in and of itself, qualify it under the Take Care Clause.[182] At most, such a declaration, if persuasive, acknowledges the rule's international standing and, consequently, its domestic legal effect; were it treated as having decisive effect, it would more closely resemble the creation of law than its execution, in tension with cases like *Brown*, *Youngstown*, and *Medellín*.[183] Likewise, employing discretion afforded by customary international law—for example, utilizing U.S. capacity, compatible with the law of the sea, to establish an exclusive economic zone[184]—should not depend

---

[178] *See* Memorandum from John C. Yoo, Deputy Assistant Attorney General and Robert J. Delahunty, Special Counsel to Alberto R. Gonzalez, Counsel to the President, Re: Treaties and Laws Applicable to the Conflict in Afghanistan And to the Treatment of Persons Captured by U.S. Armed Forces In that Conflict at 35–41 (Nov. 30, 2001) (concluding that "[r]egardless of its substance . . . customary international law cannot bind the executive branch under the Constitution because it is not federal law"); *accord* Memorandum from John C. Yoo, Deputy Assistant Attorney General for William J. Haynes II, General Counsel for the Department of Defense, Re: Military Interrogation of Alien Unlawful Combatants Held Outside the United States at 73 (Mar. 14, 2003).

[179] As noted previously, some of these memoranda were subsequently qualified, and the March 14, 2003, memorandum was withdrawn in its entirety. Memorandum for the Files, *supra* note 112, at 3; *see* Letter from Daniel B. Levin, Acting Assistant Attorney General to William J. Haynes II, Office of Legal Counsel (Feb. 4, 2005).

[180] *See also infra* this chapter text accompanying note 378 (noting memoranda concerning the FBI's authority).

[181] *See generally* Jack Goldsmith & John F. Manning, *The Protean Take Care Clause*, 164 U. PA. L. REV. 1835, 1838 (2016); Swaine, *Taking Care of Treaties*, *supra* note 41.

[182] For example, the president's declaration that the "U.S. Government will therefore choose out of a sense of legal obligation to treat the principles set forth in Article 75" of the Additional Protocol to the 1949 Geneva Convention (to which the United States is not a party) as "applicable" to particular detainees, and that it "expects all other nations to adhere to these principles as well," would not by virtue of that action alone establish binding domestic law. The White House, Office of the Press Secretary, *Fact Sheet: New Actions on Guantánamo and Detainee Policy* (Mar. 7, 2011), https://perma.cc/K459-W9T9. For further discussion, see Chapter 6 § V(C) (discussing presidential recognition of customary international law as an alternative approach to international agreements).

[183] *See supra* this chapter text accompanying notes 171–172. Other constitutional authority may, of course, justify the declaration and provide it with domestic legal significance—for example, the president's commander-in-chief authority. *See* Chapter § II(B).

[184] Proclamation No. 5030, 48 Fed. Reg. 10,605 (Mar. 10, 1983); *see President's Statement* (Mar. 10, 1983), *in* DEP'T OF STATE BULL., June 1983, at 70–71; Marian Nash Leich, *Law of the Sea*, 77 AM. J. INT'L L. 619 (1983).

on any authority conferred by the Take Care Clause. Finally, customary international law that is unsettled or indeterminate may be an inadequate basis for Take Care Clause authority. The law of expropriation at the time *Banco Nacional de Cuba v. Sabbatino* was rendered, for example, might not have supported presidential authority under the Take Care Clause.[185]

The still-controversial question is whether well-established customary international law that appears to impose determinate obligations on the executive branch may be invoked against it, or by it, under the Take Care Clause. The argument is much stronger if customary international law, or some part of it, has the status of federal law under the Supremacy Clause (a question revisited later in this chapter).[186] *Medellín v. Texas* appeared to hold that because a non-self-executing treaty provision lacks judicial enforceability, it could not augment presidential authority to displace state law;[187] it did not directly address, however, whether the president and the rest of the executive branch was nonetheless obligated by virtue of the Take Care Clause to abide by such a provision in its own conduct.[188] It is possible that the customary international law rule in *The Paquete Habana* would, if encountered today, have to be both "part of our law" and judicially enforceable federal common law in order to warrant relief against U.S. officials or provide authority for those officials to secure U.S. compliance.

C. Judicial Incorporation

As we have seen, customary international law may enter the U.S. domestic legal order by virtue of a constitutionally authorized statute or international agreement, sometimes augmented by presidential authority. Absent implementation by one or both of the political branches, what is the place of customary international law in U.S. courts? To be sure, the political branches are usually in the

---

[185] Banco Nacional de Cuba v. Sabbatino, 376 U.S. 398, 428–30 (1964); for discussion of this rule's perceived certainty in the act of state context, see Chapter 4 § III.

[186] *See supra* this chapter text accompanying notes 56–57 (discussing founding-era evidence); *infra* this chapter text accompanying note 202 (discussing status of customary international law in relation to the authority of federal courts), § III(D) (discussing limits on presidential incorporation).

[187] Medellín v. Texas, 552 U.S. 491, 532 (2008) ("This authority allows the President to execute the laws, not make them. For the reasons we have stated, the *Avena* judgment is not domestic law; accordingly, the President cannot rely on his Take Care powers here."). For further discussion in the context of non-self-executing treaties, see *infra* this chapter text accompanying notes 359–361; Chapter 6 § IV(A); and Chapter 9 §§ II(B), II(C).

[188] *See* RESTATEMENT (FOURTH) § 310 rptrs. note 13; Swaine, *Taking Care of Treaties, supra* note 41; *see* Chapter 6 § IV(A)(3). Cases like *In re Neagle* depended upon a conflict between federal law (in the form of a constitutional obligation) and state criminal law. *In re* Neagle, 135 U.S. 1, 59–62 (1890) (discussing, inter alia, *Ex parte* Siebold, 100 U.S. 371 (1880), and Tennessee v. Davis, 100 U.S. 275 (1880)); *see also* Nixon v. Fitzgerald, 457 U.S. 731, 750 (1982) (describing president's authority under the Take Care Clause as including "the enforcement of federal law").

backdrop. To entertain customary international law questions in the first place, for example, a federal court must have jurisdiction conferred by a statute consistent with Article III;[189] as *Sosa v. Alvarez-Machain* demonstrated, a jurisdictional statute may also enable claims.[190] Nonetheless, judicial authority is often an especially indispensable part of reckoning international law and transmuting it into federal law.

The genesis of federal common law is a subject that clearly transcends foreign relations law, and is beyond the scope of this volume. Nevertheless, some attention to historical questions is necessary. If *Erie Railroad v. Tompkins* and its successors did not directly resolve the general status of customary international law,[191] prior understandings may continue to govern; whether *Erie* implicitly addressed those questions may depend on how they were presented beforehand.

1. Customary International Law as General Common Law

In 1900, the Supreme Court famously declared in *The Paquete Habana* that "[i]nternational law is part of our law, and must be ascertained and administered by the courts of justice of appropriate jurisdiction, as often as questions of right depending upon it are duly presented for their determination."[192] The pronouncement's beauty lies in its ambiguity. The "international law" of which the Court spoke was clearly the law of nations, or customary international law.[193] But what "our law" meant and what "part" customary international law played within it—let alone the question of which courts were likely to have "appropriate jurisdiction" and when issues would be "duly presented"— was much less clear. To this day, the decision is a Rorschach test for views on international law's place in the U.S. constitutional scheme.

The most basic proposition in *The Paquete Habana*, that the law of nations might *sometimes* supply a rule of decision, was always beyond cavil. While founding-era discussions showed concern about the uses to which courts might put international law, such as criminalizing offenses against the law of nations

---

[189] *See generally* RICHARD FALLON ET AL., THE FEDERAL COURTS AND THE FEDERAL SYSTEM 307–25 (7th ed. 2015) (discussing, generally, congressional authority over federal jurisdiction). The Supreme Court's original jurisdiction, which encompasses "[c]ases affecting Ambassadors, other public Ministers and Consuls," U.S. CONST. art. III, § 2, cl. 2, is a different matter. FALLON ET AL., *supra*, at 267–71 (discussing congressional capacity to limit or deem nonexclusive Supreme Court original jurisdiction). Matters are also different, of course, for state courts of general jurisdiction, so long as Congress has not attempted to circumscribe their authority. *See id.* at 326–35, 412–22.

[190] Sosa v. Alvarez-Machain, 542 U.S. 692, 714, 724–25 (2004); *see infra* this chapter § IV(B).

[191] Erie R.R. Co. v. Tompkins, 304 U.S. 64 (1938).

[192] The Paquete Habana, 175 U.S. 677, 700 (1900). For further discussion, see *supra* this chapter § II(B)(3) and *infra* this chapter § III(D).

[193] As noted below, though, some regard *The Paquete Habana* as standing only for the proposition that certain types of customary international law are eligible for preemptive force. *See* Anthony J. Bellia, Jr. & Bradford R. Clark, *The Law of Nations as Constitutional Law*, 98 VA. L. REV. 729, 800–02 (2012).

without legislative instruction,[194] the idea that courts could take that law into account was uncontroversial.[195] Preratification discourse,[196] early practice,[197] and decisions by the period's leading jurists[198] are peppered with representations that customary international law mattered even in the absence of constitutional or statutory command. The Supreme Court seemed to have accepted this understanding in *Sosa v. Alvarez-Machain* in "giv[ing] the edge" to the view that, as of 1789, "torts in violation of the law of nations would have been recognized within the common law of the time."[199]

The common law reflecting the law of nations resembled what we would now call *general* common law, which was meaningfully different from our post-*Erie* categories of "state" or "federal" common law.[200] Back then there was readier acceptance that law might be a "brooding omnipresence," supplying a basis for decision in cases not otherwise resolvable, and greater willingness to tolerate ambiguity about its place in the constitutional order.[201] Even so, some found it

[194] *See supra* this chapter § II(A)(2) (noting concerns expressed during discussion of the Offences Clause as to whether the law of nations sufficed, without congressional intermediation, as a constitutionally recognized basis for criminal prosecutions).

[195] *See generally* David L. Sloss, Michael D. Ramsey, & William S. Dodge, *International Law in the Supreme Court to 1860, in* INTERNATIONAL LAW IN THE U.S. SUPREME COURT: CONTINUITY AND CHANGE 28 (2011); Dickinson, *supra* note 7.

[196] *See, e.g.,* FEDERALIST NO. 3, at 43 (John Jay) (praising the "wisdom of the convention in committing such questions"—including those involving the law of nations—"to the jurisdiction and judgment of courts appointed by and responsible only to one national government"); FEDERALIST NO. 80 (Alexander Hamilton) (describing, generally, the importance of vesting in the national judiciary matters involving foreign citizens and the law of nations).

[197] This view was evidenced, for example, in exchanges concerning U.S. efforts to maintain neutrality during the war between England and France. *See supra* this chapter text accompanying notes 45–48, 134–137. Later, writing as Camillus, Hamilton explained that the confiscatory acts violating the Jay Treaty would also violate the law of nations, and "Tis indubitable that the customary law of European Nations is as a part of the common law and by adoption that of the U States." *From Alexander Hamilton To Defence No. XX, supra* note 137, at 342; *see also supra* note 140 (quoting Who Privileged from Arrest, 1 Op. Att'y Gen. 26, 27 (1792), and Territorial Rights—Florida, 1 Op. Att'y Gen. 68, 69 (1797)).

[198] *See, e.g.,* The Nereide, 13 U.S. (9 Cranch) 388, 423 (1815) (Marshall, C.J.) (stating that until a contrary statute is enacted, "the Court is bound by the law of nations which is a part of the law of the land"); Ware v. Hylton, 3 U.S. (3 Dall.) 199, 281 (1796) (Ware, J.) (indicating that the new United States "were bound to receive the law of nations, in its modern state of purity and refinement"); Talbot v. Janson, 3 U.S. (3 Dall.) 133, 161 (1795) (Iredell, J.) (citing capture as violating "our own law (I mean the common law, of which the law of nations is a part, as it subsisted either before the act of Congress on the subject, or since that has provided a particular manner of enforcing it,) as well as of the law of nations generally"). Chief Justice Jay expressed a similar view in his grand jury practice. *See* Henfield's Case, 11 F. Cas. 1099, 1101–04 (C.C.D. Pa. 1793) (No. 6360); John Jay, *The Charge of Chief-Justice Jay, to the Grand Juries on the Eastern Circuit,* N.H. GAZETTE, June 3, 1790, at 2.

[199] Sosa v. Alvarez-Machain, 542 U.S. 692, 714 (2004); *see also id.* at 739–40 (Scalia, J., concurring in part and dissenting in part) (agreeing with depiction as general common law). For further discussion, see *infra* this chapter §§ II(C)(2), IV(B)(1).

[200] *See* FALLON ET AL., *supra* note 189, at 713 n.7 (noting broad consensus among commentators); William A. Fletcher, *The General Common Law and Section 34 of the Judiciary Act of 1789: The Example of Marine Insurance,* 97 HARV. L. REV. 1513, 1514–15 & n.9 (1984) (noting evolving terminology).

[201] *See* Fletcher, *supra* note 200, at 1517–18 (citing, inter alia, PETER S. DU PONCEAU, A DISSERTATION ON THE NATURE AND EXTENT OF THE JURISDICTION OF THE COURTS OF THE UNITED STATES 88 (1824)); Jay, *supra* note 7, at 822–24.

harder to accept that this general common law would, even when applied by federal courts, constitute supreme federal law, with all that entailed for the authority of national institutions.[202]

Subsequent practice did little to fix this law's likeness to either federal or state common law, as they presently exist. Evidence either way is limited, since it was not until 1875 that Congress provided a stable option for exercising federal question jurisdiction.[203] Pre-*Erie* case law does not, in any event, establish any clear federal (as opposed to national) component to the law of nations. The evidence is particularly negative on jurisdictional questions. *American Insurance Co. v. 356 Bales of Cotton* suggested that admiralty matters would not, because admiralty law preceded the United States, "aris[e] under the laws of the United States," suggesting the possibility that the law of nations would for similar reasons fall outside Article III.[204] Later decisions reinforced those doubts.[205] Such cases may be explained in a variety of ways—for example, by the nature of the international issue,[206] by the terms of the statute conferring judicial

---

[202] *See* Fletcher, *supra* note 200, at 1521–25. These discussions were complicated by claims that at least some of the law of nations was derived directly from the law of England. *See, e.g.,* The Rapid, 12 U.S. (8 Cranch) 155, 162 (1814) (stating that law of prize "was the law of England before the revolution, and therefore constitutes a part of the admiralty and maritime jurisdiction conferred on this Court in pursuance of the constitution").

[203] Act of Mar. 3, 1875, ch. 137, 18 Stat. 470, 470–71 (1875). Congress initially enacted such jurisdiction in 1801, see Act of Feb. 13, 1801, ch. 4, § 11, 2 Stat. 89, 92, but repealed it the next year. Act of Mar. 8, 1802, ch. 8, 2 Stat. 182 (1802). This naturally limited the inquiry into whether such a statute, if applied to the law of nations, was compatible with Article III jurisdiction over the "laws of the United States."

[204] 26 U.S. (1 Pet.) 511, 545 (1828) (also reported as *American Insurance Co. v. Canter*); *see* Bradley, *supra* note 13, at 608–16; Sloss, Ramsey, & Dodge, *supra* note 195, at 31–32; A.M. Weisburd, *State Courts, Federal Courts, and International Cases,* 20 YALE J. INT'L L. 1, 29–31 (1995); Stewart Jay, *Origins of Federal Common Law: Part Two,* 133 U. PA. L. REV. 1231, 1309–11 (1985).

[205] *See, e.g.,* N.Y. Life Ins. Co. v. Hendren, 92 U.S. 286, 286–87 (1875) (holding that statutory appellate jurisdiction was lacking over a question predicated on "the general laws of war, as recognized by the law of nations"). Even Justice Bradley, who regarded customary international law as part of the "laws of the United States," having "the force of law in our courts," depended on the conclusion that these laws of war had been "adopted and used by the United States" and not "modified as the government sees fit." *Id.* at 287–88 (Bradley, J., dissenting); *see also* Ker v. Illinois, 119 U.S. 436, 444 (1886) (holding that whether forcible seizure abroad of a person is grounds to object to trial in state court is "a question of common law, or of the law of nations" within the province of either a state or federal court, which the Supreme Court had no right to review).

[206] For example, Huntington v. Attrill, 146 U.S. 657 (1892), characterized a "question of international law" as appropriate for resolution in the court in which suit might be brought. The Court indicated that were the case brought in federal court, it would be "one of those questions of general jurisprudence which that court must decide for itself, uncontrolled by local decisions," *id.* at 683, which might have been consistent with the supremacy of customary international law. *See* David J. Bederman, *Law of the Land, Law of the Sea: The Lost Link Between Customary International Law and the General Maritime Law,* 51 VA. J. INT'L L. 299, 329–30 (2011). By the same token, though, if suit was brought in state court, it was not open to Supreme Court review. *Huntington,* 146 U.S. at 683. But this might have turned on the law merchant, which was more subject to local variation than the traditional interstate species of international law. Carlos M. Vázquez, *Customary International Law as U.S. Law: A Critique of the Revisionist and Intermediate Positions and a Defense of the Modern Position,* 86 NOTRE DAME L. REV. 1495, 1526 (2011).

authority,[207] or as verifiable errors[208]—but there is little evidence that the law of nations would reliably be considered as federal law for jurisdictional purposes.[209]

Beyond these jurisdictional matters, courts wrestled with the law of nations as a rule of decision, but these cases were also inconclusive. *The Lottawana* stressed the importance of national uniformity in at least some transnational matters (like maritime law, in which the Constitution established specific Article III authority), and indicated concern about potential inconsistencies induced by state courts and state law, but did not squarely address supremacy.[210] Other cases in kindred areas suggested supremacy-like effect.[211] But there were caveats as well. Proponents of the general common law, skeptical of federal authority, believed that sufficient uniformity could be achieved without supremacy.[212] States also retained an acknowledged capacity to introduce state-law variations,[213] much like the United States as a whole.[214] Notwithstanding the reputation of the *Swift*

---

[207] *See, e.g.*, Oliver Am. Trading Co. v. Mexico, 264 U.S. 440, 442–43 (1924) (deeming a foreign sovereign immunity issue—certified for Supreme Court review as a potential jurisdictional error—to be a matter of "general law"); Vázquez, *supra* note 206, at 1526–27 (arguing that the certificate was held improper because jurisdiction had actually been predicated on diversity, such that the immunity issue did not concern "the question of the jurisdiction of the district court as a federal court") (quoting *Oliver Am. Trading*, 264 U.S. at 442). Cases like *Hendren* and *Wulfsohn v. Russian Socialist Federated Soviet Republic*, 266 U.S. 580 (1924), for their parts, involved writs depending on a statutory grant over cases dependent on certain claims "under the constitution, or any treaty or statute of, or commission held or authority exercised under the United States." *See* Judiciary Act of 1789, ch. 20, § 25, 1 Stat. 83, 85–87, amended by Act of Feb. 5, 1867, ch. 28, 14 Stat. 385 (applicable in *Hendren*); *see also* Act of Sept. 6, 1916, ch. 448, § 2, 39 Stat. 726, 727 (1916) (codified at 28 U.S.C. § 1257 (2018)) (applicable in *Wulfsohn*) (detailing similar terms).

[208] *See, e.g.*, Vázquez, *supra* note 206, at 1530–31 (noting possibility that *Hendren* depended on a subsequently recognized mistake concerning the reviewability of state court applications of federal common law).

[209] David J. Bederman, *Customary International Law in the Supreme Court, 1861–1900, in* INTERNATIONAL LAW IN THE U.S. SUPREME COURT, *supra* note 195, at 118 (acknowledging that "the post–Civil War Court was emphatic that customary international law was not federal law for purposes of establishing federal question jurisdiction").

[210] The Lottawanna, 88 U.S. 558, 575 (1874). The explicit creation of Article III jurisdiction over "all cases of admiralty and maritime jurisdiction," which the Court emphasized, was not easily extrapolated to the whole law of nations. *Id.* at 574–75.

[211] In some interstate cases, the Supreme Court invoked customary international law while constraining state conduct—though the contribution of that law to the judgments was unclear. *See* Kansas v. Colorado, 206 U.S. 46, 97 (1907); Kansas v. Colorado, 185 U.S. 125, 146–47 (1902). And in some maritime cases, like *Southern Pacific Co. v. Jensen*, 244 U.S. 205 (1917), supremacy seemed to hinge on the constitutional status of maritime law (*id.* at 216, 218)—reflecting uncertainty as to whether pre-*Erie* case law really equated maritime and admiralty cases, the law merchant, and all areas included within or touched on by the law of nations. For discussion, see Michael D. Ramsey, *Customary International Law in the Supreme Court, 1901–1945, in* INTERNATIONAL LAW IN THE U.S. SUPREME COURT, *supra* note 195, at 229–34.

[212] Fletcher, *supra* note 200, at 1517–25.

[213] *The Lottawanna*, 88 U.S. at 579–81.

[214] *Id.* at 576 (noting attention to "our own legal history, constitution, legislation, usages, and adjudications as well").

CUSTOMARY INTERNATIONAL LAW 361

v. Tyson era, the cases suggested judicial caution about any automatic judicial in-corporation of international rules.[215]

On the whole, the pre-*Erie* regime was limited in its capacity to conform the general common law to the law of nations, or to imbue the law that it incorpo-rated with federal characteristics. The prospects for the law of nations as fed-eral common law do not, however, necessarily stand or fall with the rest of the *Swift* regime. Cases like *The Paquete Habana* showed the law of nations playing a stronger role in constraining federal actors than would state law, even if its equivalence to federal law was unclear.[216] It seems fairest to conclude that when *Erie* was decided, the relationship between the law of nations and other parts of the general common law was not fixed, at least not in any way that can easily be recovered. This makes suspect any claim that the federal law status of customary international law is continuous with the pre-*Erie* regime—or, for that matter, any claim that *Erie* renounced a well-defined law of nations regime.

2. Customary International Law as Federal Common Law

A (slightly) more proximate question is what *Erie* resolved in 1938.[217] The Court was not at all focused on international law.[218] Nonetheless, its statutory analysis took Congress to have directed federal courts sitting in diversity to apply state law "in all matters except those in which some federal law is controlling," and its constitutional analysis equated this exception with "matters governed by the Federal Constitution or by acts of Congress." On its face, this approach either overlooked the law of nations or relegated it to a nonfederal status.[219]

It seems somewhat unlikely that the Court meant to change, without dis-cussion, how the law of nations was treated. Conceivably international matters were regarded as another matter entirely; *Erie* also failed to mention treaties as an example of controlling federal law, though these would surely afford a rule of decision in appropriate cases. Its reasoning about the *Swift v. Tyson* regime, too, applies unevenly. The Court's doubts about that regime's ability to achieve uniformity and the Court's concerns about discrimination against state citizens

---

[215] *See, e.g., id.* at 576–77 ("[W]e must always remember that the court cannot make the law, it can only declare it. If, within its proper scope, any change is desired in its rules, other than those of proce-dure, it must be made by the legislative department.").

[216] The Paquete Habana, 175 U.S. 677 (1900); *see supra* this chapter text accompanying notes 163, 173.

[217] The critical literature is extensive. For a recent assessment, see Caleb Nelson, *A Critical Guide to Erie Railroad Co. v. Tompkins*, 54 WM. & MARY L. REV. 921 (2013); for a classic, see Henry J. Friendly, *In Praise of Erie—And of the New Federal Common Law*, 39 N.Y.U. L. REV. 383 (1964).

[218] *See* Erie R.R. Co. v. Tompkins, 304 U.S. 64, 69–70 (1938) (describing nature of tort claim); *see also id.* at 75–76 (describing additional, problematic subjects of "general law" addressed by federal courts); Reply Brief on Behalf of Petitioner Erie Railroad Company at 7–10, *Erie R.R.*, 304 U.S. 64 (No. 367) (identifying decisions countermanding state courts in diversity cases).

[219] *Erie R.R.*, 304 U.S. at 72, 78.

unable to invoke diversity of citizenship and seek federal jurisdiction were germane to the law of nations only if it had in fact been treated as ordinary general common law.[220] However, the Court's concerns about the impact of judicial authority on federalism and on separation of powers applied a bit more readily to the law of nations.[221] Jurisprudential objection to law existing "without some definite authority behind it" might be reduced if the United States and foreign sovereigns moved cautiously in developing the law of nations. Still, that safeguard might be of little comfort if federal courts were themselves significant participants in such development.[222]

Complicating matters further, after *Erie*, the Court recognized federal common law in limited circumstances where federal interests were particularly acute.[223] Most prominently, in *Banco Nacional de Cuba v. Sabbatino*,[224] the Court indicated that the Act of State doctrine enjoyed the status of federal law, and suggested that international law, and matters of international relations concerning the separation of powers, were not contemplated by *Erie*.[225] But

[220] *Id.* at 74–77.

[221] *Erie* evinced concern with the prospect that federal courts would use general common law to invade the states' domain even where Congress could not. *Id.* at 72, 78; *see also* John Hart Ely, *The Irrepressible Myth of Erie*, 87 HARV. L. REV. 693, 703 n.62 (1974); Nelson, *supra* note 217, at 974 n.184. *But cf.* Harold Hongju Koh, Commentary, *Is International Law Really State Law?*, 111 HARV. L. REV. 1824, 1831 (1998) (emphasizing that the Offences Clause established national authority over the law of nations).

[222] *Erie R.R.*, 304 U.S. at 78–79 (quoting Black & White Taxicab v. Brown & Yellow Taxicab, 276 U.S. 518, 533 (1928)). *Compare* Weisburd, *supra* note 204, at 49, 51 (arguing that customary international law is "the joint product of the lawmaking activity of many sovereigns"), *and* Vázquez, *supra* note 206, at 1510–12 (describing dependence of federal courts on others to establish customary international law), *with* Curtis A. Bradley & Jack L. Goldsmith, *Customary International Law as Federal Common Law: A Critique of the Modern Position*, 110 HARV. L. REV. 815, 853–54 (1997) (arguing that *Erie* requires a *domestic* source of authority), *and* Lea Brilmayer, *Untethered Norms After Erie Railroad Co. v. Tompkins: Positivism, International Law, and the Return of the "Brooding Omnipresence,"* 54 WM. & MARY L. REV. 725 (2013) (likening customary international law to general common law).

[223] The Court's first qualification, announced on the same day as *Erie*, was part of a distinctive line of cases involving the settlement of interstate disputes. *See* Hinderlider v. La Plata River & Cherry Creek Ditch Co., 304 U.S. 92 (1938). But there were other examples of what Judge Friendly called the "new," or "specialized," federal common law. Henry J. Friendly, *In Praise of Erie—And of the New Federal Common Law*, 39 N.Y.U. L. REV. 383, 405 (1964); *see also* Tex. Indus., Inc. v. Radcliff Materials, Inc., 451 U.S. 630, 640 (1981) (explaining that federal common law is appropriate when "a federal rule of decision is necessary to protect uniquely federal interests," and when "Congress has given the courts the power to develop substantive law") (internal quotation marks omitted); City of Milwaukee v. Illinois (Milwaukee II), 451 U.S. 304, 314 (1981) (describing federal common law as applicable where courts are "compelled to consider federal questions [that] cannot be answered from federal statutes alone") (internal quotation marks omitted).

[224] 376 U.S. 398 (1964).

[225] *Id.* at 425 (stating that "[i]t seems fair to assume that the Court did not have rules like the act of state doctrine in mind when it decided *Erie*"); *id.* (noting contemporaneous warnings about the danger were *Erie* "extended to legal problems affecting international relations," and that "rules of international law should not be left to divergent and perhaps parochial state interpretations") (citing Philip C. Jessup, *The Doctrine of* Erie Railroad v. Tompkins *Applied to International Law*, 33 AM. J. INT'L L. 740 (1939)); *id.* at 425 (stressing "that an issue concerned with a basic choice regarding the competence and function of the Judiciary and the National Executive in ordering our relationships

Sabbatino did not exactly decide that question, and other elements of the opinion suggested narrower rationales.[226] Indeed, the Court applied the Act of State doctrine so as to *supersede* a claim that itself tried to rely on customary international law, without suggesting that it was resolving a clash between two instances of federal law.[227]

Gradually, competing schools of thought emerged concerning the position of customary international law after *Erie*.[228] Accepting the need to describe customary international law as federal or state law, and recoiling from the latter, the "modern position" suggested that customary international law must be regarded as federal common law.[229] On this view, *Erie* had effectively resolved the jurisdictional status and supremacy of customary international law.[230] In *Filartiga v. Pena-Irala*, the Second Circuit pronounced that "the law of nations . . . has always been part of the federal common law."[231] The *Restatement (Third)* spoke in similarly sweeping terms.[232] Pushing back, so-called "revisionists"—including the work of Curtis Bradley and Jack Goldsmith—accepted the alternatives

with other members of the international community must be treated exclusively as an aspect of federal law").

[226] For example, *Sabbatino* explained that pre-*Erie* cases had suggested the federal status of the act-of-state doctrine, *see id.* at 426, and cited doctrine-specific constitutional and statutory provisions. *Id.* at 427 n.25.

[227] *Id.* at 428–32; *see also infra* note 342 (discussing influence of a customary international law norm's strength). Possibly the Court was driven by a conflicts-like principle that U.S. law, including both international law and the Act of State doctrine, would not apply to acts by a foreign state in its own territory. Louis Henkin, *International Law as Law in the United States*, 82 MICH. L. REV. 1555, 1561 (1984).

[228] For a leading (and critical) evaluation of these approaches, see BELLIA & CLARK, THE LAW OF NATIONS AND THE UNITED STATES CONSTITUTION, *supra* note 17, at 149–88.

[229] *See, e.g.,* Koh, *supra* note 221, at 1861 (describing "International law is federal law" as conventional wisdom); *accord id.* at 1824, 1825.

[230] *See, e.g.,* Friendly, *supra* note 217, at 405 (claiming that *Erie* led to "the emergence of a federal decisional law in areas of national concern that is truly uniform").

[231] Filartiga v. Pena-Irala, 630 F.2d 876, 885–86 (2d Cir. 1980). That said, the court was focused on Article III and statutory jurisdiction, rather than the status of customary international law as a rule of decision. *See id.* at 889 (stating that "[our] holding on subject-matter jurisdiction decides only whether Congress intended to confer judicial power, and whether it is authorized to do so by Article III," whereas "[t]he choice of law inquiry is a much broader one, primarily concerned with fairness" which "looks to wholly different considerations"). Nonetheless, *Filartiga* was widely regarded as addressing federal-law status for Supremacy Clause purposes as well. *See, e.g.,* Fletcher, *supra* note 200, at 657.

[232] RESTATEMENT (THIRD) § 111(1) (stating that "[i]nternational law and international agreements of the United States are law of the United States and supreme over the law of the several States"); *accord id.* § 111 cmt. d ("Customary international law is considered to be like common law in the United States, but it is federal law. A determination of international law by the Supreme Court is binding on the States and on State courts."); *id.* § 111 cmt. e (describing cases arising under customary international law as "within the Judicial Power of the United States under Article III, Section 2 of the Constitution," and like other federal law . . . part of the 'laws . . . of the United States' "); *id.* § 115 cmt. e (concluding that "[s]ince . . . any rule of customary international law, is federal law," it "supersedes inconsistent State law or policy whether adopted earlier or later"). For a critique, see Bradley & Goldsmith, *supra* note 222, at 830–31, 834–37.

presented by *Erie*, but chose a different path, depicting customary international law as state common law.[233] Yet others resisted the dilemma. For them, customary international law was neither federal nor state law, but rather a potential rule of decision that resembled a post-*Erie* general common law.[234]

The Supreme Court's decision in *Sosa v. Alvarez-Machain* had something for every camp.[235] The opinion reinforced the continuing status of the law of nations as part of "the domestic law of the United States" and characterized actions for its enforcement as a potential component of post-*Erie* federal common law.[236] At the same time it amplified *Erie*'s concerns about lawmaking by federal courts.[237] This tension aside, *Sosa*'s value is constrained by the issues the Court addressed and the nature of the ATS. The decision did not directly discuss Article III jurisdiction (as opposed to statutory jurisdiction under the ATS) nor customary international law's supremacy (as opposed to its capacity to provide a rule of decision).[238] Moreover, the Court stressed that it was relying on a jurisdictional statute that specifically entailed implementing the law of nations, and cautioned that the capacity to develop customary international law as federal common law

---

[233] *See, e.g.*, Curtis A. Bradley & Jack L. Goldsmith, *The Current Illegitimacy of International Human Rights Litigation*, 66 FORDHAM L. REV. 319, 349–50 (1997) (concluding that "in most cases, states would rarely incorporate CIL into state law," with the result that customary international law "simply would not be a rule of decision in federal court"); *see also* Bradley & Goldsmith, *supra* note 222; Curtis A. Bradley & Jack L. Goldsmith, Commentary, *Federal Courts and the Incorporation of International Law*, 111 HARV. L. REV. 2260 (1998).

[234] *See, e.g.*, MICHAEL D. RAMSEY, THE CONSTITUTION'S TEXT IN FOREIGN AFFAIRS 348–55 (2007) (arguing for status as nonpreemptive, federal law); T. Alexander Aleinikoff, *International Law, Sovereignty, and American Constitutionalism: Reflections on the Customary International Law Debate*, 98 AM. J. INT'L L. 91, 97–100 (2004) (urging consideration of customary international law as "nonpreemptive, nonfederal law" in federal, but not state, courts); Michael D. Ramsey, *International Law as Non-Preemptive Federal Law*, 42 VA. J. INT'L L. 555, 577, 584 (2002) (same); Weisburd, *supra* note 204, 29–35, 51 (same); Ernest A. Young, *Sorting Out the Debate over Customary International Law*, 42 VA. J. INT'L L. 365 (2002) (arguing for reviving status of customary international law as general common law).

[235] Sosa v. Alvarez-Machain, 542 U.S. 692 (2004). For varied reactions to how *Sosa* resolved preexisting debates, see, for example, Curtis A. Bradley, Jack L. Goldsmith, & David H. Moore, *Sosa, Customary International Law, and the Continuing Relevance of Erie*, 120 HARV. L. REV. 869 (2007); William S. Dodge, *Bridging Erie: Customary International Law in the U.S. Legal System After Sosa v. Alvarez-Machain*, 12 TULSA J. COMP. & INT'L L. 87 (2005).

[236] *See, e.g., Sosa*, 542 U.S at 732 (concluding that "federal courts should not recognize private claims under federal common law for violations of any international law norm with less definite content and acceptance among civilized nations than the historical paradigms familiar when [the ATS] was enacted"); *see also id.* at 726 (describing other recognition of "federal common law rules in interstitial areas of particular federal interest"); *id.* at 730 (same).

[237] *See id.* at 725–28 (citing, inter alia, changing conceptions of the common law and the role of federal courts, modern reluctance to create private rights of action, non-interference with foreign relations, and deference to the legislative branch). Justice Scalia would have held that these concerns foreclosed the judicial creation of causes of action. *See id.* at 739–42, 744–51 (Scalia, J., concurring in part and concurring in the judgment).

[238] The Court did, however, cite *Filartiga* approvingly for the general proposition that federal courts could recognize ATS claims. *See Sosa*, 542 U.S. at 725, 731, 732; Chapter 4 § I(C) (describing adoption of First Judiciary act and noting unresolved Article III issues).

might be less robust for more general jurisdictional statutes.[239] Accordingly, some lower courts have inferred that the judiciary lacks similar authority under other statutes.[240]

The lack of closure regarding judicial incorporation of customary international law is illustrated by the Supreme Court's later treatment, in *Samantar v. Yousuf*, of immunity for foreign officials.[241] The Court acknowledged that enactment of the FSIA in 1976 had displaced "the pre-existing common law" for determining the sovereign immunity of foreign states.[242] By contrast, it held, the FSIA did not address the immunity of individual foreign officials, leaving that immunity governed by the uncodified "common law" of official immunity.[243] Although clarity as to the relationship between this immunity and customary international law, and its status as *federal* common law, might have been material to the Court's statutory analysis, it left such matters to the lower courts to resolve on remand.[244] Lower courts may defensibly assume that foreign official immunity is at least partly derived from customary international law,[245] and that it has

---

[239] *Sosa*, 542 U.S. at 731 n.19 (denying that "every grant of jurisdiction to a federal court carries with it an opportunity to develop common law"); *id.* (noting that the ATS "was enacted on the congressional understanding that courts would exercise jurisdiction by entertaining some common law claims derived from the law of nations; and we know of no reason to think that federal-question jurisdiction was extended subject to any comparable congressional assumption"); *id.* (stating that, while the power to imply common law under the ATS was consistent with the responsibilities of federal and state courts, "a more expansive common law power related to 28 U.S.C. § 1331 might not be").

[240] For example, the Ninth Circuit interpreted *Sosa* as denying to customary international law its status as Article III federal law under ordinary circumstances. Sarei v. Rio Tinto, 671 F.3d 736, 752 (9th Cir. 2011) (en banc) [hereinafter *Rio Tinto V*] ("[T]he norms *Sosa* recognizes as actionable under the ATS *begin* as part of international law—which, without more, would not be considered federal law for Article III purposes—but they *become* federal common law once recognized to have the particular characteristics required to be enforceable under the ATS.") (emphases in original), *vacated and remanded on other grounds*, 569 U.S. 945 (2013) (mem. op.); *see also* Ali v. Rumsfeld, 649 F.3d 762, 791 (D.C. Cir. 2011) (Edwards, J., dissenting) (stating that absent the ATS, "federal courts would have no authority today to recognize common law causes of action for violations of customary international law, such as torture"); *id.* at 792 ("[I]t is section 1350, not international law, that gives federal courts the authority to enforce international norms that a federal court can properly recognize as within the common law enforceable 'without further statutory authority'") (quoting *Sosa*, 542 U.S. at 729); Mohamad v. Rajoub, 634 F.3d 604, 609–10 (D.C. Cir. 2011) (distinguishing 28 U.S.C. § 1331).

[241] 560 U.S. 305 (2010). For more extensive discussion of the common-law immunity owed foreign officials, see Chapter 4 § V(D).

[242] *Samantar v. Yousuf*, 560 U.S. at 313; *see* Foreign Sovereign Immunities Act (FSIA), 28 U.S.C. §§ 1330, 1602.

[243] *Samantar v. Yousuf*, 560 U.S. at 325–26.

[244] *Id.* at 325–26. The Court was invited to consider these issues, in relation to canons of construction, but it avoided the questions. *Id.* at 319–20 & n.14 (declining to address argument that the need to preserve consistency with international law warranted broader construction of the FSIA, so as to secure immunity); *id.* at 320 (holding inapplicable the canon of construction that statutes should be interpreted consistently with the common law).

[245] *See, e.g.*, Yousuf v. Samantar, 699 F.3d 763, 773 (4th Cir. 2012) (noting that "immunity decisions turn upon principles of customary international law and foreign policy"); *id.* at 773 ("[W]e must draw from the relevant principles found in both international and domestic immunity law, as well as the experience and judgment of the State Department").

the status of federal common law,[246] while others may perpetuate the Supreme Court's more ambiguous depiction.[247]

As matters stand, courts appear most likely to treat customary international law as federal common law in two, or possibly three, circumstances. First, political branch measures may be deemed to authorize courts to treat customary international law as federal common law. *Erie* specifically reserved a role for federal common law in matters governed by statutes,[248] and such lawmaking does not seem confined to directly construing an enactment's terms.[249] Accordingly, just as in *Sosa*, federal courts may be authorized to apply customary international law not only when a federal statute explicitly creates a claim but also when a statute establishes jurisdiction predicated on customary international law and a cause of action is otherwise wanting.[250] In principle, the same authority may be inferred from nonjurisdictional statutes, treaties and congressional-executive agreements, or executive branch measures that have the force of law. In none of these cases, though, is customary international law being enforced as federal common law purely of its own accord.[251]

Second, treating customary international law as federal common law may be required by some aspect of the Constitution (separate, that is, from the judicial

---

[246] *See, e.g.*, United States v. Sinovel Wind Grp. Co., 794 F.3d 787, 792 (7th Cir. 2015) (noting that *Samantar v. Yousuf* "recognized some residual federal common law of foreign sovereign immunity").

[247] *See, e.g.*, Doğan v. Barak, 932 F.3d 888, 893–94 (9th Cir. 2019) (holding that permitting a Torture Victim Protection Act (TVPA) claim to proceed against an Israeli Defense Minister "would be to enforce a rule of law against the sovereign state of Israel," such that the minister "would therefore be entitled to common-law foreign sovereign immunity"). The characterization arguably bears on questions like the capacity of courts to develop an exception to that immunity for violation of peremptory (*jus cogens*) norms. The executive branch argued, concerning that question, that "courts have no authority to create federal common-law principles of foreign-official immunity, absent Executive Branch guidance," see Brief for United States as Amicus Curiae Supporting Affirmance at 25, Dogan v. Barak, 932 F.3d 888 (9th Cir. 2019) (No. 16-56704), but the court resolved against it on other grounds. *See Dogan*, 932 F.3d at 896–97.

[248] Erie R.R. Co. v. Tompkins, 304 U.S. 64, 78 (1938).

[249] Indeed, the point is that the "substance of th[e] rule is not clearly suggested by federal enactments." Martha A. Field, *Sources of Law: The Scope of Federal Common Law*, 99 HARV. L. REV. 881, 890–91 (1986) (emphasis omitted); *see* Am. Elec. Power Co. v. Connecticut, 564 U.S. 410, 421 (2011) (alluding to "subjects within national legislative power where Congress has so directed") (internal quotation marks omitted); Tex. Indus., Inc. v. Radcliff Materials, Inc., 451 U.S. 630, 640 (1981) (referencing matters "in which Congress has given the courts the power to develop substantive law").

[250] *See* Sosa v. Alvarez-Machain, 542 U.S. 692, 728 (2004) (citing "clear mandate" for federal claims under the Torture Victim Protection Act); *id.* at 729 (concluding that ATS was one of the "limited enclaves in which federal courts may derive some substantive law in a common law way"). On this view, *Sosa* is simply an example of the broader phenomenon of the "new" post-*Erie* federal common law. *See* Friendly, *supra* note 217, at 412–13 (describing premises of *Textile Workers v. Lincoln Mills*, 353 U.S. 448 (1957), in which federal jurisdiction over labor suits entailed authority to develop federal common law). *But cf. Sosa*, 542 U.S. at 726 (describing *Lincoln Mills* more narrowly as an example of a "haven of specialty" based on "express congressional authorization to devise a body of law directly").

[251] Thus, as declared in *Sosa*, federal courts were entrusted to "not recognize private claims under federal common law for violations of any international law norm." *Sosa*, 542 U.S at 732.

authority that Article III generally confers).[252] Courts may understand these requirements quite differently. On a broad view, the Constitution establishes an "assumed competence to make judicial rules of particular importance to foreign relations,"[253] which could entail substantial judicial authority to recognize the supremacy of customary international law.[254] Alternatively, courts may consider that the more fundamental constitutional norm, even for areas of profound national interest, is that the judiciary's role in foreign relations is subordinate to that of the political branches, which would suggest a much more minimal role in recognizing customary international law as federal common law.[255] Indeed, on such a view, claims for a constitutional basis are difficult to distinguish from a requirement of authorization by the political branches.[256]

Courts may seek to resolve this puzzle by reverting to how the Constitution and the law of nations were understood at the founding, something that authoritative scholarship by A.J. Bellia and Bradford Clark has explored.[257] The

[252] See, e.g., Am. Elec. Power Co., 564 U.S. at 421 (stating that federal common law is appropriate for "subjects within national legislative power . . . where the basic scheme of the Constitution so demands").

[253] This was how Sosa characterized Banco Nacional de Cuba v. Sabbatino, 376 U.S. 398, 427 (1964), while stating that "we have even assumed competence" on such occasions. Sosa, 542 U.S. at 726 (emphasis added); see also Tex. Indus., Inc., 451 U.S. at 641.

[254] See, e.g., RESTATEMENT (THIRD) § 111 rptrs. note 2 (suggesting that the reasoning in United States v. Belmont, 301 U.S. 324, 331 (1937), regarding national authority over foreign relations, "would apply" to establish supremacy of customary international law).

[255] Thus, Sosa cautioned that, notwithstanding the occasional "assumed competence" to establish rules of decision, that "the general practice has been to look for legislative guidance before exercising innovative authority over substantive law." Sosa, 542 U.S. at 726. Sabbatino suggested that the more sensitive the international matter, the greater the need for judicial deference or for leaving the matter exclusively to the political branches. See Sabbatino, 376 U.S. at 428; cf. Zschernig v. Miller, 389 U.S. 429, 432 (1968) (indicating that "the field of foreign affairs [is one] the Constitution entrusts to the President and the Congress").

[256] See, e.g., Al-Bihani v. Obama, 619 F.3d 1, 34 (D.C. Cir. 2010) (Kavanaugh, J., concurring in the denial of rehearing en banc) 34 ("After Erie and particularly after Sosa . . . it is clear that customary-international-law norms, like non-self-executing treaties, are not part of domestic U.S. law," since "when Congress does not act to incorporate those norms into domestic U.S. law, such non-incorporation presumably reflects a deliberate congressional choice"); Buell v. Mitchell, 274 F.3d 337, 376 (6th Cir. 2001) (holding that determining "whether customary international law prevents a State from carrying out the death penalty," when doing so would be constitutional, "is a question that is reserved to the executive and legislative branches of the United States government, as it their constitutional role to determine the extent of this country's international obligations and how best to carry them out").

[257] As they explain, this understanding distinguished the law merchant, the law maritime, and the law of state-state relations, with particular focus on the third—largely because the law of state-state relations entailed respect for "perfect rights," which if neglected and violated would have given just cause for war. BELLIA & CLARK, THE LAW OF NATIONS AND THE UNITED STATES CONSTITUTION, supra note 17, at 41–71. While the consequences of violating the law of nations were widely appreciated, see supra this chapter § I(A), the distinction of perfect rights is largely due to publicists like Vattel, whose influence on the founding generation is prone to being overstated. See supra this chapter text accompanying notes 8, 64–67. The case law, at least until recently, did not map onto these distinctions, nor describe particular kinds of rights as preconditions for the enforcement by federal courts of the law of nations. Indeed, as Bellia and Clark acknowledge, some foundational cases correspond imperfectly with perfect rights. See Bellia & Clark, The Federal Common Law of Nations, supra note 17, at 68 (noting that United States v. Peters, 3 U.S. (3 Dall.) 121 (1795), involved "a right derived

constitutional authority for judicial enforcement of customary international law might vary by the nature of the rule involved; this would warrant application of customary international law in U.S. law to respect traditional rights of U.S.-recognized foreign states, including against the United States and the states, but perhaps little else.[258] While this view is compatible with some modern rules,[259] it does not easily accommodate enforcing rules against foreign states, including on behalf of their own nationals,[260] and to date its appeal for the Supreme Court has been strongest for founding-era rights.[261] In any event, deciding which rules correlate sufficiently with constitutional design to warrant treatment as federal common law, and which do not, is prone to being criticized as the kind of judicial creativity and discretion that animated *Erie*'s critique of *Swift*-era jurisprudence.[262]

Including because modern authorities like *Sabbatino*, *Filartiga*, and the *Restatement (Third)* have suggested a more welcoming approach, courts are likely to entertain additional arguments for applying customary international law as federal common law. A third circumstance seems basic but plausible: customary international law may be applied as a federal rule of decision when both

---

from a perfect right," and *The Schooner Exchange v. McFaddon*, 11 U.S. (7 Cranch) 116 (1812), "that went beyond clearly defined perfect rights," but potentially averted war).

[258] *See* BELLIA & CLARK, THE LAW OF NATIONS AND THE UNITED STATES CONSTITUTION, *supra* note 17, at 188–268. In an earlier summary, they explained:

> [T]he best reading of Supreme Court precedent dating from the founding to the present is that the law of nations does not apply as preemptive federal law by virtue of any general Article III power to fashion federal common law, but only when necessary to preserve and implement distinct Article I and Article II powers to recognize foreign nations, conduct foreign relations, and decide momentous questions of war and peace.

Bellia & Clark, *The Federal Common Law of Nations, supra* note 17, at 9.

[259] *See* BELLIA & CLARK, THE LAW OF NATIONS AND THE UNITED STATES CONSTITUTION, *supra* note 17, at 218 (citing Paquete Habana, 175 U.S. 677 (1900)).

[260] *See* BELLIA & CLARK, THE LAW OF NATIONS AND THE UNITED STATES CONSTITUTION, *supra* note 17, at 199–211; *id.* at 270 (explaining that "[m]odern customary international law restricts how nations treat their own citizens within their own territory, and did not exist at the founding," with the consequence that "the Constitution contains no provisions designed to facilitate the application of such law in the U.S. legal system").

[261] *See* Nestlé USA, Inc. v. Doe, 141 S. Ct. 1931, 1941 (2021) (Gorsuch, J., concurring) (citing Bellia & Clark, *The Alien Tort Statute and the Law of Nations, supra* note 12, with regard to the need to provide judicial recourse for violation of perfect rights that might permit foreign states to engage in reprisals or war); Jesner v. Arab Bank, PLC, 138 S. Ct. 1386, 1416–17 (2018) (Gorsuch, J., concurring in part and concurring in the judgment) (same).

[262] As Bellia and Clark note, a broader view of the original constitutional allocation of foreign affairs powers might enable federal courts to "seek to preserve amicable relations by applying customary international law at least until the political branches direct otherwise." Bellia & Clark, *The Federal Common Law of Nations, supra* note 17, at 91. That suggestion has been embraced by those urging a broad approach to the federal-law character of customary international law. *Compare* Vázquez, *supra* note 206, at 1597–1609 (suggesting compatibility of Bellia-Clark position with the "modern position"), *with* BELLIA & CLARK, THE LAW OF NATIONS AND THE UNITED STATES CONSTITUTION, *supra* note 17, at 226–31, 263–65 (responding to Vázquez).

the need for a federal rule and capacity for uniformity is compelling, yet action by the political branches is wanting. A sufficient need may arise not only when U.S. culpability is at stake but also when the customary international law in question directly implicates interstate relations and interstate responsibility.[263] The capacity for uniformity is clearest when the rule is longstanding and well established, so as to mitigate concerns about discretionary lawmaking or inadvertent deviation from international obligations.[264] Enforcing longstanding and well-established customary international law is consistent with *Sosa*'s requirement that federal law claims under the ATS meet historical standards for definiteness, specificity, and universality.[265] Such caution would also ameliorate *Erie*-based concerns about the limited authority of federal courts.

[263] *Cf.* Clark & Bellia, *The Federal Common Law of Nations, supra* note 17 (emphasizing the significance of particular international norms to the friendly relations of the United States). This is arguably reflected in the criterion, most widely employed in the Second Circuit, that customary international law must be related to transgressions "of mutual, and not merely several, concern" to states. *See* Flores v. Southern Peru Copper Corp., 414 F.3d 233, 249–50 (2d Cir. 2003) (quoting Filartiga v. Pena-Irala, 630 F.2d 876, 888 (2d Cir. 1980)); *id.* at 249, (citing IIT v. Vencap, Ltd., 519 F.2d 1001, 1015 (2d Cir. 1975) (Friendly, J.) (defining customary international law as those "standards, rules or customs (a) affecting the relationship between states or between an individual and a foreign state, and (b) used by those states for their common good and/or in dealings inter se")); *accord* United States v. Bellaizac-Hurtado, 700 F.3d 1245, 1252, 1256 (11th Cir. 2012) (distinguishing drug trafficking and, generally, private criminal activity from matters of "mutual concern"). One component of that inquiry is whether such wrongs are not only of mutual concern in some abstract sense but are also—even if ostensibly internal in character, as in official torture, extrajudicial killings, and genocide—"capable of impairing international peace and security." *Flores*, 414 F.3d at 249; *see* Abdullahi v. Pfizer, 562 F.3d 163, 185 (2d Cir. 2009) (describing this as "[a]n important, but not exclusive, component" of the inquiry).

[264] The availability of well-developed rules has been understood as an important safeguard for federal common lawmaking authority. *See* Am. Elec. Power Co. v. Connecticut, 564 U.S. 410, 422 (2011) (noting that "'[a]bsent a demonstrated need for a federal rule of decision, the Court has taken 'the prudent course' of 'adopt[ing] the readymade body of state law as the federal rule of decision until Congress strikes a different accommodation,'" and that "where . . . borrowing the law of a particular State would be inappropriate, the Court remains mindful that it does not have creative power akin to that vested in Congress") (quoting United States v. Kimbell Foods, Inc., 440 U.S. 715, 740 (1979)).

[265] Sosa v. Alvarez-Machain, 542 U.S. 692, 725, 732 (2004). *Sosa* also cited with approval lower court ATS opinions consistent with this approach. *Id.* at 732–33. As *Filartiga* itself noted, that court's confidence in the universal and specific condemnation of torture was "diametrically opposed to the conflicted state of law that confronted the *Sabbatino* Court." *Filartiga*, 630 F.2d at 881 (citing Banco Nacional de Cuba v. Sabbatino, 376 U.S. 398, 428–30 (1964)). Indeed, *Sabbatino* and other non-ATS cases appear to make customary international law's relative clarity relevant in determining whether federal courts should confer federal status. *See Sabbatino*, 376 U.S. at 428 (explaining that "the greater the degree of codification or consensus" regarding a customary international law rule, "the more appropriate it is for the judiciary to render decisions regarding it, since the courts can then focus on the application of an agreed principle to circumstances of fact rather than on the sensitive task of establishing a principle not inconsistent with the national interest or with international justice"); *see also* Hamdan v. United States, 696 F.3d 1238, 1250 n.10 (D.C. Cir. 2012) (suggesting that "imposing liability on the basis of a violation of 'international law' or the 'law of nations' or the 'law of war' generally must be based on norms firmly grounded in international law") (citing *Sosa*, 542 U.S. at 724–38, and Hamdan v. Rumsfeld, 548 U.S. 557, 602–03 & n.34, 605 (2006) (plurality)), *overruled on other grounds*, Al Bahlul v. United States, 767 F.3d 1 (2014) (en banc).

This third circumstance and its parameters are speculative, and it may not be widely recognized as a basis for federal common law in the near future. Many potential exercises of judicial authority can instead be premised on statutory or constitutional bases. More important, decisions applying customary international law rarely require focusing on attributes (like supremacy) uniquely associated with the status of federal common law; as before *Erie*, what typically matters is whether federal courts may draw upon customary international law as an authoritative rule of decision, rather than whether state law is preempted or general federal question jurisdiction is established.[266] Lastly, any such category is hardly free of difficulty. Distinguishing the degree of uniformity required to warrant recognition as federal law from that necessary to recognize *any* customary international law norm would be challenging. It would also require acknowledging that other customary norms *not* meeting those standards will have a lesser status within the United States. Were the present Supreme Court ever to address the question, it might regard customary international law having this lesser status as similar in character to non-self-executing treaty provisions: international law of significance to the United States, and binding on the international plane, but perhaps not sufficient by itself to resolve claims presented to federal courts for decision.[267]

III. Limits on Incorporation

Debates about how customary international law is incorporated into U.S. law pose the question, not often confronted in actual practice, of whether customary international law is limited by state law. Sorting out the relationship with other forms of domestic law is only superficially easier. If custom has only the status of state law, its subordination to the types of federal law explicitly identified in the Supremacy Clause—the Constitution, statutes, and treaties—is reasonably straightforward.[268] It is more complicated otherwise, even if it enjoys the status

---

[266] As many have observed, it is difficult to find cases directly holding inapplicable a state or local law based on a perceived conflict with customary international law. In one case, the New York Court of Appeals held that Argentina was exempt from municipal property taxes based on a customary norm protecting consular offices from taxation, but it is not clear how contested the issue of supremacy was—and the court was clearly influenced by an as-yet-unratified convention negotiated by the United States. Republic of Argentina v. City of New York, 25 N.Y.2d 252, 257–61 (1969). Even in the pioneering case of *Filartiga*, the Second Circuit eschewed other potential jurisdictional theories that did not rely on customary international law, see *Filartiga*, 630 F.2d at 887, and it may not have been necessary to conclude that the rule in question had the status of federal law. *See* Vázquez, *supra* note 206, at 1505–06.

[267] *But see supra* note 206 (noting scholarship suggesting an intermediate, nonfederal status for most or all customary international law).

[268] As noted below, this is not entirely without complications—including for non-self-executing treaties and presidential actions.

of federal common law. Because customary international law is not specifically addressed in the Supremacy Clause, and because the clause gives little indication as to the hierarchy among even those types of law it does address, considering custom's place requires more comprehensive discussion.

A. Relationship with the Constitution

Though there is little judicial precedent, it is widely assumed that the Constitution trumps any contrary requirement based on customary international law.[269] Beyond a general intuition as to the Constitution's preeminence,[270] this assumption might reflect the established primacy of the Constitution over statutes (and the perceived difficulty of arguing that customary international law has a higher status than do statutes),[271] or the surmise that customary international law's position is unlikely to be more exalted than that of treaties—a form of international law that, like statutes, is certainly subordinate to the Constitution.[272]

To the extent customary international law limits the Constitution, it is by virtue of the latter's terms. For example, any limitation of Congress' authority under the Offences Clause to preexisting offenses is a limitation informed by customary international law, but it is imposed by the Constitution.[273] Of course,

---

[269] RESTATEMENT (THIRD) § 115(3) ("A rule of international law . . . will not be given effect as law in the United States if it is inconsistent with the United States Constitution."); United States v. Yunis, 924 F.2d 1086, 1091 (D.C. Cir. 1991) ("[T]he role of judges . . . is to enforce the Constitution, laws, and treaties of the United States, not to conform the law of the land to norms of customary international law."). Chief Justice Taney's infamous opinion in *Dred Scott* reported, tangentially, that "no laws or usages of other nations . . . can enlarge the powers of the Government, or take from the citizens the rights they have reserved." Scott v. Sandford, 60 U.S. (19 How.) 393, 451 (1856). The substance of that case has, however, been thoroughly renounced. Jamal Greene, *The Anticanon*, 125 HARV. L. REV. 379, 406–12 (2011); *see also* Mark W. Janis, Dred Scott *and International Law*, 43 COLUM. J. TRANSNAT'L L. 763 (2005).

[270] *See, e.g.*, Marbury v. Madison, 5 U.S. (1 Cranch) 137, 177 (1803) (describing a written constitution as "the fundamental and paramount law of the nation").

[271] Under the Supremacy Clause, only laws "made in Pursuance" of the Constitution "shall be the supreme Law of the Land." U.S. CONST. art. VI, § 2; *see also Marbury*, 5 U.S. at 180; McCulloch v. Maryland, 17 U.S. (4 Wheat.) 316, 423 (1819). For further discussion regarding statutes, see *infra* this chapter § III(B).

[272] *See* Reid v. Covert, 354 U.S. 1, 16 (1957) (plurality op.) ("[N]o agreement with a foreign nation can confer power on the Congress, or on any other branch of Government, which is free from the restraints of the Constitution"); *id.* at 17 (noting that holding otherwise "would permit amendment of that document in a manner not sanctioned by Article V"); *see also* Boos v. Barry, 485 U.S. 312, 324 (1988) (relying in part on *Reid v. Covert* in indicating that international law is a factor, at most, in First Amendment analysis); Finzer v. Barry, 798 F.2d 1480, 1483 (D.C. Cir. 1986) (Wald, C.J., dissenting) (objecting to "recogniz[ing] *de facto* the Law of Nations as superior to the Constitution . . . a result which has been soundly rejected by the Supreme Court," apparently relying on *Reid v. Covert*), *aff'd in part and rev'd in part*, Boos v. Barry, 485 U.S. 312 (1988). For further discussion regarding treaties, see *infra* this chapter § III(C).

[273] *See, e.g.*, United States v. Bellaizac-Hurtado, 700 F.3d 1245, 1249–51 (11th Cir. 2012); *see also* United States v. Arjona, 120 U.S. 479 (1887); *supra* this chapter text accompanying notes 93.

the principle of constitutional supremacy is purely domestic in character. Any domestic impotency leaves the international obligation unaffected,[274] as U.S. law itself acknowledges.[275]

In some contemporary cases involving individual rights, such as the compatibility of the death penalty with the Eighth Amendment, the Court has drawn on foreign and international sources, including (at least arguably) customary international law, to construe provisions of the Constitution.[276] These are part of a broader practice, of longer standing, in which foreign and international law is invoked by U.S. courts to buttress constitutional interpretation.[277] The merits of this revival, its significance to resolving particular cases, and the consistency of the Court's practice were hotly debated.[278] For immediate purposes, it suffices to note that there is no general principle that potential conflicts should be resolved by interpreting the Constitution to avoid breaches of customary international

---

[274] See, e.g., Applicability of the Obligation to Arbitrate Under Section 21 of the United Nations Headquarters Agreement of 26 June 1947, Advisory Opinion, 1988 I.C.J. 12, 34 ¶ 57 (Apr. 26) (recalling, in treaty context, "the fundamental principle of international law that international law prevails over domestic law").

[275] RESTATEMENT (THIRD) § 111 cmt. a; id. § 115 cmt. b; cf. Medellín v. Texas, 552 U.S. 491, 520 (2008) (noting that, even if international judgments were not domestic law, they "would still constitute international obligations, the proper subject of political and diplomatic obligations").

[276] See Chapter 10 § II(F). The Court's opinions do not identify or distinguish among those sources with particular care. See, e.g., Graham v. Florida, 560 U.S. 48, 80–81 (2010) (citing "the global consensus against the sentencing practice in question," and citing U.N. Convention on the Rights of the Child while noting that the United States was one of only two nations not to have ratified that treaty); Roper v. Simmons, 543 U.S. 551, 575–78 (2005) (citing "the laws of other countries" and "international authorities" as "instructive"); id. at 604–05 (O'Connor, J., dissenting) (asserting that the Court had "consistently referred to foreign and international law as relevant to its assessment of evolving standards of decency," and that "[a]t least, the existence of an international consensus of this nature can serve to confirm the reasonableness of a consonant and genuine American consensus"); Atkins v. Virginia, 536 U.S. 304, 316 n.21 (2002) (noting indicia of global disapproval of imposing the death penalty for crimes committed by the mentally disabled); see also Lawrence v. Texas, 539 U.S. 558, 573 (2003) (citing European Court of Human Rights opinion concerning invalidity of criminal prosecution of consensual homosexual conduct under the European Convention on Human Rights); Grutter v. Bollinger, 539 U.S. 306, 344 (2003) (Ginsburg and Breyer, JJ., concurring) (citing the International Convention on the Elimination of All Forms of Racial Discrimination, to which the United States was party, and the Convention on the Elimination of All Forms of Discrimination Against Women, to which it was not, regarding affirmative action).

[277] See generally Cleveland, supra note 141.

[278] The most extensive objection, Justice Scalia's dissent in Roper, emphasized the selective use. Roper, 543 U.S. at 608, 622–28 (Scalia, J., dissenting). Other opinions expressed the view that that such evidence was "meaningless" and the method "dangerous." Lawrence, 536 U.S. at 598 (Scalia, J., dissenting); see also Graham, 560 U.S. at 114 n.12 (Thomas, J., dissenting); Atkins, 536 U.S. at 324–25 (Rehnquist, C.J., dissenting); id. at 347 (Scalia, J., dissenting). There is an extensive academic discussion. See, e.g., Agora: The United States Constitution and International Law, 98 AM. J. INT'L L. 42 (2004). Both foreign and international standards have largely been ignored since, even in sharply contested cases. See, e.g., Jones v. Mississippi, 141 S. Ct. 1307 (2021) (upholding state statutory scheme permitting sentences of life without parole for juvenile offenders, over dissent by three justices); Brief of Amicus Curiae Amicus Populi in Support of Respondent at 28, Jones v. Mississippi, No. 18-1259, 141 S. Ct. 1307 (2021) (contrasting "American sentencing policy with that of other nations," in view of approach in Roper and Graham).

law, quite unlike the approach taken to statutory interpretation.[279] Instead, the premise of such interpretation is that it helps illuminate, or verify, the best reading according to U.S. constitutional methods, such as by lending clarity to what "cruel and unusual" means.[280]

B. Relationship with Federal Statutes

The Offences Clause envisions a harmonious relationship between domestic authority and the law of nations, according to which Congress discharges the nation's interest in punishing offenses against international law. So far as can be recovered, the possibility of *conflict* between statutes and international law was not carefully considered.

Following the Constitution's adoption, as potential conflicts emerged, so too did strategies for mediating them—with the unintended consequence that the rules concerning direct conflicts remains underdeveloped. The *Restatement (Third)* eventually described a simple, symmetrical later-in-time principle: an act of Congress prevails over an extant principle of customary international law, and a newly developed customary international law rule should, at least in principle, likewise prevail over a preexisting statute.[281] As explored in the following subsections, while the former position seems established, the latter has less support. Even a later-in-time statute remains tempered, however, by the canon that statutes should be construed, to the extent possible, so that they are consistent with international law.

1. Later-in-Time Statutes

Early constitutional discourse emphasized the significance to the United States of adhering to the law of nations. As part of that discourse, cases and commentary often asserted that congressional statutes could not alter the law of nations. While such assertions could be taken to indicate supremacy of the law of nations and to undermine the subsequent emergence of a later-in-time principle,[282] the premises seem to have been different. In part, commentators were working out potential distinctions between binding and more discretionary strands of the law

---

[279] See *infra* this chapter text accompanying notes 326–330 (discussing the *Charming Betsy* principle).

[280] See, e.g., *Graham*, 560 U.S. at 81 (noting that "[t]he question before us is not whether international law prohibits the United States from imposing the sentence at issue in this case"; rather, "[t]he question is whether that punishment is cruel and unusual").

[281] RESTATEMENT (THIRD) § 115 cmt. d. As finalized, the *Restatement (Third)* stated the first position with greater conviction. See *infra* this chapter text accompanying note 317.

[282] See, e.g., Jordan J. Paust, *Rediscovering the Relationship Between Congressional Power and International Law: Exceptions to the Last in Time Rule and the Primacy of Custom*, 28 VA. J. INT'L L. 393, 418–43 (1988).

of nations;[283] in part, they were unpacking a distinction between permissible national variations at the margins and core, unalterable principles.[284] In the main, though, these early accounts were stressing that Congress was unable to alter international rules as such on the *international* plane—not that it lacked the capacity, on the *domestic* plane, to alter the internal application of those rules.[285] Deviations were hardly encouraged, and those urging fidelity to the law of nations did sometimes suggest that it was unalterable in every regard, but mostly while relying on interpretive techniques to reconcile U.S. law with international law.[286]

[283] Vattelian distinctions between "voluntary" (binding) norms and merely "customary" rules based on state practice may have been at work; the appeal of such distinctions faded over time as the later-in-time rule emerged. *See* Dodge, *supra* note 65, at 536–44; *see also supra* this chapter text accompanying note 65. In *Ware v. Hylton*, for example, Justices Chase and Iredell indicated that a Virginia state statute would be valid even if it had violated the law of nations, but only because the international norm was "customary" in Vattel's weaker sense. Ware v. Hylton, 3 U.S. (3 Dall.) 199, 223–24, 227–29 (1796) (Chase, J.); *id.* at 263–66 (Iredell, J., concurring).

[284] *See* PETER S. DU PONCEAU, A DISSERTATION ON THE NATURE AND EXTENT OF THE JURISDICTION OF THE COURTS OF THE UNITED STATES 3 (1824) (stating that "[t]he law of nations . . . stands on other and higher grounds than municipal customs, statutes, edicts or ordinances," and "[e]very branch of the national administration, each within its district and its particular jurisdiction is bound to administer it . . . whenever it is not altered or modified by particular national statutes, or usages not inconsistent with its great and fundamental principles"); *see, e.g.,* Ross v. Rittenhouse, 2 U.S. (2 Dall.) 160, 162–63 (Pa. 1792) (stating that municipal law enforcing the law of nations "may . . . facilitate or improve the execution of its decisions, by any means they shall think best, *provided* the great universal law remains unaltered" and doubting that "the law of nations is counteracted, or infringed by [jury trials relating to captures]") (emphasis added); *id.* at 163 (concluding that "the Congress and Legislature of Pennsylvania had power and authority to make the alteration, in the mode of trial of facts litigated between citizens").

[285] *See, e.g.,* Miller v. The Resolution, 2 U.S. (2 Dall.) 1, 4 (Fed. Ct. App. 1781) ("The municipal laws of a country cannot change the law of nations, so as to bind the subjects of another nation"); Who Privileged from Arrest, 1 U.S. Op. Att'y Gen. 26, 27 (1792) (stating that the "obligation [of the law of nations] commences and runs with the existence of a nation, subject to modifications on some points of indifference," but noting that "[i]ndeed a people may regulate it so as to be binding upon the departments of their own government, in any form whatever; but with regard to foreigners, every change is at the peril of the nation which makes it"). This may have been the sense employed by George Nicholas in the Virginia debates. *See* 3 THE DEBATES IN THE SEVERAL STATE CONVENTIONS ON THE ADOPTION OF THE FEDERAL CONSTITUTION, *supra* note 70, at 502 (reportedly stating that "there was no such thing as a particular law of nations, but that the law of nations was permanent and general," and that "[i]t was superior to any act or law of any nation; it implied the consent of all, and was mutually binding on all"). Justices Iredell and Wilson, who wrote in *Ware*, appears to have appreciated the distinction between international continuation and domestic effect. *James Iredell's Memorandum on Attorney General Edmund Randolph's Report on the Judiciary, in* 4 THE DOCUMENTARY HISTORY OF THE SUPREME COURT OF THE UNITED STATES, *supra* note 59, at 542 (describing "necessary Law of Nations" as being "unrepealable by the Legislative Authority," meaning that "[w]hatever effect [an Act of Legislation] may have upon the People of that Country," it "can have none on the People of any other Country."); *James Wilson's Charge to the Grand Jury* (May 23, 1791), *in* 2 THE DOCUMENTARY HISTORY OF THE SUPREME COURT OF THE UNITED STATES *supra* note 59, at 166, 179 (conceding authority of a nation to alter either the voluntary or positive law of nations by municipal legislation with effect on its own citizens, but not "any farther").

[286] In the state setting, for example, the Mayor's Court of New York appeared to shrink from endorsing Alexander Hamilton's strong claim that a New York trespass statute was void because it was inconsistent with the law of nations. *Rutgers v. Waddington (N.Y. Mayor's Court 1784), reprinted in* 1 THE LAW PRACTICE OF ALEXANDER HAMILTON: DOCUMENTS AND COMMENTARY 393, 399–406 (Julius Goebel, Jr. ed., 1964). But the court felt "bound to exempt th[e] law" from application because

Case law seemed to concede that Congress had the constitutional authority to override customary international law if it expressed itself plainly enough.[287] Likewise, well-known declarations that courts should treat the law of nations as part of the law of the land, such as Chief Justice Marshall's opinion in *The Nereide*, typically assumed in the next breath that Congress retained the capacity to divest the courts of that power by enacting a superseding statute.[288] This might have been considered an inevitable byproduct of national sovereignty.[289] In addition, the emerging view of the law of nations as a single body of law, in which all norms (not just "voluntary" law) were binding, was leavened by a developing dualism that permitted national deviation even as the international obligation for the United States remained intact.[290] Where the law of nations limited congressional authority, it was because international law informed Article I limits and because the U.S. Constitution had deemed it relevant.[291]

The result was an increasingly clear commitment to the proposition that a later-in-time statute superseded, as a matter of U.S. law, all recognized forms of the law of nations. The Court in *The Paquete Habana* famously suggested in one passage that a legislative act, as well as executive acts, might be "controlling" in cases that also involved law-of-nations issues.[292] While this dictum proved confusing, and problematic, in the context of executive acts,[293] the possibility it

---

"[t]he repeal of the law of nations, or any interference with it, could not have been in contemplation" of the legislature, without resolving whether the statute might in theory have "revoked the law of nations" and bound the judiciary. *Id.* at 417; *see id.* at 282–315 (providing background); PHILIP HAMBURGER, LAW AND JUDICIAL DUTY 346–57 (2008) (situating *Rutgers* in broader discourse concerning equitable interpretation). For further discussion, see *infra* notes 335, 337.

[287] *See* Murray v. The Schooner Charming Betsy, 6 U.S. (2 Cranch) 64, 118 (1804); Talbot v. Seeman, 5 U.S. 1, 44 (1801). Some nineteenth century cases, like *The Schooner Exchange v. McFaddon*, 11 U.S. 116, 136–46 (1812), and *Brown v. United States*, 12 U.S. 110, 123–27 (1814), are more complex because the international norms at issue—given their customary (rather than "voluntary") nature, or exemptions contained within the rules themselves—arguably made them easier to reconcile with inconsistent municipal law. Dodge, *supra* note 65, at 542–44. For further discussion, see *infra* this chapter § III (B)(3).

[288] The Nereide, 13 U.S. (9 Cranch) 388, 423 (1815) (Marshall, C.J.) (stating that "[i]f it be the will of the government to apply to Spain any rule respecting captures which Spain is supposed to apply to us, the government will manifest that will by passing an act for the purpose," but that "[t]ill such an act be passed, the Court is bound by the law of nations which is a part of the law of the land").

[289] *See* HENKIN, FOREIGN AFFAIRS, at 235.

[290] *See* Dodge, *supra* note 65, at 544–53. Thus, for example, one Attorney General opinion that has been cited to illustrate the law of nations' primacy simply stressed congressional incapacity to alter the international obligations of the United States as such, even in the event domestic law were different. *See* Right of Expatriation, 9 Op. Att'y Gen. 356, 362–63 (1859) (opinion of Attorney General Black).

[291] *See, e.g.*, Military Commissions, 11 U.S. Op. Att'y Gen. 297, 299 (1865) (opinion of Attorney General Speed); *see also* Miller v. United States, 78 U.S. 268, 316 (1871) (Field, J., dissenting) (stating that "the only limitation" on war powers is the law of nations, which in imposing particular restrictions "is no less binding upon Congress than if the limitation were written in the Constitution").

[292] The Paquete Habana, 175 U.S. 677, 700 (1900).

[293] *See supra* this chapter § II(B)(3), and *infra* this chapter text § III(D).

indicated of superseding legislative acts—if incapable of being reconciled with the law of nations—has been widely endorsed.[294] Courts have frequently recognized, for example, that Congress may legislate without regard to jurisdictional limits on U.S. authority,[295] and generally upheld the legislative capacity to prescribe different standards or directly "interdict" rights established by international law.[296]

Because Congress does not routinely defy customary international law, and because many of these decisions simply assumed *arguendo* some conflict between a statute and international law,[297] courts have rarely had cause to explore the principle's contours. Future cases may confront more nettlesome questions. For example, it has not yet been necessary to clarify how conflicts should be

---

[294] RESTATEMENT (THIRD) § 115(1)(a) ("An act of Congress supersedes an earlier rule of international law . . . as law of the United States if the purpose of the act to supersede the earlier rule . . . is clear or if the act and the earlier rule . . . cannot be fairly reconciled"); *id.* § 115 cmt. a ("An act of Congress will also be given effect as domestic law in the face of . . . a preexisting rule of customary international law"); *see, e.g.,* The Over the Top, 5 F.2d 838, 842 (D. Conn. 1925) (stating, with respect to potential conflict between tariff law and the law of the sea, that "[i]nternational practice is law only in so far as we adopt it, and like all common or statute law it bends to the will of the Congress"); Tag v. Rogers, 267 F.2d 664, 666 (D.C. Cir. 1959) (stating, with respect to potential conflict between treaty and subsequently amended congressional statute, on the one hand, and customary international law, on the other, that "it has long been settled in the United States that the federal courts are bound to recognize any ["treaty, statute, or constitutional provision"] as superior to canons of international law"); Comm. of U.S. Citizens Living in Nicar. v. Reagan, 859 F.2d 929, 939 (D.C. Cir. 1988) (same); United States *ex rel.* Pfefer v. Bell, 248 F. 992, 995 (D.C.N.Y. 1918) (explaining that international law rules are "subject to the express acts of Congress, and the courts of the United States have not the power to declare a law unconstitutional, if it be within the authority given to Congress as to legislation, even though the law itself be in contravention of the so-called law of nations").

[295] *See, e.g.,* TMR Energy Ltd. v. State Prop. Fund of Ukraine, 411 F.3d 296, 302 (D.C. Cir. 2005) (upholding personal jurisdiction over a foreign state pursuant to a federal statute and contrary to an alleged international law restriction, and observing that "[n]ever does customary international law prevail over a contrary federal statute"); United States v. Yousef, 327 F.3d 56, 93 (2d Cir. 2003) ("If a statute makes plain Congress's intent . . . , then Article III courts, . . . must enforce the intent of Congress irrespective of whether the statute conforms to customary international law."). *See generally* Chapter 4 § 4(A).

[296] *See, e.g.,* Garcia-Mir v. Meese, 788 F.2d 1446, 1454–55 (11th Cir. 1986) (finding sufficiently clear expression of congressional intent to override asserted international legal norm against prolonged arbitrary detention).

[297] *See, e.g.,* Oliva v. U.S. Dep't of Justice, 433 F.3d 229, 232, 233–36 (2d Cir. 2005) (assuming, hypothetically, that a customary international law required consideration of whether removal was consistent with the best interests of the child, federal statute limiting relief controlled outcome); Bradvica v. INS, 128 F.3d 1009, 1014 n.5 (7th Cir. 1997) (holding that congressional standards for asylum must be applied in any event, but noting that international law objection likely lacked merit); Barrera-Echavarria v. Rison, 44 F.3d 1441, 1450–51 (9th Cir. 1995) (upholding detention on the basis of the attorney general's statutory authority, executive action, and judicial doctrine, which constituted a combination of "controlling acts," but noting doubts about international law objection); United States v. Yunis, 924 F.2d 1086, 1091 (D.C. Cir. 1991) (relying on statutory authority to authorize prosecution of those who take Americans hostage abroad no matter where the offense occurs or where the offender is found," and that the court's "inquiry can go no further," but also noting genuine prospect that jurisdiction was consistent with international law); United States v. Pinto-Mejia, 720 F.2d 248, 259–60 (2d Cir. 1983) (noting that Congress may choose to "legislate with respect to conduct outside the United States, in excess of the limits posed by international law," but noting that application at issue would not violate international norms), *modified on other grounds,* 728 F.2d 142 (2d Cir. 1984).

reckoned—whether, for example, a statutory scheme might be deemed to occupy a field and comprehensively displace international law.[298]

Another area of uncertainty concerns treatment of peremptory or *jus cogens* norms, those "accepted and recognized by the international community of States as a whole as a norm from which no derogation is permitted."[299] There is no authoritative international (let alone U.S.) roster of peremptory norms, but these plausibly include the prohibitions on aggression, genocide, slavery, racial discrimination and apartheid, crimes against humanity, and torture, as well as basic rules of international humanitarian law and the right to self-determination.[300] Notwithstanding that such norms are nonderogable on the international plane, both international law and U.S. law may afford immunity for foreign governments and foreign officials who have violated them.[301] More controversially yet, it is conceivable that Congress might encroach upon those norms by, for example, authorizing or immunizing a U.S. use of force that could be portrayed as aggression, or by authorizing or immunizing use by U.S. officials of enhanced interrogation techniques resembling torture.[302] Similar tensions may also arise as

---

[298] At least one decision implied that the full spectrum used in preemption analysis, including field preemption, might be invoked. *See* Galo-Garcia v. INS, 86 F.3d 916, 918 (9th Cir. 1996) (rejecting refugees claim for safe haven and nonreturn, based on customary international law, because the "extensive legislative scheme for the admission of refugees" constituted a controlling legislative act). *Cf.* Chapter 9 § II (discussing forms of preemption).

[299] Vienna Convention on the Law of Treaties, May 23, 1969, art. 53, 8 I.L.M. 679, 1155 U.N.T.S. 331 [hereinafter VCLT]; *see* Chapter 6(III) (describing U.S. reception of the VCLT as the customary international law of treaties).

[300] *See* Int'l L. Comm'n, Peremptory norms of general international law (jus cogens): Texts of the draft conclusions and Annex adopted by the Drafting Committee on second reading, Concl. 23 Annex, 73rd Sess., A/CN.4/L.967 (2022); *see also* Int'l Law Comm'n, Rep. on the Work of Its Fifty-Third Session, U.N. Doc. A/56/10, at 85 (2001), *reprinted in* [2001] 2 Y.B. Int'l L. Comm'n 1, 85, U.N. Doc. A/CN.4/SER.A/2001/Add.1 (providing similar list, in relation to state responsibility); RESTATEMENT (THIRD) § 102 cmt. k (indicating that "the principles of the United Nations Charter prohibiting the use of force" are peremptory in character), & § 702 cmt. n (including, inter alia, "the murder or causing the disappearance of individuals," and "prolonged arbitrary detention"); Tel-Oren v. Libyan Arab Republic, 726 F.2d 774, 791 n.20 (D.C. Cir. 1984) (Edwards, J., concurring) (citing commentators as identifying "at least four acts that are now subject to unequivocal international condemnation: torture, summary execution, genocide and slavery"); *cf.* RESTATEMENT (FOURTH) § 413 (describing universal jurisdiction over "certain offenses of universal concern, such as genocide, crimes against humanity, war crimes, certain acts of terrorism, piracy, the slave trade, and torture").

[301] *See* Chapter 4 §§ V(A) (foreign sovereign immunity), V(D)(1) (head of state (status-based) immunity), V(D)(2) (official (conduct-based) immunity).

[302] *Cf.* Saleh v. Bush, 848 F.3d 880, 893–94 (9th Cir. 2017) (declaring, in holding that U.S. officials accused of crime of aggression were entitled to immunity under the Westfall Act, that "Congress also can provide immunity for federal officers for *jus cogens* violations"); Ali v. Rumsfeld, 649 F.3d 762, 774–75 (D.C. Cir. 2011) (holding that where U.S. officials were acting within the scope of their employment, the Westfall Act required substitution of the United States as the defendant, and the Federal Tort Claims Act (FTCA) required dismissal for failure to exhaust administrative remedies of claims of torture and other mistreatment brought by Afghan and Iraqi detainees). *But cf.* Al Shimari v. CACI Premier Technology, 368 F. Supp. 3d 935, 944 (E.D. Va. 2019) (holding that the United States lacked sovereign immunity for violations of *jus cogens* norms, including third-party claims brought by military contractor accused of torture).

to norms that are not now regarded as peremptory,[303] rules on the margin of recognizably peremptory norms for which the terms remain unclear,[304] or some combination.[305] While a few decisions have hesitated over conflicts between U.S. statutes and peremptory norms,[306] it is unlikely that a U.S. court would even consider holding a later-in-time statute unenforceable based on anything less than clear-cut violation of a peremptory norm that had previously been accepted as peremptory by the U.S. political branches. Even then, the complex relationship on the international plane between *jus cogens* and other species of international law,[307] and a general reluctance by U.S. courts to recognize higher international norms,[308] will probably inhibit courts from adopting an exception to the primacy of domestic statutes.[309] It is thus unsurprising, for example, that

[303] For example, the obligation to abide by judgments of the International Court of Justice, which U.S. courts have rejected as a *jus cogens* principle. Comm. of U.S. Citizens Living in Nicar. v. Reagan, 859 F.2d 929, 940 (D.C. Cir. 1988).

[304] For example, a U.S. court might have to confront the question whether cruel, inhuman, and degrading treatment was either peremptory in its own right or an entailment of the fundamental obligation to refrain from torture—even if they readily acknowledged torture as a *jus cogens* violation. *See, e.g.,* Siderman de Blake v. Republic of Argentina, 965 F.2d 699, 717 (9th Cir. 1992) (identifying torture as a *jus cogens* violation); United States v. Emmanuel, 2007 WL 2002452, at *10 (S.D. Fla. 2007) ("It is beyond peradventure that torture and acts that constitute cruel, inhuman or degrading punishment, acts prohibited by jus cogens, are similarly abhorred by the law of nations"); *cf.* Pierre v. Gonzales, 502 F.3d 109, 113–15 (2d Cir. 2007) (illustrating difference between torture and other acts for purposes of U.S. law).

[305] For example, the United States has long regarded the crime of aggression, standing alone, as poorly defined. Harold Hongju Koh & Todd F. Buchwald, *The Crime of Aggression: The United States Perspective,* 109 Am. J. Int'l L. 257, 258, 261, 264–72 (2015).

[306] *See, e.g., Comm. of U.S. Citizens Living in Nicar.,* 859 F.2d at 936 (declining to "resolve th[e] uncertainty" as to the relationship between U.S. law and peremptory norms, given the conclusion that no peremptory norm had been established, but stating that if "Congress and the President violate a peremptory norm (or *jus cogens*), the domestic legal consequences are unclear"); *In re* Agent Orange Prod. Liab. Litig., 373 F. Supp. 2d 7, 131 (E.D.N.Y. 2005) ("Customary international law is binding upon all states . . . but may be modified within a state by subsequent legislation or a treaty, provided that the customary international law was not a peremptory norm (*jus cogens*).").

[307] *See* Martti Koskenniemi, Fragmentation of International Law: Difficulties Arising from the Diversification and Expansion of International Law: Report of the Study Group of the International Law Commission, ¶¶ 361–79, U.N. Doc. A/CN.4/L.682 (Apr. 13, 2006) (depicting relationship between *jus cogens* and other international norms). The fact that norms conflicting with *jus cogens* principles are invalid appears not to resolve the legitimacy of procedural obstacles to vindicating those principles, including norms relating to jurisdiction and immunity. *Id.* ¶¶ 372–73, *citing* Al-Adsani v. the United Kingdom (No. 35763/97), 2001-XI Eur. Ct. H.R. 101-02 (upholding state immunity despite alleged *jus cogens* violations); Case Concerning the Arrest Warrant of 11 April 2000 (Dem. Rep. Congo v. Belg.), Judgement, 2002 I.C.J. 3 (Feb. 14) (upholding official immunity for sitting foreign minister of the Democratic Republic of Congo against alleged *jus cogens* violations).

[308] Charter obligations have previously been deemed not to supersede congressional statutes, see, *e.g.,* Hitai v. Immigration and Naturalization Serv., 343 F.2d 466, 468 (2d Cir. 1965) (U.N. Charter provisions deemed non-self-executing, and therefore do not invalidate provision of immigration law); Vlissidis v. Anadell, 262 F.2d 398, 400 (7th Cir. 1959) (same), or have been deemed non-self-executing and unenforceable by U.S. courts. *See* Medellín v. Texas, 552 U.S. 491 (2008); *see also* Tel-Oren v. Libyan Arab Republic, 726 F.2d 774, 809 (D.C. Cir. 1984) (Bork, J., concurring) (Articles 1 and 2 of U.N. Charter not self-executing); U.S. v. Caro-Quintero, 745 F. Supp. 599, 614–15 & n.24 (C.D. Cal. 1990) (compiling case law relating to domestic enforcement of the U.N. Charter).

[309] Interestingly, while the *Restatement (Third)* accepted the principle of peremptory norms, it advised U.S. courts not to supersede international agreements on that basis. *See* Restatement (Third)

courts have routinely rejected claims that the FSIA is inapplicable to *jus cogens* claims,[310] even as some have shown willingness to override foreign official immunity premised on federal common law.[311] Although the case law has not established any particular practice, it may be expected that peremptory norms will prove most influential in the judicial construction of ambiguous statutes.[312]

2. Later-in-Time Customary International Law

Although U.S. doctrine is often expressed more cautiously—in terms of statutes' superiority over "earlier" or "preexisting" international law[313]—there are substantial indications of a simpler rule, according to which congressional statutes are hierarchically superior over conflicting customary international law, without regard to the relative time at which they became effective.[314]

Such a view may be different than at the founding. Those developing the Constitution might have been slow to confront the possibility that Congress would legislate in the teeth of the law of nations, but they might also have

§ 331 cmt. e (explaining that the *jus cogens* doctrine is of such "uncertain scope" that a "domestic court should not on its own authority refuse to give effect to an agreement on the ground that it violates a peremptory norm"). It also suggested the political branches would be similarly reluctant. *Id.* rptrs. note 4 (explaining that, because "there are no safeguards against their abuse . . . the United States is likely to take a particularly restrictive view of these doctrines, and they can be applied as international law accepted by the United States only with caution").

[310] Matar v. Dichter, 563 F.3d 9, 14 (2d Cir. 2009); Belhas v. Moshe Ya'Alon, 515 F.3d 1279, 1287 (D.C. Cir. 2008); Sampson v. Federal Republic of Germany, 250 F.3d 1145, 1156 (7th Cir. 2001); Smith v. Socialist People's Libyan Arab Jamahiriya, 101 F.3d 239, 242–45 (2d Cir. 1996); Princz v. Federal Republic Germany, 26 F.3d 1166, 1173–74 (D.C. Cir. 1994); Siderman de Blake v. Republic of Argentina, 965 F.2d 699, 719 (9th Cir. 1992); *see supra* Chapter 4(V).

[311] *See, e.g.,* Yousuf v. Samantar, 699 F.3d 763, 775–77 (4th Cir. 2012) (concluding that foreign officials are not entitled to conduct-based immunity for *jus cogens* violations); *see supra* Chapter 4 § V(D).

[312] *See infra* this chapter § III (B)(3) (discussing *Charming Betsy* principle).

[313] *See supra* this chapter note 294 (citing authorities). This may be especially appealing when the discussion is framed as relating to both customary international law and international agreements. *See, e.g.,* RESTATEMENT (THIRD) § 115(1)(a).

[314] *See, e.g.,* Oliva v. U.S. Dep't of Justice, 433 F.3d 229, 236 (2d Cir. 2005) (stating that "clear congressional action trumps customary international law") (internal quotations and citations omitted); TMR Energy Ltd. v. State Prop. Fund of Ukraine, 411 F.3d 296, 302 (D.C. Cir. 2005) ("*Never* does customary international law prevail over a contrary federal statute.") (emphasis added); Comm. of U.S. Citizens Living in Nicar. v. Reagan, 859 F.2d 929, 939 (D.C. Cir. 1988) (stating that "no enactment of Congress can be challenged on the ground that it violates customary international law"); United States v. Pinto-Mejia, 720 F.2d 248, 259 (2d Cir. 1983) ("Congress is not bound by international law."); Appropriation of Captured Property by the War and Navy Departments, 10 U.S. Op. Att'y Gen. 519, 521 (1863) (supposing that "in case an act of Congress should happen to conflict with a dogma of the 'public law,' so-called, the dogma must yield to what our Constitution declares to be 'the supreme law of the land,'" since even though "such a conflict may lead to diplomatic reclamations, and, possibly, to war . . . . that cannot make the act of Congress cease to be the law of the land, binding upon the people and their judges"). Most often, relative timing is simply ignored. *See, e.g.,* United States v. Yousef, 327 F.3d 56, 109 n.44 (2d Cir. 2003) (repudiating dicta in United States v. Javino, 960 F. 2d 1137, 1142–43 (2d Cir. 1992)); *id.* at 108 (stating that a "claim that principles of customary international law constrain Congress's power to enact laws that proscribe extraterritorial conduct is simply wrong").

considered it unlikely that the law of nations would develop so as to challenge previously enacted legislation. Among the binding, non-elective law of nations, much was derived from unchanging precepts of natural law or dictated by long-standing reason and practice. Properly designed U.S. institutions, moreover, would anticipate international law and so limit any possibility of conflict.[315] Modern customary international law may also anticipate few instances of later-in-time customary rules, for different reasons. Claims that an international rule has only freshly emerged are likely to be rare, for fear of undermining the willingness of courts or others to recognize it at all, and the prospect of recognizing a new rule in the teeth of U.S. statutory law (and, presumably, U.S. opposition) may decrease the likelihood still further.[316]

While acknowledging the lack of precedent, the *Restatement (Third)* suggested that, in principle, later-arising customary international law could supersede an earlier statute.[317] That principle may be supported, as it argued, by the presumed equivalence of customary international law and treaties under international law (and hence a presumed equivalence under U.S. law) and the fact that, according to U.S. doctrine, treaties and statutes abide by a symmetrical later-in-time principle.[318] It might also be argued that when Congress acts in full view of a preexisting customary norm, it can (if the statute is unambiguous) be understood to

[315] *See supra* this chapter text accompanying notes 63–70.

[316] Even putting aside any application of the "persistent objector" exception, which may safeguard states which have consistently opposed the application of a rule to themselves, U.S. opposition may play an outsized role in defeating the development of a norm for all states—certainly, as to whether that norm is likely to be acknowledged by a U.S. court. *See Yousef*, 327 F.3d at 92 n.25 (noting that although "it is not possible to claim that the practice or policies of any one country, including the United States, has such authority that the contours of customary international law may be determined by reference only to that country, it is highly unlikely that a purported principle of customary international law in direct conflict with the recognized practices and customs of the United States and/or other prominent players . . . could be deemed to qualify as a bona fide customary international law principle").

[317] *See* RESTATEMENT (THIRD) § 115 cmt. d (stating that "[i]t has also not been authoritatively determined whether a rule of customary international law that developed after, and is inconsistent with, an earlier statute or international agreement of the United States should be given effect as the law of the United States"); *see also id.* rptrs. note 4 (acknowledging that "[t]here seem to have been no cases in which a court was required to determine whether to give effect to a principle of customary law in the face of an inconsistent earlier statute or international agreement of the United States"). An earlier version stated more assertively that "[a] rule of international law . . . that becomes effective as law in the U.S. supersedes any . . . inconsistent preexisting provision of the law of the U.S." RESTATEMENT (THIRD) OF THE FOREIGN RELATIONS LAW OF THE UNITED STATES (Tent. Draft No. 1, 1980) § 135(1); *see* Harold G. Maier, *The Authoritative Sources of Customary International Law in the United States*, 10 MICH. J. INT'L L. 450, 479 (1989) (describing modification of provision and quoting testimony from Professor Henkin explaining the change); *see also* Henkin, *supra* note 227, at 1561–67; *see also supra* note 232 (noting suggestions that customary international law may never be superseded by domestic enactments).

[318] RESTATEMENT (THIRD) § 115 rptrs. note 4 (suggesting that the equivalence of customary international law and international agreements in both U.S. law and international law means that "arguably later customary law should be given effect as law of the United States, even in the face of an earlier law or agreement, just as a later international agreement of the United States is given effect in the face of an earlier law or agreement"—but noting possible concerns).

have intentionally put the United States in violation of it, whereas the same can hardly be said as to later-arising norms—and courts should not themselves force the United States into conflict.[319]

Nevertheless, as matters stand, courts will be slow to endorse this approach. The predicate, that subsequent customary international law constitutes binding federal law, may be fulfilled less often than the *Restatement (Third)* envisioned.[320] Even if that is surmounted, U.S. courts have other techniques for reconciling formally coequal sources of law.[321] In the circumstances at hand, they may grasp the opportunity to accept, *arguendo*, the proposition that a customary rule exists, while likewise assuming that it entered into force prior to a statute (or, at least, balking at finding definitively that it arose subsequently).[322] It is much less likely that they would take customary international law's iterative nature to mean that it is *inevitably* later in time, and if anything, arguments to that effect probably help secure the preference for applying statutes irrespective of any temporal order.[323]

All in all, it seems improbable that U.S. courts will recognize instances in which later-arising customary international law overrides statutory law.[324] It is

---

[319] This foreshadows possible warrants for the *Charming Betsy* principle. *See infra* this chapter § III (B)(3); Chapter 2 § II(E); and Chapter 4 § IV(B)(1).

[320] *Compare* RESTATEMENT (THIRD) § 115 cmt. d & rptrs. note 4 (noting, in explaining the proposed principle, that customary international law is "law of the United States," like international agreement), *with* this chapter *supra* text accompanying notes 123–129.

[321] Later customary international law might, for example, be likened to a general statute that does not expressly repeal a prior special statute. Rodgers v. United States, 185 U.S. 83, 87-89 (1902). *See generally* 1 A NORMAN J. SINGER & J.D. SHAMBIE SINGER, SUTHERLAND STATUTES AND STATUTORY CONSTRUCTION ch. 23 (7th ed. 2011). *But see infra* text accompanying note 361 (addressing whether earlier-in-time statutes should be subject to the *Charming Betsy* principle).

[322] The previously referenced case of *Yousef* may be instructive. The statutory provision at issue was adopted as part of the Aircraft Sabotage Act of 1984, Pub. L. No. 98-473, 98 Stat. 2187-88, while the asserted multi-factored test for a reasonableness limit to jurisdiction was reported in § 403 of the *Restatement (Third)*, published in 1987. United States v. Yousef, 327 F.3d 56, 108–09 (2d Cir. 2003). That test supposedly emerged as a rule prior to 1987, but after the *Restatement (Second)*. RESTATEMENT (THIRD) § 403 cmt. a & rptrs. note 10. Courts have sometimes referenced § 403 as reflecting customary international law, see Kiobel v. Royal Dutch Petroleum Co., 569 U.S. 108, 132 (2013) (Breyer, J., concurring); F. Hoffmann-La Roche Ltd. v. Empagran S.A., 542 U.S. 155, 165 (2004); Hartford Fire Ins. Co. v. California, 509 U.S. 764, 798–99 (1993); *id.* at 818 (Scalia, J., dissenting), but it was criticized during its drafting as lacking any basis in international law. *See, e.g.*, Laker Airways Ltd. v. Sabena, Belgian World Airlines, 731 F.2d 909, 950 (D.C. Cir. 1984). It would have been very difficult for the *Yousef* court to establish whether some critical development in its gestation occurred between 1984 and 1987.

[323] *But see* Paust, *supra* note 282, at 418 (arguing that "customary international law would necessarily be 'last in time,' since custom is either constantly re-enacted through a process of recognition and behavior involving patterns of expectation and practice or it loses its validity and force as law"). Customary international law is not usually supposed to be so ephemeral. *See* David J. Bederman, *Acquiescence, Objection and the Death of Customary International Law*, 21 DUKE J. COMP. & INT'L L. 31, 35–38 (2010); *e.g.*, Continental Shelf (Tunis. v. Libya), Judgement, 1982 I.C.J. 18, 115 ¶ 53 (Feb. 24) (separate opinion of Judge Aréchaga) (explaining that judicially recognized rules of customary international law may only be abrogated by new customary rules, since "[o]nly a legal rule may abrogate a pre-existing one").

[324] The *Restatement (Third)* notes the related point that "[c]ourts in the United States will hesitate to conclude that a principle has become a rule of customary international law if they are required to

thus unsurprising, all told, that courts have stated the later-in-time principle so as to favor later statutes but not, reciprocally, customary international law norms. One of the most direct considerations of the proposition that later customary norms took precedence over a prior statute—in the D.C. Circuit's decision in *Tag v. Rogers*—squarely rejected it.[325]

3. Presumption of Consistency

A tried-and-true technique for reducing conflict between U.S. statutes and customary international law—and, inadvertently, inhibiting the development of clearer rules concerning the hierarchy between those sources—has been a canon of construction that presumes consistency between statutes and international law, better known as the *Charming Betsy* principle. As Chief Justice Marshall pronounced in the namesake case, "an act of Congress ought never to be construed to violate the law of nations if any other possible construction remains."[326]

Attributing this principle to *Charming Betsy* is somewhat unfair.[327] The canon was not much used in that case, which concerned a vessel of U.S. origin captured by a French privateer and then recaptured by the U.S. Navy—posing the issue whether a U.S. statute restricting trade with the French by any person "resident within the United States or under their protection" reached a vessel owned at the time by a U.S.-born person who was a longtime resident of a neutral state. In deciding that it did not, the Court pronounced respect for international law respecting neutrals.[328] Still, it is hard to tell whether the law-of-nations canon did much work, as the Court indicated that the statutory text itself was best read as excluding foreign subjects;[329] the opinion also disclosed strikingly little

give it effect in the face of an earlier inconsistent statute"—which seems to suggest they would resolve any conflict by doubting the provenance of the norm. RESTATEMENT (THIRD) § 115 rptrs. note 4.

[325] Tag v. Rogers, 267 F.2d 664, 666 (D.C. Cir. 1959) (stating, in response to the claim that international law authoritatively prohibited certain seizures and confiscations during wartime and rendered "null and void" provisions of the Trading with the Enemy Act, that "[t]here is no power in this Court to declare null and void a statute adopted by Congress or a declaration included in a treaty merely on the ground that such provision violates a principle of international law").

[326] Murray v. Schooner Charming Betsy, 6 U.S. (2 Cranch) 64, 118 (1804). For further discussion, see Chapter 2 § II(E) and Chapter 4 § IV(B)(1).

[327] Those studying Chief Justice Marshall's contributions to the law of nations have attributed the interpretive canon to his prior opinion in *Talbot v. Seeman*. *See, e.g.*, Edward Dumbauld, *John Marshall and the Law of Nations*, 104 U. PA. L. REV. 38, 53 & n.75 (1955).

[328] *Charming Betsy*, 6 U.S. at 118.

[329] The Court stated that statutes should not be construed so as to "violate neutral rights, or to affect neutral commerce, further than is warranted by the law of nations as understood in this country," *Charming Betsy*, 6 U.S. at 118, but how this related to the statute's interpretation was unclear. One provision, to the Court, made the propriety of seizure depend on whether a vessel was sold with the purpose of violating the statute's prohibition of trade by U.S. citizens or others under U.S. protection—since otherwise the condemnation penalty would apply to all American vessels sold to neutrals just as it would when they were American-owned, an "extraordinary intent [which] ought to have been plainly expressed." *Id.* at 119. Its reading might have been driven by international law on neutrality, or by the presumption that profitable sales to neutrals should not be affected. *Id.* at 118.

about the international law violation being avoided.[330] An earlier opinion by Chief Justice Marshall had applied the same principle to greater effect. In *Talbot v. Seeman*, the Court considered whether a different statute permitted salvage, again in the case of a neutral ship retaken from the French;[331] there, Marshall had to acknowledge that "[t]he words of the act would certainly admit of [a contrary] construction,"[332] but nevertheless construed reference to ships retaken from "the enemy" as more narrowly applying to ships retaken from a *common* enemy of the United States and the neutral state.[333] According to the Court, that "not unreasonable . . . construction" would mean that "the act of congress will never violate those principles which we believe, and which it is our duty to believe, the legislature of the United States will always hold sacred."[334]

Such cases established what is now known as the *Charming Betsy* canon of construction,[335] while leaving important questions in their wake. One question

In either case, this added little to the text's focus on illegal trade by U.S. citizens, which the Court claimed would otherwise have been pointless for Congress to have inserted. *Id.* at 119. Having determined that condemnation was permitted only for defined vessels contemporaneously associated with the prohibited wrongdoing, which had to be by the stipulated persons, the Court still had to address whether this included a U.S. citizen born in the United States who had become a Danish subject resident outside of the United States. The Court thought such application would be inconsistent with U.S. conduct and prior case law, as well as "the very expressions of the act"—placing in doubt whether any external aids to construction were necessary. *Id.* at 120.

[330] Argument for the libellant (the captor) attempted to found a right to take the vessel on the law of nations governing a state of war, *id.* at 75, 76–80, 84, and argued in favor of salvage by contending that the alternative recourse in French courts would violate the international law of prize. *Id.* at 88–91 (citing Talbot v. Seeman, 5 U.S. (1 Cranch.) 1 (1801)). The claimant debated each point on its merits. *Id.* at 91–109, 112–15. Chief Justice Marshall only alluded to a vague potential for infringing neutral rights, *id.* at 118, and as to salvage, simply expressed doubt that the risks of illegal treatment in France were sufficiently imminent. *Id.* at 121. For additional background, see Frederick C. Leiner, *The Charming Betsy and the Marshall Court*, 45 AM. J. LEG. HIST. 1, 13–18 (2001).

[331] 5 U.S. (1 Cranch) 1 (1801).

[332] *Id.* at 43. One contraindication, indeed, was that the statute nominally governed ships belonging to the "subject of *any* nation in amity with the United States, if re-taken from the enemy." Act of March 2, 1799, § 7, 1 Stat. 709, 716.

[333] *Talbot*, 5 U.S. at 44. In that case, the neutral ship's state, Hamburg, was at peace with the French (not just with the United States).

[334] *Id.* at 44.

[335] At least a few earlier decisions suggested the same approach, also without stating authority. *See* Jones v. Walker, 13 F. Cas. 1059, 1064 (C.C.D. Va. 1800) (Jay, Cir. J.) (asserting that since a Virginia state statute restricting British subjects from bringing suit in Virginia courts would, if broadly applied after such subjects had ceased to be alien enemies, be "contrary to the laws and practice of civilized nations," such a construction should not be "adopted in case one more consonant to reason and the usage of nations can be found"—and identifying "a very obvious one" that would limit application to "fraudulent and collusive assignments" that might have arisen during wartime); *supra* note 286 (discussing *Rutgers v. Waddington*, a 1784 decision by the Mayor's Court of New York). The canon may have been linked to the principle in English and U.S. courts that statutes should be construed to be consistent with the common law, of which the law of nations was a part. Curtis A. Bradley, *The "Charming Betsy" Canon and Separation of Powers: Rethinking the Interpretive Role of International Law*, 86 GEO. L.J. 479, 487–88 (1998) (discussing this theory, and citing subsequent English cases). A more direct inspiration for Chief Justice Marshall may have been cases like *Heathfield v. Chilton*, (1767) 98 Eng. Rep. 50 (K.B.), 4 Burr. 2015, 2016 (Eng.), in which Lord Mansfield opined that a particular act of Parliament "did not intend to alter, nor can alter the law of nations." Lord Mansfield's

concerns the canon's rationale. Judicial adoption of the canon might anticipate the likely preferences of the legislature, advance U.S. compliance with international law, or serve the separation of powers by making the political branches more directly responsible for determining whether to breach international law.[336] Such differences are more theoretical than practical—all boil down to a (defeasible) estimation of legislative intent,[337] and by now Congress likely legislates in view of the canon regardless of its original warrant[338]—but might matter in any doctrinal re-evaluation. For example, an internationalist emphasis might apply a different standard to avoid unintentional violations of *jus cogens* norms, while a legislative intent or separation-of-powers approach might place less weight on customary international law altogether, or focus (per *Charming Betsy*) on the law of nations "as understood in this country."[339]

A second question concerns the statutory threshold for the canon's application. According to the *Restatement (Third)*, U.S. statutes should "[w]here fairly possible . . . be construed so as not to conflict with international law or with an international agreement of the United States."[340] Although the *Restatement (Fourth)* and judicial opinions have employed the same "[w]here fairly possible" construction,[341] it remains unclear what it means. Some cases, including *Charming Betsy* (from which the *Restatement (Third)* derived its phrasing),

---

views appear to have been known to Mayor Duane, who wrote *Rutgers v. Waddington*; allegedly, Lord Mansfield later wrote to explain that his view was *not* that the law of nations could supersede a statute (as opposed, seemingly, to influencing its interpretation). *See* HAMBURGER, *supra* note 286, at 351–52; Bellia & Clark, *The Federal Common Law of Nations, supra* note 17, at 25.

[336] For a clear discussion of these three approaches, and endorsement of the third, see Bradley, *supra* note 335.

[337] *See, e.g., Talbot,* 5 U.S. at 44 (referencing the virtue of seeing that "the act of congress will never violate those principles which we believe, and which it is our duty to believe, the legislature of the United States will always hold sacred"); *Rutgers, supra* note 286, at 417 ("The repeal of the law of nations, or any interference with it, could not have been in contemplation, in our opinion, when the Legislature passed this statute; and we think ourselves bound to exempt that law from its operation"); *accord* Murray v. Schooner Charming Betsy, 6 U.S. (2 Cranch) 64, 118–19 (1804). Modern cases offer little explanation beyond alluding to presumed congressional intent. *See, e.g.,* F. Hoffman–La Roche Ltd. v. Empagran S.A., 542 U.S. 155, 164 (2004) (explaining rule that ambiguous statutes will be construed to avoid "unreasonable interference with the authority of sovereign nations," and that "[t]his rule of construction reflects principles of customary international law—law that (we must assume) Congress ordinarily seeks to follow") (citing, inter alia, *Charming Betsy*); *accord* Weinberger v. Rossi, 456 U.S. 25, 32 (1982).

[338] McNary v. Haitian Refugee Ctr., Inc., 498 U.S. 479, 496 (1991) (stating, with respect to a different canon of construction, that "[i]t is presumable that Congress legislates with knowledge of our basic rules of statutory construction"); *cf.* Bradley, *supra* note 335, at 496–97 (considering this as variant of legislative intention approach).

[339] *Charming Betsy,* 6 U.S. at 118.

[340] RESTATEMENT (THIRD) § 114 & rptrs. note 1 (citing *Charming Betsy,* 6 U.S. at 118).

[341] The *Restatement (Fourth),* which did not address customary international law generally, used the same standard for resolving conflicts between statutes and international law governing jurisdiction to prescribe. RESTATEMENT (FOURTH) § 406; *see also id.* § 309 (using "[w]here fairly possible" standard to assess the compatibility of statutes and Article II treaties).

suggest something approaching a clear statement rule.[342] The higher burden that places on Congress is most appropriate when circumstances indicate that the conflicting customary rule has the status of federal law, which would render the situation closer to one of implied repeal[343]—and to the case when a statute and a self-executing treaty must be reconciled.[344] Some lower court opinions have suggested a less accommodating approach toward international law and would require that a threshold degree of statutory ambiguity must be established before the canon is applied.[345] While the *Restatement (Third)* moved away from any ambiguity requirement,[346] that position has clearly not solidified, as the division of opinions in a recent D.C. Circuit case, *Al-Bihani v. Obama*, reflects.[347]

[342] *Charming Betsy*, 6 U.S. at 118 (stating that "an Act of Congress ought never to be construed to violate the law of nations if any other possible construction remains"); *id.* at 119 (providing that "extraordinary intent" of Congress to violate the law of nations must be "plainly expressed" to be given effect by the courts); *see also* McCulloch v. Sociedad Nacional de Marineros de Hond., 372 U.S. 10, 21–22 (1963) (stating, in connection with claimed conflict between labor statute and "well-established rule of international law stating that the law of the flag state ordinarily governs the internal affairs of a ship," that Congress will be deemed to have enacted superseding laws only if "the affirmative intention of the Congress [is] clearly expressed") (quoting Benz v. Compania Naviera Hidalgo, S.A., 353 U.S. 138, 147 (1957)); The Schooner Adeline, 13 U.S. (9 Cranch) 244, 287 (1815) (applying enactment, despite inconsistency with the law of nations, because "the statute is expressed in clear and unambiguous terms"); Federal–Mogul Corp. v. United States, 63 F.3d 1572, 1581 (Fed. Cir. 1995) ("[A]bsent express Congressional language to the contrary, statutes should not be interpreted to conflict with international obligations."); Beharry v. Reno, 183 F. Supp. 2d 584, 599 (E.D.N.Y. 2002) (stating that "in order to overrule customary international law, Congress must enact domestic legislation which both postdates the development of a customary international law norm, and which clearly has the intent of repealing that norm"), *rev'd on other grounds sub nom.* Beharry v. Ashcroft, 329 F.3d 51 (2d Cir. 2003).

[343] *See supra* this chapter §§ III(B)(1)–(2).

[344] *See, e.g.,* Trans World Airlines, Inc. v. Franklin Mint Corp., 466 U.S. 243, 252 (1984) (in connection with perceived conflict between a repealing act and the self-executing Warsaw Convention, stating that "[t]here is . . . a firm and obviously sound canon of construction against finding implicit repeal of a treaty in ambiguous congressional action"). To be clear—and as is discussed later—the better view is that the *Charming Betsy* canon should be applied in reconciling statutes and treaties regardless of whether the latter are self-executing, but the warrant is nonetheless stronger in the event they are. *See generally* Chapter 6 § (IV)(C)(2).

[345] *See, e.g.,* United States v. Yousef, 327 F.3d 56, 92 (2d Cir. 2003) (stating that "[t]he *Charming Betsy* canon comes into play only where Congress's intent is ambiguous," or "where legislation is susceptible to multiple interpretations," as when "general words" are employed); *accord* Serra v. Lappin, 600 F.3d 1191, 1199–1200 (9th Cir. 2010); Oliva v. U.S. Dep't of Justice, 433 F.3d 229, 236 (2d Cir. 2005); Sampson v. Federal Republic of Germany, 250 F.3d 1145, 1152 (7th Cir. 2001); *cf.* F. Hoffmann–La Roche Ltd. v. Empagran S.A., 542 U.S. 155, 163 (2004) ("[T]his Court ordinarily construes ambiguous statutes to avoid unreasonable interference with the sovereign authority of other nations.").

[346] *See* RESTATEMENT (THIRD) § 115(1)(a) ("An act of Congress supersedes an earlier rule of international law . . . as law of the United States if the purpose of the act to supersede the earlier rule or provision is clear or if the act and the earlier rule or provision cannot be fairly reconciled."); *id.* § 115 cmt. a ("The courts do not favor a repudiation of an international obligation by implication and require clear indication that Congress, in enacting legislation, intended to supersede the earlier agreement or other international obligation."). A requirement of showing statutory ambiguity, or at least generality in a statute's terms, would be consistent with that taken by the *Restatement (Second)*. RESTATEMENT (SECOND) § 3(3) cmt. j ("[C]ourts in the United States interpret general or ambiguous words in statutes in a manner consistent with international law as understood by them.").

[347] Al-Bihani v. Obama, 619 F.3d 1 (D.C. Cir. 2010) (denying petition for rehearing en banc). *Compare id.* at 7–8 & n.6 (D.C. Cir. 2010) (Brown, J., concurring in denial of rehearing en banc)

Going forward, the most substantial challenge may be whether the *Charming Betsy* canon persists as a general norm or is instead disaggregated. The principle has long been broadly framed as one that similarly accommodates treaties and customary international law, but that may be hard to maintain; the strength of the presumption as to customary international law is certainly more contested in' contemporary case law.[348] Even as concerns customary international law, application of the *Charming Betsy* principle may vary. One recurring context has involved whether a U.S. law regulates persons or conduct outside U.S. territory or regulates foreign vessels in U.S. waters.[349] There, application of other interpretive canons, like the presumption against extraterritoriality[350] and the presumption against regulating the internal affairs of foreign vessels (even in U.S. territory),[351] tend to diminish the added value of the broader *Charming Betsy* principle— which shares with the other principles an overarching concern with "avoid[ing] unreasonable interference with the sovereign authority of other nations."[352]

The question of how far applying the presumption against extraterritoriality exhausts the potential service of the *Charming Betsy* in cases to which both might

---

(insisting on significance of requiring a threshold finding of ambiguity), *with id.* at 53–54 (Williams, J.) (suggesting broader inquiry into statutory meaning).

[348] With regard to treaties, as just noted, there may be increased pressure to differentiate between self-executing and non-self-executing treaty provisions. *See supra* this chapter text accompanying notes 142, 187.

[349] Some cases involving the canon concerned primarily foreign conduct. *See, e.g., Hoffman–La Roche*, 542 U.S. at 164. Other cases involved the application of U.S. law to foreign vessels in U.S. waters. *See, e.g.*, McCulloch v. Sociedad Nacional de Marineros de Honduras, 372 U.S. 10, 20–22 (1963). And still others concerned the application of U.S. law outside U.S. territory and to foreign entities. *See, e.g.*, Lauritzen v. Larsen, 345 U.S. 571, 578 (1953); United States v. Palmer, 16 U.S. (3 Wheat.) 610, 631 (1818); Murray v. Schooner Charming Betsy, 6 U.S. (2 Cranch) 64, 118–19 (1804); Talbot v. Seeman, 5 U.S. (1 Cranch) 1, 43–44 (1801); *see also* Cook v. United States, 288 U.S. 102, 120 (1933) (application of U.S. law to foreign vessel outside limit to U.S. territorial waters fixed by treaty). One of the relatively few exceptions to this pattern involved application of an employment discrimination statute abroad, but for the ostensible benefit of Americans employed at a U.S. naval facility; in that case, though, the mitigating international law obligation was based on treaty commitments. Weinberger v. Rossi, 456 U.S. 25, 32 (1982).

[350] *See, e.g.*, Morrison v. Nat'l Austl. Bank Ltd., 561 U.S. 247, 255 (2010) ("When a statute gives no clear indication of an extraterritorial application, it has none."); EEOC v. Arabian Am. Oil Co. (Aramco), 499 U.S. 244, 248 (1991) (citing a "longstanding principle of American law 'that legislation of Congress, unless a contrary intent appears, is meant to apply only within the territorial jurisdiction of the United States'") (quoting Foley Bros., Inc. v. Filardo, 336 U.S. 281, 285 (1949)). *See generally* Chapter 4 § IV(B) (discussing presumption).

[351] *See, e.g.*, Spector v. Norwegian Cruise Line Ltd., 545 U.S. 119, 130 (2005) (describing, as "narrow exception" to "[t]he general rule that United States statutes apply to foreign-flag ships in United States territory," principle that "[a]bsent a clear statement of congressional intent, general statutes may not apply to foreign-flag vessels insofar as they regulate matters that involve only the internal order and discipline of the vessel, rather than the peace of the port"). As apparent from the cases relied upon in *Spector, id.* at 130–31, the internal affairs doctrine was based on "the well-established rule of international law that the law of the flag state ordinarily governs the internal affairs of a ship." McCulloch v. Sociedad Nacional de Marineros de Honduras, 372 U.S. 10, 21 (1963) (citing Wildenhus's Case, 120 U.S. 1, 12 (1887)); *id.* at 21 (citing, additionally, the general *Charming Betsy* canon).

[352] *See Hoffman–La Roche*, 542 U.S. at 164.

apply principle is a fine one.[353] But broader arguments for a revised approach—like that of then-Judge Kavanaugh, who contended that the *Charming Betsy* canon should not be applied to customary international law and that the Supreme Court's "citation" in extraterritoriality contexts did not "not support invocation of the canon outside of that narrow context"[354]—seem misplaced, and have not persuaded other judges. Concerns that the principle may thwart congressional intent might well find similar fault with the presumption against extraterritoriality.[355] In all events, it should be recalled that when Congress speaks sufficiently directly, it overrides the *Charming Betsy* canon as completely as any other.[356]

C. Relationship with Treaties

It has sometimes been postulated that a later-in-time principle also governs, symmetrically, the relationship between customary international law and international agreements to which the United States is a party. Thus, the *Restatement (Third)* indicated that either an Article II treaty or a congressional-executive agreement, and "probably" a sole executive agreement, would supersede prior customary international law as U.S. law, and that subsequent customary international law would in turn prevail over prior agreements.[357] It acknowledged, however, the lack of authority for the latter proposition, and there have been no prominent examples since.[358]

---

[353] At least one opinion clearly indicates that the *Charming Betsy* canon operates to restrict statutes that satisfy the presumption against extraterritoriality. *See* Hartford Fire Ins. Co. v. California, 509 U.S. 764, 814–16 (1993) (Scalia, J., dissenting) (discussing use of the *Charming Betsy* canon to limit the reach of statutes when "the presumption against extraterritoriality has been overcome or is otherwise inapplicable").

[354] *Al-Bihani*, 619 F.3d 1, 35 (D.C. Cir. 2010) (Kavanaugh, J., concurring in the denial of rehearing en banc); *see id.* at 10 (arguing that the *Charming Betsy* canon applied solely to international law that has been "incorporated into U.S. law," and that in the event of ambiguity, a statute's construction would be entrusted to the president, either "within the bounds of reasonableness" or subject to presidential discretion in matters relating to war-making authority); *id.* at 34 (contending that "[a]fter *Erie*, and particularly after *Sosa* and *Medellín*, courts should not invoke the *Charming Betsy* canon to conform federal statutes to non-self-executing treaties and customary international law"). *Contrast, e.g., Aramco*, 499 U.S. at 264 (Marshall, J., dissenting) (describing the *Charming Betsy* canon as a "wholly independent rule of construction" from the presumption against extraterritoriality).

[355] *See* Chapter 4 § IV(B).

[356] *See, e.g., Hartford Fire Ins.*, 509 U.S. at 815 (Scalia, J., dissenting) (acknowledging that, notwithstanding presumption, Congress "clearly has constitutional authority" to "exceed . . . customary international-law limits on jurisdiction to prescribe"); *Lauritzen*, 345 U.S. at 578 (stating that the presumed consistency with international law "is not, as sometimes is implied, any impairment of our own sovereignty, or limitation of the power of Congress").

[357] RESTATEMENT (THIRD) § 115 cmt. d.

[358] *Id.; see also id.* rptrs note 4 ("There seem to have been no cases in which a court was required to determine whether to give effect to a principle of customary law in the face of an inconsistent earlier statute or international agreement of the United States").

It would be appealing to defer to international law for governing principles, since international agreements of the United States and customary international would also require reconciling on the international plane, and it is best to harmonize the law of the United States with U.S. international obligations where possible. Unfortunately, international law offers relatively little guidance. The *lex posterior* principle suggests that the later treaty or customary law should prevail, but that rule's complexity (including consideration of whether the states concerned are all parties to the treaty concerned, and the *lex specialis* principle favoring application of more specialized rules) and the limited guidance at present do not commend it to domestic courts.[359]

International law conflicts principles would not, in any event, address idiosyncrasies of U.S. law that may affect the standing of either source of law. U.S. courts are likely to give effect to a later-arising Article II treaty or congressional-executive agreement over a conflicting, preexisting customary norm. After all, as discussed in Chapter 6, later Article II treaties and congressional-executive agreements may supersede earlier statutes; since custom has no higher status in U.S. law than statutes, the same result should obtain for earlier customary rules.[360] But whether a later non-self-executing treaty provision or sole executive agreement would be deemed to supersede an earlier-arising customary norm is more speculative. The answer depends on whether a court would perceive each of the sources involved to enjoy the equivalent status of federal law, which (in the case of customary international law) may turn on its relationship with the U.S. Constitution and whether it has been endorsed by the political branches.[361]

The converse situation, involving later customary rules, is also complex. The choice as to whether to give effect to a later customary rule over a conflicting non-self-executing treaty provision or sole executive agreement might again depend on which sources were treated as having the status of federal law. Even assuming the later customary rule was treated as federal common law, it is unlikely that a court would apply that rule in lieu of a conflicting term in a self-executing treaty or congressional-executive agreement, as either would be deemed comparable to a statute for these purposes.[362] Exceptional circumstances might exist. If

---

[359] *See generally* Int'l Law Comm'n, Rep. on the Work of its Fifty-Eighth Session, U.N. Doc. A/61/10, at 416–23 ¶¶ 24–41 (2006) (Conclusions of the work of the Study Group on the Fragmentation of International Law), *reprinted in* [2006] 2 Y.B. Int'l L. Comm'n U.N. Doc. A/CN.4/SER.A/2006/Add.1 (Part 2); NANCY KONTOU, THE TERMINATION AND REVISION OF TREATIES IN THE LIGHT OF NEW CUSTOMARY INTERNATIONAL LAW (1994); MARK E. VILLIGER, CUSTOMARY INTERNATIONAL LAW AND TREATIES 59–60, 149–223; 195–200 (2d ed. 1997); Michael Akehurst, *The Hierarchy of Sources in International Law*, 47 BRIT. Y.B. INT'L L. 273 (1975). Drafters of the Vienna Convention on the Law of Treaties considered, but ultimately deleted, provisions which would have explicitly permitted subsequent custom to modify the terms of a treaty. VILLIGER, *supra*, at 195–200; Akehurst, *supra*, at 277.

[360] *See* Chapter 6 §§ IV(C)(2)–(3).

[361] *See* Chapter 6 § IV(A)(3).

[362] *See supra* text accompanying notes 314, 320 (describing difficulties associated with position that later-arising customary norms might prevail over preexisting statutes). This appears to be

international law itself indicated the superiority of the customary norm—much like it recognizes, for example, the obligation to follow peremptory norms, irrespective of their relative timing[363]—a U.S. court might apply it, particularly if U.S. precedent or determinate political-branch practice recognized the norm as being superior in character. Likewise, if the president has determined that an emergent rule of customary international law has superseded a preexisting treaty obligation of the United States, a U.S. court is likely to maintain consistency with the international practice of the United States. For example, the executive branch concluded that a 24-nautical-mile contiguous zone had become permissible under customary international law, thereby accomplishing a "supersession" of narrower U.S. rights under the 1958 Convention on the Territorial Sea and the Contiguous Zone. Because the president was deemed to have unilateral authority to make this determination for the United States, and the domestic legal force of a displaced treaty was deemed to be "generally no greater than its international law force," that determination was thought to mean that customary international law prevailed over the treaty as a matter of domestic law as well.[364]

D. Relationship with Executive Branch Conduct

The question of whether the president and subordinate executive branch officials may act in contravention of customary international law is intimately connected with issues previously discussed in this chapter, including the status of custom as federal law and the scope of the Take Care Clause. But it also poses the question of whether the president has the capacity to defy custom that would satisfy threshold requirements for standing as federal law.

Amid plentiful early reminders of the significance of international obligations to the United States and its officials, there were qualifications of potential import for the executive branch. In *Brown v. United States*, as noted earlier, Chief Justice Marshall's opinion—in holding that the customary norm in question did not

---

consistent with the practice of international tribunals, which have shown themselves to be reluctant to give effect to supervening custom in favor of treaty rules. KONTOU, *supra* note 359, at 132–34.

[363] *See* VCLT, *supra* note 299, art. 53 (providing that "[a] treaty is void if, at the time of its conclusion, it conflicts with a peremptory norm of general international law"); *id.* art. 64 (providing that "[i]f a new peremptory norm of general international law emerges, any existing treaty which is in conflict with that norm becomes void and terminates"); *see also* Int'l Law Comm'n, Rep. on the Work of its Fifty-Eighth Session, *supra* note 359, at ¶¶ 32–33.

[364] Convention on the Territorial Sea and the Contiguous Zone, Apr. 29, 1958, 15 U.S.T. 1606, 516 U.N.T.S. 206; *see* Memorandum from David Small, Assistant Legal Adviser for Oceans, International Environmental and Scientific Issues, Regarding Territorial Sea Convention (Apr. 5, 1989), *Digest of United States Practice in International Law 1991–1999*, U.S. DEPARTMENT OF STATE, https://perma. cc/FWX7-VQVS; *see also* Response of John McGinnis, Office of Legal Counsel (July 1, 1991), available at *id.* (deferring to the analysis of the Department of State regarding international law issues).

invest the president with the power to seize enemy property on U.S. soil upon the declaration of war, because that norm was "a guide which the sovereign follows or abandons at his will"—seemed to support the notion that some international obligations served neither to empower *nor* constrain the president, absent legislative implementation.[365]

To judge by present-day analyses, early signals pale by comparison next to *The Paquete Habana*. As previously noted, that decision declared that "[i]nternational law is part of our law" and held unlawful a naval admiral's detention of foreign fishing vessels; at the same time, it suggested that such law was relevant "where there is no treaty, and no controlling executive or legislative act or judicial decision."[366] This qualification has been construed as suggesting that an executive act might inhibit a court from enforcing international law,[367] but that was not evident in the case at hand, and the Court plausibly meant nothing of the kind.[368] The issue was simply whether the owner had some legal right that might be invoked to enable the vessel's recovery. The Court's response was to survey the possible domestic bases for such a right; so, absent a treaty, statute, case, or executive act (though the president and secretary of the navy had at points themselves required that international law be observed),[369] the court turned to the law of nations.[370] In short, the Court seemed to assume that custom could serve as binding legal authority,[371] but also that it might be applied as a last resort,

---

[365]   Brown v. United States, 12 U.S. (8 Cranch) 110, 128 (1814); *see supra* notes 167–170.

[366]   The Paquete Habana, 175 U.S. 677, 700 (1900); *see supra* note 216 (discussing implications for the president's obligation to conform to international law). For further discussion of *The Paquete Habana*, see *supra* this chapter §§ II(B)(3) and II(C)(1).

[367]   That broader reading would be more easily defended as an account of the relationship between customary international law and statutes or treaties (or, for that matter, the Constitution), as well as judicial decisions based on one of those sources. *See supra* this chapter § III (B) (statutes), § III(C) (treaties); *e.g.*, Tag v. Rogers, 267 F.2d 664, 666 (D.C. Cir. 1959) (claiming, in response to invocation of international law norms, that "[w]hatever force [claimant's] argument might have in a situation where there is no applicable treaty, statute, or constitutional provision," any of those sources are superior to international law rules, but omitting mention of executive acts) (citing *The Paquete Habana*); *accord* Comm. of U.S. Citizens Living in Nicar. v. Reagan, 859 F.2d 929, 939 (D.C. Cir. 1988).

[368]   For rival interpretations of this aspect of *The Paquete Habana*, see HENKIN, FOREIGN AFFAIRS, at 240–42; Bederman, *supra* note 209, at 120–22; William S. Dodge, *The Paquete Habana: Customary International Law as Part of Our Law, supra* note 163; *Agora: May the President Violate Customary International Law?*, 80 AM. J. INT'L L. 913 (1986) (contributions by Jonathan I. Charney, Michael J. Glennon, and Louis Henkin), and *Agora: May the President Violate Customary International Law? (Cont'd)*, 81 AM. J. INT'L L. 371 (1987) (contributions by Frederick L. Kirgis, Jr., Anthony D'Amato, and Jordan J. Paust). The perspective described here is close to that in Joseph M. Sweeney, *Quousque Tandem o Paquete Habana* (Letter to the Editor-in-Chief), 81 AM. J. INT'L L. 637 (1987).

[369]   *See supra* note 216 (noting presidential proclamations to abide by international law, and admiral's exchange with secretary of the navy).

[370]   *See The Paquete Habana*, 175 U.S. at 700 (stating that in the absence of other sources, "*resort must be had* to the law of nations") (emphasis added).

[371]   Justice Fuller's dissent disagreed that some "established" or "immutable" rule bound the president, who was left free "to apply, or to modify, or to deny altogether such immunity as may have been usually extended." *Id.* at 715, 720 (Fuller, J., dissenting). Beyond addressing the particular rule in question, he also suggested uncertainty that law of nations principles bound the sovereign, relying in

perhaps because it was harder to reckon.[372] The Court did not address whether executive conduct might actually be hierarchically superior to custom; that would have been unnecessary, given its confidence that the admiral had lacked authority from his superiors to conduct the seizure in the first place.[373] On this view, the Court was describing the law of nations as a supplement to other public laws that the judiciary might employ, more an alternative than a rival.[374]

Others have favored a more internally conflicted reading of *The Paquete Habana*, in which it recognized customary international law's domestic authority while describing the capacity of the political (and judicial) branches to defy it. In *Garcia-Mir v. Reagan*, the court of appeals appeared to accept that the U.S. attorney general had violated international law prohibitions against prolonged arbitrary detention that were nominally part of U.S. law, but held that the attorney general's involvement—exercising presumptively delegated authority from the president—qualified as a "controlling executive act" under *The Paquete Habana* that effectively immunized the violation.[375] *Garcia-Mir* was immediately controversial[376] but stands as the leading contemporary decision concerning the executive power to deviate from customary international law.[377] Not long

part on Chief Justice Marshall's opinion in *Brown v. United States*. *Id.* at 715 (Fuller, J., dissenting); for the majority's view, see *id.* at 710–11.

[372] Here Justice Gray echoed his earlier opinion in *Hilton v. Guyot*, 159 U.S. 113, 163 (1893) ("The most certain guide, no doubt, for the decision of such questions is a treaty or a statute of this country. But when, as is the case here, there is no written law upon the subject, the duty still rests upon the judicial tribunals of ascertaining and declaring what the law is, whenever it becomes necessary to do so, in order to determine the rights of parties to suits regularly brought before them."); *see The Paquete Habana*, 175 U.S. at 700 (citing *Hilton*). Notably, the judicial decisions mentioned in *The Paquete Habana* could make the task easier by "recognizing and enforcing that law," enabling future courts to ascertain its content. United States v. Smith, 18 U.S. (5 Wheat.) 153, 160–61 (1820).

[373] *The Paquete Habana*, 175 U.S. at 713 (noting, after reviewing correspondence, that "[t]he admiral's despatch assumed that he was not authorized, without express order, to arrest coast fishermen peaceably pursuing their calling; and the necessary implication and evident intent of the response of the Navy Department were that Spanish coast fishing vessels and their crews should not be interfered with," absent exceptional conduct).

[374] *See also The Paquete Habana*, 175 U.S. at 708 (concluding that rule existed "by the general consent of the civilized nations of the world, and independently of any express treaty or other public act"); *id.* at 708 (observing that prize courts are bound to take notice of the law of nations "in the absence of any treaty or other public act of their own government in relation to the matter"); *cf.* First National City Bank v. Banco Nacional de Cuba, 406 U.S. 759, 763 (1972) (citing *The Paquete Habana* as supporting "the general rule that a court of the United States, where appropriate jurisdictional standards are met, will decide cases before it by choosing the rules appropriate for decision from among various sources of law including international law").

[375] Garcia-Mir v. Meese, 788 F.2d 1446, 1454–55 (11th Cir. 1986). Invoking *The Paquete Habana*, the court also concluded that Congress had exercised its power "to interdict the application of international law" for a different class of claimants, *id.* at 1454, and concluded even that circuit precedent had established a "controlling judicial decision" in a prior case involving a constitutional due process objection. *Id.* at 1455 (citing Jean v. Nelson, 727 F.2d 957, 974–75 (11th Cir. 1984)).

[376] The decision inspired a symposium on *The Paquete Habana*. *See supra* this chapter note 368 (citing contributions).

[377] *Garcia-Mir* was particularly influential with regard to detention claims. *See, e.g.*, Gisbert v. U.S. Atty. General, 988 F.2d 1437, 1447–48 (5th Cir. 1993); Fernandez Luiz v. Luttrell, 46 F. Supp. 2d 754,

afterward, the Justice Department's Office of Legal Counsel (OLC), changing its view, upheld the authority of the FBI to apprehend and abduct a fugitive residing in a foreign state, notwithstanding that it violated customary international law. Although the issue might have been resolved on the basis of statutory authority, OLC emphasized that both Congress and the president were empowered by "the sovereign's right to override international law," and both *The Paquete Habana* and *Garcia-Mir* featured prominently.[378]

Finalized amid these developments, the *Restatement (Third)* attempted a compromise. It emphasized that "international law and agreements are law of the United States" that the president is constitutionally bound to observe. Still, the reporter's notes cautioned that "the President may have power to act in disregard of international law 'when acting within his constitutional authority.'"[379] This was notionally narrower than some readings of *The Paquete Habana*, insofar as it defined the president's presumptive obligation broadly, on the premise that customary international law is federal law, then suggested an exception for matters that the Constitution itself left to the president—evidently on the assumption that the constitutional grant of authority was indifferent as to whether it was discharged in keeping with international law.[380] Depending on the breadth of the constitutional exception, the bottom line was not necessarily different from cases like *Garcia-Mir*.[381]

One challenge to carrying forward the *Restatement (Third)* compromise is that, contrary to its more generous view, U.S. courts may not regard *all* customary international law as federal law.[382] To the extent courts regard a given

---

758 (W.D. Tenn. 1999); Tartabull v. Thornburgh, 755 F. Supp. 145, 149 (E.D. La. 1990); Sanchez v. Kindt, 752 F. Supp. 1419, 1432 (S.D. Ind. 1990).

[378] Authority of the Federal Bureau of Investigation to Override International Law in Extraterritorial Law Enforcement Activities, 13 Op. O.L.C. 163, 168–81 (1989) (citing error in Extraterritorial Apprehension by the Federal Bureau of Investigation, 4B Op. O.L.C. 543 (1980)).

[379] RESTATEMENT (THIRD) § 115 rptrs. note 3 (quoting Louis Henkin, *The Constitution and United States Sovereignty: A Century of Chinese Exclusion and its Progeny*, 100 HARV. L. REV. 853, 878–86 (1987)); *accord id.* (stating that "[t]here is authority for the view that the President has the power, when acting within his constitutional authority, to disregard a rule of international law"). *But see id.* (noting possibility that political question doctrine would be invoked).

[380] In his treatise, Professor Henkin explained the argument in terms that seemed reminiscent of *United States v. Curtiss-Wright Corp.*, 299 U.S. 304, 319–20 (1936): it would be a matter of the sovereign "power," "not right," of the United States to violate international law, and "presumably the President can exercise that power for the United States, acting under one of his explicit powers or under authority he derives from the powers of the United States inherent in its sovereignty," without invariably violating the Constitution. HENKIN, FOREIGN AFFAIRS, at 236.

[381] *Garcia-Mir* applied (or attempted to apply) the *Restatement (Third)* principle, as it then stood in draft. *See Garcia-Mir*, 788 F.2d at 1454–55. *But see infra* this chapter text accompanying notes 392–397 (discussing treatment of lower-level officials).

[382] *See* RESTATEMENT (THIRD) § 111(1) (stating that "[i]nternational law and international agreements of the United States are law of the United States and supreme over the law of the several States"); *see supra* this chapter note 232 (citing similar statements). *See generally* this chapter § II(C)(2).

rule as more akin to state common law, or at any rate a status below that of federal common law, it will be hard to assert that it constrains the president under the Take Care Clause.[383] That does not mean that the president is unconstrained. The international obligation would persist in any event, and any executive branch decision could still take sober account of the consequences for U.S. compliance and for general observance of the rule. For better or for worse, this is similar to other aspects of the president's responsibility for customary international law: for example, it is widely conceded that Congress can legislate in violation of international obligations, but it is the president's decision to sign a bill that usually determines whether the U.S. law becomes effective and establishes a potential violation.[384]

Another challenge for the *Restatement (Third)* approach lies in reckoning the scope of any exception for matters within the president's constitutional foreign relations authority. Virtually any act involving customary international law can be said to relate to foreign relations; at the same time, presidential authority rarely depends on the capacity to *violate* customary international law. While such violations have been described as an essential means by which the United States may contribute to the development (or abrogation) of international norms,[385] this diminishes alternatives that remain open to the president.[386] Moreover, the president is not the only U.S. actor capable of contributing.[387] Congress, in

[383] *See supra* this chapter text accompanying notes 171–188 (discussing Take Care authority).

[384] U.S. CONST. art. I, § 7, cl. 2; *see* Eber Bros. Wine & Liquor Corp. v. United States, 337 F.2d 624, 628 (Ct. Cl. 1964) ("[The president] alone can approve or veto legislation; that authority cannot be delegated. Whatever the help a President may have, the ultimate decision must be his."); *see also* U.S. CONST. art. I, § 7, cl. 2 (providing for veto override by two-thirds majority); *cf.* United States v. Buck, 690 F. Supp. 1291, 1301 (S.D.N.Y. 1988) (noting, skeptically, submission by U.S. government that the president's failure to recommend ratification of Protocol I to the Geneva Conventions constituted a "controlling executive act").

[385] *See, e.g.*, Jonathan I. Charney, *The Power of the Executive Branch of the United States Government to Violate Customary International Law*, 80 AM. J. INT'L L. 913, 917, 921–22 (1986). A variation is the argument that the president has the capacity to perform acts that terminate a customary international obligation—such as cooperating in creating a superseding obligation—that are comparable to the constitutional authority to terminate a treaty obligation. Louis Henkin, *The President and International Law*, 80 AM. J. INT'L L. 930, 934–36 (1986). But even if one accepts that the president has constitutional authority to unilaterally terminate treaties, see Chapter 6 § VI(B), customary international law does not share the consensual, or terminable, qualify of a treaty. *See* HENKIN, FOREIGN AFFAIRS, at 243.

[386] Executive branch officials may be able to influence custom while it is developing. Michael J. Glennon, *Can the President Do No Wrong?*, 80 AM. J. INT'L L. 923, 929–30 (1986). And once custom has been established, official declarations—not just transgressive acts—may exert influence, to the extent that any state can generate a change in the law. *See* COMM. ON FORMATION OF CUSTOMARY (GEN.) INT'L LAW, INT'L LAW ASS'N, *supra* note 1, at 13–16; Int'l Law Comm'n, Rep. on the Work of its Seventieth Session, *supra* note 1, at 133 (Conclusion 6).

[387] COMM. ON FORMATION OF CUSTOMARY (GEN.) INT'L LAW, INT'L LAW ASS'N, *supra* note 1, at 17 (noting that practice by "the executive, legislative and judicial organs of the State" may contribute to state practice); Int'l Law Comm'n, Rep. on the Work of its Seventieth Session, *supra* note 1, at 132 (Conclusion 5) ("State practice consists of conduct of the State, whether in the exercise of its executive, legislative, judicial or other functions.").

particular, remains free to change U.S. law and exert international influence by means that are more easily reconciled with constitutional principles, including by delegating authority to the president.[388]

On the approach suggested here, presidential conduct should only rarely pose quandaries regarding the domestic standing of customary international law. To the extent a customary rule conflicts with a statutory or constitutional assignment of authority to the president, courts are less likely to consider that rule as having the status as federal law in the first place.[389] Conversely, if a statute or the Constitution has imbued the rule with the authority of federal law, the president's authority to resist should be at its lowest ebb.[390] The greatest prospect for a constitutional stalemate is if the president violates customary international law that the judiciary deemed deserved federal-law status based on the need for a federal rule and the capacity for uniformity, but presumably the occasions on which such conflicts might arise will be few and far between.[391]

Violations by lower-level officials are likely to be more common, and their treatment under exceptions designed to protect presidential authority remains unclear. While it has been argued that the president alone[392]—possibly, including Cabinet-level officers as well[393]—has the capacity to issue "controlling executive acts" that override customary international law, such limitations are hard to defend. If the president does have authority to override otherwise binding customary law, that authority should be delegable elsewhere within the executive branch, unless delegation is barred by the Constitution or by statute.[394]

---

[388] *See* Glennon, *supra* note 386, at 929.

[389] *See supra* this chapter text accompanying notes 268–272.

[390] *See supra* this chapter text accompanying note 172. *See generally* Youngstown Sheet & Tube Co. v. Sawyer, 343 U.S. 579, 635–38 (1952) (Jackson, J., concurring) (describing three-tiered approach to evaluating presidential authority). For further discussion of *Youngstown*, see Chapter 1 § II(B) and Chapter 8 § II(B).

[391] *See supra* this chapter text accompanying notes 186–188.

[392] In *Garcia-Mir*, the court of appeals noted that the then-current drafts of the *Restatement (Third)* appeared to have dropped earlier statements that the president alone could authorize breaches of customary international law. Garcia-Mir v. Meese, 788 F.2d 1446, 1454–55 (11th Cir. 1986). The *Restatement (Third)* reporters later observed critically that the court in *Garcia-Mir* "failed to find any constitutional authority in the President to detain the aliens in question." RESTATEMENT (THIRD) § 115 rptrs. note 3. Professor Henkin subsequently made clear that he would require presidential authorization. HENKIN, FOREIGN AFFAIRS, at 243 ("[I]t should require an act of the President, not of some lower Executive official, and it should be an act that claims justification as an exercise of Presidential Foreign Affairs power"); *see also* Charney, *supra* note 385, at 921–22 & n.28 (distinguishing the president's "special role" in government and foreign affairs from that of Cabinet and other officers, who would not be authorized to violate international and domestic law).

[393] *See Garcia-Mir*, 788 F.2d at 1454 (explaining that while "*The Paquete Habana* does not support the proposition that the acts of Cabinet officers cannot constitute controlling executive acts," it "[a]t best [] suggests that lower level officials cannot by their acts render international law inapplicable," which would not support a "challenge . . . to the acts of the Attorney General").

[394] *See* Myers v. United States, 272 U.S. 52, 117 (1926) (noting breadth of presidential authority to delegate constitutional functions); Presidential Succession and Delegation in Case of Disability, 5 Op. O.L.C. 91, 94–95 (1981) (listing nondelegable presidential authority, including the power to

Executive branch officials remain constrained by the powers of their office, and their statutory or administrative instructions may require them to abide by international law;[395] still, that possibility does not support a general precondition that the president or a Cabinet official must be directly responsible before any executive act can be excused, if such an excuse is available to anyone.[396] Indeed, focusing on each office's constraints could better explain the language in *The Paquete Habana* about "controlling executive act[s]."[397] If conduct by executive branch officials that breaches customary international law is permissible at all, that exception should be limited to acts that are "controlling" in the sense of being authorized and directed according to other U.S. constitutional and statutory law, and consistent with such customary international law as U.S. courts deem to have domestic force.

IV. Contemporary Issue Areas

While the law of nations, now customary international law, has always been relevant to U.S. law, the domains have evolved substantially. For example, its influence in admiralty and maritime law slowly tapered off. The law of nations in that area—facilitated by Article III's grant of authority to federal courts[398]—supplied

make treaties (not including the power enter into executive agreements), the power to issue formal executive orders, and the power to serve as commander in chief of the army and navy).

[395] Numerous statutes, particularly on subjects touching the law of the sea, do require U.S. officials exercising regulatory authority to abide by international law, and not merely international agreements. *See, e.g.*, 16 U.S.C. § 1435(a) (2018) (marine sanctuaries); 16 U.S.C. § 1826a (2018) (port privileges based on high-seas large-scale driftnet fishing); Pub. L. No. 107-210, div. A, tit. III, § 344(b), 116 Stat. 987 (2002) (foreign mail transiting the United States); 33 U.S.C. § 1912 (2018) (pollution from ships); 33 U.S.C. § 2622 (protecting shorelines from waste).

Various regulations also incorporate such obligations. Some, like those relating to marine sanctuaries, mirror statute injunctions. *See, e.g.*, 15 C.F.R. § 922.4 (2020); 50 C.F.R. §§ 404.12, 665.906, 665.936, 665.966 (2019). In other instances, the regulations impose fresh restrictions. *See, e.g.*, 19 C.F.R. §§ 12.73(g), 12.80(b)(6), 12.85(c)(5) (2019) (exempting from various requirements diplomat-owned vehicles designated by the State Department for free entry). Of particular moment for *The Paquete Habana*, see 32 C.F.R. § 700.705 (requiring naval commanders to observe "the principles of international law"). For historical perspective, see QUINCY WRIGHT, THE CONTROL OF AMERICAN FOREIGN RELATIONS, *supra* note 123, at 167–68.

[396] In *Hampton v. Mow Sun Wong*, 426 U.S. 88 (1976), the Supreme Court held that a Civil Service Commission rule barring noncitizens from federal civil service employment violated due process—reasoning, in part, that while Congress or the president might be presumed to have national interests like foreign policy in mind were they to have established the rule, the same could not be assumed of the Commission. *Id.* at 104–05. This seems too remote to suggest a rule in this context, and the Court's interest in whether the Commission was actually required to adopt the rule in question is appropriate on any view. *Id.* at 105–14. *But see* Charney, *supra* note 385, at 922 n.28 (invoking *Hampton*); Elena Kagan, *Presidential Administration*, 114 HARV. L. REV. 2245, 2370–72 (2001) (suggesting readings of *Hampton* that link presidential participation to judicial deference).

[397] The Paquete Habana, 175 U.S. 677, 700 (1900).

[398] U.S. CONST. art. III, § 2, cl. 1 (providing that "[t]he judicial Power shall extend to ... all Cases of admiralty and maritime Jurisdiction ...").

a substantial portion of the Supreme Court's docket through the early nineteenth century[399] and was widely understood to establish a form of general common law.[400] Admiralty was federalized before the *Erie* revolution and largely withstood it.[401] U.S. doctrine gradually parted from customary international law to become an independent body of federal common law—only later to be dominated by federal statutory law and affected, to a lesser degree, by international agreements.[402]

Other areas, such as the law merchant, became disassociated from both customary international law and federal common law and today are regulated either by more positive forms of federal law (including international agreements) or by state common law.[403] This section discusses examples of areas in which customary international law plays a larger contemporary role—piracy and terrorism, as well as human rights. Other areas in which custom plays a substantial role, like the laws of war, recognition, and the immunity of foreign officials, are discussed in other chapters.[404]

A. Piracy and Terrorism

1. Piracy

Piracy's significance under international law and to the U.S. legal system has varied over the years. A substantial diplomatic problem for early presidents, addressed at least in small part by establishing U.S. courts with appropriate

[399] Ariel N. Lavinbuk, Note, *Rethinking Early Judicial Involvement in Foreign Affairs: An Empirical Study of the Supreme Court's Docket*, 114 YALE L.J. 855, 877–78 (2005).

[400] *See, e.g.*, BELLIA & CLARK, THE LAW OF NATIONS AND THE UNITED STATES CONSTITUTION, *supra* note 17, at 113–34; Fletcher, *supra* note 200; David P. Currie, *Federalism and the Admiralty: "The Devil's Own Mess,"* 1960 SUP. CT. REV. 158.

[401] S. Pac. Co. v. Jensen, 244 U.S. 205, 215 (1917) (stating that "in the absence of some controlling statute, the general maritime law, as accepted by the federal courts, constitutes part of our national law, applicable to matters within the admiralty and maritime jurisdiction"); Louise Weinberg, *Back to the Future: The New General Common Law*, 35 J. MAR. L. & COM. 523, 539 (2004) ("After *Jensen*, when admiralty lawyers refer to 'the general maritime law' they do not mean a kind of pre-*Erie* general common law. They mean *federal* common law") (emphasis in original).

[402] THOMAS J. SCHOENBAUM, ADMIRALTY AND MARITIME LAW 95 (5th ed. 2012); FALLON ET AL., *supra* note 189, at 692–93; for discussion of custom's diminished role, see Bederman, *supra* note 206; *e.g.*, Director, OWCP v. Perini North River Associates, 459 U.S. 297, 306–24 (1983) (applying congressional enactments subsequent to *Jensen*).

[403] BELLIA & CLARK, THE LAW OF NATIONS AND THE UNITED STATES CONSTITUTION, *supra* note 17, at 19–39 (describing historical significance); William S. Dodge, *Customary International Law, Change, and the Constitution*, 106 GEO. L.J. 1559, 1560 (2018) (noting that "[s]ome subjects like the law merchant have disappeared from customary international law altogether").

[404] *See, e.g.*, Chapter 8 § III(B) (regulating the military); Chapter 3 § IV(A) (recognition of a new foreign state); and Chapter 4 § V(D) (immunity of foreign officials).

jurisdiction,[405] piracy seemed to have waned in relevance before reviving as a substantial challenge to U.S. and international security.[406]

Legally speaking, the field continues to be defined in large part by customary international law, including for the United States. The U.S. code continues to advert to the crime of piracy "as defined by the law of nations,"[407] and general statutory references to the law of nations, as in the ATS, are understood to refer indirectly to the same concept.[408] Piracy in its international sense also determines the constitutional extent of legislative authority to "define and punish piracy" (as opposed to a felony committed on the high seas, an offense against the law of nations, or something else entirely), particularly as to matters arguably at the outer bounds of Congress' reach.[409] For example, the Maritime Drug Law Enforcement Act (MDLEA) facially applies to stateless or foreign vessels on the high seas,[410] provoking examination whether drug smuggling may constitutionally be defined and punished as piracy or a felony.[411]

In the background is the fundamental question whether "piracy" should be understood as it was traditionally defined by the law of nations, or rather according to contemporary customary international law. Courts have shown a consistent impulse toward modernity, which includes acceptance that the customary international law of piracy is informed by treaties, not all of which the United States has ratified—like the U.N. Law of the Sea Convention.[412] Even

---

[405] See supra this chapter § II(A)(1); see also Chapter 7 § I(A) (discussing early attempts to address piracy through international institutions).

[406] See, e.g., S.C. Res. 1816, ¶ 7 (June 2, 2008) (authorizing states, for six-month period, to enter Somalia's territorial waters and use all necessary means to repress piracy consistent with international law); id. ¶ 9 (disclaiming any creation of new customary international law); see also S.C. Res. 2608, ¶¶ 14, 15 (Dec. 3, 2021) (extending related authority).

[407] 18 U.S.C. § 1651 (2018) (providing that "[w]hoever, on the high seas, commits the crime of piracy as defined by the law of nations, and is afterwards brought into or found in the United States, shall be imprisoned for life").

[408] Sosa v. Alvarez-Machain, 542 U.S. 692, 725 (2004).

[409] U.S. CONST. art. I, § 8, cl. 10; see supra this chapter § II(A)(1).

[410] Pub. L. No. 99-570, 100 Stat. 3207 (1986) (codified as amended at 46 U.S.C. 70501-07 (2018)). For foreign-registered vessels or vessels in foreign territorial waters, the foreign state concerned must either consent or (in the former case only) waive objection, as may be conclusively determined by State Department certification. Id. § 70502(c)(1)(C)–(E), (c)(2).

[411] See, e.g., United States v. Nueci-Peña, 711 F.3d 191, 196–98 (1st Cir. 2013); United States v. Estupinan, 453 F.3d 1336, 1338–39 (11th Cir. 2006); United States v. Moreno-Morillo, 334 F.3d 819, 824–25 (9th Cir. 2003); United States v. Martinez-Hidalgo, 993 F.2d 1052, 1056 (3d Cir. 1993); see also United States v. Suerte, 291 F.3d 366, 372–75 (5th Cir. 2002) (discussing Article I authority in resolving due process objections); United States v. Davis, 905 F.2d 245, 248–49 (9th Cir. 1990) (concluding that Constitution permitted extraterritorial application of statute, but also opining that "there must be a sufficient nexus between the defendant and the United States" to satisfy due process). The MDLEA is not alone in taking a more expansive view of U.S. jurisdiction over high-seas felonies. See, e.g., United States v. Saac, 632 F.3d 1203, 1209–11 (11th Cir. 2011) (holding that Drug Trafficking Vessel Interdiction Act of 2008 (DTVIA), 18 U.S.C. § 2285 (2018), is constitutional exercise of Article I authority over high-seas felonies regardless of nexus to the United States).

[412] See U.N. Convention on the Law of the Sea, Dec. 10, 1982, art. 101(a)–(c), 1833 U.N.T.S. 397, 436 [hereinafter UNCLOS] (defining piracy as consisting of "acts of violence or detention, or any act of depredation, committed for private ends by the crew or the passengers of a private ship or a private

courts considering statutory references to piracy "as defined by the law of nations" generally invoke contemporary customary international law,[413] as have courts considering the offense as an exemplary tort under the ATS.[414] So long as the statutes are framed in general terms, a modernized approach is encouraged by the *Charming Betsy* canon, as it better ensures the compatibility of U.S. law with international constraints.[415]

The constitutional question could be thought to invite a different approach. Article I, Section 8, Clause 10 authority over "Piracies" might be limited to that category as it was originally understood by the law of nations (as robbery on the high seas), or administered according to contemporary customary international law. Similarly, but to opposite effect, the same provision's authority over "Felonies committed on the high Seas" may adhere to the original and more expansive understanding of "high Seas," or contract due to the contemporary expansion of other maritime zones.[416] Arguably felonies jurisdiction, or any expansive understanding of piracy, should be limited to conduct enjoying some connection with the United States, as opposed to assuming the kind of universal jurisdiction associated with general piracy.[417]

aircraft," directed against a ship or aircraft, or people aboard the ship or aircraft, on the high seas or outside the jurisdiction of any state); *see also* Geneva Convention on the High Seas, Apr. 29, 1958, art. 15, 13 U.S.T. 2312, 450 U.N.T.S. 11 (providing similar definition).

[413] Thus, for example, one court concluded that acts of violence involving no taking of property and committed by those who boarded a vessel on the high seas only as captives, nonetheless fell within the modern piracy statute—providing, like the 1819 act, for punishment of those "commit[ting] the crime of piracy as defined by the law of nations"—by virtue of modern international law. United States v. Dire, 680 F.3d 446, 451, 454–69 (4th Cir. 2012) (construing 18 U.S.C. § 1651 (2018)). *But cf.* United States v. Bellaizac-Hurtado, 700 F.3d 1245, 1248 (11th Cir. 2012) (citing prior case law defining piracy as robbery on the high seas).
[414] *See* Inst. of Cetacean Research v. Sea Shepherd Conservation Soc'y, 725 F.3d 940, 943–44 (9th Cir. 2013) (holding, in light of UNCLOS, that the "private ends" required for piracy need not involve financial enrichment, and so would include acts of a political character by private parties, and that the requisite "acts of violence" could include the destruction of property).
[415] *See, e.g.,* United States v. Ali, 718 F.3d 929, 936 (D.C. Cir. 2013) (construing the general aiding and abetting (18 U.S.C. § 2(a) (2018)) and conspiracy (18 U.S.C. § 371) provisions in relation to acts connected to piracy, but not themselves taking place on the high seas, in light of the *Charming Betsy* principle and the UNCLOS definition of piracy, which the court concluded made "defining piracy . . . a fairly straightforward exercise").
[416] *See* UNCLOS, *supra* note 412, arts. 2–4, 57, 86 (defining high seas as beginning, potentially, 200 miles from the baseline, complementing the coastal state's territorial waters and exclusive economic zone). Although the U.S. understanding of the term "high seas," and the Supreme Court's construction of statutory references thereto, has narrowed over time, see *In re* Air Crash off Long Island, New York, on July 17, 1996, 209 F.3d 200, 205–15 (2d Cir. 2000), this might not be applied in construing the Constitution. *But cf.* Hoopengarner v. United States, 270 F.2d 465, 470 (6th Cir. 1959) (concluding, based on statutory precedent, that "[t]he Great Lakes come within the definition of 'the high Seas,' as used in the Constitution") (citing United States v. Rodgers, 150 U.S. 249 (1893)).
[417] *See* United States v. Cardales-Luna, 632 F.3d 731, 739–51 (1st Cir. 2011) (Torruella, J., dissenting) (arguing that the MDLEA would be unconstitutional as applied to persons and activity without any nexus to, or impact in, the United States) (citing Eugene Kontorovich, *Beyond the Article I Horizon: Congress's Enumerated Powers and Universal Jurisdiction over Drug Crimes*, 93 MINN. L. REV. 1191 (2009)).

Of course, regulation of piracies and related conduct may have other constitutional authorization, including as offenses against the law of nations, or as exercises of the treaty power or the authority over admiralty and foreign commerce.[418] Still, should the margins of the authority over piracy and felonies ever be tested, it seems questionable to limit that authority to the strict confines of their original subjects, or to hold that only conduct resembling the classic understanding of piracy is entitled to universal jurisdiction. Congress nowadays may be more willing to exceed international rules concerning jurisdiction,[419] and modern case law more readily accepts that the Constitution grants Congress the authority to violate international law.[420] The presumption against extraterritoriality, and the *Charming Betsy* canon, effectively measure whether Congress has intended to regulate more aggressively.[421] If and to the extent Congress explicitly exceeds the internationally accepted boundaries of its jurisdiction, there is no obvious reason why it should be viewed as constitutionally circumscribed.[422]

[418] *See, e.g.*, United States v. Shi, 525 F.3d 709, 720–22 (9th Cir. 2008) (supporting constitutionality of criminal prosecution under 18 U.S.C. § 2280(b)(1)(C) (2018), entailing jurisdiction over certain acts of maritime violence, on bases that the statute defined and punished a high-seas felony, that it defined and punished the international offense of piracy, and that it was necessary and proper to implement U.S. treaty obligations). *But see Cardales-Luna*, 632 F.3d at 738–51 (Torruella, J., dissenting) (considering, and rejecting, various arguments for MDLEA constitutionality).

[419] Objections to the constitutionality of the MDLEA, for example, depend heavily on passages in the Supreme Court's decision in United States v. Furlong, 18 U.S. (5 Wheat.) 184 (1820). *See Cardales-Luna*, 632 F.3d at 745 (Torruella, J., dissenting) (citing *Furlong*, 18 U.S. at 196–97). *Furlong*, however, not only emphasized the risk of foreign objection, but also estimated as a matter of statutory interpretation that Congress would not have intended to punish criminal offenses "with which they had no right to interfere." *Furlong*, 18 U.S. at 198; *see supra* this chapter § II(A)(1) (discussing *Furlong*). By contrast, Congress in enacting the MDLEA not only explicitly sought to extend its reach beyond the territorial jurisdiction of the United States, see 46 U.S.C. § 70503(b) (2018), and declined to treat U.S. jurisdiction over a vessel as an element of an offense, *id.* § 70504(a), but also denied that individuals had standing to raise international law defenses, stating that "[a] failure to comply with international law does not divest a court of jurisdiction and is not a defense to a proceeding" under the statute. *Id.* § 70505; *see* United States v. Bellaizac-Hurtado, 779 F. Supp. 2d 1344, 1347 (S.D. Fla. 2011) (explaining that preclusion of international law defenses under § 70505 was due to the fact that the statute incorporated international law standards for jurisdiction, and otherwise reserved standing to protest to foreign states rather than individuals), *rev'd on other grounds*, 700 F.3d 1245 (11th Cir. 2012).

[420] *See supra* this chapter text accompanying notes 287–296.

[421] *See* Chapter 4 § IV(B) (presumption against extraterritoriality); *see also supra* this chapter text accompanying notes 353–356 and Chapter 2 § II(E) (discussing *Charming Betsy* canon).

[422] *Cardales-Luna*, 632 F.3d at 743 n.12 (Torruella, J., dissenting) (acknowledging contrary authorities); *see, e.g.*, United States v. Suerte, 291 F.3d 366, 373–75 (5th Cir. 2002) (upholding constitutionality of MDLEA against jurisdictional nexus challenge); United States v. Saac, 632 F.3d 1203, 1209–11 (8th Cir. 2011) (upholding constitutionality of Drug Trafficking Vessel Interdiction Act of 2008 (DTVIA), without requiring jurisdictional nexus); *see also* Brief for the United States in Opposition at 4, Garcia v. United States, 549 U.S. 1110 (2007) (No. 06-236) (explaining that "[b]y its terms, the High Seas Clause authorizes Congress to punish any felony committed on the High Seas, without limitation," and "[t]here is no requirement that the felony prohibited must have some demonstrated effect on the United States' relations with foreign powers").

2. Terrorism

Although acts of terrorism are often analogized to piracy,[423] they are quite different as a matter of customary international law. Beginning in earnest with the D.C. Circuit's decision in *Tel-Oren v. Libyan Arab Republic*,[424] a number of U.S. decisions have concluded that there is an insufficient consensus concerning terrorism's definition to support recovery on the basis of international law.[425] To be sure, some violations may be distinguished.[426] But courts are likely particularly reluctant to conclude not only that international law prohibited the relevant form of terrorism but also that such prohibition satisfied the ATS, discussed in the next section, or some other statutory basis for U.S. jurisdiction.

Judicial wariness regarding international law guidance on terrorism, together with a preference for codification in criminal matters, led to congressional intervention. Unlike piracy statutes, which have incorporated law-of-nations standards, these statutes define terrorism as a matter of U.S. law (and somewhat inconsistently, at that).[427] For the short term, this means that international

---

[423] *See, e.g.*, Pub. L. No. 103-272, § 1(e), July 5, 1994, 108 Stat. 1241 (codified at 49 U.S.C. § 46502) (defining hijacking as "aircraft piracy").

[424] Tel-Oren v. Libyan Arab Repub., 726 F.2d 774, 796 (D.C. Cir. 1984) (Edwards, J.) (stating, in light of "disharmony" on the international plane, that "I cannot conclude that the law of nations . . . outlaws politically motivated terrorism, no matter how repugnant it might be to our own legal system"); *accord id.* at 806–07 (Bork, J., concurring).

[425] *See, e.g.*, Nahl v. Jaoude, 968 F.3d 173, 184–89 (2d Cir. 2020) (Walker, J., concurring) (concluding that the plaintiffs had not established that international law directly prohibits individuals, as opposed to states, from financing terrorist acts); In re Terrorist Attacks on September 11, 2001, 714 F.3d 118, 125 (2d Cir. 2013) (concluding that "because no universal norm against 'terrorism' existed under customary international law (i.e., the 'law of nations') as of September 11, 2001" the claims were without merit); United States v. Yousef, 327 F.3d 56, 106–08 (2d Cir. 2003); In re Chiquita Brands Int'l, Inc. Alien Tort Statute & S'holder Derivative Litig., 792 F. Supp. 2d 1301, 1317 (S.D. Fla. 2011).

[426] *See* Almog v. Arab Bank, PLC, 471 F. Supp. 2d 257, 285 (E.D.N.Y. 2007) (concluding that "organized, systematic suicide bombings and other murderous attacks against innocent civilians for the purpose of intimidating a civilian population are a violation of the law of nations," supporting a cause of action under the Alien Tort Statute); *cf. In re Chiquita Brands Int'l*, 792 F. Supp. 2d at 1316 n.8, 1321 (disagreeing with *Almog* and distinguishing it as concerning specific allegations of suicide bombings and assassinations of civilians, as opposed to other acts of terrorism).

[427] One provision lists something like fifty statutory criminal offenses as "Federal crimes of terrorism." 18 U.S.C. § 2332b(g)(5) (2018). *See also* 18 U.S.C. § 2331 (defining "international terrorism" under the Anti-Terrorism Act as consisting of acts that "appear to be intended (i) to intimidate or coerce a civilian population; (ii) to influence the policy of a government by intimidation or coercion; or (iii) to affect the conduct of a government by mass destruction, assassination or kidnapping"); 50 U.S.C. § 1801(c)(2) (adopting substantially the same approach under Foreign Intelligence Surveillance Act of 1978); 6 U.S.C. § 444(2)(A)–(B) (defining "acts of terrorism," for purposes of securing coordination with Homeland Security, as those that are "unlawful" and cause damage to U.S. persons, property, or entities as "further defined and specified by the Secretary"); 8 U.S.C. § 1182(a)(3)(B)(ii) (defining "terrorist activity," for purposes of admissibility of noncitizens, as any that would be unlawful where committed (or which would be unlawful were it committed in the United States) and that involves, inter alia, attacks on third parties to influence the policy of any government, attacks on aircraft and other vessels, or the use of chemical, biological, or nuclear weapons). *See generally* Nicholas J. Perry, *The Numerous Federal Legal Definitions of Terrorism: The Problem of Too Many Grails*, 30 J. LEGIS. 249 (2004).

law approaches to terrorism, while of continuing relevance to cases like those arising under the ATS, have less direct bearing on adjudication under the Anti-Terrorism Act and various criminal provisions.[428] In the longer term, any emerging customary international law regarding terrorism will confront a patchwork of U.S. definitions, posing risks of inconsistency between U.S. law and international rules.[429]

B. Human Rights

1. Alien Tort Statute (ATS)

The ATS, adopted as part of the Judiciary Act of 1789, was one of the first indications of how the United States intended to treat customary international law (then, the law of nations).[430] Since 1980, when the Second Circuit Court of Appeals revitalized the ATS in *Filartiga v. Pena-Irala*,[431] the ATS has also been understood as a central vehicle for incorporating international human rights law into U.S. law. Like everything about the statute, even its name,[432] the degree to which the ATS originally embraced this objective has been controversial. Scholars examining the statute's origins have attributed objectives ranging from a cosmopolitan interest in redressing violations of international law[433] to a narrower interest in avoiding U.S. culpability for certain wrongs committed against foreigners, such as a U.S. citizen's assault on a foreign ambassador in the United States.[434] The focus, under virtually any depiction, has been on the law of

---

[428] *See, e.g.*, Biton v. Palestinian Interim Self-Gov't Auth., 510 F. Supp. 2d 144, 146 (D.D.C. 2007) (concluding that the absence of international consensus was irrelevant, given the definition of "international terrorism" under the Anti-Terrorism Act). The Alien Tort Statute remains relevant to potential civil actions by noncitizens, as the Anti-Terrorism Act is limited to U.S. nationals. 18 U.S.C. § 2333 (2018); *see also* Rothstein v. UBS AG, 708 F.3d 82, 94–98 (2d Cir. 2013) (suggesting additional limitations concerning secondary liability and proximate cause).

[429] *Cf.* United States v. Yousef, 327 F.3d 56, 107 n.42 (2d Cir. 2003) (citing varied U.S. approaches to terrorism under domestic statutes as further confounding the definition of terrorism under international law).

[430] *See supra* this chapter § II(A) and Chapter 4 § I(C).

[431] 630 F.2d 876 (2d Cir. 1980).

[432] For a period, some preferred referring to the statute as the "Alien Tort Claims Act" (and "ATCA"), while others favored "Alien Tort Statute" or "Alien Tort Act." This dispute was effectively settled by the Supreme Court, which has steadily referred to the "Alien Tort Statute" (most thoroughly in *Sosa v. Alvarez-Machain*). *See* Corrie v. Caterpillar, Inc., 503 F.3d 974, 979 n.5 (9th Cir. 2007) (noting varying usage) (citations omitted); *see also* Argentine Republic v. Amerada Hess Shipping Corp., 488 U.S. 428, 432 (1989) (using "Alien Tort Statute").

[433] *See, e.g.*, Anne-Marie Burley, *The Alien Tort Statute and the Judiciary Act of 1789: A Badge of Honor*, 83 Am. J. Int'l L. 461 (1989); William R. Casto, *The Federal Courts' Protective Jurisdiction over Torts Committed in Violation of the Law of Nations*, 18 Conn. L. Rev. 467 (1986).

[434] The wrongs on which the statute is said to have focused range from safe conduct violations, see Thomas H. Lee, *The Safe-Conduct Theory of the Alien Tort Statute*, 106 Colum. L. Rev. 830 (2006), to a variety of intentional torts committed against a noncitizen's person or private property, see Bellia & Clark, *The Alien Tort Statute and the Law of Nations, supra* note 12.

nations. While the ATS also established jurisdiction for torts based on violation of a "treaty of the United States," such claims were much less common, even after the statute's revival in 1980,[435] and it became better known as a proving ground for customary international law in U.S. courts.

Following *Filartiga*, the Supreme Court let matters percolate in the lower courts for roughly two decades before rendering its first major decision on the ATS, *Sosa v. Alvarez-Machain*, in 2004.[436] As described previously, *Sosa* took a cautious view of the judicial capacity to develop federal common law.[437] Consistent with that approach, the Court only guardedly accepted use of the ATS to vindicate the customary international law of human rights. Describing the statute as "in terms only jurisdictional,"[438] the Court understood Congress to have provided a "limited, implicit sanction to entertain the handful of international law *cum* common law claims understood in 1789"—violation of safe conduct, infringement of the rights of ambassadors, and piracy. It also allowed, however, that courts exercising jurisdiction under the ATS might recognize other claims that "rest on a norm of international character accepted by the civilized world and defined with a specificity comparable to the features of the[se] 18th-century paradigms."[439]

Sosa thus accepted a dynamic, but conspicuously limited, role for customary international law in human rights cases. The standard it imposed seemed demanding. In calling for "definite content" (or "specificity") and "acceptance among civilized nations" like that of its paradigm norms, the Court required

---

[435] 28 U.S.C. § 1350 (2018); *see* Kenneth C. Randall, *Federal Jurisdiction over International Law Claims: Inquiries into the Alien Tort Statute*, 18 N.Y.U. J. INT'L L. & POL. 1, 46 (1985) (observing that plaintiffs alleged treaty violations less frequently, such that the treaty basis under the ATS "has been left largely unexamined"). *See generally* Chapter 6 § IV(A)(3) (citing examples). One challenge is that the United States has tended to ratify multilateral human rights treaties subject to conditions providing that key provisions are non-self-executing, which may then be taken to prevent invoking the treaty as such for ATS claims. *E.g.*, Sosa v. Alvarez-Machain, 542 U.S. 692, 735 (2004) (explaining that "the United States ratified the [International Covenant on Civil and Political Rights] on the express understanding that it was not self-executing and so did not itself create obligations enforceable in the federal courts," such that the plaintiff properly assumed the obligation to show that the relevant norm "has attained the status of binding customary international law"); Aldana v. Del Monte Fresh Produce, N.A., 416 F.3d 1242, 1247 (11th Cir. 2005) (per curiam) (same, concerning cruel, inhuman, and degrading treatment). Following *Medellín v. Texas*, 552 U.S. 491 (2008), a noncitizen with a treaty-based claim may be asked to show both that the treaty is self-executing and that it affords private rights—and, even if a treaty is being invoked to evidence customary international law, may need to overcome the argument that U.S. ratification of the treaty on a non-self-executing basis signals the will of the political branches and precludes treating even customary international law as a basis for an ATS claim. *Id.* at 524–25 (citing Youngstown Sheet & Tube Co. v. Sawyer, 343 U.S. 579, 635–38 (1952) (Jackson, J., concurring)). *See generally* Chapter 6 §§ IV(A)(3), (7).

[436] 542 U.S. at 692.

[437] *See supra* this chapter text accompanying notes 235–239.

[438] *Sosa*, 542 U.S. at 712, 725; *see also id.* at 713 (rejecting position that the ATS "was intended not simply as a jurisdictional grant, but as authority for the creation of a new cause of action for torts in violation of international law").

[439] *Id.* at 712, 725; *accord id.* at 732.

that claims be based in "binding customary international law" proved by reference to established sources,[440] as opposed to "new and debatable violations of the law of nations."[441] Some of this could be understood as simply requiring rigor in evaluating customary international law claims, much as would an international tribunal. However, the Court's insistence that the rules invoked be comparable to eighteenth-century torts imposed a more anachronistic, and distinctively national, limit. The definiteness and acceptance requirements also reflected the Court's insistence that claims be administrable by U.S. courts,[442] and addressed concerns about the consequences of opening those courts to controversial claims.[443] Sosa indicated other potential principles that might limit the availability of claims for violations of customary international law, such as an exhaustion requirement,[444] though it did not directly adopt any. Evaluating the arbitrary detention claim at issue, the Court found it too ill-defined and lacking in legal support to meet the "specificity" demanded by the ATS.[445] The Court's consideration of whether the claim was supported under international law was hard to extricate from whether the claim satisfied the statutory, U.S.-specific screen, leaving it unclear how much independent work the latter had performed.[446]

The Sosa majority stressed how its approach was consistent with lower court precedent,[447] and lower courts largely proceeded on that basis. Subsequent

[440] Id. at 735, 737 (referring to "binding customary international law" standard); id. at 736 (inquiring whether the requested rule "has the status of a binding customary norm today"); id. at 733–34 (adverting to "sources we have long, albeit cautiously, recognized") (citing The Paquete Habana, 175 U.S. 677, 700 (1900)).

[441] Id. at 728.

[442] E.g., id. at 737 (suggesting that even if "some policies of prolonged arbitrary detentions" violate international law, "it may be harder to say which policies cross that line with the certainty afforded by Blackstone's three common law offenses").

[443] Id. at 732–33 (indicating that requirement that a norm be "sufficiently definite" involved an "element of judgment about the practical consequences of making that cause available to litigants in the federal courts"); id. at 736 (warning of "breathtaking" implications of a broad rule).

[444] Id. at 733 n.21 (noting possibility of exhaustion, as well as case-specific deference to the political branches); see also id. at 732 n.20 (noting as "related consideration . . . whether international law extends the scope of liability for a violation of a given norm to the perpetrator being sued, if the defendant is a private actor such as a corporation or individual"). Other possible defenses have subsequently been suggested by other members of the Court, in part as an alternative to developing more stringent threshold standards. See, e.g., id. at 760, 760–61 (Breyer, J., concurring in part and in the judgment) (agreeing that other principles might apply, and citing international comity); Jesner v. Arab Bank, PLC, 138 S. Ct. 1386, 1430–31 (2018) (Sotomayor, J., dissenting) (noting presumption against extraterritoriality, personal jurisdiction, exhaustion, forum non conveniens, international comity, and case-specific deference).

[445] Sosa, 542 U.S. at 733–38.

[446] See, e.g., id. at 737.

[447] Id. at 731 ("The position we take today has been assumed by some federal courts for 24 years, ever since the Second Circuit decided Filartiga v. Pena-Irala"); id. at 732 (suggesting that standard "is generally consistent" with lower court precedent) (citing Filartiga v. Pena-Irala, 630 F.2d 876, 890 (2d Cir. 1980); Tel-Oren v. Libyan Arab Republic, 726 F.2d 774, 781 (D.C. Cir. 1984) (Edwards, J., concurring); and In re Estate of Marcos Human Rights Litigation, 25 F.3d 1467 (9th Cir. 1994)); see Kiobel v. Royal Dutch Petroleum Co., 569 U.S. 108, 134–35 (2013) (Breyer, J., concurring) (noting professed consistency of Sosa with Filartiga and Marcos).

decisions let proceed claims based on well-established international offenses like torture, genocide, war crimes, and crimes against humanity,[448] while taking a more skeptical view of less settled norms, including by directly or indirectly questioning their existence under international law.[449] The acid test would seem to be whether U.S. courts will decline to permit claims based on norms they *acknowledge* to be part of customary international law on the basis that they nonetheless lack sufficient definiteness, or acceptance—that is, due to a genuinely distinct, additional ATS hurdle. To date, this distinction has been suggested by few cases,[450] and the stringency of other barriers to recovery (principally extra-territoriality) mean that the occasions for confronting the question may grow still fewer.[451]

Despite the high standard set for definiteness and acceptance, and the availability of other grounds for dismissal, members of the Court remain intent on raising the substantive threshold for customary international law claims. In *Nestlé USA, Inc. v. Doe*, Justice Thomas (joined by two other justices) opined that "courts must refrain from creating a cause of action whenever there is *even*

---

[448] *See, e.g., Rio Tinto V*, 671 F.3d 736, 758–59 (9th Cir. 2011) (en banc) (genocide), *vacated and remanded on other grounds*, 133 S. Ct. 1995 (2013) (mem. op.); *id.* at 763–64 (war crimes); *see also Sosa*, 542 U.S. at 762 (Breyer, J., concurring in part and concurring in judgment) (describing a "subset" of "universally condemned behavior" for which "universal jurisdiction exists," including "torture, genocide, crimes against humanity, and war crimes"); Kadic v. Karadzic, 70 F.3d 232, 236 (2d Cir. 1995) (genocide, war crimes, and crimes against humanity). For less well-established claims that courts permitted to proceed, see, for example, Doe v. Exxon Mobile Corp., 654 F.3d 11, 17 (D.C. Cir. 2011) (assuming, based on absence of dispute between the parties, that extrajudicial killing, torture, and prolonged arbitrary detention are sufficiently established norms of customary international law); Abdullahi v. Pfizer, Inc., 562 F.3d 163, 174–88 (2d Cir. 2009) (holding that norm of customary international law prohibiting medical experimentation on non-consenting human subjects satisfied *Sosa* standard); *In re* S. African Apartheid Litig. v. Daimler AG, 617 F. Supp. 2d 228, 250–53 (S.D.N.Y. 2009) (arbitrary denationalization, but not acts of apartheid by a nonstate actor, satisfies standard).

[449] *See, e.g.*, Mora v. New York, 524 F.3d 183, 207–09 (2d Cir. 2008) (holding that claim relating to consular notification and access after arrest does not meet the *Sosa* standard); Cisneros v. Aragon, 485 F.3d 1226, 1228–31 (10th Cir. 2007) (statutory rape); Taveras v. Taveras, 477 F.3d 767, 776–82 (6th Cir. 2007) (cross-border parental child abduction). Among the offenses unsuccessfully alleged in pre-*Sosa* cases, see, for example, Flores v. Southern Peru Copper Corp., 414 F.3d 233, 254–55 (2d Cir. 2003) (right to life, right to health, and prohibition on intranational pollution); Bigio v. Coca-Cola, 239 F.3d 440, 447–49 (2d Cir. 2001) (private racial or religious discrimination); Hamid v. Price Waterhouse, 51 F.3d 1411, 1417–18 (9th Cir. 1995) (fraud, breach of fiduciary duty, and misappropriation of funds); Zapata v. Quinn, 707 F.2d 691, 692 (2d Cir. 1983) (regulatory takings).

[450] *Compare Rio Tinto V*, 671 F.3d at 768–69 (acknowledging "a great deal of support for the proposition that systematic racial discrimination by a state violates a *jus cogens* norms," but concluding that the norm was not "sufficiently specific and obligatory" to provide the basis for a cause of action under the ATS), *with id.* at 771, 777–78 (Pregerson, J., concurring in part and dissenting in part) (concluding that because the norm had *jus cogens* status, it necessarily satisfied *Sosa* and fell within the ATS). It is more common to link the two inquiries. *See, e.g., id.* at 767–68 (holding that, because an alleged food and medical blockade did not constitute a prohibited act according to definition of crimes against humanity in the statutes of international criminal tribunals, it did not "violate a specific internationally recognized norm within the meaning of *Sosa*").

[451] *See generally* Chapter 4 § IV(B) (discussing presumption).

a single sound reason to defer to Congress."[452] He echoed prior opinions in regarding *Sosa* as establishing a two-step test that claimants had to satisfy in order to have a cause of action recognized: first, identifying a "specific, universal, and obligatory norm" comparable to those recognized as torts in 1789; and second, demonstrating that "courts should exercise 'judicial discretion' to create a cause of action rather than defer to Congress," a step Justice Thomas described as "extraordinarily strict" and which essentially permitted bypassing the first inquiry altogether.[453] The opinion was not the first to attribute a two-step approach to *Sosa*,[454] but *Sosa* did not exactly establish one; what may be now termed a first step was a completely integrated inquiry, intended to incorporate judicial caution that might limit the availability of relief, and additional constraints were left for consideration in future cases.[455] Justice Gorsuch, writing separately, would simply have overruled *Sosa* so as to "jettison the misguided notion that courts have discretion to create new causes of action under the ATS."[456] For the time being, the Court has not adopted these views.

The Supreme Court, as well as the lower courts, have also wrestled with how to address the scope of ATS liability (like aiding and abetting and other forms of secondary liability) and the actors subject to liability (like corporations). It seems likely that if customary international law established not just a substantive standard for conduct (such as the prohibition of torture) but also plainly established the requisite scope of liability for the relevant actor, the ATS would at least presumptively afford a remedy. If international law instead clearly *prohibited* liability under the circumstances at issue, courts applying the ATS would almost certainly not afford relief. Between these extremes, however, U.S. courts

---

[452] 141 S. Ct. 1931, 1937 (2021) (Thomas, J., joined by Gorsuch & Kavanaugh, JJ.) (citing Hernández v. Mesa, 140 S. Ct. 735, 743 (2020)) (emphasis added). *Hernández v. Mesa,* cited for that proposition, does not actually support it. 140 S. Ct. at 743 (describing inquiry into whether "'there are sound reasons to think Congress might doubt the efficacy or necessity of a damages remedy'" and "'whether the Judiciary is well suited, absent congressional action or instruction, to consider and weigh the costs and benefits of allowing a damages action to proceed'") (quoting Ziglar v. Abbasi, 137 S. Ct. 1843, 1858 (2017)).

[453] *Id.* at 1938 (quoting Sosa v. Alvarez-Machain, 542 U.S. 692, 732, 736 n.27 (2004)); *see id.* at 1939 (stating that "[r]egardless of whether respondents have satisfied the first step of the *Sosa* test, it is clear that they have not satisfied the second").

[454] *See id.* at 1945 (Sotomayor, J., concurring in part and concurring in the judgment) (noting that, "[i]n the years since, this Court has read *Sosa* to announce a two-step test for recognizing the availability of a cause of action under the ATS"); *see also* Jesner v. Arab Bank, PLC, 138 S. Ct. 1386, 1398 (2018) (Kennedy, J.); *id.* at 1409–11 (Alito, J., concurring in part and concurring in the judgment); *id.* at 1419–21, 1429 (Sotomayor, J., dissenting); *id.* at 1938 (quoting *Sosa,* 542 U.S. at 732, 736 n.27).

[455] *Sosa,* 542 U.S. 692 at 732–33 (stating that "the determination whether a norm is sufficiently definite to support a cause of action should (and, indeed, inevitably must) involve an element of judgment about the practical consequences of making that cause available to litigants in the federal courts"); *see id.* & nn.20–21 (suggesting additional possible considerations).

[456] *Nestlé USA,* 141 S. Ct. at 1940 (Gorsuch, J., concurring); *accord id.* at 1943 (stating that "the door" to new causes of action is one that "*Sosa* should not have cracked").

have wrestled with whether customary international law or federal common law resolves these scope issues.

The Supreme Court eventually addressed whether certain actors are subject to ATS liability. Reacting to a confusing prompt in *Sosa*,[457] lower courts divided over whether international law must establish the liability of corporations,[458] or whether it leaves such questions (like the existence of a civil damages remedy in the first place) to national law.[459] After initially bypassing the issue,[460] the Supreme Court took up the question of corporate liability in *Jesner v. Arab Bank*, concluding that foreign corporations, at least, were not subject to liability under the ATS.[461] Justice Kennedy, with two other justices, prioritized whether corporate liability was sufficiently established under international law (and thought there was only "weak support" for that proposition),[462] and in view of "sufficient doubt" regarding international liability turned to the question of whether courts should defer to Congress as a matter of judicial caution—and on that ground secured a majority.[463] Four dissenters said that this misapplied *Sosa*, which

---

[457] *See Sosa*, 542 U.S. at 732 n.20 (describing as "related" to the issue of whether an international norm is sufficiently definite the consideration of "whether international law extends the scope of liability for a violation of a given norm to the perpetrator being sued, if the defendant is a private actor such as a corporation or individual" (citing Tel-Oren v. Libyan Arab Republic, 726 F.2d 774, 791–95 (D.C. Cir. 1984) (Edwards, J., concurring), and Kadic v. Karadzíc, 70 F.3d 232, 239–41 (2d Cir. 1995)). It was uncertain whether the Court meant to suggest a distinction between natural persons and corporations or, to the contrary, to imply that the two should be treated similarly. *See* Flomo v. Firestone Natural Rubber Co., 643 F.3d 1013, 1017 (7th Cir. 2011) (noting the "enigmatic footnote" and interpretive dispute); *see also* Kiobel v. Royal Dutch Petroleum Co., 621 F.3d 111, 129 n.31 (2010) (disavowing any conclusion that *Sosa* established a distinction between corporations and natural persons); *id.* at 166 (Leval, J., concurring) (suggesting that *Sosa* implied that private parties should be treated identically).

[458] The conclusion that follows from this, however, was disputed. *Compare, e.g., Rio Tinto V*, 671 F.3d 736, 748 (9th Cir. 2011) (en banc) (plurality op.) (suggesting that "[t]he proper inquiry...should consider separately each violation of international law alleged" and which actors may violate it), *and id.* at 759–60 (prohibition on genocide applies to corporations), *and id.* at 764–65 (same, for war crimes), *with Kiobel*, 621 F.3d at 127–31 (contending that international law must determine the scope of ATS liability), *and id.* at 131–45 (concluding that "imposing liability on corporations for violations of customary international law has not attained a discernible, much less universal, acceptance among nations of the world").

[459] *See* Doe v. Exxon Mobil Corp., 654 F.3d 11, 41–43 (D.C. Cir. 2011) (differentiating corporate liability as remedial matter, distinctive from the cause of action question determined by international law); *Flomo*, 643 F.3d at 1019 (same). For discussion of this approach, see Chimène I. Keitner, *Conceptualizing Complicity in Alien Torts Cases*, 60 HASTINGS L.J. 61 (2008).

[460] In *Kiobel v. Royal Dutch Petroleum Co.*, the Supreme Court had granted certiorari to review a lower court holding that the ATS did not apply to suits against foreign corporations, but ultimately resolved the case on the basis of the presumption against extraterritoriality. Kiobel v. Royal Dutch Petroleum Co., 569 U.S. 108, 114 (2013); *see* Chapter 4 § IV(B).

[461] Jesner v. Arab Bank, PLC, 138 S. Ct. 1386, 1407 (2018).

[462] *Id.* at 1402 (Kennedy, J., joined by Roberts, C.J., & Thomas, J.); *see id.* at 1399–1402.

[463] *Id.* at 1402 (2018) (Kennedy, J., joined by Roberts, C.J., & Thomas, J.); *see id.* at 1402–08. Two other justices agreed with the outcome and with the focus on domestic law, but would have taken stronger stances. *Id.* at 1408 (Alito, J., concurring in part and concurring in the judgment) (concluding that creating causes of action against foreign corporations is incompatible with the separation of powers); *id.* at 1412 (Gorsuch, J., concurring in part and concurring in the judgment)

sought definiteness and acceptance as to substantive conduct (in *Jesner*, terrorism financing), but not as to remedial or enforcement questions like whether corporations should be held liable.[464] They allowed the possibility that particular substantive rules might be framed such that corporations could not violate them, but did not explore that distinction at length.[465] All told, a majority in *Jesner* concluded, as a matter of national law, that it would be inappropriate without direction from Congress to make foreign corporations liable under the ATS.[466] By contrast, in a subsequent case, *Nestlé USA, Inc. v. Doe*, most of the justices indicated that they had no misgivings about treating U.S. corporations as liable, so long as the other ATS prerequisites were satisfied—but the Court decided that case on extraterritoriality grounds.[467]

It remains unclear how the Supreme Court will evaluate other issues, like aiding-and-abetting liability, that could also be viewed either as questions of customary international law or U.S. law.[468] The Court has touched on the issue of secondary liability but not resolved it.[469] Lower courts have generally upheld the possibility of such claims.[470] As they did with corporate liability, these courts

(concluding that courts should not create new ATS causes of action permitting recovery against any defendants).

[464] *Id.* at 1419–21 (Sotomayor, J., dissenting, joined by Ginsburg, Breyer, & Kagan, JJ.).

[465] *Id.* at 1421–22 (Sotomayor, J., dissenting) (discussing *Sosa*, 542 U.S., at 732 & n.20). The dissent also disputed the interpretation and significance of the principal evidence relied on by the plurality, namely, the charters of various international criminal tribunals. *Id.* at 1422–25.

[466] *Id.* at 1402–05 (majority op.).

[467] *Nestlé USA, Inc. v. Doe*, 141 S. Ct. 1931, 1940 (2021) (Gorsuch, J., concurring) ("The notion that corporations are immune from suit under the ATS cannot be reconciled with the statutory text and original understanding."); *id.* at 1950 (Alito, J., dissenting) ("Corporate status does not justify special immunity"); *id.* at 1947 n.4 (Sotomayor, J., concurring in part and concurring in judgment) (agreeing, and noting that five members of the Court would not treat domestic corporations as immune from suit under the ATS).

[468] Comparable issues arise with respect to conspiracy and agency claims. *See, e.g., In re* Chiquita Brands Int'l, Inc. Alien Tort Statute & Shareholder Derivative Litig., 792 F. Supp. 2d 1301, 1343 (S.D. Fla. 2011).

[469] *Nestlé USA, Inc.*, 141 S. Ct. at 1936 (noting dispute regarding aiding-and-abetting liability); *see also id.* at 1949 & n.6 (Sotomayor, J., concurring in part and concurring in the judgment) (addressing international law relevant to aiding and abetting). In *Sosa* itself, the Supreme Court reported on pending aiding-and-abetting litigation, which it used to illustrate the potential need for deference to the executive branch, but it resolved neither the choice of law question nor whether such liability was appropriate at all. Sosa v. Alvarez-Machain, 542 U.S. 692, 733 n.21 (2004). *But cf.* Oona A. Hathaway et al., *Aiding and Abetting in International Criminal Law*, 104 CORNELL L. REV. 1593, 1630 (2020) (suggesting that "[t]he Supreme Court has acknowledged the existence of aiding-and-abetting liability under the ATS—in a footnote in *Sosa*—but it did not describe the appropriate substantive standard").

[470] *E.g.*, Doe v. Exxon Mobil Corp., 654 F.3d 11, 19 (D.C. Cir. 2011) ("Virtually every court to address the issue, before and after *Sosa*, has . . . recogniz[ed] secondary liability for violations of international law since the founding of the Republic"), *vacated on other grounds*, Doe v. Exxon Mobil Corp., 527 F. App'x 7 (D.C. Cir. 2013) (mem.); *Rio Tinto V*, 671 F.3d 736, 748–49 (9th Cir. 2011) (en banc); Aziz v. Alcolac, Inc., 658 F.3d 388, 395–96 (4th Cir. 2011); Presbyterian Church of Sudan v. Talisman Energy, Inc., 582 F.3d 244, 257–59 (2d Cir. 2009).

have looked to international law as applied by international criminal tribunals for guidance, often puzzling over the precise *mens rea* standard they suggest.[471] While lower courts have certainly considered whether an additional constraint may be imposed by federal common law, a substantial focus of their opinions has been international law.[472]

The Supreme Court's treatment of corporate liability suggests that establishing secondary liability under the ATS will require more than simply establishing its availability under customary international law. One hurdle, obviously, concerns whether aiding-and-abetting or a similar issue triggers concerns about federal common law–making; opinions have suggested, for example, that comparisons with other U.S. statutory regimes might matter,[473] but also that the threshold for exercising caution could be extremely low.[474] A second, related hurdle concerns whether any recognition of secondary liability under international law will be held to *Sosa* standard for recognizing substantive causes of action—meaning that they must be sufficiently definite and widely accepted, beyond whatever international law requires.[475] Were the *Sosa* standard applied, disputes about the details of liability theories under international law (for example, the appropriate

---

[471] The Second Circuit and Fourth Circuit have required a showing that the defendant had the purpose of facilitating the underlying violation. *See Talisman*, 582 F.3d at 258–59; *Aziz*, 658 F.3d at 398–400. The Eleventh Circuit has instead required simply that the defendant have knowledge that it was assisting in the underlying violation. *See* Cabello v. Fernández-Larios, 402 F.3d 1148, 1157–58 (11th Cir. 2005); *see also Doe*, 654 F.3d at 32–39, *vacated on other grounds*, Doe v. Exxon Mobil Corp., 527 F. App'x 7 (D.C. Cir. 2013) (mem.); *infra* this chapter note 472. The Ninth Circuit has covered the waterfront. *See, e.g., Rio Tinto V*, 671 F.3d at 765–66 (plurality op.) (declining to resolve the appropriate standard, and assuming *arguendo* that the higher standard of purposive action was required); *id.* at 770–71 (Reinhardt, J., concurring) (concluding that knowledge sufficed, based on federal common law standard); *id.* at 772–74 (Pregerson, J., concurring in part and dissenting in part) (concluding that knowledge sufficed, based on international standard). *See generally* Keitner, *supra* note 459, at 86–96 (2008) (describing case law, and defending test requiring knowledge plus substantial effect on the commission of wrongdoing).

[472] For example, after initially holding that aiding and abetting was established in international law and for purposes of the ATS, see *Doe*, 654 F.3d at 15, 16, 28–32, the D.C. Circuit panel vacated its decision. Doe v. Exxon Mobil Corp., 527 F. App'x 7 (D.C. Cir. 2013) (mem.). This was based partly on the Supreme Court's decision regarding ATS extraterritoriality, see *id.* (citing Kiobel v. Royal Dutch Petroleum Co., 569 U.S. 108, 132 (2013)), but also on an intervening decision by the International Criminal Tribunal for the Former Yugoslavia regarding the standard for aiding-and-abetting liability. *Id.* (citing Prosecutor v. Perisic, Case No. IT-04-81-A, Judgment (Int'l Crim. Trib. for the Former Yugoslavia Feb. 28, 2013)).

[473] *See, e.g.,* Jesner v. Arab Bank, PLC, 138 S. Ct. 1386, 1403–05 (2018) (Kennedy, J., joined by Roberts, C.J., & Thomas, J.) (examining corporate liability under analogous statutes).

[474] *See, e.g., Nestlé USA, Inc.*, 141 S. Ct. at 1937 (Thomas, J.) (suggesting that even a single reason of some kind justifies refraining from exercising common-law rulemaking authority); *see supra* this chapter text accompanying note 452.

[475] *See supra* this chapter text accompanying notes 440–446 (discussing *Sosa*), 460–467 (discussing *Jesner* and *Nestlé*). Some lower-court decisions have indicated that secondary liability must be established according to the definiteness and acceptance standard employed for determining primary norms. *See, e.g., Doe*, 654 F.3d at 30. Others appear to regard the ATS as recognizing any liability established under international law. *See, e.g., Rio Tinto V*, 671 F.3d at 749 (describing aiding-and-abetting liability as "well-established" by international law, and adding that "the ATS itself does not bar aiding and abetting liability").

mens rea standard) might be enough to bar liability.[476] Matters might proceed differently if a secondary liability issue is instead governed entirely by federal common law, rather than being derived from international law, but there is no consensus on this approach.[477] At least post-*Sosa*, the Supreme Court has not construed federal common law generously, but that has not to this point made it disinclined to frame ATS issues as involving its possible creation.

Even if an actionable violation of international law provisionally addressed by the ATS has been established, other potential defenses remain.[478] The relationship between these defenses and customary international law varies. *Sosa* noted that at least one possible defense, the requirement that a claim first be exhausted in available foreign or international fora, might be premised on international law.[479] Like secondary liability and corporate liability, disregarding an exhaustion requirement established under international law might put the United States out of compliance with its international obligations; alternatively, the United States may regard exhaustion as an aspect of international comity. To this point, lower courts have generally declined to recognize an exhaustion requirement that would substantially limit ATS liability.[480] Another defense that *Sosa* noted, speculatively, was case-by-case

---

[476] *Cf.* Hathaway et al., *supra* note 469, at 1631–34 (describing "[f]ruitless [s]earch for [u]nity" by U.S. courts seeking to synthesize the international practice relating to aiding-and-abetting liability, resulting in "wildly different views" regarding the appropriate standard).

[477] *Compare, e.g.*, Doe v. Unocal Corp., 395 F.3d 932, 963 (9th Cir. 2002) (Reinhardt, J., concurring) (defending treatment of aiding-and-abetting liability as "ancillary legal question," governed by federal common law, as opposed to the primary international law violation by the state concerned), *with* Keitner, *supra* note 259, at 64, 73–83 (describing and advocating approach by which aiding-and-abetting liability is "a conduct-regulating rule defined by international law, rather than an ancillary question governed by domestic law"), *and* Chimene Keitner, *Not Dead Yet—Some Thoughts on Kiobel*, Opinio Juris (Sept. 21, 2010), https://perma.cc/3XFF-T9RZ (indicating that corporate liability, in contrast, is governed by U.S. law), *with* Ingrid Wuerth, *The Alien Tort Statute and Federal Common Law: A New Approach*, 85 Notre Dame L. Rev. 1931, 1932–33 (2010) (describing continuum "with certain aspects of ATS litigation governed by federal common law that is tightly linked to international law, other aspects governed by federal common law that is not derived from international norms, and still others that fall somewhere in between," applying to issues like secondary liability and corporate liability alike).

[478] Sosa v. Alvarez-Machain, 542 U.S. 692, 733 n.21 (2004); *see supra* this chapter text accompanying note 444 (citing other opinions).

[479] 542 U.S. at 732 n.21.

[480] The Ninth Circuit appeared eventually to conclude that exhaustion is a prudential doctrine that U.S. courts might, but need not invariably, invoke—inspired by international law, but perhaps not required by international law of domestic courts, or perhaps ostensibly required but countermanded by the ATS. *See* Sarei v. Rio Tinto, PLC, 550 F.3d 822, 832 n.10 (9th Cir. 2008) [*Rio Tinto III*] (en banc) (describing alignment of judges as favoring prudential rather than statutory exhaustion); *id.* at 829–31 (describing international law basis for exhaustion); *see also Rio Tinto V*, 671 F.3d at 754–55 (applying prudential approach). *Contrast Rio Tinto V*, 671 F.3d at 793, 796–97 (Bea, J., concurring in part and dissenting in part) (urging that "exhaustion of local remedies is mandatorily required by 'the law of nations'"); Sarei v. Rio Tinto, PLC, 487 F.3d 1193, 1231 (9th Cir.2007) [*Rio Tinto II*] (Bybee, J., dissenting) (same). Other courts of appeal had indicated reservation about an exhaustion defense, at least one that would require complete capitulation as a matter of international law to proceedings before a hostile judiciary. *See, e.g.*, Flomo v. Firestone Natural Rubber Co., 643 F.3d 1013, 1025 (7th Cir. 2011).

deference to the political branches to avoid undue impacts on U.S. foreign policy.[481] Unlike many other ATS issues, any such deference could not even arguably be attributed to international law. It has had only limited application and is often entangled with the political question doctrine.[482]

As the preceding discussion reflects, *Sosa* may have been more effective in raising issues than resolving them, and many of the outstanding issues implicate the continuing role of customary international law in U.S. courts. It is unlikely that they will be imminently resolved, and indeed, their relevance has plummeted. Because the Supreme Court has held, and re-emphasized, that the ATS does not apply extraterritorially, it has not had to resolve conflicts on issues like aiding-and-abetting liability or the liability of U.S. corporations;[483] indeed, the presumption against extraterritoriality may have warded off reconsideration of *Sosa* itself.[484] The same has proven true in the lower courts.[485] The ATS will remain relevant, of course, to torts committed against noncitizens in the United States—though even there, the relevance of customary international law offenses may be tempered in the unlikely event the conduct is actionable as a deprivation of their civil rights[486] or as a tort under state common law or foreign law.[487]

---

[481] *Sosa*, 542 U.S. at 733 n.21.

[482] *See, e.g.,* Doe v. Exxon Mobil Corp., 654 F.3d 11, 58–62 (D.C. Cir. 2011) (suggesting possibility for case-specific deference and dismissal on the basis of a non-justiciable political question, assuming an unambiguous submission by U.S. government expressing concern with litigation alleging human rights violations). *See generally* Beaty v. Republic of Iraq, 480 F. Supp. 2d 60, 78–85 (D.D.C. 2007) (reviewing case law regarding case-specific dismissals, framed in terms of the political question doctrine, and concluding that cases depend substantially on whether the U.S. government expressly recommends dismissal).

[483] *See* Nestlé USA, Inc. v. Doe, 141 S. Ct. 1931 (2021) (deciding on the basis of extraterritoriality, rather aiding-and-abetting liability and domestic corporate liability issues presented); Kiobel v. Royal Dutch Petroleum Co., 569 U.S. 108 (2013) (deciding on the basis of extraterritoriality, rather than foreign corporate liability, aiding-and-abetting, and case-specific deference issues presented or implicated by the proceedings below); *see also* Jesner v. Arab Bank, PLC, 138 S. Ct. 1386, 1428–31 (2018) (Sotomayor, J., dissenting) (noting that objectionable consequences relating to foreign corporate liability might have been addressed by resolving case on extraterritoriality grounds).

[484] *See supra* this chapter text accompanying notes 452–456 (discussing opinions in *Nestlé USA*).

[485] In the Ninth Circuit's long-running *Rio Tinto* litigation, its en banc decision on exhaustion was vacated and remanded by the Supreme Court on the basis of *Kiobel v. Royal Dutch Petroleum Co. See* Rio Tinto PLC v. Sarei, 569 U.S. 945 (2013) (mem.), which led the Ninth Circuit to dismiss, presumably on extraterritoriality grounds. Sarei v. Rio Tinto, PLC, 722 F.3d 1109 (9th Cir. 2013) (en banc). Similarly, in the Second Circuit's anti-apartheid litigation, which was the basis for *Sosa's* aside on case-specific deference, the court of appeals perceived further proceedings as turning on extraterritoriality. *See* Balintulo v. Daimler AG, 727 F.3d 174 (2d Cir. 2013).

[486] *See, e.g.,* 42 U.S.C. § 1983 (providing for liability to "any citizen of the United States or other person within the jurisdiction thereof to the deprivation of any rights, privileges, or immunities secured by the Constitution and laws"); Bivens v. Six Unknown Named Agents of Federal Bureau of Narcotics, 403 U.S. 388 (1971) (recognizing implied private action for damages against federal officers violating U.S. constitutional rights while acting in their official capacities). *But see* Hernández v. Mesa, 140 S. Ct. 735, 743 (2020) (construing *Bivens* narrowly, including in light of potential effect on U.S. foreign relations, in case involving shots fired from the United States by U.S. Border Patrol agent killing Mexican national in Mexico).

[487] *See, e.g.,* Donald Earl Childress III, *The Alien Tort Statute, Federalism, and the Next Wave of Transnational Litigation,* 100 GEO. L.J. 709, 712–15 (2012).

2. Other Human Rights Statutes

Although the ATS is the oldest and broadest U.S. statute addressing human rights, it is not alone. While other statutes have posed some of the same issues that have arisen with the ATS, they tend to yield answers more easily—not simply because the statutes are more modern and circumscribed in their application but also because they generally avoid unmediated incorporation of customary international law. The Supreme Court has invoked such statutes in reading the ATS restrictively, reasoning that Congress has declined to issue a comparable "clear mandate" encouraging judicial involvement in human rights suits under the ATS[488]—and that variations in the statutory schemes indicate that those issues are ripe for legislative and not judicial judgment.[489] To the extent other schemes deny liability, that has sometimes been understood as a ground for similarly limiting ATS liability.[490]

The most prominent of these statutes is the Torture Victim Protection Act (TVPA), enacted in 1991.[491] Focusing on torture and extrajudicial killing, the TVPA addresses a number of questions left unclear on the face of the ATS. It establishes a cause of action, thus precluding any understanding that it is solely jurisdictional.[492] Moreover, while the TVPA encompasses a broader class of potential claimants, including both noncitizens and U.S. citizens, it limits liability to individuals acting under actual or apparent authority or color of law of any foreign nation. This removes any question of liability for those acting under the authority of the U.S. government, or concerning whether state action was required.[493]

The TVPA might have simply incorporated prohibitions on torture and extrajudicial killing as those wrongs are defined by customary international law. Instead, it pursued a degree of statutory independence. The definition of torture was closely informed by international law, but also incorporated understandings

---

[488] *See, e.g.,* Sosa v. Alvarez-Machain, 542 U.S. 692, 728 (2004) (juxtaposing "clear mandate" of Torture Victim Protection Act (TVPA) with ATS).

[489] *See, e.g.,* Nestlé USA, Inc. v. Doe, 141 S. Ct. 1931, 1939–40 (2021) (comparing Trafficking Victims Protection Reauthorization Act of 2003 (TVPRA) to ATS).

[490] Jesner v. Arab Bank, PLC, 138 S. Ct. 1386, 1403–04 (2018) (invoking limitation of TVPA to natural persons); *see infra* this chapter text accompanying notes 498–501 (discussing TVPA limitations).

[491] Torture Victim Protection Act of 1991 ["TVPA"], Pub. L. No. 102-256, 106 Stat. 73, 28 U.S.C. § 1350 note (2018).

[492] TVPA, *supra* note 491, § 2(a) (establishing liability); *see* 28 U.S.C. § 1331 (2018) (establishing jurisdiction over federal questions); Romero v. Drummond Co., 552 F.3d 1308, 1315 (11th Cir. 2008) (contrasting ATS, a jurisdiction-conferring statute that does not create independent causes of action, with the TVPA, which creates a cause of action but does not establish jurisdiction).

[493] TVPA, *supra* note 491, § 2(a); *cf. Sosa,* 542 U.S. at 698, 699–712 (addressing claims against U.S. government, notwithstanding their superficial inclusion within the ATS, according to the Federal Tort Claims Act, 28 U.S.C. § 1346(b)(1) (2018)); *id.* at 732 n.20 (noting question whether international law extends a given norm to non-governmental actors). Insisting on state action necessarily poses issues relating to official (conduct-based) immunity. *See* Chapter 4 § V(D)(2).

established by the United States in ratifying the Torture Convention;[494] extrajudicial killing depended on international law but was carefully defined.[495] Either kind of claim, as noted previously, was permitted only with respect to state action, even if international law might ultimately afford greater latitude.[496] The more detailed statutory treatment affected other issues that proved difficult under the ATS. The TVPA's text directly confronted some issues, like the statute of limitations, and whether claimants had to exhaust remedies for claims arising overseas.[497] In other instances, courts have been able to resolve issues on the basis of statutory interpretation, letting customary international law play a secondary role. Thus, for example, whether the TVPA provides for secondary liability is considered primarily as a question of legislative intent.[498] Similarly, in deciding that TVPA liability was limited to natural persons, the Supreme Court

---

[494] TVPA, *supra* note 491, § 3(b) (defining torture); *see* S. Rep. No. 102-249, at 8 (1991) (noting "word-for-word" incorporation of understandings in statutory definition); *accord* H.R. Rep. No. 102-367, pt. 1, at 4–5 (1991). For suggestions as to how this might affect application of the TVPA, see, for example, Price v. Socialist People's Libyan Arab Jamahiriya, 294 F.3d 82, 91–93 (D.C. Cir. 2002) (relying both on Torture Convention and U.S. understandings in interpreting the application of the TVPA and the Foreign Sovereign Immunities Act as concerns the requisite degree of severity and motivation for torture); *accord* Simpson v. Socialist People's Libyan Arab Jamahiriya, 326 F.3d 230, 234 (D.C. Cir. 2003).

[495] TVPA, *supra* note 491, § 3(a) (defining extrajudicial killing, including "deliberated killing not authorized by a previous judgment pronounced by a regularly constituted court affording all the judicial guarantees which are recognized as indispensable by civilized peoples," but excluding "any such killing that, under international law, is lawfully carried out under the authority of a foreign nation"); *see* S. Rep. No. 102-249, *supra* note 494, at 6 (explaining that the TVPA "incorporates into U.S. law the definition of extrajudicial killing found in customary international law," as well as the Geneva Convention (I) for the Amelioration of the Wounded and Sick in Armed Forces in the Field, such that "only killings which are truly extrajudicial in nature and which violate international law are actionable under the TVPA"); *cf.* Mamani v. Berzain, 654 F.3d 1148, 1154 n.7 (11th Cir. 2011) ("We assume for purposes of this discussion that an extrajudicial killing falling within the statutory definition of the TVPA would also likely violate established international law. But this may not be true under all circumstances.").

[496] When the TVPA was enacted, Congress did not regard the statutory limitation to individuals "under actual or apparent authority, or color of law, of any foreign nation" to be truncating rights evident under international law. S. Rep. No. 102-249, *supra* note 494, at 8. Still, judicial opinions considering recovery for non-official torture under the ATS—and rejecting it—had earlier suggested that international law was trending in that direction. Tel-Oren v. Libyan Arab Republic, 726 F.2d 774, 795 (D.C. Cir. 1984) (Edwards, J., concurring). That prospect was extinguished by the TVPA. *See In re* Xe Servs. Alien Tort Litig., 665 F. Supp. 2d 569, 593 (E.D. Va. 2011).

[497] The TVPA's ten-year statute of limitations, see TVPA, *supra* note 491, § 2(c), has frequently been borrowed by courts for ATS claims. *See, e.g.*, Chavez v. Carranza, 559 F.3d 486, 492 (6th Cir. 2009) (citing practice, and also borrowing approach to equitable tolling). On the other hand, courts have indicated reluctance about applying the TVPA's requirement that claimants exhaust foreign legal remedies, see TVPA, *supra* note 491, § 2(b), to ATS claimants. *See, e.g.*, Jean v. Dorélien, 431 F.3d 776, 781 (11th Cir. 2005).

[498] The legislative history indicates both that Congress anticipated aiding-and-abetting liability (and command responsibility) and that it premised this expectation in part based on international law. S. Rep. No. 102-249, *supra* note 494, at 8–9 & n.16; Cabello v. Fernandez-Larios, 402 F.3d 1148, 1157–58 (11th Cir. 2005). The result, in any event, is that courts are typically quick to acknowledge the possibility of secondary liability. *See, e.g.*, Sinaltrainal v. Coca-Cola Co., 578 F.3d 1252, 1258 n.5 (11th Cir. 2009).

rejected the argument that the statute had to be construed in terms of international law, at least absent evidence that Congress knew and intended to incorporate any specialized usage, and instead pondered the meaning of the statutory term "individual" as an ordinary question of statutory interpretation.[499]

This divergence of method may ultimately pose problems. Because the ATS and the TVPA establish liability for similar conduct, but appear subject to different limitations, courts have wrestled with how to reconcile them—with at least one decision suggesting that the TVPA occupies the field for offenses that it addresses, lest the ATS be used to circumvent the TVPA's exhaustion or other requirements.[500] Other opinions have rejected this as a repeal by implication, and because the TVPA's legislative history indicates that it was not intended to affect the ATS.[501] It is possible, nonetheless, to acknowledge the anomaly that courts applying the ATS to claims by noncitizens might refrain from requiring exhaustion, while requiring it for U.S. citizens (ineligible under the ATS) who present identical claims, or that ATS claimants might come to enjoy relaxed state action requirements that are foreclosed to TVPA claimants.[502] As noted previously, though, the opportunity and effect of these anomalies will be limited by the territorial limits to the ATS, which make the TVPA the more reliable basis for proceeding against foreign conduct.

The TVPA merely illustrates the range of statutory tools for litigating human rights violations established by international law. The Trafficking Victims Protection Reauthorization Act of 2003 (TVPRA) added a private right of action for claims against the perpetrators of human trafficking.[503] In 2008, Congress added the ability to sue indirect participants, and in so doing established a *mens rea* standard.[504] Addressing the *mens rea* standard has not eliminated difficult

---

[499] *See* Mohamad v. Palestinian Auth., 566 U.S. 449, 457 n.4 (2012).

[500] Enahoro v. Abubakar, 408 F.3d 877, 884–86 (7th Cir. 2005) (concluding that TVPA occupies the field of civil remedies for claims of torture or extrajudicial killing and remanding to permit a determination whether the complaint could be amended so as to state a TVPA, rather than ATS, claim, and to assess whether the TVPA exhaustion requirement would require dismissal).

[501] *Id.* at 886–89 (Cudahy, J., dissenting) (citing legislative history and judicial precedent); *e.g.*, Kadic v. Karadzic, 70 F.3d 232, 241 (2d Cir. 1995) ("The scope of the Alien Tort Act remains undiminished by enactment of the Torture Victim Act"); Aldana v. Del Monte Fresh Produce, Inc., 416 F.3d 1242, 1250 (11th Cir. 2005) (holding that claimants may bring claims under both the TVPA and the ATS).

[502] *See Abubakar*, 408 F.3d at 889–92 (Cudahy, J., dissenting) (acknowledging appeal of interpolating exhaustion requirement for ATS claims, but disagreeing as to its application to either TVPA or ATS claims); *cf. Karadzic*, 70 F.3d at 241 (rejecting contention that the state action requirement of the TVPA was intended to apply to ATS actions).

[503] Pub. L. No. 108-193, § 4(a)(4)(A), 117 Stat. 2875 (2003) (codified at 18 U.S.C. § 1595).

[504] Pub. L. 110-457, Title II, § 221(2), Dec. 23, 2008, 122 Stat. 5067 (codified at 18 U.S.C. § 1595(a)) (adding, as person against whom a claim may be brought, "whoever knowingly benefits, financially or by receiving anything of value from participation in a venture which that person knew or should have known has engaged in an act in violation of this chapter").

legal questions, though it has perhaps reduced them.[505] The statute does not directly address its geographic application, but the statutory text and legislative history has satisfied at least one court that the civil remedy applies abroad for certain predicate offenses.[506] It is regrettable that Congress did not address the question how the TVPRA relates to invocation of the ATS for trafficking claims. As with the TVPA, however, it seems likely that the diminishing jurisdictional scope of the ATS may largely moot the question of any overlap.[507]

---

[505] *See, e.g.,* S.J. v. Choice Hotels Int'l, Inc., 473 F. Supp. 147, 152–54 (E.D.N.Y. 2020) (considering different views regarding knowledge standard).

[506] Roe v. Howard, 917 F.3d 229, 239–45 (4th Cir. 2019). The 2008 amendment added a provision that provided for extraterritorial criminal jurisdiction "[i]n addition to any domestic or extraterritorial jurisdiction otherwise provided by law. . . ." *See* 18 U.S.C. § 1596.

[507] *See, e.g.,* Velez v. Sanchez, 693 F.3d 308, 324 (2d Cir. 2012) (avoiding addressing "preemption" based on holding that jurisdiction over ATS claims was lacking, but noting that "neither the plain language nor the legislative history of the TVPRA references the ATS").

6

Treaties and Other International Agreements

While the Constitution says little about customary international law—appropriate, perhaps, for unwritten norms—it does set out the basics for treaties.[1] Article I says that the several states may not make treaties;[2] Article II explains who may make them, namely, the president and the Senate;[3] Article III describes the place of treaties in federal courts;[4] and Article VI establishes their place in U.S. law.[5]

Practice has complicated this simple scheme. The president and the Senate enjoy a partnership somewhat different from that described by Article II, since the president takes little "advice" concerning most phases of treaty-making and Senate "consent" is often conditional.[6] Non-self-execution doctrine has substantially qualified the place of treaties in federal courts and, potentially, the supremacy of treaties in U.S. law.[7] Most dramatically, the United States has diminished its reliance on Article II treaties, resorting more often to other means of approving international agreements, even for substantial national commitments.[8] Other, more subtle developments—such as the degree to which treaties and other U.S. agreements regulate matters once left to the states—have unsettled background assumptions that may have been foundational.[9]

---

[1] Some have even contended that the Constitution itself is a kind of treaty. *See generally* FRANCISCO FORREST MARTIN, THE CONSTITUTION AS TREATY: THE INTERNATIONAL LEGAL CONSTRUCTIONALIST APPROACH TO THE U.S. CONSTITUTION (2007); *cf.* Akhil Reed Amar, *The Consent of the Governed: Constitutional Amendment Outside Article V*, 94 COLUM. L. REV. 457, 465 (1994) (asserting that the Articles of Confederation, preceding the Constitution, "were nothing more than a tight treaty among thirteen otherwise independent states").

[2] U.S. CONST. art. I, § 10 ("No State shall enter into any Treaty, Alliance, or Confederation . . . .").

[3] U.S. CONST. art. II, § 2 ("[The president] shall have Power, by and with the Advice and Consent of the Senate, to make Treaties, provided two thirds of the Senators present concur . . . .").

[4] U.S. CONST. art. III, § 2 ("The judicial Power shall extend to all Cases, in Law and Equity, arising under this Constitution, the Laws of the United States, and Treaties made, or which shall be made, under their Authority . . . .").

[5] U.S. CONST. art. VI ("This Constitution, and the Laws of the United States which shall be made in Pursuance thereof; and all Treaties made, or which shall be made, under the Authority of the United States, shall be the supreme Law of the Land; and the Judges in every State shall be bound thereby, any Thing in the Constitution or Laws of any State to the Contrary notwithstanding.").

[6] *See infra* this chapter text accompanying notes 191–195.

[7] *See infra* this chapter § IV(A)(3).

[8] *See infra* this chapter § V.

[9] *See infra* this chapter § II(D).

Still, few if any of these shifts are clearly incompatible with the Constitution. The original understanding of the treaty power is elusive, particularly given uncertainty about the import of pre-constitutional experience or the records of the Constitution's drafting or ratification.[10] In a few instances, the Constitution likely was intended to settle a controversy, but *how* it was settled is unclear;[11] at least as often, it seems likely that a problem was unanticipated or that it was deliberately left unresolved. Subsequent practice by the federal government might help resolve open questions, but there is dispute about the circumstances in which such practice is probative.[12] But what is distinctive about the treaty power is the degree to which the flexibility afforded by the Constitution has entitled a wider range of actors—not just the Congress, the president, and the courts, as usual, but also the tandem of the president and the Senate, in cooperation with treaty partners—to forge constitutional and political meaning. That process has changed what was anticipated or filled in gaps (depending upon the issue and on one's perspective), but it also has left some fundamental questions open for future resolution.

This chapter discusses the range of contemporary legal issues that arise in connection with Article II and other means by which the United States enters into international agreements. As with the law of nations and customary international law, the terminology requires clarification at the outset. "Treaty" in contemporary international law refers generally to legally binding international agreements—including those regulated by the Vienna Convention on the Law of Treaties (VCLT), which has its own, narrower defined scope.[13] In U.S. law,

---

[10] *See* Methodological Preface. This uncertainty was reflected in early debates over the treaty power. During debate in 1796 over the House's role, Hamilton published essays invoking the convention's official records, which he had just deposited with the Secretary of State. *See infra* this chapter note 82 (discussing proposed amendment). Madison, defending the House's role, alluded only vaguely to his own convention notes; instead, he claimed that it was inappropriate to generalize about the convention's intentions, and indicated that the ratifying conventions were more probative. *See* MARY SARAH BILDER, MADISON'S HAND: REVISING THE CONSTITUTIONAL CONVENTION 219–20 (2015); Mary Sarah Bilder, *How Bad Were the Official Records of the Federal Convention?*, 80 GEO. WASH. L. REV. 1620, 1667–80 (2012).

[11] For example, most despair at resolving how the Constitution distinguished between the agreements categorically prohibited for the states, see U.S. CONST. art. I, § 10, cl. 1, and those subject to congressional permission, see *id.* art. I, § 10, cl. 3, or not regulated at all. *See generally* U.S. Steel Corp. v. Multistate Tax Comm'n, 434 U.S. 452, 460–63 (1978) (admitting that "[t]he Framers clearly perceived compacts and agreements as differing from treaties," but that "[w]hatever distinct meanings the Framers attributed . . . were soon lost").

[12] *See generally* Curtis A. Bradley & Trevor W. Morrison, *Historical Gloss and the Separation of Powers*, 126 HARV. L. REV. 411 (2012).

[13] The VCLT's defined term adds the qualifications (not otherwise required by international law) that, for VCLT purposes, such obligations have to be in writing and between States. Vienna Convention on the Law of Treaties, May 23, 1969, art. 2(1)(a), 8 I.L.M. 679, 681, 1155 U.N.T.S. 331 (entered into force Jan. 27, 1980, not ratified) [hereinafter VCLT]. A separate but similar Convention addresses agreements involving international organizations. *See* Vienna Convention on the Law of Treaties Between States and International Organizations or Between International Organizations, Mar. 21, 1986, U.N. GAOR, U.N. Doc. A/CONF.129/15, *reprinted in* 25 I.L.M 543 (1986). The United States is not a party to either agreement. *See generally* Duncan B. Hollis, *Defining Treaties*, *in* THE

"treaty" is usually understood to connote agreements approved according to Article II of the U.S. Constitution, which involves consent by the Senate; as discussed in Section V later, the United States also enters into international agreements by means other than consent by the Senate.[14] This overlapping terminology creates room for confusion. When describing agreements that are binding under international law, this chapter (and this volume) uses the terms "treaty," "international agreement," or "agreement."[15] Where appropriately distinguished, treaties made for the United States under Article II are described as "Article II treaties" or "advice-and-consent treaties," unless it is clear from the context. Treaties not made according to Article II are generically referred to as "non–Article II agreements" (or "agreement" if it is clear from the context); as explained in Section V, more particular forms are described as "congressional-executive agreements," "sole executive agreements," and so on.

Notwithstanding their divergent terminologies, any discussion of international agreements under U.S. foreign relations law requires heeding the international law of treaties. The focus here is on U.S. law; at the end of the day, though, any U.S. international agreement concerns law operating on the international plane, which addresses matters such as whether an agreement has been formed, how it should be interpreted, or how it might be terminated. Accordingly, this chapter will discuss the international law of treaties—including the VCLT, to which the United States is not a party, but which generally reflects customary international law[16]—to the extent it informs U.S. foreign relations law.

OXFORD GUIDE TO TREATIES ch. 1 (Duncan B. Hollis ed., 2d ed. 2020) (describing basic parameters of a "treaty" under the international law of treaties, including as distinct from the VCLT).

[14] See also infra this chapter text accompanying notes 769–773 (describing differences between varieties of congressional-executive agreements and "sole" executive agreements).
[15] The term "treaty" is used exclusively when describing the operation of VCLT rules that apply to those instruments.
[16] This is the longstanding position of the United States. See Letter of Submittal from William P. Rogers, U.S. Sec'y of State, to President Richard M. Nixon (Oct. 18, 1971), reprinted in 65 DEP'T STATE BULL. 684, 685 (Dec. 13, 1971); see also 1974 DIGEST OF U.S. PRACTICE 235 (quoting Memorandum of Charles Bevans, Assistant Legal Adviser for Treaty Affairs (June 6, 1974)) (addressing provisional application and invoking the VCLT, "which, although not yet in force, is the most recent consensus of the world community on the law of treaties"); see also RESTATEMENT (FOURTH) § 301, rptrs. note 1 ("Although the United States is not a party to the Convention, it accepts that the Convention generally reflects international practice concerning treaties and that many of its provisions are binding as a matter of customary international law."); Robert E. Dalton, The Vienna Convention on the Law of Treaties: Consequences for the United States, 78 AM. SOC'Y INT'L L. PROC. 276, 278 (1984) (reporting that "the Office of the Legal Adviser takes into account many of its provisions in dealing with day-to-day treaty problems").
The Supreme Court has rarely referred to the VCLT, but lower courts have at least sometimes depicted it as stating custom. Compare, e.g., Chubb & Son, Inc. v. Asiana Airlines, 214 F.3d 301, 308 (2d Cir. 2000) (describing VCLT as "largely a restatement of customary rules, binding States regardless of whether they are parties to the Convention," and noting U.S. acknowledgment) (internal citations and quotations omitted), with Avero Belg. Ins. v. Am. Airlines, Inc., 423 F.3d 73, 79 & n.8 (2d Cir. 2005) (treating the VCLT "not [as] a primary source of customary international law, but rather one of the secondary sources . . . that we rely upon only insofar as they rest on factual

I. Historical Emergence of the Treaty Power

A. Pre-Constitutional Experience

1. Pre-Articles Experience

Those formulating the treaty provisions of the new Constitution were not writing on a clean slate, but the challenge lies in determining what lessons they had extracted from their experience. Colonial treaty-making, while limited, hinted at the difficulty for Britain in coordinating foreign affairs relating to its colonies: while in principle treaty-making was reserved to the king, the colonies at times embarked on concluding their own agreements, such as with each other and with Indian tribes.[17] Colonists could also study how the British treaty system functioned for other matters. Still, assuming a British approach to treaty-making was discernible then, or now, it remains difficult to establish a shared understanding among the Founders—who might have considered the British approach solely as it functioned downstream for a colony such as theirs, or instead from a British (national) standpoint more appropriate to the independent statehood to which they aspired—let alone to determine the extent to which they embraced it or rebelled against it.[18]

Certainly, after the revolution, the colonists wanted to deal as peers with European powers, including Great Britain. The formal independence they pursued was not merely symbolic, but critical to their diplomatic capacity to forge

and accurate descriptions of the past practices of states") (internal citations and quotations omitted). International courts and commentators are less equivocal. *See, e.g.,* Gabcikovo-Nagymaros Project (Hung. v. Slovk.), Judgment, 1997 I.C.J. 7, ¶ 46 (Sept. 25) (noting ICJ's holdings "that some of the rules laid down in that Convention might be considered as a codification of existing customary law"); Maria Frankowska, *The Vienna Convention on the Law of Treaties Before United States Courts,* 28 VA. J. INT'L L. 281 (1988); THE LAW OF TREATIES BEYOND THE VIENNA CONVENTION (Enzo Cannizzaro ed., 2011).

[17] *See* JOHN FERLING, A LEAP IN THE DARK: THE STRUGGLE TO CREATE THE AMERICAN REPUBLIC 15–16 (2003). There were attempts to form unions among the colonies for purposes of coordinating their trade, defense, and Indian policies, such as the Albany Congress of 1754, but they faced resistance from the Crown and by colonial assemblies intent on defending their prerogatives. *See* MERRILL JENSEN, THE ARTICLES OF CONFEDERATION 108 (1940); ROBERT C. NEWBOLD, THE ALBANY CONGRESS AND PLAN OF UNION OF 1754 (1955); TIMOTHY J. SHANNON, INDIANS AND COLONISTS AT THE CROSSROADS OF EMPIRE: THE ALBANY CONGRESS OF 1754 (2002).

[18] *See generally* JACK P. GREENE, PERIPHERIES AND CENTER: CONSTITUTIONAL DEVELOPMENT IN THE EXTENDED POLITIES OF THE BRITISH EMPIRE AND THE UNITED STATES, 1607–1788 (1987) (particularly chapters four through seven); JACK P. GREENE, THE CONSTITUTIONAL ORIGINS OF THE AMERICAN REVOLUTION (2011); for a brief summary of how British developments affected U.S. perceptions, see 4 JOHN PHILLIP REID, CONSTITUTIONAL HISTORY OF THE AMERICAN REVOLUTION: THE AUTHORITY OF LAW 151–53 (1993). Of course, the Founders were also aware of other systems, past and present. *See* DAVID J. BEDERMAN, THE CLASSICAL FOUNDATIONS OF THE AMERICAN CONSTITUTION: PREVAILING WISDOM 173–74 (2008); *see also infra* this chapter § IV(A) (1) (discussing attempts to construe treaty supremacy in the United States through the lens of British parliamentary supremacy).

political and commercial treaty relations with potential allies; they also believed that treaty-making was essential to solidifying their revolution.[19] On the same date that the Continental Congress approved committees to draft the Declaration of Independence and the Articles of Confederation, it created a third, led by John Adams, to "prepare a plan of treaties to be proposed to foreign powers."[20] A sound approach to treaties, evidently, was considered essential to laying the groundwork for independence.[21]

Of the three committees, Adams' "model treaty" initiative left by far the least impression on history, but it may have been instructive in the short term. The model treaty, approved by a unanimous Congress, presumed that the U.S. interest lay in commercial alliances without political or military entanglements.[22] Congress not only helped formulate, and approved, the model treaty provisions,[23] but was also involved in appointing and instructing the commissioners entrusted with implementing the model in negotiations with France.[24] Actual negotiations followed their own course, driven partly by France's own interests.[25] In the end, while commercial aspects were consistent with the model,[26] the resulting U.S.-French treaties of 1778 created an entangling alliance of the kind the United States sought to avoid—and complicated discussions with the British that might have averted war and, later, secured peace.[27] Then, despite the commissioners'

---

[19] *See* DAVID ARMITAGE, THE DECLARATION OF INDEPENDENCE: A GLOBAL HISTORY 31–37 (2007); James H. Hutson, *The Partition Treaty and the Declaration of American Independence*, 58 J. AM. HIST. 877 (1972).

[20] *See* 5 JOURNALS OF THE CONTINENTAL CONGRESS 431 (establishing committees); *id.* at 433 (naming members to committee for model treaty).

[21] ARMITAGE, *supra* note 19, at 35; William C. Stinchcombe, *John Adams and the Model Treaty*, *in* THE AMERICAN REVOLUTION AND "A CANDID WORLD" 69 (Lawrence S. Kaplan ed., 1977).

[22] The model treaty promised peace, friendship, and cooperation with Great Britain, but focused on giving each party most-favored-nation status and protecting the shipping rights of neutral and allied states. *See* John Adams, A Plan of Treaties, *in* 4 PAPERS OF JOHN ADAMS 265–78 (Robert J. Taylor ed., 1979) (initial plan as submitted to Congress); *see also id.* at 279 (amended committee report); *id.* at 290 (plan of treaties adopted, with instructions); SAMUEL FLAGG BEMIS, THE DIPLOMACY OF THE AMERICAN REVOLUTION 45–47 (1935); ROBERT W. SMITH, AMID A WARRING WORLD: AMERICAN FOREIGN RELATIONS, 1775–1815, at 6 (2012).

[23] Adams' initial draft of a model treaty was not radically altered. *See* Editorial Note, 4 PAPERS OF JOHN ADAMS, *supra* note 22, at 263; EDMUND CODY BURNETT, THE CONTINENTAL CONGRESS 207 (1941).

[24] Commissioners were occasionally replaced. 5 JOURNALS OF THE CONTINENTAL CONGRESS 827; 6 *id.* at 897; 9 *id.* at 946–47; *id.* at 975. Their original instructions detailed which of the prescribed provisions could be conceded (and when) and which ones must be insisted upon. 5 *id.* at 813–17; *see* 4 PAPERS OF JOHN ADAMS, *supra* note 22, at 263–65, 290–302. These were later amended, and afforded some discretion. *See, e.g.*, 6 JOURNALS OF THE CONTINENTAL CONGRESS 884; *id.* at 895–96; 9 *id.* at 951–52.

[25] These interests included French concern that the United States would strike a prior peace deal with Great Britain. BEMIS, *supra* note 22, at 60–61, 67–69; JACK N. RAKOVE, THE BEGINNINGS OF NATIONAL POLITICS: AN INTERPRETIVE HISTORY OF THE CONTINENTAL CONGRESS 117 (1979).

[26] *See* BURNETT, *supra* note 23, at 207.

[27] *See* BEMIS, *supra* note 22, at 61–69; DAVID C. HENDRICKSON, PEACE PACT: THE LOST WORLD OF THE AMERICAN FOUNDING 163–65 (2003); SMITH, *supra* note 22, at 10–11; *see also* Stinchcombe,

substantial departures from their instructions, Congress approved the treaties within days of learning of them.[28] As a model for legislative direction of treaty-making, the experience was not terribly auspicious.

2. Experience Under the Articles of Confederation

The Articles of Confederation, which were approved by Congress in 1777 but only entered into force in 1781, provided the United States with its first formal foreign relations architecture, including as to treaty-making. The Articles gave the national government the exclusive authority to send and receive ambassadors and to enter into treaties and alliances,[29] signaling U.S. stability in its external relationships and providing a measure of diplomatic credibility.[30] In contrast with the national government's clearly delineated (and circumscribed) legislative authority in domestic matters, the treaty power appears to have extended to virtually every subject;[31] it could even be understood as making up for deficiencies in national authority.[32] However, the treaty power was also vested solely in Congress, which proved ineffective at delegating the power, whether to its committees or otherwise. The limited "executive authority" that emerged under the Articles was attributable to legislative disability and to the initiative and self-help of individual diplomats.[33]

---

supra note 21, at 70–81 (describing differences between the model treaty's aspirations and U.S. foreign policy conducted by the Congress and its Committee of Secret Correspondence).

[28] BEMIS, *supra* note 22, at 67–69; BURNETT, *supra* note 23, at 330–33 (noting, however, that members of Congress sought to have France rescind two of the articles).

[29] *See* ARTICLES OF CONFEDERATION of 1781, art. VI (providing in relevant part that "[n]o State, without the Consent of [Congress] . . . shall send any embassy to, or receive any embassy from, or enter into any conference, agreement, alliance, or treaty with any King, prince, or state"); *id.* art. IX (giving the United States the "sole and exclusive right and power . . . of sending and receiving ambassadors [and] entering into treaties and alliances").

[30] *See* RAKOVE, *supra* note 25, at 178–79.

[31] Such "treaties and alliances" could not, however, prevent the states from imposing nondiscriminatory duties and posts on foreigners, nor prevent them from prohibiting the export or import of goods or commodities. ARTICLES OF CONFEDERATION OF 1781, art. IX.

[32] *See* Saikrishna Bangalore Prakash, *The Boundless Treaty Power Within a Bounded Constitution*, 90 NOTRE DAME L. REV. 1499, 1506–07 (2015) (noting, in particular, that the treaty power assumed a general authority to regulate foreign commerce, although Congress lacked such legislative capacity); *see also id.* at 1503–06 (describing backdrop).

[33] *See generally* FREDERICK W. MARKS III, INDEPENDENCE ON TRIAL: FOREIGN AFFAIRS AND THE MAKING OF THE CONSTITUTION 152–53 (1973). The Articles gave the president of Congress little real authority. BURNETT, *supra* note 23, at 503; *see* RICHARD B. MORRIS, THE FORGING OF THE UNION 1781–1789, at 99–108 (1987). Congressional committees on foreign affairs also wielded little power. BURNETT, *supra*, at 118, 489–90; H. JAMES HENDERSON, PARTY POLITICS IN THE CONTINENTAL CONGRESS 270 (1974); GAILLARD HUNT, THE DEPARTMENT OF STATE OF THE UNITED STATES: ITS HISTORY AND FUNCTIONS 1–13 (1914); MORRIS, *supra*, at 95; BRADFORD PERKINS, THE CREATION OF A REPUBLIC EMPIRE, 1776–1865, at 54–55 (1993); Bestor, *supra*, at 52–55. Even the Department of Foreign Affairs—headed by a Secretary for Foreign Affairs—had limited responsibilities. HUNT, THE DEPARTMENT OF STATE, *supra*, at 14–53; Bestor, *supra*, at 56–60.

Exceptionally, Congress could appoint a quasi-executive "Committee of the States" to manage affairs during its recesses, but treaties and alliances required supermajority approval and could not be

The resulting treaty system improved on, without transforming, that of the Continental Congress. Ongoing negotiations with Great Britain were largely unaffected.[34] Despite the commissioners' defiance of congressional instructions,[35] as well as congressional delays,[36] the United States wound up securing a highly favorable result.[37] Negotiations with Spain concerning access to the Mississippi were more dispiriting.[38] Unable to secure free navigation from Spain, John Jay in 1786 took the highly controversial step of asking for authority to offer the relinquishment of U.S. rights for a period in exchange for other commercial terms.[39]

delegated. *See* ARTICLES OF CONFEDERATION of 1781, art. IX, ¶ 5; *see also* Arthur Bestor, *Respective Roles of Senate and President in the Making and Abrogation of Treaties—The Original Intent of the Framers of the Constitution Historically Examined*, 55 WASH. L. REV. 1, 52 (1979) (characterizing the Committee as "little more than a message center"); MARKS, *supra*, at 153 ("practically useless"); MORRIS, *supra*, at 97 (stating that the Committee's "ineffective efforts constitute one of the most dismal chapters in the history of the Congress").

[34] Negotiations with Britain were commenced prior to the Articles' entry into force, but Congress largely abided by the Articles from the time they were adopted. BURNETT, *supra* note 23, at 502–03. This gave John Adams a credible basis for opposing a European plan to conduct peace consultations with the United States through thirteen separate state delegations: Adams replied that under the Articles—as "universally known as any constitution of government in Europe"—the authority to negotiate with foreign powers was exclusively lodged in Congress. RICHARD B. MORRIS, THE PEACEMAKERS: THE GREAT POWERS AND AMERICAN INDEPENDENCE 208–09 (1965); *see id.* at 182–84.

[35] This may have been due in part to concerns about French domination of U.S. foreign policy. *See* WILLIAM C. STINCHCOMBE, THE AMERICAN REVOLUTION AND THE FRENCH ALLIANCE 153–82, 195–96 (1969); *e.g.*, 20 JOURNALS OF THE CONTINENTAL CONGRESS 610–17; *id.* at 617, 625–27 (instructing commissioners "to undertake nothing in the negotiations for peace or truce, without [French] knowledge and concurrence; and ultimately to govern yourselves by their advice and opinion"); *see also* BEMIS, *supra* note 22, at 189–242; MORRIS, *supra* note 34, at 193–217, 237–38, 438–41; Bradford Perkins, *The Peace of Paris: Patterns and Legacies, in* PEACE AND THE PEACEMAKERS: THE TREATY OF 1783, at 190–229 (Ronald Hoffman & Peter J. Albert eds., 1986).

[36] *See* Jack N. Rakove, *Solving a Constitutional Puzzle: The Treatymaking Clause as a Case Study*, 1 PERSP. IN AM. HIST. (n.s.) 233, 275 (1984) (concluding that "this deadlock [over setting terms] had loomed as a threat to the nation's security as well as an embarrassing example of habitual congressional indecision"); CLINTON ROSSITER, 1787: THE GRAND CONVENTION 50 (1966) (noting that "the Treaty of Paris, almost a 'steal' for the United States, lay unratified [for nearly two months] before a Congress that could not muster the nine state delegations necessary for approval").

[37] Peace with Great Britain also diminished the utility of joining a pan-European armed neutrality league, allowing Congress to recall the principle that entanglements of such a sort should be resisted. BEMIS, *supra* note 22, at 149–71; William S. Carpenter, *The United States and the League of Neutrals of 1780*, 15 AM. J. INT'L L. 511 (1921); *see* 24 JOURNALS OF THE CONTINENTAL CONGRESS 392–94.

[38] For historical summaries, see Michael Allen, *The Mississippi River Debate, 1785–1787*, 36 TENN. HIST. Q. 447 (1977); Editor's Note: *The Debate in the Virginia Convention on the Navigation of the Mississippi River, 12–13 June 1788, in* 10 DOCUMENTARY HISTORY OF THE RATIFICATION OF THE CONSTITUTION 1179 (John P. Kaminski et al. eds., 1993); for legal accounts, see Eli Merritt, *Sectional Conflict and Secret Compromise: The Mississippi River Question and the United States Constitution*, 35 AM. J. LEGAL HIST. 117 (1991); Charles Warren, *The Mississippi River and the Treaty Clause of the Constitution*, 2 GEO. WASH. L. REV. 271 (1934). *See generally* Edward T. Swaine, *Negotiating Federalism: State Bargaining and the Dormant Treaty Power*, 49 DUKE L.J. 1127, 1174–87 (2000).

[39] 31 JOURNALS OF THE CONTINENTAL CONGRESS 480; *see* BURNETT, *supra* note 23, at 655 (stating, of Jay's request, that "[a] bomb tossed into the hall of Congress and about to explode would scarcely have produced greater consternation"). For Jay's report, see 31 JOURNALS OF THE CONTINENTAL CONGRESS 537–52 (reprinting report of Aug. 17, 1786).

Congress acquiesced, by a 7 to 5 vote along sectional lines, notwithstanding that at least nine states would have to assent to any treaty[40]—giving the impression that Congress might not feel obligated to approve an agreement even if it complied with congressionally approved instructions.[41] Jay negotiated, under congressional supervision, until the eve of the constitutional convention,[42] but he knew it was fruitless.[43] To those interested in free navigation, at least, the episode demonstrated the risk that treaties devastating to minority interests might be pursued, suggesting the value in further constraints on treaty-making.[44] To others, the episode suggested the difficulty of achieving the unity necessary to bargain effectively with foreign powers.[45] Few if any perceived that the treaty's subject matter was somehow out of bounds under the Articles, and indeed treaties were concluded on a number of subjects that were not expressly enumerated as powers entrusted to the national authorities.[46]

---

[40] See 31 JOURNALS OF THE CONTINENTAL CONGRESS 574–96.

[41] See 31 JOURNALS OF THE CONTINENTAL CONGRESS 597–600 (remarks of Pinckney); see also Notes on Debates in the Continental Congress: Pinckney's Speech, in 31 JOURNALS OF THE CONTINENTAL CONGRESS 933–48.

[42] See Resolutions Reaffirming American Rights to Navigate the Mississippi (Nov. 29, 1786) (editorial note), in 9 PAPERS OF JAMES MADISON 181–82 (Robert A. Rutland & William M.E. Rachal eds., 1975) (Virginia state resolutions); 32 JOURNALS OF THE CONTINENTAL CONGRESS 152 (requiring that Jay report on negotiations); Resolution to Transfer Negotiations with Spain to Madrid (Apr. 18, 1787), in id. at 388 (moving, unsuccessfully, to transfer responsibility so that negotiations would be managed by Thomas Jefferson, the Minister at the Court of France); Notes on Debates (Apr. 18, 1787), in id. at 389–90 (same); Notes on Debates (Apr. 25, 1787), in id. at 404 (moving that Jay be informed, in essence, as to the legal nullity of the seven-state instruction).

[43] Letter from Jay to the President of Congress (Apr. 11, 1787), in 32 JOURNALS OF THE CONTINENTAL CONGRESS 184, 187–88; 32 JOURNALS OF THE CONTINENTAL CONGRESS 189, 204 (remarking that "a Treaty disagreeable to one half of the Nation had better not be made, for it would be violated, and that a War disliked by the other half, would promise but little success, especially under a Government so greatly influenced and affected by popular Opinion"); see also HENDERSON, supra note 33, at 396 (noting consensus that, absent a radical change in southern views, "the proposed treaty could never be consummated").

[44] Jay himself was accused of evading his instructions and inflating Spanish expectations. See, e.g., Letter from James Monroe to Thomas Jefferson (June 16, 1786), in 3 The EMERGING NATION: A DOCUMENTARY HISTORY OF THE FOREIGN RELATIONS OF THE UNITED STATES UNDER THE ARTICLES OF CONFEDERATION, 1780–1789, at 203 (Mary A. Guinta et al. eds., 1996); Letter from James Monroe to Thomas Jefferson (July 16, 1786), in 3 EMERGING NATION, supra, at 236. Debates at the Virginia ratifying convention criticized both Jay and Congress. See 10 DOCUMENTARY HISTORY, supra note 38, at 1231–35 (statement of Monroe); id. at 1236 (statement of William Grayson); id. at 1247 (statement of Patrick Henry). But see id. at 1240 (statement of Madison) (defending Jay and the negotiations).

[45] RAKOVE, supra note 25, at 349–50 (noting that, in light of the sectional divisions exhibited during the Mississippi debates, "southern members began to suspect what some northern delegates were in fact considering: that the impasse over this question portended the creation of two or three separate confederacies"); accord HENDERSON, supra note 33, at 394–99; PETER ONUF & NICHOLAS ONUF, FEDERAL UNION, MODERN WORLD: THE LAW OF NATIONS IN AN AGE OF REVOLUTIONS 1776–1814, at 95 (1993). Madison was acutely concerned that the Jay proposal would scuttle any attempt to foster national authority. See Letter of Madison to Jefferson (Aug. 12, 1786), in 9 PAPERS OF JAMES MADISON, supra note 42, at 93, 96–97; Letter of Madison to James Madison, Sr. (Nov. 1, 1786), in id. at 153, 154.

[46] See Prakash, supra note 32, at 1507–10 (noting, among others, Articles-era treaties that expanded U.S. boundaries, regulated foreign commerce extensively, and regulated the rights of persons).

Another issue was the frailty of national law. The Articles contained no obvious means by which Congress could establish nationwide law binding the states and their courts; there was also no federal judiciary and no capacity to enforce any judgments courts might render.[47] The United States thus was limited in what it could offer foreign powers interested in exchanging concessions and limited in being able to drive such powers to the bargaining table by imposing or threatening sanctions.[48] This tended to leave matters in the hands of the several states; in principle, the states were restricted in striking their own bargains, but could be tempted into granting concessions,[49] or if aroused might take retaliation into their own hands.[50] The resulting inhibitions on U.S. bargaining wounded national pride and threatened the nation's economic health.[51]

[47] JENSEN, *supra* note 17, at 242–44; MARKS, *supra* note 33, at 3; *see* PHILIP HAMBURGER, LAW AND JUDICIAL DUTY 587–88 (2008) (noting language of the Articles); James E. Pfander, *Rethinking the Supreme Court's Original Jurisdiction in State-Party Cases*, 82 CAL. L. REV. 555, 584–85 (1994). *But see* Chapter 4 § (I)(A) (discussing Articles-era admiralty courts).

[48] ELIGA H. GOULD, AMONG THE POWERS OF THE EARTH: THE AMERICAN REVOLUTION AND THE MAKING OF A NEW WORLD EMPIRE 126–27 (2012); NORMAN GRAEBNER, RICHARD DEAN BURNS, & JOSEPH M. SIRACUSA, FOREIGN AFFAIRS AND THE FOUNDING FATHERS: FROM CONFEDERATION TO CONSTITUTION, 1776–1787, at 85, 91–93 (2011); REGINALD HORSMAN, THE DIPLOMACY OF THE NEW REPUBLIC, 1776–1815, at 23–24 (1985); ONUF & ONUF, *supra* note 45, at 95; RAKOVE, *supra* note 25, at 345–46; Frederick W. Marks III, *Power, Pride, and Purse: Diplomatic Origins of the Constitution*, 11 DIPLOMATIC HIST. 303 (1987).

[49] MARKS, *supra* note 33, at 151 (concluding that the resumption by some states of trade with Great Britain before the war's official end was "disastrous for diplomatic efforts under way at the time to convince the British to make commercial concessions"); RAKOVE, *supra* note 25, at 346 (noting view of some congressional delegates "that the country had to be protected from its own lust for British goods"). Foreign powers appreciated the potential for pitting states against each other. *See* DANIEL GEORGE LANG, FOREIGN POLICY IN THE EARLY REPUBLIC: THE LAW OF NATIONS AND THE BALANCE OF POWER 76 (1985) (noting Lord Sheffield's view that state competition for British trade would moot any need for a treaty); Letter from Chevalier de la Luzerne to Comte de Vergennes (Apr. 15, 1783), *in* 2 EMERGING NATION, *supra* note 44, at 89–90 (forecasting the rush of states for British trade).

[50] Hamilton later observed that "[s]everal States have endeavored, by separate prohibitions, restrictions, and exclusions, to influence the conduct of [Great Britain] in this particular," warning that "the want of concert, arising from the want of a general authority and from clashing and dissimilar views in the State, has hitherto frustrated every experiment of the kind, and will continue to do so as long as the same obstacles to a uniformity of measures continue to exist." THE FEDERALIST No. 22, at 144 (Alexander Hamilton); *see also* THE FEDERALIST No. 80, at 476 (Alexander Hamilton) (proposing that "the peace of the whole ought not to be left at the disposal of a part," because "[t]he Union will undoubtedly be answerable to foreign powers for the conduct of its members"); James Madison, Vices of the Political System of the United States (Apr. 1787), *in* THE MIND OF THE FOUNDERS: SOURCES OF THE POLITICAL THOUGHT OF JAMES MADISON 83, 84 (Marvin Meyers ed., 1973) (noting that "those disputes with other nations, which being among the greatest of public calamities, it ought to be least in the power of any part of the community to bring on the whole"); *cf.* THE FEDERALIST No. 42, at 265 (James Madison) (criticizing the Articles of Confederation for "leav[ing] it in the power of any indiscreet member to embroil the Confederacy with foreign nations").

[51] HORSMAN, *supra* note 48, at 28–29, 31; Marks, *supra* note 48, at 313–19; ONUF & ONUF, *supra* note 45, at 95. Publius emphasized this threat to national pride and the nation's economic health. THE FEDERALIST No. 4, at 49 (John Jay) (stating that "[i]f [foreign powers] find us either destitute of an effectual government . . . or split into three or four independent and probably discordant republics or confederacies . . . what a poor, pitiful figure will America make in their eyes!"); *see also* THE FEDERALIST No. 5, at 53 (John Jay); THE FEDERALIST No. 15, at 107 (Alexander Hamilton) (citing "[t]he imbecility of our government"); THE FEDERALIST No. 22, at 149 (Alexander Hamilton)

The lack of national authority, moreover, meant that the United States had difficulty complying with treaties already made. The British, for example, cited state measures that frustrated efforts by British merchants to collect prewar debts, along with other violations of the peace treaty, as a basis for their own failure to vacate Great Lakes forts and fulfill other treaty obligations.[52] Even if this was pretextual,[53] the Founders were concerned with the potential effect of noncompliance on national reputation and the risk it posed for future treaty-making.[54]

Not everyone was convinced that these problems were inherent in the Articles of Confederation. Its drafters plausibly expected that the states, while preserving their discretion for complying with national measures, nevertheless intended to do so by some means, such that no enforcement mechanism was strictly necessary.[55] From there, it was just a short step toward the view that the Articles actually *required* compliance.[56] (After the Constitution was

(cautioning that "[a] nation, with which we might have a treaty of commerce, could with much greater facility prevent our forming a connection with her competitor in trade, though such a connection should be ever so beneficial to ourselves").

[52] *See* 31 JOURNALS OF THE CONTINENTAL CONGRESS 781 (reprinting report); *see also* MARKS, *supra* note 33, at 10–11 (citing peace treaty violations); *id.* at 151 (citing additional violations).

[53] For some alleged breaches, such as those respecting Article 5's obligation that Congress "earnestly recommend" action by the state legislatures, the British would have known that Congress lacked authority to command the states. *See* RAKOVE, *supra* note 25, at 343; *see also* MORRIS, *supra* note 33, at 196–97, 364 n.5. Moreover, British reluctance to vacate their forts was probably inevitable given their interest in Canadian security and the fur trade. *See, e.g.,* BEMIS, *supra* note 22, at 70–72; STANLEY ELKINS & ERIC MCKITRICK, THE AGE OF FEDERALISM 126 (1993); GOULD, *supra* note 48, at 127–28; HORSMAN, *supra* note 48, at 32; MORRIS, *supra* note 33, at 201–03.

[54] As Hamilton famously noted:

> The treaties of the United States, under the present [Articles of Confederation], are liable to the infractions of thirteen different legislatures, and as many different courts of final jurisdiction, acting under the authority of those legislatures. The faith, the reputation, the peace of the whole Union, are thus continually at the mercy of the prejudices, the passions, and the interests of every member of which it is composed. Is it possible that foreign nations can either respect or confide in such a government?

THE FEDERALIST NO. 22, at 151 (Alexander Hamilton); *see also* THE FEDERALIST NO. 42, at 264 (James Madison) (noting that under the Articles of Confederation, "treaties might be substantially frustrated by regulations of the States"); 1 FARRAND'S RECORDS 316 (Madison's notes) (noting that "[t]he files of Congs. contain complaints already, from almost every nation with which treaties have been formed," and that continued violations risked "the greatest of national calamities"); ONUF & ONUF, *supra* note 45, at 121 (contrasting the British refusal to negotiate trade concessions for America with a liberal British treaty with France, and concluding that the difference was due to America's inability to enforce its treaties).

[55] *See* Jack Rakove, *The Legacy of the Articles of Confederation*, 12 PUBLIUS: THE JOURNAL OF FEDERALISM 45, 52 (1982).

[56] Edmund Randolph (later Attorney General) suggested to Jefferson that the Articles might require enforcement notwithstanding Virginia law, while admitting that the precise means were unclear. *See* Letter to Thomas Jefferson from Edmund Randolph (Jan. 30, 1784), *in* 6 THE PAPERS OF THOMAS JEFFERSON 513, 513–15 (Julian P. Boyd ed. 1952); *see also* HAMBURGER, *supra* note 47, at 589–90. Later, Jefferson opined that a treaty granting rights to French citizens would operate as part of "the Law of the Land," and as such there would be "no Occasion for the Assemblies to pass Laws on this Subject, the Treaty being a Law, as I concieve [sic], superior to those of particular Assemblies, and repealing them where they stand in the Way of its

ratified, members of the Supreme Court, deciding in *Ware v. Hylton* whether
pre–Revolutionary War debts owed British creditors were lawfully discharged
by a Virginia statute, divided in part over whether this was inconsistent over
with the status of the Treaty of Paris under the Articles of Confederation.[57])
Some thought that Congress could at least importune states on that basis,[58]
while others insisted that Congress lacked any genuine power.[59] Consistent
with a more limited reading of the Articles, amendments to enhance congressional power were proposed early and often, but failed due to regional
divisions and due to the sense that more far-reaching reforms were needed.[60]
Many ultimately settled on the view that the Articles were not sufficient to address the problems at hand.

Operation." Thomas Jefferson, Jefferson's Amplification of Subjects Discussed with Vergennes
(circa Dec. 20, 1785), *in* 9 THE PAPERS OF THOMAS JEFFERSON, *supra*, at 110. John Jay, reporting
as the Secretary of Foreign Affairs on the subject of state violations of the Treaty of Paris, opined
that "[w]hen therefore a treaty is constitutionally made, ratified and published by Congress,
it immediately becomes binding on the whole nation, and superadded to the laws of the land,
without the intervention, consent or fiat of state legislatures." John Jay, Report (Oct. 13, 1796),
in 4 SECRET JOURNALS OF THE CONGRESS OF THE CONFEDERATION 185, 204 (1820). Hamilton's
famous 1784 argument in *Rutgers v. Waddington* arguably "move[d] the obligation of observing
treaties from . . . soft ground to the terra firma of legal imperative." JULIUS GOEBEL, JR., THE LAW
PRACTICE OF ALEXANDER HAMILTON: DOCUMENTS AND COMMENTARY 289 (1964); *see* Rutgers
v. Waddington (N.Y.C. Mayor's Ct. 1784), *reprinted in id.* at 393; *see also* John C. Yoo, *Globalism
and the Constitution: Treaties, Non-Self-Execution, and the Original Understanding*, 99 COLUM.
L. REV. 1955, 2016–18 (1999) (discussing Hamilton's *Rutgers* argument and similar opinions
expressed in his "Phocion" pamphlets of 1784).

[57] The Supreme Court reversed a divided circuit court and held for the plaintiffs seeking to recover the debt, issuing a brief opinion for the Court. Ware v. Hylton, 3 U.S. (3 Dall.) 199, 285
(1796). Individual justices wrote separately. Justice Chase opined that "treaties made by Congress,
according to the Confederation, were superior to the laws of the states; because the Confederation
made them obligatory on all the states," among other reasons. *Id.* at 236 (Chase, J.). Justice Wilson,
too, thought that "[i]ndependent . . . of the Constitution of the United States . . . the treaty is sufficient to remove every impediment founded on the law of Virginia." *Id.* at 281 (Wilson, J.). Justice
Iredell did not vote, having participated below (and in favor of the reversed decision), but he was
allowed to reprint his opinion from those proceedings. There, he had stressed that absent state
repeals, "no British creditor could have maintained a suit in virtue of the treaty, where any legislative impediment existed, until the present constitution of the United States was formed." *Id.* at 276
(Iredell, J.).

[58] *See, e.g.*, 32 JOURNALS OF THE CONTINENTAL CONGRESS 124–25 (noting resolution asserting
that state laws inconsistent with any part of a national treaty violated the binding law of the law, and
urging those laws' repeal). Congress also recommended that the states adopt acts permitting judicial
resolution of treaty-based claims notwithstanding any contrary state law. *See id.* at 177 (adopting
explanatory Letter from President of Congress to the State Governors); *see also* MORRIS, *supra* note
33, at 202 (describing Jay's letter and the resulting congressional resolution as the foundation for the
Constitution's Supremacy Clause).

[59] HAMBURGER, *supra* note 47, at 590–92; *see also id.* at 588–89 (citing objections in 1778 by
Chief Justice Drayton of South Carolina relating to the standing of congressional actions under the
Articles).

[60] Proposals were submitted as early as 1781, resumed in earnest in the spring of 1784, and included a separate convention at Annapolis in 1786. *See* MARKS, *supra* note 33, at 84–95; MORRIS,
supra note 33, at 245–57; RAKOVE, *supra* note 25, at 289–96, 345–52.

B. Constitutional Design

Foreign relations difficulties, including in negotiating and fulfilling treaties, helped catalyze the decision to design a new constitution. The founding generation continued to perceive international competence as the transcendent objective of independence and union,[61] and as 1789 approached, they became increasingly convinced that a different form of constitution was required.[62]

The breadth of the changes contemplated, particularly for the national political branches, means that deliberations over the Constitution's treaty-specific clauses tell only a fraction of the story. Indeed, treaties were not themselves a focal point of the convention's most prominent initiatives—in order of appearance, the Virginia Plan,[63] the Pinckney Plan,[64] the New Jersey Plan,[65] and Hamilton's "sketch"[66]—but rather emerged as an entailment of other choices. Ultimately, however, they received significant attention during subsequent discussions, including as to questions that remain of contemporary significance.

1. Separation of Treaty Powers

Although the Treaty Clause highlights the roles played by the president and Senate, there was little recorded consideration of the part either might play through most of the convention.[67] The proposal introduced on August 6, 1787,

---

[61] See, e.g., GOULD, supra note 48, at 10–11; HENDRICKSON, supra note 27, at 28–29; David M. Golove & Daniel J. Hulsebosch, A Civilized Nation: The Early American Constitution, the Law of Nations, and the Pursuit of International Recognition, 85 N.Y.U. L. REV. 932 (2010). For a critical review of this literature, see Tom Cutterham, The International Dimension of the Federal Constitution, 48 J. AM. STUD. 501 (2014).

[62] See RAKOVE, supra note 25, at 350 (describing conducting foreign policy as "clearly the principal responsibility that Congress would exercise in time of peace" and, thus, posing "the most alarming questions the delegates encountered between the Treaty of Paris and the calling of the Philadelphia Convention"); accord HENDRICKSON, supra note 27, at 28–29; Marks, supra note 48, at 308, 316.

[63] 1 FARRAND'S RECORDS 20–23 (Madison's notes) (Virginia Plan, as originally introduced by Randolph); see also id. at 47; id. at 61; id. at 224–25; id. at 235–36. See generally MORRIS, supra note 48, at 275–80; JACK N. RAKOVE, ORIGINAL MEANINGS: POLITICS AND IDEAS IN THE MAKING OF THE CONSTITUTION 59–63 (1996).

[64] Several versions of this plan are included in Max Farrand's records alone. See 2 FARRAND'S RECORDS 157–58; 3 id. at 595–601; id. at 604–09 (reprinting outlines and reconstructions of the Pinckney Plan); see also Jared McClain, An Analysis of Charles Pinckney's Contributions at the Constitutional Convention of 1787, 24 J. S. LEG. HIST. 1 (2016); S. Sidney Ulmer, Charles Pinckney: Father of the Constitution?, 10 S.C.L.Q. 225 (1957). The Pinckney Plan was introduced immediately after the Virginia Plan and was also referred to the Committee of the Whole, 1 FARRAND'S RECORDS 23 (Madison's notes), but went no further. See MORRIS, supra note 33, at 273, 278; William Ewald, The Committee of Detail, 28 CONST. COMMENT. 197 (2012).

[65] 1 FARRAND'S RECORDS 242, 244–45 (New Jersey Plan, introduced by William Paterson); see RAKOVE, supra note 63, at 63–66.

[66] 1 FARRAND'S RECORDS 291–92 (Hamilton Plan). For an overarching account of design issues, see Swaine, Negotiating Federalism, supra note 38, at 1162–87, 1193–1211.

[67] See Arthur Bestor, "Advice" from the Very Beginning, "Consent" When the End Is Achieved, 83 AM. J. INT'L L. 718, 719 (1989). There had been discussion regarding whether the Virginia Plan's concept of giving an executive those "Executive rights vested in Congress by the Confederation," 1 FARRAND'S RECORDS 21 (Madison's notes) (Resolution 7), might in the bargain reallocate the more

provided that the Senate should have the power to make treaties.[68] Yet some of the Framers sought to involve the House.[69] Madison, following Hamilton,[70] suggested that because the Senate "represented the States alone" (and for "other obvious reasons"), "the President should be an agent in Treaties," thereby "[a]llowing the President & Senate to make Treaties."[71] After an inconclusive discussion, the proposal was referred to committee, where it was transformed into something similar to its final version.[72]

That this drafting was done with so little controversy has been read as indicating that no significant change was intended—that the role played by the Confederation Congress was essentially transferred to the Senate.[73] That view depends on silence in the convention records that are known to be incomplete.[74] It also makes too little of the decision—while dividing legislative power between two houses—to vest legislative authority in the Senate and, exceptionally, to require Senate consent by a two-thirds supermajority. This addressed small-state

legislative powers of making war and peace, but the delegates struck out that portion of the proposal. *See* Bestor, *Advice*, *supra*, at 720–22; Bestor, *Respective Roles*, *supra* note 33, at 79–81; Arthur Bestor, *Separation of Powers in the Domain of Foreign Affairs: The Original Intent of the Constitution Historically Examined*, 5 SETON HALL L. REV. 527, 575–76 (1974).

[68] *See* 2 FARRAND'S RECORDS, *supra* note 64, at 183 (Report of the Committee of Detail, Aug. 6, Art. 9, § 1) ("The Senate of the United States shall have power to make treaties, and to appoint Ambassadors, and Judges of the supreme Court."); *accord id.* at 392 (Madison's notes).

[69] 2 FARRAND'S RECORDS, *supra* note 64, at 392 (Madison's notes) (Gouverneur Morris).

[70] Alexander Hamilton had taken the view that a chief executive should "have with the advice and approbation of the Senate the power of making all treaties." 1 FARRAND'S RECORDS 292 (Madison's notes) (Article 4); *accord id.* (Article 6) (granting to the Senate "the power of advising and approving all Treaties"). By Madison's account, Hamilton disclaimed offering this plan as a "proposition" because he estimated that it would not immediately appeal to the convention or to the people at large. *Id.* at 291.

[71] 2 FARRAND'S RECORDS 392, 394 (Madison's notes).

[72] After being sent to the Committee of Detail, see *id.* at 394 (Madison's notes), and then to the Committee of Postponed Parts, see *id.* at 473 (Journal), the proposal returned with a clause providing that "[t]he President by and with the advice and Consent of the Senate, shall have power to make Treaties . . . [b]ut no Treaty shall be made without the consent of two thirds of the members present." *Id.* at 498–99 (Madison's notes). General Charles Cotesworth Pinckney, who had been at the convention (but not himself on the Committee of Postponed Parts), later asserted that it had given "the President a power of proposing treaties, as he was the ostensible head of the Union, and to vest the Senate (where each state had an equal voice) with the power of agreeing or disagreeing to the terms proposed." 4 JONATHAN ELLIOT, THE DEBATES IN THE SEVERAL STATE CONVENTIONS ON THE ADOPTION OF THE FEDERAL CONSTITUTION, AS RECOMMENDED BY THE GENERAL CONVENTION AT PHILADELPHIA, IN 1787, at 263–65 (Burt Franklin ed., 1968) (1888) [hereinafter ELLIOT'S DEBATES]. For more impartial accounts, see Jack N. Rakove, *Making Foreign Policy—The View from 1787*, *in* FOREIGN POLICY AND THE CONSTITUTION 1, 9–10 (Robert A. Goldwin & Robert A. Licht eds., 1990); Rakove, *supra* note 36, at 242–43; R. Earl McClendon, *Origin of the Two-Thirds Rule in Senate Action upon Treaties*, 36 AM. HIST. REV. 768, 769–70 (1931).

[73] *See, e.g.,* Bestor, *supra* note 33, at 101, 118; *accord* Raoul Berger, *The Presidential Monopoly of Foreign Relations*, 71 MICH. L. REV. 1, 11 (1972); William Whitwell Dewhurst, *Does the Constitution Make the President Sole Negotiator of Treaties?*, 30 YALE L.J. 478, 483 (1921).

[74] *Cf. supra* this chapter text accompanying notes 63–66 (noting, too, variety of proposals put before the convention).

concerns about runaway treaty-making but invited in turn concerns about minority control and neglect of national interest.[75] While today the president's involvement in treaty-making under the Constitution seems like the most significant change from the Articles, involving the president was largely a byproduct of the debate concerning vesting power in the Senate, with the president's own function receiving little scrutiny throughout.[76]

Ultimately, of course, the Treaty Clause did establish some parameters for the horizontal separation of treaty powers. Even if it is implausible to suppose that it was drafted to confine the Senate merely to approving or disapproving treaties,[77] it is also implausible that it was designed to confine the president solely to carrying out the Senate's instructions, given concerns about the Articles' ineffectual scheme.[78] In fact, the president's power to "make" treaties was probably understood to include final judgment on whether ultimately to proceed with ratification,[79] thereby firmly placing the president in charge of binding the United States to an international agreement.[80] On balance, the convention neither foreclosed

[75] See, e.g., 2 FARRAND'S RECORDS 522–23 (Madison's notes) (noting James Wilson's description of the Senate's power "to make Treaties," and his objections to the Senate's "dangerous tendency to aristocracy," along with Gouverneur Morris' response).

[76] See Rakove, supra note 36, at 246–50. Madison did suggest exempting treaties of peace from the two-thirds rule and from presidential concurrence, see 2 FARRAND'S RECORDS 540 (Sept. 7) (Madison's notes), which arguably implies that the Senate was generally capable of directing negotiations and approving treaties, without or despite the president. See Bestor, supra note 33, at 129; Bestor, Separation of Powers, supra note 67, at 653–55. But Madison's position was particularly about peace treaties, and focused more on the two-thirds hurdle than on the president, and this and similar proposals were defeated. 2 FARRAND'S RECORDS 540–41, 543 (Madison's notes); id. at 544–47 (Journal); id. at 547–50 (Madison's notes).

[77] As Professor Rakove concluded, "[n]othing in this debate suggests that the framers viewed the president as the principal and independent author of foreign policy, or that they would have reduced the advice and consent required of the Senate to the formal approval of treaties negotiated solely at the initiative and discretion of the executive." RAKOVE, supra note 63, at 266–67.

[78] See Rakove, supra note 36, at 275 (noting the then evident "dangers of allowing foreign policy to be made exclusively by a Senate that would bear an unfortunate resemblance to the existing Congress"). To be sure, Madison had recommended precisely that the "President should be an agent in Treaties." 2 FARRAND'S RECORDS 392 (Madison's notes). But reading that as suggesting that Madison "merely wished to write into the new Constitution the relationship that already existed between the old Congress and its Secretary for Foreign Affairs," Bestor, supra note 33, at 109, ignores how he and others were also interested in cabining the power of the Senate and the states it then represented—rather than just perpetuating the system as in the old Congress, in which states were naturally supreme. 2 FARRAND'S RECORDS 392. In sum, it is difficult to read the convention proceedings and conclude that the president was added to the Treaty Clause "simply to serve as the agent of the Senate or to avoid violating the principle of the unitary executive." Rakove, supra note 36, at 250.

[79] As indicated below, the president's ultimate authority to decide whether to ratify was confirmed by subsequent practice, but appears never to have been in doubt. See infra this chapter text accompanying notes 163–165.

[80] The president's role in selecting U.S. diplomats, see U.S. CONST. art. II, § 2, cl. 2, and receiving those from foreign states, see id. art. II, § 3, plausibly confirmed a degree of independence—and as the Supreme Court recently noted, these textual assignments are augmented by the understanding that the president also possessed the capacity to "open diplomatic channels simply by engaging in direct diplomacy with foreign heads of state and their ministers." Zivotofsky v. Kerry, 576 U.S. 1, 13–14

legislative involvement in negotiations nor contraindicated any later assumption by the president of a leading role in those regards.

2. Treaties and the States

Perhaps because the convention paid so little attention to treaties on the whole, there was little recorded discussion of what proved during ratification to be the states' greatest concern: namely, the subjects treaties could reach. As with the Articles of Confederation, the Treaty Clause did not enumerate the kinds of treaties that could be made; unlike the Articles, however, the Treaty Clause also failed to exclude any.[81] The import was widely understood among the convention delegates. But rather than urging that this breadth be readjusted, or providing reasons to read it narrowly, those concerned proposed increasing the difficulty of achieving Senate approval (and adopting the two-thirds rule) and attempted to mitigate the Senate's power by enhancing that of the House of Representatives.[82]

By contrast, the convention paid close attention to the problem of making treaties sufficiently effective against the states. Hopes that treaty compliance might be successfully managed according to the Articles of Confederation approach had dimmed by the time of the convention.[83] Madison's Virginia Plan not only proposed broad national legislative authority but also the ability to "negative" state laws that interfered with the union—including those inconsistent with treaties.[84] The New Jersey Plan's more modest view of national authority fared poorly as a whole,[85] but its suggestion that

---

(2015). For further discussion of *Zivotofsky v. Kerry*, see Chapter 1 §§ I(B), II(A)(2), II(B); Chapter 2 § II(C); and Chapter 3 § I(D).

[81] Prakash, *supra* note 32, at 1510–12.

[82] Thus, George Mason argued that the power to originate revenue legislation should be held by the House only, since the Senate "could already sell the whole Country by means of Treaties." *See* 2 FARRAND'S RECORDS 297–98 (Madison's notes). James Wilson, supporting an amendment to make treaties binding only if "ratified by a law," cautioned that "[u]nder the clause, without the amendment, the Senate alone can make a Treaty, requiring all the Rice of S. Carolina to be sent to some one particular port." *Id.* at 393 (Madison's notes).

[83] *See, e.g.,* 1 FARRAND'S RECORDS, *supra* note 54, at 19, 24–25 (May 29) (remarks of Randolph, in favor of Virginia Plan, citing problem of treaty infractions).

[84] For background on the negative, see Charles F. Hobson, *The Negative on State Laws: James Madison, the Constitution, and the Crisis of Republican Government*, 36 WM. & MARY Q. 215 (1979). Application to state laws contravening treaties was made explicit after amendment. 1 FARRAND'S RECORDS 47; *id.* at 61; *id.* at 224–25; *id.* at 235–36 (report of the Committee of the Whole). There was debate about the necessity of national legislative authority, and the sufficiency of judicial capacity, but little about the underlying imperative. 2 FARRAND'S RECORDS 27–28 (remarks of Morris, Sherman, Martin, Madison, and Pinckney); *see* Martin S. Flaherty, *History Right?: Historical Scholarship, Original Understanding, and Treaties as "Supreme Law of the Land,"* 99 COLUM. L. REV. 2095, 2121–23 (1999).

[85] 1 FARRAND'S RECORDS 313, 322 (reporting vote against reporting the New Jersey Plan to the convention).

treaties be made the supreme law of the land outlived both Madison's proposed negative and suggestions that treaties could be made supreme only by involving the whole Congress.[86]

Instead, the convention proceeded on the assumption that treaties made for the United States—through the president and Senate, it had been decided— would by virtue of their making alone have the same force as statutes.[87] Proponents and opponents alike thought the Supremacy Clause had established the status for "all Treaties" which some had tried to develop under the Articles— status as law of the land, superior to all state law, and binding state judges.[88] No one thought treaty supremacy was a complete solution. For example, Congress also required authority to legislate in matters of foreign commerce in order to counter unfair trade practices and encourage European powers to have recourse to treaties.[89] But most understood Congress' Article I authority as a complement to treaty supremacy, rather than indicating its limits.[90] Suggestions that the Framers intended to require legislative implementation generally, or to require statutes for matters falling within Congress' Article I authority, are unpersuasive

[86] See 1 FARRAND'S RECORDS 245 (proposing treaty supremacy); 2 FARRAND'S RECORDS 27–29 (approving resolution providing for treaty supremacy). A later effort to revive the negative was narrowly defeated. Id. at 382, 390–91. Gouverneur Morris offered an amendment providing that "[t]he Senate shall have power to treat with foreign nations, but no Treaty shall be binding on the United States 'which is not ratified by a Law.'" This amendment was probably suggested more to make the House a participant in treaties, and perhaps to inhibit their making, than it was to temper their legal status, and it was supported by the Pennsylvania delegation only. See id. at 382–83 (Journal); id. at 392–94 (Madison's notes); see also Rakove, supra note 36, at 240–41, 246–47; Bestor, supra note 33, at 109–10; Bestor, Separation of Powers, supra note 67, at 637; Vasan Kesavan, The Three Tiers of Federal Law, 100 Nw. U. L. REV. 1479, 1531–34 (2006).

[87] The Committee of Detail modified the text somewhat—making it clearer, for example, that state constitutions also had to yield to treaties. 2 FARRAND'S RECORDS 177, 183 (Committee of Detail); see also id. at 137, 144–45 (Randolph-Rutledge draft); id. at 163, 169 (Wilson-Rutledge draft). Later, after further amendments to make clear the application to preexisting treaties, see id. at 409, 417 (Madison's notes), it was set in its present form by the Committee of Style. Id. at 603 (Committee of Style); see U.S. CONST. art. VI, cl. 2 ("[A]ll Treaties made, or which shall be made, under the Authority of the United States, shall be the supreme Law of the Land; and the Judges in every State shall be bound thereby, any Thing in the Constitution or Laws of any State to the Contrary notwithstanding.").

[88] Rakove, supra note 36, at 264. Even those disagreeing about whether treaty supremacy was desirable seemed to share this common understanding. See SAMUEL B. CRANDALL, TREATIES: THEIR MAKING AND ENFORCEMENT 53–63 (2d ed. 1916); see also Flaherty, supra note 84, at 2128; Kesavan, supra note 86, at 1559–60, 1591–92.

[89] See GRAEBNER, BURNS, & SIRACUSA, supra note 48, at 85, 93–96.

[90] The anti-Federalist Federal Farmer did argue that to make the treaty and foreign commerce clauses "consistent," and to make the powers of the president and Senate less "exceptionable," "the true construction is, that the president and senate shall make treaties; but all commercial treaties shall be subject to be confirmed by the legislature." Letter XI of Federal Farmer (dated Jan. 10, distributed May 2, 1788), reprinted in 17 DOCUMENTARY HISTORY, supra note 44, at 308–10. Earlier, the Federal Farmer's warnings had suggested a much more conventional, unqualified understanding of treaty supremacy under the Constitution. See Letter IV from the Federal Farmer (Oct. 12, 1787), reprinted in 14 DOCUMENTARY HISTORY, supra note 38, at 43–44.

on their own terms,[91] in addition to being irreconcilable with subsequent case law and practice.[92]

Two other issues relating to the states appeared to be resolved at the convention, though neither received prolonged consideration. The first concerned the responsibilities of the newly established federal judiciary, which was eventually given jurisdiction over cases involving treaty construction.[93] The second concerned the treaty-making capacity of the states. While the Articles of Confederation had required congressional consent before a state could enter into any "conference, agreement, alliance or treaty" with a foreign power[94]—with states violating a similar restriction on interstate compacts[95]—the Constitution

---

[91] Professor Yoo has suggested that the original understanding might be that "treaties were to take effect as internal law upon implementation by Congress." Yoo, *supra* note 56, at 1962; *see also* John C. Yoo, *Treaties and Public Lawmaking: A Textual and Structural Defense of Non-Self-Execution*, 99 COLUM. L. REV. 2218, 2219 (1999) [hereinafter Yoo, *Treaties and Public Lawmaking*] (stating that legislative implementation was required "particularly in areas within Congress's Article I powers"). But there is substantial evidence that the Framers were convinced that treaties would be judicially enforceable regardless of whether Congress possessed legislative authority over the treaty's subject matter. *See* Flaherty, *supra* note 84, at 2120–51. Professor Yoo's contrary understanding relies heavily on the idea that Article II treaties were executive in character "as under the British Constitution," see Yoo, *Treaties and Public Lawmaking*, *supra*, at 2223, but this takes a narrow view of how eighteenth-century British practice was perceived at the time. Some of the Founders, at least, understood British practice as allowing for self-executing treaties. *See, e.g.,* JEREMY BLACK, PARLIAMENT AND FOREIGN POLICY IN THE EIGHTEENTH CENTURY 1–12 (2004); Kesavan, *supra* note 86, at 1515–29; *id.* at 1525 n.226 (collecting founding-era references); THE FEDERALIST NO. 69, at 419 (Alexander Hamilton) (relying on Blackstone); Kesavan, *supra* note 86, at 1552–55 (describing Hamilton's construction). Others like James Wilson did suggest that parliamentary implementation was necessary. *See* Yoo, *supra* note 56, at 2044–48. But they could well have appreciated that British practice at the time required non-self-execution for powers exclusively held by parliament, such as appropriations or taxation, see Kesavan, *supra* note 86, at 1562–71, or functioned more as an ad hoc political accommodation, see Flaherty, *supra* note 84, at 2130–34.

Regardless, the Framers' understanding of British practice does not dictate what they understood the *U.S. Constitution* to be attempting, and anti-Federalist concerns about how treaties would usurp legislative power—and a proposed amendment, supported by Wilson on grounds of continuity with British practice, that would have required congressional consent to treaty-making—did not prevail. *See supra* this chapter text accompanying note 82; *see also* Kesavan, *supra* note 86, at 1567–69 (discussing a failed proposal during Pennsylvania convention); *cf.* HENDRICKSON, *supra* note 27, at 28–29 (noting that, while British practice was instructive for those drafting the Articles of Confederation, "that ungainly structure . . . had clearly broken down").

[92] *See, e.g.,* Carlos Manuel Vázquez, *Laughing at Treaties*, 99 COLUM. L. REV. 2154 (1999) (addressing Professor Yoo's textual, doctrinal, and structural claims); *see also* this chapter § IV (discussing self-execution and non-self-execution).

[93] The Virginia plan was silent on this subject. 1 FARRAND'S RECORDS 22 (Madison's notes). The Pinckney plan, however, would appear to have assigned appellate jurisdiction over some or all cases involving treaty construction, and that was later broadened to include treaty cases more generally. *See* U.S. CONST. art. III, § 2, cl. 1 ("The judicial Power shall extend to all Cases, in Law and Equity, arising under this Constitution, the Laws of the United States, and Treaties made, or which shall be made, under their Authority").

[94] ARTICLES OF CONFEDERATION of 1781, art. VI; *see also id.* art. IX (authorizing the United States to enter into treaties and alliances).

[95] 1 FARRAND'S RECORDS 316 (Madison's notes).

flatly prohibited any "treaty, alliance, or confederation" between a state and a foreign power, with congressional permission being required for any "agreement or
compact" with a foreign power.[96]

3. Evaluation During Ratification

Although the Constitution's treaty-related provisions seemed to garner relatively
little attention during the convention, they received considerable scrutiny afterward.[97] Critics highlighted how the new treaty power circumvented the House
of Representatives while simultaneously establishing federal law that was clearly
supreme over state law.[98] The *Federalist Papers* responded with an integrated argument concerning the need for a national profile in foreign affairs, best executed
by a president;[99] the efficiency and security of entrusting treaty-making to the
Senate and president;[100] the need to make treaties supreme and subject to federal
jurisdiction, given that they were legal obligations binding on the United States;[101]

---

[96] 2 FARRAND'S RECORDS 187 (Madison's notes); *id.* at 442 (Madison's notes). *See* U.S. CONST. art. I,
§ 10, cl. 1 ("No State shall enter into any Treaty, Alliance, or Confederation"); *id.* art. I, § 10, cl. 3 ("No
State shall, without the Consent of Congress . . . enter into any Agreement or Compact with another
State, or with a foreign Power"). For discussion of the implications for non–Article II agreements, see
infra this chapter § V(A)(3); for broader discussion of compacts, see Chapter 9 § III.

[97] "The articles relating to Treaties, to paper money, and to contracts, created more enemies than
all the errors in the System, positive & negative put together." Letter of James Madison to Thomas
Jefferson, Oct. 17, 1788, reprinted in 11 PAPERS OF JAMES MADISON 297 (Robert A. Rutland & Charles
F. Hobson eds., 1977). For an accessible summary of these proceedings, with extensive quotations,
see CRANDALL, *supra* note 88, at 53–63; *see also* EDWARD S. CORWIN, NATIONAL SUPREMACY: TREATY
POWER VS. STATE POWER 59–74 (1913).

[98] *See, e.g.,* George Mason, Objections to the Constitution (Oct. 7, 1787), *reprinted in* 13
DOCUMENTARY HISTORY, *supra* note 38, at 346, 350 (proclaiming that "[b]y declaring all Treaties
supreme Laws of the Land, the Executive & the Senate have, in many Cases, an exclusive Power of
Legislation; which might have been avoided, by proper Distinctions with Respect to Treaties, and
requiring the Assent of the House of Representatives, where it could be done with Safety"); *see also*
Letter IV from the Federal Farmer, *reprinted in* 1 THE DEBATE ON THE CONSTITUTION: FEDERALIST
AND ANTIFEDERALIST SPEECHES, ARTICLES, AND LETTERS DURING THE STRUGGLE OVER
RATIFICATION 276 (Bernard Bailyn ed., 1993); Brutus, Essays of Brutus II (Nov. 1, 1787), *in* 2 THE
COMPLETE ANTI-FEDERALIST 372, 377 (Herbert J. Storing ed., 1981).

[99] *See, e.g.,* THE FEDERALIST No. 42, at 264 (James Madison) ("If we are to be one nation in any respect, it clearly ought to be in respect to other nations."); THE FEDERALIST No. 75, at 452 (Alexander
Hamilton) (stressing how only an independent president could "enjoy the confidence and respect
of foreign powers" as "the constitutional representatives of the nation"). Similar explanations were
proffered for denying a capacity in states to make treaties or similar agreements. THE FEDERALIST
No. 44, at 280–81 (James Madison).

[100] *See, e.g.,* THE FEDERALIST No. 64, at 392 (John Jay) (emphasizing virtues of thoroughness as
well as "secrecy and despatch"); THE FEDERALIST No. 75, at 452 (Alexander Hamilton) (noting that
adding participation by the House of Representatives would risk secrecy and "dispatch," and complicate proceedings).

[101] *See, e.g.,* THE FEDERALIST, No. 22, at 151 (Alexander Hamilton) (stressing that the pursuit of
state interests could violate treaties of the nation, putting "[t]he faith, the reputation, the peace of
the whole Union" at stake); THE FEDERALIST No. 80, at 476 (Alexander Hamilton) ("[T]he peace of
the WHOLE ought not to be left at the disposal of a PART. The Union will undoubtedly be answerable to foreign powers for the conduct of its members."); THE FEDERALIST No. 75, at 450 (Alexander

and the capacity of the Senate, with the two-thirds rule, to protect state interests.[102]

Discussions during the state conventions continued to show a wide variety of views; conclusions are hard to come by, save that the Treaty Clause, however controversial, survived intact. Dividing authority between the president and the Senate was perceived by critics as offering no more security to state interests than did the existing scheme.[103] Debate about whether the House should have been excluded recognized that it had been, and clearly appreciated that treaties under the Constitution would mix legislative and executive functions.[104] And attempted assurances by Federalists that state interests were constitutionally protected did little to satisfy those concerned, perhaps because the arguments would have seemed half-hearted.[105] Amendments that would have safeguarded certain state laws, the Constitution itself, or existing federal statutes, or which would have raised the threshold for Senate approval of certain kinds of treaties, were rejected in the Maryland, New York, Pennsylvania, and Virginia ratifying conventions (or, in North Carolina's first convention, came to naught).[106] The end result, critics must have perceived, required depending on the president and two-thirds of the Senate as political safeguards—coupled with limitations that might emerge from the House, or foreign partners, in particular contexts—and otherwise to take a leap of faith.[107]

Hamilton) (recognizing the need for federal control of treaties because they "are CONTRACTS with foreign nations, which have the force of law, but derive it from the obligations of good faith," and constitute "agreements between sovereign and sovereign").

[102] See, e.g., THE FEDERALIST NO. 64, at 395 (John Jay) (emphasizing equal and capable representation of states in the Senate).

[103] See, e.g., 10 DOCUMENTARY HISTORY, supra note 38, at 1244 (statement of William Grayson); id. at 1246 (statement of Patrick Henry). The Constitution's defenders did, however, maintain that the Senate's protection of minority interests, and the presidential check on the legislature, offered the possibility of a change for the better. See id. at 1249–52 (statement of George Nicholas).

[104] For the South Carolina House of Representatives debate, see 4 ELLIOT'S DEBATES, supra note 72, at 263 (Jonathan Elliot ed., 2d ed. 1859) (statement of Pierce Butler); id. at 264–67 (statement of Charles Cotesworth Pinckney). In Pennsylvania, James Wilson—who during the convention had tried but failed to secure a role for the House of Representatives in treaty-making—argued that the House's legislative authority in practice would exercise "strong restraining influences upon both President and Senate." 2 ELLIOT'S DEBATES, supra note 72, at 505–07 (statement of James Wilson).

[105] In the Virginia debates, Randolph challenged critics of the Treaty Clause to propose a workable limit, while positing reassuringly that "neither the life nor property of any citizen, nor the particular right of any state, can be affected by a treaty," since treaties were by nature and practice only "binding on the aggregate community in its political, social capacity." 3 ELLIOT'S DEBATES, supra note 72, at 504. Madison also thought it was impossible, and probably "defective" and dangerous, to define limits to the treaty power, while suggesting that the treaty power did not include those that would "dismember the empire" or "alienate any great, essential right," and that "[t]he object of treaties is the regulation of intercourse with foreign nations." Id. at 514–15. In his view, shared with Randolph, id. at 504, and George Nicholas, id. at 507, the treaty power would have to be exercised consistent with its objectives, id. at 514. It would have been quite hard for critics to be satisfied with these depictions of a limited treaty power. See Prakash, supra note 32, at 1513–15.

[106] See CRANDALL, supra note 88, at 62–63.

[107] See, e.g., 3 ELLIOT'S DEBATES, supra note 72, at 500 (statement of Patrick Henry) (noting the risk to "territorial rights, and our most valuable commercial advantages," and stating that "if any

C. Subsequent History

After entry into force of the Constitution, the federal government's treaty practice added considerable detail to the matters addressed, or neglected, by the
Constitution's text. Aspects of this practice are discussed in particular doctrinal
contexts later in this chapter. Two episodes, though, are worth noting as broader,
tonal developments in treaty practice; because they are failures, rather than
achievements, they may otherwise be too easy to look past.

One was the failure of the United States to ratify the 1919 Treaty of Versailles,
including the Covenant of the League of Nations. Wherever responsibility for
the treaty's defeat lies—and whatever the treaty's substantive merits—the defeat deeply influence views of the treaty power. Those committed to protecting
the Senate's role in treaty-making viewed its resistance to the postwar treaties,
including its wielding of conditions as the price for ratification, as illuminating
that body's potential power. Others, however, drew the conclusion that the
United States required other means of making international agreements and
participating in world governance. The constitutional capacity for other forms
of international agreements that did not require Senate consent (congressional-
executive agreements and sole executive agreements) was pressed hard
during the next world war, and their use became one of the most important
developments in twentieth-century U.S. foreign relations law.[108]

A second consequential failure was the "Bricker Amendment," a constitu-
tional amendment considered in various forms during the 1950s. Senator John
W. Bricker and his allies sought to counter the holding of *Missouri v. Holland*.[109]
In that case, decided in 1920, the Supreme Court upheld the constitutionality
of the Migratory Bird Treaty Act, which implemented a bilateral treaty with
Great Britain (acting on behalf of Canada).[110] The Court regarded the treaty,

---

thing should be left us, it would be because the President and senators were pleased to admit it," since
"[t]he power of making treaties, by this Constitution, ill-guarded as it is, extended farther than it did
in any country in the world"); *see also id.* at 504, 514 (statements of Patrick Henry). George Mason
asserted that "there is nothing in that Constitution to hinder a dismemberment of the empire," since
"[t]he President and Senate can make any treaty whatsoever"; his proposal to change the text to require a three-fourths vote in the Senate failed. *Id.* at 508–09.

[108] *See* DEENA FRANK FLEMING, THE UNITED STATES AND THE LEAGUE OF NATIONS, 1918–1920
(1932); Bruce Ackerman & David Golove, *Is NAFTA Constitutional?*, 108 HARV. L. REV. 801, 802
(1995); Jean Galbraith, *From Treaties to International Commitments: The Changing Landscape of
Foreign Relations Law*, 84 U. CHI. L. REV. 1675, 1685 (2017) (discussing Memorandum from the
Solicitor for the Department of State to Senator Henry Cabot Lodge on International Executive
Agreements Not Submitted to the Senate (Aug. 23, 1922)); David Golove, *From Versailles to San
Francisco: The Revolutionary Transformation of the War Powers*, 70 U. COLO. L. REV. 1491, 1493–94
(1999). For more detailed discussion of issues posed by the episode, particularly those involving the
U.S. approach to international organizations, see Chapter 7 § I (C).

[109] 252 U.S. 416 (1920). For further discussion, see *infra* this chapter § II(D).

[110] For much more background, see Edward T. Swaine, *Putting* Missouri v. Holland *on the Map*,
73 MO. L. REV. 1007 (2008); *see also* Mark W. Janis, Missouri v. Holland: *Birds, Wars, and Rights, in*

which sought to protect migratory birds from extinction, as one addressing "a national interest of very nearly the first magnitude" that clearly fell within the treaty power.[111] "If the treaty is valid," the Court further posited, "there can be no dispute about the validity of the statute under Article I, § 8, as a necessary and proper means to execute the powers of the Government."[112] It upheld a statute implementing the treaty, the Migratory Bird Treaty Act, notwithstanding lower court decisions that had held unconstitutional nearly identical legislation (enacted by Congress on its own Article I authority) on the ground that the legislation had violated state sovereignty protected by the Tenth Amendment.[113] The result seemed to vindicate the federal government's strategy of using treaty-making as a means of evading the Tenth Amendment and supported the understanding that the national government had power under the Constitution to do by treaty what could not be done by Congress under its Article I powers.[114]

For Senator Bricker and his supporters, *Missouri v. Holland* meant that multilateral treaty-making—particularly human rights treaties, which potentially required dramatic changes in U.S. antidiscrimination laws—posed a danger to the autonomy of U.S. states and to the United States as a whole. Versions of their proposed constitutional amendment would have denied treaties conflicting with the Constitution any force or effect, required that treaties become effective as U.S. law only through legislation which would be valid in the absence of treaty, and subjected non–Article II agreements to the same limits imposed on treaties.[115] In 1954, their effort fell one vote short of the requisite two-thirds majority in the Senate,[116] but it was successful by other means. Though never seriously in doubt, their insistence that treaties could not contravene the Constitution was vindicated in 1957 by the Supreme

---

INTERNATIONAL LAW STORIES 207 (John E. Noyes, Laura A. Dickinson, & Mark W. Janis eds., 2007); Charles A. Lofgren, Missouri v. Holland *in Historical Perspective*, 1975 SUP. CT. REV. 77.

[111] *Holland*, 252 U.S. at 435; *see infra* this chapter § II(D) (discussing constitutional limits on the treaty power).

[112] *Holland*, 252 U.S. at 432; *see infra* this chapter text accompanying notes 684–695 (discussing the Necessary and Proper Clause and the treaty power).

[113] *See, e.g.*, United States v. McCullagh, 221 F. 288 (D. Kan. 1915); United States v. Shauver, 214 F. 154, 155 (E.D. Ark. 1914). *But cf. Holland*, 252 U.S. at 433 ("Whether the two cases cited were decided rightly or not they cannot be accepted as a test of the treaty power.").

[114] *See infra* this chapter text accompanying notes 680–683.

[115] *See, e.g.*, S. REP. NO. 83-412, at 1 (1953) (version adopted by Judiciary Committee); *see also* S.J. Res. 1, 83d Cong. (1953) (revised proposal from Sen. Bricker); S.J. Res. 43, 83d Cong. (1953) (proposal by Sen. Watkins); LOCH K. JOHNSON, THE MAKING OF INTERNATIONAL AGREEMENTS 85–110 (1984); DUANE TANANBAUM, THE BRICKER AMENDMENT CONTROVERSY: A TEST OF EISENHOWER'S POLITICAL LEADERSHIP 36–48, apps. A–M (1988). The version submitted for a floor vote in 1954 provided (1) that "[a] provision of a treaty or other international agreement which conflicts with this Constitution shall not be of any force or effect"; and (2) "[a]n international agreement other than a treaty shall become effective as internal law in the United States only by an act of the Congress." 100 CONG. REC. 2,358 (1954).

[116] 100 CONG. REC. 2,374–75 (1954).

Court in *Reid v. Covert*.[117] More significantly, President Eisenhower staved off support for a constitutional amendment by committing not to submit certain human rights treaties for Senate approval, a decision that impeded U.S. support for human rights for decades and, arguably, changed its understanding regarding the domestic effect of treaties.[118] Even when the United States finally resumed its support for human rights treaties, beginning with the ratification in 1988 of the Convention on Genocide, the treaty-makers agreed on conditions that effectively achieved Bricker's goal of limiting the domestic effect of human rights treaties, such as by requiring a delay in ratification until implementing legislation had been adopted, declaring that a treaty was non-self-executing, or adopting substantive reservations that limited U.S. obligations.[119]

The remainder of this chapter addresses longstanding and contemporary foreign relations law issues arising in relation to treaties and other international agreements of the United States. The sequence begins with how treaties are made (Section II) and ends with how these and other international agreements are unmade (Section VI); in between, it addresses how treaties are interpreted (Section III); how Article II treaties are incorporated into U.S. law (Section IV); and alternatives to Article II treaties (Section V).

II. Making Treaties

Making international agreements for the United States involves both international and national law. The international law of treaties sets out basic parameters, leaving details to be resolved by particular agreements—and, ultimately, it is left to each state to decide for itself how to express its consent to be bound.[120] Consequently, U.S. adherence to international agreements is closely informed by Article II of the U.S. Constitution, as supplemented by extensive political branch practice, operating in relation to an international law framework.

---

[117] Reid v. Covert, 354 U.S. 1 (1957); *see infra* this chapter § II(D)(2).

[118] *See generally* NATALIE HEVENER KAUFMAN, HUMAN RIGHTS TREATIES AND THE SENATE (1990); DAVID L. SLOSS, THE DEATH OF TREATY SUPREMACY: AN INVISIBLE CONSTITUTIONAL CHANGE (2016) chs. 10–11; TANANBAUM, *supra* note 110; Louis Henkin, *U.S. Ratification of Human Rights Treaties: The Ghost of Senator Bricker*, 89 AM. J. INT'L L. 341 (1995).

[119] Convention on the Prevention and Punishment of the Crime of Genocide, Dec. 9, 1948, 78 U.N.T.S. 277 (entered into force Jan. 12, 1951); *see* Multilateral Treaties Deposited with the Secretary General: Status as of May 24, 2021, https://perma.cc/6TAP-DCAF (noting entry into force for the United States). One of the declarations adopted as part of Senate approval was that the president would not deposit the instrument of ratification until after implementing legislation required by a particular Convention provision had been enacted, which accounted for the subsequent delay in U.S. ratification. U.S. Senate Resolution of Advice and Consent to Ratification of the International Convention on the Prevention and Punishment of the Crime of Genocide, 132 CONG. REC. 2,349, 2,350 (1986):

[120] As in other areas of foreign relations law, the experience of other states offers a rich set of comparisons. *See, e.g.*, OXFORD HANDBOOK OF COMPARATIVE FOREIGN RELATIONS LAW, pt. II (Curtis A. Bradley ed., 2019) (providing global surveys and case studies of how treaties are made in U.S. and foreign legal systems).

This section begins by introducing, very briefly, the most relevant rules from the international law of treaties. It then focuses on "treaty-making" and "treaties" in the sense used in Article II of the U.S. Constitution, although some of the discussion necessarily informs other means by which the United States enters into international agreements.

A. Making Treaties Under International Law

Issues addressed by international law, including what states must accomplish to make a binding international agreement, help structure the questions that U.S. law and U.S. actors must answer. As reflected in the following subsections, these questions are principally the concern of the executive branch. Yet legislators remain attentive as to how and when U.S. obligations are formed when making international agreements,[121] and courts must sometimes assess their status, including in deciding whether agreements may be invoked in court against the United States or other states.[122] At the margins, how U.S. actors address these questions may in turn influence international legal practice.

1. Capacity and Authority

A threshold question in treaty-making, infrequently posed, is whether a given entity is able to enter into the treaty at all. Treaty-making capacity is a key attribute of statehood,[123] and the United States and most of its treaty partners are universally recognized as states. Nonetheless, capacity issues may arise in several ways. Not all agreements are open to every state, so whether a particular state (including the United States) can become party to a given agreement may depend on its terms.[124] And significant questions still arise as to whether another entity is a state or will

---

[121] As one illustration, senators wrote to Iran concerning the proposed Joint Comprehensive Plan of Action concerning its nuclear program, provoked by concerns that the president was using an executive agreement to circumvent the Senate. Letter from Senate Republicans to the Leaders of Iran, March 9, 2015, *reprinted in* N.Y. TIMES (Mar. 9, 2015), https://perma.cc/T6QX-CH82.

[122] *See, e.g.*, Avero Belg. Ins. v. Am. Airlines, Inc., 423 F.3d 73 (2d Cir. 2005) (assessing whether United States and Belgium were parties to the same agreement relating to the Warsaw Convention of 1929 and whether it had entered into force by the date in question).

[123] VCLT, *supra* note 13, art. 6. It is evident from the U.S. Constitution that the federal government exercises U.S. sovereignty for treaty-making purposes. *See infra* this chapter text accompanying note 744 (discussing authority of the federal government and that of the U.S. states).

[124] For example, it is occasionally unclear whether the United States is eligible to become a party to an agreement's protocols when it has not ratified the principal or framework agreement. *See* 2002 DIGEST OF U.S. PRACTICE 183–86, S. EXEC. REP. NO. 107-4 at 80 (advising, in response to Senate inquiry, that the United States could become party to protocols to the U.N. Convention on the Rights of the Child because the protocols were open to accession by states that had *signed*, even if not *ratified*, the Convention). On some occasions, the United States may become a party to protocols of a treaty, even though it is ineligible to become a party to the main agreement. 2010 DIGEST OF U.S. PRACTICE 790–91 (Africa Nuclear-Weapon-Free-Zone Treaty (Treaty of Pelindaba) and the South Pacific Nuclear Weapons-Free-Zone Treaty (Treaty of Rarotonga)). *See generally* RESTATEMENT (FOURTH)

be treated as such in the context of a particular agreement. For example, different views exist as to whether entities such as Kosovo, Palestine, or Taiwan are "states" under international law.[125] When serving as the depositary of a treaty, or engaging with another treaty depositary, the United States may address this issue as purely a question of international law, involving questions of statehood, treaty law, and the treaty's criteria for membership.[126] By contrast, when the United States is determining its own treaty relationships with an entity, it will also take into account national law and policy relating to recognition of states.[127]

It is important to note, though, that even if an entity is not a state (and not, therefore, automatically possessed of the capacity to enter into treaties), it might be accorded that capacity by states and by the relevant treaty. Thus, a substate entity (e.g., Quebec) might be accorded the capacity by its state (under Canadian law) to enter into a treaty, and it may do so if that treaty so allows. Likewise, an international organization (e.g., the United Nations) might be accorded the capacity by its member states (under the U.N. Charter) to enter into treaties, such as with another international organization or with a state, and permitted to participate by the terms of a particular treaty.[128] Although treaties with entities other

§ 302 rptrs. note 2 (noting variety of participation conditions); THE OXFORD GUIDE TO TREATIES, *supra* note 13, at 669–89 (providing examples of participation conditions).

[125] *See* JAMES CRAWFORD, THE CREATION OF STATES IN INTERNATIONAL LAW 198–219 (2d ed. 2007) (Taiwan); *id.* at 407–08 (Kosovo); *id.* at 434–46 (Palestine). Palestine has been accorded non-Member Observer status by the United Nations. *See* G.A. Res. 67/19 (Dec. 4, 2012).

[126] *See* U.S. Dep't of State, 11 Foreign Affairs Manual § 753.4, https://perma.cc/KG6Z-FN78; *see, e.g.*, 1 CUMULATIVE DIGEST OF U.S. Practice 490–93 (describing U.S. views as depositary for the Statute of the International Atomic Energy Agency (IAEA), and contrasting its views as an IAEA member, in relation to the United Nations Council for Namibia). While the U.N. Secretary-General defers to the General Assembly as to whether an entity is a state, see U.N., Treaty Section of the Office of Legal Affairs, Summary of Practice of the Secretary-General as Depositary of Multilateral Treaties at 3, 22–27, U.N. Doc. ST/LEG/7/Rev.1 (1999), the United States has not declared any similar policy.

[127] *See* Chapter 3 § I(D) (addressing presidential authority over recognition). For example, with regard to Palestine, the United States has communicated to depositaries and other international actors its view that Palestine is not qualified to accede to various international conventions, as well as its own disposition not to consider itself in treaty relations with Palestine. *See* Relocation of the United States Embassy to Jerusalem (Pal. v. U.S.), Order, 2018 I.C.J. 708, 709 (Nov. 15) (noting U.S. position that, in light of its previously communicated views denying treaty relations with Palestine in relation to the Vienna Convention on Consular Relations and its Optional Protocol, the ICJ lacked jurisdiction); 2015 DIGEST OF U.S. PRACTICE 120–21 (communicating views on Palestinian accession to the Netherlands, as depositary for the Convention for the Pacific Settlement of International Disputes); Diplomatic Notes from the United States to the United Nations (Jan. 15, 2015), https://perma.cc/EE4A-HJHN (compiling communications to the U.N. Secretary-General in relation to various depositary notifications relating to Palestinian accession).

[128] *See* Vienna Convention on the Law of Treaties Between States and International Organizations or Between International Organizations, *supra* note 13, art. 6 (providing that an international organization's capacity to conclude agreements "is governed by the rules of that organization"). *See generally* Olufemi Elias, *Who Can Make Treaties? International Organizations, in* THE OXFORD GUIDE TO TREATIES, *supra* note 13, at ch. 5; Tom Grant, *Who Can Make Treaties? Other Subjects of International Law, in* THE OXFORD GUIDE TO TREATIES, *supra* note 13, at ch. 7. The competence of U.S. states is addressed in Chapter 9 § I.

than states were uncommon when Article II was adopted—with the arguable exception of treaties with the American Indian tribes, which were understood at the time to be *sui generis* under the Constitution[129]—there seems to be no constitutional obstacle to the United States entering into such treaty relations.[130]

Assuming a state or other entity enjoys capacity to enter an agreement, there can possibly be a separate issue as to which representatives can act on its behalf. Under the international law of treaties, a state is represented by anyone with apparent authority to do so—such as the head of state or government, the minister of foreign affairs, or (within their jurisdiction) the heads of diplomatic missions or missions to an international organization—or by those on whom the state has conferred "full powers."[131] The executive branch, as explored later, employs these alternatives when representing the United States in its own treaty practice.[132] Whether a person is authorized to represent a foreign state can also arise in the course of executive branch diplomacy, such as when there are two competing governments that seek to represent the same state at a multilateral treaty negotiation.[133]

---

[129] The treaty power was clearly understood to permit agreements with tribes. *See, e.g.,* Johnson v. M'Intosh, 21 U.S. (8 Wheat.) 543, 593–94 (1823); *see also* RESTATEMENT OF THE LAW: THE LAW OF AM. INDIANS, PROPOSED FINAL DRAFT § 5 cmt. a (AM. LAW INST. Mar. 30, 2021) ("Indian treaties are negotiated, ratified, and declared under the Treaty Power, Article II, § 2 of the Constitution."). Yet the Supreme Court did not understand tribes as states for other constitutional purposes. For example, with regard to controversies "between a state or the citizens thereof, and foreign states, citizens, or subjects," U.S. CONST. art. III, § 2, cl. 1, the Court considered whether the Cherokee nation "constitute[d] a foreign state in the sense of the constitution" and concluded that it did not. Cherokee Nation v. Georgia, 30 U.S. (5 Pet.) 1, 16–18 (1831). Likewise, the Court construed Congress' "power to regulate commerce with foreign nations, and among the several states, and with the Indian tribes," U.S. CONST. art. I, § 8, cl. 3, to imply a distinction between "foreign nations" and "Indian tribes." *Cherokee Nation,* 30 U.S. (1 Pet.) at 18–20; *accord* United States v. Kagama, 118 U.S. 375, 378–79 (1886).

[130] *See* Wang v. Masaitas, 416 F.3d 992, 996–99 (9th Cir. 2005) (upholding constitutionality of bilateral extradition treaty with Hong Kong and concluding that treaties with "non-sovereign entities" fall within Article II). *But cf. id.* at 1000, 1004 (Ferguson, J., dissenting) (concluding that this presented a political question). Such agreements, however, may fall less clearly within the federal monopoly on treaties. *See* Chapter 9 § II(A).

[131] *See* VCLT, *supra* note 13, arts. 7(2), 7(1)(a); *see also id.* art. 7(1)(b) (noting that practice may authorize others to represent states). *See generally* RESTATEMENT (FOURTH) § 302(2); *id.* cmt. b & rptrs. note 4; Carlos Iván Fuentes & Santiago Villalpando, *Making the Treaty, in* THE OXFORD GUIDE TO TREATIES, *supra* note 13, at 211–13; Peter Kovacs, *Article 7 (Convention of 1969), in* 1 THE VIENNA CONVENTIONS ON THE LAW OF TREATIES: A COMMENTARY 129–35 (Oliver Corten & Pierre Klein eds., 2011).

[132] Article II gives the president (as both the U.S. head of state and its head of government) the authority to negotiate treaties on behalf of the United States, and the president then directs similar activities by others, including the secretary of state and diplomatic representatives. *See infra* this chapter text accompanying note 156.

[133] The issue was more common in the nineteenth century, when U.S. doctrine regarded ratified treaties as retroactively effective to the point at which they were first signed by duly authorized representatives—putting a greater premium on the matter of those representatives' authority at the time of signing. Under contemporary U.S. and international doctrine, ratified treaties are not retroactive to signing; they bind states only after the point of ratification and only in relation to other states or international organizations that have ratified.

2. Consent and Entry into Force

Most agreements stipulate how consent may be manifested and when the agreement will enter into force. Bilateral agreements, typically those of lesser significance, may simply call for consent to be expressed through an exchange of diplomatic notes, or by signature of authorized representatives. For more significant bilateral agreements and for multilateral treaties, a state typically manifests consent through a process of ratification, whereby the state first signs the treaty and then, at a later stage, ratifies the signature by means of an instrument of ratification. (For this reason, describing a state as adhering to a treaty based solely on signature would often be erroneous. Where ratification is contemplated, signature signals the state's intent to pursue ratification and associated obligations, not a state's final decision on whether it is to be bound by the treaty.) Not all states use the term "ratification" for this process; for some, the terms "acceptance" or "approval" are preferred. Moreover, if a state was unable to sign the treaty during the period that it was open for signature, then its ultimate act of adherence to the treaty is typically referred to as "accession" rather than "ratification." Notwithstanding these different legal terms, the process is often referred to generically as one of "ratification," which is the approach taken in this chapter.

Ratification is made effective when instruments of ratification are exchanged with other states or when an instrument of ratification is communicated to the depositary of the treaty. Even then, however, a state's consent may not bring the agreement into force for it. Each agreement specifies how it is to comes into force, and multilateral treaties often require reaching a threshold number of ratifying states and provide for an additional period of time to elapse before entry into force (e.g., sixty days) to allow states to prepare; other rules address the timing for states who ratify after a treaty has entered into force.[134] Once the treaty has entered into force, only states that have ratified it are parties to the treaty (these are known as "states parties" or simply "parties"); states that have signed the treaty, but not ratified, are not yet parties. As explored later, however, states that have signed, or ratified, but for which an agreement has not yet entered into force, may still be subject to certain obligations under the international law of treaties.[135]

3. Reservations to Treaties

States parties to an agreement, even those similarly situated, may not assume identical obligations. Agreements may have optional articles or protocols that states may opt for (or opt out of) when they join the treaty.[136] Frequently,

---

[134] *See* VCLT, *supra* note 13, arts. 9–17, 24. *See generally* THE VIENNA CONVENTIONS ON THE LAW OF TREATIES: A COMMENTARY, *supra* note 131 (providing relevant article-specific chapters).

[135] *See infra* this chapter § II(C) (discussing obligations pending entry into force of a treaty).

[136] These may also allow states parties to exempt themselves from post-consent administrative decisions. *See, e.g.,* Protocol Concerning Specially Protected Areas and Wildlife to the Convention

states choose to consent to a treaty subject to reservations of their own devise. As used in the international law of treaties, "reservations" are unilateral
statements (whether labeled as reservations or not) which purport to qualify
that state's treaty obligations.[137] Reservations allow states considerable flexibility,
but they are not unregulated.[138] Agreements may permit, prohibit, or restrict
reservations, and agreements relating to international organizations may require
approval by a treaty body. Moreover, reservations are impermissible if they violate an agreement's object and purpose.[139]

   If a state makes a reservation when consenting to a treaty, other states parties
may react to the reservation in ways that affect the reserving state's adherence to
the treaty. Sometimes a reservation is expressly permitted by the treaty, which
obviates any need for other states to accept; in very limited circumstances, where
it appears that applying the treaty in its entirety was essential to the consent of
each state party, the reservation must be accepted by all parties.[140] Usually states
react individually by accepting or rejecting the reservation. If a state accepts the
reservation (which it may do expressly or, more commonly, tacitly, by failing
to object within twelve months), then the treaty enters into force between the
reserving state and the accepting state, with the reservation having modified
the treaty for both parties. If a state rejects the reservation, then such objection
will prevent the reserved-to provision from taking effect between objecting
and reserving states, to the extent of the reservation, unless the objection states
that the treaty is not to come into force at all as between them.[141] These rules
mean that for a multilateral treaty there may be a core of rights and obligations
pertinent to all parties, but also a network of bilateral relationships by which
reservations have affected *inter se* some aspects of those rights and obligations.

   In principle, if a reservation is incompatible with the object and purpose of
a treaty, no state should accept the reservation, nor allow the modified treaty
to enter into force between it and the reserving state. Nevertheless, reserving
states have adhered to treaties in circumstances where other states, international
courts, expert treaty bodies, or others assert that the reservation is incompatible

---

for the Protection and Development of the Marine Environment of the Wider Caribbean Region, art.
11.4(d), Jan. 18, 1990, TIAS No. 03-416; 2015 DIGEST OF U.S. PRACTICE 121–22 (noting U.S. reservation based on objection to procedure for listing additional species).

   [137] *See* VCLT, *supra* note 13, art. 2(1)(d).
   [138] The following discussion is necessarily abbreviated. *See generally* VCLT, *supra* note 13, arts.
19–23; RESTATEMENT (FOURTH) § 305(3), cmt. e & rptrs. notes 5–10; Int'l Law Comm'n, Guide to
Practice on Reservations to Treaties and Commentaries Thereto, Rep. on the Work of Its Sixty-Third
Session, U.N. Doc. A/66/10/Add.1 (2011)); Edward T. Swaine, *Treaty Reservations, in* THE OXFORD
GUIDE TO TREATIES, *supra* note 13, ch. 12; THE VIENNA CONVENTIONS ON THE LAW OF TREATIES: A
COMMENTARY, *supra* note 131 (providing chapter-length discussions of Articles 19–23 of the VCLT).
   [139] VCLT, *supra* note 13, arts. 19–20.
   [140] VCLT, *supra* note 13, art. 20(1)–(2).
   [141] VCLT, *supra* note 13, art. 20(4)–(5).

with the treaty. When this happens, an issue may arise as to whether the reservation can be regarded by others as severable, meaning that the reserving state is bound to the agreement in its entirety, without benefit of its reservation.[142] This adds complexity under international law and, as explored later, under U.S. law as well.

4. Impact of National Law on Treaty Law

Whether national law has been faithfully observed when a state consents to a treaty very rarely matters under international law. A state seeking to vitiate its consent to an international agreement on the ground that its national law has been violated can succeed only if the violation is manifest and the rule involved is both of fundamental importance and concerns competence to conclude international agreements.[143]

This principle, which the United States accepts, helps to discourage other states from invoking excuses based on national law to avoid their treaty obligations.[144] By the same token, of course, it limits the U.S. ability to invoke violations of its own law. Some rules of U.S. law, while important, are not sufficiently fundamental to render U.S. consent invalid.[145] Even violations of fundamental and conspicuous

---

[142] The United States, among others, disagrees with this view. *Observations by the United States on General Comment 24* (Mar. 28, 1995), 1 Rep. of the Human Rights Comm., U.N. Doc. A/50/40 Annex VI, at 129–30, *reprinted in* 3 INT'L HUM. RTS. REP. 265 (1996) (arguing that state objections may only result in application of the treaty without the reserved-to provision, or the treaty not coming into force at all between the relevant states); *see* Swaine, *supra* note 138, at 299–303; *see also* Guide to Practice on Reservations to Treaties and Commentaries Thereto, *supra* note 138, at 482–96, 502–42 (presuming that severability may occur and that the reserving state remains a party to the treaty, but allowing the reserving state to overcome that presumption by timely opposition, in which case the state is not a party).

[143] VCLT, *supra* note 13, art. 46; Vienna Convention on the Law of Treaties Between States and International Organizations or Between International Organizations, *supra* note 13, art. 46; *see* RESTATEMENT (FOURTH) § 302 cmt. c & rptrs. notes 6–7. There is a separate VCLT provision concerning instances in which a representative's authority is subject to a specific restriction that was notified to other negotiating states beforehand. VCLT, *supra* note 13, art. 47. Otherwise, invalidity is quite narrowly construed. *See, e.g.*, Land and Maritime Boundary Between Cameroon and Nigeria (Cameroon v. Nigeria), Judgement, 2002 I.C.J. 303, 430, ¶¶ 265–66 (Oct. 10) (noting, in holding that Nigerian law preventing its head of state from entering into binding agreements without governmental approval was insufficiently manifest to invalidate Nigeria's consent, that states were under no "general legal obligation . . . to keep themselves informed of legislative and constitutional developments in other States . . .").

[144] 1 CUMULATIVE DIGEST OF U.S. PRACTICE 1229, 1237–38 (statement by Assistant Secretary of State for Legislative and Intergovernmental Affairs); *see, e.g.*, 2003 DIGEST OF U.S. PRACTICE, 251, 251–52 (describing U.S. objection to attempt by Peru to invoke violation of its national law concerning legislative consent as a basis for invalidity under Article 46).

[145] Thus, violation of a U.S. statute or regulation designed to ensure consultation between the executive branch and the Senate, or within the executive branch, is unlikely to be of fundamental importance, even were it sufficiently manifest to other states. *See, e.g.*, Trade Act Restrictions on the Extension of Most-Favored-Nation Rights, 11 Op. O.L.C. 128, 134 & n.13 (1987) (discussing potential violation of statutory restrictions on fast-track trade agreement authorization). *But see* Jan Klabbers, *The Validity and Invalidity of Treaties, in* THE OXFORD GUIDE TO TREATIES, *supra* note 13, at 554–57 (suggesting that no rigid distinction between constitutional and non-constitutional rules is appropriate).

rules—such as Article II's requirement of Senate advice and consent—may not be sufficiently manifest in a particular case, given widespread use by the United States of non–Article II agreements,[146] just as other states' national rules relating to ratification may not be manifest to the United States.[147] Last, but not least, manifest violations of fundamental rules that do not concern treaty-making are irrelevant, notwithstanding their obvious domestic significance.[148]

The international rules on this subject are rarely relevant in domestic litigation.[149] Nonetheless, the impossibility of invoking most national law violations under international law—coupled with the principle that valid treaties bind consenting states[150]—is important to bear in mind. In principle, those international rules suggested that it could be valuable to provide international audiences with clear guidance on how the United States consents to treaties, so as to identify potentially manifest violations of them. Moreover, the rule makes clear that

[146] As discussed below, the United States has so frequently entered into non–Article II agreements that any violation of Article II is unlikely to be clear as a matter of national law, let alone obvious to other states. See infra this chapter § V. The executive branch has accordingly expressed the view that non-treaty agreements would be valid under international law even if (contrary to its views) Article II required them to be approved by the Senate. 121 CONG. REC. 36,718, 36,721 (1975) (Oct. 8, 1975 memorandum by the State Department Legal Adviser); 122 CONG. REC. 3,374, 3,378–79 (1976) (Feb. 4, 1976 memorandum by the Assistant Legal Adviser for Treaty Affairs). But see 121 CONG. REC. 36,721, 36,724 (1975) (Sept. 24 and Oct. 22, 1975 memoranda from the Senate Office of Legal Counsel, disagreeing with the Department of State's view).

[147] When the Senate discussed a revised Panama Canal Treaty, some suggested that a new Panamanian plebiscite was required to remove the risk that Panama could later claim its consent was invalid. See 124 CONG. REC. 6,545–46 (1978) (statement of Sen. Griffin); id. at 7,019–20 (statement of Sen. Griffin); id. at 10,485–88 (statement of Sen. Bartlett); S. EXEC. REP. 95-12, at 200 (1978) (minority views of Sen. Griffin). The Department of State, however, accepted the Panamanian government's view that such a process was unnecessary, including because any violation was not sufficiently "manifest" under Article 46. See Theodor Meron, Article 46 of the Vienna Convention on the Law of Treaties (Ultra Vires Treaties): Some Recent Cases, 49 BRIT. Y.B. INT'L L. 175, 184–85 (1978) (quoting correspondence of Arthur W. Rovine, Assistant Legal Adviser for Treaty Affairs). The Senate then declined to adopt a proposed reservation that would have required the president to ascertain whether the Panamanian constitution had been satisfied. 124 CONG. REC. 10,488–89 (Apr. 18, 1978); see RESTATEMENT (FOURTH) § 302 rptrs. note 6.

[148] For example, constitutional limits on the capacity of the United States to implement treaty obligations—due, for example, to the Bill of Rights, or federalism-related limits on national authority—could not qualify U.S. consent. See, e.g., Michael Bothe, Art. 46, 1969 Vienna Convention, in 2 THE VIENNA CONVENTION ON THE LAW OF TREATIES 1094, supra note 131.

[149] Courts rarely confront claims that an international agreement violates the U.S. Constitution, let alone agree with them. See, e.g., Star-Kist Foods, Inc. v. United States, 275 F.2d 472, 483–84 (C.C.P.A. 1959) (rejecting claim that trade agreement with Iceland was null and void because it lacked Senate approval). If a court were to find an agreement unenforceable under U.S. law, it would likely stop there, rather than assessing whether it also indicated invalidity under international law. Going further—or considering whether an agreement was unenforceable against another state, based on its violation of U.S. law—might overstep the judicial role. Notably, the relevant VCLT provisions would not leave the correctness of a claim of invalidity solely in the hands of the invoking state, but rather describe a process to be followed by the invoking state and by any affected state(s) for resolving any potential dispute. See VCLT, supra note 13, arts. 46, 65–68; see RESTATEMENT (FOURTH) § 302 rptrs. note 7.

[150] See VCLT, supra note 13, art. 26 (invoking the principle of pacta sunt servanda, that "[e]very treaty in force is binding upon the parties to it and must be performed by them in good faith.").

444 THE LAW OF U.S. FOREIGN RELATIONS

U.S. obligations may remain enforceable despite domestic invalidity, perhaps influencing how broadly potential grounds for domestic invalidity are construed or commending rules that provide better safeguards.[151]

B. Treaty-Making Under Article II

The Treaty Clause of Article II of the U.S. Constitution provides that "[the President] shall have Power, by and with the Advice and Consent of the Senate, to make Treaties, provided two thirds of the Senators present concur."[152] While the clause is the starting point for a wide range of legal issues concerning international agreements, its depiction of the treaty "Power" focuses on how the branches "make" treaties. This makes it the clear starting point for considering procedural issues about treaty-making, though there is little doubt that matters have changed substantially since the founding.[153]

1. Negotiation (and Advice)

By statute, responsibility for negotiating and concluding treaties and other international agreements on behalf of the United States is assigned to the secretary of state or her designate, who may then—according to the "Circular 175 Procedure"—provide authority to others to act.[154] (Based on other statutory authority, the U.S. Trade Representative (USTR) has taken the position that it need not follow the same process.[155]) Ambassadors and other diplomats may

---

[151] Cf. Made in the USA Found. v. United States, 242 F.3d 1300, 1310 n.23 (11th Cir. 2001) (suggesting that NAFTA would remain enforceable against the United States under international law even if deemed unconstitutional); Greater Tampa Chamber of Commerce v. Goldschmidt, 627 F.2d 258, 263 & n.4 (D.C. Cir. 1980) (invoking Article 46 of the VCLT to suggest that, were the court to hold that the United States unconstitutionally entered into an executive agreement on air travel with the United Kingdom, the fact that the agreement would remain binding as a matter of international law would likely compel the Senate to approve the agreement as an Article II treaty). A related VCLT provision establishes (subject to Article 46) that "[a] party may not invoke the provisions of its internal law as justification for its failure to perform a treaty." VCLT, supra note 13, art. 27. The United States also considers this to be a principle of customary international law. 1 CUMULATIVE DIGEST OF U.S. PRACTICE 1229, 1237 (statement by assistant secretary of state for legislative and intergovernmental affairs).

[152] U.S. CONST. art. II, § 2, cl. 2.

[153] For criticism of this evolution, see Bestor, Advice, supra note 67, at 725–27; Bestor, supra note 33, at 15–17; Bestor, Separation of Powers, supra note 67, at 534–41; for praise of Bestor's account of the founding, see Ackerman & Golove, supra note 108, at 809 n.21; Rakove, supra note 36, at 235 n.5.

[154] 1 U.S.C. § 112b(c) (2018); 22 C.F.R. § 181.4 (2019); 11 Foreign Affairs Manual, supra note 126 §§ 710–14, https://perma.cc/LF49-QV32; RESTATEMENT (FOURTH) § 302 rptrs. note 5. For an excellent overview of this process, see Oona A. Hathaway, Curtis A. Bradley, & Jack L. Goldsmith, The Failed Transparency Regime for Executive Agreements: An Empirical and Normative Analysis, 134 HARV. L. REV. 629, 658–65 (2020).

[155] See 19 U.S.C. § 1872. USTR's position has manifested itself in relation to procedures for determining, among other things, whether congressional approval is required, and then reporting those assessments to Congress. See Hathaway, Bradley, & Goldsmith, supra note 154, at 673 n.204 (describing disagreement between USTR and Department of State lawyers regarding whether

represent the United States by virtue of their offices. For international conferences, a document known as "full powers" may be issued that gives a specific person or persons authority to negotiate, sign, or otherwise finalize a treaty on behalf of the United States; the document discloses to interested states, however, that even after signature or finalization, the agreement is still subject to presidential approval, which may require advice or consent by the Senate.[156]

Department of State procedures provide for consulting with Congress (as well as with the broader public),[157] but assessing whether congressional involvement is constitutionally required, or (if unwelcome) constitutionally permissible, is more difficult. The Treaty Clause provides limited guidance. The president's power to "make" treaties does not unequivocally confer power to negotiate them; it could advert to the process of approving negotiated treaties,[158] or to the subsequent task of ratifying a treaty on behalf of the United States.[159] In any case, the power to "make" must be exercised "by and with" the Senate, which could be read to suggest that negotiations were to begin only when mutually agreed.[160] Given that the Senate was viewed for most of the constitutional convention as the best place to locate *all* treaty powers,[161] it seems plausible that negotiations were regarded as something that could be part of a joint enterprise, as opposed to something falling outside of the Treaty Clause altogether.[162] Among the Framers,

USTR is subject to Circular 175 or may separately approve international agreements); *U.S. Practice Regarding Acceptance of Amendments to the WTO Agreement*, 101 AM. J. INT'L L. 655, 657 & n.18 (2007) (noting USTR view, adding that "[n]o parallel procedure exists in the USTR to determine whether an amendment to a U.S. trade agreement requires congressional approval"). USTR may not be singular in this regard. *See* Hathaway, Bradley, & Goldsmith, *supra* note 154, at 673 n.204.

[156] Full powers usually do not obviate the need for further instruction on matters extending beyond the scope of the authorization granted, and usually do not constitute final authorization to sign or conclude a treaty on the nation's behalf. 1989–1990 DIGEST OF U.S. PRACTICE 142–43 (reprinting excerpts from May 5, 1989, memorandum prepared by the Office of the Assistant Legal Adviser for Treaty Affairs); *see* 11 Foreign Affairs Manual, *supra* note 126 §§ 724.1–724.3, 725.1, https://perma.cc/V6SS-YHP2; *id.* §§ 731.3, 733, https://perma.cc/P5N2-2X7T; *id.* §§ 742, 745, https://perma.cc/99DH-3CW7.

[157] *Id.* §§ 724.3(c), 725.1, https://perma.cc/V6SS-YHP2.

[158] This constraint on the meaning of "making" treaties would be consistent with the use of that term in other domestic contexts. *See, e.g.*, U.S. CONST. art. I, § 4, cl. 1 (providing that Congress may "make" rules regarding congressional elections); *id.* § 8, cl. 18 (conferring power to "make" all necessary and proper laws).

[159] This constraint on what is meant by "making" treaties is consistent with aspects, at least, of Professor Henkin's view. HENKIN, FOREIGN AFFAIRS, at 177 ("If [the president] approves what [the negotiators] have negotiated, he seeks the consent of the Senate, and if he obtains it he can 'make' the treaty."); *id.* at 177 n.*.

[160] *Cf.* Henry Cabot Lodge, *The Treatymaking Powers of the Senate, in* A FIGHTING FRIGATE AND OTHER ESSAYS AND ADDRESSES 232 (1902) ("The 'advice and consent of the Senate' are . . . coextensive with the 'power' conferred on the President, which is 'to make treaties,' and apply to the entire process of treatymaking.").

[161] *See, e.g.*, 2 FARRAND'S RECORDS 183 (August 6 Committee of Detail draft).

[162] The president's power to nominate ambassadors, U.S. CONST. art. II, § 2, cl. 2, might establish a separate basis for an exclusive negotiating authority, as those ambassadors would represent the United States in treaty affairs. But such nominations are also subject to Senate approval, and

it was common to regard negotiating as essentially executive in nature, but at the same time, to acknowledge the compromise worked by the role the Treaty Clause allocated to the Senate.[163]

Subsequent practice identified, and to some degree resolved, three intertwined questions about the roles of the president and Senate. First, practice established that the president had authority to proceed with negotiations without first seeking legislative authorization. Presidents initially deferred to the Senate, but came to seek counsel less formally and less regularly. Commentary tends to emphasize an episode in which President Washington sought the Senate's advice on a treaty, then took offense when his personal appearance before it lacked the desired effect; that instance was probably not pivotal, but Washington and his successors did quickly establish greater independence.[164] The contemporary view is that presidents are not constitutionally obligated to seek advice from the Senate as a whole "until the end of the process when [the Senate] is asked to give its advice and consent to ratification."[165]

Second, subsequent practice also rejected any inalienability position, according to which any legislative involvement might intrude unconstitutionally

---

pre-constitutional experience had suggested that either the president or the Senate could instruct them. *See supra* this chapter text accompanying note 33. Negotiation might also be an "executive Power" vested in the president, *id.* art. II, § 1, cl. 1, but whether that provision is a separate grant of authority, and how it relates to Senate authority over treaties, is controverted. *Compare* Saikrishna B. Prakash & Michael D. Ramsey, *The Executive Power over Foreign Affairs*, 111 YALE L.J. 231, 287–95 (2001) (arguing that the Vesting Clause provides a separate grant of authority), *with* Curtis A. Bradley & Martin S. Flaherty, *Executive Power Essentialism and Foreign Affairs*, 102 MICH. L. REV. 545, 589–91, 626–36 (2004) (suggesting that the Treaty Clause, rather than the Vesting Clause, assigned the president a role in negotiating treaties, with subsequent practice enhancing that assignment to the exclusion of the Senate).

[163] *See* Bestor, *supra* note 33, at 110–12; Bestor, *Separation of Powers*, *supra* note 67, at 538, 581–84 n.190; *see, e.g.*, A Native of Virginia, Observations upon the Proposed Plan of Federal Government (1788), *reprinted in* 9 DOCUMENTARY HISTORY, *supra* note 38, at 681. Those stressing Senate and executive branch expertise had common cause, for example, in resisting proposals to make senators subject to greater control by state legislatures. 2 ELLIOT'S DEBATES, *supra* note 72, at 291 (remarks of Robert Livingston); *id.* at 306 (remarks of Alexander Hamilton).

[164] Washington's reaction was at least tempered enough that he tried again, without incident, on the next business day, and the experience as a whole seems only to have soured him on conducting such business in person. JOURNAL OF WILLIAM MACLAY 130–32 (Edgar S. Maclay ed., 1890); *see also* RALSTON HAYDEN, THE SENATE AND TREATIES: 1789–1817, at 17–27 (1920) (explaining Washington's interest in Senate instruction, his preference for personal consultation, and its frustration). The Washington administration did eventually begin bypassing preliminary advice and consent from the Senate, though its practice was not uniform. *See* Jean Galbraith, *Prospective Advice and Consent*, 37 YALE J. INT'L L. 247 (2012).

[165] CONG. RESEARCH SERV., 106TH CONG., TREATIES AND OTHER INTERNATIONAL AGREEMENTS: THE ROLE OF THE UNITED STATES SENATE 106–71 (Comm. Print 2001) [hereinafter CRS, TREATIES AND OTHER INTERNATIONAL AGREEMENTS]; *see also* RESTATEMENT (FOURTH) § 303 cmt. a ("According to longstanding practice, presidents and their agents (generally from the Department of State) negotiate treaties on behalf of the United States before seeking the Senate's formal advice and consent."); *id.* § 303 rptrs. note 1; CRANDALL, *supra* note 88, at 67–72; HAYDEN, *supra* note 155, at 104–05; W. STULL HOLT, TREATIES DEFEATED BY THE SENATE 27 (1933).

on the president's exclusive power. Even those taking a limited view of Senate authority conceded that the president could invite legislative participation.[166] Indeed, the president has consulted with Senate committees during negotiations and included individual senators as advisers, observers, and sometimes even members of delegations.[167]

A third question is harder to answer: Assuming that the president is free to negotiate without first securing Senate advice, while also being free to invite legislative participation, may the legislature *insist* on having a role? The president's primacy in negotiations is often described as though it precludes any such authority.[168] The Supreme Court's most well-known discussion of these issues, in *United States v. Curtiss-Wright Export Corp.*, seemed to take that approach: the president "alone negotiates"; moreover, "[i]nto the field of negotiation the Senate cannot intrude . . . and Congress itself is powerless to invade it."[169] Subsequent decisions, invoking this dicta,[170] have emphasized that the power to negotiate falls solely to the president—implying their agreement that, even if the power is not precisely inalienable, it should at least be free from legislative regulation

---

[166] *See, e.g.,* 2 JOSEPH STORY, COMMENTARIES ON THE CONSTITUTION OF THE UNITED STATES 325 (1833) (noting the question of "whether the agency of the Senate was admissible previous to the negotiation . . . or was limited to the exercise of the power of advice and consent, after the treaty was formed," and concluding that early practice established "that the option belonged to the executive to adopt either mode"); *accord* H. Jefferson Powell, *The President's Authority over Foreign Affairs: An Executive Branch Perspective,* 67 GEO. WASH. L. REV. 527, 561 (1999).

[167] CRS, TREATIES AND OTHER INTERNATIONAL AGREEMENTS, *supra* note 165, at 6, 37, 107, 109–11; RESTATEMENT (FOURTH) § 303 rptrs. note 2. Service by senators as delegation members for a treaty negotiation may raise conflict-of-interest and separation-of-powers concerns relating to their ability simultaneously to negotiate and to provide advice and consent, thus favoring less formal participation. CRS, TREATIES AND OTHER INTERNATIONAL AGREEMENTS, *supra* note 165, at 110–11.

[168] *See, e.g.,* THOMAS J. WICKHAM, CONSTITUTION, JEFFERSON'S MANUAL, AND RULES OF THE HOUSE OF REPRESENTATIVES, H.R. Doc. No. 115-177, § 594, at 318 (2019) [hereinafter JEFFERSON'S MANUAL] ("[N]egotiations are carried on by the executive alone"); ALBERT H. PUTNEY, UNITED STATES CONSTITUTIONAL HISTORY AND LAW 293 (1908) ("Throughout the whole history of the country the share of the Senate in treaties has consisted in ratifying treaties already negotiated."); *see also* HENKIN, FOREIGN AFFAIRS, at 177 (describing the president as "decid[ing] whether to negotiate with a particular country (or countries) on a particular subject," "appoint[ing] and instruct[ing] the negotiators and follow[ing] their progress in negotiations," and deciding whether to seek Senate consent and ratification for their result, and that in practice "[t]he Senate does not formally advise on treaties before or during negotiations"); Powell, *supra* note 166, at 558–59 (asserting that "the executive's power over negotiations vests in it the discretion to determine the goals as well as the modes of diplomacy"). *But see, e.g.,* William Whitwell Dewhurst, *Does the Constitution Make the President Sole Negotiator of Treaties?,* 30 YALE L.J. 478 (1921) (reprinted as S. DOC. NO. 67-9 (1921)).

[169] United States v. Curtiss-Wright Export Corp., 299 U.S. 304, 319 (1936); *see also* Durand v. Hollins, 8 F. Cas. 111, 112 (C.C.S.D.N.Y. 1860) (No. 4186) (noting in dicta, while addressing the president's power to order the bombardment of a foreign town, that "the president is made the only legitimate organ of the general government, to open and carry on correspondence or negotiations with foreign nations, in matters concerning the interests of the country or of its citizens"). For further discussion of *Curtiss-Wright,* see Chapter 1 §§ I(D), II(A)(2).

[170] *See, e.g.,* Zivotofsky v. Kerry, 576 U.S. 1, 21 (2015) (noting that the "description of the President's exclusive power was not necessary to the holding of *Curtiss-Wright*—which, after all, dealt with congressionally authorized action, not a unilateral Presidential determination").

or interference.[171] The executive branch, unsurprisingly, concurs,[172] and sometimes it sounds like the legislative branch has even acquiesced.[173]

It is possible to distinguish different forms of treaty negotiation and different forms of legislative influence. Presidential autonomy is likely most robust in the context of direct interactions with foreign powers. This casts doubt on the constitutionality of any legislative attempt, for example, to dictate the persons representing the United States in treaty negotiations.[174] Similar reasoning likely inhibits any legislative attempt to require that the president initiate negotiation of a treaty,[175] and conversely, may be used to object to preventing the

---

[171] *See, e.g., id.* at 13 ("The President has the sole power to negotiate treaties") (citing *Curtiss-Wright*); Goldwater v. Carter, 444 U.S. 996, 1000 n.1 (1979) (Powell, J., concurring) (quoting *Curtiss-Wright*); Earth Island Inst. v. Christopher, 6 F.3d 648, 652–53 (9th Cir. 1993) (citing *Curtiss-Wright* for the proposition that "[t]he President alone has the authority to negotiate treaties with foreign countries," before concluding that "[t]his court has not and cannot lawfully order the Executive to comply with the terms of a statute that impinges upon power exclusively granted to the Executive Branch under the Constitution"); Edwards v. Carter, 580 F.2d 1055, 1075 (D.C. Cir. 1978) (MacKinnon, J., dissenting) ("It is unquestioned that the *negotiation* of treaties rests solely in the President.") (emphasis in original (citing *Curtiss-Wright*)).

[172] *See, e.g.,* Issues Raised by Foreign Relations Authorization Bill, 14 Op. O.L.C. 37, 40 (1990) ("In the conduct of negotiations with foreign governments, it is imperative that the United States speak with one voice. The Constitution provides that that one voice is the President's.") (quoting 2 PUB. PAPERS 1042, 1043 (July 31, 1989) (President George H.W. Bush's veto message of July 31, 1989)).

[173] CRS, TREATIES AND OTHER INTERNATIONAL AGREEMENTS, *supra* note 165, at 6 ("The first phase of treatymaking, negotiation and conclusion, is widely considered an exclusive prerogative of the President except for making appointments which require the advice and consent of the Senate."). Most statements are actually hard to credit to the Senate or the Congress as a whole, or relate only incidentally. For example, John Marshall's famous declaration—recirculated in *Curtiss-Wright* and elsewhere—that the executive branch "is entrusted with the whole foreign intercourse of the nation," John Marshall, Speech of March 7, 1800, *in* 4 THE PAPERS OF JOHN MARSHALL 105 (Charles T. Cullen ed., 1984), addressed the president's *execution* of an existing treaty, not a treaty's making, and implicated Take Care authority more than anything else. *See* Louis Fisher, *The Staying Power of Erroneous Dicta: From* Curtiss-Wright *to* Zivotofsky, 31 CONST. COMMENT. 149 (2016).

[174] *See, e.g.,* 14 Op. O.L.C., *supra* note 172, at 38, 41 (opining that restricting funds for U.S. delegations participating in the Conference on Security and Co-operation in Europe, on the condition that the delegations include individuals representing a legislatively-controlled entity, would be unconstitutional, invoking president's "constitutional responsibility to represent the United States abroad and thus to choose the individuals through whom the Nation's foreign affairs are conducted"); EDWARD S. CORWIN, THE PRESIDENT: OFFICE AND POWERS, 1787–1984, at 214 (Randall W. Bland et al. eds., 5th ed. 1984) ("There is no more securely established principle of Constitutional practice than the exclusive right of the President to be the nation's intermediary in its dealings with other nations." (emphasis omitted)); Myres S. McDougal & Asher Lans, *Treaties and Congressional-Executive or Presidential Agreements: Interchangeable Instruments of National Policy: I,* 54 YALE L.J. 181, 203 (1945) ("No one today doubts that the President has complete control of the actual conduct of negotiations in the making of all international agreements"). Jefferson, while secretary of state, objected to having the French consul present credentials to the U.S. Congress, declaring that the president is "the only channel of communication between this country and foreign nations, it is from him alone that foreign nations or their agents are to learn what is or has been the will of the nation, and whatever he communicates as such, they have a right and are bound to consider as the expression of the nation . . . ." Jefferson to Edmond C. Genêt (Nov. 22, 1793), *reprinted in* 9 THE WRITINGS OF THOMAS JEFFERSON 256 (Albert E. Bergh ed., 1903).

[175] *See* CRANDALL, *supra* note 88, at 74 (indicating that while "the President will always give careful consideration to the views of Congress, deliberately expressed, as to instituting negotiations, he cannot be compelled by a resolution of either house or of both houses of Congress to exercise a power entrusted to him under the Constitution"). Thus, a court of appeals held that a statute providing

president from doing so in particular fora.[176] President Wilson once opined that this asserted power to control "initiative in foreign affairs, which the President possesses without any restriction whatever," is "virtually the power to control them absolutely."[177]

Presidential autonomy in negotiations seems more tenuous when the Senate (or Congress) is weighing in on the objectives of negotiations that the president has elected to pursue. To the Framers, it might have seemed plausible that the Senate could respect the president's lead while retaining the ability to establish policy as part of its "advice" function.[178] In practice, Congress has often favored providing policy recommendations to the president over measures that

---

that the secretary of state "shall . . . initiate negotiations as soon as possible" for certain agreements protecting sea turtles would unconstitutionally "impinge[] upon power exclusively granted to the Executive Branch"—or, at least, that ordering such negotiations was beyond judicial authority. Earth Island Inst. v. Christopher, 6 F.3d 648, 649 n.1, 652–53 (9th Cir. 1993). The executive branch has regularly expressed a similar view. President Reagan, signing an authorizations bill notwithstanding provisions that would "require or prohibit the initiation of negotiations in the field of international relations," indicated that he would "construe these provisions as being subject to my exclusive authority to determine the time, scope, and objectives of any negotiations." Statement on Signing the Foreign Relations Authorization Act, Fiscal Years 1988 and 1989, 2 Pub. Papers 1541, 1542 (Dec. 22, 1987). This "time, scope, and objective" language has since been invoked in relation to other funding restrictions, including those that might be construed as requiring negotiations. See, e.g., Section 235A of the Immigration and Nationality Act, 24 Op. O.L.C. 276, 281 (2000) (declining to construe statutory provision requiring the establishment of foreign facilities as requiring diplomatic negotiations to obtain foreign consent, and citing Reagan statement); see also Chapter 7 § II(D) (describing treatment by the Office of Legal Counsel in relation to international organizations).

[176] One statutory provision purporting to limit the president's negotiating authority, enacted in 1913 and still on the books, requires the executive branch to seek statutory authorization before participating in international conferences—including, seemingly, multilateral negotiations. Act of Mar. 4, 1913, ch. 149, 37 Stat. 912, 913 (1913) (codified at 22 U.S.C. § 262). Congress and the president were evidently erratic in abiding by this law from the beginning, see Henry M. Wriston, American Participation in International Conferences, 20 Am. J. Int'l L. 33 (1926), perhaps due to concerns that it sought to regulate the president as well and failed to rely on available appropriations authority. Id. at 39–40. In any case, the executive branch now regards the law as ineffective. See Office of Legal Counsel, U.S. Dep't of Justice, Constitutionality of Section 7054 of the Fiscal Year 2009 Foreign Appropriations Act, at 7 (June 1, 2009), https://perma.cc/8NL3-8FGF; accord Restatement (Fourth) § 303 rptrs. note 3; Henkin, Foreign Affairs, at 118.

[177] Woodrow Wilson, Constitutional Government in the United States 77 (1908).

[178] Hamilton distinguished between "[t]he actual conduct of foreign negotiations," which was "peculiarly" executive, and the "management of foreign negotiations," which fell to the president "according to general principles concerted with the Senate, and subject to their final concurrence." The Federalist Nos. 72, 84, supra note 50, at 435–36, 519 (Alexander Hamilton); see also The Federalist No. 64, at 392, 393 (John Jay) (commending president-led negotiating, so as to "facilitate the attainment of the objects of the negotiation," without discussing the origin of those objects). As secretary of state, Thomas Jefferson stated that "[t]he transaction of business with foreign nations is Executive altogether," and "belongs then to the head of that department," but added "except as to such portions of it as are specially submitted to the Senate"—meaning, possibly, the Senate's advice-and-consent power with respect to treaties or ambassadorial appointments—and that "[e]xceptions are to be construed strictly." Thomas Jefferson, Opinion on the Powers of the Senate Respecting Diplomatic Appointments (April 24, 1790), reprinted in 16 The Papers of Thomas Jefferson, supra note 56, at 379.

purported to be binding,[179] occasionally suggesting that nothing more could be done.[180] On other occasions, though, Congress attempted more mandatory directions, provoking executive branch resistance and undercutting any idea of a constitutional settlement.[181] Legislators might reasonably presume that the president is usually best left to exercise discretion in negotiations, that there is usually little upside to adopting edicts that will be difficult to monitor or enforce (including due to executive branch constitutional objections),[182] or that it suffices

[179] See CRS, Treaties and Other International Agreements, supra note 165, at 109–11 (providing examples of Senate and congressional resolutions, most in the form of nonbinding recommendations).

[180] In 1816, the Senate Committee on Foreign Relations recommended against a proposed resolution that would have advised President Madison to pursue negotiations with Great Britain, citing the president's role as "the constitutional representative of the United States with regard to foreign nations" and the one "most competent to determine when, how, and upon what subjects negotiation may be urged with the greatest prospect of success." Compilation of Reports of Committee on Foreign Relations, United States Senate 1789–1901, S. Doc. No. 56-231, pt. 6, 21 (1901) [hereinafter Compilation] (reprinting report of Feb. 15, 1816); see 3 S. Exec. Journal, 14th Cong., 1st Sess. 8–9 (1815) (providing resolution). Still, neither the Senate nor the Congress seemed to regard the matter of legislative authority to be closed. Much later, after the House of Representatives tried to declare U.S. policy toward Mexico, and the secretary of state criticized the measure to the French, the House considered and narrowly defeated a resolution stating that when Congress exercised its "constitutional right to an authoritative voice" it bound the president in foreign negotiations. Cong. Globe, 38th Cong., 2d Sess. 48, 48–53 (1864). Senator Spooner later made an oft-quoted argument to the effect that the Senate had no part in treaty negotiations and could not bind the president, see 40 Cong. Rec. 1,418 (1906), but others like Senator Bacon disagreed to a degree. Id. at 2,125–32 (arguing that the president's negotiating power was implied and could be reconciled with Senate advice, although either the president or the Senate might ultimately reject the other's counsel).

[181] Typically, presidents have asserted that they will construe the offending statute as being subject to their constitutional authority or as advisory only. See, e.g., Statement on Signing the Foreign Relations Authorization Act, supra note 175, at 1542; Statement on Signing the Departments of Commerce, Justice, and State, the Judiciary, and Related Agencies Appropriations Act, 1990, 2 Pub. Papers 1570, 1571 (1989). This is not the same, however, as concerted opposition. For example, after President George H.W. Bush objected to an authorization statute an "impermissibly intrudes upon [the president's] constitutional authority to conduct our foreign relations and to appoint our Nation's envoys" and said he would treat it as expressing the sense of Congress, see Statement on Signing the Foreign Relations Authorization Act, Fiscal Years 1990 and 1991, 1 Pub. Papers 239–40 (Feb. 16, 1990), he largely abided by it. CRS, Treaties and Other International Agreements, supra note 165, at 100. Congress has also sometimes stood its ground. Thus, after the president vetoed, on constitutional grounds, a bill providing that comprehensive negotiations to end apartheid should begin and conclude promptly, Veto of H.R. 4868, H.R. Doc. No. 99-273 (1986), Congress overrode the veto. See Comprehensive Anti-Apartheid Act of 1986, § 401(b)(1), Pub. L. No. 99-440, 100 Stat. 1106 (1986), repealed by South African Democratic Transition Support Act of 1993, § 4, Pub. L. No. 103-149, 107 Stat. 1504 (1993).

[182] President Wilson refused to cooperate with a request by the Senate Committee on Foreign Relations for drafts of peace treaties still being negotiated with Germany's war allies, claiming that it "would tend to take the function of negotiating treaties out of the hands of the Executive, where it is expressly vested by the Constitution." Senator Lodge, responding as Committee chair, was conciliatory, agreeing that negotiations were "wholly in the hands of the Executive," and noting that the Senate had requested only information that could be provided consistent with the public interest, a judgment on which it might treat the president's word as final. Four Treaties Denied to Senate, N.Y. Sun, Sept. 2, 1919, at 1; cf. 4 Elliott's Debates, supra note 72, at 127 (statement of James Iredell, in North Carolina's ratifying convention, that presidents would "regulate all intercourse with foreign powers," but also were obliged to provide to the Senate "every material intelligence").

to make recommendations in light of the Senate's ultimate power to withhold consent, without conceding for all time the president's autonomy.[183]

Ultimately, though, very little can be considered settled: Congress or the Senate may attempt more comprehensive regulation, and the executive branch may object to any attempt to assert legislative authority over treaty negotiations. For example, in evaluating a proposed bill that would have established a World Trade Organization (WTO) Dispute Settlement Commission and, on its recommendation, authorize and direct the president to negotiate to amend or modify rules or procedures relating to WTO proceedings, the Justice Department's Office of Legal Counsel recalled that the executive branch had "repeatedly objected on constitutional grounds to Congressional attempts to mandate the time, manner and content of diplomatic negotiations," including any requirement that the president negotiate for "certain diplomatic objectives."[184] On the executive's view, the president's power over treaty negotiations includes "the discretion to determine the goals as well as the modes of diplomacy," and enjoys autonomy from congressional interference.[185] Such positions are unlikely to be resolved by litigation, but compromise may be required in the event the executive branch actually desires to secure approval of any treaty.

2. Consent by the Senate

As the Senate's "advice" authority has winnowed, its "consent" authority has remained substantial, and grown more complex. Formally, Senate consideration is triggered at the president's discretion. Even if the United States has signed an agreement subject to ratification (which, as discussed later, may itself give rise to international obligations), the Senate becomes charged with acting only if and when the president has taken the further step of transmitting the agreement to it for advice and consent—sometimes, after considerable times has elapsed following signature. Such transmittal entails a process by which the secretary of

---

[183] Reviewing nonbinding measures a hundred years ago, Samuel Crandall noted that in each instance "the desired negotiations either were pending at the time of the adoption of the resolution or were eventually instituted." He drew the conclusion that only nonbinding congressional measures were permissible, but the same history suggested that binding measures might have been deemed unnecessary to achieve the objective sought by Congress. CRANDALL, *supra* note 88, at 74.

[184] Memorandum from Walter Dellinger, Assistant Attorney General, Office of Legal Counsel, to Alan Kreczko, Legal Adviser, National Security Council, at 3 (Feb. 9, 1995), https://perma.cc/MPW7-HAVD (regarding WTO Dispute Settlement Review Commission Act); *see also* Office of Legal Counsel, U.S. Dep't of Justice, Unconstitutional Restrictions on Activities of the Office of Science and Technology Policy in Section 1340(A) of the Department of Defense and Full-Year Continuing Appropriations Act, 2011, at 8 (Sept. 19, 2011), https://perma.cc/P2AR-4ZX2 (objecting to statutory restrictions on participation by the Office of Science and Technology Policy in diplomatic discussions with China, among other things, as "implicat[ing] the President's exclusive authority to determine the time, scope, and objectives of discussions with China, as well as his exclusive authority to select the agent he prefers as the representative of the United States in these discussions").

[185] *See* Powell, *supra* note 166, at 558–59. For broader discussion of the president's power to conduct diplomacy, see Chapter 3.

state submits the treaty to the president along with an article-by-article analysis, which the president then transmits to the Senate with a message requesting its advice and consent. Thereafter, the treaty is typically considered by the Senate Committee on Foreign Relations and, if reported out favorably to the entire Senate, must be consented to by two-thirds of the senators present and voting. If the Senate consents to ratification of the treaty, it so notifies the president, along with any conditions, such as reservations. If the Senate does not consent, the treaty is returned to the Committee and must be reported out again before any further consideration; the president may also request the return of the treaty, in which case it is removed from the Committee's treaty calendar.[186]

This supermajority requirement for consent to ratification was designed to be a high threshold, and prevailing procedures have enhanced it. Prior to the president's transmittal, the Senate can telegraph its views, thereby discouraging the president from acting.[187] After transmittal, there are practical obstacles, in that the time available for Committee hearings or floor consideration may be scarce, and Senate rules favoring minority positions (such as the filibuster) will apply. The Senate may delay due to substantive or political concerns, or because it wishes to ensure that implementing legislation can be enacted concurrently.[188] And any delay may be extended (and made more tolerable) because—unlike bills, which expire at the end of a legislative session—a proposed treaty may remain with the Senate in perpetuity.[189] Indeed, some treaties have languished there for decades.[190]

---

[186] See CRS, TREATIES AND OTHER INTERNATIONAL AGREEMENTS, supra note 165, at 7–12; RESTATEMENT (FOURTH) § 303 & rptrs. notes 4–6.

[187] See S. Res. 98, 105th Cong. (1997) (as passed July 25, 1997) (voting 95 to 0 to express the Senate's sense that the United States should not enter into the Kyoto Protocol). The Senate has also provided consent beforehand, but modern practice is overwhelmingly to the contrary. Cf. Galbraith, Prospective Advice and Consent, supra note 164 (noting examples of prior consent, and advocating for its revival for certain agreements).

[188] Alternatively, the Senate can consent to ratification, subject to a condition that the president refrain from ratifying until an implementing law is enacted. See, e.g., 146 CONG. REC. 18,766 (2000) (Convention on Protection of Children and Co-operation in Respect of Intercountry Adoption).

[189] Indeed, even a treaty subjected to a vote, but failing to receive two-thirds approval, may later be reconsidered by the Senate, unless the Senate decides to return the treaty to the president. See STANDING RULES OF THE SENATE, S. DOC. NO. 113-18, Rule XXX, at 43 (2013); SENATE COMM. ON FOREIGN RELATIONS, BACKGROUND INFORMATION ON THE COMMITTEE ON FOREIGN RELATIONS, S. DOC. 105-28, at 23–25 (2000); CRS, TREATIES AND OTHER INTERNATIONAL AGREEMENTS, supra note 165, at 143–45; see also RESTATEMENT (FOURTH) § 303 rptrs. note 6.

[190] See, e.g., CRS, TREATIES AND OTHER INTERNATIONAL AGREEMENTS, supra note 165, at 144 (citing examples, including that of the Optional Protocol Concerning the Compulsory Settlement of Disputes, Apr. 29, 1958, 450 U.N.T.S. 170 (1958), relating to the 1958 Geneva Conventions relating to the law of the sea, which remained on the Senate Committee on Foreign Relations calendar for 40 years, after it failed to receive approval by the full Senate). As of this writing, the Senate Committee on Foreign Relations, to which treaties are initially committed or recommitted, indicates continuing responsibility for a number of International Labor Organization treaties on which the last relevant action was taken more than fifty years ago. See Treaties, UNITED STATES SENATE COMMITTEE ON FOREIGN RELATIONS, https://perma.cc/Q7YV-KQ96 (last visited May 26, 2021).

3. U.S. Reservations and Other Conditions

While the Senate's reluctance to proceed with prominent treaties looms largest, its reputation as "the graveyard of treaties" also owes something to its use of reservations and other conditions.[191] As noted previously, "reservations" modify an agreement.[192] Other conditions, not addressed by the VCLT, are nonetheless common in U.S. practice. "Understandings" propose interpretations without purporting to alter the agreement. "Declarations" are used by the United States to make policy statements or to describe the treaty's domestic status, not unlike "provisos" (sometimes called "conditions," in a nongeneric sense), which usually relate to the process by which U.S. actors make or implement the treaty.[193] In the aggregate, these conditions—sometimes called "RUDs" after their principal types—attempt to reconcile U.S. preferences with its international obligations. They also reconcile preferences among U.S. actors. Whether the executive branch initially suggests conditions or not, the Senate may decide to attach them to its resolution of advice and consent.[194] If the president then ratifies, it may only be subject to the Senate-approved conditions.[195]

As U.S. case law acknowledges, the legal effect of these conditions remains dependent on the reactions of foreign states.[196] According to the VCLT, as well

---

[191] Louis Henkin suggested that the appellation "the graveyard of treaties" was reinforced by the "searing experience" with the Treaty of Versailles, in which "the Senate purported to consent, but with numerous and radical reservations." HENKIN, FOREIGN AFFAIRS, at 178 n.†. The label was earlier popularized in relation to the Hay-Pauncefote Treaty, preliminary to creation of the Panama Canal, which the Senate approved with amendments that were unacceptable to the British—causing the treaty's failure before it was renegotiated. *The Graveyard of Good Treaties*, NATION, Mar. 15, 1900, at 199; The Hay-Pauncefote Treaty, Nov. 18, 1901, 32 Stat. 1903; *see* Galbraith, *Prospective Advice and Consent*, *supra* note 164, at 248 & n.2.

[192] *See supra* this chapter text accompanying notes 137–139. An "amendment," the term preferred in the bilateral context, instead seeks to secure a textual change with which the other party must affirmatively agree.

[193] CRS, TREATIES AND OTHER INTERNATIONAL AGREEMENTS, *supra* note 165, at 126–27; RESTATEMENT (FOURTH) § 305 rptrs. note 2. Understandings are discussed at greater length below, in relation to treaty interpretation. *See infra* this chapter text accompanying notes 464–470. Other conditions are discussed elsewhere in the context of the substantive issues to which they relate. *See infra* this chapter § IV(A)(7) (discussing self-execution and non-self-execution declarations); *see also infra* this chapter text accompanying note 355 (discussing federalism-related conditions).

[194] *See* United States v. Stuart, 489 U.S. 353, 374–75 (1989) (Scalia, J., concurring) ("[T]he Senate has unquestioned power to enforce its own understanding of treaties. It may, in the form of a resolution, give its consent on the basis of conditions."). This authority was initially confirmed for amendments to bilateral treaties. *See* Haver v. Yaker, 76 U.S. (9 Wall.) 32, 35 (1869); Fourteen Diamond Rings v. United States, 183 U.S. 176, 183 (1901) (Brown, J., concurring).

[195] *Stuart*, 489 U.S. at 374–75 (Scalia, J., concurring); RESTATEMENT (FOURTH) § 305(1)–(3); *id.* cmt. d & rptrs. note 4. Whether conditions in a treaty ratified by the United States bind the president should depend, of course, on whether the Senate intended a condition to be binding. Curiously, the Senate sometimes affirmatively notes that a condition is binding, which has the potential to put other instances in doubt. *See supra* this chapter note 188 (discussing Convention on Protection of Children and Co-operation in Respect of Intercountry Adoption); *see also infra* this chapter text accompanying note 202 (suggesting potential qualification when conditions are not communicated internationally, or if they exceed Senate authority).

[196] *Stuart*, 489 U.S. at 374–75 (Scalia, J., concurring) (noting that whether conditions "become part of the treaty and of the law of the United States" depends not only on the president's agreement,

as particular treaty regimes, other states may react to any reservations advanced by the United States and thereby affect treaty relations between themselves and the United States; states and treaty bodies may also assert that a U.S. reservation is ineffective because it is inconsistent with a treaty's object and purpose.[197] Understandings, declarations, and provisos do not purport to be altering the terms of the treaty, and thus there is no expectation that other states will react, nor do such conditions have any direct legal effect on other states. That said, another party may regard a U.S. condition as a reservation (even if that was not the U.S. label) and react to it on those terms.[198]

Other states may also ratify a treaty with their own reservations, which can alter their obligations to the United States and U.S. obligations toward them. As such, the United States also regularly reviews and reacts to the reservations to treaties proposed by foreign states. Finally, any state, including the United States, may withdraw conditions at any time.[199] The upshot is that while treaty conditions expand the Senate's options (and those of the United States) when consenting to a treaty, they also mean that U.S. treaty obligations may not be conclusively established when the Senate consents.

U.S. courts have shown little interest in these nuances, and they tend to assume that any conditions operate with the legal effect proposed by the United States.[200] Greater care is warranted. As to reservations, courts may find it difficult to evaluate whether they violate a treaty's object and purpose, but other issues—such as whether a treaty permits reservations to the relevant provision, and whether the reservation in question had been accepted by a relevant state— can be more easily determined by a court, and advice from the Department of

---

but also whether they are "accepted by the other contracting parties"); *Fourteen Diamond Rings*, 183 U.S. at 183 (Brown, J., concurring) (noting that, by itself, "[t]he Senate has no right to ratify the treaty and introduce new terms into it, which shall be obligatory upon the other power").

[197] *See supra* this chapter § II(A)(3).

[198] RESTATEMENT (FOURTH) § 305 cmt. e (noting irrelevance of a condition's label); *see supra* this chapter note 137 (quoting definition in article 2 of the VCLT). The International Law Commission's Guide to Practice on Reservations to Treaties, without using the term "understanding," addresses both "interpretative declarations" and "conditional interpretative declarations"—the former being more akin to a typical understanding, as the term is commonly used, and the latter being disguised reservations. *See* Guide to Practice on Reservations to Treaties and Commentaries Thereto, *supra* note 127, §§ 1.2–1.8.

[199] *See supra* this chapter § II(A)(3).

[200] *See, e.g.*, Beazley v. Johnson, 242 F.3d 248, 267 (5th Cir. 2001) (treating as "valid" and controlling U.S. reservations to the International Covenant on Civil and Political Rights, and citing authority); *id.* at 267 (treating as effective U.S. declaration that provisions of the International Covenant on Civil and Political Rights are non-self-executing); Clientron Corp. v. Devon IT, Inc., 35 F. Supp. 3d 665, 675 (E.D. Pa. 2014) (treating as "binding and obligatory" declarations to the U.N. Convention on the Recognition and Enforcement of Foreign Arbitral Awards that were pre-authorized by the Convention) (internal citations omitted); RESTATEMENT (FOURTH) § 305 rptrs. note 3 (reporting that "[l]ower courts have also generally given effect to . . . conditions when interpreting and applying treaties"); *see also infra* this chapter § III(B)(2).

State may always be sought.[201] Other conditions may or may not warrant similar examination. It is sometimes suggested that a condition must be communicated to and accepted by other states before it can have any domestic legal effect.[202] Given that conditions other than reservations do not purport to affect U.S. rights or obligations under a treaty, however, it may be questioned whether the failure to take steps toward that end should qualify their potential effect as a matter of U.S. law.[203]

Whether the Constitution also imposes constraints on treaty conditions is largely unresolved. Presumably conditions must respect constitutional prohibitions like the First Amendment. Presumably, too, conditions should relate in some fashion to the topic of the treaty on which Article II authority is premised.[204] For example, were the Senate to propose a condition that "Each citizen shall be provided with free health care" when consenting to ratification of an arms control treaty—and the president thereafter ratified the treaty, such that it came into force (perhaps with an additional condition providing that it was self-executing)—that would very likely exceed the scope of the treaty power.

More demanding limits are sometimes proposed. One well-known decision involved a bilateral treaty between the United States and Canada assigning each country shares of Niagara River water for power generation, to which the Senate attached a "reservation" that limited U.S. use of its share to that specifically

---

[201] See RESTATEMENT (FOURTH) § 305 cmt. e & rptrs. notes 7–8; see also id. § 305 rptrs. note 9 (highlighting possibility of withdrawal). Assuming any reservation is permissible and properly submitted, it is ordinarily deemed accepted by another state party after one year—a mechanical inquiry. VCLT, supra note 13, art. 20(5); see supra this chapter text accompanying notes 137–139. Whether another state has objected is also relatively easy to determine, but the effect on treaty relations may be more difficult to ascertain, assuming the objecting state has not objected to treaty relations in their entirety. See supra this chapter text accompanying notes 140–142.

[202] See, e.g., Stuart, 489 U.S. at 374–75 (Scalia, J., concurring) (suggesting importance of acceptance for conditions generally); see also Relevance of Senate Ratification History to Treaty Interpretation, 11 Op. O.L.C. 28, 32–33 (1987) (noting that because "express conditions" communicated to other parties "are considered to be part of the United States' position in ratifying the treaty, they are generally binding on the President, both internationally and domestically, in his subsequent interpretation of the treaty"); Answers to Questions for the Record on the Legal Status of the SALT II Documents Transmitted to the Senate, reprinted in 1979 DIGEST OF U.S. PRACTICE, at 702, 710, 714 (submitted by Herbert J. Hansell, Legal Adviser) (indicating that a contemporaneous Senate resolution setting out its understanding, but not made part of the resolution of ratification, "would not be legally binding per se" if not included and accepted by the other party to a bilateral treaty, but if provided to that party and not contradicted, might be persuasive evidence of the parties' interpretation); cf. RESTATEMENT (FOURTH) § 305 rptrs. note 8 ("Conditions that affect U.S. rights or obligations under a treaty must be communicated in writing by the President to the other treaty parties if they are to have effect under international law.").

[203] See supra this chapter text accompanying note 193.

[204] See RESTATEMENT (FOURTH) § 305(1) ("The Senate may attach reservations or other conditions to its advice and consent to a treaty as long as they relate to the treaty and are not inconsistent with the Constitution."); id. § 305 rptrs. notes 3–4; accord RESTATEMENT (THIRD) § 303 rptrs. note 4. As to constitutionality, a condition has to meet the same standard as that applied for treaties, which is not identical to that for statutes. RESTATEMENT (FOURTH) § 305 cmt. b; id. § 312 & cmt. c; see Missouri v. Holland, 252 U.S. 416, 432–43 (1920); infra this chapter text accompanying notes 211–212.

authorized by Congress. The D.C. Circuit later reviewed a state agency's application to use the U.S. share pursuant to a general statutory procedure. Observing
that the U.S. reservation related "to a matter of *purely domestic* concern," as
it was a point of indifference to Canada, the court indicated that the reservation was not properly part of the treaty.[205] This suggested a difficult role for the
judiciary—requiring that it resolve whether a reservation, like the associated
treaty as a whole, was genuinely of "international concern"[206]—and the decision was sharply criticized.[207] But the court's concerns should not be cavalierly
dismissed. It seems to be accepted that the domestic legal effect of reservations
derives from their international efficacy.[208] If a condition relates to a multilateral
treaty, however, all that requires is the indifference (and non-objection) of other
states, which seem like a low threshold for making law for the United States.[209]
(For conditions other than reservations, which neither seek nor require acceptance by other states, it is no threshold at all.[210]) Even if one assumes that a condition must relate somehow to the treaty, the power of the president and Senate
to condition acceptance remains of potential troubling breadth.[211] For example,

[205] Power Auth. of N.Y. v. Fed. Power Comm'n, 247 F.2d 538,542 (D.C. Cir. 1957) (emphasis in
original), *vacated as moot sub nom.* Am. Pub. Power Ass'n v. Power Auth. of N.Y., 355 U.S. 64 (1957)
(per curiam). Formally, the court treated the reservation as nonbinding in order to avoid resolving
whether the treaty was unconstitutional. *Id.* at 543. Its reasoning effectively undermined the Senate's
depiction of the condition as a "reservation." Insofar as the condition in question did not directly bear
on either party's treaty obligations, it resembled a declaration or proviso, which might have lacked
sufficient domestic legal effect on its face. However, the United States insisted that Canada formally
accept the condition and indicate as much in the exchange of ratifications. Canada complied; however, all this occurred after its parliament had already approved the treaty, reinforcing the condition's
irrelevance to it. *See id.* at 540–41.

[206] *Power Auth.*, 247 F.2d at 542; *id.* at 542–44; *see infra* this chapter text accompanying notes 282–
285 (discussing international concern test).

[207] *See* HENKIN, FOREIGN AFFAIRS, at 451–53 n.29; Louis Henkin, *The Treaty Makers and the Law
Makers: The Niagara Reservation*, 56 COLUM. L. REV. 1151 (1956). Treatment in the *Restatement
(Third)* was subtle. A reporters' note provided that "[a] condition imposed by the Senate that does not
seek to modify the treaty and is solely of domestic import, is not part of the treaty and hence does not
partake of its character as 'supreme Law of the Land.'" RESTATEMENT (THIRD) § 303 rptrs. note 4. At
the same time, it regarded a condition like that in *Power Authority* as fully effective in conditioning
consent, insofar as according that effect did not require treating the condition as part of the law of the
land. *Id.* The *Restatement (Fourth)* simply noted the decision, suggesting it had not influenced other
courts. RESTATEMENT (FOURTH) § 305 rptrs. note 3.

[208] *See supra* this chapter § II(A)(3).

[209] Bilaterally, a reservation is the functional equivalent of a treaty amendment. For multilateral
treaties, the VCLT's default rules provide that a proposed reservation is deemed to be accepted by
another state party if it fails to object within a year, see VCLT, *supra* note 13, arts. 20(5), and a U.S. ratification containing a reservation would be deemed legally effective once at least one other state party
had accepted the reservation. *See id.* art. 20(4)(c); *see also supra* this chapter § II(A)(3).

[210] *See supra* this chapter text accompanying notes 202–203.

[211] The *Restatement (Third)* leaned heavily on the Senate's power to condition consent, but did suggest that a condition wholly unrelated to the treaty in question would be ineffective. RESTATEMENT
(THIRD) § 303 rptrs. note 4. Professor Henkin also reasoned that "since the Senate can withhold consent for no reason, perhaps it can withhold it for any reason, and a President may have to buy that
consent at whatever price and in whatever form the Senate asks." HENKIN, FOREIGN AFFAIRS, at 182.
This was potentially in tension with his view that unconstitutional statutory conditions could be
disregarded. *Id.* at 182 & n.**; *see also* RESTATEMENT (THIRD) § 303 rptrs. note 4 (indicating that "a

U.S. treaty-makers would seem to be capable of using conditions to alter the application of federal statutes on occasions when the treaty does not require it and when Congress as a whole would not agree.[212] If a condition is to have effect as U.S. law, it does not seem much to ask that it relate to the subject matter of the treaty, and relate as well as to U.S. obligations under the treaty or their implementation, but no practicable test has been developed.

Like U.S. courts, the Senate generally shows little interest in what happens to conditions after U.S. ratification, including how other states react (and lodge their own conditions).[213] However, the Senate has objected to treaty provisions that prohibit reservations, as they place the Senate in an undesirable position of either accepting or rejecting the treaty in its entirety.[214] The Senate has also exhibited concern, as during its consideration of the U.N. Convention on the Rights of Persons with Disabilities, that a president might withdraw conditions

condition invading the President's constitutional powers—for example, his power of appointment" would be ineffective). Conceivably, one might treat the president as having accepted an unrelated condition, and as having lost the right to disregard it, without constraining third parties (like the state agency at issue in *Power Authority*) that may be affected.

[212] In the *Power Authority* case, the condition—which required that U.S. redevelopment of its share of international waters receive subsequent statutory authorization—purported to block the authority flowing from an existing statute, the Federal Power Act. *Power Auth.*, 247 F.2d at 540–41. Professor Henkin argued that since the original statute was not focused on the Niagara, the condition simply "prevent[ed] the Federal Power Act from automatically extending to a new area" and did not "take away from the act or the Commission any authority existing prior to the treaty." Henkin, *supra* note 207, at 1172–74, 1181; *cf. id.* at 1179–80 (citing other examples of implementation-related conditions). This is just a different way of saying that the condition prescribed the opposite of what a statute of general application had indicated. The result may appear similar to declarations about treaty self-execution, which seek to affect the domestic legal force of treaties, and which Professor Henkin later criticized (at least declarations of non-self-execution). Louis Henkin, *Two Hundred Years of Constitutional Confrontations in the D.C. Courts*, 90 GEO. L.J. 725, 733–34 (2002). The Niagara reservation went further, however, asserting a self-executing effect for the condition itself, rather than for a treaty provision.

[213] The executive branch has suggested that Senate consent encompasses conditions proposed by other states prior to Senate consent and, in principle, those proposed thereafter; that does not, however, absolve the executive branch of responsibility (which it has accepted) for bringing to Congress' attention any that warrant review. CRS, TREATIES AND OTHER INTERNATIONAL AGREEMENTS, *supra* note 165, at 153–54; *Contemporary Practice of the United States Relating to International Law*, 60 AM. J. INT'L L. 559, 563–64 (1966) (excerpting Department of State letter of Mar. 1, 1966). Conditions to bilateral treaties are a different matter, and it is accepted that the president would revert to the Senate in the event another state proposed an amendment after the Senate had given advice and consent. CRS, TREATIES AND OTHER INTERNATIONAL AGREEMENTS, *supra* note 165, at 153–54.

[214] *See* CRS, TREATIES AND OTHER INTERNATIONAL AGREEMENTS, *supra* note 165, at 15, 42 & n.56, 175 & nn.26–27, 274–76. Senate objections to prohibitions on reservations are usually expressed in committee reports (for example, with regard to the Protocol on Environmental Protection to the Antarctic Treaty), but sometimes are included in declarations made part of the resolution of ratification (as with the Inter-American Convention on Sea Turtles and the United Nations Convention Relating to the Conservation and Management of Straddling Fish Stocks and Highly Migratory Fish Stocks) or in something styled a sense-of-the-Senate declaration included in such a resolution (such as in connection with the Chemical Weapons Convention). *See id.* at 175 n.27.

that the Senate deemed essential.[215] Given that the Senate occasionally uses conditions to protect its perceived prerogatives,[216] it might conceivably use conditions to regulate the treatment of *other* conditions, such as by proposing a condition to a treaty that would require Senate consent before reservations to that treaty may be withdrawn.[217] This might allay Senate concerns but also raises its own difficult constitutional questions.[218]

4. Ratification by the President

"Ratification" is often misused by courts as a shorthand for Senate advice and consent (as in "the Senate ratified the treaty"),[219] but ratification is actually a separate and subsequent step. Once the Senate consents to the ratification of a treaty, it is again the president's turn to decide its fate. Ratifying usually entails an executive branch official signing the instrument of ratification and then exchanging it with other states or depositing it with a treaty depositary; substantive issues in

---

[215] *See* U.N. Convention on the Rights of Persons with Disabilities, June 30, 2009, S. TREATY DOC. No. 112-7 (2014), 2515 U.N.T.S. 3 (Dec. 13, 2006); S. EXEC. REP. 113–12, 160–62, 208, 212–13 (2014). The president has sought prior consent before withdrawing U.S. reservations, but it is hard to discern a constitutional rule. For example, prior consent was sought and obtained before withdrawing a reservation to the Patent Cooperation Treaty. *See* MESSAGE FROM THE PRESIDENT OF THE UNITED STATES, REQUEST FOR ADVICE AND CONSENT TO WITHDRAWAL OF A RESERVATION MADE TO THE 1975 PATENT COOPERATION TREATY, S. TREATY DOC. NO. 98-29 (1984); 132 CONG. REC. 29,884–85 (1986). There, however, legislative involvement was required for other reasons, since amendments to U.S. law were needed in order to satisfy the international obligations accruing in the absence of the reservation. LETTER OF TRANSMITTAL, *in id.* at (I). Other withdrawals might be distinguishable, particularly if it were plain that "continuation of the condition [wa]s no longer a material element of the Senate's original advice and consent," RESTATEMENT (FOURTH) § 305 rptrs. note 9, or if unilateral presidential action was required by exigent circumstances.

[216] *See, e.g.*, Ratification by the President of the United States, U.S.-Ger. Treaty of Peace, Oct. 21, 1921, 42 Stat. 1939, 1945, 12 L.N.T.S. 192 (1921) (understanding to a treaty that prohibited representation or participation by the United States in any body associated with a peace treaty with Germany absent statutory authorization); John H. Wigmore, Editorial Note, *May the Federal Senate Hamstring the Executive's Power to Confer with Other Nations?*, 20 ILL. L. REV. 688, 689–90 (1926) (describing executive branch resistance); Quincy Wright, *Validity of the Proposed Reservations to the Peace Treaty*, 20 COLUM. L. REV. 121, 136–37 (1920) (criticizing condition's constitutionality).

[217] In one exchange concerning the Convention on the Rights of Persons with Disabilities, a Senate Committee on Foreign Relations chair indicated interest in a nonseverability reservation. The Department of State opined that such a reservation was unnecessary and potentially counterproductive, but allowed that it might be done in such a way as to gain executive branch support. S. EXEC. REP. 113-12, *supra* note 215, at 160–62, 208, 212–13.

[218] Concerns might be particularly substantial if Senate conditions reached beyond a particular treaty—for example, conditioning consent on programmatic changes to the advice-and-consent process or addressing withdrawal from other treaties. *See supra* this chapter text accompanying notes 205–212 (discussing relatedness requirement).

[219] *See, e.g.*, Bond v. United States, 572 U.S. 844, 848–49 (2014); Massachusetts v. EPA, 549 U.S. 497, 509 (2007); Roper v. Simmons, 543 U.S. 551, 622 (2005) (Scalia, J., dissenting); El Al Isr. Airlines, Ltd. v. Tsui Yuan Tseng, 525 U.S. 155, 160, 174 (1999); Metro. Wash. Airports Auth. v. Citizens for the Abatement of Aircraft Noise, Inc., 501 U.S. 252, 276 n.21 (1991); E. Airlines Inc. v. Floyd, 499 U.S. 530, 535, 550 (1991); O'Connor v. United States, 479 U.S. 27, 28 (1986); Air Fr. v. Saks, 470 U.S. 392, 397, 403 (1985).

this regard are rare.[220] Ratification completes the treaty-making process from the U.S. standpoint,[221] enabling (if not ensuring) the treaty's entry into force for the United States.[222]

Ratification is not, however, a foregone conclusion. It may be delayed to allow the United States to adopt statutes and other means to ensure its performance of treaty obligations,[223] or for other reasons.[224] The president may also decline ratification altogether, because of changed global conditions, because a new president disfavors the negotiated agreement, or due to disagreements over conditions that the Senate has sought to impose.[225] Outright refusals by the president to ratify a

---

[220] On occasion, questions have arisen as to whether a condition, such as one relating to national law or policy, should be included with the instrument of ratification. Presidents have sometimes withheld such conditions at the Senate's request, due to the Senate's belief that the condition must be followed by the president but need not be communicated to other parties to the treaty. Rarely (and controversially), presidents have withheld such conditions on their own initiative. See RESTATEMENT (FOURTH) § 305 rptrs. note 8; CRS, TREATIES AND OTHER INTERNATIONAL AGREEMENTS, supra note 165, at 127–28. For example, with respect to the 1976 Treaty of Friendship and Cooperation with Spain, a Senate declaration concerning the need for democracy in Spain was placed by the president, for diplomatic reasons, in an annex to the instrument of ratification rather than in the instrument of ratification itself, on the premise that such a condition had no international legal effect in any event. See CRS, TREATIES AND OTHER INTERNATIONAL AGREEMENTS, supra note 165, at 126; 1976 DIGEST OF U.S. PRACTICE, at 214–17.

[221] The president formerly issued proclamations indicating that a treaty had entered into force, but no longer does so. RESTATEMENT (FOURTH) § 303 rptrs. note 5. Previously, there was uncertainty as to whether such a proclamation was an essential precondition before a treaty might be enforced within the United States. See RESTATEMENT (THIRD) § 312, cmt. k & rptrs. note 4 (citing authorities); see also John H. Jackson, The General Agreement on Tariffs and Trade in United States Domestic Law, 66 MICH. L. REV. 249, 290–92, 312 (1967) (asserting that the General Agreement on Tariffs and Trade (GATT) may have become effective as domestic law only upon presidential proclamation). In principle, a treaty might by its terms require a proclamation for it to enter into force, or a statute might treat a proclamation as a material step for certain purposes. See, e.g., 50 U.S.C. § 4302 (deeming term "end of the war" to "mean the date of proclamation of exchange of ratifications of the treaty of peace, unless the President shall, by proclamation, declare a prior date").

[222] Other steps required prior to entry into force, such as ratification by a sufficient number of states, may be required. See supra this chapter text accompanying note 134.

[223] Robert E. Dalton, National Treaty Law and Practice: United States, in NATIONAL TREATY LAW AND PRACTICE 777 (Monroe Leigh, Merritt R. Blakeslee, & L. Benjamin Ederington eds., 1999). For example, the United States delayed ratification for seven years following advice and consent to four nuclear security treaties, and has yet to ratify the Basel Convention on the Control of Transboundary Movements of Hazardous Wastes and their Disposal—which the United States signed in 1990, and for which the Senate provided advice and consent in 1992—because additional legislation remains needed. See Basel Convention on Hazardous Wastes Share, U.S. DEP'T OF STATE (Feb. 11, 2019), https://perma.cc/4KN9-U9G7. For these and other examples, see also RESTATEMENT (FOURTH) § 303 rptrs. note 5 (describing procedure after Senate advice and consent); Jean Galbraith, Making Treaty Implementation More Like Statutory Implementation, 115 MICH. L. REV. 1309, 1311, 1323 (2017) (describing examples).

[224] See Goldwater v. Carter, 617 F.2d 697, 705 (D.C. Cir. 1979), rev'd on other grounds, 444 U.S. 996 (1979); CRANDALL, supra note 88, at 97; CRS, TREATIES AND OTHER INTERNATIONAL AGREEMENTS, supra note 165, at 152.

[225] The Senate may fail to incorporate conditions the president proposed and deems necessary, may propose conditions the president deems inadvisable, or may propose conditions that the president knows another state or states will regard as unacceptable. See CRANDALL, supra note 88, at 97–99 (citing examples); CRS, TREATIES AND OTHER INTERNATIONAL AGREEMENTS, supra note 165, at 152–53 (same).

treaty consented to by the Senate are relatively rare, probably because the Senate tends to proceed with approval only when a treaty is likely to be ratified.

C. Obligations Arising Prior to Entry into Force of the Treaty

Even in advance of a treaty entering into force for the United States, it may none-theless be subject to certain obligations relating to the treaty, either because it is required by good faith under the international law of treaties or due to spe-cific provisions of the treaty or an associated agreement. The two most important types of such obligations deserve brief discussion.

1. Obligation Not to Defeat the Object and Purpose of the Treaty

Upon signing a treaty subject to ratification,[226] the United States (like other states) assumes an obligation, even prior to entry into force of the treaty, arising under international law. As described in Article 18 of the VCLT, this interim obli-gation is to "refrain from acts which would defeat the object and purpose of" the treaty.[227] The same obligation arises whenever the United States has expressed its consent to be bound to a treaty (whether or not preceded by signature) but the treaty has not yet entered into force.[228] The obligation is described as "interim" in nature because it ceases, automatically, when the agreement has entered into force for the states concerned, or for other reasons.[229]

This obligation serves U.S. interests by precluding other states, prospec-tive treaty partners, from acting in a manner that frustrates a treaty prior to the

---

[226] The same obligation arises upon exchanging instruments subject to ratification, acceptance, or approval, see VCLT, *supra* note 13, art. 18(a), but for simplicity's sake this discussion will be framed in terms of signature only.

[227] *See* VCLT, *supra* note 13, art. 18. While not a party to the VCLT, the United States recognizes this interim obligation as binding under customary international law. *See, e.g.*, 2001 DIGEST OF U.S. PRACTICE, at 212–13 (reprinting answer by Secretary of State Powell to question by Senator Helms, noting recognition by the Johnson, Nixon, Carter, Reagan, and Clinton administrations); *see also* Laurence Boisson de Chazournes, Anne-Marie La Rosa, & Makane Moïse Mbengue, *Article 18 of the 1969 and 1986 Vienna Conventions on the Law of Treaties, in* THE VIENNA CONVENTION ON THE LAW OF TREATIES, *supra* note 131, at 382–83.

[228] *See* VCLT, *supra* note 13, art. 18(b).

[229] First, if the obligation has arisen upon signature, the obligation may be terminated by notice of the signing state that it intends not to become a party to the treaty. *See id.* art. 18(a); *see also infra* this chapter text accompanying notes 241–245. Second, if the obligation has arisen based upon expres-sion of consent to be bound, then it applies pending the treaty's entry into force "provided that such entry into force is not unduly delayed." *See* VCLT, *supra* note 13, art. 18(b). This possibility for ter-mination of due to "undue delay" suggests that the obligation terminates even though a consenting state has not withdrawn its consent to be bound; the notion of "undue" delay likely gives states a substantial margin of appreciation in determining how long the obligation continues. *See* Boisson de Chazournes et al., *Article 18, supra* note 227, at 396–97. A state can also withdraw its consent to be bound by the treaty before an agreement has entered into force, which would concomitantly termi-nate any interim obligation. *See* ANTHONY AUST, MODERN TREATY LAW AND PRACTICE 109–10 (3d ed. 2013).

agreement's entry into force.[230] The constitutional concern, however, is that the executive branch, by acting on its own initiative in concluding an instrument that is subject to ratification, can create an obligation for the United States without any involvement of the Senate.[231] The concern is accentuated by the number of important treaties for which the president has triggered this interim obligation, which can exist for many years before the Senate provides its consent to ratification, if it ever does.[232]

The exact scope of the obligation "not to defeat the object and purpose of" the treaty is notoriously indeterminate.[233] Full compliance with an agreement's terms presumably satisfies the interim obligation too, but acts inconsistent with those terms do not necessarily violate it.[234] What kinds of acts, then, do? The United States has said that signatories are "at least" to "avoid actions which could render impossible the entry into force and implementation of the treaty," which

---

[230] For example, for the Strategic Arms Limitations Talks (SALT) II treaty—which the United States had signed, but for which the president had not yet sought advice and consent—the Department of State emphasized that both the United States and the Soviet Union had to "refrain from acts which would defeat the object and the purpose of the SALT II Treaty." 1980 DIGEST OF U.S. PRACTICE, at 398; *see also* 2013 DIGEST OF U.S. PRACTICE, at 646, 648 (statement joined by the United States, following fourth conference on the Comprehensive Nuclear Test Ban Treaty, calling on all states to "refrain from acts that would defeat the object and purpose of the Treaty pending its entry into force").

[231] *See, e.g.,* David H. Moore, *The President's Unconstitutional Treatymaking,* 59 UCLA L. REV. 598 (2012); *cf.* Curtis A. Bradley, *Unratified Treaties, Domestic Politics, and the U.S. Constitution,* 48 HARV. INT'L L.J. 307 (2007) (describing constitutional concerns).

[232] By one estimate, about 90 percent of treaties submitted to the Senate during a recent decade were signed by U.S. representatives subject to ratification. Moore, *supra* note 231, at 608; *see id.* at 660–72 (Table 2) (compiling treaties). As of this writing, treaties signed by the United States, and subjecting it to continuing interim obligations, include the International Covenant on Economic, Social, and Cultural Rights, Dec. 16, 1966, 993 U.N.T.S. 3 (signed by the United States Oct. 5, 1977); the American Convention on Human Rights, Nov. 22, 1969, 1144 U.N.T.S. 143 (signed June 1, 1977); Additional Protocols I, June 8, 1977, 1125 U.N.T.S. 3 (signed Dec. 12, 1977) and II, June 8, 1977, 1125 U.N.T.S. 609 (signed Dec. 12, 1977) to the 1949 Geneva Conventions; the Convention on the Elimination of All Forms of Discrimination Against Women, Dec. 18, 1979, 1249 U.N.T.S. 13 (signed July 17, 1980); the Convention on the Rights of the Child, Nov. 20, 1989, 1577 U.N.T.S. 3 (signed Feb. 16, 1995); the Agreement relating to the Implementation of Part XI of the Law of the Sea Convention, July 28, 1994, 1836 U.N.T.S. 3 (signed July 29, 1994); the Comprehensive Nuclear-Test-Ban Treaty, Sept. 24, 1996, 35 I.L.M. 1439 (signed Sept. 24, 1996); the Kyoto Protocol to the 1992 U.N. Framework Convention on Climate Change, Dec. 11, 1997, 2303 U.N.T.S. 162 (signed Nov. 12, 1998); and last but not least, the 1969 Vienna Convention of the Law of Treaties itself, which reflects the obligation not to defeat the object and purpose of a treaty, VCLT, *supra* note 13, art. 18 (signed Apr. 24, 1970). Some, like the Kyoto Protocol, have not been submitted by the president for Senate consideration. In at least some instances, interim obligations may be interwoven with political or other commitments. *See, e.g.,* 131 CONG. REC. 3,448–53 (1985) (reprinting July 2, 1984, letter from Senators Symms and East, objecting to extended U.S. compliance with SALT II).

[233] Boisson de Chazournes et al., *Article 18, supra* note 227, at 383; *accord* RESTATEMENT (FOURTH) § 304 rptrs. note 8.

[234] Memorandum from Roberts B. Owen, U.S. Dep't of State Legal Adviser (Feb. 21, 1980), *reprinted in* S. EXEC. REP. NO. 96-33, at 45, 47 (1980) (noting that "the rule seems to contemplate that . . . signatories are clearly not obliged to carry out all treaty provisions during the period prior to ratification"); *see, e.g.,* 1979 DIGEST OF U.S. PRACTICE, at 693 (statement by Ambassador Richardson) (asserting that deep-seabed mining would not violate interim obligations assumed by the United States prior to entry into force of a deep-seabed-mining agreement).

is clarifying, but also to avoid those acts "defeat[ing] its basic purpose and value to the other party or parties"—which essentially restates, without clarifying, the test in Article 18 of the VCLT.[235]

The obligation's indeterminacy probably made it easier for the United States and others to accept. But it has also heightened anxiety that treaty partners, perhaps with the acquiescence of the U.S. executive branch, might assert object-and-purpose responsibilities incumbent upon the United States—resembling comprehensive treaty obligations—even while the Senate is withholding advice and consent.[236] To date, U.S. courts have not seriously evaluated the scope of the obligation or potential constitutional limits.[237] It seems a stretch to suppose that Article II's negotiating authority entails the capacity to *begin performing* aspects of an agreement, and any such authority is presumably strained further if the interim period is prolonged, especially if delay is attributable to the president.[238] Moreover, while the obligation not to defeat the object and purpose of a treaty

---

[235] Memorandum from Roberts B. Owen, *supra* note 234, at 47. Thus, for example, a failure to destroy or dismantle a weapon as required by an agreement is unlikely to violate the obligation, because compliance could be affected later, whereas the testing of a weapon in violation of an agreement might have irreversible effects. *Id.* at 48; *see also* The President's News Conference, 2 PUB. PAPERS 1777, 1781–82 (Oct. 14, 1999) (saying, of the signed but unratified Comprehensive Test Ban Treaty, "All I can tell you is, we're not going to test. I signed that treaty. It still binds us unless I go, in effect, and erase our name. Unless the President does that and takes our name off, we are bound by it.").

[236] *See* RESTATEMENT (FOURTH) § 304 rptrs. note 9. For example, certain senators objected on constitutional grounds to any signature-based obligation that the Department of Defense "comply fully and precisely with all the provisions of the unratified SALT II treaty." 131 CONG. REC. 3,448, 3,449–53 (1985) (reprinting July 2, 1984, letter from Senators Symms and East). Others expressed concerns about obligations that might be established were the United States to sign the U.N. Convention on the Law of the Sea, indicating that signature of a treaty "will not bind [the Senate] from taking any action which anyone claims would defeat the object and purpose of the treaty." 1979 DIGEST OF U.S. PRACTICE, at 691–92; *see also* Moore, *supra* note 231, at 645–48 (providing additional examples of Senate concerns). In one case, the United States actually coordinated with other states to establish—in a nonbinding statement later noted by the Security Council—that "a nuclear-weapon test explosion or any other nuclear explosion would defeat the object and purpose of the [Comprehensive Test Ban Treaty]." *Joint Statement on the Comprehensive Nuclear-Test-Ban Treaty by the Nuclear Nonproliferation Treaty Nuclear-Weapon States*, U.S. Dep't of State (Sept. 15, 2016), https://perma.cc/UF44-QXBV; S.C. Res. 2310, ¶ 4 (Sept. 23, 2016).

[237] *See, e.g.,* Ehrlich v. Am. Airlines, Inc., 360 F.3d 366, 373 & n.7 (2d Cir. 2004) (noting, but deeming waived, party's invocation of an obligation not to defeat the object and purpose arising from U.S. signature of the Montreal Convention). A few have mistakenly implied that the United States might owe such obligations under the 1982 U.N. Convention on the Law of the Sea, which the United States has not, in fact, signed. Mayaguezanos por la Salud y el Ambiente v. United States, 198 F.3d 297, 304 n.14 (1st Cir. 1999); United States v. Kun Yun Jho, 465 F. Supp. 2d 618, 624 (E.D. Tex. 2006), *rev'd on other grounds*, 534 F.3d 398 (5th Cir. 2008); United States v. Royal Caribbean Cruises, Ltd., 24 F. Supp. 2d 155, 159 (D.P.R. 1997). The confusion probably arose because the Clinton administration did sign a subsequent, related agreement on deep seabed mining and then submitted both for Senate approval, although the 1982 Convention was solely a candidate for accession (being without signature and, correspondingly, without any obligation not to defeat its object and purpose). S. TREATY Doc. 103-39 (1994).

[238] The interim period is harder to defend, for example, if a treaty remains in limbo because it has not yet been submitted for Senate consideration. Ultimately, the United States may also avoid unnecessarily incurring the obligation through signature for any multilateral treaties that permit signature-free accession at a later point.

may appear modest as compared to the president's ability to enter into sole executive agreements, to which it is sometimes compared, the latter is limited to circumstances involving the president's plenary powers—whereas this interim obligation may be generated irrespective of the subject matter regulated by the treaty.[239] Ultimately, the issue is whether this particular type of obligation, designed to be temporary in nature, requires the Senate's authorization, or instead should be understood as preserving the Senate's role by preventing acts that might thwart its chance to consider the treaty.[240] Because the executive branch rarely clarifies its understanding of the obligation that has been created when signing a treaty, let alone its basis in U.S. law, past practice is difficult to assess.

According to the VCLT, the obligation ceases when a signatory makes clear its intention not to become a party to the treaty.[241] The best-known example of the United States taking this step has been its so-called unsigning of the Rome Statute for the International Criminal Court—in reality, the communication from the U.S. government to the depositary indicating that the United States did not intend to become a party.[242] The capacity to end the obligation, even with immediate effect, does not fully resolve separation-of-powers concerns, so long as there is an intervening (or lingering) obligation,[243] and so long as the president controls whether notice is given.[244] Nonetheless, the ease of reversal arguably makes signing-based obligations less objectionable. It is notable, finally, that the United States is likely able to retract any notice disavowing its intention

[239] See infra this chapter § V(C) (discussing sole executive agreements). Like sole executive agreements, the obligation not to defeat the object and purpose of the treaty may be premised on the president's general constitutional authority to conduct foreign relations. See, e.g., Bradley, supra note 231, at 322–27; Moore, supra note 231, at 632–34. However, the obligation might in principle merely require refraining from acts that the United States is not authorized to undertake in any event, or mandate acts already authorized by national law, such that it puts little or no strain on the president's independent constitutional authority. RESTATEMENT (FOURTH) § 304 cmt. e & rptrs. note 9.

[240] Memorandum from Roberts B. Owen, supra note 234, at 50.

[241] VCLT, supra note 13, art. 18(a); Memorandum from Roberts B. Owen, supra note 234, at 47. Notice to a depositary or to other states parties should suffice for terminating the obligation, depending on the nature of the treaty.

[242] See Letter from John R. Bolton, Under Sec'y of State for Arms Control, to Gen. Kofi Annan, U.N. Sec'y-Gen. (May 6, 2002), available at https://perma.cc/P4WW-3WWG; see 2008 DIGEST OF U.S. PRACTICE, at 136, 143 (speech by Department of State Legal Adviser John Bellinger); see also Abagninin v. AMVAC Chem. Corp., 545 F.3d 733, 738 (9th Cir. 2008) (stating afterward "the United States has neither signed nor ratified the Rome Statute"). The claimed effect was not any "unsigning," as such, but rather terminating the obligation attending signature.

[243] The Senate may have misgivings, certainly, about the obligation during the period before the executive branch decides to provide notice. And even when notice is given, it would not resolve U.S. responsibility for any prior violations of the obligation not to defeat the object and purpose of the treaty.

[244] One solution would be to withhold signature when presidential authority for the interim performance is unclear or when the treaty is not ready to be submitted for Senate consideration. Alternatively, the president might deem notice obligatory when the Senate has clearly indicated that it will not approve a treaty, as when the Senate unanimously adopted a resolution opposing ratification of the Kyoto Protocol. See S. Res. 98, 105th Cong. (1997).

to ratify an agreement. Because such notices do not, in fact, "unsign" the treaty for the United States, a depositary (like the U.N. Secretary-General, in the case of the Rome Statute) may merely record the U.S. communication without prejudice to restoring the interim obligation from signature based on a subsequent communication.[245]

2. Obligations from Provisional Application of the Treaty

Like the obligation not to defeat the object and purpose of the treaty, obligations may arise for the United States in advance of the entry into force of the treaty from its provisional application, in whole or in part. But unlike the obligation not to defeat the object and purpose of the treaty, which derives from a background rule of international treaty law, whether an agreement is to be provisionally applied depends upon an agreement among the states that have negotiated the treaty. The relevant VCLT rule simply provides that the details for whether and how provisional application commences are determined by agreement of the states that have negotiated a particular treaty; such agreement on provisional application may be contained with the text of the treaty that is being provisionally applied, or may appear in a separate instrument.[246] The United States has accepted the concept of provisional application of treaties both in principle and in its treaty practice.[247]

Although the foreign relations issues posed by provisional application vary by treaty, some generalization is possible. When provisional application for United States is triggered upon its ratification—due to a treaty article providing as much, so as to address the circumstance, for example, in which there are not yet sufficient ratifications from other states[248]—Senate advice and consent has provided legislative authorization as it would for any other treaty obligation (likely with

---

[245] The United Nations noted the U.S. communication simply as a footnote to the entry for the United States among state participants, while continuing to reflect the date of U.S. signature. Multilateral Treaties Deposited with the Secretary-General, Status of Treaties, Chapter XVIII, Penal Matters, 10. Rome Statute of the International Criminal Court, https://perma.cc/HFH9-U8ZE.

[246] *See* VCLT, *supra* note 13, art. 25; Danae Azaria, *Provisional Application of Treaties, in* THE OXFORD GUIDE TO TREATIES, *supra* note 13, ch. 10. Of particular note, the International Law Commission in 2021 adopted a Guide to Provisional Application of Treaties, including draft guidelines and a draft annex containing examples of provisions on provisional application. *See* Int'l Law Comm'n, Draft Guidelines and Draft Annex Constituting the Guide to Provisional Application of Treaties, with Commentaries Thereto, U.N. Doc. A/76/10, at 68 (2021).

[247] *See* RESTATEMENT (FOURTH) § 304 rptrs. note 7; *see, e.g.*, 2017 DIGEST OF U.S. PRACTICE, at 306, 309–10 (excerpts of remarks made by Department of State Acting Legal Adviser Richard Visek, at a Sixth Committee Meeting on Agenda Item 81: Report of the International Law Commission on the Work of its 69th Session (Oct. 25, 2017)).

[248] *See, e.g.*, Arms Trade Treaty, art. 23, Sept. 25, 2013, S. TREATY DOC. NO. 114-14 (entered into force Dec. 24, 2014, not ratified); G.A. Res. 67/234 (June 11, 2013). Per the treaty, states may declare whether they accept provisional application (of two of its articles) when signing or when depositing an instrument of ratification; the United States is a signatory, but did not declare that it accepted provisional application. The Arms Trade Treaty, *supra*, art. 23.

full contemplation of provisional application provisions).[249] Yet provisional application may also be triggered by the executive branch's agreement to accept such an obligation for the United States in advance of advice and consent.[250] For example, the president might agree to provisionally apply the obligations of an arms control treaty or of a maritime boundary delimitation immediately upon signature, well in advance of the Senate providing advice and consent. Doing so raises issues similar to those posed by the obligation not to defeat a treaty's object and purpose, given that treaty-related legal obligations are being assumed for the United States even before the Senate has acted.[251] Since the agreement is to apply (provisionally) specific written provisions of a treaty, however, the obligations arising from provisional application are typically more determinate than any interim obligation.[252]

---

[249] Foreign relations law issues may also be ameliorated by other means. For example, even though Senate advice and consent had already been provided, the United States deposited a notification to bring the 1962 International Coffee Agreement provisionally into force, explaining that ratification would be premature because implementing legislation had not yet been adopted—while also indicating that the United States would not apply any treaty obligation that would require such legislation. Richard Bilder, *The International Coffee Agreement: A Case History in Negotiation*, 28 LAW & CONTEMP. PROBS. 328, 373–74, 389 (1963); CRS, TREATIES AND OTHER INTERNATIONAL AGREEMENTS, *supra* note 165, at 114; *see* International Coffee Agreement, Sept. 28, 1962, 14 U.S.T. 1911, 469 U.N.T.S. 169.

[250] Signature of the treaty often suffices, if the treaty states that all or certain of its provisions will apply provisionally upon signature. *See, e.g.*, Treaty on Measures for the Further Reduction and Limitation of Strategic Offensive Arms, Protocol, U.S.-Russ., Apr. 8, 2010, pt. 8, § 1, T.I.A.S. No. 11-205 (available at https://perma.cc/25FC-9APE); *see also* General Agreement on Tariffs and Trade, Protocol of Provisional Application, Oct. 30, 1947, 61 Stat. A3, A2051, 55 U.N.T.S. 188, 308 [hereinafter GATT Protocol of Provisional Application] (conditioning provisional application on signature by all designated states before a certain date). Some schemes are more complex. For example, a law of the sea agreement provisionally applied to states upon their consent to the agreement's adoption in the General Assembly, upon signature, or upon specific notice to the depositary, but also allowed states presumptively subject to provisional application (because of their consent or signature) to opt out. Agreement relating to the Implementation of Part XI of the United Nations Convention on the Law of the Sea, art. 7(1), July 28, 1994, 1836 U.N.T.S. 3 [hereinafter Implementation of Part XI Agreement].

[251] *See* Draft Guidelines, *supra* note 246, at 78 (indicating, in Guideline 6, that "[t]he provisional application of a treaty or a part of a treaty produces a legally binding obligation to apply the treaty or a part thereof," save as otherwise provided); *see also* Treaty on Conventional Armed Forces in Europe (CFE), S. TREATY DOC. No. 102-8, at 196 (1991) [hereinafter CFE Treaty] (indicating that "provisional application requires the States Parties to comply with the provisions so applied to the strict letter of the law even though the Treaty as a whole has not yet entered into force"); *accord* Kardassopoulos v. Republic of Geor., ICSID Case No. ARB/05/18, Objections to Jurisdiction, ¶¶ 209–10 (July 6, 2007); 1974 DIGEST OF U.S. PRACTICE, at 234, 235–36 (statement of the Assistant Legal Adviser for Treaty Affairs concerning provisional application of the Food Aid Convention).

[252] *See, e.g.*, CFE Treaty, *supra* 251, at 32, 38, 41, 48, 54, 55, 58, 67, 69, 91, 143, 144, 147, 195, 196 (noting binding nature of the agreement to apply provisionally particular treaty provisions); *see also id.* at 188 (noting that an article not subject to provisional application was not legally binding prior to entry into force). In the case of the Arms Trade Treaty, the United States elected not to declare that it would provisionally apply the relevant articles, but would have been aware that it remained subject to the obligation not to defeat its object and purpose arising from its signature. *See supra* this chapter note 248.

Committing the United States to provisional application before legislative consent has been received is potentially problematic if legislative approval would be required for the commitment in question, were it not provisional. The key question is whether the president has other constitutional or legislative support for such an agreement,[253] and the issue somewhat resembles that for executive agreements.[254] Provisional application may be distinguished, however, on the basis of imminent need and the temporary nature of the obligation, and predicated more persuasively on the basis of the president's Article II negotiating authority.[255] Prolonged provisional application may reduce the force of that distinction, particularly when the president has not even sought advice and consent[256] or when provisional application is repeatedly renewed.[257] As with other questions involving advice and consent, potential objections may be warded off by consulting with the Senate. The Senate's tolerance for provisional application might be understood to indicate a degree of acquiescence in presidential capacity, either so as to redeem a specific instance or as a general rule.

---

[253] RESTATEMENT (FOURTH) § 304 cmt. d ("Under the U.S. law, if the advice and consent of the Senate, or congressional approval, is required, but has not yet been obtained, a commitment that an agreement shall have provisional effect for the United States must rest on another agreement, on a statute, or on the President's own constitutional authority."); see also id. rptrs. note 7.

[254] See infra this chapter §§ V(A), (C) (discussing congressional-executive and sole executive agreements); see, e.g., THREE TREATIES ESTABLISHING MARITIME BOUNDARIES BETWEEN THE UNITED STATES AND MEXICO, VENEZUELA AND CUBA, S. EXEC. REP. NO. 96–49, at 19 (1980) (testimony of Mark B. Feldman, Deputy Legal Adviser, Department of State) ("[I]n the case of these boundary treaties, we should look upon provisional application of the treaty in the same legal terms as an executive agreement," in that "[i]t could be authorized by treaty or by statute or, to the extent that it falls within the President's constitutional authority, by the Constitution."); CRS, TREATIES AND OTHER INTERNATIONAL AGREEMENTS, supra note 165, at 113–14. In practice, the executive branch has often invoked legislative bases for provisional application. See CONG. RESEARCH SERV., 93D CONG., LAW OF THE SEA TREATY: ALTERNATIVE APPROACHES TO PROVISIONAL APPLICATION, PREPARED FOR THE SUBCOMM. ON INT'L ORGS. & MOVEMENTS OF THE HOUSE COMM. ON FOREIGN AFFAIRS 2–3 (Comm. Print 1974).

[255] See THREE TREATIES ESTABLISHING MARITIME BOUNDARIES BETWEEN THE UNITED STATES AND MEXICO, VENEZUELA AND CUBA, S. EXEC. REP. NO. 96-49, supra note 254, at 25–27 (1980) (executive branch responses to additional questions submitted by Senator Javits).

[256] The United States extended provisional application of the GATT from 1947 until the advent of the WTO in 1995. See GATT Protocol of Provisional Application, supra note 250. As Professor Jackson observed during this period, "GATT has never been submitted to the Senate; in fact, there was never even a plan to do so." Jackson, supra note 221, at 253; see also Joel R. Paul, The Geopolitical Constitution: Executive Expediency and Executive Agreements, 86 CAL. L. REV. 671, 751–52 (1998) (noting that the executive branch withdrew from congressional consideration (and did not submit to the Senate) a related agreement to establish an International Trade Organization).

[257] For example, following signature by the United States and Cuba of the U.S.-Cuba Maritime Boundary Agreement, art. V, Dec. 16, 1977, T.I.A.S. No. 12-208.1, which provided for a two-year period of provisional application, the president submitted the agreement to the Senate for its advice and consent, but there has been no definitive action since. See S. EXEC. DOC. H. 96-1 (1979). Instead, the United States and Cuba have been extending provisional application of the treaty for approximately forty years through the periodic exchange of diplomatic notes. STEPHEN P. MULLIGAN, CONG. · RESEARCH SERV., RL32528, INTERNATIONAL LAW AND AGREEMENTS: THEIR EFFECT UPON U.S. LAW 11 n.82 (2018).

The extent of any domestic legal effect presents a separate issue. Provisional application of some agreements, such as arms control agreements, tends to raise few questions involving national law, and fewer still that might arise in litigation. Moreover, an agreement on provisional application of a treaty may be designed precisely in order that states can apply the treaty immediately without first changing their laws.[258] In other instances, the United States may seek to tailor its agreement to provisional application, either by indicating that it is constrained by national law or by limiting its agreement so as to provisionally apply only discretionary functions under the treaty. The executive branch has stated that "the President may not, through provisional application of treaties, change existing law," but that "treaties applied provisionally within the President's authority have full effect under domestic law pending a decision with respect to ratification."[259] This may be meant to concede only that an agreement on provisional application cannot change *federal* law, as certain sole executive agreements can preempt state and local law.[260] In any event, the executive branch or courts may also invoke prior legislative authorization as a basis for giving legal effect to any provisional application.[261]

Any agreement on provisional application of a treaty will continue to bind the United States until it is terminated in accordance with international law.[262] Subject to any rules in the agreement itself, an agreement on provisional

---

[258] *See, e.g.*, Implementation of Part IX Agreement, art. 7(2) (providing for implementation "in accordance with their national or internal laws and regulations"); GATT Protocol of Provisional Application, *supra* note 250, art. 1(b) (provisional application of Part II "to the fullest extent not inconsistent with existing legislation"); Energy Charter Treaty, art. 45(1), Dec. 17, 1994, 34 I.L.M. 360, 2080 U.N.T.S. 95 (provisional application "to the extent . . . not inconsistent with [a state's] constitution, laws or regulations"); Treaty with Ukraine on Mutual Legal Assistance in Criminal Matters, Ukr.-U.S., July 22, 1998, S. TREATY DOC. No. 106-16, at 19, 21 (1999) (exchange of notes establishing provisional application "to the extent possible under the respective domestic laws of the United States and Ukraine").

[259] THREE TREATIES ESTABLISHING MARITIME BOUNDARIES BETWEEN THE UNITED STATES AND MEXICO, VENEZUELA AND CUBA, *supra* note 254, at 27 (executive branch responses to additional questions submitted by Senator Javits).

[260] *See infra* this chapter text accompanying notes 870–873.

[261] The relative strength of any legislative basis, and the degree of emphasis upon it, vary. For example, provisional application of GATT was accorded effect in U.S. law under a number of different theories, some emphasizing congressional authorization. *See* Paul, *supra* note 256, at 751–58 (providing overview of commentary and case law). Others, like the *Restatement (Third)*, appeared to put little stock in that basis. RESTATEMENT (THIRD), pt. VIII, ch. 1 intr. Note at 264 (stating that "[d]espite some attempts by Congress to distance itself from the [GATT], its status as a commitment of the United States is not in doubt, and courts in the United States assume its binding character"); *id.* at 264–66 (acknowledging that "[t]he GATT has a status in United States law different than that . . . for international agreements generally," in view of the particular form of provisional application agreed to by states parties).

[262] *See supra* this chapter text accompanying notes 143–148 (discussing general principles of treaty law relating to constitutional violations, save for those involving manifest violations of rules of fundamental importance relating to treaty-making competence); Draft Guidelines, *supra* note 246, at 83–86 (Guidelines 10, 11, and accompanying commentary).

application terminates when the treaty enters into force for the states concerned,[263] or may be terminated by providing notice.[264] Termination is unlikely to pose novel foreign relations issues. If provisional application arises solely from signature of a treaty (containing articles that provisionally apply immediately upon signature), termination by the president should not be at odds with legislative authority.[265] Where provisional application has been triggered by U.S. ratification of an agreement (pending the treaty's entry into force, or thereafter in relation to other states that have signed but not yet ratified), the executive's termination authority is presumably at least as extensive as it would be in relation to treaties.[266]

Because the United States is not always prepared to assume international obligations, even if provisional (and terminable), it may instead make a nonbinding commitment to comply with a treaty in advance of its entry into force.[267] Even when no option for provisional application has been established by a treaty, a state may make a unilateral declaration that it will abide by a treaty's obligations prior to its entry into force for that state.[268] In certain circumstances, such a

[263] Article 25(1) of the VCLT describes provisional application as "pending [an agreement's] entry into force." VCLT, *supra* note 13, art. 25(1), but the more exact default rule may be that such application terminates only when the treaty enters into force for the states concerned—meaning that provisional application may continue, unless the agreement indicates otherwise, for those states that have not yet ratified the agreement. Draft Guidelines, *supra* note 246, at 81–83 (Guideline 9 and accompanying commentary). Some agreements are unclear as to whether termination of provisional application for all is intended upon termination. *See, e.g.,* Implementation of Part XI Agreement, *supra* note 258, art. 7(3). They may also limit the period for which provisional application is possible. *See id.*; Agreement relating to the International Telecommunications Satellite Organization, art. XX(c), Aug. 20, 1971, 23 U.S.T. 3813, 1220 U.N.T.S. 149 [hereinafter INTELSAT Agreement].

[264] Article 25(2) of the VCLT establishes a default rule according to which, in the absence of another agreement, a state may terminate provisional application "if that State notifies the other States between which the treaty is being applied provisionally of its intention not to become a party to the treaty." VCLT, *supra* note 13, art. 25(2); Draft Guidelines, *supra* note 246, at 81–83 (Guideline 9 and accompanying commentary); *see, e.g.,* GATT Protocol of Provisional Application, *supra* note 250, ¶ 5; INTELSAT Agreement, *supra* note 263, art. XX(c)(iii); THREE TREATIES ESTABLISHING MARITIME BOUNDARIES BETWEEN THE UNITED STATES AND MEXICO, VENEZUELA AND CUBA, *supra* note 254, at 27 (executive branch responses to additional questions submitted by Senator Javits) (stating generally that "provisional application is terminated if the United States or its treaty partner informs the other of its intention not to become a party to the agreement"). Agreements may, however, permit termination on different premises, including for any reason. *See, e.g.,* Agreement to Facilitate Interchange of Patent Rights and Technical Information for Defense Purposes, Ger.-U.S., art. IX, Jan. 4, 1956, 7 U.S.T. 45, 268 U.N.T.S. 143.

[265] If the legislature has in fact approved an agreement, but the president has not yet ratified, termination of provisional application asserts little more authority than the president ordinarily possesses in deciding whether to ratify following legislative approval.

[266] *See* RESTATEMENT (FOURTH) §304 rptrs. note 7; *see also infra* this chapter § VI.

[267] *See, e.g.,* 2002 DIGEST OF U.S. PRACTICE, at 186, 187, 189–90 (discussing nonbinding memorandum of understanding relating to the 1987 Treaty on Fisheries Between the Governments of Certain Pacific Island States and the Government of the United States of America, T.I.A.S. No. 11,100).

[268] For example, the Syrian Arab Republic, upon depositing its instrument of accession to the Chemical Weapons Convention, informed the Secretary-General, acting as the depositary, that it would apply the Convention provisionally pending its entry into force for it. *See* C.N.592.2013. TREATIES-XXVI.3 (Sept. 4, 2013) (Depositary Notification). Given that there was no "agreement"

unilateral declaration may be legally binding under international law,[269] but such an obligation is legally distinct from obligations arising from an agreement on provisional application of a treaty.[270]

D. Constitutional Limits on Treaty-Making

Although the Supremacy Clause sowed some confusion on this score, there has never been any serious doubt that the Constitution restricts the treaty power.[271] Even so, judicial review of the constitutionality of treaties has been essentially nonexistent. The Supreme Court has recognized the priority of the Bill of Rights, for example,[272] but it has done little to articulate, let alone apply, other substantive limits.

This lack of judicial review may be attributed in part to justiciability-related rules and principles of deference. Courts may also be especially disinclined to interfere with the domestic operation of treaties, given that international obligations will continue regardless.[273] But the result is little constitutional doctrine by which treaties can be assessed—which likely contributes to further

---

among the negotiating states of the Convention to apply it provisionally, the incident is best understood as Syria making a unilateral commitment to apply the Convention pending its entry into force, rather than provisional application of the Convention as understood in VCLT Article 25.

[269] See generally Int'l Law Comm'n, Guiding Principles Applicable to Unilateral Declarations of States Capable of Creating Legal Obligations, with Commentaries Thereto, U.N. Doc. A/61/10 (2006), reprinted in [2006] 2 Y.B. Int'l L. Comm'n 161–66, U.N. Doc. A/CN.4/SER.A/2006/Add.1 (Part 2).

[270] See 2017 DIGEST OF U.S. PRACTICE, at 310 (remarks by Department of State Acting Legal Adviser Richard Visek) (urging that unilateral commitments were exceptional and should be eliminated from guide to provisional application). But see Draft Guidelines, supra note 246, at 75 (indicating, in draft Guideline 4, that such declarations constitute another means by which provisional application may be agreed); id. at 212–13 (explaining that, to qualify, such declarations "must be expressly accepted by the other States or international organizations concerned, as opposed to mere non-objection...").

[271] In Missouri v. Holland, Justice Holmes observed that the Supremacy Clause does not specifically require that treaties be "made in Pursuance" of the Constitution, as it does for statutes, and that its application to "all Treaties made, or which shall be made, under the Authority of the United States," U.S. CONST. art. VI, cl. 2, might be read to require only "the formal acts prescribed to make the convention." Missouri v. Holland, 252 U.S. 416, 433 (1920). He disavowed; however, any suggestion that treaties could disregard the Constitution. See infra this chapter text accompanying notes 310–316. As the plurality opinion in Reid v. Covert later explained, the Constitution's wording has a more benign explanation: the language used for treaties was chosen "so that agreements made by the United States under the Articles of Confederation, including the important peace treaties which concluded the Revolutionary War, would remain in effect." Reid v. Covert, 354 U.S. 1, 16–17 (1957).

[272] Reid, 354 U.S. at 15; see infra this chapter text accompanying notes 311–314.

[273] See, e.g., Bond v. United States, 572 U.S. 844, 855 (2014) (noting government cautions about inhibiting the treaty power, and "undermin[ing] confidence in the United States as an international treaty partner," before explaining that the Court would resolve the case on statutory grounds). See also Chapter 4 § II (political question doctrine).

judicial abstention and makes any analysis tentative in nature. This subsection addresses possible subject-matter limits that would be particular to treaties. It then discusses whether other constitutional limits, applicable to other forms of national authority, might apply equally to treaties.

1. Subject-Matter Limits

Inspired by founding-era arguments,[274] commentary has long suggested subject-matter limits on treaties, though there is little agreement on any judicially enforceable limits that would seriously inhibit the preferences actually exhibited by the political branches.

It is usually assumed that international law defined, or defines, the outer bounds of an Article II "treaty." Those framing the Constitution likely used the term as it was understood by their foreign contemporaries, not least because a key objective was to enable the United States to enter into agreements with other states that would be considered binding under international law.[275] Today, U.S. foreign relations law uses the term "treaty" somewhat differently than under international law, due to its specific implications for constitutional practice,[276] but the core elements of a valid treaty under international law remain common to the U.S. form. Such an instrument need not be called a treaty at all, and it may be concluded with states or with other subjects of international law. (The VCLT is narrower—it addresses only treaties between states, and only those that are in writing—but such criteria only describe what that treaty regulates, rather than minima imposed by the international law of treaties.[277]) An Article II treaty should also be an international agreement "governed by international law," as the VCLT puts it, suggesting a mutual commitment to binding legal status.[278]

---

[274] See supra this chapter text accompanying notes 103–107.

[275] See HENKIN, FOREIGN AFFAIRS, at 184–85; Oona A. Hathaway et al., The Treaty Power: Its History, Scope, and Limits, 98 CORNELL L. REV. 239, 283–88 (2013).

[276] See supra this chapter text accompanying notes 13–14.

[277] VCLT, supra note 13, art. 2(1)(a) (defining "treaty," "[f]or the purposes of the present Convention"); Hollis, supra note 13, at 12 (describing the VCLT definition as "limited to the VCLT"); id. at 21–24 (examining VCLT focus on writing and agreements between states). As to the writing requirement, the Case-Zablocki Act implies that non–Article II agreements, at least, need not be in writing, as it indicates that "the text of any oral international agreement, which agreements shall be reduced to writing," shall be transmitted to Congress. 1 U.S.C. 112b(a) (requiring that the secretary of state transmit to Congress the text of non–Article II agreements, for purposes of notification). As to agreements with subjects of international law other than states, comparable elements for a "treaty" between the United States and an international organization may be found in the Vienna Convention on the Law of Treaties between States and International Organizations or between International Organizations, supra note 13, art. 2(a). Most states (including the United States), however, have not ratified or acceded to that treaty, and it has not entered into force.

[278] Hollis, supra note 13, at 19–21, 24–30; see also id. at 35–36 (distinguishing political commitments); cf. RESTATEMENT (FOURTH) § 312 rptrs. note 4 ("Presumably there must be an actual international agreement with another state (or with an entity, such as a public international organization, that has been given capacity to enter into an international agreement) that is intended to be legally binding.").

This supports the notion that Article II treaties must be bona fide, not sham or mock agreements that would not genuinely be governed by international law.[279] Regardless, such criteria have never proven important in a particular matter.[280]

International law does not itself impose subject-matter limits on treaties.[281] As a matter of U.S. constitutional law, it has long been suggested, in varying ways, that a treaty must address a matter of "international concern."[282] In one variant— among several limits tentatively suggested by Jefferson—the treaty power might extend only to subjects for which treaties were traditionally used (and, perhaps, for which treaties were necessary).[283] Second, one might exclude matters "which normally and appropriately were within the local jurisdiction of the States."[284] A third variant, endorsed by the *Restatement (Second)*, suggested that the treaty power is limited to "the external concerns of the nation as distinguished from matters of a purely internal nature."[285] Each variant owes less to the international law of treaties than to U.S. constitutional considerations, informed to a degree by postulates about how international law was perceived at the founding and how that understanding is best translated to the present day.

---

[279] *See* RESTATEMENT (THIRD) § 302 rptrs. note 2 (suggesting amenability to principle that "an international agreement of the United States must be a bona fide agreement with another state, serving a foreign policy interest or purpose of the United States"); HENKIN, FOREIGN AFFAIRS, at 185 (stating that "for constitutional law as for international law . . . there must be an agreement, a bona fide agreement, between states, not a 'mock-marriage'"); *id.* at 197 & nn.37 & 87; *see also* JEFFERSON'S MANUAL, *supra* note 168, § 594 at 318 ("It is admitted that [a treaty] must concern the foreign nation, party to the contract, or it would be a mere nullity . . ."). Any inquiry into the intent of states entering treaties remains problematic, at least as a matter of international law. *See* RESTATEMENT (THIRD) § 302 cmt. c (stating that international law "does not look behind the[] motives or purposes" of states entering treaties); Hollis, *supra* note 13, at 26–27 (noting disagreement concerning use of intent as to whether a treaty is "governed by international law").

[280] HENKIN, FOREIGN AFFAIRS, at 185 (acknowledging that "no 'agreement' made by the President and Senate has ever been challenged as a 'pseudo-treaty'").

[281] The international law of treaties does provide, however, that treaties violating peremptory (or *jus cogens*) norms are invalid. *See* Chapter 5 §§ III(B)(1), (C).

[282] The "international concern" expression is usually attributed to Charles Evans Hughes. *See* Charles Evans Hughes, Limitations of the Treaty-Making Power of the United States in Matters Coming Within the Jurisdiction of the States (Apr. 26, 1929), *in* 23 AM. SOC'Y INT'L L. PROC. 194, 194–96 (1929); *see also Treaties and Executive Agreements: Hearings on S.J. 1 Before a Subcomm. of the S. Comm. on the Judiciary*, 84th Cong. 183 (1955) (Secretary of State John Foster Dulles) (stating that a treaty could not regulate matters "which do not essentially affect the actions of nations in relation to international affairs, but are purely internal"). For an extensive exchange, see Curtis A. Bradley, *The Treaty Power and American Federalism*, 97 MICH. L. REV. 390 (1998) [hereinafter Bradley, *Treaty Power*]; Curtis A. Bradley, *The Treaty Power and American Federalism, Part II*, 99 Mich. L. REV. 98 (2000) [hereinafter Bradley, *Treaty Power II*]; David M. Golove, *Treaty-Making and the Nation: The Historical Foundations of the Nationalist Conception of the Treaty Power*, 98 MICH. L. REV. 1075 (2000); *see also* Hathaway et al., *supra* note 275, at 283–88 (discussing "international concern"); Duncan B. Hollis, *An Intersubjective Treaty Power*, 90 NOTRE DAME L. REV. 1415 (2015).

[283] *See* JEFFERSON, MANUAL, *supra* note 168, § 594 at 318 ("By the general power to make treaties, the Constitution must have intended to comprehend only those objects which are usually regulated by treaty, and can not be otherwise regulated.").

[284] Hughes, *supra* note 282, at 194–96. The idea closely resembles a Tenth Amendment limitation, discussed below. *See infra* this chapter text accompanying notes 337–340.

[285] RESTATEMENT (SECOND) § 117 cmt. b.

These and other versions of an asserted "international concern" requirement have long coexisted, unresolved, as possible means of addressing episodic
concerns about an unconstrained treaty power.[286] Still, palliative and rhetor-
ical uses aside, "international concern" tests gradually lost prominence and
bite. Supreme Court cases described the treaty power as one that "extends to
all proper subjects of negotiation with foreign governments," but that was not
clearly stated as a limit.[287] Likewise, the *Restatement (Third)*, which squarely
rejected the *Restatement (Second)* approach,[288] stated that the United States may
constitutionally make a treaty "on any subject suggested by its national interests
in relations with other nations,"[289] which sounded less like a limit than the absence of one.[290] Cases in the lower courts did not suggest any material limit,[291]
and some of those advocating for a restrained understanding of the treaty power
put no stock in the feasibility or desirability of reviving any "international concern" test.[292]

The tide seemed like it might turn in the Supreme Court's decision in *Bond
v. United States*, which involved federalism-related objections to the Chemical
Weapons Convention and its implementing statute.[293] The majority ultimately

---

[286] Opportunistic and unstable use of the "international concern" requirement, particularly during
the founding era, is extensively discussed in Golove, *supra* note 282.

[287] *In re* Ross, 140 U.S. 453, 463 (1891); *accord* Asakura v. Seattle, 265 U.S. 332, 341 (1924); *see also*
De Geofroy v. Riggs, 133 U.S. 258, 266 (1890) ("The treaty power of the United States extends to all
proper subjects of negotiation between our government and the governments of other nations").

[288] *See* RESTATEMENT (THIRD) § 302 cmt. c (reporting that "[c]ontrary to what was once suggested,
the Constitution does not require that an international agreement deal only with 'matters of international concern,'" and that "the United States may make an agreement on any subject suggested by its
national interests in relations with other nations").

[289] RESTATEMENT (THIRD) § 302 cmt. c. For debate over whether a "national interest" or similar
limit is meaningful, compare Golove, *supra* note 282, at 1287–91 & n.728 (describing as limit), with
Bradley, *Treaty Power II, supra* note 282, at 106 (suggesting it serves no limiting function).

[290] *See also* Santovincenzo v. Egan, 284 U.S. 30, 40 (1931) (stating that "[t]he treaty-making power
is broad enough to cover all subjects that properly pertain to our foreign relations").

[291] The court of appeals in *Bond* perceived that despite the "long history" of subject-matter limits,
they might have become obsolete—and that, on any view, the Chemical Weapons Convention
was valid. United States v. Bond, 681 F.3d 149, 161 (3d Cir. 2012). Other courts have upheld the
International Convention against the Taking of Hostages, Dec. 17, 1979, T.I.A.S. 11081, 1316 U.N.T.S.
205, as being within the "generous limits" of the Treaty Clause, on the assumption that there "must
be certain outer limits, as yet undefined." United States v. Lue, 134 F.3d 79, 82–84 (2d Cir. 1998); *accord* United States v. Ferreira, 275 F.3d 1020, 1027–28 (11th Cir. 2001); United States v. Mikhel, 889
F.3d 1003, 1024 (9th Cir. 2018). One long-marginalized precedent, however, held that a reservation
concerning a "purely domestic concern" was unenforceable, and if binding would have suggested the
constitutional invalidity of a bilateral treaty. Power Auth. of N.Y. v. Fed. Power Comm'n, 247 F.2d 538,
541–43 (D.C. Cir. 1957), *vacated as moot sub nom.* Am. Pub. Power Ass'n v. Power Auth. of N.Y., 355
U.S. 64 (1957) (per curiam); *see supra* this chapter text accompanying note 205.

[292] *See, e.g.*, Bradley, *Treaty Power I, supra* note 282, at 451–56.

[293] Bond v. United States, 572 U.S. 844 (2014); *see* Convention on the Prohibition of the
Development, Production, Stockpiling and Use of Chemical Weapons and on their Destruction,
Sept. 3, 1992, 1975 U.N.T.S. 45 [hereinafter Chemical Weapons Convention]; Chemical Weapons
Convention Implementation Act, Pub. L. No. 105-277, 112 Stat. 2681 (codified as amended in
scattered sections of the U.S. Code). For further discussion of *Bond*, see Chapter 9 § II(A).

avoided resolving the constitutionality of the convention or the implementing statute by construing the latter narrowly; its interpretation was clearly animated, however, by a reluctance to enable federal criminal prosecutions of essentially local conduct.[294] In contrast, Justice Thomas (joined by Justice Scalia and Justice Alito) called for reviving an international concern-type requirement for Article II treaties in future cases.[295] His concurrence most closely resembled the third of the variants noted previously, according to which a treaty "can be used to arrange intercourse with other nations, but not to regulate purely domestic affairs."[296] The authority on which he relied had actually espoused a wide range of pro-limitation views, and their lack of congruence—which was obvious to their exponents and their immediate audiences[297]—went undiscussed.[298] Post-ratification practice, touched on only briefly, did not seem conclusive,[299] nor did the cited precedents propose any enforceable criteria.[300]

---

[294] Bond, 572 U.S. at 857–66; see id. at 854–56 (describing preference for avoiding constitutional issues). This entailed reversing the decision of the court of appeals, which had upheld the statute's broader application, thereby requiring it to determine whether the convention was valid. United States v. Bond, 681 F.3d 149, 159 (3d Cir. 2012).

[295] Justice Thomas acknowledged, though, that the parties had not challenged (nor briefed) the constitutionality of the Chemical Weapons Convention. Bond, 572 U.S. at 883–84, 896 (Thomas, J., concurring in judgment). His opinion was joined in full by Justice Scalia, and in the main (exclusive of introductory and concluding portions, including discussion of what was properly before the Court) by Justice Alito. Id. at 882.

[296] Id. at 884 (Thomas, J., concurring in judgment); accord id. at 886–87, 891–93, 895–96.

[297] See, e.g., JEFFERSON'S MANUAL, supra note 168, § 594 at 317–18 ("To what subjects this [treaty] power extends, has not been defined in detail by the Constitution; nor are we entirely agreed among ourselves.").

[298] For example, Justice Thomas cited Professor Golove in estimating that "[a]t least until recently" the original understanding of subject-matter limitations was "widely shared." Bond, 572 U.S. at 895 (Thomas, J., concurring in judgment) (citing Golove, supra note 282, at 1288). But Professor Bradley, whom Justice Thomas cited extensively, thought Professor Golove misunderstood or diluted subject-matter limitations, see Bradley, Treaty Power II, supra note 282, at 105–11, and he rejected as unworkable and nonjusticiable something much like what Justice Thomas favored. Bradley, Treaty Power, supra note 282, at 451–56.

[299] Justice Thomas discussed the House's views on the Jay Treaty, in which some argued that intervention was unnecessary in light of the treaty power's inherent limitations, as well as Jefferson's Manual, which followed that controversy. Bond, 572 U.S. at 889–93 (Thomas, J., concurring in judgment). Yet Jefferson's views at the time were neither objective nor representative, perhaps not even of his own thinking. See Golove, supra note 282, at 1178–93 (reviewing Jefferson's views); see, e.g., Letter from Thomas Jefferson to James Madison (Mar. 27, 1796), in 16 PAPERS OF JAMES MADISON, supra note 10, at 280 ("I see no harm in rendering [the House's] sanction necessary, and not much harm in annihilating the whole treaty making power"). A more comprehensive assessment of the Jay Treaty, including the behavior of the president and Senate, probably cuts against treaty-power limits. See Golove, supra note 282, at 1157–61. Beyond the Jay Treaty incident, there are certainly pronouncements of subject-matter limits, see Hollis, supra note 282, at 1427–28, but also numerous treaties "regulating what appear to be purely domestic affairs." Bond, 572 U.S. at 883 (Thomas, J., concurring in judgment).

[300] Justice Thomas invoked cases describing the treaty power as encompassing "all proper subjects of negotiation with foreign governments." Bond, 572 U.S. at 893 (Thomas, J., concurring in judgment) (internal quotations and citations omitted); see supra this chapter text accompanying note 287. He also noted some Supreme Court cases described treaties as "dealing in some manner with intercourse between nations." See Bond, 572 U.S. at 893 (Thomas, J., concurring in judgment) (citing Holmes v. Jennison, 39 U.S. (14 Pet.) 540, 569 (1840), and Holden v. Joy, 84 U.S. (17 Wall.) 211, 242–43

Justice Thomas ultimately declined to engage in specifics, beyond endorsing the general principle of limiting the treaty power.[301] Justice Alito, however, would have gone further and found unconstitutional the application of the Chemical Weapons Convention on the facts of the case. He was satisfied that the convention mostly pursued a matter of international concern.[302] That said, if the convention was read to require U.S. legislation criminalizing conduct "typically . . . regulated by the States," it "exceed[ed] the scope of the treaty power," meaning that the implementing legislation could not constitutionally be enforced.[303] In effect, this married the third variant, requiring an object external to the United States as a whole, with an as-applied version of the second variant, requiring that the treaty power not facilitate encroachment on the internal jurisdiction of the several states.

Taken together, the separate opinions in *Bond* seemed to agree that there has to be *some* limit on the treaty power, but failed to indicate any likely candidate. The majority, for its part, noted in passing the executive branch's view that the Constitution had deliberately refrained from choosing any subject-matter limitation, and that such limitations could put the United States in jeopardy of violating its international obligations.[304] The *Restatement (Fourth)*, addressing the issue shortly after *Bond*, took the position that there was insufficient precedent or practice to support *either* the *Restatement (Second)*'s test *or* the *Restatement (Third)*'s position, leaving the continued role of the varying tests largely up in the air.[305]

As a complement to any "international concern" requirement, it has sometimes been suggested that treaties must not trench on some matters that are plainly of *national* concern: that is, they cannot address "subjects of legislation in which [the Constitution] gave a participation to the House of Representatives."[306] Jefferson, articulating various proposed limits, paused the most over this, and acknowledged that according to critics "it would leave very little for the treaty

---

(1872)). Still other cases "identified certain paradigmatic instances of 'intercourse' that were 'proper negotiating subjects' fit for treaty." *Id.* (citing *Holmes*, 39 U.S. at 569; *De Geofroy*, 133 U.S. at 266; *Asakura*, 265 U.S. at 341). None explicitly invoked these descriptions as limiting conditions.

[301] *Bond*, 572 U.S. at 896 (Thomas, J., concurring in judgment) ("acknowledg[ing] that the distinction between matters of international intercourse and matters of purely domestic regulation may not be obvious in all cases," but concluding that "hypothetical difficulties in line-drawing are no reason to ignore a constitutional limit on federal power").

[302] *Id.* at 897 (Alito, J., concurring in the judgment) (agreeing with Justice Thomas that "the treaty power is limited to agreements that address matters of legitimate international concern," but concluding that controlling "true" chemical weapons was "a matter of great international concern, and therefore the heart of the Convention clearly represents a valid exercise of the treaty power").

[303] *Id.* at 896–97 (Alito, J., concurring in the judgment).

[304] *See id.* at 855.

[305] RESTATEMENT (FOURTH) § 312 rptrs. note 8; *see id.* rptrs. note 4 (discussing the issue).

[306] JEFFERSON'S MANUAL, *supra* note 168, § 594 at 318.

power to work on," but appeared to regard it as appropriate to keep each form of national authority in its lane and to confine treaties to only those occasions for which they were distinctly necessary.[307] While similar ideas have been expressed since, they remain as controversial as when Jefferson suggested them, and they are extremely difficult to reconcile with contemporary practice.[308] Some of those most sympathetic to that perspective concede that the treaty power may be exercised in areas of congressional authority, but assert that such treaties may not be self-executing.[309]

2. Other Constitutional Limits

Putting aside subject-matter limits particular to the Treaty Clause, applying more universal constitutional standards may seem straightforward. In *Missouri v. Holland*, perhaps the high-water mark of treaty authority under U.S. law, Justice Holmes took care to note that "[t]he treaty in question does not contravene any prohibitory words to be found in the Constitution."[310] Later, in *Reid v. Covert*, the Court held that military courts conducting trials of civilian dependents of overseas armed forces service members pursuant to an international agreement had to comply with the Fifth and Sixth Amendments.[311] The plurality explained that "no agreement with a foreign nation can confer power on the Congress, or on any other branch of Government, which is free from the restraints of the Constitution."[312] *Reid* involved executive agreements, rather than treaties,[313] but the supremacy of the Constitution applies to conflicts between treaties and individual liberties as well.[314]

---

[307] *Id.; see* GARY LAWSON & GUY SEIDMAN, THE CONSTITUTION OF EMPIRE: TERRITORIAL EXPANSION AND AMERICAN LEGAL HISTORY 38 (2004) (summarizing Jefferson's position as being that "treaties cannot serve as substitutes for legislation").

[308] *See* LAWSON & SEIDMAN, *supra* note 307, at 38–40 (endorsing Jefferson's overall, "implementational" theory of the treaty power, but noting that it "has never garnered wide support," and that it "is problematic along every dimension that is relevant for constitutional meaning: historical, textual, intratextual, and structural."). *But see* HENKIN, FOREIGN AFFAIRS, at 195 (noting that "[t]reaties have dealt with many matters that were also subject to legislation," such as commercial matters); Vázquez, *supra* note 92, at 2191 (observing that "most treaties throughout our history have involved matters that plausibly fall within Article I," and that "[n]umerous Supreme Court and lower court decisions give effect to treaties on matters within Article I powers"); *id.* at 219 n.147 (citing cases).

[309] *See* John C. Yoo, *Laws as Treaties?: The Constitutionality of Congressional-Executive Agreements*, 99 MICH. L. REV. 757, 760 n.10, 73 n.17, 821 (2001); *cf. id.* at 832, 834, 836, 838, 839–42 (suggesting broader view, not limited to self-execution, concerning exclusion of treaty power from matters regulable by Congress according to Article I). *But see supra* this chapter text accompanying notes 91–92 (noting competing views regarding non-self-execution).

[310] Missouri v. Holland, 252 U.S. 416, 433 (1920). For further discussion, see *supra* this chapter § I(C).

[311] Reid v. Covert, 354 U.S. 1 (1957).

[312] *Id.* at 16.

[313] *See infra* this chapter § V.

[314] *E.g.*, Boos v. Barry, 485 U.S. 312, 324 (1988) (stating, in treaty context, that position taken by *Reid* plurality was "well established"); *accord* Martin v. Warden, Atlanta Pen, 993 F.2d 824, 829 (11th Cir. 1993); Sahagian v. United States, 864 F.2d 509, 513 (7th Cir. 1988); Oneida Indian Nation of

At the core of *Missouri v. Holland* and *Reid* is the truism that the constitutional constraints applicable to the treaty power constrain the treaty power.[315] The challenge lies in determining which constraints so apply. This can be especially difficult for structural constraints—broadly, principles concerning how the relevant institutions exercise power—which are not spelled out, or which are spelled out quite incompletely, in the constitutional text. The First Amendment literally limits actions by "Congress," but the Court appears never to have believed that this meant treaties made by the president and Senate were free to chart their own course; this suggests, at a minimum, that resolving whether and how other restrictions on the national government apply to treaty-making requires careful analysis.[316]

One potential constraint of continuing interest is state sovereign immunity, in the sense that "a federal court generally may not hear a suit brought by any person against a nonconsenting State" of the union.[317] The Eleventh Amendment, the most obvious starting point, appears quite circumscribed.[318] But the Supreme Court has gone beyond the Eleventh Amendment's text to recognize immunity in federal question cases and suits brought by foreign governments, among others.[319]

How this applies to Article II treaties is not straightforward. The Court has held that Congress may abrogate state sovereign immunity when exercising power under Section 5 of the Fourteenth Amendment,[320] but it has also held

---

N.Y. v. New York, 860 F.2d 1145, 1163 (2d Cir. 1988); *see also* Am. Ins. Ass'n v. Garamendi, 539 U.S. 396, 416 n.9 (2003) (noting that the ability of treaties and executive agreements to preempt inconsistent State law is "[s]ubject . . . to the Constitution's guarantees of individual rights"); RESTATEMENT (FOURTH) § 307 ("A treaty provision will not be given effect as law in the United States to the extent that giving it this effect would violate any individual constitutional rights.").

[315] *See also* De Geofroy v. Riggs, 133 U.S. 258, 267 (1890) ("It would not be contended that [the treaty power] extends so far as to authorize what the constitution forbids . . ."); Cherokee Tobacco, 78 U.S. (11 Wall.) 616, 620 (1871) ("It need hardly be said that a treaty cannot change the Constitution or be held valid if it be in violation of that instrument.").

[316] U.S. CONST. amend. I (providing that "Congress shall make no law" restricting certain rights relating to religion, speech, assembly, and petitioning). "Congress" was also denied the capacity to restrict the slave trade prior to 1808, without clearly resolving whether that same capacity could be exercised by treaty. *Id.* art. I, § 9, cl. 1 (providing that "[t]he Migration or Importation of such Persons as any of the States now existing shall think proper to admit, shall not be prohibited by the Congress" before 1808); *id.* art. V (prohibiting constitutional amendment of slave trade provision before 1808); *see* LAWSON & SEIDMAN, *supra* note 307, at 42–44.

[317] Allen v. Cooper, 140 S. Ct. 994, 1000 (2020).

[318] U.S. CONST. art. XI (restricting judicial power over certain suits "commenced or prosecuted against one of the United States by Citizens of another State, or by Citizens or Subjects of any Foreign State."); *see Allen*, 140 S. Ct. at 1000 (noting that, notionally, the Eleventh Amendment "applies only if the plaintiff is not a citizen of the defendant State").

[319] *See* Hans v. Louisiana, 134 U.S. 1, 14–15 (1890); Principality of Monaco v. Mississippi, 292 U.S. 313, 330 (1934).

[320] Fitzpatrick v. Bitzer, 427 U.S. 445, 456 (1976); *see* Va. Office for Prot. and Advocacy v. Stewart, 563 U.S. 247, 254 n.2 (2011); Kimel v. Florida Bd. of Regents, 528 U.S. 62, 80–92 (2000).

that Congress may *not* do so when using its Article I authority (save, apparently, for the Bankruptcy Clause).[321] The Treaty Clause falls within Article II rather than Article I, but the reasons for permitting abrogation under the Fourteenth Amendment—because it was adopted subsequent to the Eleventh Amendment and revised the preexisting balance between state and federal power, leaving "'antecedent provisions of the Constitution'" unaffected—do not commend themselves to the treaty context.[322] The Court has also noted the failure of a proposal, during Congress' consideration of the amendment in 1794, that would have exempted treaties.[323] And on a couple of occasions, the Court appears to have assumed, at least in passing, that the state sovereign immunity doctrine limits treaties.[324] Lower courts have applied the doctrine wholesale to treaty-based claims against states and state officials.[325]

Even if courts today considered the question open, they would likely reach a similar conclusion for functional reasons.[326] If immunity protects state dignity,[327] or operates as a limit on Article III jurisdiction,[328] it is not clear why the answer for treaties should be different. There is precedent that denies the "sovereignty" of the several states when it comes to matters of foreign affairs, or claims that any such sovereignty was surrendered in the constitutional plan,[329] and it

---

[321] Seminole Tribe v. Florida, 517 U.S. 44, 47, 72–73 (1996); *see, e.g.,* Florida Prepaid Postsecondary Ed. Expense Bd. v. Coll. Sav. Bank, 527 U.S. 627, 636 (1999) (holding that the Intellectual Property Clause, Art. I, § 8, cl. 8, could not be the basis for abrogating state sovereign immunity from patent infringement suits); *Allen,* 140 S. Ct. at 1002 (applying *Florida Prepaid* to copyright infringement suits, which had the same constitutional basis for statutory authority).

[322] *Seminole Tribe,* 517 U.S. at 65–66 (quoting Pennsylvania v. Union Gas Co., 491 U.S. 1, 42 (1989) (Scalia, J., dissenting)). Article II may be distinguished because it was adopted prior to the Eleventh Amendment; if that distinction were not enough, Section 5 of the Fourteenth Amendment also contains state-related prohibitions and enforcement-enabling language that Article II's text does not. *See Seminole Tribe,* 517 U.S. at 59 (noting distinctive features of § 5).

[323] *See* Alden v. Maine, 527 U.S. 706, 721 (1999) (citing 4 ANNALS OF CONG. 30–31, 476–78 (1794)); *id.* at 735.

[324] *See* Fed. Republic of Ger. v. United States, 526 U.S. 111, 112 (1999) (per curiam) (declining emergency original jurisdiction suit and stating that "a foreign government's ability here to assert a claim against a State is . . . probable contravention of Eleventh Amendment principles"); Breard v. Greene, 523 U.S. 371, 377–78 (1998) (per curiam) (noting Eleventh Amendment as "a separate reason why Paraguay's suit might not succeed").

[325] *See* Republic of Para. v. Allen, 134 F.3d 622, 629 (4th Cir. 1998) (applying Eleventh Amendment bar to remedies against state officials for past violations of treaty, at least absent evidence of ongoing violations); United Mexican States v. Woods, 126 F.3d 1220, 1222 (9th Cir. 1997) (same); Consulate Gen. of Mex. v. Phillips, 17 F. Supp. 2d 1318, 1323–27 (S.D. Fla. 1998) (same); Atl. States Legal Found. v. Babbit, 83 F. Supp. 2d 344, 346–48 (N.D.N.Y. 2000) (same).

[326] *See* Edward T. Swaine, *Does Federalism Constrain the Treaty Power?,* 103 COLUM. L. REV. 403, 433–41 (2003); Carlos Manuel Vázquez, *Treaties and the Eleventh Amendment,* 42 VA. J. INT'L L. 713 (2002); *cf.* RESTATEMENT (FOURTH) § 312 rptrs. note 6 ("This principle [of state sovereign immunity] potentially applies to claims brought under treaties or legislation implementing them.").

[327] *See* Fed. Mar. Comm'n v. S.C. Ports Auth., 535 U.S. 743, 760 (2002); *Alden,* 527 U.S. at 728. *But see Fed. Mar. Comm'n,* 535 U.S. at 770–72 (Stevens, J., dissenting) (contesting dignity rationale).

[328] *See Seminole Tribe,* 517 U.S. at 72–73.

[329] As to the former, see United States v. Curtiss-Wright Exp. Corp., 299 U.S. 304, 316–18 (1936); as to the latter, see Missouri v. Holland, 252 U.S. 416, 432–33 (1920). *Cf.* Principality of Monaco v. Mississippi, 292 U.S. 313, 322–23 (1934) (explaining that states were to be immune from being

remains of keen contemporary importance—as at the founding—to secure state compliance with treaties.[330] But the Court regards state sovereign immunity as consistent with substantial federal authority.[331] Future litigation may explore nuances in how exceptions to immunity, such as the ability to seek prospective relief and the capacity of the United States to bring suit in its own name, should apply to treaties.[332]

A second potential structural constraint on treaties is the anti-commandeering principle, which establishes that federal law cannot direct state legislatures to enact regulatory programs or compel state and local officials to enforce federal law.[333] Whether this applies in the same way to all bases for national authority remains unclear,[334] but it is plausible that the Court would apply the principle to limit certain exercises of the treaty power—notwithstanding familiar

sued without their consent, "save where there has been 'a surrender of this immunity in the plan of the convention'") (quoting THE FEDERALIST, No. 81, at 487 (Alexander Hamilton)). It has been suggested, for example, that the Treaty Clause might be likened to the Bankruptcy Clause, U.S. CONST. art. I, § 8, cl. 4, which was understood at the Convention to subordinate states so as to diminish their interference and to achieve uniformity—albeit exceptionally, and with regard mostly to *in rem* jurisdiction. *See* Philip Tassin, *Why Treaties Can Abrogate State Sovereign Immunity: Applying Central Virginia Community College v. Katz to the Treaty Power*, 101 CAL. L. REV. 755 (2013)). *But cf.* Cent. Va. Cmty. Coll. v. Katz, 546 U.S. 356, 359 (2006); *id.* at 369 n.9 (noting the "singular nature" of bankruptcy jurisdiction, and the particular history of the Bankruptcy Clause); Allen v. Cooper, 140 S. Ct. 994, 1002–03 (2020) (describing it as a "striking aspect" of *Katz* that it had the Bankruptcy Clause as itself abrogating Eleventh Amendment immunity).

330 *See supra* this chapter § I.
331 *Seminole Tribe*, 517 U.S. at 61–63 (stressing plenary authority over Indian Commerce); *see also Alden*, 527 U.S. at 732 ("The Constitution, by delegating to Congress the power to establish the supreme law of the land when acting within its enumerated powers, does not foreclose a State from asserting immunity to claims arising under federal law…").
332 *See generally* RESTATEMENT (FOURTH) § 312 rptrs. note 6. Lower court cases have assumed that the exception for prospective relief under *Ex parte* Young, 209 U.S. 123 (1908), applies to treaties as well. *See infra* this chapter text accompanying note 557. The exception for suits by the United States, see United States v. Texas, 143 U.S. 621 (1892), may also have been assumed. *Cf.* Sanitary Dist. of Chi. v. United States, 266 U.S. 405, 425 (1925) (concluding that the United States had "standing … to carry out treaty obligations to a foreign power").
333 *See* New York v. United States, 505 U.S. 144, 161–66 (1992); Printz v. United States, 521 U.S. 898, 935 (1997). Putting these strands together is largely a matter of economy, as their warrants differ—and the principle against commandeering state legislatures is generally more highly regarded. *E.g.*, Vicki C. Jackson, *Federalism and the Uses and Limits of Law: Printz and Principle?*, 111 HARV. L. REV. 2180, 2199 (1998); Saikrishna Bangalore Prakash, *Field Office Federalism*, 79 VA. L. REV. 1957, 2012–13 (1993).
334 *See* Branch v. Smith, 538 U.S. 254, 302 (2003) (O'Connor, J., concurring in part and dissenting in part) (querying "[w]hether the anticommandeering principle … is as robust in the Article I, § 4 context … as it is in the Article I, § 8, context" at issue in *New York* and *Printz*); *see also* Matthew D. Adler & Seth F. Kreimer, *The New Etiquette of Federalism: New York, Printz, and Yeskey*, 1998 SUP. CT. REV. 71, 119–33 (contending that the anti-commandeering principle is inapplicable to congressional action under the Reconstruction Amendments). However, the Court has indicated that the principle is a general reflection of state sovereignty that does not turn on the precise basis for congressional authority. Reno v. Condon, 528 U.S. 141, 149 (2000) (explaining that "we [have] held federal statutes invalid, not because Congress lacked legislative authority over the subject matter, but because those statutes violated the principles of federalism contained in the Tenth Amendment").

distinctions between foreign relations and domestic authority.[335] The ease with which the Court might take the plunge and the consequences depend very much on how it would apply potential nuances under existing doctrine, such as distinguishing national measures that apply equally to private parties and states or their officials, or distinguishing noncoercive measures and those involving conditional preemption.[336]

A third possible constraint, the Tenth Amendment,[337] is the hardest to assess. The argument for applying it is simple: the treaty power is wielded by a limited national government with residual powers reserved to the states, and should not be an unlimited means of circumventing that principle.[338] This is similar to, if not congruent with, suggestions that the treaty power must avoid subject matter usually within the jurisdiction of states.[339] Tenth Amendment case law has been unclear, however, as to whether it focuses on the scope of a claimed national authority, or instead seeks more directly to protect some "province of state power," and (if the latter) how much that reserved power varies depending on the asserted source of national authority.[340]

In *Missouri v. Holland*, Justice Holmes described the question, memorably, as being whether a treaty not violating any textual prohibition was nonetheless "forbidden by some invisible radiation from the general terms of the Tenth Amendment."[341] The Court concluded that the bilateral treaty at issue was not forbidden, given the evident need for national action and international

---

[335] *Cf.* Swaine, *supra* note 326, at 424 n.88 (noting conflicting authorities). As one measure of its uncertainty, the topic is not addressed in the *Restatement (Fourth)*.

[336] *See* Swaine, *supra* note 326, at 424–33, 480–87. This issue has been most carefully explored in relation to the Vienna Convention on Consular Relations. *See, e.g.,* Carlos Manuel Vázquez, Breard, Printz, *and the Treaty Power*, 70 U. COLO. L. REV. 1317 (1999).

[337] *See* U.S. CONST. amend. X ("The powers not delegated to the United States by the Constitution, nor prohibited by it to the States, are reserved to the States respectively, or to the people.").

[338] *See, e.g.,* JEFFERSON'S MANUAL, *supra* note 168, §594 at 318 (indicating that the treaty power "must have meant to except out of these the rights reserved to the States; for surely the President and Senate cannot do by treaty what the whole government is interdicted from doing in any way").

[339] *See, e.g.,* Golove, *supra* note 282, at 1281 ("Were the President and Senate to make a treaty on a subject inappropriate for negotiation and agreement, and thus beyond the scope of the treaty power, the treaty would be invalid under the Tenth Amendment."); *id.* at 1086 ("A treaty that violates this [subject-matter] limitation would be beyond the scope of the treaty power and thus would invade the sphere 'reserved' to the states by the Tenth Amendment."); *cf. supra* this chapter text accompanying notes 282–285 (discussing variants of international concern limits).

[340] New York v. United States, 505 U.S. 144, 155–56 (1992) (describing rival views of the Tenth Amendment, and stating that in cases involving the division of authority between the federal government and the states, "the two inquiries are mirror images of each other," insofar as "[i]f a power is delegated to Congress in the Constitution, the Tenth Amendment expressly disclaims any reservation of that power to the States; if a power is an attribute of state sovereignty reserved by the Tenth Amendment, it is necessarily a power the Constitution has not conferred on Congress"); *see* Bond v. United States, 564 U.S. 211, 226 (2011) (stating, in upholding standing to challenge a conviction under the statute implementing the Chemical Weapons Convention on Tenth Amendment grounds, that "[w]hether the Tenth Amendment is regarded as simply a "'truism' . . . or whether it has independent force of its own, the result here is the same") (internal quotations and citations omitted).

[341] Missouri v. Holland, 252 U.S. 416, 433–34 (1920).

cooperation to protect migratory birds.[342] Decisions by the Rehnquist Court and the Roberts Court, however, have made the Tenth Amendment's "radiation" more visible, if not clear.[343] The prospect that this jurisprudence might unsettle *Missouri v. Holland* inspired a rich literature,[344] and the separate opinions in *Bond v. United States* suggest the matter is not resolved.[345]

Justice Holmes's starting point, that constitutional limits on the treaty power had to be "ascertained in a different way" than those on Article I, still has much to commend it.[346] Prohibitory words of general application, like those in the Bill of Rights, are one thing. But any powers implicitly withheld under Article II, and thus reserved to the states, need not be coterminous with the powers withheld under Article I: much depends on the scope of the treaty power, and the Constitution's prohibition on state treaties suggests that the powers reserved to the states relating to international agreements are relatively narrow.[347] Some such distinction has long been in play. For example, Congress' ability to engineer the Louisiana Purchase based on its peacetime authorities under Article I was unclear; Jefferson had doubts too about whether the treaty power sufficed, but arguments that the Tenth Amendment had less purchase in relation to the treaty power, because the states were disabled from entering into similar arrangements,

---

[342] *Missouri v. Holland*, 252 U.S. at 435.

[343] *Compare, e.g.*, New York v. United States, 505 U.S. 144, 157 (1992) ("The Tenth Amendment . . . directs us to determine . . . whether an incident of state sovereignty is protected by a limitation on an Article I power"), *with* United States v. Comstock, 560 U.S. 126, 144 (2010) (discounting claim to state sovereignty when the national government is exercising powers specifically enumerated in Article I, together with Necessary and Proper authority, since "[v]irtually by definition" these are not reserved to the states and protected by the Tenth Amendment).

[344] *See generally* Bradley, *Treaty Power* I, *supra* note 282; Bradley, *Treaty Power II*, *supra* note 282; Golove, *supra* note 282; Swaine, *supra* note 326.

[345] *See supra* this chapter text accompanying notes 293–305 (discussing opinions). Another signal that the Tenth Amendment might constrain the treaty power was the Court's preceding, unanimous decision that the defendant had standing to raise the issue. *See* Bond v. United States, 504 U.S. 211 (2011).

[346] *Holland*, 252 U.S. at 433. Justice Holmes directly stated that "[w]e do not mean to imply that there are no qualifications to the treaty-making power" (*id.*); one part of the opinion did seem to imply just that, but there was a more benign explanation. *See supra* this chapter text accompanying note 271.

[347] *See, e.g.*, Reid v. Covert, 354 U.S. 1, 18 (1957) (plurality op.) (concluding that "[t]o the extent that the United States can validly make treaties, the people and the States have delegated their power to the National Government and the Tenth Amendment is no barrier"); *see also supra* this chapter text accompanying notes 11, 96 (noting the Compact Clause and related authorities); Chapter 9 § III (discussing compacts and federalism); *see also infra* this chapter text accompanying notes 765–767 (discussing relationship with non–Article II agreements). The distinctive scope of the treaty power and the power left to the states need not turn on construction of the Treaty Clause itself. Thus, even if one follows a minority view, like the argument that the treaty power simply limits a broad "executive Power" conferred by the Vesting Clause by requiring Senate advice and consent, the powers reserved to the states are then diminished by the combined force of the Vesting Clause and the treaty power. Lawson & Seidman, *supra* note 307, at 45–51.

were influential.[348] Resistance to the use of treaties to acquire territories did not long persist.[349]

The idea that the Tenth Amendment applies differently to the treaty power is consistent with case law that holds, also in keeping with *Missouri v. Holland*, that Article II treaties may constitutionally establish international obligations that do not (otherwise) fall within Congress' legislative authority.[350] While proposals that the treaty power should be confined in its domestic legal effects to the same limits attending Congress' legislative powers under Article I appeal to a sense of symmetry—because they address the intuition that the treaty power is limited, without hazarding the development of a separate body of law concerning subject-matter limits—they achieve it by de-emphasizing the symmetry between the international and domestic efficacy of treaties that was one objective of the founding.[351] A different path toward a similar end, which would sharply limit the implementation of non-self-executing Article II treaties via the Necessary and

---

[348] *See* EVERETT SOMERVILLE BROWN, CONSTITUTIONAL HISTORY OF THE LOUISIANA PURCHASE, 1803–1812, at 20–22 (1920) (quoting advice of Secretary of Treasury Gallatin that "[t]he only possible objection" to the acquisition must be the Tenth Amendment, and explaining that the objection was weaker in relation to the treaty power); *see also id.* at 20–35 (describing other executive branch discussions); *id.* at 55–61, 62–65 (describing debates in the House and Senate). *See generally* DAVID P. CURRIE, THE CONSTITUTION IN CONGRESS: THE JEFFERSONIANS, 1801–1829, at 95–101 (2001). For an argument that Jefferson should have heeded his initial doubts about even acquisition's constitutionality, see Robert Knowles, *The Balance of Forces and the Empire of Liberty: States' Rights and the Louisiana Purchase*, 88 IOWA L. REV. 343 (2003).

[349] *See, e.g.*, Am. Ins. Co. v. Canter, 26 U.S. (1 Pet.) 511, 542 (1828) ("The Constitution confers absolutely on the Government of the Union the powers of making war, and of making treaties; consequently, that Government possesses the power of acquiring territory, either by conquest or by treaty."); 3 JOSEPH STORY, COMMENTARIES ON THE CONSTITUTION OF THE UNITED STATES § 1282 (Boston, Hilliard, Gray & Co. 1833) ("[T] he constitutional right of the United States to acquire territory would seem so naturally to flow from the sovereignty confided to it, as not to admit of very serious question."); Martin S. Flaherty, *Post-Originalism*, 68 U. CHI. L. REV. 1089, 1094 (2001) (stating that "no constitutional dispute was more important at the time, nor seemingly more beside the point now, than the Louisiana Purchase").

[350] *See, e.g.*, United States v. Lara, 541 U.S. 193, 201 (2004) (citing *Missouri v. Holland*, 252 U.S. at 433); United States v. Bond, 681 F.3d 149 (3d Cir. 2012) (noting debate about the scope of limits on the treaty power, including trend toward lesser limitations, and concluding that "[w]hatever the Treaty Power's proper bounds may be . . . we are confident that the [Chemical Weapons] Convention . . . falls comfortably within them"), *rev'd on other grounds*, 572 U.S. 844 (2014); United States v. Fries, 781 F.3d 1137 (9th Cir. 2015); United States v. Lue, 134 F.3d 79 (2d Cir. 1998); RESTATEMENT (FOURTH) § 312(1) ("The treaty power conferred by Article II of the Constitution may be used to enter into treaties addressing matters that would fall outside of Congress' legislative authority in the absence of the treaty"); *see id.* cmt. c & rptrs. note 2 (citing *Missouri v. Holland*, 252 U.S. at 433). The "otherwise" in the text, like the reference in § 312(1) of the *Restatement (Fourth)* to "matters that would fall outside of Congress's legislative authority in the absence of the treaty," reflects the fact that the Necessary and Proper Clause may enhance congressional authority in the context of a particular treaty. *See id.* § 312(2); *see also infra* this chapter notes 614–615 (self-execution) and 680–687 (implementation of non-self-executing treaties).

[351] *See* Bradley, *Treaty Power*, *supra* note 282, at 451–56 (concluding that subject-matter limits are likely impracticable and ill-adapted to modern treaty-making); *id.* at 456 (advocating "subject[ing] the treaty power to the same federalism restrictions that apply to Congress's legislative powers," such that "the treaty power would not confer any additional regulatory powers on the federal government, just the power to bind the United States on the international plane").

Proper Clause, and thus constrain implementation to the scope of Article I authority and its attendant constraints, is addressed later.[352]

The extent to which Tenth Amendment and other structural limits apply to Article II treaties remains open to inquiry, but may not be of much practical significance. Even if treaties were not universally susceptible to state sovereign immunity, anti-commandeering, Tenth Amendment, or similar doctrines, the statutory implementation of any non-self-executing provisions[353]—and the congressional-executive agreements often used in lieu of treaties[354]—may be. Moreover, the treaty-makers have a number of techniques that they employ to protect state sovereignty, including negotiating federalism-related exceptions with treaty partners and employing conditions (such as declarations of non-self-execution), allowing states and localities to implement international obligations, and rejecting federalism-threatening treaties altogether.[355] These techniques may correspond inexactly with what the Constitution requires,[356] but they are also likely to protect state autonomy even when judicial protection would not. For example, when considering the Convention on the Elimination of All Forms of Discrimination Against Women, the Senate contemplated a declaration that the treaty would be non-self-executing, together with an understanding that the federal government would only implement the treaty "to the extent that it exercises jurisdiction over the matters covered therein, and otherwise by the State and local governments." Those might easily have resolved any constitutional difficulties, but the United States further decided not to proceed with advice and consent, in part due to federalism concerns that somehow persisted.[357]

Even if federalism-protecting doctrines apply to Article II treaties much as they do to domestic statutes, and even if the political branches refrain from taking prophylactic measures, relatively few Article II treaties have posed potential issues regarding state sovereign immunity or commandeering. Tenth Amendment limits, too, rarely appear germane to Article II treaties, let alone in

---

[352] See infra this chapter § IV(B).

[353] See infra this chapter text accompanying notes 680–687.

[354] See infra this chapter § V(A).

[355] For examples of the political branches declaring a treaty non-self-executing, and of examples in which federalism issues were not heeded, see Duncan B. Hollis, Executive Federalism: Forging New Federalist Constraints on the Treaty Power, 79 S. CAL. L. REV. 1327, 1369–86 (2006); see also Hathaway et al., supra note 275, at 314–24 (discussing "top-down" and "bottom-up" federalism accommodations).

[356] See Bradley, Treaty Power, supra note 282, at 440–45 (describing strengths and weaknesses of political process protections, but ultimately regarding them as insufficient); Bradley, Treaty Power II, supra note 282, at 110–11 (same). For a broader description of treaty-specific, political, and diplomatic checks, see Hathaway et al., supra note 275, at 304–14.

[357] See Convention on the Elimination of All Forms of Discrimination Against Women, S. Exec. Rep. No. 107-9, at 11–13 (2002) (text of resolution of advice and consent, with proposed reservations, understandings, and declarations); see also id. at 20–23 (additional views of Sens. Helms, Brownback, and Enzi) (stating persistent federalism and other concerns).

justiciable circumstances. It is important, in all events, to respect the different powers that were plausibly assigned to the national government under Article II.

III. Interpreting International Agreements

Whether an international agreement was constitutionally made arises much less often than questions about *what* was made: what does the agreement mean, and how does it apply to a particular controversy? Particular disputes may not endure, but much turns on an agreement's meaning—not just in resolving concrete cases but also for states considering whether to ratify the agreement or engaged in examining the performance of obligations.

The VCLT sets out a comprehensive, globally accepted approach to treaty interpretation. The United States is not a party to the VCLT, and perhaps for that reason, the Supreme Court has rarely alluded to it.[358] Yet understanding the VCLT remains vital to understanding U.S. practice and interpreting its international obligations.[359] As the executive branch has acknowledged, the VCLT's interpretive elements are consistent with customary international law and, to that extent, bind the United States and its courts.[360] Beyond this, the VCLT and the rules it reflects also inform how other states draft, interpret, and perform agreements, including those in which the United States participates. This suggests the centrality of the VCLT's approach; at a minimum, discrepancies between the U.S. and international approaches to treaty interpretation should be

---

[358] The Supreme Court has alluded to the VCLT indirectly. For example, *Sanchez-Llamas v. Oregon* quoted the *Restatement (Third)*, which was in turn a near-verbatim quotation of VCLT Article 31(1). Sanchez-Llamas v. Oregon, 548 U.S. 331, 346 (2006) (quoting RESTATEMENT (THIRD) § 325(1)). Lower courts are occasionally more direct. *See, e.g.,* Pliego v. Hayes, 843 F.3d 226, 232 (6th Cir. 2016); De Los Santos Mora v. New York, 524 F.3d 183, 196 n.19 (2d Cir. 2008); Kreimerman v. Casa Veerkamp, S.A. de C.v., 22 F.3d 634, 638 & n.9 (5th Cir. 1994).

[359] Illustratively, the *Restatement (Fourth)* section on treaty interpretation largely tracks the relevant provisions of the VCLT. RESTATEMENT (FOURTH) § 306; *see id.* cmt. a (stating that the VCLT's articles "set forth principles that one would expect any interpreter to apply in construing obligations under a treaty").

[360] *Id.* § 306 cmt. a & rprtrs. note 1. *See, e.g.,* Counter-Memorial of the United States of America, Avena and Other Mexican Nationals (Mex. v. U.S.), Written Proceedings, 2004 I.C.J. 12, at 67–68 & n.142 (Nov. 3, 2003) (describing Article 31 of the VCLT, the general rule of treaty interpretation, as "an article reflecting customary international law" and stating that Article 32, describing supplementary methods, "likewise reflects customary international law"); Brief for the United States as Amicus Curiae Supporting Petitioner at 19 & n.6, Abbott v. Abbott, 560 U.S. 1 (2010) (No. 08-645) (invoking Articles 31 and 32 and "recogniz[ing] the Convention as an authoritative guide to treaty interpretation" (citing Fujitsu Ltd. v. Fed. Express Corp., 247 F.3d 423, 433 (2d Cir. 2001)). International tribunals concur, *e.g.,* Arbitral Award of 31 July 1989 (Guinea-Bissau v. Sen.), Judgment, 1991 I.C.J. 53, ¶ 48 (Nov. 12) (stating that Articles 31 and 32 "may in many respects be considered as a codification of existing customary international law"), as do at least some U.S. courts. *See, e.g.,* Chubb & Son, Inc. v. Asiana Airlines, 214 F.3d 301, 309 (2d Cir. 2000) (stating that the VCLT is "an authoritative guide to the customary international law of treaties").

evaluated so as to avoid inadvertent disagreement between the United States and other states.

The following discussion addresses the broadly similar approaches taken in the VCLT and in U.S. practice, particularly that of U.S. courts. It then considers additional forms of interpretive evidence, such as particular positions taken by the executive branch and the Senate, on which U.S. practice leans more heavily, and other types of evidence (for example, the views of international tribunals) to which U.S. practice appears to accord less weight.

A. International (and Domestic) Elements

The basic structure of the VCLT's provisions on treaty interpretation is fairly easily stated. Article 31(1) states that treaty provisions should be understood in light of their text, in view of their context and object and purpose.[361] Article 31(2) explains what is meant by "context."[362] Article 31(3) then says that interpretation should simultaneously "take[] into account" certain additional elements, like relevant rules of international law.[363] Article 32 separately identifies pertinent "supplementary means of interpretation," such as the preparatory work (*travaux préparatoires*), which are to be invoked more sparingly.[364]

Unsurprisingly, this structure is harder to manage in practice. It has been suggested, for example, that treaty interpretation involves "a single combined operation" involving the VCLT's various "means of interpretation," or elements.[365] Still, the VCLT's sequence of provisions remains a useful basis for describing U.S. practice, even if it differs somewhat in the weight it attributes to the elements concerned.

1. Text and Context

Article 31(1) indicates that treaty provisions are to be "interpreted in good faith in accordance with the ordinary meaning to be given to the terms of the treaty in their context and in the light of its object and purpose."[366] As this suggests, the VCLT approach to interpretation, and that of international tribunals, is largely textualist.[367] This approach is generally thought to favor objective indicia

---

[361] VCLT, *supra* note 13, art. 31(1).

[362] VCLT, *supra* note 13, art. 31(2).

[363] VCLT, *supra* note 13, art. 31(3).

[364] VCLT, *supra* note 13, art. 32.

[365] Int'l Law Comm'n, Draft Conclusions on Subsequent Agreements and Subsequent Practice in Relation to the Interpretation of Treaties, With Commentaries, U.N. Doc. A/73/10, at 17 (2018) (conclusion 2(5)).

[366] VCLT, *supra* note 13, art. 31(1).

[367] *See, e.g.*, Territorial Dispute (Libyan Arab Jamahiriya/Chad), Judgment, 1994 I.C.J. 6, ¶ 41 (Feb. 3) ("Interpretation must be based above all upon the text of the treaty."); Competence of the General Assembly for the Admission of a State to the United Nations, Advisory Opinion, 1950 I.C.J. 4, 8

over a more open-ended inquiry into the intention of the parties, which might be too unpredictable and destabilizing.[368] At the same time, this textualism is not rigid.[369] Attention to the "object and purpose" and "context" of the treaty at issue means that similar words, used in different kinds of agreements, may be interpreted differently, and that a broad range of background international law rules may be invoked.[370]

Treaty interpretation in U.S. courts is broadly similar. Historically, the Supreme Court case law varied between emphasizing good faith (which may be paired with a principle favoring liberal interpretation of treaties, or favoring treaty-based rights) and placing greater emphasis on text.[371] In more recent cases, text has moved more clearly to the fore.[372] Much as with statutory interpretation,[373] the modern Court consistently stresses that interpretation must begin, if not necessarily end, with the "ordinary meaning" of a provision's words.[374]

Ordinary meaning is sometimes (perhaps even ordinarily) clear enough, but not always. Dictionaries, for example, may provide a range of possible meanings, without reliably indicating whether the parties intended any or all of those

(Mar. 3) (advisory opinion) ("If the relevant words in their natural and ordinary meaning make sense in their context, that is an end of the matter.").

[368] *See, e.g.*, RICHARD K. GARDINER, TREATY INTERPRETATION 6–9 (2d ed. 2015).

[369] *See* RESTATEMENT (FOURTH) § 306 rptrs. note 2 (citing commentaries).

[370] *See id.* § 306 rptrs. notes 5, 9. A Study Group of the International Law Commission, in a report finalized by its chairperson, suggested that Article 31(3)(c) makes relevant customary international law and general principles of law where the treaty provision is "unclear or open-textured" or the treaty's terms "have a recognized meaning" in those bodies of law, and may require consideration of "other treaty-based rules so as to arrive at a consistent meaning." *Fragmentation of International Law: Difficulties Arising from the Diversification and Expansion of International Law: Conclusions of the work of the Study Group*, U.N. Doc. A/61/10 (2006), *reprinted in* [2006] 2 Y.B. Int'l L. Comm'n 180, ¶¶ (20)–(21), U.N. Doc. A/CN.4/SER.A/2006/Add.1 (Part 2).

[371] Duncan B. Hollis, *Treaties in the Supreme Court, 1861–1900, in* INTERNATIONAL LAW IN THE U.S. SUPREME COURT: CONTINUITY AND CHANGE 55, 80–83 (David L. Sloss, Michael D. Ramsey, & William S. Dodge eds., 2011); Michael P. Van Alstine, *Treaties in the Supreme Court, 1901–1945, in id.* at 191, 209–15.

[372] Michael P. Van Alstine, *The Death of Good Faith in Treaty Jurisprudence and a Call for Resurrection*, 93 GEO. L.J. 1885 (2005). For an example of a case bucking that trend, see E. Airlines, Inc. v. Floyd, 499 U.S. 530, 532 (1991). Good faith has also been invoked to distinguish international obligations from supreme federal law. Medellín v. Texas, 552 U.S. 491, 505 (2008) (quoting THE FEDERALIST NO. 33, at 207 (J. Cooke ed., 1961) (Alexander Hamilton) (comparing "laws that individuals are 'bound to observe' as 'the *supreme law* of the land' with 'a mere treaty, dependent on the good faith of the parties'") (emphasis in original).

[373] *See, e.g., Abbott*, 560 U.S. at 10 (noting common emphasis on text). Some opinions suggest, more generally, that "[t]reaties are construed in much the same manner as statutes." Kahn Lucas Lancaster, Inc. v. Lark Int'l Ltd., 186 F.3d 210, 215 (2d Cir. 1999); *e.g., El Al Isr. Airlines*, 525 U.S. at 181 (Stevens, J., dissenting) (arguing that "a treaty, like an Act of Congress, should not be construed to preempt state law unless its intent to do so is clear"). But this is a distinct, and risky, proposition, in that it risks incongruity with interpretations by other states parties.

[374] Context is often mentioned in the same breath. *See, e.g.*, Lozano v. Montoya Alvarez, 572 U.S. 1, 11 (2014) (stating that "our 'duty [i]s to ascertain the intent of the parties' by looking to the document's text and context") (citations omitted); *Saks*, 470 U.S. at 397 (1985) ("The analysis must begin . . . with the text of the treaty and the context in which the written words are used.").

definitions to be acceptable.[375] A more basic issue—bedeviling the inquiry into ordinary meaning—is that the negotiating parties may well have had uncommon or specialized meanings in mind, and the ultimate objective is "to give the specific words of the treaty a meaning consistent with the shared expectations of the contracting parties."[376] The VCLT accommodates this by allowing, exceptionally, for a demonstration that the parties intended a "special meaning."[377] While U.S. courts do not often interpret treaties according to "special meaning" per se,[378] they may nonetheless (as in international practice) arrive at what they consider to be a treaty text's ordinary meaning by considering contextual evidence that is special in character.[379] Regardless, courts should be sensitive to how terms are used in international law and treaty practice, even if that differs from what a dictionary might indicate,[380] and the Supreme Court has not always done so.[381]

[375] The difficulty of relying on dictionaries for a fixed meaning has been stressed in WTO dispute settlement, including in cases involving the United States. See, e.g., Appellate Body Report, United States—Measures Affecting the Cross-Border Supply of Gambling and Betting Services, ¶¶ 164–66, WTO Doc. WT/DS285/AB/R (adopted Apr. 7, 2005); see also GARDINER, supra note 368, at 186–89. The latitude afforded by dictionary definitions also tends to permit inconsistent results. Several U.S. cases, wrestling with whether ne exeat rights were "rights of custody" within the meaning of the Hague Convention on the Civil Aspects of International Child Abduction, applied various dictionary definitions both of "custody" and "determine" (a term used in the Convention's definition of "rights of custody"), to conclude that they were not. See, e.g., Croll v. Croll, 229 F.3d 133, 138–41 (2nd Cir. 2000); Gonzalez v. Gutierrez, 311 F.3d 942, 949 (9th Cir. 2002). But the Supreme Court took a different view, in part because it invoked an alternative definition of "determine." Abbott, 560 U.S. at 11.

[376] Saks, 470 U.S. at 399; accord Water Splash, Inc. v. Menon, 137 S. Ct. 1504, 1512 (2017); Lozano, 572 U.S. at 12–14; BG Grp., PLC v. Republic of Arg., 572 U.S. 25, 36–37 (2014); Olympic Airways v. Husain, 540 U.S. 644, 650 (2004); El Al Isr. Airlines, Ltd. v. Tsui Yuan Tseng, 525 U.S. 155, 167 (1999); E. Airlines, 499 U.S. at 536; Stuart, 489 U.S. at 365–66; see also Ware v. Hylton, 3 U.S. (3 Dall.) 199, 237 (1796) (opinion of Chase, J.) (emphasizing the goal of effectuating the intent of the treaty parties).

[377] According to the VCLT, a "special meaning shall be given to a term" only "if it is established that the parties so intended." VCLT, supra note 13, art. 31(4); see, e.g., Legal Status of Eastern Greenland (Den. v. Nor.), Judgment, 1933 P.C.I.J., (ser. A/B) No. 53, at 49 (Apr. 5) (stating that "if it is alleged by one of the Parties that some unusual or exceptional meaning is to be attributed to [the word 'Greenland'], it lies on that Party to establish its contention"). See generally GARDINER, supra note 368, at 338–40.

[378] See Bank of N.Y. v. Yugoimport, 745 F.3d 599, 609–10, 612 n.11 (2d Cir. 2014) (applying VCLT in keeping with choice-of-law principles, and noting invocation of "special meaning" provision, but concluding that "there is no indication that the parties intended a special meaning for 'agency'"); see also Logan v. Dupuis, 990 F. Supp. 26, 29 (D.D.C. 1997) (noting lack of evidence of "special meaning").

[379] See GARDINER, supra note 368, at 155–56 (discussing example in U.S. case law of defining terms based in part on context of treaty); id. at 337–38 (noting broader tendency).

[380] See, e.g., Kasikili/Sedudu Island (Bots./Namib.), Judgment, 1999 I.C.J. 1045, ¶ 27 (Dec. 13) (determining "the ordinary meaning of the words 'main channel' by reference to the most commonly used criteria in international law and practice").

[381] In Medellín v. Texas, the Court interpreted "undertakes to comply" in Article 94 of the U.N. Charter as suggesting a need for further action before an ICJ judgment should be given effect. See Medellín v. Texas, 552 U.S. 491, 508–09 n.5 (2008); id. at 533–34 & n.1 (Stevens, J., concurring). The dissent stressed that ordinary English and Spanish dictionaries (Mexico was the other party to the ICJ proceeding) indicated unambiguously a present obligation, id. at 551–54 (Breyer, J., dissenting), but none of the opinions explored its usage in international law—which did not support the Court's view. See, e.g., Application of the Convention on the Prevention and Punishment of the Crime of Genocide (Bosn. & Herz. v. Serb. & Montenegro), 2007 I.C.J. 47, ¶ 162 (Feb. 26) (defining "[t]he

Of course, courts must also steer away from adopting an understanding peculiar to one party, even one objectively supported by its legal practice.[382]

Textualist challenges may be pronounced when an agreement is not in English. Sometimes a U.S. court will have to construe a treaty in which a non-English version is the sole authentic text (such as the frequently litigated Warsaw Convention, for which French is the official language).[383] Such circumstances may require attention to specialized legal meaning in that language.[384] More often, U.S. courts construe treaties that are equally authentic in English and at least one other language, requiring them to consider whether there are any discrepancies and, if so, to reconcile texts to develop a common meaning.[385] Multiple authoritative texts can make it easier to identify a common meaning, if the texts are not at cross purposes, but U.S. courts may be tempted to rely inordinately on the English version.[386]

ordinary meaning of the word 'undertake'" as indicating acceptance of an obligation, and stating that "[i]t is a word regularly used in treaties setting out the obligations of the Contracting Parties," "unqualified," "and it is not to be read merely as an introduction to later express references to legislation, prosecution and extradition"); Carlos Manuel Vázquez, *Treaties as Law of the Land: The Supremacy Clause and the Judicial Enforcement of Treaties*, 122 HARV. L. REV. 599, 661 (2008) ("In international law usage, an 'undertaking' is well recognized to be a hard, immediate obligation.").

[382] See VCLT, *supra* note 13, art. 31(1); Lozano v. Montoya Alvarez, 572 U.S. 1, 12 (2014) (regarding it as "particularly inappropriate" to apply a background principle of U.S. law to the interpretation of treaties, absent evidence it was shared by states parties); De Geofroy v. Riggs, 133 U.S. 258, 271 (1890) (suggesting, according to canon of liberal construction, that a treaty's "words are to be taken in their ordinary meaning, as understood in the public law of nations, and not in any artificial or special sense impressed upon them by local law, unless such restricted sense is clearly intended"). *But see infra* this chapter § III(B) (discussing deference by U.S. courts to the political branches).

[383] Convention for the Unification of Certain Rules Relating to International Transportation by Air, art. 36, Oct. 12, 1929, 49 Stat. 3000, 137 L.N.T.S. 11; *see, e.g.*, El Al Isr. Airlines, Ltd. v. Tsui Yuan Tseng, 525 U.S. 155, 167–68 (1999); E. Airlines, Inc. v. Floyd, 499 U.S. 530, 535–42 (1991); Air Fr. v. Saks, 470 U.S. 392, 397–400 (1985).

[384] *E.g.*, *E. Airlines*, 499 U.S. at 536 (deferring to the French legal meaning of Warsaw Convention terms because it "was drafted in French by continental jurists") (citing *Saks*, 470 U.S. at 399). On the other hand, the Supreme Court has also examined the "official American translation" of the relevant text, on the premise that it "was before the Senate when it ratified the Convention in 1934." *See Saks*, 470 U.S. at 397; *accord* Olympic Airways v. Husain, 540 U.S. 644, 649 n.4 (2004). While any U.S. translation may be compared to the official treaty text, the risk is that the latter will be displaced. For a good balance, see *El Al Isr. Airlines*, 525 U.S. at 162 n.4 (noting "[c]itations in this opinion are to the official English translation of the Convention," but "[w]here relevant, we set out, in addition, the Convention's governing French text"); *see also* Onyeanusi v. Pan Am, 952 F.2d 788, 791 (3d Cir. 1992) (turning to French definition of treaty term "[b]ecause the official version of the treaty is in French—the version contained in the United States Code is merely an unofficial translation").

[385] The VCLT also contains an article on interpretation of treaties authenticated in two or more languages. VCLT, *supra* note 13, art. 33. It is unclear, however, whether all of Article 33 reflects customary international law; the United States has not taken a position. RESTATEMENT (FOURTH) § 106 rptrs. note 7. Exceptionally, an agreement may translate only certain provisions or terms, permitting inferences about those not translated. Bank of N.Y. v. Yugoimport, 745 F.3d 599, 610 (2d Cir. 2014) (discussing Agreement on Succession Issues Between the Five Successor States of the Former State of Yugoslavia art. 9, June 29, 2001, 41 I.L.M. 3).

[386] Notably, the Supreme Court, in construing a bilateral treaty with Spain, focused on the English-language version to the exclusion of the equally authentic Spanish-language text, which led to an interpretation that the treaty was not self-executing. Foster v. Neilson, 27 U.S. (2 Pet.) 253 (1829).

One sound way of ascertaining the meaning of a treaty provision, whether it is in one language or more, is to consider its terms in the context of other treaty provisions or associated agreements and by examining the treaty's structure as a whole.[387] According to the VCLT, the broad range of text considered as part of the context includes any annexes or preambles.[388] U.S. practice shows some variety—as to preambles, for example, courts have sometimes deemed them to have lesser status,[389] and views in the political branches have varied[390]—but they are most often used to elucidate the context much as the VCLT would suggest.[391]

When the Court returned to the same treaty a few years later in a different case, and paid attention to the Spanish text as well, it came to the opposite conclusion. United States v. Percheman, 32 U.S. (7 Pet.) 51, 88–89 (1833); see infra text accompanying notes 525–529 (discussing non-self-execution doctrine and prior decision in Foster v. Neilson). Courts sometimes seem to privilege certain language versions. See, e.g., Kahn Lucas Lancaster, Inc. v. Lark Int'l Ltd., 186 F.3d 210, 216–18 (2d Cir. 1999) (suggesting that other equally authentic languages for the New York Convention provided "more insight into the drafters' intent" than the Russian and Chinese versions, as the former were "the working languages of the United Nations Conference on International Commercial Arbitration, which drafted the Convention"). Of course, the usual problems of "ordinary meaning" remain. For example, in Sale v. Haitian Ctrs. Council, 509 U.S. 155 (1993), the Supreme Court analyzed parallel phrasing of a term ("return ('refouler')") in the English version of the United Nations Convention Relating to Status of Refugees. See Convention Relating to Status of Refugees, art. 33, July 28, 1951, 189 U.N.T.S. 137. Following the approach taken in U.S. statutory law, the Court reasoned that "'return' ha[d] a legal meaning narrower than its common meaning," but then consulted ordinary, non-legal French-English dictionaries—rather than focusing on the legal usage of "refouler." Haitian Ctrs., 509 U.S. at 180–82.

[387] See, e.g., Water Splash, Inc. v. Menon, 137 S. Ct. 1504, 1508–10 (2017). This commitment to heeding context well precedes the VCLT. See, e.g., Ward v. Race Horse, 163 U.S. 504, 508 (1896).

[388] Thus, while a particular provision is being interpreted, the context of that provision consists of the other operative provisions in the treaty itself, the preamble, and any annexes. VCLT, supra note 13, art. 31(2).

[389] See, e.g., Jogi v. Voges, 480 F.3d 822, 834 (7th Cir. 2007) ("Courts should look to materials like preambles and titles only if the text of the instrument is ambiguous."). Compare Cornejo v. County of San Diego, 504 F.3d 853, 861 (9th Cir. 2007) (citing preamble, while noting that the Senate Committee on Foreign Relations had emphasized a preambular statement), with id. at 866–67 (Nelson, J., dissenting) (disputing interpretation of preamble and suggesting that the preamble "cannot be relied upon to create ambiguity in a statute," while also suggesting different interpretation of preamble).

[390] See Max H. Hulme, Comment, Preambles in Treaty Interpretation, 164 U. Pa. L. Rev. 1281, 1285–87, 1288–89 (2015) (reviewing disagreement among senators as to whether preambular language in the New START agreement would be legally binding, with the Department of State minimizing its significance).

[391] See, e.g., World Holdings, LLC v. Fed. Republic of Ger., 613 F.3d 1310, 1316 n.10 (11th Cir. 2010) ("The language of a treaty must be read in context . . . and the 'context' of a treaty includes its preamble.") (citations omitted); see also Medellín v. Dretke, 544 U.S. 660, 688–89 (2005) (Vienna Convention on Consular Relations); Société Nationale Industrielle Aerospatiale v. U.S. Dist. Court for S. Dist. of Iowa, 482 U.S. 522, 534 (1987) (Hague Convention on the Taking of Evidence Abroad in Civil or Commercial Matters); Mora v. New York, 524 F.3d 183, 195–97 (2d Cir. 2008) (VCLT); cf. Bond v. United States, 572 U.S. 844, 849 (2014) (citing preamble to Chemical Weapons Convention in describing background); Olympic Airways v. Husain, 540 U.S. 644, 660–61 (2004) (citing need for uniformity, indicated in preamble to Warsaw Convention, as supporting deference to subsequent practice by states parties). The executive branch regularly invokes preambles as a means of interpretation. See, e.g., 2016 Digest of U.S. Practice, at 479, 481–82 (excerpting letter of April 14, 2006, from Department of State Legal Adviser Brian Egan, regarding the amended Air Transport Agreement between the United States and the European Community and its member states); id. at 484–85 (excerpting Article 1108 submission in NAFTA proceedings); id. at 490–91. Annexes,

As previously noted, the VCLT also includes as part of the interpretive context any related agreement between all the parties, and instruments that one party has made that have been accepted by the others, when made in connection with the treaty's conclusion.[392] Since acceptance by the United States (among others) of the agreement or instrument is a prerequisite, their relevance should be un-controversial. While such agreements are not often invoked in U.S. judicial proceedings, they have been an important way for the United States to resolve outstanding issues in areas like arms control.[393]

Finally, a good-faith interpretation of a treaty term, in its context, should be rendered "in the light of its object and purpose."[394] The VCLT suggests that object and purpose should be a primary consideration during interpretation, not merely confirmatory.[395] Nonetheless, U.S. courts typically cite to a treaty's object and purpose to verify an interpretation that is based on other elements of the interpretive methodology,[396] and they show little inclination to rely on evidence of

likewise, may be invoked by U.S. courts. *See, e.g.,* Bank of N.Y. v. Yugoimport, 745 F.3d 599, 610, 612–13 (2d Cir. 2014).

[392] VCLT, *supra* note 13, art. 31(2); *see* AUST, *supra* note 229, at 210–12. To be made "in connection with the conclusion of the treaty," as that phrase is used in article 31(2), an agreement should be "made in a close temporal and contextual relation" with the finalization of a treaty's text. Int'l Law Comm'n, Draft Conclusions on Subsequent Agreements, *supra* note 365, at 28, 30; *see also* Richard Gardiner, *The Vienna Convention Rules on Treaty Interpretation, in* THE OXFORD GUIDE TO TREATIES, *supra* note 13, at 467–68. A related agreement need not be a formal "treaty" in the sense used in the VCLT, and possibly such an agreement need not be legally binding at all. *See infra* this chapter text accompanying note 405 (discussing "agreement" in the context of Article 31(3)(a)).

[393] For example, the START Agreement between the United States and the Soviet Union included thirty-eight "Agreed Statements" between the parties, albeit as part of an annex that was integral to the agreement. Treaty with the Union of Soviet Socialist Republics on the Reduction and Limitation of Strategic Offensive Arms (The START Treaty), art. XVII & annex 1, U.S.-U.S.S.R., Nov. 25, 1991, S. TREATY DOC. NO. 102-20, at 46, 48–66. At the same time, there were separate executive agreements, letters embodying executive agreements, declarations, and the like, that were not formally part of the agreement but bore on it—and, because of that, were not presented for the Senate's advice and consent, although they were submitted to it. *See generally* AUST, *supra* note 229, at 210–12 (citing as examples of treaty-related agreements conference final reports, chairman's statements, understandings, and explanatory reports).

[394] VCLT, *supra* note 13, art. 31(1). *See generally* GARDINER, *supra* note 368, at 211–22.

[395] *Compare* VCLT, *supra* note 13, art. 31(1) (object and purpose inquiry), with *id.* art. 32 (describing supplementary materials).

[396] *See, e.g., Floyd,* 499 U.S. at 552 (describing construction as "better accord[ing] with the Warsaw Convention's stated purpose"); United States v. Stuart, 489 U.S. 353, 368 (1989) (citing the "evident purpose" behind provisions of bilateral double taxation treaty as rebutting a party's nontextual arguments); Société Nationale Industrielle Aerospatiale v. U.S. Dist. Court for S. Dist. of Iowa, 482 U.S. 522, 529–30 (1987) (noting "purpose" of Hague Convention on the Taking of Evidence Abroad in Civil or Commercial Matters, after concluding that a proffered interpretation was "foreclosed by the plain language of the Convention"). One broad examination may be found in *Abbott v. Abbott,* in which the Court explained why the "objects and purposes" of the Hague Convention on the Civil Aspects of International Child Abduction—deterring child abductions to a country that provides a friendlier forum, and providing for resolution in the country of habitual residence—supported its interpretation that the Convention afforded a return remedy for *ne exeat* rights. That basis for interpreting the convention, however, was the last one discussed. Abbott v. Abbott, 560 U.S. 1, 20–22 (2010).

object and purpose to gainsay an interpretation that they view as following from the text.[397] This tendency may even be compatible with the view, expressed in some opinions, that ambiguity is appropriate before a provision's object and purpose is given substantial weight.[398]

Still, attention to object and purpose by U.S. courts is probably more common and more nuanced than this account suggests. Decisions frequently consider a treaty's object and purpose indirectly when analyzing a provision's context or intended operation; sometimes, too, the object and purpose is stipulated in the treaty (often the preamble), which also makes it part of the context.[399] Courts downplaying arguments about a treaty's object and purpose may invoke contrary text, but they may also be mindful of different (or multiple) goals or differ as to how the object and purpose is best advanced.[400] Each method is consistent with a purposive analysis, so long as it is well grounded in the treaty in question. More distinctly, U.S. courts may also emphasize object and purpose in circumstances where the political branches accorded to it special weight when making the treaty.[401]

---

[397] See United States, Fed. Reserve Bank v. Iran, Bank Markazi, Iran-US Cl. Trib. Case No. A28, ¶ 58 (suggesting that "under Article 31 of the Vienna Convention, a treaty's object and purpose is to be used only to clarify the text, not to provide independent sources of meaning that contradict the clear text"); cf. AUST, supra note 229, at 209 (suggesting that object-and-purpose evidence is "more for the purpose of confirming an interpretation"). In Sale v. Haitian Ctrs. Council, for example, the Supreme Court differed with a lower court's reliance on object and purpose. 509 U.S. 155, 169 (1993). The Court agreed that it should be guided by the "high purpose" of the treaty, id. at 187, but rested primarily on the text and negotiating history, which it found consistent with that purpose. Id. at 179–87.

[398] See Stuart, 489 U.S. at 372–73 (Scalia, J., concurring in the judgment). Justice Scalia invoked Rocca v. Thompson, 223 U.S. 317 (1912), in which the Court had responded to invocation of a treaty's object and purpose by saying that "it would have been very easy to have declared that purpose in unmistakable terms." Id. at 332. But see id. at 332–34 (stressing that the bilateral treaty at issue had eschewed language used in other, comparable treaties). Even if an ambiguity threshold is rejected, evidence of object and purpose will be most influential when the terms are ambiguous. See, e.g., Trans World Airlines, Inc. v. Franklin Mint Corp., 466 U.S. 243, 255–59 (1984) (noting "debatable" meanings of Warsaw Convention terms before turning, inter alia, to exploring treaty purposes).

[399] See, e.g., Abbott, 560 U.S. at 20 (citing preamble of Hague Convention on the Civil Aspects of International Child Abduction as basis for the controlling principle that "the best interests of the child are well served when decisions regarding custody rights are made in the country of habitual residence"); Cornejo v. County of San Diego, 504 F.3d 853, 858, 861 n.13 (9th Cir. 2007) (citing preamble to the Vienna Convention on Consular Relations as suggesting objective of improving consular functions). Courts that resort to the preamble for identifying the object and purpose may not label it as use of "context" or regard such context as controlling the interpretation.

[400] See, e.g., Abbott, 560 U.S. at 20–21 (citing as the "objects and purposes" of the Hague Convention on the Civil Aspects of International Child Abduction not only promoting custody rights decisions in the country of habitual residence, but also deterring and reducing harm from abductions); Volkswagenwerk Aktiengesellschaft v. Schlunk, 486 U.S. 694, 704–05 (1988) (describing how favored interpretation promoted some, but not all, purposes of the Hague Service Convention); cf. Appellate Body Report, United States—Import Prohibition of Certain Shrimp Products, ¶ 17, WTO Doc. WT/DS58/AB/R (adopted Oct. 12, 1998) (rejecting "one-sided view of the object and purpose of the WTO Agreement," and noting generally the possibility of "no single, undiluted object and purpose but rather a variety of different, and possibly conflicting, objects and purposes").

[401] See, e.g., Nuru v. Gonzales, 404 F.3d 1207, 1221–23 (9th Cir. 2004) (applying a U.S. understanding adopted in relation to the U.N. Convention against Torture and Other Cruel, Inhuman or Degrading Treatment or Punishment, which indicated that the Convention's exemption of "lawful

2. Subsequent Agreements, Subsequent Practice, and Relevant Rules

Beyond text and the context, as the latter is defined in Article 31(2), the VCLT indicates in Article 31(3) that additional elements should be "be taken into account, together with the context": namely, subsequent agreements between the parties relating to interpretation or application of the treaty, subsequent practice which establishes the parties' agreement as to the treaty's application, and any relevant rules of international law applicable to the parties.[402]

Unlike the collateral agreements previously discussed—agreements of any nature, made among all the parties, in connection with a treaty's conclusion, that contribute to understanding its context[403]—the agreements described in Article 31(3)(a) arise *subsequent* to the treaty's conclusion[404] and involve the parties' agreement as to its interpretation or application.[405] The United States regards such agreements as an important basis for treaty interpretation and has stressed that they need not be formal agreements.[406] (The U.S. view may at times be considered too elastic—for example, its position that unilateral actions by the North American Free Trade Agreement (NAFTA) parties together amounted to a "subsequent agreement" was rejected, with that evidence instead being accepted as showing a relevant subsequent practice under Article 31(3)(b)[407]—but it has also sought and secured more easily recognized agreements with other parties.[408])

---

sanctions" did not allow a state "through its domestic sanctions [to] defeat the object and purpose of the Convention to prohibit torture").

[402] VCLT, *supra* note 13, art. 31(3).

[403] Agreements (along with party-created instruments accepted by other parties) made in connection with a treaty's conclusion are addressed in Article 31(2). *See supra* this chapter text accompanying notes 392–393.

[404] As previously suggested, an agreement is likely "subsequent" if it is made after a treaty's text is concluded. *See supra* this chapter note 392. U.S. courts often refer to "postratification" understanding or conduct, though the demarcation as it is understood in international law is different, and there is in any event often no common ratification date. *See, e.g.*, GE Energy Power Conversion Fr. SAS v. Outokumpu Stainless USA, 140 S. Ct. 1637, 1646 (2020) (citations omitted).

[405] VCLT, *supra* note 13, art. 31(3)(a). Like Article 31(2)(a), which refers to an agreement "between all the parties," Article 31(3)(a)—which references an agreement "between the parties"—is thought to reference a single, common agreement among all the parties. Int'l Law Comm'n, Draft Conclusions on Subsequent Agreements, *supra* note 365, at 30.

[406] Response of Respondent United States of America to Methanex's Post-Hearing Submission at 2–3 (July 27, 2001), Methanex v. United States (NAFTA Ch. 11 Arb. Trib.) (stating that subsequent agreements are "authoritative" and "must [be] take[n] into account," and that an "agreement" may take any form), https://perma.cc/NPX9-4647; *see* Sean D. Murphy, *Contemporary Practice of the United States Relating to International Law*, 95 Aм. J. Iɴт'ʟ L. 887–88 (2001). The ILC has concluded that such an agreement need not necessarily be binding. Int'l Law Comm'n, Draft Conclusions on Subsequent Agreements, *supra* note 365, at 29 (commentary (6) to conclusion 4).

[407] C.C.F.T. v. United States, Award on Jurisdiction ¶¶ 174–77, 184–89 (Jan. 28, 2008) (NAFTA Ch. 11 Arb. Trib.), https://perma.cc/Y3NY-DP83; *see* Int'l Law Comm'n, Draft Conclusions on Subsequent Agreements, *supra* note 365, at 29–30 (commentaries (8)–(11) to conclusion 4).

[408] NAFTA Free Trade Commission, Interpretation of the Free Trade Commission of Certain Chapter 11 Provisions (July 31, 2001), https://perma.cc/9FQW-RLHZ; *see* Murphy, *supra* note 406, at 889.

Subsequent agreements have not, in any event, loomed especially large in U.S. courts. Case law seems sensitive to whether subsequent agreements have legal effect comparable to treaty amendments and whether they have received Senate advice and consent.[409]

Subsequent practice among the parties is more prominent in U.S. courts, but the case law does not exactly hew to the VCLT approach. Under Article 31(3) of the VCLT, subsequent practice, like subsequent agreements, is understood to require acceptance by all parties to the treaty being interpreted, the idea being that subsequent practice genuinely "establishes the agreement of the parties" as to the treaty's interpretation.[410] Acceptance by fewer states is considered as a less authoritative "supplementary means" of interpretation under Article 32, which (as discussed later) is principally relevant when the methods of interpretation under Article 31 produce an ambiguous result.[411]

U.S. case law addressing subsequent practice effectively merges these approaches. Courts do not seem to treat agreement by all states parties as a distinct threshold. Instead, evidence of subsequent practice is generally given "considerable weight,"[412] with the breadth of practice among states parties[413]—as well as the consistency of their practice and its duration—functioning as variables that enhance or detract from its significance.[414] Subsequent practice is also

---

[409] *See, e.g.*, El Al Isr. Airlines v. Tsui Yuan Tseng, 525 U.S. 155, 174–75 (1999) (relying on a protocol, ratified by the United States after Senate advice and consent, that "amends" the Warsaw Convention). In *E. Airlines, Inc. v. Floyd*, 499 U.S. 530 (1991), the Supreme Court rejected a lower court's reliance on subsequent agreements, concluding that they cast little light on the underlying Warsaw Convention, but its treatment varied based on the perceived authoritativeness of the subsequent agreement. *Compare id.* at 547–49 (considering the subsequent Hague Protocol, which "amended" the Warsaw Convention, but finding it inconclusive), *with id.* at 549–50 (considering Guatemala City Protocol of 1971, but discounting relevance because, among other things, it had not taken legal effect, and "because the United States Senate has not ratified the Protocol"), *and id.* at 549 (considering Montreal Agreement of 1966, but discounting relevance in light of the fact it was an agreement among major international carriers, not states parties to the Warsaw Convention). The ILC has explained that amendments should be treated as distinct effects from treaty interpretation. Int'l Law Comm'n, Draft Conclusions on Subsequent Agreements, *supra* note 365, at 51, 58–63 (conclusion 7 and commentaries (21)–(38)).

[410] VCLT, *supra* note 13, art. 31(3)(b); *see supra* this chapter text accompanying notes 392–393 (discussing subsequent agreements among "all" parties); Int'l Law Comm'n, Draft Conclusions on Subsequent Agreements, *supra* note 365, at 31 (commentary (16) to conclusion 4) (discussing requirement of practice by "all" states); *id.* at 33 (commentary (23) to conclusion 4) (same).

[411] VCLT, *supra* note 13, art. 32; Int'l Law Comm'n, Draft Conclusions on Subsequent Agreements, *supra* note 365, at 33 (commentary (23) to conclusion 4); *id.* at 36–37 (commentary (35) to conclusion 4); *see* RESTATEMENT (FOURTH) § 306 cmt. c & rptrs. note 4.

[412] *See, e.g.*, Monasky v. Taglieri, 140 S. Ct. 719, 727 (2020) (internal quotations and citations omitted); *see also* Abbott v. Abbott, 560 U.S. 1, 16 (2010) (stating that this approach applies to "any treaty," and citing cases).

[413] While the Court focuses on states parties, its cases have an unfortunate habit of using "sister signatories" or other potentially misleading terms. *See, e.g.*, *Monasky*, 140 S. Ct. at 727. The extent to which the practice of states that are signatories (but not states parties) should contribute to treaty interpretation is considerably more uncertain.

[414] *Compare, e.g.*, Water Splash, Inc. v. Menon, 137 S. Ct. 1504, 1512–13 (2017) (citing consistency of practice, and absence of any countervailing examples), *and* Trans World Airlines, Inc. v. Franklin

weighed more heavily when there are indications that uniformity among states was a particular goal, either by virtue of the treaty's object and purpose (as with the Warsaw Convention) or by virtue of a statutory directive (as with the Hague Convention on the Civil Aspects of International Child Abduction).[415] It should be further enhanced when interpreting bilateral agreements, given the plausibility that one state's practice has been tacitly accepted by the other, although the Supreme Court has not made that a point of emphasis.[416] Perhaps unsurprisingly, text-oriented judges are less enamored of subsequent practice. Thus Justice Thomas, for example, has shied away from describing it as anything more than "an aid"[417] and expressed particular skepticism toward later-blooming practice, reasoning that it sheds less light on the "original shared understanding" of the treaty text.[418] Even so, a striking *absence* of subsequent practice supporting a proffered interpretation is prone to be regarded as confirming a rival interpretation derived from other elements.[419]

What types of conduct count as subsequent practice? The VCLT does not provide any definition, but it appears to include not only official acts and diplomatic statements but also decisions by domestic courts and domestic legislation, among other things;[420] this element may sometimes be lumped with subsequent

---

Mint Corp., 466 U.S. 243, 255 (1984) (invoking "50 years of consistent international and domestic practices under the [Warsaw] Convention"), *with Medellín*, 552 U.S. at 516 n.10 (noting that, assuming Moroccan practice was supportive, it was "at best inconsistent"). Courts confronted with limited illustrations of subsequent practice appear to feel free to agree or disagree with it. *See, e.g., E. Airlines*, 499 U.S. at 550–52 (disagreeing with Israeli court); Air Fr. v. Saks, 470 U.S. 392, 404 (1985) (finding "few decisions ... precisely on point," but agreeing with French court).

[415] As to the former, see, for example, *El Al Isr. Airlines*, 525 U.S. at 169, 175–76 (noting that "cardinal purpose" of the Convention was to promote uniformity of rules). As to the latter, see *Abbott*, 560 U.S. at 16 (citing statutory directive to promote "uniform international interpretation of the Convention") (quoting 42 U.S.C. § 11601(b)(3)(B)); *accord Monasky*, 140 S. Ct. at 727–28.

[416] *See, e.g.*, O'Connor v. United States., 479 U.S. 27, 33 (1986).

[417] GE Energy Power Conversion Fr. SAS v. Outokumpu Stainless USA, 140 S. Ct. 1637, 1646 (2020).

[418] *Id.* at 1647 (noting that the subsequent practice "relied on by the parties occurred decades after the finalization of the New York Convention's text in 1958," which "diminishes the value of these sources as evidence of the original shared understanding of the treaty's meaning"); *see also Monasky*, 140 S. Ct. at 733 (Thomas, J., concurring in part and concurring in the judgment) ("original understanding").

[419] *See, e.g.*, Medellín v. Texas, 552 U.S. 491, 516–17 & n. 10 (2008) (citing complete, or near-complete, absence of state practice supporting view that governing treaties required treating ICJ decisions as directly enforceable in national courts); Sanchez-Llamas v. Oregon, 548 U.S. 331, 343–44 & n.3, 347 (2006) (citing complete, or near-complete, absence of state practice supporting view that the Vienna Convention on Consular Relations required judicial remedies).

[420] Under the VCLT, roughly the same approach is taken to construing subsequent practice under Article 31(3)(b) and that which counts with Article 32, save that the former must establish the parties' agreement relating to the treaty's interpretation. Int'l Law Comm'n, Draft Conclusions on Subsequent Agreements, *supra* note 365, at 31–37 (commentaries (16)–(35) to conclusion 4); *id.* at 37–51 (conclusions 5–6 and accompanying commentaries). The effects, however, are different, as is generally the case for elements considered pursuant to Article 32. *Id.* at 51–58 (conclusion 7 and commentaries (1)–(20)).

agreements, making the two difficult to distinguish.[421] A number of U.S. cases cite decisions by foreign courts as relevant practice.[422] Other cited practice includes diplomatic statements,[423] multinational commissions,[424] and foreign legislation.[425] Scholarship summarizing foreign practice may be invaluable, even if it is not given independent weight as such.[426]

Finally, "any relevant rules of international law applicable in the relations between the parties" fall within Article 31(3)(c) of the VCLT.[427] Such rules need not arise subsequent to the agreement.[428] These feature infrequently in U.S. practice, as courts appear reluctant to rely on more general rules when interpreting treaties. In one well-known case, *United States v. Alvarez-Machain*, the Supreme Court construed an extradition treaty as not prohibiting cross-border abductions, largely irrespective of their prohibition under customary international law.[429] The Court's reasoning, which regarded general norms about not using police power in another sovereign's territory as remote from extradition treaty at issue, arguably neglected the rule's relevance to the drafting of the treaty and afterward.[430] Notwithstanding this, some decisions have interpreted treaties based on general principles associated with treaty interpretation.[431]

---

[421] *Id.* at 29–30 (commentaries (7), (11) to conclusion 4).

[422] *See, e.g.*, Monasky v. Taglieri, 140 S. Ct. 719, 728 (2020) (citing decisions by the European Court of Justice and the supreme courts of the United Kingdom, Canada, and Australia); Water Splash, Inc. v. Menon, 137 S. Ct. 1504, 1512 & n.6 (2017) (citing "[m]ultiple foreign courts"). Sometimes U.S. courts will cite national precedent at the same time, perhaps with the thought that it indicates a practice to which other states parties may react. *See Saks*, 470 U.S. at 404–05 (citing accordance of U.S. decisions with those of other states parties).

[423] *Water Splash*, 137 S. Ct. at 1512 & n.7 (citing objections by states parties to service by mail as bearing on interpretation of Hague Convention on the Service Abroad of Judicial and Extrajudicial Documents in Civil and Commercial Matters).

[424] *Water Splash*, 137 S. Ct. at 1512–13 & n.8 (citing conclusions by special commissions operating within the Hague Conference on Private International Law). In another recent case, however, the Supreme Court expressed hesitation about relying on a recommendation issued by the United Nations Commission on International Trade Law, noting that "we have not previously relied on UN recommendations to discern the meaning of treaties." *GE Power Conversion*, 140 S. Ct. at 1647 (citing Yang v. Majestic Blue Fisheries, LLC, 876 F.3d 996, 1000–1001 (9th Cir. 2017)).

[425] *See, e.g.*, Zicherman v. Korean Air Lines Co., 516 U.S. 217, 227–28 (1996).

[426] *See, e.g.*, GE Power Conversion, 140 S. Ct. at 1646 (citing analysis of decisions by foreign courts); Air Fr. v. Saks, 470 U.S. 392, 404 (1985) (citing the construction of a Warsaw Convention term by European legal scholars).

[427] VCLT, *supra* note 13, art. 31(3)(c).

[428] Arguably, their interpretive significance is greater if they were apparent to the treaty negotiators, and would have been apparent to states when they became parties. Even so, later-arising rules do count. *See* AUST, *supra* note 229, at 216–17.

[429] United States v. Alvarez-Machain, 504 U.S. 655, 666–70 (1992).

[430] *Id.* at 663–64; *see also id.* at 682 & n.27 (Stevens, J., dissenting) (arguing that the treaty had to be interpreted in light of the prohibition under customary international law). It remains important, in any event, to consider whether a particular customary rule is genuinely relevant to the subject matter of the treaty so as to aid in its interpretation. *See* Oil Platforms (Iran v. U.S.), Judgment, 2003 I.C.J. 161, 237–40 (Nov. 6) (separate opinion of Higgins, J.).

[431] *See* Medellín v. Texas, 552 U.S. 491, 517 (2008) (reporting as a "general principle[] of interpretation" that "'absent a clear and express statement to the contrary, the procedural rules of the forum State govern the implementation of the treaty in that State'") (quoting Sanchez-Llamas v. Oregon,

3. Preparatory Work and Other Supplementary Means

Article 32 of the VCLT provides that "supplementary means of interpretation" may also be invoked, with more constrained effect on the interpretive enterprise.[432] As previously noted, Article 32 serves as kind of a catch-all for potential interpretive elements, including subsequent agreements or practices that do not satisfy Article 31's standards.[433] Article 32 also specifically mentions, however, "the preparatory work of the treaty and the circumstances of its conclusion."[434] This preparatory work, often called a treaty's *travaux préparatoires*, are mostly materials that evidence its negotiating history, like successive drafts and conference records.

Intuitively enough, the value of preparatory work as interpretive evidence depends on its characteristics, such as its "authenticity, completeness and availability."[435] (Availability is important not only for any judicial consideration, but may also bear on whether states not involved in negotiations could become fully informed before their ratification or accession.) Article 32 also suggests a more formal safeguard against giving excessive weight to preparatory work: such elements are supposed to be used only to confirm the meaning derived according to Article 31, or to establish that meaning when an Article 31-based interpretation is "ambiguous or obscure" or "leads to a result which is manifestly absurd or unreasonable."[436] These thresholds are difficult to maintain; for example, ambiguity may be more readily discovered after surveying those supplementary means. Still, most states and observers appreciate that "supplementary means of interpretation" are supplementary, and that they rarely qualify otherwise favored readings of the text in its context.[437]

Practice in U.S. courts arrives at a somewhat similar place by a somewhat different route. It would be unusual to prioritize preparatory materials over a treaty's text.[438] Instead, preparatory work is usually employed solely to confirm

548 U.S. 331, 351 (2006), quoting Breard v. Greene, 523 U.S. 371, 375 (1998) (per curiam)). *But cf.* Lozano v. Montoya Alvarez, 572 U.S. 1, 12 (2014) (stressing inappropriateness of invoking legal principles particular to the United States in interpreting treaties).

[432] VCLT, *supra* note 13, art. 32.

[433] For example, subsequent practice may be relevant under Article 32 even though it falls short of establishing that all parties concurred in a common agreement as to a treaty's interpretation. *See, e.g.,* Int'l Law Comm'n, Draft Conclusions on Subsequent Agreements, *supra* note 365, at 50 (commentary (24) to conclusion 6).

[434] VCLT, *supra* note 13, art. 32.

[435] AUST, *supra* note 229, at 218; *see id.* at 217–20 (discussing practical considerations).

[436] VCLT, *supra* note 13, art. 32.

[437] *See, e.g.,* MARK E. VILLIGER, COMMENTARY ON THE 1969 VIENNA CONVENTION ON THE LAW OF TREATIES 446–47 (2009) ("[A] result arrived at by the use of primary means of Article 31 will always prevail over solutions suggested by the supplementary means."). *But see* Julian Davis Mortenson, *The Travaux of Travaux: Is the Vienna Convention Hostile to Drafting History?*, 107 AM. J. INT'L L. 780 (2013) (arguing that the *travaux préparatoires,* at least, was not intended solely as a last resort).

[438] *But cf.* Sumitomo Shoji American, Inc. v. Avagliano, 457 U.S. 176, 180 (1982) ("The clear import of treaty language controls unless 'application of the words of the treaty according to their obvious

what text and context indicate, or assumed to have greater influence only when the text and context are ambiguous or otherwise confounding.[439] However—and potentially more at odds with the VCLT—such evidence is usually considered together with other "extratextual" materials.[440] The potential discrepancy, then, has more to do with the inadequate relative weight given other "extratextual" evidence (such as subsequent practice of all parties, or concerning a treaty's object and purpose), which under the VCLT are relevant irrespective of whether ambiguity has been established, than with the mistreatment of Article 32 materials.[441] Such distinctions should be of diminished significance if the text and context are considered to be straightforward, and the preparatory materials are only confirmatory, as is often the case.[442]

Maintaining this broad consistency with international practice is important, given the risk otherwise of generating treaty interpretations inconsistent with those of other states parties. To that end, U.S. practice concerning preparatory work should heed some variables used internationally. It is sounder to credit preparatory work when it is published and widely available—litigants will of course be more likely to cite it then,[443] but more important, it is more likely to be

meaning effects a result inconsistent with the intent or expectations of its signatories.' ") (citation omitted); *id.* at 189 (stating that "we discern no reason to depart from the plain meaning of the [t]reaty language"). Naturally, there may be disagreements about whether a court has demonstrated its willingness to do so. *See, e.g.*, United States v. Stuart, 489 U.S. 353, 373 (1989) (Scalia, J., concurring) (construing the majority opinion as implying that, "*had* the extrinsic evidence contradicted the plain language of the [t]reaty it would govern") (emphasis in original); *id.* at 373 ("Only when a treaty provision is ambiguous have we found it appropriate to give authoritative effect to extratextual materials.").

[439] *See, e.g.*, Water Splash, Inc. v. Menon, 137 S. Ct. 1504, 1510–11 (2017) (suggesting that, given the "strong[]" indications of text and structure, "the most" a contrary argument in those terms accomplished was to create an ambiguity—and that any such ambiguity was resolved by other evidence, including drafting history); E. Airlines, Inc. v. Floyd, 499 U.S. 530, 535 (1991) (" 'Other general rules of construction may be brought to bear on difficult or ambiguous passages.' ") (quoting *Volkswagenwerk*, 486 U.S. at 700); Chan v. Korean Air Lines, 490 U.S. 122, 134 (1989) ("[W]here the text is clear . . . we have no power to insert an amendment" based on the drafting history).

[440] *See, e.g.*, *Water Splash*, 137 S. Ct. at 1511 (stating that when a treaty provision is ambiguous, the Court " 'may look beyond the written words to the history of the treaty, the negotiations, and the practical construction adopted by the parties.' ") (quoting Volkswagenwerk Aktiengesellschaft v. Schlunk, 486 U.S. 694, 700 (1988)); Abbott v. Abbott, 560 U.S. 1, 15–22 (2010) (turning to evidence of Department of State interpretation, subsequent practice, scholarly commentary, and object and purpose of agreement); *accord* Lozano v. Montoya Alvarez, 572 U.S. 1, 21–22 (2014) (Alito, J., concurring) (following *Abbott*).

[441] Secondarily, some of the materials lumped together as "extratextual" or "nontextual," like executive branch submissions to the Senate during advice and consent, would likely not be given any weight at all under the VCLT. *See infra* this chapter §§ III(B)(1)–(2).

[442] *See, e.g.*, Monasky v. Taglieri, 140 S. Ct. 719, 727 (2020) (explaining how a treaty's negotiating and drafting history "corroborates" interpretation of its text); Zicherman v. Korean Air Lines Co., 516 U.S. 217, 226 (1996) (explaining that preparatory work and subsequent practice "confirm" textual analysis).

[443] *Saks*, 470 U.S. at 400 ("In part because the 'travaux preparatoires' of the Warsaw Convention are published and generally available to litigants, courts frequently refer to these materials to resolve ambiguities in the text.") (citing authorities).

understood (and acquiesced in, or objected to) by states parties.[444] Courts should also assess carefully the definitiveness of particular statements made within the negotiating history and whether, on the whole, the history compels rather than merely permits a particular interpretation.[445]

B. Deference by U.S. Courts When Interpreting Treaties

Whatever nuances distinguish the VCLT and U.S. interpretative approaches, most of the same considerations are in play. The potential for disagreement is greater where the U.S. approach takes into account entirely distinct considerations, particularly when doing so has the effect of discounting considerations that are prominent in international practice.

1. Judicial Deference to the Executive Branch

For over a century, U.S. courts—while retaining final authority over the interpretation of agreements, at least for purposes of U.S. law—have indicated that they afford "great weight" or its equivalent to a treaty's interpretation by the executive branch.[446] This appears not to be empty rhetoric; studies suggest that executive branch interpretations, when proffered, are a good way to predict the outcome of a treaty interpretation case.[447] Although the Supreme Court has sowed some doubt by disagreeing with the executive branch in high-profile cases,[448] and the

---

[444] See supra this chapter text accompanying note 435.

[445] See Chan, 490 U.S. at 134 n.5 ("Even if the text were less clear, its most natural meaning could properly be contradicted only by clear drafting history."); O'Connor v. United States, 479 U.S. 27, 35 (1986) (representing that "[w]hile the [lower court] may have been correct that the negotiating history does not favor the Government's position sufficiently to overcome what that court regarded as a plain textual meaning in favor of the taxpayers, it certainly does not favor the taxpayers' position sufficiently to affect our [contrary] view of the text"); El Al Isr. Airlines, Ltd. v. Tsui Yuan Tseng, 525 U.S. 155, 169, 181 (1999) (Stevens, J., dissenting) (attributing to majority, and concurring, with view that the "inference [from preparatory work] is not strong enough, in itself, to require that [textual] ambiguity be resolved in the plaintiff's favor").

[446] See, e.g., Medellín v. Texas, 552 U.S. 491, 513 (2008); Sumitomo Shoji Am., Inc. v. Avagliano, 457 U.S. 176, 184–85 (1982); Kolovrat v. Oregon, 366 U.S. 187, 194 (1961); Factor v. Laubenheimer, 290 U.S. 276, 294–95 (1933); Charlton v. Kelly, 229 U.S. 447, 468 (1913).

[447] See David J. Bederman, Revivalist Canons and Treaty Interpretation, 41 UCLA L. Rev. 953, 1015–19 (1994); Robert M. Chesney, Disaggregating Deference: The Judicial Power and Executive Treaty Interpretations, 92 Iowa L. Rev. 1723, 1755 (2007). Correlations probably overstate the matter: one would expect a high correspondence between executive branch views and outcomes if such views were well informed about the treaty and about judicial methods.

[448] See, e.g., El Al Isr. Airlines, 525 U.S. at 168 (citing "great weight" standard in allowing that "[r]espect is ordinarily due the reasonable views of the Executive Branch concerning the meaning of an international treaty") (emphases added); Hamdan v. Rumsfeld, 548 U.S. 557, 630 (2006) (omitting "great weight" standard, and stating that the "reasoning [shared by the lower court and the government] is erroneous"); id. at 718, 724 (Thomas, J., dissenting) (disagreeing, and stressing "great weight" standard). The Court has also stated simply that "[w]e do not accept the Solicitor General's view as applied to the treaty before us," since while it "respect[ed] the Government's views about the proper interpretation of treaties," it was "unable to find any other authority or precedent" for its view.

Restatement (Fourth) said only that "ordinarily" courts accord executive branch views "great weight,"[449] the Court has subsequently reiterated that "great weight" is due.[450]

The Court has acknowledged that the rationale for this deference remains unclear.[451] Some explanations rely generally on the separation of powers in foreign affairs.[452] Others focus on executive branch expertise in treaty matters, including from having been involved in the treaty's negotiation or from the executive branch's familiarity with the expectations of other parties.[453] Not surprisingly, given this uncertainty, decisions vary as to the factors they suggest should bear on deference. Some considerations might be predicted from deference to administrative agencies in the statutory construction context. Courts are least likely to defer when they regard the executive branch views as clashing with the treaty text;[454] resistance may redouble when deference would unsettle precedent or presumptions.[455] Courts have noted approvingly when executive branch positions are longstanding,[456] presumably because that reduces the risk that they

BG Grp., PLC v. Argentina, 572 U.S. 25, 37–38 (2014). For an argument that this lack of deference is part of a broader trend, see Ganesh Sitaraman & Ingrid Wuerth, *The Normalization of Foreign Relations Law*, 128 HARV. L. REV. 1897, 1958, 1968–70 (2015).

[449] RESTATEMENT (FOURTH) § 306(6).

[450] *See, e.g.*, Republic of Sudan v. Harrison, 139 S. Ct. 1048, 1060 (2019); Water Splash, Inc. v. Menon, 137 S. Ct. 1504, 1510–12 (2017); Lozano v. Montoya Alvarez, 572 U.S. 1, 22 (2014) (Alito, J., concurring); Abbott v. Abbott, 560 U.S. 1, 15 (2010).

[451] GE Energy Power Conversion Fr. SAS v. Outokumpu Stainless USA, 140 S. Ct. 1637, 1646 (2020) ("We have never provided a full explanation of the basis for our practice of giving weight to the Executive's interpretation of a treaty. Nor have we delineated the limitations of this practice, if any. But we need not resolve these issues today."); *Abbott*, 560 U.S. at 40 (Stevens, J., dissenting) (noting that the Court had afforded such deference "[w]ithout discussing precisely why").

[452] *See, e.g.*, Scott M. Sullivan, *Rethinking Treaty Interpretation*, 86 TEX. L. REV. 777, 790 (2008) (suggesting "several possible rationales for this recent deference: (1) a concern over judicial competence in matters of foreign affairs; (2) the enormous value placed in the ability of the Executive to be flexible in foreign affairs; and (3) the increasing consolidation of power into the Executive Branch and away from both the Legislative and Judicial Branches") (citations omitted).

[453] United States v. Kin-Hong, 110 F.3d 103, 110 (1st Cir. 1997) (citing deference concerning treaty interpretation as one principle helping to ensure "that the judicial inquiry does not unnecessarily impinge upon executive prerogative and expertise").

[454] *See, e.g.*, *Hamdan*, 548 U.S. at 630–31 (insisting that "not of an international character" in common Article 3 to the 1949 Geneva Conventions "bears its literal meaning"); World Holdings, LLC v. Fed. Republic of Ger., 613 F.3d 1310, 1317 n.11 (11th Cir. 2010) (refusing to give "great weight" to a foreign state's invocation of an executive branch interpretation, in part on grounds that the "plain language" of the treaty, "read in context," made resort to extrinsic views unnecessary).

[455] BG Grp., PLC v. Argentina, 572 U.S. 25, 37–38 (2014) (expressing particular reluctance to unsettle accepted precedent supporting a presumption that parties, including states parties to treaties, "intend procedural preconditions to arbitration to be resolved primarily by arbitrators"). The Court at times has suggested special solicitude toward agreements conferring rights on individuals, see Charlton v. Kelly, 229 U.S. 447, 468 (1913), but that has not had obvious traction in U.S. jurisprudence.

[456] Water Splash, Inc. v. Menon, 137 S. Ct. 1504, 1511–12 (2017) (citing consistency); Lozano v. Montoya Alvarez, 572 U.S. 1, 21–23 (2014) (Alito, J., concurring).

are driven by short-term preference, although they have also deferred to late-arising views.[457]

In principle, executive branch views should have greater weight when linked with premises—recognized in international law—that tend to justify deference. For example, although textual analysis is critical, there is no reason to defer to executive branch citations of dictionaries. By contrast, if the executive suggests that a term or concept has special meaning in international legal practice, then deference may be more justified.[458] The executive may also offer valuable insight concerning an agreement's object and purpose, which can be elusive, or concerning preparatory work (the *travaux préparatoires*).[459] The most promising basis for deference is when executive branch views rest on the subsequent practice of the parties relating to the interpretation or application of the treaty.[460] The executive branch is better situated than courts to distill both U.S. practice and the practice of other states. To the extent that its representations of that practice are public and consistent, they may themselves count as relevant practice—further minimizing potential inconsistency between deference and international interpretive methods.[461]

Forcing courts to differentiate among the interpretive elements that are the basis for deference to the executive branch may make their task more difficult. Courts will have to take care to avoid exaggerating any particular element's hierarchical significance: subsequent practice not accepted by all states parties, for example, is still valued as a supplemental means of interpretation, just like preparatory work, and thus of a lesser significance than text or context, even when reported by the executive branch. In theory, they should also avoid double

---

[457] *Compare* Abbott v. Abbott, 560 U.S. 1, 15 (2010) (according "great weight" to position taken in brief, expressing view "long understood" by Department of State (citing Sumitomo Shoji Am., Inc. v. Avagliano, 457 U.S. 176, 184–85, 184 n.10 (1982))), *with id.* at 40 (Stevens, J., dissenting) (suggesting that majority had deferred to "newly memorialized" position of Department of State that was potentially inconsistent with its prior position); *see also* Medellín v. Texas, 552 U.S. 491, 513 (2008) (reporting that the United States had "unfailingly adhered to its view" (citing Brief for United States as Amicus Curiae at 4, 27–29, Medellín v. Texas, 552 U.S. 491 (2008) (evidencing view, but not its unfailing nature))). For further discussion of *Medellín*, see *infra* this chapter § IV(A); Chapter 1 § II(B); Chapter 3 § I(D); Chapter 5 § II(B); Chapter 7 § III(C); and Chapter 9 §§ II(B), II(C).

[458] *See* VCLT, *supra* note 13, art. 31(4).

[459] As previously noted, the Court has indicated that deference is owed to "the meaning attributed to treaty provisions by the Government agencies charged with their negotiation and enforcement." *See, e.g., Sumitomo Shoji*, 457 U.S. at 184–85; *see supra* this chapter note 446 (citing additional authority). While that may have been meant abstractly, actual U.S. involvement in the negotiations of the treaty would seem relevant. *Cf.* United States v. Howard, 996 F.2d 1320, 1330 n.6 (1st Cir. 1993) (suggesting that rule of non-inquiry in extradition context stems, "at least in part," from interpretive practice in which judiciary deferred to executive branch offices that wrote and negotiated operative documents).

[460] *See supra* this chapter text accompanying notes 410–414.

[461] *Cf. Abbott*, 560 U.S. at 15 ("The Executive is well informed concerning the diplomatic consequences . . . including the likely reaction of other contracting states and the impact on the State Department's ability to reclaim children abducted from this country.").

counting, such as by weighing both deference to the executive branch and the element on which that deference is predicated as though they are completely distinct.[462] On the positive side, though, element-oriented deference would avoid assigning excessive weight to executive branch views that themselves rest on supplementary means of interpretation of limited weight, such as agreements accepted by the parties in connection with a treaty's conclusion.

2. Judicial Deference to the Senate

While the executive branch is primarily responsible for interpreting treaties on behalf of the United States and for opining about interpretation questions before U.S. courts, Senate advice-and-consent proceedings are highly influential. Such proceedings often galvanize the prevailing view of the political branches while permitting rival views to be voiced. Advice-and-consent materials help establish a treaty's metes and bounds and afford the Senate its last formal opportunity to influence a treaty's interpretation by the courts.[463]

Treaty conditions, which invariably require cooperation between the Senate and the executive branch, are one such mechanism.[464] Their relationship with interpretation depends on the type of condition. Reservations seek to nullify or modify the legal effect of a treaty provision in relation to the state making the reservation, and thus to change rather than interpret the relevant provision. Other states may respond to them and seek to deny or accept that effect.[465] Understandings, in contrast, express the U.S. interpretation of a treaty or its provisions, but with less concrete effect on treaty obligations; the VCLT does not recognize understandings, as such, as a treaty-related instrument, so long as they are not disguised reservations.[466] Unless a U.S. understanding gains meaningful acceptance by other states parties, including through views other states venture in parallel, parties may react to the understanding (or ignore it) just as they would to any other unilateral practice. Consequently, a U.S. court interpreting a treaty principally on the basis of a U.S. understanding risks incompatibility with the interpretation prevailing internationally.

---

[462] *See, e.g., Water Splash*, 137 S. Ct. at 1511–13 (citing drafting history and the views of other states in addition to the views of the executive branch).

[463] In *Fourteen Diamond Rings v. United States*, the Supreme Court disregarded a joint resolution that purported to clarify the status of the Philippines under a treaty of peace between the United States and Spain, to which the Senate had previously consented. Fourteen Diamond Rings v. United States, 183 U.S. 176, 180 (1901). Noting that the joint resolution had passed the Senate by less than a two-thirds vote—and deeming immaterial any view taken by the House—the Court advised that the resolution was "absolutely without legal significance on the question before us," because "[t]he meaning of the treaty cannot be controlled by subsequent explanations of some of those who may have voted to ratify it." *Id.*

[464] *See supra* this chapter § II(B)(3).

[465] *See* VCLT, *supra* note 13, art. 2(d); *see also supra* this chapter text accompanying note 196.

[466] VCLT, *supra* note 13, art. 2(1)(d); *see supra* this chapter text accompanying note 198.

To date, U.S. courts have not been deterred, and treat U.S. understandings as authoritative or nearly so.[467] One court of appeals went so far as to suggest that U.S. understandings were binding on U.S. courts even if they were inconsistent with the treaty or with international law more generally.[468] Possible constitutional objections aside,[469] the appeal of understandings as a device for resolving treaty interpretation questions is evident. Understandings cannot take into account practice or agreements subsequent to Senate consideration or U.S. ratification.[470] Still, because understandings are articulated during Senate advice and consent, they plausibly figured in the U.S. decision to ratify the treaty, and they are less likely than a later executive branch interpretation to be motivated by a particular controversy; moreover, they are communicated to other parties as the official position of the United States. At least absent a clear inconsistency with a treaty's text, U.S. courts will likely continue to defer to understandings.

Other advice-and-consent materials, not manifested in the form of conditions, are more difficult to assess. Courts do sometimes cite miscellaneous materials that evidence executive and Senate views, but they may have qualms about interpreting a treaty based solely on one treaty party's understanding.[471]

---

[467] See Auguste v. Ridge, 395 F.3d 123, 142 (3d Cir. 2005) ("[F]or purposes of domestic law, the understanding proposed by the President and adopted by the Senate in its resolution of ratification are the binding standard to be applied in domestic law."); accord Cherichel v. Holder, 591 F.3d 1002, 1012 (8th Cir. 2010) (citing Auguste v. Ridge); Pierre v. Attorney General of U.S., 528 F.3d 180, 187 (3d Cir. 2008) (same); see also Oxygene v. Lynch, 813 F.3d 541, 546 (4th Cir. 2016) (stating that "an express understanding [to the Convention against Torture] reflects the intent of the United States to influence how executive and judicial bodies later interpret the treaty on both the international and domestic level," meaning that the Convention "had acquired a [corresponding] gloss in the United States"); cf. United States v. Stuart, 489 U.S. 353, 374–75 (1989) (Scalia, J., concurring) (addressing conditions generally); Relevance of Senate Ratification History to Treaty Interpretation, 11 Op. O.L.C. 28, 32–33 (1987) (indicating that understandings, like other conditions, were generally binding on the president).

[468] See Auguste, 395 F.3d at 142 (stating, in dicta, that courts are obligated to give an understanding "domestic legal effect, regardless of any contention that the understanding may be invalid under international norms governing the formation of treaties or the terms of the Convention [Against Torture] itself").

[469] But see supra this chapter text accompanying notes 204–212 (describing appropriate limits to the authority of U.S. conditions not altering U.S. obligations).

[470] A U.S. understanding might take into account subsequent agreements or practice that preceded the Senate's advice and consent.

[471] Cf. RESTATEMENT (FOURTH) § 306 rptrs. note 11 (noting that "domestic materials may also illuminate the understanding of the United States in entering into the treaty," but noting potential incompatibility with international law). In United States v. Stuart, 489 U.S. 353 (1989), the majority relied on Senate proceedings and presidential communications and defended the use of Senate preratification debates and reports. Id. at 366–67, 367 n.7. Justice Scalia objected in part to looking beyond the text at all. Id. at 372 (Scalia, J., concurring). But see Bederman, supra note 356, at 999–1000 (critiquing concurrence); Detlev F. Vagts, Senate Materials and Treaty Interpretation: Some Research Hints for the Supreme Court, 83 AM. J. INT'L L. 546 (1989) (same). In addition, however, Justice Scalia cautioned that Senate materials were prone to express U.S. views rather than mutual agreement among states parties. Stuart, 489 U.S. at 373–75 (Scalia, J., concurring); see also id. at 370 (Kennedy, J., concurring) (asserting that the Court should not unnecessarily resolve "whether Senate debates on ratification are authoritative or even helpful in determining what the signatories to a treaty intended"). Although Stuart concerned the 1942 Convention Respecting Double Taxation, the case was decided amid the

In principle, advice-and-consent materials might be probative of international meaning. Such material might contribute to the subsequent practice of other states, if U.S. practice comes to the attention of other treaty parties and gains general assent.[472] They might also, indirectly, capture aspects of the treaty's preparatory work.[473]

In reality, though, advice-and-consent materials are likely to be privileged by U.S. courts not because they correspond with the international interpretation of a treaty, but rather because they indicate what the president and the Senate thought the United States had agreed.[474] A treaty's text is likely the best guide to those expectations.[475] Otherwise, advice-and-consent materials may most defensibly be given weight when the circumstances indicate a shared view by the political branches—for example, when the executive branch position is put before, and endorsed by, the Senate.[476] Practical problems in determining when a view is held by the Senate as a whole may simply result in deferring to the president's later assessment of this record.[477] Presumably, though, advice-and-consent

controversy over the executive branch's "reinterpretation" of the Anti-Ballistic Missile Treaty. *Stuart*, 489 U.S. at 376–77 (Scalia, J., concurring); *see infra* this chapter text accompanying notes 479–486.

[472] *See supra* this chapter §§ III(A)(2) (discussing subsequent practice under Article 31 of the VCLT), III(A)(3) (discussing subsequent practice under Article 32 of the VCLT).

[473] *See, e.g.*, Water Splash, Inc. v. Menon, 137 S. Ct. 1504, 1511 & n.4 (2017) (describing as part of "drafting history" representations by a member of a U.S. delegation during the negotiation of the Hague Service Convention, which were then reiterated during subsequent testimony before the Senate Committee on Foreign Relations).

[474] In *United States v. Stuart*, the majority addressed objections to using Senate materials to interpret treaties by citing those materials' superiority to the *travaux préparatoires* as a reliable guide to *Senate* understanding. *Stuart*, 489 U.S. at 367 n.7; *see also* Sale v. Haitian Ctrs. Council, 509 U.S. 155, 194–98 (1993) (Blackmun, J., dissenting) (stressing marginal significance of remarks during negotiations not certain to have been "communicated to the United States Government or to the Senate in connection with the ratification of the Convention"). Later, in *Medellín v. Texas*, the Supreme Court was content to state—in rejecting a contrary treaty interpretation—that "there is no reason to believe that the President and Senate signed up for such a result." *See* Medellín v. Texas, 552 U.S. 491, 510–11 (2008); *see also id.* at 514 (defending emphasis on text by recalling "[t]hat is after all what the Senate looks to in deciding whether to approve the treaty"). For further discussion of *Medellín*, see *infra* this chapter § IV(A); Chapter 1 § II(B); Chapter 3 § I(D); Chapter 5 § II(B); Chapter 7 § III(C); and Chapter 9 §§ II(B), II(C).

[475] *But cf. Medellín*, 552 U.S. at 514 (defending emphasis on text by recalling "[t]hat is after all what the Senate looks to in deciding whether to approve the treaty").

[476] *Water Splash*, 137 S. Ct. at 1512 (citing Secretary of State report placed before the Senate Committee on Foreign Relations); Lozano v. Montoya Alvarez, 572 U.S. 1, 21–22 (2014) (Alito, J., concurring) (attributing "great weight" to Department of State analysis provided to the Senate in connection with advice and consent); *cf.* Abbott v. Abbott, 560 U.S. 1, 15, 40–43 (2010) (Stevens, J., dissenting) (contrasting current executive branch position with, among other things, the executive's submission during the advice-and-consent process, and suggesting diminished deference to current position).

[477] Thus, the *Restatement (Third)* suggested in commentary that "[a]lthough the Senate's resolution of consent may contain no statement of understanding, there may be such statements in the report of the Senate Foreign Relations Committee or in the Senate debates," but added that "[i]n that event, the President must decide whether they represent a general understanding by the Senate and, if he finds that they do, must respect them in good faith." RESTATEMENT (THIRD) § 314 cmt. d.

materials should enjoy less weight when the Senate's views appear to diverge from those of the executive.[478]

Particularly difficult questions are posed by what has been called executive branch "reinterpretation": claims that the executive branch's interpretation as it is later manifested differs materially from the view it expressed to the Senate. This problem arose with respect to the 1972 Anti-Ballistic Missile (ABM) Treaty. In the 1980s, the executive branch under President Ronald Reagan sought to interpret the ABM Treaty as allowing for a space-based (rather than land-based) anti-ballistic missile system, including what was known as the Strategic Defense Initiative. Many members of the Senate, however, perceived such an interpretation to be contrary to a more restrictive executive branch interpretation tendered during the advice-and-consent process, leading to a heated debate between the branches.[479] Shortly afterward, the Senate adopted the "Biden condition" (or "Byrd-Biden condition") in consenting to the 1987 Intermediate-Range Nuclear Forces (INF) Treaty, which would constrain the U.S. interpretation of the treaty to a "common understanding" shared by the president and Senate at the time the latter gave its advice and consent.[480] The Senate used variants of this condition in some later treaties.[481]

---

[478] See 11 Op. O.L.C., *supra* note 467, at 33 (suggesting that, when not reflecting views held by the executive branch, statements during Senate advice and consent "have only limited probative value and therefore are entitled to little weight in subsequent interpretations of the treaty"); *id.* at 34 (same).

[479] See ABM Treaty Interpretation Resolution, S. Res. 167, 100th Cong. (1987) (stating, inter alia, that "if, following Senate advice and consent, the President proceeds to ratify a treaty, the President may ratify only the treaty to which the senate advised and consented," and that a treaty's meaning "is to be determined in light of what the Senate understands the treaty to mean when it gives its advice and consent"). The resolution was not voted on by the Senate as a whole. *Cf.* 1 CUMULATIVE DIGEST OF U.S. PRACTICE 1250-73 (excerpting developments). For evaluations at the time, compare Abram Chayes & Antonia Handler Chayes, Commentary, *Testing and Development of "Exotic" Systems Under the ABM Treaty: The Great Reinterpretation Caper*, 99 HARV. L. REV. 1956 (1986), with Abraham D. Sofaer, *The ABM Treaty and the Strategic Defense Initiative*, 99 HARV. L. REV. 1972 (1986). For later commentary, see *Arms Control Treaty Reinterpretation*, 137 U. PA. L. REV. 1351 (1989); John Norton Moore, *Treaty Interpretation, the Constitution and the Rule of Law*, 42 VA. J. INT'L L. 163 (2001), John Yoo, *Politics as Law?: The Anti-Ballistic Missile Treaty, the Separation of Powers, and Treaty Interpretation*, 89 CAL. L. REV. 851 (2001).

[480] The condition further indicated that the "common understanding is based on":

    (i) first, the text of the Treaty and the provisions of this resolution of ratification; and

    (ii) second, the authoritative representations which were provided by the President and his representatives to the Senate and its Committees, in seeking Senate consent to ratification, insofar as such representations were directed to the meaning and legal effect of the text of the Treaty.

134 CONG. REC. 12,849 (1988) (resolution of advice and consent to INF Treaty); *see also* 1 CUMULATIVE DIGEST OF U.S. PRACTICE 1257-73 (excerpting developments).

[481] See CRS, TREATIES AND OTHER INTERNATIONAL AGREEMENTS, *supra* note 165, at 128–31. These conditions were most prevalent during Senator Helms' long chairmanship of the Senate Committee on Foreign Relations. In some instances, the proposition was stated as a condition of some form that purported to "be binding upon the President." *See, e.g.,* 143 CONG. REC. 8,255, 8,257 (1997) (CFE Flank Document); *accord* 144 CONG. REC. 7,908, 7,911 (1998) (Protocols to the North Atlantic Treaty of 1949 on the Accession of Poland, Hungary, and the Czech Republic); 145 CONG. REC. 6,056, 6057 (1999) (Convention on Nuclear Safety); 146 CONG. REC. 23,077–87 (2000) (multiple bilateral

The ABM and INF treaty controversies lacked any formal resolution, undermining their ability to provide guidance. The ABM controversy presented the issue whether—as a constitutional matter, and *absent* any treaty condition—the Senate's appreciation of a treaty, as informed by the executive branch, binds the executive and the United States as a whole.[482] The Legal Adviser at the time initially expressed the view that when the Senate "gives its advice and consent to a treaty, it is to the treaty that was made, irrespective of the explanations [the Senate] is provided."[483] As he argued, a hard-and-fast rule enforcing the Senate's appreciation would be inconsistent with elements of treaty interpretation and, potentially, with the treaty binding the United States under international law.[484] This was consistent with some prior executive branch views about the weight to be given Senate interpretations,[485] and while the executive backpedaled as the ABM controversy progressed, it never fully conceded the constitutional point.[486]

investment, mutual legal assistance, extradition treaties, and other treaties). In other instances, the condition seemed to be set out separately from other conditions that were expressly made binding. 144 Cong. Rec. 18,509 (1998) (OECD Convention on Combating Bribery of Foreign Public Officials in International Business Transactions); 144 Cong. Rec. 14,581 (1998) (Grains Trade Convention and Food Aid Convention Constituting the International Grains Agreement, the Trademark Law Treaty, and Amendments to the Convention on the International Maritime Organization). In at least one instance, the condition was made simply as one of the "declarations, which express the intent of the Senate." 156 Cong. Rec. 23,472, 23,474–75 (2010) (New START Treaty).

[482] The Senate Committee on Foreign Relations resolution invoked the Constitution, see ABM Treaty Interpretation Resolution, S. Res. 167, 100th Cong. § 2 (1987), and the INF conditions were later "based on the Treaty Clauses of the Constitution." 134 Cong. Rec. 12,849 (1988); *see also* S. Exec. Rep. 100-15, at 87, 96–97 (1988) (asserting that INF condition made apparent "principles that inherently apply to the INF Treaty" (emphasis omitted)).

[483] *The ABM Treaty and the Constitution: Joint Hearings Before the Senate Comm. on Foreign Relations and the Senate Comm. on the Judiciary*, 100th Cong. 375 (1987) [hereinafter *Joint ABM Hearings*] (prepared statement of Abraham D. Sofaer, Department of State Legal Adviser). Then-Senator Biden opined that this position was "incredible" and "absolutely staggering." *Id.* at 130.

[484] This appeared to be recognized by the Senate Committee on Foreign Relations insofar as it indicated that "any subsequent practice between the parties in the application of the treaty is to be taken into account in interpreting the treaty." ABM Treaty Interpretation Resolution, S. Res. 167, 100th Cong. § 2(2)(E) (1987). Yet it was difficult to see how that element could be reconciled with privileging the treaty text and executive branch communications during the advice-and-consent process; given that subsequent practice naturally continues after the Senate provided its consent, the incompatibility was still more manifest. *See also Joint ABM Hearings, supra* note 483, at 192–94 (testimony of Arthur W. Rovine).

[485] *See* 5 Hackworth Digest 262 (describing message from Secretary of State Hughes to Ambassador Houghton of July 30, 1923, suggesting that the latter might inform the German Foreign Office that senatorial statements concerning the Treaty of Berlin, "occurring in general debate, cannot be regarded as affecting the interpretation of that treaty"); *id.* at 153 (characterizing telegrams from Secretary of State Kellogg to the U.S. Ambassadors to Great Britain and France as indicating that a report of the Senate Committee on Foreign Relations "had no legal effect whatsoever" on the Kellogg-Briand Pact). In the latter case, at least, the Senate made no claim to the contrary. 5 Hackworth Digest 152–53 (citing 70 Cong. Rec. 1,730 (1929)); *see also* 70 Cong. Rec. 1,655–56 (1929) (discussing significance of report).

[486] *See* 1 Cumulative Digest of U.S. Practice 1263–65 (excerpting March 17, 1988, letter from White House counsel, on behalf of all relevant agencies); *id.* at 1267 (excerpting May 27, 1988, statement by President Reagan, following Senate approval of the INF Treaty, noting "concerns" about constitutionality); *id.* at 1268 (excerpting June 10, 1988, letter from Reagan to the Senate, subsequent

If the Senate's appreciation of a treaty at the time it provides consent is not otherwise binding under the Constitution, everything depends on whether a Biden condition legally constrains the president following ratification.[487] Such conditions do make more explicit the problems generally posed by understandings: because they do not even purport to affect international law,[488] they risk dictating a treaty interpretation for the United States that other states parties may not share.[489] Biden conditions also remain vulnerable to constitutional objection to the extent they would limit the interpretations that the United States may espouse internationally,[490] though that objection is weaker if a condition only stymies giving domestic legal effect to a different interpretation.[491] Probably nothing in the potential efficacy of these conditions resolves the more general question of whether the Senate understanding of a treaty, absent such conditions, must prevail.[492]

The political safeguards against a future "constitutional bait-and-switch" should suffice. As the ABM Treaty dispute progressed, the executive branch was chastened by concerns that the Senate might withhold future consent to controversial treaties if it could not trust branch assurances as to their meaning;

---

to the exchange of instruments, asserting that established treaty interpretation principles "may not be limited or changed by the Senate alone, and those principles will govern any future disputes over the interpretation of the Treaty").

[487] See supra this chapter 195 (noting binding effect of conditions on the executive branch generally). Because the executive branch has ratified treaties with Biden conditions, assured the Senate that it could depend on executive branch testimony, and maintained that the executive branch would adhere to such testimony, that might be understood as accepting the efficacy of those conditions in particular. See CRS, TREATIES AND OTHER INTERNATIONAL AGREEMENTS, supra note 165, at 130 n.39 (citing The START Treaty: Hearing Before the Senate Comm. on Foreign Relations 102nd Cong., pt. 1, at 506–07 (1992) (responses of the Department of State to questions from Senator Cranston), and S. EXEC. REP. 103-5, at 16 (1993) (Open Skies Treaty)).

[488] The Senate reinforced that there was no intended effect on international law when providing advice and consent to the INF Treaty by failing to demand—in contrast with certain declarations and understandings, see 134 CONG. REC. 12,850 (1988)—that the Biden condition should be communicated to the Soviet Union in connection with the ratification.

[489] See, e.g., 1 CUMULATIVE DIGEST OF U.S. PRACTICE 1268 (Reagan letter); RESTATEMENT (FOURTH) § 306 rptrs. note 11.

[490] Thus, for example, the condition to the INF Treaty specifically stated that "the United States shall not agree to or adopt an interpretation different from th[e] common understanding except pursuant to Senate advice and consent to a subsequent treaty or protocol, or the enactment of a statute." 134 CONG. REC. 12,849 (1988).

[491] A condition precluding such domestic legal effect would resemble a declaration that the treaty was not self-executing. See infra this chapter § IV(A)(7).

[492] Professor Henkin, however, maintained in his treatise that the executive branch's concession that formal conditions were generally binding meant that "what the Senate in fact thought the treaty meant is the treaty to which it consented." HENKIN, FOREIGN AFFAIRS, at 184. By contrast, in testimony to the Senate, he would have limited any preclusive effect to the Senate's "clear understanding as to what a treaty means in an essential respect," presumably expressed through conditions. Joint ABM Hearings, supra note 483, at 90 (testimony of Louis Henkin). The Restatement (Third) was more equivocal, suggesting that the president would be entrusted to determine the Senate's view and how to respect it in good faith. See supra this chapter text accompanying note 477.

such concerns led to executive branch disclosure of treaty negotiating materials and a pledge of future fidelity to assurances contained in executive branch testimony.[493] Congress also added funding restrictions in some instances as separate insurance against changes in executive branch interpretations.[494] Such disputes remain most likely in sensitive bilateral treaties like arms control, where negotiations are not transparent—and where the Senate, if it wishes to establish a view, must secure treaty amendments rather than propose reservations.

3. Judicial Deference to International Tribunals

Courts in the United States frequently have cause to look to the decisions of other tribunals, including as regards treaties: as noted previously, other states parties' tribunals are understood to contribute to subsequent practice and thus to treaty interpretation.[495] Apart from this aggregated effect, there is little sustained obligation to recognize, or defer to, treaty interpretations by particular foreign tribunals, save to the degree they may figure in a judgment enforceable under U.S. law.[496] Likewise, the United States is obligated by the New York Convention, among other treaties, to recognize awards by certain international arbitral tribunals.[497] Still, the obligation to respect the outcome of such proceedings is not signal any overarching commitment to defer on matters of treaty interpretation by arbitral tribunals.[498]

---

[493] Originally, the Reagan administration expressed the view that the president was bound to any specific interpretation of a treaty that was "generally understood," "clearly intended," and "relied upon" by the Senate during advice and consent. *See* S. EXEC. REP. 100-15, at 90–91, 94–96, 447–48 (1988) (noting, in particular, remarks by Department of State Legal Adviser Abraham Sofaer and White House Counsel Arthur Culvahouse); *see also* 11 Op. O.L.C., *supra* note 467, at 37 (suggesting that the weight of testimony "will likely depend upon such factors as the formality of the statement, the identity and position of the Executive Branch official making the statement, the level of attention and interest focused on the meaning of the relevant treaty provision, and the consistency with which members of the Executive Branch adhered at the time to the view of the treaty provision reflected in the statement"). Eventually, the executive branch made less qualified commitments. *See, e.g.,* S. EXEC. REP. 100-15, at 442 (1988) (Feb. 9, 1988, letter from Secretary of State Schultz, describing executive branch testimony as authoritative, and indicating that administration will not depart from it); *The CFE Treaty: Hearings Before the Subcomm. on European Affairs of the Comm. on Foreign Relations,* 102d Cong. 47-49 (1991) (testimony of Secretary of State Baker stating that testimony before the committee should be "considered authoritative . . . without any need for [the Senate] to incorporate them in [a] resolution of advice and consent"). The Senate nonetheless faulted these commitments for failing to acknowledge that the testimony was legally binding. *E.g.,* S. EXEC. REP. 100-15, at 94–96, 448 (1988).
[494] National Defense Authorization Act for Fiscal Years 1988 and 1989, Pub. L. No. 100-180, § 225, 101 Stat. 1019, 1056 (1987).
[495] *See supra* this chapter § III(A)(2).
[496] To be clear, foreign judgments are frequently entitled to recognitions under state law and principles of comity, see RESTATEMENT (FOURTH) § 481, and generally entitled to the same preclusive effects as would be due in the state of origin. *Id.* § 487.
[497] *See* United Nations Convention on the Recognition and Enforcement of Foreign Arbitral Awards, June 10, 1958, 330 U.N.T.S. 38.
[498] *See* Medellín v. Texas, 552 U.S. 491, 533–34 & n.1 (2008) (citing, as exceptions, examples in which international judgments were incorporated in U.S. law, either by virtue of treaty or statute).

Historically, the United States has been particularly cautious about exposing itself to the jurisdiction of international courts, including bodies like the Permanent Court of International Justice, the American Court of Human Rights, and the International Criminal Court. As such, it is relatively rare for an international court to issue a decision calling upon the United States to take action, and it is even rarer for such decisions to implicate the jurisdiction of U.S. courts or other actors on the domestic plane. One important exception involves the International Court of Justice (ICJ). The United States has accepted, in certain circumstances, the jurisdiction of the ICJ,[499] and certain of its decisions have required U.S. courts to examine whether and to what extent those decisions are entitled to deference.

Beginning in 1998 with *Breard v. Greene* and continuing in other cases concerning the Vienna Convention on Consular Relations, the Supreme Court stated that it "should give respectful consideration to the interpretation of an international treaty rendered by an international court with jurisdiction to interpret such."[500] *Breard* involved an emergency proceeding before the Supreme Court premised on an ICJ order on interim measures of protection;[501] as such, there had been little opportunity for the ICJ to set out its interpretation of the Vienna Convention, or for the Supreme Court to engage with it. Notably, though, the *Breard* opinion immediately qualified its words about "respectful consideration" by explaining that international law established a strong presumption, in tension with the ICJ proceedings, that forum states were free to apply their procedural rules, and also that this rule was reflected in the Vienna Convention itself.[502] The Supreme Court concluded that, in light of U.S. legal principles, including those governing the procedural default of claim, it was inappropriate for the judiciary to order that Breard's execution be stayed.[503]

Subsequent Supreme Court decisions confronted similar issues regarding interpretation of the Vienna Convention, but in a different posture. In separate proceedings (known as the *LaGrand* and *Avena* cases), also involving U.S. administration of the death penalty, the ICJ issued judgments that more definitively set out its understanding of the treaty and its conclusions that the United States had violated its obligations.[504] Nevertheless, despite the Supreme Court's

---

For further discussion of this case, see *infra* this chapter § IV(A); Chapter 1 § II(B); Chapter 3 § I(D); Chapter 5 § II(B); Chapter 7 § III(C); and Chapter 9 §§ II(B), II(C).

[499] *See* Chapter 7 § II(D) (discussing ICJ jurisdiction).
[500] Breard v. Greene, 523 U.S. 371, 375 (1998) (per curiam); *see also* Sanchez-Llamas v. Oregon, 548 U.S. 331, 353 (2006) (reaffirming *Breard*); Medellín v. Texas, 552 U.S. 491, 513 n.9 (2008) (citing *Breard*).
[501] Vienna Convention on Consular Relations (Para. v. U.S.), 1998 I.C.J. 248 (Apr. 9).
[502] *Breard*, 523 U.S. at 375.
[503] *Breard*, 523 U.S. at 375–77.
[504] LaGrand (Ger. v. U.S.), Judgment, 2001 I.C.J. 466 (June 27); Avena and Other Mexican Nationals (Mex. v. U.S.), Order, 2003 I.C.J. 99 (May 22).

reiteration that it owed "respectful consideration" to the ICJ's views, and its recognition that the ICJ had undertaken to set out views subsequent to *Breard*, the Court decided in *Sanchez-Llamas v. Oregon* to hew to the interpretation it had tendered (on an expedited basis) in *Breard*.[505] Regarding the United States' international obligations, the Court reasoned that nothing in the ICJ statute indicated that its judgments were binding on U.S. courts—noting that the statute even suggested that the ICJ was not bound by its own precedent in subsequent cases.[506] Beyond that, the Court emphasized its own preeminent role within the U.S. scheme, seemingly requiring that it exercise independent judgment in interpreting treaties.[507] It also cast doubt on the deference owed the ICJ's role, given the U.S. withdrawal from its jurisdiction over Vienna Convention disputes, and said that the ICJ decisions in question were thus "only" due respectful consideration.[508] Yet later, in *Medellín v. Texas*, the Supreme Court recalled the respectful consideration standard from *Breard*, but this time queried whether "that principle would apply when the question is the binding force of ICJ judgments themselves, rather than the substantive scope of a treaty the ICJ must interpret in resolving disputes."[509]

The Vienna Convention litigation suggests that U.S. courts are unlikely to afford much weight to treaty interpretation by international tribunals.[510] One potential hurdle is whether the tribunal has "jurisdiction to interpret" the treaty in question,[511] and U.S. courts may afford little deference on the issue of whether a tribunal in fact possesses such authority.[512] In *Sanchez-Llamas*, the Supreme

---

[505] Sanchez-Llamas v. Oregon, 548 U.S. 331, 353 (2006) ("Although the ICJ's interpretation deserves 'respectful consideration' . . . we conclude that it does not compel us to reconsider our understanding of the Convention in *Breard*.") (citation omitted) (quoting *Breard*, 523 U.S. at 375).

[506] *Sanchez-Llamas*, 548 U.S. at 354–55 (discussing ICJ Statute and treatment of precedent); *accord* Medellín, 552 U.S. at 513 n.9. The Supreme Court's view regarding the ICJ's use of precedent is an oversimplification, as the ICJ tends to adhere to its precedent unless there are strong grounds for departing from it. *See generally* MOHAMED SHAHABUDDEEN, PRECEDENT IN THE WORLD COURT 134–35 (1996).

[507] *Sanchez-Llamas*, 548 U.S. at 354–55 (discussing ICJ statute and treatment of precedent); *id.* at 353–54 (citing *Marbury v. Madison* for proposition that it is "emphatically the province and duty of" U.S. courts to interpret treaties).

[508] *Id.* at 355 (citing *Breard*).

[509] Medellín v. Texas, 552 U.S. 491, 513 n.9 (2008). For discussions of *Medellín*, see *infra* this chapter § IV(A); Chapter 1 § II(B); Chapter 3 § I(D); Chapter 5 § II(B); Chapter 7 § III(C); and Chapter 9 §§ II(B), II(C).

[510] Unsurprisingly, lower courts have followed the Supreme Court in favoring its determinations over those of the ICJ. *See, e.g.*, Mora v. New York, 524 F.3d 183, 205–07 (2d Cir. 2008); Commonwealth v. Gautreaux, 458 Mass. 741, 751–52 (2011).

[511] *E.g.*, Breard v. Greene, 523 U.S. 371, 375 (1998). The ICJ's jurisdiction was not directly at issue, as the parties involved agreed that the ICJ had jurisdiction to interpret the Vienna Convention on Consular Relations and that this was binding on the United States as a matter of international law. *See, e.g.*, *Medellín*, 552 U.S. at 504.

[512] As previously noted, *Medellín* indicated that "respectful consideration" might not be due to the ICJ's view of the binding force of its own judgments, which might extend to the court's understanding of its own jurisdiction. *Medellín*, 552 U.S. at 513 n.9.

Court also indicated it was material that the ICJ lacked *prospective* authority over the United States with respect to the treaty in question.[513] The reasoning was not explained, but it suggests that weighing an international tribunal's views may be premised less on expertise than on the need to avoid continued conflicts.

Even absent special reasons for caution, it seems unlikely that U.S. courts will treat the views of international courts as having substantial value independent of the quality of their reasoning. On its face, "respectful consideration" deference is less than the "great weight" owed the executive branch's views,[514] and will likely resemble the limited deference given views of treaty bodies and other international institutions.[515] Such deference may also be comparable to the treatment of informal agency decision-making—meaning that an interpretation is "entitled to respect . . . but only to the extent that [it has] the power to persuade."[516] The most important factor bearing on the persuasiveness of an international court's interpretation, ultimately, is likely to be its compatibility with the treaty's text, which suggests a confined role for the court itself.[517]

---

[513] The United States had withdrawn from the Optional Protocol to the Vienna Convention on Consular Relations, which had been the basis for the ICJ's jurisdiction over the United States in the *Breard, LaGrand,* and *Avena* death penalty cases. *Sanchez-Llamas,* 548 U.S. at 355 ("Whatever the effect of [ICJ decisions] before this withdrawal, it is doubtful that our courts should give decisive weight to the interpretation of a tribunal whose jurisdiction in this area is no longer recognized by the United States.").

[514] *See Mora,* 524 F.3d at 206 (contrasting the "great weight" owed the views of the executive with the "respectful consideration" owed to interpretation of international bodies); *cf. Sanchez-Llamas,* 548 U.S. at 355 (noting "great weight" standard, then stating that the ICJ's judgment is "entitled only to the 'respectful consideration' due an interpretation of [a treaty] by an international court").

[515] *See, e.g.,* Commonwealth v. Judge, 591 Pa. 126, 150–51 (2007) (likening deference owed the Human Rights Committee, in its interpretation of the International Covenant on Civil and Political Rights, to the "respectful consideration" owed the ICJ). In *Cummins, Inc. v. United States,* 454 F.3d 1361 (Fed. Cir. 2006), the court of appeals concluded that a classification opinion by the World Customs Organization was, like the ICJ, "not binding and is entitled, at most, to 'respectful consideration'"—which it made clear could be satisfied by according the opinion "persuasive value, if any," and was satisfied when the district court afforded "no deference" to the opinion. *Id.* at 1366 (citation omitted); *see also* RESTATEMENT (FOURTH) § 306 rptrs. note 8 (stating that "[t]hough often not directly legally binding, the pronouncements of such expert bodies [as the Human Rights Committee] can nevertheless be important guides to the treaty in question," while noting misgivings of U.S. government). As with international tribunals, issues of jurisdiction may arise. *Cf. Judge,* 591 Pa., at 150–51 (noting Committee limitations, but affording minimal deference).

[516] *Mora,* 524 F.3d at 206 (quoting Christensen v. Harris County, 529 U.S. 576, 587 (2000)); *see also* Skidmore v. Swift & Co., 323 U.S. 134, 140 (1944) (citing, as factors bearing on the degree of deference to an informal administrative agency decision, "the thoroughness evident in its consideration, the validity of its reasoning, its consistency with earlier and later pronouncements, and all those factors which give it power to persuade, if lacking power to control").

[517] *See, e.g., Sanchez-Llamas,* 548 U.S. at 356 (indicating conflict between the ICJ interpretation and the "plain import" of the treaty text); *cf.* Abbott v. Abbott, 560 U.S. 1, 43–44 (2010) (Stevens, J., dissenting) (discussing subsequent practice by states parties, and invoking *Breard* to the effect that "the interest in having our courts correctly interpret the [treaty] may outweigh the interest" in having the relevant provision "resolved in the same way that it is resolved in other countries").

IV. Incorporation, Implementation, and Hierarchical Status

If the United States is a party to an international agreement that imposes binding obligations under international law, what effect does that agreement have in the U.S. legal system? This question is a central concern of U.S. foreign relations law, and more within its control than issues of treaty interpretation. Yet it remains unsettled in key respects, even as to Article II treaties—though these are the agreements with which the United States has the clearest constitutional instruction.

This section first addresses the topic of treaty self-execution and non-self-execution, which concerns the circumstances in which an Article II treaty is effective automatically as U.S. law. It then addresses how a treaty can be implemented by other domestic law. The final portion considers the hierarchical status of Article II treaties in U.S. law, both relative to one another and relative to other forms of law.

A. Incorporation by Treaty Self-Execution

The Constitution provides that "all" treaties of the United States are the "supreme Law of the Land."[518] One entailment, seemingly, is that a treaty of the United States is part of U.S. law. As such, a treaty should be applicable by courts in justiciable cases just as would any other relevant source of U.S. law, be it a federal statute or state common law rule.[519] This suggests that treaties are "self-executing," in the sense that they are enforceable, as such, in U.S. courts, without the need for prior implementation by the U.S. Congress or other actors.

Yet qualifications immediately suggest themselves. What if the treaty by its text or context calls for a different means of incorporation by the parties, such as through implementing legislation? If that is the case, then perhaps self-execution would be inconsistent with the treaty obligation. Or what if the Constitution assigns lawmaking concerning a matter addressed by a treaty to Congress exclusively, thus making it inappropriate for the president (even with the advice and consent of the Senate) to "make" such law? If the treaty is vague, indeterminate,

---

[518] U.S. CONST. art. VI, cl. 2 ("This Constitution, and the Laws of the United States which shall be made in Pursuance thereof; and all Treaties made, or which shall be made, under the Authority of the United States, shall be the supreme Law of the Land; and the Judges in every State shall be bound thereby, any Thing in the Constitution or Laws of any State to the Contrary notwithstanding.").

[519] See Chapter 4. The Constitution establishes that the judicial power of federal courts includes cases arising under treaties. U.S. CONST. art. III, § 2, cl. 1. The Constitution also sets out the Supreme Court's original jurisdiction, which does not include treaties as such, though it does touch on matters (like "Cases affecting Ambassadors") that are prone to do so. Id. § 2, cl. 2. Subject-matter jurisdiction in the lower federal courts is exclusively the product of statute. See 28 U.S.C. § 1331 (2018); RESTATEMENT (FOURTH) § 301 cmt. c.

or aspirational in nature, should it be treated as automatically enforceable in U.S. law? The challenge is how to reconcile these and similar qualifications with the ostensibly unqualified Supremacy Clause. The resulting doctrine, addressing self-executing and non-self-executing treaty provisions, remains one of the most complicated in U.S. foreign relations law.[520]

1. Beginnings of Self-Execution and Non-Self-Execution

The Supremacy Clause was intended to effect a dramatic change in the legal status of treaties. The United States had suffered serious embarrassment, and risked war, when the national government proved unable to compel the states to abide by treaties. At least in part, this was because under the Articles of Confederation, a treaty did not itself establish domestic law—being "binding in moral obligation" only, as Justice Iredell wrote in the *Ware v. Hylton* proceedings[521]—even while Congress' ability to compel states to comply was also seriously in doubt.[522]

Ware v. Hylton allowed individual justices the opportunity to share diverse views about the Articles and about how to interpret the Treaty of Paris, but they agreed that the Supremacy Clause changed the import of U.S. treaties for U.S. law: the U.S. Constitution was the supreme law of the land, and its Supremacy Clause automatically conferred comparable status on treaties in turn.[523] By contrast with the Articles, Justice Iredell explained in his circuit court opinion, "so far as a treaty constitutionally is binding, upon principles of moral obligation, it is also *by the vigour of its own authority to be executed in fact*."[524]

Chief Justice Marshall reinforced this view, for a more unified Court, in *Foster v. Nielsen*, a case involving whether a provision in a bilateral treaty between the United States and Spain, providing that certain land grants "shall be ratified and confirmed" by the United States, was judicially enforceable as such or required legislative implementation first.[525] Given the diverse national schemes of the

---

[520] *See, e.g.*, United States v. Postal, 589 F.2d 862, 876 (5th Cir. 1979) ("The self-execution question is perhaps one of the most confounding in treaty law").

[521] Ware v. Hylton, 3 U.S. (3 Dall.) 199, 277 (1796) (Iredell, J.). For background on *Ware*, see *supra* this chapter text accompanying note 57.

[522] *See supra* this chapter § I(B)(2).

[523] Justice Cushing spoke to the question most directly. *See Ware*, 3 U.S. (3 Dall.) at 282 (Cushing, J.) (describing the Treaty of Paris as "having been sanctioned, in all its parts, by the constitution of the United States, as the supreme law of the land"); *id.* at 284 (stating that "there is no want of power, the treaty being sanctioned as the supreme law, by the constitution of the United States, which nobody pretends to deny to be paramount and controlling to all state laws, and even state constitutions, wheresoever they interfere or disagree," and that "[t]he treaty . . . is of equal force with the constitution itself; and certainly, with any law whatsoever"); *see also id.* at 236–37 (Chase, J.) (stating that state constitutions, and state laws, must be "prostrate" before a treaty); *cf. id.* at 281 (Wilson, J.) (concluding that "the treaty annuls" Virginia's confiscatory statute, independent of the Constitution).

[524] *Ware*, 3 U.S. at 277 (Iredell, J.) (emphasis added).

[525] Foster v. Neilson, 27 U.S. (2 Pet.) 253, 314 (1829); *see also* Treaty of Amity, Settlement and Limits, Spain-U.S., Feb. 22, 1819, 8 Stat. 252 (Adams-Onis Treaty of 1819). For more comprehensive discussions of *Foster*, see SLOSS, *supra* note 118, ch. 4; Carlos M. Vázquez, *Foster v. Neilson and United*

United States' treaty partners, like Great Britain,[526] Chief Justice Marshall did not suppose that the automatic efficacy of treaties was required by international law; indeed, he took a treaty's "nature" to be "a contract between two nations, not a legislative act." Accordingly, he reasoned, a treaty "does not generally effect, of itself, the object to be accomplished, especially so far as its operation is infra-territorial; but is carried into execution by the sovereign power of the respective parties to the instrument."[527] This meant that the approach under the Articles of Confederation was compatible with international law, had the United States been capable of imposing legislation on its several states, or if the states had simply effectuated the change themselves.

The U.S. Constitution, Marshall explained, had ultimately established a "different principle." The Supremacy Clause meant not just that treaties were, upon some further implementation by Congress, supreme over state law, but also that a treaty is "to be regarded in courts of justice as equivalent to an act of the legislature, *whenever it operates of itself, without the aid of any legislative provision*."[528] That qualification made a substantial difference, for "when the terms of the stipulation import a contract, when either of the parties engages to perform a particular act," then "the treaty addresses itself to the political, not the judicial department; and the legislature must execute the contract, before it can become a rule for the Court."[529]

The Court almost immediately reconsidered *Foster's* application of this approach,[530] and *Foster* itself seems to have occasioned few doubts about the enhanced status of treaties under the Constitution.[531] For most of the next

States v. Percheman: Judicial Enforcement of Treaties, *in* INTERNATIONAL LAW STORIES 151 (John E. Noyes et al. eds., 2007). For further discussion of *Foster*, see *infra* this chapter § IV(A)(4).

[526] *See supra* this chapter note 91 (discussing non-self-execution under British constitution). In *Foster* itself, Great Britain's treaty practice was indirectly relevant, as a condition precedent to the treaty between Spain and the United States. *Foster*, 27 U.S. at 300–01.

[527] *Foster*, 27 U.S. at 314.

[528] *Foster*, 27 U.S. at 314 (emphasis added).

[529] *Foster*, 27 U.S. at 314. For further discussion of this qualification, see *infra* this chapter § IV(A) (2).

[530] United States v. Percheman, 32 U.S. (7 Pet.) 51, 88–89 (1833); *see supra* this chapter note 386.

[531] *See, e.g.*, Lessee of Pollard's Heirs v. Kibbe, 39 U.S. (14 Pet.) 353, 388 (1840) (Baldwin, J., concurring) (noting *Foster*-like qualification, but adding that "if a treaty made under its authority, is a supreme law of the land, it would be a bold proposition, that an act of Congress must be first passed in order to give it effect as such; and equally bold to assert . . . that its stipulations may be performed or not, at the discretion of Congress"). Even just after *Foster*, and prior to the about-face in *Percheman*, assessments seemed to put greater emphasis on judicial enforceability. *See, e.g.*, 3 JOSEPH STORY, COMMENTARIES ON THE CONSTITUTION OF THE UNITED STATES § 1832 (1833) (stating that it was indispensable that treaties "have the obligation and force of a law, *that they may be executed by the judicial power*") (emphasis added); *id.* at 695 ("If they are supreme laws, courts of justice will enforce them directly in all cases, to which they can be judicially applied, in opposition to all state laws . . . ."); *id.* at 695–96 n.3 (discussing "different principle" pronouncement in *Foster*); *id.* at 696–97 & n.1 (noting that, in virtue of non-self-execution, that "[t]here are, indeed, still cases, in which courts of justice can administer no effectual redress").

century, the "different principle" established by the Supremacy Clause, and the automatic enforceability of treaties, was the dominant takeaway. There was at least one case in which the Supreme Court arguably held that a treaty was un-enforceable because it was non-self-executing,[532] and others in which non-self-execution was referenced more peripherally—as the presumed predicate for subsequent legislation implementing treaty obligations.[533] As a general matter, though, U.S. courts entertained treaty-based claims and defenses without asking whether the treaties involved were self-executing, or noted in a conclusory fashion that they were.[534]

Following World War II, however, matters gradually changed. Litigation invoking multilateral human rights treaties and the U.N. Charter excited the non-self-execution doctrine. Initially, indications that courts might find some of the treaties self-executing featured prominently in attempts to advance the Bricker Amendment movement to inhibit the efficacy of treaties.[535] Subsequently, some lower court decisions, and then the *Restatement (Second)*, came to regard non-self-execution as a basis for refusing to afford relief to claimants and, seemingly, as a qualification to the supremacy of treaties.[536] Eventually, U.S. treaty-makers sought to control the issue by including non-self-execution conditions in Senate resolutions of advice and consent.[537]

[532] Cameron Septic Tank Co. v. Knoxville, 227 U.S. 39, 44, 50 (1913) (holding both that a treaty did not apply to a particular patent, and that it was "certainly the sense of Congress that [the treaty] was not" self-executing); *see* Medellín v. Texas, 552 U.S. 491, 545 (2008) (Breyer, J., dissenting) (citing *Cameron Septic Tank Co.* as an exceptional instance of a non-self-execution holding); RESTATEMENT (FOURTH) § 310 rptrs. note 1 (same).

[533] *See, e.g.,* Head Money Cases, 112 U. S. 580, 597–99 (1884) (noting that "so far as a treaty made by the United States with any foreign nation can become the subject of judicial cognizance in the courts of this country, it is subject to such acts as congress may pass for its enforcement, modification, or repeal"). For similar references, see Fok v. United States, 185 U.S. 296, 303 (1902); United States v. Lee Yen Tai, 185 U.S. 213, 220–23 (1902); De Lima v. Bidwell, 182 U.S. 1, 195–96 (1901).

[534] *See, e.g.,* Cook v. United States, 288 U.S. 102, 119 (1933) (stating, with regard to a bilateral treaty, that "in a strict sense the Treaty was self-executing, in that no legislation was necessary to authorize executive action pursuant to its provisions," and citing view of the secretary of state); Asakura v. City of Seattle, 265 U.S. 332 (1924) (stating, of bilateral treaty, that "[i]t operates of itself without the aid of any legislation, state or national; and it will be applied and given authoritative effect by the courts"); *see also Medellín,* 552 U.S. at 545 (Breyer, J., dissenting) (stating that "this Court has frequently held or assumed that particular treaty provisions are self-executing, automatically binding the States without more"); *id.* at 568 (detailing examples in appendix A); RESTATEMENT (FOURTH) § 310 rptrs. note 1 (citing examples of treaty provisions applied, without direct consideration of self-execution, so as to supersede state or local law); *id.* § 310 rptrs. note 1 (citing examples of the direct enforcement of treaties in various subject areas).

[535] These developments, and the development of non-self-execution more generally, are expertly discussed in SLOSS, *supra* note 118. As Professor Sloss recounts, a 1950 decision by a California state court, which relied on the U.N. Charter to invalidate a state statute discriminating against Japanese nationals, was cited as "exhibit number one" by supporters of the Bricker Amendment. *Id.* at 174; *see* Fuji v. California, 217 P.2d 481 (Cal. App. 2d 1950). The California Supreme Court subsequently held that the relied-upon provisions of the Charter required legislative action before they could be enforced. Fujii v. State, 242 P.2d 617, 621 (Cal. 1952).

[536] *See* SLOSS, *supra* note 118, chs. 12–13.

[537] RESTATEMENT (FOURTH) § 310 rptrs. note 9.

Foster's bookend was the Supreme Court's 2008 decision in *Medellín v. Texas*, which also confronted distinctive facts.[538] *Medellín* addressed the enforceability in U.S. courts of a judgment of the ICJ, which had held that the United States was obligated to provide review and reconsideration of state-court convictions and sentences of fifty-one named Mexican nationals.[539] The decision came to be binding on the United States by virtue of three treaties: the Optional Protocol Concerning the Compulsory Settlement of Disputes to the Vienna Convention, which provides for the "compulsory settlement" of disputes arising under the Vienna Convention on Consular Relations;[540] the ICJ Statute, which establishes ICJ jurisdiction over cases specially provided for in treaties and states that its decisions have "binding force" between the parties with respect to a particular case;[541] and the U.N. Charter, which provides that a state party "undertakes to comply with the decision of the International Court of Justice in any case to which it is a party."[542]

The Supreme Court held that because the treaty obligation to abide by the ICJ judgment was not self-executing, it could not prevail over state law. With respect to the treaties particularly at issue, it reasoned that the U.N. Charter "call[ed] upon governments to take certain [future] action" rather than establishing an intent "to vest ICJ decisions with immediate legal effect in domestic courts,"[543] and emphasized the understanding of U.S. treaty-makers.[544] The Court also suggested that non-self-execution had a pervasive effect on treaty enforcement insofar as it dismissed the president's attempt to execute the ICJ judgment.[545] The circumstances were unusual—given the Court's prior decisions disagreeing with the ICJ's reading of the underlying Vienna Convention on Consular Relations,[546]

---

[538] 552 U.S. 491 (2008). For discussions of *Medellín*, see *supra* this chapter § III(B); Chapter 1 § II(B); Chapter 3 § I(D); Chapter 5 § II(B); Chapter 7 § III(C); and Chapter 9 §§ II(B), II(C).

[539] Case Concerning Avena and Other Mexican Nationals (Mex. v. U.S.), Judgment, 2004 I.C.J. 12 (Mar. 31).

[540] Optional Protocol Concerning the Compulsory Settlement of Disputes to the Vienna Convention, Apr. 24, 1963, art. I, 500 U.N.T.S. 241; *see* Vienna Convention on Consular Relations, Apr. 24, 1963, art. 36, 21 U.S.T. 77, 596 U.N.T.S. 261.

[541] Statute of the International Court of Justice arts. 36(1), 59, June 26, 1945, 59 Stat. 1055, T.S. No. 993.

[542] U.N. Charter, art. 94(1).

[543] *Medellín*, 552 U.S. at 508 (internal quotations and citations omitted); *see also id.* at 508–09, 511–13, 516 n.10, 517–18 (discussing applicability of ICJ decisions in domestic courts).

[544] *Id.* at 509, 513, 523.

[545] *Id.* at 523–32; *see* Memorandum from President George W. Bush to the Attorney General Regarding Compliance with the Decision of the International Court of Justice in Avena (Feb. 28, 2005), https://perma.cc/Q6G7-RQ7E; *see also* Brief for the United States as Amicus Curiae Supporting Respondent, Medellín v. Dretke, 544 U.S. 660 (2005) (No. 04-5928) (reprinting original memorandum); *infra* this chapter text accompanying notes 583–586.

[546] *Medellín*, 552 U.S. at 513 n.9 (noting that the Court gives "respectful consideration to the interpretation of an international treaty rendered by an international court with jurisdiction to interpret [the treaty]" (quoting Breard v. Greene, 523 U.S. 371, 375 (1998) (per curiam)); *see supra* this chapter text accompanying notes 514–517 (discussing "respectful consideration" standard).

and the potential for disrupting state-level administration of criminal law, including the death penalty[547]—but the Court's sweeping reasoning, after years of relative silence on the subject of self-execution, ensured its immediate influence.[548]

The following subsections discuss the implications of self-execution and non-self-execution for the status of treaties in U.S. law, then explore different means for identifying self-execution and non-self-execution. For better or for worse, courts typically approach non-self-execution as a unified doctrine: a conclusion, reached for any of several different reasons, that has similar implications for the judicial enforceability of a treaty.[549] The nature of those conclusions is explored immediately following, but some preliminary guidance may be helpful. First, the issue of self-execution is controlled by U.S. law and concerns the domestic status of a treaty that concededly binds the United States as a matter of international law.[550] Concomitantly, whether the treaty is non-self-executing does not affect whether the treaty continues to bind the United States internationally.[551] Second, while it is a common shorthand (used here as well) to say that a treaty is self-executing or non-self-executing, some of a treaty's provisions may be self-executing and others not.[552] Third, notwithstanding the Supremacy Clause, case law has not established any clear presumption favoring or disfavoring self-execution.[553] As the following subsections reflect, courts *have* generally tended to identify premises for non-self-execution, rather than identifying grounds for

[547] *Medellín*, 552 U.S. at 518, 522–23, 528–30.

[548] The *Restatement (Fourth)* stressed the case's distinctive features and arguably overbroad language but acknowledged its prominence. RESTATEMENT (FOURTH) § 310 rptrs. note 2.

[549] However, leading commentators have long pushed to disentangle the doctrine, so that the non-self-execution drawn from different premises would also have different consequences. The seminal article is Carlos Manuel Vázquez, *The Four Doctrines of Self-Executing Treaties*, 89 AM. J. INT'L L. 695 (1995); *see also* SLOSS, *supra* note 118; David L. Sloss, *Taming Madison's Monster: How to Fix Self-Execution Doctrine*, 2015 BYU L. REV. 1691 (2016); Carlos Manuel Vázquez, *Four Problems with the Draft Restatement's Treatment of Treaty Self-Execution*, 2015 BYU L. REV. 1747 (2016).

[550] RESTATEMENT (FOURTH) § 310 cmt. c. A treaty might, however, require a certain domestic act or status before it can enter into force or before its provisions become operative. *See, e.g.*, Convention on Commercial Reciprocity, Haw.-U.S., art. V, June 3, 1875, 19 Stat. 625 (providing that convention would enter into force upon approval and proclamation by the king of the Hawaiian Islands and ratification and proclamation by the United States, "but not until a law to carry it into operation shall have been passed by the Congress of the United States of America").

[551] RESTATEMENT (FOURTH) § 301(3) & cmt. d; *id.* § 310(1); *see, e.g.*, Medellín v. Texas, 552 U.S. 491, 522 (2008) (summarizing holding that "while the ICJ's judgment in *Avena* creates an international law obligation on the part of the United States," the treaty provision establishing that obligation is nonetheless not self-executing); *id.* at 504 ("No one disputes that the *Avena* decision . . . constitutes an *international* law obligation on the part of the United States") (emphasis in original).

[552] RESTATEMENT (FOURTH) § 310 & cmt. b (citing United States v. Postal, 589 F.2d 862, 884 n.35 (5th Cir. 1979); *see, e.g.*, United States v. Noriega, 808 F. Supp. 791, 797 (S.D. Fla. 1992); *Treaty on Outer Space: Hearings Before the S. Comm. Foreign Relations*, 90th Cong. 35 (1967) (testimony of Ambassador Arthur Goldberg); *cf. id.* at 33 (Senator Gore) (noting that this made the treaty's operability "ambiguous").

[553] RESTATEMENT (FOURTH) § 310 cmt. d & rptrs. note 3.

self-execution, which suggests that self-execution is a starting point. At the same time, some of the inquiries would, if taken to their logical extreme, suggest that it is hard for a treaty provision to be deemed self-executing. If so, that is a relatively new development in U.S. law.

2. Consequences of Self-Execution

Under the Supremacy Clause, a self-executing treaty provision is binding, judicially enforceable federal law, applicable in court notwithstanding any contrary state law.[554] These seemingly straightforward implications are subject to important qualifications. The most important are hierarchical principles, explored later, that attempt to reconcile treaties (both self-executing and non-self-executing) with other federal law. Treaties are subordinate, for example, to the U.S. Constitution. Judicial enforceability is also subject to justiciability limitations explored in Chapter 4.

Even beyond such limits, however, self-execution does not mean enforceable by every means. The Supremacy Clause is understood to secure automatically certain benefits for private parties, including the ability of litigants to invoke the treaty provision "defensively" to avoid application of conflicting state and local law[555]—and, by virtue of the later-in-time rule, over conflicting, earlier-arising federal statutes.[556] Litigants may also

---

[554] See Medellín, 552 U.S. at 506 n.3; accord RESTATEMENT (FOURTH) § 310 rptrs. note 9; id. § 311(a) cmt. a & rptrs. note 1; RESTATEMENT (THIRD) § 111 cmt. h.

[555] See Sanchez-Llamas v. Oregon, 548 U.S. 331, 346 (2006) (noting that because "a self-executing treaty binds the States pursuant to the Supremacy Clause . . . the States therefore must recognize the force of the treaty in the course of adjudicating the rights of litigants"); Kolovrat v. Oregon, 366 U.S. 187, 198 (1961); Clark v. Allen, 331 U.S. 503, 508 (1947). See generally Armstrong v. Exceptional Child Ctr., Inc., 575 U.S. 320, 326 (2015). The scope of such "defensive" use is not precisely settled. See Georges v. United Nations, 834 F.3d 88, 97–98 (2d Cir. 2016) (noting description of a private party's ability to invoke a treaty provision "(1) 'to defend against a claim by the United States government' or (2) 'to defend against a claim by another private party under state or federal law'" (quoting Oona A. Hathaway, Sabria McElroy, & Sara Aronchick Solow, International Law at Home: Enforcing Treaties in U.S. Courts, 37 YALE J. INT'L L. 51, 84 (2012))).
Exceptionally, individuals may not be entitled to invoke a self-executing provision, even defensively. For example, after being extradited to the United States, an individual might invoke before a U.S. court the "rule of specialty" found in the relevant extradition treaty, whereby the U.S. prosecution may not exceed the scope of the extradition agreement, and the individual may not be tried on charges other than those for which he or she was extradited. Some courts hold that such claims, even if arising under a treaty directly benefiting private persons, and invoked by them as a defense, may be raised exclusively by the extraditing state, see, e.g., United States v. Garavito-Garcia, 827 F.3d 242, 246–47 (2d Cir. 2016), or may be waived by that state. See, e.g., United States v. Stokes, 726 F.3d 880, 889–90 (7th Cir. 2013). For descriptions of the issue, see United States v. Fontana, 869 F.3d 464, 468–70 (6th Cir. 2017); United States v. Puentes, 50 F.3d 1567, 1571–75 (11th Cir. 1995); cf. S. EXEC. REP. No. 109-4, at 3 (2005) (Senate Committee on Foreign Relations statement that "the lack of a private right of action [under the U.N. Convention against Transnational Organized Crime] does not affect the ability of persons whose extradition is sought to raise any available defenses in the context of the extradition proceeding").

[556] See infra this chapter text accompanying notes 715–718 (elaborating later-in-time rule).

obtain injunctive or declaratory relief, assuming they meet the relevant requirements.[557]

The Supreme Court has stressed, however, the distinction between a litigant's defensive use of a "rule of decision," which flows directly from the Supremacy Clause, and a "private right of action" or "cause of action"—meaning the capacity, having identified an individual right provided by federal law, for a litigant to initiate a judicial action—which does not.[558] Likewise *Medellín*, in dicta, stated that a self-executing treaty provision does not necessarily confer "privately enforceable rights" in this sense.[559] Pre-*Medellín* decisions did not emphasize this distinction, so as to merge the issue of privately enforceable rights with the threshold question of self-execution, and so may offer little helpful guidance about how post-*Medellín* decisions should decide whether such rights have been conferred.[560]

Whether a self-executing treaty provision creates a private right of action depends on the treaty in question; some treaties may well be drafted to do so, while others may not. However, because treaties often depend on interstate mechanisms for their enforcement (such as by allowing states to bring a claim for violation before an international court or an expert treaty body), it is also fair to say, as the *Restatement (Third)* did, that "[i]nternational agreements, even those directly benefiting private persons, generally do not create private rights or provide for a private cause of action in domestic courts."[561] *Medellín* mistook this empirical observation as proposing a "background presumption" against private rights of action, and noted some lower court authority to that effect.[562] While the Court did not directly endorse such a presumption, it has sometimes been understood to support one.[563]

---

[557] *See, e.g.*, Asakura v. City of Seattle, 265 U.S. 332, 340 (1924) (allowing private business owner to sue a city and its officials to stop them from enforcing a city ordinance that violated a treaty). Courts have generally assumed that this right to seek prospective relief applies to treaties. *See, e.g.*, Republic of Paraguay v. Allen, 134 F.3d 622, 627 (4th Cir. 1998); United Mexican States v. Woods, 126 F.3d 1220, 1223 (9th Cir. 1997).

[558] *Armstrong*, 575 U.S. at 324–27; *see* RESTATEMENT (FOURTH) § 311(a), cmt. a & rptrs. note 1.

[559] *See Medellín*, 552 U.S. at 506 n.3; *accord* RESTATEMENT (FOURTH) § 310 rptrs. note 9; RESTATEMENT (FOURTH) § 311(a), cmt. a & rptrs. note 1; RESTATEMENT (THIRD) § 111 cmt. h.

[560] Mora v. New York, 524 F.3d 183, 201 n.25 (2d Cir. 2008) (describing pre-*Medellín* precedent).

[561] RESTATEMENT (THIRD) § 907 cmt. a.

[562] RESTATEMENT (FOURTH) § 311 rptrs. note 1; *see* Medellín v. Texas, 552 U.S. 491, 506 n.3 (2008) (quoting *Restatement (Third)*, construing it as stating a "background presumption," and explaining that "[a]ccordingly" lower courts "have presumed that treaties do not create privately enforceable rights in the absence of express language to the contrary") (citations omitted); *see also* Cornejo v. San Diego, 504 F.3d 853, 858–59 (9th Cir. 2007) ("While treaties *may* confer enforceable individual rights . . . most courts accept a 'presumption' against inferring individual rights from international treaties.") (emphasis in original; citations omitted).

[563] For cases citing *Medellín* to this effect, see, for example, Georges v. United Nations, 834 F.3d 88, 97 (2d Cir. 2016) (Convention on Privileges and Immunities of the United Nations); United States v. Sedaghaty, 728 F.3d 885, 917 (9th Cir. 2013) (U.S.-Egypt Mutual Legal Assistance Treaty); Katel Ltd. Liab. Co. v. AT&T Corp., 607 F.3d 60, 67–68 (2d Cir. 2010) (International Telecommunications Regulations); McKesson v. Islamic Republic of Iran, 539 F.3d 485, 488–89 (D.C. Cir. 2008) (U.S.-Iran

The fact that most international agreements do not create privately enforceable rights provides a flimsy basis for a presumption relevant to the kinds of treaties that are typically invoked by private claimants in U.S. courts. A sounder approach would simply bear in mind the nature of international agreements while construing a particular treaty's intention with respect to private rights of action and remedies.[564] A treaty might indicate that it was not intended to create such rights, making any presumption irrelevant.[565] Conversely, a treaty might provide indications that treaty-based claims may be pursued before domestic courts. The question of remedies is both related and distinct. If the treaty specifies a remedy for individuals, it suggests both self-execution and a private right;[566] if it does not specify any remedy, some courts have inferred that the treaty itself does not establish a private right, but that seems more speculative.[567]

U.S. courts are often reluctant to add national remedies to an international instrument based on their own authority.[568] However, laws other than the treaty

---

Treaty of Amity); *Mora*, 524 F.3d at 201 (Vienna Convention on Consular Relations). *But cf.* Sanchez-Llamas v. Oregon, 548 U.S. 331, 376 (2006) (Breyer, J., dissenting) (stating that "no such presumption exists"). The *Restatement (Fourth)* indicated that most such cases involved requests for a damages remedy, and consistent with a presumption against damages under statutory schemes. RESTATEMENT (FOURTH) § 311 rptrs. note 1. Still, some post-*Medellín* cases concern other remedies. *See, e.g., Sedaghaty*, 728 F.3d at 917 (right of discovery). It is also not clear whether the reasons to presume that Congress did not create a damages remedy for a statute should apply equally to treaties—which may advert to private damages less frequently, but which are also harder to amend to correct any judicial error.

[564] *See, e.g.*, Gross v. Ger. Found. Indus. Initiative, 549 F.3d 605, 615–16 (3d Cir. 2008) (disavowing application of a "strict presumption in this case," but construing Joint Statement of the Berlin Accords for evidence regarding "the intentions of the signing participants").

[565] *See, e.g., In re* Price, 685 F.3d 1, 11–12 (1st Cir. 2012) (explaining that "the US-UK [Mutual Legal Assistance Treaty] contains no express language creating private rights," but "[t]o the contrary, the treaty expressly states that it does not give rise to any private rights").

[566] For example, air liability conventions—the 1999 Convention for the Unification of Certain Rules for International Carriage by Air (Montreal Convention) and its 1929 predecessor (the Warsaw Convention)—expressly refer to actions for damages. *See, e.g.*, Baah v. Virgin Atl. Airways Ltd., 473 F. Supp. 2d 591, 593 & n.4 (S.D.N.Y. 2007) (concluding that "the Montreal Convention is self-executing and creates a private right of action in U.S. courts"). However, an obligation among states to provide compensation for certain wrongs does not by itself imply a cause of action in U.S. court for private parties to seek compensation in their own right. Even if such a cause of action is created, it may not overcome foreign sovereign immunity from U.S. jurisdiction, see Argentine Republic v. Amerada Hess Shipping Corp., 488 U.S. 428, 442 (1989), or overcome the sovereign immunity of the United States in its own courts. Goldstar (Panama) S.A. v. United States, 967 F.2d 965, 968 (4th Cir. 1992).

[567] Even if a treaty fails to provide an express remedy, a claimant nevertheless may be able to invoke rights established by the treaty so long as the remedies are predicated on a separate, statutory basis. *See* Gandara v. Bennett, 528 F.3d 823, 838 & n.19 (11th Cir. 2008) (Rodgers, J., specially concurring) (suggesting distinction and possible disagreement both with majority and with Cornejo v. San Diego, 504 F.3d 853, 861 n.14 (9th Cir. 2007)).

[568] Thus, U.S. courts have refused to establish remedies in U.S. law for violations of Article 36 of the Vienna Convention on Consular Relations, including the dismissal of indictments or the exclusion of evidence. *E.g.*, United States v. Duarte-Acero, 296 F.3d 1277, 1281–82 (11th Cir. 2002). As the Supreme Court explained in *Sanchez-Llamas*, even if the Convention conferred an individual right, it must also (absent a basis in some other treaty or statute) "provide a particular remedy, either

may establish supplementary relief. For example, under U.S. civil rights law, a civil action may be brought in federal court under 42 U.S.C. § 1983 seeking a remedy for those deprived by state government employees and other acting under "color of law" of "rights, privileges, or immunities secured by the Constitution and laws."[569] Treaties (at least when self-executing) are presumably "laws" for this purpose, but that leaves the important question as to whether a treaty establishes an individual "right" that is entitled to a section 1983 remedy.[570] Separately, a civil action may be brought in federal court under the Alien Tort Statute (ATS) by a noncitizen for a tort committed "in violation of the law of nations or a treaty of the United States." ATS plaintiffs have rarely invoked violations of self-executing treaties, but that path remains open, subject to the statute's narrow construction in recent Supreme Court jurisprudence.[571] These potential paths for invoking a

expressly or implicitly." Sanchez-Llamas v. Oregon, 548 U.S. 331, 346–47 (2006). The Court was unconvinced the parties intended a remedy like the exclusion of evidence, which would have been unfamiliar to many states parties. *Id.* at 344. *But see id.* at 346–47 (acknowledging that a treaty-provided remedy would pose "no issue of intruding on the constitutional prerogatives of the States or the other federal branches," since "[c]ourts must apply the remedy as a requirement of federal law").

[569] 42 U.S.C. § 1983 (2018).

[570] The Supreme Court has held that plaintiffs suing under § 1983 do not have to establish that a statute intended to create a private remedy, but must establish that it intended to establish some right for the class of persons in question. Gonzaga Univ. v. Doe, 536 U.S. 273, 283–86 (2002). Courts have differed, however, as to whether plaintiffs may recover under § 1983 for violations of Article 36 of the Vienna Convention on Consular Relations. Some have relied on indications in the Convention's preamble and elsewhere that its purpose is not to benefit individuals, and have credited the executive branch's view that Article 36 is merely part of an interstate scheme. *See, e.g., Gandara,* 528 F.3d at 826–29; Mora v. New York, 524 F.3d 183, 193–207 (2d Cir. 2008); *Cornejo,* 504 F.3d at 857–64. Others have stressed that the Convention confers individual rights. *See, e.g.,* Jogi v. Voges, 480 F.3d 822, 831–35 (7th Cir. 2007); *Cornejo,* 504 F.3d at 865–72 (Nelson, J., dissenting); United States v. Li, 206 F.3d 56, 72 (1st Cir. 2000) (Torruella, J., concurring in part and dissenting in part) (stating, outside § 1983 context, that Article 36 "unequivocally establishes that the protections . . . belong to the individual national"); *cf. Sanchez-Llamas,* 548 U.S. at 343 ("find[ing] it unnecessary," outside § 1983 context, "to resolve the question whether the Vienna Convention grants individuals enforceable rights"). The ICJ concluded that there was "no doubt" that Article 36 confers individual rights, LaGrand (Ger. v. U.S.), Judgment, 2001 I.C.J. Rep. 466, ¶¶ 76–77 (June 27), but some U.S. courts found its treaty analysis conclusory. *See, e.g., Mora,* 524 F.3d at 206–07. Disagreement among U.S. courts has also turned on the clarity with which individual rights must be conferred in the treaty in order to satisfy § 1983. *Compare Cornejo,* 504 F.3d at 858–61, *with id.* at 864–66, 869–73 (Nelson, J., dissenting). *See generally* RESTATEMENT (FOURTH) § 311 rptrs. note 4.

[571] 28 U.S.C. § 1350 (2018) (providing jurisdiction in district court over "any civil action by an alien for a tort only, committed in violation of the law of nations or a treaty of the United States"); *see* Chapter 5 § IV(B)(1). For rare examples, see Jogi v. Voges, 425 F.3d 367, 373 (7th Cir. 2005) (indicating that claimed breach of Article 36 of the Vienna Convention on Consular Relations could be pursued under the ATS), *opinion withdrawn on reh'g,* 480 F.3d 822, 824 (7th Cir. 2007); Bolchos v. Darrel, 3 F. Cas. 810 (D.C.S.C. 1795) (No. 1607) (finding actionable, based on predecessor provision, cargo seizure violating a treaty of the United States with France). Of course, the treaty in question must be one that bound the United States at the relevant time. *See* Vietnam Ass'n for Victims of Agent Orange v. Dow Chem. Co., 517 F.3d 104, 118 (2d Cir. 2008) (rejecting Vietnam War–era claims based on the 1925 Geneva Protocol in part because the United States did not ratify the Protocol until 1975, after the alleged tort had occurred). Courts have also held that in such a case the treaty must be self-executing. M.C. v. Bianchi, 782 F. Supp. 2d 127, 129 n.1 (E.D. Pa. 2011) (dicta, citing Sosa v. Alvarez-Machain, 542 U.S. 692, 734–35 (2004)); *see, e.g.,* Ruiz v. Fed. Gov't of Mexican Republic,

self-executing treaty are not exhaustive; the key point is that a treaty's provisions are not the sole basis for relief.[572]

3. Consequences of Non-Self-Execution

The core import of non-self-execution for relevant treaty provisions is that affected parts of the treaty are not judicially enforceable as such.[573] Beyond this, the consequences are unsettled. The primary question involves what the United States must do to incorporate the treaty provision. *Medellín* indicated that "[w]hether [a non-self-executing treaty] has domestic effect depends upon implementing legislation passed by Congress."[574] While that may have been true in the case at hand, it is not a sound generalization. To begin with, treaty non-self-execution does not always require *future* congressional action: nothing is required if federal legislation already suffices to implement what the treaty envisages.[575] And if preexisting federal legislation can obviate the need for future congressional action, so too might executive branch measures or state law; it stands to reason that noncongressional implementation might also satisfy any need for future measures, so long as they were sufficiently certain. If Congress in particular must act, that conclusion needs to be justified by the specific reason a treaty is regarded as non-self-executing—if the treaty itself specifies that legislative implementation is a prerequisite, or the Constitution requires congressional lawmaking[576]—or

---

No. EP-07-CV-079-PRM, 2007 WL 2978332, at *4 (W.D. Tex. Sept. 28, 2007) (U.N. Charter); Torrez v. Corr. Corp. of Am., No. CV 07-1551-PHX-SMM (JRI), 2007 WL 3046153, at *5 (D. Ariz. Oct. 16, 2007) (International Covenant on Civil and Political Rights).

[572] *See* RESTATEMENT (FOURTH) § 311 rptrs. note 5 (noting potential bases in the federal habeas statute (22 U.S.C. § 2241), the Administrative Procedure Act (5 U.S.C. § 701 et seq.), and common law).

[573] *See* RESTATEMENT (FOURTH) § 310(1); *see also* Medellín v. Texas, 552 U.S. 491, 498, 504–06 (2008).

[574] *Medellín,* 552 U.S. at 505 n.2. As the *Restatement (Fourth)* suggests, the Court's language might be explained as a product of the president's evident lack of other authority. RESTATEMENT (FOURTH) § 310 rptrs. note 13; *see infra* this chapter text accompanying notes 583–586 (discussing presidential authority). Other cases, however, contain similar dicta. *Medellín,* 552 U.S. at 525–26 (citing *Foster,* 27 U.S. at 315, Whitney v. Robertson, 124 U.S. 190, 194 (1888), and Igartua–De La Rosa v. United States, 417 F.3d 145, 150 (1st Cir. 2005) (en banc)); Doe v. Holder, 763 F.3d 251, 257 (2d Cir. 2014) (stating that "[a]s a non-self-executing treaty provision, Article 24 [of the U.N. Convention against Transnational Organized Crime] could not be enforced absent implementing legislation").

[575] RESTATEMENT (FOURTH) § 310(1) ("Even when a treaty provision is not self-executing, compliance with the provision may be achieved through judicial application of preexisting or newly enacted law, or through legislative, executive, administrative, or other action outside the courts."). As a matter of terminology, whether existing law suffices does not affect whether a treaty provision is described as "non-self-executing," as the latter inquiry focuses on the direct effect of the treaty rather than the overall legal situation in U.S. law at the time the treaty enters into force for the United States.

[576] *See infra* this chapter § IV(A)(5). The inclination to regard non-self-executing treaty provisions as invariably requiring legislative implementation (as opposed to, for example, executive branch implementation) may be a modern tendency. *See* Galbraith, *supra* note 223, at 1332–33.

because other actors simply lack sufficient authority due to broader constitutional principles.[577]

Another important question, made more vexing by *Medellín*, concerns the legal effect of the non-self-executing treaty provision itself. The Supreme Court implied at points that a non-self-executing provision lacks the status of federal law,[578] but at other points (perhaps because it was the question directly at issue) it suggested only that a non-self-executing provision could not be judicially enforced.[579] The *Restatement (Fourth)* noted the ambiguity, but favored the latter, narrower, reading.[580] Either position invites objection. If a non-self-executing treaty wholly lacks the status of federal law, that accentuates the doctrine's tension with the Supremacy Clause.[581] If, on the other hand, a non-self-executing treaty is "supreme law" but cannot be judicially enforced at all, it is harder to fathom what supremacy means, and risks undermining supremacy's essential attributes in other areas.[582] Perhaps the answer turns on the specific reason why the treaty is not self-executing, but the Court did not say so.

---

[577] *See infra* this chapter notes 583–586 (discussing implications for presidential authority); *infra* this chapter § IV(B) (discussing means of incorporating non-self-executing treaties).

[578] *Medellín*, 552 U.S. at 504 (stating that non-self-executing treaties "do not by themselves function as binding federal law"); *id.* at 505 n.2 (defining self-execution as entailing "that the treaty has automatic domestic effect as federal law upon ratification," whereas a " 'non-self-executing' treaty does not by itself give rise to domestically enforceable federal law"); *id.* at 510 (contrasting self-executing judgments that "were instead regarded as automatically enforceable domestic law" and "immediately and directly binding on state and federal courts pursuant to the Supremacy Clause"); *id.* at 516 (noting conclusion that a non-self-executing obligation "does not by itself constitute binding federal law"); *id.* at 520 (stating that "the particular treaty obligations . . . do not of their own force create domestic law"); *id.* at 522 (concluding that the ICJ's judgment "does not of its own force constitute binding federal law"); *id.* at 527 (describing a non-self-executing treaty as one without "domestic effect of its own force").

[579] *Medellín*, 552 U.S. at 504 (noting that not all international obligations "automatically constitute binding federal law enforceable in United States courts"); *id.* (asking "whether the *Avena* judgment has automatic *domestic* legal effect such that the judgment of its own force applies in state and federal courts") (emphasis in original); *id.* at 513 (whether implementation is "through direct enforcement in domestic courts"); *id.* at 519 (whether obligation is "directly enforceable as domestic law in our courts"); *id.* at 523 (whether obligation is "a rule of domestic law binding in state and federal courts"); *see also* Bond v. United States, 572 U.S. 844, 850–51 (2014) (stating that the Chemical Weapons Convention "creates obligations only for State Parties and 'does not by itself give rise to domestically enforceable federal law' absent 'implementing legislation passed by Congress' ") (quoting *Medellín*, 552 at 515 n.2).

[580] RESTATEMENT (FOURTH) § 310 rptrs. note 12 (concluding that "there is no clear reason at present to conclude that non-self-executing provisions are, as a general matter, less than supreme law"); *see id.* § 310(1) (describing self-execution as addressing whether "[a] treaty provision is directly enforceable in courts in the United States"). As the *Restatement (Fourth)* noted, the *Restatement (Third)* had—well before *Medellín*—indicated in some ambiguous comments that non-self-executing treaty provisions were not supreme law in any respect. *Id.* § 310 rptrs. note 14.

[581] Vázquez, *supra* note 381, at 648–49.

[582] *Id.* at 649–51. To say that a non-self-executing treaty provision has the force of national law, but is just directed to the political branches, is not convincing. *Id.* at 649 (conceding that "a treaty addressed to the legislature lacks virtually all of the attributes that we usually associate with a 'law' "). If it lies within Congress' discretion, as a matter of U.S. law, whether to implement a treaty, its status as law seems overly contingent.

This lack of clarity about the status of a non-self-executing treaty has implications for presidential authority. *Medellín* considered a presidential memorandum that attempted to implement the ICJ judgment, issued after more informal attempts to cajole states into compliance had failed. Medellín (but not the United States) argued that this overrode state criminal law by virtue of the president's "take care" authority: even if the relevant treaties relating to the ICJ judgment were not self-executing, the argument went, they were still federal law which the president was authorized to execute.[583] The Court described the decision of the U.S. government not to rely on the Take Care Clause as "a wise concession,"[584] explaining breezily that "the *Avena* judgment is not domestic law; accordingly, the President cannot rely on his Take Care powers here."[585] Assuming the Court's reasoning is not confined to *Medellín's* facts, its dismissal of the "take care" argument suggests that—even if a non-self-executing treaty provision somehow remains part of the supreme law of the land, despite being "not domestic law"—its diminished status cannot give the president capacity to act with the full force of federal law.[586]

The Court also rejected the U.S. government's alternative bases for asserting presidential power to override state criminal law—that the relevant treaties implicitly authorized the president to implement the ICJ decision[587] and that the president had independent constitutional authority[588]—for reasons sounding partly in federalism, and partly having to do with limits to the president's dispute-resolution authority.[589] But the Court's reasoning also suggested a surprising consequence of non-self-execution. Evaluating the implicit authorization claim, the Court emphasized again that responsibility for implementing a

---

[583] *Medellín,* 552 U.S. at 532; *see* U.S. Const. art. II, § 3 (stating that the president "shall take Care that the Laws be faithfully executed").

[584] That concession could also have been motivated by prudential considerations: it may have seemed against the U.S. government's interests to argue that the president has what might be a nondiscretionary obligation to heed non-self-executing treaties. Edward T. Swaine, *Taking Care of Treaties,* 108 Colum. L. Rev. 331, 342 (2008).

[585] *Medellín,* 552 U.S. at 532.

[586] The Court appeared to acknowledge that some kind of presidential authority would exist even if the treaty was not self-executing. *See id.* at 523 n.13 (agreeing that it was " 'difficult to believe that in the exercise of his Article II powers pursuant to a ratified treaty, the President can *never* take action that would result in setting aside state law' " (quoting *id.* at 564 (Breyer, J., dissenting))) (emphasis in original); *id.* (describing "more limited" questions being decided as to whether the president "may unilaterally create federal law . . ."); Restatement (Fourth) § 310 rptrs. note 13 (stating that, in principle, "the President may rely on appropriate constitutional authority to implement a non-self-executing treaty obligation").

[587] *Medellín,* 552 U.S. at 525–30.

[588] *Id.* at 530–32.

[589] *See* Chapter 9 § II(C) (discussing related federalism issues); *infra* this chapter text accompanying notes 864–866 (discussing presidential capacity to settle disputes, including by sole executive agreements).

non-self-executing treaty "falls to Congress," not the president,[590] adding the (largely unpersuasive) claim that this derived from the text of Article II.[591] The Court added that "the non-self-executing character of the relevant treaties not only refutes the notion that the ratifying parties vested the President with the authority to unilaterally make treaty obligations binding on domestic courts, but also implicitly prohibits him from doing so," putting the president's authority into the third (and least favorable) of Justice Jackson's *Steel Seizure* categories.[592] Assuming the president and Senate expected Article 94 of the U.N. Charter (and the other relevant treaties) to be non-self-executing, it was error to attribute to them, retroactively, the Court's particular understanding of non-self-execution—namely, that consent to the treaty was intended to divert all relevant implementing authority to Congress—as the "express or implied will of Congress."[593]

Despite all this, the Court stressed that even "the combination of a non-self-executing treaty and the lack of implementing legislation" need not necessarily preclude the president from acting to comply with the treaty. Rather, the president "cannot unilaterally execute" the obligation "by giving it domestic effect," which "constrains" the president's ability to comply with the international obligation "by unilaterally making the treaty binding on domestic courts."[594] One might then differentiate presidential compliance measures that require "internal" compliance by officials within the executive branch, rather than seeking conformity by state or local governments or private parties. But it is not clear how such measures would fare were they challenged in court, if the treaty obligations themselves are not judicially enforceable. Moreover, any such measures must still be "consistent with the Constitution," and otherwise lawful, and directions to executive branch officials may be cast into doubt if (per the Court) the meaning of non-self-execution is that congressional action is required in the first instance.[595]

---

[590] *Medellín*, 552 U.S. at 525–26. Elsewhere, though, the Court stated more carefully that a non-self-executing treaty is "one that was ratified with the understanding that it is not to have domestic effect *of its own force*," without stipulating that legislation was required. *Id.* at 527 (emphasis added).

[591] The idea was that the president's power to "make" a treaty, see U.S. CONST., art. II, § 2, provides an opportunity (evidently, the exclusive one) for "ensuring that it contains language plainly providing for domestic enforceability." *Medellín*, 552 U.S. at 526. Among other things, this presumes that treaty partners have nothing to say on the matter.

[592] *Medellín*, 552 U.S. at 527 (citing Youngstown Sheet & Tube Co. v. Sawyer, 343 U.S. 579, 637–38 (1952) (Jackson, J., concurring)).

[593] Edward T. Swaine, *The Political Economy of Youngstown*, 83 S. CAL. L. REV. 263, 329–32 (2010) (quoting *Youngstown*, 343 U.S. at 637 (Jackson, J., concurring)); Swaine, *supra* note 584, at 349–59. For further discussion of *Youngstown*, see Chapter 1 § II(B) and Chapter 8 § II(B).

[594] *Medellín*, 552 U.S. at 530; *see also id.* at 530 (stating that the president "may not rely upon a non-self-executing treaty to 'establish binding rules of decision that preempt contrary state law'") (quoting Brief for United States as Amicus Curiae at 5, *id.* (No. 04-5928)).

[595] *Medellín*, 552 U.S. at 530 ("The President may comply with the treaty's obligations by some other means, so long as they are consistent with the Constitution."); *see also Reopening the American Frontier: Exploring How the Outer Space Treaty Will Impact American Commerce and Settlement in Space: Hearing before the Subcomm. on Space, Science, and Competitiveness of the S. Comm. on*

If a treaty is not judicially enforceable and is not law that the president is charged with executing, the degree to which it enables presidential action may also be doubted.

4. Treaty-Based Inquiry

Cases like *Foster v. Nielsen* and *Medellín v. Texas*, among others, suggested that non-self-execution is treaty-based. When a treaty provision, properly interpreted, contemplates initial action of a kind inconsistent with immediate self-execution—action that normally would be taken by one or the other of the political branches—then the treaty will be regarded as non-self-executing. Ordinarily this means legislation, but that is not invariably the case; a treaty may require action by the executive branch or require implementation that in the U.S. system can only be discharged by executive branch action.[596] For example, a treaty might contemplate the United States first negotiating and ratifying another treaty, steps that can only be taken by the president.[597] Conversely, if a treaty appears to contemplate immediate implementation without any such further action, it will tend to be regarded as self-executing (although it remains subject to other reasons for non-self-execution, such as any constitutional limits).[598]

Foster illustrated right away the potential difficulty of such inquiries. Chief Justice Marshall first asked whether the treaty obligation—that land grants "shall be ratified and confirmed"—"act[s] directly on the grants, so as to give validity to those not otherwise valid," or instead "pledge[s] the faith of the United States to

---

Commerce, Science, and Transportation, 115th Cong. 26 (2017) [hereinafter *Reopening the American Frontier*], at 42 (statement of Sen. Cruz) (stating that "the Executive certainly has the authority to recognize international law obligations and to make discretionary decisions consistent with those obligations, even if a particular treaty is not self-executing," but "[w]hat the Executive cannot do is violate United States law").

[596] *See* Republic of Marshall Islands v. United States, 865 F.3d 1187, 1194 n.4 (9th Cir. 2017) (noting that "[a]lthough courts often frame this analysis as concerning future legislative steps by Congress, this approach is equally applicable to impending executive action by the President or the agencies charged with fulfilling a treaty's objectives," and citing authority); *see also infra* this chapter text accompanying notes 698–701 (describing incorporation of treaties by executive branch action).

[597] *See, e.g.,* Rodriguez v. Pan American Health Organization, 29 F.4th 706 (D.C. Cir. 2022) (noting that because the Constitution of the World Health Organization (WHO), an international agreement, called for the WHO's privileges and immunities to be defined in a separate agreement, it was non-self-executing); *Republic of Marshall Islands,* 865 F.3d at 1195 (explaining that Article VI of the Nuclear Non-Proliferation Treaty, stating that "[e]ach of the Parties to the Treaty undertakes to pursue negotiations in good faith on effective measures," was non-self-executing in part because it is "addressed to the executive, urging further steps only the executive can take—negotiation with other nations").

[598] *See, e.g., Republic of Marshall Islands,* 865 F.3d at 1194 (explaining that "[s]ome treaties reveal their self-execution by expressly calling for direct judicial enforcement," and citing Article 28 of the Warsaw Convention, which specifies the terms of an "action for damages" against air carriers); *cf. Medellín,* 522 U.S. at 508 (stating that "Article [94] is not a directive to domestic courts"); *infra* this chapter notes 614, 660 (discussing examples). In all events, constitutional limits on self-execution would remain. *See infra* this chapter § IV(A)(5).

pass acts which shall ratify and confirm them."[599] Noting that the treaty did not say that the land grants "shall be valid" or were "hereby confirmed," the Court read it as suggesting an executory obligation, one requiring a further step before it was fully realized. This reading prompted the next question: Executed by whom?[600] Under the U.S. scheme, as the Court construed the treaty's English-language version, it had to be Congress.[601]

On the Court's premises, at least, this approach was faithful both to the treaty text and to the Supremacy Clause. Some interpolation was involved. Even assuming the provision required further acts before taking domestic effect, it did not precisely require *legislative* action; rather, the treaty "addresse[d] itself to the political, not the judicial department," and fell to Congress by virtue of U.S. separation-of-powers principles. The Court did not commit to whether this was anticipated by the treaty parties. (Because the obligation in question concerned the United States only, the parties might indeed have understood a phrase like "ratified and confirmed" to mandate action by the U.S. Congress,[602] though it seems unlikely that Spain could have objected if the United States had "ratified and confirmed" the grants through executive or judicial acts if those were effective as a matter of U.S. law.) The provision was deemed non-self-executing, in any event, because the measure it contemplated was one that, in the U.S. system, had to be discharged by a political branch.

Application of *Foster's* textual approach was soon second-guessed, after the Court realized that the equally authoritative Spanish translation stated that the grants "shall *remain* ratified and confirmed," so that the treaty "operate[d] of itself" and did not require legislative implementation.[603] Still, the textualist approach survived, and was applied in *Medellín*.[604] There, Article 94 of

[599] Foster v. Neilsen, 27 U.S. (2 Pet.) 253, 314 (1829). For further discussion of *Foster*, see *supra* this chapter § IV(A)(1).

[600] *Id.*

[601] *Id.*

[602] Any such interpretation is less plausible in multilateral treaties, or even in bilateral agreements involving obligations for dualist states parties. Thus, in *Missouri v. Holland*, Justice Holmes assumed that the Migratory Bird Treaty with the United Kingdom was non-self-executing, in light of its provision that the parties "agree themselves to take, or propose to their respective appropriate law-making bodies, the necessary measures for insuring the execution of the present Convention." Convention Between the United States and Great Britain for the Protection of Migratory Birds, Gr. Brit.–U.S., art. VIII, Aug. 16, 1916, 39 Stat. 1702; *see* Missouri v. Holland, 252 U.S. 416, 431 (1920). However, that language would have been warranted by Great Britain's scheme (as well as its dependence on Canadian implementation, and by Canada's own dependence on its provinces), which casts doubt on whether it required that the treaty be non-self-executing for the United States. *See* Swaine, *supra* note 110, at 1018–26. For further discussion of *Missouri v. Holland*, see *supra* this chapter §§ I(C) and II(D)(2).

[603] United States v. Percheman, 32 U.S. (7 Pet.) 51, 88–89 (1833) (emphasis added); *see supra* this chapter text accompanying notes 386, 530.

[604] *See* Medellín v. Texas, 552 U.S. 491, 514 (2008) (noting "our obligation to interpret treaty provisions to determine whether they are self-executing," invoking *Foster* and *Percheman*). For earlier decisions, see, for example, Robertson v. Gen. Elec. Co., 32 F.2d 495, 500 (4th Cir. 1929) (explaining the text of section 308 of the Versailles Treaty, stating that "the rights of priority . . . shall be extended

the U.N. Charter stated that each member state "undertakes to comply" with ICJ judgments, rather than saying that each "shall" so undertake or the like. The Court took this to suggest future action by states through their political branches—and took the fact that Article 94 referenced enforcement through the Security Council to be trading the option of domestic judicial enforcement for international diplomacy.[605] The Court's reading of the Charter's text was questionable,[606] and it gave little real cause to think states parties would have regarded an international mechanism to be exclusive of the right to resort to domestic judicial enforcement. (It did note how that might be favored by the United States and other permanent members of the Security Council, which could veto international enforcement, leaving them vulnerable only to domestical enforcement.[607]) As a matter of U.S. constitutional law, however, the Court asserted that automatic judicial enforcement would be "particularly anomalous" in light of the assignment of foreign relations to the political branches.[608]

The potential breadth of this reasoning was striking. Medellín suggested that if a treaty establishes another recourse, even of a potentially political nature, such recourse is in tension with a conclusion that the treaty is self-executing. If the Security Council pathway for enforcing the ICJ's decision undermined claims that the obligation to abide by that decision was self-executing, then the ICJ's own availability to resolve disputes would suggest that the underlying treaty provisions (there, the Vienna Convention on Consular Relations) with which it was entrusted were *also* not self-executing—and so on, for other international

by each of the high contracting parties," as "not only us[ing] language of futurity, 'shall be extended,'" but also "provid[ing] that the extension shall be made, not by the instrument itself, but 'by each of the high contracting parties'"); Sei Fujii v. California, 242 P.2d 617, 621 (Cal. 1952) (explaining that Articles 55 and 56 of the U.N. Charter, by which member states "promote" general objectives and "pledge to take joint and separate action," contemplated "that future legislative action by the several nations would be required . . ."); *id.* at 622 (citing negotiations).

[605] U.N. Charter arts. 94(1) & 94(2); *see Medellín*, 552 U.S. at 509 (describing this "express diplomatic—that is, nonjudicial—remedy" as "itself evidence that ICJ judgments were not meant to be enforceable in domestic courts").

[606] *Medellín*, 552 U.S. at 553–54 (Breyer, J., dissenting). But *cf. id.* at 533–35 (Stevens, J., concurring in the judgment) (construing Article 94 as sufficiently ambiguous that U.S. courts should leave "the choice of whether to comply with ICJ judgments, and in what manner, 'to the political, not the judicial department'") (quoting *Foster*, 27 U.S. at 314).

[607] *Medellín*, 552 U.S. at 509–11. Only permanent members that required self-execution under their national laws would share precisely the same concerns. In any event, lower courts had previously assumed that obstacles to international dispute settlement favored finding that a treaty *was* self-executing. *See* Saipan v. U.S. Dep't of Interior, 502 F.2d 90, 97–98 (9th Cir. 1974) (citing obstacles to using Security Council as alternative forum as supporting self-execution); United States v. Noriega, 808 F. Supp. 791, 799 (S.D. Fla. 1992) (citing limitations to treaty-based protest recourse in determining that provisions of the Third Geneva Convention should be considered self-executing).

[608] *Medellín*, 552 U.S. at 511; *see also id.* at 510–11, 514–16, 517–18 (addressing constitutional considerations); *id.* at 525–27 (emphasizing assignment to Congress). The Court's reference to the "option of noncompliance," *id.* at 511, was confusing in light of its acknowledgment that the ICJ decision was binding under international law. *Id.* at 522.

mechanisms and the treaties to which they related. Nominally, the Court resisted attempts to generalize about international tribunals,[609] and stressed that the fact "that an ICJ judgment may not be automatically enforceable in domestic courts does not mean the particular underlying treaty is not."[610] But the larger point remains: contrary to the Court's reasoning, providing for international recourse, even if it deemed it to be the exclusive remedy on the international plane, does not readily imply that the parties intended to foreclose domestic options.[611]

International mechanisms factor aside, there is good reason to proceed gingerly with any treaty-based inquiry into self-execution. Treaties, particularly multilateral treaties, anticipate diverse constitutional schemes. As Justice Breyer noted in his *Medellín* dissent, states are unlikely to negotiate terms that require self-execution when that is a nonstarter for a state like the United Kingdom, which requires parliamentary implementation.[612] It also seems unlikely that states would require domestic legislation notwithstanding the possibility that the treaty could be automatically judicially enforceable under national law, as in the United States and elsewhere. Even for treaties with a limited number of potential states parties, it may be difficult to ascertain what national schemes permit or require.[613]

[609] *Compare id.* at 552–53, 569–75 (Breyer, J., dissenting) (detailing concerns about other treaty provisions involving the ICJ), *and id.* at 546 (noting precedent holding enforceable in U.S. courts decisions by international tribunals interpreting treaties) (citing Comegys v. Vasse, 26 U.S. (1 Pet.) 193, 211–12 (1828), *and* Meade v. United States, 76 U.S. (9 Wall.) 691, 725 (1870)), *with id.* at 519 (majority op.) ("We do not suggest that treaties can never afford binding domestic effect to international tribunal judgments"), *and id.* at 519–20 ("Our holding does not call into question the ordinary enforcement of foreign judgments or international arbitral agreements."), *and id.* at 533–34 (Stevens, J., concurring in the judgment) (suggesting that some other international decisions, at least, would be regarded as self-executing).

[610] *Id.* at 520–21 (majority op.); *see also id.* at 506 n.4 (bypassing question whether the Vienna Convention on Consular Relations, the treaty affording the rights that were at issue before the ICJ, was self-executing). Again, however, it may be difficult to reconcile this caution with the Court's suggestion that providing an international mechanism for resolving disputes was inconsistent with allowing domestic judicial recourse. *See, e.g.,* Safety Nat'l Cas. Corp. v. Certain Underwriters at Lloyd's, London, 587 F.3d 714, 727 (5th Cir. 2009) (noting that "*Medellín* could be read to imply that the Convention [on the Recognition and Enforcement of Foreign Arbitral Awards] in its entirety is not self-executing" (citations omitted)).

[611] Sometimes, treaties may establish remedies that *do* appear inimical to U.S. judicial enforcement. *See, e.g.,* Holmes v. Laird, 459 F.2d 1211, 1222 (D.C. Cir. 1972) (holding nonjusticiable an attempt to enforce the 1951 NATO Status-of-Forces Agreement, providing in part that "'[a]ll differences . . . relating to the interpretation or application of this Agreement shall be settled by negotiation *without recourse to any outside jurisdiction*'") (emphasis added).

[612] *Medellín,* 552 U.S. at 547–49 (Breyer, J., dissenting); *see* Ian Sinclair, Susan J. Dickson, & Graham Maciver, *National Law Treaty and Practice: United Kingdom, in* NATIONAL TREATY LAW AND PRACTICE 733 (Duncan B. Hollis, Merritt R. Blakeslee, & L. Benjamin Ederington eds., 2005) (noting that "[g]enerally speaking, in the United Kingdom . . . no treaty is self-executing . . ."); *accord* Shaheed Fatima, *The Domestic Application of International Law in British Courts, in* OXFORD HANDBOOK OF COMPARATIVE FOREIGN RELATIONS LAW, *supra* note 120, at 490–97; *cf. supra* this chapter text accompanying note 91 (noting complexity of British practice at the time of the founding).

[613] *See* Oona Hathaway, *A Comparative Foreign Relations Law Agenda, in* OXFORD HANDBOOK OF COMPARATIVE FOREIGN RELATIONS LAW, *supra* note 120, at 91–92 (noting diverse state practices); Duncan B. Hollis, *A Comparative Approach to Treaty Law and Practice, in* NATIONAL TREATY LAW

Absent such unlikely indications, it seems better to assume that treaty drafters and potential parties intend for a treaty to take effect in each party's domestic legal system by the means that system affords: for some states, treaties will be directly applicable; for others, implementation will require further steps. To the extent states have a general preference, it seems likeliest that they would want the treaty to take advantage of supremacy wherever possible, such that construing a treaty as foreclosing self-execution is relatively implausible.[614] It is therefore only an exceptional treaty, and an even more exceptional *multilateral* treaty, that will explicitly demand legislative (or executive) implementation or measures that, when translated into U.S. constitutional terms, are best understood that way.[615] Likewise, references in a treaty to adoption of national measures should not generally be taken to mean that the United States must eschew direct judicial enforcement of the treaty, let alone require congressional implementation in particular.[616]

AND PRACTICE, *supra* note 612, at 39–47 (describing diverse state practices); Yuji Iwasawa, *The Doctrine of Self-Executing Treaties in the United States, A Critical Analysis*, 26 VA. J. INT'L L. 627 (1986) (examining U.S. doctrine in light of other states).

[614] *See Medellín*, 552 U.S. at 552 (Breyer, J., dissenting) (stating that "the language [of Article 94 of the U.N. Charter] in effect tells signatory nations to make an ICJ compulsory jurisdiction judgment 'as binding as you can'"). Quite unusually, a treaty may even oblige states parties to take advantage of self-execution where available. *See* Bacardi Corp. of Am. v. Domenech, 311 U.S. 150, 159–63 (1940) (treating as self-executing the General Inter-American Convention for Trade Mark and Commercial Protection art. 35, Feb. 2, 1929, O.A.S.T.S. No. 15, which stipulated in part that its provisions "shall have the force of law in those States in which international treaties possess that character, as soon as they are ratified by their constitutional organs"). *See generally* RESTATEMENT (FOURTH) § 310 rptrs. note 7.

[615] One potential example is the Outer Space Treaty, which provides in Article VI that outer space activities of non-governmental entities "shall require authorization and continuing supervision by the appropriate State Party to the Treaty." Treaty on Principles Governing the Activities of States in the Exploration and Use of Outer Space, Including the Moon and Other Celestial Bodies, Jan. 27, 1967, 18 U.S.T. 2410, 610 U.N.T.S. 205. In post-*Medellín* hearings before Congress, it was asserted that because "[i]n the United States, Congress determines the nature of the authorization," this provision was non-self-executing. *Reopening the American Frontier*, *supra* note 595, at 28 (statement of Laura Montgomery, Ground Based Space Matters, LLC).

[616] *But see, e.g., Medellín*, 552 U.S. at 534 (Stevens, J., concurring) (citing as "unambiguous language foreclosing self-execution" a provision of the International Plant Protection Convention, providing that states parties "undertake to adopt the legislative, technical and administrative measures specified in this Convention"); United States v. Ionia Management S.A., 555 F.3d 303, 307 (2d Cir. 2009) (indicating that provision in the 1973 International Convention for the Prevention of Pollution from Ships and its 1978 Protocol (MARPOL) that parties "undertake to give effect" to their obligations meant that it was non-self-executing). References to the adoption of legislation are often better interpreted as meaning adoption of any *necessary* legislation: some states may already have in place sufficient legislation to implement the treaty, some states may simulate legislation through self-execution, and still others may be constitutionally required to adopt implementing legislation.

For example, following *Medellín*, lower courts, concluding that some provisions of the United Nations Convention against Transnational Organized Crime, Nov. 15, 2000, 2225 U.N.T.S. 209, are not self-executing, have depended overmuch on language in its Article 34 that "[e]ach State Party shall take necessary measures, including legislative and administrative measures . . . to ensure the implementation of its obligations." *See* Sanjaa v. Sessions, 863 F.3d 1161, 1167 (9th Cir. 2017); Doe v. Holder, 763 F.3d 251, 256 (2d Cir. 2014). Yet the parties appeared to have in mind that states would

Two related positions suggested by *Medellín* require caution. First, *Medellín* may have made treaty-based inquiries as to self-execution seem conventional by stressing how the treaty would have been understood by U.S. treaty-makers, much as U.S. courts might approach ordinary treaty interpretation.[617] But this is prone to conflate interpretation of what the treaty itself provides (on which U.S. treaty-makers may have valuable insight) with the import of that interpretation for self-execution within the U.S. constitutional system (on which the treaty-makers lack any privileged or decisive vantage). As *Medellín* itself stated, self-execution "is, of course, a matter for this Court to decide."[618] Treaty-makers are best viewed as an audience whose understanding should be compatible with the Court's conclusions.[619]

Second, *Medellín*'s remarks about how treaties could provide for their self-execution could be read to signal a presumption against self-execution.[620] But the Court should be taken at its word that some treaty provisions are self-executing while others are not, and that no particular language is necessary—as might have been required were a presumption at work.[621]

---

fulfill the Convention in varied ways, such that "[m]onist systems could ratify the Convention and incorporate its provisions into domestic law by official publication, while dualist systems would require implementing legislation." *See* U.N. Office on Drugs and Crime, Div. for Treaty Affairs, *Legislative Guides for the Implementation of the United Nations Convention Against Transnational Organized Crime and the Protocols Thereto*, pt. 1, at 6, ¶ 6 (2004). Non-self-execution will follow more naturally when some provisions of a treaty require enactment of additional measures and others do not. *See, e.g.,* British Caledonian Airways, Ltd. v. Bond, 665 F.2d 1153, 1160–61 (D.C. Cir. 1981) (distinguishing among provisions of the Chicago Convention on International Civil Aviation and concluding that those which "set forth rights or obligations of the contracting states and their flag carriers that require no legislation or administrative regulations to implement them" were self-executing).

[617] *E.g., Medellín*, 552 U.S. at 519 (indicating that a treaty is self-executing "when the textual provisions indicate that the President and Senate intended for the agreement to have domestic effect"); *accord id.* at 508, 521, 523; *cf. supra* this chapter § III(B) (discussing deference in treaty interpretation). *But see* Sloss, *supra* note 549, at 1723–33 (reviewing evidence concerning U.S. treaty-makers' understanding of Article 94 of the U.N. Charter in particular).

[618] *Medellín*, 522 U.S. at 519. On whether focusing on U.S. treaty-makers is compatible with the Supremacy Clause, compare Michael D. Ramsey, *A Textual Approach to Treaty Non-Self-Execution*, 2015 BYU L. REV. 1639, 1660–61; Vázquez, *Four Problems, supra* note 549, at 1770; Vázquez, *supra* note 381, at 638–41, with Curtis A. Bradley, *Self-Execution and Treaty Duality*, 2008 SUP. CT. REV. 131, 149–57.

[619] *See also* RESTATEMENT (FOURTH) § 310(2) ("Courts will evaluate whether the text and context of the provision, along with other treaty materials, are consistent with an understanding by the U.S. treatymakers that the provision would be directly enforceable in courts in the United States."); *accord id.* cmt. c & rptrs. note 4.

[620] *See, e.g., Medellín*, 552 U.S. at 513–14 (noting that because "[t]he pertinent international agreements . . . do not provide for implementation of ICJ judgments through direct enforcement in domestic courts," federal courts refrain from doing so); ESAB Grp., Inc. v. Zurich Ins. PLC, 685 F.3d 376, 387 (4th Cir. 2012) (claiming "an emerging presumption against finding treaties to be self-executing").

[621] *E.g., Medellín*, 552 U.S. at 518 (arriving at "the unremarkable proposition that some international agreements are self-executing and others are not"); *id.* at 520 (same); *id.* at 521 (denying any "require[ment] that a treaty provide for self-execution in so many talismanic words"); *see also* RESTATEMENT (FOURTH) § 310 cmt. d & rptrs. note 3 (concluding that there is no general presumption for or against self-execution).

5. Constitution-Based Inquiry

The Constitution speaks to the issue of self-execution—favorably—through the Supremacy Clause, and inferring contrary messages seems hazardous. Still, in principle, a treaty may be regarded as non-self-executing for the United States because the Constitution requires preliminary implementation based on the subject matter addressed, irrespective of what the treaty itself may indicate. Treaty-based inquiries may themselves implicate the Constitution, including in favor of non-self-execution. In a case like *Foster*, for example, the treaty's (supposed) requirement that land grants "shall be ratified" was understood to call for acts of the kind performed by Congress.[622] In other cases, even though the treaty does not itself invite reflection on whether it is immediately enforceable by the judiciary, the Constitution might impose an independent limit. More particularly, the Constitution may be understood in some instances to require that Congress, and not merely the Senate and president, act, and thus to prevent courts from deeming the treaty to be enforceable as such.[623] Non-self-execution of this type would be consistent with the Supremacy Clause because, like statutes, treaties are unenforceable if they infringe another part of the Constitution.[624]

The challenge lies in determining what such constitutional limits are. The allocation of the appropriations power to Congress, and the requirement that revenue-raising bills originate in the House of Representatives, is the example most often cited. The Constitution provides that "No Money shall be drawn from the Treasury, but in Consequence of Appropriations made by Law . . ."[625] If "by Law" is understood to require using statutes—although treaties are hardly nonlegal and, like statutes, avoid "Executive usurpations" of funding by the president[626]—then a treaty could not directly "draw[] [money] from the Treasury." On this logic, courts have suggested they would regard a treaty provision that purported to require U.S. funding as non-self-executing.[627] The same

---

[622] *See supra* this chapter text accompanying notes 599–601.

[623] The Constitution might also be deemed to require non-self-execution if the obligation involved the exercise of power reserved to the states; however, federalism-related objections have not been conceived of in this way.

[624] Marbury v. Madison, 5 U.S. (1 Cranch) 137 (1803); *see also supra* this chapter § II(D)(2).

[625] U.S. CONST. art. I, § 9, cl. 7. *See generally* Chapter 2 § III.

[626] 3 ANNALS OF CONG. 938 (1793) (Rep. Madison); *see also* 3 JOSEPH STORY, *supra* note 531, § 1342; 1 ST. GEORGE TUCKER, BLACKSTONE'S COMMENTARIES 362 (1803) (Ed.'s App., Note D).

[627] *See* Edwards v. Carter, 580 F.2d 1055, 1058–59, 1063–64 & n.22 (D.C. Cir. 1978) (distinguishing between a treaty that disposed of United States property in the Panama Canal Zone, which could be self-executing, from one involving the expenditure or transfer of money); Turner v. Am. Baptist Missionary Union, 24 F. Cas. 344, 345–46 (C.C.D. Mich. 1852) (supporting similar distinction). This is consistent with the congressional practice of enacting appropriations statutes to assist in implementing treaties. RESTATEMENT (FOURTH) § 310 rptrs. note 11; *cf.* De Lima v. Bidwell, 182 U.S. 1, 198 (1901) ("express[ing] no opinion as to whether Congress is bound to appropriate the money" in light of the fact that "Congress made prompt appropriation of the money stipulated in the treaty"). On this approach, a treaty might be regarded as self-executing for purposes functionally equivalent to an authorization statute (authorizing particular action), but not self-executing for purposes functionally equivalent to an appropriations statute (appropriating the funds for that action).

reasoning applies to any treaty provision that might be perceived to be in tension with the direction that "[a]ll Bills for raising Revenue shall originate in the House of Representatives."[628]

A far broader claim concerning constitution-based non-self-execution relies on the mere assignment of a subject to Congress, from which it has been asserted that treaty provisions touching on that subject must be treated as not self-executing.[629] This position is not always stated categorically, but its implications would be sweeping. Since many types of treaties overlap with what Congress is empowered to do under Article I of the Constitution, the approach would suggest that a wide range of treaties should be deemed non-self-executing.[630] Such an approach is difficult to reconcile with the constitutional scheme, historical practice, or judicial precedent, which instead indicate that Article I authority generally coexists peacefully with self-executing treaties irrespective of potential subject-matter overlap.[631]

In practice, the political branches have treated subject-matter assignments as requiring congressional implementation in a very few areas. Congress routinely enacts implementing legislation when a treaty requires criminal liability or

[628] U.S. CONST. art. I, § 7, cl. 1. For dicta suggesting that such treaty provisions would be non-self-executing, see Edwards, 580 F.2d at 1058; Swearingen v. United States, 565 F. Supp. 1019, 1022 (D. Colo. 1983); see also The Over the Top, 5 F.2d 838, 845 (D. Conn. 1925) (asserting non-self-execution for treaty that would "enact the fiscal or criminal law of a nation"); Rebecca M. Kysar, On the Constitutionality of Tax Treaties, 38 YALE J. INT'L L. 1 (2013) (arguing that the Origination Clause should be read to constrain self-executing tax treaties). Notably, the constitutional text does not itself address measures for raising revenue that are not "Bills." Further, at least some treaty provisions concerning tax and revenue matters have been assumed by U.S. courts to be self-executing. RESTATEMENT (FOURTH) § 310 rptrs. note 11; cf. Lidas, Inc. v. United States, No. CV–98–4503–DT(RCX), 1999 WL 164409 (C.D. Cal. Feb. 5, 1999) (holding that treaties aimed at avoiding double taxation and preventing fiscal evasion were consistent with the Origination Clause), aff'd on other grounds, 238 F.3d 1076 (9th Cir. 2001).

[629] See, e.g., Yoo, supra note 56, at 2093 (arguing that "it appears that the President and Senate cannot use the Treaty and Supremacy Clauses to exercise powers that ordinarily would fall within the scope of Congress's authority over legislation"); id. at 2094 (suggesting that "federal courts . . . could refuse to enforce, pursuant to the modern doctrine of non-self-execution, treaties that infringe on Congress's enumerated powers under Article I").

[630] See Yoo, supra note 56, at 2094 (suggesting that this approach "would render non-self-executing many of the multilateral regulatory treaties under consideration in areas such as the environment, the economy, or human rights"). Professor Yoo also suggests, in the alternative, a "soft" rule, in which courts might require that the treaty-makers "issue a clear statement if they want a treaty to be self-executing." Yoo, Treaties and Public Lawmaking, supra note 91, at 2220.

[631] See supra this chapter text accompanying notes 91–92 (assessing Professor Yoo's argument). For example, as the Restatement (Fourth) notes, congressional authority over foreign commerce is understood to coexist peacefully with numerous friendship, commerce, and navigation treaties. RESTATEMENT (FOURTH) § 310 rptrs. note 11. Such treaties have also generally been considered to be self-executing, see, e.g., McKesson Corp. v. Islamic Republic of Iran, 539 F.3d 485, 488 (D.C. Cir. 2008), and Medellín v. Texas indicated that the issue is one of their language—not some insuperable constitutional obstacle. 552 U.S. 491, 520–21 (2008); see also Edwards v. Carter, 580 F.2d 1055 (D.C. Cir. 1978) (holding the Panama Canal Treaty properly conveyed property to another nation, notwithstanding Congress' power to "dispose of and make all needful Rules and Regulations respecting the Territory or other Property belonging to the United States" under U.S. CONST. art. IV, § 3, cl. 2).

punishment.[632] This practice (and, presumably, the need for specificity in criminal law) has led courts to speculate that treaty provisions of that sort must be non-self-executing,[633] and U.S. treaty-makers generally accept that limit in practice.[634] It is also likely that a treaty seen as touching on Congress' ability to declare war, such as a treaty that commits the United States to declare war upon a state who attacks an ally, would be seen as non-self-executing. Since contemporary U.S. practice no longer involves "declaring war," and the nature of the forcible action that would require congressional authorization is contested, it is unclear which treaties of this kind should be deemed non-self-executing.[635]

With the possible exception of appropriations and revenue-raising, which have distinct warrants, courts should approach constitution-based inquiries into self-execution with a healthy skepticism.[636] There is little logical or

---

[632] *See* RESTATEMENT (FOURTH) § 310 rptrs. note 11 (citing examples but noting too that state criminal law may be relied upon to implement treaty obligations).

[633] *See, e.g.*, Hopson v. Krebs, 622 F.2d 1375, 1380 (9th Cir. 1980) ("Treaty regulations that penalize individuals . . . are generally considered" non-self-executing); United States v. Postal, 589 F.2d 862, 877 (5th Cir. 1979) (reporting that it "appears to be the case" that obligations respecting "criminal sanctions" are non-self-executing; *Over the Top*, 5 F.2d at 845 (a treaty that would "enact . . . criminal law" is non-self-executing). This has not seemed to inhibit prosecutions in military tribunals based on treaty offenses relating to the laws of war, *see* RESTATEMENT (FOURTH) § 310 rptrs. note 11 (citing *Ex parte* Quirin, 317 U.S. 1, 30 n.7, 35 (1942) and *In re* Yamashita, 327 U.S. 1, 7–8, 14–16 (1946)), nor treaty provisions that speak to the extraterritorial reach of criminal provisions, *see id.* (citing Cook v. United States, 288 U.S. 102, 120–21 (1933)).

[634] Practice does not, however, delineate the scope of this exception. *Compare* S. EXEC. REP. 111-5, at 11 (2010) (statement by Senate Committee on Foreign Relations criticizing assertion of self-execution as "substantively suspect in that it purported to rule out the use of legislation to make clear the federal government's authority to impose criminal or civil penalties for violations of the treaties, their implementing arrangements, and regulations issued to implement the treaties"), *with id.* at 86 (responses of Associate Deputy Attorney General James A. Baker) ("Although a treaty generally cannot itself establish a Federal criminal offense . . . we are not aware of any authority for the view that treaties may not exempt certain actors from, or have the practical effect of narrowing the scope of, criminal culpability under other Federal law.") (citations omitted).

[635] *Compare* RESTATEMENT (THIRD) § 111 cmt. i ("It has been commonly assumed that an international agreement cannot itself bring the United States into a state of war"), *and id.* § 111 rptrs. note 6, *with* RESTATEMENT (FOURTH) § 310 rptrs. note 11 (omitting discussion); *see also* 2 FARRAND'S RECORDS 318–19 (indicating concerns about placing authority to declare war in the hands of the president and Senate, in part to keep it separate from treaty power); Chapter 8 § I. Support is drawn from the North Atlantic Treaty, Apr. 4, 1949, arts. 5 & 11, 63 Stat. 2241, 34 U.N.T.S. 243, which provides that the "Parties agree that an armed attack against one or more of them in Europe or North America shall be considered an attack against them all," and that each of them "will assist the Party or Parties so attacked," but then provides that "[t]his Treaty shall be ratified and its provisions carried out by the parties in accordance with their respective constitutional processes." *See* RESTATEMENT (THIRD) § 111 rptrs. note 6; HENKIN, FOREIGN AFFAIRS, at 201 & n.97. This scheme was indeed understood as leaving the existing U.S. constitutional allocations of power unaltered. *See, e.g., North Atlantic Treaty: Hearings Before the S. Comm. on Foreign Relations*, 81st Cong. 80 (testimony of Secretary of State Dean Acheson). But it presumably did not speak to the United States alone.

[636] *See, e.g.*, RESTATEMENT (FOURTH) § 310 & cmt. f & rptrs. note 11 (describing category in largely contingent terms); RESTATEMENT (THIRD) § 111 rptrs. note 6 (acknowledging lack of "definitive authority"). *But cf.* David H. Moore, *Do U.S. Courts Discriminate Against Treaties?: Equivalence, Duality, and Non-Self-Execution*, 110 COLUM. L. REV. 2228, 2231 (2010) (describing opponents of non-self-execution as agreeing on a principle of constitutional preclusion but disagreeing on its components).

precedent-driven basis for distinguishing among the Article I authorities for these purposes. Practice by the political branches may reflect their assessment that implementing certain treaties requires political, rather than judicial, judgment.[637] Still, particularly if treaty-makers adopt a treaty of the same general type as has been adopted before, on terms and in a context that are otherwise consistent with self-execution, courts should require implementing legislation only if presented with a very strong, and distinctive, case for congressional exclusivity.

6. Justiciability-Based Inquiry

The most frequently relevant inquiry concerns whether a treaty provision is insufficiently precise, obligatory, or immediate to be judicially enforceable in the absence of initial implementation by the political branches. The issue is reminiscent of the political question doctrine, and likewise is concerned with constitutional limits on the judicial function.[638] It also overlaps with, but remains distinct from, other self-execution inquiries. Unlike the constitution-based inquiry (as it has been explored to date), the justiciability-based inquiry does not suppose that the Constitution has assigned implementation to ordinary congressional lawmaking; instead, it considers whether implementation is appropriate for the judiciary.[639] This takes a treaty's terms and U.S. separation-of-power rules into account, and a treaty provision might well be regarded similarly under a treaty-based inquiry. But justiciability in the sense used here may remain an issue even where a treaty provision was clearly intended by the treaty parties to be judicially enforced without need for prior implementation.

Courts have been most concerned about the specificity and determinacy of the treaty provision concerned. If they regard a provision as vague, overly general, or indeterminate in content—much as if it left "a lack of judicially discoverable and manageable standards for resolving" a treaty-based claim[640]—the provision may be considered non-self-executing.[641] On the other hand, a provision that

---

[637] For the nonjusticiability basis for non-self-execution, see the next subsection.

[638] *See, e.g.,* Republic of Marshall Islands v. United States, 865 F.3d 1187, 1192 (9th Cir. 2017) (describing non-self-execution, standing, and the political question doctrine as supporting "the same separation-of-powers principle—enforcement of this treaty provision is not committed to the judicial branch"); British Caledonian Airways, Ltd. v. Bond, 665 F.2d 1153, 1159 (D.C. Cir. 1981) (framing issue as "Non-Self-Executing Treaty Raising Political Questions"). *See generally* Chapter 4 § II(A).

[639] *See* Vázquez, *Four Problems, supra* note 549, at 1756.

[640] Baker v. Carr, 369 U.S. 186, 217 (1962) (applying political question doctrine).

[641] *See, e.g.,* Rodriguez v. Pan American Health Organization, 29 F.4th 706 (D.C. Cir. 2022) (concluding that a provision in the WHO Constitution, which called for privileges and immunities necessary for the fulfillment of the organization's objectives, "does not provide an enforceable rule-of-decision," being too general in character); Frolova v. Union of Soviet Socialist Republics, 761 F.2d 370, 373–74 (7th Cir. 1985) (holding non-self-executing provisions of the U.N. Charter that were "phrased in broad generalities..."); *cf.* Diggs v. Richardson, 555 F.2d 848, 851 (D.C. Cir. 1976) (holding non-self-executing a Security Council resolution that did not "provide specific standards" but instead one "foreign to the general experience and function of American courts"). *Compare* United States

is specific and determinate will likely pass muster, barring some other basis for non-self-execution.[642] Treaty obligations that involve determining what is best, appropriate, or feasible,[643] especially if they qualify a would-be obligation so much as to make it precatory or hortatory,[644] may be prone to entail what political question doctrine describes as "an initial policy determination of a kind clearly for nonjudicial discretion."[645] It may be difficult to distinguish a justiciability-based inquiry from other ways that a U.S. court is likely to construe a treaty in relation to self-execution, but in some circumstances it may be sounder.[646]

It is unclear whether courts apply, or should apply, the same justiciability standards as for statutory law. That seems like a plausible starting point, given the parallelism in the Supremacy Clause.[647] Courts have been more inclined to view international obligations and foreign relations matters as nonjusticiable in character, but that distinction (to the extent it still holds true) may be of limited relevance.[648] At a minimum, in any case, treaty provisions that simply extend

---

v. Noriega, 746 F. Supp. 1506, 1533 (S.D. Fla. 1990) (suggesting that invoked provisions of the U.N. Charter, O.A.S. Charter, and Hague Convention "set forth broad general principles . . . and do not by their terms speak to individual or private rights"), with United States v. Noriega, 808 F. Supp. 791, 797–99 (S.D. Fla. 1992) (indicating that, because the Third Geneva Convention differed from the "language . . . of a broad and general nature" in those treaties, its provisions would likely be deemed self-executing).

[642] Smith v. Canadian Pac. Airways, Ltd., 452 F.2d 798, 801 (2d Cir. 1971) (treating a provision of the Warsaw Convention as "absolute and mandatory" and self-executing), abrogated on other grounds by Benjamins v. British European Airways, 572 F.2d 913 (2d Cir. 1978); Commonwealth v. Hawes, 76 Ky. (13 Bush) 697, 702–03 (1878) ("When it is provided by treaty that certain acts shall not be done, or that certain limitations or restrictions shall not be disregarded or exceeded by the contracting parties, the compact does not need to be supplemented by legislative or executive action") (cited in United States v. Rauscher, 119 U.S. 407, 427–28 (1886)). See generally RESTATEMENT (FOURTH) § 310 rptrs. note 5.

[643] See, e.g., Doe v. Holder, 763 F.3d 251, 256 (2d Cir. 2014) (observing that witness-protection obligation in the U.N. Convention against Transnational Organized Crime was non-self-executing provision, in part because it "left to the [party]'s discretion to determine what measures are 'appropriate' and 'within its means,' and what protection is sufficiently 'effective,' suggesting that the provision has no immediate legal effect").

[644] See, e.g., INS v. Stevic, 467 U.S. 407, 417, 429 n.22 (1984) (describing article 34 of the Convention Relating to the Status of Refugees, July 28, 1951, 19 U.S.T. 6259, 189 U.N.T.S. 150, which provides in relevant part that "[t]he Contracting States shall as far as possible facilitate the assimilation and naturalization of refugees," as "precatory and not self-executing").

[645] Baker, 369 U.S. at 217.

[646] Much of Medellín, for example, concerned the difficult determinations that enforcing ICJ decisions under the U.N. Charter would entail, which sounded in nonjusticiability terms—and might have been more convincing than the Court's contention that the U.N. Charter actually mandated enforcement by political processes only. Medellín v. Texas, 552 U.S. 491, 504–05, 508–09 (2008).

[647] Vázquez, supra note 381, at 667 (arguing that the Supreme Court's decisions in Foster and Percheman indicate that "a treaty is judicially enforceable in the same circumstances as constitutional or statutory provisions of like content . . .").

[648] See Chapter 4 § II.

otherwise justiciable domestic prerogatives to foreigners should be presumed to be self-executing.[649]

Any comprehensive inquiry into the suitability of judicial enforcement for purposes of determining whether a treaty provision was self-executing might include, as Justice Breyer's dissent in *Medellín* suggested, not just the treaty's text and drafting history, but also its subject matter (with matters of war and peace being less justiciable, and less likely to be self-executing, than matters relating to private rights); whether it confers "specific, detailed individual rights" or provides other definite standards; whether courts would be required to create a new cause of action, particularly of a controversial nature; and perhaps other factors.[650] This would likely be difficult to administer. The *Medellín* majority cautioned that more complex assessments about non-self-execution might "'jettiso[n] relative predictability for the open-ended rough-and-tumble of factors,'" and that uncertainty might undermine U.S. involvement in future agreements.[651] Of course, if the justiciability-based inquiry expands the grounds for non-self-execution, it might also heighten tensions with the Supremacy Clause.

7. Declarations by the Treaty-Makers
For much of U.S. history—consistent with the limited profile of the self-execution question generally—the president and the Senate did not formally address self-execution during the advice-and-consent process. An increasingly common means of addressing self-execution, however, has been through declarations that are adopted by the Senate (sometimes, having been suggested by the president) when granting consent to the treaty.

Declarations that a treaty is not intended to be self-executing came into vogue with the U.S. ratification of core multilateral human rights treaties,[652] but they

---

[649] *See, e.g.*, Asakura v. City of Seattle, 265 U.S. 332, 340–41 (1924) (treaty providing that citizens of the other state "shall have" and "shall receive" certain rights).

[650] *See Medellín*, 552 U.S. at 549–51 (Breyer, J., dissenting); *see also* Saipan v. U.S. Dep't of Interior, 502 F.2d 90, 97 (9th Cir. 1974) (citing as relevant factors "the purposes of the treaty and the objectives of its creators, the existence of domestic procedures and institutions appropriate for direct implementation, the availability and feasibility of alternative enforcement methods, and the immediate and long-range social consequences of self- or non-self-execution") (internal citations omitted).

[651] *Medellín*, 552 U.S. at 514 (quoting Jerome B. Grubart, Inc. v. Great Lakes Dredge & Dock Co., 513 U.S. 527, 547 (1995)).

[652] *See, e.g.*, S. Res. of Advice and Consent to Ratification of the Convention on the Elimination of All Forms of Racial Discrimination, S. Exec. Rep. No. 107-9, 140 Cong. Rec. 14,326 (1994) (attaching declaration "[t]hat the United States declares that the provisions of the Convention are not self-executing"); S. Res. of Advice and Consent to Ratification of the International Covenant on Civil and Political Rights, S. Treaty Doc. No. 95-20, 138 Cong. Rec. 8,070 (1992) (similar, but limiting non-self-execution to Articles 1–27 of the treaty); S. Res. of Advice and Consent to Ratification of the Convention Against Torture and Other Cruel, Inhuman or Degrading Treatment or Punishment, S. Treaty Doc. No. 100-20, 136 Cong. Rec. 36,198 (1990) (similar, but limiting non-self-execution to Articles 1–16 of the treaty).

are used in other contexts as well.[653] Courts have routinely deferred to such declarations, though most stop short of calling them decisive.[654] Indeed, even while deferring, some cases have stressed that whether a treaty is self-executing is a matter for courts to decide.[655] In some cases, moreover, the declarations almost certainly reinforced what would have been a determination of non-self-execution on other grounds.[656] Such declarations are most interesting when they would change the result: that is, when they would prevent a treaty provision that otherwise would be self-executing from having domestic legal effect, including being judicially enforced.

The capacity of declarations of non-self-execution to have this kind of decisive effect is far from obvious. Certainly U.S. treaty-makers may refuse to make a treaty at all, from which some assert a lesser power of denying a treaty that is made any domestic effect. The problem is that a treaty with a declaration is not really a lesser authority than a refusal to make a treaty at all, since in the former case, the United States is still subject to an international obligation (and with a potentially compromised capacity to abide by it).[657] Nor are limits on the domestic legal effects of statutes analogous: the political branches enjoy plenary authority to enact, and temper, a constitutional statute, but the U.S. government lacks any capacity to ratify a treaty with itself.[658] Further, the argument that a

---

[653] See, e.g., S. Res. of Advice and Consent to Ratification of the Hague Convention on International Recovery of Child Support and Family Maintenance, S. Exec. Rep. No. 111-2, 156 Cong. Rec. 17,230 (2010); S. Res. of Advice and Consent to Ratification of the U.N. Convention Against Corruption, S. Exec. Rep. No. 109-18, 152 Cong. Rec. 17,143 (2006).

[654] Restatement (Fourth) § 305 rptrs. note 6; id. § 310(2) cmt. e, & rptrs. note 9. The Supreme Court has expressed its views only indirectly. Sosa v. Alvarez-Machain, 542 U.S. 692, 735 (2004) (noting that, given the U.S. declaration that the International Covenant on Civil and Political Rights (ICCPR) was non-self-executing, the treaty did not "establish the relevant and applicable rule of international law" to be applied as customary international law in U.S. court). At least one lower court, however, has given "judicial effect" to the declaration that the ICCPR was not self-executing. Renkel v. United States, 456 F.3d 640, 644 (6th Cir. 2006); see also Wang v. Ashcroft, 320 F.3d 130, 140 (2d Cir. 2003) (noting, with approval, concession that the Convention against Torture provisions are not self-executing, in light of U.S. declaration and presidential letter of transmittal).

[655] See, e.g., Renkel, 456 F.3d at 643 (quoting Frolova v. Union of Soviet Socialist Republics, 761 F.2d 370, 373 (7th Cir. 1985)); Medellín, 522 U.S. at 519 (self-execution "is, of course, a matter for this Court to decide").

[656] For example, cases have noted the Senate's declaration that provisions of the Convention against Torture are not self-executing, while also noting that its implementing legislation references the Senate's conditions in establishing regulatory authority. See, e.g., Auguste v. Ridge, 395 F.3d 123, 133–34, 141–43 (3d Cir. 2005); Castellano-Chacon v. I.N.S., 341 F.3d 533, 551 (6th Cir. 2003); Saint Fort v. Ashcroft, 329 F.3d 191, 202 (1st Cir. 2003).

[657] Indeed, treaty supremacy was supposed to resolve discontinuity between international obligations and the law of the land; avoiding that discontinuity by refraining from international obligations is a completely different approach. See Foster v. Neilson, 27 U.S. (2 Pet.) 253, 314 (1829). Compare Vázquez, supra note 381, at 675–77, with Curtis A. Bradley & Jack L. Goldsmith, Treaties, Human Rights, and Conditional Consent, 149 U. Pa. L. Rev. 399, 405–09 (2000).

[658] See also Vázquez, supra note 381, at 676 (expressing doubts as to treaty authority being analogous to statutory authority). But see Bradley & Goldsmith, supra note 657, at 447–48. The question is not whether the Senate and the president are entitled to employ conditions (like understandings, other declarations, and provisos) that are not part of an international obligation, but whether these

declaration is the functional equivalent of a reservation regarding non-self-execution, which is presumptively acceptable, is unpersuasive. Unlike a declaration, a reservation (if accepted) mitigates any contrary operation of the Supremacy Clause by changing the international obligation on which it operates;[659] if a treaty provision would otherwise be deemed self-executing, a declaration of non-self-execution dubiously purports to qualify that provision by a unilateral decision of the U.S. treaty-makers.[660] Particularly if a declaration of non-self-execution would have the effect of sustaining otherwise-superseded national law, it is uncomfortably akin to a legislative veto exercised by the Senate and president.[661]

---

modify the effect of the treaty under the Supremacy Clause. *See supra* this chapter text accompanying note 629.

[659] Concerns about declarations of non-self-execution have been likened to objections previously made to "domestic" reservations. Vázquez, *supra* note 381, at 676–85; *see supra* this chapter text accompanying notes 205–212 (discussing *Power Authority* case). But one can accept the inevitability of "domestic" conditions while differentiating among them. A *reservation* would amend the international obligation and thereby ensure that any failure to meet it could not breach international law; correspondingly, it allows other states the opportunity to object, which could defeat a reservation or prevent treaty relations altogether. In contrast, a *declaration* lacks any international efficacy; if "non-self-execution declarations are in fact part of the terms of the treaties," as some assert, it is only in the trivial sense that they are notified to other parties. Bradley & Goldsmith, *supra* note 657, at 448 (citing *Four Treaties Relating to Human Rights: Hearings before the S. Comm. on Foreign Relations*, 96th Cong. 40 (1979) (statement of Jack Goldklang, Department of Justice)); *see also* COMM. ON FOREIGN RELATIONS, INTERNATIONAL CONVENTION ON THE PREVENTION AND PUNISHMENT OF THE CRIME OF GENOCIDE, S. EXEC. REP. No. 99-2, at 16–17 (1985). In fact, the United States may decide not even to communicate to other states a declaration that a treaty is not self-executing, or may do so notwithstanding the Senate's own intentions. Vázquez, *supra* note 381, at 670 n.318; *see also* Igartúa v. United States, 654 F.3d 99, 109–10 (1st Cir. 2011) (Torruella, J., op. concerning denial of en banc consideration) ("Such declarations are, of course, not the Law of the Land; only reservations are part of the treaty and become the Law of the Land.").

[660] In at least one instance, the political branches appear to have agreed that a U.S. declaration that a treaty is not self-executing is problematic if the treaty itself obligates self-execution. The executive branch negotiated two bilateral treaties with preambles providing that "the provisions of this Treaty are self-executing in the United States." Treaty Concerning Defense Trade Cooperation, Austl.-U.S., Sept. 5, 2007, S. TREATY DOC. No. 110-10 (2007); Treaty Concerning Defense Trade Cooperation, U.K.-U.S., June 21 & 26, 2007, S. TREATY DOC. No. 110-7 (2007). Reacting to Senate concerns, the president submitted, and the Senate adopted, declarations indicating that each treaty "is not self-executing in the United States, notwithstanding the statement in the preamble to the contrary." 156 CONG. REC. 17,232-33, 17,235 (2010); *see also id.* at 17,233, 17,235 (addressing private rights). The Senate Committee on Foreign Relations explained that "[i]f the assertion of self-execution had been contained in the body of these treaties," treaty amendment would have been warranted, but because "[t]he assertion is made only in each treaty's preamble . . . such language is not legally binding on the parties." S. EXEC. REP. No. 111-5, at 11, 22, 27, 34, 41 (2010). The implication was that a declaration might not have sufficed to overcome a legal obligation of self-execution embedded in the text of the treaty. *See also* Galbraith, *supra* note 223, at 1357–58 (discussing implications for interbranch cooperation).

[661] The Supreme Court distinguished a line-item veto from a "return," or traditional veto, on grounds of its timing (after a bill becomes a law), its incompleteness (cancelling only a part of what a veto would prevent), and the Constitution's silence on such nullifying or amending authority—and the latter two objections seem relevant to a declaration that a treaty is not self-executing. Clinton v. City of New York, 524 U.S. 417, 439 (1998).

In practice, the treaty-makers will continue to employ declarations of non-self-execution—often as a prerequisite for Senate consent—and courts will continue to accept such declarations as highly instructive or conclusive. Deference may be based on a separation-of-powers logic, or perhaps the sense that the political branches are establishing a gloss on the Treaty Clause and the Supremacy Clause. Deference also avoids the quandary that could arise from deeming unenforceable a declaration of non-self-execution, were it to call into question (under U.S. law) whether the United States has entered into the treaty at all.

Some of these issues are not unique to declarations of non-self-execution. After the 2008 *Medellín* decision highlighted the importance of confronting self-execution issues before ratification, declarations by the U.S. treaty-makers that a treaty is intended to be self-executing have become more frequent.[662] These declarations may serve modest ambitions, such as negating any presumption against self-execution that might be asserted. Still, the constitutional power of the political branches to render self-executing a treaty provision that would otherwise be non-self-executing seems doubtful. Presumably such a declaration could not gainsay a treaty provision that explicitly called for initial legislative implementation, or portray as self-executing a provision that, for constitutional reasons, was nonjusticiable or required an act of Congress as a whole. More generally, treating such a declaration as decisive supposes that the treaty-makers can enact federal law when the treaty of its own accord does not, and substitutes their declaration for legislative implementation by Congress as a whole.[663] Nonetheless, as with declarations of non-self-execution, courts are likely to defer to declarations of self-execution.[664] This may be desirable as a matter of parity and to prevent undue non-self-execution. Courts would also be wary, presumably, of placing the United States in a position of being subject to international obligations that the political branches have assumed need not be separately implemented into U.S. law.

Declarations of either form pose interpretive issues. Typically, they have said simply that the treaty as a whole, or specified provisions, are "not self-executing"

---

[662] *See, e.g.,* EXTRADITION TREATIES WITH THE EUROPEAN UNION, S. EXEC. REP. NO. 110-12, at 9–10 (2008) (noting as a new development Senate Committee on Foreign Relations' inclusion of proposed declarations of self-execution, and noting that *Medellín* "has highlighted the utility of a clear statement regarding the self-executing nature of treaty provisions"); *e.g.,* S. Res. of Advice and Consent to Ratification of the Agreement on Extradition Between the United States of American and the European Union, S. EXEC. REP. NO. 110-12, 154 CONG. REC. 20,167 (2008) (providing in declaration that "[t]his Treaty is self-executing"). For a brief account of post-*Medellín* declarations, see Sloss, *supra* note 549, at 1699–1702.

[663] *See* RESTATEMENT (FOURTH) § 310 rptrs. note 9 (noting misgivings but suggesting that "it seems likely that courts will also give substantial weight to declarations of self-execution ... subject to any constitutional obstacles to self-execution").

[664] *Cf. id.* § 310 rptrs. note 9 (suggesting likelihood of deference).

(or, more recently, "self-executing").[665] This may seem straightforward, but such declarations may have meant to say something less than it would now appear. Prior to *Medellín*, which stated that even a self-executing treaty provision did not necessarily create a private right or cause of action,[666] the treaty-makers sometimes seem to have understood a declaration of non-self-execution as a way to communicate that they did not intend to enable private claims[667]—without necessarily anticipating the broader effects of non-self-execution attributed by *Medellín*, such as an implied intent to constrain executive branch implementation.[668] Accordingly, courts might appropriately construe older declarations of non-self-execution, barring any contrary indications, as narrowly addressing private enforceability, and thus as permitting enforcement by public authorities or even defensive invocation in judicial proceedings.[669] Post-*Medellín* declarations of self-execution, conversely, should probably not be presumed to create private rights.[670]

Whatever interpretation is placed on, or weight given to, declarations concerning self-execution, less weight should be given to other evidence regarding the intentions of U.S. treaty-makers. Statements or testimony by executive branch officials, or reports by the Senate Committee on Foreign Relations, are a familiar touchstone from the treaty interpretation context,[671] and they may well be cited by courts in relation to self-execution, but they may be less apt in that context. Such evidence may provide insight regarding the treaty's construction

---

[665] *See supra* this chapter note 652 (quoting declaration relating to Convention on the Elimination of All Forms of Racial Discrimination); *supra* this chapter note 662 (quoting declaration relating to Agreement on Extradition Between the United States of American and the European Union).

[666] *See infra* this chapter text accompanying notes 555–567.

[667] *See, e.g.,* S. Exec. Rep. No. 102-23, at 19 (1992) (stating, of declaration of non-self-execution, that "[t]he intent is to clarify that the [ICCPR] will not create a private cause of action in U.S. courts," and suggesting a similar objective in relation to Convention against Torture declaration).

[668] *See infra* this chapter text accompanying notes 583–595.

[669] *Sosa v. Alvarez-Machain*, 542 U.S. 692 (2004), may be read as suggesting a broader construction of the ICCPR's declaration of non-self-execution. *See* Restatement (Fourth) § 310 rptrs. note 9. However, *Sosa* was addressing whether to recognize private claims under federal common law for violations of international law. *See Sosa*, 542 U.S. at 735. Other declarations, of course, may warrant a different (and broader) interpretation, and post-*Medellín* declarations are likely to routinely require it. *See, e.g.,* S. Exec. Rep. No. 112-6, at 6 (2012) (proposing a declaration that "[t]he provisions of the Convention [on the Rights of Persons with Disabilities] are not self-executing," such that "they cannot be directly enforced by U.S. courts or give rise to individually enforceable rights in the United States"). For discussions of *Sosa* generally, see Chapter 5 §§ II(C)(2), IV(B)(1).

[670] It is notable, nonetheless, that some declarations do explicitly address private rights, posing a potential interpretive question in the event other resolutions of advice and consent do not. *See, e.g.,* S. Exec. Rep. No. 110-22, at 10–14 (2008) (providing declarations of self-execution for three protocols to the 1980 Convention on Certain Conventional Weapons, but stressing that—while domestically enforceable as federal law—the protocols do not "confer private rights enforceable in United States courts."); Senate Resolution of Advice and Consent to The Hague Convention, S. Treaty Doc. No. 106-1A, 154 Cong. Rec. 21,776 (2008) (declaration stating that, with exceptions, the Convention was self-executing, but also stating that "[t]his Convention does not confer private rights enforceable in United States courts").

[671] *See infra* this chapter §§ III(B)(1)–(2).

and bear on any treaty-based inquiry into self-execution.[672] Otherwise, however, they attempt (like a declaration) to affect the operation of federal law without being required to do so by a treaty, and (unlike a declaration) such statements are not formally approved by the Senate as a whole nor by the president in depositing an instrument of ratification.[673]

Courts should also take care before making inferences based on whether Congress has enacted treaty-related legislation. Congress may have refrained from doing so because existing law sufficed, not because it regarded a treaty provision as self-executing. Conversely, Congress may adopt new legislation to assist with treaties it considers self-executing.[674] Of course, the argument for either kind of inference may be strengthened if there is evidence regarding Congress' purpose in legislating or refraining from doing so.[675] Courts pursuing the question of the treaty-makers' intentions relating to self-execution should also consider, for more recent treaties, whether the treaty-makers failed to adopt a declaration, at least if a declaration was considered but not adopted.[676]

B. Implementation of Treaty Obligations by Other Means

Particularly for treaties that are partly or wholly non-self-executing, the United States may implement its treaty obligations through domestic law other than the treaty itself. Little if anything may be necessary, even for treaties that require effectuation through domestic law: U.S. treaty-makers may have anticipated the creation of treaty obligations and successfully negotiated the treaty so as to be

---

[672] *See, e.g., Medellín,* 552 U.S. at 510 (citing executive branch testimony during congressional hearings relating to Security Council proceedings to enforce ICJ judgments); *id.* at 513 (giving "great weight" to fact that "[t]he Executive Branch has unfailingly adhered to its view that the relevant treaties do not create domestically enforceable federal law").

[673] *See* RESTATEMENT (FOURTH) § 310 rptrs. note 9.

[674] In *Foster v. Neilson,* the Supreme Court took the adoption of legislation after conclusion of the treaty as a signal that the political branches regarded the treaty as non-self-executing. *See* 27 U.S. (2 Pet.) 253, 315 (1829). The Court's later reversal of its interpretation in *Foster* strongly suggested that the earlier reading of Congress' understanding was wrong. United States v. Percheman, 32 U.S. (7 Pet.) 51, 88–89 (1833). The *Restatement (Fourth)* also argued against such inferences, at least in reasoning from the legislative implementation of one provision to another. *See* RESTATEMENT (FOURTH) § 310 rptrs. note 8. For further discussion of *Foster, see supra* this chapter §§ IV(A)(1) and IV(A)(4).

[675] For example, the argument for an inference that the treaty is not self-executing is strong when there is compelling evidence that U.S. legislation was adopted following a diagnosis that existing law was inadequate, an understanding that courts would regard the treaty as not self-executing, and a legislative initiative designed to ensure that the United States complied with its obligation. *See, e.g.,* Cameron Septic Tank Co. v. Knoxville, 227 U.S. 39, 47–50 (1913) (Brussels Treaty of 1900).

[676] *But see* Doe v. Holder, 763 F.3d 251, 256–57 (2d Cir. 2014) (concluding that provision of the U.N. Convention against Transnational Organized Crime was not self-executing, despite failure of the Senate to adopt a declaration proposed by the Secretary of State, in light of other evidence of the treaty-makers' intentions). *Compare* S. TREATY DOC. NO. 108-16, at XVIII (2004) (letter of submittal proposing declaration), *with* S. EXEC. REP. NO. 109-4, at 8 (2005) (proposing instead declaration indicating that, in light of sufficiency of existing law, no new legislation was contemplated).

consistent with existing U.S. law, warranting only maintenance of the status quo;[677] alternatively, the U.S. treaty-makers may have ratified the treaty with reservations that harmonized the treaty obligations with existing U.S. law.[678] In addition, however, the United States may also adopt new legislation, relying on it to fulfill the treaty obligations. As previously noted, the president will avoid ratifying a treaty until any necessary legislation is in place, even at the cost of delay.[679] Whether any such measures are necessary is typically considered by the executive branch at the outset of the negotiations, possibly in consultation with the Congress.

Congress' authority to adopt legislation implementing treaties is broad.[680] Its enumerated authority under Article I is extensive, including as to matters involving interstate commerce[681] and foreign commerce;[682] notably, the

[677] See, e.g., S. TREATY DOC. No. 106-23, at XII (1997) (letter of submittal from Secretary of State Albright, indicating that existing legislation "provides sufficient authority to implement U.S. obligations under the revised [International Plant Protection Convention]").

[678] See, e.g., 151 CONG. REC. 22,643 (2005) (declarations, contained in the Senate resolution of advice and consent, providing in identical terms that "current United States law, including the laws of the States of the United States, fulfills the obligations of the Protocol for the United States [and] [a]ccordingly, the United States of America does not intend to enact new legislation to fulfill its obligations" under the U.N. Convention against Transnational Organized Crime and its protocol on trafficking in persons).

[679] See supra this chapter text accompanying note 223. For example, while drafting implementing legislation for the Environmental Protocol to the Antarctic Treaty, the executive branch discovered existing legislation that allowed it to discharge its obligation through the simpler means of issuing new regulations. Dalton, supra note 223, at 789.

[680] Extrinsic constitutional limits, like those imposed by federalism or the Bill of Rights, have already been addressed. See supra this chapter § II(D)(2).

[681] U.S. CONST. art. I, § 8, cl. 3. Admittedly, the case law has not been consistent. See United States v. Lopez, 514 U.S. 549, 552–59 (1995) (reviewing case law). Compare, e.g., Nat'l Fed'n of Indep. Bus. v. Sebelius, 567 U.S. 519 (2012) (holding that forcing individuals to participate in interstate commerce by purchasing health insurance exceeded both the Commerce Clause and the Necessary and Proper Clause, but that Congress had sufficient authority under its taxing power), with Gonzales v. Raich, 545 U.S. 1 (2005) (holding that Congress had Commerce Clause authority to regulate the intrastate manufacture and possession of marijuana).

[682] U.S. CONST. art. I, § 8, cl. 3. See generally Chapter 2 § IV. The case law regarding the Foreign Commerce Clause is less extensive, but suggests that this authority is broader than the power over interstate commerce. See, e.g., Japan Line, Ltd. v. County of Los Angeles, 441 U.S. 434, 448 & n.13 (1979); Buttfield v. Stranahan, 192 U.S. 470, 492–93 (1904) (noting "exclusive and absolute" power of Congress over foreign commerce); Scott Sullivan, The Future of the Foreign Commerce Clause, 83 FORDHAM L. REV. 1955, 1968 (2015) (discussing cases declaring power of Foreign Commerce Clause to be broader than Interstate Commerce Clause); see also Baston v. United States, 137 S. Ct. 850 (2017) (Thomas, J., dissenting from the denial of certiorari) (urging review of expansive construction by lower courts of foreign commerce authority); cf. United States v. Lara, 541 U.S. 193, 200 (2004) (describing analogous power over Indian commerce as conferring a "plenary and exclusive" power to regulate tribal matters). Professor Colangelo has distinguished between an "inward-looking" foreign commerce power entailing domestic regulation, which he characterizes as more robust in some regards than Congress' power over interstate commerce, and an "outward-looking" foreign commerce power entailing extraterritorial regulation, which is in respects weaker. Anthony J. Colangelo, The Foreign Commerce Clause, 96 VA. L. REV. 949, 953–54 (2010). Significantly, concerns regarding this latter power are partly due to Congress' limited authority to regulate commerce inside foreign nations. Id. at 954–55. When a treaty is being implemented, "the potential for sovereign interference" is ameliorated. Id. at 1013.

federal government's treaty authority has tended to be scrutinized only when the Commerce Clause is put to one side, as in *United States v. Bond*.[683] Even so, because the other enumerated authority of Congress under Article I may not perfectly correspond to the breadth of subjects of modern treaties, Article I's Necessary and Proper Clause is an important complement to the treaty power.[684] In *Missouri v. Holland*, Justice Holmes vindicated its use in implementing treaties, declaring that "[i]f the treaty is valid there can be no dispute about the validity of the statute under Article I, § 8, as a necessary and proper means to execute the powers of the Government."[685] That view has been criticized in a dissent by Justice Scalia, who would construe what is necessary and proper "for carrying into Execution . . . [the] Power . . . to make Treaties" as more narrowly allowing Congress only to adopt laws to help "make" treaties, such as by funding negotiations, but not to implement a treaty that "has been *made* and is not susceptible of any more making."[686] That critique, however, has itself been criticized,[687] and has not yet influenced case law or congressional practice.

According to prevailing law, then, Congress may implement treaties by enacting laws even if they would not otherwise fall within its enumerated Article I legislative authority.[688] Necessary and proper authority supports legislation that bears a rational relationship to the constitutional power concerned, or is " 'convenient,' " " 'useful,' " or " 'conducive' " to its " 'beneficial exercise.' "[689] Arguably, this authority is "nowhere broader and more important than in the

---

[683] *See* Bond v. United States, 572 U.S. 844, 854–55 (2014) (noting U.S. government's disavowal of Commerce Clause authority); *see supra* this chapter text accompanying notes 293–305 and Chapter 9 § II(A) (discussing *Bond v. United States*). In *Missouri v. Holland*, 252 U.S. 416 (1920), the lower courts had decided that Commerce Clause authority was wanting; whether the Supreme Court would have agreed is unclear, as it did not reopen the matter. *Id.* at 432–33; *see supra* this chapter text accompanying notes 109–114, 341–345 (discussing *Missouri v. Holland*).

[684] U.S. CONST. art. I, § 8, cl. 18 (giving Congress the power "[t]o make all Laws which shall be necessary and proper for carrying into Execution . . . all other Powers vested by this Constitution in the Government of the United States or in any Department or Officer thereof"). For pre-*Missouri v. Holland* cases applying this authority to treaties, see, for example, Keller v. United States, 213 U.S. 138, 147 (1909); Neely v. Henkel, 180 U.S. 109, 121 (1901); Prigg v. Pennsylvania, 41 U.S. (16 Pet.) 539, 619 (1842).

[685] *Holland*, 252 U.S. at 432.

[686] *Bond*, 572 U.S. at 873–76 (Scalia, J., concurring in the judgment, joined by Thomas, J.) (emphasis in original) (quoting U.S. CONST. art. I, § 8, cl. 18 & art. II, § 2, cl. 2). The analysis cites and relies heavily on Nicholas Quinn Rosenkranz, *Executing the Treaty Power*, 118 HARV. L. REV. 1867 (2005).

[687] *See, e.g.*, Swaine, *supra* note 110, at 1012–18; *see also* Jean Galbraith, *Congress's Treaty-Implementing Power in Historical Practice*, 56 WM. & MARY L. REV. 59 (2014) (addressing practice); Michael D. Ramsey, *Congress's Limited Power to Enforce Treaties*, 90 NOTRE DAME L. REV. 1539, 1540–51 (2015) (textual and structural arguments).

[688] RESTATEMENT (FOURTH) § 312(2).

[689] *See* United States v. Comstock, 560 U.S. 126, 133–34 (2010) (quoting McCulloch v. Maryland, 17 U.S. (4 Wheat.) 316, 413, 418 (1819)); *see also* Nat'l Fed'n of Indep. Bus. v. Sebelius, 567 U.S. 519, 537 (2012) ("great latitude"); Armstrong v. Exceptional Child Ctr., Inc., 575 U.S. 320, 325 (2015) ("broad discretion"); United States v. Kebodeaux, 570 U.S. 387, 394–95 (2013) (same).

realm of foreign relations."[690] Courts have noted instances in which a statutory provision closely conforms to a treaty's language or does not materially expand on it,[691] or where Congress could rationally have concluded that a federal solution is necessary,[692] or where the subject matter lies at the core of the treaty power,[693] but none of these factors has been presented as a strict precondition. Nor need Congress expressly invoke the treaty power or the Necessary and Proper Clause.[694] Legislation that goes beyond what a treaty requires, such as by exceeding a minimum standard in pursuit of a treaty's ultimate objective, is more debatable; resolution of the issue will turn as much on treaty interpretation as it does the scope of Congress' constitutional authority.[695]

Were *Missouri v. Holland* revisited, such that the Necessary and Proper clause was not available to support treaty-implementing legislation, and if Congress' other powers were found wanting, the Offences Clause might come into play. Leading commentators have suggested that this clause affords legislative authority to punish not only offenses arising under customary international law

---

[690] United States v. Belfast, 611 F.3d 783, 805 (11th Cir. 2010).

[691] *See, e.g.,* United States v. Mikhel, 889 F.3d 1003, 1024 (9th Cir. 2018) (noting that the Hostage Taking Act, 18 U.S.C. § 1203 (2018), "tracks the [International Convention Against the Taking of Hostages] language in all material respects"); United States v. Lue, 134 F.3d 79, 84 (2d Cir. 1997) (same); *see also* United States v. Bond, 681 F.3d 149, 165 (3d Cir. 2012) (stating that "the [Chemical Weapons Convention Implementation] Act is within the constitutional powers of the federal government under the Necessary and Proper Clause and the Treaty Power, unless it somehow goes beyond the [Chemical Weapons] Convention" or has "materially expanded on" it), *rev'd sub nom.,* Bond v. United States, 572 U.S. 844 (2014). Thus "identicality is not required," and "slight variances" (at least) are not impermissible. *Belfast,* 611 F.3d at 806.

[692] *See, e.g.,* United States v. Santos-Riviera, 183 F.3d 367, 373 (5th Cir. 1999) ("Congress rationally concluded that a hostage taking within our jurisdiction involving a noncitizen is sufficiently likely to involve matters implicating foreign policy or immigration concerns as to warrant a federal criminal proscription."). Thus, after the Supreme Court's decision in *Bond v. United States,* a court of appeals upheld the constitutionality of the Chemical Weapons Convention Implementation Act under the Necessary and Proper Clause, in part based on the "substantial interest" the federal government had in addressing the greater risks at issue in that case. United States v. Fries, 781 F.3d 1137, 1149 (9th Cir. 2015) (quoting *Bond,* 572 U.S. at 864).

[693] *See Bond,* 681 F.2d at 166.

[694] *See generally* EEOC v. Wyoming, 460 U.S. 226, 243–44 n.18 (1983) (citing authorities); *see, e.g.,* United States v. Georgescu, 723 F. Supp. 912, 918 (E.D.N.Y. 1989) (noting that Congress had not explained the basis for criminalizing sexual abuse aboard certain foreign aircraft outside U.S. airspace, but upholding in part on the basis of international conventions and Necessary and Proper Clause). Direct engagement, however, might increase the prospect that the judiciary will defer to congressional judgment on the proper implementation of a non-self-executing treaty.

[695] In *United States v. Belfast,* the court of appeals held that Congress' implementation of the Convention against Torture was a valid exercise of its Necessary and Proper authority. Although it emphasized the similarity of the statute to the Convention, it also emphasized that "the [Convention] created a floor, not a ceiling," and that "the arguably more expansive definition of torture adopted by the United States is that much more faithful to the [Convention]'s purpose of enhancing global efforts to combat torture." *Belfast,* 611 F.3d at 806, 809. Likewise, a court of appeals upheld a provision of the Prosecutorial Remedies and Other Tools to End the Exploitation of Children Today Act, 18 U.S.C. § 2423 (2018) (PROTECT Act) against the argument, endorsed by a district court, that it had exceeded Congress' authority by reaching noncommercial conduct, reasoning that the statute's broader prohibition closed "enforcement gaps that otherwise could have hindered" treaty objectives. United States v. Park, 938 F.3d 354, 368 (D.C. Cir. 2019).

but also offenses relating to treaties, since the latter also fall within the meaning of "Offences against the Law of Nations."[696] There have been few opportunities to test that proposition as an independent basis for treaty implementation.[697]

As emphasized earlier, legislation is not the only means of implementing a non-self-executing treaty.[698] The U.S. government frequently opts to implement such an obligation through a combination of statutory and administrative meas-ures, potentially involving the delegation of substantial authority to the executive branch.[699] Moreover, sometimes the United States opts to forgo statutory imple-mentation altogether in favor of administrative measures.[700] Courts have en-forced these measures, even when appear more restrictive than the full measure of treaty-based rights.[701]

---

[696] U.S. CONST. art I, § 8, cl. 10. Professors Cleveland and Dodge would permit legislation establishing civil or criminal penalties in "at least the following circumstances":

> (1) a treaty operates directly on individuals to prohibit the conduct; (2) a treaty requires do-mestic legislation punishing the conduct; (3) a treaty clearly proscribes the conduct, even if it does not operate directly on individuals or expressly mandate punishment; and (4) a treaty authorizes punishment of the conduct, even if it does not require it.

Sarah H. Cleveland & William S. Dodge, *Defining and Punishing Offenses Under Treaties*, 124 YALE L.J. 2202, 2264 (2015). The last of these circumstances (the inclusion of optionally proscribed con-duct) would address conduct at the margins of what the Necessary and Proper Clause may address. *See id.* at 2264–65.

[697] Case law has been mixed. *Compare* United States v. Bellaizac-Hurtado, 700 F.3d 1245 (11th Cir. 2012) (holding that the Offences Clause solely encompasses offenses under customary international law, and since drug trafficking was not prohibited by customary international law, prosecution under the Maritime Drug Law Enforcement Act (MDLEA) involving trafficking in foreign territorial waters lacked a constitutional basis), *with* United States v. Clark, 266 F. Supp. 3d 573 (D.P.R. 2017) (con-struing Offences Clause as including treaty offenses, and upholding application of MDLEA to activi-ties in international waters on the basis of treaty obligations), *and* United States v. Balbuena-Peguero, No. 16-CR-656, 2017 WL 1399696 (D.P.R. Apr. 18, 2017) (same). In other circumstances, it may be difficult to discern whether judicial references to Offences Clause authority concerns treaty violations or parallel offenses under customary international law; the availability of other constitu-tional authority also means that the Offences Clause basis is usually untested.

[698] *See supra* this chapter text accompanying notes 598, 614–616.

[699] *See, e.g.,* United States v. Ionia Mgmt. S.A., 555 F.3d 303, 307 (2d Cir. 2009) (describing the 1973 International Convention for the Prevention of Pollution from Ships and its 1978 Protocol (MARPOL) as non-self-executing treaties, which are implemented by a statute authorizing the Coast Guard to "prescribe any necessary or desired regulations to carry out the provisions"); Alaska v. Kerry, 972 F. Supp. 2d 1111, 1140–41 (D. Alaska 2013) (holding that based on U.S. ratification of MARPOL, which was non-self-executing, and related legislation, "Congress should be presumed to have intended" that once amendments to MARPOL are accepted by the Secretary of State, they "would constitute enforceable domestic law without further implementation by Congress").

[700] This kind of direct regulatory implementation was most common during the nineteenth and early twentieth centuries, in relation to treaties that involved a prosecutorial function, Indian treaties, and some immigration matters. Galbraith, *supra* note 223, at 1334–41.

[701] *See* Fok Yung Yo v. United States, 185 U.S. 296, 301–03 (1902) (holding that, where treaty with China established transit privilege "subject to such regulations by the government of the United States as may be necessary to prevent said privilege of transit from being abused," executive branch regulations were "operative without an act of Congress to carry [them] into effect"); for background, see Galbraith, *supra* note 223, at 1339–41. *But cf.* Doe v. Holder, 763 F.3d 251, 256–57 (2d Cir. 2014) (concluding that, because the relevant provision of the U.N. Convention against Transnational Organized Crime was non-self-executing, and thus required legislation, neither the courts nor the Board of Immigration Appeals could provide relief based on the Convention).

C. Hierarchical Status

To some degree, the status of U.S. treaties in relation to other sources of U.S. law is a matter of perspective. From the international law standpoint, so long as a treaty remains in force for the United States, it is superior to conflicting national law—in the sense that such law cannot detract from the obligations set forth in the treaty.[702] From the national standpoint, however, the status of treaties within U.S. law is determined by U.S. law alone.[703] By and large, U.S. courts appreciate this distinction, notwithstanding its anomalies. Just as courts can accept that a treaty binds the United States internationally but still find that the treaty is non-self-executing within U.S. law, which then may leave courts without a basis for enjoining U.S. violation, they recognize that a treaty may be displaced as a matter of national law even if that puts the United States in breach of the treaty vis-à-vis its treaty partners.[704] All the same, these tensions have influenced the nature of the rules concerning the place of treaties in the U.S. legal order.

1. Conflicts Between Treaties and the Constitution

While the Supremacy Clause does not directly address the hierarchy among the three types of "supreme Law of the Land"—the U.S. Constitution, statutes, and treaties—the Supreme Court early on established that the Constitution is "the fundamental and paramount law of the nation."[705] The Constitution's primacy has always been understood to include its priority over both statutes and treaties; of particular relevance here, any treaty conflicting with the Constitution cannot be applied as law within the United States.[706]

Because international law excuses a state from its treaty obligations based on domestic-law conflicts only under narrowly defined circumstances,[707] the primacy of constitutional obligations under U.S. law may impair U.S. compliance with treaties. U.S. treaty-makers try to reduce this risk by avoiding conflicting treaty obligations, including by using reservations.[708] Judicial techniques for

---

[702] *See* VCLT, *supra* note 13, art. 27.

[703] *See generally* Edward T. Swaine, *Treaty Conditions and Constitutions: Walls, Windows, or Doors?, in* WHITHER THE WEST?: INTERNATIONAL LAW IN EUROPE AND THE UNITED STATES 146 (Chiara Giorgetti & Guglielmo Verdirame eds., 2021) (noting tension between international and national law perspectives).

[704] *See, e.g.,* Pigeon River Improvement, Slide & Boom Co. v. Charles W. Cox, Ltd., 291 U.S. 138, 160 (1934) (noting that, although a federal statute "would control in our courts as the later expression of our municipal law, . . . the international obligation [would] remain[] unaffected").

[705] Marbury v. Madison, 5 U.S. (1 Cranch) 137, 177 (1803).

[706] *See supra* this chapter text accompanying notes 310–314.

[707] *See supra* this chapter § II(A)(4). Of particular note, the domestic provisions must concern the "competence to conclude treaties," and not other matters, such as whether the treaty violates individual liberties. VCLT, *supra* note 13, art. 46; *supra* this chapter text accompanying notes 145–146; *see* RESTATEMENT (FOURTH) § 302; *id.* § 307 rptrs. note 4.

[708] RESTATEMENT (FOURTH) § 307 cmt. d. Thus, for example, in ratifying the International Covenant on Civil and Political Rights, the United States proposed a reservation to an article

addressing tensions between the Constitution and a treaty are more limited. At least in theory, courts may consider the need to abide by a treaty obligation in assessing alleged constitutional violations. For example, compliance with a treaty obligation might be regarded as a compelling governmental interest in individual rights balancing tests, though such arguments have had limited success to date.[709]

Courts have not embraced a treaty-oriented version of the constitutional avoidance canon, according to which federal statutes are construed to avoid constitutional conflicts,[710] and it seems better on balance not to go down that road.[711] To be sure, treaties, just like statutes, are inferior to the Constitution. But bending a treaty's interpretation so as to conform to the Constitution, while solving a domestic problem, is prone to generate an international one by deviating from the understanding of the treaty accepted by other states parties. While the constitutional avoidance canon aligns with a belief that Congress would not intentionally craft a statute that departs from the U.S. Constitution, no such

---

regulating propaganda for war and hate speech, stating that the article "does not authorize or require legislation or other action by the United States that would restrict the right of free speech and association protected by the Constitution and laws of the United States." S. EXEC. REP. NO. 102-23, at 21–22 (1992), *as reprinted in* 138 CONG. REC. 8,070 (1992); *see also* S. EXEC. REP. NO. 103-29, at 33 (1994), *reprinted in* 140 CONG. REC. 14,326 (1994) (similar reservation in resolution of advice and consent to for the Convention on the Elimination of All Forms of Racial Discrimination).

[709] In *Boos v. Barry*, a First Amendment case, the Court acknowledged the United States' "vital national interest in complying with international law," and that "protecting foreign emissaries has a long history and noble purpose"—one incorporated in the Vienna Convention on Diplomatic Relations. 485 U.S. 312, 322–23 (1988). But the Court stated that "the fact that an interest is recognized in international law does not automatically render that interest 'compelling' for purposes of First Amendment analysis," and declined to decide "whether, or to what extent, . . . international law could ever require that First Amendment analysis be adjusted to accommodate the interests of foreign officials," because the statute was not narrowly tailored to serve that interest. *Id.* at 324; *see* Chapter 10 § II(A)(1); *see also* Gonzales v. O Centro Espirita Beneficente Uniao do Vegetal, 546 U.S. 418, 438 (2006) (reasoning, in relation to a statute requiring the government to show a compelling interest before limiting religious practices, that regulation of drug-derived tea by the 1971 U.N. Convention on Psychotropic Substances does not "automatically" establish a compelling interest in applying implementing legislation to related practices).

[710] But cf. CRS, TREATIES AND OTHER INTERNATIONAL AGREEMENTS, *supra* note 165, at 70–72 (suggesting that "the courts, in lieu of express declarations of unconstitutionality, evidence a proclivity merely to refuse full effectuation of specific treaty provisions that might offend constitutional requirements") (citing, *inter alia*, City of New Orleans v. United States, 10 Pet. (35 U.S.) 662 (1836), and Rocca v. Thompson, 223 U.S. 317 (1912)). In *Nat'l Res. Def. Council v. Envtl. Prot. Agency*, 464 F.3d 1, 9–10 (D.C. Cir. 2006), the court held that a critical use decision by the Meeting of the Parties of the Montreal Protocol on Substances that Deplete the Ozone Layer did not constitute "law" for purposes of domestic statutory review of EPA action, noting the desirability of avoiding nondelegation objections. *Id.* at 9. The court construed both the Clean Air Act and the Montreal Protocol as instead creating only nonbinding (political) commitments, as opposed to "judicially enforceable domestic law." *Id.* at 10; *see* Chapter 7 § III(B) (discussing decision).

[711] But see John K. Setear, *A Forest With No Trees: The Supreme Court and International Law in the 2003 Term*, 91 VA. L. REV. 579, 630 & n.196 (2005) (suggesting that "the interpretation of a treaty to avoid constitutional violation seems as prudent as does employing the constitutional avoidance doctrine").

belief can be imputed to treaty-makers of other nations, who are unlikely to have the U.S. Constitution front of mind when negotiating the treaty.[712] Moreover, although it would be difficult to correct an errant judicial construction of the Constitution designed to accommodate a treaty, it is also not easy to renegotiate a major multilateral treaty to overcome a potentially idiosyncratic reading of the treaty designed to conform it to U.S. law. For similar reasons, as explored later, courts typically do not construe treaties, or other international law, so as to avoid conflict with preexisting statutes, whereas they will avoid constructions of statutes that would violate treaties or other international law.[713]

It is better, in general, to entrust the task of reconciling treaties with the U.S. Constitution to the political branches. The U.S. treaty-makers may (and do) seek to avoid such conflicts when negotiating treaties and in deciding whether to approve U.S. participation, including through the use of conditions. If conflicts with the U.S. Constitution later manifest themselves, the political branches are also positioned to withdraw from the treaty in a manner and timing most consistent with the international obligations of the United States.

2. Conflicts Between Treaties and Statutes

As with treaties and the Constitution, the Supremacy Clause is silent concerning the hierarchical relationship between treaties and federal statutes, and the basic ground rules are more contested. Arguments persist that one form of law or the other—some say statutes, some say self-executing treaties—should be deemed superior in the event of a conflict.[714]

Case law has taken neither side. Instead, courts have favored the later arising form of law, whichever it may be, according to what is known as the "later-in-time" or "last-in-time" rule.[715] In the more robust line of precedent, courts

---

[712] The constitutional avoidance principle was derived from the principle that courts should avoid construing U.S. law in a way that would violate international law. *See* Edward J. DeBartolo Corp. v. Fla. Gulf Coast Bldg. & Constr. Trades Council, 485 U.S. 568, 575 (1988); *infra* this chapter text accompanying notes 730, 823 (discussing *Charming Betsy* principle of interpretation).

[713] *See, e.g.*, RESTATEMENT (FOURTH) § 309 rptrs. note 4 (addressing whether treaties should be interpreted so as to conform to federal statutes); *infra* this chapter text accompanying notes 729–733.

[714] *Compare, e.g.*, AKHIL REED AMAR, AMERICA'S CONSTITUTION: A BIOGRAPHY 302–07 (2005) (questioning whether treaties may ever supersede earlier-enacted statutes), *and* Vasan Kesavan, *supra* note 86 (same), *with* Louis Henkin, *Treaties in a Constitutional Democracy*, 10 MICH. J. INT'L L. 406, 425–26 (1989) (suggesting that the later-in-time rule relies on a "misconstruction of Article VI," and suggesting "an argument for the supremacy of international law and treaties in our jurisprudence, subject to the Constitution"). *But cf.* HENKIN, FOREIGN AFFAIRS, at 211 (concluding that "[a]t the end of the twentieth century, the power of Congress to enact laws that are inconsistent with U.S. treaty obligations, and the equality of treaties and statutes in U.S. domestic law, appear to be firmly established").

[715] *See, e.g.*, The Cherokee Tobacco, 78 U.S. (11 Wall.) 616, 621 (1871) ("A treaty may supersede a prior act of Congress, and an act of Congress may supersede a prior treaty."). Numerous lower-court decisions have also referred to the later-in-time rule. *See, e.g.*, Peterson v. Islamic Republic of Iran, 758 F.3d 185, 190 (2d Cir. 2014); United States v. Kelly, 676 F.3d 912, 916 (9th Cir. 2012); Fund for

have given effect to statutes that conflict with earlier-in-time treaties.[716] These cases recognized Congress' capacity to change laws, and that U.S. sovereignty requires the ability to act inconsistently with treaties, even if doing so places the United States in violation of its treaty obligations;[717] they also noted the virtues of allowing the whole Congress to resolve conflicts, and the perils of any rule that would allow courts to ignore legislative results.[718] Courts have also applied self-executing treaty provisions notwithstanding earlier statutes, but less frequently. (Indeed, only one modern Supreme Court case, *Cook v. United States*, involving Prohibition, has done so.[719]) This lower frequency could reflect more qualified enthusiasm for treaties, but U.S. treaty-makers may simply be vigilant in avoiding conflicts with existing statutes—by refraining from entering into treaties that might pose such conflicts, or by amending existing law so as to comport with the new treaty obligations.

Although the rule has been justified as a means by which courts defer to the lawmakers, the political branches also pay heed to the rule when considering applicable law. Thus, the executive branch uses the later-in-time rule to resolve

Animals, Inc. v. Kempthorne, 472 F.3d 872, 878–79 (D.C. Cir. 2006); Ntakirutimana v. Reno, 184 F.3d 419, 426 (5th Cir. 1999).

[716] *See, e.g.*, Breard v. Greene, 523 U.S. 371, 376 (1998) (per curiam, on denial of certiorari) (taking view that Antiterrorism and Effective Death Penalty Act, being later enacted, "prevents [a criminal defendant] from establishing that the violation of his Vienna Convention rights prejudiced him"); Whitney v. Robertson, 124 U.S. 190, 193–95 (1888) (applying later-enacted statute authorizing collection of duties, notwithstanding earlier treaty with Dominican Republic); Edye v. Robertson (Head Money Cases), 112 U.S. 580, 596–99 (1884) (holding that later-enacted immigration-related statute would be applied, notwithstanding alleged conflict with earlier treaties still in force). The Court appeared to hedge slightly in *Chae Chan Ping v. United States* (also known as *The Chinese Exclusion Case*), noting that there was "nothing in the treaties between China and the United States to impair the validity of the [later] act of congress"—suggesting a kind of vested sovereign right. 130 U.S. 581, 602–03 (1889). For further discussion of *The Chinese Exclusion Case*, see Chapter 1 § I(D); Chapter 8 § I(C)(1); and Chapter 10 § III(A)(1).

[717] Justice Curtis, riding circuit, provided a lengthy and influential analysis on the later-in-time rule. Taylor v. Morton, 23 F. Cas. 784 (C.C.D. Mass. 1855); *see, e.g., id.* at 786 (describing power to override treaty as a "prerogative, of which no nation can be deprived, without deeply affecting its independence," and that there was "no doubt that it belongs to congress"); for later invocations of the decision, see *Chae Chan Ping*, 130 U.S. at 602; *Whitney*, 124 U.S. at 194–95; *Head Money Cases*, 112 U.S. at 599; Restatement (Fourth) § 309 rptrs. note 2.

[718] As to the value of adding congressional input, see, for example, *Head Money Cases*, 112 U.S. at 599; *Whitney*, 124 U.S. at 194–95. As to the role of judiciary, see Botiller v. Dominguez, 130 U.S. 238, 247 (1889) (declining to assume judicial authority "for enforcing the provisions of a treaty with a foreign nation which the government of the United States, as a sovereign power, chooses to disregard").

[719] *See* Cook v. United States, 288 U.S. 102, 118–19 (1933) (holding that statute establishing U.S. maritime jurisdiction over vessel seized outside U.S. territorial waters was superseded by a 1924 treaty between the United States and Great Britain, "being later in date than the Act of 1922"). Other cases, to be sure, have made clear the equivalence of treaties to statutes when applying the later-in-time rule. *See, e.g.*, United States v. The Schooner Peggy, 5 U.S. (1 Cranch) 103, 110 (1801) (noting that "where a treaty is the law of the land, and as such affects the rights of parties litigating in court, that treaty as much binds those rights and is as much to be regarded by the court as an act of congress").

which law to follow in the event of a conflict.[720] Congress, naturally, may work around the rule,[721] but it has also specifically directed that it be followed in the event conflicts arise.[722] Whether Congress (or the treaty-makers) may delegate to the executive branch authority through administrative measures to override a treaty has not been conclusively resolved.[723]

Prosaic details can be important. Courts should apply whichever law reflects the "latest expression of the sovereign will"[724]—but when the "will" is expressed, and whether it remains effective, require careful evaluation. A statute may be effective upon enactment or at a later point; a statute is also deprived of force, eliminating any potential conflict, when it expires according to its terms or if another statute repeals it.[725] Treaties are less straightforward. The *Restatement (Fourth)* deems the United States to have expressed its will (for purposes of determining

---

[720] For example, the executive branch has long recognized the superseding power of later-in-time treaties. *See* Canadian Boundary Waters, 30 Op. Att'y. Gen. 351, 354 (1915) (concluding that statutory provision was superseded to the degree it conflicted with a later treaty, meaning that it is "the duty of the officials, whose function it is to administer the laws and regulations relating to commerce upon the Great Lakes, to fulfill . . . the requirements of the treaty and it is not necessary that the statute should be expressly repealed"); *see also* Power of the Sec'y of the Treasury Respecting Certain Fla. Claims, 5 Op. Att'y Gen. 333, 345 (1852); Copyright Convention with Gr. Brit., 6 Op. Att'y Gen. 291, 293 (1856).

[721] Courts, and Congress itself, occasionally invoked what appeared to be a moral or ethical obligation to adhere to treaties, but that was not a basis for courts to refuse enforcement of a later statute. *Cf. Chae Chan Ping*, 130 U.S. at 602–03 ("This court is not a censor of the morals of other departments of the government; it is not invested with any authority to pass judgment upon the motives of their conduct.").

[722] *See* 26 U.S.C. § 7852(d)(1) (2018) ("For purposes of determining the relationship between a provision of a treaty and any law of the United States affecting revenue, neither the treaty nor the law shall have preferential status by reason of its being a treaty or law."). Section 7852(d)(1) was intended to change the preexisting statutory provision privileging treaty rules against inadvertent statutory change in the 1954 U.S. Code. *See* S. REP. No. 100-445, at 317 & 316–28 (1988); *see also* 26 U.S.C. § 7852(d)(2) (2018) (savings clause for treaties in effect in 1954); Jamieson v. Comm'r of Internal Revenue, 95 T.C.M. (CCH) 1430 (2008).

[723] Thus the question whether the Internal Revenue Code could, and has, delegated to the Internal Revenue Service the authority to override tax treaty obligations respecting conduit financing arrangements. 26 U.S.C. § 7701(l) (2018); 26 C.F.R. § 1.881-3(a)(3)(ii)(C); *see* Timothy S. Guenther, *Tax Treaties and Overrides: The Multiple-Party Financing Dilemma*, 16 VA. TAX REV. 645, 675 (1997) (concluding that, as a matter of statutory interpretation, including by virtue of constitutional concerns, that § 7701(l) does not allow the Treasury to override treaties); Richard L. Doernberg, *Treaty Override by Administrative Regulation: The Multiparty Financing Regulations*, 2 FLA. TAX REV. 521, 550–51 (1995).

[724] Whitney v. Robertson, 124 U.S. 190, 195 (1888); *accord Chae Chan Ping*, 130 U.S. at 600; *see also* Power of the Sec'y of the Treasury Respecting Certain Fla. Claims, 5 Op. Att'y Gen. 333, 345 (1852) ("The last expression . . . of the law giving power must prevail"). Less mystically, courts are to heed "the latest expression of the will of the U.S. political branches." RESTATEMENT (FOURTH) § 309(2).

[725] The branches' "wills" are expressed, and the law generally takes effect, either when the president signs a bill into law or upon a successful vote by Congress to overrule a veto. RESTATEMENT (FOURTH) § 309 cmt. c (citing U.S. CONST. art. I, § 7); *id.* § 309 rptrs. note 5. A statute may also contain a provision delaying its effect (as might a statute repealing a prior statutory provision). If a statute delegates the authority to override a treaty, and it is exercised, the effective date of the statute, rather than that of the regulation or other executive action, should be determinative. *See* Doernberg, *supra* note 723, at 551.

whether it is last in time) when the president ratifies a treaty, but regards a treaty as entering into force (to determine whether there is any conflict at all) according to its terms, which can be much later.[726] As with statutes, a treaty may lose its capacity to pose a conflict, as when the United States has validly terminated, suspended, or withdrawn from it.[727] A treaty provision must also be self-executing in order to prevail over an earlier-in-time statute. Thus, any conflict between a non-self-executing treaty provision and a federal statute is resolved in favor of the statute, regardless of timing.[728]

Considering a later-in-time statute, as is more often the case, courts avoid some conflicts through an interpretive presumption designed to avoid conflict with treaties. As the presumption is typically formulated, courts are supposed to construe statutes to avoid treaty conflicts "where fairly possible,"[729] but that phrasing is not very instructive.[730] A different formulation is derived from the canon against implicit repeal, which requires that a later-in-time statute "clearly express" Congress' intention to override a prior treaty.[731] Neither formulation

---

[726] See RESTATEMENT (FOURTH) § 309 cmt. c (citing U.S. CONST. art. II, § 2); id. § 309 rptrs. note 5. To illustrate, the United States might manifest its will for a treaty when it deposits the instrument of ratification, making it potentially later-in-time relative to a preexisting statute; no conflict would exist, however, until that treaty acquired legal force by its own terms, which might await ratification by additional states parties or fulfillment of some other condition. See supra this chapter text accompanying note 134. It seems to follow that if the president signed a statute into law at any point after that treaty was ratified (and nothing in the statute indicated it had delayed legal effect), the statute would be later-in-time, and courts would apply that statute as law even if the previously ratified treaty assumed international legal force after the statute took effect. Cf. RESTATEMENT (FOURTH) § 309 rptrs. note 6 (suggesting related modification of Restatement (Third) approach).

[727] See RESTATEMENT (FOURTH) § 309 cmt. c & rptrs. note 5; see infra this chapter § VI.

[728] See Medellín v. Texas, 552 U.S. 491, 505–06 (2008) ("Only '[i]f the treaty contains stipulations which are self-executing, that is, require no legislation to make them operative, [will] they have the force and effect of a legislative enactment." (citations omitted)); id. at 518 (citing Cook v. United States, 288 U.S. 102, 119 (1933), for proposition that a "later-in-time self-executing treaty supersedes a federal statute if there is a conflict"); see also Whitney, 124 U.S at 194 (noting that if a treaty and a statute are inconsistent, "the one last in date will control the other, provided always the stipulation of the treaty on the subject is self-executing"); Treaties—Chinese, 21 Op. Att'y Gen. 347, 348 (1896) ("As the treaty is subsequent to the statute, and as its provisions are self-executing, I am of the opinion that it does modify the requirement of the statute . . ."). Whether a treaty is self-executing is irrelevant in applying a subsequent statute. Medellín, 552 U.S. at 509 n.5 (noting simply that "a later-in-time federal statute supersedes inconsistent treaty provisions" (citations omitted)).

[729] See RESTATEMENT (THIRD) § 114; RESTATEMENT (FOURTH) § 309(1), cmt. b & rptrs. note 1 (citing Roeder v. Islamic Republic of Iran, 646 F.3d 56, 61 (D.C. Cir. 2011), and Munoz v. Ashcroft, 339 F.3d 950, 958 (9th Cir. 2003)).

[730] The phrasing is derived from the standard used in interpreting statutes to avoid constitutional conflicts. RESTATEMENT (FOURTH) § 309 rptrs. note 1; see, e.g., Ashwander v. Tenn. Valley Auth., 297 U.S. 288, 348 (1936) (Brandeis, J., concurring). A similar principle, though put more sharply, was the rule of Murray v. Schooner Charming Betsy, 6 U.S. (2 Cranch) 64, 118 (1804), that "an act of Congress ought never to be construed to violate the law of nations if any other possible construction remains." RESTATEMENT (FOURTH) § 309, rptrs. note 1; see also id. § 406 (discussing the principle); supra this chapter text accompanying note 712 (same).

[731] See Cook v. United States, 288 U.S. 102, 120 (1933) ("A treaty will not be deemed to have been abrogated or modified by a later statute, unless such purpose on the part of Congress has been clearly expressed."); accord Trans World Airlines v. Franklin Mint Corp., 466 U.S. 243, 252 (1984) (quoting Cook); see also Weinberger v. Rossi, 456 U.S. 25, 32 (1982) (requiring "some affirmative expression

means that Congress has to expressly reference a treaty in order to abridge it as a matter of national law.[732] At the same time, there is no great clarity as to whether a statute's text must be ambiguous before it can be construed in a manner compatible with the treaty.[733]

Generally speaking, the interpretive presumption should apply to the same conflicts between statutes and treaties addressed by the later-in-time rule, with two exceptions. First, the interpretive presumption is narrower, insofar as it should not be applied when construing later-in-time treaties; attempting to harmonize the treaty with earlier U.S. law would risk conflict with the treaty interpretation generally accepted by other states parties.[734] Second, the interpretive

of congressional intent to abrogate the United States' international obligations . . ."); Washington v. Wash. State Commercial Passenger Fishing Vessel Ass'n, 443 U.S. 658, 690 (1979) (recalling that "[a]bsent explicit statutory language, we have been extremely reluctant to find congressional abrogation of treaty rights"). The analogy to the canon for statutory repeals by implication seems appropriate, insofar as self-executing treaties and statutes have equal status under the Supremacy Clause. *See, e.g.*, Epic Sys. Corp. v. Lewis, 138 S. Ct. 1612, 1624 (2018) (requiring a "heavy burden" of showing "a clearly expressed congressional intention," one that is "clear and manifest," to overcome the strong presumption against statutory repeals by implication) (internal quotations and citations omitted).

[732] In *Trans World Airlines*, the Supreme Court did remark that neither the would-be statutory repeal nor its legislative history made reference to the prior treaty, and the repeal had other objectives; it further remarked that "[l]egislative silence is not sufficient to abrogate a treaty." 466 U.S. at 252 (citing Weinberger v. Rossi, 456 U.S. 25, 32 (1982)); *cf.* United States v. Palestine Liberation Org., 695 F. Supp. 1456, 1468–69 (1988) (holding that later-in-time statute had not superseded obligations toward foreign mission under an international agreement, when the statute had not explicitly mentioned the mission or the agreement, the statute's "notwithstanding" clause mentioned "any provision of law to the contrary" but not "treaties" per se, and the legislative history failed to evidence any "clear and unequivocal intent" by members of Congress to override) (discussed further in Chapter 3 § II(B)). Still, earlier cases had suggested that courts should enforce a later-in-time statute even if Congress had accidentally abrogated a treaty. *See* Taylor v. Morton, 23 F. Cas. 784, 785 (C.C.D. Mass. 1855) ("If the act of congress, because it is the later law, must prescribe the rule by which this case is to be determined, we do not inquire whether it proceeds upon a just interpretation of the treaty, or an accurate knowledge of the facts of likeness or unlikeness of the articles, or whether it was an accidental or purposed departure from the treaty"); *accord* Chae Chan Ping v. United States, 130 U.S. 581, 602 (1889); Whitney v. Robertson, 124 U.S. 190, 195 (1888); *see also* Alvarez y Sanchez v. United States, 216 U.S. 167, 175–76 (1910) ("assum[ing]" that Congress did not intend a later statute to modify a treaty, "but, if that act were deemed inconsistent with the treaty, the act would prevail; for an act of Congress, passed after a treaty takes effect, must be respected and enforced . . .").

[733] The *Restatement (Fourth)* noted, but declined to resolve, whether there was such a threshold. RESTATEMENT (FOURTH) § 309 rptrs. note 1 (comparing Fund for Animals, Inc. v. Kempthorne, 472 F.3d 872, 878 (D.C. Cir. 2006) ("The canon applies only to ambiguous statutes . . ."), with Owner-Operator Indep. Drivers Ass'n v. U.S. Dep't of Transp., 724 F.3d 230, 234 (D.C. Cir. 2013) ("[A]bsent some clear and overt indication from Congress, we will not construe a statute to abrogate existing international agreements even when the statute's text is not itself ambiguous.")).

[734] *See* RESTATEMENT (FOURTH) § 309 rptrs. note 4. Nevertheless, some decisions have applied the presumption against repeals by implication when construing treaties, much as they would in relating a later statute to an earlier one. *See, e.g.*, Johnson v. Browne, 205 U.S. 309, 321 (1907) (stating that "a later treaty will not be regarded as repealing an earlier statute by implication unless the two are absolutely incompatible and the statute cannot be enforced without antagonizing the treaty"); United States v. Lee Yen Tai, 185 U.S. 213, 222 (1902) ("Like principles must control when the question is whether an act of Congress has been superseded in whole or in part by a subsequent treaty"); Whitney v. Robertson, 124 U.S. 190, 194 (1888) ("When [a statute and a treaty] relate to the same subject, the courts will always endeavor to construe them so as to give effect to both, if that can be

presumption has in another sense broader application, as it should be applied in interpreting later statutes that conflict with existing self-executing *or* non-self-executing treaties alike. In either case, Congress is assumed to be reluctant to legislate so as to violate an international obligation. Whether the earlier treaty provision automatically established judicially enforceable national law should not be relevant.[735]

3. Conflicts Between Treaties and Other International Law

Conflicts among treaties or between treaties and other forms of international law rarely arise in U.S. court.[736] Under international law, when two treaties conflict and certain conditions are met (for example, that the relevant states are parties to both treaties), then the later-in-time treaty controls.[737] This *lex posterior derogat legi priori* rule may be qualified if treaties establish their own conflicts rules.[738] Although the *lex posterior* rule also applies as a matter of U.S. foreign relations law,[739] non-self-execution may add other complications. While a later-in-time treaty may be superior to an earlier treaty according to international law, the later treaty may nevertheless lack enforceability in U.S. courts if it is non-self-executing; if the earlier-in-time treaty were, by contrast, self-executing, a court might deem it to retain the force of law, though it should not do so if it is properly deemed to have been terminated under international law. Courts have added other glosses as to how to interpret and reconcile conflicting treaty provisions.[740]

---

done without violating the language of either"); Canadian Boundary Waters, 30 Op. Att'y Gen. 351, 354 (1915) (citing *Johnson v. Browne*, and presumption against repeal by implication, in relation to conflict posed by later-in-time treaty).

[735] Chew Heong v. United States, 112 U.S. 536, 539 (1884) ("[T]he court should be slow to assume that congress intended to violate the stipulations of a treaty"); *see* RESTATEMENT (FOURTH) § 309 rptrs. note 1 (citing Ma v. Ashcroft, 257 F.3d 1095, 1114 (9th Cir. 2001) (applying the principle to avoid contravention of the International Covenant on Civil and Political Rights, which was ratified with a declaration that it was not self-executing)). *But see Trans World Airlines*, 466 U.S. at 252 (emphasizing, in applying implicit repeal approach, that the Warsaw Convention "is a self-executing treaty").

[736] Probably the most extensive experience involves superseding treaties between the United States and Indian tribes. *Cf.* RESTATEMENT OF THE LAW: THE LAW OF AM. INDIANS, PROPOSED FINAL DRAFT, *supra* note 129, § 5(c) (noting that such treaties could be abrogated if "the treaty signatories agree to amend the treaty").

[737] *See generally* VCLT, *supra* note 13, art. 30; AUST, *supra* note 229, at 192–204.

[738] VCLT, *supra* note 13, art. 30(2); *Fragmentation of International Law: Difficulties Arising from the Diversification and Expansion of International Law: Conclusions of the work of the Study Group*, U.N. Doc. A/61/10 (2006), *reprinted in* [2006] 2 Y.B. Int'l L. Comm'n, pt. 2, at 181–82, U.N. Doc. A/CN.4/ SER.A/2006/Add.1 (Part 2).

[739] *See, e.g.*, Iwanowa v. Ford Motor Co., 67 F. Supp. 2d 424, 459 (D.N.J. 1999) ("[I]f there is an irreconcilable conflict between a subsequent treaty and a prior treaty between the same nations, relating to the same subject matter, the new treaty is controlling and must be deemed to abrogate the prior inconsistent treaty or provision therein.").

[740] *See, e.g.*, Fotochrome, Inc. v. Copal Co., Ltd., 517 F.2d 512, 518 n.4 (2d Cir. 1975) (regarding multilateral convention as controlling notwithstanding earlier bilateral treaty, and notwithstanding later convention's savings clause preserving bilateral agreements, because "inasmuch as both

The relationship between treaties and conflicting customary international law as a matter of U.S. law is more speculative. If a treaty provision is self-executing, courts are likely to apply it even if it conflicts with a later-developing rule of customary international law. If a treaty provision is not self-executing, the relative priority courts give as between it and a rule of customary international law will likely depend, among other things, on whether the political branches have taken steps to incorporate either obligation into U.S. law.[741]

As considered later in this chapter, the relationship between self-executing treaties and congressional-executive agreements is likely governed by a later-in-time rule.[742] The capacity of a later-in-time sole executive agreement to override a prior self-executing treaty provision is considerably more doubtful. Like other international agreements, the domestic enforceability of a sole executive agreement should not be affected by conflicting non-self-executing treaty provisions, but—as discussed later—that leaves the question whether the executive agreement itself has the status of federal law.[743]

4. Conflicts Between Treaties and State and Local Law

The Supremacy Clause establishes both that state courts are bound to apply treaties and that treaties supersede conflicting state law.[744] These principles were an essential objective of the Constitution, given genuine concerns that the states were frustrating the performance of international obligations and risking reprisals against the United States.[745]

As case law has developed, certain complications have emerged. One complication, predictably, concerns non-self-executing treaties. Early decisions were emphatic on the force of the supremacy of treaties vis-à-vis state law. In *Ware v. Hylton*, for example, the Supreme Court held that a provision of the 1783 Treaty of Paris respecting debts owed British creditors should be applied in lieu of a conflicting Virginia law, with one justice stating that under the U.S. Constitution, "every treaty made, by the authority of the United States, shall be superior to

---

agreements further the same purpose, the one tending to further that purpose most forcefully, the Convention, should be given effect"); Sayne v. Shipley, 418 F.2d 679, 683–84 (5th Cir. 1969) (treating earlier bilateral agreement as not superseded by later one, given differing degrees of generality, savings clause in later agreement, and view of the Department of State that the relevant provision in the earlier treaty was still in effect).

[741] *See supra* this chapter § IV(B).
[742] *See infra* this chapter text accompanying note 792.
[743] *See infra* this chapter text accompanying note 853.
[744] U.S. CONST. art. VI, cl. 2; RESTATEMENT (FOURTH) § 310 & cmt. a; Chapter 9 § II(B). The same principles apply to municipal and other non-federal law, for which "state law" is a conventional shorthand.
[745] *See supra* this chapter § I.

the Constitution and laws of any individual State."[746] Even after *Foster v. Nielsen*, the Supreme Court was quick to apply treaty provisions in lieu of state law,[747] leaving some to think the Court understood the issue of non-self-execution differently in those days.[748] Yet the doctrine of non-self-executing treaties, as it now exists, has surely complicated matters. Nowadays, a threshold question for courts assessing whether a treaty provision prevails over state law is whether the provision is self-executing. If a treaty provision conflicts with state law, but the treaty provision is non-self-executing, courts will treat the state law as though it is not preempted.[749] Instead, preemption will depend on any federal law implementing the treaty;[750] absent preemption, state courts may also apply state-law principles in seeking to reconcile other state and local law with treaty obligations.[751] If a treaty provision is self-executing, however, it will be applied by federal and state courts, and prevail in any conflict with state law, regardless of whether it is later in time.[752]

---

[746] Ware v. Hylton, 3 U.S. (3 Dall.) 199, 237 (1796) (Chase, J.); *see id.* at 285 (opinion of the Court); *supra* this chapter text accompanying notes 57, 521–524 (providing additional background); *see also* RESTATEMENT (FOURTH) § 308 rptrs. note 1 (citing additional early case law).

[747] *See, e.g.*, Asakura v. City of Seattle, 265 U.S. 332, 341 (1924) (describing treaty as "binding within the State of Washington," such that its rule "cannot be rendered nugatory in any part of the United States by municipal ordinances or State laws," because "[i]t operates of itself without the aid of any legislation, state or national," such that "it will be applied and given authoritative effect by the courts"); *see* RESTATEMENT (FOURTH) § 308 cmt. b & rptrs. note 1 (noting routine application of treaties rather than conflicting state law); *supra* this chapter text accompanying notes 532–534 (same).

[748] *See supra* this chapter text accompanying notes 530–534. For example, Professor Sloss has argued that the Supreme Court long understood non-self-execution of treaties as a separation-of-powers question, not as one relating to supremacy. *See, e.g.*, SLOSS, *supra* note 118, at 7.

[749] *See* RESTATEMENT (FOURTH) § 308 rptrs. note 3 (stating that "non-self-executing treaty provisions are not themselves directly judicially enforceable" so as to preempt state law). The *Restatement (Third)* was less categorical. RESTATEMENT (THIRD) §115 cmt. e ("Even a non-self-executing agreement of the United States, not effective as law until implemented by legislative or executive action, may sometimes be held to be federal policy superseding State law or policy."). After *Medellín*, it was clear that—at least insofar as judicial enforceability was concerned—the capacity of non-self-executing treaty provisions to supersede state law was limited. *See, e.g.*, Medellín v. Texas, 552 U.S. 491, 522-23 (2008) (concluding that "while the ICJ's judgment in *Avena* creates an international law obligation on the part of the United States, it does not of its own force constitute binding federal law that pre-empts state restrictions on the filing of successive habeas petitions."). It is less clear whether other actors, in other settings, may treat the state law as preempted. *See supra* this chapter text accompanying note 336.

[750] RESTATEMENT (THIRD) § 111 cmt. h (explaining that, if a treaty provision is non-self-executing, "it is the implementing legislation, rather than the agreement itself, that is given effect as law in the United States"); Safety Nat'l Cas. Corp. v. Certain Underwriters at Lloyd's, London, 587 F.3d 714, 739–42 (5th Cir. 2009) (en banc) (Elrod, J., dissenting) (discussing implications, in a reverse preemption case); *cf.* RESTATEMENT (FOURTH) § 310(1) (implying that legislative implementation of non-self-executing treaty provisions would resolve the enforceability of treaties).

[751] RESTATEMENT (FOURTH) § 308 rptrs. note 3 (citing cases); *see also* Commonwealth v. Fernandes, 148 N.E.3d 361, 377–80 (Mass. 2020) (holding that, while Massachusetts law indicated that individual rights were conferred by the Vienna Convention on Consular Rights, their violation did not warrant a new trial).

[752] RESTATEMENT (FOURTH) § 308 (stating that "when there is a conflict between State or local law and a self-executing treaty provision, courts in the United States will apply the treaty provision"); *id.*

A second complication involves how preemption doctrine, which was developed principally in cases involving federal statutes, applies to preemption of state law by treaty.[753] As explored more extensively in Chapter 9, statutory cases describe several different types of preemption, though the categories are not precise or wholly distinct.[754] Treaty cases have typically considered "direct" conflicts between a treaty and state law, in which it is impossible to comply with both.[755] State law may also pose a conflict when it "stands as an obstacle to the accomplishment and execution of the full purposes and objectives of Congress."[756] One leading decision—*American Insurance Association v. Garamendi*—held that California law was preempted because it posed an obstacle to the policy evidenced by a sole executive agreement;[757] the Supreme Court presumably would have reached a similar decision were a treaty involved. Cases in which a treaty expressly preempts state law are less common.[758] Likewise, treaty-related cases where the federal government has "occupied the field" are uncommon, save to the extent that treaties are subsumed within the broader doctrine of dormant foreign relations power preemption.[759]

Statutory preemption case law should be borrowed only with considerable care. Such cases are likely to inquire into matters like the nature of Congress' enumerated authority and the framework of federal regulation,[760] features less apposite to preemption by treaty, which generally involves more piecemeal regulation via Article II. Uncertainty in statutory cases is more easily resolved, furthermore,

cmt. b ("When there is a conflict between a State or local law and a self-executing treaty provision, the State or local law is displaced, and courts are obligated to apply the treaty provision.").

[753] *See, e.g., In re* World War II Era Japanese Forced Labor Litig., 164 F. Supp. 2d 1160, 1166–67 (N.D. Cal. 2001) (explaining that "[a]lthough the Supreme Court has written extensively about when congressional acts have preemptive effect . . . it has provided little guidance on the preemptive effect of treaties," and "has not established a similar detailed framework for courts to utilize when analyzing preemption by treaties") (citations omitted).
[754] *See* Chapter 9 § II(A); *e.g.,* Crosby v. Nat'l Foreign Trade Council, 530 U.S. 363, 372 & n.6 (2000).
[755] *Compare, e.g.,* Volkswagenwerk Aktiengesellschaft v. Schlunk, 486 U.S. 694, 699 (1988) (noting that mandatory provision in the Hague Service Convention "pre-empts inconsistent methods of service prescribed by state law in all cases to which it applies"), *with* Ventress v. Japan Airlines, 486 F. 3d 1111, 1115 (9th Cir. 2007) (reversing district court holding that provision in U.S.-Japan Friendship, Commerce, and Navigation Treaty, permitting Japanese employers to engage specialists "of their choice," conflicted with and preempted California employment law).
[756] Hines v. Davidowitz, 312 U.S. 52, 67 (1941); *see* Crosby, 530 U.S. at 372.
[757] Am. Ins. Ass'n v. Garamendi, 539 U.S. 396, 421–27 (2003); *see infra* this chapter text accompanying note 853 (discussing supremacy of executive agreements).
[758] *See Garamendi,* 539 U.S. at 416–17 (stating that if an executive agreement, or treaty, "expressly preempted" the state law in question, it would be preempted, but noting absence of preemption clause); El Al Isr. Airlines v. Tseng, 525 U.S. 155, 167–76 (1999) (Warsaw Convention precluded damages action under New York tort law).
[759] *See* Chapter 9 § II(B). The *Restatement (Third)* suggested "in principle" the possibility of field preemption for treaties, but allowed that "the matter has apparently not been adjudicated." RESTATEMENT (THIRD) § 115 cmt. e; *accord id.* § 1 rptrs. note 5.
[760] *See, e.g.,* Arizona v. United States, 567 U.S. 387, 394–415 (2012).

by a presumption that federal statutes are not intended to preempt state law, which (as explored in Chapter 9) may not apply at all in the foreign relations context, let alone in treaty cases.[761]

At a minimum, applying preemption principles to treaties requires sensitivity to the principles explored elsewhere in this chapter. The increased recognition of non-self-executing treaties may be consistent with avoiding "cavalier" assumptions that treaties preempt state law,[762] but by the same token, applying a presumption against preemption to treaty provisions that *are* established as self-executing seems odd and akin to a second bite of the apple. Applying a presumption against preemption to treaties would also be distinctly difficult to overcome. Satisfying the statutory presumption against preemption can require showing that preemption was "the clear and manifest purpose of Congress,"[763] whereas it is unlikely that other states parties involved in drafting treaty provisions would exhibit any purpose directly related to the allocation of authority within the United States. U.S. treaty-makers would likely only be able to meet that standard by imposing conditions when ratifying the treaty or, more definitively, by enacting legislation—steps that were supposed to be unnecessary for self-executing treaty provisions. While federalism-related concerns warrant due consideration when considering treaty preemption, the distinct risks of noncompliance with the treaty obligations and the distinct difficulties in counteracting any presumption against preemption counsel against applying one in this context.[764]

V. Agreements Other than Article II Treaties

The Constitution only details one means by which the United States can enter into international agreements, which is the making of "Treaties" under Article II by the president with the advice and consent of the Senate. Other kinds of agreements are mentioned, but only in terms of what *states* may or may not do; states may enter into "agreements" or "compacts" with congressional consent, while they are foreclosed altogether from entering into "treaties," "alliances,"

---

[761] *See* Chapter 9 §§ II(A)–(B).

[762] *Cf.* Wyeth v. Levine, 555 U.S. 555, 565 n.3 (2009) (explaining presumption against preemption as being based on the notion that because states are "independent sovereigns in our federal system," Congress "does not cavalierly pre-empt" state law) (quoting Medtronic, Inc. v. Lohr, 518 U.S. 470, 485 (1996)).

[763] *Wyeth*, 555 U.S. at 565 (internal quotations and citations omitted). The Court has held that this need not depend on statutory text where its interpretation poses particular difficulties, see De Buono v. NYSA-ILA Med. and Clinical Servs. Fund, 520 U.S. 806, 813–14 (1997) (explaining approach in ERISA cases), which might be advisable in the treaty context.

[764] For further discussion of preemption-related issues, see Chapter 9 §§ II(B)–(C).

or "confederations"[765] Whether this implies that the *federal government*, with its predominant role in U.S. foreign relations (and supervisory role regarding agreements and compacts), should likewise be entitled to enter into similar non-"treaty" agreements, or rather lacks such authority because it is omitted, is unclear. So too are the substantive differences among these types of agreements, and whether (if available to the federal government) they necessarily imply a process for making those agreements different from that described by Article II. The Supreme Court has said that it cannot recover what distinguishes the various types of agreements from one another, let alone what they might mean for federal authority.[766]

Nonetheless, the distinctions drawn by the Constitution remain with us to some degree; for example, they figured in the debates over U.S. entry into the 1994 NAFTA.[767] Still with us, too, are murky claims about whether the Constitution conferred on the federal government a capacity to conclude agreements simply as an inherent attribute of nationhood.[768] Many, however, treat the relevant issues—regarding the scope and consequences of the federal government's authority to enter into international agreements by means other than an Article II treaty—as best addressed by subsequent practice. As that practice has developed, the terms the Constitution uses to characterize non–Article II agreements, such

---

[765] *Compare* U.S. CONST. art. I, § 10, cl. 3 ("No State shall, without the consent of Congress... enter into any Agreement or Compact with another State, or with a foreign Power"), *with id.* art. I, § 10, cl. 1 (prohibiting states from entering into any treaty, alliance, or confederation).

[766] *See, e.g.*, United States Steel Corp. v. Multistate Tax Comm'n, 434 U.S. 452, 460–63 (1978) (stating that while "[t]he Framers clearly perceived compacts and agreements as differing from treaties," and that the various terms each had "precise meanings," these distinctions "were soon lost"); *cf.* Virginia v. Tennessee, 148 U.S. 503, 520 (1893) (suggesting that "we do not perceive any difference in the meaning" of compact or agreement," save that " 'compact' is generally used with reference to more formal and serious engagements than is usually implied in the term 'agreement' "). *See generally* Chapter 9 § III.

[767] North American Free Trade Agreement Implementation Act, Pub. L. No. 103-182, 107 Stat. 2057 (1993) (codified as amended in scattered sections of 19 U.S.C.). As to whether the constrained state-related authority regarding non-treaty agreements implied national authority (or its lack), see Ackerman & Golove, *supra* note 108, at 921 n.514; David M. Golove, *Against Free-Form Formalism*, 73 N.Y.U. L. REV. 1791, 1917 n.378 (1998). Some in the NAFTA debate took the Compact Clause to indicate that congressional authority was limited to matters other than "treaties." *See* Laurence H. Tribe, *Taking Text and Structure Seriously: Reflections on Free-Form Method in Constitutional Interpretation*, 108 HARV. L. REV. 1221, 1270–72 (1995). Others considered whether the Constitution's terminology defined mutually exclusive or even consistent categories—with "treaties" being a general term and "agreements" or "compacts" a subset of arrangements that were permitted states, and "treaty" being used less restrictively in the Article II context. *See* Golove, *supra*, at 1909–17; *see also* Whether Uruguay Round Agreements Required Ratification as a Treaty, 18 Op. O.L.C. 232 (1994); MICHAEL D. RAMSEY, THE CONSTITUTION'S TEXT IN FOREIGN AFFAIRS 179–80, 192–93 (2007); Bradford R. Clark, *Domesticating Sole Executive Agreements*, 93 VA. L. REV. 1573 (2007).

[768] United States v. Curtiss-Wright Exp. Corp., 299 U.S. 304, 318 (1936) (noting "the power to make such international agreements as do not constitute treaties in the constitutional sense" is "inherently inseparable from the conception of nationality") (citations omitted). For further discussion, see Chapter 1 §§ I(D), II(A)(2).

as "alliances" or "confederations," are not much in use; instead, the focus is on whether and how they have earned legislative endorsement.

Three types of non–Article II agreements seem to have emerged.[769] First, "congressional-executive agreements" are negotiated and concluded by the executive branch, much as with an Article II treaty. However, instead of receiving consent by a two-thirds vote in the Senate, congressional-executive agreements depend either on prior (*ex ante*) or subsequent (*ex post*) approval by both houses of Congress through simple majority votes. *Ex ante* congressional-executive agreements occur when Congress adopts a statute that allows the president to conclude future agreements with foreign states that fall within the statute's parameters, such as with agreements on the export of nuclear material.[770] The NAFTA was a good example of an *ex post* congressional-executive agreement, in that the president negotiated the NAFTA with Canada and Mexico, then submitted the agreement to both houses of Congress, which then approved it by majority vote in both houses.

Second, "treaty-implementing" agreements are concluded solely by the president based on the existence of a treaty that appears to contemplate follow-on agreements. As such, treaty-implementing agreements resemble *ex ante* congressional-executive agreements, but they derive authority from an Article II treaty rather than a statute. For example, after the Senate gave advice and consent to the 1951 NATO Status of Forces Agreement, which contemplated certain privileges and immunities for U.S. forces deployed to NATO allies,[771] the president concluded bilateral status of forces agreements with those allies, invoking as his authority to do so the 1951 treaty.[772]

"Sole executive agreements" rely exclusively on the president's own constitutional authority. Thus, under Article II of the Constitution the president is the commander-in-chief of U.S. armed forces; this might be sufficient license for the president to conclude an agreement with a foreign ally during an armed conflict regarding transit of U.S. forces through that ally's territory en route to a battlefield, or to provide for the passage of foreign troops through the United States.[773]

---

[769] In principle, a non–Article II agreement might bear more than one character: a given provision might be authorized by a statute or treaty, while another might depend on the president's constitutional authority to enter into sole executive agreements.

[770] Atomic Energy Act of 1954, Pub. L. No. 83-703, § 123, 68 Stat. 919, 940 (codified as amended at 42 U.S.C. § 2153); *see infra* this chapter text accompanying notes 798–801 (noting limitations on this authority); *see also infra* this chapter text accompanying note 797 (noting widespread use of *ex ante* authorization for foreign assistance measures).

[771] NATO Status of Forces Agreement, June 19, 1951, 4 U.S.T. 1792, T.I.A.S. 2846, 199 U.N.T.S. 67.

[772] *See* R. CHUCK MASON, CONG. RESEARCH SERV., Rl34531, STATUS OF FORCES AGREEMENT (SOFA): WHAT IS IT, AND HOW HAS IT BEEN UTILIZED? 2 (2012); *see also infra* this chapter text accompanying note 847 (discussing comparable agreement with Japan, and related decision in Wilson v. Girard, 354 U.S. 524 (1957)).

[773] McDougal & Lans, *supra* note 174, at 247; Craig Mathews, *The Constitutional Power of the President to Conclude International Agreements*, 64 YALE L.J. 345, 352–59 (1955).

This tripartite taxonomy of non–Article II agreements has been sharply contested, but it remains an established part of foreign relations discourse.[774] Their shared history, in any event, is important.[775] The long employment of non–Article II agreements, and their cumulative weight, makes it difficult to claim that Article II is the exclusive means for the United States to enter into international agreements. Not only can non–Article II agreements be traced back to the founding, but they also comprise over 90 percent of the international agreements entered into by the United States since 1939.[776]

The changing mix among these agreements also affects arguments about the legitimacy of non–Article II agreements as a whole. It was once possible to concede the president's capacity to conclude certain sole executive agreements, but to object to allowing Congress to usurp the Senate's role (particularly as to *ex post* congressional approval, which more closely resembles Senate advice and consent).[777] Congressional-executive agreements have flourished, however, and the modern sensibility is to more readily accept non–Article II agreements that receive legislative endorsement. Nonetheless, it is widely understood that the range of options for concluding an international agreement serves to enhance presidential power, given the executive's discretion (within political constraints) to choose the type of instrument that is most apt or most feasible for any given occasion.[778] This range of options has only been increased by the executive branch's significant use of nonbinding agreements—agreements that are not *legally* binding, though they may be politically binding, and even ripen into legal obligations over time—for important arrangements.[779]

---

[774] For criticisms of this standard taxonomy—particularly as to the value of distinguishing between congressional-executive agreements and sole executive agreements—see Daniel Bodansky & Peter Spiro, *Executive Agreements+*, 49 VAND. J. TRANSNAT'L L. 885 (2016); Harold Hongju Koh, *Triptych's End: A Better Framework to Evaluate 21st Century International Lawmaking*, 126 YALE L.J.F. 337 (2017).

[775] *See generally* Ackerman & Golove, *supra* note 108; Oona A. Hathaway, *Treaties' End: The Past, Present, and Future of International Lawmaking in the United States*, 117 YALE L.J. 1236 (2008).

[776] For a recent compilation of figures, see Curtis A. Bradley & Jack L. Goldsmith, *Presidential Control over International Law*, 131 HARV. L. REV. 1201, 1210 (2018); *see id.* at 1209 n.17 (citing sources).

[777] Military and claims settlements concluded by the president alone were fairly common from the beginning of the United States. *See* Ackerman & Golove, *supra* note 108, at 816–17. Congressional-executive agreements, in contrast, were rarer, the important exception being statutory authority, first enacted in 1792, licensing the Postmaster General to make postal agreements with foreign states. *Id.* at 826–27; *see* Act of Feb. 20, 1792, ch. 7, § 26, I Stat. 232, 239. For discussion of how these alternatives may have been viewed relative to Article II, see Ackerman & Golove, *supra* note 108, at 814, 853–56, 867–69.

[778] *See, e.g.*, Bradley & Goldsmith, *supra* note 776, at 1206–20; Jean Galbraith, *From Treaties to International Commitments: The Changing Landscape of Foreign Relations Law*, 84 U. CHI. L. REV. 1675 (2017); Oona A. Hathaway, *Presidential Power over International Law: Restoring the Balance*, 119 YALE L.J. 140 (2009).

[779] *See infra* this chapter § V(D).

Finally, the varied forms of non–Article II agreements, and the evolving balance between the executive and legislative branches, are reflected in the procedure for choosing among the instruments. In accordance with its Circular 175 procedure, the Department of State evaluates whether to pursue an international agreement as an Article II treaty or on some other basis.[780] The formal criteria for this evaluation offer limited guidance, and they are not binding, but they do indicate some of the relevant values, including several bearing on the need for congressional action.[781]

Congress, for its part, has tried to improve the transparency of non–Article II agreements along with congressional oversight. The Case-Zablocki Act of 1972 requires the executive branch to report to Congress any non–Article II agreements it has concluded.[782] Due to tardy and incomplete reporting, this regime has occasionally been revisited and strengthened.[783] In addition, Congress requires the publication of both Article II treaties and non–Article II agreements.[784] These publication requirements have also been repeatedly revised in light of delays and omissions, but they remain narrower in their application than the rules governing nonpublic reporting to Congress.[785]

---

[780] *See* 11 Foreign Affairs Manual, *supra* note 126, § 723.1 et seq.; *see supra* this chapter text accompanying notes 154–155 (noting statutory and regulatory authority relating to the Circular 175 procedure).

[781] Eight factors are enumerated "[i]n determining a question as to the procedure which should be followed for any particular agreement":

(1) The extent to which the agreement involves commitments or risks affecting the nation as a whole;
(2) Whether the agreement is intended to affect state laws;
(3) Whether the agreement can be given effect without the enactment of subsequent legislation by the Congress;
(4) Past U.S. practice as to similar agreements;
(5) The preference of the Congress as to a particular type of agreement;
(6) The degree of formality desired for an agreement;
(7) The proposed duration of the agreement, the need for prompt conclusion of an agreement, and the desirability of concluding a routine or short-term agreement; and

(8) The general international practice as to similar agreements.

11 Foreign Affairs Manual, *supra* note 126, § 723.3. How these are to be taken into account is not entirely clear. They are also tempered by any constitutional restrictions. *Id.* (referencing need for "due consideration" of factors in § 723.2); *id.* (stating, in addition, that "the utmost care is to be exercised to avoid any invasion or compromise of the constitutional powers of the President, the Senate, and the Congress as a whole"). For discussion, see Hathaway, *supra* note 775, at 1249–52.

[782] They are to be reported as soon as practicable after conclusion, and in all events within sixty days afterward. Pub. L. No. 92-403, 86 Stat. 619 (1972) (codified as amended at 1 U.S.C. § 112b (2018)); for background, see Hathaway, Bradley, & Goldsmith, *supra* note 154, at 648–50.

[783] *See* Hathaway, *supra* note 778, at 166–67 (noting compliance issues); Hathaway, Bradley, & Goldsmith, *supra* note 154, at 650–56 (describing statutory and regulatory reforms). The regulations implementing the statute, see 22 C.F.R. § 181.8 (2020), have also been periodically revised to reduce the regulatory burden and improve compliance. *See, e.g.*, 79 Fed. Reg. 68116 (Nov. 14, 2014); 1991 DIGEST OF U.S. PRACTICE, at 679, 679–82. However, reporting shortfalls reportedly continue. Hathaway, Bradley, & Goldsmith, *supra* note 154, at 676.

[784] Act of Sept. 23, 1950, c. 1001, § 2, 64 Stat. 980 (codified as amended at 1 U.S.C. § 112a (2018)).

[785] Hathaway, Bradley, & Goldsmith, *supra* note 154, at 645–48, 651.

A. Congressional-Executive Agreements

In essence, a congressional-executive agreement involves both a statute (or statutes) and an international agreement, but the sequence varies. As previously suggested, its two principal forms take distinct paths: Congress either enacts a statute that authorizes the executive branch to negotiate, conclude, and ratify an international agreement, or instead approves of an agreement after it has been negotiated by the president. The first accounts for many more agreements. By some estimates, *ex ante* congressional-executive agreements comprise approximately 80 to 85 percent of all international agreements concluded by the United States; in contrast, the United States has in recent decades finalized about one *ex post* congressional-executive agreement per year.[786] Highly significant agreements continue to be established by *ex post* means (including the NAFTA or the Uruguay Round agreements that established the World Trade Organization),[787] but by the numbers, *ex ante* congressional authorization is the dominant alternative to advice-and-consent treaty-making.

Congressional-executive agreements of both types present common issues, and many are comparable to those already considered for Article II treaties. Apart from issues of statutory interpretation relating to the authorizing legislation, the agreement itself may require interpretation, which may be conducted according to ordinary treaty-law principles.[788] The domestic legal effect of such agreements is distinct, but not radically so. Because congressional-executive agreements involve congressional authorization, it is sometimes said that they entirely bypass the doctrine of self-executing and non-self-executing treaties,[789] but that may be a bit hasty. Congress could indicate directly that an agreement is not itself judicially enforceable.[790] An *ex ante* congressional-executive

---

[786] Bradley & Goldsmith, *supra* note 776, at 1212–13.

[787] Uruguay Round Agreements Act, Pub. L. No. 103-465, 108 Stat. 4809 (1994) (codified as amended in scattered sections of 19 U.S.C.); North American Free Trade Agreement Implementation Act, *supra* note 767.

[788] *See, e.g.*, Eshel v. Comm'r of Internal Revenue Serv., 831 F.3d 512, 518 (D.C. Cir. 2016) (stating that "[e]xecutive agreements"—there, one authorized by statute—"must be interpreted under the same principles applicable to international treaties," and noting that "it is inappropriate to make the United States' maxims for statutory construction unilaterally dispositive"). Naturally, any deference ordinarily owed to Senate views would be qualified by those expressed in Congress as a whole. *See supra* this chapter text accompanying notes 474–478 (noting, and questioning, reliance on Senate views).

[789] *See* Henkin, Foreign Affairs, at 217 (stating that "[t]he Congressional-Executive agreement also eliminates issues about self-executing and non-self-executing agreements"); *see also* Gary Born, *Customary International Law in the United States*, 92 Wash. L. Rev. 1641, 1684 (2017) (describing as "rules of international law, with the status of federal law," certain customary rules, "self-executing treaties, congressional executive agreements, or sole executive agreements").

[790] *See* Bradley, *supra* note 618, at 164 (stating that congressional-executive agreements "reduce[] the issue of self-execution, since Congress often specifies the level of judicial enforceability that it wants when approving the agreements (sometimes substantially limiting such enforceability)," and suggesting they are most easily analogized to statutes); *see also* Henkin, Foreign Affairs, at 217 n.** (allowing that "[i]n approving a Congressional-Executive agreement, Congress can limit its

agreement could also be non-self-executing because the subsequent agreement requires (further) domestic implementation before it is judicially enforceable, because the Constitution requires additional implementation by Congress, or because the obligation is nonjusticiable.[791] Whether an agreement is itself judicially enforceable may affect other questions, such as whether an *ex ante* congressional-executive agreement establishes a later-in-time authority that overrides U.S. obligations under a prior Article II treaty.[792]

1. *Ex Ante* Agreements

Ex ante agreements arise in two sets of circumstances, broadly speaking. In the first, the executive branch, having determined that prior legislative authorization is advisable but does not yet exist, attempts to secure it. Securing congressional authorization for an agreement is somewhat like enacting a conventional domestic statute, but (as with other forms of international agreement) the international element is distinctive. Such authorization may or may not be finalized before the agreement's negotiation, but it should precede any U.S. ratification, as that binds the United States and presumes domestic authority.[793]

effect as law of the land"). Congress may also indicate to the contrary. *See* B. Altman & Co. v. United States, 224 U.S. 583, 601 (1912) (stating, which regard to an *ex ante* congressional-executive agreement, that "the purpose of Congress was manifestly to permit rights and obligations of that character to be passed upon in the Federal court of final resort"). It seems fair to say that "[c]ongressional-executive agreements are generally presumed self-executing unless specified otherwise." Hathaway, *supra* note 775, at 1321.

[791] *See generally supra* this chapter §§ IV(A)(4)–(6); *see, e.g.*, Canadian Lumber Trade All. v. United States, 30 C.I.T. 391, 432 (Ct. Int'l Trade 2006) (stating that self-execution analysis "is equally applicable to congressional-executive agreements"), *aff'd in part, vacated in part*, 517 F.3d 1319 (Fed. Cir. 2008). In Weinberger v. Rossi, 456 U.S. 25 (1982), the Court noted in passing that congressional-executive agreements—in that case, of the *ex ante* form—may "in appropriate circumstances have an effect similar to treaties in some areas of domestic law." *Id.* at 30 n.6; *see* Al-Bihani v. Obama, 619 F.3d 1, 35 n.17 (2010) (Kavanaugh, J., concurring in the denial of rehearing en banc) (construing *Weinberger v. Rossi* as concerning "a statute's interaction with a congressional-executive agreement, the language of which made the agreement self-executing and thus domestic U.S. law").

[792] The relative priority in U.S. law of an Article II treaty and an *ex ante* congressional-executive agreement likely depends on the terms of the agreement and those of the statutory authorization. One executive branch opinion indicated that "it lies within the power of Congress to authorize the President substantially to modify the United States' obligations under a prior treaty, including an arms control treaty," when that authorization was coupled with the president's own constitutional authority over foreign affairs. Validity of Congressional-Executive Agreements that Substantially Modify the United States' Obligations Under an Existing Treaty, 20 Op. O.L.C. 389, 389 (1996); *accord id.* at 395. The opinion presupposed that "[a]n international agreement negotiated by the President and concluded with prior, or subsequent, authorization from Congress has 'the force and effect of an act of Congress.'" *Id.* at 399 (quoting The President—Authority to Participate in International Negotiations—Trade Act of 1974 (19 U.S.C. § 2101)—Participation in Producer-Consumer Fora, 2 Op. O.L.C. 227, 229 (1978)). The scope of authorization also matters. 2 Op. O.L.C., *supra*, at 229 ("If the agreement is submitted to the full Congress and is approved by joint resolution or is implemented by statute, it is likewise entitled to the force and effect of an act of Congress *to the extent of the approval or implementation*.") (emphasis added).

[793] A statute that provides authority for an international agreement might make itself contingent in whole or in part on ratification of the resulting agreement. *See, e.g.*, International Dolphin

In a second, more routine situation, legislative authorization already exists, leaving only the task of negotiating and concluding the agreement itself. The United States has long authorized by statute the conclusion of bilateral agreements in areas like postal regulations,[794] law enforcement,[795] and other areas.[796] Probably the greatest number of agreements, however, are those authorized by the Foreign Assistance Act of 1961, as amended.[797]

The threshold question—when considering an agreement that was not proposed for congressional approval nor submitted to the Senate for advice and consent—is whether preexisting statutory authorization is even being claimed. The executive branch has not always clearly disclosed its authority for non–Article II agreements, even those reported to Congress. The regulations implementing the Department of State's publication and reporting obligations do commit to providing Congress with specific authority for each non–Article II agreement;[798] the cited authorities, however, are not always precise or discriminating.[799] In public accounts, too, it is not always easy to distinguish between executive branch representations that an agreement is *consistent* with

Conservation Program Act, Pub. L. No. 105-42, § 6, 111 Stat. 1122, 1129 (1997) (codified as amended at 16 U.S.C. § 1412 (2018)) (providing that executive branch officials "shall seek to secure a binding international agreement to establish an International Dolphin Conservation Program"); *id.* § 8 (codified as amended at 16 U.S.C. § 1362 note (2018)) (providing that, subject to certain exceptions and conditions, relevant statutory sections of the statute become effective upon certification by the Secretary of State that a "legally binding instrument establishing the International Dolphin Conservation Program has been adopted and is in force"); *see also* Def. of Wildlife v. Hogarth, 25 C.I.T. 1309 (Ct. Int'l Trade 2001) (highlighting provision); Richard W. Parker, *The Use and Abuse of Trade Leverage to Protect the Global Commons: What We Can Learn From the Tuna–Dolphin Conflict,* 12 GEO. INT'L ENVTL. L. REV. 1 (1999) (providing background).

[794] *See supra* this chapter note 777 (noting postal precedent); *infra* this chapter note 803 (noting present-day statute); Postal Conventions with Foreign Countries, 19 Op. Att'y Gen. 513, 520 (1890) (discussing postal authority); Hathaway, *supra* note 775, at 1289 & n.138 (calculating that by 2000, the United States had entered into over four hundred such agreements).

[795] *See* Seizure of Foreign Ships on the High Seas Pursuant to Special Arrangements, 4B Op. O.L.C. 406, 407–09 (1980) (discussing modern authority for agreements relating to drug trafficking on the high seas) (citing 22 U.S.C. § 2291(a) (2018)).

[796] These include agreements relating to areas as diverse as international fisheries, 16 U.S.C. § 1822(a) (2018), and religious freedom, 22 U.S.C. § 6445(c) (2018). For a discussion and tabulation of examples, see Hathaway, *supra* note 778, at 155–67.

[797] Foreign Assistance Act of 1961, Pub. L. No. 87-195, 75 Stat. 424 (codified in scattered sections of 22 U.S.C.). According to one study, the Foreign Assistance Act accounted for at least eight hundred executive agreements in fields as diverse as debt, defense, economic cooperation, judicial assistance, and narcotics. Hathaway, *supra* note 775, at 1256 & n.48.

[798] *See* 22 C.F.R. § 181.1–.9 (2019); Hathaway, Bradley, & Goldsmith, *supra* note 154, at 650. The citation of supporting authorities, made part of cover memos accompanying the agreements, are not made public by the U.S. government, but many were disclosed in response to FOIA requests. Oona A. Hathaway, Curtis A. Bradley, & Jack L. Goldsmith, The Failed Transparency Regime for Executive Agreements: An Empirical and Normative Analysis: Executive Agreements, https://dataverse.harv ard.edu/dataverse/executiveagreements (providing database of disclosed cover memos).

[799] *See* Hathaway, Bradley, & Goldsmith, *supra* note 154, at 677–79 (noting nature of cited authority); *id.* at 715–16 (describing "kitchen sink" approach to citations).

existing statutes and assertions that the agreement is affirmatively *authorized* by statute,[800] even though the distinction seems constitutionally significant.[801]

Assuming, however, that statutory authorization is genuinely being claimed, the question becomes whether the statute being invoked (or some other statute) authorizes with sufficient specificity the conclusion of international agreements.[802] Some statutes do so explicitly.[803] But authorization may also be claimed when a statute presupposes the existence of agreements and so might be understood to imply the capacity to negotiate and conclude them.[804] Authority

[800] For example, in relation to the Minamata Convention on Mercury, Nov. 6, 2013, T.I.A.S. No. 17-816, the Department of State stated simply that the United States "can implement Convention obligations under existing legislative and regulatory authority." U.S. Dep't of State, Press Release on United States Joins Minamata Convention on Mercury (Nov. 6, 2013), https://perma.cc/BE9S-225S. *Compare* Bradley & Goldsmith, *supra* note 776, at 1216 (citing this as an example of how "the purported statutory bases for some executive agreements have grown so tenuous as to be nonexistent"), *with* Bodansky & Spiro, *supra* note 774, at 910–11 (citing the Minamata Convention as an example of an "executive agreement+," being supported but not authorized by Congress). Based on the later-disclosed cover memo reciting authorities, one statute provided "at least plausible authorization," see Hathaway, Bradley, & Goldsmith, *supra* note 154, at 712, but it is not clear whether that statute was considered important in the decision to proceed.

[801] It has been argued that the Supreme Court's decision in *Japan Whaling Ass'n v. Am. Cetacean Soc'y* accepted the president's authority to enter into an agreement that was consistent with (rather than authorized by) a domestic regulatory statute, but the Court did not address the question. *Compare* David A. Wirth, *Executive Agreements Relying on Implied Statutory Authority: A Response to Bodansky and Spiro*, 50 VAND. J. TRANSNAT'L L. 741, 748 (2017), *with Japan Whaling Ass'n*, 478 U.S. 221, 230 (1986) (describing the challenge as presenting "a purely legal question of statutory interpretation"); *see also* Brief for the Federal Petitioners at 44, Japan Whaling Ass'n v. Am. Cetacean Soc'y, 478 U.S. 221 (1986) (Nos. 85-954 and 85-955) (characterizing the agreement with Japan as an "executive agreement," without suggesting it was supported by congressional authority). It is easier to perceive how tacit indications of congressional approval may influence the standard of judicial review or develop constitutional practice. *See supra* this chapter text accompanying note 592 (discussing *Youngstown*); *infra* this chapter text accompanying notes 858–865 (discussing *Dames & Moore*). Congress may try to countermand any such inferences. *See, e.g.*, National Commitments Resolution, S. Res. 85, 91st Cong. (1969); 115 CONG. REC. 17,245 (1969) (resolving, in precursor to War Powers Resolution, that certain commitments to use U.S. armed forces properly "result[] only from affirmative action . . . by means of a treaty, statute, or concurrent resolution of both Houses of Congress specifically providing for such commitment").

[802] *See generally* RESTATEMENT (THIRD) § 303(2); *supra* this chapter text accompanying notes 794–797 (noting examples). The *Restatement (Fourth)*, in its initial phase of work, did not address non–Article II agreements, meaning that the *Restatement (Third)* remains the American Law Institute's most authoritative resource. RESTATEMENT (FOURTH), pt. I note, at 3.

[803] The classic example remains postal agreements. *See, e.g.*, Postal Reorganization Act, Pub. L. No. 91-375, § 2, 84 Stat. 719, 724 (1970) (codified as amended at 39 U.S.C. § 407) ("The Postal Service, with the consent of the President, may negotiate and conclude postal treaties or conventions"); *see also supra* this chapter notes 777, 794. Another important, but more complex, example is the Foreign Military Sales Act of 1968, Pub. L. No. 90-629, § 3, 82 Stat. 1320, 1322 (codified as amended at 22 U.S.C. § 2753), which in some sense authorizes agreements and requires them as a condition precedent—stating that before selling or leasing defense articles to any state or international organization, or entering into agreements for cooperative projects with NATO member states, see 22 U.S.C. § 2767, the United States must first obtain the agreement of the state or international organization that it will not transfer those articles. *Id.* § 2753(2).

[804] *See, e.g.*, Barquero v. United States, 18 F.3d 1311, 1315 (5th Cir. 1994) (holding that 1986 amendments to the Internal Revenue Code, by referring to exclusions of certain corporations per bilateral or multilateral agreements, implicitly "constitute[d] specific congressional authorization" to the president to enter into United States–Mexico tax information exchange agreement);

may also be inferred from statutes that authorize cooperation with foreign states, or establish international programs, but which do not advert directly to international agreements.[805] Of greater concern, a comprehensive review found that about one-third of the statutory authorities cited in cover memos for the Department of State's Case-Zablocki reports to Congress did not even arguably delegate authority to make international agreements—and that about one-sixth of the memos invoked nothing that plausibly delegated such authority.[806]

If the executive branch is invoking statutory authorization, and if Congress has actually authorized making international agreements, then a third question is presented: whether a particular agreement, or its operative provision, falls within the scope of that authorization. The Supreme Court has spoken only indirectly to these kinds of delegations,[807] but lower courts' decisions suggest that legislative authority will be generously construed.[808] A similar generosity is likely

CRS, TREATIES AND OTHER INTERNATIONAL AGREEMENTS, *supra* note 165, at 79 n.75 (citing authorizations examples). As one study observed, some statutes might authorize the *negotiation* of agreements without clearly assigning responsibility to *conclude* them. *See* Hathaway, Bradley, & Goldsmith, *supra* note 154, at 680–81 (citing 22 U.S.C. § 2656d(a)(1), which assigned the Secretary of State "primary responsibility for coordination and oversight" over "all major science or science and technology agreements and activities between the United States and foreign countries," coupled with a statutory policy expressing support for bilateral and multilateral agreements, *id.* § 2656b(2)).

[805] Implicit authorization might be attributed to statutes conferring the ability to manage an aspect of foreign relations, *e.g.*, Foreign Assistance Act of 1961, Pub. L. No. 87-195, § 503, 75 Stat. 424, 435 (codified as amended at 22 U.S.C. § 2311 (2018)) ("The President is authorized to furnish military assistance on such terms and conditions as he may determine"), or suggesting broad programmatic responsibility, *e.g.*, International Anti-Corruption and Good Governance Act of 2000, 22 U.S.C. § 2152c(a)(1) (2018) (authorizing the president to "establish programs that combat corruption, improve transparency and accountability, and promote other forms of good governance in [eligible] countries"). *See* RESTATEMENT (THIRD) § 303 cmt. e ("Congress may enact legislation that requires, or fairly implies, the need for an agreement to execute the legislation."); Bradley & Goldsmith, *supra* note 776, at 1215; Hathaway, *supra* note 778, at 156–65; Hathaway, Bradley, & Goldsmith, *supra* note 154, at 681–82.

[806] *See* Hathaway, Bradley, & Goldsmith, *supra* note 154, at 683–85.

[807] Several Supreme Court cases have, however, sustained unilateral presidential actions under the authority of trade statutes, and in the process rejected arguments sounding in the nondelegation doctrine. *See* Field v. Clark, 143 U.S. 649, 691–94 (1892); J.W. Hampton, Jr. & Co. v. United States, 276 U.S. 394, 406–11 (1928).

[808] *See, e.g.*, Libas, Ltd. v. United States, 20 C.I.T. 1215, 1216–17 (Ct. Int'l Trade 1996) (construing "[t]he President's authority to negotiate [textile trade] agreements . . . as a broad grant of authority"); *cf.* Star-Kist Foods, Inc. v. United States, 275 F.2d 472, 481–82 (C.C.P.A. 1959) (suggesting that a foreign trade agreement was within the authority conferred by Trade Agreements Act of 1934). Courts have applied the same approach to claims that a trade agreement's particular term, or legal effect, exceeds statutory authority. *E.g.*, Von Damm v. United States, 90 F.2d 263, 267–69 (C.C.P.A. 1937) (terms in reciprocal trade agreement with Cuba fall within statutory tariff authority); Marianao Sugar Trade v. United States, 29 Cust. Ct. 275, 282–88 (1952) (same). A subgenre of these cases grapples with whether a statutory reference to "treaty" or "treaties" includes other types of international agreements; these suggest that courts will construe such statutes generously because they "touch upon the United States' foreign policy." *See, e.g.*, Weinberger v. Rossi, 456 U.S. 25, 31–32 (1982) (construing exemption for employment discrimination permitted by "treaty" to include congressional-executive agreement, and noting other ambiguous statutes); B. Altman & Co. v. United States, 224 U.S. 583, 600–01 (1912) (equating congressional-executive agreement with treaties for purposes of jurisdictional statute).

to be employed in construing whether such statutory authority also supports administrative actions that implement the agreement.[809]

Because *ex ante* authorization does assign substantial responsibility to the executive branch for international agreements, and because statutory obligations to report and to publish already concluded agreements are weak in principle and even weaker in practice, Congress has experimented with other safeguards. Its ability to rely on treaty-like reservations and other conditions is limited, insofar as *ex ante* authorization is broader and precedes an agreement's conclusion, so authorizing statutes may establish limiting criteria for any agreements that the executive concludes.[810] Congress has also tried to condition the effectiveness of resulting international agreement on subsequent legislative approval, or the lack of legislative disapproval, by one or both houses. After the Supreme Court struck down legislative vetoes, some of these provisions were revised (and, inevitably, weakened),[811] while others remain constitutionally suspect.[812] In practice, the most effective legislative check is probably a combination of congressional information-gathering and political pressure.[813]

---

[809] *See* Defs. of Wildlife v. Hogarth, 25 C.I.T. 1309, 1316–18 (Ct. Int'l Trade 2001); *cf. Star-Kist Foods*, 275 F.2d at 481–82 (noting that, according to statute, a presidential adjustment of duties must advance congressional policy and be "'required or appropriate' to carrying out the [statutorily authorized] trade agreement as well").

[810] *See, e.g.*, Magnuson Fishery Conservation and Management Act of 1976, Pub. L. No. 94-265, §§ 201(c), 203, 90 Stat. 331, 339–42 (codified as amended at 16 U.S.C. §§ 1821(c), 1823 (2018)) (describing "sense of the Congress" that each authorized "governing international fishery agreement" must "include a binding commitment, on the part of such foreign nation and its fishing vessels, to comply" with specified terms and conditions); Atomic Energy Act of 1954, Pub. L. No. 83-703, § 123, 68 Stat. 919, 940 (codified as amended at 42 U.S.C. § 2153 (2018)) (prohibiting certain international activities involving the transfer of nuclear materials unless pursuant to an agreement which requiring certain safeguards by other parties).

[811] *See generally* CRS, TREATIES AND OTHER INTERNATIONAL AGREEMENTS, *supra* note 165, at 79–80 (describing statutory restrictions and adaptation following *INS v. Chadha*, 462 U.S. 919 (1983)). For example, as amended, certain fishery and atomic energy agreements are subject to a joint resolution of disapproval. *See* 16 U.S.C. § 1823 (2018); 42 U.S.C. § 2153(d) (2018). But because joint resolutions, like statutes—but unlike concurrent resolutions—are presented for presidential signature, a joint resolution of disapproval may be stymied by the executive.

[812] Social Security totalization agreements (which protect the benefits of workers with careers in more than one country) remain authorized by statute, subject to a delayed entry-into-force date following transmittal to the Congress, and subject to disapproval by one house. 42 U.S.C. § 433(e) (2018); *see* Eshel v. Comm'r of Internal Revenue Serv., 831 F.3d 512, 518 (D.C. Cir. 2016). This right of disapproval has not been exercised, but a controversial agreement with Mexico has apparently not been transmitted. *See* Allison Christians, *Taxing the Global Worker: Three Spheres of International Social Security Coordination*, 26 VA. TAX. REV. 81, 90–91 (2006). Were it tested, it seems likely that it would not pass muster. CONG. RESEARCH SERV., R41009, INTERNATIONAL SOCIAL SECURITY AGREEMENTS 13–15 (2010) (noting litigation risk and severability issues), https://perma.cc/EYW4-R6S5.

[813] For example, the Anti-Counterfeiting Trade Agreement (ACTA), May 1, 2011, 50 I.L.M. 243, was criticized on the assumption that it was being pursued as a sole executive agreement, although the executive maintained that it was supported by legislation inviting international cooperation. Conclusion of the agreement was stymied. *See* Bodansky & Spiro, *supra* note 774, at 908–10; *see also* Koh, *supra* note 774, at 343 (noting defenses of the ACTA, during service as the Department of State Legal Adviser, as being based on "consistent executive practice," "legal landscape," and "general preauthorization"—as distinct from claim that Congress had "expressly pre-authorize[d] this particular agreement").

2. *Ex Post* Agreements

In principle, the procedure for *ex post* congressional-executive agreements makes congressional authorization easier to identify. After the executive has completed the negotiation of an agreement but prior to ratification (or otherwise bringing the agreement into force for the United States),[814] Congress authorizes it and thereby provides the basis for ratification. The process for adopting *ex post* congressional-executive agreements may also be specially structured in advance of the negotiation of the agreement. In areas like trade, Congress has enacted statutory procedures which provide that conforming agreements that meet substantive, reporting, and consultative requirements may be presented for congressional approval through an accelerated procedure sometimes called "fast track" authority (more recently, "trade promotion" authority).[815] Even here, though, congressional authorization of the agreement, and its statutory implementation, are provided only after negotiation of the agreement. Leading examples include the NAFTA and the agreements that established the WTO.[816]

The sequence for *ex post* agreements also means that Congress can more easily adopt tools like those used by the Senate for Article II treaties. Congress may approve an agreement subject to conditions,[817] so long as it has not previously

---

[814] Exceptionally, authorization may be attributed to legislation enacted after an agreement has actually been made on behalf of the United States and even after it enters into force—such that it appears, initially, to be a sole executive agreement. This may arise when indirect authorization is claimed through appropriations measures, as for U.S. participation in the Pan American Union, 48 Stat. 534 (1934), see HENKIN, FOREIGN AFFAIRS, at 216 & 492 n.152, Ackerman & Golove, *supra* note 108, at 829 n.116, or the United Nations Relief and Rehabilitation Administration (UNRRA). H.J. Res. 192, 78th Cong., 58 Stat. 122 (1944); *see* Ackerman & Golove, *supra* note 108, at 880; Herbert W. Briggs, *The UNRRA Agreement and Congress*, 38 AM. J. INT'L L. 650 (1944); *see also* 19 U.S.C. § 3471 (2018) (authorizing U.S. participation in the Commission for Labor Cooperation "in accordance with the North American Agreement on Labor Cooperation," a supplemental agreement not otherwise approved by Congress, and authorizing appropriations).

[815] *See* Trade and Tariff Act of 1984, Pub. L. No. 98-573, § 401(a), 98 Stat. 2948 (1984) (codified as amended at 19 U.S.C. § 2112(b) (2018)); Trade Act of 1974, Pub. L. No. 93-618, § 102, 88 Stat. 1978 (1975) (codified as amended at 19 U.S.C. § 2112(e) (2018)); Omnibus Trade and Competitiveness Act of 1988, Pub. L. No. 100-418, § 1103, 102 Stat. 1107 (1988) (codified at 19 U.S.C. § 2903 (2018)); Bipartisan Trade Promotion Authority Act of 2002, Pub. L. No. 107-210, 116 Stat. 933 (codified at 19 U.S.C. §§ 3801–13 (2018)); Bipartisan Congressional Trade Priorities and Accountability Act of 2015, Pub. L. No. 114-26, 129 Stat. 320 (2015) (codified at 19 U.S.C. §§ 4201–10 (2018)). Because such authority applies for finite periods, the executive branch may seek renewal for the purposes of particular negotiations; while awaiting renewal, the executive might fulfill the preexisting requirements while initiating negotiations. Request for Comments Concerning Proposed Trans-Pacific Partnership Trade Agreement, 74 Fed. Reg. 66,720 (Dec. 16, 2009).

[816] North American Free Trade Agreement Implementation Act, *supra* note 767; Uruguay Round Agreements Act, *supra* note 787.

[817] *See* S.J. Res. 144, 61 Stat. 756, 757–58 (1947) (joint resolution authorizing the U.N. Headquarters Agreement subject to conditions); S.J. Res. 77, 80th Cong., 61 Stat. 214, 214–15 (1947) (joint resolution authorizing the International Refugee Organization Agreement subject to conditions). Statutory conditions will be awkward if the president has already accepted a binding international obligation according to the agreement's terms. *See* Ackerman & Golove, *supra* note 108, at 880 (noting anomaly of reservation to U.S. adherence to the 1943 Agreement for the United Nations Relief and Rehabilitation Administration); Briggs, *supra* note 814, at 655–57 (suggesting irrelevance of late reservations under international law).

bound itself not to do so (as in fast track, or trade promotion, processes, in which it bars amendments and limits itself to an up-or-down vote in order to enhance the president's credibility when negotiating with other states).[818] It may also limit domestic application, though this may confuse U.S. courts. Congress appears to distinguish between an international agreement itself, Congress' approval of an agreement, and Congress' enactment of a statute or other measures to implement an agreement;[819] addressing the judicial enforceability of one (such as the agreement itself) does not necessarily address treatment of the others (such as the statute).[820] Absent statutory instruction, it should probably be assumed that when Congress adopts implementing legislation *ex post*, it intends those terms to be judicially enforceable, but does not intend the agreement itself to have direct domestic legal effect as if it were self-executing.[821]

Statutory limits may affect other domestic legal consequences, such as the effect on prior agreements.[822] They may also affect interpretation. Ordinarily, the agreement approved by Congress will be the focus in interpreting the international obligations of the United States. On the other hand, inquiries into U.S. law—as before U.S. courts—may focus on interpreting the agreement's

---

[818] See *supra* notes 145–146; *see, e.g.,* 19 U.S.C. § 4205(b)(2) (2018).

[819] Multiple components may be referenced in the same breath. *E.g.,* North American Free Trade Agreement Implementation Act, *supra* note 767, § 101(a) (codified at 19 U.S.C. § 3311(a) (2018)) (separately approving the NAFTA itself, as well as the statement of administrative action); Uruguay Round Agreements Act, *supra* note 787, § 101(a) (codified at 19 U.S.C. § 3511(a) (2018)) (similar provision); *see also* 19 U.S.C. § 2903(a)(1) (2018) (detailing conditions for entry into force of certain trade agreements, and differentiating among components); 19 U.S.C. § 2191(b)(1)(A) (2018) (defining various components of an "implementing bill" for such agreements). For thorough discussion, see Canadian Lumber Trade All. v. United States, 30 C.I.T. 391, 427–34 (Ct. Int'l Trade 2006), *aff'd in part and vacated in part,* 517 F.3d 1319, 1341–42 (Fed. Cir. 2008).

[820] The leading case regarding the NAFTA's preclusion provision concluded that statute-based claims were, for this reason, not included within a statutory reference to "any cause of action or defense under . . . the Agreement or by virtue of Congressional approval thereof." North American Free Trade Agreement Implementation Act, *supra* note 767, § 102(c) (codified at 19 U.S.C. § 3312(c) (2018)); *see Canadian Lumber Trade All.,* 517 F.3d at 1341–42. A previous case, construing a nearly identical provision relating to the Uruguay Round Agreements, reached the opposite conclusion. Uruguay Round Agreements Act, *supra* note 787, § 102(c) (codified at 19 U.S.C. § 3512(c) (2018)); *see* Bronco Wine Co. v. Bureau of Alcohol, Tobacco and Firearms, No. 98-15444, 1999 WL 68632, 1999 U.S. App. LEXIS 2130 (9th Cir. Feb. 11, 1999), *aff'ng* Bronco Wine Co. v. U.S. Dep't Treasury, 997 F. Supp. 1318 (E.D. Cal. 1997). *But see* NSK Ltd. v. United States, 3, 28 C.I.T. 1535, 1544 (Ct. Int'l Trade 2004) (holding that § 102(c) did not bar challenge relating to interpretation and application of U.S. statute as inconsistent with the agreement).

[821] See H.R. REP. No. 103-826, pt. 1, at 25 (1994) (reporting that provisions relating to the Uruguay Round Agreements, the Tokyo Round, the NAFTA, and bilateral trade agreements with Israel and Canada, which indicated that U.S. laws prevailed over any conflicting international provisions in those agreements, were "consistent with the Congressional view that necessary changes in Federal statutes should be specifically enacted, not preempted by international agreements"). Such limits are on a surer footing than declarations that Article II treaties are not self-executing, since the plenary authority of Congress and the president over enactment of federal statutes is clearer than the authority of the Senate and president to act autonomously in altering the effect of a treaty within the U.S. legal system. *See supra* this chapter § IV(A)(7).

[822] 20 Op. O.L.C., *supra* note 792, at 400 (noting that "Congress has also ratified, by legislation, Executive acts that substantially modified pre-existing treaty (or other international) obligations").

statutory implementation by Congress and the executive branch. This distinction should be minimal. Statutory interpretation of a congressional-executive agreement should bear in mind not only the general principle that U.S. law should be construed in light of international law, but also take due account when the law in question was enacted for the exact purpose of discharging a particular international obligation of the United States.[823]

While congressional authority over *ex post* congressional-executive agreements seems substantial, and akin to its ordinary legislative authority, the distinctive degree of executive branch authority also bears emphasis. Even when Congress has not limited its own capacity to impose conditions, as through fast-track authority, it will be presented with an agreement that has already been negotiated and, in the view of other states, finalized. As compared to a statute, the president also has greater authority over whether to execute the final effectuation of congressional-executive agreement. Unlike domestic legislating, in which the president's (regular) veto of a bill might be overcome by a congressional supermajority, the president retains the capacity to frustrate a fully authorized congressional-executive agreement by refusing to ratify it, just as with an Article II treaty.[824]

3. Constitutional Limits

Given the broad use of congressional-executive agreements and their frequent invocation before courts, it is fair to presume generally that they can be used in lieu of Article II treaties.[825] Still, it would be rash to assume complete "interchangeability" in this regard. The idea that congressional-executive agreements could replace Article II treaties was pushed aggressively in support of developing practice during World War II, and the degree of historical continuity with preceding agreements was probably exaggerated.[826] In any event, interchangeability largely prevailed afterward, and eventually the *Restatement (Third)* came close

---

[823] Interpreting statutes that further implement *ex post* congressional-executive agreements should, for this reason, resemble the approach to interpreting statutes that implement non-self-executing Article II treaties. *See supra* this chapter text accompanying notes 789–791.

[824] Hathaway, *supra* note 775, at 1329.

[825] *See* HENKIN, FOREIGN AFFAIRS, at 215–18; 20 Op. O.L.C., *supra* note 792, at 398 ("The constitutionality of such 'congressional-executive agreements' is firmly established.").

[826] Ackerman & Golove, *supra* note 108, at 806–08. There were, naturally, variations in the arguments for interchangeability, and not everyone agreed that non–Article II agreements could be used in every circumstance—or, for that matter, that treaties might also be used whenever a congressional-executive agreement is possible. *See, e.g.,* EDWARD S. CORWIN, THE CONSTITUTION AND WORLD ORGANIZATION 31–54 (1944); CORWIN, *supra* note 174, at 232–40; WALLACE MCCLURE, INTERNATIONAL EXECUTIVE AGREEMENTS: DEMOCRATIC PROCEDURE UNDER THE CONSTITUTION OF THE UNITED STATES (1941); Myres S. McDougal & Asher Lans, *Treaties and Congressional-Executive or Presidential Agreements: Interchangeable Instruments of National Policy: II*, 54 YALE L.J. 534 (1945); Quincy Wright, *The United States and International Agreements*, 38 AM. J. INT'L L. 341 (1944).

to accepting the complete fungibility of legislatively approved agreements.[827] But not long after the *Restatement (Third)* was published, controversy over the congressional-executive agreements for the NAFTA and the Uruguay Round Agreements suggested the matter was not wholly resolved. Are there limits, and if so, what are they?

One position is that only Article II treaties may be used for particularly important or "significantly sovereignty-altering commitments."[828] That view requires condemning some prominent agreements as having been unconstitutionally made.[829] It is somewhat more appealing as a generalization, but too vague to function as a justiciable standard. When it was argued in the debate over the NAFTA's constitutionality that congressional-executive agreements could not be used for "major and significant" agreements or those impinging on national, state, or local sovereignty, one court concluded that the issue was a political question.[830] Neither Congress nor the Senate was ultimately persuaded, either.[831] If the claim is destined to be resolved only (if at all) by the political branches, it is doubtful any clear standard will emerge.

It has also been contended that, whatever an agreement's supposed significance, certain subject matters remain the exclusive province of Article II treaties.[832] Because these subjects are not article clearly specified in the Constitution and rely more on construing past practice by the political branches,

---

[827] RESTATEMENT (THIRD) § 303(2) (indicating that "the President, with the authorization or approval of Congress, may make an international agreement dealing with any matter that falls within the powers of Congress and of the President under the Constitution"); *id.* § 303 cmt. e (stating that "any agreement concluded as a Congressional-Executive agreement could also be concluded by treaty," that "either method may be used in many cases," and that "[t]he prevailing view is that the Congressional-Executive agreement can be used as an alternative to the treaty method in every instance"); *see also* HENKIN, FOREIGN AFFAIRS, at 217 (concluding that "it is now widely accepted that the Congressional-Executive agreement is available for wide use, even general use, and is a complete alternative to a treaty").

[828] Tribe, *supra* note 767, at 1277; *see also* Bradley & Morrison, *supra* note 12, at 476 (2012) (suggesting that "major" agreements, "at least in certain subject areas," must be addressed by Article II treaties).

[829] *See, e.g., supra* this chapter text accompanying notes 767, 787 (noting examples of the NAFTA and Uruguay Round agreements); *cf.* Tribe, *supra* note 767, at 1250 (conceding diversity in practice, but disputing significance).

[830] *See* Made in the USA Found. v. United States, 242 F.3d 1300, 1315 & n.33 (11th Cir. 2001). The district court had rejected that claim on its merits. Made in the USA Found. v. United States, 56 F. Supp. 2d 1226, 1317–23 (N.D. Ala. 1999).

[831] Although the NAFTA, unlike the Uruguay Round Agreements, failed to receive the two-thirds vote that would have been required of an Article II treaty, the court of appeals reported that no member of the Senate opposed approval on the ground that it was necessary to make the agreement according to Article II. *Made in the USA Found.*, 242 F.3d at 1319. This lack of opposition within the Senate may reflect a broader concession as to the permissibility of significant congressional-executive agreements. *See* CRS, TREATIES AND OTHER INTERNATIONAL AGREEMENTS, *supra* note 165, at 5, 85–86 (noting widespread legislative use).

[832] Conversely, it has been contended that certain subject-matters are the exclusive province of congressional-executive agreements, and cannot be concluded by Article II treaties. *See supra* this chapter § II(D)(2).

the ground rules are hard to discern. At least occasionally, agreements on subjects often said to require Article II treaties—such as arms control[833] and the extradition of U.S. citizens[834]—are made outside Article II. Others, like multilateral human rights agreements, have essentially unblemished records as Article II treaties, but with fewer examples on which to base any rule.[835]

Ideally, practice-based claims would coincide with a conceptual justification. One such argument might be that Congress' capacity to authorize congressional-executive agreements is limited by its enumerated powers,[836] most of which are in

[833] See, e.g., Peter J. Spiro, Treaties, Executive Agreements, and Constitutional Method, 79 TEX. L. REV. 961, 996–1000 (2001); Yoo, supra note 309, at 804–06. As these accounts stress, almost all arms control treaties have been made pursuant to Article II treaties. See, e.g., Treaty on Measures for Further Reduction and Limitation of Strategic Offensive Arms, Russ.-U.S., Apr. 8, 2010, T.I.A.S. No. 11-205 (2010); Convention on the Prohibition of the Development, Production, Stockpiling and Use of Chemical Weapons and on Their Destruction, Jan. 13, 1993, T.I.A.S. No. 97-525, 1975 U.N.T.S. 45. But, as these accounts also acknowledge, Congress has endorsed making such agreements by other means. See Arms Control and Disarmament Act of 1961, Pub. L. No. 87-297, § 33, 75 Stat. 631, 634 (codified as amended at 22 U.S.C. § 2573(b) (2018)) (prohibiting the president from assuming "militarily significant" arms control obligation "except pursuant to the treaty making power of the President under the Constitution or unless authorized by further affirmative legislation by the Congress of the United States") (emphasis added). The original Strategic Arms Limitation Talks Agreement (SALT I), which limited certain strategic offensive arms on an interim basis, was entered into as a congressional-executive agreement. U.S.-USSR Strategic Arms Limitation Joint Resolution, Pub. L. No. 92-448, 86 Stat. 746 (1972); Interim Agreement Between the United States of America and the Union of Soviet Socialist Republics on Certain Measures with Respect to the Limitation of Strategic Offensive Arms, U.S.-U.S.S.R., May 26, 1972, 23 U.S.T. 3462, T.I.A.S No. 7504. Still, recent arms control agreements have all been made as Article II treaties, the Senate repeatedly has stated its intent to maintain that practice, and the president appears to have acquiesced. See Bradley & Morrison, supra note 12, at 473–75 (2012); see, e.g., S. EXEC. REP. NO. 102-22, at 81 (1991) (declaration of Senate intent "to approve international agreements that would obligate the United States to reduce or limit the Armed Forces or armaments of the United States in a militarily significant manner only pursuant to the Treaty Power as set forth in Article II, Section 2, Clause 2 of the Constitution," in regard to Resolution of Advice and Consent to the Treaty on Conventional Armed Forces in Europe, Nov. 19, 1990, 30 I.L.M. 1); 137 CONG. REC. 34,348 (1991) (same).

[834] See Hathaway, supra note 775, at 1346–48; see also Yoo, supra note 309, at 808–09 (extradition generally); MICHAEL JOHN GARCIA & CHARLES DOYLE, CONG. RESEARCH SERV., 98-958, EXTRADITION TO AND FROM THE UNITED STATES: OVERVIEW OF THE LAW AND RECENT TREATIES, App. A (2016) (listing bilateral extradition treaties to which the United States is a party). During the 1990s, Congress enabled, in certain circumstances, the extradition of noncitizens to foreign countries even in the absence of an Article II treaty. See Antiterrorism and Effective Death Penalty Act of 1996, Pub. L. No. 104-132, § 443(a) (1996) (codified at 18 U.S.C. § 3181 (2018)). Congress also adopted a statute permitting the surrender of U.S. citizens to face prosecution before the international criminal tribunals for Rwanda and for the former Yugoslavia. See National Defense Authorization Act for Fiscal Year 1996, Pub. L. No. 104-106, § 1342, 110 Stat. 186, 486 (1996). A court of appeals decision upheld executive branch authority to surrender a U.S. citizen to an international criminal tribunal pursuant to a congressional-executive agreement, holding that resort to an Article II treaty was not constitutionally required. Ntakirutimana v. Reno, 184 F.3d 419, 425–27 (5th Cir. 1999). But see Yoo, supra note 309, at 809 (criticizing decision).

[835] Spiro, supra note 833, at 1000–02; Yoo, supra note 309, at 806–08.

[836] Cf. RESTATEMENT (THIRD) § 303(2) (accepting congressional-executive agreements "dealing with any matter that falls within the powers of Congress and of the President under the Constitution"). The reporters' notes appear to go further, at least tentatively. Id. § 303 rptrs. note 7 ("It has been suggested that the authority to make a Congressional-executive agreement may be broader than the sum of the respective powers of Congress and the President; that in international matters the President and Congress together have all the powers of the United States inherent in its sovereignty

Article I, § 8.[837] The explanatory power of such a limit, however, may be doubted. Most controversial agreements, like multilateral trade agreements, clearly fall within Article I.[838] Other areas in which treaties appear to be preferred, like human rights, are not unambiguously excluded from congressional authority.[839] Unless a narrower view of Congress' Article I authority (and other powers) is established, the only topics plausible for an agreement between the United States and a foreign partner, and yet justifiably excluded from congressional-executive agreements on this particular basis, would seem to occupy narrow niches—such as cession of U.S. territory—where confirmatory practice is unlikely to emerge.[840]

If constitutional limits on the use of congressional-executive agreements were both relevant and, in principle, judicially enforceable, difficult questions would remain. Courts would have to resolve whether any constitutional limit concerns Congress' approval of the agreement or the implementing statute, and perhaps confront severability issues. To the extent a limit is assumed, it has been argued that it is mooted in the event that support for a congressional-executive agreement within the Senate exceeds two-thirds,[841] but that seems dubious. Aside from any influence that treaty-specific legislative procedures might have had, it will rarely be clear whether a two-thirds approval would also have been secured

and nationhood, and they can therefore make any international agreement on any subject.") (referencing United States v. Curtiss-Wright Exp. Corp., 299 U.S. 304, 318 (1936)).

[837] U.S. CONST. art. I, § 8. Other provisions, of course, assign important authority to Congress. *See id.* amend. XIV, § 5 ("The Congress shall have power to enforce, by appropriate legislation, the provisions of this article.").

[838] Trade agreements not only involve foreign commerce, but may also concern tariffs, thereby implicating the role reserved for the House of Representatives in revenue-raising. *See* RESTATEMENT (THIRD) § 303 rptrs. note 9.

[839] *Compare* Yoo, *supra* note 309, at 812 & n.221 (suggesting that "the implementation of the substantive terms of human rights treaties may rest outside of Congress's enumerated powers . . ."), *with* Hathaway, *supra* note 775, at 1270–71, 1342–43 (considering human rights obligations as falling within Article II).

[840] *See* Hathaway, *supra* note 775, at 1344–48. Some areas, like extradition, depend very much on how narrowly the area is defined, which also affects how one assesses the density of practice. *See supra* this chapter text accompanying note 781; Hathaway, *supra* note 775, at 1346–48 (suggesting a need for the agreement to be in the form of a treaty, so long as it involves extradition of U.S. citizens).

[841] *See, e.g.,* Tribe, *supra* note 767, at 1227 (noting that because "the WTO Agreement received more than the requisite supermajority support in the Senate . . . from a practical perspective; it seems largely irrelevant whether the agreement was processed through the Treaty Clause of Article II"); *id.* at 1227 n.18 (observing that "[a]rguably, the difference in process is of constitutional significance regardless of the ultimate vote"). Similar suggestions might be made in relation to Senate support for *ex ante* authorization or procedural measures. *See* JANE M. SMITH, DANIEL T. SHEDD, & BRANDON J. MURRILL, CONG. RESEARCH SERV., 97-896, WHY CERTAIN TRADE AGREEMENTS ARE APPROVED AS CONGRESSIONAL-EXECUTIVE AGREEMENTS RATHER THAN TREATIES 2 n.6 (2013) (suggesting that "Senate deference to the use of the congressional-executive agreement for the Uruguay Round agreements may arguably be inferred from its 76–16 vote to amend the [Omnibus Trade and Competitiveness Act of 1988] to extend the date by which the President could enter into the agreements pursuant to this statute, the yeas constituting more than two-thirds of that body") (citation omitted).

if the higher threshold had been appreciated during deliberations. If using congressional-executive agreements is constitutionally objectionable, apparent approval in the Senate does not cure it.

B. Executive Agreements Pursuant to Treaty

Executive agreements pursuant to Article II treaties are a small proportion of U.S. agreements,[842] but they are a critical tool in particular contexts.[843] Their making is straightforward. Following entry into force of an Article II treaty, the executive branch—without further legislative authorization—enters into an executive agreement that implements some aspect of the treaty.[844] This type of international agreement has also been uncontroversial.[845] In theory, they are subject to objections generally raised against agreements that are not made pursuant to Article II, since the Senate is not directly providing advice and consent for the new agreement. But given that consent was afforded for the initial Article II treaty, that plausibly extends to any subsequent implementing agreement fairly contemplated by the terms of that treaty.

Naturally, executive agreements pursuant to a treaty remain prone to objection where they arguably exceed the scope of the authority conveyed by that treaty.[846] The Supreme Court examined such a question in *Wilson v. Girard*, which held that a protocol concluded between the United States and Japan fell within the provision of an earlier security treaty that authorized making certain administrative agreements, relying in part on the Senate's awareness of the subsequent agreement in question.[847] If an executive agreement has a looser relationship with its precursor treaty, including less clarity about whether additional

---

[842] By one informal estimate, executive agreements pursuant to a treaty comprised about 1 to 3 percent of recent U.S. agreements. Bradley & Goldsmith, *supra* note 776, at 1214.

[843] For example, Secretary of State John Foster Dulles estimated in 1953 that ten thousand executive agreements had been concluded to implement the 1949 North Atlantic Treaty. *See* CRS, TREATIES AND OTHER INTERNATIONAL AGREEMENTS, *supra* note 165, at 86 & n.116 (citing Hearings before the Subcomm. on Constitutional Amendments of the S. Comm. on the Judiciary on S.J. Res. 1 and S.J. Res. 43, 83d Cong. 877 (1953)).

[844] CRS, TREATIES AND OTHER INTERNATIONAL AGREEMENTS, *supra* note 165, at 5, 86.

[845] The *Restatement (Third)* devotes only a few sentences to such agreements, without querying their constitutional authority. RESTATEMENT (THIRD) § 303(3) cmt. f & rptrs. note 6 (citing Wilson v. Girard, 354 U.S. 524 (1957)).

[846] As with *ex ante* congressional-executive agreements, executive agreements pursuant to treaty may in theory pose delegation issues, but those have not materialized.

[847] Wilson v. Girard, 354 U.S. 524 (1957). Two aspects suggested Senate awareness. First, when ratifying the 1951 bilateral security treaty, the Senate had before it a signed administrative agreement that the later protocol was to amend. Second, the Senate subsequently ratified the 1951 NATO Status-of-Forces Agreement (also a treaty), and knew at that time of the U.S. commitment to establish the later protocol, which was to correspond with the terms of the NATO treaty—and necessarily found those terms acceptable. *Id.* at 528–29.

agreements were necessary,[848] then the authority for the agreement may also rely on the president's own authority under Article II and the Take Care Clause, which invites an inquiry resembling that for a sole executive agreement.[849] Agreements pursuant to a treaty will be most vulnerable when an executive agreement is at the outermost bounds of a particular treaty's authorization and creates commitments of a kind that would usually be made by an Article II treaty; as a practical matter, the Senate's reaction will be important.[850]

Other potential issues relating to agreements pursuant to a treaty are fairly conventional. Because such an agreement is equivalent to an Article II treaty under international law, it should be interpreted much as would a treaty,[851] although a court may pay less attention to Senate views regarding the agreement than if the court were charged with interpreting the precursor treaty.[852] Few cases have addressed the domestic legal force of executive agreements pursuant to a treaty. While it has been assumed that such agreements, like treaties, have the force of federal law,[853] not all treaties are judicially enforceable as such; a

---

[848] The Restatement (Third), for example, states that "[a]n executive agreement may be made by the President pursuant to a treaty . . . when the executive agreement can fairly be seen as implementing the treaty, especially if the treaty contemplated implementation by international agreement," which strongly implies that an executive agreement may be sustained even though the treaty did not contemplate any agreement being made. RESTATEMENT (THIRD) § 303 cmt. f (emphasis added).

[849] See infra this chapter § V(C) (discussing sole executive agreements). Indirect Senate approval may be significant. See, e.g., United States v. Walczak, 783 F.2d 852, 855–56 (9th Cir. 1986) (concluding that although Congress had not "specifically authorize[d]" by statute a civil aviation agreement, and although an Article II treaty did not "literally authorize the President to enter into agreements implementing it," the agreement is "among those which the President may conclude on his own authority" because it "was designed to implement the goals of . . . an Article II treaty, and [because] Congress contemplated that agreements having to do with civil aviation would be negotiated by the executive branch").

[850] See, e.g., Executive Agreements with Portugal and Bahrain: Hearings on S. Res. 214 Before the S. Foreign Relations Comm., 92d Cong. 11 (1972) (statement of Sen. Case, describing as "somewhat farfetched" the claim that the 1949 North Atlantic Treaty licensed the president to make a 1971 base agreement with Portugal); S. REP. No. 92-632 (1972) (favoring bill that would require base agreements with Portugal and Bahrain to be submitted for consideration as Article II treaties); John F. Murphy, Treaties and International Agreements Other Than Treaties: Constitutional Allocation of Power and Responsibility Among the President, the House of Representatives, and the Senate, 23 U. KAN. L. REV. 221, 225–29 (1975) (describing controversy, including Department of State replies and legislative attempts to cut off funding).

[851] Harris v. United States, 768 F.2d 1240, 1242 (11th Cir. 1985) ("We apply the same rules of treaty interpretation to executive agreements implementing treaty provisions.").

[852] See supra this chapter § III(B)(2) (discussing use of U.S. "legislative history" in treaty interpretation). This is distinct from the question, just discussed, regarding whether an executive agreement pursuant to treaty was in fact authorized by the treaty, as to which the views of views of the U.S. treaty-makers regarding the meaning of the precursor treaty may be considered valuable.

[853] One decision stated simply that "[i]t is not disputed that, as an international executive agreement," the U.S.–South Korea Status of Forces Agreement, S. Kor.–U.S., July 9, 1966, 17 U.S.T. 1677, "may be regarded as equivalent to a treaty and therefore as federal law." Dep't of Def. v. Fed. Labor Relations Auth., 685 F.2d 641, 648 (D.C. Cir. 1982) (citing B. Altman & Co. v. United States, 224 U.S. 583, 601 (1912)). Elsewhere, the court made clear that the executive agreement was based on a mutual defense treaty. Id. at 643 (citing Mutual Defense Treaty, S. Kor.–U.S., Oct. 1, 1953, 5 U.S.T. 2368, T.I.A.S. No. 3097).

safer assumption might be that agreements pursuant to a treaty have the same domestic-law status as do the treaties they implement, although that, too, is a generalization.[854]

C. Sole Executive Agreements

Sole executive agreements—binding international agreements that lack statutory or treaty authorization, whether by design or in fact—are not mentioned in the Constitution. They are nonetheless a significant part of U.S. foreign relations law. By one estimate, they comprise 5 to 10 percent of the international agreements entered into by the United States.[855] Many are of a minor or temporary nature, but some facilitated milestones in U.S. foreign policy, including in recent memory the Paris Peace Accords, which ended the Vietnam War in 1973, and the Algiers Accords, which ended the Iran hostage crisis in 1981.[856]

The broadest constitutional objection to this type of agreement is predictable: that under the Constitution, Article II treaties are the exclusive way to enter into international agreements. Equally predictable is the dominant answer, which is that constitutional practice long ago cemented the availability of sole executive agreements. That answer is of limited value. Practice has almost certainly not resolved the legality of all agreements for all purposes;[857] indeed, recent case

---

[854] See RESTATEMENT (THIRD) § 303 cmt. f ("Such an executive agreement has the same effect and validity as the treaty itself, and is subject to the same constitutional limitations as the treaty."). This generalization might err on either of two scores. A non-self-executing treaty provision might be non-self-executing precisely because it awaited the implementing executive agreement—augmenting the argument for the latter's enforceability. Conversely, an executive agreement implementing a self-executing treaty provision may contain qualifications or enjoy characteristics that would make the executive agreement non-self-executing, or at least nonjusticiable.

[855] Bradley & Goldsmith, *supra* note 776, at 1214–15. Estimates as to the number of sole executive agreements vary depending, among other things, on views as to whether an agreement is in fact authorized under Article II or is a binding international agreement. *Id.* at 1215 n.37. One commentator estimated that nearly fifteen thousand sole executive agreements were concluded over the fifty-year period ending in 2005. Michael P. Van Alstine, *Executive Aggrandizement in Foreign Affairs Lawmaking*, 54 UCLA L. REV. 309, 319 (2006).

[856] See Agreement on Ending the War and Restoring Peace in Viet-Nam, Jan. 27, 1973, 24 U.S.T. 115, 935 U.N.T.S. 2; Declaration of the Government of the Democratic and Popular Republic of Algeria Relating to Commitments Made by Iran and the United States, Iran-U.S., Jan. 19, 1981, 20 I.L.M. 224; *see also* CRS, TREATIES AND OTHER INTERNATIONAL AGREEMENTS, *supra* note 165, at 88 (providing other notable examples, such as the Litvinov Agreement of 1933, recognizing the Soviet Union, and the Destroyers-for-Bases Exchange with Great Britain preceding U.S. entry into World War II).

[857] Those accepting the relevance of practice as a gloss on the Constitution were sometimes more inclined to accept sole executive agreements than congressional-executive agreements, but perhaps only for minor matters. Edwin Borchard, *Shall the Executive Agreement Replace the Treaty*, 53 YALE L.J. 664, 670, 673–75 (1944); *see also* Edwin Borchard, *Treaties and Executive Agreements: A Reply*, 54 YALE L.J. 616 (1945).

law has suggested that such agreements may be meaningfully distinguished from one another.

The key question is whether a sole executive agreement can be attributed to one of the president's independent constitutional powers. The Supreme Court has recognized "some measure of power to enter into executive agreements without obtaining the advice and consent of the Senate,"[858] but it has not been precise about that power's sources or extent.[859] Prefatory agreements supplementary to treaty-making, such as temporary arrangements pending agreement (*modi vivendi*) and agreements to negotiate, may be entailments of the president's treaty power.[860] Depending on their scope, security-related agreements, such as status-of-forces agreements, may relate solely to the commander-in-chief power.[861] Other agreements might be attributable to different Article II powers and their entailments[862] and to the president's overall authority to conduct foreign relations on behalf of the United States.[863] The leading judicial precedents have involved claims settlement agreements, which resolve claims between the United States (and its nationals) and a foreign state (and its nationals). Such agreements have sometimes been justified in terms of the president's recognition power,[864] but that was less central in later cases, like *Dames & Moore v. Regan*[865]

---

[858] Dames & Moore v. Regan, 453 U.S. 654, 682 (1981).

[859] *See generally* Bradford R. Clark, *Domesticating Sole Executive Agreements*, 93 VA. L. REV. 1573 (2007) (criticizing *Dames & Moore* in this regard).

[860] U.S. CONST. art. II, § 2; *see also id.* art II, § 3 (Take Care authority); QUINCY WRIGHT, THE CONTROL OF AMERICAN FOREIGN RELATIONS 239–40, 243 (1922); McDougal & Lans, *supra* note 174, at 248 n.150. A similar capacity to make temporary arrangements may support other treaty-based commitments, such as the obligation not to defeat a treaty's object and purpose, or the provisional application of a treaty pending its entry into force. *See supra* this chapter § II(C).

[861] U.S. CONST. art. II, § 2, cl. 1. Such agreements have concerned armistices (more relevant for declared wars), cessation of hostilities, and prisoners of war. *See, e.g.*, McDougal & Lans, *supra* note 174, at 246–47.

[862] *See* 11 Foreign Affairs Manual, *supra* note 126, § 723.2-2(C) (stating that constitutional sources for sole executive agreement "include," non-exclusively, "[t]he President's authority as Chief Executive to represent the nation in foreign affairs," the power to send and receive ambassadors and recognize foreign government, the commander-in-chief power, and take care authority).

[863] This fallback position may itself be traced to textual assignments, such as the authority to send and receive ambassadors. U.S. CONST. art. II, § 3; *see also id.* art. II, § 1, cl. 1 (assigning the "executive Power"). *See generally* Chapter 3. But it is also associated with *Curtiss-Wright's* famous description of the "very delicate, plenary and exclusive power of the President as the sole organ of the federal government in the field of international relations," although that did not directly concern international agreements. United States v. Curtiss-Wright Export Corp., 299 U.S. 304, 320 (1936); *see* Chapter 1 §§ I(B), II(A)(2).

[864] *See* Chapter 3 § IV(D); *see also* McDougal & Lans, *supra* note 174, at 247–48; United States v. Belmont, 301 U.S. 324, 330 (1937) (explaining that, in light of the executive's "sole organ" authority, sole executive agreements recognizing the USSR and assigning claims did not require Senate advice and consent); United States v. Pink, 315 U.S. 203, 229 (1942) (describing this as a "modest implied power of the President"). The centrality of recognition to these cases was recognized in *Zivotofsky v. Kerry*, 576 U.S. 1, 17–20 (2015) (*Zivotofsky II*); *see* Chapter 1 §§ I(B), II(A)(2), II(B); Chapter 2 § II(C); and Chapter 3 § I(D).

[865] In *Dames & Moore*, the Court described the claims settlement authority at issue as "a necessary incident to the resolution of a major foreign policy dispute between our country and another," and concluded that Congress had "acquiesced in the President's action." *Dames & Moore*, 453 U.S. at 688.

and *American Insurance Association v. Garamendi*,[866] neither of which involved establishing U.S. relations with a foreign state or its government.

Beyond proximity to some identifiable presidential power, a sole executive agreement is more likely to be considered appropriate—within the executive branch, at least—if it is of short duration, responds to an exigency, poses few constraints or risks for the United States, and if Congress has previously acquiesced in such agreements in similar circumstances.[867] Presidential authority that might warrant a sole executive agreement is not incompatible with employing other types of agreements to similar ends if the president so chooses.[868] Still, prior use of Article II treaties and congressional-executive agreements to address a given issue may undermine the case for sole executive authority in comparable circumstances. For example, security agreements based on the president's commander-in-chief authority may give rise to objections when they too closely resemble agreements traditionally done with legislative approval, or contain broader obligations than those typically included in sole executive agreements.[869]

---

[866] In *Garamendi*, the Court noted the president's "authority to make 'executive agreements' with other countries," of which "[m]aking executive agreements to settle claims of American nationals against foreign governments [was] a particularly longstanding practice," while approving extension of judicial acceptance to settling claims against foreign corporations—the better to avoid "hamstring[ing] the President in settling international controversies." Am. Ins. Ass'n v. Garamendi, 539 U.S. 396, 415–16 (2003). For a pre-*Garamendi* criticism of this extension, see Ingrid Brunk Wuerth, *The Dangers of Deference: International Claim Settlement by the President*, 44 HARV. INT'L L.J. 1 (2003).

[867] *See supra* this chapter text accompanying note 781 (noting Circular 175 considerations regarding choice of agreement type); *accord Iraq After the Surge: Hearings Before the S. Comm. on Foreign Relations*, 110th Cong. 451 (2008) (Joint Responses of Ambassador Satterfield and Assistant Secretary Mary Beth Long to Questions Submitted for the Record by Senator Robert P. Casey, Jr.); *see also* Michael D. Ramsey, *Executive Agreements and the (Non)Treaty Power*, 77 N.C. L. REV. 133 (1998) (arguing that minor, short-term agreements, lacking in domestic legal effect, were consistent with the original understanding).

[868] For example, it is not incompatible for Congress to legislate, or for the Senate to provide advice and consent to an Article II treaty, in *support* of an exclusive presidential power such as recognition. Indeed, the president's decision to conclude a sole executive agreement notwithstanding these possibilities is fully consistent with the idea that "it is for the President alone to determine which foreign governments are legitimate." *Zivotofsky II*, 576 U.S. at 19; *id.* at 15–17. *But cf.* Bodansky & Spiro, *supra* note 774, at 902–03 (suggesting that adoption of the 1951 NATO Status of Forces Agreement, *supra* note 771, as an Article II treaty, and the connection of other agreements with existing treaties or legislation, was inconsistent with claims that such agreements could be based on commander-in-chief authority).

[869] The 2008 U.S.-Iraq Status of Forces Agreement (SOFA), for example, was criticized due to unusual provisions—for example, providing authority for U.S. troops to engage in certain military operations—that went beyond the normal bounds of a sole executive agreement addressing the status of U.S. forces abroad. *E.g.*, M. Cherif Bassiouni, *Legal Status of US Forces in Iraq from 2003–2008*, 11 CHI. J. INT'L L. 1, 9–15, 27 (2010); Bodansky & Spiro, *supra* note 774, at 902 & n.90; Bradley & Goldsmith, *supra* note 776, at 1247–48; Hathaway, *supra* note 778, at 143 n.4; *see* Agreement on the Withdrawal of United States Forces from Iraq and the Organization of Their Activities during Their Temporary Presence in Iraq, Iraq-U.S., Nov. 27, 2008, https://perma.cc/QR9P-3UGH [Iraq-U.S. SOFA]; *see also* Strategic Framework Agreement for a Relationship of Friendship and Cooperation Between the United States and the Republic of Iraq, Iraq-U.S., Nov. 17, 2008, T.I.A.S. No. 09-101.1 [Iraq-U.S. Strategic Framework Agreement]. While critics portrayed the Iraq-U.S. SOFA as predicated solely on the president's authority, its defenders portrayed it simply as an "executive agreement"

Sole executive agreements would be quite controversial, of course, if they established international obligations in tension with those assumed via other
U.S. agreements.[870]

A distinct and substantial question is whether—assuming a sole executive
agreement is constitutionally valid—it establishes national law that may displace
conflicting state and federal law. Early claims settlement cases, predicated on the
recognition power, established the potential preemptive effect of sole executive
agreements.[871] In *Garamendi*, the Court stated more generally that "valid executive agreements are fit to preempt state law."[872] The subsequent decision in
Medellín v. Texas suggested possible limits, describing the Court's claims settlement agreement cases as involving a "narrow set of circumstances" and a " 'particularly longstanding practice' of congressional acquiescence."[873] The Court
did not question the validity of sole executive agreements in other areas, but did
seem to imply that they might not displace contrary state law.

Happily, there have been few opportunities to test how sole executive
agreements relate to other federal law. Most authority suggests that such
agreements should be regarded as inferior to statutes and yield in the event of
conflict, because of a sense that law created by both political branches, especially
one with "legislative Powers,"[874] is superior to any made by one.[875] A similar logic

---

used in lieu of an Article II treaty and requiring no additional legislative authority, while invoking
preexisting statutory authority. *See Iraq After the Surge: Hearings Before the S. Comm. on Foreign
Relations*, 110th Cong. 371 (2008) (statement of Hon. David M. Satterfield, Senior Adviser to the
Secretary of State and Coordinator for Iraq).

[870] This tension would be more acute in the unlikely event that a sole executive agreement created
an international obligation that was inconsistent with an existing Article II treaty or congressional-
executive agreement. As a matter of international law, the sole executive agreement might prevail irrespective of whether it would be deprived of force according to U.S. law. *See infra* this chapter § V(E);
see also supra this chapter § II(A)(1).

[871] Professor Clark has emphasized that the act of state doctrine, and the formerly absolute immunity of foreign sovereigns, also help explain why the Supreme Court conferred supremacy on those
agreements. *See* Clark, *Domesticating, supra* note 767, at 1618–52. For a different act of state analysis
(to which Professor Clark responds), see RAMSEY, CONSTITUTION'S TEXT, *supra* note 767, at 295–99;
Ramsey, *supra* note 867, at 147 n.52.

[872] Am. Ins. Ass'n v. Garamendi, 539 U.S. 396, 416 (2003). *Garamendi* itself did not apply the agreement in question directly, but the rather the federal policy embodied in it; this was enough, if a state
law posed a "clear conflict," to "require state law to yield." *Id.* at 425. Lower courts have also applied
claims settlement agreement principles more generally. *See, e.g.*, United States v. Walczak, 783 F.2d
852, 856 (9th Cir. 1986) (stating that "constitutionally valid executive agreements are to be applied
by the courts as the law of the land" and that "the Agreement on Air Transport Preclearance has the
full force of law") (citing United States v. Pink, 315 U.S. 203, 230 (1942)). For further discussion, see
Chapter 9 § II(C).

[873] Medellín v. Texas, 552 U.S. 491, 531, 532 (2008). For further discussion of *Medellín*, see *supra*
this chapter §§ III(B), IV(A); Chapter 1 § II(B); Chapter 3 § I(D); Chapter 5 § II(B); Chapter 7 §
III(C); and Chapter 9 §§ II(B), II(C).

[874] U.S. CONST. art I, § 1.

[875] United States v. Guy W. Capps, Inc., 204 F.2d 655, 658 (4th Cir. 1953) (describing an executive
agreement, the basis for a government contract, as "void because it was not authorized by Congress
and contravened provisions of a statute"), *aff'd*, 348 U.S. 296 (1955); 11 Foreign Affairs Manual, *supra*

suggests that treaties, which also enjoy legislative approval and clear constitutional recognition, are also hierarchically superior. Still, some have suggested that a constitutionally valid sole executive agreement might prevail over earlier treaties, congressional-executive agreements, or even statutes,[876] given that it is an exercise of constitutional authority allocated to the president, and is not inherently inferior to other exercises of power. In the unlikely event such arguments were accepted, they might be confined to sole executive agreements that rest on *exclusive* presidential authority, meaning authority that the president alone may exercise.[877] Finally, one might speculate that U.S. courts would likely give a sole executive agreement effect notwithstanding preexisting customary international

---

note 126, § 723.2-2(C) (explaining, in relation to Circular 175 procedure, that presidential authority to conclude sole executive agreements assumes "the agreement is not inconsistent with legislation enacted by the Congress in the exercise of its constitutional authority"); *see also* Waiver of Claims for Damages Arising Out of Cooperative Space Activity, 19 Op. O.L.C. 140, 155 n.29 (1995) (stating that, "unlike treaties, a sole executive agreement may not be effective in the face of prior inconsistent legislation"); CRS, TREATIES AND OTHER INTERNATIONAL AGREEMENTS, *supra* note 165, at 93–95 (describing courts as "reluctant to enforce" sole executive agreements over prior statutes, but that "the law on this point may yet be in the course of further development"); *cf.* Seery v. United States, 127 F. Supp. 601, 606–07 (Ct. Cl. 1955) (explaining that it would be "incongruous if the Executive Department alone, without even the limited participation by Congress which is present when a treaty is ratified, could . . . nullify the Act of Congress consenting to suit on Constitutional claims" and so interfere with constitutional rights"). *But cf.* RESTATEMENT (THIRD) § 303 cmt. j (describing the status of sole executive agreements relative to earlier statutes as "not . . . authoritatively determined"). The position that sole executive agreements would yield to a conflicting statute may also be predicated on a view that they would lack efficacy against contrary state law. *E.g.*, Swearingen v. United States, 565 F. Supp. 1019, 1021 (D. Colo. 1983) (stating in dicta that "executive agreements do not supersede prior inconsistent acts of Congress because, unlike treaties, they are not the 'supreme Law of the Land'").

[876] Etlimar Societe Anonyme of Casablanca v. United States, 106 F. Supp. 191, 195–96 (Ct. Cl. 1952) (indicating that a sole executive agreement was equivalent to a treaty for Supremacy Clause purposes), *overruled in part*, Seery v. United States, 127 F. Supp. 601, 606 (Ct. Cl. 1955); HENKIN, FOREIGN AFFAIRS, at 228 (suggesting later-in-time effect, but acknowledging that "[t]he issue remains unresolved"); Derek Jinks & David Sloss, *Is the President Bound by the Geneva Conventions?*, 90 CORNELL L. REV. 97, 138 (2004) ("Since sole executive agreements 'have a similar dignity' as treaties, a later sole executive agreement arguably supersedes an earlier treaty under the later-in-time rule."). Some such authority may conflate different forms of international agreement. *See, e.g.*, Risinger v. SOC LLC, 936 F. Supp. 2d 1235, 1252 (D. Nev. 2013) (citing authority concerning agreements pursuant to treaties); Hawkins v. Comparet-Cassani, 33 F. Supp. 2d 1244, 1256 (C.D. Cal. 1999) (citing authority concerning later-in-time statutes).

[877] The *Restatement (Third)*'s reporters' notes observe that—at least for a presidential power like recognition—one might resist giving the president power to overturn a congressional act, but also resist differentiating between species of federal law. RESTATEMENT (THIRD) § 115 rptrs. note 5 (quoting THE FEDERALIST No. 64, at 394 (John Jay) ("All Constitutional acts of power, whether in the executive or in the judicial department, have as much legal validity and obligation as if they proceeded from the legislature")); *accord* United States v. Pink, 315 U.S. 203, 230 (1942); Constitutionality of Legislative Provision Regarding ABM Treaty, 20 Op. O.L.C. 246, 250–51 (1996) (suggesting "serious doubts" about the constitutionality of proposed legislation that would deny binding effect to a sole executive agreement recognizing the succession of new states to the rights and obligations of their predecessors under Article II treaties).

law and that they would certainly do so relative to a prior sole executive agreement involving the same states parties.[878]

D. Nonbinding Agreements

Nonbinding, or "political," agreements are a longstanding phenomenon. They structured critical geopolitical relationships during the United States' rise as a global power—from the Atlantic Charter among Allied powers during World War II, to the Shanghai Communique developed by President Nixon and Chairman Mao and the Helsinki Accords. Now they feature prominently in attempts to address contemporary problems like climate change.[879]

The appeal of these arrangements stems in large part from their capacity to be *politically* binding, which may achieve some or all of the ends sought by more conventional agreements, while at the same time avoiding *legally* binding obligations. Given their nature, the law has relatively little to say about them. The VCLT does not address them,[880] nor does the customary international law of treaties.[881] Because they are nonbinding internationally, they would not qualify as Article II treaties—and, accordingly, need not be concluded as such.[882] It is also fairly assumed that they lack any domestic legal effect, so they are subordinate to federal and state law.[883] To the extent such policy instruments require a

[878] RESTATEMENT (THIRD) § 115 cmt. d ("A sole executive agreement that is within the President's constitutional authority . . . would supersede a prior sole executive agreement and probably a preexisting rule of customary law as United States law").

[879] Duncan B. Hollis & Joshua J. Newcomer, *"Political" Commitments and the Constitution*, 49 VA. J. INT'L L. 507, 510–11, 563–66 (2009); Bradley & Goldsmith, *supra* note 776, at 1217–20; CRS, TREATIES AND OTHER INTERNATIONAL AGREEMENTS, *supra* note 165, at 61–63; *see also* Anthony Aust, *The Theory and Practice of Informal International Instruments*, 35 INT'L & COMP. L.Q. 787 (1986); Oscar Schachter, *The Twilight Existence of Nonbinding International Agreements*, 71 AM. J. INT'L L. 296, 303 (1977). It has been suggested that it would be premature to regard nonbinding agreements as a constitutional custom, see Hollis & Newcomer, *supra*, at 563–64, but there were arguably analogous activities early in U.S. history. Michael D. Ramsey, *Evading the Treaty Power?: The Constitutionality of Nonbinding Agreements*, 11 FIU L. REV. 371, 375 (2016).

[880] *See* VCLT, *supra* note 13, art. 2 (defining "treaty"); Schachter, *supra* note 879, at 301 & n.19 (discussing *travaux préparatoires* of the Vienna Convention on the Law of Treaties).

[881] *Cf.* Schachter, *supra* note 879, at 300–01 (discussing the paradox of states concluding such agreements, sometimes in great detail, yet eschewing any legal consequences). States, including the United States, operate on this premise. *See, e.g.,* Transmittal of the Treaty with the U.S.S.R. on the Reduction and Limitation of Strategic Offensive Arms (The START Treaty), Nov. 25, 1991, S. TREATY DOC. NO. 102-20, at 1086 (proclaiming that "[a] 'political' undertaking is not governed by international law").

[882] Hollis & Newcomer, *supra* note 879, at 548–50; Ramsey, *supra* note 879, at 375.

[883] *See* Ramsey, *supra* note 879, at 375 (concluding that "nonbinding agreements . . . should have no domestic legal effect in U.S. courts nor impose any legal obligations on U.S. domestic entities"); *cf.* RESTATEMENT (THIRD) § 301 cmt. e & rptrs. note 2 (concluding that nonbinding agreements were outside the scope of its part on international agreements).

constitutional basis, they have been associated with the president's general foreign affairs powers.[884]

The recent prominence of nonbinding agreements has renewed attention regarding their legal implications. Agreements such as the 2015 Joint Comprehensive Plan of Action (JCPOA), drawn between several countries, the European Union, and Iran, appear to have been made as nonbinding instruments at least in part to avoid any constitutional obligation to seek Senate or congressional approval.[885] Such agreements (and nonbinding provisions in otherwise binding agreements) may not themselves create legal obligations for the United States, but can establish a framework for harnessing existing domestic authority toward the agreement's objectives, not unlike a non-self-executing treaty.[886] The galvanizing capacity of nonbinding agreements, and the possibility that they were carefully drawn to avoid requiring legislative approval while achieving similar results, has invited more careful scrutiny.

Of course, a threshold concern is whether a given agreement is, in fact, not legally binding. Negotiating states may make their intent apparent by using terms like "political" or "nonbinding," by disclaiming a legally binding nature, or by avoiding language that evokes obligation (such as "shall" or "agree," as opposed to "should").[887] Unsurprisingly, they often leave matters ambiguous or internally inconsistent, and state appraisals of an agreement may differ.[888]

---

[884] *But cf.* Hollis & Newcomer, *supra* note 879, at 550–54 (discussing, but resisting, attributing nonbinding agreements to the Constitution's foreign affairs powers); *id.* at 554–72, 570 (suggesting a nonplenary power rooted in constitutional custom, or "in the structure of the Constitution, constructed as a delegated, if unenumerated, sovereign power of the federal government").

[885] *See* Joint Comprehensive Plan of Action, July 14, 2015, https://perma.cc/U7WT-9VQ7. For depictions of the JCPOA as a political commitment, see, for example, Letter from Julia Frifield, Assistant Sec'y, Legislative Affairs, U.S. Dep't of State, to Rep. Mike Pompeo (Nov. 19, 2015), https://perma.cc/ESW2-LKSU; Letter from Denis McDonough, Assistant to the President and Chief of Staff, to Sen. Bob Corker (Mar. 14, 2015), 2015 DIGEST OF U.S. PRACTICE 123. JCPOA was endorsed, however, in a legally binding Security Council resolution. *See* S.C. Res. 2231, ¶ 1 (July 20, 2015); STEPHEN P. MULLIGAN, CONG. RESEARCH SERV., R44761, WITHDRAWAL FROM INTERNATIONAL AGREEMENTS: LEGAL FRAMEWORK, THE PARIS AGREEMENT, AND THE IRAN NUCLEAR AGREEMENT 20–28 (2018) [hereinafter CRS, WITHDRAWAL FROM INTERNATIONAL AGREEMENTS]; *see also infra* this chapter text accompanying notes 907–908.

[886] An example of (important) nonbinding provisions being contained in a binding agreement is the 2015 Paris Agreement on climate change. *See* U.N. Framework Convention on Climate Change Conference of the Parties, Report of the Conference of the Parties on its Twenty-First Session, add. at 21, U.N. Doc. FCCC/CP/2015/10/Add.1 (Jan. 29, 2016) [hereinafter Paris Agreement]; *see also* Daniel Bodansky, *The Paris Climate Change Agreement: A New Hope?*, 110 AM. J. INT'L. L. 288, 290 (2016). *But cf.* Jack Goldsmith, *The Contributions of the Obama Administration to the Practice and Theory of International Law*, 57 HARV. INT'L L.J. 455, 466 (2016) (noting invocation of "independent domestic law authorities that were not designed to effectuate or approve international agreements" at all); Hollis & Newcomer, *supra* note 879, at 545–48 (noting this and other forms of domestic significance).

[887] Hollis & Newcomer, *supra* note 879, at 523–24 (noting various techniques); Schachter, *supra* note 879, at 297–99 (same); *see also infra* this chapter text accompanying notes 909–912.

[888] *See* Schachter, *supra* note 879, at 297 (noting resistance to explicit resolution); *see, e.g.*, Hollis & Newcomer, *supra* note 879, at 510–11 n.13 (noting Russian appraisal of agreements among Allied Powers as "very important rules of international law"); *cf.* Alexandria Zavis & Ramin Mostaghim,

The basic problem is that nonbinding and binding agreements share important features: both encourage conforming behavior, often without enforcement mechanisms, and both disrupt any expectation that a subject is solely a domestic concern.[889] Despite calls for greater clarity, the executive branch doubtless enjoys discretion as to how best to draft a nonbinding agreement.[890] Where uncertain, courts in the United States should defer to executive determinations as to whether an agreement is nonbinding, though the status of the agreement under international law remains governed by that law.[891]

The weight given nonbinding agreements within U.S. law may also pose issues. Courts sometimes take nonbinding agreements into account in evaluating claims as to customary international law.[892] Courts also may conflate nonbinding agreements with non-self-executing treaties,[893] but—apart from their quite distinct characters under international law—non-self-executing provisions matter for domestic law in ways that nonbinding provisions likely do not, such as by factoring into the interpretation of potentially conflicting statutes.[894] The limited role of nonbinding agreements in U.S. law may be complicated by *American Insurance Association v. Garamendi*, which suggested that an executive *policy* involving cooperation with other states might preempt California law.[895] While

Iran Leader Says GOP Senators' Letter Implies U.S. "Not Trustworthy," L.A. Times, Mar. 10, 2015 (comments by Iranian foreign minister indicating that Iran anticipated that the JCPOA would establish binding international law). Some international lawyers may presume that an agreement is internationally binding. Hollis & Newcomer, *supra* note 879, at 524 & n.65.

[889] *See generally* Hollis & Newcomer, *supra* note 879, at 539–44 (noting similarities between binding and nonbinding agreements); Schachter, *supra* note 879, at 303–04.

[890] Some have suggested that the executive branch "has a constitutional obligation to assure that a purportedly nonbinding agreement is clearly and unequivocally nonbinding under international law." Ramsey, *supra* note 879, at 376. The basis is unclear, and it might seriously encroach on presidential authority—especially if other states resisted language that would satisfy the standard, and thereby foreclose the use of such agreements.

[891] Recent cases involving the JCPOA suggest that courts do not always pay heed. *See, e.g.,* Leibovich v. Islamic Republic of Iran, 297 F. Supp. 3d 816, 822 (N.D. Ill. 2018) (describing JCPOA as "deal" imposing "obligations"); Peterson v. Obama, No. 15-cv-411-PB, 2015 WL 8526551, 2 & n.1 (D.N.H. 2015) (acquiescing in description of JCPOA as an Article II treaty). For general guidance, see State Dep't Office of the Legal Adviser, *Treaty Affairs, Guidance on Non-Binding Documents,* https://perma.cc/SX8V-V2M9; *see also* Memorandum from Robert E. Dalton, Assistant Legal Adviser for Treaty Affairs, *International Documents of a Non-Legally Binding Character* (Mar. 18, 1994), https://perma.cc/JE5X-34FL.

[892] *See, e.g.,* United States v. Kakwirakeron, 730 F. Supp. 1200, 1202 (N.D.N.Y 1990) (treating the Helsinki Accords as "indicative of the status of international law on self-determination of peoples and of the duty of nations to abide by their international obligations"); Ctr. for Indep. of Judges and Lawyers of U.S., Inc. v. Mabey, 19 B.R. 635, 647 (D. Utah 1982) (noting that Helsinki Accords "do not have the force of treaty law within the United States," but might conceivably evidence customary international law).

[893] *See, e.g.,* Frolova v. U.S.S.R., 761 F.2d 370, 375–76 (7th Cir. 1985) (concluding that the Helsinki Accords are non-self-executing).

[894] *See supra* this chapter text accompanying notes 574–582.

[895] That policy was "embod[ied]" in a binding executive agreement, but the agreement's significance was minimized because it lacked preemptive force. Am. Ins. Ass'n v. Garamendi, 539 U.S. 396, 417 (2003).

the Court's reasoning might support giving domestic legal force to a nonbinding agreement or to a nonbinding provision in an otherwise binding agreement, it is likely qualified by the reasoning of *Medellín v. Texas*, in which the Supreme Court refused to give effect to an executive policy that went beyond any domestically effective, internationally binding obligation.[896] Whether a federal policy, embodied in a nonbinding obligation, might under some circumstances contribute to federal law, is probably best regarded as unresolved.

As with countless other foreign relations law issues, the principal mechanism for addressing legal concerns about presidential resort to nonbinding agreements is through interbranch action, reaction, and mutual accommodation. On occasion, following congressional pressure, the executive branch has (with cooperation by U.S. partners) developed what was envisioned as a nonbinding agreement into something that is binding.[897] In other instances, after it has become evident that Congress would not approve a formal, binding agreement, the executive branch has developed a nonbinding agreement instead.[898] Congress has also acted both to inhibit and to encourage U.S. compliance with particular nonbinding agreements.[899] These dialogues relate to substantive preferences as much as, or more than, the legal character of any agreement. They may be stymied, however, when a nonbinding agreement is not made public, and it bears mention that the executive branch is only required by law to report *binding* agreements to Congress.[900]

---

[896] 552 U.S. 491, 532 (2008); *cf. id.* at 523, 530 (holding open prospects attributing domestic effects to presidential actions under other circumstances). For further discussion of *Medellín*, see *supra* this chapter §§ III(B), IV(A); Chapter 1 § II(B); Chapter 3 § I(D); Chapter 5 § II(B); Chapter 7 § III(C); and Chapter 9 §§ II(B), II(C).

[897] *See* Hollis & Newcomer, *supra* note 879, at 508–10 (discussing evolution of Iraq-U.S. SOFA into a sole executive agreement); *see also supra* this chapter text accompanying note 869 (discussing Iraq-U.S. SOFA and Iraq-U.S. Strategic Framework Agreement).

[898] This is one narrative of the JCPOA. Goldsmith, *supra* note 886, at 466. On another narrative, the review mechanism that Congress adopted—the Iran Nuclear Agreement Review Act of 2015—inadvertently "cede[d]" the President authority to conclude a legally binding nuclear agreement, not just an informal political pact," whether or not President Obama actually availed himself of that authority. David Golove, *Congress Just Gave the President Power to Adopt a Binding Legal Agreement with Iran*, JUST SECURITY, May 14, 2015 https://perma.cc/7QCZ-BCX2; *accord* Bruce Ackerman & David Golove, *Can the Next President Repudiate Obama's Iran Agreement?*, THE ATLANTIC (Sept. 10, 2015), https://perma.cc/WR3Q-LQE3. In light of the Trump administration's withdrawal from the JCPOA, the issue may be moot, unless the United States subsequently rejoins. *See infra* this chapter text accompanying notes 967–968.

[899] Hollis & Newcomer, *supra* note 879, at 567–68 (citing examples).

[900] 22 C.F.R. § 181.2(a) (2020) (providing that, for purposes of defining the international agreements subject to required reporting under the Case-Zablocki Act, "[t]he parties must intend their undertaking to be legally binding, and not merely of political or personal effect. Documents intended to have political or moral weight, but not intended to be legally binding, are not international agreements."). For concerns on this front, see CRS, TREATIES AND OTHER INTERNATIONAL AGREEMENTS, *supra* note 165, at 231–32.

E. Establishing Commitments by Means Other than Agreement

Just as Article II treaties are not the only forms of international agreement for the United States, agreements are not the only means by which the United States can establish international obligations. These alternative means afford the executive branch yet more options—potentially at the expense of Congress. Three deserve brief mention.

As discussed in Chapter 5, the United States participates in establishing customary international law, and the president's interpretation or recognition of a customary rule may be decisive for other U.S. actors. Because customary rules may correlate with multilateral agreements to which the United States is not a party, and for which congressional approval is withheld or unlikely, presidential recognition of principle of customary international law might be regarded as simulating U.S. ratification by the United States and as an executive branch end-around.[901] Possible examples—the 1969 VCLT,[902] the 1977 Additional Protocols I[903] and II[904] to the 1949 Geneva Conventions, and the 1982 U.N. Convention on the Law of the Sea[905]—suggest at most that the executive is prone to endorse

[901] For arguments to this effect, see Bradley & Goldsmith, *supra* note 776, at 1226–33; Eric Talbot Jensen, *Presidential Pronouncements of Customary International Law as an Alternative to the Senate's Advice and Consent*, 2015 BYU L. REV. 1525.

[902] *See supra* this chapter note 16 (discussing U.S. position).

[903] The United States long supported Article 75 of Additional Protocol I, but its view regarding the legal status of that provision was unclear. Michael J. Matheson, *The United States Position on the Relation of Customary International Law to the 1977 Protocols Additional to the 1949 Geneva Conventions*, 2 AM. U. J. INT'L L. & POL'Y 419, 422–23, 427 (1987). The Obama administration indicated it would "choose out of a sense of legal obligation to treat the principles set forth in Article 75 as applicable" to certain detainees, while noting continuing, "significant concerns" with Protocol I. The White House, Office of the Press Secretary, *Fact Sheet: New Actions on Guantánamo and Detainee Policy* (Mar. 7, 2011), https://perma.cc/K459-W9T9. The executive branch cited U.S. law as contributing to "crystallization" of the Article 75 principles as customary international law, without recognize it as such. *Libya and War Powers: Hearing Before the S. Comm. on Foreign Relations*, 112th Cong. 57 (2011) (responses of Department of State Legal Adviser Harold Koh to questions submitted by Sen. Richard G. Lugar); U.S. Dep't of Def., Law of War Manual, ¶ 8.1.4.2, at 512 (June 2015, updated Dec. 2016), https://perma.cc/QA5T-ATP8; *see* Bradley & Goldsmith, *supra* note 776, at 1233 n.131 (observing that the Legal Adviser's statement "stopped short of claiming that Article 75 was binding as a matter of" customary international law).

[904] It has been suggested that President Obama declared Additional Protocol II to be customary international law and regarded "its provisions as binding on the United States, regardless of the Senate's advice and consent." Jensen, *supra* note 901, at 1538–39 (citing The White House, Office of the Press Secretary, *Fact Sheet: New Actions on Guantanamo and Detainee Policy* (Mar. 7, 2011), https://perma.cc/K459-W9T9). The cited statement only indicated that U.S. practice is already consistent with Additional Protocol II, while advocating, not dispensing with, advice and consent.

[905] *See* Bradley & Goldsmith, *supra* note 776, at 1231–32; Jensen, *supra* note 901, at 1534–38. Some statements indicate simply that the United States would act in a manner consistent with international law, including as might be reflected in the Convention. *See* White House, Office of the Press Secretary, *Fact Sheet of March 10, 1983, on United States Oceans Policy*, 22 I.L.M. 461, 462 (1983); *see also* Presidential Statement on United States Oceans Policy, 1 PUB. PAPERS 378–79 (Mar. 10, 1983); Proclamation No. 5030, 48 Fed. Reg. 10,605 (Mar. 10, 1983); Pres. Proclamation No. 5928, 54 Fed. Reg. 777 (Dec. 27, 1988). Nothing suggested that the United States was abiding by international

particular rules as customary rather than the agreement in its entirety. The operative effect of a U.S. statement that a treaty provision reflects customary international law is hard to state definitively. Such statements could serve as agreement alternatives only when the rules are plausibly customary—yet not so clearly as to make presidential subscription immaterial—and when treaty-based reciprocity and any procedural mechanisms are peripheral. Executive branch statements and practice are more likely to contribute to custom's formation, without fully substituting for an agreement's ratification and entry into force.[906]

Second, as discussed in Chapter 7, U.S. participation in international organizations may also produce decisions establishing international and U.S. law. For example, the president may facilitate the adoption by the U.N. Security Council of a binding resolution under Chapter VII of the U.N. Charter, which contains obligations that would normally be embedded in a binding agreement. This scenario is striking in part because it displaces the usual multilateral treaty-making process (and involves 15 nations imposing obligations on all 193 U.N. member states), but also because the executive branch may by this means effectuate binding international law without any role for Congress. The United States rarely pursues (and the Security Council rarely adopts) resolutions of this "treaty-like" quality, and such resolutions may not be enforceable as a rule of law in U.S. courts.[907] Most important, to the extent they have been contemplated as a means for circumventing Congress, Congress has been swift to object and has at times been successful in its objections.[908]

A third alternative to agreements is unilateral declarations by the United States that are regarded as legally binding under international law. Such "[d]eclarations

---

law distinctly *established* by the Convention, let alone electing to do so, and any domestic effect was specifically disclaimed. Presidential Statement on United States Oceans Policy, 1 PUB. PAPERS 379 (Mar. 10, 1983); Proclamation No. 5928, 54 Fed. Reg. 777 (Dec. 27, 1988). The Justice Department's Office of Legal Counsel, considering an assertion of jurisdiction and sovereignty over the territorial sea, noted that the proclamation itself lacked domestic legal effect and recalled that "the most legally secure method" would be entering into a treaty. Legal Issues Raised by Proposed Presidential Proclamation to Extend the Territorial Sea, 12 Op. O.L.C. 238, 238–39, 253 (1988).

[906] This is consistent with the position that the *Restatement Third* took with respect to the U.N. Convention on the Law of the Sea. RESTATEMENT (THIRD) pt. V, intr. note, at 5–8.

[907] *See* Diggs v. Richardson, 555 F.2d 848, 851 (D.C. Cir. 1976) (holding Security Council resolution non-self-executing); *accord* Tarros S.p.A. v. United States, 982 F. Supp. 2d 325, 340–43 (S.D.N.Y. 2013).

[908] On one telling, this was the fate of presidential attempts to pursue a Security Council resolution relating to the Comprehensive Test Ban Treaty, which—after protest led by the chair of the Senate Committee on Foreign Relations—was downgraded to a nonbinding resolution. Bradley & Goldsmith, *supra* note 776, at 1245–47; *see* S.C. Res. 2310, ¶ 4 (Sept. 23, 2016). According to executive branch officials, no binding resolution was ever pursued, and they (ultimately, at least) disavowed any such intention. *The Administration's Proposal for a U.N. Resolution on the Comprehensive Nuclear Test-Ban Treaty: Hearing Before the S. Comm. on Foreign Relations*, 114th Cong. 44–45 (2016) (letter of Sept. 7, 2016, from Sec'y of State Kerry and Assistant Sec'y of State for Legislative Affairs Frifield to Sen. Corker); *see id.* at 43 (letter of Aug. 12, 2016, from Sen. Corker to President Barack Obama).

publicly made and manifesting the will to be bound may have the effect of creating legal obligations," even absent any mutuality or reciprocity.[909] If such a declaration creates legal obligations, it has been asserted that they may create reliance interests and "cannot be revoked arbitrarily," save in circumstances similar to those for the revocation of international agreements.[910]

The United States is among the states which have pressed for a restrictive understanding of unilateral declarations, in part out of concern that a state might inadvertently assume international obligations.[911] Unilateral declarations might also be faulted for creating an additional mechanism by which the president might circumvent domestic safeguards on international commitments. Internationally, authority for making declarations is clearly vested in executive branch officials, and legislatures appear to play no particular role.[912] But, as a matter of U.S. foreign relations law, circumventing Congress is problematic; unsurprisingly, interest in such declarations seems to increase when congressional opposition to an international agreement appears substantial.[913] Even so, the risk of strategic (mis)use seems low. Unilateral declarations are relatively untested, and there are probably few circumstances in which they have concrete advantages over sole executive agreements.[914] The relative disadvantages are fairly clear, given that the domestic legal effect is almost wholly speculative, and—as with other agreement alternatives—political countermeasures can scarcely be avoided.

---

[909] *Guiding Principles Applicable to Unilateral Declarations of States Capable of Creating Legal Obligations, With Commentaries Thereto,* 2 Y.B. Int'l Law Comm'n 161, 162 (2006), U.N. Doc. A/CN.4/SER.A/2006/Add.1 (Part 2) [hereinafter *Guiding Principles*] (Guiding Principle 1); *see* Nuclear Tests (Austl. v. Fr.; N.Z. v. Fr.), Judgment, 1974 I.C.J. 253, 267–70 (Dec. 20); Case Concerning the Frontier Dispute (Burk. Faso v. Mali), Judgment, 1986 I.C.J. 554, 573–74 (Dec. 22).

[910] *See Guiding Principles, supra* note 909, at 161, 166 (Guiding Principle 10).

[911] *See* U.S. Statement to U.N. General Assembly, Sixth Committee, on the Report of the International Law Commission on its 58th Session, *excerpted in* 2006 DIGEST OF U.S. PRACTICE 281–82. *But see Guiding Principles, supra* note 909, at 161–66 (stressing, in Guiding Principles 1, 3, 7, and 10 and accompanying commentary, bases for a restrictive reading); Michael J. Matheson, *The Fifty-Eighth Session of the International Law Commission,* 101 AM. J. INT'L L. 407, 421–23 (2007) (noting evolution of ILC approach toward a more conservative approach).

[912] *Guiding Principles, supra* note 909, at 161, 166 (Guiding Principle 10).

[913] *See, e.g.,* David A. Koplow, *Nuclear Arms Control by a Pen and a Phone: Effectuating the Comprehensive Test Ban Treaty Without Ratification,* 46 GEO. J. INT'L L. 475, 511–15 (2015) (suggesting unilateral commitments, including by the United States, as a means of reviving the Comprehensive Test Ban Treaty, which the United States has signed but not ratified); Frédéric Gilles Sourgens, *Climate Commons Law: The Transformative Force of the Paris Agreement,* 50 N.Y.U. J. INT'L L. & POL. 885 (2018) (arguing that despite the attempted U.S. withdrawal from the Paris Agreement, the United States has already made an internationally binding unilateral commitment to reduce carbon emissions); *see also* Suyash Paliwal, *The Binding Force of G-20 Commitments,* 40 YALE J. INT'L L. ONLINE 1 (2014) (suggesting that G-20 commitments may also constitute binding unilateral declarations).

[914] A unilateral declaration might have appeal in the unusual instance in which no other appropriate state party is available to conclude an agreement, or where a wider obligation was required but a multilateral agreement was infeasible. Yet there would be a substantial cost in terms of international and domestic legal uncertainty.

VI. Exiting Treaties

Even if a treaty is properly made, interpreted, and incorporated in U.S. law, a wide range of performance-related questions remain. These questions do not receive extensive consideration in U.S. courts. Instead, the administration of treaties is understood to be the responsibility of the political branches, especially the executive branch, and restrained mostly by U.S. interests and international law. For example, the United States appears to accept the material breach standard that exists in the international law of treaties, but entrusts the president with primary responsibility for applying it, and (as elsewhere) generally expects the president to abide by customary international law governing treaties and governing state responsibility.[915] To date, however, there is little evaluation of the effect of breaches on the enforceability of treaties in U.S. courts.

The question of whether and when the United States can withdraw from, terminate, or suspend its treaties has also received relatively little judicial attention, but that may change. Unlike the making of agreements (which Article II addresses in part, at least), there is no constitutional text regarding exit, and courts have resisted opportunities to develop clear doctrinal solutions. As a result, U.S. law continues to be unsettled, relying on inferences from constitutional structure, from political practice, and from international law, to inform a subject that bears closely on the entire corpus of treaty law. Prominent U.S. decisions to withdraw from major agreements, such as the 2015 Paris Agreement on climate change,[916] the Iran nuclear deal,[917] and the Open Skies Treaty,[918] and to suspend and then withdraw from the INF Treaty,[919] mean that the subject continues to receive extensive attention.[920]

---

[915] *See, e.g., infra* this chapter text accompanying notes 929 (indicating U.S. acceptance of international rules), 919 (discussing INF suspension); *see also supra* this chapter text accompanying note 360 (discussing scope of presidential obligation to abide by customary international law).

[916] U.S. Dep't of State, Office of the Spokesperson, Communication Regarding Intent to Withdraw From Paris Agreement (Aug. 4, 2017), https://perma.cc/DR7U-D9NV. *But see* Press Statement by Sec'y of State Antony J. Blinken, The United States Officially Rejoins the Paris Agreement (Feb. 19, 2021), https://perma.cc/D5HY-UHNK.

[917] President Donald Trump, Remarks on the Joint Comprehensive Plan of Action (May 8, 2018), https://perma.cc/6ZYC-WN8L.

[918] U.S. Dep't of State, Press Statement by Principal Deputy Spokesperson, Treaty on Open Skies (Nov. 22, 2020), https://perma.cc/U8QJ-89EY.

[919] Secretary of State Michael R. Pompeo, Press Statement on U.S. Intent to Withdraw from the INF Treaty (Feb. 2, 2019), https://perma.cc/6NVY-J6AD.

[920] The declared intention to seek the return of the U.N. Arms Trade Treaty from the Senate, and to notify U.S. intent not to ratify, seem distinct but comparable issues. Missy Ryan & John Hudson, *During NRA Speech, Trump Drops Out of Another Global Arms Treaty*, WASH. POST. (Apr. 16, 2019), https://perma.cc/MX49-BGRL; *see supra* this chapter text accompanying notes 226–229 (discussing interim obligation and its termination).

A. Exit Under International Law

Under the VCLT, a party may, under certain circumstances, "suspend" an agreement's operation with respect to one or more parties. More decisively, a party may end its obligations under the treaty (sometimes called a "denunciation" of the treaty). This can take the form of "withdrawal" from a multilateral treaty (with the treaty likely continuing for other states parties) or "termination" of a bilateral treaty.

As the VCLT indicates, these options are appropriate to different circumstances, including as may be indicated by the governing treaty or by some other means reflecting the consent of the parties. A treaty may, for example, details the conditions under which a party may exit. It may also permit exit without limiting the grounds for doing so, though it is often subject to advance notice of a prescribed period of time.[921] Alternatively, after entry into force of the treaty, the parties collectively might decide to allow exit,[922] or to conclude a subsequent agreement that expressly or implicitly limits the continued force of the treaty.[923]

Naturally, a state may wish to pursue exit when the treaty does not address the issue and when other states appear unlikely to collectively assent to it. The law of treaties generally disfavors exit under these circumstances unless it can be established that the parties intended to allow exit or exit can be implied by the nature of the treaty.[924] At the same time, treaty law also establishes certain bases for excusing exit, subject to any limits within any particular agreement. For example, a party may invoke another party's material breach as a basis for terminating an agreement or suspending its operation in whole or in part.[925] Additionally, a party may invoke a supervening impossibility of performance or a fundamental change of circumstances as grounds for suspending, terminating, or withdrawing from obligations.[926] Significantly, however, parties are not supposed to terminate, withdraw from, or suspend the operation of a treaty entirely on their own. Instead, the VCLT envisages that a state will provide notice of its intent to exit to all the other parties, who then may either accept the exit or reject it—in the latter case triggering international dispute resolution procedures.[927]

---

[921] *See* VCLT, *supra* note 13, art. 54(a) (termination or withdrawal); *id.* at 57(a) (suspension).

[922] *Id.* art. 54(b) (termination or withdrawal), art. 57(b) (suspension).

[923] *Id.* art. 58 (suspension following agreement by certain parties only), art. 59 (termination or suspension implied by conclusion of a later agreement).

[924] *Id.* art. 56(1). In the case of an implied termination or withdrawal option (or one that seems to have been intended by the parties), the VCLT requires at least twelve months' notice is required. *Id.* art. 56(2).

[925] *Id.* art. 60.

[926] *Id.* arts. 61–62.

[927] *Id.* arts. 65–67. *See generally* RESTATEMENT (FOURTH) § 313 cmt. a & rptrs. note 1.

The VCLT's approach in this regard is generally consistent with customary international law,[928] and the United States regards the substance of these rules as legally binding.[929] Naturally, these rules also provide parameters in which the president operates. That said, it is important to stress that international law does not pretend to resolve which domestic institutions act for a state in effectuating exit, nor whether any domestic preconditions must be satisfied first.[930] The VCLT also contains no provision that would allow the United States (or other states) to invoke the manifest violation of domestic legal rules as a basis for disregarding a U.S. suspension, withdrawal, or termination.[931] Although other parties may be free to accommodate reconsideration of U.S. exit on such grounds, the most effective means for resolving a constitutionally problematic exit would appear to be for the United States to revoke a presidential notification of the intent to withdraw, terminate, or suspend during any relevant notice period.[932]

B. Presidential Authority to Bring About Exit

While the U.S. Constitution does not directly address how to unmake Article II treaties—let alone how to unmake other types of agreements—its provisions and overall structure provide suggestions of a sort.[933] Based on the Treaty Clause, one might argue that the president's ultimate capacity to decide whether to "make" a

---

[928] See, e.g., Gabcikovo-Nagymoros Project (Hung. v. Slovk.), Judgment, 1997 I.C.J. 7, ¶ 46 (Sept. 25) (stating that VCLT provisions on suspension and termination "in many respects" reflect customary international law); cf. Military and Paramilitary Activities in and against Nicaragua (Nicar. v. U.S.), Judgment on Jurisdiction and Admissibility, 1984 I.C.J. 392, ¶ 63 (Nov. 26) (stating that customary international law of treaties "requires a reasonable time for withdrawal from or termination of treaties that contain no provision regarding the duration of their validity").

[929] See, e.g., Treaty Termination: Hearings Before the S. Comm. on Foreign Relations on S. Res. 15, Resolution Concerning Mutual Defense Treaties, 96th Cong. (1979), reprinted in 1979 DIGEST OF U.S. PRACTICE 751, 758 (describing customary rules regarding termination as "reflected generally" in the Vienna Convention on the Law of Treaties); Letter of Submittal from William P. Rogers, U.S. Sec'y of State, to President Richard M. Nixon (Oct. 18, 1971), reprinted in 65 DEP'T STATE BULL. 684, 687–88 (Dec. 13, 1971) (endorsing material breach, impossibility-of-performance, and fundamental-change-of-circumstances rules, as well as procedures for suspension, termination, and withdrawal).

[930] See also infra this chapter text accompanying note 973 (addressing whether an agreement's withdrawal clause may be properly construed as delegating authority to the president).

[931] See Hannah Woolaver, Domestic and International Limitations on Treaty Withdrawal: Lessons from South Africa's Attempted Departure from the International Criminal Court, 111 AJIL UNBOUND 450, 454 (2018) (suggesting "this is a lacuna in international law that should be filled").

[932] Cf. R (Miller) v. Secretary of State for Exiting the European Union [2017] UKSC 5 (requiring approval by U.K. parliament of "Brexit" notice); Democratic Alliance v. Minister of International Relations and Cooperation 2017 (3) SA 212 (S. Afr.) (requiring approval by South African parliament of notice of withdrawal from the Rome Statute of the International Criminal Court).

[933] For a brief review of textual and structural arguments, see Curtis A. Bradley, Treaty Termination and Historical Gloss, 92 TEX. L. REV. 773, 779–83 (2014); see also DAVID ADLER, THE CONSTITUTION AND THE TERMINATION OF TREATIES (1986); HENKIN, FOREIGN AFFAIRS, at 211–14; Arthur Bestor, supra note 33; Powell, supra note 166, at 562–63. See generally RESTATEMENT (FOURTH) § 313 cmts. b–d.

treaty—by exercising discretion as to whether or not a Senate-approved treaty should be ratified—is consistent with the president possessing the sole capacity to exit from the treaty thereafter.[934] The implication of a presidential prerogative is also consistent with the president's power to send and receive ambassadors, insofar as managing exit has a diplomatic character; indeed, the president's "recognition" power may be pertinent if withdrawing recognition of a foreign government or state upends treaty relations with that state and requires exit.[935] As discussed elsewhere, these and related executive functions are sometimes extrapolated into descriptions of the president as the "sole organ" for conducting U.S. foreign policy,[936] which may support the president's ability to exit from treaties on his or her own initiative. Even the president's "executive power" might be invoked.[937]

There are also grounds for arguing that legislative cooperation is indispensable. The legislative role in making an agreement arguably requires a comparable role in unmaking it: statutes, for example, can only be terminated by replicating the statutory process, and the president has no unilateral capacity to change the law.[938] The likeness to statutes may seem particularly acute for self-executing treaties—conceivably the only kind of agreement contemplated at the

[934] Cf. Zivotofsky v. Kerry, 576 U.S. 1, 13 (2015) (Zivotofsky II) (noting, in relation to recognition authority, that "[t]he President has the sole power to negotiate treaties . . . and the Senate may not conclude or ratify a treaty without Presidential action."). For discussion of Zivotofsky II, see Chapter 1 §§ I(B), II(A)(2), III(B); Chapter 2 § II(C); and Chapter 3 § I(D).

[935] Zivotofsky II, 576 U.S. at 28 (stating conclusion that "the power to recognize or decline to recognize a foreign state and its territorial bounds resides in the President alone"). See generally Chapter 3 § IV. Whether the president may unilaterally terminate a treaty as an incident of recognition, however, has not been conclusively settled. See infra this chapter text accompanying notes 942–946 (discussing Goldwater v. Carter, 444 U.S. 996 (1979)).

[936] See 10 ANNALS OF CONG. 613 (1800) (Rep. John Marshall, describing president as the "sole organ" of the United States in foreign relations); United States v. Curtiss-Wright Exp. Corp., 299 U.S. 304, 320 (1936) (adopting "sole organ" depiction); see also Zivotofsky II, 576 U.S. at 21 (stating that the president has "a unique role in communicating with foreign governments."). See generally Chapter 1 § II(A)(2).

[937] See, e.g., Zivotofsky II, 576 U.S. at 35–36 (Thomas, J., concurring in part and dissenting in part) (stating that "founding-era evidence reveals that the 'executive power' included the foreign affairs powers of a sovereign State"); RAMSEY, THE CONSTITUTION'S TEXT, supra note 767, at 157–60 (emphasizing termination authority as "executive" in this sense). This robust vision of the "executive power" is controversial, for reasons having little to do with treaties. See, e.g., Julian Mortenson, Article II Vests Executive Power, Not the Royal Prerogative, 119 COLUM. L. REV. 1169 (2019) (arguing that such executive power was confined to executing law, rather than vesting foreign relations authority). On almost any view, whether an authority is "executive" assumes it has not been assigned elsewhere. See generally Chapter 3 § I(B).

[938] See, e.g., RAMSEY, THE CONSTITUTION'S TEXT, supra note 767, at 158 (addressing, in originalist terms, principle that "when a power is given to do an act, the power is also given to repeal it") (internal quotations omitted). As to statutes, see INS v. Chadha, 462 U.S. 919, 954 (1983) (stating that "repeal of statutes, no less than enactment, must conform with Art. I"); Clinton v. City of New York, 524 U.S. 417, 438 (1998) ("There is no provision in the Constitution that authorizes the President to enact, to amend, or to repeal statutes.").

founding—which similarly accomplish national lawmaking.[939] Even if there are limits to the statutory analogy,[940] Congress is surely entitled to override treaties in their domestic legal effect, and perhaps that capacity warrants recognizing its indispensable role in authorizing exit from international aspects as well.[941]

The courts have not resolved these competing perspectives. *Goldwater v. Carter* gave the Supreme Court its first real opportunity,[942] after President Carter gave notice that the United States would terminate the 1954 Mutual Defense Treaty with the Republic of China (based in Taiwan). Availing themselves of the ensuing one-year notice period, and intent on prevent U.S. termination from taking final effect, members of Congress sued. The district court held that termination required "the advice and consent of the United States Senate or the approval of both houses of Congress,"[943] emphasizing concerns

---

[939] In his *Manual of Parliamentary Practice*, Jefferson wrote that "[t]reaties being declared, equally with the laws of the United States, to be the supreme law of the land, it is understood that an act of the legislature alone can declare them infringed and rescinded." JEFFERSON'S MANUAL, *supra* note 168, § 599, at 319.

[940] *See generally* RESTATEMENT (FOURTH) § 313 cmt. d. Article II treaties are certainly more in the president's wheelhouse than Congress'. Unlike statutes, consent is vested solely in the Senate, rather than the legislature as a whole. The more relevant parallel for this purpose is to the appointment of officers (which Article II, § 2, cl. 2 likewise addresses), and there it is well settled that no legislative involvement in termination (i.e., dismissal) is required. *See* Myers v. United States, 272 U.S. 52 (1926); *see also infra* this chapter text accompanying note 982. *But see* Humphrey's Ex'r v. United States, 295 U.S. 602 (1935) (holding Congress can, by statute, limit the president's removal of inferior officers to "just cause" reasons). The end game for treaties is, in all events, materially different from that of statutes, since—following Senate consent—the president alone decides whether to ratify, and no legislative supermajority can override a presidential determination not to do so. *See supra* this chapter text accompanying notes 220–225; *see also infra* this chapter text accompanying note 962 (discussing proposed "mirror" principle for termination generally).

[941] Case law clearly establishes the domestic legal capacity of Congress to override a treaty. *See, e.g.,* Breard v. Greene, 523 U.S. 371, 376 (1998) (plurality opinion) (per curiam) (citing Reid v. Covert, 354 U.S. 1, 18 (1957)); Whitney v. Robertson, 124 U.S. 190, 193–95 (1888); *see also supra* this chapter text accompanying notes 715–717. But any such statute does not itself affect the international obligation created by the treaty, suggesting that a separate capacity is required. *See, e.g.,* Pigeon River Improvement, Slide & Boom Co. v. Charles W. Cox, Ltd., 291 U.S. 138, 160 (1934) (observing that a definitively conflicting, later federal statute "would control in our courts as the later expression of our municipal law" while "the international obligation remained unaffected"). *But cf.* La Abra Silver Mining Co. v. United States, 175 U.S. 423, 460 (1899) (representing that Congress could—"so far as the people and authorities of the United States are concerned"—by legislation "abrogate a treaty made between this country and another country . . .") (citations omitted).

[942] Long before, in *Charlton v. Kelly*, the Court remarked that the executive branch had "elected to waive any right to free itself from the obligation to deliver up its own citizens" although Italy had refused to surrender its own citizens under the same treaty. 229 U.S. 447, 476 (1913). Arguably this "suggest[ed] in dicta that the Executive Branch could decide whether to stop complying with a bilateral treaty in response to a breach by the other party," see Bradley, *supra* note 933, at 802–03, but the Court explained the point (plausibly) as concerning treaty interpretation. *Charlton*, 229 U.S. at 476. An earlier lower court case, *Ropes v. Clinch*, 20 F. Cas. 1171 (C.C.S.D.N.Y. 1871) (No. 12,041), had enumerated in dicta different ways that "congress" could interfere with a treaty's operative effect in the United States, including that "the government of the United States" had the power to "disregard even [a treaty term governing termination], and declare that 'the treaty shall be, from and after this date, at an end.'" *Id.* at 1174.

[943] Goldwater v. Carter, 481 F. Supp. 949, 951 (D.D.C. 1979). The court changed its earlier view that the plaintiffs lacked standing, concluding that a preliminary Senate vote that rejected unilateral presidential authority—but without a final vote on the affected resolution—evidenced "at least

about permitting a president to single-handedly set aside the supreme law of the land.[944] The court of appeals, however, concluded that presidential termination was lawful, stressing the treaty's termination provision and that the president's action was part of a broader process of recognizing the People's Republic of China (based in Beijing).[945] The Supreme Court, hearing the case on an expedited basis, held that the suit was nonjusticiable.[946] Lower courts have since held that challenges to President Ronald Reagan's termination of a 1956 Treaty of Friendship, Commerce, and Navigation with Nicaragua and President George W. Bush's withdrawal of the United States from the 1972 Anti-Ballistic Missile Treaty also presented political questions.[947]

Absent clear resolution by the courts, political practice has held sway, and it has charted more than one course. Both Congress as a whole and the Senate played substantial roles at least through the nineteenth century—authorizing (sometimes after the fact), and occasionally directing, presidential termination of treaties.[948] Beginning around World War II, however, presidents more frequently assumed independent authority to exit treaties, sometimes asserting that this was an exclusive constitutional prerogative.[949] While individual members

some congressional determination to participate in the process whereby a mutual defense treaty is terminated, and clearly falls short of approving the President's termination effort." *Id.* at 954; *see also id.* at 951–56.

[944] *Id.* at 962–64.

[945] Goldwater v. Carter, 617 F.2d 697, 707–09 (D.C. Cir. 1979) (en banc) (per curiam).

[946] Four justices regarded the president's power to terminate the treaty as a political question, Goldwater v. Carter, 444 U.S. 996 (1979); *id.* at 1003 (Rehnquist, J., concurring in the judgment), and a fifth concluded that the case lacked ripeness pending more concrete disagreement between the political branches. *Id.* at 998 (Powell, J., concurring); *see* Chapter 4 § II(A) (discussing political question aspects), § II(B)(2) (discussing ripeness). A dissent would have held that the president could unilaterally terminate the treaty as a "necessary incident" of the president's power to decide whether to recognize Taiwan and mainland China. *Id.* at 1006–07 (Brennan, J., dissenting).

[947] Beacon Prods. Corp. v. Reagan, 633 F. Supp. 1191, 1198–99 (D. Mass. 1986) (dismissing on political question grounds a challenge to termination of treaty with Nicaragua); Kucinich v. Bush, 236 F. Supp. 2d 1, 2 (D.D.C. 2002) (dismissing on standing, ripeness, and political question bases a challenge to withdrawal from the Anti-Ballistic Missile Treaty).

[948] Details of the history have been contested. *Compare, e.g.*, Memorandum from Herbert J. Hansell, Legal Adviser, U.S. Dep't of State, to Cyrus R. Vance, U.S. Sec'y of State (Dec. 15, 1978), *in* S. COMM. ON FOREIGN RELATIONS, 95TH CONG., TERMINATION OF TREATIES: THE CONSTITUTIONAL ALLOCATION OF POWER 395, 400–23 (Comm. Print 1978) (compiling evidence favoring presidential authority), *with Goldwater*, 617 F.2d at 723–34 (MacKinnon, J., dissenting in part and concurring in part) (critically evaluating evidence supporting presidential authority), *and* Bradley, *supra* note 933, at 811 n.218 (citing sources criticizing Hansell memorandum). For recent summaries, see RESTATEMENT (FOURTH) § 313 rptrs. note 2; CRS, TREATIES AND OTHER INTERNATIONAL AGREEMENTS, *supra* note 165, at 201–08; Bradley, *supra* note 933.

[949] The clearest example during the early twentieth century was the Coolidge administration's unilateral termination in 1929 of a smuggling convention with Mexico. *See* Bradley, *supra* note 933, at 805–06. The Franklin Roosevelt administration followed suit, but executive authority usually had some form of legislative support. *Id.* at 806–07; *Goldwater*, 617 F.2d at 728–32 (MacKinnon, J., dissenting in part and concurring in part). Executive branch legal advice in support of unilateralism gradually became less equivocal, even though actual assertions of presidential authority remained rare. *See* Bradley, *supra* note 933, at 801–10 (citing Department of State memoranda and

of Congress occasionally initiated lawsuits, the legislature as a whole did little to formally challenge such initiatives, and at times toyed with accepting their legitimacy, as with termination of the Taiwan mutual defense treaty.[950] In principle, such practice might establish presidential authority,[951] and courts and others have relied on the modern trend in evaluating the issue—meaning that, presidential assertions of authority have been determining whether treaties continue to be effective as U.S. law.[952] In the *Restatement (Fourth)*, "established practice" was cited as the basis for concluding that the president could act on behalf of the United States in proceeding with suspension, termination, or withdrawal from Article II treaties.[953]

Any such conclusion, however, risks overshadowing some important qualifications. Practice supports the president's capacity to act without prior congressional authorization, but this power of initiative does not establish that the president is free to disregard properly enacted legislative limits.[954] (How exactly Congress might react to a presidential determination, or inhibit unilateral presidential action with respect to a particular agreement, is discussed in the

other executive branch guidance); *see, e.g.,* International Load Line Convention, 40 Op. Att'y Gen. 119, 123 (1941) (distinguishing between a fundamental change in circumstances, which would entitle the president to declare a convention inoperative or suspended, and simple denunciation or abrogation, which it was implied would by contrast require "action by the Senate or by the Congress"); *see also infra* this chapter text accompanying note 964 (citing additional authorities claiming that the president's authority was not only independent, but exclusive).

[950] Prior to termination, Congress expressed the sense that consultation was appropriate, but it did not require legislative consent. *See* International Security Assistance Act of 1978, Pub. L. No. 95-384, § 26(b), 92 Stat. 730, 746. After extensive hearings, the Senate Committee on Foreign Relations reported a resolution that would have recognized more than a dozen potential grounds on which the president might unilaterally terminate a treaty. 125 Cong. Rec. 13,685 (1979). The Senate then reverted to previously drafted language that denied any unilateral authority and asserted that Senate consent was necessary; that substituted resolution, however, was never brought to a vote. S. Res. 15, 96th Cong. (1979); *see* Goldwater v. Carter, 481 F. Supp. 949, 954–55 (D.D.C. 1979); CRS, Withdrawal from International Agreements, *supra* note 883, at 13–14; Bradley, *supra* note 933, at 811–12.

[951] The feasibility of congressional regulation, discussed below, might affect whether legislative inaction should count as acquiescence. And unilateral presidential measures are less precedent-setting if *post hoc* legislative authorization was potentially available but proved lacking in fact; in that case, the president's initiation of exit was not necessarily an assertion of independent authority. *Cf.* Bradley, *supra* note 933, at 794–96 (citing examples of *ex post* congressional and Senate consent).

[952] CRS, Treaties and Other International Agreements, *supra* note 165, at 201 (describing unilateral presidential authority as "an open question," but conceding that "[a]s a practical matter . . . the President may exercise this power since the courts have held that they are conclusively bound by an executive determination with regard to whether a treaty is still in effect"); *see, e.g.,* Goldwater, 617 F.2d at 706 (en banc) (per curiam) (emphasizing presidential determination). *But see id.* at 723 (MacKinnon, J., concurring in part and dissenting in part) (emphasizing congressional participation in past practice); *Goldwater,* 481 F. Supp. at 964 (emphasizing that "the predominate United States' practice in terminating treaties . . . has involved mutual action by the executive and legislative branches").

[953] Restatement (Fourth) § 313(1).

[954] *See infra* this chapter § VI(C); Restatement (Fourth) § 313 cmt. d & rptrs. note 6.

next subsection.) Moreover, practice has only established the executive's power to initiate exit from a treaty when doing so would be compatible with international law.[955] U.S. notifications of intended exit generally have highlighted how the exit is compatible with the treaty's terms, suggesting that international law is regarded as a constraint.[956]

It has been suggested that, as a matter of domestic law, congressional-executive agreements are different, such that the president might lack even the presumptive capacity to initiate exit. There is little evidence of this distinction being recognized,[957] and the claimed differences do not seem compelling. One suggestion has been that exiting congressional-executive agreements is more akin to terminating statutes, since the agreement was approved by both houses of Congress and therefore depends on Congress' legislative authority.[958] But exiting from a congressional-executive agreement is not much like terminating a statute. Such agreements are not finalized in the same way: after legislative approval is secured, the president has complete discretion as to whether or not to enter into any international agreements. Afterward, the statute itself need not be affected by any presidentially directed exit, which only concerns the accompanying international obligation; assuming Congress has not already addressed the possibility of exit,[959] it can choose to change the statute or leave it be.[960] It is unclear, then,

---

[955] See RESTATEMENT (FOURTH) § 313(1) (stating that "the President has the authority to act on behalf of the United States in . . . withdrawing the United States from treaties, either on the basis of terms in the treaty allowing for such action (such as a withdrawal clause) or on the basis of international law that would justify such an action."); see also supra this chapter text accompanying note 915.

[956] See, e.g., Diplomatic Note to the Ambassador of Sweden, U.S. Dep't of State (June 7, 2007), https://perma.cc/G6TU-6YQH (notifying termination of bilateral tax treaty and citing both termination provision and vestigial legal operation of the treaty); Press Release, U.S. Dep't of the Treasury, United States Terminates Estate and Gift Tax Treaty with Sweden (June 15, 2007), https://perma.cc/2G4D-545C (noting functional basis for termination). The United States appears only rarely to have notified exit from an agreement that lacks a provision on termination; it can finesse any interpolation of an advance-notice requirement by avoiding any claim of immediate effect. See Letter from Condoleezza Rice, U.S. Sec'y of State, to Kofi Annan, U.N. Sec'y-Gen. (Mar. 7, 2005), https://perma.cc/23KS-QVAZ (noting withdrawal from the Optional Protocol to the Vienna Convention on Consular Relations).

[957] See Curtis A. Bradley, Exiting Congressional-Executive Agreements, 67 DUKE L.J. 1616, 1639–40 (2018) (citing examples of terminating both ex post and ex ante congressional-executive agreements, including trade agreements and membership in the International Labour Organization and UNESCO).

[958] See, e.g., Joel P. Trachtman, Power to Terminate U.S. Trade Agreements: The Presidential Dormant Commerce Clause Versus an Historical Gloss Half Empty, 51:3 INT'L LAW. (2018), at 445; Yoo, supra note 309, at 814–16 (emphasizing kinship with statutes).

[959] Congress may, as with a treaty, provide that implementing legislation cease upon the agreement's termination, but then termination has domestic effect as Congress had intended—not due to the president's unilateral decision to strike an otherwise operative statute. See infra this chapter text accompanying note 969 (citing examples).

[960] Indeed, because any statute remains undisturbed, setting a higher bar for congressional-executive agreements would be odd: it is the president's termination of a self-executing treaty, in which the effect under U.S. law is derived directly from the international obligation, which has the more radical effect of automatically expunging national law.

why there should be special solicitude for Congress' Article I or other legislative powers, which need not be affected at all.[961]

It has also been suggested that different forms of agreement should require different means of exit, in each case mirroring the paths by which they were entered.[962] This does not seem to correspond with U.S. treaty practice (nor with other Article II authority for which initial legislative consent is required, like the appointment and removal of officers).[963] For sole executive agreements, however, it is assumed that when the president properly relies on the Constitution itself for authority to enter into an agreement, that same authority permits the president to exit that agreement unilaterally.[964] Even then, though, it may be hard to resolve whether an agreement has also secured legislative support, and making this decisive in establishing the legality of exit seems problematic.[965] As with Article II treaties, the executive branch appears to regard international law as a constraint.[966]

---

[961] Exit may still unsettle Congress' expectations in enacting a statute, but Article I does not generally protect these independent of Congress' enactments—save as against state interference, as with the dormant Foreign Commerce Clause doctrine. *See also* Bradley, *supra* note 957, at 1629–32 (noting that congressional authority, where detailed, is established in lieu of state power, not relative to executive authority). Congressional authority does bear on its affirmative attempts to regulate exit. *See infra* this chapter text accompanying note 971.

[962] Harold Hongju Koh, *Presidential Power to Terminate International Agreements*, 128 YALE L.J.F. 432, 436 (2018) (urging "commonsense 'mirror principle,'" whereby absent exceptional circumstances, the degree of congressional participation constitutionally required to exit any particular agreement should mirror the degree of congressional participation that was required to enter that agreement in the first place").

[963] *See supra* this chapter text accompanying note 940 (noting that officers need not be removed by the same means that they are appointed). *But see* Koh, *supra* note 962, at 458–59 (urging bases for distinguishing removal of officers).

[964] RESTATEMENT (THIRD) § 339 rptrs. note 2 ("No one has questioned the President's authority to terminate sole executive agreements."); CRS, TREATIES AND OTHER INTERNATIONAL AGREEMENTS, *supra* note 165, at 173–74 (concluding that it "seems to be invariably true" that the president may terminate "executive agreements concluded by virtue of exclusive Presidential authority").

[965] *See supra* this chapter text accompanying notes 897–900. The 2015 Paris Agreement on climate change, *supra* note 886, from which the United States indicated its intent to withdraw before deciding to rejoin, see *supra* this chapter text accompanying note 916, is a case in point. President Obama did not articulate the basis for entering into that agreement originally, leaving unresolved whether authority was premised on a Senate-approved treaty, see United Nations Framework Convention on Climate Change art. 25, May 9, 1992, 1771 U.N.T.S. 107 [hereinafter UNFCCC], on the Clean Air Act, or on the president's constitutional authority. CRS, WITHDRAWAL FROM INTERNATIONAL AGREEMENTS, *supra* note 885, at 16–17. *But see* Koh, *supra* note 962, at 467–72 (discussing application of "mirroring principle" to Paris Agreement).

[966] The 2015 Paris Agreement on climate change, again, serves as an example. International law indicated that the United States might effectuate its objective by withdrawing from the Paris Agreement itself or from the underlying UNFCCC, but each option required a year's notice that could be lodged only after the agreement in question had been in effect for three years already—which was the case for the UNFGCC but not for the Paris Agreement. *See* Paris Agreement, *supra* note 886, art. 28; UNFCCC, *supra* note 965, art. 25. The executive branch chose the least expeditious means (notifying, after the required delay, its future withdrawal from the Paris Agreement itself) and complied with it, rather than asserting greater capacity for unilateral decision-making based on the nature of the agreement.

Nonbinding agreements naturally present fewer exit-related concerns. By hypothesis, such agreements involve no international obligation for which U.S. exit rules would have to account. Any national law relating to the agreement would remain in place and could even require the United States to perform consistent with the terms of the agreement after exit. Adaptation is usually easier, as illustrated by U.S. withdrawal from the JCPOA, an agreement concerning Iran's nuclear program, which the U.S. executive branch depicted as a political agreement that neither bound the United States internationally nor required legislative approval.[967] The United States implemented the agreement through executive action, with the lifting of sanctions on Iran (as called for by the agreement) governed by a statute that assigned waiver authority to the president.[968] Had U.S. law gone further and required that the United States abide by the JCPOA, it might have impeded the reimposition of sanctions by the Trump administration.

C. Congressional Regulation of Exit

As previously noted, the practice according to which the president decides whether to exit from international agreements does not mean that Congress lacks any potential role. It is taken for granted, for example, that in adopting relevant national law—either in connection with an Article II treaty or in legislating before or after the negotiation of a congressional-executive agreement— Congress may decide whether U.S. law should survive U.S. exit.[969] Beyond that, though, the legislature can also potentially play a role in authorizing, compelling, or restricting exit.

---

[967] See supra this chapter note 885.

[968] See Exec. Order No. 13,716, 81 Fed. Reg. 3,693 (Jan. 21, 2016); Dep't of the Treasury & Dep't of State, *Guidance Relating to the Lifting of Certain U.S. Sanctions Pursuant to the Joint Comprehensive Plan of Action on Implementation Day* 34–37 (Jan. 16, 2016), https://perma.cc/RR8H-U5HN; *cf.* KENNETH KATZMAN ET AL., CONG. RESEARCH SERV., R44942, U.S. DECISION TO CEASE IMPLEMENTING THE IRAN NUCLEAR AGREEMENT (2018) (describing domestic means for ceasing compliance). Termination was further complicated by a Security Council resolution. *See* S.C. Res. 2231 (July 20, 2015), https://perma.cc/C7JP-LLSW.

[969] Such decisions may be provided for in framework legislation. Thus, under Section 125 of the Free Trade Act of 1974, import restrictions established according to related trade agreements generally survive for one year after termination or withdrawal of such an agreement. 19 U.S.C. § 2135(e) (2018); *see also* 18 U.S.C. § 3181(a) (2018) (providing that the "provisions of this chapter relating to the surrender of persons who have committed crimes in foreign countries shall continue in force only during the existence of any treaty of extradition with such foreign government"). Congress may also address the question in particular implementing statutes. *See, e.g.,* United States–Korea Free Trade Agreement Implementation Act, Pub. L. No. 112-41, § 107(c), 125 Stat. 428, 432 (2011) ("On the date on which the Agreement terminates, this Act . . . shall cease to have effect"). These examples suggest how it may be orderly to link statutory expiration to treaty termination; at the same time, requiring statutory continuity might diminish the incentive for the executive branch to initiate termination in the first place.

The first possible role, authorizing exit, has not been controversial. Legislative consent was common before presidents began initiating exit unilaterally,[970] and it should be easier to defend any executive branch decision supported by the legislative branch.[971] Congressional authorization of exit may indeed be critical if exit would be inconsistent with international law, since it is established that Congress can change U.S. law in contravention of international law—while the president's unilateral capacity to breach international law is more doubtful.[972] But ascertaining when Congress has conferred authority on the executive may not be straightforward. Approving an agreement that itself provides for withdrawal, termination, or suspension may be read to imply an assignment of like authority to the president, but only if one regards the Senate or Congress as fully acquiescing in the idea that any U.S. authority falls to the president.[973] Congressional references to the possibility of future authorization may also be misconstrued as requiring legislative approval.[974]

A second possibility, that Congress might during the life of the treaty compel the president to exit from an agreement, would likely prove much more

---

[970] *See* Bradley, *supra* note 933, at 789–93 (citing examples of consent by Congress); *id.* at 793–94 (citing examples of Senate consent); *see also id.* at 794–96 (citing examples of *ex post* consent).

[971] *See* Youngstown Sheet & Tube Co. v. Sawyer, 343 U.S. 579, 635–38 (1952) (Jackson, J., concurring). For further discussion of *Youngstown*, see Chapter 1 § II(B) and Chapter 8 § II(B). In principle, legislative authorization would be constrained by the nondelegation doctrine, though that has been applied narrowly in foreign affairs. *See* Chapter I § II(A)(1). Treaty termination would also be distinguishable to the extent that the president has independent constitutional authority that is simply being supplemented or confirmed.

[972] *See supra* this chapter text accompanying notes 717–723. That said, an open-ended delegation by Congress would arguably add little, as Congress would not then itself be making a deliberate decision to place the United States in violation of international law. *See supra* this chapter text accompanying note 793.

[973] In the Article II context, the executive branch has asserted that such provisions "constitute the Senate's authorization to the President to terminate the treaty." 1979 DIGEST OF U.S. PRACTICE 769 (written reply by the Department of State to questions from the Senate Committee on Foreign Relations), which view was adopted by the D.C. Circuit majority in *Goldwater*. Goldwater v. Carter, 617 F.2d 697, 708 (D.C. Cir. 1979) (stating that "the President's authority as Chief Executive is at its zenith when the Senate has consented to a treaty that expressly provides for termination on one year's notice, and the President's action is the giving of notice of termination"). As the dissent noted, the treaty conferred an entitlement on the United States rather than addressing "who can act for [it]." *Id.* at 737 (MacKinnon, J., dissenting in part and concurring in part).

[974] Section 125 of the Uruguay Round Agreements Act describes circumstances under which "approval of the Congress . . . shall cease to be effective," 19 U.S.C. § 3535 (2018), and specially enables a joint resolution to withdraw congressional approval from the WTO—with the evident purpose of avoiding procedural roadblocks in Congress that might prevent a withdrawal initiative. *See generally* CONG. RESEARCH SERV., RL32700, SEEKING WITHDRAWAL OF CONGRESSIONAL APPROVAL OF THE WTO AGREEMENT: BACKGROUND, LEGISLATIVE PROCEDURE, AND PRACTICAL CONSEQUENCES (2005); CONG. RESEARCH SERV., R41291, WORLD TRADE ORGANIZATION (WTO): ISSUES IN THE DEBATE ON U.S. PARTICIPATION (2010). As a joint resolution, presidential approval would be required, so the approach is not a means by which withdrawal could be compelled. *See, e.g.,* WITHDRAWING THE APPROVAL OF THE UNITED STATES FROM THE AGREEMENT ESTABLISHING THE WORLD TRADE ORGANIZATION, H.R. Rep. 109-100 (2005) (discussing proposed H.J. Res. 27). This approach does not appear intended to require congressional consent for any U.S. withdrawal, though that position has been asserted. *See, e.g.,* Trachtman, *supra* note 958, at 463.

controversial. The executive branch has sometimes asserted an exclusive power over exit, derived from the president's general authority over the conduct of foreign relations,[975] but that view is not supported by practice.[976] Congress has on rare occasions directed the president to terminate an agreement;[977] when the president has resisted, it has tended to be because a particular directive is inconsistent with international law.[978] Any conclusion about the constitutionality of this practice might depend on whether core diplomatic or legislative functions were at stake,[979] whether Congress was acting in an area of its traditional

---

[975] *See, e.g.*, 5 HACKWORTH DIGEST, ch. XVI, § 509, at 331–32 (1943) (quoting 1939 Department of State memorandum suggesting that "the power to denounce a treaty inheres in" the president as chief executive, conveying "full control over the foreign relations of the nation, except as specifically limited by the Constitution."); Memorandum from Herbert J. Hansell, *supra* note 948, at 395, 399 (suggesting similar view—at least when a treaty contains an exit provision—and suggesting that Senate authority was "fulfilled when the treaty is made"). The Department of Justice once made a similar claim to exclusive executive power over suspension of a treaty. *See* Memorandum from John C. Yoo, Deputy Assistant Att'y Gen. & Robert J. Delahunty, Special Counsel, Office of Legal Counsel, U.S. Dep't of Justice, to John Bellinger III, Senior Assoc. Counsel to the President & Legal Adviser to the Nat'l Sec. Council, Authority of the President to Suspend Certain Provisions of the ABM Treaty 15–16 (Nov. 15, 2001), https://perma.cc/T42P-K82P. That opinion was later withdrawn. Office of Legal Counsel, U.S. Dep't of Justice, Memorandum for the Files Re: Status of Certain OLC Opinions Issued in the Aftermath of the Terrorist Attacks of September 11, 2001, at 8–9 (Jan. 15, 2009), https://perma.cc/TAK6-9GBT.

[976] RESTATEMENT (FOURTH) § 313 rptrs. note 6 ("Although historical practice supports a unilateral presidential power to suspend, terminate, or withdraw the United States from treaties, it does not establish that this is an exclusive presidential power"); *accord* rptrs. notes 2, 3. There is soft support for presidential responsibility for mediating any inconsistencies. For example, after a maritime statute requested and directed the president to give notice to treaty partners of termination of treaties inconsistent with that law, a private party objected to termination of a particular treaty provision supposedly in violation of congressional direction. The Supreme Court responded that

> it was incumbent upon the President, charged with the conduct of negotiations with foreign governments and also with the duty to take care that the laws of the United States are faithfully executed, to reach a conclusion as to the inconsistency between the provisions of the treaty and the provisions of the new law.

Van Der Weyde v. Ocean Transp. Co., 297 U.S. 114, 118 (1936).

[977] Bradley, *supra* note 933, at 791–92 (citing examples in 1883 and 1915 of congressional directions of termination, and noting presidential cooperation). One modern instance was the Comprehensive Anti-Apartheid Act of 1986, Pub. L. No. 99-440, 100 Stat. 1086, 1100, passed over President Reagan's veto, which directed the Secretary of State to terminate a bilateral air services agreement between the United States and South Africa. *Id.* § 306(b)(1) ("The Secretary of State shall terminate the Agreement Between the Government of the United States of America and the Government of the Union of South Africa Relating to Air Services Between Their Respective Territories, signed May 23, 1947, in accordance with the provisions of that agreement"); *id.* § 313 (providing in similar terms for the termination of a double taxation treaty). The president later gave notice of termination, though the basis is not immediately evident. Current Actions, DEP'T STATE BULL., Dec. 1986, at 84, 87; *see* Bradley, *supra* note 933, at 844 n.244; *cf.* S. Afr. Airways v. Dole, 817 F.2d 119, 126 (D.C. Cir. 1987) (upholding immediate revocation of air services in accordance with statute, including on the basis of the foreign commerce power and Necessary and Proper Clause).

[978] Bradley, *supra* note 933, at 792–93 (citing examples in 1879 and 1920 of presidential resistance when congressional directives sought, in effect, to modify existing treaties).

[979] *See generally* Zivotofsky v. Kerry, 576 U.S. 1 (2015). It would be harder to defend congressional intervention that usurped any diplomatic role for the president in carrying out the termination. The only known example of a legislative attempt to terminate a treaty directly, rather than through the president's agency, was a 1798 statute declaring that treaties with France were not "legally obligatory

competence,[980] and whether legislative authority was expressed authoritatively via a statute or joint resolution.[981]

A third possible role is one in which the legislature provides, in its approval of a treaty or congressional-executive agreement, for legislative participation in any exit decision. Limiting exit options would, again, likely elicit objections that the legislature has intruded upon an exclusive presidential authority. More distinctly, the means for affording congressional participation in an exit decision could pose issues. If the Senate, when approving a treaty, required further legislative consent prior to exit, it would evoke precedent indicating that the Senate lacked authority to require its consent for the dismissal of officers.[982] (That authority would be more readily distinguishable in the context of an attempt to require congressional approval for exit from a congressional-executive agreement.) Alternatively, a statute that authorized the president to proceed unless the legislature disapproved, without vesting a negative in the president on that legislative disapproval, might be vulnerable as a legislative veto.[983] (Here, the more challenging question would involve extrapolating legislative veto principles to a condition in the Senate's resolution of advice and consent for an Article II

on the government or citizens of the United States." That statute might be defended, however, given that it was enacted amid the "quasi-war" with France and hence implicated Congress' power to declare war. Bradley, *supra* note 933, at 789.

[980] For example, reviewing Section 6(a)(2) of the proposed WTO Dispute Settlement Review Commission Act, which provided that "upon adoption of a joint resolution withdrawing Congress' approval of the WTO Agreement, 'the United States shall cease to be a member of the WTO,'" the Justice Department's Office of Legal Counsel concluded that it was "not prepared to say that section 6(a)(2) is unconstitutional—in part because it did not directly order the president "to do or say anything," but largely because "the express grant to Congress of the authority to regulate foreign commerce provides substantial support for Congressional authority in this area." Memorandum from Walter Dellinger, Assistant Attorney General, Office of Legal Counsel, to Alan Kreczko, Legal Adviser, National Security Council, *supra* note 184, at 5.

[981] Against less authoritative enactments, like a concurrent resolution or Senate-only resolution, a recalcitrant president could defensibly invoke the constitutional obligation to execute the preexisting treaty or congressional-executive agreement; that objection might be less powerful in relation to a sole executive agreement. Perhaps more controversially, it seems dubious even to attribute formal authority to a Senate resolution adopted by a two-thirds supermajority. As discussed earlier, the Senate's advice-and-consent role arguably entails authority to approve any exit decision. *See supra* this chapter text accompanying notes 938–943. But that is different from understanding the Senate's role—situated within Article II, and exercised in cooperation with the president—as entailing a *unilateral* power to end them, let alone supporting any such power for congressional-executive agreements.

[982] *See* Myers v. United States, 272 U.S. 52 (1926). It might be possible to defend a "for-cause requirement" on presidential action, like that upheld in the context of appointment of officials. Yet it would be difficult to specify in advance the permissible grounds for termination, other than perhaps those permissible under international law. *See generally* Humphrey's Ex'r v. United States, 295 U.S. 602 (1935); Kristen E. Eichensehr, *Treaty Termination and the Separation of Powers*, 53 VA. J. INT'L L. 247 (2013).

[983] INS v. Chadha, 462 U.S. 919 (1983) (holding that a one-house veto violated constitutional requirements of bicameralism and presentment).

treaty.[984]) Probably the cleanest means of asserting legislative authority would be for Congress to react to a presidential notice before it took full effect under international law—for example, reacting to the president's notice of withdrawal, given in advance of U.S. withdrawal, by adopting legislation that purports to require the president to retract or otherwise nullify that notice. Even if the president did not immediately comply, such an effort would more likely establish a justiciable case regarding separation of powers issues.[985]

---

[984] Article II is one of the exceptional instances in which one house of Congress may exercise authority, see *Chadha*, 462 U.S. at 955, but presentment or its analogue may remain an issue. Senate consent to an Article II treaty that was conditioned by reservation or declaration to a Senate role in exiting from the treaty would purport to assign to the Senate the right to "approve or disapprove executive acts," Constitutionality of Proposed Legislation Affecting Tax Refunds, 37 Op. Att'y Gen. 56, 56 (1933); moreover, it would do so without allowing the president a final negative, as the executive branch possesses with respect to ratification of any Article II treaty (or, for that matter, any congressional-executive agreement). At the same time, it is notable that conditions like those affecting self-execution of a treaty already facilitate highly unorthodox means of establishing and disestablishing national law. *See supra* this chapter § IV(A)(7).

[985] *Cf.* Goldwater v. Carter, 444 U.S. 996, 996 (1979) (Powell, J., concurring) (stating that "a dispute between Congress and the President is not ready for judicial review unless and until each branch has taken action asserting its constitutional authority").

7

International Organizations

Chapter 6 addressed generally the means by which the United States enters into international agreements, as well as the limitations on their effectiveness under national law. When the United States enters into an agreement concerning an international organization (referred to here as an "international organization agreement"), distinct issues may arise. Some of these issues manifest themselves at the threshold of U.S. engagement, or while suspending or terminating U.S. involvement. Just as frequently, they result from an international organization's capacity to generate international and domestic obligations.[1]

U.S. foreign relations law offers no authoritative definition of "international organizations," which are treated here as being roughly synonymous with intergovernmental organizations.[2] Neighboring subjects—instances in which parties to a treaty accord authority to autonomous institutional arrangements such as meetings of the parties or conferences of the parties,[3] or agree to ad hoc arbitration under treaties such as the North American Free Trade Agreement (NAFTA) and its successor, the United States–Canada–Mexico Agreement (USMCA),[4] for example—are often part of the same conversation, and are touched on here as well. These and comparable arrangements challenge, to varying degrees,

---

[1] For a survey, see Paul B. Stephan, *Constitutionalism and Internationalism: U.S. Participation in International Institutions, in* THE OXFORD HANDBOOK OF COMPARATIVE FOREIGN RELATIONS LAW 373 (Curtis A. Bradley ed., 2018); for instructive comparisons, see Paul Craig, *Engagement and Disengagement with International Institutions: The U.K. Perspective, in id.* at 393; Andreas Paulus & Jans-Hendrik Hinselmann, *International Integration and Its Counter-Limits: A German Constitutional Perspective, in id.* at 411.

[2] U.S. law does define "international organization" and similar terms in certain limited contexts, such as for purposes of establishing privileges and immunities. *See, e.g.,* 22 U.S.C. § 288 (2018) (defining "international organization" as being any organization for which U.S. participation is licensed by treaty or statute and which the president has designated by executive order as being entitled to privileges and immunities); *see also* RESTATEMENT (THIRD) § 221 (defining "international organization" as "an organization that is created by an international agreement and has a membership consisting entirely or principally of states").

[3] The seminal account is Robin R. Churchill & Geir Ulfstein, *Autonomous Institutional Arrangements in Multilateral Environmental Agreements: A Little-Noticed Phenomenon in International Law,* 94 AM. J. INT'L L. 623 (2000).

[4] *United States–Mexico–Canada Agreement (USMCA),* OFFICE OF U.S. TRADE REP. (Nov. 30, 2018), https://perma.cc/ATV7-B4PL; United States–Mexico–Canada Agreement Implementation Act, Pub. L. 116-113, 134 Stat. 11 (2020); *see* North American Free Trade Agreement (NAFTA), Dec. 17, 1992, Can.-Mex.-U.S., 32 I.L.M. 289; North American Free Trade Agreement Implementation Act, Pub. L. No. 103-82, 107 Stat. 2057 (1993) (codified as amended in scattered sections of 19 U.S.C.).

constitutional principles that limit or divide national authority, and factor into U.S. decisions about whether and how to participate. For instance, U.S. consideration of participation in the World Trade Organization (WTO) surfaced claims that doing so would transfer national decision-making to international authorities, thereby arrogating treaty-making authority that belonged to the president and Senate, legislative authority that belonged to Congress, and judicial authority that could be exercised only by U.S. courts.[5]

This chapter begins with an overview of how these issues were addressed in constitutional design and formative practice, before analyzing significant issues that international organizations continue to pose under U.S. foreign relations law.

I. Historical Perspectives

Contemporary discussions of international organizations and their consistency with U.S. constitutional norms occasionally suggest that the founding generation aspired to establish an international organization,[6] or at the opposite extreme (and more frequently), that contemporary organizations were largely beyond the founding generation's reckoning.[7] Unsurprisingly, reality lies somewhere in between. The founding generation and their successors grappled with issues analogous to those now being confronted, but they did not resolve them. Indeed, it may be fair to say that the constitutional scheme, even as elaborated by

---

[5] For discussion of these and related objections to the WTO, see Curtis A. Bradley, *International Delegations, the Structural Constitution, and Non-Self-Execution*, 55 STAN. L. REV. 1557, 1573–74 (2003); Julian G. Ku, *The Delegation of Federal Power to International Organizations: New Problems with Old Solutions*, 85 MINN. L. REV. 71, 71, 96–98, 124, 125 (2000); Edward T. Swaine, *The Constitutionality of International Delegations*, 104 COLUM. L. REV. 1492, 1506–11, 1517–18, 1519–20, 1570–71, 1589–90 (2004); *see also infra* this chapter text accompanying notes 152, 161, 179.

[6] *See, e.g.*, FRANCISCO FORREST MARTIN, THE CONSTITUTION AS TREATY 1–17 (2007) (arguing that the U.S. Constitution was essentially an intergovernmental organization agreement). This theme tended to be revived when the United States considered major international commitments, as when it contemplated joining the League of Nations. *See* JAMES BROWN SCOTT, THE UNITED STATES OF AMERICA: A STUDY IN INTERNATIONAL ORGANIZATION 145–68 (1920) (depicting constitutional convention as an "international conference"); *id.* at 268–82 (describing the Supreme Court as a "prototype of a court of international justice"); HERBERT ARTHUR SMITH, THE AMERICAN SUPREME AS AN INTERNATIONAL TRIBUNAL 106–207 (1920)); *cf.* MERRILL JENSEN, THE NEW NATION: A HISTORY OF THE NEW NATION DURING THE CONFEDERATION, 1781–1789, at x–xiv (1950) (noting and criticizing attempts to invoke early history in pursuit of such causes).

[7] This is sometimes just descriptive. *See, e.g.*, HENKIN, FOREIGN AFFAIRS, at 254 ("The Framers may not have anticipated, or even conceived of, international organizations and 'international governance'"). But the novelty of international organizations for U.S. constitutional analysis is for others part of a critique. *See, e.g.*, JEREMY RABKIN, WHY SOVEREIGNTY MATTERS (1998); Ku, *supra* note 5, at 86–87; Jed Rubenfeld, *The Two World Orders*, WILSON Q., Autumn 2003, at 22; John C. Yoo, *The New Sovereignty and the Old Constitution: The Chemical Weapons Convention and the Appointments Clause*, 15 CONST. COMMENT. 87, 130 (1998); Ernest A. Young, *The Trouble with Global Constitutionalism*, 38 TEX. INT'L L.J. 527, 544–45 (2003).

subsequent practice, anticipated continued debate over issues that seem to arise afresh today.

A. Articles of Confederation

Those finding an immanent internationalism in the U.S. Constitution often begin their account a bit beforehand. The First Continental Congress, for example, appeared to operate (during its two months of existence) as a quasi-international assembly. Each colony's delegation voted as a single unit.[8] The form and authority of that assembly was also strictly limited: decision-making required unanimity,[9] and compliance with its measures was essentially voluntary.[10]

The longer-lived and more powerful Second Continental Congress has also been described as international in character. The Declaration of Independence was issued by the "thirteen united States of America," which suggested both unity and autonomy, but it concluded by declaring the existence of "Free and Independent States." The Articles of Confederation (proposed in 1777 and entering into force in 1781) maintained this tension. What the Articles styled as "The United States of America" was also referred to as a "Confederacy" (Article I), a "Confederation" (Articles II, VI, XI–XIII), and a "league" (Article III), terms that at the time arguably connoted an international organization more than a single nation.[11] The Articles also required approval by each state before any would be bound (and unanimous approval of any amendments) (Article XIII), not unlike a traditional treaty, and the representatives of each state were appointed, instructed, and compensated as if they were part of an international delegation (Article V).[12] Yet the confederation government wielded authority more akin to that of a state,[13] including (once fully operational) by non-unanimous,

[8] *See* AKHIL REED AMAR, AMERICA'S CONSTITUTION 22 (2005).

[9] CALVIN C. JILLSON & RICK K. WILSON, CONGRESSIONAL DYNAMICS: STRUCTURE, COORDINATION, AND CHOICE IN THE FIRST AMERICAN CONGRESS, 1774–1789, at 134–35 (1994).

[10] Thus, the Articles of Association adopted in 1774 provided that "a committee be chosen in every county, city, and town" to police the Association's boycott (art. 11), and in its penultimate paragraph recommended "to the provincial conventions, and to the committees in the respective colonies, to establish such farther regulations as they may think proper, for carrying into execution this association." 1 JOURNALS OF THE CONTINENTAL CONGRESS 79–80.

[11] *See* AMAR, *supra* note 8, at 25–27; David Golove, *The New Confederalism: Treaty Delegations of Legislative, Executive, and Judicial Authority*, 55 STAN. L. REV. 1697, 1703–06 (2003); *see also* DAVID C. HENDRICKSON, PEACE PACT: THE LOST WORLD OF THE AMERICAN FOUNDING 47–48 (2003).

[12] *See* AMAR, *supra* note 8, at 26; *see also* ANDREW C. MCLAUGHLIN, A CONSTITUTIONAL HISTORY OF THE UNITED STATES 126–27 (1935) (noting that the Articles' provisions relating to the privileges and immunities of individuals, and extradition, resembled those in international pacts).

[13] *See* ARTICLES OF CONFEDERATION OF 1781, art. IX (detailing powers of the United States in Congress).

if supermajority, decision-making.[14] The nature of state sovereignty within this scheme is, unsurprisingly, the subject of an extensive literature.[15]

Extrapolating from the Articles of Confederation to the question of how the United States should consider today's international organizations is impossible. The founding generation could easily have perceived a difference between their confederation and how that confederation (and its members) might engage further with other, distinct states, including in the form of a (different) international organization.[16] Moreover, even if the Constitution's precursors resembled international arrangements, the analogy depends not only on whether the Confederation Congress had features akin to the international organizations of its day but also how well those feature resemble characteristics of modern arrangements, like the capacity of the U.N. Security Council to make certain legally binding decisions by a qualified majority.[17] Finally, as discussed later, the Constitution was intended to depart in relevant regards from Articles of Confederation.

Nevertheless, the Articles do suggest that the Founders were open to experimenting with the location of sovereignty along lines that prefigured modern international organizations. This was demonstrated by an early attempt to address piracy, one of the most persistent foreign policy challenges confronting the young United States. Years before being forced, as president, to go to war with the Barbary pirates, Thomas Jefferson—in service as Minister

---

[14] See id. art. IX (requiring assent by nine states for most substantive matters); see also KEITH L. DOUGHERTY, COLLECTIVE ACTION UNDER THE ARTICLES OF CONFEDERATION 28–32 (2001) (discussing sovereignty-protecting aspects of Articles).

[15] See, e.g., JACK N. RAKOVE, THE BEGINNINGS OF NATIONAL POLITICS: AN INTERPRETIVE HISTORY OF THE CONTINENTAL CONGRESS 173 n.* (1979) (endorsing conclusion that "'the central government alone possessed those attributes of external sovereignty which entitled it to be called a state in the international sense, while the separate States, possessing a limited or internal sovereignty, may rightly be considered a creation of the Continental Congress, which preceded them in time and brought them into being'") (quoting Richard B. Morris, The Forging of the Union Reconsidered: A Historical Refutation of State Sovereignty over Seabeds, 74 COLUM. L. REV. 1056, 1088–89 (1974)); see also AMAR, supra note 8, at 25–28 & n.61; SAMUEL BEER, TO MAKE A NATION: THE REDISCOVERY OF AMERICAN FEDERALISM 195–206 (1993); RICHARD B. MORRIS, THE FORGING OF THE UNION, 1781–1789, at 55–79 (1987); cf. GORDON S. WOOD, THE CREATION OF THE AMERICAN REPUBLIC, 1776–1787, at 354–59 (1969) (noting resemblance of 1776 confederation to European concepts of international assembly, but also noting nationalist rhetoric and degree of unity).

[16] The evidence was at least ambivalent with regard to Great Britain and its other subjects. The peace treaty with Great Britain itself indicated that the states were sovereign and independent and would be treated with as such. See Definitive Treaty of Peace (Treaty of Paris), Gr. Brit.–U.S., art. I, Sept. 3, 1783, 8 Stat. 80; FORREST MCDONALD, NOVUS ORDO SECLORUM: THE INTELLECTUAL ORIGINS OF THE CONSTITUTION 150 (1985) (noting relevance of provision to sovereignty debate). At the same time, the Articles did provide that Canada, and perhaps other British colonies, could join the Confederation. ARTICLES OF CONFEDERATION OF 1781, art. XI.

[17] But cf. AMAR, supra note 8, at 26 (invoking William Paterson's description of unanimity under the Articles of Confederation as in "the nature of all treaties") (quoting 1 FARRAND'S RECORDS, at 250); id. at 516 n.61 (arguing that "the Confederation Congress resembled a traditional assemblage of ambassadors, akin to today's United Nations").

Plenipotentiary at Versailles—had to address the raids by Mediterranean pirates against U.S. merchant ships. While Jefferson preferred military reprisals to the European practice of paying tribute, neither option seemed feasible, given limited U.S. naval power and the state of its finances. Jefferson instead proposed in 1786 a "special confederation" between the United States and European powers to address the problem.[18]

Jefferson recognized that the impossibility of resolving operational questions in advance and the physical distances involved posed the question "whether it will not be better for them to give full powers . . . to their Ambassadors, or other Ministers resident at some one court of Europe, who shall form a Committee, or Council, for carrying this convention into effect."[19] The influential Marquis de Lafayette made the case to U.S. audiences, writing to George Washington and John Jay[20]—with Jay relaying Lafayette's letter to the Confederation Congress, after which it was favorably reported to the secretary for foreign affairs (which is to say, to Jay himself).[21] The proposal eventually withered on the vine, apparently due to the difficulty of compelling the states to provide financial support.[22] Even so, no one seems to have objected that vesting this special confederation with control over U.S. naval (or financial) resources would be legally problematic.[23]

[18] See Editorial Note: Jefferson's Proposed Concert of Powers Against the Barbary States, in 10 THE PAPERS OF THOMAS JEFFERSON 560 (Julian P. Boyd ed., 1955) [hereinafter Editorial Note]; for discussions relating to the legal significance, see Golove, supra note 11, at 1727–29; Paul C. Szasz, Thomas Jefferson Conceives an International Organization, 75 AM. J. INT'L L. 138 (1981).

[19] Thomas Jefferson, Proposed Convention Against the Barbary States (July 4, 1786), art. 7, in 10 THE PAPERS OF THOMAS JEFFERSON, supra note 18, at 566. Decision-making in the committee might have been conducted by majority voting, with voting weighted by each member's contribution to the naval force (or, alternatively, the equivalent in financial support). Id. art 7. Although unclear, this contribution might have been subject to determination by the committee itself, which would certainly manage other operations and appoint those who were to serve on the contributed naval vessels. See id. arts. 5, 6, 8.

[20] Editorial Note, supra note 18, at 562–63 (quoting Lafayette correspondence to both Washington and Jay). Jefferson evidently preferred employing Lafayette in order to avoid an overt clash with his colleague and fellow commission member John Adams, whom he knew to prefer ransoming. Id. at 562, 564.

[21] See 32 JOURNALS OF THE CONTINENTAL CONGRESS 65–66 (transmittal by John Jay); 33 JOURNALS OF THE CONTINENTAL CONGRESS 419–20 (reporting support by nine of ten state delegations).

[22] This was Jefferson's diagnosis, at least. Editorial Note, supra note 18, at 562 (quoting Jefferson's autobiography). But see id. at 565–66 (suggesting, as another explanation, divisions in Congress between the pro-English and pro-French factions). Jefferson reported, in any event, that the European powers were generally supportive (with the exception of England and also Spain, which had recently paid Algiers a substantial sum), and that the only element missing was subscription by the United States. 1 THE WRITINGS OF THOMAS JEFFERSON 93–94 (Paul Leicester Ford ed., 1892).

[23] Congress did only have Lafayette's brief summary before it—which omitted the details about adherence, voting, and the like, and was more open to being understood as a treaty-based confederacy in which all decisions were resolved by more standard diplomatic means. Letter from Marquis de Lafayette to John Jay (Oct. 28, 1786), in DEP'T OF STATE, 1 DIPLOMATIC CORRESPONDENCE OF THE UNITED STATES OF AMERICA 319, 320 (1837) (text of the letter); Editorial Note, supra note 18, at 563 (noting discrepancies between versions of Lafayette's text). A motion by Virginia delegate William Grayson provided additional details that suggested greater autonomy. 33 JOURNALS OF THE CONTINENTAL CONGRESS 419.

B. Constitutional Design

The most fundamental limit to pre-constitutional precedent concerning international organizations is that the Constitution was designed to change things. Madison bemoaned the lack of sanction and coercion in the Confederation government and likened it disparagingly to a mere treaty;[24] Hamilton damned international leagues with faint praise, adding that the states' inconsistent ambitions made the Articles of Confederation unworkable.[25] The resulting Constitution broke from any existing international templates in numerous regards, including in establishing the supremacy of constitutional and federal law over state lawmaking (Article VI) and permitting amendment by a supermajority to bind all members (Article V).[26]

At the same time, the new Constitution seemed to place few overt constraints on entering into international alliances. Comparing the Treaty Clause with the provisions addressing state authority permits various conjectures. Article I, Section 10 allows the states, with congressional permission, to enter an "agreement or compact with another state or with a foreign power," but prohibits them from entering "any Treaty, Alliance, or Confederation."[27] The distinction in Article I, Section 10 between a "Treaty" and an "Alliance, or Confederation," and the fact that Article II grants the national government only the authority to enter into "treaties"[28] might be read to imply that the federal government was denied the authority to enter into any "alliance" or "confederation," potentially including some international organizations. But perhaps the express prohibition to the states meant only that the national government, which was supposed to have greater capacity than the Confederation Congress, was left to effectuate any such arrangements,[29] and Article I, Section 10 was intent only on demonstrating the breadth of the prohibition for states.[30]

---

[24] James Madison, Observations (Apr. 1787), *in* 2 THE WRITINGS OF JAMES MADISON 361, 363 (Gaillard Hunt ed., 1900) (arguing that the lack of sanction and authority meant that the system "wants the great vital principles of a Political Cons[ti]tution . . . it is in fact nothing more than a treaty of amity of commerce and of alliance, between independent and Sovereign States").

[25] THE FEDERALIST No. 15, at 108–13 (Alexander Hamilton).

[26] *See* AMAR, *supra* note 8, at 34–37.

[27] U.S. CONST. art. I, § 10. For more extensive discussion of compacts, see Chapter 9 § III.

[28] U.S. CONST. art. II, § 2, cl. 2.

[29] *See* Golove, *supra* note 11, at 1732–34. Professor Golove noted that if "confederations" are implicitly excluded from the Treaty Power, "alliances" must be as well, although no one seemed to think that. *Id*; *cf.* George Washington, Farewell Address (Sept. 17, 1796), *in* PRESIDENTIAL DOCUMENTS 18, 24 (J.F. Watts & Fred L. Israel eds., 2000) ("It is our true policy to steer clear of *permanent* alliances with any portion of the foreign world . . .") (emphasis added); Thomas Jefferson, First Inaugural Address (Mar. 4, 1801), *in* WRITINGS 492, 494 (Merrill D. Peterson ed., 1984) (calling for "peace, commerce, and honest friendship with all nations, *entangling* alliances with none") (emphasis added). The issue also has significance for the capacity of the national government to enter into non–Article II agreements. *See* Chapter 6 § V.

[30] The upshot might have been to deny states the ability to enter into agreements that governed relations of greater significance over longer periods of time. *See* St. George Tucker, *Appendix, in* 1

Unfortunately, what "confederations" and "alliances" meant to the Framers has largely been forgotten, and the Supreme Court appears to have abandoned any inquiry.[31] Moreover, even if the power to enter into confederations and alliances is implicitly vested in the national government, that does not mean that *all* confederations and alliances are permissible—any more than the explicit inclusion of "treaties" means that all treaties are permissible.[32] Clarity about the constitutionality of international organization agreements lies, if anywhere, beyond the Constitution's text.

C. Subsequent Practice

Post-founding-era engagements with international organizations resist easy characterization, but the United States has displayed both international leadership and a tendency to be hamstrung by idiosyncrasies of domestic law and politics. The U.S. acceptance, with Great Britain, of the procedures for the *Alabama* claims arbitration—which addressed British neutrality violations during the Civil War resulting from allowing its dockyards to construct armed ships for the Confederacy—was a pathbreaking advance toward acceptance of significant decision-making by an international body.[33] The United States took more of a back seat on some initiatives due to the difficulty of reconciling international decision-making with authority the United States placed in the private sector and in state-level regulations. Such was the case for the first true international organization, the International Telegraph Union, although the United States effectively behaved as though it were a member long before formally acceding in 1932.[34]

WILLIAM BLACKSTONE, COMMENTARIES 310 (St. George Tucker ed., 1803); David E. Engdahl, *Characterization of Interstate Arrangements: When Is a Compact Not a Compact?*, 64 MICH. L. REV. 63, 75–81 (1965). Justice Story, however, did not accept this distinction. 3 JOSEPH STORY, COMMENTARIES ON THE CONSTITUTION OF THE UNITED STATES § 715 (1833); *see also* Abraham C. Weinfeld, *What Did the Framers of the Federal Constitution Mean by "Agreements or Compacts"?*, 3 U. CHI. L. REV. 453, 460–64 (1936) (explaining how Story misunderstood Tucker and Vattel).

[31] *Cf.* United States Steel Corp. v. Multistate Tax Comm'n, 434 U.S. 452, 459–64 (1978) (recounting the interpretations of the words "treaty," "compact," and "agreement" by the Framers and the Court, and concluding that the distinct meanings were lost by 1833).

[32] *Cf.* Missouri v. Holland, 252 U.S. 416, 433 (1920) ("We do not mean to imply that there are no qualifications to the treaty-making power; but they must be ascertained in a different way."). For discussion of *Missouri v. Holland*, see Chapter 6 §§ I(C), II(D)(2).

[33] *See* Tom Bingham, *The Alabama Claims Arbitration*, 54 INT'L COMP. L.Q. 1, 23 (2005); Charles H. Brower II, *The Functions and Limits of Arbitration and Judicial Settlement Under Private and Public International Law*, 18 DUKE J. COMP. & INT'L L. 259, 272–74 (2008); Mary Ellen O'Connell, *Arbitration and the Avoidance of War: The Nineteenth-Century American Vision, in* THE SWORD AND THE SCALES: THE UNITED STATES AND INTERNATIONAL COURTS AND TRIBUNALS 34–37 (Cesare P.R. Romano ed., 2009).

[34] *See* MARK MAZOWER, GOVERNING THE WORLD: THE HISTORY OF AN IDEA 102 (2012); BOB REINALDA, ROUTLEDGE HISTORY OF INTERNATIONAL ORGANIZATIONS: FROM 1815 TO THE PRESENT

In addition, after serving as a key participant in the creation of the Permanent Court of Arbitration,[35] the United States led, with mixed success, two campaigns in a very short period of time—resulting in the conclusion of more than two dozen nonaggression treaties from 1908 to 1909 (known as the Root arbitration treaties), with further expansion championed by President Taft in 1911—to vest that institution with decision-making authority over vital global affairs.[36]

The domestic politics of these and other initiatives dominated any legal issues, but at least some initiatives precipitated debate on constitutional issues posed by U.S. engagement with international organizations. One episode of particular note involved the Treaty of Versailles, one of the peace treaties that ended World War I. Part I of the treaty consisted of the Covenant of the League of Nations, an international organization designed to deter armed conflict and to help arbitrate international disputes.[37] The U.S. Senate, famously, rejected the Treaty of Versailles and hence the League as well.[38] Unsurprisingly, given that the treaty aimed not only to end the war with Germany but also to achieve a more enduring peace, constitutional objections focused on the League's compatibility with Congress' power to declare war and the president's authority as commander in chief.[39] Other objections related to the treaty power without necessarily implicating the League's function as an international organization.[40] These included

DAY 86–87 (2009); RITA LAURIA WHITE & HAROLD M. WHITE, JR., THE LAW AND REGULATION OF INTERNATIONAL SPACE COMMUNICATION 37 (1988).

[35] See MAZOWER, *supra* note 34, at 81–93; REINALDA, *supra* note 34, at 68–71. *See generally* MANUEL INDLEKOFER, INTERNATIONAL ARBITRATION AND THE PERMANENT COURT OF ARBITRATION (2013).

[36] See John P. Campbell, *Taft, Roosevelt, and the Arbitration Treaties of 1911*, 53 J. AM. HIST. 279 (1966). *See generally* Stephen Wertheim, *The League That Wasn't: American Designs for a Legalist-Sanctionist League of Nations and the Intellectual Origins of International Organization, 1914–1920*, 35 DIPLOMATIC HIST. 797 (2011).

[37] Treaty of Peace between the Allied and Associated Powers and Germany, June 28, 1919, 225 Consol. T.S. 188; Covenant of the League of Nations, June 28, 1919, 225 Consol. T.S. 195 [hereinafter Covenant].

[38] On November 19, 1919, the Senate rejected the treaty with Senator Lodge's initial package of fourteen reservations. 58 CONG. REC. 8,786 (1919); *see also id.* at 8,802 (reporting failure of second vote); *id.* at 8,803 (reporting rejection, later that day, of the treaty as a whole, without reservations). On March 19, 1920, the Senate again rejected the proposed treaty, this time with a package of fifteen reservations. *See* 59 CONG. REC. 4,599 (1920). The United States later concluded several bilateral peace agreements. Treaty of Peace Between the United States and Austria, Austria-U.S., Aug. 24, 1921, 42 Stat. 1946; Treaty of Peace Between the United States and Germany, Ger.-U.S., Aug. 25, 1921, 42 Stat. 1939; Treaty of Peace Between the United States and Hungary, Hung.-U.S., Aug. 29, 1921, 42 Stat. 1951.

[39] The Covenant established both an obligation to refrain from war-making and, more overtly, an obligation to assist victims. Covenant, *supra* note 37, arts. 10, 11, 16.

[40] Defenders of the Covenant, indeed, frequently said it raised conventional issues concerning the treaty power. Percy L. Edwards, *Are the Terms of the Covenant for the Proposed League of Nations Repugnant to the Constitution?*, 89 CENT. L.J. 244 (1919).

concerns about how the executive branch negotiated the treaty,[41] its effect on other treaties,[42] and whether the United States could effectively exclude domestic matters from being treated as international disputes.[43]

The Covenant also presented more general questions involving how its organs—initially an Assembly (consisting of representatives from all members), a Council (a smaller body consisting of certain permanent and rotating members), and a Secretariat (with a Secretary General)—would discharge more dynamic treaty commitments.[44] In addition to superintending the League's ambitious dispute settlement system,[45] the Council assumed responsibility for fixing armament limits that members could exceed only with its blessing,[46] and the Assembly could apportion responsibility for the League's expenses.[47] The Permanent Court of International Justice (PCIJ), to be planned by the Council (and ultimately brought into being by a separate treaty), was to resolve disputes that the members put before it and issue advisory opinions.[48]

U.S. consideration of the League raised questions of continuing relevance to international organization agreements today.[49] First and foremost, by what

---

[41] *See* J.M. Mathews, *The League of Nations and the Constitution*, 18 MICH. L. REV. 378, 378–80 (1920) (evaluating objections).

[42] The Covenant limited League members as to both their existing and future treaties. Covenant, *supra* note 37, art. 20 (providing that members "solemnly undertake that they will not hereafter enter into any engagements inconsistent with the terms thereof," and that if they have previously done so, "it shall be the duty of such Member to take immediate steps to procure its release from such obligations"). In addition, it commanded members to register future treaties with the League Secretariat, on pain of rendering them nonbinding without compliance. *Id.* art. 18. Some otherwise inclined to defend the Covenant found that unacceptable. *E.g.*, H. St. George Tucker, *Constitutionality of the Covenant of Covenant of the League of Nations*, 89 CENT. L.J. 79, 81 (1919).

[43] Covenant, *supra* note 37, art. 15; *see* Leo Gross, *The Charter of the United Nations and the Lodge Reservations*, 41 AM. J. INT'L L. 531, 538–39 (1947).

[44] *See*, respectively, Covenant, *supra* note 37, arts. 3, 4, 6, & 14; *see also* Quincy Wright, *Validity of the Proposed Reservations to the Peace Treaty*, 20 COLUM. L. REV. 121, 124 n.15 (1920) (noting additional commissions and organs created by the Covenant and the Treaty of Versailles).

[45] Members agreed to submit any disputes between them "likely to lead to a rupture" to arbitration, judicial settlement, or Council inquiry, and to refrain from war in the meantime. Covenant, *supra* note 37, art. 12. They also agreed to submit other suitable disputes to arbitration or judicial settlement (including by the Permanent Court), to carry out any award or decision in good faith, and to refrain from resorting to war against any member that so complied. *Id.* art. 13. The Council assumed responsibility for proposing steps to resolve any noncompliance and to address serious disputes itself, through the Assembly, or by leaving them to the members to take action as they saw fit. *Id.* arts. 12, 15.

[46] *Id.* art. 13; *see also id.* art. 10 (providing for Council role in advising how to fulfill the obligation to prevent external aggression).

[47] *Id.* art. 6.

[48] *Id.* art. 14.

[49] For background, see DENNA FRANK FLEMING, THE UNITED STATES AND THE LEAGUE OF NATIONS, 1918–1920 (1932); W. STULL HOLT, TREATIES DEFEATED BY THE SENATE 249–307 (1933); HERBERT F. MARGULIES, THE MILD RESERVATIONISTS AND THE LEAGUE OF NATIONS CONTROVERSY IN THE SENATE (1989); RALPH A. STONE, THE IRRECONCILABLES: THE FIGHT AGAINST THE LEAGUE OF NATIONS (1970); for an account by one of the chief participants, see HENRY CABOT LODGE, THE SENATE AND THE LEAGUE OF NATIONS (1925). *See also* Chapter 6 § I(C) (briefly noting relevance for development of the treaty power).

means could the United States join agreements creating an international organization, or adhere to one of its institutions? President Wilson sought Senate approval of the Treaty of Versailles containing the Covenant, but considered entering into a provisional arrangement, solely on his own authority, that would have bound the United States to the League of Nations created by the Covenant.[50] Later, after attempts to join the PCIJ by separate treaty ran aground,[51] members of the House and Senate introduced measures that would have provided legislative authorization for U.S. membership in the Court and in the League as a whole while avoiding the treaty process.[52] Ultimately, none of these efforts bore fruit.

Second, what made an international organization obligation constitutionally problematic or, at least, worth evaluating? Widely varied views surfaced. Some suggested distinguishing between measures of the international organization that were legally binding on the international plane and those that were legally nonbinding or only "moral."[53] Others would have discounted any such international obligations on the premise that the U.S. Constitution secured sovereign authority to disregard external constraints.[54] To the opposite effect, yet others regarded the constitutional problem of international obligations as being largely inescapable, insofar as any treaty commitment pressured U.S. institutions to comply with measures subsequently adopted by the international organization.[55] Some thought that a key consideration was whether a treaty reassigned functions to an international organization that would ordinarily fall to a U.S. domestic institution. Perhaps it was permissible, the thinking went, for a provision of the Covenant to constrain congressional authority over the war-making power, but

[50] Kurt Wimer, *Woodrow Wilson's Plans to Enter the League of Nations through an Executive Agreement*, 11 WESTERN POL. Q. 800 (1958).

[51] These efforts, and the campaign to enlist the United States in the PCIJ as a whole, are discussed extensively in MICHLA POMERANCE, THE UNITED STATES AND THE WORLD COURT AS A "SUPREME COURT OF THE NATIONS": DREAMS, ILLUSIONS AND DISILLUSION 65–138 (1996).

[52] James W. Garner, *Acts and Joint Resolutions of Congress as Substitutes for Treaties*, 29 AM. J. INT'L L. 482, 484–85 (1935).

[53] *See, e.g.*, QUINCY WRIGHT, THE CONTROL OF AMERICAN FOREIGN RELATIONS 114–15 (1922) [hereinafter WRIGHT, CONTROL]; Mathews, *supra* note 41, at 380, 384, 386; Quincy Wright, *Effects of the League of Nations Covenant*, 13 AM. POL. SCI. REV. 556, 572–73, 575 (1919). President Wilson repeatedly stressed that various Covenant obligations were "moral" rather than "legal" in character. By his reckoning, a legal obligation "specifically binds you to do a particular thing under certain sanctions," whereas a moral obligation involved judgment and lacked clear sanction; Wilson indicated that "a moral obligation is of course superior to a legal obligation and . . . has a greater binding force." S. COMM. ON FOREIGN RELATIONS, TREATY OF PEACE WITH GERMANY: REPORT OF THE CONFERENCE BETWEEN MEMBERS OF THE SENATE COMMITTEE ON FOREIGN RELATIONS AND THE PRESIDENT OF THE UNITED STATES, S. DOC. NO. 66-76, at 19, 21 (1st Sess. 1919).

[54] *See, e.g.*, William Howard Taft, Constitutionality of the Proposals: Address to the First Annual Assemblage of the League to Enforce Peace (May 26, 1916), *reprinted in* TAFT PAPERS ON THE LEAGUE OF NATIONS 52, at 58–60 (Theodore Marburg & Horace E. Flack eds., 1920); Mathews, *supra* note 41, at 385–86; Tucker, *supra* note 42, at 80–81.

[55] *See, e.g.*, George Wharton Pepper, *The Objections to the League of Nations Covenant*, 8 PROC. ACAD. POL. SCI. CITY OF N.Y. 28, 34–35 (1920).

it was quite another thing for a League organ to exercise discretion in Congress' place;[56] others wrestled instead with whether the PCIJ would unconstitutionally displace the U.S. Supreme Court.[57]

Third, to what extent could any potential constitutional infirmities be mediated through an international organization agreement, or by U.S. safeguards established when adhering to such agreement? In the case of the Covenant, some thought constitutional sovereignty was adequately protected by the unanimity requirement for substantive action by the Council (suggesting a U.S. veto),[58] or by Covenant provisions allowing the United States to opt out of initiatives or to withdraw from the treaty altogether should new obligations arise.[59] In addition, many in the Senate favored reservations requiring separate congressional assent before Covenant-based measures would take effect for the United States.[60]

---

[56] *Compare, e.g.,* 57 CONG. REC. 4,691-92 (1919) (statement of Sen. Knox), *with* 58 CONG. REC. 3,137-39 (1919) (statement of Sen. Smith); *see also* WRIGHT, CONTROL, *supra* note 53, at 113 (discussing constitutional concerns relating to the League of Nations Covenant); C.A. Hereshoff Bartlett, *The Constitution or the League of Nations—Which?*, 53 AM. L. REV. 513, 514–15 (1919) (same); William Howard Taft, *The Paris Covenant for a League of Nations*, 13 AM. POL. SCI. REV. 181, 195 (1919) (same).

[57] *See, e.g.,* Mathews, *supra* note 41, at 380–82; William G. Ross, *Constitutional Issues Involving the Controversy Over American Membership in the League Of Nations, 1918-1920,* 53 AM. J. LEGAL HIST. 1, 36 (2013).

[58] Article 5's unanimity requirement for Council and Assembly decisions exempted procedural matters and also required only the agreement of those members represented at the relevant meeting. Covenant, *supra* note 37, art. 5; *see also id.* art. 1 (requiring two-thirds vote of the Assembly to approve new members); *id.* art. 15 (permitting the Council and the Assembly to publish or adopt reports, under certain conditions, by majority vote). For discussion, see 58 CONG. REC. 3,688-89 (1919) (colloquy between Senator Hitchcock and Senator Kellogg); *see also* WRIGHT, CONTROL, *supra* note 53, at 113–14 (discussing constitutional concerns); Gilbert N. Hitchcock, *In Defense of the League of Nations,* 84 ANNALS AM. ACAD. POL. & SOC. SCI. 201, 205 (1919) (stressing significance of unanimity requirement as safeguarding U.S. interests); John Fischer Williams, *The League of Nations and Unanimity,* 19 AM. J. INT'L L. 475 (1925) (exploring ambiguities relating to unanimity requirement for Assembly and Council actions).

[59] These options were functionally similar. Amendments to the Covenant proposed by the Council would not take effect against any member that dissented from them—but the consequence was that such a member would cease to be part of the League. Covenant, *supra* note 37, art. 26; *see* Manley O. Hudson, *Amendment of the Covenant of the League of Nations,* 38 HARV. L. REV. 903 (1925); *cf.* FRANCIS BOWES SAYRE, EXPERIMENTS IN INTERNATIONAL ADMINISTRATION 25, 31 n.† (1919); L.S. WOOLF, INTERNATIONAL GOVERNMENT 194–95 (1916) (discussing similar ratify-or-exit provision relating to the Universal Postal Union). While the Covenant also provided for voluntary withdrawal, see Covenant, *supra* note 37, art. 1, there was disagreement as to that afforded much comfort to the United States—given that a departing party would first have to fulfill "all its international obligations and all its obligations under th[e] Covenant." *Id.; see, e.g.,* 58 CONG. REC. 3,688-89 (1919) (remarks of Senator Kellogg).

[60] Such reservations would have required congressional consent as a condition precedent to acknowledging any obligation to use military force, accepting any mandate, or permitting participation by the United States or its representative in any League organ, and would have conditioned U.S. financial contributions on congressional appropriations. They would also have made the United States the sole judge of whether a matter fell within its domestic jurisdiction, accommodated the Monroe Doctrine, and reserved the right to increase armaments if the United States was threatened with invasion or engaged in war. *See* 58 CONG. REC. 8,777–78 (1919) (detailing fourteen Lodge Reservations subject to 1919 vote); 59 CONG. REC. 4,599 (1920) (detailing fifteen reservations

Others, though, thought the reservations themselves gave rise to constitutional objections,[61] and a number expressed doubt as to whether the reservations would be effective internationally,[62] though certain conditions—such as a later-proposed understanding regarding the Permanent Court, which appeared to require Senate advice and consent before the president could submit disputes for resolution—might nevertheless constrain U.S. practice.[63]

It is hard to draw definitive conclusions from the U.S. experience with the League of Nations. Many of the constitutional objections to the Covenant involved vague concerns about U.S. sovereignty.[64] The outcome provided little added clarity. In rejecting the Versailles Treaty, the Senate did not rest on legal concerns; tellingly, it declined to consent to the treaty even with reservations that would have defused many, if not all, of the constitutional objections.[65] The details risk obscuring a potentially enduring question: did President Wilson's decision to avoid fixed legal obligations in favor of decision-making by international organizations allow for greater compatibility with the U.S. Constitution, or did it instead open the door to dynamic rulemaking that posed an even greater threat?[66]

The U.N. Charter provided an opportunity to revisit many of these issues. The legal and political climate had changed appreciably. Evolving Supreme Court case law,[67]

---

subject to 1920 vote); Wright, *supra* note 44 (reviewing some of the reservations considered in 1919); WRIGHT, CONTROL, *supra* note 53, at 113.

[61] *See, e.g.*, Wright, *supra* note 44, at 125–42.

[62] At the time, the use of reservations for multilateral treaties was less certain, and the Lodge reservations simply asserted that they would become effective upon approval by "at least three of the four principal allied and associated powers, to wit, Great Britain, France, Italy, and Japan." 58 CONG. REC. 8,777–78 (1919); *see also* 58 CONG. REC. 3,690–92 (1919) (reflecting exchange of views).

[63] William Hays Simpson, *The Use of Executive Agreements in the Settlement of International Reclamations*, 8 DET. L. REV. 23, 33–34 (1938). This was one manifestation of a longer-running debate about whether it was necessary to enter into a separate, Senate-approved agreement in order to initiate arbitrations and similar proceedings before international tribunals. *See generally* WRIGHT, CONTROL, *supra* note 53, at 108–10; James Oliver Murdock, *Arbitration and Conciliation in Pan America*, 23 AM. J. INT'L L. 273, 285–88 (1929). James L. Tryon, *A World Treaty of Arbitration*, 20 YALE L.J. 163, 173–74 (1911); Robert R. Wilson, *Clauses Relating to Reference of Disputes in Obligatory Arbitration Treaties*, 25 AM. J. INT'L L. 469, 473, 475–76, 478, 488 (1931).

[64] 58 CONG. REC. 3,136 (1919) (statement of Sen. Smith) (attacking attempts to invoke "the scarecrow of a super-State"); Mathews, *supra* note 41, at 388 (noting that "the Covenant has been attacked, not because of any particular provisions, but because, taking it by and large, it establishes a super-government over the contracting parties"); Quincy Wright, *Effects of the League of Nations Covenant*, 13 AM. POL. SCI. REV. 556, 568 (1919) ("The real concern, however, has been lest the league itself become a second Holy Alliance, arrogating to itself jurisdiction in the domestic affairs of its members.").

[65] *See supra* this chapter note 38.

[66] *See* Wertheim, *supra* note 36; *see also* Stephen Wertheim, *The League of Nations: A Retreat from International Law?*, 7 J. GLOBAL HIST. 210 (2012).

[67] *See, e.g.*, HENKIN, FOREIGN AFFAIRS, at 514 n.38 (invoking as "major constitutional change (or clarification) . . . *Curtiss-Wright, Missouri v. Holland* and the New Deal Commerce clause and Due Process cases").

compromised Senate prerogatives,[68] and a greater U.S. appetite for international governance following another world war (and attendant regret over the U.S. rejection of the League) all improved the prospect for U.S. adherence to the Charter.[69] Still, Congress remained vigilant about the separation of powers,[70] and President Roosevelt and President Truman were intent on accommodating them.[71]

Like the Covenant, the Charter addressed areas traditionally monopolized by domestic actors, and created an institutional structure with genuine decision-making capacity. Its shift toward universal membership arguably made that commitment more dramatic.[72] But potential U.S. objections were also addressed. For example, while the League's unanimity principle was weakened in order to make the United Nations more effective,[73] U.S. autonomy was preserved by means of a virtual Security Council monopoly over legally binding measures (in contrast to other U.N. organs, like the General Assembly, which acted primarily through nonbinding means), coupled with a U.S. ability to block any nonprocedural decisions by the Council.[74] Withdrawal was at least arguably more seamless.[75]

---

[68] See Bruce Ackerman & David Golove, Is NAFTA Constitutional?, 108 HARV. L. REV. 799 (1995) (providing historical account of the surge in interchangeability doctrine concurrent with the New Deal).

[69] See, e.g., 91 CONG. REC. 7,968–69 (Senator Barkley); id. at 8,067–68 (Senator Pepper); Ackerman & Golove, supra note 68, at 883 n.385 (citing speeches by President Roosevelt and his opponent Thomas Dewey that criticized isolationism and criticized rejection of the League); Myres S. McDougal & Asher Lans, Treaties and Congressional-Executive or Presidential Agreements: Interchangeable Instruments of National Policy: I, 54 YALE L.J. 181, 183 (1945) (noting popular support for "a foreign policy which continues our war-time alliances and which seeks to create upon that foundation both a new general security organization . . . and all the other supporting institutions").

[70] The House and Senate each enacted resolutions urging that the United States cooperate in creating an international authority to deter aggression and preserve peace, but only through "constitutional processes"—meaning, at a minimum, approval of a treaty by the Senate. H.R. Res. 25, 78th Cong., 89 CONG. REC. 7655 (1943); S. Res. 192, 78th Cong., 89 CONG. REC. 9222 (1943); see Louis Fisher, The Korean War: On What Legal Basis did Truman Act?, 89 AM. J. INT'L L. 21, 24– 25 (1995). Professors Ackerman and Golove situate these resolutions in the context of a broader tide toward interchangeability, see Ackerman & Golove, supra note 68, at 881–83, and note (as did Professor Corwin) the Senate's lack of dogmatism on the question, see EDWARD S. CORWIN, THE CONSTITUTION AND WORLD ORGANIZATION 52–53 (1944).

[71] Half of the delegation to the San Francisco Conference consisted of members of Congress. The Charter of the United Nations: Hearings Before the S. Comm. on Foreign Relations, 79th Cong. 165 (1945); again, see Fisher, supra note 70, at 26–27.

[72] Cf. Stephen Wertheim, Instrumental Internationalism: The American Origins of the United Nations, 1940–3, 54 J. CONTEMP. HIST. 265 (2019) (explaining the evolution in U.S. views, and regarding them as consistent with U.S. aspirations to global leadership).

[73] See Clyde Eagleton, Covenant of the League of Nations and Charter of the United Nations: Points of Difference, 13 DEP'T STATE BULL. 263, 263 (1945) (stressing that under the U.N. Charter, "[t]he over-all rule of unanimity is abandoned" in favor of "a more flexible system"). In practice, the League had gravitated away from unanimity in the Assembly, which increasingly employed a type of resolution that required only a majority vote. See Leland Goodrich, From League of Nations to United Nations, 1 INT'L ORG. 3, 9–10 (1947); see also supra this chapter note 58 (noting limits to unanimity principle for Council decisions).

[74] See infra this chapter text accompanying note 166.

[75] Unlike the Covenant, the Charter was silent as to withdrawal. However, a separate document adopted at the San Francisco Conference declared that "if . . . a Member because of exceptional circumstances feels compelled to withdraw . . . it is not the purpose of the Organization to compel

Sovereigntists might even regard the new International Court of Justice (ICJ) with ambivalence. Unlike the PCIJ, which was the subject of a distinct treaty, the ICJ Statute was made an integral part of the Charter. Even so, a state would only be exposed to binding ICJ decision-making when the state had separately accepted the court's jurisdiction, which blunted the import of the change.[76]

On the whole, while U.S. membership in the United Nations advanced its engagement with international organizations, U.S. ratification did more to create an ongoing opportunity to address issues of U.S. foreign relations law than it did to resolve them. Contemporaries stressed, indeed, how the Charter had merely ducked the questions posed by the Covenant.[77] Before long, operation of the United Nations excited political opposition not wholly unlike that which undermined President Wilson's League, but it was deferred and attenuated as the Charter received swift and overwhelming approval.[78]

Similar tensions surfaced in relation to at least some of the other international organizations that emerged after World War II. Some of these organizations focused on traditional concerns, like security (for example, the North Atlantic Treaty Organization (NATO)),[79] economic cooperation (for example, the International Monetary Fund (IMF)),[80] and trade (like the General Agreement on Tariffs and Trade (GATT)) and the GATT's successor, the WTO).[81] They also surfaced in relation to newer types of organizations, like those focusing on environmental protection (such as the International Whaling Commission or the

that Member to continue its co-operation in the Organization." U.N. Conference on International Organizations, *Verbatim Minutes of the Ninth Plenary Session*, at 5–6, Doc. 1210, P/20 (June 25, 1945). Because this dropped the Covenant's requirement that international obligations would have to be satisfied as a condition precedent for withdrawal, see *supra* note 59, it was thought to allay concerns that the organization would be impossible to exit. *See, e.g.*, Goodrich, *supra* note 73, at 11.

[76] U.N. Charter, arts. 92–93; Statute of International Court of Justice, June 26, 1945, 59 Stat. 1055, 33 U.N.T.S. 993; for discussion of this change, see POMERANCE, *supra* note 51, at 138–65.

[77] Some were less positive about this, positing a conspiracy of silence designed to conceal the Charter's resemblance to the League, see Goodrich, *supra* note 73, at 3–4, while others saw the Charter's terms as a transparent attempt to anticipate and avoid the objections to the Covenant. *See* Gross, *supra* note 43, at 531–32.

[78] *See, e.g.*, Clyde Eagleton, *The United States and the United Nations*, 28 N.Y.U. L. REV. 17 (1953) (describing early U.N. excesses and U.S. backlash); *cf.* Robert E. Riggs, *Overselling the UN Charter—Fact and Myth*, 14 INT'L ORG. 277 (1960) (evaluating claims that U.S. backers of U.N. participation misled the public). In the short term, the U.S. appetite for international governance was undeterred. *See, e.g.*, Burton Andrews, *Amending the Constitution to Provide for Participation in a World Government*, 14 ALB. L. REV. 125, 125–31 (1950) (citing numerous post-Charter state and federal resolutions embracing broader forms of world government).

[79] North Atlantic Treaty, Apr. 4, 1949, 63 Stat. 2244 (1949), T.I.A.S. No. 1964; for a brief account of this and similar security-oriented organizations, see REINALDA, *supra* note 34, ch. 23.

[80] Articles of Agreement of the International Monetary Fund, Dec. 27, 1945, 2 U.N.T.S. 39.

[81] Final Act Embodying the Results of the Uruguay Round of Multilateral Trade Negotiations, Apr. 15, 1994, Legal Instruments—Results of the Uruguay Round vol. 1, 33 I.L.M. 1125 (1994); for a brief account of this and similar economics-oriented organizations, see REINALDA, *supra* note 34, ch. 25, 35, 39.

U.N. Environment Program (UNEP)).[82] Some of the cross-cutting issues these organizations pose are reviewed in the following.

II. U.S. Participation in International Organizations

A. Method for Admission

The means by which the United States may permissibly join an international organization is closely linked with a broader debate about the interchangeability of treaties, congressional-executive agreements, and sole executive agreements.[83]

As with other international agreements, the less controversial course for joining an international organization is to secure legislative authorization, whether by Article II treaty (as with the United Nations or, unsuccessfully, the League of Nations), by prior congressional authorization (initiated as a bill, as with the IMF,[84] or as a joint resolution, as with the International Labour Organization (ILO)[85]), or by post hoc congressional approval of an executive agreement (as with the Headquarters Agreement concluded with the United Nations).[86] Even before the broader growth of congressional-executive agreements, U.S. adherence to many important international organizations was

---

[82] While the International Whaling Commission is a conventional treaty-based organization, see International Convention for the Regulation of Whaling, Dec. 2, 1946, 62 Stat. 1716, 161 U.N.T.S. 72, UNEP was established as a subsidiary organ of the U.N. General Assembly, see G.A. Res. 2997 (XXVII), (Dec. 15, 1972). For overviews of these and other environmental organizations, see REINALDA, *supra* note 34, at 517–20, 646–62; Churchill & Ulfstein, *supra* note 3.

[83] *See generally* Chapter 6 § V. The *Restatement (Third)* cites examples of agreements relating to international organizations, without further distinction, as evidence of interchangeability. RESTATEMENT (THIRD) § 303 rptrs. note 8; *see also* CONG. RESEARCH SERV., TREATIES AND OTHER INTERNATIONAL AGREEMENTS: THE ROLE OF THE UNITED STATES SENATE 5 (Comm. Print 2001) [hereinafter CRS, TREATIES AND OTHER INTERNATIONAL AGREEMENTS] (citing, inter alia, participation in international organizations as an example of the kind of functions authorized by joint resolution, and concluding that "[t]he constitutionality of this type of agreement seems well established and Congress has authorized or approved them frequently").

[84] Bretton Woods Agreement Act of 1945, 22 U.S.C. § 286 (2018).

[85] 48 Stat. 1182 (1934). For additional examples of this method, see Ackerman & Golove, *supra* note 68, at 892 & nn.424–25 (citing the Food and Agriculture Organization, UNESCO, the International Refugee Organization, the WHO, and the Caribbean Commission). The ILO is perhaps more remarkable because it had been rejected by the Senate when presented as part of the Treaty of Versailles and the Covenant of the League of Nations, only to be resuscitated later via joint resolution. *See* WALLACE MCCLURE, INTERNATIONAL EXECUTIVE AGREEMENTS 125–27 (1941); Manley O. Hudson, *The Membership of the United States in the International Labor Organization*, 28 AM. J. INT'L L. 669 (1934). In contrast, when an attempt was made to adhere to the Protocol and Statute of the Permanent Court of International Justice, the advice and consent of the Senate was sought—not, ultimately, effectively. *See* MICHAEL DUNNE, THE UNITED STATES AND THE WORLD COURT, 1920–1935 (1988); DENNA FRANK FLEMING, THE UNITED STATES AND THE WORLD COURT, 1920–1966 (rev. ed. 1968).

[86] 22 U.S.C. § 287 (2018).

authorized by both houses of Congress rather than by a supermajority of the Senate.[87] Nonetheless, sustained public examination of interchangeability was revived when the United States used such congressional-executive agreements to join the WTO and to adhere to the decision-making processes of NAFTA. The choice to bypass the Senate suggested that the political branches view themselves as enjoying broad latitude in choosing how to afford legislative consent to decision-making by international institutions. While it may yet be maintained that Article II treaties are required for certain significant, sovereignty-affecting commitments, the practice particular to international organizations does as much to detract from that principle as to support it,[88] and courts are unlikely to second-guess the political branches' choices.[89]

Resort to sole executive agreements is meaningfully different. The executive branch has not asserted the ability to join significant international organizations based solely on independent presidential authority, although there are instances in which claimed legislative authorization has been debatable.[90] Perhaps the closest call, in practical terms, was the Algiers Accords, creating the Iran-U.S. Claims Tribunal, which the Supreme Court accepted as an agreement having domestic legal effect based both on the president's claims settlement authority and a degree of legislative authorization.[91] Were the executive branch to seek to join

[87] See McCLURE, supra note 85, at 248–49 & n.81 (citing the ILO and Universal Postal Union as examples); see also McDougal & Lans, supra note 69, at 270 (claiming that "[a]s a matter of practical expediency, the executive agreement has almost always been the procedure utilized for effecting American adherence to international organizations"); id. at 270–73 (citing examples of the ILO, the Pan-American Union and agreements negotiated under its aegis, and others).

[88] Cf. John H. Jackson, The General Agreement on Tariffs and Trade in United States Domestic Law, 66 MICH. L. REV. 250, 270–74 (1967) (considering, and ultimately rejecting, argument that because the GATT evolved into an international organization, it was separately objectionable).

[89] See Chapter 4 § II(A) and Chapter 6 § V; see, e.g., Made in the USA Found. v. United States, 242 F.3d 1300, 1311–20 (11th Cir. 2001) (concluding that to challenge the use of a congressional-executive agreement for NAFTA presented a nonjusticiable political question).

[90] For example, the executive branch took the position that Congress implicitly authorized the General Agreement on Tariffs and Trade (GATT), Oct. 30, 1947, 61 Stat. A-11, 55 U.N.T.S. 194, through the preceding Reciprocal Trade Agreements Act, but that position was not universally accepted. See Ackerman & Golove, supra note 68, at 896 n.441 (describing political controversy); Jackson, supra note 88, at 274 (concluding, after analysis, that the executive agreement was implicitly authorized). A second example is the Pan American Union (later, the Organization of American States), which was authorized after the fact (if at all) "by inference from the recurrent Congressional acts appropriating funds to defray the American portion of the organization's expenses or to meet the cost of sending delegates to conferences." McDougal & Lans, supra note 69, at 344; see H.R. Exec. Doc. No. 53-116, at 2–4 (1894); McCLURE, supra note 85, at 12; LAURENCE F. SCHMECKEBIER, INTERNATIONAL ORGANIZATIONS IN WHICH THE UNITED STATES PARTICIPATES 77–79 (1935); Ackerman & Golove, supra note 68, at 829 n.116.

[91] Declaration of the Government of the Democratic and Popular Republic of Algeria Relating to Commitments Made by Iran and the United States, Iran-U.S., Jan. 19, 1981, 20 I.L.M. 224. In Dames & Moore v. Regan, 453 U.S. 654 (1981), the Supreme Court upheld the president's authority to nullify the attachment of Iranian assets per the Accords in part on the basis of the International Emergency Economic Powers Act (IEEPA), Pub. L. No. 95-223, 91 Stat. 1626 (1977) (codified as amended at 50 U.S.C.A. §§ 1701–06 (2018)), which it held "constitutes specific congressional authorization to the President." Id. at 675. In contrast, the Court held that the legislation invoked by the executive branch

an international organization while conceding that neither a Senate superma-jority nor Congress as a whole had approved the commitment, it would likely be forging new ground. Justiciability doctrines might frustrate legal challenges to any such effort. Still, suits that have unsuccessfully challenged congressional-executive agreements are readily distinguishable: judicial intervention as to a sole executive agreement potentially interferes with one political branch, but would presumably be defending the constitutional prerogatives of the other, and courts might be particularly inclined to reach the merits if there were an impasse between the executive branch and Congress.[92]

Adherence to an international organization agreement also poses ancillary questions distinct from those attending other international agreements. One issue involves the terms of U.S. ratification. While ratification (or accession) to any multilateral agreement may be subject to the approval of other states parties, international organization agreements can require approval by the international organization in its own right, which may frustrate the U.S. ratification process.[93] A second issue is posed by the ability to simulate formal membership by partic-ipating indirectly in the ongoing work of an international organization. A de-cision by the president to maintain observer status for the United States at an international organization could be controversial—particularly in the wake of indications by Congress that it will not support becoming a party, or following

did not "constitute[] specific authorization of the President's action suspending claims" and referring them for resolution by the Iran-U.S. Claims Tribunal, but that—in addition to some presidential au-thority to enter into sole executive agreements—"[c]rucial" to its decision was "the conclusion that Congress has implicitly approved the practice of claim settlement by executive agreement." *Id.* at 677, 680. For further discussion, see Chapter 1 § II(B); Chapter 3 § IV(D); and Chapter 6 § V.

[92] *See Made in the USA Found.*, 242 F.3d at 1318 (concluding that for "'[p]rudential consider-ations. . . a dispute between Congress and the President is not ready for judicial review unless and until each branch has taken action asserting its constitutional authority'" (quoting Goldwater v. Carter, 444 U.S. 996 (1979) (Powell, J., concurring))); *id.* at 1319 ("'[t]he Judicial Branch should not decide issues affecting the allocation of power between the President and Congress until the po-litical branches reach an impasse'" (quoting *Goldwater*, 444 U.S. (Rehnquist, J., concurring))); *see also* Dole v. Carter, 569 F.2d 1109, 1110 (10th Cir. 1977) (rejecting on political question grounds a challenge based on "distinctions which may be drawn between executive agreements and treaties," in a suit brought by a senator concerning an executive agreement committing to return crown jewels to Hungary). For further discussion, see Chapter 4 § II.

[93] Having failed to become a member of the League of Nations, the United States nonetheless con-sidered ratifying, with reservations, the Protocol of Signature to which was annexed the Statute of the Permanent Court of International Justice. While the United States initially hoped that it would suffice to secure consent to these reservations from three or four allies, it became evident that it would be necessary to gain the express assent by all the other states that were party to the Statute. FLEMING, *supra* note 85, at 73–74.) The Senate's proposed reservations, accordingly, were predicated on a series of bilateral exchanges of notes. However, the League Council considered that approach as inappro-priate, viewing Council approval as necessary; further, the Council proposed modifications to the U.S. reservations that were unacceptable to the United States, and hence doomed the U.S. bid to join. POMERANCE, *supra* note 51, at 104–08.

U.S. withdrawal[94]—as might any congressional attempts to restrict observer status.[95] As yet, however, any controversy has been muted, probably because a nonparty tends only to shape the scope of future, potential obligations.[96] A third issue, involving complications posed by the presence or absence of a right to withdraw, is discussed in the following.

B. Method for Withdrawal/Suspension

Withdrawing from international organization agreements, or suspending U.S. participation in them, raises many of the same issues addressed in Chapter 6.[97] As elsewhere, the president has assumed the ability to withdraw on the basis of independent authority. While some of these withdrawals have attracted substantial attention—such as the withdrawals from the ILO[98] and the U.N. Educational, Scientific and Cultural Organization (UNESCO) (twice),[99]

---

[94] As noted immediately later, the United States has withdrawn from several international organizations, such as UNESCO and the ILO, as a means of registering its objections to the organization's functioning. *See infra* this chapter § II(B). Nevertheless, it has sometimes elected to maintain its status as an observer—which organizations like UNESCO have permitted notwithstanding the absence of provisions expressly addressing the issue. *See* Director-General of the U.N. Educ., Sci., and Cultural Org. (UNESCO), *Consequences of the Withdrawal of a Member State From UNESCO*, ¶¶ 60–69, UNESCO Doc. 4 X/EX/2 (Jan. 28, 1985), *reprinted in* 24 I.L.M. 493, 504–06 (1985); UNESCO Exec. Board, UNESCO Doc. 4 X/EX/Decisions of February 22, 1985, *reprinted in* 24 I.L.M. 528, 529–30 (1985).

[95] *Cf.* Departments of Commerce, Justice, and State, the Judiciary, and Related Agencies Appropriations Act, 2002, Pub. L. No. 107-77, § 630 (2001) (limiting U.S. cooperation with the International Criminal Court). *But see* Statement on Signing the Departments of Commerce, Justice, and State, the Judiciary, and Related Agencies Appropriations Act, 2 Pub. Papers 1459 (Nov. 28, 2001) (indicating that restrictions "must be applied consistent with [the president's] constitutional authority in the area of foreign affairs").

[96] *Cf.* Steven Kuan-Tsyh Yu, *The Relationship Between the Republic of China and United Nations Specialized Agencies*, 12 Chinese (Taiwan) Y.B. Int'l L. & Aff. 42, 61–63 (1992–1994) (describing eligibility of states for observer status at various specialized U.N. agencies and attendant rights, consisting principally of the ability to participate in the deliberations of the plenary body).

[97] *See generally* Chapter 6 § VI.

[98] *See United States Withdrawal from the International Labor Organization*, 16 I.L.M. 1561 (1977); Letter from Secretary of State Henry Kissinger to Director-General Francis Blanchard (Nov. 5, 1975), *reprinted in* 14 I.L.M. 1582 (1975) (providing two-year notice of U.S. intentions); *see also* William P. Alford, *The Prospective Withdrawal of the United States from the International Labor Organization: Rationales and Implications*, 17 Harv. Int'l L.J. 623 (1976); Stephen I. Schlossberg, *United States' Participation in the ILO: Redefining the Role*, 11 Comp. Lab. L.J. 48 (1989). The United States later rejoined. *See* International Labor Organization: Statement on the U.S. Decision to Rejoin the Organization, 1 Pub. Papers 306 (Feb. 13, 1980).

[99] The United States announced its withdrawal from UNESCO in 1983. Letter from Secretary of State George Schultz to UNESCO Director-General Amadou Mahtar M'Bow (Dec. 28, 1983), *reprinted in* 23 I.L.M. 220 (1984) (containing also the response by Director-General M'Bow); *see* Peri A. Hoffer, Note, *Upheaval in the United Nations System: United States' Withdrawal from UNESCO*, 12 Brook. J. Int'l L. 161 (1986). It announced that it would return in 2002. *See* Address to the United Nations General Assembly in New York City, 2 Pub. Papers 1572 (Sept. 12, 2002); Sean D. Murphy, United States Practice in International Law: Volume 2, 2002–2004, at 115–16 (2006). It then announced in 2017 that it would once again withdraw, while noting that it desired "to remain

and initiation of that process with respect to the World Health Organization (WHO)[100]—they have not been especially controversial in purely legal terms. In part this may be due to the withdrawals having a sufficient degree of legislative support,[101] but it may also derive from the failure of objections to presidential withdrawal authority in *Goldwater v. Carter*.[102]

That said, the stability of international organizations—such that, like many broad-based multilateral agreements, one state's withdrawal is unlikely to cause the agreement to terminate—and, at the same time, their adaptive nature, pose distinct challenges. When the president is exercising delegated authority to accept membership in an international organization, continuation of the international organization after U.S. withdrawal presumably means that U.S. re-entry remains authorized.[103] This appears to have been the premise, in any event, of the procedure by which the United States departed from and then rejoined the ILO and UNESCO.[104]

Assuming a capacity to recommit exists, it confers greater discretion on the executive branch than the power simply to terminate treaties. The evolutionary tendency of international organizations, including their ability to change the

---

engaged with UNESCO as a non-member observer state." Press Release, Heather Nauert, State Dep't Spokesperson, The United States Withdraws from UNESCO (Oct. 12, 2017), https://perma.cc/ PQ2X-EAWJ; see *United States Gives Notice of Withdrawal from UNESCO, Citing Anti-Israel Bias*, 112 AM. J. INT'L L. 107 (2018).

[100] The United States announced in 2020 that it would withdraw, effective mid-2021. Press Release, Morgan Ortagus, State Dep't Spokesperson, Update on U.S. Withdrawal from the World Health Organization (Sept. 3, 2020), https://perma.cc/UVE4-3WWU. The United States retracted that notice of withdrawal before it took effect. *See* Letter from President Joseph R. Biden Jr. to Sec'y-Gen. Antonio Guterres (Jan. 20, 2021), https://perma.cc/BT74-R37G. For other examples, and a broader discussion, see Marian Nash (Leich), *Contemporary Practice of the United States Relating to International Law*, 91 AM. J. INT'L L. 93 (1997) (noting U.S. withdrawal from the U.N. Industrial Development Organization (UNIDO), Apr. 8, 1979, S. TREATY DOC. NO. 97-19); *see also* MARK F. IMBER, THE USA, ILO, UNESCO AND IAEA: POLITICIZATION AND WITHDRAWAL IN THE SPECIALIZED AGENCIES (1989).

[101] *But see* Hoffer, *supra* note 99, at 195 n.180 (noting bills introduced that would have prohibited the president from terminating U.S. participation in UNESCO); *U.S. Withdrawal from UNESCO: Hearings Before the Subcomms. On Human Rights & Int'l Orgs. & on Int'l Operations of the Comm. on Foreign Affairs*, 98th Cong. 345–65 (1984) [hereinafter *UNESCO Hearings*] (report by David M. Sale, *Constitutionality of Legislation Prohibiting Unilateral Executive Withdrawal of U.S. Membership in the United Nations Education, Scientific, and Cultural Organization (UNESCO)*) (same). *Cf.* Eric A. Posner, *International Law and the Disaggregated State*, 32 FLA. ST. U. L. REV. 797, 828 n.103 (2005) (noting bills decrying, or proposing measures designed to reverse, U.S. withdrawal of compulsory ICJ jurisdiction).

[102] 444 U.S. 996 (1979); *see* Chapter 4 § II(A) and Chapter 6 § VI(B).

[103] *See* Jean Galbraith, *Rejoining Treaties*, 106 VA. L. REV. 73 (2020) (contending that Senate resolutions of advice and consent, and congressional authorizations, should be presumed to authorize rejoining).

[104] This appeared consistent with the *ex ante* statutory authorizations for joining UNESCO and the ILO. *See* Pub. L. No. 79-565, 60 Stat. 712 (1946), codified at 22 U.S.C. § 287m (2018) (authorizing acceptance of UNESCO); Act June 30, 1948, ch. 756, § 1, 62 Stat. 1151 (codified at 22 U.S.C. § 271) (authorizing acceptance of ILO); Galbraith, *supra* note 103, at 98–99.

international obligations attending to membership, means that a decision to rejoin the organization at a later point could benefit from fresh legislative scrutiny; that argument may even be enhanced if withdrawal has actually been successful in altering the organization's policies or the terms of U.S. membership.[105] Pursuing such ends may be defended as exercising the president's constitutional authority to negotiate international agreements,[106] but negotiation is conventionally exercised either pursuant to *ex ante* statutory authorization or in anticipation of an *ex post* approval by statute or Senate advice and consent. At some point, an asserted capacity to re-enter an international organization that involves different obligations than those existing at the time of the original legislative consent becomes difficult to distinguish from a claim that the president has authority to change advice-and-consent terms after the fact.[107] Naturally, any such concerns will be ameliorated, at least in part, when U.S. re-entry effectively requires congressional approval, as when return to the international organization effectively requires legislative appropriation of unpaid dues or other financial contributions.[108]

C. Method for Engaging in Rulemaking

The terms by which the United States participates in the work of an international organization vary by the treaty in question, as modified by any U.S. reservations, understandings, and declarations. At the national level, Congress routinely exercises control over the executive branch's engagement with international organizations—and, derivatively, over the organizations themselves—through the appointments and appropriations processes. The U.N. Participation Act is an important, and not unrepresentative, example. It requires Senate advice

---

[105] The international complications posed by the capacity to withdraw and then rejoin—for example, with additional reservations—present different questions. *See* Laurence R. Helfer, *Not Fully Committed? Reservations, Risk, and Treaty Design*, 31 YALE J. INT'L L. 367, 371–72 (2006) (noting instances of rejoining maneuvers).

[106] *UNESCO Hearings, supra* note 101, at 358–59; *see* United States v. Curtiss-Wright Export Co., 299 U.S. 304, 319 (1936). For further discussion of *Curtiss-Wright*, see Chapter 1 §§ I(D), II(A)(2).

[107] *See* Chapter 6 § III (B)(2) (noting controversies concerning presidential reinterpretation of treaties). This suggests that the negotiating authority argument may be stronger in instances of *ex ante* authorization, in which case the international organization's hypothesized revision—which enticed the United States to rejoin after withdrawal—may be just as much within Congress's original compass as the prior agreement.

[108] In the case of UNESCO, the United States had not provided funding since 2011, based on its objections to Palestinian membership. The prevailing assumption is that congressional authorization for at least some proportion of membership dues is a condition precedent for rejoining. *See,* *e.g.,* Alexa Oleson, *Biden Should Rejoin UNESCO—But Not Without Getting Something in Return,* FOREIGN POLICY (Jan. 21, 2021), https://perma.cc/W52F-RF7A; *see also* MURPHY, *supra* note 99, at 116 (noting requests for congressional funding prior to previous resumption of U.S. membership).

and consent for the appointment of high-ranking U.S. representatives to the United Nations (and its specialized agencies) while delegating to the president the authority to employ others as well. All representatives follow the president's instructions, as relayed by the secretary of state, but Congress is entitled to detailed annual reports. Congress also authorizes U.S. spending through the usual annual appropriations process, deferring for the most part to the U.N. General Assembly's reckoning of the U.S. share of expenses.[109] As described later, Congress retains some control over the results of U.N. rulemaking, at least relating to legislative prerogatives like the war power.[110]

Deeper legislative intrusions into rulemaking by international organizations have been controversial. With increased vigor, Congress has sought to direct by statute the U.S. "voice and vote" within certain organizations, so as to require opposing measures by which the international organization would provide assistance to a particular state[111] (or to states having particular characteristics[112]), to favor assistance for particular states,[113] to promote particular objectives through the international organization,[114] or to seek reform of an organization's practices.[115] Such provisions may be the price of securing legislative approval

[109] 22 U.S.C. §§ 287–287l (2018).

[110] See infra this chapter § III(B).

[111] See, e.g., 22 U.S.C. § 5811 note (providing that the secretary of the treasury should instruct the U.S. executive directors of international financial institutions to use the U.S. voice and vote to oppose financial assistance to Belarus).

[112] For example, Congress instructed the directors of specified international financial institutions to oppose assistance to states that commit human rights abuses, expropriate, or foment terrorism. See, e.g., 22 U.S.C. § 262d(a) (addressing assistance to states "other than those whose governments engage in . . . a pattern of gross violations of internationally recognized human rights" or providing refuge to terrorist hijackers); id. §§ 262d(e), (g) (providing non-exclusive criteria for identifying states committing gross violations of human rights); id. § 262d (f) (addressing non-assistance to states committing gross violations of human rights, subject to exceptions); id. §§ 262p-4q, 262p-4r, & 262p-11 (addressing non-assistance to states engaged in terrorism); id. §§ 283r, 284j, 285o, 290g-8, & 2370 (addressing non-assistance to states engagement in nationalization, expropriation, or related activities). Sometimes domestic interests are in the foreground. See, e.g., 22 U.S.C. § 262h (directing U.S. executive directors at specified international institutions to oppose assistance for the production of commodities or minerals in surplus on the world market, where production would hurt U.S. producers); accord id. § 262h note (citing similar provisions in numerous appropriations acts); id. §§ 262k & 262n-2 (codified voice and vote provisions relating to commodities and minerals).

[113] See, e.g., 22 U.S.C. § 7511 (stating the sense of Congress that the United States should use its voice and vote in support of international commitments to Afghanistan).

[114] See, e.g., 22 U.S.C. § 262f (requiring that the United States use its voice and vote in certain international financial institutions to promote the use of light capital technologies); id. § 262p-7 (requiring the secretary of the treasury to direct the U.S. executive directors at the World Bank and the IMF to "promote the establishment of poverty reduction strategy policies and procedures"). Cf. 22 U.S.C. § 262g (establishing policy to use the U.S. voice and vote in certain international financial institutions to combat malnutrition and promote economic development in developing countries, but directing opposition to financial assistance relating to the "export of palm oil, sugar, or citrus crops" in the event it would injure U.S. producers).

[115] See, e.g., 22 U.S.C. § 262p-4p (providing for the secretary of the treasury to direct U.S. directors at certain international financial institutions to use their voice and vote to urge the institution to adopt various policies favoring worker rights); id. § 262p-9 (similar provision aimed at labor-related reforms of World Bank reporting); Kristina Daugirdas, Congress Underestimated: The Case of The World

of an international agreement, as with the case of the U.S.-Mexico-Canada Agreement Implementation Act.[116] Even so, the president has objected to some such provisions on grounds that they interfere with the foreign affairs power,[117] while Congress has defended its prerogatives.[118]

Although there has been no clear institutional settlement and justiciability hurdles remain prominent,[119] some guidance may be possible. Statutory terms that do less to constrain the executive branch are likely to be more welcome and less prone to pose constitutional concerns. Hortatory provisions suggesting how U.S. officials "should" vote or what they must "encourage" seem less intrusive,[120] as do those that defer to executive branch judgment.[121]

Bank, 107 AM. J. INT'L L. 517, 560–61 (2013); Charles Tiefer, *Adjusting Sovereignty: Contemporary Congressional-Executive Controversies About International Organizations*, 35 TEX. INT'L L.J. 239, 249–51 (2000).

[116] *See* United States–Mexico–Canada Agreement Implementation Act, Pub. L. 116-113, §§ 832–34, 134 Stat. 11 (2020) (directing the secretary of the treasury to direct U.S. representatives to the Board of Directors of the North American Development Bank to use voice and vote to seek preferences for certain projects, efficiencies, and development of performance measures).

[117] *See, e.g.*, Constitutionality of Section 7054 of the Fiscal Year 2009 Foreign Appropriations Act, 33 Op. O.L.C. 1 (2009), https://perma.cc/EX9S-6YR6 (noting objections by successive presidents to recurring provision prohibiting the use of funds for expenses for U.S. delegations to specialized U.N. agencies, bodies, or commission chaired or presided over by a state determined by the secretary of state to be one supporting international terrorism).

[118] For example, following President Obama's release of a signing statement objecting to voice-and-vote provisions in the fiscal 2009 supplemental appropriations act, the House of Representatives adopted an amendment to a 2010 fiscal year spending bill designed to reiterate its position and mitigate the signing statement. 155 CONG. REC. 17302, 17304 (2009) (remarks of Rep. Frank). Congress has also considered preempting the effect of any signing statement by insisting on seeing reforms before money will be authorized for institutions in question. *See* S. COMM. ON FOREIGN REL., 111TH CONG., THE INTERNATIONAL FINANCIAL INSTITUTIONS: A CALL FOR CHANGE 20 (Comm. Print 2010), https://perma.cc/S67X-YRQC.

[119] *See, e.g.*, Atl. Tele-Network Inc. v. Inter-American Dev. Bank, 251 F. Supp. 2d 126 (D.D.C. 2003) (dismissing challenge to vote by the executive branch on Inter-American Development Bank loan, allegedly in violation of federal statute, on grounds that, inter alia, the plaintiff lacked standing and lacked a private cause of action, and citing favorably defendants' argument that the claim presented a nonjusticiable political question); *id.* at 129–30 (citing precedent).

[120] *See, respectively*, Pub. L. No. 109-456, § 202, 120 Stat. 3384 (2006) (providing that the President "should" instruct U.S. officials at U.N. voluntary agencies to use their voice and vote to pursue certain humanitarian policy objectives for the Democratic Republic of the Congo); 22 U.S.C. § 262j (2018) (directing that United States "shall" use its voice and vote in certain regional development organizations to "shall encourage such institutions [to] promote the decentralized production of renewable energy"). There is yet more variety. *See, e.g., id.* § 262n-3 (providing that the secretary of the treasury "shall instruct" the U.S. director at the IMF "to use aggressively" the U.S. voice and vote "to vigorously promote" opening agricultural commodities markets).

[121] Daugirdas, *supra* note 115, at 528–30; *see, e.g.*, 22 U.S.C. § 262p-4r (2018) (voice and vote provision permitting secretary of the treasury to instruct U.S. executive directors in the event the president determines that a potential beneficiary country may frustrate U.S. efforts against terrorism); *id.* § 262p-4q (voice and vote provision requiring that the secretary of the treasury instruct U.S. executive directors at international financial institutions to oppose loans to countries designated as terrorist states by the secretary of state pursuant to other provisions). Waivers may also be available. *See, e.g.*, div. A, tit. XV, Pub. L. No. 103-60, §§ 1511(c), (d), 107 Stat. 1839 (1993) (codified at 50 U.S.C. § 1701 note) (requiring that the secretary of the treasury instruct the U.S. executive directors of international financial institutions to use the U.S. voice and vote to oppose financial assistance to Serbia

Stricter provisions present difficult questions, and have divided even commentators sympathetic to congressional prerogatives.[122] Executive branch objections resemble those made against congressional attempts to regulate the negotiation of international agreements and seek to preserve the president's exclusive power to conduct diplomacy notwithstanding Congress' power of the purse.[123] Voice-and-vote provisions may be distinguishable. Executive participation in the work of an international organization has a more attenuated relation to treaty-making than do negotiations preliminary to the organization's creation or U.S. adherence: once the United States has adhered to the international organization agreement, the executive branch is less engaged in making the agreement than in executing the law, in which role it is subordinate to Congress. Moreover, Congress' stake in at least some of the decisions taken by the organization may also be more easily defended in terms of the spending power. When authorizing or appropriating funds, Congress may generally allocate funds to be spent in relation to a particular country; when financial assistance is being authorized or appropriated for use by an international organization, mandatory instructions to U.S. delegates similarly constrain how the executive branch (through the organization) spends U.S. money.[124] When statutory limitations relate directly to the international organization's use of its budget—as when Congress insisted on constraining what it perceived as bloated bureaucracy at the United Nations, even when that forced the United States into arrears—it

or Montenegro, subject to presidential waiver). Congressional restrictions may also seem more discretionary if they coincide with executive branch preferences and have only short-term effect. In 1945, Congress adopted legislation that required the U.S. governor and executive director of the IMF and the IBRD to obtain certain interpretations from those institutions of their respective powers. 22 U.S.C. §§ 286i–j (2018). These instructions appear to have been acceptable to the executive branch, and their objective was in any event shortly achieved. Daugirdas, *supra* note 115, at 556–58.

[122] *Compare, e.g.*, HENKIN, FOREIGN AFFAIRS, at 249 (suggesting that "[a]ttempts by Congress to instruct U.S. representatives [to international organizations] are highly questionable as a matter of constitutional separation of powers, and are usually only hortatory or are likely to be treated as such by the President," but noting pragmatic value of heeding Congress given its ultimate control over funding), *with* Lori Fisler Damrosch, *Treaties and International Regulation*, 98 AM. SOC'Y INT'L L. PROC. 349, 351 (2004) (describing Justice Department opposition to voice-and-vote provisions as "wrong as a matter of democratic political theory, historical experience, common sense, and constitutional law," and citing to precedent supporting congressional authority to establish "broad contours of national foreign policy"). The leading discussion of these questions, albeit focused on the World Bank, is Daugirdas, *supra* note 115, at 525–26, 544–49.
[123] *See, e.g.*, 33 Op. O.L.C., *supra* note 117; *see also* Unconstitutional Restrictions on Activities of the Office of Science and Technology Policy in Section 1340(A) of the Department of Defense and Full-Year Continuing Appropriations Act, 2011, 35 Op. O.L.C. 1 (2011), https://perma.cc/P2AR-4ZX2 (treating as similar). The issue of these restrictions, and the extent of Congress's appropriations power, is discussed extensively in Chapter 2 §§ II(C) and III; *see also* Chapter 3 § III(E) and Chapter 6 § II(B)(1).
[124] *See, e.g.*, 22 U.S.C. § 262h (2018) (voice-and-vote provision "oppos[ing] any assistance by such institutions, using funds appropriated or otherwise made available pursuant to any provision of law," for certain export activities).

may seem straightforward as a matter of national law, even if not in keeping with U.S. international obligations.[125]

This said, spending power defenses of congressional involvement do not seem entirely decisive. U.S. financial support is comingled with the contributions of other states, and the decision with respect to the use of those funds is collaborative rather than unilateral. Some voice-and-vote provisions, moreover, only incidentally concern the expenditure of appropriated funds per se, but rather express a legislative view on substantive positions that may be taken by representatives of the U.S. executive branch. Consequently, some measures to instruct U.S. positions at international organizations, or to govern U.S. positions on fundamental governance or operations questions, may only be defended as entailments of Congress' general legislative power or on a very broad conception of its ability to condition spending. At least where mandatory provisions bear directly on traditional executive branch authority—for example, where they involve the admission of other states to membership in an international organization, which may even have the effect of reducing U.S. financial obligations—they test the separation of powers.[126] According to the executive branch, voice-and-vote instructions may be still less defensible if they are attempted by the Senate as part of advice and consent.[127]

---

[125] See, e.g., SEAN D. MURPHY, 1 UNITED STATES PRACTICE IN INTERNATIONAL LAW: VOLUME 1, 1999–2001, at 113–19 (2002) (describing international and domestic bargaining over payments by the United States to the United Nations).

[126] See, e.g., 22 U.S.C. § 6034 (providing that, subject to limited exceptions, the secretary of the treasury "shall instruct the United States executive director of each international financial institution to use the voice and vote of the United States to oppose the admission of Cuba as a member of such institution," until such point as the president "submits a determination . . . that a democratically elected government in Cuba is in power"); see also id. § 7424 (providing that the president "should use the voice and vote of the United States in the United Nations Security Council to ensure that each resolution of the Security Council authorizing any peacekeeping operation" or "peace enforcement" exempts permanently "at a minimum, members of the Armed Forces of the United States participating in such operation from criminal prosecution or other assertion of jurisdiction by the International Criminal Court for actions undertaken by such personnel in connection with the operation").

[127] The Justice Department's Office of Legal Counsel (OLC) objected to a proposed voice-and-vote "condition" that would have required the U.S. commissioner on the North Pacific Fur Seal Commission to vote against taking fur seals for commercial purposes within U.S. jurisdiction. Constitutionality of Proposed Conditions to Senate Consent to the Interim Convention on Conservation of North Pacific Fur Seals, 10 Op. O.L.C. 12 (1986); see Protocol Amending the Interim Convention on Conservation of North Pacific Fur Seals Between the United States, Canada, Japan, and the Soviet Union, Oct. 12, 1984, S. TREATY DOC. No. 99-5 (1985). OLC reasoned that the condition interfered with the president's executive power, which extended to his function in carrying out international agreements. One premise was that the conditions, unlike treaty reservations, would not have any effect on U.S. international legal obligations under the Protocol—and thus could not be derived from the Senate's role in making treaties via its advice-and-consent function. Id. at 16–18 & n.14; see also id. at 17–18 (noting, more generally, its problematic "limitation on the discretion of the President's representative"). The protocol was later returned to the president without consent, after the interim convention expired. S. Res. 267, 146 CONG. REC. 2480 (2000).

D. Method for Engaging in Dispute Resolution

While international dispute resolution mechanisms have multiplied,[128] the United States has found it persistently difficult to participate in them. To be sure, the United States has sometimes championed the creation of arbitral institutions. As of 1908, not long after creation of the Permanent Court of Arbitration, it was even said that "[t]he United States has been and is a partisan—we might almost say a violent partisan—of international arbitration."[129] But the United States later refused to join the PCIJ, and this and other contemporaneous episodes offer meaningful insight into U.S. legal and political tastes—much as did the prominent U.S. role in later creating the United Nations and its International Court of Justice.[130]

Historically, one source of U.S. ambivalence has been the method for engaging in dispute resolution. It has been accepted that a treaty, congressional-executive agreement, or (in some circumstances) a sole executive agreement might be employed to commit a specific matter to arbitration.[131] Disagreements arose, however, during Senate consideration of *general* arbitration treaties submitted for its approval. Because these treaties described potentially arbitrable questions more capaciously—including, potentially, matters of interest to the Senate—battle was joined over whether separate consent by the Senate, in the form of a supplemental treaty, was necessary prior to submitting particular cases for arbitral resolution.

The problem became evident not long after Congress itself called for general arbitration treaties.[132] President Cleveland negotiated an 1897 general arbitration treaty with Great Britain, and President McKinley asked for Senate approval. The Senate then proposed that the special agreement (or *compromis*) required to proceed with any particular dispute would itself be in the form of treaty, requiring approval by two-thirds of the Senate; such proposal, by defeating the purpose of a general arbitration treaty, doomed its successful conclusion.[133] Later, when the Senate proposed similar amendments to general arbitration treaties, Theodore Roosevelt refused to seek their renegotiation,[134] but his administration later

---

[128] Jenny S. Martinez, *Towards an International Judicial System*, 56 STAN. L. REV. 429, 430 (2003).

[129] Editorial Comment, *The American Theory of International Arbitration*, 2 AM. J. INT'L L. 387 (1908); *see* JOHN BASSET MOORE, THE UNITED STATES AND INTERNATIONAL ARBITRATION (1896); *supra* this chapter note 35.

[130] *See supra* this chapter notes 48–52.

[131] *See* Charles Cheney Hyde, *Agreements of the United States Other than Treaties*, 17 GREEN BAG 229 (1905); John Bassett Moore, *Treaties and Executive Agreements*, 20 POL. SCI. Q. 385 (1905).

[132] *See* WRIGHT, CONTROL, *supra* note 53, at 108–10; Myres S. McDougal & Asher Lans, *Treaties and Congressional-Executive or Presidential Agreements: Interchangeable Instruments of National Policy: II*, 54 YALE L.J. 534, 558–62 (1945) (citing initial congressional interest in general arbitration treaties, but also their exemplification of "death by Senate"); Wilson, *supra* note 63.

[133] *See* HOLT, *supra* note 49, at 154–62 (reviewing defeat of Olney-Pauncefote Treaty).

[134] *See id.* at 204–12 (discussing Hay treaties). The Senate's amendment to a proposed agreement with France, which served as kind of a stalking horse for those agreements, would have required that

negotiated general arbitration treaties that expressly required a special agreement for a particular dispute for which Senate consent was necessary.[135] This approach proved unsustainable. President Taft wound up abandoning such general arbitration treaties when it became apparent that some intended for the Senate's role in consenting to a special agreement to be more than perfunctory, such that it would have a genuine capacity to determine whether a particular matter was arbitrable.[136] Still later, the Senate insisted on maintaining the special agreement requirement in the form of a reservation to the General Treaty of Inter-American Arbitration, notwithstanding attempts to differentiate that treaty as involving a more narrowly drawn class of potential disputes.[137]

The executive branch decried the Senate's approach, but at the same time, absorbed the underlying message.[138] The continuing constitutional significance is

a special "treaty" be concluded prior to any arbitration, appearing to impose a restriction on how France could properly commit a matter to arbitration, as opposed to regulating only the U.S. process. See James F. Barnett, *International Agreements Without Advice and Consent of the Senate*, 15 YALE L.J. 63, 79–81 (1905); Editorial Comment, *The American Theory of International Arbitration, supra* note 129, at 388.

[135]   These were known as the Root Treaties. Chandler P. Anderson, *The New Arbitration Treaty with France*, 22 AM. J. INT'L L. 362, 363–64 (1928).

[136]   Each of the treaties, signed with Great Britain and France in 1911, would have enabled a joint high commission of inquiry to determine whether the scope of a particular dispute was justiciable. Because of the commission's composition and voting rules, U.S. sovereign interests appeared to be protected by U.S. nationals. That did not, however, necessarily protect the interests of the Senate. *See* 48 CONG. REC. 1066 (remarks of Sen. McCumber). *See generally* John P. Campbell, *Taft, Roosevelt, and the Arbitration Treaties of 1911*, 53 J. AM. HIST. 279 (1966); E. James Hindman, *The General Arbitration Treaties of William Howard Taft*, 36 HISTORIAN 52 (1973); for the proposed treaties themselves, see *General Arbitration Treaty Between the United States of America and the French Republic*, 5 AM. J. INT'L L. 249 (Supp. 1911); *General Arbitration Treaty Between Great Britain and the United States*, 5 AM. J. INT'L L. 253 (Supp. 1911).

[137]   General Treaty of Inter-American Arbitration, Jan. 5, 1929, 49 Stat. 3152, 130 L.N.T.S. 135; *see* James Oliver Murdock, *Arbitration and Conciliation in Pan America*, 23 AM. J. INT'L L. 273, 285–88 (1929); John B. Whitton & John Withrow Brewer, *Problems Raised by the General Treaty of Inter-American Arbitration*, 25 AM. J. INT'L L. 447, 463–68 (1931) (discussing the *compromis*). This was despite the executive branch's success in persuading the Senate to withdraw one of its previously approved reservations. *See* Denys P. Myers, *Acceptance of the General Treaty of Inter-American Arbitration*, 30 AM. J. INT'L L. 57 (1936); *see also* James W. Garner, *The Senate Reservations to the Inter-American General Treaty of Arbitration*, 26 AM. J. INT'L L. 333 (1932) (discussing exemptions in regard to public consular property).

[138]   Theodore Roosevelt remarked, "I think that this amendment makes the treaties shams, and my present impression is that we had better abandon the whole business rather than give the impression of trickiness and insincerity which would be produced by solemnly promulgating such a sham." 2 CORRESPONDENCE OF THEODORE ROOSEVELT AND HENRY CABOT LODGE 111 (1925), *cited in* Whitton & Brewer, *supra* note 137, at 468 n.115; *see also* Letter from Charles Hughes to the U.S. President, Mar. 21, 1923, Ann. 1 to Memorandum by Lord Chelmsford (First Lord of the Admiralty), July 21, 1924, PRO W 6062/338/98 FO 371/10573 (concluding that "it would seem to be entirely clear that until the Senate changes its attitude it would be a waste of effort for the President to attempt to negotiate treaties with the other powers providing for an obligatory jurisdiction of the scope stated in [the Optional Clause]"), *quoted in* Lorna Lloyd, *"A Springboard for the Future": A Historical Examination of Britain's Role in Shaping the Optional Clause of the Permanent Court of International Justice*, 79 AM. J. INT'L L. 28, 33 n.21 (1985).

uncertain. The United States was not alone in favoring, for general arbitration treaties, that further special agreements be required for the resolution of specific disputes, but it was more insistent that such agreements comply with ordinary domestic constitutional requirements (meaning, for the United States, Article II).[139] Senators sometimes insisted that advice and consent for each special agreement was essential to avoiding unconstitutionally delegating the Senate's advice-and-consent authority,[140] while at other times resistance seemed grounded more on caution about particular U.S. commitments.[141] Still, these early episodes plausibly reflected the Senate's perceived prerogative to decide whether particular disputes could be resolved pursuant to a general arbitration treaty.[142]

Gradually, the special agreements mechanism took a back seat to an approach in which categories of cases were simply excluded from international adjudication.[143] The most notable example involved the compulsory jurisdiction of the ICJ. The executive branch agreed that for the United States, such recognition required approval by two-thirds of the Senate, or a majority of both houses.[144] Ultimately, the Senate consented, but subject to three qualifications: one that put aside disputes which the parties had entrusted to other tribunals; another for disputes relating to "matters which are essentially within the domestic jurisdiction of the United States of America as determined by the United States of America" (known as the "Connally reservation"); and a third for disputes under a multilateral treaty, unless all the parties to the treaty affected by the decision were parties to the ICJ's proceedings, or the United States specially agreed to jurisdiction (the "Vandenberg reservation").[145] The self-judging Connally reservation was particularly controversial because it appeared to substantially compromise

[139] For example, special agreements were a feature of the pathbreaking Anglo-French arbitration agreement of 1903. Wilson, *supra* note 63, at 476. The United States was, however, a distinctive proponent of provisions that insisted on ratification of special agreements according to domestic constitutional law. UNITED NATIONS, SYSTEMATIC SURVEY OF TREATIES FOR THE PACIFIC SETTLEMENT OF INTERNATIONAL DISPUTES, 1928–1948, at 70–78 (1949).

[140] *See* S. COMM. ON FOREIGN RELATIONS, REPORT UPON THE GENERAL ARBITRATION TREATIES WITH GREAT BRITAIN AND FRANCE, SIGNED ON AUGUST 8, 1911, AND THE PROPOSED COMMITTEE AMENDMENTS, S. DOC. NO. 62-98, at 4–8 (1911) (prepared by Sen. Lodge).

[141] *See, e.g.*, 48 CONG. REC. 646-47 (1912) (remarks of Sen. Hitchcock); *id.* at 2823–24 (remarks of Sen. Heyburn).

[142] *See, e.g.*, MAX HABICHT, POST-WAR TREATIES FOR THE PACIFIC SETTLEMENT OF INTERNATIONAL DISPUTES 1044–45 (1931); Wilson, *supra* note 63, at 488.

[143] For a survey of reservations employed by the United States and others, see HABICHT, *supra* note 142, at 992–1000.

[144] S. Rep. No. 79-1835, at 9–10 (1946) (describing concessions by the legal adviser of the Department of State, the secretary of state, and the president).

[145] Declaration Respecting Recognition by the United States of the Compulsory Jurisdiction of the International Court of Justice, Aug. 14, 1946, U.S.-U.N., 61 Stat. 1218, 1 U.N.T.S. 9; *see* 92 Cong. Rec. 10,618, 10,621 (1946) (Vandenberg reservation); *id.* at 10,694 (Connally reservation); Louis Sohn, *American Acceptance of the Jurisdiction of the International Court of Justice: Experiences and Prospects*, 19 GA. J. INT'L & COMP. L. 489, 490 (1989) (describing these as "reservations . . . added at the last minute on the floor of the Senate"); *see* POMERANCE, *supra* note 51, at 206–63.

the ICJ's jurisdiction, potentially to the point of rendering it a nullity.[146] The executive branch came to recognize its downsides, as it impaired the United States' own ability to invoke jurisdiction,[147] and weakened the ICJ as an institution.[148] It was also an incomplete solution. In view of the ICJ's finding of jurisdiction in 1984 over a case brought by Nicaragua against the United States for military and paramilitary activities in Central America, the United States (which did not in that case invoke the Connally reservation) terminated its recognition of compulsory jurisdiction altogether.[149]

Despite curtailing the ICJ's compulsory jurisdiction, the United States remains party to many treaties that authorize the ICJ to resolve treaty-related disputes.[150] Even where the United States has insisted on U.S. consent as a precondition for a tribunal's jurisdiction over any particular matter, it does not appear to have secured any continuing Senate role.[151] Acquiescence in other tribunals (like the U.S. commitment to binding resolution of disputes by the WTO's Dispute Settlement Body)[152] and consideration of others (as with the Convention on the Law of the Sea),[153] as well as mixed-claims commissions and binational panels

[146] See, e.g., Interhandel Case (Switz. v. U.S.), Preliminary Objections, 1959 I.C.J. 6, 95 (Mar. 21) (Lauterpacht, J., dissenting) (regarding the Connally reservation as invalid, and as invalidating the U.S. declaration as a whole, such that the United States was not subject to ICJ compulsory jurisdiction).

[147] For example, in one proceeding initiated by the United States against Bulgaria, the United States had to address Bulgaria's ability to invoke, reciprocally and for its own advantage, the United States' exclusion of matters falling within its domestic jurisdiction; ultimately, the ICJ dismissed the proceeding with the consent of both parties. Observations and Submissions of the United States on the Preliminary Objections of Bulgaria, Aerial Incident of 27 July 1955 (U.S. v. Bulg.), 1959 I.C.J. Pleadings 301 (Feb. 1960); Aerial Incident of 27 July 1955 (U.S. v. Bulg.), 1960 I.C.J. 146 (May 30).

[148] In 1976, the legal adviser of the Department of State conveyed to the Senate a study recommending that the United States retract the so-called Connally reservation. 1976 DIGEST OF U.S. PRACTICE 650, 651. See generally POMERANCE, supra note 51, at 264–332 (discussing these and similar efforts).

[149] See Letter from George P. Schultz, U.S. Sec'y of State, to Dr. Javier Perez de Cuellar, U.N. Sec'y-Gen. (Apr. 6, 1984), 23 I.L.M. 670 (1984) (modifying U.S. declaration); Letter from George P. Schultz, U.S. Sec'y of State, to Dr. Javier Perez de Cuellar, U.N. Sec'y-Gen. (Oct. 7, 1985), 24 I.L.M. 1742 (1985) (terminating U.S. declaration). See generally POMERANCE, supra note 51, at 333–81.

[150] Medellín v. Texas, 552 U.S. 491, 569–70 (2008) (Breyer, J., dissenting) (compiling appendix of then effective provisions).

[151] In setting out its conditions for ratification of the Genocide Convention, for example, the Senate adopted a reservation requiring separate U.S. consent before any matter concerning the Convention might be put before the International Court of Justice. It did not, however, insist on a Senate role in such consent; in contrast, an understanding regarding the future establishment of an international penal tribunal declared that the United States "reserve[d] the right to effect its participation in any such tribunal only by a treaty entered into specifically for that purpose with the advice and consent of the Senate." Marian Nash Leich, Contemporary Practice of the United States Relating to International Law: Protection of Human Rights, 80 AM. J. INT'L L. 612 (1986) (quoting S. Exec. Rep. No. 2, 99th Cong. (1985)).

[152] Understanding on Rules and Procedures Governing the Settlement of Disputes art. 22, Apr. 15, 1994, Marrakesh Agreement Establishing the World Trade Organization, Annex 2, 1869 U.N.T.S. 401 [hereinafter DSU].

[153] U.N. Convention on the Law of the Sea, opened for signature Dec. 10, 1982, 1833 U.N.T.S. 397 (entered into force on Nov. 16, 1994) [hereinafter LOS Convention]. U.S. discussions have focused

(for example, Chapters 11 and 19 of NAFTA),[154] have sometimes proven controversial, but objections have typically turned more on the consequences of dispute resolution than on the procedure for submitting disputes. U.S. adherence to agreements providing for the international arbitration of non-interstate disputes—like the International Centre for Settlement of Investment Disputes (ICSID) Convention, the U.N. Convention on the Recognition and Enforcement of Foreign Arbitral Awards (or New York Convention), and the Inter-American Convention on International Commercial Arbitration (the Inter-American or Panama Convention)[155]—have not posed similar issues.

III. Incorporation of International Organization Lawmaking into U.S. Law

As with other states, U.S. incorporation of international organization lawmaking turns both on international processes—which establish, through the founding treaties or otherwise, the methods and required consequences of rulemaking—and on domestic law, mainly the statutes and regulations that implement U.S. international obligations. These processes defy easy generalization.[156] Nevertheless, it is useful to identify some common forms of international lawmaking—changes to treaties, international legislation, and international

---

attention on, *inter alia*, the potential employment of the International Tribunal for the Law of the Sea, the International Court of Justice, arbitral tribunals, and the Deep Seabed Disputes Chamber. *See* Swaine, *supra* note 5, at 1533–35.

[154] *See* NAFTA, *supra* note 4, arts. 1115–38, Annexes 1120.1, 1138.2 (describing binational investor-state dispute arbitration for violations of Chapter 11, which protects foreign investors); *id.* arts. 1904–05, Annexes 1901.2, 1903.2, 1904.13 (describing binational investor-state dispute arbitration under Chapter 19 for review of anti-dumping and countervailing duty determinations). As noted previously, NAFTA has been succeeded by the USMCA. *See supra* this chapter text accompanying note 4. While NAFTA's Chapter 19 was retained via the USMCA's Chapter 10, NAFTA's Chapter 11–type procedure was confined under the USMCA's new Chapter 14 to the United States and Mexico—with some alterations—and limited to transitional and legacy application for Canadian enterprises and those investing in Canada. *See* USMCA, *supra* note 4, arts. 10.8–10.18 (with accompanying annexes), *id.* Annexes 14-B & 14-C; David A. Gantz, *The United States–Mexico–Canada Agreement: Settlement of Disputes*, BAKER INST. POL'Y REP. (May 2, 2019), https://perma.cc/ZB6N-PBD2; Daniel Garcia-Barragan, Alexandra Mitretodis, & Andrew Tuck, *The New NAFTA: Scaled-Back Arbitration in the USMCA*, 36 J. INT'L ARB. 739 (2019).
[155] See, respectively, Convention on the Settlement of Investment Disputes between States and Nationals of Other States art. 1, *opened for signature* Mar. 28, 1965, 17 U.S.T. 1270; Inter-American Convention on International Commercial Arbitration, Jan. 30, 1975, O.A.S.T.S. No. 42, 1438 U.N.T.S. 245; New York Convention on the Recognition and Enforcement of Foreign Arbitral Awards, June 10, 1958, 21 U.S.T. 2517, 330 U.N.T.S. 38. *See also infra* this chapter note 253 (discussing implementation of these conventions).
[156] *See generally* JOSE E. ALVAREZ, INTERNATIONAL ORGANIZATIONS AS LAW-MAKERS (2005).

dispute resolution[157]—and describe, briefly, how they have been reflected in
U.S. law, before describing delegation-related concerns that have been posed.

A. Treaty Changes

In principle, treaties bind only those states that accept them. In principle, the
same holds true for amendments to treaties (which usually must be ratified just like the original treaty), but the underlying treaty may provide otherwise.[158] Some leading international organization agreements explicitly permit
the adoption of amendments by a majority or supermajority of members, and
some admit the further possibility that the amended terms will bind even those
member states that have not ratified the amendment.[159] Sometimes, as with the
U.N. Charter, assent by the United States to the amendment is indispensable, in
that case because it has a privileged roles as a permanent member of the Security
Council.[160] In other instances—for example, the WTO, the IMF, and the ILO—
U.S. treaty obligations may be changed notwithstanding U.S. objections, so long
as other states muster sufficient support.[161]

Other means of changing treaties may also truncate state consent. The first
involves so-called "tacit amendment" procedures, which permit new international obligations—usually technical in character and developed by consensus—
to be imposed on states that fail to object within the requisite period. Such
procedures are common in the environmental field, and feature as well as in

---

[157] This puts to one side many international organization activities, such as internal reforms and
soft law, that have less well-defined extrinsic legal effect—though the distinction between internal
and external effects is somewhat unsatisfying. *See id.* at 143–45.

[158] Vienna Convention on the Law of Treaties, art. 40, May 23, 1969, 1155 U.N.T.S. 331 [hereinafter
Vienna Convention].

[159] *See* RESTATEMENT (THIRD) § 334 rptrs. note 1.

[160] Amendments take effect for all members so long as they have first been approved by two-thirds
of General Assembly members and ratified by two-thirds of the member states, including all permanent members of the Security Council. U.N. Charter art. 108; *see also id.* art. 109 (describing alternative amendment process pursuant to a general conference). *See generally* Carolyn L. Willson,
Changing the Charter: The United Nations Prepares for the Twenty-First Century, 90 AM. J. INT'L L. 115
(1996).

[161] Each treaty differs somewhat. Amending some WTO provisions does require assent by all
members, see Marrakesh Agreement Establishing the World Trade Organization, art. X, § 2, Apr. 15,
1994, 1867 U.N.T.S. 154 [hereinafter Marrakesh Agreement], and those affecting a member's rights
and obligations must generally be accepted by a particular member before it can be invoked against
it. Swaine, *supra* note 5, at 1508 n.49 (explaining operation of provisions); *see* Marrakesh Agreement,
supra, art. X, § 1. Amendments to the IMF's Articles of Agreement are not so limited. Swaine, *supra*
note 5, at 1508 & n.50. In the case of the ILO, the United States has a privileged position—so long as
it remains among the "Members of chief industrial performance"—but only half of such privileged
members need assent to a change, and there is again no suggestion that a particular member's assent
is necessary in order to make an amendment effective against it. *See id.* at 1506–07 n.45; HENRY G.
SCHERMERS & NIELS M. BLOKKER, INTERNATIONAL INSTITUTIONAL LAW §§ 1173–86 (5th ed. 2011)
(citing additional examples and discussing voting rules).

other organizations like the International Maritime Organization (IMO) and the International Atomic Energy Agency (IAEA).[162] The regime for the Montreal Protocol on Substances That Deplete the Ozone Layer is more complex. The protocol may be formally amended by a process that requires a two-thirds majority of the Meeting of the Parties (MoP) and ratification by two-thirds of the states parties; such amendments are ultimately effective only against states that ratify the amendment.[163] However, "adjustments" to the protocol (which concern targets and timetables for substances already subject to control under the protocol) may be made more easily. Adjustments also require two-thirds approval by the MoP, as well as majority support from both the developed and developing states parties, but they lack any requirement that a state indicate assent before it is bound—indeed, a state may be bound even if it voted against the adjustment.[164]

A second method involves the ability of an international organization (or a subsidiary body) to authoritatively interpret its foundational treaties. As a formal matter, interpretations do not change the treaty text, but in practice they may serve similar same ends.[165] The U.N. Security Council famously developed through practice an interpretation by which an abstention by a permanent member qualifies as the "concurrence" called for the U.N. Charter, permitting the Council to more easily render substantive decisions.[166] Some interpretive

---

[162] See CRS, Treaties and Other International Agreements, supra note 83, at 182–83; Helfer, supra note 105; David A. Koplow, When Is an Amendment Not an Amendment?: Modifications of Arms Control Agreements Without the Senate, 59 U. Chi. L. Rev. 981, 1029–31 (1992); Swaine, supra note 5, at 1512–15. With regard to the environmental area, see particularly Bernhard Boockmann & Paul W. Thurner, Flexibility Provisions in Multilateral Environmental Treaties, 6 Int'l Envtl. Agreements 113 (2006); Jutta Brunnée, COPing with Consent: Law-Making Under Multilateral Environmental Agreements, 15 Leiden J. Int'l L. 1, 7 (2002); Churchill & Ulfstein, supra note 3. With regard to the traditional leader, the IMO, see particularly A.O. Adede, Amendment Procedures for Conventions with Technical Annexes: The IMCO Experience, 17 Va. J. Int'l L. 201 (1977); Lei Shi, Successful Use of the Tacit Acceptance Procedure to Further Progress in International Maritime Law, 11 U.S.F. Mar. L.J. 299 (1999).

[163] See Vienna Convention for the Protection of the Ozone Layer, art. 9, Mar. 22, 1985, T.I.A.S. No. 11,097, 1513 U.N.T.S. 324 (detailing framework rules for amendment of protocols); Montreal Protocol on Substances that Deplete the Ozone, art. 11(4)(h), Sept. 16, 1987, T.I.A.S. No. 89-101.

[164] Montreal Protocol, supra note 163, art. 2; for background, see Andrew D. Finkelman, Note, The Post-Ratification Consensus Agreements of the Parties to the Montreal Protocol: Law or Politics? An Analysis of Natural Resources Defense Council v. EPA, 93 Iowa L. Rev. 665, 673–76 (2008); Annecoos Wiersema, The New International Law-Makers? Conferences of the Parties to Multilateral Environmental Agreements, 31 Mich. J. Int'l L. 231 (2009). It is thus one of the few international organization agreements that can be amended without permitting an individual veto either at the adoption or ratification phases—although in practice, the parties have insisted on consensus. Laurence R. Helfer, Nonconsensual International Lawmaking, 2008 U. Ill. L. Rev. 71, 85–86 (2008).

[165] See Alvarez, supra note 156, at 65–108; Jose E. Alvarez, Constitutional Interpretation in International Organizations, in The Legitimacy of International Organizations 104, 113, 137–38 (Jean-Marc Coicaud & Veijo Heiskanen eds., 2001); Swaine, supra note 5, at 1509–10.

[166] The Charter requires "[d]ecisions of the Security Council on all [non-procedural] matters shall be made by an affirmative vote of nine members including the concurring votes of the permanent members." U.N. Charter, art. 27(3) (emphasis added); The Charter of the United Nations; A Commentary 447–48 (Bruno Simma ed., 3d ed. 2013) (noting departure from original expectations); see Leo Gross, Voting in the Security Council: Abstention from Voting and Absence from

authority even resembles newly proposed treaties. The ILO issued interpretive declarations deriving various workplace rights from mere adherence to the ILO's constitution, notwithstanding that the rights at issue were also articulated in conventions that some ILO members had not ratified.[167]

Third, and finally, international organizations may assume responsibility for evaluating treaty reservations. The Vienna Convention on the Law of Treaties contemplates that a competent organ of the international organization must accept any reservation proposed to a constituent instrument of that organization;[168] expert treaty bodies, like the Human Rights Committee, have sought to assume the role of reviewing reservations for compatibility with the object and purpose of the treaty with which they are concerned.[169] If a U.S. reservation is authoritatively deemed incompatible, the effect may be to preclude U.S. membership in the treaty, or to change the terms on which the United States becomes a party to the treaty.[170]

The means of incorporating changes to treaties within U.S. law reflect these distinctions, at least to some extent. For a formal treaty amendment, U.S. law changes automatically only if the treaty, together with all its future iterations, is deemed self-executing. Where the Senate has separately provided advice and consent to the treaty amendment, consideration of whether it is self-executing should be much the same as for any treaty.[171] Where the Senate has not had that opportunity, however, the situation may differ. To the extent self-execution depends on the understanding of the treaty-makers, a court may be unlikely to presume that an amendment not known to the political branches when the underlying treaty was approved is one that they would have expected to have immediate effect.[172] Advice and consent or U.S. legislation may anticipate and incorporate such changes to a treaty regime, as does the Clean Air Act with respect

---

Meetings, 60 YALE L.J. 209 (1951); *see also* Legal Consequences for States of the Continued Presence of South Africa in Namibia (South West Africa) Notwithstanding Security Council Resolution 276 (1970), Advisory Opinion, 1971 I.C.J. 16, 22 (June 21) (relying on this "consistent[] and uniform[]" interpretation, and its acceptance by U.N. members, as establishing an authoritative general practice).

[167] ILO Declaration on Fundamental Principles and Rights at Work, art. 2, June 18, 1998, 37 I.L.M. 1237 (1998).

[168] Vienna Convention, *supra* note 158, art. 20(3).

[169] ICCPR Human Rights Comm., General Comment 24(52) on Issues Relating to Reservations Made upon Ratification or Accession to the Covenant or Optional Protocols Thereto, or in Relation to Declarations Under Article 41 of the Covenant, Fifty-Second Session, at 10, U.N. Doc. CCPR/C/21/Rev.1/Add.6 (1994); *see* Chapter 6 § II(A)(3).

[170] *See* Swaine, *supra* note 5, at 1511–12. Reservations, when permissible, alter treaty relations between the reserving state and other states parties, depending on whether the other state accepts the reservation or objects to it. Vienna Convention, *supra* note 158, art. 21. For discussion, *see* Chapter 6 §§ II(A)(3) and II(B)(3).

[171] *See generally* Chapter 6 § IV(A).

[172] *See* Medellín v. Texas, 552 U.S. 491, 509, 513, 523 (2008); Chapter 6 § IV(A)(1).

to treaties addressing ozone depletion.[173] Otherwise, the political branches may decide that recourse to approval by the Senate or by Congress as a whole is most practical.[174]

The consequences for U.S. law of other means of changing treaty obligations are more difficult to sort out. For tacit amendment procedures, the presumption should be that the political branches have, in assenting to the original treaty, assented equally to the treaty-based process for elaborating it.[175] Nevertheless, the Senate has expressed disquiet with any circumvention of its advice-and-consent role and has experimented with remedies—including requiring the executive branch to object to proposed tacit amendments in order to prevent them from having force against the United States,[176] or even assuming some vague capacity within the Senate to object itself, at least at the national level.[177]

Other types of changes to existing treaty obligations are less conspicuous and less easily addressed as a matter of incorporation. Authoritative treaty interpretation,

---

[173] The act actually defines the term "Montreal Protocol" to mean "the Montreal Protocol on Substances that Deplete the Ozone Layer, a protocol to the Vienna Convention for the Protection of the Ozone Layer, including adjustments adopted by Parties thereto and amendments that have entered into force." 42 U.S.C. § 7671(9) (2018).

[174] See CRS, TREATIES AND OTHER INTERNATIONAL AGREEMENTS, supra note 83, at 178–79 (citing examples of amendments to ILO Constitution and START Treaty being adopted via advice and consent); id. at 179–80 (citing example of ABM Treaty and dispute concerning whether designation of successor parties was a matter of executive branch discretion or rather a treaty amendment); id. at 180–81 (citing disagreement between the executive branch and Senate concerning whether the CFE Flank Document and the Agreed Statement Regarding Demarcation relating to the ABM Treaty could instead be approved by means of a statute, in each case resolved in favor of the treaty form).

[175] See id. at 183; see also id. at 182 (citing examples of the INF Treaty, the CFE Treaty, the START agreement, the U.S.-Japan Convention for the Protection of Migratory Birds, the Montreal Protocol on Substances that Deplete the Ozone Layer, the International Convention on Safety of Life at Sea, and the U.N. Charter).

[176] See 1973 DIGEST OF U.S. PRACTICE 183–84 (describing Senate understanding relating to the 1973 Protocol to the 1949 International Convention for the Northwest Atlantic Fisheries directing that the president object to any proposed amendment, preventing its entry into force for the United States, if the Senate had not provided advice and consent at such time as the amendment had received the requisite three-fourths approval of member states). Similarly, while the president is statutorily authorized to proclaim as U.S. law amendments to the Convention on the International Regulations for Preventing Collisions at Sea, he or she is also obligated to notify Congress of any proposed amendments and—if Congress passed a concurrent resolution of disapproval—relay to the International Maritime Organization that the United States objects to the amendment, preventing its entry into force for the United States. International Navigation Rules Act of 1977, Pub. L. No. 95-75, 91 Stat. 308 (codified at 33 U.S.C. §§ 1602(c)–(d) (2018)); see also Pub. L. 104-66, § 3003 (codified as amended at 31 U.S.C. § 1113 note) (amending reporting requirements); 1977 DIGEST OF U.S. PRACTICE 399–401 (noting objection to constitutionality in signing statement by President Carter); William Alan Shirley, Note, Resolving Challenges to Statutes Containing Unconstitutional Legislative Veto Provisions, 85 COLUM. L. REV. 1808, 1823 (1985) (noting objection to provision under INS v. Chadha and concluding that, given legislative history, it should be regarded as not severable).

[177] See S. Exec. Rep. 96-36, 96th Cong., 2d Sess. at 2 (1980) (reporting expectation of Senate Foreign Relations Committee that it will be informed of proposals for the tacit amendment of the Convention on the Prevention of Maritime Pollution by Dumping of Wastes and other Matter so as to facilitate its objection in appropriate cases); CRS, TREATIES AND OTHER INTERNATIONAL AGREEMENTS, supra note 83, at 183 (noting "fundamental questions" regarding whether the Foreign Relations Committee could stand in for the Senate as a whole).

even effectively changing the meaning of a treaty, may be effective under U.S. law if consistent with the interpretive methods applied by U.S. courts and other domestic actors.[178] The basic expectation in all events is that interpretive tools will not be used to circumvent the formal amendment process.[179] As to treaty reservations, various pronouncements by international organizations regarding their validity have not yet had any substantial effect on U.S. implementation; indeed, more broadly, the international or constitutional validity of U.S. reservations has had little impact on their treatment by U.S. courts or other domestic institutions.[180] The United States might plausibly distinguish between circumstances in which a specific authority to interpret a treaty or pronounce on reservations is conveyed by the original treaty and circumstances in which an international organization or expert treaty body has simply assumed the function. Where the authority itself is disputed, it is especially unlikely that the U.S. government would concede either an international or domestic legal effect to its application.[181]

B. International Legislation

International legislation by international organizations is far more common than the various species of treaty changes discussed previously, but by the same token defies easy generalization. As used here, international legislation (or rulemaking) occurs when an international organization adopts a measure that does not change the international organization agreement but instead creates new, autonomous rules that are binding upon the member states of the international

---

[178] *See* Chapter 6 § III.

[179] *See, e.g.*, URUGUAY ROUND AGREEMENTS ACT: STATEMENT OF ADMINISTRATIVE ACTION, H.R. REP. NO. 103-316 (1994), *reprinted in* 1994 U.S.C.C.A.N. 4040, 4044–45, 1994 WL 16137731 (explaining that "[t]he Ministerial Conference and the General Council are the sole WTO bodies empowered to issue authoritative, binding interpretations of the WTO Agreement and MTAs," but indicating that they "may not, however, use their authority to issue interpretations that would undermine the amendment provisions set out in Article X"); *id.* at 4053–54 (stressing that the United States is not to base actions to enforce the WTO on any panel or Appellate Body report, and that courts are to reach their "own, independent interpretation of the relevant provisions in the light of the agreement's negotiating and legislative history," including the Statement of Administrative Action). For one illustration of the controversial line between amendment and interpretation, see Charles H. Brower II, *Why the FTC Notes of Interpretation Constitute a Partial Amendment of NAFTA Article 1105*, 46 VA. J. INT'L L. 347 (2006).

[180] *See* Chapter 6 §§ II(A)(3) and II(B)(3); Louis Henkin, *The Treaty Makers and the Law Makers: The Niagara Reservation*, 56 COLUM. L. REV. 1151, 1176–77 (1956) (asserting, in the course of criticizing an exception, that—previously—"[n]o 'reservation' by the Senate in giving advice and consent to the ratification of any treaty has ever been declared invalid and disregarded by any court or authority in the United States"); *see, e.g.*, Beazley v. Johnson, 242 F.3d 248, 264–68 (5th Cir. 2001) (interpreting narrowly criticism by the Human Rights Committee of U.S. reservation to the Covenant on Civil and Political Rights).

[181] *Cf.* Observations by the United States on General Comment 24, 3 INT'L HUM. RTS. REP. 265, 265–69 (1996) (contesting authority asserted by the Human Rights Committee with respect to reservations to the Covenant on Civil and Political Rights).

organization. Some international legislation is significant and highly visible, like binding measures adopted by the U.N. Security Council under Chapter VII of the U.N. Charter,[182] but there is considerable variety. States may spell out an international organization's legislative capacity in the international organization agreement—or it may be supplied only by a separate, later treaty,[183] or assumed over time by the organization and its members.[184] The purported legal effect may also vary. Legislation may be presented as legally binding, merely advisory, or left unclear, sometimes all for the same organization.[185] Additional legal effects may be indirectly conferred by other organizations or agreements.[186] Procedures for the adoption of legislation, naturally, vary widely.[187]

[182] U.N. Charter art. 41 (authorizing the Security Council to adopt measures calling for, inter alia, the "complete or partial interruption of economic relations" or "the severance of diplomatic relations"); id. arts. 48–49 (obliging members to carry out such decisions); see also Legal Consequences for States of the Continued Presence of South Africa in Namibia (South West Africa) Notwithstanding Security Council Resolution 276 (1970), Advisory Opinion, 1971 I.C.J. 16, 51–53 (June 21) (establishing member state obligation to comply with Security Council Resolution—adopted outside of Chapter VII context but of comparable gravity—declaring illegal South African presence in Namibia). The WTO is another example, see Marrakesh Agreement, supra note 161, arts. IV(1), IX(1), and arguably the Organisation for Economic Co-operation and Development (OECD), see Convention on the Organisation for Economic Co-operation and Development, art. 5(a), Dec. 14, 1960, 12 U.S.T. 1728, 1734, 888 U.N.T.S. 179, 185 (compiling decisions); id. art. 6 (noting that absent unanimous agreement to the contrary, decisions must be reached by consensus).

[183] Professor Alvarez suggests the IMO and WHO as examples. See ALVAREZ, supra note 156, at 219–20. The WHO, at least, also seems to have legislative powers per its charter. Constitution of the World Health Organization, arts. 20–21, July 22, 1946, 62 Stat. 2679, 14 U.N.T.S. 185, available at https://perma.cc/G96R-BM36 (describing adoption of regulations by Health Assembly, which are to take effect for members in the absence of timely rejection or reservations).

[184] The Montreal Protocol, for example, mentions amendments and adjustments, see supra note 163, but the notion of other types of "Decisions" appears to have developed from the practice of the MoP. Finkelman, supra note 164, at 676–77. In particular circumstances, however, the Protocol attributes significance to determinations by the parties without describing the procedures for their adoption. See, e.g., Montreal Protocol, supra note 163, art. 2H(5) ("This paragraph will apply save to the extent that the Parties decide to permit the level of production or consumption [of methyl bromide] that is necessary to satisfy uses agreed by them to be critical uses.").

[185] See, e.g., Convention on International Civil Aviation, art. 12, Dec. 7, 1944, 61 Stat. 1180, 15 U.N.T.S. 295 (providing that "[e]ach contracting State undertakes to keep its own regulations in these respects uniform, to the greatest possible extent, with those established from time to time under this Convention"); id. arts. 37–38 (establishing authority to promulgate standards and recommended practices); see ALVAREZ, supra note 156, at 223–24 (discussing varied authorities for the International Civil Aviation Organization); THOMAS BUERGENTHAL, LAW-MAKING IN THE INTERNATIONAL CIVIL AVIATION ORGANIZATION (1969).

[186] For example, Article 3 of the Agreement on the Application of Sanitary and Phytosanitary Measures, Marrakesh Agreement Establishing the World Trade Organization, creates a presumption that regulatory measures adopted by WTO members based on international standards established elsewhere are not discriminatory and violative of the WTO. ALVAREZ, supra note 156, at 221.

[187] Security Council resolutions adopted under Chapter VII, famously, require the consent of all permanent members, including the United States. See supra this chapter text accompanying note 166. Under the Chicago Convention, in contrast, the Council may adopt annexes and amendments thereto, memorializing particular standards and recommended practices, by a two-thirds majority, and become effective within a specified time unless a majority of the contracting states register disapproval. Convention on International Civil Aviation, supra note 185, art. 90.

Further variety is evident in how such international legislation is incorporated in U.S. law. In some cases, U.S. law essentially registers the fact of international legislation—for example, by keying the operation of a U.S. statute to certain exercises of international authority.[188] Other times, international legislation has more complex effects. Congress may treat international legislation as conferring discretionary authority on the executive branch—as with the U.N. Participation Act, which authorizes the president to adopt and apply national measures to enforce most (but not all) binding Security Council resolutions.[189] Congress may also treat international legislation as imposing a duty on the executive branch, or as limiting otherwise-conferred authority.[190] More exotically, U.S. law may regard international legislation as the basis for transferring regulatory authority to or from other states, as with the regulation of aircraft.[191] Changes in international legislation may also be incorporated automatically according to regulation.[192]

---

[188] See, e.g., Iran and Libya Sanctions Act of 1996, 110 Stat. 1541, amended by ILSA Extension Act of 2001, Pub. L. No. 107-24, §§ 2(a), 3–5, 115 Stat. 199, 200 (codified at 50 U.S.C. § 1701 note (2018)) (requiring president to notify relevant congressional committee when a listed nation adopts sanctions on Iran or Libya and to provide additional details, including the results of any WTO or GATT review of the sanctions); Swaine, supra note 5, at 1519–20 (discussing controversy over assimilation of Security Council and WTO determinations for purposes of administering the Clean Diamond Trade Act, and similar concerns regarding EPA listing of new persistent organic chemicals in administering implementation of the Stockholm Convention on Persistent Organic Pollutants).

[189] United Nations Participation Act, 22 U.S.C. § 287c (2000). But see id. § 287d (limiting presidential authority to make armed forces available to the Security Council).

[190] For example, Congress directed the secretary of transportation to require compliance with noise standards either of the secretary's own design or as developed by the International Civil Aviation Organization (if compatible with the secretary's standards). 49 U.S.C. § 47508 (2018). Similarly, the EPA administrator was authorized under the Clean Air Act to promulgate a methyl bromide phaseout "in accordance with" the Montreal Protocol, and to promulgate critical-use exemptions only "to the extent consistent with the Montreal Protocol." 42 U.S.C. § 7671c(d). A subsequent legal challenge contended that the EPA was bound under the Protocol and the Clean Air Act to heed a decision adopted by a MoP, and its failure to do so was thus not in accordance with law; the EPA agreed that some provisions in the relevant decisions were cognizable in U.S. law, but not the particular ones invoked against it. Finkelman, supra note 164, at 683–85. As discussed later, the D.C. Circuit disagreed with both positions. Nat. Res. Def. Council (NRDC) v. Envtl. Prot. Agency (EPA), 464 F.3d 1, 11 (D.C. Cir. 2006).

[191] 49 U.S.C. 44701(e)(1) (providing that the FAA administrator may—under the Convention on International Civil Aviation and by a bilateral agreement with another country—"exchange with that country all or part of their respective functions and duties with respect to registered aircraft under the following provisions of the Convention").

[192] See, e.g., 14 C.F.R. § 91.703(a) (2020) (providing that U.S.-registered aircraft operated over the high seas must comply with annex 2 (Rules of the Air) to the Convention on International Civil Aviation); id. § 91.703(b) (providing that annex 2 "is incorporated by reference into this section"); 14 C.F.R. § 129.5(b) (2019) (requiring that foreign carriers within the United States conduct their operations in accordance with Annex 6 on the operation of aircraft); 40 C.F.R. § 87.60 (2019) (establishing that sampling and measurement of smoke emissions must be as specified in Appendix 2 to Annex 16). As noted previously, such annexes are subject to amendment by a supermajority of the Council for International Civil Aviation Organization, thus infusing federal regulations with a dynamic element.

Most commonly, though, U.S. statutes or regulations are adopted on a post hoc, ad hoc basis to keep up with evolving U.S. international obligations.[193]

C. International Dispute Resolution

As a general matter, U.S. law incorporates the result of international dispute resolution processes as required—and, at least in major cases, through legislation. The Supreme Court held in *Medellín v. Texas* that while Article 94 of the U.N. Charter, the ICJ Statute, and the Optional Protocol to the Vienna Convention on Consular Relations created a binding international obligation for the United States to abide by an adverse decision by the ICJ, the relevant treaty provisions were not self-executing and required congressional legislation before such a decision could be enforceable as domestic law in U.S. courts.[194] However, the Court disavowed any "suggest[ion] that treaties can never afford binding domestic effect to international tribunal judgments," and even stated that its decision did "not call into question the ordinary enforcement of foreign judgments or international arbitral agreements."[195] Another dispute resolution agreement could be distinguished on the ground that it lacked any alternative to enforcement in domestic court (unlike the U.N. Security Council mechanism for enforcing ICJ decisions, emphasized in *Medellín*), appeared less exclusively interstate in character, lacked consistent executive branch opposition, or differed as a matter of treaty interpretation.[196]

In any event, the Court was undoubtedly correct in indicating that the judgments of other international and foreign tribunals are enforceable in U.S. courts by virtue of implementing legislation. For example, statutory provisions implement U.S. obligations to enforce contractual obligations to arbitrate and to enforce foreign arbitral awards rendered pursuant to the ICSID Convention, the New York Convention, and the Panama Convention.[197] Congress also provided for the

---

[193] *See, e.g.,* Transfrontier Shipments of Hazardous Waste for Recovery Within the OECD, 40 C.F.R. §§ 262.80–262.89 (2010) (adopting waste lists established according to the Organisation of Economic Co-operation and Development Council [OECD], *Decision of the Council Concerning the Control of Transfrontier Movements of Wastes Destined for Recovery Operations*, C(92)39/Final (Mar. 30, 1992)); News Release, Dep't of Health & Human Servs., United States Officially Accepts New International Health Regulations (Dec. 13, 2006), https://perma.cc/6EUD-AYZ6 (noting incorporation of World Health Organization [WHO], International Health Regulations, WHA 58.3, Fifty-Eighth World Health Assembly (2005), https://perma.cc/6HKC-F4LV)).

[194] Medellín v. Texas, 552 U.S. 491, 506–19 (2008); *see* RESTATEMENT (FOURTH) § 310 & rptrs. note 2. For discussions of *Medellín*, see Chapter 1 § II(B); Chapter 3 § I(D); Chapter 5 § II(B); Chapter 6 §§ III(B), IV(A); and Chapter 9 §§ II(B), II(C).

[195] *Medellín*, 552 U.S. at 519; *id.* at 519–20.

[196] *See*, respectively, *id.* at 509; *id.* at 511–12; *id.* at 509, 513; *id.* at 517.

[197] RESTATEMENT (THIRD) OF THE U.S. LAW OF INTERNATIONAL COMMERCIAL ARBITRATION § 5.1 (Proposed Final Draft (Apr. 24, 2019)); for discussion of the conventions themselves, see *supra* this chapter § II(D). As to implementation of the ICSID Convention, see 22 U.S.C. § 1650a (2018). *But cf.* Mobil Cerro Negro, Limited v. Bolivarian Republic of Venezuela, 863 F.3d 96 (2d Cir. 2017) (holding that, notwithstanding legislative implementation of ICSID, the Foreign Sovereign Immunities Act provides the only basis for subject-matter jurisdiction to enter judgment against foreign sovereigns

implementation of Chapter 19 of NAFTA, and later its successor in the USMCA.[198] Particular issues relating to these provisions are explored in the following.[199]

D. Execution by International Organizations

In addition to conferring legal status on the lawmaking of international organizations, international law—and, derivatively, U.S. law—may assign responsibility for the execution of such lawmaking. The circumstances under which international agreements constitute law that the president and other federal officials are obliged to execute have been addressed previously.[200] Even where it may not be obligatory as a matter of domestic law, the executive branch commonly takes steps to ensure conformity with international organization agreements, as with other international obligations.[201]

Officials of international organizations may also be assigned responsibility for executing international law under circumstances that touch on U.S. interests.[202] The clearest examples involve the inspection regimes sometimes used in bilateral or multilateral arms control regimes.[203] Under the Chemical Weapons Convention, for example, the Technical Secretariat of the Organization for the Prohibition of Chemical Weapons (OPCW) is charged with conducting inspections of U.S. facilities within the United States.[204] The United States accommodates this approach through the

---

based on arbitration awards). As to implementation of the New York Convention, see 9 U.S.C. §§ 201–08; *see, e.g.*, BG Group, PLC v. Republic of Argentina, 572 U.S. 25 (2014) (applying Federal Arbitration in considering petition to vacate or modify award under New York Convention). As to the Panama Convention, see 9 U.S.C. §§ 301–07; *see, e.g.*, Productos Mercantiles E Industriales, S.A. v. Faberge USA, Inc., 23 F.3d 41, 45 (2d Cir. 1994) (explaining that the legislative history "clearly demonstrates that Congress intended the [Panama] Convention to reach the same results as those reached under the New York Convention" so "'that courts in the United States would achieve a general uniformity of results under the two conventions'") (quoting H.R. Rep. No. 501, 101st Cong., 2d Sess. 4 (1990)).

[198] *See* Pub. L. 116-113, tit. IV, § 421, Jan. 29, 2020, 134 Stat. 61, *amending* 19 U.S.C. § 1516a(g) (providing for implementation and limited review of Chapter 19 panel decisions).

[199] *See infra* this chapter § III(E)(3).

[200] *See* Chapter 6 § IV(A).

[201] *See* Chapter 6 § IV(B).

[202] As explained later, the characterization of this activity as executive, as opposed to being legislative or judicial, may be debated, at least in the absence of a clear correspondence with domestic categories. *See infra* this chapter § III(E).

[203] *See generally* DENNIS S. ARONOWITZ, LEGAL ASPECTS OF ARMS CONTROL VERIFICATION IN THE UNITED STATES (1965); LOUIS HENKIN, ARMS CONTROL AND INSPECTION IN AMERICAN LAW (1958) [hereinafter HENKIN, ARMS CONTROL]; HENKIN, FOREIGN AFFAIRS, at 264–65; *cf.* David A. Koplow, *Arms Control Inspection: Constitutional Restrictions on Treaty Verification in the United States*, 63 N.Y.U. L. REV. 229, 239–88 (1988) (describing comparable issues relating to inspection by the other party to a bilateral agreement); *id.* at 293 n.399 (noting, peripherally, possibility of internationalized regimes). For discussion of implications for individual rights, see Chapter 10 § II(C)(5).

[204] Convention on the Prohibition of the Development, Production, Stockpiling, and Use of Chemical Weapons and on Their Destruction, art. IX, Jan. 3, 1993, T.I.A.S. No. 97-525.

Chemical Weapons Convention Implementation Act, which establishes a national focal point for coordinating with both the OPCW and other states parties, including through accompanying regulations.[205] At the opposite end of the spectrum, the American Service Members' Protection Act, adopted following U.S. signature of the Rome Statute, prohibits U.S. cooperation with representatives of the International Criminal Court (ICC), and bars investigative activities by agents of the ICC within the United States or a territory subject to its jurisdiction, in part based on concern that the United States (through its signature) might have assumed an obligation to abide by the Rome Statute's object and purpose.[206] Subject to certain restrictions, that prohibition might be waived by the president.[207] Nonetheless, it is unusual insofar as it both anticipates and forecloses cooperation with an international organization pursuant to a treaty which the United States had not ratified and of which it is not a member.

E. Delegation Concerns

The delegation of legislative, judicial, and executive authority to international organizations has long been controversial in the United States. Recent decades have seen sustained scrutiny, spurred in part by the Security Council's active agenda, a spate of death penalty cases before the ICJ, the expanding international trade regime, and repeated consideration of whether to join the Convention on the Law of the Sea, among other things. Despite this interest, there are few established legal impediments.

Challenges to international delegations face several common substantive difficulties that deserve highlighting. First, the legal force of most anti-delegation objections depends on the status of domestic anti-delegation doctrines. If the nondelegation doctrine (and Article III limits on assigning judicial power, or Appointments Clause limits on assigning enforcement authority outside the executive branch) remain underenforced in purely domestic cases, this diminishes the force of objections to international variants.[208] The exception, as noted later,

---

[205] Pub. L. No. 105-277, div. I, tit. I, § 101, 301–09, Oct. 21, 1998, 112 Stat. 2681 (codified at 22 U.S.C. §§ 6711, 6721–29 (2018)); Exec. Order No. 13,128, 64 Fed. Reg. 34,703 (June 25, 1999); *e.g.*, 15 CFR §§ 716.1–716.10, 717.1–717.5 (Commerce Department regulations concerning inspections of nongovernmental facilities, including their coordination with the Organization for the Prohibition of Chemical Weapons).

[206] Pub. L. No. 107-206, tit. II, § 2004, Aug. 2, 2002, 116 Stat. 902 (codified at 22 U.S.C. 7423 (2018)); *see id.* § 2002 (codified at 22 U.S.C. § 7421) (noting signature by President Clinton, despite expressed reservations). The United States had since notified the treaty depositary that it did not intend to become a party to the Rome Statute and that it would not assume legal obligations under it. Letter from John R. Bolton, Under Sec'y of State for Arms Control, to Gen. Kofi Annan, U.N. Sec'y-Gen. (May 6, 2002), available at https://perma.cc/P4WW-3WWG. For discussion of interim obligations, see Chapter 6 § II(C)(1).

[207] 22 U.S.C. §§ 7422 (c)–(d).

[208] *See infra* this chapter text accompanying notes 227–228.

concerns objections to delegations of the treaty-making authority, which are meaningfully distinct from any domestic analogy.[209]

Second, even if domestic anti-delegation doctrines remain robust, their application to international organizations is plagued by comparability problems. Assuming that Congress is prohibited from redistributing its legislative authority, is the power exercised by international organizations "legislative" in the same sense? For example—given that Congress cannot by itself adopt sanctions legislation that binds all states worldwide not to trade with a targeted state—if the U.N. Security Council adopts such a decision (which inter alia affects the international legality of U.S. trade with that target), has the Security Council exercised a legislative power delegated by the United States, or has it exercised a *sui generis* power? Similarly, do international tribunals exercise something like the judicial power that is vested in Article III courts, or is the capacity of the former to resolve international disputes under international law sufficiently distinctive? Is executive activity by international organizations properly understood as the kind that may only be vested in officers appointed by the president? These translation issues permeate delegation debates.[210]

Third, assuming that domestic forms of authority are otherwise comparable, the international context may be distinguishable. Foreign affairs are sometimes said (most famously in *United States v. Curtiss-Wright Exp. Corp.*) to require a different approach to delegation, either because the Constitution grants the president greater independent authority or for functional reasons involving the type of decision-making.[211] Treaty-based delegations may also be more easily tolerated if any consequent legal obligations or enforcement are purely international in character, or if the United States retains a capacity to veto changes with which it

---

[209] *See infra* this chapter § III(E)(1).

[210] *See, e.g.,* Bradley, *International Delegations, the Structural Constitution, and Non-Self-Execution, supra* note 5, at 1575 (noting that "[a]t least some of the [NAFTA Chapter 19] panel members, however, will not be Article III judges. Nor is their selection subject to the Article II appointments process."). Chapter 10 of the USMCA is comparable. *See supra* this chapter note 154.

[211] United States v. Curtiss-Wright Exp. Corp., 299 U.S. 304, 320 (1936) (stressing that to avoid embarrassment in international affairs, "congressional legislation which is to be made effective through negotiation and inquiry within the international field must often accord to the President a degree of discretion and freedom from statutory restriction which would not be admissible were domestic affairs alone involved"). For further discussion of *Curtiss-Wright,* see Chapter 1 §§ I(D), II(A)(2). In a more recent case, *Gundy v. United States,* 139 S. Ct. 2116 (2019), Justice Gorsuch's dissent (for himself, Justice Thomas, and Chief Justice Roberts)—which generally urged a relatively stringent application of the nondelegation doctrine—noted that "Congress may assign the President broad authority regarding the conduct of foreign affairs or other matters where he enjoys his own inherent Article II powers." *Id.* at 2144 (Gorsuch, J., dissenting); *accord id.* at 2137; *see* Curtis A. Bradley & Jack L. Goldsmith, *Presidential Control over International Law,* 131 HARV. L. REV. 1201, 1264 (2018) (noting differentiated treatment of foreign affairs distinction, but stressing diminished significance of nondelegation doctrine generally); Ganesh Sitaraman & Ingrid Wuerth, *The Normalization of Foreign Relations Law,* 128 HARV. L. REV. 1897, 1970–74 (2015) (describing, and critiquing, differentiated treatment).

disagrees, or the capacity to pretermit adverse consequences by withdrawing.[212] International delegations may, on the other hand, be more objectionable in light of concerns about sovereignty costs or antidemocratic decision-making. These questions turn on, and contribute to, broader normative issues concerning the authority of international law and organizations, but they do not translate easily into domestic case law. The following discussion will, for the most part, assume the possibility that an international organization may adopt measures with which the United States disagrees and that (at least temporarily) will bind it.

1. Delegation of Authority to Change U.S. Treaty Obligations

The anti-delegation objection most distinctive to the international context concerns treaty amendments and comparable means for altering a treaty commitment itself. Two kinds of objections may be made. One hinges on the degree to which an international organization asserts authority to change international obligations of the United States. Thus, the plainer the assertion of treaty-amending authority or something comparable—and the plainer the ability to exercise that authority without U.S. consent, or the opportunity for a U.S. veto— the more pronounced the concern. The safeguard of U.S. assent, however, raises its own potential concerns. Any U.S. control over the application to the United States of a treaty amendment is typically exercised unilaterally by the executive branch; this safeguard effectively transforms concerns about the loss of U.S. sovereign authority into a delegation issue more typical of the modern administrative state—but in a multilateral context where the ability of Congress to recapture that authority is likely to be much more limited.

To date, no court has held that a treaty is unconstitutional because it allows an international body to change U.S. treaty obligations. One decision, though, intimated that it might pose serious issues. In *NRDC v. EPA*, the D.C. Circuit considered whether decisions by the MoP of the Montreal Protocol on Substances that Deplete the Ozone Layer, which affected U.S. obligations under the protocol with respect methyl bromide production, constituted "law" against which the Environmental Protection Agency's (EPA) subsequent implementation should be tested.[213] The case did not directly involve treaty "amendments" or the amendment-like "adjustments" under the protocol, which the legislative branch had substantially accommodated: the Senate had given advice and consent to the Copenhagen Amendment to the Montreal Protocol, and Congress had

---

[212] *See, e.g.*, William J. Davey, *The Appointments Clause and International Dispute Settlement Mechanisms: A False Conflict*, 49 WASH. & LEE L. REV. 1315, 1316–19 (1992) (defending dispute settlement provisions of the United States–Canada Free Trade Agreement Act on grounds that, inter alia, binational panels were exercising authority solely pursuant to an international agreement, not under U.S. law, and that panel decisions were not enforceable domestically).

[213] NRDC v. EPA, 464 F.3d 1, 7–10 (D.C. Cir. 2006); *see* Montreal Protocol, *supra* note 163.

defined the "protocol" in implementing legislation as including amendments that had entered into force (like the Copenhagen Amendment, which had added methyl bromide as a regulated chemical) and adjustments (like that scheduling the elimination of methyl bromide).[214] Rather, the case concerned certain MoP "decisions" that afforded the United States certain limited exemptions, thereby allowing continued use of methyl bromide. The court balked at treating those decisions as binding law—reasoning that doing so would mean that "Congress either has delegated lawmaking authority to an international body or authorized amendments to a treaty without presidential signature or Senate ratification, in violation of Article II of the Constitution." To avoid possible delegation objections, the court construed the Clean Air Act and the Montreal Protocol "as creating an ongoing international political commitment rather than a delegation of lawmaking authority to annual meetings of the Parties."[215]

Although largely in dicta,[216] the court's concerns about "post-ratification side agreements" also called into question the legal effects of amendments and adjustments.[217] The decision anticipated *Medellín v. Texas*, in which the Supreme Court, addressing whether certain treaty provisions were self-executing, resisted construing an international tribunal's interpretation of a U.S. treaty as binding under domestic law.[218] But unlike *Medellín*, which accepted the binding nature of the tribunal's decision on the international plane while denying the decision

---

[214] *See generally NRDC v. EPA*, 464 F.3d at 3 & n.2. For the international component, see U.N. Env't Programme, *Report of the Fourth Meeting of the Parties to the Montreal Protocol on Substances That Deplete the Ozone Layer*, at Annex III, art. I(I), UNEP/OzL.Pro.4/15 (Nov. 25, 1992), https://perma.cc/2NED-A4PH (adopting Article 2H); United Nations: Montreal Protocol on Substances that Deplete the Ozone Layer—Adjustments and Amendments, art. 2H, Nov. 23–25, 1992, 32 I.L.M. 874, 880 (1993); *see also supra* this chapter note 184 (describing means of altering the Montreal Protocol). For the domestic component, see Clean Air Act Amendments of 1990, tit. VI, Pub. L. No. 101-549, 104 Stat. 2399, 2648 (codified as amended at 42 U.S.C. § 7671(9) (2018)).

[215] *NRDC v. EPA*, 464 F.3d at 7–10; *see also id.* at 9 ("A holding that the Parties' post-ratification side agreements were 'law' would raise serious constitutional questions in light of the nondelegation doctrine, numerous constitutional procedural requirements for making law, and the separation of powers.").

[216] At several junctures, the court acknowledged that—notwithstanding the opinion's broader reasoning—it was most acutely focused on MoP decisions. *See, e.g., NRDC v. EPA*, 464 F.3d at 5, 8, 9. There was also an easy alternative basis for avoiding the delegation issue as to the decisions: the EPA's position, to which the court did not directly respond, was that the particular decisions at issue in the case were not by their nature binding, and were in any event fully satisfied by the agency's decision. *Id.* at 8 (noting EPA view that unfulfilled aspects of the decisions were "hortatory"); Finkelman, *supra* note 164, at 683–85.

[217] *See NRDC v. EPA*, 464 F.3d at 9–10.

[218] In *NRDC v. EPA*, the D.C. Circuit directly analogized the MoP to the ICJ and the doctrine of non-self-executing treaty provisions. 464 F.3d at 8–9 (citing Medellin v. Dretke, 544 U.S. 660, 682–84 (2005) (O'Connor, J., dissenting)). For discussion of the subsequent decision in *Medellín v. Texas*, 552 U.S. 491 (2008), see *supra* this chapter § III(C); Chapter 1 § II(B); Chapter 3 § I(D); Chapter 5 § II(B); Chapter 6 §§ III(B), IV(A); and Chapter 9 §§ II(B), II(C).

immediate legal effect domestically,[219] the D.C. Circuit seemed disposed to treat the MoP's work (whether in the form of amendments, adjustments, or decisions) as political commitments on *both* the international and domestic planes, without providing much by way of explanation.[220]

A future case might more squarely consider the constitutionality of a treaty that by its terms (and as consented to by the political branches) permits amendment through acts by an international organization and its members, even over the opposition of the United States. In such circumstances, it would be difficult to credit the idea that the Senate and president altogether lacked the power to vest future alterations of an Article II treaty in extrinsic authorities. Unlike Article I, which vests "[a]ll legislative Powers" in Congress,[221] Article II does not explicitly assert any monopoly in the president and Senate (and in practice, a nearly interchangeable authority has been assumed for congressional-executive agreements, and to a more limited degree for agreements in which the president acts alone).[222] Moreover, treaty-making by definition vests power outside the U.S. political branches: making a treaty requires international partners; a treaty's meaning may evolve through its interpretation by others; and a treaty typically vests in another state party the capacity to suspend, withdraw from, or terminate a treaty, or for that matter to obstruct U.S. termination of its own obligations. In short, quite unlike national legislation, treaties routinely entail the loss of unilateral authority, meaning there is cause to doubt the capacity of anti-delegation objections to establish a treaty's unconstitutionality.

Alternative means of amending treaty obligations generally raise fewer concerns yet. Tacit amendment procedures entrust to the executive branch the decision whether to subject the United States to new obligations or, alternatively, to object on its behalf; the dynamic is largely similar to that for international legislation, discussed later. A treaty's assignment of interpretative authority to an international organization may be thought to undermine the judiciary's authority under Article III to say what the law is—an issue also addressed later—but to the extent such power is genuinely enabled by a treaty, the treaty has essentially altered the law that the U.S. judiciary is charged with applying. Finally, to the extent that a treaty genuinely assigns to an expert treaty body responsibility for evaluating U.S. treaty reservations, that seems largely similar in character to the way international law permits other states parties to object, on any basis, to

---

[219] *Medellín*, 552 U.S. at 504 ("No one disputes that the *Avena* decision . . . constitutes an international law obligation on the part of the United States. But not all international law obligations automatically constitute binding federal law enforceable in United States courts.").

[220] *See, e.g., NRDC v. EPA*, 464 F.3d at 9. For criticism, see John H. Knox, *Natural Resources Defense Council v. EPA*, 101 Am. J. Int'l L. 471, 475–76 (2007).

[221] U.S. Const. art. 1, § 1; *see infra* this chapter § III(E)(2).

[222] *See* Chapter 6 § V.

U.S. reservations, and thereby render a treaty provision (or even the treaty as a whole) inapplicable in their treaty relations *inter se*. The capacity of states to object to reservations has, on the whole, been strongly favored by both the Senate and the executive branch, and this naturally supports the capacity of other states to object to reservations by the United States itself.[223]

2. Delegation of Legislative Authority

While Article II does not explicitly govern "all" treaties (or all international agreements), nor dictate the proportion of the treaty power that needs to be retained by the Senate, Article I's Vesting Clause may seem more determinative with regard to legislation.[224] This textual grant is often cited as the basis for the nondelegation doctrine, a principle that Congress cannot generally assign its legislative power to any other entity, and must make sure that any party exercising delegated authority does so according to an "intelligible principle."[225] The court in *NRDC v. EPA* suggested that—to the extent the international decisions at issue in that case were likened to legislation, as opposed to treaty amendments—they raised equally serious issues, problems best avoided by construing the decisions as lacking legal effect.[226]

Some issues relating to the core nondelegation doctrine seem equally germane to this international variant. There are substantial objections concerning the doctrine's basis in the Constitution's original understanding, to which it is often attributed.[227] The doctrine has also suffered long stretches of near desuetude, given that the Supreme Court (by its own admission) has "'almost never felt qualified to second-guess Congress'" as to how much discretion may permissibly be entrusted to a statute's enforcers.[228]

---

[223] *See* Chapter 6 §§ II(A)(3) and II(B)(3).

[224] U.S. CONST. art. I, § 1 (vests "[a]ll legislative [p]owers herein granted" to the full Congress).

[225] Gundy v. United States, 139 S. Ct. 2116, 2123 (2019) (plurality op.) ("Accompanying that assignment of power to Congress is a bar on its further delegation."); *see* Whitman v. Am. Trucking Ass'ns, 531 U.S. 457, 472 (2001); J.W. Hampton, Jr., & Co. v. United States, 276 U.S. 394, 409 (1928).

[226] NRDC v. EPA, 464 F.3d 1, 8–10 (D.C. Cir. 2006); *see supra* this chapter text accompanying notes 213–220.

[227] *Compare* Julian Davis Mortenson & Nicholas Bagley, *Delegation at the Founding*, 121 COLUM. L. REV. 277 (2021) (concluding that, as an originalist matter, Congress could delegate legislative power, so long as that power was not permanently alienated by making it nonrecoverable), *with* Ilan Wurman, *Nondelegation at the Founding*, 130 YALE L.J. 1490 (2021) (defending plausibility of nondelegation doctrine on originalist premises).

[228] Whitman v. American Trucking Ass'ns, Inc., 531 U.S. 457, 474–75 (2001) (quoting Mistretta v. United States, 488 U.S. 361, 416 (1989) (Scalia, J., dissenting)). More recently, in Gundy v. United States, 139 S. Ct. 2116 (2019), a majority agreed that the Sex Offender Registration and Notification Act (SORNA) did not violate the existing nondelegation doctrine. *Id.* at 2129–30. Justice Alito would have preferred to reconsider the doctrine, to the end of making it more stringent, see *id.* at 2130 (Alito, J., concurring in the judgment), and three other justices would have struck down the act based on their view of the doctrine. *Id.* at 2131 (Gorsuch, J. dissenting). None showed an appetite for disregarding the doctrine altogether. For a prior discussion of the landscape, see Swaine, *supra* note 5, at 1536–37, 1544–54.

More important for immediate purposes, the nondelegation doctrine may apply differently in the international context. International organizations do not exercise "legislative powers herein granted."[229] As Louis Henkin stressed, assuming the power these organizations exercise is otherwise legislative in character, it is power granted by the United States, in tandem with other states parties, pursuant to an international agreement rather than through any instrument that could be fashioned by Congress alone. International legislation also binds other states parties, an authority that Congress entirely lacks. Even when a resulting rule establishes law for the United States alone—as, for example, when the United States receives a special exemption for its phaseout of ethyl bromide— such delegations conceivably "creat[e] law *for* the United States not *of* the United States," because they only directly concern the question of whether the United States will be violating its international law obligations.[230] Finally, the remedy of interpreting U.S. law to avoid nondelegation problems, while familiar from the domestic context,[231] is nowhere near as seamless in the international context. Interpreting international legislation as nonbinding risks misconstruing that law, on a parochial basis, in a way that excuses noncompliance by other states, while interpretations designed solely to deny that legislation any domestic effect may imperil U.S. compliance with binding international law.[232]

To be sure, these distinctions may not be dispositive. If international legislation was deemed to be "legislative" in an Article I sense, the nondelegation doctrine could be broadly understood as preventing Congress from vesting it elsewhere, such that the precise identity of the recipient, and whether it also derives authority from other sources, may be deemed immaterial.[233] (The fact that it depends upon the agreement and cooperation of others may be particularly unpersuasive to those suspicious of foreign authority.) Article II treaties may be sufficiently different in kind from ordinary legislation to merit nonapplication

---

[229] U.S. Const. art. I, § 1.

[230] Henkin, Foreign Affairs, at 263–64.

[231] *See, e.g.*, John F. Manning, *Textualism as a Nondelegation Doctrine*, 97 Colum. L. Rev. 673 (1997); Cass R. Sunstein, *Nondelegation Canons*, 67 U. Chi. L. Rev. 315 (2000).

[232] As previously noted, the decision in *NRDC v. EPA* appeared to construe narrowly both international and domestic law. *See supra* this chapter text accompanying notes 213–220.

[233] Carter v. Carter Coal Co., 298 U.S. 238, 310–11 (1936) (invalidating delegation to coal producers and miners party under Bituminous Coal Conservation Act); A.L.A. Schechter Poultry Corp. v. United States, 295 U.S. 495, 537 (1935) (critiquing delegation under the National Recovery Act to "trade or industrial associations or groups"). Any delegation to a nonfederal entity, domestic or international, involves assigning authority to an entity that also depends on other outside bodies either to consent to the grant or to create the entity in the first place. *Carter v. Carter Coal* describes the delegation in question as "legislative delegation in its most obnoxious form; for it is not even delegation to an official or an official body, presumptively disinterested, but to private persons whose interests may be and often are adverse to the interests of others in the same business"—a claim that others might make against foreign authority as well. *Carter Coal Co.*, 298 U.S at 311.

of the doctrine,[234] but congressional-executive agreements are somewhat harder to distinguish from ordinary legislation,[235] and the nondelegation doctrine arguably controls the disposition of all legislative powers available to the federal government.[236] Finally, while a precondition of U.S. consent (or its failure to veto) may be considered as redeeming international delegations, that is not readily compatible with the Supreme Court's insistence that "Congress must 'lay down by legislative act an intelligible principle to which the person or body authorized to [act] is directed to conform.' "[237] The idea seems to be that limitations have to be imposed in the original delegation, rather than by the international organization or by the president on behalf of the United States.[238]

Despite these cautionary notes, it appears unlikely that the nondelegation doctrine will be used to invalidate a treaty or congressional-executive agreement, and any distinctive effect for international organizations may be hard to discern. Notwithstanding *NRDC v. EPA*, some courts have proven willing to treat international legislation as binding U.S. law without pausing over delegation objections.[239] Other courts may construe international legislation, or may limit its effect under U.S. law, in such a way as to avoid giving such legislation dispositive force, but that may only loosely correspond with the nondelegation

---

[234] Most would view the treaty power itself as neither purely legislative nor executive in character. *See, e.g.*, THE FEDERALIST NO. 75, at 450–51 (Alexander Hamilton). The issue at hand, however, is whether a treaty might constitutionally permit some entity other than Congress to *itself* exercise something akin to legislative power.

[235] *See, e.g.*, United States v. Curtiss-Wright Export Corp., 299 U.S. 304, 315–18 (1936). To be sure, congressional-executive agreements in some ways transcend Article I. *Cf.* Oona A. Hathaway, *Treaties' End: The Past, Present, and Future of International Lawmaking in the United States*, 117 YALE L.J. 1236, 1327–30 (2008) (describing disagreement as to relationship between such agreements and Article I).

[236] *Cf.* Thomas W. Merrill, *Rethinking Article I, Section 1: From Nondelegation to Exclusive Delegation*, 104 COLUM. L. REV. 2097, 2109–14 (2004) (identifying an "exclusive delegation doctrine" limiting the capacity of agencies to issue binding legislative rules unless Congress has authorized them to do so).

[237] Whitman v. Am. Trucking Ass'ns, 531 U.S. 457, 472 (2001) (quoting J.W. Hampton, Jr., & Co. v. United States, 276 U.S. 394, 409 (1928)); *see id.* at 473 (emphasis in original) ("The idea that an agency can cure an unconstitutionally standardless delegation of power by declining to exercise some of that power seems to us internally contradictory. The very choice of which portion of the power to exercise—that is to say, the prescription of the standard that Congress had omitted—would *itself* be an exercise of the forbidden legislative authority.").

[238] Mistretta v. United States, 488 U.S. 361, 373–79 (1989) (identifying limits to concededly "significant discretion" granted U.S. Sentencing Commission that sufficed to resolve nondelegation issue).

[239] Conservation Council for Hawaii v. National Marine Fisheries Serv., 154 F. Supp. 3d 1006, 1023 (D. Haw. 2015); *see* Conservation and Management of Highly Migratory Fish Stocks in the Western and Central Pacific Ocean, Sept. 5, 2000, T.I.A.S. No. 13,115, and the Western and Central Pacific Fisheries Convention Implementation Act ("Implementation Act"), tit. V, Pub. L. 109-479, § 501, 120 Stat. 3656. As the court stressed, the convention on fish stocks gave its commission the authority to make the relevant decisions and provide that they would be binding, the Implementation Act authorized the U.S. National Marine Fisheries Service to promulgate regulations to carry out those decisions, and the relevant rules had deliberately done so—making the international measures "domestically enforceable." *Id.* at 1025; *see id.* at 1023–25 (citing "critical differences" between that scheme and the one at issue in *NRDC v. EPA*).

doctrine—and the results depend on the nature of the international and domestic schemes. Thus, one court of appeals rejected the Coast Guard's attempt to defend a regulatory process as "one controlled by an international organization," the IMO, "with the State Department acting as an intermediary . . . leaving the Coast Guard with a minor and purely ministerial role."[240] Rather than a delegation of authority to the IMO, one sanctioned by the treaty or by Congress, the court took the Coast Guard *itself* to be improperly "delegating its congressionally given authority" to the IMO. On this view, the problem was the lack of legislative authorization for this "subdelegation," not its constitutional impermissibility.[241] Another court permitted the Animal and Plant Health Inspection Service (APHIS), in adopting a pest-treatment rule, to employ standards promulgated by the Interim Commission on Phytosanitary Measures, a body of the International Plant Protection Convention. APHIS had explained that those standards would further U.S. adherence to its obligations under the WTO's Agreement on the Application of Sanitary and Phytosanitary Measures. The court accepted APHIS's statutorily-permitted, but discretionary, reliance, without questioning its constitutionality.[242]\

3. Delegation of Judicial Authority

While treaty changes and international legislation by international organizations present similar delegation issues, adjudication is more distinctive. Article III of the U.S. Constitution defines the scope of the judicial power, including as to treaties to which the United States is a party. It also describes the institutions fit for its exercise (namely, the Supreme Court and inferior courts that Congress may create) and the characteristics of federal judges, the appointment of which is governed by the Appointments Clause.[243] The basic limitation said to follow from these provisions is that "the U.S. Congress may not delegate to another tribunal 'the essential attributes of judicial power,'" including (but not limited to) the power "to say what the law is."[244] As discussed later, case law establishes that

---

[240] Defs. of Wildlife v. Gutierrez, 532 F.3d 913, 926 (D.C. Cir. 2008).

[241] *Id.* at 926–27. The treaty concerned, the International Convention for the Safety of Life at Sea ("SOLAS"), Nov. 1, 1974, 32 U.S.T. 47, T.I.A.S. 9700, had sought adherence by states party to IMO-adopted routes. *Id.* ch. 5, reg. 8(d); *see also* Convention on the Intergovernmental Maritime Consultative Organization, art. 2, Mar. 6, 1948, 9 U.S.T. 621, T.I.A.S. 4044 (establishing IMO). But the relevant statutes then in effect, as construed by the court, had assigned responsibility solely to the Coast Guard. *Defs. of Wildlife*, 532 F.3d at 926–27.

[242] NRDC *ex rel.* Lockyer v. Dep't of Agric., 613 F.3d 76, 85–86 (2d Cir. 2010); *see* International Plant Protection Convention, Dec. 6, 1951, 23 U.S.T. 2770, T.I.A.S. 7465; WTO Agreement on the Application of Sanitary and Phytosanitary Measures, Apr. 15, 1994, 1867 U.N.T.S. 493.

[243] See, respectively, U.S. CONST. art. III; *id.* amend. XI; and *id.* art. II, § 2, cl. 2.

[244] See, respectively, Sandra Day O'Connor, *Federalism of Free Nations*, 28 N.Y.U. J. INT'L L. & POL. 35, 42 (1995) (quoting Commodity Futures Trading Comm'n v. Schor, 478 U.S. 833, 851 (1986)), and Marbury v. Madison, 5 U.S. (1 Cranch) 137, 177 (1803).

the political branches under some circumstances may establish non–Article III courts, but it has not addressed whether international tribunals unconstitutionally derogate from Article III and its restraints.

History establishes a kind of precedent. The United States has long assumed the capacity to vest international tribunals with the power to issue decisions that determine U.S. interests in international disputes. There have been few instances of any sustained constitutional inquiry, but that may itself be revealing. The 1788 Consular Convention with France is a good example. Hamilton, later invoking the convention as precedent, described it as involving "actual transfers" to French consuls "of portions of the internal jurisdiction and ordinary judiciary power of the Country the exercise of which our Government is bound to aid with its whole strength"; while conceding that "all reflecting men" might doubt the propriety of its provisions but for their necessity, he noted that Congress had assisted in executing its provisions "by making our judicial tribunals and the public force of the country auxiliary to the decrees of the foreign tribunals which they authorize within our territory," and claimed that "no question has been heard about their constitutionality."[245]

On other occasions, questions were posed but not resolved, arguably suggesting that any objections were not deemed fatal. After Article VI of the Jay Treaty established mixed commissions to assess claims by British subjects for losses due to legal impediments to contractual debts, the House debated the treaty's compatibility with Article III of the U.S. Constitution, but the United States proceeded with ratification.[246] During the nineteenth century, the executive branch initially refused, after internal debate over Article III objections, to

---

[245] Alexander Hamilton, *The Defence No. XXXVIII* (Jan. 9, 1796), *in* 20 THE PAPERS OF ALEXANDER HAMILTON 22, 28, 32 (Harold C. Syrett & Jacob E. Cooke eds., 1962); Convention Defining and Establishing the Functions and Privileges of Consuls and Vice Consuls, Fr.-U.S., Nov. 14, 1788, *reprinted in* 2 TREATIES AND OTHER INTERNATIONAL ACTS OF THE UNITED STATES OF AMERICA 228 (Hunter Miller ed., 1931). For discussion, see *Editorial Note: The Consular Convention of 1788*, 14 THE PAPERS OF THOMAS JEFFERSON 67 (Julian P. Boyd ed., 1958); Golove, *supra* note 11, at 1744–45; David Golove, *The Hamiltonian Constitution and Foreign Affairs*, 95 AM. SOC'Y INT'L L. PROC. 107, 111 (2001). *Cf.* Glass v. Sloop Betsey, 3 U.S. (3 Dall.) 6, 25 (1794) (declaring, in assessing whether an admiralty matter exceeded the jurisdiction of federal district courts because it fell within the scope of French consular courts, that "no foreign power can of right institute, or erect, any court of judicature of any kind, within the jurisdiction of the United States, but such only as may be warranted by, and be in pursuance of treaties").

[246] Treaty of Amity Commerce and Navigation, between His Britannic Majesty; and The United States of America art. VI, Gr. Brit.-U.S., Nov. 19, 1794, 1 Stat. 459 [hereinafter Jay Treaty]; *see* DAVID P. CURRIE, THE CONSTITUTION IN CONGRESS: THE FEDERALIST PERIOD, 1789–1801, at 212 n.46 (1997); Henry Paul Monaghan, *Article III and Supranational Judicial Review*, 107 COLUM. L. REV. 833, 853–54 (2007). The commission became stymied for other reasons, which also limited the potential for challenge. *See* 1 JOHN BASSETT MOORE, HISTORY AND DIGEST OF THE INTERNATIONAL ARBITRATIONS TO WHICH THE UNITED STATES HAS BEEN A PARTY 275–98 (1898) [hereinafter MOORE, HISTORY AND DIGEST]; 3 JOHN BASSETT MOORE, INTERNATIONAL ADJUDICATIONS 233–26 (1931) (reprinting background documents relating to commission disputes).

join a British proposal to form a joint international court to address slave trading, but agreed to a similar proposal several decades later.[247]

These and other precedents were invoked, much later, in an extensive public debate over dispute resolution arising under the NAFTA. NAFTA's Chapter 19 permitted the convening of binational panels on a state-to-state basis to conduct binding review of anti-dumping and countervailing duty determinations by U.S. agencies for consistency with U.S. federal law—deviating from what would otherwise be judicial review by the Court of International Trade, an Article III court.[248] The NAFTA Implementation Act permitted constitutional challenge, but such challenges produced no definitive result.[249] Even so, it seems significant that similar mechanisms were employed in both Chapter 19's predecessor, Chapter 19 of the U.S.-Canada Free Trade Agreement (FTA), and its successor, Chapter 10 of the USMCA.[250] Certainly the political branches appear unconvinced that such delegation is unconstitutional.

For its part, the Supreme Court has acknowledged that binding and non-binding interstate dispute resolution, claims resolution processes, and recognizing foreign and international judgments are a well established part of the U.S. legal tradition.[251] *Dames & Moore v. Regan* accepted, at least provisionally,

[247] For varied appraisals, compare Eugene Kontorovich, *The Constitutionality of International Courts: The Forgotten Precedent of Slave-Trade Tribunals*, 158 U. PA. L. REV. 39 (2009) (suggesting that the nineteenth-century slave-trade tribunals cast doubt on U.S. participation in certain modern tribunals, like the International Criminal Court), with Jenny S. Martinez, *International Courts and the U.S. Constitution: Reexamining the History*, 159 U. PA. L. REV. 1069 (2011) (contending that, properly construed, U.S. opponents were more concerned with subjecting Americans to trial in foreign courts for violations of U.S. law, or vesting authority in international tribunals before international law clearly prohibited the slave trade).

[248] NAFTA, *supra* note 4, arts. 1902, 1904; 28 U.S.C. § 1581(i) (2018) (exempting Chapter 19 from exclusive jurisdictional grants to the U.S. Court of International Trade); *see* Ontario Forest Indus. Ass'n v. United States, 444 F. Supp. 2d 1309, 1311–16 (Ct. Int'l Trade 2006) (describing scheme); *see also* Monaghan, *supra* note 246, at 837–39; James E. Pfander, *Article I Tribunals, Article III Courts, and the Judicial Power of the United States*, 118 HARV. L. REV. 643, 766–67 (2004).

[249] 19 U.S.C. § 1516a(g)(4)(A); *see* Coal. For Fair Lumber Imports, Exec. Comm. v. United States, 471 F.3d 1329, 1333 (D.C. Cir. 2006) (dismissing constitutional challenge to treaty scheme in light of subsequent bilateral agreement revoking the underlying anti-dumping and countervailing duty orders process).

[250] *See* Chapter 19 of the U.S.–Canada Free Trade Agreement (FTA), Can.-U.S., Jan. 2, 1988, 27 I.L.M. 293 (1988); as to the USMCA, see *supra* this chapter text accompanying notes 4, 154, 198. In first evaluating the FTA, Congress considered the constitutional issues, but not extensively. H.R. Rep. No. 100-816, pt. 4, at 4–5 (1988); *see also U.S.-Canada Free-Trade Agreement: Hearing Before the S. Comm. on the Judiciary*, 100th Cong. (1988) [hereinafter *U.S.-Canada Free-Trade Agreement: Hearing*].

[251] Some of this history was distinguished in *Medellín v. Texas*, 552 U.S. 491, 519 & n.11 (2008) (citing cases); *see* Comegys v. Vasse, 26 U.S. 193, 212 (1828) (construing as "conclusive and final" and "not re-examinable" decision rendered by claims commission pursuant to 1819 Adams-Onis Treaty between the United States and Spain); United States v. La Abra Silver Mining Co., 29 Ct. Cl. 432 (1894) (upholding "general and fundamental principle" that "the award of an arbitration whether sitting between individuals or nations, in the absence of fraud or mistake, is binding upon the parties to such arbitration," in context of U.S.-Mexico Convention of 1868); *see also* Meade v. United States, 76 U.S. (9 Wall.) 691, 725 (1870) (affirming the notion that a decision under the U.S.-Spain Treaty of 1819 "was final and conclusive, and bar[red] a recovery upon the merits" in American court);

the Iran-U.S. Claims Tribunal,[252] and courts have subsequently enforced the Tribunal's awards—pursuant to a separate treaty and federal statute.[253] In *Medellín v. Texas*, the Court acknowledged that, in a variety of contexts, a treaty may provide that the judgment of an international tribunal binds U.S. courts, in principle including matters between the United States and a foreign state that were otherwise fit for Article III—and with potential application to the conviction and sentencing of individuals in state court.[254]

Were courts earnestly to attempt the application of case law concerning non–Article III to international tribunals, the framing would pose challenges at the threshold. If the basic objection is that the U.S. political branches have assigned "[t]he judicial [p]ower of the United States" to international tribunals, despite precedents limiting the transfer of Article III authority to Article I tribunals, the basic answer is that this is different: international tribunals are neither created solely by the United States nor answerable to it, and it is inconceivable that the Supreme Court would play its conventional domestic role in overseeing them.[255] At the same time, the fact that the assent of other states is required may offer little comfort to those perceiving that the Constitution generally limits the ability of the United States to employ alternatives to Article III courts. Even U.S. authority

---

Frelinghuysen v. Key, 110 U.S. 63, 71 (1884) (upholding the president's capacity to withhold the payment of money awarded by mixed claims commission under the U.S.-Mexico Convention of 1868 in light of subsequently negotiated agreement with Mexico, while noting that absent bilateral negotiation "[t]here is no doubt that the provisions of the convention as to the conclusiveness of the awards are as strong as language can make them"); 1 RICHARD B. LILLICH & BURNS H. WESTON, INTERNATIONAL CLAIMS: THEIR SETTLEMENT BY LUMP SUM AGREEMENTS 26–27 (1975); Moore, *supra* note 131, at 398–417.

[252] Dames & Moore v. Regan, 453 U.S. 654 (1981) (upholding presidential authority to nullify the attachment of Iranian assets and transfer them, pursuant to specific congressional authorization, as well as presidential authority to suspend claims pending in U.S. courts); *see id.* at 679–88 (citing extensive U.S. claims settlement practices). The legality of this arrangement was reviewed by OLC, see Legality of the International Agreement with Iran and Its Implementing Executive Orders, 4A Op. O.L.C. 302, 310–13 (1981) (opinion of Jan. 19, 1981), then reaffirmed after a change in administration, see Review of Domestic and International Legal Implications of Implementing the Agreement with Iran, 4A Op. O.L.C. 314, 314–21 (1981) (opinion of Jan. 29, 1981). *See generally* Introduction and Summary to Opinions of the Office of Legal Counsel Relating to the Iranian Hostage Crisis, 4A Op. O.L.C. 71 (1981).

[253] Ministry of Defense of Islamic Republic of Iran v. Gould, Inc., 969 F.2d 764, 770 (9th Cir. 1992); *see supra* this chapter text accompanying note 155 (noting the Convention on the Recognition and Enforcement of Foreign Arbitral Awards (New York Convention) and its statutory implementation).

[254] Medellín v. Texas, 552 U.S. 491, 519 & n.11 (2008). For further discussion of *Medellín*, see *supra* this chapter § III(C); Chapter 1 § II(B); Chapter 3 § I(D); Chapter 5 § II(B); Chapter 6 §§ III(B), IV(A); and Chapter 9 §§ II(B), II(C).

[255] *See, e.g.*, Pfander, *supra* note 248, at 768 ("Unlike Article I tribunals, the NAFTA panels are not in a legal sense the creatures of Congress, they do not act as agents of the United States in resolving litigated disputes, and they do not answer to the Supreme Court in the interpretation of the Agreement or in the resolution of disputes."); *see also* CURRIE, *supra* note 246, at 212 n.46 (suggesting similar answer for objections to Jay Treaty mixed tribunals); HENKIN, FOREIGN AFFAIRS, at 267 (suggesting similar answer for international tribunals generally). *But cf.* Monaghan, *supra* note 246, at 867–68.

or influence on the tribunal, while bearing directly on its political appeal and advisability, has only the most indirect influence on its constitutionality.[256]

Assuming, nonetheless, that the domestic jurisprudence with respect to the role of Article III courts can be applied *mutatis mutandis* to the international sphere, at least three factors appear critical. One factor concerns whether the right of the United States or some other actor to proceed before an Article III tribunal has essentially been waived.[257] Individuals pursuing an international claim, for example, may be asked to waive their right to proceed in national courts.[258] It appears, however, that structural or separation-of-powers flaws may not be waived—necessitating inquiry into, inter alia, whether a non–Article III tribunal "exercises the range of jurisdiction and powers normally vested only in Article III courts, the origins and importance of the right to be adjudicated, and the concerns that drove [the federal government] to depart from the requirements of Article III."[259] Applying these factors to international tribunals, one can imagine a court attaching substantial weight to the international origin or character of any claims, the need to engineer neutral adjudication to satisfy foreign states, and the values and foreign policy interests promoted by international adjudication.[260]

A second factor involves the nature of the law and the parties. The Supreme Court has exhibited particular concern about relegating traditional common-law

---

[256] Thus, for example, while the claims commission accepted in Comegys v. Vasse, 26 U.S. 193 (1828), consisted of three U.S. citizens selected by the president, see Treaty of Amity, Settlement, and Limits, Between the United States of America and His Catholic Majesty (Adams-Onís Treaty), Spain-U.S., art. 11, Feb. 22, 1819, 8 Stat. 252, it should be of little moment to any formal Article III or Appointments Clause analysis: if the commission exercised "[t]he judicial Power of the United States," there was a different prescribed institution and means for appointment.

[257] *See* Commodity Futures Trading Comm'n v. Schor, 478 U.S. 833, 848–50 (1986) (recognizing possibility of express and implicit waiver). Courts may sustain a constitutional objection, however, if "the litigant 'did not truly consent to' resolution of the claim against it in a non–Article III forum." Wellness Int'l Network Ltd. v. Sharif, 575 U.S. 665, 681 (2015) (quoting Stern v. Marshall, 564 U.S. 462, 493 (2011)).

[258] *See, e.g.,* NAFTA, *supra* note 4, art.1121 (providing that investors commencing Chapter 11 arbitration may submit a claim only if they "waive their right to initiate or continue before any administrative tribunal or court under the law of any Party, or other dispute settlement procedures, any proceedings with respect to the measure of the disputing Party that is alleged to be a breach" of certain provisions, subject to exceptions); *cf.* Loewen Group, Inc. v. U.S., ICSID Case No. ARB(AF)/98/3, Objections to Jurisdiction (June 26, 2003), 42 I.L.M. 811, 812 (2003) (construing art. 1121). In other circumstances, the United States may espouse a U.S. national's claim before an international tribunal; this removes the claim from the national's control and denies them the capacity to pursue the claim before U.S. courts, foreign courts, or other venues. RESTATEMENT (THIRD) § 713 rptrs. note 9 (describing U.S. practice with regard to claims by its nationals); *id.* § 902 & cmt. 1 & rptrs. note 8 (describing U.S. interstate claims practice). Because it is non-elective, this should not be deemed to waive the U.S. national's Article III challenge.

[259] *Schor,* 478 U.S. at 851; *see also* Al Bahlul v. United States, 792 F.3d 1, 3–7 (D.C. Cir. 2015) (applying same analysis to alleged forfeiture of structural Article III objection).

[260] *But cf.* Al Bahlul, 792 F.3d at 19–22 (finding balance of factors wanting in holding that a statute permitting the executive branch to try crimes of inchoate conspiracy before military commission violated Article III and the separation of powers).

claims, particularly between private actors, to non–Article III courts; some international tribunals have been entrusted with such claims.[261] By contrast, actions against government entities, or regulatory or administrative matters like trade and customs, may fall within the so-called public rights exception, according to which congressionally-created rights entail greater capacity to select the judicial forum.[262] The distinction between private and public rights is not easy to apply nor, apparently, decisive, as some cases seem to ignore the distinction in favor of a broader balancing approach.[263] Arguably the focus could be refined by asking whether the legal rights of U.S. nationals are compromised by an international scheme, but that distinction only partly addresses the interest in preserving the judicial power.[264]

A third factor concerns whether the scheme permits appellate review by an Article III court. For particular rights, appellate review (if not more) may be a minimum condition for satisfying Article III.[265] Requiring any such review would seem to be a substantial hurdle for international tribunals, given that

[261] Mixed commissions, including those under Article VI of the Jay Treaty, have often resolved domestic law issues. Jay Treaty, *supra* note 246, art. VI; Monaghan, *supra* note 246, at 853–54; *see* Moore, *supra* note 131, at 398–417 (citing additional examples).

[262] Oil States Energy Servs. LLC v. Greene's Energy Group LLC, 138 S. Ct. 1365, 1373 (2018) (noting Congress has "significant latitude to assign adjudication of public rights to entities other than Article III courts"); *see, e.g., Ex parte* Bakelite Corp., 279 U.S. 438, 452 (1929); United States v. La Abra Silver Mining Co., 29 Ct. Cl. 432, 456 (1894).

[263] *See* Oil States, 138 S. Ct. at 1373 (noting doctrinal ambiguity); Monaghan, *supra* note 246, at 873–75. For contrasting views concerning the decisiveness of the public-private distinction, *compare* N. Pipeline Constr. Co. v. Marathon Pipe Line Co., 458 U.S. 50, 70 (1982) (plurality op.) (indicating that "only [public rights] controversies . . . may be removed from Art. III courts and delegated to legislative courts or administrative agencies for their determination"), *with Schor*, 478 U.S. at 854 (suggesting that "searching" examination is appropriate, rather than automatic disqualification, "where private, common law rights are at stake"); for contrasting views on this distinction, *compare Schor*, 478 U.S. at 851 (explaining aversion to "formalistic and unbending rules" and deemphasizing the category of public rights), *with* Granfinanciera v. Nordberg, 492 U.S. 33, 54 (1989) (re-emphasizing public-private distinction but declining to limit public rights to cases involving government parties).

[264] *See* Monaghan, *supra* note 246, at 877–79. Professor Monaghan noted, with approval, that this would distinguish NAFTA Chapter 11 proceedings (which involved complaints by foreign investors against expropriation and similar practices) as well as Chapter 19 proceedings (which are intergovernmental in character, though they risked interests secured by American nationals under U.S. trade law), but it is not evident why the formal identity of the parties should matter for purposes of Article III.

[265] N. *Pipeline Constr. Co.*, 458 U.S. at 86 n.39 (plurality op.) (rejecting suggestion by litigants that "Article III is satisfied so long as some degree of appellate review is provided"); *see* Pfander, *supra* note 248, at 646–71 (reviewing Article III theories, including those emphasizing the significance of appellate review). Professor Martinez has offered a contrary view:

> Nor would a treaty agreeing to submit certain kinds of disputes under international law to international courts violate Article III's grant of the judicial power to the federal courts, at least so long as those courts retained some measure of discretion in deciding whether to enforce a particular judgment and there were no other factors that suggested that the particular delegation dramatically infringed on the integrity of the judicial branch. . . . So long as courts retain a certain amount of discretion—as they would under a presumption but not an absolute rule of enforcement—and so long as the jurisdiction of the international court

other parties to a dispute would consider it unwelcome (and unprecedented) to permit supervision by U.S. courts.[266]

Unsurprisingly, then, existing schemes do not enable such appellate review. Indeed, quite to the contrary, some international tribunals have been granted the capacity to gainsay, directly or indirectly, prior judgments of U.S. courts. NAFTA's Chapter 11—and going forward, USMCA's Chapter 14—permit foreign investors to initiate review before international panels of whether U.S. jurisdictions, including their judiciary, have complied with important international obligations.[267] The authority these panels exercise, which offers the possibility of money damages against federal authorities, does not actually entail appellate review of U.S. court judgments.[268] More important, though, the grounds available to U.S. courts for refusing or deferring recognition or enforcement of panel awards is too limited to constitute appellate review, if that were actually required to satisfy Article III.[269] There is precedent for such inversions of review by Article III courts—such as the Treaty of Washington, according to which the United States and Great Britain espoused their respective nationals' claims arising out of the Civil War, permitted a mixed commission to review prize decisions of the Supreme Court and the House of Lords[270]—but the situation remains distinctive enough to attract scrutiny.

The Supreme Court's cases concerning the Vienna Convention on Consular Relations established an indirect solution of sorts to these problems: namely, maintaining the supremacy of Article III courts by limiting the domestic effect of international decisions. The Supreme Court in *Sanchez-Llamas v. Oregon* was clearly discomfited by the idea that the ICJ could effectively countermand its decisions, either by imposing a different treaty interpretation or by directing a result in a particular case, regarding this as a threat to the "judicial power"

was not so broad as to usurp a major part of the domestic courts' regular work, there should be no Article III problem.
Martinez, *Towards an International Judicial System*, *supra* note 128, at 502.

[266] *Cf. supra* this chapter text accompanying notes 248–249 (noting limited opportunity for constitutional review of Chapter 19 panels).

[267] *See* NAFTA, *supra* note 4, art. 1102 (equality of treatment); *id.* art. 1110 (expropriation); *id.* arts. 1115–16 (denials of justice).

[268] *See* Robert B. Ahdieh, *Between Dialogue and Decree: International Review of National Courts*, 79 N.Y.U. L. Rev. 2029 (2004) (depicting NAFTA Chapter 11 review process as "dialectical review," neither a nonbinding "dialogue" among national and supranational tribunals nor traditional binding judicial review).

[269] 9 U.S.C. § 207 (2018) (providing for confirmation of awards in accordance with the New York Convention); *see* Pfander, *supra* note 248, at 767–68 (noting limitation, but finding appellate review unnecessary in light of international character of the NAFTA scheme).

[270] Treaty Between the United States and Great Britain: Claims, Fisheries, Navigation of the St. Lawrence, American Lumber on the River St. John, Boundary, Gr. Brit.–U.S., May 8, 1871, 17 Stat. 863; *see* 4 Moore, History and Digest, *supra* note 246, at 4057–78; Monaghan, *supra* note 246, at 860–62.

contemplated by Article III.[271] As the international and national perspectives on the convention continued to diverge, the Supreme Court in *Medellín v. Texas* confronted what it acknowledged was a determinative judgment by the ICJ that established a binding international legal obligation for the United States.[272] It defused the conflict in part by observing that the individual parties to the U.S. litigation before it (José Ernesto Medellín and the state of Texas) were not parties to the international litigation (those being Mexico and the United States)—a distinction that may not always be available.[273] *Medellín* ultimately dissolved the potential tension between its Article III power and the delegation of dispute resolution authority to the ICJ under treaties by construing those treaties as non-self-executing. It remains to be seen whether this is the kernel of a broader solution. Invocation of the non-self-execution doctrine probably defers the potential problem of delegating judicial power to any implementing statute, and absent such implementation, leaves the United States at risk of defaulting on its international obligations by being unable to harness the U.S. legal system to establish compliance.

Beyond Article III, a collateral objection sometimes made against U.S. participation in international tribunals concerns whether it violates the Appointments Clause. That provision assigns to the president the power to appoint (with the advice and consent of the Senate) ambassadors, other public ministers and consuls, and Supreme Court justices, as well as "all other Officers of the United States."[274] Officers of the United States include "any appointee exercising significant authority pursuant to the laws of the United States."[275] For "inferior Officers," Congress may vest appointment in "the President alone," "the Courts of Law," or "the Heads of Departments"; non-officer employees, as well as non-employees, raise no Appointments Clause issues.[276]

While there has been disagreement about whether contemporary dispute resolution obligations pose Appointments Clause issues,[277] there are significant

---

[271] *See* Sanchez-Llamas v. Oregon, 548 U.S. 331, 353–54 (2006) (stating that while the ICJ's treaty interpretation deserves "respectful consideration," it did not "compel" reconsideration of the Court's previous understanding, since "[i]f treaties are to be given effect as federal law under our legal system, determining their meaning as a matter of federal law 'is emphatically the province and duty of the judicial department,' headed by the 'one supreme Court' ") (internal citations omitted).

[272] *See supra* this chapter text accompanying note 254.

[273] *See* Medellín v. Texas, 552 U.S. 491, 511–12 (2008).

[274] U.S. CONST. art. II, § 2, cl. 2.

[275] Buckley v. Valeo, 424 U.S. 1, 125–26 (1976); *see* Freytag v. C.I.R., 501 U.S. 868, 880–82 (1991) (making clear that "significant authority" distinguishes both principal and inferior officers from non-officer employees).

[276] U.S. CONST. art. II, § 2, cl. 2; *see* Lucia v. Securities & Exchange Comm'n, 138 S. Ct. 2044, 2051 n.3 (2018); Edmond v. United States, 520 U.S. 651, 659–60 (1997).

[277] *Compare, e.g.,* Jim C. Chen, *Appointments with Disaster: The Unconstitutionality of Binational Arbitral Review under the United States–Canada Free Trade Agreement,* 49 WASH. & LEE L. REV. 1455, 1479–96 (1992), *and* Alan B. Morrison, *Appointments Clause Problems in the Dispute Resolution*

problems with any such challenge. Members of international arbitral panels or judges appointed in connection with an international organization in which the United States participates may not be operating as officers of the United States at all. On some occasions, such positions have been distinguished as only temporary or limited in character.[278] Alexander Hamilton also described them as operating in "a different mode" altogether, apparently because of the international character of their appointment.[279] If the typical distinction is "between federal officers—officers exercising power of the National Government—and nonfederal officers—officers exercising power of some other government," it is fair to say that "other governments" are involved.[280] Alternatively, much like the Court's recent distinguishing of the work of officials as concerning "primarily local duties" relating to Puerto Rico, it might consider the function of international tribunals to be primarily international in character.[281] Such persons would require neither Senate advice and consent nor appointment appropriate to an inferior officer.[282]

Were any substantial Appointments Clause issue posed, it has been suggested that the absence of binding legal effect under U.S. law for any resulting decisions—which may be evident from the treaty or the statutory scheme—might cure any

Provisions of the United States-Canada Free Trade Agreement, 49 WASH. & LEE L. REV. 1299 (1992), with Davey, *supra* note 212, at 1319–22.

[278] United States v. Hartwell, 73 U.S. (6 Wall.) 385, 393 (1868); *see, e.g.,* Office—Compensation, 22 Op. Att'y Gen. 184, 187–88 (1898) (concluding that a presidentially appointed commissioner, designated to arbitrate claims concerning the seizure of British vessels in the Bering Sea, did not hold an "office" because "the temporary character of the employment, which was to consist of and to terminate at the end of the examination of a limited number of specified claims"); Members of the General Board of Arbitration, 23 Op. Att'y Gen. 313, 315 (1900) (same).

[279] Addressing constitutional objections to the commissioners appointed for Jay Treaty arbitrations, Hamilton responded:

> [T]hey are not in a strict sense OFFICERS. They are arbitrators between the two countries. Though in the Constitutions, both of the United States and of most of the Individual states, a particular mode of appointing officers is designated, *yet in practice it has not been deemed a violation* of the provision to appoint Commissioners or special Agents for special purposes in a different mode.

A. Hamilton, *The Defence No. 37 (Jan. 6, 1796), reprinted in* 20 THE PAPERS OF ALEXANDER HAMILTON 13, 14, 20 (H. Syrett ed., 1974) (emphasis added); *see also* Office—Compensation, *supra* note 278, at 188 ("[I]t seems clear that a person employed solely as a sworn judge of a joint international commission would not be spoken of as an officer of either country, although, under a treaty requiring it, selected and sent to his post by one of them").

[280] Fin. Oversight and Mgmt. Bd. for Puerto Rico v. Aurelius Inv., LLC, 140 S. Ct. 1649, 1658 (2020).

[281] In *Financial Oversight and Management Board for Puerto Rico,* the Court held that a board established with authority (inter alia) to modify the laws of Puerto Rico and its instrumentalities was not composed of officers of the United States; what mattered was not whether the officers exercised authority concerning Puerto Rico, as an Article IV territory of the United States, but rather that the officers were exercising "primarily local duties." *Id.* at 1661–63.

[282] *See generally* Brief for Respondents at 48–52, Coal. For Fair Lumber Imports, Exec. Comm. v. United States, 374 F.3d 1329 (D.C. Cir. 2006) (No. 05-1366), 2006 WL 638136.

constitutional difficulty.[283] This suggests the appeal of employing constitutional avoidance doctrines to construe domestic legal effect narrowly. Doing so would likely not inhibit the capacity of the executive branch to conform to those decisions for matters falling within its discretionary authority,[284] but it might prevent any executive branch implementation from having legal force in the absence of legislative authorization.[285]

4. Delegation of Executive Authority

The United States is party to few international organization agreements today that raise issues as regards the exercise of executive authority. This may be because few agreements go so far as to accord executive authority to an international organization, or because the United States is averse to joining those that do. Occasionally, however, delegations of authority to international officials— such as to the Technical Secretariat of the OPCW, which is authorized to conduct inspections of U.S. public and private facilities—are viewed as raising constitutional concerns.[286]

The issues raised in this context may be similar to those previously discussed. Indeed, historical precedents involving the use of U.S. courts to facilitate evidence-gathering by international bodies might be characterized as delegating either judicial *or* executive functions to such bodies,[287] and the Appointments Clause in this context raises familiar issues relating to whether international

---

[283] *Cf. U.S.-Canada Free-Trade Agreement: Hearing, supra* note 250, at 81–82 (testimony of John O. McGinnis, Deputy Assistant Att'y Gen., Office of Legal Counsel) (suggesting that were implementing legislation to confer binding domestic legal effect to panel decisions under the U.S.-Canada Free Trade Agreement—conceded to be binding under international law—it would pose Appointments Clause issues).

[284] *Id.* at 81–82 (testimony of John O. McGinnis, Deputy Assistant Att'y Gen., Office of Legal Counsel). Professor Monaghan suggested doubt as to the basis for such authority, even as to discretionary activities, and cited other OLC advice that seemed to share that view. Monaghan, *supra* note 246, at 864–65, *citing United States–Canada Free-Trade Agreement: Hearing before the Subcomm. on Courts, Civil Liberties, and the Administration of Justice of the H. Comm. on the Judiciary,* 100th Cong. 504, 505 (1988) (letter from Thomas M. Boyd, Acting Assistant Att'y Gen., Office of Legal Counsel) (explaining, in relation to proposed formulation that the President would "advise" government agencies of international obligations incurred by virtue of binational panels, that "Government agencies that had merely been 'advised' of panel and committee decisions would be under no legal obligation to implement those decisions. Indeed, they probably would lack the legal authority to do so.").

[285] For discussion of comparable approaches in *Medellín v. Texas,* 552 U.S. 491 (2008), and *NRDC v. EPA,* 464 F.3d 1 (D.C. Cir. 2006), see *supra* this chapter text accompanying notes 217–220.

[286] For a few other possible examples, see Ku, *supra* note 5, at 110 & n.131; Yoo, *supra* note 7, at 130; *see also* Swaine, *supra* note 5, at 1530–33. For broader discussion of constitutional issues raised by the Chemical Weapons Convention, see Ronald D. Rotunda, *The Chemical Weapons Convention: Political and Constitutional Issues,* 15 CONST. COMMENT. 131 (1998).

[287] *See* HENKIN, ARMS CONTROL, *supra* note 203, at 56–58.

officials are exercising "significant authority."[288] Interference with executive authority may also be styled as violating the nondelegation doctrine. For example, according to the Henry J. Hyde United States–India Peaceful Atomic Energy Cooperation Act of 2006, the United States was only permitted to ship nuclear fuel to India if it were consistent with the then governing transfer guidelines issued by the Nuclear Suppliers Group, a multilateral export regime.[289] President George W. Bush's signing statement indicated that the executive branch would regard this provision as advisory, because if it were construed to prohibit the executive branch from transferring items to India "a serious question would exist as to whether the provision unconstitutionally delegated legislative power to an international body."[290]

As with other forms of delegation, executive branch checks on the authority that international organizations or their officials exercise may reduce the perceived gravity of any concerns. Indeed, control by executive branch officials directly addresses whether any constitutional violation has occurred.[291] In the case of the Chemical Weapons Convention, for example, one concession to varied constitutional and political objections has been to assume federal responsibility for the discharge of the international obligations, as by employing U.S. government officials to accompany and assist international inspectors.[292]

Responses to Appointments Clause critiques concerning executive functions have also pressed the argument that the clause is inapposite when the officials concerned are not federal officials at all—as when delegations to state, private, or international actors are concerned.[293] That argument might be used to justify sweeping circumvention of the Appointments Clause.[294] The narrower case

---

[288] *See, e.g.*, Ku, *supra* note 5, at 107–10; Yoo, *supra* note 7, at 117–29; for a description of the academic and political debate, see Jeremy B. Zucker, *The Instance of Chemical Weapons Control*, in DELEGATING STATE POWERS: THE EFFECT OF TREATY REGIMES ON DEMOCRACY AND SOVEREIGNTY 95, 127–31 (Thomas M. Franck ed., 2000).

[289] Henry J. Hyde United States–India Peaceful Atomic Energy Cooperation Act of 2006, Pub. L. No. 109-401, § 104(d)(2), 120 Stat. 2726 (2006) (codified at 22 U.S.C. § 8003(d)(2) (2018)).

[290] *See* Statement on Signing the Henry J. Hyde United States–India Peaceful Atomic Energy Cooperation Act of 2006, 42 WEEKLY COMP. PRES. DOC. 2179 (Dec. 18, 2006); *see also* Statement on Signing the Clean Diamond Trade Act, 1 PUB. PAPERS 386 (Apr. 25, 2003) (taking similar view concerning whether future changes to the Kimberley Process Certification Scheme could be construed to bind executive branch).

[291] For an illustration of how these values coincide, see, for example, Yoo, *supra* note 7.

[292] Chemical Weapons Convention Implementation Act of 1998, Pub. L. No. 105-277, 112 Stat. 2681 (codified at 22 U.S.C. §§ 6721–29). For a useful description of the Convention's implementation, see Barry Kellman, *The Advent of International Chemical Regulation: The Chemical Weapons Convention Implementation Act*, 25 J. LEGIS. 117 (1999).

[293] *See, e.g.*, Neil Kinkopf, *Of Devolution, Privatization, and Globalization: Separation of Powers Limits on Congressional Authority to Assign Federal Power to Non-Federal Actors*, 50 RUTGERS L. REV. 331, 392–95 (1998).

[294] *See* Yoo, *supra* note 7, at 120–23.

for exempting such delegations may turn on the extent of executive branch or even judicial checks on the exercise of authority by international organization officials.[295] Unfortunately, authoritative guidance on what safeguards are constitutionally required is hard to come by.

---

[295] *Compare* Kinkopf, *supra* note 293, at 395, *with* Yoo, *supra* note 7, at 122–23 (providing divergent views of accountability under the Chemical Weapons Convention, albeit in advance of its implementing legislation).

8

War Powers

The Supreme Court observed in *Haig v. Agee* that it "is 'obvious and unarguable' that no governmental interest is more compelling than the security of the Nation."[1] To that end, the U.S. Constitution accords to the federal government a wide range of powers that collectively may be characterized as the "war powers." Indeed, Justice Robert Jackson noted that "out of seventeen specific paragraphs of congressional power [in Article I, Section 8 of the Constitution], eight of them are devoted in whole or in part to specification of powers connected with warfare."[2] Not only are these war powers viewed as wide-ranging, but they perhaps are not exhaustive of federal power in this area and have been employed over history in various ways to protect U.S. national security and U.S. interests.[3]

To Congress, in particular, the Constitution grants several express war powers: (1) provide for the common defense of the United States; (2) define and punish offenses against the law of nations, to include the law of war; (3) declare war; (4) grant letters of marque and reprisal; (5) make rules concerning captures on land and water; (6) raise and support armies, "but no Appropriation of Money to that Use shall be for a longer Term than two Years"; (7) provide and maintain a navy; (8) make rules for the government and regulation of the land and naval forces; (9) provide for calling forth the militia to execute the laws of the union, suppress insurrections, and repel invasions; (10) provide for organizing, arming, training, and disciplining the militia; and (11) exercise exclusive authority over all federal forts, magazines, arsenals, dockyards, and other needful buildings.[4] Congress also, of course, has the power to appropriate funds for the U.S. government and to enact all laws "necessary and proper" to execute any federal power.[5]

---

[1] Haig v. Agee, 453 U.S. 280, 307 (1981) (citing Aptheker v. Sec'y of State, 378 U.S. 500, 509 (1964)).

[2] Johnson v. Eisentrager, 339 U.S. 763, 788 (1950); *see* MICHAEL D. RAMSEY, THE CONSTITUTION'S TEXT IN FOREIGN AFFAIRS 218 (2007) ("[T]he Constitution's text devotes as much space to war and military power as it does to any other foreign affairs subject.").

[3] *See* Hamilton v. Regents of the Univ. of California, 293 U.S. 245, 264 (1934) (indicating that the federal government's war powers are "well-nigh limitless"); Miller v. United States, 78 U.S. (11 Wall.) 268, 305 (1870) ("Upon the exercise of these powers no restrictions are imposed. Of course the power to declare war involves the power to prosecute it by all means and in any manner in which war may be legitimately prosecuted."); Stewart v. Kahn, 78 U.S. (11 Wall.) 493, 506 (1870) ("The measures to be taken in carrying on war . . . are not defined [in the Constitution]. The decision of all such questions rests wholly in the discretion of those to whom the substantial powers involved are confided by the Constitution.").

[4] U.S. CONST. art. I, § 8.

[5] *Id.* §§ 7, 8.

By contrast, the Constitution grants to the president just two express war powers: (1) to be commander in chief of the U.S. Army and Navy and (2) to be commander in chief of the militia of the several states, when called into federal service.[6] Of course, as a general matter, the "executive Power shall be vested in" the president, and "he shall take Care that the Laws be faithfully executed . . . ."[7] The Constitution also addresses the position of the several states in this regard, denying to them the power to: (1) grant letters of marque and reprisal; (2) keep troops or ships of war in time of peace; or (3) engage in war, unless actually invaded, or in such imminent danger as will not admit of delay.[8]

In some situations, actions taken by the federal government have been supported by a loose reference to a collective federal "war power." For example, when the federal government during World War II imposed curfews upon[9] and interned[10] Japanese-Americans, such actions were premised upon statute,[11] executive order,[12] and military orders.[13] In upholding such actions, the Supreme Court referred generally to the "war power" of Congress and the executive.[14] For the most part, however, actions by the federal government are analyzed on the basis of one or more of the specific enumerated powers, especially in situations where there is a confrontation or potential confrontation between the political branches.

Constitutional text is a critical starting point for assessing the law in this area and is best assessed with an understanding of what came before 1789, including the powers of the British government, the powers of the Continental Congress, and the powers under the Articles of Confederation. Yet, even then,

---

[6] *Id.*, art. II, § 2. Comparing this allocation, Michael Glennon finds that the president's powers are "paltry in comparison with, and are subordinate to, [the Constitution's] grants to Congress." MICHAEL J. GLENNON, CONSTITUTIONAL DIPLOMACY 72 (1990).

[7] U.S. CONST. art. II, §§ 1, 3.

[8] *Id.*, art. I, § 10.

[9] *See* Hirabayashi v. United States, 320 U.S. 81 (1943).

[10] *See* Korematsu v. United States, 323 U.S. 214 (1944). The conviction in *Korematsu* was later set aside on writ of *coram nobis*, 584 F. Supp. 1406 (N.D. Cal. 1984). The Court invalidated detention of citizens whose loyalty was conceded by the government. *Ex parte* Endo, 323 U.S. 283 (1944). As noted in Chapter 1 § III, *Korematsu* and *Hirabayashi* were heavily criticized outside the Court for an unwillingness to examine the true reasons that motivated the government's action (racial hostility and discrimination), and instead for dispensing with civil liberties in a time of crisis. Ultimately, in 2018, the Court that declared that "*Korematsu* was gravely wrong the day it was decided, has been overruled in the court of history, and—to be clear—'has no place in law under the Constitution.'" Trump v. Hawaii, 138 S. Ct. 2392, 2423 (2018).

[11] *See* Act of March 21, 1942, ch. 191, Pub. L. No. 77-503, 56 Stat. 173.

[12] *See* Exec. Order No. 9,066, 7 Fed. Reg. 1407 (Feb. 19, 1942), later rescinded by Proclamation No. 4417, 41 Fed. Reg. 7741 (Feb. 19, 1976) (codified at 3 C.F.R. pt. 2714 (1977)).

[13] *See, e.g.*, Civilian Exclusion Order No. 34, Western Defense Command and Fourth Army Wartime Civil Control Administration (May 3, 1942).

[14] *See, e.g.*, *Korematsu*, 323 U.S. at 217–18 (finding that "we are unable to conclude that it was beyond the war power of Congress and the Executive to exclude those of Japanese ancestry from the West Coast war area at the time they did").

the constitutional text accords powers to both political branches in a manner that does not wholly exclude either from decision-making in this area, and otherwise leaves much unsaid as to how exactly these powers are to be exercised. As such, historical practice since 1789 is extraordinarily relevant; indeed, it seems likely that this is consistent with the expectations of the Framers, who would have anticipated that much of the line-drawing would only be worked out over time. Further, the relatively small and militarily weak nation that emerged in 1789 has been transformed over time into today's military superpower with political and economic interests, and military alliances, that span the globe. In the course of the historical development of the United States as a military power, attitudes of all three branches regarding the exercise of U.S. war powers have evolved, especially in the willingness to accord to the president significant discretion as the initiator of actions deemed necessary to protect U.S. national security.

In that respect, a central focus in public and academic discourse has been on who gets to decide whether to *resort to armed force*, sometimes in the form of deploying U.S. military forces abroad and other times projecting force by missile attacks or other means. The Constitution allocates to Congress the power to "declare war" and case law since that time has interpreted the power as according to Congress considerable power in this area. Yet even at the Philadelphia convention it was recognized that the president, who is accorded the commander-in-chief power, was constitutionally permitted to act quickly to defend the United States from sudden internal or external threats. Over time, the president's power as a practical matter has grown considerably to address various kinds of threats without prior congressional authorization. That, in turn, has led to efforts by Congress to cabin the president's power, notably in the 1973 War Powers Resolution, and to exert a constraining influence on the president in less direct ways, including through the exercise of its oversight and appropriations powers.[15]

Other, less discussed areas of the war powers, however, are also important. Some powers concern the *conduct* of armed conflict, notably the commander-in-chief power, the power to make rules concerning captures on land and water, and the power to grant letters of marque and reprisal. Still other powers concern *establishment and regulation of the military*, which includes powers to raise revenues to provide for the common defense, to raise and support the military, and to purchase and regulate military installations; and the *power to call forth*, organize, arm, and discipline *the militia*.

In the background of the exercise of these powers lie various rules of international law relating to the *jus ad bellum* (law concerning when a state may resort

---

[15] *See generally* DAVID J. BARRON, WAGING WAR: THE CLASH BETWEEN PRESIDENTS AND CONGRESS, 1776 TO ISIS (2016).

to armed conflict) and the *jus in bello* (law concerning how a state must conduct itself during an armed conflict). As a matter of U.S. law, these rules of international law are inferior to the U.S. Constitution, but they nevertheless play a very important role in the exercise of U.S. war powers. In some instances, these rules of international law are incorporated into U.S. law by treaty or statute, while in other instances they are not directly incorporated but serve to influence the rules set forth in U.S. statutes or regulations. Moreover, they can play an important role in influencing the discretion exercised by political decision makers within U.S. law; for example, the willingness to resort to armed conflict in a particular situation may depend on whether the action will be supported by allies, which in turn may depend on whether the action is perceived as consistent with international law. As such, this chapter pays attention as well to the most salient rules of international law in this area.

I. Power to Resort to Armed Force

Perhaps the most studied and most contentious of the war powers concerns the power to "declare war." Yet, given the disappearance today of declarations of war, the more salient issue is the power to resort to armed force, whether that occurs based on a declaration of war or by some other means. Such force may occur between the United States and a foreign state, or between the United States and a nonstate actor, such as a terrorist organization. It may concern large deployments of U.S. forces or lesser projections of force, such as through missile strikes, perhaps using unmanned drones. However exercised, it is clear that the power is almost exclusively a federal power; the several states may not engage in "war" except when Congress consents or when the state is "actually invaded, or in such imminent Danger as will not admit of delay."[16] Yet beyond that, much remains debated as to the power to resort to armed force, though in practice the president has become dominant as the first mover, while Congress often operates on the sidelines, especially with respect to temporary and relatively low-level projections of force.

A. Pre-Constitutional Origins of the Power

In the period immediately prior to the American Revolution, the power to initiate war rested with the British monarchy, a power referred to by John Locke as

---

[16] U.S. CONST. art. I, § 10, cl. 3.

"federative" and resting with the "executive" and by William Blackstone as one of the direct prerogatives that are "rooted in and spring from the king's political person."[17] Further, the king alone had the power to raise the army and navy and to issue letters of marque and reprisal by which private persons could pursue military action.[18] Parliament controlled the "power of the purse," but the king's power to wage war was considered absolute, with "no legal authority that can either delay or resist him."[19] While some formal declarations of war were issued in this period, "war" often arose without any such declarations.[20]

At the outset of the American rebellion, it was the Second Continental Congress in 1776 that took the decisive step (issuance of the Declaration of Independence) that placed the colonies in a position of armed conflict with Britain. Neither side "declared war" on the other; the colonies were content to secure independence without any armed conflict, while Britain viewed the situation as an internal rebellion, not a war against a belligerent of comparable status. As such, the outbreak of the rebellion sheds little light on the location of power in the new republic to commence war, other than highlighting that the momentous decision to declare independence was taken collectively by the representatives of the colonies.[21] The post-independence establishment of "republican" governments in the several states also resulted in an allocation of the power to commence war to the new state legislatures, not to their governors.[22]

The Articles of Confederation, which were approved by the Continental Congress in 1777 and entered into force in 1781, took a similar approach. Article 9 provided: "The United States in Congress assembled, shall have the sole and exclusive right and power of determining on peace and war, except in cases mentioned in the sixth article . . . ."[23] The sixth article precluded the states from engaging in war unless approved by Congress, unless the "State be actually invaded by enemies," or it "shall have received certain advice of a resolution being formed by some nation of Indians to invade such State, and the danger is so imminent as not to admit of a delay till the United States in Congress assembled can be consulted . . . ."[24]

---

[17] JOHN LOCKE, TWO TREATISES OF GOVERNMENT §§ 146–47 (Peter Laslett ed., 1988) (1690); 1 WILLIAM BLACKSTONE, COMMENTARIES *233.
[18] 1 WILLIAM BLACKSTONE, COMMENTARIES *250–51.
[19] Id. at *243.
[20] See infra this chapter § I(D)(1).
[21] While the exact status of the Continental Congress as a legislative or executive (or both) body is not entirely clear, see JACK N. RAKOVE, THE BEGINNINGS OF NATIONAL POLITICS: AN INTERPRETIVE HISTORY OF THE CONTINENTAL CONGRESS 383–85 (1979); RAMSEY, supra note 2, at 29–46 (finding the Congress to be primarily an executive body), there is no question that it was a body of representatives from the several states, not a single person or office like the King of England.
[22] Curtis A. Bradley & Martin S. Flaherty, Executive Power Essentialism and Foreign Affairs, 102 MICH. L. REV. 545, 582 (2004).
[23] ARTICLES OF CONFEDERATION OF 1781, art. IX, ¶ 1.
[24] Id., art. VI, ¶ 5.

Further, the sixth article denied to the states any ability to maintain military forces or vessels of war, unless approved by Congress for defense of the state, but the states were required to "always keep up a well-regulated and disciplined militia . . . ."[25] Finally, the states could not grant commissions to warships or issue letters of marque or reprisal, "unless such State be infested by pirates, in which case vessels of war may be fitted out for that occasion, and kept so long as the danger shall continue, or until the United States in Congress assembled shall determine otherwise."[26] Thus, for the most part, the Articles sought to embed the war powers in the Confederation Congress, while denying such powers to the several states, but with the recognition that the states would need to defend themselves against imminent threats even in the absence of congressional approval.

At the time it was understood that some wars were more formal and extensive than other forms of armed conflict, which led some commentators and courts to draw a distinction between "perfect" and "imperfect" war.[27] That distinction, however, was not expressly incorporated into the Articles of Confederation, such that · the authority of the Continental Congress appears to have embraced all forms of war. Some contemporary commentators have associated the power to grant letters of marque and reprisal as covering all uses of force short of "war," but that distinction also is not expressly captured in the Articles of Confederation or in the analogous provisions of the Constitution.[28]

B. Power as Expressed in the U.S. Constitution

At the 1787 Constitutional Convention in Philadelphia, a desire quickly emerged in favor of establishing a national executive. Even so, several delegates asserted that the war power should not be given to the president for fear that it would transform the office into something approaching a monarch.

The initial "Virginia Plan" would have placed with the executive "the Executive rights vested in Congress by the Confederation."[29] Charles Pinckney, however, expressed fear at giving to the executive the powers over war and peace that resided in the Confederation Congress, since doing so would make the "Executive a Monarchy, of the worst kind . . . ."[30] John Rutledge agreed, saying

---

[25] *Id.,* ¶ 4.
[26] *Id.,* ¶ 5.
[27] *See, e.g.,* Miller v. Ship Resolution, 2 U.S. (2 Dall.) 19, 21 (1781).
[28] *See* Jules Lobel, *"Little Wars" and the Constitution,* 50 U. Miami L. Rev. 61, 70 (1995). *But see* C. Kevin Marshall, *Putting Privateers in Their Place: The Applicability of the Marque and Reprisal Clause to Undeclared Wars,* 64 U. Chi. L. Rev. 953, 954 (1997).
[29] 1 Farrand's Records 21.
[30] *Id.* at 64–65.

that "he was not for giving" the new executive "the power of war and peace."[31] James Wilson then attempted to mediate the issue by arguing that "Executive powers" did not include powers of war and peace, a position that James Madison supported.[32] Even Alexander Hamilton, who famously spoke in favor of the British system as "the best in the world," asserted in his June 18 speech that the Senate should have the "sole power of declaring war," while the president would have "the direction of war when authorized or begun . . . ."[33]

In light of these prior discussions, the formulation of the war power produced by the Committee of Detail in August assigned to Congress the power to "make" war.[34] At a key debate held on August 17, that power was changed to be a power to "declare" war, an important shift in terminology that presumably speaks to the distribution of powers as between the political branches.[35] On one reading, the shift was intended to accord to the president an ability to repel sudden attacks, even in the absence of congressional authorization, and in that sense (and only that sense) to be able to "make war."[36] While that may be so, the evidence from the debate is fragmentary and inconclusive. At the same time, and given the original decision (as reflected in the Committee of Detail's text) to lodge with Congress a general power to "make war," it is implausible to posit that the Framers suddenly decided, during a very brief debate, to restrict that power solely to the issuance of a formal proclamation of war, something that they were fully aware had largely disappeared from international practice.[37] Brien

---

[31] *Id.* at 65.

[32] *Id.* at 65–67.

[33] *Id.* at 288, 292.

[34] 2 FARRAND'S RECORDS 182.

[35] *Id.* at 314, 318–19. For efforts to interpret the debate, see, for example, H. JEFFERSON POWELL, THE PRESIDENT'S AUTHORITY OVER FOREIGN AFFAIRS: AN ESSAY IN CONSTITUTIONAL INTERPRETATION 115–18 (2002); W. TAYLOR REVELEY III, WAR POWERS OF THE PRESIDENT AND CONGRESS: WHO HOLDS THE ARROWS AND OLIVE BRANCH? 81–85 (1981); Arthur Bestor, *Separation of Powers in the Domain of Foreign Affairs: The Intent of the Constitution Historically Examined,* 5 SETON HALL L. REV. 527, 602–10 (1974); Philip Bobbitt, *War Powers: An Essay on John Hart Ely's* War and Responsibility: Constitutional Lessons of Vietnam and Its Aftermath, 92 MICH. L. REV. 1364, 1378–81 (1994); Charles A. Lofgren, *War-Making Under the Constitution: The Original Understanding,* 81 YALE L.J. 672, 675–77 (1972); William Michael Treanor, *Fame, The Founding, and The Power to Declare War,* 82 CORNELL L. REV. 695, 713–19 (1997).

[36] *See* FRANCIS D. WORMUTH & EDWIN B. FIRMAGE, TO CHAIN THE DOG OF WAR: THE WAR POWER OF CONGRESS IN HISTORY AND LAW 18 (2d ed. 1989) ("The power to initiate war was left to Congress, with the reservation that the President need not await authorization from Congress to repel a sudden attack on the United States."); Raoul Berger, *War-Making by the President,* 121 U. PA. L. REV. 29, 41 (1972) ("Pretty plainly, when Madison and Gerry proposed to *leave* to the President power 'to repel sudden attacks' they reflected Sherman's view that the 'Executive should be able to repel and not to commence war.' ").

[37] *See* REVELEY, *supra* note 35, at 55 (finding that "undeclared war was the norm in eighteenth-century European practice, a reality brought home to Americans when Britain's Seven Years' War with France began on this continent. Thus, the Framers and Ratifiers knew that war might be limited or general, that marque and reprisal were a means of waging limited hostilities, and that even major conflict generally began without prior declaration."); Lofgren, *supra* note 35, at 695 ("It seems

Hallett observes: "[T]he simple fact is that the custom of formally declaring war had gone out of fashion at least a hundred years before the Federal Convention met in Philadelphia. By 1789 no nation was regularly and consistently declaring war formally."[38] Indeed, in the course of the state ratification conventions, Alexander Hamilton observed that "the ceremony of a formal denunciation of war has of late fallen into disuse ...."[39]

Likewise, viewing the power to "declare war" as referring solely to situations where a "formal" or "perfect" state of "war" arose (in other words, a full-scale armed conflict that engaged traditional international law rules applicable to belligerents and neutrals),[40] leaving to the president "imperfect" wars of varying levels of hostility,[41] seems counterintuitive based on the evidence at hand, since no such distinctions were discussed. Rather, of those who spoke at the debate, Pierce Butler was the only Framer who favored lodging with the president a general power to act, and in doing so, he made no distinctions as between different kinds of wars. Everyone else who spoke apparently wanted to keep the power out of the president's hands and in those of Congress, except as necessary to repel sudden attacks. Further, the decision to accord to Congress the power to "grant Letters of Marque and Reprisal," which is essentially a power over whether to unleash a limited form of hostilities against another state, does not sit easily with the idea that it was left to the president to decide whether to pursue hostilities short of "perfect" war.[42]

In sum, the better view is that "declare war" was generally understood by the Framers to be synonymous with "initiating a state of war by a public act" and that "war" can be declared either by "formal announcement" or by "commencing armed hostilities" (i.e., "by Word or Action").[43] Indeed, Michael Ramsey cites to

unlikely, however, that an observer in 1787–88 would have concluded that the Constitution would leave such an important power [the power to wage undeclared war] unvested.").

[38] BRIEN HALLETT, THE LOST ART OF DECLARING WAR 34 (1998); see also BRIEN HALLETT, DECLARING WAR: CONGRESS, THE PRESIDENT, AND WHAT THE CONSTITUTION DOES NOT SAY (2012) ("By 1789 the realities of international practice and custom had already rendered the power to declare war with due ceremony vacuous.").

[39] THE FEDERALIST NO. 25, at 165 (Alexander Hamilton).

[40] See, e.g., Eugene V. Rostow, Great Cases Make Bad Law: The War Powers Act, 50 TEX. L. REV. 833, 850–51 (1972).

[41] See JOHN YOO, THE POWERS OF WAR AND PEACE: THE CONSTITUTION AND FOREIGN AFFAIRS AFTER 9/11, at 148–49 (2005) ("the framers thought of the power to begin hostilities as different from the power to declare war"). See generally John C. Yoo, War and the Constitutional Text, 69 U. CHI. L. REV. 1639 (2002).

[42] U.S. CONST. art. I, § 8, cl. 11.

[43] Michael D. Ramsey, Textualism and War Powers, 69 U. CHI. L. REV. 1543, 1545 (2002) [hereinafter Ramsey, Textualism and War Powers]; see RAMSEY, supra note 2, at 237–38; Michael D. Ramsey, Text and History in the War Powers Debate: A Reply to Professor Yoo, 69 U. CHI. L. REV. 1685 (2002).

several sources, including John Locke,[44] William Blackstone,[45] and Vattel,[46] who regarded the concept of "declare war" as embracing either words or action, and who likely influenced the views of the Framers.[47] At the same time—assuming that the change in language was meant to generally leave with Congress the power to initiate hostilities, while allowing the president the power to repel sudden attacks—the debate did little to clarify exactly where in the constitutional text the president's power to repel sudden attacks could be found and, perhaps more importantly, its exact range.[48]

As the several states contemplated ratification of the Constitution, some attention was paid to the power to make war, as one touchstone for the level of power that would be granted to the new executive.[49] None of these statements indicated that Congress' power was limited solely to the issuance of a formal declaration of war or to placing the United States in a formal or "perfect" state of war. Rather, the dominant claim was that the president was being denied the power on his own to enmesh the nation in hostilities with other nations at whatever level of formality. In *Federalist No. 4*, John Jay indicated the reason for denying extensive war powers to the president: "[A]bsolute monarchs will often make war when their nations are to get nothing by it, but for purposes and objects merely personal, such as a thirst for military glory, revenge for personal affronts, ambition, or private compacts to aggrandize or support their particular families or partisans."[50] Hamilton likewise downplayed the president's powers to take the nation to war. He explained in *Federalist No. 69* that the president's powers were inferior to those of the king and even, to a certain extent, inferior to those of the governor of New York, as the latter always has command of a militia.[51] At the state ratifying conventions, some comments were made on the war power along the lines of *Federalist No. 4* and *No. 69*.[52] Though perhaps ironic today,

---

[44] LOCKE, *supra* note 17, at § 16 ("The *State of War* is a State of Enmity and Destruction; And therefore declaring by Word or Action, not a passionate and hasty, but a sedate setled Design, upon another Mans Life, *puts him in a State of War* with him against whom he has declared such an Intention ....").

[45] 4 WILLIAM BLACKSTONE, COMMENTARIES *71 ("... the crime of *piracy*, or robbery and depredation upon the high seas, is an offence against the universal law of society.... As therefore [a pirate] has renounced all the benefits of society and government, and has reduced himself afresh to the savage state of nature, by declaring war against all mankind, all mankind must declare war against him ....").

[46] 3 EMMER. DE VATTEL, THE LAW OF NATIONS 463, § 225 [1758] (James Brown Scott ed., Charles G. Fenwick trans., 1820) ("For a nation taking up arms against another from that instant declares itself an enemy to all the individuals of the latter, and authorizes them to treat it as such.").

[47] RAMSEY, *supra* note 2, at 227–29.

[48] *See* Bobbitt, *supra* note 35, at 1375–77.

[49] *See* BARRON, *supra* note 15, at 17–33.

[50] THE FEDERALIST No. 4, at 46 (John Jay) ("These and a variety of other motives, which affect only the mind of the sovereign, often lead him to engage in wars not sanctified by justice or the voice and interests of his people.").

[51] *Id.* No. 69, at 417–18 (Alexander Hamilton).

[52] *See, e.g.,* 2 THE DEBATES IN THE SEVERAL STATE CONVENTIONS ON THE ADOPTION OF THE FEDERAL CONSTITUTION 528 (Jonathan Elliot ed., 2d ed. 1901) (James Wilson at Pennsylvania

some Anti-Federalists attacked the Constitution for concentrating too much of the war power in Congress. Patrick Henry complained: "The Congress can both declare war, and carry it on; and levy your money, as long as you have a shilling to pay."[53]

Important statements by the Framers in later years, including those that generally represented opposing views, may help shed light on what was meant by the power to declare war. Madison, the co-author of the "declare war" amendment at the Philadelphia convention, would five years later note that those "who are to *conduct a war* cannot in the nature of things, be proper or safe judges, whether *a war ought* to be *commenced, continued,* or *concluded.*"[54] Moreover, in a letter to Thomas Jefferson a decade after the Philadelphia convention, Madison maintained that "[t]he constitution supposes, what the History of all Govts demonstrates," that the executive is "the branch of power most interested in war, & most prone to it." Therefore, the Constitution had "accordingly with studied care, vested the question of war in the Legisl."[55] Alexander Hamilton, a strong proponent of presidential power, seemed largely in agreement, though protective of the president's power to respond to attacks. Hence, in the context of arguing that President Jefferson could respond to attacks on U.S. vessels by Tripoli, Hamilton explained that the Constitution affirmatively provided Congress the power to declare war, "the plain meaning of which is, that it is the peculiar and exclusive province of Congress, *when the nation is at peace,* to change that state into a state of war; ... in other words, it belongs to Congress only, *to go to war.*"[56]

As discussed later in this chapter, the Constitution more directly allocates the commander-in-chief power to the president in Article II.[57] It is important to acknowledge, though, that this authority was not solely interposed against Congress. Rather, it was commonly understood as ensuring that there would be civilian control over U.S. armed forces; the president was not accorded the power because he (or she) was expected actually to take command in the field, but because the military, including militias, must be controlled by elected and hence accountable officials, who are capable of balancing military strategy with

convention); 4 *id.* at 107–08 (James Iredell at North Carolina convention); *id.* at 287 (Charles Pinckney at South Carolina convention).

[53] 9 THE DOCUMENTARY HISTORY OF THE RATIFICATION OF THE CONSTITUTION 1069 (John P. Kaminski & Gaspare J. Saladino eds., 1990).
[54] James Madison, *Letters of Helvidius No. I, in* 6 THE WRITINGS OF JAMES MADISON 148 (Gaillard Hunt ed., 1900–1910).
[55] Letter from James Madison to Thomas Jefferson (Apr. 2, 1797), *in id.* at 312.
[56] Alexander Hamilton, *Examination of Jefferson's Message to Congress of December 7, 1801, in* 8 THE WORKS OF ALEXANDER HAMILTON 249 (Henry Cabot Lodge ed., 1904).
[57] U.S. CONST. art. II, § 2. For discussion of the commander-in-chief power, see *infra* this chapter § II(B).

political strategy.[58] As such, the vesting of this power in the president did not establish the primacy of the president as a military tactician, much less as the strategic military thinker to whom decisions on initiating armed conflict must be entrusted. James Madison as Helvidius explained how, notwithstanding the commander-in-chief power, the constitutional scheme did not accord to the president power to judge whether to make war. Rather, the "declaring of war is expressly made a legislative function" and the "judging of the obligations to make war, is admitted to be included as a legislative function," such that whenever "a question occurs, whether war shall be declared, or whether public stipulations require it, the question necessarily belongs to the department to which those functions belong—and no other department can be in *the execution of its proper functions*, if it should undertake to decide such a question.[59]

Reflecting on these materials, most commentators are in accord that by locating the power to declare war with Congress, the Framers intended to vest the power to initiate armed conflict with Congress and not the president. For example, Taylor Reveley argues that the Constitution's grant of authority to Congress to declare war and to issue letters of marque and reprisal demonstrates the intent to vest in Congress all control over the resort to force other than to repel sudden attacks.[60] Similarly, Charles Lofgren concludes that "the grants to Congress of power over the declaration of war and issuance of letters of marque and reprisal likely convinced contemporaries even further that the new Congress would have nearly complete authority over the commencement of war."[61] In his study of the subject, John Hart Ely observes that often the "'original understanding' of the document's framers and ratifiers" is hard to divine, but, in the context of the war power, the evidence was clear: "The power to declare war was constitutionally vested in Congress. The debates, and early practice, establish that this meant that all wars, big or small, 'declared' in so many words or not— most weren't, even then—had to be legislatively authorized."[62] Likewise, William Casto notes that "there is no record of any member of the founding generation even stating that the president may lawfully start a war."[63] Jack Rakove finds in the records of the convention "that the framers believed that questions of war and peace—that is, the most critical subjects of foreign policy—were appropriate

[58] The most famous example of the exercise of civilian control over the military may be President Harry Truman's decision to relieve General Douglas MacArthur of command of U.S. forces in Korea during the Korean War, due to concern that MacArthur's strategy would embroil the United States in armed conflict with communist China.

[59] Madison, *supra* note 54, at 153 (emphasis in original).

[60] REVELEY, *supra* note 35, at 63.

[61] Lofgren, *supra* note 35, at 700.

[62] JOHN HART ELY, WAR AND RESPONSIBILITY: CONSTITUTIONAL LESSONS OF VIETNAM AND ITS AFTERMATH 3 (1993) (footnote omitted).

[63] WILLIAM R. CASTO, FOREIGN AFFAIRS AND THE CONSTITUTION IN THE AGE OF FIGHTING SAIL 189 (2006).

subjects for legislative determination rather than an inherent prerogative of executive power."[64] Abraham Sofaer maintains that "[t]he power to 'declare' war could not tenably be read, after examining both the Convention and ratification processes, as limiting Congress' control to formal war-making. Congress was seen by all who commented on the issue as possessing exclusive control of the means of war."[65] Stephen Griffin concludes that "there was no one in the early republic who even attempted to make the case that the war power was executive in nature."[66]

C. Historical Practice

On eleven occasions and during five wars—beginning in 1812 and most recently in 1942—Congress has declared war, in each instance after receiving a request to that effect from the president. Nevertheless, as indicated in the following subsections, the United States has initiated or responded to armed conflict many times without a declaration of war, sometimes on the basis of other forms of statutory authorization by Congress, sometimes on the basis of implied authorization from Congress, and sometimes on the basis of presidential decision alone. This section recounts some of the key historical practice in initiation of armed conflict by the United States since 1789.

1. Early Precedents: 1789 to the Civil War

Early Conflicts with Indian Tribes. The earliest use of the war power under the U.S. Constitution concerned actions against Indian tribes along the new nation's western frontier. Congress adopted in 1789 a statute providing for the pay of officers and privates in the service of the United States and providing that "the said troops shall be governed by the rules and articles of war which have been established by the United States in Congress assembled, or by such rules and

[64] Jack N. Rakove, *Solving a Constitutional Puzzle: The Treatymaking Clause as a Case Study*, 1 PERSP. AM. HIST. 233, 239 (1984).

[65] ABRAHAM D. SOFAER, WAR, FOREIGN AFFAIRS AND CONSTITUTIONAL POWER: THE ORIGINS 56 (1976) (citation omitted).

[66] STEPHEN M. GRIFFIN, LONG WARS AND THE CONSTITUTION 22 (2013); *see also* LOUIS FISHER, PRESIDENTIAL WAR POWER 8–9 (3d ed. 2013) ("The President never received a general power to deploy troops whenever and wherever he thought best, and the framers did not authorize him to take the country into full-scale war or to mount an offensive attack against another nation."); HAROLD HONGJU KOH, THE NATIONAL SECURITY CONSTITUTION: SHARING POWER AFTER THE IRAN-CONTRA AFFAIR 76 (1990) (finding that the Framers rejected "the English model of a king who possessed both the power to declare war and the authority to command troops"); WORMUTH & FIRMAGE, *supra* note 36, at 17–31 (discussing the war clause); David Gray Adler, *Courts, Constitution, and Foreign Affairs, in* THE CONSTITUTION AND THE CONDUCT OF AMERICAN FOREIGN POLICY 19 (David Gray Adler & Larry N. George eds., 1996) (finding that the Constitution "makes Congress the sole and exclusive repository of the ultimate foreign relations power—the authority to initiate war").

articles of war, as may hereafter by law be established."[67] Initially, there were only a few hundred men directly serving in the U.S. military; instead, reliance was principally on using the militias of the several states.[68] Consequently, the same statute authorized the president "to call into service from time to time, such part of the militia of the states respectively, as he may judge necessary" for the purpose of "protecting the inhabitants of the frontiers of the United States from the hostile incursions of the Indians."[69] The following year a more comprehensive statute created a permanent military establishment, organizing U.S. forces into regiments and battalions, though the state militias remained the primary source for obtaining troops.[70]

President Washington used these authorities in 1791 to instruct the governor of the Northwest Territory (territory west of Pennsylvania and northwest of the Ohio River), Arthur St. Clair, to pursue a peace treaty with the relevant Indian tribes if possible, but to use force, if necessary, to protect U.S. settlements. Although St. Clair was a major general in the Revolutionary War, he proceeded to lead U.S. Army components and detachments from the militias of Pennsylvania and Virginia to the worst defeat the U.S. Army ever experienced in the Indian wars.[71] The defeat spawned an investigation in which Congress reviewed executive branch documents, interviewed department heads and other witnesses, and obtained a written statement from General St. Clair, a process that triggered the first claims of executive privilege to withhold sensitive information.[72]

Despite that defeat, President Washington continued efforts to secure the safety of U.S. nationals from Indian attacks, though the correspondence of the period establishes that he drew a distinction between "defensive" measures and "offensive" operations, with the latter having to be authorized by Congress.[73] For example, writing in 1793 to Governor William Moultrie of Georgia, he maintained: "The Constitution vests the power of declaring war with Congress; therefore no offensive expedition of importance can be undertaken until after they shall have deliberated upon the subject, and authorized such a measure."[74]

[67] Act of Sept. 29, 1789, ch. 25, §§ 2, 4, 1 Stat. 95, 96. The statute thus maintained rules previously established by the Continental Congress for regulation of its military forces.

[68] For a discussion of the federal government's powers as they relate to militias, see *infra* this chapter § III(C).

[69] Act of Sept. 29, 1789, § 5, 1 Stat. at 96.

[70] Act of Apr. 30, 1790, ch. 10, 1 Stat. 119.

[71] More than six hundred soldiers and many women and children were killed in what became known as the Battle of Wabash, near the headwaters of the Wabash River. *See* WILLIAM H. GUTHMAN, MARCH TO MASSACRE: A HISTORY OF THE FIRST SEVEN YEARS OF THE UNITED STATES ARMY 1784–1791, at 243–44 (1970).

[72] FISHER, *supra* note 66, at 17–18.

[73] *Id.* at 18–20; SOFAER, *supra* note 65, at 121–27. *See generally* WILEY SWORD, PRESIDENT WASHINGTON'S INDIAN WAR: THE STRUGGLE FOR THE OLD NORTHWEST, 1790–1795 (1985).

[74] *Letter from President George Washington to Governor William Moultrie (Aug. 28, 1793), in* 33 THE WRITINGS OF GEORGE WASHINGTON 73 (John C. Fitzpatrick ed., 1940); *see also* ALEXANDER DECONDE, THE QUASI-WAR: THE POLITICS AND DIPLOMACY OF THE UNDECLARED WAR WITH

Even so, as Louis Fisher notes, "[a]s the years progressed, the distinction between defensive and offensive actions on Indian policy gradually blurred ... Presidential policies of restraint carried only so much weight in a country that was expanding in size and highly decentralized."[75]

Washington's Neutrality Proclamation. Worried that private actions might entangle the United States in the war between England and France, President Washington issued his Proclamation of Neutrality in 1793, which both declared U.S. neutrality in that conflict and threatened legal action against any U.S. national providing assistance to either foreign state. Issuance of the proclamation sparked the famous "Pacificus/Helvidius" debate between Alexander Hamilton and James Madison over whether such action intruded upon Congress' war powers. Hamilton argued that the proclamation was a permissible act by the president as the *"organ* of intercourse between the Nation and foreign Nations," as well as the "interpreter" of existing treaties—an act designed to maintain peace.[76] Madison rebuked the assertion of any broad presidential power relating to matters of war and peace, saying that such matters were assigned to Congress.[77] Despite the difference, both writers assumed that, under the Constitution, the authority to resort to war resided with the Congress.[78] In any event, since actual efforts to pursue prosecutions failed on grounds that any crime cannot be based solely on a presidential proclamation,[79] involvement of the Congress became necessary, leading to the adoption in 1794 of the Neutrality Act and its successors.[80]

Quasi-War with France. During the "quasi-war" with France in the late 1790s there occurred a considerable expansion of the U.S. military establishment in anticipation of a possible invasion.[81] Moreover, there emerged the precedent of

FRANCE 1797–1801, at 122 (1966) (recounting that former President Washington—in response to a possible invasion of Louisiana and the Floridas—said that he "opposed all offensive operations against Spanish territory without a declaration of war").

[75] FISHER, *supra* note 66, at 20.
[76] Alexander Hamilton, Pacificus No. 1 (June 29, 1793), *reprinted in* 15 THE PAPERS OF ALEXANDER HAMILTON 38 (Harold C. Syrett & Jacob E. Cooke eds., 1969).
[77] Madison, *supra* note 54, at 152.
[78] *See* GRIFFIN, *supra* note 66, at 22. Hamilton's position is best conceived as arguing that the president could *affect* Congress' power to declare war when exercising executive functions, such as when determining U.S. obligations under treaties. *See* SOFAER, *supra* note 65, at 112–13.
[79] *See, e.g.,* Henfield's Case, 11 F. Cas. 1099 (D. Pa. 1793) (No. 6,360), in which the jury proved unwilling to convict Henfield based on arguments that he had violated a common law crime.
[80] Neutrality Act of 1794, ch. 50, 1 Stat. 381; *see* Glass v. Sloop Betsey, 3 U.S. (3 Dall.) 6 (1794); Application of the Neutrality Act to Official Government Activities, 8 Op. O.L.C. 58, 59–72 (1984); WILLIAM R. CASTO, THE SUPREME COURT IN THE EARLY REPUBLIC: THE CHIEF JUSTICESHIPS OF JOHN JAY AND OLIVER ELLSWORTH 82–84 (1995); Martin S. Flaherty, *The Story of the Neutrality Controversy: Struggling Over Presidential Power Outside the Courts, in* PRESIDENTIAL POWER STORIES 21 (Christopher H. Schroeder & Curtis A. Bradley, eds. 2008).
[81] *See* Act of Mar. 2, 1799, ch. 31, §§ 1–9, 1 Stat. 725, 725–26; Act of July 16, 1798, ch. 76, § 2, 1 Stat. 604, 604; Act of May 28, 1798, ch. 47, 1 Stat. 558. *See generally* Dean Alfange, Jr., *The Quasi-War and*

congressional support for the recourse to force against a foreign state by means of statutory authorizations on funding, naval armament, raising of forces, and the use of force, rather than by means of a formal declaration of war.[82] Indeed, this period confirms the allocation to Congress of the power to decide whether the nation should formally declare war or should instead pursue aggressive measures short of such a declaration.[83]

Thus, rather than request a formal declaration of war, President John Adams in May 1797 and March 1798 asked Congress for statutory authority to use the U.S. Navy to protect U.S. shipping.[84] Congress granted the request by authorizing the president to instruct his commanders to bring into port any "armed vessels" operating under the authority of France found "hovering" off the U.S. coast "for the purpose of committing depredations" on U.S. commercial vessels (and to retake any U.S. commercial vessels that had been seized).[85] In a subsequent statute, the president was authorized to condemn the goods found on those vessels, provided they had not been previously seized by the French from U.S. nationals.[86] Shortly thereafter, Congress authorized the president to instruct his commanders "to "subdue, seize and take *any* armed French vessel, which shall be found within the jurisdictional limits of the United States, or elsewhere, on the high seas . . ." and to commission private U.S. vessels to engage in comparable actions.[87]

During this period, the Supreme Court weighed in, through several significant cases, concerning the executive–congressional roles in the exercise of the war power. In *Talbot v. Seeman*, Chief Justice John Marshall wrote for a unanimous Court that "[t]he whole powers of war [are], by the constitution of the United States, vested in congress . . ." and that "congress may authorize general hostilities . . . or partial hostilities . . . ."[88]

In *Bas v. Tingy*, the Supreme Court determined whether a 1799 statute that used the term "enemy" should apply to circumstances arising during the U.S.-France "quasi-war." Justice Bushrod Washington noted that the case raised the general question of whether the United States was at "war" at all. He found that where Congress declares war upon a foreign state there is a "perfect" war, but that Congress can also authorize the use of military force through statutes, thereby

---

Presidential Warmaking, in THE CONSTITUTION AND THE CONDUCT OF AMERICAN FOREIGN POLICY, *supra* note 66, at 274; BARRON, *supra* note 15, at 35–55.

[82] For early statutory authorizations providing for the purchasing, arming, and manning of naval vessels, see Act of July 1, 1797, ch. 7, 1 Stat. 523; Act of Mar. 27, 1794, ch. 12, 1 Stat. 350.

[83] *See* SOFAER, *supra* note 65, at 139–66.

[84] *See* 1 A COMPILATION OF THE MESSAGES AND PAPERS OF THE PRESIDENTS 233–39, 264–65 (James D. Richardson ed., 1904) (messages of President Adams to Congress).

[85] Act of May 28, 1798, ch. 48, 1 Stat. 561.

[86] Act of June 28, 1798, ch. 62, § 1, 1 Stat. 574, 574.

[87] Act of July 9, 1798, ch. 68, §§ 1–2, 1 Stat. 578, 578–79 (emphasis added).

[88] Talbot v. Seeman, 5 U.S. (1 Cranch) 1, 28 (1801).

establishing a war that is "limited" or "imperfect."[89] Thus, Justice Washington advanced a broad notion of "war"; he maintained that "public war" "is an external contention by force, between some of the members of the two nations, authorised by the legitimate powers."[90] In this situation, given that Congress had raised an army, suspended commerce with France, and terminated a treaty with France, an "imperfect war" existed, allowing France to be qualified as an enemy under the 1799 statute. In such a situation, "those who are authorised to commit hostilities, act under special authority, and can go no farther than to the extent of their commission."[91]

That last assertion was directly confirmed in *Little v. Barreme*. There, the Court made clear that congressional restrictions contained within war-related statutes limited the president's discretion, such as only authorizing the executive to seize U.S. vessels on the high seas that were sailing *to* French ports and not those sailing *from* French ports to the United States.[92] Chief Justice Marshall noted in dicta that, even if the president might have acted this way (e.g., seizing U.S. vessels sailing from French ports) in the absence of congressional authority on the basis of his own constitutional power, once Congress imposed a restriction on the president's action then the president must conform to that restriction.[93] Similar statutory restrictions on presidential authority resided in the Neutrality Act, including restricting the president from authorizing certain types of private military actions.[94]

Barbary Pirates. During the 1790s, the United States slipped into a practice of paying "tributes" (or bribes) to pirate chieftains located along the Barbary Coast of North Africa, in exchange for their leaving U.S. commercial vessels alone.[95] Determined to cease these payments, President Jefferson in May 1801 directed

---

[89] Bas v. Tingy, 4 U.S. (4 Dall.) 37, 40–41 (1800) (Washington, J.). Justice Chase concurred that "Congress is empowered to declare a general war, or congress may wage a limited war; limited in place, in objects, and in time. If a general war is declared, its extent and operations are only restricted and regulated by the *jus belli*, forming a part of the law of nations; but if a partial war is waged, its extent and operation depend upon our municipal laws." *Id.* at 43.

[90] *Id.* at 40.

[91] *Id.* Justice Paterson agreed that Congress may authorize war "as to certain objects, and to a certain extent...." *Id.* at 45.

[92] *See* Little v. Barreme, 6 U.S. (2 Cranch) 170 (1804) (applying Act of Feb. 9, 1799, ch. 2, § 1, 1 Stat. 613, 613–14).

[93] *See id.* at 177–78. For statutory restrictions relating to the treatment of French nationals and other persons detained by U.S. forces, see Act of Feb. 28, 1799, ch. 18, 3 Stat. 624; Act of Mar. 3, 1799, ch. 45, 3 Stat. 743; Act of July 9, 1798, ch. 68, § 8, 2 Stat. 578, 580; Act of June 28, 1798, ch. 62, § 4, 2 Stat. 574, 575.

[94] *See* United States v. Smith, 27 Fed. Cas. 1192, 1229–30 (D.N.Y. 1806) (No. 16,342) (denying that an alleged presidential authorization to pursue private military actions against Spain could supersede the Neutrality Act); Overview of the Neutrality Act, 8 Op. O.L.C. 209, 211 (1984).

[95] SOFAER, *supra* note 65, at 208–24; Gerhard Casper, *The Washington Administration, Congress and Algiers, in* THE CONSTITUTION AND THE CONDUCT OF AMERICAN FOREIGN POLICY, *supra* note 66, at 259. For discussion of an earlier attempt to establish a "special confederation" between the United States and European powers to address this problem, see Chapter 7 § I(A).

U.S. Navy frigates to go to the Mediterranean to protect U.S. vessels and, in the event that the Barbary powers declared war on the United States, to use force against the pirate vessels "to protect our commerce & chastise their insolence."[96] The president indicated that he was acting based on an existing statute, but there was no express authority from Congress in that statute to engage in such military action.[97] In December 1801, the president asked Congress for authorization to use U.S. naval vessels to protect U.S. shipping in the Mediterranean, including "offensive" naval action.[98] Congress then adopted a statute, in February 1802, authorizing the use of U.S. naval vessels "for protecting effectually the commerce and seamen thereof on the Atlantic ocean, the Mediterranean and adjoining seas" and "to subdue, seize and make prize of all vessels, goods and effects, belonging to the Bey of Tripoli, or to his subjects . . . and also cause to be done all such other acts of precaution or hostility as the state of war will justify, and may, in his opinion, require."[99]

Thereafter, armed conflict did occur, including ultimately the Battle of Derne at Tripoli in 1805. Over the years, many have debated the significance of the initial stages of this conflict, with some emphasizing the president's action as unilateral in nature and others emphasizing the existence of statutes supporting the president's authority.[100] The most salient point, however, may be that President Jefferson, while acknowledging that he had sent the squadron to the Mediterranean, informed Congress that he was "[u]nauthorized by the Constitution, without the sanction of Congress, to go beyond the line of defense" and that it was for Congress to authorize "measures of offense."[101] President Jefferson's cautionary assertion triggered a strong reaction from Alexander Hamilton, writing as Lucius Crassus, to the effect that the president was being

---

[96] 1 Naval Documents Related to the United States Wars with the Barbary Powers 467 (1939).

[97] Act of Mar. 3, 1801, ch. 20, § 2, 2 Stat. 110, 110 (1801) (authorizing six frigates to be "officered and manned as the President of the United States may direct . . .").

[98] See 1 A Compilation of the Messages and Papers of the Presidents, supra note 84, at 326–27 (message of President Jefferson to Congress).

[99] Act of Feb. 6, 1802, ch. 4, §§ 1–2, 2 Stat. 129, 129–30. The statute accorded the president authority to commission private U.S. vessels to engage in comparable actions. For a similar statutory authority granted by Congress in 1815 to President Madison to suppress pirate actions against U.S. commercial vessels off the coast of Algeria, see Act of Mar. 3, 1815, ch. 90, 3 Stat. 230. Pirate attacks on U.S. commercial vessels in the Caribbean and Latin America prompted Congress to adopt in 1819 a more general authority for the president to use "the public armed vessels" of the United States as he deemed necessary to protect "the merchant vessels of the United States and their crews from piratical aggressions and depredations." That authority now appears at 33 U.S.C. § 381 (2018).

[100] Compare Presidential Power to Use the Armed Forces Abroad Without Statutory Authorization, 4A Op. O.L.C. 185, 187 (1980) (finding President Jefferson's action as early confirmation of the president's power to act without congressional authorization), with Fisher, supra note 66, at 35 (finding that "in at least ten statutes, Congress explicitly authorized military action by Presidents Jefferson and Madison" against the Barbary powers).

[101] 1 A Compilation of the Messages and Papers of the Presidents, supra note 84, at 327.

far too deferential to congressional prerogatives, given that the Barbary Powers had declared war on the United States.[102] Both leaders appeared to agree that the president could act alone defensively and that offensive action required congressional consent, but they disagreed as to what constituted "defensive" action, with Hamilton arguing that once another nation declares war, the U.S. response is defensive.

War of 1812. Congress' first declaration of war came in 1812, after President Madison informed it in June of various hostile actions by England, principally concerning the treatment of U.S. merchant vessels and seamen on the high seas and the blockading of U.S. ports.[103] The declaration took the form of a bill enacted by both Houses and signed into law by President Madison.[104] In the course of prosecuting the war, President Madison called up the militias of the several states pursuant to a 1795 statute that authorized doing so "to execute the laws of the Union, suppress insurrections, and repel invasions," an authority later confirmed by the Supreme Court.[105] In anticipation of significant military encounters, Congress adopted various statutes concerning the treatment of British prisoners.[106] Further, a statute originally adopted amidst the "quasi-war" with France (commonly known as the Alien Enemies Act) was used to detain and deport male British nationals older than thirteen found in the United States.[107] The war, however, proved costly to the United States; it severely damaged the U.S. economy and entailed a British invasion that burned the U.S. Capitol, the White House, and numerous executive branch buildings. The Treaty of Ghent signed in December 1814 and ratified in February 1815 ended the war.[108]

One important case that arose from the war concerned the president's power to condemn five hundred tons of timber in the United States that belonged to enemy aliens (i.e., British nationals). While seizure of the property of enemy

---

[102] 7 THE WORKS OF ALEXANDER HAMILTON 745–47 (John C. Hamilton ed., 1851); 25 THE PAPERS OF ALEXANDER HAMILTON 454–56 (Harold C. Syrett & Jacob E. Cooke, eds., 1977).

[103] For Madison's request to Congress, see 1 A COMPILATION OF THE MESSAGES AND PAPERS OF THE PRESIDENTS, *supra* note 84, at 499–505; *see* BARRON, *supra* note 15, at 83–97.

[104] Act of June 18, 1812, ch. 102, 1 Stat. 755. The vote in the House on June 4 was 79 to 49. The vote in the Senate on June 17 was 19 to 13.

[105] Act of Feb. 28, 1795, ch. 36, 2 Stat. 424 [hereinafter Militia Act of 1795]; Martin v. Mott, 25 U.S. (12 Wheat.) 19, 29 (1827).

[106] *See* Act of Mar. 3, 1813, ch. 61, § 1, 2 Stat. 829, 829–30; Act of July 6, 1812, ch. 128, 1 Stat. 777; Act of June 26, 1812, ch. 107, § 7, 1 Stat. 759, 761.

[107] Act of July 6, 1798, ch. 66, 2 Stat. 577 (codified as amended at 50 U.S.C. §§ 21–24 (2018)). The statute required the president to allow such noncitizens to remove or dispose of their property.

[108] Treaty of Peace and Amity, Between his Britannic Majesty and the United States of America, Dec. 24, 1814, 8 Stat. 218. Despite the obvious vulnerability of the United States to the European powers, as demonstrated in the War of 1812, within just a few years President James Monroe would articulate what would become "The Monroe Doctrine." The 1823 doctrine warned European nations that, as a matter of policy, the United States would not accept any further colonization or puppet monarchs in the Western Hemisphere. 2 A COMPILATION OF THE MESSAGES AND PAPERS OF THE PRESIDENTS 218 (James D. Richardson, ed., 1904).

aliens in time of war was fully permitted under international law at that time, Chief Justice Marshall found that such power did not reside in the president, at least when the property was located in the United States. Rather, in *Brown v. United States*, Justice Marshall found that such a seizure required statutory authorization: "[I]n this country, from the structure of our government, proceedings to condemn the property of an enemy found within our territory at the declaration of war, can be sustained only upon the principle that they are instituted in execution of some existing law . . . ."[109] With no such statutory authorization in existence, and with Congress' declaration of war alone being insufficient authorization, the president's action was invalid and the condemnation of the property was annulled. The case indicated an early belief that war powers permitted to a sovereign under international law do not rest, under U.S. law, solely with the president, even in circumstances where Congress has declared war.

This period also demonstrated the possibility of the president seeking a declaration of war from Congress, but instead being provided with statutory authorization to use force without such a declaration. President Madison in 1815 wished to pursue military action against Algeria, which had been seizing U.S. commercial vessels operating in the Mediterranean, and to that end sought a declaration of war against "the Dey and Regency of Algiers."[110] Rather than issue a formal declaration of war, Congress adopted legislation authorizing the president to use the U.S Navy to protect U.S. commerce and seamen, to seize all vessels, goods, and effects belonging to Algeria, "and, also, to cause to be done all such other acts of precaution or hostility, as the state of war will justify, and may in his opinion require."[111]

In the following years, Congress adopted statutes authorizing the president to use public armed vessels as necessary to protect U.S. commercial vessels from piracy, a particular problem in Caribbean and Latin American waters, including by attacking and seizing pirates and their vessels.[112] As such, Congress' ability to authorize uses of force could be seen operating, even during this early period, in the context of U.S. use of force against nonstate actors.

Mexican-American War. As the United States expanded its territory to encompass lands claimed by other nations, resort to the war power became a recurrent

---

[109] Brown v. United States, 12 U.S. (8 Cranch) 110, 123 (1814). A different result may arise if the seizure occurs outside U.S. territory, such as during enforcement of a blockade. *See* HENKIN, FOREIGN AFFAIRS, at 104. Moreover, *Brown* may no longer be good law, given that the Court, in *The Prize Cases*, 67 U.S. (2 Black) 635, 671–74 (1863), sustained President Lincoln's ability on his own authority to seize enemy property in war, even when found in the United States. The most famous "seizure" of such "property" during wartime may be President Lincoln's January 1863 Emancipation Proclamation, which freed all the slaves in the ten states that were still in rebellion.

[110] For Madison's request to Congress, see 1 A COMPILATION OF THE MESSAGES AND PAPERS OF THE PRESIDENTS, *supra* note 84, at 554.

[111] Act of March 3, 1815, ch. 90, § 2, 3 Stat. 230, 230.

[112] Such statutes remain largely intact in 33 U.S.C. §§ 381–87.

phenomenon. In 1836, Texas announced its secession from Mexico, but the latter continued to view the former as its province. In 1845, the United States annexed Texas, sparking tensions between the two nations. In May 1846, President Polk ordered General Zachary Taylor to move U.S. forces into territory along the U.S.-Mexico border that was in dispute. Thereafter, a military clash between U.S. and Mexican forces—which included battles at Palo Alto and Resaca de la Palma—prompted President Polk to inform Congress that Mexico "has passed the boundary of the United States, has invaded our territory and shed American blood upon the American soil," and hence to request a declaration of war.[113]

After a heated debate in Congress, in which opponents lamented that the president's own actions had triggered the hostilities, Congress approved on May 11–12 its second declaration of war, a bill entitled "providing for the Prosecution of the existing War between the United States and the Republic of Mexico," which was signed into law by President Polk.[114] The declaration was a recognition that war already existed and essentially served to vindicate the president's actions in responding to that war.[115] Two years of war ensued, the first U.S. war fought principally on foreign soil. The war ended with the 1848 Treaty of Guadalupe Hidalgo, by which Mexico lost more than one-third of its territory (including present-day Arizona, California, and New Mexico), and the Rio Grande became the southern boundary of Texas.[116] Despite those gains, congressional concern (principally by the Whig Party) that the president had "unnecessarily and unconstitutionally" precipitated the war resulted in an 1848 vote of censure by the House of Representatives.[117]

Greytown Incident. In the wake of the Mexican–American War, the U.S. role as a power in the Western Hemisphere grew dramatically. A vivid example of that power was the 1854 bombardment by the *U.S.S. Cyane* of Greytown (presently San Juan del Norte), a port town of Nicaragua where U.S. nationals and the U.S. consulate had purportedly suffered injuries and losses. When the town leaders declined to make amends, the *Cyane* bombarded the city for a day and then sent forces ashore to destroy the town. Foreign states roundly condemned the bombardment, but President Franklin Pierce defended it as an appropriate measure for protecting U.S. nationals and property.[118] In a civil suit by a town

---

[113] 4 A COMPILATION OF THE MESSAGES AND PAPERS OF THE PRESIDENTS 442 (James D. Richardson ed., 1904); *see* CAROL CHRISTENSEN & THOMAS CHRISTENSEN, THE U.S.-MEXICAN WAR (1998).

[114] Act of May 13, 1846, ch. 16, 9 Stat. 9. The vote in the House on May 11 was 174 to 14. The vote in the Senate on May 12 was 40 to 2.

[115] For the Supreme Court's characterization of the declaration years later, see The Prize Cases, 67 U.S. (2 Black) 635, 668 (1863).

[116] Treaty of Peace, Friendship, Limits, and Settlement between the United States and the Republic of Mexico, Feb. 2, 1848, 9 Stat. 922.

[117] CONG. GLOBE, 30th Cong., 1st Sess. 95 (1848). The vote was 85 to 81.

[118] 5 A COMPILATION OF THE MESSAGES AND PAPERS OF THE PRESIDENTS 280–84 (James D. Richardson ed., 1904).

resident brought in U.S. courts, a federal circuit court upheld the president's actions, noting that "as it respects the interposition of the executive abroad, for the protection of the lives or property of the citizen, the duty must, of necessity, rest in the discretion of the president."[119] Indeed, the court observed that "[a]cts of lawless violence, or of threatened violence to the citizen or his property, cannot be anticipated and provided for; and the protection, to be effectual or of any avail, may, not unfrequently, require the most prompt and decided action."[120]

The incident evoked concerns from some members of Congress, who claimed that the president was overstepping his authority by engaging in such reprisals.[121] In 1868, Congress enacted the Hostage Act, which directs the president to pursue diplomacy to secure the release of any U.S. national deprived of his or her liberty, failing which he may only use means "not amounting to acts of war."[122] That statute, with some modification, remains in force today.[123]

The Greytown bombardment may be contrasted with a different incident, arising in the same time frame, regarding presidential power to secure U.S. interests abroad. In *Chae Chan Ping v. United States (The Chinese Exclusion Case)*, the Supreme Court recounted how, in 1856, the president had been asked to provide U.S. naval forces for a British-led military expedition to secure French, U.K., and U.S. commercial interests in China. According to the Court, "England requested of the President the concurrence and active co-operation of the United States similar to that which France had accorded, and to authorize our naval and political authorities to act in concert with the allied forces."[124] Yet, because doing so would involve the United States participating in existing hostilities, the request was denied, "and the Secretary of State in his communication to the English government explained that the war-making power of the United States was not vested in the President but in Congress, and that he had no authority, therefore, to order aggressive hostilities to be undertaken."[125]

2. Civil War to 1950: Emergence as a Global Military Power

U.S. Civil War. Faced with the secession of several southern states, as well as the seizure of and attack on federal installations, President Abraham Lincoln upon assuming office in April 1861 exercised a range of war powers without waiting for Congress to return from recess,[126] including blockading southern ports,[127]

---

[119] Durand v. Hollins, 8 F. Cas. 111, 112 (S.D.N.Y. 1860) (No. 4,186).
[120] *Id.*
[121] *See, e.g.*, CONG. GLOBE, 33d Cong., 2d Sess. 951 (1855).
[122] Act of July 27, 1868, ch. 249, § 3, 15 Stat. 223, 224.
[123] *See infra* this chapter text accompanying note 482.
[124] Chae Chan Ping v. United States (The Chinese Exclusion Case), 130 U.S. 581, 591 (1889). For further discussion of this case, see Chapter 1 § I(D) and Chapter 10 § III(A)(1).
[125] *The Chinese Exclusion Case*, 130 U.S. at 591.
[126] *See* BARRON, *supra* note 15, at 131–59.
[127] *See* The Prize Cases, 67 U.S. (2 Black) 635, 665–71 (1863).

suspending[128] the writ of habeas corpus,[129] and raising military forces from state militias.[130]

In 1863, the Supreme Court considered the legality of seizures made during the president's blockade prior to congressional approval. In *The Prize Cases*, the Court sought to delineate the roles of the Congress and the president in the context of an internal insurrection by advancing several propositions: (1) "Congress alone has the power to declare a national or foreign war"; (2) Congress "cannot declare war against a State, or any number of States, by virtue of any clause in the Constitution"; (3) the Constitution confers on the president the executive power, and he is bound to take care that the laws are faithfully executed; (4) moreover, the president is commander-in-chief of the army and navy and of the militia of the several States when called into service; (5) on the one hand, the president "has no power to initiate or declare a war either against a foreign nation or a domestic State"; and (6) on the other hand, by virtue of statutes adopted in 1795 and 1807, the president "is authorized to call out the militia and use the military and naval forces of the United States in case of invasion by foreign nations, and to suppress insurrection against the government of a State or of the United States."[131]

In some instances, the exercise of such powers prompted challenges in U.S. courts to the effect that the president had acted unconstitutionally. A notable example concerned Lieutenant John Merryman, an officer of the Maryland militia, who was alleged to have committed treasonous acts, such as cutting telegraph wires and burning bridges to impede the movement of Union forces. After Merryman was detained in May 1861 at Fort McHenry in Baltimore, a Maryland judge issued a writ of habeas corpus to the commander of the fort, who responded that the writ had been suspended by the president. In *Ex parte Merryman*, Chief Justice Roger Taney, sitting as a federal circuit court judge, confirmed the issuance of the writ, finding that the president lacked any authority to suspend habeas corpus, including an authority based on presidential war powers. According to Chief Justice Taney, "if the authority which the constitution has confided to the judiciary department and judicial officers, may thus,

---

[128] The president and his military officials are not able to "suspend" the power of courts to issue writs; what is actually meant by such a "suspension" is that executive officials will not follow normal procedural requirements for detention of persons and will not enforce orders by courts relating to writs of habeas corpus. *See* David J. Barron & Martin S. Lederman, *The Commander in Chief at the Lowest Ebb—A Constitutional History*, 121 HARV. L. REV. 941, 999 (2008).

[129] For the president's order of April 27, 1861, see 7 A COMPILATION OF THE MESSAGES AND PAPERS OF THE PRESIDENTS 3219 (James D. Richardson ed., 1904). Subsequent orders expanded the locations where the writ could be suspended.

[130] President Lincoln's action in calling up the militia appears to have been based on the Militia Act of 1795, discussed *supra* note 105, among others.

[131] *The Prize Cases*, 67 U.S. (2 Black) at 668. For the referenced statutes, see the Militia Act of 1795, *supra* note 105, and the Insurrection Act of 1807, ch. 39, 2 Stat. 443 (codified at 10 U.S.C. §§ 251–55 (2018)).

upon any pretext or under any circumstances, be usurped by the military power, at its discretion, the people of the United States are no longer living under a government of laws . . . ."[132]

President Lincoln disregarded the ruling, arguing that the Suspension Clause in the Constitution empowered the president to suspend the privilege of the writ of habeas corpus, at least when Congress was not in session. Upon Congress' return in July, he explained the necessity for taking such action, whether viewed as legal or illegal. Tacitly conceding that the suspension order was constitutionally suspect, he famously (and rhetorically) asked: "Are all the laws *but one* to go unexecuted, and the Government itself go to pieces lest that one be violated?"[133] At the same time, President Lincoln accepted that his conduct was subject to congressional control; Congress could approve, disapprove, or limit the president's action.[134] Indeed, President Lincoln asked for Congress' approval of the various actions he had taken.[135] Congress responded in August 1861 by adopting a statute approving, legalizing, and making valid "all the acts, proclamations, and orders of the President" since March 4, 1861, "respecting the army and navy of the United States . . . with the same effect as if they had been issued and done under the previous express authority and direction of the Congress of the United States."[136]

Thereafter, much of President Lincoln's actions during the Civil War fell within the ambit of statutory authorizations, with Congress conducting considerable oversight of executive actions through its Joint Committee on the Conduct of the War. Moreover, limitations set by Congress on the exercise of presidential war powers were later upheld by the Supreme Court.[137] As for the detention of suspected Southern sympathizers, in February 1862 the president (through the

---

[132] *Ex parte* Merryman, 17 F. Cas. 144, 152 (D. Md. 1861) (No. 9,487). For commentary, see BRIAN McGINTY, THE BODY OF JOHN MERRYMAN: ABRAHAM LINCOLN AND THE SUSPENSION OF HABEAS CORPUS (2011); JONATHAN W. WHITE, ABRAHAM LINCOLN AND TREASON IN THE CIVIL WAR: THE TRIALS OF JOHN MERRYMAN (2011); Daniel A. Farber, *Lincoln, Presidential Power, and the Rule of Law*, 113 Nw. U. L. REV. 667, 681–85 (2018).

[133] 6 A COMPILATION OF THE MESSAGES AND PAPERS OF THE PRESIDENTS 25 (James D. Richardson ed., 1909).

[134] *Id.* ("Whether there shall be any legislation upon the subject, and, if any, what, is submitted entirely to the better judgment of Congress.").

[135] *Id.* at 31.

[136] Act of Aug. 6, 1861, ch. 63, § 3, 12 Stat. 326, 326. The statute did not expressly address suspension of the writ of habeas corpus, leading some to express uncertainty as to whether it did so. *See* NOAH FELDMAN, THE BROKEN CONSTITUTION: LINCOLN, SLAVERY, AND THE REFOUNDING OF AMERICA 210 (2021) (finding only that it was "conceivable" that the president's directive to General Winfield Scott regarding military arrests without charge counted as an order "respecting the army"). Congress only expressly addressed the issue some two years later in the Habeas Corpus Suspension Act, 12 Stat. 755 (1863), in language that was ambiguous as to retroactivity. *See* FELDMAN at 223–24.

[137] *Ex parte* Milligan, 71 U.S. (4 Wall.) 2 (1866) (finding that trials of civilians by presidentially created military commissions are unconstitutional, since martial law cannot exist where the civil courts are operating).

secretary of war) ordered the release of almost everyone held as a political prisoner "on their subscribing to a parole engaging them to render no aid or comfort to the enemies in hostility to the United States."[138]

Spanish-American War. The third time that the United States declared war occurred in 1898 with respect to Spain. For several years, U.S. legislators, newspapers, and others had been calling for U.S. action against Spain for its treatment of U.S. nationals and commercial interests in Cuba, and in support of rebellion by the Cuban people. After the U.S. battleship *Maine* blew up in Havana harbor, President William McKinley informed Congress on April 11 that the explosion was caused by a submarine mine, implying that Spain attacked the vessel (later investigations established that the explosion was internal).[139] President McKinley stated that intervention in Cuba "may be justified" and requested authority "to take measures to secure a full and final termination of hostilities between the Government of Spain and the people of Cuba . . . ."[140]

On April 20, Congress approved a joint resolution asserting that the Cuban people had the right to independence and that Spain should withdraw its military forces from Cuba. Further, the joint resolution authorized the president to "use the entire land and naval forces of the United States, and to call into the actual service of the United States the militia of the several States, to such extent as may be necessary to carry these resolutions into effect."[141] One important condition of the bill (referred to as the Teller Amendment) stated that the United States "hereby disclaims any disposition or intention to exercise sovereignty, jurisdiction, or control over said Island except for the pacification thereof, and asserts its determination, when that is accomplished, to leave the government and control of the Island to its people."[142]

President McKinley signed the joint resolution into law on April 20 and transmitted it to Spain, prompting the latter on April 21 to break diplomatic relations with the United States and the U.S. Navy to commence a blockade of Cuba. On

---

[138] VII COMPLETE WORKS OF ABRAHAM LINCOLN 103 (John G. Nicolay & John Hay, eds., 1894). Professor Feldman notes, however, that the February 1862 order provided discretion to continue detention of persons deemed spies or threats to public safety. FELDMAN, *supra* note 136, at 213. Further, he argues that the president ignored the limitations set forth in the 1863 Habeas Corpus Suspension Act, *id.* at 228, and that, over the course of the war, he authorized arrests without charge not just of persons posing an immediate threat (such as John Merryman), but persons who resisted being drafted into the army, who spoke against the draft, and who were simply viewed as disloyal. *Id.* at 217. Further, Professor Feldman notes that *Ex parte* Milligan was only decided in 1866, after the war was over. *Id.* at 244. Although estimates vary, at least 13,535 civilians were detained by the military during the course of the war, and likely far more. *See* MARK E. NEELY, JR., THE FATE OF LIBERTY: ABRAHAM LINCOLN AND CIVIL LIBERTIES 115, 130 (1991).

[139] 13 A COMPILATION OF THE MESSAGES AND PAPERS OF THE PRESIDENTS 6281–92 (James D. Richardson ed., 1909).

[140] *See id.*

[141] H.R.J. Res. 24, 55th Cong., 30 Stat. 738, 738–39 (1898).

[142] *Id.* at 739.

April 23, Spain declared war on the United States.[143] President McKinley then requested Congress to declare war on Spain.[144] On April 25, Congress adopted a bill declaring the existence of a state of war since the commencement of the blockade, which was then signed by the president.[145]

Though the Spanish-American War lasted less than a year, it had dramatic consequences, including the independence of Cuba, and the subsequent acquisition by the United States from Spain of Guam, the Philippines, and Puerto Rico.[146] U.S. control of the Philippines was thereafter marked by repeated hostilities with Philippine rebels, which continued until 1913, with U.S. actions both authorized and funded by Congress.[147]

Boxer Rebellion. The American desire for a presence in the Philippines arose in part from greater interest in Asia generally, especially China. Hoping to develop trade relations with China and to avoid exclusionary policies by the powers already present there, Secretary of State John Hay engineered the 1899 "Open Door Policy." Yet resentment within China to such "foreign imperialism" helped fuel the Boxer Rebellion, which, among other things, threatened foreign nationals, who fled to the various foreign legation compounds in Beijing and elsewhere for protection. In 1900, President McKinley authorized some five thousand U.S. troops and associated naval vessels to join an allied expedition in China to help rescue the foreign legations, since the Chinese imperial government proved unable or unwilling to do so. The eight-nation alliance deployed some twenty thousand forces to China, where they defeated the Imperial Army, suppressed the Boxer Rebellion, and captured various Chinese cities, including Beijing.[148] The president's action was undertaken without the approval of Congress, which was in recess.[149] Upon Congress' return, the president asserted that the action was necessary to rescue U.S. nationals and their property, to obtain redress for

[143] *See* DAVID F. TRASK, THE WAR WITH SPAIN IN 1898, at 57 (1981).

[144] For McKinley's request to Congress, see 13 A COMPILATION OF THE MESSAGES AND PAPERS OF THE PRESIDENTS, *supra* note 139, at 6296–97.

[145] Act of Apr. 25, 1898, ch. 189, 30 Stat. 364. The votes in the House and in the Senate on April 25 were both voice votes.

[146] The war ended with the Treaty of Peace between the United States of America and the Kingdom of Spain, Apr. 11, 1899, 30 Stat. 1754.

[147] *See generally* PAUL A. KRAMER, BLOOD OF GOVERNMENT: RACE, EMPIRE, THE UNITED STATES, AND THE PHILIPPINES (2006).

[148] *See* 14 A COMPILATION OF THE MESSAGES AND PAPERS OF THE PRESIDENTS 6417–25 (James D. Richardson, ed., 1909); *see also* JOSEPH W. ESHERICK, THE ORIGINS OF THE BOXER UPRISING 271–314 (1987) (providing background information).

[149] *See* ARTHUR M. SCHLESINGER, JR., THE IMPERIAL PRESIDENCY 89 (1973) ("The intervention in China marked the start of a crucial shift in the presidential employment of armed force overseas. In the nineteenth century, military force committed without congressional authorization had been typically used against nongovernmental organizations. Now it was beginning to be used against sovereign states ...").

wrongs to them, and to restore order.[150] Congress generally supported the action and at least one court viewed Congress' appropriation of funds as a form of authorization.[151]

Latin American Interventions. After the turn of the century, there were a series of U.S. interventions in Latin America: Colombia (1901, 1903); the Dominican Republic (1905, 1916); Cuba (1906); Honduras (1907); Nicaragua (1909, 1912); Mexico (1914, 1916); and Haiti (1915).[152] These interventions had congressional sanction in some instances (often after the fact),[153] but at times occurred solely on the basis of presidential authority. One aspect of the U.S. actions seems to have been a desire to stave off European interventions in support of their own creditors; if the Monroe Doctrine was to be maintained, it was thought necessary for the United States itself to exercise an international police power to curb "[c]hronic wrong-doing," as President Theodore Roosevelt put it.[154] After leaving the presidency, but before becoming chief justice of the Supreme Court, William Howard Taft (who had served as governor-general of the Philippines from 1900 to 1904 and briefly as civil governor of Cuba in 1906) also characterized such interventions as a form of "police" action as opposed to "war."[155] Yet such actions were not always temporary in nature: President Wilson's intervention in Haiti in 1915 led to an American military presence there for some twenty years, while his 1916 intervention in the Dominican Republic led to an eight-year military occupation.

World War I. President Wilson's reelection campaign in 1916 stressed that he had kept the United States out of war in Europe; he had already in 1914 issued proclamations of U.S. neutrality.[156] By 1917, however, Germany's policy of unrestricted submarine warfare against commercial vessels, including U.S. vessels and vessels carrying U.S. persons and property, in conjunction with the public outcry over the Zimmermann telegram, provoked the United States to war.[157]

---

[150] 14 A COMPILATION OF THE MESSAGES AND PAPERS OF THE PRESIDENTS, *supra* note 148, at 6417–25.

[151] Hamilton v. McClaughry, 136 F. 445, 451 (D. Kan. 1905).

[152] *See* R. ERNEST DUPUY & WILLIAM H. BAUMER, THE LITTLE WARS OF THE UNITED STATES 123–68 (1968).

[153] For congressional authorization regarding interventions in Colombia/Panama that began in 1901, see Convention for the Construction of a Ship Canal to Connect the Waters of the Atlantic and Pacific Oceans, Pan.-U.S., Nov. 18, 1903, 33 Stat. 2234; in Mexico in 1914, see H.R.J. Res. 251, 63d Cong., 38 Stat. 770 (1914) renewed by Act of July 1, 1916, Pub. L. No. 64-133, ch. 210, 39 Stat. 337; in Haiti in 1915, see Act of June 12, 1916, ch. 140, 39 Stat. 223; and in the Dominican Republic in 1916, see Act of Feb. 11, 1918, ch. 15, 40 Stat. 437.

[154] 15 A COMPILATION OF THE MESSAGES AND PAPERS OF THE PRESIDENTS 6923–24 (James D. Richardson, ed., 1909). President Roosevelt's view became known as the "Roosevelt Corollary" to the Monroe Doctrine.

[155] WILLIAM HOWARD TAFT, OUR CHIEF MAGISTRATE AND HIS POWERS 95 (1916).

[156] 18 COMPILATION OF THE MESSAGES AND PAPERS OF THE PRESIDENTS 7969–77 (James D. Richardson, ed., 1908).

[157] The German Foreign Minister, Arthur Zimmermann, sent a telegram to the Mexican government inviting it to join the war as an ally against the United States, in exchange for Germany financing

President Wilson ended diplomatic relations with Germany in February 1917 and sought authority from Congress to arm U.S. commercial vessels.[158] When Congress adjourned without taking action, the president proceeded to arm the vessels on his own authority strictly for them to take "defensive" action.[159] As German submarine attacks on U.S. vessels continued to inflict serious losses, the mood shifted away from just armed neutrality and toward offensive military action. In April, the president called Congress into an extraordinary session and asked it to declare war on Germany.[160] Congress proceeded to do so by means (for the first time) of a joint resolution, which was signed into law by the president in April.[161] Eight months later, upon another request by President Wilson, Congress also declared war on Austria-Hungary by joint resolution, marking the fifth time the United States had declared war.[162]

The U.S. involvement in World War I came only in the war's final year, with U.S. naval forces guarding merchant vessels and U.S. ground forces principally operating in France as the American Expeditionary Forces. Most fighting ended by late 1918 and the basic terms of peace were established by the Treaty of Versailles in June 1919. The U.S. declarations of war, however, were only formally terminated by Congress in 1921, which in turn were acknowledged in bilateral treaties.[163]

Interwar Period. An important element of the aftermath of World War I, with implications for U.S. war powers, was the establishment of the League of Nations.[164] Article X of the Covenant of the League of Nations provided that members "undertake to respect and preserve as against external aggression the territorial integrity and existing political independence of all Members of the League," and that in "case of any such aggression or in case of any threat or danger of such aggression the Council shall advise upon the means by which this obligation shall be fulfilled."[165]

Mexico in recovering Texas, California, and other former Mexican territories. *See generally* BARBARA W. TUCHMAN, THE ZIMMERMANN TELEGRAM (2d. ed. 1966); BARRON, *supra* note 15, at 205–27.

[158] 17 COMPILATION OF THE MESSAGES AND PAPERS OF THE PRESIDENTS 8211–12 (James D. Richardson ed., 1897).

[159] *Id.* at 8228.

[160] For Wilson's request to Congress with respect to Germany, see *id.* at 8226–33.

[161] Act of Apr. 6, 1917, ch.1, 40 Stat. 1. The vote in the Senate on April 4, 1917 was 82 to 6, while the vote in the House on April 6, 1917 was 373 to 50.

[162] Act of Dec. 7, 1917, ch.1, 40 Stat. 429. The vote in the Senate was 74 to 0 and in the House was 365 to 1, both on December 7, 1917. For Wilson's request to Congress regarding Austria-Hungary, see 18 COMPILATION OF THE MESSAGES AND PAPERS OF THE PRESIDENTS, *supra* note 156, at 8399–8406.

[163] Act of July 2, 1921, ch. 40, 42 Stat. 105; Treaty of Peace, Hung.-U.S., Aug. 29, 1921, 42 Stat. 1951; Treaty of Peace, Ger.-U.S., Aug. 25, 1921, 42 Stat. 1939; Treaty of Peace, Austria-U.S., Aug. 24, 1921, 42 Stat. 1946.

[164] On the League of Nations generally, F.S. NORTHEDGE, THE LEAGUE OF NATIONS: ITS LIFE AND TIMES, 1920–1946 (1986).

[165] League of Nations Covenant, art. 10.

President Wilson thought that such language preserved Congress' prerogative with respect to declaring war and returned home from the negotiations believing he could secure the Senate's consent to ratification of the new treaty. Yet opponents of the treaty argued that Article X undermined congressional authority, making it unclear and even unlikely that the president would seek congressional authority prior to resorting to war. For that reason, the chairman of the Senate Foreign Relations Committee, Henry Cabot Lodge, insisted upon a reservation to the article stating that the "United States assumes no obligation . . . to employ the military or naval forces of the United States under any article of the treaty" unless authorized by Congress, since Congress "has the sole power to declare war or authorize the employment of the military or naval forces of the United States . . . ."[166] President Wilson accepted the principle expressed in the reservation, but opposed the reservation itself (along with others); the Senate ultimately rejected the treaty, in part due to concerns about the meaning of Article X.[167] This difficulty in having a U.S. treaty obligation arguably allowing the president to resort to war without any congressional check was known to and avoided by those who later crafted the U.N. Charter.[168]

The period leading up to U.S. entry into World War II is striking, at least by today's standards, given the general acceptance by President Roosevelt and all other leading decision makers that the president lacked the power to take important steps to prepare the nation and to assist its allies—let alone use actual military force—in response to what the president regarded as a dangerous threat to U.S. security.[169] Congress adopted, and President Roosevelt reluctantly signed into law, Neutrality Acts in 1935–1937 and 1939 that prohibited most U.S. export of arms and ammunition, or loans to foreign states that were at war (such as Italy and Ethiopia) or to parties involved in a civil war (such as in Spain), making no distinction between aggressors and victims.[170] One popular proposal at the time would have amended the U.S. Constitution to require a national referendum on

---

[166] 58 CONG. REC. 8,777 (1919).

[167] See THOMAS J. KNOCK, TO END ALL WARS: WOODROW WILSON AND THE QUEST FOR A NEW WORLD ORDER 205 (1992); MARGARET MACMILLAN, PEACEMAKERS: THE PARIS CONFERENCE OF 1919 AND ITS ATTEMPT TO END WAR 92–106 (2001).

[168] See Michael J. Glennon, The Constitution and Chapter VII of the United Nations Charter, 85 AM. J. INT'L L. 74, 76–77 (1991); Leo Gross, The Charter of the United Nations and the Lodge Reservations, 41 AM. J. INT'L L. 531, 550 (1947).

[169] See, e.g., DAVID M. KENNEDY, FREEDOM FROM FEAR: THE AMERICAN PEOPLE IN DEPRESSION AND WAR, 1929–1945, at 393–406, 426–64 (1999); WARREN F. KIMBALL, THE JUGGLER: FRANKLIN ROOSEVELT AS WARTIME STATESMAN 11–13 (1991); DAVID REYNOLDS, FROM MUNICH TO PEARL HARBOR: ROOSEVELT'S AMERICA AND THE ORIGINS OF THE SECOND WORLD WAR 42–50 (2001); BARRON, supra note 15, at 229–55.

[170] S.J. Res. 173, Pub. L. No. 74-67, 49 Stat. 1081 (1935); H.R.J. Res. 491, 74th Cong., 49 Stat. 1152 (1936); S.J. Res. 3, 75th Cong., 50 Stat. 3 (1937); H.R.J. Res. 306, Pub. L. No. 76-54, 54 Stat. 4 (1939) (codified at 22 U.S.C. §§ 441–57 (2018)). An exception did exist in some of the statutes for "cash and carry" sales, whereby the foreign belligerent paid up front and transported the war materiel itself.

any declaration of war by Congress, other than in cases where the United States had been attacked (the Ludlow Amendment).[171] Indeed, the need for congressional authorization with respect to all major decisions that might implicate the United States in war was commonly accepted in the years leading up to Pearl Harbor, with the president's "bases-for-destroyers" scheme an example of legally contorted efforts to skirt the practiced constitutional scheme.[172] Further, the insistence by isolationist elements in Congress that war abroad did not threaten U.S. security, and that war with Germany and Japan was not likely, would be remembered by executive policymakers in the years to come, sowing their doubts upon the wisdom of leaving the decision on initiation of war exclusively with the legislative branch.[173]

With the Lend-Lease Act of March 1941, the U.S. stance of neutrality ended.[174] Congress authorized the sale, lending, or giving of war materials to any foreign state whose defense the president deemed vital to the United States, including Britain and China. Attacks by German U-boats on U.S. vessels prompted President Roosevelt to take a series of steps in 1941 based on his own authority: sending U.S. naval patrols halfway across the Atlantic to find and report to Britain on the locations of German submarines; signing agreements with Denmark and Iceland for the basing of U.S. forces in those states; freezing the assets of the Axis governments; seizing of private facilities relevant to defense needs, such as an aviation plant in California; and declaring in September 1941 that U.S. naval vessels would attack German and Italian naval vessels when necessary in "waters which we deem necessary for our defense."[175] By November 1941, most aspects of the 1930s Neutrality Acts were repealed.

World War II. On December 7, 1941, Japanese aircraft launched from aircraft carriers in the Pacific attacked the U.S. naval base at Pearl Harbor, Hawaii; within hours, Japan also attacked U.S. forces in the Philippines. Simultaneously, Japan declared war on the United States. On December 8, President Roosevelt

---

[171] *See, e.g.*, H.R.J. Res. 167, 74th Cong. (1935). *See generally* ERNEST C. BOLT, JR., BALLOTS BEFORE BULLETS: THE WAR REFERENDUM APPROACH TO PEACE IN AMERICA, 1914–1941 (1977).

[172] *See generally* David Golove, *From Versailles to San Francisco: The Revolutionary Transformation of the War Powers*, 70 U. COLO. L. REV. 1491 (1999). Defending the bases-for-destroyers scheme, Attorney General Robert Jackson stated that the president's commander-in-chief power required him to "use all constitutional authority which he may possess to provide adequate bases and stations for the utilization of the naval and air weapons of the United States at their highest efficiency in our defense." Acquisition of Naval and Air Bases in Exchange for Over-Age Destroyers, 39 Op. Att'y Gen. 484, 486 (1940); *see* Edwin Borchard, *The Attorney General's Opinion on the Exchange of Destroyers for Naval Bases*, 34 AM. J. INT'L L. 690 (1940); Herbert W. Briggs, *Neglected Aspects of the Destroyer Deal*, 34 AM. J. INT'L L. 569 (1940); Quincy Wright, *The Transfer of Destroyers to Great Britain*, 34 AM. J. INT'L L. 680 (1940).

[173] *See* GRIFFIN, *supra* note 66, at 58.

[174] An Act to Further Promote the Defense of the United States, ch. 11, 55 Stat. 31 (1941).

[175] 1941 THE PUBLIC PAPERS AND ADDRESSES OF FRANKLIN D. ROOSEVELT 391 (Samuel I. Rosenman ed., 1950).

addressed Congress with his "day of infamy" speech, asking for a declaration of war against Japan.[176] Within an hour, Congress obliged, adopting the declaration in the form of a joint resolution, which was immediately signed into law by the president.[177]

By declaring war on Japan, the United States triggered reactions from the two other members of the 1940 Tripartite Pact, in which Germany, Italy, and Japan agreed to assist one another in the event that one of them was attacked by a nation not already involved in the existing armed conflict (excluding the Soviet Union).[178] In light of the U.S. declaration of war, Germany and Italy declared war on the United States. Consequently, after receiving a request from President Roosevelt, on December 11 Congress responded by declaring war on Germany and on Italy, again by means of a joint resolution adopted by Congress and signed into law by the president.[179] Six months later, in June 1942, again after receiving a request from President Roosevelt, the last three declarations of war in U.S. history (making a total of eleven) were issued against Bulgaria, Hungary, and Romania, again by means of a joint resolution adopted by Congress and signed by the president.[180]

The wartime status allowed the president to invoke a series of war-related statutes, as well as obtain new authorities from Congress, such as the ability to seize plants, mines, or facilities deemed necessary for the war effort that were threatened with labor strikes.[181] Those powers lingered for years after the fighting ended, given that the U.S. declaration of war was only terminated with Germany and Japan in 1951.[182]

---

[176] For Roosevelt's request with respect to Japan, see *id.* at 514–16.

[177] S.J. Res. 116, 77th Cong., Pub. L. No. 77-328, 55 Stat. 795 (1941). The votes were 82 to 0 in the Senate and 388 to 1 in the House.

[178] Tripartite Pact, Ger.-It.-Japan, Sept. 27, 1940, 204 L.N.T.S. 381 (1942).

[179] For Germany, see S.J. Res. 119, 77th Cong., Pub. L. No. 77-331, 55 Stat. 796 (1941). The votes were 88 to 0 in the Senate and 393 to 0 in the House. For Italy, see S.J. Res. 120, 77th Cong., Pub. L. No. 77-332, 55 Stat. 797 (1941). The votes were 90 to 0 in the Senate and 399 to 0 in the House. The declaration against Italy was terminated by the Treaty of Peace, It.-U.S., Feb. 10, 1947, 61 Stat. 1245. For Roosevelt's request with respect to Germany and Italy, see 1941 THE PUBLIC PAPERS AND ADDRESSES OF FRANKLIN D. ROOSEVELT, *supra* note 175, at 532.

[180] For Bulgaria, see H.R.J. Res. 319, 77th Cong., 56 Stat. 307 (1942). The vote on June 3 in the House was 357 to 0 and in the Senate on June 4 was 73 to 0. The declaration was ultimately terminated by the Treaty of Peace, Bulg.-U.S., Feb. 10, 1947, 61 Stat. 1915. For Hungary, see H.R.J. Res. 320, 77th Cong., 56 Stat. 307 (1942). The vote on June 3 in the House was 360 to 0 and in the Senate on June 4 was 73 to 0. The declaration was ultimately terminated by the Treaty of Peace, Hung.-U.S., Feb. 10, 1947, 61 Stat. 2065. For Romania, see H.R.J. Res. 321, 77th Cong., 56 Stat. 307 (1942). The vote in the House on June 3 was 361 to 0 and in the Senate on June 4 was 73 to 0. The declaration was ultimately terminated by the Treaty of Peace, Rom.-U.S., Feb. 10, 1947, 61 Stat. 1757. For Roosevelt's request with respect to Bulgaria, Hungary, and Rumania, see 1942 THE PUBLIC PAPERS AND ADDRESSES OF FRANKLIN D. ROOSEVELT 257 (Samuel I. Rosenman ed., 1950).

[181] *See* War Labor Disputes Act, ch. 144, 57 Stat. 163 (1943).

[182] *See, e.g.*, Woods v. Cloyd W. Miller Co., 333 U.S. 138 (1948) (upholding the continuation of wartime rent controls). For termination of the war with Germany, see H.R.J. Res. 289, Pub. L. No. 82-181, 65 Stat. 451 (1951). For termination of the war with Japan, see Treaty of Peace, Japan-U.S., Sept. 8, 1951, 3 U.S.T. 3169.

Birth of the United Nations. At the conclusion of the war, the U.N. Charter was adopted by some fifty nations meeting in San Francisco. The scheme of the Charter included the creation of a U.N. Security Council, consisting of five permanent members (China, France, Soviet Union, United Kingdom, and United States), plus six non-permanent members (which was later expanded to ten non-permanent members).[183] In Chapter VII of the Charter, the Security Council was authorized by Article 39 to determine the existence of a threat to the peace, breach of the peace, or act of aggression, and to respond to the situation under Article 41 with nonforcible measures or under Article 42 with forcible ones.[184] Further, Article 43 envisaged that states would enter into agreements with the United Nations for the provision of military forces when called upon by the Security Council.[185]

At the time that the U.S. Senate consented to ratification of the Charter, "Article 43 agreements" were viewed as the device by which the United States (and other nations) would commit to providing some, limited support to the United Nations in the form of troops and equipment, which would be "on call" for a U.N. "police action" (as opposed to a large-scale deployment).[186] Once an Article 43 agreement between the United States and the United Nations was concluded, the president would be able to deploy some U.S. forces at the request of the United Nations within the scope of the Article 43 agreement, without needing further congressional approval. Hence, the debate in Congress in 1945 centered on whether any Article 43 agreement that the United States would wish to conclude with the United Nations must first secure consent from either the Congress as a whole (by joint resolution) or the Senate (by consent to a treaty).[187] Only after assurances from President Truman and other members of the executive branch that any Article 43 agreement would require congressional approval did the Senate provide its consent to ratification of the Charter.[188] The issue of whether such a process would constitute an unconstitutional delegation of congressional power was heatedly debated. Yet most senators ultimately concluded,

---

[183] U.N. Charter art. 23.

[184] *Id.* arts. 39, 41, 42.

[185] *Id.* art. 43.

[186] 91 CONG. REC. 8,190 (1945). The vote in the Senate was 89 to 2. For background, see *The Charter of the United Nations: Hearings on the Charter of the United Nations for the Maintenance of International Peace and Security, Submitted by the President of the United States on July 2, 1945 Before the S. Comm. on Foreign Relations,* 79th Cong. 1 (1945); EDWARD R. STETTINIUS, JR., U.S. DEP'T OF STATE, PUB. NO. 2349, CHARTER OF THE UNITED NATIONS, REPORT TO THE PRESIDENT ON THE RESULTS OF THE SAN FRANCISCO CONFERENCE (1945).

[187] *See* Jane E. Stromseth, *Rethinking War Powers: Congress, the President, and the United Nations,* 81 GEO. L.J. 597, 601–14 (1993); *see also* Jane E. Stromseth, *Treaty Constraints: The United Nations Charter and War Powers, in* THE U.S. CONSTITUTION AND THE POWER TO GO TO WAR 83 (Gary M. Stern & Morton H. Halperin eds., 1994) (discussing the implications for U.S. constitutional war powers of the adoption of the U.N. Charter).

[188] FISHER, *supra* note 66, at 90–94.

as Jane Stromseth observes, that the "limited delegation of U.S. forces to the Security Council by special agreement, protected by the U.S. veto, was constitutionally acceptable both because Congress initially would approve any special agreement *and* because these forces would be used only in U.N. authorized 'police actions' of limited scope," as opposed to "full-scale mobilization of U.S. forces in war."[189]

After ratification of the Charter, Congress adopted the U.N. Participation Act (UNPA),[190] designed in part to indicate the conditions upon which U.S. forces might participate in U.N. actions. Section 6 of the UNPA authorizes the president to negotiate special agreements with the Security Council (subject to the approval of Congress) that provide for "the numbers and types of armed forces, their degree of readiness and general location, and the nature of facilities and assistance, including rights of passage, to be made available to the Security Council on its call for the purpose of maintaining international peace and security" under the Charter.[191] Once negotiated, the president "shall not be deemed to require the authorization of the Congress to make available to the Security Council on its call in order to take action under article 42 of said Charter and pursuant to such special agreement or agreements the armed forces, facilities, or assistance provided for therein . . . ."[192]

Thus, consistent with the U.S. ratification history of the U.N. Charter, the UNPA provided that the president must seek congressional approval of any Article 43 agreements that would make U.S. forces, facilities, or assistance available to the U.N. Security Council "on its call." Reflecting on this statute and its legislative history, Edwin Corwin asserted that "the controlling theory of the act is that American participation in United Nations shall rest on the principle of departmental collaboration, and not on an exclusive presidential prerogative in the diplomatic field."[193]

As it turns out, the United States has never concluded an Article 43 agreement with the United Nations, nor has any other state, such that the United Nations

---

[189] Stromseth, *Rethinking War Powers, supra* note 187, at 608; *see also id.* at 617–18 (similar debate in the context of passage of the UNPA).

[190] United Nations Participation Act of 1945 (UNPA), ch. 583, Pub. L. No. 79-264, 59 Stat. 619 (codified at 22 U.S.C. §§ 287–287e (2018)). The UNPA was amended in 1949 so as to allow the president to detail U.S. military personnel to the United Nations for purposes other than use of force under Chapter VII, such as noncombatant observers or guards. Act of Oct. 10, 1949, ch. 660, Pub. L. No. 81-341, 63 Stat. 734 (codified at 22 U.S.C. § 287d).

[191] UNPA, § 6, 59 Stat. at 621. Separately, Section 7 of the UNPA authorizes the president to provide no more than 1,000 U.S. military personnel to serve in a noncombatant capacity for U.N. peacekeeping operations. UNPA, § 7, 63 Stat. at 735–36.

[192] UNPA, § 6, 59 Stat. at 621.

[193] EDWIN S. CORWIN, THE PRESIDENT: OFFICE AND POWERS 1787–1957, at 221 (4th rev. ed. 1957); *see* LELAND M. GOODRICH & ANNE P. SIMONS, THE UNITED NATIONS AND THE MAINTENANCE OF INTERNATIONAL PEACE AND SECURITY 398 (1955).

does not have any ability to "call up" military forces to address threats to the peace. Rather, after adoption of the Charter, disagreements emerged among the major powers regarding the nature and scope of the military forces that would be on call for the United Nations—disagreements that hardened with the onset of the Cold War and that prevented any Article 43 agreements.[194]

Since 1945, the United Nations has deployed "blue-helmeted" forces in many situations to maintain a peace between two states (or between two factions within a state), but these U.N. "peacekeeping" forces—seconded by states to the United Nations on a temporary basis—are usually relatively small numbers of lightly armed military personnel who are deployed with the consent of the host state or states.[195] When coercive armed force is determined to be necessary, the Security Council instead authorizes (but does not compel) the use of such force by states for those purposes that are established by the Council. States then individually decide whether to participate in such a use of force and, if they do, those states operate under national command-and-control, not as part of a U.N.-organized and -controlled operation.[196]

3. Cold War: Swing to Executive Dominance

A confluence of developments in the wake of the Second World War altered the relationship between the president and Congress concerning the power to resort to armed force.[197] Whereas prior to Pearl Harbor it was commonly accepted that Congress must take any major decision that might embroil U.S. forces in armed conflict, the desire for "no more Pearl Harbors" called into question the wisdom of allocating solely to Congress the responsibility for preparing for and responding to threats to U.S. security.[198] Further, the United States emerged from the war as a global military power, the leader of an alliance of states that looked to the United States for extensive military and economic assistance, and welcomed the permanent basing of U.S. forces on their soil as the vanguard of future attacks. Threats to the United States now meant not just threats to U.S. territory but threats to U.S. allies and U.S. forces stationed around the globe. Communism

---

[194] See 2 THE CHARTER OF THE UNITED NATIONS: A COMMENTARY 1354–56 (Simma et al., eds., 3d ed. 2012).

[195] See generally ALEX J. BELLAMY ET AL., UNDERSTANDING PEACEKEEPING (2d ed. 2010); HITOSHI NASU, INTERNATIONAL LAW ON PEACEKEEPING: A STUDY OF ARTICLE 40 OF THE UN CHARTER (2009); ANDRZEJ SITKOWSKI, UN PEACEKEEPING: MYTH AND REALITY (2006).

[196] See U.N. Charter art. 44.

[197] For the most sustained treatment of this argument, see GRIFFIN, supra note 66; see also David Gray Adler, The Constitution and Presidential Warmaking, in THE CONSTITUTION AND THE CONDUCT OF AMERICAN FOREIGN POLICY, supra note 66, at 183.

[198] See, e.g., David P. Auerswald & Peter F. Cowhey, Ballotbox Diplomacy: The War Powers Resolution and the Use of Force, 41 INT'L STUD. Q. 505, 511 (1997) ("The ill-fated Neutrality Acts made Congress wary of blanket prohibitions on U.S. involvement in foreign conflicts, for fear of being blamed for allowing another Holocaust.").

and its spread became viewed as the principal threat to U.S. security, yet it was perceived as a threat emanating not from a single foreign state, one that could be fought in a classic war, but instead a hydra-headed threat, emerging across the globe, that had to be "contained" overtly and covertly through a wide range of diplomacy and coercion in a "cold war" (much as the threat of terrorism is viewed today).[199] As an example of this perception, in 1957 Congress adopted a statute indicating that the United States was prepared to use force in the Middle East to assist any foreign state faced with armed aggression from a communist state.[200] Further, the advent of nuclear weapons, especially after they were secured by the Soviet Union and then China, changed perceptions about the ability to wait for Congress to act when faced with a threat; now the necessary response time could be measured not in months or weeks, but in hours or even seconds. Indeed, by the late 1940s, isolationism in the United States was largely dead.

As such, the default position for the projection of military power was no longer U.S. inaction unless authorized by Congress; rather, it was constant action entailing projection of U.S. military power worldwide of differing magnitudes. While Congress was a partner in establishing the Marshall Plan, the North Atlantic Treaty Organization (NATO), and other key initiatives, "wise men" in positions of power and influence believed that complex decisions on U.S. security policy could only be based on a well-informed, thoughtful, decisive, and coherent strategy, playing to the president's inherent institutional strengths.[201]

Korean War. Thus, when North Korea invaded South Korea in June 1950, President Truman evinced none of the caution and deference to Congress that characterized the actions of President Wilson and President Roosevelt in the years leading up U.S. involvement in two world wars. President Truman decided to send some three hundred thousand U.S. forces to assist South Korea, without any declaration of war or express authorization to use military force from Congress, shattering the "long-standing legislative-executive consensus" on the war power.[202] Further, the president's decision was not just to push North

---

[199] *See United States Objectives and Programs for National Security,* U.S. Dep't. of State Policy Planning Staff (Apr. 7, 1950) (commonly referred to as NSC-68) (declassified in 1975), https://perma.cc/NSL7-XHDW.

[200] H.R.J. Res. 117, Pub. L. No. 85-7, 71 Stat. 5 (1957) (codified at 22 U.S.C. §§ 1961–65 (2018)). The statute was adopted at the request of President Eisenhower. *See* Special Message to the Congress on the Situation in the Middle East, 1 Pub. Papers 6, 11–15 (Jan. 5, 1957).

[201] *See generally* John Lewis Gaddis, Strategies of Containment: A Critical Appraisal of Postwar American National Security Policy (1982); Walter Isaacson & Evan Thomas, The Wise Men: Six Friends and the World They Made (2013); Gordon Silverstein, Imbalance of Powers: Constitutional Interpretation and the Making of American Foreign Policy (1996); *see also* Michael Beschloss, Presidents of War 586 (2018) (concluding that the "Founders would probably be thunderstruck" to see the power of modern presidents to initiate major military conflicts).

[202] Ely, *supra* note 62, at 10; *see* Louis Fisher, *Truman in Korea, in* The Constitution and the Conduct of American Foreign Policy, *supra* note 66, at 320; Barron, *supra* note 15, at 289–311. *But see* Robert F. Turner, *Truman, Korea, and the Constitution: Debunking the "Imperial President"*

Korean forces back to their prior position at the thirty-eighth parallel but to move north of that parallel in an effort to unite Korea, a decision that precipitated counterintervention by China.[203] Congress as a whole did not challenge the president's action, either as a matter of substance or of process, although a few members—such as Senators Robert Taft and Kenneth Wherry—objected to the president's failure to obtain congressional approval.[204] Even so, this swing to comparative advantage for the executive was not decisive; Congress continued to adopt statutory restrictions on the president's ability to wage war and the Supreme Court remained protective of Congress' role, most famously in *Youngstown Sheet & Tube Co. v. Sawyer*.[205]

A new feature of the war power in this conflict was the existence of the United Nations. After Japan lost control of the Korean peninsula at the end of World War II, U.S. forces administered the territory south of the thirty-eighth parallel, while Soviet forces administered the territory north of that parallel. In 1948, in conjunction with the withdrawal of most U.S. and Soviet forces, a "Republic of Korea" was established in the south based on an election conducted under the auspices of the United Nations, while a "Democratic Republic of Korea" was established in the north sponsored by the Soviet Union, with both regimes claiming sovereignty over the entire peninsula. When North Korean forces attacked across the thirty-eighth parallel in June 1950, the U.N. Security Council adopted a resolution declaring the attack to be a breach of the peace, calling for the immediate cessation of hostilities and the withdrawal of the invading troops to the thirty-eighth parallel, and asking members of the United Nations to assist in implementation of the resolution.[206] As the North Korean forces advanced deeper into South Korea, the Security Council adopted a second resolution, this time recommending that members of the United Nations furnish to the Republic of Korea such aid as might be necessary to repel the attack and to restore international peace and security in the area.[207] A third resolution then recommended

---

Myth, 19 Harv. J.L. & Pub. Pol'y 533 (1996). Notably, in August of 1950 Congress appropriated $12 billion for the military action in Korea. *See* Elizabeth D. Schafer, *Louis Arthur Johnson, in* 1 U.S. Leadership in Wartime: Clashes, Controversy, and Compromise 716 (Spencer C. Tucker ed., 2009).

[203] *See* Gary R. Hess, Presidential Decisions for War: Korea, Vietnam and the Persian Gulf 8–40 (2001).

[204] *See* 96 Cong. Rec. 9,318–23 (1950).

[205] 343 U.S. 579 (1952). For discussion of *Youngstown*, see *infra* this chapter § II(B) and Chapter 1 § II(B).

[206] S.C. Res. 82 (June 25, 1950). Adoption of these resolutions was possible because the Soviet Union absented itself from meetings of the Security Council, in protest at the failure to allow the communist government to represent China at the United Nations. Had the Soviet Union been present, it could have voted against the resolutions and thereby, as a permanent member, blocked their adoption.

[207] S.C. Res. 83 (June 27, 1950).

that members providing military forces and other assistance to South Korea "make such forces and other assistance available to a unified command under the United States of America," and requested the United States to "designate the commander of such forces."[208] The United States then organized a unified command structure for the multinational military forces, known as the "United Nations Command," and named General Douglas MacArthur as commander.

The question that arose was whether the existence of the United Nations and U.S. membership in it altered or in some way added to the authority of the president to resort to armed force. A Department of State memorandum addressed the legal authority for the president's action in Korea, stressing his constitutional role as commander in chief, his historic role in previously deploying U.S. forces, and the foreign policy interests of the United States in supporting the United Nations. The memorandum noted the president's constitutional role in conducting U.S. foreign relations and commanding U.S. armed forces; that "[s]ince the beginning of United States history, he has, upon numerous occasions, utilized these powers in sending armed forces abroad"; that the "preservation of the United Nations for the maintenance of peace is a cardinal interest of the United States"; and finally that "[b]oth traditional international law and article 39 of the United Nations Charter and the resolution pursuant thereto authorize the United States to repel the armed aggression against the Republic of Korea."[209]

The breadth of this legal argument contrasts sharply with assertions of the president's power to resort to war prior to 1945. Little reliance had been placed previously on the various relatively minor incidents involving U.S. forces abroad, certainly not in the context of the president's ability to authorize a large-scale deployment of the U.S. Army, Navy, and Air Force. While the president's inherent power had been recognized as supporting the president's ability to repel an attack on the United States, it had not been extended to the repelling of attacks on an ally. Nevertheless, the legal argument advanced by the Truman administration was not thereafter rejected by any U.S. president; rather, since that time, Department of Justice memoranda concerning the war power have repeatedly cited to the Korean deployment as a precedent in support of a broad power of the president to resort to war.[210]

---

[208] S.C. Res. 84 (July 7, 1950).

[209] *Authority of the President to Repel the Attack in Korea*, 23 DEP'T ST. BULL. 173 (1950); see Collective Self-Defense, 5 WHITEMAN DIGEST, at 1113–18; Independence, *id.*, at 102–09; Nonaggression, *id.*, at 789–95; Edwin C. Hoyt, *The United States Reaction to the Korean Attack: A Study of the Principles of the United Nations Charter as a Factor in American Policy-Making*, 55 AM. J. INT'L. L. 45 (1961). For a bibliography of executive branch opinions relating to war powers since 1950, see Stephen M. Griffin, *A Bibliography of Executive Branch War Powers Opinions Since 1950*, 87 TUL. L. REV. 649 (2013).

[210] *See, e.g.*, The President and the War Power: South Vietnam and the Cambodian Sanctuaries, 1 Op. O.L.C. 321, 329, 331 (1970); 4A Op. O.L.C., *supra* note 100, at 187–88.

The Department of State memorandum noted that U.S. actions in Korea were authorized by the U.N. Security Council and were in support of the United Nations, but it did not argue that the U.N. Charter or Security Council resolutions were a source of *presidential* authority. Nor did President Truman make such a claim in his public comments, though he referred to Security Council resolutions when explaining why he was deploying military force. For example, he stated: "The Security Council called upon all members of the United Nations to render every assistance to the United Nations in the execution of [the Council's] resolution. In these circumstances I have ordered United States air and sea forces to give the [South] Korean Government troops cover and support."[211] As previously noted, while the U.S. ratification of the U.N. Charter signaled Senate consent to membership in a certain institutional structure, the clear understanding at the time of ratification and during the enactment of the UNPA was that U.S. forces would only be provided in support of the United Nations pursuant to further consent from Congress.

Threats to Taiwan. Immediate post-Korea practice, seemed to confirm that Congress remained relevant to decisions regarding the resort to force. President Truman's expansive claims to a presidential war power ran into congressional resistance in the context of the stationing of U.S. forces in Europe in 1951.[212] No doubt aware of that resistance, President Eisenhower, noting certain provocative actions in the Strait of Taiwan by the (unrecognized) communist government on mainland China that posed a threat to the (U.S.-recognized) nationalist government on Taiwan (Formosa), requested in 1955 that Congress adopt a resolution that "would clearly and publicly establish the authority of the President as Commander-in-Chief to employ" U.S. armed forces as necessary to deal with the situation.[213] At the same time, President Eisenhower indicated that authority for "some of the actions which might be required would be inherent in the authority of the Commander-in-Chief."[214]

Congress responded with a resolution noting that an attack would endanger "the vital interests of the United States and all friendly nations in or bordering upon the Pacific Ocean" and therefore that the president was authorized to employ U.S. armed forces "as he deems necessary for the specific purpose of securing and protecting Formosa and the Pescadores against armed attack," with "this authority to include the securing and protection of such related positions

---

[211] Statement by the President on the Situation in Korea, 1 PUB. PAPERS 492 (June 27, 1950).

[212] Stromseth, *Rethinking War Powers, supra* note 187, at 635–38.

[213] Special Message to the Congress Regarding United States Policy for the Defense of Formosa, 1 PUB. PAPERS 209–10 (Jan. 24, 1955).

[214] *Id.* With respect to the "provocative actions," the communist government in 1954 attacked the islands of Kinmen and Matsu in the Taiwan Straits, which had been controlled by the nationalist government on Formosa.

and territories of that area now in friendly hands and the taking of such other measures as he judges to be required or appropriate in assuring the defense of Formosa and the Pescadores."[215] Diplomatic efforts, however, resolved the immediate tensions in the Taiwan Strait, such that the United States did not actually employ any forcible measures. Although the resolution provided that it would expire when the president determined that the peace and security of the area was reasonably assured, Congress ultimately repealed the resolution in 1974.[216]

Vietnam War. The Korean precedent loomed large in the 1960s as a similar scenario played out in Vietnam, this time with the United States supporting South Vietnamese forces and communist China supporting North Vietnamese forces. In August 1964, a U.S. destroyer was conducting a patrol in the waters of the Gulf of Tonkin when it was reportedly attacked by three North Vietnamese Navy torpedo boats. President Johnson requested and secured from Congress a joint resolution authorizing the president "to take all necessary steps, including the use of armed force, to assist any member or protocol state of the Southeast Asia Collective Defense Treaty requesting assistance in defense of its freedom."[217] The Gulf of Tonkin Resolution thereafter served as a key basis for President Johnson's (and later President Nixon's) escalation of U.S. forces in Vietnam, as well as in Laos and Cambodia, which ultimately led to the death of some fifty thousand U.S. servicemen and -women.

The unpopularity of the war encouraged many to question its constitutionality and ultimately led to repeal of the Gulf of Tonkin Resolution in 1971, yet the legal basis advanced by the executive branch never turned exclusively on the existence of that resolution.[218] Rather, the Korean precedent featured in the arguments by the Johnson and then Nixon administrations, with Under Secretary of State Nicholas Katzenbach, in 1967, going so far as to argue that the constitutional authority "to declare war" was obsolete in the era of the U.N. Charter, since the resort to war was barred by the Charter, leaving only actions either in self-defense or under the authority of the U.N. Security Council.[219] Such claims were never

---

[215] H.R.J. Res. 159, Pub. L. No. 84-4, 69 Stat. 7 (1955). The vote in the Senate was 85 to 3 and in the House 410 to 3.

[216] Act of Oct. 26, 1974, Pub. L. No. 93-475, 88 Stat. 1439.

[217] H.R.J. Res. 1145, Pub. L. No. 88-408, 78 Stat. 384 (1964) (commonly referred to as the Gulf of Tonkin or Tonkin Gulf Resolution). The vote in the House of Representatives was 416 to 0 and in the Senate was 88 to 2. For President Johnson's justification and request, see Radio and Television Report to the American People Following Renewed Aggression in the Gulf of Tonkin, 2 PUB. PAPERS 927 (Aug. 4, 1964).

[218] Act of Jan. 12, 1971, Pub. L. No. 91-672, § 12, 84 Stat. 2053, 2055; *see* Alexander M. Bickel, *The Constitution and the War*, 54 COMMENT. 49, 49 (1972) (charging President Lyndon Johnson with starting "an unconstitutional war").

[219] *U.S. Commitments to Foreign Powers, Hearing on S. Res. 151 Before the S. Comm. on Foreign Relations*, 90th Cong. 71–82 (1967) (statement of Hon. Nicholas Katzenbach, Under Secretary of State); *see* STAFF OF S. COMM. ON FOREIGN RELATIONS, 91ST CONG., DOCUMENTS RELATING TO THE WAR POWER OF CONGRESS, THE PRESIDENT'S AUTHORITY AS COMMANDER-IN-CHIEF AND THE WAR IN INDOCHINA (Comm. Print 1970); Leonard C. Meeker, *The Legality of United States Participation in*

successfully tested in U.S. courts, which invariably viewed them as presenting nonjusticiable political questions.[220]

4. Congress' Efforts to Reclaim Authority: War Powers Resolution

Congressional unhappiness with the war in Vietnam, and a belief that it was waged without adequate congressional approval, promoted efforts to reclaim authority for Congress to decide on the U.S. resort to armed force.[221] In 1969, the U.S. Senate adopted the "National Commitments Resolution," which asserted the sense of the Senate that "a national commitment by the United States to a foreign power necessarily and exclusively results from affirmative action taken by the executive and legislative branches" of the U.S. government.[222] Moreover, the Senate sought a year later to limit the presence of U.S. troops in Cambodia by means of an amendment to the Foreign Military Sales Act (the "Cooper-Church amendment").[223] The 1970 amendment would have barred funds necessary to keep U.S. troops in Cambodia after June 30 and would have prohibited "any combat activity in the air above Cambodia in direct support of Cambodian forces" without further congressional approval, but that amendment was not adopted in the House of Representatives. A different amendment (the "Hatfield-McGovern amendment") would have required an end to all U.S. military operations in Vietnam during 1971, but that amendment was not adopted in either House.[224]

Even so, such efforts presaged the 1973 War Powers Resolution, adopted by Congress at a time when President Nixon was on the verge of impeachment

---

the Defense of Viet-Nam, 54 DEP'T ST. BULL. 474, 484–85 (1966); see also John N. Moore, The National Executive and the Use of the Armed Forces Abroad, Lecture Delivered at the Naval War College (Oct. 11, 1968), 22 NAVAL WAR C. REV. (Jan. 1969), at 28 (discussing the historical controversies over the president's treaty and war powers); Quincy Wright, The Power of the Executive to Use Military Forces Abroad, 10 VA. J. INT'L L. 43 (1969) (discussing executive-congressional relations in terms of the military following World War I).

[220] See DaCosta v. Laird, 471 F.2d 1146 (2d Cir. 1973); Mitchell v. Laird, 488 F.2d 611 (D.C. Cir. 1973); Orlando v. Laird, 443 F.2d 1039 (2d Cir. 1971); Luftig v. McNamara, 373 F.2d 664 (D.C. Cir. 1967); Atlee v. Laird, 347 F. Supp. 689 (E.D. Pa. 1972); Gravel v. Laird, 347 F. Supp. 7 (D.D.C. 1972); Berk v. Laird, 317 F. Supp. 715 (E.D.N.Y. 1970); Velvel v. Johnson, 287 F. Supp. 846 (D. Kan. 1968). On justiciability for foreign affairs cases generally, see Chapter 4 § II.

[221] See BARRON, supra note 15, at 313–31.

[222] S. Res. 85, 91st Cong., 1st Sess., 115 CONG. REC. 17,279 (1969) (enacted); see also S. REP. NO. 91-129 (1969) (report from Senate Committee on Foreign Relations recommending passing S. Res. 85); U.S. Commitments to Foreign Powers: Hearings on S. Res. 151 Before the S. Comm. on Foreign Relations, 90th Cong., 1 (1967) (discussing S. Res. 151 and evaluating the roles of Congress and the executive when making foreign policy). The vote was 70 to 16.

[223] S. REP. NO. 91-865 (1970). The vote was 58 to 37 in favor of the amendment.

[224] The amendment was number 605 to H.R. 17,123, 91st Cong., 116 CONG. REC. 13,547 (1970) (a military procurement authorization bill). The amendment was defeated in the Senate by a vote of 55 to 39. 116 CONG. REC. 30,683 (1970).

due to the Watergate scandal.[225] The resolution was adopted over the veto of the president, who asserted that "the restrictions which this resolution would impose upon the authority of the President are both unconstitutional and dangerous to the best interests of our Nation."[226] Most but not all subsequent presidents apparently agreed that the resolution was unconstitutional; President Carter, for example, characterized the resolution as an "appropriate reduction" in the president's power.[227] Further, the Justice Department's Office of the Legal Counsel (OLC) indicated in 1980 that key restrictions in the resolution are constitutional.[228] Even so, subsequent practice (as discussed later) is such that it is probably "not possible to say flatly either that Presidents have complied with the War Powers Resolution or that they have not."[229]

By its terms, the purpose of the resolution is "to fulfill the intent of the framers of the Constitution of the United States and insure that the collective judgment of both the Congress and the President will apply to" (1) "the introduction of United States Armed Forces into hostilities, or into situations where imminent involvement in hostilities is clearly indicated by the circumstances," and (2) "to the continued use of such forces in hostilities or in such situations."[230]

Section 2(c) of the resolution asserts that the president may only introduce U.S. forces into hostilities where there exists "(1) a declaration of war, (2) specific statutory authorization, or (3) a national emergency created by attack upon the United States, its territories or possessions, or its armed forces."[231] The president is instructed under Section 3 to consult with Congress before introducing U.S. forces into hostilities,[232] but "there has been very little consultation with

---

[225] H.R.J. Res. 542, Pub. L. No. 93-148, 87 Stat. 555 (codified at 50 U.S.C. §§ 1541–49 (2018)) [hereinafter War Powers Resolution]. For the vote in each house, see 119 CONG. REC. 36,198 (1973) (Senate); *id.* at 36,221–22 (House). For legislative history, see H.R. REP. NO. 93-287 (1973); S. REP. NO. 93-220 (1973); H.R. REP. NO. 93-547 (1973) (Conf. Rep.). The term "resolution" is potentially misleading in that the measure is a "law" adopted by both Houses (by means of a joint resolution) and then enacted over the president's veto. For a compendium of materials, see STAFF OF H. COMM. ON FOREIGN AFFAIRS, 103D CONG., THE WAR POWERS RESOLUTION: RELEVANT DOCUMENTS, REPORTS, CORRESPONDENCE (Comm. Print 1994). For an overview, see Overview of the War Powers Resolution, 8 Op. O.L.C. 271 (1984). For background by leading architects of the resolution, see Thomas F. Eagleton, *Congress and the War Powers*, 37 MO. L. REV. 1 (1972); William B. Spong, Jr., *Can Balance Be Restored in the Constitutional War Powers of the President and Congress?*, 6 U. RICH. L. REV. 1 (1971).

[226] *See* Veto of the War Powers Resolution, 1 PUB. PAPERS 893 (Oct. 24, 1973).

[227] "Ask President Carter": Remarks During a Telephone Call-in Program on the CBS Radio Network, 1 PUB. PAPERS 291 (Mar. 5, 1977).

[228] 4A Op. O.L.C., *supra* note 100, at 196 ("We believe that Congress may, as a general constitutional matter, place a 60-day limit on the use of our armed forces as required by the provisions of § 1544(b) of the Resolution.").

[229] Ellen C. Collier, *Statutory Constraints: The War Powers Resolution, in* THE U.S. CONSTITUTION AND THE POWER TO GO TO WAR, *supra* note 187, at 55.

[230] War Powers Resolution, 50 U.S.C. § 1541(a) (2018).

[231] *Id.* § 1541(c).

[232] *Id.* § 1542.

Congress under the Resolution when consultation is defined to mean seeking advice prior to a decision to introduce troops. Presidents have met with congressional leaders after the decision to deploy was made but before commencement of operations."[233]

Section 4(a) of the resolution requires that, in the absence of a declaration of war, the president must report to Congress, within forty-eight hours (sometimes referred to as "48-hour reports"), if he or she introduces U.S. armed forces:

(1) into hostilities or into situations where imminent involvement in hostilities is clearly indicated by the circumstances;

(2) into the territory, airspace or waters of a foreign nation, while equipped for combat, except for deployments which relate solely to supply, replacement, repair, or training of such forces; or

(3) in numbers which substantially enlarge United States Armed Forces equipped for combat already located in a foreign nation .... [234]

Among other things, the report must explain the circumstances necessitating the deployment and the "estimated scope and duration of the hostilities or involvement."[235] Section 5(b) of the resolution then provides that within sixty days (extendable by the president to ninety days) after a report under Section 4(a)(1) is submitted (or required to be submitted), the president shall terminate the use of U.S. forces, unless Congress has declared war or authorized the use of force, has extended the deadline, or is unable to meet as the result of an armed attack upon the United States.[236]

Section 5(c) of the resolution purports to require that the president remove U.S. forces at any time Congress adopts a concurrent resolution, but this provision may be unconstitutional (as a form of "congressional veto") in the wake of *INS v. Chadha*.[237] Alternatively, Section 5(c) may be constitutional since it is not purporting to nullify an earlier statutory enactment by Congress that delegates power to the president but, rather, to make clear that Congress is not acquiescing to a presidential exercise of power that is constitutionally allocated to Congress

---

[233] RICHARD F. GRIMMETT, CONG. RESEARCH SERV., RL33532, WAR POWERS RESOLUTION: PRESIDENTIAL COMPLIANCE 23 (2012).

[234] War Powers Resolution § 1543(a).

[235] *Id.*

[236] *Id.* § 1544(b).

[237] *Id.* § 1544(c); INS v. Chadha, 462 U.S. 919 (1983). The Supreme Court in *Chadha* did not expressly address whether Section 5(c) of the resolution was unconstitutional, though the district court judge in *Crockett v. Reagan*, 558 F. Supp. 893 (1982), indicated that Section 5(c) may be unconstitutional. By contrast, a U.S. district court judge in 1990 indicated that Congress could prevent the president from using military force by means of a concurrent resolution. Dellums v. Bush, 752 F. Supp. 1141, 1152 (D.D.C. 1990).

under Article I of the Constitution.[238] In any event, Section 9 of the resolution provides that if any provision of the resolution is invalid, the remainder of the resolution is unaffected.[239]

Finally, Section 8 of the resolution purports to preclude any inference that a statute or treaty authorizes the introduction of U.S. forces into hostilities unless such instrument specifically provides for such action.[240] As a consequence, contemporary statutes to authorize the use of force typically indicate that they satisfy this section. For example, the 2001 Authorization for Use of Military Force Statute authorized the president "to use all necessary and appropriate force" in response to the attacks of September 11, 2001, and then asserted that "[c]onsistent with section 8(a)(1) of the War Powers Resolution" the above language was "intended to constitute specific statutory authorization within the meaning of section 5(b) of the War Powers Resolution."[241] Likewise, Congress' resolution in favor of using force against Iraq in response to its 1990 invasion of Kuwait stated that the resolution constituted specific statutory authorization within the meaning of the resolution.[242] Even so, the executive branch has asserted that this part of the resolution does not bind future Congresses from impliedly authorizing hostilities, and therefore Congress' enactment of appropriations legislation in a given context can constitute authorization for hostilities.[243]

By its terms, the resolution arguably provides the president with an ability to introduce U.S. forces into "hostilities" for two months (with an additional month if required by military necessity), but thereafter, in the absence of congressional approval at that point, requires the withdrawal of such forces.[244] In practice, however, the resolution has not resulted in presidential withdrawal of U.S. forces from hostilities after sixty (or ninety) days, nor ensured "that the collective judgment of both the Congress and the President" is brought to bear on the deployment of U.S. forces abroad. Indeed, critics of the resolution assert that it contains highly imprecise terms ("hostilities," "imminent") and carveouts that allow presidents essentially to circumvent the resolution's requirements.[245] In particular, the president can reflexively report that his action falls under Section

---

[238] *See* ELY, *supra* note 62, at 119–20; G. Sidney Buchanan, *In Defense of the War Powers Resolution: Chadha Does Not Apply*, 22 HOUS. L. REV. 1155 (1985); Louis Fisher, *Congressional Checks on Military Initiatives*, 109 POL. SCI. Q. 739, 752 (1994–95) ("The War Powers Resolution does not delegate legislative authority to the president. No legislative veto exists as a condition on that authority.").

[239] War Powers Resolution § 1548.

[240] *Id.* § 1547(a).

[241] S.J. Res. 23, Pub. L. No. 107-40, § 2(a)–(b), 115 Stat. 224, 224 (2001) (codified at 50 U.S.C. § 1541 note (2018)).

[242] H.R.J. Res. 77, Pub. L. No. 102-1, § 2(c), 105 Stat. 3, 4 (1991) (codified at 50 U.S.C. §1541 note).

[243] *See, e.g.*, Authorization for Continuing Hostilities in Kosovo, 24 Op. O.L.C. 327 (2000).

[244] *See* 4A Op. O.L.C., *supra* note 100, at 191, 191 n.13.

[245] *See, e.g.*, Oona A. Hathaway, *How to Revive Congress' War Powers* (Yale L. & Econ. Rsch. Paper, Sept. 10, 2019), https://perma.cc/RVP7-8ZPW (proposing inclusion of a definition for "hostilities").

4(a)(2) (introduction of forces that are "equipped for combat") or Section 4(a)(3) (adding forces to those already deployed abroad),[246] rather than under Section 4(a)(1),[247] and thereby avoid triggering the sixty-day clock for withdrawal set forth in Section 5.[248]

For example, in October 1983, after a military coup that led to unrest in the Caribbean island-state of Grenada, President Reagan ordered an invasion by approximately 1,900 Marines and armed airborne troops, which increased to about 5,600 troops. The president's report to Congress, consistent with the War Powers Resolution, simply stated that he had deployed troops "equipped for combat." Similar reports were issued in the context of the 1986 bombing campaign against Libya and the 1989 invasion of Panama.[249]

Efforts in the aftermath of the resolution's adoption to secure judicial review of the president's compliance with the resolution were not successful. For example, in *Crockett v. Reagan*, members of Congress challenged President Reagan's failure to report on his decision to send military advisers to El Salvador, but the district court found that Congress, not the court, must resolve whether those forces were introduced "into hostilities or into situations where imminent involvement in hostilities is clearly indicated by the circumstances," thereby triggering the reporting requirement under the resolution.[250] In *Sanchez-Espinoza v. Reagan*, a suit by members of Congress, Nicaraguan citizens, and U.S. citizens for violations of U.S. law, including the resolution, in relation to President Reagan's support for paramilitary operations in Nicaragua, was dismissed on political question grounds.[251] In *Lowry v. Reagan*, a challenge to President Reagan's decision to send U.S. naval forces to the Persian Gulf to protect oil tankers was dismissed on

---

[246] War Powers Resolution, 50 U.S.C. § 1543(a)(2)–(3). *See supra* this chapter note 225.

[247] *Id.* § 1543(a)(1)).

[248] *Id.* § 1544. For a systematic analysis of presidential notifications to Congress consistent with the resolution, see Tess Bridgeman, Reiss Center on Law and Security, *War Powers Resolution Reporting: Presidential Practice and the Use of Armed Forces Abroad, 1973–2019* (2020), https://perma.cc/NET7-ZSDV.

[249] Letter to the Speaker of the House of Representatives and the President Pro Tempore of the Senate on the United States Strike Against Libya, 1 PUB. PAPERS 478 (Apr. 16, 1986); Letter to the Speaker of the House of Representatives and the President Pro Tempore of the Senate on United States Military Action in Panama, 2 PUB. PAPERS 1734 (Dec. 21, 1989).

[250] Crockett v. Reagan, 558 F. Supp. 893, 895 (D.D.C. 1982), *aff'd per curiam*, 720 F.2d 1355 (D.C. Cir. 1983). The district court did assert that "were Congress to pass a resolution to the effect that a report was required under the [resolution], or to the effect that the forces should be withdrawn, and the President disregarded it, a constitutional impasse appropriate for judicial resolution would be presented." *Id.* at 899; *see also* Chapter 4 § II(A)(2) (noting application of political question doctrine in *Crockett* and other War Powers Resolution challenges).

[251] 568 F. Supp. 596 (D.D.C. 1983), *aff'd*, 770 F.2d 202 (D.C. Cir. 1985); *see also* Dornan v. Sec'y of Def., 851 F.2d 450 (D.C. Cir. 1988) (affirming dismissal of complaint alleging that the president allowed Congress to usurp his foreign policy responsibilities unconstitutionally).

similar grounds.[252] In *Conyers v. Reagan*, members of Congress challenged the invasion of Grenada as a violation of both the Constitution and the resolution, but the district court dismissed the case on the ground that the plaintiffs had other remedies, while the circuit court affirmed on grounds that the case was moot (by that time, most U.S. troops had been withdrawn from Grenada).[253]

As of 2019, presidents had submitted 105 "48-hour" reports to Congress that were said to be "consistent with" (rather than required by or pursuant to) the resolution.[254] Those reports, which are sent to the speaker of the House and the president *pro tempore* of the Senate, virtually never cite to Section 4(a)(1) or otherwise state that U.S. military forces had been "introduced into hostilities or imminent hostilities," thereby avoiding the sixty-day limitation imposed by Section 5(b).[255] Rather, the reports typically indicate that U.S. forces "equipped for combat" have been deployed to a foreign state, and further that they have deployed for limited purposes, such as to support the security of U.S. personnel, peacekeeping, or maritime interception operations. In some instances, a report consolidates several different deployments that collectively relate to a particular purpose, such as counterterrorism.

Still, as noted previously, Congress habitually invokes the resolution when authorizing the deployment of U.S. forces and, in doing so, sets forth specific purposes for which those forces may be used. For example, the Authorization for Use of Force against Iraq Resolution of 2002, which expressly invoked the War Powers Resolution, authorized the president to use U.S. military force (1) to "defend the national security of the United States against the continuing threat posed by Iraq," and (2) to enforce all relevant U.N. Security Council resolutions relating to Iraq.[256] Moreover, prior to using military force under the statute, the

---

[252] Lowry v. Reagan, 676 F. Supp. 333 (D.D.C. 1987). *See generally* MICHAEL JOHN GARCIA, CONG. RESEARCH SERV., RL30352, WAR POWERS LITIGATION INITIATED BY MEMBERS OF CONGRESS SINCE THE ENACTMENT OF THE WAR POWERS RESOLUTION (2012).

[253] Conyers v. Reagan, 578 F. Supp. 324 (D.D.C. 1984), *aff'd*, 765 F.2d 1124 (D.C. Cir. 1985).

[254] *See* GRIMMETT, *supra* note 233; Bridgeman, *supra* note 248, at 16–17. For summaries of most of these reports, see ELLEN C. COLLIER & RICHARD F. GRIMMETT, CONG. RESEARCH SERV., R426999, THE WAR POWERS RESOLUTION: CONCEPTS AND PRACTICE (2019).

[255] War Powers Resolution, 50 U.S.C. §§ 1543(a)(1), 1544(b). The one exception related to the *Mayaguez* incident in 1975. In that incident, President Ford submitted a report to Congress after he ordered U.S. armed forces to retake the *Mayaguez*, a U.S. merchant vessel that had been seized by Cambodia. *See* Letter to the Speaker of the House and the President Pro Tempore of the Senate Reporting on United States Actions in the Recovery of the SS *Mayaguez*, 1 PUB. PAPERS 669 (May 15, 1975) ("In accordance with my desire that the Congress be informed on this matter and taking note of Section 4(a)(1) of the War Powers Resolution, I wish to report to you . . . ."). President Ford's report triggered the sixty-day period, but the U.S. operation was completed before that period had elapsed. For discussion, see John C. Cruden, *The War-Making Process*, 69 MIL. L. REV. 35, 124–30 (1975); William B. Spong, Jr., *The War Powers Resolution Revisited. Historic Accomplishment or Surrender?*, 16 WM. & MARY L. REV. 823, 855–56 (1975). For a discussion of Congress' overall acceptance of the *Mayaguez* operation, see Thomas E. Behuniak, *The Seizure and Recovery of the S.S. Mayaguez: A Legal Analysis of United States Claims, Part 1*, 82 MIL. L. REV. 41, 61 n.78 (1978).

[256] H.R.J. Res. 114, §§ 3(a), 3(c), Pub. L. No. 107-243, 116 Stat. 1498 (2002).

president was required to communicate to Congress his determination that the use of diplomatic and other peaceful means would not "adequately protect the national security of the United States . . . or . . . lead to enforcement of all relevant United Nations Security Council resolutions,"[257] and further that the use of force was "consistent" with fighting terrorism.[258]

Congress sometimes has taken the further step of authorizing the deployment of U.S. military forces for only a fixed period of time. For example, in the context of President Reagan's decision in 1982 to deploy U.S. forces as part of a multinational force to Lebanon during its civil war, which led to U.S. casualties, Congress in mid-1983 passed a provision, as part of the Lebanon Emergency Assistance Act of 1983, which required statutory authorization for any substantial expansion in the number and role of that deployment.[259] Then, in October 1983, Congress passed a joint resolution—using the expedited procedures of the War Powers Resolution—which provided that the deployment constituted an introduction of forces into hostilities or imminent hostilities within the meaning of Section 4(a)(1), thereby requiring congressional authorization.[260] The joint resolution provided such authorization, but limited the duration of the deployment to no more than eighteen months, and provided for even earlier termination if certain contingencies occurred, such as the assumption by the United Nations or the government of Lebanon of the responsibilities of the multinational force.[261] President Reagan signed the joint resolution into law but in doing so declared that he was not ceding any of his authority under the Constitution, was not recognizing the constitutionality or wisdom of the War Powers Resolution, and was not acknowledging that additional congressional authority was required once the authorization in the joint resolution lapsed.[262] The temporal limitation was never tested, as shortly thereafter an attack on the U.S. Marine barracks in Beruit killed 241 Marines, prompting withdrawal of all U.S. forces from Lebanon by February 1984 before the eighteen-month period expired. After President Bill Clinton in October 1993 announced an intention to withdraw U.S. forces from Somalia by the end of March 1994, Congress invoked the War Powers Resolution in late 1993 when asserting that U.S. military forces should depart from Somalia by that time.[263] U.S. forces were withdrawn in early March 1994.

---

[257] *Id.* § 3b(1).

[258] *Id.* § 3b(2).

[259] Lebanon Emergency Assistance Act of 1983, Pub. L. No. 98-43, 97 Stat. 214.

[260] Multinational Force in Lebanon Resolution, S.J. Res. 159, 98th Cong., Pub. L. No. 98-119, § 2(b), 97 Stat. 805, 805 (1983).

[261] *Id.* § 6, 97 Stat. at 807.

[262] Statement on Signing the Multinational Force in Lebanon Resolution, 2 Pub. Papers 1444–45 (1983).

[263] Address on Somalia, 2 Pub. Papers 1703 (Oct. 7, 1993); Act of Nov. 11, 1993, Pub. L. No. 103-139, 107 Stat. 1418.

The resolution has been criticized as at best having had little effect, and at worst as displacing "good faith dialogue between the co-equal branches with after the fact litigation,"[264] or as an unconstitutional encroachment on executive authority.[265] Some observers sympathetic to its objectives nevertheless have called for its repeal.[266] Even so, the resolution remains facially pertinent for both the executive and legislative branches whenever an issue arises concerning the deployment of the U.S. military into situations where combat may occur. Even if the president acts and Congress remains silent (in other words, does not authorize the use of force), some observers characterize it as a "short-term contract" by Congress with the president that still has a conditioning effect upon the latter. On this account, the "contract" purportedly shifts political risk to the president during an armed conflict pursuant to certain parameters, but retains for Congress an ultimate check on presidential policy.[267] As such, the resolution helps to minimize the problem of collective action within Congress in the face of a need for immediate action, as well as the electoral repercussions that could arise from confronting the president when a conflict arises. Importantly, the resolution by its mere existence is said to condition the behavior of the executive branch, principally with respect to the duration of the use of force, since "presidents have a strong interest in resolving military conflicts by short-term but decisive use of force, tailored to the [resolution's] specifications, rather than risk the international ramifications of domestic infighting."[268]

5. Post–Cold War Uses of Force

Resort to armed force by the United States since the end of the Cold War has had some of the same characteristics as in earlier times: the scope and intensity of the use of force can vary considerably; Congress may expressly or tacitly authorize the force; the president may have proceeded without congressional authorization; and both branches pay some heed to the War Powers Resolution as a relevant instrument. Yet there are some differences in the character of

---

[264] Michael A. Newton, *Inadvertent Implications of the War Powers Resolution*, 45 CASE W. RES. J. INT'L L. 173, 173 (2012).

[265] *See, e.g.*, ROBERT F. TURNER, REPEALING THE WAR POWERS RESOLUTION: RESTORING THE RULE OF LAW IN U.S. FOREIGN POLICY (1991); Rostow, *supra* note 40; Abraham D. Sofaer, *Remarks: The War Powers Resolution: Fifteen Years Later (Oct. 4, 1988)*, 62 TEMP. L. REV. 317, 320–25 (1989); Robert F. Turner, *The War Powers Resolution at 40: Still an Unconstitutional, Unnecessary, and Unwise Fraud That Contributed Directly to the 9/11 Attacks*, 45 CASE W. RES. J. INT'L L. 109 (2012); Robert F. Turner, *The War Powers Resolution: Unconstitutional, Unnecessary, and Unhelpful*, 17 LOY. L.A. L. REV. 683 (1984).

[266] *See, e.g.*, Michael J. Glennon, *Too Far Apart: Repeal the War Powers Resolution*, 50 U. MIAMI L. REV. 17 (1995).

[267] *See, e.g.*, Auerswald & Cowhey, *supra* note 198.

[268] *Id.* at 507 ("Since the Act's passage, presidents have only used force once for more than sixty days without congressional authorization.").

contemporary resort by the United States to armed force and three factors in particular stand out.

a. Emergence of the U.N. Security Council as a Factor

In August 1991, Saddam Hussein's Iraq invaded and wholly occupied Kuwait, later announcing that Kuwait was annexed as a province of Iraq. Immediately after the invasion, the U.N. Security Council adopted a resolution condemning Iraq's action and demanding that Iraq immediately and unconditionally withdraw its military forces from Kuwait.[269] When Iraq failed to do so, the Security Council adopted a series of resolutions over the course of the fall of 1990 that, inter alia, imposed economic sanctions upon Iraq (and occupied Kuwait), provided for the maritime enforcement of those sanctions, and prevented transit of aircraft to and from Iraq and Kuwait.[270] Ultimately, in Resolution 678, the Security Council authorized U.N. member states co-operating with the government of Kuwait "to use all necessary means to uphold and implement" those resolutions and "to restore international peace and security in the area" unless Iraq, by January 15, 1991, fully implemented the Council's resolutions.[271]

Concomitantly, the George H.W. Bush administration deployed naval forces to the region to ensure compliance with the sanctions regime and deployed some five hundred thousand U.S. troops to the Arabian Peninsula (primarily in Saudi Arabia) in anticipation of an air and ground assault into Kuwait. The Bush administration asserted that, while it welcomed the political support of Congress, the president already had the power to use U.S. military forces to assist Kuwait even in the absence of congressional authorization.[272] Although some observers advanced the argument that the president was authorized to "take care" that the U.N. Charter (a treaty of the United States) was "faithfully executed,"[273]

---

[269] S.C. Res. 660 (Aug. 2, 1990).

[270] For the economic sanctions, see S.C. Res. 661 (Aug. 6, 1990). For maritime enforcement of the economic sanctions, see S.C. Res. 665 (Aug. 25, 1990). For transit of aircraft, see S.C. Res. 670 (Sept. 25, 1990).

[271] S.C. Res. 678, ¶¶ 1–2 (Nov. 29, 1990).

[272] See, e.g., Remarks at Dedication Ceremony of the Social Sciences Complex at Princeton University in Princeton, New Jersey, 1 PUB. PAPERS 496, 497 (May 10, 1991); JAMES A. BAKER III, THE POLITICS OF DIPLOMACY: REVOLUTION, WAR AND PEACE, 1989–1992, at 338–39 (1995); GEORGE BUSH & BRENT SCOWCROFT, A WORLD TRANSFORMED 397–98, 441 (1998); BOB WOODWARD, THE COMMANDERS 325 (1991); Adam Clymer, 102d Congress Opens, Troubled on Gulf but Without a Consensus, N.Y. TIMES, Jan. 4, 1991, at A1 (reporting on a high-level meeting between the president and senior congressional leaders at which the president maintained that he did not need congressional authorization). Perhaps most notoriously, President Bush said in 1992: "I didn't have to get permission from some old goat in the United States Congress to kick Saddam Hussein out of Kuwait." Remarks at the Texas State Republican Convention in Dallas, Texas, 1 PUB. PAPERS 993, 995 (June 20, 1992).

[273] See, e.g., The Constitutional Roles of Congress and the President in Declaring and Waging War, Hearings Before the S. Judiciary Comm., 102d Cong. 230, 237–41 (1991) (statement of Eugene Rostow, former Dean of Yale Law School). This argument was difficult to maintain given that Security

the administration only went so far as saying that a "declaration of war" was not appropriate when the United States participates in a U.N.-authorized international force.[274] President Bush said: "I don't think I need it . . . I feel that I have the authority to fully implement the United Nations resolutions."[275] Such a view prompted some members of Congress to sue the president in federal court seeking injunctive relief; while the district court found that the case was justiciable, it dismissed the suit as not sufficiently ripe since the position of Congress as a whole on the use of force against Iraq was not yet known, and because there was not yet a definitive course of action by the executive branch.[276]

Ultimately, President Bush was persuaded that prudence dictated requesting Congress to adopt a resolution in "support" of such action.[277] On January 12, 1991, Congress did so by means of a joint resolution stating that "[t]he President is authorized . . . to use United States Armed Forces pursuant to United Nations Security Council Resolution 678 (1990) in order to achieve implementation of Security Council Resolutions 660, 661, 662, 664, 665, 666, 667, 669, 670, 674, and 677."[278] During the debate, those in Congress who addressed the point uniformly took the position that Security Council authorization to use force did not alter the obligation for congressional authorization required under the Constitution.[279] At the same time, Congress conditioned its authorization by providing that the president, before using such force, must report to Congress that the United States had used, without success, all appropriate diplomatic and other peaceful means to obtain Iraqi compliance with the Security Council resolutions.[280] As such, Congress used the objectives of the Security Council resolutions to establish the scope of its authorization to use military force. Further, the joint resolution provided that it was specific statutory authorization within the meaning of Section

---

Council Resolution 678 did not require the United States to act; it simply authorized states to act if they wished to do so.

[274] *See Crisis in the Persian Gulf Region: U.S. Policy Options and Implications: Hearings Before the S. Comm. on Armed Servs.*, 101st Cong. 701, 703 (1990) (statement of Richard Cheney, Secretary of Defense).

[275] The President's News Conference on the Persian Gulf Crisis, 1 PUB. PAPERS 17, 20 (Jan. 9, 1991); *see* Edward Keynes, *The War Powers Resolution and the Persian Gulf War, in* THE CONSTITUTION AND THE CONDUCT OF AMERICAN FOREIGN POLICY, *supra* note 66, at 241, 241–42.

[276] Dellums v. Bush, 752 F. Supp. 1141, 1151 (D.D.C. 1990); *see also* Ange v. Bush, 752 F. Supp. 509 (D.D.C. 1990) (finding that soldier's claim that the president's deployment of him was a violation of the War Powers Clause was a nonjusticiable political question).

[277] The President's News Conference on the Persian Gulf Crisis, *supra* note 275, at 19–20.

[278] Authorization for Use of Military Force Against Iraq Resolution, H.R.J. Res. 77, Pub. L. No. 102-1, § 2(a), 105 Stat. 3, 3 (1991) (codified at 50 U.S.C. § 1541 note (2018)). For President Bush's signing statement, see Statement on Signing the Resolution Authorizing the Use of Military Force Against Iraq, 1 PUB. PAPERS 40, 40 (Jan. 14, 1991).

[279] *See* Stromseth, *Rethinking War Powers, supra* note 187, at 651–52.

[280] Authorization for Use of Military Force Against Iraq Resolution, § 2(b), 105 Stat. at 3–4.

5(b) of the War Powers Resolution, and that the president must make periodic reports to Congress on matters within the scope of the joint resolution.

On January 16, President Bush reported to Congress that peaceful means had been exhausted.[281] Thereafter, a U.S.-led coalition of forces pursued an air and ground campaign that succeeded in expelling Iraqi forces from Kuwait and that pushed several kilometers into Iraqi territory.[282] By late February, Iraq was willing to accept a provisional ceasefire, followed thereafter by a Security Council ceasefire resolution (Resolution 687) imposing a series of obligations upon Iraq, including acceptance of international demarcation of the Iraq-Kuwait border, identification and destruction of Iraqi weapons of mass destruction, and payment of compensation.[283] Further resolutions in the following years would continue to apply and adjust these obligations upon Iraq, especially with respect to weapons of mass destruction, and at times were referenced by the United States when sporadically engaging in military actions in Iraq.[284] Hence, as with the outset of the conflict, the Security Council's resolutions became the means by which the terms of peace were established; there was no postconflict armistice or peace agreement between the United States and Iraq.

The Security Council and its resolutions featured again in 2002–2003 when the United States sought to pursue forcible measures against Iraq for failure to abide by its obligations regarding weapons of mass destruction. President George W. Bush made a speech in September 2002 to the U.N. General Assembly calling for expeditious action by the Security Council in addressing Iraq's failure.[285] Although executive branch officials maintained that the president could proceed with a use of force against Iraq even in the absence of congressional authorization,[286] President Bush requested that Congress support the use of military force against Iraq.[287]

In October 2002, Congress adopted a joint resolution authorizing the use of force, which thereafter was commonly referred to as the "2002 AUMF" statute.

---

[281] Letter to Congressional Leaders Transmitting a Report Pursuant to the Resolution Authorizing the Use of Force Against Iraq, 1 PUB. PAPERS 42 (Jan. 16, 1991).

[282] President Bush reported to Congress that such combat operations were undertaken "consistent with the War Powers Resolution." Letter to Congressional Leaders on the Persian Gulf Conflict, 1 PUB. PAPERS 52 (Jan. 18, 1991).

[283] S.C. Res. 687 (Apr. 3, 1991).

[284] S.C. Res. 1284 (Dec. 17, 1999); S.C. Res. 986 (Apr. 14, 1995); S.C. Res. 715 (Oct. 11, 1991); S.C. Res. 707 (Aug. 15, 1991); S.C. Res. 688 (Apr. 5, 1991); see SEAN D. MURPHY, UNITED STATES PRACTICE IN INTERNATIONAL LAW: VOLUME 1: 1999–2001, at 408–16 (2002).

[285] U.N. GAOR, 57th Sess., 2d plen. mtg. at 5, U.N. Doc. A/57/PV.2 (Sept. 12, 2002).

[286] See, e.g., Applying the War Powers Resolution to the War on Terrorism: Hearing Before the Subcomm. on the Constitution, Federalism, and Prop. Rights of the S. Comm. on the Judiciary, 107th Cong. 8 (2002) (statement of John C. Yoo, Deputy Assistant Att'y Gen., Office of Legal Counsel, U.S. Department of Justice).

[287] Remarks Following a Meeting with Congressional Leaders and an Exchange with Reporters, 2 PUB. PAPERS 1611–12 (Sept. 18, 2002).

The statute provided that the president is "authorized to use the Armed Forces of the United States as he determines to be necessary and appropriate in order to (1) defend the national security of the United States against the continuing threat posed by Iraq; and (2) enforce all relevant United Nations Security Council resolutions regarding Iraq."[288]

As was the case for the 1990 authorization, the joint resolution required that the president first determine that diplomatic and other peaceful means had been exhausted, asserted that the joint resolution was specific statutory authorization within the meaning of Section 5(b) of the War Powers Resolution, and required the president to make periodic reports to Congress on matters within the scope of the joint resolution. President Bush signed the joint resolution into law, but said that doing so did not "constitute any change in the long-standing positions of the executive branch on either the President's constitutional authority to use force to deter, prevent, or respond to aggression or other threats to U.S. interests or on the constitutionality of the War Powers Resolution."[289] The joint resolution contained no termination clause.

Thereafter, the United States was unsuccessful in securing a Security Council resolution authorizing the use of force, but Resolution 1441 did declare that Iraq was in "material breach" of its disarmament obligations.[290] The executive branch then developed a position that, under international law, the earlier Security Council resolution (Resolution 678) authorizing the use of force against Iraq remained available to the United States for addressing Iraq's material breach of the ceasefire resolution (Resolution 687).[291] In March 2003, the United States (in alliance with a few other states) commenced an air campaign against Iraq, followed by an invasion of ground forces that toppled the government of Saddam Hussein, leading to an occupation of Iraq by U.S. and U.K. forces and ultimately the establishment of a provisional and then permanent government of Iraq. U.S. forces remained in Iraq for several years as part of a Multinational Force in Iraq authorized in 2003 by a U.N. Security Council resolution and then

---

[288] Authorization for Use of Military Force against Iraq Resolution of 2002, Pub. L. No. 107-243 § 3(a), 116 Stat. 1498, 1501 (2002) (codified at 50 U.S.C. § 1541 note (2018)). The joint resolution was adopted in the House by a vote of 296 to 133 and in the Senate by a vote of 77 to 23. For the legislative history of the resolution, see JENNIFER K. ELSEA & MATTHEW C. WEED, CONG. RESEARCH SERV., RL31133, DECLARATIONS OF WAR AND AUTHORIZATIONS FOR THE USE OF MILITARY FORCE: HISTORICAL BACKGROUND AND LEGAL IMPLICATIONS 16–19 (2014).

[289] Statement on Signing the Authorization for use of Military Force Against Iraq Resolution of 2002, 2 PUB. PAPERS 1814 (Oct. 16, 2002).

[290] S.C. Res. 1441 (Nov. 8, 2002).

[291] See Sean D. Murphy, Assessing the Legality of Invading Iraq, 92 GEO. L.J. 173 (2004); William H. Taft IV & Todd F. Buchwald, Preemption, Iraq, and International Law, 97 AM. J. INT'L L. 557, 563 (2003).

terminated in 2008.[292] Thereafter, U.S. forces remained in Iraq during 2009–2011 pursuant to a U.S.-Iraq agreement.[293]

Just prior to the commencement of hostilities against Iraq in March 2003, a coalition of U.S. soldiers, parents of U.S. soldiers, and members of Congress filed suit challenging the constitutionality of the president's action. The complaint advanced two principal arguments that were at tension with one another: first, that there existed a confrontation between Congress and the president because the president was allegedly not acting in conformity with Congress' joint resolution and, second, that Congress and the president were in collusion with Congress' unconstitutional delegation to the president of the decision on whether to declare war on Iraq. The First Circuit Court of Appeals found that there was no "constitutional impasse" between Congress and the president regarding the use of force against Iraq, and that "the mere fact that the October Resolution grants some discretion to the President fails to raise a sufficiently clear constitutional issue."[294]

Other circumstances have provided an opportunity to test the significance of U.N. Security Council authorizations to use force when congressional authorization is absent. In such circumstances, the executive branch typically has not relied upon the Security Council's authorization for states to use force or on U.S. obligations arising under the U.N. Charter as the legal basis for the president's authority. For example, after a military coup in Haiti in 1990 that ousted its democratically elected leader, Jean-Bertrand Aristide, both the Organization of American States and the United Nations imposed economic sanctions on Haiti, demanding Aristide's reinstatement. After years of unsuccessful efforts at diplomacy, the U.N. Security Council authorized U.N. "Member States to form a multinational force under unified command and control . . . to use all necessary means to facilitate the departure from Haiti of the military leadership . . . ."[295] President Clinton ordered the U.S. military to deploy, and, literally as U.S. warplanes were in the air and U.S. naval craft were deploying to the region, the leaders of the military coup decided to step aside.[296]

No express authorization existed from Congress for this operation. In a joint resolution adopted by Congress and signed into law by the president, Congress

---

[292] See S.C. Res. 1511 (Oct. 16, 2003); see also S.C. Res. 1723 (Nov. 28, 2006) (discussing the situation in Iraq); S.C. Res. 1637 (Nov. 8, 2005) (same); S.C. Res. 1546 (June 8, 2004) (same). The termination was in the form of no longer renewing the mandate. See S.C. Res. 1790 (Dec. 18, 2007) (extending the mandate of the multinational force in Iraq until December 31, 2008).

[293] Agreement on the Withdrawal of United States Forces from Iraq and the Organization of Their Activities during Their Temporary Presence in Iraq, Iraq-U.S., Nov. 27, 2008, https://perma.cc/QR9P-3UGH.

[294] Doe v. Bush, 323 F.3d 133, 137, 143 (1st Cir. 2003). For discussion of ripeness in foreign relations generally, see Chapter 4 § II(B)(2).

[295] S.C. Res. 940 (July 1, 1994).

[296] See Address to the Nation on Haiti, 2 PUB. PAPERS 1571 (Sept. 18, 1994).

expressed the sense that "the President should have sought and welcomed congressional approval before deploying United States Armed Forces to Haiti."[297] In justifying the legality of the president's action, the executive branch did not rely upon the Security Council's authorization or on U.S. obligations under the U.N. Charter. Rather, OLC opined that the president possessed broad power in this area[298] and that the operation was permissible for three reasons: (1) there existed a 1994 Department of Defense Appropriations Act expressing a sense of Congress that funds should not be expended for military operations in Haiti in the absence of certain findings by the president (findings which were duly made);[299] (2) the War Powers Resolution recognized an ability of the president to deploy armed forces into "hostilities or into situations where imminent involvement in hostilities is indicated by the circumstances"; and (3) given the nature, scope and duration of the deployment and the consent of the recognized (albeit in exile) president of Haiti, President Clinton could regard the deployment as not constituting "war" within the meaning of the Declare War Clause.[300]

b. Uses of Force in Response to Terrorist Threats

The use of U.S. armed forces abroad when responding to threats in recent years has "shifted significantly from responding to state actors to responding to terrorist organizations."[301] Indeed, actions in the 1990s by al-Qaeda against the United States, culminating in the terrorist attacks of September 11, 2001, demonstrated a threat to the United States from nonstate actors on a scale that had not previously been widely understood. The nature of the threat introduced new elements to the war powers debate: the threat often invited a quick, covert, and targeted response by the United States, in situations where there had been loss of U.S. life; the threat was not from the direct actions of a foreign state (though addressing the threat potentially required using force in other states); the "enemy" was far less cohesive, consisting of a loosely affiliated series of cells operating in multiple states; and the duration of hostilities appeared far more indeterminate and open-ended. Such conditions made action by the president on an

---

[297] S.J. Res. 229, 103d Cong. § 1(b), 108 Stat. 4358 (1994).

[298] Deployment of United States Armed Forces into Haiti, 18 Op. O.L.C. 173, 178 (1994) ("Such a pattern of executive conduct, made under claim of right, extended over many decades and engaged in by Presidents of both parties, 'evidences the existence of broad constitutional power.'" (quoting 4A Op. O.L.C., *supra* note 100, at 187)).

[299] Act of Nov. 11, 1993, Pub. L. No. 103-139, 107 Stat. 1418.

[300] 18 Op. O.L.C., *supra* note 298, at 178–79; *see* Phillip R. Trimble, *The President's Constitutional Authority to Use Limited Military Force*, 89 Am. J. Int'l L. 84 (1995). For critiques of this position, see Letter of Ten Law Professors, *reprinted in* Marian Nash (Leich), *Contemporary Practice of the United States Relating to International Law*, 89 Am. J. Int'l L. 96, 127–30 (1995); Lori Fisler Damrosch, *Agora: The 1994 U.S. Action in Haiti: The Constitutional Responsibility of Congress for Military Engagements*, 89 Am. J. Int'l L. 58 (1995).

[301] Bridgeman, *supra* note 248, at 19.

emergency basis a likely phenomenon and made less likely action by Congress to challenge the president, or even (given the fluidity of the situation) the adoption by Congress of authorizations to use force.[302]

For example, in August 1998, bombs exploded at the U.S. embassies in Nairobi, Kenya, and Dar es Salaam, Tanzania, killing nearly three hundred people, including twelve U.S. nationals.[303] After an investigation into the coordinated attacks led U.S. officials to suspect the involvement of al-Qaeda (under the leadership of Osama bin Laden, who was living in Afghanistan), President Clinton ordered the launch of cruise missiles against al-Qaeda paramilitary training camps in Afghanistan and against a Sudanese pharmaceutical plant that the United States identified as an al-Qaeda-related chemical weapons facility.[304] In reports to Congress, President Clinton stated that the "United States acted in exercise of our inherent right of self-defense consistent with Article 51 of the United Nations Charter" and that "I directed these actions pursuant to my constitutional authority to conduct U.S. foreign relations and as Commander in Chief and Chief Executive."[305]

At a White House press conference, National Security Advisor Samuel R. Berger also referred to a 1996 statute as authority for disrupting and destroying "those kinds of military terrorist targets."[306] That statute, the Antiterrorism and Effective Death Penalty Act of 1996, contains a congressional finding that "the President should use all necessary means, including covert action and military force, to disrupt, dismantle, and destroy international infrastructure used by international terrorists, including overseas terrorist training facilities and safe havens."[307] No steps were taken by Congress in opposition to the president's action.

---

[302] *See generally* CHRIS EDELSON, EMERGENCY PRESIDENTIAL POWER: FROM THE DRAFTING OF THE CONSTITUTION TO THE WAR ON TERROR (2013); CURTIS A. BRADLEY, INTERNATIONAL LAW IN THE U.S. LEGAL SYSTEM 293–344 (3d ed. 2020).

[303] Other incidents attributed to al-Qaeda in this period include: the 1993 bombing of the World Trade Center that killed 6 persons and wounded more than 1,000; the 1996 bombing of a U.S. military housing complex in Dhahran, Saudi Arabia that killed 19 U.S. servicemen and wounded 372 other persons; and the October 2000 bombing of the *USS Cole* in the harbor of Aden, Yemen that killed 17 U.S. sailors and wounded 39. *See generally* ROHAN GUNARATNA, INSIDE AL QAEDA: GLOBAL NETWORK OF TERROR (2002).

[304] Remarks in Martha's Vineyard, Massachusetts, on Military Action against Terrorist Sites in Afghanistan and Sudan, 2 PUB. PAPERS 1460 (Aug. 20, 1998); Address to the Nation on Military Action Against Terrorist Sites in Afghanistan and Sudan, *id.*

[305] Letter to Congressional Leaders Reporting on Military Action Against Terrorist Sites in Afghanistan and Sudan, *id.* at 1464 (Aug. 21, 1998). The United States also notified the U.N. Security Council of the missile attacks. *See* U.N. SCOR, 53d Sess., 22d mtg., U.N. Doc. S/1998/780 (Aug. 20, 1998).

[306] The White House, Office of the Press Secretary, Press Briefing on U.S. Strikes in Sudan and Afghanistan (Aug. 20, 1998), https://perma.cc/872V-8UXE.

[307] Antiterrorism and Effective Death Penalty Act of 1996, Pub. L. No. 104-132, § 324(4), 110 Stat. 1214, 1255 (codified at 22 U.S.C. § 2377 note (2018)).

On September 11, 2001, nineteen al-Qaeda operatives boarded four U.S. commercial passenger jets in Boston, Newark, and Washington, hijacked the aircraft minutes after takeoff, and crashed them into the World Trade Center in New York, the Pentagon in northern Virginia, and the Pennsylvania countryside. All told, some three thousand persons were killed in the incidents, the worst single-day casualties for the United States since the Battle of Antietam during the U.S. Civil War.[308]

The U.S. government regarded the September 11 actions as comparable to a military attack. In the week following the attacks, President George W. Bush declared a national emergency and called to active duty the reserves of the U.S. armed forces.[309] Furthermore, negotiations between the two political branches led to Congress adopting and President Bush signing into law a joint resolution that, after noting that "the President has authority under the Constitution to take action to deter and prevent acts of international terrorism against the United States," provided in Section 2 that "the President is authorized to use all necessary and appropriate force against those nations, organizations, or persons he determines" (1) "planned, authorized, committed, or aided the terrorist attacks that occurred on September 11, 2001," or (2) "harbored such organizations or persons, in order to prevent any future acts of international terrorism against the United States by such nations, organizations or persons."[310]

The breadth of this authorization is notable: the president was delegated authority to determine whether an entire foreign state (or organization or person) has a sufficient connection to the September 11 attacks—perhaps by "aiding" those responsible for the attacks—in which case force may be used against that foreign state, organization, or person.[311] Among other things, this statute authorizing the use of military force (or "2001 AUMF" statute) stated that it constituted specific statutory authorization within the meaning of Section 5(b) of the War Powers Resolution.[312]

---

[308] *See generally* NAT'L COMM'N ON TERRORIST ATTACKS UPON THE U.S., THE 9/11 COMMISSION REPORT (2004).

[309] Exec. Order No. 13,223, 66 Fed. Reg. 48,201 (Sept. 14, 2001); Proclamation 7463, 66 Fed. Reg. 48,199 (Sept. 18, 2001).

[310] Authorization for Use of Military Force, S.J. Res. 23, 107th Cong., Pub. L. No. 107-40, § 2(a), 115 Stat. 224, 224 (2001) (codified at 50 U.S.C.§ 1541 note). The resolution was adopted in the Senate by a vote of 98 to 0 and in the House by a vote of 420 to 1. For the debate in Congress, see 147 CONG. REC. 17,040–45, 17,110–56 (2001). *See generally* RICHARD F. GRIMMETT, CONG. RESEARCH SERV., RS22357, AUTHORIZATION FOR USE OF MILITARY FORCE IN RESPONSE TO THE 9/11 ATTACKS (P.L. 107-40): LEGISLATIVE HISTORY (2007); David Abramowitz, *The President, the Congress, and Use of Force: Legal and Political Considerations in Authorizing Use of Force Against International Terrorism*, 43 HARV. INT'L L.J. 71 (2002).

[311] For analyses of the statute and its implications, see Curtis A. Bradley & Jack L. Goldsmith, *Congressional Authorization and the War on Terrorism*, 118 HARV. L. REV. 2047 (2005); Jennifer Daskal & Stephen I. Vladeck, *After the AUMF*, 5 HARV. NAT'L SECURITY J. 115 (2014).

[312] Authorization for Use of Military Force § 2(a) (referring to 50 U.S.C. § 1544(b)). In signing the joint resolution, however, President Bush maintained "the longstanding position of the executive

The U.N. Security Council unanimously adopted on September 12 a resolution condemning "the horrifying terrorist attacks," which the Council regarded, "like any act of international terrorism, as a threat to international peace and security."[313] The resolution did not expressly authorize the use of force by the United States, but did affirm in light of the attacks the U.S. inherent right of individual and collective self-defense, as well as the need "to combat by all means" the "threats to international peace and security caused by terrorist acts."[314]

After unsuccessfully asking the *de facto* government of Afghanistan, the Taliban, to hand over the leaders of al-Qaeda, the United States on October 7 commenced an air and then ground campaign in Afghanistan, which by 2002 succeeded in toppling the Taliban government from power and in killing, capturing, or forcing al-Qaeda operatives into hiding.[315] A new Afghan government was established, but U.S. forces remained in Afghanistan to address continuing security threats, both from al-Qaeda and the Taliban, and were joined in August 2003 by NATO forces organized as an International Security Assistance Force. The 2001 AUMF statute was repeatedly cited not just in support of the president's ability to engage in military operations in Afghanistan but also to detain "enemy combatants" captured in Afghanistan or elsewhere (including U.S. nationals),[316] to prosecute such persons before military commissions,[317] and to support a variety of other measures incidental to the use of force, such as electronic surveillance of communications, including in the United States.[318] In 2014, the United States and NATO formally ended combat operations in Afghanistan.

U.S. actions, however, were not limited to Afghanistan, instead unfolding in various other locations as part of what President Bush asserted was a "global war on terrorism" directed against militant forces associated with al-Qaeda. Thus, U.S. military forces: deployed in 2002 to the Philippines to advise and assist the Philippine Armed Forces in combating Filipino Islamist groups linked with

---

branch regarding the President's constitutional authority to use force, including the Armed Forces of the United States and regarding the constitutionality of the War Powers Resolution." Statement on Signing the Authorization for Use of Military Force, 2 PUB. PAPERS 1124, 1125 (Sept. 18, 2001).

[313] S.C. Res. 1368, ¶ 1 (Sept. 12, 2001); *see also* S.C. Res. 1373 (Sept. 28, 2001) (reaffirming resolutions 1269 and 1368).

[314] S.C. Res. 1373, pmbl. (Sept. 28, 2001); S.C. Res. 1368, pmbl. (Sept. 12, 2001).

[315] *See* Address Before a Joint Session of the Congress on the United States Response to the Terrorist Attacks of September 11, 2 PUB. PAPERS 1140, 1141 (Sept. 20, 2001). For the Taliban's response, see Rajiv Chandrasekaran, *Afghan People are Urged to Prepare to a Holy War*, WASH. POST, Sept. 19, 2001, at A1; Rajiv Chandrasekaran, *Taliban Rejects U.S. Demand, Vows a "Showdown of Might*," WASH. POST, Sept. 22, 2001, at A1. The United States informed the U.N. Security Council that it was taking such action in self-defense. *See* U.N. SCOR, 56th Sess., 4392d mtg., U.N. Doc. S/2001/946 (Oct. 7, 2001).

[316] *See* Chapter 10 § II(D)(7).

[317] *See infra* this chapter § III(B) and Chapter 10 § II(E)(4).

[318] *See infra* this chapter note 409.

al-Qaeda; deployed in that same year to the Horn of Africa to disrupt and detect militant al-Qaeda affiliates in the region; engaged in numerous drone attacks
in the federally administered tribal areas of western Pakistan against al-Qaeda
operatives, as well as a nighttime raid on Abbottabad, Pakistan, in May 2011 that
resulted in the death of Osama bin Laden; conducted a series of military strikes
on al-Qaeda militants in Yemen, including through the use of drone aircraft; and
deployed in 2012 to northern Mali to provide support to the government in combating radical Islamists affiliated with al-Qaeda.[319] The 2001 AUMF statute continued to be invoked in support of such actions and, when reporting to Congress
"consistent with the War Powers Resolution," the president invariably explained
the connection of the targeted forces with al-Qaeda.[320]

During their administrations, Presidents Obama and Trump undertook
extensive measures, including air strikes and deployment of ground forces,
against the self-proclaimed "Islamic State" (ISIL or ISIS), a nonstate organization that straddled the border of Syria and Iraq.[321] In a report to Congress in
2014, President Obama stated that, after consulting with allies, he had decided
upon "implementation of a new comprehensive and sustained counterterrorism
strategy to degrade, and ultimately defeat, ISIL."[322] To that end, he ordered additional U.S. armed forces to Iraq "to provide training, communications support,
intelligence support, and other support, to select elements of the Iraqi security forces," and also "a systematic campaign of airstrikes and other necessary
actions against these terrorists in Iraq and Syria."[323] He asserted that such actions
were pursuant to his "constitutional and statutory authority as Commander in
Chief" (including pursuant to the 2001 and 2002 AUMF statutes) "and as Chief
Executive, as well as my constitutional and statutory authority to conduct the

---

[319] *See generally* PETER L. BERGEN, THE LONGEST WAR: THE ENDURING CONFLICT BETWEEN
AMERICA AND AL-QAEDA (2011); RICHARD A. CLARKE, AGAINST ALL ENEMIES: INSIDE AMERICA'S
WAR ON TERROR (2004). On the standards applied by the Obama administration with respect to
drone strikes, see The White House, Office of the Press Secretary, *Fact Sheet: U.S. Policy Standards
and Procedures for the Use of Force in Counterterrorism Operations Outside the United States and
Areas of Active Hostilities* (May 23, 2013), https://perma.cc/F3K6-HVKP.

[320] *See, e.g.*, Letter to Congressional Leaders on the Deployment of United States Combat-
Equipped Armed Forces, 1 PUB. PAPERS 804, 805 (June 15, 2012) (asserting that, in the context of
actions taken in Somalia, "the U.S. military has worked to counter the terrorist threat posed by al-
Qa'ida and al-Qa'ida–associated elements of al-Shabaab").

[321] The legal basis advanced for such action under international law differed depending on the
location of the actions. U.S. actions in Iraq were based upon Iraqi consent. U.S. actions in Syria were
based on the exercise of a U.S. right of individual and collective (with Iraq) self-defense, given that
the Syrian government was "unwilling or unable to prevent the use of its territory for such attacks."
Letter of Samantha J. Power, U.S. Representative to the United Nations, to Ban Ki-moon, U.N. Sec'y-
Gen. (Sept. 23, 2014), https://perma.cc/CUZ2-7VVD.

[322] Letter to Congressional Leaders Reporting on the Deployment of United States Armed Forces
Personnel to Iraq and the Authorization of Military Operations in Syria, 2014 DAILY COMP. PRES.
DOC. 1, 1 (Sept. 23, 2014).

[323] *Id.*

foreign relations of the United States."[324] Thereafter, U.S. forces engaged in extensive bombing operations of ISIL in both Iraq and Syria and provided training and
support for Kurdish and Arab fighters against it.[325]

Although some commentators rejected the legal justification for the
president's action,[326] arguing that ISIL was not an affiliate of al-Qaeda and therefore did not fall within the scope of the 2001 AUMF statute, Congress did not
challenge the president, and instead secured from him in 2015 draft language for
a new authorization to use force.[327] That authorization, however, was not enacted
into law, because it proved too difficult for Congress to agree upon whether to
include a geographical limitation, whether terms such as "associated persons or
forces" were sufficiently precise, and other matters.[328]

As is clear from the U.S. actions indicated here, resort to force against nonstate actors implicates the rights and obligations of foreign states, given that
foreign nonstate actors are invariably located in the territory of a foreign state.
Consequently, while the resort to force against a nonstate actor may seem to
be of a lesser significance than U.S. resort to force against a foreign state, using
force against the nonstate actor risks conflict with the government of the foreign
state where the nonstate actor is located, or even with that of a third state that is
supporting the nonstate actor. For example, in late 2019, U.S. forces in Iraq were
the target of certain Iraqi-based militant groups believed by the United States
to be supported by Iran. In January 2020, the Trump administration launched
a missile strike at a two-car convoy departing Baghdad airport that killed a visiting Iranian general, Qasem Soleimani, who was believed to be supporting and

---

[324] *Id.; see also* WHITE HOUSE, REPORT ON THE LEGAL AND POLICY FRAMEWORKS GUIDING THE
UNITED STATES' USE OF MILITARY FORCE AND RELATED NATIONAL SECURITY OPERATIONS 3–7, 16
(Dec. 2016), https://perma.cc/2ZS3-MZRF (reiterating such authorities and further claiming sup-
port from congressional authorization of assistance to the Syrian opposition); Office of the Legal
Counsel, U.S. Dep't of Justice, Authority to Order Targeted Airstrikes Against the Islamic State of
Iraq and the Levant (Dec. 30, 2014), https://perma.cc/E6DU-XVMV (describing president's actions
as constitutional). During President Trump's administration, similar measures were taken against
ISIL. *See, e.g.*, Letter to Congressional Leaders on the Global Deployment of United States Combat-
Equipped Armed Forces, 2020 DAILY COMP. PRES. DOC. 1 (June 9, 2020).

[325] *See* CARLA E. HUMUD & CHRISTOPHER M. BLANCHARD, CONG. RES. SERV. RL33487, ARMED
CONFLICT IN SYRIA: OVERVIEW AND U.S. RESPONSE (2020).

[326] *See, e.g.*, Bruce Ackerman, *Congress Must Act as Obama's War Against the Islamic State Hits
an Expiration Date*, WASH. POST, Nov. 7, 2014, at A19; Editorial Board, *Legal Authority for Fighting
ISIS*, N.Y. TIMES, Sept. 12, 2014, at A30 ("Mr. Obama . . . is now putting forward unjustifiable interpretations of the executive branch's authority to use military force without explicit approval from
Congress.").

[327] *See* Message to Congress on Submitting Proposed Legislation to Authorize the Use of Military
Force Against the Islamic State of Iraq and the Levant (ISIL) Terrorist Organization, 2015 DAILY
COMP. PRES. DOC. 1 (Feb. 11, 2015).

[328] *See* MATTHEW C. WEED, CONG. RESEARCH SERV., R43760, A NEW AUTHORIZATION FOR USE
OF MILITARY FORCE AGAINST THE ISLAMIC STATE: ISSUES AND CURRENT PROPOSALS 9–10 (Feb.
21, 2017).

coordinating the militant attacks.[329] According to the Department of Defense, General Soleimani was targeted because he was "responsible for the deaths of hundreds of American and coalition service members and the wounding of thousands more."[330] The cited legal bases for the strike were the president's commander-in-chief power[331] and the 2002 AUMF statute,[332] which according to the administration authorized "the use of force for the purpose of establishing a stable, democratic Iraq and addressing terrorist threats emanating from Iraq."[333] A few days later, Iran launched sixteen ballistic missiles against U.S. and coalition facilities in Iraq that caused traumatic brain injury to more than one hundred U.S. troops, but no fatalities.[334]

This time Congress did react to the U.S. use of force. A resolution was introduced in Congress directing "the President to terminate the use of United States Armed Forces for hostilities against the Islamic Republic of Iran or any part of its government or military, unless explicitly authorized by a declaration of war or specific authorization for use of military force against Iran."[335] At the same time, the resolution provided that the law did not "prevent the United States from defending itself against imminent attacks."[336] After passing in both the Senate and the House,[337] President Trump vetoed the bill in May 2020 saying it was unnecessary because, given the passage of time, the United States "is not engaged in the use of force against Iran," and further that it "incorrectly implies that the military airstrike" was conducted without statutory authority, when it

---

[329] For President Trump's comments, see Remarks on the Death of Islamic Revolutionary Guard Corps Major General and Quds Force Commander Qasem Soleimani of Iran in Palm Beach, Florida, 2020 DAILY COMP. PRES. DOC.1 (Jan. 3, 2020). For the justification under U.S. and international law, see Paul C. Ney, U.S. Dep't of Def. Gen. Counsel, Legal Considerations Related to the U.S. Air Strike Against Qassem Soleimani (Mar. 4, 2020), https://perma.cc/G754-ZHJE; Letter from Ambassador Kelly Craft, Permanent Representative, United States Mission to the United Nations, to Ambassador Dang Dinh Quy, President, United Nations Security Council (Jan. 8, 2020), https://perma.cc/E377-8EXY.

[330] U.S. Dep't of Def., Press Statement (Jan. 2, 2020), https://perma.cc/48KJ-KXGT.

[331] U.S. CONST. art. II § 2, cl. 1.

[332] Authorization for Use of Military Force Against Iraq Resolution of 2002, Pub. L. No. 107-243, 116 Stat. 1498 (2002) (codified at 50 U.S.C. § 1541 note (2018)).

[333] White House, Notice on the Legal and Policy Frameworks Guiding the United States' Use of Military Force and Related National Security Operations (Feb. 2020), https://perma.cc/R489-D9FU. The notice was provided to Congress in response to reporting called for by the National Defense Authorization Act for Fiscal Year 2018, Pub. L. No. 115-91, § 1264, 131 Stat. 1283 (2017), as amended, National Defense Authorization Act for Fiscal Year 2020, Pub. L. No. 116-92, § 1261, 133 Stat. 1198 (2019).

[334] See Jean K. Galbraith, Contemporary Practice of the United States Relating to International Law, 114 AM. J. INT'L L. 288, 321 (2020); Loren DeJonge Schulman & Paul Scharre, The Iranian Missile Strike Did Far More Damage Than Trump Admits, N.Y. TIMES (Feb. 12, 2020), https://perma.cc/8BBV-RNDN.

[335] S.J. Res. 68, 116th Cong. § 2(a) (2020).

[336] Id. § 2(b).

[337] The vote in the Senate was 55 to 45. 166 CONG. REC. S1061 (daily ed. Feb. 13, 2020). The vote in the House was 227 to 186. 166 CONG. REC. H1637 (daily ed. Mar. 11, 2020).

was supported by the 2002 AUMF.[338] While he acknowledged the bill's allowance for action against "imminent attacks," President Trump asserted that there was a need for the president to be able to respond to broader threats: "Protecting the national security of the United States involves taking actions to de-escalate threats around the world. . . . This resolution would impede the President's ability to counter adversarial forces by anticipating their next moves and taking swift actions to address them decisively."[339] Although the Senate voted to override the president's veto, the vote fell short of doing so, and consequently the bill did not become law.[340]

c. Uses of Force Principally for Humanitarian Objectives
A number of factors may explain why the United States since the end of the Cold War has repeatedly considered (and occasionally engaged in) significant uses of force for humanitarian objectives. The relative decline of East-West tensions has decreased the dangers to global stability of such actions, the human rights movement has placed increased emphasis on protecting vulnerable groups from atrocities by their government, and the dramatic increase in communications technologies through the internet and social media has sometimes prompted public desire to act. Even so, when such incidents arise and the president is inclined to act, Congress appears less able to garner political support for authorizing (or rejecting) the president's action, perhaps because of the lack of a direct threat to U.S. national security.

Humanitarian operations often involve an armed conflict that threatens a civilian population, leading the president to consider measures to ameliorate that suffering, including through the use of force. For example, in the aftermath of the Iraq-Kuwait War, the United States (in conjunction with France and the United Kingdom) engaged in a humanitarian relief operation in northern Iraq ("Operation Provide Comfort") designed to protect Iraqi Kurds who had fled into the mountains along the border of Turkey to escape oppressive acts by the Iraqi government in the form of air, missile, and artillery attacks. With death rates among the Kurdish refugees estimated at as many as one thousand per day, the United States declared a "no-fly" zone in northern Iraq prohibiting all flights north of the thirty-sixth parallel and "commenced an extensive relief operation, consisting of air dropping tons of food, water, coats, tents, blankets, and medicines into Iraq."[341] Ultimately, safe havens were established, protected by

---

[338] Statement on Vetoing Legislation to Terminate the Use of United States Armed Forces in Hostilities Against Iran, 2020 DAILY COMP. PRES. DOC. 1 (May 6, 2020).

[339] Message to the Senate Returning Without Approval Legislation To Terminate the Use of United States Armed Forces in Hostilities Against Iran, 2020 DAILY COMP. PRES. DOC. 1, 2 (May 6, 2020).

[340] The vote in the Senate was 49 to 44. 166 CONG. REC. S2313 (daily ed. May 7, 2020).

[341] *See* SEAN D. MURPHY, HUMANITARIAN INTERVENTION: THE UNITED NATIONS IN AN EVOLVING WORLD ORDER 168, 172 (1996).

as many as twenty thousand forces from thirteen states, including the United States, though by mid-July those forces were replaced by U.N. peacekeepers.[342] No express congressional authorization existed for such action; the use of force statute adopted by Congress in November 1990 authorized the use of force to uphold various Security Council resolutions, but none of the identified resolutions in that authorization related to such a humanitarian operation. There did exist a different Security Council resolution relating to the plight of the Kurds, but Congress' use of force statute did not refer to that resolution, which, in any event, did not authorize or call for states to intervene in Iraq for this purpose.[343] Arguably a provision contained in a 1991 appropriations law provided some authority for the humanitarian operation, although that provision confusingly only supported action "consistent" with the 1990 use of force statute and prior Security Council resolutions, which provided no such authority.[344]

Similarly, in response to the armed conflict that broke out in the Balkans in the early 1990s, the United States undertook various measures, including airdrops of food and medicine, which President Clinton described as "a massive effort, running longer than the Berlin airlift, which has relieved starvation and suffering for tens of thousands of Bosnians," and as including "enforcement of a no-fly zone to stop the parties from spreading the war with aircraft."[345] Moreover, in the latter part of the armed conflict, U.S. military forces participated in a NATO bombing campaign against Bosnian Serbs to achieve humanitarian objectives, such as to force a withdrawal of heavy weapons from around Sarajevo. While President Clinton kept Congress informed of such actions, none of them were expressly authorized by Congress.

In this same time period, civil war in Somalia led to chaotic conditions, in which thousands of persons were killed, hundreds of thousands were displaced from their homes, the nation's infrastructure was severely diminished, and government had all but disappeared. Although various organizations sought to provide food and medicine, such supplies were largely stymied by interclan warfare.[346] After a U.N. peacekeeping operation failed to improve conditions, the United States offered in November 1992 to deploy some twenty thousand troops

[342] Id. at 174, 176.
[343] See S.C. Res. 688 (Apr. 5, 1991).
[344] See National Defense Authorization Act for Fiscal Years 1992 and 1998, Pub. L. No. 102-190, § 1096, 105 Stat. 1290, 1489 (1991) ("[T]he Congress supports the use of all necessary means to achieve the goals of United Nations Security Council Resolution 688 consistent with all relevant United Nations Security Council Resolutions and the Authorization for Use of Military Force Against Iraq Resolution....").
[345] The President's Radio Address and an Exchange with Reporters, 1 PUB. PAPERS 283, 284 (Feb. 19, 1994).
[346] See generally TERRENCE LYONS & AHMED I. SAMATAR, SOMALIA: STATE COLLAPSE, MULTILATERAL INTERVENTION, AND STRATEGIES FOR POLITICAL RECONSTRUCTION (1995).

to help ensure distribution of food and aid in Somalia.[347] The U.N. Security Council then adopted a resolution in essence authorizing a U.S.-led force to enter Somalia to help safeguard relief operations.[348] By January 1993, some 24,000 U.S. Marines had been deployed to Somalia as the core of a multinational "United Task Force." The deployment initially did much to restore relief operations but was unable over the long term to lead to political stability in Somalia. Ultimately, U.S. efforts to capture a Somali warlord led to the disastrous October 1993 raid recounted in *Black Hawk Down* and a loss of support in the United States for continuing the intervention.[349]

When U.S. forces began deploying to Somalia in December 1992, President George H.W. Bush did not seek any express authorization from Congress. In February 1993, the Senate adopted a joint resolution stating that, in order to avert further starvation in Somalia, the "President is authorized to use United States Armed Forces pursuant to United Nations Security Council Resolution 794 in order to implement the Resolution, which authorizes the use of 'all necessary means to establish as soon as possible a secure environment for humanitarian relief operations in Somalia.' "[350] The House did not take up the matter until several months later, in May 1993, at which time it adopted a slightly revised version of the resolution.[351] Yet a reconciled version never passed both Houses of Congress and events on the ground in Somalia ultimately overtook any statutory authorization for the use of force.

There did arguably exist implied authorization for U.S. force in Somalia in the form of a statute adopted to address relief operations in the Horn of Africa. Among other things, that statute provided that it was "the sense of the Congress that the President should . . . ensure, to the maximum extent possible and in conjunction with other donors, that emergency humanitarian assistance is being made available to those in need . . . ."[352] Further, the statute indicated that U.S. policy should be "to assure noncombatants . . . equal and ready access to all food, emergency, and relief assistance," and that the United States should "redouble its commendable efforts to secure safe corridors of passage for emergency food and relief supplies in affected areas . . . ."[353] Although the Department of Justice noted such statutory authority, the attorney general justified the

---

[347] *See* U.N. Secretary-General, *The Situation in Somalia: Rep. of the Secretary-General*, U.N. Doc. S/23829 (Apr. 21, 1992).

[348] S.C. Res. 794 (Dec. 3, 1993) (authorizing states to use all necessary means to establish "a secure environment for humanitarian relief operations"); *see also* S.C. Res. 837 (June 6, 1993).

[349] *See* MARK BOWDEN, BLACK HAWK DOWN: A STORY OF MODERN WAR (1999).

[350] S.J. Res. 45, 103d Cong. (1993). The resolution passed on a voice vote.

[351] *See* 139 CONG. REC. 11,037 (1993). The vote was 243 in favor, 179 opposed, and 10 abstentions.

[352] Horn of Africa Recovery and Food Security Act, Pub. L. No. 102-274, § 3(b)(3), 106 Stat. 115, 116 (1992) (codified at 22 U.S.C. § 2151 note (2018)).

[353] *Id.* §§ 4(a)(1), 4(b)(1), 106 Stat. at 117.

intervention principally on the basis that, even without express prior authorization from Congress, the president—as commander in chief and as chief executive—"may reasonably and lawfully determine that the protection of those engaged in relief work in Somalia, including members of the United States Armed Forces who have been and will be dispatched to Somalia to assist in that work, justifies the use of United States military personnel in this operation."[354]

Moreover, the attorney general maintained that such power included using "those military personnel to protect Somalians and other foreign nationals in Somalia," given prior U.S. deployments to China during the Boxer Rebellion in 1900–1901 and to the Dominican Republic in 1965, which also involved protecting non-U.S. nationals.[355] Even so, after public support for the U.S. intervention collapsed in the fall of 1993, Congress enacted legislation providing that funds for the operation could be obligated beyond March of 1994 only "to protect American diplomatic facilities and American citizens, and noncombat personnel [there] to advise the United Nations commander in Somalia."[356] President Clinton then announced that all U.S. forces would be withdrawn from Somalia by March 1994.

Similar challenges for congressional action arose with respect to the U.S. air strikes in 1999 against the Federal Republic of Yugoslavia (FRY, consisting of Serbia and Montenegro). Although the United States said that it had considered "numerous" factors in deciding to use force against the FRY, the primary objective was to prevent Serb military and police forces from committing human rights abuses within Serbia's province of Kosovo against Kosovar Albanians.[357] In the lead-up to the conflict, talks among the interested parties were unsuccessfully held in Rambouillet, France, in February 1999. At that time, the U.S. House of Representatives passed a resolution supporting the deployment of U.S. forces to Kosovo in the event of a peace agreement.[358] After the Rambouillet talks failed, on March 23 the U.S. Senate passed a resolution stating that "the President of the United States is authorized to conduct military air operations and missile strikes in cooperation with our NATO allies against the Federal Republic of Yugoslavia (Serbia and Montenegro)."[359] Although the resolution was transmitted to the

---

[354] Authority to Use United States Military Forces in Somalia, 16 Op. O.L.C. 6, 6 (1992).

[355] *Id.* at 6, 11.

[356] Appropriations Act of 1994, Pub. L. No. 103-139, § 8151(b)(2)(B), 107 Stat. 1418, 1476 (1993).

[357] *See* U.S. Dep't of State, Daily Press Briefing of James P. Rubin (Mar. 16, 1999), https://perma.cc/4AG5-V8NZ.

[358] *See* H.R. Con. Res. 42, 106th Cong. (1999) was enacted by the House of Representatives on March 11, 1999, by a vote of 219 to 191. The resolution authorized the deployment of U.S. forces to Kosovo as part of a NATO peacekeeping operation up to a level of 15 percent of the total NATO force, subject to certain notification and reporting requirements to Congress.

[359] S. Con. Res. 21, 106th Cong. (1999).

House of Representatives for concurrence, the House did not vote on the matter for more than a month.

On March 24, U.S. air strikes commenced, operating under a NATO umbrella but without U.N. Security Council authorization.[360] On March 26, President Clinton formally notified congressional leaders, charging that the FRY had "failed to comply with U.N. Security Council resolutions, and its actions are in violation of its obligations under the U.N. Charter and its other international commitments." The president stated that he had taken these actions pursuant to his "constitutional authority to conduct U.S. foreign relations and as Commander in Chief and Chief Executive," and that he was keeping Congress informed "consistent" with the War Powers Resolution of 1973.[361]

On April 12, Representative Tom Campbell introduced two resolutions in the House of Representatives, one requiring the termination of U.S. military involvement in Kosovo and, alternatively, one declaring that a state of "war" exists between the United States and the FRY. On April 28, the House held four votes on the conflict with the FRY. The House voted against terminating U.S. military involvement in Kosovo,[362] against declaring "war" with the FRY,[363] in favor of requiring the president to seek congressional approval before introducing ground troops into Kosovo,[364] and deadlocked on a vote regarding the Senate resolution supporting the air campaign.[365]

Despite the unwillingness of the House to declare explicitly its support for the air campaign, the House passed on May 18, by a vote of 269 to 158, and the Senate passed on May 20, by a vote of 64 to 36, a $15 billion emergency appropriation to support U.S. military activities in Kosovo and refugee assistance, as well as other matters unrelated to Kosovo.[366] OLC determined that such an appropriation constituted congressional authorization for continued U.S. military action after the expiration of sixty days under Section 5(b) of the War Powers Resolution.[367]

---

[360] Remarks on the NATO Airstrikes Against Serbian Targets and an Exchange With Reporters, 1 PUB. PAPERS 462 (Mar. 28, 1999); see also William Jefferson Clinton, A Just and Necessary War, N.Y. TIMES, May 23, 1999, at WK17 (discussing instability in the Balkans).

[361] Letter to Congressional Leaders Reporting on Airstrikes Against Serbian Targets in the Federal Republic of Yugoslavia (Serbia and Montenegro), 1 PUB. PAPERS 459, 459–60 (Mar. 26, 1999); see also Letter to Congressional Leaders Reporting on Airstrikes Against Serbian Targets in the Federal Republic of Yugoslavia (Serbia and Montenegro), 1 PUB. PAPERS 516 (Apr. 7, 1999).

[362] H.R. Con. Res. 82, 106th Cong. (1999). The resolution was defeated by a vote of 290 to 139.

[363] H.R.J. Res. 44, 106th Cong. (1999). The resolution was defeated by a vote of 427 to 2.

[364] H.R. Res. 1569, 106th Cong. (1999) (enacted). The resolution passed by a vote of 249 to 180.

[365] A further effort in the Senate by Senator John McCain to pass a resolution authorizing the president "to use all necessary force and other means" to accomplish U.S. and NATO objectives was set aside on May 4, largely due to opposition from the White House, which did not wish to promote the idea of U.S. ground troops being introduced into the conflict. See Helen Dewar, Senate Shelves McCain Proposal on Kosovo, WASH. POST, May 5, 1999, at A27.

[366] Act of May 21, 1999, Pub. L. No. 106-31, 113 Stat. 57.

[367] 24 Op. O.L.C., supra note 243.

Based on the unwillingness of the House to join the Senate in explicitly supporting the air campaign, as well as its vote against the resolution declaring a state of war against the FRY, Representative Campbell and sixteen other members of the House of Representatives on April 30 filed a federal lawsuit challenging President Clinton's ability to continue the air campaign against the FRY without authorization from Congress. Plaintiffs argued that they had standing since the president's action "violated the War Powers clause of the Constitution" as well as the War Powers Resolution. In light of this allegation, the plaintiffs requested the court to issue declaratory relief that the president's actions were unconstitutional and that "the President was required to withdraw the United States Armed Forces from the Federal Republic of Yugoslavia by May 25, 1999."[368] Both the district court (in June 1999) and the circuit court (in February 2000) dismissed the case, finding that the plaintiffs lacked standing. The circuit court found no nullification of the plaintiffs' votes in Congress because Congess "could have passed a law forbidding the use of U.S. forces," and "could have cut off funds for the American role in the conflict," but in both respects failed to do so.[369]

Ultimately, the use of air strikes alone to engage in humanitarian actions has been defended by the executive branch as not requiring congressional authorization. For example, in reaction to the outbreak of civil war in Libya in early 2011, the U.N. Security Council passed a resolution imposing an arms embargo on Libya, freezing the assets of its leader Muammar Gaddafi and ten members of his inner circle, and restricting their travel.[370] When the violence continued, the Council adopted a second resolution demanding an immediate ceasefire and characterizing the violence as possibly "crimes against humanity." Further, the resolution established a ban on all flights within Libya (a "no-fly zone"), other than flights transporting humanitarian aid, evacuating foreign nationals, enforcing the no-fly zone, or those "deemed necessary for the benefit of the Libyan people." Importantly, the resolution authorized member states "acting nationally or through regional organizations or arrangements, and acting in cooperation with the Secretary-General, to take all necessary measures . . . to protect civilians and civilian populated areas under threat of attack in [Libya], while excluding a foreign occupation force in any form on any part of Libyan territory . . . ."[371] Thereafter, a multistate coalition commenced military operations against Libya to implement the resolution, with NATO assuming control of some aspects.

While other NATO member states conducted most of the air strikes in Libya against Gaddafi's forces, U.S. forces flew most of the missions related to

---

[368] Campbell v. Clinton, 52 F. Supp. 2d 34, 39 (D.D.C. 1999).
[369] Campbell v. Clinton, 203 F.3d 19, 23 (D.C. Cir. 2000). For discussion of congressional standing generally, see Chapter 4 § II(B)(1).
[370] See S.C. Res. 1970 (Feb. 26, 2011).
[371] See S.C. Res. 1973 (Mar. 17, 2011).

reconnaissance, surveillance, and refueling (comprising approximately one-fourth of the missions flown each day by NATO), as well as occasional air strikes using drone (unmanned) aircraft.[372] No U.S. ground troops or trainers were deployed into Libya. In March 2011, President Obama transmitted to Congress a report "as part of my efforts to keep the Congress fully informed, consistent with the War Powers Resolution." In it, he stressed that the "United States has not deployed ground forces into Libya. United States forces are conducting a limited and well-defined mission in support of international efforts to protect civilians and prevent a humanitarian disaster."[373] Specifically, in support of U.N. Security Council resolution 1973, "U.S. military forces, under the command of Commander, U.S. Africa Command, began a series of strikes against air defense systems and military airfields for the purposes of preparing a no-fly zone. These strikes will be limited in their nature, duration, and scope."[374]

Thereafter, OLC issued an opinion defending the lawfulness of the action, stating that prior congressional approval was not required given that the limited military operations contemplated did not constitute "war" in the constitutional sense. Comparing the action to the 1995 no-fly zone patrols and periodic air strikes in Bosnia, as well as the 1999 NATO bombing campaign in respect of Kosovo (which had no congressional authorization), the Office noted that the Libyan action also would be limited to air strikes and associated support missions. Therefore, the operation would avoid the "difficulties of withdrawal and risks of escalation that may attend commitment of ground forces," which were "two factors that this Office has identified as 'arguably' indicating 'a greater need for approval [from Congress] at the outset,' to avoid creating a situation in which 'Congress may be confronted with circumstances in which the exercise of its power to declare war is effectively foreclosed.' "[375] Further, like the prior operations, "the anticipated operations here served a 'limited mission' and did not 'aim at the conquest or occupation of territory.' "[376] In any event, if the War Powers Resolution required authorization from Congress within sixty days (or

---

[372] See, e.g., John R. Crook, *Contemporary Practice of the United States Relating to International Law*, 58 AM. J. INT'L L. 568, 574 (2011).

[373] See Letter to Congressional Leaders Reporting on the Commencement of Military Operations Against Libya, 1 PUB. PAPERS 280–81 (Mar. 21, 2011); see also Letter to Congressional Leaders on the Global Deployments of United States Combat-Equipped Armed Forces, *id.* at 678 (June 15, 2011) (describing reasons for the start of the military operation in Libya as being "to prevent a humanitarian catastrophe and address the threat posed to international peace and security by the crisis in Libya and to protect the people of Libya from the Qadhafi regime.").

[374] Letter to Congressional Leaders Reporting on the Commencement of Military Operations Against Libya, *supra* note 373, at 280; see also Remarks on the Situation in Libya, *id.* at 247 (Mar. 18, 2011).

[375] Authority to Use Military Force in Libya, 35 Op. O.L.C. 1, 13 (Apr. 1, 2011) (quoting 19 Op. O.L.C. at 333).

[376] *Id.* (quoting 19 Op. O.L.C. at 332).

cessation of U.S. military operations), that deadline passed without congressional action.[377]

In June 2011, ten members of the House of Representatives sued President Obama, claiming that the ongoing military action violated Congress' Article I powers and the requirements of the War Powers Resolution. Among other things, the plaintiffs requested a declaration that U.S. military action against Libya was a "war" for purposes of the Constitution and was unconstitutional absent authorization from Congress. The district court, however, dismissed the case on grounds of standing,[378] noting that under *Raines v. Byrd*[379] the Supreme Court had held "that generalized injuries that affect all members of Congress in the same broad and undifferentiated manner are not sufficiently 'personal' or 'particularized,' but rather are *institutional*, and too widely dispersed to confer standing."[380] Here, the plaintiffs had not brought the case on behalf of the House of Representatives as a whole, and prior case law had "all but foreclosed the idea that a member of Congress can assert legislative standing to maintain a suit against a member of the Executive Branch."[381]

6. Threatening Armed Conflict

Presidential action has not been limited to the actual resort to armed force. Over the course of U.S. history, presidents have threatened foreign states with military force if certain demands are not met. In several of the incidents discussed previously, the president has issued threats prior to the pursuit of armed conflict. In such situations, Congress has rarely authorized the president to take such action, even though the threat may well place the United States in a position where resort to armed force becomes almost inevitable.

Yet in some situations Congress has supported the president in issuing such threats. For example, in April 1914, after U.S. sailors were mistakenly detained by Mexican federal troops in Tampico, Mexico, President Woodrow Wilson demanded that the Mexican government apologize, raise the U.S. flag in a prominent place, and give it a twenty-one-gun salute. When the Mexican government apologized but declined to give the salute, the president went before Congress seeking support in extracting Mexico's compliance. On April 22, Congress adopted a joint resolution stating that "the President is justified in the employment of the armed forces of the United States to enforce his demand for

---

[377] *See* Eileen Burgin, *War Over Worlds: Reinterpreting "Hostilities" and the War Powers Resolution,* 29 BYU J. Pub. L. 99 (2014); Charlie Savage, *Libya Effort Is Called Violation of War Act,* N.Y. Times, May 26, 2011, at A8.
[378] Kucinich v. Obama, 821 F. Supp. 2d 110, 125 (D.D.C. 2011).
[379] 521 U.S. 811 (1997).
[380] *Kucinich,* 821 F. Supp. 2d at 118 (quoting Kucinich v. Bush, 236 F. Supp. 2d 1, 7 (D.D.C. 2002)).
[381] *Id.* at 115–16.

unequivocal amends for certain affronts and indignities committed against the United States" by Mexico.[382] The resolution further stated that "the United States disclaims any hostility to the Mexican people or any purpose to make war upon Mexico."[383] Alas, events on the ground in Mexico overtook the situation, with U.S. Marines landing on April 21 at Veracruz, forcibly seizing the city and occupying it for seven months.[384]

The issuance of such threats continues today. During 2012–2013, President Obama made various statements indicating that he might use military force against Syria if it used chemical weapons against its people[385] and against Iran if it continued to pursue a nuclear program that many feared would result in nuclear weapons.[386] Likewise, President Trump made various statements (and "tweets" on the social networking site Twitter) that threatened or appeared to threaten Iran, North Korea, Syria, and Venezuela with military action if they did or did not take certain actions.[387]

D. Contemporary Issues

1. Method and Consequences of Congressional Authorization

Traditional international law distinguished between rules that applied in times of "peace" and rules that applied in times of "war"; the latter included rules that allowed for killing or capturing of enemy combatants, seizure of enemy property, expulsion of enemy aliens, and obligations of neutral states to refrain from assisting either belligerent.[388]

---

[382] H.R.J. Res. 251, 63d Cong., 38 Stat. 770 (1914).

[383] *Id.*; *see* Modes of Redress, 6 HACKWORTH DIGEST, at 152; States, Territories, and Governments, 1 HACKWORTH DIGEST, at 151.

[384] *See* JOHN S.D. EISENHOWER, INTERVENTION! THE UNITED STATES AND THE MEXICAN REVOLUTION, 1913–1917, at 79–124 (1993).

[385] *See, e.g.*, Address to the Nation on the Situation in Syria, 2 PUB. PAPERS 1020, 1023 (Sept. 10, 2013).

[386] *See, e.g.*, Remarks at the American Israel Public Affairs Committee Conference, 1 PUB. PAPERS 249, 253 (Mar. 5, 2012).

[387] *See* Donald J. Trump (@realDonaldTrump), Twitter (Jan. 2, 2018, 7:49 PM), https://perma.cc/C9Y5-3F77 (North Korea); Brian Ellsworth, *Trump Says U.S. Military Intervention in Venezuela "An Option;" Russia Objects*, REUTERS, Feb. 3, 2019; Donald J. Trump (@realDonaldTrump), Twitter (July 22, 2018, 11:24 PM), https://perma.cc/2TBJ-LPDK (Iran); Ryan Pickrell, *US Warns Syria Response will be "Stronger" Than Ever Before if Assad Uses Chemical Weapons Again*, BUSINESS INSIDER (Sept. 10, 2018, 8:32 PM), https://perma.cc/MU95-E9MK.

[388] *See generally* 8 ANNALS OF CONG. 1980 (1798) (Joseph Gales ed., 1834) (remarks of Rep. Gallatin); Clyde Eagleton, *The Duty of Impartiality on the Part of a Neutral*, 34 AM. J. INT'L L. 99 (1940); Quincy Wright, *The Present Status of Neutrality*, 34 AM. J. INT'L L. 391 (1940); HUGO GROTIUS, DE JURE BELLI AC PACIS (OF THE LAW OF WAR AND PEACE) (Francis W. Kelsey trans., 1925) (1625); VATTEL, *supra* note 46.

Historically, a formal declaration of war clearly established a state of "war" between two belligerents.[389] Yet, as previously noted, by the 1700s states habitually resorted to armed conflict without issuance of formal declarations of war.[390] Indeed, one study concluded that from 1700 to 1870 there were 107 cases of war, but not more than 10 involved a declaration of war.[391] Perhaps for that reason, the existence of a declaration of war does not appear to have been a *sine qua non* for triggering the law of war. The 1878 edition of Kent's *Commentary* explained that "[s]ince the Peace of Versailles in 1763, formal declarations of war of any kind seem to have been discontinued, and all the necessary and legitimate consequences of war flow at once from a state of public hostilities, duly recognised, and explicitly announced, by a domestic manifesto or State paper."[392] By way of example, the *Commentary* noted that the war between England and France that broke out in 1793, triggering President Washington's declaration of neutrality, involved no declaration of war by either belligerent (nor did the wars between them in 1778 or 1803).[393]

As indicated in the prior section, Congress has "declared war" eleven times in U.S. history, the last being in 1942. The exercise of this power of Congress, however, has not been limited to formal declarations of war. Beginning with the "quasi-war" against France in the late 1700s, and continuing today, Congress has viewed its power as including the authority to approve or disapprove of other ways that the United States might resort to armed force against another state or nonstate actor. That is not to say that all decisions to resort to armed force lay exclusively with Congress; the president has often acted without securing any authority from Congress.[394] But Congress' power to "declare" has not been viewed as limited solely to a decision of whether to formally declare war.[395] As such, while formal declarations of war may now be largely a thing of the past, that

---

[389] *See* Clyde Eagleton, *The Form and Function of the Declaration of War*, 32 Am. J. Int'l L. 19 (1938).

[390] *See supra* this chapter § I(C).

[391] J.F. Maurice, Hostilities Without Declaration of War: From 1700 to 1870, at 4 (1883); *see also* Hallett, The Lost Art of Declaring War, *supra* note 38, at 34; Treanor, *supra* note 35, at 709 (discussing the Founders' understanding of "declare war" as compared to what it meant in international law).

[392] Kent's Commentary on International Law 170–71 (J.T. Abdy ed., 2d ed. 1878).

[393] *Id.* at 171.

[394] Michael Ramsey argues that declarations of war remain prevalent but are now mostly issued by the president in the form of public announcements "that the nation has entered a state of war, together with the reasons for, and objectives of, the conflict." Michael D. Ramsey, *Presidential Declarations of War*, 37 U.C. Davis L. Rev. 321, 325 (2003).

[395] *See, e.g.*, Mitchell v. Laird, 488 F.2d 611, 615 (D.C. Cir. 1973) ("[I]t is constitutionally permissible for Congress to use another means than a formal declaration of war to give its approval to a war . . . ."); United States v. Castillo, 34 M.J. 1160, 1164 (N-M. Ct. Crim. App. 1992) ("Congress may assent to the waging of war by means other than a formal declaration of war, and what form it chooses to record that assent is within its discretion to decide.").

development cannot fairly be said to have obviated Congress' Article I powers in this area.

A few commentators have argued that Congress should only act by "declaring war" and should not simply authorize the use of force when exercising its Article I power.[396] Yet the president, Congress, the Supreme Court, and most commentators all appear to regard "use of force" resolutions by Congress as a form of Congress' power under Article I.[397] Thus, in *Hamdan v. Rumsfeld*, the Court assumed that the authorization contained in the 2001 AUMF statute "activated the President's war powers."[398]

A congressional authorization to use force may also be implied from the authorization and appropriation of funds, though some caution must be exercised in that regard.[399] John Hart Ely suggested applying "first-order common sense" to the issue: "If there is no reason to infer that Congress knew what the agency or program in question was about, the fact that it was buried in an appropriations measure is typically not taken to constitute authorization of it. If the program was conspicuous, it is."[400]

Congress has from the outset supported presidential uses of force by means of appropriations statutes, such as those adopted during the "quasi-war" with France in the late 1790s.[401] Similar authority existed during the Vietnam War[402] and, more recently, during the 1999 military campaign against Serbia with respect to Kosovo.[403] One contemporary impediment to the use of appropriations statutes to authorize military operations, however, is that the War Powers Resolution purports, in Section 8(a)(1), to bar Congress from doing so unless the

---

[396] *See* HALLETT, THE LOST ART OF DECLARING WAR, *supra* note 38, at 145–68; J. Gregory Sidak, *To Declare War*, 41 DUKE L.J. 27 (1991).

[397] *See, e.g.*, Peter Raven-Hansen, *Constitutional Constraints: The War Clause*, *in* THE U.S. CONSTITUTION AND THE POWER TO GO TO WAR, *supra* note 187, at 43; Bradley & Goldsmith, *supra* note 311, at 2059; Alexander M. Bickel, *Congress, the President and the Power to Wage War*, 48 CHI.-KENT L. REV. 131, 139–40 (1971).

[398] Hamdan v. Rumsfeld, 548 U.S. 557, 594 (2006) (citing to Hamdi v. Rumsfeld, 542 U.S. 507 (2004)). For further discussion of *Hamdan*, see *infra* this chapter §§ II(A), II(B), III(B); Chapter 1 § II(B); Chapter 5 § II(A)(2); and Chapter 10 § II(E)(4).

[399] *See* Note, *Congress, The President, and the Power to Commit Forces to Combat*, 81 HARV. L. REV. 1771, 1801 (1968). A few commentators do not regard appropriation statutes as sufficient authority to use armed force. *See, e.g.*, WORMUTH & FIRMAGE, *supra* note 36, at 225–34.

[400] ELY, *supra* note 62, at 27.

[401] *See supra* this chapter text accompanying note 74.

[402] *See* Da Costa v. Laird, 448 F.2d 1368, 1369 (2d Cir. 1971) (". . . there was sufficient legislative action in extending the Selective Service Act and in appropriating billions of dollars to carry on military and naval operations in Vietnam to ratify and approve the measures taken by the Executive, even in the absence of the Gulf of Tonkin Resolution."); Orlando v. Laird, 443 F.2d 1039, 1042 (2d Cir. 1971) (citing the same as showing that "Congress and the Executive have taken mutual and joint action in the prosecution and support of military operations in Southeast Asia from the beginning of those operations"); WILLIAM C. BANKS & PETER RAVEN-HANSEN, NATIONAL SECURITY LAW AND THE POWER OF THE PURSE 119 (1994).

[403] *See* 24 Op. O.L.C., *supra* note 243.

appropriation measure "states that it is intended to constitute specific statutory authorization within the meaning of this chapter . . . ."[404] A prior Congress, however, cannot bind a future Congress as to the means by which the latter authorizes the president to use military force; thus, it cannot require a future Congress to include in its statute a reference to the War Powers Resolution.[405] Everything, then, turns on whether the present-day Congress is in fact authorizing a use of force, which is possible through an appropriations statute that is sufficiently targeted at the military operation being pursued by the president.

Further, when Congress expressly authorizes a use of force, the authorization may contain conditions and restrictions. When construing the statutes adopted by Congress for the "quasi-war" with France, U.S. courts regarded such authorization as more circumscribed than would be a general declaration of war.[406] Similar conditions or restrictions may be seen in contemporary statutes authorizing the use of force. Thus, the authorization may be limited to the achievement of specific objectives, may be limited in time and place, and may be unavailable if further diplomatic measures for peaceful settlement exist.[407]

Regardless of the method used to authorize the use of force, consequences arise or can arise for the United States under international law depending on the circumstances, including the level of hostilities and the reactions of the other belligerent and third-party states. Large-scale hostilities have been regarded as engaging traditional rules of the law of war; indeed, contemporary treaties (such as the 1949 Geneva Conventions) apply in situations of "armed conflict" not just "war," and hence operate in any circumstance where armed conflict is deemed to have arisen between two belligerents. For low levels of coercion, the matter is less clear, especially if the coercion is of short duration.

As a matter of U.S. statutory law, however, there may be a difference if Congress "declares war" as opposed to authorizes a use of force, since under several statutes a "declaration of war" by Congress automatically has an effect that does not arise with respect to other types of congressional action. For example, under the Alien Enemy Act, the president is authorized to deport, detain, or otherwise regulate enemy aliens located in the United States in cases of "declared war" or an invasion of the United States; the simple adoption of a use of force authorization

---

[404] 50 U.S.C. § 1547(a)(1) (2018). This provision (which originally appeared at S. 440, 93d Cong. § 3(4) (1973)) was intended "to counteract the opinion in the *Orlando v. Laird* decision of the Second Circuit Court holding that passage of defense appropriations bills, and extension of the Selective Service Act, could be construed as implied Congressional authorization for the Vietnam war." S. Rep. No. 93-220, at 25 (1973).

[405] *See* Banks & Raven-Hansen, *supra* note 402, at 131; Bobbitt, *supra* note 35, at 1399 ("If Congress can constitutionally authorize the use of force through its appropriations and authorization procedures, an interpretive statute that denies this inference—as does . . . the original War Powers Resolution—is without legal effect.").

[406] *See, e.g.,* Gray v. United States, 21 Ct. Cl. 340, 373 (Ct. Cl. 1886).

[407] *See supra* this chapter note 89.

by Congress does not appear to meet the terms of the statute.[408] Other statutes, however, are activated whenever a "war" exists, which could arise either from a declaration of war or from a use of force authorization that leads to a state of "war." For example, the Trading with the Enemy Act authorizes the president "during the time of war" to investigate, regulate, and prohibit any financial or property transactions in which any foreign state or its nationals have any interest.[409] Rather than "war," some statutes refer instead to "armed hostilities." Hence, the International Emergency Economic Powers Act (IEEPA) authorizes the president "when the United States is engaged in armed hostilities or has been attacked by a foreign country or foreign nationals" to seize any of their property that is subject to U.S. jurisdiction.[410] Sometimes the statute expressly refers to situations where Congress has authorized the use of force. For example, the running of statutes of limitations for certain federal offenses is suspended when "the United States is at war or Congress has enacted a specific authorization for the use of the Armed Forces, as described in section 5(b) of the War Powers Resolution (50 U.S.C. 1544 (b)) . . . ."[411] In many instances, these statutes are also available if the president issues a declaration of national emergency, while certain other statutes are *only* activated if the president issues a declaration of national emergency.[412]

2. Consequences of International Law

As noted in the introduction to this chapter and by the preceding discussion regarding the emergence of the U.N. Security Council as a factor with respect to the use of force, various rules of international law relating to the *jus ad bellum* (law concerning when a state may resort to armed conflict) reside in the background of the rules on U.S. constitutional war powers. As a matter of U.S. law, these rules of international law are inferior to the U.S. Constitution, but they nevertheless play a very important role in the exercise of U.S. war powers.

The core *jus ad bellum* rules are found in the U.N. Charter. Article 2(4) sets forth what is widely regarded as a prohibition on all uses of force (or threats to use force) by one state against another, although disagreements often arise as to whether certain types of actions (such as a rescue of one's nationals from a grave threat) do in fact violate the prohibition.[413] Two exceptions to this prohibition

---

[408] 50 U.S.C. § 21.

[409] 50 U.S.C. §§ 4301–41.

[410] 50 U.S.C. § 1702(a)(1)(C) (2018).

[411] 18 U.S.C. § 3287.

[412] For example, under the National Emergencies Act, 50 U.S.C. § 1631 (2018), the president, upon declaring a national emergency, must publish it in the *Federal Register* and report to Congress which emergency powers he is exercising.

[413] U.N. Charter art. 2(4) ("All Members shall refrain in their international relations from the threat or use of force against the territorial integrity or political independence of any state, or in any other manner inconsistent with the Purposes of the United Nations.").

are expressly set forth in the Charter. First, a state may act in self-defense on its own behalf or in collective self-defense on behalf of another state.[414] Here, too, disagreements arise as to whether the conditions meriting self-defense have arisen and whether the defensive action is necessary and proportionate to the threat it is addressing.[415] Second, a state may use force when so authorized by the U.N. Security Council under Chapter VII of the Charter. For the Security Council to issue such an authorization, it must determine that there exists a threat to the peace, a breach of the peace, or an act of aggression, and it may authorize either nonforcible action (such as economic sanctions) or forcible action.[416]

While the U.N. Charter contains the core rules, other instruments also set forth relevant rules. For example, several regional defense agreements provide for collective self-defense, such as the North Atlantic Treaty, which is the charter for NATO.[417] Under Article 5 of the North Atlantic Treaty, the parties agree that an armed attack against one party shall be considered an attack against all NATO parties, such that all parties will assist the attacked party by taking action as they deem necessary. NATO's North Atlantic Council invoked Article 5 for the first time in the aftermath of the September 2001 terrorist incidents.[418] While such treaties help foster cooperation among states for engaging in collective self-defense, they are not drafted in a manner that commits the United States to necessarily use military force (the NATO Charter only calls for actions by NATO members "as they deem necessary") and, in any event, are not regarded under

---

[414] Article 51 of the U.N. Charter provides:

Nothing in the present Charter shall impair the inherent right of individual or collective self-defence if an armed attack occurs against a Member of the United Nations, until the Security Council has taken measures necessary to maintain international peace and security. Measures taken by Members in the exercise of this right of self-defence shall be immediately reported to the Security Council. . . .

U.N. Charter art. 51.
[415] An important source of interpretation and clarification of these rules has been the International Court of Justice. *See* Armed Activities on the Territory of the Congo (Dem. Rep. Congo v. Uganda), Judgment, 2005 I.C.J. 168 (Dec. 19); Oil Platforms (Iran v. U.S.), Judgment, 2003 I.C.J. 161 (Nov. 6); Legality of the Threat or Use of Nuclear Weapons, Advisory Opinion, 1996 I.C.J. 226 (July 8); Military and Paramilitary Activities in and Against Nicaragua (Nicar. v. U.S.), Judgment, 1986 I.C.J. 14 (June 27).
[416] U.N. Charter arts. 39, 41, 42. For recent literature on the Charter's use of force rules, see OLIVIER CORTEN, THE LAW AGAINST WAR: THE PROHIBITION ON THE USE OF FORCE IN CONTEMPORARY INTERNATIONAL LAW (2010); THE OXFORD HANDBOOK OF THE USE OF FORCE IN INTERNATIONAL LAW (Marc Weller ed., 2015); YORAM DINSTEIN, WAR, AGGRESSION AND SELF DEFENCE (6th ed. 2017).
[417] North Atlantic Treaty, Apr. 4, 1949, 63 Stat. 2241, 34 U.N.T.S. 243. As of 2022, NATO consists of thirty European states, Canada, and the United States.
[418] *See* Statement by NATO Secretary General, Lord Robertson, Oct. 2, 2001, 40 I.L.M. 1268 (2001). Similar action was taken under the Inter-American Treaty of Reciprocal Assistance (Rio Pact) art. 3, Sept. 2, 1947, 62 Stat. 1681, 21 U.N.T.S. 77, which embodies a comparable collective self-defense commitment within the American hemisphere.

U.S. law as an advance authorization by Congress as a whole for the president to use military force on his own initiative.[419]

In some instances, these rules of international law are incorporated into U.S. law by treaty or statute. For example, as noted previously, recent statutes by Congress authorizing the use of force have limited the authority to the objective of upholding Security Council resolutions, which requires analysis of the terms of those resolutions in order to understand the scope of the congressional authorization. In other instances, such rules of international law are not directly incorporated into U.S. law but serve to influence the rules set forth in U.S. statutes or regulations. Moreover, these rules of international law can play an important role in influencing the discretion exercised by political decision makers; for example, the willingness to resort to armed conflict in a particular situation may depend on whether the action will be supported by allies, which in turn may depend on whether the action is perceived as consistent with international law. Indeed, a key value in securing authorization to use force from the U.N. Security Council lies in the galvanizing of global support for using force or other sanctions against a state or nonstate actor.[420]

3. Theories of Balancing

The United States stations U.S. military forces abroad as a regular matter, in foreign states such as Germany, the Republic of Korea, Japan, and the United Kingdom. The president also orders temporary deployments of U.S. military forces to foreign states, at their request, for various types of training, humanitarian, and other operations. Deployment of U.S. forces for such "peaceful" operations is not regarded as encroaching upon Congress' war powers, though any such deployments must conform with conditions or restrictions established under U.S. law.

Instead, conflicts between the political branches arise when the president orders U.S. military forces into situations where armed hostilities exist or may exist. In assessing the permissibility of such deployments, various theories have emerged, which can be generally reduced to the following five categories.[421]

---

[419] See S. EXEC. REP. NO. 95-12, at 66 (1978) ("A treaty may not declare war because the unique legislative history of the declaration-of-war clause . . . clearly indicates that that power was intended to reside jointly in the House of Representatives and the Senate."); GLENNON, supra note 6, at 205.

[420] See supra this chapter § I(C)(5).

[421] The theories discussed below emphasize textual, historic and functional arguments. For a political theory emphasizing the incentives of the political branches, see Jide Nzelibe, A Positive Theory of the War Powers Constitution, 91 IOWA L. REV. 993 (2006) (finding, inter alia, that the president's ex ante beliefs regarding the outcome of the conflict and possible adverse public reaction are what determine whether to seek congressional authorization).

a. President May Not Use Armed Force Without Congressional Authorization Except to "Repel Sudden Attacks"

One common theory is that, except to "repel sudden attacks," the president may not act without congressional authorization. Perhaps the most eloquent proponent of this theory is John Hart Ely in his book *War and Responsibility*.[422] Ely argues that Congress in all instances must authorize the use of force before it may be undertaken, though (relying heavily on Madison's notes at the Philadelphia convention as to why the power "to declare war" was accorded to Congress) he accepts that the president can act to repel sudden attacks when advance congressional approval is not possible, a notion sometimes referred to as "defensive" war.[423] Given that normally the individual states of the United States may not engage in war without the consent of Congress, but may do so when the state is "actually invaded, or in such imminent Danger as will not admit of delay,"[424] one argument is that *a fortiori* the president may also engage in war without the consent of Congress when the United States is actually invaded or in such imminent danger as will not admit of delay.

Otherwise, Ely maintains, the text of the Constitution, the reasoning of the Framers, and U.S. history up until the Korean War all support the proposition that the president may not act in the absence of congressional authorization.[425] The concept of "repel attacks" was probably understood narrowly by the Framers;[426] by contrast, Ely would construe the president's "reserved authority" more functionally as embracing the ability to respond militarily—while simultaneously seeking congressional authorization—"to genuine and serious threats to our national security beyond attacks on U.S. territory."[427] Various statements by U.S. courts, all dicta, play into this theory of leaving to Congress the war power except that the president may act to "repel sudden attacks."[428]

[422] ELY, *supra* note 62.

[423] *Id.* at 5 (interpreting the constitutional drafting as reserving "to the president the power, without advance congressional authorization, to 'repel sudden attacks'"); *see* Michael Stokes Paulsen, *Youngstown Goes to War*, 19 CONST. COMMENT. 215, 237–41 (2002); RAMSEY, *supra* note 2, at 239; Henry P. Monaghan, *Presidential War-Making*, 50 B.U. L. REV. 19, 28 (1970).

[424] U.S. CONST. art. I, § 10, cl. 3.

[425] Ely, *supra* note 62, at 3–10

[426] *See* RAMSEY, *supra* note 2, at 241–42; Berger, *supra* note 36, at 43; Leonard G. Ratner, *The Coordinated Warmaking Power—Legislative, Executive, and Judicial Roles*, 44 S. CAL. L. REV. 461, 467 (1971).

[427] ELY, *supra* note 62, at 5–7; *see also* S. REP. NO. 92-606, at 4 (1972) (citing testimony of Alexander M. Bickel); Michael Stokes Paulsen, *The War Power*, 33 HARV. J.L. & PUB. POL'Y 113 (2010) (discussing the application of the constitutional war powers to the war on terror).

[428] *See, e.g.*, United States v. Verdugo-Urquidez, 494 U.S. 259, 273 (1990); Haig v. Agee, 453 U.S. 280, 292 (1981) (noting "the changeable and explosive nature of contemporary international relations, and the fact that the Executive is immediately privy to information which cannot be swiftly presented to, evaluated by, and acted upon by the legislature") (quoting Zemel v. Rusk, 381 U.S. 1, 17 (1965)); The Prize Cases, 67 U.S. (2 Black) 635, 668 (1863) ("If a war be made by invasion of a foreign nation, the President is not only authorized but bound to resist force by force ... without waiting for any special legislative authority."); *see also* 4A Op. O.L.C., *supra* note 100, at 187 (asserting that the

For Ely, discrepant post-Korea practice is essentially unconstitutional and the product of a tacit bargain between the political branches whereby the president gets to deploy force but takes responsibility for adverse repercussions, while Congress avoids difficult and politically risky decisions, but can scold the president if things go wrong for acting without authorization.[429] A solution to this unconstitutional practice, according to Ely, is to revisit the War Powers Resolution, so as to devise a better means for forcing the president to seek congressional authorization before committing U.S. forces to combat. Further, Ely believes that U.S. courts should be more willing to scrutinize presidential conduct so as to restore the balance of power originally envisaged in the Constitution. Other scholars, as well as politicians, have also advanced proposals for amending or replacing the War Powers Resolution so as to bring contemporary practice back into line with the constitutional framework.[430] An alternative solution is to acknowledge that presidents will act in an emergency situation that may extend beyond repelling a sudden attack, but to expect them to "come later to Congress to explain what they did, why they acted, and request Congress to provide retroactive authorization."[431]

This theory fits well within the original constitutional design; it is textually oriented in recognizing that the power to "declare war" (as well as a significant number of other war powers) was expressly assigned to Congress and no comparable power was expressly assigned to the president.[432] One problem with this theory, though, is that it fails to draw obvious lines as to what the president can and cannot do. To the extent that the president may not only "repel sudden attacks" but may also act to address "genuine and serious threats to our national security," the theory potentially opens the door to a wide range of unspecified presidential action. Perhaps mitigating this problem is the fact that the theory still requires the president to secure authorization from Congress as soon as possible; in other words, flexibility is accorded to the president only because of a perceived difficulty in expeditiously convening and securing authorization

president holds "the implicit advantage . . . over the legislature under our constitutional scheme in situations calling for immediate action").

[429] ELY, *supra* note 62, at 52–54, 87–88.

[430] *See, e.g.*, Senators Byrd-Nunn-Warner-Mitchell proposal, contained in S. 2, 101st Cong., 135 CONG. REC. 465–66 (1989), and S.J. Res. 323, 100th Cong., 134 CONG. REC. 11,648 (1988), to establish a permanent consultation group of eighteen members; *Presidential Decision Directive 25*, THE WHITE HOUSE (May 3, 1994), https://perma.cc/H8MD-RREG (supporting legislative changes); Joseph R. Biden, Jr., & John B. Ritch III, *The War Power at a Constitutional Impasse: A "Joint Decision Solution,"* 77 GEO. L.J. 367 (1988); Michael J. Glennon, *Strengthening the War Powers Resolution: The Case for Purse-Strings Restrictions*, 60 MINN. L. REV. 1 (1975); Tim Kaine, *A Better Approach to War Powers*, 5 PRISM SEC. STUD. J. 3 (2014).

[431] Fisher, *supra* note 238, at 743–44.

[432] *See* RAMSEY, *supra* note 2, at 241.

from Congress. Once Congress can be convened, it retains the power to decide whether the president's action was proper and should be maintained.

A second problem with this theory is that it is not a good fit for historical practice since World War II, and therefore poorly maps onto contemporary discourse between the president and Congress. For the past several decades, the president has used military force in circumstances that do not involve an immediate threat to the United States (either in the sense of a sudden attack on U.S. territory or a threat functionally equivalent), nor does the president habitually seek authorization from Congress concomitant with his use of force.

b. In Addition to Repelling Attacks, the President May Use Armed Force to Address Low-Intensity Armed Conflict, Subject to Congressional Restrictions
A second theory is that the president may use armed force not just to repel sudden attacks but to address any low-intensity armed conflict, measured by its nature, scope, and duration, albeit subject to whatever limitations Congress may have enacted. The core of this theory is that such measures do not constitute "war" in the sense meant by Article I and therefore do not require congressional authorization.[433] This theory is generally built on several propositions, as may be seen in memoranda issued by OLC, such as its opinion regarding U.S. military intervention in Libya in 2011.[434]

First, because of his role as chief executive for foreign, military, and national security affairs, and as commander in chief, the president has a power to undertake U.S. military action abroad for the purpose of protecting important national interests, such as the preservation of regional stability or maintaining the credibility of the U.N. Security Council. Second, the Constitution expressly provides for a sharing of war powers as between the two political branches, requiring therefore some interpretive gloss to understand where the lines of authority are to be drawn[435] (in this sense, there is common ground with the first theory just stated, which accepts that the president may act on his own in some circumstances).

Third, an important aspect of that gloss is U.S. historical practice, given the president's repeated use of military force abroad without prior congressional approval. In that regard, OLC has pointed to the "bombing in Libya (1986), an intervention in Panama (1989), troop deployments to Somalia (1992), Bosnia (1995), and Haiti (twice, 1994 and 2004), air patrols and airstrikes in Bosnia (1993–1995), and a bombing campaign in Yugoslavia (1999), without specific

---

[433] *See generally* Walter Dellinger, *After the Cold War: Presidential Power and the Use of Military Force*, 50 U. MIAMI L. REV. 107 (1995).
[434] 35 Op. O.L.C., *supra* note 375.
[435] *Id.* at 6–7.

prior authorizing legislation."[436] According to OLC, this historical practice was an important "indication of constitutional meaning, because it reflects the two political branches' practical understanding, developed since the founding of the Republic, of their respective roles and responsibilities with respect to national defense, and because '[m]atters intimately related to foreign policy and national security are rarely proper subjects for judicial intervention.'"[437]

Fourth, in the War Powers Resolution,[438] Congress itself has recognized an ability of the president to act in advance of congressional authorization, both in the provision calling upon the president to report to Congress within forty-eight hours of taking certain actions[439] and in the provision requiring withdrawal of U.S. forces after sixty days (extendable to ninety days) in the absence of congressional authorization.[440] As such, while the resolution does not purport to provide any authorization to the president, its structure indicates acceptance by Congress of the president's power to act in certain situations.[441] In short, the president may act in such situations even without specific prior authorization from Congress, but only "insofar as Congress has not specifically restricted it."[442]

Finally, what the president may do turns on the *nature, scope, and duration* of the proposed use of force. According to OLC, "determining whether a particular planned engagement constitutes a 'war' for constitutional purposes . . . requires a fact-specific assessment of the 'anticipated nature, scope, and duration' of the planned military operations," with the standard of "war" only being met "by prolonged and substantial military engagements, typically involving exposure of U.S. military personnel to significant risk over a substantial period."[443]

This theory has the benefit of mapping more closely than the first theory onto existing practice by the political branches, as a means of addressing the imprecision of the relevant constitutional text. Doing so is a respectable means of constitutional interpretation: thus Justice Felix Frankfurter, in *Youngstown*, referred to a "gloss" on executive power arising from "a systematic, unbroken, executive practice, long pursued to the knowledge of the Congress and never before questioned, engaged in by presidents who have also sworn to uphold the Constitution, making as it were such exercise of power part of the structure of our government . . . ."[444]

---

[436] *Id.* at 7.
[437] *Id.* (quoting Haig v. Agee, 453 U.S. 280, 292 (1981)).
[438] 50 U.S.C. §§ 1541–49 (2018) (discussed at *supra* note 225).
[439] *Id.* § 1543(a).
[440] *Id.* § 1544(b).
[441] 35 Op. O.L.C., *supra* note 375, at 8.
[442] *Id.* at 6, 10–12.
[443] *Id.* at 8.
[444] Youngstown Sheet & Tube Co. v. Sawyer, 343 U.S. 579, 610–11 (1952) (Frankfurter, J., concurring); *see* Zivotofsky v. Kerry, 576 U.S. 1, 23 (2015) (placing "significant weight" on "accepted understandings and practice" when evaluating the division of authority between the president and

Further, this theory takes account of functional considerations. If the first, more limited, theory noted here is correct, then the president would be denied the "ability to warn of, or threaten, the use of military force," even though doing so "is an ordinary and essential element in the toolbox of that branch of government empowered to formulate and implement foreign policy."[445] Finally, the theory allows for a check on presidential power, both because uses of force that rise to a certain threshold of "war" (i.e., prolonged and substantial military engagements) still require advance congressional authorization and because uses of force below that threshold are still subject to any congressional restrictions.

With respect to the kinds of military operations that are envisaged, four types of operations seem to fall readily within the theory's added scope. The president,[446] Congress,[447] and the judiciary[448] all appear to agree that the president may engage in short-term use of U.S. military forces abroad, without

---

Congress); NLRB v. Canning, 573 U.S. 513, 524 (2014) (noting that "long settled and established practice is a consideration of great weight in a proper interpretation of constitutional provisions regulating the relationship between Congress and the President" (internal quotation marks and alterations omitted)); Dames & Moore v. Regan, 453 U.S. 654, 678–86 (1981) (describing "a history of congressional acquiescence in conduct of the sort engaged in by the President"); Koh, *supra* note 66, at 70–71 (characterizing historical precedent as "quasi-constitutional custom" in foreign affairs). For further discussion of *Youngstown*, see *infra* this chapter § II(B) and Chapter 1 § II(B).

[445] Powell, *supra* note 35, at 119; *see also* Matthew C. Waxman, *The Power to Threaten War*, 123 Yale L.J. 1626 (2014) (discussing "allocation of legal power to threaten military force or war").

[446] *See* 4A Op. O.L.C., *supra* note 100, at 187 ("Presidents have repeatedly employed troops abroad in defense of American lives and property."); Presidential Powers Relating to the Situation in Iran, 4A Op. O.L.C. 115, 121 (1979) ("It is well established that the President has the constitutional power as Chief Executive and Commander-in-Chief to protect the lives and property of Americans abroad."); 1 Op. O.L.C., *supra* note 210, at 326 (noting that the president as commander in chief has authority "to commit military forces of the United States to armed conflict . . . to protect the lives of American troops in the field"); *Statement on U.S. Policy*, 53 Dep't St. Bull. 20 (1965) (regarding President Lyndon Johnson ordering U.S. military intervention in the Dominican Republic "to preserve the lives of American citizens and citizens of a good many other nations"); Training of British Flying Students in the United States, 40 Op. Att'y Gen. 58, 62 (1941) ("[T]he President's authority has long been recognized as extending to the dispatch of armed forces outside of the United States, either on missions of goodwill or rescue, or for the purpose of protecting American lives or property or American interests.").

[447] *See, e.g.*, 55 Comp. Gen. 1081, 1084 (1976) ("[T]he President does have some authority to protect the lives and property of Americans abroad even in the absence of specific congressional authorization.").

[448] *See, e.g.*, United States v. Verdugo-Urquidez, 494 U.S. 259, 273 (1990) ("The United States frequently employs Armed Forces outside this country—over 200 times in our history—for the protection of American citizens or national security."); Cunningham v. Neagle, 135 U.S. 1, 64 (1890) (noting that among the president's "rights, duties, and obligations growing out of the constitution itself, our international relations, and all the protection implied by the nature of the government under the constitution" is the obligation to protect U.S. nationals abroad); Durand v. Hollins, 8 F. Cas. 111, 112 (C.C.S.D.N.Y. 1860) ("Acts of lawless violence, or of threatened violence to the citizen or his property, cannot be anticipated and provided for; and the protection, to be effectual or of any avail, may, not unfrequently, require the most prompt and decided action.").

congressional authorization, to protect U.S. nationals and U.S. property.[449] Such protection and rescue operations are challenging to catalog,[450] but probably began with President Jefferson's efforts in the early 1800s to stop the preying on U.S. vessels off the Barbary Coast[451] and include incidents such as President McKinley's decision in 1900 to send some five thousand U.S. troops and associated naval vessels to China to protect Americans during the Boxer Rebellion,[452] the 1975 military operation by U.S. armed forces to retake the *Mayaguez*,[453] the 1980 attempt to rescue U.S. diplomatic and consular personnel being held hostage in Iran,[454] the 2013 deployment of U.S. forces to South Sudan to protect U.S. personnel there from internal armed conflict,[455] the 2014 attempt to rescue U.S. nationals being held hostage by the self-proclaimed Islamic State in Syria/Iraq,[456] and the 2016 attempt to rescue hostages being held in Afghanistan.[457] Such operations, though not always successful, have employed a modest number of U.S. forces, acting abroad for less than a few days, to accomplish a specific and limited objective, and have met with virtually no adverse reaction from Congress.

A second type of operation falling within the scope of this theory would be where the president orders U.S. military forces to assist in humanitarian relief operations, in situations where there is a potential for aircraft to be shot down or for U.S. forces to come under fire. As previously noted, examples include the humanitarian relief operations in northern Iraq from April to July 1991,[458] the establishment and protection of safe havens in Bosnia in 1994–1995,[459] the intervention in Somalia in 1993–1994,[460] and more recently the deployment of

---

[449] *See* RAMSEY, *supra* note 2, at 247 ("[T]he President's commonly asserted power to rescue U.S. citizens abroad (at least where the menace does not come from the foreign sovereign) does not involve use of force directed at a foreign sovereign and thus does not declare war.").

[450] Studies attempting to identify such actions include, Memorandum of the Solicitor for the Department of State, Right to Protect Citizens in Foreign Countries by Landing Forces (Oct. 5, 1912); JAMES GRAFTON ROGERS, WORLD POLICING AND THE CONSTITUTION: AN INQUIRY INTO THE POWERS OF THE PRESIDENT AND CONGRESS, NINE WARS AND A HUNDRED MILITARY OPERATIONS, 1789–1945 (1945); MILTON OFFUTT, THE PROTECTION OF CITIZENS ABROAD BY THE ARMED FORCES OF THE UNITED STATES (Johns Hopkins Univ. Stud. in Hist. and Pol. Sc., Ser. 46, No. 4, 1928) (listing seventy-six instances between 1813 and 1927).

[451] *See supra* this chapter note 100.

[452] *See supra* this chapter notes 148–150.

[453] *See supra* this chapter note 255.

[454] *See* MARK BOWDEN, GUESTS OF THE AYATOLLAH: THE FIRST BATTLE IN AMERICA'S WAR WITH MILITANT ISLAM 409–68 (2006).

[455] Letter to Congressional Leaders on the Deployment of United States Armed Forces Personnel to South Sudan, 2 PUB. PAPERS 1377 (Dec. 19, 2013).

[456] *See* Karen DeYoung, *The Anatomy of a Failed Hostage Rescue Deep in Islamic State Territory*, WASH. POST (Feb. 14, 2015), https://perma.cc/TU8N-LUNQ.

[457] Matthew Rosenberg & Adam Goldman, *U.S. Rescue Attempt in Afghanistan Missed Western Hostages by Hours*, N.Y. TIMES (Sept. 8 2016), https://perma.cc/XLK3-DP7K.

[458] *See supra* this chapter text accompanying notes 341–344.

[459] *See supra* this chapter text accompanying note 345.

[460] *See supra* this chapter text accompanying notes 346–351.

U.S. military aircraft in Iraq in 2014 to conduct air strikes and drop humanitarian aid to assist Iraqi civilians being targeted by "Islamic State" militants.[461] Such efforts have not been expressly authorized by Congress, but are invariably justified by indicating that U.S. government personnel and private citizens are engaged in the relief effort and must be protected, the president may deploy U.S. forces to protect those persons, and, as an ancillary matter, the same troops may protect non-U.S. nationals.[462]

A third type of military operation falling within the scope of this theory would be U.S. military deployments in the form of "peacekeeping" missions—undertaken at the consent of the host state and conducted either through the United Nations or by the United States directly—where there is some possibility that the U.S. forces may come under fire.[463] For example, when U.S. military forces deployed to Bosnia-Herzegovina in 1995 to assist an international force in the implementation of the Dayton Peace Accords that ended the Balkans War, there was some chance that the U.S. forces might become embroiled in lingering animosities among the warring factions. Even so, the executive branch took the position that "considerable weight should be given to the consensual nature and protective purposes of the operation," in particular that the "deployment is intended to be a limited mission that will ensure stability while the peace agreement is put into effect" and that, because "the mission is in support of an agreement that the warring parties have reached and is at the invitation of those parties, it is reasonably possible that little or no resistance to the deployment will occur."[464]

All told, by 1996 the United States deployed about 16,500 troops to Bosnia-Herzegovina, as well as about 6,000 support personnel in Croatia, Hungary, and Italy.[465] Congress, at times prior to this deployment, expressed a view that

---

[461] See, e.g., Letter to Congressional Leaders Reporting on the Commencement of Military Operations in Iraq, 2014 DAILY COMP. PRES. DOC. 1 (Sept. 1, 2014); see also Janine di Giovanni, Inside the Islamic State's Siege of Mount Sinjar, NEWSWEEK (Aug. 14, 2014), https://perma.cc/3JSV-42YF ("In the past few days, the U.S. has mounted a number of humanitarian aid drops, as well as air strikes to counter Islamic State (IS) militants . . .").

[462] See, e.g., 16 Op. O.L.C., supra note 354, at 8 ("[W]here, as here, United States government personnel and private citizens are participating in a lawful relief effort in a foreign nation, we conclude that the President may commit United States troops to protect those involved in the relief effort."); id. at 10 ("He may also decide to send sufficient numbers of troops so that those who are primarily engaged in assisting the United Nations in noncombatant roles are defended by others who perform a protective function."); id. at 11 ("Past military interventions that extended to the protection of foreign nationals provide precedent for action to protect endangered Somalians and other non-United States citizens.").

[463] See RAMSEY, supra note 2, at 247 ("A peacekeeping mission approved by the relevant territorial sovereign or sovereigns, for example, would not be a declaration of war against anyone.")

[464] Proposed Deployment of United States Armed Forces into Bosnia, 19 Op. O.L.C. 327, 332 (1995).

[465] STEVEN R. BOWMAN, CONG. RESEARCH SERV., IB93056, BOSNIA: U.S. MILITARY OPERATIONS 10 (updated July 8, 2003).

U.S. forces should not be deployed to enforce a Balkans peace settlement.[466] After the deployment, Congress expressed the view that U.S. ground forces should not remain in Bosnia-Herzegovina indefinitely and that the president should work with other nations to allow their withdrawal, favoring instead an intelligence and logistical support role.[467] Even so, Congress supported the deployment through a combination of annual Department of Defense budget appropriations and supplemental appropriations over a period of several years.[468] More limited deployments have occurred in other countries. For example, at the request of the government of Jordan, President Obama in June 2016 sent 2,200 U.S. forces there to support the security of Jordan and promote regional stability.[469] Yet such peacekeeping or stability operations pose risks for involvement in low-intensity conflict, such as President Obama's deployment in October 2015 of U.S. troops to Cameroon, again with the consent of the government, to assist in that country's fight against Boko Haram, an Islamist militant group.[470]

A fourth type of military operation falling within the scope of this theory would be covert operations other than rescues of U.S. nationals that amount to a temporary use of force against another nation or a projection of force by proxy. Examples of such action might include the clandestine U.S. military assistance for the 1961 "Bay of Pigs" invasion of Cuba,[471] for the Afghan mujahedeen after the 1979 Soviet invasion[472] or, more recently, for rebels in Syria.[473] Since covert actions remain subject to congressional regulation, one important issue is the extent to which existing law imposes any constraints with respect to such actions and whether the executive branch has conformed to those constraints.[474] For example, U.S. law requires the president to issue a written finding before

[466] See, e.g., Department of Defense Appropriations Act, 1995, Pub. L. No. 103-335, § 8100, 108 Stat. 2599, 2643 (1994) (sense of Congress that no funds appropriated under Act should be available to deploy U.S. armed forces to participate in a Bosnian peace settlement).

[467] See, e.g., Strom Thurmond National Defense Authorization Act for Fiscal Year 1999, Pub. L. No. 105-261, § 1202, 112 Stat. 1920, 2147 (1998).

[468] BOWMAN, supra note 465, at 3–4.

[469] Letter to Congressional Leaders on the Global Deployment of United States Combat-Equipped Armed Forces, 2016 DAILY COMP. PRES. DOC. 4 (June 13, 2016).

[470] Letter to Congressional Leaders Reporting on the Deployment of United States Armed Forces Personnel to Cameroon, 2015 DAILY COMP. PRES. DOC. 1 (Oct. 14, 2015).

[471] See generally PETER WYDEN, BAY OF PIGS: THE UNTOLD STORY (1979).

[472] See generally GEORGE CRILE, CHARLIE WILSON'S WAR: THE EXTRAORDINARY STORY OF HOW THE WILDEST MAN IN CONGRESS AND A ROGUE CIA AGENT CHANGED THE HISTORY OF OUR TIMES (2004).

[473] See Ernesto Londoño & Greg Miller, CIA Begins Weapons Delivery to Syrian Rebels, WASH. POST (Sept. 11, 2013), https://perma.cc/HX3H-SP9H.

[474] See Abraham D. Sofaer, The Power over War, 50 U. MIAMI L. REV. 33, 52 (1995) ("To the extent Congress sees fit to regulate covert uses of force, the President must comply, absent some extraordinary limitation that unduly restricts the power to conduct military operations, or otherwise prevents the President from performing the executive function."); see also Gary M. Stern & Morton H. Halperin, "Covert" Paramilitary Action and War Powers, in THE U.S. CONSTITUTION AND THE POWER TO GO TO WAR, supra note 187, at 149.

authorizing any covert action and further provides that such finding "shall be reported in writing to the congressional intelligence committees as soon as possible after such approval and before the initiation of the covert action," except in certain limited circumstances.[475]

A common thread of these types of operations is that, in context, it does not appear that U.S. forces will directly encounter significant hostilities and, if they do, it would be purely incidental to the operation. Thus, with respect to Haiti, the Justice Department concluded that "the President was entitled to take into account the anticipated nature, scope, and duration of the planned deployment, and in particular the limited antecedent risk that United States forces would encounter significant armed resistance or suffer or inflict substantial casualties as a result of the deployment."[476] Likewise, in the context of Somalia, the Justice Department viewed as central to the legal analysis whether the deployment "appears primarily aimed at providing humanitarian assistance, and will only involve combat as an incident to that humanitarian mission."[477]

This theory accepts that the deployment of U.S. military forces into low-intensity armed conflict (or potential armed conflict) is subject to whatever limitations Congress may have enacted. If so, it would appear to allow for a congressional decision to *block* a presidential initiative of this type, raising the question of what type of decision is necessary to do so. If the power to resort to force is one generally held by Congress, but one which also may be exercised by presidential initiative for low-intensity armed conflict subject to congressional check, then it should be possible for Congress to block the president's action by a concurrent resolution (as contemplated by the War Powers Resolution) and possibly even by a simple resolution in either House, on the basis that either House is entitled to refuse to authorize a declaration of war.[478] Following the decision in *INS v. Chadha*,[479] however, Congress appears now to approach the matter as calling for a joint resolution of Congress, to be presented to the president for signature, and, if vetoed, to be sustained by a two-thirds vote in both Houses before entering into force.[480]

---

[475] *See, e.g.*, 50 U.S.C. § 3093b(c) (2018).

[476] 18 Op. O.L.C., *supra* note 298, at 179.

[477] 16 Op. O.L.C., *supra* note 354, at 8 n.1.

[478] *See, e.g.*, Dellums v. Bush, 752 F. Supp. 1141, 1149 (D.D.C. 1990) (opining in dicta that Congress could prevent the president from using military force by means of a concurrent resolution); Fisher, *supra* note 238, at 749 (". . . Congress could pass a concurrent resolution disapproving of a presidential war, automatically triggering a point of order against any measure that contains funds to perpetuate the conflict."); TURNER, *supra* note 265, at xiv (finding that one of the checks "incorporated to protect against executive abuse . . . [is] the power of either house of Congress to veto a decision to initiate a war").

[479] 462 U.S. 919 (1983); for discussion, see Chapter 2 § II(B).

[480] *See* 50 U.S.C. § 1546a (2018).

This theory, however, also encounters significant challenges. As Justice Frankfurter once noted (albeit not in *Youngstown*), "Illegality cannot attain legitimacy through practice."[481] The fact that the president did not seek congressional authorization in many situations and that Congress did not react as a body does not necessarily establish constitutional authority; indeed, in some instances, the incident at issue was over long before Congress was in a position to react.

Further, depending on how one gauges congressional acquiescence, there is some evidence that Congress does not favor robust presidential authority of this kind. For example, to address a foreign government's unjust detention of a U.S. citizen, a statute originally adopted in 1868, and amended in 1989, calls for the president to "use such means, not amounting to acts of war and not otherwise prohibited by law, as he may think necessary and proper to obtain or effectuate the release"; such language would seem to cast some doubt on Congress' acceptance of presidential power to rescue U.S. nationals through the use of military force.[482]

Moreover, the theory appears susceptible to abuse, given that the executive branch has viewed the "nature, scope, and duration" standard as enabling fairly substantial military action. Any resort to force that does not involve deployment of ground forces (thus, any use of air strikes) and that is not intended to continue for a long time would apparently be deemed permissible, in the absence of congressional restriction. Thus, the theory was used to justify air strikes on Syria in 2017 (against a military airfield) and 2018 (against a scientific research center, a storage facility, and a bunker) for the purpose of degrading Syria's chemical weapons facilities.[483] Further, the "scope, nature and duration" theory embraces the ability of the president on his or her own to attack the foreign state in circumstances where the United States and its nationals are not at risk; the focus of the theory is solely upon qualitative aspects of the force being used, and not on its purpose. Thus, with respect to the air strikes against Syria, the stated rationale was not to protect the United States or its nationals (at least not directly), but instead involved broad assertions about promoting regional stability, preventing a worsening humanitarian catastrophe, and deterring the use and proliferation of chemical weapons.[484] Moreover, this theory accords considerable discretion to the president in determining whether the use of force might lead to large-scale

---

[481] Inland Waterways Corp. v. Young, 309 U.S. 517, 524 (1940); *see* Gerhard Casper, *Constitutional Constraints on the Conduct of Foreign and Defense Policy: A Nonjudicial Model,* 43 U. CHI. L. REV. 463, 479 (1976) (". . . unconstitutional practices cannot become legitimate by mere lapse of time.").

[482] 22 U.S.C. § 1732.

[483] Letter to Congressional Leaders on United States Military Operations in Syria, 2017 DAILY COMP. PRES. DOC. 1 (Apr. 8, 2017); Letter to Congressional Leaders on United States Military Operations in Syria, 2018 DAILY COMP. PRES. DOC. 1 (Apr. 15, 2018).

[484] Office of the Legal Counsel, U.S. Dep't of Justice, April 2018 Airstrikes Against Syrian Chemical-Weapons Facilities, 11 (May 31, 2018), https://perma.cc/4PLW-AQMH.

armed conflict. For the air strikes against Syria, the assumption was that a relatively weak Syrian government would not be able to respond, and hence that the
"anticipated hostilities would not rise to the level of a war in the constitutional
sense."[485] Yet presumably there existed at least some potential for enmeshing
the United States in armed conflict not just with Syria but with Syria's principal
backers at that time, Russia and Iran, an assessment that might warrant congressional involvement.

Finally, the theory apparently embraces even the large-scale deployments of
U.S. forces into potential armed conflict, such as the sending of twenty thousand
U.S. troops to Haiti to oust a military regime. Such a deployment clearly is not of
the same nature as a military raid to rescue a few U.S. hostages or a temporary
incursion into another state to provide humanitarian relief. Rather, U.S. military
interventions for the purpose of toppling *de facto* governments have historically
entailed quite significant commitments to the affected states in both "blood and
treasure." Similar points might be made with respect to the large-scale and relatively lengthy deployments of U.S. forces to Somalia in 1992–1993 and Bosnia
starting in 1995, where direct engagement in armed hostilities was not an objective of the deployments, but where the risk of such engagement was far from *de
minimis*. In any event, although cast in terms suggestive of significant limits, the
theory appears potentially available to support an extremely wide range of presidential uses of force.

c. In Addition to Repelling Attacks, the President May Use Armed Force When Authorized by the U.N. Security Council

Some commentators have maintained that the president can use force not just
to repel sudden attacks but also when there exists an authorization to use force
issued by the Security Council under the U.N. Charter. Central features of this
argument are: the U.N. Charter obligates the United States to abide by decisions
of the U.N. Security Council issued under Chapter VII; U.S. ratification of the
U.N. Charter has established the obligations arising under the Charter as part of
the supreme law of the United States; and the president is charged with faithfully
executing that law.[486] As such, it is said to follow, the president may act to use
force as authorized by the U.N. Security Council.

This argument is unconvincing. The text of the U.N. Charter itself does
not, of course, directly address U.S. presidential authority to deploy military

---

[485] *Id.* at 1.

[486] *See* U.N. Charter art. 25 ("The Members of the United Nations agree to accept and carry out
the decisions of the Security Council in accordance with the present Charter."). For reference to such
views, see Stromseth, *Rethinking War Powers, supra* note 187, at 613–14 (referring to arguments by
Senators Scott Lucas and Warren Austin at the time of the Senate's consent to ratification of the U.N.
Charter, though noting that even they qualified their comments under questioning by others).

forces.[487] Rather, the Charter speaks to the authority of the Security Council to make decisions regarding the use of force vis-à-vis U.N. member states. When the Security Council acts, such decisions are never cast in terms of *ordering* a U.N. member state to use military force, which might be the strongest basis for maintaining that the president must "faithfully execute" U.S. law in the form of an obligation to use force arising under a U.S. treaty.[488] Rather, such authorizations are cast in terms of authorizing U.N. members to use military force in a given situation, *should they choose to do so.* As such, when these resolutions are issued, the United States is placed in a position where, as a matter of its political discretion, it may or may not use military force, which would seem not to change the distribution of the war power between the political branches that otherwise exists.[489] When it has addressed the matter, the executive branch appears to take the position that such resolutions impose no duty upon the United States.[490]

Moreover, the constitutional allocation of power as between the Congress and the president with respect to war cannot be altered by a treaty; any treaty that purports to do so is unconstitutional.[491] If the argument is, alternatively, that the Senate's consent to the treaty constitutes a form of congressional authorization to use force, then the problem is that the power to declare war is not allocated just to the Senate; it is allocated to the Congress as a whole, such that the Senate alone could not by treaty satisfy whatever involvement of Congress is necessary under the Constitution. The claim might be that the degree of constitutional uncertainty was such that a nonauthoritative measure makes a measurable difference.[492] Still,

---

[487] *See Congress, the President, and the Power to Commit Forces to Combat, supra* note 399, at 1800 (noting that the "language [of] the United Nations Charter ... clearly illustrates the neutrality of their obligations with respect to the internal distribution of the war-making power"). To the contrary, in the context of indicating that member states may enter into Article 43 agreements with the United Nations for the provision of armed forces, the Charter expressly recognizes that this is to be done in accordance with the constitutional processes of those states. *See* U.N. Charter art. 43(3).

[488] An interesting question is whether the Security Council *could* order a state to use force against another state, if there was political will within the Council to adopt such a resolution. Arguably Article 43 of the U.N. Charter only gives the Security Council power to call up armed forces of a state to achieve Chapter VII objectives after that state has concluded an agreement with the United Nations for the provision of such assistance. *See* Glennon, *supra* note 168, at 77 ("Various commentators, both inside and outside the United Nations, have ... observed that the Security Council is unable under the United Nations Charter to require a member state to make its armed forces available for use in hostilities.").

[489] *See id.* at 75, 81–82 ("... that a *right* exists under international law to take certain action says nothing about whether a *power* exists under domestic law to exercise that right.").

[490] *See, e.g.,* 16 Op. O.L.C., *supra* note 354, at 12 n.5 ("We do not conclude that a Security Council resolution calling on member States to provide troops to assist the United Nations by itself imposes any legal *duty* on the President to act in accordance with the resolution.").

[491] GLENNON, *supra* note 6, at 192–205. The same problem arises with respect to arguments that U.S. treaties on mutual defense, such as the NATO treaty, provide authority for the president to use military force.

[492] This may be suggested by Justice Jackson's famous three-tiered approach, in which implied authorization by Congress, or at least "congressional inertia, indifference or quiescence," may salvage presidential action. Youngstown Sheet & Tube Co. v. Sawyer, 343 U.S. 579, 637–38 (1952) (Jackson, J., concurring); for discussion, see Chapter 1 § II(B).

it seems to be widely accepted, and relevant, that treaties attempting to exercise an authority vested in Congress as a whole (including, it is thought, agreements that would have the effect of declaring war) are prone to be regarded as non-self-executing, and that non-self-executing treaties do not provide the president with Take Care authority that would establish federal law.[493]

Rather than approaching this issue as "faithful execution" of the law, some commentators have instead stressed the *nature* of action taken pursuant to authorization of the U.N. Security Council: that is, that such actions are not a resort to "war" in the sense originally understood by the Framers of the Constitution. The Framers were concerned about a president embarking unilaterally on a use of force that might place the United States at odds with foreign states, triggering a state of "war" as understood under classic international law. By contrast, a use of force in support of the United Nations entails the United States operating in harmony with other nations to address collectively a threat; rather than sparking "war," such a use of force is more in the nature of a global or regional "police action," which simply does not engage the "declare war" power of Congress in the same way.[494] The purpose of the Declare War Clause "was to ensure that this fateful decision did not rest with a single person," but the "new system vests that responsibility in the Security Council, a body where the most divergent interests and perspectives of humanity are represented and where five of the fifteen members have a veto power."[495] On this theory, in consenting to ratification of the U.N. Charter, the U.S. Senate understood "that the Charter empowered the Council to authorize the sending of U.S. forces into a police action and that this authority would empower the President without his having to seek the specific consent of Congress."[496] Such a theory explains and is confirmed by Congress' passivity to President Truman's large-scale deployment of U.S. forces during the Korean War, given the authorization to use force issued by the Security Council in that context.[497] At the time, several senators spoke in favor of Truman's unilateral action given that it was a "police action," not "war."[498]

There are substantial counterarguments. First, as previously discussed, the dominant view at the time of the ratification of the U.N. Charter was that the president would be able to use U.S. forces without congressional authorization in support of U.N. "police actions" only pursuant to a U.N. Charter Article 43 agreement, to which the Senate had given advice and consent. While the debate at the

---

[493] For discussion, see Chapter 6 §§ IV(A)(3), IV(A)(5).

[494] *See* Thomas M. Franck & Faiza Patel, *UN Police Action in Lieu of War: "The Old Order Changeth,"* 85 AM. J. INT'L L. 63 (1991).

[495] *Id.* at 74.

[496] *Id.* at 68.

[497] *Id.* at 70–72.

[498] *Id.*; *see also* Stromseth, *Rethinking War Powers, supra* note 187, at 627–30 (discussing several senators' statements of support for President Truman's actions).

time did not directly address what would happen in the absence of an Article 43 agreement, the participants clearly envisaged that ratification of the U.N. Charter alone would not provide the president with a form of congressional authorization to use force.[499] Indeed, one might ask "why would the United States insist at the time of ratification upon one procedure that requires congressional authorization, while inferentially permitting an alternative procedure, invocable by the President alone, that dispenses with that requirement?"[500] Further, an inference in favor of sole presidential power arising from the Senate's ratification of the U.N. Charter would appear to be nullified by an inference against sole presidential power arising from Congress' adoption of the War Powers Resolution, especially Section 8(a).[501]

Second, while the Korean precedent represents an expansive interpretation of presidential power, the dominant position espoused by the Truman administration regarding the president's constitutional authority was not dependent on the nature of the action being a U.N. "police action." As previously noted, the position instead turned on an assertion of inherent presidential authority to use force, based on the president's constitutional powers and on past practice. While support of the United Nations and the existence of Security Council resolutions inviting U.S. actions were reasons politically favoring a decision to pursue force, they were not invoked as the source of presidential power; indeed, some decisions by the president to deploy U.S. forces to Korea appear to have occurred in advance of such resolutions.[502]

Third, as the Security Council began to issue authorizations to use force in 1990 and thereafter, the executive branch has not argued that the president's authority to use military force derives from the fact that U.N. "police action" is at issue.[503] Rather, the president continues to rely on existing presidential power, though often maintaining that the use of such power is justified given decisions reached by the Security Council or given U.S. interests in maintaining the credibility of the United Nations.[504] In other words, authorizations by the Security Council are simply invoked as a reason why the exercise of existing presidential power is politically appropriate and justified in a given context. Even then, such claims are not uniformly accepted by Congress; the 1990–1991 Iraq-Kuwait War

---

[499] Stromseth, *Rethinking War Powers, supra* note 187, at 614 (". . . virtually everyone in Congress—including Senators Lucas and Austin—assumed that Congress, by virtue of its final say over any agreement making U.S. forces available for U.N. military actions, would be actively involved in implementing U.S. obligations under the Charter.").

[500] Glennon, *supra* note 168, at 77–78.

[501] *See supra* this chapter text accompanying notes 264–268.

[502] Stromseth, *Rethinking War Powers, supra* note 187, at 623–24, 638.

[503] GRIFFIN, *supra* note 66, at 86 ("A review of presidential decisions regarding major wars after 1945 shows no indication that the U.N. theory was generally accepted by the executive branch.").

[504] *See, e.g.,* 16 Op. O.L.C., *supra* note 354, at 12; *see also Authority of the President to Repel the Attack in Korea, supra* note 209, at 177.

and the 2003 Iraq War demonstrate that Congress does not regard the president as empowered to resort to the use of force simply because the Security Council has or may authorize such force.

Fourth, and finally, the theory masks a very substantial grant of authority to the president. While decision-making by the U.N. Security Council helps to blunt the unilateral nature of presidential action, the unique U.S. role at the U.N. Security Council (where the United States wields considerable influence and power) makes the Security Council an unreliable check on the exercise of presidential power. Moreover, classifying all actions authorized by the U.N. Security Council as "police actions" lumps together a broad range of coercive activity. Such U.N. authorized actions may entail the deployment of just a few thousand U.S. Marines for humanitarian relief operations or may entail the deployment of a million U.S. soldiers for active combat duty. Treating all such actions as being of the same nature, for the purpose of determining whether the president may act upon his own authority, would deviate from the original constitutional design, from past practice, and from the overall thrust of the War Powers Resolution, and, as such, is unpersuasive.

Even so, the existence of an authorization to use force from the U.N. Security Council has important political consequences. In such circumstances, the president is well positioned to characterize the resort to force as an imperative for U.S. foreign policy, both to address a threat recognized by the diverse interests represented on the Council and to uphold U.S. commitments to the United Nations and to its allies, even in the absence of congressional authorization. Moreover, Congress' ability as a political matter to deny authorization to the president or to demand that the president secure such authorization appears diminished, since it is less easy to assert that the president is acting unilaterally or precipitously. When congressional authorization is granted in the context of an authorization by the Security Council, Congress is inclined to incorporate in its joint resolution a reference to the Council's action, both in identifying the threat to the peace and the steps to be taken in addressing that threat. Hence, although authorization by the Security Council does not resolve the constitutionality of presidential action, it can serve as an important political touchstone for the two branches in addressing such action.

d. President May Resort to Any Armed Force (Including Large-Scale Deployments), Subject to Congressional Restrictions

Although the executive branch has not historically asserted that the president may use armed force for *any* armed conflict (including large-scale and lengthy deployments)—albeit subject to congressional restrictions—it acts at times as though it has assumed such authority. For example, the administration of President George H.W. Bush in the fall of 1990 appears to have believed that it required no authorization from Congress for a full-scale air and ground campaign in Kuwait for the purpose of expelling from it the world's fourth largest army.[505] Similarly, in the fall of 2002, President George W. Bush's administration took the position that it needed no authorization from Congress to engage in a full-scale air and ground campaign in Iraq for the purpose of toppling the Iraqi government.[506] In both instances, the president ultimately requested congressional support and congressional authorization was provided, but the starting point appears have been a presidential belief that force may be used even in the absence of such authorization.

This theory may be based on the idea that the Framers designed a system in which it was expected that the president would take the initiative in matters concerning armed force, and would be able to act without prior congressional approval, but would always be subject to Congress' ultimate control. One justification for this theory might be that the decision to use U.S. armed forces abroad is principally political and not constitutional. On this view, a president's decision to do so without congressional authorization may be unwise foreign policy, but would not be considered illegal; it would remain the case that Congress could repudiate that policy, such as by refusing to fund it.[507] Another justification, ostensibly narrower and more focused on the constitutional text, is to claim that only "Congress, not the President, has the power *to place the nation in a state of war* through words (issuing formal proclamations) or action (directing armed attacks)";[508] yet, the president may take all steps falling short of "initiating war," such as "defensive war" or "provocative actions that might incite another nation into war with the United States."[509] On this reading, much then turns on what it means for the president to be proscribed only from "initiating" a "state of war" between the United States and a foreign state. In practice, the distinction between the president not being able to "strike the first blow" but being able to "incite the striking of such a blow" against the United States[510] is so elusive as to call into question whether any limitation on presidential action really exists.

Ultimately, this theory accepts that the political branches share power in this area, such that in any given situation whether the president can act will depend on a constellation of factors, not upon a bright-line, predetermined standard.[511] Abraham Sofaer suggests that where "Congress specifically instructs the President, expressly or impliedly, to refrain from using force, both Congress and

---

[505] *See supra* this chapter text accompanying note 272.
[506] *See* Mike Allen & Juliet Eilperin, *Bush Aides Say Iraq War Needs No Hill Vote; Some See Such Support as Politically Helpful*, WASH. POST, Aug. 26, 2002, at A1.
[507] Monaghan, *supra* note 423, at 32–33.
[508] RAMSEY, *supra* note 2, at 237–38 (emphasis added).
[509] *Id.* at 255.
[510] *Id.* at 256.
[511] *Id.* (noting that the president's power is "limited by important congressional powers.").

the courts have ample authority and incentive to enforce the law."[512] Likewise, where "the President acts secretly and fails to inform or consult with Congress, similar remedies are available. In such circumstances, the President uses force at his or her peril."[513] By contrast, where "the President acts openly but without prior, explicit approval, the legality of that conduct should continue to depend upon its consistency with the practices and expectations developed over the last two hundred years."[514] For Sofaer, the president's conduct will be conditioned by inevitable consultations with and informal approvals by members of Congress, a need to be responsive to the American people, and a need to act in accordance with international law.[515]

Arguably, at least, this theory best captures the reality of many instances of presidential-congressional decision-making regarding the use of force. The "nature, scope, and duration" standard favored by OLC, and set forth previously,[516] may be more constitutionally sound, but it appears to explain poorly the president's ability to deploy tens of thousands of U.S. troops into environments where armed conflict exists or is highly likely to exist (Bosnia, Somalia, Haiti), and does not explain at all the apparent belief by at least some presidents that authority exists for even large-scale military operations (such as in Iraq). By contrast, a theory that the president can resort on his own even to large-scale armed conflict is highly functional and adaptive in nature: it accepts the existence of a strong executive capable of acting decisively and expeditiously, accepts the need for an ultimate check on such presidential power by the other branches, and acknowledges inescapable political currents that exist more broadly within American society that condition the behavior of the political branches.

The clear and substantial disadvantage of this theory is that the law seems to disappear. Certainly the Constitution and its rather conspicuous allocation of the war powers to Congress recedes into the background, overwhelmed by contemporary practicalities, making it perhaps even more difficult for Congress to play the gatekeeping role that the Framers appear to have envisaged.

e. President Has Preclusive Authority to Resort to Armed Conflict, But Can Be Impeached or Denied Funding

Some commentators have argued that the president has preclusive authority to act and that Congress may not interfere with such exercise of presidential power,

---

[512] Sofaer, *supra* note 474, at 52.

[513] *Id.*

[514] *Id.*

[515] *Id.* at 52–54; *see* Monaghan, *supra* note 423, at 33 ("No president could survive politically if he is seen acting in lawless defiance of a congressional command to end the war, even if he could escape impeachment.").

[516] *See supra* this chapter text accompanying notes 433–485.

other than by impeaching the president or declining to appropriate funds for uses of force. On this account, the "Framers established this system because they were not excessively worried by the prospect of unilateral executive action," since the "President was seen as the protector and representative of the People," whereas "the Framers expressed a deep concern regarding the damage that Congress, and the interest groups that could dominate it, might cause in the delicate areas of war and foreign policy."[517]

By this reading, the power to "declare war" in Article I does not accord to Congress *any* power to decide on the recourse to armed force; rather, it only provides Congress a power to recognize formally whether the United States is in a legal state of war for purposes of U.S. national law, which has the collateral effect "of ousting the courts from war powers disputes . . . ."[518] Rather, it is the president who has the power to resort to armed force, based on his "powers over foreign relations and the military," because the Framers placed all executive power, as it was then understood in Britain, in the president, with the exception of powers expressly enumerated for the other branches.[519]

This is a difficult position to maintain, especially given that it is grounded in a purported shared understanding of the Framers. As discussed previously, the pre-constitutional history as compared with the text of the Constitution, the debates at the Philadelphia convention, comments made at the state ratifying conventions, and the common understandings expressed in the writings of the time, all strongly indicate a different view, one in which the power to "declare war" was not limited to mere formalities.[520] Further, early decisions of the Supreme Court, such as in *Bas v. Tingy*, *Talbot v. Seeman*, and *Little v. Barreme*, appear to acknowledge that it is for Congress to authorize either a full-fledged "war" or a more limited "imperfect" war, while at "no point during the first forty years of activity under the Constitution, did a President or any other important participant claim that Presidents could exercise force independently of congressional control."[521] As such, it is no surprise that the argument in favor of a preclusive presidential power to resort to armed force has been subject to strong criticisms, including that it is based on a highly selective use of evidence from

---

[517] John C. Yoo, *The Continuation of Politics by Other Means: The Original Understanding of War Powers*, 84 CAL. L. REV. 167, 174 (1996). *See generally* JOHN YOO, CRISIS AND COMMAND: THE HISTORY OF EXECUTIVE POWER FROM GEORGE WASHINGTON TO GEORGE W. BUSH (2009); JOHN YOO, THE POWERS OF WAR AND PEACE: THE CONSTITUTION AND FOREIGN AFFAIRS AFTER 9/11, *supra* note 41.

[518] Yoo, *The Continuation of Politics by Other Means*, supra note 517, at 295.

[519] *Id.*

[520] *See supra* this chapter § I(A)–(B); *see also* Saikrishna Prakash, *Unleashing the Dogs of War: What the Constitution Means by "Declare War,"* 93 CORNELL L.J. 45, 84 (2007) ("there is no evidence that anyone, either in Philadelphia or in the states, read 'declare war' in the Constitution as only authorizing Congress to issue formal declarations of war.").

[521] Sofaer, *supra* note 474, at 50–51.

the period of the founding and evinces an unwillingness to confront squarely the Framers' basic rejection of monarchical prerogatives when designing the executive power.[522]

Distinctly, Michael Ramsey has argued that the president can wage war in response to another state's declaration of war against the United States, since at that point a state of "war" already exists such that Congress' power to "declare war" power is irrelevant.[523] The issue is not likely to arise often, given that declarations of war rarely feature in contemporary interstate practice; rather, states invariably declare that they are acting in self-defense when they use military force.[524] Yet it should be noted that the evidence from the eighteenth century indicates an understanding that, in response to another state's declaration of war, there might or might not be a resort to war-like action. Hence, as a part of its power to "declare war," it seems plausible that the Framers intended for Congress to retain the power to choose not to fight back or to accept whatever terms for peace are set by the other state. If so, Congress' power to declare war embraces not just the decision to resort to war-like action against another state but to decide the purposes, objectives, and general means for pursuing such action.[525]

---

[522] See, e.g., GRIFFIN, supra note 66, at 43 ("... the most serious problem with Yoo's argument is that he is unable to find a single person in the Convention or ratification debates who advocated the kind of presidential war-initiation power he favors."); Louis Fisher, The Law: John Yoo and the Republic, 41 PRESIDENTIAL STUD. Q. 177, 180 (2011) (finding that numerous Framers "vigorously repudiated the British war powers model" at the Constitutional Convention because they "were deeply concerned about unilateral executive commitments to war"); Julian Davis Mortenson, Executive Power and the Discipline of History, 78 U. CHI. L. REV. 377, 381 (2011) (finding that Yoo "misstates crucial facts, misunderstands important episodes, and misrepresents central primary sources"); Stuart Streichler, Mad About Yoo, or Why Worry About the Next Unconstitutional War?, 24 J.L. & POL. 93, 108 (2008) ("Yoo's argumentative strategy, in short, is to draw inferences from the text and historical context for evidence of what the founders must have believed the Declare War Clause meant, even if that contradicts their actual statements about what they understood it to mean."). For a lively exchange, see Robert J. Delahunty & John Yoo, Making War, 93 CORNELL L. REV. 123 (2007); Saikrishna Prakash, Reply, A Two-Front War, 93 CORNELL L. REV. 197 (2007); Prakash, supra note 520.

[523] See, e.g., RAMSEY, supra note 2, at 239–45.

[524] For an interesting recent example, see SEAN D. MURPHY ET AL., LITIGATING WAR: ARBITRATION OF CIVIL INJURY BY THE ETHIOPIA CLAIMS COMMISSION 126–27 (2013) (arbitral commission finding that an Ethiopian declaration that it would act in self-defense was not a "declaration of war" that could serve as a casus belli). It should also be noted that a purported declaration of war sometimes may be better understood as more in the nature of a declaration of a state of emergency (i.e., addressing a situation internal and not external to the declaring state). On this point with respect to the declaration issued by the Panamanian legislative body in 1989 concerning the deteriorating relations with the United States, see MURPHY, supra note 341, at 112 n.77.

[525] These points are developed in Prakash, supra note 520, at 94–112; see also Prakash, A Two-Front War, supra note 522 (replying to various professors' critiques and reiterating stance that any decision to wage war is exercising constitutional "declare war" power and therefore Congress' role); Michael D. Ramsey, Response, The President's Power to Respond to Attacks, 93 CORNELL L. REV. 169 (2007) (discussing stance that Constitution gave the president the ability "to respond if another nation created a state of war with the United States").

II. Power to Conduct Armed Conflict

A. Consequences of International Law

As noted at the outset of this chapter, in the background of the exercise of U.S. constitutional war powers lie various rules of international law relating to the *jus in bello* (law concerning how a state must conduct itself during an armed conflict). Again, as a matter of U.S. law, these rules of international law are inferior to the U.S. Constitution, but they nevertheless can play a very important role with respect to U.S. conduct of warfare after an armed conflict begins.

While originally the *jus in bello* were rules that operated in time of "war" between two states, today such rules apply whenever an "armed conflict" has arisen between two states—or, to a more limited extent, whenever there exists a "non-international" armed conflict (NIAC), meaning a conflict between a state and a nonstate actor (or between two nonstate actors). If such an armed conflict exists, the *jus in bello* regulates how the relevant actors should conduct themselves, including rules on the regulation of means and methods of warfare, the treatment of prisoners and injured participants, the treatment of enemy nationals and their property, the treatment of the populations of occupied territories, and the relations between neutral states and belligerent states.[526]

Many customary rules relating to the law of armed conflict were codified at the Hague Peace Conferences of 1899 and 1907, notably in the 1907 Hague Regulations.[527] Such rules were further strengthened after the world wars, in particular in 1949 through the four Geneva Conventions[528] and in 1977 with two additional protocols to the 1949 Geneva Conventions.[529] Conventions on

---

[526] For recent literature in this area, see JONATHAN CROWE & KYLIE WESTON-SCHEUBER, PRINCIPLES OF INTERNATIONAL HUMANITARIAN LAW (2013); INGRID DETTER, THE LAW OF WAR (3d ed. 2013); THE HANDBOOK OF INTERNATIONAL HUMANITARIAN LAW (Dieter Fleck ed., 4th ed. 2021).

[527] Hague Convention Respecting the Laws and Customs of War on Land, with annexed Regulations, Oct. 18, 1907, 36 Stat. 2277 [hereinafter Hague Convention IV]. The United States is a party to this Convention.

[528] Geneva Convention for the Amelioration of the Condition of the Wounded and Sick in Armed Forces in the Field, Aug. 12, 1949, 6 U.S.T. 3114, 75 U.N.T.S. 31 [hereinafter Geneva Convention I]; Geneva Convention for the Amelioration of the Condition of Wounded, Sick, and Shipwrecked Members of the Armed Forces at Sea, Aug. 12, 1949, 6 U.S.T. 3217, 75 U.N.T.S. 85 [hereinafter Geneva Convention II]; Geneva Convention Relative to the Treatment of Prisoners of War, Aug. 12, 1949, 6 U.S.T. 3316, 75 U.N.T.S. 135 [hereinafter Geneva Convention III]; Geneva Convention Relative to the Protection of Civilian Persons in Time of War, Aug. 12, 1949, 6 U.S.T. 3516, 75 U.N.T.S. 287 [hereinafter Geneva Convention IV]. The United States is a party to these conventions.

[529] Protocol Additional to the Geneva Conventions of 12 August 1949, and Relating to the Protection of Victims of International Armed Conflicts, June 8, 1977, 1125 U.N.T.S. 3 [hereinafter Additional Protocol I]; Protocol Additional to the Geneva Conventions of 12 August 1949, and Relating to the Protection of Victims of Non-International Armed Conflicts, June 8, 1977, 1125 U.N.T.S. 609 [hereinafter Additional Protocol II]. The United States is a party to neither protocol. There is also a third protocol, entitled Protocol Additional (III) to the Geneva Conventions of 12 August 1949, and Relating to the Adoption of an Additional Distinctive Emblem, Dec. 8, 2005, 2404

particular issues, such as the treatment of cultural property during armed conflict, also exist.[530] The United States, as a party to many (but not all) of these treaties, has accepted an obligation under international law to act in accordance with them.

Further, such treaties are sometimes incorporated into U.S. law when developing U.S. statutes and regulations. For example, U.S. law allows for the prosecution for a "war crime" in any situation where the person committing the war crime or the victim of the war crime is either a U.S. national or a member of the U.S. armed forces.[531] A "war crime" is then defined to mean conduct defined as a "grave breach" of any of the 1949 Geneva Conventions (or any protocol to which the United States is a party); conduct prohibited by specified articles of the 1907 Hague Regulations; conduct that constitutes a grave breach of common Article 3 to the 1949 Geneva Conventions, when it occurs in the context of a NIAC; and certain conduct contrary to the provisions of a treaty relating to mines and booby traps.[532]

Even where a U.S. statute does not expressly refer to a treaty, the statute may incorporate both treaty and customary rules of the *jus in bello*. For example, in *Hamdan v. Rumsfeld*, a detainee held by the United States at Guantánamo Bay, Cuba, challenged his prosecution before a military commission established pursuant to a military order of President George W. Bush.[533] The Supreme Court accepted that the president, as commander in chief, could convene military commissions to try war crimes, given the 2001 AUMF statute. Yet the Court also found that Congress had regulated such commissions pursuant to the Uniform Code of Military Justice (UCMJ).[534] The UCMJ set forth provisions for the convening of court martials, then stated in Article 21 that the "provisions of this chapter conferring jurisdiction upon courts-martial do not deprive military

---

U.N.T.S. 261. The third protocol establishes an additional emblem (the red crystal); the United States is a party to this protocol.

[530] Hague Convention for the Protection of Cultural Property in the Event of Armed Conflict, May 14, 1954, T.I.A.S. No. 09-313.1, 249 U.N.T.S. 215; First Protocol to the Hague Convention of 1954 for the Protection of Cultural Property in the Event of Armed Conflict, May 14, 1954, 249 U.N.T.S. 358; Second Protocol to the Hague Convention of 1954 for the Protection of Cultural Property in the Event of Armed Conflict, Mar. 26, 1999, 2253 U.N.T.S. 172. The United States is a party to the 1954 convention, but not to its two protocols.

[531] 18 U.S.C. § 2441(a)–(b) (2018).

[532] 18 U.S.C. § 2441(c)–(d); *see* Protocol on Prohibitions or Restrictions on the Use of Mines, Booby-Traps and Other Devices (Protocol II), May 3, 1996, S. TREATY DOC. No. 103-25, 2048 U.N.T.S. 93.

[533] Hamdan v. Rumsfeld, 548 U.S. 557 (2006). For discussion of *Hamdan* in the context of the commander in chief's power to convene military commissions, see *infra* this chapter § II(B); for *Hamdan* in relation to Congress' power to regulate the military, see *infra* this chapter § III(B); *see also* Chapter 1 § II(B); Chapter 5 § II(A)(2); and Chapter 10 § II(E)(4). On the ability of Guantánamo detainees to bring actions before U.S. courts challenging their detention, see Chapter 10 § II(D)(7).

[534] For discussion of the UCMJ, see *infra* this chapter § III(B).

commissions, provost courts, or other military tribunals of concurrent jurisdiction with respect to offenders or offenses that by statute *or by the law of war* may be tried by military commissions, provost courts, or other military tribunals."[535] Since Hamdan was before a military commission that was convened by a military order (and not a statute), the Court found that Article 21 required that the commission operate in accordance with the "law of war," which inter alia meant consistent with the 1949 Geneva Conventions. The Court then found that the proceedings against Hamdan were defective under the laws of war both in terms of the substantive charges against Hamdan[536] and in terms of the procedures of the commission.[537] After the Court's ruling, Congress responded by adopting a new statute that broadly authorized the president to pursue prosecutions by war commissions, and that asserted the *president's* constitutional authority to interpret any applicable standards of international law.[538]

The *jus in bello* is also incorporated by the executive branch. Among the most important examples are the numerous military manuals adopted to regulate the conduct of U.S. armed forces. For example, the Department of the Army Field Manual is replete with references to the 1907 Hague Regulations, 1949 Geneva Conventions, and other sources of both treaty and customary law in this area and has served for decades as a cornerstone for training and guiding U.S. military personnel with respect to field operations.[539] Moreover, even in the absence of statutes or regulations, the *jus in bello* may inform internal U.S. government deliberations. For example, when considering the legality of targeting U.S. nationals for military air strikes in the conflict with al-Qaeda, the Justice Department apparently considered one of the relevant factors in a due process analysis to be whether the operation was to be conducted "in a manner consistent with applicable law of war principles."[540]

The extent to which treaty rules have passed into customary international law, binding upon the United States even in the absence of U.S. ratification of the treaty concerned, and the extent to which those rules apply not just to international armed conflicts but to NIACs as well, are frequently contested.[541] Even

---

[535] 10 U.S.C. § 821 (emphasis added).

[536] *Hamdan*, 548 U.S. at 595–613.

[537] *Id.* at 625–28.

[538] Military Commissions Act of 2006, Pub. L. No. 109-366, § 6(a)(3), 120 Stat. 2600, 2632.

[539] DEP'T OF THE ARMY, FIELD MANUAL 27-10, THE LAW OF LAND WARFARE (1956).

[540] U.S. Dep't of Justice, Draft White Paper: Lawfulness of a Lethal Operation Directed Against a U.S. Citizen Who Is a Senior Operational Leader of Al–Qa'ida or An Associated Force (Nov. 8, 2011), https://perma.cc/98HL-AEJK.

[541] For a study under the auspices of the International Committee of the Red Cross, see JEAN-MARIE HENCKAERTS & LOUISE DOSWALD-BECK, CUSTOMARY INTERNATIONAL HUMANITARIAN LAW (2005). For the U.S. government's reaction to the study's methodology, particularly as regards the practice of nonstate actors, see U.S. Joint Letter from John Bellinger III, Legal Adviser, U.S. Department of State, and William J. Haynes, General Counsel, U.S. Department of State to Dr. Jakob Kellenberger, President, International Committee of the Red Cross, Regarding Customary

so, such rules may provide a basis for the shaping of U.S. policies and may, over time, "harden" into legal obligation. For example, while the United States is not a party to Protocol I to the 1949 Geneva Conventions, it has regarded various provisions of that protocol as reflecting customary international law.[542] Article 75 of Protocol I sets forth a series of "fundamental guarantees" for the protection of all persons in an international armed conflict. In 2011, the Obama administration announced new actions relating to treatment of detainees being held in the armed conflict between the United States and al-Qaeda, which included the assertion that "Article 75 is a provision of the treaty that is consistent with our current policies and practice and is one that the United States has historically supported."[543] Moreover, the statement maintained that the U.S. government will "choose out of a sense of legal obligation to treat the principles set forth in Article 75 as applicable to any individual it detains in an international armed conflict, and expects all other nations to adhere to these principles as well."[544]

B. Commander-in-Chief Power

Article II of the Constitution provides: "The President shall be Commander in Chief of the Army and Navy of the United States, and of the Militia of the several States, when called into the actual service of the United States."[545] Assuming that there is authority to resort to war, it is generally accepted that the president's commander-in-chief power carries with it at least two core attributes upon which Congress may not intrude.

International Law Study, 46 I.L.M. 511 (2007). For a response, see Response of Jean-Marie Henckaerts to the U.S. Joint Letter, 46 I.L.M. 957 (2007); see also PERSPECTIVES ON THE ICRC STUDY ON CUSTOMARY INTERNATIONAL HUMANITARIAN LAW (Elizabeth Wilmshurst & Susan Breau eds., 2007) (discussing how to identify customary international humanitarian law).

[542] The 1977 additional protocols have received impressive (although not universal) international support, with 174 parties to Additional Protocol I and 169 to Additional Protocol II as of mid-2022. Although not a party to Additional Protocol I, the United States regards much, but not all, of it as reflecting customary international law. See Michael J. Matheson, Session One: The United States Position on the Relation of Customary International Law to the 1977 Protocols Additional to the 1949 Geneva Conventions, 2 AM. U.J. INT'L L. & POL'Y 419 (1987); William H. Taft IV, The Law of Armed Conflict After 9/11: Some Salient Features, 28 YALE J. INT'L L. 319, 322 (2003). The United States is also not a party to Additional Protocol II, but that protocol has evoked sufficient controversy that its status as customary international law is uncertain.

[543] Press Release, The White House, Fact Sheet: New Actions on Guantanamo and Detainee Policy (Mar. 7, 2011), https://perma.cc/K459-W9T9.

[544] Id.

[545] U.S. CONST. art. II, § 2, cl. 1. The text provides no real guidance as to the meaning of the power. See David Luban, On the Commander-in-Chief Power, 81 S. CAL. L. REV. 477, 483 (2008) ("On its face, the clause tells us where the commander in chief authority is located: in the president. But the clause tells us nothing about what the commander in chief power encompasses.").

First, the president and the president alone is to be the commander in chief: Congress cannot by statute establish some other person or Congress itself as the commander in chief, nor constrain the president's discretion in supervising the military.[546] It is the president and the president alone, as commander in chief, who "superintend[s] the military."[547] "[O]nce war is commenced, Congress cannot conduct a campaign; it cannot 'deprive the President of command of the army and navy.'"[548] One important advantage of placing this power with the president—a civilian leader—is that it serves to deny such power to the military. In the midst of the U.S. Civil War, Attorney General Edward Bates noted that the president is not necessarily "skilled in the art of war and qualified to marshal a host in the field of battle," but by serving in this role the military becomes subordinate to the orders of civilian authority.[549]

Second, it is also generally accepted that the president alone (and not Congress) is to make tactical judgments involving when, where, and how to attack the enemy.[550] This view has been expressed at regular intervals. Thus, Hamilton explained in *Federalist No. 69* that, as commander in chief, the president possesses "the supreme command and direction of the military and naval forces"; as he further noted in *Federalist No. 74*, it made sense for the president to be commander in chief because directing the war "most peculiarly demands those qualities which distinguish the exercise of power by a single hand."[551] In the context of the Mexican-American War, the Supreme Court stated in *Fleming*

[546] *See* Barron & Lederman, *supra* note 128, at 1102–06 (referring to this as the "superintendence prerogative").

[547] Loving v. United States, 517 U.S. 748, 772 (1996); *see also* Placing of United States Armed Forces Under United Nations Operational or Tactical Control, 20 Op. O.L.C. 182, 184 (1996) (stating the Constitution grants the president the sole responsibility "to select the particular personnel who are to exercise tactical and operational control over U.S. forces"). In *Loving*, the Supreme Court concluded that there was no concern in having Congress delegate to the president an authority to prescribe aggravating factors to be taken into account during court martials at the death penalty phase, since the "delegated duty . . . is interlinked with duties already assigned to the president by express terms of the Constitution" as commander in chief. *Loving*, 517 U.S. at 772.

[548] Berger, *supra* note 36, at 77.

[549] 10 Op. Att'y Gen. 74, 79 (1861).

[550] *See* Banks & Raven-Hansen, *supra* note 402, at 150, 154–57; Ely, *supra* note 62, at 25 (". . . it was the point of the Commander in Chief Clause to keep Congress out of day-to-day combat decisions once it had authorized the war in question."); Glennon, *supra* note 6, at 84 (finding that the president's sole powers "do extend to operational battlefield decisions concerning the means to be employed to achieve ends chosen by Congress"); Henkin, Foreign Affairs, at 103–04 ("It would be unthinkable for Congress to attempt detailed, tactical decision, or supervision, and as to these the President's authority is effectively supreme."); Ramsey, *supra* note 2, at 253–55; David J. Barron & Martin S. Lederman, *The Commander in Chief at the Lowest Ebb—Framing the Problem, Doctrine, and Original Understanding*, 121 Harv. L. Rev. 689, 705 (2008); David M. Golove, *Against Free-Form Formalism*, 73 N.Y.U. L. Rev. 1791, 1855 (1998).

[551] The Federalist No. 69, at 418 (Alexander Hamilton); *id.*, No. 74, at 447 (Alexander Hamilton); *see* United States v. Sweeny, 157 U.S. 281, 284 (1895) (finding that the purpose in the power "is evidently to vest in the president . . . such supreme and undivided command as would be necessary to the prosecution of a successful war").

v. Page that as "commander-in-chief, he is authorized to direct the movements of the naval and military forces placed by law at his command, and to employ them in the manner he may deem most effectual to harass and conquer and subdue the enemy."[552] Robert Jackson, serving as attorney general on the eve of World War II, maintained that "the President's responsibility as Commander in Chief embraces the authority to command and direct the armed forces in their immediate movements and operations designed to protect the security and effectuate the defense of the United States."[553]

President Lincoln famously exercised extensive powers as commander in chief during the Civil War. At the outset of the war, for example, Lincoln declared a blockade of southern ports and commenced seizing vessels that violated the blockade as well as "enemy" vessels and cargo, without any authorization from Congress. The Supreme Court found such action lawful, given his role as commander in chief, when confronted with an insurrection.[554] Like most other assertions of commander-in-chief authority, during the Civil War and otherwise, the blockade presented little opportunity to resolve the extent to which such applications of presidential power were not merely constitutional in the absence of congressional authority but also immunized from congressional interference. There were contemporary indications, however, that at least some tactical decisions might be exclusively for the president. For example, Chief Justice Chase, in his concurring opinion in *Ex Parte Milligan*, stated that Congress has extensive powers during a time of war, but may not enact legislation that "interferes with the command of the forces and the conduct of campaigns" and may not "direct the conduct of campaigns."[555]

Various acts by the president closely associated with directing such military movements that appear akin to this core power include the gathering of intelligence on the enemy,[556] issuing rewards for the capture of deserters,[557] enacting measures to extract local resources in occupied territory,[558] and constituting courts-martial.[559] President Lincoln, again, afforded an example when emancipating slaves in the areas of the United States under rebellion. In September 1862, the president declared that, on January 1, 1863, "all persons held as slaves within any state, or designated part of a state, the people whereof shall then be

---

[552] Fleming v. Page, 50 U.S. (9 How.) 603, 615 (1850); *see* 1 Op. O.L.C., *supra* note 210.

[553] 40 Op. Att'y Gen., *supra* note 446, at 61–62.

[554] The Prize Cases, 67 U.S. 635, 670 (1863).

[555] *Ex parte* Milligan, 71 U.S. (4 Wall.) 2, 139 (1866) (Chase, C.J., concurring); *see also* Hamdan v. Rumsfeld, 548 U.S. 557, 591–92 (2006) (quoting *Ex parte Milligan* 71 U.S. (4 Wall.) at 139–40); Hamilton v. Dillin, 88 U.S. (21 Wall.) 73, 87 (1875) (finding that the president alone is "constitutionally invested with the entire charge of hostile operations").

[556] Totten v. United States, 92 U.S. 105, 106 (1876).

[557] Kurtz v. Moffitt, 115 U.S. 487, 503 (1885).

[558] Fleming v. Page, 50 U.S. 603, 616 (1850).

[559] Swaim v. United States, 165 U.S. 553, 557–58 (1897).

in rebellion against the United States shall be then, thenceforward, and forever free."[560] When that date arrived, the president designated the relevant areas, stating that his action was "by virtue of the power in me vested as Commander-in-Chief, of the Army and Navy of the United States in time of actual armed rebellion against the authority and government of the United States, and as a fit and necessary war measure for suppressing said rebellion . . . ."[561]

There is some disagreement, however, as to the range of associated activities that fall within this core of authority, and more particularly whether they share the characteristic of being exclusive of congressional power—particularly given that Congress "throughout our history has adopted intrusive measures regulating executive war powers, including some in the midst of battle."[562] The potential range and assertedly preclusive effect of the commander-in-chief power were particularly evident in the wake of the attacks of September 11, 2001. The administration of President George W. Bush asserted that the power to direct military activities in the "war on terror" extended to a wide range of decisions about how best to engage al-Qaeda and the Taliban, including implementing a secret "terrorist surveillance program" that included warrantless interception of international communications into and out of the United States[563] and aggressive measures with respect to the detention, interrogation, and trial of suspected enemy combatants.[564] One OLC memorandum sweepingly asserted that the president holds "the plenary authority, as Commander in Chief and the sole organ of the Nation in its foreign relations, to use military force abroad" and to make decisions about the amount, method, timing, and nature of the use of military force.[565] Perhaps the most notorious of those claims was set forth in the 2002 OLC memorandum, which asserted that a statute criminalizing state-sponsored torture outside the United States could not apply to the treatment of

[560] Preliminary Emancipation Proclamation, *in* 5 THE COLLECTED WORKS OF ABRAHAM LINCOLN 434 (Basler ed., 1953).

[561] Emancipation Proclamation, *in* 6 THE COLLECTED WORKS OF ABRAHAM LINCOLN 29 (Basler ed., 1953); *see* Michael Stokes Paulsen, *The Emancipation Proclamation and the Commander in Chief Power*, 40 GA. L. REV. 807 (2006).

[562] Barron & Lederman, *supra* note 128, at 1106; *see* EDWARD S. CORWIN, THE PRESIDENT: OFFICE AND POWERS 1787–1984, at 293–96 (5th ed. 1984); Berger, *supra* note 36, at 75–82; Henry P. Monaghan, *The Protective Power of the Presidency*, 93 COLUM. L. REV. 1, 31 (1993).

[563] *See, e.g.*, Legal Authorities Supporting the Activities of the National Security Agency Described by the President, 30 Op. O.L.C. 1, 2 (2006) ("The [National Security Agency] activities are supported by the President's well-recognized inherent constitutional authority as Commander in Chief and sole organ for the Nation in foreign affairs to conduct warrantless surveillance of enemy forces for intelligence purposes to detect and disrupt armed attacks on the United States."). For litigation relating to this program, see Clapper v. Amnesty Int'l USA, 568 U.S. 398 (2013).

[564] On the ability of detainees in military detention abroad to bring actions before U.S. courts challenging their detention, see Chapter 10 § II(D)(7); on their trial by military commission, *see infra* this chapter § III(B) and Chapter 10 § II(E)(4).

[565] The President's Constitutional Authority to Conduct Military Operations Against Terrorists and Nations Supporting Them, 25 Op. O.L.C. 188, 188 (2001).

detainees in Guantánamo Bay, Cuba, since "Congress can no more interfere with the President's conduct of the interrogation of enemy combatants than it can dictate strategic or tactical decisions on the battlefield."[566]

Such broader claims of presidential power that is immunized from congressional control are unpersuasive. Certainly, the constitutional text itself does not suggest a wide-ranging presidential power to the exclusion of Congress whenever there exists war or armed conflict. Nor do other sources that shed light on the meaning of the text. The term "commander in chief" in pre-1776 Britain appears to have referred to a purely military appointee who was subject to the complete direction and control of Parliament or the king.[567] After the outbreak of the American rebellion, the Continental Congress exercised such direction and control over its commander in chief, instructing George Washington in 1775 "punctually to observe and follow such orders and directions, from time to time, as you shall receive from this, or a future Congress of these United Colonies, or committee of Congress."[568] Throughout the Revolutionary War, Congress used committees to direct the war effort, including instructions regarding the deployment of troops, the interception of ships, and even the method of the army's retreat (e.g., denying Washington's request that he be allowed to burn New York City while insisting that he defend Fort Washington).[569] Though Congress soon found that it was not feasible to keep General Washington on too tight a leash, instructing him that "whereas all particulars cannot be foreseen . . . many things must be left to your prudent and discreet management . . . ," Congress never relinquished its general prerogative to give Washington specific instructions regarding the conduct of the war.[570]

Similarly, as the several states after 1776 adopted their new constitutions and accorded to an executive official (sometimes designated as "commander in chief") control over the state's militia, in each instance the power of the legislature to control that official remained intact. David Barron and Marty Lederman maintain that "not a single one of the new state constitutions expressly conferred such preclusive authority [upon the executive], nor did any of them suggest that the legislative branch would be prevented from interfering with the Commander in Chief's conduct of military operations."[571] Rather, "five of them—including the Massachusetts Constitution, which likely was the primary model for the

---

[566] Memorandum from Jay S. Bybee, Assistant Attorney Gen., Office of the Legal Counsel, to Alberto R. Gonzales, Counsel to the President (Aug. 1, 2002), *reprinted in* THE TORTURE PAPERS: THE ROAD TO ABU GHRAIB 172, 207 (Anthony Lewis, Karen J. Greenberg, & Joshua L. Dratel eds., 2005).

[567] Barron & Lederman, *supra* note 550, at 772–73; *see* Luban, *supra* note 545, at 502–05.

[568] 2 JOURNALS OF THE CONTINENTAL CONGRESS 96.

[569] Barron & Lederman, *supra* note 550, at 775.

[570] 2 JOURNALS OF THE CONTINENTAL CONGRESS 101.

[571] Barron & Lederman, *supra* note 550, at 782.

federal Commander in Chief Clause in 1787—stated expressly that the governor would have to exercise his military powers in conformity with state law."[572]

The sparse records of the Constitutional Convention also do not reveal any sense that the commander-in-chief power allocated to the president wide-ranging authority preclusive of congressional control.[573] Indeed the relative silence about the clause suggests that the clause was viewed as simply allocating to the president the ability to control the armed forces; were it meant to be a grant of preclusive power on a potentially broad range of issues, one would have expected greater debate as to its propriety.[574] Of course, by structuring the new government so that the commander in chief was chosen by the people (through electors) rather than by Congress and by according to that person the ability to veto laws enacted by Congress, the Framers no doubt understood that the practical ability of Congress to control the commander in chief had inherent limits. Nevertheless, the possibility of such control remained intact. Finally, the evidence from the ratification of the Constitution by the states also suggests no belief that the president, other than having a preclusive right to serve as commander in chief, would operate beyond the control of the Congress.[575]

Since 1789, Congress has imposed significant constraints upon the president's actions as commander in chief of U.S. forces, even in times of armed conflict.[576] For the most part, the executive branch appears to have accepted the constitutionality of such constraints, with the president regularly signing such statutes into law. Further, in litigation, the executive branch at times has acknowledged an obligation of the president to operate as commander in chief both in accordance with the law of war and with statutory limitations. For example, in the *Prize Cases*—which concerned the validity of the North's blockade of Southern ports during the civil war—the executive branch argued that, while the function of using the army and navy rested with the president, "the mode of using them, within the rules of civilized warfare, and *subject to established laws of Congress*, must be subject to his discretion as a necessary incident to the use, *in the absence of any act of Congress controlling him*."[577]

---

[572] *Id.*

[573] *See* Luban, *supra* note 545, at 508–32. Luban argues that the underlying theory of the commander-in-chief power at the founding was "separationist" in simply placing civilian control over the military; "it contemplated a civilian commander in chief whose military competence could be near zero and whose exercise of the command function would be circumscribed by hiving off crucial military powers and giving them to Congress or the states." *Id.* at 532.

[574] Barron & Lederman, *supra* note 550, at 785–91.

[575] *Id.* at 792–99.

[576] For an extensive gathering of the adoption of such statutory constraints over the course of U.S. history, see VIOLET L. TURNER & MADDOX M. WATSON, CONGRESSIONAL LIMITS ON MILITARY OPERATIONS (2012); Barron & Lederman, *supra* note 128.

[577] Br. for the U.S. and Captors, *The Prize Cases*, 67 U.S. (2 Black) 635 (1863), *in* 3 LANDMARK BRIEFS AND ARGUMENTS OF THE SUPREME COURT OF THE UNITED STATES: CONSTITUTIONAL LAW 517 (Philip B. Kurland & Gerhard Casper eds., 1978) (cited in Barron & Lederman, *supra* note

The Supreme Court appears repeatedly to have accepted the constitutionality of such statutory constraints. In *Little v. Barreme*, the Court made clear that congressional restrictions contained within a war-related statute limited the president's discretion, in that instance by authorizing the executive to seize U.S. vessels sailing *to* French ports and not those sailing *from* French ports.[578] In *Brown v. United States*,[579] the Court found during the War of 1812 that, while the laws of war permit a belligerent to seize in its territory enemy belligerent property, under U.S. law such seizure required statutory authorization; the president's commander-in-chief power alone was not sufficient, notwithstanding the existence of a declaration of war by Congress. Most famously, in *Youngstown*, a dominant theme of the Court's decision was whether President Truman's seizure of the steel mills to maintain the flow of arms to Korea was contrary to the express or implied will of Congress; even the dissenters accepted that the president's actions were "subject to congressional direction."[580] Justice Jackson's concurrence observed that the power is sometimes invoked "as support for any Presidential action, internal or external, involving use of force, the idea being that it vests power to do anything, anywhere, that can be done with an army or navy."[581] In that context, Jackson warned about such excessive claims, saying that nothing would be "more sinister and alarming than that a President whose conduct of foreign affairs is so largely uncontrolled, and often even is unknown, can vastly enlarge his mastery over the internal affairs of the country by his own commitment of the Nation's armed forces to some foreign venture."[582] As noted, in *Hamdan v. Rumsfeld*, the Court accepted that the president as commander in chief may in time of war convene military commissions to try war crimes, but held that Congress could regulate by statute such commissions, in that case by means of the UCMJ.[583] Among other things, the Court in *Hamdan* stated that

---

550, at 761, n.213) (emphasis added). The blockade was indirectly authorized by Congress by two prior statutes that authorized the president to use U.S. naval forces to suppress insurrection against the U.S. government. The blockade was directly authorized subsequently by Congress as well. *The Prize Cases*, 67 U.S. (2 Black) at 668–70; *see* Thomas H. Lee & Michael D. Ramsey, *The Story of the Prize Cases: Executive Action and Judicial Review in Wartime, in* PRESIDENTIAL POWER STORIES 53 (Christopher H. Schroeder & Curtis A. Bradley eds., 2008).

[578] Little v. Barreme, 6 U.S. (2 Cranch) 170, 179 (1804) (applying Act of Feb. 9, 1799, ch. 2, § 1, 1 Stat. 613, 613–14).

[579] 12 U.S. (8 Cranch) 110 (1814).

[580] Youngstown Sheet & Tube Co. v. Sawyer, 343 U.S. 579, 710 (1952) (Vinson, C.J., dissenting). For further discussion of *Youngstown*, see Chapter 1 § II(B).

[581] *Youngstown*, 343 U.S. at 641 (Jackson, J., concurring).

[582] *Id.* at 642.

[583] *See* Military Order of November 13, 2001: Detention, Treatment, and Trial of Certain Non-Citizens in the War Against Terrorism, 66 Fed. Reg. 57,831 (Nov. 16, 2001). On the UCMJ, see *infra* this chapter § III(B).

the president "may not disregard limitations that Congress has, in proper exercise of its own war powers, placed on his powers."[584]

One explanation for the general acceptance of Congress' ability to place constraints on the commander-in-chief power is that the president is rarely, in fact, capable of operating independent of other constitutional powers. Once the president moves beyond a core, preclusive domain of deciding matters relating directly or closely to troop deployments, other constitutional powers typically come into play, which must be considered capable of mitigating the commander-in-chief power.[585] For example, Congress' express power to "raise" the army would appear to carry with it some ability to condition the use of that army.[586] Other congressional powers not typically associated with war powers also may be engaged during a time of armed conflict, and these too will be implicated in any assessment of the contours of the commander-in-chief power. Such congressional powers include the general power to appropriate funds for the "general Welfare of the United States,"[587] the power to "define and punish . . . Offences against the Law of Nations,"[588] and the power to "make all Laws which shall be necessary and proper for carrying into Execution the foregoing Powers, and all other Powers vested by this Constitution in the Government of the United States, or in any Department or Officer thereof."[589] To these might be added the Senate's power to withhold consent to the appointment and promotion of military officers, as well as political appointments to the Department of Defense and other agencies concerned with national security.[590]

The direct relevance of these other constitutional powers may explain, in part, why the executive branch normally accepts that the commander-in-chief power must be exercised in accordance with the laws of war, including treaties such as the 1907 Hague and the 1949 Geneva Conventions.[591] Not only are such treaties part of the supreme law of the land, but many aspects of them fall within the

---

[584] Hamdan v. Rumsfeld, 548 U.S. 557, 593 n.23 (2006). For further discussion of *Hamdan*, see *supra* this chapter § II(A); *infra* this chapter § III(B); Chapter 1 § II(B); Chapter 5 § II(A)(2); and Chapter 10 § II(E)(4).

[585] *See* Moore, *supra* note 219, at 32 ("Presidential power, even in the exercise of the Commander in Chief power, is not autonomous . . . .").

[586] *See infra* this chapter § III(A).

[587] U.S. CONST. art. I, § 8, cl. 1; *see* Chapter 2.

[588] U.S. CONST. art. I, § 8, cl. 10; *see* Chapter 5.

[589] U.S. CONST. art. I, § 8, cl. 18; *see* Kennedy v. Mendoza-Martinez, 372 U.S. 144, 160 (1963) (". . . Congress has broad power under the Necessary and Proper Clause to enact legislation for the regulation of foreign affairs.").

[590] U.S. CONST. art. II, § 2, cl. 2 (the Appointments Clause).

[591] *See, e.g.*, Harold Hongju Koh, Legal Adviser, U.S. Dep't of State, The Obama Administration and International Law, Address to the Annual Meeting of the American Society of International Law (Mar. 25, 2010), https://perma.cc/GE5D-M8VH (asserting that all operations by the U.S. government must comply with international humanitarian law).

scope of matters that Congress can regulate under Article I.[592] Hence, the presence of these other congressional powers may be seen as conditioning the discretion that might otherwise exist for the president as commander in chief.[593]

In addition, whatever the precise relationship between the president's commander-in-chief power and congressional authority, the president's power (like Congress' war powers) is constrained by constitutional and statutory rights protective of the individual. As a general matter, the executive cannot act in a manner that denies persons their life, liberty, or property without due process of law.[594] Further, numerous statutes protect individuals by criminalizing murder, assault, theft, and so on. In time of war, such rules change, not in the sense of disappearing but in the sense of being conditioned by the laws of war. For example, whereas the president normally cannot order the killing of a U.S. national, in a time of war the president can order the killing of an enemy combatant, even if he or she happens to be a U.S. national. An important question with respect to Congress' authorization of the use of force against al-Qaeda and associated operatives was whether the president could target by drone strikes persons away from the original "battlefield" of Afghanistan (such as in Yemen), including persons who were U.S. nationals.[595] OLC approached the question largely by asking whether such a killing would constitute "murder" or "unlawful killing" under the relevant statutes, and concluded that it would not, since a public authority justification existed; the operation was lawful under the laws of war.[596]

In short, the considerable powers assigned to Congress under the Constitution that continue to operate during a period of armed conflict, the apparent

---

[592] For an argument that the president, as commander in chief, cannot violate the Geneva Conventions because Congress has the authority under Article I to enact legislation superseding or implementing such treaty obligations, see Derek Jinks & David Sloss, *Is the President Bound by the Geneva Conventions?*, 90 CORNELL L. REV. 97 (2004).

[593] For other arguments that the commander-in-chief power is circumscribed by international law, see Jean Galbraith, *International Law and the Domestic Separation of Powers*, 99 VA. L. REV. 987 (2013); David Golove, *Military Tribunals, International Law, and the Constitution: A Franckian-Madisonian Approach*, 35 N.Y.U. J. INT'L L. & POL. 363, 364 (2003); Stephen I. Vladeck, *Military Courts and Article III*, 103 GEO. L.J. 933, 993–96 (2015); Ingrid Brunk Wuerth, *International Law and Constitutional Interpretation: The Commander in Chief Clause Reconsidered*, 106 MICH. L. REV. 61, 63–64 (2007).

[594] *See generally* Chapter 10.

[595] *See* Al-Aulaqi v. Panetta, 35 F. Supp. 3d 56, 74 (D.D.C. 2014) (dismissing the case, after U.S. national's death, due to "special factors" counseling hesitation under the *Bivens* doctrine); Al-Aulaqi v. Obama, 727 F. Supp. 2d 1 (D.D.C. 2010) (dismissing the case, prior to U.S. national's death, due to plaintiff father's lack of standing).

[596] Office of Legal Counsel, U.S. Dep't of Justice, Applicability of Federal Criminal Laws and the Constitution to Contemplated Lethal Operations Against Shaykh Anwar al-Aulaqi (July 16, 2010), https://perma.cc/6XV2-NXGC; *see* Lawfulness of a Lethal Operation, *supra* note 540; *see also* Michael Stokes Paulsen, *Drone On: The Commander in Chief Power to Target and Kill Americans*, 38 HARV. J. L. & PUB. POL'Y 43 (2015) (discussing stance that during the "time of constitutionally authorized war, [the president] has the plenary power and discretion under the U.S. Constitution to target and kill specific individuals that he in good faith determines to be active enemy combatants engaged in lawful or unlawful hostilities against the United States.").

understanding in 1787–1789 that a "commander in chief" remains constrained by the law, and the myriad statutory constraints that, since the founding, have operated during armed conflict and been upheld by U.S. courts as against presidential power, all support the conclusion that the commander-in-chief power does not generally displace statutory limits, even in times of armed conflict. And even though it is conventionally understood that the president enjoys a core substantive and preclusive prerogative as commander in chief, commentators have struggled to establish any agreed line beyond which Congress may not go in regulating the conduct war. In their extensive study, David Barron and Marty Lederman identified three general methods that have been suggested for such line-drawing: distinguishing between nonbattlefield regulations (permissible) and battlefield regulations (impermissible);[597] distinguishing between negative prohibitions upon the president (permissible) and affirmative commands to the president (impermissible);[598] or distinguishing between *ex ante* framework measures applicable to all armed conflicts (permissible) and *post hoc* restrictions aimed at a particular conflict (impermissible).[599] In each instance, Barron and Lederman persuasively conclude that such distinctions are vague, illusory, susceptible to manipulation, and hence ultimately unsatisfactory.

For example, consider the Detainee Treatment Act, adopted in 2005, which contained regulations relating to the treatment of persons in the custody of the Department of Defense and the administration of detainees held in Guantánamo Bay, Cuba.[600] Among other things, the statute prohibited "cruel, inhuman, or degrading treatment or punishment" of any prisoner of the U.S. government, required that military interrogations be performed in accordance with the U.S. Army Field Manual for Human Intelligence Collector Operations,[601] and directed the Department of Defense to establish "Combatant Status Review Tribunals" to determine whether each detainee held at Guantánamo Bay was properly designated as an enemy combatant.[602] This statute could be viewed as a permissible nonbattlefield regulation prohibiting the president from denying certain rights to detainees as part of a framework measure relevant to all U.S. conflicts. Alternatively, it could be viewed as an impermissible battlefield

[597] Barron & Lederman, *supra* note 550, at 753–55. For an argument favoring such a distinction, see Jinks & Sloss, *supra* note 592.

[598] Barron & Lederman, *supra* note 550, at 755–56. For an argument favoring such a distinction, see AKHIL REED AMAR, AMERICA'S CONSTITUTION: A BIOGRAPHY 188 (2005).

[599] Barron & Lederman, *supra* note 550, at 756–59. For an argument along these lines, see BANKS & RAVEN-HANSEN, *supra* note 402, at 156–57.

[600] 42 U.S.C. § 2000dd (2018).

[601] DEP'T OF THE ARMY, FIELD MANUAL 2-22.3, HUMAN INTELLIGENCE COLLECTOR OPERATIONS (superseding FM 34-52) (2006).

[602] On the ability of Guantánamo detainees to bring actions before U.S. courts challenging their detention, see Chapter 10 § II(D)(7); on their trial by military commission, see *infra* this chapter § III(B) and Chapter 10 § II(E)(4).

regulation (since it is relevant to persons detained on an actual battlefield and since the "battlefield" in the war on terror is a malleable concept) that commands the president to take certain actions and was adopted in the context of specific concerns about specific treatment in a specific place (Guantánamo Bay).

Consequently, such distinctions may best be understood as factors relevant in determining whether a statute impermissibly intrudes upon the commander-in-chief power, but not as providing bright-line tests. The lack of any such test may be acceptable given that, as a practical matter, the most obvious examples of substantive prerogatives in this area—such as the president's discretion to order an attack to commence at first light, rather than under cover of darkness—are simply not issues that Congress is likely to regulate. Further, in practice, Congress and the president are usually not operating at cross-purposes, but either in cooperation or in the "twilight" zone in which the president takes an initiative to which Congress is acquiescent. In such circumstances, Justice Jackson's concurrence in *Youngstown* provides yet again a means for assessing the strengths of the president's position, leaving a space for both presidential discretion if the president proceeds conscientiously and cautiously, and congressional veto if he does not.[603]

C. Power to Make Rules Concerning Captures on Land and Water

The power to "make Rules concerning Captures on Land and Water" is assigned by the Constitution to Congress as a part of the same provision that contains the "declare War" and "grant Letters of Marque and Reprisal" powers.[604]

The exact meaning of this clause has elicited debate among scholars, for courts typically refer to the clause as part of a cluster of War Powers Clauses, making it difficult to ascertain exactly what work this particular clause is doing.[605] Notably, some commentators construe the Captures Clause as addressing only the seizure and conversion of enemy property,[606] while other commentators view it as addressing seizures of property and of persons.[607] Of those that view the

---

[603] *See generally* H. JEFFERSON POWELL, THE PRESIDENT AS COMMANDER IN CHIEF: AN ESSAY IN CONSTITUTIONAL VISION (2013). *But see* Robert Bejesky, *War Powers Pursuant to False Perceptions and Asymmetric Information in the "Zone of Twilight,"* 44 ST. MARY'S L.J. 1 (2012).

[604] U.S. CONST. art. I, § 8, cl. 11.

[605] *See, e.g.,* Hamdan v. Rumsfeld, 548 U.S. 557, 591 (2006); Al Odah v. United States, 321 F.3d 1134, 1136 (D.C. Cir. 2003), *rev'd,* Rasul v. Bush, 542 U.S. 466 (2004).

[606] *See, e.g.,* Saikrishna Bangalore Prakash, *The Separation and Overlap of War and Military Powers,* 87 TEX. L. REV. 299, 319–21 (2008); Ingrid Wuerth, *The Captures Clause,* 76 U. CHI. L. REV. 1683, 1689 (2009); John Yoo, *Transferring Terrorists,* 79 NOTRE DAME L. REV. 1183, 1201–02 (2004).

[607] *See, e.g.,* Barron & Lederman, *supra* note 550, at 735–36 n.143; Jules Lobel, *Conflicts Between the Commander in Chief and Congress: Concurrent Power over the Conduct of War,* 69 OHIO ST. L.J. 391, 402 (2008); Michael D. Ramsey, *Torturing Executive Power,* 93 GEO. L.J. 1213, 1240 (2005).

Captures Clause as only addressing property, some construe it even more narrowly as only addressing private seizures and conversion of property, not those
undertaken by the government.[608]

Emmerich de Vattel used "capture" as a term relevant to both property and
persons,[609] and Richard Lee's *A Treatise of Captures in War*, published in 1759,
addressed both seizures of property and persons.[610] Certainly such works may
have influenced the Framers' concept of the term. On the other hand, in 1775,
the Continental Congress adopted a resolution expressing a concern that "unless
some laws be made to regulate, and tribunals erected competent to determine the
propriety of captures," then rebel armed vessels might end up preying on those
who were not loyal to Britain.[611] The resolution then provided that only "armed
vessels as are or shall be employed in the present cruel and unjust war against the
United Colonies" may be "seized and forfeited."[612] The focus of the resolution on
establishing "laws . . . to regulate . . . captures" of British government property
and the similarity of its language to the Captures Clause ultimately included in
the U.S. Constitution may suggest that the latter too is oriented solely toward
property.[613] The following year, Congress adopted a resolution using "captures"
in the prologue, and thereafter corresponding orders, which authorized privateering against public or private vessels and their goods belonging to inhabitants
of Britain.[614] Further, Congress sought to provide for the disposition of the proceeds from such prizes, such as by recommending that the several states establish
courts (or empower existing courts) to address such captures.[615] Yet Congress
also adopted resolutions addressing the capture of persons, such that the term
was not used exclusively in the context of property.[616]

The Articles of Confederation provided to its Congress the power "of
establishing rules for deciding in all cases, what captures on land or water shall
be legal, and in what manner prizes taken by land or naval forces in the service
of the United States shall be divided or appropriated . . . ."[617] This language is ambiguous; while parts of it are focused on captures of property, there is no obvious
exclusion of persons from the phrase "captures on land or water," nor any obvious restriction of the term to captures conducted by private persons. Certainly,
the Confederation Congress did adopt acts and resolutions addressing the public

---

[608] Prakash, *supra* note 606, at 319–20.
[609] VATTEL, *supra* note 46, at 344, § 132.
[610] *See* RICHARD LEE, A TREATISE OF CAPTURES IN WAR (1759).
[611] 3 JOURNALS OF THE CONTINENTAL CONGRESS 373.
[612] *Id.*
[613] *See* Wuerth, *supra* note 606, at 1713.
[614] 4 JOURNALS OF THE CONTINENTAL CONGRESS 230–31; *see* Wuerth, *supra* note 606, at 1714–16.
[615] *See* Wuerth, *supra* note 606, at 1720–21.
[616] *Id.* at 1722–24.
[617] ARTICLES OF CONFEDERATION OF 1781, art. IX.

and private seizure of persons, and such power was either grounded in this pro-vision or in some other ambiguous power, such as its power to grant letters of marque and reprisal or its power to make "rules for the government and regula-tion of the said land and naval forces, and directing their operations."[618]

At the Philadelphia convention, the initial proposals with respect to "captures" concerned the categories of cases that could be heard by federal courts.[619] The first draft text for the powers of Congress referred to a power to "declare the law of piracy, felonies and captures on the high seas, and captures on land,"[620] and then changed to a power to "make rules concerning captures on land and water,"[621] before ultimately being consolidated by the Committee of Style with the Declare War and Marque and Reprisal Clauses. While one might project intentions based on these changes in wording,[622] there appears to be no evidence as to the intentions of the Framers from the debates themselves or from the state ratifica-tion conventions. Certainly, in the decade following the entry into force of the Constitution, Congress adopted statutes that provided for the seizure and dis-position of both property and persons, whether by public or private means, but invariably without specifying exactly what part of the Constitution supported such actions. Examples would include statutes adopted in 1799 during the "quasi-war" with France authorizing President John Adams to "exchange or send away" French nationals "that have been, or may be captured and brought into the United States" or to "retaliate" against such nationals as "may be captured."[623]

The Supreme Court has weighed in only to a limited extent, and provided little clarity. As previously noted, the case of *Brown v. United States* concerned the president's power to condemn timber in the United States that belonged to British nationals during the War of 1812.[624] Chief Justice Marshall found that such power did not reside in the president, at least when the property was located in the United States, due to the Captures Clause. According to Marshall, even the "declaration of war has only the effect of placing the two nations in a state of hos-tility, of producing a state of war, of giving those rights which war confers," but does not have the effect "of operating, by its own force, any of those results, such as a transfer of property, which are usually produced by ulterior measures of gov-ernment . . . ."[625] Given that the Constitution accords to Congress the power to "to declare war, grant letters of marque and reprisal, and make rules concerning

---

[618] *Id.*
[619] *See* Wuerth, *supra* note 606, at 1728–29.
[620] 2 FARRAND'S RECORDS 143.
[621] *Id.* at 320.
[622] *See* Wuerth, *supra* note 606, at 1731.
[623] *See* Act of Mar. 3, 1799, ch. 45, 1 Stat. 743, Act of Feb. 28, 1799, ch. 18, 1 Stat. 624 (both noted in Wuerth, *supra* note 606, at 1734).
[624] *See supra* this chapter text accompanying note 109.
[625] Brown v. United States, 12 U.S. (8 Cranch) 110, 125–26 (1814).

captures on land and water," Justice Marshall found that it would be too re-strained to interpret the clause as being confined to extraterritorial captures; and if "it extends to rules respecting enemy property found within the territory," then he "perceive[d] an express grant to congress of the power in question as an inde-pendent substantive power, not included in that of declaring war."[626]

The Court's decision in *Brown* clearly regarded the Captures Clause as sus-taining a power of Congress to adopt rules regarding the seizure and disposition of enemy property, to the exclusion of the president, even after any declaration of war. *Brown* may be distinguishable from circumstances in which the president seeks to seize and dispose of such property when located outside the United States, such as during enforcement of a blockade or when occupying foreign territory.[627] Yet it is also possible that *Brown* is no longer good law, given that the Court, in *The Prize Cases*, sustained President Lincoln's ability on his own authority to seize enemy prop-erty in war (vessels bound for Confederate ports), even when found in the United States.[628] The majority—which did not expressly refer to the Captures Clause—was clearly influenced by the fact that Congress was not in session at the time that the president acted, and upon reconvening in July 1861, promptly approved all the president's actions.[629] By contrast, the dissenters did describe the Captures Clause as empowering Congress and not the president, to the effect that the president had no power to establish a blockade under the law of nations and that the capture of the vessels and cargo that occurred before Congress' authorization (either for breach of blockade or as enemy property) was illegal and void.[630]

To a large extent, issues relating to seizure of enemy property are now addressed through statutes. The first, the Trading with the Enemy Act, was enacted in 1917, and restricts trade between the United States and enemy na-tions.[631] Among other things, the law gives the president the power to oversee or restrict any and all trade between the United States and its enemies in times of war. The second is the IEEPA,[632] which can be invoked when the president finds that there exists an "unusual and extraordinary threat . . . to the national secu-rity, foreign policy, or economy of the United States" that originates "in whole or substantial part outside the United States."[633] Once such a finding is made, the president may block transactions and freeze assets as necessary to deal with the threat.[634] Further, if the United States is attacked, the president is authorized to

---

[626] *Id.* at 126.
[627] *See* HENKIN, FOREIGN AFFAIRS, at 104.
[628] The Prize Cases, 67 U.S. (2 Black) 635 (1863).
[629] *Id.* at 670–71.
[630] *Id.* at 688, 698–99 (Nelson, J., dissenting).
[631] 50 U.S.C. § 4305 (2018); 50 U.S.C. app. §§ 1–44 (2012).
[632] 50 U.S.C. §§ 1701–08 (2018).
[633] *Id.* § 1701(a).
[634] *Id.* §1702(a)(1)(B).

confiscate properties associated with the attacking nation or a group or person who aided in the attack.[635] Both statutes fall within the scope of the National Emergencies Act, which requires that the declared emergency be renewed annually to remain in effect.[636] In terms of property found on the battlefield, except as provided in regulations, "enemy material captured or found abandoned shall be turned over to appropriate United States or allied military personnel . . . ."[637]

D. Power to Grant Letters of Marque and Reprisal

Originally, a "letter of marque and reprisal" was a letter provided by the government in peacetime to a private person (a privateer) authorizing him or her to make a lawful capture of property abroad as a means of righting a specific wrong that a foreign state had failed to remedy.[638] Over time, the concept became almost exclusively associated with the seizure by privateers of property on the high seas, and by the late 1700s it was mostly associated with licensing a private vessel to make lawful captures of enemy vessels during a time of hostilities, in exchange for the private vessel receiving a portion of the captured property.[639] During the Revolutionary War, the several states—lacking significant naval capabilities—relied heavily upon privateers to prey upon British commerce; by one account, there were sixty-four public vessels employed by the rebels, but nearly eight hundred private vessels sailing under letters of marque and reprisal.[640]

Under the Articles of Confederation, the power to grant letters of marque and reprisal was lodged with the Confederation Congress in times of peace, but entrusted to the several states, subject to regulation by Congress, if Congress had issued a declaration of war or if such letters were being used to respond to piracy.[641] By contrast, the power to "grant letters of Marque and Reprisal" is assigned by the U.S. Constitution exclusively to Congress, and the several states are expressly denied any such power.[642] The original proposals at the Philadelphia

---

[635] *Id.* § 1702(a)(1)(C).

[636] National Emergencies Act, 50 U.S.C. §§ 1601–51.

[637] 10 U.S.C. § 2579(b)(2).

[638] *See* STEPHEN C. NEFF, WAR AND THE LAW OF NATIONS: A GENERAL HISTORY 77–78 (2005).

[639] *Id.* at 80–81, 109; *see* HENRY WHEATON, A DIGEST OF THE LAW OF MARITIME CAPTURES AND PRIZES 14 (1815).

[640] Marshall, *supra* note 28, at 958–77; *see* EDGAR STANTON MACLAY, A HISTORY OF AMERICAN PRIVATEERS 7–9 (1899).

[641] *See* ARTICLES OF CONFEDERATION OF 1781, art. IX, § 1 ("The United States, in Congress assembled, shall have the sole and exclusive right and power . . . of granting letters of marque and reprisal in times of peace . . . ."). The power was denied to the states under Article VI with some exceptions, such as when a state was "infested by pirates." *See id.*, art. VI.

[642] U.S. CONST. art. I, § 8, cl. 11; *id.*, art. I, § 10, cl. 1.

convention did not address this power. It was only immediately after the change of "make war" to "declare war" in August 1787 that Elbridge Gerry proposed the inclusion of a power to grant such letters and that it be accorded to Congress.[643] His proposal was unanimously accepted, but otherwise there was apparently little discussion of the matter.[644]

The decision by the Framers to place the power with the federal government under the U.S. Constitution in time of peace or war is clear, as well as its express denial to the several states. What is less clear is the exact scope of the clause. Potentially, it only addresses Congress' power to license private vessels to make lawful captures of enemy vessels.[645] On this account, Congress' power to authorize *public* vessels to make lawful captures of property, as well as the power to determine exactly which kinds of enemy or neutral property could be seized once a public or private capture occurs, resides not in this clause but in the Captures Clause.[646] Alternatively, the clause may address more broadly Congress' power to authorize public and private vessels to make lawful captures and its power to determine what property may be seized.[647]

A third possibility is that the clause addresses more broadly still Congress' power to initiate and control low-intensity armed conflict, including such captures and seizures of property.[648] In other words, the terms "marque and reprisal" may have had a certain generic meaning in the late seventeenth century that covered coercive action falling short of war—but that was closely associated with and might lead to war. In support of this view, one may point to scholars who influenced the Framers such as Matthew Hale, who, in reflecting on British practice in the century prior to the American Revolution, maintained: "[S]pecial kinds of war are that, which we usually call *marque* or reprisal . . . ."[649] Similarly, Blackstone asserted that the prerogative of granting letters of marque and reprisal "is nearly related to, and plainly derived from, that other of making war; this being indeed only an incomplete state of hostilities, and generally ending in a formal denunciation of war."[650] The inclusion

---

[643] 2 FARRAND'S RECORDS 326.

[644] *Id.* at 328.

[645] *See* J. Andrew Kent, *Congress's Under-Appreciated Power to Define and Punish Offenses Against the Law of Nations*, 85 TEX. L. REV. 843, 920 (2007); Marshall, *supra* note 28, at 954.

[646] *See* Wuerth, *supra* note 606, at 1736.

[647] *See* Ramsey, *Textualism and War Powers, supra* note 43, at 1613–18; Wuerth, *supra* note 593, at 90.

[648] *See* ELY, *supra* note 62, at 66–67; REVELEY, *supra* note 35, at 16–22; Lobel, *supra* note 28, at 67–70; Lofgren, *supra* note 35, at 699–700; Abraham D. Sofaer, *The Presidency, War, and Foreign Affairs: Practice Under the Framers*, 40 L. & CONTEMP. PROBS. (Spring 1976), at 12, 27.

[649] 1 MATTHEW HALE, HISTORIA PLACITORUM CORONAE: THE HISTORY OF THE PLEAS OF THE CROWN 162 (P.R. Glazebrook, ed., 1971).

[650] 1 WILLIAM BLACKSTONE, COMMENTARIES *250.

of the power at the Philadelphia convention immediately after the "make war/ declare war" debate might suggest an effort "to ensure that only Congress would have the power to commence armed hostilities against foreign nations, whether those hostilities constituted full-scale war or some lesser or imperfect warfare."[651] Thomas Jefferson, as the first secretary of state, noted that the making of "a reprisal on a nation is a very serious thing . . . [I]t is considered an act of war, and never failed to produce it in the case of a nation able to make war . . . ."[652] Joseph Story, citing to Blackstone, said that the power to issue letters of marque and reprisal was " 'plainly derived from that of making war.' "[653] In light of such authorities, Charles Lofgren subsequently opined that the Marque and Reprisal Clause "could easily have been interpreted as serving as a kind of shorthand for vesting in Congress the power of *general* reprisal outside the context of declared war. "[654]

However understood, invocation of the power for the purpose of actually granting letters of marque and reprisal seems to have crested with the War of 1812.[655] Since that time, such practice has fallen into disuse, replaced instead by the dramatic rise in U.S. naval and coast guard capabilities.[656] Contemporary use of private military contractors to engage in military and security operations on behalf of the U.S. government has reawakened scholarly consideration of this power, with attendant concerns as to whether the U.S. government is regulating such contractors sufficiently to uphold its obligations under U.S. and international law.[657]

---

[651] Lobel, *supra* note 28, at 69; *see* REVELEY, *supra* note 35, at 86 (finding that Elbridge Gerry's "concern suggests a desire to make it absolutely clear that congressional control covered minor as well as major uses of American armed force").

[652] Opinion of Thomas Jefferson, Sec'y of State, May 16, 1793, *quoted in* 7 MOORE DIGEST, at 1, 123 (1906).

[653] 3 JOSEPH STORY, COMMENTARIES ON THE CONSTITUTION OF THE UNITED STATES 64 (1833) (quoting 1 WILLIAM BLACKSTONE, COMMENTARIES *258–59).

[654] Lofgren, *supra* note 35, at 696–97.

[655] At the outset of the War of 1812, Congress both declared war and authorized the president to grant letters of marque and reprisal. *See* Act of June 18, 1812, ch. 102, 2 Stat. 755; *see also* GEORGE COGGESHALL, HISTORY OF THE AMERICAN PRIVATEERS AND LETTERS-OF-MARQUE, DURING OUR WAR WITH ENGLAND IN THE YEARS 1812, '13 AND '14 (1856).

[656] The post–Crimean War peace conference in 1856—the Congress of Paris—formally abolished by treaty the practice of issuing letters of marque and reprisal. While European nations signed the treaty, the United States did not. *See* Nicholas Parrillo, *The De-Privatization of American Warfare: How the U.S. Government Used, Regulated, and Ultimately Abandoned Privateering in the Nineteenth Century*, 19 YALE J.L. & HUMAN. 1 (2007).

[657] *See* LAURA A. DICKINSON, OUTSOURCING WAR & PEACE: PRESERVING PUBLIC VALUES IN A WORLD OF PRIVATIZED FOREIGN AFFAIRS (2011); William R. Casto, *Regulating the New Privateers of the Twenty-First Century*, 37 RUTGERS L.J. 671 (2006); Antenor Hallo de Wolf, *Modern* Condottieri *in Iraq: Privatizing War from the Perspective of International and Human Rights Law*, 13 IND. J. GLOBAL LEGAL STUD. 315 (2006); Jules Lobel, *Covert War and Congressional Authority: Hidden War and Forgotten Power*, 134 U. PA. L. REV. 1035 (1986).

III. Power to Establish and Regulate the Military

A. Power to Raise Revenues to Provide for the Common Defense, to Raise and Support the Military, and to Purchase and Regulate Military Installations

While Congress may not deny to the president the command of U.S. military forces, Congress *can* deny to the president U.S. military forces to command. The policy questions presented by creating and maintaining such forces were very apparent to those drafting the Constitution. Indeed, among the complaints lodged in the Declaration of Independence was that King George III had "kept among us, in times of peace, Standing Armies without the Consent of our legislatures," had quartered "large bodies of armed troops among us," and had "affected to render the Military independent of and superior to the Civil power."[658]

With such history in mind, the Framers decided in the Constitution to assign to Congress certain appropriation powers that are expressly associated with war-making. First, Congress is given the power to raise revenues so as to "provide for the common Defence."[659] Second, Congress is given the power to "raise and support Armies, but no Appropriation of Money to that Use shall be for a longer Term than two Years."[660] Third, Congress has the power to "provide and maintain a Navy."[661] Such powers are largely a federal power; only with the consent of Congress may the several states "keep Troops, or Ships of War in time of Peace."[662]

To all of this should be added Congress' power to "exercise exclusive Legislation in all Cases whatsoever . . . over all Places purchased by the Consent of the Legislature of the State in which the Same shall be, for the Erection of Forts, Magazines, [and] Arsenals . . . ."[663] This clause basically supports the idea of federal "enclave" jurisdiction over military installations in the United States, much in the same way that Congress exercises such jurisdiction over the District of Columbia or federal installations generally.[664] As a general matter, such areas are subject to the "special maritime and territorial jurisdiction of the United States"

---

[658] DECLARATION OF INDEPENDENCE (U.S. 1776).

[659] U.S. CONST. art. I, § 8, cl. 1. These Revenues Clauses operate in tandem with Article I, § 9, Clause 7, which states that "No money shall be drawn from the Treasury, but in Consequence of Appropriations made by Law . . . ." *Id.* art. I, § 9, cl. 7. For more general discussion of Congress' power of the purse, see Chapter 2 § III.

[660] *Id.* art. I, § 8, cl. 12.

[661] *Id.* art. I, § 8, cl. 13.

[662] *Id.* art. I, § 10, cl. 3.

[663] *Id.* art. I, § 8, cl. 17.

[664] *See generally* David E. Engdahl, *State and Federal Power over Federal Property*, 18 ARIZ. L. REV. 283 (1976).

and not to the jurisdiction of the several states, although substantive criminal offenses may be grounded in the host state's law.[665]

As previously noted, Congress adopted in 1789 a statute providing for the pay of officers and privates in the service of the United States and providing that "the said troops shall be governed by the rules and articles of war which have been established by the United States in Congress assembled, or by such rules and articles of war, as may hereafter by law be established."[666] The following year a more comprehensive statute created a permanent military establishment, organizing U.S. forces into regiments and battalions, though the state militia remained the primary source for obtaining troops for many years.[667]

Since that early period, Congress has adopted annually or biennially statutes authorizing and appropriating funds to sustain U.S. military forces, as well as other parts of the government responsible for national security affairs. For example, the Department of Defense Appropriations Act for 2021 appropriated approximately $700 billion to that Department for national defense–related activities.[668] The result of allocating such powers to Congress is that it may decide whether the United States shall have armed forces and, if so, of what size, nature, and structure.[669] Those powers appear to be plenary in nature. When President Lincoln at the outset of the Civil War on his own initiative began enlisting volunteers into a Union Army, the Supreme Court found that he acted unconstitutionally, at least until Congress authorized such action by statute in August 1861.[670]

Over the course of U.S. history, Congress has created important positions such as the Chairman of the Joint Chiefs of Staff (who, although the highest-ranking U.S. military official, is prohibited by law from having operational command authority), as well as important ranks, such as five-star generals or admirals, that affect in significant ways the structure and chain-of-command within the U.S. military.[671] Perhaps the most sweeping of congressional reforms

---

[665] 18 U.S.C. § 7 (2018); see, e.g., Assimilative Crimes Act, 18 U.S.C. § 13(a). There are some exceptions, either because the host state reserved rights at the time of cession, or because federal law so provides. See, e.g., Evans v. Cornman, 398 U.S. 419 (1970) (finding that federal enclave residents have an Equal Protection Clause right to vote as residents of the host state).

[666] Act of Sept. 29, 1789, ch. 25, §§ 2, 4, 1 Stat. 95, 96. The statute thus maintained rules previously established by the Continental Congress for regulation of its military forces. See supra this chapter I(C)(1).

[667] Act of Apr. 30, 1790, ch. 10, 1 Stat. 119; see also Act of May 30, 1796, ch. 39, 1 Stat. 483 (organizing the structure of the military); Act of Dec. 23, 1791, ch. 3, § 4, 1 Stat. 226, 228 (discussing military payments); Act of Mar. 3, 1791, ch. 28, 1 Stat. 222 (adding another regiment to the military).

[668] See Consolidated Appropriations Act, 2021, div. C, Pub. L. No. 116-260, 134 Stat. 1182, 1286 (2020).

[669] WORMUTH & FIRMAGE, supra note 36, at 89–106.

[670] United States v. Hosmer, 76 U.S. (9 Wall.) 432 (1870); see Act of Aug. 6, 1861, ch. 63, § 3, 12 Stat. 326, 326.

[671] With respect to the Chairman of the Joint Chiefs of Staff, see 10 U.S.C. § 152(c) (2018) (". . . he may not exercise military command over the Joint Chiefs of Staff or any of the armed forces.").

occurred in the late 1940s, with the renaming of the Department of War as the Department of the Army, the creation of the Department of the Air Force from the Army's air forces, and then the merger of the Departments of Army, Navy, and Air Force into a federated Department of Defense, headed by a secretary of defense.[672] Congressional regulation may also be detail-oriented. For example, the Department of Defense Appropriations Act for 2015 provided that the Department of Defense may not use any appropriated funds to move prisoners from the Guantánamo Bay detention camp in Cuba to the United States.[673] The requirement that no appropriation for U.S. military forces shall be for a longer term than two years establishes that Congress must continually be reviewing and reconsidering such decision-making.

Once U.S. military forces are "raised," may Congress place restrictions on the location of those forces? On the one hand, once it has "raised" U.S. military forces, it might be argued that Congress cannot direct the president as to where such forces should be deployed, because doing so intrudes excessively upon the president's own powers, especially as commander in chief. On the other hand, Congress' powers are not just to raise such forces but also to "support" them and to raise revenues to provide for the common defense, which carries attendant possibilities of restricting the use of such funds. A classic example of such a restriction arose in a 1909 appropriations provision, which denied appropriations for Marine Corps forces unless they were serving "on board all battleships and armored cruisers, and also upon such other vessels of the navy as the President may direct, in detachments of not less than eight per centum of the strength of the enlisted men of the navy on said vessels."[674] In considering this restriction, the U.S. Attorney General opined that "Congress has power to create or not to create . . . a marine corps, make appropriation for its pay, [and] provide that such appropriation shall not be available unless the marine corps be employed in some designated way . . . ."[675]

Bearing in mind as well Congress' power to declare war, some congressional restrictions on deployments of U.S. forces appear designed to minimize the likelihood of U.S. forces inciting hostilities that Congress wishes to avoid. Here a classic example is the Selective Training and Service Act of 1940, which established the first peacetime draft in U.S. history, and which required all U.S. males between twenty-one and thirty-six years of age to register.[676] The statute provided that all

---

[672] Such reforms occurred principally by means of the National Security Act of 1947, Pub. L. No. 80-253, 61 Stat 495, as amended in August 1949.

[673] See Consolidated and Further Continuing Appropriations Act, 2015, Pub. L. No. 113-235, § 528 (2014).

[674] Act of Mar. 3, 1909, ch. 255, 35 Stat. 753, 773–74.

[675] Appropriations—Marine Corps—Service on Battle Ships, Etc., 27 Op. Att'y Gen. 259, 260 (1909).

[676] Pub. L. No. 76-783, 54 Stat. 885 (1940) (also known as the Burke-Wadsworth Act).

drafted soldiers had to remain in the Western Hemisphere or in U.S. possessions or territories located in other parts of the world; the president was not permitted to station such soldiers in other parts of the world even in the event of armed conflict. President Roosevelt signed the statute into law without any reservations as to its constitutionality, and followed its strictures until a new statute was adopted in the wake of the attack on Pearl Harbor that brought the United States into World War II.[677] Other "location" restrictions have targeted specific foreign states, especially those experiencing an internal armed conflict. Thus, in 1976, Congress prohibited the Central Intelligence Agency from conducting military or paramilitary operations in Angola, and further denied the use of any funds to finance directly or indirectly military assistance to Angola.[678] Likewise, in 1984, the "Boland Amendment" prohibited assistance of any kind to support the *contras* in Nicaragua.[679]

When authorizing a use of force, Congress may indicate geographically where that force may be used, and in so doing indirectly instruct the president as to the general deployment of U.S. forces as a part of that armed conflict. Thus, Congress has authorized the president to seize French vessels located near the U.S. coast,[680] to seize and occupy Florida from Spanish rule,[681] to protect Formosa and the Pescadores from a Chinese attack,[682] or to use force to expel Iraqi forces from Kuwait.[683] Further, once hostilities have commenced, congressional restrictions may be structured to limit the expansion of such hostilities or to extract the United States from them. For example, during the Vietnam War, Congress famously prohibited the use of funds "to finance the introduction of United States ground combat troops into Cambodia."[684] As previously discussed, Congress provided that funds could no longer be used for U.S. troops in Lebanon in 1984 and in Somalia in 1994.[685]

[677] *See supra* this chapter text accompanying note 177.

[678] *See* International Security Assistance and Arms Export Control Act of 1976, Pub. L. No. 94-329, § 404, 90 Stat. 729, 757–58.

[679] *See* Department of the Interior and Related Agencies Appropriations Act, 1985, Pub. L. No. 98-473, § 8066(a), 98 Stat. 1838, 1935.

[680] *See* Act of May 28, 1798, ch. 48, 1 Stat. 561.

[681] Act of Mar. 3, 1819, ch. 93, § 1, 3 Stat. 523, 523–24.

[682] *See supra* this chapter note 215.

[683] *See supra* this chapter note 242.

[684] Special Foreign Assistance Act of 1971, Pub. L. No. 91-652, § 7(a), 84 Stat. 1942, 1943. Such location restrictions raise the sharpest debates in the context of armed conflict but are a common feature of peacetime regulations. *See, e.g.*, Consolidated and Further Continuing Appropriations Act, 2015, § 8019, Pub. L. No. 113-235 (2014) ("No more than $500,000 of the funds appropriated or made available in this Act shall be used during a single fiscal year for any single relocation of an organization, unit, activity or function of the Department of Defense into or within the National Capital Region....").

[685] *See supra* this chapter text accompanying notes 259–262, 354; *see also* Peter Raven-Hansen & William C. Banks, *From Vietnam to Desert Shield: The Commander in Chief's Spending Power*, 81 IOWA L. REV. 79 (1995) (discussing the relationship between war powers and Congress' power of the purse).

While at times questions arise as to whether such measures unconstitutionally encroach upon executive authority, the Supreme Court generally has characterized Congress' appropriations powers as "broad and sweeping,"[686] and in *Youngstown*, Justice Jackson stated that "Congress alone . . . may determine in what manner and by what means [revenues] shall be spent for military and naval procurement."[687]

B. Power to Regulate the Military

Under the Articles of Confederation, Congress was empowered to make "rules for the government and regulation of the said land and naval forces, and directing their operations."[688] This power was largely carried over to the U.S. Constitution, but without the clause "and directing their operations," given the creation of the office of the president and his role as commander in chief. As such, the Constitution empowers Congress to "make Rules for the Government and the Regulation of the land and naval Forces."[689] The language suggests a robust authority; Raoul Berger maintained that the "word 'government' connotes a power to control, to administer the government of the armed forces; the word 'regulate' connotes a power to dispose, order, or govern."[690] The Supreme Court has found that this power gives Congress "plenary control over the rights, duties, and responsibilities in the framework of the Military Establishment, including regulations, procedures, and remedies related to military discipline."[691] Further, the Court has confirmed that this power is "no less plenary" than Congress' other Article I powers.[692]

In June 1775, the Second Continental Congress established the "Articles of War," which was essentially a set of regulations governing the conduct of the Continental Army.[693] The Congress under the Constitution in 1789 adopted a statute providing that U.S. "troops shall be governed by the rules and articles of war which have been established by the United States in Congress assembled,

---

[686] Rumsfeld v. Forum for Acad. & Institutional Rights, Inc., 547 U.S. 47, 58 (2006); United States v. O'Brien, 391 U.S. 367, 377 (1968).

[687] Youngstown Sheet & Tube Co. v. Sawyer, 343 U.S. 579, 643 (Jackson, J., concurring). For a thoughtful treatment of this subject, see BANKS & RAVEN-HANSEN, *supra* note 402. For discussion of *Youngstown*, see *supra* this chapter § II(B) and Chapter 1 § II(B).

[688] ARTICLES OF CONFEDERATION OF 1781, art. IX.

[689] U.S. CONST. art. I, § 8, cl. 14.

[690] Berger, *supra* note 36, at 80.

[691] Chappell v. Wallace, 462 U.S. 296, 301 (1983).

[692] Loving v. United States, 517 U.S. 748, 767 (1996).

[693] *See American Articles of War of 1775, in* WILLIAM WINTHROP, MILITARY LAW AND PRECEDENTS 953 (2d ed. 1920).

or by such rules and articles of war, as may hereafter by law be established."[694] Those Articles of War were periodically revised for the next 150 years, with significant supplementation during the Civil War by the "Lieber Code" imposed by President Lincoln's military order.[695] In parallel, starting in 1800, "rules and regulations . . . for the government of the navy" were developed to regulate the conduct of the U.S. Navy.[696] In May 1951, Congress replaced such rules with the UCMJ, which remains in force today.[697]

In general, the UCMJ serves as a system of criminal law applicable in the military context. Subject to this system are all members of the U.S. uniformed services, members of the military reserve components when they are on active full-time duty, members of the National Guard when activated for federal duty, and others, such as cadets of the various U.S. military academies.[698] In addition to general and miscellaneous provisions,[699] subchapters of the UCMJ address apprehension and restraint;[700] nonjudicial punishment;[701] court-martial jurisdiction;[702] composition of courts-martial;[703] pre-trial procedure;[704] trial procedure;[705] sentences;[706] post-trial procedure and review of courts-martial;[707] punitive articles (which sets forth various types of violations, such as desertion, failure to obey an order, aiding the enemy, or espionage);[708] and the Court of Appeals for the Armed Forces.[709] Separate from the UCMJ, the executive branch has developed both the Rules of Court Martial (analogous to the Federal Rules of Criminal Procedure) and the Military Rules of Evidence (analogous to the Federal Rules of Evidence), which are collected in the *Manual for Courts Martial*.[710]

---

[694] Act of Sept. 29, 1789, ch. 25, § 4, 1 Stat. 95, 96. The statute thus maintained rules previously established by the Continental Congress for regulation of its military forces.

[695] *See* General Orders No. 100 by President Lincoln (Apr. 24, 1863), *in* INSTRUCTIONS FOR THE GOVERNMENT OF ARMIES OF THE UNITED STATES IN THE FIELD (1863) (reprinted by Government Printing Office, 1898).

[696] *See* Act of Apr. 23, 1800, ch. 33, 2 Stat. 45.

[697] Uniform Code of Military Justice, 10 U.S.C. §§ 801–946a (2018).

[698] *Id.* § 802.

[699] *Id.* §§ 801–06, 935–40.

[700] *Id.* §§ 807–14.

[701] *Id.* § 815.

[702] *Id.* §§ 816–21.

[703] *Id.* §§ 822–29.

[704] *Id.* §§ 830–35.

[705] *Id.* §§ 836–54.

[706] *Id.* §§ 855–58.

[707] *Id.* §§ 859–76.

[708] *Id.* §§ 877–934.

[709] *Id.* § 941.

[710] *See* MANUAL FOR COURTS-MARTIAL, UNITED STATES (2012 ed.), https://perma.cc/T77V-B6WY. The Manual is periodically amended by executive order. *See, e.g.,* Exec. Order No. 13643, 78 Fed. Reg. 29,559 (May 21, 2013).

The basic process for a court-martial of a U.S. service member typically entails a commanding officer (the convening authority) referring a case for trial by court-martial. At that trial, various protections are accorded to the accused, such as the right against self-incrimination and the right to qualified defense counsel.[711] If the trial leads to a conviction, the conviction and sentence are reviewed by the convening authority, which can set aside the conviction, reduce the sentence, or remand the case for a rehearing. If the conviction and sentence are approved, they may be reviewed by an intermediate court if they entail punishment in the form of death, a bad conduct discharge, a dishonorable discharge, dismissal of an officer, or confinement for one year or more.[712] From there, the case may be appealed to the U.S. Court of Appeals for the Armed Forces. In certain circumstances, the Supreme Court has discretion to review UCMJ cases on direct appeal or through collateral (habeas) review.[713]

Other federal law is also relevant to certain acts committed by or against the U.S. military (or, for that matter, any U.S. national). In particular, the War Crimes Act criminalizes certain conduct prohibited by the 1907 Hague Regulations, criminalizes both "grave breaches" of the 1949 Geneva Conventions and violations of "common Article 3" to those conventions, and criminalizes conduct prohibited by certain other law of war treaties to which the United States adheres.[714]

Congress' power to regulate the military might be viewed as extending not just to rules and regulation of U.S. forces but also to how the president is to treat enemy forces as well.[715] Certainly, the Continental Congress adopted resolutions regulating the treatment of persons captured by U.S. military forces, as did Congress in the early years under the Constitution, though it is not entirely clear what part of Article I supported those initiatives.[716] Today, the 1907 Hague

---

[711] Uniform Code of Military Justice, §§ 831, 838(b).

[712] The intermediate courts are the Army Court of Criminal Appeals, the Navy-Marine Corps Court of Criminal Appeals, the Air Force Court of Criminal Appeals, or the Coast Guard Court of Criminal Appeals.

[713] See 28 U.S.C. § 1259.

[714] War Crimes Act, 18 U.S.C. § 2441; see Hague Convention IV, supra note 527. "Grave breaches" are defined in each of the four Geneva Conventions and generally refer to willful killing, torture or inhuman treatment of persons protected by the relevant convention. Geneva Convention I, supra note 528, art. 50; Geneva Convention II, supra note 528, art. 51; Geneva Convention III, supra note 528, art. 130; Geneva Convention IV, supra note 528, art. 147. "Common Article 3" refers to an article that is common to all four Geneva Conventions and that applies with respect to both international and non-international armed conflicts. The Military Commissions Act of 2006 amended this portion of the War Crimes Act so as to cover only torture, cruel or inhumane treatment, murder, mutilation or maiming, intentionally causing serious bodily harm, rape, sexual assault or abuse, and the taking of hostages. See Military Commissions Act of 2006, Pub. L. No. 109-366, § 6(b), 120 Stat. 2600, 2633–35.

[715] Prakash, supra note 606, at 338–40.

[716] See, e.g., 4 JOURNALS OF THE CONTINENTAL CONGRESS 254 (barring the killing, torturing, or mistreating of prisoners by privateers); Act of Mar. 3, 1813, ch. 61, 2 Stat. 829; Act of July 6, 1812, ch. 128, 2 Stat. 777; Act of Mar. 3, 1799, ch. 45, 1 Stat. 743; Act of Feb. 28, 1799, ch. 18, 1 Stat. 624; Act of

Regulations and 1949 Geneva Conventions set forth standards of treatment for enemy prisoners of war, and those standards are implemented for the United States primarily through Department of Defense regulations.[717]

Since the founding, the Articles of War or UCMJ have allowed military courts to prosecute both U.S. military forces and enemy combatants.[718] Prosecuting U.S. nationals before military courts has sometimes proven controversial because they do not include judges with the lifetime tenure of Article III judges nor do they provide for a grand or petit jury.[719] In general, prosecutions of active duty U.S. personnel have been upheld, regardless of whether the alleged offense is connected to their service.[720] Prosecutions of persons who are not on active military service have been more problematic. For example, in *United States ex rel. Toth v. Quarles*, the Supreme Court found that Article III and the right to a jury trial barred the court-martial of a former U.S. military service member charged with committing a murder while serving in the U.S. military abroad; having been discharged from the military, his trial by court-martial was unconstitutional.[721] Likewise, in *Reid v. Covert*, a plurality of the Court found that Congress could not use military courts to try spouses of U.S. military personnel for conduct committed abroad.[722] Concurring in the decision, Justices Felix Frankfurter and John Marshall Harlan suggested that in other circumstances similar prosecutions might be possible. Justice Frankfurter proposed a balancing test that would require a court to weigh all the factors involved to decide whether military dependents "are so closely related to what Congress may allowably deem essential for the effective" regulation of military forces that such dependents may be subjected to court-martial jurisdiction in capital cases, even if they were to lose their constitutional protections as a consequence.[723]

July 9, 1798, ch. 68, § 8, 1 Stat. 578, 580; Act of June 28, 1798, ch. 62, § 4, 1 Stat. 574, 575; Act of June 25, 1798, ch. 60, § 4, 1 Stat. 572, 573.

[717] *See* DEP'T OF THE ARMY REGULATION 190-8, ENEMY PRISONERS OF WAR, RETAINED PERSONNEL, CIVILIAN INTERNEES AND OTHER DETAINEES (1997); DEP'T OF DEFENSE DIRECTIVE 2310.1, DOD PROGRAM FOR ENEMY PRISONERS OF WAR (EPOW) AND OTHER DETAINEES (1994); DEP'T OF THE ARMY FIELD MANUAL 27-10, *supra* note 539. *See generally* OFFICE OF GENERAL COUNSEL, DEPARTMENT OF DEFENSE LAW OF WAR MANUAL 511-643 (updated 2016).

[718] *See, e.g.,* Guénaël Mettraux, *US Courts-Martial and the Armed Conflict in the Philippines (1899–1902): Their Contribution to National Case Law on War Crimes*, 1 J. INT'L CRIM. JUST. 135 (2003).

[719] Constitutional protections distinguish between civilians and military personnel for purposes of prosecuting serious crimes. The Fifth Amendment of the U.S. Constitution provides: "No person shall be held to answer for a capital, or otherwise infamous crime, unless on a presentment or indictment of a Grand Jury, except in cases arising in the land or naval forces, or in the Militia, when in actual service in time of War or public danger . . . ." U.S. CONST. amend. V.

[720] *See* Solorio v. United States, 483 U.S. 435 (1987).

[721] *See* United States *ex rel.* Toth v. Quarles, 350 U.S. 11 (1955).

[722] *See* Reid v. Covert, 354 U.S. 1 (1957) (Warren, C.J.; Black, J.; Douglas, J.; Brennan, J., plurality opinion).

[723] *Id.* at 44 (Frankfurter, J., concurring in result).

A contemporary version of this issue is whether U.S. military courts may be used to prosecute civilian contractors working for the U.S. military who are charged with committing offenses abroad. Although not active-duty personnel, such persons might be viewed as having purposefully affiliated themselves with, and directly benefited from, U.S. military operations, thus justifying the exercise of jurisdiction over them by U.S. military courts.[724]

In times of armed conflict, the Articles of War or UCMJ have also preserved the ability of the president to convene military *commissions* in place of civilian courts in areas where martial law has been declared or in U.S.-occupied territory, or to try enemy combatants for violations of the laws of war.[725] A notable early example was the military commission convened by General George Washington during the Revolutionary War to try Major John Andre, who was captured behind rebel lines in civilian dress after a meeting with General Benedict Arnold, but such commissions have featured in virtually all U.S. wars, including the Civil War.[726]

The use of such commissions has been controversial, because they typically do not possess the same protections for defendants as may be found in either military or civilian courts. Nonetheless, the Supreme Court rejected a challenge to such commissions in *In re Yamashita*, a case involving prosecution for war crimes before a U.S. military commission in the Philippines of the commanding general during World War II of the Imperial Japanese Army.[727] Moreover, the Court unanimously found in *Ex Parte Quirin* that such prosecutions may be held in the United States to prosecute unprivileged enemy combatants, including those who are U.S. nationals.[728] In that case, the Court found that an incident of Congress' "power to wage war" was the authority to create military commissions to try enemy belligerents, that Congress' power to "define and punish offenses against the law of nations" allowed Congress to empower those commissions

---

[724] *See* United States v. Ali, 71 M.J. 256, 272–73 (C.A.A.F. 2012) (Baker, J., concurring).

[725] *See* John M. Bickers, *Military Commissions Are Constitutionally Sound: A Response to Professors Katyal and Tribe*, 34 TEX. TECH L. REV. 899 (2003); David Glazier, *Precedents Lost: The Neglected History of the Military Commission*, 46 VA. J. INT'L L. 5 (2005); *see also* Lewis L. Laska & James M. Smith, *"Hell and the Devil": Andersonville and the Trial of Captain Henry Wirz, C.S.A., 1865*, 68 MIL. L. REV. 77 (1975).

[726] *See* 1 HALLECK'S INTERNATIONAL LAW OR RULES REGULATING THE INTERCOURSE OF STATES IN PEACE AND WAR 573–74 (Sherston Baker ed., 3d ed. 1893); JOHN FABIAN WITT, LINCOLN'S CODE: THE LAWS OF WAR IN AMERICAN HISTORY 219–30, 264–73, 289–304 (2012).

[727] *In re* Yamashita, 327 U.S. 1 (1946). For commentary supporting such commissions so long as they are trying individuals for recognized international law violations, see Jonathan Hafetz, *Policing the Line: International Law, Article III, and the Constitutional Limits of Military Jurisdiction*, 2014 WIS. L. REV. 681; Vladeck, *supra* note 593.

[728] *Ex parte* Quirin, 317 U.S. 1, 37–38 (1942); *see also* Hamdi v. Rumsfeld, 542 U.S. 507, 519 (2004) ("There is no bar to this Nation's holding one of its own citizens as an enemy combatant."). For scholarly commentary on *Quirin*, see LOUIS FISHER, NAZI SABOTEURS ON TRIAL: A MILITARY TRIBUNAL AND AMERICAN LAW (2d ed. 2005); A. Christopher Bryant & Carl Tobias, Quirin Revisited, 2003 WIS. L. REV. 309; BARRON, *supra* note 15, at 258–67, 277–83.

to try belligerents who "in their attempt to thwart or impede our military effort have violated the law of war," and that Congress had sanctioned through
the Articles of War (specifically Article 15) the use of military commissions to
try offenders for offenses against the law of war whatever their nationality.[729] In
comparing such commissions to civilian courts, the Court found that military
commissions are "in the natural course of events . . . usually called upon to function under conditions precluding resort to" "familiar parts of the machinery for
criminal trials in the civil courts" and that military commissions are simply not
"courts in the sense of the Judiciary Article" of the Constitution.[730]

At the same time, the power to establish and regulate military commissions is
hardly unlimited.[731] During the post–Civil War period of Reconstruction, when
military commission proceedings were brought against Indiana residents for
conspiracy and treason, the Supreme Court in *Ex parte Milligan* struck down
their use. Employing military commissions to try civilian noncombatants, it held,
was unconstitutional unless no civilian courts were available; such commissions
could not be used as a surrogate for the civilian courts to try persons unaffiliated
with an enemy force.[732]

In November 2001, President George W. Bush issued a military order authorizing the establishment of military commissions to try persons associated with
al-Qaeda and other individuals who "engaged in, aided or abetted, or conspired
to commit, acts of international terrorism, or acts in preparation therefor, that
have caused, threaten to cause, or have as their aim to cause, injury to or adverse effects on the United States, its citizens, national security, foreign policy,
or economy," as well as those who harbor such individuals.[733] (In *Hamdi
v. Rumsfeld*, as discussed elsewhere, a plurality of the Court concluded that the
detention of enemy combatants was properly incident to the 2001 congressional
statute authorizing the use of force, but also that U.S. nationals had a due process
right to contest their detention as an "enemy combatant" before a neutral decision maker.)[734]

Subsequently, in *Hamdan v. Rumsfeld*,[735] the Court considered whether
President Bush lacked the power to convene military commissions, since
Congress had neither formally declared war nor expressly authorized such

[729] *Ex parte Quirin*, 317 U.S. at 26, 28–29.
[730] *Id.* at 39.
[731] *Cf.* Hamdan v. Rumsfeld, 548 U.S. 557, 597 (2006) (plurality op.) (stating that "*Quirin* represents
the high-water mark of military power to try enemy combatants for war crimes").
[732] *Ex parte* Milligan, 71 U.S. (4 Wall.) 2 (1866).
[733] Military Order of November 13, 2001: Detention, Treatment, and Trial of Certain Non-Citizens
in the War Against Terrorism, 66 Fed. Reg. 57,833, 57,834 (Nov. 16, 2001).
[734] Hamdi v. Rumsfeld, 542 U.S. 507, 509 (2004) (plurality op.). For discussion of *Hamdi*, see
Chapter 1 § III and Chapter 10 § II(D)(7).
[735] Hamdan v. Rumsfeld, 548 U.S. 557 (2006). For further discussion of *Hamdan*, see *supra* this
chapter §§ II(A), II(B); Chapter 1 § II(B); Chapter 5 § II(A)(2); and Chapter 10 § II(E)(4).

commissions,[736] or rather whether such commissions were authorized by the 2001 authorization to use military force.[737] The Court emphasized Congress' constitutional authority to sanction the use of military commissions in appropriate circumstances. Further, the Court concluded that *Quirin*, on which the president relied heavily, was consistent with the proposition that Congress could also regulate the use of such commissions—and that Congress had "at most" acknowledged presidential authority to convene military commissions where justified under the Constitution and laws, including the law of war.[738] In this instance, the Court held, President Bush's military commissions were defective because their structure and procedures violated the UCMJ, which had not been overridden by any other statutes. Specifically, the UCMJ provided that military commissions should not deviate unnecessarily from the procedures by which courts martial operate and, further, that such commissions must operate in accordance with either a statute or the "law of war," of which the 1949 Geneva Conventions and customary international law is a part.[739] The Court found that the procedures of President Bush's military commissions deviated from courts-martial in significant ways and without justification (such as by allowing the accused to be excluded from the proceedings even in the absence of any disruptive conduct). Moreover, the laws of war (specifically Common Article 3 to the 1949 Geneva Conventions) prohibit "the passing of sentences and the carrying out of executions without previous judgment pronounced by a regularly constituted court,"[740] and President Bush's military commissions were not such a "court" since they had not been established by statute. To remedy these defects, Congress enacted the Military Commissions Act of 2006,[741] so as to authorize the existing military commissions.[742]

The ability of foreign nationals to challenge their military detention (even in the absence of prosecution before a military commission) has been the subject of Supreme Court jurisprudence. In *Johnson v. Eisentrager*, the Court found that U.S. courts had no jurisdiction over German war criminals held in a U.S.-administered prison in Germany, where the prisoners had at no time been in

---

[736] For an academic elaboration of such arguments, see Neal K. Katyal & Laurence H. Tribe, *Waging War, Deciding Guilt: Trying the Military Tribunals*, 111 YALE L.J. 1259 (2002).

[737] For an academic elaboration of such arguments, see Bradley & Goldsmith, *supra* note 311, at 2129–33.

[738] *Hamdan*, 548 U.S. at 590–95.

[739] 10 U.S.C. §§, 821, 836 (2018).

[740] *See, e.g.*, Geneva Convention III, *supra* note 528, art. 3.

[741] Military Commissions Act of 2006, Pub. L. No. 109-366, 120 Stat. 2600 (codified as amended in scattered sections of 10, 18, 28 and 42 U.S.C.).

[742] For discussion of the commander-in-chief power to convene military commissions, see *supra* this chapter §II(B); for further discussion of the prosecution of enemy combatants before military commissions, see Chapter 10 § II(E)(4).

U.S. territory.[743] By contrast, in *Rasul v. Bush*, the Court found that the control exercised by the United States over its base in Guantánamo Bay, Cuba, was sufficient to trigger the application of statutory habeas corpus rights.[744] A provision of the Military Commissions Act of 2006 sought to deny to those detainees the ability to bring habeas actions in U.S. federal courts, but was struck down by the Supreme Court in *Boumediene v. Bush* as an unconstitutional suspension of the writ of habeas corpus.[745] Since that time, federal courts have sought to develop standards for reviewing habeas petitions from Guantánamo detainees, while denying such petitions relating to U.S. military detentions elsewhere.[746]

C. Power to Call Forth, Organize, Arm, and Discipline the Militia

Under Article I of the Constitution, Congress is also assigned the power to "provide for calling forth the Militia to execute the Laws of the Union, suppress Insurrections and repel Invasions."[747] Moreover, Congress has the power to "provide for organizing, arming, and disciplining the Militia, and for governing such Part of them as may be employed in the Service of the United States, reserving to the States respectively, the Appointment of Officers, and the Authority of training the Militia according to the discipline prescribed by Congress."[748] Under Article II, the "President shall be Commander in Chief . . . of the Militia of the several States, when called into the actual Service of the United States . . . ."[749] The Second Amendment provides that a "well regulated Militia, being necessary to the security of a free State, the right of the people to keep and bear Arms, shall not be infringed."[750]

The American colonies formed militias, which played a critical role during the American Revolution.[751] Upon independence, those colonial militias transformed into state militias and, at the Philadelphia convention, it was

---

[743] 339 U.S. 763 (1950). The prisoners were detained and convicted in China by an U.S. military commission for violating the laws of war. They were then transported to the U.S.-occupied part of Germany and imprisoned by the U.S. Army.

[744] 542 U.S. 466 (2004).

[745] 553 U.S. 723 (2008). For discussion of *Boumediene*, see Chapter 10 §§ I(B), II(D)(7).

[746] For further discussion, see Chapter 10 § II(D)(7).

[747] U.S. CONST. art. I, § 8, cl. 15.

[748] *Id.* art. I, § 8, cl. 16.

[749] *Id.* art. II, § 2.

[750] *Id.* amend. II.

[751] *See* DANIEL J. BOORSTIN, THE AMERICANS: THE COLONIAL EXPERIENCE 345–72 (1958); John W. Shy, *A New Look at Colonial Militia*, 20 WM. & MARY Q. 175 (1963); Allan R. Millett, *The Constitution and the Citizen-Soldier, in* THE UNITED STATES MILITARY UNDER THE CONSTITUTION OF THE UNITED STATES, 1789–1989, at 100 (Richard H. Kohn ed., 1991).

understood that they would continue to function to help protect the United States. Alexander Hamilton, in *Federalist No. 29*, argued that "a well-regulated militia [is] the most natural defense of a free country"; moreover, allowing the federal government to call forth the militia would obviate the need for a federal army, which would be "dangerous to liberty."[752]

As previously noted, the earliest use of the war power under the U.S. Constitution concerned actions against Indian tribes along the new nation's western frontier. In using force against the Indians, considerable reliance was placed upon using the militias of the several states since there was no significant standing army. Hence, Congress adopted in 1789 a statute authorizing the president "to call into service from time to time, such part of the militia of the states respectively, as he may judge necessary" for the purpose of "protecting the inhabitants of the frontiers of the United States from the hostile incursions of the Indians."[753]

In this early period, militias were also heavily relied upon to address internal threats. In the First Militia Act of May 2, 1792, Congress authorized the president to call up the state militias if necessary, not just to repel invasions but also to suppress insurrections or to execute the laws of the United States.[754] Yet the president could only call up state militias to suppress insurrections when requested by a state's legislature or executive or to assist in executing the laws when requested by a federal judge.[755] The Second Militia Act of May 8, 1792, provided for the organization of the state militias, and conscripted every "free able-bodied white male citizen" between the ages of eighteen and forty-five.[756]

Use of the militias under these two statutes was tested in July 1794, when the "Whiskey Rebellion" reached its climax, sparked by a federal excise tax designed by Alexander Hamilton to help pay off the national debt. Farmers in western Pennsylvania who sold their grain in the form of whiskey violently resisted federal efforts to collect the tax. Relying on the First Militia Act of 1792, President Washington provided evidence to Associate Justice James Wilson of the violence, whereupon Wilson certified to the president that the normal means for

---

[752] THE FEDERALIST No. 29, at 183 (Alexander Hamilton).

[753] Act of Sept. 29, 1789, ch. 25, § 5, 1 Stat. 95, 96.

[754] Act of May 2, 1792, ch. 28, 1 Stat. 264. This statute was the first of a series of statutes that relate to the president's power to "call forth" state militias for different purposes, several which remain in force today. *See* Ku Klux Klan (Civil Rights) Act of 1871, ch. 22, §§ 3–4, 17 Stat. 13, 14–15 (codified in part at 10 U.S.C. § 253 (2018)); Suppression of the Rebellion Act of 1861, ch. 25, 12 Stat. 281 (codified at 10 U.S.C. §§ 251–55); Insurrection Act of 1807, ch. 39, 2 Stat. 443 (codified at 10 U.S.C. §§ 251–55); Act of February 28, 1795, ch. 36, 1 Stat. 424 (codified as amended at 10 U.S.C. §§ 251–55). For discussion, see Stephen I. Vladeck, *Emergency Power and the Militia Acts*, 114 YALE L.J. 149 (2004).

[755] Act of May 2, 1792, ch. 28, §§ 1, 2, 1 Stat. 264, 264.

[756] Act of May 8, 1792, ch. 33, § 1, 1 Stat. 271, 271. These terms were later expanded to cover all males, regardless of race, between the ages 18–54. *See* The Militia Act of 1862, ch. 201, § 1, 12 Stat. 597, 597.

upholding U.S. law were inadequate. President Washington then called up and led into western Pennsylvania some fifteen thousand members of the militias of Maryland, New Jersey, Pennsylvania, and Virginia to suppress the rebellion. Faced with the imminent arrival of such forces, the insurrectionists dissipated; some twenty were arrested, but were later acquitted or pardoned.[757] The judicial certification requirement in the 1792 statute was replaced in the Militia Act of 1795 with a requirement that the militia be used to assist in executing the laws only until thirty days after the commencement of the next session of Congress,[758] at which point Congress would be able to authorize such action.

These statutes would be used throughout the nineteenth century to call up the militias, both for handling internal matters—such as suppressing election disorders or quelling riots—as well as for deployment in wars alongside regular U.S. armed forces.[759] The term "National Guard" apparently was used first in New York in 1824 by some militia units, who decided to name themselves after the French National Guard in honor of the Marquis de Lafayette.[760] The term "National Guard" became a more common expression nationwide with the 1903 passage of the Efficiency in Militia Act (also known as the "Dick Act").[761] That act required the several states to divide their militias into two sections, one of which should be called the "National Guard" (an organized militia) and the other known as the "Reserve Militia." Further, the act authorized federal funds to the National Guard units to pay for equipment and training, in exchange for those units being organized and trained in a manner similar to the U.S. Army.

The 1933 National Defense Act amendments required that all federally funded soldiers be dual-enlisted in both the state National Guard and the National Guard of the United States, a newly created federal reserve force, resulting in National Guard reserve forces under mixed state and federal control.[762] Further,

---

[757] See generally THOMAS P. SLAUGHTER, THE WHISKEY REBELLION: FRONTIER EPILOGUE TO THE AMERICAN REVOLUTION (1988). Keen to avoid any repetition, Congress in November 1794 authorized the president to call forth the military as necessary "in the four western counties of Pennsylvania" in order "to suppress unlawful combinations" and "to cause the laws to be duly executed" there. Act of Nov. 29, 1794, ch. 1, §§ 1–2, 1 Stat. 403, 403.

[758] See Act of February 28, 1795, ch. 36, § 2, 1 Stat. 424, 424.

[759] See, e.g., The Prize Cases, 67 U.S. (2 Black) 635, 668 (1863); Luther v. Borden, 48 U.S. (7 How.) 1 (1849); Martin v. Mott, 25 U.S. (12 Wheat.) 19, 28–33 (1827); see also JERRY COOPER, THE RISE OF THE NATIONAL GUARD: THE EVOLUTION OF THE AMERICAN MILITIA, 1865–1920, at 47 (1997); David E. Engdahl, Soldiers, Riots, and Revolution: The Law and History of Military Troops in Civil Disorders, 57 IOWA L. REV. 1 (1971). For an example from the Spanish-American War, see Act of Apr. 25, 1898, ch. 189, 30 Stat. 364.

[760] MICHAEL D. DOUBLER, THE NATIONAL GUARD AND RESERVE: A REFERENCE HANDBOOK 50 (2008).

[761] Efficiency in Militia Act, ch. 196, 32 Stat. 775 (1903).

[762] Act of June 15, 1933, ch. 87, §§ 5–7, 48 Stat. 153, 155–56.

the Act provided that Congress could call those reserve forces into federal service in the event of an emergency.[763]

Today the "National Guard of the United States" is a reserve military force, composed of National Guard military members or units of each state, the District of Columbia, and the territories of Guam, Puerto Rico, and the Virgin Islands. Most National Guard members have a full-time civilian job and only serve part-time in the National Guard, unless called into active duty.[764] Separately, some states also maintain "naval militias," which are reserve military forces administered under the authority of the state government, which can be called up into federal service as the Naval Militia. Moreover, persons may be part of a state "militia" without being a part of that state's National Guard and may even fall within the scope of an "unorganized" militia. Hence, there are two classes of the militia: "(1) the organized militia, which consists of the National Guard and the Naval Militia; and (2) the unorganized militia, which consists of the members of the militia who are not members of the National Guard or the Naval Militia."[765]

---

[763] For general histories of the National Guard and militias, see ELBRIDGE COLBY, THE NATIONAL GUARD OF THE UNITED STATES: A HALF CENTURY OF PROGRESS (1977); JIM DAN HILL, THE MINUTE MAN IN WAR AND PEACE: A HISTORY OF THE NATIONAL GUARD (1964); JOHN K. MAHON, HISTORY OF THE MILITIA AND THE NATIONAL GUARD (1983); ROBERT K. WRIGHT, JR. & RENEE HYLTON-GREENE, A BRIEF HISTORY OF THE MILITIA AND THE NATIONAL GUARD (1986).

[764] See generally DOUBLER, supra note 760.

[765] 10 U.S.C. § 246 (2018).

9

Federalism and Foreign Relations

The Founders who met in Philadelphia in 1787 had two broad and overlapping objections to the vertical distribution of foreign relations authority under the Articles of Confederation.[1] One concerned the absence of sufficient centralized authority, such as the inability of the central government to regulate foreign commerce or to pay off foreign debts contracted by the United States. Another involved state violations of the law of nations and of U.S. treaties; violations of the 1783 Treaty of Paris with Great Britain, for example, risked giving cause for war under the law of nations as it stood at the time.[2] As such, a key objective of the new Constitution was to correct such deficiencies.[3]

The consequence, as explained throughout this volume, is that the Constitution places the foreign relations powers in the hands of the federal government. Concomitantly, it expressly denies certain of these powers to the states, save in some circumstances where Congress consents.[4] Thus, the Constitution's structure, seen from afar, is suggestive that the states have no or very little role in U.S. foreign relations. Yet, as will be discussed in Section I, that is not the case. Not only are the states recognized by the Constitution as having some role with respect to U.S. foreign relations, in myriad other ways they are very important for those relations, such as by influencing the conduct of the federal government or by helping to implement U.S. international obligations. Even so, Section II explains that conflicts do arise between the states and the federal government in this area, and when they do some of the most important veins of foreign relations law doctrine address how federal law preempts state law. This chapter concludes in Section III with discussion of one way that the Constitution expressly acknowledges a role for the state: their ability to conclude "compacts" with foreign states and sub-state entities.

---

[1] *See* THE FEDERALIST NOS. 1, 6, 8–9, 11, 21 (Alexander Hamilton), NOS. 2–5 (John Jay), No. 49 (James Madison); *see also* Richard B. Bilder, *The Role of States and Cities in Foreign Relations, in* FOREIGN AFFAIRS AND THE U.S. CONSTITUTION 115 (Louis Henkin et al. eds., 1990) (and in 83 AM. J. INT'L L. 821 (1989)).

[2] *See infra* this chapter text accompanying notes 167–170; *see also* Chapter 5 § I(A) and Chapter 6 § I(A).

[3] *See* Martin S. Flaherty, *Are We to Be a Nation?: Federal Power vs. "States' Rights" in Foreign Affairs*, 70 U. COLO. L. REV. 1277, 1312 (1999); Michael D. Ramsey, *The Power of the States in Foreign Affairs: The Original Understanding of Foreign Policy Federalism*, 75 NOTRE DAME L. REV. 341, 403–18 (1999).

[4] *See* Chapter 1 § I(E); HENKIN, FOREIGN AFFAIRS, at 151–55.

I. Role of States in Foreign Relations

To a degree, the Constitution expressly addresses the role of the states with respect to U.S. foreign relations. The Constitution provides that no state shall enter into any "Treaty, Alliance, or Confederation," nor shall any state grant letters of marque and reprisal.[5] No state without the consent of Congress may "lay any Imposts or Duties on Imports or Exports," except as necessary for its inspection laws.[6] No state shall, without the consent of Congress, "keep Troops, or Ships of War in time of Peace";[7] "enter into any Agreement or Compact with another State, or with a foreign Power";[8] "or engage in War, unless actually invaded, or in such imminent Danger as will not admit of delay."[9] Further, according to the Supremacy Clause, foreign relations developments at the federal level that constitute federal law—including treaties, customary international law that operates as federal common law, and certain presidential acts—are binding upon the states as "the supreme Law of the Land."[10]

All this suggests that other provisions of the Constitution limiting the national government's authority (at least in principle) apply differently in foreign relations law, perhaps by design. While in theory the Ninth Amendment establishes a rule of strict construction of federal enumerated powers,[11] and the

---

[5] U.S. CONST. art. I, § 10, cl. 1. By contrast, the president is assigned the power to make treaties, with the advice and consent of the Senate. *See* U.S. CONST. art. II, § 2. *See generally* Chapter 6. Further, Congress is given the power to "grant Letters of Marque and Reprisal." U.S. CONST. art. I, § 8, cl. 11. *See generally* Chapter 8 § II(D).

[6] U.S. CONST. art. I, § 10, cl. 2. By contrast, Congress is authorized "[t]o lay and collect Taxes, Duties, Imposts and Excises" to pay debts and provide for the common defense and general welfare. *Id.* art. I, § 8, cl. 1, *See generally* Chapter 2 § III. For discussion of how the truncation of state authority, in favor of national authority, helped address "[o]ne of the major defects of the Articles of the Confederation," see Michelin Tire Corp. v. Wages, 423 U.S. 276, 283–94 (1976) (distinguishing, however, nondiscriminatory *ad valorem* state property taxes).

[7] U.S. CONST. art. I, § 10, cl. 3. By contrast, Congress is given authority "[t]o raise and support Armies" (while limiting appropriations for that purpose to a term no longer than two years) and "[t]o provide and maintain a Navy," among other powers of war and peace. *Id.* § 8, cls. 12, 13. *See generally* Chapter 8 § III(A).

[8] U.S. CONST. art. I, § 10, cl. 3; *see infra* this chapter § III. Again, by contrast, the national government is granted the power to make treaties, *see supra* note 7, but curiously is not expressly given any capacity to make agreements or compacts. *See* Chapter 6 § V.

[9] U.S. CONST. art. I, § 10, cl. 3. By contrast, Congress is given the authority to declare war, *see id.* § 8, cl. 11, and the president is designated as the commander in chief. *Id.* art. II, § 2, cl. 1. *See generally* Chapter 8 §§ I, II(B).

[10] U.S. CONST. art. VI, cl. 2. For analysis of the original meaning of the clause, see Henry Paul Monaghan, *Supremacy Clause Textualism*, 110 COLUM. L. REV. 731 (2010); Peter L. Strauss, *The Perils of Theory*, 83 NOTRE DAME L. REV. 1567 (2008); Michael D. Ramsey, *The Supremacy Clause, Original Meaning, and Modern Law*, 74 OHIO ST. L.J. 559 (2013).

[11] U.S. CONST., amend. IX ("The enumeration in the Constitution, of certain rights, shall not be construed to deny or disparage others retained by the people."); AKHIL REED AMAR, THE BILL OF RIGHTS: CREATION AND RECONSTRUCTION 123–24 (1998) (defending the view that the Ninth Amendment "sounds in part in federalism," while noting that this "had faded considerably" after adoption of the Fourteenth Amendment). On individual rights and foreign relations, see generally Chapter 10.

Tenth Amendment provides residually a role for states in matters not delegated by the Constitution to the federal government,[12] in reality the expansive federal foreign affairs powers under the Constitution, and the powers specifically foreclosed to the states, appear to leave very little power in this area for the states to exercise. The Ninth Amendment has had no noticeable value in restricting the national government,[13] and Justice Holmes pronounced in *Missouri v. Holland* that an otherwise valid treaty would not be "forbidden by some invisible radiation from the general terms of the Tenth Amendment."[14] Not long afterward, the Supreme Court in *United States v. Belmont* famously opined: "[I]n respect of our foreign relations generally, state lines disappear. As to such purposes the State of New York does not exist."[15]

Upon more careful reflection, however, most everyone—including, but not limited to, the State of New York—would agree that this is an exaggeration: states actually play a substantial role in foreign relations, and it is not an altogether bad thing that they do.[16] Indeed, one might argue that an enduring and constitutionally acknowledged role for states is an important structural feature of separation of powers, with the states serving as a counterweight to the broad power enjoyed by the national government, and particularly the executive branch, in foreign relations.[17] This continued, residual importance of the states with respect to foreign relations takes a number of forms. Appreciating some of the different kinds

[12] *Id.* amend. X ("The powers not delegated to the United States by the Constitution, nor prohibited by it to the States, are reserved to the States respectively, or to the people."); Gregory v. Ashcroft, 501 U.S. 452, 457 (1991) ("The Constitution created a Federal Government of limited powers.... The States thus retain substantial sovereign authority under our constitutional system.").

[13] *See* HENKIN, FOREIGN AFFAIRS, at 277. Some have argued that the Ninth Amendment should be harnessed as a vehicle for incorporating human rights into U.S. law, *see* Jordan J. Paust, *Human Rights and the Ninth Amendment: A New Form of Guarantee*, 60 CORNELL L. REV. 231 (1975), but those arguments have not had purchase. *See, e.g.,* United States v. Morales, 464 F. Supp. 325, 326 (E.D.N.Y. 1979) (rejecting claim that the Ninth Amendment incorporates " 'the Law of Nations and the Laws of War' as set forth in the Geneva Convention").

[14] Missouri v. Holland, 252 U.S. 416, 433–34 (1920). For discussion, see Chapter 6 §§ I(C), II(D) (2).

[15] United States v. Belmont, 301 U.S. 324, 331 (1937); *see* Zschernig v. Miller, 389 U.S. 429, 436 (1968) (suggesting that "foreign affairs and international relations [are] matters which the Constitution entrusts solely to the Federal Government"); Hines v. Davidowitz, 312 U.S. 52, 63 (1941) ("The Federal Government ... is entrusted with full and exclusive responsibility for the conduct of affairs with foreign sovereignties."); Holmes v. Jennison, 39 U.S. (14 Pet.) 540, 575 (1840) (finding that it "was one of the main objects of the Constitution to make us, so far as regarded our foreign relations, one people and one nation...."); HENKIN, FOREIGN AFFAIRS, at 150. For discussion of *Belmont*, see *infra* this chapter § II(C) and Chapter 3 § IV(D).

[16] *See* MICHAEL J. GLENNON & ROBERT D. SLOANE, FOREIGN AFFAIRS FEDERALISM: THE MYTH OF NATIONAL EXCLUSIVITY xviii, 35–76 (2016); *see also* David H. Moore, *Beyond One Voice*, 98 MINN. L. REV. 953 (2014); Daniel Abebe & Aziz Z. Huq, *Foreign Affairs Federalism: A Revisionist Approach*, 66 VAND. L. REV. 723 (2013); Robert B. Ahdieh, *Foreign Affairs, International Law, and the New Federalism: Lessons from Coordination*, 73 MO. L. REV. 1185 (2008); Sarah H. Cleveland, *Crosby and the "One-Voice" Myth in U.S. Foreign Relations*, 46 VILL. L. REV. 975 (2001); Edward T. Swaine, *The Undersea World of Foreign Relations Federalism*, 2 CHI. J. INT'L L. 337 (2001).

[17] *See* Ramsey, *supra* note 3, at 429.

of state and local activities is vital to understanding the importance of the federal doctrines designed to limit some of those activities, which are discussed in the remainder of this chapter.

First, in a few respects, the Constitution actually envisages a role for the states; they are not entirely excluded.[18] Thus, as previously noted and discussed in greater depth later,[19] states are permitted to enter into "compacts" with foreign states and substate entities. Such compacts may include modest undertakings, such as the construction or maintenance of a transboundary bridge or road, but they need not be so confined. In principle, the Constitution also contemplates that, with congressional consent, the states might also keep troops or ships of war in times of peace, or engage in war. If actually invaded or in imminent danger, the states may resort to "war" even without the consent of Congress;[20] this may seem archaic, but it has been invoked, albeit not always under compelling circumstances.[21] The list of such roles for the states is not long, but one must bear them in mind, along with an awareness that the enumerated foreign relations powers of the federal government have notable omissions that may afford other opportunities for the states.[22]

Second, as a political (if not legal) matter,[23] the presence of the states and their role in regulating vast areas of U.S. law at the local level has a conditioning effect upon the executive when negotiating, accepting, and interpreting international

---

[18] *See* MICHAEL D. RAMSEY, THE CONSTITUTION'S TEXT IN FOREIGN AFFAIRS 259–317 (2007).

[19] *See infra* this chapter § III.

[20] U.S. CONST. art. I, § 10, cl. 3.

[21] *See, e.g.,* Op. Att'y Gen. Mark Brnovich (Ariz.), Re: The Federal Government's Duty to Protect the States and the States' Sovereign Power of Self Defense When Invaded, Op. I22-001 (R21-015), Feb. 7, 2022, https://perma.cc/ZW3F-3WLB (concluding that because the federal government is failing to defend the state of Arizona from invasion, in the sense of unauthorized noncitizen immigrants, drugs, and associated violence attributed to Arizona's border with Mexico, the state's constitutional authority to use self-defense due to being "actually invaded" under art. I, § 10, cl. 3, is triggered, together with its right to execute its inspection laws under art. I, § 10, cl. 2).

[22] For example, the Constitution makes only limited reference to the "law of nations." U.S. CONST. art. I, § 8, cl. 10. *See generally* Chapter 5.

[23] The conventional understanding has been that the federal treaty power operates free from federalism limits. *See* Missouri v. Holland, 252 U.S. 416 (1920); RESTATEMENT (THIRD) § 302 cmt. d. Recently, however, some scholars have maintained that the power is limited, at a minimum by the anticommandeering doctrine under the Tenth Amendment (which prevents the federal government from requiring states or state officials to enforce federal law) and by state sovereign immunity under the Eleventh Amendment, if not as well by subject-matter limits that parallel those of the Commerce Clause. *See* HENKIN, FOREIGN AFFAIRS, at 166; Curtis A. Bradley, *The Treaty Power and American Federalism,* 97 MICH. L. REV. 390 (1998); Curtis A. Bradley, *The Treaty Power and American Federalism: Part II,* 99 MICH. L. REV. 98 (2000); Nicholas Q. Rosenkranz, *Executing the Treaty Power,* 118 HARV. L. REV. 1867 (2005); Edward T. Swaine, *Does Federalism Constrain the Treaty Power?,* 103 COLUM. L. REV. 403 (2003). *But see* Michael D. Ramsey, Missouri v. Holland *and Historical Textualism,* 73 MO. L. REV. 969 (2008) (finding full support for *Holland's* conclusion in the Constitution's original meaning). For discussion of the scope of the treaty power, see Chapter 6 § II.

obligations.[24] The federal government is often disinclined to enter into international commitments that would displace state authority, given that doing so may create difficulties in securing either Senate consent to ratification of a treaty or necessary implementing legislation.[25] While maintaining that the Tenth Amendment does not limit the exercise of the treaty power, the executive branch has sought to negotiate treaty provisions that avoid federalism concerns, has attached understandings when adhering to treaties to avoid obligations that require action beyond existing federal law, has attached reservations or understandings clarifying that the treaty's obligations will be implemented "at the appropriate government level," or has sought inclusion of a "federalism clause" in the treaty that allows deviation from obligations based on competences between the federal government and its constituent units.[26] For instance, when ratifying the 1948 Charter of the Organization of American States, the U.S. instrument of ratification contained a reservation—included at the Senate's insistence—that none of the charter's provisions "shall be considered as enlarging the powers of the Federal Government of the United States or limiting the powers of the several states of the Federal Union with respect to any matters recognized under the Constitution as being within the reserved powers of the several states."[27] Not long afterward, Senate receptiveness to federalism concerns, reflecting state resistance to antidiscrimination principles, played a key role in the so-called Bricker Amendment proposals and resulted in a truce that stymied ratification of multilateral human rights treaties for over a quarter century.[28]

This conditioning effect has considerable contemporary relevance. The status of the United States as the only nation not to have ratified the U.N. Convention on the Rights of the Child may be attributed, at least in part, to an unwillingness on the part of Congress to preempt broadly state-level decisions in the area of family law.[29] Likewise, efforts to pursue U.S. ratification of the Hague Choice of

[24] See Duncan B. Hollis, Executive Federalism: Forging New Federalist Constraints on the Treaty Power, 79 S. CAL. L. REV. 1327 (2006) (analyzing how the executive has devised mechanisms for accommodating federalism in U.S. treaties); HENKIN, FOREIGN AFFAIRS, at 167–69.

[25] See, e.g., Curtis A. Bradley, Federalism, Treaty Implementation, and Political Process: Bond v. United States, 108 AM. J. INT'L L. 486 (2014).

[26] See U.S. Dep't of State, Office of the Legal Adviser, Memorandum Summarizing U.S. Views and Practice in Addressing Federalism Issues in Treaties (Nov. 8, 2002), https://perma.cc/67D4-MXWX. The rationale for such approaches appears to vary between genuine concerns about possible constitutional limits, considered concessions to improve domestic political prospects, and largely independent preferences for greater leeway under a treaty. See Swaine, supra note 23, at 445–47 & nn.170–74 (discussing examples).

[27] See ORGANIZATION OF AMERICAN STATES (OAS), Charter of the OAS, Signatories and Ratifications, https://perma.cc/T9AR-8NV3; see also Hollis, supra note 24, at 1379 (noting genesis of reservation and its acceptance, with some resistance, by other member states).

[28] See Chapter 6 § I(C).

[29] See, e.g., Susan Kilbourne, Student Research, The Convention on the Rights of the Child: Federalism Issues for the United States, 5 GEO. J. ON FIGHTING POVERTY 327 (1998); David P. Stewart, Ratification of the Convention on the Rights of the Child, 5 GEO. J. ON FIGHTING POVERTY 161, 176–78, 182–83

Courts Convention in recent years have foundered on the difficulties presented in displacing state law.[30] For that reason, the federal government must carefully consider whether state and local law operates in a manner that allows the United States to ratify or accede to a treaty. After an international agreement has been entered into, the manner in which the agreement (or its implementing statute) is interpreted may well be affected by consideration of state interests. The Supreme Court's decision in *Bond v. United States*, interpreting a federal statute implementing the Chemical Weapons Convention not to reach purely local crimes, may be understood in this way.[31]

Third, the federal government cooperates with the states, to one degree or another, in implementing U.S. foreign relations law.[32] States often freelance, engaging on their own in foreign affairs in areas where the federal government is inactive or indifferent; in at least some of these instances, though, the federal government is at least marginally supportive.[33] For example, states regularly send trade missions to foreign countries, consisting of government officials and representatives of local businesses, to discuss exports to and investment from those countries; indeed, many state governments have "international trade and

---

(1998). Some discrete areas of family law have been addressed through treaties ratified by the United States. *See* Chapter 10 § III(B).

[30] For varying views on how these difficulties might be surmounted, *compare, e.g.*, David P. Stewart, *Implementing the Hague Choice of Court Convention: The Argument in Favor of "Cooperative Federalism*," *in* FOREIGN COURT JUDGMENTS AND THE UNITED STATES LEGAL SYSTEM (Paul B. Stephan III ed., 26th Sokol Colloquium, Vol. 7, 2014), *with* Stephen B. Burbank, *Federalism and Private International Law: Implementing the Hague Choice of Court Convention in the United States*, 2 J. PRIV. INT'L L. 287 (2006); *and* Linda J. Silberman, *The Need for a Federal Statutory Approach to the Recognition and Enforcement of Foreign Country Judgments, in* FOREIGN COURT JUDGMENTS AND THE UNITED STATES LEGAL SYSTEM, *supra; and* Peter D. Trooboff, *Implementing Legislation for the Hague Choice of Court Convention, in id.; cf.* Ronald A. Brand, *New Challenges in the Recognition and Enforcement of Judgments, in* PRIVATE INTERNATIONAL LAW: CONTEMPORARY CHALLENGES AND CONTINUING RELEVANCE 360 (F. Ferrari & Diego P. Fernandez Arroyo eds., 2019) (assessing the problems presented by having judgments recognition law largely determined at the state, rather than the federal, level); Stephen B. Burbank, *A Tea Party at the Hague?*, 18 Sw. J. INT'L L. 629 (2012) (assessing federalism challenge to private law treaties generally); Paul R. Dubinsky, *Private Law Treaties and Federalism: Can the United States Lead?*, 54 TEX. INT'L L.J. 39 (2018) (same).

[31] Bond v. United States, 572 U.S. 844, 857–58 (2014); *see infra* this chapter text accompanying notes 157–164; *see also* Chapter 6 § II(D)(1).

[32] *See* Jean Galbraith, Book Review, *Cooperative and Uncooperative Foreign Affairs Federalism*, 130 HARV. L. REV. 2131 (2017); Johanna Kalb, *The Persistence of Dualism in Human Rights Treaty Implementation*, 30 YALE L. & POL'Y REV. 71, 99–104 (2011); Julian G. Ku, *The State of New York Does Exist: How the States Control Compliance with International Law*, 82 N.C. L. REV. 457, 501–10 (2004); Julian G. Ku, *The Crucial Role of States and Private International Law Treaties: A Model for Accommodating Globalization*, 73 Mo. L. REV. 1063, 1065 (2008); *see also* Oona A. Hathaway et al., *The Treaty Power: Its History, Scope, and Limits*, 98 CORNELL L. REV. 239, 320–22 (2013) (recounting state action that allows for treaty compliance).

[33] *See generally* EARL H. FRY, THE EXPANDING ROLE OF STATE AND LOCAL GOVERNMENTS IN U.S. FOREIGN AFFAIRS (1998); Julian G. Ku, *Gubernatorial Foreign Policy*, 115 YALE L.J. 2380 (2006).

investment" offices, not just within the state but overseas as well.[34] Comparable efforts may actually owe their origin to the federal government: for example, hundreds of U.S. cities have "sister city" relationships with cities abroad that are essentially self-directed,[35] though the origins of the program lie in an initiative by President Dwight D. Eisenhower.[36] In other instances, state and local governments may initiate activities that are later acknowledged and accommodated by the federal government, including as an aspect of national policy. For example, when state and local governments in the 1980s began adopting laws that precluded local governments from buying from or investing in companies doing business in apartheid-era South Africa, the federal government adopted a statute that imposed federal sanctions but expressly preserved the state and local measures.[37] A similar approach was taken with respect to the federal "Buy America" requirements for government procurement of rail or road transportation, which bars the secretary of transportation from restricting states that receive federal funding from imposing even more stringent "Buy America" procurement requirements.[38] Federal laws imposing sanctions on a foreign government, such as those concerning Sudan[39] and Iran,[40] sometimes include a provision authorizing certain kinds of state and local sanctions.[41]

In what is often called "cooperative federalism," the federal government more clearly relies on and seeks to harness the states' regulatory, administrative, and law enforcement infrastructure to promote national objectives. One

---

[34] *See, e.g.,* VIRGINIA ECONOMIC DEVELOPMENT PARTNERSHIP, https://perma.cc/AG6P-WYTQ (noting its offices in Virginia, Germany, Japan, and South Korea).

[35] *See* GLENNON & SLOANE, *supra* note 16, at 62, 68–69. *But see* Galbraith, *supra* note 32, at 2141–43.

[36] *See* Judith Resnik, *Foreign as Domestic Affairs: Rethinking Horizontal Federalism and Foreign Affairs Preemption in Light of Translocal Internationalism,* 57 EMORY L. REV. 31, 48 (2007).

[37] *See, e.g.,* Comprehensive Anti-Apartheid Act of 1986, Pub. L. No. 99-440, § 606, 100 Stat. 1086 (1986); *cf.* Constitutionality of South African Divestment Statutes Enacted by State and Local Governments, 10 Op. O.L.C. 49 (1986) (opining, prior to the act's passage, that state and local divestment statutes and ordinances were constitutional).

[38] 49 U.S.C. § 5323(j)(9) (2018); *see* Mabey Bridge & Shore, Inc. v. Schoch, 666 F.3d 862, 873 (3d Cir. 2012) (finding that such a provision precludes a claim that state law has been preempted).

[39] *See, e.g.,* Sudan Accountability and Divestment Act of 2007, Pub. L. No. 110-174, 121 Stat. 2516 (2007) (codified as amended at 15 U.S.C. § 80a–13, 50 U.S.C. § 1701 (2018)) (permitting states and municipalities to adopt and enforce measures that divest state and local government assets or that prohibit the investment of state and local government assets, from certain business operations in Sudan). For concern by President George W. Bush that such authorization might interfere with the federal government's "exclusive authority to conduct foreign relations," see Statement on Signing the Sudan Accountability and Divestment Act of 2007, 43 WEEKLY COMP. PRES. DOC. 1646 (Dec. 31, 2007).

[40] *See, e.g.,* Comprehensive Iran Sanctions, Accountability, and Divestment Act, Pub. L. No. 111-195, § 202(f), 124 Stat. 1312 (2010) (allowing certain state and local sanctions against the government of Iran so long as they are "not preempted by any Federal law or regulation").

[41] When such accommodations are not made, state and local sanctions may not survive review. *See infra* this chapter text accompanying notes 144–152 (discussing litigation concerning Myanmar (Burma)).

prominent area is immigration law, where federal efforts rely heavily on local law enforcement officials.[42] What may be less evident is the routine reliance of the federal government on states and localities for implementation of obligations assumed by the United States under international law.[43] A treaty entered into by the United States may be self-executing, or it may be implemented entirely by means of a federal statute.[44] Yet some treaties adhered to by the United States are implemented primarily through existing state and local law, where that law is sufficient for upholding the relevant obligations.[45]

By way of example, when the United States was considering ratification of the 1984 Convention against Torture,[46] the Department of State analyzed to what extent it was necessary to adopt federal implementing legislation. The department concluded that acts of torture committed within the United States were already criminal under existing state statutes (such as assault or murder) and, in limited circumstances, under federal statutes (such as on interstate kidnapping or hostage-taking). As such, federal legislation was only needed to address two relatively narrow issues: jurisdiction over offenses committed by U.S. nationals outside the United States and jurisdiction over noncitizen offenders who commit torture abroad and then turn up in U.S. territory.[47] To take another example, protection of foreign investment under bilateral investment treaties or free trade agreements typically requires that the foreign investor receive "fair and equitable treatment," be treated no less favorably than U.S. investors, and (sometimes) be treated no less favorably than investors from other countries. These obligations are typically implemented through business-friendly state and local laws and regulations, though due process and equal protection rules of the U.S. Constitution serve as an important backdrop. Arbitration claims brought by foreign investors against the United States under international agreements almost

---

[42] See, e.g., ADAM B. COX & CRISTINA M. RODRÍGUEZ, THE PRESIDENT AND IMMIGRATION LAW 133–61 (2020) (explaining how the executive branch cannot escape a bureaucratic reliance on state-level institutions); Adam B. Cox & Thomas J. Miles, Policing Immigration, 80 U. CHI. L. REV. 87, 93 (2013) (empirically evaluating a federal program that enlisted local police for screening persons); Galbraith, supra note 32, 2145–46 (summarizing such cooperation); Cristina M. Rodríguez, The Significance of the Local in Immigration Regulation, 106 MICH. L. REV. 567 (2008) (urging greater use of such cooperation); Michael J. Wishnie, State and Local Police Enforcement of Immigration Laws, 4 U. PA. J. CONST. L. 1084 (2004) (detailing federal efforts to enlist, or even conscript, state and local police in routine immigration enforcement).

[43] See, e.g., Chad G. Marzen, The Application of International Law in State Courts: The Case of Florida, 49 U. TOLEDO L. REV. 205 (2018).

[44] See Chapter 6 § IV(A)–(B).

[45] See generally Ku, The State of New York Does Exist, supra note 32.

[46] Convention against Torture and Other Cruel, Inhuman or Degrading Treatment or Punishment, Dec. 10, 1984, S. TREATY DOC. NO. 100–20, 1465 U.N.T.S. 85.

[47] U.S. Dep't of State, Summary and Analysis of the Convention Against Torture and Other Cruel, Inhuman, or Degrading Treatment or Punishment, May 23, 1988, S. TREATY DOC. NO. 100-20, at 8–10 (1988).

always concern the alleged failure of state and local governments to protect the foreign investor under their laws.[48]

In other instances, implementation depends less on the adoption or continuation of state and local laws as such and more on cooperative behavior by state and local officials. For example, as discussed previously, U.S. obligations under the International Covenant on Civil and Political Rights are usually fulfilled through compliance by local police, prosecutors, and courts operating within the confines of preexisting state law (accommodated, to a degree, by a federalism understanding).[49] The limits of cooperation may be more apparent when the international legal obligation requires behavior genuinely distinct from ordinary U.S. practices—as in the obligation of state and local law enforcement authorities to advise a noncitizen, when arrested, that his or her consulate in the United States may be informed of the arrest and may have access to the detainee so as to provide assistance, which is derived from U.S. obligations under the Vienna Convention on Consular Relations.[50] As discussed later in this chapter, the failure of officials to adhere to these Vienna Convention obligations has led to extensive domestic and international litigation,[51] prompting the federal government to pursue extensive efforts to educate state and local law enforcement authorities regarding rights of consular assistance.[52]

Fourth, states sometimes engage foreign relations–related activities that resist or oppose federal law and policy, a phenomenon that might be characterized as "uncooperative federalism."[53] This phenomenon arguably encompasses a wide variety of conduct that reflects varying degrees of noncooperation. Modest forms of noncooperation may be seen in criticisms by state and local governments of federal foreign relations policies. The numerous resolutions adopted by cities

---

[48] *See* Chapter 2 § IV(C); Chapter 10 §§ II(D), II(G).

[49] International Covenant on Civil and Political Rights, Dec. 16, 1966, S. TREATY DOC. No. 95-20, 999 U.N.T.S. 171; *see also* S. EXEC. REP. NO. 102-23, at 17–18 (explaining U.S. federalism understanding); Chapter 1 § I(E). In some instances, state and local law has been amended in a manner that indirectly reflects developments in the field of human rights law. *See, e.g.*, Vicki C. Jackson, *Constitutional Dialogue and Human Dignity: States and Transnational Constitutional Discourse*, 65 MONT. L. REV. 15, 21–27 (2004) (explaining how Montana Constitution was inspired by the Puerto Rican Constitution, which was in turn influenced by international human rights); *see also* COLUMBIA LAW SCH., HUMAN RIGHTS INST., BRINGING HUMAN RIGHTS HOME: HOW STATE AND LOCAL GOVERNMENTS CAN USE HUMAN RIGHTS TO ADVANCE LOCAL POLICY (2012) (noting parallels between state and local laws and human rights); Martha F. Davis, *The Spirit of Our Times: State Constitutions and International Human Rights*, 30 N.Y.U. REV. L. & SOC. CHANGE 359 (2006) (urging greater use of international standards).

[50] Vienna Convention on Consular Relations art. 36, Apr. 24, 1963, 21 U.S.T. 77, 596 U.N.T.S. 261.

[51] *See infra* this chapter note 190 and accompanying text.

[52] *See, e.g.*, U.S. Dep't of State, Consular Notification and Access: Instructions for Federal, State and Local Law Enforcement and Other Officials Regarding Foreign Nationals in the United States and the Rights of Consular Officers to Assist Them (5th ed. 2018).

[53] *See* Jessica Bulman-Pozen & Heather K. Gerken, Essay, *Uncooperative Federalism*, 118 YALE L.J. 1256 (2009); Galbraith, *supra* note 32.

criticizing the 2003 U.S. intervention in Iraq, for example,[54] echo the 1798 Virginia and Kentucky Resolutions that protested the Alien and Sedition Acts—enacted during the administration of President John Adams purportedly to strengthen national security during the "quasi-war" with France.[55] States have also occasionally adopted state laws (or even amended their constitutions) to restrict the application of all or some foreign or international law by state courts.[56] This, too, is largely expressive in character, although such laws might conflict with federal foreign relations law if they prevent state courts from applying federal law derived from, or depending upon, the foreign or international law in question.[57] And even if state or local laws are essentially expressive, they may raise issues under the dormant foreign affairs doctrine.[58]

State-level initiatives that adopt rules that the federal government has not embraced are a mixed lot, and at least in the foreign-relations context, may verge on the uncooperative. For example, a state or municipal endorsement of a treaty that the federal government has declined to ratify may be inconsistent with federal policy; in other instances, however, the federal position may be driven by a desire not to remove decision-making from the states, and so might not begrudge them the opportunity to decide for themselves. Thus, although the United States has declined to ratify the Convention on the Elimination of Discrimination against Women (CEDAW), that decision does not necessarily signal a conflict with a measure such as San Francisco's 1998 ordinance implementing CEDAW within the city.[59] Indeed, assuming the existence of a conflict may be doubtful given the proposal of a federalism understanding during the Senate's

---

[54] See, e.g., Peter Slevin, *Wisconsin Voters Prepare to Weigh In On the War in Iraq*, WASH. POST, Mar. 18, 2006, at A3 (reporting that "three years after the U.S. invasion, 76 cities have passed resolutions calling for troops to come home").

[55] See STANLEY ELKINS & ERIC MCKITRICK, THE AGE OF FEDERALISM 588–94, 719–26 (1993).

[56] For example, a "Save our State Amendment" was adopted for the Oklahoma Constitution that forbade state courts from considering either "international law" or "Sharia law" when deciding cases. H.R.J. Res. 1056, 52d Leg., 2d Sess. (Okla. 2010). Tennessee adopted a statute restricting application of foreign law generally, but under narrower circumstances. See 2010 Tenn. Pub. Acts 983 (restricting reliance on "any foreign law, legal code or system against a natural person in this state" if "the decision rendered either violated or would violate any right of the natural person in this state guaranteed by the Tennessee Constitution or the United States Constitution or any statute or decision under those constitutions"). For scholarly analysis, see Aaron Fellmeth, *U.S. State Legislation to Limit Use of International and Foreign Law*, 106 AM. J. INT'L L. 107 (2012); Holly Tao, *Congress, Courts, and Control over Persuasive Sources of Law*, 51 GONZ. L. REV. 235 (2015–16).

[57] In the case of Oklahoma's "Save our State Amendment," the law was also found to violate the Establishment Clause. Awad v. Ziriax, 670 F.3d 1111 (10th Cir. 2012) (affirming preliminary injunction); Awad v. Ziriax, 966 F. Supp. 2d 1198 (W.D. Okla. 2013) (entering permanent injunction).

[58] See *infra* this chapter § II(E).

[59] For a brief account of the ordinance and its implementation, as well as similar efforts in other jurisdictions, see Gaylynn Burroughs, *More than an Incidental Effect on Foreign Affairs: Implementation of Human Rights by States and Local Governments*, 30 N.Y.U. REV. L. & SOC. CHANGE 411, 416–18 (2006).

consideration of the treaty.[60] Moreover, it might be said that the "relevant international norms have created a focal point for sub-national participation" in transnational coordination.[61]

Likewise, federal decisions not to pursue, under international law, legally binding targets and timetables regarding greenhouse gases have led to attempts by several states to pursue policies that simulate those objectives. Thus, after the Trump administration announced in 2017 its intention to withdraw from the 2015 Paris Agreement on climate change,[62] the states of California, New York, and Washington established the "United States Climate Alliance," a coalition committed to reducing greenhouse gas emissions consistent with the goals of the Paris Agreement.[63] As of 2022, the coalition consisted of twenty-five governments representing 56 percent of the U.S. population; the alliance estimated that its shared policy would achieve a combined 50 to 52 percent reduction in greenhouse gas emissions below 2005 levels by 2030.[64] This initiative followed similar state efforts undertaken following the U.S. failure to ratify the 1997 Kyoto Protocol,[65] and preceding the 2015 Paris Agreement, but those efforts were supported by the Obama administration.[66]

Stronger forms of noncooperation, however, have been evident in certain areas. In immigration law, for example, localities have established themselves as "sanctuary cities" for undocumented noncitizens,[67] and states have pursued litigation to overturn federal immigration policies affecting Muslims[68] and to prevent the separation of migrant families who crossed illegally at the border.[69]

---

[60] S. Exec. Rep. No. 103-38, at 51 (1994) (proposing understanding that "this Convention shall be implemented by the Federal Government to the extent that it exercises jurisdiction over the matters covered therein, and otherwise by the State and local governments. To the extent that State and local governments exercise jurisdiction over such matters, the Federal Government shall, as necessary take appropriate measures to ensure the fulfillment of this Convention").

[61] Ahdieh, *supra* note 16, at 1208.

[62] Rep. of the Conference of the Parties on its Twenty-First Session, U.N. Doc. FCCC/CP/2015/10/ Add.1, Addendum, at 21 (Jan. 29, 2016).

[63] *See* United States Climate Alliance, https://perma.cc/ZU3P-VTT4.

[64] U.S. Climate Alliance, *Fact Sheet* 1–2 (Jan. 12, 2022), https://perma.cc/3R32-LQB4.

[65] Kyoto Protocol to the United Nations Framework Convention on Climate Change, Dec. 11, 1997, 37 I.L.M. 22, 2303 U.N.T.S. 162.

[66] *See* Galbraith, *supra* note 32, at 2150; *see, e.g.,* Regional Greenhouse Gas Initiative, https://perma.cc/EB2R-B2VT (cooperative effort among the states of Connecticut, Delaware, Maine, Maryland, Massachusetts, New Hampshire, New York, Rhode Island, and Vermont to cap and reduce carbon-based emissions); *see also* David Hodas, *State Law Responses to Global Warming: Is It Constitutional to Think Globally and Act Locally?*, 21 Pace Envtl. L. Rev. 53 (2004); Judith Resnik et al., *Ratifying Kyoto at the Local Level: Sovereigntism, Federalism, and Translocal Organizations of Local Actors (TOGAs)*, 50 Ariz. L. Rev. 709 (2008). For discussion of ongoing climate compacts between U.S. states and Canadian provinces, see *infra* this chapter § III.

[67] *See, e.g.,* Ming H. Chen, *Trust in Immigration Enforcement: State Noncooperation and Sanctuary Cities After Secure Communities*, 91 Chi.-Kent L. Rev. 13 (2016); Glennon & Sloane, *supra* note 16, at 300–06.

[68] Trump v. Hawaii, 138 S. Ct. 2392 (2018).

[69] *See, e.g.,* L. v. U.S. Immig. & Customs Enf't, 310 F. Supp. 3d 1133 (S.D. Cal. 2018) (creating a nationwide class of separated parents and issuing a preliminary injunction requiring the government

States legalizing marijuana have also put the United States at risk of breaching its obligations under international narcotics treaties to which it is a party.[70] After lower-level state and local officials had failed to inform noncitizens of their ability to seek consular assistance, as required under the Vienna Convention on Consular Relations, several state governors rejected presidential entreaties to comply with preliminary orders issued by the International Court of Justice (ICJ), and the Supreme Court upheld their capacity to do so.[71] Eventually, as discussed later, Texas refused to comply with a more formal request by the president to abide by an ICJ judgment, and the Supreme Court also upheld that refusal.[72]

Whether it is deemed cooperative or uncooperative, federalism in foreign relations is shaped by the recourses that are constitutionally available to the federal government. One possible option, requiring that states adopt legislation at the insistence of the federal government, appears foreclosed by the anti-commandeering doctrine; that doctrine has also been extended to preclude the federal government from requiring state and local officials to enforce federal law, and it seems likely that both doctrines operate in the foreign relations sphere.[73] The federal government is also limited in its ability to abrogate state sovereign immunity, and the Supreme Court has implied that this applies equally in the foreign relations context.[74] And members of the

to reunite families); de Nolasco v. U.S. Immig. & Customs Enf't, 319 F. Supp. 3d 491 (D.D.C. 2018) (ordering an injunction to reunite the parents and children of a family separated at the border).

[70] *See* Jonathan Remy Nash, *Doubly Uncooperative Federalism and the Challenge of U.S. Treaty Compliance*, 55 COLUM. J. TRANSNAT'L L. 3, 21–23 (2016).

[71] Breard v. Greene, 523 U.S. 371, 378 (1998) (per curiam) (noting that "[l]ast night the Secretary of State sent a letter to the Governor of Virginia requesting that he stay Breard's execution. If the Governor wishes to wait for the decision of the ICJ, that is his prerogative. But nothing in our existing case law allows us to make that choice for him"); *see* Letter from Madeleine K. Albright, U.S. Sec'y of State, to James S. Gilmore III, Governor of Va. (Apr. 13, 1998), *reprinted in* Jonathan I. Charney & W. Michael Reisman, *Agora:* Breard: *The Facts*, 92 AM. J. INT'L L. 666, 671–72 (1998).

[72] Memorandum of President George W. Bush to the U.S. Attorney General Alberto Gonzales, 44 I.L.M. 950 (2005); Medellín v. Texas, 552 U.S. 491, 525–32 (2008); *see infra* this chapter text accompanying notes 237–250.

[73] *See, respectively*, New York v. United States, 505 U.S. 144, 188 (1992) (holding that "[t]he Federal Government may not compel the States to enact or administer federal regulatory programs"); Printz v. United States, 521 U.S. 898, 935 (1997) (finding that Congress cannot temporarily require state law enforcement officers to regulate handgun purchases as called for by federal law). Translating the anti-commandeering principles to the foreign affairs context is complex, but a number of leading commentators regard them as applicable, including in relation to exercise of the treaty power. *See, e.g.*, Carlos Manuel Vázquez, Breard, Printz, *and the Treaty Power*, 70 U. COLO. L. REV. 1317, 1350–59 (1999); Oona A. Hathaway et al., *The Treaty Power: Its History, Scope, and Limits*, 98 CORNELL L. REV. 239, 272–74 (2013); HENKIN, FOREIGN AFFAIRS, at 467 n.75. For additional discussion, see Swaine, *supra* note 23, at 423–33, 480–87; Chapter 6 § II(D)(2).

[74] Federal Republic of Germany v. United States, 526 U.S. 111, 112 (1999) (per curiam) (stating that a foreign state's capacity to establish a claim in original jurisdiction against a state "is without

Court recently emphasized that the federal government may not condition federal funding in an overly coercive way.[75] The application of each of these doctrines to the foreign relations sphere is unsettled and complicated, but much of the complexity mirrors the challenges of applying the doctrines in wholly domestic contexts. As discussed later, the more conventional means of constraining uncooperative foreign relations–related behavior by states and localities is to argue that the activity is expressly or implicitly preempted by federal law.[76]

The continuing role of the states in U.S. foreign relations may seem surprising, but it is a natural consequence of the fact that the Constitution presumes that the states retain broad, unenumerated authority, and at no point affirmatively excludes the states from engaging in acts implicating foreign affairs. Rather than starting from the position that "in respect of our foreign relations generally . . . the State of New York does not exist,"[77] it would be sounder to start with the general assumption that, unless a foreign relations matter is expressly forbidden to the states, the Constitution allows concurrent exercise of power by the federal and state governments until such time as the former acts to preempt the latter.[78] In other words, while the federal government's power is supreme in this area of the law, it is not exclusive, and it was never intended to be.[79]

evident support in the Vienna Convention and in probable contravention of Eleventh Amendment principles"); *Breard*, 523 U.S. at 377 (describing the Eleventh Amendment as "a separate reason why Paraguay's suit [against Virginia state officials] might not succeed"); RESTATEMENT (FOURTH) § 312 rptrs. note. A number of commentators suggest that it applies to treaties and in the foreign relations context generally, albeit with limitations. *See, e.g.*, HENKIN, FOREIGN AFFAIRS, at 166; Mitchell N. Berman, R. Anthony Reese, & Ernest A. Young, *State Accountability for Violations of Intellectual Property Rights: How to "Fix" Florida Prepaid (and How Not To)*, 79 TEX. L. REV. 1037, 1189; Carlos Manuel Vázquez, *Treaties and the Eleventh Amendment*, 42 VA. J. INT'L L. 713, 741 (2002); Hathaway et al., *supra* note 73, at 269–71. For additional discussion, see Swaine, *supra* note 23, at 433–41, 487–92; Chapter 6 § II(D)(2).

[75] *See, e.g.*, Nat'l Fed. of Indept. Business v. Sebelius, 567 U.S. 519, 580–82 (2012) (opinion of Roberts, C.J.) (finding that a provision withholding all federal Medicaid funding from states that do not adopt Medicaid expansion under the Affordable Care Act was unconstitutionally coercive); *id.* at 625 (Ginsburg, J., concurring in part, concurring in the judgment in part, and dissenting in part) ("The Chief Justice therefore—*for the first time ever*—finds an exercise of Congress' spending power unconstitutionally coercive."); *see* Kathleen M. Sullivan, *Unconstitutional Conditions*, 102 HARV. L. REV. 1413, 1430–32 (1989) (describing federalism-based limits on coercion as "more theoretical than real").

[76] *See infra* this chapter § II.

[77] United States v. Belmont, 301 U.S. 324, 331 (1937); *see supra* this chapter note 15 and accompanying text.

[78] *See* Jack L. Goldsmith, *Federal Courts, Foreign Affairs, and Federalism*, 83 VA. L. REV. 1617, 1642 (1997).

[79] *See, e.g.*, Ramsey, *supra* note 3, at 418.

II. Methods of Preempting State Law

Preemption issues have become especially salient for U.S. foreign relations law over the course of the past century, principally due to two historical trends. First, as is well known, the power of the federal government to regulate matters that traditionally were left to the states has grown tremendously, especially since the New Deal. A key element in this growth has been the expansive interpretation of Congress' power under the Commerce Clause, allowing the federal government to regulate almost any matter on which it chooses to regulate. Recent case law suggests, anew, that such power is not unlimited,[80] and that it has limited capacity to encroach on state sovereignty.[81] Even so the federal government remains robustly engaged in various matters, such as health, education, environment, energy, labor, and transportation, that are prone to conflict with state and local laws.

Second, concomitant with the growth of federal power vis-à-vis the states, international affairs (and international law) has embraced topics for regulation that extend beyond traditional interstate diplomacy and touch on previously domestic affairs. As transnational harms became more apparent, whether from the theft of intellectual property, the expropriation of foreign investment, the loss of endangered species, or pollution of the oceans, so too did attempts by governments worldwide to address those harms by international regulation, principally through multilateral treaties and international organizations. Moreover, the human rights revolution has meant that the regulation by a government (at any level) of its own people became the subject of international law, generating international obligations for the United States regarding, inter alia, racial discrimination, the right to life, religious freedom,

---

[80] *See* United States v. Morrison, 529 U.S. 598 (2000) (holding that Congress lacked the power to adopt a federal civil remedy for gender-motivated crimes); City of Boerne v. Flores, 521 U.S. 507 (1997) (Congress is limited in its ability to restrict a state's freedom to enforce a federal statute on religious freedom); United States v. Lopez, 514 U.S. 549 (1995) (holding that Congress lacked the power to criminalize the "purely intrastate" possession of a gun near a school, since the matter was noneconomic in nature and not part of a larger regulation of economic activity, and since the statute contained no jurisdictional element that would ensure a case-by-case inquiry into whether a particular firearm possession affected interstate commerce). *But see* Gonzales v. Raich, 545 U.S. 1 (2005) (holding that the Commerce Clause gives Congress authority to prohibit the local cultivation and use of marijuana, despite state law to the contrary); *id.* at 22 (noting that the Necessary and Proper Clause permits Congress to regulate some purely intrastate activity in pursuit of interstate commerce).

[81] Seminole Tribe of Fla. v. Florida, 517 U.S. 44 (1996) (holding that Congress lacked the power under the Commerce Clause to abrogate a state's constitutional immunity from suit under the Eleventh Amendment).

and treatment of detainees. This second development meant that as the federal government was becoming a more dominant actor vis-à-vis the states, it was also participating in a foreign relations realm that increasingly embraced regulation of topics that previously were largely local, or at least national, in nature—even while, as previously noted, states and cities became increasingly engaged in global affairs.

One consequence of these developments is that the opportunities for conflict between the federal and state governments became far greater, requiring both sides (including federal courts) to consider where the lines should be drawn. A further consequence is that in drawing such lines, traditional rules of thumb were undermined. As a historical matter, the nationalist perspective drew on the dogma of *United States v. Curtiss-Wright Export Corp.* concerning the federal government's primacy in the field of foreign relations.[82] Yet, over time, the globalization that has brought federal and state governments into greater potential conflict has undermined the case for treating as different and discrete what *Curtiss-Wright* regarded as "external affairs" and "internal affairs." As such, a bald dichotomy that state and local activities conducted within their traditional domain should survive, while those perceived as regulation of foreign policy should be struck down, has become increasingly difficult to sustain.[83] Even so, such dichotomy possesses an enduring attraction and can be observed in the more granular theories of preemption employed in foreign relations matters.

[82] United States v. Curtiss-Wright Export Corp., 299 U.S. 304 (1936); *see* Chapter 1 §§ I(D), II(A) (2). As previously noted, the scope of *Curtiss-Wright* has been substantially qualified—with particular concern for preserving a role for Congress, but with evident import for other actors as well. Zivotofsky v. Kerry (*Zivotofsky II*), 576 U.S. 1, 21 (2015) (describing portions of *Curtiss-Wright* as dicta and stating that "[i]t is not for the President alone to determine the whole content of the Nation's foreign policy"). For further discussion of *Zivotofsky II*, see Chapter 1 §§ I(B), II(A)(2), II(B); Chapter 2 § II(C); and Chapter 3 § I(D).

[83] For example, the claim that immigration matters are solely within the domain of the federal government appears no longer sustainable. *See generally* PRATHEEPAN GULASEKARAM & S. KARTHICK RAMAKRISHNAN, THE NEW IMMIGRATION FEDERALISM (2015); Peter H. Schuck, *Taking Immigration Federalism Seriously*, 2007 U. CHI. LEGAL F. 57; Cristina M. Rodríguez, *The Significance of the Local in Immigration Regulation*, 106 MICH. L. REV. 567 (2008); Juliet P. Stumpf, *States of Confusion: The Rise of State and Local Power over Immigration*, 86 N. CAR. L. REV. 1557 (2008); Jennifer M. Chacón, *Immigration Federalism in the Weeds*, 66 UCLA L. REV. 1330 (2019); Shayak Sarkar, *Financial Immigration Federalism*, 107 GEO. L.J. 1561 (2019). Likewise, matters relating to international trade demonstrably implicate matters of concern to the states. *See, e.g.*, MICHELLE SAGER, ONE VOICE OR MANY? FEDERALISM AND INTERNATIONAL TRADE 94, 104–11 (2002); Charles Tiefer, *Free Trade Agreements and the New Federalism*, 7 MINN. J. GLOB. TRADE 45 (1998). Arguably divining overarching principles in this area from constitutional provisions (or silences) is not helpful, given that the Constitution is probably best understood as representing compromises of various interests. *See* John F. Manning, *Federalism and the Generality Problem in Constitutional Interpretation*, 122 HARV. L. REV. 2003 (2009).

802   THE LAW OF U.S. FOREIGN RELATIONS

A. Preemption by Federal Statute

In accordance with the Supremacy Clause, federal statutes, as "Laws of the United States,"[84] preempt state laws where the two conflict. As implied by the requirement that such statutes be made "in Pursuance of" the Constitution, they must be grounded in a constitutional power accorded to the federal government. This test is often easily met when the statute concerns foreign relations, given the federal government's range of enumerated authorities—such as the Foreign Commerce Clause, the Offenses Clause, or the treaty power, which are all supplemented by the Necessary and Proper Clause—and the occasional identification of implied powers.[85] As always, the federal statute must be able to withstand any limitations imposed on the federal government, such as those appearing in the Bill of Rights and the Fourteenth Amendment.[86]

For example, in the years following the Civil War, at a time when the U.S. military was deployed in several southern states as a part of Reconstruction, the Supreme Court in *Tarble's Case*[87] was confronted with a clash between federal military law and state law, potentially threatening the ability of the army to function. Federal military law allowed for custody over an army enlistee who had allegedly deserted, while Wisconsin law allowed the enlistee's father to obtain a writ of habeas corpus from the Wisconsin courts, based on the father's claim that his son was too young to enlist on his own. The Court attempted to acknowledge that the federal and state government each enjoyed inviolable authority in their respective spheres, even in the same territorial space, "except so far as such intrusion may be necessary on the part of the National government to preserve its rightful supremacy in cases of conflict of authority."[88] To determine whether that supremacy was indeed rightful, the Court nevertheless deemed it necessary to consider the source of the federal government's power and whether the federal law at issue was an exercise of that power.[89] It had little difficulty in identifying Congress' powers "to raise and support armies" and "to make rules for the government and regulation of the land and naval forces,"[90] and held that those powers embraced laws and regulations on "how the armies shall be raised, whether by voluntary enlistment or forced draft, the age at which the soldier shall

---

[84] U.S. CONST. art. VI, cl. 2 ("This Constitution, and the Laws of the United States which shall be made in Pursuance thereof; and all Treaties made, or which shall be made, under the Authority of the United States, shall be the supreme Law of the Land . . . .").

[85] *See generally* Chapter 2 § I.

[86] *See generally* Chapter 10 § II.

[87] 80 U.S. (13 Wall.) 397 (1871).

[88] *Id.* at 407.

[89] *Id.* at 408.

[90] U.S. CONST. art. I, § 8, cls. 12, 14.

be received, and the period for which he shall be taken."[91] As such, Wisconsin law had to give way to federal authority.

Assuming a federal statute is constitutionally sound, modern case law may treat it as preempting state law on any of three different bases—though the Supreme Court has acknowledged that these categories are not "rigidly distinct"[92] and perhaps even that attempts at precision are fruitless.[93] *Express preemption* entails an explicit direction from Congress that the indicated types of state law are displaced. When such a direction exists, the central issue is how far the scope of that direction extends.[94] In the absence of express preemption, *conflict preemption* arises where compliance with both the federal statute and the state law is impossible,[95] or where the state law would frustrate the attainment of federal objectives, bearing in mind the purpose of the federal statute and the extent to which that purpose is impaired by the state law.[96] *Field preemption* arises when a federal statutory scheme is so pervasive as to make reasonable an inference that Congress has preempted the state law within that field.[97] For field preemption, a salient issue is whether the federal interest in the regulated area is dominant (as opposed to being an area traditionally regulated by the states, like education). Historically, subjects like immigration law, and sometimes the entirety of foreign relations, have been treated as among those where the federal interest is dominant and thus field preemption is likely.[98] Yet as foreign relations law has expanded to cover an enormous range of areas, many of which were previously regarded as within the domain of states, field preemption on a purported foreign relations matter at times may be less obvious.

[91] *Tarble's Case*, 80 U.S. (13 Wall.) at 408.

[92] *See* Crosby v. National Foreign Trade Council, 530 U.S. 363, 372 n.6 (2000); *see, e.g.*, Murphy v. Nat'l Collegiate Athletic Ass'n, 138 S. Ct. 1461, 1480 (2018); Arizona v. United States, 567 U.S. 387, 398–400 (2012). *But cf.* Kansas v. Garcia, 140 S. Ct. 791, 801 (2020) (distinguishing between federal statutes that expressly preempt state law, preemption occurring "by virtue of restrictions or rights that are inferred from statutory law," and implied preemption).

[93] *See* Hines v. Davidowitz, 312 U.S. 52, 67 (1941) ("This Court, in considering the validity of state laws in the light of treaties or federal laws touching the same subject, has made use of the following expressions: conflicting; contrary to; occupying the field; repugnance; difference; irreconcilability; inconsistency; violation; curtailment, and interference. But none of these expressions provides an infallible constitutional test or an exclusive constitutional yardstick. In the final analysis, there can be no one crystal clear distinctly marked formula.").

[94] *See* Altria Group, Inc. v. Good, 555 U.S. 70, 76 (2008) ("If a federal law contains an express preemption clause, it does not immediately end the inquiry because the question of the substance and scope of Congress' displacement of state law still remains."); *e.g.*, Riegel v. Medtronic, Inc., 552 U.S. 312 (2008).

[95] *See, e.g.*, Florida Lime & Avocado Growers, Inc. v. Paul, 373 U.S. 132, 142–43 (1963).

[96] *See, e.g.*, *Crosby*, 530 U.S. at 373; *Hines*, 312 U.S. at 67.

[97] *See, e.g.*, United States v. Locke, 529 U.S. 89, 115 (2000); English v. General Elec. Co., 496 U.S. 72, 79 (1990); California v. ARC America Corp., 490 U.S. 93, 100 (1989).

[98] For a brief discussion of the development of federal power in this area, see Chapter 10 § III(A)(1).

The common focus in all three types of preemption concerns congressional purpose.[99] That purpose may be hard to discern and courts may invoke a presumption against preemption.[100] In domestic contexts—at least in cases not involving express preemption[101]—the Court has said that courts should not assume that Congress intended to preempt traditional powers of the states, unless there is a "clear and manifest purpose of Congress" to do so.[102] It has allowed, however, that the presumption against preemption is not as strong in areas where the states have not traditionally legislated, most particularly in areas that are "inherently federal in character."[103]

The Court has been cautious about transposing the presumption against preemption to the foreign relations context,[104] and there is a sound argument that doing so would be inappropriate[105]—if nothing else, as a reflection of the predicate that the presumption is apt for areas traditionally regulated by the states.[106] For example, in *United States v. Locke*,[107] the Supreme Court stated that such a

---

[99] *Altria Group*, 555 U.S. at 76 (citing Medtronic, Inc. v. Lohr, 518 U.S. 470, 485 (1996)).

[100] Invocation of such a presumption is somewhat unpredictable. *See* Arizona v. Inter Tribal Council of Ariz., Inc., 570 U.S. 1, 13 (2013) (noting "the presumption against pre-emption sometimes invoked in our Supremacy Clause cases").

[101] When a statute contains an express preemption clause, courts are likely to treat that as the best guide to congressional intent. *See, e.g.,* Puerto Rico v. Franklin Cal. Tax-Free Trust, 579 U.S. 115, 125 (2016) (citations omitted).

[102] *See, e.g.,* Rice v. Santa Fe Elevator Corp., 331 U.S. 218, 230 (1947) (courts should assume that "the historic police powers of the States" are not superseded "unless that was the clear and manifest purpose of Congress."); *Medtronic, Inc. v. Lohr*, 518 U.S. at 485 (same); Wyeth v. Levine, 555 U.S. 555, 565 (2009) (same); Hillman v. Maretta, 569 U.S. 483, 490 (2013) (same).

[103] Buckman Co. v. Plaintiffs' Legal Comm., 531 U.S. 341, 347 (2001).

[104] *See, e.g.,* Crosby v. National Foreign Trade Council, 530 U. S. 363, 374 n.8 (2000) ("We leave for another day a consideration in this context of a presumption against preemption."); United States v. Locke, 529 U.S. 89, 108 (2000) (indicating that where "state laws . . . bear upon national and international maritime commerce . . . there is no beginning assumption that concurrent regulation by the State is a valid exercise of its police powers."). *But cf.* Bond v. United States, 572 U.S. 844, 858 (2014) (noting the presumption against preemption, and invoking the "[c]losely related" but distinct "well-established principle that 'it is incumbent upon the federal courts to be certain of Congress' intent before finding that federal law overrides' the 'usual constitutional balance of federal and state powers'") (citations omitted).

[105] *See, e.g.,* Abebe & Huq, *supra* note 16 (arguing that the presumption should depend on the circumstances of the case); *see also* Jack Goldsmith, *Statutory Foreign Affairs Preemption*, 2000 SUP. CT. REV. 175, 200 (concluding that "courts should perform preemption analysis without recourse to the presumptive canons"); Harold G. Maier, *Preemption of State Law: A Recommended Analysis*, 83 AM. J. INT'L L. 832 (1989).

[106] Hines v. Davidowitz, 312 U.S. 52, 67–68 (1941) (stressing, for purposes of conflict analysis, that "this legislation is in a field which affects international relations, the one aspect of our government that from the first has been most generally conceded imperatively to demand broad national authority."). *Compare, e.g.,* Hillman v. Maretta, 569 U.S. 483, 490 (2013) (suggesting that because regulating domestic relations was traditionally a state-law domain, "[t]here is therefore a 'presumption against pre-emption' of state laws governing domestic relations") (citations omitted), *with Wyeth*, 555 U.S. at 565 ("'In all pre-emption cases, and *particularly* in those in which Congress has 'legislated . . . in a field which the States have traditionally occupied,' . . . we 'start with the assumption that the *historic police powers* of the States were not to be superseded by the Federal Act unless that was the clear and manifest purpose of Congress.'") (emphases added) (citations omitted).

[107] 529 U.S. 89 (2000).

presumption was inappropriate in the context of state law restrictions affecting international maritime commerce. An association of tanker owners had challenged a state of Washington regulatory regime aimed at preventing, and providing remedies for, oil spills by oceangoing oil tankers. The Court found that the federal government's overall regulatory regime occupied the field, clearly invalidating various regulations of the state of Washington; in doing so, it held that any "assumption" of concurrent regulatory authority was inapposite, given that the area involved "national and international maritime commerce," in which "Congress has legislated in the field from the earliest days of the Republic."[108]

Immigration law has presented numerous cases involving preemption.[109] In *Hines v. Davidowitz*,[110] the Court considered a Pennsylvania statute passed in 1939 that required noncitizens to register each year with the state and to carry a registration card that had to be shown to police when requested; failure to comply risked criminal penalties. In 1940, Congress enacted the Federal Alien Registration Act, which provided for federal registration, but with no requirement that noncitizens carry a registration card.[111] The Supreme Court passed over the question of whether federal power in this field was exclusive, focusing instead on "the supremacy of the national power in the general field of foreign affairs, including power over immigration, naturalization and deportation,"[112] the sensitivity for foreign relations of the protection of noncitizens in the United States,[113] the existence of treaties that reciprocally called for such protection,[114] efforts throughout U.S. history to resist laws that "singl[e] out aliens as particularly dangerous and undesirable groups,"[115] and the fact that Congress had now adopted a noncitizen registration statute.[116] Among other things, the Court explained, field preemption in international affairs was in the interests of states too, given that one "of the most important and delicate of all international relationships . . . has to do with the protection of the just rights of a country's own

[108] *Id.* at 108 (indicating that where "state laws . . . bear upon national and international maritime commerce . . . there is no beginning assumption that concurrent regulation by the State is a valid exercise of its police powers").

[109] For discussion, see authorities cited *supra* note 83.

[110] 312 U.S. 52 (1941).

[111] Current federal law requires both registration and the carrying of proof of status. *See* 8 U.S.C. §§ 1301–06 (2018).

[112] Hines v. Davidowitz, 312 U.S. 52, 63 (1941). When confronted with such cases, the Court typically grounds federal power in this area on Congress' power to "establish a uniform Rule of Naturalization," U.S. Const. art. I, § 8, cl. 4, and the federal government's inherent power as sovereign to control and conduct relations with foreign nations. United States v. Curtiss-Wright Export Corp., 299 U. S. 304, 318 (1936). *See generally* Chapter 10 § III(A).

[113] *Hines,* 312 U.S. at 64; *see* Chy Lung v. Freeman, 92 U.S. 275–80 (1876) (emphasizing the need for foreign states to communicate with one national sovereign regarding the treatment of noncitizens in the United States).

[114] *Hines,* 312 U.S. at 69.

[115] *Id.* at 70

[116] *Id.*

nationals when those nationals are in another country," and "that international controversies of the gravest moment, sometimes even leading to war, may arise from real or imagined wrongs to another's subjects inflicted, or permitted, by a government."[117]

While stressing the importance of federal supremacy in the field of immigration, *Hines* left open whether states could enact statutes that regulated noncitizens other than through registration. In *Toll v. Moreno*,[118] the Court considered the preferential treatment accorded by the state-operated University of Maryland for purposes of tuition and fees to students with "in-state" status. Maryland allowed lawful permanent residents to obtain in-state status, but denied it to nonimmigrant noncitizens. The question presented was whether such status could be denied to noncitizens whom Congress had allowed to be domiciled in Maryland and elsewhere—more particularly, noncitizen officers or employees of certain international organizations and members of their immediate families holding a special G-4 visa.[119] The Court struck down the state law as applied, maintaining that Maryland's decision to deny in-state status to such noncitizens, solely on account of their federal nonimmigration status, amounted to an ancillary burden not contemplated by Congress when admitting them to the United States.[120]

In recent years, some states have adopted laws that seek to discourage undocumented noncitizens from traveling to and working in their jurisdictions. A pair of cases arising out of Arizona are illustrative. In *Chamber of Commerce v. Whiting*,[121] business and civil rights organizations challenged an Arizona statute that provided for the suspension or revocation of licenses of state employers who knowingly or intentionally employ undocumented noncitizens, potentially in tension with the federal Immigration Reform and Control Act (IRCA), which regulated the employment of noncitizens.[122] While federal law made it unlawful for employers to hire noncitizens known to be undocumented,[123] it only expressly preempted "any State or local law imposing civil or

---

[117] *Id.* at 63–65 (emphasis added).

[118] 458 U.S. 1, 10 (1982).

[119] Under U.S. immigration law, persons admitted temporarily to the United States with nonimmigrant status normally have difficulty becoming permanent residents and then citizens. By allowing nonimmigrant noncitizens with G-4 visas to obtain domicile, Congress determined that it was not a violation of U.S. law for such noncitizens to develop a subjective intent to stay in the United States indefinitely. Moreover, although a G-4 visa lapses on termination of employment with an international organization, a G-4 noncitizen does not necessarily have to leave the United States. Absent an adverse factor (*e.g.*, commission of a crime), such noncitizens who have been present in the United States for several years usually can have their status adjusted to permanent resident without difficulty.

[120] *Toll*, 458 U.S. at 9–10.

[121] 563 U.S. 582 (2011).

[122] Immigration Reform and Control Act (IRCA), Pub. L. No. 99-603, 100 Stat. 3359 (1986) (codified at 8 U.S.C. § 1324a (2018)); *see also* Illegal Immigration Reform and Immigrant Responsibility Act (IIRIRA), 110 Stat. 3009-546 (note following 8 U.S.C. § 1324a).

[123] 8 U.S.C. § 1324a(a)(1)(A).

criminal sanctions (*other than through licensing and similar laws*) upon those who employ, or recruit or refer for a fee for employment, unauthorized aliens."[124] A majority of the Court held that Arizona's licensing provision fell within the "other than" exemption to the preemption provision.[125] A plurality also held that the law was not implicitly preempted, given that it appeared that Congress had preserved for the states the authority to impose sanctions upon employers of undocumented noncitizens by means of licensing laws—illustrating how the limitations to an express preemption provision may create something like a safe harbor for state law, even in a largely nationalized area.[126] As to whether Arizona's statute had upset the balance struck by IRCA, the plurality deemed that concern apposite only to "uniquely federal areas of regulation," whereas the statute in question was addressing licensing of in-state businesses (rather than immigration); it also distinguished prior cases of preemption as involving direct interference by the state with the federal program.[127]

In *Arizona v. United States*,[128] the Court addressed four statutory provisions enacted by Arizona, which (as the Court acknowledged) had a significant interest in immigration policy, given that by one estimate undocumented noncitizens constituted six percent of Arizona's population.[129] The Court found three of those provisions preempted: (1) one that made it a crime for a noncitizen to fail to complete or carry a registration document, given that Congress (like in *Hines*) already had established a framework for such registration;[130] (2) another making it a crime for an undocumented noncitizen to seek or perform work in Arizona, given that Congress had imposed criminal penalties on employers of such noncitizens, but not on the noncitizens themselves, such that the state law would interfere with the balance struck by Congress on this issue;[131] and (3) one that allowed Arizona officers to arrest, without a warrant, a person who an officer had probable cause to believe had committed an offense making him removable from the United States, given that the provision usurped the discretion of the federal government with respect to removal.[132] In contrast, the Court upheld,

---

[124] *Id.* § 1324a(h)(2) (emphasis added).

[125] *Whiting*, 563 U.S. at 594–600.

[126] *Id.* at 600–01 (Roberts, C.J., plurality).

[127] *Id.* at 603–04 (Roberts, C.J., plurality). The Court also upheld the Arizona law's requirement that employers verify employment eligibility through a federally created verification scheme (E-Verify), finding that it was not impliedly preempted. *Id.* at 607–10 (majority opinion).

[128] 567 U.S. 387 (2012). For commentary, see Lucas Guttentag, *Immigration Preemption and the Limits of State Power: Reflections on* Arizona v. United States, 9 STAN. J. CIV. RTS. & CIV. LIBERTIES 1 (2013); Catherine Y. Kim, *Immigration Separation of Powers and the President's Power to Preempt*, 90 NOTRE DAME L. REV. 691 (2014).

[129] *Arizona*, 567 U.S. at 397.

[130] *Id.* at 400–03 (§ 3 of the Arizona law).

[131] *Id.* at 403–07 (§ 5(C)).

[132] *Id.* at 407–10 (§ 6).

against a facial challenge, a provision that required Arizona officers to make a reasonable attempt to determine the immigration status of persons stopped, detained, or arrested on some legitimate purpose, if there was reasonable suspicion that the person was an undocumented noncitizen, and requiring the officers to check with federal authorities regarding an arrestee's immigration status prior to their release.[133] Such mere communication with federal authorities during otherwise lawful police activity was not preempted, but the Court indicated that such a provision might be found unconstitutional as applied.[134]

The Court's overall approach means that immigration law is not off limits to the states; much depends on the nature of the state law, both on its face and as applied. Lower courts have found preempted various state laws relating to immigration where, for example, they took what were previously only federal crimes, subject to federal enforcement and prosecution, and made them also state crimes subject to state enforcement and prosecution;[135] effectively expelled undocumented noncitizens from the state, such as by prohibiting them from entering into contracts;[136] criminalized the "harboring" of undocumented noncitizens, such as by renting them housing;[137] required public schools to collect documents on immigration status;[138] or prohibited employment of undocumented noncitizens.[139] At the same time, the lower courts have upheld less stringent laws, such as a prohibition on undocumented noncitizens entering into specific public records transactions;[140] a city ordinance requiring prospective tenants to obtain occupancy licenses identifying their citizenship and immigration status;[141] a law instructing police officers as to what forms of identification (or what affirmations) constitute acceptable verification of immigration status;[142] or authorizing an officer to transport a lawfully detained undocumented noncitizen to an in-state federal facility.[143]

---

[133] Id. at 411–15 (§ 2(B)).

[134] The Court emphasized state provisions that protected individual rights, including a requirement that the check must be implemented in a manner consistent with federal law. Id. at 411.

[135] United States v. South Carolina, 840 F. Supp. 2d 898, 915–19 (D.S.C. 2011); see also United States v. South Carolina, 906 F. Supp. 2d 463, 467–68 (D.S.C. 2012) (reaffirming preliminary injunction in material respects).

[136] United States v. Alabama, 691 F.3d 1269, 1292–97 (11th Cir. 2012).

[137] Id. at 1285–88; United States v. South Carolina, 840 F. Supp. 2d at 919–20; see also United States v. South Carolina, 906 F. Supp. 2d at 468–69 (reaffirming preliminary injunction in material respects).

[138] United States v. Alabama, 691 F.3d at 1297.

[139] Lozano v. City of Hazleton, 724 F.3d 297 (3d Cir. 2013); see Mary D. Fan, Rebellious State Crimmigration Enforcement and the Foreign Affairs Power, 89 WASH. U. L. REV. 1269 (2012) (describing state laws that seek to incorporate federal standards relating to criminalization of immigration, but that diverge from federal enforcement policy).

[140] United States v. Alabama, 691 F.3d at 1297–1301.

[141] Keller v. City of Fremont, 719 F.3d 931 (2013).

[142] Utah Coalition of La Raza v. Herbert, 26 F. Supp. 3d 1125, 1138–40 (D.C. Utah 2014).

[143] Id. at 1140–42

Statutory preemption has also been a prominent, and to a degree unexpected, issue with regard to sanctions affecting foreign states. *Crosby v. National Foreign Trade Council* considered a Massachusetts statute, adopted in June 1996, that restricted the authority of its government agencies to purchase goods or services from companies doing business with Myanmar (Burma).[144] In September 1996, Congress adopted a statute imposing a set of mandatory sanctions on Myanmar, as well as conditional sanctions that the president could impose or lift as part of a strategy, in coordination with foreign states, to encourage democracy and improvements in human rights in Myanmar.[145] President Clinton thereafter imposed conditional sanctions as authorized by the federal statute.[146] A nonprofit trade organization sued Massachusetts, asserting that its statute was preempted by federal law. Lower courts granted declaratory and injunctive relief on a variety of bases, including the dormant foreign affairs power and the dormant Foreign Commerce Clause, methods of preemption discussed further later.[147]

The Supreme Court affirmed on statutory preemption grounds, but its reasoning suggested the affinity among these methods. The Massachusetts statute was not expressly preempted by the federal statute, although members of Congress were likely aware of it when they took action. Moreover, the federal statute neither addressed state government procurement activities nor private trade in goods and services (though it did address U.S. investment in Myanmar). Nevertheless, the Court held that the state's statute served "as an obstacle to the accomplishment of Congress' full objectives under the federal Act."[148] Specifically, the Court concluded "that the state law undermine[d] the intended purpose and 'natural effect'" of several provisions of the federal statute: (1) "its delegation of effective discretion to the President to control economic sanctions against" Myanmar, imposing or lifting them as deemed necessary; (2) "its limitation of sanctions solely to United States persons and new investment" in Myanmar, as opposed to all persons and other forms of business activity; and (3) "its directive to the President to proceed diplomatically in developing a comprehensive, multilateral strategy" toward Myanmar.[149]

An important element in the Court's reasoning was the need to prevent state interference in federal foreign policy when the United States negotiates

---

[144] 530 U.S. 363 (2000).

[145] *See* Foreign Operations, Export Financing, and Related Programs Appropriations Act, 1997, Pub. L. No. 104-208 § 570, 110 Stat. 3009-166-167 (enacted by the Omnibus Consolidated Appropriations Act, 1997, § 101(c), 110 Stat. 3009-121-172).

[146] Exec. Order No. 13047, 3 C.F.R. § 202 (1998), *reprinted in* 50 U.S.C. § 1701 (2018).

[147] *See* Nat'l Foreign Trade Council v. Natsios, 181 F.3d 38, 45, 53 (1st Cir. 1999), *aff'd sub nom.* Crosby v. Nat'l Foreign Trade Council, 530 U.S. 363 (2000).

[148] *Crosby*, 530 U.S. at 373.

[149] *Id.* at 373-74.

with foreign states, both Myanmar itself and other foreign states who also were seeking to influence Myanmar. Among other things, the Court said that the state law intruded upon the president's ability "to speak for the Nation with one voice in dealing with other governments."[150] As such, the Court's reasoning seemed to extend beyond conventional statutory preemption to a broader, protective approach to federal foreign policy, one that leans heavily on a "one voice" doctrine,[151] constituting an "extra-statutory solicitude for formal diplomatic interaction with foreign powers, and for the President's presumptively exclusive ability to engage in it."[152] The implications are unclear, in that most state-level sanctions on foreign countries—whether or not a federal statute exists—have the potential to interfere with federal efforts to negotiate toward a particular political solution for human rights or other concerns with that state.[153]

At least in areas that routinely present the potential for conflict, Congress could clarify matters by pursuing a more systematic scheme for statutory preemption. To that end, various proposals have been advanced, such as for general and absolute statutory bans on state laws in certain areas (for example, on all state laws that facially distinguish between citizens and noncitizens, or that discriminate based on foreign law), or for constructing a method for clearance with the Department of State prior to adopting a state measure (similar to the preclearance regime under the Voting Rights Act).[154] Adoption of such general bans, however, may well have a complementary but unintended effect of blessing all state laws falling outside their scope. Moreover, the likelihood of Congress pursuing any such scheme, and the enthusiasm of the Department of State about assuming a supervisory and politically fraught role, would appear low.

The question of treaty-based preemption, meaning preemption based directly on a treaty itself, is considered in the following section; it is worth noting, however, that the courts have not devised a meaningfully distinct approach to preemption by purely domestic statutes as compared to preemption by statutes that implement treaty obligations.[155] In *United States v. Locke*, for example, the Court did not find it necessary to decide whether international treaties and instruments had a direct preemptive effect on the state regulatory scheme. The Court noted simply that "[t]he existence of the treaties and agreements on standards of

---

[150] *Id.* at 381.

[151] Cleveland, *supra* note 16, at 976 (arguing that the "one voice" doctrine is poorly grounded and the Court's use of it in a statutory preemption analysis "contravened the federal government's long-standing deference to the states in this area").

[152] Edward T. Swaine, Crosby *as Foreign Relations Law*, 41 Va. J. Int'l L. 481, 502 (2001).

[153] *See* Carlos Manuel Vázquez, W(h)ither *Zschernig?*, 46 Vill. L. Rev. 1259, 1287–1304 (2001) (arguing that the Court's approach in *Crosby* would have led to preemption even in the absence of a federal statute).

[154] *See* Ryan Baasch & Saikrishna Bangalore Prakash, *Congress and the Reconstruction of Foreign Affairs Federalism*, 115 Mich. L. Rev. 47, 95–106 (2016).

[155] *See generally* Chapter 6 § IV(B) (discussing mechanisms for implementing treaties).

shipping is of relevance, of course, for these agreements give force to the long-standing rule that the enactment of a uniform federal scheme displaces state law, and the treaties indicate Congress will have demanded national uniformity regarding maritime commerce."[156]

The issue was indirectly presented in *Bond v. United States*, which required that the Court assess the scope of a statute implementing the Chemical Weapons Convention.[157] The Court invoked the "well-established principle" that it is "incumbent upon the federal courts to be certain of Congress' intent before finding that federal law overrides" the "usual constitutional balance of federal and state powers."[158] *Bond* did not directly involve preemption, but rather concerned whether federal law afforded a basis for prosecution. Still, the Court's reasoning arguably favors distinguishing preemption by a statute from preemption by a treaty, given both the Court's emphasis on Carol Anne Bond being prosecuted under the statute, and the Court's view that "the statute—unlike the Convention—must be read consistent with principles of federalism inherent in our constitutional structure."[159]

Yet regarding treaty-implementing statutes as ordinary instances of statutory preemption would be fundamentally erroneous. In *Bond*, a central point of contention concerned whether the statute in question was sufficiently ambiguous to merit applying a federalism-favoring clear statement rule.[160] But the more basic issue was whether the Court was right to suppose that Congress thought about state authority in this context in the same way as it does for statutes that do not implement treaties. Unlike with a purely domestic statute, the United States and its federal system are rarely primary drivers in a treaty's drafting. Of course, in many circumstances, the president and the Senate will accommodate federalism in their approach to negotiating and ratifying a treaty.[161] (For congressional-executive agreements, which are approved more like statutes, Congress often does so as well.[162]) But at least where the United States becomes a party to a treaty

---

[156] United States v. Locke, 529 U.S. 89, 103 (2000).

[157] Bond v. United States, 572 U.S. 844 (2014); *see* Convention on the Prohibition of the Development, Production, Stockpiling and Use of Chemical Weapons and on their Destruction, Sept. 3, 1992, S. TREATY DOC. NO. 103-21, 1975 U.N.T.S. 45 [hereinafter Chemical Weapons Convention]; Chemical Weapons Convention Implementation Act, Pub. L. No. 105-277; 112 Stat. 2681 (codified as amended in scattered sections of the U.S. Code). As explored in Chapter 6, the Court might instead have assessed the constitutionality of the convention or the implementing statute—as some justices urged—but proceeded instead on statutory grounds. *See* Chapter 6 § II(D)(1).

[158] *Bond*, 572 U.S. at 858 (quoting Gregory v. Ashcroft, 501 U.S. 452, 460 (1991)).

[159] *Id.* at 856; *see* Michael J. Glennon & Robert D. Sloane, *The Sad, Quiet Death of Missouri v. Holland: How* Bond *Hobbled the Treaty Power*, 41 YALE J. INT'L L. 51 (2016); GLENNON & SLOANE, *supra* note 16, at 205–20 (arguing that *Bond* is best interpreted as based on a premise that treaty-implementing statutes must conform with principles of federalism).

[160] *Compare Bond*, 572 U.S. at 860 n.2, 865–66, *with id.* at 868–72 (Scalia, J., concurring in the judgment).

[161] *See supra* this chapter § I.

[162] *See infra* this chapter notes 202–209 and accompanying text.

without a reservation, understanding, or declaration concerning federalism, *and* the implementing statute essentially transcribes the treaty's text,[163] there is no serious basis for assuming that Congress has considered and eschewed the full reach of federal law or, for that matter, preemption. Instead, the fairest assumption is that Congress has decided to implement the treaty as federal law, and that any preemptive effects follow irrespective of the presumption used for purely domestic statutes.[164]

B. Preemption by Treaty

As a deliberate corrective to the Articles of Confederation, treaties also preempt state laws where the two conflict.[165] In keeping with the Supremacy Clause, the treaty must have been ratified or acceded to in accordance with the requirements of the Constitution, and to the extent that there are any limits to the scope of the treaty power, the treaty must fall within that scope.[166] In order to be directly enforceable by U.S. courts, however, the treaty must be "self-executing"; it must be of a nature that it does not require an implementing statute in order to be enforced.[167]

An early example of preemption of state law by treaty, as noted in Chapter 6, arose in *Ware v. Hylton*, which considered the effect of the 1783 Treaty of Paris with Great Britain in relation to Virginia state law.[168] The treaty ended the American Revolution but provided certain protections to nationals of Britain, notably that British creditors would "meet with no lawful Impediment to the

---

[163] *Bond*, 572 U.S. at 851 (acknowledging that "[t]he Act closely tracks the text of the treaty").

[164] *See generally* Edward T. Swaine, *Bond's Breaches*, 90 NOTRE DAME L. REV. 1517, 1520–22 (2015).

[165] *See* Chapter 6 § I. Indeed, securing state compliance with U.S. obligations under treaties was a key problem under the Articles of Confederation. *See* THE FEDERALIST No. 22, at 147 (Alexander Hamilton) (asserting that treaties under the Articles "are liable to the infractions of thirteen different legislatures, and as many different courts of final jurisdiction, acting under the authority of those legislatures"); THE FEDERALIST No. 42, at 261 (James Madison) (asserting that treaties under the Articles "might be substantially frustrated by regulations of the States"); *see also* Carlos Manuel Vázquez, *Treaty-Based Rights and Remedies of Individuals*, 92 COLUM. L. REV. 1082, 1101–04 (1992); David M. Golove & Daniel J. Hulsebosch, *"The Known Opinion of the Impartial World": Foreign Relations and the Law of Nations*, *in* THE CAMBRIDGE COMPANION TO THE FEDERALIST 115 (Jack N. Rakove & Colleen A. Sheehan eds., 2020).

[166] *See* U.S. CONST. art. VI, cl. 2 (referring to "all Treaties made, or which shall be made, under the Authority of the United States" as "the supreme Law of the Land"); Chapter 6 § II.

[167] *See* RESTATEMENT (FOURTH) § 308 ("Treaties are supreme over State and local law, and when there is a conflict between State or local law and a self-executing treaty provision, courts in the United States will apply the treaty provisions."); RESTATEMENT (THIRD) §§ 111, 115(2); GLENNON & SLOANE, *supra* note 16, at 185–245, 307–09; *see also* Chapter 6 § IV.

[168] Ware v. Hylton, 3 U.S. (3 Dall.) 199 (1796); *see* Chapter 6 §§ IV(A)(1), IV(C)(4).

Recovery" of their debts.[169] When a British creditor sued in federal court to recover on a debt owed by a Virginia debtor, the question arose as to whether the treaty was enforceable notwithstanding a 1777 Virginia state law providing for state confiscation of debts owed to alien enemies (such that Virginian debtors paid their debts to the state rather than to their British creditors). Four of the five justices of the Supreme Court filed opinions, collectively finding that treaties take precedence over conflicting state laws, and hence the Virginia law was invalid. Justice Samuel Chase noted: "It is the declared will of the people of the United States that every treaty made, by the authority of the United States, shall be superior to the Constitution and laws of any individual State; and their will alone is to decide."[170] *Ware v. Hylton* was the first case to establish federal judicial review of state laws, and preceded by seven years the recognition in *Marbury v. Madison* of federal judicial review of federal law.[171]

A long line of Supreme Court cases thereafter reaffirmed the preemptive effects of a treaty on a state law, often on the basis that there was a direct conflict between the two that makes it impossible to comply with both. Unsurprisingly, many of these conflicts arose in areas of traditional state concern, like trusts and estates, business licensing, and torts. In *Chirac v. Chirac's Lessee*,[172] a U.S.-France treaty that enabled French nationals to hold and inherit lands in the United States within any requirement of naturalization, was held to have preempted a contrary Maryland statute. Similarly, in *Hauenstein v. Lynham*,[173] a U.S.-Switzerland treaty preempted Virginia common law that precluded noncitizens from inheriting immovable property by descent, while in *De Geofroy v. Riggs*,[174] a U.S.-France treaty preempted District of Columbia common law on land inheritance. In *Asakura v. City of Seattle*,[175] a U.S.-Japan treaty of commerce and friendship

---

[169] Definitive Treaty of Peace, art. IV, Sept. 3, 1783, Gr. Brit.–U.S., 8 Stat. 80, *reprinted in* 2 TREATIES AND OTHER INTERNATIONAL ACTS OF THE UNITED STATES OF AMERICA 151 (Hunter Miller ed., 1931).

[170] *Ware*, 3 U.S. at 237. For similar outcomes in respect to the Treaty of Paris, see Fairfax's Devisee v. Hunter's Lessee, 11 U.S. (7 Cranch) 603, 627–28 (1813); Higginson v. Mein, 8 U.S. (4 Cranch) 415, 419 (1807); Hopkirk v. Bell, 7 U.S. (3 Cranch) 454, 458 (1806).

[171] 5 U.S. (1 Cranch) 137 (1803).

[172] 15 U.S. (2 Wheat.) 259, 270–78 (1817). *But see* Todok v. Union State Bank of Harvard, 281 U.S. 449 (1930) (a U.S.-Norway treaty providing that foreign nationals in the respective states "may freely dispose of their goods and effects either by testament, donation or otherwise, in favour of such persons as they think proper" did not preempt a Nebraska law providing for certain restrictions on the conveyance of homestead property, which applied to citizens and noncitizens alike. Treaty with Sweden and Norway, Nor.-U.S., art. VI, July 4, 1827, 8 Stat. 346, 354.).

[173] 100 U.S. 483 (1879).

[174] 133 U.S. 258 (1890).

[175] 265 U.S. 332 (1924); *see* Jordan v. Tashiro, 278 U.S. 123, 127 (1928) (same treaty preempting a California statute precluding incorporation of a hospital by Japanese nationals). *But see* Ohio *ex rel.* Clarke v. Deckebach, 274 U.S. 392, 395–96 (1927) (finding that a U.S.-U.K. treaty reciprocally protecting merchants did not conflict with a Cincinnati ordinance that denied licenses for pool rooms to noncitizens).

preempted a Seattle ordinance that excluded noncitizens from engaging in business as pawnbrokers. In *Kolovrat v. Oregon*,[176] an 1881 U.S.-Serbia treaty, the 1945 Bretton Woods Agreement, and a 1948 U.S.-Yugoslavia treaty preempted an Oregon probate statute that precluded a national of communist Yugoslavia from collecting an inheritance in Oregon. In *El Al Israel Airlines v. Tseng*,[177] the multilateral Warsaw Convention[178] that establishes the circumstances in which there may be recovery for personal injury suffered on board an aircraft or in the course of any of the operations of embarking or disembarking, preempted New York tort law.[179]

Generally speaking, the judiciary's approach to resolving treaty-based conflicts has shown less concern about accommodating state powers. As with other forms of preemption, a conflict is resolved in favor of the treaty irrespective of whether it was adhered to before or after the state law was enacted (and thus irrespective of whether the treaty-makers could have acted in contemplation of the state law in question); it also immaterial whether the state law is in the form of a state constitution, statute, administrative order, or court judgment.[180]

More distinctly, any presumption against preemption in the treaty context is more difficult to support.[181] At least episodically, courts have invoked a principle that, to the extent that the state law is restricting rights that might be available under an ambiguous treaty provision, the more protective interpretation is favored,[182] which seems to mitigate such a preemption.[183] In addition, as the Court has noted, applying such a presumption in the context of a treaty poses distinct risks, given the enhanced potential for treaty violations and the ensuing

---

[176] 366 U.S. 187 (1961).

[177] 525 U.S. 155 (1999).

[178] *See* Convention for the Unification of Certain Rules Relating to International Carriage by Air, Oct. 12, 1929, art. 17, 49 Stat. 3000, 3018, T. S. No. 876 (1934) (*reprinted at* note following 49 U.S.C. § 40105 (2018)), as amended by the Montreal Protocol No. 4, Sept. 8, 1955, *reprinted in* S. EXEC. REP. No. 105-20, at 21–32 (1998).

[179] For additional cases, including examples from lower federal and state courts, see RESTATEMENT (FOURTH) § 308 rptrs. note 1.

[180] RESTATEMENT (FOURTH) § 308 cmt. b.

[181] RESTATEMENT (FOURTH) § 308 rptrs. note 2 (concluding that "[t]he case law does not clearly support any presumption regarding preemption of State law by a treaty"). *Compare, e.g.*, David H. Moore, *Treaties and the Presumption Against Preemption*, 2015 B.Y.U. L. REV. 1555, 1555 (urging greater favor toward a "presumption against preemption in the treaty context"), *with* Michael P. Van Alstine, *Federal Common Law in an Age of Treaties*, 89 CORNELL L. REV. 892, 899 (2004) (stressing that the "the federal government's exclusive authority over the creation of international obligations of the United States . . . substantially undermines the traditional presumption against preemption of state law in the treaty context"), *and* Carlos Manuel Vázquez, *Laughing at Treaties*, 99 COLUM. L. REV. 2154, 2177 (1999) (suggesting presumption of judicial enforceability).

[182] *See, e.g.*, Jordan v. Tashiro, 278 U.S. 123, 127 (1928) ("[W]here a treaty fairly admits of two constructions, one restricting the rights that may be claimed under it and the other enlarging them, the more liberal construction is to be preferred.").

[183] *See, e.g.*, Nielsen v. Johnson, 279 U.S. 47, 52 (1929) (asserting that liberal construction of treaties means that their interpretation "is not restricted by any necessity of avoiding possible conflict with state legislation and when so ascertained must prevail over inconsistent state enactments").

complications for the international relations of the United States.[184] Even so, the Supreme Court has sometimes suggested, without much explanation, that something like the standard presumption against preemption operates even in the treaty context.[185] In resolving this basic tension—between whether a treaty will be broadly construed so as to ensure that its purposes will be achieved, or more narrowly construed, so as not to transgress the traditional prerogatives of the states—more explicit attention might be paid by the courts to the process-related protections afforded by requiring the advice and consent of two-thirds of the Senate, which was designed to protect the interests of the states (and often, in point of fact, does).[186]

As explored in Chapter 6, the doctrine of non-self-executing treaties means that a treaty may impose an international obligation upon the United States without being enforceable, as such, in U.S. courts.[187] That chapter and others have also explored the Supreme Court's decision in *Medellín v. Texas*;[188] for present purposes, it illustrates one way treaties might have effects that preempt state law.[189] The issue in that case was not whether a treaty itself preempted state law, but rather whether one or more treaties had the effect of making a judgment of the ICJ against the United States directly enforceable as domestic law in Texas state courts notwithstanding state law. Mexico had pursued a case at the ICJ in which it claimed that the United States had violated its obligations under the Vienna Convention on Consular Relations (VCCR) in relation to more than fifty Mexican nationals on death row in the United States, and that the ICJ had jurisdiction over those claims under a VCCR optional protocol.[190] The ICJ found that it had jurisdiction and, further, that the United States had violated the VCCR by

---

[184] *See, e.g.*, El Al Isr. Airlines, Ltd. v. Tseng, 525 U.S. 155, 175 (1999) (finding that the standard "home-centered" analysis with its presumption against preemption "should not be applied, mechanically, in construing our international obligations"); *see* RESTATEMENT (FOURTH) § 308 rptrs. note 2 (noting concerns regarding enhanced risk of noncompliance and political process protections). *But see El Al Isr. Airlines, Ltd.*, 525 U.S. at 177 (Stevens, J., dissenting) (criticizing "novel premise that preemption analysis should be applied differently to treaties than to other kinds of federal law"); *id.* at 181 (proposing clear intent standard for treaty preemption).

[185] *See, e.g.*, United States v. Pink, 315 U.S. 203, 230 (1942) ("[E]ven treaties . . . will be carefully construed so as not to derogate from the authority and jurisdiction of the States of this Nation unless clearly necessary to effectuate the national policy."); Guaranty Trust Co. v. United States, 304 U.S. 126, 143 (1938) ("Even the language of a treaty wherever reasonably possible will be construed so as not to override state laws or to impair rights arising under them.").

[186] RESTATEMENT (FOURTH) § 308 rptrs. note 2; for further discussion of applying the presumption against preemption, see Chapter 6 § IV(C)(4).

[187] *See* Chapter 6 § IV(A).

[188] 552 U.S. 491 (2008).

[189] For discussions of *Medellín*, see *infra* this chapter § II(C); Chapter 1 § II(B); Chapter 3 § I(D); Chapter 5 § II(B); Chapter 6 §§ III(B)(3), IV(A); and Chapter 7 § III(C).

[190] Avena and Other Mexican Nationals (Mex. v. U.S.), 2004 I.C.J. 12; *see* Vienna Convention on Consular Relations, Apr. 24, 1963, 21 U.S.T. 77, 596 U.N.T.S. 261; Optional Protocol to the Vienna Convention on Consular Relations Concerning the Compulsory Settlement of Disputes, Apr. 24, 1963, 21 U.S.T. 325, 596 U.N.T.S. 487.

failing to provide required notice to Mexican nationals and Mexican officials that would have facilitated consular and legal representation of those detained and later tried and convicted.[191] As a remedy for the violations, the ICJ ordered that the United States "provide, by means of its own choosing, review and reconsideration of the convictions and sentences of the Mexican nationals."[192]

One of the detainees (José Ernesto Medellín) then filed a habeas petition challenging his Texas murder conviction and death sentence based on the denial of VCCR rights, hoping to use the *Avena* judgment as a basis for avoiding the application of Texas' procedural default rules (since Medellín had not timely raised this issue). The Texas Court of Criminal Appeals dismissed Medellín's application as an abuse of the writ, concluding that the *Avena* judgment was not binding federal law that displaced Texas' rules.[193] On appeal, the Supreme Court considered whether one of the treaties associated with the ICJ's jurisdiction or judgment provided a basis for regarding the *Avena* judgment as federal law.[194] In brief, the Court held that while the United States had an obligation under international law to comply with the ICJ's judgment,[195] none of the three treaties established that the ICJ's judgment in *Avena* was directly enforceable as domestic law in a state court in the United States,[196] nor did the defendant have any other basis for objecting to the application of Texas law.[197]

---

[191] *Avena*, 2004 I.C.J. at 71–72, ¶ 153(4)f–(7).

[192] *Id.* at 72, ¶ 153(9).

[193] *Ex parte* Medellín, 223 S.W.3d 315 (Tex. Crim. App. 2006).

[194] In *Medellín*, it was not argued that the VCCR itself provided a basis for setting aside Texas procedural default rules. In a separate case that postdated *Avena*, but predated *Medellín*, the Court concluded that (assuming without deciding that the VCCR creates judicially enforceable rights) a state may apply its procedural default rules to claims arising under the VCCR's article on consular notification and access. *See* Sanchez-Llamas v. Oregon, 548 U.S. 331 (2006); *see also* Curtis A. Bradley, *The Federal Judicial Power and the International Legal Order*, 2006 SUP. CT. REV. 59. Further, in *Breard v. Greene*, 523 U.S. 371, 375 (1998), the Court stated:

> [W]hile we should give respectful consideration to the interpretation of an international treaty rendered by an international court with jurisdiction to interpret such, it has been recognized in international law that, absent a clear and express statement to the contrary, the procedural rules of the forum State govern the implementation of the treaty in that State.

[195] The Supreme Court itself recognized this international obligation. *See Medellín*, 552 U.S. at 504 ("No one disputes that the *Avena* decision—a decision that flows from the treaties through which the United States submitted to ICJ jurisdiction with respect to Vienna Convention disputes—constitutes an international law obligation on the part of the United States.").

[196] *See id.* at 507–08 (discussing application of the VCCR's optional protocol); *id.* at 508–11 (discussing application of Article 94 of the U.N. Charter); *id.* at 511 (discussing application of the ICJ Statute) (citing Statute of the International Court of Justice (ICJ Statute), 59 Stat. 1055, T.S. No. 993 (1945)).

[197] *See infra* this chapter text accompanying notes 232–236 (discussing presidential authority). Texas executed Mr. Medellín in August 2008, five months after the Supreme Court's decision. Other executions occurred thereafter. *See, e.g.*, Kristina Daugirdas & Julian Davis Mortenson, *Contemporary Practice of the United States Relating to International Law*, 108 AM. J. INT'L L. 783 (2014). Though not viewing the *Avena* judgment as legally binding, some state courts took into account in their decisions the U.S. obligation to comply with the ICJ's judgment. *See, e.g.*, Torres v. Oklahoma, No. PCD–04–442, 2004 WL 3711623 (Okla. Crim. App. May 13, 2004), 43 I.L.M. 1227 (2004) (remanding the case

While the Court's non-self-execution analysis was cast so as to be germane to the efficacy of treaties in U.S. courts generally (sometimes concertedly so),[198] the potential intrusion into state authority is heavily emphasized in parts of the opinion.[199] And in that regard, one of the more intriguing parts of the Court's reasoning was its reiteration of the "general principle[] of interpretation . . . that 'absent a clear and express statement to the contrary,'" states parties to a treaty should be presumed to have intended that "the procedural rules of the forum State govern the implementation of the treaty in that State."[200] While this resembled, in form, the presumption against preemption, it was distinctly based on international law and related to the procedural rules of the United States as a whole; in principle, therefore, it suggested that any equivalent to the presumption against preemption, as might be applied in interpreting treaties regarding non-self-execution, was nonconstitutional and defeasible.[201]

Chapter 6 noted that most international agreements concluded by the United States are not done in the form of an Article II treaty.[202] One broad category of non–Article II agreements, congressional-executive agreements, are concluded by the president based on authorization from a majority of both houses of Congress; trade agreements, for example, are frequently concluded by this means.[203] Putting aside debates about the constitutionality of non–Article II

---

for an evidentiary hearing on the failure to provide VCCR rights); Gutierrez v. State, No. 53506, 2012 WL 4355518 (Nev. Sup. Ct. Sept. 19, 2012) (granting an evidentiary hearing to decide whether there was prejudice in the failure to provide VCCR rights); Commonwealth v. Gautreaux, 941 N.E.2d 616 (Mass. 2011) (finding that a failure to provide VCCR rights could support a motion for a new trial). Likewise, some governors acted to commute sentences in light of the *Avena* judgment. *See, e.g.*, Janet Koven Levit, *A Tale of International Law in the Heartland: Torres and the Role of State Courts in Transnational Legal Conversation*, 12 Tulsa J. Comp. & Int'l L. 163 (2005). The federal government also sought to persuade governors to commute the sentences of the relevant noncitizens from death to life imprisonment. *See, e.g.*, 2011 Digest of U.S. Practice, at 23–25. Efforts were made to pursue federal legislation to facilitate compliance with the VCCR and with the *Avena* judgment, *id.* at 11–23, but to date such efforts have not succeeded.

[198] *See, e.g., Medellín*, 552 U.S. at 518 (noting that "Medellín's interpretation would allow ICJ judgments to override otherwise binding state law; there is nothing in his logic that would exempt contrary federal law from the same fate"); *id.* at 515 (criticizing the dissent's proposed multifactor analysis for allowing "the courts [to] pick and choose which shall be binding United States law— trumping not only state but other federal law as well"). The opinion's ambiguity regarding the relationship between non-self-executing treaties and the Supremacy Clause arguably undermines the latter's essential attributes. *See* Chapter 6 § IV(A)(3).

[199] *Medellín*, 552 U.S. at 522 (reporting that "Medellín does not ask us to enforce a foreign-court judgment settling a typical commercial or property dispute," but instead "argues that the *Avena* judgment has the effect of enjoining the operation of state law," and that such "judgment would force the State to take action to 'review and reconside[r]' his case").

[200] *Id.* at 517 (quoting Sanchez-Llamas v. Oregon, 548 U.S. 331, 351 (2006) (quoting Breard v. Greene, 523 U.S. 371, 375 (1998) (per curiam))).

[201] *But cf.* Chapter 6 § IV(A)(4) (discussing general difficulty of construing treaties in relation to non-self-execution).

[202] *See* Chapter 6 § V.

[203] *See* Chapter 6 § V(A).

agreements, including the circumstances under which they may be employed, it is widely accepted that a valid congressional-executive agreement, like a statute or treaty, can establish supreme law that has preemptive effect.[204] There is less clarity, however, on the finer details, such as might bear on resolving whether a presumption of some kind is appropriate. Thus, congressional-executive agreements are often portrayed as having the same preemptive effects as treaties.[205] Yet some congressional-executive agreements, known as *ex ante* agreements—as noted in Chapter 6, accounting for the vast majority of congressional-executive agreements—receive congressional approval *prior* to the conclusion of any agreement, thus arguably distinguishing them from treaties (and from statutes that control preemption by their own force) in terms of diagnosing what Congress intended.[206] Further, congressional-executive agreements are also portrayed as having the same preemptive effects as conventional domestic statutes, given that such agreements typically are implemented by a statute that itself has the preemptive effects (not wholly unlike the Chemical Weapons Convention Implementation Act considered in *Bond*).[207] Yet a statute implementing a congressional-executive agreement is charged with the delicate task of aiding in the adherence to U.S. international obligations, thus distinguishing the situation from that of a conventional domestic statute.[208]

All things considered, it is probably sound to treat the preemptive effect of congressional-executive agreements as akin to that of treaties or statutes implementing treaties, given the international legal consequences of inadequate U.S. implementation. Moreover, and much as with treaties, congressional-executive agreements often accommodate federalism in any event. For example, the Uruguay Round Agreements Act not only barred anyone other than the United States from challenging U.S. or state action or inaction based on its consistency with the statute but also established a process by which the United States is to consult with the states and provide notice to Congress before taking legal action against a state or local government for noncompliance with the statute.[209]

---

[204] *See* RESTATEMENT (THIRD) §§ 111 cmt. d & 115 cmt. e. The most widely cited examples are in fact cases involving sole executive agreements, which almost certainly have less authority relative to those approved *ex ante* or *ex post* by Congress. *See infra* this chapter text accompanying notes 210–236.

[205] *See* RESTATEMENT (THIRD) §§ 111 cmt. d & 115 cmt. e; HENKIN, FOREIGN AFFAIRS, at 217.

[206] For this reason, some express skepticism as to whether *ex ante* congressional agreements are necessarily of the same domestic legal effect. *See* Oona A. Hathaway, *Presidential Power Over International Law: Restoring the Balance*, 119 YALE L.J. 140, 213–14, 214 n.237 (2009).

[207] *See, e.g.*, Int'l Agreement Executed by President, 40 Op. Att'y. Gen. 469, 471 (1946); *see supra* this chapter text accompanying notes 157–159 (discussing *Bond* and statutory preemption).

[208] *See also* Chapter 6 § V(A)(2) (noting potential complexity of relevant instruments in *ex post* congressional-executive agreements).

[209] Uruguay Round Agreements Act of 1994, Pub. L. No. 103-465, § 102, 108 Stat. 4809, 4815–19 (codified at 19 U.S.C. § 3512 (2018)). For discussion, see authorities cited *supra* note 83.

C. Preemption by Presidential Action

As discussed throughout this volume, the president is accorded certain powers with respect to foreign relations that are not dependent upon acts by Congress. In the exercise of those powers, the president might conclude an executive agreement with a foreign state that does not receive approval from Congress (in other words, an agreement that is not in the form of either a treaty or a congressional-executive agreement).[210] In several cases—the limits of which have been hotly debated—the Supreme Court has determined that such a "sole" executive agreement, if constitutionally valid, is capable of preempting conflicting state law.

In *United States v. Belmont*, a Russian corporation had deposited funds with a private banker (Belmont) doing business in New York. In 1917, a communist government came to power in Russia, establishing the Union of Soviet Socialist Republics (USSR), and in 1918 it expropriated the Russian corporation and all of its worldwide assets. The United States, however, did not recognize the new government and the funds remained deposited in New York. The USSR had also expropriated properties of U.S. nationals in Russia, resulting in numerous claims by those nationals against the USSR. In 1933, the new U.S. administration of Franklin D. Roosevelt decided to recognize the government of the USSR and to establish diplomatic relations. As a part of normalizing the relationship and resolving all outstanding claims between the two countries, the USSR agreed to relinquish its rights to assets found in the United States and to assign those rights to the United States,[211] via a bilateral agreement commonly referred to as the Litvinov Assignment.[212]

The Litvinov Assignment, for purposes of U.S. law, was in the form of a sole executive agreement. Upon its conclusion, the U.S. government sought access to the assigned assets, including the funds deposited with Belmont.[213] The U.S. executors of Belmont's will objected. The Second Circuit concluded that the USSR's 1918 decree had no effect on the Belmont's New York deposits, because

---

[210] *See* Chapter 6 § II.

[211] United States v. Belmont, 301 U.S. 324, 325–27 (1937). For further discussion, see Chapter 3 § IV(D).

[212] The mechanics of the assignment involved: (1) a communication dated November 16, 1933, from the USSR People's Commissar for Foreign Affairs, Maxim Litvinov, to President Roosevelt, whereby the USSR assigned to the United States amounts admitted or found to be due it as the successor of prior governments of Russia (or otherwise) preparatory to a final settlement of the claims outstanding between the two governments and the claims of their nationals; (2) a communication dated November 16, 1933, from President Roosevelt to Commissar Litvinov, accepting such assignment; and (3) execution of the assignments by the financial attaché of the USSR embassy in the United States, Serge Ughet, on August 25, 1933, and November 15, 1933. *See* 22 U.S.C. § 1641(6).

[213] In due course, the United States would use such assets to compensate U.S. nationals for their claims against the USSR. Indeed, the existence of such claims and their nonpayment had for years been one of the barriers to U.S. recognition of the USSR. *See* 1 HACKWORTH DIGEST, at 302–04.

expropriation was contrary to New York public policy.[214] As such, the USSR could not assign any rights to the United States with respect to that deposit. In reversing, the Supreme Court first noted that the act of state doctrine precluded passing judgment upon an act taken by a foreign state done within its own territory.[215] But the Court also held that the president's act of recognizing the USSR government and establishing diplomatic relations had the effect of validating all acts of the USSR government "from the commencement of its existence,"[216] while observing that the negotiation and conclusion of such an agreement were plainly within the president's competence.[217] Importantly, the Court stated that, while treaties clearly preempt state law under the Constitution, "the same rule would result in the case of all international compacts and agreements from the very fact that complete power over international affairs is in the national government and is not and cannot be subject to any curtailment or interference on the part of the several states."[218] Famously, if tendentiously, it concluded that "[a]s to such purposes, the State of New York does not exist."[219]

A slightly later case, *United States v. Pink*, presented largely similar facts.[220] The Supreme Court held that a 1937 USSR government declaration, which maintained that its 1918 decree had extraterritorial effect, was conclusive in establishing that the New York funds at issue fell within the decree.[221] The Court considered whether the fact that in *Pink*, the creditors seeking the funds were foreign was a meaningful distinction from *Belmont*. In that regard, the Court emphasized (more so than it did in *Belmont*) that the Litvinov Assignment was oriented toward resolving claims of U.S. nationals against the USSR, noting that there "is no Constitutional reason why this Government need act as the collection agent for nationals of other countries when it takes steps to protect itself or

---

[214] *Belmont*, 301 U.S. at 327.

[215] *Belmont*, 301 U.S. at 327–30. For discussion of the act of state doctrine, see Chapter 4 § III.

[216] *Id.* at 330.

[217] *Id.* The Court's opinion was written by Justice Sutherland, who also penned the Court's opinion just a year earlier in *United States v. Curtiss-Wright Export Corp.*, 299 U.S. 304 (1936). Although the opinion noted that "[t]he recognition, establishment of diplomatic relations," and the agreement and assignment were all part of the same transaction, which was within the competence of the president, Justice Sutherland also expounded more broadly on presidential power in the field of foreign relations, much as he had in *Curtiss-Wright*, asserting that "Governmental power over external affairs is not distributed, but is vested exclusively in the national government," and that "in respect of what was done here, the Executive had authority to speak as the sole organ of that government." *Id.* at 330. For further discussion of *Curtiss-Wright*, see Chapter 1 §§ I(D), II(A)(2).

[218] *Belmont*, 301 U.S. at 331.

[219] *Id. But see supra* this chapter § I.

[220] United States v. Pink, 315 U.S. 203 (1942). In *Pink*, the funds of a Russian company were held by the New York superintendent of insurance, it was state courts that had denied the U.S. government access to the funds, the competing creditors for the funds were foreign, and a key issue before the state courts was whether the USSR decree reached these particular assets. For further discussion, see Chapter 3 § IV(D).

[221] *Pink*, 315 U.S. at 220–21.

its own nationals on external debts."[222] The Court also emphasized (again, more than it did in *Belmont*) the exact source and limited nature of the president's power: the settlement of claims as part of recognizing a foreign government was a "modest implied power" of the president, for unless "such a power exists, the power of recognition might be thwarted or seriously diluted."[223] If New York law was not preempted, it would "tend to restore some of the precise impediments to friendly relations which the President intended to remove on inauguration of the policy of recognition of the Soviet Government."[224]

In *Dames & Moore v. Regan*, the executive agreements at issue were not part of a process for recognizing a new government, but it was a means for resolving a major foreign policy crisis. As discussed in Chapter 1,[225] U.S. diplomatic and consular personnel were held hostage in Iran from 1979 to 1981, a crisis that only ended with the entry into force of the Iran-U.S. Algiers Accords, concluded by President Jimmy Carter as executive agreements.[226] The Algiers Accords required, among other things, that the United States nullify all attachments of Iranian property in the United States, transfer Iranian assets from the United States to Iran, and terminate claims that had been filed by U.S. nationals in U.S. courts against Iran, in exchange for Iran's release of the hostages.[227] The Accords also provided for the establishment of a claims tribunal in The Hague to resolve, among other things, the claims of the U.S. nationals against Iran.[228] In considering the constitutionality of the executive orders that sought to implement the Algiers Accords (and doing so on an expedited basis), the Court did not focus on issues of preemption or on federalism more generally.[229] Nevertheless, the effect of the opinion was to uphold the president's authority to transfer claims pending in both U.S. federal and state courts to an international arbitral tribunal, without regard to any state laws or rules to the contrary.

Subsequently, in *American Insurance Ass'n v. Garamendi*, the Supreme Court stated that "generally . . . valid executive agreements are fit to preempt state law, just as treaties are . . . ."[230] Leading authorities have reached similar

---

[222] *Id.* at 228.

[223] *Pink*, 315 U.S. at 229–30. This less sweeping description of presidential power than existed in *Curtiss-Wright* and in *Belmont* may be due, at least in part, to Justice Sutherland's retirement from the Court in 1938, several years before the decision in *Pink*.

[224] *Id.* at 231; *see id.* at 233 ("No State can rewrite our foreign policy to conform to its own domestic policies.").

[225] *See* Chapter 1 § II(B).

[226] Dames & Moore v. Regan, 453 U.S. 654, 664 (1981).

[227] *Id.* at 665.

[228] *Id.*

[229] Nor does this appear to have been the subject of inquiry by the Office of Legal Counsel, which reviewed the Algiers Accords and related legal matters in an extraordinary series of opinions. *See generally* Introduction and Summary to Opinions of the Att'y Gen. of the U.S. and of the Off. of Legal Couns. Relating to the Iranian Hostage Crisis, 4A Op. O.L.C. 71 (1980).

[230] Am. Ins. Ass'n v. Garamendi, 539 U.S. 396, 416 (2003).

conclusions.[231] Yet there are some grounds for caution, particularly in light of dicta in *Garamendi* that was amplified by dicta in *Medellín v. Texas*—neither case having squarely presented the issue of preemption based on an agreement. In *Medellín*, the Court characterized its precedent on sole executive agreement as concerning "the authority of the President to settle foreign claims pursuant to an executive agreement."[232] Moreover, it stressed the presence in that line of authority of a "pervasive enough . . . history of congressional acquiescence."[233] (In *Dames & Moore* itself, the Court had also noted that, apart from the broader sweep of history, the same statutes that it held did not directly authorize the entirety of the executive power at issue had nonetheless "indicat[ed] congressional acceptance of a broad scope for executive action in circumstances such as those presented in this case."[234]) In effect, this suggested that the facts of those decisions (focused on claims settlement) might limit the constitutional authority to employ sole executive agreements, their preemptive effect, or both.[235] As a result, whether other types of executive agreements also have preemptive effects is unclear, but there are concrete indications that the executive branch does not consider such authority as limited to traditional instances of claims settlement.[236]

Whether presidential action in the field of foreign relations that does *not* take the form of an executive agreement also preempts inconsistent state law is less well understood. In *Medellín v. Texas*,[237] discussed previously in this chapter and elsewhere,[238] the federal government argued, in addition to invoking treaty

---

[231] *See, e.g.*, RESTATEMENT (THIRD) § 1 rptrs. note 5; *id.* § 115, rptrs. note 5; CONG. RESEARCH SERV., 106TH CONG., TREATIES AND OTHER INTERNATIONAL AGREEMENTS: THE ROLE OF THE UNITED STATES SENATE 5, 92 (Comm. Print 2001). *But see, e.g.*, Michael D. Ramsey, *Executive Agreements and the (Non)Treaty Power*, 77 N.C. L. REV. 133 (1998) (finding that sole executive agreements should not have such preemptive effect).

[232] Medellín v. Texas, 552 U.S. 491, 530 (2008). The emphasis on claims settlement authority was less pronounced in *Garamendi*, which described presidential authority broadly, *see Garamendi*, 539 U.S. at 414, but even there the Court noted that claims settlement agreements were "a particularly longstanding practice." *Id.* at 415. Indeed, Justice Ginsburg's dissent faulted the majority for failing to recognize that its precedent concerned claims settlement. *Id.* at 436–38 (Ginsburg, J., dissenting).

[233] *Medellín*, 552 U.S. at 531; *see also Garamendi*, 539 U.S. at 414 (noting "particularly longstanding" claims settlement practice).

[234] Dames & Moore v. Regan, 453 U.S. 654, 677 (1981).

[235] *See, e.g.*, Bradford R. Clark, *Domesticating Sole Executive Agreements*, 93 VA. L. REV. 1573 (2007).

[236] *See, e.g.*, Waiver of Claims for Damages Arising Out of Coop. Space Activity, 19 Op. O.L.C. 140 (1995) (concluding, in assessing proposed agreements entailing the waiver of state claims, that "sole executive agreements that purport to create legal obligations, like statutes and treaties, are 'the supreme Law of the Land' for purposes of the Supremacy Clause, U.S. Const. art. VI, cl. 2, and thus bind the states") (citing, inter alia, Memorandum for Conrad Harper, Legal Adviser, Department of State from Walter Dellinger, Assistant Attorney General, Office of Legal Counsel, Re: Enforceability of Penalty-Related Assurances Provided to Foreign Nations in Connection with Extradition Requests (Nov. 18, 1993)).

[237] 552 U.S. 491 (2008).

[238] *See supra* this chapter § II(B); *see also* Chapter 1 § II(B); Chapter 3 § I(D); Chapter 5 § II(B); Chapter 6 §§ III(B), IV(A); and Chapter 7 § III(C).

commitments that made the ICJ's judgment in the *Avena* case binding on the United States, that the judgment was also binding on state courts by virtue of a memorandum issued by President George W. Bush in February 2005. That memorandum provided:

> I have determined, pursuant to the authority vested in me as President by the Constitution and the laws of the United States of America, that the United States will discharge its international obligations under the decision of the International Court of Justice in the *Case Concerning Avena and Other Mexican Nationals (Mexico v. United States of America) (Avena)*, 2004 ICJ 128 (Mar. 31), by having State courts give effect to the decision in accordance with general principles of comity in cases filed by the 51 Mexican nationals addressed in that decision.[239]

According to the executive branch, even if the *Avena* judgment did not of its own force require domestic courts to set aside ordinary rules of procedural default, the president's memorandum required that result, either because (1) it operated in conjunction with U.S. treaty obligations, or (2) because of the president's foreign affairs authority to resolve claims disputes with foreign nations.[240]

As to the first argument, the Court did not regard the president's memorandum, in conjunction with treaty obligations, as establishing a presidential power "to establish binding rules of decision that preempt contrary state law."[241] Drawing on *Youngstown*[242] and *Dames & Moore*,[243] the Court found that the president's authority to act, as with the exercise of any governmental power, "must stem either from an act of Congress or from the Constitution itself."[244] While the United States had an obligation under its treaty commitments to comply with the *Avena* judgment, an international obligation did not by that token alone permit the president on his own authority to transform the obligation into national law; such a power could be conferred only by the Senate's consent to a self-executing treaty or by implementing legislation enacted by Congress.[245] Indeed, when the president is acting to implement an obligation that arises from a non-self-executing treaty, then he or she is acting contrary to the implicit understanding

---

[239] Memorandum of President George W. Bush to the U.S. Attorney General Alberto Gonzales, *supra* note 72.

[240] Medellín v. Texas, 552 U.S. 491, 525 (2008).

[241] *Id.* (quoting Brief for United States as Amicus Curiae Supporting Petitioner at 5, Medellín v. Texas, 552 U.S. 491 (2008) (No. 06-984); *see* Chapter 6 § IV(A)(3) (discussing consequences of non-self-execution for presidential authority).

[242] Youngstown Sheet & Tube Co. v. Sawyer, 343 U.S. 579, 585 (1952). For discussion of *Youngstown*, see Chapter 1 § II(B) and Chapter 8 § II(B).

[243] Dames & Moore v. Regan, 453 U.S. 654, 668 (1981).

[244] *Medellín*, 552 U.S. at 524.

[245] *Id.* at 525–26.

of the ratifying Senate, and thus acting within the scope of Justice Jackson's third *Youngstown* category, where the president's power is at its lowest ebb.[246] Even were indications of congressional acquiescence deemed relevant, the Court found no such acquiescence could be attributed to Congress' reaction to the president's resolution of ICJ disputes, the president's role in litigating foreign policy concerns, or the president's general (statutory) authorization to represent the United States before the United Nations.[247]

Nor was the Court convinced by the second argument—that the president's memorandum could displace Texas law based solely on the president's foreign affairs authority to resolve claims disputes with foreign nations. As previously noted, the Court took the various claims settlement cases advanced by the executive branch to involve "a narrow set of circumstances: the making of executive agreements to settle civil claims between American citizens and foreign governments or foreign nationals."[248] By contrast, the Court noted, the president could not identify "a single instance in which the President has attempted (or Congress has acquiesced in) a Presidential directive issued to state courts," let alone "one that reaches deep into the heart of the State's police powers and compels state courts to reopen final criminal judgments and set aside neutrally applicable state laws."[249] Medellín himself, but not the president, invoked the president's "take care" authority, which the Court construed as "allow[ing] the President to execute the laws, not make them," without addressing any additional hurdle that might be presented by its use to override state law.[250]

Once one moves beyond formal instruments, like sole executive agreements, and toward instruments like presidential memoranda, it becomes difficult to avoid discussing the entire range of means by which presidents establish foreign policy—for example, the agreement-related policy at issue in *Garamendi*, as discussed further later. Nonetheless, it may be useful to treat executive policies that assert their own preemptive force (as was arguably, but not definitely, the case with the presidential memorandum at issue in *Medellín*) as having greater weight than those involving a judicial inference—even if that inference is encouraged by the executive branch in the course of litigation. Of course, presidential action taken in conjunction with a foreign state, whereby political commitments are

---

[246] *Id.* at 527; *see* Chapter 6 § IV(A)(3) (noting the limits of this reasoning).
[247] *Medellín*, 552 U.S. at 528–30.
[248] *Id.* at 531.
[249] *Id.* at 532.
[250] *Id.* at 532. For further discussion, see Chapter 6 § IV(A)(3). For commentary on this part of the Court's opinion, see Margaret E. McGuinness, Medellin, *Norm Portals, and the Horizontal Integration of International Human Rights*, 82 Notre Dame L. Rev. 755 (2013); Edward T. Swaine, *Taking Care of Treaties*, 108 Colum. L. Rev. 331 (2008); Edward T. Swaine, *The Political Economy of* Youngstown, 83 S. Cal. L. Rev. 263, 329–33 (2010); Michael P. Van Alstine, *Executive Aggrandizement in Foreign Affairs Lawmaking*, 54 U.C.L.A. L. Rev. 309 (2006); A. Mark Weisburd, Medellín, *the President's Foreign Affairs Power and Domestic Law*, 28 Penn St. Int'l L. Rev. 595 (2010).

made by means of an agreement, may be viewed by courts as having yet stronger force in preempting state law than unilateral presidential action, even if the latter touches upon U.S. international commitments.

D. Preemption by Dormant Foreign Commerce Clause

As with the (interstate) Commerce Clause, U.S. courts have found that the Foreign Commerce Clause is not only a "positive" grant of power to Congress[251] but also a "negative" constraint upon the states. As such, the "dormant" Foreign Commerce Clause can have the effect of preempting state law even in circumstances where Congress has not done so through a statute.[252] In such a situation, what is "dormant" is not the Foreign Commerce Clause itself but, rather, Congress' exercise of its regulatory power.

As early as 1827, the Supreme Court struck down a licensing requirement for imports adopted by Maryland on the grounds that it violated the federal government's exclusive power over foreign commerce.[253] In *Brown v. Maryland*, Maryland had adopted a statute requiring importers of foreign goods, before being authorized to sell them, to purchase a Maryland license. Plaintiffs were indicted for failure to do so. Apparently, there was no claim that Maryland's law was preempted by a federal statute, nor by a treaty relevant to the facts of the case. After noting the existence of the Foreign Commerce Clause, Chief Justice John Marshall explained that "[t]he power [to regulate commerce] is coextensive with the subject on which it acts, and cannot be stopped at the external boundary of a state, but must enter its interior."[254] In this instance, the power "must be capable of authorizing the sale of those articles it introduces."[255] Chief Justice Marshall apparently viewed Congress, by not acting to prevent the import of the articles in question, as having "authorized" such imports, and in turn, their sale in the United States. As such, the charges imposed by Maryland "on the introduction and incorporation of the articles into" goods sold in the United States "must be hostile to the power given to Congress to regulate commerce, since an essential part of that regulation, and principal object of it, is to prescribe the regular means for accomplishing that introduction and incorporation."[256]

---

[251] U.S. CONST. art. I, § 8, cl 3 ("The Congress shall have Power . . . To regulate Commerce with foreign Nations, and among the several states, and with the Indian Tribes . . ."); *see* Chapter 2 § IV (discussing "positive" use as basis for legislation affecting foreign relations).

[252] *See* HENKIN, FOREIGN AFFAIRS, at 158–62; GLENNON & SLOANE, *supra* note 16, at 147–83.

[253] Brown v. Maryland, 25 U.S. (12 Wheat.) 419 (1827). The Court also struck down the statute as preempted by the Constitution's prescription that "no State shall lay any impost or duties on imports or exports." *Id.* at 437–45.

[254] *Id.* at 446.

[255] *Id.*

[256] *Id.* at 448.

In the present day, the dormant Foreign Commerce Clause may be implicated, for example, in connection with restrictions by states on their governments or companies from doing business with foreign nations.[257] The Supreme Court has also explored the doctrine in cases involving state taxation of multinational corporations doing business in the state. In *Japan Line, Ltd. v. County of Los Angeles*, the Court considered a California *ad valorem* property tax imposed on foreign-owned instrumentalities with respect to cargo shipping containers used for international commerce.[258] The Court applied two cumulative sets of tests. The first set was the same that applied to a state tax affecting *domestic* commerce: the tax is unconstitutional if it (1) applies to an activity lacking a substantial nexus to the taxing state; (2) is not fairly apportioned; (3) discriminates against interstate commerce; or (4) is not fairly related to the services the state provides.[259] The second set applied when the tax in question concerned the instrumentalities of foreign commerce: such a tax would also be unconstitutional if (5) there is an enhanced risk of multiple taxation due to taxation by a foreign sovereign, especially where the instrumentality of commerce is domiciled abroad;[260] or (6) the state tax tends to impair federal uniformity in an area where federal uniformity is essential.[261]

The Court found that California's tax ran afoul of the last two tests. Because under these circumstances, Japan had "the right and the power to tax the containers in full," California's tax risked double taxation.[262] Moreover, the Court concluded that California's tax prevents the nation from "speaking with one voice" with regard to the treatment of such containers.[263] It noted that the United States and Japan were parties to a treaty that granted containers "temporary admission free of import duties and import taxes and free of import prohibitions and restrictions," provided they are used solely in foreign commerce and are subject to re-exportation.[264] While the treaty did not itself preempt state-level taxation, it reflected "a national policy to remove impediments to the use of

---

[257] *See, e.g.*, National Foreign Trade Council v. Natsios, 181 F.3d 38, 44–67 (1st Cir. 1999), *affirmed on other grounds*, Crosby v. National Foreign Trade Council, 530 U.S. 363 (2000); Antilles Cement Corp. v. Acevedo Vilá, 408 F.3d 41, 46 (1st Cir. 2005) ("We regard this concern as equally vivid in non-tax dormant Foreign Commerce Clause cases.").

[258] Japan Line, Ltd. v. County of Los Angeles, 441 U.S. 434 (1979). In essence, for days of the year when a cargo shipping container used on board a vessel was present in a California port, that property would be taxed by California, just as one might impose a tax on real estate or personal property.

[259] *Id.* at 444–45 (citing to Complete Auto Transit, Inc. v. Brady, 430 U.S. 274, 279 (1977)).

[260] *Id.* at 446–48.

[261] *Id.* at 448–51.

[262] The Court noted that the "containers are owned, based, and registered in Japan; they are used exclusively in international commerce; and they remain outside Japan only so long as needed to complete their international missions." *Id.* at 451–52.

[263] *Id.* at 452–53.

[264] Customs Convention on Containers art. 2, May 18, 1956, 20 U.S.T. 301, 304, 338 U.N.T.S. 103, 106.

containers as 'instruments of international traffic.' "[265] Among other things, the Court noted the danger of not speaking with one voice: "The risk of retaliation by Japan, under these circumstances, is acute, and such retaliation of necessity would be felt by the Nation as a whole."[266]

Each of these two additional tests illustrated a dimension distinct to the dormant Foreign Commerce Clause. The "risk of multiple taxation" is not of equivalent concern under the dormant Commerce Clause because the federal government has the authority to fairly apportion taxes as among the states; by contrast, the federal government lacked the capacity to prevent Japan from taxing the containers in full.[267] The significance of "speaking with one voice" was also distinct to the foreign setting. Comparing the scope of congressional authority as it relates to interstate and foreign commerce, the Court found "evidence that the Founders intended the scope of the foreign commerce power to be the greater"; it then indicated that "[t]he need for federal uniformity [was] no less paramount" when it came to assessing a dormant power that must be left free for congressional action.[268] Uniformity seemed necessary not just for establishing a policy that could be pursued with foreign nations but also for determining when it was appropriate to avoid antagonizing them and thereby creating negative externalities that might be visited indiscriminately against the United States as a whole.[269]

In relatively short order, the Court decided several similar cases in favor of state laws,[270] but its 1994 decision in *Barclays Bank v. Franchise Tax Board of California* provides the clearest counterpoint.[271] In that case, the Court upheld a California income tax upon in-state franchises of multinational corporations that used a "worldwide combined reporting" method. Applying the same approach as *Japan Line*, the Court this time found that neither of the two tests associated with foreign commerce posed a constitutional obstacle. With respect to whether there was an enhanced risk of multiple taxation, the Court said that California's method, which was sensitive to the proportion of business activity within California, did not inevitably result in multiple taxation, and that

---

[265] *Japan Line*, 441 U.S. at 453 (quoting 19 U.S.C. § 1322(a)).
[266] *Id.*
[267] *Id.* at 446–48; *see* Anthony J. Colangelo, *The Foreign Commerce Clause*, 96 Va. L. Rev. 949, 968–69 (2010). Indeed, it is not clear how, exactly, Japan's "right" to tax the containers played into the analysis, beyond the fact that Japan had the "power" to do so and the United States had limited capacity to correct it. By contrast, in *Japan Line* the Court noted that California could plausibly argue that its own tax was fairly apportioned, given that it depended on average presence in California. *Japan Line*, 441 U.S. at 445.
[268] *Japan Line*, 441 U.S. at 448–49.
[269] *Id.* at 450–51.
[270] Container Corp. of Am. v. Franchise Tax Bd., 463 U.S. 159, 184–97 (1983) (upholding California state franchise tax against dormant Foreign Commerce Clause); Wardair Can. Inc. v. Fla. Dep't of Revenue, 477 U.S. 1, 7–13 (1986) (upholding Florida state sales tax on sale of aviation fuel against dormant Foreign Commerce Clause challenge).
[271] Barclays Bank PLC v. Franchise Tax Bd. of Cal., 512 U.S. 298 (1994).

a proposed alternative method (an "arm's-length" approach that allocates tax-able income based on accounting principles) would not eliminate whatever risk might exist.[272]

With respect to whether the tax impaired federal uniformity in an area where such uniformity is essential, the Court observed that it had previously upheld California's worldwide combined reporting method in a different context (the taxation of foreign subsidiaries of domestic corporations at issue in *Container Corp. of America v. Franchise Tax Board*), concluding that it did not unconstitu-tionally risk multiple international taxation,[273] and Congress had taken no steps since that time to enact legislation prohibiting states from taxing corporate in-come based on that method.[274] In this context, executive branch statements indi-cating concern with or opposition to the method are not sufficient, given that the "Constitution expressly grants Congress, not the President, the power to 'regu-late Commerce with foreign Nations.'"[275]

Jurisprudence concerning the dormant Commerce Clause has been criticized as lacking consistency and coherence.[276] Likewise, the approach of courts to the dormant Foreign Commerce clause has not been free from criticism, both be-cause of its reliance on the malleable criteria used in the domestic setting and because of the uncertain application of the additional criteria advanced in the foreign context. The Court's attempt to distinguish instances in which a state tax "merely has foreign resonances, but does not implicate foreign affairs," does not seem promising.[277] In particular, the role that the "speaking with one voice" test plays is unclear; some forms of congressional inaction invite a striking down of the state law (*Japan Line*), while other forms do not (*Container Corp. of America*; *Barclay's Bank*). The Court is assessing the degree of congressional engagement—somewhat as in an ordinary statutory preemption question—but in a vaguer way since, as the Court stressed, "Congress may more passively indicate" the lack of any interest in federal uniformity than it might, for example, with respect to dis-crimination against interstate commerce.[278]

By the same token, though, *Barclay's Bank* has been heralded by some obser-vers as the Supreme Court possibly stepping back from dormant preemption doctrines and instead calling upon Congress to act if it wished to preclude state measures affecting foreign relations.[279] Since *Barclay's Bank*, however, it appears

---

[272] *Id.* at 319.
[273] *See* Container Corp. of Am. v. Franchise Tax Bd., 463 U.S. 159 (1983).
[274] *Barclays Bank*, 512 U.S. at 324–28.
[275] *Id.* at 329.
[276] *See, e.g.*, Brannon P. Denning, *Reconstructing the Dormant Commerce Clause Doctrine*, 50 WM. & MARY L. REV. 417 (2008).
[277] *See Container Corp.*, 463 U.S. at 194.
[278] *Barclays Bank*, 512 U.S. at 323.
[279] *See e.g.*, Goldsmith, *supra* note 105, at 211; Peter J. Spiro, *Foreign Relations Federalism*, 70 U. COLO. L. REV. 1223, 1265–66 (1999).

that the Court remains inclined to use dormant foreign affairs doctrines even when the Foreign Commerce Clause is not at issue, as discussed in the next section.

E. Preemption by Dormant Foreign Affairs Power

Even in the absence of a statute or treaty that preempts a state law, and where there is no negative implication from the Foreign Commerce Clause, state law may be preempted under what has been referred to as the "dormant" foreign affairs power.[280] Such preemption is not common, and its rare invocation has led some to doubt whether it is a viable doctrine. In large part this is due to its potentially extensive application: were it granted the breadth with which it has sometimes been stated, a robust dormant foreign affairs power might well call into question any state law that affects U.S. foreign affairs, a possibility that seems unlikely given the transnational activities in which states are enmeshed.

The doctrine is typically ascribed to *Zschernig v. Miller*, in which an Oregon probate statute precluded a nonresident noncitizen from inheriting property unless: (1) the noncitizen's country of origin would allow a U.S. national to inherit property on the same terms as a national of that country; (2) U.S. nationals would be allowed to transfer payments from such foreign inheritance to the United States from the foreign country; and (3) the foreign country would not confiscate such inheritance.[281] Adopted in 1951, at the outset of the Cold War, the statute was generally understood to be targeting noncitizens from communist states, where U.S. nationals would not have the same rights to private property as exist in the United States. In 1947, in *Clark v. Allen*, the Supreme Court had upheld a similar California statute against a facial challenge,[282] given that it "seemed" (as *Zschernig* later put it) "to involve no more than a routine reading of foreign laws."[283] But by the time it decided *Zschernig* in 1968, the Court was concerned about the manner in which numerous state statutes of this kind were being applied. The Court asserted that the probate courts of various states—not confined to Oregon—had launched inquiries into the type of governments that existed in foreign states, had assessed whether noncitizens under the foreign state's law had enforceable rights (and whether these "so-called 'rights'" were "merely dispensations turning upon the whim or caprice of government officials"), and had made determinations as to whether representations by

---

[280] *See* HENKIN, FOREIGN AFFAIRS, at 162–65; GLENNON & SLOANE, *supra* note 16, at 87–145.
[281] Zschernig v. Miller, 389 U.S. 429, 430–31 (1968).
[282] Clark v. Allen, 331 U.S. 503 (1947).
[283] *Zschernig*, 389 U.S. at 433.

foreign officials were credible or made in good faith, and whether foreign legal systems reflected "any element of confiscation."[284] Yet the Court regarded such inquiries to be a "kind of state involvement in foreign affairs and international relations" that "the Constitution entrusts solely to the Federal Government," inquiries "not sanctioned by *Clark v. Allen*."[285] In perhaps its clearest statement of the principle it perceived, the Court said that it "seems inescapable that the type of probate law that Oregon enforces affects international relations in a persistent and subtle way," and such state "regulations must give way if they impair the effective exercise of the Nation's foreign policy."[286] These and other statements suggested that the Court was concerned, not without justification, that statutes such as that of Oregon were having an undue effect on U.S. foreign relations[287] or were even pursuing specific foreign policy objectives.[288] In either event, the states were acting at the federal government's expense, such that the state laws would have to yield, even in the absence of a clear conflict with federal policy.[289]

Zschernig has been regarded as an unusual case, given that the state law was struck down not just in the absence of a federal statute or treaty but also in the absence of an expressed policy of either Congress or the executive branch in opposition to the state law. The result was hard for many of the justices to reconcile with the Court's 1947 decision in *Clark v. Allen*.[290] Ironically, one of the apparent constants was the Court's disregard for the views expressed by the executive branch. In *Clark v. Allen*, the executive branch appears to have argued that the statute was "an extension of state power into the field of foreign affairs, which is exclusively reserved by the Constitution to the Federal Government,"[291] and yet the Court upheld the statute. In *Zschernig*, by contrast, the executive branch appeared to have acquiesced in the constitutionality of such laws, or at least those of California and Oregon,[292] and yet the statute was struck

---

[284] *Id.* at 433–34.

[285] *Id.* at 436.

[286] *Id.* at 440.

[287] *Id.* at 435 (describing the Oregon statute as creating more than a mere "diplomatic bagatelle" with a "great potential for disruption or embarrassment").

[288] *Id.* at 437–38 (describing the Oregon case law as pursuing foreign policy objectives, such as "the freezing or thawing of the 'cold war,'" although these "of course are matters for the Federal Government, not for local probate courts"); *id.* at 439 (noting claim that one provision of the Oregon statute sought to induce foreign states to ensure that their laws gave Oregonians similar inheritance-related rights abroad as they enjoyed in Oregon).

[289] Justice Harlan, in contrast, would have required a more direct conflict with the exercise of a federal policy. *Id.* at 457–58 (Harlan, J., concurring in result). He concurred because he regarded the Oregon law to be preempted by a bilateral treaty with Germany. *Id.* at 457.

[290] Edward T. Swaine, *Negotiating Federalism: State Bargaining and the Dormant Treaty Power*, 49 Duke L.J. 1127, 1144 n.53 (2000) (noting that half of the justices participating in *Zschernig* did not regard the two decisions as reconcilable).

[291] *See Clark v. Allen*, 331 U.S. at 516.

[292] *See Zschernig*, 389 U.S. at 434 (referring to the "Government's acquiescence in the ruling of *Clark v. Allen* ...").

down.[293] As such, the Court's decision in *Zschernig* appears to have been based largely on its own appreciation of the foreign policy implications of state courts' decisions rendered under such statutes, irrespective of the expressed judgment of the executive branch.

In *American Insurance Ass'n v. Garamendi*, there was no federal statute or treaty, but there was an executive branch policy at issue, which this time the Court followed. In that case, California's 1999 Holocaust Victim Insurance Relief Act of 1999 (HVIRA), required any insurer doing business in California to disclose information about all policies sold in Europe between 1920 and 1945.[294] Such disclosure could assist potential claimants in pursuing Holocaust-era claims—particularly in California, which had facilitated such claims[295]—for the theft of Jewish assets, including life insurance policies, which were a form of savings held by many Jews in Europe before the Second World War.[296] To enforce the statute, California began issuing administrative subpoenas against the subsidiaries of several European insurance companies.[297] An association of insurance companies challenged the statute as unconstitutionally interfering with the federal government's conduct of foreign relations.[298] The strength of their position turned principally on an effort by the German government and German companies to provide compensation to all those "who suffered at the hands of German companies during the National Socialist era" by means of a "foundation" set up to quickly and completely process unpaid Holocaust-era claims.

The foundation was created by an international agreement signed by the German chancellor and President Bill Clinton, which for purposes of U.S. law took the form of a sole executive agreement.[299] That agreement did not expressly preempt state law, but instead provided that whenever a German company was sued on a Holocaust-era claim in a U.S. court, the U.S. government would submit a statement to the court that "it would be in the foreign policy interests of the United States for the Foundation to be the exclusive forum and remedy for the resolution of all asserted claims against German companies arising from their involvement in the National Socialist era and World War II."[300] Though unwilling

---

[293] Justice Stewart, in his concurring opinion in *Zschernig*, noted the government's concession, but responded in part: "We deal here with the basic allocation of power between the States and the Nation. Resolution of so fundamental a constitutional issue cannot vary from day to day with the shifting winds at the State Department." 389 U.S. at 443 (Stewart, J., concurring).

[294] Am. Ins. Ass'n v. Garamendi, 539 U.S. 396, 401 (2003).

[295] At the time of the case, California had amended the state's code of civil procedure to allow state residents to sue in state court on insurance claims based on such acts perpetrated in the Holocaust, and further had extended the governing statute of limitations to 2010. *See id.* at 409.

[296] *Id.* at 401–02.

[297] *Id.* at 411.

[298] *Id.* at 412.

[299] Agreement Concerning the Foundation "Remembrance, Responsibility and the Future," Ger.-U.S., July 17, 2000, T.I.A.S. No. 13,104.

[300] *Id.*, Annex B, ¶ 1.

to guarantee that U.S. foreign policy interests would "in themselves provide an independent legal basis for dismissal," the government agreed to tell U.S. courts "that U.S. policy interests favor dismissal on any valid legal ground."[301] Further, the government promised to use its "best efforts, in a manner it considers appropriate," to secure state and local government respect for the foundation as the exclusive mechanism.[302] Fairly viewed, the agreement did not establish a binding U.S. commitment under international law that such cases would not proceed in U.S. courts, but it did establish an executive branch policy to seek to bring about that result.

After describing the potential preemptive force of sole executive agreements, the Supreme Court noted the parties' acknowledgment "that the agreements include no preemption clause," which left any claimed "preemption to rest on asserted interference with the foreign policy those agreements embody."[303] The Court reviewed the competing views expressed in *Zschernig*—the majority view, which it characterized as describing a species of field preemption, and the view expressed in Justice Harlan's concurrence, which it characterized as describing something more like conflict preemption—and found it did not have to choose between those views in the case at hand.[304] In deciding that California's law was preempted, the Court stated the "express federal policy and the clear conflict raised by the state statute are alone enough to require state law to yield."[305] Moreover, the court stated that any uncertainty about the existence of a conflict "would have to be resolved in the National Government's favor, given the weakness of the State's interest, against the backdrop of traditional state legislative subject matter, in regulating disclosure of European Holocaust-era insurance policies in the manner of HVIRA."[306] The Court acknowledged that there existed choices in how to pursue this as a matter of foreign policy, noting that the "basic fact is that California seeks to use an iron fist where the President has consistently chosen kid gloves."[307] But for the Court, regardless of which approach it saw as preferable, "our business is not to judge the wisdom of the National Government's policy."[308] Rather, the "question relevant to preemption in this case is conflict, and the evidence here is 'more than sufficient to demonstrate that the state Act stands in the way of [the president's] diplomatic objectives.'"[309]

---

[301] *Id.*, Annex B, ¶ 7.
[302] *Id.*, art. 2(2).
[303] *Garamendi*, 539 U.S. at 416–17.
[304] *Id.* at 418–20.
[305] *Id.* at 425.
[306] *Id.*
[307] *Id.* at 427 (citing to Crosby v. Nat'l Foreign Trade Council, 530 U.S. 363, 386 (2000)).
[308] *Id.*
[309] *Id.* For commentary on the case, see Brannon P. Denning & Michael D. Ramsey, American Insurance Association v. Garamendi *and Executive Preemption in Foreign Affairs*, 46 Wm. & Mary L. Rev. 825 (2004); Matthew Schaefer, *Constraints on State-Level Foreign Policy: (Re)Justifying,*

Prior to *Garamendi*, judicial neglect of the *Zschernig* decision and the dormant foreign affairs doctrine had led some observers to write the doctrine's obituary.[310] *Garamendi*, however, suggested that a version (or versions) of the doctrine survived, and it has since been invoked by the lower courts with greater vigor, along with a degree of refinement. Thus, in a series of cases before it, the Ninth Circuit has emphasized a two-part inquiry: (1) whether the state statute regulates in an area of traditional state interest (in other words, is the state interest weak?); and (2) whether the state statute intrudes upon a power reserved to the federal government (in other words, is the federal interest strong?). In *Deutsch v. Turner Corp.*,[311] the Ninth Circuit held that a California state statute allowing claims on behalf of World War II slave/forced labor victims was preempted. While the plaintiffs characterized the state statute as a purely procedural measure, in which the state extended the normal statute of limitations,[312] the court saw the measure as much more. In its view, "the California legislature chose to create a specific cause of action for persons subjected to slave labor by the Nazis and their allies and sympathizers," including by defining a class of plaintiffs who may sue, setting the method for measuring damages and establishing a special rule for corporate liability.[313] While the court considered that "a state is generally more likely to exceed the limits of its power when it seeks to alter or create rights and obligations than when it seeks merely to further enforcement of already existing rights and duties," it also made clear that not much actually turned on this; what mattered most was that California had "created" or revived "a special class of tort actions, with the aim of rectifying wartime wrongs committed by our enemies or by parties operating under our enemies' protection."[314] As such, the statute intruded upon "the power of the federal government to make and to resolve war, including the power to establish the procedure for resolving war claims."[315] Barring specific authorization from the federal government, the court reasoned, "states are prohibited from exercising foreign affairs powers, including modifying the federal government's resolution of war-related disputes."[316]

Two subsequent cases were broadly similar. In *Von Saher v. Norton Simon Museum of Art at Pasadena*, the plaintiff sought, pursuant to a California statute,

---

Refining and Distinguishing the Dormant Foreign Affairs Doctrine, 41 SETON HALL L. REV. 201 (2011); RAMSEY, *supra* note 18, at 283–99.

[310] Writing before the issuance of *Garamendi*, one commentator presciently argued that claims of the doctrine's death were premature. *See* Vázquez, *supra* note 153.

[311] 324 F.3d 692 (9th Cir. 2003).

[312] *Id.* at 707.

[313] *Id.*

[314] *Id.* at 708.

[315] *Id.* at 711.

[316] *Id.* at 714.

the return from a museum of two paintings alleged to have been looted by German Nazis during World War II.[317] The court rejected the museum's argument that the statute conflicted with any outstanding or material federal restitution policy,[318] but held that it violated the dormant foreign affairs power. The court's first inquiry was whether the statute involved a traditional state responsibility. While the plaintiff argued that extending the statute of limitations for a stolen property claim was a "quintessential state function,"[319] the court rejected that characterization, noting that the statute focused solely on Holocaust victims and their heirs.[320] In its view, "California's real purpose was to create a friendly forum for litigating Holocaust restitution claims, open to anyone in the world to sue a museum or gallery located within or without the state."[321] Moreover, as in *Deutsch v. Turner*, the statute also intruded upon the federal foreign affairs power by establishing a remedy for wartime injuries, even if in this instance the target (museums and galleries) was not a wartime enemy.[322] While emphasizing the federal government's "full and exclusive responsibility" for foreign affairs generally,[323] the court did note, further, that with regard to Holocaust survivors and their heirs, the "history of federal action is so comprehensive and pervasive as to leave no room for state legislation" and offered the potential for better addressing the claims at issue—strongly suggesting that the government had *actually*, not merely *potentially*, occupied the field.[324] The opinion concluded by putting greater emphasis on the limits of state authority: "In sum, it is California's *lack* of power to act which is ultimately fatal."[325]

In *Movsesian v. Victoria Versicherung AG*, the Ninth Circuit, sitting *en banc*, considered a California statute that extended the statute of limitations, and vested jurisdiction in state courts, for certain insurance claims brought by victims of the Armenian genocide, leading to a class action lawsuit against various insurers.[326] The court accepted that insurance regulation was generally an area of traditional state responsibility, but found that the statute was not a "garden variety" insurance regulation, as its purpose was "to provide potential monetary relief and a friendly forum for those who suffered from certain foreign events."[327] Further, the statute intruded upon the federal government's foreign

---

[317] Von Saher v. Norton Simon Museum of Art at Pasadena, 592 F.3d 954 (9th Cir. 2010).
[318] *Id.* at 961–63.
[319] *Id.* at 964.
[320] *Id.*
[321] *Id.* at 965.
[322] *Id.* at 966.
[323] *Id.* at 967 (quoting Hines v. Davidowitz, 312 U.S. 52, 63 (1941)).
[324] *Id.* at 967–68.
[325] *Id.* at 968.
[326] 670 F.3d 1067 (9th Cir. 2012). The class consisted of persons of Armenian descent who sought benefits under the defendants' life insurance policies that were issued or in effect in the Ottoman Empire between 1875 and 1923. *Id.* at 1070.
[327] *Id.* at 1076.

affairs power because it "expresses a distinct political point of view on a specific matter of foreign policy," by imposing "the politically charged label of 'genocide' on the actions of the Ottoman Empire (and, consequently, present-day Turkey)" and by expressing sympathy for "Armenian Genocide victim[s]."[328] Moreover, the statute would require state courts to determine whether the policyholder "escaped to avoid persecution," which would require "a highly politicized inquiry into the conduct of a foreign nation."[329] As such, California's statute was preempted.[330]

By contrast, in *Gingery v. City of Glendale*, the Ninth Circuit held that a city's establishment of a monument in a public park commemorating Korean women who were allegedly forced to serve as comfort women in Japan during and before World War II did not intrude upon the federal government's foreign affairs powers.[331] According to the court, such a monument advocating against violations of human rights "is well within the traditional responsibilities of state and local governments" regarding public monuments and memorials.[332] Intriguingly, the court treated such conduct as being of a piece with other expressive activities and noted that even if the city's objective was (as one city council member put it) "to 'put the city of Glendale on the international map,'" that was consistent "with the role local governments have traditionally played in public discourse related to foreign affairs."[333] Even if that were not the case, the court found it implausible that the monument had more than an incidental or indirect effect on foreign affairs.[334] To be sure, the activity at issue was of modest prominence, but the court's emphasis that, as the complaint alleged, the U.S. government had "consistently sought to avoid" taking a position on the comfort women issue[335] is somewhat in tension with idea of preemption not being warranted on the facts of the case.

The persistent difficulty in drawing a line between permissible and impermissible state and local actions according to a dormant foreign affairs power has led to criticisms that this method of preemption entails a problematic role for the

---

[328] *Id.*

[329] *Id.*

[330] For criticism of the case, see Michael D. Ramsey, *International Wrongs, State Law Remedies, and Presidential Policies*, 32 Loy. L.A. Int'l & Comp. L. Rev. 19 (2010). Subsequently, two years after the House and Senate had passed resolutions recognizing the Armenian genocide, President Joe Biden acknowledged the events as a genocide. Statement on Armenian Remembrance Day, 2021 Daily Comp. Pres. Doc. 1 (Apr. 24, 2021).

[331] Gingery v. City of Glendale, 831 F.3d 1222 (9th Cir. 2016).

[332] *Id.* at 1229.

[333] *Id.* at 1230.

[334] *Id.* at 1230–31 (noting that there was no demonstrated adverse effect on U.S.-Japan relations, and that the city had not taken stronger measures, such as creating a cause of action, or extending the statute of limitations for an existing cause of action, for comfort women victims).

[335] *Id.* at 1229 (quoting Complaint for Declaratory & Injunctive Relief at 12, Gingery v. City of Glendale, No. 2:14-cv-1291 (C.D. Cal. Feb. 20, 2014)).

judiciary and neglects the authority of the political branches—much as might be said of the dormant Foreign Commerce Clause.[336] That difficulty doubtless has contributed to irregular invocation of this method and to calls for its abandonment. Rather than relying upon courts to draw such a line, it is said, preemption should occur only through affirmative action by the political branches of the federal government, such as by legislation.[337] Yet dormant preemption might also be refined or restated in a number of ways. For example, courts might be more amenable to instances in which the state action is principally "inward-looking" rather than "outward-looking." On this view, using climate change agreements or CEDAW as a benchmark for how to regulate matters at the local level would seem to pose fewer risks of conflicts with federal policy. By contrast, action that is outward-looking, such as passing judgments on the governance of foreign states (*Zschernig*) or exposing foreign companies to Holocaust-related disclosure or litigation (*Garamendi, Movsesian*) is more problematic, given the greater potential for creating frictions for the United States with foreign states.[338]

Still, even certain "inward-looking" state action may be problematic. Thus, state-level conformance with a multilateral agreement not yet ratified by the United States might undermine the federal government's leverage to secure a better agreement through further bargaining. Further, the state's conformance might create negative externalities for other states or for the United States as a whole. Consequently, one might instead posit allowing courts to strike down those state measures that involve "direct or indirect negotiating—put less formally, bargaining—with foreign powers on matters of national concern," a concept that may be characterized as a "dormant treaty power."[339]

F. Preemption by Customary International Law

Chapter 5 discussed the manner in which customary international law, or the "law of nations," operates as a part of U.S. law, noting not just its incorporation by legislative or executive act but also by its own force.[340] While the U.S. Constitution is silent on the matter, direct incorporation of customary international law by the U.S. judiciary, when appropriate, is best conceived of as a type of

---

[336] Swaine, *supra* note 290, at 1150–61 (noting common weaknesses of the dormant doctrines).

[337] *See, e.g.,* Curtis A. Bradley & Jack L. Goldsmith, *Customary International Law as Federal Common Law: A Critique of the Modern Position,* 110 HARV. L. REV. 815, 860–70 (1997); Goldsmith, *supra* note 78, at 1624, 1690–98; Spiro, *supra* note 279, at 1226.

[338] *See generally* Burroughs, *supra* note 59. Indeed, *Von Saher* might be understood as a case where the facts presented an "inward-looking" scenario, but the state law at issue had the potential for "outward-looking" application, and for that reason was struck down.

[339] *See* Swaine, *supra* note 290, at 1138.

[340] *See* Chapter 5 § II(C).

federal common law; where that is the case, such law presumably would preempt inconsistent state law.[341]

Yet the Supremacy Clause does not expressly provide for such preemption; it does provide that "treaties" are supreme over state law,[342] but there is no reference therein to the "law of nations," even though that source of law is referenced elsewhere in the Constitution.[343] The Supremacy Clause also provides that the "Laws of the United States" are supreme over conflicting state law, but it refers to such U.S. laws as "made in Pursuance" of the Constitution. Viewing customary international law—which is made, or results from, the widespread practice of nations that they regard as compelled by law—as falling within that portion of the Supremacy Clause may be problematic, as it is not made in pursuance of the Constitution. Further, when establishing the jurisdiction of federal courts in Article III of the Constitution, the Framers apparently did not assume that certain important matters associated with the law of nations (admiralty and maritime issues) would necessarily fall within the scope of the "Laws of the United States"; rather, they made specific reference to such matters, and could have done likewise in the Supremacy Clause.[344]

The Framers were aware of the challenges facing the United States in relation to the laws of nations.[345] In *The Federalist Papers*, Alexander Hamilton spoke about the need for the federal judicial power to extend to the application of the law of nations, because "the peace of the WHOLE ought not to be left at the disposal of a PART"—warranting jurisdiction over cases in which foreign citizens were concerned, at least for "cases arising upon treaties and the law of nations."[346] Likewise, John Jay saw a need for federal courts to apply the law of nations to avoid inconsistencies by the several states.[347] Given their views and others at the time, the absence of "law of nations" from the Supremacy Clause is puzzling; why make a point of referring in that clause to "treaties" but not to "law of nations," if the objective was for both to be supreme over state law? Louis Henkin maintained the following:

---

[341] *See* Chapter 5 § II(C)(2); *see also* Sosa v. Alvarez-Machain, 542 U.S. 692, 729 (2004) (stating that "post-*Erie* understanding has identified limited enclaves in which federal courts may derive some substantive law in a common law way"); GLENNON & SLOANE, *supra* note 16, at 272 ("Customary international law is part of federal common law.").

[342] U.S. CONST. art. VI, cl. 2.

[343] *Id.* art. I, § 8, cl. 10 (according to Congress the power to "define and punish Piracies and Felonies committed on the high Seas, and Offences against the Law of Nations").

[344] *Id.* art. III, § 2, cl. 1 (extending the judicial power to "all Cases, in Law and Equity, arising under this Constitution, the Laws of the United States, and Treaties . . . ;—to all Cases of admiralty and maritime Jurisdiction"); *see* Chapter 5 § I(B)(3).

[345] *See* Chapter 5 § I(A).

[346] THE FEDERALIST No. 80, at 475–78 (Alexander Hamilton).

[347] THE FEDERALIST No. 3, at 43 (John Jay).

838   THE LAW OF U.S. FOREIGN RELATIONS

The Framers wrote treaties explicitly into the Supremacy Clause because the supremacy of treaties to state law was a major issue that had to be resolved, and accepted by the states. Cases arising under treaties were declared to be within the judicial power of the United States because such cases were to be expected; the Framers probably did not anticipate cases or controversies arising under international law until Congress defined offenses under that law or enacted other legislation to implement international law, and cases arising under international law would then be cases arising under the laws of the United States.[348]

Henkin's position is not without merit, though it might lead to a conclusion that the Framers only expected customary international law to preempt state law after it had been incorporated into a federal statute by Congress.[349] An alternative explanation is that customary international law was conceived of as part of the common law of the United States with no bright distinction between it being federal common law or state common law. In either instance, what was important was not to make clear in the Supremacy Clause that customary international law (as a form of federal law) was supreme over state law but, rather, to position federal judges in Article III so that they could apply customary international law (as a form of law present at both the federal and state levels) when resolving disputes implicating such law. The types of cases indicated in Article III, which includes those relating to foreign states, their ambassadors, ministers, and consul, and admiralty and maritime matters, were the kinds of cases where customary international law would be at issue. In other words, arguably the objective was not to make customary international law supreme over state law, because it was part of state law; the objective was to ensure that federal courts could take jurisdiction over cases in which such law would arise. Only over the past century, after the Court's decision in *Erie Railroad Co. v. Tompkins*, does U.S. law draw a sharper distinction between federal and state common law, narrowing considerably the scope of the former, while at the same time locating customary international law within its ambit.[350] As such, only today does the issue of whether customary international law is supreme over state law come into sharper focus.

Such an explanation is reinforced when considering the broader design of the Constitution, as discussed in Chapter 5. When considering the various provisions affording powers to Congress, the president, and the judiciary with

---

[348] HENKIN, FOREIGN AFFAIRS, at 237–38.

[349] In support of that conclusion, see Al-Bihani v. Obama, 619 F.3d 1, 33 (D.C. Cir. 2010) (Kavanaugh, J., concurring in the denial of rehearing en banc) ("After *Erie* and particularly after *Sosa* . . . it is clear that customary-international-law norms, like non-self-executing treaties, are not part of domestic U.S. law," since "when Congress does not act to incorporate those norms into domestic U.S. law, such non-incorporation presumably reflects a deliberate congressional choice").

[350] Erie Railroad Co. v. Tompkins, 304 U.S. 64 (1938); *see* Chapter 5 § II(C)(1).

respect to foreign relations, there is simply no evidence for the view that the Framers intended to grant exclusive authority to the legislature over customary international law, so as to preclude any executive or judicial authority. While the authority enjoyed by those other branches in this respect may not be well defined, it is sufficient to undermine any suggestion that Congress alone occupied the field.[351]

In practice, the circumstances where customary international law as such may be observed as preempting state law appear relatively limited. Until modern times, customary international law principally concerned obligations nations owed to one another, which was not an area in which state laws regulated. The best example in earlier times where such obligations might conflict with state laws concerned the area of immunity of foreign states or their officials. Today, foreign sovereign immunity is regulated by federal statute, but immunity of certain foreign officials (such as heads of state) is not so regulated, thus leaving at least this area to preemption by customary international law.[352] As customary international law has developed over time, such as in the area of human rights, there are today further possibilities for state law to conflict with customary international law.[353] Even then, however, the most likely areas may already have been addressed through U.S. constitutional rights, federal statutes, or treaties, thus obviating a need to resort to preemption by customary international law.[354]

III. Compact Clause

As explained in Section I of this chapter, the states not only retain the capacity to affect foreign relations through independent measures; the Constitution actually licenses them to engage with foreign states through certain types of agreements, at least so long as the states suffer the prospect of congressional review.

The Constitution provides that "[n]o State shall enter into any Treaty, Alliance, or Confederation."[355] At the same time, the Compact Clause provides that

---

[351] See Chapter 5 § I(B).

[352] See Chapter 4 §§ V(A)(1), V(D).

[353] For a sustained argument that the only area of modern customary international law that properly falls within federal law under the Constitution, and therefore preempts state law, is the area concerning the "traditional rights of foreign nations under the law of state-state relations," see ANTHONY J. BELLIA, JR. & BRADFORD R. CLARK, THE LAW OF NATIONS AND THE UNITED STATES CONSTITUTION 75 (2017). On this reading, while the Supreme Court has also determined that customary rules of maritime law are a form of federal law, other kinds of customary international law (such as relating to human rights) have not been incorporated into federal law, and thus have no preemptive effect.

[354] For further discussion, see Chapter 5 § II(C)(2).

[355] U.S. CONST. art. I, § 10, cl. 1. On the drafting of this clause, see Chapter 6 § I(A)(2) & (B)(2); on its significance when determining the types of agreements the federal government may conclude, see Chapter 6 § V.

"[n]o State shall, without the Consent of Congress, ... enter into any Agreement or Compact with another State, or with a foreign power ...."[356] The potential of the Compact Clause has been most extensively explored in relation to interstate compacts. But compacts with foreign states, or their subnational entities, are permitted in ostensibly parallel terms, and these are undertaken for a wide variety of purposes.[357] Among these are pedestrian matters, such as the construction or maintenance of transboundary bridges or roads, cooperation on forest fire protection, use and conservation of water resources, regulating transboundary pollution, and the development of economic ties.[358] For example, the state of California and the ministry of economy of Mexico entered into a memorandum of understanding in 2019 that seeks "to expand the current level of economic and investment cooperation between Mexico and California in, but not limited to, the field of alternative and renewable energy, environment and related clean technologies, agriculture-related technologies, micro, small and medium enterprises, innovation, workforce development, digital economy and creative industries and cybersecurity."[359] But states like California have also reached well beyond their borders to conclude, for example, an agreement with Scotland on combatting climate change,[360] as well as a compact with the World Bank on sharing good practices with other territories and cities on sustainable, low-carbon development.[361]

The Supreme Court (and, indeed, the federal government as a whole) has made only partial progress in addressing how these and other arrangements fit in the constitutional scheme. For example, in assessing whether such an arrangement is an "Agreement" or "Compact" within the meaning of the Compact Clause, one might pause over the potential distinction between those terms. Yet when addressing this issue in the context of an interstate arrangement, the Supreme Court has said that it does "not perceive any difference" in their meaning, "except

---

[356] U.S. Const. art. I, § 10, cl. 3. For commentary, see Henkin, Foreign Affairs, at 152–56; Duncan B. Hollis, *Unpacking the Compact Clause*, 88 Tex. L. Rev. 741 (2010); Glennon & Sloane, *supra* note 16, at 277–89.

[357] For examples and accompanying commentary, see Glennon & Sloane, *supra* note 16, at 277–89; Henkin, Foreign Affairs, at 152–56; Hollis, *supra* note 356, at 754; Swaine, *supra* note 23, at 493–532.

[358] *See, e.g.*, Peter R. Jennetten, Note, *State Environmental Agreements with Foreign Powers: The Compact Clause and the Foreign Affairs Powers of the States*, 8 Geo. Int'l Env't L. Rev. 141 (1995); Alexander Kazazis, Note, *The Western Climate Initiative: The Fate of an Experiment in Subnational Cross-Border Environmental Collaboration*, 37 Brook. J. Int'l L. 1177 (2012).

[359] Memorandum of Understanding between the Ministry of Economy of the United Mexican States and the Government of the State of California of the United States of America, Oct. 4, 2019, https://perma.cc/8ZHT-NTZC.

[360] *See, e.g.*, Memorandum of Understanding between the Government of Scotland and the California Energy Commission, Jan. 15, 2018, https://perma.cc/7NRK-CZW2.

[361] Memorandum of Understanding between State of California and International Bank for Reconstruction Development, International Development Association, Nov. 11, 2016, https://perma.cc/U88R-KT8E.

that the word 'compact' is generally used with reference to more formal and serious engagements than is usually implied in the term 'agreement.'"[362] The question is of little interest, in any event, insofar as the two forms merit identical treatment under the Constitution.

Instead, the first question for foreign compacts—and one that merits greater attention than with interstate compacts—is whether an arrangement is an "Agreement" or "Compact" (whatever difference there may be between the two), which a state may in principle enter into with foreign powers, as opposed to being a "Treaty, Alliance, or Confederation" (again, however those three might be distinguished from one another), all of which are flatly prohibited to the states.[363] While acknowledging that the distinctions drawn among all these terms were important to the Framers, the Court has confessed that they are now lost to us.[364] The most that can be said, at least based on case law, is that treaties and their kin are associated with greater formality than compacts and their kin, and are intended to govern for longer periods;[365] Justice Story added that treaties were also "of a political character[,] such as treaties of alliance" (but also including treaties involving general commercial privileges).[366]

This general distinction between treaties and compacts was applied recently in litigation involving a California-led climate initiative. California and several other states had joined with Canadian provinces in forming the Western Climate Initiative, a collaborative project designed to develop regional strategies for addressing climate change. California enacted laws that permitted state agencies to link the state's state cap-and-trade program with other jurisdictions; eventually, its program was linked with those of Quebec and Ontario, which was then memorialized in an agreement (although Ontario later withdrew). The U.S. federal government, which had become less supportive of climate change policies, sued in 2019, raising a number of constitutional challenges.[367]

One of those challenges contended that the agreement was a prohibited treaty. That challenge drew at least atmospheric support from Supreme Court dicta in *Massachusetts v. EPA*, in which the Court stated: "Massachusetts cannot invade Rhode Island to force reductions in greenhouse gas emissions, it cannot

---

[362] Virginia v. Tennessee, 148 U.S. 503, 520 (1893).

[363] Holmes v. Jennison, 39 U.S. (14 Pet.) 540, 571 (1840) (Chief Justice Taney, speaking for three other justices).

[364] U.S. Steel Corp. v. Multistate Tax Comm'n, 434 U.S. 452, 460–63 (1978) (suggesting "that the Framers used the words 'treaty,' 'compact,' and 'agreement' as terms of art, for which no explanation was required and with which we are unfamiliar" (footnote omitted)).

[365] *Holmes*, 39 U.S. at 570–72 (Taney, J.).

[366] 3 JOSEPH STORY, COMMENTARIES ON THE CONSTITUTION OF THE UNITED STATES §§ 1395–97 (1991) (1833); *see infra* this chapter text accompanying note 380 (discussing Supreme Court's treatment of Story's commentary).

[367] For this and further background, see United States v. California, 444 F. Supp. 3d 1181, 1183–90 (E.D. Cal. 2020).

negotiate an emissions treaty with China or India, and in some circumstances the exercise of its police powers to reduce in-state motor-vehicle emissions might well be pre-empted."[368] The district court, however, concluded that this was a "stray comment" that had little relevance[369] and held that the instrument in question fell well short of the understanding of treaties sketched by the Court on previous occasions. It was not an alliance for purposes of peace or war (unlike, for example, the Confederacy), nor a "cession of sovereignty," given that the Agreement permitted California and Quebec to set their own targets and reporting requirements.[370] Nor, although it helped to create a market of sorts, was it sufficiently extensive so as to amount to a treaty concerning "general commercial privilege."[371] The court seemed to give no deference to the judgment of the executive branch, although the United States had initiated the suit and raised the objection that the prohibition on state treaties was implicated.[372]

Assuming that an arrangement is not flatly prohibited as a treaty, the second question is whether the arrangement is a compact (or agreement) at all, or instead some lesser form of cooperation. In *Virginia v. Tennessee,* an 1893 case involving an interstate boundary between Virginia and Tennessee, the Supreme Court said that the terms compact and agreement, "taken by themselves," were capacious, being:

> [S]ufficiently comprehensive to embrace all forms of stipulation, written or verbal, and relating to all kinds of subjects; to those to which the United States can have no possible objection or have any interest in interfering with, as well as to those which may tend to increase and build up the political influence of the contracting states, so as to encroach upon or impair the supremacy of the United States, or interfere with their rightful management of particular subjects placed under their entire control.[373]

The Department of State, which at times is consulted by states on this issue, "traditionally has looked to whether the text in question is intended to be legally binding," which might be indicated by having a title, preamble, specific commitments, and a signature block.[374] If legally binding, then it appears the

---

[368]   Massachusetts v. EPA, 549 U.S. 497, 519 (2007).
[369]   *United States v. California,* 444 F. Supp. 3d at 1192.
[370]   *Id.* at 1193 (quoting Williams v. Bruffy, 96 U.S. 176, 182 (1877)).
[371]   *Id.; see* Virginia v. Tennessee, 148 U.S. 503, 519 (1893).
[372]   *United States v. California,* 444 F. Supp. 3d at 1192.
[373]   *Virginia,* 148 U.S. at 517–18.
[374]   *See* Letter of William H. Taft, IV, Legal Adviser of the Department of State, to Senator Byron L. Dorgan of North Dakota, regarding a Memorandum of Understanding signed by the State of Missouri and the Province of Manitoba (Nov. 20, 2001), attachment, https://perma.cc/9K9M-BPDP [hereinafter Taft Letter].

department would view the arrangement as a compact. Even if it is not legally binding, the arrangement might still be regarded as a compact. The department has advised that it looks to what the Supreme Court has called the "classic indicia" of a compact, which the Court has applied when reviewing related laws of two or more states: whether the states have established a joint organization or a body; whether there is some restriction on a state's ability unilaterally to modify or repeal its law; or whether limitations on state action operate only on a basis of reciprocity.[375] Applying such "classic indicia," the district court charged with reviewing California's cap-and-trade pact suggested that it was not a compact within the meaning of the Constitution, pointing inter alia to the fact that California was free to withdraw at any time (as Ontario had earlier), even if "the practical consequences of withdrawal may be steep."[376]

Assuming that the arrangement is a compact (or agreement), the Compact Clause appears to call for the consent of Congress. But the Supreme Court's case law has interpolated another, third question, easily conflated with the second one: Is the compact also the *kind* of compact that requires congressional assent? The Court has concluded that certain interstate compacts may be concluded without congressional approval, so long as they do not encroach upon the political power of the federal government. In *Virginia v. Tennessee*, Virginia sought to declare null and void its agreement on demarcation of its boundary with Tennessee, since it was a compact concluded without the consent of Congress.[377] The Court granted that the instrument in question could be deemed a compact, but thought it would be absurd to believe that all compacts would merit Congress' attention: the United States would have no interest, the Court imagined, if one state were to agree to purchase a small parcel of land in another state for a public building, or if states were to agree regarding use of the Erie Canal to transport goods to a World's Fair, or if two states would agree to drain a swamp straddling their states to address an outbreak of malaria.[378]

In the Court's view, the Compact Clause was intended to establish a "prohibition . . . directed to the formation of any combination tending to the increase of political power in the States, which may encroach upon or interfere with the just supremacy of the United States."[379] It drew upon Story's *Commentaries*, which indicated that "the consent of Congress may be properly required, in order to check any infringement of the rights of the national government, and, at the

---

[375] *Id.; see* Ne. Bancorp, Inc. v. Bd. of Governors of Fed. Rsrv. Sys., 472 U.S. 159, 175 (1985).

[376] *United States v. California*, 444 F. Supp. 3d at 1194–95.

[377] *Virginia*, 148 U.S. at 517.

[378] *Id.* at 518 ("[I]t would be the height of absurdity to hold that the threatened States could not unite in providing means to prevent and repel the invasion of the pestilence, without obtaining the consent of Congress, which might not be at the time in session").

[379] *Id.* at 519.

same time, a total prohibition to enter into any compact or agreement might be attended with permanent inconvenience or public mischief."[380]

The Court later admitted that *Virginia v. Tennessee* had furthered a misunderstanding of Story—who was distinguishing as political, and as risks to federal sovereignty, those instruments that were too akin to treaties and therefore prohibited to the states altogether—but nevertheless said that the Court's understanding had become settled law.[381] As a result, the approach taken in interstate compacts remains that only those agreements that increase the political power of the states and interfere with the supremacy of the U.S. government are deemed to fall within the Compact Clause so as to require congressional consent.[382] The case law suggests certain rules of thumb, such as whether a pact purports to authorize the states to do something they would not be free to do in the pact's absence, whether the states delegate sovereign power to a pact-created entity or whether they may reject its proposals, and whether states are free to withdraw at any time.[383]

The Court has not subsequently applied this approach to compacts between a state and a foreign power. The more comparable precedent is *Holmes v. Jennison*, an 1840 case in which a resident of Canada (Holmes) was arrested in Vermont on order of its governor (Jennison) for delivery to Canadian law enforcement authorities.[384] A divided Court held that Vermont lacked the power to surrender Holmes.[385] Chief Justice Roger Taney, speaking for three other Justices, determined that an agreement by Vermont to deliver Holmes to Canada constituted an "agreement" within the meaning of the Compact Clause.[386] He seemed to perceive no distinction between agreements or compacts that required congressional consent and those that did not; instead, he asserted that the "framers of the Constitution manifestly believed that any intercourse between a state and a foreign nation was dangerous to the Union" and "that it would open a door of which foreign powers would avail themselves to obtain influence in separate states. Provisions were therefore introduced to cut off all negotiations and intercourse between the state authorities and foreign nations."[387]

---

[380] *Virginia v. Tennessee*, 148 U.S. at 519–20 (quoting JOSEPH STORY, COMMENTARIES ON THE CONSTITUTION OF THE UNITED STATES).

[381] *See* U.S. Steel Corp. v. Multistate Tax Comm'n, 434 U.S. 452, 459–72 (1978) (providing extensive discussion of the Court's jurisprudence); *e.g., id.* at 466 & n.17 & 468 n.19 (noting mistaken understanding in *Virginia v. Tennessee* of Justice Story's approach); *id.* at 468–71 (noting ratification of *Virginia v. Tennessee* approach and indicating agreement).

[382] *See, e.g.,* Ne. Bancorp, Inc. v. Bd. of Governors of Fed. Rsrv. Sys., 472 U.S. 159, 175–76 (1985); *Multistate Tax Comm'n*, 434 U.S. at 471–72.

[383] *Multistate Tax Comm'n*, 434 U.S. at 473.

[384] Holmes v. Jennison, 39 U.S. 540 (1840).

[385] For discussion of the other opinions, see Swaine, *supra* note 290, at 1224, 1224 n.338.

[386] *Holmes*, 39 U.S. at 573.

[387] *Id.* at 573–74.

The significance of *Holmes v. Jennison* might be debated. Chief Justice Taney did not carry the majority of the Court. Further, his reasoning that the arrangement between Vermont and Great Britain, on behalf of its dominion Canada, amounted to an implicit compact or agreement of any relevant sort—through Great Britain's mere acceptance of the extradited prisoner, in the absence of an extradition treaty with the United States—seems strained.[388] Moreover, as noted previously, subsequent cases take a different approach to the scope of the Compact Clause.

Assuming, however, that *Holmes v. Jennison* remains pertinent precedent, one way to reconcile it with cases like *Virginia v. Tennessee* would note the former's emphasis on the policy of the federal government not to extradite persons who had allegedly committed offenses abroad.[389] In context, Vermont's decision to extradite could well be understood as encroaching upon or interfering with federal supremacy (hence, being the type of compact requiring congressional consent even under *Virginia v. Tennessee*) and as a compact that Congress (albeit implicitly) opposed. Yet some commentators see no need to harmonize the standards being applied in the two cases. Rather, because of greater concerns about encroaching on the treaty power, and greater risks to federal supremacy generally, foreign compacts should be treated as *always* requiring congressional consent.[390] The Court has not taken this step, nor has it directly rejected it, though it has balked at extrapolating the indiscriminate approach in *Holmes v. Jennison* to interstate compacts.[391]

Notwithstanding potential distinctions, lower courts have sometimes applied the standard articulated in *Virginia v. Tennessee* to state compacts with foreign states.[392] For example, in *United States v. California*, the district court suggested that California's cap-and-trade pact was not a compact at all, but it nevertheless proceeded to evaluate whether the pact enhanced state power at the expense of the national government's power, such that it would be deemed the kind of compact that required congressional consent under the Compact Clause. The court applied the Supreme Court's approach in *Multistate Tax Comm'n*, which asked whether the compact authorized members to "exercise any powers they

---

[388] *See* Swaine, *supra* note 290, at 1224–26.

[389] *Id.* at 574.

[390] *See* Swaine, *supra* note 23, at 507; *see also* HENKIN, FOREIGN AFFAIRS, at 154–55; Hollis, *supra* note 356, at 745.

[391] In endorsing the *Virginia v. Tennessee* approach in *Multistate Tax Comm'n*, the Court expressed concern about applying Chief Justice Taney's views so as to discourage forms of interstate cooperation. U.S. Steel Corp. v. Multistate Tax Comm'n, 434 U.S. 452, 460 (1978); *cf. id.* at 464–67, 470–71 (discussing *Holmes v. Jennison*).

[392] *See, e.g.,* McHenry County v. Brady, 37 N.D. 59 (1917) (finding that an agreement of North Dakota municipalities with Canadian municipalities regarding construction and maintenance of a drain was not the type of compact that required congressional consent, consistent with the *Virginia* standard).

could not exercise in its absence," delegated sovereign power to an outside organ-ization, and whether members states were free to withdraw.[393] Unsurprisingly, given that (in keeping with the Supreme Court precedent) the second and third factors were essentially identical to those used to determine whether the cap-and-trade pact was a compact at all, the district court concluded that it would not require congressional consent. It did, however, emphasize more plainly, in rela-tion to the first factor, that "[i]t is well within California's police powers to enact legislation to regulate greenhouse gas emissions and air pollution," and that the compact did not accordingly enhance the state's powers relative to those of the national government.[394]

Assuming that a compact rises to the level of requiring congressional con-sent, a fourth question is whether Congress has so consented. Here the Court has indicated considerable flexibility as to how such consent may be indicated; it may be provided before *or after* the compact was concluded, and the consent might be either express or implicit.[395] In *Virginia v. Tennessee*, the Court found that the compact between Virginia and Tennessee received implicit consent from Congress given that it was known to Congress, and Congress acted thereafter in a manner that suggested no objection.[396] Interestingly, the Court buttressed its conclusion by noting the importance under international law of the stability of boundaries, citing to Vattel, Wheaton and its own prior jurisprudence in support.[397]

This fourth question rarely arises in practice. According to the Department of State, only a few state compacts with foreign states actually have been sub-mitted to Congress for consent. Examples include an agreement in 1956 between New York and Canada to create a port authority for a bridge crossing the Niagara River; a 1958 Minnesota–Manitoba agreement relating to a highway; 1949 and 1952 compacts for addressing fires in the Northeast; a 1968 Great Lakes Basin Compact between U.S. states and Canada; and various compacts authorized under the 1972 International Bridge Act.[398]

The few instances in which congressional consent has been sought reflect, to some degree, the infrequency of foreign compacts that are potentially problem-atic under the Compact Clause, but it also highlights the character of the existing jurisprudence. The Department of State has stressed that, while it is often asked its views of state arrangements, the Constitution does not assign to the executive

[393] United States v. California, 444 F. Supp. 3d 1181, 1196 (E.D. Cal. 2020) (quoting *Multistate Tax Comm'n*, 434 U.S. at 473).
[394] *Id.* at 1196–97.
[395] Virginia v. Tennessee, 148 U.S. 503, 521 (1893).
[396] *Id.* at 521–22, 525.
[397] *Id.* at 523–25 (inter alia citing to Poole v. Lessee of Fleeger, 36 U.S. (11. Pet.) 185 (1837)).
[398] *See* Taft Letter, *supra* note 374.

branch the responsibility for interpreting or enforcing the Compact Clause, instead placing responsibility with Congress and the states themselves.[399] Because Congress is rarely engaged, Compact Clause jurisprudence resembles that of the dormant Foreign Commerce Clause or dormant foreign affairs power: in effect, courts take the lead, with the executive branch sometimes assisting in an advisory role. It is unsurprising, for example, that in the California cap-and-trade pact litigation, the executive branch also raised constitutional objections that leaned heavily on precedent like *Zschernig*, *Crosby*, and *Garamendi*, as well as the line of Ninth Circuit cases applying those decisions.[400] The district court held that California's initiative posed no conflict with appropriations legislation or climate treaties to which the United States was a party, nor with President Trump's withdrawal from the Paris Accord,[401] but the court also determined that the pact sufficiently addressed a matter of traditional state responsibility (environmental affairs) and did not unduly intrude on the federal government's authority.[402] The overlap between these issues and the Compact Clause component of the litigation was considerable, and for all of them the position of the executive branch was rejected.[403] As it happened, the successor administration also disagreed with the government's previous litigation position, and obtained dismissal of the appeal.[404]

[399] *Id.*

[400] United States v. California, No. 2:19-cv-02142 WBS EFB 2020 WL 4043034 (E.D. Cal. July 17, 2020); for discussion of those doctrines and this case law, see this chapter § II. The government also initiated, but then dismissed, a cause of action based on the Foreign Commerce Clause. *United States v. California*, 2020 WL 4043034 at *3 n.8.

[401] *Id.* at *5–7; *see* Global Climate Protection Act of 1987, tit. XI, Pub. L. No. 100-204, 101 Stat. 1407 (codified as amended at note following 15 U.S.C. § 2901 (2018)); United Nations Framework Convention on Climate Change, May 9, 1992, S. Treaty Doc. No. 102-38, 1771 U.N.T.S. 107; U.N. Framework Convention on Climate Change Conference of the Parties, *Report of the Conference of the Parties on its twenty-first session, held in Paris from 30 November to 13 December 2015, Addendum, Part two: Action taken by the Conference of the Parties at its twenty-first session*, annex, U.N. Doc. FCCC/CP/2015/10/Add.1 (Jan. 29, 2016) [Paris Agreement].

[402] *United States v. California*, 2020 WL 4043034 at *8–12.

[403] For an argument that greater deference was owed, see Thomas Liefke Eaton, *Reanimating the Foreign Compacts Clause*, 45 Wm. & Mary Env't L. & Pol'y Rev. 29 (2020).

[404] United States v. California, No. 20-16789, 2021 WL 4240403 (9th Cir. Apr. 22, 2021) (order dismissing appeal).

10

Individual Rights and Foreign Relations

How U.S. foreign relations and individual rights intersect depends on the type of persons, places, and rights at issue. Individual rights of U.S. citizens in the United States vis-à-vis the U.S. government usually present few issues distinct to U.S. foreign relations law. Rights of noncitizens in the United States, however, can differ considerably from those enjoyed by U.S. citizens, and these are properly considered a part of U.S. foreign relations law. Among noncitizens in the United States, moreover, rights may well differ based on the depth of connection between the noncitizen and the United States: for example, a noncitizen permanent resident enjoys greater rights than a noncitizen tourist.

Outside the United States, the rights of U.S. citizens and noncitizens alike may differ from those enjoyed within the United States; much depends on context, such as the U.S. control over the foreign territory where the governmental conduct has occurred. Certain places neither fully "home" nor "abroad"—unincorporated territories of the United States—present yet another distinct circumstance and offer a window on how rights under U.S. law are closely tied to location. Finally, the different types of rights at issue do not all operate on persons and places in the same way, thus requiring a closer look at the nature of the particular right and how it is interpreted.

Section I introduces different types of persons and places that are especially pertinent to individual rights in this area of U.S. foreign relations, specifically noncitizens in the United States; persons in unincorporated U.S. territories; and citizens and noncitizens abroad. Section I also notes that international law on the protection of persons serves as an important backdrop to this area of U.S. foreign relations law; human rights treaties and other rules can have direct or indirect effects on individual rights in U.S. law, and, in any event, U.S. law is the vehicle by which the United States upholds its international obligations on the protection of persons. Following that, this chapter considers salient individual rights, first by identifying in Section II those rights arising under the various provisions of the Bill of Rights and the Fourteenth Amendment, and then by addressing in Section III certain recurrent (and important) subject-matter areas for individuals: immigration law; transnational family law; and extradition.

I. Types of Persons and Places

A. Noncitizens in the United States

Under U.S. law, a noncitizen—often referred to by the term "alien" in statutes and regulations—is defined as "any person not a citizen or national of the United States."[1] The Constitution itself avoids any reference to "aliens" or the like. The Naturalization Clause found in Article I simply accords to Congress the power to "establish a uniform Rule of Naturalization . . . ."[2] There is one reference to foreign citizens: Article III, in addressing the judicial power of the United States, refers to jurisdiction over controversies "between a State, or the Citizens thereof, and foreign States, Citizens or Subjects."[3] In several other places, principally provisions related to requirements for political office and voting rights, the Constitution implicitly excludes noncitizens by making reference to "Citizen" or "Citizens."[4]

The Bill of Rights not only eschews terms for noncitizens but even the term "citizen."[5] Instead, the Bill of Rights makes reference to "person" or "persons" or "people," which, as broader terms, might be interpreted as including a broader class of individuals than citizens.[6] Indeed, this preference for broad terms in the Bill of Rights has led some to conclude that all the protections set forth in the Bill

---

[1] 8 U.S.C. § 1101(a)(3) (2018). As a matter of international law, being a "national" of a country generally refers to the status of a person as a member of that country and is an important concept when considering a country's rights and obligations with respect to that person (such as that country's ability to protect the person diplomatically). "Citizenship" is a different and narrower concept that describes the status of a national as being politically integrated within the country, providing to that person certain rights and responsibilities (such as the right to vote or to run for office). In U.S. law, this distinction also operates, but only to a very limited context. At present, virtually all U.S. "nationals" are U.S. "citizens." *See infra* this chapter § III(A)(1). Given that the distinction for the United States between "national" and "citizen" is largely insignificant and that the U.S. Constitution and most U.S. statutes and cases refer to "citizen" rather than "national," this chapter uses the term U.S. "citizen" to cover U.S. nationals generally.

[2] U.S. CONST. art. I, § 8, cl. 4. For further discussion of this clause, see *infra* this chapter § III(A).

[3] *Id.* art. III, § 2, cl. 1.

[4] *See id.* art. I, § 2, cl. 2; *id.* § 3, cl. 3; *id.* art. II, § 1, cl. 5; *see also id.* art. IV, § 2, cl. 1 (using "Citizens" to indicate privileges and immunities in the several states).

[5] By contrast, the Eleventh Amendment refers to foreign "Citizens" and "Subjects." *See id.* amend. XI ("The Judicial power of the United States shall not be construed to extend to any suit in law or equity, commenced or prosecuted against one of the United States by Citizens of another State, or by Citizens or Subjects of any Foreign State").

[6] *See, e.g.*, United States v. Verdugo-Urquidez, 494 U.S. 259, 265, 269 (1990) (in the context of the use of "the people" in the Fourth Amendment, a plurality of the Court found that the expression "seems to have been a term of art employed in select parts of the Constitution" extending rights "to a class of persons who are part of a national community or who have otherwise developed sufficient connection with this country to be considered part of that community," while "person" is an even broader concept); District of Columbia v. Heller, 554 U.S. 570, 580 (2008) (finding, when analyzing the Second Amendment, that "in all six other provisions of the Constitution that mention 'the people,' the term unambiguously refers to all members of the political community, not an unspecified subset.").

of Rights were intended not to differentiate between U.S. citizens and others.[7] The U.S. Supreme Court, however, has not approached the Bill of Rights in this way, preferring to acknowledge particular amendments, or particular clauses of particular amendments, as applying or not applying to categories of noncitizens,[8] as discussed in more detail in Section II.

Noncitizens present in the United States historically have received at least some constitutional protection.[9] Such treatment may function as the counterpart to the duties and obedience to U.S. law expected of them when so present.[10] Generally, the extent to which noncitizens located in the United States possess constitutional rights varies depending on how close are the ties of a particular class of noncitizens to the United States; the greater the connection of similarly situated noncitizens to the United States, the greater the constitutional protections they enjoy.[11] Closeness or connectivity are measured across a few

---

[7] See, e.g., T. Alexander Aleinikoff, Citizens, Aliens, Membership and the Constitution, 7 CONST. COMMENT. 9, 22 (1990); David Cole, Are Foreign Nationals Entitled to the Same Constitutional Rights as Citizens?, 25 T. JEFFERSON L. REV. 367, 368 (2003); Maryam Kamali Miyamoto, The First Amendment After Reno v. American-Arab Anti-Discrimination Committee: A Different Bill of Rights for Aliens?, 35 HARV. C.R.-C.L. L. REV. 183, 183 (2000).

[8] See, e.g., Plyler v. Doe, 457 U.S. 202, 210, 212 (1982) (stating that all persons within the United States are entitled to due process under the Fifth and Fourteenth Amendments and are covered by the Equal Protection Clause of the Fourteenth Amendment, regardless of status); Bridges v. Wixon, 326 U.S. 135, 148 (1945) (holding that lawful permanent residents have First Amendment rights); Wong Wing v. United States, 163 U.S. 228, 238 (1896) (holding that all persons physically within the United States are protected by the Fifth and Sixth Amendments); Yick Wo v. Hopkins, 118 U.S. 356, 369 (1886) (holding that the provisions of the Fourteenth Amendment "are universal in their application, to all persons within the territorial jurisdiction" of the United States, including all noncitizens, regardless of status). But see Kwong Hai Chew v. Colding, 344 U.S. 590, 596 n.5 (1953) ("The Bill of Rights is a futile authority for the alien seeking admission for the first time to these shores. But once an alien lawfully enters and resides in this country he becomes invested with the rights guaranteed by the Constitution to all people within our borders.").

[9] See Agency for Int'l Dev. v. All. for Open Soc'y Int'l, Inc., 140 S. Ct. 2082, 2086 (2020) ("As the Court has recognized, foreign citizens in the United States may enjoy certain constitutional rights—to take just one example, the right to due process in a criminal trial.") (emphasis in original); RESTATEMENT (THIRD) § 722(1) ("An alien in the United States is entitled to the guarantees of the United States Constitution other than those expressly reserved for citizens"). Noncitizens in the United States also benefit from certain statutory protections, such as civil rights laws that provide criminal and civil remedies for violations of rights of "persons," which is interpreted as including noncitizens. See 18 U.S.C. § 242; 42 U.S.C. §§ 1981, 1983, 1985–88; United States v. Otherson, 637 F.2d 1276 (9th Cir. 1980) (upholding criminal conviction of federal border patrol agents for beatings of undocumented noncitizens).

[10] Something akin to this "social compact" point was made by Madison during the constitutional debates. See 4 JONATHAN ELLIOT, THE DEBATES IN THE SEVERAL STATES ON THE ADOPTION OF THE FEDERAL CONSTITUTION 556 (2d ed. 1836) (stating, when discussing the relationship between noncitizens and the Constitution, that "as [noncitizens] owe, on one hand, a temporary obedience, they are entitled, in return, to their protection and advantage."); see also Cole, supra note 7, at 372; Gerald L. Neuman, Whose Constitution?, 100 YALE L.J. 909, 913–19 (1991).

[11] See Karen Nelson Moore, Aliens and the Constitution, 88 N.Y.U. L. REV. 801, 803–04 (2013); see also Johnson v. Eisentrager, 339 U.S. 763, 770 (1950) ("Mere lawful presence in the country creates an implied assurance of safe conduct and gives him certain rights . . ."); Landon v. Plasencia, 459 U.S. 21, 32 (1982) ("[O]nce an alien gains admission to our country and begins to develop the ties that go with permanent residence, his constitutional status changes accordingly.").

different dimensions, such as the noncitizen's immigration status, whether the noncitizen is regarded as holding an allegiance to a foreign country (especially in time of war), or whether the noncitizen has violated U.S. laws.[12]

Of these factors, the most significant is the noncitizen's immigration status. Noncitizens in the United States generally fall into one of three categories that will be used throughout this chapter: (1) *undocumented noncitizens* (or "aliens," in many legal instruments), meaning noncitizens who entered the United States illegally or who overstayed temporary permission to be present; (2) *nonimmigrant noncitizens*, meaning those who are lawfully present but only have permission to stay temporarily, such as for tourism or for a diplomatic assignment;[13] and (3) *lawful permanent residents* (or immigrant noncitizens), meaning noncitizens who have immigrated to, and have permission to remain in, the United States permanently and eventually to seek citizenship if they wish to do so.[14]

Persons falling within any one of these three categories often enjoy a greater degree of constitutional protection than do other noncitizens; thus, a noncitizen who falls into none of these categories and who is stopped and held at the U.S. border does not even have a right to a deportation hearing.[15] But persons falling into these three categories also receive varied treatment among them. For example, an undocumented noncitizen has a right to a deportation hearing, but generally has no right to assert a selective-enforcement claim (such as a claim of selective bias or corruption in the noncitizen's particular case) so as to avoid deportation.[16] A nonimmigrant noncitizen may be barred from making campaign contributions, whereas a lawful permanent resident may not.[17] A lawful permanent resident who is present in the United States for fewer than five years might be denied an ability to enroll in Medicare, while a lawful permanent resident present for a longer period, such as a decade, might not.[18]

Indeed, lawful permanent residents may be accorded considerable rights. Such persons—who receive an identification card as proof of their enhanced

---

[12] *See, e.g.*, United States v. Huitron-Guizar, 678 F.3d 1164, 1166–67 (10th Cir. 2012) (discussing whether an undocumented noncitizen can be part of "the people" protected by the Second Amendment); An Act Respecting Alien Enemies (Alien Enemy Act), ch. LXVI, 1 Stat. 577 (1798) (codified as amended at 50 U.S.C. §§ 21–24 (2018)) (allowing the removal from the United States of any person who is a national of a country at war with the United States).

[13] *See* Immigration and Nationality Act (INA) § 101(a)(15), 8 U.S.C. § 1101(a)(15) (2018).

[14] INA § 245, 8 U.S.C. § 1255.

[15] Shaughnessy v. United States *ex rel.* Mezei, 345 U.S. 206, 212 (1953). *See infra* this chapter § III(A)(4).

[16] Reno v. Am.-Arab Anti-Discrimination Comm., 525 U.S. 471, 488 (1999). For a broad analysis of different types of rights that undocumented noncitizens can advance across various categories (e.g., workplace remedies or right to counsel), see Hiroshi Motomura, *The Rights of Others: Legal Claims and Immigration Outside the Law*, 59 DUKE L.J. 1723 (2010).

[17] Bluman v. Fed. Election Comm'n, 800 F. Supp. 2d 281, 288 (D.D.C. 2011), *aff'd*, 565 U.S. 1104 (2012).

[18] Mathews v. Diaz, 426 U.S. 67, 82–83 (1976).

status, commonly called a "green card"—may live in the United States for years, even decades, raising children, participating in their local community, and paying federal and state taxes. Yet even these noncitizens are denied certain rights accorded only to U.S. citizens. The Supreme Court has not accepted the proposition that admission to the United States for permanent residence confers a "vested right" on the noncitizen, equal to that of a U.S. citizen, to remain within the United States, nor that the noncitizen is entitled to constitutional protections to the same extent as the citizen.[19] For example, such noncitizens usually are not eligible to vote.[20] They can also be denied certain types of employment opportunities, making it permissible, for example, for a state to form a "citizens-only" police force.[21] Further, a lawful permanent resident who is the citizen of an "enemy" nation is subject to arrest, internment, and even deportation as an "alien enemy";[22] courts will only entertain objections to custody concerning whether there exists a state of war between the United States and the other nation and whether the person is, in fact, a citizen of that nation.[23] Even a lawful permanent resident who successfully becomes a U.S. citizen has a different status than a natural-born citizen, the most famous distinction being the ineligibility of the former to serve as president of the United States.[24]

The diminished rights accorded a lawful permanent resident in the United States, as compared to those of a U.S. citizen, are derived at least in part from the fact that the noncitizen is not fully integrated into the United States as a political matter. Typically, lawful permanent residents remain the national of and (in principle) are loyal to their country of nationality. Further, as explained in *Harisiades v. Shaughnessy*, they avoid certain burdens that a U.S. citizen must bear, such as any requirements of military service.[25] As partial consolation, at

---

[19] Harisiades v. Shaughnessy, 342 U.S. 580, 584–88 (1952).

[20] Federal law prohibits noncitizens from voting in federal elections, punishing them for doing so by fines, imprisonment, inadmissibility, and deportation. *See* Illegal Immigration Reform and Immigrant Responsibility Act of 1996 § 216, 18 U.S.C. § 611 (2018). At the state level, all states require U.S. citizenship for state elections. At the local level, most cities and other localities require U.S. citizenship, but there are some exceptions. *See generally* Jamin B. Raskin, *Legal Aliens, Local Citizens: The Historical, Constitutional and Theoretical Meanings of Alien Suffrage*, 141 U. PA. L. REV. 1391 (1993).

[21] Foley v. Connelie, 435 U.S. 291, 300 (1978).

[22] Alien Enemy Act, 50 U.S.C. §§ 21–24.

[23] *See* Johnson v. Eisentrager, 339 U.S. 763, 775 (1950).

[24] U.S. CONST., art. II, § 1, cl. 5; *see also id.* art. I, § 2, cl. 2 (no person may serve as a representative unless he or she has "been seven Years a Citizen of the United States"); *id.* § 3, cl. 3 (no person may be a senator unless he or she has "been nine Years a Citizen of the United States").

[25] Harisiades v. Shaughnessy, 342 U.S. 580, 586 (1952). When the United States previously has enacted military drafts, noncitizens have been exempted. *See, e.g.*, Selective Service Amendment Act of 1969, Pub. L. No. 91-124 § 1, 83 Stat. 220 (codified as amended at 50 U.S.C. § 3801). Moreover, under international law, the United States cannot compel a noncitizen to take part in military operations directed against the person's own country. *See* Regulations Respecting the Laws and Customs of War on Land, art. 23, *annexed to* Hague Convention (IV) Respecting the Laws and Customs of War on Land, Oct. 18, 1907, 36 Stat. 2277, 2301–02, 205 Consol. T.S. 277.

least, the lawful permanent resident is protected under international law relating to injury to noncitizens, including under treaties of the United States; if injured, a claim on the noncitizen's behalf may be brought against the United States by the country of nationality.[26]

B. Persons in Unincorporated U.S. Territories

One harbinger of diminished U.S. constitutional protections abroad is their application to unincorporated U.S. territories, where only "fundamental" constitutional rights apply.[27] While such territories are under the sovereignty of the United States, they are not deemed to be "incorporated" for purposes of U.S. constitutional law, a status that was typically conferred on territories that were on a path to statehood (such as Alaska prior to 1959).[28] At present there are thirteen unincorporated U.S. territories, five of them inhabited, containing a total population of approximately four million people, most of whom are U.S. citizens.[29]

Following the U.S. acquisition of certain territories, the Supreme Court in the early twentieth century decided in a controversial series of cases—the so-called *Insular Cases*—that full constitutional protections do not apply in unincorporated U.S. territories.[30] Congress, however, may apply certain rights and protections by

---

[26] *Harisiades*, 342 U.S. at 585 (the noncitizen "may claim protection against our Government unavailable to the [U.S.] citizen. As an alien he retains a claim upon the state of his citizenship to diplomatic intervention on his behalf, a patronage often of considerable value.").

[27] RESTATEMENT (THIRD) § 721 cmt. c; *see id.* rptrs. note 3.

[28] Currently, there is just one incorporated U.S. territory, but it is not destined for statehood: Palmyra Atoll, a group of islands having no permanent residents that is located between Hawaii and American Samoa. *See* Office of Insular Affairs, *Definitions of Insular Area Political Organizations*, https://perma.cc/DA47-PWSM. Palmya Atoll is administered by the Department of the Interior. *See* Hawaii Omnibus Act, Pub. L. No. 86-624, 74 Stat. 411, 424 (1960) (codified at 48 U.S.C. § 644a); Exec. Order No. 10,967, 26 Fed. Reg. 9,667 (Oct. 10, 1961).

[29] *See* U.S. GEN. ACCOUNTING OFFICE, GAO/OGC-98-5, U.S. INSULAR AREAS: APPLICATION OF THE U.S. CONSTITUTION (1997). The territories are: American Samoa, Guam, Northern Mariana Islands, U.S. Virgin Islands, Puerto Rico, Baker Island, Howland Island, Jarvis Island, Johnston Atoll, Kingman Reef, Midway Atoll, Navassa Island, and Wake Island. Four of the territories are permanently inhabited and are under the general federal administrative responsibility of the Department of the Interior (American Samoa, Guam, Northern Mariana Islands, and U.S. Virgin Islands). Puerto Rico is also permanently inhabited, but Congress has authorized it to be governed locally. *See* Puerto Rico Federal Relations Act of 1950, Pub. L. No. 81-600, 64 Stat. 319. The remaining territories are not permanently inhabited, raising important questions about the nature of U.S. sovereignty over them. *See, e.g.*, Joseph Blocher & Mitu Gulati, *La Navassa: Property, Sovereignty, and the Law of the Territories*, 131 YALE L.J. 2390 (2022).

[30] *See* Dorr v. United States, 195 U.S. 138 (1904) (finding no requirement of a unanimous jury verdict in, then territory, the Philippines); Hawaii v. Mankichi, 190 U.S. 197 (1903) (finding that the same is true as to Hawaii); Armstrong v. United States, 182 U.S. 243 (1901) (holding that, after the cessation to the United States of Puerto Rico, imported goods from there to the mainland were no longer subject to duties, and a company was entitled to sue the United States for duties paid under protest); De Lima v. Bidwell, 182 U.S. 1 (1901) (finding that Puerto Rico should not be regarded as a foreign state for tariff purposes); Dooley v. United States, 182 U.S. 222 (1901) (holding the same as *Armstrong*); Dooley v. United States, 183 U.S. 151, 151 (1901) (same); Downes v. Bidwell, 182 U.S. 244

statute if it so chooses.[31] For example, in *Downes v. Bidwell,* the Court had to resolve whether Puerto Rico, which was ceded by Spain to the United States after
the Spanish-American War, fell within the scope of the constitutional provision
declaring that "all Duties, Imposts, and Excises shall be uniform throughout the
United States."[32] In finding that such a provision did not apply to Puerto Rico, the
Court distinguished between constitutional provisions that "go to the very root
of the power of Congress to act at all" and other provisions that "are operative
only 'throughout the United States' or among the several states."[33] According to
three of the concurring justices, "[i]n the case of the territories, as in every other
instance, when a provision of the Constitution is invoked, the question which
arises is, not whether the Constitution is operative, for that is self-evident, but
whether the provision relied on is applicable."[34] Here, "[t]he Constitution has
undoubtedly conferred on Congress" a power to govern territories, and in doing
so, Congress must operate "within the limits of [its] constitutional power."[35] Yet
the power to govern territories is broad in nature; Congress can create such municipal government as it deems fit, it can "give to the inhabitants . . . such degree
of representation as may be conducive to the public well-being," and it can even

(1901) (holding that Puerto Rico is not part of the United States for purposes of the Constitution's
revenue clauses); Fourteen Diamond Rings v. United States, 183 U.S. 176, 179 (1901) (finding that
the Philippines was not a foreign state but, rather, "under the complete and absolute sovereignty and
dominion of the United States" and items brought from there to the mainland by an individual were
not imports); Goetze v. United States, 182 U.S. 221 (1901) (finding that the same was true for the
Hawaiian Islands); Huus v. N.Y. & P.R. S.S., 182 U.S. 392 (1901) (finding that vessels traveling between the United States and Puerto Rico engaged in "coasting trade" rather than foreign trade); *see
also* Balzac v. Porto Rico, 258 U.S. 298 (1922) (finding no requirement of a Sixth Amendment jury
trial in Puerto Rico).
    These cases have since attracted considerable criticism, including from the judiciary. *See, e.g.,*
United States v. Vaello Madero, 142 S. Ct. 1539, 1552 (2022) (Gorsuch, J., concurring) (declaring
that "[i]t is past time to acknowledge the gravity of this error and admit what we know to be true: The
Insular Cases have no foundation in the Constitution and rest instead on racial stereotypes. They
deserve no place in our law"); Ballentine v. United States, No. CIV.1999-130, 2001 WL 1242571,
at *7 (D.V.I. Oct. 15, 2001) (regretting the continuing influence of this "thoroughly ossified set of
cases marked by the intrinsically racist imperialism of a previous era of United States colonial ex-
pansionism"); KAL RAUSTIALA, DOES THE CONSTITUTION FOLLOW THE FLAG? THE EVOLUTION OF
TERRITORIALITY IN AMERICAN LAW 79–86 (2009); RECONSIDERING THE INSULAR CASES: THE PAST
AND FUTURE OF THE AMERICAN EMPIRE (Gerald L. Neuman & Tomiko Brown-Nagin eds., 2015);
HENKIN, FOREIGN AFFAIRS, at 307–08. For further discussion of the *Insular Cases, see infra* this
chapter § III(A)(1).

   [31] *See, e.g.,* 48 U.S.C. § 1421b (extending certain constitutional protections to Guam); *id.* § 1561
(to Virgin Islands); *id.* § 1801 (to Northern Mariana Islands). Such laws are generally viewed as
grounded in the Territorial Clause of the Constitution. U.S. CONST., art. IV, § 3, cl. 3.
   [32] U.S. CONST. art. I, § 8, cl. 1 ("The Congress shall have Power To lay and collect Taxes, Duties,
Imposts and Excises, to pay the Debts and provide for the common Defence and general Welfare
of the United States; but all Duties, Imposts and Excises shall be uniform throughout the United
States.").
   [33] Downes v. Bidwell, 182 U.S. 244, 277 (1901).
   [34] *Id.* at 292 (White, J., Shiras, J., and McKenna, J., concurring in result).
   [35] *Id.* at 289.

"deprive such territory of representative government if it is considered just to do so."[36] Given that "Congress derives its authority to levy local taxes for local purposes within the territories, not from the general grant of power to tax as expressed in the Constitution," but from its broader power to govern territories, then Congress' right to locally tax "is not restrained by the requirement of uniformity throughout the United States."[37]

The general reasoning of cases such as *Downes* has led to diminished constitutional protections in U.S. territories. Thus, at present, U.S. citizens in Puerto Rico do not have voting representation in Congress under Article I of the Constitution, nor electoral votes for electing the president under Article II. Yet, by statute, Puerto Rico is entitled to a "resident commissioner" in the U.S. House of Representatives, who does not vote on the floor of the House but can vote on procedural matters and in House committees.[38] Moreover, the reasoning of the *Insular Cases* has continued to inform contemporary jurisprudence in relation to other geographic areas. For example, in *Boumediene v. Bush*, the Court found that detainees held at Guantánamo Naval Base in Cuba enjoyed the constitutional privilege of habeas corpus; even though the detention was outside the United States, the Suspension Clause still had full effect.[39] In reaching this conclusion, the Court discussed at some length the *Insular Cases* (including *Downes*), saying that they established "a doctrine that allowed [the Court] to use its power sparingly and where it would be most needed" and that "[t]his century-old doctrine informs our analysis in the present matter."[40]

While many aspects of the Bill of Rights have been applied to unincorporated territories,[41] their application has continued to be uneven. In *King v. Morton*,[42] the D.C. Circuit in 1975 established a framework under which fundamental rights, such as trial by jury, might be "impractical and anomalous" and thus not applicable in American Samoa, in light of local

---

[36] *Id.* at 289–90.

[37] *Id.* at 292.

[38] 48 U.S.C. §§ 891–94.

[39] Boumediene v. Bush, 553 U.S. 723 (2008); U.S. CONST. art. I, § 9, cl. 2 ("The Privilege of the Writ of *Habeas Corpus* shall not be suspended, unless when in Cases of Rebellion or Invasion the public Safety may require it.").

[40] *Boumediene*, 553 U.S. at 757–59. On the ability of Guantánamo detainees to bring actions before U.S. courts challenging their detention, see this chapter § II(D)(7); on their trial by military commission, see this chapter § II(E)(4) and Chapter 8 § III(B).

[41] *See* Torres v. Puerto Rico, 442 U.S. 465, 471 (1979) (finding that the Fourth Amendment is applicable to Puerto Rico, either directly or by operation of the Fourteenth Amendment); Ralpho v. Bell, 569 F.2d 607 (D.C. Cir. 1977) (finding that, under the Fifth Amendment, a national of a U.S. trust territory was entitled to due process of law before a Micronesian Claims Commission created by Congress); Examining Board v. Flores de Otero, 426 U. S. 572, 599–601 (1976) (finding that Puerto Rico is subject to the equal protection guarantee of either the Fifth or the Fourteenth Amendment); Calero-Toledo v. Pearson Yacht Leasing Co., 416 U. S. 663, 668–69 n.5 (1974) (finding that Puerto Rico is subject to the Due Process Clause of either the Fifth or Fourteenth Amendment).

[42] 520 F.2d 1140 (D.C. Cir. 1975).

customs.[43] In *Califano v. Torres*,[44] a 1978 case, the Supreme Court held that persons residing in the United States may be denied by Congress supplemental Social Security benefits upon moving to Puerto Rico. In *Harris v. Rosario*,[45] a 1980 decision, the Court held that Congress needs only a rational basis to support less beneficial treatment for Puerto Rico and its citizens than is provided to the states and their citizens; more heightened scrutiny under the equal protection guarantee of the Fifth Amendment is not required. In *Wabol v. Villacrusis*,[46] the Ninth Circuit in 1992 upheld, against an equal protection challenge, the validity of race-based land alienation laws in the Commonwealth of the Northern Marianas Islands, with the court seeking "a delicate balance between local diversity and constitutional command."[47] In *Torres v. Sablan*,[48] the Supreme Court in 2000 issued a summary affirmance of the decision by the District Court for the Northern Mariana Islands that "one person, one vote" was not a fundamental right guaranteed in unincorporated territories, even to U.S. citizens there.[49] While such judgments are infrequent, they demonstrate how quickly constitutional rights begin to lose their salience on the "periphery" of the United States, presaging the approach taken to their application beyond U.S. borders.

C. Citizens and Noncitizens Abroad

The U.S. Constitution creates the U.S. government and, to that extent, regulates the actions of the U.S. government, both in the United States and abroad.[50] Even so, at one time it was not clear whether the constraints contained in the Bill of Rights applied to U.S. governmental action taken outside the United States. In 1891, the Supreme Court said in *In re Ross* that they did not apply, broadly asserting that "[t]he Constitution can have no operation in another country"[51]—

---

[43] *Id.* at 1148. On remand, however, the district court found it unconstitutional for American Samoa to deny the plaintiff the right to a jury trial. King v. Andrus, 452 F. Supp. 11, 17 (D.D.C. 1977).

[44] 435 U.S. 1 (1978).

[45] 446 U.S. 651 (1980).

[46] 958 F.2d 1450 (9th Cir. 1992).

[47] *Id.* at 1461.

[48] 528 U.S. 1110 (2000) (mem.).

[49] *Id.*; *see* Northern Mariana Islands v. Atalig, 723 F.2d 682, 690 (9th Cir. 1984) (rejecting a Sixth and Fourteenth Amendment challenge to restrictions on the jury trial right by the Commonwealth for the Northern Mariana Islands).

[50] *See* RESTATEMENT (THIRD) § 721. For a general discussion of extraterritoriality in U.S. law and history, see RAUSTIALA, *supra* note 30.

[51] *In re Ross*, 140 U.S. 453, 464 (1891); *see* RAUSTIALA, *supra* note 30, at 68 ("*Ross* is frequently held to be a defining case for the nineteenth-century vision of strict territoriality."). The Court in *Ross* concluded that the Constitution's protections "apply only to citizens and others within the United States, or [those] who are brought there for trial for alleged offences committed elsewhere, and not to residents or temporary sojourners abroad." *In re* Ross, 140 U.S. at 464.

notwithstanding that the United States in that case was clearly exercising governmental authority abroad by applying U.S. law, through its consular courts, to foreign sailors on U.S.-flagged ships in Japan.[52]

That broad position, however, has not endured. In 1957, in *Reid v. Covert*,[53] a plurality of the Court, in an opinion by Justice Hugo Black, rejected "the idea that when the United States acts against citizens abroad it can do so free of the Bill of Rights,"[54] and dismissed *In re Ross* as "a relic from a different era."[55] *Reid* concerned an attempt by Congress to subject the wives of U.S. servicemen to trial by military tribunals for capital crimes under the Uniform Code of Military Justice, which at the time denied them the protections of the Fifth and Sixth Amendments. The plurality held that this was unconstitutional, stating that the "United States is entirely a creature of the Constitution" and when "the Government reaches out to punish a citizen who is abroad, the shield which the Bill of Rights and other parts of the Constitution provide to protect his life and liberty should not be stripped away just because he happens to be in another land."[56]

The *Reid* plurality suggested that were the Court to treat constitutional protections as inoperative when inconvenient, all rights would be at risk; if such a "dangerous doctrine" were "allowed to flourish," it "would destroy the benefit of a written Constitution and undermine the basis of our Government."[57] Yet the holding in *Reid* scarcely eliminated that risk. While agreeing with the ultimate outcome, the concurring opinions of Justices Frankfurter and Harlan resolved the case on much narrower grounds, declining to hold that U.S. citizens were entitled to the full range of constitutional protections in all overseas criminal prosecutions.[58] As such, since *Reid*, the dominant view has been that the Bill of Rights protects U.S. citizens abroad from actions of the U.S. government, but

---

[52] *In re* Ross, 140 U.S. at 464; *see* HENKIN, FOREIGN AFFAIRS, at 305 ("Why the Justices thought the Constitution was 'territorial', like a deity of old, is not clear.").

[53] 354 U.S. 1 (1957).

[54] *Id.* at 5 (Black, J., plurality).

[55] *Id.* at 12.

[56] *Id.* at 5–6 (footnotes omitted); *see* Kinsella v. United States ex rel. Singleton, 361 U.S. 234, 249 (1960) ("[A civilian dependent stationed abroad] is protected by the specific provisions of Article III [of the Constitution] and the Fifth and Sixth Amendments....").

[57] *Reid*, 354 U.S. at 14; RAUSTIALA, *supra* note 30, at 140–48.

[58] *See Reid*, 354 U.S. at 45–46 (Frankfurter, J., concurring in result) (rejecting the view that Congress was precluded from mandating the court martial of civilians in all cases and calling instead for a balancing of constitutional protections as against essential regulation of military forces); *id.* at 74 (Harlan, J., concurring in result) (finding that "there are provisions in the Constitution which do not necessarily apply in all circumstances in every foreign place"). Just five years earlier, the Supreme Court had let stand the prosecution of a U.S. civilian dependent (who killed her military spouse stationed in Germany) before the U.S. Court of the Allied High Commission for Germany, in a decision that focused largely on whether that court had jurisdiction. Madsen v. Kinsella, 343 U.S. 341 (1952).

the context in which such rights operate may result in some diminution of those rights.[59]

Equally important, *Reid* did little to shore up the rights afforded noncitizens abroad in relation to U.S. government action. Well before *Reid*, the Supreme Court indicated that "[o]ur Constitution, laws and policies have no extraterritorial operation, unless in respect of our own citizens."[60] Further, in *Johnson v. Eisentrager*, the Court asserted that applying the Fifth Amendment to noncitizens abroad would necessarily mean doing so for all other constitutional rights, as "none of them is limited by its express terms, territorially or as to persons. . . . Such extraterritorial application of organic law would have been so significant an innovation in the practice of governments that, if intended or apprehended, it could scarcely have failed to excite contemporary comment."[61] More recently the Court stated, equally categorically, that "it is long settled as a matter of American constitutional law that foreign citizens outside U.S. territory do not possess rights under the U.S. Constitution."[62] According to the Court: "If the rule were otherwise, actions by American military, intelligence, and law enforcement personnel against foreign organizations or foreign citizens in foreign countries would be constrained by the foreign citizens' purported rights under the U.S. Constitution. That has never been the law."[63]

Such sweeping statements are not the whole story. Although case law in this area is relatively limited,[64] it appears that while constraints upon U.S. government action contained within the Constitution do not *generally* apply to noncitizens abroad, they may apply in certain circumstances. Thus, some constitutional

---

[59] *See, e.g.*, United States v. Barona, 56 F.3d 1087, 1091 n.1 (9th Cir. 1995) (considering the applicability of the exclusionary rule when U.S. government agents engage in a joint investigation abroad with a foreign government).

[60] United States v. Belmont, 301 U.S. 324, 332 (1937). For discussion of *Belmont*, see Chapter 3 § IV(D) and Chapter 9 § II(C).

[61] Johnson v. Eisentrager, 339 U.S. 763, 784–85 (1950).

[62] Agency for Int'l Dev. v. All. for Open Soc'y Int'l, Inc., 140 S. Ct. 2082, 2086 (2020) (asserting that "it [was] long settled as a matter of American constitutional law that foreign citizens outside U.S. territory do not possess rights under the U.S. Constitution."); *see also* DHS v. Thuraissigiam, 140 S. Ct. 1959, 1982 (2020) (suggesting that application of Due Process Clause to nonresident aliens would be "contrary to more than a century of precedent").

[63] *All. for Open Soc'y Int'l*, 140 S. Ct. at 2086–87. For criticism of the Court's sweeping statement in this case, see Leading Cases, *First Amendment—Freedom of Speech—Extraterritoriality*—Agency for International Development v. Alliance for Open Society International, Inc., 134 HARV. L. REV. 490, 494–95 (2020).

[64] In 1987, the *Restatement (Third)* cautiously maintained that "[a]lthough the matter has not been definitively adjudicated, the Constitution probably governs also at least some exercises of authority by the United States in respect of some aliens abroad." *See* RESTATEMENT (THIRD) § 721 cmt. b; *compare* Jules Lobel, *The Constitution Abroad, in* FOREIGN AFFAIRS AND THE U.S. CONSTITUTION 167 (Louis Henkin et al. eds., 1990) (favoring application of the U.S. Constitution to all U.S. government actions abroad against noncitizens), *and* Alec Walen, *Constitutional Rights for Nonresident Aliens: A Doctrinal and Normative Argument*, 8 DREXEL L. REV. 53 (2015) (arguing that U.S. case law was never clearly against such application), *with* Paul Stephan, *Constitutional Limits on the Struggle Against International Terrorism: Revisiting the Rights of Oversea Aliens*, 19 CONN. L. REV. 831, 834–42 (1987) (disfavoring such application).

protections may apply depending on whether the noncitizen has a substantial connection to the United States, such as a lawful permanent resident who happens to be abroad.[65] By contrast, as discussed further later, the Fourth Amendment does not apply to the search and seizure by U.S. government agents of property that is owned by a noncitizen (who is not a lawful permanent resident) and located in a foreign country.[66] Some constitutional protections may apply depending on whether the noncitizens are detained abroad in places "within the constant jurisdiction" of the government.[67] For example, nonresident enemy aliens who are captured and imprisoned abroad by the U.S. government in places where there is weak or temporary U.S. jurisdiction or control have no right to a writ of habeas corpus in a court of the United States.[68] By contrast, noncitizens do have such a right in places where U.S. jurisdiction and control are strong and long-term, such as at Guantánamo Naval Base as seen in *Boumediene v. Bush*.[69]

As such, like the application of the Bill of Rights to noncitizens in the United States, application of the Bill of Rights to persons abroad requires careful consideration as to the context, notably the status of that person, the degree of jurisdiction exercised by the United States over the territory in question, the context in which the right arises, and the specific right at issue.

D. U.S. Obligations Under International Law as a Backdrop

International law features, to a degree, in the creation, interpretation, and enforcement of individual rights relating to foreign affairs, such as in the interpretation of "cruel and unusual punishment,"[70] the concept of the "refugee,"[71] or defenses that might be raised in the context of extradition.[72] International law

---

[65] *See* Landon v. Plasencia, 459 U.S. 21, 32 (1982) (lawful permanent resident who travels abroad temporarily and seeks re-entry to the United States is accorded due process rights, including the right to a hearing and to be informed of and respond to any charges against him).

[66] *See infra* this chapter § II(C)(1) (discussing United States v. Verdugo-Urquidez, 494 U.S. 259 (1990)).

[67] Boumediene v. Bush, 553 U.S. 723, 769 (2008) (noncitizens detained at U.S. naval base in Cuba have a constitutional right to the writ of habeas corpus). For further discussion of *Boumediene*, see *supra* this chapter § I(B) and *infra* this chapter § II(D)(7).

[68] Johnson v. Eisentrager, 339 U.S. 763, 777–81 (1950) (finding no writ of habeas corpus right for nonresident enemy aliens who were captured in China by the U.S. army, convicted in China by a U.S. military commission for violations of the laws of war, and then transported to U.S.-occupied Germany for imprisonment by the army).

[69] *Boumediene*, 553 U.S. at 768, 771 (finding that the Constitution reached U.S. government conduct at Guantánamo Naval Base in Cuba where, despite *de jure* Cuban sovereignty, the U.S. government has "indefinite" and "complete and total control"); *see* United States v. Tiede, 86 F.R.D. 227 (1979) (noncitizen tried in Berlin by U.S. Court for Berlin (established under U.S. postwar occupation authority) constitutionally entitled to a jury trial).

[70] *See infra* this chapter § II(F).

[71] *See infra* this chapter § III(A)(3).

[72] *See infra* this chapter § III(C).

classically is a system of law concerned dominantly with interstate rights and obligations, but the system has always paid some attention to the treatment of individuals, such as the privileges and immunities of foreign diplomats, or the seizure and punishment of pirates found on the high seas. Over time, the treatment of all noncitizens became a matter of concern to the field of international law, resulting today in a robust area of international law addressing minimum and comparative standards of treatment for noncitizens, grounded in treaty and customary international law. Moreover, during the past century, the field of human rights has blossomed to address the treatment by a state of *all* persons within its territory or jurisdiction, whether they are noncitizens or the state's own citizens.[73]

The United States has adhered to several global human rights agreements, notably the International Covenant on Civil and Political Rights (ICCPR);[74] the Convention on the Elimination of All Forms of Racial Discrimination (CERD);[75] the Convention against Genocide;[76] the Convention against Torture;[77] two optional protocols on the rights of children;[78] and miscellaneous labor conventions.[79] Such agreements may establish a committee of experts charged with scrutinizing implementation by states parties, such as the ICCPR's Human Rights Committee,[80] and at times U.S. courts have found statements by such committees as persuasive or at least helpful.[81] When adhering to

---

[73] *See* RESTATEMENT (THIRD) §§ 701–03. *See generally* CHRISTOF HEYNS & FRANS VILJOEN, THE IMPACT OF THE UNITED NATIONS HUMAN RIGHTS TREATIES ON THE DOMESTIC LEVEL (2002); *see also* David L. Sloss, *Incorporation, Federalism, and International Human Rights, in* HUMAN RIGHTS AND LEGAL JUDGMENTS: THE AMERICAN STORY (Austin Sarat ed., 2017) (arguing that the Supreme Court's selective incorporation doctrine can be explained and justified by reference to rights found in both the U.S. Bill of Rights and in international human rights law).

[74] Dec. 16, 1966, S. TREATY DOC. No. 95-20 (1978), 999 U.N.T.S. 171.

[75] Dec. 21, 1965, S. TREATY DOC. No. 95-18 (1978), 660 U.N.T.S. 195, 5 I.L.M. 350.

[76] Convention on the Prevention and Punishment of the Crime of Genocide, Dec. 9, 1948, S. EXEC. DOC. No. O, 81-1 (1949), 78 U.N.T.S. 277.

[77] Convention against Torture and Other Cruel, Inhuman or Degrading Treatment or Punishment, Dec. 10, 1984, S. TREATY DOC. No. 100-20 (1988), 1465 U.N.T.S. 85.

[78] G.A. Res. 54/263, annexes I & II, Optional Protocol on the Involvement of Children in Armed Conflict, and Optional Protocol on the Sale of Children, Child Prostitution and Child Pornography (May 25, 2000).

[79] *See, e.g.,* Convention Concerning the Prohibition and Immediate Action for the Elimination of the Worst Forms of Child Labour, June 17, 1999, ILO No. C182, 38 I.L.M. 1207.

[80] *See* Rüdiger Wolfrum, *The Committee on the Elimination of Racial Discrimination,* 3 MAX PLANCK Y.B. U.N. L. 489 (1999). Thomas Buergenthal, *The U.N. Human Rights Committee,* 5 MAX PLANCK Y.B. U.N. L. 341 (2001); Vera Shikhelman, *Implementing Decisions of International Human Rights Institutions—Evidence from the United Nations Human Rights Committee,* 30 EUR. J. INT'L L. 753 (2019).

[81] *See, e.g.,* Igartúa v. United States, 86 F. Supp. 3d 50, 59 n.6 (D.P.R. 2015); Beazley v. Johnson, 242 F.3d 248, 265 (5th Cir. 2001) (holding that the Human Rights Committee expressing "concern" about the incompatibility of a U.S. reservation to the ICCPR did not amount to "an attempt either to void or sever the reservation"); United States v. Duarte-Acero, 208 F.3d 1282, 1287 (11th Cir. 2000); United States v. Benitez, 28 F. Supp. 2d 1361, 1364 (S.D. Fla. 1998).

human rights agreements, the United States has often included reservations, understandings, or declarations (RUDs) with its instrument of ratification, modifying or interpreting the instrument in important ways, an approach taken by many other states as well.[82] RUDs allow the United States to shape the obligations so as to accommodate existing U.S. law or policy, and they often include a statement that the convention is not self-executing.[83] At the same time, the United States has declined to join certain global human rights agreements, notably the two optional protocols to the ICCPR;[84] the International Covenant on Economic, Social and Cultural Rights;[85] the Convention on Discrimination against Women;[86] the Convention on the Rights of the Child;[87] the Convention Persons with Disabilities;[88] and the Convention on Enforced Disappearance.[89]

Further, the United States has supported numerous human rights resolutions adopted by the U.N. General Assembly, notably the Universal Declaration of Human Rights,[90] as well as such resolutions adopted by the U.N. Human Rights Council (or its predecessor, the Human Rights Commission),[91] or other international bodies.[92] These resolutions themselves are not regarded as legally binding, but may codify existing customary international law or may influence

[82] *See* RESERVATIONS TO HUMAN RIGHTS TREATIES AND THE VIENNA CONVENTION REGIME: CONFLICT, HARMONY OR RECONCILIATION (Ineta Ziemele ed., 2004); Eric Neumayer, *Qualified Ratification: Explaining Reservations to International Human Rights Treaties*, 36 J. LEGAL STUDS. 397 (2007).

[83] Curtis A. Bradley & Jack L. Goldsmith, *Treaties, Human Rights, and Conditional Consent*, 149 U. PA. L. REV. 399, 402–03 (2000). For a critique of this practice by the United States, see Eric Chung, Note, *The Judicial Enforceability and Legal Effects of Treaty Reservations, Understandings, and Declarations*, 126 YALE L.J. 170 (2016).

[84] First Optional Protocol to the ICCPR, Dec. 16, 1966, 999 U.N.T.S. 302, 6 I.L.M. 383 (creating a procedure for individuals to send a communication to the ICCPR Human Rights Committee); Second Optional Protocol to the ICCPR, Dec. 15, 1989, 1642 U.N.T.S. 414, 29 I.L.M. 1464 (abolishing the death penalty).

[85] Dec. 16, 1966, 993 U.N.T.S. 3. The economic, social, and cultural rights in this agreement are generally not recognized in the U.S. Constitution, though many have now been established through statutes on matters such as the minimum wage, education, Social Security, and healthcare.

[86] Convention on the Elimination of All Forms of Discrimination against Women, Dec. 18, 1979, 1249 U.N.T.S. 13.

[87] Nov. 20, 1989, 1577 U.N.T.S. 3.

[88] G.A. Res. 61/106, annex I, Convention on the Rights of Persons with Disabilities (Dec. 13, 2006).

[89] G.A. Res. 61/177, annex, International Convention for the Protection of All Persons from Enforced Disappearance (Dec. 20, 2006). *See generally* NATALIE H. KAUFMAN, HUMAN RIGHTS TREATIES AND THE SENATE: A HISTORY OF OPPOSITION (1990).

[90] G.A. Res. 217 (Dec. 10, 1948).

[91] *See, e.g.*, U.N. Human Rights Council Res. 15/21 (Oct. 6, 2010) (addressing "the rights of all individuals to assemble peacefully and associate freely, including in the context of elections").

[92] *See, e.g.*, the United Nations Standard Minimum Rules for the Treatment of Prisoners originally adopted in 1955 by the First U.N. Congress on the Prevention of Crime and revised thereafter, which is now referred to as the "Nelson Mandela Rules." G.A. Res. 70/175 (Jan. 8, 2016). U.S. courts have regularly referred to these rules. *See, e.g.*, Estelle v. Gamble, 429 U.S. 97, 103, n.8 (1976); United States v. D.W., 198 F. Supp. 3d 18, 141 (E.D.N.Y. 2016); Santos v. Holland, 2017 WL 111627, at *14, n.11 (E.D. Cal. Jan. 10, 2017).

the development of such law or the adoption of new treaties. In any event, they have been referred to by U.S. courts when considering individual rights.[93]

On the regional level, the United States supported the adoption of the 1948 American Declaration of Rights and Duties of Man[94]—which it regards as a non-legally binding resolution—and is a party to the 1948 Charter of the Organization of American States (OAS).[95] In 1960, the OAS established the Inter-American Commission on Human Rights, an autonomous entity consisting of seven nongovernmental human rights experts that scrutinizes the implementation of human rights in OAS member states, including the United States.[96] The U.S. government and U.S. courts do not regard the reports, recommendations, or requests (such as for implementation of precautionary measures) issued by the Commission as having any legally binding effect,[97] but in some instances,

[93] Compare Zemel v. Rusk, 381 U.S. 1, 14, n.13 (1965) (citing Article 13 of the Universal Declaration when analyzing the requirements of due process), Kennedy v. Mendoza-Martinez, 372 U.S. 144, 161, n.16 (1963) (citing Article 15 of the Universal Declaration when discussing the "drastic consequences of statelessness"), Velez v. Sanchez, 693 F.3d 308, 319–20 (2d Cir. 2012) (identifying slavery as a violation of customary international law and looking to the International Labour Organization's interpretations of forced labor to determine that plaintiff-appellant had not established a violation as part of an Alien Tort Statute claim), Filartiga v. Pena-Irala, 630 F.2d 876, 882 (2d Cir. 1980) (finding that the right to be free from torture "has become part of customary international law, as evidenced and defined by the Universal Declaration of Human Rights"), and Levy v. Weksel, 143 F.R.D. 54, 56 (S.D.N.Y. 1992) (invoking Article 10 of the Universal Declaration in determining whether the court should take into consideration documents subject to a protective order), with Sosa v. Alvarez-Machain, 542 U.S. 692, 734–35 (2004) (concluding that the Universal Declaration was not legally binding at its inception and could not "establish the relevant and applicable rule of international law"), United States v. Chatman, 351 Fed. App'x 740, 741 (3d Cir. 2009) (holding that "the Universal Declaration of Human Rights is a non-binding declaration that provides no private rights of action").
[94] OAS Res. XXX (May 2, 1948), reprinted in BASIC DOCUMENTS PERTAINING TO HUMAN RIGHTS IN THE INTER-AMERICAN SYSTEM, OAS/Ser.L/V/I.4 Rev. 9 (2003).
[95] Apr. 30, 1948, 2 U.S.T. 2394, 119 U.N.T.S. 3, as amended by protocols of 1967, 1985, 1992, and 1993.
[96] See, e.g., Dann v. United States, Case 11.140, Inter-Am. Comm'n H.R., Report No. 75/02 (2002) (government interference with the use and occupation of ancestral lands by a U.S. Indian tribe); Detainees at Guantánamo Bay, Cuba, Inter.-Am. Comm'n H.R., Precautionary Measure 259/02, 41 I.L.M. 532 (Mar. 12, 2002) (classification and treatment of detainees at Guantánamo Bay Naval Base in Cuba); Statehood Solidarity Comm. v. United States, Case 11.204, Inter-Am. Comm'n H.R., Report No. 98/03 (2003) (denial to residents of the District of Columbia of the opportunity to vote for members of the U.S. Congress).
[97] Mitchell v. United States, 971 F.3d 1081, 1084 (9th Cir. 2020) (concluding that the Commission lacks the "power to make binding rulings with respect to nations, like the United States, that have not ratified the American Convention," and instead it is "limited to making nonbinding recommendations for human-rights improvements"); Flores-Nova v. Att'y Gen., 652 F.3d 488, 493–95 (3d Cir. 2011) (determining "that the [Commission]'s decision does not create an obligation binding on the United States" because the OAS Charter and Commission's governing statute do not make the Commission's decisions binding on the United States, and because the Commission's "decisions are not enforceable domestically"); Garza v. Lappin, 253 F.3d 918, 925 (7th Cir. 2001) (holding that "based on the language of the OAS Charter and the Commission's Statute, . . . the United States has not obligated itself to be bound by the Commission's decisions—or more accurately not to the degree that would be required to create privately enforceable rights"); Workman v. Sundquist, 135 F. Supp. 2d 871, 872–73 (M.D. Tenn. 2001) (relying on Fourth Circuit precedent in determining that no U.S. treaty obligations would require U.S. court enforcement of a decision of the Commission (citing Roach v. Aiken, 781 F.2d 379 (4th Cir. 1986))).

U.S. courts have viewed information compiled by the Commission as pertinent to an issue before the court.[98] The United States signed in 1977, but never ratified, the American Convention on Human Rights establishing the Inter-American Court of Human Rights.[99] Consequently, the U.S. government and U.S. courts also do not view the judgments of the Court as binding upon the United States or as enforceable in U.S. courts.[100] Yet, here too, the Court's judgments might be seen a relevant to a particular issue before a U.S. court, such as the meaning of "extrajudicial killing" under international law.[101]

Obligations under human rights agreements ratified by the United States apply to all persons within U.S. territory, regardless of their nationality or legal status. The question whether such obligations also apply with respect to persons outside U.S. territory over whom the United States exercises some degree of jurisdiction has proven more contentious. The text of any given agreement obviously informs the analysis, but differences of interpretation have arisen. For example, the United States has taken the position that its obligations under the ICCPR only apply within U.S. territory, and not in places such as Guantánamo Naval Base in Cuba, whereas the Human Rights Committee and the International Court of Justice have concluded that the ICCPR does apply extraterritorially, in places where the state party exercises jurisdiction.[102]

---

[98] See, e.g., Aguilar v. Garland, 29 F.4th 1208 (10th Cir. 2022) (considering Commission's report on threats to transgender population in Honduras in reversing denial of asylum for Honduran transgender woman).

[99] Nov. 22, 1969, 1144 U.N.T.S. 123, 9 I.L.M. 673, as amended by protocols of Nov. 14, 1988, 28 I.L.M. 156, and June 8, 1990, 29 I.L.M. 1447; see JO M. PASQUALUCCI, THE PRACTICE AND PROCEDURE OF THE INTER-AMERICAN COURT OF HUMAN RIGHTS (2d ed., 2012).

[100] See, e.g., Garza, 253 F.3d at 925 (acknowledging that although the "Court's decisions are potentially binding on member nations," the United States "has not ratified [the Convention], and so that document does not yet qualify as one of the 'treaties' of the United States that creates binding obligations"); United States v. Li, 206 F.3d 56, 64 n.4 (1st Cir. 2000) (paying attention not to Court's position but U.S. government's contrary position before the Court, in an advisory proceeding, that the Vienna Convention on Consular Relations "does not require the domestic courts of State parties to take any actions in criminal proceedings, either to give effect to its provisions or to remedy their alleged violation." (quoting Written Observations of the United States of America, Request for Advisory Opinion OC-16, June 1, 1998 (corrected June 10, 1998))).

[101] Mamani v. Sánchez Bustamante, 968 F.3d 1216, 1239 (11th Cir. 2020) (citing the Court in a Torture Victims Protection Act case to determine what constitutes an "extrajudicial killing" under international law); see Han Kim v. Democratic People's Republic of Korea, 774 F.3d 1044, 1049 (D.C. Cir. 2014) (citing the Court—with the D.C. Circuit acknowledging that "the United States is a signatory to the Court's underlying treaty, though not a state party"—for the use of circumstantial evidence "in cases of forced disappearance").

[102] Compare Michael J. Dennis, Application of Human Rights Treaties Extraterritorially in Times of Armed Conflict and Military Occupation, 99 AM. J. INT'L L. 119 (2005) (ICCPR does not apply outside U.S. territory), with Human Rights Committee, General Comment No. 31, U.N. Doc. CCPR/C/21/Rev.1/Add.13, ¶ 10 (2004) (ICCPR obligations apply with respect to all individuals "who may find themselves in the territory or subject to the jurisdiction of the State Party"); Legal Consequences of the Construction of a Wall in the Occupied Palestinian Territory, Advisory Opinion, 2004 I.C.J. 136, ¶ 109 (July 9) (finding that the ICCPR's object and purpose call for its application outside national territory). See generally MARKO MILANOVIC, EXTRATERRITORIAL APPLICATION OF HUMAN RIGHTS TREATIES: LAW, PRINCIPLES, AND POLICY (2011).

Similarly, a U.S. reservation when ratifying the human rights treaty may lead to an interpretation regarding the agreement's application to U.S. conduct abroad. For example, when the United States ratified the Convention against Torture, it filed a reservation to Article 16—which obliges the Party "to prevent in any territory under its jurisdiction . . . acts of cruel, inhuman or degrading treatment or punishment"—stating that the United States was only bound insofar as the term "cruel, inhuman or degrading treatment or punishment" was treatment or punishment prohibited by the Fifth, Eighth, and/or Fourteenth Amendments to the U.S. Constitution.[103] The U.S. attorney general–designate in 2005 took the position that noncitizens interrogated outside the United States enjoyed no substantive rights under those amendments and therefore, per the reservation, the United States had no Article 16 obligations with respect to its conduct abroad, such as in relation to the Guantánamo detainees.[104] That position prompted Congress, led by former prisoner of war Senator John McCain, to adopt the Detainee Treatment Act, which provided: "No individual in the custody or under the physical control of the United States Government, regardless of nationality or physical location, shall be subject to cruel, inhuman, or degrading treatment or punishment."[105]

The remainder of this chapter dominantly focuses on the role of the U.S. Constitution and pertinent U.S. statutes for protecting individual rights relating to foreign relations. Nevertheless, international law on the treatment of persons remains a relevant backdrop. On occasion, individual rights identified in a treaty or customary rule feature directly in U.S. law, such as the invocation of an extradition treaty to advance a right in a removal proceeding. Yet there are often impediments to directly applying international law in that way—such as whether the international obligation is self-executing (in the case of treaties)[106] or has the

---

[103] Convention against Torture, *supra* note 77, art. 16; 136 CONG. REC. 36193-99 (1990).

[104] Confirmation Hearing on the Nomination of Alberto R. Gonzales To Be Attorney General of the United States: Hearings Before the S. Comm. on the Judiciary, 109th Cong. 121 (2005); *see* Craig Forcese, *A New Geography of Abuse? The Contested Scope of U.S. Cruel, Inhuman, and Degrading Treatment Obligations*, 24 BERKELEY J. INT'L L. 908 (2006).

[105] Detainee Treatment Act of 2005, tit. X, Pub. L. No. 109-148 § 1003(a), 119 Stat. 2680, 2739 (codified at 42 U.S.C. § 2000dd(a) (2018)). For discussion of the ability of noncitizens to raise challenges in U.S. court concerning their military detention abroad, see this chapter § II(D)(7).

[106] *See, e.g.*, Sosa v. Alvarez-Machain, 542 U.S. 692, 734–35 (2004) (determining that the ICCPR is not self-executing and therefore "did not itself create obligations enforceable in the federal courts"); Igartua v. United States, 654 F.3d 99, 100 (1st Cir. 2011) (same); Carloni v. Birmingham Jefferson Cnty. Transit Auth., 2018 WL 3418214, at *5 (N.D. Ala. July 13, 2018) (same); Hitai v. Immigr. and Naturalization Serv., 343 F.2d 466, 468 (2d Cir. 1965) (non-self-executing U.N. Charter provision cannot invalidate immigration law); *see* Chapter 6 § IV(A).

status of federal law (in the case of customary international law),[107] whether the claimed right is justiciable,[108] and whether the party invoking international law requires (and lacks) a private right of action.[109]

More commonly, international law on the treatment of persons may feature indirectly in U.S. law, such as through a U.S. statute or regulation specifically adopted to implement a treaty obligation,[110] or use of international law to aid the interpretation of a closely aligned concept in U.S. constitutional or statutory law.[111] In any event, U.S. constitutional and statutory law is the primary means by which the United States upholds the obligations to which it is bound for the protection of persons, including under international human rights law. For example, even if CERD[112] does not directly (or even indirectly) feature in U.S. law, the United States fulfills its obligations under that Convention to other states parties by means of the relevant U.S. constitutional and statutory regimes that prevent and punish racial discrimination.[113]

---

[107] See Chapter 5 § II(C).

[108] See, e.g., Sei Fujii v. State, 242 P.2d 617, 621–22 (Cal. 1952) (California Supreme Court finding that the human rights provisions of the U.N. Charter "lack[ed] the mandatory quality and definiteness which would indicate an intent to create justiciable rights"); see Chapter 4 § II.

[109] See, e.g., Shibeshi v. United States, 920 F. Supp. 2d 105, 107–08 (D.D.C. 2013) (dismissing plaintiff's causes of action based upon the Universal Declaration of Human Rights and ICCPR because neither can be enforced by private actors before U.S. courts); Ali v. Rumsfeld, 649 F.3d 762, 791 (D.C. Cir. 2011) (Edwards, J., dissenting) (stating that absent the Alien Tort Statute, "federal courts would have no authority today to recognize common law causes of action for violations of customary international law, such as torture").

[110] See, e.g., Genocide Convention Implementation Act of 1987, 18 U.S.C. § 1091 (2018); Torture Convention Implementation Act, 18 U.S.C. §§ 2340, 2340A, & 2340B; War Crimes Act of 1996, 18 U.S.C. § 2441.

[111] See, e.g., United States v. Duarte-Acero, 208 F.3d 1282, 1285–87 (11th Cir. 2000) (relying on the text of the ICCPR, the travaux préparatoires of the relevant provision, and Human Rights Committee interpretations in rejecting appellant's argument that conviction in U.S. courts would violate double jeopardy protections based on a previous conviction for the same offense in Colombia); Grutter v. Bollinger, 539 U.S. 306, 344 (2003) (Ginsburg, J., concurring) (referring to the CERD when acknowledging that race-conscious admissions policies must have a "logical end point"); Mamani v. Sánchez Bustamante, 968 F.3d 1216, 1237–38 (11th Cir. 2020) (referencing the Human Rights Committee's interpretation of the ICCPR Article 6 right to life when determining what constitutes an "extrajudicial killing" under customary international law for purposes of interpreting the Torture Victim Protection Act); Nahl v. Jaoude, 968 F.3d 173, 185 (2d Cir. 2020) (citing recent International Court of Justice jurisprudence and a U.N. Security Council resolution for the premise that financing terrorism is a violation of international law for states but not individuals, in the context of an Alien Tort Statute claim).

[112] Supra note 75.

[113] See U.S. Dep't of State, Initial Report of the United States of America to the United Nations Committee on the Elimination of Racial Discrimination 2, ¶ 6 (2000). See generally BETH STEPHENS ET AL., INTERNATIONAL HUMAN RIGHTS LITIGATION IN U.S. COURTS (2008); JEFFREY DAVIS, JUSTICE ACROSS BORDERS: THE STRUGGLE FOR HUMAN RIGHTS IN U.S. COURTS (2008).

II. Rights Arising Under the Bill of Rights and
Fourteenth Amendment

The Bill of Rights—the first ten amendments of the U.S. Constitution, which were adopted not long after the Constitution itself—represent a series of restraints upon the federal government in its treatment of persons.[114] The rights contained therein are equally protected from infringement by Congress, the executive, or the judiciary, including by means of a treaty or executive agreement.[115] Moreover, by virtue of the Reconstruction amendments and their subsequent interpretation,[116] many of the same restraints also apply to the conduct of state governments in the United States.[117] While this chapter focuses on federal law, it is worth noting that state constitutional (and statutory) protections also deserve consideration, particularly given that they may be even more protective in constraining state governmental action.[118]

As is the case in other areas of U.S. constitutional law, the rights set forth in the Bill of Rights, while often expressed in absolute terms, are never absolute. The political branches and the courts have always recognized that other interests are at stake, which must be taken into account when applying such rights. When foreign relations are at issue, those interests may include national security, preservation of friendly relations with other states, and the desire that other states reciprocate with favorable conduct vis-à-vis U.S. citizens under their jurisdiction or control. The significance of such interests has led some scholars to argue that, when individual rights come into conflict with matters of foreign relations, such rights are often depreciated, a consequence of not just the potential gravity of

---

[114] See U.S. CONST. amends. I–X. See generally AKHIL REED AMAR, THE BILL OF RIGHTS: CREATION AND RECONSTRUCTION Part I (1998) (describing Bill of Rights).

[115] See Reid v. Covert, 354 U.S. 1, 17 (1957) ("The prohibitions of the Constitution were designed to apply to all branches of the National Government and they cannot be nullified by the Executive or by the Executive and the Senate combined.") (Black, J., plurality); id. at 16 ("no agreement with a foreign nation can confer power on the Congress, or on any other branch of Government, which is free from the restraints of the Constitution."); RESTATEMENT (FOURTH) § 307 ("A treaty provision will not be given effect as law in the United States to the extent that giving it this effect would violate any individual constitutional rights."). On incorporation of treaties in U.S. law, see Chapter 6 § IV; on executive agreements, see Chapter 6 § V).

[116] See U.S. CONST. amends. XIII–XV. See generally AMAR, supra note 114, Part II (describing Reconstruction Amendments); infra this chapter § II(G) (discussing Fourteenth Amendments).

[117] See McDonald v. City of Chicago, 561 U.S. 742, 759–63 (2010) (describing the Supreme Court's varied approaches to incorporation, concluding with a "selective incorporation" approach); AMAR, supra note 114, at 7. The Constitution's amendments do not exhaust the constitutional protections afforded individuals, including noncitizens, against the several states. For example, Article I, Section 10, of the Constitution forbids states from passing any bill of attainder, any ex post facto law, or any law impairing the obligation of contracts. U.S. CONST. art. I, § 10, cl. 1.

[118] For a seminal account, see William J. Brennan, Jr., State Constitutions and the Protection of Individual Rights, 90 HARV. L. REV. 489 (1977); see also William J. Brennan, Jr., The Bill of Rights and the States: The Revival of State Constitutions as Guardians of Individual Rights, 61 N.Y.U. L. REV. 535 (1986).

issues of foreign relations but also the tendency of U.S. courts to be cautious in an area where their perceived expertise is minimal.[119] Further, as discussed later, the level of scrutiny applied by a court when considering laws that deny rights may turn on whether the rights being harmed are those of a noncitizen and, if so, on that noncitizen's legal status.[120]

Finally, in some instances it may not be possible even to secure judicial review of alleged harm to an individual's rights. For example, the effort by a father to secure review of a claim that his son (a U.S. citizen) was being unlawfully targeted by the U.S. government to be killed in Yemen, as part of a "global war on terrorism," was deemed as presenting a nonjusticiable political question, given that "national security, military matters and foreign relations are 'quintessential sources of political questions.'"[121] Similarly, a U.S. journalist based in opposition-held northwestern Syria—Bilal Abdul Kareem—alleged in U.S. court that he was placed by the United States on a "kill list" and was being targeted with air strikes in violation of his due process rights. Again, U.S. district and circuit courts dismissed the case, this time on grounds relating to standing and the state secrets privilege.[122] In *United States v. Zubaydah*, a noncitizen was captured by

---

[119] *See, e.g.*, Louis Henkin, Constitutionalism, Democracy, and Foreign Affairs 71–73 (1990); Norman Dorsen, *Foreign Affairs and Civil Liberties, in* Foreign Affairs and the U.S. Constitution 134 (Louis Henkin et al. eds., 1990). *See generally* Chapter 4.

[120] When courts consider the constitutionality of certain laws, they may engage in different forms of judicial review. In areas such as equal protection of the law or restrictions on content-based speech, courts normally will scrutinize the challenged law in one of three ways: strict scrutiny, intermediate scrutiny (or "heightened scrutiny"), and rational basis scrutiny. For a law to pass strict scrutiny, it must further a compelling governmental interest and be narrowly tailored to achieve that interest. To pass intermediate scrutiny, the law must further an important government interest and do so by means that are substantially related to that interest. To pass rational basis scrutiny, the law must be rationally related to a legitimate government interest, whether real or hypothetical. *See* Erwin Chemerinsky, Constitutional Law: Principles and Policies § 6.5 (6th ed. 2019).

[121] Al-Aulaqi v. Obama, 727 F. Supp. 2d 1, 44–45, 48–49 (D.D.C. 2010) (quoting El-Shifa Pharm. Indus. Co. v. United States, 607 F.3d 836, 841 (D.C. Cir. 2010)). The father was also deemed to lack standing to bring the claim on behalf of his son. The son was thereafter killed in a U.S. drone strike, along with another U.S. citizen. *See* Ruairi McDonnell, Note, *The Vice of Prudence: Judicial Abstention and the Case of* Al-Aulaqi v. Obama, 74 U. Pitt. L. Rev. 759, 762 (2013). For discussion of the administrative process behind such targeted killings and associated efforts before U.S. courts, see Elena Chachko, *Administrative National Security*, 108 Geo. L.J. 1063, 1079–89 (2020).

[122] The district court initially denied the government's motion to dismiss on standing and political question grounds, declaring that Kareem had pleaded a plausible claim and had a right as a U.S. citizen to invoke the Fifth Amendment and demand due process before the government could terminate his life. Zaidan v. Trump, 317 F. Supp. 3d 8 (D.D.C. 2018). The government then invoked the state secrets privilege and again moved to dismiss on the grounds that whether Kareem had been targeted for death is a state secret and the government need not reveal it. The district court dismissed the claim on that basis, while the circuit court found that Kareem lacked standing to sue, finding that—on the available evidence—there was no plausible basis to conclude that Kareem had been targeted. Kareem v. Haspel, 412 F. Supp. 3d 52 (D.D.C. 2019), *vacated and remanded*, 986 F.3d 859 (D.C. Cir. 2021). The state secrets privilege originated in *United States v. Reynolds*, in which the Court found that the executive branch could bar evidence from being used in court—even if it results in termination of the proceedings—if the executive deems that release of the information would impair national security. United States v. Reynolds, 345 U.S. 1 (1953); *see also* Tenet v. Doe, 544 U.S. 1 (2005) (concluding that espionage agents cannot sue the government to enforce an espionage contract, as doing so would

the United States in Pakistan as an alleged member of al-Qaeda and was allegedly transferred to multiple "black sites" where he was subjected to torture.[123] When Zubaydah sought disclosures from two contractors as to their role in his detention, he initially prevailed before lower courts, but the Supreme Court dismissed his case due to the state secrets privilege. According to a fractured majority, the type of information that Zubaydah sought "would tend to confirm (or deny) the existence of a CIA detention site in Poland," and thus there was reasonable cause for the government to consider any further confirmation a matter of national security, potentially exposing the existence of black sites in other foreign states.[124]

A. Speech, Religion, and the Press (First Amendment)

Conduct of U.S. citizens in the United States is fully protected by the First Amendment, even if such conduct touches upon U.S. foreign relations.[125] For example, in *Lamont v. Postmaster General*, the Supreme Court struck down a statute authorizing the post office to retain all mail from abroad determined to be "Communist political propaganda" and to forward it to addressees only upon their request.[126] According to the Court, imposing such an obligation on the addressee was "almost certain to have a deterrent effect" on the receipt of literature and thus constituted an unconstitutional limitation on the addressee's rights under the First Amendment.[127]

Noncitizens residing in the United States are also entitled to First Amendment protections.[128] In *Bridges v. Wixon*,[129] the Court held that, in light of the First Amendment, a federal statute could not constitutionally authorize the

---

jeopardize the protection of state secrets); Gen. Dynamics Corp. v. United States, 563 U.S. 478, 479 (2011) (finding that "when full litigation of that defense 'would inevitably lead to the disclosure of' state secrets, neither party can obtain judicial relief" (quoting Totten v. United States, 92 U.S. 105, 107 (1876))).

[123] United States v. Zubaydah, 142 S. Ct. 959, 963–65 (2022).
[124] *Id.* at 968. On nonjusticiability in foreign relations cases generally, see Chapter 4 § II.
[125] The First Amendment provides: "Congress shall make no law respecting an establishment of religion, or prohibiting the free exercise thereof; or abridging the freedom of speech, or of the press; or the right of the people peaceably to assemble, and to petition the government for a redress of grievances." U.S. CONST. amend. I. Moreover, although the First Amendment begins with the phrase "Congress shall make no law," the rights it describes are equally protected from infringement by the executive or the judiciary. *See, e.g.*, HENKIN, FOREIGN AFFAIRS, at 284 & n.4 (explaining that First Amendment freedoms apply to congressional, executive, and judicial actions). For a general discussion of the First Amendment, see ERWIN CHEMERINSKY, CONSTITUTIONAL LAW: PRINCIPLES AND POLICIES §§ 11, 12 (6th ed. 2019).
[126] 381 U.S. 301 (1965).
[127] *Id.* at 307.
[128] *See* RESTATEMENT (THIRD) § 722 cmt. a.
[129] 326 U.S. 135 (1945).

U.S. government to deport a noncitizen on the basis of literature he had published that "revealed a militant advocacy of the cause of trade-unionism," but that "did not teach or advocate or advise . . . subversive conduct."[130] Similarly, in *Bello-Reyes v. Gaynor*, an undocumented noncitizen who lived for decades in the United States was arrested and then released on bond pending removal proceedings.[131] Thereafter, the noncitizen became active in publicly opposing government immigration policies, at which point the government again arrested him and increased his bond. When the noncitizen asserted that his rearrest and detention were in retaliation for his protected speech, the Ninth Circuit found that once a petitioner—even an undocumented noncitizen—makes a showing of a First Amendment retaliation claim, the burden shifts to the government to show that it would have taken the same action even in the absence of the protected conduct.[132] By contrast, at least in the era of McCarthyism, lawful permanent residents have been deported for conduct that implicates free speech, such as joining an organization (the Communist Party) that advocates the overthrow of the U.S. government by force.[133]

Interestingly, the strength of First Amendment protections in the United States has led to the phenomenon of "libel tourism," whereby plaintiffs secure judgments in foreign courts that apply more plaintiff-friendly defamation law, and then seek to enforce the judgments in the United States. To limit such actions, the federal government in 2010 adopted the SPEECH Act, designed to prevent enforcement of foreign libel judgments unless they comply with the standards of U.S. law, including the First Amendment.[134]

U.S. citizens operating abroad continue to enjoy the protections of the First Amendment with respect to conduct of the U.S. government. For example, in *Agency for International Development v. Alliance for Open Society International, Inc.*, the Court found that the First Amendment forbids the government from distorting speech by requiring, as a condition of receiving federal funds, that U.S. nongovernmental organizations operating abroad "pledge allegiance" to a state-sponsored message.[135] By contrast, the Court has recently stated that nonresident noncitizens abroad possess no First Amendment rights. In a second round of *Agency for International Development*, the Court found that, because

---

[130] *Id.* at 148.

[131] Bello-Reyes v. Gaynor, 985 F.3d 696 (9th Cir. 2021).

[132] *Id.* at 702.

[133] Harisiades v. Shaughnessy, 342 U.S. 580, 591–92 (1952) ("We think the First Amendment does not prevent the deportation of these aliens"); *see infra* this chapter § III(A)(1). While *Harisiades* has never been overruled, developments in First Amendment jurisprudence might lead to a different result today.

[134] Securing the Protection of our Enduring and Established Constitutional Heritage (SPEECH) Act, Pub. L. No. 111-223, 124 Stat. 2380 (2010) (codified at 28 U.S.C. § 4101 note (2018)).

[135] Agency for Int'l Dev. v. All. for Open Soc'y Int'l, 570 U.S. 205 (2013).

the *foreign* affiliates of U.S. nongovernmental organizations possess no First Amendment rights, the U.S. government's statutory requirement requiring such organizations to have "a policy explicitly opposing prostitution and sex trafficking" in order to receive funding did not violate the Constitution.[136]

Although in principle free speech protections apply equally to the realm of foreign relations,[137] some courts and observers identify a "national security" exception to such protections,[138] informed by a long history of governmental reactions to perceived foreign threats and wartime dangers.[139] While a government invocation of "national security" does not result in complete deference by the courts, it does factor heavily in balancing free speech interests of individuals against the broader public interest.[140] Indeed, the Supreme Court has considered it "obvious and unarguable that no governmental interest is more compelling than the security of the Nation."[141]

As discussed in the following subsections, the First Amendment has notably featured in a few areas of U.S. foreign relations law: (1) the regulation of protests near embassies or consulates; (2) the denial of the entry of noncitizens to the United States; (3) the unlawful disclosure of classified foreign relations information; (4) public access to foreign relations information; and (5) the provision of material support to foreign terrorist organizations.

---

[136] Agency for Int'l Dev. v. All. for Open Soc'y Int'l, 140 S. Ct. 2082 (2020) (relating to funding under the United States Leadership Against HIV/AIDS, Tuberculosis, and Malaria Act, Pub. L. No. 108-25, 117 Stat. 711 (codified as amended in scattered sections of 22 and 42 U.S.C.)).

[137] N.Y. Times Co. v. United States, 403 U.S. 713, 714 (1971) (per curiam).

[138] *See, e.g.*, United States v. Rosen, 445 F. Supp. 2d 602, 632 (E.D. Va. 2006), *amended* 2006 WL 5049154 (E.D. Va. Aug. 16, 2006), *aff'd*, 557 F.3d 192 (4th Cir. 2009); Worthy v. Herter, 270 F.2d 905, 908 (D.C. Cir. 1959) ("In case of a clear and present danger to the national security, even so generally unrestrictable a right as speech can be restricted. In case of a reasonably anticipated threat to security or to law and order, many acts by individuals can be restricted."). *See generally* GEOFFREY R. STONE, PERILOUS TIMES: FREE SPEECH IN WARTIME: FROM THE SEDITION ACT OF 1798 TO THE WAR ON TERRORISM (2004); Geoffrey R. Stone, *Free Speech and National Security*, 84 IND. L.J. 939, 954 (2009) [hereinafter Stone, *Free Speech and National Security*].

[139] Such measures include the Alien and Sedition Acts of the late eighteenth century, the Wilson administration's prosecution of some two thousand persons opposed to U.S. involvement in World War I, and Senator Joseph McCarthy's attacks on persons in the 1950s for vague ties to communism.

[140] *See Rosen*, 445 F. Supp. at 632–33; *see also* HENKIN, FOREIGN AFFAIRS, at 286.

[141] Haig v. Agee, 453 U.S. 280, 307 (1981) (internal quotation marks and citations omitted). *But see* Andrew V. Moshirnia, *Valuing Speech and Open Source Intelligence in the Face of Judicial Deference*, 4 HARV. NAT'L SEC. J. 385 (2013). Such concerns animated the views of some Supreme Court justices when considering permissible procedures for prosecuting detainees in the post-9/11 period. *See, e.g.*, Hamdan v. Rumsfeld, 548 U.S. 557, 723 (2006) (Thomas, J., dissenting) (citing *Haig* when stating "this Court has concluded, in the very context of a threat to reveal our Nation's intelligence gathering sources and methods, that '[i]t is "obvious and unarguable" that no governmental interest is more compelling than the security of the Nation' "); Hamdi v. Rumsfeld, 542 U.S. 507, 595 (2004) (Thomas, J., dissenting) ("[A] meaningful ability to challenge the Government's factual allegations will probably require the Government to divulge highly classified information to the purported enemy combatant, who might then upon release return to the fight armed with our most closely held secrets.").

1. Regulation of Protests Near Embassies or Consulates

According to First Amendment jurisprudence, content-based governmental restraints on speech and association are strongly disfavored, while content-neutral regulation of time, place, or manner of expression is scrutinized less rigorously.[142] In *Boos v. Barry*,[143] the Court struck down as facially invalid a D.C. statutory provision declaring it unlawful to "display . . . any sign within 500 feet of a foreign embassy . . . that tends to bring that foreign government into 'public odium' or 'public disrepute.'"[144] The Court viewed the provision as a content-based restriction on political speech in a public forum that was not narrowly tailored to serve a compelling state interest, including the desire to protect the dignity of foreign diplomatic personnel as required under international law.[145] Among other things, the Court compared the D.C. statute with a federal criminal statute that applied in places other than the District of Columbia, which was focused not on types of speech, but narrowly on acts that "intimidate, coerce, threaten, or harass a foreign official"—language specifically intended to avoid concerns arising under the First Amendment.[146]

At the same time, the Court held that a D.C. statutory provision prohibiting persons from congregating within 500 feet of a foreign embassy, and that required persons to obey a police dispersal order, was not facially invalid. Here the Court emphasized that the provision was a content-neutral restriction on the place and manner of speech.[147]

2. Right to Receive Foreign Speech

Citizens have sometimes invoked the First Amendment as a basis for their ability to invite noncitizens to travel to the United States for the purpose of receiving information and exchanging ideas. As a general matter, the Constitution does not accord a right of entry for noncitizens seeking admission to the United States.[148] In *Kleindienst v. Mandel*,[149] however, the U.S. claimants contended that their First and Fifth Amendment rights were being violated by the government's denial of entry to a Belgian professor of Marxist theory who had been invited to speak at the claimants' universities. More specifically, the claimants challenged the attorney general's decision not to issue a discretionary waiver under a statutory

---

[142] ERWIN CHEMERINSKY, CONSTITUTIONAL LAW: PRINCIPLES AND POLICIES §§ 11.3, 11.4 (6th ed. 2019); HENKIN, FOREIGN AFFAIRS, at 287.

[143] 485 U.S. 312 (1988); *see* Frend v. United States, 100 F.2d 691 (D.C. Cir. 1938) (upholding a D.C. law prohibiting picketing within 500 feet of an embassy); RESTATEMENT (THIRD) § 721 cmt. d & rptrs. note 4.

[144] *Boos*, 485 U.S. at 315.

[145] *Id.* at 318–29.

[146] *Id.* at 324–26 (discussing 18 U.S.C. § 112(b)(2) (2018)).

[147] *Id.* at 329–32; *see* HENKIN, FOREIGN AFFAIRS, at 288.

[148] *See infra* this chapter § III(A).

[149] 408 U.S. 753 (1972).

provision barring noncitizens from obtaining a U.S. visa if they advocated or published communist doctrine.[150]

While the district court held the noncitizen had no personal right of entry to the United States, it concluded that U.S. citizens *do* have a First Amendment right to have the noncitizen enter and to hear him—in essence, a right to receive foreign speech.[151] In reversing, the Supreme Court acknowledged the First Amendment implications of the visa denial. Yet the Court declined even to balance those rights against governmental regulatory interests, on the predicate that the attorney general's decision was a valid exercise of a plenary power relating to admission of noncitizens that Congress had delegated to the executive.[152] It held that "when the Executive exercises this power [to exclude a noncitizen] on the basis of a facially legitimate and bona fide reason, the courts will neither look behind the exercise of that discretion, nor test it by balancing its justification against the [plaintiffs'] First Amendment interests."[153] Lower courts have often applied this "facially legitimate and bona fide" test when accepting or rejecting challenges to individual visa denials.[154]

This right under the First Amendment to receive speech or information from abroad can feature in more usual contexts. For example, in *Thunder Studios*, Australian citizens—following a business deal that went sour—sent hundreds of emails to employees of California-based Thunder Studios, hired protesters to picket the studio, and hired vans to drive around Los Angeles with messages against the studio. Thunder Studios successfully sued the Australians

---

[150] *Id.* at 756–60.

[151] Mandel v. Mitchell, 325 F. Supp. 620 (E.D.N.Y. 1971); *see* Joseph Thai, *The Right to Receive Foreign Speech*, 71 OKLA. L. REV. 269 (2018).

[152] *Kleindienst*, 408 U.S. at 769–70.

[153] *Id.* at 770; *see also* Burrafato v. U.S. Dep't of State, 523 F.2d 554, 556–57 (2d Cir. 1975) (citing *Mandel* to "require justification for an alien's exclusion" and finding that, because the noncitizen was present in the United States illegally, "no constitutional rights of American citizens over which a federal court would have jurisdiction are 'implicated' here.").

[154] *See, e.g.,* Cardenas v. United States, 826 F.3d 1164, 1172–73 (9th Cir. 2016); Am. Acad. of Religion v. Napolitano, 573 F.3d 115, 125 (2d Cir. 2009); Marczak v. Greene, 971 F.2d 510, 517 (10th Cir. 1992) (finding that a consular official's "decision must be at least reasonably supported by the record"); Allende v. Shultz, 605 F. Supp. 1220, 1224–25 (D. Mass. 1985), *aff'd,* 845 F.2d 1111 (1988) (holding that U.S. officials did not exhibit a "facially legitimate" justification for prohibiting the entrance of a public speaker when they argued that her entrance would be "prejudicial to the public interest"); Harvard L. Sch. F. v. Shultz, 633 F. Supp. 525, 531–32 (D. Mass. 1986), *vacated,* 852 F.2d 563 (1st Cir. 1986) ("The public interest in preserving free and open debate on" policies that are in conflict with those of the U.S. government "must be regarded as of overwhelming priority, as mandated by the First Amendment, and as being at the heart of our survival as a free people."); NGO Comm. on Disarmament v. Haig, No. 82 Civ. 3636, slip op. (S.D.N.Y. June 10, 1982), *aff'd,* 697 F.2d 294 (2d Cir. 1982) (applying the *Mandel* test to hold that the court could not examine the government's discretion in not permitting a group of 320 foreign nationals to come to the United States for a U.N. conference); Am. Socio. Ass'n v. Chertoff, 588 F. Supp. 2d 166, 173 (D. Mass. 2008) (plaintiffs had a right to "'*Mandel* review' to determine whether the visa denial at issue had been supported by a 'facially legitimate and bona fide reason'" (quoting Adams v. Baker, 909 F.2d 643, 650 (1st Cir. 1990); Allende v. Shultz, 845 F.2d 1111, 1116 (1st Cir. 1988))).

in U.S. district court for the tort of stalking under California law, but the Ninth Circuit reversed. Although the Australians were located at all relevant times outside the United States, their conduct was protected under the First Amendment, given that the First Amendment "includes the right to receive information from outside the United States" and the "speech and speech-related activity" were "directed at and received by California residents."[155]

Not all such situations have yet to be litigated. For example, the U.S. government engages in cyber operations that seek to defend against covert foreign government influence operations that target the U.S. electorate with disinformation. While *Kleindienst* stands for the proposition that the U.S. government may incidentally burden the right to receive information from foreign sources, and while there is a compelling government interest in protecting U.S. elections from foreign interference,[156] any government actions based on the content of speech is suspect. Consequently, the government must analyze various factors when embarking on such cyber operations, including whether the operation can be undertaken in a "content neutral" manner.[157]

3. Denial of Entry of Noncitizens with Respect to Religion and Free Exercise

The First Amendment's Establishment Clause and Free Exercise Clause have also been invoked in litigation concerning admission of noncitizens to the United States. By a series of executive decisions, President Trump imposed travel restrictions on noncitizens coming from specified countries whose populations were principally Muslim, arguing that such action was necessary as a matter of addressing terrorist threats.[158] Opponents alleged, among other things, that such "travel bans" or "Muslim bans" violated the Establishment Clause by inhibiting U.S. citizens in their interactions with noncitizens of the Muslim faith and by stigmatizing the Islamic religion (through singling out Muslim immigrants and refugees), which they supported by citing various public comments by President Trump and his advisers.[159]

---

[155] Thunder Studios, Inc. v. Kazal, 13 F.4th 736, 743–44 (9th Cir. 2021).

[156] Bluman v. FEC, 800 F. Supp. 2d 281, 288 (D.D.C. 2011), *aff'd*, 565 U.S. 1104 (2012) (upholding statute forbidding foreign nationals campaign contributions and expenditures, since "[i]t is fundamental to the definition of our national political community that foreign citizens do not have a constitutional right to participate in, and thus may be excluded from, activities of democratic self-government").

[157] *See* Paul C. Ney, Jr., *Some Considerations for Conducting Legal Reviews of U.S. Military Cyber Operations*, 62 HARV. INT'L L.J. ONLINE 22, 33 (2020) (speech by general counsel of the Department of Defense).

[158] The president invoked his authority under immigration-related statutes, notably 8 U.S.C. § 1182(f) (2018) and 8 U.S.C. § 1185(a). On these travel restrictions in relation to presidential power concerning immigration, see *infra* this chapter § III(A)(2).

[159] *See* Jennifer Lee Barrow, *Trump's Travel Ban: Lawful But Ill-Advised*, 41 HARV. J. L. & PUB. POL. 691, 702–15 (2018); *First Amendment—Establishment Clause—Judicial Review of Pretext—Trump v.*

The first executive order, signed shortly after President Trump assumed office, barred for ninety days entry to the United States of all nationals from seven predominantly Muslim countries, regardless of whether they were lawful permanent residents or already had visas to enter the United States, further barred entry for Syrian refugees indefinitely, and barred all other refugees from any country for 120 days.[160] This was challenged by several states, which invoked the interests of their residents as well as their independent governmental interests.

In *Washington v. Trump*, a district court issued a nationwide temporary restraining order on the enforcement of the executive order, on grounds that it "adversely affects the States' residents in areas of employment, education, business, family relations, and freedom to travel.[161] These harms extend to the States by virtue of their role as *parens patriae* of the residents living within their borders."[162] Further, the executive order harmed "the operations and missions of their public universities and other institutions of higher learning," as well as injured "the States' operations, tax bases, and public funds."[163] Another district court, in *Aziz v. Trump*, also issued an injunction against the first executive order, but focused on the issue of religious freedom.[164] According to the court, the executive order likely violated the First Amendment's prohibition on the government singling out a particular religion for disfavor. The court reviewed public comments by President Trump and by his advisers and found that they illustrated an animus toward Islam, including an intention to impose a "complete shutdown" on the entry of Muslims into the United States. As such, the court concluded that the executive order was meant to target one religion, in violation of the principle of religious freedom, thereby causing harm to the state of Virginia and its residents.[165]

The second executive order extended the ban for another ninety days and was substantially similar, but dropped the indefinite ban on Syrian refugees

---

Hawaii, 132 HARV. L. REV. 327 (2018); Eunice Lee, *Non-Discrimination in Refugee and Asylum Law (Against Travel Ban 1.0 and 2.0)*, 31 GEO. IMMIGR. L.J. 459 (2017).

[160] Exec. Order No. 13,769, 82 Fed. Reg. 8,977 (Jan. 27, 2017).

[161] No. C17-0141JLR, 2017 WL 462040 (W.D. Wash. Feb. 3, 2017).

[162] *See id.* at *2. The Ninth Circuit declined the government's emergency motion for a stay. Washington v. Trump, 847 F.3d 1151 (9th Cir. 2017) (per curiam).

[163] Washington v. Trump, 2017 WL 462040, at *2 (W.D. Wash. Feb. 3, 2017). While the district court's decision was appealed, a panel of the Ninth Circuit declined to stay the order. Washington v. Trump, 847 F.3d 1151 (9th Cir. 2017). The proceeding was eventually dismissed as moot when the executive order was replaced with a second executive order. Washington v. Trump, 2017 WL 3774041 (9th Cir. Mar. 8, 2017).

[164] 234 F. Supp. 3d 724, 739 (E.D. Va. 2017).

[165] *Id.* at 730, 737–39. After the first executive order was replaced, the district court dismissed the action without prejudice, ending the injunction, while noting that the "dismissal does not vacate the Memorandum Opinion issued by this Court on February 13, 2017." Stipulation of Dismissal Without Prejudice, Aziz v. Trump, No. 1:17-cv-116 (E.D. Va. June 1, 2017).

and exempted certain noncitizens, such as those who were lawful permanent residents or who already had been issued visas.[166] Section 1 of the revised order stated its purpose was to "protect U.S. citizens from terrorist attacks, including those committed by foreign nationals[,]" and that "[e]ach of these countries is a state sponsor of terrorism, has been significantly compromised by terrorist organizations, or contains active conflict zones."[167] In *Hawai'i v. Trump*,[168] a district court found that "a reasonable, objective observer—enlightened by the specific historical context, contemporaneous public statements, and specific sequence of events leading to its issuance—would conclude that the Executive Order was issued with a purpose to disfavor a particular religion, in spite of its stated, religiously-neutral purpose."[169] In *International Refugee Assistance Project v. Trump*,[170] a district court issued a similar temporary restraining order based solely on the plaintiff's Establishment Clause claim.[171] The Fourth Circuit affirmed, finding first that the deference to the decisions of the political branches called for in *Kleindienst v. Mandel* "does not completely insulate those decisions from *any* meaningful review."[172] In the court's reckoning, the plaintiffs had plausibly alleged that the government's stated purpose of protecting national security was not in good faith, but instead was a pretext for its religious purpose;[173] accordingly the court declined to defer and applied the three-part Establishment Clause test set forth in *Lemon v. Kurtzman*.[174] The Supreme Court later vacated the decision on mootness grounds when the executive order expired.[175]

A third executive action, this time in the form of a presidential proclamation, indefinitely suspended the entry of nationals—other than lawful permanent residents and noncitizens who already possessed visas—from six predominantly Muslim countries (Chad, Iran, Libya, Somalia, Syria, and Yemen), but also banned the entry of North Korean nationals, and barred certain Venezuelan government officials and their families from obtaining tourist and temporary

---

[166] Exec. Order No. 13,780, 82 Fed. Reg. 13,209 (Mar. 6, 2017).

[167] *Id.* § 1(d).

[168] 241 F. Supp. 3d 1119 (D. Haw. 2017).

[169] *Id.* at 1134. After the challenged provisions of the executive order expired, the Supreme Court remanded the case with instructions to dismiss it as moot. *Trump v. Hawaii*, 138 S. Ct. 377 (mem.) (2017).

[170] 241 F. Supp. 3d 539 (D. Md. 2017).

[171] *Id.* at 566.

[172] Int'l Refugee Assistance Project v. Trump, 857 F.3d 554, 591 (4th Cir. 2017) (emphasis in original); *see supra* this chapter note 149 (discussing *Kleindienst*).

[173] *Int'l Refugee Assistance Project*, 857 F.3d at 592.

[174] *Id.* at 592–97 (applying Lemon v. Kurtzman, 403 U.S. 602 (1971)). To prevail under the *Lemon* test, the government must show that the challenged action: (1) "ha[s] a secular legislative purpose"; (2) that "its principal or primary effect [is] one that neither advances nor inhibits religion"; and (3) that it does "not foster 'an excessive government entanglement with religion.'" 403 U.S. at 612–13 (citations omitted).

[175] Trump v. International Refugee Assistance, 138 S. Ct. 353 (2017).

business visas.[176] While lower courts also acted to enjoin this action,[177] the Supreme Court, by a 5–4 decision, upheld the constitutionality of the executive proclamation in *Trump v. Hawaii*.[178] According to the Court, the proclamation was on its face a valid exercise of the broad presidential discretion accorded under U.S. immigration law for determining that noncitizens are inadmissible.[179] Notwithstanding the president's public statements, the Court, subjecting the proclamation to the deferential rational basis review, found that it was neutral on its face and was "plausibly related to the Government's stated objective to protect the country and improve vetting processes" for noncitizens traveling to the United States, because it was "expressly premised" on "preventing entry of nationals who cannot be adequately vetted and inducing other nations to improve their practices."[180]

Justice Breyer, dissenting, found that the facts tended to show "evidence of antireligious bias" that formed "a sufficient basis to set the Proclamation aside."[181] And Justice Sotomayor's dissent argued that the Proclamation's "façade of national-security concerns . . . [did] little to cleanse [it] of the appearance of discrimination that the President's words have created" and that "a reasonable observer would conclude that the Proclamation was motivated by anti-Muslim animus" in violation of the Establishment Clause.[182] She recounted numerous statements made by the president during his campaign for the presidency and thereafter, such as that "Islam hates us. . . . [W]e can't allow people coming into this country who have this hatred of the United States . . . [a]nd of people that are not Muslim."[183]

The Court's decision suggests that, so long as the executive asserts a national-security rationale for imposing a travel ban, then notwithstanding highly objectionable public statements by a president, the ban likely will survive challenges that it is motivated by improper religious considerations. Of particular note, the

---

[176] Proclamation No. 9645, 82 Fed. Reg. 45,161 (Sept. 24, 2017). For subsequent changes, see Proclamation No. 9723, 83 Fed. Reg. 15,937 (Apr. 10, 2018) (removing Chad from the list); Proclamation No. 9983, 85 Fed. Reg. 6,699 (Jan. 31, 2020) (expanding the coverage to include six more foreign states—of which three were predominantly Muslim (Kyrgyzstan, Nigeria, and Sudan)—on public safety or national security grounds, with restrictions tailored to each state, and no application to nonimmigrant groups).

[177] Ali v. Trump, No. C17-0135JLR, 2017 U.S. Dist. LEXIS 181208 (W.D. Wash. Nov. 1, 2017); Washington v. Trump, No. C17-0141JLR, 2017 U.S. Dist. LEXIS 178606 (W.D. Wash. Oct. 27, 2017); Exodus Refugee Immigration, Inc. v. Holcomb, No. 1:15-cv-01858-TWP-DML, 2017 U.S. Dist. LEXIS 175748 (S.D. Ind. Oct. 24, 2017).

[178] 138 S. Ct. 2392 (2018).

[179] Trump v. Hawaii, 138 S. Ct. 2392 (2018); *see* 8 U.S.C. § 1182(f) (2018). For further discussion, see *infra* this chapter § III(A).

[180] *Id.* at 2420–21.

[181] *Id.* at 2433 (Breyer, J., dissenting).

[182] *Id.* at 2433 (Sotomayor, J., dissenting).

[183] *Id.* at 2436.

Court maintained that applying a limited review of facially neutral government action in the face of establishment clause claims " 'has particular force' in admission and immigration cases that overlap with 'the area of national security.' "[184] Indeed, the majority was dismissive of the plaintiffs' reliance "on Establishment Clause precedents concerning laws and policies applied *domestically*," thus suggesting a view that a more lenient approach may be warranted with respect to all foreign relations laws and policies that touch upon national security.[185]

In any event, immediately upon assuming office, President Joe Biden signed a presidential proclamation ending the travel restrictions under the existing presidential proclamation, and directed the Department of State to pursue the processing of visa applications for individuals from affected countries consistent with otherwise applicable law and visa processing procedures.[186]

4. Access to and Unlawful Disclosure of Foreign Relations Information

The Supreme Court has never construed the First Amendment as establishing a constitutional right of individuals to know or to access information held by the U.S. government.[187] Still, several federal statutes create rights to such information;[188] one of the most important of these, the Freedom of Information Act (FOIA), provides for the release of information held by the U.S. government. Yet FOIA also allows for governmental withholding of information pursuant to exemptions that may apply to foreign relations information,[189] and courts have generally deferred to the executive branch on such decisions when they implicate national security concerns.[190] In the context of criminal prosecutions, foreign

---

[184] *Id.* at 2419 (citing to Kerry v. Din, 576 U.S. 86, 104 (Kennedy, J., concurring)).

[185] *Id.* at 2417 (emphasis added); *see also id.* at 2418 ("The case before us differs in numerous respects from the conventional Establishment Clause claim. Unlike the typical suit involving religious displays or school prayer, plaintiffs seek to invalidate a national security directive regulating the entry of aliens abroad.").

[186] Proclamation No. 10141, 86 Fed. Reg. 7,005 (Jan. 20, 2021).

[187] *See* Stone, *Free Speech and National Security*, *supra* note 138, at 959.

[188] *See, e.g.*, Privacy Act of 1974, 5 U.S.C. § 552a (2018) (allowing access to governmental records pertaining to the requesting individual); Government in the Sunshine Act, *id.* § 552b (establishing requirements that certain governmental meetings be open to the public so as to promote more informed public debate of an agency's policies); Federal Advisory Committee Act, *id.* app. §§ 1–16 (requiring access to meetings and records of federal advisory committees, so as to avoid the use of such committees to further the goals of any special interest group) [hereinafter FACA].

[189] *Id.* § 552. FOIA establishes procedures for any member of the public to obtain copies of agency documents and records, unless the request falls within one of nine exemptions. The most salient exemption for foreign relations matters is FOIA exemption 1, which covers information "specifically authorized under criteria established by an Executive order to be kept secret in the interest of national defense or foreign policy." *Id.* § 552(b)(1)(a). In the event of nondisclosure, FOIA provides for judicial review, which takes place even in situations concerning information relating to foreign relations. *Id.* § 552(a)(4)(B).

[190] *See, e.g.*, Ctr. for Nat'l Sec. Studies v. U.S. Dep't of Justice, 331 F.3d 918, 926–27 (D.C. Cir. 2003) (concluding in a FOIA case that it is "well established that the judiciary owes some measure of deference to the executive in cases implicating national security, a uniquely executive purview."); *see also* HENKIN, FOREIGN AFFAIRS, at 287.

relations matters that the U.S. government prefers to remain secret may be governed by the procedures for dealing with classified information found in the Classified Information Procedures Act.[191]

As a general matter, First Amendment freedom of speech restraints do not protect U.S. government employees who disclose classified information,[192] and such persons have been successfully criminally prosecuted.[193] The Espionage Act of 1917, for example, enables prosecution for disclosures made to a foreign government or for purposes connected with aiding an enemy.[194] Other statutes address different types of disclosure.[195] Further, U.S. government employees who publish a work in violation of a nondisclosure agreement with the government have no First Amendment right to receive royalties based on the publication.[196]

Persons who are not U.S. government employees may also be prosecuted for disclosing what they know to be classified foreign relations information. In *United States v. Rosen*,[197] a Department of Defense employee communicated classified information to the defendants, who were lobbyists for the American-Israel Public Affairs Committee; the defendants then communicated the information to members of the media and foreign government officials. They were charged under the Espionage Act for conspiring to transmit "information relating to the national defense" to individuals "not entitled to receive" such information.[198] Defendants argued the statute was unconstitutional because, inter alia, it violated their First Amendment rights to free speech and to petition the government. While accepting that case law was sparse in addressing application of the statute

---

[191] 18 U.S.C. app. III §§ 1–16 (2018). For further discussion, see Chapter 2 § II(G)(1).

[192] *See* Stone, *Free Speech and National Security*, *supra* note 138, at 959.

[193] *See, e.g.*, United States v. Manning, 78 M.J. 501 (A. Ct. Crim. App. 2018) (upholding conviction of a U.S. soldier for violation of the Espionage Act and other offenses for downloading and releasing classified government information to the public via WikiLeaks). President Obama commuted the soldier's sentence in 2017. U.S. Dep't of Justice, Office of the Pardon Attorney, *Commutations Granted by President Barack Obama (2009–2017)*, https://perma.cc/399P-HMKS.

[194] 18 U.S.C. §§ 792–94; *see* Robert D. Epstein, *Balancing National Security and Free-Speech Rights: Why Congress Should Revise the Espionage Act*, 15 COMMLAW CONSPECTUS 483 (2007); *see, e.g.*, Josh White, *Sailor from Oregon Charged with Espionage*, WASH. POST, Aug. 10, 2006, at A6 (reporting on espionage charges against a U.S. Navy petty officer who allegedly stole classified information from his submarine and attempted to pass it to foreign government officials in three countries—Austria, Bahrain, and Mexico—while on active duty).

[195] *See, e.g.*, 18 U.S.C. § 798 (prohibiting the disclosure of the nature, preparation, or use of any government code, cipher, cryptographic system, or communication intelligence); Atomic Energy Act of 1946, 42 U.S.C. §§ 2161–63, 2165, 2274 (providing criminal penalties for disclosing atomic energy data).

[196] *See* Snepp v. United States, 444 U.S. 507 (1980). In *Snepp*, the Supreme Court agreed that the U.S. employee had breached the "constructive trust" between him and the government, which was especially significant in the case of a former Central Intelligence Agency (CIA) agent, as it "impairs the CIA's ability to perform its statutory duties" and potentially jeopardizes the safety of current CIA operatives (and even Snepp himself). *Id.* at 512.

[197] 445 F. Supp. 2d 602 (E.D. Va. 2006), *amended*, No. 1:05CR225, 2006 WL 5049154 (E.D. Va. Aug. 16, 2006), *and aff'd*, 557 F.3d 192 (4th Cir. 2009).

[198] *See* 18 U.S.C. § 793(e).

to persons other than U.S. government employees, the district court still concluded that, notwithstanding the First Amendment, "both common sense and the relevant precedent point persuasively to the conclusion that the government can punish those outside of government for the unauthorized receipt and deliberate retransmission of information relating to national defense."[199] The court pointedly drew a distinction, in this regard, between national security secrets and "ordinary secrets," whereby in the latter instance the individual is disclosing information for the purpose of identifying incompetence or corruption.[200]

By contrast, when the press receives classified foreign relations information and the government seeks to secure a judicial order restraining publication, there is a "heavy presumption" against the constitutional validity of such an order.[201] The seminal case of *New York Times Co. v. United States*,[202] which grew out of the disclosure of portions of the "Pentagon Papers,"[203] pitted the rights of newspapers under the First Amendment against the authority of the executive branch over foreign relations and national security information. After the *New York Times* and the *Washington Post* began publishing excerpts, the government sought an injunction against any further publication, arguing that "the President's power to conduct foreign affairs and his position as Commander in Chief give him authority to impose censorship on the press to protect his ability to deal effectively with foreign nations and to conduct the military affairs of the country."[204] The Court, however, in a *per curiam* decision, affirmed the lower courts' denial of the injunction, quoting[205] its prior jurisprudence that "[a]ny system of prior restraints of expression comes to this Court bearing a heavy presumption against its constitutional validity,"[206] and that the government "thus carries a heavy burden of showing justification for the imposition of such a restraint."[207] The concurring justices expressed different rationales. According

---

[199] *Rosen*, 445 F. Supp. at 637. The court rejected the defendants' First Amendment right to petition argument for essentially the same reason. *See id.* at 641–43.

[200] *Id.* at 639.

[201] Bantam Books, Inc. v. Sullivan, 372 U.S. 58, 70 (1963).

[202] 403 U.S. 713 (1971). For analysis, see George Freeman, *The First Amendment and The Times*, 17 COMM. & L. 21 (1995); Louis Henkin, *The Right to Know and the Duty to Withhold: The Case of the Pentagon Papers*, 120 U. PA. L. REV. 271 (1971); David McCraw & Stephen Gikow, *The End to an Unspoken Bargain? National Security and Leaks in a Post-Pentagon Papers World*, 48 HARV. C.R.-C.L. L. REV. 473 (2013).

[203] Officially titled "Report of the Office of the Secretary of Defense Vietnam Task Force, History of U.S. Decision-Making Process on Viet Nam Policy," the "Pentagon Papers" was a report commissioned by Secretary of Defense Robert McNamara in 1967 to provide a history of U.S. political and military involvement in Vietnam. Among other things, information contained within the report indicated that at various times the executive branch was not truthful to Congress and to the U.S. public about such involvement. In June of 1971, small portions of the report were leaked to the press and widely distributed.

[204] N.Y. Times Co. v. United States, 403 U.S. 713, 741 (1970) (Marshall, J., concurring).

[205] *Id.* at 714.

[206] *Bantam Books, Inc.*, 372 U.S. at 70; *see* Near v. Minnesota *ex rel.* Olson, 283 U.S. 697 (1931).

[207] Org. for a Better Austin v. Keefe, 402 U.S. 415, 419 (1971).

to Justice Stewart, for example, the publication of classified information may only be restrained if the government can show that its disclosure would result in "direct, immediate, and irreparable damage to our Nation or its people," a burden which had not been met in the case.[208] Justice Black was more sweeping, expressing concern about any invocation of national security to justify the denial of First Amendment rights: "The word 'security' is a broad, vague generality whose contours should not be invoked to abrogate the fundamental law embodied in the First Amendment. The guarding of military and diplomatic secrets at the expense of informed representative government provides no real security for our Republic."[209]

5. Provision of Support to Terrorist Groups

Federal law criminalizes the provision of material support to foreign terrorist organizations designated as such by the U.S. government.[210] In *Holder v. Humanitarian Law Project*,[211] several U.S. citizens and organizations challenged the constitutionality of the relevant statute on the ground that it violated their First Amendment rights to free speech and association. The plaintiffs had sought to provide financial and other tangible support for the humanitarian and political activities of the Kurdistan Workers Party (PKK) in Turkey and the Liberation Tigers of Tamil Eelam (LTTE) in Sri Lanka. According to the plaintiffs, the statute violated their freedoms of speech and association because it criminalized their provision of material support to the PKK and the LTTE without requiring the government to prove they specifically intended to further the unlawful ends of those organizations.[212]

Although urged by the government to apply an intermediate scrutiny test (on the basis that the statute was regulating conduct),[213] the Supreme Court decided that more rigorous scrutiny was warranted as "the conduct triggering coverage under the statute consist[ed] of communicating a message."[214] Even so, the Court upheld the statute as applied. The Court accepted congressional factual findings that providing foreign terrorist groups with material support in any form not only furthers terrorism but also strains U.S. relationships with its allies

---

[208] *New York Times Co.*, 403 U.S. at 730 (Stewart, J., concurring).

[209] *Id.* at 719 (Black, J., concurring). But see Justice Blackmun's dissent, maintaining that the "First Amendment, after all, is only one part of an entire Constitution." *Id.* at 761 (Blackmun, J., dissenting).

[210] 18 U.S.C. § 2339B(a)(1) (making it a federal crime to "knowingly provide[] material support or resources to a foreign terrorist organization"). The authority to designate an entity as a "foreign terrorist organization" rests with the secretary of state. 8 U.S.C. §§ 1189(a)(1), (d)(4).

[211] 561 U.S. 1 (2010).

[212] *Id.* at 10–11.

[213] *See* United States v. O'Brien, 391 U.S. 367 (1968) (rejecting a First Amendment challenge to a conviction under a generally applicable prohibition on destroying draft cards, even though O'Brien had burned his card in protest against the draft).

[214] *Humanitarian Law Project*, 561 U.S. at 28.

and undermines international cooperation in preventing terrorist attacks.[215] Indeed, the Court noted that, when adopting the statute, Congress found that "foreign organizations that engage in terrorist activity are so tainted by their criminal conduct that any contribution to such an organization facilitates that conduct."[216] Further, the particular types of "speech" that the plaintiffs proposed to undertake—direct training on dispute settlement, education on how to acquire "relief," and even general political advocacy coordinated with and on behalf of the organizations—are not protected speech, given that such support can be used to advance terrorist objectives.[217] The Court also found that Congress had avoided restricting independent advocacy or any activities not directed to, coordinated with, or controlled by foreign terrorist groups, including independent speech in support of the group or even membership—therefore, the statute equally did not impermissibly burden the freedom of association.[218]

Holder represents an extraordinary degree of deference to a statute that, in essence, criminalizes nonviolent speech based solely on a link to foreign groups deemed terrorist in nature.[219] Perhaps sensitive to the potential implications of its judgment, the Court asserted (albeit vaguely) that there were limits to what the government may do, including that "we in no way suggest that a regulation of independent speech would pass constitutional muster, even if the Government were to show that such speech benefits foreign terrorist organizations," nor "that Congress could extend the same prohibition on material support at issue here to domestic organizations."[220]

Even so, the outcome in *Holder* is striking. Rather than conducting the usually rigorous review of content-based restrictions on speech, the Court essentially employed an ends-justifies-the-means analysis, in which reducing advocacy in support of foreign terrorist groups was permissible simply because it was deemed helpful in stopping terrorism.

B. Keep and Bear Arms (Second Amendment)

The Second Amendment identifies a right "to keep and bear Arms" and the Supreme Court determined in *District of Columbia v. Heller* that this guarantees

---

[215] *Id.* at 32.

[216] Antiterrorism and Effective Death Penalty Act of 1996, Pub. L. No. 104-132, § 301(a)(7), 110 Stat. 1247 (codified at 18 U.S.C. § 2339B note (findings and purpose)).

[217] *Humanitarian Law Project*, 561 U.S. at 36–39.

[218] *Id.* at 24, 40.

[219] *See* Andrew V. Moshirnia, *Valuing Speech and Open Source Intelligence in the Face of Judicial Deference*, 4 HARV. NAT'L SEC. J. 385 (2013).

[220] *Humanitarian Law Project*, 561 U.S. at 39.

"the individual right to possess and carry weapons in case of confrontation."[221] While the Second Amendment is normally discussed in a purely domestic context, there are at least three ways the amendment relates to foreign affairs: defense against a foreign attack, the right of noncitizens in the United States to keep and bear arms, and the relationship to arms controls treaties entered into by the United States.

1. Defense Against a Foreign Attack

The central dispute in *Heller* concerned whether the Second Amendment substantially concerned the rights of individuals (the view ultimately adopted by the Court) or rather centered on the right to form militias (expressed in the dissents of Justices Stevens and Breyer[222]). No one appeared to contest the proposition that the Second Amendment was designed, in part, to help the United States defend against a foreign attack. Article I of the Constitution expressly accords Congress the power to call forth the militia to "repel invasions";[223] the Second Amendment's famous subordinate clause—"being necessary to the security of a free State"—suggests that the amendment's protection relates, at least in part, to defense against a foreign attack.[224]

At the time of the founding, the United States was exposed to the possibility of attacks from tribes of American Indians and from European powers (Britain, France, and Spain) who continued to possess territory in North America. The ability of individual Americans to possess arms, which could be harnessed by calling up militias, was viewed as a cornerstone of the ability to defend against any such attacks,[225] while simultaneously decreasing the pressure to maintain a large standing army.[226] The British invasion of 1812, leading to the burning of

---

[221] District of Columbia v. Heller, 554 U.S. 570, 592 (2008). The Second Amendment provides: "A well regulated Militia, being necessary to the security of a free State, the right of the people to keep and bear Arms, shall not be infringed." U.S. Const. amend. II. For a general discussion of the Second Amendment, see Erwin Chemerinsky, Constitutional Law: Principles and Policies § 10.10 (6th ed. 2019).

[222] See id. at 651 (Stevens, J., dissenting) ("When each word in the text is given full effect, the Amendment is most naturally read to secure to the people a right to use and possess arms in conjunction with service in a well-regulated militia."); id. at 681 (Breyer, J., dissenting) ("[T]he Second Amendment protects militia-related, not self-defense-related, interests.").

[223] U.S. Const. art. I, § 8, cl. 15. For further discussion of the power to call up militias, see Chapter 8 § III(C).

[224] See Heller, 544 U.S. at 597 ("It is true that the term 'State' elsewhere in the Constitution refers to individual States, but the phrase 'security of a free state' and close variations seem to have been terms of art in 18th-century political discourse, meaning a ' "free country" ' or free polity."); see also Eugene Volokh, Necessary to the Security of a Free State, 83 Notre Dame L. Rev. 1, 5 (2007).

[225] See Heller, 544 U.S. at 597 (finding that the Founders viewed militias as necessary, inter alia, for "repelling invasions"); United States v. Miller, 307 U. S. 174, 179 (1939) (explaining that at the founding "the Militia comprised all males physically capable of acting in concert for the common defense."); The Federalist No. 46, at 329, 334 (James Madison) ("near half a million of citizens with arms in their hands").

[226] See, e.g., Perpich v. Dep't of Defense, 496 U. S. 334, 340 (1990) ("there was a widespread fear that a national standing Army posed an intolerable threat to individual liberty and to the sovereignty

the U.S. Capitol and the White House, was the kind of attack that threatened the United States in its early years. No doubt with that incident in mind, Justice Story in his 1833 *Commentaries on the Constitution of the United States* noted: "The militia is the natural defence of a free country against *sudden foreign invasions*, domestic insurrections, and domestic usurpations of power by rulers."[227]

2. Right of Noncitizens to Bear Arms in the United States

The Court in *Heller* regarded "the people" in the text of the Second Amendment as "all members of the political community," relying on *United States v. Verdugo-Urquidez*.[228] As discussed later in relation to the Fourth Amendment,[229] the Court in *Verdugo-Urquidez* defined the phrase "the people" as "a class of persons who are part of a national community or who have otherwise developed sufficient connection with this country to be considered part of that community."[230]

What constitutes a "sufficient connection" with the United States to afford a noncitizen rights under the Second Amendment is an open question. It seems likely that lawful permanent residents enjoy such a connection. Moreover, pursuant to the Fourteenth Amendment, they benefit from strict scrutiny under an equal protection analysis whereby a state would have to demonstrate a compelling state interest in imposing arms-related regulations on lawful permanent residents, but not on U.S. citizens. For example, in *Fotoudis v. Honolulu*,[231] a lawful permanent resident challenged Honolulu's statutory prohibition on granting firearm permits to noncitizens. In finding that such denial constituted a violation of the Second Amendment, the court reasoned that lawful permanent residents are on a path to citizenship, "entitled to a wide array of constitutional rights," and "a class of persons who are part of a national community."[232] As such, they are "among the people" of the United States for purposes of the

---

of the separate States"). For historical accounts of the Amendment's origins, see SAUL CORNELL, A WELL-REGULATED MILITIA: THE FOUNDING FATHERS AND THE ORIGINS OF GUN CONTROL IN AMERICA (2006); H. RICHARD UVILLER & WILLIAM G. MERKEL, THE MILITIA AND THE RIGHT TO ARMS (2002).

[227] 2 JOSEPH STORY, COMMENTARIES ON THE CONSTITUTION OF THE UNITED STATES § 1897 (4th ed. 1873) (emphasis added). Justice Story's perspective on the individual rights view of the Second Amendment was sharply disputed in Heller. *Compare* 544 U.S. at 668 (Stevens, J., dissenting) (stating that [t]here is not so much as a whisper" of the individual rights view in Story's account), *with id.* at 608–09 (disagreeing, and quoting Story).

[228] *Heller*, 544 U.S. at 579–81.

[229] *See infra* this chapter text accompanying notes 301–321.

[230] United States v. Verdugo-Urquidez, 494 U.S. 259, 265 (1990) (citing United States *ex rel.* Turner v. Williams, 194 U.S. 279, 292 (1904), which denied First Amendment protection to excludable noncitizen).

[231] 54 F. Supp. 3d 1136 (D. Haw. 2014).

[232] *Id.* at 1144 (quoting Fletcher v. Haas, 851 F. Supp. 2d 287, 299 (D. Mass. 2012), and *Verdugo-Urquidez*, 494 U.S. at 265).

Second Amendment, and thus possess an individual right to keep and bear arms.[233] The court noted uncertainty about whether a Second Amendment analysis employed intermediate scrutiny or strict scrutiny, but even assuming that Honolulu's statute implemented either an "important government objective" (intermediate scrutiny) or a "compelling state interest" (strict scrutiny), the court found that the statute was neither "substantially related" nor "narrowly tailored" to such interests.[234] The Court also found that the statute violated the Equal Protection Clause of the Fourteenth Amendment.[235] The court reasoned that, while Honolulu had "a sufficient general interest in requiring permits to acquire firearms," denying the plaintiff such an opportunity merely because he was a lawful permanent resident was "not a narrowly tailored means of achieving [Honolulu's] goal."[236]

It is less likely that the Second Amendment protects all nonimmigrant noncitizens and undocumented noncitizens. The federal Firearms Owners' Protection Act of 1986,[237] which amended the Gun Control Act of 1968,[238] provides in part that it is unlawful for an undocumented noncitizen or, with certain exceptions, a nonimmigrant noncitizen to transport or receive firearms or ammunition via interstate or foreign commerce.[239] The distinctions drawn by Congress in the statute may be suggestive of its belief that undocumented noncitizens and nonimmigrant noncitizens (unlike citizens and lawful permanent residents) are not entitled to Second Amendment rights.[240] Alternatively, the distinctions might be viewed as accepting that Second Amendment rights extend to all noncitizens in the United States, but that it is nevertheless permissible

---

[233] *Id.* (quoting *Verdugo-Urquidez*, 494 U.S. at 273).

[234] *Id.* (internal quotation marks omitted).

[235] *Id.* at 1141–42.

[236] *Id.* at 1143 (quoting Smith v. South Dakota, 781 F. Supp. 2d 879, 886 (D.S.D. 2011)); *see Fletcher*, 851 F. Supp. at 303 ("Although Massachusetts has an interest in regulating firearms to prevent dangerous persons from obtaining firearms . . . the statute here fails to distinguish between dangerous non-citizens and those non-citizens who would pose no particular threat if allowed to possess handguns."); *Smith*, 781 F. Supp. at 886 (granting motion for preliminary and permanent injunction by lawful permanent resident against enforcement of South Dakota citizenship requirement for state permit to carry a concealed weapon); Say v. Adams, No. 3:07-CV-377-R, 2008 WL 718163, at *3 (W.D. Ky. Mar. 14, 2008) (granting an injunction against enforcing a Kentucky law limiting the issuance of a license to carry concealed weapons to U.S. citizens, reasoning in part that "[a] blanket prohibition discriminating against aliens is not precisely draw[n] to achieve the goal of facilitating firearms purchases when there exists a nondiscriminatory way to achieve the same goals").

[237] Firearms Owners' Protection Act of 1986, Pub. L. No. 99-308, 100 Stat. 449 (codified as amended in scattered sections of 18 and 26 U.S.C.).

[238] Gun Control Act of 1968, Pub. L. No. 90-618, 82 Stat. 1213 (codified as amended at 18 U.S.C. § 921 (2018)).

[239] 18 U.S.C. § 922(g)(5); *see id.* § 922(y)(2)–(3) (noting exceptions, such as for designated foreign officials and foreign law enforcement officers).

[240] *See* United States v. Huitron-Guizar, 678 F.3d 1164, 1169 (10th Cir. 2012) ("That Congress saw fit to exclude illegal aliens from carrying guns may indicate its belief, entitled to our respect, that such aliens, as a class, possess no such constitutional right.").

for the government to impose regulation on the exercise of that right to certain noncitizens due to factors pertinent to their status.[241]

In any event, in challenges to the federal statute, the Fourth, Fifth, and Eighth Circuits have held that Second Amendment protection does not extend to undocumented noncitizens.[242] For example, in *United States v. Carpio-Leon*,[243] the Fourth Circuit maintained that the such noncitizens were "not law-abiding members of the political community" and, by entering "the United States unlawfully[,] have no more rights under the Second Amendment than do aliens outside of the United States seeking admittance."[244] The Fifth Circuit, for its part, held that "[w]hatever else the term means or includes, the phrase 'the people' in the Second Amendment of the Constitution does not include aliens illegally in the United States."[245] By contrast, the Seventh Circuit, in *United States v. Meza-Rodriguez*, held that an undocumented noncitizen can develop sufficiently substantial connections to the United States to receive protection from the Second Amendment,[246] although in that case the federal statute at issue did not impermissibly restrict such rights.[247] The Ninth Circuit in *United States v. Torres*[248] and the Tenth Circuit in *United States v. Huitron-Guizar*[249] refrained from resolving whether undocumented noncitizens did not fall within the scope of the Second Amendment but, for the sake of analysis, assumed that they did, before then upholding the contested statute.[250]

3. Relationship to U.S. Arms Controls Treaties
To date, arms control treaties entered into by the United States have not resulted in Second Amendment challenges (although they have posed issues

[241] For example, the basis for forbidding arms to undocumented noncitizens may be that Congress has concluded that such individuals are harder to trace, are more likely to assume a false identity, or (having violated U.S. law) are more likely to defy other laws and therefore should not be armed. *Id.* at 1170.

[242] *See* United States v. Carpio-Leon, 701 F.3d 974 (4th Cir. 2012); United States v. Portillo-Munoz, 643 F.3d 437 (5th Cir. 2011); United States v. Flores, 663 F.3d 1022 (8th Cir. 2011); *see also* United States v. Yanez-Vasquez, No. 09-40056-01-SAC, 2010 WL 411112, at *2 (D. Kan. Jan. 28, 2010).

[243] 701 F.3d 974 (4th Cir. 2012).

[244] *Id.* at 976.

[245] *Portillo-Munoz*, 643 F.3d at 442. The court distinguished the term in the Second Amendment from its use in the Fourth Amendment, by noting that the former "grants an affirmative right," while the latter "is at its core a protective right against abuses by the government." *Id.* at 441. For an argument that the Supreme Court should find that undocumented noncitizens fall within "the people" for purposes of the Second Amendment, see Anjali Motgi, *Of Arms and Aliens*, 66 STAN. L. REV. ONLINE 1 (2013).

[246] *See* United States v. Meza-Rodriguez, 798 F.3d 664, 671 (7th Cir. 2015).

[247] *Id.* at 673.

[248] 911 F.3d 1253 (9th Cir. 2019).

[249] 678 F.3d 1164 (10th Cir. 2012).

[250] *Id.*; *see* Charlotte Nichols, *Second Amendment Rights Come Second to Citizenship: Why Illegal Immigrants Are Not Included in "The People" of the Second Amendment*, 50 U. MEMPHIS L. REV. 509 (2019).

under the Fourth, Fifth, and Tenth Amendments).[251] Presumably, this is because the kinds of weapons regulated by those treaties are not the kinds of weapons that individuals in the United States seek lawfully to possess, and even if they were, the government would likely be able show a compelling interest for strict regulation.

An arms control treaty recently adopted by the United Nations is arguably different in character. The objective of the Arms Trade Treaty (ATT), which entered into force in 2014, is to establish common international standards for regulating the international trade in conventional arms and to eradicate the illicit trade in conventional arms.[252] Among other things, it obligates parties to establish and maintain an effective national control system for the export, import, transit, and transshipment of and brokering activities related to the eight categories of conventional arms covered by the treaty, as well as exports of related ammunition and parts.[253] Although the United States signed the treaty (during the administration of President Obama), it notified the United Nations (during the administration of President Trump) that it did not intend to pursue ratification.[254] According to President Trump, doing so was necessary because "[w]e will never allow foreign bureaucrats to trample on your Second Amendment freedom."[255] Supporters of the agreement, however, noted that the preamble of the treaty reaffirms "the sovereign right of any State to regulate and control conventional arms exclusively within its territory, pursuant to its own legal or constitutional system,"[256] and further noted that the ATT was silent as to control or regulation of the domestic sale of arms.[257] Accordingly, constitutional objections to the treaty would likely have to be predicated upon an assertion that the Second Amendment applied extraterritorially, which seems unlikely.[258]

---

[251] See infra this chapter § II(C)(5); see also Chapter 6 § II(D)(1), Chapter 9 § II(A) (discussion of Bond v. United States, 572 U.S. 844 (2014)).

[252] Arms Trade Treaty, Apr. 2, 2013, 52 I.L.M. 988. As of mid-2022, the treaty has 110 parties.

[253] Id. arts. 3, 4, 5.2.

[254] See Communication from the United States of America to U.N. Secretary-General (July 19, 2019), https://perma.cc/44PF-SK5J. On the legal significance of "unsigning" a treaty, see Chapter 6 § (II)(C)(1).

[255] Remarks at the National Rifle Association Institute for Legislative Action Leadership Forum in Indianapolis, Indiana, 2019 DAILY COMP. PRES. DOC. 243 (Apr. 26, 2019).

[256] Arms Trade Treaty, supra note 252, pmbl.

[257] See, e.g., Message to the Senate Transmitting the Arms Trade Treaty, 2016, DAILY COMP. PRES. DOC. 840 (Dec. 9, 2016) ("The Treaty is fully consistent with the domestic rights of U.S. citizens, including those guaranteed under the U.S. Constitution.").

[258] See George Rutherglen, The Rights of Aliens under the United States Constitution: At the Border and Beyond, 57 VA. J. INT'L L. 707, 718 (2018).

C. Unreasonable Searches and Seizures (Fourth Amendment)

The Fourth Amendment provides that all searches and seizures by the government must be reasonable;[259] this normally requires a warrant and probable cause for searches and seizures, as well as the exclusion from trial of illegally obtained evidence.[260] Yet there are some exceptions to these requirements, the precise scope of which continues to be litigated.[261] Perhaps unsurprisingly, there also remain unresolved questions as to application of the Fourth Amendment in the context of foreign relations law. Notably, the Fourth Amendment uses the words "the people," as opposed to the words "person" in the Fifth Amendment and the "accused" in the Sixth Amendment, and that difference has proven critical to case law considering the rights of noncitizens.

The following considers various ways in which the Fourth Amendment features in U.S. foreign relations law: (1) the Fourth Amendment's application to surveillance within the United States of U.S. citizens for collection of foreign intelligence; (2) its application to searches and seizures of noncitizens in the United States; (3) its application to searches and seizures by the U.S. government of citizens and noncitizens outside the United States; (4) the availability of *Bivens* actions by noncitizens against the U.S. government; and (5) its relationship to inspection regimes required by arms control treaties.

---

[259] The Fourth Amendment provides:

> The right of the people to be secure in their persons, houses, papers, and effects, against unreasonable searches and seizures, shall not be violated, and no Warrants shall issue, but upon probable cause, supported by Oath or affirmation, and particularly describing the place to be searched, and the persons or things to be seized.

U.S. CONST. amend. IV. For a general discussion of the Fourth Amendment, see 2 WAYNE R. LAFAVE ET AL., CRIMINAL PROCEDURE § 3 (4th ed. 2015). For some, this reasonableness, rather than warrants or probable cause, is the fundamental value underlying the Fourth Amendment. *See, e.g.,* Akhil Reed Amar, *Fourth Amendment First Principles*, 107 HARV. L. REV. 757, 768–69 (1994); AKHIL REED AMAR, THE CONSTITUTION AND CRIMINAL PROCEDURE: FIRST PRINCIPLES 1–45 (1997). *But see, e.g.,* Thomas Y. Davies, *Recovering the Original Fourth Amendment*, 98 MICH. L. REV. 547 (1999) (disputing reasonableness-oriented accounts of the Fourth Amendment); Donald Dripps, *Akhil Amar on Criminal Procedure and Constitutional Law: "Here I Go Down that Wrong Road Again,"* 74 N.C. L. REV. 1559 (1996) (contesting overall approach to constitutional criminal procedure).

[260] *See, e.g.,* Brigham City v. Stuart, 547 U.S. 398, 403 (2006) (finding that "it is a basic principle of Fourth Amendment law that searches and seizures inside a home without a warrant are presumptively unreasonable.") (quoting Groh v. Ramirez, 540 U.S. 551, 559 (2004)); Ornelas v. United States, 517 U.S. 690, 699 (1996) (finding that the Fourth Amendment has a "strong preference for searches conducted pursuant to a warrant") (quoting Illinois v. Gates, 462 U.S. 213, 236 (1983)).

[261] Commonly accepted exceptions to the warrant requirement include consensual searches, administrative searches, searches incident to arrest, and "exigent circumstance" searches, such as when evidence is being destroyed or officers are in "hot-pursuit" of a suspect. *See, e.g.,* Georgia v. Randolph, 547 U.S. 103, 118–19 (2006) (emergency aid); United States v. Santana, 427 U.S. 38, 42–43 (1976) (hot pursuit); Ker v. California, 374 U.S. 23, 39 (1963) (destruction of evidence). *But see, e.g.,* Caniglia v. Strom, 141 S. Ct. 1596 (2021) (rejecting broad exception for "community caretaking").

1. Foreign Intelligence Surveillance in the United States

U.S. citizens in the United States enjoy considerable protection under the Fourth Amendment from search and seizure by the U.S. government. In one area relating to foreign relations, however, that protection is significantly diminished. From at least World War II to 1978, on the basis of what several circuit courts characterized as a "national security" or "foreign intelligence" exception to the Fourth Amendment,[262] U.S. citizens in the United States were subjected to surveillance by the U.S. government without a warrant if there was probable cause to suspect that the individual was an agent of a foreign power and if the investigation was not for the purpose of enforcement of criminal law.[263]

In 1978, Congress adopted the Foreign Intelligence Surveillance Act of 1978 (FISA),[264] which is now the applicable law in this area, and which requires intelligence officials to obtain authorization from the attorney general and a warrant from the Foreign Intelligence Surveillance Court (FISC) before conducting surveillance in the United States for foreign intelligence purposes.[265] The constitutional balancing struck by FISA is that, even if the president has an inherent constitutional power to authorize foreign intelligence surveillance, Congress may regulate it by means of a reasonable warrant procedure.[266] If authorized, surveillance may be conducted of an agent of a "foreign power," defined as including any foreign government or foreign-based political organization that is

---

[262] See United States v. Truong Dinh Hung, 629 F.2d 908, 913 (4th Cir. 1980) (finding "that the Executive Branch need not always obtain a warrant for foreign intelligence surveillance"); United States v. Buck, 548 F.2d 871, 875 (9th Cir. 1977) (finding that "[f]oreign security wiretaps are a recognized exception to the general warrant requirement"); United States v. Butenko, 494 F.2d 593, 605–06 (3d Cir. 1974) (finding that "prior judicial authorization was not required since the district court found that the surveillances . . . were conducted and maintained solely for the purpose of gathering foreign intelligence information'" and further that the surveillance was reasonable); United States v. Brown, 484 F.2d 418, 426 (5th Cir. 1973) (finding that the president's authority to conduct "warrantless wiretaps for the purpose of gathering foreign intelligence" is inherent in the constitutional "duty to act for the United States in the field of foreign relations, and . . . to protect national security"). By contrast, warrants were required when wiretapping "a domestic organization that [was] neither the agent of nor acting in collaboration with a foreign power, even if the surveillance" was authorized by "presidential directive in the name of foreign intelligence gathering." Zweibon v. Mitchell, 516 F.2d 594, 614 (D.C. Cir. 1975) (internal citation omitted); see United States v. U.S. Dist. Court, 407 U.S. 297 (1972) (concluding that the Fourth Amendment's warrant requirement applies to investigations of wholly domestic threats to security, such as domestic political violence and other crimes).

[263] See L. Rush Atkinson, The Fourth Amendment's Security Exception: Its History and Limits, 66 VAND. L. REV. 1343, 1346–47 (2013) (describing the pre-1978 situation).

[264] Pub. L. No. 95-511, 92 Stat. 1783 (codified as amended 50 U.S.C. ch. 36 (2018)). The primary authority by which the government conducts such foreign intelligence surveillance is Executive Order 12,333. See Exec. Order No. 12,333, 3 C.F.R. 200 (1982), reprinted as amended in 50 U.S.C. § 3001 note (2018). See generally Peter P. Swire, The System of Foreign Intelligence Surveillance Law, 72 GEO. WASH. L. REV. 1306 (2004).

[265] 50 U.S.C. § 1803. Although originally limited to electronic surveillance, FISA is now available for the purpose of physical surveillance and searches, access to limited forms of business records, and pen register and "trap and trace" orders. See Swire, supra note 264, at 1328. The eleven judges of the FISC are district court judges designated by the chief justice of the Supreme Court.

[266] H.R. REP. NO. 95-1283, pt. 1, at 24 (1978).

not substantially composed of U.S. citizens or lawful permanent residents (to include foreign terrorist organizations).[267] A U.S. citizen or lawful permanent resident can qualify as an agent of a foreign power if the citizen knowingly engages in certain listed activities, such as clandestine intelligence activities for the foreign power,[268] but cannot be considered such an agent solely on the basis of activities protected by the First Amendment.[269]

While the original statute required that the attorney general find that "the purpose" of the search was to obtain foreign intelligence information (which federal courts interpreted as meaning "primary purpose"),[270] the 2001 Patriot Act changed that standard so as to require that obtaining foreign intelligence information be only a "significant purpose," thereby allowing searches that are expected to uncover some criminal investigative information.[271] This development meant that the "wall" originally thought to exist between law enforcement and foreign intelligence investigations was largely set aside, leading to interpretations by the FISC that were hospitable to the sharing of information between foreign intelligence and law enforcement officers.[272]

In the aftermath of the terrorist attacks of 9/11, it was revealed that the national security agency had engaged in a program of wiretapping communications between persons located in the United States and persons located abroad, for the purpose of thwarting further terrorist attacks, without any court approval as contemplated by FISA.[273] The president maintained that such wiretapping

---

[267] 50 U.S.C. § 1801(a). The FISC can issue an order approving the surveillance upon finding a number of factors, notably that "there is probable cause to believe that the target of the electronic surveillance is a foreign power or an agent of a foreign power." Id. For reporting requirements, see USA PATRIOT Improvement and Reauthorization Act of 2005, Pub. L. No. 109-177, § 118, 120 Stat. 192, 217–18 (codified in scattered sections of 8, 15, 18, 21, 28, and 42 U.S.C.) (requiring semiannual reporting to the House Permanent Select Committee on Intelligence and to the Senate Select Committee on Intelligence, among others); 50 U.S.C. § 1807 (requiring the attorney general to transmit to the Administrative Office of the U.S. Court and to Congress an annual report setting forth the previous year's total number of applications of orders and order extensions, as well as the number of such orders and extensions that were granted, modified, and denied).

[268] 50 U.S.C. § 1801(b)(2).

[269] Id. § 1805(a)(2)(A).

[270] See, e.g., United States v. Johnson, 952 F.2d 565, 572 (1st Cir. 1991); United States v. Badia, 827 F.2d 1458, 1464 (11th Cir. 1987); United States v. Pelton, 835 F.2d 1067, 1075–76 (4th Cir. 1987); United States v. Duggan, 743 F.2d 59, 77–78 (2d Cir. 1984).

[271] Uniting and Strengthening America by Providing Appropriate Tools Required to Intercept and Obstruct Terrorism (Patriot) Act of 2001, Pub. L. No. 107-56, 115 Stat. 272; see 50 U.S.C. §§ 1804(a)(6)(B), 1823(a)(6)(B).

[272] See In re Sealed Case No. 02-001, 310 F.3d 717, 743 (FISA Ct. Rev. 2002). For criticism of the change, see Erwin Chemerinsky, Losing Liberties: Applying a Foreign Intelligence Model to Domestic Law Enforcement, 51 UCLA L. REV. 1619, 1627 (2004).

[273] See James Risen & Eric Lichtblau, Bush Lets U.S. Spy on Callers Without Courts, N.Y. TIMES (Dec. 16, 2005), https://perma.cc/7WFS-MYP9. For commentary, see Memorandum from Elizabeth B. Bazan & Jennifer K. Elsea, Cong. Research Serv., Presidential Authority to Conduct Warrantless Electronic Surveillance to Gather Foreign Intelligence Information (Jan. 5, 2006); John Cary Sims, What NSA Is Doing . . . and Why It's Illegal, 33 HASTINGS CONST. L.Q. 105 (2006); John Yoo, The Terrorist Surveillance Program and the Constitution, 14 GEO. MASON L. REV. 565 (2007); Neal Katyal & Richard

was "fully consistent with my constitutional responsibilities and authorities" and was "a vital tool in our war against the terrorists."[274] According to the Justice Department's Office of the Legal Counsel (OLC), the president has the authority to gather information necessary to fulfill his constitutional responsibilities, including as commander in chief and when conducting U.S. foreign affairs.[275] Further, Congress' authorization for the use of military force (AUMF) enacted in the wake of the 9/11 attacks, while not expressly addressing the issue of electronic surveillance, "confirms and supplements the President's constitutional authority to protect the Nation, including through electronic surveillance, in the context of the current post-September 11th armed conflict with al Qaeda and its allies."[276] Finally, in OLC's view, FISA expressly contemplated "that a later legislative enactment could authorize electronic surveillance outside the procedures set forth in FISA itself" and the "AUMF constitutes precisely such an enactment."[277] Initial court challenges to the executive action were inconclusive,[278] but ultimately the FISC reportedly found (in a classified opinion) that certain aspects of the government program were not lawful.[279] In any event, this warrantless surveillance program prompted amendments to FISA in 2008. Those amendments included FISA Section 702, which allows the government without a warrant to target the communications of noncitizens abroad to collect foreign intelligence information, but *not* to target intentionally communications of any person located in the United States.[280] Even so, while U.S. citizens in the United

Caplan, *The Surprisingly Stronger Case for the Legality of the NSA Surveillance Program: The FDR Precedent*, 60 STAN. L. REV. 1023 (2008); CHARLIE SAVAGE, POWER WARS: INSIDE OBAMA'S POST-9/11 PRESIDENCY 162–223 (2015).

[274] Presidential Radio Address, 2005, 41 WEEKLY COMP. PRES. DOC. 1880-81 (Dec. 17, 2005).

[275] Legal Authorities Supporting the Activities of the National Security Agency Described by the President, 30 Op. O.L.C. 1 (2006).

[276] *Id.* at 12–13; *see* Authorization for the Use of Military Force, Pub. L. No. 107-40, 115 Stat. 224 (2001) (codified at 50 U.S.C. 1541 note); Chapter 8 § I(C)(5)(b).

[277] 30 Op. O.L.C., *supra* note 275, at 21. The relevant FISA provision is 50 U.S.C. § 1809(a)(1), which bars any person from "intentionally engag[ing] in electronic surveillance under color of law except as authorized by . . . express statutory authorization . . . ."

[278] *See, e.g.*, Am. Civil Liberties Union v. Nat'l Sec. Agency, 438 F. Supp. 2d 754 (E.D. Mich. 2006) (finding that the NSA's program violated the Fourth Amendment, the First Amendment, and the separation-of-powers doctrine, and that the AUMF did not authorize the program), *stayed*, Am. Civil Liberties Union v. Nat'l Sec. Agency, 467 F.3d 590, 591 (6th Cir. 2006), *vacated*, Am. Civil Liberties Union v. Nat'l Sec. Agency, 493 F.3d 644 (6th Cir. 2007) (finding that plaintiff journalists, academics, and lawyers lacked standing, having failed to plead direct injuries).

[279] *See* Michael C. Miller, *Standing in the Wake of the Terrorist Surveillance Program: A Modified Standard for Challenges to Secret Government Surveillance*, 60 RUTGERS L. REV. 1039 (2008); Arwen Mullikin & Syed M. Rahman, *The Ethical Dilemma of the USA Government Wiretapping*, 2 INT'L J. MANAGING INFO. TECH. 32 (2010).

[280] 50 U.S.C. §§ 1881a(a), 1881a(b)(1) (2018). By also providing that FISA § 702 surveillance may not intentionally target citizens and lawful permanent residents reasonably believed to be located outside the United States, a collateral consequence of these amendments was to expand FISA's standard protections to foreign intelligence surveillance of citizens and permanent residents abroad. *Id.* § 1881a(b)(3); *see* Jonathan D. Forgang, *"The Right of the People": The NSA, the FISA Amendments*

States may not be the intended target, they may still be caught up indirectly in the surveillance; the degree to which that has occurred, which is unclear, has raised civil liberty concerns.[281]

2. Searches and Seizures of Noncitizens in the United States

Noncitizens entering the United States at a border or point of entry (such as an airport) may be searched, along with their belongings, without any requirement of consent or a warrant.[282] However, once lawfully within the United States, the noncitizen benefits from the protection of the Fourth Amendment. The Supreme Court concluded in its 1973 decision in *Almeida-Sanchez v. United States* that the warrantless seizure of a noncitizen legally present in the United States violated the Fourth Amendment.[283] In that case, the U.S. Border Patrol engaged in a warrantless search of a Mexican national's automobile some twenty-five miles north of the Mexican border, as part of a roving patrol, without probable cause or consent.[284] After the search uncovered marijuana, the noncitizen was charged and convicted of a federal crime. While the government sought to cast the search as a permissible type of surveillance conducted along the border,[285] the Court found that the search was not a "border search" and violated the Fourth Amendment. By contrast, stopping, visually inspecting, and briefly questioning persons at reasonably located permanent check points, even sixty-six miles from a national border, without a warrant or any probable cause does not violate the Fourth Amendment.[286] To similar effect, U.S. immigration authorities that entered a

Act of 2008, and Foreign Intelligence Surveillance of Americans Overseas, 78 FORDHAM L. REV. 217, 237–38 (2009).

[281] *See, e.g., Fact Sheet: Impact of Warrantless Section 702 Surveillance on People in the United States*, HUM. RTS. WATCH (Mar. 1, 2017, 3:10 PM), https://perma.cc/LKD4-56XQ.

[282] *See* Carroll v. United States, 267 U.S. 132, 154 (1925); Boyd v. United States, 116 U. S. 616, 623–24 (1886).

[283] 413 U.S. 266 (1973); *see also* United States v. Brignoni-Ponce, 422 U.S. 873 (1975) (holding that a roving patrol may not stop a vehicle near the Mexican border and question occupants about their citizenship simply because they appear to be of Mexican ancestry); *Carroll*, 267 U.S. at 154; RESTATEMENT (THIRD) § 722 cmt. a; James G. Connell III & René L. Valladares, *Search and Seizure Protections for Undocumented Aliens: The Territoriality and Voluntary Presence Principles in Fourth Amendment Law*, 34 AM. CRIM. L. REV. 1293 (1997).

[284] Instead of a roving patrol, the border patrol has also engaged in warrantless searches of private vehicles at permanent traffic checkpoints removed from the border. Such searches also have been found to violate the Fourth Amendment. *See* United States v. Ortiz, 422 U.S. 891 (1975).

[285] At the time, and still today, § 287(a)(3) of the Immigration and Nationality Act, 8 U.S.C. § 1357(a)(3) (2018), provided for warrantless searches of automobiles and other conveyances "within a reasonable distance from any external boundary of the United States," as authorized by regulations to be promulgated by the attorney general. The attorney general's regulation at the time, 8 CFR § 287.1, defined "reasonable distance" as "within 100 air miles from any external boundary of the United States." The regulation maintains the same definition today, but with the addition of "or any shorter distance which may be fixed by the chief patrol agent for CBP, or the special agent in charge for ICE . . . ." *Id.*

[286] United States v. Martinez-Fuerte, 428 U.S. 543 (1976).

factory in southern California and questioned employees to determine if any were undocumented noncitizens did not engage in a detention or seizure proscribed by the Fourth Amendment.[287]

Cases such as *Almeida-Sanchez* suggest that citizens and noncitizens in the United States are protected equally from warrantless searches under the Fourth Amendment. Such a broad application of Fourth Amendment protections might be doubted given the Court's opinion in *United States v. Verdugo-Urquidez*, which, as discussed in the next section, held that without "substantial connections" to the United States (that would render a noncitizen suspect one of "the people"), a noncitizen is not part of "the people" protected by the Fourth Amendment.[288] Yet *Verdugo-Urquidez* concerned a search *abroad* of a noncitizen who had no voluntary connection to the United States. Noncitizens present in the United States necessarily have a voluntary connection with it, irrespective of their immigration status; some, like lawful permanent residents, may have additional reasons for supposing a particularly strong connection. The location of the search in the United States would also be seen as an important factor for independent reasons: not applying Fourth Amendment protections has the potential to erode such protections more generally in the United States, given that the exact status of the person being searched may not be known at the outset.[289]

Search and seizure of evidence from a noncitizen in the United States that violates the Fourth Amendment, however, is not a basis for exclusion of such evidence in a removal proceeding brought against a noncitizen.[290] The exclusionary rule prevents the government, with certain exceptions, from using evidence gathered in violation of the Constitution (whether it be of the Fourth Amendment,[291] Fifth Amendment,[292] or Sixth Amendment[293]), but the rule only applies in criminal cases.[294] In *INS v. Lopez-Mendoza*,[295] the Court assumed that the Fourth Amendment applied to undocumented noncitizens in the United States, but found that even if the defendants had been unlawfully arrested, their ensuing admissions of illegal entry need not be excluded from their removal hearing.[296] Among other things, the Court noted that the application of the rule

[287] INS v. Delgado, 466 U.S. 210 (1984).

[288] *See* United States v. Verdugo-Urquidez, 494 U.S. 259, 265–66, 271 (1990); *see infra* this chapter text accompanying notes 301–321.

[289] *See* Michael Scaperlanda, *The Domestic Fourth Amendment Rights of Aliens: To What Extent Do They Survive* United States v. Verdugo-Urquidez?, 56 Mo. L. Rev. 213 (1991).

[290] On removal proceedings generally, see *infra* this chapter § III(A)(4).

[291] *See* Mapp v. Ohio, 367 U.S. 643 (1961).

[292] *See* Miranda v. Arizona, 384 U.S. 436 (1966).

[293] *See* Gilbert v. California, 388 U.S. 263 (1967).

[294] *See, e.g.*, United States v. Janis, 428 U.S. 433, 447 (1976) ("In the complex and turbulent history of the [exclusionary] rule, the Court never has applied it to exclude evidence from a civil proceeding, federal or state.").

[295] 468 U.S. 1032 (1984).

[296] *Id.* at 1040–50.

894 THE LAW OF U.S. FOREIGN RELATIONS

in removal proceedings "would compel the courts to release from custody persons who would then immediately resume their commission of a crime through their continuing, unlawful presence in this country."[297] The Court also noted that the "body" or "identity of a defendant or respondent in a criminal or civil proceeding is never itself suppressible as a fruit of an unlawful arrest, even if it is conceded that an unlawful arrest, search, or interrogation occurred."[298] In this instance, the defendants did not contest what the challenged evidence indicated, which was that they were undocumented noncitizens.[299]

The same rules under FISA that apply with respect to surveillance of U.S. citizens for foreign intelligence purposes apply to noncitizens in the United States, except for one important difference. As indicated in the prior section, FISA precludes governmental surveillance of citizens and permanent residents when undertaken solely in relation to activities protected by the First Amendment.[300] By contrast, there is no comparable preclusion for other noncitizens engaged in such activities in the United States.

3. Searches and Seizures of Citizens and Noncitizens Abroad

Different standards apply with respect to U.S. government search and seizures of citizens and noncitizens conducted outside the United States. The principal case is *United States v. Verdugo-Urquidez*, in which the Supreme Court found that Fourth Amendment protections do not apply to searches and seizures by U.S. government agents of property owned by a nonresident noncitizen in a foreign country. Verdugo-Urquidez was a Mexican who was apprehended in Mexico by Mexican police and transported to the United States, where he was arrested on narcotics charges. Thereafter, an agent of the U.S. Drug Enforcement Agency obtained permission from the Mexican government to search the Mexican residences of Verdugo-Urquidez but did not obtain a search warrant from a U.S. judge or magistrate before doing so.[301]

Reviewing the argument that the search violated the Fourth Amendment, Chief Justice Rehnquist, writing for the majority, stated that the Fourth Amendment's reference to "the people" refers "to a class of persons who are part of a national community or who have otherwise developed sufficient connection with this country to be considered part of that community."[302] Further, the Court was convinced by historical evidence that "the purpose of the Fourth

---

[297] *Id.* at 1050.

[298] *Id.* at 1039.

[299] *Id.* at 1040.

[300] *See supra* this chapter text accompanying note 269.

[301] United States v. Verdugo-Urquidez, 494 U.S. 259, 262–63 (1990); *see* RAUSTIALA, *supra* note 30, at 157–58, 169–77.

[302] *Verdugo-Urquidez*, 494 U.S. at 265 (citing U.S. *ex rel.* Turner v. Williams, 194 U.S. 279 (1904)).

Amendment was to protect the people of the United States against arbitrary action by their own Government; it was never suggested that the provision was intended to restrain the actions of the Federal Government against aliens outside of the United States territory."[303] Verdugo-Urquidez had no voluntary connection with the United States that might place him among "the people." Given that, "[a]t the time of the search, he was a citizen and resident of Mexico with no voluntary attachment to the United States, and the place searched was located in Mexico, . . . the Fourth Amendment has no application."[304] The Court noted, among other things, that application of the Fourth Amendment under such circumstances would affect not only U.S. law enforcement activities abroad, but also military operations; while such restrictions might be imposed by the political branches, they are not to be found in the Constitution.[305]

Justice Kennedy's concurrence did not "place any weight on the reference to 'the people' in the Fourth Amendment as a source of restricting its protections."[306] Rather, he focused on the particular circumstances that would "make adherence to the Fourth Amendment's warrant requirement impracticable and anomalous,"[307] which related more to the fact that the search was occurring in another state's territory.[308] Notwithstanding Justice Kennedy, most lower courts have followed the majority's approach, focusing on whether the nonresident noncitizen has a significant voluntary connection to the United States.[309] Less clear, is whether the rationale of the majority in *Verdugo-Urquidez* equally applies to lawful permanent residents whose property is searched abroad and, if so, whether the fact of their immigration status automatically satisfies

---

[303] *Id.* at 266.

[304] *Id.* at 274–75.

[305] *Id.* at 273, 275.

[306] *Id.* at 276 (Kennedy, J., concurring).

[307] *Id.* at 278.

[308] Justice Kennedy noted, inter alia, the absence of local magistrates available to issue warrants, the differing conceptions of reasonableness, and the need to cooperate with foreign officials. *Id.*

[309] *See, e.g.*, Rasul v. Myers, 563 F.3d 527, 529 (D.C. Cir. 2009) (holding that four British nationals captured in Afghanistan and transported to a U.S. naval base in Cuba were not among "the people" protected under the Fourth Amendment); United States v. Bravo, 489 F.3d 1, 9 (1st Cir. 2007) (holding that the Fourth Amendment does not apply to the U.S. Coast Guard's search of nonresident noncitizens on what was determined to be a "stateless" vessel on the high seas); United States v. Davis, 905 F.2d 245, 251 (9th Cir. 1990) (holding that the Fourth Amendment does not apply to nonresident noncitizens aboard a foreign vessel on the high seas); United States v. Larrahondo, 885 F. Supp. 2d 209, 221 (D.D.C. 2012) (holding that the Fourth Amendment does not apply to wiretap evidence collected from a Colombian national in Colombia); United States v. Defreitas, 701 F. Supp. 2d 297, 304 (E.D.N.Y. 2010) (holding that the searches and seizures of nonresident noncitizens abroad by non-U.S. law enforcement officers were not protected by the Fourth Amendment); United States v. Fantin, 130 F. Supp. 2d 385, 390 (W.D.N.Y. 2000) (holding that the nonresident noncitizen defendants did not meet the prerequisites of Fourth Amendment protection when Canadian and Mexican properties were searched). For an analysis concluding that the defendant could satisfy both the "connection" and "location" tests, see *Martinez-Aguero v. Gonzalez*, 459 F.3d 618, 624–25 (5th Cir. 2006).

the "connectivity" test.[310] Attorneys at the Department of Justice, however, regard permanent residents located abroad as "likely" falling within "the people" protected by the Fourth Amendment, and so caution that overseas "investigators should make every effort to determine if the targets of an investigation are U.S. citizens, resident aliens, or have other significant connections to the United States."[311]

The consequences of *Verdugo-Urquidez* for federal law enforcement and other activities abroad that affect noncitizens are not entirely settled, but the case appears to diminish severely Fourth Amendment rights of most noncitizens abroad. Further, the U.S. government is authorized by FISA Section 702 to conduct electronic surveillance of communications by nonresident noncitizens located abroad for intelligence purposes, so long as there is no targeting of communications involving citizens or persons in the United States.[312] While Section 702 provides that such collection must be "conducted in a manner consistent with the Fourth Amendment,"[313] the surveillance of nonresident noncitizens abroad appears to be conducted without any requirement that there be an individualized suspicion of criminal wrongdoing or even a threat to U.S. national security.[314] Efforts to challenge the constitutionality of such surveillance have been impeded both because the data collected is usually not used in subsequent criminal prosecutions—where standing would clearly exist—and because broad challenges have been set aside due to lack of standing.[315]

The Supreme Court has never directly addressed the applicability of the Fourth Amendment to U.S. citizens abroad,[316] so as to restrict the actions of U.S. officials

---

[310] *See* United States v. Omar, No. 09-242, 2012 WL 2277821, at *3–4 (D. Minn. June 18, 2012) (declining to reach the question "whether a lawful permanent resident, subject to a search and seizure on foreign soil, is entitled to the protections of the Fourth Amendment," but noting that it is an open issue in the Eighth Circuit).

[311] Christopher J. Smith, Anthony Aminoff, & Kelly Pearson, *Gathering Gang Evidence Overseas*, 68:5 DOJ J. FED. L. & PRAC. 47, 53 (2020) (article by attorneys in the office of international affairs and in the criminal division).

[312] 50 U.S.C. § 1881a(a) (providing that, notwithstanding FISA's usual restrictions on surveillance, "the Attorney General and the Director of National Intelligence may authorize jointly . . . the targeting of persons reasonably believed to be located outside the United States to acquire foreign intelligence information"); *id.* § 1881a(b)(3) (precluding such targeting with respect to citizens outside the United States). For more detailed discussion of FISA in the context of surveillance within the United States, see *infra* this chapter text accompanying notes 264–269.

[313] 50 U.S.C. § 1881a(b)(6).

[314] For an argument that nonresident noncitizens are protected under the Fourth Amendment from unreasonable searches and seizures, see Alec Walen, *Fourth Amendment Rights for Nonresident Aliens*, 16 GERMAN L.J. 1131 (2015) (also *in* PRIVACY AND POWER: A TRANSATLANTIC DIALOGUE IN THE SHADOW OF THE NSA-AFFAIR 282 (Russell A. Miller ed., 2017)).

[315] Clapper v. Amnesty Int'l USA, 568 U.S. 398 (2013) (finding that a reasonable likelihood that respondents' communications would be intercepted under FISA is not enough to show future injury for standing purposes, and finding no present injury stemming from the respondents' choice to take costly measures to protect their confidential communications).

[316] *But see* United States v. Verdugo-Urquidez, 494 U.S. 259, 283 n.7 (1990) (Brennan, J., dissenting) (recognizing "the rule, accepted by every Court of Appeals to have considered the question, that the

involved in searches and seizures. Lower courts, however, have maintained, or at least strongly suggested, that the Fourth Amendment does so apply,[317] and the executive branch may have conceded as much.[318] Further, *Reid v. Covert's* assertion that when "the Government reaches out to punish a citizen who is abroad, the shield which the Bill of Rights and other parts of the Constitution provide to protect his life and liberty should not be stripped away just because he happens to be in another land,"[319] arguably supports the proposition that the Fourth Amendment fully applies to searches and seizures relating to U.S. citizens abroad. The rationale of *Verdugo-Urquidez*, whereby "the people" protected by the Fourth Amendment are persons "who are part of a national community or who have otherwise developed sufficient connection with this country," is also suggestive that all U.S. citizens are so protected. Indeed, in *Verdugo-Urquidez*, Chief Justice Rehnquist (writing for the plurality) and Justices Kennedy and Stevens all seemed to restrict their views on the limitations of the Fourth Amendment to nonresident noncitizens.[320] Finally, in explaining why Verdugo-Urquidez could be treated differently than citizens abroad, notwithstanding the equal protection clause of the Fifth Amendment, the Court did not maintain that citizens abroad also fell outside the scope of the Fourth Amendment's protections. Rather, the Court noted that U.S. constitutional provisions "were not intended to extend to aliens in the same degree as to citizens."[321]

Fourth Amendment applies to searches conducted by the United States Government against United States citizens abroad").

[317] *See* United States v. Juda, 46 F.3d 961, 968 (9th Cir. 1995) ("[T]he Fourth Amendment's reasonableness standard applies to United States officials conducting a search affecting a United States citizen in a foreign country."); Rosado v. Civiletti, 621 F.2d 1179, 1189 (2d Cir. 1980) (in a Fourth Amendment case concerning a search conducted abroad by foreign authorities, observing in dicta that "the Bill of Rights does apply extraterritorially to protect American citizens against the illegal conduct of United States agents"); Powell v. Zuckert, 366 F.2d 634 (D.C. Cir. 1966) (holding that the Fourth Amendment applied to a U.S. search, with Japanese participation, of an off-base dwelling of a U.S. citizen air force employee).
[318] United States v. Bin Laden, 126 F. Supp. 2d 264, 270 (S.D.N.Y. 2000) ("The Government seems to concede the general applicability of the Fourth Amendment to American citizens abroad, but asserts that the particular searches contested in this case (which were conducted overseas to collect foreign intelligence) call for a more limited application of the Amendment.").
[319] Reid v. Covert, 354 U.S. 1, 5–6 (1957) (Black, J., plurality); *see supra* this chapter text accompanying notes 53–59.
[320] *See* United States v. Verdugo-Urquidez, 494 U.S. 259, 261 (1990); *id.* at 278 (Kennedy, J., concurring); *id.* at 279 (Stevens, J., concurring in judgment); *see also* HENKIN, FOREIGN AFFAIRS, at 306 ("It seems unlikely that a majority of the Court [in *Verdugo*] would have held the Fourth Amendment inapplicable had the accused been a U.S. citizen.").
[321] *Verdugo-Urquidez*, 494 U.S. at 273. In analyzing constraints on FBI apprehension and abduction of a fugitive residing in a foreign state, the Office of the Legal Counsel opined that a violation of foreign or customary international law would not violate the Fourth Amendment; it did not, however, indicate that the Fourth Amendment simply had no application abroad. Authority of the Federal Bureau of Investigation to Override International Law in Extraterritorial Law Enforcement Activities, 13 Op. O.L.C. 163, 181–83 (1989).

Yet even if the application of the Fourth Amendment to U.S. citizens abroad requires that any search or seizure be reasonable, there are limits to that protection. The Department of Justice's Office of the Legal Counsel has maintained that an arrest in violation of foreign law or customary international law does not necessarily violate the Fourth Amendment.[322] Further, a search or seizure of a U.S. citizen abroad may not require that a warrant be obtained. In *In re Terrorist Bombings of U.S. Embassies in East Africa (Fourth Amendment Challenges)*,[323] a U.S. citizen living in Kenya and suspected of terrorist acts was subject to telephone wiretaps and a warrantless search by U.S. officials in cooperation with Kenyan authorities. The Second Circuit concluded (relying in part on *Reid*) that the Bill of Rights generally does apply extraterritorially to protect U.S. citizens against conduct of the U.S. government,[324] but that the Fourth Amendment's *warrant* requirement "does not govern searches conducted abroad by U.S. agents," and that "such searches of U.S. citizens need only satisfy the Fourth Amendment's requirement of reasonableness."[325] In finding that the Fourth Amendment warrant requirement does not apply to any U.S. government searches abroad of U.S. citizens, the court of appeals stressed the lack of precedent for requiring a warrant in such circumstances, the inadvisability of requiring the U.S. government to obtain warrants from foreign magistrates, and the absence of any mechanism for obtaining a U.S. warrant granting authority for such a search.[326] At the same time, the court found that these particular searches were reasonable, emphasizing several factors: the complex and decentralized nature of al-Qaeda; the difficulty of determining at the outset the value of intelligence information that is sought; the tendency for conspirators to speak in code; and the foreign language challenge.[327]

A further issue is whether the Fourth Amendment applies at all—even to the limited extent of a reasonableness requirement—if the search of the U.S. citizen abroad is conducted *by a foreign government*.[328] Generally, Fourth Amendment principles do not apply to searches by foreign authorities in their own countries,

---

[322] 13 Op. O.L.C., *supra* note 321, at 181–83.
[323] United States v. Odeh (*In re* Terrorist Bombings of U.S. Embassies in E. Afr. (Fourth Amendment Challenges)), 552 F.3d 157 (2d Cir. 2008).
[324] *Id.* at 167.
[325] *Id.*
[326] *Id.* at 172. For analysis, see Carla Crandall, *Bombed Away: How the Second Circuit Destroyed Fourth Amendment Rights of U.S. Citizens Abroad*, 2010 BYU L. Rev. 719 (2010); Orin S. Kerr, *The Modest Role of the Warrant Clause in National Security Investigations*, 88 Tex. L. Rev. 1669, 1680 (2010).
[327] *In re Terrorist Bombings*, 552 F.3d at 175–76; *see also* United States v. Stokes, 726 F.3d 880, 892–94 (7th Cir. 2013) (agreeing with the Second Circuit in *In re Terrorist Bombings* that Fourth Amendment warrant requirement does not apply to searches of U.S. citizens abroad and finding the search in this case, concerning alleged illegal sexual conduct with a minor, was reasonable).
[328] United States v. Peterson, 812 F.2d 486, 490 (9th Cir. 1987).

even if the targets of the search are U.S. citizens and evidence obtained thereafter is introduced in a U.S. court.[329] There are, however, two exceptions to this general rule. First, if the conduct of the foreign government "shocks the conscience" of the U.S. court, evidence procured by that conduct might not be admitted.[330] Second, if the U.S. government "substantially participates" in a search of a U.S. citizen that is conducted by a foreign government, such that the search is a "joint venture," the "reasonableness" requirement of the Fourth Amendment protections applies.[331] But if the U.S. government's involvement is of a lesser degree, such as passing information to the foreign government that leads to the search (or merely receiving and using evidence that results from such a search), then the reasonableness requirement does not apply.[332]

In some instances, searches of U.S. citizens by the U.S. government have occurred on the high seas, outside the territory of either the United States or a foreign nation. A threshold issue is that the United States—usually through a coast guard or navy vessel—must assert jurisdiction over a vessel, which might be done with the consent of a foreign flag state.[333] Circuit courts have applied the Fourth Amendment's "reasonableness" standard in such situations, maintaining that in such circumstances a warrant is not required, given that the location of the search and the practical difficulties of obtaining a warrant present exigent circumstances.[334] Further, in *United States v. Peterson*,[335] the court held that a U.S. government search of a U.S. citizen on the high seas, which was allegedly tainted by unlawful wiretaps by the Philippine government in the Philippines and in which the United States participated, would be reasonable if the wiretaps

---

[329] *See id.*; United States v. Morrow, 537 F.2d 120, 139 (5th Cir. 1976); United States v. Rose, 570 F.2d 1358, 1361 (9th Cir. 1978).

[330] *See, e.g., Morrow*, 537 F.2d at 139.

[331] *See, e.g.*, United States v. Barona, 56 F.3d 1087, 1091 (9th Cir.1995); United States v. Rose, 570 F.2d 1358, 1362 (9th Cir. 1978); Stonehill v. United States, 405 F.2d 738, 743 (9th Cir. 1968); *Stokes*, 710 F. Supp. 2d at 697; RESTATEMENT (THIRD) § 433(3).

[332] *See* Birdsell v. United States, 346 F.2d 775, 782 (5th Cir. 1965) ("[T]he Fourth Amendment does not apply to arrests and searches made by [foreign] officials in [a foreign country] for violation of [foreign] law, even if the persons arrested are Americans and American police officers gave information leading to the arrest and search."); *see also* United States v. Janis, 428 U.S. 433, 455 n.31 (1976); United States v. Rose, 570 F.2d 1358, 1362 (9th Cir. 1978); Stonehill v. United States, 405 F.2d 738, 746 (9th Cir. 1969).

[333] Assertion of Jurisdiction by the United States Over Foreign Vessels Seized Pursuant to a Special Arrangement, 4B Op. O.L.C. 572, 573–74 (1980) (noting the flag state's primary jurisdiction, which may be renounced in favor of the United States, after which evidence obtained in violation of the Fourth Amendment may not be relied upon).

[334] *See, e.g.*, Juda v. United States, 46 F.3d 961, 968–69 (9th Cir. 1995) (holding, inter alia, that a stateless vessel on the high seas from which U.S. law enforcement seized drugs fell within the jurisdiction of the United States, and that the U.S. Coast Guard acted within its authority to inspect the vessel on the high seas); United States v. Tinoco, 304 F.3d 1088, 1116–17 (11th Cir. 2002) (determining "that the Coast Guard had reasonable suspicion to believe that the vessel here was engaged in illegal smuggling activities" because it was "unmarked [and] flagless," and the Coast Guard observed its crew members "throw[] bales and fuel drums into the water").

[335] 812 F.2d 486 (9th Cir. 1987).

conformed to Philippine law.[336] Moreover, even if the wiretaps did not conform with Philippine law (which the court assumed), the Fourth Amendment claim is defeated where U.S. authorities have relied on foreign law enforcement officers' representations that there has been compliance with their law.[337]

4. *Bivens* Actions by Noncitizens Against the U.S. Government

In the 1971 opinion in *Bivens v. Six Unknown Named Agents of Federal Bureau of Narcotics*,[338] the Supreme Court held that a U.S. citizen may bring a lawsuit for damages against a federal officer for violations in the United States of the Fourth Amendment. While the Court has extended such a "*Bivens* remedy" to violations of the Fifth and Eighth Amendments,[339] it has refrained from doing so for any constitutional violations in the context of noncitizens located abroad or undocumented noncitizens located in this United States.

For example, in *Ziglar v. Abbasi*,[340] the Supreme Court declined to extend such a *Bivens* remedy to certain undocumented noncitizens who were detained in the United States and who sued for alleged constitutional harms suffered during detention. In that case, the plaintiffs were six undocumented noncitizens—most of whom were Muslim and of Middle Eastern origin—who were detained after the 9/11 terrorist attacks and treated as "of interest" in the government's investigation of those attacks. The plaintiffs sued various government officials, arguing that the government used their status as noncitizens to detain them, when the government's real purpose was to investigate whether they were terrorists, and that the conditions of their confinement violated their constitutional rights to due process and equal protection. The Court did not assert that a *Bivens* remedy was unavailable simply because the individuals were undocumented noncitizens. Rather, the Court viewed the constitutional right at issue in the case (treatment during detention) as meaningfully different from the rights at issue in *Bivens* (involving FBI agents handcuffing an individual in his home without a warrant).[341] In addition, the Court concluded that there were special factors

---

[336] *Id.* at 490–91.

[337] *Id.* at 492; *see* United States v. Stokes, 710 F. Supp. 2d 689, 703 (N.D. Ill. 2009) (noting that "U.S. law enforcement officers who reasonably rely on a foreign authority's representations of applicable foreign law have not engaged in any culpable police misconduct"); *Juda*, 46 F.3d at 968 (DEA reasonably relied on a representation from Australian police that no warrant was required under Australian law for installation of a transmitter on a vessel; accordingly, the good faith exception to the exclusionary rule applies).

[338] 403 U.S. 388 (1971).

[339] *See* Carlson v. Green, 446 U.S. 14 (1980) (for constitutionally inadequate prisoner medical care in violation of the Eighth Amendment); Davis v. Passman, 442 U.S. 228 (1979) (for gender discrimination against a public employee in violation of the equal protection component of the Fifth Amendment).

[340] 137 S. Ct. 1843 (2017).

[341] *Id.* at 1860.

weighing against such a remedy, including the fact that the noncitizens were challenging a government policy (rather than an individual officer's action); the detention was in the aftermath of a major terrorist attack on U.S. soil; allowing a suit in damages would interfere with "sensitive functions of the Executive Branch," including its responsibility to implement national security policies; and, given that national security policy is a field for the political branches, such a remedy would raise separation of powers issues.[342]

In *Hernandez v. Mesa*,[343] the Court declined to recognize a *Bivens* claim in the context of a cross-border incident involving the shooting death of a foreign national. In that case, a U.S. border patrol agent, standing on U.S. soil, shot and killed a fifteen-year-old Mexican national who was on Mexican soil, having just returned back across the border following entry into U.S. territory. The teenager's family pursued a *Bivens* remedy in U.S. court, alleging that the agent had violated the teenager's Fourth and Fifth Amendment rights. The Court's refusal to recognize a remedy was predicated on a two-step inquiry: first, examining whether the remedy arose in a new context or for a new category of defendants; and second, if so, whether there are any factors that counseled hesitation about extending the remedy. It deemed the cross-border situation to be a new context.[344] Further, several factors weighed against the extension of *Bivens* to that context: (1) the "potential effect on foreign relations," given that a "cross-border shooting is by definition an international incident," which "may lead to a disagreement between [two] countries" that is best resolved through diplomacy;[345] (2) the connection to national security, in that the executive protects the United States in part by controlling the movement of persons across the border;[346] and (3) that statutes addressing analogous claims, such as a statute permitting the recovery of damages for constitutional violations by officers acting under color of state law, are limited to U.S. citizens or other persons within U.S. jurisdiction.[347] While concerns about judicial intervention are a constant in *Bivens* cases, and may be particularly acute in the foreign relations context, the Court's reasoning is peculiar in at least one regard: all things being equal, one would assume that affording a damages remedy to injured foreign nationals would generally reduce not inflame international tensions.

By contrast, the Ninth Circuit in *Lanuza v. Love* allowed a *Bivens* remedy for a nonimmigrant noncitizen pursuing lawful permanent resident status, where a

---

[342] *Id.* at 1861; *see also* Mirmehdi v. United States, 689 F.3d 975 (9th Cir. 2012) (declining to allow a noncitizen not lawfully in the United States to sue for monetary damages claiming constitutionally invalid detention).
[343] 140 S. Ct. 735 (2020).
[344] *Id.* at 743.
[345] *Id.* at 744.
[346] *Id.* at 746.
[347] *Hernandez*, 140 S. Ct. at 747–49 (citing 42 U.S.C. § 1983 (2018)).

government immigration attorney intentionally submitted a forged document in an immigration proceeding for the purpose of bringing about the noncitizen's removal.[348] The court found that *Ziglar v. Abbasi* did not foreclose extending *Bivens* remedies to immigration cases,[349] and distinguished the context of that case—involving the detention of suspected terrorist—from the claimed violation of due process rights in a routine immigration proceeding.[350] While the *Lanuza* case presented a new context for a *Bivens* remedy,[351] the court found no special factors suggesting that a *Bivens* remedy was inappropriate. The noncitizen was suing a particular federal officer for wrongful behavior (not for a broader governmental policy);[352] such litigation did not appear burdensome to the government, nor a threat to "the political branches' supervision of national security and foreign policy";[353] and the case had not garnered any executive or congressional attention such that it risked interference with foreign affairs or diplomacy more generally.[354]

5. Inspection Regimes Required by Arms Control Treaties

The United States has ratified a wide range of multilateral and bilateral arms control treaties establishing limitations on nuclear,[355] biological,[356] and chemical weapons,[357] on missiles,[358] and on specific conventional weapons that are excessively injurious or indiscriminate.[359] Such treaties sometimes contain verification

---

[348] 899 F.3d 1019 (9th Cir. 2018).

[349] *Id.* at 1021.

[350] *Id.* at 1027.

[351] *Id.* at 1028.

[352] *Id.* at 1029.

[353] *Id.* at 1030.

[354] *Id.*

[355] *See, e.g.,* Treaty Banning Nuclear Weapon Tests in the Atmosphere, in Outer Space and Under Water, Aug. 5, 1963, 14 U.S.T. 1313, 480 U.N.T.S. 43; Treaty on the Non-Proliferation of Nuclear Weapons, July 1, 1968, 21 U.S.T. 483, 729 U.N.T.S. 161.

[356] Convention on the Prohibition of the Development, Production, and Stockpiling of Bacteriological (Biological) and Toxin Weapons, and on Their Destruction, Apr. 10, 1972, 26 U.S.T. 583, 1015 U.N.T.S. 163.

[357] Convention on the Prohibition of the Development, Production, Stockpiling and Use of Chemical Weapons and on Their Destruction, Jan. 13, 1993, S. TREATY DOC. No. 103-21 (1993), 1975 U.N.T.S. 45 [hereinafter Chemical Weapons Convention].

[358] *See, e.g.,* Treaty on the Limitation of Anti-Ballistic Missile Systems, U.S.-U.S.S.R., May 26, 1972, 23 U.S.T. 3435 [hereinafter ABM Treaty]; Treaty on the Elimination of Intermediate-Range and Shorter-Range Missiles, U.S.-U.S.S.R., Dec. 8, 1987, 1657 U.N.T.S. 2 [hereinafter INF Treaty]. The United States withdrew from the ABM Treaty in 2002 and from the INF Treaty in 2019.

[359] Convention on Prohibitions or Restrictions on the Use of Certain Conventional Weapons Which May Be Deemed to Be Excessively Injurious or to Have Indiscriminate Effects, Oct. 10, 1980, S. TREATY DOC. No. 103-25 (1994), 1342 U.N.T.S. 137. The United States is also a party to the first two protocols. *See* Protocol on Non-detectable Fragments (Protocol I), Oct. 10, 1980, S. TREATY DOC. No. 103-25 (1994), 1342 U.N.T.S. 168; Protocol on Prohibitions or Restrictions on the Use of Mines, Booby-Traps and Other Devices (Protocol II), Oct. 10, 1980, as amended May 3, 1996, S. TREATY DOC. No. 105-1 (1997), 2048 U.N.T.S. 133.

provisions, which call for inspections in the United States of facilities by an international organization or a foreign state (and allow, in return, inspections of other state parties). When such inspections include nongovernmental facilities, issues may arise with respect to potential violations of the search and seizure provision of the Fourth Amendment.[360]

For example, the United States ratified the Chemical Weapons Convention (CWC)[361] in 1997 and adopted an implementing statute[362] and regulations.[363] The CWC calls for two types of verification inspections. "Routine inspections" may be conducted with respect to all facilities, whether public or private, that are "declared" by the United States as producing chemicals contained in the convention's three schedules.[364] For these routine inspections, the secretariat of the Organization for the Prohibition of Chemical Weapons selects the facilities to be inspected; the inspections are then limited to determining the accuracy of U.S. declarations regarding the activity at such facilities, as well as whether such activities are consistent with the CWC. Separately, the CWC establishes a system of "challenge inspections" whereby a CWC state party may make immediate inspections of any facility within the jurisdiction of another party, including an undeclared facility, subject to specified procedures.[365]

While concerns have been raised as to the constitutionality of such inspections in the United States when conducted of nongovernmental facilities,[366] the

---

[360] *See generally* LOUIS HENKIN, ARMS CONTROL AND INSPECTION IN AMERICAN LAW (1958); HENKIN, FOREIGN AFFAIRS, at 265–66, 288; Robert F. Greenlee, *The Fourth Amendment and Facilities Inspections under the Chemical Weapons Convention*, 65 U. CHI. L. REV. 943 (1998). Ratification of a 2002 human rights protocol would raise similar issues. The Optional Protocol to the Convention against Torture and Other Cruel, Inhuman or Degrading Treatment or Punishment, Dec. 18, 2002, 2375 U.N.T.S. 237, provides for visits to the detention facilities of States Parties, such as prisons, by independent international and national bodies, for the purpose of strengthening protections against torture and other inhuman treatment. At the time of its adoption, the United States noted search-and-seizure and federalism concerns with the protocol. *See* John Davison, Deputy U.S. Representative to the U.N. Economic and Social Council, *Explanation of Vote on the Optional Protocol to the Convention Against Torture and Other Cruel, Inhuman and Degrading Treatment or Punishment*, U.S. DEP'T OF STATE (July 24, 2002), https://perma.cc/NTN9-YUXV. Since that time, the United States has taken no steps to pursue ratification. *See, e.g.*, U.S. Dep't of State, U.S. Periodic Report to the U.N. Committee against Torture 89 (2013), https://perma.cc/H467-YTPG (response to Question 44(a)).

[361] Chemical Weapons Convention, *supra* note 357.

[362] Chemical Weapons Convention Implementation Act of 1998, div. I, Pub. L. No. 105-277, 112 Stat. 2681-856. Among other things, the statute establishes criminal and civil penalties for the development, production, acquisition, stockpiling, transfer, possession, or use of chemical weapons.

[363] Exec. Order No. 13,128, 3 C.F.R. § 199 (1999); Chemical Weapons Convention Regulations, 15 C.F.R. § 710-29 (2020).

[364] *See* Chemical Weapons Convention, *supra* note 357, Annex on Implementation and Verification, Part VI, § E (listing the verification regime for Schedule One chemicals); *id.* Part VII, § B (listing the verification regime for Schedule Two chemicals); *id.* Part VIII, § B (listing the verification regime for Schedule Three chemicals).

[365] Chemical Weapons Convention, *supra* note 357, art. IX.

[366] *See, e.g., Constitutional Aspects of the Chem. Weapons Convention: Testimony before the Subcomm. on the Constitution of the S. Comm. on the Judiciary*, 104th Cong. (1996) (statement of Roger Pilon, Senior Fellow and Director, Center for Constitutional Studies, Cato Institute); Jonathan P. Hersey & Anthony F. Ventura, *Challenging Challenge Inspections: A Fourth Amendment Analysis of*

U.S. government normally conducts such inspections with the consent of the owner or operator of the facility, such that no warrant is required.[367] To that end, the Department of Commerce has developed guidance and briefings for industry to plan in advance for potential inspections,[368] and technical assistance is available to assist the facility with an inspection.[369] If consent is not forthcoming, however, then the government may seek an administrative warrant to inspect the facility. When this is done for a commercial facility, "probable cause justifying the issuance of a warrant may be based not only on specific evidence of an existing violation but also on a showing that 'reasonable legislative or administrative standards for conducting an . . . inspection are satisfied with respect to a particular [establishment].' "[370] Moreover, if the facility is part of a closely regulated industry, then this "expectation is particularly attenuated."[371] In the United States, the chemical manufacturing industry is highly regulated, due to health, safety, and environmental concerns.[372] If an administrative warrant cannot be obtained, then it may be possible to secure a criminal search warrant, if there is probable cause to believe that the statute implementing the CWC is being violated. If none of the preceding steps are available, the CWC contains a "constitutional savings provision" designed to allow the inspected state to take account of any constitutional obligations that it may have.[373]

the Chemical Weapons Convention, 25 FLA. STATE U. L. REV. 569, 589–617 (1998); Ronald D. Rotunda, The Chemical Weapons Convention: Political and Constitutional Issues, 15 CONST. COMMENT. 131 (1998); Robert F. Greenlee, The Fourth Amendment and Facilities Inspections Under the Chemical Weapons Convention, 65 U. CHI. L. REV. 943 (1998).

[367] See Fourth Amendment Issues Raised by Chemical Weapons Inspection Regime: Statement before the Subcommittee on the Constitution, Federalism, and Property Rights of the Senate Committee on the Judiciary, 20 Op. O.L.C. 310 (1996) (statement by Richard L. Shiffrin, Deputy Assistant Attorney General).
[368] U.S. DEP'T OF COMMERCE, CWC INDUSTRY INSPECTION PREPARATION HANDBOOK (n.d.), https://perma.cc/XJ4B-98X3.
[369] 50 U.S.C. § 1525(a) (2018).
[370] Marshall v. Barlow's, Inc., 436 U.S. 307, 320 (1978) (footnote omitted) (quoting Camara v. Municipal Court, 387 U.S. 523, 538 (1967)).
[371] New York v. Burger, 482 U.S. 691, 700 (1987).
[372] See, e.g., Resource Conservation and Recovery Act of 1976, 42 U.S.C. § 6901 (2018); Toxic Substances Control Act of 1976, 15 U.S.C. §§ 2601–29; Clean Air Act, 42 U.S.C. §§ 7401–7515; Clean Water Act, 33 U.S.C. §§ 1251–1387.
[373] Chemical Weapons Convention, supra note 357, Annex on Implementation and Verification, Part X, ¶ 41 ("[T]he inspected State Party member shall be under the obligation to allow the greatest degree of access taking into account any constitutional obligations it may have with regard to proprietary rights or searches and seizures."). The transmittal package to the Senate explained that "the Convention provides a system for the inspected State Party to manage access to a challenged site in a manner that allows for protection of its national security, proprietary, and constitutional concerns." 103 CONG. REC. 32228, 32229 (1993).

D. Due Process, Equal Protection, and Taking of Property
(Fifth Amendment)

The Fifth Amendment addresses a range of issues, mostly related to criminal trials, due process, and the taking of property.[374] In describing those it protects, the amendment refers to "person" rather than to "citizen" or "the people," suggesting that the protections stated therein apply broadly. In practice, the amendment appears to apply fully to all persons, citizens and noncitizens alike, and their property, in the United States.[375] In the 1896 case of *Wong Wing v. United States*, the Supreme Court found that the U.S. government could deport an undocumented noncitizen without a jury trial, but could not punish him without a jury trial, as it would violate the Fifth and Sixth Amendments.[376] Such reasoning has allowed noncitizens in the United States to benefit from various Fifth Amendment criminal law protections, including the grand jury guarantee[377] and the privilege against self-incrimination.[378] Noncitizens presumably also benefit from the prohibition on double jeopardy; notably, however, the "dual-sovereignty doctrine" provides that the laws of two sovereigns (such as a foreign state and the United States) create two offenses, such that prosecution by those sovereigns for the same conduct does not violate the Double

---

[374] The Fifth Amendment of the U.S. Constitution provides:

> No person shall be held to answer for a capital, or otherwise infamous crime, unless on a presentment or indictment of a Grand Jury, except in cases arising in the land or naval forces, or in the Militia, when in actual service in time of War or public danger; nor shall any person be subject for the same offence to be twice put in jeopardy of life or limb; nor shall be compelled in any criminal case to be a witness against himself, nor be deprived of life, liberty, or property, without due process of law; nor shall private property be taken for public use, without just compensation.

U.S. CONST. amend. V. For a general discussion of the Fifth Amendment, see ERWIN CHEMERINSKY, CONSTITUTIONAL LAW: PRINCIPLES AND POLICIES §§ 7.3, 8.4, 9 (6th ed. 2019); 1 WAYNE R. LAFAVE ET AL., CRIMINAL PROCEDURE § 2.7 (4th ed. 2015); 2 LAFAVE ET AL. at §§ 6.5–6.10; 2 LAFAVE ET AL. at § 8.10; 3 LAFAVE ET AL. at § 15.1; 4 LAFAVE ET AL. at § 25.

[375] RESTATEMENT (THIRD) § 722 cmt. a.

[376] 163 U.S. 228 (1896) (finding that in criminal proceedings, noncitizens must be accorded the protections of the Fifth and Sixth Amendments); *see* Mathews v. Diaz, 426 U.S. 67, 77 (1976) (finding that "[t]here are literally millions of aliens within the jurisdiction of the United States. The Fifth Amendment ... protects every one of these persons"); RESTATEMENT (THIRD) § 721 cmt. h.

[377] *Wong Wing*, 163 U.S. at 238 (holding that all noncitizens are entitled to Fifth Amendment protections in a criminal trial, including indictment of a grand jury). The grand jury guaranty is required in federal prosecutions, not in all state prosecutions. *See* Hurtado v. California, 110 U.S. 516 (1884).

[378] *See* Sanchez-Llamas v. Oregon, 548 U.S. 331, 350 (2006) (finding that "[a] foreign national detained on suspicion of crime ... is protected against compelled self-incrimination."); *In re* Gault, 387 U.S. 1, 47–48 (1967) (holding that the protection against self-incrimination applies in all types of cases and against all defendants); *see also* Padilla v. Kentucky, 559 U.S. 356 (2010) (holding that an attorney for a lawful permanent resident in a criminal proceeding is required to notify their client that pleading guilty makes them deportable, and not doing so is a Sixth Amendment violation).

Jeopardy Clause.[379] Most broadly, in both criminal and civil contexts, the Fifth and Fourteenth Amendments require due process—that "the application of federal and State statutes must be neither arbitrary nor fundamentally unfair."[380] Further, noncitizens in the United States may invoke the writ of habeas corpus to test the legality of their restraint, as can noncitizens detained abroad in places where the U.S. government exercises a high degree of control.[381]

Application of the many dimensions of the Fifth Amendment to government conduct in relation to activities or persons outside the United States, however, is less clear. A plurality of the Supreme Court in *Reid v. Covert* advanced the broad proposition that, when the United States acts against its citizens abroad, it can do so only in accordance with all the limitations imposed by the Constitution, including the Fifth Amendment.[382] In that instance, this meant that the government could not expose U.S. citizens accompanying military personnel abroad to trial by military tribunal, under military regulations and procedures, rather than trial in civilian courts with all the safeguards of the Fifth and Sixth Amendments.

Even so, the exact contours by which the Fifth Amendment applies in relation to activities abroad of both citizens and noncitizens is largely unsettled. To date, Fifth Amendment issues have arisen in several ways: (1) U.S. criminal investigation of noncitizens abroad; (2) U.S. abduction of noncitizens abroad for prosecution in the United States; (3) U.S. civil actions against noncitizens located abroad; (4) equal protection for noncitizens in the United States; (5) taking of property without just compensation; (6) liberty to travel to and from the United States; and (7) military detention of noncitizens abroad.

---

[379] *See* Gamble v. United States, 139 S. Ct. 1960, 1967 (2019) ("The murder of a U.S. national is an offense to the United States as much as it is to the country where the murder occurred and to which the victim is a stranger. . . . [C]ustomary international law allows this exercise of jurisdiction."); Heath v. Alabama, 474 U.S. 82, 92 (1985) ("This Court has plainly and repeatedly stated that two identical offenses are not the 'same offence' within the meaning of the Double Jeopardy Clause if they are prosecuted by different sovereigns.").

[380] RESTATEMENT (FOURTH) § 403 cmt. c.

[381] Nishimura Ekiu v. United States, 142 U.S. 651, 660 (1892) (holding that noncitizens, including undocumented noncitizens, are entitled to petition for habeas corpus); Rasul v. Bush, 542 U.S. 466 (2004) (holding that noncitizens who were not nationals of countries at war with the United States, who denied engaging in acts of aggression against the United States, and who have not been afforded access to any tribunal, but who were being held at the U.S. naval station in Guantánamo Bay, Cuba, where the United States exercised "complete jurisdiction and control," were entitled to file statutory habeas corpus petitions); Boumediene v. Bush, 553 U.S. 723 (2008) (finding that the 2006 Military Commissions Act, which eliminated federal courts jurisdiction to hear habeas applications from detainees who have been designated as enemy combatants, was an unconstitutional suspension of the writ of habeas corpus for noncitizen detainees at Guantánamo).

[382] Reid v. Covert, 354 U.S. 1 (1957). *See supra* this chapter text accompanying notes 53–55. While the Fourteenth Amendment contains a comparable due process requirement, activity by state governments abroad that implicates due process appears minimal.

1. U.S. Criminal Investigation of Noncitizens Abroad

The Fifth Amendment Due Process Clause is understood as a procedural and substantive safeguard against the U.S. government's ability to deprive persons of "life, liberty, or property" in both criminal and civil contexts and has important ramifications, especially in the context of criminal investigations and prosecutions.[383] To what extent such protections apply to U.S. criminal investigations abroad of noncitizens, however, is unclear.[384]

On the one hand, the premises on which the Supreme Court has limited the application of constitutional rights to noncitizens abroad apply awkwardly to Fifth Amendment violations. The Supreme Court's analysis in *Verdugo-Urquidez*, which denied the protection of the Fourth Amendment to the search of a noncitizen's residence abroad, stressed that the Fourth Amendment operated differently than the Fifth Amendment, in that the Fourth Amendment violation occurs at the time of the search and seizure, while the Fifth Amendment violation occurs at the time of the trial in the United States.[385] As such, arguably any violations of the Fifth Amendment that lead to the introduction of incriminating evidence in a U.S. criminal trial actually transpire in (and are thus closely connected to) the United States.[386] On the other hand, the Court, or at least individual justices, in cases such as *Reid v. Covert*,[387] *Verdugo-Urquidez*,[388] and *Boumediene*[389] have repeatedly signaled concern about applying constitutional

---

[383] *See, e.g.*, Mathews v. Eldridge, 424 U.S. 319, 335 (1976) (procedural due process requires government action to be implemented in a fair manner, even if it survives the stricter standards of substantive due process); Rochin v. California, 342 U.S. 165, 172 (1952) (holding that substantive due process prohibits government conduct that "shocks the conscience"); *see also* HENKIN, FOREIGN AFFAIRS, at 289–91.

[384] Such protections do not operate in relation to criminal proceedings by a foreign state. For example, in *United States v. Balsys*, 524 U.S. 666 (1998), the U.S. government subpoenaed a lawful permanent resident to testify about his wartime activities between 1940 and 1944 and his immigration to the United States. The noncitizen invoked the Fifth Amendment privilege against self-incrimination, based on his fear of prosecution by a foreign state. The Supreme Court held that concern with foreign prosecution falls outside the scope of the Self-Incrimination Clause.

[385] United States v. Verdugo-Urquidez, 494 U.S. 259, 264 (1990); *see supra* this chapter text accompanying notes 301–315.

[386] This approach to due process might also be consistent with *Boumediene v. Bush*, 553 U.S. 723 (2008), in which the Court recognized the habeas corpus rights of noncitizens in U.S. detention on foreign soil. Such consistency would make sense given that the concept of due process and the writ of habeas corpus are closely related. *See, e.g.*, Fay v. Noia, 372 U.S. 391, 402 (1963) ("Thus there is nothing novel in the fact that today habeas corpus in the federal courts provides a mode for the redress of denials of due process of law. Vindication of due process is precisely its historic office."). Courts, of course, have viewed the right to habeas corpus as arising exclusively under the Suspension Clause, not the Fifth Amendment. *See, e.g.*, Ali v. Rumsfeld, 649 F.3d 762, 771 (D.C. Cir. 2011); Igartúa v. United States, 626 F.3d 592, 600 (1st Cir. 2010); Rasul v. Myers, 563 F.3d 527, 529 (D.C. Cir. 2009).

[387] *See supra* this chapter text accompanying notes 53–55.

[388] *See supra* this chapter text accompanying notes 301–320.

[389] *See Boumediene*, 553 U.S. at 762–64 (stating that "questions of extraterritoriality turn on objective factors and practical concerns, not formalism"). For further discussion of *Boumediene*, see *supra* this chapter § I(B) and *infra* this chapter § II(D)(7).

protections to U.S. government activities abroad, in light of difficult issues that arise when operating in foreign territory. Certainly, that has been the case when dealing with investigation and prosecution of enemy aliens abroad.[390]

In the absence of clear rulings by·the Supreme Court on the exact extent of Fifth Amendment protections for noncitizens abroad, lower courts have forged ahead in at least three important areas: the privilege against self-incrimination; the introduction of evidence secured from coerced testimony; and the right to counsel.

With respect to the privilege against self-incrimination, some U.S. courts have held that the privilege, including the requirement of *Miranda* warnings (or a comparable warning given the constraints of custodial interrogation in a foreign country),[391] applies to a noncitizen interrogated abroad by U.S. law enforcement for the purpose of prosecution in U.S. courts when the noncitizen's statement is then offered at a U.S. trial against the defendant.[392] Yet other courts have found such statements admissible, even in the absence of a *Miranda* or comparable warning, so long as the statement is made voluntarily.[393]

As was the case for searches and seizures under the Fourth Amendment, this issue often arises in the context of U.S. government participation in the interrogation of a noncitizen by a foreign government. Here too, the Fifth Amendment

---

[390] *See, e.g.*, Johnson v. Eisentrager, 339 U.S. 763 (1950) (holding that the Fifth Amendment does not apply to enemy aliens abroad).

[391] *See, e.g.*, U.S. v. Zaitar, 858 F. Supp. 2d 103, 115 (D.C. Cir. 2012) (finding that adapted *Miranda* warnings were sufficient, even through somewhat of a language barrier, so long as the defendant understood their meaning); Cranford v. Rodriguez, 512 F.2d 860, 863 (10th Cir. 1975) (holding that a "good faith effort to comply with the *Miranda* doctrine" was sufficient); United States v. Dopf, 434 F.2d 205, 207 (5th Cir. 1970) (finding that the oral warning against self-incrimination by the FBI during an interrogation in Mexico was sufficient, despite the lack of a written waiver, because the waiver would have no application in Mexico).

[392] *See, e.g.*, United States v. Odeh (*In re* Terrorist Bombings of U.S. Embassies in E. Afr.), 552 F.3d 177, 201 (2d Cir. 2008) (holding that "foreign nationals interrogated overseas but tried in the civilian courts of the United States are protected by the Fifth Amendment's self-incrimination clause."); *see generally* Mark A. Godsey, *Miranda's Final Frontier—The International Arena: A Critical Analysis of* United States v. Bin Laden, *and a Proposal for a New* Miranda *Exception Abroad*, 51 DUKE L.J. 1703 (2002) (concluding that courts should not require FBI agents to adhere strictly to the requirements of *Miranda* abroad).

[393] *See, e.g.*, United States v. Abu Ali, 528 F.3d 210, 227 (4th Cir. 2008) (holding that, because "the United States cannot dictate the protections provided to criminal suspects by foreign nations," voluntary statements made to Saudi interrogators are admissible even without *Miranda* warnings); United States v. Yousef, 327 F.3d 56, 145 (2d Cir. 2003) (holding that defendant's statements to Jordanian officials were admissible despite the lack of *Miranda* warnings because statements taken by foreign officials need only be voluntary); Kilday v. United States, 481 F.2d 655, 656 (5th Cir. 1973) (holding that, because the defendant's statements to INTERPOL while in Argentina were not coerced, and because "the United States Constitution cannot compel such specific, affirmative action by foreign sovereigns," they were admissible even without *Miranda* warnings). For an argument that such courts have engaged in a far less rigorous assessment of whether the defendant's confession is truly voluntary (as compared with domestic interrogations), even when the government involved has a history of torturing detainees, see Jenny-Brooke Condon, *Extraterritorial Interrogation: The Porous Border between Torture and U.S. Criminal Trials*, 60 RUTGERS L. REV. 647 (2008).

does not generally apply to interrogations by a foreign government, even when information so obtained is introduced in a U.S. criminal proceeding. Yet there are two exceptions. First, if the conduct of the foreign government "shocks the conscience" of the U.S. court, the evidence may not be admitted.[394] Second, when U.S. law enforcement officials are intimately involved with the actions of foreign officials, either under a "joint venture" theory (which requires active or substantial participation of U.S. law enforcement officials) or under an "agency" theory (where foreign officials act as agents of U.S. law enforcement), courts have found the *Miranda* protection to apply.[395]

With respect to the introduction of evidence secured from coerced testimony, normally such information is suppressed as a violation of the Fifth Amendment.[396] For U.S. foreign relations law, this issue typically arises in the context of alleged torture by foreign officials that leads to a confession by a noncitizen. In these cases, lower courts have analyzed whether the testimony was involuntary and coerced and, if so, suppressed the information.[397]

---

[394] *See, e.g.,* United States v. Fernandez, 559 F.3d 303, 330 (5th Cir. 2009) (finding that the "shocks the conscience" standard requires "conduct [that] is 'brutal and offensive to human dignity'" and Mexican agents encouraging the defendant to lie and exaggerate his story, with the knowledge of U.S. law enforcement, did not "sink to the required depths").

[395] *See, e.g.,* United States v. Straker, 800 F.3d 570, 615–16 (D.C. Cir. 2015); *Abu Ali,* 528 F.3d at 227–28; *see also* United States v. Maturo, 982 F.2d 57, 60–62 (2d Cir. 1992) (analyzing whether wiretaps initiated solely by the Turkish National Police, attained with information and equipment provided by U.S. law enforcement agents, were excludable as evidence under "joint venture" and "agent" theories).

[396] *See, e.g.,* Arizona v. Fulminante, 499 U.S. 279 (1991) (holding that information obtained by state agents and used to convict defendant was barred by the Due Process Clause of the Fifth and Fourteenth Amendments since the defendant was motivated to confess by fear of physical violence); *see also* Brown v. Mississippi, 297 U.S. 278 (1936) (holding that convictions of murder which rest solely upon confessions shown to have been extorted by state officers through torture of the accused are void under the Due Process Clause of the Fourteenth Amendment).

[397] *See, e.g.,* Al-Hajj v. Obama, 800 F. Supp. 2d 19, 27 (D.D.C. 2011) (holding that some of petitioner's statements must be suppressed because taint of prior coercion outside of U.S. custody had not yet dissipated, but that other statements were admissible); United States v. Karake, 443 F. Supp. 2d 8, 86 (D.D.C. 2006) (concluding that defendant's statements to Rwandan officials were the product of coercion, and therefore "involuntary and inadmissible"); *see also* Al-Qurashi v. Obama, 733 F. Supp. 2d 69, 94 (D.D.C. 2010) (concluding that "[b]ased on the totality of the circumstances" the government "sustained [its] burden to show that these incriminating statements were made voluntarily and are therefore admissible"); United States v. Abu Ali, 395 F. Supp. 2d 338, 379 (E.D. Va. 2005) (stating, despite finding that there was insufficient evidence of torture to hold that a defendant's statements were involuntary, that "the Court would like to make a very clear statement that torture of any kind is legally and morally unacceptable, and that the judicial system of the United States will not permit the taint of torture in its judiciary proceedings"). The exact constitutional doctrine being applied in such cases is not always clear. For an analysis that noncitizens abroad cannot claim the protection of the due process "involuntary confession rule" of the Fifth and Fourteenth Amendments, but can invoke the Fifth Amendment's prohibition of "compelled" confessions, which arises under the privilege against compulsory self-incrimination, see Mark A. Godsey, *The New Frontier of Constitutional Confession Law—The International Arena: Exploring the Admissibility of Confessions Taken by U.S. Investigators from Non-Americans Abroad,* 91 Geo. L.J. 851 (2003).

With respect to the right to counsel, since *Edwards v. Arizona*,[398] U.S. courts have recognized a Fifth Amendment right to counsel during custodial interrogations in the United States (in addition to the post-indictment Sixth Amendment right to counsel).[399] In criminal investigations abroad, at least one court has found that the Fifth Amendment right to counsel applied to the custodial interrogation of a noncitizen in a foreign state by U.S. law enforcement, when conducted jointly with foreign officials.[400]

2. U.S. Abduction of Noncitizens Abroad for U.S. Prosecution

Arguably, the Due Process Clause of the Fifth Amendment (or of the Fourteenth Amendment in state proceedings) should be construed so as to put restraints on U.S. officials abroad acting unlawfully to bring defendants to the United States, such as through abduction abroad in violation of foreign law, customary international law, or a treaty of the United States. For some time, common law jurisdictions generally followed the rule that a person brought into the jurisdiction of a court as a result of an international abduction (or some form of state-sponsored deception) could not challenge the court's jurisdiction based on the illegality of the arrest. The rule is referred to as the *male captus bene detentus* ("badly captured, well detained") rule, famously displayed by the exercise of jurisdiction by Israeli courts over Adolf Eichmann after his kidnapping in Argentina.[401] Beginning in the 1970s, however, that practice evolved in many countries, such that an abduction undertaken without regard to a formal extradition process is now more likely to serve as a basis for a court to stay the proceedings before it.[402]

In the United States, however, the *male captus bene detentus* rule—often referred to as the *Ker-Frisbie* rule—persists.[403] In *Ker v. Illinois*,[404] the defendant

---

[398] 451 U.S. 477 (1981).

[399] *See infra* this chapter § II(E)(2).

[400] *See* United States v. Osorio-Arellanes, No. CR-11-00150-004-TUC-DCB (BPV), 2019 WL 357933 at *4 (D. Ariz. Jan. 29, 2019) ("The Court finds that there was no violation of [the defendant's] Fifth Amendment right to remain silent or be advised by counsel during questioning.").

[401] Att'y Gen. v. Eichmann, 36 I.L.R. 5, 70–71 (D.C. Jer. 1961), *aff'd*, 36 I.L.R. 277 (S. Ct. Isr. 1962).

[402] *See, e.g.*, R. v. Hartley [1978] 2 N.Z.L.R. 199 (CA) (N.Z.); Levinge v. Director of Custodial Services and others (1987) 9 N.S.W.L.R. 546 (Austl.); State v. Ebrahim 1991 (2) S.A. 553 (A) (S. Afr.); R. v. Horseferry Rd. Magis. Ct., *Ex parte* Bennett [1994] 1 AC (HL) 42 (appeal taken from Eng.); R. v. O'Connor, [1995] S.C.R. 411 (Can.); *see also* RESTATEMENT (FOURTH) § 427 rptrs. note 7. Whether such a trend might result in formation of a rule of customary international law or general principle of law is unclear; as it happens, ad hoc international criminal tribunals have maintained the *male captus bene detentus* rule. *See, e.g.*, Prosecutor v. Barayagwiza, Case No. ICTR-97-19, Decision on the Extremely Urgent Motion by the Defence for Orders to Review and/or Nullify the Arrest and Provisional Detention of the Suspect, ¶ 74 (Nov. 3, 1999); Prosecutor v. Dragan Nikolić, Case No. IT-94-2-Pt, Decision on Defence Motion Challenging the Exercise of Jurisdiction by the Tribunal (Int'l Crim. Trib. for the Former Yugoslavia Oct. 9, 2002).

[403] *See* RESTATEMENT (FOURTH) § 427 rptrs. note 5.

[404] 119 U.S. 436 (1886).

was abducted in Peru by an individual and brought before an Illinois court, where he was tried and convicted for larceny. Although a Peru-U.S. extradition treaty existed, the defendant was not brought to the United States by means of the treaty's procedures. The Supreme Court rejected the defendant's argument that the failure to abide by the treaty's terms divested U.S. courts of jurisdiction, saying broadly that "such forcible abduction is no sufficient reason why the party should not answer when brought within the jurisdiction of the court which has the right to try him for such an offence, and presents no valid objection to his trial in such court."[405] In *Frisbie v. Collins*,[406] the Court applied the rule in *Ker* to a domestic, interstate context, involving a defendant who had been kidnapped in Chicago by Michigan state officers and brought to trial before a Michigan court.[407]

While in *Ker* the abduction was not viewed as having U.S. government involvement, and the government of Peru did not object to the prosecution, neither of those redeeming features was present in the *Alvarez-Machain* case.[408] The defendant was a citizen of Mexico, abducted there by agents of the U.S. Drug Enforcement Administration and brought to the United States for trial on federal kidnapping and murder charges. The U.S. government did not follow the procedures of a U.S.-Mexico extradition treaty in securing custody of the defendant,[409] and Mexico protested the abduction—as did the defendant. The Ninth Circuit held that although forcible abductions were not expressly prohibited by the treaty, they did violate the treaty's purpose, and that such treaty

---

[405] *Id.* at 444; *see* United States v. Romero-Galue, 757 F.2d 1147, 1150 n.10 (11th Cir. 1985) (noting that "[j]urisdiction over the person of a defendant 'in a federal criminal trial whether citizen or alien, whether arrested within or beyond the territory of the United States,' is not subject to challenge on the ground that the defendant's presence before the court was unlawfully secured").

[406] 342 U.S. 519 (1952).

[407] In upholding the conviction over objections based on the Due Process Clause of the Fourteenth Amendment (and a federal statute), the Court explained that the rule "rest[s] on the sound basis that due process of law is satisfied when one present in court is convicted of crime after having been fairly apprized of the charges against him and after a fair trial in accordance with constitutional procedural safeguards" and that there is "nothing in the Constitution that requires a court to permit a guilty person rightfully convicted to escape justice because he was brought to trial against his will." *Id.* at 522.

[408] United States v. Alvarez-Machain, 504 U.S. 655 (1992). As late as 1980, OLC concluded that a forcible abduction, when coupled with a protest from the country of the abduction, was a violation of international law and an "impermissible invasion of the territorial integrity of another state." Extraterritorial Apprehension by the Federal Bureau of Investigation, 4B Op. O.L.C. 543, 549 (1980). Less than a decade later, however, OLC opined that a statute (18 U.S.C. § 3052) granted the Federal Bureau of Investigation broad investigative and apprehension authority involving crimes against the United States, including permission to undertake an extraterritorial capture of an individual without the cooperation or consent of the custodial state. Moreover, this was the case even if the actions would be in violation of customary international law, of unexecuted treaty obligations (such as Article 2(4) of the U.N. Charter), or of an extradition treaty. Authority of the Federal Bureau of Investigation to Override International Law in Extraterritorial Law Enforcement Activities, 13 Op. O.L.C. 163 (1989).

[409] Extradition Treaty, Mex.-U.S., May 4, 1978, 31 U.S.T. 5059.

violation (along with the formal protest of Mexico) divested the district court of jurisdiction.[410] The Supreme Court disagreed. In its view, the treaty neither expressly nor impliedly prohibited such an abduction, and thus under the rule of *Ker v. Illinois*, Mexico's protest was not decisive.[411] By contrast, Justice Stevens charged the Court with "fail[ing] to differentiate between the conduct of private citizens, which does not violate any treaty obligation, and conduct expressly authorized by the Executive Branch of the Government, which unquestionably constitutes a flagrant violation of international law, and in my opinion, also constitutes a breach of our treaty obligations."[412]

The Court's reasoning in *Alvarez-Machain* does confirm one exception to the *Ker-Frisbie* rule, which is that an abduction abroad by the U.S. government in violation of a treaty of the United States *would* divest a U.S. court of jurisdiction over the defendant.[413] The Court had previously signaled the existence of such an exception,[414] and lower courts had assumed it. For example, in *United States v. Postal*, the Fifth Circuit concluded that "that self-executing treaties may act to deprive the United States, and hence its courts, of jurisdiction over property and individuals that would otherwise be subject to that jurisdiction."[415] Another possible exception, concerning whether an abduction that violated customary international law would divest a U.S. court of jurisdiction, is unresolved. Some lower courts have concluded that "a defendant must demonstrate, by reference to the express language of a treaty and/or the established practice thereunder, that the United States affirmatively agreed not to seize foreign nationals from the territory of its treaty partner";[416] on this premise, a violation of customary international law standing alone would not be sufficient,[417] nor would the violation of

---

[410] United States v. Alvarez-Machain, 946 F.2d 1466 (9th Cir. 1991).

[411] *Alvarez-Machain*, 504 U.S. at 699. The Court's decision evoked considerable commentary. *See* HENKIN, FOREIGN AFFAIRS, at 306–07; Michael J. Glennon, *State-Sponsored Abduction: A Comment on* United States v. Alvarez-Machain, 86 AM. J. INTL. L. 746 (1992); Jacques Semmelman, United States v. Alvarez-Machain, 86 AM. J. INTL. L. 811 (1992); John Quigley, *Our Men in Guadalajara and the Abduction of Suspects Abroad: A Comment on* United States v. Alvarez-Machain, 68 NOTRE DAME L. REV. 723 (1993).

[412] *Alvarez-Machain*, 504 U.S. at 682 (Stevens, J., dissenting) (footnote omitted).

[413] *See* RESTATEMENT (FOURTH) § 427 rptrs. note 6.

[414] *See* Cook v. United States, 288 U.S. 102, 121 (1933) (acknowledging that the government may limit its own jurisdiction by entering into a treaty); Ford v. United States, 273 U.S. 593, 605–06 (1927) (explaining that "the *Ker* case does not apply here" because "a treaty of the United States is directly involved," but then finding that the jurisdictional issue had not been timely raised).

[415] 589 F.2d 862, 875 (5th Cir. 1979). The qualification relating to whether a treaty is "self-executing" is potentially significant, save that a treaty concerning extradition is likely to be deemed self-executing. *See infra* Chapter 6 § IV (A).

[416] United States v. Noriega, 117 F.3d 1206, 1213 (11th Cir. 1997); *see* United States v. Rezaq, 134 F.3d 1121, 1130 (D.C. Cir. 1998).

[417] *See* United States v. Best, 304 F.3d 308, 314 (3d Cir. 2002) ("unless the government's seizure of Best was in violation of a treaty between the United States and Brazil, the District Court has jurisdiction over Best in spite of the potential violation of international law."); *Postal*, 589 F.2d at 884 (a defendant "cannot rely upon a mere violation of international law as a defense to the court's jurisdiction").

a treaty to which the United States or the state of the abduction is not a party.[418] However, in *Alvarez-Machain* itself, the Supreme Court did not consider the argument that the kidnapping had violated customary international law, instead focusing exclusively on the issue of whether the treaty was violated.[419] On remand in that case, the Ninth Circuit did not resolve whether the Supreme Court's opinion had foreclosed considering additional bases for objection, but stated instead that "[t]o the extent that customary international law may arguably provide a basis for an exception to the *Ker-Frisbie* Doctrine, the exception has been recognized only in a situation in which the government's conduct was outrageous."[420] It may be difficult to resolve the question definitively in the absence of a clearly understood violation of customary international law.

In *United States v. Toscanino*, the Second Circuit identified a different exception to the rule of *Ker-Frisbie*.[421] In that case, the defendant alleged that, during his abduction from Uruguay by U.S. officials, he was subjected to torture and abuse. The Second Circuit held that due process concerns required the trial court to divest itself of jurisdiction "where it has been acquired as the result of the government's deliberate, unnecessary and unreasonable invasion of the accused's constitutional rights."[422] The court argued that the U.S. government should not have the power to bring defendants to the jurisdiction of the United States by any means, no matter how inhumane or brutal, and then be permitted to enjoy the fruits of its lawless behavior.[423] Whether the *Toscanino* exception has survived

---

[418] *Best*, 304 F.3d at 315 (finding that Brazil and the United States were not both parties to three treaties pled).

[419] Counsel for Alvarez-Machain asserted at oral argument that "there are strong arguments for the authority of the courts to enforce a customary prohibition in international law in this case." When asked by Justice O'Connor, "Well, if we were to conclude the treaty doesn't cover this, do you fall back on some violation of international law?", counsel replied that these had been presented to, but not ruled upon, by the lower courts, and "presumably those would be litigated if this Court finds that there is no provision in the treaty." Transcript of Oral Argument at 34–35, United States v. Alvarez-Machain, 504 U.S. 655 (1992) (No. 91-712).

[420] United States v. Alvarez-Machain, 971 F.2d 310, 311 (9th Cir. 1992) (citing United States v. Reed, 639 F.2d 896, 901 (2d Cir. 1981); United States v. Toscanino, 500 F.2d 267 (2d Cir. 1974)). The court treated this as a distinct objection from whether "the circumstances of his kidnapping were so shocking that the abduction constituted a denial of due process." *Id.* *Cf.* United States v. Verdugo-Urquidez, 1994 WL 279226 *1 (9th Cir. June 22, 1994) (concluding that "[o]utrageous government conduct is a prerequisite to [both] international law and due process claims" of the kind at issue before the court of appeals in *Alvarez-Machain*).

[421] 500 F.2d 267 (2d Cir. 1974); *see* RESTATEMENT (FOURTH) § 427 rptrs. note 5; RAUSTIALA, *supra* note 30, at 165–69.

[422] *Toscanino*, 500 F.2d at 275. *But see* United States v. Darby, 744 F.2d 1508, 1531 (11th Cir. 1984) (rejecting *Toscanino's* reasoning).

[423] For cases finding the conditions of the exception not to have been met, see United States v. Rosenthal, 793 F.2d 1214, 1232 (11th Cir. 1986) (reaffirming that the Eleventh Circuit "declined to adopt the *Toscanino* approach, but even if *Toscanino* was applicable Rosenthal would not benefit from it since there is no evidence of conduct which shocks the conscience," nor did the United States violate the extradition treaty with Colombia); United States v. Lira, 515 F.2d 68 (2d Cir. 1975) (holding that the defendant's forcible abduction in Chile did not impair criminal charges because there was no evidence of cruel or inhuman conduct).

Alvarez-Machain is unclear, given that the Court in *Alvarez-Machain* appears to have viewed the means by which a defendant is brought before the court as irrelevant to the question of whether the court has jurisdiction.[424]

3. U.S. Civil or Criminal Actions Against Noncitizens Located Abroad

Noncitizens and foreign corporations (understood as legal "persons") abroad regularly are accorded due process protections under the Fifth and Fourteenth Amendments in the context of civil claims brought against them in U.S. courts, including personal jurisdiction limits based on the minimum contacts requirement and "traditional notions of fair play and substantial justice."[425] Such protections also have been raised in the context of subjecting foreign states and their state-owned enterprises to civil actions in the United States. Indeed, the issue has become more salient in recent years, as Congress has repeatedly modified the Foreign Sovereign Immunities Act to allow civil litigation against foreign sovereigns.[426] Yet the Supreme Court has intimated that foreign states are not "persons" within the meaning of the Fifth Amendment,[427] and lower courts have so found, thereby denying them its protections.[428] By contrast, lower courts have

---

[424] *See* United States v. Best, 304 F.3d 308, 312 (3d Cir. 2002) ("Subsequent decisions of the Supreme Court indicate that there is reason to doubt the soundness of the *Toscanino* exception, even as limited to its flagrant facts."); United States v. Matta-Ballesteros, 71 F.3d 754, 763 (9th Cir. 1995) (noting that "[i]n the shadow cast by *Alvarez-Machain*, attempts to expand due process rights into the realm of foreign abductions, as the Second Circuit did in [*Toscanino*], have been cut short"). *But see id.* at 772 (Noonan, J., concurring) (noting, inter alia, that the holding in *Matta-Ballesteros* did not, unlike *Toscanino*, require addressing any violation of due process rights of the abducted, and that unlike *Alvarez-Machain* "[t]his case does not turn on an alleged violation of international customary law") (citations omitted).

[425] Daimler AG v. Bauman, 571 U.S. 117, 126 (2014). Such cases fall into the category of what the Court has called "specific jurisdiction," as opposed to "general jurisdiction," which is predicated on the idea that the defendant is "essentially at home" in the forum. Ford Motor Co. v. Mont. Eighth Jud. Dist. Ct., 141 S. Ct. 1017, 1024–25 (2021); *see, e.g., Daimler AG*, 571 U.S. at 126 (detailing the Court's history of personal jurisdiction cases); RESTATEMENT (FOURTH) §§ 421–23 (2018).

[426] The issue of whether a foreign state is entitled to due process under the Fifth Amendment is distinct from the question of whether there exists a sufficient nexus between the foreign state and the United States to satisfy the requirements of a U.S. statute. In some instances, the necessary statutory nexus might be measured by whether constitutionally based due process standards have been met. For purposes of the Foreign Sovereign Immunities Act, courts have regarded personal jurisdiction over the foreign state to exist so long as there is an applicable exception to the state's immunity and the state has been properly served. *See* RESTATEMENT (FOURTH) § 451 cmt. b; *id.* § 454 rptrs. note 9; RESTATEMENT (THIRD) OF U.S. LAW OF INTERNATIONAL COMMERCIAL AND INVESTOR-STATE ARBITRATION § 4.26 rptrs. note a(ii) (AM. L. INST., Proposed Final Draft Apr. 24, 2019). For the FSIA generally, see Chapter 4 § V(A).

[427] Republic of Argentina v. Weltover, Inc., 504 U.S. 607, 619 (1992) (suggesting in dicta that foreign states are not "persons").

[428] *See, e.g.,* Corporacíon Mexicana de Mantenimiento Integral, S. de R.L. de C.V. v. Pemex-Exploración y Producción, 832 F.3d 92, 102 (2d Cir. 2016) (noting that foreign nations have no Fifth Amendment due process rights); Price v. Socialist People's Libyan Arab Jamahiriya, 294 F.3d 82, 96 (D.C. Cir. 2002) ("[F]oreign nations . . . are entirely alien to our constitutional system . . . ."). *Compare* RESTATEMENT (FOURTH) § 454 cmt. f (noting that "several lower courts have held that foreign states are not constitutionally protected by the Fifth Amendment."), *with* RESTATEMENT (THIRD) § 721 cmt. l ("A foreign state or an international organization is not a 'person' enjoying rights under the United

accorded Fifth Amendment due process to foreign organizations that they do not deem to be governing a sovereign state, notably the Palestinian Authority.[429]

Due process concerns have also been raised in the context of criminal actions brought in the United States against noncitizens for conduct abroad that has little or no effect on the United States.[430] Any such concerns may be regarded as addressed in specific contexts, such as where the conduct occurs on board a stateless vessel on the high seas,[431] or where there exists a U.S. treaty placing offenders on notice that the United States is obligated to submit to prosecution (or to extradite) alleged offenders even when the offense has been committed in another state party.[432] Such treaties address offenses such as piracy on the high seas[433] or violence against diplomats.[434]

States Constitution generally, but foreign states are accorded procedural due process and may claim also the minimum due process requirements for the exercise of *in personam* jurisdiction by courts in the United States."). For a scholarly argument that Fifth Amendment protections should apply to foreign states as "persons," see Ingrid Wuerth, *The Due Process Clause and Other Constitutional Rights of Foreign Nations*, 88 FORDHAM L. REV. 633 (2019); *see also* Gerald Neuman, *Whose Constitution?*, 100 YALE L.J. 909 (1991); Lori Fisler Damrosch, *Foreign States and the Constitution*, 73 VA. L. REV. 483, 522 (1987).

[429] *See, e.g.*, Livnat v. Palestinian Auth., 851 F.3d 45, 48–54, 58 (D.C. Cir. 2017) (holding that the Palestinian Authority has Fifth Amendment due process rights); Waldman v. Palestine Liberation Org., 835 F.3d 317, 344 (2d Cir. 2016) (overturning a $655.5 million judgment because the district court lacked personal jurisdiction over the defendants due to insufficient contacts). As the court noted in *Livnat*, "[n]othing in *Price*, other precedent, or the appellants' arguments compels us to extend the rule in *Price* to all foreign government entities. And no party here argues that the Palestinian Authority is a *sovereign* foreign state." 851 F.3d at 49.

[430] *See, e.g.*, United States v. Perlaza, 439 F.3d 1149 (9th Cir. 2006) (reversing for lack of due process convictions of noncitizens prosecuted for smuggling cocaine where conduct occurred on a Colombian vessel off the coasts of Colombia, Ecuador, and Peru and, while consent to boarding and seizure was secured from Colombian government, U.S. government provided no evidence of any nexus to the United States); United States v. Medjuck, 48 F.3d 1107, 1111 (9th Cir. 1995) (due process requires the government to demonstrate that there exists "a sufficient nexus between the conduct condemned and the United States" such that the application of a U.S. statute would not be arbitrary or fundamentally unfair to the defendant).

[431] United States v. Caicedo, 47 F.3d 370, 372 (9th Cir. 1995) (concluding that due process does not require a nexus when noncitizen defendant is apprehended on a stateless vessel because such vessels "are 'international pariahs'" that, "[b]y attempting to shrug the yoke of any nation's authority, . . . subject themselves to the jurisdiction of all nations" (quoting United States v. Marino-Garcia, 679 F.2d 1373, 1382 (11th Cir. 1982))); United States v. Moreno-Morillo, 334 F.3d 819, 829 (9th Cir. 2003) (same).

[432] *See, e.g.*, United States v. Shi, 525 F.3d 709, 723 (9th Cir. 2008); *see also* Jennifer K. Elsea, *Substantive Due Process and U.S. Jurisdiction over Foreign Nationals*, 82 FORDHAM L. REV. 2077, 2095–96 (2014).

[433] *See, e.g.*, United States v. Ali, 718 F.3d 929, 944 (D.C. Cir. 2013) (finding sufficient notice to the defendant given the 1958 Convention on the High Seas).

[434] *See, e.g.*, United States v. Bello Murillo, 826 F.3d 152, 157–58 (4th Cir. 2016) (finding sufficient notice to the defendant given the 1973 Convention on the Prevention and Punishment of Crimes against Internationally Protected Persons, including Diplomatic Agents).

4. Equal Protection for Noncitizens in the United States

The text of the Fifth Amendment contains no Equal Protection Clause of the kind found in the Fourteenth Amendment, which constrains the states.[435] Nevertheless, the Fifth Amendment's admonition that no person can be deprived of life, liberty, or property without due process of law has been viewed as embracing a guarantee that persons receive equal protection under the law, and thus imposes such an obligation on federal government as well.[436] As a general matter, the standards are the same for equal protection analyses of state and federal government actions.[437]

For federal and state laws regulating noncitizens, however, the equal protection guarantee of the Fifth Amendment requires only a rational basis review, rather than strict scrutiny.[438] For example, in *Hampton v. Mow Sun Wong*,[439] the Court considered the constitutionality of a rule adopted by the federal civil service commission barring all noncitizens, including lawful permanent residents, from employment in the competitive federal civil service. The Court stated that when the federal government "asserts an overriding national interest as justification for a discriminatory rule which would violate the Equal Protection Clause if adopted by a State, due process requires that there be a *legitimate basis* for presuming that the rule was actually intended to serve that interest."[440] According to the Court, such a basis can be assumed to be valid if (1) "the agency which promulgates the rule has direct responsibility for fostering or protecting that interest," or (2) "if the rule were expressly mandated by the Congress or the President."[441] The Court found the rule at issue to be unconstitutional, since the

---

[435] For a discussion of the Equal Protection Clause under the Fourteenth Amendment, see *infra* this chapter § II(G).

[436] *See, e.g.*, Schneider v. Rusk, 377 U.S. 163 (1964) (invalidating under the Fifth Amendment, as discriminatory, a federal statute that penalized foreign residency by naturalized U.S. citizens but not natural-born U.S. citizens). In *Schneider*, the Court stated that "while the Fifth Amendment contains no equal protection clause, it does forbid discrimination that is 'so unjustifiable as to be violative of due process.'" *Id.* at 165 (quoting *Bolling*, 347 U.S. at 499); *see also* Bolling v. Sharpe, 347 U.S. 497, 499 (1954) ("[D]iscrimination may be so unjustifiable as to be violative of due process."); HENKIN, FOREIGN AFFAIRS, at 292–93.

[437] *See* Buckley v. Valeo, 424 U.S. 1, 93 (1976) ("Equal protection analysis in the Fifth Amendment area is the same as that under the Fourteenth Amendment.") (citing Weinberger v. Wiesenfeld, 420 U.S. 636, 638 n.2 (1975)); *see also* Adarand Constructors, Inc. v. Pena, 515 U.S. 200, 217 (1995) (detailing the Court's treatment of "the equal protection obligations imposed by the Fifth and Fourteenth Amendments as indistinguishable"); ERWIN CHEMERINSKY, CONSTITUTIONAL LAW: PRINCIPLES AND POLICIES § 9.1 (6th ed. 2019).

[438] *See* Mathews v. Diaz, 426 U.S. 67, 81–82, 84–85; *see also* RESTATEMENT (THIRD) § 722 cmt. d ("Unlike discriminations by the States, . . . courts have not declared that discriminations by Congress are suspect, requiring strict scrutiny and a compelling national interest to sustain them."). In some circumstances, state regulations of noncitizens will also be analyzed under rational basis review. *See infra* this chapter § II(G)(4).

[439] 426 U.S. 88 (1976).

[440] *Id.* at 103 (emphasis added).

[441] *Id.*

civil service commission was not the agency charged with fostering or protecting the interests that the rule purportedly protected, nor had it been expressly mandated by Congress or the president.[442] Thereafter, however, the president issued an executive order excluding noncitizens from the civil service, which was upheld in the lower courts.[443]

For matters relating to U.S. foreign relations, "overriding national interests" will often be at stake. Indeed, to the extent that equal protection challenges are brought by noncitizens for differential treatment by the federal government as between citizens and noncitizens,[444] or as among noncitizens,[445] courts defer much more readily to the political branches of the federal government than they would to the states.[446] There are many examples of federal rules that discriminate between citizens and noncitizens, including limiting jury service to citizens;[447] restricting the promotion of noncitizens in the armed services and merchant marine;[448] denying communications licenses to noncitizens;[449] prohibiting noncitizens from service as national bank directors;[450] and limiting issuance of air carrier certificates to corporations that are majority U.S. owned and controlled.[451] When confronted with such rules, the Supreme Court has "firmly and repeatedly endorsed the proposition that Congress may make rules as to noncitizens that would be unacceptable if applied to citizens."[452] Often

---

[442] *Id.* at 116–17.

[443] *See* Vergara v. Hampton, 581 F.2d 1281 (7th Cir. 1978); Jalil v. Campbell, 590 F.2d 1120 (D.C. Cir. 1978); Mow Sun Wong v. Campbell, 626 F.2d 739 (9th Cir. 1980).

[444] Mathews v. Diaz, 426 U.S. 67, 79–80 (1976) (finding that Congress regularly makes rules for noncitizens "that would be unacceptable if applied to citizens"); United States v. Lopez-Flores, 63 F.3d 1468 (9th Cir. 1995) (finding that a federal statute with an "alienage" qualification, including the Hostage Taking Act at issue in the case, "enacted pursuant to Congress' immigration or foreign policy powers, is therefore subject to the lowest level of judicial review. Only classifications that 'arbitrarily subject all resident aliens to different substantive rules from those applied to citizens' will fail to survive that scrutiny.") (quoting *Hampton*, 426 U.S. at 101).

[445] *See, e.g.,* Poveda v. U.S. Att'y Gen., 692 F.3d 1168, 1177 (11th Cir. 2012) ("Congress has plenary power to pass legislation concerning the admission and exclusion of aliens, and federal classifications that distinguish among groups of aliens are subject only to rational basis review.") (quoting Resendiz-Alcaraz v. Ashcroft, 383 F.3d 1262, 1271 (11th Cir. 2004)); *see also infra* this chapter § III(A). *See generally* Stephen H. Legomsky, *Immigration Law and the Principle of Plenary Congressional Power*, 1984 SUP. CT. REV. 255 (1984).

[446] *See* RESTATEMENT (THIRD) § 722 cmt. d; Motomura, *supra* note 16, at 1733; Cristina M. Rodrıguez, *The Significance of the Local in Immigration Regulation*, 106 MICH. L. REV. 567, 628 (2008).

[447] 28 U.S.C. § 1861 (2018).

[448] 10 U.S.C. § 532; 46 U.S.C § 8103.

[449] 47 U.S.C. § 310.

[450] 12 U.S.C. § 72.

[451] 49 U.S.C. §§ 40102, 41102.

[452] Demore v. Kim, 538 U.S. 510, 522 (2003) (finding that Congress, justifiably concerned with evidence that removable criminal noncitizens who are not detained continue to engage in crime and fail to appear for their removal hearings in large numbers, may require that such persons be detained for the period necessary for their removal proceedings; such detention even without a determination specific to the detained noncitizen did not violate due process under the Fifth Amendment); *see* RESTATEMENT (THIRD) § 722(2); HENKIN, FOREIGN AFFAIRS, at 295.

the discriminatory rule will be found sufficiently tied to federal regulation or management of immigration or naturalization,[453] to statutory benefits being conferred that are relevant to U.S. residency,[454] or to management of a foreign relations crisis.[455]

Even so, such federal power is not unlimited. For example, in *Faruki v. Rogers*,[456] a district court invalidated, on equal protection grounds, a federal statute requiring a naturalized citizen to be a U.S. citizen for ten years in order to be eligible for the U.S. Foreign Service. The court found that the statute was designed to ensure that such foreign service officers possess strong knowledge of the United States, yet there was no requirement that birthright citizens have lived in the United States prior to applying, nor any requirement that naturalized citizens do so during or after the ten-year period.[457]

Equal protection is not accorded to noncitizens of the nationality of a foreign belligerent (often referred to as "enemy aliens") who happen to be present in the United States at the outbreak of or during war.[458] The Alien Enemies Act authorizes the U.S. government to apprehend, detain, or remove enemy aliens in the United States by presidential proclamation when there is a declared war between the United States and a foreign state (or an actual or threatened invasion of the United States).[459] Invoking that statute at the outset of World War II, President Franklin Roosevelt issued three presidential proclamations authorizing the United States to detain German, Italian, or Japanese nationals in the United States, including lawful permanent residents.[460] As a consequence, the

---

[453] *See* David A. Martin, *Graduated Application of Constitutional Protections for Aliens: The Real Meaning of* Zadvydas v. Davis, 2001 SUP. CT. REV. 47, 87–88 (2002) (seeing the Court as skeptical of federal government distinctions based on alienage if not sufficiently linked to regulation of immigration or naturalization); *contra* Anna C. Tavis, Note, *Healthcare for All: Ensuring States Comply with the Equal Protection Rights of Legal Immigrants*, 51 B.C. L. REV. 1627, 1648 (2010) (maintaining that challenges to restrictions on noncitizens' access to federal benefits under the 1996 Personal Responsibility and Work Opportunity Reconciliation Act generally were unsuccessful in limiting the federal government's power to make such distinctions).

[454] *See, e.g.*, Mathews v. Diaz, 426 U.S. 67 (1976) (upholding a statutory provision that conditioned participation in a federal Medicare program on permanent residency status and continuous residence in the United States for five years).

[455] *See, e.g.*, Narenji v. Civiletti, 617 F.2d 745 (D.C. Cir. 1979) (upholding, in the wake of the seizure of U.S. hostages in Iran, executive regulations requiring all Iranian nationals in the United States holding student visas to report their current status and whereabouts to the government).

[456] 349 F. Supp. 723 (D.D.C. 1972).

[457] *Id.* at 735.

[458] *See* RESTATEMENT (THIRD) § 722 cmt. h.

[459] Alien Enemies Act, 40 Stat. 531 (codified at 50 U.S.C. §§ 21–24 (2018)); *see* 50 U.S.C. § 21. The act was originally adopted as one of the well-known Alien and Sedition Acts in 1798, see Act of 25 June 1798, ch. 58, 1 Stat. 570, and modified only incidentally in 1918. Act of April 16, 1918, ch. 55, 40 Stat. 531.

[460] Proclamation No. 2525, 6 Fed. Reg. 6,321 (Dec. 7, 1941) (Japanese nationals); Proclamation No. 2526, 6 Fed. Reg. 6323 (Dec. 8, 1941) (German nationals); Proclamation No. 2527, 6 Fed. Reg. 6324 (Dec. 8, 1941) (Italian nationals). Separately, the U.S. government detained thousands of *U.S. citizens* of Japanese descent during World War II based on an interpretation of the federal war power. *See* Chapter 1 § III, Chapter 8, intro (discussing Korematsu v. United States, 323 U.S. 214 (1944)).

FBI and other law enforcement agencies arrested or detained thousands of such noncitizens. While many were released or paroled after hearings before a local alien enemy hearing board, others remained interned throughout the war.[461] Moreover, for stated reasons of hemispheric security, the United States offered to intern allegedly dangerous enemy aliens living in Latin American countries. Some fifteen Latin American countries accepted the offer and sent more than 6,600 individuals of Japanese, German, and Italian nationality, along with some of their families, to the United States for internment.[462] Several thousand internees chose to or were forced to repatriate to their country of nationality.[463] In *Ludecke v. Watkins*, the Supreme Court found that the removal from the United States, without judicial review, of a German national detained during World War II was a permissible exercise of the war power by the political branches and did not violate the Constitution.[464]

5. Taking of Property Without Just Compensation

Under the Takings Clause of the Fifth Amendment, the U.S. government may not deprive citizens in the United States of their property without compensation.[465] The provision also protects the property of noncitizens in the United States. In *Russian Volunteer Fleet v. United States*,[466] the U.S. Shipping Board Emergency Fleet Corporation requisitioned, from a Russian corporation, contracts for the construction of two vessels in New York. The Supreme Court found that the "petitioner was an alien friend"—meaning, presumably, not a national of a state with which the United States was at war—"and as such was entitled to the protection of the Fifth Amendment of the Federal Constitution."[467] The Court noted that the relevant U.S. statute providing for such claims against the U.S. government did not seek to exclude noncitizens[468] and stated that

---

[461] *See generally* ROGER DANIELS, CONCENTRATION CAMPS, NORTH AMERICA: JAPANESE IN THE UNITED STATES AND CANADA DURING WORLD WAR II (1971); ARNOLD KRAMMER, UNDUE PROCESS: THE UNTOLD STORY OF AMERICA'S GERMAN ALIEN INTERNEES (1997).

[462] *See generally* MAX PAUL FRIEDMAN, NAZIS AND GOOD NEIGHBORS: THE UNITED STATES CAMPAIGN AGAINST THE GERMANS OF LATIN AMERICA IN WORLD WAR II (2003); Edward N. Barnhart, *Japanese Internees from Peru*, 31 PACIFIC HISTORICAL REV. 169 (1962). For a personal account, see HEIDI GURCKE DONALD, WE WERE NOT THE ENEMY: REMEMBERING THE UNITED STATES' LATIN-AMERICAN CIVILIAN INTERNMENT PROGRAM OF WORLD WAR II (2006).

[463] With respect to forcible removal, President Truman, on July 14, 1945, directed the removal from the United States of all alien enemies "who shall be deemed by the Attorney General to be dangerous to the public peace and safety of the United States." Proclamation No. 2655, 10 Fed. Reg. 8947 (July 14, 1945).

[464] 335 U.S. 160 (1948).

[465] U.S. CONST. amend. V ("[N]or shall private property be taken for public use, without just compensation.").

[466] 282 U.S. 481 (1931).

[467] *Id.* at 489.

[468] *Id.* at 490–91.

reciprocal rights were not a precondition for the exercise of Fifth Amendment rights.[469]

The Takings Clause also protects U.S. citizen property abroad. For example, in *Seery v. United States*,[470] a U.S. citizen owned property in Austria that was seized in July 1945 by the U.S. Army and used for several years as an officers' club. When the citizen sued the U.S. government for the loss of personal property and damage to the buildings, the U.S. government contended that the Takings Clause did not apply because the property was not in the United States when it was taken. In rejecting that contention, and while acknowledging the lack of relevant precedents, the Court of Claims said that "since the Constitutional provision could be applied, without inconvenience, to such a situation, it ought to be so applied."[471] The government alternatively argued that the property was "enemy property" and therefore could be seized, but the court noted that it was private property not being used by or for an enemy of the United States, and moreover was seized after the end of hostilities.[472]

Lower courts have found that the Takings Clause protection extends to actions abroad by the U.S. government involving property owned by noncitizens, but only if there is a "substantial connection" between the noncitizen and the United States.[473] For example, in *Atamirzayeva v. United States*,[474] the plaintiff was an Uzbekistan national who had no connection to the United States other than possessing a cafeteria located adjacent to a U.S. embassy in Tashkent. The plaintiff alleged that embassy officials demanded that local authorities tear down the cafeteria in order to increase embassy security, which those authorities did. The Court of Claims found that the plaintiff had no connection to the United States that would entitle her to compensation under the Takings Clause.

[469] *Id.* at 491–92; *see* United States v. Pink, 315 U.S. 203, 228 (1942) (nonresident noncitizens owning property in the United States are entitled to the protection of the Fifth Amendment); Sardino v. Federal Reserve Bank of New York, 361 F.2d 106, 111 (2d Cir. 1966) (finding the Fifth Amendment fully applicable to protection of a noncitizen's bank account in New York); RESTATEMENT (THIRD) § 721 rptrs. note 7.

[470] 127 F. Supp. 601 (Ct. Cl. 1955).

[471] *Id.* at 603; *see* Turney v. United States, 115 F. Supp. 457 (Ct. Cl. 1953); Wiggins v. United States, 3 Ct. Cl. 412 (U.S. 1867).

[472] *Seery*, 127 F. Supp. at 605–06; *see* RESTATEMENT (THIRD) § 721 rptrs. note 7.

[473] *See, e.g.*, Doe v. United States, 95 Fed. Cl. 546, 553 (2010) (finding no substantial connection with respect to a Fifth Amendment claim by an Iraqi citizen whose home was occupied by U.S. forces during the Battle of Fallujah, where the only connection with the United States was the " 'unique relationship' created between the United States and Iraq"); Ashkir v. United States, 46 Fed. Cl. 438 (2000) (finding no substantial connection with respect to a Fifth Amendment claim by a Somalian citizen for physical occupation and destruction of his property in Mogadishu by U.S. armed forces); Rosner v. United States, 231 F. Supp. 2d 1202 (S.D. Fl. 2002) (finding no substantial connection with respect to a Fifth Amendment claim on behalf of Hungarian Jews, and their descendants, whose personal property and valuables were allegedly stolen and loaded onto the "Hungarian Gold Train" by the pro-Nazi Hungarian government during World War II, and later seized by the U.S. Army in Austria).

[474] 77 Fed. Cl. 378 (2007), *aff'd*, 524 F.3d 1320 (Fed. Cir. 2008).

Further, the U.S. government is not responsible for a foreign government's taking of property of either a U.S. citizen or a noncitizen in which the U.S. government does not directly participate and from which it does not benefit. In *Anglo Chinese Shipping Co. v. United States*,[475] the supreme commander for the Allied Powers after World War II directed that Japan retain a vessel owned by a Hong Kong corporation that Japan had seized during its conquest of Hong Kong, so as to use the vessel for laying and repairing submarine cables. In finding that such action was not a taking by the U.S. government in violation of the Fifth Amendment, the court focused on the minimal nature of the U.S. involvement, which was simply a pro forma approval made necessary because the postwar Japanese government was powerless to act without Allied consent.[476]

As discussed in Chapter 4, a question of justiciability may arise in the course of securing judicial review of an alleged U.S. government taking abroad, if the claim is viewed as challenging a U.S. foreign policy decision.[477] For example, in *El-Shifa Pharmaceutical Industries Co. v. United States*,[478] the plaintiff owners of a Sudanese pharmaceutical plant brought a takings claim against the United States for destroying the plant through a missile attack, which was launched in response to the 1998 bombings of U.S. embassies in Kenya and Tanzania.[479] The Federal Circuit found that the claim raised a nonjusticiable political question, saying that, where the president has concluded that the United States is at risk of imminent attack, "we cannot find in the Constitution any support for judicial supervision over the process by which the President assures himself that he has in fact targeted that part of the enemy's wealth of property that he thinks, if it were destroyed, would most effectively neutralize the possibility of attack."[480]

In *Ramirez de Arellano v. Weinberger*,[481] however, the D.C. Circuit found justiciable a takings claim by U.S. citizens seeking injunctive relief for an alleged occupation (amounting to effective seizure and destruction) of a privately owned

---

[475] 127 F. Supp. 553 (Ct. Cl. 1955).

[476] *Id.*; *see* Best v. United States, 292 F.2d 274 (Ct. Cl. 1961) (finding no taking under the Fifth Amendment for actions in postwar occupied Germany taken by the Allied High Commission for Germany, as opposed to by the U.S. government). Consideration of the connection of the U.S. government to the foreign government appears analogous to the connection required between the U.S. government and a private actor that takes property. *See* Nat'l Bd. of YMCA v. United States, 395 U.S. 85, 93 (1969) ("[I]n any case where government action is causally related to private misconduct which leads to property damage—a determination must be made whether the government involvement in the deprivation of private property is sufficiently direct and substantial to require compensation under the Fifth Amendment."); Langenegger v. United States, 756 F.2d 1565, 1571 (Fed. Cir. 1985) ("When considering a possible taking, *the focus is not on the acts of others, but on whether sufficient direct and substantial United States involvement exists.*") (emphasis in original).

[477] *See* Chapter 4 § II.

[478] 378 F.3d 1346 (Fed. Cir. 2004).

[479] *Id.* at 1361–70.

[480] *Id.* at 1366. For rejection of plaintiffs' claims based on the Federal Tort Claims Act and other bases, see El-Shifa Pharm. Indus. Co. v. United States, 607 F.3d 836 (D.C. Cir. 2010).

[481] 745 F.2d 1500 (D.C. Cir. 1984) (en banc).

cattle ranch in Honduras by the U.S. military for training of Salvadoran soldiers. Among other things, the court noted that the plaintiffs did not challenge the U.S. military presence in Honduras or in Central America, nor did they object to U.S. sponsorship of a training center in Honduras. Rather, "[p]laintiffs' claim, properly understood, is narrowly focused on the lawfulness of the United States defendants' occupation and use of the plaintiffs' cattle ranch."[482]

Likewise, in *Langenegger v. United States*,[483] U.S. plaintiffs pursued a claim against the U.S. government for El Salvador's expropriation of a coffee plantation. The Federal Circuit upheld the justiciability of the claim, stating that "[c]onsideration of land taking claims are clearly the role of the judiciary" under the Fifth Amendment, "ascertainment of 'just compensation' is a judicial function," and "the Constitution does not provide for a foreign affairs exception."[484] Among other things, the court noted that "this case does not require a judicial determination of El Salvador's sovereignty or the appropriateness of its actions, . . . nor does the case question the executive's authority to undertake any action."[485] Yet, on the merits, the court found that a U.S. government foreign policy that advocated for agrarian reform in El Salvador was too remote to sustain a takings claim against the U.S. government.[486]

Four types of U.S. government conduct in the area of U.S. foreign relations feature prominently in takings cases; in each, the claims are usually unsuccessful. First, takings claims will sometimes arise with respect to conduct by the U.S. military during armed conflict, as was the case in *El-Shifa Pharmaceutical Industries Co. v. United States*. To the extent that the case is justiciable, one basis to deny such claims—even of a U.S. citizen—is the "enemy property doctrine." The origins of the doctrine may be traced to the 1854 U.S. naval assault on Greytown, Nicaragua, which destroyed the town, including private property of U.S. citizens therein. When U.S. plaintiffs sued in the Court of Claims for the destruction of

---

[482] *Id.* at 1512. While the case was on appeal to the Supreme Court, Congress passed a law prohibiting funding of the training center until the president certified to Congress that the Honduran government recognized "the need to compensate as required by international law the United States citizen who claims injury from the establishment and operation of the existing Center." Foreign Assistance and Related Programs Appropriations Act, 1985, Pub. L. No. 98-473, 98 Stat. 1884, 1893–94 (1984). Thereafter, the Supreme Court vacated the judgment and remanded the case to the circuit court "for reconsideration of its opinion and judgment in light of the [statute] and other events occurring since October 5, 1984." Weinberger v. Ramirez de Arellano, 471 U.S. 1113 (1985). On remand, the D.C. Circuit reversed the district court's decision and remanded with instructions that the complaint be dismissed. According to the circuit court, since the United States had discontinued its participation in the military center, plaintiff's request for injunctive relief was no longer equitable for it "would not halt an asserted, ongoing violation but would merely forestall a potential violation." De Arellano v. Weinberger, 788 F.2d 762, 764 (D.C. Cir. 1986).
[483] 5 Ct. Cl. 229 (1984), *aff'd*, 756 F.2d 1565 (Fed. Cir. 1985).
[484] *Langenegger*, 756 F.2d at 1569.
[485] *Id.*
[486] *Id.* at 1570–73.

their property, the court noted that "[n]o government, except as a special favor bestowed, has ever paid for the property of even its own citizens in its own country destroyed in attacking or defending against a common public enemy," and "much less is any government bound to pay for the property of neutrals domiciled in the country of its enemy, which its forces may chance to destroy in its operations against such enemy."[487] Even if the property owners are not hostile to the United States, the claims are not meritorious, for "one who takes up a residence in a foreign place and there suffers an injury to his property by reason of belligerent acts committed against that place by another foreign nation, must abide the chances of the country in which he chose to reside . . . ."[488] This "enemy property doctrine" was also applied by the Supreme Court to cases involving destruction of property by the Union Army during the U.S. Civil War.[489] Similarly, in the aftermath of World War II, three oil companies presented takings claims for the destruction by the U.S. military of oil terminal facilities in the Philippines in December 1941, so as to deprive them of falling into Japanese hands.[490] The Supreme Court rejected the claims, finding that the "terse language of the Fifth Amendment is no comprehensive promise that the United States will make whole all who suffer from every ravage and burden of war" and that the "Court has long recognized that in wartime many losses must be attributed solely to the fortunes of war, and not to the sovereign."[491] At the same time, the doctrine may not shield the U.S. government from claims by U.S. citizens for private property seized for use by the army, as demonstrated by cases arising in the Mexican-American War and the U.S. Civil War.[492]

---

[487] Perrin's Case, 4 Ct. Cl. 543, 547–48 (U.S. 1868), aff'd, Perrin v. United States, 79 U.S. (12 Wall.) 315 (1871).

[488] Id. at 548–49; see Juragua Iron Co. v. United States, 212 U.S. 297, 305–06 (1909) (finding no compensable taking where government destroyed suspected source of infectious disease located on enemy soil).

[489] See, e.g., United States v. Pacific R.R., 120 U.S. 227, 233–39 (1887) (finding that the U.S. government was not responsible under the Takings Clause for destruction of a number of railroad bridges by Union forces operating in Missouri during the Civil War).

[490] United States v. Caltex (Phil.), Inc., 344 U.S. 149, 154–55 (1952).

[491] Id. at 155–56; see Nat'l Bd. of YMCA v. United States, 396 F.2d 467, 470 (Ct. Cl. 1968) ("It is axiomatic that the fifth amendment is not suspended in wartime, but it is equally well recognized that a destruction of private property in battle or by enemy forces is not compensable."); Juragua Iron Co., 212 U.S. at 305–08 (finding that property of U.S. citizens in Cuba during the Spanish-American War could be regarded as enemy property subject to the laws of war, and to be destroyed whenever military necessity so demanded).

[492] Id. at 239; see, e.g., United States v. Russell, 80 U.S. (13 Wall.) 623 (1871) (upholding a takings claim for requisitioning three private steamboats to ferry Union soldiers during the Civil War); Mitchell v. Harmony, 54 U.S. (13 How.) 115 (1851) (upholding a takings claim for U.S. military use of plaintiff's wagons and mules during the Mexican-American War). In the context of the U.S. Civil War, the doctrine was affected by the Abandoned and Captured Property Act, 12 Stat. 820 (1863), which codified rules for the treatment of "enemy" property found to be abandoned or captured by Union forces. For discussion, see Thomas H. Lee & David L. Sloss, International Law as an Interpretive Tool in the Supreme Court, 1861-1900, in INTERNATIONAL LAW IN THE U.S. SUPREME

Second, takings claims will sometimes arise when the U.S. government seizes the property of an enemy, enemy allies, or enemy aliens during a period of war; here, too, unless Congress decides otherwise, such claims are usually unsuccessful, notwithstanding the Fifth Amendment. Such seizures typically occur pursuant to the Trading with the Enemy Act (TWEA),[493] which delegates to the president extensive powers for economic regulation during war.[494] In *Cummings v. Deutsche Bank und Disconto-Gesellschaft*,[495] the Supreme Court found that, pursuant to the war power and "untrammeled by the due process or just compensation clause," Congress may enact laws (such as TWEA) granting executive power to direct seizure, use, and disposition of alien enemy property in the United States, leaving to the postwar period whether and how to reconcile any claims by former owners.[496] Even so, courts will review whether the executive has properly designated property as being that of an enemy alien.[497]

Third, the U.S. government is also able to block or "freeze" the transactions and assets of noncitizens, notwithstanding the Fifth Amendment, when necessary for addressing a national emergency under the International Emergency Economic Powers Act (IEEPA) and related statutes.[498] IEEPA authorizes the president to declare the existence of an "unusual and extraordinary threat . . . to the national security, foreign policy, or economy of the United States" that originates "in whole or substantial part outside the United States."[499] Following such a declaration, the president may block transactions and assets to deal with the threat.[500] If the United States is attacked, the president may confiscate property connected

---

COURT: CONTINUITY AND CHANGE 124, 131–32 (David L. Sloss, Michael D. Ramsey, & William S. Dodge eds., 2011).

[493] Trading with the Enemy Act (TWEA), Pub. L. 65-91, 40 Stat. 411 (1917) (codified as amended at 50 U.S.C. §§ 4301–41 (2018)).

[494] TWEA § 5(b), 50 U.S.C. § 4305.

[495] 300 U.S. 115 (1937).

[496] *Id.* at 120; *see* Tran Qui Than v. Regan, 658 F.2d 1296, 1304 (9th Cir. 1981) (upholding U.S. government's authority under TWEA in the post–Vietnam War era to block funds owed by the U.S. government to a Vietnamese bank). Originally enacted in 1917, TWEA was also available from 1933 to 1977 to address national emergencies. *See, e.g.,* Sardino v. Federal Reserve Bank of N.Y., 361 F.2d 106, 111 (2d Cir. 1966) (upholding U.S. government's authority under TWEA to prevent funds in a New York bank account to be remitted to Cuban national residing in Cuba, noting that "only in a technical sense were we at peace" with Cuba). In 1977, however, it was limited to invocation during war, *see* An Act with Respect to the Powers of the President in Time of War or National Emergency, Pub. L. No. 95-223, 91 Stat. 1625 (1977), with the exception of existing sanctions programs. On TWEA's constitutionality, see Zittman v. McGrath, 341 U.S. 446 (1951) (upholding the constitutionality of TWEA based on the U.S. government's foreign affairs powers); Propper v. Clark, 337 U.S. 472 (1949) (same); Freedom to Travel Campaign v. Newcomb, 82 F.3d 1431 (9th Cir. 1996) (same).

[497] *See, e.g.,* Societe Internationale v. Rogers, 357 U.S. 197, 211 (1958).

[498] Tit. II, Pub. L. No. 95-223, 91 Stat. 1626 (1977) (codified at 50 U.S.C. §§ 1701–08 (2018)); *see* Chapter 2 § IV(E).

[499] 50 U.S.C. § 1701(a).

[500] *Id.* § 1702(a)(1)(B).

with any foreign state, group, or person that aided in the attack.[501] U.S. courts have concluded that such blocking of noncitizen transactions and assets do not constitute a seizure of property for purposes of the Fifth Amendment,[502] so long as the action does not eliminate all economically valuable use from the asset or is not continued indefinitely.[503] Likewise, imposition of sanctions that interfere in the contractual rights of noncitizens generally are not regarded as constituting a compensable taking of contractual rights.[504]

Finally, takings claims may arise out of attempts to assist private claimants. The executive branch may espouse claims of U.S. nationals against foreign governments for the purpose of settling them diplomatically or by means of an international dispute resolution body.[505] A U.S. government decision as to whether to espouse the claim of a citizen is discretionary and is not reviewable by courts,[506] nor is the citizen's consent necessary.[507] Nonetheless, a decision to espouse has the effect of taking the claim out of the citizen's hands, such that

---

[501] *Id.* § 1702(a)(1)(C).

[502] *See, e.g.*, Chichakli v. United States, 141 Fed. Cl. 633, 641 (2019) (upholding against a takings claim the blocking of plaintiff's property by an executive order under IEEPA that targeted individuals associated with Liberian President Charles Taylor, in implementation of U.N. Security Council sanctions); Paradissiotis v. United States, 304 F.3d 1271, 1274 (Fed. Cir. 2002) (finding that the imposition of sanctions under IEEPA in relation to Libya "substantially advance[d] the national security of the United States and that the frustration of contract rights resulting from the application of those [sanctions] does not constitute a Fifth Amendment taking."); Holy Land Found. for Relief & Dev. v. Ashcroft, 219 F. Supp. 2d 57, 78 (D.D.C. 2002), *aff'd*, 333 F.3d 156 (D.C. Cir. 2003) (holding that a U.S. foundation whose assets were blocked under IEEPA when it was designated as a terrorist organization did not have a valid takings claim).

[503] *See, e.g., Holy Land Found. for Relief & Dev.*, 219 F. Supp. 2d at 78 (owner of property frozen eight months may "some day" have a more viable takings claim) (citing Tahoe-Sierra Pres. Council v. Tahoe Reg'l Planning Agency, 535 U.S. 302 (2002)); Nielsen v. Sec'y of the Treasury, 424 F.2d 833, 843–44 (D.C. Cir. 1970) (blocking of foreign assets raises takings issue if continued indefinitely).

[504] *See, e.g., Paradissiotis*, 304 F.3d at 1274 (effect of IEEPA sanctions on stock option contract); 767 Third Ave. Assocs. v. United States, 48 F.3d 1575 (Fed. Cir. 1995) (leasehold contract); Chang v. United States, 859 F.2d 893 (Fed. Cir. 1988) (employment contract).

[505] *See* Shanghai Power Co. v. United States, 4 Ct. Cl. 237, 243–45 (1983), *aff'd mem.*, 765 F.2d 159 (Fed. Cir. 1985) (discussing the history of claim espousal); RESTATEMENT (THIRD) § 713; *id.* § 721 cmt. g & rptrs. note 8; RESTATEMENT (SECOND) §§ 205, 211–14; HENKIN, FOREIGN AFFAIRS, at 299–302; Robert C. Kelso, *Espousal: Its Use in International Law*, 1 ARIZ. J. INT'L & COMPAR. L. 233 (1982).

[506] *See, e.g.*, Chytil v. Powell, 15 F. App'x 515, 517 (9th Cir. 2001) (considering effort by naturalized citizen to have U.S. government espouse his claim, finding that "[e]spousal seems particularly unsusceptible to resolution in the judicial branch"); Marik v. Powell, 15 F. App'x 517, 519 (9th Cir. 2001) (same).

[507] *See, e.g.*, Meade v. United States, 76 U.S. (9 Wall.) 691, 724–25 (1869) (finding that, regardless of the U.S. citizen's attitude, the citizen lacked the power to deprive the government of settlement authority); Dames & Moore v. Regan, 453 U.S. 654, 679–80 (1981) (finding it undisputed that the U.S. government has sometimes disposed of citizen claims without their consent); Asociacion de Reclamantes v. Mexico, 735 F.2d 1517, 1523 (D.C. Cir. 1984) (when considering private claims against government of Mexico that had been espoused by U.S. government, "[t]his authority to espouse claims does not depend on the consent of the private claimholder").

the person can no longer pursue the claim through other means.[508] In any given instance, the executive's authority to espouse claims of U.S. nationals might be anchored in statutory authority, but there is ample historical precedent for a power of the president to espouse claims—a power associated with international law on "diplomatic protection of nationals" and to which Congress has acquiesced—especially when done in the context of recognizing a foreign government, ending an armed conflict, or resolving a foreign relations crisis.[509] While such espousal may relate to a single or few private U.S. claims, it may also relate to an entire class of claims by citizens against a foreign state for a particular period of time, in which case a global claims settlement agreement might be reached by which a "lump sum" amount is provided to the United States (sometimes drawn from the foreign state's assets that are "frozen" in the United States).[510] Congress has repeatedly authorized the Foreign Claims Settlement Commission within the Department of Justice to operate quasi-judicial programs that receive and distribute such funds to meritorious U.S. claimants.[511]

When claims are espoused and settled by the U.S. government, they are effectively extinguished, rather than merely regulated. In considering whether such a settlement has given rise to a compensable taking, the Federal Circuit has said that courts should consider several factors: (1) "the degree to which the property owner's rights were impaired," (2) "the extent to which the property owner is an incidental beneficiary of the governmental action," (3) "the importance of the public interest to be served," (4) "whether the exercise of governmental power can be characterized as novel and unexpected or falling within traditional boundaries," and (5) "whether the action substituted any rights or remedies for those that it destroyed."[512]

In considering whether a property owner's "rights were impaired," the case law is animated by the deep uncertainty that usually exists in vindicating any claim of a U.S. citizen against a foreign state: actions in U.S. courts may not be

---

[508] *See, e.g., Asociacion de Reclamantes*, 735 F.2d at 1523 (finding that "the fact that a claim has been espoused provides a complete defense for the defendant sovereign in any action by the private individual...").

[509] *See Dames & Moore*, 453 U.S. at 679–82 (in the context of resolving hostages crisis with Iran, finding historical support for the constitutionality of presidential espousal and settlement of claims, and relying on Congress' implicit acquiescence to such conduct); *see also* Roman Pipko & Jonathan S. Sack, *Rediscovering Executive Authority: Claims Settlement and Foreign Sovereign Immunity*, 10 YALE J. INT'L L. 295, 320–28 (1985) (arguing in favor of an independent presidential authority under Article II of the Constitution).

[510] *See generally* RICHARD B. LILLICH & BURNS H. WESTON, INTERNATIONAL CLAIMS: THEIR SETTLEMENT BY LUMP SUM AGREEMENTS (1975) (2 vols.); BURNS H. WESTON ET AL., INTERNATIONAL CLAIMS: THEIR SETTLEMENT BY LUMP SUM AGREEMENTS, 1975–1995 (1999).

[511] *See* 22 U.S.C. § 1621 (2018). Decisions of the Commission are not reviewable in U.S. court. *See* 22 U.S.C. § 1623(h). For information on the Commission, see U.S. Dep't of Justice, Foreign Claims Settlement Commission of the U.S., https://perma.cc/TKQ2-DZFC.

[512] *See Belk v. United States*, 858 F.2d 706, 709 (Fed. Cir. 1988) (citations omitted).

available due to sovereign immunity and, if available, may face great difficulty in enforcement; actions in foreign courts, or international fora, may not be available or effective. Moreover, when such claims arise and are not resolved, they frequently become irritants in the relations between the two states concerned. These prospects encourage espousal and interstate settlement of claims.[513]

Unsurprisingly, then, efforts to convince courts that claims settlement by the government constitutes a taking of property generally have not been successful.[514] For example, in *Alimanestianu v. United States*, U.S. plaintiffs were pursuing claims against the government of Libya in U.S. courts for the bombing of UTA flight 772 by terrorists of the Abu Nidal Organization in 1989, and had received damages awards totaling $6.9 billion.[515] While on appeal, the United States entered into a settlement agreement with Libya, which removed the claims from U.S. courts, espoused the claims against Libya, and required Libya to deposit $1.5 billion into a humanitarian fund, of which $681 million was "to ensure the fair compensation for the claims of nationals of the United States for wrongful death or physical injury in those cases described in the Act which were pending against Libya . . . as well as other terrorism-related claims against Libya."[516] When the U.S. plaintiffs challenged the settlement as a taking of property, the Federal Circuit rejected the claim, noting the executive's responsibility for conducting foreign affairs; the lack of the plaintiffs' investment-backed expectation in their claims and in a nonfinal judgment, for which payment would require cooperation of Libya;[517] and that the plaintiffs' recovery from the settlement was

---

[513] As the Federal Circuit has noted, "those who engage in international commerce must be aware that international relations sometimes become strained, and that governments engage in a variety of activities designed to maintain a degree of international amity." Abrahim-Youri v. United States, 139 F.3d 1462, 1468 (Fed. Cir. 1997).

[514] *See* Shanghai Power Co. v. United States, 4 Ct. Cl. 237 (1983), *aff'd mem.*, 765 F.2d 159 (Fed. Cir. 1985); Aris Gloves, Inc. v. United States, 420 F.2d 1386 (Ct. Cl. 1970). *But see* Gray v. United States, 21 Ct. Cl. 340, 392–93 (1996) (U.S. citizen entitled to compensation for a taking where his claim was set off by the U.S. government when addressing claims by France against the United States; "the citizen whose property is thus sacrificed for the safety and welfare of his country . . . has a right to compensation."); *In re* Aircrash in Bali, 684 F.2d 1301 (9th Cir. 1982) (finding that plaintiffs have a right to compensation if their claims have been unreasonably impaired by limitation on liability in Warsaw Convention).

[515] 888 F.3d 1374, 1377 (Fed. Cir. 2018).

[516] *Id.* at 1378 (quoting U.S. Dep't of State, Certification Under Sec. 5(a)(2) of the Libyan Claims Resolution Act Relating to the Receipt of Funds for Settlement of Claims Against Libya 2 (2008)); *see* Agreement, Libya-U.S., Aug. 14, 2008, T.I.A.S. No. 08-814 ("Claims Settlement Agreement"). Congress codified the Claims Settlement Agreement through the Libyan Claims Resolution Act, Pub. L. No. 110-301, 122 Stat. 2999 (2008) (codified at 28 U.S.C. § 1605A note (2018)), which provided that, upon receipt of the funds pursuant to the Claims Settlement Agreement, Libya's sovereign immunity would be restored.

[517] On this issue, the court noted that Congress had only amended the Foreign Sovereign Immunities Act in 1996 so as to permit claims against foreign states designated as supporters of terrorism. While Libya was designated as such a terrorist state, the executive could have revoked the designation at any time. *Alimanestianu*, 888 F.3d at 1383–84 (citing Republic of Iraq v. Beaty, 556 U.S.

likely more than they could have expected by enforcing any U.S. judgment themselves.[518]

In some instances, the executive may extinguish a claim not just for less than face value, but without securing any compensation for the U.S. claimant at all.[519] In *Belk v. United States*,[520] the U.S. claimants were held hostage in Iran during 1979 to 1981. The United States concluded with Iran a set of agreements, known as the Algiers Accords, which inter alia brought about the release of the hostages, but which also required the United States to espouse and extinguish any claims by the hostages against the government of Iran for damages during their captivity.[521] The Court of Claims found that given the extensive powers of the federal government with respect to foreign affairs, and since the claimants were the intended beneficiaries of the Algiers Accords and lacked any investment-backed expectations, the claimants did not suffer a compensable taking.[522]

Further, in the context of the conclusion (by executive agreement) of the Algiers Accords, the act of placing the espoused claims before an international dispute resolution body, even to the extent of removing them from U.S. courts, was found constitutionally permissible. In *Dames & Moore v. Regan*, the Supreme Court set aside constitutional objections by citizens regarding the suspension of their claims in U.S. courts in favor of their resolution before the Iran-U.S. Claims Tribunal (an arbitral body based in The Hague), given the past claims resolution practice of the executive, which had been endorsed or acquiesced to by Congress.[523] In this regard, two factors bear emphasis. First, the Court relied on Congress' acquiescence to past executive conduct, rather than on the president's sole constitutional authority under Article II. Second, the Court's acceptance of sending the claims to an international tribunal was influenced by a quid pro quo; the Court noted that the "fact that the President has provided such a forum here means that the claimants are receiving something in return for the suspension of their claims, namely, access to an international tribunal before which they may well recover something on their claims."[524]

848, 864–65 (2009) (finding that the status of foreign sovereign immunity "generally is not something on which parties can rely in shaping their primary conduct")).

[518] *Alimanestianu*, 888 F.3d at 1383–84.

[519] Asociacion de Reclamantes v. Mexico, 735 F.2d 1517, 1523 (D.C. Cir. 1984) ("Once it has espoused a claim, the sovereign has wide-ranging discretion in disposing of it. It may compromise it, seek to enforce it, or waive it entirely.").

[520] 858 F.2d 706 (Fed. Cir. 1988).

[521] *Id.* at 707–08; *see* Belk v. United States, 12 Ct. Cl. 732, 734 (1987).

[522] *Belk*, 858 F.2d at 709–10.

[523] *See* Dames & Moore v. Regan, 453 U.S. 654, 675–88 (1981).

[524] *Id.* at 687.

6. Liberty of Travel to and from the United States

Within the United States, U.S. citizens have a right to travel from state-to-state that is protected against state interference by the Privileges and Immunities Clause of the Fourteenth Amendment.[525] U.S. citizens also possess a freedom to travel that is considered a form of liberty protected under the Due Process Clauses of the Fifth and Fourteenth Amendments.[526] While this freedom to travel includes travel outside the United States, the Supreme Court has been careful to distinguish such freedom from the right of interstate travel. The latter is "virtually unqualified," but the former is "no more than an aspect of the liberty protected by the Due Process Clause ... [and] can be regulated within the bounds of due process."[527] Indeed, the freedom to travel outside the United States "is subordinate to national security and foreign policy considerations."[528]

Cases upholding this freedom of travel typically arise in connection with the issuance of passports.[529] In *Kent v. Dulles*,[530] the Court held that Congress had not authorized the secretary of state to deny passports to citizens based on their affiliation with the Communist Party. The Court stated that whatever broad statutory authority may have been provided to the executive with respect to issuance of passports, it did not extend to the denial of passports on this basis.[531] Moreover, in *Aptheker v. Secretary of State*,[532] the Court struck down a statutory provision forbidding the issuance of a passport to a member of the Communist Party,[533] saying that it "sweeps too widely and too indiscriminately across the liberty guaranteed in the Fifth Amendment."[534] The Court was troubled that the

---

[525] U.S. CONST. amend. XIV, § 1 ("No State shall make or enforce any law which shall abridge the privileges or immunities of citizens of the United States"); *see* Griffin v. Breckenridge, 403 U.S. 88, 105–06 (1971). There is some discrepancy in the case law as to which constitutional provision provides the source of this right, but Justice Stewart in *United States v. Guest* noted that such differences are unimportant, given that all courts recognize the existence of the right. 383 U.S. 745, 758–59 (1966).

[526] U.S. CONST. amend. V; *id.* amend. XIV, § 1; *see* Kent v. Dulles, 357 U.S. 116, 125 (1958) ("The right to travel is a part of the 'liberty' of which the citizen cannot be deprived without due process of law under the Fifth Amendment.").

[527] Haig v. Agee, 453 U.S. 280, 307 (1981) (quoting Califano v. Torres, 435 U.S. 1, 4 n.6 (1978)); *see* RESTATEMENT (THIRD) § 721 cmt. i (quoting *Haig v. Agee*). *But see* Jeffrey Kahn, *International Travel and the Constitution*, 56 UCLA L. REV. 271 (2008) (making the case for a fundamental right to international travel based on the 14th Amendment Citizenship Clause rather than the Due Process Clauses).

[528] *Agee*, 453 U.S. at 306.

[529] Some cases concern U.S. treasury regulations that prevent citizens from engaging in financial transactions with a foreign country, such as Cuba, which in effect precludes travel to such a state. The Court has upheld such regulations as constitutional. *See* Regan v. Wald, 468 U.S. 222 (1984) (finding treasury regulations preventing travel to Cuba as not violating the due process clause of the Fifth Amendment).

[530] 357 U.S. 116 (1958).

[531] *Id.* at 130.

[532] 378 U.S. 500 (1964).

[533] Subversive Activities Control Act of 1950, Pub. L. No. 81-831, 64 Stat. 987 (codified at 50 U.S.C. § 781 et seq. (2018)).

[534] *Aptheker*, 378 U.S. at 514.

statute (like the executive policy in *Kent*) denied passports based solely on political beliefs, thereby establishing "an irrebuttable presumption that individuals who are members of the specified organizations will, if given passports, engage in activities inimical to the security of the United States."[535] Prohibiting such travel had only "a tenuous relationship" with the safeguarding of national security, the objective purportedly sought by Congress.[536]

While the Court has recognized that revocation of a passport "undeniably curtails travel," and does not necessarily promote national security to the requisite degree, it has found that "the freedom to travel abroad with a 'letter of introduction' in the form of a passport issued by the sovereign is subordinate to national security and foreign policy considerations; as such, it is subject to reasonable governmental regulation."[537] For example, in *Haig v. Agee*,[538] the Court held that the president, acting through the secretary of state, has authority to revoke the passport of a U.S. citizen on the ground that the citizen's activities in foreign countries are causing, or are likely to cause, serious damage to the national security or foreign policy of the United States.[539] (In that case, the citizen was a former employee of the Central Intelligence Agency (CIA) engaged in activities, including abroad, that sought to reveal the identifications of alleged undercover CIA agents and intelligence sources in foreign countries.) The Court rejected the plaintiff's argument that the freedom to travel abroad implicated the First Amendment's freedom of speech. First, the Court found that such "speech" simply was not protected, any more than would be the publication of "the sailing dates of transports or the location of troops."[540] Second, the Court concluded that, "[t]o the extent the revocation of [respondent's] passport operates to inhibit [him], 'it is an inhibition of *action*,' rather than of speech."[541]

The refusal to validate passports for all U.S. citizens to travel to a particular country, on foreign policy grounds, has also been upheld. Thus, in *Zemel v. Rusk*,[542] the Court upheld the refusal of the secretary of state to validate the passports of all U.S. citizens for travel to Cuba. Among other things, the Court noted that the secretary of state had made no effort selectively to deny passports on the basis of political belief or affiliation, but simply imposed a general ban on travel to Cuba following the U.S.-Cuba break in diplomatic and consular relations after 1961.[543] The Court said that the Fifth Amendment right to travel,

---

[535] *Id.* at 511.
[536] *Id.* at 514.
[537] Haig v. Agee, 453 U.S. 280, 306 (1981).
[538] 453 U.S. 280 (1981).
[539] *Id.* at 306.
[540] *Id.* at 308–09 (quoting Near v. Minnesota *ex rel.* Olson, 283 U.S. 697, 716 (1931)).
[541] *Id.* at 309 (citing Zemel v. Rusk, 381 U.S. 1, 16–17 (1965) (emphasis in original).
[542] 381 U.S. 1 (1965).
[543] *Id.* at 13.

standing alone, was insufficient to overcome the foreign policy justifications supporting the restriction.[544] Similarly, the Court in *Regan v. Wald*[545] found that restrictions on travel-related transactions with Cuba imposed by Congress did not violate the freedom to travel protected by the Fifth Amendment. The Court concluded that, given the traditional deference to executive judgment in the realm of foreign policy, "there is an adequate basis under the Due Process Clause of the Fifth Amendment to sustain the President's decision to curtail the flow of hard currency to Cuba—currency that could then be used in support of Cuban adventurism—by restricting travel."[546] In recent years, the establishment of security watch lists and no-fly lists for national security purposes that impede the travel of U.S. citizens and permanent residents have also spawned Fifth Amendment challenges.[547]

As for the travel of noncitizens to the United States, noncitizens generally have no such right under the Constitution.[548] Lawful permanent residents returning to the United States, however, have some due process rights under the Fifth Amendment if the government seeks to deny them entry.[549] Moreover, even nonresident noncitizens may have such rights if they have significant voluntary connections to the United States. For example, the Ninth Circuit found that a nonresident noncitizen located abroad, but who was previously legally present in the United States for four years on a student visa, had "significant voluntary connections" to the United States, such that she had a right to bring substantive due process claims under the Fifth Amendment,[550] including her right to travel to the United States, the right to be free from incarceration, and the right to be free from the stigma and humiliation of her status on a government "no-fly list."[551]

7. Military Detention of Noncitizens Abroad

When armed conflict breaks out between the United States and a foreign state or nonstate actor, noncitizens may be placed in military detention outside the

---

[544] *Id.* at 16.

[545] 468 U.S. 222 (1984).

[546] *Id.* at 243 (quoting *Zemel v. Rusk*, 381 U.S. at 14–15).

[547] Latif v. Holder, 28 F. Supp. 3d 1134, 1160–61 (D. Or. 2014) (finding that the available procedures for civilians and permanent residents to challenge placement on the government's No-Fly List "falls far short of satisfying the requirements of due process"); Elhady v. Kable, 391 F. Supp. 3d 562, 568 (E.D. Va. 2019) (finding that the inclusion of U.S. citizens on a consolidated government watch list violated their due process rights), *rev'd*, 993 F.3d 208 (4th Cir. 2021).

[548] *See infra* this chapter § III(A)(2).

[549] *See, e.g.*, Landon v. Plasencia, 459 U.S. 21 (1982).

[550] *See* Ibrahim v. Dep't of Homeland Sec., 669 F.3d 983, 997 (9th Cir. 2012).

[551] *See* Ibrahim v. Dep't of Homeland Sec., 62 F. Supp. 3d 909, 928 (N.D. Cal. 2014) (citing Hamdi v. Rumsfeld, 542 U.S. 507, 529 (2004); Paul v. Davis, 424 U.S. 693, 701 (1976); Kent v. Dulles, 357 U.S. 116, 125 (1958)).

United States, and further may be prosecuted before a U.S. military commission.[552] In *Johnson v. Eisentrager*, the respondents were "nonresident enemy aliens" captured in China by the U.S. Army, where they were tried and convicted by a U.S. military commission for violations of the laws of war committed in China.[553] Thereafter, they were transported to U.S.-occupied Germany and imprisoned there in U.S. Army custody. At no time were they within the territorial jurisdiction of any U.S. civil court. Claiming that their trial, conviction, and imprisonment violated various constitutional rights, they petitioned U.S. courts for a writ of habeas corpus. The U.S. Supreme Court, however, found that a nonresident enemy alien has no right to access to U.S. courts in wartime, even to ascertain the existence of a state of war or to ascertain whether the person is in fact an enemy alien.[554] Among other things, the Court noted the practical difficulties of transporting the prisoners and any witnesses "across the seas for [a] hearing" in the United States, which in time of war "would hamper the war effort and" give "aid and comfort to the enemy."[555] Ultimately, the Court found that the term "any person" in the Fifth Amendment and "the accused" in the Sixth Amendment do not extend to alien enemies everywhere in the world engaged in hostilities against the United States.[556]

In the aftermath of 9/11, considerable attention was paid to whether noncitizens captured abroad—mostly during the armed conflict in Afghanistan—and held in military detention at Guantánamo Naval Base in Cuba could challenge in U.S. court the government's basis for their detention. The George W. Bush administration maintained that it could constitutionally capture and detain such noncitizens based on the statute enacted after 9/11 authorizing the use of force against al-Qaeda and its supporters.[557] In *Hamdi v. Rumsfeld*, five justices of the Court recognized that detention of individuals who fought against the United States in Afghanistan "for the duration of the particular conflict in which they were captured, is so fundamental and accepted an incident to war as to be an exercise of the 'necessary and appropriate force' Congress has authorized the

---

[552] On the prosecution of enemy combatants before military commissions, see *infra* this chapter § II(E)(4) and Chapter 8 § III(B); on the commander-in-chief power to convene military commissions, see Chapter 8 § II(B).

[553] 339 U.S. 763, 776 (1950); *see* RAUSTIALA, *supra* note 30, at 136–38, 199–200.

[554] *Eisentrager*, 339 U.S. at 776 (stating that "the nonresident enemy alien, especially one who has remained in the service of the enemy, does not have . . . access to our courts, for he neither has comparable claims upon our institutions nor could his use of them fail to be helpful to the enemy").

[555] *Id.* at 778–79.

[556] *Id.* at 782–83 (noting that "[i]f the Fifth Amendment protects them from military trial, the Sixth Amendment as clearly prohibits their trial by civil courts" and yet "[t]he Court of Appeals has cited no authority whatever for holding that the Fifth Amendment confers rights upon all persons, whatever their nationality, wherever they are located and whatever their offenses, except to quote extensively from a dissenting opinion in *In re Yamashita*, 327 U.S. 1" (1946), the holding of which was "to the contrary").

[557] Authorization for Use of Military Force, Pub. L. No. 107-40, 115 Stat. 224 (2001).

President to use."[558] Although such detentions entailed deviation from normal criminal procedures, a plurality of the Court held that the Due Process Clause required that the detainee's interest in liberty, together with the risk of erroneous detention and the value of procedural safeguards, be weighed against national security interests and the costs of those safeguards—and required notice of the factual basis for classification as an enemy combatant and an opportunity to challenge that classification before a neutral fact-finder.[559] After *Hamdi*, the Department of Defense established combatant status review tribunals to determine whether individuals detained at Guantánamo were "enemy combatants," and later the process for such determinations was regulated by statute.[560]

In *Rasul v. Bush*, the Court found that the extensive control exercised by the United States over Guantánamo was sufficient to trigger the application of statutory habeas corpus rights to detainees held there, thereby allowing them to contest in U.S. court that they were enemy combatants in the U.S. armed conflict with al-Qaeda.[561] After issuance of the decision in *Rasul*, Congress enacted a provision in the 2006 Military Commissions Act (MCA) eliminating federal court jurisdiction to hear habeas applications from detainees who have been designated as enemy combatants.[562] The Supreme Court then struck down that provision in *Boumediene v. Bush*, finding it to be an unconstitutional suspension of the right of habeas corpus, given that writ may be suspended only when public safety requires it in times of rebellion or invasion.[563] According to the Court, various factors weighed in favor of finding a constitutional right to habeas corpus in this instance: the accused's denial that they were enemy combatants;

---

[558] 542 U.S. 507, 518 (2004) (O'Connor, J., plurality op.), *id.* at 588–89 (Thomas, J., dissenting). For further discussion, see Chapter 1 § III and Chapter 8 § III(B).

[559] 542 U.S. 507, 524–35 (plurality op.). *But see id.* at 575–76 (Scalia, J., dissenting, joined by Stevens, J.) (objecting to applying a balancing test to address the process due under the Due Process Clause); *id.* at 589 (Thomas, J., dissenting) (rejecting balancing approach, and indicating that in the context of wartime detentions, executive classifications should be "virtually conclusive").

[560] The Detainee Treatment Act, tit. X, Pub. L. No. 109-148, 119 Stat. 2739 (2005) (codified as amended in scattered statutes of the U.S. Code) established certain procedural requirements for executive review of the detainees' status. Among other things, it directed the Department of Defense to develop and report on procedures for determining whether each detainee held at Guantánamo was properly designated as an enemy combatant through the "Combatant Status Review Tribunals" (CSRTs) that the Department of Defense had established. After a one-time review by the CSRTs, Administrative Review Boards (ARBs) conducted an annual status review for each detainee. Both the CSRTs and the ARBs consisted of military personnel. In 2011, the responsibilities of the CSRTs and ARBs were transferred to Guantánamo Periodic Review Boards (PRBs), an interagency process staffed by civilians. *See* Exec. Order No. 13,567, 3 C.F.R. 227 (2012); Exec. Order No. 13,823, 3 C.F.R. 321 (2019).

[561] 542 U.S. 466 (2004). For a reflection on *Rasul*, and the significance of the individuals being noncitizens who were held outside the United States, see Richard H. Fallon Jr. & Daniel J. Meltzer, *Habeas Corpus Jurisdiction, Substantive Rights, and the War on Terror*, 120 HARV. L. REV. 2029 (2007).

[562] Military Commissions Act of 2006, Pub. L. No. 109-366, § 7, 120 Stat. 2600, 2635 (codified at 28 U.S.C.A. § 2241(e) (Supp. 2007)).

[563] Boumediene v. Bush, 553 U.S. 723, 743, 792 (2008); U.S. CONST., art. I, § 9, cl. 2. For further discussion of *Boumediene*, see *supra* this chapter § I(B).

the government's "absolute" and "indefinite" control over the naval base; and the lack of credible arguments that the military mission at Guantánamo would be compromised if habeas courts had jurisdiction.[564]

Thereafter, Congress amended the MCA such that habeas petitions in U.S. courts challenging the basis of the detentions at Guantánamo were no longer prohibited.[565] Various challenges to such detention have been brought before the District Court for the District of Columbia and then appealed to the D.C. Circuit Court of Appeals. Indeed, the judges of the District Court for the District of Columbia developed a standing case management order used in many Guantánamo habeas cases to manage discovery and to protect classified information from unwarranted disclosure.[566] The jurisprudence of these decisions has not been entirely consistent and remains evolving,[567] addressing issues such as the standard for who may be detained,[568] access of detainees to information,[569] injunctive relief regarding conditions in detention,[570] and the scope of habeas

[564] *Boumediene*, 553 U.S. at 766–69.

[565] Military Commissions Act of 2009, tit. XVIII, Pub. L. No. 111-84, 123 Stat. 2190, 2574.

[566] *In re* Guantanamo Bay Detainee Litig., Misc. No. 08-442, 2008 WL 4858241 (D.D.C. Nov. 6, 2008), *as amended*, 2008 WL 5245890 (D.D.C. Dec. 16, 2008).

[567] *Compare* Qassim v. Trump, 927 F.3d 522, 527–30 (D.C. Cir. 2019) (concluding that Fifth Amendment due process rights are available for Guantánamo detainees in habeas proceedings), *with* Al Hela v. Trump, 972 F.3d 120, 147–48 (D.C. Cir. 2020) (holding that "the protections of the Due Process Clause" simply "do not extend" to Guantánamo), *vacated, reh'g en banc granted sub nom.* Al Hela v. Biden, No. 19-5079, 2021 WL 6753656 (D.C. Cir. Apr. 23, 2021). The D.C. Circuit in *Qassim* denied rehearing en banc but issued opinions that fundamentally disagreed regarding the application of the Fifth Amendment. Qassim v. Trump, 938 F.3d 375 (D.C. Cir. 2019) (per curiam); *compare id.* at 376 (Millet, Pillard, & Edwards, JJ., concurring in the denial of rehearing en banc), *with id.* (Henderson & Rao, JJ., dissenting). For an initial analysis of the jurisprudence of federal courts regarding habeas petitions from Guantánamo Bay detainees, see Benjamin Wittes et al., The Emerging Law of Detention: The Guantánamo Habeas Cases as Lawmaking 1 (2010); Benjamin Wittes et al., The Emerging Law of Detention 2.0: The Guantánamo Habeas Cases as Lawmaking 1 (2012).

[568] For initial cases that grappled with the standard by which individuals might be detained, see Barhoumi v. Obama, 609 F.3d 416, 432 (D.C. Cir. 2010); Al-Bihani v. Obama, 590 F.3d 866, 872 (D.C. Cir. 2010); Hamlily v. Obama, 616 F. Supp. 2d 63, 78 (D.D.C. 2009) (finding that the president has the authority to "detain persons who are or were part of Taliban or al Qaeda forces or associated forces that are engaged in hostilities against the United States"). Ultimately, the National Defense Authorization Act for Fiscal Year 2012, Pub. L. No. 112-81, § 1021(b)(2), 125 Stat. 1298, 1562 (2011), authorized the detention of a "person who was a part of or substantially supported al-Qaeda, the Taliban, or associated forces that are engaged in hostilities against the United States or its coalition partners, including any person who has committed a belligerent act or has directly supported such hostilities in aid of such enemy forces." For an application of that standard, see Hussain v. Obama, 718 F.3d 964, 967 (D.C. Cir. 2013). *See generally* Stephen I. Vladeck, *Detention After the AUMF*, 82 Fordham L. Rev. 2189 (2014).

[569] *See, e.g.*, *Qassim*, 927 F.3d at 528–30 (finding that Guantánamo detainees can claim procedural due process violations, but that detainees' effort to see classified information supporting his detention was premature); *id.* at 530–32 (declining to resolve, and remanding for further consideration, whether due process required that the detainee and his counsel be provided with access to classified information concerning the government's detention decision, as might relate to further habeas proceedings).

[570] *See, e.g.*, Aamer v. Obama, 742 F.3d 1023 (D.C. Cir. 2014) (determining that Guantánamo detainees' challenge to force-feeding was not entitled to preliminary injunctive relief).

proceedings.[571] Among other things, such courts have refrained from recognizing a Fifth Amendment substantive due process right that would require the release into the United States of detainees that the government conceded it could not lawfully hold, but who could not be returned to their country of origin due to fears of torture or execution.[572] Further, such detainees or their families have unsuccessfully pursued *Bivens* claims for their detention and treatment while in custody at Guantánamo and elsewhere abroad.[573] Persons held in military detention in places other than Guantánamo, such as in Afghanistan and Iraq, have not been found to have constitutional rights.[574]

E. Trials (Sixth Amendment)

As a general matter, the procedural protections of the Sixth Amendment— which include, for example, the right to a speedy trial and the right to confront witnesses[575]—apply broadly to criminal prosecution within the United States, including of noncitizens.[576] U.S. prosecutions held outside of the United States, however, present a more complicated picture. The Sixth Amendment was thought, at one time, not to apply at all to such prosecutions, even of U.S. citizens.

---

[571] *See, e.g.*, Al-Zahrani v. Rodriguez, 669 F.3d 315 (D.C. Cir. 2012) (holding that action relating to a deceased detainee at Guantánamo is not a habeas action).

[572] *See* Kiyemba v. Obama, 561 F.3d 509 (D.C. Cir. 2009) (concerning detention of Chinese citizens who were ethnic Uighurs and were no longer deemed to be enemy combatants).

[573] *See, e.g.*, Hamad v. Gates, 732 F.3d 990 (9th Cir. 2013) (concluding that Congress had deprived district courts of subject-matter jurisdiction over such claims); Al-Zahrani v. Rodriguez, 669 F.3d 315, 319–20 (D.C. Cir. 2012) (finding that money damages are "not constitutionally required" and as the sole remedy sought in this case, *Bivens* claims are precluded).

[574] *See, e.g.*, Ali v. Rumsfeld, 649 F.3d 762, 772 (D.C. Cir. 2011) (holding that, because Afghanistan and Iraq were in an "active theater of war," the detainees in U.S. military facilities in those places did not have any Fifth or Eighth Amendment rights) (quoting Boumediene v. Bush, 553 U.S. 723, 770 (2008)); Al Maqaleh v. Gates, 605 F.3d 84 (D.C. Cir. 2010) (jurisdiction of U.S. courts does not extend to noncitizens held in detention by U.S. military forces at U.S. military base in the Afghan "theater of war"); Rasul v. Myers, 563 F.3d 527 (D.C. Cir. 2009) (same as *Ali v. Rumsfeld*).

[575] The Sixth Amendment provides:

> In all criminal prosecutions, the accused shall enjoy the right to a speedy and public trial, by an impartial jury of the State and district wherein the crime shall have been committed, which district shall have been previously ascertained by law, and to be informed of the nature and cause of the accusation; to be confronted with the witnesses against him; to have compulsory process for obtaining witnesses in his favor, and to have the Assistance of Counsel for his defence.

U.S. CONST. amend. VI. For a general discussion of the Sixth Amendment, see 3 WAYNE R. LAFAVE ET AL., CRIMINAL PROCEDURE § 11.1(a) (4th ed. 2015).

[576] *See* Wong Wing v. United States, 163 U.S. 228 (1896) (imprisonment at hard labor camp of noncitizen in the United States without a jury trial constitutes a violation of the Fifth and Sixth Amendments); RESTATEMENT (THIRD) § 722 cmt. a. Such protections do not operate in civil proceedings, which include proceedings for the removal of a noncitizen. *See infra* this chapter § III(A) (4).

Thus, in *In re Ross*, the Supreme Court rejected a habeas corpus petition by a U.S. citizen that his conviction by a U.S. consular court in Japan violated the Sixth Amendment right to a jury trial,[577] saying that the "Constitution can have no operation in another country."[578] Among other things, the Court in *Ross* also noted that giving extraterritorial effect to the right to a jury trial "would be impracticable from the impossibility of obtaining a competent grand or petit jury" abroad.[579]

The rigid view expressed in *Ross*, in which the Constitution was entirely bounded by territory, has not endured, especially under the influence of the plurality's decision in *Reid v. Covert*.[580] In *Reid*, the plurality maintained that "[t]he *Ross* case is one of those cases that cannot be understood except in its peculiar setting" (meaning trial under a statute authorizing U.S. consuls to try U.S. citizens charged with committing crimes in Japan and certain other "non-Christian countries"), and further that "it seems highly unlikely that a similar result would be reached today."[581] In *Kinsella v. United States ex rel. Singleton*, a 7–2 majority of the Court held that a U.S. civilian dependent tried by a U.S. military court in Germany was "protected by the specific provisions of Article III [of the Constitution] and the Fifth and Sixth Amendments"[582] In doing so, the Court only made reference to the "*Ross* doctrine" as having been found in *Reid* as "neither applicable nor controlling."[583]

Even so, to the extent that such trials occur outside the United States, practical difficulties of the kind noted in *Ross* come to the fore, presenting uncertainty as to how the full panoply of Fifth and Sixth Amendment trial protections might apply. The following sections briefly address four issues that have arisen with respect to the Sixth Amendment under U.S. foreign relations law: (1) the right to a speedy (U.S.) trial for a noncitizen who is located abroad; (2) the post-indictment right of counsel for a noncitizen who is located abroad; (3) the right to confront and compel testimony of witnesses located abroad; and (4) the lack of Fifth and Sixth Amendment rights in trials by military commission.

---

[577] 140 U.S. 453 (1891).
[578] *Id.* at 464.
[579] *Id.*
[580] *See* 354 U.S. 1, 5–6 (1957) (plurality holding that, in times of peace and for capital offenses committed abroad, civilian dependents of members of the U.S. armed forces overseas could not constitutionally be tried by court-martial, rather than in civilian courts before a jury of peers); *see also supra* this chapter text accompanying notes 53–58.
[581] *Id.* at 10.
[582] 361 U.S. 234, 249 (1960).
[583] *Id.* at 237.

1. Right to a Speedy U.S. Trial for Noncitizen Located Abroad

U.S. courts have concluded that the right of criminal defendants to appear in person at their trial, as a matter of due process, is guaranteed by the Fifth, Sixth, and Fourteenth Amendments.[584] As such, if an individual is not present in the indicting jurisdiction, a trial cannot proceed unless the person waives the right to be present or voluntarily leaves after the trial has commenced, or in other limited circumstances.[585] At the same time, a defendant in a criminal case has the right to a speedy trial under the Sixth Amendment. This means that the prosecution has a limited period in which to bring a defendant to trial after they have been formally charged. A person who flees the indicting jurisdiction cannot take advantage of the right, as the "clock" is paused if the defendant is evading justice. But for noncitizens resident outside the United States, perhaps living in their own country, a failure by the prosecution diligently to pursue extradition after indictment could require dismissal of any subsequent criminal proceedings.[586]

While the Supreme Court has not addressed the question, most courts have found that a noncitizen residing abroad benefits from a right to a speedy trial, and that an undue delay in pursuing extradition may violate that right.[587] Other courts have avoided directly addressing the issue by assuming arguendo that such a right exists but finding that no unreasonable delay occurred.[588] One district court, however, has held that the right does not attach until the noncitizen enters the United States.[589]

---

[584] See, e.g., Hopt v. Utah 110 U.S. 574, 579 (1884) ("If he be deprived of his life or liberty without being so present, such deprivation would be without that due process of law required by the Constitution.").

[585] For some exceptions to the general rule, consistent with constitutional principles, see Fed. R Crim. P. 43.

[586] See generally Roberto Iraola, Due Process, the Sixth Amendment, and International Extradition, 90 Neb. L. Rev. 752 (2012).

[587] See, e.g., United States v. Diacolios, 837 F.2d 79, 84 (2d Cir. 1988) (noncitizen defendant living abroad benefits from speedy trial right, but the government "satisfied its burden of demonstrating due diligence in seeking defendant's return for trial without unnecessary delay"); United States v. Dionisio, No. 04-cr-30-bbc, 2008 WL 4949914 (W.D. Wis. Nov. 17, 2008) (four-year delay in arrest of noncitizen defendant living abroad, due to unjustified concerns about seeking extradition, violated defendant's speedy-trial rights).

[588] See, e.g., United States v. Wanigasinghe, 545 F.3d 595, 597 (7th Cir. 2008) (avoiding "broad pronouncement" on the extraterritorial reach of a speedy-trial right); United States v. Tchibassa, 452 F.3d 918, 921 n.1, 927 (D.C. Cir. 2006) (assuming arguendo that a noncitizen defendant living abroad was entitled to a speedy trial right, but not deciding the issue).

[589] See United States v. Koch, No. 03-144, 2011 WL 284485, at *3 (W.D. Pa. Jan. 25, 2011) (a noncitizen residing outside the United States "has no Sixth Amendment right to a speedy trial or to other constitutional protections"); cf. United States v. Kashamu, 15 F. Supp. 3d 854, 859 (N.D. Ill. 2014) (indicating sympathy for U.S. position that "the Fifth and Sixth Amendments are inapplicable to a foreign national living abroad who is not in the United States and has never appeared before this Court on the indictment against him," but exercising caution regarding unnecessarily "broad pronouncements" regarding extraterritorial application of constitutional rights) (quoting United States v. Wanigasinghe, 545 F.3d 595, 597 (7th Cir.2008)).

2. Post-Indictment Right of Counsel for Noncitizen Located Abroad

The Sixth Amendment right to counsel commences upon indictment and guarantees a defendant the right to have counsel present at all "critical stages" of the criminal proceedings.[590] Whereas there may be some flexibility under the Fifth Amendment as to the admissibility of evidence obtained from a noncitizen located abroad prior to indictment,[591] admissibility of evidence obtained post-indictment in such circumstances may be less flexible. For example, one federal court has found that, once indicted, the noncitizen must be informed of the right to counsel prior to interrogation abroad and, if the noncitizen invokes a right to counsel, it cannot be thereafter waived.[592]

3. Right to Confront and Compel Testimony of Witnesses Located Abroad

The Sixth Amendment's Confrontation Clause provides that a person accused of a crime has the right to confront a witness against him or her in a criminal action, while the Compulsory Process Clause allows the defendant to secure witnesses through the issuance of a court-ordered subpoena. By statute, a federal court may subpoena a U.S. citizen or lawful permanent resident who is located abroad to appear before it or a grand jury.[593] In *Blackmer v. United States*, the Supreme Court explained that a U.S. citizen, even while residing in another country, owes allegiance to the United States, and is bound by its laws, including a subpoena to testify in a criminal case.[594]

However, federal courts ordinarily have no authority to subpoena nonresident noncitizens who are located abroad.[595] For this reason, U.S. mutual legal assistance treaties (MLATs) typically contain provisions facilitating the voluntary travel of noncitizens to the United States for testimony in a criminal case,[596] and

---

[590] Montejo v. Louisiana, 556 U.S. 778, 786 (2009) ("Interrogation by the State is such a stage.").

[591] *See supra* this chapter notes 391–395.

[592] *See* United States v. Osorio-Arellanes, No. CR-11-00150-004-TUC-DCB (BPV), 2019 WL 357933, at *5 (D. Ariz. Jan. 29, 2019). Applying the law to the facts, the court initially found that the noncitizen's counsel was not present, *id.*, but on reconsideration of the facts found that he was. *See* United States v. Osorio-Arellanes, No. CR-11-00150-004-TUC-DCB (BPV), 2019 WL 417039 (D. Ariz. Jan. 31, 2019).

[593] *See* 28 U.S.C. § 1783 (2018). Further, 28 U.S.C. § 1784 authorizes contempt sanctions if the subpoenaed person fails to appear or otherwise comply with the subpoena.

[594] 284 U.S. 421, 436–38 (1932).

[595] *See, e.g.,* United States v. Abu Ali, 528 F.3d 210, 239 (4th Cir. 2008) (finding that noncitizen witnesses abroad were beyond the subpoena power of the district court); United States v. Duran Samaniego, 345 F.3d 1280, 1283 (11th Cir. 2003) (same); United States v. Olafson, 213 F.3d 435, 441 (9th Cir. 2000) (same); United States v. Groos, 616 F. Supp. 2d 777, 791 (N.D. Ill. 2008) (same); United States v. Ozsusamlar, 428 F. Supp. 2d 161, 177 (S.D.N.Y. 2006) (same).

[596] *See, e.g.,* Treaty on Mutual Legal Assistance in Criminal Matters, Leich.-U.S., art. 10, July 8, 2002, S. TREATY DOC. 107-16. As of 2022, the United States has bilateral MLATs in force with virtually every member state of the European Union, many of the member states of the Organization of American States, and many other countries. For information on U.S. MLATs, see U.S. Dep't of State, Treaties in Force: A List of Treaties and Other International Agreements of the United States in Force

providing for a transfer of custody of noncitizens imprisoned in a foreign nation for such testimony.[597] In the absence of an MLAT, a prosecutor or court may use letters rogatory to secure evidence,[598] proceeding on the basis of comity rather than a treaty obligation.[599]

The inability of federal courts to compel the testimony of noncitizens located abroad, however, raises Sixth Amendment concerns, as such witnesses may not be able or willing to travel to the United States. For that reason, the Federal Rules of Criminal Procedure authorize overseas depositions under "exceptional circumstances" and "in the interest of justice."[600] Such depositions must be in conformity with the Confrontation Clause, meaning that the defendant must be given the opportunity to attend government depositions taken abroad, the defendant or counsel must be allowed to cross-examine the witness, and the deposition must be taken under oath and recorded.[601] Occasionally courts have admitted depositions that did not meet all of these conditions, due to the limitations present in the country where the deposition took place.[602] In *United States v. McKeeve*,[603] the First Circuit found that "the confrontation clause requires, at a minimum, that the government undertake diligent efforts to facilitate the defendant's presence. We caution, however, that although such efforts must be undertaken in good faith, they need not be heroic."[604]

on January 1, 2020 (2020) and Supplement (2021–2022) (bilateral treaties are listed under individual country headings).

[597] *See, e.g.*, Treaty on Mutual Legal Assistance in Criminal Matters, Fr.-U.S., art. 18, Dec. 10, 1998, S. Treaty Doc. No. 106-17.

[598] *See* 28 U.S.C. §§ 1781–82. The U.S. court may transmit such letters directly to a foreign or international tribunal or may do so through the Department of State.

[599] *See In re* Commissioner's Subpoenas, 325 F.3d 1287, 1290–91 (11th Cir. 2003) (indicating that law enforcement authorities found letters rogatory "to be an unattractive option in practice" as compared to MLATs because the former "provided wide discretion in the district court to refuse the request and did not obligate other nations to return the favor").

[600] Fed. R. Crim. P. 15(a)(1).

[601] *See* Fed. R. Crim. P. 15(c)–(e).

[602] *See, e.g.*, United States v. Cooper, 947 F. Supp. 2d 108, 110–16 (D.D.C. 2013) (accepting court-ordered depositions taken in Indonesia even though the government could not guarantee that a written record would be created, but where: an oath or affirmation would be administered; both sides would be allowed to examine and cross-examine the witnesses; an official translator would be used; the defendant would be allowed to have his own translator; the depositions would be videotaped; the parties would be allowed to make objections on the record; the defendant, although not present, would be allowed to view the proceedings by video and audio link and to consult with his attorney by telephone during the proceedings; and the court would entertain challenges to use the depositions at trial "[i]f the actual procedures vary from the procedures outlined"); United States v. Sturman, 951 F.2d 1466, 1480–81 (6th Cir. 1991) ("Depositions taken in foreign countries cannot at all times completely emulate the United States methods of obtaining testimony. Here, all steps were taken to ensure the defendants' rights while respecting the legal rules established in a different country.").

[603] 131 F.3d 1 (1st Cir. 1997).

[604] *Id.* at 8 (citations omitted) (finding constitutionally sufficient a district court's order that the government transport the defendant's attorney to the deposition abroad, and to install two telephone lines; one that would allow the defendant to monitor the deposition from his prison cell, and another that would allow him to consult privately with counsel during the deposition).

4. Trial by Military Commission

As discussed in greater depth in Chapter 8,[605] Congress has used its authority to make rules regulating U.S. armed forces[606] to enact the Uniform Code of Military Justice (UCMJ), which allows for prosecution of U.S. service members before U.S. military courts (courts-martial) for violations of both U.S. law and the laws of war.[607] The rules and procedures before such military courts have become, over time, highly developed.[608] By contrast, military commissions convened in time of armed conflict or military occupation, usually for the purpose of prosecuting noncitizens who are enemy combatants for violations of the laws of war, historically have been less regulated. Even so, Congress has exercised its authority under the Constitution to define and punish offenses against the law of nations so as to allow for such commissions.[609]

Trial by military commission may occur either in the United States or abroad. In *Ex Parte Quirin*,[610] eight German residents (two of whom claimed to be U.S. citizens) received training in World War II Germany and then traveled to the United States covertly via submarine for the purpose of engaging in sabotage. All eight were subsequently arrested, tried in the United States by military commission, found guilty, and sentenced to death (the sentences of two were later commuted to life in prison). Several challenged their convictions in U.S. court arguing, inter alia, that the Fifth and Sixth Amendments required a regular trial.[611]

In rejecting that challenge, the Supreme Court noted that various types of offenses against the United States (such as petty offenses and criminal contempt triable at common law without a jury) do not require trial by jury and are not deemed to be within the provisions of the Fifth and Sixth Amendments governing "crimes" and "criminal prosecutions."[612] Likewise, the Court decided that "the Fifth and Sixth Amendments cannot be taken to have extended the right to

---

[605] *See* Chapter 8 § III(B).

[606] U.S. CONST. art. I, § 8, cl. 14.

[607] Uniform Code of Military Justice, 10 U.S.C. §§ 801–946a (2018).

[608] Constitutional protections available in civilian courts do not operate fully in these military courts. For example, the Fifth Amendment expressly states that the grand jury requirement does not apply to "cases arising in the land or naval forces, or in the Militia, when in actual service in time of war or public danger . . . ." U.S. CONST. amend. V. Such exception is deemed implied in the Sixth Amendment as well. *See Ex parte* Milligan, 71 U.S. (4 Wall.) 2, 138–39 (1866). Nevertheless, the UCMJ contains numerous protections that accord a form of due process and other rights. *See* RESTATEMENT (THIRD) § 721 rptrs. note 10 ("When [members of the armed forces are] tried by court martial, they are entitled to 'due process' and other rights conferred in the" UCMJ).

[609] U.S. CONST. art. I, § 8, cl. 10. On the commander-in-chief power to convene military commissions, see Chapter 8 § II(B).

[610] 317 U.S. 1 (1942).

[611] *See generally* LOUIS FISHER: NAZI SABOTEURS ON TRIAL: A MILITARY TRIBUNAL AND AMERICAN LAW (2005).

[612] *Ex Parte Quirin*, 317 U.S. at 40.

demand a jury to trials by military commission, or to have required that offenses against the law of war not triable by jury at common law be tried only in the civil courts."[613] The reasoning applied equally to U.S. citizens and noncitizens: such offenders are "outside the constitutional guaranty of trial by jury, not because they [are] aliens, but only because they [have] violated the law of war by committing offenses constitutionally triable by military tribunal."[614]

Most trials by military commission, however, have taken place abroad during or in the aftermath of an armed conflict, as was the case in *Johnson v. Eisentrager*.[615] In the aftermath of the attacks of 9/11, considerable attention was paid to the establishment of military commissions at Guantánamo Naval Base in Cuba to prosecute enemy combatants in the U.S. armed conflict with al-Qaeda. In *Hamdan v. Rumsfeld*, the Supreme Court determined that the military commission system that had been established at Guantánamo solely by military order of President George W. Bush was unlawful.[616] According to the Court, the president had established military commissions that were inconsistent the UCMJ, which required that military commissions either be created by statute or be sanctioned by the "law of war,"[617] and further required that that military commissions should not deviate unnecessarily from the procedures by which courts martial operate.[618] After determining that no statute existed authorizing these military commissions,[619] the Court found that the procedures of the military commissions deviated from courts martial in significant ways and without justification (such as by allowing the accused to be excluded from the proceedings even in the absence of any disruptive conduct).[620] Moreover, the laws of war (specifically Common Article 3 to the 1949 Geneva Conventions) prohibit "the passing of sentences and the carrying out of executions without previous judgment pronounced by a regularly constituted court,"[621] and yet the president's

---

[613] *Id.*

[614] *Id.* at 44.

[615] For discussion of *Eisentrager* in the context of the ability of noncitizens to challenge before U.S. courts their military detention abroad, see *supra* this chapter § II(D)(7).

[616] 548 U.S. 557 (2006); Military Order of Nov. 13, 2001, 66 Fed. Reg. 57,831-36 (Nov. 16, 2001). For further discussion of *Hamdan*, see Chapter 1 § II(B); Chapter 5 § II(A)(2); and Chapter 8 §§ II(A), II(B), and III(B).

[617] 10 U.S.C. § 821 (2018) (stating that "[t]he provisions of this chapter conferring jurisdiction upon courts-martial do not deprive military commissions . . . of concurrent jurisdiction with respect to offenders or offenses that by statute or by the law of war may be tried by military commissions").

[618] *Id.* § 836.

[619] *Hamdan*, 548 U.S. at 590-95.

[620] *Id.* at 614 (noting that the "accused and his civilian counsel may be excluded from, and precluded from ever learning what evidence was presented during, any part of the proceeding that either the Appointing Authority or the presiding officer decides to 'close'").

[621] *See, e.g.*, Geneva Convention Relative to the Treatment of Prisoners of War, art. 3, Aug. 12, 1949, 6 U.S.T. 3316, 75 U.N.T.S. 135.

military commissions were not such a "court" since they had not been established by statute.[622]

Thereafter, Congress provided for such commissions by means of the 2006
Military Commissions Act (MCA), as amended.[623] Under the statute, an accused
detainee may appeal a final decision of the military commission to a U.S. Court
of Military Commission Review (a body consisting of persons who meet the
same qualifications as military judges or comparable qualifications for civilian
judges).[624] The accused may then appeal any final decision to the D.C. Circuit
Court of Appeals.[625] Those decisions, in turn, may be reviewed by the Supreme
Court under writ of certiorari.[626] While the MCA, as amended, has provided
a greater degree of regulation of the military commissions at Guantánamo, including with respect to protections for the accused, the Guantánamo proceedings nevertheless have been criticized for allowing the admission of secret
evidence, hearsay, and certain evidence obtained through coercion, as well as
obstruction of access to counsel.[627]

F. Prohibition on Cruel and Unusual Punishment
(Eighth Amendment)

The Eighth Amendment states: "Excessive bail shall not be required, nor excessive fines imposed, nor cruel and unusual punishments inflicted."[628] Like other
provisions of the Bill of Rights, it is framed in terms of a negative restriction on
the government rather than a positive right; further, it is not expressly predicated on citizenship or on the "people." As such, the amendment protects both
U.S. citizens and noncitizens from excessive bail, excessive fines, or cruel and
unusual punishment. Certain protections for noncitizens, however, might be different. For example, in *Carlson v. Landon*, the Supreme Court upheld a decision
by the attorney general, as executive head of the Immigration and Naturalization

---

[622] *Hamdan*, 548 U.S. at 632–33 (finding that "[a]t a minimum, a military commission 'can be "regularly constituted" by the standards of our military justice system only if some practical need explains
deviations from court-martial practice'" (quoting Kennedy, J., concurring in part, *infra* at 645)).

[623] Military Commissions Act of 2006, Pub. L. No. 109-366, 120 Stat. 2600; Military Commissions
Act of 2009, Pub. L. No. 111-84, §§ 1801–07, 123 Stat. 2190, 2574.

[624] 10 U.S.C. § 950f (2018).

[625] *Id.* § 950g. The appellate court may take action only with respect to matters of law, including the
sufficiency of the evidence to support the verdict.

[626] *Id.*

[627] *See generally* JESS BRAVIN, THE TERROR COURTS: ROUGH JUSTICE AT GUANTANAMO BAY (2013);
GUANTÁNAMO AND BEYOND: EXCEPTIONAL COURTS AND MILITARY COMMISSIONS IN COMPARATIVE
PERSPECTIVE (Fionnuala Ní Aoláin & Oren Gross eds., 2013).

[628] U.S. CONST. amend. VIII. For a general discussion of the Eighth Amendment, see ERWIN
CHEMERINSKY, CONSTITUTIONAL LAW: PRINCIPLES AND POLICIES § 7.3 (6th ed. 2019); 4 WAYNE R.
LAFAVE ET AL., CRIMINAL PROCEDURE §§ 12.2, 12.3(c) (4th ed. 2015).

Service, to detain resident aliens without bail, pending a determination on deportability.[629]

In considering what constitutes "cruel and unusual" punishment, the Supreme Court has referred to "evolving standards of decency."[630] In that regard, the Court at times has found relevant whether a particular type of punishment is regarded as impermissible in foreign countries or under international law.[631] Yet the Court's reference to foreign and international law for this purpose has waxed and waned, driven by each justice's own assessment of whether the Eighth Amendment is sufficiently open-textured as to invite—as one indicator of contemporary standards of decency—consideration of such law.

For example, when considering whether the death penalty is "cruel and unusual," the Court has—after considering U.S. laws and practice—at times looked to foreign and international law for further guidance. In *Coker v. Georgia*,[632] the Court stated that it is "not irrelevant here that out of 60 major nations in the world surveyed in 1965, only 3 retained the death penalty for rape where death did not ensue."[633] In *Enmund v. Florida*,[634] when considering the constitutionality of the death penalty for the driver of a getaway car, the Court observed that "the doctrine of felony murder has been abolished in England and India, severely restricted in Canada and a number of other Commonwealth countries, and is unknown in continental Europe."[635] In *Thompson v. Oklahoma*,[636] the Court noted the abolition of the death penalty for juveniles under sixteen years of age "by other nations that share our Anglo-American heritage, and by the leading members of the Western European community," and observed that "[w]e have previously recognized the relevance of the views of the international community in determining whether a punishment is cruel and unusual."[637] By contrast, in *Stanford v. Kentucky*, the Court emphasized "that it is *American* conceptions of decency that are dispositive" in interpreting the Eighth Amendment and rejected "the contention... that the sentencing practices of other countries are relevant."[638] In *Atkins v.*

---

[629] Carlson v. Landon, 342 U.S. 524, 544–45 (1952). In dissent, Justice Black maintained that the government's action violated the Eighth Amendment (and the First and Fifth Amendments as well). *Id.* at 557–58 (Black, J., dissenting); *see id.* at 569 (Burton, J., dissenting) (agreeing that the Eighth Amendment precluded the government's action).

[630] *See* Trop v. Dulles, 356 U.S. 86, 100–01 (1958) (plurality opinion in case involving revocation of citizenship).

[631] *See, e.g., id.* at 102–03 ("The civilized nations of the world are in virtual unanimity that statelessness is not to be imposed as punishment for crime.").

[632] 433 U.S. 584 (1977).

[633] *Id.* at 596 n.10 (plurality opinion).

[634] 458 U.S. 782 (1982).

[635] *Id.* at 796–97 n.22.

[636] 487 U.S. 815 (1988).

[637] *Id.* at 830–31 n.31 (plurality opinion).

[638] Stanford v. Kentucky, 492 U.S. 361, 369 n.1 (1989). That contention was expressed by Justice Brennan. *Id.* at 389 (Brennan, J., dissenting).

Virginia,[639] the Court recognized that "within the world community, the imposition of the death penalty for crimes committed by mentally retarded offenders is overwhelmingly disapproved."[640]

Most recently, in *Roper v. Simmons*,[641] the Court struck down as unconstitutional under the Eighth Amendment the death penalty for juveniles under the age of eighteen. After reviewing U.S. law and practice on the issue, the Court stated that "[o]ur determination that the death penalty is disproportionate punishment for offenders under 18 finds confirmation in the stark reality that the United States is the only country in the world that continues to give official sanction to the juvenile death penalty."[642] In particular, the Court noted that the U.N. Convention on the Rights of the Child (CRC),[643] "which every country in the world has ratified save for the United States and Somalia, contains an express prohibition on capital punishment for crimes committed by juveniles under 18," and "no ratifying country has entered a reservation to the provision prohibiting the execution of juvenile offenders. Parallel prohibitions are contained in other significant international covenants . . . ."[644] In dissent, Justice Scalia strongly criticized the Court's use of these "foreign sources," arguing inter alia that the U.S. failure to ratify the CRC "can only suggest that *our country* has either not reached a national consensus on the question, or has reached a consensus contrary to what the Court announces."[645]

Critics of such jurisprudence object to the use of foreign and international law when determining the meaning of the U.S. Constitution. At the extreme, it is even claimed that such law is being used to overturn law that otherwise exists in the United States.[646] The Court, however, has been careful in maintaining that the use of such law is not because it is directly binding upon the United States, but because it provides guidance on the nature of what constitutes "cruel and unusual" punishment.[647] In the wake of the controversy stirred by *Roper*, the Court found in *Graham v. Florida* that life without parole for juvenile nonhomicide

---

[639] 536 U.S. 304 (2002).

[640] *Id.* at 317 n.21.

[641] 543 U.S. 551 (2005).

[642] *Id.* at 575.

[643] U.N. Convention on the Rights of the Child, Nov. 20, 1989, 1577 U.N.T.S. 3.

[644] *Roper*, 543 U.S. at 576.

[645] *Id.* at 623, 628.

[646] Thus, in *Roper*, Justice Scalia charged that foreign sources were being "cited *to set aside* the centuries-old American practice—a practice still engaged in by a large majority of the relevant States—of letting a jury of 12 citizens decide whether, in the particular case, youth should be the basis for withholding the death penalty." *Id.* at 628.

[647] For general perspectives on the use by the Court of international and foreign authorities in reaching conclusions on contested issues of constitutional law, see essays by Mark Tushnet, Roger P. Alford, and Melissa A. Waters, *in* INTERNATIONAL LAW IN THE U.S. SUPREME COURT: CONTINUITY AND CHANGE, *supra* note 492, at 507–29; Melissa A. Waters, *Creeping Monism: The Judicial Trend Toward Interpretive Incorporation of Human Rights Treaties*, 107 COLUM. L. REV. 628 (2007); Sarah H. Cleveland, *Our International Constitution*, 31 YALE J. INT'L L. 1 (2006); Vicki C. Jackson, *Constitutional Comparisons: Convergence, Resistance, Engagement*, 119 HARV. L. REV. 109 (2005);

offenders would violate the Eighth Amendment.[648] Among other things, the Court noted that the United States was the only country with such a sentence and, further, that such a sentence was inconsistent with the CRC. But the Court reiterated: "The question before us is not whether international law prohibits the United States from imposing the sentence at issue in this case. The question is whether that punishment is cruel and unusual."[649]

G. Equal Protection Under the Law (Fourteenth Amendment)

Section 1 of the Fourteenth Amendment, in its opening clause, sets forth the basic rule as to who is to be regarded as a "citizen" of the United States (and of the state in which the person resides).[650] The second clause of that section provides that no "State shall make or enforce any law which shall abridge the privileges or immunities of citizens of the United States."[651] That clause has some salience for U.S. foreign relations law, in that the privileges and immunities of U.S. citizens that may not be denied by any state include "free access to [U.S.] seaports, through which operations of foreign commerce are conducted,"[652] and the privilege "to demand the care and protection of the Federal government over [a citizen's] life, liberty, and property when on the high seas or within the jurisdiction of a foreign government."[653]

The third clause provides that no state shall deprive any "person" of life, liberty, or property without due process of law.[654] Due process of law in relation to both the Fifth and Fourteenth Amendments was addressed previously.[655] Finally, the last clause provides that no state shall "deny to any person within its jurisdiction the equal protection of the laws."[656] The Supreme Court has read this notion of equal protection into the Fifth Amendment's Due Process Clause, thus extending its reach to action of the federal government.[657] The following

Lori Fisler Damrosch & Bernard H. Oxman, *Agora: The United States Constitution and International Law*, 98 AM. J. INT'L L. 42 (2004).

[648] 560 U.S. 48 (2010).

[649] *Id.* at 81.

[650] U.S. CONST. amend. XIV, § 1, cl. 1; *see infra* this chapter text accompanying notes 711–722. For a general discussion of the Fourteenth Amendment, see ERWIN CHEMERINSKY, CONSTITUTIONAL LAW: PRINCIPLES AND POLICIES § 9 (6th ed. 2019).

[651] U.S. CONST. amend. XIV, § 1, cl. 2.

[652] Slaughter-House Cases, 83 U.S. (16 Wall.) 36, 79 (1873) (quoting Crandall v. Nevada, 73 U.S. 35, 44 (1868)).

[653] *Id.* at 79.

[654] U.S. CONST. amend. XIV, § 1, cl. 3.

[655] *See supra* this chapter § II(D).

[656] U.S. CONST. amend. XIV, § 1, cl. 4; *see* HENKIN, FOREIGN AFFAIRS, at 292–97, 309–10.

[657] *See supra* this chapter § II(D)(4).

addresses the Equal Protection Clause in relation to action by state and local governments.

1. Lawful Permanent Residents

The Equal Protection Clause has featured in various U.S. foreign relations law cases in the context of rights owed to noncitizens in the United States. In particular, it has arisen in relation to lawful permanent residents. Worded in broad terms, the clause guarantees equal protection to any *person* within a state's jurisdiction, and therefore has been read to accord equal protection to all noncitizens in the United States.

For example, in the 1886 case of *Yick Wo v. Hopkins*,[658] the City of San Francisco adopted an ordinance making it illegal to operate a laundry in a wooden building without a permit, which a board of supervisors had discretion to grant. Virtually all persons of Chinese ancestry (mostly lawful permanent residents) were denied permits, while virtually all others were granted permits. In finding that the administration of the statute violated the Equal Protection Clause,[659] the Supreme Court stated that the Fourteenth Amendment "is not confined to the protection of citizens" but, rather, its "provisions are universal in their application to all persons within the territorial jurisdiction, without regard to any differences of race, of color, or of nationality . . . ."[660]

In the 1915 case of *Truax v. Raich*,[661] Arizona had enacted a statute requiring that employers only employ a specified percentage of noncitizens. Based on the statute, a lawful permanent resident was dismissed from employment purportedly to bring the employer into compliance with the statute. While the Supreme Court acknowledged the power of the state to make reasonable legislative classifications to promote the health, safety, morals, and welfare of those within its jurisdiction, the Court found that such legislative discretion "does not go so far as to make it possible for the State to deny to lawful inhabitants, because of their race or nationality, the ordinary means of earning a livelihood."[662] Among other things, the Court found that "[i]t requires no argument to show that the right to work for a living in the common occupations of the community is of the very essence of the personal freedom and opportunity that it was the purpose of the [Fourteenth] Amendment to secure"; further, "[i]f this could be refused

---

[658] 118 U.S. 356 (1886).

[659] *Id.* at 374 ("No reason for [such distinction] is shown, and the conclusion cannot be resisted, that no reason for it exists except hostility to the race and nationality to which the petitioners belong, and which in the eye of the law is not justified.").

[660] *Id.* at 369; *see also* Wong Wing v. United States, 163 U.S. 228, 242 (1896) (finding "[a] resident, alien born, is entitled to the same protection under the laws that a citizen is entitled to."); United States v. Wong Kim Ark, 169 U.S. 649, 695 (1898) (same).

[661] 239 U.S. 33 (1915).

[662] *Id.* at 41.

solely upon the ground of race or nationality, the prohibition of the denial to any person of the equal protection of the laws would be a barren form of words."[663]

Moreover, the Court indicated that such unequal treatment would intrude upon federal power with respect to immigration, for the "assertion of an authority to deny to noncitizens the opportunity of earning a livelihood when lawfully admitted to the State would be tantamount to the assertion of the right to deny them entrance and abode, for in ordinary cases, they cannot live where they cannot work."[664] Other employment-related restrictions targeting noncitizens have also been struck down.[665]

With respect to lawful permanent residents, such discriminatory laws or regulations are reviewed under a strict scrutiny test, whereby there must be a compelling governmental interest for drawing distinctions between citizens and lawful permanent residents (or among lawful permanent residents) that the law is narrowly tailored to achieve.[666] As such, classifications based on citizenship status are "suspect" for purposes of analyzing a violation of the Equal Protection Clause. In *Graham v. Richardson*,[667] the Court held that such "aliens as a class are a prime example of a 'discrete and insular' minority for whom . . . heightened judicial solicitude [strict scrutiny] is appropriate."[668] Such scrutiny may be warranted given the long history of discrimination in the United States against noncitizens, often based on prejudice or economic protectionism, and the fact

---

[663] *Id.*

[664] *Id.* at 42; *see* Graham v. Richardson, 403 U.S. 365, 377–80 (1971); RESTATEMENT (THIRD) § 722 cmt. b.

[665] *See, e.g.*, Examining Bd. of Eng'rs, Architects & Surveyors v. Flores de Otero, 426 U.S. 572 (1976) (striking down a Puerto Rican statute preventing a lawful permanent resident from working as an engineer); *In re* Griffiths, 413 U.S. 717 (1973) (striking down a Connecticut statute preventing lawful permanent resident from membership in the Connecticut bar); Sugarman v. Dougall, 413 U.S. 634 (1973) (striking down a New York law that prevented noncitizens from holding civil service jobs). As discussed earlier in this chapter, the federal government is accorded greater leeway when imposing employment restrictions. In *Hampton v. Mow Sun Wong*, 426 U.S. 88 (1976), the U.S. Civil Service Commission promulgated a regulation that required applicants for most positions in the federal competitive civil service to be U.S. citizens, or persons owing permanent allegiance to the United States. The Supreme Court found that overriding national interests might justify a citizenship requirement in the federal civil service, even though an identical requirement could not properly be enacted by a state in a comparable situation. Yet, if this is to be done, it must be properly authorized by Congress or the president, or justified with reasons by the Commission. *Id.* at 116. The Court found no express mandate from Congress or the president to the Commission to issue such a prohibition, nor any sufficient justification by the Commission, and therefore held the regulation to be invalid. Thereafter, however, President Gerald R. Ford issued Exec. Order No. 11,935, 5 C.F.R. § 7.4 (1976), which again barred noncitizens from virtually all positions in the federal civil service for certain reasons, including a desire to encourage naturalization by noncitizens. Lower courts upheld the constitutionality of the executive order. *See* this chapter § II(D)(4).

[666] *See* RESTATEMENT (THIRD) § 722 cmt. c.

[667] 403 U.S. 365 (1971).

[668] *Id.* at 371–72 (striking down, under the strict scrutiny test, Arizona and Pennsylvania laws that restricted the eligibility of noncitizens for welfare benefits) (citing United States v. Carolene Prods. Co., 304 U.S. 144, 152–53 n.4 (1938)).

that noncitizens cannot vote and thus cannot protect themselves through the political process.[669] Moreover, given that lawful permanent residents pay taxes, denying them access to financial resources made available by the government to citizens is deemed problematic.[670] Even so, it has been pointed out that courts continue to uphold certain forms of discrimination that arguably do not meet the standard set forth in *Graham*, such as discrimination with respect to the ability of noncitizens to own land or to rent property.[671]

In order to provide protections to U.S. nationals (including investors) operating abroad, the United States historically has entered into certain types of treaties, often styled as treaties of "friendship, commerce and navigation," treaties of "amity," or bilateral investment treaties, that contain within them standards of treatment that protect U.S. nationals in particular areas, such as operating a business or making and benefiting from an investment.[672] Such standards might be absolute in nature (for example, that there be no expropriation of the national's property without prompt, adequate and effective compensation) or may be tied to the treatment accorded to others, such as the treatment accorded by the foreign state to its own nationals (a national treatment standard) or to the most favorable treatment accorded to the nationals of a third state (a most-favored-nation standard).[673] Such treaties, however, are typically reciprocal in nature, meaning that the United States commits to provide the same standards of treatment to nationals of the treaty partner when they come to or invest in the United States. Where such treaties require that the United States accord national treatment to foreign nationals of the treaty party for a particular subject-matter area, the treaty essentially calls for an equal protection standard in that area. For example, the U.S.-Japan Treaty of Commerce and Navigation at issue in *Asakura*

---

[669] *See* David Cole, *Rights Over Borders: Transnational Constitutionalism and Guantanamo Bay*, 2008 CATO SUP. CT. REV. 47, 60 (2008).

[670] *See, e.g.*, Nyquist v. Mauclet, 432 U.S. 1 (1977) (striking down a New York statute on equal protection grounds because the statute barred lawful permanent residents who were not intending to become U.S. citizens from qualifying for state financial aid for higher education). In *Nyquist*, the Court stated: "Resident aliens are obligated to pay their full share of the taxes that support the assistance programs. There thus is no real unfairness in allowing resident aliens an equal right to participate in programs to which they contribute on an equal basis."). *Id.* at 12.

[671] *See* Allison Brownell Tirres, *Property Outliers: Non-Citizens, Property Rights and State Power*, 27 GEO. IMMIGR. L.J. 77, 81 (2012) (surveying and critiquing noncitizen land laws in the United States and finding that "*Graham* has not been consistently applied to state limitations on alien land ownership or leasing rights").

[672] *See* KENNETH J. VANDEVELDE, THE FIRST BILATERAL INVESTMENT TREATIES: U.S. POSTWAR FRIENDSHIP, COMMERCE AND NAVIGATION TREATIES (2017); KENNETH J. VANDEVELDE, U.S. INTERNATIONAL INVESTMENT TREATIES (2009). Most recently, investment protections may be found in a section (or chapter) of U.S. free trade agreements.

[673] For general discussion of such standards, see, for example, Jeswald W. SALACUSE, THE LAW OF INVESTMENT TREATIES (2015); MIRA SULEIMENOVA, MFN STANDARD AS SUBSTANTIVE TREATMENT (2019); AUGUST REINISCH & CHRISTOPH SCHREUER, INTERNATIONAL PROTECTION OF INVESTMENTS: THE SUBSTANTIVE STANDARDS (2020).

v. City of Seattle required that citizens of either party "shall have liberty to enter, travel, and reside in the territories of the other to carry on trade, wholesale and retail, ... and generally to do anything incident to or necessary for trade upon the same terms as native citizens or subjects."[674] When Seattle imposed an ordinance that effectively precluded a Japanese national from operating as a pawnbroker but allowed U.S. citizens to do so, the Court struck down the ordinance as a violation of the treaty.[675]

2. Nonimmigrant Noncitizens

Less clear is whether nonimmigrant noncitizens benefit from the heightened strict scrutiny test. The Supreme Court has not directly addressed this issue (though its jurisprudence has spoken generally of "aliens," not just lawful permanent residents), but the Fifth and Sixth Circuits have found that the strict scrutiny test is not applicable to nonimmigrant noncitizens, given that they lack citizen-like features. As such, state statutes need only survive a rational basis test. When employing that test, the Fifth Circuit in *LeClerc v. Webb*[676] upheld a state statute preventing nonimmigrant noncitizens from sitting for the state bar exam,[677] while the Sixth Circuit in *LULAC v. Bredesen*[678] upheld a state statute preventing such noncitizens from obtaining driver's licenses.[679]

Dissents in both cases noted that the Supreme Court has drawn no such distinction between classes of noncitizens and that the concern about noncitizens not having any influence in the political process applies equally to lawful permanent residents and to nonimmigrant noncitizens.[680] Those dissents appear to have influenced the Second Circuit in *Dandamundi v. Tish*,[681] where the court struck down a New York statute which provided that only citizens and lawful permanent residents could apply to be licensed as a pharmacist.[682] According to the Second Circuit, there was no compelling reason to distinguish between lawful

---

[674] Treaty of Commerce and Navigation, U.S.-Japan, Feb. 21, 1911, art. I, *in* U.S. DEP'T OF STATE, FOREIGN RELATIONS OF THE UNITED STATES 414 (1911); 5 AM. J. INT'L L. SUPP. 100 (1911).

[675] Asakura v. City of Seattle, 265 U.S. 332, 343 (1924).

[676] 419 F.3d 405 (5th Cir. 2005).

[677] *Id.*; *see also* Van Staden v. St. Martin, 664 F.3d 56 (5th Cir. 2011) (reaffirming *LeClerc*).

[678] 500 F.3d 523 (6th Cir. 2007).

[679] *Id. See generally* Jenny-Brooke Condon, *The Preempting of Equal Protection for Immigrants?*, 73 WASH. & LEE L. REV. 77 (2016); John Harras, *Suspicious Suspect Classes—Are Nonimmigrants Entitled to Strict Scrutiny Review Under the Equal Protection Clause? An Analysis of Dandamundi and LeClerc*, 88 ST. JOHN's L. REV. 849 (2014).

[680] *See LULAC*, 500 F.3d at 543–44 (Gilman, J., dissenting); *LeClerc*, 419 F.3d at 426 (Stewart, J., dissenting).

[681] 686 F.3d 66 (2d Cir. 2012).

[682] *Id.*; *accord* Adusumelli v. Steiner, 740 F. Supp. 2d 582 (S.D.N.Y. 2010) (reaching the same conclusion); Kirk v. N.Y. State Dep't of Educ., 562 F. Supp. 2d 405 (W.D.N.Y. 2008) (same); *see also* Finch v. Commonwealth Health Ins. Connector Auth., 959 N.E.2d 970, 974 (Mass. 2012) (striking down a state provision limiting state healthcare benefits for nonimmigrant noncitizens on state equal protection grounds).

permanent residents and nonimmigrant noncitizens, both of whom lacked political influence.[683] Further, the court noted that nonimmigrant noncitizens may be present in the United States for long periods of time, and in some instances may seek permanent residence and citizenship.[684]

3. Undocumented Noncitizens

Undocumented noncitizens in the United States are protected by the Equal Protection Clause, but do not benefit from a strict scrutiny test when exposed to discriminatory governmental laws and regulations.[685] In *Plyler v. Doe*,[686] the Court declared unconstitutional a Texas law that provided free grade school education for children of citizens and lawful permanent residents, but required that undocumented noncitizens pay for their schooling.[687] While it was argued that undocumented noncitizens are not "persons within the jurisdiction" of a state, and therefore do not benefit from the Equal Protection Clause, the Supreme Court rejected that argument, finding: "Whatever his status under the immigration laws, an alien is surely a 'person' in any ordinary sense of that term. Aliens, even aliens whose presence in this country is unlawful, have long been recognized as 'persons' guaranteed due process of law by the Fifth and Fourteenth Amendments."[688]

The *Plyler* Court did not articulate a specific level of scrutiny but held that such noncitizens are not members of a suspect class, nor are they entitled to the benefits of strict scrutiny.[689] Even so, at least in this particular context, the Court appeared to apply a standard different and higher than a mere rational basis review. Rather than focus on Texas' rationale, the five-justice majority stressed the blamelessness of the children, particularly given that their presence in the country is not a "product of their own unlawful conduct," as compared with the conduct of their parents.[690] As such, the Court found it "difficult to conceive of a rational justification for penalizing these children for their presence within the United States."[691] Among other things, the Court emphasized the "importance of education in maintaining our basic institutions," "the lasting impact of its deprivation on the life of the child," and the "significant social costs borne by our Nation when select groups are denied the means to absorb the values and skills

---

[683] *Dandamudi*, 686 F.3d at 75.
[684] *Id.* at 78.
[685] *See* Craig v. Boren, 429 U.S. 190 (1976) (articulating the intermediate scrutiny test in the context of gender-based discrimination).
[686] 457 U.S. 202 (1982).
[687] *Id.* at 210.
[688] *Id.*
[689] *Id.* at 216–18.
[690] *Id.* at 219–20.
[691] *Id.* at 220.

upon which our social order rests."[692] The Court went on to say that the statute "can hardly be considered rational unless it furthers some substantial goal of the State,"[693] and yet no such goal was articulated; rather, Texas' principal argument was simply that the children were undocumented.[694] The Texas statute did not correspond to any identifiable congressional policy when classifying undocumented noncitizens, such as a congressional desire to conserve state educational resources.[695]

In his dissent, Chief Justice Burger maintained that a rational basis review was the appropriate standard and that Texas was due judicial deference on matters relating to the allocation of its educational resources. He further argued that the heightened scrutiny applied by the majority was inappropriate, given that the law did not impinge upon any fundamental right and that the classification at issue was established by the federal government in its immigration laws and policies.[696] Various state statutes since *Plyler* have imposed restrictions that target or indirectly affect undocumented noncitizens (such as imposing penalties on landlords who provide housing or employers who provide jobs to undocumented noncitizens), but to date those cases have been addressed on federal preemption grounds rather than on equal protection grounds.[697]

4. Possible Application of Rational Basis Review

Despite all the above, the Court has applied the lower test of rational basis review to state regulation of all noncitizens (including lawful permanent residents) based on three exceptions. First, under the "political function" exception, alienage classifications related to self-government and the democratic process are upheld so long as a rational basis can be articulated for the classification. Thus,

---

[692] *Id.* at 221.

[693] *Id.* at 224; *see id.* at 230 ("If the State is to deny a discrete group of innocent children the free public education that it offers to other children residing within its borders, that denial must be justified by a showing that it furthers some substantial state interest.").

[694] *Id.* at 224.

[695] *Id.* at 225–26; *see* Holley v. Lavine, 529 F.2d 1294 (2d Cir. 1976) (declining to dismiss summarily equal protection claims of an undocumented noncitizen who was denied welfare benefits for minor children). By contrast, the Supreme Court has recognized that the states have some authority to act with respect to undocumented noncitizens where such action mirrors federal objectives and furthers a legitimate state goal. *See* Arizona v. United States, 567 U.S. 387 (2012); De Canas v. Bica, 424 U.S. 351 (1976), *partially superseded by statute*, Immigration Reform and Control Act, Pub. L. No. 99-603, 100 Stat. 3359 (1990) (upholding state program that reflected Congress' intention to bar from employment all noncitizens except those possessing a grant of permission to work in the United States). For discussion of *Arizona v. United States*, see Chapter 9 § II(A).

[696] *Plyler*, 457 U.S. at 244–45 (Burger, C.J., dissenting).

[697] *See, e.g.*, Ga. Latino All. for Hum. Rts. v. Governor of Ga., 691 F.3d 1250, 1269 (11th Cir. 2012) (finding certain sections of a Georgia immigration bill incongruous with the Immigration and Nationality Act, and therefore enjoined because "when state laws intrude into areas of overwhelming federal interest and erode the discretion implicit in the sovereignty of the country, we must recognize the supremacy of federal law"); Chamber of Com. of U.S. v. Edmondson, 594 F.3d 742 (10th Cir. 2010) (finding an Oklahoma employment eligibility act is in large part preempted by federal law).

a state may deny noncitizens the right to vote, to hold political office, or to serve on juries.[698] According to the Supreme Court, "the 'political function' exception . . . applies to laws that exclude aliens from positions intimately related to the process of democratic self-government."[699]

Second, restrictions have been upheld under a closely allied "public function" exception, which concerns government employment of noncitizens in positions that fulfill fundamental obligations of government, such as police officers,[700] probation officers,[701] and elementary or secondary school teachers.[702] At the same time, a restriction on the employment of noncitizens as notaries public was struck down because the function of a notary does not "implicate responsibilities that go to the heart of representative government."[703]

Third, restrictions have been upheld under the "special public interest" exception, which concerns regulation or distribution of the common property or resources of the people of the state, the enjoyment of which may be limited to its citizens as against not just noncitizens, but also the citizens of other states.[704] In the 1876 case of *McCready v. Virginia*,[705] the restriction to the citizens of Virginia of the right to plant oysters in one of its rivers was sustained on the ground that such tidewaters are "owned" by Virginia and thus are the common property of the citizens of the state. Likewise, in the 1914 case of *Patsone v. Pennsylvania*,[706] discrimination against noncitizens was upheld by the Court in the context of protecting and preserving wild game for the benefit of Pennsylvania citizens.[707]

Whether such older cases retain their vitality, however, is unclear. In *Missouri v. Holland*,[708] the Court cast doubt upon a state's right of "title" to wild birds, finding that to "put the claim of the State upon title is to lean upon a slender

---

[698] *See* Michael Scaperlanda, *Partial Membership: Aliens and the Constitutional Community*, 81 IOWA L. REV. 707, 736–37 (1996).

[699] Bernal v. Fainter, 467 U.S. 216, 220 (1984); *see* Cabell v. Chavez-Salido, 454 U.S. 432, 439 (1982) ("The exclusion of aliens from basic governmental processes is not a deficiency in the democratic system but a necessary consequence of the community's process of political self-definition."); Foley v. Connelie, 435 U.S. 291, 297 (1978) ("The essence of our holdings to date is that although we extend to aliens the right to education and public welfare, along with the ability to earn a livelihood and engage in licensed professions, the right to govern is reserved to citizens.").

[700] *Foley*, 435 U.S. at 292. *But see* Sugarman v. Dougall, 413 U.S. 634 (1973) (striking down New York law that prevented noncitizens from holding civil service jobs).

[701] *Cabell*, 454 U.S. at 433.

[702] Ambach v. Norwick, 441 U.S. 68 (1979).

[703] Bernal v. Fainter, 467 U.S. 216, 225 (1984).

[704] RESTATEMENT (THIRD) § 722 cmt. c ("A State may probably deny to aliens what it may deny to citizens of other States, e.g., access to its public parks and lands, publicly owned game, and other natural resources.").

[705] 94 U.S. 391, 396 (1876).

[706] 232 U.S. 138 (1914).

[707] *Id.*; *see also* Geer v. Connecticut, 161 U.S. 519 (1896) (sustaining under the Commerce Clause a Connecticut law that, in order to restrict the use of game to the people of the state, prohibited the out-of-state transportation of game killed within the state).

[708] 252 U.S. 416 (1920). For further discussion of this case, see Chapter 6 §§ I(C), II(D)(2).

reed."[709] Moreover, in the 1948 case of *Torao Takahashi v. Fish and Game Commission*,[710] the Court found that California could not, under the Equal Protection Clause, deprive a Japanese national of a permit to fish in coastal waters based on his lack of U.S. citizenship.

III. Rights Arising in Certain Subject-Matter Areas

Any attempt to explore in depth individual rights as they operate across specific subject-matter areas is challenging in scale, as such rights arise in many different contexts. Moreover, attempting to do so in a single volume, let alone a single chapter, would invariably miss important contextual details, particularly those arising from statutes, treaties, and other nonconstitutional sources. For these reasons, this section addresses just three specific areas that have been of recurrent interest, especially before U.S. courts, and that provide important perspectives on how such rights operate within U.S. foreign relations law.

Part A of this section addresses individual rights in the context of immigration law, as an example of a traditional field of foreign relations law dominated by the federal government and federal statutes. Part B considers transnational aspects of family law, an area of private law traditionally allocated to the states, but that has relatively recently been the focus of certain international regulation. Part C explores individual rights in the context of extradition, an area in which the national government dominates, but in which individual rights have long been secured by self-executing treaties.

A. Immigration Law

1. Constitutional Underpinnings

The Constitution provides that the "Congress shall have the power . . . [t]o establish a uniform rule of naturalization,"[711] which speaks expressly to Congress' power to regulate who may acquire U.S. citizenship. With adoption of the Fourteenth Amendment in 1868, the Constitution also clarifies which persons are "citizens" of the United States: "All persons born or naturalized in the United States, and subject to the jurisdiction thereof, are citizens of the United States and of the State wherein they reside."[712]

---

[709] *Missouri v. Holland*, 252 U.S. at 434.
[710] 334 U.S. 410 (1948).
[711] U.S. Const. art. I, § 8, cl. 1, 4.
[712] *Id.* amend XIV, § 1.

Based on such provisions, Congress has adopted various laws clarifying the persons who are citizens of the United States at birth, whether in the United States[713] or abroad.[714] This birthright citizenship applies even if the parents of the child are noncitizens[715] and apparently even if they are undocumented noncitizens.[716] Because Native American tribes in the United States have been accorded a special sovereignty status, for a long time they were not regarded as "subject to the jurisdiction" of the United States, and thus not considered U.S. citizens at birth (although they could become naturalized).[717] In 1924, however, the Indian Citizenship Act granted birthright citizenship to Native Americans.[718] As the United States incorporated new territory throughout the 1800s and early 1900s, treaties and legislation made most persons within those territories U.S. citizens.[719] In the *Insular Cases*, however, the Supreme Court determined that unincorporated U.S. territories and commonwealths are only "appurtenant" to the United States, rather than part of the United States, thereby limiting the application of the U.S. Constitution to those places.[720] Even so, Congress has conferred birthright citizenship by statute to all persons born in unincorporated U.S. territories,[721] with the exception of American Samoa and an atoll administered as a part of American Samoa known as Swains Island (such persons are U.S. nationals but not U.S. citizens).[722]

---

[713] For the most part, persons born in the fifty states and District of Columbia are, at birth, U.S. citizens. *See* INA § 301(a), 8 U.S.C. § 1401(a) (2018).

[714] *See* INA § 301(c), 8 U.S.C. § 1401(c) (birth abroad to two U.S. citizen parents); INA § 301(g), 8 U.S.C. § 1401(d) (birth abroad to one citizen and one noncitizen parent in wedlock); INA § 309(a), 8 U.S.C. § 1409(a) (birth abroad out-of-wedlock to a U.S. citizen father); INA § 309(c), 8 U.S.C. § 1409(c) (birth abroad out-of-wedlock to a U.S. citizen mother); *see also* Sessions v. Morales-Santana, 137 S. Ct. 1678 (2017) (finding that the differing requirements for unwed mothers and fathers violate the Equal Protection Clause).

[715] *See* United States v. Wong Kim Ark, 169 U.S. 649 (1898).

[716] *See* U.S. Dep't of State, 8 Foreign Affairs Manual § 301.1–1(d), https://perma.cc/C58D-4UG8 ("All children born in and subject, at the time of birth, to the jurisdiction of the United States acquire U.S. citizenship at birth even if their parents were in the United States illegally at the time of birth."). Exceptionally, children born in the United States to accredited foreign diplomats and consular officers do not acquire citizenship because they are not "born . . . subject to the jurisdiction of the United States." *See* 8 C.F.R. 101.3(a)(1) (2018); RESTATEMENT (THIRD) § 212 rptrs. note 1; Muthana v. Pompeo, 985 F.3d 893 (D.C. Cir. 2021) (child of Yemeni diplomat born in the United States did not obtain U.S. citizenship).

[717] *See* Elk v. Wilkins, 112 U.S. 94, 102 (1884).

[718] Pub. L. No. 68-175, 43 Stat. 253 (1924) (codified as amended at 8 U.S.C. § 1401(b)).

[719] For example, the Treaty of Guadalupe Hidalgo, Mex.-U.S., Feb. 2, 1848, 9 Stat. 922, which ended the Mexican-American War, extended U.S. citizenship to approximately 60,000 Mexican residents of the New Mexico Territory and some 7,500 living in California. Richard L. Nostrand, *Mexican Americans Circa 1850*, 65 ANNALS ASS'N AM. GEOGRAPHERS 378, 382 (1975). For Alaska, see 8 U.S.C. § 1404. For Hawaii, see 8 U.S.C. § 1405.

[720] *See supra* this chapter text accompanying notes 30–49.

[721] *See* 8 U.S.C. § 1402 (Puerto Rico); *id.* § 1406(b) (Virgin Islands); *id.* § 1407(b) (Guam); 48 U.S.C. § 1801 note (Covenant to Establish a Commonwealth of the Northern Mariana Islands in Political Union with the United States of America).

[722] *See* 8 U.S.C. §§ 1101(a)(29), 1408; RESTATEMENT (THIRD) § 212 cmt. a & rptrs. note 1. That exception can have consequences. *See* Fitisemanu v. United States, 1 F.4th 862 (10th Cir. 2021) (denying

The Constitution does not, however, expressly address Congress' power to regulate the admission of noncitizens to the United States, their status while present in the United States, the procedures for removing noncitizens from the United States, or related matters.[723] As such, the existence and contours of federal power in this area is found principally in the laws enacted by the federal government and associated case law, which have to some degree ventured ahead of any constitutional prescription.

Prior to 1875, the federal government did not regulate immigration to the United States.[724] As immigration increased, however, anti-immigrant attitudes emerged and so did government regulation, including at the national level. In 1875, Congress enacted the first federal immigration law, which prohibited entry into the United States of subjects of "China, Japan, or any Oriental country" for contract service or "for the purposes of prostitution."[725] In 1882, Congress enacted the Chinese Exclusion Act,[726] which excluded entry of all Chinese laborers. So as to administer immigration regulation, Congress in 1881 established a commissioner of immigration in the Department of Treasury.[727]

This authority of the federal government to regulate immigration, at least in times of peace, was challenged in federal court. In the aftermath of the U.S. Civil War, some state governments started to pass their own immigration laws, leading the Supreme Court to pronounce in 1876 that regulation of immigration was exclusively a federal responsibility.[728] Not long after, in *Chae Chan Ping v. United States* (*The Chinese Exclusion Case*), which addressed the Chinese Exclusion Act of 1882, the Supreme Court stated: "That the government of the United States, through the action of the legislative department, can exclude aliens from its territory is a proposition which we do not think open to controversy. Jurisdiction over its own territory to that extent is an incident of every independent nation."[729]

birthright citizenship to American Samoans, on grounds that the guarantee of citizenship in the Fourteenth Amendment does not apply to unincorporated U.S. territories); Tuaua v. United States, 788 F.3d 300 (D.C. Cir. 2015) (same). *See generally American Samoa and the Citizenship Clause: A Study in Insular Cases Revisionism*, 130 HARV. L. REV. 1680 (2017).

[723] The Constitution also does not address the basis for a U.S. citizen to lose the status of "citizen," and thereby become a noncitizen. *See infra* this chapter § III(A)(5).

[724] For discussion of the emergence of Congress' power in this regard, see Chapter 1 § I(D), Chapter 2 § I(B).

[725] Page Act of 1875, ch. 141, Pub. L. No. 43-141, 18 Stat. 477 (1875) (also known as the Asian Exclusion Act).

[726] Chinese Exclusion Act of 1882, ch. 126, Pub. L. No. 47-126, 22 Stat. 58 (1882). While the ban initially was to last for just ten years, it was renewed in 1892, then made permanent in 1902, and only repealed in 1943. *See* Chinese Exclusion Repeal Act of 1943, ch. 344, Pub. L. No. 78-199, 57 Stat. 600 (1943) (also known as the Magnuson Act).

[727] Immigration Act of 1891, ch. 551, 26 Stat. 1084 (1891).

[728] Chy Lung v. Freeman, 92 U.S. 275 (1876).

[729] 130 U.S. 581, 603 (1889); *see* Chapter 1 § I(D), Chapter 8 § I(C)(1).

As the Court perceived it, the source of federal power in this regard arises not from express provisions of the Constitution but from the fact that "the United States, in their relation to foreign countries and their subjects or citizens, are one nation, invested with powers which belong to independent nations, the exercise of which can be invoked for the maintenance of its absolute independence and security throughout its entire territory."[730] The racial orientation of the statute did not trouble the Court in *Chae Chan Ping*; it stated that if Congress viewed the "presence of foreigners of a different race in this country, who will not assimilate with us, to be dangerous to its peace and security, their exclusion is not to be stayed because at the time there are no actual hostilities with the nation of which the foreigners are subjects."[731]

Almost immediately, a pair of decisions reinforced the scope of federal authority. In *Ekiu v. United States*,[732] the Court found that an immigration inspector's decision—within the authority conferred upon him by statute—that a noncitizen is not permitted entry to the United States, is final and conclusive, other than by appeal as permitted within the executive branch, and is not subject to habeas corpus review in federal court. In *Fong Yue Ting v. United States*, the Court confirmed that the political branches had "the power to exclude or to expel aliens," which was "to be regulated by treaty or by an act of Congress, and to be executed by the executive authority according to the regulations so established, except so far as the judicial department has been authorized by treaty or by statute, or is required by the paramount law of the Constitution."[733]

Much time has passed since these decisions were rendered, and they have been subject to sharp criticism for making sweeping statements about federal power in the context of federal policies that were plainly race-based.[734] Nonetheless, they seem to retain precedential value with respect to federal power to regulate immigration (and removal), and they continue to be cited in contemporary immigration cases.[735] These and other cases are associated with the view that Congress has *plenary* power to regulate the admission, exclusion, and removal of noncitizens;[736] to regulate categories of noncitizens present in the United

---

[730] *The Chinese Exclusion Case*, 130 U.S. at 604.

[731] *Id.* at 606; *see* T. Alexander Aleinikoff, *Federal Regulation of Aliens and the Constitution*, 83 Am. J. Int'l L. 862 (1989).

[732] 142 U.S. 651 (1892).

[733] 149 U.S. 698, 713 (1893); *see* United States *ex rel.* Knauff v. Shaughnessy, 338 U.S. 537, 542 (1950) (reaffirming).

[734] *See, e.g.*, Louis Henkin, *The Constitution and United States Sovereignty: A Century of Chinese Exclusion and Its Progeny*, 100 Harv. L. Rev. 853, 862–63 (1987).

[735] *See, e.g.*, Arizona v. United States, 567 U.S. 387, 422 (2012) (citing Fong Yue Ting v. United States, 149 U.S. 698 (1893), and Ekiu v. United States, 142 U.S. 651 (1892)).

[736] *See, e.g.*, Oceanic Steam Navigation Co. v. Stranahan, 214 U.S. 320, 339 (1909) ("[O]ver no conceivable subject is the legislative power of Congress more complete than it is over" the admission of noncitizens); Lem Moon Sing v. United States, 158 U.S. 538, 547 (1895) (Congress' power "to exclude aliens altogether from the United States, or to prescribe the terms and conditions upon which

States; and to regulate naturalization,[737] a view sometimes referred to as the "plenary power doctrine."[738] Indeed, as a leading commentator stated, the Supreme Court's approach has been that U.S. immigration laws and policies are "not subject to the Bill of Rights, including its requirements of due process of law and the equal protection of the laws."[739]

Congress was slow to adopt rights-enhancing reforms of its own volition. The Chinese Exclusion Act of 1882 was novel at the time and comprehensive in its targeted rejection of a particular race, but it was subsequently renewed, expanded in some regards in 1924, and when repealed by the 1943 Magnuson Act (as part of a war-related appeal to China), it was replaced with a national quota that permitted only a trivial number of immigrants, all from China, to enter the United States.[740] Direct racial barriers were finally dropped in 1952, when Congress adopted the Immigration and Nationality Act (INA),[741] which remains today the central statute in this area.[742]

they may come to this country, and to have its declared policy in that regard enforced exclusively through executive officers, without judicial intervention, is settled by our previous adjudications."). Considering perhaps the most poignant possibility, the *Restatement (Third)* noted that "in the past the Supreme Court ruled that the United States had authority to deport an alien even if the person had been admitted for permanent residence and had peacefully resided in the United States for many years." RESTATEMENT (THIRD) § 722 cmt. i. *See, e.g.*, Carlson v. Landon, 342 U.S. 524, 534 (1952) (if "aliens fail to obtain and maintain citizenship by naturalization, they remain subject to the plenary power of Congress to expel them under the sovereign right to determine what noncitizens shall be permitted to remain within our borders.").

[737] *See, e.g.*, Galvan v. Press, 347 U.S. 522, 530 (1954) ("The power of Congress over the admission of aliens and their right to remain is necessarily very broad, touching as it does basic aspects of national sovereignty, more particularly our foreign relations and the national security"); United States v. Hernandez-Guerrero, 147 F.3d 1075, 1077 (9th Cir.1998) (in exercising this power, which falls into the arena of foreign affairs, "Congress is not subject to the rigid constraints that govern its authority in domestic contexts").

[738] *See, e.g.*, Mathews v. Diaz, 426 U.S. 67, 82 (1976) (describing the "narrow standard of [judicial] review of decisions made by the Congress or the President in the area of immigration and naturalization"); Boutilier v. INS, 387 U.S. 118, 123 (1967) (sustaining Congress' "plenary power to make rules for the admission of aliens and to exclude those who possess those characteristics which Congress has forbidden"); *see also* Aleinikoff, *supra* note 7, at 10–11.

[739] HENKIN, FOREIGN AFFAIRS, at 304.

[740] It was not until the mid-1960s that large-scale immigration of Chinese nationals was permitted into the United States. The Senate ultimately passed a resolution expressing regret for having enacted the Chinese Exclusion Act and maintaining exclusionary rules for six decades; the House subsequently adopted a similar, but less detailed, expression of regret. S. Res. 201, 112th Cong. (Oct. 6, 2011); H.R. Res. 683, 112th Cong. (June 18, 2012).

[741] Immigration and Nationality Act of 1952, Pub. L. No. 82-414, 66 Stat. 163 (1952) (codified as amended in scattered sections of 8 U.S.C. (2018)).

[742] Subsequent statutes have further shaped U.S. regulation of immigration. *See, e.g.*, Immigration and Nationality Act of 1965, Pub. L. No. 89-236, 79 Stat. 911 (1968) (creating, inter alia, a seven-category preference system that gives priority to relatives of U.S. citizens and lawful permanent residents, as well as to professionals and other individuals with specialized skills); Immigration Reform and Control Act of 1986, Pub. L. No. 99-603, 100 Stat. 3359 (1986) (legalizing most undocumented immigrants who had arrived in the United States prior to 1982, but making it illegal to knowingly hire undocumented noncitizens, and establishing financial and other penalties for companies that employed such noncitizens); Illegal Immigration Reform and Immigrant Responsibility Act of

Although the INA substantially changed U.S. immigration law, nothing altered the Supreme Court's deferential approach to the authority of the political branches over immigration, even in matters involving civil liberties. The same year the INA was adopted, the Court decided in *Harisiades v. Shaughnessy*[743] that Congress could authorize the removal of a lawful permanent resident solely because of membership in the Communist Party, even when that membership had terminated prior to enactment of the Alien Registration Act (which made deportation mandatory for all aliens who, at any time past, had been members of certain proscribed organizations).[744] Although the case involved lawful permanent residents who had opted not to become naturalized U.S. citizens, the Court's finding appears relevant to all noncitizens in the United States. After confirming that the power to remove noncitizens is inherent in every sovereign state,[745] the Court deployed a further rationale for federal power in this area, which was that by "withholding his allegiance from the United States," a permanent resident who declines to become a citizen "leaves outstanding a foreign call on his loyalties which international law not only permits our Government to recognize but commands it to respect" and that "to protract this ambiguous status within the country is not his right but is a matter of permission and tolerance;" moreover, the government's "power to terminate its hospitality has been asserted and sustained by this Court since the question first arose."[746] On this reasoning, the power of the federal government to remove a noncitizen due to certain conditions (such as prior membership in a prescribed organization) derives, in part, from the view that noncitizens who are not on a path to citizenship are guests in the United States, who can be disinvited if the government wishes to do so.

The plenary power theory approach has been repeatedly reaffirmed. In 2012, in *Arizona v. United States*, the Court stressed the federal government's "broad, undoubted power over the subject of immigration and the status of aliens," "rest[ing], in part, on the . . . constitutional power to 'establish a uniform Rule of Naturalization,'" partly on the national government's "inherent power as sovereign to control and conduct relations with foreign nations," and partly on the functional reasons for placing responsibility with a national sovereign capable of

---

1996, div. C, Pub. L. No. 104-208, 110 Stat. 3009-546 (1996) (imposing, inter alia, criminal penalties for racketeering, noncitizen smuggling, and the use or creation of fraudulent immigration-related documents and increasing law enforcement authority); Real ID Act of 2005, Pub. L. No. 109-13, 119 Stat. 302 (2005) (inter alia addressing various immigration issues pertaining to terrorism).

[743] 342 U.S. 580 (1952).
[744] Alien Registration (Smith) Act, Pub. L. No. 76-670, 54 Stat. 670 (1940).
[745] *Harisiades*, 342 U.S. at 587–88 (removal "is a weapon of defense and reprisal confirmed by international law as a power inherent in every sovereign state").
[746] *Id.* at 585–87 (citing to *Fong Yue Ting v. United States*, 149 U.S. 698 (1893), and similar cases).

managing relations with other nations about the treatment of their nationals.[747] This plenary power seems firmly anchored not just in the federal government but in Congress, as indicated in *Chae Chan Ping*. Indeed, the Supreme Court has stated on multiple occasions that "[o]ver no conceivable subject is the legislative power of Congress more complete."[748]

All the same, the scope of this authority, including Congress' ability to act wholly arbitrarily, or with racial or religious animus, has not been entirely settled.[749] Only very rarely have federal statutory provisions relating to the admission, exclusion, removal, or naturalization of noncitizens, or of their categorization, been struck down by the Court. But it remains subject to general structural limitations that may bear on individual rights, as in *INS v. Chadha*.[750] Another case, *Sessions v. Dimaya*, held that a residual clause used elsewhere in the criminal code, adverting to "crimes of violence," was unconstitutionally vague as incorporated in the INA's definition of aggravated felony and applied on that basis during the removal proceedings of a long-term permanent resident.[751] That outcome may be explained as a cross-application of the Court's more general void-for-vagueness precedent, which commonly occurs in rights-based challenges. It is notable that although the Court was badly fractured, there was no mention of the plenary power doctrine, not even in the U.S. government's briefs; Justice Thomas did suggest that "[e]ven assuming the Due Process Clause prohibits vague laws, this prohibition might not apply to laws governing the removal of aliens," but that part of his dissent was not joined by any other justice.[752]

The power of the president in this regard is also wide-ranging, given the steady delegation of power by Congress and the executive's day-to-day control over when and how to enforce immigration law.[753] Even so, as compared with Congress, the president's power appears more limited. Not only must the president act in accordance with the relevant immigration statutes but the exercise

---

[747] 567 U.S. 387, 394–95 (2012) (quoting U.S. CONST. art. I, § 8, cl. 4).

[748] Oceanic Steam Navigation Co. v. Stranahan, 214 U.S. 320, 339 (1909); *accord* Fiallo v. Bell, 430 U.S. 787, 792 (1977) (adding that "[t]his Court has repeatedly emphasized" this principle). *See generally* David A. Martin, *Why Immigration's Plenary Power Doctrine Endures*, 68 OKLA. L. REV. 29 (2015).

[749] *See, e.g., Fong Yue Ting*, 149 U.S. at 738 (Brewer, J., dissenting) (inter alia "deny[ing] that there is any arbitrary and unrestrained power to banish residents, even resident aliens"); Henkin, *supra* note 734, at 862–63; Kevin R. Johnson, *Bringing Racial Justice to Immigration Law*, 116 NW. U. L. REV. ONLINE 1 (2021).

[750] 462 U.S. 919 (1983) (holding that INA § 244(c)(2) was an unconstitutional violation of separation of powers because it allowed the House of Representatives to act unilaterally to invalidate removal decisions by the Executive); *see* Chapter 1 § II(A)(1), Chapter 2 § II(B).

[751] 138 S. Ct. 1204 (2018) (holding that "crime of violence" as defined in 18 U.S.C. § 16 was "unconstitutionally vague," and that INA § 101(a)(43)(f), which cites to that section of the criminal code, was unconstitutional as applied).

[752] *Id.* at 1245 (Thomas, J., dissenting).

[753] *See* ADAM B. COX & CRISTINA M. RODRÍGUEZ, THE PRESIDENT AND IMMIGRATION LAW 17–46, 162–88, 215–37 (2020).

of his or her discretionary power under the law is subject to review, including under the Administrative Procedure Act (APA).[754] In *Shaughnessy v. Mezei*, the Court maintained that a lawful permanent resident, who was seeking to return to the United States, cannot be excluded by the attorney general in a manner that "captiously" deprives him "of his constitutional rights to procedural due process."[755] At the same time, this standard appears to afford the executive branch considerable latitude. In *Mezei*, for example, the Court found it permissible for the executive to exclude the permanent resident for security reasons, given that he had spent nineteen months in a communist country, even though such exclusion resulted in the noncitizen's long-term detention at Ellis Island (twenty-one months) because no other country was willing to receive him.

The limits of presidential authority may be seen in efforts by two administrations to address the issue of undocumented noncitizens brought to the United States as children. Although U.S. law provides that undocumented noncitizens, once discovered, should be removed from the United States, the Obama administration in 2012 implemented a policy known as Deferred Action for Childhood Arrivals (DACA),[756] which allowed some undocumented noncitizens who were brought into the United States as children to receive a renewable, two-year period of deferred action from removal (and to be eligible for a work permit but not for citizenship). Ultimately, more than 700,000 persons entered the program. In 2014, after President Obama announced an intention to follow the same policy for some 4.3 million undocumented noncitizens who were parents of U.S. citizens and lawful permanent residents (DAPA),[757] Texas and several other states sued, obtaining a preliminary injunction from a federal district court against the program's expansion.[758] The Fifth Circuit Court of Appeals affirmed the injunction.[759] The court noted that the executive branch had failed to follow the notice-and-comment procedure of the APA.[760] Moreover, the court

---

[754] *See* Administrative Procedure Act, Pub. L. No. 79-404, 60 Stat. 237 (1946) (codified at 5 U.S.C. §§ 500–96 (2018)); *see* Cox & Rodríguez, *supra* note 753, at 191–214 (identifying meaningful constraints legislation imposes on the president when superintending the immigration system).

[755] 345 U.S. 206, 213 (1953); *see also* Kwong Hai Chew v. Colding, 344 U.S. 590 (1953) (temporary absence from the United States cannot constitutionally deprive a lawful permanent resident, who seeks to return, of his right to be heard).

[756] Memorandum from Janet Napolitano, Sec'y of Homeland Sec., to David V. Aguilar, Acting Comm'r, U.S. Customs and Border Patrol, et al. (June 15, 2012), https://perma.cc/9NWJ-HM4W. Such undocumented noncitizens who were raised in the United States were referred to as "Dreamers," a name derived from the Development, Relief, and Education for Minors Act (DREAM Act), which was introduced unsuccessfully several times in Congress to allow such persons to become permanent residents.

[757] Memorandum from Jeh Johnson, Sec'y, Dep't of Homeland Sec., to Leon Rodríguez, Dir., USCIS, et al. (Nov. 20, 2014), https://perma.cc/TZ4E-JM4V.

[758] Texas v. United States, 86 F. Supp. 3d 591 (S.D. Tex. 2015).

[759] Texas v. United States, 809 F.3d 134 (5th Cir. 2015); *see also* Texas v. United States, 787 F.3d 733 (5th Cir. 2015) (declining to stay the injunction).

[760] *Id.* at 177, 178.

said that DAPA was more than just a policy of not enforcing the law with respect to undocumented noncitizens; rather, the policy would confer "lawful presence" and associated benefits on a class of unlawfully present noncitizens.[761] While the INA accords broad deference to the executive in matters of enforcement, the court found that such conferral was beyond the scope of what the INA could reasonably be interpreted to authorize.[762] In an unsigned, one line *per curiam* opinion, an equally divided Supreme Court affirmed.[763]

Subsequently, the Trump administration announced initially that DAPA would be rescinded and then that DACA would be rescinded as well, which also prompted several challenges in U.S. court that the latter decision was arbitrary and capricious in violation of the APA and infringed the equal protection guarantee of the Fifth Amendment's Due Process Clause.[764] While the administration argued that the decision to rescind DACA was not subject to judicial review because it fell within the executive's discretionary enforcement power, the Supreme Court concluded that that the decision was reviewable in federal court, and further was "arbitrary and capricious" under the APA.[765] The Court found that the government "was required to assess whether there were reliance interests, determine whether they were significant, and weigh any such interests against competing policy concerns" before rescinding.[766]

2. Admission of Nonimmigrants and Immigrants

All noncitizens seeking admission to the United States are classified as either nonimmigrants or immigrants. Generally speaking, "nonimmigrants" seek only a temporary presence in the United States, while "immigrants" seek permanent residence in the United States, often as a prelude to pursuing U.S. citizenship. Both categories, as nonresident noncitizens, have no constitutional right of entry to the United States, nor a right to have their petition for entry heard by a court of law.[767] Indeed, even a noncitizen seeking asylum in the United States, present at

---

[761] *Id.* at 166.

[762] *Texas v. United States*, 809 F.3d at 169.

[763] United States v. Texas, 579 U.S. 547 (2016) (per curiam).

[764] U.S. Dep't of Homeland Sec., Rescission of Memorandum Providing for Deferred Action for Parents of Americans and Lawful Permanent Residents ("DAPA") (June 15, 2017), https://perma.cc/FF4Q-ULRF; U.S. Dep't of Homeland Sec., Memorandum on Rescission of Deferred Action for Childhood Arrivals (DACA) (Sept. 5, 2017), https://perma.cc/98S6-JY72. For the lower courts' decisions, see Regents of the Univ. of Cal. v. Dep't of Homeland Sec., 279 F. Supp. 3d 1011 (N.D. Cal. 2018); Batalla Vidal v. Nielsen, 279 F. Supp. 3d 401(E.D.N.Y. 2018); NAACP v. Trump, 298 F. Supp. 3d 209 (D.D.C. 2018); Regents of the Univ. of Cal. v. Dep't of Homeland Sec., 908 F.3d 476 (9th Cir. 2018).

[765] Dep't of Homeland Sec. v. Regents of the Univ. of Cal., 140 S. Ct. 1891, 1914 (2020).

[766] *Id.* at 1915; *see* COX & RODRÍGUEZ, *supra* note 753, at 174–88, 219–31.

[767] *See* Kleindienst v. Mandel, 408 U.S. 753, 766 (1972). By contrast, a lawful permanent resident who travels abroad temporarily and seeks re-entry to the United States is accorded due process rights, including the right to a hearing and to be informed of and respond to any charges against him or her. *See* Landon v. Plasencia, 459 U.S. 21, 32 (1982); Kwong Hai Chew v. Colding, 344 U.S. 590 (1953) (lawful permanent resident who works four months on a vessel at sea is entitled to due

the border (or a short distance inside the border if attempting to enter illegally), cannot claim due process rights.

For example, a Sri Lankan citizen, Vijayakumar Thuraissigiam, crossed the southern U.S. border in 2017 without inspection or an entry document, but was stopped and arrested by the border police within 25 yards of the border. Thereafter, he was placed in expedited removal proceedings.[768] Although Thuraissigiam sought asylum due to a fear of persecution in Sri Lanka,[769] an asylum officer, his supervisor, and an immigration judge all determined on an expedited basis that he had not established a credible fear of persecution.[770] Thuraissigiam then filed a habeas petition in federal district court, arguing that the expedited removal order violated his constitutional, statutory, and regulatory rights. The district court, however, dismissed the petition for lack of subject-matter jurisdiction, concluding that U.S. law—specifically 8 U.S.C. Section 1252(e)(2)[771]—precluded federal court jurisdiction over Thuraissigiam's claims, and further concluding that the expedited removal process did not effectively suspend the writ of habeas corpus, in violation of the Suspension Clause.[772] Although the Ninth Circuit reversed, finding that, as applied, Section 1252(e)(2) violated the Suspension Clause and the Due Process Clause, the Supreme Court did not agree.[773] With respect to the Suspension Clause, the Court found that its application in this context "would extend the writ of habeas corpus far beyond

process). However, if the lawful permanent resident travels abroad for an extended period of time, such as nineteen months, the noncitizen may be denied due process by being "assimilated" to a non-citizen seeking entry for the first time. *See* Shaughnessy v. United States *ex rel.* Mezei, 345 U.S. 206, 213 (1953); INA § 101(a)(13)(C), 8 U.S.C. § 1101(a)(13)(C) (2018). An individual outside the United States who claims to be a U.S. citizen, but is not able to prove it to the satisfaction of the Department of State, may seek lawful entry to the United States by applying at a U.S. diplomatic or consular office for a certificate of identity, and then travelling to a U.S. port of entry and applying for admission. A determination at the port of entry that the person is not entitled to admission to the United States, on grounds that the person is not a U.S. national, is subject to habeas review in a U.S. court. *See* 8 U.S.C. § 1503(b)–(c); Kwock Jan Fat v. White, 253 U.S. 454 (1920).

[768] On expedited removal proceedings generally, see *infra* this chapter § III(A)(4).

[769] On refugees and asylum seekers generally, see *infra* this chapter § III(A)(3).

[770] Immigration judges are Article II administrative judges who fall within a subagency of the Department of Justice, known as the Executive Office for Immigration Review. That office contains three adjudicative components: the immigration judges sitting in sixty-nine immigration courts throughout the United States, under the auspices of an Office of the Chief Immigration Judge; a fifteen-member Board of Immigration Appeals; and an Office of the Chief Administrative Hearings Officer (which handles specialized issues, such as claims of unfair employment practices). *See* U.S. Dep't of Justice, *Executive Office for Immigration Review Organization Chart*, https://perma.cc/6CGC-EJCM.

[771] *See* 8 U.S.C. § 1252(e) (providing that judicial review of expedited removal orders is narrowly limited, such as in situations where the petitioner can prove by a preponderance of the evidence that the petitioner is an alien lawfully admitted for permanent residence).

[772] Thuraissigiam v. Dep't. of Homeland Sec., 287 F. Supp. 3d 1077 (S.D. Cal. 2018), *rev'd*, 917 F.3d 1097 (2019).

[773] *See* Dep't of Homeland Sec. v. Thuraissigiam, 140 S. Ct. 1959 (2020).

its scope 'when the Constitution was drafted and ratified," and that "[h]abeas has traditionally been a means to secure *release* from unlawful detention," whereas Thuraissigiam "invokes the writ to achieve an entirely different end, namely, to obtain additional administrative review of his asylum claim and ultimately to obtain authorization to stay in this country."[774] With respect to the Due Process Clause, the Court found that, while aliens who have established connections to the United States have due process rights in removal proceedings, "the Court long ago held that Congress is entitled to set the conditions for an alien's lawful entry into this country and that, as a result, an alien at the threshold of initial entry cannot claim any greater rights under the Due Process Clause."[775]

U.S. immigration law establishes administrative processes for noncitizens to seek entry into the United States, yet these admission processes accord applicants no significant substantive or procedural rights. Nonimmigrants seeking to enter the United States need to obtain a visa from a U.S. embassy or consulate that is specific to their situation, such as business visitors, investors, students, or tourists.[776] Most categories of nonimmigrant visas do not have annual quotas, and the standards for admission are less rigorous than for immigrants, but the visa allows presence in the United States for only a limited period of time. Such nonimmigrants include representatives of foreign states and international organizations who must travel to the United States as a part of their official functions.[777] Noncitizens seeking admission to the United States, but who do not fall within the INA's categories of "nonimmigrants," are considered immigrants. The INA sets forth various categories of "preference immigrants,"[778] such as employment-based immigrants, diversity immigrants,[779] and family-sponsored

---

[774] *Id.* at 1963 (citing to Boumediene v. Bush, 553 U.S. 723, 746 (2008) (emphasis in original)).

[775] *Id.* at 1963–64 (citing to Nishimura Ekiu v. United States, 142 U.S. 651, 660 (1892)).

[776] *See* 8 U.S.C. § 1101(a)(15)(A)–(V). *See generally* ROBERT C. DIVINE & R. BLAKE CHISAM, IMMIGRATION PRACTICE (15th ed. 2014).

[777] With respect to diplomats, visas are granted to ambassadors, other diplomats, and consular officers (and their immediate family members) who have been accredited by a foreign government that is recognized *de jure* by the United States and who have been accepted by the president or by the secretary of state. 8 U.S.C. § 1101(a)(15)(A)(i). The same is true for other officials and employees of the foreign government, if done on a basis of reciprocity. 8 U.S.C. § 1101(a)(15)(A)(ii). For U.S. treatment of foreign ambassadors and other public ministers, see Chapter 3 § II and Chapter 4 § I(C). Similarly, visas are available to foreign officials (and immediate family members) serving as a representative to an international organization that is based in the United States. 8 U.S.C. § 1101(a)(15) (G). Moreover, under 8 U.S.C. § 1101(a)(15)(C), visas may be granted to "an alien in immediate and continuous transit through the United States, or an alien who qualifies as a person entitled to pass in transit to and from the United Nations Headquarters District and foreign countries, under the provisions of" Section 11 of the Headquarters Agreement, U.N.-U.S., June 26, 1947, 61 Stat. 3416. For discussion of U.S. obligations under the agreement in the context of an effort by Congress to restrict the presence of offices of the Palestinian Authority in the United States, see United States v. Palestine Liberation Organization, 695 F. Supp. 1456 (S.D.N.Y. 1988). For more discussion of the case, see Chapter 3 § II(B).

[778] INA § 203, 8 U.S.C. § 1153.

[779] Diversity immigrants are those applying from countries or regions that have not seen large numbers of emigrants to the United States in recent years. 8 U.S.C. § 203(c).

immigrants; for such categories there are typically annual quotas for different countries.[780] Immigrants lawfully admitted into the United States are referred to as "lawful permanent residents" (also known as "green card" holders because of the documentation that they receive). Unlike nonimmigrants, lawful permanent residents may stay in the United States indefinitely, so long as they do not engage in removable conduct.[781] They are also eligible to work in the United States, may own property, may join the U.S. armed forces, and may eventually seek U.S. citizenship if they meet certain eligibility requirements.[782] In addition to meeting the preceding qualifications, all noncitizens seeking admission to the United States must not otherwise be ineligible. Noncitizens may be deemed "inadmissible" before entering the United States for various reasons, such as a threat to national security, a risk for spreading communicable disease, poverty ("public charge"), prior criminal activity, association with terrorist activity, adverse consequences for U.S. foreign policy, or protection of the U.S. work force.[783]

Under the doctrine of "consular nonreviewability," a person who is denied a nonimmigrant or immigrant visa generally cannot seek judicial review of the decisions by the Department of State or its consular officers. This doctrine has its origins in the "plenary power" doctrine, whereby Congress has plenary power to regulate the admission, exclusion, and removal of noncitizens, and that power in turn has been delegated to the president subject to statutory constraints.[784] Courts sometimes describe the consular nonreviewability doctrine as having no exceptions,[785] and there may even be some statutory prescription to the exercise

---

[780] See generally RYAN BAUGH, U.S. LAWFUL PERMANENT RESIDENTS: 2018 (Dep't of Homeland Sec., 2019) (summarizing the "annual flow" of all lawful permanent residents in the United States, categorized by visa type, geographic region, and other demographics). Some immigrants are exempt from these quotas, notably "immediate relatives" (spouses, children, or parents) of U.S. citizens. INA § 201(b)(2)(A)(i), 8 U.S.C. § 1151. Applications are initially screened by U.S. embassies and consulates, and then processed by the Department of Homeland Security's U.S. Citizenship and Immigration Services (USCIS).

[781] As of 2019, there were about 13.6 million lawful permanent residents in the United States. Bryan Baker, Estimates of the Lawful Permanent Resident Population in the United States and the Subpopulation Eligible to Naturalize: 2015–2019 (Dep't of Homeland Sec., 2020).

[782] Such requirements include: lawful admission to the United States; completion of a period of residency (typically at least five years, or three years if filing as a spouse of a U.S. citizen); literacy in English; a showing of allegiance to the United States; and good moral character.

[783] INA § 212(a), 8 U.S.C. § 1182(a).

[784] See supra text accompanying footnotes 736–748. Even in the absence of congressional authorization, there is precedent for the proposition that the exclusion of noncitizens is an inherent part of the president's general foreign affairs powers. See United States ex rel. Knauff v. Shaughnessy, 338 U.S. 537, 542 (1950) (holding that "there is no question of inappropriate delegation of legislative power involved here. The exclusion of aliens is a fundamental act of sovereignty. The right to do so stems not alone from legislative power but is inherent in the executive power to control the foreign affairs of the nation.").

[785] See Knauff, 338 U.S. at 543 (finding that "it is not within the province of any court, unless expressly authorized by law, to review the determination of the political branch of the Government to exclude a given alien"); Kleindienst v. Mandel, 408 U.S. 753, 765 (1972) (reaffirming the doctrine); Loza-Bedoya v. INS, 410 F.2d 343, 347 (9th Cir. 1969) (concluding that the doctrine of consular nonreviewability applies even if the record demonstrates that a visa denial was based on clearly

of such judicial review.[786] Some applications for visas that are denied by consular officers abroad receive administrative review by the Department of State, but this review is generally limited to purely legal questions, is advisory on factual questions, and only occurs when requested by the consular officer; hence, a visa applicant has no right to request such review.[787]

Even so, limited exceptions to the consular nonreviewability doctrine might be discerned from the case law, such as when review is sought by a U.S. citizen that there is no "facially legitimate and bona fide reason" for the denial of the visa to a noncitizen,[788] review is sought on the basis that the underlying statute or regulation applied by the consular officer is unconstitutional,[789] review is sought claiming that the consular officer made a procedural error,[790] or a statute or treaty exists calling for such review.[791] Of particular note in this regard, INA Section 202(a)(1)(A) expressly provides for the nondiscriminatory issuance of immigrant visas; it mandates that, with limited exceptions, "no person shall receive any preference or priority or be discriminated against in the issuance of an immigrant visa because of the person's race, sex, nationality, place of birth, or place of residence."[792] That said, the Supreme Court has found that

erroneous information); Ngassam v. Chertoff, 590 F. Supp. 2d 461, 466–67 (S.D.N.Y. 2008) (concluding that a "[c]ourt does not have jurisdiction to review a consular official's decision, even if its foundation was erroneous, arbitrary, or contrary to agency regulations").

[786] See Saavedra Bruno v. Albright, 197 F.3d 1153, 1162 (D.C. Cir. 1999) (interpreting the 1996 Illegal Immigration Reform and Immigrant Responsibility Act (IIRIRA), div. C, Pub. L. No. 104-208, 110 Stat. 3009-546, as statutorily precluding lawsuits challenging consular actions); see also Stephen H. Legomsky, Fear and Loathing in Congress and the Courts: Immigration and Judicial Review, 78 TEX. L. REV. 1615, 1623–24 (2000) (discussing jurisdiction-stripping provisions of IIRIRA).

[787] See, e.g., Van Ravenswaay v. Napolitano, 613 F. Supp. 2d 1, 5 (D.D.C. 2009) (finding that the Department of State "advisory opinion is an optional step in the visa decision-making process and is neither necessary nor required for a consular determination").

[788] See supra this chapter text accompanying notes 149–154.

[789] See, e.g., Martinez v. Bell, 468 F. Supp. 719, 725–26 (S.D.N.Y. 1979) (concluding that "the [c]ourt may . . . without violating the consular non-reviewability doctrine, examine the constitutionality of the statute employed by the Secretary [of State] in exercising his discretion"); Alexis v. U.S. Att'y Gen., 431 F.3d 1291, 1294–95 (11th Cir. 2005) (allowing such review only when there is a "substantial constitutional challenge" (quoting Gonzalez-Oropeza v. U.S. Att'y Gen., 321 F.3d 1331, 1333 (11th Cir. 2003)).

[790] See, e.g., Patel v. Reno, 134 F.3d 929 (9th Cir. 1998) (allowing such review where consular officer refused to act on visa applications for eight years, since the challenge was not to a decision within the discretion of the consular officer, but to the existence of any authority to suspend the applications); Amidi v. Chertoff, No. 07cv710 (AJB), 2008 WL 2662599, at *3 (S.D. Cal. Mar. 17, 2008) (finding judicial review available since the challenge concerns "the consulate's decision to terminate or cancel the application, as opposed to the discretionary decision of whether to approve or deny the application").

[791] See, e.g., Baan Rao Thai Rest. v. Pompeo, 985 F.3d 1020 (D.C. Cir. 2021) (accepting in principle that a statute or treaty might call for such review but finding in this instance that the U.S.-Thailand Treaty of Amity and Economic Relations only concerned procedural rights, and consular reviewability is not a procedural matter).

[792] INA § 202(a)(1)(A), 8 U.S.C. § 1152(a)(1)(A) (2018).

the noncitizen is not even owed a detailed explanation of the reasons for the denial.[793]

Moreover, Congress has accorded considerable discretion to the president in the implementation of U.S. law concerning admission, such as determining the number of refugees who may be admitted to the United States.[794] For example, in 2019, President Trump determined that the number of refugees allowed to resettle in the United States for fiscal year 2020 be reduced by 40 percent, from 30,000 to 18,000.[795] Yet the exercise of discretion concerning admission to the United States evoked controversy when President Trump, by a series of executive decisions, sought broadly to prevent entry of noncitizens from certain predominantly Muslim countries, purportedly as presenting heightened terrorism-related risks. Section 212(f) of the INA gives the president authority to suspend "entry of any aliens or of any class of aliens" if he finds that entry "would be detrimental to the interests of the United States."[796] While lower federal courts struck down two initial executive orders on grounds that they targeted immigration by Muslims,[797] a subsequent presidential proclamation, which broadly restricted entry to the United States by citizens of eight countries (six of which were predominantly Muslim)[798] was upheld by the Supreme Court in *Trump v.*

---

[793] Kerry v. Din, 576 U.S. 86 (2015) (finding that no constitutional rights were violated by the Department of State denying a full explanation of why a noncitizen's visa was denied).

[794] INA § 207, 8 U.S.C. 1157 (providing that the number of refugees who may be admitted in any fiscal year shall be such number as the president determines, after appropriate consultation with Congress). As broad as such discretion may be, it is not unbounded. For example, a lawful permanent resident who travels outside the United States temporarily must be accorded due process, including a hearing, when being denied reentry to the United States. *See supra* note 767.

[795] *See* Presidential Determination on Refugee Admissions for Fiscal Year 2020, 2019 DAILY COMP. PRES. DOC. 1 (Nov. 1, 2019). At the same time, the number of individuals obtaining the status of lawful permanent resident has remained relatively consistent as between administrations. *See Persons Obtaining Lawful Permanent Resident Status: Fiscal Years 1820 to 2018*, DEP'T HOMELAND SEC. (Oct. 2019), https://perma.cc/KV7E-34GV.

[796] INA § 212(f), 8 U.S.C. § 1182(f); *see also* U.S. Dep't of State, 9 Foreign Affairs Manual § 302.11-3(B)(1), https://perma.cc/NE58-UY9N; Abourezk v. Reagan, 785 F.2d 1043, 1049 n.2 (D.C. Cir. 1986) (finding that Section 212(f) ensures that "the Executive would not be helpless in the face of" a noncitizen who posed a danger to the United States), *partially superseded by statute*, INA § 279, 8 U.S.C. § 1329, as amended. For invocation of INA Section 212(f) by other presidents, see Kate M. Manuel, Cong. Research Serv., R44743, Executive Authority to Exclude Aliens: In Brief 7-10 (2017) (detailing categories of noncitizens excluded under INA § 212(f) chronologically from President Reagan to President Obama).

[797] *See* Exec. Order No. 13,769, 82 Fed. Reg. 8,977 (Jan. 27, 2017) (inter alia barring for ninety days entry to the United States of all nationals from seven predominantly Muslim countries, regardless of whether they were lawful permanent residents or already had visas to enter the United States, and barring entry for Syrian refugees indefinitely); Exec. Order No. 13,780, 82 Fed. Reg. 13,209 (Mar. 6, 2017) (inter alia extending the ban for another ninety days but dropping the indefinite ban on Syrian refugees and exempting certain noncitizens, such as those who were lawful permanent residents or who already had been issued visas). For discussion of the lower court decisions on these two executive orders, see *supra* this chapter text accompanying notes 161–175.

[798] Proclamation No. 9645, 82 Fed. Reg. 45,161 (Sept. 24, 2017) (indefinitely suspending the entry of nationals from six predominantly Muslim countries (Chad, Iran, Libya, Somalia, Syria, and Yemen), and from North Korea, as well as certain Venezuelan government officials and their

Hawaii.[799] Among other things, the Court relied upon the fact that Section 212(f) accorded "the President broad discretion to suspend the entry of" noncitizens into the United States.[800] While INA Section 202(a)(1)(A), as noted previously,[801] bars discrimination based on nationality in the issuance of immigrant visas, the Court found the section did not limit the president's authority to block the immigration of nationals of specified countries. According to the Court, the president's action was a determination of admissibility of noncitizens for immigration to the United States and not, once that determination was made, to the allocation of immigrant visas, which was the focus of Section 202(a)(1)(A).[802] The Court also did not regard the proclamation as violating the Establishment Clause.[803]

In 2020, in view of a national emergency declared concerning the COVID-19 pandemic,[804] President Trump issued proclamations suspending entry of virtually all immigrants, without regard to their country of origin, subject to certain exceptions.[805] The stated reasons did not directly concern the health and safety of U.S. residents, but rather concerned the need to conserve Department of State resources for providing services to U.S. citizens abroad and to control any excess supply of labor that might inhibit economic recovery following the pandemic.[806]

---

families, other than lawful permanent residents and noncitizens who already possessed visas). In 2018, the president removed Chad from the list. Proclamation No. 9723, 83 Fed. Reg. 15,937 (Apr. 10, 2018). In 2020, the president expanded the coverage to include six more countries—of which three were predominantly Muslim (Kyrgyzstan, Nigeria, and Sudan)—on public safety or national security grounds, but the restrictions were tailored to each country and did not apply to nonimmigrant groups. Proclamation No. 9983, 85 Fed. Reg. 6699 (Jan. 31, 2020).

[799] 138 S. Ct. 2392 (2018). For the lower court decisions on this executive proclamation, see *supra* this chapter note 177.

[800] *See id.* at 2408. For discussion of this case in relation to Korematsu v. United States, 323 U.S. 214 (1944), see Chapter 1 § III.

[801] *See supra* note 792 and accompanying text.

[802] *See Trump v. Hawaii*, 138 S. Ct. at 2414–15 (finding that the determination of "the universe of aliens who are admissible to the United States" operates in a different sphere than "the allocation of immigrant visas," which occurs after the determination is reached). As the Court noted, prior presidents have also determined that noncitizens from certain countries were not admissible for immigration. *See, e.g.*, Proclamation No. 5517, 51 Fed. Reg. 30470 (1986) (barring immigration by Cuban nationals); Exec. Order No. 12,172, 3 C.F.R. 461 (1979), as amended by Exec. Order No. 12,206, 3 C.F.R. 249 (1980) (barring immigration by Iranian nationals).

[803] *See supra* this chapter § II(A)(2).

[804] In March 2020, President Trump declared that the COVID-19 outbreak in the United States constituted a national emergency. *See* Proclamation No. 9994, 85 Fed. Reg. 15,337 (Mar. 13, 2020).

[805] Proclamation No. 10014, § 1, 85 Fed. Reg. 23,441 (Apr. 22, 2020) ("Suspension of Entry of Immigrants Who Present a Risk to the U.S. Labor Market During the Economic Recovery Following the 2019 Novel Coronavirus Outbreak"); Proclamation No. 10052, 85 Fed. Reg. 38,263 (June 22, 2020) ("Suspension of Entry of Immigrants and Nonimmigrants Who Present a Risk to the United States Labor Market During the Economic Recovery Following the 2019 Novel Coronavirus Outbreak"). Among the exceptions were those for lawful permanent residents, medical personnel, and spouses of U.S. citizens. *See* Proclamation No. 10014, *supra* § 2.

[806] Proclamation No. 10014, *supra* note 805.

President Biden subsequently lifted the suspension, while noting (as is typical) that the new proclamation did not create any rights or benefits enforceable against the United States.[807]

3. Refugees and Asylum Seekers

Certain individuals seeking to immigrate to the United States maintain that they merit special consideration as "refugees" or persons seeking "asylum." Prior to attaining that status, however, such individuals go through an entirely different procedure from other immigrants and in the process receive meaningfully different protections. If successful in being granted asylum or refugee status, the individuals become lawful permanent residents and thereafter can become naturalized U.S. citizens.

a. Refugees

The Refugee Act of 1980 established the current procedures for admission to the United States of refugees, and for their resettlement and absorption, by amending the INA and the Migration and Refugee Assistance Act of 1962.[808] As amended, the INA defines a "refugee" as any "person who is outside any country of such person's nationality" and who is "unable or unwilling to return to, and is unable or unwilling to avail himself or herself of the protection of, that country because of persecution or a well-founded fear of persecution on account of race, religion, nationality, membership in a particular social group, or political opinion."[809]

Under the statute, the president, in consultation with Congress, decides on the total number of refugees that the United States will admit annually.[810] Persons who apply for admission to the United States as refugees undergo a screening by the U.S. Customs and Immigration Service (USCIS).[811] In conducting such screening, the highest priority normally is given to persons identified as potentially eligible by a U.S. embassy, by the U.N. High Commissioner for Refugees, or by nongovernmental organizations.[812] Priority is also given to persons coming from groups of "special concern" that have been identified by the Department of State, such as a persecuted minority in a particular country.[813] To be admitted

---

[807] Proclamation No. 10149, 86 Fed. Reg. 11,847 (Feb. 24, 2021).

[808] Refugee Act of 1980, Pub. L. No. 96-212, 94 Stat. 102 (1980) (codified in scattered sections of 8 U.S.C. and 22 U.S.C. § 2601 (2018)); Migration and Refugee Assistance Act of 1962, Pub. L. No. 87-510, 76 Stat. 121 (1962). For analysis of the Refugee Act of 1980, see Deborah E. Anker & Michael H. Posner, *The Forty Year Crisis: A Legislative History of the Refugee Act of 1980*, 19 SAN DIEGO L. REV. 9 (1981); David A. Martin, *The Refugee Act of 1980: Its Past and Future*, 3 MICH. J. INT'L L. 91 (1982).

[809] INA § 101(a)(42), 8 U.S.C. § 1101(a)(42).

[810] INA § 207(a), 8 U.S.C. § 1157(a).

[811] 8 C.F.R. § 207.4 (2018).

[812] INA § 207(a)(3), 8 U.S.C. §1157(a)(3). Specific priorities can change yearly. *See, e.g., FY 2020 U.S. Refugee Admissions Program Access Categories*, U.S. DEP'T STATE, https://perma.cc/RX2K-GB2J.

[813] 8 C.F.R. § 207.5 (2018).

to the United States as a refugee, the person must prove, for that individual case, a "well-founded fear" of persecution within the meaning of the statute; must not already have "firmly resettled" in any other country; and must not be inadmissible on grounds such as health, criminal activity, or security.[814] The decision on whether to admit falls within the discretion of the attorney general or a designee.[815] Once admitted to the United States, the U.S. Office of Refugee Resettlement (of the Department of Health and Human Services) and the Bureau of Population, Refugees, and Migration (of the Department of State) provide resources for refugees to resettle, receive job training, and become economically self-sufficient.[816]

The INA definition of "refugee" is based on the definition found in the 1951 U.N. Convention on the Status of Refugees,[817] which was the first comprehensive multilateral treaty on the treatment of refugees.[818] Generally, the convention imposes obligations on states parties concerning the treatment of refugees and accords to the Office of the U.N. High Commissioner for Refugees (UNHCR) responsibilities for monitoring the convention's implementation.[819] The convention was adopted in the wake of World War II and initially applied only to individuals who fled Europe prior to 1951.[820] The convention's 1967 protocol, however, removed those geographic and temporal limitations, such that the convention now has universal coverage.[821]

The United States is not a party to the 1951 Refugee Convention. In the 1950s, various concerns, including burgeoning financial obligations relating to postwar relief activities, prompted the United States to stay out of the convention system.[822] The United States, however, did accede to the 1967 protocol to the convention,[823] which has the effect of binding the United States to the

[814] 8 U.S.C. §§ 1101(a)(42)(A), 1157(c).
[815] INA § 207(c), 8 U.S.C. § 1157(c)(1).
[816] INA §§ 411, 412, 8 U.S.C. §§ 1521, 1522.
[817] S. REP. No. 96-256, at 4 (1979), *as reprinted in* 1980 U.S.C.C.A.N. 141, 144; *see* Convention Relating to the Status of Refugees, July 28, 1951, 189 U.N.T.S. 137 (not ratified) [hereinafter Refugee Convention]. The convention defines a "refugee" as "any person who . . . owing to well-founded fear of being persecuted for reason of race, religion, nationality, membership of a particular social group or political opinion, is outside the country of his nationality and is unable or, owing to such fear, is unwilling to avail himself of the protection of that country . . . ." *Id.* art. 1(A)(2).
[818] *See generally* THE 1951 CONVENTION RELATING TO THE STATUS OF REFUGEES AND ITS 1967 PROTOCOL: A COMMENTARY (Andreas Zimmerman et al. eds., 2011); JAMES C. HATHAWAY, THE RIGHTS OF REFUGEES UNDER INTERNATIONAL LAW (2005).
[819] Refugee Convention, pmbl., Art. 35.
[820] *Id.*, art. 1(B)(I).
[821] Protocol relating to the Status of Refugees, art. 1(2), Jan. 31, 1967, 19 U.S.T. 6223, 606 U.N.T.S. 267 [hereinafter Refugee Protocol].
[822] *See* Kathryn M. Bockley, *A Historical Overview of Refugee Legislation: The Deception of Foreign Policy in the Land of Promise*, 21 N.C. J. INT'L L. & COM. REG. 253, 278 (1995).
[823] U.N. Treaty Collection, *Status of Treaties: Convention relating to the Status of Refugees*, https://perma.cc/P56K-MRU8; U.N. Treaty Collection, *Status of Treaties: Protocol relating to the Status of Refugees*, https://perma.cc/QJC8-8JU5.

convention as amended,[824] and which prompted the United States to adopt the Refugee Act of 1980.[825] As such, the negotiating history of the convention, its text and context, and post-adoption interpretation by states parties can be relevant when interpreting U.S. law in this area.[826] Further, the Supreme Court and lower federal courts have recognized that the UNHCR provides "significant guidance" in interpreting international refugee law and its incorporation into U.S. law,[827] and to that end accord weight[828] to the guidance set forth in the UNHCR's *Handbook*.[829]

b. Asylum Seekers

An asylum seeker is essentially a refugee who has already arrived in the United States or at a U.S. border or point of entry.[830] Thus, while refugees apply for admission to the United States from abroad, asylum seekers pursue admission after they have arrived at or in the United States. Unlike for refugees, there are no U.S. numerical quotas for persons granted asylum. While a person might otherwise have been denied admission to the United States as not qualifying for an

---

[824] In addition to lifting the convention's geographic and temporal limitations, the protocol binds parties to the substantive obligations of the convention and reiterates its procedural requirements. *See* Refugee Protocol, *supra* note 821, arts. 1(1), 2–11.

[825] *See* Yusupov v. Attorney Gen., 518 F.3d 185, 203 (3d Cir. 2008) ("The legislative history of the Refugee Act . . . makes clear that Congress intended to protect refugees to the fullest extent of [the United States'] international obligations."); *accord* Bringas-Rodriguez v. Sessions, 850 F.3d 1051, 1060–61 (9th Cir. 2017) (en banc).

[826] *See, e.g.*, INS v. Stevic, 467 U.S. 407, 416–18 (1984) (detailing U.S. refugee law before and after the 1967 Refugee Protocol and citing the U.S. reasoning in deciding to accede to it); Garcia v. Sessions, 856 F.3d 27 (1st Cir. 2017) (citing the Refugee Convention throughout the opinion and dissent); R-S-C v. Sessions, 869 F.3d 1176, 1188–89 (10th Cir. 2017) (citing Articles 28 and 34 of the Refugee Convention in the court's reasoning).

[827] *See, e.g.*, INS v. Cardoza-Fonseca, 480 U.S. 421, 439 n.22 (1987); Mohammed v. Gonzales, 400 F.3d 785, 798 (9th Cir. 2005); *see also* Note, *American Courts and the U.N. High Commissioner for Refugees: A Need for Harmony in the Face of a Refugee Crisis*, 131 HARV. L. REV. 1399, 1419 (2018).

[828] *See, e.g.*, United States v. Aguilar, 883 F.2d 662, 680 (9th Cir. 1989) (citing the UNHCR Handbook, *infra* note 829); *see also* Status of Persons Who Emigrate for Economic Reasons Under the Refugee Act of 1980, 5 Op. O.L.C. 264, 266 (1981) (Theodore B. Olson) ("Congress was aware of the criteria articulated in [UNHCR's] Handbook when it passed the [Refugee] Act in 1980, and . . . it is [thus] appropriate to consider the guidelines in the Handbook as an aid to the construction of the Act."); Note, *supra* note 827, at 1419 (noting that "the UNHCR was already engaged in monitoring and interpretive activities at the time that the United States joined the international refugee regime by signing the [1967] Protocol").

[829] U.N. High Commissioner for Refugees (UNHCR), *Handbook on Procedures and Criteria for Determining Refugee Status and Guidelines on International Protection: Under the 1951 Convention and the 1967 Protocol Relating to the Status of Refugees*, HCR/1P/4/ENG/REV. 4 (Feb. 2019). Among other things, the *Handbook* indicates best practices for determining refugee status, and explains the various components of the definition of "refugee" set out in the 1951 convention and the 1967 protocol.

[830] INA § 208(a)(1), 8 U.S.C. § 1158(a)(1) (2018). In *Sale v. Haitian Ctrs. Council*, 509 U.S. 155 (1993), the Court found that neither the INA nor Article 33 of the Refugee Convention prohibited the president from interdicting Haitians outside U.S. territorial waters (on the high seas) and forcing them to return to Haiti, without the benefit of a hearing to determine their refugee status.

immigrant visa, an asylum seeker may apply for asylum "irrespective of such alien's status."[831]

When a noncitizen first seeks asylum, the person must have a "credible fear of persecution,"[832] which means that there is a "significant possibility" that the person could establish eligibility for asylum.[833] If successful, the noncitizen is able to enter the United States (or, if already present, to remain in the United States) for one year.[834]

During this period, the individual can apply to USCIS under INA Section 208 for permanent asylum and thereby become a lawful permanent resident.[835] To succeed, the asylum seeker has the burden of demonstrating that the standard of being a refugee is met; thus, the noncitizen must have a "well-founded fear of persecution" in the noncitizen's home country on account of race, religion, nationality, membership in a particular social group, or political opinion.[836] To establish a well-founded fear of persecution, the applicant must demonstrate that his fear is both "objectively reasonable" and "subjectively genuine."[837] Federal regulation provides that, when establishing eligibility for asylum, a "well-founded fear" requires establishing one of two things. First, individuals can establish that they suffered past persecution in their country of origin; where that is established, the person is presumed to have a well-founded fear of persecution if returned, which can only be rebutted by USCIS showing that there has been a change in circumstances in the country of origin or that the applicant could be returned to a different part of the country to avoid future persecution.[838] Even if USCIS makes such a showing, there are discretionary grounds for the relevant decision maker nevertheless granting the asylum where the "applicant has demonstrated compelling reasons for being unwilling or unable to return to the country arising out of the severity of the past persecution" or "has established that there is a reasonable possibility that he or she may suffer other serious harm upon removal to that country."[839] Second, even in the absence of past persecution, individuals can establish "[t]here is a reasonable possibility of suffering

---

831 *Id.*
832 INA § 235(b)(1)(B)(ii), 8 U.S.C. § 1225(b)(1)(B)(ii).
833 INA § 235(b)(1)(B)(v), 8 U.S.C. § 1225(b)(1)(B)(v).
834 INA § 209(a), 8 U.S.C. § 1159(a).
835 INA § 208, 8 U.S.C. § 1158.
836 INA § 208(b)(1)(B), 8 U.S.C. § 1158(b)(1)(B); *see supra* note 809 and accompanying text.
837 *See* Fisher v. INS, 79 F.3d 955, 960 (9th Cir. 1996) (en banc).
838 8 C.F.R. § 208.13(b)(1) (2021).
839 *Id.* § 208.13(b)(1)(iii); *see, e.g.*, Lal v. INS, 255 F.3d 998, 1005 n.4, 1009 (9th Cir. 2001), *opinion amended on reh'g*, 268 F.3d 1148 (9th Cir. 2001) (applying the exception where applicant "was dragged from his home under force of arms, detained, beaten and tortured with knives and cigarettes, forced to drink human urine, deprived of food and water, subjected to religious and politically-based taunts and threats, and had his home and place of worship burned"). For the origins of this humanitarian exception, see Matter of Chen, 20 I. & N. Dec. 16 (BIA 1989).

such persecution" if returned to their country.[840] Interpretation of this standard can vary; the Ninth Circuit has held that the standard is met if, "on the basis of objective circumstances personally known to him, [the noncitizen] believes that he has at least a one in ten chance of being killed."[841] In any event, the ultimate decision on whether to grant asylum is discretionary in nature and falls within the discretion of either the secretary of homeland security or the attorney general.[842] Some noncitizens are ineligible, however, such as persons who have been convicted of a particularly serious crime.[843]

A range of issues may arise in the context of an asylum proceeding. For example, various cases have considered whether the persecution at issue falls within one of the requisite categories of "race, religion, nationality, membership in a particular social group, or political opinion." In *INS v. Elias-Zacarias*,[844] a Guatemalan was approached in his home by guerrillas seeking to recruit him for military service; when he refused, the guerrillas threatened to return to kill him. The noncitizen fled to the United States and, in the course of removal proceedings, sought asylum, claiming that he had a well-founded fear of persecution based on political opinion. The Supreme Court, however, found that a guerrilla organization's attempt to recruit a person did not constitute a qualifying form of persecution, because the guerrillas were not persecuting him on account of his political opinion. In *Matter of Acosta*,[845] a Salvadorian taxi driver was threatened by a guerrilla group with violence if he did not participate in disruptive transportation stoppages, so he fled to the United States, seeking asylum for persecution based on "membership in a particular social group."[846] The Board of Immigration Appeals, however, held that a "social group" concerns an "immutable characteristic"; being a taxi driver did not qualify because the noncitizen could change professions or move to a different area of El Salvador to conduct his business.[847]

The law governing asylum may clash with other immigration initiatives undertaken by Congress or the executive branch. For example, in 2018, the Department of Justice and Department of Homeland Security jointly adopted an interim final rule that made "migrants who enter[ed] the United States in violation of 'a presidential proclamation or other presidential order suspending or

---

[840] 8 C.F.R. § 208.13(b)(2)(i)(B).

[841] Montecino v. INS, 915 F.2d 518, 520 (9th Cir. 1990); *accord* Velarde v. INS, 140 F.3d 1305, 1310 (9th Cir. 1998).

[842] INA § 208(b)(1)(A), 8 U.S.C. § 1158(b)(1)(A).

[843] INA § 208(b)(2), 8 U.S.C. § 1158(b)(2); *see* Barahona v. Garland, 993 F.3d 1024 (8th Cir. 2021) (finding that where government seeks to bar asylum relief due to prior commission of a serious crime, government bears the burden of establishing that the bar applies).

[844] 502 U.S. 478 (1992).

[845] 19 I. & N. Dec. 211 (BIA 1985).

[846] *Id.* at 216–18.

[847] *Id.* at 233–34.

limiting the entry of aliens along the southern border with Mexico' . . . ineligible for asylum."[848] President Trump then issued a proclamation that "suspend[ed] the entry of all migrants along the southern border of the United States for ninety days, except for any migrant who 'enter[ed] . . . through a port of entry.' "[849] Challenged in U.S. courts, the rule (in conjunction with the proclamation) was held to be in conflict with the INA and was thus enjoined.[850] Separately, the Public Health Service Act authorizes the director of the Centers for Disease Control and Prevention (CDC) to suspend the admission of persons into the United States when the director determines that the existence of a communicable disease in a foreign country or place creates a serious danger of the introduction of such disease into the United States.[851] That authority was invoked by the CDC in 2020 to persons traveling from Canada or Mexico (regardless of their country of origin) who would otherwise be introduced into a "congregate setting" at a land port of entry (not airports) or border patrol station at or near the U.S. borders with Canada and Mexico, subject to certain exceptions.[852] The order provided no exception for persons arriving at the border seeking asylum, raising a question as to the relationship between the Public Health Service Act and the 1980 Refugee Act.

As discussed further later, when the government has initiated removal proceedings before an immigration judge against a noncitizen in the United States, the noncitizen can seek a different form of relief, albeit one still based on a fear of persecution in the country to which he or she is to be removed.[853] When this occurs, the petition is for "withholding of removal" under INA Section 241(b)(3). Importantly, this type of relief is mandatory not discretionary, but the standard for establishing a fear of persecution in such a proceeding is higher than under INA Section 208.[854] While the individual must still demonstrate that "life or freedom would be threatened" in the foreign country "because of the alien's race, religion, nationality, membership in a particular social group,

---

[848] East Bay Sanctuary Covenant v. Trump, 950 F.3d 1242, 1259 (9th Cir. 2020) (quoting Aliens Subject to a Bar on Entry Under Certain Presidential Proclamations; Procedures for Protection Claims, 83 Fed. Reg. 55,934, 55,952 (Nov. 9, 2018)).

[849] Id. at 1259–60 (quoting Proclamation No. 9822, 83 Fed. Reg. 57,661, 57,663 (Nov. 9, 2018)).

[850] Id. at 1284, amended sub nom. East Bay Sanctuary Covenant v. Biden, 993 F.3d 640 (9th Cir. 2021).

[851] Public Health Service Act, §§ 362, 365, 42 U.S.C. §§ 265, 268 (2018).

[852] Notice of Order Under Sections 362 and 365 of the Public Health Service Act Suspending Introduction of Certain Persons From Countries Where a Communicable Disease Exists, 85 Fed. Reg. 17,060 (Mar. 26, 2020). The CDC subsequently extended and amended this order. See 85 Fed. Reg. 22,424 (Apr. 20, 2020) (extending to May 20, 2020); 85 Fed. Reg. 31,503 (May 26, 2020) (extending the order "until the CDC Director determines that the danger of further introduction of COVID-19 into the United States from covered aliens has ceased to be a serious danger to the public health . . .").

[853] 6 U.S.C. § 521; see infra this chapter text accompanying notes 881–885.

[854] INA § 241(b)(3)(A), 8 U.S.C. § 1231(b)(3)(A) (providing that "the Attorney General may not remove an alien to a country" in which they would face persecution).

or political opinion,"[855] the Supreme Court has interpreted this standard (which arose in a different statutory and regulatory context than INA Section 208) as meaning that "it is more likely than not that the alien would be subject to persecution" in the country if returned, and thus a better than 50 percent chance of a threat to the individual's well-being.[856] Moreover, the relief granted under this process is more limited than for a grant of asylum; it does not lead to permanent resident status for the individual (or any derivative benefits for family members) and it only precludes removal to the country of nationality, but not to third countries. Finally, the ability to secure such relief is subject to certain exceptions.[857] If the immigration judge denies the relief, the decision is then appealable within the Department of Justice's adjudicatory system, with a possible final review by the attorney general.[858]

4. Removal and Non-refoulement

Once a noncitizen is within ("admitted" to) the United States, the Office of Immigration and Customs Enforcement (ICE), part of the Department of Homeland Security, may seek to "remove" the noncitizen from the United States on grounds that the person is not lawfully present, has violated a visa, has committed a criminal offense, or for certain other reasons.[859] For example, a noncitizen may be removed if the person provided material support to a terrorist organization at any point before or during his or her presence in the United States.[860] If the noncitizen entered the United States through the normal immigration process, then such removal is sometimes referred to as "deportation" (by

---

[855] *Id.* For the individual's burden of proof, see INA § 241(b)(3)(C), 8 U.S.C. § 1231(b)(3)(C).

[856] INS v. Stevic, 467 U.S. 407, 429–30 (1984); *see* INS v. Cardoza-Fonseca, 480 U.S. 421, 449–50 (1987) (citing INA § 243(h), which was amended in 1996 by div. C, tit. III, Pub. L. No. 104-208, § 307(a) (1996) and effectively replaced by INA § 241(b)(3)(A)). In *Stevic*, the Court found that the asylum standard that applies in a removal proceeding (INA § 241(b)(3)(A)) does not apply in a nonremoval proceeding (INA § 208(a)), while in *Cardoza-Fonseca*, the Court found that the standard that applied in a nonremoval proceeding does not apply in a removal proceeding.

[857] The noncitizen can be removed if: (1) the noncitizen himself or herself participated in such persecution; (2) the noncitizen convicted of a particularly serious crime is a danger to the community; (3) there are serious reasons to believe that the noncitizen committed a serious nonpolitical crime outside the United States before arriving in the United States; or (4) there are reasonable grounds to believe that the noncitizen is a danger to U.S. security. 8 U.S.C. § 1231(b)(3)(B). On the first of these exceptions, referred to as the "persecutor bar" to receiving asylum, see Negusie v. Holder, 555 U.S. 511 (2009) (holding that while the "persecutor bar" prohibits anyone who participated in torture or persecution from receiving asylum, motivation and intent in that participation are relevant).

[858] *See* 8 C.F.R. § 1003.1(b)(9), (h) (2021).

[859] INA § 237, 8 U.S.C. § 1227 (2018); *see* Harisiades v. Shaughnessy, 342 U.S. 580 (1952). On the potency and bureaucracy of this "deportation power," see COX & RODRÍGUEZ, *supra* note 753, at 79–102.

[860] INA § 212(a)(3), 8 U.S.C. § 1182(a)(3). *See, e.g., In re* S-K-, 23 I. & N. Dec. 936 (BIA 2006); Matter of A-C-M-, 27 I. & N. Dec. 303 (BIA 2018).

contrast, removal of undocumented noncitizens is sometimes referred to as "exclusion" because they were never "admitted" to the United States).[861]

In either event, if ICE decides that a noncitizen is removable, it initiates removal proceedings for which it can apprehend and detain the noncitizen.[862] Removal proceedings then take place under INA Section 240 before an immigration judge.[863] Because removal proceedings are deemed to be civil in nature, a number of the rights protected by the Fourth, Fifth, and Sixth Amendments have been held inapplicable.[864] However, noncitizens are afforded a number of procedural protections in removal proceedings, including the right to a proceeding,[865] the right to be represented by counsel at the noncitizen's own expense,[866] the right to effective translation at the hearing,[867] and the right to provide evidence and testimony.[868] Further, the government must prove by "clear, unequivocal, and convincing evidence" that the facts alleged as grounds for removal are true.[869] Moreover, the noncitizen may be authorized by statute to seek judicial review of a final order of removal in the judicial circuit in which the removal proceedings were completed,[870] such as for lack of a fair administrative hearing.[871]

---

[861] For expedited removal of arriving noncitizens who have not been admitted into the United States, see *infra* this chapter § III(A)(5). In 1996, Congress established an Alien Terrorist Removal Court to handle prosecutions of complex national security removal cases, while protecting classified information, but this Article III court has never been utilized. *See* Aram A. Gavoor & Timothy M. Belsan, *The Forgotten FISA Court: Exploring the Inactivity of the ATRC*, 81 OHIO STATE L.J. 139 (2020).

[862] INA § 239, 8 U.S.C. § 1229; INA § 236, 8 U.S.C. § 1226; *see* Shaughnessy v. United States *ex rel.* Mezei, 345 U.S. 206, 213 (1953).

[863] INA § 240, 8 U.S.C. § 1229a.

[864] *See* Abel v. United States, 362 U.S. 217, 237 (1960) (noting the different procedural protections associated with criminal proceedings and removal proceedings); *see also id.* at 217 (holding that search and seizure and use of evidence in removal hearing cannot violate Fourth or Fifth Amendments); INS v. Lopez-Mendoza, 468 U.S. 1032, 1038 (1984) (holding that the exclusionary rule of the Fourth Amendment did not apply in a deportation hearing because it "is a purely civil action to determine eligibility to remain in this country, not to punish an unlawful entry"). The Sixth Amendment's guarantee of effective assistance of counsel, however, requires that in criminal proceedings against noncitizens, their counsel communicate to them the immigration-related consequences of a conviction, including advising them whether a guilty plea may result in removal. Padilla v. Kentucky, 559 U.S. 356 (2010). For an argument that a removal proceeding should not be viewed as solely civil (or criminal) in nature but rather is a unique type of proceeding that should attract a range of constitutional rights, see Peter L. Markowitz, *Deportation Is Different*, 13 U. PA. J. CONST. L. 1299 (2011).

[865] INA § 240, 8 U.S.C. § 1229a(a); *see, e.g.*, Kwong Hai Chew v. Colding, 344 U.S. 590, 598 (1953) (noting that once an alien has been admitted to lawful residence, "not even Congress may expel him without allowing him a fair opportunity to be heard").

[866] INA § 240(b)(4)(A), 8 U.S.C. § 1229a(b)(4)(A).

[867] Augustin v. Sava, 735 F.2d 32 (2d Cir. 1984); Gonzalez v. Zurbrick, 45 F.2d 934 (6th Cir. 1930).

[868] INA § 240(b)(4)(B), 8 U.S.C. § 1229a(b)(4)(B); 8 C.F.R. § 1240.7 (2018).

[869] Woodby v. INS, 385 U.S. 276, 282–86 (1966).

[870] INA § 242(b)(2), 8 U.S.C. § 1252. In order to be reviewable, the removal order needs to be administratively final, meaning all administrative remedies have been exhausted, and the petition is then filed within thirty days. INA §§ 242(a)(1), (b).

[871] *See* Wong Yang Sung v. McGrath, 339 U.S. 33, 50 (1950); U.S. *ex rel.* Vajtauer v. Comm'r of Immigration, 273 U.S. 103, 106 (1927).

Thus, as contrasted with rights possessed by noncitizens not yet admitted to the United States, these proceedings afford noncitizens considerable due process rights. Further, these rights may be buttressed by judicial sensitivity to the potentially grave consequences of removal in construing governmental authority. The Supreme Court has resolved statutory ambiguity in favor of the applicant, given that removal "is a drastic measure and at times the equivalent of banishment or exile," and that "since the stakes are considerable for the individual, we will not assume that Congress meant to trench on his freedom beyond that which is required by the narrowest of several possible meanings of the words used."[872]

If a noncitizen has been convicted of certain specified crimes, that person must be detained during the removal proceedings,[873] given the concern that the noncitizen may continue to engage in crime and fail to appear for their removal hearings. Such "mandatory detention," even if prolonged (and to a degree that would be impermissible were it visited upon citizens) is constitutionally permissible for the duration of the noncitizen's removal proceedings.[874] Once a final removal order is issued, the noncitizen may continue to be detained for a ninety-day period,[875] and thereafter may be detained only for such time as is reasonably necessary to secure the removal.[876]

In the course of challenging removal, the noncitizen may request one or more types of relief. For example, the noncitizen might request voluntary departure, by which the noncitizen departs at the noncitizen's own expense, avoiding the stigma of formal removal;[877] cancellation of removal, which is available to certain lawful permanent residents and other noncitizen residents, based on the length of their presence in the United States and other factors;[878] or adjustment of status from nonimmigrant to lawful permanent resident.[879]

Two recurrent forms of relief from removal relate to the international law principle of *non-refoulement*, whereby a state is obligated not to return a person

---

[872] Fong Haw Tan v. Phelan, 333 U.S. 6, 10 (1948) (finding that a statute, which provides that "[a]n alien who is 'sentenced more than once' to imprisonment for a term of one year or more because of conviction of a crime involving moral turpitude committed after entry shall" be removed, does not apply to an alien who, in a single trial, has been convicted on two different counts of a single indictment); *accord* INS v. Errico, 385 U.S. 214, 225 (1966).

[873] INA § 236(c), 8 U.S.C. § 1226(c).

[874] Demore v. Kim, 538 U.S. 510 (2003).

[875] INA § 241(a)(6), 8 U.S.C. § 1231(a)(6).

[876] Zadvydas v. Davis, 533 U.S. 678 (2001). The same applies with respect to noncitizens who have not yet been admitted to the United States. *See* INA § 241(a)(1)(A), 8 U.S.C. § 1231(a)(1)(A); Clark v. Suarez Martinez, 543 U.S. 371 (2005).

[877] INA § 240B, 8 U.S.C. § 1229c.

[878] INA § 240A(a), 8 U.S.C. § 1229(b). Cancellation of removal is precluded if the lawful permanent resident, during the initial seven years of U.S. residency, commits certain offenses, *see* 8 U.S.C. § 1182(a)(2), even if the conviction occurred after that period. *See* Barton v. Barr, 140 S. Ct. 1442 (2020).

[879] INA § 245, 8 U.S.C. § 1255.

to another state in certain circumstances. First, as previously noted,[880] a noncitizen placed in a removal proceeding can petition for "withholding of removal" under INA Section 241(b)(3) if, by returning the individual to their country of origin, "the alien's life or freedom would be threatened in that country because of the alien's race, religion, nationality, membership in a particular social group, or political opinion."[881] The Supreme Court has interpreted this standard as meaning that "it is more likely than not that the alien would be subject to persecution" if returned.[882] This form of relief derives from the U.S. obligation of *non-refoulement* that arises under Article 33(1) of the 1951 Convention on Refugees, which states: "No Contracting State shall expel or return ('refouler') a refugee in any manner whatsoever to the frontiers of territories where his life or freedom would be threatened on account of his race, religion, nationality, membership of a particular social group or political opinion."[883] Given that the Convention on Refugees (and its protocol) defines "refugee" as someone who has a "well-founded fear" of such persecution, and given that proving a well-founded fear is less demanding than proving that persecution is "more likely than not," it was argued after the adoption of the Refugee Act of 1980 that the United States should adopt the lower standard for removal proceedings. Yet the Supreme Court in *INS v. Stevic* found that the political branches, when deciding to accede to the 1967 protocol, regarded existing U.S. law on removal (which used the "more likely than not" standard in removal proceedings) as consistent with the requirements of the protocol.[884] Further, while the standard for admitting a refugee to the United States may be tied to the definition of "refugee," the Court found that the standard for removal associated with Article 31(1) is not.[885] And to be clear, individuals stopped by U.S. authorities *outside* the United States, such as on the high seas, do not benefit from these protections; the Court in *Sale v. Haitian Centers Council, Inc.* determined that neither the INA nor Article 33 called for extraterritorial application, but rather indicated protections only once the individuals are within in the United States.[886]

---

[880] *See supra* this chapter text accompanying notes 853–858.

[881] INA § 241(b)(3)(A), 8 U.S.C. § 1231(b)(3)(A).

[882] *See supra* note 856 and accompanying text.

[883] Refugee Convention, *supra* note 817, art. 33(1). The same article establishes certain narrow exceptions, by providing that the protection may not "be claimed by a refugee whom there are reasonable grounds for regarding as a danger to the security of the country in which he is, or who, having been convicted by a final judgement of a particularly serious crime, constitutes a danger to the community." *Id.*, art. 33(2).

[884] 467 U.S. 407, 417–18 (1984).

[885] *Id.* at 424–30.

[886] Sale v. Haitian Ctrs. Council, Inc., 509 U.S. 155 (1993); *see* Harold Hongju Koh & Michael J. Wishnie, *The Story of* Sale v. Haitian Centers Council: *Guantánamo and Refoulement, in* HUMAN RIGHTS ADVOCACY STORIES 385 (Deena R. Hurwitz & Margaret L. Satterthwaite eds., 2009); Harold Hongju Koh, *The Enduring Legacies of the Haitian Refugee Litigation*, 61 N.Y.L. SCH. L. REV. 31 (2016–2017). On how presidents have managed migration crises, large and small, see COX & RODRÍGUEZ, *supra* note 753, at 47–78.

Second, a noncitizen placed in a removal proceeding can petition for "withholding of removal" if it is more likely than not that the individual will be tortured in the proposed country of removal. This form of relief derives from the U.S. obligation of *non-refoulement* that arises under the 1984 Convention against Torture and Other Cruel, Inhuman or Degrading Treatment or Punishment.[887] Article 3 of the convention provides: "No State Party shall expel, return ('refouler') or extradite a person to another State where there are substantial grounds for believing that he would be in danger of being subjected to torture."[888] When ratifying the convention, the United States lodged an "understanding" that "the phrase 'where there are substantial grounds for believing that he would be in danger of being subjected to torture,' as used in Article 3 of the convention, [means] 'if it is more likely than not that he would be tortured.'"[889] Thus, the U.S. understanding sought to clarify that existing U.S. law on removal was in harmony with the Article 3 obligation. Congress implemented the U.S. obligation under Article 3 through a portion of the Foreign Affairs Reform and Restructuring Act,[890] which in turn is implemented by regulation.[891] A range of cases have interpreted such rules.[892]

A further form of relief may be available that is unrelated to a U.S. treaty obligation. In the Immigration Act of 1990,[893] Congress created a "temporary protected status" (TPS) for nonimmigrants who are already in the United States, allowing them to remain temporarily, if there is a compelling humanitarian reason for doing so.[894] The noncitizen must be a national of a country that has received a TPS designation from the secretary of homeland security, which is typically issued due to an ongoing armed conflict, an environmental disaster, or other extraordinary but temporary conditions in the country.[895] During a designated period, the TPS holder is not removable from the United States, is not detainable by the Department of Homeland Security on the basis of immigration

---

[887] Convention against Torture, *supra* note 77.

[888] *Id.*, art. 3(1).

[889] For the U.S. reservations, declarations, and understandings to the convention, see 136 CONG. REC. 36,192-93 (1990), or see U.N. Treaty Collection, *Status of Treaties: Convention against Torture and Other Cruel, Inhuman or Degrading Treatment or Punishment*, https://perma.cc/YF67-8ZCW.

[890] Foreign Affairs Reform and Restructuring Act, div. B, title XXII, Pub. L. No. 105-277, § 2242, 112 Stat. 2681-822 (1998) (codified at 8 U.S.C. § 1231 note (2018)).

[891] 8 C.F.R. §§ 208.16(c), 208.18 (2018).

[892] *See, e.g.*, Nasrallah v. Barr, 140 S. Ct. 1683 (2020) (holding that the INA does not preclude judicial review over a noncitizen's factual challenges to an immigration judge's finding on the likelihood of torture, even when the noncitizen has committed a crime under 8 U.S.C. § 1252(a)(2)(C)); *see generally* Trent Buatte, *The Convention against Torture and Nonrefoulement in U.S. Courts*, 35 GEO. IMMIGR. L.J. 701 (2021) (discussing certain splits among the circuit courts and recommending greater use of the Convention drafting history and its interpretation by international bodies as a means of harmonizing divergent U.S. interpretations).

[893] Immigration Act of 1990, Pub. L. No. 101-649, § 302, 104 Stat. 4978 (Nov. 29, 1990).

[894] INA § 244, 8 U.S.C. § 1254a.

[895] *Id.* § 1254a(b)(1).

status, is eligible for an employment authorization document, and may be authorized to travel outside the United States.[896]

The INA sets forth a separate and expedited removal process for noncitizens who have not been admitted into the United States. A noncitizen arriving at the U.S. border or a port of entry must be inspected by an immigration official[897] and, unless he is found "clearly and beyond a doubt entitled to be admitted,"[898] generally undergoes an expedited removal proceeding to determine admissibility.[899] Under this expedited proceeding, INA Section 235(b)(1) provides that the noncitizen may be removed from the United States without further hearing or review, so long as the noncitizen lacks valid entry documents or has attempted to procure admission by fraud or misrepresentation.[900] Such noncitizens, however, may seek asylum based on a credible fear of persecution.[901]

5. Loss of U.S. Citizenship

The Constitution does not expressly address the circumstances under which an individual may lose U.S. citizenship. Under the INA, a U.S. citizen, whether by birth or through naturalization, can lose citizenship by expressly renouncing that citizenship or by voluntarily performing certain acts with the intention of relinquishing citizenship.[902] For example, the intention can be presumed based on acceptance of a foreign nationality that requires renunciation of U.S.

---

[896] *Id.* § 1254a(f).

[897] INA § 235(a)(3), 8 U.S.C. § 1225(a)(3).

[898] 8 U.S.C. § 1225(b)(2)(A).

[899] The Department of Homeland Security implements expedited removal for not just noncitizens at a port of entry or at a border who are seeking entry into the United States but also: (1) noncitizens who entered the United States by sea, were not admitted or paroled, and have been in the United States for less than two years; and (2) noncitizens who, within fourteen days of entering the United States, were apprehended within 100 miles of a border, and who have not been admitted or paroled. *See* HILLEL R. SMITH, CONG. RESEARCH SERV., LSB10150, IMMIGRATION LAWS REGULATING THE ADMISSION AND EXCLUSION OF ALIENS AT THE BORDER 2 (2020).

[900] INA § 235(b)(1), 8 U.S.C. § 1225(b)(1). Accompanied noncitizen children are generally treated in the same manner as adults and may be subject to expedited removal. INA § 235(b)(1)(A). Unaccompanied noncitizen children are not subject to expedited removal, but instead normally are placed in regular removal proceedings under INA Section 240, regardless of whether the child is found at the border or in the interior of the United States. INA § 240(c)(7)(C)(iv), 8 U.S.C. § 1229a(c) (7)(C)(iv). During such proceedings, the child is placed in the custody of the Department of Health and Human Services' Office of Refugee Resettlement. 6 U.S.C. § 279(b).

[901] *See supra* this chapter § III A(3)(b). For an early, favorable assessment of the expedited removal process, see David A. Martin, *Two Cheers for Expedited Removal in the New Immigration Laws*, 40 VA. J. INT'L L. 673 (2000). For a more recent, critical assessment, see Jennifer Lee Koh, *When Shadow Removals Collide: Searching for Solutions to the Legal Black Holes Created by Expedited Removal and Reinstatement*, 96 WASH. U.L. REV. 337 (2018).

[902] Those acts, which mostly require that the person be at least eighteen years old, include applying for and obtaining naturalization in a foreign country, or serving in the military of a foreign country as an officer or when the foreign state is engaged in hostilities against the United States. INA § 349, 8 U.S.C. § 1481; *see* RESTATEMENT (THIRD) § 212(3)(a).

citizenship.[903] Yet other acts, such as acquiring a foreign nationality at birth, are not a basis for presuming an intention to lose U.S. citizenship.[904] The fact of *intention to relinquish* the U.S. citizenship is central; it is not the mere performance of the aforementioned acts. Thus, an act such as bearing arms against the United States "may be highly persuasive evidence in the particular case of a purpose to abandon citizenship," but cannot be "treat[ed] . . . as conclusive evidence of the indispensable voluntary assent of the citizen."[905] Furthermore, the government must prove, by a preponderance of evidence, that the citizen both voluntarily committed the expatriating act and intended to relinquish citizenship in the process.[906]

Although not expressly addressed in the Constitution, the INA's requirement that there be an intent to relinquish citizenship is constitutionally driven. The Supreme Court first upheld, in *Perez v. Brownell*, a version of the statute that permitted revoking U.S. citizenship based on the citizen's voluntary performance of specified actions (in that instance, voting in a foreign election) without requiring any intent or desire on the person's part to lose citizenship.[907] Only nine years later, in *Afroyim v. Rusk*, the Court repudiated its earlier decision, holding that the Fourteenth Amendment's Citizenship Clause guaranteed a U.S. citizen's right to keep his citizenship; mere voting in a foreign election, as in that case, was an insufficient basis for loss of citizenship.[908] Thereafter, the INA was amended to require an intention to relinquish citizenship.[909]

U.S. citizens who have obtained citizenship through naturalization (and not by birth) can have their naturalization revoked if the naturalization was "illegally procured" or "procured by concealment of a material fact or by willful misrepresentation."[910] Famously, in *United States v. Demjanjuk*, the

---

[903] *See* Vance v. Terrazas, 444 U.S. 252 (1980). Mere naturalization in a foreign state, however, does not automatically result in loss of U.S. citizenship; to be certain, the U.S. citizen should seek and obtain a certificate of loss of nationality. *See* Farrell v. Blinken, 4 F.4th 124 (D.C. Cir. 2021).

[904] Certain reasons for denying U.S. citizenship may be unconstitutional. For example, stripping an individual of U.S. citizenship as a form of punishment, such as for deserting during wartime, is cruel and unusual punishment prohibited by the Eighth Amendment. Trop v. Dulles, 356 U.S. 86, 101–02 (1958).

[905] Vance v. Terrazas, 444 U.S. 252, 261 (1980) (quoting Nishikawa v. Dulles, 356 U.S. 129, 139 (1958) (Black, J., concurring)).

[906] *Id.* at 267; *see* INA § 349(b), 8 U.S.C. § 1481; Survey of the Law of Expatriation, 26 Op. OL.C. 56 (2002) (maintaining that "[e]xpatriating a U.S. citizen . . . on the ground that, after reaching the age of 18, the person has obtained foreign citizenship or declared allegiance to a foreign state generally will not be possible absent substantial evidence, apart from the act itself, that the individual specifically intended to relinquish U.S. citizenship").

[907] 356 U.S. 44 (1958).

[908] 387 U.S. 253 (1967); *see* Schneider v. Rusk, 377 U.S. 163 (1964) (finding three years of continuous residence by a naturalized citizen in his country of origin is an insufficient basis for loss of citizenship); Kennedy v. Mendoza-Martinez, 372 U.S. 144 (1963) (evasion of draft is insufficient).

[909] *See* Immigration and Nationality Act Amendments of 1986, Pub. L. No. 99-653, § 18, 100 Stat. 3655 (codified at 8 U.S.C. § 1481).

[910] INA § 340(a), 8 U.S.C. § 1451(a); *see* RESTATEMENT (THIRD) § 212(3)(b) & rptrs. note 4.

defendant was stripped of his U.S. citizenship based on fraudulent statements at the time of his naturalization, which failed to disclose that he served as a guard at several Nazi training and concentration camps during World War II.[911] However, such "denaturalization" may only occur if the government can satisfy with "clear, unequivocal, and convincing proof" before an Article III court that the certificate of citizenship was unlawfully or fraudulently procured.[912] Given the fundamental rights at stake, "the facts and the law should be construed as far as is reasonably possible in favor of the citizen."[913] For example, in *Schneiderman v. United States*, the Court struck down the denaturalization of a U.S. citizen based solely on the government's view that the person was not "attached to the principles of the Constitution" given his membership in the Communist Party of America.[914]

When an individual takes an oath of allegiance to the United States in order to become a naturalized citizen, the individual is required to renounce any other citizenship.[915] Yet U.S. law does not otherwise address dual nationality and thus does not require individuals who already possess U.S. citizenship to renounce a second citizenship. For example, a child born in a foreign state to U.S. citizen parents may be both a U.S. citizen and a citizen of the state of birth; likewise, an individual having U.S. citizenship at birth may naturalize at a later date in a foreign state without necessarily relinquishing U.S. citizenship. As such, U.S. citizens can possess dual nationality, thereby owing allegiance to two states, though doing so may preclude certain U.S. protections for the individual vis-à-vis the foreign state and may pose risks in the event of an armed conflict between the United States and the other state of nationality.[916]

---

[911] 367 F.3d 623 (6th Cir. 2004); *see* United States v. Daifullah, 11 F.4th 888 (8th Cir. 2021) (citizenship revoked on grounds of misrepresentations made when applying for visa and asylum concerning identity and immigration history); Fedorenko v. United States, 449 U.S. 490 (1981) (citizenship revoked from individual who willfully concealed that he had served as an armed guard at Treblinka concentration camp, where he had committed crimes against inmates). Such persons are not eligible to obtain U.S. citizenship pursuant to the Displaced Persons Act, Pub. L. No. 80-774, 62 Stat. 1009 (1948).

[912] Schneiderman v. United States, 320 U.S. 118, 125 (1943) (quoting Maxwell Land-Grant Case, 121 U.S. 325, 381 (1887)); *see* Baumgartner v. United States, 322 U.S. 665, 671 (1944).

[913] *Schneiderman*, 320 U.S. at 122.

[914] 320 U.S. 118, 135 (1943).

[915] 8 U.S.C. § 1448(a)(2); *see* Harisiades v. Shaughnessy, 342 U.S. 580, 585 (1952) ("Each has been offered naturalization, with all of the rights and privileges of citizenship, conditioned only upon open and honest assumption of undivided allegiance to our Government.").

[916] *See, e.g.,* Kawakita v. United States, 343 U.S. 717 (1952) (holding that a dual national who worked in Japan during World War II owed allegiance to the United States and could be tried for treason).

B. Transnational Family Law

Family law within the United States is principally governed by state and not federal law, but the United States is a party to certain treaties relating to family law
that have led to rights and obligations under U.S. law. Such treaties have emerged
from the work of the Hague Conference on Private International Law (Hague
Conference), an international organization based in the Netherlands, of which
the United States is a member.[917] The following addresses three areas where
Hague Conference treaties feature in U.S. law: (1) international child abduction;
(2) international adoption; and (3) international child support and maintenance
obligations.

1. International Child Abduction

The 1980 Hague Convention on the Civil Aspects of International Child
Abduction seeks to "protect children internationally from the harmful effects of
their wrongful removal or retention and to establish procedures to ensure their
prompt return to the State of their habitual residence . . . ."[918] The convention
defines what is meant by a wrongful removal or wrongful retention of a child by
reference to whether such removal or retention is in breach of "rights of custody"
attributed to a person under the law of the state in which the child was "habitually resident immediately before the removal or retention."[919] If a wrongful removal or retention has occurred, the convention obligates states parties to take
all appropriate measures, inter alia, to: "discover the whereabouts of a child who
has been wrongfully removed or retained"; "prevent further harm to the child"
by taking provisional measures; "secure the voluntary return of the child . . ."; initiate "judicial or administrative proceedings with a view to obtaining the return
of the child . . ."; and "provide such administrative arrangements as may be necessary and appropriate to secure the safe return of the child."[920] Each state party

---

[917] *See* Statute of the Hague Conference on Private International Law, Pub. L. No. 88-244, 77 Stat.
775 (1963) (codified at 22 U.S.C. § 269g (2018)). The United States has been a member of the Hague
Conference since 1964. For information on the Hague Conference, see HAGUE CONFERENCE ON
PRIVATE INTERNATIONAL LAW, https://perma.cc/LEC3-8YBN.

[918] Hague Convention on the Civil Aspects of International Child Abduction, pmbl., Oct. 25, 1980,
T.I.A.S. No. 11,670, 1343 U.N.T.S. 89 [hereinafter Hague Convention].

[919] *Id.,* art. 3(a). This standard can require a U.S. court to inquire into the rights possessed by each
parent under foreign law. *See, e.g.,* Ogawa v. Kang, 946 F.3d 1176 (10th Cir. 2020) (finding that petitioner father had not demonstrated that his child's removal from Japan, the place of the child's habitual residence, to the United States was in breach of his custody rights under the law of Japan). The
premise of the convention is "that the interests of children . . . in matters relating to their custody" are
best served when custody decisions are made in the child's country of "habitual residence." Hague
Convention, *supra* note 918, pmbl.

[920] Hague Convention, *supra* note 918, art. 7.

must designate a "central authority" to fulfill the state's obligations and to cooperate with other states parties.[921]

The convention sets forth procedures for an individual (usually a parent) to make an application for assistance in addressing wrongful removal or retention.[922] In the event of such removal or retention, the "judicial or administrative authorities of Contracting States shall act expeditiously in proceedings for the return of children" and set a period of time for explaining any delay.[923] Importantly, the convention is designed so that the court (or administrative authority) where the child is located is largely limited to determining whether the child is under the age of sixteen and has been removed from the child's habitual residence in violation of the custody rights of the left-behind parent; the court is not entrusted with reviewing on the merits the validity of those custody rights.[924] The court, however, may "request that the applicant obtain from the authorities of the State of habitual residence of the child a decision . . . that the removal or retention was wrongful . . . ."[925] Further, the court may find that specified exceptions to return exist, such as that "there is a grave risk that his or her return would expose the child to physical or psychological harm or otherwise place the child in an intolerable situation," or that "the child objects to being returned and has attained an age and degree of maturity at which it is appropriate to take account of its views."[926]

In 1988, the United States ratified the convention, which it implements by means of the International Child Abduction Remedies Act (ICARA).[927] As a general matter, ICARA sets forth the structure for U.S. hearings on these issues, including the applicable burdens of proof, relaxed rules for admissibility of documents, and guidelines for the award of fees and costs.[928] In so doing, the statute confers original jurisdiction on both state and federal courts to hear convention cases.[929] Further, the statute designates the Department of State as the

---

[921] *Id.*, art. 6; *see id.*, arts. 9–10.

[922] *Id.*, art. 8.

[923] *Id.*, arts. 11–12.

[924] *Id.*, art. 16.

[925] *Id.*, art. 15.

[926] *Id.*, art. 13; *see, e.g., In re ICJ*, 13 F.4th 753 (9th Cir. 2021) (despite allegations that father in France, the place of habitual residence, viewed child pornography and was abusive to mother, district court erred in not considering whether there were remedies available that both protect the child and permit her return to France, as required by the convention); Avendano v. Balza, 985 F.3d 8 (1st Cir. 2021) (district court did not err in determining that the mature child exception to the presumption of return to the child's country of habitual residence applied).

[927] International Child Abduction Remedies Act, Pub. L. No. 100-300, 102 Stat. 437 (1988) (codified at 22 U.S.C. §§ 9001–11 (2018)).

[928] 22 U.S.C. §§ 9003(e), 9005, 9007; *see* JAMES D. GARBOLINO, THE 1980 HAGUE CONVENTION ON THE CIVIL ASPECTS OF INTERNATIONAL CHILD ABDUCTION: A GUIDE FOR JUDGES (2d ed. 2015).

[929] 22 U.S.C. § 9003.

central authority under the convention,[930] a function that is performed by its Office of Children's Issues.

There is a substantial body of U.S. federal and state case law dealing with the convention.[931] As suggested by the preceding, two key issues in such cases are the identification of the "habitual residence" of the child and, then, who has "rights of custody" under the law of that jurisdiction. For example, in *Monasky v. Taglieri*, the Supreme Court considered the standard for determining a child's habitual residence.[932] An Italian father and U.S. mother lived in Italy, but two months after their daughter was born, the mother returned to the United States without the father's consent (alleging that the father had repeatedly assaulted her before and during her pregnancy).[933] Lower courts had previously found that a child habitually resides where the child has become "acclimatized" to her surroundings.[934] Yet, in *Monasky*, the district court found that the child was too young to have acclimatized to her surroundings, and therefore inquired into whether there was an agreement of the parents as to residence. Finding that there was a shared intent to live in Italy, the district court determined that Italy was the child's habitual residence, a finding affirmed by the Sixth Circuit.[935]

The Supreme Court, however, found that the determination of habitual residence should not turn solely on either "acclimatization" or on the existence of an agreement of the parents. Rather, a child's habitual residence depends on a fact-intensive inquiry into the entirety of the circumstances of each case, which may include those and other factors.[936] In reaching this conclusion, the Court

---

[930] *Id.* § 9006 note.

[931] *See, e.g.*, Lozano v. Montoya Alvarez, 572 U.S. 1 (2014) (finding that a one-year statute of limitation on a petition to return an abducted child under the convention remains in effect even when one parent has deliberately concealed the child's whereabouts from the other parent); Chafin v. Chafin, 568 U.S. 165 (2013) (finding that a district court may rule on a petition to return a child to the child's foreign state of residence according to the convention's articles even after the child has returned to that foreign state); Moore v. Moore, 349 P.3d 1076 (Alaska 2015) (finding the convention to be only one factor to consider in determining whether to limit visitation by a parent solely from countries that have ratified the convention); Noergaard v. Noergaard, 197 Cal. Rptr. 3d 546 (Cal. Ct. App. 2015) (finding that due process requires a trial court to consider allegations of a parent's abuse and death threats when considering the parent's demand for custody under the convention). Cases also arise relating to foreign states that are not parties to the convention, in which case issues of comity may be central. *See, e.g.*, Mohsen v. Mohsen, 5 So. 3d 218 (La. Ct. App. 1st Cir. 2008) (vacating part of trial court's judgment ordering the surrender of child's passport because Nicaragua was not party to the convention).

[932] 140 S. Ct. 719 (2020). The Court also considered the standard for reviewing a lower court's determination on appeal, finding that it is subject to a deferential, clear-error standard of review. *Id.* at 730.

[933] Domestic violence has featured in a number of cases under the convention. *See* Brenda Hale, *Taking Flight—Domestic Violence and Child Abduction*, 70 CURRENT LEGAL PROBS. 3 (2017).

[934] *See* Taglieri v. Monasky, 907 F.3d 404 (6th Cir. 2018) (quoting Robert v. Tesson, 507 F.3d 981, 992 n.4 (6th Cir. 2007)).

[935] *Id.* at 411; *see* Ahmed v. Ahmed, 867 F.3d 682 (6th Cir. 2017) (holding that, when determining a child's habitual residence, shared parental intent should be considered when the child is especially young).

[936] *Monasky*, 140 S. Ct. at 727–28.

considered ICARA,[937] the text of the convention,[938] the convention's negotiating history,[939] and in particular, the convention's interpretation by foreign courts.[940] Indeed, the Court noted that "ICARA expressly recognizes 'the need for uniform international interpretation of the convention,'"[941] and further that "the understanding that the opinions of our sister signatories to a treaty are due 'considerable weight,'... has 'special force' in Hague Convention cases."[942]

In *Abbott v. Abbott*, the issue of custodial rights was central.[943] In that case, a U.K. father and U.S. mother were divorced in Chilean courts, which awarded custody of their son to the mother and visitation rights to the father but prohibited each from removing the child from Chile without the other's consent. Nevertheless, the mother moved the child to Texas. The father requested an order from a Texas federal district court for the son to be returned pursuant to the convention, but the court declined, finding that the child's removal did not constitute a breach of the father's "rights of custody," as defined in the convention. The Supreme Court, however, found that a *ne exeat* right (a right to restrain someone from leaving a country) is a right of custody under the convention, which the father possessed, and which required application by U.S. courts under the convention and ICARA. As was the case in *Monasky*, the Court addressed the text of the convention,[944] the convention's negotiating history,[945] and its interpretation by foreign courts,[946] as well as the views of the Department of State regarding interpretation of the convention[947] and Chilean law.[948]

2. International Adoption

The 1993 Hague Convention on Protection of Children and Co-operation in Respect of Intercountry Adoption creates a transparent process for international adoptions to ensure that they proceed in a manner that serves the "best interests

---

[937] *Id.* at 727.

[938] *Id.* at 723–24, 726.

[939] *Id.* at 726–27. In particular, the Court relied upon commentary of the official reporter of the negotiating sessions that led to the adoption of the convention. *See* Elisa Pérez-Vera, 1980 Hague Child Abduction Convention, *Explanatory Report*, 3 Actes et Documents de la Quatorzième Session, 425–73 (1982) (commonly referred to as the Pérez-Vera Report).

[940] *Monasky*, 140 S. Ct. at 728. *See generally* Linda Silberman, *Interpreting the Hague Abduction Convention: In Search of a Global Jurisprudence*, 38 U.C. DAVIS L. REV. 1049 (2005).

[941] *Monasky*, 140 S. Ct. at 727 (quoting 22 U.S.C. § 9001(b)(3)(B) (2018)).

[942] *Monasky*, 140 S. Ct. at 727 (quoting El Al Israel Airlines, Ltd. v. Tsui Yuan Tseng, 525 U.S. 155, 176 (1999)); *see* Ann Laquer Estin, *Where Is the Child at Home? Determining Habitual Residence after Monasky*, 54 FAMILY L.Q. 127 (2020).

[943] 560 U.S. 1 (2010).

[944] *Id.* at 20–21.

[945] *Id.* at 19–20 (relying on the Pérez-Vera Report).

[946] *Id.* at 16–18.

[947] *Id.* at 15.

[948] *Id.* at 10; *see* Ann Laquer Estin, *The Hague Abduction Convention and the United States Supreme Court*, 48 FAMILY L.Q. 235 (2014).

of the child and with respect for his or her fundamental rights as recognised in international law."[949] The convention establishes detailed procedures for the adoption of the child,[950] so as to help safeguard against the abduction, sale, or trafficking of children.[951] Further, the convention obligates states parties to co-operate among themselves for implementing those procedures[952] and, if the adoption proceeds in accordance with such standards, to recognize the validity of the adoption.[953] The convention only applies where the child is habitually res-ident in one state party (the state of origin) and then is moved to another state party (the receiving state) by persons habitually resident in the latter, either after or for the purpose of adoption.[954] The state of origin is required to make critical determinations regarding a child's adoptability,[955] and for its part, the receiving state must make determinations regarding the suitability of a particular adop-tion.[956] To fulfill such responsibilities, each state party must designate a "central authority."[957] There is also a process for accreditation of entities to assist states in carrying out these tasks.[958]

The United States signed the convention in 1994, but only ratified it in 2007. In the course of pursuing ratification, the United States adopted the Intercountry Adoption Act of 2000.[959] The statute designates the Department of State as the central authority for purposes of the convention,[960] but then focuses principally on the process for U.S. accreditation and oversight of entities qualified to assist in such adoptions,[961] which has been the subject of litigation in U.S. courts.[962]

---

[949] *See* Convention on Protection of Children and Cooperation in Respect of Intercountry Adoption, art. 1(a), May 29, 1993, 1870 U.N.T.S. 167, S. TREATY DOC. No. 105-51 (1998).

[950] *Id.* arts. 14–22.

[951] *Id.* art. 1(b).

[952] *Id.* arts. 7, 9.

[953] *Id.* arts. 23–27.

[954] *Id.* art. 2(1).

[955] Among other things, the authorities in the state of origin must establish that the child is adopt-able; must give "due consideration" to the possibilities for placement of the child instead in the state of origin; must ensure that the persons who consent to the adoption have been counseled about the legal effects of adoption; and must ensure that such persons have given their consent freely, without being induced by compensation of any kind. *Id.* art. 4.

[956] Such determinations include "that the prospective adoptive parents are eligible and suit[able]" for the adoption, and "that the child is or will be authorized to enter and reside permanently in that State." *Id.* art. 5.

[957] *Id.* art. 6.

[958] *Id.* arts. 10–13.

[959] Intercountry Adoption Act, Pub. L. No. 106-279, 114 Stat. 825 (2000) (codified at 42 U.S.C. §§ 14901–54 (2018)). When ratifying the convention, the United States declared that its provisions were not self-executing.

[960] 42 U.S.C. § 14911(a).

[961] *Id.* §§ 14921–24.

[962] *See, e.g.,* Faith Int'l Adoptions v. Pompeo, 345 F. Supp. 3d 1314 (W.D. Wash. 2018) (enjoining the Department of State's suspension of plaintiffs' accreditation when the Council of Accreditation had deferred its decision until after the accreditation renewal had expired); Fingerson v. Dep't of Homeland Sec., 198 F. Supp. 3d 786, 793 (W.D. Ky. 2016) (granting a motion to dismiss because

The statute also provides for recognition under U.S. law of adoptions of foreign children and their immigration to the United States,[963] and for the emigration of U.S. children for adoption abroad.[964] According to the Hague Conference, for the period of 2005 to 2018, U.S. citizens adopted approximately one-half of all children adopted through the convention system.[965]

3. International Child Support and Maintenance Obligations

The 2007 Hague Convention on the International Recovery of Child Support and Other Forms of Family Maintenance seeks to guarantee international recovery of child support and family maintenance by creating a system of cooperation among states parties.[966] To that end, the convention establishes a system whereby an individual (the creditor) may submit an application to the "central authority" of the individual's state, for transmittal to a state where there is a person (the debtor) who owes (or is alleged to owe) maintenance.[967] The application might be for recognition or enforcement of an existing decision on maintenance or, where there exists no such decision, establishment of a decision in the requested state.[968] As necessary, the requested state must provide the creditor with effective access to procedures, including enforcement and appeal procedures.[969]

One of the convention's key objectives is to allocate decision-making authority among the states parties. Thus, decisions by a state in which the creditor is habitually resident may not be modified, at behest of the debtor, in any other state, at least so long as the creditor maintains its habitual residence.[970] Further, courts (or a relevant administrative authority) in the requested state are not to review the merits of an existing decision.[971] Moreover, they are obligated to recognize and enforce decisions rendered in other states parties, subject to certain limitations,[972] such as where "recognition and enforcement of the decision is manifestly incompatible with [that state's] public policy ('*ordre public*')."[973]

USCIS's classifications for a "child from a Convention country who enters the United States as a non-immigrant" are reasonable and Congress has not spoken directly on the issue).

[963] 42 U.S.C. § 14931.

[964] *Id.* § 14932.

[965] Peter Selman, *Global Statistics for Intercountry Adoption: Receiving States and States of origin 2005–2018*, HAGUE CONFERENCE ON PRIVATE INTERNATIONAL LAW, Table 1 (Dec. 20, 2019), https://perma.cc/U77B-NSDS.

[966] Hague Convention on the International Recovery of Child Support and Other Forms of Family Maintenance, Nov. 23, 2007, S. TREATY DOC. NO. 110-21 (2008), 2955 U.N.T.S. 81.

[967] *Id.* arts. 4–6, 9.

[968] *Id.* art. 10.

[969] *Id.* art. 14.

[970] *Id.* art. 18(1).

[971] *Id.* art. 28.

[972] *Id.* arts. 20, 22.

[973] *Id.* art. 22(a).

Enforcement measures may include wage withholding, garnishment from bank accounts and other sources, deductions from social security payments, or a forced sale of property.[974]

The National Conference of Commissioners on Uniform State Laws in the United States developed a model law in 2000, known as the Uniform Interstate Family Support Act (UIFSA),[975] which addresses recognition and enforcement of child support and maintenance obligations at both the interstate level within the United States and vis-à-vis foreign states. UIFSA was amended by the National Conference in 2008 to accommodate changes necessary for U.S. implementation of the convention. A federal statute was then enacted requiring all states receiving federal funds for use in enforcing child support obligations to adopt the model law as amended,[976] which they proceeded to do.[977] Thereafter, the United States ratified the convention in 2017 and now implements its obligations principally through state not federal law.

In circumstances where the foreign country is not a party to the convention, recognition and enforcement may also be available under the UIFSA based on reciprocity. Such reciprocity may arise from mutual declarations made by a U.S. authority and a foreign state; for the United States, such declarations are issued either by the Department of State or by one of the several states.[978] If reciprocity has not been established through mutual declarations, recognition and enforcement nevertheless may proceed on the basis of comity, which may require demonstrating that the foreign court had jurisdiction over the matter and that enforcement of its judgment would not offend public policy in the United States.[979]

---

[974] *Id.* art. 34.

[975] Unif. Int'l Family Support Act, 9 U.L.A. 253 (2000).

[976] Preventing Sex Trafficking and Strengthening Families Act, tit. III, Pub. L. No. 113-183, § 301(f), 128 Stat. 1943 (2014). The act amends 42 U.S.C. § 666(f) (2018) to require that "each state must have in effect the Uniform Interstate Family Support Act, as approved by the American Bar Association on Feb. 9, 1993, including any amendments officially adopted as of Sept. 30, 2008 by the National Conference of Commissioners on Uniform State Laws."

[977] *See, e.g.,* Uniform Interstate Family Support Act, N.J. STAT. ANN. §§ 2A:4-30.124-30.201 (West 2019).

[978] Personal Responsibility and Work Opportunity Reconciliation Act of 1996 (PRWORA), Pub. L. No. 104-193, § 371, 110 Stat. 2105 (1996). The statute authorizes the secretary of state, with the concurrence of the secretary of health and human services, to make federal-level declarations of reciprocity for child support establishment and enforcement. It further authorizes states to enter into their own arrangements with foreign jurisdictions that have not been declared to be foreign reciprocating countries under the act, to the extent consistent with federal law.

[979] *See, e.g.,* Country of Luxembourg *ex rel.* Ribeiro v. Canderas, 768 A.2d 283, 288–89 (N.J. Super. Ct. Ch. Div. 2000) (finding no reciprocity between Luxembourg and the United States and holding that while "principles of comity must be examined," no comity was afforded because "it would offend our public policy to enforce a judgement which is inconsistent with due process under our state and federal constitutions.").

C. Extradition

The Supreme Court has found that the power to regulate extradition is "a national power," not a power residing with the states.[980] Such power, however, is not vested solely in the executive branch; rather, extradition from the United States to another country may only proceed when authorized by a treaty or (much less commonly) a statute,[981] such as a statute relating to terrorist acts[982] or to an international criminal tribunal.[983] Given that virtually all extraditions occur on the basis of a treaty, extradition proceedings are viewed as grounded in the treaty power,[984] and the courts typically defer to the executive branch on whether an extradition treaty is in force.[985] If so, the extradition is conducted pursuant to procedures set forth in the relevant treaty and by statute.[986] Although some countries never extradite their own citizens, the United States has done so since its inception,[987] whether or not obligated by the relevant treaty to do so.[988]

---

[980] United States v. Rauscher, 119 U.S. 407, 412–14 (1886). *See generally* M. CHERIF BASSIOUNI, INTERNATIONAL EXTRADITION: UNITED STATES LAW AND PRACTICE (6th ed. 2014); RONALD J. HEDGES, INTERNATIONAL EXTRADITION: A GUIDE FOR JUDGES (2014).

[981] *See* 18 U.S.C. §§ 3181(a), 3184; Valentine v. United States *ex rel.* Neidecker, 299 U.S. 5, 8 (1936) (the power "is not confided to the Executive in the absence of treaty or legislative provision"), *partially superseded by statute*, 18 U.S.C. § 3196; Charlton v. Kelly, 229 U.S. 447, 463 (1913) (same); Grin v. Shine, 187 U.S. 181, 191 (1902) (same). Given the relevance of statutes and, even more, treaties, characterizing extradition as largely or exclusively an executive function is not accurate. *See* John T. Parry, *The Lost History of International Extradition Litigation*, 43 VA. J. INT'L L. 93, 105–24, 150–53 (2002) (demonstrating that international extradition from the United States has never been an exclusively executive function).

[982] *See* 18 U.S.C. § 3181(b) (authorizing the surrender of persons other than citizens and lawful permanent residents who commit violent acts against U.S. nationals abroad).

[983] *See, e.g.*, National Defense Authorization Act, Pub. L. No. 104-106, § 1342, 110 Stat. 186 (1996). Section 1342(a)(1) of the statute provides that the federal extradition statutes shall apply to the surrender of persons by the United States to the International Criminal Tribunal for Rwanda (ICTR). In *Ntakirutimana v. Reno*, 184 F.3d 419 (5th Cir. 1999), the Fifth Circuit found that there was no constitutional requirement that a treaty exist for extradition and that it was sufficient that Congress had conferred authority on the president to surrender fugitives to the ICTR.

[984] U.S. CONST. art. II, § 2.

[985] *See, e.g.*, Arias Leiva v. Warden, 928 F.3d 1281, 1283–84 (11th Cir. 2019) (determining that "[u]nder the separation of powers established in and demanded by our Constitution, the Judicial Branch cannot second-guess" the executive branch's determination of whether an extradition treaty remains in force); Hoxha v. Levi, 465 F.3d 554, 562 (3d Cir. 2006) (holding that the validity of an extradition treaty "is a political question" for the executive branch). *But see* Galanis v. Pallanck, 568 F.2d 234, 239 (2d Cir. 1977) (determining that "[w]hile the views of the State Department [in interpreting an extradition treaty] are entitled to respect, they are not controlling" (citation omitted)).

[986] 18 U.S.C. §§ 3181–96.

[987] *See* United States v. Robins, 27 F. Cas. 825 (D.S.C. 1799).

[988] 18 U.S.C. § 3196 ("If the applicable treaty or convention does not obligate the United States to extradite its citizens to a foreign country, the Secretary of State may, nevertheless, order the surrender to that country of a United States citizen whose extradition has been requested . . . ."); *see* Charlton v. Kelly, 229 U.S. 447, 467–69 (1913) (discussing the modern practice of some states not extraditing their own citizens, and that U.S. extradition treaties sometimes exempt citizens from its obligations and other times are silent on the matter).

A foreign state may initiate an extradition request by submitting to the Department of State those documents required by the relevant treaty, which typically would include a foreign arrest warrant and evidence establishing probable cause that the individual committed the crime charged.[989] The request is then transmitted to the Department of Justice for review, and then to the U.S. attorney's office for the district where the individual is located. That office initiates an extradition proceeding before a judicial officer,[990] such as a magistrate, who issues an arrest warrant.[991] The judicial officer then conducts the hearing to determine if the individual is extraditable.[992] The hearing is not a trial on the merits of the charges; rather, the purpose is to determine whether the individual is, in fact, the person sought for extradition, to confirm that a valid treaty (or statute) exists allowing such an extradition, to determine whether the evidence is "sufficient to sustain the charge under the provisions of the" treaty or statute,[993] and to consider a limited number of defenses to extradition available to the individual. Such defenses are usually specified by the extradition treaty; as such, it is important that U.S. extradition treaties have been regarded as self-executing in U.S. law, at least in the sense that they may be invoked defensively by an individual even in the absence of a statute.[994] If there are no valid defenses, the court then certifies to the secretary of state that the extradition may occur,

---

[989] RESTATEMENT (THIRD) § 478 cmt. a.

[990] Traditionally, the judicial officer has been regarded as acting under special authority conferred by treaties or by statute to individual judges or magistrates, rather than under authority granted to courts generally. On this view, while the proceeding is in form judicial, it is "not an exercise of any part of what is technically considered the judicial power of the United States." In re Muller, 10 Op. Att'y Gen. 501, 506 (1863); see In re Kaine, 55 U.S. (14 How.) 103, 120 (1853) (Curtis, J., concurring) (finding that the authority is not based on "any part of the judicial power of the United States"); United State v. Ferreira, 54 U.S. (13 How.) 40 (1852) (same). But see CHRISTOPHER H. PYLE, EXTRADITION, POLITICS, AND HUMAN RIGHTS 301, 305 (2001) (finding the claim that extradition magistrates do not exercise the judicial power of the United States as one of the "unwarranted assumptions, fictions, delusions, and myths" of extradition law).

[991] 18 U.S.C. § 3184.

[992] 18 U.S.C. §§ 3184, 3189–90. The individual may waive the right to extradition proceedings. See U.S. Dep't of State, 7 Foreign Aff. Manual § 1631.4, https://perma.cc/X7S5-R76X. If the treaty lacks a waiver provision, however, and the foreign government insists upon formal extradition, then a request for waiver may be denied. See Blaxland v. Commonwealth Dir. of Public Prosecutions, 323 F.3d 1198 (9th Cir. 2003).

[993] 18 U.S.C. § 3184.

[994] See Johnson v. Browne, 205 U.S. 309, 317–22 (1907) (indicating that extradition treaties, generally, are self-executing); United States v. Rauscher, 119 U.S. 407, 410–11, 429–30 (1886) (same); RESTATEMENT (FOURTH) § 310 rptrs. note 1 (noting that extradition treaties have historically been treated as self-executing). The modern Supreme Court has behaved consistently, without speaking so sweepingly. In Medellín v. Texas, the Court invoked Rauscher as a case vindicating the need to interpret the particular terms of a treaty. 552 U.S. 491, 519 n.11 (2008). The decision did not appear to cast doubt on how extradition treaties, invoked defensively, would fare under its approach to non-self-execution, but separate opinions by some of the justices invoked the prior treatment of extradition treaties as seemingly inconsistent with the majority's approach. See id. at 545, 556 (Breyer, J., dissenting).

a certification that is not appealable.[995] The final decision to extradite then lies with the secretary.[996]

One type of defense sometimes raised in the hearing arises from the "dual criminality" (or "double criminality") doctrine, which requires that the conduct at issue be a crime in both the requested and requesting states. A standard provision in most extradition treaties,[997] the dual criminality doctrine serves the purpose of ensuring that the offense is serious and that a requested state will not be embarrassed by assisting in the punishment of an act that the requested state tolerates under its own law. Some U.S. extradition treaties address this doctrine by incorporating a list of offenses regarded by both parties as crimes; these lists must then be regularly updated. Modern treaties typically contain broad, catch-all clauses that simply acknowledge the principle, leaving it to the requested state to determine whether the principle is satisfied with regards to a particular request. In any event, an individual in the United States seeking to avoid extradition may seek to argue that the offense charged is not a serious offense prohibited in both the United States and the requesting state.[998] Likewise, an individual extradited to the United States from another state may also invoke the doctrine as a basis for setting aside a U.S. conviction.[999] Courts have accorded weight to the view of the executive branch on whether a crime is covered by a treaty, but have also engaged in their own review of the treaty.[1000]

---

[995] The individual, however, can pursue a writ of habeas corpus before a federal district court, but the scope of the court's review is limited to determining whether: (1) the judge reviewing the extradition request has jurisdiction; (2) whether the offense charged falls within the extradition treaty; and (3) whether probable cause exists to believe the accused was guilty of the underlying offense. *See* Fernandez v. Phillips, 268 U.S. 311, 312 (1925). For example, the district court cannot inquire into whether the foreign state complied with its own law, including on statute of limitations, when pursuing the extradition. *See* Skaftouros v. United States, 667 F.3d 144 (2d Cir. 2011). It is expected that other types of challenges will be brought instead in the foreign jurisdiction.

[996] 18 U.S.C. § 3186; *see, e.g., In re* United States, 713 F.2d 105, 109 (5th Cir. 1983) ("[T]he court lacked the authority to order final extradition; [this] could only be accomplished by the Secretary of State."); Shapiro v. Sec'y of State, 499 F.2d 527, 531 (D.C. Cir. 1974) ("[E]xtradition is ordinarily a matter within the exclusive purview of the Executive."), *aff'd sub nom.* Comm'r v. Shapiro, 424 U.S. 614 (1976).

[997] *See* United States v. Lui Kin-Hong, 110 F.3d 103, 114 (1st Cir. 1997).

[998] One district court, however, found that "exhaustive research discloses precious few cases in which a federal court held there was not dual criminality." *In re* Zhenly Ye Gon, 768 F. Supp. 2d 69, 82 (D.D.C. 2011).

[999] *See, e.g.,* United States v. Khan, 993 F.2d 1368, 1372–73 (9th Cir. 1993) (setting aside a U.S. conviction for the use of a telephone to facilitate the commission of a drug felony, given that use of a telephone during the commission of a drug offense is not a crime in Pakistan, which had extradited the defendant to the United States).

[1000] *See, e.g., In re* Salazar, No. 09MJ2545-BLM, 2010 WL 2925444, at *4 (S.D. Cal. July 23, 2010) (finding that government's "uncontested opinion" that "the offense for which extradition is sought is punishable in accordance with the laws of both contracting parties" provides "substantial evidence of extraditability," but also conducting its own review of the treaty (quoting Amended Complaint, ECF. No. 4, Ex. 1)). Such according of weight appears to be anchored in the deference given to the executive with respect to the interpretation of treaties. *See, e.g.,* Kolovrat v. Oregon, 366 U.S. 187, 194 (1961) (stating that "[w]hile courts interpret treaties for themselves, the meaning given

A second type of defense arises for extradition treaties that do not allow extradition for "political offenses," meaning an offense that has been pursued by a foreign state to achieve political goals. The reason for the "political offense exception" is that the requesting state may have charged the individual with a crime, such as treason, sedition, or espionage, and yet the individual's conduct was motivated by an intent to achieve political change, such as through protest or even violent acts.[1001] For example, in *Ornelas v. Ruiz*, Mexico sought U.S. extradition of an individual for murder, arson, robbery, and kidnapping that was allegedly committed as part of a raid on a village in Mexico at a time when revolutionary activity was occurring.[1002] In allowing the extradition, the Court indicated that it was proper to look at various aspects of the raid: "the character of the foray, the mode of attack, the persons killed or captured, and the kind of property taken or destroyed."[1003] In this instance, the Court was unwilling to set aside a determination that, although the raid may have been contemporaneous with a revolutionary uprising, it was essentially unrelated, and thus not of a political character.[1004] Under the influence of *Ornelas*, U.S. courts have generally looked to satisfy two factors (sometimes called the "incidence" test): (1) that the conduct at issue occurred during a political revolt, disturbance, or uprising involving a certain level of violence;[1005] and, if so, (2) that the conduct was incidental to that revolt, disturbance, or uprising in seeking to accomplish associated political change.[1006] The test, however, appears malleable, not the least in determining the requisite level of violence that is suggestive of political activity. In *United States v. Pitawanakwat*, a member of an Indigenous group defending native lands discharged a weapon at a police helicopter during the occupation of private property in Canada.[1007] When Canada sought extradition of the individual from the United States, the district court found the conduct to be a non-extraditable

---

them by the departments of government particularly charged with their negotiation and enforcement is given great weight"); *see also* Chapter 6 § III(B)(1).

[1001] *See* Quinn v. Robinson, 783 F.2d 776 (9th Cir. 1986). For criticism of the rule, see Barbara Ann Banoff & Christopher H. Pyle, *"To Surrender Political Offenders"; The Political Offense Exception to Extradition in United States Law*, 16 N.Y.U. J. INT'L & POL. 169, 172 (1984); Miriam Sapiro, Note, *Extradition in an Era of Terrorism: The Need to Abolish the Political Offense Exception*, 61 N.Y.U. L. REV. 654, 692 (1986).

[1002] 161 U.S. 502, 510 (1896).

[1003] *Id.* at 511.

[1004] *Id.* at 512.

[1005] *See, e.g.*, Quinn v. Robinson, 783 F.2d 776, 806–07 (9th Cir. 1986) (indicating that the political offense exception is "applicable only when a certain level of violence exists and when those engaged in that violence are seeking to accomplish a particular objective"); Jimenez v. Aristeguieta, 311 F.2d 547, 560 (5th Cir. 1962) (indicating that there must exist "a revolutionary uprising or other violent political disturbance").

[1006] *See, e.g.*, *Quinn*, 783 F.2d at 809 (holding "that there [must] be a nexus between the act and the uprising").

[1007] 120 F. Supp. 2d 921 (D. Or. 2000).

political offense, because it was "part of a broader protest in 1995 aimed at the Canadian government in support of sovereignty by the native people over their land."[1008] Further, determining whether the conduct incidental to that violence seeks "political" change may be difficult, especially when the conduct is only tangentially connected to political opposition.[1009]

A third type of defense arises when the alleged offender argues that, if extradition occurs, there is a substantial likelihood of mistreatment of the individual or of an unfair trial in the requesting state. Under the "rule of non-inquiry,"[1010] the court determining whether a defendant is extraditable may *not* examine the requesting state's criminal justice system, including taking into account evidence that the individual was tried in absentia,[1011] will be exposed to physical danger[1012] or double jeopardy,[1013] will be tried using illegally obtained

---

[1008] *Id.* at 938.

[1009] *See, e.g.,* Nezirovic v. Holt, 779 F.3d 233 (4th Cir. 2015) (finding that the alleged conduct of war crimes was not subjectively motivated by a political aim, and that the offenses were not political in nature when viewed objectively); Koskotas v. Roche, 931 F.2d 169, 172 (1st Cir. 1991) (allegations of financial fraud and political corruption that have just some connection to political opposition do not qualify as political offenses); Ahmad v. Wigen, 910 F.2d 1063 (2d Cir. 1990) (an attack on a commercial bus full of innocent civilians was not a political offense despite the existence of a political motivation); *see also* Barapind v. Enomoto, 400 F.3d 744, 751 (9th Cir. 2005) (finding that the individual bears the burden of proving the nexus between the crime underlying the extradition request and the alleged political activity); David M. Lieberman, Note, *Sorting the Revolutionary from the Terrorist: The Delicate Application of the "Political Offense" Exception in U.S. Extradition Cases,* 59 STAN. L. REV. 181 (2006).

[1010] The rule originated in *Neely v. Henkel,* which found that when a U.S. citizen commits a crime in another country, "he cannot complain if required to submit to such modes of trial and to such punishment as the laws of that country may prescribe for its own people, unless a different mode be provided for by treaty stipulations between that country and the United States." 180 U.S. 109, 123 (1901). For analysis and defense of the rule, see Jacques Semmelman, *Federal Courts, the Constitution, and the Rule of Non-Inquiry in International Extradition Proceedings,* 76 CORNELL L. REV. 1198 (1991). For criticism of the rule, including in the context of the emergence of human rights treaties to which the United States is a party, see John T. Parry, *International Extradition, the Rule of Non-Inquiry, and the Problem of Sovereignty,* 90 BOSTON U. L. REV. 1973 (2010); John Quigley, *The Rule of Non-Inquiry and Human Rights Treaties,* 45 CATH. U. L. REV. 1213 (1996); 2 VED P. NANDA & DAVID K. PANSIUS, LITIGATION OF INTERNATIONAL DISPUTES IN U.S. COURTS § 10:21 (2d ed. 2013).

[1011] *See, e.g.,* Gallina v. Fraser, 278 F.2d 77, 78–79 (2d Cir. 1960) (finding that the rule prevents inquiry into the foreign procedures awaiting the defendant upon extradition, including a conviction in absentia).

[1012] *See, e.g.,* Hoxha v. Levi, 465 F.3d 554, 563–64 (3d Cir. 2006) (using non-inquiry doctrine to dismiss a claim of potential torture and extrajudicial killing). The Foreign Affairs Reform and Restructuring Act of 1998 (FARRA), Pub. L. No. 105-277, § 2242, 112 Stat. 2681-822 (codified at 8 U.S.C. § 1231 note (2018)) provides that the United States will not extradite "any person to a country in which there are substantial grounds for believing the person would be in danger of being subject to torture." To the extent that defenses to extradition have been brought in U.S. court on the basis of torture by the requesting state if extradited, courts have viewed the matter as premature, as no final agency decision had yet been reached on whether to extradite. *See, e.g., Hoxha,* 465 F.3d at 564–65; Cornejo-Barreto v. Siefert, 218 F.3d 1004, 1016 (9th Cir. 2000), *rev'd,* 379 F.3d 1075 (9th Cir. 2004), *vacated as moot,* 389 F.3d 1307 (9th Cir. 2004). Whether such a challenge may be brought after a decision of the secretary of state to extradite is not fully settled, but some courts have conducted such a review. *See* Trinidad y Garcia v. Thomas, 683 F.3d 952, 957 (9th Cir. 2012) (en banc) (per curiam); Prasoprat v. Benov, 622 F. Supp. 2d 980, 983–88 (C.D. Cal. 2009).

[1013] *See, e.g., In re* Ryan, 360 F. Supp. 270, 274 (E.D.N.Y. 1973), *aff'd,* 478 F.2d 1397 (2d Cir. 1973).

evidence,[1014] or other due process concerns in the foreign court.[1015] In *Munaf v. Geren*, for example, the Supreme Court relied upon the rule when considering the transfer in Iraq of two U.S. citizens from U.S. military custody to Iraqi custody, stating that "it is for the political branches, not the Judiciary, to assess practices in foreign countries and to determine national policy in light of those assessments."[1016] Thus, the alleged offender may seek relief on such bases only from the secretary of state, who ultimately has the discretion to deny the extradition request. Serving in such a role, the secretary may condition extradition upon assurances from the requesting state that the individual will be treated properly and receive a fair trial.[1017]

When a U.S. prosecutor at the state or federal level seeks extradition to the United States of an offender located abroad, the prosecutor must obtain an arrest warrant from a U.S. court under a statute that allows extradition when there "is a treaty or convention for extradition between the United States and any foreign government . . . ."[1018] An extradition request is then transmitted through the Department of Justice and Department of State to the foreign government in whose territory the offender is located. The extradition then moves forward under the processes set forth in the extradition treaty; if the alleged crime was committed abroad, then venue in the United States "shall be in the district in which the offender . . . is arrested or is first brought."[1019] Once the alleged offender arrives in the United States, a defense sometimes raised in U.S. court concerns the "rule of specialty," which requires that alleged offenders only be tried for the crime for which they were extradited. Thus, if the extradition request was for a charge of murder, but the individual is later tried for some other offense, the individual may raise as a defense that a trial may not proceed on the basis of any charge other than murder.[1020] U.S. courts of appeals have split, however, on whether the alleged *offender* may raise the rule of specialty as a defense, as opposed to the state from which the offender was extradited.[1021] Although

---

[1014] *See, e.g.*, Magisano v. Locke, 545 F.2d 1228, 1230 (9th Cir. 1976).

[1015] *See, e.g.*, Basso v. Pharo, 278 Fed. Appx. 886, 887 (11th Cir. 2008) (declining to consider the individual's "assertion that he would be subjected to due process violations if extradited.").

[1016] 553 U.S. 674, 700–01(2008).

[1017] *See, e.g.*, Emami v. District Court, 834 F.2d 1444, 1454 (9th Cir. 1987) ("[T]he State Department alone has the power to condition the extradition of Emami on an agreement with Germany not to deport Emami to Iran."); Demjanjuk v. Petrovsky, 776 F.2d 571, 584 (6th Cir. 1985) ("A decision to attach conditions to an order of extradition is within the discretion of the Secretary of State . . . ."); *see also* RESTATEMENT (THIRD) § 478 cmt. d.

[1018] 18 U.S.C. § 3184 (2018); *see* RESTATEMENT (FOURTH) § 312.

[1019] 18 U.S.C. § 3238; *see* United States v. Ghanem, 993 F.3d 1113 (9th Cir. 2021) (person arrested in Greece and extradited to the United States, who arrived first in New York for a connecting flight, must be tried there and not in California).

[1020] United States v. Rauscher, 119 U.S. 407 (1886).

[1021] The Second and Eleventh Circuits permit standing for the individual to raise the defense. *See* United States v. Baez, 349 F.3d 90, 93 (2d Cir. 2003); United States v. Puentes, 50 F.3d 1567, 1572 & n.2 (11th Cir. 1995) ("We hold that a criminal defendant has standing to allege a violation of the principle

less common, an individual being extradited by the United States to a requesting state may also raise the rule of specialty in U.S. extradition proceedings, if the offense charged in the foreign state is not the offense contained in the extradition request.[1022]

Given that the death penalty is available in certain U.S. jurisdictions, foreign states where such a penalty is impermissible may refuse their extradition requests for capital crimes, absent an express assurance or agreement that a capital sentence will not be pursued or imposed. Thus, in *Soering v. United Kingdom*, the European Court of Human Rights found that the United Kingdom could not extradite a German national to the United States on murder charges in Virginia unless the relevant authorities agreed that he would not be exposed to the death penalty.[1023] Thereafter, such agreement was reached and the individual was extradited from the United Kingdom, tried in Virginia, and sentenced to life imprisonment.[1024]

of specialty. We limit, however, the defendant's challenges under the principle of specialty to only those objections that the rendering country might have brought."). Several other circuits, however, do not view the individual as having standing to raise the defense. *See* United States *ex rel.* Saroop v. Garcia, 109 F.3d 165, 168 (3d Cir. 1997); United States v. Van Cauwenberghe, 827 F.2d 424 (9th Cir. 1987); *Demjanjuk*, 776 F.2d at 583–84; *In re* Extradition of Hurtado, No. EP-13-MC-00166-ATB, 2013 WL 4515939, at *3 (W.D. Tex. Aug. 21, 2013).

[1022] *See, e.g., In re* Extradition of Lahoria, 932 F. Supp. 802, 820 (N.D. Tex. 1996) (considering but rejecting an argument that the offenses to be tried in India are not the offenses for which extradition is sought under the India-U.S. extradition treaty).

[1023] No. 14038/88, 11 Eur. H.R. Rep. 439 (1989); *see* United States v. Burns, [2001] 1 S.C.R. 283, 296 (Can.) (finding that assurances against the imposition of the death penalty were "constitutionally required in all but exceptional cases" before Canada could extradite a prisoner to the United States in accordance with Article 6 of the extradition treaty between the United States and Canada).

[1024] *See* Stephan Breitenmoser & Gunter E. Wilms, *Human Rights v. Extradition: The Soering Case*, 11 MICH. J. INT'L L. 845 (1990); *see also* Bharat Malkani, *The Obligation to Refrain from Assisting the Use of the Death Penalty*, 62 INT'L & COMP. L.Q. 523 (2013).

Index

For the benefit of digital users, indexed terms that span two pages (e.g., 52–53) may, on occasion, appear on only one of those pages.

Abbott v. Abbott, 985
access to U.S. courts
  foreign state/government inability to, 156–
    59, 157n.322, 232, 232n.360
  by nationals of foreign entity, 159
  recognition powers and, 159, 232, 232n.360
Acosta, Matter of, 972
acquisition of territory
  Congress powers to regulate, 55n.35
  constitutional protections in U.S.
    territories, 854–56
  expropriations cases, 200, 200n.162
  property acquisition by foreign state, 127
  recognition of new states, 147–49
act of state doctrine, 9–10, 199–210, 200n.162,
    201–2nn.174–77, 203–4nn.182–87,
    205n.194, 206n.196, 206–7n.200,
    207n.206, 362–63, 362–63n.225
Administrative Procedure Act (APA, 1946), 74,
    196–97, 959–60
admiralty/maritime law. *See* maritime
  law; piracy
adoption/international, 985–87, 986n.955
AECA (1976), 96
Afghanistan
  al-Qaeda-related strikes in, 711
  atrocity crimes investigation, 100–1
  commander-in-chief power, 762
  covert operations, 739–40
  drone strikes, 762
  foreign assistance provision, 60, 87–88
  non-recognition of government, 155
  self-defense rights, 711
  U.S. military interventions in, 713, 736–37
  withdrawal of U.S. troops from, 87–88
Afroyim v. Rusk, 980
Agency for International Development, 59
Agency for International Development v.
    Alliance for Open Society International,
    Inc., 870–71
agency regulation, 23, 23n.147
air defense identification zones, 55–56

al-Qaeda. *See* September 11, 2001 attacks;
  terrorism
Alabama Claims arbitration, 607–8
Alfred Dunhill of London, Inc. v. Republic of
    Cuba, 205–6, 206n.196
Algiers Accords (1981), 36–37, 37n.231, 166,
    616–17, 821–22, 928
Alien Enemy Act (1798), 728–29, 918–19
Alien Registration Act (1940), 958
Alien Tort Statute (ATS, 1789), 182–83,
    183n.51, 228–29, 241, 335–36, 364–65,
    401–10, 406–7n.463, 407–8nn.468–72,
    409n.477, 410n.482, 410n.486, 413, 518–20
aliens. *See* noncitizens
Alimanestianu v. United States, 927–28,
    927–28n.517
allocation/balance of powers
  concepts, definitions, 1–2
  Congress, 2, 3–5, 21–22, 25–26, 28
  Congress/president balance, 30–42, 32n.200,
    33n.208, 38n.245, 40n.259, 40–41n.260,
    743–44, 743n.492, 746–48
  constitutional law, xxi–xxii, xxin.10, 1–
    2, 3, 31
  federalism, 17–19
  foreign relations generally, 2–19
  foreign relations powers not derived from
    Constitution, 11–16, 11n.74, 12n.77,
    14nn.88–89
  judiciary, 4–5, 6–7, 9–11, 21–22, 21n.133,
    22n.137
  national emergency, 42–49, 47n.303, 49n.315
  president, 5–9
  president's advantages generally, 20–23
  president's advantages unique to foreign
    relations, 23–30, 25n.160, 26n.164,
    30n.190
Almeida-Sanchez v. United States, 892–93
ambassadors/ministers/consuls, U.S. *See*
    *also under*president, appoint-and-
    receive powers
  Ambassador at Large, 135, 139

ambassadors/ministers/consuls, U.S. (*cont.*)
   ambassadors not subject to Senate
     consent, 139–40
   appointing/law of nations, 133–34,
     133–34n.182
   Appointments Clause, 133
   classification of posts, 140
   congressional powers, 52–53, 112–13, 134–
     36, 136n.192, 140–44, 142–43n.226
   funding of missions, 141–43, 142–43n.226
   Ineligibility Clause, 136–38, 137n.197
   law of nations, 133–34, 133–34n.182
   persona non grata designation, 119–20, 119–
     20nn.79–80, 131–32
   personal rank of ambassador, 139–40
   presidential powers, 5, 24–25, 135–36,
     136n.192
   qualifications for office, 135–36
   receiving foreign, 125–32, 125n.113
   regulation of diplomatic posts/positions,
     140–44, 142–43n.226
   removal of, 133, 138–39, 138n.206
   salary increase, 137–38
   selection of, 133–36, 136n.192, 139
American Banana v. United Fruit Co., 236
American Declaration of Rights and Duties of
   Man (1948), 863–64
American Insurance Association v. Garamendi,
   555, 576–77, 577n.866, 578, 582–83, 821–
   22, 831–33, 846–47
*American Insurance Co. v. 356 Bales of
   Cotton*, 359–60
American Insurance v. Garamendi, 122, 166–67
American Service Members' Protection Act
   (2002), 638–39
Andean Trade Preference Act (2002), 95–96
Anglo Chinese Shipping Co. v. United States, 921
Antarctic Treaty (1959), 213–14, 214n.241
Anti-Ballistic Missile (ABM) Treaty (1974), 169,
   169n.386, 503–4
Anti-Counterfeiting Trade Agreement (ACTA,
   2011), 566n.813
Anti-Deficiency Act (1884), 84–85
Anti-Terrorism Act (ATA, 1987), 129–31,
   130n.156, 221–22
Anti-Terrorism Clarification Act (ATCA,
   2018), 131
Antiterrorism and Effective Death Penalty Act
   (1996), 711
Appointments Clause, 133
Aptheker v. Secretary of State, 929–30
arbitration/act of state doctrine, 208–9,
   209n.213

Arizona v. United States, 807–8, 958–59
arms control treaties
   inspections required/Fourth Amendment,
     902–4, 903n.360, 904n.373
   Second Amendment relationships, 886–87
Arms Export Control Act (AECA, 1976), 59
arms sales prohibitions, 27, 62, 85, 96–97
Arms Trade Treaty (ATT, 2013), 887
Articles of Confederation
   conducting foreign relations, 109–10
   foreign coin valuation, 101–2
   foreign commerce powers, 88
   Foreign Emoluments Clause, 171n.396
   foreign relations powers not derived from
     Constitution, 13–16
   importance, xix–xx
   international organizations, 603–5, 603n.10,
     604n.16, 604n.17, 605nn.19–23
   judiciary role under, 176–77
   land/water capture rule making
     powers, 765–66
   letters of marque/reprisal, 768–69
   military establishment/regulation, 775
   preemption, 812
   study methodology, xxiv
   treaty power, 418–20, 420–21n.33, 423–24nn.49–
     51, 424nn.53–54, 424–25nn.56–58, 511
   war powers, 663–64
Artukovic v. Boyle, 170
Asakura v. City of Seattle, 813–14, 948–49
asylum seekers, 961–63, 961–62n.767,
   962n.770, 970–74, 970n.830, 971n.839
Atamirzayeva v. United States, 920
Atkins v. Virginia, 372n.276, 943–44
Austria v. Altmann, 160
authorization express or implied, 34–36
Avena case, 121–22, 816, 822–24
Aziz v. Trump, 875

Baker v. Carr, 185, 185n.61, 189–91, 190n.92
Balkans War, 738
Banco Nacional de Cuba v. Sabbatino, 152,
   200, 200n.162, 205–8, 355–56, 362–63,
   363n.226
*Barclays Bank v. Franchise Tax Board of
   California*, 827–29
Bas v. Tingy, 673–74, 749–50
Belk v. United States, 928
Bello-Reyes v. Gaynor, 869–70
Blackmer v. United States, 56–57, 938
Bond v. United States, 472–74, 473–74nn.294–
   300, 474–15nn.301–2, 479–80, 543n.692,
   791–92, 811–12, 817–18

Boos v. Barry, 872
Bosnia-Herzegovina
    air strikes, 723–24
    anticipated hostilities, 748
    collective nonrecognition, 150–51
    humanitarian interventions in, 718
    nature, scope, and duration standard, 748
    peacekeeping missions, 738
    U.S. military interventions in, 718, 734–35,
        737–39, 748
Boumediene v. Bush, 781–82, 856, 859–60, 907–
    8, 933–34
Bowsher v. Synar, 138–39
Breard v. Greene, 507–8
Bretton Woods Agreement (1945), 813–14
bribery, 200
Bridges v. Wixon, 869–70
Brown v. Maryland, 825
Brown v. United States, 352–53, 352n.167, 355–
    56, 389–90, 676–77, 760–61, 766–67
Budget and Impoundment Control Act (ICA,
    1974), 84–86

Califano v. Torres, 856–57
cap-and-trade compact, 845–46
Captures Clause, 764–68
Carlson v. Landon, 942–43
Case-Zablocki Act (1972), 560,
    560n.782, 564–65
Central American Free Trade Agreement–
    Dominican Republic (CAFTA-DR,
    2004), 94–95
*Chae Chan Ping v. United States (Chinese
    Exclusion Case)*, 12–13, 12n.78, 15–16,
    679, 955–56, 955n.726, 958–59
Chamber of Commerce v. Whiting, 806–7
Charlton v. Kelly, 591–92, 591n.942
*Charming Betsy. See Murray v. Schooner
    Charming Betsy*
Chemical Weapons Convention (1993), 472–74,
    473–74nn.294–300, 474–15nn.301–2,
    481–82, 481nn.350–51, 638–39, 811
Chemical Weapons Convention
    Implementation Act (1998), 638–39
Chevron deference, 23, 23n.147
children
    abduction/international, 982–85, 982n.919,
        983n.926, 984n.931
    adoption/international, 985–87, 986n.955
    support/maintenance obligations, 987–88,
        988n.978
Chinese Exclusion Act (1882), 955–56,
    955n.726, 957

Chinese Exclusion case, 12–13, 12n.78, 15–16,
    679, 955–56, 955n.726, 958–59
Chirac v. Chirac's Lessee, 813–14
citizenship
    birthright citizenship, 954,
        954–55nn.714–22
    intention to relinquish, 979–81
    loss of U.S. citizenship, 979–81,
        979–80nn.902–3
claims settlement
    conclusion of executive agreements
        incidental to recognition, 163–67
    foreign-owned, 177, 177–78n.18, 178–79,
        812–13, 819–22, 819n.212, 819n.213,
        820n.217
    Holocaust-era, 166–67, 831–34
    slave/forced labor victims, 833
Clark v. Allen, 829–31
classified information
    congressional powers, 74–76
    presidential powers, 26–27
Classified Information Procedures Act (CIPA,
    1980), 75–76
Clean Air Act (1963), 632–33
Coker v. Georgia, 943–44
Commerce Clause, 800, 800n.80
commerce regulation powers/Congress, 52, 58,
    88–101, 88n.267
commercial activity exception
    FSIA, 268–72, 268n.595, 270–176nn.606–7,
        271–72nn.611–12, 272n.616, 289–91,
        290nn.727–28, 291nn.735–38, 296–97,
        297–98n.778
    VCDR, 296–97, 297–98n.778
Committee on Foreign Investment in the
    United States (CFIUS), 97–98
Compact Clause, 839–47
conducting foreign relations
    generally, 105–8
    constitutional design, 110–15
    constitutional practice, 115–20
    diplomatic credentials, 125–26, 126n.119
    embassies/consulates/foreign
        missions, 126–31
    liability insurance for foreign
        missions, 128–29
    litigation involving foreign missions, 129–31,
        129n.142, 130n.153
    persona non grata designation, 119–20, 119–
        20nn.79–80, 131–32
    power to conduct, 108–24
    pre-constitutional experience, 108–10,
        108n.14

conducting foreign relations (*cont.*)
  presidential waivers/foreign missions, 130–
    31, 130n.159
  privileges/immunities of foreign
    missions, 128–29
  property acquisition by foreign state, 127
  protection of foreign missions, 128
  receiving foreign ambassadors, 125–32,
    125n.113
  reopening of foreign missions, 130–31,
    130n.159
  solidification of president's power, 121–24
  travel restrictions for foreign
    missions, 128–29
Congress
  admission of states/powers to regulate, 52–53
  allocation/balance of powers, 2, 3–5, 21–22,
    25–26, 28
  Compact Clause consent, 839–47
  contempt, 73–74, 74n.162
  customary international law, 327–29, 338–44,
    338n.92, 375–77, 375n.287, 380–81, 384–
    85, 385n.346
  enumeration of powers, 17
  foreign relations powers generally, 788,
    788nn.5–10
  Habeas Corpus Clause, 43
  international organization agreements, 620–
    29, 621–22nn.112–18, 622–23nn.119–21,
    624nn.126–27
  international organizations
    admission, 615–16
  judicial deference to Senate, 497–509,
    500n.463, 501n.467, 501–2n.471,
    502nn.474–76, 503nn.479–80, 504–
    5nn.484–86, 505n.492, 506n.493
  land/water capture rule making
    powers, 764–68
  legislative powers (*see* legislative powers/
    Congress)
  letters of marque/reprisal, 659–60, 661,
    662–63, 664, 666, 669–70, 766, 768–70,
    770nn.655–56
  military establishment/regulation, 771–85,
    774n.684, 777n.714, 778n.719
  neutrality statute of 1794, 117
  power to appoint ambassadors/public
    ministers/consuls, 112–13
  recognition powers, 148
  spending power generally, 4
  statute-treaty conflicts, 547–52,
    548nn.716–19, 550–51nn.730–33,
    551–52nn.734–35

  treaty exit regulation, 596–600, 596n.969,
    597nn.973–74, 598–99nn.975–81,
    599–600nn.982–85
  treaty power, 112–13, 442–43, 443nn.146–48,
    444–52, 446nn.164–65, 447nn.166–67,
    447–48nn.168–73, 448–49nn.174–75,
    449–51nn.178–83, 452nn.187–90, 466,
    466nn.253–57, 542–43, 543nn.691–95
  voice-and-vote provisions/international
    agreements, 621–24, 622–23nn.119–21
  war powers, 3–4, 661, 662, 665–66, 665–
    66nn.36–37, 668–70, 673–74, 677, 697–
    704, 731–50, 759–63
congressional-executive agreements, 94–95,
  561–73, 570n.827, 570n.831, 571nn.833–
  34, 571–72n.836, 615–17, 811–12, 817–18
  ex ante agreements, 558, 561–66, 561–
    62nn.788–92, 562–63n.793, 563–
    64nn.798–801, 564–415nn.803–5,
    565nn.808, 566nn.812–13, 817–18
  ex post agreements, 558, 561, 567–69,
    567nn.814–15, 567–68nn.817–21
constitutional law
  admission of states, 52–53
  allocation/balance of powers, xxi–xxii,
    xxin.10, 1–2, 3, 31
  Appointments Clause, 133
  Articles of War, 775–79
  Bill of Rights, 47
  Captures Clause, 764–68
  Commerce Clause, 800, 800n.80
  Compact Clause, 839–47
  conducting foreign relations, 105–8
  congressional-executive agreements,
    94–95, 558, 559, 559n.777, 561–73,
    561–62nn.788–92, 570n.827, 570n.831,
    571nn.833–34, 571–72n.836, 599–600,
    599–600nn.982–84, 811–12, 817–18
  customary international law relationships,
    327–35, 366–68, 367nn.255–56, 368n.258,
    371–73, 371n.272, 372nn.276–78
  Declare War Clause, 744
  denial of funds, 85–87
  Due Process Clause, 907–10, 907n.384,
    907n.386
  Eighth Amendment, 942–45, 944n.646
  Emoluments Clause, 171–73, 171n.396,
    173n.409
  Establishment Clause, 874–78
  First Amendment, 869–82
  Fifth Amendment, 905–35, 905nn.374–78,
    906n.381, 911n.407
  Foreign Commerce Clause, 802, 825–29

Foreign Emoluments Clause, 171–73, 171n.396, 173n.409
foreign relations powers, 1–2
foreign state/government inability to access U.S. courts, 156–59, 157n.322, 931–32
Fourteenth Amendment, 476–77, 905–35, 911n.407, 945–53
Fourth Amendment, 859–60, 888–904, 888nn.259–61, 907–8
Free Exercise Clause, 874–78
Habeas Corpus Clause, 43
Ineligibility Clause, 136–38, 137n.197
judiciary design, 178–81, 178–79nn.23–26, 179n.28, 181n.39, 181n.44
jurisdiction limits, 230–31
Naturalization Clause, 850
Necessary and Proper Clause, 802
non-self-execution of treaties, 531nn.629–31, 532nn.632–35
Offences Clause, 338–44, 338n.92, 339nn.95–96, 340n.100, 341n.108, 343n.116, 344n.122, 371–72, 373, 543–44, 544nn.696–97, 761, 802
personal rank of ambassador, 139–40
raise and support armies, 3–4
Reception Clause, 105
states' rights, 606–7
Second Amendment, 882–87
Sixth Amendment, 935–42, 935n.575
Supremacy Clause, 179, 179n.28, 370–71, 371n.271, 430–31, 469, 511–12, 516–17, 534–35, 534n.647, 536–38, 802, 837–38
Suspension Clause, 856
Take Care Clause, 7–9, 7n.49, 8n.53, 38–39, 38n.245, 329–30, 352–56, 352n.163, 352–53nn.167–70, 353–54nn.171–74, 354n.176, 355n.182, 356n.187, 389, 392–93
Takings Clause, 919–28, 920n.473
Tenth Amendment impacts on treaty power, 479–82, 479nn.339–40, 480nn.342–45, 480nn.346–47
Treaty Clause, xvi, 426–36, 444–60, 469–83, 469n.271, 606–7 (see also treaty power)
treaty self-execution, 530–33, 530–31nn.627–28
Vesting Clause, 6–7nn.43–44, 12n.77, 38–39, 38n.245
consulates. See embassies/consulates
consultation fees/Emoluments Clause, 172
Container Corp. of America v. Franchise Tax Board, 828
contempt/Congress, 73–74, 74n.162

Conventions of United Nations. See under U.N. Conventions
Conyers v. Reagan, 701–2
Cook v. United States, 547–48
Cooper-Church amendment (1970), 697
corporate liability
  customary international law, 404–5, 406–9, 406–7n.463, 409n.477
  U.S. civil/criminal actions against noncitizens located abroad, 914–15, 914–15nn.426–29, 915n.430
counterfeiting, 102–3, 103n.379, 222–23, 222–23n.293
Country Reports on Human Rights Practices, 68
Court of International Trade, 52–53, 53n.18
courts. See judiciary
Crimes Act (1790), 336–37, 346–47
crimes against humanity, 227–28, 403–4, 403n.447
Crockett v. Reagan, 701–2
Crosby v. National Foreign Trade Council, 29–30, 35, 809, 846–47
cruel and unusual punishment (Eighth Amendment), 942–45, 944n.646
Cummings v. Deutsche Bank und Disconto-Gesellschaft, 924
customary international law. See also law of nations
  generally, 323–24
  adjudicative jurisdiction, 231–33, 231–32n.356, 232n.360, 232–33n.363, 233nn.366–67
  admiralty/maritime law, 359–60, 395–96, 396n.401
  aiding-and-abetting liability, 407–9, 407–8nn.468–72
  arbitrary detention, 391–92, 391n.375, 741
  ATS liability scope, 405–7, 406nn.457–60, 406–7n.463
  authority in U.S. law, 333
  case-specific deference, 409–10, 410n.482
  congressional powers, 327–29, 338–44, 338n.92, 375–77, 375n.287, 380–81, 384–85, 385n.346
  consistency presumption, 382–87, 382–83nn.329–33, 383–84n.335, 384n.337, 385nn.344–46, 386nn.349–51, 387nn.353–56
  constitutional relationships, 327–35, 366–68, 367nn.255–56, 368n.258, 371–73, 371n.272, 372nn.276–78
  corporate liability, 404–5, 406–9, 406–7n.463, 409n.477

customary international law. (*cont.*)
establishing commitments by means other
than agreement, 584–86, 584–585nn.903–
5, 585n.908
executive branch conduct relationships,
389–95, 390n.367, 391nn.372–74,
391n.375, 392nn.379–81, 393nn.384–87,
394–95nn.392–96
executive branch deference, 350–52,
350n.156, 352n.163
exhaustion requirement, 409–10, 409n.480, 413
extraterritoriality, 386, 386n.350
as federal common law, 361–70, 362nn.221–
22, 362–63n.225, 363nn.231–32,
364–65nn.236–40, 365n.244, 366n.247,
366nn.249–50, 367nn.255–56, 368n.258,
369nn.263–65, 370n.266
federal statutes, relationship to, 373–87
foreign sovereign immunity, 255–57,
255n.509, 259n.531, 274–75, 275nn.631–
33, 284, 312–14, 312–14nn.852–55, 365–
66, 365n.244, 366n.247
foreign vessels internal affairs, 386, 386n.351
as general common law, 357–61, 357n.193,
358nn.197–98, 359–24nn.203–7, 360n.211
human rights, 401–14, 402n.435, 403n.444,
403–4nn.447–50, 405nn.452–56,
406nn.457–60, 406–7n.463, 410n.486
international law-treaty conflicts, 552–53,
552–53n.740
judiciary powers, 330–33, 330–31n.50,
356–70, 357n.193, 358nn.197–98,
359–24nn.203–7
jurisdiction, 325–26, 331–32, 332nn.57–59,
336–37, 336n.77, 361–62, 381n.322
jus cogens norms, 377–79, 377–79nn.300–9
later-in-time hierarchal superiority, 379–82,
379n.314, 380n.315, 380nn.316–17,
381nn.321–23, 381–82nn.324–25
later-in-time statutes, 373–79, 374–
75nn.283–86, 375n.287, 376nn.294–95,
376–77nn.297–98, 377–79nn.300–9
law merchant, 396
legislative incorporation, 335–46
lex posterior principle, 388
limits on incorporation, 370–95
making/interpreting, 348–52, 349n.151,
350n.155, 350n.156
methodology, xxii–xxiii
Necessary and Proper Clause, 342–43
nonbinding agreements, 582–83
offenses against (Offences Clause), 338–
44, 338n.92, 339nn.95–96, 340n.100,

341n.108, 343n.116, 344n.122, 371–72,
373, 543–44, 544nn.696–97, 761
piracies/felonies, 3, 327–29, 328n.35,
328–29n.38, 336–38, 337n.81, 337n.84,
396–99, 397nn.410–11, 397–98nn.412–15,
398nn.416–17
power to conduct armed conflict, 751–54,
754n.542
pre-constitutional experience, 324–27
preemption by, 836–39
presidential powers, 329–30, 346–56,
347nn.137–40, 355n.178, 389–95,
390n.367, 391nn.372–74, 391n.375,
392nn.379–81, 393nn.384–86,
394–95nn.392–96
property seizure, 352–56, 352–53nn.167–70
residual authority, 344–46
rights of belligerents/neutrals, 334–35,
334n.69
Supremacy Clause, 370–71, 371n.271
Take Care Clause/authority, 7–9, 7n.49,
8n.53, 38–39, 38n.245, 329–30, 352–56,
352n.163, 352–53nn.167–70, 353–
54nn.171–74, 354n.176, 355n.182,
356n.187, 389, 392–93
territorial/effects jurisdiction, 213–16,
213nn.234–37, 214n.241, 214–15nn.244–
45, 215nn.247–49, 216nn.254–55
territorial jurisdiction, 212–13
terrorism, 399–400nn.422–25, 400–1,
400nn.426–27
torture, 403–4, 403n.447
treaties relationships, 387–89
treaty law, impacts on, 387–89, 442–44,
442nn.142–43, 442nn.144–45, 443nn.146–
48, 443n.149, 444n.151
treaty making according to, 437–44
treaty offenses, 343–44, 344n.122
treaty power, 437–44, 471–72, 471n.282
treaty power, consent/entry into force
under, 440
treaty power capacity/authority under,
437–39, 437–38n.124, 438n.127, 439n.129,
439nn.132–33
treaty reservations under, 440–42,
440–41n.136
war powers, 728, 729–31, 729n.413,
730n.414, 780–81
cybercrime, 222

Dames & Moore v. Regan, 36–38, 37n.231,
37n.234, 39–40, 42, 100, 122, 166, 576–77,
576n.865, 649–50, 821–22, 928

Dandamundi v. Tish, 949–50
Dayton Peace Accords (1995), 738
De Geofroy v. Riggs, 813–14
death penalty, 372n.276, 943–44
Declare War Clause, 744
defense against foreign attack/Second
    Amendment, 883–84
Defense Production Act (1950), 97
Deferred Action for Childhood Arrivals
    (DACA, 2012), 960–61
Deferred Action for Parents of Americans and
    Lawful Permanent Residents (DAPA,
    2014), 960–61
Department of State
    Compact Clause, 842–43, 846–47
    congressional reporting, 68–69
    diplomatic/consular immunity, 299–305,
        299–300nn.790–93, 301n.796, 304nn.812–
        14, 304–5nn.815–16
    diplomatic credentials, 126, 126n.119
    foreign assistance provision, 60, 68, 80–88,
        85n.243
    House committee authority, 59
    ICARA administration, 983–84
    official (conduct-based/functional)
        immunity, 314–15, 314–15n.859
detained noncitizens rights, 296–97
Detainee Treatment Act (2005), 763–64, 865
Deutsch v. Turner Corp., 833–34
Diplomatic Relations Act (1978), 296–98
disasters, major, 43–44
disclosure/executive privilege, 76–80,
    79–80n.202
District of Columbia powers to regulate, 52–
    53, 55–56
District of Columbia v. Heller, 882–83
doctrines
    act of state doctrine, 9–10, 199–210,
        200n.162, 201–2nn.174–77, 203–4nn.182–
        87, 205n.194, 206n.196, 206–7n.200,
        207n.206, 362–63, 362–63n.225
    Charming Betsy doctrine, 71, 235–36,
        245–46, 256, 284, 382–87, 383–84n.335,
        384n.337, 385n.342, 386nn.349–51,
        387nn.353–56, 399
    dual/double criminality doctrine, 991,
        991–92nn.998–1000
    dual-sovereignty doctrine, 905–6
    effects doctrine, 243–44
    enemy property doctrine, 922–23
    forum non conveniens doctrine, 242
    jus cogens doctrine (*see jus cogens* doctrine)
    international comity doctrine, 9–10

non-delegation doctrine, 21–22, 21n.133
one voice doctrine, 809–10
political question doctrine, 9–10, 184–92,
    184nn.56–57, 185n.61, 188nn.80–84,
    189nn.85–87, 189n.90, 190n.92, 191n.101,
    191–92nn.105–6, 201, 921–23, 951–52
plenary powers doctrine, 958–59
preemption doctrine, 555–56
Downes v. Bidwell, 854–56
due process, 38–39, 38n.245, 48–49, 49n.315,
    905–35, 905nn.374–78
Due Process Clause, 907–10, 907n.384,
    907n.386

Edwards v. Arizona, 910
EEOC v. Arabian American Oil Co., 236, 240–
    41, 241n.413
effects doctrine, 243–44
Eighth Amendment, 942–45, 944n.646
Ekiu v. United States, 956
El Al Israel Airlines v. Tseng, 813–14
*El-Shifa Pharmaceutical Industries Co. v. United
    States*, 921, 922–23
embassies/consulates/foreign missions
    generally, 126–31
    establishing in U.S., 126–31, 129n.142,
        130n.153, 130n.156
    liability insurance for, 128–29
    litigation involving, 129–31, 129n.142,
        130n.153
    presidential waivers, 130–31, 130n.159
    privileges/immunities of, 128–29
    protection of, 128
    regulation of protests near, 872
    reopening of, 130–31, 130n.159
    travel restrictions for, 128–29
Emoluments Clause, 171–73, 171n.396,
    173n.409
employment
    equal protection/Fourteenth Amendment,
        476–77, 946–47, 947n.665
    FSIA impacts, 290–91, 290n.728
    naturalized citizen/U.S. Foreign
        Service, 918
    noncitizens in federal civil service, 394–95,
        395n.396, 916–17, 947, 947n.665
    preemption, 806–7
    of undocumented noncitizens, 806–7, 957,
        957–58n.742
enemy combatant treatment, 713, 763–64, 777–
    78, 778n.719, 900–1
enforcement jurisdiction, 234–35, 234n.372
Enmund v. Florida, 943–44

equal protection
 Fifth Amendment, 905–35, 906n.381,
  911n.407
 Fourteenth Amendment, 905–35,
  911n.407, 945–53
 lawful permanent residents, 946–49
 for noncitizens in U.S., 916–19
 nonimmigrant noncitizens, 949–50
 undocumented noncitizens, 950–51,
  951nn.695–97
Erie Railroad v. Tompkins, 357, 361–64,
 362nn.221–22, 362–63n.225, 366,
 366n.249, 838
espionage, 222
Espionage Act of 1917, 879
Establishment Clause, 874–78
exclusive economic zones, 55–56
executive agreements
 Algiers Accords (1981), 36–37, 37n.231, 166,
  821–22, 928
 conclusion of executive agreements
  incidental to recognition, 163–67
 congressional-executive agreements (*see*
  congressional-executive agreements)
 international organizations admission, 615–
  16, 616–17nn.90–91
 Litvinov Assignment (1933), 164
 nonbinding, 580–83, 581n.886, 581–
  82nn.888–91, 583n.898, 583n.900, 596
 preemption of state law, 821–22
 prohibitory words in Constitution, 475–76,
  476n.316
 pursuant to Article II treaties, 573–75,
  574–75nn.852–54
 sole, 575–80, 575n.857, 576–77nn.862–66,
  577–78nn.867–70, 595, 616–17, 616–
  17nn.90–92, 821–22, 822n.236, 831–32
executive orders
 admission of nonimmigrants/immigrants,
  966–67, 966nn.796–97, 967n.802
 asset freezes, 100, 819–20, 819n.212,
  819n.213, 820n.217, 924–25
 authorization express or implied, xxin.10,
  32–41, 37n.231, 37n.234, 38n.245,
  40n.259, 67
 classified information, 74–76
 denial of entry to U.S., 874–78, 876n.174
 internment of personnel, 44–46, 45n.282,
  660, 660n.10
 Japanese internment/WWII, 44–46, 45n.282,
  49, 49n.315, 660, 918–19
 non-self-executing treaties, 39–40
 sanctions against foreign persons, 100–1

 seizures of property and persons, xxin.10,
  32–39, 33n.208, 38n.245, 42, 67, 123–24,
  353–54, 353–54n.172, 355–56, 522–23,
  692–93, 735, 735–36n.444, 760–61,
  764, 823–24
 war powers, 44–46, 45n.282
executive privilege, 76–80, 79–80n.202
extradition
 generally, 989–95
 arrest/extradition of foreign national/
  Compact Clause, 844–45
 congressional powers relating to, 57–58
 death penalty, 995
 deportation hearings, 852, 869–70
 dual/double criminality doctrine, 991,
  991–92nn.998–1000
 equal protection/Fourteenth Amendment,
  905–35, 911n.407
 incidence test, 992–93
 political offense exception, 992–93,
  992n.1005, 993n.1009
 power to regulate, 989
 proceedings, 990–91, 990–91nn.990–95
 request for initiation, 990–91
 rule of non-inquiry, 993–94,
  993–852nn.1010–12
 rule of specialty, 994–95, 994–95n.1021
 treaty power, 170, 570–72, 571n.834,
  572n.840, 911–13

F. Hoffmann-La Roche Ltd. v. Empagran S.A.,
 244–45, 244n.437, 381n.322
Falsification of official documents, 222
family law/transnational
 generally, 982–88
 adoption/international, 985–87, 986n.955
 child abduction/international, 982–85,
  982n.919, 983n.926, 984n.931
 child support/maintenance obligations, 987–
  88, 988n.978
 custody rights, 984, 985
 habitual residence of child, 984–85
Faruki v. Rogers, 918
Federal Alien Registration Act (1940), 805–6
Federal Arbitration Act (1926), 209n.213
Federal Republic of Germany v. Philipp, 274–75,
 274–75n.630, 276
Federal Tort Claims Act (FTCA, 1946), 277–78,
 278–79n.651
federalism. *See also* states' rights
 compacts, 790
 cooperative federalism, 792–95
 federal funding conditions, 798–99

federal government recourses, 798–99
firearm possession, 800n.80
foreign relations authority generally, 787
government procurement, 792–93
marijuana legalization, 797–98, 800n.80
preemption (*see* preemption)
regulation by states, 790–92, 790n.23
sanctions, 792–93
sanctuary cities, 797–98
sister city relationships, 792–93
state-federal implementation, 792–95
state-level initiatives, 796–97
states' role in foreign relations, 17–19, 788–
    99, 789n.15, 798n.73
uncooperative federalism/noncooperation,
    795–98, 796n.56
war powers of states, 790
federative power (Locke), 23–24
felonies committed on the high seas, 3, 52, 70,
    327–29, 328n.35, 328–29n.38, 335–38,
    337n.81, 337n.84
Fifth Amendment, 905–35, 905nn.374–78,
    906n.381, 911n.407
Filartiga v. Pena-Irala, 363–64, 401–2, 403n.447
Firearms Owners' Protection Act
    (1986), 885–86
First Amendment, 869–82
Fleming v. Page, 755–56
Fong Yue Ting v. United States, 956
Foreign Affairs and the Constitution (Henkin),
    xvii–xviii
Foreign Affairs Reform and Restructuring Act
    (1998), 61
Foreign Assistance Act (1961), 59, 81–84, 563
foreign coin value regulation, 3, 52, 101–3,
    103n.379
Foreign Commerce Clause, 802, 825–29
Foreign Corrupt Practices Act (FCPA, 1977),
    98–99, 202–3
Foreign Cultural Exchange Jurisdictional
    Immunity Clarification Act (2016), 276
Foreign Emoluments Clause, 171–73, 171n.396,
    173n.409
Foreign Gifts and Decorations Act
    (1966), 171–73
Foreign Intelligence Surveillance Act (FISA,
    1978), 889–92, 889n.265, 890n.267,
    891–92n.280
Foreign Intelligence Surveillance Court
    (FISC), 889–92
foreign investment, 96–98, 97n.328, 793–94
foreign investors arbitration claims, 18
Foreign Military Sales Act (1970), 697

foreign missions. *See* embassies/consulates/
    foreign missions
Foreign Missions Act (1982), 126–31
foreign policy generally
    congressional authority, 29–30
    presidential powers, 25–30
Foreign Relations Authorization Act (2003),
    142–43n.226
Foreign Service Act (1980), 136
Foreign Sovereign Immunities Act (FSIA,
    1976). *See also* immunity of individuals
    absolute theory, 249–50, 249nn.465–
        67, 290–91
    acquired by succession or gift, 277,
        277nn.639–40
    acta jure imperii/acta jure gestionis, 248–49,
        251, 270, 289–90
    agencies/instrumentalities, 261–64,
        261nn.546–49, 262nn.551–53, 262–
        63n.557, 263–64nn.558–64
    arbitration exception, 267–68,
        267–68nn.586–89
    art works, 276
    attachment/execution immunity, 285–87,
        285nn.698–99, 286–175nn.701–2,
        286n.704
    attribution to foreign state criterion, 262,
        262–63n.557
    central banks, 263–64, 264nn.563–64
    charter-based waivers, 290–91, 291n.736
    civil liability/Offences Clause
        authority, 341–42
    civil RICO claims, 254n.504
    commercial activity exception, 268–72,
        268n.595, 270–176nn.606–7, 271–
        72nn.611–12, 272n.616, 289–91,
        290nn.727–28, 291nn.735–38, 296–97,
        297–98n.778
    congressional powers, 256, 276, 284, 286–87
    core function test, 263–64
    counterclaim exception, 268
    criminal matters, 254, 254n.503
    customary international law, 255–57,
        255n.509, 259n.531, 274–75, 275nn.631–
        33, 284, 365–66, 365n.244, 366n.247
    domestic takings rule, 274–75,
        274–75nn.630–31
    early development, 247–52, 247n.451,
        247nn.452–53, 248n.455, 248n.457,
        248nn.459–61, 249nn.465–67, 250n.470,
        250nn.475–76
    employment matters, 289–91, 290n.728
    exceptions to immunity, 58

Foreign Sovereign Immunities Act (FSIA, 1976) (*cont.*)

exclusive venue provision, 290, 290n.729

executive branch deference, 258–60, 260n.538, 292–93, 306–8, 307n.829, 308n.833, 310–14, 310n.844, 311n.848, 312–14nn.852–55

exhaustion of local remedies, 275–76, 276n.635

expropriation exception, 257–58, 264–65, 264n.566, 273–76, 273n.619, 273nn.622–23, 274nn.624–25, 274–75n.630, 275nn.631–33, 276n.635

federal cause of action, 281–82, 281n.672

foreign officials, inapplicability of FSIA, 302n.802, 302–3n.803

foreign state *stricto sensu*/political subdivisions, 258–61, 259–60nn.531–38, 260–61nn.539–45, 285–86

foreign state threshold question, 258–64, 258nn.526–27, 258nn.528–30

genocide, 274–75, 275n.633

gravamen, 272, 272n.616

human rights violations, 257–58, 257n.525, 274–75, 275n.633

immunity from suit, 264–84, 264–65nn.565–70

immunity of states not persons, 254, 254–176nn.501–4, 293–95, 294n.758

inability to claim immunity, 159–60

international organizations/officials/ premises, 287–95, 288n.715, 289nn.723–24, 290n.727, 290n.729, 291–92nn.740–43, 293nn.749–51

judiciary relationship to, 246–52

jus cogens offenses, 256–58, 257nn.522–25, 318–19, 318nn.873–76

majority ownership criterion, 262, 262–63n.557

nature/scope of, 252–58, 252n.492, 253–54nn.497–98, 255–56nn.507–11, 255n.509, 256n.515, 257nn.522–25

noncommercial tort exception, 277, 277nn.642–43

official (conduct-based/functional) immunity, inapplicability of FSIA 302–4

organ criterion, 263–64, 263–64nn.558–64

passive personality jurisdiction, 221–22

peacekeeping missions, contrasting FSIA and IOIA, 289–95, 289n.724, 295n.759

property/tort exceptions, 276–78, 277nn.639–41, 277nn.642–43, 277n.644, 278–79nn.650–51

restrictive immunity, 287–89, 288n.715, 291–92, 349–50

rights in immovable property, 277, 277n.641

same immunity analysis, 287–88, 290–91

Section 1604 exceptions, 267, 267nn.584–85

separate legal personality criterion, 262, 262nn.551–53

state-owned enterprise, 254

state sponsor of terrorism, 279–80, 280n.659, 284

Tate Letter (1952), 251, 251nn.478–79, 259n.535

territoriality limit, 279–80, 279n.657

terrorism, 254, 286–87

terrorism-related exceptions, 279–84, 279n.656, 279–80nn.657–65, 281nn.666–68, 283n.681, 283n.685, 284n.686, 290

waivers/related exceptions, 265–68, 265nn.574–75, 266nn.577–80, 290–91

foreign states/officials

Congress powers to regulate, 55–56

foreign sovereign recognition, 40–41, 40–41n.260

immunity in U.S. courts, 58 (*see also* immunity of individuals)

president's recognition powers, 67, 86, 107, 113–18, 114–15nn.54–55, 120–21

forum non conveniens doctrine, 9–10, 231–32, 231–32n.356, 242

Foster v. Nielsen, 511–13, 524–26, 534–35, 534n.647, 540, 540n.674, 553–54

Fotoudis v. Honolulu, 884–85

Fourteenth Amendment, 476–77, 905–35, 911n.407, 945–53

Fourth Amendment, 859–60, 888–904, 888nn.259–61, 907–8

Fr. v. Turk. Judgment (*Lotus* case), 212, 212n.228, 219, 219n.273

Francis v. United States, 141

Free Exercise Clause, 874–78

Freedom of Information Act (FOIA, 1967), 878–79

Frisbie v. Collins, 910–11

Garcia-Mir v. Reagan, 391–92, 391n.375, 392nn.379–81, 394nn.392–93

Gelston v. Hoyt, 146–47

Geneva Conventions (1949), 751–53, 761–62, 777–78, 780–81

genocide, 227–28, 403–4, 403n.447

Gingery v. City of Glendale, 835

Goldwater v. Carter, 170–71, 187–88, 189, 189nn.85–87, 591–92, 591n.942, 618–19

Graham v. Florida, 944–45
Graham v. Richardson, 947–48
Guano Islands Act (1856), 55–56
Guantánamo Bay detainees, 40, 234, 713, 752–53, 757–58, 763–64, 772–73, 781–82, 856, 859–60, 932–34, 934n.569, 941–42
Guaranty Trust Co. v. United States, 156, 158, 160
Gun Control Act (1968), 885–86

Habeas Corpus Clause, 43
Hague Choice of Courts Convention (2005), 791–92
Hague Convention on Protection of Children and Co-operation in Respect of Intercountry Adoption (1993), 985–87
Hague Convention on the Civil Aspects of International Child Abduction (1980), 982–83, 982n.919
Hague Convention on the International Recovery of Child Support and Other Forms of Family Maintenance (2007), 987
Hague Regulations (1907), 751–53, 761–62, 777–78
Haig v. Agee, 659, 930
Haiti
    Charming Betsy doctrine, 383–84, 384n.338
    covert operations, 740
    diplomatic communications/refusal to produce, 77–78
    nature, scope, and duration standard, 748
    nonrecognition of state, 102–3, 155–57
    peacekeeping missions, 294–95, 295n.759
    regime change, 742
    treaty advice-and-consent materials, 502–3, 502n.474
    treaty language, 487, 487–88n.386
    treaty object and purpose, 488–89, 488n.387
    U.S. citizen/illicit activities abroad, 92
    U.S. jurisdiction, 55–56, 55n.37
    U.S. military interventions in, 684, 709–10, 734–35, 740, 742
Hamdan v. Rumsfeld, 40, 42, 48–49, 340–41, 341n.105, 727, 752–53, 760–61, 780–81, 932–33, 941–42
Hampton v. Mow Sun Wong, 394–95, 395n.396, 916–17, 947, 947n.665
Harisiades v. Shaughnessy, 853–54, 958
Harris v. Rosario, 856–57
Hartford Fire Ins. Co. v. California, 243–44, 244n.432, 245–46
Hatfield-McGovern Amendment (1971), 697
Hauenstein v. Lynham, 813–14

Hawai'i v. Trump, 875
Hernandez v. Mesa, 901
Hilton v. Guyot, 242
Hines v. Davidowitz, 57, 805–6, 805n.112
Hirabayashi v. United States, 46
Holder v. Humanitarian Law Project, 881–82
Holmes v. Jennison, 844–45
Holocaust Victim Insurance Relief Act (HVIRA, 1999), 166–67, 831–32
Hostage Act (1868), 37
House Foreign Affairs Committee jurisdiction, 59
human rights. *See also* Alien Tort Statute (ATS)
    act of state doctrine, 203n.183, 204n.186
    crimes against humanity, 227–28, 403–4, 403n.447
    customary international law, 401–14, 402n.435, 403n.444, 403–4nn.447–50, 405nn.452–56, 406nn.457–60, 406–7n.463, 410n.486
    FSIA, 257–58, 257n.525, 274–75, 275n.633
    jurisdiction, 203–4
    preemption, 800–39
    reservations, understandings, or declarations (RUDs), 861–62
    U.S. support of resolutions regarding, 861–65, 863n.93, 863–64nn.96–101
humanitarian objectives/use of force, 717–24, 737–38, 881–82

Immigration and Nationality Act (INA, 1952), 22, 957–58, 965–66, 979
immigration law. *See also* noncitizens
    admission of nonimmigrants/immigrants, 961–68, 961–62n.767, 962n.770, 963–64nn.777–83, 966nn.796–97
    asylum seekers, 961–63, 961–62n.767, 962n.770, 970–74, 970n.830, 971n.839
    birthright citizenship, 954, 954–55nn.714–22
    Bivens remedy for noncitizens, 901–2
    conspiracy to violate immigration/customs laws, 222
    constitutional basis, 953–61, 954–55nn.714–22, 955n.726, 956–57n.736, 957–58nn.737–42
    consular nonreviewability, 964–66, 964–65nn.784–85
    employment of undocumented noncitizens, 806–7
    in-state status/G-4 visas, 806, 806n.119
    liberty to travel to and from the U.S., 929–31, 929n.525, 929n.529, 931n.547, 956–57, 956–57n.736

Immigration and Nationality Act (INA, 1952) (*cont.*)
loss of U.S. citizenship, 979–81, 979–80nn.902–3
mandatory detention, 976
Native Americans, 954
plenary power doctrine, 956–59, 956–57n.736, 964–65
preemption, 57, 803, 805–8, 805n.112, 806n.119
presidential powers, 959–61, 966–67, 967n.802
refugees, 968–70, 969n.817, 970n.829
removal/non-refoulement, 973–79, 974n.857, 975n.861, 975n.864, 979nn.899–900
restrictions, 12–16, 12n.78
temporary protected status (TPS), 978–79
treaty power, 793–94, 797–98
undocumented noncitizens statutory provisions, 807–8
visas, 963–66, 963–64nn.777–82
Immigration Reform and Control Act (IRCA, 1986), 806–7
immunity of individuals (*see also* Foreign Sovereign Immunities Act (FSIA))
accident-related exception/VCCR, 298–99
application to U.S. personnel abroad, 301–2, 301n.799
common-law, 302–3, 302–3n.803, 303n.807
conduct-based/functional (*ratione materiae*), 303–4, 312–19, 312n.850, 312n.851, 312–14nn.852–55, 314–15nn.859–60, 315n.864, 316–17nn.867–69, 318nn.873–76
consular functions/VCCR, 298–99, 298n.782
diplomatic/consular privileges/immunities, 295–302
foreign officials, other, 302–21
FSIA (*see* Foreign Sovereign Immunities Act [FSIA])
head-of-state, 303–4, 305–12, 306nn.824–26, 307nn.828–30, 308n.833, 308nn.834–36, 309n.838, 310n.844, 311n.848, 914–15
inability to claim foreign sovereign immunity from suit, 159–60
privileges/immunities of foreign missions, 128–29
special mission, 303–4, 319–21, 319–20nn.879–80, 320n.882, 320–21n.884
status-based/personal (*ratione personae*), 303–4, 305–12, 306nn.824–26,

307nn.828–30, 308n.833, 308nn.834–36, 309n.838, 310n.844, 311n.848
troika, 309, 309n.838
from U.S. jurisdiction, 246–321
waivers, diplomats/consular officials, 299, 299nn.787–88
impersonating foreign officials, congressional powers to regulate, 55–56
incorporation of treaties
beginnings of, 511–16, 511n.523, 511–12n.525, 512–13nn.531–34, 513n.535
Bricker Amendment, 434–36, 513, 513n.535, 790–91
changes, incorporation into U.S. law, 629–58, 630nn.160–61, 633nn.173–74, 633n.176
civil actions, 518–20
Constitution-treaty conflicts, 545–47, 545–46nn.708–9, 546n.710
declarations by treaty makers, 535–40, 537nn.659–61, 539nn.669–70, 540nn.674–76
domestic effect, 523–24, 523–24n.595
hierarchical status, 516, 545–56, 578–80, 578–79nn.874–77
international law-treaty conflicts, 552–53, 552–53n.740
later-in-time rule, 547–52, 549nn.720–23, 549–50nn.725–28
lex posterior rule, 552
multilateral treaties, 528, 528–29nn.614–16
non-self-execution, 511–16, 513n.532, 515nn.549–51
non-self-execution consequences, 520–24, 520n.575, 521nn.578–80, 523–24n.595
non-self-execution, Constitution-based inquiry, 530–33, 530–31nn.627–28, 531nn.629–31, 532nn.632–35
non-self-execution, justiciability-based inquiry, 533–35, 533–34nn.641–46
non-self-execution, treaty-based inquiry, 524–29, 524nn.596–97, 525n.602, 525–26nn.604–8, 527nn.609–11, 527n.612
obligations, implementing by other means, 540–44, 541–42nn.682–84, 543nn.691–95, 544nn.696–97, 544nn.699–701
re-emption doctrine, 555–56
private right of action/treaty incorporation, 517–18, 518n.566
section 1983 remedy, 518–20, 518–20nn.568–71
by self-execution, 510–40, 510nn.518–19
self-execution consequences, 516–20, 516n.555

state/local law-treaty conflicts, 553–56, 554nn.747–49

statute-treaty conflicts, 547–52, 548nn.716–19, 549nn.720–23, 549–50nn.725–28, 550–51nn.730–33, 551–52nn.734–35

individual rights

generally, 849, 865–66

access/unlawful disclosure of foreign relations information, 878–81, 878nn.188–90

alien enemy detention, 918–19, 931–34, 933n.560

alien enemy property, 924, 924n.496

arms control treaties inspections and Fourth Amendment, 902–4, 903n.360, 904n.373

arms control treaties and Second Amendment, 886–87

asset freezes, 100, 819–20, 819n.212, 819n.213, 820n.217, 924–25

Bill of Rights/Fourteenth Amendment, 849, 867–953

citizens/noncitizens abroad, 857–60, 857n.51, 858n.58, 859n.64, 863n.93, 863–64nn.96–101

cruel and unusual punishment (Eighth Amendment), 942–45, 944n.646

defense against foreign attack/Second Amendment, 883–84

denial of entry to U.S., 872–73, 873n.154, 874–78, 876n.174

double jeopardy, 905–6

dual-sovereignty doctrine, 905–6

due process/Fifth Amendment, 38–39, 38n.245, 48–49, 49n.315, 905–35, 905nn.374–78

enemy property doctrine, 922–23

equal protection/Fifth Amendment, 905–35, 906n.381, 911n.407

equal protection for noncitizens in U.S., 916–19

equal protection/Fourteenth Amendment, 905–35, 911n.407, 945–53

Establishment Clause, 874–78

evidence secured from coerced testimony, 909, 909nn.396–97

executive's authority to espouse private claims, 925–28, 925n.507, 927–28n.517

family law/transnational, 982–88

Free Exercise Clause, 874–78

immigration law (see immigration law)

interrogation by foreign government, 908–9

keep and bear arms/Second Amendment, 882–87, 885n.236, 886n.245

lawful permanent residents/equal protection, 946–49, 947n.665

liberty to travel to and from the U.S., 929–31, 929n.525, 929n.529, 931n.547, 956–57, 956–57n.736

military detention of noncitizens abroad, 931–35, 932n.556, 933n.560, 934nn.568–69

Miranda warnings, 908–9

national security exception, 871, 871nn.138–41

noncitizens (see noncitizens)

nonimmigrant noncitizens/equal protection, 949–50

overriding national interests, 917–18, 917n.444, 917n.452

persons in unincorporated U.S. territories, 854–57, 854nn.28–29, 854–55n.30

political question doctrine, 921–23, 922n.482, 951–52

post-indictment right of counsel/noncitizen located abroad, 938

provision of support to terrorist groups, 881–82

rational basis review application, 951–53

receiving foreign speech, 869, 872–74

regulation of protests near embassies/consulates/foreign missions, 872

right to confront/compel testimony of witnesses located abroad, 938–39, 939nn.602–4

right to counsel, 910, 975–76, 975n.864

right to speedy U.S. trial/noncitizen located abroad, 937, 937nn.587–89

search and seizure abroad/Fourth Amendment, 893, 894–900, 895n.309, 896nn.312–15, 896–97nn.316–21, 899n.334

search and seizure conducted by foreign government, 898–99

search and seizure/Fourth Amendment, 859–60, 888–902, 888nn.259–61, 907–8

self-incrimination, 905–6, 905nn.374–78, 908–9

special public interest exception, 952

speech/religion/press freedoms, 869–82, 869n.125, 871nn.138–41

standards of treatment protecting U.S. nationals, 948–49

surveillance of citizens/Fourth Amendment, 889–92, 889n.262, 889n.265, 890n.267, 891–92n.280

individual rights (*cont.*)
  taking of property without just
    compensation, 905–35, 920n.473,
    921n.476, 922n.482, 924n.496, 925n.507,
    927–28n.517
  travel of noncitizens to U.S., 906
  trial by military commission, 940–42,
    940n.608
  trials/Sixth Amendment, 935–42, 935n.575
  U.S. abduction of noncitizens abroad for
    prosecution in U.S., 910–14, 911n.407,
    911n.408, 913nn.419–20
  U.S. civil/criminal actions against noncitizens
    located abroad, 914–15, 914–15nn.426–29,
    915n.430
  U.S. criminal investigation/noncitizens
    abroad, 907–10, 907n.384, 907n.386
  U.S. nationals located abroad, 55–57, 70
  U.S. obligations under international
    law, 860–66
  undocumented noncitizens/equal protection,
    950–51, 951nn.695–97
Ineligibility Clause, 136–38, 137n.197
INS v. Chadha, 22, 61–62, 699–700, 699n.237,
  740, 959
INS v. Elias-Zacarias, 972
INS v. Lopez-Mendoza, 893–94
INS v. Stevic, 976–77
Insular Cases, 854–56, 854–55n.30
insurance
  Armenian genocide claims, 834–35
  Holocaust-era claims, 166–67, 831–34
  prescriptive comity, 243–44, 244n.432
Inter-American Commission on Human
  Rights, 863–64
Inter-American Court of Human
  Rights, 863–64
Intercountry Adoption Act (2000), 986–87
Intermediate-Range Nuclear Forces (INF)
  Treaty (1987), 503–4
international agreements. *See* international
  organization agreements; treaty power
International Bridge Act (1972), 846
International Child Abduction Remedies Act
  (ICARA, 1988), 983–85
international comity doctrine, 9–10
International Court of Justice (ICJ)
  compulsory jurisdiction, 627–28,
    628n.147, 797–98
  FSIA terrorism exceptions, 284, 284n.686
  head-of-state immunity, 310–11
  re-emption by treaty, 814–15
  president as representing U.S. before, 121–22

treaty non-self-execution, 513–15, 525–27
treaty-related disputes resolution, 628–
  29, 653–54
U.S. deference to, 507–9
International Covenant on Civil and Political
  Rights (ICCPR, 1966), 18, 795, 861–
  62, 864
International Covenant on Economic,
  Social and Cultural Rights (ICESCR,
  1966), 861–62
International Criminal Court (ICC)
  investigative activities by agents of, 638–39
  jurisdiction, 215, 215n.249
  U.S. deference to, 507
  war crimes investigation, 100–1
International Emergency Economic Powers
  Act (IEEPA, 1977), 37, 99–101, 728–29,
  767–68, 924–25
international organization agreements
  generally, 601–2, 601n.2
  admission method, 615–29, 615n.85, 616–
    17nn.90–92, 617–18nn.93–95
  appellate review/Article III court, 652–54,
    652–53n.265
  Appointments Clause violations, 654–56,
    655nn.278–82, 657–58
  Articles of Confederation, 603–5, 603n.10,
    604n.16, 604n.17, 605nn.19–23
  authoritative interpretation, 631–32, 633–34,
    634nn.179–80, 643–44
  constitutional design, 606–7
  delegation, 639–58
  delegation of authority to change treaty
    obligation, 641–44
  dispute resolution, 625–29, 625–26nn.134–
    37, 626n.138, 628n.147, 628n.151, 628–
    29n.153, 637–38, 637–38n.197
  establishing commitments by means other
    than agreement, 585, 585n.908
  execution, 638–39
  executive authority delegation, 656–58
  historical perspectives, 602–15
  incorporation of lawmaking into U.S.
    law, 629–58
  international dispute resolution, 637–38,
    637–38n.197
  international legislation/rulemaking, 634–37,
    635nn.182–87, 636nn.188–92
  judicial authority delegation, 647–56, 649–
    50nn.251–52, 650n.255, 651nn.257–58,
    652–53n.265, 654n.271
  legislative authority delegation, 644–47,
    645n.233

nondelegation doctrine, 644–47, 645n.233
observer status, 617–18
peacekeeping missions, 624, 624n.126
post-agreement-ratification practice,
     607–15, 608nn.38–39, 609n.42, 609n.45,
     610n.53, 611–12nn.58–60, 612n.63,
     613–14nn.73–75
post-ratification side agreements, 642–43
ratification, 617–18, 617n.93
recommit capacity, 619–20
reservations, understandings, and
     declarations (RUDs), 861–62
rulemaking engagement method, 620–29,
     621–22nn.112–18, 622–23nn.119–21,
     624nn.126–27
spending power defenses, 623–24,
     624nn.126–27
state authority, 790–91
tacit amendment procedures, 630–31
treaty changes, incorporation into U.S. law,
     629–58, 630nn.160–61, 633nn.173–74,
     633n.176
treaty reservations, 632
voice-and-vote provisions, 621–24,
     622–23nn.119–21
withdrawal/suspension method, 618–20,
     618–19nn.98–101, 620–3nn.105–8
International Organization Immunities
     Act (IOIA, 1945), 287–95, 288n.715,
     289nn.723–24, 290nn.727–28, 290n.729,
     291nn.735–38, 293nn.749–51
International Refugee Assistance Project v.
     Trump, 875
International Telegraph Union, 607–8
Iran-Contra Affair, 72–73, 85
Iran Nuclear Agreement Review Act
     (2015), 63
Iran-U.S. Claims Tribunal, 616–17, 649–50
Iran v. Gould, 157–58
Islamic State of Iraq/Levant (ISIL), 191–92,
     192n.106, 714–15, 736–38

J.P. Morgan Chase Bank v. Traffic Stream (BVI)
     Infrastructure Ltd., 159
Jam v. International Finance Corporation, 288–
     93, 289nn.723–24, 293n.751
Japan Line, Ltd. V. County of Los
     Angeles, 826–28
Japanese internment, WWII, 44–46, 45n.282
Jerusalem Embassy Act (1995), 141–43,
     142–43n.226
Jesner v. Arab Bank, 406–7, 406–7n.463
Johnson v. Eisentrager, 781–82, 859, 941–42

Joint Comprehensive Plan of Action (JCPOA,
     2015), 581–82, 581–82nn.888–91, 583,
     583n.898, 596
judiciary. *See also* Supreme Court
     act of state doctrine, 199–210, 200n.162, 201–
          2nn.174–77, 203–4nn.182–87, 205n.194,
          206n.196, 206–7n.200, 207n.206, 362–63,
          362–63n.225
     adjudicative jurisdiction, 231–33, 231–
          32n.356, 232n.360, 232–33n.363,
          233nn.366–67
     allocation/balance of powers, 4–5, 6–7, 9–11,
          21–22, 21n.133, 22n.137
     appellate authority, 176–77
     congressional powers to regulate, 52–53
     congressional role in act of state doctrine,
          208–9, 209nn.213–14
     congressional role in standing issues, 194–95,
          194n.124
     constitutional design, 178–81, 178–79nn.23–
          26, 179n.28, 181n.39, 181n.44
     criminal jurisdiction, 212–14, 212n.231,
          214n.241
     customary international law, 330–33, 330–
          31n.50, 356–70, 357n.193, 358nn.197–98,
          359–24nn.203–7
     enforcement jurisdiction, 234–35, 234n.372
     executive branch role in act of state
          doctrine, 209–10
     expropriations cases, 200, 200n.162
     foreign-owned debt collection claims,
          177, 177–78n.18, 178–79, 812–13, 819,
          819n.212, 819n.213, 820n.217, 821–22 (*see*
          also claims settlement)
     foreign sovereign immunity, 246–52 (*see also*
          Foreign Sovereign Immunities Act [FSIA])
     forum non conveniens, 242
     historical role, 176–83
     immunity from U.S. jurisdiction, 246–321
     injury-in-fact requirement, 194, 194n.124
     institutional injury, 194–95
     international agreements authority
          delegation, 647–56, 649–50nn.251–52,
          650n.255, 651nn.257–58, 652–53n.265,
          654n.271
     international rules impacts, 210–46
     jurisdiction, constitutional limits, 230–31
     jurisdictional bases, 211–35
     maritime matters historically, 176–77
     nationality (active personality) jurisdiction,
          216–19, 217n.257, 217n.259, 217n.262,
          219n.271
     nonbinding agreements, 582–83

judiciary (*cont.*)
   nonjusticiability and foreign affairs, 184–99
   passive personality jurisdiction, 219–22,
      219nn.273–75, 219–20nn.276–79,
      220–21nn.280–84
   political question doctrine, 184–92,
      184nn.56–57, 185n.61, 188nn.80–84,
      189nn.85–87, 189n.90, 190n.92, 191n.101,
      191–92nn.105–6, 201, 921–23, 951–52
   prescriptive comity, 242–46, 242n.421,
      243nn.425–26, 243nn.429–30, 244n.432,
      244n.437, 245n.442
   prescriptive jurisdiction, 212–31, 283
   presumption against extraterritoriality,
      235–41, 236n.380, 236n.388, 237n.393,
      238–39nn.397–98, 239nn.399–401,
      239nn.402–4, 240n.409, 241n.413,
      245–46
   private parties standing, 195
   protective jurisdiction, 222–24, 222n.292,
      222–24nn.293–97, 224nn.298–301
   prudential standing, 193, 194
   reasonableness, 242–46, 244n.437
   ripeness/mootness, 195–99, 196n.134,
      196n.135, 197nn.141–42, 198nn.149–50,
      198nn.151–53
   role generally, 175
   Senate, deference to, 497–509, 500n.463,
      501n.467, 501–2n.471, 502nn.474–76,
      503nn.479–80, 504–5nn.484–86,
      505n.492, 506n.493
   separation-of-powers, 193–94
   standing, 193–95, 193n.119, 194n.124, 194–
      95n.127, 230, 230n.342
   statute of limitations/foreign debt
      collection, 833–35
   territorial/effects jurisdiction, 212–16,
      213nn.234–37, 214n.241, 214–15nn.244–
      45, 215nn.247–49
   treaty power, 178–80, 179n.26, 179n.28,
      180n.37, 454–57, 454–55nn.200–2, 456–
      57nn.205–12, 492–93, 492–93nn.413–19
   treaty power, deference to executive branch,
      495–97, 498–99nn.451–57
   universal jurisdiction, 224–30, 224–25nn.302–6,
      227n.320, 229n.335, 229n.337, 230n.340,
      230n.342
   waivers/act of state doctrine, 207, 207n.206
Judiciary Act of 1789, 181–83, 181n.42, 335–36
jurisdiction
   adjudicative, 231–33, 231–32n.356,
      232n.360, 232–33n.363, 233nn.366–67
   bases of, 211–35

   civil claims, 228–29
   criminal jurisdiction, 212–14, 212n.231,
      214n.241, 240–41, 240n.411, 794–95
   detained noncitizens rights, 296–97,
      297n.775
   forum non conveniens, 231–32, 231–32n.356
   Guantánamo Bay detainees, 234
   habeas corpus actions, 933–35
   human rights, 203–4
   illicit sexual conduct, 218–19, 218n.268
   immunity from U.S. jurisdiction, 246–321
   Ker-Frisbie rule, 910–14
   law of nations, 325–26, 331–32, 332nn.57–
      59, 336–37, 336n.77, 361–62, 381n.322
   matters re-empti partially within territory,
      215, 215nn.247–49
   nationality (active personality), 216–19,
      217n.257, 217n.259, 217n.262, 219n.271
   passive personality, 219–22, 219nn.273–75,
      219–20nn.276–79, 220–21nn.280–84
   prescriptive, 212–31, 283
   protective, 222–24, 222n.292, 222–24nn.293–
      97, 224nn.298–301
   prudential exhaustion requirement, 233,
      233n.366
   taxation, 218–19, 218n.270
   territorial/effects, 212–16, 213nn.234–37,
      214n.241, 214–15nn.244–45, 215nn.247–
      49, 216nn.254–55
   terrorism, 221–22, 229
   universal, 224–30, 224–175nn.302–3,
      225–176nn.304–6, 227n.320, 229n.335,
      229n.337, 230n.340, 230n.342
   war powers, 728–29, 781–82
Jurisdictional Immunities of the State case, 284
jus cogens doctrine
   act of state doctrine, 203–4, 204n.185
   customary international law, 377–79,
      377–79nn.300–9
   FSIA offences, 256–58, 257nn.522–25, 318–
      19, 318nn.873–76
   human rights, 402, 403n.444
Justice Against Sponsors of Terrorism Act
   (JASTA, 2016), 60, 61, 279, 283n.685

keep and bear arms/Second Amendment, 882–
   87, 885n.236, 886n.245
Kent v. Dulles, 929–30
Ker-Frisbie rule, 910–14
Ker v. Illinois, 910–12
King v. Morton, 856–57
Kinsella v. United States ex rel. Singleton, 936
Kiobel v. Royal Dutch Petroleum Co., 70–71, 241

Kleindienst v. Mandel, 872–74, 875–76
Kolovrat v. Oregon, 813–14
Korematsu v. United States, 44–46, 45n.282, 49, 49n.315
Kyoto Protocol (1997), 463–64, 463n.244

labor-management relations, 33
LaFontant v. Aristide, 306n.824
Lamont v. Postmaster General, 869, 869n.125
land and naval forces regulation, 3–4
land and water captures, 3–4
Langenegger v. United States, 922
Lanuza v. Love, 901–2
law of nations. *See also* customary
    international law
    generally, 323–24
    appoint-and-receive powers, 113–14
    appointing U.S. ambassadors/ministers/
        consuls, 133–34, 133–34n.182
    authority in U.S. law, 333
    Congress powers, 3, 52, 55–56, 327–29, 338–
        44, 338n.92
    judiciary powers, 330–33, 330–31n.50
    jurisdiction, 325–26, 331–32, 332nn.57–59,
        336–37, 336n.77, 361–62, 381n.322
    noncitizen tort claims, 70–71
    offenses against (Offences Clause), 338–
        44, 338n.92, 339nn.95–96, 340n.100,
        341n.108, 343n.116, 344n.122
    pre-constitutional experience, 324–27
    president powers, 329–30
    residual authority, 344–46
    rights of belligerents/neutrals, 334–35, 334n.69
League of Nations, Covenant of the, 434,
        608–12, 609n.42, 609n.45, 610n.53, 611–
        12nn.58–60, 612n.63, 685–86
Take Care Clause, 329–30
Lebanon Emergency Assistance Act (1983), 703
LeClerc v. Webb, 949–50
legislative powers/Congress
    generally, 51–52
    antitrust, 98
    bribery of foreign officials, 98–99, 99n.345
    classified information, 74–76
    commerce regulation powers, 52, 58, 88–101,
        88n.267
    conduct solely within foreign countries, 91–93,
        91nn.283–84, 93n.297
    congressional authorization method/
        consequences, 725–29, 727–28nn.402–5
    congressional-executive agreements, 94–95,
        561–73, 570n.827, 570n.831, 571nn.833–34,
        571–72n.836, 817–18

congressional reporting, 68–69
consultation requirements, 68–69
contempt, 73–74, 74n.162
customary international law, 335–46
delegation, 21–22, 62, 62n.83
denial of funds, 85–87
enumerated/unenumerated powers, 52–
    58, 55n.35
executive acquiescence, 67–68
executive privilege, 76–80, 79–80n.202
extraterritoriality, 69–71, 70n.136, 70n.137
felonies committed on the high seas, 3, 52,
    70, 327–29, 328n.35, 328–29n.38, 335–38,
    337n.81, 337n.84
foreign assistance provision, 60, 68, 80–88,
    85n.243
foreign coin value regulation, 3, 52, 101–3,
    103n.379
foreign commerce power scope, 89–93,
    90n.276, 91nn.283–84
foreign investment, 96–98, 97n.328
funding reductions, 86–87
House/Senate committees, 59–60, 59n.61
knowing standard, 98–99
legislative veto, 22, 22n.137, 61–63
military force authorization, 673–77, 695–96,
    702–3, 706–9, 712–17, 719–22, 725–29,
    727–28nn.402–5, 732–34, 737–38, 740–41
    (*see also* war powers)
money laundering, 98
oversight methods, 71–80
presentment, 61–63
presidential emergency economic
    powers, 99–101
presidential signing statements, 63–69,
    65n.104
presumptions/foreign statute interpretation,
    69–71, 70n.136, 70n.137
report-and-wait provisions, 63
spending power, 52–53, 80–88, 85n.243
statutory authorizations, 673–77, 678–
    79, 681–82
subpoenas, 73–74, 78
trade in goods/services, 94–96
troop withdrawals, 86–88
withholding of information by executive
    branch, 74–80, 79n.196, 79–80n.202
Lemon v. Kurtzman, 875–76, 876n.174
Lend-Lease Act (1941), 687
letters of marque and reprisal, 3–4, 17
libel tourism, 870
liberty to travel to/from the U.S., 929–31,
    929n.525, 929n.529, 931n.547

Libya
air strikes, 722–24
entry of nationals to U.S., 876–77
low-intensity armed conflict
authority, 734–35
sanctions on, 636–37, 636n.188, 722
terrorism, 400
U.S. military interventions
in, 701, 714–15, 714n.321, 722–24,
723n.373, 734–35
U.S. plaintiff claims against, 927–28
Line Item Veto Act challenge, 194–95,
194–95n.127
Little v. Barreme, 674, 749–50, 760–61
Litvinov Assignment, 164, 819–21, 819n.212,
819n.213, 820n.217
Lobbying Disclosure Act (1995), 135–36
Lone Star Infrastructure Protection Act
(2021), 98
Lottawana, The, 360–61
Lotus case, 212, 212n.228, 219, 219n.273
Lowry v. Reagan, 701–2
LULAC v. Bredesen, 949–50
Luther v. Borden, 184–85, 184nn.56–57

male captus bene detentus, 910–11
Marbury v. Madison, 812–13
Maritime Drug Law Enforcement Act (MDLEA,
1986), 70, 222–23, 223–24nn.296–97, 229,
397, 397n.410, 399, 399n.419
maritime law. *See also* piracy
Captures Clause, 764–68
customary international law, 359–60, 395–96,
396n.401
felonies committed on the high seas, 3, 52,
70, 327–29, 328n.35, 328–29n.38, 335–38,
337n.81, 337n.84
judiciary matters historically, 176–77
land/water capture rule making
powers, 764–68
letters of marque/reprisal, 659–60, 661,
662–63, 664, 666, 669–70, 766, 768–70,
770nn.655–56
preemptionby federal statute, 804–5
searches of U.S. citizens by U.S. government,
899–900, 899n.334
Massachusetts v. EPA, 841–42
McCready v. Virginia, 952
Medellín v. Texas
generally, 121–22
binding international legal obligation,
582–83, 637, 642–43, 649–
50, 653–54

enforcement of ICJ rulings, 507–8, 508–
9nn.512–13, 525–27, 525–26nn.604–8,
527n.612
premption by presidential action, 38–39,
42, 107–8, 353–54, 353–54n.172,
582–83, 814–17, 816–17nn.194–97,
817n.198, 821–24
privately enforceable rights, 517
sole executive agreements re-emption state
law, 578
Take Care Clause authority, 355–56,
356n.187
treaty non-self-execution, 296–97, 297n.772,
521–24, 521nn.578–80, 523n.594, 528–29,
528–29nn.614–16, 529nn.620–21, 535
Merryman, Ex parte, 44, 680–81
methodology
American Law Institute (ALI) restatements,
xxiii–xxiv
comparative foreign relations law, xxiv–xxv
constitutional law, xix–xxii
Executive Orders, xxii
international law, xxii–xxiii
regulations, xxii
statutory law, xxii
terminology, xxvi
Mexican Debt Disclosure Act of 1995, 79
Migration and Refugee Assistance Act
(1962), 968
Migratory Bird Treaty Act (1918), 434–35
Military Commissions Act (2006), 942
military commissions/tribunals, 40, 713,
779–82, 906, 931–32, 936, 940–42,
940n.608
military detention of noncitizens abroad,
931–35, 932n.556, 933n.560,
934nn.568–69
Military Extraterritorial Jurisdiction Act
(2000), 218–19
Military Rules of Evidence, 776
militia-related war powers, 3–4, 5, 661, 667–68,
758–59, 782–85, 882–87
Millennium Challenge Corporation (MCC),
85n.243
Milligan, Ex Parte, 756, 780
Miscellaneous Receipts Act (1849), 84–85
Missouri v. Holland, 434–36, 475–76, 476n.316,
479–80, 481–82, 481nn.350–51, 541–44,
788–89, 952–53
Monasky v. Taglieri, 984
money laundering, 70, 98, 217, 217n.261, 270,
270n.606
Montevideo Convention (1933), 160

mootness/ripeness, 195–99, 196n.134, 196n.135, 197nn.141–42, 198nn.149–50, 198nn.151–53

Morrison v. National Australia Bank Ltd., 236, 238, 238–39nn.397–98

Morrison v. Olson, 6n.43

Movsesian v. Victoria Versicherung AG, 834–35

Multistate Tax Comm'n case, 845–46

Munaf v. Geren, 993–94

Murray v. Schooner Charming Betsy, 71, 235–36, 245–46, 256, 284, 382–87, 383–84n.335, 384n.337, 385n.342, 386nn.349–51, 387nn.353–56, 399

mutual legal assistance treaties (MLATs), 938–39

Myers v. United States, 138–39

NAFTA (1992), 94–95, 344–45, 491–92, 557–58, 557n.767, 561, 567–68, 568nn.819–21, 569–70, 570n.831, 601–2, 615–16, 628–29, 629n.156, 649, 653

NAFTA Implementation Act (1993), 649

National City Bank of New York v. Republic of China, 152

National Commitments Resolution (1969), 697

national emergency/national security
access/unlawful disclosure of foreign relations information, 878–81, 878nn.188–90
allocation/balance of powers, 42–49, 47n.303, 49n.315
civil liberties, 42–49, 47n.303, 49n.315
defense against foreign attack/Second Amendment, 883–84
enemy aliens, 918–19
foreign investment, 97–98
individual rights exception, 871, 871nn.138–41
president's proclamation powers, 876–78
provision of support to terrorist groups, 881–82
wiretapping/electronic surveillance, 890–92, 898

National Guard, 5, 784–85. *See also* militia-related war powers

National Petrochemical Co. of Iran v. The M/T Stolt Sheaf, 158

NATO Status of Forces Agreement (1951), 558

NATO use of force authorization, 730–31

Naturalization Clause, 850

naturalization uniform rule, 3, 52

Naval Militia, 785

navy provision/maintenance, 3–4

Necessary and Proper Clause, 54–55

needful buildings, congressional powers, 3–4

Neely v. Henkel, 993n.1010

Nestlé USA, Inc. v. Doe, 241, 404–5, 406–7, 406–7n.463, 407n.467

Neutrality Crisis, 183

New York Times Co. v. United States, 76–77, 880–81

9/11 Commission, 73

Nixon v. United States, 76–77

non-self-execution of treaties
generally, 511–16, 513n.532, 515nn.549–51
consequences, 520–24, 520n.575, 521nn.578–80, 523–24n.595
Constitution-based inquiry, 530–31nn.627–28, 531nn.629–31, 532nn.632–35
declarations by treaty makers, 535–40, 537nn.659–61, 539nn.669–70, 540nn.674–76
justiciability-based inquiry, 533–35, 533–34nn.641–46
nonbinding agreements as, 582–83
obligations, implementing by other means, 540–44, 541–42nn.682–84, 543nn.691–95, 544nn.696–97, 544nn.699–701
re-emption by treaty, 814–15
treaty-based inquiry, 524–29, 524nn.596–97, 525n.602, 525–26nn.604–8, 527nn.609–11, 527n.612
U.N. Security Council use of force authorization, 743–44, 743n.492

noncitizens. *See also* immigration law
alien enemies, 852–53, 859–60
alien enemy property, 924
arrest/extradition of foreign national/ Compact Clause, 844–45
asset freezes, 100, 819–20, 819n.212, 819n.213, 820n.217, 924–25
Bivens actions by, 900–2
closeness/connectivity, 851–53, 859–60, 884–85, 895–96, 920, 920n.473
concepts, definitions, 850–51, 850n.1, 850nn.5–6, 851n.8
constitutional protections, 850–53, 851nn.9–11, 859–60, 868–69
denial of entry to U.S., 872–73, 873n.154, 876–77, 876n.174
deportation hearings, 852, 869–70, 893–94, 974–79, 975n.864
detained noncitizens rights, 296–97, 297n.775
detention abroad, 868–69
driver's licenses, 949–50

noncitizens (*cont.*)
employment of undocumented noncitizens, 806–7
equal protection for noncitizens in U.S., 916–19
federal civil service employment, 916–17
Fifth Amendment protections, 905nn.374–78, 906n.381
First Amendment protections, 869–70
green cards, 852–53
immigration status, 852–53
in-state status/G-4 visas, 806, 806n.119
individual rights abroad, 857–60, 857n.51, 858n.58, 859n.64, 863n.93, 863–64nn.96–101
lawful permanent resident removal due to affiliation, 958–59
lawful permanent residents, 852–54, 853n.20, 875–76, 884–85, 889–90, 918–19, 963–64
lawful permanent residents/equal protection, 946–49, 947n.665
liberty to travel to and from the U.S., 933n.560
mandatory detention, 976
military detention abroad, 931–35, 932n.556, 933n.560, 934nn.568–69
nonimmigrant noncitizens, 852
nonimmigrant noncitizens/equal protection, 949–50
overriding national interests, 917–18, 917n.444, 917n.452
post-indictment right of counsel/noncitizen located abroad, 938
property inheritance by, 829–31, 831n.293
public education, 950–51, 951nn.695–97
registration of, 57, 805–6, 805n.112
right to bear arms in U.S., 884–86, 885n.236, 886n.245
right to speedy U.S. trial/noncitizen located abroad, 937, 937nn.587–89
right to travel to U.S., 931
rights in U.S., 850–54
search and seizure/Fourth Amendment, 859–60, 892–94, 892nn.283–85, 907–8
selective-enforcement claims, 852
taking of property without just compensation, 919–28, 920n.473, 921n.476, 922n.482
tort claims/law of nations, 70–71
U.S. abduction of noncitizens abroad for prosecution in U.S., 910–14, 911n.407, 911n.408, 913nn.419–20

U.S. civil/criminal actions against noncitizens located abroad, 914–15, 914–15nn.426–29, 915n.430
U.S. criminal investigation/noncitizens abroad, 907–10, 907n.384, 907n.386, 914–15nn.426–29, 915n.430
undocumented noncitizens, 852–53
undocumented noncitizens/equal protection, 950–51, 951nn.695–97
undocumented noncitizens statutory provisions, 807–8
voting rights, 852–53, 853n.20, 856, 947–48
writ of habeas corpus, 905–6, 906n.381, 931–32, 933–35, 962–63
nondelegation doctrine, 21–22, 21n.133
North American Free Trade Agreement (1992). *See* NAFTA
NRDC v. EPA, 641–43, 644

OBB Personenverkehr AG v. Sachs, 272, 272n.616
Offences Clause, 338–44, 338n.92, 339nn.95–96, 340n.100, 341n.108, 343n.116, 344n.122, 371–72, 373, 543–44, 544nn.696–97, 761, 802
Omnibus Trade and Competitiveness Act (1988), 95–96
Organization of American States (OAS), 863–64
Ornelas v. Ruiz, 992–93
Outer Space Treaty (1967), 528, 528n.615
Ozanic v. United States, 165–66

Palestine Liberation Organization (PLO), 129–31, 129n.142, 130n.153
Palestinian Authority, 83
Panama
access to U.S. courts, 156–57
extraterritoriality, 230, 230n.340
head of state immunity, 310n.844
liability of foreign state/officials, 208–9, 209n.213
non-recognition of head of state, 154, 161, 306, 306n.824
U.S. military interventions in, 145, 684, 701, 734–35
Panama Canal Treaty (1903), 442–43, 443n.147, 453, 453n.191, 531, 531n.631
Panama Convention (1975), 267–68, 267n.587, 628–29, 637–38, 637–38n.197
Paquete Habana, The, 353–54, 354nn.173–74, 357–58, 357n.193, 361, 375–76, 390–92, 390n.367, 391nn.372–74, 394–95

passport place of birth listing, 6–7, 29–30,
    30n.190, 40–41, 40n.259, 42, 66–68,
    67n.120, 107, 123, 123n.96, 147, 186–87
Patriot Act (2001), 890
Patsone v. Pennsylvania, 952
Peace Corps Amendments, 59
peacekeeping missions
    FSIA, 289–95, 289n.724, 295n.759
    international organization agreements, 624,
        624n.126
    war powers, 691, 702, 718–19, 720–21,
        720n.358, 738
Pentagon Papers, 880–81
peremptory norms. See *jus cogens* doctrine
Perez v. Brownell, 980
Permanent Court of Arbitration, 607–8
Permanent Court of International Justice
    (PCIJ), 609–12, 613–14
Pfizer, Inc. v. Government of India, 156
Philippine Independence Act (1934), 148
piracy. *See also* Maritime Drug Law
        Enforcement Act (MDLEA, 1986);
        maritime law
    customary international law, 3, 327–29,
        328n.35, 328–29n.38, 336–38, 337n.81,
        337n.84, 396–99, 397nn.410–11, 397–
        98nn.412–15, 398nn.416–17
    felonies committed on the high seas, 3, 52,
        70, 327–29, 328n.35, 328–29n.38, 335–38,
        337n.81, 337n.84
    historical perspectives, 604–5, 605nn.19–23
    Supreme Court holdings, 337–38, 337n.84
Plyler v. Doe, 950–51, 951nn.695–97
political question doctrine, 9–10, 184–92,
        184nn.56–57, 185n.61, 188nn.80–84,
        189nn.85–87, 189n.90, 190n.92, 191n.101,
        191–92nn.105–6, 201, 921–23, 951–52
power of the purse, 52–53, 80–88, 85n.243
preemption
    generally, 800–39, 800n.80
    Compact Clause, 839–47
    concurrent regulatory authority, 804–5
    conflict re-emption, 803
    congressional-executive agreements, 817–18
    congressional purpose test, 804, 817–18
    by customary international law, 836–39
    by dormant foreign affairs power, 829–
        36, 846–47
    by dormant Foreign Commerce Clause, 825–
        29, 835–36, 846–47
    employment of undocumented
        noncitizens, 806–7
    express re-emption, 803

    by federal statutes, 802–12, 803n.93,
        804nn.104–6
    field re-emption, 803
    foreign relations context, 804–5
    immigration law, 57, 803, 805–8, 805n.112,
        806n.119
    licensing of undocumented
        noncitizens, 806–7
    noncitizen registration, 805–6
    preclearance, 810
    by presidential action, 819–25, 819n.212,
        819n.213, 820n.217, 822n.236
    sanctions/government procurement, 809–10
    by treaty, 810–18, 812n.165, 816–17nn.194–
        97, 817n.198
prescriptive comity, 242–46, 242n.421,
        243nn.425–26, 243nn.429–30, 244n.432,
        244n.437, 245n.442
president
    allocation/balance of powers, 5–9
    allocation/balance of powers advantages
        generally, 20–23
    allocation/balance of powers advantages
        unique to foreign relations, 23–30,
        25n.160, 26n.164, 30n.190
    appoint-and-receive powers, 105–8, 106n.6,
        110–32, 119n.74, 119–20nn.79–80,
        125n.113, 347–48, 348nn.144–45, 445–46,
        445–46n.162
    broad grant of authority, 116–17
    classified information, 74–76, 75n.171
    commander-in-chief power, 33–35, 87–88,
        191–92, 192n.106, 347–48, 348n.143,
        354–56, 355n.183, 558, 576–78, 576n.862,
        577n.868, 668–69, 680, 686–87, 687n.172,
        695, 715–16, 736–37, 736n.446, 754–64,
        755n.547, 755n.550, 757n.563
    conducting foreign relations (*see* conducting
        foreign relations)
    congressional-executive agreements,
        94–95, 558, 559, 559n.777, 561–73,
        561–62nn.788–92, 570n.827, 570n.831,
        571nn.833–34, 571–72n.836, 599–600,
        599–600nn.982–84, 811–12, 817–18
    consultation requirements, 68–69
    customary international law powers, 329–30,
        346–56, 347nn.137–40, 389–95, 390n.367,
        391nn.372–74, 391n.375, 392nn.379–81,
        393nn.384–86, 394–95nn.392–96
    emergency economic powers, 99–101
    executive acquiescence, 67–68
    executive orders, 44–46, 45n.282
    executive privilege, 76–80, 79–80n.202

president (*cont.*)
  faithful execution of laws, 7–8, 7–8nn.49–50, 38n.245, 65–66
  foreign relations powers not derived from Constitution, 14, 14nn.88–89
  immigration law authority, 959–61, 966–67, 967n.802
  international organization agreements, 618–20, 618–19nn.98–101, 620–3nn.105–8, 623–24
  issuing directives to state courts, 122
  Japanese internment, WWII, 44–46, 45n.282
  later-in-time principle, 381–82, 382n.325
  letters of marque/reprisal, 3–4, 17, 327
  nature, scope, and duration standard, 31–32
  persona non grata designation, 119–20, 119–20nn.79–80, 131–32
  political question doctrine, 191–92, 191–92nn.105–6
  re-emption by presidential action, 819–25, 819n.212, 819n.213, 820n.217
  presidential signing statements, 63–69, 65n.104
  proclamation powers, 116, 876–78
  recognition of new foreign state, 144–47
  recognition powers, 67, 107, 113–18, 114–15nn.54–55, 120–21, 148, 163–67, 186–87
  seizures/confiscations, 381–82, 382n.325, 389–92
  Take Care authority/treaty incorporation, 522–24, 522nn.584–86, 523n.594, 573–74, 824
  trade in goods/services, 94–96
  treaty authority to exit, 589–96, 591nn.940–41, 591n.942, 592–93nn.949–52, 594–95nn.959–61, 595n.966
  treaty power, 444–51, 444–45nn.155–56, 445–46nn.162–63, 446nn.164–65, 447nn.166–67, 447–48nn.168–73, 448–49nn.174–76, 449–51nn.178–83, 522–24, 522nn.584–86, 523n.594, 573–74, 583
  treaty ratification by, xv–xvi, 18, 458–60, 459nn.220–22, 459nn.223–25, 501
  troop withdrawals, 86–88
  war powers, 666–69, 674–77, 675n.99, 680–81, 691–704, 710–17, 731–50
  war powers preclusive authority, 748–50, 750n.522, 759, 762–63
  War Powers Resolution (1973), 61–62, 191–92, 191n.105
  withholding of information by executive branch, 74–80, 79n.196, 79–80n.202

press freedoms (First Amendment), 869–82, 869n.125
presumption against extraterritoriality, 235–41, 236n.380, 236n.388, 237n.393, 238–39nn.397–98, 239nn.399–401, 239nn.402–4, 240n.409, 241n.413, 245–46
Prize Cases, The, 680, 759, 767
Proclamation of Neutrality (1793), 116
Promoting Security and Justice for Victims of Terrorism Act (PSJVTA, 2019), 131
PROTECT Act (2003), 91–93, 93n.297, 218–19
public health emergencies, 43–44
Public Interest Declassification Act (2000), 75n.171
public ministers/consuls. *See* ambassadors/ministers/consul, U.S.
Puerto Rico, 854–56

Quirin, Ex Parte, 779–81, 940–41

Raines v. Byrd, 194–95, 194–95n.127
Ralls Corporation v. CFIUS, 97–98
Ramirez de Arellano v. Weinberger, 921–22
Rasul v. Bush, 781–82, 933–34
reasonableness of interference with sovereign authority of other states in antitrust context, 242–46, 244n.437
Reception Clause, 105
Reciprocal Trade Agreements Act (1934), 94
recognition powers. *See also under* president, recognition powers
  access to U.S. courts/nationals of foreign entity, 159
  accommodating newly created foreign states, 169–71, 169n.386
  asset freezes and nonrecognition, 100, 819–20, 819n.212, 819n.213, 820n.217
  ceding territory, 148
  collective nonrecognition, 150–51
  conclusion of executive agreements incidental to recognition, 163–67
  Congress's limited role, 147–49, 158–59, 163, 308, 308n.835
  de facto approach, 152–54
  foreign belligerency/insurgency, 167–68
  foreign government coming to power extraconstitutionally, 151–56, 207–8
  foreign state/government inability to access U.S. courts, 156–59, 157n.322, 232, 232n.360
  head-of-state immunity, 306–8, 308n.833, 308nn.834–36, 309n.838

inability to claim foreign sovereign immunity
    from suit, 159–60
inability to control foreign state property
    located in U.S., 161
joint resolutions, 149, 149n.269
nonrecognition, 149–51, 154–67
popular support of government, 153
president generally, 67, 107, 113–18, 114–
    15nn.54–55, 120–21, 163–67, 186–87
presidential prerogative, 144–47, 146n.253
public/external acts/nonrecognized
    foreign entity not given effect by U.S.
    courts, 161–63
recognition of new foreign state, 144–51
of state in treaty making, 437–38, 438n.127
taxation, 165
war powers, 148
withdrawal of recognition, 151, 154, 292–93,
    293nn.749–51
Refugee Act (1980), 968, 976–77
refugees, 968–70, 969n.817, 970n.829
Regan v. Wald, 930–31
Reid v. Covert, 56–57, 435–36, 475–76,
    476n.316, 480n.347, 778, 858–59, 858n.58,
    896–97, 906, 907–8, 936
religious freedoms (First Amendment), 869–82,
    869n.125
Republic of Argentina v. Weltover, 269–70, 271,
    271–72nn.611–12
Republic of Austria v. Altmann, 252–54,
    253–54n.498
Republic of Mexico v. Hoffman, 249–50,
    250nn.475–76
ripeness/mootness, 195–99, 196n.134,
    196n.135, 197nn.141–42, 198nn.149–50,
    198nn.151–53
RJR Nabisco, Inc. v. European Community,
    236–38, 236n.388, 238–39n.398,
    239nn.401–4
Rogers Act (1924), 134–35
Rome Statute, 463–64, 463n.242
Roper v. Simmons, 372–73, 372nn.276–78, 944
Ross, In re, 857–58, 935–36
Rubin v. Islamic Republic of Iran, 286–87
Rucho v. Common Cause, 187
Rules of Court Martial, 776
Russian Volunteer Fleet v. United States, 919–20
Rutgers v. Waddington, 177–78n.18,
    374–75n.286

S.S. "Lotus" judgment (*Lotus* case), 212,
    212n.228, 219, 219n.273
Sale v. Haitian Centers Council, Inc., 976–77

Salimoff v. Standard Oil Co., 162
SALT II Treaty (1979), 460–61, 461n.230, 462–
    63, 462n.236
Samantar v. Yousuf, 302–3, 302–3n.803,
    305, 306, 312–14, 313n.854, 365–66,
    381n.322
Sanchez-Espinoza v. Reagan, 701–2
Sanchez-Llamas v. Oregon, 507–9, 653–54
Saudi Arabia v. Nelson, 270
Schneiderman v. United States, 980–81
Schooner Exchange, The, 248–49, 248n.455,
    248n.457, 248nn.459–61, 252, 265
search and seizure/Fourth Amendment
    generally, 859–60, 888–904, 888nn.259–
    61, 907–8
    abroad, 893, 894–900, 895n.309, 896nn.312–
    15, 896–97nn.316–21, 899n.334
    Bivens actions by noncitizens, 900–2
    conducted by foreign government, 898–99
    noncitizens, 892–94
    surveillance of citizens, 889–92
Second Amendment, 882–87
Second Hickenlooper Amendment, 208–9
Seery v. United States, 920
Selective Training and Service Act
    (1940), 773–74
September 11, 2001 attacks, 46–47, 63–64, 73,
    354–55, 710–11, 712–13, 890–92, 932–
    33, 941–42
Sessions v. Dimaya, 959
Shaughnessy v. Mezei, 959–60
Sherman Act (1890), 243–44
Sixth Amendment, 935–42, 935n.575
slavery/slave-trading, 227–28
Social Security totalization agreements, 566,
    566n.812
Soering v. United Kingdom, 995
sole organ power, 27–30, 30n.190
Somalia
    anti-terrorism operations, 713–14, 714n.320
    anticipated hostilities, 742, 748
    covert operations, 740
    entry of nationals to U.S., 876–77
    funding restrictions, 774
    head-of-state immunity, 314–15, 314n.858
    humanitarian interventions, 718–20, 740
    military location restrictions, 774
    nature, scope, and duration standard, 748
    piracy, 396–97, 397n.406
    U.S. military interventions, 703, 713–14,
        719–20, 734–35, 737–40, 738n.462, 742,
        748, 774
    withdrawal of U.S. troops from, 703

Sosa v. Alvarez-Machain, 228, 356–58, 364–
65, 365nn.239–40, 366n.250, 368–69,
369n.265, 402–5, 403n.444, 405nn.452–56
sovereignty
duties of U.S. citizens living abroad, 56–57
inability to claim foreign sovereign immunity
from suit, 159–60
maritime/air spaces, 55–56
powers inherent, 11–16, 11n.74, 12n.77,
27–28, 56–57
public/external acts/nonrecognized
foreign entity not given effect by U.S.
courts, 161–63
Spacil v. Crowe, 307n.829
special committee oversight methods, 72–73
SPEECH Act (2010), 870
speech freedoms (First Amendment), 869–82,
869n.125
standing, 193–95, 193n.119, 194n.124, 194–
95n.127, 230, 230n.342
Stanford v. Kentucky, 943–44
START Agreement (1991), 488–89, 489n.393
states' rights. *See also* federalism
boundaries/Compact Clause, 842–44
Compact Clause, 839–47
federalism *vs.*, 17–19
foreign relations power, 13–14, 17–19
sovereign immunity, 798–99
treaty power, 429–32, 429n.82, 430n.87, 430–
31nn.90–91, 454, 479–81, 479nn.339–
40, 556–57
war powers, 790
Steel Seizure case. *See Youngstown Sheet & Tube
Co. v. Sawyer*
Strategic Defense Initiative, 503–4
subpoenas
administrative/Holocaust-era claims, 831
congressional oversight, 71, 73–74, 78,
78nn.192–93
criminal investigations/noncitizens abroad,
907, 907n.384
immunity to, 254, 311–12, 311n.848, 314–15,
315n.860
right to confront/compel testimony of
witnesses located abroad, 938–39
of sitting presidents, 79–80, 79–80n.202
standing to issue, 194–95
Supreme Court. *See also* judiciary
access to U.S. courts/nationals of foreign
entity, 159
ad valorem property tax, 826–28
admissibility of noncitizens, 966–67,
967n.802

aiding-and-abetting liability, 407–9,
407–8nn.468–72
asset freezes and nonrecognition, 819–21
ATS liability scope, 405–7, 406nn.457–60,
406–7n.463
Bivens actions by noncitizens, 900–2
case-specific deference, 409–10, 410n.482
citizens/noncitizens rights
abroad, 857–60
classified information, 75
commander-in-chief power, 756, 760–61
common law claims relegation, 651–52
common-law immunity, 302–3, 302–3n.803,
303n.807
Compact Clause, 839–47
conclusion of executive agreements
incidental to recognition, 163–67
concurrent regulatory authority, 804–
5, 810–12
on congressional unenumerated
powers, 56–57
conspiracy/law of war, 340–41, 341n.108
Constitution hierarchical status, 545
constitutional design, 181–82, 181n.44
corporate liability, 404–5, 406–9, 406–7n.463,
409n.477
court martial/right to jury trial, 778
cruel and unusual punishment, 942–45
customary international law, 364–66,
365n.244, 390–92, 390n.367, 391nn.372–
74, 391n.375
death penalty/executions, 507–9,
508–9nn.512–13
denaturalization of U.S. citizen, 980–81
executive agreements, 576–77, 576nn.862–
65, 578, 578nn.871–72
executive branch deference, 495–97,
498–99nn.451–57
executive privilege, 76–80
extradition, 57–58
federal law supremacy, 802–3
First Amendment protections, 869–71, 872
on foreign commerce power, 88, 89–90
foreign officials immunity, 302–21
foreign-owned debt collection claims, 819–
22, 819n.212, 819n.213, 820n.217 (*see also*
claims settlement)
habitual residence of child, 984–85
human rights, 228, 356–58, 364–65,
365nn.239–40, 366n.250, 368–69,
369n.265, 402–5, 402n.435, 403n.444,
403–4nn.447–50, 405nn.452–56
immigration, 57

instrumentalities of foreign commerce, 826–28

international law binding U.S. law, 649–54, 650n.255, 654n.271

international organizations/officials/premises, 288–90, 289nn.723–24, 290n.727

lawful permanent resident removal due to affiliation, 958–60

licensing of undocumented noncitizens, 806–7

licensing requirement/imports, 825

military commissions, 780–81

military establishment/regulation, 775

non-refoulement, 976–77

nonbinding agreements, 582–83

noncitizen in-state status/G-4 visas, 806, 806n.119

noncitizen registration, 805–6, 805n.112

noncitizens, 850–51

noncitizens and overriding national interests, 917–18, 917n.444, 917n.452

noncitizens property inheritance, 829–32, 831n.293

noncitizens search and seizure/Fourth Amendment, 892–94, 892nn.283–85

one voice doctrine, 809–10

passport issuance/denial/revocation due to affiliation, 929–31

piracy/felonies, 337–38, 337n.84

plenary power doctrine, 958–59

political question doctrine, 185–89, 185–86n.63, 188nn.80–84, 189nn.85–87, 189n.90, 190n.92, 191n.101, 191–92nn.105–6, 951–52

preemption by presidential action, 821–24

preemption/foreign relations context, 804–5

preemptive effects of treaty on state law, 813–17, 816–17nn.194–97, 817n.198

president, preclusive authority, 749–50

presidential authority to exit treaty, 591–92, 591n.942

president's power to recognize foreign states/officials, 67

president's proclamation powers, 876–78

presumption against extraterritoriality, 235–41, 236n.380, 237n.393, 238–39nn.397–98, 239nn.399–401, 239nn.402–4, 240n.409, 241n.413

private right of action/treaty incorporation, 517–18, 518nn.566–67

provision of support to terrorist groups, 881–82

recognition of foreign government coming to power extraconstitutionally, 152

recognition of new foreign state, 146–47, 146n.253

right to jury trial, 935–36

rights of belligerents/neutrals, 334–35, 334n.69

risk of multiple taxation, 826–28

sanctions/government procurement, 809–10

seizures of property and persons, 766–67

state/local law-treaty conflicts, 553–54, 554nn.747–49

state sovereign immunity, 798–99

taxation, in-state franchises/multinational corporations, 827–28

termination of treaties, 170–71

treaty non-self-execution, 512–15, 513n.532, 521–24, 521nn.578–80, 522nn.584–86, 523n.594, 528–29, 529nn.620–21, 534–35, 534n.647, 541–43, 543n.692, 582–83, 637, 642–43

treaty termination, 185–86

undocumented noncitizens statutory provisions, 807–8

universal jurisdiction, 228

war powers, 680

Supremacy Clause, 179, 179n.28, 370–71, 371n.271, 430–31, 469, 511–12, 516–17, 534–35, 534n.647, 536–38, 802, 837–38

surveillance of citizens/Fourth Amendment, 889–92, 889n.262, 889n.265, 890n.267, 891–92n.280

Suspension Clause, 856

sustainable development awards/Emoluments Clause, 172

Swift v. Tyson, 361–62

Syria

  agencies/instrumentalities, 263–64, 263–64n.562

  air strikes, 191–92, 192n.106, 714–15, 715n.324, 741–42

  chemical weapons in, 468–69, 468–69n.268, 725

  entry for Syrian refugees into U.S., 875–77, 966–67, 966–67nn.797–98

  foreign assistance limits, 83, 168

  nonrecognition, 150

  as state sponsor of terrorism, 279–80, 280n.660

  treaty obligations commitment to apply, 468–69, 468–69n.268

  U.S. military interventions in, 736–40

  U.S. targeting of citizens in, 868–69

Taft-Hartley Act (1947), 33
Tag v. Rogers, 381–82, 382n.325
Taiwan Relations Act (1979), 158–59, 163
Take Care Clause, 7–9, 7n.49, 8n.53, 38–39,
    38n.245, 329–30, 352–56, 352n.163,
    352–53nn.167–70, 353–54nn.171–74,
    354n.176, 355n.182, 356n.187, 389, 392–93
Takings Clause, 919–28, 920n.473
taking of property without just compensation,
    905–35, 920n.473, 921n.476, 922n.482,
    924n.496, 925n.507, 927–28n.517
Talbot v. Seeman, 382–83, 673, 749–50
Tarble's Case, 802–3
Tariff Act (1890), 94
taxation
    ad valorem property tax, 826–28
    congressional powers, 4, 17, 52–53
    customary international law, 370, 370n.266
    in-state franchises/multinational
        corporations, 827–28
    jurisdiction, 218–19, 218n.270
    recognition powers, 165
    risk of multiple taxation, 826–28
Tel-Oren v. Libyan Arab Republic, 400, 400n.424
Tenth Amendment, impact on treaty power,
    479–82, 479nn.339–40, 480nn.342–45,
    480nn.346–47
territorial acquisition, 11–12, 11n.74, 12n.77
terrorism
    closure of foreign mission, 129–31, 129n.142,
        130n.153
    commander-in-chief power, 757–58,
        757n.563, 762
    customary international law, 399–
        400nn.422–25, 400–1, 400nn.426–27
    drone strikes, 762
    federal cause of action, 281–82, 281n.672
    foreign sovereign immunity, 254, 286–87
    jurisdiction, 221–22, 229
    military commissions, 780–81
    presidential authority, 46–47, 63–64
    provision of support to terrorist
        groups, 881–82
    state sponsor of terrorism/FSIA, 279–80,
        280n.659, 284
    taking of property without just
        compensation, 927–28, 927–28n.517
    territoriality limit, 279–80, 279n.657
    terrorism-related exceptions/FSIA, 279–84,
        279n.656, 279–80nn.657–65, 281nn.666–
        68, 283n.681, 283n.685, 284n.686, 290
    terrorist threats by nonstate actors/use of
        force, 710–17, 711n.303, 714n.321

*Terrorist Bombings of U.S. Embassies in
    East Africa, In re (Fourth Amendment
    Challenges)*, 898
Thompson v. Oklahoma, 943–44
Thunder Studios, Inc. v. Kazal, 873–74
Timberlane Lumber Co. v. Bank of America,
    242–43, 243n.426
Toll v. Moreno, 806
*Torao Takahashi v. Fish and Game
    Commission*, 952–53
Torres v. Sablan, 856–57
torture
    act of state doctrine, 208–9, 209n.214
    commander-in-chief power, 757–58
    cooperative federalism, 794–95
    customary international law, 377–79,
        378n.304, 403–4, 403n.447
    evidence secured from coerced testimony,
        909, 909nn.396–97
    state-sponsored, 757–58
    U.S. abduction of noncitizens abroad for
        prosecution in U.S., 913–14
    universal jurisdiction, 227–28
Torture Convention (1985). *See under* U.N.
    Conventions
Torture Victim Protection Act (TVPA, 1991),
    341–42, 411–14, 411n.493, 412nn.494–98
Trade Act (1974), 94
Trade Expansion Act (1962), 94
Trading with the Enemy Act (1917), 728–29,
    767–68, 924, 924n.496
trafficking, 227–28, 230n.340, 230n.342
Trafficking Victims Protection Reauthorization
    Act of 2003 (TVPRA), 413–14
transnational family law. *See* family law/
    transnational
treason, congressional power to
    punish, 52–53
Treaty of Paris (1783), 17, 177, 177–78n.18, 325,
    511, 511n.523, 553–54, 787, 812–13
Treaty of Versailles (1919), xvi, 434, 608–10
treaty power
    generally, 415–17, 416–17n.13, 417–18n.16
    accommodating newly created foreign states,
        169–71, 169n.386
    act of state doctrine, 206–7, 206–7n.200
    advice and consent of Senate, 112–13, 442–
        43, 443nn.146–49, 451–52, 452nn.187–90,
        457–58, 457–58nn.213–18, 501–3, 577–78,
        577n.868, 578nn.871–72, 624, 625–
        28, 632–33
    anti-commandeering principle, 478–79,
        478n.334, 482–83

Article I/Constitution, 531–33, 541–
    43, 571–72
Article II/Constitution, 439, 439n.132,
    442–43, 444–60, 444–45nn.155–56,
    445–46nn.162–65, 447nn.166–67,
    447–48nn.168–73, 448–49nn.174–76,
    449–51nn.178–83, 452nn.188–90, 453–
    54n.196, 454n.198, 454–55nn.200–2, 456–
    57nn.205–12, 457–58nn.213–18, 470–71,
    470n.277, 471n.279, 615–16, 643
Articles of Confederation, 418–20, 420–
    21n.33, 423–24nn.49–51, 424nn.53–54,
    424–25nn.56–58, 511
authoritative interpretation, 631–32, 633–34,
    634nn.179–80, 643–44
Bricker Amendment, 434–36, 513,
    513n.535, 790–91
Byrd-Biden condition, 503, 503nn.479–80
capacity/authority, 437–39, 437–38n.124,
    438n.127, 439n.129, 439n.132
capacity/authority under international law,
    437–39, 437–38n.124, 438n.127, 439n.129,
    439nn.132–33
changes, incorporation into U.S. law, 629–58,
    630nn.160–61, 633nn.173–74, 633n.176
civil actions, 518–20
Compact Clause, 839–47
congressional, 112–13, 442–43, 443nn.146–
    48, 444–52, 446nn.164–65, 447nn.166–67,
    447–48nn.168–73, 448–49nn.174–75,
    449–51nn.178–83, 452nn.187–90, 466,
    466nn.253–57, 542–43, 543nn.691–95
congressional-executive agreements (see
    congressional-executive agreements)
congressional regulation of exit, 596–600,
    596n.969, 597nn.973–74, 598–99nn.975–
    81, 599–600nn.982–85
Connally reservation, 627–28
consent/entry into force, 440
Constitution-treaty conflicts, 545–47,
    545–46nn.708–9, 546n.710
constitutional law, 17, 426–36, 455, 606–7
constitutional limits on, 469–83, 469n.271
continuity principle, 169
customary international law, 417, 437–44,
    471–72, 471n.282
customary international law, capacity/
    authority under, 437–39, 437–38n.124,
    438n.127, 439n.129, 439nn.132–33
customary international law, consent/entry
    into force under, 440
customary international law, making
    under, 437–44

customary international law, reservations
    under, 440–42, 440–41n.136
customary international law impacts on
    treaty law, 387–89, 442–44, 442nn.142–43,
    442nn.144–45, 443nn.146–48, 443n.149,
    444n.151
declarations by treaty makers, 535–
    40, 537nn.659–61, 539nn.669–70,
    540nn.674–76
defeating object/purpose of, 460–64,
    460nn.226–29, 461nn.230–32, 461–
    62nn.234–35, 463n.239, 463–64nn.242–45
delegation of authority to change treaty
    obligation, 641–44
domestic effect, 523–24, 523–24n.595
elements of interpretation, 484–97
establishing commitments by means other
    than agreement, 584–86, 584–585nn.903–
    5, 585n.908, 586n.914
evaluation during ratification, 432–33,
    432–34nn.98–107
ex ante agreements (see under congressional-
    executive agreements)
ex post agreements (see under congressional-
    executive agreements
executive agreements pursuant to
    Article II treaties (see under executive
    agreements)
exiting, 587–600
extradition, 170, 570–72, 571n.834,
    572n.840, 911–13
federalism clause inclusion, 790–91
foreign investment protection, 793–94
foreign relations powers not derived from
    Constitution, 14, 14nn.88–89
friendship, commerce, and navigation
    (FCN), 265, 265nn.574–75
full powers document, 444–45, 445n.156
hierarchical status, 578–80,
    578–79nn.874–77
hierarchical status in incorporation,
    516, 545–56
historical emergence of, 418–36
human rights agreements, 570–72
immigration law, 793–94, 797–98
inalienability, 446–47
incorporation by self-execution, 510–
    24, 510nn.518–19, 511n.523, 511–
    12n.525, 512–13nn.531–34, 513n.535,
    515nn.549–51
international agreement interpretation,
    483–509
international concern test, 455–57

treaty power (*cont.*)
  international law-treaty conflicts, 552–53,
    552–53n.740
  international organizations, 438–39
  judicial deference to executive branch, 495–
    97, 498–99nn.451–57
  judicial deference to international tribunals,
    506–9, 508–9nn.512–13, 509nn.514–17
  judicial deference to Senate, 497–509,
    500n.463, 501n.467, 501–2n.471,
    502nn.474–76, 503nn.479–80, 504–
    5nn.484–86, 505n.492, 506n.493
  judiciary, 178–80, 179n.26, 179n.28, 180n.37,
    454–57, 454–55nn.200–2, 456–57nn.205–
    12, 492–93, 492–93nn.413–19
  language/foreign or multiple in
    interpretation, 487, 487–88nn.383–86
  later-in-time principle, 380–81, 380n.318
  later-in-time rule, 547–52, 549nn.720–23,
    549–50nn.725–28, 550–51nn.730–33
  League of Nations, Covenant of the, 608–9,
    609n.42, 609n.45
  lex posterior rule, 552
  making generally, 436–83, 643
  making under international law, 437–44
  multilateral treaties, 528, 528–29nn.614–
    16, 627–28
  national law impacts on treaty law, 442–44,
    442nn.142–43, 442n.143, 442–43nn.144–
    48, 443–44nn.149–51
  negotiation/advice, 444–51, 444–45n.155,
    445n.156, 445–46nn.158–63, 446nn.164–
    65, 447nn.166–67, 447–48nn.168–73,
    448–49nn.174–76, 449–51nn.178–83, 466,
    466nn.253–57
  New Jersey Plan, 111–12, 178–79, 178–
    79n.25, 330–31, 426, 429–30
  non-self-executing treaties, 39–40, 121–22,
    511–16, 513n.532, 515nn.549–51
  non-self-execution consequences, 520–24,
    520n.575, 521nn.578–80, 522nn.584–86,
    523–24n.595
  non-self-execution/Constitution-based
    inquiry, 530–33, 530–31nn.627–28,
    531nn.629–31, 532nn.632–35
  non-self-execution/justiciability-based
    inquiry, 533–35, 533–34nn.641–46
  non-self-execution/treaty-based inquiry,
    524–29, 524nn.596–97, 525n.602, 525–
    26nn.604–8, 527nn.609–11, 527n.612
  non–Article II agreements, 556–86,
    557n.767, 558n.769, 559n.777, 560n.781,
    560n.782

  nonbinding agreements, 580–83,
    581n.886, 581–82nn.888–91, 583n.898,
    583n.900, 596
  object/purpose in interpretation, 489–90,
    489–90nn.396–98, 490nn.399–400
  obligations, implementing by other means,
    540–44, 541–42nn.682–84, 543nn.691–95,
    544nn.696–97, 544nn.699–701
  obligations arising prior to entry into
    force, 460–69
  Pinckney Plan, 111, 178–79, 178n.24, 330–
    31, 426
  pre-Articles experience, 418–25, 419n.22
  preemption by presidential action, 822n.236
  preemption by treaty, 812–18, 812n.165,
    816–17nn.194–97, 817n.198
  preemption doctrine, 555–56
  preparatory work in interpretation, 495–97,
    495–96nn.438–42, 499, 502–3, 502n.474
  presidential authority to exit, 589–96,
    591nn.940–41, 591n.942, 592–93nn.949–
    52, 594–95nn.959–61, 595n.966
  presidential power to make, 5, 24–25, 170–
    71, 346–47, 428–29, 428–29nn.78–80, 439,
    439n.132, 444–51, 444–45nn.155–56, 445–
    46nn.162–63, 446nn.164–65, 447nn.166–
    67, 447–48nn.168–73, 448–49nn.174–76,
    449–51nn.178–83, 522–24, 522nn.584–86,
    523n.594, 573–74, 583
  private right of action/treaty incorporation,
    517–18, 518nn.566–67
  prohibitory words in Constitution, 475–76,
    476n.316, 480–81
  provisional application obligations, 464–
    69, 464–66nn.248–57, 467nn.258–61,
    468nn.263–64, 468–69nn.268–70
  ratification by president, xv–xvi, 18, 458–60,
    459nn.220–22, 459nn.223–25, 501, 536–
    37, 537n.660
  ratification under customary international
    law, 440, 441n.139
  representatives acting on behalf of, 439,
    439nn.132–33, 444–51
  reservations evaluation, 632
  reservations/other conditions, 453–58,
    453nn.191–95, 453–54n.196, 454n.198,
    454–55nn.200–2, 456–57nn.205–12,
    457–58nn.213–18
  reservations regarding states' rights, 790–91
  reservations to treaties, 440–42,
    442n.142, 500
  reservations to treaties/Article II, 453–58,
    453nn.191–95, 453–54n.196, 454n.198,

454–55nn.200–2, 456–57nn.205–12,
457–58nn.213–18
reservations under customary international
law, 440–42, 441n.139
section 1983 remedy, 518–20,
518–20nn.568–71
self-execution consequences, 516–20,
516n.555
separation of treaty power, 426–29, 427n.72,
428n.76, 428–29nn.77–80, 463–64,
463n.243, 525
sole executive agreements (*see under*
executive agreements)
standards of treatment protecting U.S.
nationals, 948–49
state/local law-treaty conflicts, 553–56,
554nn.747–49
state sovereign immunity, 476–78, 477–
78n.329, 482–83
states' rights, 429–32, 429n.82, 430n.87, 430–
31nn.90–91, 454, 479–81, 479nn.339–
40, 556–57
statute-treaty conflicts, 547–52, 548nn.716–
19, 549nn.720–23, 549–50nn.725–28,
550–51nn.730–33, 551–52nn.734–35
study methodology, xxiii
subject-matter limits, 470–75, 470n.277,
471n.279, 471n.282, 472n.291, 473–
74nn.294–300, 474–15nn.301–2
subsequent agreements/practice/relevant
rules in interpretation, 491–94, 491n.404,
492n.409, 492–93nn.413–19, 493–
94nn.420–24, 494n.430
substate entity, 438–39, 439n.129
supplementary means of interpretation, 495–
97, 495–96nn.438–42
tacit amendment procedures, 630–31
Tenth Amendment impacts, 479–82,
479nn.339–40, 480nn.342–45,
480nn.346–47
termination, 170–71, 185–86
text/context in interpretation,
484–90, 485n.370, 486n.375, 486–
87nn.381–82, 487–88nn.383–86,
488–89nn.391–93, 489–90nn.396–98,
490nn.399–400
treaty-based preemption, 810–12
treaty-implementing agreements, 558
tribes, 438–39, 439n.129
unilateral declarations, 585–86, 586n.914
Vandenberg reservation, 627–28
Virginia Plan, 111, 330–31, 426, 429–
30, 664–65

trials/Sixth Amendment
generally, 935–42, 935n.575
court-ordered depositions, 939, 939n.602
by military commission, 940–42, 940n.608
post-indictment right of counsel/noncitizen
located abroad, 938
right to confront/compel testimony of
witnesses located abroad, 938–39,
939nn.602–4
right to speedy U.S. trial/noncitizen located
abroad, 937, 937nn.587–89
Truax v. Raich, 946–47
true conflict test, 243–44, 244n.432, 245–46
Trump v. Hawaii, 49, 49n.315, 876–78, 966–67,
967n.802
Trump v. Mazars USA, 76–77

U.N. Charter, 612–14, 613–14nn.73–75, 689–91
U.N. Conventions
Chemical Weapons Convention (1993), 903–
4, 904n.373
Convention against Genocide (1948), 213–
14, 628n.151, 861–62
Convention against Torture (1985), 219, 225–
26, 411–13, 412n.494, 794–95, 861–62,
865, 978
Elimination of All Forms of Racial
Discrimination (CERD, 1965), 861–62
Elimination of Discrimination against
Women (CEDAW, 1979), 796–97, 835–
36, 861–62
on Jurisdictional Immunities of States and
Their Property (2004), 283n.685
Law of the Sea (1982), xv–xvi, 397–98, 628–
29, 628–29n.153
Privileges and Immunities of the United
Nations (General Convention, 1946),
291–92, 291–92nn.740–43, 294–95,
294n.758
on the Rights of Persons with Disabilities
(2007), 457–58
on the Rights of the Child (1989), 372–73,
372n.276, 791–92, 861–62, 944
on the Status of Refugees (1951), 969–70,
969n.817, 976–77
U.N. Participation Act (UNPA, 1945), 620–
21, 636–37
U.S. Constitution. *See* constitutional law
*U.S. Steel Corp. v. Multistate Tax
Comm'n*, 845–46
Underhill v. Hernandez, 199
Uniform Code of Military Justice (UCMJ), 752–
53, 776, 778–79, 780–81, 858, 940

Uniform Interstate Family Support Act (UIFSA, 2008), 988
unitary executive theory, 8–9
United States Climate Alliance, 797
United States ex rel. Toth v. Quarles, 778
United States v.
  Alvarez-Machain, 235, 494, 494n.430, 911–13, 911n.408, 913nn.419–20
  Arjona, 338–40, 339n.95, 342–43, 343n.116, 344–45
  Arlington County, 165
  Arthrex, Inc., 6–7n.44
  Belmont, 122, 163–64, 788–89, 789n.15, 819–20, 819n.212, 819n.213, 820n.217
  Bollinger, 92
  Bond, 541–42
  California, 845–46
  Carpio-Leon, 886
  Clark, 91–92
  Curtiss-Wright Export Corp., 13–16, 27–30, 28n.179, 62, 107–8, 121, 164, 447–48, 447n.169, 640–41, 640n.211, 801
  Demjanjuk, 980–81
  Furlong, 336–37
  Huitron-Guizar, 886
  Locke, 804–5, 810–11
  McKeeve, 939
  Meza-Rodriguez, 886
  Microsoft, 234–35, 234n.372
  Palestine Liberation Organization, 129–31, 129n.142
  Palmer, 336–38
  Park, 92–93, 93n.297
  Pendleton, 92
  Peterson, 899–900
  Pink, 122, 163–65, 170–71, 820–21
  Pitawanakwat, 992–93
  Postal, 912–13
  Rosen, 879–80
  Stuart, 501–2n.471, 502n.474
  Torres, 886
  Toscanino, 913–14
  Verdugo-Urquidez, 884–85, 893, 894–96, 907–8
  Zubaydah, 868–69
United States–Mexico–Canada Agreement (USMCA, 2019), 94–95, 344–45, 601–2, 621–22, 653
Upright v. Mercury Business Machines Co., 162–63
Uruguay Round trade agreements (1994), 94–95, 561, 567, 569–70, 597n.974
U.S.-Japan Treaty of Commerce and Navigation (1911), 948–49

Valentine v. United States, 57–58
VCLT. See Vienna Convention on the Law of Treaties
Verlinden B.V. v. Central Bank of Nigeria, 58, 252–54
Vesting Clause, 6–7nn.43–44, 12n.77, 38–39, 38n.245
vesting of executive power, 6–7, 6–7nn.43–44
Vienna Convention on Consular Relations (VCCR, 1963), 295–302, 296–97nn.770–75, 298–99nn.782–86, 299nn.787–88, 299–300nn.790–93, 301n.796, 301n.799, 507, 526–27, 653–54, 795, 814–15
Vienna Convention on Diplomatic Relations (VCDR, 1961), 126, 294–302, 296–97nn.770–75, 298n.781, 301n.796, 301n.799
Vienna Convention on the Law of Treaties (VCLT, 1969), xv, 416–17, 416–17n.13, 453–54, 588–89. See also treaty power
Virginia v. Tennessee, 842–44, 845–46
Von Saher v. Norton Simon Museum of Art at Pasadena, 833–34

W.S. Kirkpatrick & Co. v. Environmental Tectonics Corp., Int'l, 200, 203–4, 205, 205n.194
Wabol v. Villacrusis, 856–57
waivers
  act of state doctrine, 207, 207n.206
  charter-based/FSIA, 290–91, 291n.736
  diplomats/consular officials immunity, 299, 299nn.787–88
  FSIA/related exceptions, 265–68, 265nn.574–75, 266nn.577–80, 290–91
  presidential waivers/foreign missions, 130–31, 130n.159
war crimes, 227–28, 752–53, 760–61, 777
war powers
  air strikes, 717–24, 741–42, 746–47
  Article 43 agreements, 689–91
  Articles of Confederation, 663–64
  Barbary pirates, 674–76, 675n.99
  bases-for-destroyers scheme, 686–87, 687n.172
  battlefield vs. nonbattlefield regulations, 762–64
  Boxer Rebellion, 683–84
  civilian contractors prosecution, 779–80
  civilian control of armed forces, 668–69, 755
  Cold War, 691–97
  commander-in-chief power, 33–35, 87–88, 191–92, 192n.106, 354–56, 355n.183, 558,

576–78, 576n.862, 577n.868, 668–69, 680,
686–87, 687n.172, 695, 715–16, 736–37,
736n.446, 754–64, 755n.547, 755n.550,
757n.563
conduct of armed conflict, 661
congressional, 3–4, 661, 662, 665–66, 665–
66nn.36–37, 668–70, 673–74, 677, 697–
704, 731–50, 759–63
congressional authorization method
consequences, 725–29, 727–28nn.402–5
constitutional text, 659–62, 660n.10, 664–70
court-martial, 776–78, 777n.714
covert operations, 739–40, 739n.474, 773–74
customary international law, 728,
729–31, 729n.413, 730n.414, 751–54,
754n.542, 780–81
declaration of war, 661, 662, 665–70, 665–
66nn.36–37, 671–72, 686–88, 698–99,
705–6, 725–29, 733–34, 744, 748–50,
750n.522, 766
denial of entry to U.S., 872–73, 873n.154,
874–78, 876n.174
enemy combatant treatment, 713, 763–64,
777–78, 778n.719, 900–1
establishment/regulation of military, 661
faithful execution of laws, 705–6
48-hour reports, 699–702, 702n.255, 722–23
funding, 87–88, 697, 721, 727–28, 727–
28nn.402–5, 738–39, 748–50, 772–74
Greytown incident, 678–79, 922–23
Guantánamo Bay detainees, 40, 234, 713,
752–53, 757–58, 763–64, 772–73, 781–82,
856, 859–60, 932–34, 934n.569, 941–42
Gulf of Tonkin Resolution, 696–97
humanitarian objectives/use of force, 717–24,
737–38, 881–82
impeachment, 748–50
Indian Tribes, early conflicts with, 670–79
interwar period, 685–87, 687n.172
Japanese internment, WWII, 660, 660n.10
jurisdiction, 728–29, 781–82
jus ad bellum/jus in bello, 661–62, 729–30,
751–54, 754n.542
Korean War, 692–95
land/water capture rule making
powers, 764–68
Latin American interventions, 684
letters of marque/reprisal, 659–60, 661,
662–63, 664, 666, 669–70, 766, 768–70,
770nn.655–56
location restrictions, 773–74, 774n.684
low-intensity armed conflict, 734–42, 735–
36n.444, 736n.448, 738n.462

low-intensity armed conflict powers, 734–42
Mexican-American War, 677–78
military commissions/tribunals, 40, 713,
779–82, 906, 931–32, 936, 940–42,
940n.608
military detention of noncitizens
abroad, 931–35, 932n.556, 933n.560,
934nn.568–69
military establishment/regulation, 771–85,
774n.684, 777n.714, 778n.719
militia-related, 661, 667–68, 758–59, 782–
85, 882–87
national emergencies, 728–29, 729n.412
nature, scope, and duration standard, 734,
735, 740, 741–42, 748
Neutrality Acts (1935–1939), 686–87
non-citizen challenging military
detention, 781–82
non-international armed conflict
(NIAC), 751
peacekeeping missions, 691, 702, 718–19,
720–21, 720n.358, 738
police actions/U.N., 745–46
post–Cold War uses of force, 704–24
power to conduct armed conflict, 751–70
power to interpret international law, 752–53
president, preclusive authority, 748–50,
750n.522, 759, 762–63
president, reserved authority/repel sudden
attacks, 732–34
president subject to congressional
restrictions, 746–48
presidential, 666–69, 674–77, 675n.99, 680–
81, 691–704, 710–17, 731–50
projection of military power, 691–92
protection and rescue operations, 674–76,
675n.99, 736–37
quasi-war with France, 672–74, 676, 726–27,
728, 795–96
repel sudden attacks theory, 732–34
reporting requirements, 699–702,
702n.255, 722–23
reserved authority/repel sudden
attacks, 732–34
resort to armed force, 661, 662–750
resort to armed force/pre-
constitutional, 662–64
sale/lending/giving of war materials, 686–87,
687n.172
seizures of property and persons, 764–68
self-defense actions, 729–30, 730n.414
Spanish-American War, 682–83, 854–56
of states, 790

war powers (*cont.*)
  statutory authorizations, 673–77, 678–79,
    681–82, 700, 712–17, 719–22, 728–29,
    729n.412, 762
  Taiwan, threats to, 695–96
  terrorist threats by nonstate actors/use of
    force, 710–17, 711n.303, 714n.321
  theories of balancing, 731–50
  threatening armed conflict, 724–25, 729–30
  U.N. Participation Act (UNPA, 1945), 690
  U.N. Security Council use of force
    authorization, 689nn.187–88, 705–10,
    705–6nn.272–73, 721, 722, 729–30, 742–
    46, 743n.492
  U.S. Civil War, 679–82
  U.N. resolutions, 689–91, 693–94
  Vietnam War, 696–97, 774
  War of 1812, 676–77, 676n.108, 760–61,
    766–67, 883–84
  War Powers Resolution (1973), 661, 697–704,
    697n.224, 699n.237, 701n.249,
    701nn.250–51, 702n.255, 712, 722,
    723–24, 727–28, 727–28nn.402–5, 733,
    735, 740
  Washington's Neutrality Proclamation, 672
  World War I, 684–85
  World War II, 687–88, 773–74
  writ of habeas corpus, 4–5, 44, 679–81, 781–
    82, 856, 931–32, 933–35
Ware v. Hylton, 424–25, 511, 553–54, 812–13
Washington v. Trump, 875
Williams v. Suffolk Insurance Co., 146–47
Wilson v. Girard, 573–74
Wong Wing v. United States, 905–6

Yamashita, In re, 779–80
Yick Wo v. Hopkins, 946
Youngstown Sheet & Tube Co. v. Sawyer
  executive order constitutionality, 32–39,
    33n.208, 38n.245, 42, 522–23, 823–24
  executive practice, xxi, xxin.10
  president's signing statement, 67
  Reception Clause authority, 123–24
  Take Care Clause authority, 353–56,
    353–54n.172
  war powers authority, 692–93, 735, 735–
    36n.444, 760–61, 764
Yugoslavia
  aiding-and-abetting liability, 407–8,
    408n.472
  claims settlement, 165–66
  extradition treaty, 170, 570–71, 571n.834
  military contractor conduct, 191–92,
    191n.105
  peacekeeping missions, 720–21, 720n.358
  preemption, 813–14
  U.S. derecognition of, 151
  U.S. military interventions in, 734–35
  U.S. recognition of, 146, 153, 165–66

Zemel v. Rusk, 930–31
Ziglar v. Abbasi, 900–2
Zivotofsky v. Clinton (Zivotofsky I), 186–87, 189,
    191–92, 192n.106
Zivotofsky v. Kerry (Zivotofsky II), 6–7, 29–30,
    30n.190, 40–41, 40n.259, 42, 66–68,
    67n.120, 107, 123, 123n.96, 147, 192
Zschernig v. Miller, 829–31, 831n.293, 832,
    846–47